The History of Philosophy

(1701)

Thomas Stanley

the apocryphile press
BERKELEY, CA
www.apocryphile.org

apocryphile press
BERKELEY, CA

Apocryphile Press
1700 Shattuck Ave #81
Berkeley, CA 94709
www.apocryphile.org

First published in three volumes (London, 1655-62); volumes I and II were reissued in 1656. The second edition was published in 1687. The fourth edition, also with the "Account of the Life and Writings," appeared in 1743. Apocryphile Press Edition, 2006.

Printed in the United States of America
ISBN 1-933993-09-X

P. Lilly pinxit.   Guil. Faithorne scul.

THOMAS STANLEY ARM.

THE
HISTORY
OF
PHILOSOPHY:

CONTAINING

The Lives, Opinions, Actions and Discourses

OF THE

PHILOSOPHERS

Of every SECT.

Illustrated with the EFFIGIES of divers of Them.

BY

THOMAS STANLEY, Esq;

The Third Edition.

To which is Added the Life of the Author, never before Published.

LONDON:

Printed for *W. Battersby* at *Thavy's* Inn-gate, near St. *Andrew's* Church in *Holbourn*, *Hugh Newman*, *Tho. Cockerill*, *Herbert-Walwyn* in the *Poultry*, and *A.* and *J. Churchil* in *Pater-Noster-Row*. MDCCI.

To my Honoured UNCLE
JOHN MARSHAM, Esq;

SIR,

I Send this Book to you, because you first directed me to this Design. The Learned *Gassendus* was my Precedent; whom nevertheless I have not follow'd in his Partiality: For he, tho' limited to a Single Person, yet giveth himself Liberty of Enlargement, and taketh occasion from this Subject to make the World acquainted with many excellent Disquisitions of his own. Our Scope being of a greater Latitude, affords less Opportunity to favour any Particular; whilst there is due to every one the Commendation of their own Deserts. This Benefit I hope to have received from the variety of the Subject; but far more are those I owe to your Encouragement, which if I could wish less, I should upon this Occasion, that there might seem to have been expressed something of Choice and Inclination in this Action, which is now but an inconsiderable Effect of the Gratitude of,

Dear Uncle,

Your most affectionate Nephew, and

Humble Servant,

THOMAS STANDLEY.

PREFACE

History (which by Expounding actions past teacheth to regulate the future, and furnisheth us with Wisdom at the cost of other Mens Experience) is not unlike Painting: Their scope is the same, and as in the latter it argues want of Skill to look upon the whole Draught with an indifferent eye, but to select and insist upon some chief particular is proper to an Artist; so he who rests satisfied with the general Relation of Affairs, (not fixing upon some eminent Actor in that Story) loseth its greatest benefit; since what is most particular, by its nearer affinity with us, hath greatest influence upon us.

Hence it is that there are two kinds of History; one represents general affairs of State; the other gives account of particular persons, whose Lives have rendred them Eminent. Homer hath given an Essay of each; of the first in his Iliads, a relation of a War betwixt different Nations; of the second in his Odysses, confined to the Person of Ulysses.

Now the life of Man being either practick, busied in civil Affairs of Peace and War, or Contemplative, retir'd from publick Business to Speculation and Study of Wisdom, Divine or Humane, it follows that this personal History be two-fold likewise, describing either the Actions of such Persons as are wholly interessed in the Affairs of State (properly compared to the Persons of a dramatical design, whose single Characters and Parts serve only to make up one joynt Plot. Such are most of those whose Lives are related by Plutarch, and the twelve Cæsars of Suetonius) or the Lives of such as have been excellent in some kind of Learning; thus Antipho writ of Poets; Eudemus of Astrologers; Cicero and Plutarch of Orators, Suetonius of Grammarians. They who writ of Philosophers exceeded the rest far in number, of whom to give a particular account will be unnecessary, because their Works are not extant, and therefore we shall only name them, Aetius, Anaxilides, Antigonus, Antisthenes, Aristocles, Aristoxenus, Callimachus, Clitomachus, Diocles, Diogenes Laertius, Eunapius, Heraclides, Hermippus, Hesychius, Hippobotus, Son, Idomeneus, Nicander, Nicias, Panætius, Porrius, Plutarch, Sotion and Theodorus.

Of almost all these (which is much to be deplored) there remain not any footsteps; the only Author in this kind for the more ancient Philosophers is Diogenes Laertius, for the later Eunapius. And to make the Misfortune the greater, that which Laertius gives us is so far short of what he might have done, that there is much more to be found of the same Persons dispersed among other Authors, which I have here collected and digested, with what diligence I could.

Nor is it unseasonable at this time to examine the Tenents of old Philosophers, when so great variety of Opinions daily spring up; some of which are but raked out of the Ruines of Antiquity, which ought to be restored to their first Owners; others being of late invention will receive addition, when advanced to such height we look down to the bottom from which Philosophy took her first rise, and see how great a progress she hath made, whose beginnings are almost inscrutable.

Although some Grecians have challenged to their Nation the Original of Philosophy, yet the more Learned of them have acknowledged it derived from the East. To omit the dark Traditions of the Athenians concerning Musæus, of the Thebans concerning Linus, and of the Thracians about Orpheus, it is manifest that the Original of the Greek Philosophy is to be derived from Thales, who Travelling into the East, first brought Natural Learning, Geometry, and Astrology thence into Greece, for which reason the Attribute of Wise was conferred upon him, and at the same time upon six others for their Eminence in Morality and Politicks. Thus Learning in the ancientest times was by the Greeks called Sophia (Wisdom) and the Professor thereof, who raised his Soul to an eminent degree of knowledge, Sophos (wise:) Pythagoras first named it Philosophy (love of Wisdom) and himself a Philosopher, affirming, that no Man is Wise, but only God.

* Laert. vit. Thalet.

* As concerning those who were honoured with this Attribute of Wise, Damon the Cyrenean undervalues them all, especially the seven. Anaximenes saith, They were all addicted to Poetry; Dicæarchus, that they were neither wise Men, nor Philosophers, but upright Men and Law-givers: Archetimus the Syracusian wrote concerning their meeting with Cypselus (Father to Periander) whereat he saith himself was present. Ephorus affirms they all met with Crœsus, Thales only excepted. Some say they met also at the Panionian Feast, and at Corinth, with Periander at Delphi.

There is some controversie concerning their Sentences, of which some are ascribed to several persons, as that,
Lacedæmonian Chilon this profess'd,
Nothing too much; a Mean in all is best.

† Not Leophantum Gorsiadem as the Interpreters render
* So Suidas Ἀκυσίλαος Κάβα υἱὸς Ἀργεῖος, by which Laertius is explained contrary to the Interpreters.

There is no less dissent concerning their number. Leandrius for Cleobulus and Myson, inserts Leophantus Son of † Gorsiades a Lebedian, or Ephesian, and Epimenides the Cretan. Plato (in his Protagoras) substitutes Myson for Periander: Ephorus, Anacharsis for Myson. Some add Pythagoras. Dicæarchus alledgeth four, acknowledg'd by all, Thales, Bias, Pittacus and Solon: then names six more, out of which are to be selected three, Aristodemus, Pamphilus, Chilon the Lacedæmonian, Cleobulus, Anacharsis, Periander; some add * Acusilaus Son of Caba or Scabra an Argive. Hermippus in his Treatise of the seven wise men, saith, they were in all seventeen, of which seven were variously named, which were, Solon, Thales, Pittacus, Bias, Chilon, Cleobulus, Periander, Anacharsis, Acusilaus, Epimenides, Leophantus, Pherecydes, Aristodemus, Pythagoras, Lasus of Hermionea, Son of Charmantides, or (according to Aristoxenus) of Simbrinus, Anaxagoras. Hippobotus in his Commentary of Philosophers, reckons Linus, Orpheus, Solon, Periander, Anacharsis, Cleobulus, Myson, Thales, Bias, Pittacus, Epicharmus, Pythagoras.

Laertius reckons them thus, Thales, Solon, Chilon, Pittacus, Bias, Cleobulus, Periander; whereunto he adds Anacharsis, Myson, Epimenides, and Pherecydes. These, saith he, were called the Wise Men, to whom some annex Pisistratus the Tyrant.

Among the Romans also three had the sir-name of Sapiens, M. Cato, C. Lælius, and L. Acilius.

THE

AN ACCOUNT
OF THE
Life and Writings
OF
THOMAS STANLEY, Esq;

THE Reader cannot expect to find in this Place a long Recital of Intrigues and Adventures; for as the Life of a Courtier or a Soldier is past in a Court or a Camp, so that of a Scholar is in the Solitude of his Study: And as Mr. *Stanley*'s Learning made up the brightest part of his Character, so an Account of his Life is but a Relation of his Atchievements in the Learned World.

Mr. *Stanley* was Son of Sir *Thomas Stanley*, and Born at *Cumberlow-Green* in *Hartford-Shire*, at the Age of 14 Years he was sent to *Cambridge*, and placed at *Pembrook-Hall* under the Tuition of Mr. *Balcanchol*, Brother to the Dean of *Durham*. This worthy Gentleman, who had Married the Lady *Steward* his Grand-Mother, took a more than Ordinary Care in the Education of his Pupil: He spared no Pains to Cherish and Animate those Desires of Learning which visibly appear'd the predominant Passion of his Mind.

While he continued yet in the University, his Fancy began to exert it self, and give some presages of what the World was to expect from his Genius: It was Here he composed those * *Madrigal's Poems*, and other Pieces, which together with some Translations out of the *French*, *Italian*, and *Spanish*, were published in one Volume after his Return from his Travels. As in his first Pieces he has given the World a Proof of the Fertility of his Invention; so in the latter, which are incomparably better, he has, beyond Exception, done of his Great Diligence and Learning.

* *Europa, Cupid crucified and Venus Vigils with Notes. Lond. 1649. —Anacreon, Bion, Moschus: Kisses by Secundus: Cupid crucified by Ausonius: Venus Vigils with divers other Poems, 1651. Octavo.*

Soon

Soon after his Return Home, when he had finished his Tour of *France*, *Italy*, and *Spain*, and by Travel extended his Knowledge beyond the Bounds of his Native Island, he Married *Dorothy*, Daughter of Sir *James Engan* of *Flower*, in the County of *Northampton*, whilst his Father and Mother were still living; and before he was arrived at that Age, which by the Laws of his Country put an End to his Minority. This alteration in his State and Condition of Life did not in the least change his Temper and Disposition, or abate his Affection to Learning, which was no less vigorous now than before. Neither the Cares nor Concerns for his Family, nor the Caresses and Endearments of a Young Wife, could prevail with him to intermit his ordinary Studies, on which he was obstinately bent. I will not say of him as a Learned Chancellor of *France* has spoke of himself, † who complains in Print, that upon his Wedding Day he had not more than Six Hours to employ in his Studies; but his Assiduity and Application is visible to all who shall consider the Greatness of his Works, and the short Limits of Life in which he finished them.

† *Budæus de Asse. Præf.*

The first Work which He enriched the Publick with, was this History of the Lives and Opinions of the Ancient *Greek* Philosophers. This Work was first begun after the Example of the Learned *Gassendus* who has composed the Lives of *Copernicus*, *Tycho Brahe*, *Peurbachius*, *Regiomontanus*, and other Modern Astronomers and Philosophers. Mr. *Stanley* was not the first who had attempted this Province; *Diogenes Laertius* in the Time of the Emperour *Marcus Antoninus* compiled a Volume of the Lives of the Elder Philosophers, and after him *Ennapius* writ the Lives of the Sophists. Besides what is extant, *Antisthenes* and many others, whose Volumes have perished, writ upon the same Subject. The Learned *Gerard Vossius* in our Age has writ a short Treatise of the Ancient Philosophy, and the several Sects, not to mention others; but Mr. *Stanley* has out-done all that preceded him in the Extent of his Design, and the vast Multitude of particulars He has amass'd together.

The many Editions of so large a Work are undeniable Proofs of the Approbation it has received from the Publick. To speak the Truth, the Excellence and Variety of the Matter, and the vast Reading which the Author has discover'd in every part of it, could not miss of Admiration. Besides, most Men have a relish for Discourses of this kind; and

and there are few who have not a Curiosity to know the Lives and Actions of those whose Virtues they admire. This has engaged so many Pens to write the Lives of Princes, Great Captains, Ministers of State, and other Persons who have made a considerable Figure in the World, or had a share in the Revolutions of Empires and Kingdoms. Others again have entertained the Publick with the Lives of Divines, Lawyers, Poets, Physicians, &c. which have been kindly received and judged both Useful and Diverting.

There are two ways of Instruction; the one by Precept, the other by Example; the former is dry and barren, and makes at most but a languid Effort; the latter is lively and brisk, and leaves a strong Impression, creating in the Mind Desires and Inclinations to imitate what is Good and Excellent, and a Horrour for what is Base and Ill. Mr. *Stanley* only considers Philosophers, and the Amusements and Speculations of Men retired from the Hurry and Noise of the World. He has with extreme Diligence compiled an exact History of their Lives, their Opinions and Notions of *Good* and *Evil*, of *God* and *Nature*; their *Theories* of the *Universe*, their *Thoughts* about the Principles of *Things*, their Schemes of Morality and Policy, their Conduct and Behaviour.

By this we see the Steps by which the *Arts* and *Sciences*, and all Parts of Humane Knowledge have been promoted, and the several Advances it has made from its Infancy, till it arrived at the Pitch it is at present at.

I mentioned before those Writers who preceded our Author in this Design, but none have executed it with so much advantage; his Aim is more Comprehensive, his Account is in every part Succinct, Pertinent, without Excursions, and consists of a vast Number of Fragments, which are not in others, supplied out of the vast Treasures of his Reading.

The following History consists of Nineteen Parts; the first treats of the Seven Sages or Wisemen of *Greece*, so Famous in Antiquity; the other give us an ample Account of the Twelve different Sects of Philosophers, the Lives of the most Eminent Professors, and the Opinions held by them. The last treat of the Chaldaick Philosophy, an Abstruse and Difficult Subject, and which required no less Learning than Mr. *Stanley*'s to venture on it.

Thales,

Thales, the *Milesian*, was the first who employ'd himself in Natural Enquiries, and was thought to deserve the Magnificent Title of Wise for his Noble Discoveries in Geometry, Astronomy, and the Theory of the Universe. His Principle was, that Water is the chief Material of which Natural Bodies are formed, and into which they are resolved. He imagined the *Earth* a great Mass, floating on a vast Abyss or Ocean of Water; and from hence gave the Reason of Earthquakes and Eruption of Springs. He conceived God as the Author of all Natural Motion, and the Soul which animated the Universe. Mr. *Stanley* tells us, he imagined *Loadstone* and *Jett* to have Souls, because of their Virtue of attracting Bodies to them. To him is ascribed the Invention of Measuring the Height of the Pyramids by their Shadows, and found the Natural Reason of Eclipses, which before were lookt on as Portentous, and Presages of some Calamity. Our Author tells us, he foretold that which ended the Five Years Wars between the *Lydians* and the *Medes*; when those poor People, frighted at the strange Darkness, and believing the Sun hid himself to avoid seeing the Slaughter, laid down their Arms, and Compos'd their Quarrels. Besides *Thales*, *Solon*, *Chilon*, *Pittacus*, *Bias*, *Cleobulus*, *Periander*, had the same Title bestowed on them. And as *Thales* was the first, who by his Travels into the Eastern Countreys made himself acquainted with Mathematical and Natural Learning, and introduced it into *Greece*, these were the Authors of several Excellent Laws and Schemes of Government: And as the Illustrious Title of Wise was conferr'd on the first for his Excellent Skill in Geometry, and the knowledge of Nature, it was conferr'd on the other for their Excellent Precepts in Morality and Politicks. Indeed the Attribute of Wise was given to all who professed any sort of Knowledge above the Vulgar, till *Pythagoras* changed *that* into the Name of Philosophy, piously thinking so great a Title could only be ascribed rightfully to the Infinite and Supreme Wisdom.

It will not be expected we should enter into a Detail of their Lives; this would be to anticipate the Reader, who will find all their Doctrines, Letters, Occasional Speeches, *&c.* recounted by our Author in their place.

The Sects of Philosophers had a Double Original; the one from *Anaximander* the Disciple of *Thales*; and therefore *Ionick*, and the other from *Pythagoras*, that Prince of Philosophers, which from the place where he held his School was

was called the *Italick*. *Anaximander* varied from the Doctrine of his Master, and instead of *Water* made *Infinity* the Principle of all Things, but has left us without an Explanation of his Meaning. He first discover'd the Obliquity of the *Zodiack*, made Geographical Charts, and invented Dials: Tho' Mr. *Stanley*, after *Salmasius*, thinks his Gnomon did only note the Tropick and Equinoctial Points, the division of Hours not being used till a long Time after. Of this Sect, besides him, were *Anaximenes*, *Anaxagoras*, &c.

Socrates, an Athenian, was the Author of the Second Sect: His chief Study was Virtue, Morality, and the Regulation of our Lives and Actions. He was Son of a *Statuary*, but the Greatness of his Genius raised him above his Birth and Condition. He did not confine himself to set Lectures in the Chair. Where-ever he was his Conversation was still Pleasant and Instructive. The Camp, the *Forum*, the Publick Streets, the Houses of his Friends, the Prison in which he endured great Hardship, were so many Schools of Knowledge and Virtue. For his great Wisdom, his Manly and Noble Thoughts, the Ease and Sweetness of his Expression he was admired by all Men, and esteemed the Prince of Philosophers. He had a right Notion of the Divine Nature, and Vigorously opposed *Politheism*; for which his Enemies reproach'd him as an Infidel, and an Enemy of the Gods, and Condemn'd him to Death; which he *Drank* with such Majesty of Soul, such Serenity of Mind, as shew'd the absolute Empire of his Reason over his Passions, and the impotence of his Enemies Malice; who by Death it self could not break in upon the Tranquility of his Mind, or make him Die other than *Socrates*. There are great Disputes maintain'd, not without some Heat, among Christian, as well as Pagan Writers concerning the *Dæmon* which attended *Socrates*, and gave him Presages of Events which should happen soon after: The discussion of this may be seen in an entire Chapter, in the Life of this Philosopher. Notwithstanding his Eminent Vertue and Wisdom, he could not escape the Malice and Wit of *Aristophanes*, who has exposed him in a Play called *The Clouds*, which Mr. *Stanley* has translated into English, and annexed as an Appendix to his Life.

The Succession of the *Ionick* Philosophy, which before *Socrates* was single, was soon after divided into several Schools and Sects, some of which were of less Note, and lasted but a short Time, others were more Considerable, and of longer Continuance; of the first sort were the *Cyrenaick, Megarick, Eleack,* and *Eretriack* Sects; of the latter were the *Academick* and *Cynick,* which two gave Birth to the *Peripatetick* and *Stoick.*

Aristippus, a Disciple of *Socrates,* was the Chief of the *Cyrenaick* Sect. He placed the Sovereign Good in Pleasure, and thinks Virtue only commendable as it conduces to acquire that. The Distinction of Right and Wrong, Just and Unjust, he thought Arbitrary, and not established by Nature, but Law and Custom. As his Principles were loose, his Life was suited to his Doctrine, which he past away in Jollity and Mirth. His good Humour render'd him agreeable to *Dionysius* the Tyrant of *Sicily,* while the Severity of *Plato,* which he miscall'd Moroseness, offended that haughty Prince. I cannot forbear here to recount one or two of the many Witty Replies which are recorded of that Philosopher, and which our Author has collected among the other Incidents of his Life. When *Dionysius* asked him what brought him to his Court, He replied, He came to Traffick with him, to offer him what He had, and receive from him what He wanted, meaning to Barter the Wit and Humour He was Master of for the other's Money. He did not confine himself to the Rules of Temperance, Sobriety, and Continence. Upon a certain Time entring into the House of a Famous Curtezan, He observed one of the Company to blush. *Sir,* said he, *there's no Harm in going in, but in not being able to come out.* When a certain Strumpet charged him with being with Child by him, *You know that no more,* says he, *than in passing thro' a Bush which Thorn it is that pricks you.* When *Dionysius* offered him three Beautiful Women, and bid him chuse one out of them, which he liked best; he took them all three away with him, that he might not, as he said, incurr the Fate of *Paris,* who had been so severely punished for his Indiscretion in preferring one to two. *Aristippus* owned but two Passions, Pleasure and Grief, as the Springs of all Humane Actions; and these are diversified according to the Temper and Complexion of every Person. He derided the Calmness and Serenity of Mind, or Exemption from all Passion; in which others place all Humane Happiness, regarding this as meer Inactivity, and a tiresome Indolence. He likewise derided the Plainness, Simplicity, and Course Living of his Old Friend *Antisthenes,* and admired the Plenty, Ease and Luxury of the *Sicilian* Court. Many other Pleasantries of the same Kind are mention'd in their Place, but I fear I have trespassed the Bounds I prescribed my self in descending to these Particulars. Be-

Besides the *Cyrenaick*, Mr. *Stanley* treats of *Megarick*, *Eleack*, and other Sects; but the most eminent of all those derived from *Socrates*, was the *Academick*, who took their Name from the place where their School was erected. *Plato* was the chief of these, concerning whose Birth Mr. *Stanley* relates several odd and marvellous Rumours. It was the common Fame at *Athens*, that *Apollo* had condescended to visit his Mother's Bed; and the God appearing in a Vision to his Father, required him to refrain the Company of his Wife till after her Delivery. A pretty Artifice, sometimes used by the *Pagan* Women, to delude their Credulous Husbands. He had a plentiful Fortune, and after he had been a Scholar of *Socrates* for a while, he Travelled to hear the Greatest Masters of his Time. In *Italy* he studied the *Pythagorick* Doctrines, and seems to have drawn many Things out of the Books of *Moses*, which he might probably have met with in his Voyages. He passes with some for the Inventor of Dialogue, but Mr. *Stanley* pretends he did only refine and polish it, and thinks the Analytick Way of Reasoning, a Noble Invention, ought to be ascribed to him. This is the Method of Discovering Truth, by supposing the Thing sought as true or known, and enquiring what the Consequents are.

Mr. *DesCartes* has given us an illustrious Instance of the Use of this Method in his *Meditations* and *Method*, where the chief Truths of Philosophy are demonstrated with great Force and Exactness. The Examples of this Method are to be found in the Books of *Euclid*, *Appollanius*, *Pappus*, and other places of the Old Geometers, as Mr. *Stanley* has marked. *Plato* thought Mathematical Learning of Use in all Parts of Humane Knowledge, and requires all his Scholars to be previously instructed in the Elements of Geometry.

His Philosophy was held in Veneration in the first Ages of Christianity, which Mr. *Stanley* thinks proceeded from his teaching, that God had one only begotten Son, whose Power extended over all Creatures. In short, his Notions are in many Points agreeable to the Scheme of our Religion.

Plato held the Soul was Immaterial and Immortal; that it was Free and Independent, but subject to Necessity or Fate.

He

He had a Great and Noble Genius, and surprizes the Mind with the Eloquence of his Stile, and the Abundance of his Imagination. To give us a more Compleat Idea of his Philosophy, Mr. *Stanley* presents us with an Abridgement of the Doctrines of the Old Academy out of *Cicero*, and after that a Compleat Summary. Several Collections of this Kind are found in *Plutarch*, *Laertius*, *Apuleius*, but our Author passing these by, has chosen that of *Alciucus*, as most perfect and compleat, and annexed it entire as an Appendix to the Life of this Philosopher. In the last place, to illustrate the Matter, he has inserted a Platonick Discourse, written after a Poetical manner in Italian by the Famous *John Picus*, Earl of *Mirandola*.

After the Death of *Plato*, his Disciples divided into two Sects, the first remained in the old Academy, the other took Possession of the Lycæum. The rest were call'd *Peripateticks*, of whom *Aristotle*, a Native of *Staggra*, was chief. Neither his Birth nor Education were so advantageous as *Plato*. Mr. *Stanley* denies that he ever practised as a Quack, or sold Remedies at *Athens*. This, and the pretended Divine, Honours paid to his Wife *Pythias*, and being concerned in a Plot against *Alexander*, Mr. *Stanley* rejects as Calumnies groundless and injurious to the Memory of so Great a Man. He made great Improvements in Logick as well as other Parts of Philosophy, invented Categories, formed the Syllogism, and determined several Modes and Figures, detected the Arts of Sophistry, writ a great Number of Books of Metaphysicks, Physicks, Natural History of Animals, *&c.*

The Fortune of this Philosopher is very strange; and it is surprising to find Men judge so differently of the same Person, in one Age: Men have been excommunicated and treated as Hereticks for reading him to their Disciples: At other times he has been Introduced into Schools and Universities, and no other Doctrine taught to their Scholars. His Writings in one Age have been made the Standard of Truth. He has been stiled the Genius of Nature, and his Performances the highest Pitch of humane Wit. Again, at others his Philosophy has been treated as Trifling, Verbose, Empty and Litigious. However it be, Mr. *Stanley* has given a curious and exact Abstract of his Doctrine.

Another Branch of the School of *Socrates* were the *Cynicks*. *Antisthenes* was the Chief of these, which after was made

made famous by *Diogenes* his Scholar. It is Difficult to determine whence this Name took its Rise. Mr. *Stanley* thinks partly from the *Cynosarges*, the *Gymnasium* or School of *Antisthenes*, and partly the Roughness and Severity of their Manners. *Diogenes* was the most considerable of this Sect, and made so great a Noise by the Singularity of his Maxims, that *Alexander* had the Curiosity to see him. His odd manner of living in a Tub, his seeking Honest Men with a Candle and Lantern at Noon, and the other pleasant Incidents of his Life, are all collected by Mr. *Stanley*.

The Sect of *Stoicks* had its Original from that of the *Cynicks*. *Zeno* was the Author of this, who having first been a Scholar of *Crates*, and afterwards a Hearer of other Philosophers, at last instituted this New Sect. This Philosophy has formed Great Men, and charmed a World of People by its Proud and Ostentatious Principles. It aims to fortifie Men against Bodily Torments, and Arm them against the Blows of Fortune. *Zeno* admitted only one God, whose different Powers and Operations were exprest by several Names. The Sovereign Happiness of Man he placed in Virtue as the only Means to make him Immortal, and afford him a Solid and Lasting Pleasure. He thought the Frame of the World would one Day be dissolved, and perish in Flames. That Absolute Empire of Man over his Body and Mind, which he so highly asserted, gave rise to that pernicious Doctrine, that any one might lawfully destroy himself. And yet there is some thing in this Philosophy which is bright and glorious, and capable of dazling the Sight of those who only look at the Splendor of the *Pagan* Virtues; with what an Air did *Zeno* teach his Wise Men the Contempt of Death, and an Indifference for the Things of the World?

The *Stoicks* were subtil *Logicians* as well as excellent *Moralists*, but we must not enter into particulars. Mr. *Stanley* has collected the Remains out of *Laertius*, *Cicero*, *Stobæus*, and others, and given us a Large Summary of that Philosophy at the End of the Life of this Philosopher. Besides *Zeno*, were eminent *Cleanthes*, *Chrysippus*, *Panætius*, *Posidonius*, and others, all whom have Justice done them by our Author.

The *Stoicks* were the last of all the Philosophers derived from *Thales*, and conclude the Succession of the *Ionick* School.

Pythagoras, whom most believe a *Samian*, was Chief of the *Italick* Sect. He continued a great while in *Ægypt* to learn their Mysteries. Mr. *Stanley* tells us, that He was made Prisoner by *Cambyses*, who sent him to *Babylon*, where He became familiar with the *Magi* and *Chaldeans*, and was acquainted with the Prophet *Ezekiel*. He was a Comely Man, and had a Majestick Mien proper to attract the Veneration of the People, and was thought by his Followers to be Hyperborean *Apollo*.

No Philosopher had more Disciples than *Pythagoras*. He enjoyned an exact Submission to all he said, and imposed a rigorous Silence on his Scholars for two Years. Temperance was the Virtue which he most earnestly recommended as most necessary to bring the Body to an entire Subjection. His Philosophy was Cabalistick, and full of Mysteries. He held the Pre-existence of the Soul, and its Migration from one Body to another. Thus he reported in his Writings of himself, that before the *Trojan* War he was *Æthalides* the Son of *Mercury*, then *Euphorbus*, then *Hermotimus*, then *Pyrrhus* a *Delian*, lastly, *Pythagoras*. In his Writings he reports that he came 207 Years since from the *Inferi*, and other Extravagancies. After his Life, Mr. *Stanley* has annexed an Account of his Discipline and Doctrine, his Symbolical Way of Teaching, and transcribed into his Works the Learned *Reuchlius* Explanation of the Pythagorick Doctrine. Of this Sect were *Empedocles*, *Archytus*, *Philolaus*, and to them it must be own'd we are indebted for the True System of the Universe, which places the Sun in the Center, and the Earth in the Planetary *Chorus*.

The Sects which spring from the *Italick* may be reduced to four, the *Heraclitian*, the *Eleatick*, the *Sceptick*, or *Pyrrhonian*, and the *Epicurean*.

Heraclitus, by the advantage of a Good Genius, was Master of that Knowledge, which others acquire with Difficulty and painful Researches.

His Contemplative Humour and Disdain for the World made him love Retirement and Solitude. He withdrew from the Society of Men, and spent his Time in the Solitary Top of a Mountain, in seriously bemoaning the Follies and Vanity of the World.

Democritus, the Head of the *Eleatick* Sect, was of a Temper very different from *Heraclitus*: He had a smiling Countenance, and diverted himself with Laughing at the Ridiculous Passion which Men discover'd for Trifles, the
Diligence

Diligence and Pains they used to obtain them, and the Regret and Grief they shew'd upon any Loss or Disappointment. The People of *Abdera*, among whom he lived, observing him to laugh frequently, began to doubt of his Good Sense, and sent for *Hippocrates* to cure him. But having shewn his *Diacosmus*, the Opinion they had of his Folly was soon converted into Admiration. He was the first Inventer of the Doctrine of *Atoms* and a *Vacuum*, or the *Corpuscular Phylosophy*, the Elements of which Mr. *Stanley* has deliver'd.

Pyrrho was Chief of the *Scepticks*. He affirmed Man could only Judge by Appearances of Truth and Falshood, and therefore Pretended the Mind only ought to continue in suspence, and not determine any thing. All the Subtilty of these Gentlemen lay in finding Reasons of Diffidence and Distrust in Matters which appeared Plain and Evident. The Curious will find their Entire Philosophy in its proper place.

The Author of the last Sect was *Epicurus*, whom our Author tells us writ more than any other of the Philosophers. He placed the Sovereign Good in Virtuous Pleasure. The wrong Interpretation of his Opinions, and the Abuse of them by his Disciples, has brought his Philosophy into Disrepute, and caused it to be decried as the Source of all Vice and Immorality. But Mr. *Stanley* affirms the Weakness of his Constitution, and his extreme Sobriety, ought to remove so injurious a Charge. Besides, the Altars erected to his Honour after his Death will not suffer us to believe him so voluptuous a Man as his Enemies would represent him. Every one knows he taught *Atoms* and a *Void* to be the Principles of things held, and contrary to *Aristotle* and others, that the World was not Eternal. Nay, he affirms it bears sensible Marks of its Newness; urging for Instance, the Rise of Arts and Sciences as undeniable Proofs of its small Continuance. *Lucretius* in his Elegant Poem has given us his Doctrine of the Universe, Providence, the Principles of Things; and *Gassendus*, who revived his Philosophy in this Age, has written his Life.

It is Time now to proceed to the three last parts of this large Work, which contain an Account of the *Chaldaick*, *Persian*, and *Sabæan* Learning. As the *European* Sciences had their Source in *Greece*, so the Philosophy of those People was derived from the Eastern Nations, whose Original is very obscure. The Writings of the Ancient Sages are long since perished, and *Plato* and *Pythagoras*, who have mixed ed their Tenets with their Philosophy, have done it in such manner, that it is hard to distinguish what they have borrowed from their own Inventions. This Difficulty has rather animated than discouraged Mr. *Stanley*, who with mighty care has amassed the scatter'd Fragments, and by digesting what is Genuine, has compiled an Idea of the Oriental Learning.

The *Chaldeans* in the Time of *Alexander*, pretended they had continued to observe the Stars for 470000 Years. But this must be regarded as an Empty Boast, since all the Observations they could then produce, as Mr. *Stanley* assures us, did fall short of two Thousand Years, and there is nothing extant, at present, of their *Astronomy* more ancient than the Æra of *Nabonaffar*, or the 3967th Year of the *Julian* Period.

Zoroaster is commonly own'd as the first Author of Arts and Sciences amongst the *Chaldeans*, but who He was, or in what Age He lived, is dark and uncertain. His Disciples, the *Magi*, propagated this Learning, which was introduced into *Greece* by *Berosus* before or about the Time of *Alexander*.

The Eastern Learning was not taught in Schools to a promiscous Audience, but confined to certain Families, the Father of whom instructed his Children, and by this Means convey'd his Mysterious Knowledge to Posterity. Their Wisemen were regarded by the Vulgar as sacred Persons, and had a separate Habitation, enjoying great Priviledges, and an Exemption from Publick Charges. They were divided into Several Kinds or Sects, according to the Subject of their Studies, as *Naturalists, Priests, Astrologers,* &c.

Their Great Master *Zoroaster* divided all Things into three Kinds. The first Eternal, without Beginning or End. The next Immortal, which had Beginning, but no End. And the last Mortal and Corruptible. They thought the First of all Things was Eternal and Supreme God, whom they termed Father and King, and placed his Essence in Light and Truth.

After God, were their Good and Ill *Dæmons*, which they conceived to inhabit the Regions of Fire, Air, Water, and Earth. The former they fancied to dwell in the Light of the Divine Presence, and were the
Mi-

Ministers and Messengers of God. The latter, whom they supposed to be Spirits of Darkness, did wander up and down, and were Enemies and Haters of Mankind, and continually seeking to Hurt and Destory them. Of these they thought the Earth, and Sea, and their most retired Cavities and Depths were full. Of the Ill *Dæmons* they accounted some to be worse than others. Those who kept their Residence in the Air they thought to be Wanton and Sportive, who either Diverted Men with their Capricious Tricks, or Inspired them with Sanguine and Amorous Thoughts. On the contrary, those which frequented solitary and dark places, or lodg'd in the Caverns of the Earth, were extremely Malignant and Fierce, and like wild Beasts, attacked and tore in Pieces whomsoever they met. If by the Permission of Heaven they were suffered to remove their Seats they enter'd into the Bodies of Men, threw them into Madness, Epilepsies, Convulsions, and other Dismal and Affrighting Distempers.

After the Immaterial Beings, the next Order were the Corporeal Worlds, of which they accounted Seven; one *Empyreal*, three *Etherial*, and three more *Material*, by which they meant the Terrestrial Globe compos'd of Water, Air and Earth.

We have said enough of their *Theology*, and *Physicks*, the next Branch of the *Chaldaick* Learning was their Arts of *Prognostick*, or *Presages* of *Future Events*. The chief of these were *Astrology*, *Augury*, *Interpretation of Dreams*, *Explanation of Prophecies*, and other like Mystical Sciences.

The third Part of the Wisdom these Sages were Famous for, was their *Magick Natural* and *Theurgick*. By the Help of the former they pretended to have a great Power over the Natural World, to drive away Wild-Beasts and Venomous Creatures, to preserve the Fruits of the Earth, to keep off Storms and Tempests, Thunder, and what not. By the latter they affirm'd they could command *Dæmons*, and call the Good to their Aid and Assistance, and repel and chase the Malignant ones. I shall not enter further into an Enumeration, but leave the Reader to see the Original, where Mr. *Stanley* has given us a large and ample Account of the Worship, Religions, Rites, Arts and Sciences of these Nations.

An Account of the Life and Writings

Having thus given a View of the History of Philosophy, we shall proceed to the rest of his Learned Labours, which are either Printed, or remain in Manuscript in the Hands of the Curious.

When Mr. *Stanley* had happily Finish'd this Work, and before he was Twenty Eight Years of Age, he undertook *Æschylus*, the most knotty and intricate of all the *Greek* Poets, and in the Year 1663. after a World of Pains spent in illustrating and restoring him, he published his Accurate and Beautiful Edition of that Author. This was a Work of great Difficulty, and an Enterprize worthy of Mr. *Stanley*'s Abilities and great Skill in the *Greek* Language. *Henry Stephens*, *Salmasius*, and divers other Criticks, thought the Difficulties insuperable, and despair'd of seeing this Accomplished.

<small>Quis Æschylum possit affirmare Græcè nunc scienti, magis patere explicabilem, quam Evangelia & Epistolas Apostolicas. Unus ejus *Agamemnon* superat obscuritate quantum est Librorum Sacrorum cum suis Hebraismis & Syriasmis & toto Hellenisticâ supellectile vel Farragine. CC. Salmas. de Hellenisticâ Ep. Ded. P. 37.</small>

Six Tragedies of this Poet were first of all published by *Aldus* at *Venice* in the Year 1518. After this *Adrian Turnebus* printed them with various Readings at the end in 1558. The same Year they came out at *Venice* Revised by *Roboretus*, who added his own Conjectures, together with those of *Michael Sophianus*, and in this Edition the *Choephoræ* was first added with *Scholia* out of the Ancient Copies. Not long after the whole came out all more Correct than before, by the Care of *Petrus Victorius* from the Press of *Henry Stephens*. In the last place, these Seven Tragedies were published by *G. Cauterus* at *Antwerp* in 1580. in which Edition, besides the Correction of an infinite number of Faults, there is an Account given of his Versification. *Isaac Causabon* in his Notes upon *Strabo* declares his intent to publish and illustrate *Æschylus*; but either he did nothing in it, or his Labours have perished, to the great detriment of Learning.

After these Great Men, Mr. *Stanley* engaged in this Work, and what he has done in it, may be drawn from the Account himself has premised to his Edition. The *Greek* Text he has taken from the *Cauterian* Edition, and the *Scholia* from *Victorius*, to which, that he might omit nothing, he has annext the various Readings, Epistles, Prefaces, Conjectures and Observations. He has farther Collated the former Tragedies, with Two Manuscripts, the one in the *Bodleyan*, and the other in the *Arundellian* Library, both of which were Lent him by Mr. *Selden*. By means of the first he has enriched the *Scholiast* on the first Three Tragedies, and by help of the latter published a *Scholiast* which never before saw the Light. The Account of the Versification which *Cauterus* published, he has Amended, Collected the Fragments, made a New *Latine* Translation; and lastly, Compleated the who Work with a most Learned Commentary.

Besides these Monuments of his Learning which are published, there are divers other Proofs of his unwearied Application remaining still in Manuscript, all or most of which are in the Library of the Right Reverend the Lord Bishop of *Norwich*. Here are his large Commentaries on *Æschylus* in Eight Volumes in *Folio* which were never published, his *Adversaria*, or Promiscuous Remarks, in which several Passages of *Sophocles*, *Euripides*, *Stephanus de Urbibus*, *Juvenal*, *Persius*, *Hesychius*, *Callimachus*, and other Ancient Authors are amended and explained. Besides what is mentioned, there are large Prælections on *Theophrastus* his Characters, and a Critical Essay on the First-Fruits and the Tenths of the Spoil said in the Epistle to the *Hebrews* to be given by the Prophet *Abraham* to *Melchisedeck*, all which are full of Excellent Learning, and no less justly valued by their present Possessors.

And thus you have a short Account of our Author, who was a Gentleman of a Comely Aspect, and exceeded by none of his Time for Modesty, Candour and Learning.

His Contemporaries paid that Deference to him which he so well deserved; his Works were much beyond the Number of his Years; and in this he might be accounted another *Picus Mirandola*, in that he Died about the same Age, leaving our Nation exceedingly indebted to his Family for affording Two such Illustrious English Men as Sir *John Marsham* and himself.

N° 667. Thom. Stanleii Amplissimi Commentarii in Æschyli Tragædias [quos suâ manu scripsit nondum Editi] 8 Vol. Fol.
N° 668. Tho. Stanleii Adversaria in quibus Sophoclis Euripidis Stephani de Urbibus Juvenalis Persii Achillis, Tatii, Theocriti, Aristidis, Parthenii, Hesychii, Antigoni, Caryftii, Callimachi loci plurimi emendantur & explicantur. Fol.
669. Tho. Stanleii Prælectiones ampliffimæ in Theophrasti Characteres.
670. Th. Stanleii ἀκροθίνια sive Exercitatio Philologica de Primitiis seu Decimis Prædæ ad vers. 4. c. 7. Epistolæ ad Hebræos. Qua nonnulla sacræ Scripturæ loca explicantur veteres aliquot Ritus eruuntur Auctores plurimi præsertim Græci, partim illustrantur partim emendantur Ind. Cod. Manuscript. Joh. Mori Episc. Norvicensis.

BOOKS

BOOKS Printed for and Sold by H. Walwyn, *at the* Three Legs *in the* Poultry, *the Corner of the* Old-Jury.

A Brief Exposition of the Church Catechism, with Proofs from Scripture. By the Right Reverend Father in God, Dr. *John Williams*, Lord Bishop of *Chichester*. The 12th Edition. Price 6 d.

The same in French, very proper for such as Learn either Language. Price 6 d.

The English Exercise for School-Boys to Translate into Latin, Comprizing all the Rules of Grammar, ascending gradually from the meanest to higher Capaties. By *J. Garretson*, School-Master, the Eighth Edition. Price 1 s.

Exercitia Latina; Or Latin for *Garretson*'s English Exercises for School-Boys to Translate Syntactically, with the Declension, Gender, Genitive Case of Nouns Substantives, Termination of Adjectives and Participles, Declension of Pronouns, Conjugations, Preter Tense, &c. of Verbs, and other Requisites for the more ready Translating English into Latin. Price 1 s.

A Christian Taught to Pray; or Instructions how to perform your Devotions to God in an acceptable manner, by way of Exposition of the Lord's Prayer. By *Jos. Stephens*, Late Lecturer of St. *Giles*'s *Cripplegate*, St. *Margaret*'s *Lothbury*, and St. *Michael Woodstreet*. Price 1 s.

Sermons on several Occasions. By the same Author. Price 1 s.

The *London* Spelling-Book; being a more Easie and Regular Method of Teaching to Spell, Read, and Write true English. Being easier for Children than a Primmer; and by the use of which a Person may Learn to Read without the help of any other English. Price Bound 6 d.

The Considerations of *Drexelius* upon Death. In Three Parts. First, Considerations upon Death, for such as are in Health: Containing a Well Man's Daily Thoughts upon Death. Reflections upon the various Aspects of Humane Life, on the Uncertainty, Vanity, and Misery of it; the Doctrines and Sayings of the Antient Philosophers and Fathers, concerning the present Life. A Discourse of *Assanus* a Turk. How to retain the Memory of Death in our Minds. Prayers for these Occasions. The Second Part Containing a Sick Man's Christian Behaviour. An Antidote against Grief. Examples of Pagans and Christians that have Contemn'd Death. A Mind Prepar'd for Death. The Benefit of Sickness. How we ought to Read, Pray and Think in our Sickness. The Faults of Sick People. Consolations in Sickness. Examples of Patience in Sickness. The Sick Person's Bargain with God. His perpetual Song. An Answer to all the Objections of Sick People. Prayers for the Occasions of Sick People. The Third Part Containing the Divine Art of Dying well. How to regain lost Time. What all Ages and Nations have thought of Death. How they behaved themselves at that time. Nine Wills of the Antients. Nine remarkable Epitaphs. A Dying Man's Considerations. His Farewel to the World. The Happiness of Death. The Dying Man's Invitation to Christ. Last Breathings to Heaven. His surrendring himself to God. Prayers suitable to these Occasions. This Book never before in English, now Translated by a Fellow of the Royal Society. With Cuts. Price 2 s.

Stanley's Lives of the Philosophers. *Folio*.

THE TABLE.

The First Part.

Containing those on whom the Attribute of *WISE* was conferred.

THALES.

Chap.	Page
1. THE County and Parents of Thales,	1
2. The time of his Birth,	2
3. His Travels,	3
4. How he lived at Miletus.	ibid
5. The Attribute of Wise conferred on him,	ib.
6. Of his Philosophy.	
Sect. 1. That Water is the Principle of all Things,	ib.
2. Of God.	6
3. Of Dæmons,	ib.
4. Of the Soul,	7
5. Of the World,	ib.
7. Of his Geometry,	8
Sect. 1. Propositions invented by him,	ib.
2. Of his taking the heighth of the Pyramids,	9
8. Of his Astronomy,	ib.
Sect. 1. Of the Cælestial Spheres,	ib.
2. Of the Sun, Moon and Stars,	10
3. Of Eclipses,	ib.
4. Of the Year,	11
5. His Astrological Predictions,	ib.
9. His Moral Sentences,	ib.
10. His Judgment in Civil Affairs,	12
11. Of his Writings,	13
12. His Auditors and Scholars,	ib.
13. Of his Death,	14

SOLON.

1. Solon's Parents, Country, and Children,	15
2. How by his means the Athenians took Salamis, Cyrrha, and the Thracian Chersonesus,	16
3. How he composed Differences and Seditions at Home,	17
4. What Alterations he made during his Government, and first of the Sisacthia	19
5. How he divided the People into Classes and erected Courts of Judicature,	ib.
6. His Laws,	20
7. Of the Axes, and Cyrbes, Senators, Oaths, and other Institutions of Solon,	24
8. How he entertained Anacharsis; his Travels to Ægypt, Cyprus, Miletus, Delphi, Corinth, and Creet,	25
9. The Attribute of Wise conferred on him: His moral Sentences,	26
10. How he opposed Pisistratus and reprehended Thespis,	27
11. How he travelled to Lydia and Cilicia,	28
12. His Death,	30
13. His Writings,	ib.

CHILON.

Chap.	Page
1. Chilon's Life,	33
2. His moral Sentences, Precepts, and Verses,	34
3. His Death and Writings,	35

PITTACUS.

1. Pittacus's Life,	36
2. His moral Sentences, Precepts, and Verses,	37
3. His Death, Brother, Wife, Son, Writings,	38

BIAS.

1. Bias's Life,	39
2. His moral Sentences, Precepts, and Verses,	40
3. His Death and Writings,	41

CLEOBULUS.

1. Cleobulus's Life, Death, and Writings,	42
2. His moral Sentences, Precepts, and Verses,	43

PERIANDER.

1. The Country, Ancestors, and Parents of Periander,	44
2. The time of his Birth, his Reign, and the change of his Disposition,	45
3. Of his being placed in the number of the seven Sages. His Sentences and Writings,	46
4. The Story of Arion,	47
5. Of his Wife,	ib.
6. Of his Children,	48
7. His Death,	51

SOSIADES.

His Collection of the Precepts of the seven Sophists,	ib.
Ausonii Ludus Septem Sapientum,	53

ANACHARSIS.

1. Anacharsis's Life and Writings,	55
2. His Hpothegms,	56
MYSON,	ib.
EPIMENIDES,	57
PHERECYDES,	58

[a]   The

The Table.

The Second Part.

Containing the *Ionick* Philosophers.

ANAXIMANDER.

1. Of his Life, 60
2. Of his Opinions, 61
    Sect. 1. That Infinity is the Principle of all Things, ib.
    2. Of the Heavens, ib.
    3. Of the Meteors, ib.

ANAXIMENES.

1. His Life, 62
2. His Opinions, ib.
    Sect. 1. That the Air is the principle of all Things, ib.
    2. Of the Heavens, ib.
    3. Of Meteors, ib.
1. His Country, Time, and Study of Philosophy, 63
2. Of his Opinions, ib.
    Sect. 1. Of the first Principles and Beginning of all Things, ib.
    2. Of the Heavens, ib.
    3. Of Meteors, 64
    4. Of the Earth, ib.
    5. Of living Creatures, ib.
3. His Predictions, 65
4. His Scholars and Auditors, ib.
5. Of his Tryal, Death, Sentences, and Writings, 66

ARCHELAUS, 73

The Third Part.

Containing the *Socratick* Philosophers.

SOCRATES.

1. His Country, Parents, and Time of Birth, 74
2. His first Education, 75
3. His Master, 76
4. Of his School and manner of Teaching, ib.
5. Of his Philosopy, 77
    Sect. 1. Metaphysicks, ib.
    2. Ethicks, 78
    3. Oeconomicks, 82
    4. Politicks, ib.
6. Of his Dæmon, 83
7. His Military Actions, 85
8. How he carried himself in the Democracy and the Oligarchy, 86
9. His falling out with the Sophists, and with Anytus, 87
10. His Tryal, 89
11. His Imprisonment, 91
12. The time and manner of his death, 92
13. What happen'd after his death, 94
14. Of his Person and Virtues, 95
15. His Wives and Children, 97
16. His Scholars and Auditors, 98
17. His Writings, 99
The Coulds of Aristophanes, 103

XENOPHON.

1. Xenophon's Country, Parents, and following of Socrates. 110
2. On what occasion he followed Cyrus into Asia, 115
3. How he brought off the Grcian Army, ib.
4. The end of the Retreat, 117
5. His following of Agesilaus, and Banishment, 118
6. How he lived at Scilluns and at Corinth, ib.
7. His Death, Person, Vertues, 119
8. His Writings, 120
His Epistles, 121

ÆSCHINES.

1. His Life, 123
2. His Writings, ib.

CRITO, 124
SIMON, 125
GLAUCO, ib.
SIMMIAS, ib.
CEBES, ib.
A Chronology.

The Fourth Part.

Containing the *Cyrenaick, Megarick, Eleack,* and *Eretriack* Sects.

The *Cyrenaick* Sect.

1. Aristippus's Country and Parents, 132
2. How he went to Athens and heard Socrates, 133
3. How he went to Ægina, ib.
4. His Institution of a Sect, 134.
    Sect. 1. Of Judgment and Judicatories, ib.
    2. Of the End or chief Good, ib.
    3. Of Vertue, 135
5. How he went to Dionysius's Court, ib.
6. His Æmulators, 136
7. His Apophthegms, ibid
8. His Writings, 139
9. His Death, ib.
10. His Disciples and Successors, 140

HEGESIAS.

1. His Life, 140
2. His Philosophy, ib.

ANNICERIS.

1. His Life, 141
2. His Philosophy, ib.

THEODORUS.

1. His Life, ib.
2. His Philosophy, 142
3. His Death, Writings, &c. ib.

BION.

1. His Life, 143
2. His Apophthegms, ib.
3. His Death, 144

The Table.

The MEGARICK Sect.

EUCLID.

Chap.	Page
1. His Country and Masters.	144
2. His Institution of a Sect.	ibid
3. His Apophthegm. and Writings.	ibid
EUBULIDES	145
ALEXINUS.	147
EUPHANTUS.	ibid
APOLLONIUS CHRONUS.	ibid

DIODORUS.

1. His Life,	148
2. His Philosophy.	ibid
ICHTHYAS.	148
CLINOMACHOS.	ibid

STILPO.

1. His Life.	ibid
2. His Philosophy.	150
3. His Disciples.	ibid
4. His Death and Writings.	ibid

The *Eleack* and *Eretriack* Sects.

PHÆDO.	150
PLISTHENES.	ibid

MENEDEMUS.

1. His Country, Parents, Teachers.	ibid
2. His School and Philosophy.	151
3. His manner of Living.	ibid
4. His Civil Employments.	152
5. His Vertues apophthegms.	ibid
6. His departure from *Eretria*, and Death.	153

The Fifth Part.

Containing the *Academick* Philosophers.

PLATO

1. THE Country, Parents, and time of Plato.	154
2. His first Education, Exercises, and Study.	157
3. His Masters in Philosophy, and Travels to that end.	158
4. What Authors he followed.	159
5. His School.	160
6. How he Instituted a Sect	161
Sect. 1. Ethick.	ibid
2. Physick.	ibid
3. Dialectick.	162
7. His Inventions.	ibid
8. His Distinctions.	163
9. His three Voyages to *Sicily*.	166
10. His Authority in Civil Affairs.	170
11. His Vertues and Moral Sentences.	171
12. His Will and Death.	172

Chap.	Page
13. His Disciples and Friends.	173
14. His Æmulators and Detractors.	ibid
15. His Writings.	174

The Doctrine of *Plato* delivered by *Alcinous*.

1. Of Philosophy, and how a Philosopher must be qualified.	179
2. That Contemplation is to be preferred before Action.	180
3. The trhe parts of Philosophy.	ibid
4. Dialectick.	ibid
5. The Elements and Office of Dialectick.	181
6. Of Propositions and Argumentations.	182
7. Of Theoretick Philosophy.	183
8. Of first Matter.	184
9. Of Ideas.	ibid
10. Of God.	ibid
11. Of Qualities.	185
12. Of the Causes, Generations, Elements, and Order of the World.	186
13. Of the conveniences of Figures with the Elements and World.	ibid
14. Of the Soul of the World, the Spheres, and the Stars.	187
15. Of Dæmons and Elements.	ibid
16. Of younger Gods makers of Men.	188
17. Of the Body and Parts of Men, and Powers of the Soul.	ibid
18. Of Sight,	ibid
19. Of the rest of the Senses.	189
20. Of Heavy and Light.	ibid
21. Of Respiration.	ibid
22. Of the causes of Diseases.	ibid
23. Of the three principal powers of the Soul.	ib.
24. Of the distinction of the parts of the Soul.	190
25. Of the Immortality of the Soul.	ibid
26. Of Fate and Free-will.	191
27. Ethick, of the chief good and of Virtues.	ib.
28. The definition and kinds of Vertue.	192
29. Of Virtues, Vices, and their differences.	201
30. That Virtue is Voluntary, Vice involuntary.	ibid
31. Of Love and Friendship.	ibid
32. Of Passions.	202
33. Of the Forms of Common-wealths.	203
34. Of a Sophist.	ibid
A *Platonick* Discourse written by *John Picus* Earl of *Mirandula*, in Explication of a Sonnet, by *Hieronymo Benivieni*.	204
The Second Part.	205
The Third Part.	206

SPEUSIPPUS.

1. His Life,	208
2. His Profession of Philosophy.	209
3. His Writings.	ibid
4. Of his Death.	ibid

XENOCRATES.

1. His County, Parents, living with *Plato*.	210
2. His Profession of Philosophy.	211
3. His Vertues and Apophthegms.	ibid
4. His Writings.	212
5. His Death.	ibid

POLEMO.

The Table.

Chap.	Page
POLEMO.	213
CRATES.	214
CRANTOR,	ibid

ARCESILAUS.

1. His Country, Parents, Teachers. 215
2. On what occasion he constituted the middle Academy. ibid
3. His Vertues and Apophthegms, 218
4. His Death. 219

LACYDES. ibid

CARNEADES.

1. His Country, Parents, Time, Masters. 220
2. How he constituted the new Academy. 221
3. On what Occasion he was sent on an Embassie to Rome. 223
4. His Vertues and Apophthegms. 224
5. His Death and Writings. ibid

CLITOMACHUS. 225
PHILO. ibid
ANTIOCHUS. 226

The Sixth Part.

Containing the *Peripatetick* Philosophy.

ARISTOTLE.

1. His Country, Parents, and time of his Birth. 227
2. His first Education and Studies. 228
3. How he heard Plato. 229
4. How he lived with Hermias. 230
5. How he lived with Philip and Alexander. ib.
6. His School and manner of Teaching. 231
7. His Philosophy. 232
8. His Correspondence with Alexander. 233
9. On what Occasion he left Athens and went to Chalcis. 234
10. His Apophthegms. ibid
11. His Will and Death. 235
12. His Person and Vertues. 236
13. His Wives and Children. ibid
14. His Disciples and Friends. 237
15. His detractors. 238
16. His Writings. ibid
17. His Commentators. 241
18. His Epistles. 243

The Doctrine of *Aristotle*.

The First Part.

1. Of Philosophy in General, and in Particular of Dialectick. 244
2. Of Terms. ibid
3. Of Propositions. 245
4. Of Syllogisms. ibid
5. Of Apodeictick or demonstrative Syllogism. 246
6. Of Dialectick Syllogism. 247
7. Of Sophistick Sillogism. ibid

The Second Part.

Chap.	Page
1. Of Physick.	248
2. Of the Principles of Natural Bodies.	ib.
3. Of Nature, and the cause of Natural Bodies.	ib.
4. Of the Affections of Natural Bodies, Motions, Place, and Time.	249
5. Of the kinds and properties of Motion.	ib.
6. Of the first mover.	ibid
7. Of Heaven.	250
8. Of Elements.	251
9. Of Generation, Corruption, Alteration, Augmentation and Diminution.	ibid
10. Of Action a Passion.	252
11. Of Mixtion and Temperament.	ibid
12. Of imperfect mixt Bodies.	253
13. Of perfect mixt Bodies.	254
14. Of Plants and Animals.	255
15. Of the Soul.	ibid
16. Of the Nutritive Faculty.	256
17. Of the Sensitive Faculty.	ibid
18. Of common Sense.	257
19. Of Phantasie and Cogitation.	ibid
20. Of Memory and Reminiscence.	258
21. Of Sleep and Waking.	ibid
22. Of Dreams.	ibid
23. Of the Intellectual Faculty.	ibid
24. Of the motive Faculty.	ibid
25. Of Life and Death.	259 ibid

The Third Part.

1. Of Ethick. 260
2. Of Oeconomick. 265
3. Of Politick. ibid

The Fourth Part.

1. Of Metaphysick. 266
2. Of the first Principle. ibid
3. Of the substance and accident. ibid
4. Of Power and Act. 267
5. Of True and False. ibid
6. Of one, the same, and diverse. 268
7. Of Immortal, Eternal, and Immoveable Substances. ibid
8. Of Gods. ibid
9. Of Intelligencies. 269

THEOPHRASTUS.

1. His Country, Parents, Masters. ibid
2. His profession of Philosophy and Disciples. ib.
3. His Vertues and Apophthegms. ibid
4. His Will and Death. 270
5. His Writings. 271

STRATO.

1. His Life. 272
2. His Will and Death. ibid
3. His Writings. 273

LYCO.

1. His Life. 274
2. His Will and Death. ibid

ARISTO. 375
CRITOLAUS. 276
DIODORUS. ibid

The Table.

The Seventh Part.

Containing the *Cynick* Philosophers.

ANTISTHENES.

Chap.	Page
1. His Life.	277
2. His Institution of a Sect.	278
3. His Apophthegms.	279
4. His Writings.	280
5. His Death.	281

DIOGENES.

1. His Country, Parents, Time, Banishment.	282
2. How he lived at Athens.	283
3. How he lived at Corinth.	284
4. His Philosophy.	ibid
5. His Apophthegms.	285
6. His Writings.	291
7. His Death.	ibid
MONIMUS.	292
ONESECRITUS.	ibid
CRATUS.	ibi.
METROCLES.	293
HIPPARCHIA.	294
MENIPPUS.	ibid
MENEDEMUS.	ibid

The Eighth Part.

Containing the *Stoick* Philosophers.

ZENO.

1. His Country, Parents, first Studies.	295
2. Of his Masters.	296
3. His School and Institution of a Sect.	ibid
4. What Honours were conferred on him.	297
5. His Apophthegms.	ibid
6. His Death.	299
7. His Person and Vertues.	300
8. His Writings.	301
9. His Disciples.	ib.

The Doctrine of the *Stoicks*.

Of Philosophy in General	302
1. Of Dialectick.	ibid
2. Of Instruments and Rules of Judgment.	303
3. Of Sense.	304
4. Of Phantasie.	ibid
5. Of True and Truth.	305
6. Of Comprehension.	ib.
7. Of Assent.	ibid
8. Of Notions.	306
9. Of Science and Opinion.	ibid
10. Of Voice, Speech, and Words.	ib.
11. Of Definition and Division.	307
12. Of Genus, Species, &c.	308
13. Of Things.	ibid
14. Of Subjects.	ibid
15. Of Qualitatives.	ibid
16. Of Quodammotatives.	309
17. Of Quodammotatives as to others.	ibid
18. Of Decibles.	310
19. Of Categorems,	ibid

Chap.	Page
20. Of Simple Axioms.	311
21. Of not Simple Axioms.	ibid
22. Of contrary Axioms.	312
23. Of Possible, Impossible; Necessary, and unnecessary, Probable, Paradoxal, and Reasonable Axioms..	ibid
24. Of reciprocal Axioms.	313
25. Of Signs.	ibid
26. Of Reason or Arguments.	314
27. Of conclusive Reasons.	ibid
28. Of Syllogism	ib.
29. Of Moods,	315
30. Of not Syllogistick conclusive Reasons,	ib.
31. Of not conclusive Reasons.	316
32. Of Fallacious Reasons or Sophisms.	ibid
33. Of Method.	ibid

Ethick.

1. Ethick, and the parts thereof.	317
2. Of Appetite.	ibid
3. Of first natural Appetite.	ibid
4. Of Appetites consequent to the first.	318
5. Of good and ill.	ibid
6. Of Eupathies.	319
7. Of Passions.	ibid
8. Of Sickness and Infirmities.	320
9. Of Vertue and Vice.	321
10. Of the End.	ibid
11. Of Indifferents.	322
12. Of Estimation.	ibid
13. Of Actions and Offices.	324
14. Of Præter-offices.	325
15. Of Wise and Vertuous Persons Paradoxes.	ib.

Physick.

1. Physick, and the parts thereof.	326
2. Of Bodies.	ib.
3. Principles.	ibid
4. Of Matter,	327
5. Of the World.	ibid
6. Of Elements.	328
7. Of Fire.	329
8. Of Stars.	ibid
9. Of the Sun.	330
10. Of the Moon.	ibid
11. Of Air.	ibid
12. Of Water and Earth.	331
13. Of Mistion and Temperament.	ib.
14. Of Generation and Corruption.	ibid
15. Of Motion.	332
16. Of living Creatures.	ib.
17. Of God.	333
18. Of Nature.	334
19. Of Fate.	335
20. Of Incorporeals, and first of Decibles.	336
21. Of Vacuum and Place.	ibid
22. Of Time.	ibid

CLEANTHES.

1. His Life.	337
2. His Apophthegms.	ibid
3. His Writings.	338
4. His Death.	339

The Table.

CHRYSIPPUS.

Chap.	Page
1. His Life.	ib.
2. His Apophthegms.	340
3. His Writings.	ibid
4. His Death.	343
ZENO.	ibid
DIOGENES.	344
ANTIPATER.	ibid
PANÆTIUS.	ibid
POSIDONIUS.	ibid
Francis Lord Virulam's *Judgment on the Philosophers*.	345
Mr. Montagu's.	ib.

The Ninth Part.

Containing the *Italick* Sect.

PYTHAGORAS.

1. THE Country, Parents, and Time of Pythagoras.	346
2. His first Education and Masters.	348
3. How he Travelled to Phœnicia.	349
4. How he Travelled to Ægypt.	ib
5. How he went to Babylon.	350
6. How he returned to Samus.	351
7. How he went to Delus, Delphi, Crete, and Sparta.	ib.
8. How he went to Olympia and Phlius.	352
9. How he lived at Samus.	ib.
10. His Voyage to Italy.	353
11. His arrival at Crotona, and upon what occasion he became eminent there.	354
12. His Oration to the Young Men.	355
13. His Oration to the Senators.	356
14. His Oration to the Boys.	357
15. His Oration to the Women.	ib.
16. His Institution of a Sect in Private and Publick.	358
17. His Authority in Civil Affairs.	ib.
18. Wonders related of him.	360
19. His Death.	361
20. His Person and Vertues.	364
21. His Wife, Children, Servants.	365
22. His Writings.	366
23. His Disciples.	368
24. The Succession of his School.	369

The Discipline and Doctrine of Pythagoras.

1. The great Authority and Esteem of Pythagoras among his Disciples.	371
2. The two sorts of Auditors, and first of the exoterick, how he exploded them.	372
3. Purificative Institution, by Sufferings.	ib.
4. Silence.	ib
5. Abstinence, Temperance, and other ways of Purification.	363
6. Community of Estates.	ib.
7. Admission or Rejection of the Exoterick Disciples.	ib.
8. Distinction of those that were admitted to be Esotericks.	ib.
9. How they disposed the day.	374
10. How they examined their Actions Morning and Evening.	375
11. Secrecy.	376

1. Sciences *preparative* to Philosophy.	377
2. Mathematick, its Name, Parts.	ibid

SECT. 1. Arithmetick. 378

1. Number, its kinds; the first kind Intellectual, in the Divine Mind.	ibid
2. The other kind of Number, Sciential, its Principles.	ibid
3. The two kinds of Sciential Numbers, odd and even.	379
4. Symbolical Numbers.	ibid
5. The Monad.	380
6. The Duad.	ib.
7. The Triad.	381
8. the Tetrad.	ibid
9. The Pentad.	382
10. The Hexad.	383
11. The Heptad.	ib.
12. The Ogdoad.	ib.
13. The Ennead.	384
14. The Decad.	ibid
15. Divination by Numbers.	ibid

SECT. 2. Musick. 385

1. Voice, its kind.	ib.
2. First Musick in the Planets.	386
3. Octochord.	ibid
4. The Arithmetical proportions of Harmony.	ib.
5. The division of the Diapason, according to the Diatonick kind.	387
6. The Canon of the Monochord.	388
7. Institution by Musick.	ib.
8. Medicine by Musick.	389

SECT. 3. Geometry. 390

1. Of a Point, Line, Superficies, Solid.	ib.
2. Propositions.	ib.
3. How he collected the Statues of Hercules.	391

SECT. 4. Astronomy. ib.

1. The System of the Spheres.	ib.
2. The Motions of the Planets.	392
3. The intervals and Harmony of the Spheres	393
4. Of the Planet Venus.	394
5. Philosophy, it Name, Definition, Parts Method.	ib.

SECT. 1. Practick Philosophy, its parts; and first of Pædeutick. 395

1. Institution, Silence, Abstinence.	ibid
2. Fortitude.	396
3. Temperance and Continuance.	ib.
4. Sagacity and Wisdom.	398

SECT. 2. Of Politick, the other part of Practick Philosophy. ibid

1. Comon Conversation.	ibid
2. Friendship.	ibid
3. Worship of the Gods.	399
4. Piety to the Dead.	400

Chap.

The Table.

Chap.	page
5. *Reverence of Parents, and Obedience to the Law.*	ib.
6. *Law-making.*	401

SECT. 3. *Theoretick* Philosophy, *its parts; and first of the Science concerning the intelligibles.* ibid
1. *Of the supream God.* ibid
2. *Of Gods, Dæmons, Heroes.* ibid
3. *Of Fate and Fortune.* ibid
4. *Divination.* 402

SECT. 4. Physick, ib.
1. *Principles.* ib.
2. *Of the World.* 404
3. *Of the Superior or Æthrial parts of the World.* 405
4. *Of the Sublunary parts of the World.* ib.
5. *Of living and animate creature.* ibid
6. *Of the Generation of animate Creatures.* ib.
7. *The Soul, its parts; and first of the irrational part.* 406
8. *Of the Rational part of the Soul, the Mind.* 407
9. *Of the Transmigration of the Soul.* ib.
10. *The separate life of the Soul.* 408

SECT. 5. *Medicine.* ib.
1. *Diætstick.* ib.
2. *Therapeutick.* 409

1. *Pythagoras his Symbolical way of teaching.* 410
2. *The Symbols of* Pythagoras, *according to* Jamblicus. ibid
3. *An Explication of the* Pythagorick *Symbols, by* Jamblicus. 411
4. *The same Symbols explained by others.* 416
5. *Other Simbols.* 418
The Golden Verses of Pythagoras. 419
Timæus *the Locrian, of the Soul of the World, and of Nature.* ib.
An Explication of the Pythagorick *Doctrine by* John Reuchlin. 423
1. *Of* Pythagoras *his way of teaching by Silence and Symbols.* ib.
2. *The Tripple World.* 424
3. *The Supream World.* ib.
4. *The Intelligible World.* 426
5. *The Sensible World.* 427
6. *The State of the Soul after Death.* ib.
7. *Of the Pythagorical Transmigration.* 428

EMPEDOCLES.
1. *His Country, Parents.* 429
2. *His Masters.* 430
3. *How he lived among the* Agrigentines; *his Power and Authority.* ib.
4. *Wonders related of him.* 431
5. *His Death.* 432
6. *His Writings.* ib.
7. *His Opinions.* ibid

EPICHARMUS.	433
ARCHYTAS.	434
ALCMÆON.	436
HIPPASUS.	ibid
PHILOLAUS.	ibid
EUDOXUS	437

The Tenth Part.

Chap.	Page

HERACLITUS.
1. *His Country, Parents, Masters.* 438
2. *How he lived at* Ephesus. 439
3. *His retirement.* ib.
4. *His Sickness and Death.* 441
5. *His Apophthegms.* 442
6. *His Writings.* 443
7. *His Doctrine.* ib.

Sect. 1. *That Fire is the Principle of all things.* ibid
2. *Of the Stars, Sun, Moon, Day, Night, &c.* 444
3. *Of the Ebbing and Flowing of the Sea.* ib.
4. *Of living Creatures.* ib.

The Eleventh Part.

XENOPHANES.
1. *His Life.* 445
2. *His Opinions.* 446

PARMENIDES.
1. *His Life.* 447
2. *His Opinions.* ib.
3. *Idea's.* 448

MELISSUS.
1. *His Life.* 449
2. *His Opinions.* ibid

ZENO.
1. *His Life.* 450
2. *His Inventions of Dialectick.* ibid
3. *His Opinions.* 451

LEUCIPPUS. 452

DEMOCRITUS.
1. *His Country, Parents, Brethren, Time.* 453
2. *His first Education, and Masters.* 454
3. *His Travels.* ibid
4. *How he lived at* Abdera, *after his return from Travels.* 455
5. *His Retirement.* ibid
6. *His Communication with* Hippocrates. 456
7. *His Death.* 461
8. *His Writing.* ibid
9. *Physick.* 462

Sect. 1. *Of the Principles of things, Atoms, and Vacuum.* ibid
2. *Of the motion of the Atoms in Vacuum, whereby all things are made.* 463
3. *Of the Generation, Corruption, Alterations and Qualities of Compounds.* ib.
4. *Of the World.* 464
5. *Of the Heavens.* ibid

The Table.

Chap.	Page
6. Of Air, Earth, Water.	ib.
7. Of the Generation of living Creatures.	465
8. Of the Soul.	ib.
9. Of the Gods.	ib.
10. Ethick.	ibid

PROTAGORAS.

1. His Country, Father, and the occasion upon which he studied Philosophy.	468
2. His Opinions and Writings.	ib.
3. His Death.	469

ANAXARCHUS. ibid

The Twelfth Part.

Containing the *Sceptick* Sect.

PYRRHO.

1. His Country, Parentage, Time, Masters.	470
2. His Institution of a Sect.	471
3. His manner of Life.	ibid
4. His Death and Disciples.	472

TIMON.

1. His Life.	473
2. His Death and Writings.	474
3. Succession of the School.	ib.

A Summary of Scepticism, by *Sextus Empiricus.*

1. The three differences of Philosophers in General.	475
2. The parts of Scepticism.	ib.
3. The names of Scepticism.	ib.
4. What Scepticism is.	ibid
5. The Principles of Scepticism.	476
6. Whether the Sceptick Dogmatizeth, and hath a Sect, and treats of Physick.	ibid
7. Whether the Sceptick takes away Phænomena's	ibid
8. The Criteri of Scepticism.	ibid
9. The end of Scepticism.	477
10. The general ways (or places) of Scepticism.	ibid
11. The ten common places of Suspension.	ib.
12. The first common place.	478
13. Whether the Creatures, commonly termed Irrational, have Reason.	479
14. The second common place	480
15. The third common place.	481
16. The fourth common place.	ibid
17. The fifth common place	483
18. The sixth common place.	ibid
19. The seventh common place.	ib.
20. The eighth common place.	484
21. The ninth common place	ib.
22. The tenth common place.	ibid
23. The five common places.	485
24. Two other common places.	486
25. The places for Confutation of Ætiologicks.	ib.
26. The phrases of the Scepticks.	487
27. Wherein Scepticism differs from those Philosophical Sects, which are most like it; and first wherein it differs from the Philosophy of Heraclitus.	488
28. Wherein Scepticism differs from the Philophy of Democritus.	ib.
29. Wherein Scepticism differs from the Cyrenaick Sect.	489
30. Wherein Scepticism differs from the Institution of Protagoras.	ibid
31. Wherein Scepticism differs from the Academick Philosophy.	ib.
32. Whether Empirical Medicine be the same with Scepticism.	490

Of DIALECTICK.

1. Whether a Sceptick can examine or dispute against Assertion.	491
2. From whence the Inquisition against Dogmatists should begin.	492
3. Of the Critery.	ibid
4. Whether there be any Critery of Truth?	ib.
5. Of the Critery in which.	ib.
6. Of the Critery by which.	494
7. Of the Critery according to which.	496
8. Of True and Truth.	ibid
9. Whether Truth be somthing in Nature?	497
10. Of Sign.	498
11. Whether there be any Endeictick Sign?	ib.
12. Of Demonstration.	499
13. Whether there is Demonstration?	500
14. Of Syllogisms.	501
15. Of Induction.	
16. Of Definition.	
17. Of Division.	
18. Of the Division of a word into Significations.	ibid
19. Of whole and part.	ib.
20. Of Genus and Species.	ibid
21. Of common Accidents.	507
22. Of Sophisms.	ibid
23. Of Amphibolies.	509

Of PHYSICK,

1. Of God,	511
2. Of Cause.	512
3. Whether there be any Cause of a Thing?	ib.
4. Of Material Principles.	513
5. Whether Bodies be incomprehensible?	514
6. Of Temperament.	515
7. Of Motion.	516
8. Of Local Motion.	ibid
9. Of Argumentation and Diminution.	518
10. Of Detraction and Addition.	ibid
11. Of Transposition.	519
12. Of Whole and Part.	ibid
13. Of Alteration.	ibid
14. Of Generation and Corruption.	520
15. Of Rest.	ibid
16. Of Place.	ibid
17. Of Time.	522
18. Of Number.	523
19. Of the ETHICAL part of Philosophy.	524
20. Of Goods, Ills, and Indifferents.	ibid
21. That Good is taken three ways.	ibid
22. Of Indifferents.	525

23. Whether

The Table.

Chap.	Page
23. Whether there is any thing naturally Good, Ill, or Indifferent.	ib.
24. What that *is which is* called, Art about Life.	526
25. Whether there be an Art about Life?	529
26. Whether there is in Men an Art about Life?	530
27. Whether the Art about Life can be taught?	ibid
28. Whether there be any thing taught?	ibid.
29. Whether there be a Teacher and a Learner?	531
30. Whether there be a way of Learning?	ib.
31. Whether the Art concerning Life be profitable to him that hath it?	532
32. Why the Sceptick sometimes on set purpose alledgeth weak Arguments.	ibid

The Thirteenth Part.

Containing the *Epicurean* Sect.

EPICURUS.

1. His Country, Parents, Brethren. 533
2. The time of his Birth. 534
3. Where he lived in his younger time. 535
4. His Masters. ibid
5. When, and upon what occasion he addicted himself to Philosophy, and instituted a Sect. 536
6. His School. ibid
7. How he lived with his Friends. 537
8. His Friends and Disciples. ib.
9. How much he wrote. 539
10. What Writings of his are particularly mentioned by Authors. ibid
11. His Will. 542
12. The manner of his Death. 543
13. The time of his Death. ib.
14. How dear his memory was to his followers. 544
15. With what constancy and unanimity the succession of his School flourished. ib.
16. The Successors and followers of *Epicurus*. 445
17. *Laertius, his Vindication of* Epicurus. ibid

The Doctrine of *Epicurus*.

Of *Philosophy* in General. 547

CANONICK, of the Criteries. 549
1. Of Truth and its Criteries. ib.
2. Canons of Sense, the first Critery. ib.
3. Canons of Prænotion, or Anticipation; the second Critery, 552
4. Canons of Affection or Passion, the third Critery. 554
5. Canons concerning the use of Words. ib.

PHYSICK, or of Nature. 555
§. 1. Of the Universe, or the nature of things. ib.
1. That the Universe consists of Body, and Vacuum or Place. 556
2. That the Universe is infinite, immovable, and immutable. ib.
3. Of the Divine Nature in the Universe. 557
4. Of first Matter, or of the principles of compound things in the Universe. 559
5. That there are Atoms in Nature, which are the Principles of compound Bodies. ib.

Chap.	Page
6. Of the Properties of Atoms, and first of their Magnitude.	560
7. Of the Figure of Atoms.	561
8. Of the gravity (or weight) and manifold motions of Atoms.	ibid
9. That Atoms (not the vulgar Elements or Homoiomera's) are the first principles of things.	562
10. Of the first and radical cause of Compounds, that is, of the Agent or Efficient.	563
11. Of Motion, which is the same with Action or Effection; and of Fortune, Fate, End, and Sympathetical and Antipothetical causes.	ib.
12. Of the Qualities of compound things in general	564
13. Qualities from Atoms considered according to their substance and interception of Vacuum.	565
14. Qualities springing from Attoms, considered according to the properties peculiar to each.	ib.
15. Qualities from Atoms, considered according to their properties taken together.	566
16. Of those Qualities which are esteemed the Accident of things; and particularly of Time.	567
17. Of the Generation and Corruption of Compounds.	568
18. Whence it comes, that a generated Body is in a certain kind of things, and distinguished from other things.	569

SECT. 2. Of the World. 570
1. Of the form and Figure of the World. ib.
2. Of the late beginning of the World 571
3. Of the cause of the World. ib
4. Of the Generation of the World. 572
5. Of the Vicissituds in the World. 573
6. A digression concerning Genii or Atoms. 574
7. Of the end or corruption of the World. 575
8. Of infinite Worlds. 576

SECT. 3. Of Inferiour Terrestrial things. ib.
1. Of the Earth situate in the middle of the World. 577
2. Of Earthquakes, and the Flames of Ætna. ib.
3. Of the Sea, Rivers, Fountains, and the overflowing of Nilus. 578
4. Of the properties of some Waters, and of Ice. 579
5. Of things terrestrial inanimate. ib.
6. Of the Load-stone in particular. 580
7. Of the Generation of Animals. 581
8. Of the use of Parts in Animals. 582
9. Of the Soul the intrinsick form of Animals. ib.
10. Of Sense in General, which is the Soul, (as it were) of the Soul. 583
11. Of Sight, and of the Images which glide into it. 585
12. That Seeing is performed by means of those Images. 586
13. Of Hearing. ibid
14. Of Smelling. 587
15. Of Tasting. 588
16. Of Touching. ib.
17. Of the Intellect, Mind, or Reason, and its Seat. ibid
18. That the Soul thinketh by Images which glide into it. 589

19 Of

The Table.

Chap.	Page
19. *Of the Affections or Passions of the Soul.*	590
20. *Of voluntary Motion, and particularly of Speaking, and Imposition of Names.*	591
21. *Of Sleep and Dreams.*	592
22. *Of Death.*	593

SECT. 4. *Of Superior things, as well Celestial as Aerial.* 594

1. *Of the substance and variety of the Stars.* 595
2. *Of the magnitude and figure of the Stars.* 596
3. *How the Stars move, out-run one another, and are turned round.* ibid
4. *Of the rising and setting of the Stars, and of the alternate length of days and nights.* 597
5. *Of the light of the Stars, and of the changes and spots in the Moon.* 598
6. *Of the Eclipses of the Stars, and their set periods.* ib.
7. *Of the presignifications of the Stars.* 599
8. *Of Comets, and those which are called falling Stars.* ib.
9. *Of Clouds.* 600
10. *Of Winds and Presters.* ibid
11. *Of Thunder.* ibid
12. *Of Lightning and Thunder-claps.* 601
13. *Of Rain and Dew.* 602
14. *Of Hail, Snow, and Frost.* ibid
15. *Of the Rain-bow and Halos.* 603
16. *Of Avernal places.* ibid
17. *Of Pestilence.* ibid

ETHICK, or Morals. 605

1. *Of Felicity, or the end of God, as far as Man is capable of it.* 606
2. *That Pleasure (without which, there is no notion of Felicity) is in its own Nature good.* ib.
3. *That Felicity consists generally in Pleasure.* 607
4. *That the Pleasure wherein consists Felicity is Irdolence of Body, and Tranquility of Mind.* 608
5. *Of the means to procure this Felicity; and of Vertues the chief.* 609
6. *Of Right-Reason, and Free-Will, from which the Vertues have all their praise.* 610
7. *Of the Vertues in general.* 611
8. *Of Prudence in general.* ibid
9. *Private Prudence.* 612
10. *Domestick Prudence.* 613
11. *Civil Prudence.* 614
12. *Of Temperance in general.* ibid
13. *Of Sobriety opposite to Gluttony.* 615
14. *Of Continence, opposite to Lust.* 617
15. *Of Meekness, opposite to Anger.* 618
16. *Of Modesty, opposite to Ambition.* 619
17. *Of Moderation, opposite to Avarice.* ibid
18. *Of Mediocrity, betwixt hope and despair of the future.* 620
19. *Of Fortitude in general.* 621
20. *Of Fortitude, as to fear of the gods.* 622
21. *Of Fortitude as to fear of Death.* 623
22. *Of Fortitude against corporeal pain.* 624
23. *Of Fortitude against discontent of Mind.* 625
24. *Of Justice in general.* 626
25. *Of Jus (Right) or Just, whence Justice is denominated.* ibid
26. *Of the Original of Right and Just.* 627
27. *Between whom Right and Justice is to be exercised.* 629
28. *With what right Justice is to be exercised.* 630

Chap.	Page
29. *Of Beneficence, Gratitude, Piety, Observance*	631
30. *Of Friendship.*	632
31 *Wherein Epicurus, asserting Pleasure to be the ultimate God, differs from the Cyrenaicks.*	633

The Fourteenth Part.

Of the *Chaldaick* Philosophy,

THE *Chaldæan* Philosophers, Institution and Sects. 1

SECT. I. Of the *Chaldæan* Philosophers. ib.

1. The Antiquity of the Chaldaick Learning. ib
2. That there were several Zoroasters. 2
3. Of the Chaldæan Zoroaster, institutor of the Chaldaick Philosophy. 3
4. Of Belus, another reputed Inventor of Sciences among the Chaldæans. 4
5. Other Chaldæan Philosophers. 5
6. Of Berosus, who first introduced the Chaldaick Learning into Greece. ib.

SECT. II. The *Chaldaick* Institution and Sects. 6

1. That all Professors of Learning were more peculiarly termed Chaldæans. ib.
2. Their Institution. ibid
3. Sects of the Chaldæans distinguished according to their several Habitations. 7
4. Sects of the Chaldæans distinguished according to their several Sciences. ib.

The Fifteenth Part.

The *Chaldaick* Doctrine. 8

SECT. I. Theology *and* Physick. ib.

1. Of the Eternal Being, God. ibid
2. The Emanation of Light or Fire from God ibid.
3. Of things eviternal or incorporeal. 9
4. The first Order. ibid
5. The Second Order. ibid
6. The Third Order. 10
7. Fountains and Principles. ib.
8. Unzoned God's and Zoned Gods. 11
9. Angels and Immaterial Dæmons. ib.
10. Souls. ib.
11. The Suramundane Light. 12
12. Of things Temporal or Corporeal. ib.
13. The Empyreal World. 13
14. The Æthereal Worlds. ibid.
15. The Material Worlds. ibid
16. Of Material Dæmons. 14

SECT. II. Astrology and other Arts of Divination. 16

1. Of the Stars, fixed an erratick, and of their pre-signification. ib.
2. Of the Planets. 17
3. The Divisions of the Zodiack. ib.
4. Of the Planets considered in respect of the Zodiack. 18
5. Aspects

Chap.	Page	Chap.	Page
5. *Aspects of the Signs and Planets*.	19	2. *Of* Hiſtaſpes *a great improver of the* Perſian *Learning*.	ibid
6. *Schemes*.	ibid	3. *Of* Oſthanes, *who firſt introduced the* Perſian *Learning into* Greece.	31
7. *Other Arts of Divination*.	20		

SECT. III. *Magick Natural and Theurgick*. ib.

SECT. II. *The Inſtitution and Sects of the* Perſians.

1. *Natural Magick*   21
2. *Magical Operations, their kinds.*   ib.
3. *Of the Tſilmenaia (or Teleſmes) uſed for averruncation.*   ib.
4. *Of the Tſilmenaia uſed for prediction.*   23
5. *Theurgick Magick.*   ib.
6. *Theurgick Rights.*   24
7. *Apparitions.*   ib.
8. *Material Dæmons how to be repulſed.*   25

1. *The Perſian Magi, their Inſtitution.*   ib.
2. *The Sects, Diſcipline, and Manners of the Magi.*   32

The Seventeenth Part.

The Doctrine of the *Perſians*.

1. *Theology and Phyſick.*   ib.
2. *Arts of Divination.*   33
3. *Of the Religious Rites or Magick of the Perſians.*   ibid
4. *The Gods of the* Perſians.   34

SECT. IV. *Of the Gods, and Religious Worſhip of the Chaldæans.*   ib.

1. *Of their Idolatrous Worſhip of the true God.* ib.
2. *Worſhip of other Gods, Angels, and Dæmons.* 26
3. *Worſhip of the Cæleſtial Bodies.*   ibid
4. *Of the Sun.*   ibid
5. *Of the Moon.*   27
6. *Of the Planets.*   28
7. *Of the other Stars*   29
8. *Of Fire.*   ib.
9. *Of the Air and Earth.*   ib.

The Eighteenth Part.

Of the *Sabæans*.

The *Sabæan* Philoſophers.

1. *Of the Inſtitutors of the* Sabæan *Sect.*   35
2. *Others of the* Sabæan *Sect.*   36
3. *Their Writings.*   37

The Sixteenth Part.

Of the *Perſians*.

THE *Perſian* Philoſophers, their Sects and Inſtitutions.   30

SECT. I. *Of the Perſian Philoſophers.* ib.

1. *Of the* Perſian *Zoroaſter, Inſtitutor of Philoſophy among the* Perſians.   ib.

The Nineteenth Part.

The Doctrine of the *Sabæans*.

1. *Of the Gods and Rites of the Sabæans.*   38
2. *Other Rites of the Sabæans contrary to the Levitical Law.*   39
3. *The Chaldaick Oracles of* Zoroaſter *and his Followers.*   40

The Table.

A TABLE of the PHILOSOPHERS, whose Lives, Writings, Opinions, Deaths, &c. are particularly Treated of.

A.	Page	D.		P.	Page
Alcmæon.	436	Democritus.	453	Panætius.	344
Alexinus.	147	Diogenes.	344, 282	Parmenides.	447
Anacharsis.	55	Diodorus.	148, 276	Periander.	44
Anaxagoras.	62	**E**		Phædo.	150
Anaxarchus.	469	Empedocles.	429	Pherecydes.	58
Anaximander	60	Epicharmus.	433	Philo.	225
Anaximenes.	62	Epicurus.	538	Philolaus,	436
Anniceris.	141	Epimenides.	57	Pittacus.	36
Antiochus.	226	Eubulides.	145	Plato.	154
Antipater.	344	Euclid.	144	Plisthenes.	150
Antisthenes.	277	Eudoxus.	437	Polemo.	213
Apollonius.	147	Euphantus.	147	Posidonius.	344
Arcesilaus.	215	**G**		Protagoras.	468
Archelaus.	73	Glauco.	125	Pyrrho.	470
Archytas.	434	**H**		Pythagoras.	346
Aristippus.	132, 227	Hegesias.	140	**S**	
Aristo.	375	Heraclitus.	438	Sextus Empiricus.	475
Aristotle.	227	Hipparchia.	294	Simmias.	125
Æschines.	123	Hippasus.	436	Simon.	125
B		Hystaspes.	30	Socrates.	74
Belus.	4	**I**		Solon.	15
Berosus.	5	Ichthyas.	148	The seven Sophists Precepts.	51
Bias.	39	**L**		Speucippus.	280
Bion.	143	Lacydes.	219	Stilpo.	148
C		Leucippus.	452	Strato.	272
Carmeades.	222	Lyco.	274	**T**	
Cebes.	125	**M**		Thales.	1
Chilon.	33	Melissus.	449	Theodorus.	141
Chrysippus.	339	Menedemus.	150, 150	Theophrastus.	296
Cleanthes.	337	Menippus.	294	Timæus.	419
Cleobulus.	42	Metrocles.	293	Timon.	473
Clinomachus.	148	Monimus.	292	**X**	
Clitomachus.	225	Myson.	56	Xenocrates.	210
Crantor.	214	**O**		Xenophanes.	445
Crates.	ibid	Onesicritus.	292	Xenophon.	110
Cratus.	292	Osthanes.	31	**Z**	
Crito.	124			Zeno.	292, 343, 450
Critolaus.	276			Zoroaster.	3, 30, 40

The End of the Table.

A TABLE of AUTHORS, Restored, Explained, and Noted, (or Censured) in the History of the Chaldaick and Greek Philosophy.

ANonymous Summarist of the *Chaldaick* Doctrine, frequently in the *Chaldaick* Philosophy.
Aristotle, Thal. chap. 6. sect. 1. Democr. ch. 9. sect. 6, 7, 8.
Arnobius, Chald. ch. 1 sect. 2.

Basil, Plat. ch. 1. Pyth. Doctr. sect. 1. ch. 3.
Cicero, Speusip. ch. 2. Zeno, Eleat. ch. 2.
Clemens Alexandrinus, Chald. sect. 1. c. 2. Pyth. ch. 24. Heracl. ch. 1. Democr. chap. 4.
Curtius, Chald. sect. 1. ch. 1.

Diodorus

The Table.

Diodorus Siculus, Chal. sect. 2. ch. 7. Socr. ch. 1. Pyth. doctr. ch. 10.
Diogenes, Laertius, frequently in *Greek* Philosophy.
Dinysius Halicarnassæus, Socr. ch. 16.
Epicharmus, Pla. ch. 4.
Etymologicum magnum, Solon, ch. 11.
Eustathius, Pyth. doct. sect. ch. 3. 4.
Gregor. Nazianzenus, Pyth. ch. 22.
Herodotus, Thales, ch. 10. Anacharf. ch. 1.
Hierocles, Euclid. ch. 3.
Higinus, Thal. ch. 1.
Jamblichus, frequently in the Life and Doctrine of *Pythagoras*.
Marmora Arundeliana, Chilon ch. 1. Xenophon ch. 2.
Micomachus, fequently Pyth. doctr.
Pliny, Pyth. ch. 20.
Plutarch, Pyth. ch. 19.
Porphyrius, Pyth. ch. 2. 7. doctr. ch. 1.
Proclus, Chald. doctr. sect. 2. ch. 7. Thal. ch. 7. ibid. sect. 1. Euclid ch. 3. Pyth. doctr. sect. 2. ch. 2. sect. 3. ch. 2.
Sextus Empericus, his Pyrrhonian Hypotyposes, in the Scepticism.
Socratick Epistles, Socr. Epist. 1, 5, 6, 7. Simon. Aristip. ch. 6.
Stobæus, Sto. doctr.
Strabo, Chald. sect. 2. ch. 4. Pyth. ch. 10.
Themistius, pyth. ch. 19.
Timæus, after the Life of *Pythagorus*.
Zoroastræan Oracles, after the *Chaldaick* Philosophy.

Anonymous Author of *Aristotle's* Life, Aristot. ch. 3,6, 8.
Apuleius, pyth. ch. 2.
Casaubon, Thal. ch. 1. Chilo. ch. 1.
Anaximander, sect. 2. ch. 2. Xenoph. ch. 1.
Eugubinus, pla. ch. 4.
Gassendus, Democr. ch. 9. sect. 3. Epic. ch. 2.
Kircher, Chald. sect. 1. ch. 2. and frequently in the *Chaldaick* Doctrine.
Leo Allatius, Socrat. ch. 1. 12. Epist. 1. 6. Xenoph. Epist. 5. 8. Simon. Aristip. ch. 8.
Lipsius, Zeno, Eleat. ch. 2.
Leucas Holstenius, pyth. ch. 19.
Lucian, Thal. ch. 13.
Magnenus, Democr. ch. 2, 7, 8, 9. sect. 1, 2, 4. ch. 10.
Meibomius, pythag. doct. sect. 2. ch. 3, 4.
Meursius, Thal. ch. 2. Socr. ch. 1, 12.
Naudæus, Chald. sect. 1. ch. 2.
Nunnesius, Arist. ch. 8.
Olympiodorus, Arist. ch. 3.
Patricius, Chald. sect. 1. ch. 2.
Petavius, Thal. ch. 2. 13. Carnead. ch. 5.
Pliny, pyth. ch. 10. doct. sept. 4. ch. 4.
Ramus, Thal. ch. 7. sect. 1.
Salmasius, Thal. ch. 5. pla. ch. 1. pyth. ch. 1
Scaliger, Chald. sect. 2. Thal. ch. 2. Soct. c. 12
Selden, Chilon, ch. 1. Xenoph. ch. 2.
Sigonius, Thal. ch.
Simplicius, pyth. doctr. sect. 4. ch. 1.
Stephanus, Thal. ch. 10.
Suidas, Thal. ch. 2. Zeno, ch. 6.
Valerius Maximus, plat. ch. 7.
Valla, Thales, ch. 10.
Vossius, Thales, ch. 2.
Ursinus, Chald. sect. 1. ch. 2.
Zoroastræan Oracles, after the *Chaldaick* philosophy.

NOTED.

ALdobrandinus, Thal. ch. 6. sect. 4. and frequently else-where.

The End of the Table.

A TABLE of PHILOSOPHERS mentioned in the History of the Chaldaick and Greek Philosophy.

A.

ABavis, *Pyth. ch.* 23, 24.
Abroteles, *ch.* 24.
Acmonides, *ibid.*
Aroufiladas, *ibid.*
Acusilaus, *Preface.*
Adicus, *Pyth. ch.* 24.
Adrastus, *Arist. ch.* 14. 17.
Ægeas, *Pyth. ch.* 24.
Ægon, *ibid.*
Æmon. *ibid.*
Æneas, *ibid.*
Ænesidemus, *ibid.*
Æschines.
Æschrion *Arist. ch.* 14.
Æthiops, *Aristip. ch.* 9.
Aetius, *Pyth. ch.* 24.

Agelas, *ibid.*
Agesarchus, *ibid.*
Agesidemus, *ibid.*
Agylas, *ibid.*
Alcias, *ibid.*
Alcimachus, *ibid.*
Alcimus, *Stilp. ch.* 3.
Alcuneion, *Pyth. ch.* 24.
Alexander Aphrodisæus, *Arist. ch.* 17.
Alexinus.
Aliochus, *Pyth. ch.* 24.
Alcmeon.
Alopecus, *Prth. ch.* 24.
Ammonius, *Arist. ch.* 17.
Amoetus, *Pyth. ch.* 24.
Amyclus, *Pla. ch.* 13.

Anacharsis.
Anaxagoras.
Anaxarchus.
Anaximander.
Anaximenes.
Anchypillus, *Mened. ch.* 1.
Andronicus, *Arist. ch.* 17.
Animenes, *Pyth. ch.* 24.
Anniceris.
Anthocharides, *Pyth. ch.* 24.
Antimedon, *ibid.*
Antiochus, *Tim. ch.* 3.
Antipater, *Aristip. ch.* 9.
Antipater, the *Sidonian.*
Antisthenes.
Apellico, *Arist. ch.* 16.
Apollonius Chronus.

Apol-

The Table.

Apollodorus Cepotyrannus. *Epic. ch.* 16.
Arcesilaus.
Archelaus.
Archippus, of Samus, *Pyth. c.* 24.
Archippus of Tarentum, *ibid.*
Arestades, *ibid.*
Arete, *Aristip. ch.* 8.
Arignote. *Pyth. ch.* 21.
Arimnestus, *Pyth. ch.* 21.
Aristæus, *Pyth. ch.* 24.
Aristagoras, *Socr. ch.* 3.
Aristangelus, *Pyth. ch.* 24.
Aristeas, *Chald. lib.* 1. p. §. c. 2.
Aristides, *Stilp. ch.* 3.
Aristides, *Pyth. ch.* 24.
Aristides, a Locrian. *Plat. ch.* 13.
Aristippus.
Aristippus, the younger, *Aristip. ch.* 6.
Aristippus of Tarentum, *Pyth. ch.* 24.
Aritto, *Arist. ch.* 17.
Aristoclides, *Pyth. ch.* 24.
Aristocrates, *ibid.*
Aristodemus, *Preface, Thal. c.* 5.
Aristomenes, *Pyth. ch.* 24.
Aristonymus, *Plat. ch.* 13.
Aristotle.
Aristotle, the *Cyrenæan.*
Aristoxenus, *Arist. ch.* 14.
Arytus, *Pyth. ch.* 24.
Asclepiades, *Pyth. Mened.*
Aspasia, *Socr. ch.* 3.
Aspasius, *Arist. ch.* 17.
Asteas, *Pyth. chap.* 24.
Astæus, *Pyth. ch.* 21.
Astylus, *Pyth. ch.* 24.
Athamas, *Pyth.*
Athenodorus, of Soli. *Zen. c.* 9.
Athenodorus of Tharsis, *Arist. ch.* 17.
Atnosion, *Pyth. ch.* 24.
Atticus, *Arist. ch.* 17.
Averroes, *ibid.*
Avicenna, *ibid.*
Axiothea, *Pla. ch.* 13. *Speus. ch.* 2.
Azonaces. *Chald. lib.* 1. p. 1. Sect. 1. ch. 5.

B.

Balielma, *Pyth. ch.* 24.
Basilides, *Epic. ch.* 16.
Bathilaus, *Pyth. ch.* 24.
Belus *Chald. lib.* 1. p. 1. §. ch. 4.
Berosus, *Chald. lib.* 1. p. 1. *sect. ch.* 6.
Bias.
Bio, *Pyth. ch.* 24.
Bion.
Boethius, *Arist. ch.* 17.
Brias, *Pyth. ch.* 24.
Bruthius, *ibid.*
Bryas, *ibid.*
Brontinus, *ibid.*
Bryso. *Socr. ch.* 3.
Bulagoras, *Pyth. ch.* 24.
Butherus, *ibid.*

C.

Cænias, *Pyth. ch.* 24.
Calibrotus, *ibid.*
Caliphon, *Pyth. ch.* 23.
Callippus, an Athenian, *Pla.* 13. *Arist. ch.* 14.
Callippus, a Corinthian, *Zen. ch.* 9.
Callisthenes, *Arist. ch.* 14.
Carneades.
Carophantidas, *Pyth. ch.* 24.
Cebes.
Cerambus, *Pyth. ch.* 24.
Chærephon, *Socr. ch.* 17.
Chæron, *Pla. ch.* 13.
Charondas, *Pyth. ch.* 24.
Chilas, *ibid.*
Chilon.
Chilonis, *Pyth. ch.* 24.
Chrisippus.
Chrysippus, a Thyrrhene, *Pyth. ch.* 24.
Cleæchma, *ibid.*
Cleanor, *ibid.*
Cleanthes.
Clearatus, *Pyth. ch.* 24.
Clearchus, of Soli, *Arist. ch.* 14.
Cleobulina, *Cleob. ch.* 1.
Cleobulus.
Cleon, *Pyth. ch.* 24.
Cleophron, *ibid.*
Cleosthenes, *ibid.*
Clinagoras, *ibid.*
Clinias, *ibid.*
Clinomachus.
Clitarchus, *Stilp. ch.* 3.
Clitomachus.
Clitus. *Arist. ch.* 14.
Colaes, *Pyth. ch.* 24.
Colotes, *Epic.*
Coriscus, *Pla. ch.* 13.
Cranius, *Pyth. ch.* 24.
Crantor.
Crates,
Crito.
Brito, the Ægean, *Pyth. ch.* 24.
Critolaus.

D.

Dacydes, *Pyth. ch.* 24.
Damarmenus, *ibid.*
Damascenus Jo. *Arist. ch.* 17.
Damascenus, Nicho. *ibid.*
Damascius, *ibid.*
Damocles, *Pyth. ch.* 24.
Damon, *ib.*
Damotages, *ib.*
Dardanius, *ib.*
Demetrius, of Amphipolis, *Pla. ch.* 13.
Demetrius Lacon, *Epic. ch.* 16.
Demetrius Phalereus.
Democritus.
Demon, *Pyth. ch.* 24.
Demosthenes, *ibid.*
Deonax, *ib.*
Dexippus, *Arist. ch.* 17.
Dexitheus, *Pyth. ch.* 24.
Dicæarchus, *Arist. ch.* 14.
Dicæarchus, *Pyth. ch.* 24.
Dicon, *ib.*
Dinarchus, *ib.*
Dinocrates, *ib.*
Diocles, a Phliasian, *ib.*
Diocles, a Syberite, *ib.*
Dioclides, *Stilp. ch.* 1.
Diogenes.
Diogenes, of Seleucia, *Ep. c.* 16.
Diogenes, of Tharsus, *ibid.*
Diodorus, the Aspendian, *Pyth. ch.* 24.
Diodorus Chronus.
Diodorus, the peripatetick.
Dion, *Pla. ch.* 13.
Dionysius. *Epic. ch.* 16.
Dionysius, a Colophonian, *Menip.*
Dioscorides, *Timon. ch.* 3.
Dioteles, *Arist. ch.* 14.
Diotyma, *Socr. ch.* 3.
Diphylus, *Stilp. ch.* 3.
Drymon, *Pyth. ch.* 24.
Dymas, *ib.*

E.

Eccelo, *Pyth. ch.* 24.
Echecrates, a Phlyasian, *ib.*
Echecrates, a Tarentine, *ib.*
Echecrates, a Woman, *ib.*
Echecratides, *Arist. ch.* 14.
Egesinus.
Eiriscus, *Pyth. ch.* 24.
Elicaon, *ib.*
Empedocles.
Empedus, *Pyth. ch.* 24.
Epicurus.
Epimenides.
Epiphron, *Pyth. ch.* 20.
Episylus, *ib.*
Epitimides, *Aristip. ch.* 9.
Erastus, *Pla. ch.* 13.
Eratus, *Pyth. ch.* 24.
Erus Armenius, *Chald. lib.* 1. p. 1. *sect.* 1. *ch.* 2.
Estiæus, *Pyth. ch.* 24.
Euæmon, *Pla. ch.* 13.
Euæus, *Pyth. ch.* 24.
Euagon, *Pla. ch.* 13.
Euander.
Euander, of Crotona, *Pyth. ch.* 24.
Euander, of Metapontum, *ib.*
Euander, of Tarentum, *ib.*
Euanor, *ib.*
Eubulides.
Eubulus, *Timon. ch.* 3.
Euclid.
Eucratides, *Epic. ch.* 16.
Eudemus of Cyprus, *Arist. c.* 14.
Eudemus, of Rhodes, *ib.*
Eudoxus.
Euelthon, *Pyth. ch.* 23.
Euetes, *ib.*
Eumeridias, *ib.*
Euphantus.
Euphemus, *ib.*
Euphranor, *Timon ch.* 3.
Euphratus, *Pla. ch.* 13.
Eurymedon, *Pyth. ch.* 24.

Euripha-

The Table.

Euriphamus, *ibid*
Eurycrates, *ibid*
Eurytus, *ibid*
Eustathius, *Arist. ch.* 17.
Euthenus, *Pyth. ch.* 24.
Euthycles, *ibid*
Euthymus, *ibid*
Euxithius, *Arist. ch.* 14.

G.

Glauco.
Glorippus, *Pyth ch.* 24.
Glycinus, *ibid*
Gyptius, *ibid*

H.

Hegesias.
Hegesilaus, *see* Egesinus.
Heloris, *Pyth. ch.* 24.
Heracleodorus, *Pla. ch.* 13.
Heraclides, an Ænian, *Pla. c.* 13.
Heraclides, the Peripatetick.
Heraclides, of Pontus, *Pla. ch.* 13. *Arist. ch.* 14.
Heraclides, the Sceptick. *Timon ch.* 3.
Heraclitus.
Hermachus, *Epic. ch.* 12.
Herminus, *Arist. ch.* 17.
Hermodamas, *Pyth. ch.* 2.
Hermodorus, *Pla. ch.* 13.
Herodotus, *Timon, ch.* 3.
Hestiæus, *Pla. ch.* 13.
Hieronymus, of Rhodes, *Arist. chap.* 14.
Hipparchia.
Hipparchides, *Pyth. ch.* 24.
Hipparchus, *Arist. ch.* 14.
Hippasus.
Hippochus, *Chald. l.* 4. *p. ch.* 2.
Hippomedon, *Pyth. ch.* 24.
Hippocrates, *Democa. ch.*
Hippon, *Pyth. ch.* 24.
Hippostatus, *ibid*
Hipposthenes, of Crotona, *ibid*
Hipposthenes, of Cyzicus, *ibid*
Hippothales, *Pla. ch.* 13.
Histaspes, *Chald. l.* 2. *p.* 1. *sect.* 1. *ch.* 2.

I.

Jamblicus, *Arist. ch.* 17.
Iccus, *Pyth. ch.* 24.
Ichthyas
Itanæas, *Pyth. ch.* 24.

L.

Lacon, *Pyth. ch.* 24.
Lacrates, *ibid.*
Lacydes.
Laphaon, *Pyth. ch.* 24.
Lasthenia, *Pla. c.* 13. *Speus. c.* 2.
Lasthenia, a Pythagorean, *Pyth. ch.* 24.
Lasus *Preface.*

Leocritus *Pyth. ch.* 24.
Leocydes, *ibid*
Leon. *Arist. ch.* 14.
Leon, a Pythagorean, *Pyth. c.* 24.
Leophantus, *Preface.*
Leophron, *Pyth. ch.* 24.
Leptines, *ibid.*
Leucippus.
Lyco.
Lyco, a Pythagorean, *Pyth. c.* 24.
Lysides, *ibid*
Lysias, *Epic. c.* 16.
Lysibius, *Pyth. c.* 24.
Lysiphanes. *Epic. c.* 1.
Lysis, *Pyth. ch.* 24.
Lytamnus, *ibid*

M.

Magentinus, *Arist. c.* 17
Malias, *Pyth. c.* 24.
Marinus, *Arist. ch.* 17.
Marmaradius, *Chal. l.* 1. *p.* 1. *sect.* 1. *ch.* 5.
Maximus, *Aristot. ch.* 17.
Mededimus, *Pla. ch.* 13.
Megistias, *Pyth. ch.* 24.
Menalippus, *ibid*
Melisies, *ibid*
Melissus.
Menedemus, the Cynick.
Menedemus, the Eretrian.
Menestius, *Pyth. ch.* 24.
Menippus.
Menodorus, *Epic. ch.* 10.
Menodotus, *Timon, ch.* 3.
Menon, *Pyth. ch.* 24.
Meton, *ibid*
Metopus, *ibid*
Metrocles.
Metrodorus, sirnamed the Theoretick. *Stilp. ch.* 3.
Metrodorus, the Chian. *Ep. c.* 4.
Melias, *Pyth. c.* 24.
Milo, *ibid.*
Miltiades, *ibid.*
Mimnomachus, *ibid.*
Mnason, *Arist. ch.* 14.
Mnesarchus, *Pyth. c.* 21, 24.
Mnesibulus, *Pyth. ch.* 24.
Mnesistratus, *Pla. ch.* 13.
Moschus, *Mened. ch.* 1.
Muya, *Pyth. ch.* 21.
Muyes. *Pyth. ch.* 24.
Myrmex, *Stilpo ch.* 3.

N.

Nastas, *Pyth. ch.* 24.
Nausiphanes, a Pythagorean, *Epic. ch.* 4.
Nausitheus, *Peth. ch.* 24.
Neocritus, *ibid.*
Nicanor, *Arist. ch.* 14.
Nicephorus Blemmydes, *Arist. ch.* 17.
Niolochus, *Tim. ch.* 3.

O.

Occelo, *Pyth. ch.* 24.
Occlo, *ibid*
Ocylus, *ibid*
Odius, *ibid*
Olympiodorus, *Arist. ch.* 17.
Onatus, *Pyth. ch.* 24.
Opsimus, *ibid*
Oresandrus, *ibid*
Osthanes, *Chald. lib.* 2. *p.* 1. §. 1. *chap.* 3.

P.

Pachymerius, *Geogr. Arist. ch.* 17.
Pacton, *Pyth.*
Pæonius, *Stilp. ch.* 3.
Palæphatus, *Arist. ch.* 14.
Pamphilius, *Epic. ch.* 4.
Panætius.
Parmenides.
Parmischus, *Pyth.*
Pasciles *Stilp. ch.* 1.
Pasicrates, *Arist. ch.* 14.
Periander.
Phædo.
Phœdo, a pythagorean *Pyth. c.* 24
Phæfidemus, *Stil. ch.* 3.
Phancelus, *Pyth. ch.* 24.
Phanius, *Arist. ch.* 14.
Phanton, *Pyth. ch.* 24.
Pherecydes.
Philippus, an Opuntian, *Pla. c.* 13
Philo, a Theban, *Zen. ch.* 9.
Philo, the peripatetic. *Arist. c.* 14
Philodemus, *Pyth. ch.* 24.
Philolaus.
Philolaus of Tarentum, *Pyth. ch.* 24.
Philonides, *ibid*
Philoponus, *Arist. ch.* 17.
Philtes, *Pyth. ch.* 24.
Phiatias, *ibid*
Phormio, *Pla. ch.* 13.
Phrasidemus, *Arist. ch.* 14
Phrinychus, *Pyth. ch.* 24.
Prontides, *ibid*
phyacyades. *ibid*
phytius, *ibid*
pyserrydus, *ibid*
pisicrates, *ibid*
pithon, *Pla. ch.* 13.
Pittacus.
Plato.
plato the younger, *Arist. ch.* 14.
Plisthenes.
Plutarch the younger, *Arist. c.* 17
Polemæus, *Pyth. ch.* 24.
polemarchus, *ibid*
Polemo.
Poliades, *Pyth. ch.* 24.
Polymnestus, *ibid*
Polystratus, *Epic. ch.* 17.
Posidonius.
Praxiphanes, *Epic. ch.* 4.
Praytus, *Tim. ch.* 3.
Proclus, *Arist. ch.* 17.
Proclus, a pythagorean, *Pyth. ch.* 24.

Prorus

The Table.

Prorus, *ibid.*
Protagoras.
Proturchus, *Epic. ch.* 16.
Proxenus, posidonean, *Pyth. c.* 24
Proxenus, a Sybarite, *ibid*
Psellus, *Arist. ch.* 17.
Ptolemæus, a Cyrenian, *Tim. c.* 3.
Ptolemæus the Black *Epic. c.* 15.
Palemæus the White, *ibid*
Ptolemæus, of Cyrene, *Tim. c.* 3.
Pylyctor, *Pyth. ch.* 24.
Pyrrho.
Pyrrho the younger, *Tim. ch.* 3.
Pyrrho, a pythagorean, *Pych. c.* 24
Pysirronde, *ibid*
Pythagoras.
Pythodotus.

R.

RHexibius, *Pyth. ch.* 24.
Rhodippus. *ibid.*

S.

SAlaccra. *Pyth. ch.*
Sara, *Pyth. ch.* 21.
Sarpedon, *Tim. ch.* 3.
Staturninus, *ibid*
Satyrus, *Arist. ch.* 14.
Sextus, *Tim. ch.* 3.
Sycas, *Pyth. ch.* 24.
Silius, *ibid*
Simichus, *Pyth. ch.* 23.
Simmias.
Simmias, the Megarick, *Stilp. ch.* 3.
Simon.
Simplicius, *Arist. ch.* 17.
Simus, *Pyth. ch.* 24.
Smichæas, *ibid*
Socrates.
Socrates, a Bythinian, *Arist. c.* 14
Solon.
Sofistratus, *Pyth. ch.* 24.

Sosthenes, *ibid*
Sostratius, *ibid*
Sotion, *Arist. ch.* 17.
Speusippus.
Sphærus, *Zeno, ch.* 9.
Sthenonides, *Pyth. ch.* 24.
Stilpo.
Strato.
Syrianus, *Aristot. ch.* 17.

T.

TAurus, *Arist. ch.* 17.
Telauges, *Pyth. ch.* 21.
Terpsion, *Socr. ch.* 17.
Teucer, *Chald. lib.* 1. *p.* 1. *sect.* 1. *ch.* 5.
Thales.
Theano, Wife of Brontino, *Pyth. ch.* 24.
Theano, Wife of Pythagoras, *ch.* 21, 24.
Themistius, *Arist. ch.* 17.
Theodas, *Tim. ch.* 3.
Theodectus, *Arist. ch.* 14.
Theodorus the Atheist.
Theodorus Metochita, *Arist. ch.*
Theodorus, of Cyrene, *Pyth. ch.* 24.
Theodorus of Tarentum, *ib.*
Sheophrastus.
Thoridas, *Pyth. ch.* 24.
Thrascus, *ib.*
Thrasydemus, *ibid.*
Thrasymachus, *Stilp. ch.* 1.
Thrasymedes, *Pyth. ch.* 24.
Timæus, the Crotonian, *ib.*
Timæus, the Cyzicene, *Pla. c.* 13
Timæus, the Locrian, *Pyth. c.* 24
Timæus, the Parian, *ib.*
Timagoras, *Stilp. ch.* 3.
Timaras, *Pyth. ch.* 24.
Timarchus, *Arist. ch.* 14.
Timesianax, *Pyth. ch.* 24.

Timolaus, *Pla. ch.* 13.
Timosthenes, *Pyth. ch.* 23.
Tydas, *ib.*
Tymasius, *ibid.*
Tymicha, *ibib.*
Tyrsenus.
Tyrsenus, *ibid.*

X.

XAnthus, *Tim. ch.* 3.
Xenocides, *Pyth. ch.* 24.
Xenon, *ibid.*
Xenocrates.
Perophanes.
Yenophantes, *Pyth. ch.* 24.
Xenophilus, *ibid.*
Xentas, *ibid.*

Z.

ZAbratus, *Pyth. ch.* 5.
Zaleucus, *Pyth. ch.* 24.
Zamoixis, *Pyth. ch.* 21.
Zarmocenidas, *Chald. l.* 1. *p.* 1. *Sect.* 1. *ch.* 5.
Zeno.
Zeno Eleates.
Zeno the Epicurean, *Stilp. ch.* 3. *Zen. c.* 9. *Epic. c.* 16.
Zeno, of Tarsis.
Zeuxes, *Tim. ch.* 3.
Zeuxippus.
Zopyrus, a Colophronian, *Menip*
Zopyrus, a Tarentine, *Pyth. c.* 24
Zoroaster, the Chaldean, *Chald. l.* 1. *p.* 1. *sect.* 1. *c.* 2. 3.
Zoroaster, the Babilonian, *Chal. lib.* 1. *p.* 1. *sect.* 1. *c.* 2.
Zoroaster, the Bactrian, *ib.*
Zoroaster, the Pamphilian, *ib.*
Zoroaster, the Persian, *ibid. lib.* 2. *pag.* 1. *sect.* 1. *ch.* 1.
Zoroaster, the Proconnesian, *Chal. lib.* 1. *p.* 1. §. 1. *c.* 2.
Zoromasdres, *Chald. lib.* 1. *p.* 1. *sect. c.* 5.

The

PART I.   1

THE HISTORY of PHILOSOPHY.

The First Part,
Containing those on whom the Attribute of WISE was conferred.

THALES.
CHAP. I.
The Country and Parents of Thales.

GReat wits, which have been happy in benefiting Posterity by their excellent inventions, have not always had the fortune to enjoy the just reward, their glory being intercepted oftentimes by some later disguise of alteration or addition. It were thereforec gratitude

tude in us, who find our selves instructed by the Ancients, to vindicate the memory of our Masters, by enquiring diligently the Author of those Labours whereof we reap the Harvest. This kind of injury hath happened very considerably to *THALES* the wise Man of *Miletus*, who first introduc'd Natural and Mathematical Learning into *Greece*, from whence it is derived to us; but the honour of so noble a design, the ambitious opposition of some, the industry of others hath so obscur'd, that there is little of the reputation left to the deserving Author. I have therefore esteemed it worth my pains, to digest what I could collect or observe of a person, to whom all lovers of Learning are so much oblig'd.

The Original of *Thales* is very obscurely delivered. Some conceive he was a *Phœnician* by birth, whose opinion seeming to be strongly founded upon *Laertius*, and the Authorities by him alledged, it is necessary that we begin with a disquisition upon his words, which are, as commonly rendred, these:

Now Thales was born, as Herodotus, Duris *and* Democritus *affirm, his Father being* Examius, *his Mother* Cleobulina, *of the* Thelidæ, *who were* Phœnicians, *the most illustrious of all from* Cadmus *and* Agenor, [*as* Plato *also saith.*] The Testimony of *Herodotus*, though * *Higynus* and * *Suidas* seem to understand it according to the common error, as if he were born in *Phœnicia*, expresly confirms the contrary, being thus: *Thales a Milesian, afar off by descent a Phœnician*; whence we may gather, that the other two Authorities of *Duris* and *Democritus* imported little more, or at least nothing to a contrary sense. So likewise that of *Leander*, which is by * *Clemens Alexandrinus* cited jointly with *Herodotus*, to prove him of a *Phœnician* extract.

He was made free of Miletus *when he went with* Neleus *who was banish'd out of* Phœnicia.] The learn'd ᵃ *Casaubon* to reconcile this Story with that of *Neleus*, who was not banish'd out of *Phœnicia*, when he built *Miletus*; for ὅτι ἦλθον σὺν Νηλέῳ ἐκπεσόντι φοινίκης, reads, ἐκπεσών τ̃ φοινίκης, as if *Thales* being banish'd out of *Phœnicia* had gone with *Neleus* to *Miletus*; which alteration begetteth a very great Anachronism, for this *Thales* was above four hundred years later than that *Neleus*. Therefore if *Laertius* meant the same *Neleus*, either he was strangely mistaken, or his Text is corrupt, and ought to be understood of the Ancestors of *Thales*, to which sense it may be reduc'd with little alteration, thus, ἐπολιτογραφηθεὶς ἢ ἐν Μιλήτῳ ὅτι ἦλθον σὺν Νηλέῳ ἐκπεσόντι φοίνικες· as if they being *Phœnicians*, went into *Caria*, and became Citizens of *Miletus*, at what time *Neleus* Son of *Cordrus* being put beside the Kingdom of *Athens* by his younger Brother *Medon*, led thither the *Ionian* Colonies, whereof *Miletus* (which he built) was the chief City. Of this Colony see *Herodotus*, *Strabo*, and *Ælian*.

But as most say he was born there, at Miletus, *and of a noble Race*:] So they render ἰθαγενής, but in opposition to the first opinion, which only mentions his Family, not Country, it may perhaps be understood here in the same relation: Some (saith he) think he was of a *Phœnician* extract, of those who were incorporated at *Miletus*; others that he was of a *Grecian* Family, and that noble. Of this latter opinion is *Plutarch*, who reproves *Herodotus* for making *Thales* descended afar off from a *Barbarian* stock, and ᵉ *Hermippus*, who ascribes that saying to him, that he thanked the Gods he was a *Grecian*, not a *Barbarian*.

ᵇ *De Herod. malign.*
ᶜ *Laert. in Thal.*

CHAP. II.

Of the time of his Birth.

APollodorus *saith, that* Thales *was born the first year of the thirty fifth Olympiad;* * *Demetrius Phalereus saith, that he was honoured with the title of Wise, when* Damasias *was Archon.* Damasias *was Archon according to* ᵃ *Dionysius Halicarnassæus the second year of the thirty fifth Olympiad, when* Ancus Martius *the fourth King of Rome began his Reign.*

Hereupon an Anachronism of one year is supposed by very learned Men, who would have *Thales* to be born the same year that *Damasias* was Archon. Whence ᵇ *Sigonius*, ᶜ *Vossius*, and others bring down the Birth of *Thales* to the second year of this Olympiad; ᵈ *Scaliger*, ᵉ *Meursius*. ᶠ *Petavius* and others raise *Damasius* to the first year, that they may make his Magistracy agree with *Thales*'s Birth; neither rightly; for the office of *Damasias* relateth not to the Birth of *Thales*. For the clearing whereof we must take notice, that *Damasias* in the *Athenian Fasti* is twice said to be Archon, first in the second year of the thirty fifth Olympiad, the next year after the Birth of *Thales*, and again the fourth year of the forty eighth Olympiad, when he obtained the title of *Wise*; the latter we cannot mention without acknowledgment of the great light Chronology hath received by Mr. *Selden*'s *Marmora Arundeliana*.

It will be also worth observance, that there was another of this name, whom *Eusebius* placeth at the eighth Olympiad, and *Laertius* and ᵍ *Plutarch* make contemporary with *Homer*, *Hesiod* and *Lycurgus*. ʰ *Scaliger*, who perceived the inconsistency of this account, perceived not the reason of it; for ⁱ *Lycurgus* and *Iphitus* instituted the Olympick Games twenty seven Olympiads before *Corœbus* was Victor, who according to *Eusebius* is the first. These two *Thales* are by some confounded; *Eusebius* calls the first a Natural Philosopher, whereas it is certain that kind of Learning was first introduc'd into *Greece* by the second. ᵏ *Suidas* cites *Phlegon*, that the latter *Thales* flourish'd in the seventh Olympiad, which *Phlegon* doubtless meant of the first. ˡ They who place *Thales* about the seventh Olympiad, and make him contemporary with *Romulus*, confounded the latter *Thales* with the first, and the true Epocha of the Olympiads with the vulgar. For the first *Thales* lived in the seventh Olympiad from the first of *Iphitus*; *Romulus* liv'd about the same distance from the Olympiad of *Corœbus*.

This time is mistaken by that learned Father *Clemens Alexandrinus*, to prove *Thales* younger than the later Prophets. ᵐ Thus (saith he) *it is demonstrated that they who prophesied in the time of* Darius Hystaspes *in the second year of his Reign*,

* *Laert.*
* *Laert.*
ᵃ *Lib. 3.*
ᵇ *De Atheni- ens. tempor.*
ᶜ *De scient. mathemat. 32. 8.*
ᵈ *In Euseb.*
ᵉ *Archont. 1.*
ᶠ *Rationar. temp. 2. 12.*

ᵍ *Vita Lycurg.*
ʰ *In Euseb.*
ⁱ *Phlegon. fragm.*

ᵏ *In voce Thales.*

ˡ *See St. Augustin. de civit. Dei, lib.18.cap. 24, & 27.*

ᵐ *Stromat. 1.*

Reign, that is to say, Aggæus, Zacharias, and Malachy, who was one of the twelve, seeing that they Prophesied in the first year of the forty eight Olympiad, were more ancient than Pythagoras, who is said to have been in the sixty second Olympiad; and then Thales eldest of the Greek Sages, who was about the fiftieth Olympiad; as if this were not rather an Argument to prove these Prophets contemporary with Thales, which Eusebius allows. * About the time (saith he) of Cyrus King of Persia, the seven wise Men flourished; this was the time in which the last of the Hebrew Prophets Prophecied, since Troy, above six hundred years after Moses, no less than fifteen hundred years. But if with Clemens Alexandrinus we account these Prophets coætaneous with Darius Hystaspes, they will appear much younger than Thales, for Darius began his Reign in the last year of the sixty fourth Olympiad.

* Præpar. Evangel. 10. 4.

CHAP. III.

His Travels.

HE employed the first and greatest part of his time in Travel; he went to Creet, to inform himself of the Mysteries of their Religion, (for that Island was famous for the Birth of Jupiter) as is acknowledged by himself in an *a* Epistle to Pherecydes.

That he Travelled also into Asia is affirmed in the same Epistles; some say into Phænicia, arguing from his Astrology which he is thought to have learned of the Phænicians, Masters of that Science; and particularly because he is said to have first observed the constellation of the Lesser Bear by which the Phænicians sailed. *b* Vossius, essays to prove the word Cynosura to be Phænician, not as derived from κυνὸς οὐρά but from כנס and אור as being a Collection of Light; or אורא כנס Umbilicus igneus.

His last Journey (being *c* in years) was into Ægypt, to confer (as he acknowledgeth in his Epistle to Pherecides) with Priests and Astronomers. There he was instructed by the Priests at Memphis, particularly, saith (saith * Jamblicus) by those of Jupiter. Laertius affirms he learnt Geometry of them; Plutarch implies as much of his Philosophy.

He was there in the Reign of *d* Amasis, by whom much favoured and admired for many things, especially for measuring the height of the Pyramids by the shadow; until at last accused to him of disaffection to Monarchs and that kind of Government, to which effect many bitter sayings of his were alledged concerning Tyrants. As when Molpagoras an eminent Person of Ionia demanded what was the strangest sight he ever saw, he answered, a Tyrant old. Another time being at a Feast where a question arose, what Beasts were most dangerous; of Wild, saith he, a Tyrant, of Tame, a Flatterer; and Princes (saith Plutarch) however they profess themselves far different from Tyrants, yet take no pleasure in such Apothegms: Hereupon he lost the favour of Amasis. Thus having Studied Philosophy in Ægypt, he returned to Miletus, and *e* Transported that vast Stock of Learning which he had there collected, into his own Country.

a Laert.

b De Scien. Mathemat. cap. 3 2.

c Plut. de plac. phil. 1.

* Vit. Pythag. l. 2.

d Plutarch. Symp. sept. sap. conviv.

e Cyril.

CHAP. IV.

How he lived at Miletus.

HIs Life at Miletus (as *a* Heraclitus affirms) was retired and private; some report he Married and had a Son named Cibissas, but the truer Opinion is of those who say he lived unmarried, and made his *b* Sisters Son *c* (whom Plutarch calls Cybisthus) his Heir. *d* He put off his Mother when she first moved him to Marry, by telling her it was not yet time; and when he was more in years, being again solicited by her, he answered, nor is it now time, meaning, it was then too late. Being demanded why he took not some course to have issue, he answered, διὰ φιλοτεκνίαν, which is the same in pronouncing with δι᾽ ἀφιλοτεκνίαν, and may be taken either because he loved Children, or did not love them, as *e* Casaubon conjectures; but perhaps his meaning may better be gathered out of another answer of his to the same question, *f* that he did not mean to draw voluntary cares upon his life, and disturb the quiet thereof; or from this Story related by *g* Plutarch.

Solon coming to Miletus to visit him, told him that he wondred he wholly neglected Marriage and Issue. Thales at that time answered nothing, but some few days after Suborned a Stranger to pretend that he came within ten days from Athens; Solon demanded what news from thence; nothing (answered the other as he was instructed) but the burial of a young man attended by the whole City, being as was said Son of the most eminent Person of the City, who at the same time was abroad in Travel. Unhappy Man (cries Solon) what was his name? I heard it, answered the other, but have forgot, only I remember he was very famous for Wisdom and Justice. Solon's fear encreasing upon every answer, he at last asked him, if the Father's name were not Solon? which the other affirming, he beat his own Head, and did other actions accompanied with speeches proper to such as are transported with grief; whereupon Thales smiling, and interrupting him; these things, Solon, said he, deterr'd me from Marriage, which thus disorder even thee a most constant person, but be not troubled at this news, it is counterfeit.

In this privacy of life he was solicited and sent unto by many Princes, whose invitations and amities, (Plutarch *h* saith) he refused; visited by many eminent Persons.

i He is said to have cohabited some time with Thrasibulus (a Man of excellent Wit and Judgment) who was King, (or according to the Greek Word) Tyrant of Miletus, *k* though his Reign continued but eleven months; *l* about the time *ultim.* that the Milesians entred into a League with Alyates the second, then King of Lydia.

a Laert.

b Laert. Suid. in θ τόν. *c* Vitâ Solon.

d Laert. Plut. Sympofiac. 3 6. Stob. Serm. 66.

e In Laertium.

f Stob. serm. 66.

g Vita Solon.

h Sept. Sap. conviv.

i Laert.

k Arist. pol. 5.

l Herodot. 1.

CHAP. V.

The Attribute of Wise conferred on him.

THE attribute of Wise, as *a* Plutarch and Saint Augustine † observes, was conferr'd upon the rest in respect of their moral Rules and Practice, but upon Thales particularly for his speculative

a Vit. Solon. † De Civit. Dei. s. 2.

speculative Learning. It was first bestowed on *Thales*, at what time *Damasias* was Archon, under whom (according to b *Demetrius Phalareus*) all the *seven* were called Wise. The second *Damasias* was Archon in the third year of the 49th Olympiad, which c *Salmasius* knew not, when to make the words of *Laertius* agree with the first *Damasias*, he misinterpreted *Eusebius* and *Clemens Alexandrinus*, and subverted all other accounts of the Birth and Death of *Thales*, whereas this fortunately complies with the times of all the seven.

b *Laert.*

c *Exercitat. Plinian. pag. 843.*

The first was *Thales*, justly preferred before the rest in respect of his great Learning, which he owed not to any Master. The time when this Honour was conferred on him, falls upon the fifty ninth year of his age.

The second, *Pittacus*, of *Mitylene*, who flourished in the forty second Olympiad, and died in the third year of the fifty second.

The third, *Bias*, of *Priene*, contemporary with *Pittacus*, living under *Alyattes* and *Crœsus*.

The fourth, *Solon*, who was Archon at *Athens* the third year of the forty sixth Olympiad. He died Olymp. 55.

The fifth, *Cleobulus* of *Lindus*, coetaneous with *Solon*.

The sixth, *Myson* of *Chene*.

The Seventh, *Chilon* of *Lacedæmon*, who was *Ephorus*, Olymp. 56.

The Credit and Glory of these Seven, was much encreased (saith *Plutarch*) by a Tripod sent round from one to another, by a mutual, noble, and modest concession: the occasion related thus, by Laertius and Valerius Maximus.

d *Some young Men of* Ionia *having bought a Draught of the* Milesian *Fishermen, when the Net was drawn up, there was found in it a Tripod,* [e *a Golden Delphick Table of great weight.*] f *Hereupon arose a dispute,* [g those affirming they had Bargain'd only for the Fish; the others, that they bought the Draught at a venture: by reason of the strangeness of the case, and the value of the Tripod; it was delivered to the City *Miletus.*] h *The Milesians sent to the Oracle at* Delphi *about it, and received this answer:*

d *Laert:*

e *Valer. Maxim. 4. 1.*
f *Laert.*
g *Val. Max.*

h *Laert.*

Com'st thou *Milesian* to consult my Shrine?
The Tripod to the Wisest I assign.

Hereupon the *Milesians*, by agreement, presented it to *Thales*, he sent it to *Bias*, *Bias* to *Pittacus*, he to another, till it pass'd through all the seven, coming at last to *Solon*, who affirming God to be the wisest, sent it back to *Delphi*, [i giving him at once the Title and reward of greatest Wisdom.]

i *Val. Max.*

But *Callimachus* in his *Iambicks*, (continueth *Laertius*) relates it otherwise; that *Bathycles* an Arcadian left a Cup, with order that it should be given to the wisest, whereupon it was presented to *Thales*, and pass'd about in course till it came to him again, who then dedicated it to *Apollo Didymæus*, with these Verses, according to *Callimachus*:

Thales to him that Rules th' *Ionian* State
This twice obtained prize doth consecrate.

In *Prose* thus, *Thales* the *Milesian*, Son of *Examius*, to *Delphian Apollo* of the *Grecians* offers this twice received Prize of eminence. He that carried the Cup from one to another, was Thyrion, Son to Bathycles,] whither allude these Verses of k *Phœnix Colophonius*.

k *Athen. digr.*

Thales, whose Birth his Country blest,
Esteemed of all Men the best,
Was of the Golden Cup possest.

Eudoxius of *Gnidus*, and *Euanthes* of *Miletus*, report that a Friend of *Crœsus* having receiv'd from him a *Golden Cup* to be given to the wisest of the Grecians, delivered it to *Thales*, and that at last it came to *Solon*, who sending to the Pythian Oracle to know who was the wisest, was answered *Myson*; whom *Eudoxius* substitutes for *Cleobulus*, *Plato* for *Periander*, the Oracle concerning *Myson* was this:

Octæan *Myson* I declare
Wiser than those that wisest are.

He that was sent upon the enquiry was *Anacharsis*. *Dædacus* the *Platonist*, and *Clearchus* affirm, that the Cup was sent by *Crœsus* to *Pittacus*, and so carried about. *Andron* in *Tripode*, (which seems to have been a discourse wholly upon this subject, and is likewise cited by *Clemens Alexandrinus*, to prove that *Thales* and the other six flourished about the fiftieth Olympiad) writes that the *Argives* proposed this *Tripod* as a *Prize* to the wisest of the *Greeks*, and that it was adjudged to *Aristodemus* a *Spartan*, who resigned it to *Chilon*; *Aristodemus* is mentioned by *Alchæus*.

This Speech we to *Aristodemus* owe,
Money's the Man, none's Poor and Honest too.

There are who report that a Ship richly laden, sent by *Periander* to *Thrasibulus Tyrant* of *Myletus*, was cast away in the *Coan Sea*, and the Tripod taken up by some *Fishermen*. *Phanodius* affirms it was lost in the *Athenian Sea*, and afterwards brought to the City, and upon consultation voted to be sent to *Bias*. Others say this Tripod was made by *Vulcan*, who gave it to *Pelops* as his Wives Portion, from him it came to *Menelaus*, and afterwards being taken away with *Helena* by *Paris* was by the *Lacedæmonian* [Hellen] thrown into the Sea, calling to mind [l an Oracle] that it would prove in time to come the ground of many Contentions. After this some *Lebedians* fishing thereabouts drew it up, and quarrelling with the *Fishermen* about it, it was brought to *Coos*, but the Controversie not decided, the business was told to those of *Miletus*, which is the chief City of that Country; they sent a Messenger to demand it, and finding themselves slighted, made War upon the Coans; in which many being slain on both sides, the Oracle declared that the Tripod should be given to the wisest, whereupon both Parties with joynt consent presented it to *Thales* [m the *Coans* being willing to grant that to a private Person, for which they before contested with all the *Milesians*] who Dedicated it to *Apollo Didymæus*; the effect of the Oracle to the Coans was this:

l *Plut. vit Sol.*

m *Plut. vit Sol.*

This Contestation shall continue till
The Golden Tripod's into th' Ocean cast

By *Vulcan*, you present to one whose skill,
Extends to things to come, present and past.

To

To the Milesians,

Comest thou Milesian to consult my Shrine? as before. Thus *Laertius.* n *Plutarch* adds, that *Thales said,* Bias *was wiser than himself, whereupon it pass'd to him, from him to another, as wiser, so passing in a circle from one to another, it came at last to* Thales *the second time. Finally it was sent from* Miletus *to* Thebes, *and dedicated to* Ismenian Apollo. *Theophrastus saith it was first sent to* Bias *at* Priene, *then by* Bias *to* Thales *at* Miletus, *so passing through all, it came again to* Bias; *and finally was sent to* Delphi. *This is most generally reported, saving instead of a Tripod, some say it was a Cup sent from* Crœsus; *others, that it was left there by* Bathycles.

Thus was the Priority of *Thales* confirmed by the Oracle, for which reason he is by *Cicero* and *Strabo* stiled *Prince of the Wise Men,* to whom the rest yielded the Preheminence.

n *Vit. Sol.*

CHAP. VI.

Of his Philosophy.

THales (saith *Laertius*) *is by many affirmed to be the first that made disquisitions upon Nature.* * *Cicero* (who taught the *Greek* Philosophers first to speak *Latin,*) acknowledges *Thales* to be the *first Author thereof.* † *Strabo* saith, that *he first of the* Grecians *made enquiry into natural Causes and the Mathematicks.* a *Plutarch* calls him *Inventer of Philosophy*; *Justin Martyr,* b *The most ancient of Philosophers*; c *Tertullian, first of Natural Philosophers*; d *Lactantius, the first that made enquiry afte natural Causes.*

* *Apud Lactant. & de Natura Deor.*
† *Lib. 14.*
a *De plac. phil. 1.3.*
b *Parænes. ad Græc.*
c *Apologet.*
d *De falf. rel. 1.5.*

Sect. 1. *That Water is the Principle of all things.*

IN his disquisition of the Natural Causes of things, he conceived *Water* to be the *first Principle of all natural Bodies, whereof they consist, and into which they resolve.* His Reasons (as delivered by e *Plutarch,* and repeated by f *Stobæus*) these:

First, Because Natural Seed, the Principle of all living Creatures is humid, whence it is probable that humidity is also the principle of all other things.

Secondly, Because all kinds of Plants are nourished by moisture; wanting which, they wither and decay.

Thirdly, Because Fire, even the Sun it self and the Stars are nourished and maintained by Vapors proceeding from Water, and consequently the whole World consists of the same. Whence Homer *supposing all things to be engendred of Water,* saith,

e *Placit. philos. 1.3.*
f *Eclog. Phys. 1.13.*

Ὠκεανὸς ὅσπερ γένεσις πάντεσσι τέτυκται.

The Ocean whence all things receive their Birth.

In pursuit (g as *Aristotle* saith) of this Opinion, he assigned *Water* the lowest place, holding (according to h *Seneca*) *that the whole Earth floats, and is carried above the Water, whether that we call the Ocean or great Sea, or any simple moisture of another nature, or a moist Element. By this Water* (saith he) *the Earth is sustained as a great Ship, which presseth upon the Water that bears it up, because the most weighty part of the World cannot be upheld by the Air, which is subtle and light.* Thus is i *Aristotle* to be explained, who saith, *Thales held, that the Earth being capable of swimming, resteth as Wood or the like; now of such things, none swim upon Air, but upon Water.*

g *Metaph. 1.3.*
h *Natur. quæst. 6.6.*
i *Metaphys.*

Upon this ground it was that he held *Water* (as *Laertius* saith) *to be the cause of Earthquakes.* Thus k *Seneca, He holds that the Globe of the Earth is upheld by the Water, and carried as a Barque, and floateth by the mobility thereof, at such time as it is said to quake.* One of his Reasons alledged by l *Seneca,* is this, *because in all extraordinary motions thereof some new Fountains commonly issued, which if they incline to one side, and shew their Keel asidelong, gather Water; which, if it chance the burden they bear be over weighty, raiseth it self higher towards the right or left side.*

k *Nat. quæst. 3. 13.*
l *Nat. quæst. 6. 6.*

From the Testimony of *Homer,* by which *Thales* (according to *Plutarch* and *Justin Martyr*) defended this Tenet (that Water is the Principle of all things) it is manifest it was delivered, (tho' imperfectly) by other *Grecians* before *Thales*; *Plutarch* m elsewhere producing this Authority of n *Hesiod.*

m *Ignis an aqua utilior?*
n *Theogon.*

Πάντων μετὰ πρώτιστα χάος γένετ'———

Of all things Chaos was the first.———

addeth, *the greater part of ancient Philosophers being called Water* Chaos, ἀπὸ τὴν χύσιν *from diffusion.* The Scholiast of o *Apollonius* upon these words,

o *Argonaut. 4.*

———Ἐξ ἱλύι ἐβλάστησε χθῶν ἄτη.

The Earth of Slime was made.

affirms (citing *Zeno*) that *the Chaos, whereof all things were made according to* Hesiod, *was water, which setling became Slime, the Slime condensed into solid Earth*; to which add this Testimony of *Orpheus,*

p *Cited by Athenagoras.*

Ἐκ τῶ ὕδατος ἰλὺς κατέστη.

Of Water Slime was made.

This Opinion they borrowed from the *Phœnicians,* with whom the *Græcians* had a very ancient correspondence. *Linus* came from thence; *Orpheus* had his Learning from thence: as *Thales* is conceived to have done likewise, which appears clearly in q *Numenius,* an ancient Philosopher, who cites the very words of *Moses* for this Opinion. *The Spirit of God moved on the Face of the Waters.* There is an eminent place in r *Eusebius* to prove this: *the divinity of the* Phœnicians *asserts the Principle of this World to be a dark Spiritual Air, or the Spirit of dark Air, and Chaos troubled and involved in darkness, that this was Infinite, and a long time had no bounds: but* (say they) *the Spirit being moved with the love of his own Principles, there was made a mixtion, which nexure was called Love; this was the beginning of the production of all things; but the Spirit it self had no Generation, and from this connexion of the Spirit was begotten* Μώτ, *which some call Slime, others corruption of watery mistion, and of this was made the Seed of all Creatures, and the Generation of all things.*

q *Porphyr. de antro Nymph.*
r *Præpar. Evangel. l. 10.*

f Strab.lib.15. Nor were the *Indians* ignorant of this, as *Megasthenes* delivers their Opinion. *f They are of the same mind in many things, with the* Grecians, *as that the World had beginning, and shall have end; that God its Maker and Governor goes quite through it; that all things had different beginnings, but that of which the World was made was Water.*

The word ἀρχή, *Principle*, becauſe with Philoſophers it includes, the efficient cauſe, and conſequently underſtood ſingly excludes the reſt, that being the moſt Noble, hath given occaſion to ſome to miſtake *Thales*, as if by acknowledging no other Principle, he conſequently accounted *Water* to be *God*; but that *Thales* underſtands by *Principle* only the material Cauſe, we may eaſily gather from *Plutarch*, *t* who condemneth *Thales* for confounding a *Principle* with an *Element*, and for holding them to be both one; *whereas (ſaith he) there is great difference; Elements are compounded, Principles are neither compounded, nor are any compleat Subſtance, and truly Water, Air, Earth, Fire, we term Elements, but Principles we call other Natures, in this reſpect that there is nothing precedent to them, whereof they are engendred. For otherwiſe, if they were not the firſt, they would not be Principles, but that rather ſhould be ſo termed whereof they were made. Now certain things there are precedent, whereof Earth and Water are compounded, viz. The firſt in form Matter, and the form it ſelf and privation.* Thales *therefore errs, affirming Water to be both Element and Principle of all things.* Thus we ſee by *Plutarch*, that the objection can only be as to the name, not to reaſon of the name; for the diſtinction of Principle and Element being not uſed in that time, *Thales* by *Principle*, meant nothing of the efficient cauſe, which is moſt certain from *Ariſtotle*. *Thales,* ſaith he, *affirms Water to be the Principle: wherefore he held the Earth to be above the Water*; perhaps he conceived ſo, becauſe he ſaw that the nutriment of all things, is humid, that heat it ſelf conſiſts thereof, and that every Creature lives thereby; he held that of which things are made to be the Principles of all things, for thoſe reaſons he was of this Opinion, *as alſo becauſe the Seeds of all things are of a humid Nature*, and Water is the principle of things humid.

t De placit. Philoſ. l. 2.

Sect. 2. *Of God.*

Apologet. contra gent. Metaphyſ. l. 3.

Tertullian ſaith, That *Thales* to *Crœſus* enquiring concerning the Deity, gave no certain account, but deſired ſeveral times of deliberating to no effect. He ſeems to reflect upon the ſame or a like Story to that which is reported of *Simonides* and *Hieron*.

But what the Opinion of *Thales* was concerning *God*, may be gathered from two Apothegms cited by *Laertius,* repeated with this gloſs by *a Clemens Alexandrinus*; *and what are not thoſe the ſayings of* Thales *that are derived from hence, That God is Glorified for ever and ever, and he openly confeſſes that he is called* καρδιογνώσης, *he who knoweth Hearts.* For Thales being demanded what God was, that (ſaith he) *which hath neither beginning nor end.* Another asking if a Man might do ill and conceal it from God. How, ſaid he, *when a Man that thinks it cannot?* Men ought to think (ſays *b Cicero* in his name) *that the Gods ſee all things.*

a Stromat. 5.

b De legib. 2.

He acknowledged the firſt of Beings, and Author of the World, aſſerting (according to *Laertius*) that *the moſt ancient of all things is God, for he is not begotten*; that *the faireſt is the World, for it is his Work.* This is confirmed by *Cicero*. Thales *the Mileſian* (ſaith he *) *who firſt enquired into theſe things, ſaid, that Water was the Principle of things, but that God was that Mind which formed all things of Water. If Gods may be without Senſe and Mind, why did he joyn the Mind to Water? Why Water to the Mind, if the Mind can ſubſiſt without a Body?* Thus *Cicero*, who underſtands *Thales* to intend the material Principle to be co-eternal with the efficient; which *Thales* himſelf ſeems not to mean, when he declared God to be the firſt of Beings. But that the *Mens* of *Anaxagoras*, for the annexing of which to Matter, he was ſo much famed, was no more than what he borrowed from *Thales*, the words of *Cicero* make good.

* *De natur. deor. 1.*

He affirmed that God by the immutable Decree of his Providence Governs the World. *Thales* (ſaith *Stobæus*) *being demanded what was moſt ſtrong, anſwered Neceſſity, for it Rules all the World. Neceſſity is the firm Judgment and immutable Power of Providence.* Hither we muſt likewiſe refer what is cited under his name by the ſame *Stobæus*, that *the firſt mover is immovable*, which *c Ariſtotle* hath borrowed from him, not owning the Author.

c Phiſic. 8. 7.

Something imperfectly was before delivered by *Orpheus*, concerning God, alledged by *d Clemens Alexandrinus* and others; but as *Cicero* ſaid, Thales *was the firſt among the* Grecians, *who made any Search into theſe things*; and that he brought it out of *Ægypt*, the *Grecians* themſelves deny not, *e* for they acknowledge that they received the names of their Gods from thence, and believed the *Ægyptians* to be the firſt, who looking up to the World above them, and admiring the Nature of the Univerſe, reflected upon the Deity.

d Admonit. ad gent.

e Herodot. lib 2.

Sect. 3. *Of Dæmons.*

Thales *(ſaith a Plutarch) with* Pythagoras, Plato, *and the Stoicks hold, that* Dæmons *are Spiritual Subſtances, and the Heroes Souls ſeparated from the Bodies, of which ſort, there are two, good, and bad; the good Hero's are the good Souls, the bad, the bad.* The ſame order *b Athenagoras* atteſts to be obſerved by *Thales*, ranking the three degrees thus: Firſt, that of the Immortal Gods, next Dæmons, thirdly, Heroes: This was followed by *Pythagoras*, that *the Gods were to be preferred in reverence before* Dæmons, Hero's *before* Men.

a Placit. Phiſoſ. 1. 8.

b Apolog.

He affirmed (as *Stobæus* ſaith) *the World to be full of theſe* Dæmons. This is thought the meaning of that of *c Ariſtotle*, repeated by *Cicero*, † Thales *thought that all things were full of Gods.* The ſame aſſertion *Laertius* * aſcribes to *Pythagoras, that the Air is full of Souls, which are Heroes and Dæmons.*

c De Anima. 1. 8.
† *de legib. 2.*
* *Vit. Pythag.*

This Opinion was aſſerted by the *Greeks,* before the time of *Thales*, particularly by *Heſiod*;
but

but whether that be argument enough, to deny, that *Thales* had it from the Ægyptians, I question; that they held it in the same manner, we may learn by * *Jamblichus*. Besides, *Pythagoras* and *Plato* (whom *Plutarch* joyns in the Tenet with *Thales*) drew their learning from the same fountain.

De myster. Ægypt. pub. ini-

Sect. 4. Of the Soul.

Plutarch and *Stobæus* say, that *Thales* first affirm'd the Soul to be αὐτοκινητόν, *a self-moving nature*. ᵃ *Aristotle* that he calls it κινητικόν in respect to the motion it gives to other things, in which are included both parts of the definition of the * *Platonists*, *a substance, having within it self a power to move it self and other things*: which * *Plato* argues to this effect: *The first of motions is that whereby a thing moves it self; the second, that whereby it moves another: Every thing that moves it self, lives; every living thing lives, because it moves it self, therefore the power of self-motion is the essence of that substance which we call the Soul, which Soul is the cause of the first generation and motion of things which are, were, and shall be; and of all their contraries, as of all transmutation, the principal of motion, and therefore more antient than the Body, which it moves by a second motion.* And afterwards declares these to be the names of the Souls motion, *to will, to Consider, to take Care, to Consult, to judge Rightly, and not Rightly, to Joy, to Grieve, to Dare, to Fear, to Hate, to Love,* and the like. *These which are the first motions, and suscipient of the second corporal, bring all things into augmentation, and decrease, conversion, or condemnation, and densation, or rarefaction.* This opinion first raised by *Thales*, was entertained in the Schools with the assent of * *Pythagoras, Anaxagoras, Socrates,* and *Plato*, till exploded by * *Aristotle*, whose chief arguments against it were these. 1. That nothing is moved but what is in place, nothing in place but what hath quantity, which because the soul wants none of the four kinds of motion (*viz*. Lation, Alteration, Diminution, Accretion) are competible (*per se*) to her. Secondly, That self-motion is not essential to the Soul, because she is moved accidentally, by external objects. The first, if understood of Circumscription, not only denies the motion of all things, that are definitively in place, as Spirits, but of the highest sphere, if compared with *Aristotle*'s definition of place; yet that some of these species of motion, though in a different extraordinary manner, are competent to the soul, and not accidentally, may be argued 1. From the further diffusion of the Soul, according to the augmentation of the Body. 2. From intellection, which is acknowledg'd a perfection, and consequently a kind of alteration, which that *Thales* understood to be one of the Soul's motions, is clear from that Apothegm ascribed to him by *Laertius, the swiftest of things is the mind,* for it over-runs all things: Whence ᵇ *Cicero*(confessing almost in every word of *Thales*, that *nothing is swifter than the mind, that no swiftness may compare with the swiftness of the mind*) would interpret the ἐντελέχεια of *Aristotle*, *a continued and perpetual motion*.

ᵃ *De plac. Phil.* 4. 2.

* *De anima.* l. 2.

* *Plato in Tim.*

* *Stob. Ecl. phys. lib.* 1.

* *Arist. de anima.* l. 2.

ᵇ *Tuscul. quæst.* 1.

The second reason may be questioned by comparing the acts of the *memory*, and *reminiscence*; the first occasion'd by exterior things yet *objective* only, so that the motion is within her self; but by the other she moves her self, from a privation to a habit, without the help of any exterior.

It is worth notice, that among these and other reasons alledg'd by ᶜ *Aristotle* to destroy this assertion, one is the possibility of the resurrection of the Body; but this ἐν παρέργῳ.

ᶜ *De anima.* l. 3.

From the second part of the difference in the definition (*viz*. from moving other things) *Thales* argued, that the *Load-stone*, and *Amber* had souls; the first because it draws Iron; the second straw. He further (saith *Laertius*) asserted those things we count inanimate, to have souls; arguing it from the loadstone and amber: The reason of which latter example, ᵈ *Aldobrandinus* falsely interprets its change of colour, and jarring as it were at Prison: But ᵉ *Aristotle* more plainly, *for of those whom we mentioned*, Thales *seems to have taken the Soul to be something* κινητικόν, *apt to move, since he affirmed a stone to have a Soul, because it moved Iron*.

ᵈ *In Laert.*
ᵉ *De anima.* l. 2.

He asserted likewise the Soul (of Man) to be immortal, and according to ᶠ *Cherilus*, was the first that held so. ᵍ *Cicero* ascribes the original of this opinion to *Pherecydes*, but it rather seems to have been brought by *Thales* from the Egyptians; that they held so ʰ *Herodotus* attests.

ᶠ *Laert.*
ᵍ *Tusc. quæst.* 1.
ʰ *Lib.* 2.

Sect. 5. Of the World.

THales held, (ᵃ) that *there was but one World*, and that (ᵇ) *made by God*; which truth was follow'd by all Philosophers; as ᶜ *Aristotle* confesseth, untill he rejected it, to defend, by the contrary, an assertion equally false; that the World is everlasting, *which could not be*, saith he, *if it had beginning*.

ᵃ *Plutarch de plac. phil.* 2. 1.
ᵇ *Laert.*
ᶜ *De Cœlo.* l. 10. 12.

That ᵈ *the World being God's Work, is the fairest of things, whatsoever disposed in lively order being a part thereof*, for which reason *Pythagoras* (according to ᵉ *Plutarch*) called it first κόσμος.

ᵈ *Laert.*
ᵉ *De plac. phil.* 2. 1.

That *Night is elder than Day.* This Circumstance of the Creation was held likewise by * *Orpheus*, and *Hesiod*, who had it from the *Phœnicians*: For this reason the * *Numidians*, * *Germans*, and * *Gauls* reckoned by Nights.

* *Timoth.*
* *Damascen.*
* *Tacit. de mor. Germ.*
* *Cæsar. de bello Gall.* 6.

That *the * World is animated*, and that ᵍ *God in the Soul thereof, diffus'd through every part, whose divine moving virtue penetrates through the element of Water*. Thus explained by the *Hermetick* Philosophers, the divine Spirit who produc'd this World out of the first Water, being infus'd as it were, by a continual inspiration into the works of nature, and diffus'd largely through, by a certain secret, and continual act, moving the whole, and every particular according to its kind, is the Soul of the World.

ᵍ *Laert.*

That *the* ʰ *World is contained in place.* This agrees with the definition of place by *space*; but they who with *Aristotle* define place a *superficies*, though they hold the parts of the World to be in place, as forced to deny the whole to be so.

ʰ *Laert.*
Plaut. sept. sap. conviv.

That

That *in the World there is no vacuum*, in which (as *Plutarch* observes) all Philosophers agree, who affirm the World to be animated, and govern'd by providence; the contrary defended by those who maintain that it consisteth of Atoms, is inanimate, not governed by providence.

Plut. de plac. phil. 1. 18.

That *matter is fluid and variable.*

° Plut. de plac. phil. 1. 9.

That *p Bodies are passible and devisible, in infinitum, and continuous as are also a line, superficies, place and time.*

p Plut. de pl. phil. 1. 16.

That *q Mistion is made by composition of the Elements.*

q Plut. de plac. phil. 2. 13. Achil Tat. lag in Arat.

That *r the Stars are earthly, yet fiery; s the Sun earthly.* They who *affirm the Stars to be fiery,* saith *t Aristotle,* hold so, as conceiving the whole superior Body to be Fire.

r De cœlo. 2. 7. Plut. de plac. phil. 2. 28.
s Plut. de plac. phil. 3. 9.
t Plut. de plac. phil. 3. 10.

That *the Moon is of the same nature with the Sun, that she is illuminated by him,* Plutarch, and Stobæus affirm this to be first held by *Thales,* though *Eudemus* cited by *Theon* ascribe it to *Anaximander.*

That *the monthly occultations of the Moon are caused by the nearness of the Sun shining round her.*

That *there is but u one earth, w round, in fashion of a Globe, x seated in the midst of the World,* to which relates that speech ascribed to him by *Cleodemus,* that, *if the earth were taken out of the World, there must of necessity follow a confusion of all things.*

u Plut. de plac. phil. 3. 11.
w Sept. sap. conviv.
x Laert.

That *the overflowing of* Nilus *is caused by the Etesian* (yearly) *winds,* which rise with the Dog-star, after the summer Solstice, and beginning the blow from the North, spread (as *z Aristotle* describes them) into remote quarters. These (saith *a Plutarch*) blowing directly against Ægypt, *cause the water to swell, that the Sea driven by these winds, entereth within the mouth of that River, and hindereth it, that it cannot discharge it self freely into the Sea, but is repulsed. Whereupon* (adds *b Diodorus Siculus*) *it overflowes Ægypt, which lieth low and level.* But this reason, though it seem plausible, is easily disproved; for if this were true, all the Rivers which are discharged into the Sea, opposite to the Etesian winds, should have the same overflowing. Thus Diodorus in his excellent Discourse upon this Subject, which concludes with the opinion of *Agatharchides* that it is occasion'd by rain, coming from the mountains of *Ethiopia.*

z Meteor. 2. 6.
a De plac. phil.
b Lib. 1.

CHAP. VII.

Of his Geometry.

*A*Puleius, who calls *Thales the inventer of Geometry amongst the Grecians,* is more just to his memory than *Anticlides* and others, who ascribe the honour thereof to *Mœris,* or to *Pythagoras,* who by the acknowledgment of *a Jamblichus,* a Pythagorean, learnt Mathematicks of *Thales.* The original and progress of this science, to the perfection it received from *Pythagoras* (which gave occasion to that mistake) is thus delivered by *Proclus.*

Florid. lib. 4. Laert. vit. Pythag.
a De vita Pythag. l. 2.
In Euclid. 2. 4.

Geometry was invented by the Egyptians, taking its beginning from measuring fields; it being necessary for them, by reason of the inundation of Nilus, *which washed away the bounds of their severals.* Nor is it to be wondered at, that as well this, as other sciences, should have their beginning from Commodiousness and opportunity; since, as is said in generation, it proceeds from imperfect to perfect; therefore not without reason is the transition from sence to consideration, and from consideration to the mind. As therefore among the Phœnicians, by reason of Merchandise and traffick, the certain knowledge of numbers had its beginning; so likewise among the Egyptians, Geometry was found out upon the foresaid occasion; and Thales going to Egypt, first brought over this science into Greece: *And many things he found out himself, and taught his fellows the principles of many things, declaring some more generally, other things more plainly.* Next him Ameristus, brother to Stesichorus *the Poet, is remembered c as having touched Geometry, of whom* Hippias *the* Elean *makes mention, as eminent is that knowledge:* After these Pythagoras *considering the principles therefore more highly, advanced it into a liberal science.*

Supply the breach in the text,
καὶ ἀπὸ τῆς λιπούσῃ εἰς τὸν νοῦν ἢ μετάβασις, &c. so Barocius translates

c Read, ὡς ἐφαψάμενος τῆς περὶ γεωμετρίας σπουδῆς, μνημονεύεται.

Sect. 1. Propositions invented by him.

That he improved (as *Proclus* implies) the Geometry which he learnt of the Ægyptians with many propositions of his own, is confirmed by *Laertius,* who saith, that *he much advanced those things the invention whereof Callimachus in the Iambicks, ascribes to* Euphorbus *the Phrygian, as scalenous triangles, and others.* Nor is it to be doubted, but that many of them are of those, which *Euclid* hath reduced into his Elements; whose design it was to collect and digest those that were invented by others, accurately demonstrating such as were more negligently proved, but of them only, these are known to be his.

[*d 1. Every Diameter divides its circle into two equal parts.*] This proposition which *Euclid* makes part of the definition of a Diameter, *Proclus* affirms to have been first demonstrated by *Thales.*

d Lib. 1. def. 17.
Euclid lib. 2. com. 14.

2. [*e In all Isosceles triangles, the angle at the base are equal the one to the other, and those right lines being produced, the angles under the base are equal.*]* *Proclus* saith, that *for the invention of this likewise, as of many other propositions, we are beholding to* Thales, *for he first observed and said, that of every Isosceles, the angels at the base are equal, and according to the antients called equal like.* These are three passages in the demonstration, which infer nothing towards the conclusion, of which kind there are many in *Euclid,* and seem to confirm the antiquity thereof, and that it was less curiously reformed by him.

e Euclid. lib. 1. prop. 5.
lib. 3. com. 9.

3. [*If two lines cut one the other, the verticle angels shall equal the one the other* [*h Eudemus* attests this Theorem to have been invented by *Thales,* but first demonstrated by *Euclid.*

h Euclid lib. 1. prop. 15. Procl. lib. 3. com. 19.

4. [* *If two triangles have two angles equal to two angels the one to the other and one side equal to one side, either that which is adjacent to the equal angles, or that which subtendeth one of the equal angles, they shall likewise have the other sides, equal to the other sides, both to both, and the remaining angle equal to the remaning angle*]* Eudemus *attributes this Theorem* (saith *Proclus*) *to* Thales, *for showing the distance of ships upon the Sea, in that manner as he is said to do, it is necessary that he perform it by this.*

Euclid lib. 1. prop. 26.
i Procl. lib. 3. com. 31.

Pamphila

PART I. THALES.

h Geom.

Pamphila (faith *Laertius*) affirms, that he first described the rectagle triangle of a circle.] *h Ramus* attributes to *Thales* (upon this authority of *Laertius*) the second, third, fourth, and fifth propositions of the fourth Book of *Euclid*, which are concerning the adscription of a Triangle and a Circle, and consequently takes καταγράψαι here to include both Inscription, and circumscription; whereas in all those propositions, there is nothing proper to a Rectangle Triangle; so that if the word ὀρθογώνιον be retain'd, it must relate to the 31st proposition of the third Book, whence may be deduced the description of a Rectangle Triangle in a Circle. But because there is no such proposition in *Euclid*, and this hath but an obscure reference to part of that Theorem; it is to be doubted that the Text of *Laertius* is corrupt, and the word (or mark) κύκλου inserted by accident, without which these words καταγράψαι τὸ τρίγωνον ὀρθογώνιον exactly correspond with those of *i Vetruvius, Pythagoricum trigonum orthogonium describere*: by which he means (as he at large expresseth *k* elsewhere,) the forty fifth Proposition of the first Book of *Euclid*, that in rectangle triangles, the square of the hypothenuse is equal to the square of the sides containing the right Angle. That *Vitruvius, Proclus*, and others, attribute this Invention to *Pythagoras*, confirms it to be the same here meant by *Laertius*; who adds, that *Thales for the Invention Sacrificed an Ox, though others* (faith he) *among whom is Apollodorus, ascribe it to Pythagoras*. And in the Life of *Pythagoras*, he cites the same *Apollodorus*, that *Pythagoras, Sacrificed a Hecatomb, having found out, that the hypothenuse of a right Angled Triangle, is of equal power to the two sides, including the right angle according to the Epigram.*

i Lib. 10. cap. 11.
k Lib. 9. cap. 2.

That Noble Scheme *Pythagoras* devis'd,
For which a Hecatomb he Sacrific'd.

l Procl. in Euclid. lib. 2. def. 4. where the words perhaps are inverted, and for τρεῖς γραμμὰς ἐπὶ ταὐτὸ τομαῖς εὑρὼν τὰς σφαιρικὰς εὑρών.

Cicero, tho' he differ in the Author, agrees in quantity of the Offering with *Laertius*; affirming, that *Pythagoras upon any new Invention used to Sacrifice an Ox*: which kind of gratitude begun by *Thales*, was imitated by others also, as by *Perseus*.

l Finding three Spiral Lines, in Sections five, Perseus an Offering to the Gods did give.

Sect. 2. Of his taking the height of the Pyramid.

a Polyhist.c.25.
b Idyl. 2.
c Lib. 22.
d Var. 7. form. 15.

THE Pyramids of *Egypt* are supposed by *a Solinus, b Ausonius, Ammianus c Marcellinus*, and *d Cassiodorus*, to cast no shadow at all, which (as Mr. *Greaves* hath observed in his excellent Discourse upon this Subject) must be meant either of the Summer time, or, which is nearer the Truth, that for the three quarters of the year, they have none at mid-day.

For, that *Thales* by the shadow measured their height, is acknowledged. *e Hieronymus* faith, *he measured the Pyramids by the shadow, observing when they are of equal bigness. f Pliny* affirms *he found out a way to take the height of them, and all such like, by measuring the shadow, at what time it is equal to the Body*. But *Plutarch* hath given a more regular and exact account of his manner of operation, by erecting a staff perpendicular upon

e Laert.

g Leb. 36. cap. 12.

the end of the shadow of the Pyramid, and by two triangles made by the Beams of the Sun, he demonstrated, that what proportion there was between the shadows, the same was betwixt the Pyramid and the Staff: A demonstration so rational, that it is the ordinary way of taking heights by shadows, founded upon this Theorem.

g Of equiangle triangles, the sides that are about equal angles are proportional, and the sides that subtend the equal Angles are homologous.

a g Euclid. lib. 6. prop. 4.

Which if *Proclus* had proceeded as far as the sixth Book of *Euclid*, we should in all likelihood have found ascribed to *Thales*; for the same argument wherewith *Eudemus* proves him inventor of the fourth Theorem in the foregoing Section, whereby he took distances, is of equal force in this, whereby he took altitudes.

The height of the great Pyramid (which *Thales* measured) is by its perpendicular (according to Mr. *Greaves*) 499 Feet, by its declining ascent, 693 Feet.

CHAP. XVIII.
Of His Astronomy.

OMitting the Fable of *Orpheus's* Harp alluding to the seven Planets, and the observations of *Hesiod*, which were little more than of the Rising and Setting of some principal Stars, (so imperfect, that *Plato* calls all those who satisfie themselves with such superficial knowledge, *Astronomers according to Hesiod*) we may with *Eudemus* and others affirm, that *Thales was the first of the Grecians that was skilful in Astronomy*. Which Science *a Pliny* asserts to have been brought out of *Phœnicia*; *b Aristotle*, that the Grecians owe much of it to the Egyptians, where it hath been a long time practised: Thither indeed *c Thales* acknowledgeth that he Travelled to confer with Astronomers.

a Lib. 5. Cap. 17.
b de Cœlo.2.12
c Epist. ad Pherecyd.

Sect. 1. Of the Celestial Sphere.

Thales, Pythagoras (faith * *Plutarch* repeated by * *Stobæus*) with his followers affirm, that *the Celestial Sphere is divided into five Circles* (which they call Zones) whereof one is called Artick, and is always in view to us; one of the Summer Tropicks, one the Equinoctial, one the Winter Tropick, one the Antartick Circle, never seen by us. The oblique Circle, called the Zodiack, lieth under the three middle Circles, it toucheth them all three as it passeth, and each of them is cut in right Angles by the Meridian, which goeth from Pole to Pole. Unjustly therefore is the invention of the Zones ascribed by *e* Posidonius *to* Parmenides; and that of the obliquity of the Zodiack by *f* others to Anaximander, Pythagoras, *or* Ænipodes.

* *De plac. phil.*

e Strab. lib. 1
f Plin. 2. 8.

g Eudemus faith, *that he first observ'd the Tropicks; Laertius*, that *he first found out the accession of the Son from Tropick to Tropick*. The word τροπαὶ signifies not only the Solstices, but the Equinoxes likewise: *h Sextus Empiricus. The Tropick signs are those into which the Sun coming, changeth and maketh conversions of the Air; such a sign is* Aries, *and the opposite to it* Libra, *so also* Capric. *and* Canc. *for in* Aries *is made the vernal conversion, in* Capr. *the winter, in* Canc. *the summer, in*

g Laert.

h Adverf. mathem. 5. 23

C Libra *the*

the autumnal. This Exposition *Laertius* confirms, when he saith that *Thales* composed only two Treatises, one of the Tropicks, the other of the Equinoctials, and that *he distinguished the seasons of the year.*

Sect. 2. *Of the Sun, Moon, and Stars.*

HE first observed the apparent Diameter of the Sun, which is the Angle made in the Eye, to be the 720th part of his Orb: This doubtless is the meaning of *Laertius*, his words these, καὶ πρῶτος τὸ τῦ ἡλίυ μέγεθος τῦ σελίωαίυ ἐπτακοσιοςὸν καὶ εἰκοςὸν μέρες ἀπεφήνατο· Than which reading, which implies the Sun to be 720 times lesser than the Moon, nothing is more Ridiculous; for knowing (as is granted by all) the cause of Eclipses, he must likewise know the Sun to be greater than the Moon: nor is it much mended by those who read καὶ πρὸς τὸ τῦ ἡλίυ μέγεθος τὸ τῦ σελίωαίυ, the Text seems rather to require ζωδιακὰ for σελίωαίυ, or something to that effect, of which, thus, *a Archimedes, this we suppose when Aristarchus saith, the Sun appeareth, as being the 720th part of the Circle of the Zodiack; for he considered how he might by instruments take the Angle made in the eye by the Sun's apparent Diameter: but to take any such thing exactly is not easie; for neither the sight, nor the hand, nor the instruments wherewith the Observation is made, are of Credit sufficient to demonstrate it exactly.* This Correction *Apuleius* thus confirms, *in his declining Age he made an excellent demonstration of the proportion of the Sun, which I have not only learned (saith Apuleius) but confirmed by practice, how may times the Sun's magnitude is comprehended in the Circle which his motion makes. This, as soon as he found out, Thales shewed to Mandratus of Pryene, who being infinitely delighted with this new and unexpected knowledge, bad him ask what he would in recompence for such an excellent invention: It will be reward enough for me, said Thales, if what you have learned of me, whensoever you communicate it to others, you profess me to be the Inventor.*

He first found out the Constellation of the lesser Bear, b *Callimachus*

> *He to Miletus Sail'd, invited*
> *By Thales Glory, who quick-sighted*
> *Is said t'have mark'd the lesser Bear,*
> *The Star by which Phœnicians steer.*

Hyginus affirms that he first called it Ἄρκ]Θ. the Bear.

Sect. 3. *Of Eclipses.*

HE was the first (saith *Laertius*) that foretold Eclipses, as *Eudemus affirms in his Astrologick History; for which* Xenophanes *and* Herodotus *admire him; attested also by* Heraclitus *and* Democritus. *Theon, Smyrnæus, and Clemens Alexandrinus cite the same place of Eudemus; the scope of whose Book was the History of Astrologers, and what every one found out.* Thus likewise *Pliny, amongst the Grecians, the first that searched into Eclipses, was* Thales *the Milesian.*

a Plutarch affirms, that *he was the first that observed the Eclipse of the Sun, and said, that it was occasioned by the Moon, coming in a direct Line underneath him, which may be seen in a Bason of Water, or Looking-glass.* b *That the Eclipse of the Moon is caused by the shadow of the Earth, which being placed betwixt these two Stars, darkens the lesser.*

The Testimony of *Herodotus*, alledged by *Laertius* is this: c *A five years War was raised between the* Lydians *and the* Medes, *in which, sometimes the Medes had the better of the Lydians, sometimes the Lydians of the Medes, and one Battel was fought by night: The War being thus equal on both sides, in the sixth year, the Armies being joyned, it hapned as they were fighting, the day on a sudden became night; which alteration of that day,* Thales *a Milesian had foretold the Ionians, designing the year wherein it should happen. The Lydians and Medes seeing the day turned to night, left off fighting, and laboured to conclude a mutual Peace, which by the Mediation of* Syennenses *King of Cilicia, and* Labnitus *King of Babylon (whom* Scaliger *conceives to be* Nebuchadnezzar*) was concluded, with the Marriage of* Aryæna *Daughter of* Alyattes, *with* Astyages, *Son of* Cyaxares, *Ratifi'd by drinking Blood.*

This is the Story of that memorable Eclipse, the time whereof is uncertain: d *Pliny* placeth it in the fourth year of the forty eighth Olympiad, before the Building of *Rome* 170 years: e *Solinus* in the 49th Olympiad, the 604th year after the Destruction of *Troy*; which falls upon the first year of that Olympiad. f *Clemens Alexandrinus* (citing *Eudemus*) about the fiftieth Olympiad, at what time *Cyaxares* Father of *Astyages* Reigned in *Media*: *Alyattes* Father of *Crœsus* in *Lydia*. *Eusebius* in the second year of the forty eighth Olympiad 1430 years after *Abraham*. *Cleomedes* saith, it was total in *Hellespont*; in *Alexandrina*, but of ten digits. g *Johannes Antiochenus* saith, It continued many hours; but they could not exceed three-

Of latter Writers differing Accounts thereof are delivered by these.

Ricciolus placeth it before the Incarnation 585 years, May 28 about 6 a Clock in the afternoon, the digits Eclipsed 12. 56.

Calvisius before the Incarnation 607 years Olympiad 43. 4 differing from *Pliny* 18 years.

The Learned Bishop of *Armagh*, in the Reign of *Cyaxares*, Olympiad 44. 4 the 147 year of *Nabonassar*, the fourth day of the *Egyptian* Month *Pachon*, according to the *Julian* account September 20 *feria* 1. beginning after Sun-rise 1 3m. 25s. digits Eclipsed 9. continuing almost two hours.

Petavius Olympiad 45. 4, *Julian* period 4117. before the Incarnation 597, after the Building of *Rome* 157. July 9. *feria*, 3. beginning after Midnight 4h. 45m. digits Eclipsed 9. 22m. continuance full two hours.

Kocca confutes *Petavius*, because that Eclipse suits not with the circumstances of the Story, as beginning too early in the Morning, and being defective as to the quantity in *Pontus* and lesser *Asia*.

Lansbergius

Lansbergius, Olympiad. 48. 3. the 163 year of *Nabonaſſar*, the 12th day of *Tybi*, which is *May* 28, digits Eclipſed 12. 20ᵐ· in *Helleſpont*: 10 12ᵐ· in *Alexandria*.

Kepler, Scaliger, Buntingus, and *Salianus,* follow *Pliny*: digits Eclipſed (according to *Buntingus*) 11. 30ᵐ.

Neither is it eaſie to determine whether this variety ariſes from the incertainty of the Aſtronomers, or of the Chronologers.

Sect. 4. *Of the Year.*

Laertius ſaith, that *he diſtinguiſhed the ſeaſons of the year, that, he firſt called the laſt day of every Month* τϱιακάς, *the thirtieth day, that he divided the year into three hundred ſixty and five days.*

This Calculation of the year he ſeemed to have learned in *Ægypt*, where it was in uſe, thus explained and commended by * *Herodotus. The Ægyptians were of all Men the firſt that found out the year, diſtinguiſhing it into twelve Months; this they gathered from the Stars, and more judiciouſly (in my Opinion) than the Grecians, for as much as the* Grecians *every third year, intercalate a Month to make up the time; but the* Ægyptians *to the number of 360 days, which twelve Months make, add yearly five days, whereby the account of the Circle of Time returning into it ſelf is made good.*

This was called in latter times, *the* Ægyptian *year* (perhaps becauſe uſed by *Ptolomy*, who lived in *Ægypt*) in diſtinction from the *Julian year*, which was then uſed in all the Weſtern parts, and hath the addition of ſix hours: the moſt perfect is the *Gregorian*, conſiſting of three hundred ſixty five days, five hours, forty nine minutes, twelve ſeconds.

Sect. 5. *His Aſtrological Predictions.*

a Plat.

Thales being earneſtly addicted to Aſtrology, became obnoxious to the Cenſure of ſome Perſons. *As he was led abroad one night by an old Woman,* his Maid, (a ᵃ *Thracian*) *to look upon the Stars, he fell into a Ditch* (wherein ſhe purpoſely led him) *to whom as he complained,* Thales, *ſaid ſhe, do you think, when you cannot ſee thoſe things that are at your feet, that you can undeſtand the Heavens?*

He was alſo for preferring this Study before Wealth, reproved by ſome Friends, not without Reproach to the Science, as conferring no advantage on its profeſſors; whereupon he thus vindicated himſelf and the Art from that Aſperſion. *When they upbraided him,* ſaith b *Ariſtotle, with his Poverty, as if Philoſophy were unprofitable, it is ſaid, that he by Aſtrology, foreſeeing the plenty of Olives that would be that year, before the Winter was gone* antequam florere cœpiſſent, (ſaith *c Cicero*) *gave earneſt, and bought up all the places for Oyl at* Miletus *and* Chios, *which he did with little Money, there being no other chapman at that time to raiſe the price; and when the time came that many were ſought for in haſt, he ſetting what rates on them he pleaſed, by this means got together much Mony, and then ſhew'd, that it was eaſie for Philoſophers to be Rich, if they would themſelves, but that Wealth was not their*

b Pol. l. 7.

De divinat. l 1.

aim. To this *Plutarch* alludes, when he ſays, that *Thales is reported to have practiſed Merchandize.*

CHAP. IX.

His Moral Sentences.

OF his Moral Sentences thoſe are firſt to be rememb**r**rd which *a Plutarch* mentions upon this occaſion.

a Sept. ſap. conviv.

Amaſis King of *Ægypt* entring into conteſtation with the King of *Æthiopia* concerning Wiſdom, propounded theſe queſtions to be reſolved by him; *what is oldeſt of all things, what faireſt, what greateſt, what wiſeſt, what moſt common, what moſt profitable, what moſt hurtful, what moſt powerful, what moſt eaſie?*

The anſwers of the *Æthiopian* were theſe, the oldeſt of things is Time, the wiſeſt Truth, the faireſt Light, the moſt common Death, the moſt profitable God, the moſt hurtful the Devil, the moſt powerful Fortune, the moſt eaſie that which pleaſeth. *Thales* demanded of *Niloxenus* whether *Amaſis* approved theſe ſolutions? *Niloxenus,* who was ſent by *Amaſis* into *Greece* with theſe other queſtions to be reſolved by the Sages, anſwered that with ſome he was ſatisfied, with others not; and yet, replies Thales, there is not one but is erroneous and betrays Ignorance. As for the firſt, how can it be defended that Time is the oldeſt of Things, when one part of it is paſt, the other preſent, the third yet to come, for that which is to come muſt in reaſon be eſteemed younger than all Men or Things? Next to affirm that Truth is Wiſdom, is as much as if we ſhould ſay, that the Light and Seeing is all one. Again, if he eſteem Light Fair, why doth he forget the Sun? His anſwers concerning God and the Devil are Bold and Dangerous, but that of Fortune moſt improbable, for if ſhe be ſo Powerful, how comes it that ſhe is ſo eaſily changed. Nor is Death the moſt common, for it is not common to the Living. The moſt ancient of Things is God, for he never had Beginning or Birth, the greateſt place of the World containeth all other things, place contains the World; the faireſt the World, for whatſoever is orderly diſpoſed is part thereof. The wiſeſt is Time, for it hath found out all things already deviſed, and will find out all that ſhall be; the moſt Common, Hope, for that remains with ſuch us have nothing elſe; the moſt Profitable, Virtue, for it maketh all things uſeful and commodious; b the moſt hurtful, Vice, for it deſtroyeth all good things; the moſt Powerful, Neceſſity, for that only is Invincible; the moſt Eaſie, that which agreeth with Nature, for even Pleauſres are many times given over and cloy us.

b Etiam a. pud. Stob. ſermi 109.

Etiam apud Stob. ſerm. 46.

To which Apothegms theſe are added by *Laertius*, The ſwifteſt of things is the Mind, for it over-runs all. He affirm'd that there is no difference betwixt Life and Death; being thereupon asked why he did not die, becauſe, ſaith he, there's no difference; to one who ask'd which was eldeſt, night or day, he anſwer'd, night by a day; another enquiring whether a man might do ill and conceal it from the Gods; nor think it ſaid he. To an Adulterer, queſtioning him if he might clear himſelf by Oath * Perjury, ſays he, is worſe than Adultery: Being demanded what was difficult, he anſwered, to know one's ſelf; what eaſie, to be rul'd by another; what ſweet,

* ἐ χϱέϱγ μοιχείας ἐπιοϱκία · not as councelling the latter, but reproving the former.

* Plut. dedæm. Socr.

to

to follow ones own Will; what Divine, that which hath neither beginning nor end. At his return from Travel, being demanded *what was the strangest thing he had seen*, he answered, *a Tyrant old. What will help to bear ill Fortune? to behold our Enemies in worse. How shall a Man live justly? by avoiding what he blames in others. Who is happy? he who hath a sound Body, a rich Fortune, and a docile Nature.*

^c^ Plutarch adds these; *We may well report probable News, but improbable should not be related. We ought not to believe our Enemies in credible things, nor to distrust our Friends in incredible.* Periander *being much troubled at a Monster which a Youth brought him, born of a Mare, with the head only of a Horse, the rest resembling a Man, he advised him not to take care for expiation of what the Prodigy portended,* ἐγὼ δὲ σοὶ παραινῶν (saith he) ἐδίσω τὸ μὴ χρᾶσθαι νομεῦσιν ἵππων, ἢ διδόναι γυναῖκας αὐτοῖς.

c Sympos. sept. sap.

Stobæus these; † *Being demanded how far Falshood was distant from Truth, as far saith he, as the Eyes from the Ears. It is hard but good to know our selves, for that is to live according to Nature.*

† *Serm.* 61.
† *Serm.* 104.

His Moral precepts are thus delivered by Demetrius Phalereus; † *If thou art a Surety, loss is nigh; be equally mindful of friends present and absent; study not to beautifie thy face but thy mind: enrich not thy self by unjust means.* † *Let not any words fall from thee which may accuse thee to him who hath committed any thing in trust to thee. Cherish thy Parents. Entertain not Evil. What thou bestowest on thy Parents thou shalt receive from thy Children in thy old Age. It is hard to understand well. The sweetest thing is to enjoy our desire. Idleness is troublesome. Intemperance hurtful. Ignorance intolerable. Learn and teach better things. Be not Idle tho' Rich. Conceal thy domestick ills. To avoid Envy be not pitiable. Use Moderation. Believe not all. If a Governor, Rule thy self.* I follow those Copies of Stobæus, that ascribe these to Thales rather than to Pittacus, because the greater part are confirmed by Laertius.

† *Stob. Serm.* 28.

† i. be true to thy trust.

Ausonius hath reduced these into Verse under his name.

Fear e'er thou sin, thy self tho' none else nigh;
Life fades, a Glorious Death can never die.
Let not thy Tongue discover thy intent,
'Tis Misery to dread, and not prevent.
He helps his Foes that justly reprehends.
He that unjustly praiseth, harms his Friends.
That's not enough to excess extends.

His Motto was according to Laertius, *Know thy self*; according to ^f^ Didymus and ^g^ Hyginus, *if thou be a Surety, loss is nigh*; by ^h^ Hermippus, this is ascribed to him, tho' by others to Socrates: *He gave thanks to Fortune for three things: first, that he was born Rational, not a Beast; secondly, that a Man, not a Woman: thirdly, that a Grecian, not a Barbarian.*

g Clem. Alex.
g Fab. 221.
h Laert.

There are beside cited by Laertius, under the name of ἀδομένα, or *loose Verses*, these sentences,

*Not many Words much Wisdom signifie.
Choose one thing excellent, to which apply
Thy Mind, and stop the mouth of Calumny.*

CHAP. X.

His Judgment in Civil Affairs.

POliticks were, according to Laertius, his first Study, in which his advice was of great Authority, tho' he were the only person (as *Cicero* observes) of the seven Wise Men, that was not Ruler of the City wherein he lived.

Of his Judgment herein we have two instances; the first from ^i^ Herodotus; *Good also, even before the destruction of* Ionia, *was the advice of* Thales, *a Milesian, afar off by descent a Phœnician, who commanded the* Ionians *to build one Common-Council-Hall, and that in* Teos, *for that* Teos *is in the midst of* Ionia, *and the rest of the Inhabited Cities, nevertheless, to be in Repute, according as the Citizens were.*

^i^ *Lib.* 1. τὰς δὲ ἄλλας πόλεας οἰκεομένας, μηδὲν ἧσσον νομίζεσθαι κατάπερ εἰ δῆμοι εἶεν, which Valla renders thus; Cæteras autem civitates habitatas nihilo minus huic parituras, quam aliarum civitatum tribus legibus parerent. Stephanus thus: Nihilo minus eodem loco haberi quo tribus: both (*I conceive*) amiss.

The other cited by Laertius (with no less applause) is this. In the first year of the fifty eighth Olympiad, *Crœsus* King of *Lydia*, fearing the greatness of *Cyrus*, and encouraged thereunto, as he conceived, by the Oracle, sent Ambassadors and Presents to the most considerable of the Grecians, perswading them to joyn with him in an expedition against *Cyrus*, which the *Lacedæmonians* with many others did: but *Thales* forbad the *Milesians* to enter into League with him. *It appears* (adds Laertius) *that his Advice in Civil Affairs was excellent*; *for this thing* (Cyrus *getting the better*) *preserv'd the City.*

Yet did he afford *Crœsus* his particular assistance in passing his Army over *Halys*, as the Grecians affirm, though *Herodotus* be of a contrary Opinion, who gives this account of both. When Crœsus *was come to the River* Halys, *then, I believe, by Bridges that were there, he passed over his Army; but the common report of the Grecians is, that* Thales *the* Milesian *was he who conveighed it over: For* Crœsus *being doubtful over what part of the River his Army should pass, there being in those days no Bridges,* Thales, *who was in the Field with him, is said to have caused the River that did run on the left hand of the Army, to run also on the right, which he brought to pass thus. Beginning above the Trench, he digged a deep Trench, and brought it in the fashion of a half Moon, that the River being turned into the Trench from the former Channel at the back of the Army, and passing by the Camp, came into the old Channel again, so that assoon as the River was thus divided.* (which ^k^ Lucian saith, *was done in one night*) *it became fordable on either side: some say that the old Channel was quite made up, but that I do not belive, for then, how could they in their return pass over?* That this is the meaning of *Herodotus*, mistaken by * Valla, will appear from the ^m^ Scholiast of *Aristophanes*, who relates it in the same manner, not without applauding *Thales*, for his excellency in Mechanicks.

^k^ *In Hippia.*

* Who renders ταύτην κατὰ τὴν διόρυχα ἐκτραπόμενος τῶν ἀρχαίων ῥεέθρων,
in quam cum introduxisset ex pristino alveo fluvium, iterum cum ubi exercitus trajectus esset in suum alveum refunderet. ^m^ *In Nubes.*

He

PART I. *THALES.*

He was a great Enemy to Tyrants, and accounted all Monarchy little better, as appears by *Plutarch*, who makes him speak thus: 'As 'for taking one for the other, (*viz*. A *Monarch* 'for a *Tyrant*) I am of the same mind with the 'young man, who throwing a Stone at a Dog, hit 'his Step-mother; it is no matter, said he, for 'even so, it lights not amiss, truly always estee-'med *Solon* very wise, for refusing to be King of 'his own Country: and *Pittacus*, if he had not 'taken upon him a Monarchy, would never have 'said, how hard it is to be a good man: and *Peri-*'*ander* being seized (as it were with an hereditary 'disease, derived from his Father) by the same 'Tyranny, did very well to endeavour as much 'as he could to disengage himself from it, by fre-'quenting the conversation of the best Men, in-'viting Sages, and Philosophers, and being in-'vited by them, not approving the dangerous 'Counsel of *Thrasibulus* my Country-man, who 'perswaded him to take off the heads of the 'chiefest. For a Tyrant, who chooseth rather to 'command Slaves than Free-men, is like a Hus-'band-man, who preferreth the gathering of Lo-'custs, and catching of Fowl, before reaping of 'good Corn. These Sovereign Authorities have 'only this good, in recompense of many Evils, a 'kind of Honour and Glory, if Men be so happy, 'that in ruling good Men, they themselves prove 'better; as for such, who in their office aim at 'nothing but security, without respect of Ho-'nour and Honesty, they are fitter to be set over 'Beasts than Men.

In the same *Symposion*, he gives this Account of Monarchy, Democracy, and Oeconomicks. *Stob. serm.* 147 *That Prince is happy, who lives till he is old, and Stob. serm.* 141 *dies a natural Death. That Common-wealth is best Stob. serm.* 43 *ordered, where the Citizens are neither too rich, nor too poor. That House is best, wherein the Master may live most at ease.*

CHAP. XI.
Of his Writings.

SOme affirm (saith *Laertius*) that he left nothing behind him in writing. Others, that he Writ

a De civit. Dei.
Of Natural Philosopy: St. *a Augustin*, saith, that *Thales*, to propagate his Doctrine to Succession, searched into the Secrets of Nature, and committing his Opinion to Monuments and Letters, grew Famous.

b Laert.
Of Nautick Astrology (mentioned by *b* by *Simplicius*) which is by some ascribed to *Phocus* a *Samian*.

Of the Tropicks and Equinoctials: which two Treatises *Laertius* saith, he composed, as judging the rest easie to be understood. These seem to be those Astrological Writings which *Lobon*, an *Argive*, who writ concerning the Poets, affirmeth to have extended to two hundred Verses.

Of Meteors: A Treatise in Verse, mentioned by *Suidas*.

Lib. 6.
ταῦτα δ᾽ ἱσο-
ρήσαν οἱ σο-
φώτατοι Θα-
λῆς κ᾽ Κάςωρ
κ᾽ Πολύβι-
συγγραψά-
μενοι κ᾽ μετ᾽
αὐτοὺς Ἡρό-
δοτος ὁ ἱσο-
ριογράφ.

The History of his own Times: if we may give credit to *c Johannes Antiochenus*, who saith, *These things* Thales, Castor, *and* Polybius *most wise Authors committed to writing, and after them* Herodotus *the Historian*: but perhaps this may be no more probable, than that *Polybius* and *Castor* should precede *Herodotus*

Ἀδομένα, of which those that are cited by *Laertius*; we have inserted among his Moral Sentences; for such they were, tending to the instruction of the common People, a kind of loose Verse coming near Prose, whence *Demosthenes* makes two kinds of Poets, τοὺς ἐμμέτρους κ᾽ τοὺς ἀδομένους, (as *Casaubon* observes) those that write in *metre*, and, (if we may so term it) those that write in *blank Verse*. Whatsoever *Laertius* in the Lives of the seven Wise Men produceth in this kind, seemeth not to be taken out of any Poet, but to have been written by the Wise Men themselves.

Epistles, of which two only are extant, preserved by.

Thales *to* Pherecydes

I Hear, that you first of the Ionians, are about to publish a Discourse to the Greeks concerning Religion, and * justly you conceive that your work ought rather to be laid in a publick Library than transmitted to uncertain Persons: if therefore it may any way pleasure you, I will willingly confer with you about that which you have written, and if you desire, will visit you at Syrus; for neither my self, nor Solon the Athenian should deserve the titles of wise men, if we, who Sail'd to Creet to inform our selves of matters there, and into Ægypt, to confer with Priests and Astronomers, should not likewise make a Journey to you: Solon also, if you think fit, will come. You who affect home, seldom pass into Ionia, nor care to enjoy the society of strangers; we, who write nothing, spend our time in travelling through Greece and Asia.

* *But the interpreters render this to another effect.*

Thales *to* Solon.

IF you leave Athens, you may, in my Opinion, settle your self (with those you take along with you) at Miletus, for here is nothing to trouble you. If you dislike that we Milesians are Governed by a Tyrant (for you are averse to all Monarchs, even Elective) yet may you please your self in the society and conversation of me your Friend. Bias likewise hath sent to invite you to Priene; if to abide at Priene please you better, we will also come and dwell there with you.

CHAP. XII.
His Auditors and Scholars.

THE first eminent Person of those who heard *Thales* and professed his Philosophy, was *Anaximander* Son of *Praxides* a *Milesian*, who flourished in the time of *Polycrates* Tyrant of *Samos*.

Next is *Anaximenes* a *Milesian* also, Son of *Euristratus*, (who according to *Eusebius*) flourished in the second year of the 56th Olympiad. He was Scholar to *Anaximander* and *Parmenides*; but that he heard *Thales* also, he acknowledgeth in an *a* Epistle to *Pythagoras*.

a Laert. vit. Anax.

We may (as in that Epistle *Anaximenes* doth) amongst the Disciples of *Thales* reckon *Pythagoras* the *Samian*, institutor of the Italick Sect, who being from his youth particularly
addicted

addicted to investigation of Religious Mysteries, addrest his first Journey to *Thales* at *Miletus*, as to one that could best further his design, being (according to * *Jamblicus*) not fully eighteen years old; which if we follow the account of *Eusebius* for his Birth (the fourth year of the seventieth Olymyiad) and that of *Sosicrates* for his Age, eighty years (for the rest, the farther they exceed that time, are so much the more incapable of Reconcilement) will fall about the second year of the fifty fourth Olympiad, which is the 82d. of *Thales*. From *Thales* he received the Rudiments of that excellence which he afterwards attained. This is acknowledged by † *Jamblicus*. *Thales*, saith he, *entertained him very kindly, admiring the difference between him and other Youths, which exceeded the Fame he had received of him. After that he had instructed him as well as he was able in the Mathematicks, alledging for excuse his old Age and infirmity, he advised him to go to Ægypt, and to converse with the* Memphian *Priests, especially those of* Jupiter, *of whom he himself had in his Travels learned those things, for which by many* he was esteemed wise; and, * again, *among other things* Thales *chiefly advised him to husband his time, in respect whereof he abstained from Wine and Flesh, only eating such things as are light of digestion, by which means he procured shortness of sleep, wakefulness, purity of Mind, and constant health of Body.*

* *De vita Pythag. 1, 2.*

Vit. Pythag. † *2.*

* *Vit. Pythag. 3, 3.*

CHAP. XIII.

Of his Death.

THales having now lived to a great age, being full of Honour and Wisdom, * died in the first year of the fifty eighth Olympiad (when according to *Pausanias Erxyclides* was Archon) as he was beholding the Olympick Games, opprest with heat, thirst, and the burden of his years which amounted to ninety two. *Laertius* under-reckons him to have lived but eighty seven years, having before acknowledged his Birth to have been in the first of the 35th Olympiad. † *Petavius* over-reckons, who makes him live to the end of the 58th, which could not be, because he died spectator of the Olympick Games. * *Lucian* and † *Sincellus* more, who say he lived 100 years. *Sosicrates* comes nearest to the Truth, who allows him to have lived 90 years; and to have died in the 58th Olympiad; for from the first of the 58th are 23 entire Olympiads.

‡ *Laert.*

† *Rationar. temp. 1. 12.*

* *De longævit.* † *Chronol.*

The manner of his Death gave *Laertius* occasion to favour him with this Epigram.

Viewing th' Olympick Games Elean Jove,
Thou didst wise Thales *from that his race remove
Nigher thy self; and 'twas well done, now old
He could not well from Earth the Stars behold.*

He was Buried according to his own appointment in a poor obscure part of the *Milesian* Field, where he presag'd that in futue times their *Forum* should be; upon his Tomb this Distich,

Plut. vit. Solon.

*Narrow the Tomb, the Fame than Heaven more wide,
Of wisest* Thales *whom this Earth doth hide.*

There was also a Statue erected in Honour of him bearing this Inscription,

Milesian Thales *this doth represent,
Who all in wise Astrology outwent.*

† There were five more of this Name mentioned by *Demetrius* the *Magnesian*, an Orator of *Calates*, an affected Imitator. A Painter of *Sicyonia*, of a great Spirit. The third very Ancient, contemporary with *Hesiod*, *Homer*, and *Lycurgus*; The fourth mentioned by *Duris*: The fifth of later times, by *Dionysius* in *Criticis*. * *Laertius* names *Phercydes* as a detractor from *Thales* the Philosoper.

† *Laert.*

* *Vit. Socrat.*

PART I. SOLON. 15

Solon.

CHAP. I.

Solon *his Parents, Country, and Condition.*

Plut.

*P*Hilocles, cited by *Didymus*, affirms that *Solon's* Father was named *Euphorion*, but by the unanimous consent of all other Writers he was called *Execeſtides*, a Person though of small Fortune and Account among the Citizens, yet of the moſt Noble Family in *Athens*, deſcended from *Codrus*, * *Solon* deriving himſelf from *Ne-* leus, Son of *Codrus*, and from *Neptune*: † His Mother near of kin to the Mother of *Piſiſtratus*; his Parents had another Son named *Dropides*, Archon, the year after *Solon*, from him was *Plato* deſcended.

Solon was born (according to *Laertius*) at *Salamis*, for which reaſon he deſired at his
death

* *Laert.*
Plut.

† *Laert. Vit.*
Proclus in Ti-
maeum.

death that his Body might be carried thither; but from his Parents and the place of his Residence, he was firnamed *Athenian*.

Plut. * His Father by Munificence and Liberality brought his Estate so low, as to want even necessaries: *Solon* (ashamed to receive from any being of a House which used to maintain others) betook himself to Merchandize: others say, he Travelled rather to improve his Knowledge and Experience, for he was a professed lover of Wisdom, and even to his last used to say, *I grow old in Learning*; Riches he esteemed not much, but to grow Rich like

————*him who abounds*
In heaps of Gold, as in rank Corn his Grounds
In Mules and Horses, whilst his numerous wealth
Made pleasing by uninterrupted health:
If to compleat these Joys, he be possest
Of Wife and Children, he is truly blest.

And else where,

Riches I wish, not Riches that are plac'd
In unjust means, for Vengeance comes at last.

That he was Profuse and Delicate, and more Luxurious in his Verses than beseems a Philosopher, is attributed to his practising Merchandise, such persons requiring more than ordinary Delicacies and freedoms in Recompence of their many and great dangers. That he was rather in the number of the Poor than of the Rich, is apparent from these his Verses.

Many Unjust grow Rich, and Pious Poor,
We would not change our Virtue for their store,
For constant Virtue is a solid base:
Riches from Man to Man uncertain pass.

† *Polit. 4. 11.* † *Aristotle* ranks *Solon* amongst the inferiour sort of Citizens, which (saith he) *is manifest from his Elegies*, meaning perhaps, some of
* *In Scytha.* these which *Plutarch* cites. 2 *Lucian* saith, he
* *Orat. 1.* was extreamly poor : * *Palæologus*, that he neither had nor valued Wealth.

CHAP. II.

How by his means the Athenians *took* Salamis, Cyrrha, *and the* Thracian Chersonesus.

* *Orat. de falsa legat.* MAny (saith * *Demosthenes*) *of obscure and contemptible have become illustrious by profession of Wisdom*. Solon *both living and dead flourished in extraordinary Glory, to whom the utmost honours were not denyed, for he left a monument of his Valour, the* Megaræan *Trophy, and of his wisdom, the recovery of* Salamis; the occasions these.

† *Pausan.* † The *Island* Salamis *revolted from the* Athenians *to the* Megarenses; * the *Athenians* having
* *Plut.* had a long troublesome War with the *Megarenses* for its recovery, grew at length so weary, that giving it over, they made a Law, forbidding any upon pain of death to speak or write any thing to perswade the City to re-attempt it : *Solon* brooking with much reluctance this ignominy, and seeing many young men in the City desirous to renew the War, (though not daring to move

it, by reason of the Edict) counterfeited himself mad, which he caused to be given out through the City, and having privately composed some elegiack Verses and got them by heart, came skipping into the *Forum* with his Cap (or as *Laertius* saith, *a Garland*) on; the People flocking about him, he went up into the place of the Cryer, and sung his Elegy, beginning thus :

A Cryer I, from Salamis *the fair,*
Am come in Verse this Message to declare :

* The Lines wherewith they were most exci- * *Pausan.* ted were these :

Rather than Athens *would, I ow'd my Birth*
To Pholegondrian, *or* Scinian *Earth :*
For Men where e'er I go will say this is
One of the Athenians *that lost* Salamis.
And,
Then let's to Salamis, *renew our Claim,*
And with th' Isle *recover our lost Fame.*

† This Poem was intituled *Salamis*; it con- † *Plut.* sisted of a hundred Verses, very Elegant: when he had made an end of singing, it was much applauded by his Friends, particularly by *Pysistratus*, who excited the Citizens to follow his advice : By this means the Law was Repealed, the Warre commenced, wherein *Solon* was made General : the common report is that taking *Pysistratus* along with him, (*whence it is that some ascribe the whole Glory of the Action to* Pysistratus, *of whom are* Frontinus, Æneas, *and* Justine) he Sailed to *Colias*, where finding all the Women Celebrating the Festival of *Ceres*, he sent a trusty Messenger to *Salamis*, who pretending to be a Renagade, told the *Megarenses*, that if they would surprize the principal Women of *Athens*, they should go with him immediately to *Colias*: The *Megarenses* believing what he said, Manned a Ship, and sent it along with him; *Solon*, assoon as he saw the Ship come from the Island, commanded the Women to retire, and as many Beardless young Men to put on their Gowns, Head-tyre, and Shoos, hiding Daggers under their Garments, and so danced and played by the Sea-side, till the Enemy were Landed, and their Ship at Anchor: by this time the *Megarenses*, deceived by their outward appearance, Landed in great haste, and came upon them, thinking to take them away by Force, * *but they sudden-* * *Polyæn. lib. ly drawing their Swords, shewed themselves to be* 1. *Men, not Women*; † *the Megarenses were all slain* † *Plut.* not one escaping, the *Athenians* going immediately to the Island took it.

* Others deny it was taken in this manner, but that first receiving this answer from the * *Plut.* Delphian Oracle.

Let Sacrifice be to those Heroes paid,
Who under the Asopian *Ground are laid,*
And dead, are by the setting Sun survey'd.

Solon by night Sailed to the Island, and Sacrificed Burnt-Offerings to the Heroes *Periphemus*, and *Cichris*; then he received five hundred Men of the *Athenians*, with condition, that if they gain'd the Island, the Supream Government

ment thereof should be in them: Shipping his Men in Fisher-boats, attended by one Ship of thirty Oars, they cast Anchor by *Salamis*, near a Point opposite to *Eubœa*: The *Megarenses* who were in *Salamis* hearing an uncertain rumor hereof, betook themselves confusedly to Arms, sending forth a Ship to bring them more certain intelligence from the Enemy, which *Solon*, as soon as it came near, took, and killing the *Megarenses*, manned with choice *Athenians*, whom he commanded to make directly for the City, with all possible secrecy; in the mean time, he with the rest of the *Athenians*, assaulted the *Megarenses* by Land, and whilst they were in fight, they who were in the Ship, making haste, possest themselves of the Town. This relation is confirmed by their Solemnity, an *Athenian* Ship comes thither first in silence, then falling on with cries and shouts, an armed Man leaps forth, and runs directly towards the *Sciradian* Promontory, against those that come from the Land: hard by is the Temple of *Mars*, built by *Solon*; for he overcame the *Megarenses*, and let go ransomless all those that escaped the misery of the War: † *Ælian* faith, *he took two Ships of the* Megarenses, *whereinto he put* Athenian *Officers and Soldiers, bidding them put on the Armour of the Enemy, whereby deceiving the* Megarenses, *he slew many of them unarmed*.

† *Var. Hist. 7. 19.*

* But the *Megarenses* persisting in obstinacy, to the loss of many lives on both sides, the business was referred to the *Lacedemonians* to be decided; many affirm *Solon* alledg'd the Authority of *Homer*, inserting a Verse into his Catalogue of Ships, which he thus recited at the trial,

* *Plut.*

Ajax *twelve Vessels brought to* Salamis,
And where the Athenian *Men had stood rank'd his*.

By which second Verse of his own making and addition he evinc'd, that *Salamis* of old belonged to the Athenians.) But the *Athenians* esteem this relation fabulous, affirming, *Solon* demonstrated to the Judges, that *Phylæus* and *Eurisaces*, Sons of *Ajax*, being made free Denizons by the *Athenians*, delivered this Island to them; and dwelt, one at *Branco*, in *Attica*, the other in *Melita*, whence there is a Tribe named *Philaidæ*, from *Philæus*, of which was *Pisistratus*. † *He overcame the* Megarenses *in an Oration, getting the better of them, not with specious words, but weight of argument*: * more clearly to convince them, he instanced in the burial of the dead, *and inscription of the names of Towns*, used by those of *Salamis*, ‖ *as he shewed, by digging up some Graves*, after the manner of the *Athenians*, not of the *Megarenses*; for in *Megara* they buried their dead with their Faces to the East, in *Athens*, to the West. But *Hereas* of *Megara* denying this, affirms, the *Megarenses* buried also with their Faces toward the West; for further confirmation, *Solon* alledg'd, that the *Athenians* had for each Man a several Coffin, the *Megarenses* buried three or four in the same. It is said also, that *Solon* was much helped by certain Oracles of *Apollo*, wherein he calls *Salamis Ionia*. This cause was decided by five *Spartans*, *Critolaidas*, *Amompherctus*, *Hypsechidas*, *Anaxilas*, and *Cleomenes*.

† *Elian. Var. Hist. 7. 19.*

* *Plut.*

‖ *Laret.*

† *Plut.*

† By this action *Solon* grew into great esteem and honour, but he became [*not long after*] much more admired and cried up by the *Greeks*, for speaking concerning the Temple at *Delphi*. The *Cyrrhæans committed many impieties against* Apollo, *and cut off part of the Land belonging to him*. † *Solon* declared, that it behoved them to relieve it, and not to suffer the *Cyrrhæans* to prophane the Oracle, but that they should vindicate the Gods cause. The *Amphictions* thus instigated by him, undertook the War with much eagerness, as *Aristotle* affirms, ascribing to *Solon* the honour of that Enterprise. *Æschines* faith, the motion made by *Solon* was confirmed by the Oracle. Some affirm he was made General; others *Alcmæon*: But the whole Army of the Greeks was (according to † *Pausanias*) led by *Clisthenes*, *Tyrant of* Sycionia, along with whom they sent *Solon* from *Athens* to be his Counsellor. * *Suidas* faith, *he was chosen Counsellor by those who were pickt out for the service of that War*. † Whilst *Clisthenes besieged* Cirtha, ‖ *they enquir'd concerning the Victory; and from the* Pythian *Oracle received this Answer*,

‖ *Plut.*

† *In Phoc.*

* *In voce Solon.*

† *Polyæn. lib. 3.*

‖ *Pausan.*

This City's Fort you shall not take before
B'ew *Amphitrites* swelling Billows roar
Against my Wave-wash'd Grove, and hallow'd Shoar.

Whereupon *Solon* advis'd to consecrate the *Cyrrhæan field to* Apollo, *by which means the Sea should touch sacred Land*. * *He used also another stratagem against the* Cirrhæans; *the River* Plistus *which ran through the City, he diverted another way, the Town holding out against the Besiegers, some drunk Well-water; others Rain, which they saved in Cisterns. He caused Roots of Hellebore to be thrown into* Plistus, *and when he found it was full poison'd, turned the River again into its proper channel: The* Cyrrhæans *drinking greedily of that Water, were taken with a continual Flux, and forced thereby to give over the defence of their works: The* Amphictions *being possest of the City, punished the* Cyrrhæans, *and avenge the Gods*. These two stratagems were ascribed to *Clisthenes*, the first by † *Poliænus*, the second by ‖ *Frontinus*; but the reason is apparent, he doing them by the direction of *Solon*. * *Solon* perswaded also the *Athenians* to reduce into their power the *Thracian Chersonesus*.

* *Pausan. ibid.*

† *Lib. 3.*
‖ *Lib. 3. cap. 7.*

* *Laert.*

CHAP. III.

How he composed differences and seditions at home, and was made Archon.

† THE *Cylonian* impiety had for a long time vexed the City, ever since the Complices of *Cylon*, having taken sanctuary, were perswaded by *Megacles* the Archon to put themselves upon a Trial, they laying hold of a Thread which was tied to the Image of *Pallas*; when they came near the Images of the Furies, the Thread broke of it self, whereupon *Megacles* with the other Archons fell upon them, as persons disown'd by the Goddess; those that were without the Temple they stoned, those who run to the Altars, they were murdered; they only escaped who sued to their Wives, whence being called impious, they were accounted odious

† *Plut.*

dious: those that remained of the *Cylonians* were grown very rich, and had perpetual enmity with the Family of *Megacles*; at what time this diſſention was higheſt, and the People thereby divided into factions, *Solon* being of much Authority amongſt them, taking with him the chiefeſt of the City, interpoſed betwixt them, and with intreaties and advice perſuaded thoſe who were called impious to ſubmit to the judgment of three hundred of the chief Citizens: *Miro* was their Accuſer; they were condemned, the Living to be baniſhed, the Bones of the dead to be digged up, and thrown beyond the confines of the Country.

During theſe Commotions, the *Megarenſes* took *Nyſſa*, and recovered *Salamis* from the *Athenians*; the City was full of ſuperſtitious terrors and apparitions; the Prieſts declared, that the entrails of the ſacrificed Beaſts imported great crimes and impieties, which required expiation. † *There was alſo a great Plague*; * the Oracle adviſ'd them to luſtrate the City; to this end they ſent († *Nicias*, Son of *Niceratus*, with a Ship) * to fetch *Epimenides* out of *Creet*, who coming to *Athens*, was entertained by *Solon* as a Gueſt, converſed with him as a Friend, inſtructed him in many things, and ſet him in the way of making Laws. *This luſtration of the City*, Euſebius *under-reckons, placing it in the ſecond year of the forty ſeventh Olympiad, whereas* Solon's *being Archon, which certainly happened after this, was in the third of the forty ſixth.* Suidas *ſeems to over-reckon, ranking it in the forty forth: the opinion of* † Laertius *agrees beſt with the circumſtances of the ſtory, that it was in the forty ſixth.*

† *Laert.*
* *Plut.*

† *Laert.*
* *Plut.*

† *In Epimenid.*

* *Plut.*

* The Commotions of the *Cylonei*, being thus appeaſed, and the Offenders extirpated, the People fell into their old difference about the Government of the Common-wealth, whereby they were divided into as many factions, as the Province contained diſtinctions of People; the Citizens were Democratical, the Countrymen affected Oligarchy, the Maritimes ſtood for a mixt kind of Government, and hindred both the other Parties from having the rule; at the ſame time the City was in a dangerous condition, by reaſon of a diſſenſion betwixt the rich and the poor, ariſing from their inequality, the buſineſs ſeemed impoſſible to be compoſed, but by a Monarchy; the Commons were generally oppreſſed by the Mony which they had borrowed of the rich, and either had tilled their Land, paying to them the ſixth part of the Crop, whence they were called *Hectemori*, and *Thetes*, or ingaged their Bodies to their Creditors, whereof ſome ſerved at home, others were ſold abroad, many alſo (there being no Law to the contrary) were neceſſitated to ſell their Children, and leave the City; through the cruelty of theſe Uſurers, the greateſt part (ſuch as had moſt courage amongſt them) aſſembling together, mutually exhorted one another not to indure theſe things any longer, but chuſing ſome truſty Man to be their Leader, to diſcharge thoſe that paid not their Mony at the ſet day, to ſhare the Land, and quite invert the State of the Common-wealth. The diſcreeteſt amongſt the *Athenians* looking upon *Solon* as a Perſon free from any crime, (neither ingaged in the oppreſſions of the rich, nor involved in the neceſſities of the poor) intreated him to take charge of the Commonwealth, and to compoſe the differences of the People. *Phanias* the *Lesbian* affirmeth, that for preſervation of the State, he deceived both Parties, promiſing under-hand to the poor, a diviſion of the Land; the rich, to make good their contracts; but that he firſt made ſcruples of undertaking the buſineſs, deterred by the avarice of the one, and inſolence of the other; he was choſen Archon, next after *Cleombrotus* († *in the third year of the forty ſixth Olympiad*) at what time he made his Laws alſo, being at once a Peace-maker, and a Law-giver, acceptable to the rich, as rich, and to the poor, as good; the People had often in their Mouths this ſaying of his, *Equality breeds no ſtrife*; which pleaſed alike both Parties; one ſide underſtanding it of Number and Meaſure, the other of Worth and Vertue; upon which hope, the moſt powerful of both Factions courted him much, and deſired him to take upon him the Tyranny of that Common-wealth, which he had now in his power, offering themſelves to his aſſiſtance: Many alſo of the moderate part, ſeeing how laborious and difficult it would be to reform the State by Reaſon and Law, were not unwilling to have a Prince created, ſuch an one as were moſt prudent and juſt: ſome affirm he received this Oracle from *Apollo*;

† *Laert.*

Sit at the Helm of State, their Pilot be,
The Common-wealth's glad to be Steer'd by thee.

But he was moſt of all reproved by his familiar Friends, for being deterred by the name of a Tyranny, as if the virtue of a King were not diffuſ'd through the Kingdom, inſtancing in *Tynondas*, long ſince Tyrant of *Eubœa*, and *Pittacus*, at preſent of *Mytelene*: nothing they alledg'd could move him; he told them a Tyranny was a fair poſſeſſion, but it had no paſſage out: to *Phocus* writing thus in Verſe,

That I preſerved free my Native ſoil,
Nor did with bloody Tyranny defile
My honour, I not bluſh at by this deed,
All that was done by others I exceed.

Whereby it appears, he was of great Authority before he writ his Laws. The Contumelies of ſuch as reproved him for declining the Government, he thus expreſt in Verſe:

Nor wiſe is Solon, *nor good counſel knows,*
For he reſiſts the good that God beſtows,
The prey within his power he did behold,
But would not draw the Net; thoughts meanly cold:
Had but his Soul with noble aims been fir'd,
The Kingdom for one day he had deſir'd,
Then ſplit, and all his Family expir'd.

CHAP.

CHAP. IV.

What alterations he made during his Government, and first of the Sisachthia.

*Plut.

* Though he refused the Tyranny, yet he behaved not himself remissly in the Government, not complying with the powerful, nor making Laws to please those who had chosen him; where things were tolerable, he corrected nor altered nothing; fearing, lest if he should change and confound the Common-wealth in every particular, he should want strength to settle it again, and to temper it with the best reason; but such things unto which he conceived he might perswade the obsequious, and compel the refractory, those he enacted; joyning (as he said) Force and Justice, whence, being afterwards demanded if he had given the *Athenians* the best Laws, the best (saith he) they would receive.

† Plut.
* Laert.

† The first change he made in the Government was this, he (* *introduced the* Sisachthia, *which was a discharge of Bodies and Goods; or as* Hesychius *defines it, a Law for remission of private and publick debts, so called from shaking off the oppression of Usury:* † *for at that time they engaged their Bodies for payment, and many through want were constrained to serve their Creditors, he therefore*) ordained that for the time past, all Debts should be acquitted, and for the future, no security should be taken upon the Body of any; this by a moderate term he called *Sisachthia*, there want not (of whom is *Androtion*) who affirmed he contented the Poor, not by an absolute discharge of the Debt, but by moderating the Interest, which he called *Sisachthia*; whereto he added the increase of Measures, and valuation of Money; for the Mina which was before seventy three Drachms, he made a hundred: by this means the poorer sort paid a greater summ in less Coin, which was a great ease to the Debtor, and no wrong to the Creditor: but the greater part hold it was an absolute discharge, which agreeth best with the Verses of *Solon*, wherein he boasteth he had *removed the bounds throughout the Land, freed such as were under oppression, called home those, who being forced to travel, had forgotten their native Language; and others that were at home under bondage, set at Liberty.*

† Laert.

* Lib. 1.

The same Law, * *Diodorus Siculus* observes to be among the *Egyptians*, conceiving *Solon* (tho' as yet he had not been there) derived it from them.

*Plut.

* But in this design a great misfortune befel him, whilst he endeavoured to redress the oppression of Usury, and was studying how to begin an Oration suitable to the thing, he acquainted his intimate Friends, in whom he reposed most confidence, *Conori, Clinias,* and *Hipponicus,* that he meant not to meddle with Land; but to cut off all Debts; they (preventing the Edict) borrowed of the Rich great Summs of Money, wherewith they purchased much Land; the Edict being published, they enjoyed their purchase, without satisfying their Creditors: *Solon* was much blamed, as not defrauded with the rest, but as being a defrauder with those, and a partaker of their cozenage; but this imputation was immediately washed away with five Talents, so much he had forth at Interest, which he first, according to the Law, blotted out, (*Laertius* saith six, perswading others to do the like) others, of whom is *Polyzelus* the *Rhodian,* fifteen; but his Friends were ever after called χρεωκοπίδαι.

* Plut.

* This pleased neither parts; he discontented the Rich by cancelling their Bonds, the poor more, not making good a parity of Estates, which they expected, as *Lycurgus* had done, he being the eleventh from *Hercules*, having reigned many years in *Lacedæmon*, great in Authority, Friends, and Wealth, whereby he was able to make good what he thought convenient for the State, rather by force than perswasion, even to the loss of his Eye, effected as a thing most expedient to the preservation and peace of the Common-wealth, that none of the Citizens were either rich or poor: But *Solon* attained not this in the Common-wealth, being one of the People, and of a mean degree; yet he omitted nothing within his power, carried on by his own Judgment, and the Faith which the Citizens had in him; that he displeased many, who expected other things, is thus acknowledged by himself.

Before they look'd upon me kindly, now
With Eyes, severe, and a contracted Brow:
Had any else my power, he would exact
Their Riches, and their fattest Milk extract.

But both Parties soon found how much this conduced to the general good, and laying aside their private differences, Sacrificed together, calling the Sacrifice Σεισάχθεια.

CHAP. V.

How he divided the People into Classes, and erected Courts of Judicature.

† Plut.

† Hereupon they chose *Solon* Reformer and Lawgiver of the Common-wealth, not limiting him to any thing, but submitting all to his Power, Magistracies, Convocations, Judgments, Courts to take an account of them, to prescribe what number and times he pleased; to disannul or ratifie of the present Law what he thought good.

* Plut.

* First, then he quite abolished all the Laws of *Draco*, except for Murther, because of their rigidness and severity, for he punished almost all offences with Death; as that they who were surprised in Idleness should be put to death; they who stole Herbs or Apples should undergo the same punishment with such as had committed Murther, or Sacriledge; whence *Demades* wittily said, *Draco* writ his Laws not in Ink, but Blood; he being asked why he punished all offences with Death, answered, *he conceived the least deserved so much, and he knew no more for the greatest.* Herodicus alluding to his name, said *his Laws were not of a Man, but of a Dragon, they were so rigid;* And † Aristotle saith, *there was nothing in them extraordinary and worthy of memory, but that severity and greatness of penalty* which was so excessive, that * *not by any edict or command, but by a silent unexpressed consent amongst the Athenians*

† Arist. Rhet. 2. 23.

* A. Gell. 11. 18.

nians *they were laid aside; afterwards they used the milder Laws made by* Solon, *differing even in name, the first being called* θεσμοὶ, *the latter* νόμοι. † Those of *Draco* were made in the 39th Olympiad, 47 years (as * *Ulpian* accounts) before these of *Solon*.

† Tatian.
Clem. Alex.
Suid.
*In Demost.
Timocr.
† Plut.

† Next, *Solon* (being desirous that all Offices might continue as they were, in the Hands of the Rich, but that other Priviledges of the Common-wealth, from which the People were excluded, might be promiscuously disposed) took an account and valuation of the People [† *and divided them into four orders*] those whose stock of dry and liquid Fruits amounted to 500 measures he ranked in the first place, and called *Pentacosiomedimni*, [* *these paid a Talent to the publick Treasury.*] In the second Class were those who were able to maintain a Horse, or received 300 Measures, these he called [† *for that reason*] *Horsemen*; they paid half a Talent. The third Class were *Zengitæ* (* *so called because*) they had 200 Measures of both sorts, † *these paid 10 Minæ*; the rest were all called *Thetes*, whom he suffered not to be capable of any Magistracy, neither did they pay any thing, but only had so far Interest in the Commonwealth, as to have a suffrage in the publick Convocation, and at Judgments, which at first seemed nothing, but afterwards appeared to be of great Consequence; for in whatsoever was brought before the Judges, he gave them leave (if they would) to appeal to the common *Forum*; moreover writing his Laws obscurely and perplexedly, he increased the Power of the *Forum*, for not being able to determine Controversies by the Law, they were forced to have recourse to the Judges; as Masters of the Law; this equality he himself thus expresseth,

† Pollux.

* Pollux.

† Pollux.

* Pollux.
† Pollux.

> The Commons I sufficient Power allow;
> Honour from none I took, on none bestow;
> Those who in Power or wealth the rest outshin'd,
> In bounds of Moderation I confin'd;
> To either part I was a firm defence,
> And neither did allow preheminence.

† Epist. 90.
* Lib. 2.

Hither † *Seneca* alluding faith, Solon *founded* Athens *upon equal right*; and * Justin *he carried himself with such temper between the Commons and the Senate, that he attracted equal favour from both, he suffered no Man* (saith † *Eneas Gazeus*) *to have a peculiar Law, but made all Men subject to the same.*

† In Theophrast.

† Plut.

† *He likewise* (continues *Plutarch*) *constituted the Court of the Areopagus*, consisting of the yearly *Archons*, whereof himself (being the chief) was one; perceiving the People to be much exalted and emboldened by the remission of their Debts, he ordained a second Court of Judicature, selecting out of each Tribe (which were in all four) a hundred Persons, who should resolve upon all Decrees before they were reported to the People; nor should any thing be brought to them, until it had first past the Senate: the Supreme Senate he appointed Judge and preserver of the Laws, conceiving the City would be less apt to float up and down, and the People become more setled, relying upon these two Courts, as on two Anchors; thus the greater part of Writers make *Solon* Institutor of the Court of *Areopagus*, (of whom also is † *Cicero*) which seems to be confirmed, in that *Draco* never mentions the *Areopagites*, but in Criminal Causes always names the *Ephetæ*; but the eighth Law of the thirtieth Table of *Solon* hath these words, *Those who are branded with Infamy before* Solon *was Archon, let them be restored to their fame, except such as were condemned by the* Areopagites, *or by the* Ephetæ, &c. And it is certain, That *the Court of* Areopagus *was long before* Solon'*s time, until then consisting promiscuously of such Persons as were eminent for Nobility, Power, or Riches, but* Solon *reformed it, ordaining none should be thereof, but such as had first undergone the Office of Archon*, See *Meursius, Areop. cap.* 3.

† De offic. l. 1.

† Pollux *saith, that* Solon *ordained a thousand Men to judge all Accusations*; * *Demetrius Phalerius, that he constituted the* Demarci, *first called* Nauclari,

† Lib. 8. cap. 6.
* Schol. Aristoph. in Nub.

CHAP. VI.
His Laws.

HAving thus disposed the Common-wealth, and Courts of Judicature, he in the next place applied himself to making Laws, which he performed so excellently, that he is generally remembred under that notion, with *Minos* of *Creet*, and *Lycurgus* of *Lacedæmon*, whose Laws those of *Solon* exceeded, (as † *Tacitus* saith) *both in exquisiteness and number :* * *of how much greater esteem they were than all before them, may be computed from this, That they were the last, and continued always in the City: They, for whom they were made, thought them more illustrious than their publick Ornaments, which transcended those of all other Cities, more impregnable than their Tower, which they accounted the strongest of all upon Earth, and far better than those things wherein they gloried most:* † *nor were they of less esteem among* Foreign *Nations, insomuch that the* Romans *agreeing concerning Laws in general, but differing about the Lawgiver, sent Ambassadors to* Athens, Sp. Posthumius Albus, A. Manlius, P. Sulpitius Camerinus, *commanding them to transcribe the renowned Laws of* Solon: † *which transferred out of the Books of* Solon, *the* Decemviri, *expounded in the twelve Tables*. Hence * *Ammianus Marcellinus saith, that* Solon *assisted by the Sentences of the* Egyptian *Priests, having with just moderation framed Laws, added also to the* Roman *State the greatest Foundation.*

† Annal. 3.
* Man. Palæolog. in protrept. ad d. fr.

† Liv. lib. 3.

† Aurel. Vict. de vir. illust. c. 21
* Lib. 22.

Of his Laws, these have been preserved by *Plutarch*, and others.

† *If any Man were beaten, hurt, or violently treated, whosoever had the means and will, might sue the Offender,* Thus (saith *Plutarch*) he wisely brought the Citizens to a mutual sense of one anothers hurts, as if done to a Limb of their own Body.

† Plut.

† *Of infamous Persons, let all such as were infamous before the Government of* Solon, *be restored to their fame, excepting whosoever were condemned by the* Ephetæ, *or in the* Prytanæum *by the Magistrates, banished for Murder, Theft, or aspiring to Tyranny.* This was the eighth Law of the thirteenth

† Plut.

thirteenth table. There were two kinds of infamy, by the lesser a Man was degraded and made uncapable of all honour or office in the Commonwealth; by the greater, he and his Children were lyable to be killed by any man, and he not to be questioned for it.

[h] *Plut.*

[i] *Lib. 2. cap. 12.*

[k] *Plut.*

[h] Of his laws, those seem most singular and paradoxal, which declare him infamous, who in a sedition takes neither part: it is cited out of *Aristotle* by [i] *A. Gellius* in these words: *If through discord and dissention, any sedition and difference divided the people into two factions, whereupon with exasperated minds both parties take up arms and fight; he, who at that time, and upon that occasion of civil discord shall not engage himself on either side, but solitary and separated from the common evil of the City withdraw himself, let him be deprived of house, Country and goods by banishment.* [k] He would not that any one saving himself harmless, should be insensible of the common calamity, or boast himself to have no share in the publick grief, but that instantly applying himself to the better and juster side, he should interest himself in the common danger, and assist, rather than out of all hazard, expect which side should get the better. When we did read (saith *A. Gellius*) this law of *Solon*, a person indued with singular wisdom, at first we remained in great suspence and admiration, enquiring for what reason he judged those worthy of punishment, who withdrew themselves from sedition and civil war; then one whose sight pierced more deeply into the use and meaning of the law, affirmed, the intent thereof was not to encrease, but appease sedition; and so indeed it is: for if all good persons, who in the beginning are too few to restrain a sedition, should not deter the distracted raging people, but dividing themselves, adhere to either side, it would follow, that they being separated as partakers of both factions, the parties might be temper'd and govern'd by them, as being persons of greatest authority; by which means they might restore them to peace, and reconcile them, governing and moderating that side whereof they are, and desiring much rather the adverse party should be preserved than destroyed.

[l] *ad Attic. 10. 1.*

[l] *Cicero* citing this law, avereth the punishment to have been capital, perhaps understanding infamy here of the more severe kind.

[m] *Plut.*

[n] *In præcept. conjugial.*

Absurd and ridiculous (saith *Plutarch*) seemeth that Law which alloweth *an inheritrix, if he who possesseth her by law as her Lord and Master be impotent, to admit any of her husbands nearest kindred.* But some aver it is just, as to those, who tho' they are impotent, yet will marry rich heirs for their mony, and by the priviledge of law wrong nature; for when they see it lawful for the heir to admit whom she pleaseth, either they will refrain from such marriages, or undergo them with the reproach of avarice and dishonesty: It is well ordered also, that she may not admit any one, but only whom she will of her husbands kindred, whereby the issue may be of his family and race. [m] Hitherto likewise it tends, that *the Bride be shut up in a room with the Bridegroom, and eat a Quince with him.* (Intimating, according to [n] *Plutarch's* interpretation, that the first grace of her lips and voyce should be agreeable and sweet) and that *he who marrieth an heir, be obliged to visit her thrice a Month at the least*: For though they have not children, this argues a respect due to a chast Wife, and prevents or reconciles unkindness and dissention.

Those words of the former law, *He who possesseth her by law as her Lord and Master*, have reference to another Law of his, mentioned by [o] *Diodorus Siculus*, that *the next of kin to an heir might by law require her in marriage, and she likewise might require him that was next of kin who was obliged to marry her, though never so poor, or to pay 500 Drachms for her dowry.* Hereto [p] *Terence* alludes.

[o] *Lib. 12.*

[p] *Hec. Act. 1. Scen.*

*The Law commands an heir to marry with
Her Husbands next of kin, and him to take her.*

And to the putting her off without a dowry of 500 drachms, (that is five *minæ*) [q] elsewhere.

[q] *Phorm. act. 2 scen. 3.*

*Though I be injur'd thus, yet rather than
I'le be contentious, or bound still to bear thee,
Since she's my kinswoman, take hence with her
The Dower the law enjoyns me, here's five pound.*

[r] In all other marriages he forbad Dowries, ordaining that *a Bride should bring with her no more than three gowns, and some slight Houshold-stuff, of small value*, the particulars whereof were express'd, as [s] *Pollux* seems to imply, for he would not that marriage should be mercenary or vendible, but that the Man and Woman should cohabit for Issue, love, and friendship. Hither [t] *Isidor* alludes amongst the Athenians legal marriage was said to be contracted in respect of issue.

[r] *Plut.*

[s] *1. 12. 15.*

[t] *Isi. Lib. 3. Epist. 243.*

That Law of his also was commended, as [u] *Demosthenes* and *Plutarch* attest, which forbad to revile the dead, *Let no man revile any dead person, though provoked by the revilings of his Children.* [w] To esteem the deceased holy, is pious, to spare the absent, just, to take away the eternity of hatred, civil.

[u] *Orat. in Leptin.*

[w] *Plut.*

[x] He forbad *to revile any living person at sacred solemnities, Courts of Judicature, and publick spectacles, upon penalty of three drachms to be paid to the reviled person, two more to the common treasury.* To moderate anger no where he accounted rude and disorderly, every where difficult, to some impossible. A law must be accommodated to what is possible, intending to punish some few, to advantage not many to no purpose.

[x] *Plut.*

[y] His law concerning Testaments is much approved; for before, no man had power to make a Will, but his goods, and lands continued in the family of the deceased person. *Solon* made it *lawful for him that had no Children, to give his estate to whom he pleased.* He preferred friendship before kindred, and favour before necessity, and ordered, that wealth should be at the disposal of him in whose hands it was: yet he permitted not this rashly, or absolutely, but conditionally, *If he were not wrought upon by sickness, potions, bondage, or the blandishments of a Wife.* justly he esteemed it all one whether a Man be seduced by indirect means, or violently constrained, thus comparing deceit with force, and pleasure with pain, as being of equal power to put

[y] *Plut.*

put a Man out of his right Mind. This Law is mentioned likewise by ᵍ *Demosthenes*.

ᵉ *Orat.in Lept.*

He also limited the Visits, Mournings, and Feasts of Women, by a Law which curbed their former Licentiousness. *Her who went abroad, he permitted not to carry with her above three Gowns, nor more meat and drink than might be bought with an obolus, nor a basket above a Cubit in bigness, nor to travel by Night, unless in a Chariot, and with Torch-light: He forbad them to tear their Cheeks to procure mourning and lamentation, at the Funerals of those, to whom they have no relation. He forbad to sacrifice an Ox at Funerals, and to bury more than three Garments with the dead Body; not to approach the Monuments of strangers unless at their Exequies.* Of which (saith *Plutarch*) our Laws are full: ʰ *Cicero* also affirms, that the Laws of the twelve Tables for contracting the pomp of Funerals, and concerning mourning, are transferred from those of *Solon*, who (as *Phalerius* writes) assoon as Funerals began to be solemnized with pomp and lamentation, took them away: Which Law the *Decemviri* put into the tenth table, almost in the very same words, for that of three Neighbourhoods and most of the rest are *Solon*'s, that of Mourning in his express words, *Let no Women tear their Cheeks, nor make lamentation at a Funeral.*

ʰ *De leg. lib. 2.*

ⁱ Considering that all the City grew very populous, many recurring thither from all parts of *Attica*, for liberty and security, that the Country was for the most part barren and bad, that such as trade by Sea import nothing for those, that have not wherewith to barter or exchange with them, he addicted the Citizens to Arts, and made a Law, that *the Son should not be obliged to maintain his Father, if he had not brought him up to a Trade* (mentioned also by ᵏ *Vitruvius*, *Galen*, ˡ *Theophylact*, and others) and commanded *the Court of Areopagus to examine by what gain every Man maintained himself, and to punish idle Persons, whom he made liable to the action of every Man, and at the third Conviction punished with Infamy.* This Law ⁿ *Herodotus*, and ᵒ *Diodorus Siculus* affirm to have been in use amongst the *Ægyptians*, made by *Amasis*, and from them derived by *Solon* to the *Athenians*.

ⁱ *Plat.*

ᵏ *Præfat.lib.6.*
ˡ *Exhort. Vrat.*
ᵐ *de artes.*
Epist.7.

ⁿ *Lib. 7.*
ᵒ *Lib. 1.*

ᵖ Yet more severe was that mentioned by *Heraclides* of *Pontus*, which *disengaged the Sons of Concubines from maintaining their Fathers.* He who transgresseth the bounds of marriage, professeth he doth it not out of desire of issue, but for pleasure, and therefore already hath his reward, and can expect to have no further tye upon those he begets, whose birth is their Shame.

ᵖ *Plut.*

ᑫ Most incongruous seem those Laws of *Solon*, which concern Women, for he permitted that whosoever surprised an Adulterer (with the Wife or ʳ Concubine of any) might kill him, (or exact Money of him) *he that ravished a free Woman was fined* 100 *Drachms, he that plaid the pander,* (20 ˢ *Æschines* faith, to die) *except to such women as were common.* He also forbad *any Man to give his Sister or Daughter to that profession, unless himself first surprise her with a Man.* This (saith *Plutarch*) seems absurd to punish the same offences sometimes severely with Death, sometimes with a pecuniary mulct, unless, because at that time Money was very rare in *A-*

ᑫ *Plut.*

ʳ *Lysias in Orat. de cæde Eratosth.*
ˢ *Orat. in Timarch.*

thens, the scarcity thereof aggravated the punishment.

ᵗ He assigned *five hundred Drachms to the Victor of the Isthmian Games, a hundred to the Victor of the Olympick:* attested also by *Laertius*, who faith, he contracted the Rewards of the Athleta's, judging them dangerous Victors, and that they were Crowned rather against, than for their Country.

ᵗ *Plat.*

ᵘ *Whosoever brought a he-Wolf was to receive five drachms, for a she-Wolf one;* according to *Demetrius Phalerius*, this being the price of a Sheep, that of an Ox. It is customary with the *Athenians*, that such as have grounds fitter for Pasture than Plowing, make War with the Wolves,

ᵘ *Plat.*

ʷ Forasmuch as there is such scarcity of Rivers, Lakes, and Springs in the Country, that they are constrained to dig Wells, he made a Law, *Where there was a common Well within a Hippicon, they should make use of it.* (A Hippicon is the distance of four Furlongs) 'they that 'lived further off should procure Water of 'their own, and if when they have digged ten 'Fathom deep, they find not any, they might be 'allowed to fill a Pitcher of six Gallons twice 'a Day at their Neighbours Well.

ʷ *Plat.*

ˣ These exact Rules he prescribed for planting, *Whosoever planted any young Tree in his Ground, should set it five foot distant from his Neighbours; who a Figtree or Olive-tree, nine:* Because the Roots of these spread far, nor is their Neighbourhood harmless to all, but sucks away the nourishment, and to some their blast is prejudicial.

ˣ *Plat.*

ʸ 'Whosoever diggeth any hole or ditch must 'make it so far distant from his Neighbours, as 'it is deep. These are confirmed by ᶜ *Cajus*, adding, 'Whosoever makes a Hedge to divide himself from his Neighbour, must not exceed his 'own Bounds; if a Wall, he must leave the space 'of a Foot, if a House, two Feet, if a Well, a 'Fathom.

ʸ *Plat.*

ᶜ *Lib.4.ad 12. tab.*

'Whosoever placeth a Hive of Bees, should 'observe the distance of thirty Feet, from those 'that were before placed by his Neighbour.

ᵇ He commanded *the Archons to Curse him who exported any thing out of the Country, or that he should pay a hundred drachms to the publick Treasury*, whereby they are not to be rejected, who say, that of old the exportation of figgs was prohibited, and that he who discovered an Exporter, was called a Sycophant.

ᵇ *Plat.*

ᶜ He made a Law concerning such as should be hurt by a Dog, wherein he ordained, *the Dog that bit to be bound in a Chain four Cubits long.*

ᶜ *Plat.*

ᵈ This Law concerning Denization is difficult, 'That none should be made free of the City, ex'cept such who were Banished for ever out of 'their own Country, or came to *Athens* with their 'whole Families to exercise some trade; this he did not to drive away Foreigners, but to invite them to *Athens* by certainty of admittance into the City, conceiving such would be faithful, those out of necessity, these out of good-will.

ᵈ *Plut.*

ᵉ Likewise to be feasted in the publick Hall was the peculiar Institution of *Solon*, which he called παρασιτεῖν, not permitting the same person to eat there frequently: but if he who were invited, would not accept of it, he was punished.

ᵉ *Plu.*

punished; conceiving this contempt of the publique honour, that an inordinate appetite.——

Hitherto *Plutarch*: these following are recited by *Laertius*.

Laert.
† *Orat. in Timarch.*

If any one maintain not his Parents, let him be infamous, as likewise he that *devours his patrimony*. Hitherto †*Æschines* alludes; in the fourth place with whom hath he to do? If any Man by prodigality hath consumed his patrimony or hereditary goods; for he conceived, he who had ordered his own Family ill, would in the same manner take care of the Common-wealth; neither did the Law-giver imagine it possible, that the same Person should be privately wicked, and publickly good, or that it were fitting such a one should go up into the chair, who took more care to frame an Oration, than to compose his Life.

* *Laert.*
† *In Timarch.*

* He *forbad such as haunted common Women to plead*; confirmed by *Æschines* †. In the third place with whom hath he to do? If any Man (saith he) be a haunter of common Women, or procure Mony by such means; for he conceived, such a one as sold his own fame for mony, would easily sell the business of the State. And ᵇ *Demosthenes*, it is worth inquiry and consideration, *Athenians*, how great care, *Solon*, the Author of this Law, had in the Commonwealth in all those which he made, and how particularly solicitous he was herein above all other things, which as it is evident by many other laws, so also by this, which forbids those *qui se prostituerunt*, either to plead or judge in publick.

ᵇ *In Androt.*

Laert.

ᶜ He augmented the rewards of such as should die in War, whose Sons he *ordered to be brought up and instructed at the publick charge*. *Aristides*, thou alone of all Men didst ordain these three things by Law, that such as died for their Country should be annually praised publickly at their Sepulchers; their Children, till grown Men, maintained at the publick charge, then sent back to their Fathers House with compleat Arms; likewise that infirm Citizens should be maintain'd at the publick charge. ᵈ *Plato* adds that the same indulgence was allowed to the Parents, you know the care of the Common-wealth, which in the laws concerning the Children and Parents of such as died in the War, *commands the supream Magistrate to take care, that the Parents of those that died in the War, above all other Citizens should not receive any injury*. The State brings up the Children also: hereby, saith *Laertius*, they became eager of fame and honour in War, as *Polyzelus*, as *Cynegyrus*, as all those in the *Marathonian* fight: to whom may be added *Harmodidus*, *Aristogiton*, *Miltiades*.

* *In Panathen.*

ᵈ *Menexen.*

ᵉ *Laert.*

ᵉ *Let not a Guardian marry the Mother of his ward, nor let any one be ward to him, who if he die, shall inherit his estate*, confirm'd by * *Syrianus*, † *Marcellius*, and others, who add that the same law forbad the ward to marry her Guardians Son.

* *In Hermog.*
† *In Hermog.*

ᶠ *Laert.*

ᶠ *Let not a Graver keep the impression of any Seal after he hath sold it.*

ᵍ *Laert.*

ᵍ *If any Man put out the Eye of another, who had but one, he shall lose both his own.*

His Law concerning theft, *Laertius* expresseth thus; *What thou laidst not down, take not up, otherwise the punishment death.* * *Æschines* adds, if

* *Orat. in Timarch.*

they confessed themselves guilty: others affirm the punishment was only to pay double the value, of whom is ʰ *A. Gellius* and † *Hermogenes*, who affirm, the Law made that distinction betwixt Sacriledge and Theft, punishing the first with death, the latter with double restitution. * *Demosthenes* clears this, reciting this Law exactly in these words, *If any Man steal in the day time above fifty drachms, he may be carried to the eleven Officers, if he steal any thing by night, it shall be lawful for any to kill him, or in the pursuit to wound him, and to carry him to the eleven Officers. Whosoever is convict of such offences, as are liable to chains, shall not be capable of giving bail for his theft, but his punishment shall be death, and if any one steal out of the Lyceum, or the Academy, or Cynosarges, a Garment or a small vessel of Wine, or any other thing of little value, or some vessel out of the Gymnasia, or Havens, he shall be punished with death; but if any Man shall be convict privately of theft, it shall be lawful for him to pay a double value, and it shall be also at the pleasure of the Convictor, besides payment of Mony, to put him in chains five days, and as many nights, so as all Men may see him bound.* ⁱ Even those who stole dung, were by *Solon*'s Law liable to punishment.

ʰ *Lib. 11. c. 18.*
† *Partit.*
* *Orat. in Timocr.*

ⁱ *Schol. Aristoph. ad equites.*

* That *if an Archon were taken drunk, he should be punish'd with death.*

* *Laert.*

To those recited by *Laertius*, add these collected by others.

He *allowed Brothers and Sisters by the same Father to marry, and prohibited only Brothers and Sisters of the same venture*; Whereas contrariwise (saith ᵏ *Philo*) the Lacedæmonian Lawgiver allowed these, and prohibited those. Hence ˡ *Cornelius Nepos* affirms, *Cimon* married his Sister *Elpinice*, invited, not more by love, than the Athenian custom, which allows to marry a Sister by the same Father.

ᵏ *De leg. spec. lib. 2.*
ˡ *In Proæm. & in Cimonis vita.*

ᵐ He writ according to the manner of the Antients, severally concerning the discipline of Matrons, for *a Woman taken in Adultery he permitted not to wear ornaments, nor to come into publick Temples, lest by her presence she should corrupt modest Women; if she came into a Temple, or adorned her self, he commanded every one to rend her Garments, to tear off her Ornaments, and to beat her, but not to kill or maim her:* By this means depriving such a Woman of all honour, and giving her a life more bitter than death. This is also confirmed by * *Demosthenes*, who adds, *If any Man surprise an Adulterer, it shall not be lawful for him who took them to have the Woman in marriage, if he continue to keep her as his Wife, let him be infamous.*

ᵐ *Æschin. Orat. in Timarch.*

* *In Neæram.*

ⁿ *Let the dead Body be be laid out within the house, according as he gave order, and the day following before Sun-rise carried forth; whilst the body is carrying to the Grave, let the Men go before, the Women follow; it shall not be lawful for any Woman to enter upon the goods of the dead, and follow the body to the grave, under threescore years of age, excepting those within the degree of cosens, nor shall any Woman enter upon the goods of the deceased after the body is carried forth, excepting those who are within the degree of Cosens.*

ⁿ *Demosth. Orat. in Macartat.*

* Concerning Sepulchers, he saith no more, than that *no man shall demolish them, or bring any new thing into them; and shall be punished, whosoever violates, casts down, or breaks any tomb, monument, or column.*

* *Cicer. de leg. 2.*

ᵒ *If*

SOLON. PART I.

p Ælian. var. hist. 2. 42. &c. ° If any one light upon the dead body of a Man unburied, let him throw earth upon it.

* Demoſt. in Lipton. * Whoſoever ſhall diſlike a received Law, let him firſt accuſe it, then if it be abrogated, ſubſtitute another: The manner whereof is largely expreſſed by Demoſthenes.

q Declam. 18. He ordained (according to q Libanius) that Children ſhould be obliged to perform all due offices to their Parents. † Sextus, ſaith he, made

† Pyrrh. Hipp. 3. 24. a Law of indemnity, whereby he allowed any Man to kill his Son; but * Dionyſius Halicar-

* Lib. 2. naſſeus affirms, he permitted them to turn their Children out of doors, and to diſinherit them, but nothing more.

† Æſchin. in Cteſiph. † He ordained that *all ſuch as declined to be engaged in War, or forſook the Army, or was a Coward, ſhould have all one puniſhment, to be driven out of the bounds of the Forum, not permitted to wear a Garland, or to enter into publick Temples.*

ſ Demoſt. Orat. in Timocr. ſ *If any one be ſeized on, for having abuſed his Parents, or forſaken his Colours, or being forbidden by Law, hath gone into places where he ought not, let the eleven officers take and bind him, and carry him into the Heliæa, it ſhall be lawful for any one that will to accuſe him, and if he be caſt, it ſhall be at the judgment of the Heliæa to impoſe what Puniſhment or Fine they ſhould think fit, if a Fine, let him be kept in fetters till it be paid.*

t Athenæus. deipn. lib. 15. t He permitted *not a man to ſell unguents,* as being an effeminate office.

c Æſchin. in Cteſiph. c As concerning Orators, he ordered, that *the Eldeſt of the Citizens ſhould go up firſt into the pleaders chair modeſtly without tumult and perturbation to move, he out of experience ſhould conceive beſt for the Common-wealth; then that every Citizen according to his age ſhould ſeverally by and in order declare his judgment.*

u Liban. declam. 13. u He ordered that *a Citizen of Athens ſhould be tried no where but at Athens.*

w Stob. 112. w He commanded that *no young man ſhould bear the office of a Magiſtrate, nor be admitted to council, though he were eſteemed exceeding wiſe.*

x Demoſt. in Ariſtogit. x For the common people he ordained ſlow puniſhments, for Magiſtrates and Rulers of the people ſuddain, conceiving thoſe might be puniſhed at any time, but that the correction of theſe would admit no delay.

z Maxim. Tyr. 39. z As for the Gods and their Worſhip, he decreed nothing, * nor againſt Parricides, anſwer-

* Cicer. orat. pro S. Roſc. ing thoſe who queſtioned him about it, *he did not think any could be ſo wicked.*

CHAP. VII.

Of the Axes and Cyrbes, Senators Oath, and other inſtitutions of Solon.

* Plut.
† A. Gell. 2. 12.
* Plut. Etymol.
† Pollux. 8.10.
ε Suid.

* THeſe Laws he ratified, for a hundred years; They were † carved in different Tables*. Thoſe which concerned private actions, in oblong quadrangular tables of Wood, with caſes, which reached from the ground and turned about upon a Pin like a Wheel, whence they were called Ἄξονες, † placed firſt in the Tower, then brought into the Prytanæum, that all might ſee them, where there were ſome remains of them in Plutarch's, time. Thoſe which concerned ε pub-

lick orders and ſacrifices, in b triangular tables of ſtone called κύρβεις either from c Cyrbus who took the account of every mans eſtate, or ἀπὸ τῦ ταῦτα κυρῶσθαι τοῖς γράμμασι, or ἀπὸ d τῦ κακοργυθῦσιν, or from the Corybantes, to whom the invention thereof is by ſome aſcribed. Theſe were placed in the Porticus regia; e Both the Axxs and Cyrbes were written after the ſame manner as Oxen to turn in ploughing βυςροφνδὸν γεάφην. whence Demoſthenes calls that law the loweſt which beginneth on the left ſide.

b Ammon. de differ. voc.
c Suid.
d Schol. Ariſtot in Aves.
e Didym. apud Harp. & Suid.

f The Senate took one common oath to make good the laws of Solon for a hundred years, each of the Theſmothetæ ſworn in the Forum at the Criers Stone; if he violated them, to dedicate a golden ſtatue of equal weight with himſelf at Delphi.

f Plut.

Some particulars of the oath impoſed by Solon mention'd by ſeveral Authors, (as, *not to abrogate his Laws*, by Plutarch, *to admit no young man to be judge*, by g Stobæus, *to hear impartially both the Plaintiff and Defendant*, by h Demoſthenes; argue it to be the ſame which the ſame i Author delivers in theſe words.

g Serm. 112.
h Orat. de corona.
i Demoſt.

'I will declare my opinion according to the 'laws of the Athenians, and five hundred Se-
'nators. By no aſſiſtance from me ſhall Ty-
'ranny or Oligarchy be admitted. I will never
'ſide with him who hath corrupted the People,
'intends, or indeavours it. I will never ſuffer
'any new tables or any diviſion of thoſe already
'received, or a parity of Lands or Goods. I
'will never call home any baniſhed or confined
'Perſon. I will conſent that he be expelled the
'City, who denies theſe Laws, decreed by the
'Senate, confirmed by the People; I will never
'permit any to be injured, I will never con-
'ſtitute any Magiſtrate before he hath given ac-
'count of his laſt Magiſtracy. I will never per-
'mit the ſame Man to be choſen twice in one
'year, or at once to hold two Offices. I will
'neither take, nor ſuffer any to take Bribes or
'rewards. I am thirty years old, I will hear im-
'partially both Plaintiff and Defendant, and
'condemn without excuſe thoſe that deſerve
'it. I ſwear by Jove, by Neptune and by Ceres,
'may they deſtroy me, my Houſe and Children,
'if I obſerve not all theſe particulars. Hence
'perhaps it is that * Heſychius affirms, Solon in
'his Laws to have ordained on oath by three
'Gods.

k τρεῖς Θεοὶ

Conſidering the irregularity of Months, and the courſe of the Moon, which agreed not always with the riſing and ſetting of the Sun, but ſometimes overtook and went paſt him in one day, he called that day the ἔνη ϗ νέα, *laſt and firſt*, attributing that part which precedes the conjunction to the laſt Month, the reſt to the beginning of the next. Thus l he taught the Athenians *to accommodate the reckoning of their days to the motion of the Moon:* m and was (as it appears) the firſt who underſtood rightly that of Homer.

l Laert.
m Plut.

When one Month ended and the next began,

The day following he called Νουμηνία, *The new Moon*; from the twentieth day to the thirtieth he reckon'd not by addition but by ſubſtraction, in reſpect of the Moons decreaſe: for this ſee n Ariſtophanes.

n The clouds. act. 4. ſcen.

* He

Laert. * He ordered the Verses of *Homer* to be recited successively, that where the first ended the next should begin ; whence *Diuchides* saith, he illustrated *Homer* more than *Pisistratus* (by whom the *Rhapsodies* were first collected) the principal Verses were.

They who inhabit Athens, &c.

† *Athen. deipn. 13.* † He first tolerated common Curtesans, and with the Mony they paid to the State erected a Temple to *Venus*, πανδημίῳ.

* *Sect. Empiric. advers. Mathem. 6.* * He first taught Soldiers to march by the sound of Fifes and Harps, observing a kind of measure in their pace.

CHAP. VIII.

How he entertained Anacharsis ; *his Travels to* Ægypt, Cyprus, Miletus, Delphi, Corinth, *and* Creet.

a Plut.
b Laert.
IN the forty seventh Olympiad (according to ª *Sosicrates*) *Anacharsis* came to *Athens* ; *Eucrates* being Archon, ᵇ he went immediately to the House of *Solon*, and knocking at the door, said he was a Stranger desirous of his Friendship and Hospitality : *Solon* answered, *It is better to contract friendship at home* ; *then you that are at home,* (replys *Anacharsis*) *make me your Friend and Guest*. *Solon* admiring his acuteness, entertained him kindly, and kept him some time with him, whilst he was imployed about publick affairs, and ordering his Laws ; which *Anacharsis* understanding, smiled, that he undertook to curb the injustice and covetousness of Citizens by written Ordinances, nothing differing from Cobwebs, holding fast the weak and poor, whilst the powerful and rich break through them ; whereto *Solon* answered, That *Men stand fast to those Covenants which it is not convenient for either party to break* : He gave the Citizens such Laws, as it was evident to all, that to keep were better than to transgress ; but the event agreed more with the conjecture of *Anacharsis*, than the expectation of *Solon*.

c Plut. ᶜ After his Laws were promulgated, some or other coming daily to him, either to praise, or dispraise them, or to advise to put in or out whatsoever came into their minds, the greater part to have the meaning explained, questioning how every thing was to be understood, and intreating him to unfould the sense ; he (considering, that not to satisfie them, would argue pride, to satisfie them would make him lyable to censure) determined to avoid ambiguities, importunities and occasions of blame, (for, as he said,

*In things that are not small.
'Tis hard to sing to all.*)

Colouring his travail with being Master of a Ship, and having obtained leave of the *Athenians* to be absent ten years, he put to Sea, hoping in that time his Laws would become familiar to them.

d Plut. ᵈ The first place of his arrival was *Ægypt*, where he dwelt, as himself saith,

At Nilus mouth, near the Canobian Shoar.

He studied Philosophy awhile with *Psenophis*, of *Heliopolis*, and *Sonches* of *Sais*, the most learned of those Priests, by whom, *Plato* affirms, he was taught the *Atlantick* Language, which he afterward began to explain in Verse ; when he questioned them in Antiquities the elder said to him, *O Solon, Solon, you* Greeks *are always Children, there is not one* Greek *an old Man*.

e Plut. ᵉ Thence he went to *Cyprus*, where he was much favoured by *Philocyprus*, one of the Kings of that Country, who had a little Town built by *Demophoon*, Son of *Theseus*, upon the River *Clarius*, in a strong place, but rugged and barren : *Solon* perswading him, their lying a pleasant Plain underneath it, to transfer the Town thither, making it more spacious and delightful : *Solon* being present at the doing hereof, took care it might be Peopled, and assisted the King to contrive it, as well for Health as Strength ; whereupon many came in to *Philocyprus*, whom other Kings emulated ; for this reason he ascribed the honour thereof unto *Solon*, naming the City (which before was called *Æpea*) from him *Soli*. This Foundation he mentions in his Elegies, addressing his speech to *Philocyprus*,

Mayst thou in Cyprus *long as King abide,
And o're this People and this Town preside ;
In a fleet Vessel from this Haven may
Cythera Crown'd with Violets me convey.
Her kind aspect and happiness may she
Grant to this Town, a safe return to me.*

He visited *Thales* also at *Miletus*, whose imposture towards him (related already in *Plutarch*'s words) receive from *Tzetzes*.

Solon's friend Thales *led a single life,
By* Solon *often mov'd to take a Wife ;
These a* Milesian (Thales *so contriv'd*)
Meeting, pretends from Athens *late arriv'd,*
Solon *asks curiously what news was there ;
One that's abroad, saith he, hath lost his Heir,
The City waited on his obsequies.
Was it not* Solon's *Son,* Solon *replys ?
To this the Stranger (as suborn'd) assents :
He with torn hair in cries his passion vents ;
Whom* Thales, (*tenderly embracing*) *Leave
This grief, saith he, I did thee but deceive ;
'Tis for these reasons Marriage I decline,
Which can deject so great a Soul as thine.*

Whether it belong to this deceit, or to a real loss ᶠ *Dioscorides*, and ᵍ *Stobæus* report, that weeping for the death of his Son, one told him, But this helps nothing, he answered, And therefore I weep.

f Laert.
g Serm. 121.

ʰ At *Delphi* he met with the rest of the wise Men, and the year following at *Corinth*, by *Periander*'s invitation, which was as *Plutarch* implies, long before *Pisistratus* came to Reign ; nor doth ⁱ *Dion Chrysostom* intend the contrary, though so interpreted by ᵏ a learned Person, his words importing only this ; *Solon fled not the Tyranny of* Periander, *though he did that of* Pisistratus.

h Laert.
i Orat. 37.
k J. Meursius.

CHAP. IX.

The attribute of Wise *conferred on him: His moral Sentences.*

[*] *Laert.*

WHen *Damasius* (the second was) Archon, (in the year of the 49 Olimpiad) all the seven received the attribute of *Wise*: of these was *Solon*, upon whom († *Themistius* saith, it was conferr'd as an honourable title full of dignity: * *Plutarch* avers that all of them (except *Thales*) were so called from their skill in civil affairs. And again, '† In 'Philosophy *Solon* chiefly affected (as did like-'wise most of the wise Men) that part of mo-'rality which concerns Politicks; and speaking 'of *Menesiphilus*, 'he was not (saith he) an 'Orator of those Philosophers who are called 'Natural, but embraced that Wisdom which 'teacheth government of a State, and prudence 'in publick Actions, which he retained as a 'Sect delivered by succession from *Solon*. Whence '* *Macrobius*, instanceth *Solon*, as skilful in 'that kind of learning which draweth Philoso-'phy deeper, and establisheth a State.

† *Orat.* 4.

* *Vit. Sol.*

† *Vit. Themist.*

* *Somn. Scip.* 2. 17.

Hereto may be added his moral Learning, for which (though *Socrates* reduced it first to a Science, and was thereupon honoured as the inventer thereof) the seven were so famous, that some affirm the Title of Wise was given them only for excelling others in a laudable course of life, and comprehending some moral Rules in short Sentences; of these they had three sorts, Apothegms, Precepts, and Ἀδόμενα.

Of his Apothegms *Laertius* recites these, 'Speech is the Image of Action; he is a King 'who hath power. Laws are like Cobwebs 'which intangle the lesser sort, the greater break 'through: Those who are in favour with Prin-'ces resemble Counters used in casting accounts, 'which sometimes stand for a great number, 'sometimes for a lesser; so those are sometimes 'honoured, sometimes cast down. Being de-'manded how Men might be brought to do no 'wrong, if, said he, they who have received 'none, and those who are wronged be alike 'concern'd: Satiety comes of Riches, contume-'ly of Satiety.

^a *Vit. Sol.*

^a *Plutarch* and others, these; 'He conceived 'that City to be best govern'd, where the Peo-'ple as eagerly prosecute wrongs done to o-'thers, as to themselves. ^b Being demanded 'how a City might be best ordered, he answer-'ed if the Citizens obey'd the Magistrates, 'the Magistrates the Laws; he affirmed that 'King and Tyrant should become most glorious, 'who would convert his Monarchy to Demo-'cracy. He esteemed that Family best, 'wherein wealth is gotten not unjustly, kept 'not unfaithfully, expended not with repen-'tance.

^b *Sympos. sept. Sapi.*

^c *Arist. Ethic.* 1. 8.

^c He defined 'the happy those who are com-'petently furnished with outward things, act 'honestly, and live temperately; which defini-'tion *Aristotle* approves.

'He said, 'A Common-wealth consists of 'two things, Reward and Punnishment.

^d *Cicer. Epist.* 15. *ad Brut.*

^e 'Seeing one of his Friends much grieved, 'he carried him to the Tower, and desired 'him to view all the buildings below, which 'observing the other to have done, now saith 'he, think with your self, how many sorrows 'have heretofore and do at present dwell 'under those Roofs, and shall in future Ages; 'and forbear to be troubled at the inconveni-'ences of Mortality as if they were only yours. 'He said also, that if Men should bring their 'misfortunes together in one place, every one 'would carry his own home again, rather than 'take an equal share out of the common 'stock.

^e *Val. Max.* 7. 2.

^f 'Being in drinking, demanded by *Peri-'ander*, whether he were silent through want 'of Discourse, or through Folly, answered, 'no Fool can be silent amidst his Cups. ^g He 'said, that City was best ordered, where-'in the good were rewarded, the bad pun-'ished.

^f *Stob. Serm.* 34.

^g *Stob. Serm.* 41.

^h 'He said, a Man ought to fear nothing, 'but that his end exceed not Philosophy.

^h *Johan. Salisb. polycr.* 8.

Demosthenes recites a Discourse which he used to the Judges, in accusing one who had moved a pernicious Law, to this effect; 'It is 'a Law generally received in all Cities, that 'he who makes false Mony should be put to 'Death. Then he demanded of the Judes, 'whether that Law seemed to them just and 'commendable, whereunto they assenting, he 'added, that he conceived Mony to be used 'amongst Citizens, in respect of private con-'tracts; but that Laws were the Mony of the 'Common-wealth: therefore Judes ought to 'punish those, who embased the Mony of 'the Common-wealth much more severely, 'than those who embase that of private Per-'sons: and that they might better understand 'it to be a far greater offence to corrupt 'Laws, than adulterate Coyn; he added, that 'many Cities use Money of Silver allay'd with 'Brass or Lead, without any prejudice to 'themselves; but whosoever should use Laws 'so adulterated, could not escape ruine and 'death.

ⁱ *Orat. in Timocrat.*

^k *Mimnermus* writing thus,

^k *Laert.*

From trouble and diseases free,
At threescore years let Death take me.

He reproved him, saying,

By my advice, that wish extend,
Nor for his counsel slight thy Friend.
Alter thy Song, and let it be,
At fourscore years let Death take me.

His moral Precepts are thus delivered by *Demetrius Phalereus*, some whereof are cited by *Laertius*. 'Nothing too much. Sit not as 'Judge; if thou dost, the condemned will e-'steem thee an Enemy. Fly pleasures, for it 'brings forth sorrow. Observe honesty in thy 'Conversation more strictly than an Oath. 'Seal Words with silence, silence with op-'portunity. Lie not, but speak the truth. 'Consider on serious things. Say not ought

^l *Stob. Serm.* 3.

' is juster than thy Parents. Procure not Friends
' in haste, nor procur'd, part with in haste.
' By learning to obey, you shall know how to
' command. What forfeiture you impose on
' others, undergo your self. Advise not Citi-
' zens what is pleasant, but what is best. Be
' not arrogant. Converse not with wicked per-
' sons. Consult the Gods. Cherish thy Friend.
' Reverence thy Parents. Make Reason thy
' Guide. What thou seest speak not. What
' thou knowest conceal. Be mild to those that
' belong to thee. Conjecture hidden things from
' apparent.

His particular sentence acording to ᵐ *Dydi-* ^{ᵐ Clem. Alex. Strom.}
mus and *Laertius* was, *Nothing too much*; ac-
cording to *Ausonius*, *Know thy self*, who ascribes
these also to him.

> Him I dare happy call whose end I see.
> Match with thy like, unequals not agree.
> By fortune guided, none to honour raise ;
> A friend in private chide, in publick praise ;
> Honours atchiev'd created far exceed ;
> If fates be sure, what helps it to take heed ?
> And if unsure, there is of fear less need.

Of his ἀπουρα *Laertius* mentions these.

> Of every Man be careful, lest he bear
> A Sword conceal'd within his breast, a clear
> Aspect, and double tongue, a mind severe.

CHAP. X.

How he opposed Pisistratus, *and reprehended*
Thespis.

*During the absence of *Solon*, the former ^{* Plut.}
dissention broke forth again in the Ci-
ty : *Lycurgus* was head of the Countrymen,
Megacles of the Maritimes, *Pisistratus* of the
Townsmen, who were most violent against
the rich ; *Solon*'s Laws were still observed in
the City, but the People aimed at novelty
and change, not as thinking it most just, but
in hopes to be Masters of other Men's goods
and to suppress the adverse party. *Solon* whilst
things stood thus, return'd to *Athens*, where
he was much reverenced and honoured by all,
but could not speak or act in publick, through
the weakness of his Body and Spirits, yet privately taking every one of the Commanders
apart, he endeavoured to reconcile their differences, wherein *Pisistratus* seemed the most
ready to be perswaded, with whom he had a
very ancient friendship, grounded as well upon
their kindred, as upon the good qualities of
Pisistratus, than whom (as *Solon* used to say)
there could not be a Person of more worth, if
he were cured of his ambition.

† About this time (according to *Plutarch*) ^{† Plut.}
which was in the fiftieth Olympiad, *Thespis*
began to present Tragedies (which *Suidas* erroneously accounts ten Olympiads later, as is
observed by *Meursius*) the People were much
taken with the novelty of the thing, for as
yet there were no contentions therein. *Solon*
naturally desirous to hear and learn, and by
reason of his age indulging more to ease and
pleasure, feasting and musick, went to see *Thespis* himself act, as was then the manner ; the
Play ended, he went to *Thespis*, and asked him,
if he were not ashamed to speak so many lies
before so great an Auditory ? *Thespis* answered,
it was no shame to act or say such things in
jest. *Solon* striking the ground hard with his
Staff, replyed, but in a short time we who approve this kind of jest shall use it in earnest,
in our contracts and transactions. * *In fine, he* ^{* Laert.}
*absolutely forbad him to teach or act Tragedies, con-
ceiving their falsity unprofitable, whereto he dissi-
multated the deceit of* Pisistratus, who soon after
† having wounded himself, came into the Forum ^{† Plut.}
in a Chariot, pretending to have been so used
by his Enemies in the behalf of the Common-
wealth, and inflamed the People with much
rage. *Solon* coming near to him, Son of *Hippocrates* (saith he) you act *Homer*'s *Ulysses* ill in
using the same means to deceive the Citizens,
wherewith he (whipping himself) deluded the
Enemy. Immediately the People flocked in to
defend *Pisistratus* : *Aristo* mov'd he might be
allowed a standing guard of fifty Men : *Solon*
rose up to oppose it, using speeches, the effect
whereof, he afterwards thus exprest in Verse.

> If evil your impieties befal,
> Gods not the Author of those mischiefs call,
> Your selves the causes, have given power to those,
> Who in requital, servitude impose.
> Lion whom the footsteps of the Fox pursue,
> Whose Souls deceit and vanity endue.
> The man's smooth tongue and speech you only heed,
> But never penetrate into the deed.

He also foretold them the aims of *Pisistratus*, in an Elegy to this effect.

> Vapours condens'd ingender Hail and Snow,
> And Thunder doth from radiant lightning flow.
> The Sea is troubled by the raging Wind,
> When not disturb'd by that, nothing more kind.
> A City by great Persons is overthrown.
> And taught beneath a Monarchy to groan.

But seeing the poorer sort much addicted to
Pisistratus, and tumultuous, the richer afraid,
consulting their safety by flight , he retired,
saying, *Athenians*, I am wiser than some, valianter than others, wiser than those who understand not the deceit of *Pisistratus*, valianter than
those who understand it, yet hold their peace,
through fear. The Senate being of the same
faction with *Pisistratus*, said he was mad, whereto he answered,

> A little time will to the people clear
> My madness, when'th'midst truth shall appear.

The People having granted *Pisistratus* his request concerning a guard, question'd not the
number of them, but conniv'd so long at
his pressing and maintaining as many Souldiers as he pleased, that at last he possest
himself of the Tower ; whereupon the City
being in a tumult, *Megacles*, with the rest of
the *Alcmæonidæ* fled. *Solon* now very old ,
and destitute of those that might back him,
went into the *Forum*, * armed with a Spear ^{* Laert.}
and

and Shield, and made an Oration to the People, partly accusing them of folly and cowardise, partly inciting them not to forsake their liberty, using this celebrious speech, 'It had been 'far easier to have supprest this Tyranny in the 'growth, but much more noble to cut it off 'now it is at the hight. No Man daring to hear him, he went home, and taking his Arms, set them in the Street before his Door (*Laertius* saith, *before the Magazin*) saying, 'I have 'helped my Country, and the Law as much as 'lay in me; or as *Laertius*, 'O Country, I 'have assisted thee both in Word and Deed. *Plutarch* adds, that from that time he lived retired, addicted to his study; and told by many the Tyrant would put him to Death, and demanded wherein he confided so much, he answered, in his Age: but *Laertius* affirms (which seems truer) that as soon he as had laid down his Arms, he forsook the Country: and * *A. Gellius*, that in the Reign of *Scovius Tullius*, Pisistratus was Tyrant of *Athens*, *Solon* going first away into voluntary exile.

* Lib. 17. cap. 21.

CHAP. XI.

How he travelled into Lydia, *and* Cilicia.

Solon at his departure from *Athens*, received invitations from many; by *Thales* desired to come to *Miletus*; by *Bias*, to *Priene*; by *Epimenides*, to *Creet*; by *Cleobulus*, to *Lindus*, as is evident from their several Letters to that effect: even *Pisistratus* pressed him to return home by this Epistle.

Pisistratus *to* Solon.

'Neither am I the only Person of the 'Greeks, nor am I without right to 'the Kingdom I possess, as being descended 'from *Codrus*: that which the *Athenians*, ha-'ving sworn to give to *Codrus* and his Heirs, 'took away, I have recovered; no other-'wise do I offend either God or Man; I 'take care that the Common-wealth be go-'verned according to the Laws you ordained 'for the *Athenians*, and that better than by a 'Democracy: I suffer none to do wrong, 'neither do I enjoy any priviledges of a Ty-'rant, more than Honour and Dignity, such 'Rewards only as were conferr'd upon the 'antient Kings; every Man pays the tenth 'of his Estate, not to me, but to the main-'tenance of publick Sacrifices, or other charges 'of the Common-wealth, or against time of 'War. You I blame not for discovering my 'intents, you did it more in love to the State, 'than in hate to me; besides, you knew not 'what Government I meant to establish, 'which if you had, perhaps you would have 'brooked my rule, and not banished your self; 'return therefore home, and believe me with-'out an Oath: *Solon* shall never receive any 'displeasure from *Pisistratus*, you know my ve-'ry Enemies have not, and if you will vouch-'safe to be of my Friends, you shall be of the 'first, for I never saw any thing in you de-'ceitful or False; if otherwise, you will live 'with the *Athenians*, use your Freedom, 'only deprive not your self of your Country, 'for my sake.

Solon returned this answer.

Solon *to* Pisistratus.

'I Believe I shall not suffer any harm by 'you, for before you were Tyrant, I was 'your Friend, and at present am no more your 'Enemy, than any other *Athenian* who dislikes 'Tyranny: whether it be better they be go-'verned by a single Person, or by a Democra-'cy, let both Parties determine. I pronounce 'you the best of Tyrants; but to return to *A-*'*thens* I think not fitting, lest I incur blame, 'who setled an equality in the *Athenian* Com-'mon-wealth, and would not accept of the 'Tyranny; by returning, I shall comply with 'thy actions.

Cræsus also sent to invite him, to whom he thus answered.

Solon *to* Cræsus.

'I Love your humanity towards us, and by '*Pallas*, but that I affect above all things 'to live under a Democracy, I should much 'sooner choose to live in your Kingdom, than 'at *Athens*, whilst *Pisistratus* rules there by 'force; but it is most pleasing to me to live 'where all things are just and equal; yet will 'I come over to you, being desirous to become 'your Guest.

Solon upon this invitation went to *Sandys*, where *Cræsus* (saith *Herodotus*) received him kindly: after the third or fourth day, the Officers at *Cræsus* appointment led him into the Treasuries, to shew him all their Greatness and Riches; when he had beheld all, *Cræsus* spoke thus unto him: ' *Athenian* Guest, because we 'have heard much fame of your Wisdom and 'Experience, having out of love to Philoso-'phy travelled into many Countries, I have 'a desire to enquire of you if ever you saw 'any Man whom you could call most hap-'py. This he demanded, hoping himself to be esteemed such. *Solon* nothing flattering him, answered according to the truth, saying, 'O King, *Tellus* the *Athenian*. At which 'speech *Cræsus* wondering. Why do you 'judge *Tellus* the most happy? Because (re-'plied *Solon*) in a well ordered State, he had 'Children honest and good, and saw every 'one of those have Children all living; thus 'having passed his life as well as is possible for 'Man, he ended it gloriously: a fight happen-'ing between the *Athenians* and their Neigh-'bours in *Eleusis*, he came into their succour, 'and putting the Enemy to flight, died nobly; 'the *Athenians* buried him in the place where 'he fell, with much honour. Whilst *Solon* recounted the happiness of *Tellus*, *Cræsus* being moved, demanded to whom he assign'd the next place, making no question but himself should be named a second. '*Celobis* (saith he) and '*Bito*, they were *Argives* by birth, they had 'sufficient

'sufficient wherewithal to maintain them-
'selves; and withal, so great strength of Bo-
'dy, that both were alike victors in the pub-
'lick Games, of whom it is thus reported;
'the *Argives* celebrating the Festival of *Juno*,
'it was necessary their Mother should be drawn
'to the Temple by a pair of Oxen, there be-
'ing no Oxen in the Field ready, these young
'Men, streightned in time, underwent the
'Yoke, and drew the Chariot of their Mother
'forty five Stadia, till they came to the Tem-
'ple; when they had so done, in the sight of
'all the People, they obtain'd the happiest end
'of their days, whereby the God declared it
'better for a Man to die than to live; the *Ar-
'gives*, pressing about them, the Men applau-
'ding the Piety of the Sons; the Women the
'happiness of the Mother; the Mother her
'self infinitely joyed with the action, and the
'glory thereof, standing before the Image, pray-
'ed the Goddess to give her Sons, *Cleobis* and
'*Bito*, the best thing that could happen to Man;
'after this Prayer, having sacrificed and feasted,
'they lay down to sleep in the Temple, and
'never waked more, but so ended their days;
'their Images (as of most excellent Persons)
'were made by the *Argives*, and set up at *Del-
'phi*. These *Solon* ranked the second Degree.
Hereat *Cræsus* growing angry; Stranger (said
he) 'doth our happiness seem so despicable
'that you will not rank us equal with private
'Persons? He answered, Do you enquire *Cræ-
'sus* concerning humane affairs of me, who
'know, that Divine Providenc is severe and
'full of alteration? In process of time we see
'many things we would not, we suffer many
'things we would not; let us propose seventy
'years, as the term of Mans life, which years
'consist of twenty five thousand and two hun-
'dred days, besides the additional month, if
'we make one year longer than another by
'that month, to make the time accord, the
'additional months, belonging to those seventy
'years, will be thirty five, the days of those
'months a thousand and fifty, whereof one is
'not in all things like another: so that every
'Man, O *Cræsus*, is miserable! you appear to
'me very rich, and are King over many, but
'the question you demand, I cannot resolve,
'until I hear you have ended your days happi-
'ly; he who hath much wealth is not happier
'than he who gets his living from day to day,
'unless Fortune continuing all those good
'things to him, grant that he die well. There
'are many Men very rich, yet unfortunate, ma-
'ny of moderate Estates, fortunate, of whom
'he who abounds in Wealth, and is not happy,
'exceeds the fortunate only in two things, the
'other him in many; the rich is more able to
'satisfie his desires, and to overcome great in-
'juries; yet the fortunate excels him, he can-
'not indeed inflict hurt on others, and satisfie
'his own desires, his good fortune debars him
'of these: but he is free from ills, healthful,
'happy in his Children,and beautiful, if to this
'a Man dies well, that is he whom you seek,
'who deserves to be called happy; before
'death he cannot be stil'd happy, but fortunate;
'yet for one Man to obtain all this is impossi-
'ble, as one Country cannot furnish it self
'with all things, some it hath, others it wants,
'that which hath most is best; so in Men, no
'one is perfect; what one hath, the other
'wants; he who hath constantly most, and at
'last quietly departs this life, in opinion, O
'King, deserves to bear that name. In every
'thing we must have regard to the end, whither
'it tends; for many, to whom God dispenseth
'all good fortunes, he at last utterly subverts.
This Story is related by *Plutarch*, also mentioned by *Laertius*, who adds, that '*Cræsus* be-
'ing magnificently adorned and seated one his
'Throne, asked him. *Whether he had ever seen
'any thing more glorious?* who answered,*Cocks,
'Pheasants, and Peacoks, who are much more
'beautiful in their natural flower.* † *Solon* after † *Herodot.*
his discourse with *Cræsus*, not soothing him,
or making any esteem of him, was dismissed,
and accounted unwise for neglecting the present good in regard to the future. * *Æsop*, the * *Plut.*
Writer of Fables was at that time at *Sardis*, sent
for thither by *Cræsus*, with whom he was much
in favour; he was grieved to see *Solon* so un-
thankfully dismist, and said to him, *Solon*, we
must either tell Kings nothing at all, or what
may please them. No, saith *Solon*, either nothing at all, or what is best for them. Thus
was *Solon* much despised by *Cræsus*.

† * Afterwards *Cræsus* being taken Prisoner † *Herodot.*
'by *Cyrus* was at his command fettered and set
'upon a great Pile of Wood to be burned: as
'he was in this posture, it came into his mind
'what *Solon* had divinely said to him, that no
'living Man is happy; as soon as he remem-
'bred these words,he fell into a great defection
'of Spirit, and sighing deeply, named *Solon*
'thrice, which *Cyrus* hearing, commanded the
'Interpreters to ask upon whom he called; they
'went to him and asked, he was silent; at last
'pressing him further, he answered, *Upon him
who I desire above all wealth, might have spoken
with all Tyrants*; notwithstanding, after much
pressure and importunity, he told them, Solon *an Athenian came long since to him, and beholding all his Wealth, valued it at nothing;
moreover, that all which he told him had come to
pass, nor did it more belong to him than to all
Mankind, especially, to those who think themselves
happy.* 'Whilst *Cræsus* said this, the fire began
'to kindle, and the outward parts thereof to be
'seized by the flame. *Cyrus* being informed by
'an Interpreter of all that *Cræsus* had said, be-
'gan to relent, knowing himself to be but a
'Man, who delivered another Man, nothing
'inferiour to him in Wealth, to be burned a-
'live, fearing to be punished for that act, and
'considering that nothing was certain in human
'affairs, he commanded the fire to be instantly
'quenched,and *Cræsus*,and those that were with
'him to be brought off; * whom ever after as * *Plut.*
long as he lived, he had in esteem. Thus *Solon*
gained praise, that of two Kings, his speech
preserved one, and instructed the other.

Plutarch relates this done in the former ten
years travel of *Solon*, upon the finishing of his
Laws, whence he maketh an Apology for the
incongruity thereof with the rules of Chronology, which had less needed, if with *Laertius*,
he had placed it after *Pisistratus* his usurpation
of the Tyranny.

Laertius

Laertius saith, he went from hence to *Cilicia*, and built there a City called after him *Soleis*, whither he brought also some few *Athenians*, whose Language growing corrupt by that of the Country, they were said to solœcise; of this is the Etymologist doubtless to be understood, who derives Σολοκοὶ ἀπὸ σόλων κιλικίων (so read we, not ἀπὸ Σόλων⊙ κιλιός.) This is also attested by *Suidas*, as a distinct relation from that of *Cyprus*, in confirmation whereof *Laertius* adds, the *Cilicians* were called *Solenses*, the *Cyprians Solii*.

CHAP. XII.

His Death.

† *Plut.*
* *De longævis.*

† *Plut.*

† H*Eraclides* affirms *Solon* lived long after *Pisistratus* began to Reign; * *Lucian* that his life extended to a hundred years; with whom those best agree, who said (as *Suidas* relates) he lived in the fifty sixth Olympiad; † but according to *Phanias*, Pisistratus *took the Tyranny upon him, when* Comias *was Archon, and* Solon *died,* Hegestratus *being Archon, who succeeeded* Comias, *which was in the first year of the fifty fifth Olympiad.* If this later opinion had not every where taken place of the other, the disagreement betwixt the time of *Solon*'s Death, and *Crœsus* Reign had not been urged by many, as an argument against the story of their meeting.

* *Var. Hist.*8. 16.
† *Lib.* 5. *cap.* 3.

He died (according to *Laertius*) aged eighty years (being, as * *Ælian* saith, very decrepit) in *Cyprus*, (as is likewise attested by (*Valerius Maximus*, and † *Suidas*) and left order with his Friends that they should carry his Bones to *Salamis*, and there causing them to be burnt, scatter the Ashes all over the Country; which story *Plutarch* (though he counts it fabulous) acknowledgeth to be attested by many Authors of credit, particularly *Aristotle*.

† *Leart.*

† *Laertius* confirms it by the testimony of *Cratinus*, who makes him speak thus:

The Island I inhabit, sown
As fame reports in Ajax *Town.*

‡ *Val. Max.* 8, 7.

That desire of knowledge which he usually profest, continued with him to his end, † confirmed the last day of his life, his Friends sitting about him, and falling into some discourse, he raised his weary head, and being demanded why he did so, he answered, *That when I have learnt that, whatsoever it be, whereon you dispute, I may die.* * His Brothers Son singing an Ode of *Sappho*, he delighted therewith, bad him teach him it, and being demanded why, *that*, said he, *I may learn whilst I depart out of this life.*

* *Stob.* 29.

† *Pausan. Attic.*
* *Demosth. in Arist.* 2. *Ælian. var. hist.* 8. 15.

After his Death, the *Athenians* erected his Statue in Brass, before the † checker'd Cloister * in the *Forum*: Another was set up at *Salamis*, hiding (as *Demosthenes* and *Æschines* describe it) the Hand within the Garment, in the same habit wherein he used to make Speeches to the *Athenians*, perhaps the same that carried this Inscription,

Fam'd Salamis, *the* Persian *pride cast down,*
And gave to Solon *Birth, the Laws renown.*

Laertius bestows this Epigram *upon him,*

A Foreign Cyprian *fire burn'd* Solon, *yet*
Salamis *keeps his Bones, their Ashes Wheat;*
His Soul to Heaven mounts with his Laws so light
A burthen they not clog, but help his flight.

CHAP. XIII.

His Writings.

H'IS excellency both in Rhetorick and Poetry is attested by many: *Cicero*, †' Before *Solon*'s time, no Man is recorded for Elo-' quence. * And again, *Lycurgus*, and *Solon* we ' place in the number of the Eloquent. ‖ *Dion,* ' *Chrysostom*, *Aristides*, *Lycurgus*, *Solon*, *Epa-*' *minondas*, and if there be any other of the ' same kind, ought to be esteemed Philosophers ' in the Common-wealth, or Orators, accord-' ing to ingenious true Rhetorick. * *Aristides,* ' *Solon* is said to have sung those things which ' concern the *Megarenses*, but neither his Laws ' nor Orations, which sometimes he made for ' the Rich to the Commons, sometimes for the ' Commons to the Rich, did he sing or comprise ' in Verse, but used a Rhetorical form, excel-' lently demonstrating in all these, that he de-' served to be esteemed an Orator and a wise ' Man, having attained both those titles and ' faculties.

† *In Bruto.*
* *DeOrat. lib.*1.
‖ *Orat.* 21.

* *Orat. Plat.* 2.

As to Poetry, *Plutarch* avers, ' he addicted ' himself thereto from the beginning, not in se-' rious matters, but ludicrous, used (as it seems) ' for his exercise and pastime; afterwards he ' included many Philosophical Sentences in ' Verse, and many affairs of State, not in rela-' lation to History, but to vindicate his own ' actions, sometimes also to correct and reprove ' the *Athenians*. *Plato* saith, ' ‖ That at the ' *Apaturian* Feast, the Boys used to repeat his ' Poems; and that if he applied himself to no-' thing but Poetry as others did, and had finish-' ed the History he brought out of *Egypt*, and ' had not been constrained by seditions and other ' distractions to lay aside that study, neither *He-*' *siod*, *Homer*, nor any of the Poets would ' have been more famous.

‖ *In Timæo.* ‖ 1. *Crit.*

Of his Writings in Prose, we must with *Laertius* name in the first place his

Laws; of which already.
Orations to the People.

His *Poems* are cited under that general title by ‖ *Phrynicus*, their particular subjects and titles these,

‖ *Eclog. d:E. Attic.*

Exhortations to himself, mentioned by *Laertius,* ‖ *Aristides*, and *Suidas*.

Elegies.

Salamis: of which Chap. 2.

Of the Athenian *Common-wealth*, which *Laertius* affirms to have extended to two thousand Verses, according to † *Pausanias*, and and ‖ *Philo, Elegiack.*

‖ *In Orat.* ϖρὶ κοσμϖ.

† *Attic.* ϖρὶ κοσμϖ.

Iambicks, mentioned by *Laertius*, cited by *Athenæus* and *Aristides*.

Epodes,

Epodes, mentioned by *Laertius*.
Elegies to King Cypranor, cited by the Author of *Aratus*, his life. Ἀδομένα, cited by *Laertius*.

Some, saith *Plutarch*, affirm, he began to reduce his own Laws into Verse.

The last work he undertook was concerning the Atlantick speech or fable, which beginning late, he was deterred by the greatness of the Work, as *Plutarch* saith, and prevented by Death.

Besides those Epistles already alledged, these are preserved also by *Laertius*.

Solon to Periander.

'YOU send me word, there are many who
' plot against you; if you should put
' them all to death, it would advantage you no-
' thing; some one there may be of those, whom
' you suspect not, who plots against you, either
' fearing himself, or disdaining you, or desirous
' to ingratiate himself with the City, though
' you have done him no injury; it is best, if
' you would be free from jealousie, to acquit
' your self of the cause; but if you will con-
' tinue in Tyranny, take care to provide a great-
' er strength of Strangers than is in your own
' City; so shall you need to fear no Man, nor
' to put any to death.

Solon to Epimenides.

'NEither are my Laws likely to benefit the
' *Athenians* long, nor have you advanta-
' ged the City by lustration; for Divine Right
' and Lawgivers cannot alone benefit Cities; it
' importeth much of what mind they are who
' lead the common People; Divine Rights and
' Laws, if they direct them well, are profitable,
' if they direct them ill, profit nothing; nei-
' ther are those Laws I gave in any better condi-
' tion; they who had charge of the Common-
' wealth, not preventing *Pisistratus* his usurpa-
' tion of the Tyranny, lost the City, of which,
' when I foretold them, I could not be belie-
' ved; the *Athenians* would rather credit his
' flatteries, than my truth; wherefore laying
' down my Arms before the Magazin, I said,
' that I was wiser than those who did not see
' *Pisistratus* aimed at the Tyranny; and stouter
' than those who durst not resist him: they
' reputed *Solon* a Madman. Lastly, I made
' this profession, O Country! behold *Solon* ready
' to vindicate thee in word and deed: they
' again esteem'd me mad. Thus I being the
' only Person that oppos'd *Pisistratus*, I came
' away from them; let them guard him with
' their Arms if they please; for know (dear
' Friend) the Man came very cunningly by the
' Kingdom, he complied at first with the De-
' mocracy, afterwards wounding himself, came
' into *Eliæa*, crying out, he had received those
' hurts from his Enemies, and required a guard
' of four hundred young Men, which they (not
' hearkening to me) granted; these carried
' Halberts: after this, he dissolved the popular
' Government; truly I laboured in vain to free
' the poorer sort from mercenary slavery, when
' they all now serve one *Pisistratus*.

Such fragments of his Poems as have been hitherto preserved are thus collected.

One of his Elegies

SPrung from *Mnemosyne* and *Jove*'s great line,
  Pierian Muses, to my prayer incline,
Grant that my life and actions may call down
Blessings from Heaven, and raise one Earth renown:
Sweet to my Friends, and bitter to my Foes,
To these my sight bring terror, joy to those.
Riches I wish, not riches that are plac'd
In unjust means, for vengeance comes at last.
Riches dispenc'd by Heavens more bounteous hand,
A base on which we may unshaken stand.
But that which Men by injuries obtain,
That which by arts and deeds unjust they gain
Comes slowly, swiftly by revenge pursued,
And misery like a close spark include,
Which soon to a devouring flame dilates,
Wrong is a weak foundation for estates.
Jove doth the end of every thing survey:
As suddain vernal blasts chase clouds away.
Ransack the bottom of the roaring main,
Then swiftly overrun the fertile plain,
Ruffling the wealthy ears; at last they rise
To *Jove*'s high seat, a calm then smooths the skies.
The *Sun*'s rich lustre mildly gilds the green
Enamel of the Meads, no Clouds are seen.
Such is *Jove*'s heavy anger differing far
From Men whose every trifle leads to War:
They are not hid for ever, who offend.
In secret, judgment finds them in the end.
Some in the act are punish'd, others late,
Even he who thinks he hath deluded fate:
At last resents it in just miseries,
Which Nephews for their Ancestors chastise.
We think it fares alike with good and bad;
Glory and self-conceit our Fancies glad
Till suffering comes, then their griev'd spirits bleed,
Who did before their Souls with vain hope feed.
He whom incurable diseases seize.
Sooths his deluded thoughts, with hopes of ease.
The coward's valiant in his own esteem,
And to themselves, fair the deformed seem.
They who want means, by poverty opprest.
Believe themselves of full estates possest.
All is attempted, some new seas explore
To bring home riches from a foreign shore:
Seas, on whose boisterous back secur'd they ride,
And in the mercy of the winds confide:
Others to crooked ploughs their Oxen yoke,
And Autumn with their plants and sets provoke.
Some *Vulcan*'s and *Minerva*'s arts admire,
And by their hands their livelihoods acquire.
Others the fair Olympian Muses trace,
And lovely learning studiously embrace.
One by *Apollo* is prophetick made,
And tells what mischiefs others shall invade:
With him the Gods converse, but all the skill
In Birds or Victims cannot hinder ill.
Some to Peonian knowlege are inclin'd.
Nor is the power of Simples unconfin'd.
The smallest hurts sometimes increase and rage,
More than all art of Physick can asswage;

Sometimes the fury of the worst disease,
The hand by gentle stroking will appease.
Thus good or bad arrives as fates design,
Man cannot what the Gods dispenc'd decline.
All actions are uncertain, no Man knows
When he begins a Work, how it shall close.
Some, who their business weigh with prudent care,
Oft of the issue incercepted are:
Whilst others who have rashly ought design'd,
An end successful of their labours find.
There is no bound to those who wealth acquire,
For they who are possest of most, desire
As much again, and who can all content,
Even those full blessings which the Gods have lent,
Man variously to his own harm applies,
Whom *Jove* by means as various doth chastise.

Again.

OUr City never can subverted be
By *Jove* or any other Deity:
For *Pallas* eye surveys with pious care
The Walls, which by her hand protected are:
Yet the Inhabitants of this great Town,
Fondly inclin'd to wealth, will throw it down;
And those unjust great Persons who are bent
Others to wrong, themselves to discontent;
For their infatiate fancies have not power
T'enjoy the sweetness of the instant hour,
But by all wicked means, intent or gain,
From hallowed, nor from publick things refrain.
Riches by theft and cozenage to possess,
The sacred bounds of justice they transgress.
Who silent sees the present, knows the past,
And will revenge these injuries at last:
Causing a careless rupture in the State,
And all our liberties shall captivate.
Rouse War from his long slumber, who the flower
Of all our youths shall bloodily devour.
For Cities which injuriously oppose
Their Friends, are soon invaded by their Foes.
These are the common evils: of the poor
Many transported to a foreign shore,
To bondage there, and fetters shall be sold.
Each private House thus shares the publick fate,
Nor can exclude it with a barr'd up gate;
For scaling furiously the higher walls,
On those whom beds or corners hides it falls.
My Soul, Athenians, prompts me to relate
What miseries upon injustice wait:
But justice all things orderly designs,
And in strict fetters the unjust confines.
What's sour, she sweetens, and allays what cloys.
Wrong she repels, ill in the growth destroys,
Softens the stubborn, the unjust reforms,
And in the state calms all seditious storms:
Bitter dissention by her reign supprest,
Who wisely governs all things for the best.

Another.

NO Man is blessed, bad is every one
That feels the warmth of the all-seeing Sun.

Another.

LEt me not die unpiti'd, every Friend
With sighs and tears my latest hour attend.

CHILO.

CHAP. I.

Chilon his Life.

*Laert.
†Serm. 28.

*CHilon was a Lacedæmonian, Son of Damagetus, corruptly termed in †Stobæus, Pages. He was eminent among the Greeks for two Predictions.

*Herodot. lib. I.
Laert.

The first to Hippocrates* to whom (being a private Person) happened a great prodigy at the Olympick Games: having prepared an Offering, and filled a Cauldron with Flesh and Water, it boiled over without Fire: This portent Chilon (accidentally present) beholding, advised him that he should not take a Wife by whom he might have Issue; that if he had one, he should put her away, and if a Son, turn him out of Doors: Hippocrates not following this advice, brought up his Son Pisistratus, who in the sedition of the Maritimes and Country-Men at Athens, those led by Megacles, these by Lycurgus, stirred up a third Faction, and gained the Tyranny.

F   †He

† *He was much renowned also for his Prediction concerning* Cythera, *a* Lacedæmonian *Island; examining the Situation thereof, would to God (said he) it had never been; or since it is, it might be swallowed up by the Sea, and wisely did he forsee.* Damaratus *a* Lacedæmonian *exile, counselled* Xerxes *to seize upon that Island, which advice if he had followed, would have ruined all* Greece. His words (according to a Herodotus) were these: *You may effect your desires if you send three hundred Ships to the* Lacedæmonian *Coast; there lies an Island named* Cythera, *of which* Chilon, *a Person of greatest Wisdom amongst us, said, it were better for the* Lacedæmonians *that it were under Water than above:* He, it seems, expected from it some such thing as I am now going to declare, not that he foresaw your Navy, but doubting any in the same kind; *Let your Men issue out of this Island upon the* Lacedæmonians, *to strike them into terror.* b Afterward, in the time of the *Peloponesian War,* Nicias taking the Island, placed some Athenians therein, who much infested the Lacedæmonians.

Laertius saith, that *he was old in the fifty second Olympiad, at what time* Esop *flourished:* that *he was* Ephorus *in the fifty sixth.* (Casaubon reads the fifty five) *but* Pamphila (continueth Laertius) *saith in the sixth, he was first* Ephorus, *when* Euthydemus *was* Archon, *as* Soficrates *also affirms, and first appointed the* Ephori *to be joyned with Kings, which* Satyrus *saith, was the Institution of* Lycurgus. Hence it is doubtful whether *Chilon* was Ephorus in the sixth Olympiad, or in the fifty sixth; the latter is more probable, in as much as he bore that office when *Euthydemus* was Archon at *Athens*, which was in the fifty sixth Olympiad, as appears by the *Marmor Arundelianum*, where for Ἐυϑυδήμων is corruptly read τῷ δήμῳ rendred *Archonte populo*. But it is likewise true that the Ephori were first Created about the sixth Olympiad, when *Polydorus* and *Theopompus* were Kings of *Lacedæmon*, a Hundred and thirty years after *Lycurgus*, as *Plutarch* (in his Life affirms,) from which time there were five annual Ephori chosen in *Lacedæmon*, whereof the first is called ἐπώνυμος, because the Year had its denomination from him: The first of the first Election was c *Elatus;* Chilon in the fifty sixth Olympiad was the first of the five of his year; which might perhaps give the occasion of the Mistake to them, who take him to be the first of that Institution, of whom is d *Scaliger*.

How he behaved himself in this Office, may be gathered from his Speech f *to his Brother, displeased that himself was not* Ephorus *at the same time:* I can bear Injuries, saith he, you cannot. He was so just in all his actions, g that in his old Age he professed he never had done any thing contrary to the Conscience of an upright Man, only that of one thing he was doubtful; having given Sentence against his Friend according to Law, he advised his Friend to appeal from him (his Judge) so to preserve both his Friend and the Law: h *A. Gellius* relates it thus; 'when his Life drew 'towards an end, ready to be seized by death, 'he spoke thus to his Friends about him: 'My Words and Actions in this long term of

'years, have been (almost all) such as I need 'not repent of, which perhaps you also know 'truly even at this time I am certain, I never 'committed any thing, the remembrance 'whereof begets any trouble in me, unless 'this one thing only, which whether it were 'done amiss or not, I am uncertain: I sat 'with two others as Judge upon the Life of 'my Friend; the Law was such, as the per-'son must of necessity be Condemned; so that 'either my Friend must lose his Life, or some 'deceit be used towards the Law: revolving 'many things in my Mind for relief of a con-'dition so desperate, I conceived that which 'I put in practice to be of all other the most 'easie to be born: Silently I condemned him, 'and perswaded those others who judged to 'absolve him: Thus preserving (in so great 'a business) the duty both of a Judge and 'Friend; but from that act I receive this trou-'ble, that I fear it is not free from perfidious-'ness and guilt, in the same business, at the 'same time, and in a publick affair, to per-'swade others, contrary to what was in my 'own judgment best.

CHAP. II.
His Moral Sentences, Precepts, and Verses.

OF his Apothegms, these are remembered by *Laertius*; he said 'Providence of fu-'ture things collected by reason, is the vertue of 'a Man. Being demanded wherein the Learned 'differ from the Unlearned? He answer'd in a 'good hope. What is hard? to conceal secrets, to dis-'pose of leisure well; and to be able to bear an 'Injury.

a Being invited to a Feast by *Periander*, (with the rest of the wise men) he would not promise to come before he knew what other company would be there, saying, *a Man is necessitated to brook an ill Companion in a Ship at Sea, or in a Tent in a Camp; but to mix indifferently with all sorts of People at a Feast is indiscretion.* Upon the same occasion *Plutarch* recites these Sentences of his; *A Prince must not think upon any transitory mortal things, but only upon the eternal, and immortal. That Common-wealth is best where the People mind the Law, more than the Lawyers. A Family must resemble as much as possible a City govern'd by a King.* b Hearing a Man say he had no Enemy, he asked him if he had any Friend; conceiving Love and Hate necessarily must follow one another.

His moral Precepts are thus delivered by c *Demetrius Phalerius. Know thy self. Speak not much in thy drink, for thou wilt transgress;* (or as *Laertius,* rule thy tongue, especially at a Feast.) *Threaten not free persons, for it is not just.* (*Laertius*, Threaten none, for that is like a Woman) *Speak not ill of thy Neighbour; if thou dost, thou shalt hear what will trouble thee. Go slowly to the feasts of thy Friends, swiftly to their Misfortunes;* (*Laertius*, go more readily to a Friend in adversity than in prosperity.) *Celebrate Marriage frugally. Speak well of the Dead. Reverence thy Elder;* (*Laertius* honour Age) *Hate him who is inquisitive into the business of others. Prefer loss before unjust gain* (for that (adds *Laertius*)

Laertius) brings grief but once, this for ever) *Deride not the unfortunate. If thou art strong, behave thy self mildly, that thou mayst rather be respected than feared* (Laertius, of thy Neighbours, Learn to) *Order thy House well. Let not thy Tongue run before thy Mind. Bridle thy Anger. Covet not Impossibilities. In the way hasten not forward. Shake not thy Hand* (Laertius, in Discourse) *for it is like a Mad-man. Obey the Laws. Be reconciled to those who have wronged you, but revenge Contumelies.* To which Laertius adds these, *To preserve thy self. Not to hate Divination, make use of Quietness.*

^d *Lib. 7. cap. 32.* ^d Pliny speaking of Authority, saith, that Men ranked Chilon amongst Oracles, consecrating three precepts of his at Delphi, in Golden letters, which are these: *Every Man to know himself, and to desire nothing too much; the Companion of anothers Money and strife is misery.*

^e *A. Gell.* ^e He only kept within bounds the two most fierce affections of the Soul, Love, and Hate, saying, *Love with such limitation, as if hereafter you might chance to hate: hate so far, as that perhaps you might hereafter love.*

Ausonius ascribes to him the effect of these Verses:

' Me, may the mean not fear, nor great despise,
' Have death and health alike before thy Eyes.
' The benefits thou givest remember never,
' Of those thou dost receive, be mindful ever.
' Learn of thy self and Friend t'orecome cross
' Fate,
' Age, Youth resembling, is a light Estate,
' Youth, Age resembling, is a greater weight.

His particular Sentence was, *To a surety, loss is near.*

Of his Ἀδομίνα, Laertius mentions this as most eminent.

Gold's Worth we by the Touchstone find,
Gold is the Touchstone of the Mind.

^f He asked Æsop what Jupiter was doing, ^f *Laert.* who answered, pulling down the high, and raising the low.

CHAP. III.

His Death and Writings.

HE died (according to ^a Hermippus) at ^a *Laert.* Pisa, embracing his Son Victor in the Olympick Games, of the Cæstus, the weakness of his Age overcome with excess of Joy; all who were present at that great Assembly, attended on his Funerals, as is affirmed by ^b Pliny ^b *Lib. 7. cap.* and Laertius, who hath this Epigram upon him, *32.*

To the Illustrious Pollux Thanks I pay,
That Chilon's Son the Olive bore away.
The Father died o'rejoy'd his Child to see
So Crown'd: a happy Death! such befal me.

Upon his Statue this Inscription.

The birth of Chilon Warlike Sparta grac'd,
Who of the seven, in the first rank was plac'd.

• He was short in Speech, whence Arista- ^c *Laert.* goras calls that manner of speaking Chilonian: ^d Ausonius also alludes hereto in the Speech he ^d *Lud.Sept. sap.* makes under his name.

• He writ Elegies extending almost to two ^e *Laert.* hundred Verses: there is likewise an Epistle of his extant to this effect.

Chilon *to* Periander.

' YOU send me word of an Expedition you
' are preparing against Foreigners, intend-
' ing to go in Person with your Army: a Mo-
' narch, I think hath little safety even at home.
' That Tyrant I esteem happy who dies at
' home a natural Death.

PITTACVS

CHAP. I.
Pittacus his Life.

PITTACUS was of *Mitelene* (the chief City of *Lesbos*) Son of *Caicus*, † or (rather) *Hyrrhadius*, a *Thracian*, his Mother a *Lesbian*, born in the thirty second Olympiad.

Laertius saith, he flourished in the forty second Olympiad ; * at that time he gave testimony of his great courage and love to his Country, in killing (assisted by the Brethren of *Alcæus* the Poet) *Melanchrus*, Tyrant of *Lesbos* and *Mitelene*.

[a] *Pittacus* grown eminent by this action, was by the *Miteleneans* made General, and *sent with a Fleet against the* Athenians, with whom they had a long contest concerning the *Achillæan* Field ; the ground of their difference this : [c] *Pisistratus took* Sigeum *by force from the* Mitelenæans, *and settled there (as King)* Hegesistratus *his natural Son*, by an Argive Woman, *who kept it, not without much dispute* ; *for betwixt the* Mitlenæans *and* Athenians *there was a long War*; *those sallying out of the* Achillæan *Town, those out of* Sigæum : [d] *those lay claim to the Town, as built by* Arohænacies *of* Mitelene, *of the Stones of old* Troy. (for the *Lesbians* challeng'd the greatest part of *Troas* as their Hereditary right, where they had built many Houses, some saith *Strabo*, standing at this Day, others demolished)

† *Laert. Said.*
* *So the Vatican MS. of Suidas, better than the Printed Editions, which read* Said.

[a] *Laert.*
[b] *Strab.*

[c] *Herod.* 5. 94.

PART I. PITTACVS. 37

^e *Herod. continues.*
^f *Strab. Laert.*
^g *Strab. Laert.*
^h *Saturnal.*
ⁱ *In Retiario.*
^k *Strab. Laert.*
^l *Herod. 5. 95.*
^m *Strab.*
ⁿ *Laert.*
^o *Arist. polit. 3. 14.*
^p *Val. Max. 6. 5.*
^q *Plut. Amator.*
^r *Arist. pol. 3. 1. 4.*
^s *Plut. de malig. Herod. Laert. Suid.*
^t *Laert.*
^u *Val. Max. 6. 5.*
Val. Max. 4. 1.
^x *De Legib. 2.*
^y *Polit. 2. 12.*

demolished) ^e these opposed their claim; alledging the Æolians *had no more right to this* Ilian *Country than themselves or any other of the* Greeks, *who assisted* Menelaus *in the recovery of* Hellen. ^f The *Athenians* sent thither as General, *Phryno*, a tall robust Person, who had been Victor in all the Olympick Exercises; perhaps the same whom *Eusebius* names in the thirty sixth Olympiad. ^g Pittacus *having been several times worsted in Battle, at last challeng'd* Phryno *to single Combat, and met him, being armed with the Weapons of a Fisherman, hiding a Net under his Shield, wherewith catching* Phryno *suddenly, he slew him with his Trident and Dagger, and by his Death recovered the Field.* From this stratagem of *Pittacus*, was derived the like kind of Fighting among the *Roman* Gladiators, called Retiarii (described by ^h *Lipsius*) as is expresly observed by *Polyænus* and ⁱ *Festus*.

^k But this War ended not so; until at last both Parties referred themselves unto *Periander*, ^l chusing him Umpire; he awarded that each side should keep what they were in possession of, whereby *Sigeum* fell to the *Athenians*. ^m Demetrius *argues* Timæus *of falshood, for affirming* Periander *built* Achilleum (*a small Town, where was the Tomb of* Achilles) *in opposition to the* Athenians*, of* Ilian *Stones, and thereby to have aided* Pittacus: *but neither was it built of such Stones* (saith Strabo) *nor was* Periander *the founder: how could he be chose Arbitrator, whose Actions had declared him an Enemy?*

ⁿ Hereupon *Pittacus* was highly honoured by the *Mitelenæans*, who ^o *being infested by banished Persons, under the leading of* Antimenides, *and* Alcæus *the Poet*) ^p either in obligation to his merit, or confidence in his Equity, by their free Votes _q *(though* Alcæus *deny it)* instated him in the Tyranny; ^r *with many Acclamations of Praise, and a great concourse of People* (as is manifest from *Alcæus*, who for that reason reprehends them.) ^s They also with general consent offered him great Gifts, and bad him take that Field which he recovered from the Citizens as much as he would. He darting his Spear, demanded only so much as that had passed over; which he dedicated to *Apollo*, called (even to the time of *Plutarch*, and *Laertius*) the Pittacæan Field. ^t *Sosicrates* avers, he took part of it for himself, saying, The half was more than the whole. _u Thus he *diverted his Mind from the Gift, conceiving it not fitting to diminish the glory of the Vertue, by the greatness of the Reward.*

'Being possessed of this Power, he shewed the 'moderation wherewith his Breast was furnish'd, 'towards *Alcæus* the Poet, who had behaved 'himself pertinaciously against him, with bitter 'hate and scurrilous wit (whereof see many in-'stances in *Laertius*,) *Pittacus* only inform'd 'him how able he was to oppress him.

During his Government, he made many Laws, one whereof is mentioned by * *Cicero*, forbidding *Any Man to go to the Funeral of such as he was not King to.* Another by ^y *Aristotle*, that *whosoever being drunk, should strike any Man, should pay double as much as if he had been sober*; or as *Laertius* delivers it, *whosoever offended, being drunk, should pay a double forfeit*; which he did to restrain the *Mitelenæans* from drukenness,

because their Island abounded in Wine. His usual exercise, even whilst he was King, (as *Clearchus* affirms) was to grind Corn, esteeming it a healthful Exercise, much commending a Mill, that in so little room, it afforded exercise to many. There was a Song _z called for that reason Ἐσυμυλίων, of which *Thales* * affirms he heard a She-slave in *Lesbos* sing the beginning *pos. sept. sap.* as the ground, which was thus.

_z *Pollux.*
* *Plut. Sym. pos. sept. sap.*

' Grind, grind my Mill amain,
' For *Pittacus* that *Lesbian* King
' To grind doth not disdain.

Being well in years, he was constrained to take upon himself the leading of an Army, whereupon he said, *It is hard to be good*; which † *Simonides* mentions, saying,

† Hence correct *Suidas* who saith Simon.

' Hard to be truly honest, this
' The *Pittaceian* Sentence is.

Plato also remembers it in his *Protagoras* (where *Simonides* reproves *Pittacus* for saying, it is hard to continue good, which he affirms to be easie, but to become good, hard; wherein he differs from *Laertius*'s expression of it.

† He continued in the Government of the Kingdom ten Years; * *Valerius Maximus* saith, *only as long as the War with the* Athenians *concerning* Sigeum *lasted, but afterwards as soon as Peace was obtained by Victory* (having in this time settled the affairs of the Common-wealth) *he laid it down, notwithstanding the* Mitelenæans *cried out to the contrary, lest he should continue Lord of the Citizens longer than the necessities of the Kingdom required*, and lived ten years after a private Person.

† *Laert.* * *6. 5.*

' He went to *Sardis*, at what time (as some say, though others apply it to *Bias*) *Cræsus* having 'made the *Grecians* in *Asia* tributary, had given 'order for the building of a Navy to invade the 'Islanders: as soon as he came thither, *Cræsus* 'asked him what News from *Greece*? He by his 'answer. diverted the King from going forward 'with his building Ships: the Islanders, saith he, 'have bought a world of Horses, intending an 'Expedition against *Sardis*; and *Cræsus* think-'ing he had spoken truth, answered, I wish the 'Gods would put it in their minds to come against 'the *Lydians* on Horse-back; he replied, It is not 'without reason, great King, that you wish and 'hope to catch the Islanders on Horse-back in the 'Continent; and what think you the Islanders wish 'more, than (hearing your preparation to set out a 'Navy against them) that they may catch the *Ly-*'*dians* upon the Sea, and revenge the cause of those 'inland *Grecians* whom you have reduced to ser-'vitude. *Cræsus* much delighted with this Speech, 'and dissvaded (for it seemed to him he spoke 'very ingeniously) from building a navy, gave it o-'ver, and contracted amity with the *Ionian* Islands.

Herod. 1. 27.

CHAP. II.
His moral Sentences Precepts, and Verses.

OF his Apothegms, *Laertius* recites these. 'The Gods themselves cannot resist neces-'sity. Power shews the Man. Being on a time 'demanded what is best, he answered, To do the 'present well. To *Cræsus*, who asked which was 'the greatest Government? That of various Wood (saith he) meaning the Law (carved) in
wooden

'wooden Tables. To a *Phocæan*, who said, I muſt
'ſeek an honeſt Man: though you ſeek much,
'(ſaith he) you ſhall not find him. To ſome who
'demanded what was moſt pleaſing, he anſwer'd,
'Time. He ſaid it was the part of wiſe Men to
'forſee inconveniences, and prevent them be-
'fore they came; of valiant Men, to order them
'well when they come.

† *Sympoſ. ſept. ſap.*

Add theſe from †*Plutarch*, 'That Prince is hap-
'py, who can make his Subject afraid not of him,
'but for him. That Common-wealth is beſt order-
'ed, where the wicked have no Command, and
'the good have. That Houſe is beſt ordered, which
'needs nothing either of ornament or neceſſity.

* *Athen. deipn. lib. 10.*

* He counſelled *Periander* to ſhun drunkenneſs and exceſs in feaſting, left he ſhould be
known to be what he was, not what he ſeemed.

† *Laert.*

‡ To a young Man asking his advice concerning Marriage, what directions he gave, is
thus expreſt by *Callimachus*.

'An *Acarnæan* Stranger *Pittacus*.
'*Hyrrhadius* Son of *Leſbos* queſtion'd thus;
'Father, a double Match is offered me;
'The birth and means of one with mine agree;
'The other far exceeds me, which is beſt?
'By your Advice my aim ſhall be addreſt.
'Lifting his Staff, (his Ages ſole defence)
'He pointing ſaid, go fetch advice from thence;
'(There he eſpi'd ſome boys by chance at play,
'As they were whipping Tops along the way)
'Follow their ſteps faith he. When nigh he drew,
'He heard them ſay, an equal take to you;
'By which direction guided, he forſook
'The richer Fortune, and the equal took;
'Be you (as he) by this wiſe Counſelled,
'And take an equal to your Marriage-Bed.

Prom. vinct.

Whither *Æſchylus* (as is obſerv'd by his
Scholiaſt) alluded ſaying.

'Wiſe, truly wiſe was he
'Who firſt Sententiouſly
'His Judgment thus expreſt,
'An equal Match is beſt.

His moral Precepts are thus collected by

* *Stob. 28.*

* *Demetrius Phalereus*, 'Know opportunity;
'what thou intendeſt, ſpeak not before thou
'doſt it, for being fruſtrate of thy hope, thou
'wilt be derided. Uſe thy Friends. What
'thou tak'ſt ill in thy Neighbour, do not thy
'ſelf. Reproach not the unhappy, for the
'Hand of God is on them. Reſtore what is
'committed to thy Truſt. Bear with thy Neigh-
'bour. Love thy Neighbour. Reproach not
'thy Friend, though he recede from thee a
'little; nor wiſh well to thy Enemy; it is a-
'gainſt Reaſon. It is hard to foreſee the fu-
'ture, what is paſt is certain, what is to come
'obſcure. The Earth is faithful, the Sea faith-
'leſs; Gain inſatiable. Acquire Honeſty; ſeek
'Obſequiouſneſs; love Diſcipline, Temperance,
'Prudence, Truth, Faith, Experience, Dexterity,
'Society, Diligence, Oeconomy, and Piety.

Auſonius cites theſe as his:

'None know to ſpeak who know not to refrain,
'One good Man's praiſe 'fore many ill mens gain.
'He's mad who envies in the happy, pride;
'Or grief in the unhappy doth deride.

'Who makes a Law muſt not that Law tranſgreſs:
'Purchaſe all Friends thou canſt in happineſs.
'And to the feweſt truſt in thy diſtreſs.

† Of his Ἀδουλία, theſe were moſt celebrious. † *Laert.*

Who hath a Quiver and a Bow,
Againſt a wicked Man ſhould go,
Whoſe doubtful Tongue never expreſt,
The faithleſs meaning of his Breaſt.

His particular Sentence was, *Know Opportunity.*

CHAP. III.

His Death, Brother, Wife, Son, Writings.

HE lived to a full Age, above Seventy * *Laert.*
Years, or (following the account of
Suidas for his Birth) Eighty. † *Lucian* exceeds, † *Longæv.*
who reckons him amongſt thoſe who lived one
Hundred years; for he † died when *Ariſtome-* † *Laert.*
nes was Archon, in the third Year of the fifty
ſecond Olympiad: Upon his Monument this
Epitaph,

Weep Citizens, as ſacred Lesbos *weeps*
For Pittacus; *this Tomb his Aſhes keeps.*

He had a Brother, who dying without Iſſue,
his Eſtate devolved to *Pittacus*; whereupon, re-
fuſing the Wealth *Cræſus* offered him, he ſaid,
he had more by half than he deſired.

He Married a Wife of Birth higher than himſelf, Siſter to *Draco*, Son of *Penthilus*; ſhe behaved her ſelf Imperiouſly towards him; where-
of * *Plutarch* gives this Inſtance, *Having invited* * *De anim. tranquil.*
ſome Friends, ſhe came in and overthrew the Ta-
ble; he ſeeing his Gueſts troubled, ſaid, 'Each of
'you hath ſome Misfortune, he is happieſt who hath
'no more than this. *Laertius* faith, The Advice
he gave concerning equal Marriage (Chap 2.)
was out of reſentment of his own Troubles.

* He had a Son named *Tyrrheus*, who at Cu- * *Laert.*
ma *ſitting in a Barber's Shop* (as was uſed a-
mongſt the Ancients, by ſuch as loved to diſcourſe of News) *was caſually killed by a Braſier*
with a Blow of a Hatchet; *the* Cumeans *took*
the Offender and ſent him to Pittacus; *he being*
informed of the Accident, ſet him at liberty, ſay-
ing, Pardon is better than Penitence.

Of his Writings *Laertius* mentions.

Ἀδουλία, already cited.
Elegies amounting to 600 Verſes.
Of Laws in Proſe; directed to his own
   Countrymen.

Epiſtles of which this is preſerved;
Pittacus to Cræſus.

'You command me to come to *Lydia* to be-
'hold your Wealth; without ſight whereof
'I can eaſily believe the Son of *Alyattes*, to
'be the richeſt of Kings, and therefore need
'not in that reſpect go to *Sardis*; for I want
'not Gold, but have enough even for my Friends
'alſo; yet I will come to you to enjoy your
'Converſation as a Gueſt.

* There was another *Pittacus*, called the Leſſer, a Law-giver; mentioned by *Phavorinus* * *Laert.*
and *Demetrius.*

BIAS.

BIAS.

CHAP. I.
Bias his Life.

*Laert.

*BIAS was of *Priene*, Son of *Tutamis*; some affirm he was rich, others that he had no Estate, but lived as an Inmate. *Satyrus* ranketh him first of the seven wife Men; the occasion whereby that Title was conferred on him, was this; he redeemed some Captive *Messenian* Virgins, brought them up as his Daughters, gave them Portions, and so sent them back to their Parents: A Tripod being afterwards found at *Athens* (as was related in the Life of *Thales*, the Place only different) with this Inscription in Gold, *To the Wise*. These Virgins (as *Satyrus* affirms) or (as *Phanodicus*) their Father came into the Congregation, and pronounced *Bias Wise*, declaring what he had done for them: Hereupon the Tripod was sent to him, which *Bias* beholding, averred *Apollo* to be the most wise,

and

and would not accept it; some affirm he dedicated it to *Hercules* at *Thebes*, as being descended from the *Theban* Colony, sent to *Priene*.

That he made good this attribute, there are many Instances; † *Aylattes* besieging *Priene*, *Bias* turned out of the Town two exceeding fat Mules, which coming to the Camp, *Crœsus* wondered to * see their Plenty extended to the very Beasts, and desirous of reconcilement, sent a Messenger to them. *Bias* causing many heaps of Sand to be made, and covered over with Wheat, shewed them to the Messengers, whereof *Alyattes* informed, was more eager of Peace than before, and sent immediately to desire *Bias* to come to him; but I (answered he) wish *Alyattes* may feed on Onyons, meaning to Weep.

† Some ascribe it to *Bias*, the diversion of *Crœsus* his Expedition against the *Greek* Islands, by others imputed to *Pittacus* related in his Life.

* *Cyrus* having taken *Crœsus*, sent an Army against the *Grecians*; the *Ionians* much troubled, assembled at the *Panionium*, where *Bias* gave them Wise Advice, which had they followed (saith *Herodotus*) they might have been the happiest of all the *Greeks*: He counselled them to joyn together in one Fleet, to Sail to *Sardinia*, and there build one City common to all the *Ionians*; whereby they might preserve themselves from Bondage, happy in possessing an Island far greater than all the rest, and commanding them; but if they continued in *Ionia*, there was no apparent hope of Liberty. This Advice was justified, the *Ionians* being subdued.

' † *Bias* (his Country *Priene* invaded by Enemies, all, whom the Cruelty of War suffer'd to 'escape, flying away laden with the most precious of their Wealth)being demanded why he 'carried none of his Goods with him. I (saith 'he)carry my Goods with me: He bore them(adds '*Valerius Maximus*) in his Breast, not to be seen 'by the Eye, but prised by the Soul; enclosed 'in the narrow dwelling of the Mind, not to 'be demolished by mortal hands, present with 'those who are settled,and not forsaking such as 'fly.

* He refused not the amity of Kings, (as *Thales* did) particularly, that of *Amasis*, King of *Ægypt*, who sent him a Victim, commanding him to take from it the best and worst part. *Bias* sent him the Tongue, for which ingenuity he was much admired.

† Another question of *Amasis* he resolved, whilst he was at *Corinth* (invited thither with the rest of the wise Men by *Periander*) where *Niloxenus* brought him this Letter.

' *Amasis*, King of *Egypt* saith thus to *Bias*, 'Wisest of the *Greeks*: The King of *Æthiopia* 'contendeth with me for preheminence in Wisdom; master'd in other things, he in conclusion requires an absurd, strange thing, that I 'drink up the Sea; this Proposition if I resolve, I 'shall have many of his Towns and Cities; if I 'resolve not, I must lose all those which are about *Elephantina*. Ponder it, and send *Niloxenus* 'back with all speed; whatever we can do for 'your Friends and Country, shall not be wanting.

Having read the Letter, *Bias* with a short pause, recollecting himself,and having whispered to *Cleobulus* who sat next him. ' What ' (saith he) *Naucratites*, *Amasis*, who commands so many Men, and possesseth so excellent a Country, will he for a few obscure ' contemptible Villages, drink up the Sea ? ' *Bias* (saith *Niloxenus* smiling) consider, as ' if he meant to do it, how it might be effected. Bid the *Æthiopian* (replied *Bias*) ' withhold the Rivers from running into the ' Sea, until he hath drunk off that which is ' now Sea; for the Imposition concerns that ' only which is such at present, not what shall ' be hereafter. *Niloxenus* embraced him with Joy, the rest applauding his Solution.

CHAP. II.

His moral Sentences, Precepts, and Verses.

HIS Apothegms are thus delivered by *Laertius*,and others. ' He is unfortunate,who ' cannot bear misfortune. It is a disease of the 'mind to desire such things as cannot be obtain'd, ' and to be unmindful of the miseries of others. ' To one that ask'd what is hard, he answered,to ' bear couragiously a change to the worse. Being ' at Sea in Company with wicked Men,who,a ' Storm arising,called upon the Gods; hold your ' Peace, saith he, lest they know you are here. To ' a wicked Man, enquiring what was Piety, he ' was silent, the other asking the reason of his ' silence: I answer not, saith he, because you ' enquire after that which nothing concerns you. ' Being demanded what is sweet to mankind, he ' answer'd, Hope.It is better to decide a difference betwixt our enemies than Friends, for one ' of the Friends will certainly become an Enemy, ' one of the Enemies, a Friend; being ask'd what ' a Man did with delight, he answered gain by 'Labour. We should so live, as though our life ' would be both long and short. So love, as if ' hereafter we might hate, conversing in Friendship with caution, remembring that it may ' possibly convert to Enmity.

' * To one demanding whether he should take ' a wife; she must be(saith he)either fair or foul; ' if fair, she will be common, if foul, a pennance.

' † That Tyrant shall gain most glory, who ' first himself obeys the Laws of his Country: ' That Common-wealth is best ordered, wherein ' every Man fears the Law more than a Tyrant. ' That Family is best ordered, where the Master ' behaves himself voluntarily within doors,as he ' doth without by constraint of the Law.

* Those who busie themselves in vain knowledge, resemble an Owl, which seeth only in ' the night, but is blind in the light; so is their ' mind sharp-sighted in vanity, dark at the approach of true light.

Ausonius hath these under his Name.

What is our chiefest good ? A Conscience free.
Our greatest ill ? Man's, Man's worst Enemy.
Poor ? th' avaricious. Rich ? who nought desires.
A Wives best dower ? the same chast life acquires.
Chaste? she, of whom report dare speak no ill.
Wise ? who hath power to hurt, but wants the will.
A Fool ? who wants the power,and yet would kill.

His moral Precepts, according to † *Demetrius Phalereus* these. 'Most Men are evil. '(† His particular Sentence) Before you do 'any thing, behold your Face in a Glass; if it 'seem handsom, do handsom things; if deform-'ed, supply the defects of Nature. Practise 'honesty. Undertake deliberately, but having 'once begun, go through. Abhor to speak ha-'stily [*Laer.* It is madness.] lest thou sin, for re-'pentance follows: Be neither simple nor sub-'tle. Admit not imprudence. Love Prudence. 'Every where profess there are Gods. Weigh 'what is to be done. Hear much, speak 'seasonably. If poor, reprove not the Rich, un-'less great advantage may arise thereby. Praise 'not an unworthy person for his Wealth. Ac-'quire by perswasion, not by violence. When 'thou dost good, impute it not to thy self, but 'the Gods. In thy Youth, gain Wealth, in 'thy Age, Wisdom. [Or as *Laertius*, from thy 'Youth to thy Age gain Wisdom, for it will 'be more sure to thee than all other Posses-'sions] Preserve in thy actions Remembrance, 'in opportunity, Caution; in thy Manners, In-'genuity; in labour, Patience; in fear Wari-'ness; in wealth, Love; in discourse, Per-'swasion; in silence, a Decorum; in Sentence, 'Justice; in boldness, Fortitude; in action, 'Power; in glory, Eminence; in thy Nature, 'Generosity.

† Stob. Serm. 28.
* Laert.

† Of his 'Ἀθμίνα, these were most esteem'd.

† Laert.

To all the City where thou liv'st be kind,
They who most favour show, most favour find:
But Pride is often with Destruction joyn'd.

And
Strength is a Gift, which Nature's hand bestows.
Rhetorick and Policy the Wise Soul knows,
Riches a Present that from Fortune flows.

CHAP. III.

His Death, and Writings.

HE was much addicted to Pleading, very earnest therein, but always employed in just causes; which † *Demodicus* the *Alerian* implies, saying *If thou chance to be a Judge, give Sentence on the* Prienæan *side*; and *Hipponax, to plead a Cause better than* Bias *the* Prienæan. And in that manner he died, being very old, as he was pleading, having ended his Speech he reposed his Head in the Bosom of his Sisters Son; his Adversary having ended his Defence; the Judges gave Sentence on *Bias*'s Side; the Court dismist, he was found dead in his Nephew's Bosom: The City bestowed a Magnificent Monument upon him, with this Inscription;

* Laert.
† Laert.
Δημόδικ@ ἐς Ἀλεσιεῖ@: perhaps it should be Δημόδοκ@ ὁ Ἀλεςιε@.

Bias of Prienæan *fam'd Descent*
Lies here, Ionia's *great Ornament.*

They also dedicated a Temple to him, called the *Tutmaian*.

Laertius bestows upon him this Epigram.

Bias lies hidden here, whom Hermes *led*
To th'grave, when Age had Snow'd upon his Head.
His Head, which (pleading for his Friend) enclin'd
Upon his Nephew to long Sleep resign'd.

He writ concerning *Ionia*, by what means it might be most happy (perhaps that Counsel already mentioned) Two Thousand Verses.

CLEOBULE

CHAP. I.

Cleobulus his Life, Death, and Writings.

Laert. **CLEOBULUS** was of *Lindus*, (a City of *Rhodes*) or, according to *Duris*, of *Caria*, Son of *Evagoras*, lineally descended from *Hercules*; excellent both in Wisdom, outward Beauty, and † *Strength* beyond all those of his time; learned in the Philosophy of the *Egyptians*. That he was Tyrant of *Lindus*, is manifest from * *Plutarch*. * He re-edified the Temple of *Minerva*, founded by *Danaus*.

†*Suid.*

De ei delph.

He had a Daughter *whom he named *Eumetis*, but was called commonly from her Father *Cleobulina*: She composed verses and riddles, in Hexamiters, famous for her Wisdom and Acuteness in those riddles, some of her questions having spread as far as *Egypt*, which she used jocularly, like Dice upon occasions, only contesting with such as provoked her; she was also indued with an admirable height of Mind, and a Wit both Politick,

† *Plut. conviv. sept. sap.*

Politick, and full of humanity, causing her Father to govern his People with more mildness. *Cratinus* also mentions her in a Comedy named from her *Cleobulæ*, often cited by *Athenæus*.

† *Laert.* † He died full of Years, which extended to Seventy: His Tomb carried this Inscription,

Wise Cleobulus's *Death, the* Lyndian *Shoar,*
To which his Birth was owing, doth deplore.

* *Laert.* * He Composed Verses and Riddles to the number of three Thousand; of which was this Riddle concerning the Year, (by *Suidas* ascribed to his Daughter *Cleobulina*.)

On Sire, twelve Sons, from every one a race
Of thirty Daughters with a double Face :
Their Looks are black, and white successively ;
Immortal they are all, and yet all die.

† *Laert.* † Some assert him the Author of this Epigram upon *Midas* (not Homer; who, as they account, lived long before *Midas*, though *Herodotus* otherwise.)

A brazen Virgin stretcht on Midas *Tomb,*
To last whilst Water runs, and Trees shall bloom ;
Whilst Sun and Moon dart their successive beams,
And the rough Sea supplied by gentle Streams.
I dwell upon this dismal Sepulchre,
To tell all those that pass, Midas *lies here.*

There is likewise extant under his name this Epistle:

Cleobulus to Solon.

'YOU have many Friends, and a Habitation every where; but I dare affirm, *Lindus* would be most pleasing to *Solon*, being governed by a Democracy; an Island where 'there is no fear of *Pisistrates*, thither your 'Friends will come to you from all parts.

CHAP. II.

His Moral Sentences, Precepts, and Verses.

† *Laert.* † OF his moral Sayings, are these: Employ thy self in something excellent. Be not vain and ungrateful. Bestow your Daughters, Virgins in Years, Matrons in discretion: implying, that the Virgins also should be instructed, which the *Greeks* used not, the *Romans* brought them up in the Liberal Sciences. Do good to your Friend that he may be more your Friend, your Enemy that he may become your Friend: For we should beware of the Calumny of Friends, of the Treachery of Enemies: When any Man goeth forth, let him consider what he is to do; when he returns, examine what he hath done.

† A Prince may be happy, if he trust none that † *Plut. Sympos.* are about him. That Common-wealth is best or- *sept. sap.* dered, wherein the Citizens fear Reproach more than Law. That Family is best, wherein more love than fear the Master.

His Precepts thus collected by * *Demetrius* * *Stob. Serm. 28* *Phalereus: A mean is best.* († His particular Sen- † *Laert.* tence) To reverence thy Father is Duty. Take care of thy Body and Soul. Hear willingly, but trust not hastily. (Or as *Laertius*, 'tis better to Love to hear, than to love to speak.) It is better to know many things, (*Laertius*, to love knowledge) than to be ignorant of all. Teach your Tongue to speak well. It is proper to Vertue, and contrary to Vice, to hate Injustice. (*Laertius*, be a Friend to vertue, a Stranger to Vice.) Preserve thy Piety. Advise thy Countrymen what is best. Govern thy Tongue. (*Laertius* Pleasure.) Do nothing by Violence. Instruct thy Children. Pray to Fortune. Forego Enmity. The Enemy to thy Country, esteem thy own. Fight not, nor be kind to thy Wife in the presence of others, one argues folly, the other madness. Correct not your Servants when they are drunk, it shews as if you were drunk your self. Marry with your equal, for by matching into a higher Family, you procure Masters, not Kinsmen. Laugh not in compliance with him who derides others; for you will be hated by those he derides. Rich, be not exalted; Poor, be not dejected. (*Laertius* adds, Learn to bear the changes of Fortune.)

Ausonius ascribes these to him.

The more is in thy Power, desire the less ;
Not to be envi'd is unhappiness.
None long in his impieties can thrive,
In others much, nought in thy self forgive.
All Men would spare the good, the bad cast down,
We share not in our Ancestors Renown :
But their inglorious Actions often own.

Of his Ἀδόμενα these were most noted. *Laert.*

By Ignorance most deeds are sway'd,
In many specious Words array'd ;
But all things shall by Time be weigh'd.

PERIANDER

CHAP. I.

The Country, Ancestors, and Parents of Periander.

PEriander was Son of *Cypselus* Tyrant of *Corinth*, his Mother *Cratea*, his Ancestors the *Heraclidæ*, (* descended from *Hercules* and *Jardana*) Reigned Kings of *Lydia* five hundred and five years, the Son continually succeeding the Father for two and twenty Generations. The original of *Cypselus*, and the manner of his obtaining the Kingdom receive thus from † *Herodotus*.

When *Corinth* was governed by an Oligarchy, inhabited by the *Bacchiadæ*, who never would marry out of their own Family, one of them (called *Amphion*) had a lame Daughter (by name *Labda*) whom when none of the *Bacchiadæ* would take to Wife, *Eetion* married (Son of *Echetrates* of the *Betræan* tribe, but descended afar off from *Lapithe* and *Cœnis*) having no Children, he consulted the *Delphian* Oracle

*Laert.
* Herod. I. 7.

† Lib. 5. 92.

Oracle about it; as soon as he entred, the Prophetess spake thus to him.

Eetion none will thee though great respect,
A stone from Labdas *fruitful Womb expect,*
Which shall the People Caush, Corinth *Correct.*

This Oracle to *Eetion*, agreed with another delivered to the *Bacchiadæ* (though by them not understood) to this effect.

A Lyon by an Eagle shall be laid
Upon a Rock, fierce, making all afrid.
Corinthians, what I say consider well,
Who in tall Corinth *and* Pirene *dwell.*

The *Bacchiadæ* who could not comprehend the meaning of this Oracle, when they heard that to *Eetion*, understood their own by the affinity it had with the other, and thereupon secretly design'd amongst themselves to kill *Eetion*'s Child. His Wife being delivered, they sent ten Men of their own to the tribe wherein *Eetion* dwelt, that they should murther the Infant; when they came to *Petra* to *Eetion*'s House, they demanded the Child. *Labda* (not knowing their intent, but thinking they came to congratulate with the Father,) brings her Son, and gives him into the hands of one of them: they had agreed (upon the way) that he into whose hands the Child were delivered should dash out its brains against the ground, but by divine Providence, the Child smiling upon him to whom *Labda* had given it, he was moved therewith to such compassion, that he could not find in his heart to kill it, but delivered it to another, he to a third, until at last it past through the hands of all the ten; None of them having power to kill it, they restored it to the Mother. Then going forth and standing before the door, they began to find fault with one another, but chiefly with him who took the Child first, for not performing the agreement; after some debate, they agreed to go in all and be equal sharers in the murther; but it was decreed that *Eetion*'s Child should be the oppressor of *Corinth*, for *Labda* standing at the door heard all their discourse, and fearing lest their minds changing, they should murther it, carried away the Child, and hid it in a measure of Corn (called *Cypsela*) a place which she conceived they could never search if they returned, and so it fell out: They came back and sought all about; when they could not find him, they agreed amongst themselves to tell those who sent them, they had done what they required, and returning home, did so. *Eetion*'s Son growing up was called *Cypselus* from the danger he had escaped in the Corn-measure; when he came to Man's estate, he consulted with the *Delphian* Oracle, and received a doubtful answer, in confidence whereof he attempted *Corinth* and took it, the Oracle was this,

Happy is Cypselus, *who to my fane*
This visit makes; he Corinth'*s Crown shall gain;*
He and his Sons (but not their Sons) shall Reign,

Being possest of the Kingdom, he persecuted the *Corinthians*, depriviving many of their Estates, more (by far) of their Lives; having reigned thirty years, he dyed and was succeeded by his Son *Periander*, whose Reign compleated this Tyranny, which lasted according to *Aristotle* 73 years and 6 months: so that *Cypselus* began to Reign in the second year of the thirtieth Olympiad.

CHAP. II.

The time of his Birth, his Reign, and the change of his Disposition.

PEriander (by computation from his death, which according to *Laertius* was in the eightieth year of his age, the last of the forty eighth Olympiad) was born in the last year of the tweenty ninth Olympiad. His Reign (according to * *Aristotle*'s account, lasting forty four years) begun in the fourth year of the thirty seventh Olympiad. *Suidas* saith, he succeeded in the Kingdom, † as being his Fathers eldest Son, which *Plutarch* calls, *a disease hereditary to him*, ‖ flourished in the thirty eight Olymdiad. He * was at first of a mild gentle disposition, but afterwards grew very rigid upon this occasion. His Mother, whilst he was very young, kept him much in her company, when he grew more in years, fell in love with him; with time her passion encreased to such extremity, that she could no longer suppress it; assuming confidence, she told her Son, there was a beautiful Lady fallen in love with him, and advised him not to slight her affection. He answer'd, he would not transgress Law and Vertue, by touhing a married Woman. His Mother pressed him with intreaties; at last he consented; she appointed a Night, advising him not to have any light in his Chamber, not to constrain the Lady to speak, but to excuse her for modestie's sake. *Periander* engaged himself to do all she directed. She, attired as richly as she could, went to his Chamber, and departed again before day-break: On the morrow she enquired if he were pleased, and if the Lady should come again to him. *Periander* said, it was his chiefest desire, and that he affected her excessively, from that time she visited her Son often: he, at last, was moved with a great curiosity to know who she was, and solicited his Mother very importunately that he might have some discourse and acquaintance with her, seeing he was so much taken with love of her, affirming it was unreasonable, he should be denyed the sight of one, with whom he had so often a neater acquaintance. His Mother affirm'd it could not be done, in respect to the Modesty of the Lady. Hereupon he gave one of his Servants order to hide a light in his Chamber: she came as she used, and when she was asleep, *Periander* rose, took the light, and seeing it was his Mother, was about to have killed her, but with-held by some genius or apparition, forbore: From that time forward he was troubled in mind, grew cruel, and killed many of his Subjects. His Mother, much accusing her unhappy genius, slew her self.

* Politic. 5.
† Excerpt. Nicol. Damasc. Suid.
‖ Conviv. sept. Sap.
* Laert. Suid.
* Parthen. orat. cap. 17.

self. *Laertius* saith, they were both conscious hereof, and that being discovered, he grew cruel to every one.

† *Herod.* † In the beginning of his Reign he was much more merciful than his Father, but keeping correspondence by Messengers with *Thrasibulus*
* *Laert.* Tyrant of *Miletus*, (* to whom in times past he had been a Guest, before he arrived to the Government) he became at last much more bloody than his Father. He sent an express to *Thrasibulus*, to know what course he should take to settle himself, and to govern the City in the best maner. *Thrasibulus* led the Messenger out of the Town, and as they walked together in a Corn-field, question'd him concerning his coming from *Corinth*, and in the mean time lopped off all the heads of Corn that grew higher than the rest, and threw them away; in this manner he went over the whole field, not speaking one word to the Messenger, and so sent him home; where being returned, *Periander* greedily enquired what Instructions he had brought; he answered, *Thrasibulus* had given him none, and that he wondered he would send him to a Mad-man, who destroyed his own goods. *Periander* enquired what *Thrasibulus* did, and immediately apprehended that he advised him to put the most eminent in the City to death. *Laertius* recites a Letter to that effect, which, if not suppositious, must have been sent at another time after this Messenger departed.

Thrasibulus *to* Periander.

I Gave your Messenger no answer, but carrying him into a field of Corn, lopped off with my stick such Ears as grew higher than the rest, whilst he followed me; if you enquire, he will relate all to you that he hath heard or seen: Do you so likewise, if you mean to settle your self in the Government, take off the Heads of the chiefest Citizens, whether your professed Enemies, or others. A Tyrant must suspect every Friend.

* *Sept. sap. conviv.* Though * *Plutarch* deny he followed this advice, *Herodotus* avers, that from thence forward *Periander* exercised all cruelty upon his Subjects, dispatching those that had escaped the Rigour and Persecutions of his Father.
† *Laert.* †He first appointed a guard of Halberdiers to secure his Person,
* *Suid.* * which consisted of three
† *Excerpt.Nicol. Damascen. and Suidas from him.* hundred, and converted the Government to a Tyranny († through his cruelty and violence) He forbad the Citizens to keep any Servants, or to be idle, always finding some employment for them: If any Man sat in the *Forum*, he was fined, for he feared lest they should plot against him.
* *Laert.* * The Citizens being desirous to live ἰᵥ ἄσε he would not suffer them; He was always in War, being of a martial disposition.
† *Suid.* † He made Ships with three banks of Oars, which he used in both Seas.
* *Laert.* He * attempted to dig the Isthmus off from the Continent.

Of his friendship and correspondence with *Thrasibulus*, * *Herodotus* gives another instance,
* *Lib.* I. 20. affirming he sent to inform him of the Oracles answer to *Alyattes* King of *Lydia*, concerning the re-edifying of the Temple of *Minerva*, and advised him to provide before-hand for his own security.

* He made a vow, if he were Victor in the *Laert. Chariot-race at the *Olympick* Games, to erect a statue of Gold: He chanced to be victorious, and wanting Gold, beholding upon a Festival of that Country the Women richly adorned, he took off all their ornaments, and so sent them home.

CHAP. III.

Of his being placed in the number of the Seven Sages. His Sentences and Writings.

*P*Eriander (saith † *Plutarch*) being become † *Sept. Sap.* a Tyrant by hereditary disease derived to *conv.* him by his Father, endeavoured to purge himself thereof as much as possible, by using the sound conversation of good Persons, and invited Wise-men to come to him; † to which purpose † *Laert.* he sent this Epistle to those of *Greece*, at such time as they met at *Delphi*.

Periander *to the* Wise Men.

I Give Pythian and Apollo many thanks, that you being met together there, will also by my Letters be brought to Corinth, I will entertain you as you well know very kindly. I hear that last year you met at the Lydian Kings in Sardis: delay not now to come to me, Tyrant of Corinth, for the Corinthians will look kindly upon you, if you come to the House of Periander.

Upon this invitation they went to him, not seven, but twice as many, of whom was *Diocles*, *Periander*'s Friend, in whose name *Plutarch* makes a large description of their entertainment, which was not in the City, but at the Port *Lecheon*, in a great Hall, appropriated to solemn Feasts, joyning to the Temple of *Venus*, to whom he had not sacrificed since the unhappy death of his Mother until that time, the particulars of the Feast, by reason of the largness of the Discourse, we refer to *Plutarch*.

He was also himself put into the unmber of these Wisemen, who, † *Plutarch* saith, were † *De ɇ' Delph.* originally but five, but that afterwards *Cleobulus* Tyrant of *Lindus*, and *Periander* Tyrant of *Corinth*, who had neither Vertue nor Wisdom, by the greatness of their Power, the multitude of their Friends, and the obligations they conferred upon those that adhered to them, forced a reputation, and thrust themselves violently into the usurped name of *Wisemen*; to which end, they spread abroad Sentences and remarkable Sayings throughout all *Greece*, the very same which others had said before, whereat the other first Sages were much displeased, yet would not discover or convince their vanity, nor have any publick Controversie about that title with Persons of so much Wealth and Power, but meeting together at *Delphi*, after some private debate, they consecrated there the Letter *E*, the fifth in the Alphabet, and in numeration, to testifie to the God of that Temple they were no more than five, and

that

that they rejected and excluded from their company, the sixth and the seventh, as having no right thereto.

Suid.
† *Protagor.*
• *Laert.*

Of those * who excluded him out of the number of the seven, some, (as † *Plato*) substitute in his room *Myso*: * others say there were two of this name, Cousins, one the Tyrant, the other of *Ambraica*: But *Aristotle* and others, assert him of *Corinth* to be the Wise, which Attribute seems to be conferred upon him, not in respect to his Actions, but moral Sayings and Writings, which were these.

'Do nothing for gain, that is proper to Trades-
'men. They who will rule safely, must be guard-
'ed with Love, not Arms. Being demanded why
'he continued King, because (saith he) it is dan-
'gerous willingly to refrain, or unwillingly to
'be deposed.

† *Plut. sept. sap. conv.*

† When the other six had given their opinions concerning Tyranny (at the Feast to which he invited them, he being desired to add his, answered with a troubled countenance, *Enough has been said to deter any Man of sound Judgment from Rule.* When they had in like manner declared their Opinions, concerning a Common-wealth, he added, *The result of all which had been said, commended that Democracy most, which came nearest an Aristocracy.*

‡ *Stob. 28.*
† *Stob. ibid.*
* *Laert.*

* *Being demanded what was the greatest in the least, he answered, a good mind in a humane body.*

His Precepts (according to † *Demetrius Phalereus*) were these, ' *Consideration is all* (* which
'was his particular Sentence) Quiet is good,
'Temerity dangerous. Gain sordid, the accusati-
'on of Nature. A Democracy is better than a
'Tyranny. Pleasures are mortal, Vertues Immor-
'tal. In good fortune be moderate, in bad pru-
'dent. It is better to die than to want. Study
'to be worthy of your Parents. Be praised Li-
'ving, beautified dead. To your Friends in
'Prosperity and Adversity be the same. What
'thou hast promised amiss, perform not.[*Laert.*
'keep thy word.] Betray not Secrets. So re-
'proach, as if thou shouldst e're long be a
'Friend. Use new Diet, but old Laws. Punish
'those who have Sinned : Restrain those that
'are about to Sin. Conceal thy misfortune, that
'it may not glad thy Enemies.

Ausonius ascribes these to him.

Pleasure and Profit never disagree.
As more sollicitous, more happy be.
'Tis ill to wish, but worse to fear to die,
With what Necessity enjoyns, comply.
If thou art fear'd of many, many fear.
Be not exalted when thy Fortune's clear.
Nor be dejected, if a storm appear.

† *Laert.*

† He writ two thousand Verses of Moral Instructions.

CHAP. IV.

The Story of Arion.

DUring the Feast we mentioned (by *Plutarch*'s Account) or rather according to *Eusebius*, in the fortieth Olympiad, there happened a strange accident, which (because *Herodotus* calls it a Miracle shewed to *Periander*) we shall relate in his words.

† *Arion* the most famous Lutinist of that time, having lived a long time with *Periander*, took a Voyage to *Italy* and *Sicily*, there having gotten together much wealth, he designed to return to *Corinth*: at *Tarentum* he hired a Corinthian Vessel, confiding above any in *Corinthians*; they, when they were at Sea, plotted to cast *Arion* over-board, that they might be Masters of his Wealth, which he understanding, offered to give them all so they would save his Life; they refusing, bad him lay violent hands upon himself, if he would be buried in his own Country, otherwise to leap immediately into the Sea. *Arion* reduced to this extremity, intreated them to give him leave to put on his richest Ornaments, and so standing upon the Poop of the Ship, to play a Tune, promising, as soon as he had done, to deliver himself into their hands. The Men moved with a great desire to hear the most excellent Lutinist in the World, retired from the Poop to the middle of the Ship: He put on his best Ornaments, and standing upon the Poop, began that Tune which they call the Morning Hymn, assoon as he had ended it, he threw himself into the Sea, with his Ornaments and Lute; the Ship sailed on to *Corinth*. It is reported, a Dolphin took him upon his Back, and carried him to *Tænarus*, where he landed, and took Shipping again for *Corinth*; he arriv'd there in the same Habit, and related all that passed; which *Periander* not believing, committed him to close Custody, not permitting him to go any whither, and in the mean time sent for the Mariners; when they came, he asked them News of *Arion*: They answered, he was very well in *Italy*, and that they left him safe at *Tarentum*: Immediately *Arion* appeared, attired, as when he leaped out of the Ship, whereat they were so confounded, they could not say any thing in their own defence. This is attested both by the *Corinthians* and *Lesbians*. At *Tænarus* there is a little Image given as an Offering of a Man sitting upon a Dolphins Back: That *Periander* caused such a one to be made, is evident from this Epigram of *Bianor*.

† *Lib. 1.*
See also *A. Gellius* who translates this of *Plutarch*, *Lucian*, and others.

The Statue of Arion o're the main
Sailing upon a Dolphin's Back was carv'd
By Periander's *Order. See, Men slain*
By cruel Men, by Fishes kind preserv'd.

CHAP. V.

Of his Wife.

† HIS Wife was named *Lysis*, by him called *Melissa*, Daughter to *Procleus*, Tyrant of *Epidaurus* and *Eristhenea*, the Daughter of *Aristocratis*, by the Sister of *Aristomedes*, which Persons ruled over the greatest part of *Arcadia*. * He fell in love with her seeing her in a *Peloponesian* dress, in her Petticoat, without a Gown, giving drink to her Father's Workmen: * Long after killed her in his Fury,

† *Laert.*
* *Athen. Delph.*
† *Laert.*

fury, big with Child, with a Stool, or a blow of his Foot, being wrought upon by the accusations of his Concubines, whom he afterward burnt.

† *Herod.* 5. † He sent one day to *Threspotos*, upon the River *Acheron*, to enquire by Necromancy concerning a *Depositum*. *Melissa* appearing, said, She would not tell them in what place it was laid, because she was cold and naked, the Cloths wherein she was buried doing her no good, for they were not burned, confirming the Truth whereof by *Periander's* putting bread into a cold Oven ; which answer carried to

* *Suid.* *Periander*, made good the Suspition that (*thro' excess of Love*) νεκρᾷ ἴσον Μελίσση ἐμίγη. Hereupon he caused Proclamation to be made, that all the *Corinthian* Women should come to *Juno's* Temple to celebrate a Festival, attired in their richest Ornaments : when they came, having placed a Guard of Soldiers in Ambush, he stripped them all, without any distinction (Free-women and Servants) of their Clothes, which he carried to *Melissa's* Grave, and having prayed, burnt them to her : This done, he sent Messengers to enquire the second time ; to whom *Melissa's* Ghost appeared, and told them where the *Depositum* was laid.

CHAP. VI.

Of his Children.

†*Herod. lib.* 3. 49. † HE had by *Melissa* two Sons, *Cypsalus* and *Lycophron*, the younger ingenious, the elder a Fool ; he had likewise a Daughter ; his elder Son at the time of his Mother's death was eighteen years old, the younger seventeen. These their Grandfather by the Mother's side *Procleus* (Tyrant of *Epidaurus*) sent for over to him, and loved them much, as in reason he ought, being the Children of his own Daughter ; when he was to send them back, he said to them, Do you know Children who slew your Mother? The elder took no heed to that Speech, but *Lycophron* the younger was so troubled at it, that when he came to *Corinth*, he neither spoke to his Father, nor would make him any Answer, looking upon him as the Murtherer of his Mother ; whereat *Periander* at length became so incensed, that he turn'd him out of doors. He being gone, *Periander* question'd the elder what discourse his Grandfather had with him; he related to him how kindly he used him, but told nothing of that which *Procleus* had said to them at their departure, for he had not taken any notice of it ; *Periander* said, it was not possible but that he should say something more, and pressed him more strictly ; at last he calling it to mind, told him this also ; which *Periander* resenting and not willing to use his Son more mildly, sent to the People with whom he lived in his ejection, forbidding them to receive him into any of their Houses. Turned out of that wherein he was, he sought to go into another, but was denied ; *Periander* having threatned those that should entertain him, and commanded all to drive him away : expelled thence, he went to another of his acquaintance, who knowing him the Son of *Periander*, entertain'd him, though with fear : At length *Periander* proclaimed, That whosoever received him into their House, or spoke to him, should pay what Fine to *Apollo* he should impose ; from that time none durst venture to entertain him or speak to him ; nor would he himself make trial of a thing which he knew to be desperate, but passed his time in the common Walks. Four days after, *Periander* seeing him poor and extenuated with Fasting, took Compassion of him, and laying aside his anger, drew nigh to him, and said, 'Son, which is better, to 'undergo what you now suffer, or by obey-'ing your Father to enjoy my Wealth and 'Kingdom ? You being my Son, and next 'Heir to the Kingdom of Fruitful *Corinth*, have 'made choice of the Life of a Vagabond, an-'grily opposing him whom you ought not to 'oppose ; if any unhappiness befel you in those 'things whereof you suspect me, it befel me, 'and I have so much the greater share therein, 'in being the Instrument thereof; hear how 'much better it is to be envied than to be pi-'tied, and what it is to be angry with our 'Parents or Betters. In these words *Periander* reprov'd his Son ; who made him no other Answer, than 'That he ought to pay a Fine 'to the God for speaking to him. *Periander* perceiving the Evil of his Son to be incurable, removed him out of his sight, and sending him by Ship to *Corcyra*, of which he was also Tyrant : Having thus disposed of him, he made War with his Father-in-Law, *Procleus*, as the chief cause of all that happened.

Laertius mentions an Epistle which he sent him to this Effect :

Periander *to* Procleus.

We committed unwillingly that Crime upon your Daughter, but you, if willingly, you alienate my Sons Mind from me, you do unjustly; therefore either soften his Mind towards me, or I shall revenge this Injury ; I have satisfied your Daughter by burning in her Honour the Garments of all the Women of Corinth.

† In fine he took *Epidaurus* and *Procleus* † *Herod. ibid.* therein, whom he preserved alive.

* In process of time *Periander* growing old, * *Herod. ibid.* and knowing himself to be no longer fit for the charge of the Common-wealth, sent to *Corcyra* to invite *Lycophron* to the Government of the Kingdom ; conceiving his eldest Son uncapable of that Office by reason of his Stupidity. *Lycophron* would not vouchsafe so much as to speak to the Messenger. *Periander* (affectionate to him) sent the second time his Son's Sister, his own Daughter, hoping he would be sooner perswaded by her ; she coming, said to him, 'Brother, had you rather the 'Kingdom should fall into the hands of others, 'and our Father's House be dispersed, than 'go Home and have it your self ? Return 'to your own House, injure your self no lon-'ger ; Obstinacy is an unhappy Inheritance : 'Cure not one Evil with another ; many prefer 'Compliance before Justice ; many in pursuit 'of their Mother's Right, lose their Father's Kingdom :

'Kingdom; a Kingdom is a flippery thing, coveted by many; our Father is old and feeble, give not your own Goods to others. Thus she pleaded to him as her Father had instructed her; he answered he would never come to *Corinth* whilst his Father lived there: Which as soon as *Periander* understood, he sent a Messenger the third time, to let him know, he would remove to *Corcyra*, and to command him to come to *Corinth* to take the Government upon him; to this the Son assented. *Periander* prepared for *Corcyra*, his Son for *Corinth*: the People of *Corcyra* informed hereof, that *Periander* might not come into their Country, kill'd his Son: In revenge of which Fact *Periander* sent three hundred Boys of the chief of the *Corcyræans* to *Sardis* to *Alyattes* King of *Lydia*, there to be gelt: The *Corinthians* who had charge of them, were driven upon *Samos*, the *Samians* understanding to what end they were sent to *Sardis*, advised them to take Sanctuary in the Temple of *Diana*, and would not suffer them, as being Suppliants to be pulled away: The *Corinthians* not permitting any Food to be given them, the *Samians* celebrated a Festival, which is observed (faith *Herodotus*) at this day; when Night was come, the Company of Youths and Maids danced whilst the Children were Praying, and in their dance, having made Cakes of Meal and Honey, flung them amongst the Children, whereby they were sustain'd alive; this they did so long till the *Samians*, who had charge of the Children, were fain to go away and leave them; then the *Samians* conveighed the Children home to *Corcyra*. * *Antenor* and *Dionysius* affirm, the *Gnidians* came to *Samos* with a Fleet, drove away *Periander*'s Guard from the Temple and carried the Children to *Corcyra*; for which reason the *Corcyræans* allowed the *Gnidians* many Honours and Immunities, which they gave not (even) to the *Samians*.

* *Plut. de malign. Herodot.*

CHAP. VII.

His Death.

***E**xcessive Melancholy (amidst these crosses) occasioned his death, in the last year of the forty eighth Olympiad, the eightieth Year of his Age, being desirous none should know where he was buried, he thus contrived it. He commanded two Men to go to a certain place at night, and to kill whom they first met, and bury him. After them he sent four to kill and bury the two; after the four, more: They obeyed his order, the first killed him. The *Corinthians* erected for him an empty Monument with this Inscription.

* *Laert.*

Periander lies within Corinthian *Ground,*
For power and wisdom above all renown'd.

Laertius hath this Epigram upon him:

At whatsoev'r shall happen be not sad:
Alike for all that God dispenseth glad.
Wise Periander *did through Grief expire,*
Because events not joyn'd with his Desire.

---

† *Stob.*

†SOSIADES

His Collection of

The Precepts of the seven *Sophists*.

FOllow God. Obey the Law. Worship the Gods. Reverence thy Parents. Suffer for Justice. Understand what thou learnest. Know what thou hearest. Know thy self. About to Marry, chuse opportunity. Consider mortal things. When thou art a guest, acknowledge it. Respect Hospitality: Command thy self. Relieve thy Friends. Govern thy Anger. Exercise Prudence. Honour Providence. Use not Swearing. Love Friendship. Apply thy self to Discipline. Pursue Glory. Emulate Wisdom. Speak well of that which is good. Disparage none. Praise Vertue. Do what is just. Be kind to thy Friends. Revenge upon thy Enemies. Practise generosity. Abstain from evil. Be general. Keep what is thine. Refrain from what belongs to others. Speak words of good Omen. Hear all things. Gratifie thy Friend. Nothing too much. Husband time. Regard the future. Hate Injury. Have Respect to thy Servants. Instruct thy Children. If thou hast ought, gratifie others. Fear deceit. Speak well of all. Be a lover of Wisdom. Judge according to Equity. What thou knowest, do. Abstain from Bloodshed. Wish things possible. Converse with the Wise. Examine Wits. What thou hast receiv'd, restore. Distrust none. Make use of Art. Defer not what thou intendest to give. Esteem Benefits. Envy none. Guard thy self. Approve hope. Hate Calumny. Possess justly. Reverence the good. Acknowledge thy Judge. Be moderate in Wedlock. Respect Fortune. Fly Engagements for any. Converse with all. Make use of thy like. Regulate Sumptuousness. Enjoy what thou possessest. Exercise Modesty. Return benefits. Pray for prosperity. Love Fortune. Hearing, see. Aim at things that may be acquired. Hate dissention. Abhor reproach. Curb thy Tongue. Repel Injury. Determine equally. Make use of thy Wealth. Examine without corruption. Blame the present. Speak knowing. Use no violence. Live pleasantly. Converse mildly. Go through thy Undertakings fearless. Be benign to all.

all. Confide not in thy Children. Govern thy Tongue. Do well to thy self. Be affable. Answer seasonably. Labour with Equity. Do that whereof thou shalt not repent. When thou hast sinned be penitent. Confine thy Eye. Counsel profitably. Perfect quickly. Preserve amity. Be grateful. Observe Concord. Declare no Secret. Fear what is more Powerful. Pursue what is profitable. Wait for Opportunity. Dissolve Enmities. Expect Age. Boast not of Strength. Use to speak well. Fly Hatred. Possess Wealth justly. Forsake not Glory. Hate Malice. Be not weary of Learning. Hazard thy self prudently. What thou joyest in, quit not. Admire Oracles. Love those thou maintainest. Blame not the Absent. Reverence thy Elders. Teach those that are Younger. Confide not in Wealth. Stand in awe of thy self. Begin no Injury. Crown thy Ancestors. Die for thy Country. Oppugne not Life. Deride not the Dead. Condole with the Unhappy. Gratifie without Damage. Be not troubled upon every occasion. Let thy Children be by a Free-Woman. Promise none. Wrong not the Dead. Suffer as Mortal. Trust not Fortune. Be in Childhood modest, in Youth temperate, in Manhood just, in Old Age prudent. Die untroubled.

AUSONII LUDUS
Septem Sapientum.
THE PROLOGUE

THE seven wise men,(that name Times past applied
To them, nor hath Posterity deny'd)
Themselves this day unto your view present.
Why dost thou blush Gown'd *Roman*? discontent
That such grave Men should on the Stage be brought!
Is't shame to us? 'Twas none to *Athens* thought:
Whose Council-Chamber was their Theatre.
True; here for business several places are
Assign'd, the Cirque for meetings, Courts to take
Enrolments, *Forums* in which Pleas to make:
But in old *Athens*, and all *Greece* was known
No other place for Business but this one.
   viz. the Theatre.
Which latter Luxury in *Rome* did raise,
 The Edile heretofore did build for Plays
A Scaffold-Stage, no work of Carved Stone ;
So *Gallius* and *Murena*, 'tis well known.
But after, when great Men not sparing Cost,
Thought it the highest Glory they could boast,
To build for Plays a Scene more eminent,
The Theatre grew to this vast extent ;
That *Pompey*, *Balbus*, *Cæsar* did enlarge ;
Vying which should exceed for state and charge.
 But to what end all this? we came not here
To tell you who first built the Theatre,
Forum, or City Gates, but t'usher in
Grave Sages, who by Gods approv'd have been.
Such as in pleasing and instructive Verse,
Their own Judicious Sentences rehearse,
Known to the Learned, and perhaps to you :
But if your Mem'ries cannot well renew
Things spoke so long since ; the Comedian shall,
Who better than I knows them, tell you all.

Enter Comedian.

Athenian *Solon*, Fame sings, wrote at *Delphis*
Γνῶθι σεαυτὸν, whose sense *know thy self*, is:
But this to Spartan *Chilon* must assign.
Some question *Chilon*, whether this be thine,
Τέλος ὁρᾶν μακροῦ βίου, *The close*
Of a long Life regard: but must suppose
That *Solon* this to *Lydian Cræsus* spake.
 From *Lesbian Pittacus* this Motto take,
Γίγνωσκε καιρὸν : that's *Know Time*: But he
By Καιρὸν here means *opportunity.*
Οἱ πλεῖστοι κακοί , *Bias* did proceed
From thee ; that is, *Most Men are ill.* Take heed
You not mistake him ; for by ill Men here
He means the ignorant : The next you hear
Is *Periander's* Μελέτη τὸ πᾶν,
That is,*Thought's Akin All*; a Thoughtful Man!
But *Lyndian Cleobulus* does protest
Ἄριστον Μέτρον; *Mean in all is best*.
Thales ἐγγύα πάρεστι δ' ἄτη cries,
Upon a *Surety present Damage lies.*
But this, for those who gain by it to tell,
May 'chance displease : Now *Solon* comes, farewel. *Exit.*

Enter Solon.

LO! *Solon* in his *Greeks* dress treads the Stage,
 To whom(as of the seven the greatest Sage)
Fame gave the prize of Wisdom from the rest ;
But Fame is not of Censure the strict Test.
Nor first nor last I take my self to be,
For their's no order in Equality.
Well did the *Delphick* Prophet sport with him
Who ask'd, which first of the Wise-men might seem,
Saying ; if on a Globe their names he writ,
None first or lowest he should find in it.
From midst of that learn'd Round come I, that so
What once I spake to *Cræsus*, All here now
Might take as spoken to themselves ; 'tis this :
Ὁρᾶν Τέλος μακροῦ βίου, which is,
Mark th' end of a long Life ; *till when* forbear
To say these wretched, or those happy are :
For *All till* then are in a doubtful state,
The proof of this we'll in few words relate.
 Cræsus the King or Tyrant (choose you which)
Of *Lydia*, happy thought, and strangely rich ;
Who to his Gods did Gold-wall'd Temples build,
Invites me o'er, I to his Summons yield.
His Royal Summons went to *Lydia*,
Willing his Subjects by our means might find
Their King improv'd, and better'd in his Mind.
He asks me whom I thought the happiest Man?
I said *Telana*, the *Athenian*,
Who his Life nobly for his Country gave ?
He pishes at it, will another have.
I told him then *Aglaus*, who the Bounds
Ne'er past in all his Life of his own Grounds.
Smiling, he says, What think you then of Me
Esteem'd the happiest in the whole World ? We
Reply'd, his End could only make that known.
He takes this ill : I willing to be gone,
Kiss his hand, and so leave him : For some ends,
Mean time, 'gainst *Persia* he a War intends ;
And all things ready, does in Person go.
How speeds ? he's vanish'd, Prisoner to his Foe,
And ready now to yield his latest Breath,
(For by the Victor he was doom'd to death)
Upon the Funeral Pile rounded with Flames
And smoak, he thus with a loud voice exclaims
O Solon! Solon! now I plainly see
Th'art a true Prophet ! Thrice thus naming me ;
Mov'd with which words, *Cyrus*, (the Conquerour)
Commands the Fire be quench, which by a shower
Of Rain then falling, happily was laid.
Thence to the King, by a choice Guard convey'd
And question'd who that *Solon* was? and why
He called so on his name ? He, for reply,
In order all declares : Pity at this
The Heart of *Cyrus* moves ; and *Cræsus* is
Receiv'd to Grace, who in a Princely Port
  Liv'd

H 2

Liv'd after, honour'd in the *Perſian* Court.
Both Kings approv'd and prais'd me, but what I
Said then to one, let each Man here apply
As ſpoke t'himſelf, 'twas for that end I came.
Farewel: your liking let your Hands proclaim
Exit

Enter Chilon.

MY Hips with ſitting, Eyes with ſeeing ake,
Expecting when *Solon* an end would make.
How little and how long your Atticks prate!
Scarce in three hundred lines one word of weight,
Or a grave Sentence, how he lookt on me
At going off? ——Now *Spartan Chilon* ſee!
Who with *Laconian* Brevity commends
To you *the Knowledge of your ſelves*, kind Friends!
Γνῶθι σαυτὸν carv'd in a *Delphos* Fane.
'Tis a hard work, but recompenc'd with gain.
Try your own ſtrength; examine what 'tis you
Have done already, what you ought to do.
All Duties of our Life, as Modeſty,
Honour and Conſtancy included be
In this, and glory, which we yet deſpiſe.
Farewel, your claps I not reſpect nor prize.
[*Exit*.

Enter Cleobulus.

I *Cleobulus*, though my Native Seat
Be a ſmall Iſle, am Author of a great
And glorious Sentence; Μέτρον ἄριστον,
A mean is beſt : You Sirs that ſit upon
The fourteen middle Benches next unto
Th' *Orcheſtra*, beſt may judge if this be true.
Your Nodd ſhews your aſſent: We thank you but
We ſhall proceed in order: Was it not
One *Afer* (who a Man of your own Clime is)
That ſaid once in this place, *Ut ne quid Nimis* ?
And hither does our Μηδὲν ἄγαν aim.
The Dorick and the Latin mean the ſame.
In ſpeaking, being ſilent, or in Sleep,
In good Turns, or in Bad, a mean ſtill keep,
In ſtudy, or whatever you intend.
I've ſaid, and that I mean, I keep here end.
[*Exit*.

Enter Thales.

I'M *Thales*, who maintain (as *Pindar* ſings)
Water to be the beſt and firſt of of things.
To whom by Phœbus *Mandate, Fiſhers brought
A golden Tripod, which they fiſhing caught,*
By him as Preſent to the wiſeſt meant.
Which I refus'd, and unto others ſent
In Knowledge my Superiours as I thought.
From one to th'other of the Sages brought,
By them again return'd, to me it came,
Who to *Apollo* conſecrate the ſame.
For ſince to ſeek the Wiſeſt, he enjoin'd,
I judge no Man but God by that deſign'd.
Now on the Stage (as thoſe before) I come
T'aſſert the Truth of my own Axiom.
Perhaps by ſome 'tmay be offenſive thought:
But not by thoſe by ſad Experience taught.
Ἐγγύα πάρεστι δ' ἄτη, ſay we,
Be Surety, and be ſure a loſer be.
A thouſand Inſtances I could produce
To prove Repentance is the only uſe
That can be made of it, but that we here
Examples by their Names to cite, forbear.

Make your own application, and conceive
The Damage, Men by this ſole Act receive.
Nor this our good Intention take amiſs,
You that like, Clap, you that diſlike it, Hiſs.

Enter Bias.

I Am *Priænean Bias*, who once taught
Οἱ πλεῖστοι κακοὶ, *That moſt Men are naught*.
I wiſh 't had been unſpoke; for Truth gains Hate.
But by bad Men, I mean illiterate,
And thoſe who barbarouſly all Laws confound.
Religion, Juſtice; for within this Round
I ſee none but are good: believe all thoſe
Whom I proclaim for bad among your Foes:
Yet there is none ſo partially apply'd
To Vice, but with the good will ſide,
Whether he truly be ſuch, or would fain
Of a good Man the Reputation gain:
The hated name of an ill Man all ſhun.
Then (*moſt good Men*) your praiſe, and I ha' done.

Enter Pittacus.

I'M *Pittacus*, who once this Maxim penn'd,
Γίγνωσκε καιρὸν, That's, *Time apprehend*.
But by Time we meant Time in Seaſon, as
In tempore veni is your *Roman* Phraſe.
And your own Comick Poet *Terence*, he,
Chief of all things makes Opportunity,
Where *Dromo* comes unto *Antiphila*.
I'th' nick of Time; conſider what I ſay,
And mark how great an inconvenience
Moſt ſuffer through this want of Providence
But now 'tis more than time we ſhould be gone;
Farewell, and give your Approbation.
Exit.

Enter Periander.

NOW on the Stage ſee *Periander* move!
He who once ſaid, and what he ſaid will prove,
Μελέτη τὸ πᾶν, *Thought is all in all*.
Since him a perfect Agent we may call,
Who firſt conſiders what he undergoes;
For we ſhould ſtill forecaſt, as *Terence* ſhews,
Th'event of Buſineſs, whether good or bad,
E'r w'undertake it: where may beſt be had
Conveniency for Planting, where to Build,
When to wage War, and when to pitch a Field:
Nor inconſiderately take in hand
Or great, or ſmall Things, for that makes a ſtand
In the free progreſs of all new deſigns;
Like Conſultation; hence we ſee it clear,
Who uſe it not, by chance, not Counſel ſteer,
But I retire, whilſt you with better Fate
Imploy your Thoughts how to uphold your State.

A NA-

ANACHARSIS.

CHAP. I.

Anacharsis his Life and Writings.

† Lib. 4. 46.

THose Nations (saith † Herodotus) which Border upon the Euxine Sea, are of all most Illiterate, the Scythians only excepted; we can alledge nothing relating to Learning of any People within the compass of that Sea, neither know we any Person *Learned but the Scythians Anacharsis; * Amongst these, notwithstanding the roughness of their Education, (for they fed upon Mares Milk, and dwelt in Waggons) were some who far exceeded all in Justice.

* Strab. lib. 7.

Such was Anacharsis, † Son of Gnurus, Brother of Cadovides, King of Scythia; his Mother a Grecian, by which means he had the advantage of two Languages, but was owner of no other House than the Custom of that Country allow'd, a Chariot, whence * he compared his dwelling to that of the Sun, carry'd in that manner round the Heavens.

† Laert.

* Plut.conviv. sep. Sap.

† The Scythians never Travel beyond their own Confines, but Anacharsis as a Person endu'd with more than ordinary Wisdom extended his Journey farther, * being sent by the King of Scythia to Greece. † He came to Athens in the first year of the 47th Olympiad, Eucrates being Archon: and * first met with Toxaris one of his own Country, by whom, as the most compendious way to take a Survey of Athens and Greece, he was address'd to Solon: how Solon received and entertained him is already related in his Life: he instructed him in the best Disciplines, recommended him to the Favour of Noblest Persons, and sought all means of giving him Respect and Honour: Anacharsis admired his Wisdom, continually followed him, in a short space learnt all things of him, and was kindly received by every one for his sake; being (as Theoxenus attests) the only Stranger whom they incorporated into their City.

† Ælian.var. hist. lib. 5.

* Herod. 4. 46
† Laert.

* Lucian. Scyth.

† Thus was he much Honoured by the Grecians for his Perfection, Wisdom, Temperance, wherein he excelled many of their Philosophers, whereupon they conferred the Attribute of Wise upon him, some accounting him one of the Seven: Periander invited him with the rest to Corinth, the Feast is largely described by Plutarch: There Anacharsis carrying with him Chaplets of Flowers, Ivy, and Laurel, Drunk, as the Scythians use, to great excess, * and required the Prize of Drinking to be given him, because he was first Drunk. In a Race (saith he) he wins who comes first at the Post, in Drinking, he who comes first to the End deserves the Reward.

† Strab.lib.7.
† Clem. Alex. Strom. 1.
† Clem. Alex. Strom. 5.
† Ælian.lib. 2.

† Athen.deipn. 10.

† Having seen much of the World, and improv'd his knowledg, he return'd to Scythia (as Lucian conjectures, not until Solon was dead) as he Sailed along the Hellespont, he put in at Cyricum, and finding the People Celebrating a Festival to the Mother of the Gods, with much splendor and munificence; he made a Vow, if he got safe home, to Sacrifice in the same manner as he had seen those of Cyricum, and to institute a Virgil. When he came into Scythia, he withdrew himself privately to Hylæa, near the Achyllean course, a place abounding with Trees, and performed the Rites of the Goddess with a Timbrel (and Cymbal * about his Neck) A Scythian espying him, carried word to Saulius the King, who went immediately thither, and being an eye-witness thereof, shot him through with an Arrow († to punish his Effeminacy, and prevent the infection thereof in others) * And now if any enquire concerning Anacharsis, the Scythians deny they knew him, because he Travelled into Greece, and affected the Customs of that Country. As I am informed by Timnes, Tutor of Spargapithes, he was Uncle to Indathyrsus, King of Scythia, Son of Gnurus, Son of Lycus, Son of Spargapithes: Now Anacharsis being of this Family, it is manifest he was † Slain by his Brother, (that his Brother was King of Scythia, and Slew him, is confirmed by Laertius, though he differ in the Name,) for Indathyrius was Son of Saulius, Saulius was he who slew Anacharsis, and consequently is the same whom Laertius calls Cadovides, adding, some report that he Shot him in Hunting; for being addicted to the Greek Customs, and endeavouring to alter the Laws of Scythia; whereupon he dying, said, he return'd safe out of Greece, guarded by his own Wisdom, but was slain at home by the envy of others. Upon him Laertius hath this Epigram.

* Clem. Alex. admonit. ad gent.

* Clem. Alex. ibid.
d Herod. continues.

† For ὑπὸ τῶ ἀδελφοῦ ῶν, read ἀδελφῶ Spargapithes.
I. Lycus.
I. Gnurus.
I. Anacharsis. Saulius, or Caduida.
Indathyrsus.

From Travel Anacharsis came at last,
And Scythia in a Grecian Mould was cast:
Whilst he was teaching how, by the Surprize
Of a wing'd Arrow carried to the Skies.

* There were many Statues erected in Honour of him by the Grecians, upon which was writ, Γλώσσης, γαστρὸς αἰδοίων κρατεῖν. * He was Temperate and Skilful in many things; He freely and largely discoursed of the manner of Diet and Medicine, which the Scythians used in curing the Sick. From the plain freedom he used in Speech, arose a Proverb, The Scythian Phrase. He writ eight hundred Verses of Orders for the Scythians and Greeks, concerning Frugal Living, and Martial Affairs. There are also two Epistles of his extent.

* Laert.
Plut. conviv. sep. Sap.
* Laert.

Anacharsis to Crœsus.

KIng of the Lydians, I came into Greece to be informed of their Manners and Studies; I need not Money, it is enough if I can return into Scythia bettered: but I will come to Sardis, because I highly esteem your Favour.

* Herod.4.75.

* Anacharsis

Cic. Tuscul. *Anacharsis to Hanno, Health.*
quæst. 5.

(a) *Clem. alex.* (a) MY Apparel is a Scythian Rug, my Shoes
Cites this frag- the hardness of my Feet, my Bed the
ment, doubt- Earth, my Sauce Hunger; I feed on Milk, Cheese,
less out of the and Flesh: you may come to me as to one that's
same Epistle. contented: But these gifts which you so much
Ἐμοὶ πει- esteem, bestow either on your Citizens, or the im-
βλημα,χλαῖνα mortal Gods.
δεῖπνον γάλα,
τυρὸς. (b) He is said to have Invented Tinder,
(b) *Strab.* 7. (e) the Anchor, and the Potters Wheel; but
(c) *Laert. Suid.* this latter is by *Strabo* evinced clearly to be
False, because mentioned by *Homer*, who lived
long after him, *Anacharsis* being in the time of
Cræsus.

CHAP. VII.

His Apophthegms.

(d) *Laert.* HIS Apothegms are these, (d) He said a
Vine bare three Grapes, the first of Pleasure,
the second of Drunkenness, the third of Repentance. He wondred, that amongst the Greeks, Artists contended, and they who were no Artists determined. Being demanded by what means a Man
might be brought not to love Wine, he said, by setting before his eyes the Actions of Drunken Persons. He wondred, the Grecians who punished Injuries by Law, rewarded the Athletæ at publick
Exercises for beating one another. Being told a
Ship is four inches thick, so far from Death, said
he, are they who Sail. He said Oyl was a Receipt
procuring Madness, because the Athletæ, the more
they were anointed therewith, the more fierce they
were against one another. How comes it, said he,
that they who forbid lying, themselves lye openly,
when they put off their Wares? He wondred that
the Greeks in the beginning of a Feast drank in little Cups, and when they were full in great. (e) Be-
(e) *Plut. con-* ing demanded (by Ardalus) whether there were any
viv. sept. Sap. Flutes in Scythia, he answered, not so much as
Strab. 15. Vines (which (f) *Aristotle* calls a demonstration
(f) *Analyt.* ὅτι, by the remote Cause) (g) *Ardalus* adding, are
post. 1. 13. there not Gods amongst the Scythians? yes, reply'd
(g) *Plut. con-* he, which understand all Languages. (h) Being as-
viv. sept. Sap. ked what Ship was safest, he answered, that which
(h) *Laert.* is in the Haven. He affirm'd the most remarkable

thing he had seen among the Grecians to be this,
that they left the Smoak upon the Mountains, and
carried the Wood into their Cities. Being demanded
whether the number of the dead or the living were
greatest; amongst which, saith he, do you account
those who are at Sea? To an Athenian, who Reproached him for being a Scythian, my Country,
(saith he) is a Disgrace to me, but you are a Disgrace to your Country. Being demanded what in
Man is both Good and Bad, he answered the Tongue.
He affirmed it is better to have one Friend worth
much, than many worth nothing. He said the Forum was the proper place for Cheating and unjust
Gain. To a young Man who Reproached him at a
Feast; Youth, said he, if at these years you cannot bear Wine, when you grow old, you will not
be able to bear Water.

(i) When he returned to Scythia, he told the (i) *Herod.* 4.
King who sent him, the Greeks were busied in 46.
all kinds of Wisdom, except the Lacedæmonians, who only knew how to give and receive
prudently.

(k) He said, the Greeks made no other use of (k) *Plut. de*
Money but to account with it. (l) At a Publick *profect. virtut.*
Assembly in Athens, he said, he wondred, why in *sent.*
the Greek Convocations, Wise Men propounded (l) *Plut. vit.*
Business, and Fools determin'd it. * That Prince *sol.*
is Happy who is Wise. That City is best, wherein * *Plut. conv.*
(all things else being equal) Vertue hath the bet- *Sap.*
ter Condition, Vice the worse.

(m) To one, who, as they were Drinking, said, (m) *Strob. serm.*
beholding his Wife, Anacharsis, you have Married 16.
one who is nothing Handsome: I am (answered he)
of that Opinion also; but put less Water in my
Wine, that I may make her handsome.

Relating the Qualities of the Vine to the King * *Athen. deipn.*
of Scythia, and shewing him some slips thereof, *lib.* 10.
he added, and by this time it would have reached
into Scythia, if the Greeks did not every year
cut off its Branches. * At a Feast, such being * *Athen. deipn.*
sent for, as might procure Mirth, he alone *lib.* 14.
smiled not; afterwards, an Ape being brought in, * *Athen. deipn.*
he Laughed, saying, that Beast is Ridiculous by *lib.* 14.
Nature, Man by Art and Study. * *Clem. Alex.*
strom. lib. 5.
Whilst he slept, he used κατέχειν τῇ μὲν λαιᾷ * *Clem. strom.* 1.
τὰ αἰδοῖα· τῇ δεξιᾷ δὲ τὸ στόμα, implying that a Man
ought to take great care to Govern both, but that
it is harder to restrain our Pleasure than our
Tongue. He said, that to him all the Grecians
were Scythians.

MYSON.

MYSON was (according to *Her-*
mippus) Son of *Stremon*, born at
Chene, a Village either of *Oetæa*,
or *Lacedæmonia*, his Father a Tyrant. *Anacharsis* demanding of the Oracle, if
any were wiser, was answered (as was in the
Life of *Thales* mentioned of *Chilon*.)

Oetæan Myson *I declare*
Wiser than those who Wisest are.

His Curiosity encreasing by this Answer, he
went to the Village, and finding him fitting
a Plough-share to the Plough, said, *Myso*, it
is not yet time to Plough: But it is (answered he) to prepare. Others affirm the Oracle
called him *Etean*, about which there is much
difference: *Parmenides* saith, that *Etea* is a Lacedæmonian Village, whereof *Myson* was. *Sosi-*
crates, that he was *Etean* by his Father, *Che-*
nean by his Mother. *Euthyphron*, that he was
a *Cretan*, *Etea* a City of *Creet*, *Anaxilaus* an
Arcadian. *Hipponax* mentions him in these
words

words. *And* Myso, *whom* Apollo *declared the wisest of all Men.* Aristomenus affirms he was of the same humour as *Timon* and *Apemantus*, a Man-hater. He retired from *Lacedæmon* into the Desert, and was there surprized all alone; smiling, being demanded why he smiled, no Man being present, he answered, for that reason. *Aristoxenus* saith, he was of no account, because not of the City, but of an obscure Village; whence some ascribe his sayings to *Pisistratus*, but others reckon him one of the Seven; *Plato* puts him in the room of *Periander*. He said, *we must not seek things from words, but words from things; things were not made for words, but words for things.* He died 97 years old.

EPIMENIDES.

EPimenides is by all acknowledged a *Cretan* (though contrary to the Custom of that Place he wore long Hair;) but in the Town where he was born they agree not. *Laertius* following the greater part of Writers, saith it was (*a*) *Cnosus*, *Strabo*, *Phæstus*. There is no less difference about the names of his *Parents*; some call his Father *Phæstius*, or *Phæstus*, others *Dosiades*, his Mother *Blasta*, others *Agasiarchus*; *Apollonius*, *Bolus*, *Laertius*, and *Suidas* name his Mother *Blasta*, *Plutarch* (*b*) *Balta*, supposed a Nymph.

It is reported, that when he was a Youth, being sent by his Father and Brethren to their Field to fetch home a Sheep to the City, Tyr'd with the Heat and Travel in search thereof, he withdrew himself at Noon (or as *Apollonius*, at Night) from the Common Way into a private Cave, where he slept (according to (*c*) *Theopompus*) fifty seven years, according to (*d*) *Varro*, (*e*) *Plutarch*, and (*f*) *Tertullian*, fifty, (*g*) *Pausanas* forty, in which interval of Time, most of his Kindred died; at the end hereof awaking, he betook himself again to the search of his Sheep, thinking it the same, or the next day to that wherein he lay down, and that he had slept but a little while; not finding it, he returned to the Field where he saw all things changed, and a Stranger in Possession thereof: Thence to the City much amazed; going into his own House, they questioned who he was; at last he met with his younger Brother, now grown old, by whom he was inform'd of all that passed, and the time of his absence. *Plutarch* saith, he awaked an Old Man; (*b*) *Pliny* and *Laertius*, that he grew old in as many days as he had slept years: (*i*) some affirm he slept not, but retired a while, employing himself in cutting up Roots.

Many other Wonders are keported of him; * some say, he received Food of the Nymphs, which he kept in an Oxes Hoof, and took thereof a little every day, requiring no other Sustenance, never being seen to eat, (*k*) he often counterfeited Resurrection from Death to Life; his (*l*) Soul going out of his Body whensoever he pleased, and returning again.

(*m*) He is reported to be the first that lustrated Houses and Fields, (*n*) which he performed by Verse. To this end the *Athenians* in the forty sixth Olympiad, visited with a Plague, and commanded by the Oracle to lustrate the City, sent *Nicias*, Son of *Niceratus* with a Ship to *Creet*, to desire *Epimenides* to come to them, which he did, and there contracted acquaintance with *Solon*, whom he privately instructed, setting him in the way of making Laws. He reduced the Divine Rights to a lesser Charge; he moderated the Mournings of the Citizens, he added some Sacrifices to the Ceremonies of Funerals, taking away Barbarous Customs which the Women used upon those occasions: and (which was of greatest concernment) by Propitiations, Procurations, and Offerings, he Lustrated and Expiated the City, rendring the People more obsequious to Justice and Unity, (*o*) and staied the Pestilence in this manner: He took Sheep, Black and White, and brought them into the *Areopagus*; there he let them loose, to go whither they would, giving order to those who followed them, that whensoever any of them lay down, they should Sacrifice in that place to the proper Deity, whereby the Plague ceased. Hence it is, that at this day, (saith *Laertius*) are to be seen in many *Athenian* Villages, Nameless Altars, Monuments of that Expiation. Some affirm he imputed it to the *Cylonian* Impiety (of which already in the Life of *Solon*) and assuaged it, by putting to Death two Young Men, *Cratinus* and *Ctesibius*.

(*p*) He is supposed first to have built Temples; one he Erected in *Athens* to the *Eumenides*; another he intended to Consecrate to the Nymphs, but a voice from Heaven was heard in these words, *Epimenides, not to the Nymphs, but to* Jupiter.

(*q*) Beholding the Haven *Munychia*, he said to those who stood by, how blind is Man to the future! The *Athenians* would tear this Haven in pieces with their Teeth, if they foresaw how much it will infest the City: This he foretold many years before it came to pass, which was in the second year of the 114 Olympiad, when *Antipater* put a Garrison of *Macedonians* into the *Munychia*.

The *Athenians* being afraid of the *Persian* Navy, he told them, it would not Invade them for many years, and when it did, the *Persians* should not effect the least of their Hopes, but depart home with greater Loss to themselves than they had given their Adversaries: which was fulfilled in the Fights at *Marathon* and *Salamis*.

He

He foretold the *Lacedemonians* (and *Cretans* also) the Overthrow they should receive by the *Arcadians*, which hapned when *Euricrates* and *Archidamus* Reigned in *Lacedemon*.

These Predictions, (for which the (a) *Grecians* esteemed him (b) (Divine, beloved of the Gods, (c) and put him in the number of their Sophists; the (d) *Cretans*,) whose Prophet he is stiled by (e) St. *Paul*) Sacrificed to him as a God) were either not known, or not credited by *Aristotle*, who avers, he used not to Prophesie of future things, but only such as were past and obscure.

For his Lustration of the City and other things he was much Honoured by the *Athenians*, who Offered him many Gifts, would have Rewarded him with a Talent, and appointed a Ship to Transport him back to *Creet*: he refused their Gifts and Money, nor would accept of any thing but a little Branch of Sacred Olive, out of the Tower, wherewith (having procured a League betwixt the *Cnossians* and *Athenians*) he returned home; and soon after died (f) 157 years old, or according to (g) others, 150, the *Cretans* say he wanted but one of 300. *Xenophanes* affirms he heard him when he was 154 years of Age. His Body the *Lacedemonians* kept by the direction of the Oracle. It was taken up many years after, marked all over with Characters, whence arose a Proverb concerning abstruse things, *the Skin of Epimenides*; He called himself Æacus, others named him *Cures*.

He was a great * Poet, and writ many things in Verse; the Subject of his Writings were these.

Initiations, Austrations, and other obscure matters in Verse,

The Generation and Theogony of the Curetes and Coribantes, 5000 Verses.

The Building of Argo, and Expedition of Jason to Colchos, 6500 Verses.

Of Sacrifices, in prose.

Of the Cretan Common-wealth.

Of Minos and Radamanthus.

* *Of Oracles and Responses*, out of which Saint *Paul* cites this Verse.

Κρῆτες ἀεὶ ψεῦσται, κακὰ θηρία, γαστέρες ἀργαί.

The Cretans are always Liers, Evil Beasts, Slow bellies.

There is extant under his name (saith *Laertius*) an Epistle to *Solon* concerning the Orders of Government given by *Minos* to the *Cretans*: which *Demetrius* conceives of latter date, not written in the *Cretan*, but *Athenian* Language; but I have met with another to this effect.

Epimenides *to* Solon.

BE of Comfort Friend; for if Pisistratus *were Ruler of Athenians, inured to Servitude, and void of Discipline, his way perhaps might continue for ever. But now he subjects not base People, but such as are mindful of Solon's instructions, who ashamed of their Bondage will not brook his Tyranny, And tho' he should settle himself in the Government unmoveable, yet I hope it will not devolve to his Children; for it is hard for free persons, brought up under excellent Laws, to suffer Bondage. As for you, wander not, but come to Creet to me, where you will find no Oppressive Monarch. If in Travelling up and down you should light upon some of his Friends, I fear you may suffer some Mischief*.

(b) There were two more of this name, one a Genealogist: The other writ in the Dorick Dialect concerning *Rhodes*.

PHERECYDES.

PHerecydes was of *Syrus* (one of the *Cyclades* near *Delus*) Son of *Badys*, or as others, *Babis*; Born according to *Suidas* in the 46 Olympiad; he lived in the time of *Alyattes* King of *Lydia*; contemporary with the seven Sophists by some accounted one of them. *Laertius* saith he was in the fifty ninth Olympiad (a) *Cicero* in the time of *Servius Tullus*.

There are who affirm he heard *Pittacus*; others say he had no Master, but Procured and Studied by himself the abstruse Books of the *Phœnicians*.

(b) Many strange things are related of him; (c) In *Syrus* being thirsty, he required Water of one of his Scholars, which (d) (being drawn out of a Well) he drank, and thereupon declared there would be an Earthquake within three days in that Island; which hapning as he foretold, gained him much Credit: though ascribed by *Cicero* not to a Divine, but a Natural Cause.

(e) Again going to *Juno's* Temple in *Janus*, he beheld a Ship with full Sail entring the Harbour, he said to those that were present, it would never come into the Haven; whilst he was speaking, a Storm arose, and the Ship sunk in their sight.

(f) Going by *Messana* to *Olympia*, he advised *Perilaus*, at whose House he lay, to remove thence with all his Family; which he obeyed not: *Messana* was soon after taken.

(g) He bad the *Lacedæmonians* not to esteem Gold or Silver. *Hercules* having so commanded him in a Dream, who appeared likewise to the Kings, and bad them obey *Pherecydes*: this some ascribe to *Pythagoras*.

He held Opinions contrary to *Thales*, but (b) agreed with him in that of Water, that it is principal of all things. He said the Gods called a Table

Table ϑυωεςίς. ¹ He first asserted the immortality of the Soul, according to some. ᵏ Tzetzes affirms he was Master to Thales, but that suits not with their times: That he instructed Pythagoras is generally acknowledged.

The manner of his death is variously related. ¹ Hermippus faith, in a War betwixt the Ephesians and Magnesians, he desirous the Ephesians might be Victors, demanded of one present, whence he was? Who answer'd of Ephesus: Draw me then, faith he, by the leggs into the Magnesian Territory, and bid your Countrymen, after they have gained the Battle, bury me. I am Pherecydes. This message he delivered; they overcame the Magnesians, and finding Pherecydes dead, buried him honourably: Some affirm he went to Delphi, and threw himself from the Corycean Mountain; But the more general Opinion is, that ᵐ he died most miserably, his whole body eaten up with Lice (Pliny saith, with Serpents which broke out of his Skin) whereby when his Face became deform'd, he avoided and refused the Sight of his Acquaintance; when any one came to visit him (as Pythagoras did) and demanded how he did, he putting out his Finger at the Key-Hole, consumed by his Disease, shewed them the condition of his whole Body: Saying χρὶ δῆλα, the skin sheweth: Which words the Philosophers take in an ill Sense: The Delians affirm the God of that place sent this Disease to him out of anger, because he boasted much of his own wisdom to his Disciples, saying, if he should never Sacrifice to any God, he should lead a life no less pleasant than those that offered Hecatombs. Pythagoras buried him; his Tomb carried this Inscription

i Cicer. Tusc. quæst. 1.
k Chiliad.

Laert.

ᵐ Eli.m. 4. 28. See also 5. 2.

Of wisdom I comprise the utmost bound;
Who further would be satisfied, must sound
Pythagoras, of Greeks the most renown'd.

Some affirm he was the first that writ in Prose, which others ascribe to Cadmus. He writ Heptamuchos or Thocrasia; perhaps the same with his Theology, ten Books containing the Origin and Succession of the Gods (if not mistaken for the Theogony of the Younger Pherecydes) an obscure dark work, the Allegories whereof Isidore cited by Clemens Alexandrinus conceives taken from the Prophecy of Cham.

Concerning this Book there is extant an Epistle under the name of Pherecydes, but may well be suspected to be spurious.

Pherecydes to Thales.

'Well may you die whenever your fatal hour arrives; as soon as I receiv'd your Letter I fell Sick, was over-run with Lice, and had a Fever; whereupon I gave order to my Servants, that as soon as I was Buried they should carry the Book to you; if you, with the rest of the Wise Men approve it, publish it; if you approve it not, publish it not, for me it doth not please; there is no certainty in it: whatsoever the Theologist saith, you must understand otherwise; for I write in Fables, constrain'd by my Disease. I have not admitted of any Physician or Friend, but when they came to the door, and ask'd how it was was with me, putting my Finger out at the Key-hole, I shewed them how desperate ill I was, and bespoke them to come on the Morrow to the Funeral of Pherecydes.

There was another of this name of the same Island, an Astrologer: There are more mentioned by Suidas.

THE HISTORY OF PHILOSOPHY.

The second Part,

Containing the *Ionick* Philosophers.

ANAXIMANDER.

CHAP. I.

Of his Life.

[a] *Laert. pref.*

Philosophy had a twofold beginning, one from *Anaximander*, another from *Pythagoras*. *Anaximander* was Disciple to *Thales*, whence that Philosophy was called *Ionick*; *Thales* being an *Ionian*, for he was of *Miletus*. *Pythagoras* was Disciple to *Pherecydes*; that King of Philosophy called, from the Place where he taught, *Italick*. *Thales* was succeeded by *Anaximander*, *Anaximander* by *Anaximenes*, *Anaximenes* by *Anaxagoras*, *Anaxagoras* by *Archelaus*, in whom (as *Plutarch Laertius* and others affirm) it ended, *Socrates* (the Scholar of *Archelaus*) introducing Morality.

[b] *Cic. acad. quæst. 4.*
[d] *Suid.*
[e] *Strab. lib. 1. & 4.*
[c] *Clem. Alex. Strom. 1.*
[f] *Laert.*

Anaximander a Milesian, [b] Countryman, Companion and [c] Kinsman of *Thales*; was his Disciple also, and [d] Successor in the Propagation of his Doctrine; Son of *Praxiades* (corruptly called by [e] some *Praxidamus*) born the third Year of the 42d Olympiad. [f] He flourished most in the time of *Polycrates*, Tyrant of *Samos*.

Suid.
[*] *Strab. lib. 1.*

[g] He demonstrated the Compendium of Geometry; [*] being next *Homer*, the first Master of that Science; he first set forth a Geographick Table, of which *Laertius* is to be understood, who affirms, *He design'd the Circumference of the Sea and Land.*

[§] *Plin. 2. 8.*
[i] *Laert.*
[k] *Suid.*
[l] *Laert.*

[h] In the 50th Olympiad he found out the Obliquity of the Zodiack, *that is* (saith *Pliny*) *he opened the Gates of all things*. [i] He invented the *Gnomon*, and set up the first in an open place at *Lacedæmon*. [k] He found out the Æquinoctial Solstices and Horologies; [l] He framed *Horoscopes* to denote the Topicks and Æquinoxes; whence [m] *Salmasius* conceives the use of his Dial was only to delineate the Tropick and Equinoctial points; that they did not serve to distinguish the hours or twelve parts of the day, he proveth, because the very name ὥρα in that sense or the division of the day into twelve equal parts, was not known a long time after.

[m] *Plinian. Exercit.*

[n] He advised the *Lacedæmonians* to quit their City and Houses, and to lie armed in the open Field, foretelling an Earth-quake which threw down the whole City, and tore away a piece of the Mountain *Taygetus*.

[n] *Cicer. divinat. Plin. 2. 79.*

[o] As he sung, the Boys used to deride him, whereupon he said, *We must learn to sing better for the Boys*.

[o] *Laert.*

Of his Auditors are remembred *Anaximenes* and *Parmenides*.

Of his Writings, these.

[p] Περὶ φύσεως, *Of Nature*. This Treatise perhaps *Laertius* means, who saith he digested his Opinions into Commentaries, which Book fell into the hands of *Apollodorus* the *Athenian*.

[p] *Suid.*

Τῆς περίοδος.
Περὶ τῶν ἁπλανῶν.

Of the Sphere, with other things.

He was, according to *Apollodorus* 64 years old the second year of the 58th Olympiad, and died soon after.

CHAP. II.

Of his Opinions.

Sect. 1. *That Infinity is the principle of all things.*

^a *Acad.quæst.4.*
^b *De plac.phil.1. 3.*
^c *Paren. ad Græc.*
^d *Laert.*
^e *Simplic. in Phys. l. 2. phys. 1. 5.*
^f *Plut. plac. phil. 1. 3.*
^g *Laert.*
^h *Cap. 6.*
ⁱ *Cicero Acad. quæst. 4.*
^k *Plut. plac. phil. 1. 3. Just. Mart. pa—*

THales (saith *Cicero*) ^a *who held that all things consist of Water, could not perswade his Countryman and Companion* Anaximander *thereto, for he asserted That Infinity is that whereof all things were made*, or (according to ^b *Plutarch Laertius* and ^c *Justin Martyr*, *that it is the principle and Element of things* (for these two he confounded, as was observed of his Master *Thales*) ^d *but not declared what this infinity is, whether Air, Water, Earth, or any other Body,* for which he was condemned by *Plutarch*.

That *it is* ^e *one, infinite in magnitude* (not number) whence ^f *Aristotle* reprehends him for imagining contrarieties can proceed from the same Principle. ^g That *it is for that Reason is infinite, that it may not fail.*

^h That *the parts thereof are changed; the whole is immutable.* ⁱ (*Simplicius* faith moveable) ^k That *out of it all things proceed, and resolve into it.*

That *there are infinite Worlds generated which corrupt into that whereof they were generated,*

Sect. 2. *Of the Heavens.*

^l *De nat.deor.1.*
^m *Plac. phil. 1. 7.*
ⁿ *Stob.*
^o *Stob.*
^p *Stob.*
^q *Plut. plac. phil. 2. 20.*

HIS Opinion (according to ^l*Cicero*) was, that *the Gods are nаtrve* (having a beginning) *rising and setting by long Intervals,* and that *there are innumerable Worlds*: This ^m *Plutarch* and *Stobæus* apply to the Heavens and Stars. But how can we (adds *Cicero*) understand a God that is not Eternal. ⁿ That *Heaven consists of cold and heat mixed.*

That *the Stars are globous instances consisting of Air full of Fire, respiring Flames at some certain part :* ^o *mov'd by the Circles and Spheres wherein they inhere ; which* assertion Aristotle borrowed from hence.

^p That *the Sun is seated highest, the Moon next, then the fixed Stars and Planets.*

That *the Circle of the Sun is* ^q 28 *times* (*Theodoret* saith 26) *greater than the Earth, having a hollow Circle about it like a Chariot-Wheel, full of Fire; in one part whereof there is a Mouth, at which the Fire is seen as out of the hole of a Flute, which is the Sun* ^r *equal in bigness with the Earth.*

^r *Plut. plac. phil. 2. 21.*
^s *Laert.*

^s That *the cause of the Sun's Eclipse is the stopping that hole in the midst, out of which the Fire issues.*

^t That *the circle of the Moon is 29 times greater than the Earth, like a Chariot Wheel, having a hollow Orb, in the midst full of Fire (like the Sun) and oblique, breathing Fire out at one part as out of a Tunnel.*

^t *Plut. plac. phil. 2. 24. Stob.*

^u That *the Eclipse of the Moon happens according to her Conversions, when the Mouth out of which the Fire issueth, is stopped.*

^u *Plut. plac. Phil. 2. 25.*

^w That *the Moon hath a light of her own : but very thin;* ^x that *she shineth in the Light she borroweth from the Sun;* which two assertions are so far ^y from being inconsistent, that it is the common opinion ^z both are true.

^w *Plut. plac. Phil. 2. 28.*
^x *Laert.*
^z *As a Learned Person conceives upon those words of Laert.*

Sect 3. *Of Meteors.*

^a *See Erasm. Reinholdus in Theoricas Purbachii Pag. 164.*
^b *Plut. Plac. phil. 3. 7.*
^c *Plut. plac. phil. 3. 3.*

' ^bTHat wind is a fluxion of the air, when
' the most subtle and liquid parts thereof
' are either stirred or resolved by the Sun.

' ^c *That* Thunders, Lightnings, Presters, and
' Whirl-winds are caused by the wind enclosed in
' a thick Cloud, which by reason of its lightness
' breaketh forth violently ; the Rupture of the
' Cloud maketh a crack, and the divulsion by
' reason of the blackness causeth a flashing
' Light. ^d *Seneca* more expresly, He ascribed all
' to wind. Thunder (saith he) is the sound of a
' breaking Cloud : Why unequal ? because the
' breakings are unequal. Why doth it thunder in
' a clear day ? Because even then the wind breaks
' through the thick and dry air. Why sometimes
' doth it thunder and not lighten ? Because the
' thinner and weaker Spirit is able to make a
' flame but not a sound. What is Lightning ?
' The agitation of the Air severing it self, and
' rushing down, disclosing a faint Fire. What is
' Thunder ? The motion of a piercing thick spirit.

^d *Nat. quæst: 2. 18.*

^e All things are so order'd, that some influence descend from the Æther upon inferiour things; so Fire sounds, forc'd upon cold Clouds : When it breaks them it shines; the fewer Flames beget ' Lightnings, the greater, Thunder: A great part, ' the rest was altered from its natural kind by its ' excessive Heat.

^e *Sen. nat. quæst.2.15.*

' ^f That the first Creatures were bred in humi-
' dity, and enclosed within sharp thorny Barks,
' but as they grew older, they became drier, and
' at last the Bark being broken round about them,
' they lived some little time after it.

^f *Plut. Plac. Phil.*

ANAXIMENES.

CHAP. I.

His Life.

a Laert.
b Simplic.
c Cic. acad. quæst. Plin. 2. 76.
d Suid.

e Laert.

f Lib. 2.

ANaximenes, was a *Milesian*, Son of *Euristratus*, b Friend, c Disciple and Successour to *Anaximander*. According to *Eusebius* he flourished in the second year of the 56th Olympiad. d *Suidas* saith he liv'd in the 55th Olympiad at the taking of *Sardis* when *Cyrus* overthrew *Cræsus*. So that the account of e *Apollodorus* (who affirms he was born in the 63d Olympiad) is corrupt. He heard also, as some affirm, *Parmenides*. He used the Ionick Dialect, plain, and incomposed. f *Pliny* calls him the Inventor of Gnomonicks; but perhaps it is a mistake for *Anaximander*. Of his auditors were *Anaxagoras* and *Diogenes Apollonites*.

These two Epistles of his are preserved by *Laertius*.

Anaximenes to Pythagoras.

'THales having lived happily even to old age,
' ended his days unfortunately. One night
' going out of his House (as he used) with his
' Maid, to contemplate the Stars, gazing, and not
' taking heed to the place, he lighted upon a
' precipice and fell down. This was the fate of
' the *Milesian* Astronomer. But let us who were
' his Auditors, preserve the Memory of the Per-
' son, and our Sons and Auditors after us. Let
' us still retain his Sayings, and begin all our
' Discourses with *Thales*.

Anaximenes to Pythagoras.

'YOu are more advised than we, who leav-
' ing *Samos* for *Crotona* live there in quiet;
' the *Eacides* prove injurious to others, and the
' *Milesians* want not Tyrants of their own choos-
' ing. The King of *Media* is likewise terrible to
' us, but would not be so, should we pay him
' Tribute. The *Ionians* are resolved to war with
' the *Medes* for the general Liberty, and if
' they fight we have no hope of Safety. How
' then can *Anaximenes*, perplexed with fear of
' death and Slavery apply his Mind to Celestial
' Speculations? But you are coveted by the *Cro-
' tonians*, and all *Italians* ; Auditors come to
' you as far as from *Sicily*.

CHAP. II.

His Opinions.

Sect. 1. *That the Air is the Principle of all things.*

Plut. de Plac.
Justin Martyr.
paræn. 1. 3. phil.

HE held that the *Air is the Principle of the Universe*, of which all things are engendred, and into which they resolve; *our Souls by which we live are Air, so Spirit and Air contain in being all the World, for Spirit and Air are two names signifying one thing.*

That a *the Air is God, begotten, immense, infinite, ever in motion*; b but *that those things which arise out of it are finite, First is begotten, Earth, Water, Fire, then of these all things.* That the Air is God understands of the faculties penetrating through the Elements or Bodies.

a *Cic. de nat. de r. 1.*
b *Cic. acad. quæst. 4.*

Sect. 2. *Of the Heavens.*

THat c *the outward Superficies of Heaven is Earthly.*

That *the Stars are of a fiery Substance, invisible, Earthly Bodies intermixt with them; that they are inherent, as nails in Chrystal.*

That d *they are forced back by the thick resisting Air,* e *and move not above (or under) but about the Earth.*

f That *the Sun is flat as a plate, of fiery substance.*

That g *the Signs of Summer and Winter come not by the Moon, but by the Sun only.*

That h *the Sun is eclipsed when the Mouth out of which issueth his heat, is closed.*

That the *Moon is likewise of a Fiery Nature.*

That *the Moon is eclipsed when the Mouth out of which issueth her heat, is closed.*

c *Plut. plac. phil. 2. 11.*

d *Plut. plac. phil. 2. 23.*
e *Laert.*
f *Plut. plac. phil. 2. 19.*

g *Plut. plac. phil. 2. 19.*
h *Plut. plac. phil. 2. 24.*

Plut.
Plut. plac. phil. 2. 29.

Sect. 3. *Of Meteors.*

THat *the Clouds are made by condensation of Air, Rain by condensation of the Clouds, out of which it is squeezed, Snow of Rain congeal'd in falling, and Hail of the same, contracted by a cold Wind.*

Plut. plac. phil. 3. 4.

Concerning Thunder, Lightning, &c. To the assertion of *Anaximander* he added the comparison of the Sea, *which being broken with Oars shineth*.

Stob.

That *the Rainbow is made by reflection of the Sun-beams upon a thick Cloud, which, not able to pierce it, are refracted upon it.*

Plut. de plac. phil. 3. 5.

That *Earthquakes proceed from the rarity and dryness of the Earth, one being caus'd by excessive heat, the other by excessive cold.* Further explained by i *Aristotle* thus; He held that the *Earth, as well when it is moist as when it is dry, breaketh, and by these great pieces thereof which use to fall upon it, is shaken:* Hence it is that Earthquakes happen either in droughts or great Rains : by droughts it is broken, and by great Showers excessively moistned parts likewise in sunder.

Plutarch de plac. 3. 15.
i *Meteor. 2.*
7 *Senec. nat. quæst. 6. 10.*

He called *the contraction and Condensation of matter, cold*; *the laxation and rarity thereof, heat*; whence a Man breaths out of his Mouth both hot and cold ; his breath compress'd by his Lips, and condens'd is cold ; but breathed forth with an open Mouth is hot by reason of the rarity.

Plut. de primo frig.

ANAXA-

ANAXAGORAS.

CHAP. I.
Anaxagoras's Country, time, and study of Philosophy.

Laert.

ANaxagoras was of *Glazomenæ*, Son of *Hegesibulus* or *Eubulus*, born in the 70th Olympiad according to *Apollodorus*; in the first year thereof; Eminent for his noble birth and wealthy fortunes, but more for his magnanimous Contempt of them. [a] He left his Lands and Patrimony, (saith [b] *Cicero*,) to learn and obtain the Divine delight of Philosophy: And [c] converted himself from civil Affairs to the knowledge of things. *Suidas* affirms he left his Grounds to Sheep and Camels to be eaten up: And therefore *Apollonius Tyaneus* said, he read Philosophy to Beasts rather than to Men. [d] *Plato* derides him for quitting his Estate; *Laertius* reports he assign'd it to his Friends; whereupon being by them accused of improvidence; why (answered he) *do not you take care of it?* To one who reproved him, as taking no care of his Country, *wrong me not*, saith he, *my greatest Care is my Country*, pointing to the Heavens. To another, asking for what end he was born, he answered, *to contemplate the Sun Moon, and Heavens*. [e] In fine, he withdrew himself to contemplation of natural Philosophy not regarding civil affairs. In this Study *Anaximenes* was his Master [f] from whom he received his Learning.

[g] In the twentieth year of his Age the first of the 75th Olympiad, *Colliades* being Archon (whom *Laertius* corruptly calls *Callias*) at the time of *Xerxes's* Expedition into *Greece* he went to *Athens* to study Philosophy, where he continued thirty Years, and was honoured with the Title of Νὖς *the Mind*, as being the first that added that principle to Matter; so *Amon*.

Where dwells fam'd Anaxagoras, *the Mind*,
[h] *For he that Agent first to matter joyn'd*,
Which things confused orderly design'd.

[a] *Plut. contra usar. Lysand.*
[b] *Tusc. quest. 5.*
[c] *De orator. 3.*

[d] *Hip. mai.*

[e] *Laert.*

[f] *Cicer. de nat. deor. 1.*

[g] *Laert.*

[h] *Laert. perhaps* ἃ τί δὴ νοῦ αὐτοῦς.

CHAP. II.
Of his Opinions.

Sect. 1. *Of the first principles, and beginning of things.*

HE held that *the material principle of all things is one and many* ὁμοιομερῆ *parts infinite, simular, and contrary, continuous to the touch,* [i] *sustaining themselves, not contained by any other.* His grounds these: First, because, according to the common Rule of natural Philosophers, of nothing proceeds nothing, it is not possible any thing can be made of that which is not; or that which hath a being can be resolved into that which hath none. Secondly, because contraries are made mutually of each other, therefore they were in each other before; for if it be necessary, that whatsoever is made, be made of that which is, or is not, but that it should be made of that which is not impossible, wherein all agree that ever discoursed upon Nature, it follows necessarily, that they be made of things that are, and are within these very things, though by reason of their smallness, not discernable by us: Hence it is that they say, every thing is mixt with every thing; because they see any thing made of any thing: but things seem different, and are called divers in respect to one another, by reason that the multitude of Infinites which are within aboundeth in the Mistion; for the whole is neither quite white nor black, Flesh nor Bone, but every thing seemeth to be of the Nature of that whereof it hath most [k] of simple Nourishment, as Bread, Water, and the like, are bred the Hair, Veins, Arteries, Nerves, Bones, and other parts of the Body, all things are therefore in this food, as Nerves, Bones, and the like, discernable by Reason, though not by Sense: Of these Atomes the whole World consisteth, as [l] Gold of Grains; these homogeneal parts are the matter of all things, his Opinion is thus exprest by [m] *Lucretius*.

[i] *Plut. plac. Phil. 1. 3.*
Arist. Phys. 3. 4.
Arist. phys. 3. 7.

[k] *Plut.*

[l] *Laert.*

[m] *Lib. 1.*

' Next *Anaxagoras* we must pursue,
' And his *Homoiomeria* review;
' A term that's no where mention'd but among
' The Greeks; too copious for our narrow tongue:
' Yet may the sense be in more words array'd;
' The principle of all things, entrails made
' Of smallest Entrails, bone of smallest bone,
' Blood of small sanguine drops reduc'd to one;
' Gold of small grains, earth of small Sands
 ' compacted,
' Small drops to Water, sparks to Fire contracted;
' The like in every thing suppos'd, yet he
' Nature asserted from all vacuum free;
' And held that each corporeal Being might
' Be subdivided into Infinite.

That [n] God is an infinite self-moving Mind that this divine [o] infinite Mind not enclosed in any Body, [p] is the efficient cause of all things; out of the infinite matter consisting of similar parts, every thing being made according to its Species by the divine Mind, who when all things were at first confusedly mingled together, came and reduced them to order.

[n] *Lactan. fals. rel. 1. 5.*
[o] *Cic. nat. deor. 1.*
[p] *August. cir. del. 8. 2.*

Sect. 2. Of the Heavens.

THat *the higher parts of the World are full of Fire, the Power that is there he called æther*, and that properly, saith *Aristotle*, for the Body, which is continually in quick motion, is conceived

Arist. Met. 1. 3.

ceived to be Divine by Nature, for that reason called *æther*, none of those that are here below being of that kind.

That "ᵃ the ambient *æther* being of a Fiery Nature by the swiftness of its Motion, snatcheth up Stones from the Earth, which being set on Fire, become Stars, ᵗ all carried from East to West."

That ᶠ 'the Stars are impelled by the condensation of the Air about the Poles, which the Sun makes more strong by compressing.'

That the 'Stars are Earthly, and that after the first Secretion of the Elements, the Fire separating it self, drew some parts of the Earth to its own Nature, and made them like Fire: whereupon he farther affirmed,

'The Sun is a burning Plate or Stone, ᵘ many times bigger than *Peloponnesus*, whose conversion is made by the repulse of the Northern Air, which he, by compressing, makes more strong.'

ʷ That 'the Moon is a dark Body, enlightned by the Sun, Habitable, having Plains, Hills and Waters; that ˣ the inequality in her Face proceeds from a mixture, cold and Earthly, for there is Darkness mixt with her Fiery Nature, whence she is called a Star, or false Light.' ʸ *Plato* saith, that the Moon was occasion of Dishonour to him, because he assumed the Original of this Opinion of her borrowing Light, to himself, whereas it was much more Ancient.

That ᶻ 'the milky way is the shadow of the Earth upon that part of Heaven, when the Sun, being underneath, enlightens not all: ᵃ Or as *Aristotle*, that the Milky way is the light of some Stars, for the Sun being under the Earth, looks not upon some Stars, the light of those on whom he looks is not seen, being swallowed up in his; the proper light of those which are hindred by the Earth from the Suns illumination, is the *Galaxy*; *Laertius* saith, he held the *Galaxy* to be the reflection of the light of the Sun.'

Sect. 3. *Of Meteors.*

That 'Comets are the co-apparition of wandring Stars, which approach so near each other, as that they seem to touch one another: or as *Laertius*, 'the concourse of Planets, emitting Flames.'

That 'falling Stars are shot down from the *æther*, as Sparkles, and therefore soon extinguished.'

That ' ᵇ Thunder is the Collision of the Clouds, lightning their mutual attrition: or, as *Plutarch*; the Cold falling upon the Hot, or the *ætherial* upon the *aerial*, the noise which it makes is Thunder: of the blackness of the Clouds is caused Lightning, of the greatness of the light Thunderbolts, of the more corporeal Fire, whirl-winds, of the more Cloudy Presters.'

That 'Lightning distills from the *æther*; and that from that great heat of Heaven many things fall down, which the Clouds preserve a long time enclosed.'

That the 'Rain-bow is a refraction of the Sun's light upon a thick dark Cloud, opposite to him as a Looking-glass; by the same reason (saith he) appeared chiefly in *Pontus*, two or more Suns.'

That 'Winds proceed from extenuation of the Air, by the Sun.'

That 'Earth-quakes are caused by the Air or Æther, which being of its own Nature apt to ascend, when it gets into the Veins and Caverns of the Earth, finding difficulty in the getting out, causeth that shaking; for the upper parts of the Earth contract themselves by the benefit of Rain, Nature having made the whole Body thereof alike, lax and spongy, the parts, as in a Ball, superior and inferior; the superior, that which is inhabited by us, the inferior, the other: This wind getting into the inferior parts, breaks the condensed Air, with the same force as we see Clouds broken, when, upon the collision of them, and motion of the agitated Air, Fire breaks forth a this Air falls upon that which is next, seeking to get out, and tears in pieces whatsoever it meets, untill through those narrow passages, it either finds a way to Heaven, or forceth one: which *Laertius* obscurely expresseth, the repulsion of the Air upon the Earth.'

That 'Snow is not white, but black, nor did it seem white to him, because he knew the Water whereof it is congealed to be black.'

Sect. 4. *Of the Earth.*

That 'the beginning of Motion proceeding from the mind, the heavy Bodies obtained the lowest place, as the Earth; the light the highest, as the fire: those betwixt both, the middle, as the Air and Water: thus the Sea subsists upon the superficies of the Earth, which is flat, the Humidity being rarified by the Sun.

That the primitive humidity being diffused, as a Pool was burned by the motion of the Sun about it, and the unctious part being exhaled, the remainder became Salt.

That 'as soon as the World was made, and living Creatures produced out of the World, the World enclined of it self towards the South, according to Divine Providence; that some parts thereof might be Habitable, others not Habitable, by reason of the extremities of Heat and Cold.

That 'the mistion of the Elements is by apposition.

That 'the inundation of *Nilus* is caused by the Snow of *Æthiopia*, which is dissolved in Summer, and congealed in Winter.

Sect. 5. *Of Living Creatures.*

That 'Creatures were first Generated of Humidity, Calidity, and Earthly Matter; afterwards mutually of one another, Males on the right side, Females on the left.

That 'the Soul is that which moveth, ᵃ that it is aerial, and hath a Body of the nature of Air.

That

> That ᵇ 'there is a Death of the Soul likewise, 'which is separation from the Body.
>
> That all Animals have active Reason.
>
> ᶜ That Sleep is an Action of the Body, not of the Soul.
>
> ᵈ That in the hand of Man consists all his Skill.
>
> ᵉ That 'the Voice is made by the Wind, 'hitting against firm resisting Air, returning 'the counter-blow to our Ears, which is the 'manner whereby also the repercussion of the 'Air is formed, called Eccho.
>
> That † 'the Gall is the cause of acute Diseases, which overflowing, is dispersed into the 'Lungs, Veins, and Costs.

ᵇ *Plut. plac. phil.* 5. 24.

ᶜ *Plut. plac. phil.* 5. 25.
ᵈ *Plut. plac. phil.* 5. 25.
ᵉ *Plut. de amore frat.*

† *Arist.*

CHAP. III.
His Predictions.

Suidas saith, he foretold many things: of those, two instances only have been hitherto preserved. The first thus related by *Pliny*, *The Grecians celebrate Anaxagoras of the Clozomenian, and for foretelling by his Learning and Science in the second year of the 78 Olympiad, on what day a Stone would fall from the Sun, which hapned in the day time in a part of* Thrace *at the River Agos, which Stone is at this day shewn, about the bigness of a Bean, of an adust colour, a Comet also burning in those nights.*

* *Plutarch* adds, that it was in his time not only shewn, but Reverenced by the *Peloponnesians.* *Eusebius* reckons the fall of this Stone upon the fourth of the 78. Olympiad, which is two years after *Pliny*'s Account of the Prediction. *Silenus*, cited by *Laertius*, saith, it fell when *Dymilus* was Archon, which if it be to be read *Dyphilus* (for the other name is not to be found near these times) will be the first year of the 84. Olympiad. But the Marble at *Arundel House* (graven about the 129. Olympiad, to be preferred before any other Chronological Account) expresly names the fall upon the 4th year, upon the 77. Olympiad, when *Theogenides* was Archon, two years before. *Pliny* faith it was foretold. It was believed to have portended (as *Plutarch* testifies) the great Defeat given to the *Athenians* by *Lysander* at the River *Agos* 62 years after, viz. the 4th year of the 93d. Olympiad.

Of the Wonder † *Aristotle* gives a very slight account, affirming, ' it was a Stone snatched up ' by the Wind, and fell in the day time, a Comet hapning in those nights, which is disproved by * *Plutarch*, who hath this large Discourse upon it: 'It is said that *Anaxagoras* did ' Prognosticate that one of the Bodies included ' the Heavens, it should be loosed by shaking, ' and fall to the Ground, the Stars are not in ' place where they were first created, they are ' heavy Bodies, of the Nature of Stone; shining ' by the reflection of the æther, being drawn up ' by force, and kept there by the violence of ' that circular motion, as at the beginning in the ' the first separation of things, cold and heavy ' they were restrained. There is another Opinion ' more probable which faith, those which we ' call falling Stars are not fluxions of the æther ' extinguisht in the Air almost as soon as lighted, ' nor inflammations or combustions of any part of the Air, which by it spreadeth upwards, but ' they are Cœlestial Bodies failing of their retention by the ordinary course of Heaven ' thrown down, not upon the habitable Earth, ' but into the Sea, which is the cause we do not ' see them; yet the assertion of *Anaxagoras* is ' confirmed by *Damachus*, who writeth in his ' Book of Religion, that 75 days together before this Stone fell, they saw a great body of ' Fire in the Air like a Cloud enflamed, which ' tarried not in one place, but went and came, ' uncertainly removing, from the driving whereof issued flashes of Fire that fell in many places like falling Stars; when this great Body of ' Fire fell in that part of the Earth, the ' Inhabitants emboldned, came to the place to ' see what it was, and found no appearance of ' fire, but a great Stone on the ground, nothing, ' in comparison of that Body, of Fire. Herein *Damachus* had need of favourable hearers: But ' if what he faith be true, he confuteth those ' Arguments who maintain it was a piece of a ' Rock by the force of a boistrous Wind torn ' from the top of a Mountain, and carried in the ' Air so long as this Whirl-wind continued, but ' so soon as that was laid, the Stone fell immediately; unless this Lightning Body which appeared so many days was fire indeed, which ' coming to dissolve, and to be put out, did beget this violent Storm of force to tear off the ' Stone, and cast it down.

This it is likely * *Charimander* meant, who in his Book of Comets faith, *Anaxagoras* observed in the Heavens a great unaccustomed light of the likeness of a huge Pillar, and that it shined for many days.

The other memorable Prediction of *Anaxagoras* was † of a Storm, which he signified by going to the Olympick Games, when the weather was fair, in a shaggy Gown, the Rain pouring down, all the *Grecians* (saith *Ælian*) saw and gloried that he knew more Divinely than according to Humane Nature.

* *Vit. Lysand:*

† *Meteor.* 1. 7.

* *Vit. Lysand.*

† *Senec. nat. quæst.* 7. 5.

† *Suid.*

CHAP. IV.
His Scholars and Auditors.

These are remembred as his Scholars and Auditors.

* *Pericles* Son of *Xantippus* being instructed by *Anaxagoras*, could easily reduce the exercise of his mind from secret abstrusive things to publick popular causes: ᵇ *Pericles* much esteemed him, was by him instructed in Natural Philosophy; and besides other Virtues, freed from Superstitious fears arising from ignorance of Physical Causes; whereof there is this instance, the head of a Ram with but one horn being brought to *Pericles*, was by the Southsayers Interpreted prodigious: *Anaxagoras* opening it, shewed that the Brain filled not its natural place, but contracted by degrees in an oval form toward that part where the horn grew. Afterwards *Anaxagoras* neglected and decrepit with age in a melancholy resentment thereof lay down and cover'd his face, resolving to starve himself; which *Pericles* hearing, came immediately to him, bewailing, not *Anaxagoras*, but himself, who should lose so excellent a Coun-

* *Cicer.*

ᵇ *Plut. vit. Peric.*

Counsellor: *Anaxagoras* uncovering his Face, said, They, *Pericles*, who would use a Lamp, must supply it with Oyl.

Archelaus, Son of *Apollodorus*, was Disciple to *Anaxagoras*, and, as *Laertius* affirms, called the Natural Philosopher for first bringing that kind of Learning to *Athens*; but now that consists with his Relation to *Anaxagoras*, who, as he acknowledgeth, Studied Natural Philosophy thirty years in *Athens*, *Casaubon* justly questions.

Euripides, * as the writer of his Life affirms, Son of *Mnesarchus*, born at the first time of *Xerxes*'s Expedition into *Greece*, the same day that the *Grecians* overthrew the *Persians*, was first a Painter, then an Auditor of *Anaxagoras*; but seeing him Persecuted for his Opinions, lastly converted himself to Tragick Poesie.

* His words (because never published) these: δήκκυσι δὲ χ Ἀναξαγόρου τοῦ Κλαζομενίου πραγματείαν δὲ ἐτεράν τ' Ἀναξαγόρου ἐδὸν ἱστάντι τὸ διʼ ἄφο νόητε δόγματα.

Socrates, Son of *Sophroniscus*, was, according to *Aristoxenus*, an Auditor of *Anaxagoras* till he left the City, and thereupon apply'd himself to *Archelaus*, which *Porphyrus* reckons above the 17th. year of his Age, or rather the nineteenth.

Democritus also is by some affirmed, being younger then *Anaxagoras* forty years, to have applied himself to him; but *Laertius* affirms he could not endure *Democritus*, and shunn'd his Conversation; *Phavorinus* likewise attests, that because he would not admit him, *Democritus* profess'd himself his Enemy, and denied his Opinions of the Sun and Moon, but said they were ancient, and that he stole them, as likewise his Description of the World, and the assertion concerning the Mind.

Metrodorus of *Lampsacum* is likewise mentioned by *Laertius* as friend to *Anaxagoras*.

CHAP. V.

Of his Trial, Death, Sentences, and Writings.

OF his Trial, saith *Laertius*, there are several Reports. *Sotion* in his Treatise of the Succession of Philosophers saith, he was accused by *Cleon* of Impiety, for asserting the Sun to be a burning Plate; but being defended by *Pericles* his Scholar, he was Fined five Talents and Banished.

Laert.

Satyrus, that he was Cited to the Court by *Thucydides*, who was of the contrary Faction of *Pericles*, accused not only of Impiety, but of holding Intelligence with the *Persians*, and in his Absence Condemned to Death; when news was brought him at the same time both of the death of his Sons, which (according to *Ælian*) were two, all that he had, and his own Condemnation, of the latter, he said, Nature long since Condemned both them and me to Death. Of his d Sons e (with a calm Look) f *You tell me nothing new or unexpected*; I knew that I begat them mortal, which some ascribe to *Solon*, others to *Xenophon*; *Demetrius Phalereus* saith, he buried them with his own hands.

Cic. Tusc. quæst. 3. Plut. de ira cohib.
+ Var. hist. 3.
d Plut. consol. ad Apolon.
e Simplic. in Epictet.
f Val. Max. 5. 10.
g Laert.

g *Hermippus*, he was Imprison'd to be put to Death, but *Pericles* appearing before the Judges, asked if they knew any thing in his Life that they could accuse? to which they answered nothing; but I, saith he, am his Disciple, then be not transported by *Calumnies* to kill the Man, but believe me and set him at Liberty; so he was dismissed, but not able to brook the disgrace, he killed himself.

h *Hieronymus* saith, that *Pericles* brought him into the Court in poor Garments extenuated with Sickness, an Object fitter for Compassion than Justice. And thus much saith *Laertius* of his Trial.

h Laert.

Suidas, that he was cast into Prison by the *Athenians* for introducing a new Opinion concerning God, and Banish'd the City, tho' *Pericles* undertook to plead his Cause, and that going to *Lampsacum*, he there starved himself to Death.

Josephus, that the *Athenians* believing the Sun to be God, which he affirmed to be without Sense and Knowledge, he was by the Votes of a few of them Condemned to Death.

But if we credit i *Plutarch*, he was neither Condemned nor Accused but by *Pericles*, who feared the Ordinance of *Diopithes*, which Cited those which held Prophane or Sublime Opinions sent out of the City. k Yet elsewhere he confesseth he was accused.

i Vit. Pericl.
k De superstit.

His departure from *Athens* being thirty years after his coming thither, falls the third year of the eighty second Olympiad, the sixty third of his Age. Thence he went to *Lampsacum*, where he continued the rest of his Age, which extended to twenty two more, so little mindful of *Athens*, or of his Country, as to one, who told him that he was deprived of the *Athenians*; he answered, no, but they of me; and l to his Friends who, when he fell sick, asked if he would be carried to *Glazomonæ* his Country; no, said he, there is no need, the way to the Grave is alike every where. m Before he died, the Magistrates of the City asked him if he would they should do any thing for him; he answered, that his only Request was, that the Boys might have leave to play yearly on that day of the Month, whereon he died; which Custom (saith *Laertius*) is continued to this time. Those of *Lampsacum* Buried him Magnificently, with this Epitaph.

l Cic. Tusc. quæst. 1.
m Plut. instruct. Polit.

Here lies, who thro' the truest Paths did pass
O'th' World Celestial, Anaxagoras.

Ælian mentions two Altars erected to him; one inscribed to the Mind, the other to Truth. *Laertius* concludes his Life with this *Epigram*.

Fam'd Anaxagoras *the Sun defin'd*
A burning Plate, for which to die, design'd:
Sav'd by his Scholar Pericles; *but he*
* *Abandon'd Life to seek Philosophy.*

* Ælian.

† He is observed never to have been seen either to laugh or smile.

† Laert.

* Being demanded if the Mountains of *Lampsacum* would in time become Sea; he answered, yes, if time fail not first.

* Laert.

† Beholding the Tomb of *Mausolus*, he said, a sumptuous Monument was a sign the substance was turned into Stone.

† Laert.

* He first affirmed the Poesie of *Homer* to consist of Vertue and Justice; to which *Metrodorus* added, that the Poet was skilful in Natural Philosophy.

* Laert.

n He conceived that there were two Lessons of Death, the time before our Birth, and Sleep.

n Stob.

Laertius

Laertius and *Clemens Alexandrinus* assert him first of the Philosophers that put forth a Book. He writ

Of Natural Philosophy, out of which *Aristotle* cites the fragments, *All these things were together*: which was the beginning of the Book: and, *To be such is to be changed.* ° *Plato* this, *the Mind is the disposer and cause of all things.* ᵖ *Athenæus* this, *what is commonly called the Milk of the Hen, is the White of the Egg.* ᑫ *Plato* Censures the Book as not using the Mind at all, nor assigning any Cause of the Order of Things, but Aerial, Ætherial, and Aquatick Natures, and the like incredible things for Causes.

The Quadrature of the Circle; which Treatise, ʳ *Plutarch* saith, he Composed during his Imprisonment.

ˢ There were three more of the same Name; the first an Orator, follower of *Isocrates*: the second a Statuary, mentioned by *Antigonus*: the last a Grammarian, Scholar to *Zenodotus*.

Marginalia: ° Phys. 1. 5. Plut. Georg. ᵖ Hip. mai. ᑫ Lib. 2. ʳ De exul. ˢ Laert.

ARCHELAUS.

Laert.

ARCHELAUS was either an *Athenian* or a *Milesian*; his Father *Apollodorus*, or according to some, *Mylon*; he was Scholar to *Anaxagoras*, Master to *Socrates*. He first transferr'd Natural Philosophy out of *Ionia* to *Athens* (but how that can be, when *Anaxagoras* his Master taught there thirty years, *Casaubon* justly questions) and therefore was called *the Natural Philosopher*: In him Natural Philosophy ended, *Socrates* his Scholar introducing Morality; but he seems also to have touched Moral Philosophy, for he treated of Laws, of things Honest and Just; from whom *Socrates* receiving his Learning, because he encreased it, is therefore thought to have invented it; whereas as *Gassendus* observes, Moral Philosophy was far more Ancient, that being the principal ground of the Attribute of *Wise* conferred upon the Seven, whose Learning lay chiefly that way: but *Socrates* is called the Author thereof, because he first reduced it to a Science. *Archelaus* asserted,

That *Principles of all things are twofold, one incorporeal,* † *the Mind,(not Maker of the World) the corporeal, infinite in number, and dissimiliar* * *which is the Air, and its rarefaction and condensation, whereof one is Fire, the other Water.*

That *the Universe is infinite.*

That *the Causes of Generation are two; heat and cold.*

That *the Stars are burning Iron Plates.*

That *the Sun is the greatest of Stars.*

That *the Sea is made by percolation of the hollow parts of the Earth.*

That *living Creatures are Generated of Slime or warm Earth, emitting a milky kind of Slime like the Chile*; that *this humid matter being dissolved by the Fire, that of it which settles into a fiery substance is Earth, that which evaporates is Air.*

That *the Winds getting into the hollow places of the Earth, filling all the spaces, the Air condensed as much as possible, the Wind that comes next presseth the first, forcing and disturbing it by frequent impulsions. This Wind seeking a Room through the narrow places, endeavoureth to break Prison, whereby it happens the Wind strugling for Passage, that the Earth is moved.*

Of the definition of the *Voice*, by *Plutarch* attributed to *Anaxagoras*, *Laertius* makes *Archelaus* the Author, describing it a *percussion of the Air.*

That *what is Just, or Dishonest is defined by Law, not by Nature.*

† These five, *Thales, Anaximander, Anaximenes, Anaxagoras, Archelaus*, by continu'l Descent succeeding one another, compleat the *Ionick* Sect.

*Marginalia: † Stob. * Plut. plac. phil. 1. 3. Sen. Nat. quæst. 6. 12. † Plut. Laert.*

74   SOCRATES.   PART.

THE
HISTORY of PHILOSOPHY.

The Third Part.
Containing the *Socratick* Philosophers.

SOCRATES.
CHAP. I.
Socrates his Country, Parents, and time of Birth.

Laert.

SOCRATES was by Country an *Athenian*, born at *Alopece*, a Town, according to *Suidas* and *Phavorinus*, belonging to the *Antiochian* Tribe. This was one of those small Villages scattered through *Attica*, before *Theseus* Reduc'd the People within the Walls of a City, which
notwith-

notwithstanding his Decree, were not deserted, but continued and preserved by their Inhabitants.

His Parents were very mean; *Sophroniscus* (an *Athenian*) his Father, a Statuary, or Carver of Images in Stone; *Phænareta*, his Mother a Midwife, a Woman of a Bold, Generous and quick Spirit, as is implied by the Character *Plato* gives her, (though wrested by *Athenæus*) of which Professions of his Parents, he is * observed to have been so far from being ashamed, that he often took occasion to mention them.

Apollodorus, *Laertius* and *Suidas* affirm he was born in the fourth year of the seventy seventh Olympiad; which may likewise be collected from the Marble at *Arundel-House*, which saith, *he died when Laches was Archon*, and reckons seventy years of his Life, which was compleat, because *Plato says* πάνυ ἱξδομη- κόντα and from *Demetrius Phalereus* (who was himself Archon the fourth year of the hundred and seventeenth Olympiad) who saith, *he died the first year of the ninety fifth Olympiad*, when he had lived seventy years, the seventieth year inclusively upwards, is the fourth of the seventy seventh Olympiad, when *Apsephion*, (or, as some call him, *Aphepsion*) was Archon, of whose Name, in * *Diodorus Siculus*, no more is left than * φαίν- which should be ἀψεφίων- but hath been incuriously alter'd into φαίδων- which if † *Meursius* had observed, he had not corrected *Laertius* without cause, nor he and *Allatius* followed the mistake of *Scaliger* (whom they term *Anonymus*) in placing *Aphepsion* in the fourth year of the seventy fourth Olympiad.

The day of *Socrates* Birth, was according to *Apollodorus*, the sixth of the Month *Thargelion*, memorable (saith *Laertius*) for the birth of *Diana*, according to the Traditions of the *Delians*, upon which day the *Athenians* did yearly lustrate their City. Many other good Fortunes happening to the *Athenians* upon this day are Recorded by *Ælian*. The day following, viz. the seventh of this Month was the Birth-day of *Plato*, both which were kept with much Solemnity by the *Greek* Philosophers (* even to the time of *Plotinus*) as is affirmed by *Plutarch*, who thereupon observes it as the effect rather of Providence, than of Chance, that their Birthdays should be so near, and that of the Master precede the Scholars.

To accommodate this time with our Account, is neither easie nor certain, yet in respect it may give some satisfaction by way of conjecture, we shall found it upon these Hypotheses, taking that order of Months which *Petavius* gives.

1. That after the Olympiads, the beginning of the *Grecian* year was always on the first of *Hecatombæon*, and Olympick Games on the fifteenth.

2. That the Neomenia of *Hecatombæon*, did (at least in the times wherein we enquire) never precede the Solstice, being then about the Calends, or *pridie Calendarum Julii*, they supposing them in *octavis signorum*, it did not precede the ninth of *July*. This *postulatum*, tho' it be doubly question'd by *Petavius*, yet none of his Arguments pretend beyond *Meton's* time,

3. That upon that supposition, if *Scaliger* hath rightly order'd the Neomenia in his Olympick Period (against which *Petavius* brings no one sufficient Argument) and consequently the rest, the Olmypick Period doth certainly exhibit the Neomenia of *Hecatombæon*. It is true, that *Petavius* disputes the Period of seventy six years, as having never been used till *Calippus* his time, but we take it here only proleptically, as the *Julian* year, to which we would accommodate it.

4. That this being after *Solon's* time, the Civil year was Lunary (and consisted of Months, which were alternately of twenty nine, and thirty days,) at *Athens*, though divers places of *Greece*, especially the more remote from thence, did not for a long time after part with their tricenary Months.

These things supposed the sixth of *Thargelion*, (will, according to the *Julian* Account, taken proleptically) fall upon *Tuesday* the twentieth of *May*: according to the *Gregorian*, upon *Tuesday* the thirtieth of *May*, in the year of the *Julian* Period 4247, before the Incarnation 467 years, the fourth year of the seventy seventh Olympiad, at which time *Socrates* was born.

CHAP. II.

His first Education.

PLutarch saith, * that as soon as he was born, *Sophroniscus* his Father consulting the Oracle, was by it advis'd to suffer his Son to do what he pleas'd, never compelling him to do what he disliked, nor diverting him from that whereto he was enclined; to give thanks for him by Sacrifice to *Jupiter Agoræus* and the Muses; to be no farther solicitous for him, he had one guide of his Life within him, better than five hundred Masters.

But his Father not observant of the Oracle's Direction, apply'd him to his own Trade of Carving Statues, contrary to his inclination, whereupon † some have argued him of Disobedience, reporting that often times, when his Father bad him work, he refused, and went away, following his own will.

His Father dying, left him (according to * *Libanius*) fourscore Minæ, which being entrusted with a Friend for Improvement, they miscarried. This Loss (though it were of all his Stock, and he thereby reduced to incredible Poverty) *Socrates* pass'd over with Silence, but was thereupon necessitated to continue his Trade for ordinary Subsistence. † This *Suidas* intimates when he saith he was first a Statuary. * *Duris*, † *Pausanias*, and the Scholiast of *Aristophanes* affirm three Statues of the Graces, cloathed, (for so they were most anciently made, not naked) set up before the entrance into the Tower at *Athens*, were his Work. *Pausanias* implieth as much of a Statue of *Mercury* in the same place; which † *Pliny* seems not to have understood, who saith, they were made by a certain Person named *Socrates*, but not the Painter. Hence *Timon*,

From these the Fluent Statuary came,
Honour'd through Greece, who did against the Name
Of Orator Abusively declaim.

But being naturally averse from this Profession, he only followed it when necessity enforced him: *Aristoxenus* saith, he wrought for Money, and laid up what he got till it came to a little Stock, which being spent, he betook himself again to the same course.

These intermissions of his Trade were bestowed upon Philosophy; whereunto he was naturally addicted, which being observed by *Crito* a Rich Philosopher of *Athens* † he took him from his Shop, being much in Love with his Candor and Ingenuity, and instructed, or rather gave him the means to be instructed by others; taking so * much care of him, that he never suffered him to want necessaries. And though his Poverty were at first so great as to be brought by † some into a Proverb, yet he became at last, as * *Demetrius* affirms, Master of a House, and fourscore Minæ, which *Crito* put out to Interest: But *his Mind* (saith † *Libanius*) *was raised far above his Fortune, and more to the advantage of his Country*; not aiming at Wealth, or the acquisition thereof by sordid Arts, he considered that of all things which Man can call his, the Soul is the chief; that he only is truly happy, who purifies that from Vice; That the only means conducing thereto, is Wisdom, in pursuit whereof he neglected all other ways of Profit and Pleasure.

† *Laert.*
* *Laert. vit. Crit.*
† *Ælian. var. hist.* 2. *Plut. de util. virtut.*
* *Plutarch. comparat. vit. Aristis. & Caton.*
† *Apolog.*

CHAP. III.

His Master.

THE first Master of *Socrates* was * *Anaxagoras*, whereby, amongst other Circumstances, it is demonstrable, that the account of *Laertius* is corrupt, *Anaxagoras* not dying in the seventy eighth, but eighty eighth Olympiad.

Aristoneus saith, that as soon as *Anaxagoras* left the City, he applied himself to ‖ *Archelaus*, which, according to *Porphyrius*, was in the seventeenth year of his age. * Of him he was much beloved, and Travelled with him to *Samos*, to *Pytho*, and to the *Isthmus*.

He was Scholar likewise to *Damon*, whom *Plato* calls a most pleasing teacher of Musick, and all other things that he would teach himself, to young Men. *Damon* was Scholar to *Agathocles*, Master to *Pericles*, *Clinias* and others; intimate with *Prodicus*. He was Banished by the unjust † *Ostracism* of the *Athenians* for his exellence in Musick.

He heard also (* as he acknowledgeth) *Prodicus* the Sophist a *Cian*, whom *Eusebius* ranks in the eighty sixth Olympiad, contemporary with *Gorgias*, *Hippias*, and *Hippocrates* the Physitian.

To these add *Diotyma* and *Aspasia*, Women excellently Learned, the first supposed to have been inspired with a Prophetical Spirit. By her he affirmed that he was instructed concerning Love, by Corporeal Beauty to find out that of the Soul; of the Angelical Mind, of God. See *Plato*'s *Phædrus*, and that long Discourse in his Symposium upon this Subject, which *Socrates* confesseth to be owing to her.

* *Laert.*
‖ *Cic. Tusc. quæst.* 5.
* *Laert.*
‡ *Plut.*
* *Plat. Men.*

Aspasia was a famous *Milesian* Woman, not only excellent her self in Rhetorick, but brought many Scholars to great Perfection in it, of whom were *Pericles* the *Athenian*, and († as himself acknowledgeth) *Socrates*.

* Of *Evenus* he learn'd Poetry, of *Ichomachus*, Husbandry, of † of *Theodorus* Geometry.

Aristagoras a *Melian*, is named likewise as his Master.

Last in his Catalogue is *Connus*, † *Nobilissimus fidicen*, as *Cicero* terms him, which Art *Socrates* learn'd of him in his * Old age, † for which the Boy's derided *Connus*, and called him the Old Man's Master.

† *Plut. Menex.*
† *Maxim. Tyr.*
† *Plat. Thæetet.*
* *Schol. Aristoph. in Nub.*
† *Epist.* 9. 22.
* *Quintil.* l. 10.
† *Plat. Euthyd.*

CHAP. IV.

Of his School and manner of Teaching.

THAT *Socrates* had a proper School, may be argued from † *Aristophanes*, who derides some particulars in it, and calls it his *Phrontisterium*.

* *Plato* and *Phædrus* mention as places frequented by him and his Auditors, the *Academy Lycæum*, and a pleasant Meadow without the City on the side of the River *Ilissus*, where grew a very fair Plain Tree. Thence, according to the Fable, *Boreas* snatch'd away *Orithia*, to whom, three Furlongs from thence was a Temple, and another to *Diana*.

* *Xenophon* affirms, he was continually abroad, that in the Morning he visited the places of publick walking and exercise; when it was full the Forum; and the rest of the day he sought out the most populous Meetings, where he Disputed openly for every one to hear that he would.

He did only teach, saith † *Plutarch*, when the Benches were prepar'd, and himself in the Chair, or in set hours of Reading and Discourse, or appointments of walking with his Friends, but even when he played, when he eat, or drank, when he was in the Camp or Market; finally, when he was in Prison; thus he made every place a School of Vertue.

His manner of Teaching was answerable to his Opinion, that the Soul pre-existent to the Body, in her first separate condition, endowed with perfect knowledge, by immersion into matter, became stupified, and in a manner lost, until awakened by discourse from sensible objects; whereby by degrees she recovers her first knowledge; for this reason he taught only by *Irony* and *Induction*: The first * *Quintilian* defines an absolute dissimulation of the Will more apparent than confest; so as in that, the words are different, from the words, in this the Sense from the Speech, whilst the whole confirmation of the Cause, even the whole Life seems to carry an Irony, such was the Life of Socrates, who was for that reason called είρων; that is, one that personates an unlearned Man, and is an admirer of others as Wise. † In this Irony (sait Cicero) and Dissimulation he far exceeded all Men in pleasantness and urbanity; it is a very Elegant, sweet and facete kind speech; acute with Gravity, accommodated with Rhetorick, words, and pleasant speeches; * he detracted from himself in dispute, and attributed more to those he meant to confute, so, when he said, or thought another thing, he freely used that dissimulation which the Greeks call Irony; which Annius also saith, was in *Africanus*.

† *Nub.*
* *Phædr.*
† *Epist. Socra tic.*
* *Memor.* 1.
† *Utrum. sen. ger. vesp.*
* *Lib.* 9. *cap.* 2.
† *De Orat.* 2.
* *Cicer. Acad. quæst.* 4.

Induction

<small>a *De invent. 1.*</small> *Induction is by* a *Cicero defined a manner of Discourse, which gains the assent of him with whom it is held, to things not doubtful, by which assents it causeth that he yield to a doubtful thing, by reason of the likeness it hath to those things whereunto he assented: This kind of Speech* Socrates *most used, because he would not himself use any argument of perswasion, but rather chose to work something out of that which he granted him with whom he disputed, which he, by reason of that which he had already yielded unto, must necessarily approve; of which he gives a large example in* Plato's b Meno. <small>b *Plut. Lach.* c *Liban. Apol.*</small> *Thus, whosoever disputed with him of what subject soever,* (c *his end being only to promote Vertue)was at last brought round about to give an account of his Life past and present, whereinto being once entred, he never gave him over till he had sufficiently examined those things,* <small>d *Plat. Enthyphyr.*</small> *and never let them go* (d *Proteus like) till they came at last to themselves.*

For this reason e *he used to say, his skill had* <small>e *Plat. Theætet. Plutarch. quæst. Platon. 1.*</small> *some affinity with that of his Mother, he being like a Midwife, tho' barren (as he modestly affirms) in himself, endeavour'd with a particular gift in assisting others, to bring forth what they had within themselves;* f *and this* <small>f *Schol. Aristoph. in nub. p. 129.*</small> *was one reason why he refused to take Mony, affirming that he knew nothing himself, and that* g *he was never Master to* <small>g *Plat Apol.*</small> *any.*

These disputes of Socrates were committed to writing by his Scholars, wherein h *Zenophon* <small>h *Laert. Vit. Xenph.*</small> *gave example to the rest, in doing it first, as also with most punctualness, as Plato with most Liberty, intermixing so much of his own, as it is not easie to distinguish the Master from the Scholar;* i *whence Socrates hearing him recite* <small>i *Laert. vit. Plut.*</small> *his* Lysis, *said, how many things doth this young Man feign of me? And* k *Xenophon* <small>k *Epist. ad Eschin.*</small> *denying Socrates ever disputed of Heaven, or of natural Causes, or the other Disciplines which the Greeks call* μαθήματα, *saith, they, who ascribe such dissertations to him, lye falsely, wherein (as* l *A. Gellius observes,) he intends* Plato, *in* <small>l *14.3.*</small> *whose Books Socrates discourseth of Natural Philosopy, Musick, and Geometry.*

CHAP. V.

Of his Philosophy.

<small>a *Histor. Ecclef. 10. 36.*</small> PORphyrius *(who was so abusive, as* a *Nicephorus observes, that he traduced Socrates with no less bitterness, than as if he endeavour'd to out-do his accusers, Anytus and Melitus) affirms;* b '*He was ingenious in nothing, unlearn'd* <small>b *Theodoret.*</small> '*in all, scarce able to write, which when upon any* '*occasion he did, it was to derision, and that he* '*could read no better than a stammering School-* '*boy: To which we shall oppose these Authorities: Xenophon who attests he was excellent in all kinds of Learning, instanceth in Arithmetick, Geometry, and Astrology; Plato, in Natural Philosophy; Idomeneus, in Rhetorick: Laertius in Medicine: In a word, Cicero averrs,* '*That by the testimony of learned Men, and the* '*Judgment of all Greece, as well in Wisdom,* '*acuteness, politeness and subtilty, as in elo-* '*quence variety, and copiousness, to whatsoe-* '*ver part he gave himself, he was without ex-* '*ception, Prince of all.*

Having searched into all kinds of Science, he observed these inconveniences and imperfections: c *First, That it was improper to leave* <small>c *Xen. mem. 1. pag. 710.*</small> *those affairs which concern Mankind, to enquire into things without us. Secondly, That these things are above the reach of Man, whence are occasioned all disputes and oppositions, some acknowledging no God, others worshipping Stocks and Stones; some asserting one simple Being, others infinite; some that all things are moved, others, that all things are immoveable. And thirdly, that these things, if attained, could not be practised, for he who contemplating divine Mysteries, enquires by what necessity things were made, cannot himself make any thing, or upon occasion produce Winds, Water, Seasons, or the like.*

Thus esteeming speculative knowledge as far only as it conduceth to practice, he cut off in all Sciences what he conceived of least use: d *In Arithmetick, he approved only as much as* <small>d *Xenoph. mem. 4.* e *De leg.*</small> *was necessary.* e (Plato *instanceth in Merchandise and Tacticks) but to proceed to useless operations he disallowed. In Geometry he allow'd that part which teacheth Measuring, as no less easie than useful; but to proceed to infinite propositions and demonstrations he disallow'd, as wholly unprofitable. In Astrology he approved the knowledge of the Stars, and observation of the Night, Months, and Seasons, as being easily learned, and very beneficial in Navigation, and to those who hunt by Night; but to examine the difference of Spheres, distance of Stars from the Earth, and their Circles, he disswaded as useless.*

f *Finally, Noting how little advantage Spe-* <small>f *Laert.*</small> *culation brought to the Life and Conversation of Mankind, he reduced her to action. He first,* saith g Cicero, *called Philosophy away from things in-* <small>g *Acad. quæst. 1.*</small> *volved by Nature in Secrecy, wherein, until his time all Philosophers had been employed, and brought her to common Life, to enquire of Vertues, and Vices, Good and Evil.*

Man, who was the sole subject of his Philosophy, having a twofold relation of divine Speculation, and humane Conversation, his Doctrines were in the former respect Metaphysical, in the latter Moral.

Sect. 1. *Metaphysicks.*

HIS *Metaphysical Opinions are thus colle-* <small>Plat. Phæd.</small> *cted and abridged out of* Plato, Xenophon, Plutarch, *and others.*

' *Philosophy is the way to true Happiness,* ' *the Offices whereof are two, to contemplate* ' *God, and to abstract the Soul from corporeal* ' *Sense.*

' *There are three Principles of all things, God,* <small>*Plutarch plat. phil 1. 3.*</small> ' *Matter, and Ideas; God is the universal intel-* ' *lect; Matter the Subject of Generation and* ' *Corruption; Idea an incorporeal substance, the* ' *Intellect of God; God the Intellect of the* ' *World.*

' *God is one* τὸ ὂν ἀυτῷ ἔχρον ἔχον, ἀυτὸ τὸ ' κάλον, ἀυτὸ τὸ ζῶον ὄν⊙, *perfect in himself, giv-* <small>Plat. Phæd.</small> ing

'ing the being, and well-being of every Crea-
'ture; what he is, (faith he) I know not, what
'he is not, I know.

Xen. memor. 1. '* That God, not chance, made the World
'and all Creatures, is demonstrable from the
'reasonable disposition of their parts, as well
'for use as defence; from their Care to preserve
'themselves, and continue their Species, that he
'particularly regards Man in his Body, from
'the excellent upright form thereof, from the
'gift of Speech, from allowance τὰς τῶν ἀρθ-
'ρῶν ἠδονὰς συνεχῶς παρέχειν in his Soul, from
'the excellency thereof above others; in both
'for divinations, predicting dangers; that he
'regards particulars; from his care of the
'whole Species; that he will reward such as
'please him, and punish such as displease him;
'from his Power to do it, from the belief he
'hath imprinted in a Man, that he will do it;
'profest by the most wise and civilized Cities
'and Ages; that he at once seeth all things,
'from the instances of the Eye, which at once
'over-runs many Miles; and of the Mind, which
'at once considereth things done in the most
'distant places. Finally, that he is such, and
'so great, that he at once sees all, hears all,
'is every where, and orders all. This is the sum
'of his Discourse with *Aristodemus*, to which we
may annex what is cited under his name (if
not mistaken) by *Stobæus*,

Care, if by Care ought may effected be;
If not, why car'st thou, when God cares for thee?

† *Xen. memor.*
I. pag. 711.
Xen. memor. 4.

† He held, 'that the Gods knew all things,
'said, done, or silently desired.
'* That God takes care of all Creatures, is
'demonstrable from the benefits he gives them
'of Light, Water, and Fire, seasonable produ-
'ction of Fruits of the Earth, that he hath
'particular Care of Man, from the nourish-
'ment of all Plants, and Creatures for Man's
'Service, from their Subjection to Man, though
'they excused him never so much in Strength,
'from the variety of Mans Sense, accommo-
'dated to the variety of Objects, for necessity,
'use, and pleasure; from Reason, where-
'by he discoursed through reminiscence, from
'sensible Objects, from Speech, whereby he
'communicates all that he knows, gives Laws,
'and governs States; that God, notwithstand-
'ing he is invisible, hath a Being, from the
'instances of his Ministers, invisible also, as
'Thunder and Wind, from the Soul of Man
'which hath something with the divine nature
'in governing those that cannot see it. This is
'the effect of his discourse with *Euthidemus*.

Schol. Aristoph. in nub. p. 128.
'The Soul is immortal, for what is always
'moveable is immortal; but that which moveth
'another, or is moved by another, hath a
'Cessation of Motion and Life.
'The Soul is præ-existent to the Body, en-
'dued with knowledge of eternal Ideas, which
'in her union to the Body she loseth, as stu-
'pified, until awakened by discourse from sen-
'sible Objects. Thus is all her Learning only re-
Plat. phæd. 'miniscence, a recovery of her first knowledge.
'The Body being compounded, is dissol-
'ved by Death, the Soul being simple pas-
'seth into another Life, incapable of Corruption.

'The Souls of Men are divine, to whom, *Cic. de amicit.*
'when they go out of the Body, the way of
'their return to Heaven is open, which to the
'best and most just is the most expedite.
'The Souls of the good after Death, are in *Plat. phæd.*
'a happy Estate, united to God in a blessed in-
'accessible place; the bad, in convenient pla-
'ces, suffer condign Punishment; but to define
'what those Places are, is *hominis νοῦν μὴ* *Stob. Eth. 262.*
ἔχοντος; whence being demanded what things
'were in the other World, he answered, nei-
'ther was I ever there, nor ever did I speak
'with any that came from thence.

Sect. 2. *Ethicks.*

HIS Morals, consider a Man either as a
single Person, or as the Father of a Family, or as a Member of the Common-wealth;
In the first respect are his Ethicks, wherein
such Sentences as have been preserved by *Xenophon, Diogenes, Laertius, Stobæus,* and others,
are thus collected.

Of Vertue and Vice.

HE exhorted his Friends to endeavour to *Xen. mem. 1.*
'be the most wise and beneficial, be-*p. 720.*
'cause, what wants reason, wants respect, as
'the Bodies of Dead Friends, and Hair, Nails,
'and the like, which are cut off and cast a-
'way.
'To be employed is good and beneficial, to *Xen. mem. p.*
'be idle, hurtful and evil: They that do good *p. 720.*
'are employed, they that spend their time in
'vain Recreations, are idle.
'He that hath most advantage by Gifts of *Xen. mem. 3.*
'Nature, as well as he that hath least, must learn *p. 778.*
'and meditate on those things wherein he would
'be excellent.
'He only is idle who might be better im-
'ployed. *Xen. mem. 3,*
'To do good, is the best course of Life, *p. 779.*
'therein fortune hath share. *Xen. mem. 3.*
p. 78.
'They are best, and best pleasing to God, *Xen. mem. 3.*
'who do any thing, with any Art or Calling; *p. 780.*
'who followeth none, is useless to the Publick,
'and hated of God.
* He taught every where, 'That a just Man * *Clem. Alex.*
'and a happy were all one, and used to Curse *Strom. 2. 417.*
'him who first by opinion divided Honesty
'and Profit (which are coherent by Nature) *Cicer. de offic.*
'as having done an impious act, for they are *3. & de leg. 1.*
'truly wicked who separate profitable and just,
'which depends on Law. The *Stoicks* have
'followed him so far, that whatsoever is ho-
'nest, the same they esteem profitable.

He asked *Memnon*, a *Thessalian*, who thought *Plut. de amicor.*
himself very Learned, and that he had reached *multit. p. 93.*
(as *Empedocles* faith) the top of Wisdom,
'What is Vertue? He answered readily and
'boldly, that there is one Vertue of a Child,
'another of an old Man, one of a Man, ano-
'ther of a Woman, one of a Magistrate, ano-
'ther of a private Person, one of a Master,
'another of a Servant. Very good, replies *So-
'crates*: I ask for one vertue, and you give us
'a whole swarm; truly conceiving, that he
'knew not one Vertue, who named so many.

Being

Plat. de lib. educ. Being demanded by *Gorgias* 'if he accounted not the great King of *Persia* happy? I know not, answered he, how he is furnished with Learning and Vertue: as conceiving that true happiness consisteth in these two, not in the frail gifts of Fortune.

Laert. *Euripides* in his *Auge* saying of Vertue; 'It is best carelesly to part with these; he rose up and went away, saying, 'It was ridiculous to seek a lost Servant, or to suffer Vertue so to go away.

Laert. He said, 'he wondered at those who carve Images of Stone, that they take such care to make Stones resemble Men, whilst they neglect, and suffer themselves to resemble Stones.

Laert.

What περὶ μικρῶν means is explained by *Aristotle, polit.* 5. 3. & *Physic.* 5. 4. He advised 'Young-Men to behold themselves every day in a Glass, that if they were beautiful, they might study to deserve it; if deformed to supply or hide it by Learning.

* *Clem. Alex. strom.* 5. He said, 'to begin well is not a small thing, * but depending on a small Moment.

He said 'Vertue was the beauty, vice the deformity of the Soul.

† *Nonn. in Greg. Stelieut.* † He said, 'outward Beauty was a sign of inward Beauty, and therefore chose such Auditors.

Stob. Ecl. serm. 1. 'In the Life of Man, as in an Image, every part ought to be beautiful.

Stob. 1¾ 'Incense to God, Praise is due to Good Men.

Stob. 1. 'Who are undeservedly accused ought to be defended; who excel others in any good quality, to be praised.

Stob. 1. 'A Horse is not known to be good by his Furniture, but qualities, a Man by his Mind, not Wealth.

Stob. 37. : It is not possible to cover Fire with a Garment, sin with time.

Stob. 46. Being demanded *who live without perturbation?* he answered, *They who are conscious to themselves of no Ill.*

Stob. 218. To one who demanded *what Nobility is*, He answered, *A good temper of Soul and Body.*

Of Affections, Love, Envy, Grief, &c.

Xen. mem. 2. THat 'two Brothers God meant should be more helpful to each other than two Hands, Feet, Eyes, or whatsoever Nature hath formed; doubtless because if they love, they may at great distance mutually help one another is the scope of his Discourse with *Chæracrates.*

Xen. mem. 3. That 'all things are good and fair to those things wherewith they agree, but ill and deformed in respect of those things, with which they agree not, is the conclusion of his second Discourse with *Aristippus.*

Xen. mem. 3. 'Envy is a grief, not at the adversity of Friends, nor the prosperity of Enemies, but at the prosperity of Friends; for many are so foolishly enclined as to malign those in good Fortune, whom in misfortune they pitied.

Stob. 1. 'A Ship ought not to trust to one Anchor, nor Life to one Hope.

Stob. 16. 'To ground Hopes on an ill Opinion is to trust a Ship to a flight Anchor.

'The beauty of Fame is blasted by Envy as by a Sickness. *Stob.* 139.

'Many adorn the Tombs of those, whom living, they persecuted with Envy. *Stob.* 139.

'Envy is the Saw of the Soul. *Stob.* 139.

'Nothing is pleasant or unpleasant by nature, but by custom. *Stob.* 144.

'Unseasonable Love is like Hate. *Stob.* 215.

Being demanded, 'what is grievous to the good, he answered, The prosperity of the Wicked. *Stob.* 240.

Being demanded 'how a Man might live without Trouble, he answered, it was not possible but that he who lives in a City or a Family must sometimes be afflicted. *Stob.* 240.

'Wicked Hopes, like ill guides, deceive a Man, and lead him into sin. *Stob.* 258.

'A Woman cannot conceive without a Man, nor a good hope produce any benefit without Labour. *Stob.* 261.

'Winter had need of Garments, old age of disingagement from grief. *Stob.* 269.

'In Life as in a Theatre, we should continue so long as the sight of things, and actions of Life seem delightful. *Stob.* 892.

'The mad should be bound, the ignorant instructed. *Xen. mem.* l. p. 719.

That 'we should endeavour to shun the censorious, and to apply our selves to such as are candid, that we should undertake only such things as we can perform, and decline such as we cannot; That whensoever we undertake any thing, we should employ therein our utmost study and endeavour, is the sum of his advice to *Eutherus.* *Xen. mem.* 2.

He said, 'the office of a wise Man is to discern what is good and honest, and to shun that which is dishonest. *Xen. mem.* 3.

'They who know what they ought to do, and do it not, are not wise and temperate, but Fools and stupid. *Xen. mem.* 3.

'Justice and every other Vertue is Wisdom. *Xen. mem.* 3.

'To be ignorant of our selves, to seem to know those things whereof we are ignorant, is next to Madness. *Xen. mem.* 3.

That 'a Pious Person is rightly defined, such a one as knows what is Lawful as to the Gods, just, he that knows what is lawful to Men, that a Man is wise as far as he knows, that what is profitable is fair to that whereto it is profitable, that they who know how to use terrible things and dangerous are valiant, the contrary timorous, is the sum of his Discourse with *Euthidamus.* *Xen. mem.* 4.

He conceived 'the only wisdom of Man to consist in not thinking he understands those things which he doth not understand. *Cicer.*

To one that complained he had not benefited himself by travel, *and not without Reason,* saith he, *because thou didst travel with thy self.* *Senec. Epist.* 1 103.

He affirmed 'There is but one good thing, Knowledge, one ill, Ignorance; but that Riches and Nobility had nothing in them of worth, but on the contrary all Evils. *Laert.*

'When a wise Man openeth his Mouth, his Vertues are as manifest, as Images in a Temple. *Stob.* 1.

'In Navigation we ought to be guided by the Pilot, in the course of Life, by those of better Judgment. *Stob.* 28. & 42.

Being

Stob. 28.   Being demanded what Wisdom was, he answered, *The composure of the Soul*; being demanded who were wise, they said he, *who do not easily err.*

Stob. 28.   'The Soul's Reason augmenteth it self as 'in a Play, the wisest, not the richest ought to 'bear the Prize.

Stob. 32.   'Fugitives fear though not pursued, Fools 'though not in Adversity, are troubled.

Stob. 32.   Seeing a young Man rich, and unlearned, '*behold* (faith he) *a Golden Slave.*

Stob. 32.   'The Luxurious is hardly cured in Sickness, 'the Fool in Adversity.

Sthb. 32.   'The Coward useth Arms against himself, 'the Fool Money.

Stob. 32.   '*Achilles* Armour fits not *Thersites*, nor the 'good habits of the Soul a Fool.

Stob. 87.   'Be not forward in Speech, for many times 'the Tongue hath cut off the Head.

Stob. 211.   'In War, Steel is better than Gold, in Life, 'wisdom excelleth wealth.

Of Piety and Obedience.

Xen. mem. 2.   THat the 'greatest of Vices is Ingratitude, 'of obligations that to Parents, that a 'disobedient Son the Gods will not bless, nor 'Men love, as doubting his return of either, 'knowing he doth it not where so much is 'due; is the sum of his Discourse with *Apiles*.

Xen. mem. 1. 722, 4. 804.   'Our Prayers should be for Blessings in ge-'neral, for God knows best what is good for 'us; our offerings proportioned to our a-'bilities, for he considers Integrity, not mu-'nificence.

Xen. mem. 1. 722.   He said (with the *Pythian* Oracle) that 'the Gods are to be worshipped according to 'the Law of the City where a Man lives, they 'who do otherwise, he thought Superstitious 'and vain.

Xen. mem. 4. 803.   'The best way of worshiping God, is 'to do what he commands.

Stob. 43.   'Superstition is obedient to Pride, as its Pa-'rent.

Stob. 193.   'A harsh Father, like a severe Law, must 'notwithstanding be obeyed.

Stob. 201.   'The reproof of a Father is a kind Remedy; 'it brings more ease than pain,

Of Fortitude and Imbecillity.

Xen. mem. 1.   THat 'a Man ought to inure himself to vo-'luntary labour and sufferance, so as what 'shall be imposed by Necessity, may appear in 'him not compulsive but free; that soft ways 'of living in Pleasures beget no good consti-'tution of Body, nor knowledge of the 'mind; that tolerance raiseth us to high 'Attempts, is the effect of his Discourse with '*Aristippus*.

Xen. mem. 3.   To one who was fearful to go so far on foot as *Olympia, he demonstrated* (to make the journey seem easie) *that it was no more than his daily walk within doors, if extended at length, would easily reach.*

† *Xen. mem.* 3.   † One that complained he was weary of a journey, 'He reproved him for being more wea-'ry than his Servant that followed him laden.

Plut. consol. ad Apollon.   He said, 'Death resembled either a deep 'sleep, or a long journey out of our Native 'Country, or an absolute annihilation of Soul 'and Body, examining all which he affirmed, 'Death to be in none of those respects Evil; 'as to the first, faith *Plutarch*, it is not ill with 'those that sleep, and we esteem that sleep 'sweetest which is deepest; and if we look on 'it as a Journey, it is rather a Blessing, for there-'by we are freed from the slavery and affections 'of the Flesh which possess and infatuate the 'Mind; in the last respect, it makes us insen-'sible of ill and pain, as well as of good and 'pleasure.

Stob. 1. & 296.   'A Statue stands firm on its Base, a vertuous 'Man on firm resolutions.

Stob. 5.   'Voluntary labours are delighted with as-'surance of Ease; Idleness, and transitory Plea-'sures beget neither a good constitution of Bo-'dy, nor any good habit in the Soul.

* *Stob.* 48.   * Being demanded, 'what is Strength? He 'answered, the motion of the Soul with the 'Body.

Stob. 49.   'Seeing the Gates of *Corinth* strongly barr'd, 'he asked, Dwell Women here?

Stob. 269.   'An honest Death is better than a dishonest 'Life.

Ælian. var. Hist.   He used to say, 'Liberty is Sister to Sloth. 'instancing in the *Indians* and *Persians*, both 'lazy; the *Phrygians* and *Lydians* very in-'dustrious, as being under Servitude.

Of Temperance, Continence, and Contentedness.

Xen. mem. 1.   HE advised 'to shun all occasions of in-'continence, affirming that such as con-'versed much with fair Women could not ea-'fily be continent.

Xen. mem. 1.   That 'the fight and kisses of the Fair, in-'fuse a Poison more dangerous than that of 'Scorpions and Spiders, is the sum of his dis-'course to *Xenophon* and *Critobulus*.

Xen. mem. 1.   That 'a free Man ought not to entertain a 'Servant addicted to Pleasures, that he which 'is slave to Pleasures, should pray to the Gods 'for better Masters, is the Conclusion of his dis-'course *de continentia*.

Xen. mem. 1.   That 'Happiness consists not in Luxury and 'Pride, that to want nothing is Divine, to want 'the least next to divine, is the conclusion of his 'discourse with *Antipho*.

Xen. mem. 3.   'He advised such as could not easily abstain 'at Feasts, to take heed of such things as per-'swade those that are not hungry to eat,and those 'that are not thirsty to drink, for they destroy-'ed the Appetite, the Head, and the Soul. He used to say merrily, '*Circe* turned Men 'into Swine, by feasting them with such Meats; 'but that *Ulysses*, partly through *Minerva*'s ad-'vice, partly through his own Temperance, re-'fraining from such things, remained un-'changed.

Xen. mem. 3.   That 'health of Body ought diligently to 'be preserved, as that whereon all knowledge 'of the Soul depends, is sum of his discourse 'with *Epigenes*.

Xen. mem. 3.   He advised one that complained he had no 'delight in his Meat, 'to refrain from Eating, 'whereby his diet would become more pleasant, 'cheap, and wholesome.

Xen. mem. 3.   In the word ἐυωχῆσθαι (*to feast*) the particle ἐυ implies, that we should eat only such things as 'as will not hurt the Mind nor the Body, and are easie to be gotten.

'That only Temperate persons, that discern and choose the best things, refraining from the worst; that by Temperance Men become the most Excellent, and most Happy, fittest for Discourse: is the summ of his Discourse with Euthidemus.

Hearing one of his Friends say, 'this Town is exceeding dear, Chiar Wine costs a Mina, Purple three, a pint of Honey five Denaries, he carried him to the Meal-men, here, saith he, a pint is sold for an Obolus; it is cheap living in this Town: then to those that sold Olives, a Chœnix two Farthings; thence to the Frippery, a Suit ten Drachms; things are cheap in this Town.

'He said, the Hungry wanted no Sauce, the Thirsty no choice of Wines.

'He commended Quiet and Leisure above all things.

'He said, they who buy early fruits at dear rates, believe they will not come in their due season.

Being asked what was a young man's Vertue, he answered, to do nothing too much.

Seeing one eat Broth very greedily, he said, 'which of you here present useth Bread for Broth, and Broth for Bread? Of which, see more at large, Xenophon his *Memorab. Lib.*

One saying, that it was a great matter to abstain from what a Man desires, he answered, but it is much a greater not to desire at all.

'A clear Fire becomes the Chimney, Serenity the Mind.

He said, 'We ought not to seek Pleasures in others, but in our selves, the Body being predisposed according as it ought.

He said, 'It is the property of God to need nothing, to need least, nighest to God.

Being demanded from what things we ought to refrain most, he answered, 'from Sordid Unjust Pleasures.

'Contentedness is like a short and pleasant way, it hath much Delight, little Toil.

'He that would see Vertue as his Country, must pass by Pleasures, as *Syrens*.

Being demanded whom he thought Richest, he answered, him who is contented with least, for Content is the Riches of Nature.

Being demanded what Continence is, he answered, 'Government of Corporeal Pleasures.

'He said the Wicked live to Eat, but the Good Eat to Live.

When a Woman saith she Loveth thee, take heed of those words, more than when she Revileth thee.

Of Liberality, Prodigality, and Covetousness.

HE conceived, that they who took Money of any, owned them for their Masters in the meanest degree of Servitude.

That Wisdom is Prostituted as well as Beauty, by taking Money for it; that he who meets with an Ingenious Person, ought to acquaint him with all the Good he can, gratis, whereby he acquires a Friend, and doth the part of a good Member of a Common-wealth; is the summ of this second discourse with Antipho.

He said, if a Rich Man be proud of his Wealth, that he could not Praise him till he knew how he would imploy it.

None can safely manage a Horse without a Bitt, nor Riches without Reason.

He compared Covetous Persons to Birds, one devoureth whatever it meets till it Choaks it self, the rest falling upon what the first left, are one after another choaked also.

The Wealth of Covetous Persons is like the Sun after he is Set, delights none.

He that gives to a Rich Man, throws Water into the Sea.

The Life of a Covetous Person is like the Feasts made for the Dead, he hath all, but enjoys nothing.

He compared the Wealth of Prodigals to Fig-Trees, growing on a Precipice: for these none are the better, but Kites and Crows; for those only Harlots and Flatterers.

Being demanded who were Covetous, he answered, such as seek after Sordid Gain, and neglect their necessary Friends.

Wine changeth with the Vessel, Riches follow the Manners of the Owner.

Of Magnanimity and Pride.

TO one angry for having Saluted a Man that returned not his Salutation; it is Ridiculous saith he, if you are not angry with every one you meet of worse Shape or Form than your self, to be angry with any for having less Manners.

Pride, like an ill Potter, or Statuary, represents the Forms of things inverted.

Wind puffs up empty Bladders, Opinion Fools.

To be exalted with good Fortune, is to run in a slippery way.

Of Patience.

'THere is less danger in drinking intemperately of Troubled Water, than with a Troubled Mind full of Wrath, before it be allayed and Purified, to satisfie thy Anger in the Punishment of a Kinsman or Coutry-man.

'If every one should bring his Misfortunes into the Publick Stock to be shar'd alike amongst all men, the greater part of those that now complain so much, would be contented and glad to keep their own.

'It is all one if a Man being overcome in any gymnick Sports should sue his Adversary, as for a Man over-master'd by Fortune to accuse her; not knowing upon what conditions we entred into the contests of Life.

Of Veracity and Flattery.

'THere is no better way to Glory than to endeavour to be good, as well as to seem such.

'The kindness of Flatterers is chased away by Adversity.

L

'Hunters take Hares with Hounds, many take Fools with their own Praises.' — *Stob. 64.*

'Wolves resemble Dogs, and Flatterers Friends, but their aims are quite contrary.' — *Stob. 64.*

'Flattery is like a painted Armour, only for shew, not use.' — *Stob. 64.*

'Think not those Faithful who Praise all thy Words and Actions, but those who Reprove thy Faults.' — *Stob. 69.*

'Suffer not a Talker and Slanderer, for he tells not thee any thing out of good will; but as he discourseth the secrets of others so will be thine to others.' — *Stob. 71.*

'Good Men must let the World see that their Manners are more firm than an Oath.' — *Stob. 114.*

Of Urbanity and Conversation.

'A Little Hall will serve to dance in, and every place and posture to speak.' — *Plut. de sanit. tuend.*

'Wind kindles Fire, Conversation, Love.' — *Stob. 37.*

'Freedom of Discourse like the seasons of the year, is best in its proper time.' — *Stob. 67.*

'It is Arrogance to speak all, and to be unwilling to hear any thing.' — *Stob. 134.*

'Converse at distance, and softly with those that are in Authority.' — *Stob. 296.*

Of Justice.

'That the Gods prescribe just things by Law, and that Just and Lawful is to them the same thing, is the summ of his Discourse with *Hippias*.' — *Xen. mem. 4.*

'They who convert goods ill gotten to good uses in a Common-wealth, do like those who who make Religious use of Sacriledge.' — *Stob. 52.*

Of Friendship.

'That a Discreet Vertuous Friend is of all Possessions the most Fertile, and ought chiefly to be regarded, is the scope of his discourse, *de amicitia*.' — *Xen. mem. 2.*

'That every Man should examine himself of what value he is to his friend, and endeavour to be of the most worth he can to him, is the effect of his Discourse with *Antisthenes*.' — *Xen. mem. 2.*

'That Wicked Men cannot be Friends, either amongst themselves, or with the good: That the way to procure friends is first, to endeavour to be good, wherein he would seem good; that all vertues may be augmented by Study and Learning, is the scope of his discourse with *Critobulus*.' — *Xen. mem. 2.*

'That we ought to our atmost Abilities to relieve the Necessities of our Friends, is the effect of his Discourse with *Aristarchus*.' — *Xen. mem. 2.*

'He said, he had rather have *Darius* to his Friend, than his *Dariks*, a Coyn so named from him.' — *Plut. de frat. amore.*

'He wondred that every Man kept an inventory of his Goods, none of his Friends.' — *Laert.*

'They who violate Friendship, though they escape the Punishment of their Friends, shall not escape the Vengeance of God.' — *Stob. 213.*

'They who forsake their own Brethren to seek out other Friends, are like those who let their own Grounds lie Fallow to till anothers.' — *Stob. 213.*

'Fear not a Friend in Adversity.'

'We esteem not that Corn best which grows on the fairest Ground, but that which nourisheth best, nor him a good Person or Friend who is of highest Birth, but most noble in Qualities.' — *Stob. 213. Stob. 212.*

'Physicians must relieve the Sick, Friends the Afflicted.' — *Stob. 258.*

'It is pleasant to grow Old with a good Friend and sound Sense.' — *Stob. 263.*

Sect. 3. Oeconomicks.

IN the second respect are his Oeconomicks, which he learned of *Ischomachus*, by *Xenophon* expresly delivered in a Treatise upon that Subject, to which add these few Sentences.

'So contrive the Building of your House, as that those parts which are towards the South may be highest, that the Winter Sun be not excluded: those toward the North lowest, that they may be less subject to the Wind; In fine, so order it that a Man may live in every Quarter thereof with most Delight and Safety: Pictures and Colours take away more Pleasantness than they afford.' — *Xen. mem. 3.*

To one who beat his Servant for being Gluttonous, Covetous, and Idle, he said, *did you at any time consider whether you deserve not more to be beaten your self?* — *Xen. mem. 3. p. 7. 88. see more there Laert.*

To one that asked his advice about taking a Wife, *whether you do or not*, saith he, *you will repent it*. — *Stob. 183.*

To others that asked his Opinion concerning Marriage, he said, *As Fishes in a Net would fain get out, and those without would get in, take heed young Men it be not so with you*. — *Stob. 183.*

Men must obey the Laws of their Countrey, Wives their Husbands. — *Stob. 193.*

Sect. 4. Politicks.

IN the 3d. Respect are his Politicks, which *Hesychius Illustrius* makes to be the same which *Plato* hath delivered under this name, where you may have them though disguised with the Language and Additions of *Plato*, to which may be annexed those Sentences of his in that kind out of *Xenophon*, *Stobæus*, and others,

'They who cannot upon occasion be useful either to an Army, a City, or a Commonwealth; yet have Confidence of themselves, ought, though never so Rich, to be under restraint.' — *Xen. mem. 1.*

'*Antipho* demanding how he might make others skilful in Politicks whilst himself medled not therein, altho' he knew that he could manage them, which way saith he? *Antipho*. I do most act the business of the Commonwealth, if I practise it only, or if I endeavour to make many able to act therein.' — *Xen. mem. 1.*

'That place is fittest for Temples and Altars which is most open, and yet retired; for it is fitting that they who pray, see, and no less fitting that they come thither pure.' — *Xen. mem. 3.*

They

PART. III. SOCRATES. 83

Xen. mem. 3. 779.
'They are not Kings, who are in Possession of
'a Throne, or come unjustly by it, but they
'who know how to Govern.

Xen. mem. 4. 813.
'A King is a Ruler of willing Subjects according to the Laws, a Tyrant is a Ruler of Subjects against their Will, not according to the
'Laws, but Arbitrary; an Aristocracy is that
'Government wherein the Magistrates are.

Xen. mem. 4.
'The Offices of a good Citizen are in Peace,
'to enrich the Common-wealth, in War to
'Subdue the Enemies thereof, in Embassie to
'make Friends of Foes, in Sedition to appease
'the People by Eloquence.

Laert.
'Of Common People he said, they were as
'if a Man should except against one piece of
'bad Money, and accept a great summ of the
'same.

Clem. Alex. strom. 4.
Stob. 141.
He said, 'the Law was not made for the good.
'Deserving Persons ought to be sharers in the
'good Fortunes of the Common-wealth.

Stob. 141.
Being demanded *What City is strongest?* he
said, *that which hath good Men.*

Stob. 141.
Being demanded *what City is best Ordered?* he
said, *that wherein the Magistraets friendly agree.*

Stob. 141.
Being demanded *what City was best?* he said,
that wherein are proposed most Rewards of Virtue.

Stob. 141.
Being demanded *what City lives best?* he said,
*that which liveth according to Law, and punisheth
the unjust.*

CHAP. VI.

Of his Dæmon.

a Sup. cap. 2.
THat Socrates had an attendant Spirit (meant as *Plutarch* conceives by the *a Oracles* answer to his Father) which diverted him from Dangers, is impugned by *Athenæus*, not without much prejudice, which the bitterness of the Discourse Betrays. Souls that are not candid, and think ill of the Best, saith *Origen*, never refrain from Calumny, seeing that they mock even the Genius of *Socrates* as a feigned thing. On the contrary, we have the Testimony of *Plato*, *Xenophon* and *b Antisthenes* contemporary with him, confirmed by *Laertius*, *Plutarch*, *Maximus*, *Tyrius*, *Dion*, *Chrysostomus*, *Cicero*, *Apuleius* by Fathers, *Tertullian*, *Origen*, *Clemeas Alexandrinus* and others, whereof a great many instances (as *Cicero* saith) were Collected by *Antipater*: these only preserv'd by other Authors.

b Apud. Athenæum.

De divinat. lib. 1

c Plut. de Gen. Socr.
'*Theocritus* going to consult *Euthyphron* a
'Sooth-sayer, found him with much Company
'walking in the Streets, amongst whom were *Simius* and *Socrates*, who was very busie, asking
'him many questions. In the midst of his Discourse he made a sudden stop, and after some
'pause, turned back and went down another
'Street, calling out to the rest of the Company
'to return and follow him, as being warned by
'the *Dæmon*. The greater part did so, the rest
'went forward, on purpose to confute the *Dæmon*, and drew along with them one *Charillus*
'that played on the Flute; but in the way, which
'was so narrow, as not to give them room to
'pass by, they were met, and overturned in the
'Dirt by a great herd of Swine; by repetition
'of which accident, *Charillus* often afterwards
'defended the *Dæmon*.

Nor did the advice of this Spiritual Attendant only respect the good of *Socrates*, but extended to such friends as conversed with him, whereof himself gives these instances.

c Plato. Theog. Ælian. v.a. hist. 8. 1
'*c Charmides* Son of *Glauco*, going to Exercise
'in the *Nemean* Race, as he was discoursing with
'*Socrates*, was by him upon notice of the Voice
'disswaded from going, to which he answered,
'that perhaps the Voice meant that he should
'not get the Victory, but, *saith he*, however, I
'shall advantage my self by exercising at this time;
'which said, he went to the Games; where he
'met with some accident, which tho' it be not related, is acknowledged to have justifi'd the coun-
'sel given him by the *Dæmon*.

Plat. Theog.
Timarchus *and* Philemon *Son of* Philemonides having Plotted together to Murther Nicias, Son of Hircoscomander, *were at the same time drinking with* Socrates. Timarchus *with intention to execute what they had determined, offer'd to rise from the Table, saying to* Socrates, we'll Socrates, *drink you on, I will but step a little way and return immediately.* Rise not, *said* Socrates, (*hearing the Dæmon as soon as he spake*) *for the Dæmon hath given me the accustomed Sign; whereupon he sate still, presently after he offered again to be gone;* Socrates *hearing the Voice, withheld him. At last, as* Socrates *was diverted by something, and did not mind him, he stole away, and committed the Murther, for which being brought to Execution, his last words to his Brother* Clitomachus *were, that he was come to that untimely end for not obeying* Socrates.

c c. de divinat. 3.
Another time, *seeing his friend* Crito's *Eye ty'd up, he ask'd him the reason, who answering, that as he walk'd in the field, one pulling a Bough, it gave a jerk back, and hit him in the eye; then you did not take my advice,* replies Socrates. *for I call'd you back making use, as I have accustomed, of divine presage.*

d Plat. Theog.
That it had likewise a great influence upon the Souls of those who conversed with him, and lived with him, d he alledgeth as Examples *Aristides* Son of *Lysimachus*, and *Thucydides* Son of *Melissus*. The first leaving *Socrates* to go to the Wars, lost, with his Company, the habit of Learning, which he acknowledged to have gained, not by any verbal instructions, of which he had none from him, but by being near him, seeing him, and sitting in the same Room with him. The second as easily, by the same means attained the same habit.

And not only to particular persons, but to general Affairs did these Predictions extend: He foretold some Friends the defeat of the *Athenian* Army in *Sicily*, as is attested by *Plutarch*, and mentioned by himself in *Plato*, where he gives another fair Example, or rather Trial of the Truth of the *Dæmon*'s Predictions, speaking of a business, whereof the event was at that time doubtful: e *You will hear*, saith he, *from many in Sicily, to whom it is known what I foretold concerning the destruction of the Army, and we may now have an experiment if the* Dæmon *speak true.* Samionus, Son of Calus, *is gone in an expedition, the sign came to me: he goes with* Thrasylus *to War against* Ephesus *and* Ionia: *my Opinion is, that he will either be slain, or at least in much danger, I greatly fear the whole design.* These are his words in *Plato*, deliver'd before the event of that Action, which fell out according to his prediction; g for *Thrasilus* was repuls'd and beaten by the *Ephesi-*

f Plat. Theog.

g Xenoph. hist. Græc. 1.

L 2 ans

the *Athenians* put to flight with the loss of four hundred Men; of which Victory the *Ephesians* erected two Trophies: This was in the one and twentieth year of the *Peloponnesian* War.

We have alledged the Universal Consent of Authors, that *Socrates* had such a Spiritual attendant; yet is there some disagreement concerning the name, more concerning the nature of it.

It is commonly named his *Dæmon*, by which Title, he himself owned it: *Plato* sometimes calls it his Guardian; *Apuleius* his God, because (saith Saint * *Augustine*) the name of Dæmon at last grew odious. But we must observe, that he did not account it a God, but sent from God, and in that sense affirmed the Signs to come from God, to wit, by Mediation of this Spirit. This, besides other places, we may argue from his first Epistle, where he speaks of the Sign it self; he useth the word *Dæmon*, when of the advice, whereof that sign was the instrument, he names God. Thus are we to understand these, and all other places of the same nature in *Plato*, where *Socrates* speaking of the *Dæmon*, saith, *if it please God, you shall learn much, and the Sign from God did not offer to stay me.*

* *De civ. dei.* 8. 4.

As for the Sign or manner of the Prediction, † some affirm it was *by Sneezing*, either of himself or others; if any chanced to Sneeze standing before him, behind him, or on his right hand, he went immediately about that which he intended; if on the left hand, he refrained or desisted: if he sneezed himself before the enterprize, it was applausive, if in the Action, disswasive. There needs not much Argument to prove this Opinion. If this sternutation proceeded either from Chance, or his natural Constitution, it could not have that provident supernatural effect; if it proceeded from some more excellent outward cause, we recur to the Genius.

† *Plutarch. de gen. Socr.*

Others confine this Prescience within the Soul of *Socrates* himself, that he said, *his Genius advised him*, they interpret it, as we usually say, *his mind gave him, or so inclined him*: In this Sense indeed *Dæmon* is not seldom taken; but this is inconsistent with the Description which *Socrates* gives of a Voice and Signs *ab exteriore*, besides, this Knowledge is not above Humane Nature.

Plutarch having exploded the Opinion of *Terpsion* concerning Sneezing, conjectured first, that it might be some Apparition; but at last concludes, that it was his Observation of some inarticulate unaccustomed sound, (or voice) conveighed to him by some extraordinary way, as we see in Dreams. This avoids not the inconvenience of the former; if *Socrates* did first of himself interpret this Sound, it is the same with the last Opinion, that his Soul had a Prophetick Inspiration, if by any help, it will come at last to the Genius.

Some conceive it to be one of those Spirits which have a particular care of Men; which *Maximus Tyrius*, and *Apuleius* describe in such manner, that they want only the name of a good Angel.

But there want not those who give it that appellation: * *Lactantius* having proved that God sends Angels to Guard Mankind, adds, *and* Socrates *affirmed that there was a Dæmon constantly near him, which kept him company from a Child, by whose Beck and Instruction he guided his Life.* Eusebius upon these words of the Psalmist, *He hath given his Angels charge over thee, that they should keep thee in all thy ways.* We learn out of *Scripture* (saith he) *that every Man hath a Guardian appointed him from above*; and Plato doubteth not to write in this manner: *All Souls having chosen a condition of Living, they proceed in order thereto, being moved by the* Dæmon, *which is proper to every one, and is sent along with them to preserve them in this Life, and to perfect those things whereof they have made choice.* And immediately after; *You may believe*, saith he, *that* Socrates *meant this, when he often affirmed that he was Governed by a* Dæmon. More plainly † *Eugubinus*, the Dæmon *of* Socrates, saith he, *mentioned so often by* Plato *(seeing that* Socrates *was a good Man, and exhorted all Men to Vertue, and by the* Dæmon *was always excited to that which was good) may perhaps not unjustly be thought his Angel, as that which appeared to* Baalam *the Prophet, and diverted him from his wickedness.* * But *Ficinus* expresly; *if you are not pleased*, saith he, speaking of this Spirit, *to call the familiar Guide of a Man his Spirit, call it if you please, his good Angel.*

* De Orig. er- ror. 2. 15.

° *De civ. dei.* 8. 4.

In *Psalm* 91.

† *De perenn. philo.* 25.

* *Argum. ad Apol. Soc.*

The chiefest Argument of * *Collius*, who opposeth this Opinion, and endeavours to prove it was an evil Spirit, is, that the *Dæmon* never disswaded or diverted from Vice, but only from outward Danger, whereas the contrary is evident enough from the foregoing Story of *Timarchus* and *Philemon*.

* *De anim. pa- gan.* 5. 14.

True it is, that the advice of the *Dæmon* was always disswasive, *never*, * as *Cicero* saith, *impulsive, often coercive*. *Apuleius* flatters *Socrates* with this Reason; *Socrates*, saith he, *as being a Man Absolute and Perfect of himself, ready in all Offices that concerned him, never needed any exhorter, but sometimes a prohibitor, if it hapned there were any danger in that which he went about, that being forewarned he might take heed, and decline the undertaking for that time; which afterwards he might re-assume, or at-attempt some other way.*

* *De divinat.* I.

CHAP. VII.

His Military Actions.

† IT is observed by many, that *Socrates* little affected Travel, his Life being wholly spent at home, saving when he went out in Military Service.

† *Lacrt.*

In the second year of the eighty sixth Olympiad broke forth a War, the greatest that ever hapned amongst the *Grecians*, betwixt the *Lacedemonians* and the *Athenians*, the Occasions and Pretexts of it arising from the Controversies of the *Athenians* with the *Corinthians*, concerning *Corcyra*, and *Polydæa*, both which being Revolted from the *Athenians*, to whom they had been Tributary, sought for Aid from the *Lacedemonians*, who sent Forces to the Relief of *Polydæa*.

In this War was *Socrates* thrice Personally engaged; first at the Siege of *Polydæa*, in the year of the   Olympiad, against which the *Athenians* sent one thousand six hundred choice Men of Arms, under the Conduct of *Phormis*, who Besieged it from the Sea by his Gallies, and on the Land side by a Wall: amongst these were *Socrates* and *Alcibiades*: *Laertius* saith, *they were on the Sea side, and that there was no means to come on the Land side further*: [a] *Plato, that they Served both on Foot*, which disagrees with the other; for there was not any Sett Battle during all the time of the Siege, only Sallies and Skirmishes. Here [b] *Alcibiades* his Comrade, attests, *Socrates outwent all Soldiers, in hardiness; and if at any time*, faith he, *as it often happens in War, the Provisions failed, there was none could bear the want of Meat and Drink like him, yet on the other side in times of Feasting, he only seem'd to enjoy them, and though of himself he would not Drink, yet being invited, he far out-drank all others, and which is strangest of all, never any Man saw him Drunk. The Excesses of Cold in the Winter, which in that Country are extraordinary, he as wonderfully endured, when the Frost was so sharp, that very few durst go out of their Tents, and those wraping their Legs and Thighs in Skins, and Furs, he went along with them, having no more Cloaths than those he usually wore. He walked bare-footed upon the Ice with less tenderness than others in Shoos, to the wonder of the Soldiers, who thought themselves Reproached by his hardiness. His Contemplative Rapture at the same time was no less worthy Admiration; he fell into a deep Contemplation one Morning, and continued all the while standing in the same Posture; at Noon it was taken notice of by the Souldiers, who told it from one another, that Socrates had stood still in the same place all that Morning: in the Evening some Ionian Souldiers wraping themselves warm, came and lay down by him in the open Field, to watch if he would continue all night in the same Posture, which he did, untill the Morning, and as soon as the Sun arose, Saluted it, and retired.* Of these kind of Raptures *A. Gellius* saith he had many. We must not omit how he behaved himself there in Fight; [b] seeing his friend *Alcibiades* deeply engaged, and much wounded, he stepped before him, defended him and his Arms from the Enemy, and brought him safely off. Nor was his Modesty inferiour to his Love or Courage, for whereas after the Battel, the Generals were to bestow an Honourable Reward upon him that had fought best, the Judges assigned it to *Socrates*, he declined it, and by his earnest intercession, procured that it might be conferred upon *Alcibiades*.

The second Action of *Socrates* was in the first year of the eighty ninth Olympiad at *Delium*, a Town in *Boetia*, which the *Athenians* took. The *Boetians* (faith *Thucydides*,) *Led by Pagondas, followed them, and bid them Battel, the left Wing of the Boetians, to the very middle of the Army was overthrown by the Athenians, and fled to the other parts, where they were yet in fight; but the Right had the better of the Athenians, and by little and little forced them to give ground, and followed them from the very first. Pagondas, whilst the left Wing of his Army was in Distress, sent two Companies of Horse secretly about the Hill, whereby that Wing of the Athenians which was Victorious, apprehending upon their sudden appearing that they had been a fresh Army, was put into a Fright, and the whole Army of the Athenians, now doubly terrified by this Accident, and by the Thebans that continually won Ground, and broke their Ranks, betook themselves to Flight, some fled towards Delium and the Sea, others the Mountain Parnes, and others other ways, as to each appeared hope of Safety. The Boetians, especially their Horse, and those Locrians that came in after the Enemy was Defeated, followed, killing them.* Socrates in this Engagement behaved himself with his accustomed Valour (so well, that [c] *Laches* confesseth, if the rest had fought like him, they had not lost the day) and care of his Friends; [d] for seeing *Xenophon unhorsed in the Flight, and thrown down on the ground (himself likewise having his Horse slain under him, fought on foot) he took him upon his Shoulders, and carried him many a stadia, and defended him till they gave over the Pursuit.* And being thus at the loss of the day, with others disperse'd in Flight (amongst whom was *Laches* the Archon, and *Alcibiades*) [e] *in the constant slowness of his Retreat expressed a Courage far above Laches, frequently looking back and round about, as greedy to be Revenged of the Enemy, if any should Pursue them;* which was the means that brought him off more safely, for they who express least fear in their Retreat, are less Subject to be Assaulted, than such as repose their confidence in Flying.

[f] As they came to a way that was divided into two, *Socrates* made a Stand, and advised those that were with him not to take that way which they were going into, along the Mountain *Parne*, but the other by the way *Retiste*, for, faith he, I heard the *Dæmon's* Voice. The greater part were Angry, as if he had trifled at a time so serious; some few were perswaded to go along, amongst whom were *Laches* and *Alcibiades*, and got safely home; the rest were met by some Horsemen, who returning from the Pursuit, fell upon them; they at first resisted, but at last enclosed by the Enemy who exceeded them in number; they gave back, and were in the end opprest, and all kill'd; except one who by the help of his Shield getting away, brought the news to *Athens*, and *Pyrilampes* Son of *Antiphon*, who being wounded by a Javelin, was taken Prisoner; and when he heard by those that were sent from *Athens* to *Thebes* to treat of Peace, that *Socrates* and the rest with him got safe home; he openly profess'd to the *Thebans*, that *Socrates* had often called him and others of his company back, who not following the advice of his Genius were slain.

The last Military Engagement was the same year at [g] *Amphipolis*, [h] which was then taken by *Brasidas* the *Lacedæmonian* General.

CHAP.

CHAP. IX.

How he carried himself in the Democracy, and the Oligarchy.

SOcrates forbore to accept any Office in the Common-wealth, (except in his latter years that of Senator) either (as * Ælian saith) because he saw the *Athenian* Government, though under the form of a Democracy, was yet nearer to a Tyranny or Monarchy, or† as himself professeth, being dissuaded by his Genius from medling in publick affairs, which Advice was his Preservation, being too honest to comply with the Injustices of the Commonwealth, and to oppose them was extreamly dangerous, as he found experimentally in that short time.

* *Var. hist.* 3.

† *Plat. Apol.*

* He was chosen to the Senate for the *Antiochian* Tribe, whereunto († as we have said) *Alopece* the Town where he was born belonged, * and in order thereto took the Oath which *Solon* appointed to be given to every Senator, to give Sentence according to the Laws, nor biassed either by favour, hatred, or any other Pretext: In the third year of the 93d Olympiad († the preheminence coming in course to the *Antiochian* Tribe, and *Socrates* thereupon becoming President of the People) he had this occasion of manifesting his Constancy. * There hapned a Sea-fight between the *Athenians* and the *Lacedæmonians* at *Arginusæ*: The *Athenian* Commanders were ten; the *Lacedæmonians* Commander in chief, *Callicratidas*; the *Lacedæmonians* were overthrown, their Admiral sunk; the *Athenians* went back to *Arginusæ* with the loss of twenty five Ships, and all the Men in them except some few that escaped to Land; the ten Commanders ordered *Theramenes* and *Thrasibulus* (Captains of the Galleys) to look out after the Vessels that were Shipwrackt, which as they were going to do, a sudden Tempest arose and hindred them; six of those Commanders returned to *Athens*, where they no sooner came, but upon the Account they gave of the Fight, the Senate committed them to Prison; *Theremenes* was their Accuser, who urg'd that they might be questioned for not relieving those that were lost by Shipwrack; the Commanders justly answer'd, that they had given order for their Relief, and that *Theramenes* and *Thrasibulus*, on whom that Charge was imposed, were (if any) to be condemned; but that they would not retort the Fault on their accusers, for the Tempest sufficiently excused them. This satisfied the Senate for that time, but at the next feast being the *Apaturia*, some Friends of *Theremenes*, by his instigation shaving their Hair, and putting on Mourning Apparel, pretending to be Kinsmen of those that were drowned, came in that habit to the Senate, and causing the Charge against the ten Commanders to be renewed, so much incensed the People, that they by menaces contrary to all Law, enforced the Senate to condemn them. *Socrates* being ordered to write the decree against them, avoided it by pretending he could not write, and knew not the Form, which occasioned Laughter in the Senate (and perhaps

* *Plat. Apol. Gorg.*
† *Chap.* 1.
* *Xen. memor.* 1. p. 711.

† *Plat. Apol.*

* *Xenoph. hist. Græc.* 1.

that Aspersion of *Porphyrius*, that he was scarce able to Write, which when he did, it was to Derision) but the true reason is by *Athenæus* acknowledged to be his constant fortitude, in that he would not violate the Laws of the Common-wealth contrary to the Oath he had taken, * to which he took more heed than to the violence wherewith he was threatned; for when the Senate proceeded to their condemnation, * he alone opposed it with his suffrage, whereupon many Orators prepared to accuse him, and the People cried out with loud Clamours, that he might be brought to answer for it: But he chose rather to hazard himself for Law and Justice, than through fear of Imprisonment and Death to consent to injustice, as the death of these Men was afterwards known to be, even to the *Athenians* themselves: and was soon after punished in *Theramenes* by the like, wherein *Socrates* gave the same Testimony of his Courage upon this occasion.

* *Xenoph. memor.* 1.

* *Laert.* Ἀλλὰ καὶ μόνος (perhaps μόνον ἐπι-ψηφίσασθαι τ᾽ ἐκαστράτηγον.

Athens after a long War with the *Lacedæmonians* of 27 years, being taken at last by *Lysander*, the *Lacedæmonian* General in the first year of the 94th Olympiad, there grew some debate concerning the alteration of the Government, from a Democracy to an Oligarchy; *Theramenes* stood for the continuance of the Democracy, but being oversway'd by the power and threats of *Lysander*; yielded to the constitution of thirty Persons, † by title Governours, in effect Tyrants, of which number was *Theramenes* (whom they took, in regard of his known Moderation and Equity, to bridle the Rapine and Avarice of others) *Critias* (first a Friend, but now a great Enemy to *Socrates* for reproving his love of *Euridamus*) *Charicles* and others, whose names are set down by *Xenophon*, as are also their murders, unjust Sequestrations of Lands, and confiscations of Goods; they began with punishment of the worst Persons, proceeded the richest, and ended with the best. Never (saith *Seneca*) was any City more miserable; 1300. (*Æschines* saith, 1500.) of the best Persons they put to death without any legal Tryal, nor was their Fury thereby asswaged, but more exasperated; that City where was the *Areopagus*, the most Religious Court of Judicature, where the Senate and People like the Senate used to assemble, was daily made a sad Colledge of Executioners, an unhappy Court too narrow for the Tyrants without rest from Oppression, without hope of Liberty or Remedy. All fled the City but *Socrates*, who *all this while set not his Foot out at the Gates*; he was continually amongst the People, comforted the lamenting Fathers, encouraged those that despaired of the State, reproached the Rich, that had lived in fear to lose their Wealth, the late repentance of their dangerous avarice, and to those that would imitate him, gave great Examples, whilst he walked free amidst the thirty Oppressors.

† *Diod. Sic. lib.* 14.

Theramenes opposing this cruelty and Injustice, was accused by *Critias* for betraying the trust of the Common-wealth, whereof he acquitted himself to the satisfaction of the Senate; but *Critias* and his Faction, fearing he might overthrow the Oligarchy, seized upon him with a Troop of Soldiers; *Theramenes* run to the Altar,

tar, but being dragged from thence by the Officers, he behaved himself like (faith Diodorus) the Disciple of *Socrates* ; the People pitied him, but none of them durst offer to help him, because he was compass'd in by the Soldiers, except *Socrates* and two of his companions, who ran to him and endeavoured to rescue him out of the hands of the Officers; *Theramenes* desired them to forbear, telling them that he much loved and commended their Kindness and Vertue, but that it would be the greatest misfortune he could have, if their love to him should occasion their deaths; whereupon *Socrates* and his Companions seeing none come in to join with them in his Aid, and that the contrar Party was too strong for them, gave over: *Theramenes* was carried to Prison, and there (being sentenced to drink Hemlock) died.

These outrages of the thirty Tyrants *Socrates* did not forbear to censure: || *Seeing many eminent Persons put to death, and the rich circumvented and betray'd to excessive punishments*, he said to Antisthenes, *Doth it repent thee that we have done nothing in our whole lives great and remakable, as those Monarchs who are described in Tragedies*, Atreus's, Thyestes's, Agamemnon's *and* Egisthus's ? *They are in those Plays beheaded, feasted with their own Flesh, and generally destroyed; but no Poet was ever so bold and impudent as to bring a Hog killed upon the Stage.*

† To another, *who murmured because he was not looked upon since they began to rule, Are you sorry for it*, said he ? He said likewise, * *that it were strange if a Neatherd who diminished and impoverished his herd, should not confess himself an ill Neatherd, but more strange that one who being set over the City, made the Citizens worse, and their number less, should not confess himself an ill Governour.* This came to their Knowledge, whereupon Critias and Charicles sent for him, and forbad him strictly to teach or discourse with any of the young Men. Socrates asked them *if in acts of prohibition he might be permitted to question what he understood not, which they granting; Then* (continues he) *I am ready to obey the Laws, but lest I trangress them thro' Ignorance, I desire to be informed, whether when you forbid me the act of Speaking, this act be to be understood of things spoken rightly or not rightly; if of the first, I must abstain from speaking what is right; if of the Second, I must take care to speak nothing but what is right.* Hereupon Charicles being displeased, said, *Since you understood not that*, Socrates, *we command you what is easier to be understood, that henceforward you speak not at all with any of the Young Men; To take away all ambiguity*, replies Socrates, *that I may not exceed my limitation; let me know expresly at what years you call a Young Man:* So long, saith Charicles, *as he is uncapable of being Senatour, and hath not attained to the heighth of his Judgment; you are not to speak with any under thirty*; May I not buy, answers Socrates, *of any under that age, nor ask them the price of any thing?* That you may, saith Charicles, *but your custom is to ask questions of things which you know very well; forbear those: And shall I not then*, replies Socrates, *make answer if any one ask me where* Charicles *dwells, or where* Critias *is ?* To such questions, saith Charicles, you

|| Ælian. var. hist. 2.

† Laert.

* Xenoph. memor. 1.

may. *You must* (continues Critias) *refrain from the Artificers, whose Ears you have sufficiently grated with your impertinent Discourse; I must then abstain* (saith Socrates) *from Justice, Piety, and the like; even from the very Neatherds*, replies Charicles, *which unless you do, take heed your Herd come not short home.*

This ill will and jealousie which they had conceived against *Socrates* was increased by the secret departure of some Friends of his out of the City, which was reported to be done by his contrivement, to give intelligence to the *Thebans*: nor was that suspicion without reason, as is manifest by his last Epistle: Hereupon they summoned him into the Court, where some Complaints were brought against him, of which having acquitted himself, they (to get a better Cause of quarrel against him) gave order to him and four more to go to the *Pyræum*, and to apprehend *Leon*, whom they meant to put to Death, that they might possess his Estate: But Socrates refused, adding, that he would never willingly assist an unjust act; whereupon *Charicles* said, *Dost thou think* Socrates, *to talk thus peremptorily, and not to suffer ? A thousand ills* answered Socrates, *but none so grievous as to do unjustly.* Charicles made no reply, nor any of the rest; the other four went for *Leon*, *Socrates* directly to his House; but from thenceforward, the Jealousie they had of him was so much encreased, that * if their Power had not been soon dissolved, they would have gone near to have taken away his Life.

* Plat. Apol.

CHAP. XI.

His falling out with the Sophists, and with Anytus.

THE Sophists *Masters of Language in those times*, saith † *Cicero* (whereof was Gorgius of Lecontium, Thrasimachus of Chalcedon, Protagoras of Abdera, Prodicus a Cian, Hippias an Elian, *and many others*) profest *in Arrogant Words to teach, how an inferiour Cause* (such was their Phrase) *might by Speaking, be made Superiour*, * and used *a sweet fluent kind of Rhetorick, argute in Sentence, lofty in words, fitter for Ostentation than pleading, for the Schools and Academies, rather than the Forum*, were so highly esteemed, that † *wheresoever they came, they could perswade the young Men to forsake all other Conversation for theirs.* * These Socrates opposed, and often by his subtilty of disputing, refelling their Principles, † *with his accustomed Interrogatories, demonstrated that they were indeed much beneath the Esteem they had gained, that they themselves understood nothing of that which they undertook to teach others; he withdrew the young Men from their empty Conversation: These, who till then had been looked upon as Angels for Wit and Eloquence, he proved to be vain affecters of Words, ignorant of those things which they professed, and had more need to give Mony to be taught, than to take* (as they used) *Mony for Teaching. The Athenians taken with these Reproofs which* Socrates *gave them, derided them, and excited their Children to the study of solid Vertue.*

† Brut.

* Cic. Orator.

† Liban. Apol.

* Cic. Burt.

† Liban. Apol.

Another

Another quarrel Socrates had of long continuance, for it was the occasion of his Death, but begun many years before, with *Anytus* an Orator by Profeſſion, privately mantained and enriched by Leather-ſellers: He had put two of his Sons to *Socrates* to be taught, but not being pleaſed, that whilſt they were in that way, they had not learn'd ſo much, as to be able thereby to get their living; he took them from *Socrates*, and put them to that trade which himſelf was aſhamed to own; wherewith *Socrates* being much diſpleaſed in reſpect of the two Youths, whoſe Ruin he preſaged, (and truly, for they fell afterwards into Debaucheries which occaſioned it) ſpared not to reproach *Anytus* in diſcourſing to his Scholars, * telling them, 'That the Trade of dreſſing Leather 'was not fit to be ſpoken of amongſt young 'Men; for they who benefit themſelves by 'any Art, cheriſh and profeſs it, as *Acumenus* '*Phyſick*, *Damon* and *Connus* Muſick; even *A-* '*nytus*, whilſt his Sons were his Scholars, was 'not aſhamed of that which they learned, 'though it were not ſufficient to maintain 'them by pleading; but for himſelf, he gloried 'that he walkt inviſible with *Pluto*'s Helmet, or '*Gyges*'s Ring, concealing from the People the 'true means of his ſubſiſtence, which indeed 'was by dreſſing Leather, which was not juſt; 'to be aſhamed of the Trade, and not of the 'Profit; for he ought to own this, or to diſclaim 'that.

* Socratic. Epiſt. 14.

'*Anytus* (ſaith *Ælian) to anſwer this re'proach, ſtudied all occaſions and ways of re'venge; but feared the *Athenians*, doubting if 'he ſhould accuſe *Socrates*, how they would 'take it, his name being in high eſteem for 'many reſpects, chiefly for oppoſing the *Sophiſts*, 'who neither taught nor knew any ſolid Learn'ing. He † adviſed with *Melitus*, a young 'Man, an Orator, unknown to *Socrates*, deſcrib'd 'by * *Plato*, with long plain Hair, a high Noſe, 'and a thin Beard, one that for a Drachm 'might be bought into any thing, by whoſe 'Counſel * ' He begins by making trial in leſſer 'things, to ſound how the *Athenians* would en'tertain a charge againſt his Life; for to have 'accuſed him upon the very firſt, he conceived 'unſafe, as well for the reaſon already menti'oned, as left the Friends and followers of *So-* '*crates* ſhould divert the anger of the Judges 'upon himſelf, for falſly accuſing a Perſon ſo 'far from being guilty of any wrong to the 'State, that he was the only ornament thereof. 'To this end he ſuborns *Ariſtophanes*, a Co'mick Poet, whoſe only buſineſs was to raiſe 'mirth, to bring *Socrates* upon the Stage, tax'ing him with Crimes which moſt Men knew 'him free from, impertinent Diſcourſe, making 'an ill Cauſe by Argument ſeem good, intro'ducing new and ſtrange Deities, whilſt him'ſelf believed and reverenced none; hereby 'to inſinuate an ill opinion of him, even into 'thoſe who moſt frequented him. *Ariſtophanes* 'taking this Theme, interweaves it with much 'abuſive Mirth; the beſt of the *Grecians* was 'his Subject, not *Cleon*, the *Lacedæmonians*, the '*Thebans*, or *Pericles* himſelf, but a Perſon dear 'to all the Gods, eſpecially *Apollo*. At firſt '(by reaſon of the novelty of the thing, the

x *Var. hiſt.*

† *Schol. Ariſtoph.*
* *Liban.*

< *Ælian.*

'unuſual perſonating of *Socrates* upon the Stage) 'the *Athenians*, who expected nothing leſs, were 'ſtruck with wonder: Then, (being naturally 'envious, apt to detract from the beſt Perſons, 'not only of ſuch as bore Office in the Com'mon-wealth, but any that were eminent for 'Learning and Vertue) they begun to be taken 'with the *Clouds*, (ſo was the Play named) 'and cried up the Actor that perſonated *So-* '*crates* with more applauſe than ever any be'fore, giving him with many ſhouts the Victo'ry, and ſending word to the Judges, that they 'ſhould ſet down no name but that of *Ariſto-* '*phanes*. *Socrates* came ſeldom to the Theatre, 'unleſs when *Euripides* conteſted with any new 'Tragedian, there, or in the *Pyræum*, then he 'went, for he affected the Wiſdom, Goodneſs, 'and ſweetneſs of his Verſe; ſometimes *Al-* '*cibiades* and *Critias* would invite him to a Co'medy, and in a manner compel him; for he 'was ſo far from eſteeming Comedians, that 'he contemn'd them as lying, abuſive, and un'profitable; whereat they were much diſpleaſ'ed: Theſe (with other things ſuggeſted by '*Anytus* and *Melitus*) were the ground of *Ari-* '*ſtophanes* his Comedy, who, it is likely, got a 'great ſum of Money by it, they being eager 'in proſecution of their deſign, and he prepa'red by want, and malice, to receive their im'preſſion: In fine, the Play got extraordinary 'Credit, that of *Cratinus* being verified,

*The Theatre was then
Fill'd with malicious Men.*

'It being at that time the Feaſt of *Bacchus*, 'a multitude of *Grecians* went to ſee the Play: '*Socrates* being perſonated on the Stage and of'ten nam'd, (nor was it much the Players ſhould 'repreſent him, for the Potters frequently did 'it upon their Stone Juggs) the Strangers that 'were preſent (not knowing whom the Co'medy abuſed) raiſed a hum and whiſper, 'every one aſking who that *Socrates* was? which 'he obſerving (for he came not thither by 'chance, but becauſe he knew himſelf ſhould be 'abuſed in the Play, had choſen the moſt 'conſpicuous Seat in the Theatre) to put the 'Strangers out of doubt, he roſe up, and all 'the while the Play laſted, continued in that 'Poſture, (* Laughing) † one that was preſent 'aſked him if it did not vex him to ſee him'ſelf brought upon the Stage? *Not at all*, (an'ſwered he) *methinks I am at a Feaſt where 'every one enjoys me.* * This Comedy was firſt act'ed when *Iſarchus* was Archon, *Cratinus* Victor 'in the firſt year of the eighty ninth Olympiad: *Ariſtophanes* being by ſome reprehended for it, to vindicate himſelf, cauſed it to be acted again the Year following, *Amintas* being Archon, but with worſe order than at firſt.

* *Ælian. var. hiſt.* 5.
† *Plut. de educand. lib.*
* *Schol. Ariſtoph.*

* *Amipſias* alſo (another Comick Poet) derided him thus in *Tribone*.

* *Laert.*

*O Socrates, the beſt of few, the vaineſt
Of many Men; and art thou come amongſt us?
Where is thy Gown? Did not this great misfortune
Befal thee by the Leather-dreſſer's help?*

CHAP.

CHAP. X.

His Trial.

Plat. Apol.
Liban. Apsl.

* MAny years paſt ſince the firſt falling out betwixt *Socrates* and *Anytus*, during which time one continued openly reproving the other, ſecretly undermining, until at length *Anytus* ſeeing the time ſute with his deſign, procured *Melitus* to prefer a Bill againſt him to the Senate in theſe terms.

Melitus Son of *Melitus*, a *Pythean*, accuſeth *Socrates* Son of *Sophroniſcus an Alopecian*. *Socrates violates the Law, not believing the Deities which this City believeth, but introducing other new Gods. He violates the Law likewiſe in corrupting Youth; the puniſhment Death.*

† See Suidas upon that word.
* Liban. Apol. p. 644.

This Bill being preferred upon Oath (*Plato* † ἀνωμοσία) *Crito* became bound to the Judges for his appearance at the day of Trial. * Soon after *Anytus* ſent privately to him, deſiring him to forbear the mention of his Trade, and aſſuring him that he would thereupon withdraw his Action; but *Socrates* return'd him anſwer, that he would never forbear ſpeaking truth as long as he lived, that he would always uſe the ſame ſpeeches concerning him; that his accuſation was not of force enough to make him refrain from ſpeaking thoſe things which he thought himſelf before obliged to ſay

* Xenoph. Apol. & memor. 4.

* The interval of time betwixt his accuſation and trial, he imployed in his uſual Philoſophical exerciſes, not taking any care to provide his defence, for which being obſerved and queſtion'd by *Hermogenes*, Son of *Hipponicus*, 'I 'provide Apology enough (ſaith he) in conſider- 'ing and purſuing the conſtant courſe of my life; '*Hermogenes* demanding how that could be? 'becauſe (ſaith he) I never did any unjuſt act, 'which I conceive the beſt Apology: But we 'often ſee Judges (ſaith *Hermogenes*) overſway'd 'by Rhetorick, to condemn the innocent, and ac- 'quit the guilty: The truth is, (replied *Socrates*) 'going about to make my Apology, I was twice 'withheld by the *Dæmon*, whereat *Hermoge-* '*nes* wondring, Is it ſtrange (continues he) 'that God ſhould think it fit for me to dye at 'this time? hitherto no Man hath lived more 'uprightly; which as it is now my greateſt com- 'fort, ſo it was the greateſt delight to my ſelf 'and Friends; if I live longer, I know I muſt 'undergo what is proper to old Age, defects of 'hearing and ſight, ſlowneſs to apprehend, 'aptneſs to forget, how can I then be pleaſed 'to live longer and grow worſe: It is likely God 'in his love to me hath ordained that I ſhould 'die in the moſt convenient Age, and by the 'gentleſt means; for if I die by Sentence, I am 'allowed the benefit of the moſt eaſie kind of 'death; I ſhall give my Friends the leaſt trouble, 'I ſhall do nothing unſeemly before thoſe that 'are preſent, and ſhall depart ſound in Body 'and Soul; is not this very deſirable? God with 'much reaſon forbids me to make any defence: 'If I could effect it, I ſhould only ſtay longer 'to be taken away by the torment of Diſeaſes, 'and imperfections of Age, which truly *Her-* '*mogenes* I deſire not; If when I give an account 'of my actions towards God and Men, the 'Judges think fit to Condemn me, I will rather 'chuſe to die than beg *of them a Life worſe than* '*Death*. Other Friends uſed the ſame perſwaſi- 'ons to him with aſſurance of Victory. † *Lyſias* 'an excellent Orator, offered him an Oration, 'which he had written in his defence, deſiring 'him if he thought good to make uſe of it at 'his Tryal; *Socrates* peruſed it, and told him, 'that it was a good one, but not fit for him. '*Lyſias* asking how that could be? Why (ſaith 'he) may not a Garment or Shooes be rich, yet 'not fit for me? If you ſhould bring me *Sicioni-* '*an* Shooes, I would not wear them though they 'were fit for my feet, becauſe they are effemi- 'nate: He conceived the Oration to be ingeni- 'ous and eloquent, but not ſtout and manly; * for 'though it were very bitter againſt the Judges, 'yet † was it more Rhetorical than became a 'Philoſopher.

† Cicer. de O-rat. 1. Laert.
* Plut.
† Laert.

The day of Tryal being come, * *Anytus*, *Lyco*, and *Melitus* prepared to accuſe him, one in behalf of the People, the ſecond of the Orators, the laſt of the Poets: *Melitus* firſt went up into the Chair proper for that purpoſe, and there ſpoke an Oration which was in it ſelf mean enough, but withal delivered ſo unhappily and School-boy like, that ſometimes he was out with fear, and turned about to be prompted like a Player, enough to beget Laughter even in thoſe that were moſt concerned in ſo ſerious a cauſe: Part of the effect whereof ſeems to be the ſame which is thus by *Xenophon* diſperſedly deliver'd, ſome particulars whereof are confirmed by *Libanius*.

* Plat. Apol.

'That *Socrates* perſwaded his Auditors to 'contemn the receiv'd Laws, ſaying it was fit 'only for Fools to be governed by a Bean, '(meaning the ſuffrages of the Senate ſo ga- 'thered.)

'That he was intimately converſant with '*Critias* and *Alcibiades*, one moſt Covetous and 'Violent in the Oligarchy, the other Ambitious 'of Tyranny.

'That he taught Diſreſpect and Diſobedience 'to Parents, telling his Scholars he would make 'them wiſer than their Fathers, and that it was 'Lawful for any one to bind his Father if he 'were mad, and for thoſe that were the more 'Wiſe, to do as much as thoſe that were leſs 'Wiſe.

'That he taught alſo diſreſpect of all other 'Kinſmen, ſaying they were not uſeful to the 'Sick, or to the accuſed, the firſt being in more 'need of a Phyſician, the latter of an Orator; 'that the good will of unable Friends was no- 'thing worth, that only the moſt knowing per- 'ſons were moſt worthy of Honour; by which 'means he would arrogate all reſpect to himſelf.

'That he ſelected out of the Poets ſome ill 'Places, and perverted others that were not 'ſo, to excite his Friends to impious actions; 'as that of *Heſiod*,

There is no work purſued Shame :
'Tis Idleneſs that merits blame.

'He expounded, as if the Poet meant all 'acts might be committed for gain.
'That he often repeated and miſ-interpreted 'theſe words of *Homer*, as if the Poet allow- 'ed the Poor to be beaten.

*When he a Prince, or some great Person meets,
Such with soft language kindly thus he greets;
Happy above the reach of fear are you;
Sit down, and bid your followers do so too.
But of the lower sort when any speaks,
Forth these words with blows his anger breaks,
Be quiet; to thy betters wretch submit;
For action and advice alike unfit.*

Melitus (his Oration ended) came down; * next him came *Anytus* with a long malicious speech, and last of all *Lyco* with all the Artifice of Rhetorick concluded the accusation.

Socrates † would not (as was the Custom) procure an Advocate to plead for him; all the while his Accusers were speaking, he seemed to employ his Mind about nothing less: as soon as they had done, he went up into the Chair, (* in which action he observed that the Dæmon did not withhold him) and with † an angry smile begun this * unpremeditated answer,† not as a Suppliant, or guilty Person, but as if Master of the Judges themselves, with a free contumacy proceeding not from Pride, but the greatness of his Mind.

* Liban. Apol.
† Cic. Tusc. quæst. 1.
* Cic. de divinat. 1.
† Socratic. Epist. 14.
* Plat. Apol.
† Cic. Tusc. quæst. 1.
· Xenoph.

'* But I wonder first (*Athenians*) how *Me-*
'*litus* came by this knowledge, that (as he saith)
'I do not worship those Gods the City wor-
'ships? Others have seen me, (and so might
'*Melitus* if he had pleas'd) Sacrifice at common
'Festivals on the Publick Altars; How do I
'introduce new Deities when I profess to be di-
'rected in all my actions by the Voice of God?
'They who observe the Notes of Birds, or an-
'swers of Men, are guided by the voice: None
'doubts of Thunder whether it be loud or ora-
'culous: Doth not the Priestess on the Tripod
'convey to us by voice what the God delivers
'to her? and that he foreknows events, commu-
'nicating them to whom pleaseth him, all Men
'(as well as I) believe and profess: Others call
'those that foretel Events, Augurs, Sooth-
'sayers, and Diviners, I the Dæmon, and (I
'conceive) more religiously than they who af-
'cribe a divine power to Birds: That I am no
'Impostor herein, many can attest who have af-
'ked my Advice, and never found it fail. Here
there arose a murmur in the Senate, some not believing, others envying what he said, that he should surpass them in such a particular favour of the Deity: 'Let such as are incre-
'dulous hear this also to confirm their Opinion
'that I am not favour'd of the Gods; when
'*Chærephon* in the presence of many witnesses,
'question'd the *Delphian* Oracle concerning me,
'*Apollo* answered, that no Man was more free,
'more just, or more wise; (here another mur-
'mur arose amongst the Judges: he proceeded)
'Yet the same God said more of *Lycurgus* the
'*Lacedæmonian* Law-giver, that he knew not
'whether to call him a God or a Man; me he
'compared not with the Gods, though he gave
'me the priority amongst Men. But trust not
'the God herein, consider me exactly your
'selves; whom know you less a Servant to
'corporeal pleasures? whom more free? I accept
'not either rewards or gifts; who more just than
'he who so conforms himself to the present time,
'as he needs not the help of any other; who
'will say he deserves not the title of wise,
'who since he was able, never desisted to learn
'by enquiry all good possible: and that I took
'not this pains in vain, is evident in that, many
'Citizens and strangers studious of Vertue, pre-
'fer my Conversation above all others: What
'is the reason that tho' all Men know I have
'no Wealth to requite them, so many desire
'to oblige me by gifts? That I require no re-
'turn from any, yet engage so many? That
'when the City being besieg'd, every one lament-
'ed his condition, I was no more mov'd than when
'it was most flourishing? That whilst others
'lay out Money on outward things to please
'themselves, I furnish my self from within, my
'self with things that please me better? If none
'can disprove what I have said, deserve I not
'the commendations both of Gods and Men?
'And yet you *Melitus* pretend that with these
'Instructions I corrupt Youth; Every one knows
'what it is to corrupt Youth: Can you name
'but one that I of Religious have made Impi-
'ous, of modest, impudent, of frugal, prodigal,
'of sober, debauch'd, of hardy effeminate, or
'the like? But I know those, answered *Meli-*
'*tus*, whom you have perswaded to be more
'obedient to you than to their own Parents:
'That as far as concerns Instruction, replied
'*Socrates*, I confess this they know to be my
'proper Care: For their Health Men obey
'Physicians before their Parents, in Law-suits
'Counsellors before their Kindred; Do you
'not in War prefer the most experienc'd Soldi-
'ers to command before your own Allies? Yes,
'answers *Melitus*, 'tis fit we should; and do
'you think it reason, then, replies *Socrates*, if
'others are preferr'd for such things as they are
'excellent in, that because in the opinion of
'some, I have an advantage beyond others in
'educating Youth, which is the greatest Be-
'nefit amongst Men, I ought therefore to die.
'*Anytus* and *Melitus* (saith he, addressing him-
'self to the Judges) may procure my Death,
'hurt me they cannot: † To fear death is to
'seem wise, and not to be so; for it is to pre-
'tend to understand that which we understand
'not: No Man knows what death is, whether
'it be not the greatest happiness that can arrive
'to a Man, and yet all fear and shun it as if they
'were sure it were the greatest Misfortune.

† Plat. de tranqu. anim.
* Plat. de ext. fol. ad Apol.

This and more (saith *Xenophon*) was said both by himself and his Friends, but the Judges were so little pleased with his unusual manner of pleading, that † as *Plato* went up into the Chair, and began a Speech in these words, *Though I, Athenians, am the youngest of those that come up in this place,* they all cried out, *of those that go down,* which he thereupon was constrain'd to do, and they proceeding to Vote, *Socrates* was cast by 281 voices; it was the custom of *Athens*, as *Cicero* observes, when any one was cast, if the Fault were not capital, to impose a pecuniary mulct; when the Judges had voted in that manner, the guilty Person was asked the highest rate whereat he estimated his offence; the Judges willing to favour *Socrates*, propounded that demand to him, He answered 25 (or as *Eubulides* saith, 100 Drachms, nor would he suffer * his Friends, † *Plato*, *Crito*, *Critobulus*, and *Apollodorus* (who desired him to estimate it at 50 minæ

† Laert.
* Xenoph.
† Plat. Apol.

minæ, promising to undertake the sum) to pay any thing for him, saying, That to pay a Penalty, was to own an offence, and telling the Judges that (for what he stood accused) he deserved the highest honours and rewards, and daily Sustenance at the publick charge out of the *Prytanæum*, which was the greatest honour that was amongst the *Grecians*; with this answer the Judges were so exasperated, that they Condemned him to Death by eighty Votes more.

* *Xen. Apol.*

* The Sentence being past, he could not forbear smiling, and turning to his Friends, saith thus, They who have suborned false Witnesses against me, and they who have born such Testimonies, are doubtless, conscious to themselves of great Impiety and Injustice; but as for me, what should more deject me now than before I was Condemned, being nothing the more guilty; they could not prove I named any new Gods for *Jupiter*, *Juno*, and the rest, or swore by such: How did I corrupt young Men by innuring them to sufferance and frugality? Of capital offences, as Sacriledge, Theft, and Treason, my very Adversaries acquit me; which makes me wonder how I come to be condemned to dye; yet that I dye unjustly will not trouble me, it is not a reproach to me, but to those who Condemned me; I am much satisfied with the example of *Palamedes*, who suffered Death in the like manner; he is much more commended than *Ulysses* the procurer of his Death; I know both future and past times will witness, I never hurt or injured any, but on the contrary have advantaged all that conversed with me to my utmost Ability, communicating what good I could, *gratis*. This said, he went away, his carriage answerable to his words, his Eyes, Gesture, and Gate expressing much chearfulness.

CHAP. XI.

His Imprisonment.

† *Consol. ad Helv.*

SOcrates (saith † *Seneca*) *with the same resolved Look, wherewith he singly opposed the thirty Tyrants entred the Prison, and took away all ignominy from the place, which could not be a Prison whilst he was there*: Here (* being

* *Maxim. Tyr.*
† *Xen. memor.* 4.
* *Plat. Phæd.*

fetter'd by the eleven Officers) he continued † thirty days after he was Condemned upon this occasion: * The Ship which carried *Theseus* and fourteen more Persons into *Creet*; he vowed if they got safe home (as it fortuned they did) to dedicate to *Apollo*, and to send it every year with a Present to *Delos*, which Custom the *Athenians* religiously observed; before the Solemnity, they used to lustrate their City, and all Condemned Persons were repreived till it retured from *Delos*, which sometimes, the Wind not serving, was a long time. The Priest of *Apollo* began the Solemnity, by Crowning the Poop of the Ship, which happening the day before *Socrates* was Condemned, occasioned his lying in Prison so long after.

In this Interval he was visited by his Friend, with whom he past the time in dispute after his usual manner: he was often solicited by them to an escape, some of them offered to carry him away by force, which he not only refused, but derided, asking, If they knew any place out of *Attica*, whither Death could not come? * *Crito*, two days before his death,

a *Plat. Crit.*

came very early in the Morning to him to the same purpose, having by his frequent Visits and Gifts gained some Interest in the Jaylour, but finding him asleep, sat still by him, admiring in the soundness of his Sleep, the happy equality of his Mind; as soon as he waked, he told him that he came to bring sad News, if not such to him, yet to all his Friends, that the Ship would certainly be at home to morrow at furthest (some that came from *Sunium* affirming they had left it there) but that in all likelyhood it would come that day, and he should dye the next. In good time be it, answered *Socrates*, but I do not believe it will come to day; for the day following I must dye, as they say, who have the Power in their Hands; but that I shall not dye to Morrow, but the day after, I guess by a Dream I had this Night, that a Woman very beautiful, in a white Garment, saluted me by my Name, saying.

Thou, ere three days are told,
Rich Phithya shalt behold.

(The same relation, according to *Laertius*, he made to *Æschines*) this occasion *Crito* took to perswade him to save himself, which he prest with many arguments; 'That his Friends 'would be accused of Covetousness, as more 'desirous to spare their Wealth, than to redeem him; that it might be effected with little trouble and expence to them who were provided for it; that himself was rich enough to do it, or if not, *Simmias*, *Cebes*, and others would joyn with him; 'That he ought not vo-'luntarily to thrust himself into destruction, 'when he might avoid it; that he should leave 'his Children in an uncertain mean Estate; 'that it would not be construed Constancy, 'but want of Courage. Consider well these 'reasons saith he, or rather (for it is now no 'time to stand considering) be perswaded, 'what is to be done, must be done this Night, 'or it will be too late. *Socrates* answered, 'that his chearful readiness to relieve him 'was much to be esteemed, if agreeable to 'Justice, otherwise, the less just, the more 'blameable: That opinion and censure ought 'not to be regarded, but Truth and Equity; 'that wrong must not be required with wrong; 'that Faith should be kept more strictly with a 'City than with private Persons; that he 'had voluntarily subjected himself to the 'Laws of his Country, by living under their 'Government, and to Violate them at last, 'were great injustice: That by breaking Pri-'son, he should not only draw his Friends into 'many Inconveniences, but himself also in-'to many Dangers, only to live and dye in 'Exile; that in such a condition, he should be 'nothing more capable to bring up his Chil-

'dren well, but dying honestly, his Friends would take the more care of them: That whatsoever inconvenience might ensue, nothing was to be preferred before Justice; that if he should escape by Treachery, the remainder of his Life would be never the more happy, nor himself after Death better entertain'd in the next World. These things (saith he) I hear like the *Corybantian* Pipes, the sound of these Words makes me deaf to every thing else; therefore whatever you shall say to the contrary, will be to no purpose; but if you have any other Business, speak. *Crito* answering, he had not any else; as for this then (concludes he) speak no more of it, let us go the way which God points out to us.

CHAP. XII.

The time and manner of his Death.

THE time of *Socrates*'s Death is formerly touched; the Marble at *Arundel-House*, saith he, died when *Laches* was Archon, aged seventy years, which (according to *Plato*) were compleat, for he faith πλέω ἑβδομηκόντα. * *Demetrius Phalerius* saith, he died the first year of the ninety fifth Olympiad, having lived Seventy Years. † *Diodorus Siculus* avers, it was done in that Year, *Laches* being Archon.

* *Laert.*

† *Laert.*

Although there be not any thing in the *Greek* Story settled by better Authority, than the Years of *Socrates*; *Leo Allatius* with much Confidence, and little Reason, controverts the received Chronology of his Life and Death, the occasion is this; the fourteenth of the *Socratick* Epistles published by him, mentioneth an Oration of *Polycrates*, as spoken at the Arraignment of *Socrates*; but the Walls of *Athens* repaired by *Conon* six Years after the Death of *Socrates*, being spoken of in that Oration, the Epistle is thereby rendred suspicious, the Truth seems to be this: After the death of *Socrates*, it became an ordinary Theme in the Schools of Rhetorick (which was at that time much studied at *Athens*) to speak for and against *Socrates*. *Polycrates*, a Sophister, to exercise his wit, wrote an Invective: *Lysius*, a famous Orator, who died about the hundredth Olympiad, had written (as we have already said) an Apologetick, which is by the Scholiast of *Aristides* cited in answer to *Polycrates*. Apologies were in like manner written by *Plato*, * *Xenophon*, and (long after by) *Libanius*; although *Isocrates* admonished *Polycrates* of certain Errors in his Oration against *Socrates*, yet the Anachronism continued, for Chronology was not yet studied in *Athens*; and thence it is that *Plato* himself is in that respect so much reprehended by *Athenæus*, *Aristides*, *Macrobius*, and others: The Writer of the *Socratical* Epistle admits *Polycrates* as the Accuser at the Trial, and the Oration as then, and there spoken, so also doth *Hermippus* whom *Laertius* cites to the same Effect; but *Phavorinus*, a Critick of later times, when Chronology was more exact, detects the Error by Computation of

* *Memorab. lib. 1.*

times: *Allatius* will by no means have the criticism of *Phavorinus* allowed, and labours to introduce an uncertainty of the time, to the end he may perswade that *Socrates* lived beyond the reparation of the Walls of *Athens*: the great Engine wherewith he labours to demolish all that hath been asserted by the Ancients, is the Testimony of *Suidas*, who (I know not upon what Authority) saith, he lived Eighty Years: His smaller Artillery are the groundless emendation of *Meursius*, and the mistake of *Scaliger* before noted; the absurd Metachronism of the *Chronicum Alexandrinum*, which makes *Socrates* die in the one hundred and fourth Olympiad, and in the ninetieth Year of his Age; the anistoresie of the unknown Writers of *Aristotle*'s Life, who supposeth him in the seventeenth Year of his Age, to have heard *Socrates* three Years, and which is most ridiculous, the notorious Anachronisms of *Plato* must serve as irrefragable Arguments to impugn the Truth. With these proofs in the Sophistical disguise of a Dialogue, he endeavours to puzzle the unwary Reader.

The manner of his Death receive from *Plato* in the Person of *Phædo* an Eye-witness; 'Every 'day (saith he) I went with other Friends 'of his to visit him; we met in the Court 'where he was tried, it being near the Prison; 'where we entertained our selves with discourse 'till the Prison was opened, then went in unto 'him and spent many times the whole day 'with him. But that day we met sooner than 'ordinary, for the Evening before as we came 'out of the Prison, we heard the Ship was 'come from *Delos*, and thereupon we appoint-'ed to meet early the next Morning at the u-'sual place, where being come, the Porter came 'out to us, and told us that we must stay a 'while before we could be admitted, for the 'eleven Officers were there taking off his 'Fetters, having brought him word that he 'must die to day: Not long after he came 'out again, and told us we might go in, where 'when we came, we found *Socrates*'s Fet-'ters newly taken off, and *Xantippe* sitting 'by him with a Child in her Arms: She as 'soon as she saw us, burst forth into Tears, 'and cried out, Ah, *Socrates*, this is the 'last time thy Friends shall ever speak to 'thee, or thou to them. *Crito* (saith *Socrates*, 'addressing himself to him) let some body 'carry her home; whereupon some of *Crito*'s 'servants led her away exclaiming, and beat-'ing her Breast. *Socrates* who was sitting up-'on the Bed, drew up his Leg and rubbed it, 'saying the whilst, How strange a thing, Friends, 'is that which Men call Pleasure, how near 'a Kin to Pain, to which it seems so contrary? 'They arrive not indeed together, but he that 'takes one, is immediately overtaken by the 'other, as if they were tied together: If Æ-'sop had observed this, certainly he would 'have made some Fable of it, as if God wil-'ling to compose their difference, had join-'ed them by the end, not being able to make 'them absolutely one; so that whosoever hath 'one, must straight have the other also; as 'it happens to me at this time, the Pain my
Fetters

'Fetters even now gave me, is now turned to
'a kind of Pleasure, and tickles me. You have
'opportunely (said *Cebes*) put me in mind to
'ask, why since your Imprisonment (which
'you never did before) you have writ Po-
'ems, a Hymn to *Apollo*, and *Æsop*'s Fables
'rendred into Verse; many have questioned
'me about it, particularly *Euenus*; if he repeat
'this demand, what answer shall I give him?
'Tell him (answers *Socrates*) that truly I did
'it not to contend with him and his Verses,
'but to comply with a Dream (which I have
'had more than once) enjoyning me to pra-
'ctise Musick; in obedience whereunto I first
'made Verses in honour of the God whose
'Feast this was; Then, conceiving it essential
'to a Poet to write Fictions, which of my self,
'I use not, I made use of some of *Æsop*'s,
'which I had in memory, as they first came
'into fancy; tell *Euenus* this, and bid him from
'me farewel, and if he be wise, follow me, for
'it seems I must go hence to day, the *Athenians*
'have so ordered it. What is that, said *Simmias*,
'which you bid *Euenus* do? I have often con-
'versed with him, but as far as I understand
'him, he will not be at all ready to be rul'd by
'you; what, saith he, is he not a Philoso-
'pher? He seems so, answers *Simmias*; then
'he will (replied *Socrates*) and so will all
'who deserve that name; but perhaps he will
'not lay violent hands upon himself, that is
'not Lawful: And as he was speaking thus, he
'set down his Leg again to the Ground, and
'fitting so, continued all the rest of the di-
'spute. Then *Cebes* asking why, how it could
'be that it should be prohibited to ones self,
'yet that a Philosopher ought to desire to
'follow a dying Person? He answered, Men
'are the Possessions of God, would you not be
'angry if your Slave should kill himself against
'your will, and if it were in your Power pu-
'nish him? We must expect a Summons from
'God, an inevitable necessity (such as I have
'at this time) to take us hence. This is truth,
'replied *Cebes*, but what you asserted even
'now is inconsistent with it; God taking care
'of us as his Possessions, can a wise Man de-
'sire to be out of his Protection? He cannot
'think to mend his condition by freeing himself
'from so excellent a Government. *Socrates*
'seemed much pleased with the subtlety of
'*Cebes*, and turning to us said, *Cebes* is always
'inquisitive, nor will easily admit any thing:
'To me, said *Simmias*, what he hath said seems
'reason, how can wise Men endure, much
'less endeavour to part with those that are so
'much better than themselves? But *Cebes* here-
'in reflects upon you, who are so ready to
'leave us, and the Gods whom you acknow-
'ledge good Governours: You say well, an-
'swers *Socrates*, I suppose you would have
'me answer as in a Court of Judicature; by all
'means, saith *Simmias*; well then, replies he,
'I will endeavour to defend my self better a-
'gainst you than I did before the Judges: Tru-
'ly did I not believe I should go to just gods,
'and to Men better than any living, I were
'inexcusable for contemning Death; but I am
'sure to go to the Gods, very good Masters,
'and hope to meet with good Men, and am

'of good Courage, hoping that something of
'Man subsists after Death, and that it is then
'much better with the good than with the
'bad. Here *Crito* interrupting him, told him
'that he who was to administer the Poyson,
'advised him to speak little, and not heat him-
'self with dispute, for it agreed not with that
'kind of Poison, which some neglecting,
'had been constrained to take it two or three
'times: Mind him not, said *Socrates*, let him
'provide as much as may serve twice or thrice,
'if need be. Then he proceeded in a large
'Discourse to declare that the chief office of
'a Philosopher is to meditate on Death; there-
'fore he ought not to fear the approach of
'it; That as Death is the Solution of the Soul
'from the Body, so is it the office of a Philo-
'sopher to free the Soul from Corporeal
'Affections; That if we understand the bet-
'ter, the more the Soul is disengaged from
'Sense, we shall understand most perfectly
'when she is wholly freed from the Body by
'Death, which Perfection of Knowledge is the
'sole end of Philosophy.

This part of the Discourse ended, *Cebes* occasions the renewing of it by the desiring him
to prove the immortality of the Soul, which
he doth first from the necessary succession of
Generation and Corruption as contraries, the
ground of the *Pythagorean* Transmigration; next
from the Soul's manner of reasoning, which
being only by reminiscence argues it had a
Being before the Body (when it had perfect
knowledge of those Ideas which upon occasion of sensible objects it recovers) and consequently shall subsist after it; much more is
spoken by *Plato* under his name, whereof almost all is manifestly *Plato*'s own, nor is it
possible to select that which is not from the
rest; the conclusion of his Discourse (as contracted by *Cicero*) was, 'That there are two *Tusc. quæst. pag.*
'ways, and a twofold course of Souls when 127.
'they go out of the Body: For such as have
'defiled themselves with humane Vices given
'over to Pleasures wherewith they are blind-
'ed, according as they are polluted with do-
'mestick Sins, or have used inexpiable deceits
'to wrong the Publick, take a by-way seclu-
'ded from the Counsel of the Gods: But they
'who have preserved themselves intire and
'chaste from the least Contagion of their Bodies,
'having always withdrawn themselves from
'them, and in humane flesh imitated the Lives
'of Gods, find a ready way open for them,
'leading them to those from whom they came:
'and as Swans are (not without reason) sa-
'cred to *Apollo*, because they seem to have
'learnt Divination from him, whereby foresee-
'ing the good that is in Death, they dye with
'Songs and delight; so ought all good and * *Plat.*
'knowing Persons to do: * Let every one
'therefore prepare for this Journey against the
'time that Fate shall call him away; You *Sim-
'mias*, *Cebes*, and the rest here present shall go
'at your appointed Hour, me Fate now sum-
'mons (as the Tragedian saith) and perhaps
'it is time that I go into the Bath, for I think
'it best to wash before I take the Poison, that
'I may save the Women the Labour of washing
'me when I am dead.

When

'When he had made an end of speaking, 'Crito asked him what Directions he would 'leave concerning his Sons and other Affairs, 'and if they could do any thing that might 'be acceptable to him? I desire no more '(faith he) than what I have often told you, 'if you take care of your selves, whatsoever 'you do will be acceptable to me and mine, 'though you promise nothing; if you neg- 'lect your selves and Vertue, you can do no- 'thing acceptable to us, though you pro- 'mise never so much; that, answered Crito, 'we shall observe; but how will you be Bu- 'ried? as you think good, faith he, if you can 'catch me, and that I give you not the slip, 'then with a Smile applying himself to us, I 'cannot perswade Crito, faith he, that I am 'any thing more than the Carkass you will a- 'non behold, and therefore he takes this care 'for my Enterrment; it seems that what 'even now I told him that as soon as I have ta- 'ken the Poison, I shall go to the Joys of the 'Blessed, hath been to little purpose; he was 'my Bail, bound to the Judges for my Appear- 'ance, you must now be my Sureties to him that 'I am departed; let him not say that Socrates is 'carried to the Grave, or laid under Ground, 'for know, dear Crito, such a mistake were a 'wrong to my Soul; be not dejected, tell the 'World my Body only is Buried, and that af- 'ter what manner thou pleasest. This said, he 'arose and retired into an inward Room, ta- 'king Crito with him, leaving us discoursing 'upon our own Misery, shortly to be deprived 'like Orphans of so dear a Father. After his 'Bathing, came his Wife and the other Wo- 'men of his Family with his Sons, two of 'them Children, one a Youth; when he had 'taken Order with these about his Domestick 'Affairs, he dismist them and came out to us.

'It was now Sun-set (for he had staid long 'within) when the Officer entred, and after a 'little pause said, I have not, Socrates, observ'd 'that Carriage in you which I have found in 'others, but as I thought you the most generous 'the mildest and best of all Men that ever came 'into this place, so I now see you hate me, not 'for that whereof others are the cause: you 'know the Message I bring, farewell; bear what 'you cannot remedy: with that he departed 'weeping, and fare thee well, (said Socrates) 'I will: how Civil is this Man? I found him 'the same all the time of my Imprisonment, he 'would often Visit me, Discourse with me, used 'me always Courteously, and now see how kind- 'ly he weeps for me: but come, Crito, let us do 'as he bids us, if the Poison be ready, let it be 'brought in; the Sun is yet scarce Set, answers 'Crito: others take it late after a plentiful Sup- 'per and full Cups; make not so much haste, 'there is time enough; he replies, they who do 'so think they gain time, but what shall I gain 'by drinking it late? only deceive my self as 'covetous of life, and sparing of that which is 'no longer mine; pray let it be as I say; then 'Crito sent one of the Attendants, who imme- 'diately returned, and with him the Man that 'was to administer the Poison, bringing a Cup 'in his hand, to whom Socrates, prethee honest 'friend (for thou art well verst in these busi-

'nesses) what must I do? nothing, said he, but 'as soon as you have drunk, walk till you 'find your Legs begin to fail, then lie down, 'and in so saying, he gave him the Cup, Socra- 'tes took it chearfully, not changing either 'Countenance or Colour, and looking pleasantly 'upon him, demanded whether he might spill 'any of it in libation, who answered, he had 'made no more than would just serve; yet, 'faith Socrates, I may pray to God, and will, 'that my passage hence may be happy, which 'I beseech him to grant, and in the same in- 'stant drank it off easily without any distur- 'bance; many of us who till now had refrained 'from Tears, when we saw him put the Cup 'to his Mouth and drink off the Poison, were 'not able to contain any longer; which Socrates 'observing, friend, (faith he) what mean you? *for this reason I sent away the Women lest they* *should be so unquiet: I have heard we should die* *with gratulation and applause, be quiet then and* *take it patiently*; 'These words made us with 'shame suppress our Tears; when he had walk- 'ed a while, perceiving his Legs to fail, he lay 'down on his back as the Executioner directed 'him, who looking on his feet pinched them 'hard, asked him if he felt it, he answer- 'ed no, he did the like to his legs, and shewing 'us how every part successively grew cold and 'stiff, told us when that chilness came at his 'heart he would die; not long after he spake these his last words, *O Crito, I owe Æsculapius a Cock, pay it, neglect it not*. It shall be done, 'faith Crito; will you have any thing else? He 'made no answer, lay still a while, then stretch- 'ed himself forth; with that the Executioner 'uncovered him, his Eyes were set, Crito closed 'them. This (faith Plato) was the end of 'the best, the wisest, and most just of Men: 'A Story, which Cicero professeth, he never 'read without Tears.

Aristotle saith, that a *Magus* coming from *Syria* to *Athens*, not only reprehended *Socrates* for many things, but foretold him also that he should die a violent Death. *Laertius* closeth his Life with this Epigram,

Drink Socrates *with* Jove, *next whom enthron'd,*
By Gods, and Wisdom's self as wisest own'd.
Thee, the Athenians *gave a Pois'nous draught,*
But first the same they from thy Lips had quaft

CHAP. XIV.

What hapned after his Death.

HE was Buried with Tears and much So- lemnity, (contrary to his own direction) by his Friends, amongst whom † the excessive †*Plut. de cot.* Grief of *Plato* is observed by *Plutarch*, and *mor.* the Mourning Habit of *Isocrates*: As soon as *Plut. vit. dec.* they had performed that last Service, fearing *Orat.* the Cruelty of the Tyrants, they stole out of the City, the greater part to *Megara* to *Euclid*, where they were kindly received, † the rest to †*Libar.* other Parts.

† Soon after, a *Lacedæmonian* Youth, who had never more acquaintance with *Socrates* than what Fame gave him, took a Journey to *Athens*, intending to become his Disciple; being come as far as the City Gates, and ready to enter, with Joy, to be so near the end at which he aimed, instead of *Socrates*, he meets there the news of his Death, whereat he was so troubled, that he would not go within the City Gates, but enquiring the place where he was Buried, went thither, and breaks forth into a Passionate Discourse, accompanied with many tears, to the enclosed dead Body; when night was come, he fell asleep upon the Sepulchre; the next Morning, affectionately kissing the Dust that lay upon it, and with much Passion taking leave of the place, he returned to *Megara*.

Suidas tells a like Story, (for that there were more examples than one in this kind, *Libanius* implies) of a *Chian* named *Cyrsas*, who coming to *Athens* to hear *Socrates*, went to his Tomb, and slept there, to whom *Socrates* appeared in a Dream, and Discoursed with him; with which only satisfaction he went directly home again.

† By these Accidents the *Athenians* were awakened into a Sense of their Injustice, considering they were obnoxious to the Censure of the *Lacedæmonians* by extraordinary Crimes, whose Children were so Affectionate to the Philosophers whom they had Murdered, as to take such long Journeys to see *Socrates*, whom they would not keep when he was with them; hereat they became so exasperated, that they were ready to tear those wicked Men that were the occasion of his Death piecemeal with their Teeth, the whole City cried out, they disclaimed the Act, and that the Authors thereof ought to be put to Death, † *Antisthenes* furthered their Rage by this means, *Some young Men of* Pontus *invited to* Athens *by the Fame of* Socrates, *met with* Antisthenes, *who carried them to* Anytus, *telling them he was much wiser than* Socrates; *whereupon those that were present, with much Indignation, turned* Anytus *out of the City*: thence he went to *Heraclea*, where some say the Citizens also Expelled him, * others that they Stoned him to Death: *Melitus* was by the *Athenians* Condemned and put to Death * others affirm the like of all his Accusers without Tryal, & * *Plutarch*, that they so much hated them, as they would not suffer them to kindle fire at their Houses, they would not answer them any question, they would not wash with them, but threw away the water they had touched as impure, until unable to brook this Hatred, they hanged themselves.

In further Testimony of their Penitence, they called home his Friends to their former Liberty of Meeting, they forbad publick Spectacles of Games and wrestling for a time, they caused his Statue, made in Brass by *Lysippus*, to be set up in the *Pompeum*, and (a Plague ensuing, which they imputed to the injustice of this Act) they made an Order that, that no Man should mention *Socrates* publickly, or on the Theatre, that so they might forget what they had done: *Euripides* (restrained by this Order from doing it directly) Reproached them overtly in a Tragedy, named *Palamedes* (in whom he alluded to *Socrates*) particularly in these Verses.

A Philomele ne'r Mischief knew;
Is Slain, alas! is Slain by you.

At which words, all the Spectators understanding they were meant of *Socrates*, fell a weeping.

The Death of this sole Person (saith † *Eunapius*) brought a general Calamity upon the City; for it may easily be Collected by Computation of Times, that from thenceforward the *Athenians* did nothing Considerable, but the City by degrees Decayed, and with it all *Greece*.

CHAP. XV.

Of his Person and Vertues.

AS to his Person, he was a very unhandsome, of a Melancholy Complexion, Bald, b a flat Nose, Eyes sticking out, a severe down-cast look, difficult in Speech, and d too concise, his Language rough and careless, but more efficacious than all the Eloquence of *Themistocles*, *Pericles*, or any other; so acute, that he could maintain either side in any Question, therefore is Reproached by *Aristophanes*, as having two Languages, whereof one was to defend Wrong; fervent in Dispute, often so Transported, that he would Beat himself, and Tear his Beard, to the Derision of the standers by, which he took quietly: Patient to be redargued; e sometimes he covered his Face in Discourse, that he might not be Diverted by any Object of Sight: f his Constitution strong and hardy, g which he preserved such, by taking diligent care of his Health; h well bearing Cold, Hunger, and upon occasion, Excess, of Wine without disturbance: i his Habit the same in Winter as in Summer, having but one Garment a year; (k) no Shooes, his Diet sparing. In fine, his countenance promised so little, that (l) *Zopyrus* a Physiognomist who undertook to discover the dispositions of Men by their looks, said he was stupid, because there were obstructions in his jugular parts; adding, he was given to Women and many other vices; whereat *Alcibiades*, and other friends of his that were present, knowing him free from those imputations, fell alaughing; but *Socrates* justified his skill, answering, he was by nature prone to those vices, but supprest his inclinations by reason, whenc (m) *Alcibiades* used to say, he resembled the image of *Silenus* ((n) as he did indeed in his countenance, baldness, and flat nose) carved on the outside of little Boxes, fitting, and playing on a Pipe; for as those Boxes within held images of the Gods, so was he adorned with chastity, integrity, and all inward beauty, ravished, as o *Plutarch* saith, with a Divine Zeal to Vertue, in all kinds whereof *Xenophon*, *Laertius* and others, assert these Instances.

p *He was so wise, that he never erred in judging betwixt better and worse, nor thereto needed any other help:* Yet he constantly professed, that he only knew that he knew nothing: q for which Reason he was by the Oracle of *Apollo* at *Delphi*, declared of all Men the most Wise in this manner to *Charephon*, many witnesses being present;

> [a] *Wise* Sophocles, *wiser* Euripides,
> But *wisest* of all Men is Socrates.

[a] *Schol. Aristoph.*

Apollo (saith *Cicero*) conceiving the only wisdom of Mankind to consist in not thinking themselves to know those things whereof they are ignorant. [c] This Oracle, though he were nothing exalted with it himself, procured him much envy.

[b] *Academ. quæst. 1.*

[c] *Laert.*

[u] *He was so Religious, that he never did any thing, without advising, first with the Gods,* [w] *never was known to attempt or speak any Impiety.* [x] He bare a Reverence to the Gods, not Humane, but such as transcended the greatest Fear: [y] Some say it was out of his great Reverence to the Divinity that he used to Swear by a [z] (Cock) a Dog, and a Plain Tree, (under which they used to sit) though it were interpreted Atheism.

[u] *Xen. memor. 4. pag. 818.*
[w] *Xen. mem. 1. p. 710.*
[x] *Plut. Philib.*
[y] *Suid.*
[z] *Schol. Aristoph.*

[a] *He was Constant, and a lover of the Publick Good, as appears in his acquitting the ten Captains, in his denying thirty Tyrants to fetch Leon in, his refusing to escape out of Prison, and Reproving such as grieved for his Death.* [b] *Xantippe* used to say, that when the State was oprest with a thousand Miseries, he always went abroad and came home with the same look, [c] never more chearful, or more troubled, for he bore a mind smooth and chearful upon all occasions, far remote from Grief, and above all fear: In his declining Age, falling sick, he was asked by one that came to visit him, how he did? very well (saith he) either way, if I live, I shall have more Emulation, if I die, more Praise.

[a] *Laert.*
[b] *Elian. Cic. Tusc. quæst. 3. Offic. 1.*
[c] *Plin. 7. 19.*

[d] *He was so Temperate, that he never preferred that which is pleasant before that which is wholsome.* He never did eat more then Appetite (which was his Sauce) made delightful; all drink was pleasing to him, because he never drank but when he was thirsty, and then with such Temperate Caution, that [e] he poured out the first draught of Water upon the Ground, and if he were at any time invited to a Feast, he, which to others is very difficult, with much ease took care not to eat more than consisted with his health, [f] whereof he was very careful, because the Exercises of the Soul depend thereon, and in order thereto, used to walk constantly before Meals, whereupon being asked by one that observed it, what he did? I get Broth, saith he, for my Supper. To this Temperance it is imputed, though [*] *Athens* were often in his time visited with the Pestilence, he alone escaped it.

[d] *Xenoph. mem. 4. 818.*
[e] *Plut.*
[f] *Xen. mem. 1. p. 712.*
[*] *Elian. 13.*

[†] *He was so frugal, that how little soever he had, it was always enough.* [h] Wanting the means to live splendidly, he taught not anxiously how to acquire more, but how to accommodate his manner of Life to that which he had, [i] wherewith he was so contented, that he affirmed himself to come nearest the Gods, because he wanted least. Seeing the great variety of things exposed to Sale, he would say to himself, how many things there are that I need not; and often had in his Mouth these Verses.

[†] *Xenoph. mem. 711. Liban. 1.*
[i] *Laert.*

> Purple, which Gold and Gems adorn,
> Is by Tragedians to be worn.

Alcibiades ambitiously munificent, sent him many great Presents; *Xantippe* admiring their value, desired him to accept them: We, (answered *Socrates*) will contest in Liberality with *Alcibiades*, not accepting, by a kind of munificence what he hath sent us.

[Ælian. 9.]

[k] To the same, who offered him a large plot of Ground to Build an House upon: And if I wanted shoos, (saith he) would you give me Leather to make them? but deserve I not to be derided if I accepted it?

[k] *Laert.*

[l] He slighted *Archelaus* King of *Macedonia*, and *Scopas*, Son of *Cranonias*, and *Eurilocus*, Son of *Larisæus*, not accepting their Money, nor going to them. *Archelaus* sending to him to desire his Company; he said, he would not go to one, from whom he should receive benefits, which he could not equal with return. [n] To *Perdiccas*, who demanded why he would not come to him, he answered, lest I die the most ignoble Death; that is, lest I receive a Benefit which I cannot requite.

[l] *Laert.*
[m] *Senec. de benefic. 5. 6.*
[n] *Anton. vit. lib. 11.*

Coming home late one night from a Feast, some wild young men knowing of his return, lay in wait for him, attired like Furies, with Vizards and Torches, whereby they used to affright such as they met; *Socrates* as soon as he saw them, nothing troubled, made a stand, and fell to questioning them, according to his usual manner, as if he had been in the *Lyceum*, or *Academy*.

[Elian. 6.]

[o] *He despised those that Cavilled at him*. [p] Being told that such an one had reviled him behind his back: Let him beat me, saith he, whilst I am not by: And that another spoke ill of him: He hath not yet learnt, said he, to speak well.

[o] *Laert.*
[p] *Stob. 71.*
[p] *Laert.*

[q] Being kicked by an insolent young fellow, and seeing those that were with him much incensed, ready to pursue him; he said, what if an Ass kick me, would you have me kick again, or sue him? but the Fellow escaped not unpunished, for every one Reproached him for this Insolence, and called him the Reviler, so that at last for Vexation, he Hanged himself.

[q] *Plut. de educ. liber.*

Another striking him a Box on the Ear, he said no more, but that it was hard a Man knew not when to go abroad with a Helmet.

[Seneca de ira.]

Another fell upon him with much Violence, which he endured without the least disturbance, suffering him to vent his Anger, which he did so long, till he made his Face all swelled and brused.

[D. Basil.]

Whensoever he perceived himself to grow incensed with any of his Friends,

[Plut. de ira, cohib.]

> Before the Storm arose,
> He to the Harbour goes.

He used to moderate his Voice, to look smilingly and moderately upon them, reserving himself untainted with Passion, by recourse to the contrary.

[r] He taught not such as conversed with him to be Covetous, for he took no Money of his Scholars, therein expressing his own Liberality.

[r] *Xenoph. mor. pag. 712.*

Hunger

Hunger or Want could never force him to flatter any: Yet was he very complaisant and facete in Company: as he one day openly at Dinner reproved one of his Friends something harshly, *Plato* said to him, had not this been better told in private? *Socrates* immediately answered, and had not you done better, if you had told me so in private? being demanded what Countriman he was? He answered, neither of *Athens*, nor *Greece*, but of the World. Sometimes he would Feast in a fine Robe, as *Plato* describes him, and when the time allowed, learned to Sing, saying, it was no shame to learn any thing which one knew not: He also Danced every day, conceiving that Exercise healthful; nor was he ashamed to play with little Children.

He was so just, that he never in the least wronged any Man, but on the contrary, benefited all such as conversed with him, as much as he could.

His Continence was Invincible: He despised the Beauty of *Alcibiades*, derided *Theodota* and *Califte*, two eminent Courtezans of that time.

He took great delight in the Conversation of good Men; to such he communicated whatsoever he knew; with them he studied the writings of the ancient wise men, selecting what was good out of them, (which confirms what was said before in the life of *Solon*, that Moral Philosophy was commenced by the Sophy) and esteemed this mutual friendship which he contracted with them above all Treasure. Towards this his outward endeavour was so affected and desired by them, as much as he affected and desired them.

CHAP. XVI.
His Wives and Children.

HE had two Wives, the first *Xantippe*, a Citizens Daughter of *Athens*, as *Theodoret* affirms, who adds, that she was Dishonest before he Married her, even with himself, besides others: *Athenæus* also saith, that after he was Married, he lent her to a Friend, and that *Alcibiades* lay with her: But *Aristoxenus*, and *Porphyrius*, from whom these Aspersions are derived, have been noted of too much malignity, to be of any Authority.

She was (according to the Character *A. Gellius* gives her) Curst, Froward, Chiding and Scolding always both day and night, and for that reason he chose her, as he profest to *Antisthenes*, from observing, that they who would be excellent in Horsemanship, chose the roughest Horses, knowing, if they are able to manage them, they may easily Rule others: He, desirous to use much conversation with Men, took her to Wife, knowing, if he could bear with her, he might easily converse with all Men. To *Alcibiades*, who said, her Scolding was intolerable, he profest it was nothing to him, being used to it, like such as live in the continual noise of a Mill: Besides, saith he, cannot you endure the cackling of Hens? but they, answered *Alcibiades*, bring me Eggs and Chickens: and my *Xantippe*, replies *Socrates*, Children.

Of her Impatience, and his Sufferance, there are several instances; one day before some of his Friends, she fell into the usual Extravagancies of her Passion, whereupon he not answering any thing, went forth with them, but was no sooner out at the door, when she running up into the Chamber, threw down Water upon his head, whereat turning to his Friends, did I not tell you saith he, that after somuch Thunder we should have Rain?

Another time she pull'd his Cloak off from his Shoulders in the open *Forum*; some friends present counselled him to beat her: Yes, saith he, that whilst we two fight, you may all stand by, and cry, well done *Socrates*, to him *Xantippe*.

To some other Story of the same kind, *Antoninus* alludes in these words: *how Socrates looked when he was fain to gird himself with a Skin*, *Xantippe* having taken his Cloaths away, and carried them forth with her, and what he said to his Friends, who out of a modest respectfulness, went back, seeing him so attired.

Having brought *Euthydemus* from the *Palæstræ* to Dine with him, *Xantippe* running to the Table, Angry, overturned it; *Euthydæmus* much troubled, rose up, and would have gone away, when *Socrates*: did not a Hen the other day saith he, the very same thing at your House, yet I was not angry thereat?

Alcibiades having sent him a curious Marchpane, *Xantippe* (furiously, as her Manner was) threw it out of the Basket, and trod upon it, whereat *Socrates* laughing, *and shall not you* (saith he) *lose your share in it*?

Another time she offered to go to a publick Show, attired undecently; take heed, said he, you be not rather the Spectacle than the Spectator.

With reason thereof he said, I had three Evils, Grammar, Poesie, and an ill Wife; two I have shaken off, but my ill Wife I cannot.

His other Wife was named *Myrto*, Niece to *Lysimachus* Daughter of *Aristides*, not the Just, as *Laertius*, and from him *Suidas* affirms, but another of that name, the third from him, as is observed by *Athenæus*, for the two Daughters of *Aristides* the Just, could not but be of great Age before the 77th Olympiad, wherein *Socrates* was born, long before which time *Aristides* died an Old Man in Exile; for that *Themistocles* died the second year of the 77th Olympiad is certain, and as *Æmilius Probus* affirms, *Aristides* died four years before *Themistocles* was Banished *Athens*, hereupon *Plutarch* more cautiously calls her not the Daughter, but Niece of *Aristides*.

Some, because *Xantippe* (as is manifest from *Plato*) out-lived him, believe he was first Married to *Myrto*, but that he had both these Wives at the same time, which is attested by *Demetrius Phalereus*, *Aristoxenus* (to whom *Athenæus* saith, that *Aristotle* gave the ground) *Calisthenes* and *Porphyrius*: whence *Aristippus* in his Epistle to his Daughter *Myrto*, advised her to go to *Athens*, and above all to honour *Xantippe* and *Myrto*, and to live with them as he with *Socrates*.

The occasion, whereupon the *Athenians*, who from the time of *Cecrops* had strictly observed single Marriage, allowed bigamy, in the time of *Socrates*, was this; In the second year of the 87 Olympiad, and the third of the 88. *Athens* was Visited extreamly with the Pestilence, which attended by War and Famine, occasioned so great a scarcity of Men, that they made an Edict it might be Lawful for any that would to take two Wives. *Euripides* made use of this Indulgence, and that *Socrates* also did so, is attested by *Satyrus* the peripatetick, and *Hieronymus* the *Rhodian*, who Recorded the Order; to which *Athenæus* imputes the silence of the Comick Poets in this particular, who omitted no grounds of Reproach. *Plutarch* implies, that he took her out of Charity, for she was a Widow [g] (without any Portion or Dowry) extreamly in want.

[g] *Laert.*

[h] *Theodoret.*

[h] *Porphyrus* reports, that when these two (*Xantippe* and *Myrto*) quarrell'd, they would at last fall both upon *Socrates*, and beat him, because he stood by and never parted them, but laughed as well when they fought with him, as with one another.

By *Xantippe* he had a Son, named *Lamprocles*, who could not brook her impatience so well as his Father, and being vex'd by her into Disobedience, was reclaim'd by *Socrates*; he died young, as may be gathered from *Plutarch*, who saith, *Timarchus* of *Chæronea*, dying very young, desired earnestly of *Socrates* that he might be Buried near his Son *Lamprocles*, who died but few days before, being his dear Friend, and of the same Age. It appears from *Plato*, that he had more Sons by her, for in his Apology he mentions three, two grown Men, the other a Child, which seems to be the same, brought by *Xantippe* to him in Prison the day of his Death, and as *Plutarch* describes it, held in her Lap.

By *Myrto* he had two Sons: the eldest *Sophroniscus*, the youngest *Menedemus*, or *Menexenus*, tho' some say he had *Menedemus* by *Xantippe*.

CHAP. XVII.

His Scholars and Auditors.

De Orator. lib. 3.

WHereas (saith *Cicero*) many *springing from* Socrates *by reason that out of his several various Disputes diffused every where, one laid hold of one thing, another of another; there were some, as it were, so many several Families differing amongst themselves, much disjoyned and disagreeing; yet all these Philosophers would be called, and conceived themselves to be* Socraticks: *Of these were.*

Plato, *from whom came* Aristotle *and* Xenocrates, *the first taking the name of* Peripatetick, *the other of* Academic.

Antisthenes, *who chiefly affected the Patience and Hardiness in* Socrates *his discourse, from whom came first the* Cynics, *then the* Stoicks.

Aristippus, *who was more delighted with his more voluptuous disputations, from him sprung the* Cyrenaick *Philosophy.*

Others there were who likewise called themselves Socraticks, *but their Sects by the strength and Arguments of the former are broken and quite extinct: such were*

Phædo, *an Elean, who instituted a particular School, from him called* Eliack, *which afterwards was called* Eretriack, *from* Menedemus, *who taught at* Eretria, *from him* Pyrrho, *thence the* Pyrrhonians.

Euclid *of* Megara, *institutor of the* Megarick *School, so named from* Clinomachus *his Disciple called the Dialectick, ending in* Zeno *the* Citian, *who introduced the* Stoick.

The Herillians *are named also, as a Scot that would be called* Socratick. To these recited by *Cicero*, *Suidas* adds

Bryso *of* Heraclea, *who together with* Euclid *invented disputative Logick.*

Theodorus *sirnamed the Atheist, who invented a peculiar Sect called* Theodorean, *the Opinion which he taught was* ἀδιαφορία, *indifference.*

Other Disciples of *Socrates* there were, who followed his Philosophy, not appropriating out of it any particular Sect, and therefore most properly deserve the Title of *Socraticks*, such are *Crito*, *Chærephon*, *Xenophon*, *Æschines*, *Simias*, *Cebes*, *Glauco*, and *Terpsion*.

The last kind of his Auditors were those who made no profession of Philosophy, of whom were

Critias and *Alcibiades*, who afterwards proved the most Ambitious Spirits of the *Athenians*, but it was discovered in neither whilst they conversed with *Socrates*, either that their youth was not capable of expressing their Vice, or that they cunningly complied (as *Xenophon* conjectures) with *Socrates*, in hopes of being by his conversation enabled to manage their former designs, which as soon as they attempted they left off their Friendship with *Socrates*. *Critias* fell from him and converted his affection into hate, because he reproved his Love to *Euthydemus*; *Alcibiades* naturally dissolute, was reclaimed by *Socrates*, and continued such whilst he conversed with him, He was of Form so exquisite as gave occasion to some to calumniate the friendship betwixt him and *Socrates*, to which effect *Aristoxenus* is cited by *Laertius* and *Athenæus*, and some verses of *Aspasia* by the latter; his Vindication we refer to *Plato* and *Xenophon*.

Of *Socrates* his Instructions to *Alcibiades* there are these instances.

[b] He told him he was nothing of what a Man ought to be, that he had no advantage by the greatness of his Birth above an ordinary Porter; whereat *Alcibiades* much troubled, with tears besought him to instruct him in Virtue, and to reform his Vices.

[b] *Cicer. Tusc. quæst. Plat. conviv. Plutarch.*

[c] Perceiving *Alcibiades* to be exceeding proud of his Riches and Lands, he shewed him a Map of the World, and bad him find *Attica* therein; which done, he desired that he would shew him his own Lands, he answered, that they were not there. Do you boast, replies *Socrates*, of that which you see is no (considerable) part of the Earth?

[c] *Ælian. 3. 28.*

[d] *Alcibiades* being by reason of his youth bashful and fearful to make an Oration to the People, *Socrates* thus encouraged him, Do you not esteem (saith he) that Shoomaker (naming him) an inconsiderable Fellow? *Alcibiades* assenting; and so likewise (continues he) that Crier and that Tent-maker. *Alcibiades* granting this, doth not, saith he, the *Athenian* Common-wealth consist of these? if you contemn them single, fear them not in an Assembly. To these add

[d] *Ælian. 2. 1*

e The four Sons of *Crito* the Philosopher; the eldest *Critobulus* [f] exceeding handsome and rich, but by *Socrates* (who valued his own Estate at five minæ) [g] demonstrated to be poorer than himself.

[e] *Laert. vit. Crit.*
[f] *Macro. Saturn. 7. 3:*
[g] *Xenoph. mem.*

The

PART III.   SOCRATES.   99

h Xenoph. mem. The second *Hermogenes*, [h] who falling into Poverty, *Socrates* perswaded *Diodorus* his friend to entertain.

i Xenoph. mem. 4. p. 786. The third *Epigenes*, a young Man of an infirm Body, whom *Socrates* advised to study his own health, as that wherein consisted the well-being and knowledge of his Mind.

The Youngest *Crossippus*.

ἴτα μαθη- Of Poets, *Euripides* (as the Writer of his Life τὴς ἐν τοῖς affirms) and *Euenus*.
ῥητορικοῖς, Σωκράτης δὲ ἐν τοῖς ἠθικοῖς καὶ φιλοσοφικοῖς.

k Ὡς ἀναγι- νωσκόμενον, μὴν οὐχ ὅλον (read εὔκολον, to which effect also Plutarch) νομίζε- θαι, χαλεπὸν δ᾽ ἐνεστκέναι Of Orators *Lysias*, eminent in that kind [k] easie to be understood, hard to be imitated, he came to *Athens* in the second year of the 82d. Olympiad. *Lysis*, whom of refractory he made pliant, and *Isocrates*, of whom when very young, *Socrates* presaged great things. In the number of his Scholars and Auditors were also ζηλοῦν πειραμένοις. *Dion. Halicarn. in Critio.*

l Plat. Apol.
m Xenoph. mem. 3. p.772. & p. 774. Laert.
[l] *Adimantus* and [m] *Glauco* Sons to *Aristo*, Brothers to *Plato*: and *Charmides* Son of *Glauco*. *Glauco* before he was twenty years old had taken upon him to be an Orator, and aimed at some great Office in the Common-wealth, not to be wrought off from this fancy which made him every where appear Ridiculous, until address'd by some Friends to *Socrates*, who made him acknowledg his own Error and Ignorance of that which he had undertaken. On the contrary, his Son *Glauco* of excellent Parts, fit for any Office in the Common-wealth, yet timerously shunning all publick Affairs, was by *Socrates* induced to undertake the Magistracy.

n Plat. Apol. [n] *Nicostratus* Son of *Theodotides* and his Brother *Theodotus*.

o Plat. ibid. [o] *Æantodorus*, and his Brother *Apollodorus*. *Lysanias*, Father of *Æschines*.

p Xenoph. mem. 2. p. 743. [p] *Chærecrates*, brother to *Chærephon*, betwixt whom there was a great Quarrel, but reconcil'd by *Socrates*.

q Plat. Apol. [q] *Paralus*, Son of *Demodocus* whose Brother was *Theages*.

r Plat. Apol. [r] *Antipho*, a Cephisiean, Father of *Epigenes*: with whom he discourses of self-sufficience, teaching *gratis*, and of veracity in [s] *Xenophon*.

s Memor. 1. p. 729, 731, 732. *Eumares* a Phliasian, and *Xenomedes*, an Athenian. Besides these, there are with whom *Socrates* discoursed and instructed.

t Xenoph. mem. 1. p. 725. [t] *Aristodemus* firnamed *the little*, who would not Sacrifice, Pray, or use Divination, but derided all such as did, was by *Socrates* convinced.

u Xen. mem. 2. [u] *Aristarchus* troubled that he had a charge of Kindred lying upon him, by *Socrates* converted to a willing Liberality towards them.

Xen. mem. 2. *Eutherus*, who returning from Travel, his Lands taken away, his Father having left him nothing, chose rather to follow a Trade than to apply himself to Friends, but diverted by *Socrates*.

Xen. mem. 2. *Diodorus*, whom *Socrates* perswaded to take *Hermogenes*.

Xen. mem. 4. *Euthydemus*, who had collected many Sentences of Poets and Sophists, thought he excelled all his equals, and hoped no less of his superiours, who was by *Socrates* constrained to acknowledge his own Error and Ignorance, and departed much troubled.

Hippias, an *Elean*, with whom *Socrates* di- *Xen. mem. 4.* scoursed of Justice.

[w] *Nicomedes*, *Pericles*, and *Iphicrates*, with *w Xenoph.* whom he discoursed concerning the Office of a General. [x] Into the last he infused Courage, *x Laert.* by shewing him the Cocks of *Midas* [y] bristling *y Περισσό- τερόν ἐστι quod gallinas Indicas facere videmus aliquando tumentes & caudam pandentes.* against those of *Callias*.

[z] *Theætetus* disputing of Knowledge, he dismist, Inspired as it were with Divine Wisdom.

[a] *Euthyphron* who intended to accuse his *mentes & cau-* own Father, he disswaded.

With *Pharrhasius* a Painter, *Clito* a Statuary, *z Plat. Laert.* and *Pistias* an Armourer: He disputes in [b] *Xe-* *a Plat. Laert.* *nophon* concerning their several Arts. *b Mem. 3.*

CHAP. XVII.

His Writings.

THey who affirm that *Socrates* writ nothing (as *Cicero*, *Plutarch*, *Dion*, *Chrysostom*, *Aristides*, *Origen*, and others) mean in respect to his Philosophy, in which kind he never wrote any thing himself, but what he discoursed was committed to writing by *Xenophon*, *Plato* and others of his Scholars. Hence the Works of *Plato* (particularly *Phædo*) went under the name of *Socrates*, and are so cited by *Aristotle*; But that some things were written by *Socrates* himself, is evident from those who affirm.

[c] He writ, together with *Euripides*, and aided *c Laert.* him in making Tragedies, whence *Mnesilochus*,

The Phrygians is Euripides *new Play.*
But Socrates *gave it the best Array.*

And again, Euripides *is steer'd by* Socrates *and* Callias.

Now thou with Pride and Self-conceit o'erflow'st;
But all the cause to Socrates *thou owest.*

Hither refer we that of [d] *Cicero*, who saith, *d Tusc.* when *Euripides* made his Play *Orestes*, *Socrates quæst. 4.* revoked the three first Verses. He writ also some Fables of *Æsop* in Verse, not very Elegant, mentioned by *Plato*, *Plutarch* and *Laertius*, beginning thus:

To those who dwelt in Corinth, *Æsop said,*
Virtue with Vulgar Wisdom be not weigh'd.

A *Pæan* or *Hymn* in honour of Apol. *and* Diana: One that went under his name beginning thus:

Dælian Apollo, *and thou fair,*
Diana, *hail; immortal pair.*

is by *Dyonisidorus* denied to be his: This is mentioned also by *Plato*, to which some add

The Encomium of *Gryllus* Son of *Xenophon*, *e Laert. vit.* slain in the *Mantinean* Fight, which the disa- *Xenoph.* greement of times will not allow; more certain it is he framed

[f] *Dialogues*, which he gave to *Æschines*, see- *f Laert. vit.* ing him in want, that he might get Money by *Æschin.* them; to these add

Epistles, some whereof are published by *Leo Allatius*; that he writ more is implied by *Arrian* and *Athenæus*.

Socrates his Epistles:

Epistle I.

YOU seem unacquainted with my resolutions, else you would not have sent the second time, and enlarged your Offers; but you believe *Socrates*, as well as the Sophists, Mercenary of his Counsel, [a] and that what I writ before was not real, but only to draw great overtures from you: therefore now you promise wonders, in confidence to oblige me by your many Presents to quit my interest and commerce with the *Athenians*, and to come over to you: I think it most unseeming a Philosopher to sell his advice, and extreamly contrary to my Practice; for ever since by God's command I first entred into Philosophy, I was never known to take any thing, but keep my Exercises in publick, [b] for every one to hear that will; I neither lock the door when I teach, as is reported of *Pythagoras*, nor go abroad to the Multitude, and exact Money of the Hearers, as some heretofore have done, and some in our times yet do; I have enough from within my self, should I accept of more from others, I know not where to deposite it, nor whom to trust better than the givers themselves, whose Faith if I suspect, I shall be thought improvident to confide in, if honest, I can receive from them, though I lay up nothing with them; for they that would be faithful keepers of Money, will not be unfaithful preservers of their own gratitude, and they will never go about to defraud me of what they would have given; but receiving that of me *gratis*, for which others take Money, they will [c] consider me when I want. In a word, if friends, they will, [d] like you, impart of their own to us; if not Friends, they will seek to deprive us of what is ours.

Besides, I have not leisure to hoard up Money, but wonder at them that say, they get Riches [e] for their own sake, and have a high Opinion of themselves for their means, who neglect Learning to addict themselves to Gain, and so become admired for their Riches, derided for their Ignorance, esteemed for all things except themselves. [f] But if we so much abhor to have recourse to Friends, [g] to depend on others to eat their Bread, how comes it that we are not ashamed to suffer the same from Money? do we not know that these Men are not suspected only for their Wealth, and if Fortune turn, they live in all disrespect? they are not fully contented when they are in esteem, because it is not for their own sakes, but in disesteem are much more discontented, being themselves the cause of their own dishonour.

First, therefore you were mistaken, if you did imagine *Socrates* would do that for Money which he would not without, not knowing that many occasions, but chiefly the necessities of my Country detain me: Wonder not that I say I discharge my Countries Business, being not imployed either in Army or Court, every one ought to apply himself to that which he is capable of; [h] things above his reach he must leave to others, and perform those that are within his compass: And in such Cities as this, not only counsellors or commanders for Sea or Land are requisite, but some likewise, that may admonish others in their Offices; for it is [k] nothing strange, that they fall as it were asleep, under the weight of their charge, and need a Goad to waken them: Over these God hath placed me, for which I become, and not without cause, Odious to them.

But he, in whom I most confide, will not suffer me to go, he knows better than my self what is good for me; when I resolved to come to thee, he with-held me, and when thou sentest the second time, forbid me; I dare not disobey him. *Pindar* taught this Wisdom, saying, *When God points out the beginning of any work, it is the direct way to obtain Virtue, the end Glorious*: The Verses are much to this purpose. Other Poets have said as much of the Gods, that what is undertaken with their advice, succeeds well; but what without God, is unprofitable to the undertakers. The wisest Cities of *Greece* consult the Oracle of *Delphi*, and as many as follow it have good success, who do not, most commonly receive prejudice.

Yet I shall not wonder, if you give no Faith to what I deliver of the *Dæmon*, for I have met with not a few alike incredulous; most of those that were in the *Delian* Fight did not believe me; I was then in Arms, and Sallied out of the City with the People to skirmish, many of us were dispersed in Fight, and as we came to a certain way, the accustomed sign came upon me; I stopt, and said, in my opinion, friends, we should not go this way, for I heard the *Dæmon*'s Voice: the greater part were angry, as if I had trifled at a time so serious; some few were perswaded to go along with me another way, and got safe home; one that came from the others brought word they were all slain: some Horse-men returning from the pursuit, had fallen upon them, whom they at first resisted, but being at last enclosed by them, who were more in number, they gave back, and were in the end oppressed and killed; he that brought this News was dangerously wounded, and escaped only by the help of his Shield. I have also by instructions from God, foretold many events to particular persons.

You offer part of your Kingdom, and invite me to it, not as to a changed Government, but to Rule both your Subjects and your self: but I confess, I have not learned to Command, and would no more undertake to Rule, not knowing how, than to play at Dice, having never been taught: And doubtless if other Men were of the same mind, there would be fewer troubles in life; whereas now the confidence of such as are ignorant, undertaking things they do not understand, occasions these many disturbances: hence is it, they make Fortune greater than she is, and by their own Folly, increase her Power. Besides, I am not Ignorant, that a King ought to be more Honoured and Admired than a private Person, and as I would not undertake to be a Horseman having no skill in Horsemanship, but had much rather be a Footman, tho' the

the charge be less honourable: the same is my Opinion as touching Kings and private Persons, nor puffed up by Ambition will I desire more glorious Afflictions: they who invented the Fable of *Bellerophon* seemed to imply something to this purpose, for he was opprest with misfortunes, not because he sought to rise higher in place, but for aiming at things above him, and being thrown down from his hopes, led the rest of his life poorly and ignominiously, driven by mocks out of Cities into the Wilderness, and shunning pathways, not what we commonly call so, but the freedom wherewith every one orders his life. But let this be taken how the Poets please, my resolution you now hear again, that I will not change this place for that, *l* conceiving this fittest for me: nor is God willing I should, who hath been ever untill now, my Counsellor and Guide.

l 'Αμείνω δοκῶν Others, ἀμείνειν δοκῶν. Perhaps ἀμείνον εἶναι δοκῶν. Or ἐμμένειν δοκῶν.

Epist. II.

YOU are not ignorant how great esteem we have of *Chærephon*, who being chosen Ambassador by the City to the *Peloponnesians*, will perhaps come to you; a Philosopher is entertained with small trouble, but the Journey is dangerous, especially because of the tumults that are there at this time, from which, if thou protect him, thou wilt preserve our friend and infinitely engage us.

Epist. III.

A *Neso* of *Amphipolis* was commended to me at *Potidæa*, he is now coming to *Athens*, being thrown out of his House by the People, for at present, Affairs are much Embroiled and Clouded there, but I believe within a little while they will clear up. In assisting him, you will oblige a deserving person, and benefit both the Cities; *Amphipolis*, left by Rebelling it incurr irremediable danger: Ours, left we be involved in their troubles as at this present we are reduced almost to extremity for *Potidæa*.

Epist. IV.

MEeting with *Critobulus*, I perswaded him to study Philosophy, but I think he is of another mind, and more addicted to affairs of State, in which he intends to make choice of the fittest method, and best instructor, for the most exellent sojourn now in *Athens*, and with many of them we are intimate. Thus much concerning him; as for us, *Xantippe* and the Children are well, and I continue to do, as when you were with me.

Epist. V.

WE hear you are at *Thebes*, and *Proxenus* gone into *Asia*, to take part with *Cyrus*; whether your designs will prosper God knows, they are here condemned by many, for it is conceived unfit the *Athenians* should assist *Cyrus*, through whose means they were deprived of Command by the *Lacedæmonians* and fight for him, who fought against them. It is not therefore strange if the State being altered, some be ready of themselves to accuse you of temporising, and the better your success is, the greater will be their Calumnies; for I am well acquainted with the dispositions of some: but since we have undertaken this, let us prove our selves honest men, and call to mind what we use to say of Virtue, accounting this one of the best sentences of the Poet, Our Fathers house must not be discredited. Know therefore, that to War,

m Read Προξενόν ᾗ καταλαβεὸν τὴν Ἀσίαν, or διαβαλεῖν εἰς τὴν Ἀσίαν.

these two are requisite, Courage and Bounty; for this we are loved of our Friends; for that, feared of our Enemies: of both, thou hast domestick precedents.

Epist. VI.

I Have taken such care of your Strangers as you desired, and retained one to plead their cause before the People, *n* a Friend of ours, who professt himself the readier to undertake it, out of his desire to serve thee.

n Perhaps Lysias.

As for that which you write in jest concerning wealth, and such as are solicitous for it, perhaps it is not unreasonable. First, because whilst others Studie to be Rich, I choose to live meanly. Then though I might receive many Gifts and Legacies from living and dead friends; yet I freely disclaim them, and for a man thus enclined, to be by others judged mad, is nothing strange: But we must examine not this only, but the rest of our life; and since we disagree in the use, no wonder that we differ in the acquisition of *o* Riches; my Diet is very sparing, my Habit the same in Winter as in Summer: I never wear shoos, I am not taken with Popular Applause, but with the study of Wisdom and Integrity. But they who are intemperate, Luxurious in Meat, not every year, but every day putting on new Apparel, are transported with unlawful delights, and as they who lose their natural Complexion have recourse to Paint. So these losing the true glory of Virtue which every one ought to have, flie to that which depends upon Complaisance with others, courting vulgar Applause with Largesses and Feasts. Hence I suppose it comes, that they need much Wealth; They themselves cannot live upon a little, nor will others admit them into their Society, unless they receive a Salary for commending them.

o For σωμάτων read χρημάτων.

But my life is well as to both these: I will not deny but in some things I may fail, I know that wisest Men prefer those, most Men these; Reflecting sometimes within my self upon God; I find that he exceeds us, in that he hath need of nothing; it is the property of a most excellent Nature not to want any thing, and to comprehend within himself all that he enjoys. Thus is he wiser than others, who imitates the most Wise, *p* and Happier, who resembles the most Happy. If Riches could do this, Riches were to be preferred; but since Vertue only can obtain it, it were folly to forsake the real good to pursue the seeming. Hence I cannot easily be perswaded but that my Condition is better than theirs.

p Read κρατιώτατον ὑπάρχειν, &c. *q* Perhaps πρὸς οἷς ἐτύχησεν, ἤδη γε τῶν ὄντως ἀνθρωπίνων περὶ ἀγαθῶν περισπεσεῖνται, &c. or, πρὸς οἷς ἠτύχει ἤδη κᾳ τῶν ὄντως ἀνθρωπίνων ἀγαθῶν περιπεπτεσεῖνται τὴν ἐπὶ τῶν μᾶλλ. &c. Certainly Allatius cannot evince πρὸς οἷς to be used for πρὸς ἃ δι᾽ ὥ.
r Others ἐὰν, ἃ λόγοις μόνον, &c. which I choose, reading immediately after for δηλώσαντες, δηλῶσαί τις.

q As for Children, who as you say ought to be provided for, the care that I take for them, all Men may see, I know but one ground of happiness, Wisdom. The Fool who reposeth his trust in Gold, possesseth not that which he hath, and is withal so much more miserable than others, in that they who are oppressed with poverty may grow Wise hereafter. But he out of an Opinion of his own Happiness, neglecting true Gain is, corrupted with Plenty. *r* Besides that he never yet obtained Man's essential good, is depriv'd of hope thereof for the future. Nor is it possible that such a Man can go on securely to Virtue, who is entangled in the flateries of those who are Masters in all insinuating Arts, and in the Charms of Pleasures which glide into the Soul through every Sense, and

and drive out all wife and found Judgment. How then can he choose but give his his Children occasion of Folly rather than Instruction, who not only in words but actions expresseth that in these things he hath placed his hope, who not proving good, their Subsistence fails, and they die miserably for want of Food: Justly punished for their Idleness; Parents are by Law enjoyned to bring up their Children till they are Men. But you, perhaps some Citizen may say to his Sons greedy to inherit, spare me not dying, and whilst you live relie for maintenance upon me, tho' dead not asham'd to lead a life more lazy than death; you expect that my fortunes should extend to others even after my decease, but your own are not competent for your selves whilst you are yet alive. Such rough Speeches happily he will use to his Children, taking the liberty both of a Father and a Patriot. My Fortunes in the estimate of other Men are mean, but in the effect nothing inferiour to the Rich. I will not leave my Children Money, but a more honourable Heritage, discreet Friends, whom as long as they keep they can want as necessaries, and if they use them ill, doubtless they would use their Money worse.

But if to you, who know the negligence of Friends, I seem to give ill advice; I answer, that all Men are not alike affected to their Friends, for some take care of them after they are dead, and it is likely that ours are not of a neglectful humour, but pleas'd with the past advantage they have received by us, no less than with the present of a short benefit, the requital is short; lasting benefits produce a return equal to their profit, and I foresee that what is mine, will hereafter appear more gracious to my Friends, and therefore I exact no rewards of them. I account nothing of equal value in exchange with Philosophy but Friendship, nor like the Sophists, have I any diffidence of those things that are mine, for being old they renew, and in their decaying ⁵ age flourish, which makes them more acceptable to the Disciples, and their Father more esteemed; ᵗ Living he obtains honour, dead is thought worthy of memory, and if he leave a Kinsman behind him, they will respect him like his Nephews, and Brethren, and shew him all kindness, as being allied to him by more than a natural affinity; neither if they would, can they neglect him in misfortunes; no more than we can slight them, who are near to us in Blood; for affinity in Soul forceth them to relieve the Son of the dead as if he were their own Brother; when they call to mind his Father, whose dishonour they account their own.

Now judge if I order my affairs ill, or take no care for my Children, so as when I die they shall be destitute of necessaries, who leave them not wealth, but such Guardians as will have a care of them and Wealth. No History makes mention of any Man that hath been made better by riches; a tried Friend in this is to be preferred before tried Gold, that he is not beneficial to every one who desires him, but to those he loves best. Nor does he supply only the necessities of Life, but is serviceable as well to the Soul of him that hath him, and is most conducing to vertue, without which nothing profit-

ˢ Perhaps ἀναθαρσῆσαι. So Allatius seems to read. ᵗ For περὶ ὧν reading πέσων.

eth; but we will consider more exactly upon these things when we meet; thus much may serve as a cursory answer to your demand.

Epist. VII.

I wonder not at what you write, that you do suspect the thirty continue the same mind to us since your departure, which they had when you were here. As soon as you were gone, they began to have a Jealousie of me, and there past amongst them a murmur that these things were not done without *Socrates*; within few days they cited me to the Court, where some complaints were preferred against me, and when I defended my self, they commanded me to go to the *Pyræum* to apprehend *Leon*, their intention was to put him to death, that they might enjoy his Estate, and make me partner in their Injustice; when I refused, and said something to this effect that I would never willingly subscribe to an unjust act; *Charicles* was present, and inwardly vext, *Socrates*, saith he, dost thou think to talk thus peremptorily, and not suffer ten thousand Ills? *Charicles*, said I, but none so hainous as to do unjustly. He answered not a word, nor any of the rest, but ever since they have liked me the worse.

As for you, some were then present, reported that your affairs succeed to your wish, that the *Thebans* in your Exile received you kindly, and will assist your return to their utmost. Some were troubled at this News, and the more because it lessened their hopes of supply from *Lacedæmon*, for they who came along with the Ambassadous, affirmed, that the *Lacedæmonians* were engaged in a great War, and the *Ephori* hearing of these Troubles, were discontented, and said, that the *Lacedæmonians* had not intrusted them with the City to see it destroy'd; ᵘ for if they would have done so, it were most easie for them who had the Command, being withal instigated thereunto by the *Corinthians* and *Thebans*; and that the City might be better governed under an *Oligarchy* than a *Democracy*. If all this be true, and your affairs succeed as they report, there is great liklyhood that upon your coming in with the *Thebans*, the *Lacedæmonians* not aiding these, all things here may be easily composed. Besides, many of the Natives who now are quiet through Fear, if they perceived never so little that ye were firm, will readily forsake this Party, because in this government of the City nothing is left them entire but through many and continual Enormities all is in Confusion; the greater part is revolted as well as you, the rest if they had the least encouragement from abroad would suffer the same that you have. So that if no other, yet this Example would manifest that the greatest unhappiness of Cities is the wickedness of their Rulers, for they are so blinded with self-interest, that they will not desist, tho' they see all things go to ruin, but with what they first troubled, think to settle affairs, continuing Banishments, Sequestrations, and unjust deaths; not considering he is an ill Physician who prescribes for a Remedy the cause of the Disease. But those are incurable; you shall do well to have a care of your self, for all that are here have but this hope left, if you act wisely, to be freed from a heavy and grievous Tyranny.

ᵘ Perhaps σφίσιγε κρατήσασι, πεποιηκέναι ἐβούλοντο, &c.

THE

THE CLOUDS OF ARISTOPHANES:

Added (not as a Comical Divertisement for the Reader, who can expect little in that kind from a Subject so antient, and particular, but) as a necessary supplement to the Life of Socrates.

ACT I. SCENE I.

Strepsiades, Phidippides, Servant.

Streps. OH, oh,
Great *Jove*, how long a night is this, how endless!
Will't ne'r be Day? I heard the Cock again,
Yet still my Servants snore; 'tis but of late They durst do thus: [a] curse o'this War that awes me,
And will not suffer me to beat the Rogues.
My good Son sleeps too, wrapt o're Head and Ears:
Well, let me try to bear them company;
Alas, I cannot, so perplext and tortur'd
With charges, Bills for Horse-meat, Interest:
All for this hopeful Son, who in's curl'd locks,
Aids matches, keeps his Coach, and dreams of Horses,
Whilst I (unhappy!) see th' unwelcome Moon
Bring on the Quarter-Day, and threaten Use-Money.
Boy, snuff the Light, bring my Account-book hither,
That I may summ my Debts and Interest:
Let's see, twelve Pound to *Pasia*, ha! twelve Pound
To *Pasia*, how laid out? to buy [b] *Coppatia*:
Would I had paid this Eye for him.
 Phid. Hold *Philo*,
You'r out of the way, begin again.
 Streps. Ay, this,
This is the misery that ruins me;
His very Sleeps are taken up with Horses.
 Phid. How many courses will the manage hold?
 Streps. Many a weary course thou lead'st thy Father:
But how much more owe I than this to *Pasia*?

Three pound t'*Aminias* for Chariot Wheels.
 Phid. Go Sirrah, take that Horse and turn him out.
 Streps. Ay, thou hast turn'd me out of all my means.
Charges at Law will Eat me up, my Creditors
Threaten to sue me to an Execution.
 Phid. Why do you wake all Night, and toss so, Father?
 Streps. I cannot sleep, the Scrivener doth so bite me.
 Phid. Yet let me rest a little longer.
 Streps. Do so.
All these will one day light upon thy head,
Curs'd be the hour when I first saw thy Mother,
I liv'd before most sweetly in the Country,
Well stockt with Sheep and Bees, Olives and Grapes,
Till from the *Megaclean* house took I
This Niece of *Megacles* out of the City,
Well fashion'd, highly bred, and richly Cloathed;
We Married, as I said, and lay together:
I smelling strong of Drugs and greasie Wool;
But she of Unguents, *Crocus*, wanton Kisses,
Of vain expence, dainties and Luxury;
I will not tell the idle Life she led,
And yet she spun, that I have often told her,
Shewing this Coat, you spin a fair thread, Woman.
 Scrv. Sir all the Oyl i'th' Lamp is wasted.
 Streps. Ha?
Why didst thou put in such a drunken Wiek?
If thou wert near me I would beat thee.
 Serv. Why Sir?

Streps.

---

[a] The *Athenians* in time of War with the *Lacedæmonians* made an Edict, that no Man should beat his Servants, left they should go' over to the Enemy. *Schol.*

[b] Their Horses were named from the marks they had, if a K, *Copatias*; if an S, *Samphoras*. *Schol.*

σπαθᾶν λίαν τρυφᾶν καὶ σπαταλᾶν. *Sch. M. S.*

Streps. Because the Wiek is thicker than the Oyl.
Well, my good Wife, and I betwixt us got
At last this Son; about his name we differ'd;
Shee'd have it something that belong'd to Horses,
Callippides, Xantippus, or *Charippus*;
I from his Grandfather; *Phidonides.*
Long time we wrangled thus, at last agreed
He should be called *Phidippides*; this Son
She takes, and stroaking kindly, thus instructs him,
' When thou art grown a Man, frequent the
  ' City,
' Follow the fashion, keep a Coach and Horses,
' Like *Megacles* thy Uncle. No, said I,
' Go in a homely Coat, and drive thy Goats
' Into [a] *Phelleus,* as thy Father doth.
But my advice prevailed so little on him,
That now he wastes my means in keeping Horses,
Which all this night I have been thinking how
To remedy, and now have found the way;
To which could I perswade him, I were happy.
  Phidippides, Phidippides,
  Phid. Your Will Sir.
  Streps. Kiss me, give me thy Hand.
  Phid. Here, Sir.
  Streps. Dost love me?
  Phid. By *Neptune* God of Horses.
  Streps. Do not name
That God, for 'tis from him springs all my
  ' Sorrow.
But if thou lov'st me truly, heartily.
O Son, be rul'd.
  Phid. In what should I be rul'd?
  Streps. Change without more delay thy course of Life,
And do as I would have thee.
  Phid. What is that?
  Streps. But wilt thou do it?
  Phid. Yes by *Bacchus* will I.
  Streps. Come hither then, seest thou that little door?
That is the [e] *Phrontisterium* of wise Souls,
Of learned Men, that tell us Heaven's an Oven,
And we the Coals inclosed in the wide Arch:
They, if we give 'em but a little Money,
Will teach us to gain all causes, right or wrong.
  Phid. Who can these be?
  Streps. Their names I know not; good
They are, and busied in continual Study.
  Phid. Oh now I know the Wretches that you mean,
The meager, wan, proud, bare-foot, begging Fellows,
Whose evil Genius's are *Socrates*
And *Chærephon.*
  Streps. Peace, talk no more so idly;
If you'l obey a Father, let me see you
Give o're your Horses and turn one of these.
  Phid. Not I, by *Bacchus,* no though you should tempt me
With all [f] *Legoras's* Breed of Racers.
  Streps. Dear Son be rul'd and learn.
  Phid. What should I learn?
  Streps. 'Tis said they have two tongues, and one of them
Able to prove any injustice reason;
Could'st thou but learn that Language, we were made,

[a] *A stony Craggy place in Attica, in such Goats delight most.* Soli M. S.

[e] Ἐν ᾧ δη-λονότι καθή-μενοι φροντί-ζουσι περὶ θεῶν καὶ με-γάλου πρα-γμάτων. Schol. M. S.

[f] ἄριστος ἱπποτρόφος. Schol. M. S.

And might dispute our stubborn Creditors
Out of the debts I have incurr'd for thee;
They get not then a penny more than words.
  Phid. I cannot do't, were I so lean and pale,
I durst not look a Jockey in the Face.
  Streps. By *Ceres* then you stay with me no longer.
You, nor your Coach-Horse, nor your *Samphoras.*
But all together pack out of my doors.
My Uncle *Megacles* will neither see
Me nor my Horses want, so long I care not.
                                          Exit.

SCENE II.

Strepsiades, Scholar.

  Streps. THough I have faild, I'll not give over thus,
But say my Prayers, and go my self to School
To learn this Art: But how can I, by Age
Dull and forgetful, reach such subtleties?
Yet on I will, why should I doubt? Ho, Friend.
  Schol. A mischief on you, who's that knocks at Door?
  Streps. Strepsiades, Cecinnian Phædo's Son.
  Schol. 'Twas rudely done to knock so hard, y'have made
My labouring Brain miscarry of a Notion.
  Streps. Forgive me, I was bred far off i'th' Country:
But pray what Notion was't that prov'd Abortive?
  Schol. 'Tis Lawful to discover that to none
But Fellow-Scholars.
  Streps. Then you may tell me,
For I come hither to be one of you.
  Schol. I will; so will value't as a Mystery.
Socrates t'other day asked *Chærephon*
How many of her feet a Flea could leap,
For one by chance had bit *Chærephon's* Eye-brow,
And leapt from thence upon the Head of *Socrates.*
  Streps. How could he measure this?
  Schol. Most dexterously.
Both Feet o'th' Flea he dipt in melting wax,
Which strait congeals to Shooes; these he plucks off,
And with them more exactly measures it.
  Streps. Great *Jupiter,* how subtle are these Wits!
  Schol. If you should hear their other Speculations.
You would say so indeed.
  Streps. Pray what was that?
  Schol. This *Chærephon* the *Sphettian* ask'd him once,
If a Gnat sounded from her Mouth or Tail.
  Streps. And what said he?
  Schol. It had a strait thin Gut,
At end of it a Bladder, into which
The Air being forc'd, sounded in breaking forth.
  Streps. Then I perceive that a Gnat's Tail's a Trumpet;
How blest is this Anatomist of Gnats!
Sure he can hide himself from purblind justice,
That knows so well these dark intestine ways.
Why should we cry up *Thales* any longer?
                                          Come

Come open me your *Phrontisterium*
And quickly let me see this *Socrates*,
I long tong to learn, open the Door — * O *Hercules*,
What strange Beasts have we here?
　Schol. Why do you wonder?
Whom do they look like think you?
　Strepf. Like the poor
Lacedæmonian Captives ta'n at † *Pylus*.
Why look they so intently on the Ground?
These seek out things that appertain to Earth!
Oh they seek Leeks; trouble your selves no more, Friends,
For I know better where are good and great ones.
　Schol. Come let's go in.
　Strepf. Let's stay a little while and talk with 'em.
　Schol. No, no, they cannot long endure the air.
　Strepf. What's this, for Heavens sake say?
　Schol. This is Astronomy.
　Strepf. And this?
　Schol. Geometry.
　Strepf. But what is it good for?
　Schol. To measure Land.
　Strepf. What, Arable, or Pasture?
　Schol. No, the whole Earth.
　Strepf. A pretty Jest indeed.
That were a mighty help to Husbandmen.
　Schol. Here's all the World, and this is *Athens*.
　Strepf. How?
I'll scarce believe that; what's become o'th' Judges?
Where the *Cicynnians* my Country-men?
　Schol. Here; this *Eubæa*; see how far 'tis stretch'd.
　Strepf. Ay, almost stretcht in pieces betwixt us,
And *Pericles*; and where is *Lacedæmon*?
　Schol. Here.
　Strepf. 'Tis too nigh us, why with all your Skill
Do you not help to thrust it farther off?
　Schol. It is not possible.
　Strepf. No? you will rue it then.
But what Man's that hangs yonder in the Basket?
　Schol. That's he?
　Strepf. He, what he?
　Schol. *Socrates*.
　Strepf. How, *Socrates*?
Call him.
　Schol. Call him your self, I'm not at leisure.

SCENE III.

Strepsiades, *Socrates*.

　Strepf. HO *Socrates.*
　Socr. * Why dost thou call me mortal?
　Strep. First I would gladly know what thou dost there?
　Socr. I walk i'th' Air, and gaze upon the Sun.
　Strepf. Why in a Basket dost thou view the Gods,
Not from the Ground?
　Strepf. I could not elevate
My thoughts to contemplation of these Mysteries,
Unless my Intellect were thus suspended,
Where my thin thoughts melt into Air (their likeness)
Stood I upon the ground, I should find nothing,
Though I sought ne'er so strictly up and down,
For the magnetick vertue of the Earth
Would draw away the humour of my Brain,
Just as we see in Nose-smart.
　Strepf. How, how's that?
Doth the Brain draw the humour out of Nose-smart?
Come down, sweet *Socrates*, and teach me quickly
The knowledge of those things for which I came.
　Socr. What camest thou for?
　Strepf. To learn the Art of Speaking.
With debts and usury I'm torn in pieces,
Tost up and down, forc'd to pawn all my Goods.
　Socr. On what occasion did you run in debt?
　Strepf. By Horses eaten into this consumption;
And I would learn of you other Language
Which teacheth Men to pay nothing: for which
By all the Gods I'll give you what you'll ask.
　Socr. By all what Gods? we do not here allow
Those Gods the City worships.
　Strepf. How then swear you,
By Copper Farthings like the *Byzantines*?
　Socr. Wouldst thou be skilful in Divine affairs?
　Strepf. By *Jove* (if any such there be) I wou'd.
　Socr. You must be then aquainted with the Clouds.
Our reverend Goddesses.
　Strepf. With all my heart.
　Socr. Sit down upon this Couch then.
　Strepf. Well.
　Socr. Now take
This Garland.
　Strepf. Why a Garland? alas, *Socrates*,
D'ye mean (like *Athamas*) to Sacrifice me?
　Socr. No, these are Rites that every one performs
At his admission.
　Strepf. But what shall I gain by't?
　Socr. Thou shalt be made most voluble in Speech,
A very Rattle, bolting words words as fine as Flower.
　Strepf. Th'art right by *Jove*, I shall be powdered.
　Socr. Silence, old man, and listen to our Prayer.
' Great King, unbounded Air, whose Arms are
' hurl'd
' About the surface of this pendant World,
' Bright Æther, reverend Clouds, that from your Sphear
' Thunder and Lightning dart, rise and appear.
　Strepf. Not yet, not yet, till I have wrapt my self
Close in my Cloak, lest I be wet: twas ill
That I forgat to bring my Riding-hood.
　Socr. ' Your power great Clouds, make to
' this Suppliant known
' Whether now seated on *Olympus* Throne,
' Or whether you your secret Revels keep
' In the wide Gardens of your Sire the Deep:
' Or of his flowing Chrystal seven mouth'd *Nile*,
' In golden Ewers wantonly beguile:
' Or in *Mauritian* Marshes keep your Court;
' Or on the snowy top of *Mimas* sport.
' Come, to our fervent Vows propitious be,
' Grace with your Presence our Solemnity.
' We humid fleeting Deities,
' The bright unbounded Clouds thus rise
' From

Chorus from Clouds.

'From our old Sire, the grumbling Flood,
'Above the tallest Hill or Wood,
'To those high Watch-Towers, whence we may
'The hollowed fruitful ground survey;
'Rivers that in soft murmurs glide,
'And the loud Seas rebellious tide;
'From thence Heavens restless Eye displays
'The splendour of his glorious rays,
'Chasing all dusty mists, that we
'In shapes divine may Mortals see.
   Socr. Thanks reverend Clouds for favouring thus our Prayer.
Did you not hear 'em speak in Thunder to us?
   Streps. Great Clouds I worship too, but am so frighted,
I scarce can hold from answering your Thunder.
   Socr. Jest not profanely in such sacred Rites:
Peace, for the swarm of Gods come singing.
   Chor. 'Come Virgin Mistresses of showers,
'Let's visit *Pallas* pregnant Bowers,
'The far renown'd *Cecropian* Plain
'Where shines the * *Eleusinian* Fane,
'Where are the most retir'd aboads,
'Statues and Temples of the Gods:
'Where Altars blaze with Incense, where
'The Holy-day lasts all the Year;
'Where the brisk Graces every Spring,
'And Youths with Virgins Dance and Sing.
   Streps. Tell me good *Socrates*, what things are these
That speak so finely? Are they Ladies?
   Socr. No,
They're *Clouds*, the Deities of Idle Men;
From these we have our Sense, Discourse, and Reason,
Our high Capricio's, and elaborate whimseys.
   Streps. My Soul, my thought did leap, while they were speaking,
And now most subtly would dispute of smoak,
Sharply confute opinion with opinion:
Oh how I long to see them once again.
   Soc. Look yonder, towards *Parnes*, look how gently
They glide to Earth.
   Streps. Where? shew me.
   Socr. See in Shoals
They creep into the Caverns of the Mountain.
   Streps. What things are these? I cannot yet behold 'em,
   Socr. There in the Entrance, look.
   Streps. Yet I scarce see them.
   Socr. Either thou seest them now, or thou art blind.
   Streps. I do by *Jove*, great Clouds, for you hold all!
   Socr. Didst thou not know these Deities before?
   Streps. Not I, I thought them only mists and vapours.
   Socr. Thou knewest not then those who maintain the Sophists.
   Streps. If these be Clouds, how comes it that they look
Like Women? For the Clouds have no such Shape.
   Socr. No, what shape have they then?
   Streps. I know not justly;
They look like flying Fleeces, but by *Jove*,
Nothing at all like Women; these have Noses.

   Socr. * Answer to what I ask.
   Streps. Ask me quickly.
   Socr. Didst ere behold a Cloud shap'd like a Centaur,
A Leopard, Bull, or Wolf?
   Streps. I have, what then?
   Socr. The Clouds can take what form they list, as when
They see a hairy Fellow curl'd like *Clitus*.
They mock his madness in a Centaur's shape.
   Streps. And when they see one that defrauds or plunders
The Commonwealth, like *Sinon*, what then do they?
   Socr. They do resemble him, turn ravenous Wolves,
This was the reason yesterday, when they
Beheld * *Cleonymus*, they fled like Deer:
And seeing † *Clisthenes*, are now turn'd Women.
   Streps. Great Queens, if you are design'd to speak to Mortals,
Make me acquainted with your rumbling voice.
   Chor. 'All hail old Man, who dost on Wisdom prey,
'And thou the Priest of subtle trifles say,
'What wouldst thou have with us, to none but thee,
'Of all the Meteor Sophists thus stoop we;
'Save *Prodicus*, to him as grave and wise,
'To thee, because thou walk'st upright, thy Eyes
'Rowling on every side, thy look severe
'And barefoot many miseries dost bear.
   Streps. Good Heavens, what voice is this, how strange and stately?
   Socr. These are our Goddesses, the rest are toys.
   Streps. Is then Olympian *Jove* no Deity?
   Socr. What *Jove*, There's no such thing; meer fancy.
   Streps. How?
Whence then proceeds all * Rain?
   Socr. Only from these.
Didst thou ere see a shower without them? take
The Clouds away, and Heaven must rain fair Weather.
   Streps. By *Phœbus* thou hast clear'd it well; till now
I thought *Jove* made Water through a sieve.
But whence comes Thunder? when I'm sick, that frights me.
These thunder as they tumble up and down.
How can that be?
   Socr. † When they are full of water,
By their own weight driven upon one another,
They roar and break.
   Streps. But who is it that drives them,
Is not that *Jove*?
   Socr. No, an ætherial Whirlwind.
   Streps. A Whirlwind, hum! I knew not that till now.
But whence comes Lightning then, that glittering Fire
Which terrifies and burns us? *Jupiter*
Useth to dart this down on Perjur'd Men.
   Socr. And how (thou plegmatick dull Saturnine,)
If darted on the Perjur'd, how comes *Sinon*,
Theorus, and *Cleonymus* to scape it?
No, his own Temple, or the *Sunian* Promontory,
Or

Marginal notes:

* μυςἰοδόκος δόμος at *Eleusis* in *Attica* were celebrated the mysteries of *Ceres*, to which *Athenians* only were admitted, not strangers; if any one discovered them to a Person not initiated, they were both put to Death. *Schol. M. S.*

* The *Socratick* way of dispute by Question.

* Coward.
† Effeminately attired.

* Whereof *Jupiter* was the particular Deity; thence firnamed Τῆς ὀμβρεύς.

† Deriding *Socrates* as Ignorant in Natural Philosophy.

Or sturdy Oaks he strikes, did they e'r wrong him?
Did the Oak e'r forswear it self?
Streps. I know not:
That which you say seems reason; but what then
Is Lightning?
Socr. When the winds are shut up close,
They swell the Clouds like Bladders, and at last
Break out with violence and horrid noises;
And by contrition kindle one another.
But thou who searchest amongst us for wisdom
How happy wilt thou be above all *Grecians*
If thou conceive well, and remember, and
Canst suffer much, and never wilt be tired
Standing or walking, nor have sense of Frost,
Nor care for dining, and refrain from Wine,
From exercises, and all other toys.
Streps. O for a solid Soul restless with cares.
Sparing, self-torturing, one that can feast
Upon a dish of Herbs, you never could
Be better fitted; a meer Anvile I.
Socr. Dost thou believe no God but those we teach?
The Chaos, Clouds and Tongue, only these three.
Streps. I'll not so much as speak of any other,
Much less bestow an Offering on their Altars.
Chor. ' Say boldly then, say what is thy request,
' For if thou honour us thou shalt be blest.
Streps. Great Queens I sue for a small matter, that
I may out-talk all *Greeks* a hundred Furlongs.
Chor. ' To thee alone this gift we will allow,
' None speak such mighty Sentences as Thou.
Streps. I do not care for mighty sentences,
But subtle ones to cheat my Creditors.
Chor. ' It is not much thou askest, and shalt obtain it,
' Learn of our Ministers and thou shalt gain it.
Streps. I shall, relying on your promise; forc'd
By want, *Coppatia* and a luckless match.
Now let 'em use me as they list, beat, starve me,
Burn, freeze, or flea me, so I escape my debts:
I care not though Men call me Impudent,
Smooth-tongu'd, audacious, petulant, abominable,
Forger of words and lies, contentious Barretour,
Old, winding, bragging, testy, crafty Fox.
Socr. Said like a Man of Courage: if thou Learn
Of me, thy fame shall spread wide as the Heavens.
Streps. What shall I do?
Socr. Thou shalt spend all thy time
With me! a Life the happiest in the World.
Streps. I long to see that day.
Socr. Thy door shall always
Be throng'd with Clients that will come to thee
For Counsel, and discourse of Cases worth
The wealth of Kingdoms, to thy hearts desire.
Chor. ' Try this old Man; first see if he be ' fit;
' Put him to th'test, and sound the depth of's wit.

Socr. Come tell me now your disposition,
That when I know it I may fit my Machines Accordingly.
Streps. You will not undermine me.
Socr. No, I would know if you have any memory.
Streps Yes, when another owes me any thing,
I can remember very well, but what
I owe my self, I'm ready to forget.
Socr. Hast thou a natural faculty in speaking?
Streps. No, I can mar words sooner far than make 'em.
Socr. How wilt thou learn then?
Streps. Fear me not, I tell you
Well, when I make some Learned deep Discourse.
Socr. † You must be sure to catch't up presently.
Streps. What, must I snap at Learning like a Dog?
Socr. This is a very Fool, an unknown Clown;
I am afraid old Man thou wilt need whipping.
What if thou shouldst be beaten?
Streps. Then I am beaten.
Socr. But what wouldst do?
Streps. I would take witness on't
And sue them on an Action of Battery.
Socr. Off with your Cloak.
Streps. Why, how have I offended?
Socr. No; but our Orders admit none but naked.
Streps. I came not hither to steal any thing.
Socr. Down with your Cloak, why dost thou trifle?
Streps. Now
Tell me if I prove apt and diligent,
Of all your Scholars who shall I come nighest?
Socr. Thou mayst perhaps be like our *Chærephon*.
Streps. Alas, alas! what an Anatomy?
Socr. No, no: But if thou wilt be any thing
Follow me without more delay.
Streps. I want
A Cake for your *Cerberus*; I go methinks
As if 'twere into the *Trophonian* Cave.
Socr. On, on, why stayest thou gazing at the door?
Chor. ' Go, for thy courage blest whose aged ' mind
' To wisdom soars, and leaves the young behind.

ACT II.

Socrates, Strepsiades.

Socr. BY *Chaos*, and this Air I breath, I never Met any thing so stupid as this fellow,
So clownish and oblivious; easie toys
He learns not half so fast as he forgets 'em,
I'll call him forth; what, ho *Strepsiades*;
Come out and bring your Bed along with you.
Streps. The fleas will hardly let me bring my self.
Socr. Quick, down with't there; and mark what I say to you.
Streps. I am ready.
Socr. What have you most mind to learn,
Measures, or Verse, or Rhyme?
Streps. By all means Measures;

† As the Scholars of *Socrates* used, especially *Xenophon* and *Plato*.

For I was cheated by a Meal-man lately
Two pecks.
   Socr. That's not the thing that I demand;
I'de know which you conceive the fairest measure,
The *Trimeter*, or the *Tetrameter*.
   Streps. The fairest measure in my mind is a Bushel.
   Socr. 'Tis nothing that you say.
   Streps. What will you lay
That your *Tetrameter* holds not a Bushel?
   Socr. Away, away, how dull thou art, and blockish.
But thou wilt be perhaps more apt at Rhime.
   Streps. What help can Rhimes afford me in my meal?
   Socr. First, they will make thee pleasant in all Company.
Then thou shalt know which suits with Anapæstick,
And which with Dactyles.
   Streps. Dactyles? I know that sure.
   Socr. Why what's a Dactyle.
   Streps. What, but this same Finger,
T'has been a Dactyle ere since I was Child.
   Socr. Th'art an unprofitable Dunce.
   Streps. I care not
For learning these devices.
   Socr. What then wouldst thou?
   Streps. That, unjust and cheating Sophisty.
   Socr. But there are things that must be learnt before
You come to that; what Creatures are there Masculine?
   Streps. Sure I know that, or I were mad indeed.

* *Deriding Socrates as Ignorant in Grammar.*

A Ram, a Bull, a Goat, a Dog, a Pigeon.
   Socr. * See how thou err'st, that call'st both Male and Female
A Pigeon.
   Streps. Right by *Neptune*, how then must I?
   Socr. Call this a Cock-pigeon, and that a Hen.
   Streps. A Pigeon, Cock and Hen, ha! by this Air,

† *A meal-trough, the Greek word hath a masculine termination but feminine Article.*

For this sole document, I will replenish
Your † *Cardopus*, with meal.
   Socr. Again th'art wrong;
Thou call'st it *Cardopus*, but 'tis *hæc Cardopus*,
And therefore henceforth call it *Cardopa*.
Next it is fit you know which names are Masculine,
And which are Feminine.
   Streps. I know well which
Are feminine, I'm sure.
   Socr. Let's hear.
   Streps. *Philina*,
Cletagora, Demetria, and *Lysinna*
   Socr. And which are Masculine?
   Streps. A World, *Philoxenus*,
Melesias, and *Aminias*.
   Socr. Thou art out.
   Streps. Are not these Masculine with you?
   Socr. * By no means.

x *Effeminate Cowards.*

How if you saw *Amynias*, would you call him?
   Streps. *Amynia*, ho!
   Socr. What, make a Woman of him?
   Streps. And reason good, h'has thrown away his Arms,
And will not fight. But to what purpose learn I
These common trifles?

   Socr. Not so common neither,
But come, lie down.
   Streps. What must I do?
   Socr. Consider
Within your self the business that concerns you.
   Streps. Not in this Bed, I thank you, if I must
Lie down, I'll meditate upon the Ground.
   Socr. But here's no room besides.
   Streps. Wretch that I am.
How shall I be tormented with these fleas!
   Socr. Now think into the depth of thy affairs,
Try every turn and winding, every double;
And if you stick at any thing: giv't ore,
And to some other; but be sure you sleep not.
   Streps. Oh, oh.
   Socr. How now, the matter?
   Streps. I am kill'd
By these Blood-suckers, these *Corinthians*.
   Socr. Do not torment your self.
   Streps. How can I choose
When I have neither money left, nor colour,
Scarce Life, no Shooes, grown almost to a
Ghost with watching?
   Socr. Now what think y'on, nothing?
   Streps. Yes
By *Neptune*.
   Socr. What?
   Streps. I'm thinking if the Fleas
Will leave a piece of me or not.
   Socr. Death on thee.
   Streps. You might have spar'd your Curse,
I'm dead already.
   Socr. Fy, fy, you must not be so tender, cover
Your Face, and study for some subtle cheat.
   Streps. Would I could learn to cheat these wicked Fleas.
   Socr. Let's see, what does he? what asleep, ha'ye thought
Of nothing yet?

** *So Socrates disputes in Plato's Phædrus, that exteriour Objects might not divert him; which Aristophanes here derides.*

   Streps. What would you have me think on?
   Socr. What would you learn?
   Streps. I have told you that already
A thousand times; I'de learn to pay no Use-Money.
   Socr. Come then, cover your self, and subtilize
Your thoughts, Dissect your Business into Atomes.
   Streps. Alas!
   Socr. Lye still, and if you stick at any thing,
Pass by it a while, and come to it again.
   Streps. Ho, my dear *Socrates*.
   Socr. What is't old Man?
   Streps. I have found out what will do it.
   Socr. As how.
   Streps. First tell me
Where I may meet with some *Thessalian* witch;
For I would steal the Moon one of these nights,
And having got her, lock her in a Chest
As charily as I would keep a Glass.
   Socr. What wilt thou get by that?
   Streps. What, if the Moon
Ne'r rise again, I'm bound to pay no use.
   Socr. How so?
   Streps. 'Cause use you know is paid by th' Month.

Socr.

Socr. 'Tis well, but I'll propound another Business;
Suppose that you were tied upon a Statute
To pay five Talents, could you raise Figures?
Streps. I know not, but I'll try.
Socr. You must not limit
Your thoughts so narrowly within your self,
But like a Beetle fetter'd in a thread,
Allow them play, and flutter in the Air.
Streps. I ha't, I ha't; the rarest way to cancel
A deed, as you'l confess when you have heard it.
Socr. What is't?
Streps. Did you nere see at any Grocers
A clear transparent stone, with which they use
To kindle fire?
Socr. You mean a Burning-glass.
Streps. The very same.
Socr. What wouldst thou do with it?
Streps. Whilst that the Scrivener writes the deed, d'ye mark,
Thus standing by him with my Burning-glass
Against the Sun, I'll burn out every letter.
Socr. Wisely, by all the Graces.
Streps. How long
To cancel thus a bond of fifty pound.
Socr. 'Tis well, now tell me if thy adversary
Sue thee, and thou art like to be overthrown
For want of witnesses, how wilt thou void His suit?
Streps. Most easily.
Socr. Which way?
Streps. Before
It comes to Judgment, I would hang my self.
Socr. Pish, thou sayst nothing.
Streps. Yes by *Jove* there's none
will prosecute a Suit against the Dead.
Socr. Away, thou fool'st, I'll teach no more.
Streps. Dear *Socrates*
Why?
Socr. Thou forget'st as fast as thou canst learn.
Tell me the first thing thou wert taught to day.
Streps. The first; stay let me see; the first thing say you?
How call you that we use to put our Meal in?
Wretch I have forgot it!
Socr. See, deservest thou not
Forgetful to be punisht for a Dunce.
Streps. Alas what shall I do? for if I learn not
The cheating language, I'm quite undone?
Good Clouds advise me what course I shall take.
Cho. 'If an ingenious Son thou hast at home,
'Thou hadst best send him hither in thy room.
Streps. I have a Son, and he's ingenious too;
But will not learn, the more my misery.
Cho. And wilt thou suffer it?
Streps. Of a promising person
His Mother is a Woman of great Spirit:
Once more I'll try; if he refuse, Ill make
No more ado but turn him out of doors;
Stay but a while, I'll be quickly back.

ACT. III.

Strepsiades, Phidippides, Socrates.

Streps. NOW by the Clouds thou staist no longer here?
Hence, and go feed in *Megacles* his Stable.

Phid. Alas what fury hath possest you Father?
By *Jove* I think you are besides your self.
Streps. See, see, he swears by *Jove*, art thou not mad
At these years to believe there is a *Jove*?
Phid. Is truth to be derided?
Streps. Well, I see
Th'art still a Child, and creditest old wives Tales.
Come, and I will tell thee what shall make thee
A Man, so you be sure to tell it no body.
Phin. Pretty; what is it?
Streps. Thou swor'st e'n now by *Jove*.
Phid. I did so.
Streps. See how good it is is to learn;
There's no such thing as *Jove*.
Phid. What then?
Streps. A Whirl-wind
Hath blown *Jove* quite away, and rules all Heaven.
Phid. What fooleries are these?
Streps. They are serious truth, Son.
Phid. Who tells you so?
Streps. Our *Socrates* the * Melian,
And *Chærephon*, that trace the steps of Fleas.
Phid. How are you grown to such a height of Madness
As to believe such Melancholy Dreamers?
Streps. Good words: Defame not Men of such deep Wisdom
And subtle Spirits; these live sparingly,
Are never at the charges of a Barber,
Unguents, or Baths, whereas thou wastest my means
As freely as if I were dead already.
Come then, and be their Scholar in my room.
Phid. What can be learnt that's good of such as they are?
Streps. All things that are accounted wisdom, Boy;
And first to know thy self, and what a dunce
Thou art, how blockish rustick, and forgetful.
But stay a little, cover thy face a while.
Phid. Alas! my Father's mad, what shall I do,
Accuse him to the Court of Folly, or
Bespeak a Coffin for him, for he talks
Idly, as he were drawing on?
Streps. Come on now.
Lets see, what's that?
Phid. A Pigeon.
Streph. Good; and that?
Phid. A Pigeon.
Streps. Both the same? ridiculous.
Take heed you make not such mistakes hereafter.
This you must call a Cock, and that a Hen.
Phid. A Hen? Is this the goodly learning, Father,
You got since your admission amongst these Earth-worms?
Streps. This and a great deal more; but being old,
I soon forget what I am taught.
Phid. I think
Twas want of Memory made you lose your Cloak.
Streps. No, 'tis hung up upon the Arts and Sciences.

* As if he should say, the Atheist: for the *Melians* were infamous for *Atheism* from *Diagoras* who profest it: *Socrates* was Scholar to *Aristagoras* a *Melian*. See Chap. 3.

Phid. And where your Shooes?
Strepſ. Loſt for the common good,
Like *Pericles*: But let's be gone, and ſee
You learn to obey me, and to wrong all elſe.
Remember that I bought thee, when thou wert
But ſix years old, a little Cart to play with.
   Phid. Alas you'll be the firſt that will repent this.
   Strepſ. Take you no care for that, do as I bid you.
Ho, *Socrates*, I've brought my Son at laſt,
Though much againſt his Will.
   Socr. Ay, that's becauſe
He's rude, untaught, a Child of Ignorance,
And unaquainted with our hungry Baskets.
   Phid. Go hang your ſelf in one of them.
   Strepſ. How Impudence! doſt thou talk thus to thy Maſter?
   Socr. So go hang, with what a ſeeming grace was that pronounc'd!
How do you think that he ſhould ever learn
To overthrow a nimble Adverſary,
Or win a Judge's Heart with Rhetorick?
   Strepſ. Fear not, but teach him; he's ingenious
By nature; for when he was but a little one,
He'd build you Houſes, and make Leather Coaches,
And Ships, and cut Frogs out of Apple parings.
What's your Opinion then? Do you not think
He's capable to learn both Languages?
Or if not both, be ſure he learn the worſe.
   Socr. Well, we ſhall try what may be done with him.
   Strepſ. Farewell, and ſo remember that in all I ſay that's juſt, you learn to contradict me.

ACT. III.

SCENE I. *Strepſiades.*

Strepſ. THe * fifth, the fourth, the third, the ſecond! hum;

[† From the twentieth day of the mouth they reckoned backward, ſee the life of *Solon*. Chap.]

The moſt abhorr'd and dreadful day's at hand,
The old and new; all I owe Money to
Threaten to ſue, and vow my utter ruin;
Yet I require nothing but what is juſt reaſon:
My friend forbear me till ſome other time;
But they all anſwer me, words are no payment,
Revile me, ſwear they'll put their Bonds in ſuit,
And let 'em, what care I, ſo my *Phidippides*
Have learnt the art of cheating: I ſhall know ſtraight;
It is but knocking at the School; ho Son!

SCENE II. *Strepſiades, Socrates.*

   Socr. SAve you, *Strepſiades.*
   Strepſ. The like to you.

[† Such gifts *Socrates* ſometimes accepted, though not money. See Chap.]

† Firſt take this Bag of Meal, for it is fit
We pay our duty to our reverend Maſter.
Now tell me, has my Son attain'd the Art
For which I plac'd him with you?
   Socr. Yes exactly.
   Strepſ, Thanks to Deceit, the Queen that governs all things.
   Socr. Now you may overthrow all Adverſaries.
   Strepſ What though a Witneſs ſwear that I have borrowed.
   Socr. Ay, though a thouſand ſwear it.
   Strepſ. Io. Io.
Triumph my Boys, woe to you Money-mongers,
You and your Bonds, your uſe on uſe may hang now,
You'll trouble me no more! O what a Son
Have I, that fenceth with a two-edg'd Tongue,
My Houſes Prop, and Guardian, my Foes terrour,
Quickly come forth, and meet my glad Embraces,
Come forth and hear thy Father.
   Socr. See the Man.
   Strepſ. O my dear Boy!
   Socr. Away, and take him with you.

SCENE III.

Strepſiades, Phidippides.

Strepſ. IO my Son! O how I joy to ſee
Thy chang'd Complexion! Thou look'ſt now methinks
As thou wert inſpir'd with contraction,
I read croſs queſtions in thy very Face,
Thy very Eyes methinks ſay, how, how's that?
Thou canſt perſwade the World that thou art wrong'd,
When thou art, he that does the wrong. I ſee't,
I plainly ſee't; a very Attick mine;
Now let it be thy ſtudy to recover
Him, whom thou almoſt haſt undone.
   Phid. Why, what
Is't that you fear?
   Strepſ. The old and the new day.
   Phid. Can one and the ſame day be old and new?
   Strepſ. I know that: I'm ſure my Creditors
By joint-conſent that day threaten to ſue me.
   Phid. They'll loſe by it if they do: For, 'tis impoſſible
To make two days of one.
   Strepſ. How is't impoſſible?
   Phid. As for a Woman to be old and young At once.
   Strepſ. But Law has ſo determined it
   Phid. But theſe Men know not what the Law doth mean.
   Strepſ. Why what's the meaning of it.
   † *Phid.* Antient *Solon.*

[† See the life of *Solon*. Chap.]

Was naturally a Lover of the People.
   Strepſ. What's that to this?
   Phid. He did appoint two days,
The laſt day of the old month for citation,
The firſt o'th' new for payment of the Money.
   Strepſ. But why the laſt day for citations?
   Phid. That
The debtor having thus one day of warning
Might fly and ſhun the trouble of the next.
   Socr. Why do the Magiſtrates then take all forfeits
Upon the old and new day?
   Phid. They are hungry.
And taſte their Meat before they ſhould fall to.
   Strepſ. Io, Ye fools that ſit ſtill and do nothing,
We that are wiſe and quick have done the buſineſs;
Ye Blocks, ye Stones, ye Sheep, ye empty Bubbles;

Let

Let me congratulate this Son of mine,
My self and my Good Fortune in a Song.
' Now *Strepsiades* th' art blest,
' Of the most discreet the best,
' What a Son thou hast, now may
' All my æmulous Neighbours say,
' When they hear that he alone
' Hath my Creditors o'rthrown.
But come my Boy, now thou shalt feast with me.

Sect. 4. *Pasias, Strepsiades, Witness.*

Pas. AND must a Man be outed of his own thus?
Better take any course than suffer this.
You must assist me in this business neighbour,
That I may call my debtor to account;
There's one Friend made a Foe; yet I'll not shame
My Country, ere I do it, I'll give him warning.
Strepsiades.
  Streps. How now, what would you have?
  Pas. The old and new day's come.
  Streps. Bear witness Friend,
He nam'd two days. What sum is't you demand?
  Pas. Twelve pounds you borrow'd when you bought your Son
A Race-horse; with the Interest.
  Streps. A Race-horse!
You know I neer car'd for em in my Life.
  Pas. And swor'st by *Jove* and all the Gods to pay it.
  Streps. By *Jove*? 'twas then before my Son had learnt
The all-convincing Speech.
  Pas. You'll not deny it.
  Streps. What have I got but that for all this Learning?
  Pas. Dar'st thou deny it, if I should put thee to
Thy Oath, and make thee call the Gods to witness it?
  Streps. What Gods d'ye mean?
  Pas. Jove, Mercury, and *Neptune.*
  Streps. By *Jove*? Yes that I will I hold thee three-pence.
  Pas. Curse on thee for this Impudence.
  Streps. If thou wert rubbed with Salt,'twould make thy Wit the quicker,
  Pas. D'ye Laugh at me?
  Streps. Thou wilt take up six Bushels.
  Pas. So help me *Jupiter*, and all the Gods,
I will be even with you for this scorn.
  Streps. I'm extreamly taken with your Gods,
And this same *Jupiter* you swear by, they
Are excellent Pastime to a knowing Man.
  Pas. Well, you will one day answer for these words.
But tell me whether I shall have my Money
Or not, give me my Answer, and I am gone.
  Streps. Stay but a little, I will answer presently,
And plainly.
  Pas. Sure he's gone to fetch the Money.
  Streps. Where is the Man that comes to ask me Money?
Tell me, what's this?
  Pas. That which it is, a *Cardopus.*
  Streps. You ask for Money, and so very a Dunce!
I'll never whilst I live pay him a Penny,
That calls a *Cardopa* a *Cardopus.*
  Pas. You will not pay then?
  Streps. Not for ought I know:
You'll stay no longer, pray about your Business.
  Pas. Yes I'll be gone, but in the mean time know
I'll have my Money, if I live this day.
  Streps. You may chance go without it; yet I'm sorry
You should be punish'd so for a mistake,
For saying *Cardopus* for *Cardopa.*

SCENE VIII.

Amynias, Strepsiades, Witness.

Amyn. OH, oh, alas!
  Streps. Who's that keeps such a bawling?
What art thou? one of * *Karkinus's* Sons?
  Amyn. 'Tis I, unhappy I!
  Streps. Keep it to thy self.
  Amyn. Unlucky chance, oh cruel Destiny,
To spoil at once my Cart and all my Horses!
† Oh *Pallas,* how unkindly hast thou used me?
  Streps. What hurt did ever *Tlepolemus* do thee?
  Amyn. Deride me not, but rather bid your Son
Pay me the Money which he had of me,
For I was never in more need of it.
  Streps. What Money, Man?
  Amyn. That which he borrowed of me.
  Streps. Then I perceive you're in a sad condition.
  Amyn. I had a scurvy fall driving my Horses.
  Streps. Thou dost but jest, 'twas driving an Ass rather.
  Amyn. I do not jest when I demand my Money.
  Streps. Upon my word thou art not right.
  Amyn. How so?
  Streps. Thy Brain methinks is troubled.
  Amyn. Either pay me
My Money strait, or I will trouble you.
  Streps. Tell me, Doth *Jove* beget and send down Rain,
Or doth the Sun exhale it from the Sea?
  Amyn. I neither know nor care.
  Streps. What? are you fit
To receive Money, and so ignorant
Of these sublime and subtle Mysteries?
  Amyn. Well, if you cannot let me have the Principal,
Pay me the Interest.
  Streps. Interest, what kind
Of Creature's that?
  Amyn. What, but the increase of Money
By Months and Days, as time runs on.
  Streps. 'Tis well.
And do you think the Sea is fuller now
Than 'twas at first?
  Amyn. No, not a drop, it is
Not fit it should.
  Streps. The Sea by your Confession
Is nothing grown; then with what Conscience Can

* Which were *Xenocles, Xenotimus,* and *Demotimus,* Tragick Poets and Actors.

† This and the following line are taken from *Xenocles* the Tragedian, which is the reason of *Strepsiades* his Answer.

Can you desire your Money should encrease.
Go get you from my Doors, fetch me a whip there.

Witn. Well, I'll bear witness for him.

Strepf. Why d'ye not go, will you move * *Samphoras*?

[margin: * The Horse's name which he bought of him.]

Amyn. Is not this riotous?

Strepf. Will you be gone?
Or shall I lead you in a Chain, and make you
Shew tricks? If you stay but a little longer,
I'll send you, and your Cart and Horses packing.

Chor. Now observe what it is to bend
'Studies to an evil end.
'This old Man, that is intent
'Creditors to Circumvent,
'Foolishly himself hath crost,
'And will find so to his cost;
'That in this false Art his Son
'Hath attain'd perfection:
'Justice cunning to refute,
'That at last he'll wish him mute.

ACT V.

SCENE I.

Strepsiades, Phidippides.

Strepf. O Neighbours, Kinsmen, Countrymen, help, help,
I'm beat, all, all over, oh my head, my back!
Thou strik'st thy Father, Rogue.

Phid. I do so, Father.

Strepf. See, see, he stands in it too.

Phid. I do indeed.

Strepf. Thief, Villain, Parricide.

Phid. More I beseech you,
I am much taken with these pretty Titles.

Strepf. Rascal.

Phid. Pray stick me fuller of these Roses.

Strepf. Dost beat thy Father?

Phid. Yes by *Jove*, and justly.

Strepf. Oh Rogue, what Justice can there be in that?

Phid. I will demonstrate it by Argument.

Strepf. By Argument?

Phid. Most easily, which Language shall I dispute in?

Strepf. Language?

Phid. Yes, the greater
Or lesser?

Strepf. I have bred thee well indeed
If thou canst make this good, that any Son
May beat his Father.

Phid. You'll confess as much
If I so prove it, that you cannot answer it.

Strepf. Well, I will hear for once what you can say.

SCENE II.

Chorus, Strepf. Phidip.

Chor. OLD Man, it much concerns you to confute
'Your Son, whose confidence appears to suit
'With a just cause; how happen'd this dispute?

Strepf. I shall relate it from the first; as soon
As we had dined, I took a Lute and bid him
Sing the Ship-shearing of *Simonides*:
He told me 'twas an old and ugly Fashion
To sing at dinner like a Miller's Wife.

Phid. And was not this sufficient to deserve
A beating; when you'd make Men chirp like † Grass-hoppers?

[margin: At Noon. *Virg. ecl.* 2.]

Strepf. Just so he said within; and added that
Simonides was an unpleasant Poet.
I must confess I hardly could forbear him;
But then I bid him take a Myrtle-branch
And act some piece of *Æschylus*: That *Æschylus*,
Saith he, is of all Poets the absurdest,
The harshest, most disorderly, and bombast.
Did not my heart pant at this Language think you?
Yet I represt it; then said I, rehearse
A learned Speech out of some modern wit;
He strait repeats out of *Euripides*
A tedious long Oration, how the Brother
(Good Heavens) did violate the Sister's Bed.
Here I confess I could contain no longer
But chid him sharply; to dispute we went,
Words upon words, till he at last to blows,
To strike, to pull, to tear me.

Phid. And not justly?
You that would discommend *Euripides*,
The wisest of all Poets.

Strepf. Wisest? ah
What did I say? I shall be beat again.

Phid. By *Jove* and you deserve it,

Strepf. How, deserve it?
Ungrateful Wretch, have I not brought thee up
Fed, and maintain'd thee from a little one,
Supplied thy wants? How then can I deserve it?

Chor. 'Now I believe each youthful breast
'With expectation possest,
'That if the Glory of the Day
'Be from the Plantiff born away,
'By this Example they may all
'Upon the Old Men heavy fall;
'What you have done with utmost art,
'To justifie is now your part.

Phid. How sweet it is to study, sage new things;
And to contemn all fundamental Laws!
When I applied my mind to Horse-coursing
I could not speak three words but I was out;
Now since I gave it ore, I am acquainted
With ponderous Sentences, and subtle Reasons,
Able to prove I ought to beat my Father.

Strepf. Nay, follow Racing still, for I had rather
Maintain thy Horses, than be beaten thus.

Phid. I will begin where you did interrupt me,
And first will ask, Did you not beat me when
I was a Child?

Strepf. But that was out of Love.

Phid. 'Tis very right, tell me then, ought not I
To recompence your Love with equal Love?
If to be beaten be to be belov'd,
Why should I suffer stripes, and you have none?
I am by nature born as free as you;
Nor is it fit the Sons should be chastiz'd,
And not their Parents.

Strepf. Why?

Phid. You urge the Law,
That doth allow all Children to be beaten:
To which I answer, old Men are twice Children,
And therefore ought when they offend, be punished
As well as we.

Strepf. But there's no Law that says
The

The Parents should be punished.
  Phid. Was not he
Who made that Law a Man as you and I?
He form'd a Law, which all the old Men followed.
Why may not I as well prescribe another,
And all the young Men follow my advice?
But all the Blows before this Law was made
Must be forgiven without all dispute.
Besides, mark how the Cocks and other creatures
Fight with their Sires, who differ not at all
From us, save only that they make no Laws.
  Streps. Why then if you will imitate the Cocks,
Do you not dine upon a Dunghil, and
Lodge in a Hen-roost?
  Phid. 'Tis not all one case,
Our *Socrates* doth not approve so far.
  Streps. Approve not then their fighting, but in this
Thou pleadest against thy self.
  Phid. How so?
  Streps. Because
Th'authority I exercise ore thee
Will be thine own, when ere thou hast a Son.
  Phid. But if I nere have any, then I never
Shall have Authority, and you will go
To th' Grave deriding me.
  Streps. 'Tis too much reason.
  Phid. Hear now another Argument.
  Streps. I'm lost.
  Phid. And then perhaps you'll take the blows I give you
Not half so ill.
  Streps. What good shall I get by them?
  Phid. I'll beat my Mother too.
  Streps. What sayst thou?
Why this is worse than t'other.
  Phid. What if I
Prove by the second Language that I ought?
  Streps. Why then you will have nothing more to do.
But prove that you, and your wife *Socrates*,
And wiser Language may hang all together.
O Clouds, all this I suffer through your means,
For I in you wholly repos'd my trust.
  Chor. ' Thy self art Author of this misery,
Because to ill thou didst thy mind apply.
  Streps. Why did you then give me no warning of it?
You know I was a rude and aged Man.
  Chor. ' This is our Custom whensoe'r we find
' Any to malice or deceit inclin'd,
' Into some dreadful mischief such we thrust,
' That they may fear the Gods, and learn what's
' just.
  Streps. Alas, this is a mischief, and a just one,
For ought I not, when I had borrowed Money,
To seek out ways t'avoid restoring it.
Come then my Son, let's be reveng'd
Upon that wicked *Socrates* and *Chærephon*,
Who have abus'd us both.
  Phid. I will not wrong
My Masters.

  Streps. Reverence Celestial *Jove*.
  Phid. Celestial *Jove*, see how you rave now Father:
There's no such thing as *Jove*.
  Streps. There is.
  Phid. * A Whirle-wind   * Act. III.
Hath blown *Jove* quite away, and rules all Heaven.
  Streps. No Son, he's not expell'd, I was but fool'd
To worship in his room a fictile Deity.
  Phid. Nay if you will needs be mad, be mad alone.

SCENE III.

Strepsiades.

Streps. MAD that I was to trust in *Socrates*, and cast off all our Gods; good *Mercury*,
Be not displeas'd, or punish, but forgive me,
That took such pains, and studied to talk idly,
And tell me what I'd best do with these Fellows,
Sue them or punish 'em some other way —
Th'art in the right, I will not sue them then,
But as thou bidst me, set their Nest on Fire;
Come *Xanthias*, come, a Fork and a Ladder quickly.
Get up and pluck the House about their Ears,
Quick if thou lovest thy Master; one of you
Go light a Torch, and bring it hither strait
Proud as they are I mean to bring 'em lower

SCENE IV.

Scholar, Strepsiades, Socrates, Chærephon.

  Schol. OH, oh!
  Streps. Torch to thy work; set Fire apace.
  Schol. What art thou doing, Man?
  Streps. That which I am doing;
Disputing somewhat hotly with your School here.
  Schol. Alas, who's this that sets our House on Fire?
  Streps. He whom you cousen'd of his Cloak.
  Schol. Thou kill'st,
Thou kill'st us, Man.
  Streps. That is the thing I mean,
If my Fork hold, and Ladder do not fail me.
  Socr. How now, what do you make on our House-ridge.
  Streps. † I walk in the Air and gaze upon the † Act II.
Sun.   Scene III.
  Socr. Alas I'm choak'd.
  Streps. Why dost thou scorn the Gods then?
  Chær. Oh me, I burn;
  Streps. Now you may calculate
The motions of the Moon; tear, pluck, beat, burn 'em.
For many reasons they deserve the Flame,
But most because they did the Gods disclaim.

XENOPHON.

CHAP. I.

Xenophon, his Country, Parents, and following of Socrates.

Laert.
* Laert.
‡ De Longæv.

* Animadv. 5.
32.

XEnophon was an *Athenian*, Son of *Gryllus*, of the *Erchiean* Tribe: the time of his birth is no where expresly delivered :* *Stesiclides* affirms *he died the first year of the one hundred and fifth Olympiad.* † Lucian *that he outlived ninety Years*: whence it is evident he was born at or before the first year of the Eighty second Olympiad, which if the learned *Casaubon* had observed, he had not * altered *Athenæus* upon sup- position, that he was but ten years old, the 4th year of the eighty ninth Olympiad (the time of his *Symposium*) whereas he was then no less than thirty six years of age. L*aertius* saith, *he flourished the fourth year of the ninety fourth Olympiad.* (*Suidas* reads *of the ninety eight*) Or, according to others, that *he flourished in the eighty ninth Olympiad with the rest of the* Socratick *Philosophers*; of whom he became one upon this Accident.

* Meeting

† Meeting *Socrates* in a narrow Lane, he stopt him with his Staff, and asked him where all kind of Meats were to be sold; to which *Socrates* made a serious Answer: And then demanded of him, where it was that Men were made good and vertuous? whereat *Xenophon* pausing, *follow me then*, faith he, *and learn*; from thenceforward he became a Disciple of *Socrates*.

In the time of that great War betwixt the *Lacedæmonians* and *Athenians*, called the *Peloponnesian War* (the natural forwardness of his Spirit, being perhaps excited by the example of his Master *Socrates*) he was personally engaged in the fight before *Delium*, the first year of the 89th Olympiad, wherein the *Bæotians* overcame the *Athenians*; in which defeat * *Xenophon* in the flight, unhorsed and thrown down, *Socrates* (who, his Horse being likewise slain under him, fought on foot) took him upon his Shoulders, and carried him many furlongs, until the Enemy gave over the pursuit. This was the first essay of his Military Profession, which he afterward resumed upon this occasion.

† *Laert.*

* *Strab. 9. Laert.*

CHAP. II.

Upon what occasion he follow'd Cyrus *into Asia.*

† *Xenoph. expedit. Cyr. lib. 1.*

† ARtaxerxes succeeded *Darius* his Father, in the Kingdom of *Persia*, *Cyrus* his younger Brother having been sent for out of his Government of *Lydia* upon his Father's sickness, which is that first ἀνάβασις: plac'd by the *Arundelian* stone in the second year of the 93d Olympiad (confounded by * a Learned Person with the latter, six years after) was imprison'd by his Brother upon the accusation of *Tissaphernes*, but released by the mediation of his Mother *Parysatis*. Being return'd to his Government, he used all secret means to strengthen himself. The *Ionian* Cities were deliver'd to *Tissaphernes* by *Artaxerxes*, but revolted to him, all except *Miletus*. His Pretences for levying Forces were, the Garrisoning of those Cities, and his opposing *Tissaphernes*: *Clearchus* likewise raised for him many in *Chersonesus*, upon pretence of warring against the *Thracians*. He privately also kept an Army on foot in *Thessaly* under *Aristippus*: and *Proxenus of Bæotia* brought him Forces as against the *Pisidians*; this *Proxenus* (who had been Scholar to *Gorgias* the *Leontine*, and † guest to *Xenophon*) sent to invite him to *Cyrus*, assuring him he should be of more esteem with him than of his own Country: *Xenophon* consulted with *Socrates* about this Letter, who doubting that if he took part with *Cyrus*, the *Athenians* should be displeased with him (*Cyrus* having before aided the *Lacedæmonians* against them) counselled him to ask the advice of the *Delphian* Oracle, *Xenophon* went thither, and demanded of *Apollo* to which of the Gods he should address his vows, and sacrifice for the good success of his intended Journey. He was answered, that he should sacrifice to those Gods to whom it was due: Returning to *Athens*, he imparted this Oracle to *Socrates*, who blam'd him, because he had not demanded whether it was best to stay or no, but (as already determin'd to go) how he might best perform his journey; Nevertheless

* *Ad Græc. Epoc. can. Chron. pag. 113.*

† *Xen. lib. 3.*

(faith he) since you have so proposed your demand, you must do as the Gods command: *Xenophon* having sacrificed according to the Oracles Direction, took Shipping, and at *Sardis* found *Proxenus* and *Cyrus* ready for their expedition into *Asia*; and was immediately recommended to *Cyrus*, being by both earnestly intreated to stay: He continued with him * not in any command, but as a Voluntier. † In which condition he did not any thing misbeseeming a Soldier, whereupon he was in the number of those whom *Cyrus* esteem'd most.

* *Xen. lib. 3.*

† *Chio. Epist. ad Metrid.*

* *Cyrus* having drawn all his Forces together, marched up and gave Battle to *Artaxerxes* (in the beginning of the fourth Year of the ninety fourth Olympiad, when *Zenenetus* was Archon) at *Cunaxa*, five hundred Stadia from *Babylon*, by the River *Euphrates*. Whilst he was viewing both Armies, he told *Xenophon*, who rode up to him, that the Sacrifices were auspicious; then *Xenophon* gave him the *Grecians* word, *Jupiter the Preserver*. The *Greeks* prevailed against *Tissaphernes*, but *Cyrus* assaulting, the King was thro' his too much forwardness, slain; the *Grecians* thinking themselves Masters of the Field, and *Cyrus* to be alive, return'd to their Camp, which they found rifled by the Enemy. * The next day the King sending *Phalinus* to them to deliver their Arms, *Xenophon* answered 'That they had nothing left but their Arms 'and Valour; as long as they kept their Arms, 'they might use their Valour, surrendring them, 'they were not Masters of themselves: It were 'Indiscretion (faith he) to surrender what we 'have left, since thereby perhaps we may make 'our selves Masters of what you have. *Phalinus* smiling, replyed, Young Man, you look 'and speak like a Philosopher; but assure 'your self your Valour will not over-master the King's Power. *Clearchus* returned this Answer for the whole Army, 'If we be esteem'd friends, 'it will be better for him that we are arm'd, if 'Enemies, better for our selves. *Tissaphernes* having made a Truce with *Clearchus*, perfidiously got him with four other Commanders, *Proxenus*, *Menon*, († with whom *Xenophon* had particular Enmity) *Agias*, and *Socrates*, twenty Captains of Cohorts, and two hundred common Soldiers into his Power; and delivering them up to the King, they were beheaded. The *Greeks* being summoned to lay down their Arms, pretending that *Clearchus* was executed for Treason discovered by *Menon* and *Proxenus*, who were very highly rewarded. *Xenophon* required to have them sent who were fittest to direct them, being Friends to both; whereto the *Persians* not able to answer, departed.

* *Xenoph. lib. 1. Laert.*

* *Xenoph. lib. 2.*

† *Laert.*

CHAP. III.

How he brought off the Grecians *Army.*

* THE *Greeks* finding themselves in such a strait, were in despair ever to see their Country again. *Xenophon* calling together the Officers of *Proxenus*, told them, 'They were 'not to expect any Mercy from the King, 'who had shewn none to the body of his dead 'Brother, having fastned his head and hand to 'a Gib-

* *Xenoph. lib. 3.*

'a Gibbet, and that they muſt reſolve to put 'their ſafety in their Arms. *Apollonides* a *Bœotian* alledg'd, that there was no means of ſafety but in the King's Favour, and began to reckon the dangers wherewith they were ſurrounded. *Xenophon* anſwered.' That when upon the death 'of *Cyrus*, they marched up to the King's 'Armies, he laboured for a ceſſation, but when 'their Captains went to him unarm'd, he abu-'ſed them; and that *Apollonides* deſerved to be 'caſhiered, as the diſhonour of his Nation, *Agaſthias* replied, (which words *Laertius* aſcribes to *Xenophon*) 'he was an inconſiderable Fellow, whoſe Ears were bored as the 'Slaves of *Lydia* : So they turned him out. Having called together all the Commanders, *Xenophon* adviſed them to chooſe new in the room of thoſe that were loſt, of whom he was elected in the place of *Proxenus* : Hereupon he put on his richeſt habit,as fitteſt either for death or victory, for his † greateſt delight was in fair poliſhed arms, affirming, that if he overcame, he deſerved ſuch; if he were overcome, and died in the Field, they would decently expreſs his Quality, and were the fitteſt Sepulchral Ornaments of a Valiant Man. His Shield was of *Argos*, his Breaſt-plate of *Attica*, his Helmet of *Bœotia*, his Horſe of *Epidaurium*; whereby *Ælian* argued the Elegance of the Perſon, in chooſing ſuch things as were fair, and eſteeming him worthy of ſuch. Thus adorned, he made an Oration to the Army, adviſing them (from the Examples of their late Commanders) not to truſt the Enemy, but in order to their return, to burn their Carriages and Tents : This advice was put in Execution ; *Cheriſophus* a *Lacedæmonian*, had charge of the Van, *Xenophon* of the Reer, choſen (ſaith *Chio*) as well for his Courage as Wiſdom, being in both excellent : betwixt theſe two there grew ſo great a friendſhip, that in all the time of the Retreat, they never had but one difference ; their March was directed towards the heads of thoſe great Rivers which lay in their way, that they might paſs them where they were fordable ; having croſſed the River *Zathe*, *Mithridates* came up to them, and galled the Reer with Shot, which the *Greeks* not able to requite, *Xenophon* provided two hundred Slings, and finding fifty Horſes fit for Service, imployed among the Carriages, mounted Men upon them, whereby having fruſtrated the ſecond attempt of *Mithridates*,they march'd to *Lariſſa*, ſeated upon *Tygris*, thence to *Miſpila* ; in their march from thence, *Tiſſaphernes* overtook them with a great Army, but was twice worſted ; whereupon (as the ſecureſt Courſe) he ſeized on a Mountain under which they muſt of neceſſity paſs ; *Xenophon* with a Party gained by another way the top of that Mountain, not without much difficulty of paſſage and trouble ; and to animate his Soldiers, one of them, named *Soteridas*, murmured that he was on Horſeback, whereas himſelf marched on Foot, oppreſſed with the weight of his Shield; which *Xenophon* hearing, alighted, took his Shield from him, and thruſting him out of his Rank, marched (notwithſtanding he had alſo a Horſe-man's Cuiraſs) in his room : But the Soldiers beat and revi-led *Soteridas*, till they conſtrained him to take again his Shield and place. When they had gained the top, the Enemy, being prevented, fled, and ſet fire on the Villages. * The *Grecians*(intercepted by the River *Tygris*) marched over the Mountains into the Country of the *Carduchi*,a People Enemy to the *Perſians*,rough and Warlike, from whom they found ſuch Oppoſition, that in ſeven days March through their Country, they were put to continual fights, and ſufferedmore diſtreſſes than the *Perſian* had put them to. Fording the River *Kentrites*, which bounds that Country, they paſſed into *Armenia*,where having put to flight ſome troops of Horſe,raiſed by the King's Deputies in theſe Parts to oppoſe their paſſage, they marched without diſturbance to the Heads of *Tygris*, which they paſſed ; thence to the River of *Teleboa* in *Weſt Armenia*,moleſted with extream Snows,loſing many by extremity of cold, till they came to the River *Phaſis*, near which liv'd the *Phaſiani*, *Tacchi*, and the *Chalybes* ; the *Tacchi*, into whoſe Country they firſt came, conveying their Proviſions into ſtrong holds, reduced the *Greeks* to great want, until with much Pains they forced one of them, where they took as much Cattle as maintained them in their Paſſage through the Country of the *Chalybes*, a ſtout Nation, of whom they could get nothing but blows: Thence they marched to the River *Harpaſus*,ſo to the *Scythidi*, where the Lord of *Gymnias*, a Town in thoſe Parts led them through the Enemies Country (which he willed them to burn as they went) to the Mountain *Theches*,from whence they might behold the Sea, to the great Joy of the Soldiers. Paſſing friendly through the Country of the *Macrones*, to the *Colchian* Mountains, diſcomfiting the *Colchi*, who oppoſed them, they arrived at *Trapezond*,a City upon the *Euxine* Sea, where was a *Greek Colony* ; here they ſacrificed and celebrated Games :† *Cheriſophus* they ſent to *Anaxibius*, the *Lacedæmonian* Admiral,(with whom he was intimate)to procure Ships for their tranſportation home. Whilſt they ſtayed in expectation of his return, they maintained themſelves by Incurſions upon the *Colchi*, and *Drylani* ; but he not coming, and their Proviſion failing,*Xenophon* perſwaded the Cities adjoyning to clear them a paſſage by Land, which they took to *Ceraſus*, a *Greek* City, where muſtering their Men, they found but eight thouſand ſix hundred left of ten thouſand that went up with *Cyrus*, the reſt conſum'd by Enemies, Snow, Sickneſs : They ſhared the Money that had been made by the ſale of Captives, reſerving a tenth for an Offering to *Apollo*, and *Diana* : *Xenophon* preſerved his to be diſpoſed at *Delphi* and *Epheſus*.From *Ceraſus* they paſſed through the Country of the *Moſynæci*, a barbarous People,divided into Factions ; the ſtronger part deſpiſing their Friendſhip, they joyned with the weaker, whom they left Maſters of all : Then they marched to the *Chalybes*, thence to the *Tibarenes*,paſſing quietly through their Country to *Cotiora*, a *Greek* Town and Colony of the *Sinopians*.Thus far the Army marched on Foot ; the diſtance of the place where they fought with *Artaxerxes* to *Cotyora*, being one hundred twenty two Encampings, ſix hundred twenty paraſangs, ten thouſand

† *Ælian. var. hiſt.* 3. 24.

* *Xenophon lib.* 4.

† *Xenophon lib.* 5.

thousand eight hundred twenty furlongs, the time eight Months.

Those of *Cotyora* refusing to afford them a Market, or entertainment for their Sick, they entred the Town by force, and took Provision, partly out of *Paphlagonia*, partly out of the Territory of the *Cotionytes*; whereupon the City of *Sinope*, to which *Cotyora* was tributary, sent Ambassadors to them, complaining of this dealing, and threatning to join with *Corylas* and the *Paphlagonians*; whereto *Xenophon* answered, *That they feared not, if need were, to War against them both, but could, if they pleased, gain the Friendship of* Corylas *and the* Paphlagonians *as well as they*. Upon which Answer, the Ambassadors growing calm, promised them all Friendship from the State of *Sinope*, and to assist them with Shipping for the whole Army, it being impossible to go by Land, by reason of the Rivers *Thermodon, Halys, Iris,* and *Parthenius*.

Xenophon had designed to plant a *Colony* there, but his intention being divulged by *Silanus*, a Sooth-sayer, those of *Sinope* and *Heraclea*, sent to the *Grecians*, promising them not only a sufficient Fleet, but desiring under-hand *Timasion*, a *Greek* Commander to promise the Army a good Sum of Money to convey them to *Troas*; which offers *Xenophon* (who only desired the common good) perswaded them to accept, and to engage mutually, not to forsake one another till they were all in safety : Those of *Heraclea* sent Shipping, but not the Money; whereupon *Timasion* and other Commanders fearing the Soldiers, desired *Xenophon* the Army might go to *Phasis*, which he refused, but thereby was occasioned a suspicion that he should Plot to deceive the Army, and to bring them back to *Phasis*, whereof he acquitted himself. Here a general Inquisition was made of all offences since the death of *Cyrus*, and they were punished; some accused *Xenophon* for beating them, all which proved for just causes, one for offering to bury his sick Companion alive; some for forsaking their Ranks; others for lying on the Ground in the Snow, or lingring behind. Thus were all things quietly settled.

CHAP. IV.

End of the Retreat.

Xenoph. lib. 6. THE *Greeks*, as soon as their Fleet was ready, set sail for *Harmond*, the Port of *Sinope*, when *Chirisophus* met them with some Galleys, from *Anaxibius*, who promised them pay as soon as they should come into *Greece*. The Army desirous of a General, intreated *Xenophon* (with extraordinary Testimony of affection) to accept that Command: *Xenophon* refused, either disswaded by inauspicious Sacrifice, or unwilling to displease the *Lacedæmonians*, in putting by *Chirisophus*, who was thereupon chosen, but soon after deposed, for refusing to extort a great Sum from *Heraclea*, a *Greek* City, their Friends : *Xenophon* also denying to be employed therein, the Army thereupon became divided; they chose ten Captains out of themselves; with *Chirisophus* remained two thousand one hundred, with *Xenophon* two thousand foot, and forty Horse; *Chirisophus* went by land to meet *Cleander* Governour of *Byzantium*, at the Mouth of the River *Calphas*, leaving such Shipping as he had to *Xenophon*, who landing in the Confines of *Thrace*, and of the *Heraclean* Country, marched quietly through the midst of the Land : The Mutineers landing at *Calphas*, surprised and spoiled the Country thereabout ; the *Thracians* rising up against them, cut off two Regiments, and besieged the Hill where the rest encamped. *Xenophon* on the way being inform'd of the desperate condition of these *Greeks*, went directly to the place, setting on fire as he went all that was combustible ; the Enemy fearing to be set upon in the Night, stole away, as did the *Greeks* also, whom *Xenophon* overtaking in the way to the Port of *Calphas*, they embrac'd him with great Joy, and arriving at the Haven, made a Decree that it should be Death for any man to propound to divide the Army, and that they should depart the Country in their first order. The former Commanders being restored in the room of *Chirisophus*, who died, they substituted *Neon*, who going forth with two thousand Men to Pillage the Country, was discomfited by *Pharnabazus*, Lieutenant to the King of *Persia*, and lost five hundred Men; the rest rescued by *Xenophon*, the Army by his encouragement marched through a large Forrest defeating *Pharnabazus*, who opposed their Passage there. *Cleander* came over to them, and having expressed much kindness to *Xenophon*, and contracted Hospitality with him, departed. The Army marched through *Bythinia* to *Chrysopolis*, in the Territories of *Chalcedon*.* Thence *Anaxibius* the *Lacedæmonian* Admiral transported them to *Byzantium*, where he had promised they should as soon as they arrived, receive Pay, without which he sent them out of the City, whereat the Soldiers incensed, returned and entred the City by force, intending to spoil it : But *Xenophon* thrusting himself amongst the Crowd, disswaded them, and appeased the Tumult, as is particularly attested by † *Chio*, an Eye-witness. By this means they were brought to depart the City quietly, which as soon as they had done, *Xenophon* desirous to go home, took leave of the Army, and returned to *Byzantium* with *Cleander*. *Anaxibius* being put out of the Admiralship, and thereupon slighted by *Pharnabazus* (at whose Instigation he had treated the *Greeks* so hardly) desired *Xenophon* to return to the Army to lead 'em to *Perinthus*, whence they should be transported into *Asia* ; the Army received him with much Joy : When they came to *Perinthus*, *Aristarchus* the Governour would not suffer them to be Transported : *Seuthes* King of *Thrace* had invited them to aid him against *Medocus*, Usurper of his Kingdom, with large offers of Money to every Soldier, of his Daughter to *Xenophon*: To him therefore, not knowing where to winter, they went. At Supper every one (according to the custom) drank to the King, and made him a Present : *Xenophon*, who sate next him, rising up, and taking the Cup, told him he gave him himself and all his Companions to be his faithful Friends, and ready
Servants

* *Xenoph. lib. 7.*

† *In Epistola ad Metridem.*

'Servants in the recovery of his Kingdom: 'Herein their Assistance did much advantage *Senthes*, The Army wanting Pay, *Xenophon* reproved *Heraclides* for not taking order about it; who thereupon endeavoured to work him out of Favour with *Senthes*, to whom he brought the rest of the Commanders, counselling them to say, that if need were, they could lead the Army upon Service as well as *Xenophon*; but they jointly protested unto *Senthes*, they would not serve at all without him: So he sent for *Xenophon* also, and being agreed to proceed, they marched towards the Country of the *Melinophagi*, as far as *Salmydesson*: which Places having reduc'd, they returned to the Plains of *Selybria*, thither came *Chaminus* a *Lacedæmonian*, *Polinicus* sent from *Thymbro*, who told them that the *Lacedemonians* had designed War against *Tissaphernes*, the charge thereof was committed to *Thymbro*, who desir'd this Army of *Greeks* to assist them, promising them good Pay. *Seuthes* willingly yielded the Army into their Hands; they sent *Xenophon* to demand their Arrears, which not without much importunity he obtained. Thence they sailed to *Lampsacus*, where *Euclides* a Soothsayer of *Xenophon*'s acquaintance ask'd him, how much Gold he had brought? *Xenophon* protested he had not enough to carry him Home, but that he sold his Horse and other things which he had about him. The next day they marched to *Ophrynium*, whither came *Brito* and *Euclides* to pay the Army; they being *Xenophon*'s Friends, restored (refusing the price of Redemption) his Horse which he much lov'd, and had pawned at *Lampsacus*. Then Marching forward by *Attramyttium*, and *Kertonium*, not far from *Atarna*, to the Plain of *Caicus*, they reacht *Pergamus*, a City of *Lydia*. Here *Hellas*, Wife of *Gongylus* an *Eretrian*, Mother of *Gorgion*, and *Gongylus* entertain'd *Xenophon*: By her Information *Xenophon* surprised *Asidates* a rich *Persian*, with his Wife and Children, and all his Goods: Returning to *Pergamus*, the *Lacedæmonians*, Captains and Soldiers, by agreement gave him also an extraordinary share of Horses, Oxen, and other things; then came *Thymbro*, and taking the Army, joyn'd it to the rest of the *Grecian* Forces, wherewith he made a War against *Tissaphernes*.

Of the King's Provinces, through which they passed, the Governours were these; *Artimas* of *Lydia*, *Artacamus* of *Phrygia*, *Mithridates* of *Lacaonia*, and *Cappadocia*; of *Cicilia*, * *Syennesis*: of *Phœnicia* and *Arabia*, *Dernes*; of *Syria* and *Assyria*, *Belesis*: Of *Babylonia*, *Roparis*: of *Media*, *Arbacas*, of the *Physiani* and *Hesperita*, *Teribazus*, the *Carduchi*, *Chalybes*, *Chaldæans*, *Macrones*, *Colchi*, *Mosynæchi*, *Cœti*, and *Tibareni*, are free Nations; *Paphlagonia*, governed by *Corylas*; the *Bithynians* by *Pharnabazus*, the *European Thracians* by *Senthes*: The total number of the Ascent and Descent is two hundred and fifteen encampings, one thousand one hundred and fifty parasangs, thirty four thousand two hundred fifty five Furlongs; the time of the Ascent and Descent one Year and three Months.

* Which perhaps was a common name to the Kings of that Country, as *Ptolomy* to those of Egypt. See *Thales*. Chap.

CHAP. V.

His following of Agesilaus, *and Banishment.*

AFter this Expedition the defeat in *Pontus*, and breach of promise of *Senthes King of the Odrysians*; *Xenophon* went into *Asia* with *Agesilaus King of the Lacedæmonians, to whom he deliver'd for a sum of money the Soldiers of* Cyrus, *and beloved infinitely,* εἰς ὑπερβολὴν: Æmilius Probus *saith, he conversed intimately with him*: Cicero, *that he instructed him.* Plutarch *affirms, that by his advice* Agesilaus *sent his Sons to be Educated at* Sparta, *to learn and art them, which none was more excellent, how to obey and command.* Agesilaus *passed into* Asia, the first year of the 96th Olympiad; he warr'd successfully with the *Persian*, but the year following was call'd home by the *Lacedæmonians* to help his Country invaded by the *Thebans*, and their Allies, whom the *Persian* had corrupted, thereby to withdraw the War out of his Country. *Xenophon* in his returning with *Agesilaus* out of *Asia* into *Bœotia*, apprehending the danger of the War they were entring into, when he came to *Ephesus* left one half of the Gold ‡ which he had reserved for an offering out of his share (of the Money which the Army divided at *Cerasunt* in their return from the expedition of *Cyrus*) with *Megabyzus*, *Diana*'s Priest, willing that if he escaped the danger of that War, it should be restored to him, if he miscarried, consecrated to *Diana*, and either made into an Image dedicated to the Goddess, or disposed some way that he should conceive most acceptable to her: The other half he sent an offering to the *Athenian* treasury at *Delphi*, inscribing thereon both his own name and that of *Proxenus*, his Predecessor in the command of that Regiment. *Agesilaus* returning, wasted *Bœotia*, and overcame the *Thebans* and their Allies in a great Battle at *Coronea* † particularly describ'd by *Xenophon*, who was there present.

* Laert.

† Supr. chap. 3.

* Xenoph. lib. 5.

† Agesil.

During the absence of *Xenophon* out of his own Country, the *Athenians* (because he took part against the King of *Persia*, their Friend, and followed *Cyrus*, who had assisted the *Lacedæmonians* against them, * supplying *Lysander* their General with Money for a Navy) proclaimed a decree of Banishment against him: † *Ister* saith, he was banished by the decree of *Eubulus*, and called home by the same: *Laertius*, that he was banished for *Laconism*, upon his going to *Agesilaus*; Some place this Decree in the third year of the 96th Olympiad, but the writer of the History of *Cyrus* his Expedition implieth, that it was before his first return out of *Asia*, affirming that before the delivery of the Army to *Thymbro*, *Xenophon* ignorant of this Decree, intended to have gone home.

* Pausan.

† Laert.

CHAP. VI.

How he lived at Scilluns, *and at* Corinth.

THE *Lacedæmonians* to requite him for suffering in their cause, maintained him at the publick charge; and chasing *Scilluns* of the *Eleans*, built a Town there, and bestowed

stowed a fair house and land upon *Xenophon*, whereupon he left *Agesilaus*, and went thither, carrying with him his Wife named *Philesia*, and his two Sons, which he had by * her, *Diodorus* and *Gryllus*, called the Dioscury. † Thither *Pelopidas* a Spartan, sent him Captives for Slaves from *Dardanus* for a Present, to dispose of them as should please him.

Scilluns was near *Olympia*, eminent for celebration of the Games, which *Megabyzus* coming to see, restor'd to *Xenophon* the Money which he had left in his Custody, wherewith * by advice of the Oracle he purchased a portion of Land, and consecrated it to *Diana*, in a place designed by *Apollo*, through which ran the River *Selinus*, of the same name with that at *Ephesus*, running by *Diana's* Temple; the River was stored as well with shell-Fish as others, the Land with all kind of Beasts for game; he built also a Temple, and after with the consecrated Money offering the Tythes of the fruits of the Land to *Diana*, all the Citizens and Neighbours, Men and Women, were invited to the Feast, where they had from the Goddesses allowance, Bread, Wine, and part of the Flesh of such Beasts as were either taken out of the consecrated ground, and sacrificed, or killed in hunting with the Sons of *Xenophon* and other Citizens, exercised against the time of the Feast out of the sacred ground; and out of *Phaloe* were taken wild Boars, Goats, and Staggs; the place lies in the way betwixt *Lacedæmonia* and *Olympia*, twenty *Stadia* from the Temple of *Olympian Jupiter*. In the sacred ground were woods and hills, stored with Trees sufficient to maintain Swine, Goats and Sheep, whereby the Beasts of carriage of such Merchants as come to the Feast are maintained plentifully: About the Temple a Grove of Fruit trees of all sorts. The Temple was an imitation in little of that at *Ephesus*: an Image of Cypress here resembling that of Gold there: A Pillar near the Temple bare this inscription, GROUND SACRED TO DIANA. HE WHO POSSESSETH IT LET HIM PAY THE TYTHE OF HIS YEARLY ENCREASE, AND WITH THE SURPLUSAGE MAINTAIN THE TEMPLE, IF HE NEGLECT, THE GODDESS WILL TAKE ORDER FOR IT. † At this place of retirement *Xenophon* employed his time in Hunting, and writing Histories, inviting his Friends thither, * of whom amongst others came *Phædo*, and *Aristippus*, much delighted with the Situation, building, and Trees planted by the hand of the owner.

† At length a War arising betwixt the *Eleans* and *Lacedæmonians*, the *Elians* invaded *Scilluns* with a great Army, and before the *Lacedæmonians* came to their relief, seized on the house and lands of *Xenophon*; his Sons with some few Servants got away privately to *Lepreum*; *Xenophon* first to *Elis*, then to *Lepreum* to his Sons, and lastly with them to *Corinth*, where he took a house, and continued the rest of his life. During this time the *Argives*, *Arcadians*, and *Thebans*, jointly opprest the *Lacedæmonians*, and had almost opprest them, when the *Athenians* made a publick decree (* mention'd by *Xenophon*) to succour them; *Xenophon* sent his Sons upon the expedition to *Athens* to fight for the *Lacedæmonians*; for (as *Diocles* affirms) they had been educated at *Sparta*, in the discipline of that Place.

This enmity ended in a great Battle at *Mantinea* in the 2d Year of the hundred and fourth Olympiad: *Diodorus* without acting any thing memorable, gave off safe, and had afterwards a Son of his Brother's Name. *Gryllus* was rank'd opposite to the *Theban* Horsemen: The *Thebans* having by the valour of their General *Epaminondas* got the better of the day, a resolute company of *Spartan* Horsemen broke in upon him, of whom was *Gryllus*, who flew *Epaminondas* with his own Hand, as *Pausanius* affirms to have been attested both by the *Athenians*, and the *Thebans*, adding, that he had seen at *Athens* a picture of the Battle at *Mantinea*, confirming the same; and that at *Mantinea* was erected a Pillar with the Statue of *Gryllus* on horse-back. In this noble action *Gryllus* lost his life, the news of whose death came to *Xenophon* at *Corinth*, as he was Sacrificing, crown'd with a Garland; as soon as he heard his Son was slain, he took off his Garland and laid it aside; then demanding after what manner he died, it was answered, fighting stoutly in the midst of his Enemies, of whom having slain many, he fell at last himself: Hereupon *Xenophon* took again his Garland, and putting it upon his Head, proceeded to Sacrifice, not so much as shedding one tear, only saying, *I knew that I had begot a Mortal*; † and calling the Gods to whom he sacrific'd, to witness, that the vertue of his Son gave him more content, than his death sorrow. * Innumerable were the Epitaphs and Encomiums that were written upon *Gryllus* to please *Xenophon*, whence may be collected in how great esteem he was.

That he made a visit to *Dionysius* Tyrant of *Sicily* (but at what time is uncertain) is implied by † *Athenæus*, who relateth, that being at a Feast of his, compelled by the Cup-bearer to drink, he called the Tyrant by Name: *What is the matter* Dionsius, *(saith he) your Cook, though excellent in that Art, doth not enforce us to eat against our Inclination?*

CHAP. VII.

His Death, Person, Vertues.

XEnophon being * *full of years* (which according to † *Lucian* exceeded ninety) died at *Corinth*, in the first of the hundred and fifth Olympiad, *Callidemus*, or *Callimedes* being Archon, at what time *Philip*, Son of *Amintus*, began his Reign in *Macedonia*. He had an ingenious modest look, long, thick Hair, handsome (to use the words of *Laertius*) beyond expression, *Adroit in every thing, particularly addicted to Horses and hunting, skilful in Tacticks, as his Writings attest; devout, a great lover of Sacrifices, skilful in interpreting them; an exact imitator of* Socrates, *temperate, as* appears from his saying, that * *It is pleasant hungry, to eat Herbs; thirsty, to drink Water*. So candid and ingenious, that * when he might have stolen the Writings of *Thucydides*, which lay concealed, he chose rather to publish them with Honour.

In a word, he was a person every way absolute, as well for action, as contemplation. Xenophon (saith * *Eunapius*) *was the only Man of all the Philosophers who adorn'd Philosophy with his words and actions; he describes Moral Vertue in his discourses and writings: In his actions he was singular; as to his conduct, a most excellent General. Alexander had not been great, if Xenophon had not said, even the perfunctory actions of valiant Persons ought to be recorded.*

*Proœm.

† He was the first that committed the disputes of *Socrates* his Master, to writing, and that with much Fidelity, not inserting excursions of his own, as *Plato* did, whom for that reason, as * *A. Gellius* observes, he argueth of Falshood; that there was a great enmity betwixt these two is affirmed by the same Author, who, as a proof thereof alledgeth, that neither of them names the other in any of their writings: † *Vossius* only observes, that *Xenophon* mentions *Plato* once in his ἀπομνημονεύματα, overseen by *A. Gellius*. This enmity is further acknowledged by † *Athenæus* and *Laertius*, confirmed by the Epistle of *Xenophon* to *Æschines*, wherein he condemns *Plato*, that not being satisfied with the Doctrine of *Socrates*, he went to the *Pythagoreans* in *Italy*, and to the *Ægyptian* Priests; arguments of a mind not constant to *Socrates*. That he was at difference with * *Aristippus* also, argued from his Writings.

† Laert.

* Lib. 14.

† De histor. Grec. l. 5.
* Lib. 3.
† Deipnos. 11.

* Laert. vit. Aristipp.

Laertius hath two Epigrams concerning him, the first upon his going with *Cyrus* into upper *Asia*

Great Xenophon at once made two ascents,
To Asia in Person, and to Heaven by fame:
His stile and action (lasting Monuments)
Lay to Socratick Wisdom equal claim.

The other upon his Banishment.

Thee the Cecropians, noble Xenophon,
Banisht their Land 'cause Cyrus thou didst aid;
But strangers prov'd far kinder than thy own:
What Athens ow'd thee, was by Corinth paid.

Laertius reckons seven *Xenophons*, this the first, the second an *Athenian*, Brother to *Nicostratus*, Author of the *Theses*; besides many other things, he writ the lives of *Pelopidas* and *Epaminondas*; the third, a Physician of *Coos*; the fourth, writer of the History of *Hannibal*: The fifth, writer of fabulous Monsters: the sixth, of *Paros* a Statuary: the seventh, an old Comick Poet: *Suidas* reckons three more; one of *Antioch*, the second of *Ephesus*, the third of *Cyprus*; Historians, or rather writers of Romances; that of the first called *Babylonica*, of the second *Ephesica* in ten Books; of the third *Cypriaca*: The Story of *Cynarus*, *Myrrha*, and *Adonis*.

CHAP. VIII.
His Writings.

Dionysius Halicarnassæus saith, that *Xenophon* was a studious Æmulator of *Herodotus*, both in words and language: His stile (according to *Cicero*) * *soft* and † *sweet* (melle dulcior) *far differing from the noise of Orators in the Forum: In his voice, * the Muses seem to speak*, whence he was sirnamed *the Attick Muse*; or according to others, *the Attick Bee*, a title formerly conferred on † *Sophocles*. His stile and manner of writing is at large discoursed upon by *Aristides Adrianensis* in an express Tract, erroneously ascribed to *Hermogenes*.

*Brut. & de Oratore. lib. 2.
* Orator.
* Cic. Orat.

† Vit. Sophocl.

The Books of *Xenophon* (which * *Scipio Africanus* had always in his hand, and † *Cicero* adviseth to read, as very profitable in many things) were (as reckoned by *Lartius*) forty, which several Persons distinguish severally; the general titles these

* Cicer. Tusc. quæst. 3.
† De senect.

Κύρου παιδεία; *the life and discipline of* Cyrus (as *Cicero* renders it) in eight Books, written *non ad historiæ fidem* (though * *Diodorus Siculus* seems to take it in that quality) *sed ad effigiem justi imperii*; not as a faithful History, but the description of an exact Prince: Whence † *Ausonius* saith, *in relating the vertues of* Cyrus, *he hath given rather a wish than a History, describing, not what he was, but what he ought to have been*.

* Lib. 15.

‡ Grat. act.

Κύρου ἀνάβασις; *the going up of* Cyrus *the younger into* Asia, in seven Books; each of which (as *Laertius* observes) hath a Proœm, the whole none: *Masius* suspects that *Xenophon* was not the Author of this Book; the Bishop of * *Armach* ascribes it to *Themistogenes*, though own'd as *Xenophon's* by *Plutarch*, *Cicero*, *Dionysius Halicarnassus*, *Hermogenes*, *Laertius*, *Athenæus*, and others.

*Annal.

Ἑλληνικα; *the Greek History*, in seven Books, continuing where *Thucydides* left; the same was done by *Theopompus*, but he went no further than sixteen Years, *Xenophon* to forty eight.

Agesilaus, of which piece *Cicero* saith, that *Agesilaus would not suffer his Picture or Statue to be made, this Book alone surpasseth all Pictures or Images in his Praise.*

The Republick of the Lacedæmonians, *and the Republick of the* Athenians, which *Demetrius* denieth to be *Xenophon's*.

† Laert.

The defence of Socrates, *and the memorials of* Socrates, which perhaps is that *History of Philosophers* mentioned by *Suidas*.

Oeconomicks, the last Book of the memorable discourses, wherewith * *Cicero* was so much delighted, that in his younger years he translated it.

Offic. 2.

Symposium, accommodated to the fourth year of the eighty ninth Olympiad, for which reason reprehended by *Athenæus*, as erroneous in Chronology; vindicated by the learned *Casaubon*.

Hiero, Or, *of a Kingdom*.
The accounts of Revenues.
Of Horses.
Of Horsemanship.
Of Hunting,
Epistles.

Besides these which are extant, *Xenophon* seems to have written other things; * *Valerius Maximus* and † *Pliny* cite his *Periplus*.

* 8. 13.
† 7. 48.

There is a Treatise of Æquivokes under *Xenophon's* name, but made and imposed upon the World by *Annius*.

XENO-

Xenophons Epistles.

To Æschines. Epist. I.

Meeting with *Hermogenes*, amongst other things I asked him what Philosophy you followed, he answered, the same as *Socrates*. For this inclination I admired you, when you lived at *Athens*, and now continue the same admiration for your Constancy above other Students of Wisdom; the greatest Argument to me of your Vertue, is your being taken with that Man, if we may call the Life of *Socrates* Mortal. That there are Divine Beings over us, all know: We Worship them as exceeding us in Power; what they are is neither easie to find, nor lawful to enquire. It concerns not Servants to examine the Nature and Actions of their Masters, their Duty is only to Obey them; and which is most considerable, the more admiration they deserve who busie themselves in those things which belong to Man; the more trouble this brings them, who affect Glory in vain unseasonable Objects: For when (*Æschines*) did any Man hear *Socrates* discourse of the Heavens, or advise his Scholars to Mathematical Demonstrations? we know he understood Musick no farther than the Ear: But was always discoursing to his Friends of something excellent; what is Fortitude and Justice and other Virtues. These he called the proper good of Mankind; other things he said Men could not arrive at; or they were of kin to Fables, such ridiculous things as are taught by the superciliuos Professors of Wisdom. Nor did he only teach this; his practice was answerable; of which I have written at large elsewhere, what I hope will not be unpleasing to you, (though you know it already) to peruse. Let * those who are not satisfied with what *Socrates* delivered, give over upon this conviction, or confine themselves to what is probable. Living, he was attested wise by the Deity; Dead, his Murderers could find no expiation by Repentance: But these extraordinary persons affect *Ægypt* and the prodigious Learning of *Pythagoras*, which unnecessary Study argueth them of Inconstancy towards *Socrates*, as doth also their Love of Tyrants, and preferring the Luxury of a *Sicilian* Table before a frugal Life.

* Meaning *Plato*, who added much of his own to the discourses of *Socrates*, and went to *Ægypt, Italy,* and *Sicily*.

To Crito. Epist. II.

Stob. serm. 201.

Socrates often told us, that they who provide much Wealth for their Children, but neglected to improve them by Virtue, do like those that feed their Horses high, and never train them to the Manage: by this means their Horses are the better in Case, but the worse for Service, whereas the commendations of a Horse consists not in his being fat, but serviceable in War. In the same kind err they who purchase Lands for their Children, but neglect their Persons; their Possessions will be of great value, themselves of none, whereas the owner ought to be more honourable than his Estate. Whosoever therefore breeds his Son well, though he leave him little, gives him much: It is the Mind which makes him great or small: whatsoever they have, to the good seems sufficient, to the rude too little. You leave your Children no more than necessity requires, which they being well educated, will esteem plentiful. The Ignorant though free from present trouble, have nothing the less fear for the future.

To Sotira. Epist. III.

† Death in my Opinion is neither good nor ill, but the end of the Life, not alike to all, for as stronger or weaker from their Birth, their years are unequal; sometimes Death is hastned by good or evil causes: and again : * neither is it fitting to grieve so much for Death, knowing that Birth is the beginning of Man's Pilgrimage, Death the end. He died as all Men (though never so unwilling) must do: but to die well, is the part of a willing and well educated person. Happy was *Gryllus*, and whosoever else chooseth not the longest life, but the most virtuous: though his (it pleased God) was short.

† *Stob. serm. 892.*

* *Stob. serm. 278.*

To Lamprocles. Epist. IV.

You must first approve the excellent assertion of *Socrates*, that *Riches are to be measured by their use*. He called not large Possessions Riches, but so much only as is necessary: in the judgment whereof he advised us not be deceived, these he called truly rich, the rest poor, labouring under an incurable poverty of mind, not estate.

Stob.

*Epist. V.

They who † write in praise of my Son *Gryllus*, did as they ought: and you likewise do well in writing to us the actions of *Socrates*; we ought not only to endeavour to be good our selves, but to praise him who lived chastly, piously, and justly, and to blame Fortune, and those who plotted against him, who ere long will receive the punishment thereof. The *Lacedæmonians* are much incensed at it, (for the ill news is come hither already) and reproach our People, saying, they are mad again, in that they could be wrought upon to put him to death whom *Pythia* declared the wisest of Men. If any of *Socrates*'s Friends want those things which I sent, give me notice, and I will help them, for it is just and honest: you do well in keeping *Æschines* with you, as you send me word. I have a design to collect the Sayings and Actions of *Socrates*, which will be his best Apology, both now and for the future, not in the Court where the *Athenians* are Judges, but to all who consider the Virtue of the Man. If we should not write this freely, it were a sin against Friendship, and the Truth. Even now there

* *Epist. Socratick. 18.*

† *Allatius otherwise.*

there fell into my hands a Piece of *Plato*'s to that effect, wherein is the name of *Socrates*, and some Discourses of his not unpleasant. But we must profess that we heard not, nor can commit to writing any in that kind, for we are not Poets as he is, though he renounce Poetry; for amidst his entertainments with beautiful persons, he affirmed that there was not any Poem of his extant, but one of *Socrates*, young and handsome. Farewell, both, dearest to me.

Epist. VI.

Epist. Socr. 21. INtending to celebrate the Feast of *Diana*, to whom we have erected a Temple, we sent to invite you hither; if all of you would come, it were much the best, otherwise, if you send such as you can conveniently spare to assist at our Sacrifice, you will do us a favour. *Aristippus* was here, (and before him) *Phædo*, who were much pleased with the Situation and Structure, but above all, with the Plantation which I have made with mine own hands. The place is stored with Beasts convenient for hunting, which the Goddess affects; let us rejoyce and give thanks to her who preserved me from the King of the *Barbarians*, and afterwards in *Pontus* and *Thrace* from greater evils, even when we thought we were out of the Enemies reach. Though you come not, yet am I obliged to write to you. I have composed some Memorials of *Socrates*, when they are perfect you shall have them. *Aristippus* and *Phædo* did not disapprove of them; salute in my name *Simon* the Leather-dresser, and commend him that he continueth *Socratick* Discourses, not diverted by Want, or his Trade, from Philosophy, as some others, who decline to know and admire such discourses and their effects.

Epist. VII.

Epist. Socr. 19 COme to us dear friend, for we have now finished the Temple of *Diana*, a Magnificent Structure, the place set with Trees, and consecrated, what remains will be sufficient to maintain us; for as *Socrates* said, if they are not fit for us, we will fit our selves to them; I write to *Gryllus* my Son and your Friend, to supply your occasions; I write to *Gryllus*, because, of a little one you have profess'd a kindness for him.

To *Xantippe*. Epist. VIII.

†*Epist. Socr.*21. † TO *Euphron* of *Megara* I delivered six measures of Meal, eight Drachms, and a new Rayment for your use this Winter: accept them, and know, that *Euclid* and *Terpsion* are exceeding good, honest persons, very affectionate to you and *Socrates*; if your Sons have a desire to come to me, hinder them not, for the Journey to *Megara* is neither long nor incommodious: Pray forbear to weep any more, it may do hurt, but cannot help. Remember what *Socrates* said, follow his Practice and Precepts; in grieving you will but wrong your self and Children; they are the young ones of *Socrates*, whom we are obliged not only to maintain, but to preserve our selves for their sakes: lest, if you or I, or any other, who after the death of *Socrates* ought to look to his Children, should fail, they might want a Guardian to maintain and protect them. I studie to live for them, which you will not do unless you cherish your self. Grief is one of those things which are opposite to Life, for by it the Living are prejudiced. *Apollodorus* † sirnamed *the soft*, and *Dion* praise you, that you will accept nothing from any, professing you are Rich; it is well done, for as long as I and other friends are able to maintain you, you shall need none else. Be of good courage, *Xantippe*, lose nothing of *Socrates*, knowing how great that Man was, think upon his Life, not upon his Death: yet that to those who consider it will appear noble and excellent, Farewel.

† The reason manifest from *Xenophon* and *Laertius*, who describe him such: *Xenophon* calls him ἐυθυνους, *Apolog. Socrat.* in all things but his affection to *Socrates*. *Leo Allatius* is much perplext concerning this appellation.

To *Cebes* and *Simmias*. Epist. X.

IT is commonly said, nothing is Richer than a poor Man. This I find true in my self, who have not so much, but whilst you my friends take care of me, seem to possess much: and it is well done of you to supply me as often as I write: As concerning my Commentaries, there is none of them but I fear should be seen by any in my absence, as I profest in your hearing, at the house where *Euclid* lay. I know dear friends a writing once communicated to many is irrecoverable. *Plato*, though absent, is much admired throughout *Italy* and *Sicily* for his Treatises; but we cannot be perswaded they deserve any Study: I am not only careful of losing the honour due to Learning, but tender also of *Socrates*.lest his Vertue should incur any prejudce by my ill relation of it. I conceive it the same thing to caluminate, or not praise to the full those of whom we write: This is my fear (*Cebes* and *Simmias*) at present, until my Judgment shall be otherwise informed. Fare ye well.

Epist. Socr. 22.

ESCHI-

ÆSCHINES.

CHAP. I.
His Life.

*Laert.
*Luc. micarum furtoris.

ÆSCHINES was Son of *Charinus* ἀλλαντοποιοῦ, or as *Plato* and others, of *Lysanias*, an *Athenian*, of the *Sphettian* Tribe: He was from his childhood very industrious; addressing himself to *Socrates*, he said to him, I am poor, and have nothing to give you but my self: Do you not know, answered *Socrates*, that you have made me a Rich Present? He was the most diligent of all his Scholars, and never quitted him; whereupon *Socrates* said, that he only, ὁ ἀλλαντοποιοῦ valued him: He was not beloved of *Plato*, nor *Aristippus*: *Idomeneus* faith, it was he who counselled *Socrates* to escape out of Prison, which *Plato* ascribes to *Crito*. Being very poor, *Socrates* bad him take some of his Dialogues and make Money of them, which *Aristippus* suspecting when he read them at *Megara*, derided him, saying, how came you by these, Plagiary? Another time † *Aristippus falling out with him, was questioned what became of his friendship, he answered, it is asleep, but I will wake it; and meeting with* Æschines, *do I seem so inconsiderable to you, said he, and unfortunate, as not to deserve Correction? It is no wonder,* answers Æschines, *if your nature exceeding mine in every thing, find out first what is expedient.* *Instigated by Poverty, he went to *Sicily*, to *Dionysius* the Tyrant, at what time *Plato*, and *Aristippus* were there: *Plato* being out of favour with the Tyrant, took occasion, by presenting Æschines, to ingratiate himself: † *He desired he might be admitted to speak with him, which the Tyrant granted, supposing he would alledge something in defence of himself: as soon as he came into his Presence, he began thus: If you knew,* Dionysius, *of any that came with a hostile intent to do you hurt, tho' he fail'd of the occasion, would you suffer him to depart unpunished? nothing less,* answered Dionysius: *for not only the ill actions, but designs of enemies deserve to be chastized.* Then (replies Plato) *if any Man should come hither out of an intent to do you a good office, and you not give him leave, ought you to neglect and despise him?* Dionysius demanded who he meant: Æschines (*said he*) *a Person of as great integrity as any of* Socrates *his friends, able to reform those with whom he converseth, who having undertaken a great voyage by Sea to come hither, and discourse Philosophically with you, is neglected.* Dionysius *was so pleased at this, that he embraced* Plato, *admiring his candor and greatness of Spirit, and entertained* Æschines *bountifully and magnificently.* Thus *Plutarch*, but *Laertius* saith, that Æschines coming thither, was despised by *Plato*, and recommended by *Aristippus*, the latter, the Socratic Epistle confirms: to *Dionysius* he imparted some Dialogues, and was gratified by him, with whom he lived untill he was deposed, and *Dion* brought into the Kingdom; then returned to *Athens*, where not daring to profess his Philosophy, because the names of *Plato* and *Aristippus* were so great, he taught and * took Money pri-

vately, at last apply'd himself to framing Orations for the Forum, in which, *Timon* faith, he was very persuasive: *Lysias* wrote one Oration in answer to him, intituled, περὶ συκοφαντίας, according to *Athenæus*, περὶ Αἰσχίνου τὸν Σωκρατικὸν χρέους, wherein he asperseth him for many things, which are not any way probable, as (besides patronising an unjust cause, and borrowing without intent to restore) for pretending to sell Unguents contrary to the Laws of *Solon*, and precepts of *Socrates*, and for injuring *Hermæus* his Wife and Children; see *Athenæus*. *Aristotle* sirnamed ὁ Μῦθος was his intimate friend. *Laertius* reckons eight of this name; the first, this Æschines the Philosopher; the second wrote of Rhetorick, the third an Orator, contemporary with *Demosthenes*, the fourth an *Arcadian*, Scholar to *Isocrates*, the fifth of *Mitilene*, sirnamed *Rhetoromastix*, the sixth a *Neopolitan*, an *Academick* Philosopher, Disciple to *Melanthius* a *Rhodian*; the seventh a *Milesian*, who wrote *Politicks*, friend to *Cicero*, the eighth a Statuary.

CHAP. II.
His Writings.

HE wrote *Dialogues*, *Orations*, and *Epistles* by the first *Athenæus* affirms, he gained a great esteem of Temperance, Humanity, and Integrity: *Menedemus* accuseth him of owning many Dialogues of *Socrates*, which he had of *Xantippe*; *Panetius* believes them to be his own, not counterfeit: those (faith *Laertius*) which express the *Socratic* habit, are seven; the first, *Miltiades*, written in a lower style: the second, *Callias*, wherein he is blamed by *Athenæus* for treating of the enmity betwixt *Callias* and his Fathers, and for deriding *Anaxagoras* and *Prodicus* in their Scholars *Theramenes*, *Philoxenus*, and *Ariphrades*. The third, *Rhinon*, the fourth, *Aspasia*, cited by *Athenæus* and *Harpocration*, the fifth *Alcibiades*, cited also by * *Athenæus*, the sixth *Axiochus*, wherein (saith † *Athenæus*) *he traduceth* Alcibiades *as given to Wine and Women*; which particular not being to be found in that *Axiochus* extant amongst the spurious *Platonick* Dialogues, argues contrary to the Opinion of *Vossius* that it is not the same. The last, *Telauges*, the scope whereof was a Satyrical derision of the Vices of that Person, as appeareth from *Demetrius Phalereus*, and * *Athenæus*.

† There were seven other Dialogues, stiled ἀκέφαλοι, which went under the name of Æschines, very loose, and not expressing enough the *Socratick* Severity; whence *Pisistratus* the *Athenian* denied that they were his, and *Perseus* faith, the greatest part were written by *Pasiphon* of *Eretria*, falsely mingled with the Dialogues of Æschines: their names (according to *Suidas*) *Phædon*, *Polyænus*, *Dracon*, *Erixias*, (perhaps that which is extant) *of Vertue*, *Frasistratus*, the *Scythians*.

* His *Orations* gave full testimony of his perfection in *Rhetorick*, in confirmation whereof,

Laertius

Laertius instanceth, that *in defence of the Father of* Phæacus *the General, and those wherein he chiefly imitated* Gorgius *the Leontine;* of *Philostratus* cites that *concerning Thargelia.*

† *Epist. ad Jul. August.*

Of his *Epistles,* one to *Dionysius* the Tyrant is mentioned by *Laertius,* as extant in his time; another there is under his name amongst the * *Socratick* Epistles in these words;

* *Epist.* 23.

As soon as I arrived at Syracuse *Aristippus met me in the Forum, and taking me by the hand, carried me immediately to* Dionysius, *to whom he said,* Dionysius, *if a Man should come hither to insinuate folly into you, did he not aim at your hurt? to which* Dionysius *consenting, what then, continues* Aristippus, *would you do to him? the worst, answers* Dionysius, *that could be: But if any one, saith he, should come to improve you in wisdom, did he not aim at your good? which* Dionysius *acknowledging: behold then (continues he)* Æschines, *one of* Socrates's *Disciples, come hither to instruct you, he aims at your good, therefore on him confer the benefits you confess due to such.* Dionysius *(said I, interrupting him,)* Aristippus *expresseth an admirable Friendship in this address, but we are owners only of so much wisdom as restrains us from abusing those with whom we converse.* Dionysius *hereat pleased, commended* Aristippus, *and promised to make good what he had confest due to me: He heard our* Alcibiades, *and delighted it seems therewith, desired if we had any other Dialogues, that we would send them to him, which we promised to do, and therefore dear friends we intend to be shortly with you. Whilst I read,* Plato *was present (which I had almost forgot to tell you) and whispered something in my behalf privately to* Dionysius, *by reason of* Aristippus; *for assoon as he was gone out, he told me that he never spoke freely when that Man (naming* Aristippus*) was present, but for what I said to* Dionysius *concerning you, I refer my self to him: The next day* Dionysius *in the Garden confirmed his speech as said of me, with many sportive sayings (for they were no better) I advised* Aristippus *and* Plato *to cease their emulation, because of their general fame; for we shall be most ridiculous, if our Actions correspond not with our Profession.*

CRITO

θ *Suid.*

CRITO was an *Athenian*† Scholar to *Socrates*: whom he loved so entirely that he never suffered him to want necessaries, of which more hath been said in the Life of *Socrates*: * Being much troubled and sued by those who had not received any injury from him, but abus'd the quietness of his disposition, which would sooner part with Mony upon no ground than go to Law, *Socrates* advised him to entertain one of the same busie, troublesome humour, to keep off the rest; *Crito* in pursuit of this Counsel made choice of *Archidamus*, an excellent Lawyer, but poor, who being obliged by his gifts and kindness, persecuted eagerly all such as molested not him only, but any of his friends: *Crito* wrote seventeen Dialogues comprised in one volumn, thus reckon'd by *Laertius*. *That the good are not made such by Learning. Of having most. What is expedient, or the Politician. Of Honesty, of Wickedness, of Security, of Law, of Divinity, of Arts, of Conversation, of Wisdom;* Protagoras *or the Politick, of Letters, of Poetry, of what is Honest,*

: *Xen.*

of Learning, of Knowing or Science, what it is to know. He writ also *an Apology for* Socrates.

† He had four Sons, *Critobulus, Hermogenes, Epigenes,* and *Ctesippus,* all Auditors of *Socrates*, of whom already.

† *Suid.*

* *Suidas* reckons three more of this name: One wrote *Getic* Stories; the second was of *Pieria* a City in *Macedonia*; the third of *Naxus*, both Historians.

* *Laert.*

SIMON

SIMON was an *Athenian*, a Leather-dresser: *Socrates* coming to his Shop, and disputing there, he committed to writing all that he remembred thereof, whence his Dialogues were called σκυτικοί. They were three and thirty, all in one Volumn: *Of Gods, of Good, of Honest, what is Honest. Of Just,* the first; the second *of Virtue, that it cannot be taught. Of Fortitude,* the first, second, third; *Of Law, of Popularity, of Honour, of Poetry, of Health, of Love, of Philosophy, of Knowledge, of Musick, of Poetry: what is Honest. Of Doctrine, of of Disputation, of Judgment, of that which is, of Number, of Diligence, of Labour of Avarice, of Boasting, of Honesty, or according to others, of Counsel, of Discourse, of Expedients, of doing ill.* He is reported the first that used the *Socratick* Discourses. *Pericles* promising that if he would come to him, he should want nothing, he answered, that he would not sell his freedom of Speech. There is extant amongst the *Socratick* Epistles, this under his name, as in answer to *Aristippus*.

Laert.

*I hear that you * deride our Learning to* Dionysius: *I confess I am a Leather-dresser, and work upon that Trade to the* † *reproof of indiscreet Persons, who think to follow* Socrates, *yet live Luxuriously. As for your Children,* Antisthenes *will correct them, to whom you writ scoffing at my manner of Life: But of this mirth enough, only be mindful of me and of thirst: These conduce much to the wise.*

* Περὶ ψε.
ταυθάζειν rather θαυμάζειν.
† νεθεσίαν. which *Allatius* renders in *derisionem*.

GLAUCO

GLAUCO was an *Athenian*: he writ nine Dialogues, comprised in one Book: *Phidylus, Euripides, Amyntichus, Euthias, Lysithides, Aristophanes, Ephalus, Anaxiphemus, Menexenus.* There are two and thirty more falsly ascribed to him.

Laert.

SIMMIAS

SImmias was a *Theban*, he writ three and twenty Dialogues in one Book: *Of Wisdom, of Ratiocination, of Musick, of Verse, of Fortitude, of Philosophy, of Truth, of Letters, of Doctrine, of Art, of Conduct, of Decency, of what is to be chosen, and what to be shunned: of Friendship, of Knowledge, of the Soul, of well-living, of Possibility, of Wealth, of Life, what is Honest, of Industry, of Love.*

† *Laert.*

CEBES

* CEbes was of *Thebes*, a Philosopher, Disciple to *Socrates*: He writ three Dialogues, *The Tablet* (which is extant) the seventh. *Phrynichus*, he writ also *an Infernal Narrative*, and other things. These are the Philosophers who did not distract the Doctrine of their Master into Sects, in which respect they may more properly be termed *Socratic*, tho' the rest also assume that Title.

* *Laert.*

A

A
CHRONOLOGY.

Olympiads.	Archontes.	
xxxv	Damasias 1. *Halic.*	*Thales* Born. *Laert*
2		*Solon* born about this time: by compute from his death.
3		*Phryno* Victor in all the Olympick Exercises, *Euseb.*
4		probably the same with whom *Pittacus* fought.
xxxvi		
2		
3		
4		
xxxvii		
2		
3		
4		
xxxviii		*Periander* began to Reign at *Corinth.*
2		
3		
4		
xxxix	Draco *Tatian. Clem. Suid.*	*Draco* makes Laws at *Athens.*
2		
3		
4		
xl		*Arion*'s Story. *Euseb.*
2		
3		
4	Heniochides *Hal.*	
xli		
2		
3		*Pittacus* flourished. *Laert.*
4		*Alyattes* King of *Lydia* began to Reign. *Anaximander*
xlii	Aristocles *Marm.*	Born. *Laert.*
2		
3		
4		
xliii		
2		
3		
4		
xliv		
2		
3		
4		
xlv		
2	Critias. 1. *Marm.*	
3		
4		
xlvi		*Epimenides* lustrates the City of *Athens*: *Laert. E-*
2	Philombratus. *Plat. Sol.*	*pimenides* Born. *Suid.*
3	Solon *Laert.*	*Solon* made Archon. His Laws.
4	Dropides. *Phil. in Critia.*	
xlvii	Eucrates. *Laert.*	*Anacharsis* came to *Athens*, to visit *Solon.* *Laert.*
2	Simon. *Marm.*	
3		
4		

xlviii

CHRONOLOGY.

		Æra Philoſ.	
xlviii	Philippus. *Clem.*		
2			
3			
4			*Periand.* died having Reinged 40 years, *Ariſt.*
xlix			*Polit.* 5. *Laert.*
2			
3	Damaſius. *Marm.*	1	The Attribute of *Wiſe* conferr'd on *Thales*, and
4		2	the other ſix.
l		3	About this time *Theſpis* began to preſent his
2		4	Tragedies. *Anaximander* found the obliquity
3	Archeſtratides. *Hal.* 4.	5	of the Zodiack. *Plin.*
4		6	
li		7	
2		8	
3		9	
4		10	
lii		11	
2		12	
3	Ariſtomenes. *Laert.*	13	*Pittacus* died. *Laert.*
4		14	
liii		15	
2		16	
3		17	
4		18	
liv		19	
2		20	*Pythagoras* viſits *Thales*. *Collected from* Jamblic.
3		21	
4	Conias *Plut. Sol.*	22	
lv	Hegeſtratus. *Plut.*	23	
2		24	
3		25	
4		26	
lvi	Euthydemus. *Laert.*	27	*Chilon* was *Ephorus*. *Laert.*
2		28	*Anaximenes* flouriſhed,
3		29	*Euſebius.*
4		30	
lvii		31	
2		32	
3		33	
4		34	
lviii		35	*Thales* died. *Laert.*
2	Etydemus. *Pauſ*	36	
3		37	
4		38	*Cyrus* takes *Sardys* and *Cræſus.*
lix		39	
2		40	
3		41	
4		42	
lx		43	
2		44	
3		45	
4		46	
lxi		47	
2		48	
3		49	
4	Heracles. *Hal.* 4.	50	
lxii		51	
2		52	
3		53	
4		54	
lxiii		55	*Piſiſtratus* died, having Reigned 17 years; *A-*
2		56	*riſt. Polit.* 5.
3		57	
4		58	
liv	Miltiades. *Hal.* 7.	59	
2		60	
3		61	
4		62	
lxv		63	*Darius* began his Reign.
2		64	

CHRONOLOGY.

3		65	
4		66	
lxvi		67	
2		68	
3		69	
4		70	
lxvii		71	
2		72	
3		73	
4		74	
lxviii	Lysagoras. *Marm.*	75	
2		76	
3		77	
4		78	
lxix	Acestorides. 11. *Hal.* 5.	79	
2		80	
3		81	
4		82	
lxx	Myrus. *Hal.* 5.	83	Anaxagoras Born. *Laert.* by compute.
2		84	
3		85	
4		86	Pythagors died. *Euseb.*
lxxi	Hipparchus *Hal.* 6.	87	
2	Pithocritus. *Marm.*	88	
3		89	
4		90	
lxxii	Diognetus. *Hal.* 6.	91	The *Marathonian Fight.*
2	Hybrilides. *Hal.* 7. *Pauf.*	92	
3	Phanippus. *Plut. Arist.*	93	
4		94	
lxxiii	Archises. *Hal.* 8.	95	
2		96	
3	Aristides. *Marm.*	97	Darius Died. Xerxes Succeeded,
4	Philocrates. *Marm.*	98	
lxxiv	Leostratus. *Hal.* 8.	99	
2	Nicodemus. *Hal.* 8.	100	
3		101	
4		102	
lxxv	Calliades. *Marm.*	103	Xerxes cross'd the Hellespont: the Fight at
2	Xantippus. *Marm.*	104	Salamis. Anaxagoras went to Athens.
3	Timosthenes. *Marm.*	105	
4	Adimantus. *Marm.*	106	
lxxvi	Phædon. *Diod. Sic.*	107	
2	Dromoclides	108	
3	Acestorides	109	
4	Menon	110	
lxxvii	Chares	111	
2	Praxiergus	112	
3	Demotion	113	
4	Apsephion	114	Socrates Born.
lxxviii	Theagenides	115	A Stone fell down from Heaven at Ægos Pota-
2	Lysistratus	116	mus; foretold by Anaxagoras.
3	Lysanias	117	
4	Lysitheus	118	
lxxix	Archedemides	119	
2	Tlepolemus	120	
3	Conon	121	
4	Euippus	122	
lxxx	Phrasiclides	123	
2	Philocles	124	
3	Bion	125	
4	Mnesithides	126	
lxxxi	Callias 1.	127	
2	Sosistratus	128	
3	Ariston	129	
4	Lysicratis	130	Xenophon Born about this time.
lxxxii	Chærephanes *Hal.*	131	
2	Antidotus	132	Anaxagoras (having Profess'd Philosopy 30 years at *Athens*,)
3	Eutidemus	133	Condemned and Banished; Collected from *Laert.*
4	Pedicus	134	

CHRONOLOGY.

lxxxiii	Philiscus *Hal.*	135	
2	Timarchides	136	
3	Callimachus	137	
4	Lysimachides	138	
lxxxiv	Praxiteles	139	
2	Lysanias	140	
3	Diphilus	141	
4	Timocles	142	
lxxxv	Murichides	143	
2	Glaucides	144	
3	Theodorus	145	
4	Euthemenes	146	
lxxxvi	Nausimachus	147	
2	Antilochides	148	
3	Achares	149	
4	Apseudas *Ptol.*	150	
lxxxvii	Pythodorus. *Thuc.*	151	
2	Euthidemus *Athen.* 5.	152	1 Year of the *Peloponnesian* War: *Thucid. lib.* 2.
3	Apollodorus. *Athen.* 5.	153	2
4	Epaminondas	154	3
lxxxviii	Diotimus	155	4 *Anaxagoras* died, by compute from *Laert.*
2	Euclides	156	5
3	Euthydemus	157	6
4	Stratocles	158	8 The fight at *Delium*, wherein *Socrates* and *Xenophon* fought. The Clouds of *Aristophanes* Acted.
lxxxix	Isarchus	159	9 The Clouds of *Aristophanes* Acted the second time.
2	Amynias	160	10
3	Alcæus	à 161	
4	Ariston	162	11 The time of *Xenophon's* symposium.
xc	Aristophilus	163	12
2	Archias	164	13
3	Antiphon	165	14
4	Euphemus	166	15
xci	Aristomnestus	167	16
2	Chabrias	168	17
3	Pisander	169	18
4	Cleocritus	170	19
xcii	Callias	171	20
2	Theopompus	172	21 *Thucydides* ends his History; *Xenophon* begins where he left.
3	Glaucippus	173	22
4	Diocles	174	23
xciii	Euctemon *Marm.*	175	24
2	Antigenes *Marm.*	176	25 The first ascent of *Cyrus* into *Asia*. *Marm.*
3	Callias *Marm.*	177	62 *Dionys.* made K. of *Syrac. Diod.* the fight at
4	Alexias	178	27 *Arginusæ*: the ten Captains put to Death. The thirty Tyrants. *Theramenes* put to Death.
xciv	Pythodorus *Athen.*	179	
2	Euclides	180	
3	Micon	181	The ascent of *Cyrus* into *Asia* against his Brother: his death *Xen.* retreats with the Army. The 30 Tyrants put down. *Socrates* put to death. *Thimbro* sent into *Asia* against *Tissaphernes* by the *Lacedæmonians*; and of *Xenophon's* Retreat.
4	Exenætus	182	
xcv	Laches	183	
2	Aristocrates	184	
3	Ithicles	185	
4	Lysiades	186	
xcvi	Phormio	187	*Agesilaus* goes into *Asia* against the *Persian*.
2	Diophaneus	188	*Agesilaus* called home; fights with the *Boeotians* at *Coronæa*.
3	Eubilides	189	
4	Demostratus	190	*Conon* re-edifies the Walls of *Athens*.
xcvii	Philocles	191	
2	Nicoteles	192	
3	Demostratus	193	
4	Antipater	194	
xcviii	Pyrrhio	195	
2	Theodorus	196	
3	Mistichides	197	
4	Dexitheus	198	
xcix	Diotrephes	129	*Aristotle* Born. *Laert.*
2	Phanostratus	200	
3	Menander	201	
4	Demophilus	202	
c	Pytheus *Marm.*	203	
2	Nico *Hal.*	204	

Nausinicus

CHRONOLOGY.

3	Nausinicus *Hal.*	205	
4	Calleas *Hal.*	206	
ci	Chariander	207	
2	Hippodamus	208	
3	Socratides	209	
4	Asteius *Pauf.*	210	
cii	Alcisthenes *Hal.*	211	
2	Phrasiclides *Marm.*	212	
3	Discinetus *Pauf.*	213	
4	Lycistratus	214	
ciii	Nausigenes *Marm.*	215	
2	Polyzelus *Hal.*	216	
3	Cephisodorus *Hal.*	217	
4	Chion	218	
civ	Timocrates *Hal.*	219	
2	Cariclides	220	
3	Molon. *Hal. dinar*	221	
4	Nicophemus	222	
cv	Callimedes	223	*Xenophon* died. *Laert.*
2	Euchariftus	224	
3	Cephisodotus	225	
4	Agathocles *Pauf. Marm.*	226	
cvi	Elpines	227	
2	Callistratus *Marm.*	228	
3	Diotimus	229	
4	Eudemus	230	
cvii	Aristodemus	231	
2	Thessalus	232	
3	Apollodorus	233	
4	Callimachus *Athen.*	234	
cviii	Theophilus *Pauf. Athen.*	235	
2	Themistocles	236	*Plato* died 82 years old. *Athen. lib.* 5.
3	Archias	237	
4	Eubulus	238	
cix	Liziscus	239	*Aristotle* went to *Mitilene*. *Laert.*
2	Pithodorus	240	
3	Sosigenes	241	*Aristotle* went to King *Philip*; *Alexander* be-
4	Nicomachus	242	ing fifteen years old. *Laert.*
cx	Theophrastus	243	
2	Lysimachides	244	
3	Charonidas	245	
4	Phrynichus	246	
cxi	Pythodorus *Arr.*	247	
2	Euænetus	248	
3	Ctesicles	249	*Aristotle* teacheth in the *Lycæum* 13 years.
4	Nicocrates	250	
cxii	Niceratus	251	
2	Aristophanes *Arr.*	252	
3	Aristophon *Ar.*	253	
4	Cephisophon	254	
cxiii	Euthycritus	255	
2	Hegemon *Hal. Ar.*	256	
3	Cremes	257	
4	Anticles	258	
cxiv	Hegesias *Arr.*	259	
2	Cephisodorus	260	
3	Philocles *Laert.*	261	
4	Archippus *Laert.*	262	*Aristotle* went to *Chalcis*, and died there near
cxv	Neæchmus *Hal.*	263	63 years old. *Laert. Theophraftus* succeeded.
2	Apollodorus	264	
3	Archippus	265	
4	Demogenes	266	
cxvi	Democlides	267	
2	Praxibulus	268	*Polemo* President of the Academy.
3	Nicodorus	299	
4	Theophrastus	270	
cxxvii	Polemo	271	
2	Simonides	272	
3	Hieromnemon	273	
4	Demetrius Phalereus		

CHRONOLOGY.

cxviii	Carinus	274	
2	Anaxicrates	275	
3	Corœbus	276	
4	Xenippus	277	
cxix	Phericles *Hal.*	278	
2	Leostratus	279	
3	Nicocles	280	
4	Calliarchus	281	
cxx	Hegemachus *Laert.*	282	
2	Euctemon	283	
3	Mnesidemus	284	
4	Antiphanes	285	
cxxi	Nicias	286	
2	Nicostratus	287	
3	Olympiodorus	288	
4	Philippus	289	
cxxii		290	
2		291	
3		292	
4		293	
cxxiii		294	
2		295	
3		296	
4		297	
cxxiv		298	
2		299	
3		300	
4		301	
cxxv		302	
2		303	
3		304	
4		305	
cxxvi		306	
2		307	
3		308	
4		309	
cxxvii	Pytharatus *Cic.*	310	
2		311	
3		312	
4		313	
cxxviii		314	
2		315	
3		316	
4		317	
cxxix	Diognetus *Marm.*	318	
2		319	
3		320	
4		321	
cxxx		322	
2		323	
3		324	
4		325	
cxxxi		326	
2		327	
3		328	
4		329	
cxxxii		030	
2		331	
3		332	
4		333	
cxxxiii		334	
2		335	
3		336	
4		337	
cxxxiv		338	*Lacydes* President of the Academy 26 years. *Laert.*
2		339	
3		340	
4		341	
cxxxv		342	
2		343	

CHRONOLOGY.

3	344	
4	345	
cxxxvi	346	
2	347	
3	348	
4	349	
cxxxvii	350	
2	351	
3	352	
4	353	
cxxxviii	354	
2	355	
3	356	
4	357	
cxxxix	358	
2	359	
3	360	
4	361	
cxl	362	
2	363	
3	364	
4	365	*Lacydes* resigns the School to *Evander* and *Te-*
cxli	366	*lecles*. *Laert.*
2	367	
3	368	
4	369	
cxlii	370	
2	371	
3	372	*Charnerdes* Born.
4		

THE HISTORY of PHILOSOPHY.

The Fourth Part.

Containing the Cyrenaick, Megarick, Eleack, Eretriack Sects.

ARISTIPPVS.

THE *CYRENAICK* SECT.
CHAP. I.

Aristippus, his Country and Parents.

THE estimation which Philosophers had daily gain'd among the Grecians about this time caused it exceedingly to multiply, whilst every Professor ambitious to be held wiser

wiser than his Master, and teaching something new, desired to have the Honour to be Author of a Sect.

The Succession of the *Ionick* Philosophy, which before *Socrates* was single: after him was divided into many Schools, whereof some were but of short continuance, others had longer succession. Of the less durable were the

- *Cyrenaick.*
- *Megarick,*
- *Eleack,*
- *Eretriack.*

so called from the places where the Professors flourished. Others of longer Succession, the

Academick, *Cynick,* out of which came the *Peripatetic.* *Stoick.*

We shall first dispatch those which were of shortest continuance, whether that they were founded upon less Reason, and *were in short time broken, as* * *Cicero* saith, *and quite extinct by the strength and Arguments of the others*; or that being instituted and founded in more obscure parts; they were not so lasting as those which were profess'd in the most flourishing City so *Athens.*

Aristippus a Disciple of *Socrates*, after his death, returned home into his Country at *Cyrene* in *Africa*, from whence the Doctrine which his Scholars retained had the name of *Cyrenaick.* † He was Son of *Aretades,* * *Cyrene.*

De Oratore lib. 3.

§ *Suid.* ‡ *Laert.*

CHAP. II.

How he went to Athens, and heard Socrates.

FROM *Cyrene Aristippus* went first to *Athens,* invited by the fame of † *Socrates, concerning* whom he fell into discourse with Ischomachus, meeting him casually at the *Olympick Games,* and enquiring what disputes they were wherewith *Socrates* prevailed so much upon the young Men, he receiv'd from him some little seeds and scatterings thereof, wherewith he was so passionately affected, that he grew pale and lean, till, to asswage his fervent thirst, he took a Voyage to *Athens,* and there drunk at the Fountain, satisfying himself with the Person, his discourse and Philosophy, the end whereof was to know our evils, and to acquit our selves of them. * *Aristotle* said, *Philosophy doth harm to those who misinterpret things well said.* *Aristippus* † chiefly delighted with the more voluptuous disputes of *Socrates,* asserted Pleasure to be the ultimate end wherein all happiness doth consist. * *His Life was agreeable to the Opinion, which he employed in Luxury, sweet Unguents, rich Garments, Wine and Women*; maintain'd by a course as different from the Precepts and Practice of *Socrates* as the things themselves were. For, notwithstanding he had a good Estate (and three Country Seats) † he first of the *Socratick* Disciples took Money for Teaching. Which *Socrates* observing, asked him *how he came to have so much?* he reply'd, *how came you to have so little?*

‡ *Plut. de curiosit.*

° *Cic. de Nat. Deor.*
† *Cic. de Orat. 3.*

* *Athen. Deipn. 12.*

† *Laert.*

A further dislike of this course *Socrates* expressed, when *Aristippus* sending him twenty *minæ,* he returned it, saying, *his Dæmon would not suffer him to take it.*

CHAP. III.

How he went to Ægina.

LEaving *Socrates,* * he went to *Ægina,* where he lived with more freedom and Luxury than before: *Socrates* sent exhortations to reclaim him, frequent but fruitless, and to the same end published that discourse which we find in *Xenophon.* Here he became acquainted with *Lais* the famous *Corinthian* Courtezan, † who came thither yearly at the Feast of *Neptune,* and was as constantly frequented by *Aristippus,* for whose sake * *Hermesianax* saith, he took a Voyage to *Corinth* (mentioned among his *Apothegms.*)

* *Athen. deipn. 12.*
† *Athen. deipn. 12.*
* *Athen. deipn. 13.*

To *Corinth* Love *the* Cyrenean *led,*
Where he enjoyed Thessalian Lais *bed;*

No Art the subtil Aristippus *knew*
By which the power of Love *he might eschew.*

† Whilst he was upon his Voyage to *Corinth,* a great Tempest arose, whereat he was much troubled: one of the Passengers saying unto him, *we ordinary people are not afraid, but you Philosophers fear* (or as * *Ælian, are you afraid like other people?*) † *our Souls,* answered he, *are not of equal value,* * *you hazard a wicked and unhppy life,* ‡ *Felicity and Beatitude.*

† *Laert.*
* *Var. Hist. 9.*
† *A. Gel. 19. 1.*
‡ *Ælian. ibid*

† To those who blamed him for frequenting *Lais, I possess her,* faith he, *not she me:* * *Lais* in emulation of *Phryne* gave admittance to all sorts of People, Rich and Poor, whereupon *Aristippus* reprehended by his Servant for bestowing so much on her, who entertained *Diogenes* the *Cynick gratis, I give her Money,* saith he, *that I may enjoy her, not that others may not.* * *Diogenes* reproached him for frequenting the company of *Lais,* saying, *Aristippus, you and I converse with the same Woman, either give over, or be like a Cynic: Do you think it absurd,* faith he, *to dwell in a House, wherein others lived before, or to Sail in a Ship that hath carrid other Passengers? It is no more absurd to affect a Woman whom others have enjoyed.*

† *Laert.*
* *Athen. deipn. 13.*
† *Athen. deipn. 13.*

At *Ægina* he continued till the death of *Socrates,* as (besides the testimony of † *Plato*) appeareth by this * Epistle of his written upon that occasion.

* *In Phædone.*
† *Socratic. Epist. 16.*

Of the death of Socrates, *I and* Cleombrotus *have received information, and that when I might have escaped from the eleven Officers, he said he would not, unless he was acquitted by Law; for that were as much as in him lay to betray his Country. My Opinion is, he being unjustly committed, he might have got his Liberty any way, conceiving that all which he could do ill or inconsiderately must be just. From whence again I blame him not, as if he had done ill even in this. You write me word that all the friends and Disciples of* Socrates *have left* Athens, *out of fear the like should befall any of you; it is well done; and we being at present at* Ægina *will*

will continue here a while, then come to you, and wherein we are able, serve you.

CHAP. IV.

His Institution of a Sect.

ARistippus returning at length to his own Country, *Cyrene*, professed Philosophy there, and Instituted a Sect called * *Cyrenaick* from the place, by some † *Hedonick*, or voluptuous from the Doctrine. *a* They who followed the Institution of *Aristippus*, and were called *Cyrenaick*, held thus,

* *Lvert.*
† *Galen. Hist. Phil.*
a Laert.

They rejected *Physick* and natural disquisitions from the seeming incomprehensibilty thereof. *Logick* they handled because of its great usefulness. But *Meleager* and *Clitomachus* affirm they despised both Physick and Dialectick alike, as unuseful; for that without these, a Man who hath learned what things are good, what evil, and able to discourse well, and to shake off Superstition and the fear of Death.

Sect. 1. Of Judgment and Judicatories.

b They held that *the Senses inform not always truly*, * *that nothing extrinsecal can be perceived, those things only can be perceived, which are felt by inward touch, as grief and pleasure, neither know we what colour any thing is, nor what sound it makes, but only that we feel our selves affected after such a manner*; *c* that *passions are comprehensive, that objects not comprehensive.* * That *nothing judgeth but by interior promotion, and the judgment of true and false consists of inward touch.*

b Laert.
a Cicer. Acad. Quæst. li. 4.

c Laert. Cic.

c *Sextus Empericus* more fully. They assert that Passions or Affections are the Judges and the only things that may comprehend, and not *fallacious*, but of those things which cause Passions, there is nothing which is comprehensible, or that may not deceive us. For, that we are made white, or affected with sweet, may be said expresly and firmly, but that the thing which causeth this affection is white or sweet, cannot in like manner be asserted. For it is possible that we be affected with whiteness from a thing that is not white, and with sweetness from a thing that is not sweet, as to him who is dim-sighted or hath the yellow-jaundice, all things seem yellow to one, duskish to the other, and he who pincheth his eye, thinketh he sees things double, he who is mad fancies two *Thebes*'s, two Suns, in all these, they that are so affected, to wit, with yellowness or duskishness, or duplicity, is true, but that the thing which moveth them is yellow or duskish, or double, is conceived to be false: so it is most consonant to reason, that we comprehend nothing more than our own passions. For we must hold that the things seen are either the passions themselves, or the causes of those passions; if we say our passions are the things seen, we must likewise affirm all things seen, to be true and comprehensive: if we say the things seen are the causes of those passions, we must confess all things seen to be false and incomprehensible. For that Passion which hapneth to us, sheweth us its self and nothing more, so that to speak truly, the Passion or Affection it self is the only thing that is apparent to us, and for that reason, in their proper affections none err, but in the external object, all. The first are comprehensive, the second incomprehensive, the Soul being weak in the discernment thereof, by reason of places, intervals, motions, mutations, and many other causes.

c Laert.

Hence they assert, that there is not in man any one common thing which judgeth, but they impose common names on the judgments; all commonly name white and sweet, but something common that is white and sweet they have not, for every Man apprehends his own affection. Now whether the same affection hapneth to any one, and to him that is next him from white, neither is he able to say, as not receiving the affection of the other, neither can the other that is next him say, as not receiving his affection. There being therefore no common affection in us, it were a rash thing to assert, that whatsoever seemeth such to me, seemeth also such to him that is next me; for perhaps my constitution is such as to be whitened from that which externally incurreth, another hath his Sense so ordered, as that he is affected otherwise. That therefore which is seen and appeareth is not common.

That by reason of the differing constitutions of the sense we are not moved alike nor in the same manner, is manifest from those who have the *Jaundice*, and those that are *Pur-blind*, and those that are *affected according to Nature*. For as from the same object, some are so affected as to be *Black*, others *Red*, others *White*: so is it likewise consonant to Reason, that they who are affected according to Nature, by reason of the different constitution of Senses, are not moved alike by the same things, but one way the White, another way the Black, another way he whose eyes are Blue, another way he whose eyes are black, whence we impose common names on things, having our selves proper and particular affections.

Sect. 2. Of the End, or chief Good.

TO these assertions (continueth *Sextus Empericus*) concerning the Judicatories, agreeth what they assert concerning Ends.

Of affections, some are *pleasant*, some *harsh* and troublesome, some *mean*: the harsh and troublesome are *ill*, whose end is *grief*; the *pleasant*, *good*, whose end, which cannot be deceived, is *pleasure*: the mean are neither good nor ill, whose end is neither good nor ill, which is an affection between pleasure and grief. Affections therefore are the judges and ends of all things, and we live, say they, observing evidence and liking, evidence in the rest of the affections, liking in pleasure.

Laertius saith, they assert two passions or affections, Grief and *Pleasure*: Pleasure, a soft smooth motion, Grief, a harsh motion. One Pleasure differeth not from another Pleasure, nor is one Pleasure sweeter than another Pleasure: this Pleasure is coveted by all living creatures, the other shunned.

They assert coporeal pleasure to be our ultimate end, as *Panætius* saith in his Book of *Sects*, not catastematick, permanent pleasure, which consisteth in privation of Grief and a quiet void of all disturbance, which *Epicurus* held.

The

The *End* differeth from *Beatitude*, for the End is some *particular* pleasure: Beatitude is that which consisteth of *all* particular pleasures, wherein are included both the *past* and *future*. Again, particular pleasure is expetible *in it self*, Felicity, *not* in it self, but for particular pleasures.

That Pleasure is our chief end is manifest, in that from our first infancy, without any instruction of others, we naturally aim thereat, and having obtained it, seek nothing else. Moreover, we avoid not any thing so much as its contrary, grief.

Pleasure is good, though proceeding from the most sordid dishonest thing, as *Hippobotus* in his Book of *Sects*: for, although the action be dishonest, yet the pleasure thereof is expetible in it self, and good.

Indolence, which *Epicurus* held, they esteem not pleasure, nor want of pleasure, grief, for both these consist in motion, but indolence and want of pleasure consists not in Motion, for Indolence is like the state of a sleeping Man.

They hold, that some Men may not desire pleasure, through perversity of mind.

All Spiritual Pleasures and Pains arise not from corporeal pleasures and pains: for from the simple prosperity of our Country or our self, we are affected with Joy.

But neither the remembrance of past goods, nor expectation of future compleat pleasure, as *Epicurus* thought, for by time and expectation the motion of the Soul is dissolved. † Pleasure, according to *Aristippus*, is μονόχρονος, consisteth only in one part of time, the present: for the remembrance of past pleasures, or expectation of the future, is vain and frivolous, and nothing appertaineth to Beatitude: but that only is good which is present. With those pleasures which he received heretofore, or shall receive hereafter, *Aristippus* said, he was nothing at all moved, the first being gone, the other not yet come, and what it will prove when it is come, is uncertain. Hence * he argued, that Men ought not to be sollicitous either about things past or future, and that not to be troubled at such things is a sign of a constant clear Spirit. He also advised to take care only for the present day, and in that day, only of the present part thereof, wherein something was done or thought: for he said, the present is only in our power, not the past or future, the one being gone, the other uncertain whether ever it will come.

Neither do pleasures consist meerly in simple sight or hearing, for we hear with delight those who counterfeit Lamentation, and those who lament truly, we hear with displeasure. This privation of Pleasure and Grief they called *mean states*.

The Pleasures of the Body are much better than those of the Soul, and the Pains or Griefs thereof much worse; for which reason those who offend actually, are most grievously punished.

To grieve is more unnatural to us, to delight, more natural: for which reason, much more care is requisite for the ordering of one than of the other, yet, many times we reject things which effect pleasure, as being grievous,

† *Athen. deipn.* 12.

* *Ael. var. Hist. lib.* 14. 6.

so that the concurrence of Pleasures which effecteth Beatitude, is very difficult.

Moreover they hold, that every wise Man doth not live pleasantly, nor every wicked Man unpleasantly, but so for the most part: for it is enough that a Man be affected and reduced by incidence of one single pleasure.

They held, that † Grief is the greatest Ill; that Grief is not effected by every ill, but by the unexpected and unforeseen: that one Man is more grieved than another.

They assert, that Riches are efficient causes of pleasure, yet not expetible in themselves.

† *Cic. Tusc. Quaest.* 4.

Sect. 3. *Of Virtue.*

ALL good consisteth in *Pleasure*, Virtue it self is only laudable, as being an efficient cause of Pleasure.

† Nothing is just, honest, or dishonest by *Nature*, but by *Law* and *Custom*: yet a good Man will do nothing that is evil, because of the censure or esteem which would fall upon his actions, and * that such a one is wise.

Prudence is a good, yet not expetible in it self, but for the sake of those things which proceed from it.

A Friend is to be embraced for the use we may have of him, as the Body cherisheth every part thereof as long as it remaineth sound.

Of Virtues, some are in the *unwise*.

Corporeal exercise conduceth to the acquisition of Vertue.

A *wise Man* is not subject to *Envy*, *Love*, or *Superstition*, for all these proceed from the vanity of *Opinion*: but he is subject to *Grief* or *Fear*, as being *Natural* accidents.

° *Cic. de Offic.* 3.

† *Laert.*

* So *Casaubon* reads, but doubtless there is a defect in the Text.

CHAP. V.

How he went to Dionysius *his Court.*

ABout this time *Dionysius*, the *Sicilian* Tyrant flourished, * to whom resorted many Philosophers, amongst the rest *Aristippus* invited by his Sumptuous Magnificence. † *Dionysius* asked him the reason of his coming: he answered, *To give what I have, and to receive what I have not*, or, as others, *when I wanted wisdom, I went to* Socrates, *now I want Money, I come to you*. He soon insinuated into the favour of *Dyonysius*, for he could conform himself to every place, time, and person, act any part, construe whatsoever hapned to the best: and thus enjoying present Pleasure, never troubled himself for the absent. As *Horace*,

* *Philostr. vit. Apol.*

† *Laert.*

Every Condition, Habit, and Event,
With Aristippus *suits with all Content.*

Of his Compliance with *Dionysius*'s Humour there are these Instances. † *Dionysius* at a Feast commanded, that all should put on Purple Robes: *Plato* refused, saying,

† *Laert.*

I will

I will not with a formal Robe disgrace,
My self, who am a Man of manly Race.

But *Aristippus* took it, and beginning to Dance, said,

If it come pure, a mirthful Feast
Never corrupts a modest Breast.

* *Laert.*   * Another time suing to *Dionysius* in the behalf of his Friend, he would not hear him; at last he threw himself at his feet, and his Petition was granted; for which being reprehended, *Blame not me,* faith he *but* Dionysius, *whose ears are in his feet*.

† *Laert.*   † *Dionysius* shewed him three Courtezans, bidding him take his choice: he leading them all three away, said, Paris *was punished for preferring one before the other two.* But, having brought them to the door, he dismist them, as ready to contemn as accept: whereupon *Strato* (or as others *Plato*) told him, *You only can wear old Garments and Rags,* for which likewise they admired him that he would wear a threadbare, and a rich *Milesian* Cloak with equal decorum, accommodating himself to both.

When *Dionysius* did spit upon him, he took it patiently: for which being reproved, *Fishermen said he, suffer themselve to be wet all over that they may catch* [κωβιον] *a Gudgeon, and shall I be troubled at a little Spittle, who mean to take* * βλενον ?

° Which being pronounced is equivocal; for, βλενος signifieth a Fish like a Gudgeon, and βλη-νος a Tyrant: as I find in a M.S. Lexicon communicated by my learned friend Mr. *John Pearson,* βλινος ὁ τύραννος, βλενος ὁ ἰχθύς; and again, Βαυνιχθὺς ὁ κ) κλίνος (read βλίνος) ὡς παλησιος κωβίῳ, confirmed by *Athenæus, deipn. 7. 10.*

† *Laert.*   † He begged Money of *Dionysius,* who said to him, you told me a wise man wanted nothing: give me, and we will talk of this afterward. When *Dionysius* had given it him, *Now,* saith he, *you see I do not want.*

By this complaisance he gained so much upon *Dionysius,* that he had a greater esteem for him than all the rest of the Philosophers, tho' sometimes he spoke so freely to *Dionysius,* that he incurr'd his displeasure.

* *Laert.*   * To *Dionysius* asking why Philosophers haunted the Gates of Rich Men, but Rich Men not those of Philosophers: Because, faith he, the one knows what he wants, the other not.

† *Laert.*   † To *Dionysius,* urging him to treat of Philosophy: *It is ridiculous,* saith he, *if you learn of me what it is, to teach me when it should be said.* Whereat *Dionysius* displeased, bad him take the lowest place, which he did quietly, saying, *You have a mind to make this Seat more Honourable.* * The next day the Tyrant asked him what he thought of that place wherein he then sate, in respect of that wherein he sate the night before? He answered, they were alike to him: to day, faith he, because I left it, it is contemned, what yesterday was esteemed the most Honourable, that where I sit to day esteemed most honourable, which yesterday, without me was, was accounted the lowest.

‡ *Athen. dcipn. 12. citing Hegesander.*

† Being asked why *Dionysius* fell out with him, he answered, for the same reason he falleth out with others.   † *Laert.*

* *Dionysius's* saying, (out of *Sophocles* as *Plutarch* affirms, who ascribes this to *Zeno.*)   *Laert.*

Who e'er goes to a Tyrant, he
A Servant is, tho' he came free

He immediately answered,

No Servant is if he came free.

Dionysius offering *Plato* a great summ of Money, which he refused: *Aristippus* being at the same time in the Court of *Dionysius,* said, *Dionysius* bestows his Liberality upon good grounds, to us who ask much, he giveth little, to *Plato,* who requireth nothing, he offereth much.

† Another time *Helicon* of *Cyzicus,* one of *Plato*'s Friends, having foretold an Eclipse of the Sun, which when it fell out accordingly, he was much honoured for it: *Aristippus* jesting with the other Philosophers, said, he could foretel a stranger thing: they demanding what it was: I Prognosticate, faith he, that *Plato* and *Dionysius* will ere long be at variance, and so it hapned.   † *Plut. vit. Dion.*

CHAP. VI.

His Æmulators.

THIS favour which he found with *Dionysius,* was perhaps the occasion, for which he was maligned by the rest of the Philosophers, amongst whom was,

* *Xenophon,* who out of ill will to him, published the † discourse between him and *Socrates* about Pleasure.   * *Laert.* † *Memorab. lib. 2.*

† *Plato* likewise, through the same disaffection tacitly reprehends him, in *Phædone,* for being in Ægina at the time of *Socrates* his Death. † *Plato* being in *Dionysius* his Court, when he was there, reproved his sumptuous life: Whereupon *Aristippus* asked him, whether he thought *Dionysius* a good Man or not: *Plato* affirmed, he thought him good: Yet he, reply'd *Aristippus,* liveth much more sumptuously; therefore it is not incompatible with goodness.   † *Laert.* † *Laert.*

† *Phædo* likewise seemed to deride him, demanding who it was that smell'd so strong of Unguents: It is I, unhappy Man that I am, answered *Aristippus,* and the *Persian* King, who is more unhappy than I. But as other things are not the worse for this, neither is a Man. * A Curse on those effeminate Persons who brought a Scandal upon so good a thing.   † *Laert.* * *Laert.* † *Senec. de benefic. Clem. Alex.*

† *Æschines* also and he were sometimes at difference: Once, after some falling out betwixt them, *Aristippus* said to him, shall we not be Friends, shall we not give over Fooling? Or, do you expect some Body should kick us into kindness? Willingly, answered *Æschines.* Now, saith *Aristippus,* remember, that though I am the Elder, yet I yielded first. *Æschines* reply'd, and justly, for you are better than I; I begun the enmity, you the reconcilement   † *Laert.*
* *Plutarch*

* *De ira cohib.* * *Plutarch* relates it thus; being fallen out with *Æschines*, he met one who asked him, *Where is now your old Friendship*, Aristippus? *It is asleep*, saith he; *but I will awake it*: and going straight to *Eschines*, *Am I so unhappy*, saith he, *and so inconsiderable in your esteem, as not to deserve Correction? Æschines* answered, *It is nothing strange, that exceeding by Nature in all things, you should first know what is fit to be done*.

Antisthenes is to be numbred also amongst those, who were displeased at his manner of Life, as appeareth by an Epistle of his to that effect, extant amongst the Socratick Epistles, to which *Aristippus* returned this Answer.

† *Socratic. Epist. 9.*
* *Ironically answering a former letter of* Antisthenes.

† Aristippus *to* Antisthenes.

WE are, *Aristippus*, *unhappy beyond measure; how can we be otherwise, living with a Tyrant, daily eating and drinking deliciously, perfumed with choicest Unguents, attired in rich loose Garments brought from* Tarentum: *And none will deliver me from the cruelty of Dionysius, who detains me, not as a rude person, but one that is verst in Socratick learning ; supplying me (as I said) with Meat, Unguents, Garments, and the like; fearing neither the judgments of Gods nor Men. And now the misfortune is much increased; He hath bestowed on me three* Sicilian *Virgins of extraordinary beauty, and many Utensils of Silver; and when this Man will give over doing such things I know not, you do well therefore to be concerned for the miseries of others; in the requital whereof I rejoice in your happiness, and return you thanks; Farewel*.

The Figs which you have, lay up against winter, and the Cretan *meal, for these things seem to be better than* † *riches; wash and drink of the fountain of* Enneacrunus; *wear the same Garment in winter as in summer, and that sordid, as becomes a free person living under the* Athenian *Democracy. As for me, I knew as soon as I came into the City and Island govern'd by a Monarch, I should suffer those ills of which you write to me; Now the* Syraqusians, Agrigentines, Geloans, *and the rest of the* Sicilians * *compassionately admire me; but* † *for my madness in coming inconsiderately to these unseemly things, I wish this curse to fall upon me, that I may never be quit of these evils;* * *because being of years of discretion, and pretending to wisdom, I would not undergo hunger and cold, nor contemn glory, nor wear a long beard; I will send you some great white Lupines to eat, after you have acted* Hercules *to the Boys ; of which things it is reported you esteem it not absurd to discourse and write : But if any man should speak of Lupines to* Dionysius, *I think it were against the rules of Tyranny: Of the rest, go and discourse with* Simon *the Leather-dresser, than whom you esteem nothing more wise; for I am not allowed familiarity with Artificers, because I live under obedience to others*.

† For χρηματος reading χρεμαδίος instead of χρημαδιος, as χρημα the last word of the following Epistle, ἀντὶ χρημάδιον, Sceptice.
* make a point at γελοιος, and read νῦν δὲ ἐλεοῦντες με περιβλέποντα, Dorice; a ridiculous and acute Irony; for περιβλέπειν signifieth to look on a thing with admiration, which is not proper to Compassion.
† Read τᾶς δὲ μανίας πέρι, ἃς ἑαυλων.
* Perhaps ὅτι δή.

Notwithstanding this jarring betwixt them, *Aristippus* was nothing backward in employing the Interest he had at Court, for some friends of *Antisthenes*, to preserve them from death; as this Letter of his to *Antisthenes* doth manifest.

Socratic Epist. 11.

† *The* Locrian *young Men of whom you write to me, will be set at liberty, neither put to death, nor fined, though they were very near death.* * *Let not* Antisthenes *know I have saved his Friends, for he loves not to converse with Tyrants, but with Mealmen and Victuallers, such as sell Meat and Drink at* Athens *without fraud, and such as sell thick Cloaths in cold weather, and such as serve* † Simon, *these are not Riches*.

* The Letter seems to be written to *Antisthenes*; and this meant ironically.
† The Leather-dresser.

Diogenes followed the example of his Master *Antisthenes* in deriding *Aristippus*, * calling him the Court-Spaniel. As *Aristippus* passed by, *Diogenes* busied about washing Herbs, called to him, saying, *If you had learned to do thus, you needed not have followed the Courts of Princes;* and you, said he, *if you had known how to converse with Men, needed not to have washed Herbs*; thus expressed by † *Horace*.

* *Laert.*
† *Epist.* 1. 17.

Diog. *On herbs if* Aristippus *could have din'd,*
The Company of Kings he had declin'd.

Arist. *He who derides me, had he wit to use*
The Company of Kings, would herbs refuse.

I mine own Jester; thou the Peoples art,
My choice is of the better, nobler part,
I by a King maintain'd, on Horseback ride,
Thou by the meanest people art supply'd,
Than those that do maintain thee thou art less;
Yet to want nothing vainly dost profess.

* *Theodorus* in his Book of Sects, reproached *Aristippus*, and *Alexis* the Comick Poet, in his *Galatea* bringeth in a Servant speaking thus of one of his Disciples;

* *Laert.*
† *Athen. Deipn.* l. 2.

My Master young on Rhetorick first intent,
Next to Philosophy his Study bent:
A Cyrenæan *liv'd at* Athens *then,*
Nam'd Aristippus, *justly first of Men,*
Esteem'd for subtlety and Luxury,
A Talent him my Master gave to be
His Scholar, but of Arts he none was taught,
Save only Cookery; that away he brought.

CHAP. VI.
His Apothegms.

OF Apothegms (in * which kind he was conceived to have an acuteness beyond all the other Philosophers,) these are remembred.

* *Suid.*

† He once gave fifty drachms for a Patridge, for which being reproved by another; *you would have given a Peny for it*, saith he, which the other granting; *so much*, saith he, *are fifty drachms to me*.

† *Laert.*

Being demanded what was the greatest benefit he had received by Philosophy ; he answered, *To converse freely with all Men*.

Being reproached for living high ; if *Magnificence were a Sin*, saith he, *it would not be practised upon days of Festival to the Gods*.

To one who asked wherein Philosophers excelled other Men; *Though all Laws were abolished*, faith he, *we should lead the same Lives*.

Being demanded how the Learned differ from the unlearned, he answered, *as Horses unbackt from such as are well managed*.

Going into the house of a Courtezan, a young Man of the Company blushed, to whom he said,

said, *It is not ill to go in, but not to be able to come out.*

To one who desired him to resolve a Riddle, Thou fool, saith he, *why wouldst thou have me resolve that which unresolved finds us such entertainment?*

He said, *it is better to be a Beggar than unlearned, for one wants only Riches, the other Humanity.*

Being reviled, he went aloof off; he that reviled, asked why he fled; *Because* saith he, *to speak ill is in your power, not to hear is in mine.*

One saying, he saw Philosophers at the gates of rich Men, *and Physicians*, saith he, *at the gates of the Sick*; *but no Man would for that reason choose to be sick rather than a Physician.*

To one who boasted he learned much; *As they*, saith he, *who eat and exercise much, are not better than those who eat only to satisfie Nature, neither are they Learned who make large, but profitable Collections.*

An Oratour pleading for him, and gaining the Cause, asked him, *What are you the better for* Socrates? *So much*, saith he, *as that I make good those things which you alledged in my defence.*

He instructed his Daughter *Arete* to contemn all that is too much.

To one who demanded what his Son would be the better for Learning; *If in nothing else, in this*, saith he, *that in the Theatre one stone shall not sit upon another.*

Of one who would have preferred his Son to him, he demanded 500 Drachms, *For so much*, saith the other, *I can buy a Slave*; *Do so*, answered he, *and then you will have two (* your Son, and him you buy.)*

⁰ Plut. de puer. educ.

He said he took money of his friends, not to make use of it himself, but to let them know the right use of it.

Being reproached for entertaining an Oratour to plead his Cause; *and when I would feast*, saith he, *I hire a Cook.*

To one who boasted of his swimming, *Are not you ashamed*, saith he, *to glory in the property of a Dolphin.*

Being demanded wherein the Learned differ'd from the Unlearn'd; *Send them naked to strangers*, saith he, *and you shall see.*

To one who boasted he could drink much without being drunk; *So*, saith he, *can a Mule.*

Being blam'd that he took Money being the Disciple of *Socrates*, and justly, saith he, for Socrates, *when they sent him Wheat and Wine, took a little for his present use, and sent back the rest, the chief of all the Athenians were his Purveyors, mine* Eutichydes, *a mercenary Servant.*

Being reprov'd by *Plato* for buying a great quantity of Fish; *They cost me*, saith he, *but an Obolus, would not you have given so much for them?* To which *Plato* assenting, *It is not that I am profuse then*, saith he, *but that you are covetous.*

Simon Pantler to *Dionysius*, a Phrygian; a Man of ill conditions, brought him to his house paved curiously with marble; *Aristippus* spits in his face, whereat the other growing angry, *I could not find*, saith he, *a fitter place.*

Being demanded how *Socrates* died; *As I would wish to do*, saith he.

Polyxenus the Sophist coming to his house, and seeing there Women and a great feast, reproved him. *Aristippus* gave him way, and after a little pause, *will you dine with me*, saith he? whereto he consenting: *Why then*, continues he, *do you reprove me?* 'Tis not the feast, but the cost which you condemn.

His Servant being upon a Journey, weary with carrying of Money; *Throw away*, saith he, *what is too much, and carry as much as you can.*

† *He bad his slaves away his Money throw, Because ore-charg'd with weight they went too slow.* † Horat. Sat. 2. 3.

* Being at Sea, and understanding the owners of the Vessel were Pyrates, he took his Money and counted it, then let it fall into the Sea, as unwillingly, and sighed: Some affirm, that he said, *It is better these Perish for Aristippus, than Aristippus for them.* * Laert. Cic. de invent.

He reproved Men for *looking upon Goods exposed to sale, and taking no care to furnish their Minds*; others ascribe this to *Diogenes*.

Living in *Asia*, he was seized by *Antaphernes* the King's Lieutenant, whereupon one saying to him, and where is now your confidence? *When*, said he, *you fool, should I be confident, if not now, when I shall meet with* Antiphernes.

Those who forsook Philosophy, to apply themselves to *Mechanical* Sciences, he compar'd to *the Suitors of* Penelope, *they could get the good wills of* Melantho, Polydora, *and others of the Servants, but could not obtain the Mistress in marriage.* Not unlike is that of *Aristo*, who said, that *Ulysses*, when he went to Hell, saw all the Dead, and spoke to them, but could not come so much as to the Sight of the Queen.

Being demanded what Boys ought to learn; *That*, saith he, *which they ought to practise when they are Men.*

To one who accused him for going from *Socrates* to *Dionysius*: *To Socrates*, saith he, *I went for* παιδεία, *Education*; *to Dionysius for* παιδία, *Recreation*.

To a Courtezan who told him she was with Child by him: *You know that no more*, said he, *than if passing through a Bush, you should say this Thorn pricked you.*

To one who blamed him, that he took Money of *Dionysius*, *Plato* a Book; he answer'd, *I want Money*, Plato *Books*.

† Having lost a great Farm, he said to one, who seemed excessively to compassionate his loss, *You have but one field, I have three left; why should not I rather grieve for you?* It is madness (adds *Plutarch*) to lament for what is lost, and not rejoice for what is left. † Plut. de tranq. anim.

* When one told him, the Land is lost for your sake; *Better*, saith he, *is it that the Land be lost for me, than I for the Land.* * Stob. Eth. 46.

† Seeing one angry vent his Passion in words; *Let us not*, saith he, *suit words to our anger, but appease our anger with words.* † Stob. Eth. 99.

* Seeing a little Woman exceeding fair; *This* saith he, *is a little Evil, but a great Beauty.* They who invert these words, and read, a little fair one, but great evil, mistake the meaning of *Aristippus*, who plays upon that ordinary Saying, applying the inversion to his own luxurious humour. * Stob. Eth. 128.

† To one, who demanded his advice whether he should Marry or no: He said no, *If you take a fair Wife*, saith he, *she will be common, if foul, a fury.* † Stob. Eth. 185.

* He

He used to advise young Men to carry such Provision, as in a Ship-wrack they might swim away withal.

Stob. Eth. 210.

† *As a Shooe that is too big is unfit for use, so is a great estate; the bigness of the Shooe troubles the wearer; Wealth may be used upon occasion either wholly, or in part.*

† *Stob. Eth. 229.*

CHAP. VIII.

His Writings.

• *Laert.*

*SOme affirm (of whom is Soſicrates) that he wrote nothing at all: others that he wrote, *The Libyan History*, three Books dedicated to Dionyſius.

Dialogues twenty five (or rather twenty three; for the number seems corrupt) in one Book; some in the *Attick* Dialect, others in the *Dorick*: their Titles these: 1. *Artabazus.* 2. *To the ship-wrackt.* 3. *To Exiles.* 4. *To a poor man.* 5. *To Lais.* 6. *To Porus.* 7. *To Lais concerning a Looking-glass.* 8. *Hermias.* 9. *The Dream.* 10. *To the Cup-bearer.* 11. *Philomelus.* 12. *To Servants.* 13. *To those who reproved him for using old wine, and common Women.* 14. *To those who reproved him for feasting.* 15. *An epistle to Arete.* 16. *To the Olympick exerciſer.* 17. *An Interrogation.* 18. *Another Interrogation.* 19. † *A Chria to Dionyſius.* 20. *Another on an Image.* 21. *Another on Dionyſius's Daughter.* 22. *To one who conceived himself dishonoured.* 23. *To one who endeavoured to give advice.*

† *A Chria is a short commemoration, aptly relating the speech or action of some Person. The third of these (viz. to Dionyſius's Daughter) Voſſius inſerts amongst the Greek Histories; if that were Historical, it is likely this to Dionyſius was of the same Nature.*

Exercitations six Books.

• *Laert.*

* *Of Pleaſure* mentioned by *Laertius* in the Life of *Epicurus*.

Of Phyſiology, out of which *Laertius* cites, that *Pythagoras* was so named, because he spake no less truth than *Pythius*.

Of the Luxury of the Antients, four Books, containing examples of those who indulged in love and pleasure; as, the love of † *Empedocles* to *Pauſanias*, in the first Book; of *Cratea* to her Son *Periander*, of *Aristotle* to the Concubine of *Hermias* in the fourth, of *Socrates* to *Alcibiades*, *Xenophon* to *Clineas*, *Plato* to *Aſter*, *Xenocrates* to *Ptolemo*. But, these latter instances shew, that these Books were not writ by this *Ariſtippus*.

† *Laert. in vit-Emped. Peri-and. Ariſtot. &c.*

Epiſtles, four are extant under his name, in the *Socratick* Collection, put forth by *Leo Allatius*.

* *L*æ*t.*

* *Socion* and *Panætius* reckon his Treatiſes thus,

Of Diſcipline.
Of Vertue, an Exhortation.
Artabazus.
The Shipwrackt.
The Baniſh'd.
Exercitations ſix.
Chria three.
To Lais.
To Porus.
To Socrates.
Of Fortune.

CHAP. IX.

His Death.

HAving lived long with *Dionyſius*, at laſt his Daughter *Arete* ſent to him, to deſire him that he would come to *Cyrene* to her, to order her Affairs; for, that ſhe was in danger of oppreſſion by the Magiſtrates. *Ariſtippus* hereupon took leave of *Dionyſius*, and being on his Voyage, fell Sick by the way, and was forced to put in at *Lipara*, an *Æolian* Iſland, where he dyed, as may be gathered from this Epiſtle, which he then ſent to his Daughter.

† *Ariſtippus* to * *Arete.*

† *Socr. Epiſt. 27.*
* *So ſupplied by Leo Allatius.*

I Received your Letter by *Teleus*, wherein you deſire me to make all poſſible haſte to *Cyrene*, becauſe your buſineſs with the Præfects goeth not to your Mind, and your Husband is unfit to manage your domeſtick affairs, by reaſon of his baſhfulneſs, and being accuſtomed to a retired life, remote from the publick. Wherefore as ſoon as I got leave of *Dionyſius*, I ſail'd towards you, and being upon my journey, fell ſick by the way at *Lipara*, where the friends of *Sonicus* provide carefully for me, with ſuch humanity, as is needful for one near death. As for your demand, what reſpect you ſhould give thoſe whom I manumiſed, who profeſs they will never deſert *Ariſtippus* whilſt they have ſtrength; but, ever ſerve him and you; truſt them in all things, they have learned from me not to be falſe. For your ſelf, I adviſe you to apply your ſelf to the Magiſtrates, which counſel will profit you, if you affect not rather to have much: You will live moſt at eaſe, if you contemn exceſs; for, they cannot be ſo unjuſt as to leave you in want. You have two Orchards left ſufficient to maintain you plentifully: and that poſſeſſion in *Bernicia*, if alone left you, were ſufficient to ſupply you fully. I do not counſel you to neglect ſmall things; but, not to be troubled for ſmall things, ſince vexation is not good even for great. If when I am dead, you want my advice for the education of young *Ariſtippus*, go to *Athens*, and above all, eſteem *Xantippe*, and *Myrto*, who have often ſpoke to me to bring you to the *Eleuſinian* Feſtivals. Whilſt you lead this pleaſant life with theſe, let the *Cyrenæan* Præfects be as unjuſt as they pleaſe, in your natural † end they cannot prejudice you. Endeavour to live with *Xantippe* and *Myrto*, as I did heretofore with *Socrates*, compoſing your ſelf to their Converſation; for, Pride is not proper in that place. If * *Tyrocles*, the Son of *Socrates*, who lived with me at *Megara*, come to *Cyrene*, it will be well done to ſupply him, and to reſpect as your own Son. If you will not nurſe a Daughter, becauſe of the great trouble it gives you, ſend for the Daughter of *Eubois*, to whom you have heretofore expreſt ſo much kindneſs, and nam'd after my Mother, and I have alſo often called her my friend. Above all, take care of little *Ariſtippus*, that he may be worthy of us, and of Philoſophy: For this I leave him as his true Inheritance, the reſt of his eſtate finds the *Cyrenæan* Magiſtrates adverſaries. But you writ me not word that any offered to take that away from you. Rejoice dear Daughter, in the poſſeſſion of thoſe Riches which are in your power, and make your ſon poſſeſs 'em likewiſe: I wiſh he were my ſon; but, being diſapointed of that hope, I depart with this aſſurance,

† *Pleaſure.*

* *Leo Allatius reads Lamprocles; but, that cannot be; for Lamprocles was dead long before; See Life Socratic. Chap. 15.*

Stob. Eth. 195.

assurance, that you will lead him in the paths trodden by good Men. Farewell, and grieve not for us.

*Of his Children, besides this *Arete* his Daughter, whom he educated in Philosophy, is remembred also a Son, whom for his stupidity he dis-inherited, and turned out of doors; for which being reproved by his Wife, who alledged, that he came from himself; he, spitting said, *This comes from me too, but profiteth me nothing.* Or, as *Laertius.* We cast τὸ φλέγμα ϰ ̀ τὰς φθεῖρας, all unnecessary things as far as we can from us.

Arete had a Son named from his Grandfather *Aristippus*, and from his Mothers instructing him in Philosophy, surnam'd μητροδιδακτος.

Besides these two (*Aristippus* the Grandfather and the Grandson) *Laertius* reckons two more of the same name: One writ the History of *Arcadia*: the Other was of the new Academy.

CHAP. IX.

His Disciples and Successors.

OF the Auditors of *Aristippus*, besides his Daughter *Arete*, (whom he taught with much care, and brought up to great Perfection in Philosophy) are remembred *Æthiops* of *Ptolomais*, and *Antipater* of *Cyrene*.

Arete communicated the Philosophy she received from her Father, to her Son *Aristippus the younger*: *Aristippus* transmitted it to *Theodorus* the *Atheist*, who instituted a Sect, call'd *Theodorean*.

Antipater communicated the Philosophy of *Aristippus* to *Epitimides* his Disciple; *Epitimides* to *Parœbates*; *Parœbates* to *Hegesias* and *Anniceris*; these two last improving it by some additions of their own, obtained the honour each of them, to have a Sect named after them, *Hegesiack* and *Annicerick*.

HEGESIAS.

CHAP. I.

His Life.

† Cic. Tusc. qu. I.

Val. Max. 8. 9.

HEGESIAS, Disciple to *Parœbates*, was surnamed πεισιθάνατος, Death's Oratour, from a † Book he writ, entituled Ἀποκαρτερῶν, upon occasion of one who had famished himself nigh to death, but was call'd back to life by his Friends, in answer to whom, he in this Book demonstrated that death takes us away from ill things, not from good, and reckoned up the incommodities of Life, and represented the Evils thereof* with so much Rhetorick, that the sad Impression thereof penetrated so far into the breasts of many hearers, that it begot in them a desire of dying voluntarily, and many laid violent hands upon themselves. Whereupon he was prohibited by *Ptolomy* the King to discourse any more upon this Subject in the Schools.

CHAP. II.

His Philosophy.

Laert.

HIS Disciples were from him called *Hegesians*. They held the same chief good and Evil with the *Cyreneans*; further asserting,

That *Kindness, Friendship, and Benevolence are in themselves nothing; not expetible, but in respect of those Benefits which cannot consist without those Persons.*

That *Perfect Felicity is absolutely impossible, because the Body is disordered by many troubles,* in which the Soul shares, and most of those things which we hope are prevented by chance.

That *Life and Death are in our choice.*

That *nothing is by Nature pleasant or unpleasant, but by the rarity and unusualness of things, or satiety; some are delighted therewith, others not.*

That *Poverty and Wealth confer nothing to Pleasure, neither are the rich poor affected with Pleasure several ways. Servitude and Liberty, Nobility and Meanness, Glory and ignominy differ nothing in this respect.*

That *to live is advantagious for a Fool, indifferent to a Wise Man.*

That *a Wise Man ought to do all things in consideration of himself, and prefer none before himself, for though possibly, he may receive benefits from others very great in outward appearance; yet are they nothing in comparison of those which he dispenseth.*

That *Sense confers nothing to certain knowledge, for all act by the rules of their own reason.*

That *Offences ought to be pardoned, for no Man offends willingly, but compell'd by some affection.*

That *we should hate no Man, but instruct him better.*

That *a wise Man should not insist so much upon choice of good things, as upon evil, making it his scope and end to live neither in Labour nor Grief; which they do, who are inclined neither way to the objects of Pleasure.*

ANNICE-

ANNICERIS.

CHAP. I.
His Life.

°*Laert.*

†*Æl.var.hist. 2. 27.*

*ANNICERIS was of *Cyrene*, Disciple to *Paræbates*. *Suidas* faith, he was an *Epicurean*, and that he lived in the time of *Alexander*. †He was excellent in Charriot-Racing, of which one day he gave a Testimony before *Plato*, and drove many Courses round the Academy, so exactly, that his Wheels never went out of the Track, to the admiration of all that were present, except *Plato*, who reprehended his too much industry, saying, It was not possible but that he who employed so much Pains about things of no value, must neglect those of greater concernment, which are truly worth admiration.

* *Laert. vit. Plat.*

* When *Plato*, by the command of *Dionysius*, was sold as a Slave in *Ægina*, *Anniceris* fortuned to be present, who redeemed him for twenty, or according to others, thirty, *Minæ*, and sent him to *Athens* to his Friends, who presently returned the Money to *Anniceris*, but he refused it, saying, They were not the only Persons that deserved to take care of *Plato*.

†*Suid.*

†He had a Brother named *Nicoteles*, a Philosopher; he had likewise the famous *Posidonius* to be his Disciple.

CHAP. II.
His Philosophy.

HIS Disciples were called *Annicerians*; †they as the rest placed all good in pleasure, and conceived Vertue to be only commendable as far as it produced pleasure. *They agreed in all things with the *Hegesians*, but they abolished not Friendship, good-will, duty to Parents, and actions done for our Country. They held,

†*Cic.de offic.3.*

**Laert.*

That *although a Wise Man suffer trouble for those things, yet he will lead a Life, nothing the less happy, tho' he enjoy but few Pleasures.*

That *the felicity of a Friend is not expetible in it self; for to agree in Judgment with another, or to be raised above, and fortified against the general Opinion, is not enough to satisfie reason, but we must accustom our selves to the best things; because of our innate vicious Inclinations.*

That a Friend is not be entertained out of useful or necessary Ends, nor when such fail, is to be cast off, but out of an intimate good will, for which we must also undergo trouble. For though they placed (as the rest) the chief end and good in Pleasure, and professed to be grieved at the loss thereof, yet they affirm that we ought to undergo voluntarily labours, out of Love to a Friend.

THEODORUS.

CHAP. I.
His Life.

**Laert.*
†*Suid.*

**Plut. Plac. Phil. 17. Cic. de nat. deor 1.*

*THEODORUS heard *Anniceris*, *Dionysius* the Logician, *Zeno* the †Cittiean, and *Pyrrho* the Ephectick. He was called the *Atheist*, because *he held there was no God, and wrote a Treatise (*Suidas* faith many) wherein he endeavoured to refel all Arguments to the contrary, out of which *Epicurus* borrowed much. Afterwards was abusively called θεὸς, upon occasion of a Dispute with *Stilpo*, to this Effect. *Do you believe*, faith *Stilpo*, *you are whatsoever you affirm your self to be*? *Theodorus* granting; *Then*, continues *Stilpo*, *if you should say you were a God, were you so*? To which *Thodorus* assenting, *Stilpo* replied; *Then impious Man, you are a Bird, or any thing else by the same Reason*.

He was ejected out of *Cyrene* by the Citizens, whereupon he said pleasantly; *You do not well*, Cyreneans, *to thrust me out of* Lybia *into* Greece. Thence he went to *Athens*, where he should have been cited to the Court of *Areopagus*, and lost his Life, but that he was freed by *Demetrius Phalereus*. Being likewise banished

banished thence, he went to Ptolomy the Son of *Lagus*, with whom he lived, and was by him sent on Embassy to *Lysimachus*, to whom speaking Atheistically; *Lysimachus* said, *Are not you that Theodorus that was banished* Athens? He answered, *It is true, the Athenians when they could bear me no longer, as* Semele Bacchus, *cast me out.* Lysimachus replied, See that you come no more to me. No, answered he, *unless* Ptolomy *send me.* Mythro Son of *Lysimachus* being present, said, *You seem not only ignorant of the Gods but of Kings.* How saith he, *Am I ignorant of the Gods, who believe you an Enemy to them?* Lysimachus threatned him with Death; * *You glory,* saith he *in a great matter, a* Cantharides *can do as much.* Or as *Stobæus, I knew not that you had not the power of a King but of Poison.* Hereat incensed, he commanded he should be crucified. *Threaten,* saith he, *those things I pray to your purple Nobles; it is all oe to* Theodorus *whether be rot above, or under Ground.*

* Sen. de tranq. anim. 6. Cic. Tusc. qu. 1. Plut. am. vitios. ad infel. suff.

Finally he went to *Cyrene,* and lived with *Marius* in much repute, in that City out of which he was first ejected.

Disputing with *Euryclides* a Priest, he ask'd, what persons those were who defile mysteries: *Euryclides* answered, *Those who communicate them to persons not initiated.* Then, replied he, *you do impiously, in declaring them to such.*

What others ascribe to *Aristippus* and *Diogenes,* some attribute to *Theodorus* and *Metrocleus,* a *Cynick,* who saying, *You would not want Disciples if you washed Herbs:* Theodorus answered, *Neither would you wash Herbs, if you knew how to converse with Men.*

He said of *Hipparchia* the Wife of *Crates; This is she who hath given over the Shuttle to put on a Cloak.*

CHAP. II.

His Philosophy.

† Suid. in Socrat.

HE taught all manner of Learning, and instituted a Sect, called *Throdorean.* † He asserted *Indifference,* that there is no difference of things.

‡ Laert.

‡ That *our end, or chief good and greatest ill, are joy and sorrow; one consisting in Prudence, the other in Imprudence.*

That *Prudence and Justice are good things, the contrary Habits ill, the mean, pleasure and grief.*

He took away Friendship, because it is neither in fools nor wise Men; those being uncapable to make use of it, the thing it self vanisheth; these not needing it, as being sufficient to themselves.

That *it is reasonable that a Wise Man expose not himself to danger for his Country; Wisdom ought not to be lost for the preservation of Fools.*

That *the World is our Country.*

That *a Man upon occasion may commit Theft, Adultery, and Sacriledge, there being nothing in these naturally evil, if that Opinion were taken away which is built upon the agreement of fools.*

That *a wise Man may publickly without shame* ἐϱωμένοις χρῆσϑαι.

He used such Inductions as these: *Is not a Woman that is skilful in Grammar, profitable in that respect as a Grammarian? Yea. Is not the same of a Youth? Yes. Is not a beautiful Woman then profitable, as being handsome? Yes: Then she who makes right use of it doth not amiss.* In these kinds of Questions he was very subtle.

CHAP. III.

His Death, Writings, &c.

AMphicrates saith, that he was condemned by the Law for Atheism, and drunk Hemlock. Laert.

He wrote, besides that which appertained to his Sect, many other things.

Laertius reckons twenty of this name: The *first* a *Samian,* Son of *Rhæcus,* who advised to lay the Foundation of the Temple at *Ephesus,* upon Embers: For, the place being wet, he said, that Coals, when they forsake the nature of Wood, acquire a solidity not to be violated by Moisture.

The *second* of *Cyrene,* a Geometrician, whose Disciple *Plato* was.

The *third* this Philosopher.

The *fourth* writ of exercising the Voice, a famous Book.

The *fifth* writ of Law-givers, beginning with *Terpander.*

The *sixth* a Stoick.

The *seventh* writ the Roman History.

The *eighth* a *Syracusian,* writ Tacticks.

The *ninth* a *Byzantine,* a Sophist, * eminent for Civil Pleas. *Suid.*

The *tenth* of the same Country, mention'd by *Aristotle* in his Epitome of Oratours.

The *eleventh* of *Thebes,* a Statuary.

The *twelfth* a Painter, mentioned by *Polemon.*

The *thirteenth* of *Athens,* a Painter, of whom writes *Menodotus.*

The *fourteenth* of *Ephesus,* a Painter, of whom *Theophanes* in his Treatise of Painting.

The *fifteenth* a Poet, who wrote Epigrams.

The *sixteenth* wrote of Poets.

The *seventeenth* a Physician, Disciple to *Athenæus.*

The *eighteenth* of *Chios,* a Stoick.

The *nineteenth* of *Miletus,* a Stoick.

The *twentieth* a Tragick Poet.

BION.

BION.

CHAP. I.

Bion *His Life*.

* Laert.

OF the *Thodorean* Sect was BION, a *Boristhenite*. What his Parents were, and what his Employments, he diverting himself to Philosophy, related to *Antigonus*, King of *Macedonia*, in this manner. *Antigonus* asked *Whence art thou? Who thy Parents? What thy Town? Bion* perceiving himself to be reproached, answered thus, My Father was a Freeman, τῶ ἀγκῶνι ἀπομυσσόμενος, implying he was a seller of Salt-Fish, a *Boristhenite*; he had not a Face, but instead thereof a Brand-mark, which declared the ill disposition of the owner: My Mother he married out of a common Brothel-

† *Athen. deipn.*

house; [† *a* Lacedæmonian *Curtezan*, named Olympia,] being such a Woman as such a Man could get. My Father for couzening the State, was sold, and all our Family for Slaves. I being a young likely Youth, was bought by an Oratour, who died, and left me all he had. I tore and burnt his Papers, went to *Athens*, and there applied my self to Philosophy. *This is the Blood and Race I boast to own.* Thus much concerning my self: Let *Perseus* therefore, and *Philonides* forbear to enquire after these things, and look you upon me, as I am in my self. You do not use, O King, when you send for Archers, to enquire of what Parentage they are; but, set them up a mark to shoot at: Even so of Friends you should not examine whence, but what they are.

Bion indeed, setting this aside, was of a versatile wit, a subtle Sophist, and gave many furtherances to the Exercisers of Philosophy: In some things he was ———

He first heard *Crates* the Academick; but, despising that Sect, took a sordid Cloak and Scrip, and became a *Cynick*: To which *Laertius* ascribes his constancy, expert of perturbation. Then he followed *Theodorus* the Atheist, who profest all manner of Learning; to whose Opinions he addicted himself, and was called a *Theodorean*: Afterwards he heard *Theophrastus* the *Peripatetick*.

CHAP. II.

His Apothegms.

HE left many Memorials, and profitable Apothegms; as, being reproved for not endeavouring to catch a young Man; New Cheese, faith he, will not stick to the Hook.

Being demanded what Man is most perplexed? He, saith he, who aims at the highest Content.

To one who asked his Advice whether he should Marry or not, (for this some ascribe to *Bion*, which *A. Gellius* to *Bias*, the mistake perhaps grounded upon the nearness of their Names) he answered, If you take a foul Wife, she will be a Torment; if a fair, Common.

He said, That *Age is the Haven to which all Ills have recourse*; That *Glory is the Mother of years*; that *beauty is a good which concerns others, not our selves*; that *riches are the sinews of things*.

To one who had consumed his Patrimony, *Earth*, saith he, *devoured* Amphiaraus, *but you devour Earth.*

He said, *It is a great ill, not to be able to bear ill.*

He reproved those who burn Men, as having no Sense, and again burn them as having Sense.

He used to say, It is better to yield our own Youth and Beauty to others, than to attempt anothers; for he that doth so, injures both his Body and Soul.

He vilified *Socrates*, saying, if he could enjoy *Alcibiades*, and did not, he was a Fool; if he could not, he did no great matter.

He said the way to the next World is easie, for we find it blindfold.

He condemned *Alcibiades*, saying, When he was a Boy, he drew away Husbands from their Wives, when a Man, Wives from their Husbands.

At *Rhodes*, whilst the *Athenians* exercised Rhetorick, he taught Philosophy; for which being reproved, I bought Wheat, faith he, and shall I sell Barley?

He said, they who are punished below would be more tormented if they carried Water in whole Vessels, than in Vessels full of holes.

One that was extreamly talkative, desiring his assistance in a business, I will do what I can for you, saith he, if you send a Messenger to me, and come not your self.

Travelling with very ill Company, they fell amongst Thieves; We shall be undone, faith he, unless we be known.

He said, Arrogance is the obstruction of Vertue.

Of a rich Man covetous, He hath not Money, faith he, but Money him.

He said, Covetous Persons keep their wealth so strictly, that they have no more use of their own than of anothers.

He said, When we are young, we use Courage, when old, Wisdom. Wisdom excels other Vertues, as the Sight the other Senses.

He said, No Man should be reproached for old Age, that being a Condition all pray they may arrive at.

To

To an envious Man said, I know not saith he, whether some ill hath befaln you, or some good another.

He said, Impiety is an ill companion to bold Language;

For though his Speech be free,
To Bondage yield must be.

That Friends whatsoever they prove ought to be retain'd: Lest we seem to have conversed with wicked Persons, or to shun good.

Being demanded if there were any Gods, he said, *Old man, wilt thou not drive this croud away.*

He conceived that he might make a Field fertile sooner by praising than by manuring it.

He said, They who love to be flattered, are like Pots carried by the Ear.

To one who asked him what folly is, he said, the obstruction of Knowledge.

He said, good Men, though Slaves, are free, but wicked Men though free, are Slaves to many Pleasures.

He said, Grammarians whilst they enquire after the Errors of *Ulysses*, mind not their own, nor see that they themselves go astray as well as he, in taking pains about useless things.

He said, Avarice is the *Metropolis* of all Evil.

* *Athen.* * Seeing a Statue of *Persus*, under which was written, ΠΕΡΣΑΙΟΣ ΞΗΝΩΝΟΣ Ο ΚΙΤΤΕΥΣ, *Persæus*, of Zeno, a *Cittiean*, he said, the writer mistook; for it should be, οἰκέτης, *Zeno's Servant*; as indeed he was.

CHAP. III.

His Death.

* *Laert.* AT last falling sick (as those of *Chalcis* say, for he died there) he was perswaded to suffer ligatures (by way of charm) he recanted and profest repentance for all he had said offensive to the Gods. He was reduced to extream want of such things as are most necessary to sick Persons, until *Antigonus* sent to him two Servants; and himself followed in a litter, as *Phavorinus* affirms in his various History, of that Sickness he died; on whose death thus *Laertius.*

Bion the Boristhenite,
By his Birth to Scythia known,
Did Religious duties slight,
Gods affirming there were none.

If to what he then profest,
Firm he had continued still,
Then his Tongue had spoke his breast,
And been constant though in ill.

But the same who Gods deny'd,
He who sacred fanes despis'd,
He who Mortals did deride,
When to Gods they sacrific'd;

Tortur'd by a long Disease,
And of Death's pursuit afraid,
Gifts their anger to appease
On their Hearts and Altars laid.

Thus with smoak and incense tries
To delight their sacred scent;
I have sinn'd, not only cries,
And what I profest repent:

But unto an old Wives Charms
Did his willing Neck submit,
And about his feeble Arms
Caus'd them Leather Thongs to knit.

And a youthful sprig of bays
Did set up before his gate:
Every means and way essays
To divert approaching fate.

Fool to think the Gods might be
Brib'd with gifts, their favours bought,
Or the sacred Deity,
Were, and were not, as he thought.

But his Wisdoms Titles (now
Turn'd to Ashes) not avail
With stretched Arms, I know not how,
Hail he cry'd, great Pluto Hail.

Of this name *Laertius* reckons ten; The *first* contemporary with *Pherecydes* the *Syrian*, of *Proconnesus*; who writ two Books extant in his time.

The *second* a *Syracusian* wrote of the Art of Rhetorick.

The *third* this Philosopher.

The *fourth* an Abderite of the Family of *Democritus*; a Mathematician: He wrote in the *Attick*, and *Ionick* Dialect: He first said there we some habitable parts of the Earth, where it was six Months day and six Months night.

The *fifth* of *Soleis*; he wrote the *Æthiopick History.*

The *sixth*, an Orator, who wrote nine Books entituled by the names of the Muses.

The *seventh* a Lyrick Poet.

The *eighth* a *Milesian* Statuary; mentioned by *Polemon.*

The *ninth* a Tragick Poet, one of those who were called *Tarsici.*

The *tenth* a Statuary of *Clazomene* or *Chios*, mentioned by *Hipponax.*

THE MEGARICK SECT.

EUCLID.

CHAP. I.

His Country and Masters.

Laert. *EUCLID (institutor of the Megarick Sect) was born at *Megara*, a Town adjacent upon the *Isthmus*; though others say at *Geta*, a City of *Sicily*.

He first studied the Writings of *Parmenides*, then went to *Athens* to hear *Socrates*: Afterwards the † *Athenians* made an order that *if any Citizen of* Megara *came into the City of* Athens, *he should be put to death*: So great was the hatred the *Athenians* bore to the *Megarenses*. * *Thucydides* mentions this Decree, whereby the *Megarenses* were prohibited *to make use of any Laws within the Athenian Jurisdiction, or the Attick Forum*: Which order the *Lacedæmonians* requiring to be repealed, and not prevailing, the *Peloponnesian* War ensued thereupon, the cruelest and longest that ever was amongst the *Grecians*.

† A Gel. 6. 10.

* Lib. 1.

A. Gel. 6. 10. *Euclid*, who was of *Megara*, and before that Decree used to go to *Athens*, and hear *Socrates*, after it was promulgated, came by night in a long Woman's Gown, and Cloak of several colours, his head attired in a Woman's Veil (so *Varro* expounds *Rica*) from his house in *Megara* to *Athens*, to *Socrates*, that he might be in that time partaker of his Counsel and instructions, and went back again before that day in the same habit twenty thousand paces.

*Laert. * Upon the death of *Socrates*, *Plato* and the rest of the Philosophers, fearing the cruelty of the Tyrants, went to *Megara* to him, who entertained him kindly.

CHAP. II.

His Institution of a Sect.

† Laert.
* Laert. vit. Socr.

† HE affected litigious Disputes, and * was therefore told by *Socrates*, that he *knew how to contend with Sophists, but not with Men*: Suitable to his contentious humour, he instituted a Sect, † first called *Megarick* from the place, afterwards *Eristick*, from the Litigious Sophistical Nature thereof: Whence * *Diogenes* said; it was not χολὴ a School, but χολὴ anger : † thus reproved by *Timon*,

† Laert.

* Laert. vit. Diog.
† Laert.

*Of all these trifles, I not value ought,
Which Phædo nor Litigious Euclid caught,
Who the Megareans mad contention taught.*

Lastly, it was called Dialectick; which name *Dionysius*, a *Carthaginian* first gave them, because their Discourse consisted of question and answer.

He affirmed, that *there is but one good, which is called by several names; sometimes Prudence, sometimes God, sometimes the Mind, and the like*: He took away all things opposite to good, saying, *there was no such thing*.

He used Arguments not by Assumption, but by Inference.

He took away disputation by Similitude, saying, that it consisted either of like or unlike; if of like, it were better to examine the things themselves to which they are like: if of unlike, the comparison is to no purpose.

CHAP. III.

His Apothegms, Writings.

HE was famous in the Schools (saith * *Plutarch*) forasmuch as hearing his Brother in a rage, say, *Let me perish, if I be not revenged*: he answered, *And I, unless I perswade you to lay aside your anger, and love me as at first*. If † *Hierocles* (who relates the same Story) for τῦ Σωκράτης writ not as *Plutarch* τῦ Σωκρατικῦ, that Epithete occasioned the mistake.

* De fraterno amore.

† Stob. serm. 81.

*. He said, *that there is one kind of Sleep, a young pliant Deity, easie to be driven away; the other gray and aged, chiefly frequenting old Men: Pertinacious and inexorable, from this God, if he once come, it is hard to get lose; words avail nothing, for he is deaf, nor can you shew him any thing that may move him, for he is blind.*

*. Stob. Eth. 38.

† Being demanded what the Gods are, and wherein they delight: *Of all things else concerning them*, saith he, *I am ignorant but of this, I know they hate curious Persons.*

† Stob. Eth. 47.

* He wrote (besides other things) six Dialogues. († *Panætius* doubts whether they were genuine or spurious) titles these,

* Laert.
† Laert. vit. Æschin.

Lamprias.
Æschines.
*Phœnix; or (as *Suidas*) the Phœnixes.
Crito.
Alcibiades.
The Erotick.

* In voce Euclides.

Of the same names are numbred
Euclid the Mathematician, a *Megarean* also, whence confounded by † *Valerius Maximus* with the Philosopher: Plato (saith he) sent the undertakers

† Lib. 8. cap. 13.

takers of the sacred Altar (who came to confer with him concerning the manner and form thereof) to Euclid the Geometrician, yielding to his skill and profession: That these undertakers came to Plato is evident from the testimony of many others; but, that he remitted them to *Euclid* the Geometrician, or that *Euclid* the Philosopher own'd that profession, is no where to be prov'd. On the contrary, * *Proclus* affirms, that *Euclid* the Mathematician was of the *Platonick* Sect; and that †*Ptolomy* King of Ægypt, asking if there were any shorter way to Geometry, he answer'd, *Not any King's-high-way*. From the death of *Socrates* to the first of the *Ptolomys* are 95 years. So that *Euclid* the *Mathematician* was much later than the Philosopher.

* *In Euclid. lib. 2 cap. 4.*
† *The Text is imperfect, read* Καὶ μέν τοι καὶ φασὶν ὅτι Πτολεμαῖος ἤρετο ποτὲ αὐτὸν εἴ τις ἐςὶ περὶ γεωμετρίαν τῆς ςοιχειώσεως βραχίων μέθοδος; ὁ δὲ μία φησίν ὦ βασιλεῦ πρὸς γεωμετρίαν βασιλικὴ ὁδὸς νεωτέρος, &c. and (so well nigh) *Barocius*.

Euclid the Archon in the second year of the 88th Olympiad, according to * *Diodorus Siculus*; but † *Aristotle* names the Archon for that year *Euclees*, confirmed by his Commentators, and by * *Suidas*, who only errs a little in the distance of Years betwixt him and *Euclid* the other *Archon*. † *Salmasius* not knowing the name *Euclees* to be any where found amongst the *Archontes*, and expresly affirming the contrary, endeavours to corrupt the Text of *Suidas* reading *Diocles*.

* *Lib.*
† *Meteor. 1. 6.*
* Σαμίων ὁ δῆμος.
† *Inscript. p. 235.*

Euclid the Archon, in the second year of the 94th Olympiad,

Euclid the Soothsayer, Friend to *Xenophon*, who * mentions him.

* *Exped. Cyr. Lib. 7.*

Euclid the Stone-cutter, named in † *Plato's* Will.

† *Laert. vit. Plat.*

EUBULIDES.

† *Laert.*

†**E**UBULIDES a *Milesian* succeeded *Euclid*. Some affirm, that *Demosthenes* the Orator was his Scholar, and that *Demosthenes* not being able to pronounce the Letter R, he taught him by continual Exercise to do it. He was a great Enemy to *Aristotle*, and much aspersed him.

In *Dialectick* he invented many kinds of Interrogation or Argument, ψευδόμενον the Lying; διαλανθάνοντα, the occult; ἠλέκτραν, Electra; ἐγκεκαλυμμένον, the Vailed; Σωρείτην, Sorites; Κερατίνην, the Horned; φαλακρὸν, the Bald: Of which thus *Demosthenes*,

The Orators sharp Eubulides *knows*
With subtle forked questions how to pose,
Speech from Demosthenes *not sweeter flows.*

These are several kinds of Sophisms, which * *Aristotle* in general defines *Eristick Syllogisms*; from this School borrowed and enlarged afterwards by the *Stoicks*.

* *Top. 8. 4.*

ψευδόμενος, termed by † *Athenæus* ψευδολόγος, by * *Cicero mentions*, is a captious reasoning, not to be dissolved; named as most of the rest, not from the form, but matter; the ordinary example being this, † *If you say that you lye when you speak truth, you lye: But you say that you lye when you speak truth; therefore you lye*. Such is that in * *Africanus, a man having four hundred (Crowns) disposeth in Legacies three hundred; next he bequeaths to you a piece of ground worth 100 Crowns: provided his Will be not liable to the Falcidian Law, [by which all Legacies are made void, if the surplusage remaining for the Heirs, amount not at least to the fourth part of the goods] The question is what right you have*. I say, the question is not to be resolved, being of that kind which the Dialecticks call ψευδόμενον, what part soever we take for true will prove false. If we say the Legacies are valid, the Will comes within compass

† *Deipn. 8. Divinat. 2.*
‡ *Cic. Lucul.*
* *Lib. 5. quæst.*

of the Falcidian Law, whereby the condition being defective, the Legacy is invalid. Again, if because the condition is defective, the Legacies are valid, it is not liable to the Falcidian Law; and if the Law take not place upon the condition, you are not to have what was bequeathed you. So much was this *Sophism* esteemed, that * *Seneca* affirms, many Books to have been written upon it: † *Laertius* reckons six distinct Treatises of *Chrysippus*. * *Athenæus* and *Suidas* averr, that *Philetus* a *Choan*, died of a Consumption, occasion'd by excessive study upon this Question only.

* *Epist. 6. 45.*
† *Vit. Chrysipp.*
* *Deipn. 8.*

Electra, named (likewise) from the chief Examples; of which thus *Lucian*: Electra *the illustrious Daughter of* Agamemnon, *knew and knew not the same thing*. Orestes *unknown standing by her, she knew that* Orestes *was her Brother, but she knew not that he was* Orestes.

Ἐγκεκαλυμμένος, the Vailed; named also from the matter, thus instanced by *Lucian*. CHR. *Answer me, Do you know your Father?* MERC. *Yes.* CHR. *What if I should bring one unto you vailed, what would you say, that you know him or not?* MERC. *That I did not know him.* CHR. *And yet that Man proves to be your Father, therefore if you knew not the Man, you knew not your Father.* MERC. *No truly; but, pull off his vail, and I shall discover the Truth.* Of the same kind is that of the *Sophists*, which † *Aristotle* affirms *Socrates* (in *Plato's Meno*) vainly labours to resolve; *Do you know all pairs are even or not? The other answering he knew it. The Sophist brings forth a pair of something which he had held hidden under his Cloak, and asks, did you know that I had this even pair or not? the other confessing he knew not, Then saith he, you know and know not the same thing.*

† *Analyt. pr. stev. 1. 1.*

Sorites, By *Cicero* termed * a *Cervalis*, who defines it to be † *when any thing by degrees is added or taken away: As a heap* (Σωρὸς) *is made by adding a grain*, or rather as * *Julianus, when from things evidently true, by very short mutations the dispute*

* *Divin. 2.*
† *Cic. Lucul.*
* *Digest. lib. 15.*

dispute is led to such things as are evidently false, the same, † *Ulpian*, The common Example mentioned by * *Cicero*, † *Laertius* * *Sextus Empiricus*, and others in this : *Are not two a few ? Are not three so likewise ? Are not four the same? So on to ten.* But two are a few, and therefore ten.

Κερατίνη *the horned*; Denominated as the rest from the Example, *What you lost not you have, you lost not Horns, therefore you have Horns.* Repeated by *Seneca*, *A. Gellius* and others. Of this kind * *St. Hierom* observes that to be which the Pharisees objected to our Saviour. He came (saith he) *from* Galilee *to* Judea, wherefore the faction of Scribes and Pharisees asked him whether it were lawful for a man to put away his wife for any cause, that they might entrap him by a Horned Syllogism, whatsoever he would answer being liable to exception : If you should say, a Wife might be put away for any cause, and another taken; he being a Professor of modesty should contradict himself; but if he should answer, a wife ought not to be put away for any cause, he should be accounted guilty of Sacriledge, and judg'd to do contrary to the Doctrine of Moses, and by Moses of God. Our Lord therefore so tempers his answer, that he passeth by their trap, alledging for testimony the sacred Scripture and natural Law, opposing the first sentence of God to the second, which was granted not from the will of God, but necessity of Sin. The same Father instances another of the same kind proposed to him, * *I was assaulted at* Rome *by a very Eloquent person, with that which they call a Horned Syllogism, so as which way soever I turn'd I was more entangl'd. To marry a wife, saith he, is it a sin or not ? I plainly not thinking to avoid his ambush, said, it is not a Sin; he then propounded another question, in Baptism. Are good works remitted or Evil? I with the like simplicity answered, Sins are remitted : When I thought my self secure, Horns began to bud out on each side on me, and the hidden forces to discover themselves. If, saith he, to marry a Wife be not a Sin, and that Baptism remitteth Sins, whatsoever is not remitted is reserved.*

† Lib. 48. ad Sabin. in tit. de verb. & rer. signific.
* In Lucullo.
‡ In Chrysip.
* Adv. Logic.

* lib. 5. in Mat.

* Epist. 83.

ALEXINUS.

§ Laert.

† Amongst the many Disciples of *Eubulides* was *Alexinus* an *Elean*, a great lover of Contention, and therefore called Ἐλέγξινος from redarguing; he most opposed *Zeno*.

Hermippus saith, he went to *Olympia*, and there profest Philosophy; his Disciples questioning why he lived there, he answered, he meant to institute a Sect, and call it *Olympick*, but his Disciples wanting subsistence, and disliking the Air, departed, he continued there solitary with one Servant only, and swimming in the River *Alphæus*, was hurt with a Reed, whereof he dyed.

He wrote against other Philosophers besides *Zeno*. And against *Ephorus* the Historian.

EUPHANTUS.

* Laert.

* From *Alexinus* came *Euphantus* an *Olinthian*, Master to King *Antigonus*, Father of *Demetrius*, Grandfather of *Antigonus Gonatus*; He died of Age; he writ
The *History of that time*.

Tragedies many, which upon their publick Representations were much much applauded.

An Oration upon a Kingdom, to *Antigonus*, very celebrious.

APOLLONIUS CRONUS:

* Laert.
† lib. 14.

* Of the Disciples of *Eubulides*, was *Apollonius Cronus*; † *Strabo* saith, he was a *Cyrenæan* by Birth, and calls him *Cronus* *Apollonius*, implying the latter to be a sir-name, from *Apollonia*, a Town of *Cyrene*.

DIODORUS.

CHAP. I.

His Life.

Laert. Diodorus was of *Jossus* a City of *Caria*, Son of *Ameinias*; *Laertius* saith, he heard *Eubulides*; †*Strabo* that he heard *Apollonius Cronus*, after whom he was called *Cronus*; the name of the Master being transmitted to the disciple, by reason of the obscurity of the true *Cronus*; *of *Diodorus* thus *Callimachus*;

†*Lib.* 14. & 17.

Laert.

———ev'n *Momus* writ
Upon the Walls, *Cronus* hath wit.

He lived with *Ptolomeus Soter*, in whose presence being questioned by *Stilpo*, in such things as upon the sudden he could not answer; he was not only punished by the King, but reproached with the name of *Cronus*: whereupon he went from the Feast, and having written an Oration upon that question, died of grief.

CHAP. II.

His Philosophy.

Lib.
†*Lucul.*

Strabo and *Laertius* affirm he was a Dialectick; Tho Dialecticks (saith †*Cicero*) teach in their Elements whether a connex (a proposition which hath the conjunction *if*) be true or false; as this, *if it be day, it is light, how much is it controverted?* Diodorus *is of one opinion,* Philo *of another,* Chrysippus *of a third: That* Diodorus *laboured much herein, appears from an Epigram of* Callimachus, *cited and explained by** Sextus Empiricus.

Advers.Gram

Concerning these propositions, the Disagreement of *Diodorus* from *Philo* and *Chrysippus*, (already mentioned by *Cicero*) is thus explained by †*Sextus Empiricus* ; *But when, saith he, or how it followeth they disagree among themselves, and those things whereby they determine a consequence to be judged, oppugn one another: as* Philo *said, It is a true* Connex, *when it beginneth not from true, and ended in false. So that according to his opinion, a true* Connex *may be true several ways, a false only one way. For when it beginneth from true, and endeth in true, it is true; as this,* If it be day, it is light. *Again, when it beginneth from false and endeth in false, it is true: As this,* If the Earth flies, the earth hath wings. *Likewise that which beginneth from false, and endeth in true is true, as this, if the* Earth flies it is Earth *: That only is true which beginneth from true, and endeth in false. Such is this,* if it be day it is night. *For if it be day, that it is day is true*, *which is the Antecedent. But that it is night is false, which was the Consequent.* Diodorus *faith, that is a true Connex which is not contingent, beginning from true, and ending in false. This is contrary to the opinion of* Philo, *for such a* Connex *as this,*

†*Pyrrh.Hyp.2.*

if it be day I discourse, and if at present it be day, and I discourse, is according to Philo's *opinion, a true* Connex *: for it begins from true, it is day, and ends in true, I discourse. But according to the opinion of* Diodorus *it is false : for it may so happen, that though it begin from true, to wit, it is day, yet it may end in false, to wit, that I discourse when I am silent. Thus by Contingency it may begin in true, and end in false ; for before I began to discourse, it began from true, to wit, it is day: but ended in false, to wit, I discourse.*

And again, * *for that we examine not many opinions concerning a* Connex, *let us say that Connex is in it self right, which beginneth not from true, and endeth in false.This, if there be motion, there is vacuity according to* Epicurus's *opinion, beginning from true, to wit, there is motion, and ending in true, will be true. According to the* Peripateticks, *beginning from true, to wit, there is motion, and ending in false, to wit, there is vacuity, will be false ; according to* Diodorus, *beginning from false; to wit, there is motion, and ending in false, to wit, there is vacuity, will be true, for the assumption, to wit, there is motion, he denies as false*,

Cap. eodem.

† Some affirm, he invented *the vailed and horned Arguments* (of which already in the life of *Eubulides*)* *Alexander Aphrodiscus*, faith he used Κυειευον]αλογον, *the dominative Argument* : Of whose original and efficacy thus †‛*Epictetus*; the dominative argument seems to have ‛been interrogated and collected upon such like ‛occasions as these : for, there being a common ‛fight amongst these three propositions to one ‛another : The first, that every thing past is ‛necessarily true. The second, that possibility ‛follows not impossibility. The third, that what ‛is not possible, neither is nor shall be true. This ‛fight *Diodorus* observing, made use of the two ‛first, to prove, that nothing is possible, which ‛is not: nor shall be. And * *Alexander*, for that ‛I be at *Corinth*, is possible, if that I have been, ‛or ever shall be there; but if neither, it is not ‛possible. It is possible, that a Child be made a ‛Grammarian, if he be made such, in confirmation ‛hereof *Diodorus* interrogated by the Dominative Argument.

†*Lacrt.*

In lib. 1. Prior.

Lib. 2. cap. 19.

In lib. 1. Prior.

He held, that nothing is moved, † arguing thus : ‛*If a thing be moved, it is neither mov'd ‛in the place wherein it is, or in the place where-‛in it is not* : But not in that wherein it is ; for ‛it resteth in the place wherein it is: nor in ‛that wherein it is not ; for where a thing is ‛not, there it can neither act nor suffer. There-‛fore nothing is moved : And * consequently ‛nothing is corrupted or perisheth.

Sext. Empir. Pyrrhon. hyp. 3. 8.

† He asserted, that the principles of things are least indivisible Bodies, in * number infinite, in magnitude finite.

Sext. Empir. advers. Gram.

†*Sext. Empir. Pyrh. hyp.3. 4.*
**Stob. Ecl. phys. 13.*

ICHTHYAS,

ICHTHYAS

Laert. *ICHTHYAS Son of *Metallus*, an eminent person, is remembred amongst these Philosophers that are derived from *Euclid*: To him *Diogenes* the *Cynick* dedicated a Dialogue.

CLINOMACHUS.

†*Laert.* † Amongst these descended from *Euclid*, was likewise *CLINOMACHUS*, a *Thurian*: He first wrote concerning *Anaxiomes*, [Propositions] *Catogorems*, [that part of a Proposition which is predicated of the other] and the like.

STILPO.

CHAP. I.

Stilpo His Life.

Laert. *STILPO was of *Megara* in *Hellas*; he lived in the time of the first *Ptolomy*: Of the Masters which he heard are reckoned,

Euclid the founder of this School: But this agrees not with his time, as was before observed.

Some followers of *Euclid*,

Thrasymachus of *Corinth*, Friend to *Ichthyas*: So *Heraclides* attesteth.

†*Laert. vit. Diogenis.* † *Diogenes* the *Cynick*.

Pasicles, a *Theban*, who heard *Crates* the *Cynick*, his own Brother.

Dioclides of *Megara*.

Lib. 4 *Cicero* saith, he was very acute, much approved by those times: His Friends (saith he) writ, he was much inclined to Wine and Women, yet relate not this in his dispraise; but, rather in his commendations, that he by Learning so subdued and represt his vicious Nature, that none ever saw him drunk, none ever discovered any Lasciviousness in him. *Plutarch* magnifies his height of Courage, mixed with meekness and temperance.

He was much addicted to civil Affairs. Besides his Wife, he kept company with *Nicareta*, a Courtezan: He had a Daughter of ill fame, whom *Simmias*, a *Syracusian*, his intimate friend, Married; she living incontinently, one told *Stilpo* she was a dishonour to him: *No more*, saith he, *than I am an honour to her*.

Ptolomeus Soter much esteemed him, and when he took Possession of *Megara* by Conquest, gave him money, and invited him along with him to *Egypt*: Of the money he took a little, but absolutely refused the Journey: Going to *Ægina*, he stayed there till *Ptolomy*'s return. *Demetrius* Son of *Antigonus*, upon the taking of *Megara*, gave order that his house might be preserved, and whatsoever belonged to him, restored; and bidding him give them an inventory of such things as he had lost, he said that he had lost nothing that belonged to him, for none had taken away his Learning; his Learning and knowledge were both left.

With *Demetrius* he disputed of Humanity so efficaciously, that he became a studious Auditor of him.

Concerning *Minerva*'s Statue, carv'd by *Phidias*, he asked a Man whether *Minerva*, Daughter of *Jove* were a God; he affirmed she was: But this, saith he, is not of *Jove*, but of *Phidias*; to which the other assented: Then, saith he, she is not a God. Hereupon being cited to the Court of *Areopagus*, he denied it not, but justified it, averring she was not a God, but a Goddess: But the *Areopagites* nothing satisfied with this evasion, ordered that he should depart the City. Hereupon *Theodorus* sirnam'd θεὸς, said in derision, How came *Stilpo* to know this, did he put aside her vail, and look upon her breast? *Theodorus* was bold of Speech, but *Stilpo* reserved, in so much, as being demanded by *Crates*, whether the Gods delighted in bent knees and Prayers: Thou fool, saith he, do not question me in publick, but when we are alone together.

He was sincere and plain, void of all artifice. *Crates* the *Cynick*, not answering him, but ἀποπερδόντος, I knew faith he, you would speak any thing rather than that which is decent.

Crates in propounding a question delivered a Fig to him, which he took and eat: *Crates* presently cryed out, that he had lost his fig: Yes, saith he, and your question also, of which that was in earnest.

Seeing *Crates* half frozen in cold weather, *Crates*, saith he, *methinks you want* ἱμάτιν καινῦ, (which one way implies a *new Garment*, another way *both a Garment and Wit*) *Crates* ashamed, answered thus.

Stilpo at Megara I saw opprest,
Where vast Typhœus lies with weight opprest.
To hear him wrangle many Scholars came,
Fair Truth to chase away was all their aim.

At *Athens* he wrought so much upon the People that they would run out of their Shops too see him: *They wonder at thee,* Stilpo (said one to him) *as a Monster*: No, saith he, *but as a true Man.*

As he was speaking with *Crates*, in the midst of their discourse he went away to buy Fish; *Crates* pursued him, crying out, that he gave over the Discourse: No, saith he, *I carry along the Discourse with me; but I leave you, the Discourse will stay, the Fish must be bought.*

Stob.

Being asked, what is harder than a Stone, he answered, *a Fool.*

CHAP. II.
His Philosophy.

* Laert.

*HE was Master of the *Megarick* School, excellent in *Eristick* Disputes, by his subtle Tenents and Discourses beautifying himself, his Country and Friends.

He took away all Species (Universals) affirming, that he who saith, a Man, denotes not any Man, the Term being not proper to this or that person, for why to one rather than to another, therefore not to this; and again, that which we see is not an Herb, for an Herb was many years ago, Therefore this was not an Herb.

† Plut.

† He likewise denied one thing to be predicated of another, arguing thus; 'If running be 'predicated of an Horse, the subject is not the 'same with the predicate; the definition of man 'is one thing, that of good another, so an Horse 'is a differing thing from running, for upon de-'mand, we give several definitions of each; 'for if a Man, and good, or an Horse, and run-'ning were the same, how could good be 'predicated of Food or Physick, and running 'of a Horse, which are things so different? Thus he admitted no conjunction with the Subject, in things which are in a subject, or predicated of a subject, but conceived that both these, unless they be the very same with the subject, cannot be predicated of it, even not as an Accident. This, though it were one of those little Sayings which *Stilpo* sportively used to cast out amongst the Sophisters, *Colotes* the Epicurean opposed so eagerly, that he framed a large discourse against *Stilpo*, grounded only upon this assertion, (which yet he neither refelled nor resolved) affirming that by holding one thing is not predicated of another, he takes away good Life; *But that* Stilpo (saith Plutarch) *was offended only at some words, and op-*posed the manner of speaking, but took not away the course of life, or abolished things, is most evident.

* He asserted the chief good to be a mind not subject to Passion.

* Senec. Epist. 9.

CHAP. III.
His Disciples.

† Laert.

† HE far exceeded others in fluent discourse and learning, that he converted almost all *Greece* to the *Megarick* Sect. *Philippus* of *Megara* saith he drew

Metrodorus sirnamed the *Theoretick*, and *Timagoras* the *Geloan*, from *Theophrastus*.

Clitarchus and *Simmias* from *Aristotle* the *Cyrenæan*,

Of Dialecticks, *Pæonius*, from *Aristides*.

Diphilus, Son of *Euphantus*, and *Myrmex*, Son of *Exenætus* coming to dispute against him, became both followers of him: Thus far *Philippus*: He likewise attracted

Phæsidemus the *Peripaterick*, excellent in Natural Philosophy.

Alcimus, the most eminent Oratour at that time in *Greece*.

Zeno the *Phœnician*, an Epicurean Philosopher.

Crates, and others; in a word, whomsoever he would himself.

Heraclides saith, that *Zeno* the *Citiean*, founder of the Stoical Sect, was his Disciple.

CHAP. IV.
His Death, Writings.

HErmippus affirmeth that he died of Age; but drank a draught of Wine to hasten his end.

Suidas saith, he wrote 20 Dialogues, *Laertius* but nine; and those not very efficacious; their Titles these,

Moschus,
Aristippus or *Callias*,
Ptolemæus,
Chærecrates,
Mitrocles,
Anaximenes,
Epigenes,
To his Daughter,
Aristotle.

He had a Son named *Dryso*, a Philosopher also.

THE
ELEACK and ERETRIACK *SECTS*.

PHÆDO.

* Laert.

*THE *Eleack* Sect was instituted by *Phædo*, an *Elean* of a noble Family; it chanced that he was taken by Thieves or Pyrates, and sold to a House of common dishonest Resort; where being forced to sit at the door, he was observed by *Socrates* in passing, who noting the ingenuity of his countenance (which was extraordinary) perswaded (as *Laertius* saith) *Alcibiades* or *Plato*, or (as *A. Gellius*,) *Cebes* to buy him, from which time he addicted himself diligently to Philosophy, and was a constant Disciple of *Socrates*; so much affected by *Plato*, that he called that most excellent

cellent discourse of the immortality of the Soul, after him, *Phædo.*

He instituted a Sect called from him *Eleack*; The Dialogues ascribed to him were

Zopyrus,
Medus,
Simon,
Antimachus, or the *Old Man,*
Nicias,
Simmias,
Alcibiades,
Critolaus.

† *Panætius* doubts whether any of these were written by *Phædo*; *Medus* is by some ascribed to *Æschines,* and by others to *Poliænus*; as are also *Antimachus* and the *Scythian* discourses.

† *Laert. vit. Æsch.*

PLISTHENES.

* *Laert.*

† THE *Eleack* Sect was continued by *Plisthenes* an *Elean,* Successor to *Phædo*; *Plisthenes* was succeeded by *Menedemus* and *Asclepiades.*

MENEDEMUS.

CHAP. I.

His Country, Parents, Teachers.

* *Laert.*

MEnedemus was one of those Philosophers that continued the School of *Phædo,* which hitherto was called *Eleack,* but from *Menedemus* was termed *Eretriack*: he was an *Eretrian,* Son of *Clisthenes*; *Clisthenes* was of the Family of the *Theopropidæ*; yet tho' noble by descent, Mechanick by profession and indigent, some affirm he was a maker of Tents (*Hesychius Illustris* terms him an Architect) adding that he taught both Arts to his Son *Menedemus,* so that when *Menedemus* wrote a decree, an *Alexinian* Philosopher reproved him, saying, *It becomes not a Wise Man to frame both Tents and decrees.*

Menedemus being sent by the *Eretrians* with a command of Soldiers to *Megara,* went from thence to *Athens* to hear *Plato* at the Academy, with whom he was so taken, that he gave over his Military Employment.

By *Asclepiades* a *Phlyasian,* his intimate Friend, he was carried to *Stilpo* at *Megara,* whom they both heard; thence taking a Journey to *Elis,* they met with *Anchypillus* and *Moschus,* who belonged to the School of *Phædo.*

Some affirm he despised *Plato* and *Xenocrates,* and *Paræbates* the *Cyrenæan*; but admired *Stilpo,* concerning whom being demanded his opinion, he only answered that *he was free.*

CHAP. II.

His School and Philosophy.

† *Laert.*

* BEing returned home to *Eretria,* he set up a School, and taught Philosophy there: the *Eliack* School being thus transferred to *Eretria,* was from thenceforward call'd *Eretriack.*

In his School there was no order of place, no Seats round about it; but as every Man chanced to be sitting, or standing, or walking, in the same postures they heard him.

He held, that *there was but one vertue and good,* reprehending those who affirmed more; whence of one who held there were many Gods, he demanded ironically *how many? and whether he thought there were more than an hundred?*

He was of a versatile wit, and in composure of his Speech a difficult adversary; he turned himself every way, and found something to say for every thing: He was very Litigious, as *Antisthenes* in his successions affirms and used this question, *What is not the same, is different from that with which it is not same?* Yes. *To benefit is not the same with good, therefore good doth not benefit.* He took away Negative Propositions, leaving only the *Affirmative*; and of these he admitted the Simple, only; but rejected those which were *not simple,* calling them *conjoyned* and *complex.*

Heraclides saith, he was a *Platonick,* and derided *Dialectick.* *Hexinus* asking, whether he had given over beating his Father; *I neither did beat him,* saith he, *nor have given over.* The other replied, *Either say yes or no, to dissolve the Ambiguity. It is ridiculous,* saith he, *to follow your Laws, when a Man may withstand them in the very entrance.*

He writ not, or composed any thing, because (saith *Antigonus Carystius*) he was of no certain opinion; yet in dispute he was so vehement, that he many times went away with black and blue Eyes.

CHAP. III.

His manner of Living.

† HE contracted a strict friendship with *Asclepiades,* nothing inferiour to that of *Pilades* to *Orestes*: *Asclepiades* was the Elder, whence there went a common saying, that he was the Poet, *Menedemus* the Player.

† *Laert.*

* When they were yet both young Philosophers, and indigent, they were cited to the Court of *Areopagus,* to give account († according to *Solon*'s Law) by what means (spending the whole day amongst Philosophers without any Labour, and having no Estate) they subsisted, and were in so good a condition: They desired that one of the Masters of the common Prison might be sent for; who, when he came, attested, that they went down every night in-

* *Athen. Deip.*
† *See Life of Solon.*

to

to the Prison, where the common Malefactors ground, and did their grind, and in pay of their Labour, received two drachms: At which the *Areopagites* much wondring, bestowed as an honourable reward upon them, two hundred Drachms.

They had other Patrons that bestowed Gifts upon them; *Archepolides* gave them three thousand pieces of Silver; they both contended which should receive last, and in conclusion, neither accepted it. The chief persons that received them were *Hipponicus*, a *Macedonian*, and *Ægetor* a *Lamiean*. *Ægetor* gave each of them thirty *Minæ*. *Hipponicus* gave *Menedemus* two thousand drachms towards the marriage of his Daughters, which, as *Heraclides* saith, were three, by his Wife *Oropia*.

For *Asclepiades* and *Menedemus* took each of them a Wife; *Asclepiades* married the Daughter, *Menedemus* the Mother: *Asclepiades*'s Wife dying, took the Wife of *Menedemus*: *Menedemus* being made a chief Magistrate, married a rich Wife; notwithstanding, he allow'd his first Wife an equal interest in the government of the House. *Asclepiades* having liv'd with *Menedemus* in great plenty; yet with great temperance, died old at *Eretria*. At that time, one, whom *Asclepiades* much loved, coming late at night, intending to have feasted with him, the Servants shut him out of doors: But *Menedemus* bad them let him in, saying *Asclepiades* would admit him even under Ground.

Menedemus was much given to Entertainments, and, because the Country was unwholesome, made many Feasts: What order he observed therein is thus delivered by *Antigonus Carystius*, and out of him (though not cited) by *Laertius*. He dined but with one or two Companions at the most; if any came to him, they were admitted after dinner was ended; if they came sooner than the set time, they walked short turns before the door, and demanded of the Servants what course was carried in; if they told them fish-broth (with which they began their Dinner) they went away; if any Flesh, they went into a room prepared for that purpose. In Summer time, *Menedemus* had the Couches or Beds of his Dining-room covered with Flags and Rushes, in Winter with Sheeps-skins. Every guest brought a Cushion; the Cup they had was no bigger than a large Spoon: instead of Sweet-meats they had *Lupines*, and Beans: sometimes such fruit as the Season afforded; in Summer Pomgranates, in Spring, Pulse, in Winter, Figgs. This *Lycophron* the *Chalcidian* confirms in his Satyrical Comedy upon *Menedemus*, where *Silenus* speaks thus to the Satyrs.

Sons impious of a pious Father, I
(You see) with your delights and sports comply:
But never by the Gods at such a Feast
In Caria, Rhodes, or Lydia was a Guest.
How plentiful!

And not long after,

A little Pot half full of Water clear,
Rated at Farthings five a boy did bear
To every guest; about vile Lupines went,
With which the Beggar's Tables scarce content.

Whilst they drank (after the feast *Menedemus* proposed questions, and instead) of a desert gave them discourse, which excited all to temperance and continence: These continued sometimes till the crowing of the Cock broke them off, much against the will of his guests, who never thought they had enough of them.

CHAP. IV.

His civil Employments.

HE was first contemned by his Countrymen, and called Dog and Fool; but at last so much honoured by them, that they committed the government of the Commonwealth to his charge, †and paid him yearly two hundred Talents, whereof he sent back fifty.   *Laert. †Laert.

After he applied himself to civil business, he was so thoughtful, that going to put Incense into a Censer, he put it besides. *Crates* reproaching him for undertaking publick employments, he sent him to Prison; whereupon as he chanced to pass by, *Crates* rose up and saluted him with the Title of *Agamemnonian*, *Leader of the City*.

He was sent Ambassador from the *Eratrians* to *Ptolomy*, and to *Lysimachus* (much honoured wheresoever he came) and to *Demetrius*, *all three Kings of *Macedonia*, of whom *Demetrius* first reigned, then *Lysimachus*, and after him (*Pyrrhus* intervening) *Ptolomy*.   *Euseb.

Some accused him to *Demetrius*, that he would betray his City to *Ptolomy*, of which charge he acquitted himself by an Epistle, beginning thus, *Menedemus to King Demetrius, Health. I hear that you are informed many things concerning us,* &c. advising him to take heed of one of those that were his Enemies, named *Æschylus*. When he was on Embassy to *Demetrius*, he spoke very earnestly and effectually concerning *Oropus*.

Antigonus also, King of *Macedonia*, loved him exceedingly, and profest himself his Disciple: In his behalf he made a Decree, clear and void of ostentation, beginning thus; *Forasmuch as King Antigonus, having overcome the Barbarians in Fight, returneth into his own Country, having good success in all his undertakings: The Senate and People have thought good,* &c.

CHAP. V.

His Vertues and Apothegms.

MENEDEMUS was of exceeding gravity, for which *Crates* deriding him, said, *Asclepiad the Philiasian, and the proud Eretrian, and Timon.*

His supercilious bumbast speech begins. In severity he was so awful, that *Eurylocus* being invited by *Antigonus*, together with *Clippides*, a youth of *Cyzicum*, refused to go, fearing *Menedemus* should know it.

In

In reproof he was bitter and bold, of which Laertius instanceth his Sayings to a young Man over-confident, to *Hierocles*, &c. To an Adulterer boasting, &c. To a young Man crying, &c.

Antigonus asking, whether he should go to a Luxurious Banquet; not speaking whether he should go or not, he bad him send them word that he was a King's Son.

One who intruded himself upon him, and discoursed very absurdly, he asked if he had a Farm; he answered, many: Go then, saith he, and look after them, lest in losing your Rusticity, you lose them also.

To one asking, whether a good Man may take a Wife, he said, Do you think I am good or not? The other assenting; but I (saith he) have taken one.

Not able to limit the Prodigality of one who invited him to Supper, he silently reproved him, eating nothing but Olives.

This freedom brought him into danger when he was in *Cyprus* with *Nicocreon*, together with his Friend *Asclepiades*; for, the King having invited him with the rest of the Philosophers to a Monthly Feast, *Menedemus* said, this convention if it be good, ought to be every day; if otherwise, this day is too much: The Tyrant answered, that he had set apart that day to converse with Philosophers. *Menedemus* persisting in his assertion, demonstrated from what he had said of the Sacrifice, that Philosophers ought to be heard at all times. Whereupon if one of the Musicians had not helped them to escape, they had been put to death, whence the Ship being endangered by a Storm, *Asclepiades* said, that the humanity of the Musician preserved them, the roughness of *Menedemus* had undone them.

He was negligent, and (as we said) careless in every thing that concerned the order of his School; likewise high-minded, and covetous of Glory: insomuch that when he and *Asclepiades* first exercised the trade of Building, *Asclepiades* was seen upon the house top carrying Clay; but *Menedemus*, if he espied any Man passing by, hid himself.

He was somewhat enclined to Superstition; having eaten in a Cook's Shop the Flesh of something that had died of it self ignorantly with *Asclepiades*, as soon as he knew it, he grew Sick, and looked Pale, till *Asclepiades* reproved him, saying, *He was not sick of the Meat, but of Fancy*.

In all other respects he was a person of a great and free Soul, in strength even in his old age equal to those who wrestled in Exercise; strong made, swarthy of Complexion, fat and corpulent; but of indifferent stature, as appears (saith *Laertius*) by his Statue in *Eretria*, in the old Stadium, so exactly carved, that it expresseth the naked proportion of his Limbs.

He loved *Aratus* and *Lycophron* the Tragick Poet, and *Antagoras* the *Rhodian*, but above all he was studious of *Homer*; next of the *Lyricks*; then of *Sophocles*: In *Satyrs* he assign'd the second place to *Achæus*; the first to *Æschylus*, whence to those in the State who defended the contrary part, he said thus,

The swift in time outstript are by the slow,
A Tortoise thus an Eagle may outgo.

These are Verses of *Achæus*: they therefore are mistaken, who say he read nothing but the *Medea* of *Euripides*, which is put among the Poems of *Neophron* the *Sicyonian*.

Of *Bion*, who spoke with much diligence against Prophets, he said, *he murthered the dead*.

To one who said, the greatest good is to enjoy those things which we desire; *it is a much greater*, saith he, *to desire those things which are fitting*.

He was violent (as we said) in controversie, but most affable in conversation and Action: *Alexinus*, whom in dispute he had often circumvented and bitterly derided, he gratified in deed; taking care for the safe Conduct of his Wife from *Delphi* to *Chalcis*, the way being much infested with Thieves.

He was an excellent Friend, as is manifest from his affection to *Asclepiades*, of which we have already spoken, only to *Persæus*, he was constantly a profest Enemy; for it was known that when *Antigonus* for *Menedemus* his sake would have restored the *Eretrians* to their first Liberty, *Persæus* withstood it: whereupon at a Feast *Menedemus* openly inveighed against him, using amongst many others this expression; *He is indeed a Philosopher, but of all Men that are, were, or ever shall be, the most wicked.*

CHAP. VI.

His departure from Eretria, *and Death*.

THE friendship he held with *Antigonus*, made him suspected by his own Country-men, as if he meant to betray the City to him; of which being accused by *Aristodemus*, he fled, and lived a while at *Oropus* in the Temple of *Amphiaraus*: Thence some golden Cups chancing to be stollen, he was by a publick decree of the *Beotians* forbidden to stay there any longer, whereupon he returned privately into his Country, and taking his Wife and Children along with him, went from thence to *Antigonus*, where he died of grief.

But *Heraclides* on the contrary affirmeth, that whilst he was Præfect of the *Eretrians*, he often defended his Country against those who would have made *Demetrius* Tyrant thereof; Neither would he therefore have betrayed it to *Antigonus*; but that was falsly laid to his charge; he afterwards went to *Antigonus*, petitioning that he would restore his Country to their Liberties; which *Antigonus* denying, he out of Grief fasted seven days, and so died. The same relation is delivered by *Antigonus Carystius*. *Heraclides* saith, he lived 84 years.

THE HISTORY of PHILOSOPHY.

The Fifth Part.
Containing the *Academick* Philosophers.

PLATO.
CHAP. I.

The Country, Parents, and Time of PLATO.

THE most eminent of all the Sects derived from *Socrates* was the *Academick*, so call'd from the *Academy*, a place in *Athens*, where the Professors thereof taught: This Sect was instituted by *Plato*, continued by *Speusippus*, *Xenocrates*, *Polemon*, *Crates*, *Crantor*, thus far called

PART V.   PLATO.

called the *first* or *old Academy*. *Arcesilaus*, succeeding *Crantor*, instituted *the middle Academy*, continued by *Lacydes*, *Telecles*, *Evander*, and *Hegesinus*. *Carneades* founded the *new Academy*, of which was also *Clitomachus*: Some reckon a *fourth Academy* instituted by *Philo* and *Charmidas*: a *fifth* by *Antiochus*.

• Laert.
† Tzetz. Chiliad II. 390.
* Laert.
† Laert. Suid.

* *Plato* was out of doubt an *Athenian*, nor are they to be credited who relate him † a *Theban*, born at *Cynocephalus*; * *Antileon* affirms his Parents to be of *Collyttus*. † He was *born* (according to *Phavorinus*) *in the Island Ægina*, *in the House of* Phidiades, *Son of Thales*; *his Father sent with others thither at the division of the Land* (upon their defection from, and subjection by the *Athenians*, at the beginning of the *Peloponnesian* War) *and returned to* Athens, *at what time those* Athenians *were ejected by the* Lacedæmonians, *in aid of the Æ*ginetæ.

• Laert. Apul. Suid.

* He was of an eminent Family; his Father *Aristo* (Son of *Aristoteles*) of the Race of *Codrus*, Son of *Melanthus*, who (as *Thrasilus* affirms) derived themselves from *Neptune*. *Melanthus* flying *Messena*, came to *Athens*, where afterwards by a Stratagem killing *Xanthus*, he was made King after *Thymocles*, the last of the *Theseidæ*. His Mother *Perictione*, by some called *Potone*, whose Kindred with *Solon* is thus described by *Laertius* and ‡ *Proclus*. *Execistides* had two Sons, *Solon* and *Dropides*: *Dropides* had *Critias*, mentioned by *Solon* in his Poems.

‡ In Timæum.

Bid fair hair'd Critias *his Sire observe,*
A wandring mind will from his Leader swerve.

Critias had *Calleschrus*, *Calleschrus* had *Critias*, one of the thirty Tyrants, and *Glaucon* (whom *Apuleis* calls *Glaucus*) *Glaucon* had *Charmides* and *Perictione*; *Perictione* by *Aristo* had *Plato*, the sixth from *Solon*; *Solon* was descended from *Neptune* and *Neleus*, [Father of *Nestor*] Thus *Laertius*, from whom *Proclus* dissents only in that, that he makes *Glaucon* Son of the first *Critias*, Brother to *Calleschrus*, which *Critias* manifestly (saith he) in *Plat*. *Charmides* confirms, calling *Glauco* (Father of *Charmides*) his Uncle. Thus was *Plato* descended both ways from *Neptune*.

There are (saith * *Apuleius*) *who assert* Plato *of a more sublime Race*: *Aristander*, followed by many Platonists, thinks, *he was begotten on his Mother by some* Spectrum *in the shape of A*pollo: † *Speusippus* in his Treatise, entituled *Plato*, or περὶ δείπνυ, *Clearchus* in his Eulogy of *Plato*; *Anaxilides* in his second Book of Philosophers; *Plutarch*, *Suidas*, and others, affirm it to have been commonly reported at *Athens*, that he was the Son of *Apollo*, who appearing in vision to her (being a Woman of extraordinary Beauty) * *Perictione se miscuit*, she thereupon conceived: *Aristo* (her husband) having often attempted to enjoy her, but in vain; at last *Apollo* appearing to him in a Vision or Dream, and a voice commanding him to refrain the company of his Wife for ten Months, until her delivery were past, he forbore; whence *Tyndarus*,

* Diog. Plat.
† Laert.
τῷ ἐπιγραφομένῳ Πλάτων ἢ περὶ δείπνυ: perhaps it should be Πλάτων, Amongst the writings of *Speusippus* is mentioned Πλάτων ἐγκώμιον.
* Sympos.
† Apul. Plat.

He did not issue from a mortal Bed;
A God his Sire, a God-like life he led.

Some thereupon (as * Saint *Hierom* saith) affirmed, he was born of a Virgin, and † it was a common Speech among the *Athenians* that *Phœbus begat* Esculapius *and* Plato, *one to cure Bodies, the other Souls*.

* Advers. Ju...
† Laert.

* *Aristo* had afterwards by *Perictione*, two Sons, *Adimaretus* and *Glauco*, and a Daughter *Potone*, Mother to *Speusippus*: These Relations of *Plato* will be more conspicuous in this Genealogical Table.

* Laert. Suid.

U 2   Neptune.

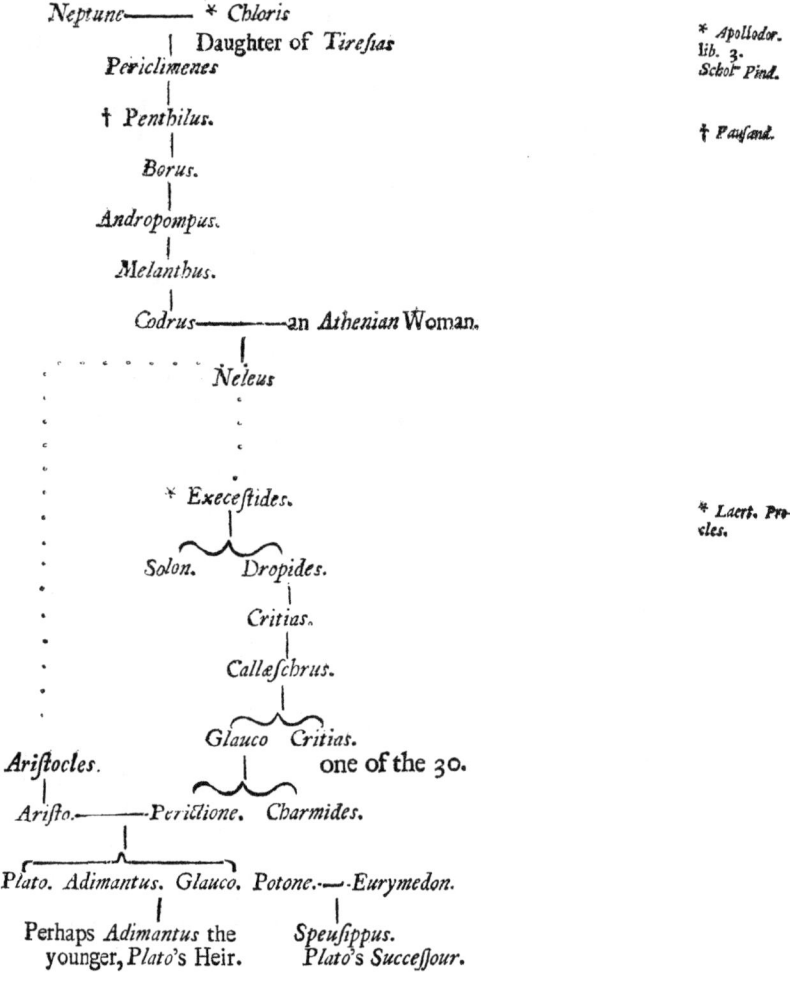

For the year of his Birth, (to omit the mistakes of *Eusebius*, who placeth it in the fourth Year of the eighty eighth Olympiad, in the Archonship of *Stratocles*, and of the *Chronicon Alexandrinum*, that placeth it the year following) *Laertius* saith, *he was Born, according to the Chronology of* Apollodorus, *in the eighty eighth Olympiad*, which seems to be towards the beginning of the first year, whilst *Aminias* was yet Archon. For *Laertius* elsewhere saith, That *he was six years younger than* Isocrates; for *Isocrates* (saith he) *was born when* Lysimachus, Plato, *when* Aminias *was Archon, under whom* Pericles *died:* in the third year of the Peloponnesian War. This *Aminias* is by the * *Scholiast* of *Euripides* called *Ameinon*, by † *Athenæus*, *Epaneimon*, by * *Diodorus Siculus*, *Epaminondas*. The various reading occasioned either by addition or detraction of the preposition ἐπὶ, but by which of these two cannot easily be evinced. † *Salmasius* endeavouring to prove the name to be Ἀμείνων, positively affirms, that the *Greeks* never name an Archon without the Preposition ἐπὶ; but that error * *Petavius* confutes, whose Opinion is confirmed by the ancient Marble at *Arundel-House*, which addeth not the Preposition to the Names of the Archons.

Neither is the Opinion of † *Athenæus* much different, who affirms, *Plato* was born (the year before) *Apollodorus* being Archon, who succeeded *Euthydemus*, who was Archon the third year of the 87th Olympiad, and that under *Euphemus*, in the fourth year of the 90th Olympiad, he was fourteen years old. For both *Laertius* and *Athenæus* agree in the year of his death, *viz.* in the first of the 108th Olympiad, when *Theophilus*, the Successor of *Callimachus*, was Archon; *Athenæus* only differeth in this, that, computing 82 Archons, he attributes so many years to *Plato's* Life, whereas 'tis certain, he lived but eighty one.

The day of his Birth, * according to *Apollodorus*, was the seventh of *Thargelion*, at which time the *Delians* did celebrate the Feast of *Apollo*. So likwise *Florus*, cited by † *Plutarch*, who adds, that the Priests and Prophets call *Apollo* ἑβδομαγένης, as being born upon this seventh day; whence perhaps was occasioned the Fiction, that he was the Son of *Apollo*, which *Plutarch* esteems no Disparagement to his Deity. In the first year of the 88th Olympiad, the *Neomenia* of *Hecatombæon* fell upon *August*, 2d. and (upon those Hypotheses which we laid down formerly in the * *Life of* *Socrates*) the Dominical Letter for that year being E. the seventh of *Thargelion* will (according to the *Julian* account taken proleptically

proleptically) fall upon *Friday*, the thirtieth of *May*: according to the *Gregorian*, upon *Friday* the ninth of *June*, in the year of the *Julian* period, 4286.

This is according to the Faith of the Hiſtorians, with whom the Aſtrologers do not agree; for * *Julius Firmicus* hath erected the Scheme of his Nativity after this manner. * *Aron.*

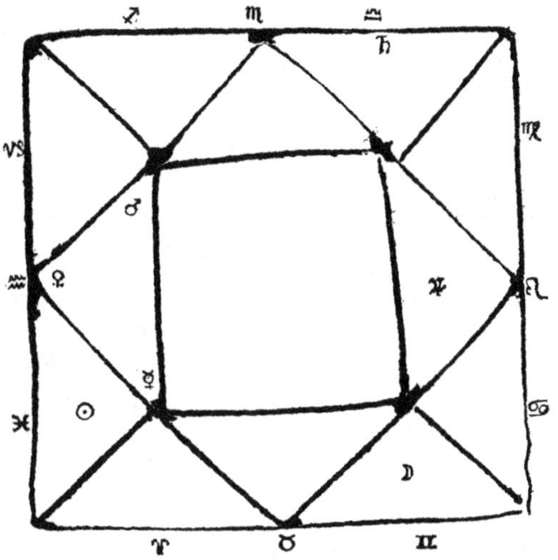

If the Aſcendent, ſaith he, ſhall be ♒, ♂ ☿ and ♀ therein poſited; and if ♃ if then be placed in the ſeventh, having ♌ for his Sign, and in the ſecond the ☉ in ♓ and the ☾ in ♊ in the fifth Houſe beholding the Aſcendent with a △ aſpect, and ♄ in the ninth from the Aſcendent in ♎. This Geniture renders a Man Interpreter of Divine and Heavenly Inſtitutions, who endued with inſtructive Speech, and the power of Divine Wit, and formed in a manner by a celeſtial Inſtitution, by the true Licenſe of Diſputations ſhall arrive at all the ſecrets of Divinity. Thus *Firmicus*, whoſe Scheme agreeth not with the other Calculation, as being betwixt the midſt of *February* and of *March*, during which time the ☉ is in ♓.

Hence will appear the great Anachroniſm of thoſe, who affirm, that *Plato* went to *Ægypt*, in the time of the Prophet *Hieremie* (whom *Euſebius* placeth in the thirty ſixth Olympiad) and heard him there. *Hieremie* at the Captivity of the *Jews* into *Babilon*, was carried by *Johanan* Son of *Caree* into *Ægypt*: The *Jews* were carried away by *Nebuchadnezzar*, at what time *Tarquinius Priſcus* Reigned at *Rome*, *Vaphres* in *Ægypt*, to whom the reſt of the *Jews* fled, which was in the forty ſeventh Olympiad, 160 years before *Plato* was Born. This Opinion * once held, was afterwards retracted by Saint *Auguſtine*, in his Book of Retractions, and confuted *de Civit. Dei*, 8. 11.

* *De Doctr. Chriſt.* 2. 28.

CHAP. II.

His firſt Education, Exerciſe, and Studies.

† WHilſt *Plato* was yet an Infant carried in the Arms of his Mother *Perictione*, *Ariſto* his Father went to *Hymettus* (a Mountain in *Attica* eminent for abundance of Bees and Honey) to Sacrifice to the Muſes or Nymphs taking his Wife and Child along with him; as they were buſied in the Divine Rites, ſhe laid the Child in a Thicket of Myrtles hard by; to whom, as he ſlept (* *in cunis dormienti*) came a ſwarm of Bees, Artiſts of Hymettian Honey, flying and buzzing about him, and (as it is reported) made a Honey-comb in his Mouth. This was taken for a preſage of the ſingular ſweetneſs of his diſcourſe; his future Eloquence foreſeen in his Infancy.

† *Ælian. var. hiſt.* 10. 21.

* *Cic. divinat. lib.* 1.

His Parents (ſaith † *Alexander*) named him *after his Grandfather*, Ariſtocles: * Speuſippus *(inſtituted in his Domeſtick Documents) extolleth his ſharpneſs of Apprehenſion, whilſt yet a Child, and the admirable Modeſty of his Diſpoſition* († which was ſuch, that he was never, even all thoſe years, ſeen to laugh immoderately) *affirming, that the beginnings of his Youth were ſeaſon'd with Labour and Love of Study; which Vertues encreaſed and met with all the reſt when he came to Man's Eſtate.*

† *Laert.*
* *Apul. dogm. Plat.*
† *Laert.*

† Of *Dionyſius* the Grammarian (mentioned in his ἀντερασταῖ) he received the firſt Rudiments of Learning. Of *Ariſto*, an *Argive*, he learned the Art of Wreſtling (at that time much in eſteem, as being one of the Olympick Exerciſes) wherein he became ſo great a Proficient, that ſome affirm, he wreſtled at the *Iſthmus* in the *Pythian* Games.

† *Laert.*

* As in years and Vertue, ſo likewiſe he encreaſed extraordinarily in outward proportion and ſhape, inſomuch, that *Ariſto* named him *Plato* (which implieth Latitude) in alluſion to the largeneſs of his Perſon: others ſay, to the wideneſs of his Shoulders; *Neanthes* of his Forehead: ſome, to his large Eloquence. Whatſoever the occaſion were, this name wore out and diſplaced the other. That he was called alſo *Sarapis*, is affirmed by † *Heſychius*. There was not any imperfection throughout his perſon, except a gibboſity in the hinder part of his Head, and (as *Timotheus* affirms) a kind of † Heſitation in his Speech.

* *Laert.*

† *In verbo* Σαραπις. *Laert.*

† ἰσχνόφωνος: which (beſides λεπτοφωνία ſmalneſs of Voice, in which ſenſe it is here taken by the Interpreters and *Ficinus*) ſignifieth an imperfection of Speech by ſtammering: *Ariſt. Prob.* 11. 30 unleſs there and here we would read ἰσχόφωνος.

He

*He learned also (as *Dicearchus* relates) to Paint: He addicted himself much to Poetry, and wrote many Poems: First, *Dithyrambs*; then Epick Poetry, which comparing with *Homer*, and finding far short of him, he burned. Then he betook himself to writing Tragedies: He made a compleat Tetralogy (four Drama's, as the manner was, when they contested, to be presented at four several Festivals, *Lenæan, Panathenæan, Chytræan*, the fourth Satyrical) and gave it to the Players to be Acted, intending to contest for the Palm upon the Olmpick Theatre: But the day before it should have been presented, chancing to hear *Socrates* Discourse at the Olympick Theatre († before the Bacchanals) he was so taken with that *Syren*, that he not only forbore to contest at that time, but wholly gave over all Tragick Poesy, and burned all his Poems, saying that of *Homer*,

Vulcan come hither, Plato *needs thy aid*.

From that time (the twentieth year of his age, which falls about the 4th of the 92d Olympiad) he became a follower of *Socrates*, and studied Philosophy.

Some affirm (of the Truth of which report, * *Ælian* justly doubts) *he was driven by Poverty to betake himself to the Wars, but intercepted by Socrates, and instructed in that which concerns Mankind, he sold his Arms, and through his perswasion, addicted himself to Philosophy*.

That he fought for his Country is certain, express'd in his answer to † *Crobylus* the Sycophant: * *Aristoxenus* and *Ælian* affirm, he was engaged thrice: First, at † Tanagara: *the second time at* Corinth: *and lastly at* Delium, *where he fought best of all the Soldiers*. Thus *Aristoxenus*. But that this is false, may be easily evinced by computation of times. The first Fight of the *Athenians* at *Tanagra*, was in the 4th year of the 80th Olympiad, 17 years before *Plato* was Born: The second, in the first of the 89th when he was but six years old. The Fight at *Delium*, was in the first of the 89th, at what time he was but four years old; from the last words of *Aristoxenus*, ἔνθα κȣ ἀϱιϛεῦσαι (implying, that *at* Delium *he had the prize for fighting best*) may be conjectured, that this was meant of *Socrates*, who was thrice personally engaged and at * *Delium* should have had the prize for fighting best, but that his Modesty procured it to be conferred upon *Alcibiades*.

CHAP. III.

His Masters in Philosophy, and his Travels to that end.

*SOcrates, the night before *Plato* was recommended to him, dreamed, that a young Swan fled from *Cupid*'s Altar in the Academy, and sate in his lap, thence fled up to Heaven, it delighted both Gods and Men with its Musick. As *Socrates* [the next day] was relating this to some of his Auditors, *Aristo* came at the same time, and presented his Son *Plato* to him, to be his Disciple. As soon as *Socrates* saw him, reading in his looks his Ingenuity: Friends, saith he, this is the Swan of *Cupid*'s Academy.

Eight years he lived with *Socrates*, in which time, he committed (as others of his Disciples) the effect of his Masters Discourse to Writing: hereof he composed Dialogues, but with so great additions of his own, † that *Socrates* hearing him recite his *Lysis* cry'd out, Oh! *Hercules*, how many things doth this young Man feign of me? for not a few things (adds *Laertius*) of those which he writ, *Socrates* never spoke.

At the time of *Socrates*'s Arraignment, the first year of the 95th Olympiad, he was one of the Senate, the youngest of the Convention. That he was a Senator, implies he was full thirty years old at that time, according to *Solon*'s Law. This argues * *Hermodorus* of a mistake, who saith, he was twenty eight years old when he fled to *Megara*, upon the Death of *Socrates*, and subverts the accounts of those who under-reckon his Birth. † The Judges being much displeased with *Socrates*, *Plato* went up into the Orators Chair, intending to Plead in his Defence, and begun thus: *Though I (*Athenians*) am the youngest of those that come up into this place*. But all the Senate crying out *of those who go down*, he was thereupon constrained to do so. *Socrates* being Condemned, *Plato* offered him to procure so much Money as might purchase his Liberty, but *Socrates* refused the Offer. * About that time, *Socrates*'s Friends being met together to condole his Death, *Plato encouraged them, and bid them not despair, for that himself was capable to Govern the School*: and in so saying, drank to Apollodorus, who answered, he would sooner take up the Cup of Poison from the hand of *Socrates*, than *Pledge him upon that Condition*. Upon the Death of *Socrates*, *Plato* (whose excessive Grief upon that Occasion is observed by † *Plutarch*) with others of his Disciples, fearing the Tyranny of those Persons, who put their Master to Death, * fled to *Euclid* at *Megara*, who friendly entertained them, till the Storm was blown over.

† *Apuleius* saith, that before he came to *Socrates*, he was initiated in the Sect of Heraclitus. But more likely is that which is affirmed by *Laertius*, that after *Socrates*'s death, he applyed himself to *Cratylus*, a follower of *Heraclitus*, and to *Hermogenes*. He conceived, saith * St. *Austine*, that his own Invention, and *Socrates*'s Instructions came short of the true aim of Philosophy: He considered with himself what course he should take to benefit himself most, for this purpose he determined to travel to any place, where report told him he might drink of the Spring of Leaning, even to the farthest parts of the Earth, saith † Cicero: * First, to *Italy*, where he addicted himself to the Discipline of *Pythagoras*, which, though he saw replenished with curious and high reason, yet, he chiefly affected to imitate the Continence and Chastity thereof, though the † *Pythagorians* themselves affirm he had all his Natural Philosophy from thence.

Perceiving the knowledge of the *Pythagoreans* to be assisted with other Disciplines, he went to *Cyrene*, to learn Geometry of *Theodorus*
the

the Mathematician: thence to Ægypt (which was then under the Empire of *Artaxerxes Mnemon*) * under pretence of selling Oyl, but the scope of his Journey was to fetch Astrology from thence: *To learn Arithmetick and Celestial Speculations of the Barbarians,* (saith † *Cicero*) * and to be instructed in the rites of the Prophets. † *He travelled over the Country, informing himself all the way by their Priests, of the multiplicious proportions of Geometry, and the observation of Celestial Motions.* At what time young Students at Athens were enquiring for Plato to instruct them, he was busied in surveying the inexplicable banks of Nilus, *the vast extent of a Barbarous Country, and the winding compass of their Trenches, a Disciple to the Ægyptian old Men.* * Having taken a full survey of all the Country; he at last setled himself in the Province of *Sais,* learning of the wise men there, what they held concerning the Universe, whether it had a beginning, and whether it is moved at present, wholly or in part, according to Reason. From these, † *Pausanias* affirms, he learn'd the Immortality of the Soul, which that they held, as likewise the transmigration thereof into several bodies, is affirmed by * *Herodotus*. † Some say, that *Euripdes* followed him to Ægypt and falling sick, was cured by the Priests with Sea water, whereupon he said,

The Sea doth wash away all ills of Man.

But this agrees not with the time of his death, which was before that of *Socrates, viz.* in the 93th Olympiad.

From Ægypt Plato returned to *Tarentum* in Italy, at what time *L. Camillus* and *P. Claudius* were Consuls at *Rome,* as * *Cicero* affirmeth. What *Fasti* he used, I know not; for in those which are now with us received as authentick, there are no such Consuls during the whole Life of *Plato*. And indeed, in those times, *Rome* was for the most part, Govern'd by Tribunes. † Here he conversed with *Eurytus* of *Tarentum,* the Elder, *Archytas* the Elder (at whose discourse concerning Pleasure he was Present) and with the rest of the *Pythagoreans, Echecrates, Timæus, Acrio* (corruptly in a *Valerius Maximus, Ario*) and *Coetus, Locrians*. Thus to the Learning of *Socrates* he added that of *Pythagoras,* and informed himself in those things which *Socrates* neglected: He would have gone also to the *Indians,* and to the *Magi,* but that the Wars which at that time were in *Asia* hindred him.

CHAP. IV.

What Authors he followed.

†**E**Ugubinus affirms, that *Plato* borrowed the mystick part of his Philosophy from *Hermes Trismegistus:* particularly, that concerning the Divine Goodness: which, I suppose, he rather asserts from his own Conjecture, in regard *Plato* had been long in Ægypt, than from any good Authority. He was induced thereunto by those Books, which are now commonly, but falsely, vented under the name of *Hermes Trismegistus*: whereas, the Learned *Casaubon,* in his b *Exercitations upon Baronius,* hath sufficiently taught us the Forgery of those Books, which seem by some Impostor, to have been compiled out of the Works of *Plato,* and the Divine Scripture.

That *Plato* received some light from *Moses,* is affirmed with much greater Authorities of several Nations and Religions: Of *Jews* by c *Aristobulus, Plato* (saith he) *he followed our Law in many things, his various allegations evince him a curious observer thereof: for the Volums of Moses were Translated before Alexander's time.* And d *Josephus, Plato chiefly followed our Lawgiver.* Of Philosophers; by e *Numenius, What is Plato* (saith he) *but* Moses *speaking Greek ?* Of Fathers, by f *Justin Martyr,* g *Clement* Alexandrinus, h *Eusebius, Theodoret,* i *Saint Augustine,* &c.

k When *Plato* went to *Sicily,* he bought the Books of *Philolaus,* a *Pythagorean,* which were three, of *Natural Philosophy,* the first that ever were published out of that School: Some say, he had them of *Dionysius's* friends, for four *Alexandrian Minæ*: Others, that *Dionysius* had them of a young Man, one of *Philolaus's* Disciples, and gave them to *Plato*. Others, that he sent to *Dion* at *Siracuse* to buy them for him, which he did for 100 *Minæ*: l *A. Gellius* saith, ten thousand Denaries: For having received of *Dionysius* above eighty Talents, he was very full of Money, Out of these, he is said (as *A. Gellius* and *Laertius* affirm) to have taken a great part of his *Timæus,* for which derided by *Timeon (in Sillis)* thus:

You (Plato) *with the same affections caught,
With a great Summ a little Treatise bought,
Where all the knowledge, which you own, was taught.*

m *Alcimus* in his four Books to *Amintas,* affirms, that *Plato* borrow'd much from the Writings of *Epicharmus,* the Comick Poet; in the first Book he hath these words: *In Sensibiles* (saith *Plato*) *neither magnitude nor quality is permanent, but in continual fluxion and mutation: as if we should substract number from them, which are neither equal, nor certain, nor quantitive, nor qualitative; these are they where Generation is always, their Essence never. To Insensibles nothing can be added, nothing taken away. This is the nature of Eternal Beings, the like and same ever.* Thus *Plato* cited by *Alcimus*. Indeed, he teacheth this in many places, particularly in *Timæo,* where he at large explaineth what is that which never is, and never had beginning, and that which hath beginning but no being. He concludes the first comprehensible, by the intellect with Reason, the other by Sense and Opinion. But the citation of *Alcimus* seems to refer to *Plato's Theætetus,* the subject of which Dialogue is *Science*: there he examines some Definitions of Science by the Antients, amongst the rest, the assertion of *Protagoras, that Science is Sense:* against which he disputes laregly, the sum this: That the Soul apprehends some things by mediation of the Body, others without: of the first kind are things *warm, light, dry, sweet,* &c. of the other, *Essence, and not Being, Similitude and Dissimilitude, Identity and Diversity, Unite and Number*

ber: Hence it follows, that Senfe apprehends not Effences, and confequently not Truths, for Effence and Truth are convertible. This affertion of *Plato* * *Alcimus* deduceth from *Epicharmus, who*, (faith he) *hath plainly fpokn of things fubject to Senfe and Reafon, in thefe words:*

* *Laert.*

> *Gods always were, to be, defifted never,*
> *Like them Eternal, ftill the fame perfever.*
> *Chaos the firft begotten Deity*
> *Is ftil'd: of fomething, how can nothing be?*
> *Thence not the firft nor fecond nothings are,*
> *How we efteem of thofe we thus declare:*
> *If we can even or uneven fumm*
> *Alter, by adding or fubtracting one,*
> *Seems it to you the fame? to me not fo,*
> *If a continu'd Meafure fhrink or grow,*
> *It is not the fame Meafure: fuch the lives*
> *Of Men are, one decays, another thrives;*
> *That Nature, which new being ever takes*
> *Is different from the being it forfakes,*
> *Not yefterday the fame were I and you,*
> *Nor fhall to morrow be what we are now.*

† *Laert.*

† Again, *Alcimus*, *The wife fay, that the Soul apprehends fome things by mediation of the Body, as when fhe hears or fees; others, fhe conceiveth within her felf, without ufing the Body, whence of beings, fome are fubject to Senfe, others, comprehenfible by the Intellect. Therefore* Plato *faith, that they who defire to know the principles of the Univerfe, muft firft diftinguifh the Ideas in themfelves, as* Similitude, Unity, Multitude, Magnitude, Reftauration. *Secondly, add in it felf,* Honeft, Good, Juft, *and the like. Thirdly, examines what Ideas cohere mutually with one another, as* Science, Magnitude, Power: *and withal, to think that thofe who are amongft us, becaufe they participate of them, fhould be called by the fame name, as for inftance, juft things are thofe which participate of* Juft, Honeft *which of* Honeft: *one of every Species is eternal, perceptible by the mind, and confequently free from perturbation. Wherefore, he afferts Idea's in Nature as Exemplars, after whofe likenefs other things are made.* Thus *Alcimus*: the firft part whereof feems to be taken out of *Plato's Theætetus*, the latter out of his *Parmenides*. The words of *Epicharmus* concerning Gods and Idea's, to which *Alcimus* refers this of *Plato*, are thefe:

> *Is Mufick then a thing? It is: The Man*
> *Mufick? no: what then? a Muficien*
> *A Man or not? he is the fame of good,*
> *Good from the thing a part is underftood:*
> *Whoever learns good by that art is made,*
> *Who Mufick, Muficien: of each Trade,*
> *As Dancing, Weaving, and the like the fame,*
> *The Art, and Artift have a different name.*

* *Laert.*

* Again, *Alcimus*: *Plato in his Opinion of Idea's faith thus: if there is memory, there muft be alfo Idea's; for Memory is of a quiet permanent thing, but nothing is permanent except Idea's, for how,* faith he, *could living creatures be preferved unlefs by their Idea and receiving a natural mind? Now they remember Similitude and their nourifhment: fhewing that all Creatures have an innate underftanding of their own fimilitude, and therefore perceive things belonging to their kind.* Thus *Alcimus*: What place of *Plato* he means I know not, † *Scaliger* reads, Πλάτων ἐν τῇ περὶ ἰδεῶν ὑπο- λήψει φησὶν εἶναι ὅτι; ταῖς ἰδέαις, &c. omitting μνήμη, as if he made a doubt whether that both of the Opinions of Idea's were *Plato's*; but I rather think *Alcimus* meant not the title of any Book, having named none in the reft of his Citations, but what himfelf abftracts out of *Plato's* Opinion concerning Idea's. *Plato* in *Philedo*, teacheth this concerning Memory, that Senfe is a motion common to the Soul and Body; this Suffering from external Senfes, the other acting and dijudicating: that Memory is a confervatory or repofitory of the Senfes. For the Soul, as oft as fhe in her felf, or by affiftance of the Body, calls to mind what fhe hath fuffered, fhe is faid to remember. To *Plato's* affertion, *Alcimus* applieth this of *Epicharmus*:

† *In Arift. de animal.*

> *Eumæus Wifdom's not to one confin'd;*
> *Various in every living knowing Mind.*
> *The Hen firft doth not living things beget,*
> *But Sits and Hatches with enlivening Heat:*
> *This Wifdom only Nature's friend difcerns,*
> *Of whom (her Miftrefs) fhe this Leffon learns.*

And again,

> *This is not ftrange, for every thing we find*
> *Is to its proper Species moft enclin'd;*
> *To Dogs a Bitch feems faireft, and to Kine*
> *A Bull, an Afs to Affes, Swine to Swine.*

Thefe things *Laertius* cites out of *Alcimus*, adding that *there are more of the fame kind in thofe four Books*, whereby he intimates the help that *Plato* received by the writings of *Epicharmus*, neither was *Epicharmus* himfelf ignorant of his own *Wifdom*, *as may be collected from thefe Verfes, Predicting that he fhold have a Follower*:

> *This I affert, and what I now maintain,*
> *Shall Monuments to future times remain,*
> *Some one hereafter will my Verfe review,*
> *And Cloathing it in Language Rich and New*
> *Invincible himfelf, others Subdue.*

* Moreover *Phavorinus* alledgeth the whole Form of *Plato's* Common-wealth in *Protagoras's* Antilogicks, others fay, he borrowed his Politicks from *Socrates*.

* *Laert.*

† Laftly, it is related, that much of *Plato's* Morality was in the Books of *Sophron* the Minograph, which having been long neglected, were by him firft brought to *Athens*, and were found lying under his Head, when he was Dead.

† *Laert.*

CHAP. V.

His School.

* **B**Eing returned to *Athens* from his Journey to *Ægypt*, he fetled himfelf in the Academy, a *Gymnafium* or place of Exercife in the Suburbs of that City, befet with Woods, taking Name from *Ecademus* one of the Heroes, as *Eupolis*.

* *Laert.*

In

In Sacred Hecademus *shady walks.*

And *Timon*,

The fluent sweet-tongu'd Sage first led the way,
Who writes as smoothly as from some green spray
Of Hecademe, *Grashoppers chirp their lay.*

Hence it was first called Ecademy, the occasion of his living here, was, that he was poor and had nothing but one Orchard in or adjoyning to the Academy, which was the least part of his Successours. This Orchard at first yielded but three *aurei nummi* of yearly Rent to the Owners, afterwards the whole Revenue amounted to a thousand or more. It was in process of time much enlarged by well-willers, and Studious Persons, who dying, bequeathed by Will something to the Professors of Philosophy, their Riches to maintain the Quiet and Tranquility of a Philosophical Life. *Plato* (the Academy being said to be a sickly place, and Phisicians advising him to transfer his School to the *Lyceum*) would not be perswaded, but answered, I would not live on the top of *Athos* to linger my Life. The unwholsomeness of the place brought him to a quartan Ague, which lasted eighteen Months, but at length by sobriety and care he master'd it, and recover'd his strength more perfect than before.

First, he taught Philosophy in the Academy, and after in the Gardens of *Colonus*. At the entrance of his School in the Academy was written, *Let none Ignorant of Geometry enter here,* meant, not only of the Measure and Proportion of Lines, but also of the inward Affections.

CHAP. VI.

How he Instituted a Sect.

HAving thus setled himself in the Academy, he began out of the Collection he had made from others, and his own invention to institute a Sect, called from the place where he taught, *Academick.* * He mixed the *Heraclitian* Discourses, with the *Socratick* and *Pythagoric*, following in Sensibles *Heraclitus*, in Intelligibles *Pythagoras*, in Politicks *Socrates*. Whereas Philosopy, † saith S. Agustine, *concerns either action or contemplation (thence assuming two names, Contemplative and Active) the Active consisting in practice of moral Actions, the Contemplative, in penetration of abstruse Phisical causes, and the nature of the Divinity*; Socrates *excelled in the Active*, Pythagoras *in the Contemplative. But Plato joyn'd them into one perfect kind, which he subdivided into three several parts; Moral, consisting chiefly in Action, Natural, in Contemplation, Rational in Distinction of true and false, which tho' useful in both the other, yet belongeth more particularly to Contemplation. So that this* Trichotomy *contradicts not the other* Dickotomy, *which includeth all within Action and Contemplation.* * And as of Old in a Tragedy, the *Chorus* Acted alone, then *Thespis* making some intermissions of the *Chorus* introduc'd one Actor, *Æschilus* a second, *Sophocles* a third: in like manner Philoso-

* *Laert.*

† *De Civit. dei lib. 8.*

‡ *Laert.*

phy was at first but of one kind, Phisick; then *Socrates* added *Ethick*; thirdly, *Plato* inventing *Dialectick*, made it perfect.

Of these three parts as they were held by *Plato*, and the rest of the old Academy, we cannot have a general better account than this of † *Cicero*.

† *Acad. quæst. 1.*

Sect. 1. *Ethick.*

The first, concerning well-living they sought in Nature, affirming that she ought to be obeyed: and that in nothing else but Nature was to be had that chief good whereto all things should be referred, that the ultimate being of desirable things, and end of all good in the mind, body and life were acquired by Nature. Those of the Body they placed in the whole, and in the parts: Health, Strength Beauty in the whole; in the parts, sound Sense, and, a certain Excellence of particular parts, as in the feet swiftness, strength in the hands, clearness in the voice, in the tongue plainness of expression. Of the mind were those which are proper to comprehend the power of Wit, which they divided into Nature and Manners. To Nature they ascribed quickness of apprehension, and Memory, both proper to the Mind and Wit; To Manners belonged Study and a kind of Wisdom formed partly by a continual Exercise, partly by Reason, in which consisted Philosophy it self, wherein that is begun and not perfected, is called progression to Virtue, what is perfected, Virtue; perfection of Nature of all things in the Mind, the most excellent. Thus of Minds: The adjuncts of Life, that was the third, they asserted such things as conduced to the practice of Virtue.

Sect. 2. *Physick.*

Of Nature (for that was next) they so treated as to divide it into two things: One the efficient, the other giving it self to this, that, thereof might be made something. In that they conceived to be a power, in this a certain matter to be effected: in both, matter could not cohere, unless contained by some power, nor the power without some matter, for there is nothing which is not enforced to be somewhere: That which consists of both, they called Body and Quality: Of Qualities, some are primary, others arising from these: the primary are uniform and simple; those which arise from these are various, and as it were multiform. Air, Fire, Water, and Earth are primary, of these arise forms of living creatures, and of those, things which are made of the Earth. These principles are called Elements, of which Air and Fire have a faculty to move and effect; the other parts, Water and Earth to suffer. To all these there is subjected a certain matter without form, destitute of quality, out of which all things are expressed and formed: It is capable of admitting all; and of changing all manner of ways, in the whole, and in every part: This resolves nothing to nothing, but into its own parts, which are divisible into infinite, there being in Nature no least which cannot be divided. Those which are moved, are all moved by intervals, which intervals likewise may be divided infinitely, and that power which we call quality, being moved and agitated every way, they conceive the whole matter to be througly changed, and by that means those things, which they call qualitative, to be produced, of which, in all coherent nature continued with all its parts, was effected the World, beyond which there is not any part of Matter or Body: The parts of the World are all things therein, kept together by a sensitive nature, wherein is likewise perfect Reason: It is also sempiternal, for there is nothing more strong whereby it may be dissolved: This power they call the Soul of the World, God, a certain Providence over all things subjected to him, regarding in the first place heavenly things, next on the Earth those things which appertain to Man. The same they sometimes call Necessity, because nothing can be otherwise than is by him Ordained: a fatal immutable continuation of Eternal Order: sometimes Fortune, as producing many things not foreseen or expected by by us, by reason of the obscurity and our ignorance of the Causes.

Sect. 3. *Dialectick*.

Of the third part of Philosophy, consisting in Reason and dissertation, they treated thus. Tho' Judgment arise from the Sense, yet the Judgment of Truth is not in the Senses. The Mind they affirmed to be Judge of things, conceiving her only fit to be credited, because she alone seeth that which is simple, and uniform, and certain: This they called Idea. All Sense they conceived to be obtuse and slow, and no way able to perceive those things which seem subject to Sense, which are so little, as that they cannot fall under Sense, so moveable and various, that nothing is one, constant, nor the same, because all things are in continual alteration and fluxion. All this part of things, they called Opinative: Science they affirmed to be no where but in the Reasons and Notions of Mind, whence they approved definitions of things, and applied them to all whereon they discoursed. They approved likewise explications of words by Etymogies: They used Arguments and Marks for things, to prove and conclude what they meant to explain: In this consisted all the discipline of Dialectick, that is, of Speech concluded by Reason.

This Account in general *Cicero* gives of the old Academy: *Plutarch*, *Laertius*, *Apuleius*, and others have made Collections more particular, we shall make choice of that of *Alcinous*, as most full and perfect, which by reason of the length is referred as an Appendix to *Plato*'s Life.

CHAP. VIII.

His Inventions.

HE added much to Learning and Language by many Inventions, as well of things as of words. To omit *Dialectick*, of which we treated last, * *Phavorinus* attributes to his invention, discoursing by way of a Question: but *Aristotle* ascribes it to *Alexamenus*, a *Stirian* or *Teian*, and it appears by the Dialogues of *Plato*, that *Socrates* also used that form of arguing. *Laertius* informs us, that *Zeno Eleates was the first composer of Dialogues, yet in my Opinion*, saith he, *Plato hath so much refined the form thereof, that he deserves to be preferred before all others, as well for invention as Reformation.*

More properly may be attributed to him the invention of † *Analytical Method*, *which reduceth the thing sought unto its principle*, *the best of Methods*. He taught it to *Leodamas*, and by it found out many things in Geometry: *Analysis*, as defined by the * Scholiast upon *Euclid*, is *a sumption of the thing sought*, *by the consequents*, (*as if it were already known*) *to find out the truth*. Examples thereof we find in the five first propositions of the 13th Book of *Euclid*, besides several others, that occur in *Apollonius Pergæus*, and *Pappus Alexandrinus*.

Amongst his Geometrical Inventions also must be remembred *the duplication of a Cube*, the occasion and manner whereof is related by † *Plutarch* and * *Philoponus*. The *Delians* afflicted with the Pestilence consulted the Oracle of *Apollo*, he answered, the Plague would cease if they doubled their Altar, which was of a Cubick figure. *Plutarch* saith, that hereupon the Overseers of the Altar, made all the four sides double to what they were before, so instead of doubling the Altar, they made it octuple to what it was. *Philoponus* saith, they caused another Cube of the same bigness with the former to be set upon it, whereby they changed the Figure of the Altar, which was no longer a Cube, but Δόκις, *a quadrilateral Pillar*. The first way it was Cubical, but not double; the second way double, but not Cubical. The Plague not ceasing, they consulted the Oracle again. *Apollo* answered, they had not fulfilled his Command, which was to build a Cubical Altar as big again as the former. Hereupon they went to *Plato*, as most skilful in Geometry, to learn of him the Oracle's meaning, and how they should find out the way of doubling a Cube, retaining the Cubick Figure. *Plato* answered, that the God mocked the *Grecians* for their neglect of Philosophy and Learning, insulting over their Ignorance, that he commanded them seriously to addict themselves to Geometry, that this could not be done any other way, than by finding out two mean proportionals between two right Lines in a Duple proportion, (*Plato*'s particular Method is delivered by *Eutochius* in his Comment upon the first Proposition of the second Book of *Archimedes de Sphæra & Cylindro*.) He added that *Eudoxus* the *Gnidian*, or *Helico* the *Cyzicene* would do it for them. That the God needed not this duplication of his Altar, but commanded all the *Grecians*, that avoiding War and the Miseries wherewith it is attended, they should apply themselves to the Muses; and having setled the turbulent Commotions of their Minds, converse harmlesly and beneficially with one another. *Philoponus* adds, that *Plato* expounded *this Problem to his Disciples*, *who writ much upon this Subject*, *though nothing thereof be extant*. Of the Antients, laboured in this Problem besides *Plato*, *Archytas* the *Tarentine*, *Menæchmus*, *Eratosthenes Philo* of *Byzantium*, *Hero*, *Apollonius*, *Pergæus*, *Nicomedes*, *Diocles*, and *Sporus*: † *Valerius Maximus* saith, that *Plato remitted the Overseers of the Sacred Altar to Euclid the Geometrician*, *as submitting to his Science and Profession*; but this is an Error, because *Euclid* the Geometrician was much later than *Plato*, and the other *Euclid*, *Plato*'s Contemporary, nothing eminent in Mathematicks, as hath

hath been before me observed by Sir *Henry Savile*.   * *Prel. 1.*

That *Plato* invented many other things in the Mathematicks, (more than appears from those Writings of his that are extant) and was most eminent therein, may be argued from the three Books of *Theon Smyrnæus*, the first *Arithmetick*, the second, *Harmonicks*, the last, (not yet published) *Astronomy*. Those Books contained many things, singular and choice, not to be met with elsewhere. The design is acknowledged by the Author, to be as an introduction necessary to the understanding of *Plato*'s Writings.

There are also divers words of which he is esteemed to be the first Author, † as *Antipodes*, a word by him first introduced into Philosophy, to signifie those People whose feet are diametrically opposite.   † *Laert.*

* Στοιχεῖον, *Element*, until his time was confounded with ἀρχὴ, *Principle*, by all Philosophers from *Thales*. *Plato* distinguish'd them thus, Ἀρχὴ, *Principle*, is that which hath nothing before it whereof it might be generated; στοιχεῖα, *Elements*, are compounded.   * *Laert.*

† The word *Poem* also, though since very trivial, was not used by any before him.   † *Laert.*

* He first used this term, τῷ ἀριθμᾷ τὸν περμηκῆ, *oblong number*, [*in Theæteto*] thereby signifying the product of a greater number muliplied by a lesser.   * *Laert.*

† He also first introduced the word Ἐπιφάνεια, *Superficies*, for which before was used ἐπίπεδον a *Plane*. Thus *Laertius*, though * *Proclus* implies, that neither *Plato* nor *Aristotle* use the word, but for it, ἐπιπεδόν. Divine *Plato* saith, he, *calls Geometry, the contemplatrix of Planes, opposing it to Stereometry, as if Plane and Superficies were the same*. So likewise doth *Aristotle*. But *Euclid* and *those who succeeded him, make Superficies the Genus, Plane a Species thereof.*   † *Laert.*   * *In Euclid. lib. 2.*

† θεοῦ πρόνοια, *Divine Providence*, a Word since much used by Christians, was first the expression of *Plato*.   † *Laert.*

* He first of Philosophers wrote against *Lysias*, Son of *Cephalus*, in *Phædro*.   * *Laert.*

† He first considered the force and efficacy of Grammar.   † *Laert.*

* He first wrote against all that were before him, whence it is wondred at, that he never mentions *Democritus*.   * *Laert.*

CHAP. VIII.

His Distinctions.

OF his Distinctions *Aristotle* made this Collection in some pieces not Extant, cited by *Laertius*.

Good is threefold.	In the Soul, as Justice, Prudence, Fortitude, Temperance, and the like. In the Body, as Beauty, good Habit. External, as Friends, Prosperity of our Country: Wealth.
Friendship is threefold.	Natural, which Parents bear to their Children, and Kindred to one another; which kind also is amongst Beasts. Sociable, begotten by conversation, without any Relation of Kindred; such as was that betwixt *Pylades* and *Orestes*. Hospitable, towards Guests, or wherewith we affect Strangers even upon Letters of Recommendation. Some add a fourth kind, *amatory*
Government is of five kinds.	Democratical: a Democracy is that wherein the People Rules and have power to make Magistrates and Laws. Aristocratical: an Aristocracy is that wherein neither Rich nor poor nor Nobles Govern, but the best Persons of the whole City. Olygarchical: An Oligarchy is when Governors are Elected by the Votes of Magistrates, for they are fewer than the Poor. Regal: { Elective by Law: as that of the *Carthaginians*: for it is Civil. Successive in a Family; as that of the *Lacedæmonians* and *Macedonians* who confine themselves to a certain Race. Tyrannical, Tyranny is that wherein Men are brought to Subjection either by Fraud or Force.
Justice is threefold.	Towards the Gods: they who Sacrifice as the Law requires, and perform the Divine Rites, are just towards the Gods. Towards Men: They who restore what was lent or committed to their Trust, are just towards Men. Towards the Dead: They who take care of Sepulchres are just toward the dead.
Science is threefold.	Practice, as playing on the Flute, Lute, and the like; which affect nothing visible. Mechanick, As Architecture of Houses, Ships, or the like: which produceth a visible effect. Theoretick, as Geometry, Harmonick Astronomy, which act not, neither produce any thing. The Geometrician considers the proportion of Lines to one another, Harmonick sounds: Astronomy, Stars, and the World.

Medicine is of five kinds.
- *Pharmaceutick*, cureth Diseases by application of Medicine.
- *Chyrurgick*, by incision or cauterising.
- *Diætetick*, by Diet.
- *Nosognomonick*, discerns Diseases.
- *Boethetick*, removeth Diseases.

Law is twofold.
- *Written*: such are those by which States are Governed.
- *Not written*, grounded upon Custom; as that no Man shall go naked into the *Forum*, habited like a Woman, is not forbidden by any written Law, but forborn because of the unwritten.

Speech is of five kinds.
- *Political*, used in Orations by such as Govern States.
- *Rhetorical*, used by Lawyers in Pleading either to Confirm, Praise, Dispraise, or Accuse.
- *Vulgar*, used by People in common Discourse.
- *Dialectical*, used by such as discourse in short questions and answers.
- *Artificial*, used by Tradesmen in their several Professions.

Musick is threefold.
- Of the Voice only.
- Of the Voice and Hands, as singing to the Lute.
- Of the Hand only, as the Harp.

Nobility is of four kinds.
- If the Predecessors were upright, just, and honest.
- If the Predecessors were Rulers of Princes.
- If the Predecessors acquired Honours, as the Command of an Army, or were Crown'd in Publick Games: those who are descended from such as we call Noble.
- If a Man be endued with a Generous Mind; this is the best kind of Nobility.

Beauty is threefold.
- *Commendable*, as a fair form.
- *Useful*, as an Instrument, House, or the like.
- *Beneficial*, as all that belongs to institution of Laws.

The *Soul* hath three parts.
- *Rational*, the Principle whereby we Judge, Discourse, and the like.
- *Concupiscible*, whereby we desire meat, coition, and the like.
- *Irascible*, whereby we are emboldned, joyed, grieved, enraged.

Perfect Virtue hath four kinds.
- *Wisdom*, the Principle of doing things right.
- *Justice*, the Principle of doing things equal in private Conversation and Publick Affairs.
- *Fortitude*, the Principle of not flying Danger through Fear, but meeting it.
- *Temperance*, the Principle of subduing Desires, and yielding to no Pleasures, but living Moderately.

Government is of five kinds.
- *By Law*: Those who are chosen Magistrates in a City Governed by Law.
- *By Nature*: The Males not only of Mankind, but of most other Creatures are predominant over the Fe-males by Nature.
- *By Custom*, as that which Masters have over their Disciples.
- *By Descent*, as the *Lacedæmonian* Kings, who succeed out of one Family: and in *Macedonia* they use the same Custom.
- *By Force*, as those who Rule a Kingdom against the will of the People.

Of *Rhetorick* are six kinds.
- *Adhortation*, as when we perswade a War against any.
- *Dehortation*, as when we disswade from War.
- *Accusation*, when we declare that we have been injured by one whom we prove cause of our Misfortune.
- *Defence*, When a Man proves he did not any Injury or Offence.
- *Encomium*, when we speak well of another.
- *Vituperation*, when we declare a Man to be wicked.

Of *Right Speaking* are four kinds; when we speak
- *What is requisite*: those things which will benefit both the hearer and speaker.
- *As much as is requisite*: if we speak neither more nor less than concerns the business.
- *To those to whom it is requisite*: as when we speak to old men that have done amiss in such terms as are fit for old Men, or to young as becomes young.
- *When it is requisite*: neither too soon nor too late; for if that be not observed, nothing can be spoken aright.

Beneficence,

Beneficence is of four kinds.	*In Wealth*, when we relieve the wants of any according to our Means. *In Body*, when we succour those who are beaten. *In Knowledge*, when we instruct, cure, teach any good. *In Speech*, he, who pleadeth in defence of another, helpeth him in words.
The *end* of things is of four kinds.	*Legal*, imposing an end to things by Decree. *Natural*, such as days, years, and hours have. *Artificial*, as the building of a House. *Accidental*, by chance, unexpected.
Of *Powers* are four kinds.	One *in the mind*, to think and conjecture. Another *of the Body*, to walk, give, receive, and the like. A third, consisting in a Multitude of Souldiers, and store of Wealth, in which respect, Princes are called Powerful. The fourth, as to suffer good or evil to be done to us; as as to be capable of Sickness, Learning, Health or the like.
Of *Humanity* are three kinds.	*In Calling*, as those who call all they meet, and salute them, taking them by the hand. *In relieving*, in relieving the misfortunes of another willingly. *In Feasting and Conversation*.
Felicity is divided into five parts.	*Prudent Counsel*, acquired by Learning and Experience. *Soundness of Senses*, consisting in the parts of the Body, as to see with the Eyes, to hear with the Ears, to smell and taste. *Prosperity of Affairs*, when those things which a Man intendeth, he performeth fully. *Good Reputation*, among Men, when a Man is well spoken of. *Plenty of Riches*, and things necessary to Life, so as to be able to supply Friends, and to perform Works of publick Magnificence: He who hath all these five kinds is perfectly Happy.
Arts are of three kinds.	The first diggeth out Metals, and fells Wood. The second gives variety of shape to things, as Wood-work and Iron-work. The third maketh use of these, as Horsemanship of Bridles, Souldiery of Arms, Musick of Instruments.
Good is of four kinds.	One, as when we call a Man good from his proper goodness. A second, as we call Virtue and Justice it self good. A third, as we say, Food, Exercise, and Medicines are beneficial. The fourth good we call the act of playing on Musick, or acting in a Play.
Of *things* some are	*Ill*, always capable to do Hurt, as Ignorance, Imprudence, Injustice and the like. *Good*, the contrary to the former. *Indifferent*, which sometimes may benefit, sometimes hurt, as walking, fitting, eating; or cannot do hurt at all, being neither good nor bad.
Good Government is threefold.	If the Laws be good. If the Laws be well kept. If without Laws the People live orderly by custom.
Ill Government is threefold.	If the Laws be bad for Natives and Foreigners. If the Laws in being are not observed. If there are no Laws at all.
Contraries are of three kinds.	*Good to ill*, as Justice to Injustice, Wisdom to Imprudence, and the like. *Ill to Ill*, as Prodigality to Avarice, unjust Torments to just. *Neither to neither*, as heavy to light, swift to slow, black to white.
Good is of three kinds.	Some we have, as Justice and Health. Of some we participate, as Good it self cannot be had, but may be participated. Some are Fixt, which we can neither have, nor participate, as to be virtuous and just.

Consultation

Consultation is threefold.	{ *From the Past*, by Example; as what befell the *Lacedemonians* through overmuch Confidence. *From the Present*, as considering the Timorousness of Men, weakness of Walls, scarcity of Provision, and the like. *From the Future*, as that Ambassadors should not be injured upon Suspicion, lest it cast Infamy upon all *Greece*.
Voice is	{ *Animate*, of living Creatures. *Articulate*, of Men. *Inanimate*, Sounds and Noise. *Inarticulate*, of Beasts.
Things are	{ *Divisible*, compounded as Syllables, Symphonies, living creatures, Water, Gold. *Homogeneous*, consist of similar parts, differing from the whole only in number, as Water, Gold, and all liquid things. *Indivisible*, compounded of nothing, as a point, sound. *Heterogeneous*, consist of dissimular parts.
Things are	{ *Absolute*, requiring nothing else to express them, as a Man, a Horse, and other creatures. *Rlatives*, which imply another thing, as greater- (than others) swifter, fairer, and the like; for what is greater relates to something lesser, and the like.

These according to *Aristotle* were *Plato*'s divisions of first things.

CHAP. IX.

His three Voyages to Sicily.

* *Laert.*
† *Plat. Epist.*

PLato made three Voyages to *Sicily*; the first to see the fiery ebullitions of *Ætna*, † and to improve the knowledge of States, and Philosophy, which he got by his other Travels;

* *Laert.*

This was about the 40th year of his age, * at what time *Dionysius* the elder, Son of *Hermocrates*, Reigned in *Syracuse*; † *Plutarch* faith, he was led thither by Providence, not Fortune, and that some good Genius, designing afar off the Liberty of the People of *Syracuse*, brought him acquainted with *Dion* then very young, who entertained him as his † Guest: He much disliked the Luxury of that place, Feasting, Nocturnal Lucubrations and the like; conversed frequently with *Dion*, discoursed with him of those things which were best in Man, and with his best Arguments exhorted him thereto: by which he seemed to lay grounds for the subversion of that Tyranny, which afterwards hapned ; * *Dion*, though young, was the most ingenious of all *Plato*'s followers, and most eager in pursuit of Virtue, as appears as well by the Testimony of *Plato*, as his own Actions. Tho he had been brought up by the King in an effeminate Luxurious kind of Life; yet as soon as he tasted of Philosophy, the guide to Virtue, his Soul was inflamed with love thereof, and from his own Candor and Ingenuity was perswaded that *Dionysius* would be no less affected therewith: And therefore desired him when he was at leisure, to admit and hear *Plato*: Hereupon the Tyrant sent for him, at that meeting all their Discourse was concerning Fortitude: *Plato* affirmed none was further from that Virtue than a Tyrant, and, proceeding to speak of Justice, asserted the Life of the Just to be Happy, of the Unjust, Miserable. *Dionysius* was displeased at this Discourse (as reflecting upon himself) and with the standers by for approving it, at last, much exasperated, he asked *Plato* why he came

† *In Dion.*

† *Plat. Epist.* 3. & 7.

* *Plut. in Dione.*

into *Sicily?* *Plato* answered, to seek a good Man: It seems, reply'd *Dionysius*, you have not yet found him. *Laertius* faith, *Plato* Disputed with him concerning Tyranny, affirming, that is not best which benefits our selves, unless it be excellent also in Virtue; whereat *Dionysius* incensed, said to him, your discourse savours of old age: and yours, answered *Plato*, of Tyranny. *Dionysius*, enraged, commanded him to be put to Death: I will have, said he, your head taken off: At which words *Xenocrates* being present, answered, *He that doth it must begin with mine*: but *Dion* and *Aristomenes* wrought with him to revoke that Sentence. *Dion* thinking his Anger would have proceeded no farther, sent *Plato* away at his own request in a Ship which carried *Pollis* (whom *Laertius* calls *Polis*, *Ælian*, *Pólis*,) a *Lacedemonian* Captain (who at that time had been sent to Embassador to *Dionysius*) back to *Greece*: *Dionysius* secretly desired *Pollis* to kill him whilst he was on Shipboard; or if not, by all means to sell him, alledging, it would be no injury to *Plato*, for he would be as Happy in Bondage as at Liberty, as being a just Man. Some affirm the occasion of *Dionysius* his Anger was, because, that when he asked what was the best Brass, *Plato* answered, that whereof the Statues of * *Aristogiton* and *Harmodius* were made. Others, that it was because he was overmastered in Learning. But *Tzetzes* rejecting these as idle Fictions of Philosophers, and Falsifiers, affirms the true Reason to have been, that he perceived, he advised *Dion* to possess himself of the Kingdom: *Pollis* Transported him to *Ægina*; there *Charmander*, Son of *Charmandrites*, accused him, as meriting Death, by a Law they had made, that the first *Athenian* that should come to that Island, should, without being suffered to speak for himself, be put to Death : Which Law, as *Phavorinus* affirms, he himself made. One that was present, saying in sport, he is a Philosopher, they set him at liberty: Some say, they brought him to the publick Assembly, to plead for himself, where he would not speak a word, but underwent all with a great Courage. Then they altered their intent

* Who slew *Hipparchus*, Brother of *Hippias* the Tyrant of *Athens*; upon which the *Pisistratides* were expelled.

intent of putting him to death, and agreed to sell him for a Slave. *Plutarch* saith, that upon a decree of the *Æginetæ*, that all the *Athenians* taken in that Island, should be sold for Slaves; *Pollis* sold him there; *Anniceris*, a *Cyrenaick* Philosopher, being accidentally present, redeemed him for twenty, or as others, thirty *Minæ*, and sent him to *Athens* to his Friends; they immediately return'd the Money to *Anniceris* but he refused it, saying they were not the only persons concerned in *Plato*'s welfare: Some say, *Dion* sent the Money, which he would not accept, but bought therewith a little Orchard in the Academy. *Pollis* was defeated by *Chabrias*, and afterwards drowned in *Elice*. The report goes that an Apparition told him, he suffered those things for the Philosophers sake. *Dionysius* understanding what had happened, writ to *Plato*, to desire him not to speak ill of him; *Plato* returned answer, that he had not so much time vacant from Philosophy, as to remember *Dionysius*. To some detractors who upbraided him, saying, *Dionysius* hath cast off *Plato*; no, saith he, but *Plato Dionysius*.

Dion continued to live, not according to the ordinary luxury of the *Sicilians* and *Italians*, but in vertue, until *Dionysius* died, for which maligned by those who lived after Tyrannical institutions. Then considering, that these documents were not practised by himself alone, but by some others, though few, he entertained a hope, that *Dionysius* the younger, who succeeded his Father in the Government, might become one of those, to the extraordinary happiness of himself, and the rest of the *Sicilians*. To this end he used many exhortations to invite him to Vertue, intermixed with some Sentences of *Plato*, with whom *Dionysius*, upon this occasion, became extreamly desirous to be acquainted: To that effect, many Letters were sent to *Athens* to him, some from *Dionysius*, others from *Pythagoreans* in *Italy*, desiring *Plato* to go to *Syracuse*, who, by prudent counsel might govern the young Man, transported by his own power to Luxury. *Plato*, as himself affirmeth, fearing to be thought a Person only of words, and not willing to engage in action, and withal, hoping, by purging one principal part, to cure the disease of all *Sicily*, yielded; *Laertius* saith, upon a promise made to him by *Dionysius*, of a place and People that should live according to the Rules of his Commonwealth; which he made not good. Hence *Athenæus* accused *Plato* of Ambition. In the mean time the Enemies of *Dion* fearing a change in *Dionysius*, perswaded him to call home from Banishment *Philistus* (a person very rational, but educated in Tyrannical Principles) as an Antidote against *Plato*'s Philosophy; but *Dion* hoped, the coming of *Plato* would regulate the licentious Tyranny of *Dionysius*.

Plato at his arrival in *Sicily*, (placed by *A. Gellius*, betwixt the beginning of *Philip*'s Reign, four hundred years from the building of *Rome*, and the *Chæronean* fight) was received by *Dionysius* with much respect: One of the King's magnificent Chariots stood ready to receive him as soon as he landed, and carried him to the Court. The King offered Sacrifice to the Gods for his coming, as a great blessing upon his government. The temperance of their Feasts, alteration of the Court, meekness of the King, gave the *Syracusians* great hopes of Reformation. The Courtiers addicted themselves to Philosophy so much, that the Palace was full of Sand (wherein they drew Geometrical figures) not long after *Plato*'s coming, at a Sacrifice in the Castle, the Herald, according to the usual manner, made a solemn Prayer, that the Gods would long preserve the Kingly Government: *Dion* standing by, said, *Will you never give over praying against me?* This troubled *Philistus* and his Friends, who feared *Plato* would insinuate into the favour of *Dionysius* so much, as that they should not be able to oppose him, since in so short time, he had effected so great an alteration in him: Hereupon they all jointly accused *Dion*, that he wrought upon *Dionysius*, by the eloquence of *Plato*, to resign his Government that it might be transferred to the Children of his Sister, to quit his command for the Academy, where he should be made happy by Geometry, resigning his present happiness to *Dion*, and his Nephews. With these and the like Instigations, *Dionysius* was so incensed, that he caused *Dion* to be unexpectedly carried on Shipboard in a little Bark, giving the Mariners order to Land him in *Italy*. This happened four Months after *Plato*'s coming. * *Plato*, * * Plat. Epist.* and the rest of *Dion*'s Friends, feared to be put to some punishment, as partakers of his offence. A report was raised, that *Plato* was put to death by *Dionysius*, as Author of all that happened: but, on the contrary, *Dionysius* doubting, lest something worse might happen from their fear, treated them all kindly, comforted *Plato*, bid him be of good chear, and intreated him to stay with him: † He caused him to be lodged † *Plutarch.* in his Castle, * in the Orchards adjoyning to his * *Plat. Epist. 7.* Palace, where not the Porter himself could go out without *Dionysius* his leave; thus cunningly, under pretence of Kindness, he watch'd him, that he might not return into *Greece*, to give *Dion* notice of the wrong done to him. *Dionysius* by frequent conversation with *Plato* (as wild Beasts are tamed by use) fell into so great liking of his discourse, that he became in love with him; but, it was a Tyrannical affection, for, he would not that *Plato* should love any but him, offering to put the power of the Kingdom into his hands, if he would value him above *Dion*. With this passion, troublesome to *Plato*, *Dionysius* was sometimes so far transported, as Men jealous of their Mistresses, that he would upon the sudden fall out with him, and as suddenly be reconciled, and ask him pardon. He had indeed a great desire of *Plato*'s Philosophy, but a great respect likewise on the other side for those who disswaded him from it, telling him, that it would ruin him to be too far ingaged therein. * In the mean time there hap- * *Plat. Ep.6.* pening a War, he sent *Plato* home, promising, that the next Spring (as soon as there was Peace) he would send back for him and *Dion* to *Syracuse*: But he kept not his promise, for which he desired *Plato* to excuse him, protesting the War to be the occasion thereof, and that as soon as it were ended, he would send for *Dion*, whom he desired in the mean time to rest satisfied, and not attempt any thing against him, nor to speak ill of him to the *Grecians*. This

Plato

Plato endeavoured to effect; he instructed *Dion* in Philosophy, in the Academy: *Dion* lay in the City at the House of *Calippus*, with whom he had been long acquainted. He purchased a Country House for Pleasure, whither he sometimes went; this he bestowed afterward, at his return to *Sicily*, upon *Speusippus*, with whom he conversed most intimately, as being so advised by *Plato*, who knew the cheerful humour of *Speusippus* to be a fit divertisement for the reserved disposition of *Dion*. *Plato* had undertaken the expence of some Plays and Dances by some Youths; *Dion* took the pains to teach them, and paid the whole charge: By this liberality which *Plato* suffered him to confer upon the *Athenians*, he gained more Love than *Plato* Honour.

In the mean time, *Dionysius*, to acquit himself of the disesteem he had gained amongst Philosophers in *Plato*'s Cause, invited many Learned Men, and in a vain Ostentation of Wisdom, applied improperly the Sentences he had learned of *Plato*: Hereupon he began to wish for *Plato* again, and to blame himself, for not knowing how to use him well when he had him, and that he had not learned so much of him as he might: and being like a Tyrant transported with uncertain passions and changes, a sudden vehement desire came upon him of seeing *Plato* again. The peace being now concluded, he sent to *Plato* to come to him (but not (as he had promised) to *Dion*) writing to him, that he would have him to come immediately, and that afterwards he would send for *Dion*. Hereupon *Plato* refused to go, notwithstanding the intreaties of *Dion*; alledging for excuse his old Age, and that nothing was done according to their agreement. In the mean time, *Architas*, whom, with others of *Tarentum*, *Plato*, before his departure, had brought into the acquaintance of *Dionysius*, came to *Dionysius*; there were also others there, Auditors of *Dion*. *Dionysius* being refused upon a second Invitation, thought his Honour deeply concerned, and thereupon sent the third time a Gally of three banks of Oars († trimmed with Fillets) and other Ships, and with them *Archidemus*, whom he conceived *Plato* most affected of all his Friends in *Sicily*, and some *Sicilian* Noblemen: * He had by all means obliged *Archytas* the *Pythagorean*, to let *Plato* know, he might come without danger, and that he would engage his word on it. † As soon as they came to *Plato*, they all protested, that *Dionysius* was much inclined to Philosophy, and delivered an Epistle from him to this effect:

Plat.Epist.3.

† *Plin.*

* *Plut.*

† *Plat.Epist.7.*

Dionysius to Plato.

(After the accustomed way of Preface) nothing (saith he) *should you do sooner, than come to Sicily at my request. First, as concerning Dion, all shall be done as you will; for I think you will only moderate things, and I will condescend: But, unless you come, you shall not obtain any thing which you desire for Dion, nor in any thing else, not in those which chiefly concern your own particular.*

* Other Epistles were sent from *Archytas*, and other *Italians* and *Tarentines*, praising *Dionysius* for his love of Learning; adding, that if *Plato* came not, it would reflect upon his Friends, as well as on himself. † Many Letters and Intreaties were sent to *Dion*, from his Wife and Sister: * to these were joyned the importunities of some Friends of *Plato*'s at *Athens*, † insomuch that *Dion* brought it to pass, that *Plato* (* lest he should desert him and the *Tarentines*,) yielded to *Dionysius*, without any excuse; and, as he writeth himself, was driven the third time to the *Sicilian* Straits,

* *Plat. Epist.*

† *Plutarch*

* *Plat. Epist.*

† *Plut.*

* *Plat.*

Once more Charybdis dangers to essay.

At his arrival in *Sicily*, *Dionysius* met him with a Chariot, drawn by four white Horses, † whereinto he took him, and made him sit, whilst himself plaid the Coach-man: whereupon a facete *Syracusian*, well vers'd in *Homer*, pleased with the sight, spoke these Verses out of the Iliads, with a little alteration:

† *Ælian. var. Hist. 4. 18.*

The Chariot groan'd beneath its weight,
Proud that the best of Men there sate.

And as *Dionysius* was much joyed at his coming, so were the *Sicilians* put in great hopes, being all desirous, and endeavouring, that *Plato* might supplant *Philistus*, and subvert Tyranny by Philosophy: The Ladies of the Court entertained *Plato* with all Civility; But above all, *Dionysius* seemed to repose more Confidence in him, than in any of his Friends; for, whereas he was jealous of all others, he had so great respect for *Plato*, that he suffered him only to come to him unsearched (* though he knew him to be *Dion*'s intimate Friend) and offered him great sums of Money, but *Plato* would not accept of any: († yet *Onetor* saith he received eighty Talents of him, wherewith enriched, he purchased the Books of *Philolaus*) whence *Aristippus* the *Cyrenæan*, who was at the same time in the Court, said, *Dionysius bestowed his Bounty on sure grounds; he gives little to us who require much, and much to *Plato* who requireth nothing*. And being blamed that he received Money of *Dionysius*, *Plato*. *Books, I want Money,* saith he, *Plato Books*. So untrue it is, as * *Xenophon* asperseth him, that he went thither to share in the *Sicilian* Luxury: Or, as † *Tzetzes*, that *he studied the art of Cookery, and lived with* Dionysius *as his Pensioner and Parasite*. So far was he from any Sordid Compliance, that at a Feast, * *Dionysius* commanding every one to put on a Purple Gown, and Dance, he refused, saying,

* *Ælian. var. Hist. 4. 18.*

† *Laert.*

* *Epist. ad Æschin.*

† *Chiliad.*

* *Laert. vit. Aristip.*

I will not with Female Robe disgrace
My self, who am a Man, of Manly Race.

Some likewise ascribe this to him, which others to *Aristippus*, that *Dionysius* saying,

Who ere comes to a Tyrant, he
A Servant is, though he came free.

He answered immediately,

No Servant is, if he came Free.

† *Plato.*

† *Plato*, after a while, began to put *Dionysius* in mind of the City he had promised him to be governed by his rules; but *Dionysius* retracted his Promise: He moved him also in the behalf of *Dion*; *Dionysius* at the first delayed him, afterwards fell out with him, but so secretly, that none saw it, for he continued to confer as much honour on him as he could possibly, thereby to make him forsake his Friendship to *Dion*. *Plato* from the beginning perceived there was no trust to be reposed in what he said or did, but that all was deceit; yet concealed that thought, and patiently suffered all; pretending to believe him. Thus they dissembled with each other, thinking they deceived the Eyes of all Men besides; *Helicon* of *Cyzicum*, a Friend of *Plato*, foretold an Eclipse of the Sun, which falling out according to his Prediction, the Tyrant much honoured him, and gave him a Talent of Silver: Then *Aristippus* jesting with other Philosophers, said he could tell them of a stranger thing that would happen; they desiring to know what that was. I foretel, saith he, *Plato and* Dionysins *will be at difference ere long*; and it came to pass. * *Dionysius* detained *Dion*'s Rent which he used to send yearly to him to *Peloponnesus*, pretending he kept it for his Nephew, *Dion*'s Son. *Plato* discontented hereat, desired he might go home, saying, he could not stay, *Dion* being used so ignominiously: *Dionysius* spoke kindly to him, desiring him to stay: He thought it not convenient to let *Plato* go so soon to divulge his actions; but being not able to prevail with him, he told him, he would provide a means for his passage; *Plato* had designed to go with the Passage-boats; *Dionysius* seeing him bent upon his Voyage, the next day spoke thus kindly to him; That *the differences betwixt* Dion *and me may be composed, I will for your sake condescend thus far,* Dion *shall receive his Revenues living in* Peloponnesus, *not as a banished person, but as one that may come hither when he and I, and you his friends shall think convenient. The Trustees for this business shall be your self, and your, and his Friends who live here*; Dion *shall receive his Rents, but through your hands, otherwise I shall not dare to trust him; in you and yours I have more confidence; stay for this reason a Year here, and then you shall carry along with you his Money, wherein you will do* Dion *a great Courtesy*. To this *Plato*, after a days deliberation consented; and writ to that effect to *Dion*; but as soon as the Ships were gone, that *Dionysius* saw he had no means to get away, forgetting his promise, he made sale of *Dion*'s Estate.

† At this time happened a Mutiny amongst the Soldiers of *Dionysius*, of which *Heraclides* a friend of *Plato*'s was reported the Author: *Dionysius* laid out to take him, but could not light on him: Walking in his Garden he called *Theodotes* to him; *Plato* being accidentally walking there at the same time; after some private Discourse with *Dionysius*, *Theodotes*, turning to *Plato*, *Plato*, saith he, *I perswade* Dionysius *that I may bring* Heraclides *to him to answer the Crimes wherewith he is charged, and then if* Dionysius *will not suffer him to live in* Sicily, *that he at least permit him to take his Wife and Children along with him to* Peloponnesus, *and live there, and whilst he shall not plot any thing against* Dionysius, *that he may there enjoy his Revenues. With this assurance I have sent to* Heraclides, *and will send again to him to come hither*; *but if he come either upon the first or second notice, I have made an agreement with* Dionysius, *and obtained a promise from him that he shall receive no harm, either in or without the City*; *but, if he be so resolved, that he send him away beyond the Confines of this Country until he shall be better satisfied with him*; Do not you Dionysius *consent hereto*, saith he? *I do*, answered *Dionysius*, *neither shall he be in your House, shall he receive any prejudice*. The next day (about twenty days before *Plato* left *Sicily*) came *Euribius* and *Theodotes* to *Plato* in much hast and trouble; *Plato*, said *Theodotes*, you were Yesterday present at the agreement betwixt *Dionysius and me, concerning* Heraclides. *I was so*, answer'd *Plato*, but since, continues *Theodotes*, *He hath sent out Officers to apprehend him, and I fear he is somewhere very nigh*; *therefore go along with us to* Dionysius, *and let us use our utmost endeavour with him*: They went; when they came before him, *Plato* (the rest standing silent by, and weeping) began thus, *These Men*, Dionysius, *are afraid lest you should do something against* Heraclides *contrary to the agreement you made Yesterday, for I suppose he is come near hereabouts*. *Dionysius* at this grew angry, his Colour often changed with Rage; *Theodotes* fell at his Feet, and taking him by the hand, besought him not to do any such thing: *Plato* continuing his Speech; *Be of good chear*, saith he, Theodotes, *for* Dionysius *will not do any thing contrary to the promise he made yesterday*. Dionysius looking severely upon *Plato*, *to you* saith he, *I made no promise*; *Yes by the Gods* answered *Plato, you promised not to do those things which* Theodotes *now beseecheth you not to do*. *Archedemus* and *Aristocratus* being present; he told *Plato* (as he had done once before, when he interceeded for *Heraclides*,) That he cared for *Heraclides* and others more than for him: and asked him before them whether he remembred that when he came first to *Syracuse*, he counselled him to restore the *Græcian* Cities? *Plato* answered, he did remember it, and that he still thought it his best course, and withal asked *Dionysius* whether that were the only counsel he had given him? *Dionysius* returned an angry contumelious Reply, and asked him, laughing scornfully, whether he taught him those things as a School-boy. To which *Plato* answered, *You well remember: What*, replies he, *as a Master in Geometry, or how?* *Plato* forbore to reply, fearing it might occasion a stop of his Voyage; but immediately went away; *Dionysius* resolved to lay wait for *Heraclides*; but he escaped to the *Carthaginian* Territories.

From this displeasure against *Plato*, *Dionysius* took occasion to forbear to send for *Dion*'s Money; and first sent *Plato* out of his Castle, where, till then, he had lain next the Palace, pretending that the Women were to celebrate a Feast ten days in the Gardens where he dwelt; For that time he commanded *Plato* to live without the Castle with *Archedemus*; during which time *Theodotes* sent for him, and complained to him of *Dionysius*'s Proceedings. *Dionysius* receiving Information that *Plato* had
Y   gone

gone to *Theodotes*, took a new occasion of displeasure against him, and sent one to him, who asked him whether he had gone to *Theodotes*. *Plato* acknowledged that he had, then, saith the Messenger, *Dionysius* bad me tell you, you do not well to prefer *Dion* and his Friends before him. Never from that time did he send for *Plato* to the Court, looking upon him as a profest friend to *Theodotes* and *Heraclides*, and his profest Enemy: * *Plato* lived without the Castle amongst the Soldiers of the Guard: who, as *Dionysius* well knew, had born him ill-will long and sought to murder him, because he counsell'd *Dionysius* to give over the Tyranny, and live without a Guard. † Some, who came to visit him, gave him notice that Calumnies were spread against him amongst the Soldiers * as if he excited *Dion* and *Theonides* to restore the Island to Liberty, and that some of them threatned, when they could light upon him to kill him. Hereupon *Plato* began to think of some means of Escape, which he effected in this manner; He sent to *Archytas* at *Tarentum*, and to other Friends, advertising them of the danger wherein he was; They, under pretence of an Embassy in the name of the Country, sent *Lamascus* (whom *Laertius* calls *Lamiscus*) one of their Party with a Galley of three Banks of Oars to redemand *Plato*, declaring that his coming to *Syracuse* was upon the Engagement of *Archytas*: His Letter was to this Effect.

* *Plut.*

† *Plat. Epist.*

* *Laert.*

Archytas to *Dionysius*, Health.

WE all Plato's Friends, have sent Lamiscus and Photides *to re-demand the Man according to your agreement with us: You will do well to consider with what importunity you prevail'd with us to invite* Plato *to you, promising to yield to all things, and to give him liberty to go and come at his pleasure; remember how much you prized his coming, and preferred him before all others: If there hath hapen'd any difference betwixt you, it will befit you to treat him courteously, and restore him safe to us. This if you do, you will do justly, and oblige us.*

† *Dionysius* to excuse himself, and to shew he was not angry with *Plato*, feasted him magnificently, and then sent him home with great Testimonies of Affection: One day amongst the rest he said to him, *I am afraid,* Plato, *you will speak ill of me when you are amongst your friends The Gods forbid,* answered *Plato* smiling, *they should have such scarcity of matter in the Academy, as to be constrained to discourse of you.* *Dionysius* at his departure, desired him to find out whether *Dion* would be much displeased if he should dispose of his Wife to another, there being at that time a report that he did not like his match, and could not live quietly with his Wife. *Plato* In his return came to *Peloponnesus*, at what time the Olympick Games were celebrated; where the Eyes of all the *Grecians* were taken off from the sports, and fixed upon him as the more worthy object: Here he found *Dion* beholding the Exercises, to whom he related what had happened. *Dion* protested to revenge the discourtesie of *Dionysius* towards *Plato*, from which *Plato* earnestly disswaded him: Being

† *Plutarch vit. Dion.*

come home to *Athens*, he wrote to *Dionysius*, and gave him a plain account of every thing, but that concerning *Dion's* Wife, he set it down so darkly, that he alone to whom the Letter was directed, could understand him; letting him know that he had spoken with *Dion* about the business which he knew, and that he would be very much displeased if *Dionysius* did it: So that at that time, because there was great hopes of Reconciliation between them, the Tyrant forbore a while to dispose of his Sister *Arete*, *Dion's* Wife, as soon after, when he saw the Breach irreconcilable, he did, Marrying her against her will to one of his Friends named *Timocrates*. *Dion* thence-forward prepared for War against *Plato's* advice, who endeavoured to disswade him from it, as well for respect of *Dionysius's* good reception of him, as for that *Dion* was well in years; though *Ælian* saith, he put *Dion* upon that War, which *Plutarch* imputes to the instigations of *Speusippus*.

CHAP. X.

His Authority in Civil Affairs.

AT home he lived quietly in the Academy, * not engaging himself in publick affairs, (though he were a person very knowing therein, as his Writings manifest,) because the *Athenians* were accustomed to Laws different from his Sense.

* *Laert.*

† His Fame spreading to the *Arcadians*, and *Thebans*, they sent Ambassadours earnestly to request him to come over to them, not only to instruct their young Men in Philosophy, but which was of higher concernment, to ordain Laws for *Megalopolis*, a City then newly built by the *Arcadians*, upon occasion of the great defeat given them by the *Lacedæmonians*, in the first year of the 103d Olympiad. *Plato* was not a little pleased at this Invitation, but asking the Ambassadours how they stood affected to a parity of Estates, and finding them so averse from it, as not to be by any means induced thereto, he refused to go: but sent *Aristonimus* his familiar friend.

† *Ælian. var. hist. 2. 41.*

The *Cyrenæans* likewise sent to him, desiring him to send them Laws for their City, but he refused, saying, it was difficult to prescribe Laws to Men in Prosperity.

Plutarch ad princip. ineruditi.

Yet to several People upon their Importunities he condescended.

To the *Syracusians* he gave Laws upon the ejection of their King:

To the *Cretans* upon their building of *Magnesia*, he sent Laws digested into twelve Books.

To the *Ilians* he sent *Phormio*; to the *Pyrrheans*, *Mededimus* (his familiar friends) upon the same design.

This is enough to justifie him against those who * accuse him of having written a form of Government, which he could not perswade any to practise, because it was so severe: And that the *Athenians*, who accepted the Laws of *Draco* and *Solon*, derided his.

* *Athan.*

CHAP.

CHAP. XI.

His Vertues and Moral Sentences.

*Laert.
†Suid.

*HE lived single, yet soberly and †chastly, insomuch as in his old Age (in compliance with the vulgar opinion) he Sacrificed to Nature, to expiate the crime of his continence. So constant in his composure and gravity, that a Youth brought up under him, returning to his Parents, and hearing his Father speak aloud, said, *I never found this in* Plato. He eat but once a day, or if the second time, very sparingly; he slept alone, and much discommended the contrary manner of Living. Of his Prudence, Patience, Magnanimity, and other Vertues, there are these instances.

*Plut.

* *Antimachus* a *Colophonian*, and *Niceratus* a *Heracleot*, contending in a Poetick Panegyrick of *Lysander*, the prize was bestowed upon *Niceratus*: *Antimachus* in anger tore his Poem; *Plato*, who at that time was young, and much esteemed *Antimachus* for his Poetry, comforted him, saying, *Ignorance is a Disease proper to the Ignorant, as Blindness to the Blind.*

†Senec. de ira. 3. 12.

† His Servant having offended him, he bad him put off his Coat, and expose his Shoulders to be beaten, intending to have corrected him with his own hand; but perceiving himself to be angry, he stopt his hand, and stood fixt in that posture; a Friend coming in asked him what he was doing, *Punishing an angry Man*, saith he.

*Senec. de ira. 3. 12.

* Another time being displeased at his Servant for some offence, *Do you* (saith he to *Speusippus* (or as *Laertius* to *Xenocrates*) accidentally coming in) *beat this Fellow, for I am angry*. And another time to his Servant he said, *I would beat thee if I were not angry*.

†Val. Max.

†Fearing to exceed the limits of Correction, and thinking it unfit the Master and Servant should be alike faulty.

*Laert.

* *Chabrias* the General being arraigned for his Life, he alone shewed himself on his side, not one of the Citizens else appearing for him. *Crobulus* the Sycophant met him, accompanying *Chabrias* to the Tower, and said unto him, *Do you come to help others, you know not that the poyson of* Socrates *is reserved for you?* Plato answered, *When I fought for my Country, I hazarded my Life, and will now in duty to my Friend.*

†Ælian. var. hist. 4.

† At the Olympick Games, he fell into Company with some Strangers, who knew him not, upon whose affections, he gained much by his affable Conversation, Dining, and spending the whole day with them, not mentioning either the Academy or *Socrates*, only saying, his name was *Plato*. When they came to *Athens*, he entertained them courteously. *Come*, Plato, said the Strangers, *shew us your namesake*, Socrates *his Disciple; bring us to the Academy, recommend us to him, that we may know him.* He smiling a little, as he used, said, *I am the Man*: Whereat they were much amazed, having conversed so familiarly with a Person of that eminence, who used no boasting or ostentation; and shewed, that besides his Philosophical discourse, his ordinary conversation was extreamly winning.

When he went out of the School, he always said, *See (Youths) that you employ your idle hours usefully.*

At a Feast he blamed those that brought in Musicians to hinder Discourse.

Laert.

Seeing a young Man play at Dice, he reproved him; he answered, *What, for so small a matter?* Custom (replies Plato) *is no small thing.*

Laert.

Being demanded, whether there should be any record to Posterity of his Actions, or Sayings, as of others before him? *First*, saith he, *we must get a Name, then many things will follow.*

Laert.

Getting on Horseback, he immediately lighted again, saying, he feared lest he should be carried away ἱππηλασία by a high wilful conceit, a Metaphor taken from a Horse.

Laert.

He advised drunken and angry Men to look in a Glass, and it would make them refrain from those Vices.

Laert.

He affirmed, that to drink to the excess of drunkenness was not allowable at any time, unless upon the festival of that God who gives Wine.

Laert.

Sleep also much displeased him, whence he saith in his Laws, *No Man sleeping is worth any thing.*

Laert.

That Truth is more pleasing to all, than any feigned story, so of Truth he saith, *de legibus*: *Truth, O Guest, is an excellent thing and durable, but to this we are not easily perswaded.*

Val. Max. 4. 1.

Being told, that *Xenocrates* had spoken many unjust things against him, he presently rejected the accusation; the Informer persisting, asked why he would not believe him? He added, it was not probable, that he whom he loved so much, should not love him again. Finally, the other swearing it was thus; he, not to argue him of Perjury, affirmed, that *Xenocrates* would never have said so, but that there was reason for it.

Senec. de ira 1. 16.

He said, *No Wise Man punisheth in respect of the fault past, but in prevention of the future.*

Ælian.

Seeing the *Agrigentines* magnificent in Building, luxurious in Feasting, *These People* (saith he) *build, as if they were to live for ever, and eat as if they were to die instantly.*

Stob.

Hearing a wicked Person speak in the defence of another, *This Man*, saith he, *carries his Heart in his Tongue.*

Stob.

Being told, that some spake ill of him, he answered, *'Tis no matter, I will live so that none shall believe them.*

Stob.

Seeing a Young Man of a good Family, who had waited all his means, sitting at the door of an Inn, feeding upon Bread and Water, he told him, *If you had dined so temperately, you would never have needed to sup so.*

Stob.

To *Antisthenes*, making a long Oration, *You know not*, saith he, *That Discourse is to be measured by the Hearer, not the Speaker.*

Stob.

Seeing a Youth over-bold with his Father, *Young Man*, saith he, *will you undervalue him, who is the cause you over-value your self?*

To one of his Disciples, who took too much care of his Body, he said, *Why do you labour so much in building your own Prison?*

Of a Prisoner Fettered, he said, *That Man is dead in his own Body, he lives in another.*

He said, that *whosoever neglected himself for another, was the most happy of all persons, for he enjoyed neither.*

One *Leo*, an eminent Citizen, being blamed for loud and immoderate clamour in the Senate, *This is,* saith he, *to be a Lyon indeed.*

His Disciples wondring, that *Xenocrates*, severe all his life time, had said something that was pleasant, *Do you wonder* (saith he) *that Roses and Lilies grow among Thorns?*

Laert. vit. Xen.

Xenocrates by reason of his severe Conversation, he advised to Sacrifice to the Graces.

He used to say, Prefer Labour before Idleness, unless you esteem Rust above Brightness.

He exhorted the Young Men to good Life, thus; Observe the different nature of Vertue and Pleasure; the momentany sweetness of the World is immediately followed by eternal Sorrow and Repentance, the short pain of the other by Eternal Pleasure.

He said, that it was a great matter in the education of Youth, to accustom them to take delight in good things; otherwise, he affirmed Pleasure to be the bait of Evil.

He affirms Philosophy to be the true help of the Soul, the rest ornaments; that nothing is more pleasing to a sound Mind, than to speak and hear truth, than which nothing is better or more lasting.

To some, who demanded what kind of possessions were best to be provided for Children: Those (saith he) which fear neither storms, nor violence of Men, nor *Jove* himself.

To *Demonicus* asking his advice concerning the education of his Son : The same care (saith he) that we have of Plants, we must take of our Children ; the one is Labour, the other Pleasure. But we must take heed that in this we be not too secure, in that too vigilant.

To *Philedonus*, who blamed him that he was as studious to learn as to teach, and asked him *how long he meant to be a Disciple ; as long,* saith he, *as I am not ashamed of growing better and wiser,*

Being demanded what difference there is betwixt a Learned Man and an Unlearned, *the same,* saith he, *as betwixt a Phisician and a Patient.*

He said, *Princes had no better Possessions than the familiarities of such Men who could not flatter, that Wisdom is as necessary to a Prince, as the Soul to the Body. That Kingdoms would be most happy, if either Philosophers rule, or the Rulers were inspired with Philosophy, for nothing is more pernicious than Power and Arrogance accompanied with Ignorance. That Subjects ought to be such as Princes seem to be.* That *a Magistrate is to be esteemed a publick, not a private good. That not a part of the Common-wealth, but the whole ought to be principally regarded.*

Plut. Sympos. 6. præfat. Ælian. var. hist.

Being desirous to take off *Timotheus* Son of *Conon*, General of the *Athenians*, from sumptuous Military Feasts; he invited him into the Academy to a plain moderate Supper, such as quiet pleasing sleeps succeed with a good temper of Body. The next day *Timotheus* observing the difference, said, They who feasted with *Plato*, were the better for it the next day ; and meeting *Plato*, said unto him ; *Your Supper*, Plato, *is as pleasant the next morning as over night,* alluding to the excellent discourse, that had past at that time.

Hence appears the truth of the Poet's saying, who being derided for acting a Tragedy, none being present but *Plato*, answered, *but this one Person is more than all the* Athenians *besides.*

CHAP. XII.

His Will and Death.

THus continuing a single Life to his End, not having any Heirs of his own, he bequeathed his Estate to young *Adimantus,* (probably the Son of *Adimantus*, his second Brother) by his Will; thus recited by *Laertius.*

These things Plato *hath bequeathed and disposed, The Eniphistidæan Grounds bordering North, on the high-way from the Cephisian Temple, South on the Heracleum of the Eniphistiades, East on* Archestratus *the Phrearian, West* Philip *the Cholidian, this let it not be lawful for any Man to sell or alienate, but let young* Adimantus *be possessor thereof in as full and ample manner as is possible. And likewise the* Enerisiadæan *Farm which I bought of* Callimachus, *adjoining on the North to* Eurymedon *the Myrrinusian, on the South to* Demostratus Xypeteron, *on the East to* Eurymedon *the Myrrinusian, on the West to* Cephissus; *Three Minæ of Silver; a Golden Cup weighing* 160, *a Ring of Gold, and an ear-ring of Gold, both together weighing four drachms and three oboli;* Euclid *the Stone-cutter oweth me three Minæ,* Diana *I remit freely, I leave Servants,* Ticho, Biêtas, Apolloniades, Dionysius *Goods, whereof* Demetrius *keepeth an Inventory. I owe no Man any thing, Executors,* Sosthenes, Speusippus, Demetrius, Hegias, Eurimedon, Callimachus, Thrasippus.

If this Will be not forged, that of *Apuleius* is false, who averrs *the Patrimony he left was a little Orchard adjoyning to the Academy, two servants, and a Cup wherein he supplicated to the Gods; Gold no more than he wore in his Ear when he was a Boy, an Emblem of his Nobility.*

Dogm. Plat.

He died on the 13th year of the Reign of *Philip*, King of *Macedon*, in the first of the 108th Olympiad; the 81st (according to *Hermippus, Cicero, Seneca,* and others) of his Age (not as *Athenæus* the 82.) which number he compleated exactly, dying that very day whereon he was born ; For which reason the Magi at *Athens* sacrificed to him, as conceiving him more than Man, who fulfilled the most perfect number, nine multiplied into it self.

Laert.

He died only of Age, which *Seneca* ascribes to his Temperance and Diligence ; *Hermippus* saith, at a Nuptial Feast; *Cicero* saith, as he was writing; they therefore who affirm he dyed (as *Pherecydes*) of Lice, do him much Injury ; upon his Tomb these Epitaphs.

Epist. 1. 58

Laert.

The first.

Whose Temperance and Justice all envies,
The fam'd Aristocles *here buried lies ;*
If Wisdom any with renown indued,
Here was it 'most, by envy not pursued.

The

The second.

Earth in her bosom Plato's body hides,
His Soul amongst the deathless Gods resides.
Aristo's Son whose Fame to Strangers spread,
Made them admire the sacred life he lead.

Another later.

Eagle, why art thou percht upon this Stone,
And gazest thence on some Gods starry throne?
I Plato's Soul to Heaven flown represent,
His Body buried in this Monument.

Phavorinus saith, that *Mithridates* the Persian set up *Plato's* Statue in the Academy with this Inscription;

MITHRIDATES SON OF RHODOBATES, THE PERSIAN, DEDICATED THIS IMAGE OF PLATO, MADE BY SILANION TO THE MUSES.

CHAP. XIII.

His Disciples and Friends.

THE Fame of this School attracted Disciples from all parts: Of whom were

Speusippus an Athenian, *Plato's* Sisters Son, whom he said reformed by the Example of his own Life.

Xenocrates a Chalcedonian, *Plato's* beloved Disciple, an imitator of his gravity and magnanimity: *Athenæus* saith, he was first the only Disciple of *Æschines*, and relief of his poverty, seduced from him by *Plato*.

Aristotle a Stagirite, whom *Plato* used to call a Colt, foreseeing that he would ungratefully oppose him, as a Colt, having suckt, kicks at his Dam: *Xenocrates* was flow, *Aristotle* quick in extremity, whence *Plato* said of them, What an Ass have I, and what a Horse to yoak together!

Philippus, an *Opuntian*, who transcribed *Plato's* Laws in Wax; to him some ascribe *Epinomis*.

Hestiæus a Perinthian.

Dion a Syracusian, whom *Plato* exceedingly affected, as is evident from his Epigrams; seeing him in the height of honour, all Mens Eyes fixt upon his noble Actions, he advised him to take heed of that vice, which makes Men care only to please themselves; a consequent of Solitude.

Amyclus (or as *Ælian, Amyclas*) a Heracleote. *See also Stob. lib. 13.*
* *Erastus* and *Coriscus* Scepsians.
Temilaus a Cyzicene.
Euæmon a Lampsacene.
Pithon, whom *Aristotle* calls *Paron*, and *Heraclides* Ænians.
Hippothales and *Callippus*, Athenians.
Demetrius of *Amphipolis*.
Heraclides of *Pontus*,

Two Women, *Lasthenia* a Mantinean, and *Axiothia* a Phliasian, who went habited like a Man.

Theophrastus, as some affirm.

Orators, *Hyperides, Lycurgus, Demosthenes.* *Lycurgus* (saith *Philistus*) was a person of great parts, and did many remarkable things, which none could perform, who had not been *Plato's* Auditor. *Demosthenes*, when he fled from *Antipater*, said to *Archias*, who counselled him to put himself into his Hands, upon promise to save his Life; far be it from me to choose rather to live ill, than to die well, having heard *Xenocrates* and *Plato* dispute of the Souls immortality.

Menesistratus a Thasian.

To these reckoned by *Laertius*, add *Aristides*, a Locrian.

Eudoxus a Gnidian, who at a great Feast made by *Plato*, first found out the manner of sitting in a circular form.

Hermodorus, of whom the Proverb, *Hermodorus traffiques in Words*. *Zenob.*

Heracleodorus, to whom *Demosthenus* writing, reprehends him, that having heard *Plato*, he neglected good Arts, and lived disorderly.

† *Euphrates*, who lived with *Perdiccas* King of *Macedonia*, in so great favour, that he in a manner shared command with him. † *Athen. deipn. lib. 11.*

Euagon of *Lampsacum.*
Timæus of *Cyzicum.* *Athen. Ibid.*
Chæron of *Pellene* *Athen. Ibid.*
Athen. Ibid.

* *Isocrates* the Oratour, with whom *Plato* was very intimate: *Praxiphanes* published a discourse they had together, in a Field of *Plato's* who at that time entertained *Isocrates* as a Guest. * *Laert.*

Aster, Phædrus, Alexis, Agato, young Men, whom *Plato* particularly affected, as appears by his Epigrams.

† *Aristonymus, Phormio, Mededimus,* his familiar Friends, already mentioned. † *Cap. 10.*

CHAP. XIV.

His Emulators and Detractors.

AS *Plato's* eminent Learning gained on one side many Disciples and Admirers, so on the other side, it procured him many Emulators, especially amongst his fellow Disciples, the followers of *Socrates*; amongst these,

Xenophon was exceedingly disaffected towards him; they emulated each other, and writ both upon one Subject, a Symposium; *Socrates* his Apology, Moral Commentaries: One writ of a Common-wealth, the other, the Institution of *Cyrus*: which Book * *Plato* notes as commentitious, affirming *Cyrus* not to have been such a person as is there exprest. Though both writ much concerning *Socrates*, yet neither makes mention of the other, except *Xenophon* once of *Plato*, in the third of his Commentaries. * *In Legib.*

Antisthenes being about to recite something that he had written, desired *Plato* to be present; *Plato* demanding what he meant to recite, he answered, that to contradict is not Lawful.

How

How come you, faith *Plato*, to write upon that Subject? And thereupon demonstrating that he contradicted himself, *Antisthenes* writ a Dialogue against him entituled *Satho*.

Aristippus was at difference with him, for which reason (in *Phædone*) he covertly reproves *Aristippus*, that being near at *Ægina* when *Socrates* died, he came not to him. He writ a Book of the Luxury of the Antients; some ascribe the amatory Epigrams to his Invention, his design in that Treatise being to detract from eminent persons, amongst the rest from *Socrates* his Master, and *Plato* and *Xenophon* his fellow-Disciples.

Æschines and *Plato* also disagreed: Some affirm, that when *Plato* was in favour with *Dionysius*, *Æschines* came thither very poor, and was despised by *Plato*, but kindly entertained by *Aristippus*: But the Epistle of *Æschines* put forth by *Allatius*, expresseth the contrary. The discourse which *Plato* relates, betwixt *Crito* and *Socrates* in Prison, *Idomeneus* saith, was betwixt *Socrates* and *Æschines*; by *Plato*, out of ill will to *Æschines*, attributed to *Crito*. But of *Æschines* he makes not any mention in all his Works, except twice slightly; once in *Phædone*, where he names him amongst the persons present at *Socrates* his Death; and again in his Apology, speaking of *Lysanius*'s Father.

Phædo, if we credit the detractions of *Athenæus*, was so much maligned by *Plato*, as that he was about to frame an Indictment against him, to reduce him to that condition of Servitude, out of which, by the procurement of *Socrates*, he had been redeemed; but his design being discovered, he gave it over. Besides his Condisciples,

Diogenes the *Cynick* derided his Laws, and assertion of Ideas; concerning the first, he asked if he were writing Laws; *Plato* assented. Have you not written already a Commonwealth, faith *Diogenes*? Yes, answered *Plato*. Had that Common-wealth Laws, faith *Diogenes*? *Plato* affirmed it had. Then replied *Diogenes*, what need you write new? [a] Another time, *Diogenes* saying, he could see the things of the World, but not Ideas: *Plato* answered, that is no wonder, for you have, and use those eyes, which behold such things: But the mind, which only can see the other, you use not.

[b] *Molon*, in detraction from him, said, *It was not strange, Dionysius should be at Corinth, but that Plato should be at Sicily*.

From these private differences, arose many scandalous imputations, forged and spread abroad by such as envied or maligned him: as [c] That he profest one thing and practised another: [d] That he loved inordinately *After*, *Dion*, *Phædrus*, *Alexis*, *Agatho*, and *Archeanassa*, a Curtesan of *Colopho*: [e] That he was a Calumniator, envious, proud, a gluttonous lover of Figgs: [f] That he was the worst of Philosophers, a parasite to Tyrants, and many other accusations alike improbable: From these the Comick Poets and others took liberty to abuse him; [g] *Theopompus* in *Autochare*.

— *for one is none,*
And two (as Plato *holds) is hardly one.*

[a] Laert. vit. Diog.
[b] Laert.
[c] Senec. 1.
[d] Laert.
[e] Athen.
[f] Tretz. Chiliad.
[g] Laert.

Anaxandrides in *Theseo*;

When Olives he (live Plato*) doth devour;*

Timon.

As Plato *feigns, in framing* † *Wonders skill'd.* † So.

Alexis *in* Meropide,

Aptly thou comest, I walking round could meet
(Like Plato*) nothing wise; but tir'd my feet.*

And in Achilione,

Thou speak'st of things thou understandst not, go
To Plato, *Thence Nile and Onions know.*

Amph. *In* Amphicrate,

What good from hence you may expect to rise,
I can no more than Plato's *good comprise;*

And in Dexidemide,

Plato, *thou nothing know'st, but how*
To look severe, and knit the Brow,

Cratylus *in* Pseudobolymæo,

A Man thou art, and hast a Soul, but this
With Plato *not sure, but Opinion is.*

Alexis *in* Olympiodoro.

My Body Mortal is grown dry,
My Soul turn'd air that cannot die;
Taught Plato *this Philosophy?*

And *in* Parasito.

Or thou with Plato *ravest alone.*

[h] *Ephippus* in *Naufrago* objects to *Plato* and some Friends of his, *that corrupted with Mony they detracted from many persons; that they went proudly habited, and they took more care of their outward Beauty, than the most Luxurious*: See *Athenæus*, *Lib.* 11.

[h] Athen. lib. 11.

CHAP. XV.

His Writings.

THe Writings of *Plato* are by way of Dialogue; of the Invention of Dialogue we have † already spoken; now of the Nature thereof.

† Chap.

A Dialogue is composed of questions and answers Philosophical or Political, aptly expressing the Characters of those persons that are the speakers in an elegant Stile; Dialectick is the Art of Discourse, whereby we confirm or confute any thing by Questions and Answers of the Disputants.

Of *Platonick* discourse there are two kinds, *Hyphegetick*, and *Exegetick*, subscribed thus,

Hyphegetick {
  Theoretick. { *Logick.*
                  Physick.
  Practick.   { *Ethick.*
                  Politick.
}

Exegetick {
  Gymnastick, { *Majeutick.*
                  Physick.
  Agonistick, { *Endeictick.*
                  Anatreptick.
}

We know there are other divisions of Dialogues; as into Dramatick Narrative mixt: But that division is more proper to Tragedy than to Philosophy.

Of *Plato*'s Dialogues are

Physick. { *Timæus.*

Logick, { The *Politick.*
            Cratylus.
            Parmenides.
            The *Sophist.*

Ethick. { Apology of *Socrates.*
            Crito.
            Phædo.
            Phædrus.
            Symposium.
            Menexemus.
            Clitophon.
            Epistles.
            Philebus.
            Hipparchus.
            The *Rivals.*

Politick, { The *Commonwealth.*
              The *Laws.*
              Minos.
              Epinomis.
              The *Atlantick.*

Majeutick, { *Alcibiades.*
               Theages.
               Lysis.
               Laches.

Pirastick, { *Euthyphron.*
               Menon.
               Ion.
               Charmides.
               Theætetus.

Endeictick, { *Protagoras.*

Anatreptick, { *Euthydemus.*
                 Hippias 1.
                 Hippias 2.
                 Gorgias 1.
                 Gorgias 2.

It being much controverted (continueth *Laertius*) whether *Plato* doth dogmatize, some affirming, others denying it, it will be necessary to say something thereupon. Δογματίζειν to dogmatize is to impose a Doctrine, as νομοθετειν to impose a Law, a Doctrine is taken two ways, either for that which is decreed, or the Decree it self; that which is decreed is a Proposition, the Decree it self an Imposition. *Plato* expounds those things which he conceiveth true: Confutes those which are false, suspends his opinion in those which are doubtful. He asserts what he conceiveth true under one of these four Persons, *Socrates*, *Timæus*, an *Athenian* Guest, an *Ælian* Guest; The Guests are not as some conceive, *Plato* and *Parmenides*, but imagined nameless Persons, as what *Socrates*, *Timæus* speak, are the Decrees of *Plato*. Those whom he argueth of falsehood are *Thrasymachus*, *Callicles*, *Polus*, *Gorgias*, *Protagoras*, *Hippias*, *Euthydemus*, and the like.

In Argument he often used Induction of both sorts. Induction is a discourse, which from certain truths collects, and inferreth a truth like to those: Of Induction there are two kinds, one from Contraries, another from Consequents: From Contraries, as when he who is questioned, answereth in all things contrary to himself, as thus; My Father is either the same with yours, or not the same; if therefore thy Father be not the same with mine, he is not my Father: And again, if a Man be not a living Creature, he is Stone, Wood, or the like; but he is neither Stone nor Wood, for he hath a Soul, and moveth himself, therefore he is a living Creature; if a living Creature, a Dog and an Ox. This kind of Induction by Contraries, serves not for assertion, but confutation: Inductions by Consequents is two-fold; one, when a singular being sought, is concluded from a singular, the first proper to Oratours, the second to Logicians; as in the first, the question is, Whether such an one were a Murtherer, it is proved from his being Bloody at the same time. This Induction is Rhetorical, for Rhetorick is conversant in singulars, not in universals; it inquireth not after Justice, but after the several parts thereof: The other is Dialectick, whereby Universals are concluded from Singulars, as in this question; Whether the Soul be immortal, and whether the living are of the dead, which is demonstrated in his Book of the Soul, by a general Maxim, that contraries proceed from contraries, this being general, is proved by singulars, as waking succeeds sleeping, the greater the lesser, and so on the contrary. Thus he useth to confirm what he asserts.

Thrasilus saith, he published his Dialogues according to the tragick Tetralogy: His genuine Dialogues are fifty six, his Commonwealth divided into ten, they make nine Tetralogies, reckoning his Common-wealth one Book, his Laws another. The first Tetralogy hath a common Subject, declaring what is the proper Life of a Philosopher: every Book hath a two-fold Title; one from the Principal Person, the other from the Subject.

The first
- *Euthypron*, or of Piety : *Piraſtick*.
- *Socrates* his Apology : *Ethick*.
- *Crito*, or of that which is to be done : *Ethick*.
- *Phædo*, or of the Soul : *Ethick*.

The second
- *Cratylus*, or, of right naming : *Logick*.
- *Theætetus*, or, of Science : *Piraſtick*.
- *The Sophiſt*, or, of Ens : *Logick*.
- *The Politick*, or, of a Kingdom : *Logick*.

The third
- *Parmenides*, or, of Idea's : *Logick*.
- *Philebus*, or, of Pleaſure : *Ethick*.
- *The Sympoſium*, or, of Good : *Ethick*.
- *Phædrus*, or, of Love : *Ethick*:

The fourth
- *Alcibiades* 1. or, of Humane Nature : *Majeutick*.
- *Alcibiades* 2. or, of Prayer : *Majeutick*.
- *Hipparchus*, or, the Covetous : *Ethick*.
- *The Rivals*, or, of Philoſophy : *Ethick*.

The fifth
- *Theages*, or of Philoſophy : *Majeutick*.
- *Charmides*, or, of Temperance : *Piraſtick*.
- *Laches*, or, of Fortitude : *Majeutick*.
- *Myſis*, or, of Friendſhip : *Majeutick*.

The sixth
- *Euthydemus*, or, the Litigious : *Anatreptick*.
- *Protagoras*, or, the Sophiſt : *Endeictick*.
- *Gorgias*, or, of Rhetorick : *Anatreptick*.
- *Menon*, or, of Vertue : *Piraſtick*.

The seventh
- *Hippias*, firſt, or, of Honeſt : *Anatreptick*.
- *Hippias*, ſecond, or, of Falſe : *Anatreptick*.
- *Io* : or, of Ilias : *Piraſtick*.
- *Menexenus*, or, the Funeral Oration. *Ethick*.

The eighth
- *Clitophon*, or, the Exhortation : *Moral*.
- *The Commonwealth*, or, of Juſt : *Politick*.
- *Timæus*, or, of Nature : *Phyſick*.
- *Critias*, or, the Atlantick : *Ethick*.

The ninth
- *Minos*, or, of Law : *Politick*.
- *Laws*, or, of Legiſlation : *Politick*.
- *Epinomis*, or, the Nocturnal Convention ; or, the Philoſophers : *Politick*.
- *Epiſtles* thirteen, Ethick, in the Inſcriptions whereof he uſeth τῶ διάγειν. *Cleon.* χαίρει. to *Ariſtodemus* one ; to *Architas* two ; to *Dionyſius* four ; to *Hermias*, *Eraſtus*, and *Coriſcus* one ; to *Leodamus* one ; to *Dion* one ; to *Dion's* Friends two. Thus *Thraſilaus*.

Others, of whom is *Ariſtophanes* the Grammarian, reduce his Dialogues to Trilogies, placing in

The first
- The Common-wealth.
- Timæus.
- Critias.

The second
- The Sophiſter.
- The Politick.
- Cratylus.

The third.
- Laws.
- Minos.
- Epinomis.

The fourth.
- Theætetus.
- Euthyphron.
- Apology.

The fifth
- Crito,
- Phædo.
- Epiſtles. The reſt ſingle without order.

Some, as we said, begin with *Alcibiades Major*, others from *Theages*, others from *Euthyphron*, others from *Clitiphon*, others from *Timæus*, others from *Phædrus* (which they say was the first Dialogue he wrote, as the Subject it self seemeth to confirm, which favours of Youth; and therefore *Dicearchus* condmns it as too light: to which Censure * *Cicero* agreeth, as conceiving, he ascribed too great a power to Love) others begin with *Theætetus*, many with his Apology.

* Cicer. Tusc. quæst. 2.

He mentions not himself in all his Writings, except once in his *Phædo*, and another time in his Apology for *Socrates*. At the recital of his *Phædo*, all but *Aristotle* rose, and went away. The efficacy of that Dialogue which treats of the Immortality of the Soul, is evident from *Cleombrotus* of *Ambracia*, who, as soon as he had read it was so disaffected to Life, that he threw himself from a high Wall into the Sea; upon whom thus † *Callimachus*,

† *Epigr.*

Cleombrotus cries out, farewell this light,
And headlong throws himself int' endless night:
Not that he ought had done, deserving death,
But Plato *read, and weary grew of Breath:*

The Dialogues generally noted as spurious (not to say any thing of his *Epinomis*, tho' some ascribe it to *Philippus* the *Opuntian*) are these,

Midon, or the Horse-courser,.
Erixias, or *Erasistratus*.
Alcyon.
Acephali, or the *Sisyphi*.
Axiochus.
Phæaces.
Demodochus.
Chelidon,
The *seventh*.
Epimenides.

Of these *Alcion* is ascribed by *Phavorinus* to *Leon*.

His Style, *Aristotle* saith, is betwixt Prose and Verse. He useth variety of Names, that his Works may not easily be understood by the Unlearned. He conceiveth Wisdom properly to be of Intellectual things, Knowledge of real Beings conversant about God, and the Soul separate from the Body. Properly, he calleth *Philosophy Wisdom*, being the appetition of Divine *Knowledge*; but, *commonly* he calleth all Skill Knowledge, as an Artificer, a Wise Man. He likewise used the same Names in divers significations; φαῦλος, which properly signifies Evil, he useth for of simple; as *Euripides* in his *Lycimnius* of *Hercules*,

φαῦλον ἄκομψον τὰ μέγις ἀγαθον.

The same words *Plato* sometimes takes for *Honest*, sometimes for *Little*. He likewise useth divers names to signifie the same thing: Idea he useth both for Species and Genus; Exemplar, both Principle and Cause. Sometimes he useth contrary expressions to signifie the same thing; Sensible he calleth a Being and no Being; a Being as having been produced; no Being in respect of its continual Mutation. Idea, neither Moveable nor Permanent, the same both one and many. The like he useth often in other things.

The method of his Discourse is three-fold: first, to declare what that is which is taught; then for what reason it is asserted, whether as a principal cause, or as a comparison, and whether to defend the Tenent, or oppugn the contrary. Thirdly, whether it be rightly said.

The marks which he usually affixed to his Writings, are these,

Χ denotes *Platonick* Words and Figures.
διπλῆ, Doctrines and Opinions proper to *Plato*.
περιεστιγμένον, choice Expressions.
διπλῆ περιεστιδμήνη, Corrections.
ὀβελὸς περιεστιγμένος, Things Superfluous.
ἀντισίγμα περιεστιγμένον, Double sigification or use.
κεραύνιον, Philosophical Institution.
ἀστερίσκος, Agreement of Opinions.
ὀβελὸς, Improbation. Hithrto *Laertius*.

There are two Epistles under *Plato*'s name, besides those in in his Works already mentioned, one in *Laertius* his Life of *Architas*.

Plato *to* Architas. εὐπράττειν.

THE *Commentaries which came from you, we received with extraordinary content, infinitely admiring the Writer, who appears to us a person worthy of those ancient predecessors; for those Men are said to be* Myræans *of those* Trojans, *which were Banished in the time of* Laomedon, *good Men, as Tradition speaks them. Those Commentaries of mine, concerning which you write, are not yet Polished; however, as they are, I have sent them to you, in the keeping of them we agree both, so as I need not give you any directions. Farewell,*

Another Published by *Leo Allatius* amongst the *Socratick* Epistles.

I had not any of those things to send to Syracuse *which* Architas *desired to receive by you; as soon as possible I will send to you. Philophy hath wrought in me I know not whether good or bad, a hatred of conversing with many Persons, justly, I think, since they err in all kind of Folly, as well in private as publick Affairs; but if unjustly, yet known I can hardly live and breath otherwise. For this reason I have fled out of the City, as out of a Den of Wild Beasts, living not far from the* Epheftiades, *and the places thereabouts. I now see, that* Timon *hated not Men, he could not affect Beasts, therefore he lived alone by himself, perhaps not without danger. Take this as you please; my resolution is to live far from the City, now and for ever hereafter, as long as God shall grant me Life.*

In Poesie he writ
Dithyrambs.
An *Epick Poem,*
Four *Tragedies,* all which (as we said) he Burned.

The *Atlantick Story,* of which thus Plutarch; Solon *began the Atlantick Story (which he had learnt of the Priests of* Sais, *very proper for the* Athenians*)* but gave it over by reason of his Old Age, and the largeness of the Work. Plato took the same Argument, as a wast piece of fertile Ground fallen to him by hereditary right; He manured it, refined it, enclosed it with large Walls, Porches, and Galleries, such as never any Fable, or Poem had before; but because he underoook it late, he was prevented by Death. The more things written delight, the more their not being perfected is   For as the Athenian City left the Temple of Jupiter; so Plato's *Wisdom amongst many excellent Writings, left the Atlantick alone imperfect.*

Epigrams, of which these are extant in *Laertius* and the Anthology.

Upon one Named *After.*

* *Laert.Anthol.* 3. 6, 27.

* The Stars, my Star, thou viewest; Heav'n I would be,
That I with thousand eyes might gaze on thee.

Upon his Death.

† *Laert.*

† A Phospher 'mongst the Living, late wert thou,
But Shin'st among the Dead a Hesper now.

Epitaph on *Dion,* Engraved on his Tomb at *Syracuse.*

† *Laert.Anthol.* 4. 33, 26.

* Old Hecuba the Trojan *Matron's* years
Were interwoven by the Fates with Tears;
But thee with blooming hopes my Dion deckt,
God's did a Trophy of their Power erect.
Thy honour'd Reliques in their Country rest,
Ah Dion! whose Love rages in my Breast.

On *Alexis.*

† *Laert. Antol.* 3. 33, 44.

† Fair is Alexis, I no sooner said,
When every one his eyes that way convey'd:
My Soul (as when some Dog a Bone we show,
Who snatcheth it) lost we not Phædrus so?

On *Archæanassa.*

* *Laert.*

* To Archæ'nassa, on whose furrow'd Brow
Love sits in Triumph, I my Service vow;
If her declining Graces shine so bright,
What flames felt you who saw her noon of light?

On *Agathon.*

My Soul, when I kiss'd Agathon, did start
Up to my Lip, just ready to depart.

‡ *Laert.*

To *Xantippe.*

† An Apple I (Love's Emblem) at thee throw,
Thou in exchange thy Virgin-zone bestow.

If thou refuse my Sute, yet read in this,
How short thy years, how frail thy Beauty is.
I cast the Apple, loving those love thee,
* Xantippe yield, for soon both old will be.   * *Anthol.*

† On the *Eretrians* vanquish'd by the *Persians.*   † *Herod. lib.*6.

* We in Eubœa born Eretrians are   * *Laert.*
Buried in Susa from our Country far.

Venus and the *Muses.*

† Virgins (said Venus to the Muses) pay   † *Laert.*
Homage to us, or Love shall wound your hearts:
The Muses answer'd, take these Toys away,
Our Breasts are proof against his childish darts.

Fortune Exchang'd.

* One finding Gold, in change, the Halter quits,   * *Laert. Anthol.*
Missing his Gold, 'tother the Halter knits.   84. 1.

On *Sappho.*

† He, who believes the Muses Nine, mistakes,   † *Ath.* 1. 67,
For Lesbian Sappho ten their number makes.   13.

Time.

* Time all things brings to pass, a change creates   * *Anth.*1. 19.
In Names, in Forms, in Nations and in States.

Death.

† That is a Plough-man's Grave, a Sailor's this;   † *Anthol.* 3.
To Sea and Land alike Death common is.   22, 3.

On one Ship-wreck'd.

* The cruel Sea, which took my Life away,   * *Anth.*3.22,6.
Forbore to strip me of my last Array:
From this a Covetous Man did not refrain,
Acting a Crime so great for so small gain;
But let him wear it to the Shades, and there
Before great Pluto in my Cloaths appear.

Another.

† Safely (O Sailors) press the Land, and wave   † *Anth.*3.22,7.
Yet know, ye pass a Ship-wreck'd person's Grave.

On the Statue of *Venus.*

* Paphian Cythera, swimming cross the Main,   * *Anth.*4.12.8.
To Gnidas came her Statue there to see.
And from on high, surveying round the Plain
Where could Praxiteles me spy? (saith she)
He saw not what's forbidden mortal Eyes,
'Twas Mars's Steel that Venus did incize.

Another.

† Not carv'd by Steel, or Praxitele's fam'd hand: † *Anth.*4.12.9.
Thus naked before the Judges didst thou stand.

Love Sleeping.

* Within the covert of a shady Grove   * *Anth.* 4. 12
We saw the little red-cheek'd God of Love.   19.
He had nor Bow nor Quiver, those among

The

The Neighbouring Trees upon a Bough were
Upon a Bank of tender Rose-buds laid (hung:
He (smiling) slept; Bees with their noise invade
His Rest, and on his lips their Honey made.

Pan Piping.

* Anth. 4. 12, 74.

* Dwell awful silence on the shady Hills,
Among the bleating Flocks, and purling rills,
When Pan the Reed doth to his Lip apply,
Inspiring it with Sacred Harmony,
Hydriads, and Hamadryads at that sound,
In a well order'd measure beat the Ground.

On the Image of a Satyr in a Fountain, and Love Sleeping.

† Anth. 4. 12, 96.

† A skilful hand this Satyr made so near
To Life, that only Breath is wanting here:
I am attendant to the Nymphs; before
I fill'd out purple Wine, now Water pour;
Who ere thou art com'st nigh, tread softly, lest
You waken Love out of his pleasing rest.

Another.

* Anth. 4. 12, 97.

* On Horned Lyæus I attend,
And pour the streams these Nayads lend,
Whose noise Love's slumber doth befriend.

Another.

† Anth. 4. 12, 102.

* This Satyr Diodorus did not make,
But charm asleep; if prick'd he will awake.

On a Seal.

* Anth. 4. 18, 6.

* Five Oxen grazing in a flowry Mead,
A Jasper Seal done to the Life doth hold,
The little Herd away long since had fled,
We'rt not inclos'd within a pale of Gold.

THE
DOCTRINE
OF
PLATO.
Delivered by
ALCINOUS.

CHAP. I.

Of PHILOSOPHY, and how a Philosopher must be Qualified.

SUCH a Summary as this may be given of the Doctrine of *Plato*. Philosophy is the desire of Wisdom, or solution of the Soul from the Body, and a Conversion to those things, which are true and perceptible by intellect. *Wisdom* σοφία, is the Science of things Divine and Humane. A *Philosopher* is he who takes denomination from Philosophy, as a Musician from Musick. He who is to be a Philosopher, must be thus qualified; First, he must have a Natural Capacity of all such Learning as is able to fit and bring him to the knowledge of that Essence which is perceptible by Intellect, not of that which is in continual fluxion or mutation. Then he must have a natural Affection to Truth, and an aversion from receiving Falshood, and besides this, Temperate in a manner by Nature; for those parts which use to be transported with Passions, he must have reduced to Obedience by Nature. For whosoever hath once embraced those Disciplines which are conversant in consideration of such things as truly exist, and hath addicted all his study thereunto, little valueth corporeal pleasure. Moreover, a Philosopher must have a Liberal Mind, for the estimation of mean things is contrary to a Man who intended to contemplate the truth of things. Likewise he must naturally love Justice, for he must be studious of Truth, Temperance, and Liberality. He must also have an accute Apprehension, and a good Memory, for these inform a Philosopher; those gifts of Nature, if improved by Discipline and Education, make a Man perfect in Vertue, but neglected are the cause of the worst ills. These *Plato* used to call by the same Names with the Virtues, *Temperance, Fortitude,* and *Justice.*

CHAP.

CHAP. II.

That Contemplation is to be preferred before Action.

Whereas Life is twofold, *Contemplative* and *Active*, the chief Office of the Contemplative consisteth in the knowledge of truth, as of the Active, in the practice of those things which are dictated by Reason. Hence the contemplative Life is first, after which as necessary followeth the Active. That it is so, may easily be proved thus. Contemplation is an Office of the Intellect in the understanding of Intelligibles: Action is an operation of the rational Soul, performed by mediation and service of the Body. For the Soul, when it contemplateth the Divinity and the notions thereof, is said to be best affected. This Affection is called φρόνησις *Wisdom*, which is nothing else but an assimulation to the Deity. This therefore ought to be esteemed the first and principal, as being most expetible and proper to Man; for there are no impediments that can hinder it from being within our power, and it is cause of our proposed end. But Active Life, and the practice thereof, chiefly making use of the mediation of the Body, are many times obstructed; Whereof those things which the contemplative Life considers in order to the Reformation of the Manners of Men, a Philosopher, as often as necessity requireth, shall transfer to action. Then shall a good Man apply himself to the administration of Civil Affairs, when he seeth them ill managed by others. He must look upon the Leading of an Army, Administration of Justice and Embassies, as things necessary. The Institution of Laws, the compressure of Seditions, Education of Youth in Discipline, are the chiefest, and, among those things which relate to Action of greatest consequence. Hence is it manifest, that a Philosopher must not only be perseverant in Contemplation, but also cherish and increase it, sometimes giving himself to Action as an Attendant upon Contemplation.

CHAP. III.

The three parts of Philosophy.

The Study of a Philoper seemeth according to *Plato* to be conversant chiefly in three things, in the *Contemplation* and Knowledge of of things, in the Practice of Vertue, and in *Disputation*. The Science of things that are, is called *Theoretick*; of those which pertain to Action, *Practick*; the disputative part *Dialectick*.

Dialectick is divided into *Division, Definition, Induction* and *Syllogism*; *Syllogism* into the *Apodeictick*, which concerneth necessary ratiocination; and *Rhetorical*, which concerneth *Enthymeme*, called an imperfect ratiocination; and lastly into *Sophisms*. This the Philosopher must look upon, not as the chiefest but a necessary part.

Of *Practick* Philosophy, one part is conversant about *Manners*, another orders *Families*, the last takes care of a *Common-wealth*. The first called *Ethick*, the second *Oeconomick*, the third, *Politick*.

Of *Theoretick* Philosopy, one part enquires into things Immutable and Divine, and the first causes of things; this is called *Theology*; another the Motion of the Stars, the Revolution and Restitution of Cœlestial Bodies, and the Constitution of the World. This is called *Physick*. That whereby we enquire Geometrically, and those other Disciplines which are called μαθήματα, is termed *Mathematick*.

Philosophy being thus divided, we must first, according to *Plato*, speak of the *Dialectick* part, and in that, first of the *Judiciary*.

CHAP. IV.

DIALECTICK.

Of the Judiciary part.

Whereas there is something that judgeth, something which is judged, it is necessary also that there be something which is made of both these, properly called *Judgment*. This Judgment may not unfitly be termed Judiciary, but more commonly that which Judgeth. This is twofold; one, *from which*, another *by which* judgment is made. That is Intellect; this the natural Organ accommodated for Judgment; primarily of *true* things; secondarily of *false*; neither is it any thing but natural reason. To explain this more fully, of things which are, a Philosopher who judgeth the things themselves, may he called a *Judge*; reason likewise is a *Judge*, by which Truth is judged, which even now we called an Organ,

Reason is twofold, one *incomprehensible* and true; the other is *never deceived* in the knowledge of those things which are. The first is in the power of God, not of Man; the second in that of Man also. This likewise is twofold, the first *Science*, and Scientifick reason; the second *Opinion*. The first hath *Certitude*, and *Stability*, as being conversant in things certain and stable. The second *similitude of truth* and *opinion*, as being conversant in things subject to mutation. Of Science in Intelligibles, and Opinion in sensibles, the Principles are *Intellection* and *Sense*.

Sense is a passion of the Soul by the mediation of the Body, first, declaring a passive faculty; when through the Organs of Sense, the Species of things are impressed in the Soul, so, as they are not defaced by time, but remain firm and lasting, the conservation thereof is called *Memory*.

Opinion is the Conjunction of Memory and Sense; for, when some object occurreth, which can first move the Sense, thereby Sense is effected in us, and by Sense, the Memory. Then again is the same thing objected to our Sense, we joyn the precedent with the consequent Sense, and now say within our selves, *Socrates*, a Horse, Fire, and the like: this is termed opinion, when we joyn the precedent Memory with the late Sense; when these agree within themselves, it is a *true opinion*, if they disagree, a *false*; for, if a man, having the species of *Socrates* in his memory, meet with *Plato*, and think, by reason of some likeness betwixt

twixt them, he hath met *Socrates* again, and afterwards joyn the senfe of *Plato*, which he took, as it were, from *Socrates*, with the memory which he preferved of *Socrates*, there will arife a falfe Opinion.

That wherein fenfe and memory are formed, *Plato* compareth to *a Tablet of Wax*, but when the Soul by cogitation reforming thefe things, which are conceived in Opinion by Memory and Senfe, looketh upon thefe as things from which the other are derived : *Plato* fometimes calleth this a *Picture and Phantafie*. *Cogitation* he calleth the Souls difcourfe within her felf: *Speech*, that which floweth from the Cogitation through the Mouth by Voice. *Intellection* is an operation of the Intellect, contemplating firft Intelligibles. It is two-fold, one of the Soul, beholding Intelligibles before fhe cometh into the Body; the other of the fame, after fhe is immers'd in the Body: The firft is properly called *Intellection*; the other, whilft fhe is in the Body, is termed *Natural Knowledge*, which is nothing but an Intellection of the Soul confined to the Body. When we fay, intellection is the principle of Science, we mean not this latter, but the other, which is competible to the Soul in her feparate State, and as we faid, is then called Intellection, now Natural Knowledge. The fame *Plato* termeth *fimple Knowledge the wing of the Soul*; fometimes *Reminifcence*.

Of thefe fimple Sciences confifteth *Reafon*; which is born with us, the efficient of natural Science; and as Reafon is twofold, Scientifick, and opinionative, fo Intellection and Senfe. It is likewife neceffary that they have their objects, which are *Intelligibles* and *Senfibles* : And forafmuch as of *Intelligibles*, fome are *Primary*, as Ideas, others *Secundary*, as the Species, that are in matter, and cannot be feparated from it. *Intellection* likewife muft be two-fold, one *of Primaries*, the other *of Secondaries*. Again, forafmuch as *in Senfibles*, fome are *Primary*, as qualities, colour, whitenefs, others by *accident*, as white coloured, and that which is concrete, as fire : in the fame manner is *Senfe*, firft, *of Primaries*, fecond, *of Secondaries*. Intellection judgeth primary Intelligibles, not without Scientifick knowledge, by a certain comprehenfion without Difcourfe. Secondaries the the fame Scientifick reafon judgeth, but not without Intellection. Senfibles, as well Primary as Secondary Senfe, judgeth, but not without opinionative reafon. That which is concrete, the fame reafon judgeth, but not without fenfe. And fince the Intelligible World is the primary Intelligible, the fenfible fomething concrete, the firft Intellection judgeth with Reafon, that is, not without Reafon; The other Opinionative reafon not without fenfe, whereas there is both Contemplation and Action; right Reafon difcerneth not in the fame manner thofe which are fubject to Contemplation, and thofe which are fubject to Action : In contemplation, it confidereth what is true, what falfe; in things that belong to Action, what is proper, what improper, what that is which is done. For having an innate knowledge of that which is good and honeft, by ufing reafon, and applying it to thofe natural notions, as to certain Rules, we judge whether every thing be good or bad.

CHAP. V.

The Elements and Office of Dialectick.

OF Dialectick, the firft and chiefeft Element according to *Plato*, is, firft, to confider the *Effence* of every thing; next the *Accidents* thereof. What a thing is, it confiders, either from its Superiours, by *divifion* and *definition*, or contrariwife by *Analyfis*. *Accidents* which adhere to Subftances, are confidered, either from thofe things which are contained by *induction*, or from thofe which do contain by *Syllogifm*.

Hence the parts of *Dialectick* are thefe, *Divifion*, *Definition*, *Analyfis*, *Induction*, *Syllogifm*. Of *Divifions*, one is a diftribution of the Genus into Species, and of the whole into parts; as when we divide the Soul into the rational part, and the irrational; and the latter, into the concupifcible and the irafcible. Another is of a word into divers fignifications, when the fame may be taken feveral ways. A *third* of accidents, according to their fubjects; as when we fay of Good, fome belong to the Soul, fome to the Body, fome are external. The *fourth* of fubjects, according to their *Accidents*; as of Men, fome are good, fome ill, fome indifferent. Divifion of the Genus into its Species, is firft to be ufed, when we examine the effence of a thing, this cannot be done but by definitions.

Definition is made by Divifion in this manner, we muft take the Genus of the thing to be defined, as that of Man, living Creature; that we muft divide by the next differences, defcending to its fpecies, as rational, and irrational, mortal, and immortal. Thus by adding the firft difference to the Genus, is made the definition of Man.

Of *Analyfis* there are three kinds, *one* by which we afcend from Senfibles to primary Intelligibles, *another*, whereby we afcend by demonftrates and fubdemonftrates, to indemonftrable immediate propofitions. The *laft*, which from fuppofition proceedeth to thofe principles which are taken without fuppofition.

The firft kind is thus, as if from that Beauty which is in the Body, we fhould proceed to that of the Mind, from that to another converfant in the Offices of Life, thence to that of Laws, and fo at laft to the vaft Ocean of Beauty, that by thefe fteps, as it were, we may arrive at the fight of the fupream Beauty.

The fecond kind of Analyfis is thus; We muft fuppofe that which we feek, and confider thofe which are precedent, demonftrating them by progreffion, from inferiours to fuperiours, untill we arrive at that which is firft and generally granted : From which, beginning anew, we return fynthetically to that which was fought. As for example, I enquire whether the Soul be Immortal, and fuppofing it to be fo, I enquire whether it be always moved. This being demonftrated, I again enquire, whether that which is always moved, is moved by it felf; which being again demonftrated, we examine, whether that which is moved by its felf, self, be the principle of Motion. Lastly, whether a Principle is ingenerate; this, as most certain, is admitted by all. That which is ingenerate, is also incorruptible; whence, as from a thing most certain, we collect this demonstration. If a Principle be ingenerate and incorruptible, that which is moved by it self, is the principle of Motion; but the Soul is moved by it self, therefore the Soul is Incorruptible, Ingenerate, and Immortal.

The third kind of *Analysis* upon supposition, is this; He who enquireth after a thing, first, supposeth that thing, then observes what will follow upon that supposition. If a reason for the supposition be required, assuming another supposition, he enquireth, whether that which was first supposed, follow again upon another supposition: This he always observeth, untill he come at last to that Principle, which is not taken upon supposition.

Induction is every method by reason, which proceedeth either from like to like, or from Singulars to Universals: It is of great efficacy to excite natural notions.

CHAP. VI.

Of Propositions and Argumentations.

OF that Speech which we call *Proposition*, there are two kinds; *Affirmation* and *Negation*; Affirmation, as *Socrates* walketh; Negation, as *Socrates* walketh not.

Of Affirmative and Negative Propositions, some are *Universal*, others *Particular*: A particular Affirmative is thus, Some Pleasure is good; a particular Negative is, Some Pleasure is not good. An *Universal Affirmative*, all dishonest things are ill; an *Universal Negative*, no dishonest thing is good.

Of Propositions, some are *Categorical*, some *Hypothetical*: the Categorical are simple, as every just thing is good: Hypothetical import consequence or repugnance.

Syllogisms are used by *Plato*, either to *confute* or *demonstrate*; to confute, what is false by interrogation, to demonstrate, what is true by declaration. *Syllogism* is a Speech, wherein some things being laid down, another thing besides those which are laid down, is necessarily inferred from them.

Of Syllogisms some are *Categorical*, some *Hypothetical*, some *Mixt*: Categorical are those whose sumptions and conclusions are simple propositions. *Hypothetical* are those which consist of *Hypothetical* Propositions: *Mixt*, which conclude both.

Plato useth *demonstrative* Arguments in those Dialogues, wherein he explaineth his own Doctrine; *Probable* against Sophists and young Men; *Litigious* against those who are properly called Eristick, as *Euthydemus* and *Hippias*.

Of Categorical *Syllogisms* there are three *Figures*; the first is, that wherein the common extreme is first the prædicate, then the subject. The second, when the common extream is prædicate in both: the third wherein the common extream is subject in both. *Extreams* are the parts of a Proposition, as in this, a *Man is a living Creature*, *Man* and *living Creatures* are the extreams. *Plato* often argueth in the first, second, and third Figures; in the first, as in *Alcibiades*;

Just things are honest,
Honest things are good,
Therefore Just things are good.

In the *second*, as *in Parmenides* as,

That which hath no parts is neither straight nor crooked,
But whatsoever hath Figure is either straight or crooked,
Therefore, whatsoever hath not parts, hath not figure.

In the *third* thus, in the same Book,

Whatsoever hath figure is qualitative,
Whatsoever hath figure is finite,
Therefore whatsoever is qualitative is finite.

Likewise by *Hypothetical* Syllogism *Plato* often disputeth, chiefly *in Parmenide* thus,

If one hath not parts, it hath neither beginning, end nor middle,
But if it have neither beginning, end, nor middle, it hath no bound, and if no bound, no figure,
Therefore if one hath no parts, it hath no figure.

In the *second* Hypothetical figure, ordinarily called the third, wherein the common extream is subject in both, he argueth thus,

If one hath not parts, it is neither straight nor crooked,
If it hath a figure, it is either straight or crooked,
Therefore if it hath no parts, it hath no figure.

In the *Third* figure by some called the second, wherein the common extream twice precedes the other two, he thus argues, in *Phædone*,

If having the knowledge of Equality we forget it not, we know, but if we forget it, we have recourse to Reminiscence, &c.

Mixt Syllogisms which conclude by consequence, he useth thus;

If one is whole and finite, that is, having beginning, middle and end; it hath figure also;
But the Antecedent is true,
Therefore the Consequent.

Of those also which overthrow by Consequence, the differences may be gathered out of *Plato*.

Thus when a Man hath diligently understood the faculties of the Mind, the various differences of Men, the several kinds of Reasoning which may be accommodated to this or that, and to what persons such and such reasons are to be used, he, meeting with an opportunity suiting with his purpose, will become a perfect Orator.

The reasons of *Sophisms* and captious Arguments are, if we observe narrowly, expressed by *Plato* in *Euthydemo*, for there is declared which are in words, which in things, and how they are to be solved.

The ten *Prædicaments* are touched by *Plato in Parmenide*, and in his other Dialogues; the place of Etymologies is fully set down *in Cratylo*. To conclude, he was singularly admirable for division and definition, wherein the greatest force of Dialectick consisteth.

The Summ of that which he saith *in Cratylo*, is this; he enquireth whether *Names* are by the power and reason of *Nature*, or by *Imposition*. He concludeth that the rectitude of names is by a certain imposition, not temerarious or casual, but seemingly to follow the nature of the things themselves; for rectitude of names is nothing but an imposition consonant to the nature of the thing: Hence every imposition of names is not sufficient for rectitude, neither the nature nor first sound of the voice, but that which is composed of both; so as every name is conveniently and properly applyed to the thing. For any name applyed to any thing will not signifie rightly, as if we should impose the name of Horse upon Man. To speak is a kind of Action: Not he that speaketh any way speaketh rightly, but he who speaketh so as the nature of the thing requireth. And for as much as expression of Names is a part of speaking, as Noun is a part of Speech, to name rightly, or not rightly, cannot be done by any imposition of names, but by a natural affinity of the name with the thing it self. So that he is a right imposer of names who can express the Nature of the things in their names; for a Name is an Instrument of the thing, not every inconsiderate name, but that which agreeth with its Nature. By this benefit we communicate things to one another whence it followeth, that it is nothing else but an instrument accommodated to the teaching and discerning of a thing, as a Weavers shuttle to his Webb. It belongeth therefore to a Dialectick to use Names aright; for as a Weaver useth a Shuttle rightly, knowing the proper use thereof after it hath been made by the Carpenter; so the Dialectick rightly useth that name which another hath made. And as to make a Helm, is the Office of a Ship-wright, but to use it rightly of a Pilot; so he who frameth names, shall impose them rightly, if he do it as if a Dialectick were present, who understandeth the nature of those things which are signified by the names. Thus much for Dialectick.

CHAP. VII.

Of Theoretick Philosopy.

WE come next to *Theoretick* Philosophy, whereof one part is *Theologick*, another *Physick*, a third, *Metaphysick*. The end of *Theology* is the knowledge of primary Causes: Of *Physick*, to understand the nature of the Universe, what kind of Creature Man is, what place he holdeth in the World; whether there be a Divine Providence over all things, to which there are other Gods subordinate; how Men are in respect of them. The end of *Mathematicks* is, to know the nature of a Superficies and a solid, and to consider the Motion and Revolution of Cœlestial Bodies, the contemplation whereof must first be proposed in brief. Thus *Plato* used to confirm the acuteness of the Mind, for it sharpneth the understanding, and rendreth it more ready towards the contemplation of Divine things. That which considereth *Numbers*, being likewise a part of Mathematics, confereth not a little to the understanding of things that are; it frees us from the error and ignorance which attend sensible things, and conduceth to the right knowledge of the essence of things: It likewise renders a Man expert in Military Affairs, especially towards the ordering of an Army by the science of *Tacticks*. *Geometry* also confereth much towards the understanding of good it self, if a Man pursue it not only for Mechanical dimension, but that he may by the help thereof ascend to things which are not, busying himself about those which are in continual Generation and Motion. *Stereometry* likewise is exceeding useful, for after the second accretion followeth this contemplation, which holdeth the third room. *Astronomy* also is useful as a fourth Discipline, whereby we consider the Motions of the Heavens and the Stars, and the Author of Night and Day, Months and Years. Thus by a familiar kind of way, finding out him who made all these, and by these Disciplines, as from certain rudiments or Elements proceeding to things more Sublime. Likewise *Musick* is to be learnt, which relateth to hearing; for, as the eyes are created for Astronomy, so are the ears for Harmony: and as when we apply our selves to Astronomy, we are led from visible things, to the Divine invisible Essence; so when we receive the Harmony of Voice in at our ears, from audible things, we ascend by degrees to those which are perceived by Intellect, unless we pursue Mathematical Disciplines to this end, the contemplation thereof will be imperfect, unprofitable, and of no value. We must therefore presently proceed from those things which are perceived by the eyes and ears to those which reason only discerneth; for, Mathematick is only a preface to divine things. They who addict themselves to Arithmetick and Geometry, desire to arrive at the knowledge of that which is, which knowledge they obtain no otherwise than as by a Dream, but really they cannot attain it because they know not the Principles themselves, nor those things which are compounded of the Principles: nevertheless, they conduce to those things which we mentioned; wherefore *Plato* will not have such Disciplines to be called Sciences. Dialectick method proceeds in such manner, that by Geometrical *Hypotheses*, it ascendeth to first Principles, which are not taken upon *Hypotheses*. For this reason he calleth Dialect a Science; but, neither Mathematick, nor Opinion, because it is more perspicuous than sensible things; nor a Science, because 'tis more obscure than first Intelligibles: But, the Opinion of Bodies the Science of Primaries, the Contemplation of Mathematicks.

He likewise asserteth *Faith* and *Imagination*: *Faith*, of things subject to Sense; *Imagination* of Images and Species.

Because Dialectick is more efficacious than Mathematick, as being conversant about Divine Eternal things, therefore it is put before all Mathematicks, as a Wall and Fortification of the rest.

CHAP. VIII.

Of first Matter.

WE must next give a brief account of *Principles*, and those things which belong to *Theology*, beginning at the first, and from thence descending to the Creation of the World, and Contemplation thereof, whereby, at last we come to the Creation and Nature of Man.

To begin with *Matter*; this he calleth the *Receptacle, Nurse, Mother, Place*, and *subject of all Images*, affirming that *it is touched without Sense, and comprehended by an Adulterate kind of Reason*. The property thereof is to undergo the Generation of all things, and to cherish them like a Nurse, and to admit all Forms, being of her own Nature expert of all Form, Quality and Species: These things are imprinted and form'd in her as in a Table, and she admitteth their Figures, not having of her self any Figure or Quality. For, she could not be fit to receive the impressions of several Forms, unless she were wholly void of all Quality and of those Forms which she is about to receive. They who make sweet Unguents of Oyl, make choice of that Oyl which hath the least scent; they who would imprint any Figures in Wax, first smooth and polish the Matter, defacing all former Figures. It is requisite that matter capable of all things, if it must receive all Forms, must not have the nature of any one of them, but must be subjected to all forms, without any quality or figure: and being such, it is neither a Body nor Incorporeal, but a Body potentially, as Brass is potentially a Statue, because then it becomes a Statue, when it puts on the Form thereof.

CHAP. IX.

Of Ideas.

WHereas Matter is a Principle, *Plato* likewise introduceth other Principles beside Matter. One as an *Exemplar*, Ideas; another *Paternal*, God, the Father and Author of all things. *Idea*, as to God, is the *Notion* of God, as to us, the *primary Intelligible*, as to matter, a *manner*, as to this sensible World an *Exemplar*, as to it self, *Essence*. For whatsoever is made with understanding, must necessarily be referred to something, as if something be made from another, as my Picture from me, the exemplar thereof must be presupposed, and if there be nothing Eternal, every Artist conceiveth it first within himself, then transferreth the Forms thereon into Matter.

They define *Idea* an Eternal Exemplar of things which are according to Nature; for, the greater part of Platonists will not allow an *Idea* to be of things that are made by Art, as of a Shield, or Lute, nor of things that are præternatural, as of a Fever, or unnatural Choler; nor of singulars, as of *Socrates* or *Plato*; nor of vile abject things, as of Filth or Straws; nor of relatives, as of greater and longer: For *Idea's* are the Eternal Notions of God, perfect in themselves.

That there are *Idea's*, they prove thus: whether God be Intellect or something Intelligent, he must have his Intelligibles, and those Eternal and Immoveable; if so, there are *Idea's*. For, if matter it self be in it self void of measure, it is necessary that it receive measure from some Superiour, that is wholly remote from matter: But the Antecedent is true, therefore the Consequent; and if so, there are *Idea's*, certain measures void of matter. Again, if the World were not made by Chance, it must not only be made of something, but by something, and not only so, but after the likeness of something; but, that after whose likeness it was made made, what is it but an *Idea?* Whence it followeth, that there are *Idea's*. Again, if Intellect differ from true Opinion, that which is Intelligible differeth from that which is Opinionable; and if so, there are Intelligibles distinct from Opinionables, wherefore there are first Intelligibles, as well as first Sensibles, whence we conclude there are *Idea's*.

CHAP. X.

Of God.

WE come next to speak of the third Principle, which *Plato*, though he think it almost ineffable, conceiveth may be expressed in this manner. If there are intelligibles, and those neither sensibles, nor coherent with sensibles; but adherent to first Intelligibles, then are there first simple Intelligibles, as there are first sensibles; the Antecedent is true, therefore the consequent. But Men subject to perturbation of Sense, when they would contemplate something intelligible, presently fall upon the thought of something sensible, whereby at the same time they imagine Magnitude, or Figure, or Colour; and therefore cannot understerstand this sincerely: But the Gods being void of Corporeal mixion understand purely and sincerely. Now because the Intellect is better than the Soul, and that Intellect which is always in act, and at once understandeth all things, is better than that Intellect which is in power, and of these, that is most excellent which is the cause of the other, and superior to all; This can be nothing else but God, whom we call the first, as being the Cause that the Intellect of the World always acteth. He, being himself immoveable, acteth upon the Intellect of the World, as the Sun upon the Eye, when it turneth towards him. And as that which is desired moveth the Appetite, it self remaining immoveable; so doth this Intellect move the Intellect of all Heaven.

Now

Now this first Intellect being most fair, must have the most fair Intelligible; but nothing is fairer than it self, therefore it always understandeth it self, and its own notions, which Act is called Operation.

Moreover, *God is first, eternal, ineffable, perfect in himself*; that is, needing none; *and ever perfect*, that is, absolute in all times, and *every way perfect*, that is, absolute in every part, *Divinity, Essence, Truth, Harmony, Good*. Neither do we so name these, to distinguish one from the other, but rather by them all to understand one. He is said to be *Good*, because he bestoweth his benefits upon all according to their several Capacities, and so is the cause of all good-*Fair*, because he is in his essence both more and equal. *Truth*, because he is the principle of all truth, as the Son of all light. And *Father*, as being cause of all things, and adorning the mind of Heaven, and Soul of the World after his own exemplar and notions. For according to his own Will he filled all things with him self, exciting the Soul of the World, and converting it to himself, for he is cause of that Intellect, which being adorned by the Father, adorneth also the nature of all this World. He is likewise *ineffable*, and as we said, can only be perceived by the Mind, for he is neither Genus nor Species, nor difference, neither can any accident be applied to him. He is *not ill*, for that it were Impiety to affirm; *nor good*, for so he should be termed if he were meanly or highly participant of goodness. Nor *difference*, for that cannot be made according to the notion of him. Nor qualited, for he is not made that which he is by quality, nor perfected thereby. Nor *void of quality*, for he is not deprived of any quality that appertaineth to him. *Nor part of any thing, nor as a whole* constituted of parts, *nor as the same or divers*, for nothing can happen to him whereby he may be distinguished from others, Neither doth he *move*, or is he *moved*.

Hence the first apprehension of him is by *Abstraction* from these things, as we understand a Point by Abstraction from Sensibles, considering first a Superficies, then a Line, then a Point. The second is by *Analogy* in this manner. As the Sun is to sight and visible things, himself not being sight, yet affording the one to see, the other to be seen, so is the first Intellect to that Intellect, which is in our Soul, and to those things which it understandeth. For, it self is not the Intellect, yet it perfecteth in these the Act of Intellection, to those it affordeth that they are understood, enlightning that truth which is in them. The third way to understand him is thus: When a Man beholdeth that Beauty which is in Bodies, he proceederh to that which is in the Soul, then to that which is in Offices and Laws: Lastly, to the vast Ocean of Beauty, after which, he considereth that which is good it self, amiable it self, expetible it self, which shineth like a Light, and meeteth the Soul, that which ascends unto it by these degrees. By this he comprehendeth God himself through reason of that Excellence, which consisteth in adoration of him. He considereth God void of parts, for nothing was before him a part, and that of which something consisteth is precedent to that whereof it is part, for a Superficies is before a Body, and a Line before Superficies. Moreover God not having many parts, can neither be locally moved, nor altered by qualities. For if he be altered, it must be done by himself, or some other; if by some other, that other must be of greater Power than he; if by himself, it must be either to better or to worse, both which are absurd.

From all these it followeth that *God is incorporeal*, which may likewise be proved thus. If God were a Body, he should consist of matter and form; for every Body consisteth of matter, and its form joins to that matter, which is made like unto the *Idea's*, and in an ineffable manner participant of them; But that that should consist of matter and form is absurd; for then he could not be either simple or a Principle; therefore he is incorporeal. Again, if he be a Body, he consisteth of matter, and consequently is either Fire or Air, or Earth or Water, or something made out of these; but none of these is Principle by it self; besides he must then be later than matter, as consisting of it, which being absurd, it is necessary that God be incorporeal. Moreover, if he were a Body, it would follow that he must be generable, corruptible, mutable, which to affirm of God were intolerable.

CHAP. XI.

Of Qualities.

THat *Qualities* are *incorporeal*, may be proved thus: Every Body is a Subject, quality is not a Subject, but an Accident, therefore quality is not a Body. Again, no Body is in a Subject; every quality is in a Subject, therefore quality is not a Body. Again, quality is contrary to quality, but no Body as no Body is contrary to a Body; therefore qualities are not Bodies. To omit, that is most agreeable to Reason, that as matter is void of quality, so quality should be void of matter, and if quality be void of matter, it must likewise be void of Corporeity, for if qualities were Bodies, two or three Bodies might be together in the same place, which is absurd.

Qualities being incorporeal, the maker of them must be incorporeal also; moreover there can be no efficients, but in corporeals, for Bodies naturally suffer and are in mutation, not continuing always in manner, nor persevering in the same state. For whensoever they seem to effect any thing, we shall find that they suffer it long before. Whence as there is something which wholly suffereth, so must there be something which wholly acteth; but such only is incorporeal.

Thus much concerning Principles as far as they relate to Theology; we proceed next to Physical Contemplations.

CHAP. XII.

Of the Causes, Generation, Elements, and Order of the World.

FOrasmuch as of sensible and singular things there must of necessity be some Exemplars, *viz.* Idea's, of which are Sciences and Definitions (for besides all particular Men, we conceive a Man in our Mind, and besides all particular Horses a Horse, and likewise besides all living Creatures, a living Creature immortal and unbegotten: As from one Seal are made many prints, and of one Man there may be many Pictures, of all which, the *Idea* it self is cause that there are such as it self is) 'tis necessary that this Universe, the fairest Fabrick of God's making, be so made by God, that in the making thereof he looked upon an *Idea* as its exemplar, whilst by a wonderful Providence and most excellent design God applied himself to the building of this Frame, because he was good.

God therefore made it of all matter, which being before the Generation of Heaven, disorderly scattered; he from a deformed confusion reduced to beautiful order, and adorned every way the parts thereof with fit numbers and figures, until at last he so distinguished them, as now they are, Fire and Earth to Air and Water, of which there were then only the footsteeps, and a certain aptitude to admit the power of Elements, and so without any reason or order, they justled matter, and were justled again by matter.

Thus God framed the World of four entire Elements, of whole Fire and Earth, Water, and Air; omitting no Power or part of any of them. For, he saith, it must be corporeal and generated, and subject to touch and sight; but without Fire and Earth nothing can be touched or seen; wherefore justly he framed it of *Fire and Earth*, and because it was requisite there should be some Chain to unite these, there is a Divine Chain, which according to the proportion of Reason maketh one of it self, and those things which are united to it, and the World could not be plain (for then one medium would have served) but Sphœrical, therefore there was need of two mediums to the constitution thereof. Betwixt Fire and Earth, by the prescription of this reason is interposed *Air* and *Water*, that as Fire is to Air, so is Air to Water, and as Air is to Water, so is Water to Earth; and again, as Earth is to Water, so is Water to Air, and as Water is to Air, so is Air to Fire.

There being nothing remaining beyond the World, God made the World *one*, conformable to this *Idea*, which is one. He likewise made it such, as that is *uncapable of sickness or age*. For, besides that nothing can befal it whereby it may be corrupted, it is so sufficient to it self, that it hath not need of any exteriour thing. He bestowed upon it a *Spherical* Figure, as being the fairest, the most capacious and aptest to motion, and because it needeth not hearing or sight, or the rest of the Senses, he gave it not any Organs of Senses. He denied all kinds of Motion to be compitible to it, except the circular, which is proper to the Mind and to Wisdom.

CHAP. XIII.

Of the convenience of Figures, with the Elements and World.

THe World thus consisteth of two parts, a *Soul* and a *Body*; this visible and corruptible, that neither subject to sight nor touch: The power and constitution of each is different, the Body consisteth of Fire, Earth, Water, and Air; which four, the maker of the Universe (there being until then nothing more confused than the Elements) formed in a *Pyramid*, a *Cube*, an *Octaedron*, and an *Icosaedron*; but chiefly in a *Dodecaedron*. Matter, as far as it put on the Figure of a *Pyramid*, became Fire, and mounted upward: For, that Figure is the most apt to cut and to divide, as consisting of fewest Triangles; and therefore is the rarest of all Figures. As far as it is an *Octaedron*, it took the quality of *Air*: Where it took that of an *Icosaedron*, it became *Water*; The figure of a *Cube Earth*, as being the most solid and stable of all the Elements. The figure of a *Dodecaedron*, he used in the fabrick of the *Universe. Superficies* come nigher the nature of Principles than all these, for they are before Solids. Of its Nature, the two Parents (as it were) are two *Triangles* most fair and rectangular; one a *Scalenum*, the other an *Isosceles*; a Scalenum is a triangle having one right angle, the other of two thirds, the last of one third. A *Scalenum* therefore is the element of a *Pyramid*, and an *Octaedron*, and an *Icosaedron*. A Pyramid consisteth of four Triangles, having all sides equal to one another, each whereof is divided as we said, into six scalenous Triangles. The *Octaedrons* consist of eight like sides, whereof each is divided into six *Scalenums*. The *Icosaeders* of twenty in the same manner; but the Element of a *Cube* is an Isosceles Triangle, for four such Triangles concurring make a Square, and six Squares a *Cube*. God made use of a *Dodecaedron* in the construction of the Universe, whence there are twelve Figures of Living Creatures in the *Zodiack*, whereof each is divided into thirty parts. Likewise in a *Dodecaedron*, which consisteth of twelve *Pentagons*, if each be divided into five Triangles, there are in every one six Triangles, so that in the whole *Dodecaedron*, there will be 360 Triangles, as many as there are degrees in the *Zodiack*.

When matter was put into those Figures by God, first it was moved rudely without order, until at last he reduced it to order, each being conjoyned to one another, and Composed in due Proportion: Neither are these distinct in Place, but are in Perpetual Motion, which they give likewise into Matter. For being straitned by the Compass of the World, and agitated by Mutual Justlings, they are driven, the

rare

rare always into the region of the solid, whence nothing is left vacuous, nothing void of Body. The inequality which remaineth amongst them causeth Convulsion, for matter is agitated amongst them, and they reciprocally by matter.

CHAP. XIV.

Of the Soul of the World, the Sphears and Stars.

FROM Bodies he alloweth that we collect the powers of the *Soul*, for seeing that we discern all things by the Soul, he justly placed the principles of all things therein, that whatsoever should occur, we might contemplate it by that which is of Kin and Neighbour unto it, and attribute an Essence thereunto consonant to the functions. Then therefore he called one substance intelligible and indivisible; he placed another divisible amongst Bodies, to signifie that the knowledge as well of the one as of the other may be had by Intellect. And knowing that in things intelligible and sensible, there is identity and diversity, he fitly composed the Soul out of all these. For, either the like is known by the like, as the *Pythagoreans* hold, or as *Heraclitus the Naturalist*, unlike always by unlike.

That he would that the World should be *generate*, we must not so understand as if there shall be any time wherein the World is not, but in as much as it always perisheth in Generation, and declareth, that there is some more excellent and principal cause of its essence.

The Soul of the World which was from all Eternity, was not made by God, but only adorned by him, in which respect he is sometimes said to have made it, for that he exciteth it, and converteth the Mind thereof, as out of a profound Sleep unto himself, that beholding his intelligibles, and affecting his notions, it should from thence receive Species and Form; whence it is manifest, that the World was endued by God, both with a Soul and Mind. For, intending it to be the best, he must have made it animate and intelligent, since an animate thing is more excellent than an inanimate, and an intelligent than an unintelligent; perhaps the Mind also could not subsist without a Soul.

This Soul, being diffused from the Centre of the World to the extreams, *comprehendeth* the whole body of the World, so as it is extended throughout the Universe, and in that manner joyneth and conserveth the whole. The external preside over the internal, for they are not divided, but these are divided into seven Circles; from the first distributed according to duple and triple Intervals. That which is comprehended by the indivisible Sphear, is correspondent to it, that which is divided to the other. For the motion of Heaven which comprehendeth all things, being not uncertain, is one and ordinate, but that of the things within it, is changeable, varied by rising and setting, whence called Planetary. The outermost Sphear moveth to the Right-Hand from *East* to *West*, the innermost contrariwise, to the Left-Hand from *West* to *East*, meeting the World.

God framed also the Stars and Constellations; some *fixed* for the ornament of Heaven and might, very many in number. The *Erratick* are seven, serving for number and time, and the illumination of all things; for time is an interval of the motion of the World, as an Image of Eternity, which is the measure of the state of the Eternal World. The Planets are not of equal Power, the *Sun* is the leader of all, who illuminateth, and sheweth all things to the Eye. Next the *Moon*, which in respect of her Power hath the second place. The rest of the Planets each according to their several Proportions. The Moon maketh the measure of a *Month*, in that space compleating its Circle, and overtaking the Sun. The Sun measureth the *Year*, for running through the circle of the *Zodiack*, he compleateth the Seasons of the Year. Of the other Stars each hath its proper revolution, with which all Men are not acquainted, but only the Learned. By all those revolutions *the absolute number of time* is compleated, when coming all to the same point, they are in such order, as if we should imagine a right line to be drawn from the Sphear of fixed Stars to the Earth, the Centers all would be seen in that line.

There being seven Orbs in the Planetary Sphear, the maker of the World, framed in them seven conspicuous bodies of matter for the most part fiery, and inserted them into the Sphears belonging to the other *Erratick* Circle. The *Moon* he placed in that Circle which is next the Earth, the *Sun* in the second, the *Morning-Star*, and the Sacred Star of *Mercury*, in that *Orb* which is equal in swiftness with the Sun. The rest higher, each in its proper Sphear. That of *Saturn* the slowest of all, he placed in that *Orb* which is next to the fixed Stars. Second to this is that which they call the Sphear of *Jupiter*, next that of *Mars*; the eigth, which is the *Supream Power*, includeth all. These are all living intelligent Creatures, and Gods endued with a Spherical Figure.

CHAP. XV.

Of Dæmons and Elements.

THere are other *Dæmons* also which we may call intelligent Gods, in each of the Elements partly visible, partly invisible, in the *æther*, Fire, Air and Water, that there be not any part of the World void of Soul, or of an animate Creature more excellent than humane Nature. Below these are all Earthly sublunary things; God is maker of the World, of all Gods and *Dæmons*. This Universe by his Divine Will shall not be dissolved. Over the rest his *Sons* preside, who by his Command and Example order whatsoever they do. By these *Lots*, *Nocturnal Visions*, *Dreams*, *Oracles*, *and whatsoever Men refer to divination*, is artificially wrought.

The *Earth* is fixed in the midst of all, round about the Axle-tree, which passeth through the midst of the World. It is the observer of Night and Day, the most ancient of all Gods in Heaven. Next the Soul of the World it affordeth us most Nutriture; about it the Heavens move, and it self is a kind of Star: It remaineth in its proper place, which by reason of its even weight is the Centre; the Æther exterior is divided into the Sphear of fixed Stars, and that of Planets. Next to these is the Air; in the midst the Earth with its Humidity.

CHAP. XVI.

Of the Younger Gods makers of Men.

AFter that all these were framed, there remained three kinds of living Creatures which were to be Mortal, *Volatile*, *Aquatile*, and *Terrestrial*; the generation whereof he committed to his *Son*, lest if he himself had begotten them, they should have been Immortal as well as the rest. They borrowing some little parts from first matter for a certain time, formed mortal living Creatures, and because of Mankind, as being next to the Gods, both the Father of all things, and his Sons likewise have a particular care, the Maker of all things sent down himself their Souls into the Earth equal in number to the Stars, and having imposed each one his proper Star, as a Vehiculum, like a Law-giver, he pronounced decrees unto them, that he himself might be inculpable, which was that there should arise Mortal affections from the Body, first Senses, next Pleasure, then Grief, and Fear, and Anger, which those Souls that should overcome, and not suffer themselves to be transported by them, should justly be accounted Victors, and at the last return to their proper Star, though they which should be transported by Injustice, should in the second Generation undergo the lives of Women, wherein if they ceased not from their Wickedness, they should at last transmigrate into the nature of Brute Beasts, the end of these Labours shall then be, when they have overcome the innate affections of the Body, and then return to their proper Habit.

CHAP. XVII.

Of the Body, and parts of Man, and Powers of the Soul.

THE Gods first formed Man of Earth, Fire, Air, and Water, borrowing some parts from matter (to be restored in their due time) which they so connected to one another by secret ties, as that of all these they framed one Body. The most excellent part of the Soul that was sent down from Heaven, they placed in the *Head*, for which as a manured Field they prepared the *Brain*. About the Face they disposed Organs proper for Sense; *Marrow* they made of smooth straight Triangles, of which the Elements were formed, that it should be the Origin of prolifick Seed. *Bones* they formed of Marrow and Earth, the Earth moistned, and often dipt in Water and Fire. *Flesh* is compounded of Salt and Sharp, as of a kind of ferment. Marrow they enclosed with *Bones*, Bones with *Sinews* instead of Chains, that by these Inflexions the knitting of the Joints might be pliant. Over these as a cover is extended the *Skin*, partly white, partly black, for beauty and use. Of these likewise consist the Internal *Bowels*, and the Belly, and the Intestines, every where rolled about it. And from the Mouth, above the *aspera Arteria*, and the *œsophagus*, of which one cometh down to the Stomach, the other to the Lungs. Meat is digested in the Belly by Spirit and Heat, and thence distributed to the whole Body according to their several Constitutions. The two Veins passing along the Spine of the Back, meet, and cross at the Head, where they spread into many parts.

Thus when the Gods had made Man, and given him a Soul as the Mistress of his Body, they placed the principal part of that Soul to which Reason appertaineth, in the head. Whence is derived Marrow and Sinews, and by the different affection of this, the Mind likewise is altered. Moreover they gave him Senses, as the attendants of Reason, and the power of judging and contemplating with Reason. Those parts of the Soul, which are moved by meaner affections, they seated in lower places; the irascible part in the Heart, the concupiscible about the Belly, and the parts next to the Navel, of which hereafter.

CHAP. XVIII.

Of Sight.

AFter that the Gods had placed the Eyes (Conduits of Light) in the Face, they included in them a Fiery Light, which being smooth, and in some manner thick, they conceived of Kin to Diurnal Light. This breaketh forth every where at the Eyes, but chiefly through the Eye-Balls, as being there most pure and clear. This agreeing with the external Light, as like with like affordeth the sense of Sight, whence in the night, when the light vanisheth and is obscured, this ray of ours no longer mingleth with the immediate Air; but, on the contrary, withdrawing it self inward, smooths and diffuses the motions that are in us, and so bringeth on Sleep, whereby the Eye-lids are shut. If it bring much rest, the sleep is little disturbed with Dreams, but if there remain any motions behind, we are troubled with many illusions. In this manner, Phantasies, whether true or false, arise. Of the same Nature are Images, which we see in Glasses, or other smooth pellucid Bodies, which exist only by reflection. For, as the Glass is concave or convex, or oblong, the object is differently represented to the Beholder. The light being reflected to other parts, those which are dispersed in convex meet in the concave, for in some, the right and left sides seem quite inverted, in others alike; in others, those which are upwards seem downwards, and on the contrary, those which are downwards, upwards.

CHAP.

CHAP. XIX.

Of the rest of the Senses.

HEaring is given for the perception of Voice, it ariseth from a Motion made about the Head, and setteth in the Liver. Voice is that which passeth through the Ear, Brain, and Blood to the Soul. A sharp Voice is that which is moved swiftly, deep which slowly, great which much, small which little.

Next followeth the Sense proper to the Nostrils, perceptible of Odour. Odour is an affection which passeth from the Veins of the Nostrils to the parts of the Navel. The Species thereof have no name, except the two that are most common, pleasant, and unpleasant, commonly called sweet and stinking. All Odour is more thick than Air, more thin than Water, for Odour is properly said to be of those things which have not yet received perfect Mutation, but consist of a communion of Air and Water, as smoke and mists. For, by the resolution of these into one another, the sense of Smelling is made.

Taste was made by the Gods to be judge of different savours. Hence are Veins extended to the Heart, by which several savours are examined. These Veins by dilating or contracting themselves severally according to the Sapors presented to them, discern the differences. The differences of Sapors are seven, sweet, sharp, sour, picquant, salt, acid, bitter; the nature of sweet Sapor is contrary to all the rest, for by its Power it sootheth and pleaseth the moisture of the Tongue, whereas of the rest some disturb and dispel it, as acute Sapors; some heat, and fly upwards, as the hot; others being abstersive, dissolve it; as the bitter; others are by degrees purgative and abstersive, as the Salt. Of these some contract the passages; they which do it more roughly, are called acid, they which more gently, austere.

The sense of Touching was formed by the Gods, to discern hot and cold, soft and hard, light and heavy, smooth and rough, and to judge the differences of each of these; *Yielding* Bodies, we call those which yield to the touch, *resisting* those which yield not; this proceedeth from the bases of Bodies: Those which have large Bases, are firm and solid, these which have narrow Bases are yielding, soft and easily changed. Rough is that which is uneven and hard, smooth, that which is plain and thick: As warm and cold qualities are most opposite, so they proceed from the most different causes. That which cutteth by the acuteness and roughness of its parts, begetteth a hot affection, that which is more thick, in penetration, a cold, whilst the more rare are expelled, and the more dense compelled to penetrate into their room. Thence ariseth a Concussion and trepidation, and (an affection which is from hence begotten in Bodies,) rigor.

CHAP. XX.

Of Heavy and Light.

HEavy and Light ought not to be defined by higher or lower place, nothing is high or low; for Heaven being absolutely round, and its convex extremity even, we cannot term any thing higher or lower, yet may we call that heavy, which is hardly drawn to a place different from its Nature; light which easily; or, heavy is that which consisteth of most parts, light of fewest.

CHAP. XXI.

Of Respiration.

WE breathe after this manner. The external Air compasseth us round about, and passeth in at our Mouth, Nostrils, and invisible Pores of the Body, where being warmed, it floweth back again to the external air, by that part out of which it flowed, it again thrusteth the external Air to the interiour. Thus there is an unintermitted succession of inspiration and expiration.

CHAP. XXII.

Of the Causes of Diseases.

OF Diseases *Plato* alledgeth many causes The first is defect, or excess of the Elements, and a change of places which agree not with their Nature. The second a preposterous generation of homogeneal parts, as when of Flesh is made Blood, or Choler, or Flegm; for all these are nothing but colliquation, or putrefaction. Flegm is a new colliquation of Flesh; swet and tears are a kind of Serum of Flegm. Flegm intercepted in the outward parts, begetteth scurf and leprosie, in the inward being mingled with Melancholy, it causeth the falling sickness. Sharp and salt Flegm engender those affections which consist in rigour, for all Bodies that are inflamed with Choler must suffer that. A World of various Diseases are engendred by Choler and Flegm. As concerning Fevers; *Plato* conceived that a continual Fever proceedeth from excess of Fire, a quotidian from excess of Air, a Tertian from excess of Water, a Quartan from excess of Earth. It remaineth that we here begin to speak of the Soul, though not without some danger, of repeating the same things.

CHAP. XXIII.

Of the three principal Powers of the Soul.

THE Gods, the makers of Mortal Creatures, having received from the first God the Soul of Man Immortal, added unto it two Mortal Parts; yet lest the Immortal Divine part might be infected with Mortal Extravagances, they seated as Prince of all in the Tower, as it were of the Body, the Head, in figure resembling the Universe. The rest of the Body they appointed as a vehiculum to serve this. To each mortal part they assigned its proper Habitation, placing the irascible in the Heart, the concupiscible in the midst betwixt the Navel and the Diaphragma, binding it there as a furious savage Beast. They framed the Lungs in respect of the Heart, soft, bloodless, hollow, and spungy, that the Heart being somewhat heated with Anger, might thereby be refrigerated and asswaged; the Liver to excite and allay the concupiscible part, having both sweetness and bitterness, as likewise for the clearing of Divinations which are given by Dreams: for as much as in it by reason of its smoothness, shining and brightness, the power which proceedeth from the mind doth shine forth. The Spleen was made for the benefit of the Liver, to purge and cleanse it; so that those corruptions, which by some diseases, are contracted about the Liver, retire thither.

CHAP. XXIV.

Of the distinction of the parts of the Soul.

THat the Soul and parts thereof according to their proper faculties are three fold; every part appointed by reason their several places, is manifest from hence. Those things which are separated by Nature, are divers; passionate and reasonable are separated by Nature; this being conversant in Intelligibles, that in things sad or joyful, to omit the passive part which is common likewise to brute Beasts. Now these two being distinct by Nature, must likewise be distinguished by place, because for the most part they disagree, and are repugnant to one another; but nothing can be repugnant to it self, neither can those things which are contrary to one another consist together in the same. In *Medea* anger seemeth to contest thus with reason;

I know what I intend is ill,
But anger over-rules my Will.

In *Laius* when he ravished *Chrysippus*, Concupiscence contested with reason; for so he saith;

Men to this Crime the Gods confine,
To know the Ill that they decline.

That the rational power is different from the passive, is evident from this, that they are ordered by several means, one by discipline, the other by habitual Practice.

CHAP. XXV.

Of the Immortality of the Soul.

THat the Soul is Immortal *Plato* proveth by these Arguments. The Soul to every thing, wherein it is, conferreth Life, as being naturally innate in her self, but that which conferreth Life to others never admitteth death, but what is such is immortal.

The Soul being Immortal, is likewise incorruptible, for it is an incorporeal Essence which cannot be changed substantially, and is only perceptible by the Intellect, not by the Eyes, and is uniform. Hence it must be simple, neither can be at any time dissolved or corrupted. The Body is contrary, for it is subject to sight and other Sensess and as it is compounded, so shall it again be dissolved, and it is multiform. When the Soul adhereth to those things which are perceptible by Intellect, it acquiesceth; Now to that by whose Presence she is disturbed, she cannot possibly be like, wherefore she is more like to those things which are perceptible by Intellect; but what is such, is such by Nature incorruptible and perishable.

Again, the Soul doth naturally preside over the Body, not the Body over the Soul, but that which by Nature ruleth and commandeth is of Kin to Divinity, wherefore the Soul being next unto God, must be Immortal, not subject to Corruption.

Again, Contraries which have no *medium*, not by themselves, but by some accident are so ordered by nature, that they may be mutually made of one another. But that which Men call Life is contrary to that which they call Death; as therefore Death is a separation of the Soul from the Body; so is Life a conjunction of the Soul with the Body, pre-existent to the Body. But if she be pre-existent, and shall subsist after the Body, it followeth that she be sempiternal, for there cannot any thing be imagined whereby she may be corrupted.

Again, if Learning be Reminiscence, the Soul must be Immortal, but that it is Reminiscence we prove thus: Learning cannot otherwise consist than by remembrance of those things we formerly knew. For, if from *Singulars* we understand *Universals*, how could we discourse by Singulars which are Infinite? Or how from a few perceive Universals? We should therefore necessarily be deceived, as if we judged that only to be a living Creature which breatheth; or how could the Notions themselves have the reason of Principles? By Reminiscence therefore, from some few which we have conceived in our our Mind, we understand the rest, and from some occurrent particulars we remember those which we knew long before, but were then given over to oblivion, when the Soul first descended into the Body.

Again, if the Soul be not corrupted by its own proper ill, neither can it be destroyed by that or any other, nor simply by any ill, and being such, shall remain uncorrupted.

Again, that which is moved in it self, as being the principle of Motion in those things which are moved, is always moved; that which is such is immortal; but the Soul is moved of it self; that which is moved of it self is the principle of all motion and generation, and a principle is expert of generation and corruption, wherefore the Souls of Men, and of the Universe it self are such, for both partake of the same mistion. He affirmeth the Soul to be moveable in her self, because it hath an innate Life, always operating by its Power.

That

That rational Souls are immortal, may clearly be asserted out of *Plato*; but whether the irrational be such seemeth doubtful; yet is it probable that being guided only by Phantasie, not endued with Reason or Judgment, neither do they contemplate any thing, or discern, or collect from it, nor can they discern ills, but generally understand nothing, nor are of the same nature with those Souls which have Intellect and Reason, but are capable of dying and being corrupted. For as much as they are immortal, it followeth that they are put into Bodies, being planted into the formed Nature of Embrio's, and transmigrate into several Bodies, as well humane as others, either according to some certain numbers which they expect, or by the Will of the Gods, or for intemperance of Life, or for love of the Body. For the Body and Soul have a kind of affinity, as Fire and Brimstone.

Moreover the Souls of the Gods have a dijudicative Faculty, called Gnostick, and impulsive to some action, called Parastatick, which faculties being likewise in humane Souls, become changed as soon as they come into the Body, the assistent into the concupiscible, the impulsive into the irascible.

CHAP. XXVI.

Of Fate and Free-will.

Concerning *Fate, Plato* held thus: All things are in Fate, yet all things are not decreed by Fate. For Fate, though it be like a Law, yet it useth not to speak in this manner, that this Man shall do thus, and to that Man, that shall befal (which were to proceed into infinite, there being an infinite Generation of Men, and infinite accidents happening daily to them; besides that this would take away our Freewill, our praise or dispraise, and whatsoever is of that kind) but rather thus; Whatsoever Soul chooseth such a Life, and doth such things, these shall follow, the Soul therefore is free, and it is left within its Power to do or not to do, without any compulsion or necessity. But that which followeth the Action is performed by Fate. As from *Paris*'s ravishing of *Helene*, (which it is within his Power to do or not to do) shall follow that the *Grecians* contend with the *Trojans* about *Helene*. Thus *Apollo* foretold *Laius*;

If thou beget a Son, that Son shall kill thee.

In the Oracle are comprehended both *Laius* and the begetting of a Son, that which shall follow upon the begetting of the Son depends on *Plato*.

That which may be done is of a middle kind betwixt true and false, and being so indefinite by Nature; That which is in our Power, is carried on as it were unto it. That which is done by our election, is presently either true or false; that which is in power is different from that which is said to be in habit and act. That which is in power, declareth an aptitude in that thing, wherein the habit is not yet perfect. So a Boy may be said to be a Grammarian, a Musician, a Carpenter in power. He is in habit of one or more of these when he hath acquired that habit. He is said to be in act, when he operateth according to that acquired habit. That which we call possible to be done, is none of these. Indeterminate is that which is in our Power, and to which part soever it enclineth, will be true or false.

CHAP. XXVII.

ETHICK.

Of the chief Good, and of Vertues.

We must next give a short account of *Plato*'s *Ethicks*. That which is worthy of all Honour, and is the Supream Good, he conceived not easie to be found, and if found, not safe to be declared. For this reason, he communicated the Contemplation of the chief good to very few, and those of his most intimate Acquaintance, of whom his Judgment made choice for this purpose. But our good, if we examine his Books diligently, we shall find he placed in the knowledge of the first Good, which may rightly be called God, and the first Mind. For all things which Men call good, he conceiveth to be called good in this respect, for as much as they derive something from that good, as all sweet and hot things are termed such from some Participation of the first sweet and the first hot. Of those things which are in us, only the Mind and reason have a similitude of the first good. Wherefore he calleth our good, Fair, Venerable, Amiable, Proportionate, and lastly Beatitude. Of those which are commonly called good, as Health, Beauty, Strength, there is none good, unless it be employed towards the practice of Vertue. For being separated from Vertue, they are like Matter only, and to those who make ill use of them, only ill. Yet these *Plato* sometimes calleth Mortal Goods. Beatitude he reckoneth not amongst humane goods, but amongst the Divine and Immortal. Whence he asserteth that the Souls of true Philosophers are replenished with vast admirable goods, and after the dissolution of their Mortal Body, are admitted to the Table of the Gods, and with them walk over and survey the Field of Truth, because they did see they used the utmost endeavours of their Souls to know it, and esteemed it the most precious of all things, by the Benefit whereof they illustrated, and excited their Mind as a lost or blinded Sight, preferring the conservation thereof before many corporeal Eyes. Foolish Men are like those who lead all their Life in some Cave under ground, where they never saw the light of the Sun, but only some empty thin Shadows of such Bodies as are with us upon the Earth, which seeing, they think they see true Bodies. As these, if ever they should be brought out of darkness into the clear light, would questionless despise all things which they saw before, and themselves much more, as having been absolutely deceived; So they who rise up out of the darkness of this life

life to those things which are divine and fair, in all likelihood will contemn what before they most esteemed, and love more vehemently this contemplation. Thus it appeareth, that only what is good is honest, and that Vertue sufficeth to Felicity.

Moreover, that good and fair consist in knowledge of the first good, he declareth in whole Volumes. As concerning those which are good by participation, he speaketh thus in his first Book of Laws. Good is two-fold, Humane and Divine, &c. If any thing be disjoyned from the first good, and void of the essence thereof, that is called good by the foolish, which in *Euthydemo*, he affirmeth to be a greater ill to the Possessor.

That he conceiveth the Vertues to be eligible in themselves, is manifest, in as much as he affirmeth that only to be good which is Honest, which he demonstrateth in many Dialogues, particularly in those of the Commonwealth.

Hence he conceiveth that Man to be most happy and blessed, who hath attained the Science we mentioned; yet not in respect of the Honours which attend such a Person, nor of any other reward; for though he be unknown to all Men, and such things, as are commonly accounted Ills, as dishonour, banishment, and death happen unto him; he is notwithstanding happy. On the contrary, a man who wants this knowledge, though he possess all things commonly esteemed good, Riches, Power, Health, Strength and Beauty, he is nothing the more happy.

He asserteth an ultimate end, conformable to all these which is to be made like unto God, as far as Humanity is capable of being such. This he expounds variously, sometimes as in *Theæteto*, he affirms our resemblance to God to consist in being Prudent, Just, and Holy; wherefore we must endeavour to fly with all possible Celerity from hence to those. This flight is the resemblance to God, as much as is possible: The similitude consisteth in Prudence, Justice, and Sanctity; sometimes in Justice only, as in his last Book of the Commonwealth. For a Man is never deserted by God, whilst he endeavoureth to be just, and by the very act of Vertue, as much as a Man is capable of, he is rendred like unto God. In *Phædone* he asserteth, that this resemblance to God is acquired by Temperance and Justice, thus. *Are not they Blessed and happy, and from hence shall go into the best place, who have practised the popular civil Vertue which they call Temperance and Justice?* Again, sometimes he affirmed, that the end of Life is to be like unto God, sometimes to follow God, as when he saith, God indeed according to the old Saying, *containing the beginning, middle and end of all things*, &c. Sometimes he joineth both together, as when he saith, *The Soul following God, and being rendred like unto him*, &c. The Principle of Utility is good it self, but this is said of God, therefore the end conformable to the Principle, is to become like unto God, to the Celestial, or rather superceletial God, who hath not Vertue, but is more excellent than all Vertue. Wherefore it is rightly said, that κακοδαιμονία, Misery, is a perversity of the the Genius, εὐδαιμονία, Beatitude is a good habit of the Genius.

This similitude to God we shall obtain, if we enjoy convenient Nature, in our Manner, Education and Sense, according to Law, and chiefly by Reason, and Discipline, and institution of Wisdom, withdrawing our selves as much as possible from Humane Affairs, and being conversant in those things only which are understood by Contemplation: The way to prepare, and, as it were, to cleanse the Demon that is in us, is to initiate our selves into higher Disciplines, which is done by Musick, Arithmetick, Astronomy and Geometry, not without some respect of the Body, by Gymnastick, whereby it is made more ready for the actions both of War and Peace.

CHAP. XXVIII.
The Definition and kinds of Vertue.

VErtue being divine, is the perfect and best affection of the Soul, which adorneth a Man, and rendreth him more excellent and ready, as well for Speech as Action, whether he do it alone or with others.

Of the Vertues, some are placed in the rational part, some in the irrational. For whereas the Nature of the rational part is one, that of the irascible another, that of the concupiscible another, the perfection of these must likewise be different. That of the rational is *Prudence*, of the irascible, *Fortitude*, of the concupiscible, *Temperance*.

Prudence is the Science of things, good, bad, and betwixt both.

Temperance is an apt moderation of Desires and Appetites; when we call Temperance a moderation and obedience, we mean only this, that it is a faculty causing all Appetites to be subjected unto it, in decent order and submiss obedience to be commanded by Nature. This is the rational part.

Fortitude is a Lawful Observation of command difficult, or not difficult, that is, it is a faculty which keepeth a Lawful Precept.

Justice is an agreement amongst all these, which causeth that the three parts of the Soul agree with one another, and that each be worthily conversant in those things which are proper, and belong unto it.

Thus it is a common intire Perfection of these three Vertues, *Prudence, Fortitude* and *Temperance*, in such manner that Reason commandeth, and the rest of the parts each according to its several Property, are restrained by Reason, and obey it.

Hence it followeth that the Vertues are mutually consequent to one another; Fortitude being the conservation of a lawful precept, is likewise conservative of right Reason. Right Reason proceedeth from Prudence; Prudence cohereth with Fortitude, for it is the Knowledge of good things; but no Man can discern that which is good, if he be distracted by Fear, or involved in the like troubles. In like manner, neither can any Man be Wise, and intemperate, for then he is

CHAP. XXIX.

Of Vertues, Vices, and their differences.

THE gifts of Nature and progress in them are called Vertues also, by reason of their Similitude with the perfect Vertues, assuming the same name. In this Sense we call all Soldiers stout, and sometimes call Imprudent and Rash persons stout, when we speak not of the perfect Vertues, for the perfect neither increase nor decrease; but Vices are intended and remitted. One Man is more imprudent and more unjust than another, neither do all the Vices follow one another, for they are certain contraries which are not compatible to the same. Such is Fury to Cowardice, and Prodigality to Covetousness, nor can there be any Man at once possessed of all Vices, no more than a Body Tormented by all Diseases.

Moreover, there is a mean affection which inclineth not plainly either to Vice or Vertue, for it is not necessary that all men must be good or bad; they are such, who have arrived at the height of these; for it is not easie to pass suddenly from Vertue to Vice, because betwixt extreams there is a great interval and distanc.

Of Vertues some are principal, others concomitant; principal are those which are in the rational part of the Soul, and by which the other Vertues are perfected. Concomitant are those which are in the other part which are subject to Affections. These act honest things according to Reason, not that which is in them, for they have none, but that which they receive from Prudence, which is confirmed in them by Custom and Exercise.

Now for as much as neither Science nor Art consisteth in any part of the Soul, but in the Rational, those Virtues which are in the other part, that is subject to Affections, cannot be taught, because they are neither Arts nor Sciences, neither have they a peculiar Doctrine. Prudence is a Science, which prescribeth unto every one what is proper to him, as a Pilot, or Master of a Ship, to inferiour ignorant Sailors. The like in a common Souldier and a General.

For as much as Ills are intended and remitted, Offences cannot be equal, but some must be greater, others lesser, for which Reason, they, who make Laws, Punish some more gently, others more severely. And though Vertues are certain Heights, as being perfect, and like unto that which is right, yet in another respect they are called Mediocrities, because all or the most of them are placed betwixt two Vices, whereof one sinneth in excess, the other in defect; as on the one side of *Liberality* is *Covetousness*, on the other *Prodigality*. For in Affections we recede from the Mean, when we relinquish that which is placed in Virtue, either by excess or defect. But neither he, who beholding his Parents wronged is nothing moved thereat, nor he who is incensed at the smallest matters void of Passion or Moderate, but the quite contrary. He who at the death of his Parents grieveth not, is void of Passion; He who destroyeth himself with grieving, is over-passionate and immoderate; he who grieveth moderately, is moderately passionate. In like manner, he, who feareth upon all occasions, and more than needs, is Timerous; he who feareth nothing is rash; He only is Stout that can keep a mean betwixt Fear and Rashness; the like in all the rest. And forasmuch as that which is mean in Affections is likewise best, and Mediocrity is nothing but a mean betwixt Excess and Defect, there are these Vertues termed Mediocrities, because in Humane perturbations and passions they affect us a middle kind of way.

CHAP. XXX.

That Vertue is Voluntary, Vice involuntary.

VErtue being chiefly of those things which are in our power, not compulsive (for it could not deserve praise, if it came either by Nature or Divine Decree) it followeth, that Vertue is voluntay, begotten by a fervent, generous, and firm impulsion.

From this, that Vertue is voluntary, it followeth that Vice is involuntary. For, who, in the most excellent part of himself would ever voluntarily choose that which is the greatest of all Ills? When a Man is carried on to Vice, he first enclineth to it, not as if it were ill, but good, and if he fall into ill, doubtless he is deceived with thinking, that this way by a lesser ill, he may arrive at a greater good, and goeth in this manner unwillingly to it. For, it is not possible, a Man should pursue ill as it is ill, without any hope of good, or fear of a greater ill. All ill things therefore, which an ill man doth, are involuntary, for, injustice being involuntary, to act unjustly is so much more involuntary, as the action of Vice is beyond the idle habit thereof. Yet, though wicked actions are involuntary, the wicked nevertheless ought to be punished, and that not after one manner; but, according to the variety of hurt which they do to those they wrong. That which is involuntary consisteth in ignorance of perturbations, all which may be diverted, either by Reason, or civil Custom, or Diligence.

CHAP. XXXI.

Of Love *and* Friendship.

FRiendship, properly so termed, is made by a mutual reciprocal benevolence. This is, when either is as much concerned for the happiness of the other, as of his own, which
equality

equality is preserved only by fimilitude of Manners: For, the like is friend to its like, if they be both Moderate; but, the intemperate cannot agree, either with themfelvs or the Moderate.

There are other things which are thought friendfhips, but are not fuch, in which there appeareth fome fhew of Vertue. Of thefe, is the natural good will of Parents to their Children, and of Kindred one to another, as alfo that which is called Civil and Sociable: Thefe are not always accompanied with mutual Benevolence. Likewife, the Amatory Art is a kind of Friendfhip. That which is Honeft is proper to a Generous Soul, Difhoneft to a Perverfe; mean, to one meanly affected. For, as the habit of the Rational Soul is threefold, Right, Difhoneft, and Mean; fo many different kinds are there of Love, which appeareth moft clearly in the difference of the ends they propofe unto themfelves. The Difhoneft aims only at Corporeal Pleafure, and therefore is abfoluetly Bruitifh. The Honeft confidereth the Mind only, as far as Vertue appeareth in it. The Mean defireth both the Beauty of the Soul and of the Body; of which Love, he who is worthy, is mean likewife; that is, neither abfolutely Honeft nor Difhoneft. Hence that love which aimeth only at the Body, ought to be termed a *Demon* (rather than a Deity, which never defcendeth to an Humane Body) tranfmitting Divine things to Men, and Humane to God.

Of the three kinds of Love, that which is proper to a good Man, being remote from Vicious Affections, is Artificial, whence it is placed in the rational part of the Soul. The Contemplations thereof are thefe, to difcern who is worthy of Love, and to contract Friendfhip with him, and enjoy it: This difcernment is made from his Aims or Defires, whether they are Generous, and directed to a good end, or Violent and Fervent. The contraction, or acquifition of Friendfhip, is made, not by wanton exceffive Praife, but rather by reprehenfion, fhewing him, that it is not convenient he fhould live in that manner he doth; when he enjoyeth the love of him whom he affects, he muft always exhort him to thofe things, by exercife whereof, he may arrive at perfect habit. Their end is that of Lover and Beloved, they may at laft become friends.

CHAP. XXXII.

Of Paffions.

INjuftice is fo great an ill, that it is better to fuffer wrong than to do wrong; for one belongeth to a wicked Man, the other to a weak Man: both are Difhoneft, but to do wrong is worfe, by how much it is more Difhoneft. It is as expedient that a wicked Man be punifhed, as that a fick man fhould be cured by a Phyfician; for all Chaftifement is a kind of Medicine for an offending Soul.

Since the greater part of Virtues are converfant about Paffions, it is neceffary that we define Paffion. Paffion is an irrational motion of the Soul, arifing out of fome good or ill; it is called an irrational motion, becaufe neither Judgments nor Opinions are Paffions; but motions of the irrational parts of the Soul. For in the irrational part of the Soul, there are motions, which though they are done by us, are yet nothing the more in our power. They are often done therefore contrary to our inclination and will; for fometimes it falleth out, that though we know things to be neither pleafing nor unpleafing, expetible nor avoidable, yet we are drawn by them, which could never be if fuch paffions were the fame with Judgment. For we reject Judgment when we difapprove it whether it ought to be fo or otherwife. In the definition is added, arifing from fome good or fome ill, becaufe of that which is mean or indifferent betwixt thefe, no Paffion is ever excited in us. All Paffions arife from that which feemeth good or ill. If we fee good prefent, we rejoyce, if future, we defire. On the contrary, if ill be prefent, we grieve, if imminent, we fear.

The fimple Affections, and, as it were, Elements of the reft are two; *Pleafure* and *Grief*; the reft confift of thefe. Neither are Fear and Defire to be numbred among the principal Paffions, for he who feareth, is not wholly deprived of Pleafure, nor can a Man live the leaft Moment, who defpaireth to be freed or eafed of fome ill. But it is more converfant in Grief and Sorrow, and therefore he, who Feareth, Sorroweth. But he who Defireth, like all thofe who defire or expect fomething, is delighted; infomuch as he is not abfolutely confident; and having not a firm hope he is grieved. And if defire and fear are not principal Paffions, it will doubtlefs follow, that none of the other Affections are fimple; as Anger, Love, Emulation and the like; for in thefe, Pleafure and Grief are manifeft, as confifting of them.

Moreover of Paffions, fome are rough others mild; the mild are thofe, which are naturally in Men, and if kept within their bounds, are neceffary and proper to Man, if they exceed vitious. Such are Pleafure, Grief, Anger, Pity, Modefty; for it is proper to Man to *delight* in thofe things which are according to Nature, and to be grieved at their contraries. *Anger* is neceffary to repel and punifh an Injury. *Mercy* agreeth with Humanity. *Modefty* teacheth us to decline fordid things. Other Paffions are rough, and preternatural, arifing from fome depraved or perverfe Cuftom. Such are exceffive Laughter, Joy in the Misfortunes of others, Hatred of Mankind. Thefe, whether intenfe or remifs, after what manner foever they are, are always Erroneous, and admit not any laudable mediocrity.

As concerning Pleafure and Grief, *Plato* writeth thus. Thefe Paffions are excited in us by Nature. Grief and Sorrow happen to thofe who are moved contrary to Nature; Pleafure to thofe who are reftored to the proper conftitution of their Nature. For he conceiveth the natural ftate of Man to confift sist in a mean betwixt Pleasure and Grief, not moved by either, in which state we live longest. He asserteth several kinds of Pleasure, whereof some relate to the *Body*, others to the *Soul*. Again, of Pleasures some are *mix'd* with Grief, some are *pure*. Again, some proceed from the *remembrance* of things past, others from *Hope* of things to come. Again, some are *dishonest*, as being intemperate and unjust; others *moderate*, and joyned with good, as joy for good things, and the Pleasure that followeth Vertue. Now because most Pleasures are naturally dishonest, he thinks it not to be disputed whether Pleasure can be simply and absolutely a good, that being to be accounted poor and of no value, which is raised out of another, and hath not a principal primary essence. For Pleasure cohereth even with its contrary Grief, and is joyned with it, which could not be, if one were simply good, the other simply ill.

CHAP. XXXIII.

Of the Forms of Common-wealths.

OF the Forms of Commonwealths, some are supposed only, and conceived by abstract from the rest. These he delivers in his Book of a Commonwealth, wherein he describeth the first Concordant, the second Discordant, enquiring which of these is the most excellent, and how they may be constituted. He also divideth a Common-wealth like the Soul into three parts, *Keepers*, *Defenders*, and *Artificers*. The Office of the first is to Counsel, to Advise, to Command; of the second, to Defend the Common-wealth, upon occasion, by Arms, which answereth to the irascible power; To the last belong Arts and other Services. He will have Princes to be Philosophers, and to contemplate the first good, affirming that so only they shall Govern rightly. For Mankind can never be freed from ill, unless either Philosophers Govern, or they who Govern be inspired with Philosophy after a Divine manner. A Common-wealth is then Governed best, and according to Justice, when each part of the City performeth its proper Office. So that the Princes give Laws to the People; the Defenders obey them, and fight for them, the rest willingly submit to their Superiours.

Of a Common-wealth he asserteth five kinds, the first, *Aristocracy*, when the best Rule: the second, *Timocracy*, when the Ambitious; the third, *Democracy*, when the People; the fourth, *Olygarchy*, when a few; the last, *Tyranny*, which is the worst of all.

He describeth likewise other supposed Forms of Common-wealth, as that in his Book of Laws; and, that which reformeth others, in his Epistles, which he useth for those Cities that in his Books of Laws he saith are sick. These have a distinct place, and Select Men out of every Age, as according to the diversity of their nature and place, they require different Institution, Education, and Arms. The Maritime People are to study Navigation and Sea-fight; the Island fighting on foot; those in Mountainous Countries to use light Armour, those on the Shore heavy. Some of these to exercise fighting on Horse-back. In this City he alloweth not a Community of Women. Thus is Politick a Virtue conversant both in Action and Contemplation; the end whereof is to constitute a City, Good, Happy, and Convenient to it self. It considers a great many things, amongst the rest, whether War be to be waged or not.

CHAP. XXXIV.

Of a Sophist.

HItherto we have spoken of a *Philosopher*, from whom a *Sophist* differeth; In *Manners*, because he teacheth young Men for gain, and desireth rather to *seem* than to *be* good. In *matter*, for a Philosopher is conversant in those things which always are, and continually remain in the same manner; but a Sophist in that which is not, for which reason he seeketh darkness, that he may not be known to be what he is. To things that are, that which is not, is not opposed as contrary, for it neither existeth, nor is participant of any Essence, nor can be understood. So that if any Man endeavour to express it in words, or comprehend it by thought; he is deceived, because he putteth together things contrary and repugnant. Yet that which is not, as far as it is spoken, is not a pure negation of that which is, but implieth a relation to another, which in some manner is joyned to *Ens*. So that unless we assume something from that which is, to that which is not, it cannot be distinguished from other things, but thus, as many kinds as they are of *Ens*, so many are there of *Non-Ens*, because that which is not an *Ens* is a *Non-Ens*.

Thus much may serve for an Introduction into *Plato*'s Philosophy: Some things perhaps are said orderly; others dispersedly, or confusedlly; yet is all so laid down, that by those which we have delivered, the rest of his Assertions may be found out and Contemplated.

After so serious a Discourse, it will not be amiss to give the Reader a Poetical Entertainment upon the same Subject,

Being A

PLATONICK DISCOURSE

Written in *Italian*, By

JOHN PICUS Earl of *MIRANDULA*,

In Explication of a Sonnet, By

HIERONIMO BENIVIENI.

The First PART.

SECT. I.

IT is Principle of the *Platonists*, That every created thing hath a three-fold being; Casual, Formal, participated. In the Sun there is no heat, that being but an Elementary Quality, not of Cœlestial Nature: Yet is the Sun the Cause and Fountain of all Heat. Fire is hot by Nature, and its proper form: Wood is not hot of it self, yet is capable of receiving that quality by Fire. Thus hath heat its Casual being in the Sun, its Formal in the Fire, its Participated in the Fuel. The most Noble and Perfect of these is the Casual: and therefore *Platonists* assert, That all Excellencies are in God after this manner of being; That in God is nothing, but from him all things; That Intellect is not in him, but that he is the Original Spring of every Intellect. Such is *Plotinus*'s meaning when he affirms, * *God neither understands nor knows*; that is to say, after a formal way, As *Dionysius Areopagita, God is neither an Intellectual nor Intelligent Nature, but unspeakably exalted exalted above all Intellect and Knowledge.*

* Ennead. 6. lib. 7. 37.

Sect. 2.

Platonists distinguish Creatures into three degrees. The first comprehends the Corporeal and visible; as Heaven, Elements, and all compounded of them: The last the invisible, incorporeal, absolutely free from Bodies, which properly are called Intellectual (by Divines, Angelical) Natures. Betwixt these is a mid-nature, which tho' incorporeal, invisible, immortal, yet moveth Bodies, as being obliged to that Office; called, the Rational Soul; inferiour to Angels, superiour to Bodies; subject to those, regent of these: above which is God himself, Author and Principal of every Creature, in whom Divinity hath a casual being; from whom, proceeding to Angels, it hath a formal being, and thence is derived into the rational Soul by participation of their lustre: below which, no Nature can assume the Title of Divine.

Sect. III.

THAT the first of these three Natures cannot be multiplied, who is but one, the Principal and Cause of all other Divinity, is evidently proved by *Platonists, Peripateticks*, and our Divines. About the second, (*viz.* The Angelick and Intellectual, *Platonists* disagree. Some (as *Proclus, Hermias, Syrianus*, and many others) betwixt God and the rational Soul place a great number of Creatures; part of these they call Νόϵἷα, νοϵρα, Intelligible, part Intellectual; which Terms, *Plato* sometimes confoundeth, as in his *Phædo. Plotinus, Porphyrius*, and generally the most refined *Platonists*, betwixt God and the Soul of the World, assign only one Creature, which they call the Son of God, because immediately produced by him. The first Opinion complies most with *Dionysius Areopagita*, and Christian Divines, who assert the number of Angels to be in a manner Infinite. The second is the more Philosophick, best suiting with *Aristotle* and *Plato*, whose Sense we only purpose to express; and therefore will decline the first Path (tho' that only be the right) to pursue the latter.

Sect. IV.

WE therefore, according to the Opinion of *Plotinus*, confirmed not only by the best *Platonists*, but, even by *Aristotle*, and all the *Arabians*, especially *Avicenne*, affirm, that God from Eternity produced a Creature of Incorporeal and Intellectual Nature, as perfect as is possible for a Created Being, beyond which,

he

he produced nothing; for, of the most perfect cause, the effect must be most perfect, and the most perfect can be but one; for, of two or more, it is not possible but that should be more or less perfect than the rest, otherwise they would not be two, but the same. This reason for our Opinion I rather choose, than that which *Avicen* alledges, founded upon this Principle, That from one Cause, as one, can proceed but one Effect. We conclude therefore, that no Creature but this first Mind proceeds immediately from God: for, of all other effects issuing from this Mind, and all other second Causes, God is only the mediate efficient. This by *Plato*, *Hermes*, and *Zoroaster*, is called the *Daughter of God*, the *Mind*, *Wisdom*, *Divine Reason*, by some interpreted *the Word*; not meaning (with our Divines) the Son of God, he not being a Creature, but one Essence co-equal with the Creator.

Sect. V.

ALL understanding Agents have in themselves the form of that which they design to effect: as an Architect hath in his mind a Figure of the Building he undertakes, which as his Pattern he exactly strives to imitate: This *Platonists* calls the Idea, or Exemplar, believing it more perfect than that which is made after it: and this manner of Being, Ideal, or Intelligible, the other Material and Sensible: So that when a Man Builds a House, they affirm there are two, one Intellectual in the Workman's Mind; the other Sensible, which he makes in Stone, Wood, or the like; expressing in that Matter the Form he hath conceived: to this *Dante* alludes.

———*None any Work can frame,*
Unless himself become the same.

Hereupon they say, tho' God produced only one Creature, yet he produced all, because in it he produced the Ideas and Forms of all, and that in their most perfect Being, that is, the Idea, for which reason they call this Mind, the Intelligible World.

Sect. VI.

AFter the pattern of that Mind they affirm this Sensible World was made, and the Exemplar being the most perfect of all Created things, it must follow that this Image thereof be as perfect as its Nature will bear. And since Animate things are more perfect than the Inanimate; and of those the Rational than the Irrational, we must grant, this World hath a Soul perfect above all others. This is the first Rational Soul, which, tho' Incorporeal, and Immaterial, is destin'd to the Function of Govering and moving Corporeal Nature: not free from the Body as that Mind whence from Eternity it was derived, as was the Mind from God. Hence *Platonists* argue the World is Eternal; its Soul being such, and not capable of being without a Body, that also must be from Eternity; as likewise the Motion of the Heavens, because the Soul cannot be without moving.

Sect. VII.

THE ancient Ethnick Theologians, who cast Poetical Veils over the Face of their Mysteries, express these three Natures by other names. *Cœlum* they call God in himself; he produced the first Mind, *Saturn*: *Saturn*, the Soul of the World, *Jupiter*. *Cœlum* implies Priority and Excellence, as in the Firmament, the first Heaven. *Saturn* signifies Intellectual Nature, wholly imployed in Contemplation; *Jupiter* Active Life, consisting in Moving and Governing all subordinate to it. The Properties of the two latter agree with their Planets: *Saturn* makes Men Contemplative, *Jupiter* Imperious. The Speculative busied about things above them; the practick beneath them.

Sect. VIII.

WHich three names are promiscuously used upon these Grounds: In God we understand first his Excellence, which as Cause, he hath above all his effects; for this he is called *Cœlus*. Secondly, the production of those effects, which denotes Conversion towards inferiours; in this respect he is sometimes called *Jupiter*, but with an addition, *Optimus, Maximus*. The first Angelick Nature hath more names, as more diversity. Every Creature consists of Power and Act: the first, *Plato* in *Philebo*, calls Infinite: the second, finite: all imperfections in the Mind are by reason of the first: all perfections, from the latter. Her Operations are threefold. About Superiours, the Contemplation of God; about the knowledge of her self; about inferiours, the production and care of this sensible World: these three proceed from Act. By Power she descends to make inferiour things; but in either respect is firm within her self. In the two first, because Contemplative, she is called *Saturn*: in the third, *Jupiter*, a name principally applied to her power, as that part from whence is derived the Act of Production of things. For the same reason is the Soul of the World, as she contemplates her self or superiours, termed *Saturn*; as she is imployed in ordering wordly things, *Jupiter*: and since the Government of the World belongs properly to her; the Contemplation to the Mind; therefore is the one absolutely called *Jupiter*, the other *Saturn*.

Sect. IX.

THIS World therefore (as all other creatures) consisteth of a Soul and Body: the Body is all that we behold, compounded of of the four Elements. These have their casual being in the Heavens, (which consist not of them, as sublunary things; for then it would follow that these inferiour parts were made before the Cœlestial, the Elements in themselves being simple, by concourse causing such things as are compounded of them:) Their former being from the Moon down to the Earth: Their participate and imperfect under the Earth, evident in the Fire, Air, and Water, experience daily finds there evinced by natural Philosophers: to which the which the ancient *Theologians* ænigmatically allude by their four Infernal Rivers, *Acheron, Cocytus, Styx,* and *Phlegeton.*

We may divide the Body of the World into three parts: Cœlestial, Mundane, Infernal: The Ground why the Poets feign the Kingdom of *Saturn* to be shared betwixt his three Sons, *Jupiter, Neptune,* and *Pluto:* implying only the threefold variation of this corporeal World; which as long as it remains under *Saturn,* that is, in its Ideal Intellectual being, is one and undivided; and so more firm and potent: but falling into the hands of his Sons, that is, changed to this material Being, and by them divided into three parts, according to the triple existence of Bodies, is more infirm and less potent, degenerating from a Spiritual to a Corporeal estate. The first part, the Heavenly, they attribute to *Jupiter*; the last and lowest to *Pluto*; the middle to *Neptune.* And because in this Principality is all Generation and Corruption, the *Theologians* express it by the Ocean, Ebbing or Flowing continually: by *Neptune* understanding the Power or Deity that presides over Generation. Yet must we not imagine these to be different Souls, distinctly informing these three parts: The World her self being one, can have but one Soul; which as it animates the subterraneal parts, is called *Pluto*; the sublunary *Neptune*; the Cœlestial, *Jupiter.* Thus *Plato* in *Philebo* avers *by Jove is understood a Regal Soul,* meaning the principal part of the World which Governs the other. This Opinion, tho' only my own, I suppose is more true than the exposition of the *Grecians.*

Sect. X.

NExt that of the World, Platonists assign many other Rational Souls, The eight Principal are those of the Heavenly Spheres; which according to their Opinion exceeded not that number; consisting of the seven Planets, and the Starry Orb. These are the nine Muses of the Poets: *Calliope* (the Universal Soul of the World) is first, the other eight are distributed to their severl Spheres.

Sect. XI.

*Timæo.

PLato asserts, * That *the Author of the World made the Mundane, and all other Rational Souls, in one Cup; and of the same Elements; the universal Soul being most perfect, ours least:* whose parts we may observe by this division: Man, the chain that ties the World together, is placed in the midst: and as all *mediums* participate of their extreams, his parts correspond with the whole World; thence called *Microcosmus.* In the World is first Corporeal Nature, eternal in the Heavens; Corruptible in the Elements, and their Compounds, as Stones, Metals, &c. Then Plants. The third degree is of Beasts. The fourth Rational Souls. The fifth Angelical Minds. Above these is God, their Origine. In Man are likewise two Bodies; one eternal, the Platonists *Vehiculum Cœleste,* immediatly informed by the Rational Soul: The other Corruptible, subject to sight, consisting of the Elements: Then the vegetative faculty, by which Generated and nourished. The third part is Sensitive and Motive. The fourth Rational; by the Latine *Peripateticks* believed the last and most Noble part of the Soul: Yet, above that is the Intellectual and *Angelick*; the most excellent part whereof, we call the Souls Union, immediately joyning it to God, in a manner resembling him; as in the other Angels, Beasts, and Plants. About these Platonists differ, *Proclus* and *Porphyrius* only allow the Rational part to be Immortal; *Zenocrates* and *Speusippus* the sensitive also; *Numenius* and *Plotinus* the whole Soul.

Sect. XII.

IDea's have their casual being in God, their Formal in the first Mind, their participated in the rational Soul. In God they are not, but produced by him in the *Angelick* Nature; through this communicated to the Soul, by whom illuminated, when she reflects on her intellectual parts, she receives the true forms of things, *Ideas.* Thus differ the Souls of Men from the Cœlestial: These in their bodily functions recede not from the Intellectual, at once Contemplating and Governing, Bodies ascend to them, they descend not. Those employed in Corporeal Office are deprived of Contemplation, borrowing Science from Sense, to this wholly enclined, full of Errors: Their only means of release from this Bondage, is, the amatory life; which by sensible Beauties, exciting in the Soul a remembrance of the Intellectual, raiseth her from this terrene life, to the eternal; by the flame of Love refined into an Angel.

The Second PART.

SECT. I.

THe apprehensive Faculties of the Soul are employed about Truth and Falshood; assenting to to one, dissenting from the other. The first is affirmation, the second negation. The desiderative converse in good and ill, inclining to this, declining to that. The first is Love, the second Hate. Love is distinguished by its objects; if of Riches, termed Covetousness; of Honour, Ambition; of Heavenly things, Piety; of equals, friendship: these we exclude, and admit no other signification, but *the desire to possess what in it self, or at least in our esteem, is fair:* of a different nature from the love of God to his Creatures, who comprehending all, cannot desire or want the Beauty and perfections of another: and from that of Friends which must be reciprocal. We therefore with *Plato* define it, ὄρεξις τῶ καλῶ *The desire of Beauty.* Desire is an inclination to real or apparent good. As

Love

there are divers kinds of good, so of desire. Love is a Species of desire, Beauty of good. Desire is Natural or Knowing. All creatures have a particular perfection by participation of the Divine Goodness. This is their end, including that degree of Felicity, whereof they are capable, to which Center they tend. This desire we call Natural; a great Testimony of Divine Providence, by which they are unwittingly (as an Arrow by the Archer) directed to their mark. With this all Creatures desire God, as being the Original good imprinted, and participating in every particular. This is in every Nature, as more or less capable; addressed to ends more or less Noble; yet, is the ultimate end of all the same, to enjoy God, as far as they may: Thus as the Psalmist, *Every thing Worships and Praiseth God*; like suppliants, *turning and offering themselves up to him*, saith *Theodoret*.

Sect. II.

THE other Species of Desire is employed only about things known, given by Nature, that to every apprehensive faculty, there might be a desiderative; to embrace what it judgeth good, to refuse what it esteemeth evil; in its own nature enclin'd to good: None ever desires to be miserable; but, the apprehensive Vertue many times mistaking Evil for Good, it oft falls out that the desiderative (in it self blind) desires Evil. This in some sense may be said voluntary, for none can force it; in another sense, not voluntary, deceived by the judgment of its Companion. This Is *Plato*'s meaning, when he saith, * *No Man Sins willingly.*

* In Timæo, Κακὸς μὲν γὰρ ἑκὼν ὀδεὶς.

Sect. III.

IT is the property of every desiderative Vertue, that he who desires, possesseth in part the thing he desires, in part not: for, if he were wholly deprived of its Possession, he would never desire it: This is verified two ways. First, nothing is desired unless it be known; and to know a thing is in some part to possess it. So *Aristotle*, † *The Soul is all, because it knows all*. And in the Psalmist God saith, *All things are mine, I know them*. Secondly, there is always some convenience and resemblance betwixt the desirer and desired: Every thing delights and preserves it self by that, which by natural affinity is most conformable to it; by its contrary is grieved and consumed. Love is not betwixt things unlike; Repugnance of two opposite natures is natural hate. Hate is a Repugnance with Knowlege. Hence it followeth, that the nature of the desired, is in some manner in the desirer; otherwise there would be no similitude betwixt them: yet imperfectly; else it were vain for it to seek what it entirely possesseth.

† De Anima, 3. 9.

Sect. IV.

AS Desire generally follows Knowledge, so several knowings are annexed to several desiring Powers. We distinguish the knowing into three degrees; Sense, Reason, Intellect; attended by three desiderative Vertues, Appetite, Election, Will. Appetite is in Bruits, Election in Men, Will in Angels. The Sense knows only corporeal things, the Appetite only desires such; the *Angelick* Intellect is wholly intent on Contemplation of Spiritual Conceptions, not inclining to Material Things, but when divested of Matter, and Spiritualiz'd, their Will is only fed with intemporal spiritual good. Rational Nature is the mean betwixt these Extreams; sometimes descending to Sense, sometimes elevated to Intellect; by its own Election complying with the desires of which she pleaseth. Thus it appears, that Corporeal Objects are desired, either by Sensual Appetite, or Election of Reason inclining to Sense: Incorporeal by Angelick Will, or, the Election of Reason, elevated to Intellectual Height.

Sect. V.

BEauty in general, is a *Harmony resulting from several things proportionably concurring to constitute a third*: In respect of which temperament, and mixture of various Natures, agreeing in the composition of one, every Creature is fair; and in this sense no simple Being is Beautiful, not God himself; this Beauty begins after him, arising from contrariety, without which is no composition; it being the union of contraries, a friendly enmity, a disagreeing concord; whence *Empedocles* makes discord and concord the Principles of all things; by the first, understanding the variety of the Natures compounding; by the second, their Union: adding, that in God only there is no discord, He not being the Union of several Natures; but, a pure uncompounded Unity. In these compositions the Union necessarily predominates over the contrariety, otherwise the Fabrick would be dissolved. Thus in the Fictions of the Poets, *Venus* loves *Mars*: This Beauty cannot subsist without contrariety; she curbs and moderates him, this temperament allays the strife betwixt these contraries. And in Astrology, *Venus* is placed next to *Mars*, to check his destructive influence; as *Jupiter* next *Saturn*, to abate his Malignancy. If *Mars* were always subject to *Venus* (the contrariety of Principles to their due temper) nothing would ever be dissolved.

Sect. VI.

THis is Beauty in the largest sense, the same with Harmony; whence God is said to have framed the World with musical Harmonious temperament. But harmony properly implies a melodious agreement of voices; and Beauty in a strict acception relates to a proportionable concord in visible things, as Harmony in audible. The desire of this Beauty is Love; arising only from one knowing faculty, the Sight; and that gave *Plotinus*, (*Ennead* 3. *lib.* 5, 3.) occasion to derive ἔρως Love, from ὅρασις Sight. Here the Platonist may object; If Love be only of visible things, how can it be applied to *Ideas*, invisible Natures? We answer, sight is twofold, Corporeal and Spiritual; the first is that of sense, the other the Intellectual faculty, by which we agree with Angels; this Platonists call Sight, the Corporeal being only an Image of this. So *Aristotle*, *Intellect is that to the Soul which sight is to the Body.* Hence is *Minerva* (Wisdom) by *Homer* called γλαυκῶπις, *Bright-ey'd.* With this sight *Moses*, St. *Paul*, and, other Saints, beheld the face of God; this Divines call Intellectual, intuitive cognition, the Beatifical vision, the Reward of the Righteous.

Sect. VII.

AS Sight, so Beauty (its Object) is twofold the two *Venus's* Celebrated by *Plato*, [*Sympos.*] and our Poet) Sensible, called Vulgar *Venus.* Intellectual in *Ideas* (which are the Object of the Intellect, as colour of sight) named Celestial *Venus.* Love also is twofold, Vulgar and Celestial; for as *Plato* saith * *There must necessarily be as many Lovers as Venus's.*

* *Sympos.*

Sect. VIII.

VEnus then is Beauty, whereof Love is generated: properly his Mother, because Beauty is the cause of Love, not as productive Principle of this Act, to Love, but as its object: the Soul being the efficient cause of it as of all his Acts; Beauty the material: for in Phylosophy the efficient is assimilated to the Father, the material to the Mother.

Sect. IX.

CElestial Love is an Intellectual desire of Ideal Beauty: *Ideas*, (as we said before) are the Patterns of things in God, as in their Fountain; in the *Angelick* Mind, Essential; in the Soul by participation, which with the Substance partakes of the *Ideas* and Beauty of the first Mind. Hence it follows, that Love of Celestial Beauty in the Soul, is not Celestial Love perfectly, but the nearest Image of it. Its truest being is with the desire of Ideal Beauty in the first Mind, which God immediately adorns with *Ideas.*

Sect. X.

LOve (saith *Plato*) was begot on *Penia*, by *Porus* (the Son of *Metis*) in *Jupiter's* Orchard, being drunk with Nectar, when the Gods met to celebrate *Venus's* Birth. Nature in it self inform, when it receives form from God is the *Angelick* Mind; this form is *Ideas*, the first Beauty; which in this descent from their Divine Fountain, mixing with a different nature, become imperfect. The first Mind, by its opacousness eclipsing their lustre, desires, that Beauty which they have lost; this desire is love; begot when *Porus* the affluence of *Ideas* mixed with *Penia* the indigence of that inform nature we termed *Jupiter* (1. 8.) *In whose Garden the Ideas are Planted*, with those the first Mind adorned, was by the Antients named *Paradise* ; to which contemplative life and eternal felicity *Zoroastres* inviting us, saith, *Seek, seek Paradise:* Our Divines transfer it to the *Cælum Empyræum*, the seat of the happy Souls, whose blessedness consists in contemplation and perfection of the Intellect, according to *Plato.* This Love *begot on Venus's Birth-day*, that is, when the Ideal Beauty, though imperfectly, is infused into the *Angelick* Mind; *Venus* yet as a Child, not grown to Perfection. *All the Gods assembled at this Feast*,that is,their Ideas, (as by *Saturn* we understand both the Planet and his *Idea*) an expression borrowed from *Parmenides.* These Gods then are those *Ideas* that precede *Venus* (she is the Beauty and Grace resulting from their variety.) *Invited to a Banquet of Nectar and Ambrosia:* those whom God Feasts with *Nectar* and *Ambrosia* are Eternal Beings, the rest not; These *Idea's* of the *Angelick* Mind are the first Eternals; *Porus was drunk with Nectar*,this Ideal affluence fill'd with Eternity; other *Idea's* were not admitted to the Feast,nor indued with Immortality.

Orpheus upon the same grounds saith, Love was born before all other Gods, in the bosom of *Chaos* : Because Nature full of indistinct imperfect forms (the Mind replenished with confused *Idea's*) desires their perfection.

Sect. XI.

THE *Angelick* Mind desires to make these *Idea's* perfect; which can only be done by means opposite to the causes of their imperfection, these are Recession from their Principle, and mixtion with a contrary Nature : Their Remedy, Separation from the unlike Nature, and return and conjunction (as far as possible) with God. Love, the desire of this Beauty, excites the Mind to Conversion and re-union with him. Every thing is more perfect as nearer its Principle; This is the first Circle. The *Angelick* Mind, proceeding from the Union of God, by Revolution of intrinsecal Knowledge returneth to him. Which with the Antients is *Venus adulta*, grown to perfection. Every Nature that may have this conversion, is a Circle; such alone are the Intellect and Rational, and therefore only capable of Felicity, the obtaining their first Principle, their ultimate end and highest good. This is peculiar to Immortal Substances, for the Material (as both *Platonists* and *Peripateticks* grant) have not this reflection upon themselves, or their Principle. These, (the *Angelick* Mind and Rational Soul) are the two intelligible Circles; answerable to which in the Corporeal World are two more ; the tenth Heaven immovable Image of the first Circle; the Celestial Bodies, that are moveable, Image of the second : The first *Plato* mentions not, as wholly different and irrepresentable by corporeal Nature : Of the second *in Timæo* he saith, That *all the Circles of this visible Heaven* (by him distinguished into the fixed Sphere and seven Planets*) represent as many Circles in the Rational Soul.*

Some attribute the name of Circle to God ; by the ancient Theologists called *Cœlus*; being a Sphere which comprehends all ; as the utmost Heaven includes the World.

In one respect this agrees with God, in another not; the property of beginning from a point and returning to it, is repugnant to him; who hath no beginning, but is himself that indivisible point from which all Circles begin, and to which they return : And in this sense it is likewise inconsistent with material things, they

they have a beginning, but cannot return to it.

In many other Properties it agrees with God; He is the most perfect of Beings; this of Figures; neither admit addition: The last Sphere is the place of all Bodies, God of all Spirits: the Soul (say Platonists) is not in the Body, but the Body is in the Soul, the Soul in the Mind, the Mind in God, the utmost place; who is therefore named by the Cabalists. מקום

Sect. XII.

THE three Graces are Handmaids to *Venus* *Thalia*, *Euphrosyne*, *Aglaia*; Viridity, Gladness, Splendour; properties attending Ideal Beauty. *Thalia*, is the permanence of every thing in its entire being; thus is Youth called green, Man being then in his perfect state; which decays as his years encrease, into his last dissolution. *Venus*, is proportion, uniting all things. Viridity, the duration of it; In the Ideal World, where is the first *Venus*, is also the first Viridity; for no Intelligible Nature recedes from its Being by growing old. It communicates this Property to sensible things as far as they are capable of this *Venus*, that is, as long as their due proportion continues. The two other properties of Ideal Beauty are Illustration of the Intellect, *Aglaia*, Repletion of the Will with desire and joy, *Euphrosyne*.

Of the Graces one is painted looking toward us; The continuation of our being is no reflex act. The other two with their Faces from us, seeming to return; the operations of the Intellect and Will are reflexive; *What comes from God to us, returns from us to God.*

Sect. XIII.

VEnus is said to be born of the Sea; Matter, the Inform Nature whereof every Creature is compounded, is represented by Water, continually flowing, easily receptable of any Form. This being first in the Angelick Mind, Angels are many times exprest by Water, as in the Psalms, *The Waters above the Heavens praise God continually,* so Interpreted by *Origen*; and some *Platonists* expound the Ocean (stiled by *Homer* Father of Gods and Men) this Angelick Mind, Principle and Fountain of all other Creatures; *Gemistius*, *Neptune*; as Commander of all Waters, of all Minds, Angelical and Humane. This is that living Fountain, whereof he that drinketh shall never thirst: These are the Waters whereon (*David* saith) God hath founded the World.

Sect. XIV.

POrus (the Affluence of *Ideas* proceeding from God) is stiled by *Plato* the Son of *Metis* (Counsel,) in Imitation of the Scripture: whence our Saviour by *Dionysius Areopagus* is termed the Angel of Counsel, that is, the Messenger of God the Father; so *Avicen* calls the first Cause conciliative, the Mind not having *Ideas* from it self but from God, by whose Counsel she receiveth Knowledge and Art to frame this visible World.

Sect. XV.

LOve * according to *Plato*, is *Youngest and* *Symposium.* *Oldest of the Gods*; They, as all other things, have a two-fold Being, Ideal and Natural. The first God in his natural Being was Love, who dispenc'd theirs to all the rest; the last in his Ideal. Love was born in the Descent of the *Ideas* into the Angelick Mind, which could not be perfect till they, its Essence, were made so, by Love's Conversion to God. The Angelick Mind owing its Natural Being to *Love*, the other Gods who succeeded this Mind, necessarily are younger than He in their natural Being, though they precede him in their Ideal, as not born till these *Ideas*, though imperfectly, were joyned to the informed Nature.

Sect. XVI.

THE *Kingdom of Necessity is said to be* *Plat. Sympos.* *before that of Love.* Every Creature consists of two Natures, Material, the imperfect, (which we here understand by Necessity) and Formal the occasion of Perfection. That whereof it most partakes is said to be predominant, and the Creature to be subject to it. Hence is Necessity (Matter) supposed to Reign when the *Idea*'s were Imperfect, and all Imperfections to happen during that time: all Perfections after Love began his Reign; for, when the Mind was by him Converted to God; that which before was imperfect in her, was perfected.

Sect. XVII.

† VEnus *is said to commend Fate.* The Order † *Plat. Sympos.* and Concatenation of Causes and Effects in this sensible World, called Fate, depends on the Order of the Intelligible World, Providence. Hence Platonists place Providence (the ordering of *Ideas*) in the first Mind, depending upon God, its ultimate end, to which it leads all other things. Thus *Venus*, being the Order of those *Ideas*, whereon Fate, the World's Order, depends, Commands it.

Fate is Divided into three parts, *Clotho*, *Lachesis*, and *Atropos*: That which is one in Providence, indivisible in Eternity, when it comes into Time and Fate, is divisible into Past, Present, and Future. Others apply *Atropos* to the fixed Sphere, *Clotho*, to the seven Planets, *Lachesis* to sublunary things.

Temporal Corporeal things only are subjected to Fate; the Rational Soul being Incorporeal, predominates over it; but is subjected to Providence, to serve which is true Liberty, by whom the Will (obeying its Laws) is led to the Acquisition of her desired end. And as often as she endeavours to loose her self from this Servitude, of Free, she becomes a Servant and Slave to Fate, of whom before she was the Mistress. To deviate from the Laws of Providence, is, to forsake Reason to follow Sense and Irrational Appetite, which being Corporeal, are under Fate; he that serves these, is much more a Servant than those he serves.

Sect. XVIII.

AS from God *Ideas* descend into the *Angelick* Mind, by which the Love of Intellectual Beauty is begot in her, called *Divine Love*; so the same Ideas descend from the Angelick Mind into the Rational Soul, so much the more imperfect in her, as she wants of Angelical Perfection: From these Springs *Humane Love*. *Plato* discourseth of the first, *Plotinus* of the latter: who by the same Argument, whereby he proves *Ideas* not Accidental but Substantial in the *Angelick* mind, evinceth likewise the specifical Reasons, the *Ideas* in the Soul to be substantial, terming the Soul *Venus*, as having a specious spendid Love, in respect of these splecifical Reasons.

Sect. XIX.

VUlgar Love is the Appetite of sensible Beauty through corporeal sight. The cause of this Beauty is the visible Heaven by its moving power. As our Motive Faculty consists in Muscles and Nerves (the Instruments of its Operation,) so the Motive Faculty of Heaven is fitted with a Body proper for Circular Sempiternal Motion: Through which Body the Soul (as a Painter with his Pencil) changeth this inferiour Matter into various Forms. Thus vulgar *Venus* (the Beauty of material Forms) hath her casual being from the moving power of the Heavens, her formal from colour, enlightned by the visible Sun, as *Ideas* by the invisible; her participate in the Figure and just order of parts communicated to sight by mediation of Light and Colour, by whose interest only it procures Love.

Sect. XX.

AS when the *Ideas* descend into the Mind, there ariseth a desire of enjoying that from whence this Ideal Beauty comes; so when the species of sensible Beauty flow into the Eye, there springs a twofold Appetite of Union with that, whence this Beauty is derived: one Sensual, the other Rational; the Principles of Bestial and Humane Love. If we follow Sense, we judge the Body wherein we behold this Beauty, to be its Fountain; whence proceeds a desire of Coition, the most intimate union with it: This is the Love of irrational Creatures. But Reason knows, that the Body is so far from being its Original, that it is Destructive to it, and the more it is severed from the Body, the more it enjoys its own Nature and Dignity: we must not fix with the Species of Sense in the Body, but refine that Species from all Reliques of Corporeal Infection.

And because Man may be understood by the Rational Soul, either considered apart, or in its union to the Body; in the first sense, Humane Love is the Image of the Celestial; in the second, desire of sensible Beauty; this being by the Soul abstracted from Matter, and (as much as its Nature will allow) made Intellectual. The greater part of Men reach no higher than this; others more perfect, remembring that more perfect Beauty which the Soul (before immers'd in the Body) beheld, are inflamed with an incredible desire of reviewing it, in pursuit whereof, they separate themselves as much as possible from the Body, of which the Soul (returning to its first Dignity) becomes absolute Mistress. This is the Image of Celestial Love, by which Man ariseth from one Perfection to another, till his Soul (wholly united to the Intellect) is made an Angel. Purged from material dross, and transformed into spiritual flame by this Divine Power, he mounts up to the Intelligible Heaven, and happily rests in his Fathers Bosom.

Sect. XXI.

VUlgar Love is only in Souls immerst in matter, and overcome by it, or at least hindred by perturbations and passions. *Angelic* Love is in the Intellect, Eternal as it. Yet but inferr'd, the greater part turning from the Intellect to sensible things, and corporeal cares. But so perfect are these Celestial Souls, that they can discharge both Functions, Rule the Body, yet not be taken off from Contemplation of Superiors: These the Poets signifie by *Janus* with two Faces, one looking toward upon Sensible things, the other on Intelligible: less perfect Souls have but one face, and when they turn that to the Body, cannot see the Intellect, being deprived of their Contemplation: when to the Intellect, cannot see the Body, neglecting the care thereof. Hence those Souls that must forsake the Intellect, to apply themselves to Corporeal Government, are by Divine Providence confined to caduque, Corruptible Bodies, loosed from which, they may in a short time, if they fail not themselves, return to their Intellectual felicity. Other Souls not hindred from Speculation, are tied to Eternal Incorruptible Bodies.

Celestial Souls then (designed by *Janus*, as the Principles of Time, Motion intervening) behold the Ideal Beauty in the Intellect, to love it perpetually; and inferiour sensible things, not to desire their Beauty; but to communicate this other to them. Our Souls before united to the Body, are in like manner double-faced; but, are then as it were, cleft asunder, retaining but one; which as they turn to either object, Sensual or Intellectual, is deprived of the other.

Thus is vulger Love inconsistent with the Celestial; and many Ravished at the sight of Intellectual Beauty, become blind to sensible; imply'd by *Callimachus*, Hymn 5. in the Fable of *Tyresias*, who viewing *Pallas* naked, lost his sight; yet by her was made a Prophet, closing the Eyes of his Body, she opened those of his Mind, by which he beheld both the present and future. The *Ghost* of *Achilles* which inspired *Homer* with all Intellectual Contemplations in Poetry, deprived him of corporeal sight.

Though Celestial Love liveth eternally in the Intellect of every Soul; yet only those few make use of it, who declining the care of the Body, can with St. *Paul* say, *Whether in the Body, or out of the Body they know not.* To which state a Man sometimes arrives; but continues there but a while, as we see in *Ecclesiastes*.

Sect.

Sect. XXII.

THus in our Soul (naturally indifferent to Sensible or Intelligible Beauty) there may be three Loves; one in the Intellect, Angelical; the second Humane; The third Sensual: The two latter are conversant about the same object, Coporeal Beauty; the sensual fixeth its Intention wholly in it; the Humane separates it from Matter. The greater part of Mankind go no further than these two; but they whose understandings are purified by Philosophy, knowing Sensible Beauty to be but the Image of another more perfect, leave it, and desire to see the Celestial, of which they have already a Tast in their Remembrance, if they persevere in this Mental Elevation, they finally obtain it: and recover that which though in them from the beginning, yet they were not sensible of, being directed by other Objects.

The Sonnet.

I.

LOve, (whose Hand guides my Heart's strict Reins,
Nor, tho' he Govern it, disdains
To feed the Fire with pious care
Which first himself enkindled there.)
Commands my backward Soul to tell
What Flames within her Bosom dwell;
Fear would perswade her to decline
The Charge of such a high Design;
But all her weak Reluctance fails,
'Gainst greater Force no Force avails.
Love to advance her Flight will lend
Those Wings by which be did descend
Into my Heart, where he to rest,
For ever, long since built his Nest:
I, what from thence he dictates, write,
And Draw him thus by his own Light.

II.

LOve, flowing from the Sacred Spring
Of uncreated good, I sing:
When Born; how Heaven he moves; the Soul
Informs; and doth the World controul;
How closely lurking in the heart,
With his sharp Weapons subtle art
From heavy Earth he Man unties,
Enforcing him to reach the Skies.
How kindled, how he flames, how burns;
By what Laws guided now he turns
To Heaven, now to the Earth descends
Now rests 'twixt both, to neither bends.
Apollo, Thee I Invocate,
Bowing beneath so great a weight.
Love, Guide me through this dark design,
And imp my shorter wings with thine.

III.

WHen from true Heaven the Sacred Sun
Into th' Angelick Mind did run,
And with enliven'd Leaves adorn,
Bestowing Form on his first-born;
Inflaming by innate desires,
She to her chiefest good aspires;
By which Reversion her rich Breast
With various Figures is imprest;
And by this Love exalted turns
Into the Sun, for whom she burns,
This flame, rais'd by the Light that shin'd
From Heaven, into th' Angelick Mind,
Is Eldest Love's Religious Ray,
By Wealth and Want begot that Day,
When Heav'n brought forth the Queen, whose Hand
The Cyprian Scepter doth Command.

IV.

THis Born in Amorous Cypris Arms,
The Sun of her bright Beauty warms.
From this our first desire accrues,
Which in new Fetters caught, pursues
The honourble path that guides
Where our Eternal good resides.
By this the Fire, through whose fair Beams
Life from above to Mankind streams,
Is kindled in our hearts, which glow
Dying, yet dying greater grow;
By this th' Immortal Fountain flows,
Which all Heaven forms below, bestows;
By this descends that shower of Light
Which upwards doth our minds invite;
By this th' Eternal Sun inspires,
And Souls with Sacred lustre fires.

V.

AS God doth to the Mind dispence
Its Being, Life, Intelligence,
So doth the Mind the Soul acquaint
How t' Understand, to Move, to Paint;
She thus prepar'd, the Sun that shines
In the Eternal Breasts designs,
And here what she includes diffuses,
Exciting every thing that uses
Motion and Sense (beneath her State)
To Live, to Know, to Operate.
Inferiour Venus hence took Birth;
Who shines in Heaven, but lives on Earth,
And o'er the World her shadow spreads:
The Elder in the Sun's Glass reads
Her Face, through the confused skreen
Of a dark shade obscurely seen;
She Lustre from the Sun receives,
And to the Other Lustre gives;
Celestial Love on this depends,
The Younger, vulgar Love attends.

VI.

FOrm'd by th' Eternal Look of God.
From the Sun's most sublime abode.
The Soul descends into Man's Heart,
Imprinting there with wondrous Art
What worth she borrow'd of her Star,
And brought in her Celestial Carr;
As well as Humane Matter yields,
She thus her Curious Mansion Builds;
Yet all those Flames from the Divine
Impression differently decline:
The Sun, who's Figur'd here, his Beams
Into another's Bosom streams;
In whose agreeing Soul he stays,
And Gilds it with his Virtuous Rays,
The Heart in which Affection bred,
Is thus by pleasing Error fed.

VII.

The heart where pleasing Error reigns,
   This Object as her Child maintains,
By the fair Light that in her shines
   (A rare Cœlestial Gift,) refines;
And by degrees at last doth bring,
   To her first splendours sacred spring:
From this Divine Look, one Sun passes
   Through three refulgent Burning-glasses,
Kindling all Beauty, which the Spirit,
   The Body, and the Mind inherit.
The rich spoils, by th' Eye first caught,
   Are to the Souls next Handmaid brought,
Who there resides: She to the Breast
   Sends them; reform'd, but not express'd:
The heart from Matter Beauty takes,
   Of many one Conception makes;
And what were meant by Nature's Laws,
   Distinct, She in one Picture draws.

VIII.

The heart by Love allur'd to see
   Within her self her Progeny;
This, like the Sun's reflecting Rays
   Upon the Waters face, surveys;
Yet some Divine, though Clouded Light
   Seems here to twinkle, and invite
The Pious Soul, a Beauty more
   Sublime, and perfect to adore,
Who sees no longer his dim shade
   Upon the Earth's vast Globe display'd,
But certain Lustre, of the true
   Sun's truest Image now in view.
The Soul thus entring in the Mind,
   There such uncertainty doth find.
That she to clearer Light applies
   Her aims, and near the first Sun flies:
She by his Splendour Beauteous grows,
   By Loving whom all Beauty flows
Upon the Mind, Soul, World, and All
   Included in this spacius Ball.

IX.

But hold! Love stops the forward Course
   That me beyond my scope would force.
Great Power! if any Soul appears
   Who not alone the Blossoms wears,
But of the rich Fruit is possest,
   Lend him thy Light, deny the rest.

The Third PART.

To treat of both Loves belongs to different Sciences; Vulgar Love to Natural or Moral Philosophy; Divine, to Theology or Metaphysicks. *Solomon* discourseth excellently of the first in *Ecclesiastes*, as a Natural Philosopher; in his *Proverbs* as a Moral: Of the second in his *Canticles*, esteemed the most Divine of all the Songs in Scripture.

Stanza. I.

The chief Order Established by Divine Wisdom in created things, is, that every interiour Nature be immediatly Governed by the Superiour; whom whilst it obeys, it is guarded from all ill, and led without any obstruction to its determinate Felicity; but, if through too much Affection to its own Liberty, and desire to prefer the Licentious Life before the profitable, it Rebel from the Superiour Nature, it falls into a double inconvenience. First, like a Ship, given over by the Pilot, it lights sometimes on one Rock, sometimes on another, without hope of reaching the Port. Secondly, it loseth the Command it had over the Natures subjected to it, as it hath deprived its Superiour of his. Irrational Nature is Ruled by another, unfit for its Imperfection to Rule any. God by his ineffable Excellence provides for every thing, himself needs not the Providence of any other: Betwixt the two extreams, God and Bruits, are Angels and Rational Souls, Governing others, and Governed by others. The first Hierarchy of Angels immediately illuminated by God, enlighten the next under them; the last (by Platonists termed *Dæmons*, by the Hebrews אלהים, as Guardians of *Men*) are set over us as we over Irrationals. So *Psal.* 8. Whilst the Angels continued subject to the Divine Power, they retained their Authority over other Creatures; but when *Lucifer* and his Companions through inordinate love of his own Excellence, aspired to be equal with God, and to be conserved, as He, by their own strength, they fell from Glory to extream Misery; and when they lost the Priviledge they had over others, seeing us freed from their Empire, enviously every hour insidiate our Good. The same Order is in the lesser World, our Soul: the inferiour Faculties are directed by the Superiour, whom following they err not. The imaginative corrects the mistakes of outward Sense; Reason is illuminated by the Intellect, nor do we at any time miscarry, but when the Imaginative will not give Credit to Reason, or Reason confident of it self, resists the Intellect. In the desiderative the Appetite is Governed by the Rational, the Rational by the Intellectual, which our Poet implies, saying,

[*Love*

[*Love, whose Hand guides my Heart's strict Reins.*]

The Cognoscitive Powers are seated in the *Head*, the Desiderative in the *Heart* : In every well ordered Soul, the Appetite is Governed by Intellectual Love; implied by the Metaphor of *Reins*, borrowed from *Plato* in his *Phædrus*.

[*Love to advance my flight, will lend The Wings by which he did ascend Into my heart*———]

When any Superiour Vertue is said to *descend*, we imply not, that it leaves its own heigth to come down to us, but draws us up to it self; its descending to us, is our ascending to it; otherwise such conjunction would be the imperfection of the Vertue, not the perfection of him who receives it.

II.

[*Love flowing from the Sacred Spring Of uncreated good*———]

From the Fountain of Divine Goodness into our Souls, in which that influx is terminated.

[*When Born.* &c.]

The Order, Participation, conversion of Ideas see Part 2, Sect.

[———*how Heaven he moves, the Soul Informs, and doth the World controul.*]

Of these three properties, Love is not the efficient : God produceth the Ideas in the Angelick Mind, the Mind illustrates the Soul with Ideal Beauty ; Heaven is moved by its proper Soul : But, without Love, these Principles do not operate: He is the cause of the Mind's conversion to God, and of the Soul's to the Mind ; without which, the Ideas would not descend into the one, nor the Specifick Reasons into the other : the Soul not illuminated by these, could not elicite this sensible form out of Matter, by the motion of Heaven.

III.

When the first emanation from God (the plenty of Ideas) descended into the Angelick Mind, she, desiring their perfection, reverts to God, obtaining of him what she covets ; which the more fully she possesseth, the more fervently she loves. This desire, (Celestial Love,) born of the obscure Mind and Ideas is explained in this *Stanza* :

[—*true Heaven*—]

God who includes all created beings, as Heaven all sensible, *lib.* 2. Sect. Only Spiritual things, according to *Platonists*, are *true* and real, the rest but shadows and images of these.

———[*the Sacred Sun*———]

The light of Ideas streaming from God.

[———*enlivened Leaves*———]

The Metaphor of *Leaves* relates to the Orchard of *Jupiter*, where these Ideas were planted, 2. 10. *Enlivened*, as having in themselves the principle of their operation, Intellection the noblest life, as the Psalmist, *Give me understanding, and I shall live*. So the *Cabalist* to the second *Sephira*, which is *Wisdom*, attributes the name of *Life*.

[———*adorn bestowing form*———]

To *Adorn* denotes no more than accidental perfection, but Ideas are the substance of the Mind, and therefore he adds, *bestowing form* ; which though they come to her from without, she receives not as accidents, but as her first intrinsecal act : Which our Author implies, terming her *desires innate*.

[*And by this Love exalted turns Into the Sun, for whom she burns.*]

Love transforms the Lover into the thing loved.

[———*Wealth and Want*———]

Porus and *Penia*, 2. 10.

IV.

The properties of *Celestial Love* are in this *Stanza* discovered.

[—*In new Fetters caught*—]

The Soul being opprest by the Body, her desire of Intellectual Beauty sleeps; but awakened by Love, is by the sensible Beauty of the Body, led at last to their Fountain, God.

[———*which glow Dying, yet glowing greater grow.*]

Motion and Operation are the signs of Life, their privation of Death : in him who applies himself to the Intellectual part, the rational and the sensitive fail ; by the Rational he is Man, by the Intellectual Communicates with Angels : As Man he dies, revived an Angel. Thus the Heart dies in the flames of Intellectual Love ; yet consumes not, but by this death *grows greater*, receives a new and more sublime Life. See in *Plato* the Fables of *Alcestes* and *Orpheus*.

V. This

V.

This *Stanza* is a Description of Sensible Beauty.

[*The elder in the Sun's glass reads*
Her Face, through the confused screen
Of a dark shade obscurely seen.]

Sensible Light is the act and efficacy of Corporeal; Spiritual Light of Intelligible Beauty. Ideas in their descent into the inform Angelisk Mind, were as Colours and Figures in the Night: As he who by Moonlight seeth some fair Object, desires to view and enjoy it more fully in the day; so the Mind, weakly beholding in her self the Ideal Beauty dim and opacous (which our Author calls the *Screen of a dark shade*) by reason of the Night of her Imperfection, turns like the Moon) to the Eternal Sun, to perfect her Beauty by him; to whom addressing her self, she becomes Intelligible Light; clearing the Beauty of Celestial *Venus*, and rendring it visible to the eye of the first Mind.

In Sensible Beauty we consider first the Object in it self, the same at Midnight as at Noon: Secondly, the light, in a manner the Soul thereof: the Author supposeth, that as the first part of the Sensible Beauty (Corporeal Forms) proceeds from the first part of Intellectual Beauty (Ideal forms) so sensible light flows from the Intelligence, descending upon Ideas.

VI, VII, VIII.

Corporeal Beauty implies, first, the material disposition of the Body, consisting of Quantity in the proportion and distance of parts, of quality in Figure and Colour: Secondly, a certain quality which cannot be exprest by any term better than Gracefulness, shining in all that is fair: This is properly *Venus*, Beauty, which kindles the Fire of Love in Mankind: They who affirm it results from the disposition of the Body, the Sight, Figure, and Colour of Features, are easily confuted by experience. We see many Persons Exact and unaccustomable in every part, destitute of this Grace and Comeliness; others less perfect in those particlar conditions, excellently graceful and comely; Thus *Catullus*,

Many think Quintia *Beauteous, Fair, and tall,*
And streight she is, apart I grant her all:
But altogether Beauteous I deny;
For, not one Grace doth that large shape supply.

He grants her Perfection of Quality, Figure, and Quantity; yet not allows her handsome, as wanting this Grace. This then must by consequence be ascribed to the Soul, which when perfect and lucid, transfuseth even into the Body some Beams of its Splendor. When *Moses* came from the Divine Vision in the Mount, his Face did shine so exceedinly, that the People could not behold it unless veiled. *Porphyrius* relates, that when *Plotinus*'s Soul was Elevated by Divine Contemplation, an extraordinary brightness appeared in his looks. *Plotinus* himself avers, that there was never any Beautiful Person wicked, that this Gracefulness in the Body, is a certain sign of Perfection in the Soul, *Proverbs* 17. 24. *Wisdom shineth in the Countenance of the Wise.*

From Material Beauty we ascend to the first Fountain by six Degrees: The Soul through the Sight represents to her self the Beauty of some particular Person, inclines to it, is pleased with it, and while she rests here, is in the first, the most Imperfect material degree. 2. She reforms by her Imagination the Image she hath received, making it more Perfect as more Spiritual; and separating it from Matter, brings it a little nearer Ideal Beauty. 3. By the light of the Agent Intellect abstracting this Form from all singularity, she considers the Universal Nature of Corporeal Beauty by it self: This is the highest degree the Soul can reach whilst she goes no further than Sense. 4. Reflecting upon her own Operation, the knowledg of Universal Beauty, and considering that every thing founded in Matter is particular, she concludes this Universality proceeds not from the outward Object, but her Intrinsecal Power; and Reasons thus: If in the dim Glass of material Phantasms this Beauty is represented by virtue of my Light, it follows, that beholding it in the clear Mirror of my substance divested of those Clouds, it will appear more perspicuous: thus turning into her self, she finds the Image of Ideal Beauty communicated to her by the Intellect, the Object of Celestial Love. 5. She ascends from this Idea in her self, to the place where Celestial *Venus* is, in her proper Form; who in fulness of her Beauty not being comprehensible, by any particular Intellect, she, as much as in her lies, endeavours to be united to the first Mind, the chiefest of Creatures, and general Habitation of Ideal Beauty, obtaining this, she terminates and fixeth her Journey: this is the sixth and last degree: They are all imply'd in the 6, 7, and 8 *Stanza's*.

[*Form'd by th' Eternal look,* &c.]

Platonists affirm some Souls are of the Nature of *Saturn*, others of *Jupiter*, or some other Planet; meaning, one Soul hath more Conformity in its Nature with the Soul of the Heaven of *Saturn*, than with that of *Jupiter*, and so on the contrary; of which there can be no Internal Cause assigned; the External is God, who (as *Plato* in his *Timæus*) Soweth and Scattereth *Souls, some in the Moon, others in other Planets and Stars, the Instruments of Time.*

Many imagine the Rational Soul descending from her Star, in her *Vehiculum Cœleste*, of her self forms the Body, to which by that Medium she is united: Our Author upon these grounds supposeth, that into the *Vehiculum* of the Soul, by her endued with Power to form the Body, is infused from her Star a particular formative vertue, distinct according to that Star; thus the Aspect of one is *Saturnine*, of another Jovial,

Jovial, &c. in their looks were read the nature of their Souls:

But because inferiour Matter is not ever obedient to the Stamp, the Virtue of the Soul is not always equally exprest in the visible Effigies: hence it happens that two of the same Nature are unlike; the Matter whereof the one consists being less disposed to receive that Figure than the other; what in that is compleat is in this imperfect; our Author infers, that the Figures of two Bodies being formed by vertue of the same Star, this Conformity begets Love.

[*From the Sun's most Sublime abode.*]

The Tropick of *Cancer*; by which Souls according to the *Platonists* descend, ascending by *Capricorn*. *Cancer* is the House of the Moon, who predominates over the vital parts, *Capricorn* of *Saturn*, presiding over Contemplation.

[*The Heart in which Affection's bred
Is thus by pleasing Error fed.*]

Frequently, if not always, the Lover believes that which he loves more Beauteous than it is, he beholds it in the Image his Soul hath formed of it; so much fairer as more separate from Matter, the Principle of Deformity; besides, the Soul is more indulgent in her Affection to this Species, considering it is *her own Child*, produc'd in her Imagination.

[———*one Sun passes
Through three refulgent Burning-glasses*]

One Light flowing from God, Beautifies the Angelick, the Rational Nature, and the Sensible World.

[———*the Soul's first Hand-maid*———]

The Imaginative

[—*to the Breast*]

The *Breast* and *Heart* here taken for the Soul, because her nearest Lodging; the Fountain of Life and Heat.

[*Reform'd but not exprest.*]

Reform'd by the Imagination from the Deformity of Matter; yet not reduc'd to perfect Immateriality, without which, true Beauty is not exprest.

SPVSIPPVS.

CHAP. I.

His Life.

Laert.

SPEUSIPPUS was an *Athenian*, born at *Mirrhynus* [wich belonged to the *Pandionian* Tribe] his Father named *Eurymedon*, his Mother *Potone*, Sister to *Plato*.

* *Apul. dogm. Plat.*

* He was brought up in the Domestick Documents of his Uncle *Plato*, † who (as he used to say) Reformed *Speusippus*'s *Life after the Pattern of his own.*

† *Plut. de adulat. & amici discrim*

* *Chio, Epist. ad Madrid.*

* *Plato* had four Kinswomen, Daughters of his Nieces; the eldest of these he Married to *Speusippus*, with a small Portion, thiry *Minæ*, which *Dionysius* had sent him: To this summ *Chio*, glad of the Occasion, added a Talent, which *Speusippus* earnestly refused, until at last, he was overcome by the just importunities of the other to receive it, alledging that he gave it not as Money, but as Kindness; that such gifts were to be entertained, for they encreased Honour,

honour, the rest were dishonourable; that he ought to accept of the good-will, though he despised the Money. The rest of those Virgins were married richly to *Athenians*, only *Speusippus*, who best deserved, was poor. With these Arguments *Speusippus* was induced to accept of *Chio*'s gift; whereat *Chio* much congratulated his own good Fortune, as having laid hold of an occasion, *such, as perhaps*, saith he, *I shall not meet again in all my Life*.

Plut. vit. Dion. When *Dion* came to *Athens*, *Speusippus* was continually in company with him, more than any other Friend there, by *Plato*'s Advice, to soften and divert *Dion*'s Humour, with a facile Companion, such as he knew *Speusippus* to be; and that withal, he knew discreetly how to observe time and place in his Mirth: whence *Timon* (in *Sillis*) calls him, *a good Jester*.

The last time that *Plato*, upon the importunity of *Dionysius*, went to *Sicily*, *Speusippus* accompanied him. Whilst they lived at *Syracuse*, *Speusippus* kept more Company with the Citizens than *Plato* did, and insinuating more into their Minds, at first they were afraid to speak freely to him, mistrusting him to be one of *Dionysius*'s Spies: But within a while they began to confide in him, and all agreed in this, to pray *Dion* to come to them, and not to take care for Ships, Men or Horses, but to hire a Ship for his own Passage; for the *Sicilians* desired no more, than that he would lend them his Name and Person against the Tyrant.

Speusippus at his return to *Athens*, perswaded *Dion* to War against *Dionysius*, and deliver *Sicily* from the Bondage of Tyranny, assuring him the Country would receive him gladly. *Dion* upon this Information received such encouragement, that he began secretly to levy Men: The Philosophers much advanced his Design. When he went to *Sicily*, he bestowed a Country-House, which he had purchased since his coming to *Athens*, upon *Speusippus*.

CHAP. II.

His Profession of Philosophy.

† *Laert.* *P*Lato dying in the first year of the 108th Olympiad, *Theophilus* being Archon, *Speusippus* succeeded him in the School of the Academy, † whom he followed also in his Doctrine.

† *Laert.* He first, as *Theodorus* affirms, looked into the Community, and mutual assistance of Mathematical Disciplines, as *Plato* did into that of the Philosophical.

* *Laert.* * He first, according to *Cineas*, declared those things, which *Isocrates* conceived not to be divulged, the same perhaps which † *Cicero* calls μυεστήκιον of *Isocrates*.

† *Epist. ad At.* 2. 1.
* *Stob. Phys.* 1. 1.

* He affirmed, that the Mind was not the same, either with *Good* or *One*; but of a peculiar Nature proper to it self.

* *Laert.* * He set up in the School which *Plato* had built, the Images of the Graces.

He exacted Money of his Disciples, contrary to the custom of *Plato*.

The two Women who were *Plato*'s Auditors, *Lasthenia* the *Mantinean*, and *Axiothea* the *Phliasian*, heard *Speusippus* likewise.

Having continued *Master* of the School eight years, he at last, by reason of his infirm Disposition, much debilitated by the Palsie, sent to *Xenocrates*, desiring him to come and take from him the Government of the School, which *Xenocrates* did.

CHAP. III.

His Writings.

HE wrote † many things, chiefly in Philosophy, Commentaries and Dialogues, of which were † *Laert. Suid.*

Aristippus the Cyrenaick.
Of Riches 1.
Of Pleasure 1.
Of Justice 1.
Of Philosophy 1.
Of Friendship 1.
Of the Gods 1.
The Philosopher 1.
To Cephalus 1.
Cephalus 1.
Clinomachus, or Lysias 1.
The Citizen 1.
Of the Soul 1.
To Gryllus 1.
Aristippus 1.
The Confutation of Arts 1.
Commentary Dialogues.
Artificial 1.
Dialogues of likeness in things 10.
Divisions and Arguments to things like.
Of the Genus's and Species of Examples.
To Amartirus.
Encomium of Plato.
Epistles to Dion, Dionysius, Philip.
Of Law.
The Mathematician.
Mandrobulus.
Lysias.
Definitions, of all these Writings the only extant.
Orders of Commentaries.
Verses.

* *Phavorinus*, in the second of his Commentaries, saith, That *Aristotle* paid three Talents for his Books. * *Laert.*

CAAP. IV.

His Death.

HE was (as † *Timotheus* saith) very infirm of Body, * insomuch that he was fain to be carried up and down the Academy in a kind of a running Chair: Riding in this manner, he one day met *Diogenes*, whom saluting, he said, Joy be with you: But not with you, answered *Diogenes*, who can endure to live being in that condition. At length he dyed willingly through Grief, as *Laertius* affirms, who elsewhere citing *Plutarch in the Lives of* Lysander *and* Scylla, saith, He died of the *Phthiriasis*; but there is no such thing extant in *Plutarch*.

† *Laert.*
* *Laert.*

Though

c Laert.

c Though he followed *Plato* in his Opinions; yet he did not imitate his Temper, for he was austere, cholerick, and had not so great command over his Pleasures. In anger he threw a Dog into a Well, and indulging to Pleasure, he went to the Marriage of *Cassander*, in *Macedonia*: He was also so great a Lover of Money, that some Poems which he had written, not very good, he sung publickly for gain: For which Vices, *Dionysius* writing to him, thus derides him: *And we may learn Philosophy from our* Arcadian *She-Scholar*. *Plato* took no Mony of his Scholars, you exact it whether they are willing or not. *d Athenæus* cites the same Epistle, after he had reproached him for Avarice and Voluptuousness, he objects his Collections of Money from many Persons; his Love to *Lasthenia*, the Sardian Curtezan; after all this adding, *Why do you accuse us of Avarice, who your self omit not any sordid way of gain? Did not you after* Hermias's *Debt was satisfied, make Collections in his Name amongst his Friends, to your own use?*

d Deipn. lib.

To a rich Man in love with a deformed Person; *What need you her*, faith he? *for ten Talents you may have a handsomer.*

Laert.

To him *Simonides* wrote Histories, wherein he related the actions of *Dion* and *Bion*.

There was another *Speusippus*, a Physician of *Alexandria*.

XENOCRATES.

CHAP. I.

His Country, Parents, and living with Plato.

a Laert.
b Suid.

Xenocrates was of *Chalcedon*, Son of ª *Agatho*, or ᵇ *Agathenor*. From the Years of his Life 82. which in all probability ended when *Polemo* succeeded in the School, the first Year of the 116th Olympiad: It may be gathered that he was born in the fourth Year of the 95th Olympiad. He heard *Plato* from his Childhood. He was dull of Apprehension; whence *Plato* comparing him with *Aristotle*, said, *One needs a Spur, the other a Bridle; what an Ass and what an Horse have I to Yoak together!* He was severe, and had a sad Look, for which reason *Plato* oft said to him, *Xenocrates, Sacrifice to the Graces*, which was an usual Phrase to Melancholy People.

c Ælian. 14. 9.

ᶜ Another time *Plato* sharply reprehended the roughness of his Disposition, which he took quietly and unmoved; saying to one that instigated him to reply in his own defence, *No, this is an Advantage to me.*

d Laert.
e Ath. Deipn.

ᵈ He accompanied *Plato* in his Voyage to *Sicily*, ᵉ where at a drinking Feast, with *Dionysius*, being honoured with a Wreath of Gold, instead of a Garland of Flowers; which were bestowed upon the Guests upon such Occasions, when he went away, he put it upon the Statue of *Mercury*, where they used to leave their ordinary Garments.

f Laert.

ᶠ when *Dionysius* fell out with *Plato*, and threatned to find one that should cut off his Head, *Xenocrates* made answer, *not before he hath cut off this*, shewing his own.

g Var. hist. 3. 19.

ᵍ *Ælian* saith, that *Xenocrates* having taken a Journey into his own Country, *Aristotle* with his Disciples came to *Plato*. *Speusippus* was at that time sick, and therefore could not be with *Plato*. *Plato* being fourscore years old, (which falls upon the fourth Year of the 107th Olympiad, the Year before his Death) his Memory through Age much decay'd, *Aristotle* fell upon him with subtle Sophistical questions, whereupon *Plato* gave over walking in publick and retired with his Friends to his own House. At the end of the three Months *Xenocrates* returning from his Travel, finds *Aristotle* walking where he had left *Plato*, and seeing that he and his Friends, when they went out of the School went not to *Plato*, but to some other part of the City, he asked one there present, what was become of *Plato*, thinking he had been Sick; the other answered, he is not Sick, but *Aristotle* hath molested him, and driven him out of the School, so that now he teacheth Philosophy in his own Garden. *Xenocrates* hearing this, went immediately to *Plato*, whom he found discoursing to his Disciples, persons of great worth and eminence. As soon as he had ended his Discourse, he saluted *Xenocrates*, as he used, very kindly, and *Xenocrates* him. When the Company was dismist, *Xenocrates*, without speaking a word of it to *Plato*, getting his Friends together, after he had chid *Speusippus* for permitting *Aristotle* to possess the School, made a Head against *Aristotle*, and opposed him with his utmost force, until at last he re-instated him in the School. Thus *Ælian*. But this Story, which he acknowledgeth to have taken up no better Authority than vulgar Report, disagrees with many Circumstances of *Aristotle*'s Life, supported by far more credible Testimonies.

CHAP.

CHAP. II.

His Profession of Philosophy.

After *Speusippus* had held the School eight years, finding himself not able to continue that charge any longer, he sent to *Xenocrates*, intreating him to take it upon him, which *Xenocrates* did ^a in the second year of the 110th Olympiad, *Lysimachides* being Archon, not without emulation and dissension with the Peripateticks, for ^b *Aristotle*, at his return out of *Macedonia*, finding *Xenocrates* possessed of the Academy, instituted a School in opposition to him, in the Lycæum saying,

Silent to be now most disgraceful were,
And see Xenocrates *possess the Chair.*

^c Some affirm, that *Alexander* falling out with *Aristotle*, to vex him, sent a Present to *Xenocrates*, ^d of fifty Talents, whereof *Xenocrates* took but 3000 Atticks, and sent back the rest, saying, That *he needed it most that was to maintain so many.* Or, as ^e *Stobæus* relates it, having entertained the Messenger after his usual Fashion, Go and tell *Alexander*, saith he, that after the rate I live, I shall not need fifty Talents in all my Life. ^f The Money being brought back to *Alexander*, he asked, if *Xenocrates* had not any Friend, adding that as for his own Friends, the Wealth of *Darius* was too little for them.

† He asserted *Unity* and *Duality* to be *Gods*; the first as it were Masculine, in the nature of a Father, reigning in Heaven, whom he called also *Jupiter*, the *Odd*, and the *Mind.* The other, as it were Female, and the Mother commanding all things under Heaven. This he called the Mind of the Universe. He likewise asserts Heaven to be Divine, and the fiery Stars to be Olympian Gods, the rest sublunary invisible Deities, which permeate through the Elements of Matter, whereof that which passeth through the Air is called *Juno*, that which through the Water, *Neptune*, that which through the Earth, *Ceres*. This the *Stoicks* borrowed from him, as he the former from *Plato*.

* He continued Master of the School twenty five years, until the first year of the hundred and sixth Olympiad; then his Disciple *Polemo* succeeded him. During that time, he lived very retired in the Academy; and if at any time he went into the City, all the Tradesmen and other People thronged to see him.

CHAP. III.

His Vertues and Apothegms.

† Amongst his other Vertues, he was very remarkable for his Continence, of which there is this Instance: *Phryne*, a famous *Athenian* Curtezan, having laid a Wager with some Young Men his Disciples, that she could not resist her Enticements, stole privately into his Bed: The next Morning being question'd and laught at by his Disciples, she said, the Wager they laid was of a Man, not of a Stone. To this end he used to mortifie himself by incision, and cauterising of his Flesh.

† His Wisdom and Sanctity was much reverenced by *Athenians*; for being to give his Testimony, and to swear, as the custom was, that he spoke nothing but truth, the Judges all rose up, and cried out, that he should not Swear, indulging that to his Sincerity, which they did not allow to one another.

* Being sent with others to *Philip* on an Embassy, the rest received Gifts from him, and went to treat in private with him; *Xenocrates* did neither, and for that part was not invited by him: The Ambassadours returning to *Athens*, said, that *Xenocrates* went along with them to no purpose: Whereupon the *Athenians* were ready to impose a mulct upon him; but when they understood by him, that they were at that time to consider chiefly concerning the Common-wealth, *Philip* having corrupted the rest with Gifts, and that he would not accept any, they bestowed double Honours upon him. *Philip* said afterwards, that of those who came to him, only *Xenocrates* would not take any Gifts.

Being sent in the time of the *Lamiack* War (which was about the second year of the hundred and fourth Olympiad) Ambassador to *Antipater*, about the redemption of some *Athenian* Prisoners, *Antipater* invited him to sit down to Supper, whereto he answered in the words of *Ulysses* in *Homer*:

O Circe, *what Man is there that is good,*
Before his friends are freed can think of food.

Antipater was so pleased with the ingenious application of these Verses, that he caused the Prisoners immediately to be set at Liberty.

† His Clemency, saith *Ælian*, extended not only to Men, but, often to irrational Creatures, as once, when a Sparrow, pursued by a Hawk, flew to his Bosom, he took it, much pleased, and hid it till the Enemy were out of Sight; and when he thought it was out of Fear and danger, opening his Bosom, he let it go, saying, that he had not betrayed a Suppliant.

* *Bion* deriding him, he refused to make any answer in his own Defence; for, a Tragedy, saith he, being mocked by a Comedy, needs not a Reply.

To one, who though he neither had learned Musick, Geometry, nor Astronomy; yet desired to be his Disciple: *Away*, saith he, *you have not the handles of Philosophy.* Some affirm he said, *I teach not to card Wool.*

Antipater coming to *Athens*, met and saluted him; which Salute he returned not, until he had made an end of the Discourse he was about.

† He was nothing proud; he assigned a particular Business to every part of the Day, a great part thereof to Meditation, one part to Silence.

* Whensoever he pierced a Vessel of Wine, it was soured before he spent it, and the Broths that were made for him were often thrown

thrown away the next day; whence proverbially was used, *the Cheese of* Xenocrates, of things that last well, and are not easily consumed.

† *Val. Max. 7. 2.*

† Holding his Peace at some detractive discourse; they asked him why he spoke not? Because, saith he, I have sometimes repented of speaking, but never of holding my Peace.

Yet, this Man, saith *Laertius*, because he could not pay the Fine imposed upon Aliens, the *Athenians* sold. *Demetrius Phalerius* bought him, contenting both Parties, the *Athenians* with their Tribute, *Xenocrates* with his Liberty.

CHAP. IV.

His Writings.

† *Laert.*

†HE left many Writings, Verses, exhortations, and Orations, their Titles these.

Of Nature 6 Books.
Of Wisdom 6.
Of Riches 1.
Arias 1.
Of Indefinite 1.
Of a Child 1.
Of Continence 1.
Of Profitable 1.
Of Free 1.
Of Death 1. which some conceive to be the same with that which is extant amongst the spurious *Platonick* Dialogues, under the Title of *Axiochus*.
Of Voluntary 1.
Of Friendship 2.
Of Equity 1.
Of Contrary 2.
Of Beatitude 2.
Of Writing 1.
Of Memory 1.
Of False 1.
Callicles 1.
Of Prudence 2.
Oeconomick 1.
Of Temperance 1.
Of the Power of Law 1.
Of a Commonwealth 1.
Of Sanctity 1.
That Vertue may be taught 1
Of Ens 1.
Of Fate 1.
Of Passions 1.
Of Lives 1.
Of Concord 1.
Of Disciples 2.
Of Justice 1.
Of Vertue 2.
Of Species 1.
Of Pleasure 2.
Of Life 1.
Of Fortitude 1.
Of One 1.
Of Ideas 1.
Of Art 1.
Of Gods 2.
Of the Soul 2.
Of Science 1.
Politick 1.
Of Scientificks 1.
Of Philosophy 1.
Of Parmenides Opinions 1.
Archidemus, or of Justice 1.
Of Good 1.
Of things which pertain to Intellect 8.
Solutions concerning Speech 1.
Physical Auscultation 6.
A Summary. 1.
Of Genus's and Species 1.
Pythagorean Assertions 1.
Solutions 2.
Divisions 8.
Positions 3.
Of Dialectick 14, & 15, & 16.
Of Disciplines concerning Distinctions 9.
Concerning Ratiocination 9.
Concerning Intelligence 4.
Of Disciplines 6.
Concerning Intelligence 2.
Of Geometry 5.
Commentaries 1.
Contraries 1.
Of Numbers 1.
Theory of Arithmetick 1.
Of Intervals 1.
Astrologick 6.
Elements, to Alexander *concerning a Kingdom* 4.
To Tribas.
To Hephæstion.
Of Geometry 2.
Verses 345.

CHAP. V.

His Death.

HE died in the 82 year of his age by a fall in the Night into the Basin (wherein he was drowned) probably in the first year of the 116th Olympiad, for in that Year *Polemo* his Successor took upon him the School.

Laertius saith, there were six more of his Name, but mentions only five. One, very ancient, skilful in *Tacticks*; another of the same City and Family with this Philosopher, Author of the Oration upon the Death of *Arsinoe*; the fourth saith he, a Philosopher, who writ in Elegiack Verse, but not happily, perhaps the same, who, *Suidas* saith, was nothing inferiour to this *Xenocrates* for Continence; the fifth, a Statuary, the sixth a Writer of Songs, as *Aristoxenus* affirms.

POLEMO.

POLEMO.

Laert. POLEMO was an *Athenian* of *Oca*, [a Town belonging to the *Oenian* Tribe,] his Father *Philostratus* (who
† *Laert.* according to † *Antigonus Carystius*) was a Citizen of great account; and kept a Chariot and Horses.

Laert. *Polemo* in his Youth was very Intemperate, and dissolute; he frequently took a sum of Money, and hid it in a private corner of some Street, to supply his Extravagances upon occasion. Even in the Academy were found three *oboli*, which he had hid under a Pillar, upon the same account. This Wildness caused discontent betwixt him and his Wife, who, thinking herself not not well used by him, accused him ὡς μειρακίοις συνών]α.

* 6. 7. * Neither did he delight (saith *Valerius Maximus*,) in Luxury only, but even in the infamy thereof. On a time, coming from a Feast, not after the setting but rising of the Sun; and seeing the Door of *Zenocrates* the Philosopher open, full of Wine, smelling sweet of Unguents, crowned with Garlands, richly attired, he rushed into his School, which was filled with a Croud of Learned Persons. Not contented with so rude an Intrusion, he sate down also, intending to make sport at his excellent Eloquence, and prudent Precepts. Hereupon all were offended as the Affront deserved, only *Zenocrates*, continuing the same Countenance and Gesture, fell from the Discourse in which he was, and began to speak of Modesty and Temperance, with the gravity of whose Discourse, *Polemo* being reduced to Repentance, first took his Garland off from his Head, and flung it on the Ground; soon after he withdrew his Arm within his Cloak; Next he laid aside the cheerfulness of that look which he had, formerly, when he affected feasting; lastly, he wholly divested himself of Luxury, and being thus cured by the wholesome Medicine of one Discourse, he, from an infamous Prodigal became a most excellent Phi-
* *Laert.* losopher, being * from that time forward so addicted to study, that he surpassed all the rest, and succeeded *Xenocrates* in the Government of the School, which he began in the first Year of the 116th Olympiad.

After he began to study Philosophy, he had such a constant Behaviour, that he retained always the same Countenance, and kept the same tone in all his Speech, whereby *Crantor* was taken with him. A Mad Dog having bit him by the Knee, he alone of all the Company seem'd to be unconcerned in it, and a Tumult happening thereupon in the City, he asked without any disturbance, what was the matter? In the Theatres also, he was nothing moved. When *Nicostratus* the Poet, sirnamed *Clytemnestra*, recited something to him and *Crates*, *Crates* was much taken therewith, but he made no more show than as if he had heard nothing, and was altogether such as *Melanthius* the Painter in his Books of Picture hath described him, for he saith in his actions was expressed a stubbornness and hardness.

Polemo used to say, we ought to exercise our selves in things, not in Dialectick Disciplines, lest, satisfying our selves with the taste and meditation of the superficial parts of Science, we become admired for subtilty in Discourse, but contradict our selves in the practice of our Life.

He was facete and ingenious, shunning that which *Aristophanes* imputes to *Euripides*, fowerness and harshness. He taught, not sitting, but, walking. The *Athenians* much honour'd him for his great Integrity, he took great delight in Solitude, whence for the most part he dwelt in a Garden, about which his Disciples built themselves little Lodges, near to his School. He was a studious imitator of *Xenocrates* (who, *Aristippus* saith, much loved him) always remembring his Innocence, severity and gravity, to which, like a Dorick Measure, he conformed his own Steps.

Ath. Deipn. lib. 2. *Antigonus Carystius* saith, that from the thirtieth year of his Age to his Death, he drank nothing but Water.

Stob. Phys. l.3. He held that the World is God.

He much affected *Sophocles*, chiefly in those places where (to use the Phrase of the Comick Poet) *a Molossian Dog seemeth to have written together with him.* And whereas *Phrynicus* saith he was

Not sweet, nor flat, but gently smooth; he said, that *Homer* was an Epick *Sophocles*, *Sophocles* a Tragick *Homer*.

He died very old of a Consumption, and left behind him many Writings. *Laertius* hath this Epigram upon him;

Wert thou not told, that Polemo lies here.
On whom slow sickness (man's worst passion) prey'd?
No, 'tis the Robe of Flesh he us'd to wear,
Which ere to Heaven he mounted, down he laid.

Of his Disciples are remembred *Crates*, *Zeno* the Stoick, and *Arcesilaus*.

CRATES.

Laert.

CRATES was a *Thriasian*, Son of *Antigenes* ; he was an Auditor of *Polemo*, and loved by him ; he succeeded him in the Government of his School. They both profited so much by one another, that living they not only followed the same institutes, but even to their last ends were alike, and being dead, were buried in the same Sepulchre. Upon which occasion *Antagorus* writ thus upon them both,

Who ere thou art, say ere thou passest by,
Crates and Polemo here buried lie;
Both for their mutual Love no less admir'd,
Than for their Eloquence, by which inspir'd,
O th' wisdom they profess'd the Age was proud,
Yet gladly to their sacred Precepts bow'd.

Hence *Arcesilaus*, when he went from *Theophrastus*, and applied himself to them, said, *They were Gods, or certain Reliques of the Golden Age.*

They were nothing popular, but what *Dionysiodorus* an ancient Musician was wont to say, may be applied to these, when he boasted, that none had ever heard him sing, as they had *Ismenius*, nor had ever seen him in a Ship, or at the Fountains.

Antigonus saith, that he sojourned at *Crantor*'s, when he and *Arcesilaus* lived most friendly, and that *Arcesilaus* dwelt with *Crantor*, *Polemo* with *Crates*, together with *Lysicles*, who was one of the Citizens, and truly, *Polemo*, as is before-mentioned, loved *Crates* ; *Crantor*, *Arcesilaus*. But *Crates* dying, as *Apollodorus* in the third of his Chronicle, left Books which he had written, partly of Philosophy, partly of Comedy ; Orations suited for publick pleading, or Embassie.

He had many eminent Disciples, of whom was *Arcesilaus*, and *Bion* the *Boristhenite*, afterwards called a *Theodorean* from that Sect.

There were ten of this Name. The *First* an antient Comick Poet.

The *Second*, an Oratour of the Family of *Isocrates*.

The *Third*, an Ingineer, that went along with *Alexander* in his Expeditions.

The *Fourth*, a Cynick.
The *Fifth*, a Peripatetick.
The *Sixth*, this Academick.
The *Seventh*, a Grammarian.
The *Eighth* writ of Geometry.
The *Ninth*, an Epigrammatick Poet.
The *Tenth*, of *Tarsis*, an Academick Philosopher.

CRANTOR.

Laert.

Crantor was of *Soli*, much admired in his own Country. He came to *Athens*, where he heard *Xenocrates*, and studied with *Polemo*.

He writ *Commentaries*, 3000 *Verses*, whereof some ascribe part to *Arcesilaus*.

Being asked how he came to be taken with *Polemo*, he answered from the tone of his Speech, never exalted nor depressed.

Falling Sick, he went to the Temple of *Æsculapius*, and walked there ; where many resorted to him from several parts, not thinking he stayed in respect of his Sickness, but that he meant to erect a School in that place ; amongst the rest came *Arcesilaus*, whom, tho' he loved him very much, he recommended to *Polemo*, whom he himself after his recovery heard also, and was extreamly taken with him.

He bequeathed his Estate, amounting to twelve Talents to *Arcesilaus*, who asking him where he would be buried, he answered,

In Earth's kind Bosom happy 'tis to lie.

He is said to have written Poems, and to have deposited them, sealed up in his own Country, in the Temple of *Minerva*; of him thus *Theætetus.*

Pleasing to Men, but to the Muses more.
Crantor too soon of Life was dispossest,
Earth his cold Body we to thee restore,
That in thy Arms he peacefully may rest.

Crantor above all admired *Homer* and *Euripides*, saying it was hard in proper Language to speak at once tragically and passionately, and quoted this Verse out of his *Bellerophon*.

Alas, yet why alas,
Through such Fate Mortals pass.

Antagoras the Poet alledgeth these Verses, as written by him.

* *My Soul's in doubt, for doubtless is his race,*
Whether I Love first of all Gods shall place,
Which drew from Erebus their old descent,
And Night beyond the Ocean's vast extent ;
Or whether to bright Venus, or to Earth,
Thou owest thy double form, and sacred birth.

ἀμφήκες]ον. one doubtless imitating the other, which both the Interpreters not observing, have strangely rendred this place.

* Read Ἐν δοιῇ μοι θυμός, ὁποῖ, &c. as Callimachus hymn. 1. Ἐν δοιῇ μάλα θυμός, ἐπεὶ γένος

He was very ingenious in imposing apt names. He said of an ill Poet that his Verses were full of Moths; and of *Theophrastus*, that his Theses were written in a Shell.

He wrote a Treatise concerning Grief, which was generally much admired, as *Cicero* and *Laertius* attest.

He died before *Polemo* and *Crates* of the Dropsy.

ARCESILAUS.

CHAP. I.

His Country, Parents, Teachers.

ARcesilaus (whom *Cicero* calls *Acesilas*) was a *Pitanean* of *Æolis*; his Father, according to *Apollodorus*, in the third of his Chronologicks, named *Seuthus*, or as others *Scythus*. He was the youngest of four Brethren, two by the same Father, only the other by the same Mother; the eldest was named *Pylades*: Of those who had the same Father, the eldest was *Mæreas*, Guardian to his Brother *Arcesilaus*.

He was born by computation from his death (which was in the fourth year of the * hundred thirty and fourth Olympiad, the seventy fifth of his Age) in the first Year of the hundred and sixteenth Olympiad.

* *Aldobrandinus* his edition reads the 130.

He first heard *Autolychus* the Mathematician, his Country-man, before he came to *Athens*, with whom he travelled to *Sardis*.

Next he heard *Xanthus* an *Athenian*, a Master of Musick.

He heard also *Hipponicus* the Geometrician, who, excepting his Skill in that Art, was otherwise a gaping dull Fellow, for which *Arcesilaus* deriding him, said, Geometry flew into his Mouth as he gaped. Of *Hipponicus* falling mad, he took so great care that he brought him to his own House, and kept him there until he was quite cured.

He likewise, by the compulsion of his Brother, studied Rhetorick, and being by Nature vehement in Discourse, and of indefatigable Industry, he addicted himself likewise to Poetry. There is an Epigram of his extant upon *Attalus* to this effect;

For Arms and Horses oft hath been the Name
Of Pergamus *through* Pisa *spread by Fame:*
But, now shall (if a mortal may divine)
To future times with greater Glory shine.

There is another Epigram of his *upon Menodorus, Son of Eudemus*.

Far hence is Thyatire, *far Phrygian Earth,*
Whence Menodore *thou didst derive thy Birth.*
But down to Acheron unpierc'd by Day,
From any place thou knew'st the ready way.
To thee this Tomb Eudemus *dedicates,*
Whom Love hath wealthy made, tho' poor the Fates.

Although his Brother *Mæreas* would have had him professed Rhetorick, yet was he naturally more enclined to Philosophy; to which end, he first became a hearer of *Theophrastus*, in which time *Crantor* being much taken with him, spoke that Verse of *Euripides* to him, out of his *Andromeda*:

Maid, if I save thee, wilt thou thankful be?

He answered in the following Verse,

Stranger, for Wife or Slave accept of me.

From thence-forward they lived in intimate Friendship, whereat *Theophrastus* troubled, said, *He had lost a Youth of extraordinary Wit, and quickness of Apprehension*.

He emulated *Pyrrho*, as some affirm, and studied Dialectick, and the Eretriack Philosophy, whence *Aristo* said of him,

Pyrrho *beyond,* Plato *before,*
And in the middle Diodore.

And *Timon*,

Next leaden Menedemus *he pursues,*
And Pyrrho *doth, or* Diodorus *choose.*

And soon after maketh him say thus;

I'll swim to Pyrrho, *and crook'd* Diodore.

He was a great admirer of *Plato*, whose Books he had.

CHAP. II.

Upon what occasion he constituted the middle Academy.

† CRates dying, *Arcesilaus* took upon him the Government of the School, which was yielded to him by *Socratides*. Being possessed of that place, he altered the Doctrine and manner of Teaching, which had been observed by *Plato* and his Successors, upon this occasion.

† *Laert.*

Plato and his followers down to to *Arcesilaus*, held, (as was said) That there are two kinds of things, some perceptible by *Sense*, others perceptible only by † *Intellect*: That from the latter ariseth *Science*, from the former *Opinion*: That the *Mind* only seeth that which always is simple, and in the same manner, and such as it is, that is, *Ideas*. But that the *Senses* are all dull and slow, neither can they perceive those things which seem subjected to Sense, because either they are so little, that they cannot fall beneath Sense, or so moveable and transient, that not one of them is constant or the same; but, all are in continual Lapse and Fluxion. Hence they called all this part of things *Opinionable*, affirming that Science is no where, but, in the Notions and Reasons of the Mind.

† *Acad. quæst. lib. 1.*

* Yet, did they profess against those, who said, the Academy took away all Sense; for they affirmed not, that there was no such thing as colour, or taste, or sapor, or sound; but, only maintained, there was no proper mark of true and certain in the Senses, there being no such any where.

* *Cic. Acad. quæst. 4.*

† Hence they allowed, that we make use of the Senses in Actions, from the reason that appeareth out of them; but, to trust them as absolutely true and infallible, they allowed not.

† *Plut. cont. Colos.*

Thus held the *Academicks* down to *Polemo*, * of whom *Arcesilaus* and *Zeno* were constant Auditors; but *Zeno* being older than *Arcesilaus*, and a very subtle Disputant, endeavoured to Correct his Doctrine, not that, as *Theophrastus* saith, he did enervate Vertue; but on the contrary, he placed all things that are reckoned among the good, in Vertue only: And this he called *Honest*, as being simple, sole, one good: Of the rest, though neither good nor evil, he held that some were *according to Nature*, others *contrary to Nature*, others *mediate*: Those which are according to Nature, he held to be *worthy Estimation*, the contrary *contrary*; the Neuter he left *betwixt both*, in which he placed no value. Of those which are Eligible, some were of more Estimation, some of less; those which were of more he called *preferred*, those of less *rejected*. And as in these, he did not change so much the things themselves as the words, so betwixt a *Rectitude* and a *Sin*, an *Office* and a *Preter-office*: He placed some things mediate, holding that Rectitudes consisted only in good Actions, Sins in Evil; but, Offices either performed or omitted, he conceived mediate things. And whereas the Philosophers of the *old Academy* did not hold all Vertue to consist in Reason, but some Vertues to be perfected by Nature or Custom; *Zeno* on the contrary placed all Vertue in Reason; and whereas the *Academicks* held, as we said [in the Life of *Plato*,] That all those Vertues may be separated, *Zeno* maintained that could not be, averring, that not only the use of Vertue (as the *Academicks* held) but the Habit thereof was excellent in it self; neither had any one Vertue, who did not always make use of it. And whereas the *Academicks* took not away Passion from Man, affirming that we are subject to Compassion, desire, fear, and joy, by Nature; but, only contracted them, and reduced them within narrower limits; *Zeno* affirmed,

* *Cic. Acad. quæst. 1.*

that from all these, as from so many Diseases, a wise Man must be free. And whereas *they* held, that all Passions were natural and irrational, and placed in one part of the Soul, Concupiscence, in the other Reason: Neither did *Zeno* herein agree with them, for he asserted, that Passions are voluntary, that Opinions are taken up by Judgment, that immoderate Intemperance is the Mother of all Passion. Thus much for *Ethicks*.

† As for *Physick*, he did not allow that fifth Nature besides the four Elements, of which the *Academicks* held Sense and Mind to be effected; for he asserted Fire to be that Nature which begetteth every thing, both Mind and Sense. He likewise dissented from *them*, in that he held, nothing can be made by a thing which hath no Body, (of which Nature, *Xenocrates*, and the *old Academicks* thought the Soul to be) and that whatsoever made any thing, or was it self made, must of necessity be a *Body*.

† *Cic. ibid.*

* He likewise asserted many things in the *third part of Philosophy*, wherein he asserted some things new of the Senses themselves, which he conceived to be joined by a certain extrinsecal impulsion, which he called *Phantasie*. To these Phantasies received by the Senses, He added *Assent* of the Mind, which he held to be placed in us, and voluntary. He did not allow all Phantasies to be faithful and worthy Credit; but, only those which have a proper Declaration of those things which they seem, which Phantasie when it is seen, is called *comprehensible*, when received and approved, he calleth it *comprehension*. That which was comprehended by Sense, he calleth *Sense*, and, if it were so comprehended, that it could not be pulled away by reason, *Science*; if otherwise, *Ignorance*; of which kind was Opinion, infirm and common to false or unknown things. Betwixt Science and Ignorance he placed that comprehension we mentioned, not reckoning it among the good nor the bad; but affirming that only was to be credited; whence he likewise attributed Faith to the Senses, for as much as he conceived the comprehension made by the Senses to be true and faithful, not that it comprehended all things that are in being; but that it omits nothing that can fall beneath it, as also, because Nature hath given it as a rule of Science and principle of it self, whence notions are afterwards imprinted in the Mind, from which not only Principles, but certain larger ways towards the invention of Reason, are found out. Errour, timerity, ignorance, opination, suspicion, and in a word, whatsoever is not of firm and constant assent, he took away from Vertue and Wisdom. In these things consisteth almost all the change and dissention of *Zeno* from the *old Academicks*.

* *Cic. ibid.*

Zeno thus maintaining many things contrary to *Plato*, as that the Soul is Mortal, and that there is no other World but this, which is subject to Sense. *Arcesilaus* perceiving this Doctrine to spread and take much, prudently concealed the Doctrine of the Academy, lest the mysteries of *Plato* being divulged and made too common, should become despicable; and *therefore* saith † St. *Augustine*) he thought it fitter to unteach the Man that was not well taught, than to teach those, whom by Experience he found not to be docile enough.

† *Contra Acad. Lib.*

Here-

*Hereupon Arcesilaus undertook to oppose and contest with *Zeno*, not out of any pertinacity or desire of Glory, but led thereunto by that obscurity of things, which had brought *Socrates* to a confession of his own Ignorance; as likewise *Democritus*, *Anaxagoras*, *Empedocles*, and almost all the ancient Philosophers, who affirmed, *That* nothing could be understood, nothing perceived, nothing known: *That* the Senses are narrow, our Minds weak, our Lives short, and *Truth* (as *Democritus* faith) *drowned in an Abyss*. That all things are held by opinion and institution, nothing left to Truth: and finally, *That* all things are involved in darkness.

† Thus *Arcesilaus* denied there is any thing that can be known, not so much as that which *Socrates* reserved, [*that he knew nothing*] conceiving all things to be hid in such darkness, that there is nothing which can be seen or understood. For these reasons we ought not to profess or affirm any thing, or to approve any thing by assent; but always to restrain and withhold our Hastiness from Errour, which then proveth great, when it approveth a thing false or unknown. Neither is there any thing more vile, than by assent and approbation to prevent Knowledge and perception.

* He did, as was agreeable to this Tenet, dispute against all Assertions and Doctrines; and having found, that in the same thing the reasons of two Opinions directly opposite, were of equal weight, he thence inferred, that we ought to with-hold our assents († ἐπέχειν) from both: [This *Laertius* means, when he faith, that *he took away propositions, by reason of the repugnance of Speech, and was the first that taught to argue on both sides.*] * And that neither the Senses nor Reason are to be credited. He therefore praised that Apophthegm of *Hesiod*: *The Gods all knowledge have conceal'd from Men.*

But this † Saint *Augustine* affirms was only done, to conceal mysteriously the meaning of *Plato*; but, they nevertheless had and held his Doctrins and Decrees, which they used to unfold to those who liv'd with them till they were old.

He likewise, as *Laertius* faith, *first altered the manner of disputing which* Plato *delivered, and made it more litigious by question and answer*, of which, thus * *Cicero*: *Socrates* used to find out by question and answer, the opinions of those with whom he discoursed, that if there were occasion, he might say something upon that which they answered: This custom not retained by his Successors, was taken up by *Arcesilaus*, who instituted, that they who would learn of him should not question him; but, themselves tell him what they thought, which when they had done, he disputed against it; but, his Auditors were to maintain their own opinion as much as they could possibly. This course took *Arcesilaus*, contrary to all other Philosophers, amongst whom, he that would learn held his Peace; which course, faith *Cicero*, is at this time held in the Academy, where he that will learn, speaks in this manner; Pleasure seems to be the chief good, whereupon in a long Oration it is disputed against it, whereby may easily be understood, that they who say, a thing seemeth to me to be so, are not really of that opinion, but desire to hear the contrary maintained.

This School constituted by *Arcesilaus*, was called the *second Academy*, in relation to its descent from *Plato*; or the *middle Academy*, in respect of the *new* one, which was afterwards set up by *Carneades*; though † *Cicero* seemeth to make no distinction between this and that, but calleth this the new Academy: But, though 'tis likely, that it was not at first so called; yet, upon the introduction of a newer, it was afterwards more generally known by the title of the *middle*, or, *second Academy*.

These *Academicks* differ from the *Scepticks*, in as much, as, though they affirmed that nothing can be comprehended; yet they took not away *true* or *false* from things. On the contrary, they held that some Phantasies were true, others false; but the *Scepticks* hold that they are both indifferent; alike defensible by Reason. The *Academicks* assert some things to be wholly improbable, some more probable than others, and that a Wise Man, when any of these occur, * may answer *yes* or *no*, following the probability, provided that he with-hold from assenting. But the *Scepticks* hold all things to be alike indifferent, not admitting Judgment, nor allowing that either our Senses or Opinions can perceive true or false, and therefore no faith is to be given to them, but we ought to persist firm and unmoveable without Opinion, or saying of any thing that it is, any more than that it is not.

CHAP. III.
His Vertues and Apophthegms.

HE preferred *Homer* above all Writers, of whom he constantly read some piece before he went to Bed, and as soon as he rose in the Morning. When he went to read any thing in him, he said, he went to his *Mistress*.

Pindar also he said was proper to raise the Voice, and give us supply of Words.

He was sententious and succinct in Speech, often using Expressions of doubtful meaning. He used to reprehend and chide sharply, and freely, whence *Timon* faith of him,

When thou chid'st young Men, think thou once wert young.

In this kind, *Laertius* instances his Sayings to a Young Man, speaking confidently, &c. to an immodest young Man, &c.

Emo a *Chian*, who, though very deformed, thought himself very handsom, asking him as he put on a rich Cloak, whether he thought a Wife Man might not love? *Arcesilaus* answered, do you mean if he be as handsome and as fine as you.

To an effeminate Person, upbraiding him as it were of Pride, he spoke this Verse,

Shall we demand Great Sir, or Silent be?

He immediately answered,

Woman, why speakest thou these harsh Words to me?

Being troubled with the talk of an inconsiderable mean Person, he said,

The Sons of Slaves intemperately speak.

Of another who talked impertinently, and loudly, he said, he had a peevish Nurse. For some he would make no answer at all.

To an Usurer, who said there was something he knew not, he answered in these Verses out of *Sophocles*'s *OEnomaus*,

The course of Storms hid from the Bird doth lie,
Until the time that she must lay draw nigh.

To a Dialectick Philosopher of *Alexinus*'s School, who was not able to say any thing worthy *Alexinus*, he related what *Philoxenus* did to a maker of Bricks, who over-hearing him sing his Verses false, trod upon his Bricks and broke them, saying, as you spoil mine, so I yours.

He was angry at those who learned not the liberal Sciences in due time.

In dispute he used this word, *I say, and will not such a one,* (naming the Person) *assent to this?* which many of his Disciples affected to imitate, as also his manner of speaking and gesture.

He was most acute in answering appositely, and converting his discourse to the present subject, and fitting it for every time.

He was very efficacious in perswasion, whence many Disciples resorted to him, though sometimes he sharply touched them, which they took patiently.

He was very good, and much excited hope in his Auditors.

As to the necessaries of Life, he was liberal and communicative, ready to do good, and much endeavouring to conceal it, avoiding all that kind of vain-glory. Visiting *Ctesibius*, who was sick, and perceiving him to be poor, he privately put a Purse under his Pillow, which when he found; This, saith he, is the sport of *Arcesilaus*. Another time he sent him 1000 Drachms. * *Plutarch* relates this as done to *Apelles* the *Chian* Painter, whom *Arcesilaus* besides many other testimonies of kindness coming to visit as he lay sick, and perceiving how poor he was, departed, and returning soon after, bringing twenty Drachms with him, then sitting close to *Apelles*'s Bed-side, *Here is nothing*, says he, *besides Empedocle's Four Elements, Fire, Water, Earth, and Æther mounting high, but methinks you lie not at your Ease,* and with that taking occasion to remove his Pillow, he conveyed the Purse privately under it, which when the old Woman that tended him found, and wondring, shewed to *Apelles*, he laughing, said, *This is one of* Arcesilaus's *Thefts*.

† He recommended *Archias*, an Arcadian to *Eumenes* King of *Pergamus*, by whom he was exalted to great Dignity.

He was very liberal, and free from Covetousness, as appeared by his Utensils of Silver, and vying with *Athecrates*, and *Callicrates*. He had many Vessels of Gold, which he lent unto many upon occasion of Feasting. These Silver Vessels a certain Man borrowed to entertain his Friends withal; *Arcesilaus* knowing him to be poor, would never send for them back: Others report he lent them to him on purpose, and when he brought them back, because he was poor, he freely bestowed them on him.

He had a fair Estate at *Pitane*, from which *Pylades* his Brother continually supplied him. *Eumenes* also Son of *Philcterus*, gave him many large Presents, whence to him only of all Kings he applied himself.

* *Quom. discern. adul. ab amic.*

† *Laert.*

When *Antigonus* was much followed, and many Persons thronged to his House, he forbore, declining his acquaintance. He was intimate with *Hierocles*, the Governour of *Munichia*, and *Pireum*, and constantly, on Holidays, went thither to visit him: *Hierocles* often entreated him to visit *Antigonus*, but he refused, and went along with him as far as the Door, and there parted with him. After *Antigonus*'s fight at Sea, many writing consolatory Epistles to him, *Arcesilaus* was silent. Being sent by his Country on an Embassy to *Antigonus* at *Demetrias*, he returned frustrate of his design.

He lived the greatest part of his time in the Academy, avoiding to meddle with publick Business; but sometimes went to the *Pireum*, as we said, out of Love to *Hierocles*; for which some reproved him.

He was very magnificent (indeed a second *Aristippus*) in the entertainment of his Friends. He openly professed Love to *Theodote* and *Philota*, Curtezans of *Elis*, for which being reprehended, he rehearsed the *Chrias* of *Aristippus*. He was very amorous, and much affected the Company of young Men, whence *Aristo* of *Chios*, a Stoick, called him a corrupter of Youth, temerarious, and impudent. Of those whom he affected are mentioned *Demetrius* and *Leochares*; *Demochares*, Son of *Laches*, and *Pythocles* Son of *Bugerus*, much affected him.

For these things he was much inveighed against at the House of *Hieronymus* the *Peripatetick*, who had invited his Friends to celebrate the Birth-Day of *Alcyoneus*, Son of *Antigonus*, for the keeping of which Feast, *Antigonus* sent yearly much Money. At this Feast *Arcesilaus* would not dispute amidst the Cups; and when *Aridelus* propounded a question to him, requiring that he would say something to it, he answered it is the best property of a Philosopher to know the Seasons of all things.

But, he was so free from Pride, that he counselled his Disciples to go and hear other Masters; and when a certain *Chian* Youth of his School declared, that he was not pleased with what he said so much as with the Discourses of *Hieronymus*, he took him by the hand and led him to the Philosopher, desiring him to cherish him according to his quality.

To one that asked why Men went from other Sects to the *Epicureans*, but never from the *Epicureans* to other Sects: Because, saith he, of Men, some are made Eunuchs, but of Eunuchs never any are made Men.

* He said, Where there are many Medicines, and many Physicians, there are most Diseases; and where there are many Laws, there is most Iniquity.

† He advised to shun Dialectick, because it turneth all things upside down.

* He compared Logicians to Gamesters that play at Dice, who take delight whilst they are cosened.

† He affirmed, that Poverty is rugged as *Ithaca*, but good to bring up a Child, in that it inureth to Frugality and Abstinence, and is generally a good School of Vertue.

* *Stob. Se. 143.*

† *Stob. Se. 212.*

* *Stob. Se. 212.*

† *Stob. Se. 235.*

CHA

CHAP. IV.

His Death.

Laert. *WHen he drew nigh the end of his Life, he bequeathed all his Estate to his Brother *Pylades*; to which end, *Mæreas* not knnowing it, he sent him first to *Chios*, and from thence sent for him back again to *Athens*. He sent three Copies of his Will, one to *Amphicritus* at *Eretria*, another to some Friends of his at *Athens*, the third to *Thaumasius* his near Kinsman, to be kept by them; with the last he sent this Letter.

Arcesilaus to *Thaumasias*, health.

I gave Diogenes *my Will to bring to you, for being often sick and infirm of Body, I thought fit to make my Will, lest if any sudden Accident should befal me, I should depart this Life with some Injury done to you, whom I have found so bountiful towards me. I desire that you, the most faithful of all my Friends, will take it into your Custody. Approve your self just to that extraordinary trust which I have reposed in you, that it may appear I have made a right choice.*

He died, as *Hermippus* saith, in a kind of Phrenzy, after he had drunk much Wine, 75 years old, in the fourth Year of the 134th Olympiad, as may be conjectured from the succession of *Lacydes*, in the School which began at that time. The *Athenians* buried him with such Solemnity as never any was before.

He took not any Women into the House with him, neither had he any Children. He flourished according to *Apollodorus* in 120th Olympiad.

There were three more of this Name, one an ancient Comick Poet, the second an Elegiack Poet, the third a Statuary.

LACYDES.

Laert. LACYDES succeeded *Arcesilaus*; he was a *Cyrenean*, (his Father named *Alexander*,) a person of much gravity, and had many Emulators. He was from his youth much given to study, poor, but pleasing to all company, and of a delightful Conversation.

As concerning his managing his Houshould affairs, it is reported that when he took any thing out of the place where he kept his provisions, he locked the Door, and threw the Key in at a hole that none might steal ought from him; which his Servants observing, frequently took it, and opening the Door, carried away what they thought good, and then put it into the same place again, in which Fact they were never discovered.

Euseb. præp. Evang.lib.14. But the most pleasant part of the Story, is, that (as † *Numenius* affirms) he was thereby perswaded to be of the Opinion of the middle Academicks; that nothing is comprehended by sense, arguing thus; Why should I think that Sense can comprehend any thing certainly, when I know that my own Senses are so often deceived, for when I go abroad, I think that I see with my Eyes those things which I leave in my Storehouse; when I return I find none of them; which could not be unless our Senses were fallible and uncertain.

Lacydes upon the Death of *Arcesilaus*, being made Master of the School in the fourth year of the 134th Olympiad, taught in the Academy, in the Gardens which were made by *Attalus* the King, which from him were called the *Lacydean* Gardens: *Laertius*, and, from him, *Suidas*, make him Institutor of the new Academy; but erroneously. He continued this Charge 26 Years, at the end whereof he resigned it, whilst he was yet alive, to *Telecles* and *Euander*, *Phocians*, his Disciples, in the second year of the 141st Olympiad.

Attalus sending for him to come to him, he returned him answer, *That Pictures make the best shew at a distance*.

Studying Geometry in his old Age, one said to him, Is it now time? he answered, When, if not now?

Athenæus saith, That *Lacydes* and *Timon* Philosophers, being invited by one of their Friends to an entertainment of two days, and desirous to suit themselves to the Company, drank very freely. *Lacydes* went away first, half Drunk, and perceiving *Timon* to steal away too, said Il. x. out of *Homer*,

To our great Glory Hector *we have Slain*.

The next day meeting *Timon* again at the same place, and seeing him not able to take off his Cups at once, made a pause, when he put it to his Mouth the second time, he said out of Il. ξ. another place of *Homer*,

Those are unhappy who contest with me.

Var. hist Ælian likewise numbers these two amongst the great drinkers, and perhaps not unjustly; for by excess of Wine he fell into the Palsie, of which he died in the second Year of the one hundred Forty first Olympiad.

He wrote Philosophicks, and of Nature.

In the School, he was succeeded, as is said by EVANDER, *Evander*, by his Disciple, EGESINUS, whom *Clemens Alexandrinus* calleth *Hegesilaus* of *Pergamus*, *Egesinus*, by CARNEADES.

CARNEADES.

CHAP. I.

His Country, Parents, Time, Masters.

CARNEADES (Successor of Egesinus) was * Cyrene, whence † Cicero saith, he was an acute Person, as being an African. He was Son of *Epicomus,* or *Philocomus. Apollodorus,* as cited by *Laertius* affirmeth he died in the 162d Olympiad; but there is a mistake in the Text; for the words of *Apollodorus* relate doubtless to the time of his Birth, which upon that Authority, we may affirm to have been in the first Year of the 162th Olympiad. *Florus* (cited by * *Plutarch*) adds, he was born on the seventh day of *Thargelion,* at what time the *Carnean* Festivals were celebrated at *Cyrene,* whence perhaps he took his Name.

This time falling after the *Callippical* Period, we shall compute it according to † *Petavius*'s Method, which although it be not exempt from question, yet is better than that of *Scaliger*,

* Laert.
† Acad. quæst. 4.

* Sympos. quæst. 8. 1.

† Doctr. temp. p.

liger, whose Method is not reconcilable to Ptolomy's Observations.

The 4th of the 164th Olympiad was
Of the *Julian* Period   4585
Epoche of the *Callippick* period   4383

Which subducted, there remains   202.
Subduct two periods more   152.

remains   50.

The Year propounded therefore is the 50th of the third period. The *Neomenian* of *Hecatombæon, June* 26. which is 177th day of the *Julian* Year; the 7th of *Thargelion* (according to *Petavius*) at that time was the 302d of the Attick Year.

To   177.
add   302.

Summ   479.
Subduct   365.

Remains   114.

The 114th day of the *Julian* year is the 24th of *April,* on which fell the 7th of *Thargelion*; which the *Dominical* Letter being B. fell on Sunday, Proleptically taken.

* He was Disciple to *Egesinus* the *Academick,* and learned Logick of *Diogenes* the *Stoick*, whence in arguing he would many times say, *If I have concluded right, the cause is my own*; *if not right*, Diogenes *must return the* Mina *he had of me*; which was the price the Dialectick Philosphers took.

*Laert.
†Cic. Acad. quæst. 4.

CHAP. II.

How he constituted the new Academy.

HE succeeded *Egesinus* in the School, and is by *Cicero* reckoned the fourth from *Arcesilaus*, (who constituted the *middle Academy*, introducing a suspension of Assent, grounded upon the uncertainty of things:) *Carneades*, constituted the *new Academy*, maintaining the same kind suspension, with no less eagerness; yet upon more moderate grounds: * For he held that the incomprehensibility of things, proceeded not from the nature of the things themselves, as *Arcesilaus* maintained; for as much as every thing really existeth in it self, and if any thing be affirmed, or denied of another, it is true or false, as to the thing it self; but the things themselves remaining firm, we derive from them a Phantasie and Similitude, which for the most part, like false Messengers lie and deceive us. To all true things there are some false adjoyned, and those so like, that there is no certain note of Judication and Assent, wherefore we cannot perceive any thing to be true.

But he was nothing less rigid as to the Academical suspension, for † he denied that any thing could be perceived, not so much as that very Maxim; *Nothing can be perceived*, arguing thus.

* Numen. apud Euseb.

† Cic. Acad. quæst. 4.

All Phantasms are of two kinds; the first included the perceptible and imperceptible; the second kind, the probable, and the improbable. Those which are contrary to Sense and Evidence, pertain to the former division; against the latter we ought not to say any thing. Wherefore there is no Phantasie followed by perception, but by approbation many; for it were contrary to Nature that nothing should be probable.

More fully * *Sextus Empericus. Carneades*, saith he, did not only oppose the *Stoicks*, but all that went before him, as to *Judgment*. His first and common Argument against all, is, that by which he sheweth absolutely, that there is nothing from which truth can be judged; not *Reason*, not *Sense*, nor *Phantasie*, nor any thing, for all these in a word deceive us. His second Argument is that whereby he shews, that altho there be something that doth judge, yet it cannot exist without an Affection from Evidence. For an Animal differeth from inanimate things by the sensitive faculty, it apprehendeth thereby both it self and external things; but Sense remaining immovable, impassible, and immutable, is not Sense, nor apprehendeth any thing, but being changed, and after some manner affected by incursion of Evidences, then it declareth things. In that affection therefore of the Soul which ariseth from Evidence, we are to seek that which judgeth. This Affection is declared when that appeareth from which it proceedeth, which Affection is nothing else but Phantasie. *Phantasie* therefore is a certain affection in an animal, which sheweth both it self and some others, as when we see any thing, our Sight is affected in some manner, so, as it was not before that act of Seeing. By this alteration we apprehend two things: First, the alteration it self, that is the Phantasie. Secondly, that from which this alteration proceeds, the thing visible. The like in the rest of the Senses. As therefore Light manifesteth it self and all things in it, so Fancy being the chief guide of Knowledge in an Animal, must like unto Light, manifest both it self, and that evident object which effecteth it. But because it doth not always shew that which is true, but often erreth, and differeth from the thing whence it proceedeth, like ill Messengers, it necessarily followeth that all Phantasies cannot leave a judgment of Truth, but only if it be true. Again, because there is no Phantasie so true, but it may be false; and of all Phantasies that seem true, there are some false, which differ little from them; that which judgeth must consist in common phantasie of true and false. But the common Phantasie of these comprehendeth not, and if it comprehendeth not, neither is there any thing that judgeth. And if Phantasie have not a Judicative Power, neither can Reason judge, for that is derived from Phantasie and justly: For that whereof it judgeth, ought first to appear unto it, but nothing can appear but through Sense void of Reason; therefore neither Sense void of Reason, nor Reason it self is that which judgeth.

Thus disputeth *Carneades* against all other Philosophers, to shew there is not any thing that judgeth. But being demanded what
judgeth,

*Adv. Mathem.

judgeth, as to the leading of Life, and acquisition of Beatitude, he hath recourse to *probable* Phantasie; and together with probable, *undistracted* and *circumcurrent*, their differences these. Phantasie is the phantasie of something, *viz.* of that which it is made, and of that *in* which it is made: That of which it is made is the external sensible *Object*; that in which the *Man*. It hath two relations, one to the Object phansied, the other to the phantasm derived from that Object. From the relation to the object it is either true or false; true, when it agreeth with the object; false, when it disagreeth. From its relation to the Phantasm, there is one which seemeth true, another false. That which seemeth true is by the *Academicks* called *Emphasis* and *Probability*, and *probable Phantasie*; that which seemeth not true, is called *Apemphasis*, *Improbability*, and *not-probable* phantasie. For, neither that which seemeth false, and is such; nor that which is true, and seemeth not such, have any thing in their Nature perswasive. But, of these Phantasies, that which is manifestly false, and seemeth not true, limiteth the Judicatory, but is not that which judgeth, as likewise produceth from that which is, but differs from it, such as was that of the Fury proceeding from *Electra* to *Orestes*. Of that which seemeth true, one kind is *tenuious*, as that which is in a thing so little, as that it is not visible, either because it takes not up room enough, or by reason of the weakness of Sight, which receiveth things confusedly, and not distinctly. The other is that which hath this common property with the true, that it seemeth to be very true. Now of these, the tenious, loose, remiss Phantasie cannot be that which judgeth; for that which cannot clearly manifest it self, nor the thing that effected it, cannot attract us, nor invite assent; but that which seemeth true and is manifest enough, that according to *Carneades*, is the Judge of Truth.

This being that which judgeth, it hath a great Latitude, and being extended into another Species, hath a more probable and vehemently affected Phantasie. Probable is taken three ways; First, for that which is true, and seemeth true; Secondly, for that which is false and seemeth true; Thirdly, for that which is true, common to both. Whence that which judgeth must be that phantasie which seemeth true, which the Academicks call probable. Sometimes the false incurreth; so that it is necessary to use the common phantasie of true and false; yet not because that more seldom incurreth, I mean that which imitateth the Truth, we are not to give credit to that which is for the greater part true, whereby it happeneth our Judgment and Actions are for the most part directed.

That which first and commonly Judgeth, *Carneades* held to be this. But forasmuch as phantasie sometimes is not of one kind, but like a Chain, one dependeth on another, there must therefore be a second Judge, which is *probable* and *undistracted* phantasie. As he who receiveth the phantasie of a Man, necessarily receiveth the phantasie of such things as are about him, and without him; of the things about him, as colour, magnitude, figure, motion, speech, cloathing, Shooes; of things without him, as Air, Light, Day, Heaven, Earth, Companions, and the like. When therefore none of these phantasies seems false, but all agree in seeming true, we credit it the more. That such a one is *Socrates* we believe, because he hath all those things which *Socrates* useth to have, as Colour, Magnitude, Figure, Gesture, Cloak, in none of these disagreeing with it self. And as some Physicians argue a Man to be in a Fever, not from one symptom, as from a high Pulse, or great heat; but from the concurrence of that heat with the Pulse, as as also from ulcerous touch, redness, thirst, and the like, all agreeing together. So the *Academick* maketh a Judgment of Truth, from a concurrence of phantasies, and when none of all his phantasies that join in the concurrence retract him as false, he saith that which incurreth is true.

That there is a credible *undistracted* concurrence, is manifest from *Menelaus*: Having left in his Ship an Image of *Helene* which he had brought from *Troy*, as if it had been *Helene* her self, landing at the Island *Pharos*, he there met with the true *Helene*, and from her attracted a true phantasie, but would not believe that phantasie, being distracted by the other, which told him that he had left *Helene* in the Ship. Such is undistracted phantasie therefore, which likewise seemeth erroneous, forasmuch as there are some more undistracted than others. Of *undistracted* phantasies, that is most credible and perfect which maketh a Judgment.

Moreover there is a *Circumcurrent* phantasie, the form whereof is next to be declared. In the *undistracted* we only enquire whether none of those phantasies which join in concurrence, attract us as false, but that they all seem true, and not improbable. But in that which is made by concurse, which useth *circumcurrence*, strictly examines every phantasie which is in that concurrence, as in Assemblies, when the People take account of every particular person that stands for the Magistracy, whether they deserve that power and right of judging. In the place of Judgment, there is that which judgeth, and that by which the judgment is made, the distance and interval, figure, time, manner, affection, and operation, each of which we examine strictly. That which judgeth, whether the Sight be dim, for if it be, it is too weak for judgment; that which is judged, whether it be not too little; that through which whether the Air be obscure; the distance, whether it be too great; the *medium* whether confused; the place, whether too wide and vast; the time, whether too sudden; the Affection, whether not phrenetick; the operation, whether not unfit to be admitted. For if all these be in one, that which judgeth is *probable* phantasie, and together, *probable*, *undistracted*, and *circumcurrent*. Wherefore as when in Life we enquire concerning some little thing, we examine of Witness; when we enquire into something of greater consequence, we examine more; but when of a thing most necessary, we examine each of the Witnesses by the joint testimony of all. So saith *Carneades*, in light

incon-

inconsiderable matters, we make use of *probable* Phantasie, only for Judgment; in things of some moment, of *undistracted* Phantasie; in things that concern well and happy Living *circumcurrent* Phantasie.

And as in things of great moment they take divers Phantasies, so in different Circumstances they never follow the same; for they say, they attend only probable Phantasie in such things wherein the circumstance of time alloweth not a strict Examination: As for instance: The Enemy pursues a Man; he coming to a Cave, takes a Phantasie, that there are some Enemies there lying in wait: Transported by this Phantasie as probable, he shunneth and flyeth from the Cave, following the probability of that Phantasie, before he accurately and diligently examine whether there really be any Enemies in Ambush in that Cave or no. *Probable* Phantasie is followed by *circumcurrent*, in those things in which time allows a curious Examination of each particular, to use judgment upon the incurring thing. As a Man coming into a dark Room, and seeing a Rope rolled up, thinking it to be a Serpent, he flies away; but afterwards returning, he examines the truth, and perceiving it not to stir, begins to think it is not a Serpent; but withal considering, that Serpents are sometimes frozen or nummed with the cold, he strikes it with his Staff: And having thus by *Circumcurence* examined the Phantasie which incurred to him, he assenteth that the Phantasie he had taken of that Body as a Serpent, is false. And again, as I said, when we manifestly behold, we assent that this is true, having first over-run in our Thoughts that our Senses are all entire, and that we behold this waking, not in a dream; that the Air is perspicuous, and a convenient distance from the Object. Hereby we receive a creditable Phantasie, when we have time enough to examine the particulars concerning the thing seen. It is the same in *undistracted* Phantasie, which they admit, when there is nothing that can retract us, as we said of *Menelaus*. Hitherto *Sextus*.

Cic. Acad. quæst. 4.

Yet though nothing can be perceived, a wise Man may consent to that which is not perceived; that is, he may *opinionate*; but so as he knoweth himself to opinionate, and that there is nothing which can be comprehended and perceived.

De fin. lib. 2.

He asserted the ultimate end to be the enjoyment of Natural Principles, which saith *Cicero*, he maintained, not that he really thought so, but in opposition to the *Stoicks*.

Laert.

He read the Books of the *Stoicks* very diligently, and disputed against them with so good success, that it gave him occasion to say; *If Chrysippus had not been, I had not been*.

Cic. Acad. quæst. 4.

Clitomachus used to say of him, he could never understand what he really held; for he would sometimes argue on one side, sometimes on the other; and by the *Calumny* of his Wit, saith *Cicero*, many times deride the best causes. Of the *Sorites* used by him, See *Sextus Empiricus*.

CHAP. III.

Upon what occasion he was sent on an Embassy to Rome.

*THE *Athenians* being fined by the *Romans* about 500 Talents, at the suit of the *Oropians* and *Sicyonians*, for destroying *Oropus*, a City of *Bæotia*, sent three Philosophers on an Embassie to the Roman Senate, to procure a mitigation of this fine, which had been imposed upon them without hearing their defence; *Carneades* the *Academick*, *Diogenes* the *Stoick*, and *Critolaus* the *Peripatetick*. About the time of this Embassie, there is much disagreement amongst Authors. *A. Gellius* saith, they came after the second *Punick* War, and maketh *Ennius* later than their coming; which *Petavius* justly conceiveth to be false, for as much as *Ennius* died in the 585th year from the building of the City. But *Cicero* affirmeth this Embassy to have been when *P. Scipio* and *M. Marcellus* were Consuls, which was the 599th Year. *Pausanias* reckoneth it upon the 603d Year of the City, which *Casaubon* approveth.

* *Plut. vit. Cat. A. Gel. 7. 14. Macr. Sat. tur. 1. 5.*

Each of these Philosophers, to shew his Learning, made choice of many eminent parts of the City, where they discoursed before great multitudes of people to the admiration of all. The Eloquence of *Carneades* was violent and rapid; that of *Critolaus*, neat and smooth, that of *Diogenes* modest and sober. *Carneades* one day disputed copiously concerning Justice before *Galba* and *Cato*, the greatest Orators of that time. The next day he subverted all he had said before by contrary Arguments, and took away that Justice which he had so much commended. This he did the better to confute those, that asserted any thing. That dispute whereby he overthrew Justice is recorded in *Cicero*, by *L. Furius*.

Lact. nt. Inst. lib. 52.

To these three Philosophers resorted all the studious young Men, and frequently heard and praised them. Chiefly the sweetness of *Carneades*, which was of greatest power, and no less fame than power, attracting eminent and benign Hearers, filled the City with noise like a great Wind; and it was reported that a *Grecian* person, qualified to Admiration, attracting all, had infused a serious Affection into the young Men, whereby forgetting other divertisements and pleasures, they were carried on as it were with a kind of madness to Philosophy. This pleased all the *Romans*, who gladly beheld their Sons instructed in *Greek* Learning by such excellent Men. Only *Cato* at the first noise of Admiration of the *Greek* Learning, was troubled, fearing the young Men should apply themselves that way, and so prefer the glory of Eloquence before Action and Military Discipline. The fame of Philosophers encreasing in the City, and *C. Acilius*, (whom *A. Gellius* and *Macrobius* call *Cecilius*) an eminent person, having at his own Request been the Interpreter of their first Oration to the Senate; *Cato* (who was then very old) under a fair pretence, moved, that these Philosophers might be sent out of the City, and

Plut.

coming

coming into the Senate-house, blamed the Magistrates, that they had so long suffered such Ambassadors to continue amongst them without any answer, who were able to perswade them to any thing: wherefore he first desired that something might be determined concerning their Embassie, that they might be sent back again to their own Schools, and instruct the Sons of *Græcians*, and that the *Roman* youth might, as they did before, apply themselves to the observance of their own Laws and Magistrates. This he did not out of anger to *Carneades*, as some though, but out of an Ambitious Emulation of the *Greek* Humanity and Literature.

CHAP. IV.

His Vertues *and* Apophthegms.

Lib. 8. c. c. 7. HE was a Person infinitely Industrious, less conversant in Physick than Ethick, and so studious that he neglected to cut his Hair and Nails. *Valerius Maximus* saith, he was so studious, that when he lay down at Meals, his Thoughts were so fixt, that he forgot to put his Hand to the Table, and that *Melissa*, who lived with him as a Wife, was fain to put him in mind thereof, and help him.

He was so eminent for Philosophy, that the Oratours themselves would many times break up their Schools, and come and hear him.

He had a great and loud Voice, whereupon the Gymnasiarch sent to him not to speak so loud, whereto he answering, *send me the Measure by which I should speak*; the other wisely and appositely replied, *You have a Measure, your Hearers*.

He was sharply invective, and in Argument almost invincible. He avoided Feasting, out of the reason we mentioned, his great studiousness.

One named *Mentor* a *Bithynian*, as *Phavorinus* saith, who had endeavoured to seduce a Mistress that he kept, coming into the School, he presently jested at him, in turning these words of *Homer*,

*Hitherto comes one opprest with hoary Years,
Like* Mentor *in his Voice and Looks appears,
Who from the School I charge you turn away.*

The other rising up replied,

He thus proclaim'd, the rest did strait obey.

Being to dispute with *Chrysippus*, he purged himself by white Hellebore to sharpen his Wit, lest any corrupt Humours in his Stomach might oppress the vigour and constancy of his mind.

Stob. Ser. 212. He compared *Dialectick* to the Fish *Polypus*, which when its Claws grow long, bites them off; so Logicians, growing subtle, confute their own assertions.

Plut. de tranq. anim. He advised Men in their greatest Prosperity to be mindful of a change, for that which is unexpected is most grievous.

He said the Sons of Rich Men and Kings learn nothing well but Riding, for their Masters *Plut. de edal.* flatter them; they who contest with them, willingly yield to them; but a Horse considers not whether a private Man or a Prince, a poor Man or a Rich be on his Back, but if he cannot rule him, he throws his Rider.

He seemed to be extreamly averse from Death, whence he often said, *The same Nature* *Laert.* *which hath put us together will dissolve us*; and hearing that *Antipater* died by drinking Poison, he was a little animated by his constancy in Death, and said, *Then give me too*, they asking what, *Wine*, saith he.

In the midst of the Night he was struck *Laert.* blind, and knew not of it, but waking, bid his Servant bring a Light; the Servant did so, telling him he had brought one, then, said he, read you.

CHAP. V.

His Death and and Writings.

HE lived according to *Laertius* 85 years, or according to *Cicero*, 90. The words † *Laert.* of * *Apollodorus* that he died in the fourth year of the 162d Olympiad, which falleth upon the 626th Year from the building of *Rome*, may easily be evinced to be false, by the greatest part of the Circumstances of his Life; particularly from this; that *Antonius* in *Cicero* saith, when he went Pro-consul into *Asia*, he found *Carneades* the *Academick* at *Athens*, who opposed all in dispute, according to the manner of his Sect. The Year of *Antonius*'s Proconsulship was the 652d Year from the building of *Rome*. But this account, as we said before, is to be applied to the time of his Birth, from which the 85th falleth upon the first year of the 184th Olympiad, the 90th upon the second of the 185th.

Laertius saith, at his death there was a great Eclipse of the Moon, which some interpreted to proceed from a Sympathy with his Loss. Upon this Eclipse I conceive *Petavius* grounded his computation of *Carneades*'s Death, when † *Do Δ. temp.* he saith, † it was upon *the first year of the* 163d *Olympiad. May* 2. *fer.* 2. *hora* 5. 46. *at Athens*. But there being a mistake of the Year, there is consequently a greater in the account of the *feria* and hour.

Carneades, as *Cicero* saith, wrote four Books of *suspension of Assent*. He wrote likewise *Epistles* to *Ariarathes*, King of *Cappadocia*, the only Monument left behind him, extant in *Laertius*'s time. Whatsoever else went under his Name, *Laertius* saith, was written by his Disciples, of whom he had many, the most eminent *Clitomachus*.

There are remembred two more of this Name, one a Philosopher, Disciple to *Anaxagoras* mentioned by *Suidas*, the other an *Epigrammatick* Poet, mentioned by *Laertius*.

CLITOMACHUS.

*CLITOMACHUS was a *Carthaginian*, Son of † *Diognetus*. He was first called *Asdrubal*, as *Plutarch* and *Laertius* affirm,* and professed Philosophy in his own Country, and native Language. Being forty Years old he went to *Athens*, and heard *Carneades*, who being much taken with his Industry, instructed and exercised him in Philosophy. With *Carneades*, *Cicero* saith he lived until he was old, and succeeded him in the School, and chiefly illustrated his Doctrins by his Writings, the number of which Books being above Four Hundred, were a sufficient Testimony of his † Industry, and that he had no less of Wit, than *Carneades* of Eloquence. He was well versed in three Sects, the *Academick*, *Peripatetick*, and *Stoick*.

Of his Books are remembred by *Cicero*, one * of *Consolation* to his Captive Country-Men, *Carthage* being then subdued by the *Romans*; another to † *Cajus Lucilius* the Poet, wherein he explained and defended the *Academick* suspension of Assent, having written before of the same things to *L. Censorinus*, who was Consul with *M. Manilius*, the sum of which Discourse was this.

*The *Academicks* hold there are such dissimilitudes of things, that some seem probable, others on the contrary. But this is not ground enough to say that some things may be perceived, others cannot, because there are many false that are probable, but no false can be perceived and known. Those therefore extreamly err, who affirm the *Academicks* to take away sense; for they say not, there is no *Colour*, *Sapor*, or *Sound*, but dispute, that there is not any proper inherent *note* in these of true and certain: (which having expounded, he adds) A Wise Man suspends Assent two ways; one, when [as we know] he absolutely refuseth to assent to any thing; another, when he with-holds from answering, either in approbation, or improbation of something, so that he neither denieth nor asserteth it. In the first way he assents to nothing, in the second he will follow Probability, and according as he finds it or not, answers yes or no. He who with-holdeth his assent from all things, is yet moved, and acteth something. He reserves therefore these phantasies by which we are excited to Action, and those of which being questioned, we may answer on either part, only as of a thing that seemeth to us so, but without assent; neither are all such phantasies approved, but only those which are not obstructed by any thing.

† In asserting good, he joined pleasure with honesty, as *Callipho* also did.

* He was a great Enemy to *Rhetorick*, as *Critolaus* the *Peripatetick*, and *Charmidas* were also. Arts they did not expel out of Cities, knowing them to be very profitable to Life, no more than they would drive *Oeconomick* out of Houses, or Shepherds from their Flocks; but they all persecuted, and every where ejected the Art of Speaking, as a most dangerous Enemy.

† He compared Dialectick to the Moon, which is in continual encrease or decrease.

* Falling sick he was taken with a Fit of a Lethargy, out of which he no sooner came, but he said, *Love of Life shall flatter me no longer*; and thereupon with his own hands ended his life.

PHILO.

†PHILO was of *Larissa*, he heard *Clitomachus* many years, and is nam'd by *Sextus Empericus*, as Constitutor of a *fourth Academy*; but *Cicero* affirms, he disallowed the distinction of Academies, and wrote expresly to prove the *first* and the *new* Academy to be both one. *Whilst he lived, the Academy wanted not a Patron. † The *Romans* admir'd him, as *Plutarch* affirms, above all *Clitomachus*'s Scholars, for his excellent discourse, and loved him for the sweetness of his disposition. *Cicero* no sooner went out of the first Schools and rudiments of Learning, but he became an Auditor of *Philo*, as he acknowledgeth himself.

Amongst other excellent things (saith * *Stobaeus*) he gave this Division of *Philosophy*. He compared *Philosophy* to a *Physician*; As the office of a Physician is first to perswade the sick person to permit himself to be cured; next to confute the reasons of his Adversary: So is it of a Philosopher, both which consist in Exhortation. Exhortation is a discourse inciting to Vertue; whereof one part explaineth its great use, the other refelleth Adversaries, or such as any way calumniate Philosophy. The comparison holds in a second manner, thus: As the part of a Physician, after he hath perswaded the patient to admit of Cure, is to apply the means thereof, as well to remove the causes of the Disease, as to induce and settle Health; so is it in this Science. After Exhortation, he endeavoureth to apply the cure, by removing false opinions wherewith the Soul is infected, and by substituting true. In the second place therefore it treats of good and evil, for the sake of which the Exhortation was made. Thirdly, the comparison holds thus: As all Medicines refer to one end, health, so all Philosophy to Beatitude. That part which treats of ends is joyned with another which treats of Life: For as in Medicine, it is not sufficient to restore health, unless it likewise deliver Rules by which it may be preserved; so in Life, some Precepts are required for conservation of the end: And this part also is twofold; private, or common: One considers the affairs of particular persons, as, whether a wise Man should manage a Common-wealth, whether he may live with Princes, whether he may Marry: The other considers the business of all in general; as, what Common-wealth is best, how Magistrates are to be chosen. This common part is called *Politick*, and is treated of distinctly by it self, as being of greatest Latitude. Now if all were wise Men, there would be no need of more Places, for the more subtle divisions would emerge from the Precedent. But because there must likewise be a care of the middle sort of Men, who cannot apply themselves to long disputations, either through want of time, or diversion of Business, there must not be omitted a Treating of Precepts, which delivereth short Rules concerning the use of each.

As to the *Stoical* Judicatory, *comprehensive Phantasie*, he held all things to be incomprehensible; as to the nature of the things themselves, comprehensible. Thus he took away the *comprehensive Phantasie* asserted by *Zeno*. _{Sext. Emp. Pyrrh. Hyp. 1. 33.}

He held that to be a good connex, which beginneth from true and endeth in false, as (if it be day, and I dispute) this, *If it is day, I dispute*: According to which tenet there may be true axioms three ways, a false only one way: For, when it beginneth from true, and endeth in true, it is true; as *If it is day, it is light*: And when it beginneth from false, and endeth in false, it is true; as, *If the Earth flies, the Earth hath Wings*. Likewise if it beginneth from false and endeth in true, it is true; as, *If the Earth flies, it is Earth*. That which is false, is that which beginneth from true, and endeth in false; as, *If it is day, it is night*; for, the antecedent, *it is day*, is true; but the consequent, *it is night*, is false. _{Sext. Emp. Pyrrh. Hyp. 2. 11.}

He appointed, that the precepts of Oratours should be delivered at one time, those of Philosophers at another. _{Tusc. Qu. l. 2.}

ANTIOCHUS.

_{* Plut. vit. Cicer.}
_{* Cic. Ac. qu. 1.}
_{† Acad. Qu. 4.}
_{* Cic. de Leg. lib. 2.}
_{† Vit. Cicer.}
_{* Cic. Acad. quæst. 4.}
_{† Sext. Empir. Pyrrh. Hypot. l. 33.}

ANTIOCHUS was an *Ascalonite*, † Brother of *Aristus*, Disciple of *Philo*. He lived with L. * *Lucullus*, the Quæstor, and General; he was also a great Friend to * *Atticus*, whom he invited to the Academy. He is named by *Sextus Empericus*, as Constitutor of a *fifth Academy*: For, as † *Plutarch* saith, he fell off from the Sect of *Carneades*, either moved by the evidence of Sense, or, as some thought, by ambition, and dissention with the Disciples of *Clitomachus* and *Philo*. So that with some little alteration, he made use of the Doctrins of the *Stoicks*; and * though he were called an *Academick* he had been, but for some alterations, an absolute *Stoick*; † whence it was said of him, *He taught the Stoical Philosophy in the Academy*; for he manifested, that the Doctrins of the *Stoicks* were in *Plato*. In his old age, saith * *Cicero*, he betook himself to the old *Academicks*, forsaking the *new*, † and diligently enquiring into the opinion of the Antients, * endeavoured to follow *Aristotle* and *Xenocrates* †, professing, that the *Stoicks* and *Peripateticks* agreed in the thing, and differed only in words. To which effect *Cicero* mentions a Book which he sent to *Balbus*: He wrote also another against his Master *Philo*, entituled *Sosus*. † *Cicero* being at *Athens* heard him, and was much taken with the eloquence and volubility of his Discourse, (* declaring him to be the most polite and accute of all Philosophers in his time) † but not with the new Doctrine which he introduced.

_{* Acad. quæst. 4.}
_{† Cic. de finib. lib. 5.}
_{* Acad. quæst. 4.}
_{† Cic. de nat. Deor. l. 1.}
_{† Cic. Acad. quæst. 4.}
_{* Plut. vit. Cicer.}
_{* Cic. Acad. quæst. 4.}
_{† Plut.}

Thus far there is a continued series of the *Academick* Philosophers.

The

THE HISTORY of PHILOSOPHY.

The Sixth Part.
Containing the *PERIPATETICK* Philosophers.

ARISTOTELES.

CHAP. I.
His Country, Parents, and time of his Birth.

Upon the death of *Plato*, his Disciples separated themselves into two Sects. The first continued in the same School, where he taught, the *Academy*: The other possess'd the *Lyceum*. The first was known by the general name of *Academicks*, or *Peripateticks of the Academy* ; the other

[a] *Ammon. sub finem. comment. in proæm. Porphyr.*

other by the general name of *Peripateticks*, or more particularly, *Peripateticks of the Lyceum*. Of the first we have discoursed already; we come now to the other, of which *Aristotle* was the Head.

^b *Aristotle* was born at *Stagira*, a City of *Thrace*, according to ^c *Herodotus* ^d *Thucydides*, ^e *Pausanias* and *Suidas*, by others placed in *Macedonia*, to take from him the imputation of a Barbarian. It was seated upon *Strymon*, a River which parts those two Countries, having a Haven called καπςθ, and a little Island of the same name belonging to it. This place, to which *Aristotle* owed his Birth, he afterwards requited with extraordinary Gratitude.

^f His Father was named *Nicomachus*, descended from *Nicomachus*, Son of *Machaon* (whose Skill in Medicine is celebrated by *Homer*) Son of *Æsculapius*, from whom *Nicomachus*, *Aristotle's* Father, deriv'd not only his Pedigree, but his Art also, for he was a Physician. *Suidas* saith, he wrote six Books of Medicine, and one of Physick. ^g *Galen* alledgeth a Plaister of one *Nicomachus*, either this or the elder. This *Nicomachus* (^h whom some affirm to have been Grandson to *Hippocrates* the Physician) lived in the time of *Amintas*, King of *Macedonia*, (Father of *Philip*) a Prince (as *Justine* witnesseth) eminent for all Royal Vertues. To him *Nicomachus* was not only Physician, but Friend and Favourite. ⁱ *Tzetzes* forgot these Relations of *Aristotle* (as *Nunnesius* observes) when he affirmed that he was called an *Æsculapian* figuratively, in respect of his Skill in Medicine, though it be true also that he did profess that Art.

His Mother, *Laertius* and *Suidas* name *Phæstias*, ^k *Dionysius Halicarnassæus*, and *Ammonius*, *Phæstis*. ^l *Ammonius* faith, she also was descended from *Æsculapius*, alledging in testimony thereof this Epigram,

His Mother Phæsis, *Sire* Nicomachus,
Descended both from Æsculapius.

But *Dionysius Halicarnassæus* faith, she was Daughter of a *Chalcidian*, one of the Colony which was sent from *Chalcis* to *Stagira*. Her Picture, *Aristotle*, in piety to her Memory, caused to be made by *Protogenes* an eminent Painter of that time, which Picture ^m *Pliny* reckons amongst the choicest pieces of that Master.

Aristotle (as *Suidas* affirms) had a Brother named *Arimnestas*, and Sister *Arimneste*. His Brother died before him without Issue, as appears by his Will.

Aristotle was born according to the testimonies of ⁿ *Apollodorus*, ^o *Dionysius Halicarnassæus* and others, in the first year of the 99th Olympiad, at what time *Diotrephes* was Archon at *Athens*, 44 years after the Birth of *Plato*, as ^p *Athenæus* accounts more justly than *Ammonius* and *Suidas*, who reckon but 42 before the Birth of *Demosthenes*, three years. ^q *Agellius* affirms, he was born the seventh year after the recovery of the City of *Rome* from the *Gauls* by *Camillus*; ^r but because (as *Plutarch* saith) it is hard to find out on what year the City was taken, it will be hard also to find upon what year it was recovered. The recovery was seven Months after its taking, but in the following Year, for it was taken in *July*, recovered in *February*. If therefore as *Valerius Flaccus*, *Agellius*, and *Cassius Hemine* account, the taking of the City was in the 363d year from the building thereof, it was recovered in 364th. Thus *Aristotle* was born in the first year of the 99th Olympiad, the 370th from the building of *Rome*.

But, if as *Livy* affirms, the taking of *Rome*, was in the 365th year from the building thereof, and its recovery in the 366th, *Aristotle* according to that account must have been born in the third year of the 99th Olympiad, in the 372d year from the building of the City. Again, if the City were taken in the 364th year after the building thereof, and recovered in the 365th Year, as *Varro*, *Pliny*, *Dionysius Halicarnassæus* account, whom *Scaliger* followeth, *Aristotle* must have been born in the second year of the 99th Olympiad, the 371 from the building of the City, reckoning always ten Months for a Year, and not casting them off, as *Pliny* and others seem to do, and beginning immediately the next year, which Months being reckoned, the account will agree with ours; hitherto *Nunnesius*.

CHAP. II.

His first Education and Studies.

^a *Nicomachus* and *Phæstis* the Parents of *Aristotle* being both dead, he was brought up by *Proxenus* an *Atarnean*, during which time being yet very young, he learned the Liberal Sciences, as appeareth, faith *Ammonius*, from those Writings of his which partly concern Poetry, partly the Poets themselves, as likewise from his *Homerical Questions*, and several Books concerning the Art of *Rhetorick*.

^b In gratitude for this care taken by *Proxenus* in his Education, *Aristotle* afterwards, not only bred up in like manner *Nicanor*, the Son of *Proxenus*, in all kinds of Learning, but adopted him his Son, and with his Estate bequeathed his Daughter to him. ^c He likewise caused the Statues of *Proxenus* and his Wife, to be made and set up in Honour of them, as is manifest by his Will.

^d *Athenæus* (citing an Epistle of *Epicure*.) and ^e *Elian* relate, that having consumed the Inheritance left by his Father in Prodigality and Luxury; he betook himself to the Wars, wherein having ill success, he professed Medicine, and by chance coming into *Plato's* School, and hearing their disputes, being of a Wit far beyond the rest, he addicted himself to Philosophy, and became Famous therein. But this agrees not well with the circumstance of his Story, as related by Authors of greater Credit, and less Prejudice.

CHAP.

CHAP. III.

How he heard Plato.

a Ammon.

a Having attained the Age of 17 years, he went (in obedience to the *Pythian* Oracle, which advised him to addict himself to Philosophy) to *Athens*, *Laertius* saith (out of *Apollodorus*) that he was then but seventeen years old, in which year *Naufigenes* was Archon, *Dionysius Halicarnasseus* saith, it was the year following, at what time *Polyzelus* was Archon, perhaps it was upon *Naufigenes*'s going out of his Office, whom *Polyzelus* succeeded. But *b* *Eumenus* is much mistaken, who saith, he was thirty years old when he came first to *Plato*, perhaps (as *Nunnesius* conjectures) because he had read in *Plato*, that Dialectick ought not to be studied till the thirtieth Year. And no less err *Ammonius*, (if he be Author of that Life) and *Olympiodorus*, who affirm, that *Aristotle* coming to *Athens* in the seventeenth year of his Age, heard *Socrates* three years, whereas *Socrates* was put to Death when *Laches* was Archon, thirty two years before *Naufigenes*, under whom *Aristotle* was seventeen years old.

b Laert.

Being recommended to *Plato*, he became his Disciple, and so continued twenty years, as an Epistle of his to *Philip* (cited by the old Interpreter of his Life) did testifie.

Plato much loved him, and admired his acuteness of Apprehension, and diligence in study; for which (*c* *Philoponus* saith) *Plato* used to call him the Mind of the School, and when *d* he was not at his Lectures, he would say, *The Intellect is not here*; or, as *Rhodiginus*, *the Philosopher of Truth is absent.* And comparing his acuteness with the dulness of *Xenocrates*, *Plato* was wont to say, *e* *What an Horse, and what an Ass have I to yoak together?* Xenocrates *needs a Spur*, Aristotle *a Bit.*

c De mundi Æternit.
d Vet. Interp.

e Laert.

f Ammon.

f Whilst he lived with *Plato*, he was extreamly studious, and given to Reading, insomuch that *Plato* called his house, *the house of the great Reader*, and would often say, *g Let us go to the great Reader's House.* This may be confirmed by that great number of ancient Authors which are cited in his Works. And though *h* *Laertius* (either in his own, or *Carneades*'s words) faith, that *Aristotle* hath thrust in as many sentences of old Authors in his writings, as both *Zeno* and *Chrysippus*; yet every one that is acquainted with the Writings of *Aristotle*, knoweth how judiciously and concisely he giveth an account of their Opinions, not for Ostentation, but disquisition.

g Interp.

h Vin. Epic.

i Elian. 3. 19.

Some report there was a great enmity betwixt *Plato* and *Aristotle*; which first arose from *Plato*'s dislike of his manner of Habit: For, *Aristotle* wore rich Garments, and rich Shooes, and contrary to *Plato*'s rule, cut his hair short, and wore Rings. He had likewise (say they) a scornful derision in his look, and tenacious contradiction in his discourse, which *Plato* not approving, preferred before him *Xenocrates, Speusippus, Amyclas* and others, to whom he communicated his Doctrine and many favours, but repudiated *Aristotle*, who thereupon, whilst *Plato* was yet alive, set up a Shcool in opposition to him, in the

k Laert.

Lyceum; at which ingratitude, *Plato* much troubled, said, *Aristotle kicks at us as young Colts at the Damm that foaled them, when they have sucked their fill*, and *l* for that reason, usually called *Aristotle* the Colt.

l Ælian. var. hist. 5. 9. Heladius, apud Photium, in biblioth.

m They add, that *Xenocrates* being gone into his Country, and *Speusippus* not well, *Aristotle* came into *Plato*'s School with some of his followers, and circumvented him with fallacious arguments, whereupon *Plato* retired to his own house, and there taught privately, leaving *Aristotle* in possession of the School, which he kept till *Xenocrates* returning, ejected him, and re-instated *Plato*. The chief Author of this report seems to have bee *Aristoxenes*, cited by *n* *Eusebius*, who as *o* *Suidas* observes, assoon as *Aristotle* was dead, cast many Aspersions upon him, out of a malicious revenge, because *Aristotle* preferred *Theophrastus* before him in the succession of the School, notwithstanding that *Aristoxenus* had gained a great name and credit among the Disciples.

m Ælian.

n Præpar. Evang. lib. 15.
o In Aristox.

But as *Ammonius* argues, it is not likely that *Aristotle*, if he would, could have ejected *Plato* out of the School, or have obtained License to erect a new one in opposition to him, for as much as at the same time *Chabrias* and *Timotheus*, *Plato*'s kinsmen, were in great power, and Generals of the *Athenian* Forces. Yet some there are, who affirm this, grounding it only on *Aristotle*'s contradicting of *Plato* in many things; to which *Ammonius* answers, that *Aristotle* doth not simply contradict *Plato*, but those who misinterpret his Writings. For if he do sometimes contradict *Plato*, what wonder? Seeing that therein he followeth *Plato* his Author, whose saying it was, that Truth ought to be preferred before all things; as also that Saying, *Socrates* indeed is dear, but Truth most dear. And elsewhere. What *Socrates* saith, we must not so much regard, as we ought to be solicitous concerning Truth. The same course *Aristotle* took, if at any time he confuted *Plato*'s Assertion, therein obeying him by following the Truth; and it is observed by *p* some, that he is very sparing in naming him, where he opposeth his Doctrine, and that thrice he makes honourable mention of him in his *q* *Rhetorick*, his Book of the World, (if that be his) and his *r* *Problems.*

p Licetus de pict. Aristot.

q Lib. 1. c. 17.
r Probl. 1. 30.

True therefore it is, (*s* as *Apollodorus, Dionysius Halicarnassæus*; but especially *Aristotle* himself, in his *t* Epistle to *Philip*, affirm) that he was a constant, sedulous hearer of *Plato* twenty Years, " unto the thirty seventh of his Age, even until *Plato* died, and then was so great an honourer of his Memory, that in testimony of his extraordinary Affection, he erected an Altar to him, bearing this Inscription:

s Laert.

t Vet. Interp.

u Vet. Interp.

x This Altar Aristotle*'s Hand did raise*
To Plato, *whom the Impious must not praise.*

x Ammon.

y *Olympiodorus* speaking of the honour which *Aristotle* gave to his Master, confirmeth it by this Argument, that he writ a whole Oration in commendation of *Plato*, wherein he first made a relation of his Life, then praised him. He adds, that *Aristotle* in his Elegies to *Eudemus*, extols him thus:

y Comment. in Gorg. Plat.

And

And coming to the fam'd Cecropian Town,
In sign of Friendship did an Altar raise
To him, whom impious persons must not praise:
Who straying Man to vertue did restore
Much by his Precept, by Example more.
One to the Gods so pious, good to Men,
No future Age must think to see again.

[1 Athen. deipn. 8. Ælian. 9. 22 & 5. 9. a Euseb. præpar. Evang.]

² Some affirm, that whilst he lived with *Plato*, he professed Medicine, and kept a Shop: But those [a] *Aristocles* confutes.

CHAP. IV.

How he lived with Hermias.

[a Laert. Suid.] ᵃ **P**Lato dying in the first year of the 108th Olympiad, and *Speusippus* his Nephew succeeding in the School, *Aristotle* went to *Hermias* the Eunuch, King of *Atarna*, a City of *Mysia* in *Asia*, who heretofore had been his fellow-Disciple under *Plato*, and had a particular kindness for him. *Hermias* receiv'd him with great testimonies of Love and respect. With him he lived three Years, [ᵇ instructing him in Philosophy] at the end whereof, *Hermias* was (as ᶜ *Strabo* saith) surprised by *Memnon* a *Rhodian*, and sent to *Artaxerxes*, King of *Persia*, who put him to Death. *Pythais* his Sister, a Woman of extraordinary vertue, (whom *Hermias*, having no Children, had design'd his Heir) being upon this accident reduced to great extremities and afflictions, *Aristotle*, in a pious gratitude to the memory of his Friend, (as his own a Letter to *Antipater* attesteth) took her to Wife, and ᵉ set up the Statue of *Hermias* in the Temple of *Delphi*, with this Inscription.

[b Suid.]
[c Lib. 13.]
[d Euseb. cont. Philos.]
[e Laert.]

This Man the Persian *King against all right*
A Sacrifice to his fierce Anger made;
Not like a Foe by Martial Arms in Fight;
But as a Friend by shew of Love betray'd.

He wrote likewise a Hymn to *Vertue*, in memory of his Friend, to this Effect.

Vertue, whom we all obtain
With much Labour, but more Gain,
For your sake to dye would please,
Toyl and Torments were but ease.
You direct Men in pursuit
Of immortal sacred Fruit,
Richer far than Gold refin'd,
Soft as Sleep, as Parents kind;
Great Alciades for your sake
Labours vast did undertake:
Leda's valiant twins made known
More your Glories than their own;
Ajax and Achilles too
Only dy'd for Love of you;
Ah! for you Atarna's Pride,
Hermias untimely dy'd.
But his name we will revive;
That our Muse shall keep alive,
Paying Hospitable Jove
Pious thanks for a Friend's Love.

There wanted not those who cast many aspersions and calumnies upon this Vertuous friendship: some affirm'd that *Hermias* lov'd *Aristotle* inordinately (an imputation not well suiting with an Eunuch,) and that for for this Reason he gave him *Pythais* to wife, whom *Suidas* and the Greek *Etymologist* affirm to have been his Daughter either by Nature or Adoption, *Demetrius Magnesius*'s Neice, *Aristippus*'s Concubine, so little do they agree in their Relation: They add that *Aristotle* was so passionately in love with her, that he Sacrificed to her after the same manner as the *Athenians* to *Ceres* at *Eleusis*. This *Laertius* relates as done whilst she was alive; but *Lyco*, first Author of this Calumny, that it was after her death. Moreover that *Aristotle* in a thankful acknowledgment of his Bounty, wrote a Pæan in praise of *Hermias*, meaning the Hymn last mentioned, which ᶠ *Athenæus*, proveth against the Calumiations of *Demophilus* not to be a sacred Hymn or Pæan, but a *Scholion* or Festival Song. Hence *Theocritus* the *Chian* derides him in this Epigram.

[f Deipn. l. 15.]

To the slave Eunuch who Atarna *sway'd*
An empty Tomb empty Aristotle *made,*
Who from the Academy did retire
To wallow in vain pleasures faithless mire.

In answer to these Calumnies (first raised by *Lyco*, dispersed further by *Aristippus*, and continued by those that malign the memory of *Aristotle*) *Apelleio* writ certain Books wherein he accurately confutes those who durst in this manner impudently Blaspheme (such are his words) the name of *Aristotle*; so much prejudice and malice being in the Accusation, as might easily argue the falseness thereof.

ᵍ Upon the Death of *Hermias*, *Aristotle* (with *Xenocrates*) fled from *Atarna* to *Mytylene*, as *Apollodorus* and *Dionysius Halicarnasseus* affirm in the fourth year of the 108th Olympiad, *Eubulus* being Archon.

[g Laert.]
[h Strab. l. 13.]

CHAP. V.

How he lived with Philip *and* Alexander.

ABout this time *Philip* King of *Macedonia*, Father of *Alexander*, taking care for the Education of his Son, now growing towards Man's Estate, and unwilling (saith ᵃ *Plutarch*) to commit his Education to Professors of Musick, or any other of the Liberal Sciences, as knowing him fit for higher designs, sent to *Aristotle* the most famous and Learned of Philosophers, to come and instruct him. ᵇ *Agellius* recites his Epistle, which was to this effect.

[a Vit. Alex.]
[b Lib. 9. c. 3.]

Philip to Aristotle, *Health*.

KNow that I have a Son, I render the gods many thanks: not so much for his Birth as that he was born in your time, for I hope that being educated and instructed by you, he will become worthy both of us, and the Kingdom which he shall inherit.

Aristotle at this request of *Philip*, went to *Macedonia* to him, in the 4th year of the 108th Olympiad, as ᶜ *Apollodorus* and *Dionysius Halicarnassæus*

[c Laert.]

carnassæus affirm, at what time *Alexander* was fifteen years old.

d Ammon.
[d] He lived there infinitely esteemed and beloved of *Philip* and *Olympia* his Wife, *Alexander*'s Mother, [e] They caused his Statue to be made and set up in honour of him. *Philip* had a kindness so particular for him, that he allowed him in a manner an equal share in the Government of the Kingdom; which interest *Ammonius* saith, he employed to the advantage as well of private persons, as of the publick, as appeareth (saith the Latin Interpreter of his Life) by his Epistles to *Philip*. [f] *Plutarch* affirms that *Philip* as a recompence to *Aristotle*, re-edified the Town where he was born, *Stagira*, which he had before laid waste. He likewise assigned him a School and Study, near *Mieza*, a Town of *Macedonia* not far from thence, where, unto this day (saith *Plutarch*) they shew the stony Seats, and shady Walks of *Aristotle*.

e Vet. Interp.

f Vit. Alex.

g Plut.
[g] He instructed *Alexander* in the deepest parts of Learning, not only in Ethicks and Politicks, but his most reserved and solid Doctrins, called *Acroatick* and *Epoptick*; never communicated to the Vulgar.

That he taught him likewise the Art of Medicine, *Plutarch* argueth, forasmuch as *Alexander* was not only exceedingly delighted with the Theory thereof, but practised it successfully upon many of his Friends, to whom he prescribed Receipts and Diets, as appeareth, saith he, by his Epistle.

h Plut.
[h] Perceiving *Alexander* to be much taken with *Homer*'s Iliads, as conceiving and calling it *the best institution of military Vertue*, he took much pains in correcting and restoring the Text, and then gave it to *Alexander*, which Copy he infinitely prized.

He writ a Book to *Alexander*, entituled: *Of a Kingdom*, mentioned by *Laertius* and *Ammonius*, wherein he instructed him how to rule.

i Vet. Interp.
[i] So much did he incline the Mind of *Alexander* to do good, that he used to say, if any day passed wherein he had not conferred some benefit, *I have not reigned to day*.

k Plut. vit. Alex.
[k] *Alexander* so much affected him, that he professed he admired and loved him no less than his Father; because his Father, he said, only gave him being, but *Aristotle* well-being.

The love which *Philip* and *Alexander* bore him was so great, that *Theocritus* the *Chian* cast the same Aspersion upon it, as he did on his Friendship with *Hermias*.

In the first year of the 111th Olympiad, *Pythodorus* being Archon, *Philip* died, and was succeeded by his Son *Alexander*, whose active Spirit, soon after his coming to the Crown, designed an Expedition against the King of *Persia*. Hereupon *Aristotle* having now lived with *Alexander* eight years, though *Justin* saith but five which some interpret of the time before *Philip*'s death, but not without some violence, (for that was above seven) preferring the quiet of a Contemplative Life before the troubles of War, took leave of him, returned to *Athens*, leaving in his room *Callisthenes* an *Olynthian*, his Kinsman (Son of his Cousin *Hero*) and Disciple; [l] whom before his departure, observing to speak with too much liberty and obstinacy to the King, he reproved in these words,

l Laert.

Son, if thou thus employ thy Tongue,
Thy thread of Life cannot be long.

And so it came to pass not long after upon this occasion. *Hermolaus*, Son of *Sopolis*, a youth of a noble Family, that studied Philosophy under *Callisthenes*, hunting the Wild Boar with *Alexander*, prevented the King by casting his dart first at him, for which he was by the King's command punished with many stripes. Troubled at the ignominy thereof, he conspired with *Sostratus*, *Antipater*, and some other Companions of his, to murther *Alexander*, which Treason being discovered by *Epimenes*, one of the Conspirators, they were all put to death. *Aristobulus* and *Ptolemæus* Son of *Lagus* affirm, they accused *Callisthenes*, as him who instigated them to this attempt. Hereupon *Callisthenes* was put into an Iron Cage, and so carried up and down in a miserable sordid condition, and at last, as *Laertius* relates (though others otherwise) thrown to Lyons and devoured.

CHAP. VI.
His School and manner of Teaching.

Thus *Aristotle* having lived eight years with *Alexander*, returned to *Athens*, as [a] *Apollodorus* and [b] *Dionysius Halicarnassæus* affirm, in the second year of the hundred and eleventh Olympiad, *Pythodorus* being Archon, where he found *Xenocrates* teaching in the Academy, which place was resigned unto him by *Speusippus*, in the fourth year of the hundred and ninth Olympiad.

a Laert.
b Epist. ad Ammon.

Hence it appeareth, that [c] *Hermippus* erreth, in affirming, that *Xenocrates* took upon him the School of *Plato*, at what time *Aristotle* was sent by the *Athenians* on an Embassy to *Philip*. For as [d] *Patricius* hath observed, it can no way agree in time, it being certain, as *Laertius* attests, that *Speusippus* succeeded *Plato* in the School in the first year of the Hundred and Eighth Olympiad, immediately upon *Plato*'s Death, and continued therein eight years, that is, to the end of the hundred and ninth Olympiad; in the second year of which Olympiad, *Aristotle*, as we said, went to *Philip*, not on an Embassy, but upon his Invitation, to educate *Alexander*.

c Laert.

d Discuss. Perip.

Neither is the Author of *Aristotle*'s Life less mistaken, who saith, that upon the Death of *Speusippus*, the *Athenians* sent to *Aristotle*, and that both of them, *Aristotle* and *Xenocrates*, took upon them *Plato*'s School, *Xenocrates* in the Academy, *Aristotle* in the Lyceum. But this error is easily detected by the same computation; for at the time of *Speusippus*'s death, *Aristotle* was with *Alexander*, nor did he leave him until six years after, all which time *Xenocrates* professed Philosophy in the *Academy*.

[e] The *Academy* being prepossess'd by *Xenocrates*, *Aristotle* made choice of the *Lyceum*, ([f] a place in the Suburbs of *Athens*, built by *Pericles* for the exercising of Soldiers.) Here he taught and discours'd of Philosophy, to such as came to him, *walking* constantly every day till the hour of anointing, which the *Greeks* usually did before Meals, whence he and his followers are called ἀπὸ τῦ περιπατεῖν, *from walking*, *Peripateticks*. Others say, he was called *Peripatetick* from walking

e Laert.
f Suid.

walking with *Alexander*, newly recovered of a sickness, in which manner he used to discourse of Philosophy with him.

(*g*) *Laert.*

(*g*) The number of his Auditors encreasing very much, he gave over walking, and taught sitting, saying,

*Now to be silent most disgraceful were,
And see* Xenocrates *possess the Chair.*

Though *Cicero* and *Quintilian* affirm, he used this Verse against *Isocrates*, in emulation of whom he taught Rhetorick to his Disciples every Morning. (*h*) So many Disciples resorted to him, that he made Laws in his School, as *Xenocrates* did in the *Academy*, creating *Archons* that Rul'd ten days.

(*h*) *Laert.*

(*i*) *Agel. lib. 21. cap. 5.*

(*i*) The Discourse and Doctrine which he delivered to his Disciples was of two kinds. One he called *Exoterick*, the other *Acroatick*. *Exoterick* were those who conduced to Rhetorick, Meditation, nice Disputes, and the knowledge of civil things. *Acroatick* those in which more remote and subtile Philosophy was handled, and such things as pertain to the Contemplation of Nature and Dialective Disceptations. *Acroatick* Discipline he taught in the *Lyceum* in the Morning, not admitting every one to come and hear them, but those only, of whose Wit and principles of Learning, and diligence and Study, he had before made Trial. His *Exoterick* Lectures were in the Afternoon and Evenings; these he communicated to all young men without any distinction, calling the latter his *Evening Walk*, the former his *Morning Walk*.

CHAP. VII.
His Philosophy.

(*a*) *Vit. Ar.*

IN *Philosophy* (saith (*a*) *Ammonius*) he seems to have done more than Man, for there's not any part of Philosophy whereof he treated, but he doth it most accurately, and many things he himself (such was his Sagacity and Acuteness) finding out, compleated and finished.

(*b*) *Ammon. vit. Ar.*

(*b*) In *Logick* it was his Invention, that he separated the Precepts of Disputation from the things themselves of which we Dispute, and taught the Manner and Reason of Disputation. For they who went before, tho' they could Demonstrate, yet they knew not how to make a Demonstration; as they who cannot make Shoes, but only wear 'em. *Alexand. Aphrodisæus* affirms, that he first reduced Syllogisms to *Mood* and *Figure*. *Philoponus*, that he invented all Dialectick Methods, whence *Theodorus* calls him *both Inventor and Perfecter of Logick*, which he indeed in a manner challengeth (but modestly) to himself, in the last Chapter of his *Elenchs*, affirming nothing had been done in that kind before, but what the Eristicks and Sophists taught. As for the *Categories*, the invention whereof some ascribe to the *Pythagoreans*, it is much more probable that they were wholly his own; for those Books entituled καθόλε λόγοι, under the Name *Archytas*, from which some conceive *Aristotle* to have borrowed much, the particulars whereof are instanced by (*c*) *Patricius*, *Themistius* affirms to have been written, not by the *Pythagorean* (neither hath *Laertius* made mention of any writings of his, for the *Pythagoreans* at that time wrote but little, the first that wrote any

(*c*) *Dissertat. Peripat.*

thing being *Philolaus*) but by some *Peripatetick*, who thought his work might pass with greater credit, if published in the name of so antient a Philosopher.

In *Physick* the *fifth Essence*, whereof Celestial Bodies consist, distinct from the four Elements, is generally ascrib'd to his invention, only *Simplicius* citeth the Authority of *Xenocrates*, in his Book of the Life of *Plato*, that *Plato* constituted five simple Bodies, Heaven and the four Elements, asserting, they differ no less in Nature than in Figure; for which reason he assign'd the Figure of a *Dodecadron* to Heaven, offering from the Figure of the four Elements. But these, as the Learned *Nunnesius* observes, seem to be rather Symbolical, and Pythagorical, than the true meaning of *Plato*. For *Plato* in his *Timæus* expresly avers, that the Heavens are of their own Nature Dissoluble, but by the Divine Will is kept together, as it were, by a tye from being dissolved. *Xenarchus*, a Philosopher, wrote against the fifth Essence, introduced by *Aristotle*, whom *Alexander Aphrodisæus* exactly answereth. *Theodorus* calleth *Aristotle*, *The Perfecter of Physick*, adding, that only his Writings upon that Subject were approv'd by following Ages, who rejected whatsoever others had written in the same kind, as appeareth by their loss. What *Epicure* and others have objected against him as a fault, *That he enquired with such diligence into the minute, and meanest things of Nature*, is a sufficient Testimony of his Excellence and Exactness in this Study.

(*d*) In *Ethick*, whereas *Polyænus* placed Felicity in External Goods, *Plato* in those of the Soul only, *Aristotle* placed it chiefly in the Soul; but affirmed it to be *defiled* and *streightned* if it want exterior goods, properly using these terms. For those things which are *defiled*, have the same Beauty within, but their Superficies only is hidden; and those which are streightned have the same real magnitude.

(*d*) *Vet. Interp.*

(*e*) In *Metaphysick*, which he calleth *First-Philosophy* and *Wisdom*, and (as the more antient Philosophers before him) *Theology* (*f*) tho' there be not any invention of his extant, yet, he perfectly went through all the Parts thereof. For he was not only acquainted, as some falsly imagine, with Terrestrial things, and those which belong to this World; but even with those things which are above this World, as may appear from the eighth Book of his *Physick*, where he saith, that *the first cause is not subject to motion, neither in it self, nor by accident*, in which words he declareth, that *God* is not a Body, nor any way passible. And in his 12th. Book of *Wisdom*, or *Metaphysicks*, he discourseth accurately of *God* and *Intelligences*, in a rational clear way, not involv'd in Fables, or Pythagorical Symbols; but founding his Assertion upon Reason and Demonstration, as much as the Subject, and Humane Reason alloweth. (*g*) *Patricius* labours much to prove that whatsoever he had in this kind excellent, he borrow'd from *Hermes Trismegistus*. But (*h*) as we have already said, Mr. *Casaubon* hath fully evinced that Book to have been imposed upon the World by some later Writer.

(*e*) *Ammon.*

(*f*) *Ammon.*

(*g*) *Dissert. Peripat.*

(*h*) *In the Life of Plato, cap.*

What is added by the acient Latin Interpreter concerning *Aristotle*'s Sentence of that *visual Hexagonal Pyramid*, (which (*i*) a Learned Person,

(*i*) *Nunnes. Vit. Arist.*

son hath observed to be chosen as a middle way betwixt the Sentence of those who made the Optick Pencil a Pyramid of a quadratick base, and those who made it of a Conick Figure) is very obscure; and hardly admits of an Interpretation worthy so great an Author.

CHAP. VIII.
His Correspondence with Alexander.

Whilst *Aristotle* taught Philosophy at *Athens*, his Disciple *Alexander* was employed in an expedition to *Asia* against *Darius* King of *Persia*, incited thereunto by the principles of Honour, which were infused into him by *Aristotle*, particularly from the Presidents of *Achilles, Ajax*, and other *Heroes* celebrated by *Homer*, whose Iliads *Aristotle* had so carefully recommended unto him. He began this Expedition in the third year of the 111th Olympiad, at which time *Ctesicles* was Archon at *Athens*, immediately after the departure of *Aristotle*, who (it is probable) came only for this reason from him, as preferring a quiet and studious Life before the troubles of War.

The first thing that *Alexander* did, was to visit the Tomb of *Achilles* in the *Sigæum*, at the sight whereof he broke forth into these words ; *O fortunate young Man that hadst a* Homer *to celebrate thy praise! for had it not been for his Iliads*, adds a *Cicero*, in the same Tomb where *Achilles's* Body lay, his Name also would have been buried. He took with him the Iliads of *Homer* corrected by *Aristotle*, and made it his constant companion, insomuch that he laid it every night with his dagger, under his Pillow. And in a Victory over *Darius*, having taken a Casket of Unguents of extraordinary Value amongst the Spoils of *Darius*, beset with Pearls and precious stones (as b *Pliny* describes it) his Friends telling him how many uses it might be put to, because Unguents did not become a Soldier; Yes, saith he, it shall serve to keep the Books of *Homer*, that the most precious work may be kept in the richest Case ; hence was this correct Copy called, as *Plutarch* saith, ἐκ τῦ ναρθηκος.

Whilst he was in *Asia*, engaged in the Wars against *Darius*, in the midst of his continual Victories and Business, hearing that *Aristotle* had published his Acroacick Books of Natural Philosophy, he sent this Letter to him ;

d *Alexander to* Aristotle, *Health*.

YOU have not done well in publishing your Acroatick *discourses, for wherein shall we excel others, if this Learning wherein we have been Instituted, be made common to all? As for me, I had rather excel others in Knowledge than in Power,* Farewel.

To which *Aristotle* returned this Answer.

e *Aristotle to* Alexander, *Health*.

YOU *wrote to me concerning my* Acroatick *Discourses that they ought not to have been communicated, but kept secret. Know, that they are made publick, and not publick ; for none but they who have heard us can understand them.* Farewell.

Thus, notwithstanding *Alexander* was busied in the Wars, yet he forgot not his Master *Aristotle*, but kept a friendly correspondence with him. So constant was he in his Love to Learning, and particularly so much enflamed, (as f *Pliny* saith) with a curious desire of understanding the natures of living Creatures, that he sent thousands of Men, throughout all *Asia* and *Greece*, to procure all kinds of living Creatures, Birds, Beasts and Fishes, at an excessive charge, g *Athenæus* saith, 800 Talents, which according to h *Budæus*'s account is 840000 Crowns: These Men he sent with what they took to *Aristotle*, that he might not be ignorant of any thing that any Nation afforded ; by which information, he composed, as *Pliny* affirmeth, fifty excellent Volumes, *of Living Creatures*, of which ten are only left, unless we put into the same number, those Books of his which have some near relation to this Subject : As *of the going of living Creatures*. 1, *Of the parts of living Creatures, and their Causes. Of the Generation of living Creatures*. If this were done by *Alexander*, as *Pliny*, and *Athenæus* attest (though i *Ælian* ascribe it to *Philip*) it must necessarily have been whilst he was in his Asiatick Expedition. For *Aristotle*, as hath been already proved, stayed but a very short time with him after the death of his Father.

Aristotle made the same use of his correspondence with *Alexander*, as he had done of the Interest he before had with *Philip*, the advantage not only of particular persons, but of whole Cities.

This the City of *Stagira*, the place of his Birth, did acknowledge, which, at the suit of *Aristotle*, *Alexander* caused to be re-edified, and re-peopled and restored to its former state, having before by *Philip* been laid level with the Ground. For, though *Plutarch* relate this as done in the time of *Philip, Laertius, Ammonius, Dion, Chrysostome, Ælian*, and others hold, that it was done by *Alexander*, to which *Valerius Maximus* adds, that it was not long before. *Aristotle's Death*. In memory of which Benefit, the People of *Stagira* used to celebrate a yearly Festival, which they called the *Aristotelian Feast*, naming the Month in which it fell, *Stagarites*.

k *Erestus* likewise, the Country of *Theophrastus*, which *Alexander* determined to punish very severely ; by the mediation of *Aristotle* was pardoned.

That he benefited many particular persons is evident, saith *Ammonius*, from his Epistles to the King, yet extant, wherein he recommends several Persons to him,

Hence it is manifest, that the Author of his Life is mistaken, when he affirms, that in *Alexander's Asiatick expedition, Aristotle accompanied him to the Brachmanes, where he writ that noble piece of the Laws and Institutions of* 255 *Cities. That likewise he travelled over all* Persia *with* Alexander, *where during the War,* Alexander *died, and* Aristotle *returned into his own Country*. This relation agrees not with the other Circumstances of *Aristotle's* Life. *Alexander* died in the fourth year of the hundred and thirteenth Olympiad, two years before *Aristotle's* departure from *Athens*.

But as it is apparent, that this Mistake proceeded only from Ignorance (yet that so great, that l *Patricius* argues from thence neither *Ammonius* nor *Philoponus* to be Authors of his Life) so are there some other Errors, which no less [m Laert.] [m] Some affirm that *Alexander*, upon the Treason of *Calisthenes*, took a great displeasure against *Aristotle*, for having recommended him to him. For tho' at first, Writing to *Criterus*, *Attalus*, and *Alcetas* immediately upon this accident, he sent them word, that the Youths had confessed the Plot proceeded only from themselves, not by the instigation of any other. [n] Yet afterwards, in an Epistle to *Antipater*, he imputes the same Crime to *Calisthenes*, not without this sharp Reflection upon *Aristotle*: *The Youths, said he, were Stoned to Death by the Macedonians, but as for the Sophist, I will punish him my self, and those who sent him, and those who entertain in their Cities such as are Traitors to me.* Hereupon they Interpret the Bounty of *Alexander* to *Xenocrates*, and Favour to *Anaximenes*, as not proceeding from the Magnificence of his Disposition, [o] but from the displeasure he had conceiv'd against *Aristotle*, whom he endeavour'd to Vex, by obliging his Adversaries and Æmulators.

[n Plut. vit. Alex.]

[o Laert.]

Upon this supposed Displeasure was grounded another report, that [p] *Aristotle* Conspiring with *Cassander* against *Alexander*, sent him, by *Antipater*, some of the Water of *Styx*, wherewith he poisoned *Alexander*. But the Relators hereof differ not a little amongst themselves: *Diodorus Siculus* and *Suidas* affirm, that *Alexander* was poisoned by *Cassander* Son of *Antipater*; *Arianus* by *Jolla* his younger Son: *Porphyrius* saith, That nothing but the horn of an Ass, such as the Asses of *Scythia* had, would contain the poyson: *Justin* and *Pausanius*, the Hoof of a Horse; *Pliny* and *Arrian*, of a Mule, *Plutarch* and *Zonaras*, of an Ass. They differ no less about the place whence the Water was fetch'd. Neither indeed can it be expected there should be a better harmony amongst the Relators of this Fable, when there is so great Dissention and variety of Relations concerning the occasion and manner of his Death. But the most credible is that of *Ephippus* [q] (cited by *Athenæus*) [r] *Orosius*, [s] *Justine*, and otherers, who aver, that *Alexander* died of a Fever, caused by excess of Drinking.

[p Plut. Alex.]

[q Deip. 10.11.]
[r Lib. 3. c. 23.]
[s Lib. 12.]

CHAP. IX.
Upon what Occasion he left Athens, *and went to* Chalcis.

[a Laert.] Twelve years *Aristotle* professed Philosophy in the *Lyceum*, not molested by any; for tho' his eminence in Learning procured him many Æmulators and Enemies, yet the Favour he had with *Alexander*, while he lived, awed them so much, that they durst not make any Discovery of the ill will they bore him. No sooner was *Alexander* dead (according to *Dionysius Halicarnassæus*) but some of them conspired against his Life. To which end, *Eurymedon*, a Priest, or (according to *Phavorinus*) *Demophilus*, accused him of Impiety; *That he introduced some Philosophical assertions, contrary to the Religion of the Athenians; that he celebrated Hermias as a God, with a Hymn, and had caused his Statue to be set up in the Delphian Temple, with an honourable Inscription.* Some affirm hereupon, he made an Oration in defence of himself, at the Court of *Areopagus*, wherein he openly pronounced this Verse, made out of two in [b] *Homer*.

[b Odyss.]

Pears upon Pears, and Figs on Figs grow here.

By σῦκον ἐπὶ σύκα, (*Figs on Figs*) reflecting upon the Multitude of *Sicophants*, which sprung up every day in the City. Hence *Phavorinus* saith, he was the first Philosopher that pleaded for himself; and there was an Oration to that purpose went about many years after under his Name. But, of the truth hereof, *Athenæus* maketh question.

[c] Others affirm, that *Aristotle* perceiving the Conspiracy that was against his Life, stole privately out of *Athens*, and went to *Chalcis*, where he spent the rest of his days, returning to his Friends, who demanding the reason of his going, made this answer, [d] *We left* Athens, *that we might not give the* Athenians *occasion to commit again the same wickedness* [e] *they committed against* Socrates, *that they might not be guilty of a double Crime against Philosophy.* To *Antipater* he wrote the forementioned Verse,

[c Laert.]
[d Ælian. var. hist.]
[e Origen. contr. Celsum. lib. 1.]

Pears upon Pears, and Figs on Figs grow here.

Giving him to understang how dangerous it was for him to live in *Athens*, since the *Athenians* were wholly addicted to Sycophantism and Calumny. This departure of *Aristotle* from *Athens*, *Dionysius Halicarnassæus* placeth in the second year of the 114th Olympiad: *Apollodorus* a year latter, perhaps less rightly.

[f] Being near sixty two years of Age, very Sickly, and without hope of living much longer, the whole company of his Followers came to him, and besought him to make choice of a Successor, whom after his Death they might look upon as the Perfecter of those Studies wherein to he had brought them. There were at that time many excellent Scholars in his School, but especially two, *Theophrastus* and *Menedemus*, or rather as *Patricius* reads, *Eudemus*. These excelled the rest in Wit and Learning. The first was of *Lesbos*, *Eudemus* of *Rhodes*. *Aristotle* answered them, he would do as they requested, when he saw it convenient. Soon after the same persons being present who had made this request to him, he complained the Wine he then drunk did not agree with his Health, but was unwholsome and harsh; and therefore desired they would send for other sorts, both *Rhodian* and *Lesbian*, saying, he would make use of that which he should find best for him, they go, seek, find, bring. *Aristotle* first calls for the *Rhodian*, tasts it, A strong Wine, saith he, and pleasant; then calls for the *Lesbian*, which having tasted, *Both*, saith he, *are good, but ἡδίων ὁ Λέσβιος, the Lesbian is the sweeter*; whereby every one understood that his choice was not of the Wine, but of his Successor, which was *Theophrastus* of *Lesbos*, a Man of extraordinary sweetness in Discourse and Conversation: Whence not long after, as soon as *Aristotle* was dead, all his Disciples applied themselves to *Theophrastus*.

[f Angel. 13 6.]

CHAP. X.
His Apothegms.

Of his Apothegms are remembred these.
Being demanded what a Man got by Lying, he answer'd, *not to be believed when he spoke truth.*
Being

hath many Friends, hath none; which is likewise extant in the seventh Book of his *Ethicks*.

Stob. Ser. 28. He said, *When things happen not as we would, we must will as they happen.*

Ser. 45. Seeing a youth very self-conceited, and withal ignorant; *Young Man*, saith he, *I wish I were what you think your self, and my Enemies, what you are.*

Ibid. Seeing a young Man proud of a fine Cloak, *Why boast you*, saith he, *of a Sheep's Fleece?*

Ser. 46. He said, *They who demonstrate plain things, light a Candle to see the Sun.*

Ser. 101. Being reviled by an Impudent Person; *Thou*, saith he, *Who art vers'd to bear all things, speakest them with delight; I who am not us'd to speak them, take no delight in hearing them.*

Ser. 128. Being demanded why he who taught others to speak, himself held his Tongue; *A Whetstone*, saith he, *cannot cut, yet it sets an edge upon Swords.*

Ibid. Being asked who can keep a Secret; *He*, saith he, *that can hold a glowing coal in his mouth.*

Ser. 161. Seeing a young man very neatly dress'd, *Are you not asham'd*, saith he, *when Nature hath made you a Man, to make your self a Woman?*

Ibid. A handsome young man, much Courted, said to him, *If I were hated of the Citizens as you are, I would hang my self*; and I, reply'd he, *would hang my self if I were lov'd by them as you are.*

Serm. Being demanded how a Man should come to be Rich; he answered, *by being Poor in Desire.*

Serm. 305. It repented him of three things; that he had ever committed a Secret to a Woman; that he had Rid when he might have gone a Foot; that he had live one day not having his Will made.

CHAP. XI.

His Will and Death.

FRom that Speech of *Aristotle* last mention'd, may be gather'd how careful he was to make his Will, but more from the exact form thereof, which was thus:

(a) *Laert.* (a) BE *all well; but if it happen otherwise*, thus Aristotle *maketh his Will. Be* Antipater *my sole Executor during the Minority of* Nicanor. *Let* Aristomenes, Timarchus, Hipparchus, Dioteles, *(and if he please, and have leisure)* Theophrastus, *be Guardians of the Children and of* Herpylis, *and all that I leave. I Will, that my Daughter, as soon as she shall be Marriageable, be given* Nicanor *to Wife. If any thing happen otherwise (which God forbid) before she be Married, or after she be Married before she hath any Children, let* Nicanor *have the ordering of my Son, and the disposal of all other things, for his Reputation and mine. Let therefore* Nicanor *take care of the Maid* Pythais, *and my Son* Nicomachus, *and order their Estates according to their Conditions, as a Father and a Brother. If in the mean time any thing shall happen to* Nicanor *(which God forbid) either before my Daugter be Married, or if Married, before she hath any Children, if he make any Will, as he appointeth, so let it be. Otherwise, if* Theophrastus *approve of it, let him Marry the Maid, and have the same power that* Nicanor *should have had. Otherwise, let the Estates as well of the Maid as the Boy be disposed with the joynt consent of the Guardians, and* Antipater, *as they shall think fit. Let likewise the Executors of* Nicanor *take care to remember us and* Herpylis, *since that she hath been faithful to me, and if she will take a Husband, that such a one be given unto her as may be no disparagement unto us. Let them give her out of my Estate, besides what is already mentioned, a Talent of Silver, three Maid-servants, if she so please, and the Hand-maid which she hath, and the Boy* Pyrrheus. *And moreover, if she will dwell at* Chalcis, *let her have that Habitation which joyneth to the Garden; if at* Stagyra, *our Patrimonial Seat; which howsoever* Herpylis *shall choose, let the Executors furnish it, as they shall think convenient and proper for* Herpylis. *Let likewise* Nicanor *take charge of the Boy* Mirmax, *that he may be restored honourably, as becometh us, unto his own, with all his goods which we delivered to our Trust. Let likewise* Ambracis *be a free Woman, and have bestowed upon her at her Marriage, fifty Drachms, and the Girl which she hath. I Will likewise, that to* Thales *be given, besides the Handmaid he hath bought, a thousand Drachms, and another Handmaid. Likewise to* Simo, *besides that Money which he hath already received to buy a Servant, let another Servant be bought, or the like Sum be given again, wherewith he may purchase one. As soon as my Daughter shall be Married, let* Tycho, Philo, Olympias *and his Son be free men. Of those Boys which served me, let none be sold, but let my Heirs make use of their Service, and when they come to Age let them be manumitted. Let the Executors take care of those Statues of* Nicanor, *and his Mother, and* Proxenus, *which I gave order for to* Gryllius, *as soon as they are perfected, be set up. Let likewise the Statue of* Arimnestus *be set up, that this Monument may remain of him, since he died without Children. I Will likewise that the Statue of my Mother be Consecrated to* Ceres, *in the* Numæan Temple, *or where else shall be thought fitting. Wheresoever my Body is Buried by the Executors, thither let the Bones of* Pythias *according as she desired, be brought and laid with mine. Let likewise* Nicanor, *if he continue well in health, dedicate at* Stagyra, *to* Jupiter Soter, *and* Minerva Sotira, *Statues of Beasts, of Stone of four Cubits, in performance of the Vow which we Vowed for him.*

He died at *Chalcis*, in the third year of the 114. Olympiad, *Philocles* being Archon, in the 63*d*. and great Climacterical year of his Age (not as (b) *Eumelus*, 70 years old) as appeareth by the computation of *Apollodorus* and *Dionysius Halicarnassus*; thus,

(c) *Laert.*

	years.
He came to *Athens* at	18
Heard *Plato*	20
Lived with *Hermias*	3
With *Philip* and *Alexander*	8
Taught in the *Lyceum*	12
Lived at *Chalcis*	2
In all	63

The manner of his Life is variously related, (*c*) *Strabo, Hesychius, Illustris,* and from him *Suidas*, relate that he drank Hemlock, either being condemn'd thereunto by the *Athenians*, as *Socrates* was, or to prevent their Judgment.

(*d*) *Justin Martyr*, (*e*) *Gregory Nazianzen*, (*f*) *Cælius Rhodoginus*, the Greek *Etymologist*, *Nonnus*, and others, follow the common Report, that a Question was proposed to him of the wonderful Nature of *Euripus*, an Arm of the Sea, coming into *Chalcis* (as *Lucian* avers) which Ebbeth and Floweth seven times in twenty four hours. Not being able to resolve it, he died of Shame and Anxiety. Some affirm that as he sate on the Bank, having considered long upon it, he at last threw himself headlong into the River, saying, *Since* Aristotle *could not take* Euripus, Euripus *take thou* Aristotle.

But the Authors of greatest Credit, (*g*) *Apollodorus*, (*h*) *Dionysius Halicarnassæus*, (*i*) *Censorinus, Laertius* and others affirm, That he died of a pain in his Stomach, caused by over-watching, and excess of Study. For *Laertius* affirms he was a most indefatigable Student, and when he went to Bed, he held a Brazen Ball in his hand, that when he fell asleep, the noise of it falling into a Basin set under it for that purpose, might awake him, which *Alexander* his Disciple imitated. To this pain of his Stomach he was very subject, and sometimes asswaged it by applying a Bottle of hot Oyl to his Breast. *Notwithstanding this natural infirmity of his Stomach*, saith *Censorinus, and the frequent Indisposition of a sickly Constitution, he preserv'd himself a long time through his Vertue and Temperance; for it is much more strange that he attain'd the Age of 63 years*, than *that he lived no longer*.

The Author of the Book *de Pomo*, affirmeth, That when he was dying, he said to his Disciples, standing about him, it was not without Reason that *Homer* said, the Gods came down to Earth to relieve Mankind. (*k*) *Coelius Rhodoginus* adds from the same Author, that when he felt the Pangs of Death to come upon him, weeping between grief and hope, he often repeated these words, *Thou Cause of Causes have Mercy on me*: And his Disciples, when they saw he was departing, said, *He who receiveth the Souls of Philosophers, may he take thine likewise, and lay it up in his own Treasury, as the Soul of a right and perfect Man, as we have known thee to be*. Of this there is no Testimony more Ancient than that of the Author of the Book *de Pomo*, who (as *Patricius* clearly observes from his Writings) was a Christian.

(*l*) The *Stagirites* fetch'd his Body from *Chalcis* to *Stagira*, where they Buried it with much Solemnity, Building a Magnificent Tomb for him, and erecting an Altar to his Memory.

(*b*) *Lib.* 1.

(*d*) *Paræn. ad gent.*
(*e*) *Stelieut.* 1.
(*f*) *Ant. lect.* 19. 8.

(*g*) *Laert.*
(*h*) *Epist. ad Amm.*
(*i*) *De die natali.*

(*k*) *Antiq.* 18. 31.

(*l*) *Vet. Interp.*

was shaven, his Hair cut short; he had a high Nose, Nose, if we credit the Head put up by *Fulvius Ursinus*, found at *Rome*, at the bottom of the *Quirinal* Hill. He was of a sickly Constitution, troubled with a natural weakness of Stomach, and frequent Indispositions, which he over-mastred by his Temperance.

St. *Hierom* affirmeth, he was the Prince of Philosophers, an absolute Prodigy, and great Miracle in Nature, into whom seemeth to have been infused whatsoever Mankind is capable of.

He was extreamly pious towards God and Man, upon which Subject, *Fortunus Licetus* hath lately written two Books.

Eusebius, Cassiodorus, and others affirm, that many Persons, Eminent for Sanctity, especially followers of School-Learning, have, through the means of *Aristotle's* Philosophy, been carri'd on to Inspection into the highest Doctrins of true Faith; as, that there is one God, &c.

As concerning his gratitude to Men, besides those Instances already mentioned, to *Proxenus* and his Son, to *Hermias* and his Sister, to his Master *Plato*, to his own *Mother, Brother* and *Country*, and infinite others; many Philosophers, whose Opinion he takes occasion to alledge, he mentions with their due Praise; of which were his Master *Plato* (of whom we have already spoken) whom, as we have said, he sometimes mentioned honourably, and sometimes concealeth his Name, where he preferreth his own Opinion. Amongst others, of whom he maketh Honourable mention, are observed *Democritus* in his first Book, *de Generatione*; *Diogenes, Apolloniates*, in the same Book; *Anaxagoras*, in the first of his Metaphysicks.

For that he was very moderate, the Interpreter of his Life confirms, instancing in his Book of *Categorems*, where he saith, *We ought not to determine any thing hastily; but to consider often, and to doubt of every thing, is not unuseful*. And again, in his Book of Good, *We must remember, being Men, not only that we are happy, but that we ought to be able to prove it by firm Reason*. And, again, in his Ethicks to *Nicomachus*: *Man is our Friend, Truth our Friend; but above all, we ought to honour Truth*. And in his Meteorologicks: *As concerning these, we doubt of some of them, others we touch superficially*. And in the same, not once or twice, but infinite times, *Men do happen upon the same Opinions, therefore we ought not to be proud of our own Wisdom, in any thing whereof we conceive our selves to be the Inventers*.

The common report therefore (grounded upon no Authority) that he collected the Books of the Antient Philosophers, and having taken out of them what he intended to confute, burnt them, is manifestly false; for any one that reads *Cicero*, will find, they were most of them extant in his time.

CHAP. XII.

His Person and Virtues.

(*) *Laert.*

(†) *Ælian. ver. hist.*

* AS concerning his Person, he was Slender, having little Eyes, and a small Voice. When he was Young, *Laertius* and *Plutarch* affirm, he had a great hesitation in his Speech. † He went in a Rich Habit, and wore Rings; his Beard,

CHAP. XIII.

His Wives and Children.

HE had two Wives, the first *Pythais*, Sister to *Hermias*, the Eunuch, Tyrant of *Atarna*, and his adopted Heir. Of the Scandals that were cast upon him by this Marriage, *Aristotle* fully

acquits

acquits himself in his Epistles to *Antipater*, where he professeth, that he Married her only out of the good will which he bore unto *Hermias*, and out of a compassion for the great misfortunes that had hapned to her Brother; adding, that she was a Woman endowed with extraordinary Modesty, and all other Vertues.

His second Wife was named *Herpilis*, a Woman of *Stagira*, whom *Apellico* (cited by *Euseb.*) and (perhaps from him) *Suid.* affirm, he Marry'd after the death of *Pythais*: With her he lived to his end, as *Hermippus*, cited by *Athenæus*, and *Timothæus*, by *Laert.* affirm. *Timæus*, a profess'd calumniator of *Aristotle* saith, she was his Concubine, and that *Aristotle* lived with her, following the Counsel of *Hesiod* in his *Georgicks*; from which Calumny, *Hesiod* is fully vindicated by *Proclus*.

_{a *Euseb. præpar. Evang.*}

By *Herpylis* he had one Son, as ᵃ *Apellico* affirmeth, whom he named after his own Father, *Nicomachus*: To him he dedicated his *great Morals*, which ᵇ *Cicero* thinks to have been written by *Nicomachus* himself: For *I see not*, saith he, *why the Son might not be like the Father*.

_{b *De fin. l.* 5.}

_{c *Euseb.*}

ᶜ This *Nicomachus* was a Disciple of *Theophrastus*, and much beloved by him; under whom he profited exceedingly in Philosophy, and arriv'd at much Eminence therein. *Suidas* saith, he writ eight Books of Physick, four of Ethicks. *Cicero* compares him both with his Tutor and Father. *Aristocles* cited by *Eusebius* affirmeth he was bred up an Orphan, by *Theophrastus*, afterwards died young in the Wars, which relation agreeth not with *Aristotle*'s Will, nor with *Suidas* or *Cicero*, who aver that he writ Books, out of which *Laertius* brings a citation, *in Eudoxo*.

He had a Daughter also called *Pythais*, who, as *Sextus Empericus* affirms, was thrice Marry'd. First to *Nicanor* the *Stagirite*, Friend to *Aristotle*. Secondly, to *Procles*, who derived his Pedigree from *Demaratus* King of *Lacedæmonia*. By him she had two Sons, *Procles* and *Demaratus*, who Studied Philosophy under *Theophrastus*. Her last Husband was *Metrodorus*, Disciple of *Chrysippus* the *Cnidian*, Master of *Erasistratus*. By him she had a Son, named after her Father, *Aristotle*. Of this *Aristotle* there is mention in the Will of *Theophrastus*, where he is called the Son of *Midias*, not *Metrodorus*. *Suidas* affirms he died before his Grandfather.

CHAP. XIV.

His Disciples and Friends.

THE Disciples of *Aristotle* were so many and so eminent, that *Nicanor* of *Alexandria* wrote an express Book upon that Subject, which had it been extant, would doubtless have given us an exact account of them, whereas now we must rest satisfied with an imperfect Catalogue.

To omit the three Princes that were his Disciples, *Hermias*, *Alexander* (of whom already) and *Antipater*, Successor to *Alexander* in *Macedonia* (who amongst other things wrote two Books of *Epistles*, in one whereof he related the Death of *Aristotle*) in the first place is mentioned.

Theophrastus of *Eressus*, a City of *Lesbos*, the most Eloquent of his Disciples. Him he appointed to Succeed him in the School.

Phanias of *Eressus* also. He wrote many Books often cited by *Athenæus*; amongst the rest, *Ammonius* cites his *Categories*, *Analyticks*, and *of Interpretation*.

Eudemus of *Rhodes*, esteemed by *Aristotle* in the second place next to *Theophrastus*. His Life was written by *Damias*, as *Simplicius* affirms, who often mentions him. He wrote *Analyticks*, and a *Geometrical History* (both cited by *Simplicius*) and some other Histories cited by *Laertius*, wherein he said the *Magi* were of Opinion, that Men should Rise again after Death. He Survived *Aristotle*.

Eudemus of *Cyprus*, who died in *Sicily* where he took *Dion*'s part, as appeareth from *Plutarch*. *Aristotle* in honour of him, call'd his Dialogue *of the Soul*, afer his Name.

Pasicrates, Brother of *Eudemus* the *Rhodian*. To him some ascribe the first lesser Book of *Metaphysicks*, as *Philoponus* affirmeth,

Theodectes; to him *Aristotle* dedicated some Books of Rhetorick, mentioned by *Valerius Maximus*, which he afterward retracted. *Patricius* conceives he was rather a Companion than a Disciple of *Aristotle*, because he mentions him seven times in his Rhetorick, which he is never observed to have done of any Disciple.

Clearchus of *Soli*. He wrote many Books often cited by *Athenæus*.

Dicæarchus, Son of *Phidias* of *Messena* in *Sicily*, a Philosopher, Orator, and Geometrician, as *Suidas* affirmeth. He is cited by *Cicero*, mentioned often by *Plutarch* amongst the best Philosophers.

Aristoxenus, Son of *Mnesias* a Musician of *Tarentum* in *Italy*, who going to *Mantinia*, there Studied Philosophy and Musick. He heard his Father, and *Lamprus* an Erythræan, and *Xenopholus* a Pythagorean, and last of all *Aristotle*, whom after his death he calumniated and wronged much, because he had left *Theophrastus* his Successor in the School, whereas himself was in great esteem amongst the Disciples. Thus *Suidas*.

Nicanor, mentioned in his Will.

Philo, who wrote against one *Sophocles*, who caused the Philosophers to be voted out of *Attica*.

Plato the younger, mentioned by *Laertius* and *Philoponus*. _{*In Platone.*}

Socrates a *Pythinian*, mentioned by *Laertius*. _{*In Sxrate.*}

Mnason, a *Phocian*, mentioned by *Ælian* as one of those who assisted *Aristotle* in the ejection of *Plato* out of the Academy. *Galen* likewise mentions him as Author of some Medicinal Writings ascribed to *Aristotle*.

Phrasidemus, a *Phocian*, mention'd by *Laertius*, as a Peripatetick Philosopher. It is likely he was a Disciple of *Aristotle*, for he was contemporary with *Theophrastus*.

Palæphatus, of *Abydas*, an Historian much, beloved of *Aristotle*.

Calisthenes, an *Olynthian*, *Aristotle*'s Sister's Son, of whom already.

Hipparchus, a *Stagirite*; of kin to *Aristotle*. He wrote, as *Suidas* affirmeth, *of the distinctions of Sexes amongst the Gods*, *of Marriage*, and the like.

Leon,

Leon, a *Byzantine*, a Peripatetick Philosopher and Sophist. Some affirm he was a Disciple of *Aristotles*. He was so excessively fat, that coming to *Athens*, upon an Embassie, the People laught at him; to whom he said, do you laugh to see me thus fat? I have a Wife a great deal fatter; yet when we agree, one Bed will hold us both, but when we disagree, not the whole House. The People suspecting him of Confederacy with *Philip*, upon a Letter of his, came in a Tumult to his House, whereupon fearing to be Stoned, he Strangled himself.

Æschiron of *Mitylinc*, an Heroick Poet, loved much by *Aristotle*, as *Suidas* saith.

Calippus an *Athenian*, who also heard *Plato*.

Satyrus, whose Books *of Lives and Characters* are cited by *Athenæus*.

Hieronymus the *Rhodian*, eminent in Philosophy. That he was *Aristotle*'s Disciple is acknowledged by *Athenæus*.

Heraclides of *Pontus*, a great *Philologist*.

To these add of less note, *Echecratides* a *Methymnæan*, and *Adrastus* a *Macedonian*, both mentioned by *Stephanus*. *Eusebius*, mentioned by *Plutarch*. *Clitas* a *Milesian*: *Menon* the Historian; *Dioteles* and *Timarchus*.

CHAP. XV.

His Detractors.

AS the Friends and Followers of *Aristotle* were more in number than those of any other Philosopher, so were also his Detractors, of whom having already had occasion to make some mention, we shall not need to give any further account than this of *Aristotle*'s, alledged by * *Eusebius*.

* *Præpar. E- vang. lib. 15.*

How then is it possible, that what *Epicure* relates of *Aristotle* can be true, that when he was a young Man, he wasted prodigally all the Means his Father left him, whereby he was necessitated to betake himself to the Wars; but therein being unfortunate, he set up an Apothecaries Shop, and *Plato* keeping open School, amongst the rest admitted him?

And who will credit *Timæus* the *Tauromenite*, who writes, that being come to riper years, he shut up his poor Shop, and gave over his Mercenary Profession?

Who can be perswaded to believe what *Aristoxenus* the Musician saith in the Life of *Plato*, that when he was from home, some Strangers rose up, and set up a School in opposition to him, which words some interpret of *Aristotle*, but Erroneously; for *Aristoxenus* always commendeth *Aristotle*; [yet *Suidas*, as we said, avers the contrary.]

Who does not esteem the Commentaries of *Alexinus* ridiculous? For he bringeth in *Alexander* as a Youth talking with his Father *Philip*, slighting the Instructions of *Aristotle*, but approving those of *Nicagoras*, surnamed *Hermes*.

Eubulides manifestly falsifies in the Book he wrote against *Aristotle*. For first, he bringeth in some dull Poems as written by others, upon his Marriage and Affinity with *Hermias*; then he saith, that he injured *Philip*, that he was not present with *Plato* at his Death, and that he corrupted his Writings.

As for the Accusation of *Demochares* against Philosophers it is not worth the mention; for he Asperseth not only *Aristotle*, but all the rest; and whosoever looks upon his Calumnies, will say they are trivial; for he affirms, that some Letters of *Aristotle*'s, against the City of *Athens* were intercepted and discovered; that he betrayed his own Country, *Stagira* to the *Macedonians* that when *Olynthus* was taken, he informed *Philip* upon the Sale and Ransom of the Goods and Prisoners, which were the most Wealthy of the *Olynthians*.

No less foolishly doth *Cephisodorus*, Disciple of *Isocrates*, Calumniate him as an effeminate Person, and a Glutton, with many other Aspersions of the same kind.

But of all, the most foolish is that of *Lyco*, who professed himself a *Pythagorean*, for he saith, That *Aristotle* Sacrificed to his Wife after she was dead, as the *Athenians* to *Ceres*; and that using to bathe himself in warm Oyl, he afterwards sold it; and that when he went to *Chalcis*, those who bought his Goods, found in one bark 75 brass Pots. Indeed near so many were the Calumniators of *Aristotle*, from whom sprung up others, some in the same Age, others a little after, all Sophists, Litigious Persons and Orators; of whose Names and Books no more remains than of their Bodies.

As for those who Flourished after these, some repeat only what these had said before, and therefore we need not take any notice of them; much less of those, who not lighting upon those Books, have framed some Inventions of their own; such as they, who affirm, he had 300 Pots, for there was not any Author of that time who made mention thereof, but *Lyco*, and he saith, there were found only 75 Pots.

And not only from Computation of time, and from the Persons who assert these Calumnies, may any Man perceive all they say to be but false; but also from this, that not any two of them lay the same thing to his Charge, but every one hath a particular Calumny different from the rest. But, if any one of these had been true *Aristotle* should have heard of it, not only once from them, but a thousand times.

It is manifest therefore, the same thing befel *Aristotle*, which hapned to many others, that as well for the Respect and Friendship he had with Princes, as for the exellency of his Dissertations, the Envy of the Sophists of that Age persecuted him. But such as are Ingenious ought not to mind Calumniators, but those who have praised and imitated him, whom they will find to fall nothing short of the others, either for number or worth. Hitherto *Aristocles*.

CHAP. XVI.

His Writings.

LAertius hath given a large Catalogue of his *Writings*, as a Testimony of his Excellency in all kinds of Learning. Their Titles, as reduced to their several Heads, by *Patricius*, are these,

Logick.

Logick.

The Sophist 1.
Of Sciences 1.
Sophistick distinctions 4.
Of Eristick 2.
Of Eristick solutions 4.
Of Genus and Species 1.
Of Proprium 1.
Epichirematick Commentaries 1.
Instances 1.
Of those which are said many ways, as according to the propositum 1.
For Science 1.
Distinctions 17.
Diæreticks 1.
Of Interrogation and answer 2.
Propositions 1.
Eristick Propositions 4.
Syllogisms 1.
First Analyticks 9.
Second Analyticks 2.
Of Problems 1.
Methodics 6.
Terms Antetopical 7.
Syllogisms 2.
Syllogistick and Terms 1.
Ante-Topicks 1.
Topicks to Terms 1.
Diæretick 1.
Definitions 13.
Argumentations 2.
Propositions 1.
Epichiretick Theses 25.
Methodic 1.
Of Speech 1.
Categories 1.
Of Interpretation 1.

Physick.

Of the Soul 1.
Of Suffering and being Passive 1.
Of Elements 3.
Of Motion 1.
Theses of the Soul 1.
Of Nature 3.
Physick 1.
Of Animals 9.
Anatomy 7.
Anatomick selections 1.
Of compound Animals 1.
Upon not Generating 1.
Of Plants 2.
Physiognomick 1.
Signs of Tempest 1.
Physicks by Elements 38.
Perspective Problems 2.
Of Stone 1. In all 75.

Ethick.

Of Justice 4.
Of Philosophy 3.
Politicks 2.
Of Riches 1.
Of Nobility 1.
Of Pleasure 1.
Alexander; or, of Colonies 1.
Of a Kingdom 1.
Of Education 1.
Of Good 3.
Oecomomick 1.
Of friendship 1.
Propositions concerning Vertue 3.
Of the Passions of Anger 1.
Ethicks 4.
Of the Better 1.
Of Elegible and Accident 1.
Of Pleasure 1.
Of Voluntary 1.
Of Fair 1.
Amicable Theses, 2.
Politicks 2.
Laws 4.
Constitutive Law 1.
Politick Auscultation 8.
Of Just 2.
Of Consultation 1.
Jurisdictions 1.
Passions 1.
Governments of Cities 158.
Proper Democracies.
Oligarchicks.
Aristocraticks.
Tyrannicks. In all 217.

Metaphysick.

Of Contraries 1.
Of Principle 1.
Of Idea 1. In all 3.

Mathematick.

Mathematicks 1.
Of Magnitude 1.
Of Unity 1.
Astronomick 1.
Optick 1.
Of Musick 1.
Mechanicks 1. In all 7.

Phylologick.

Of Poets 3.
Gryllus of Rhetorick.
Works of Rhetorical Art 2.
Collection of the Theodectick Art, 1.
Rhetorical Enthymemes 1.
Homerical Difficulties 6.
Poeticks 1.
Comparisons 1.
The Olympionicæ 1.
Pythionick Musick.
Pythick 1.
Pythionick Elenchs 1.
The Dionysiack Victories 1.
Of Tragedies 1.
Poems, 3. So Hermias to Democritus,
Elegies. In all 27.

Uncertain or Extraordinary.

Nerinthus 1.
Menexenus 1.
Erotick 1.
Symposium 1.
Protreptick 1.
Of Prayer 1.

Collection of Arts 12.
Art 1.
Another Art 1.
Collection 2.
Of Fabulous Living Creatures 1.
Medicine 2.
Memorials 1.
Encyclicks 2.
Inordinate 12.
Expounded by their Genus 14.
Doctrines 1.
Proverbs 1.   In all 46.

Epistles.

TO Philip and Alexander 4.
To Antipater 3.
To Mentor 1.
To Aristo 1.
To Olympias 1.
To Hæpheftion 1.
To Themistagoras 1.
To Philoxenus 1.   In all 19.

Against the ancient Philosophers.

OUT of Plato's Laws 2.
Out of Plato's Commonwealth 2.
Out of Timæus and Archytas their Writings 1.
Problems out of Democritus 2.
Against Melissus 1.
Against Alcmæon 1.
Against Gorgias 1.
Against Xenophanes 1.
Against Zeno 1.
Of the Philosophy of Archytas 3.
Of the Philosophy of Speusippus and Xenocrates 1.   In all 19.

The Sum of all these Books, excepting the Epistles, is 513. *Laertius* reckons them to be near 400. perhaps accounting the several Books that are upon the same subject for one. But of these the greatest part is lost, and of many that are extant the titles altered; of the extant there are only these:

Logick.

CAtegories 1.
Of Interpretation 1.
First Analyticks 2.
Second Analyticks 2.
Topicks 8.
Elenchs 1.

Physick.

OF Natural Auscultation 8.
Of Heaven 4.
Of Generation and Corruption 2.
Of Meteors 4.
Of the World 1. *suspected*.
Of the Soul 3.
Of Sense and Sensibles 1.
Of Memory and Reminiscence 1.
Of Sleep and waking 1.
Of Dream 1.
Divination by Dreams 1.
Of the motion of Living Creatures 1.
Of the length and shortness of Life 1.
Of youth and age, life and death 1.
Of Respiration 1.
Of the going of Animals 1.
Of Breath 1.
Of the generation of Animals 5.
Of the parts of Animals 4.
The History of Animals 10.
Of Colours 1.
Of Physiognomy 1.
Spurious 2.

Ethick.

EThick, to Nicomachus 10.
Great Ethick 2.
Ethick to Eudemus 7.
Of Vertues 1.
Oeconomick 2.
Politick 8.

Metaphysick.

MEtaphysick 14.
Of the abstruse part of Divine wisdom according to the Ægyptians, Translated out of Arabick; but suspected to be spurious, 14.

Mathematicks.

MAthematicks 2.
Mechanick 1.
Of insecable Lines.

Phylologicks.

RHetorick 3.
Rhetorick to Alexander 1.
Poetick 1.

Extraordinary.

PRoblems 38.
Wonders 1.
Of Zenophanes; Zeno and Gorgias 1.

Besides these, there are many other Books cited for his, under these titles.

Magick, Laert. Proæm.
Epitome of Oratours, Laert. Aristip.
Of Beans, Laert. Pythag.
Of Mixtion, Aristot. de sensu. cap. 3.
Of Sapors, Arist. de sensu. cap. 4.
Physical History, Arist. de incess. Animal. cap. 2.
Of Nutriment, Arist. de Somno, cap. 3.
Selection of Contraries, Arist. Metaph. lib. 3. cap. 2.
Division of Contraries, Arist. Metaph. lib. 10. c. 3.
Of Opposites, Simplic. in cap. de Opposit. Comm. 8.

Collection

Collection of *Pythagorick Opinions*; Simplic. in lib. 2. de Cœlo. Com. 4.

Of *Idea's*, Alexand. in lib. 1. Metaphyſ. Comm. 59. where he cites the fourth Book, tho' *Laertius*, but one, as if there were no more.

Of *Enunnciation*, Alexand. in lib. 4. Metaphyſ. Com. 25. & 44.

Homerical Difficulties. 6.

Of *Platonick aſſertions*. Plut. contra. Colot.

Eudemus, Plut. Conſol. ad Apollon.

Of *Drunkenneſs*, Plut. Sympoſiac. 3. *Athenæus* cites the tenth Book hereof.

Animal, or of *Fiſhes*, Athen. Deipn. 7.

Of *living Creatures, and of things pertaining to living Creatures*, Athen.

Of *the manners of living Creatures*. Athen.

Of *Pheaſants*, Athen.

Of *Conſanguinity*, Athen.

Of *wonderful Luxury*, Athen.

Apology, Athen.

Histories, Athen.

Barbarous Juriſdictions.

Of *Audibles*, Porphyr. Comm. in Ptol.

Mus. Proclus in Timæum Plat.

The *Cohabitant*, Proclus. Proæm. in Repub. Platon.

Θεολογυμένα, Macrob. Saturnal. lib. 1.

Of *Nature*, Clem. Alexandrin. Strom. lib. 6.

We ſhall not add the *Peplus* cited by *Nicephorus*, and the *Chriæ* by *Stobæus*, under his Name, ſince it is manifeſt they belong not to the ſame *Ariſtotle*, as *Patricius* hath evinced.

Theſe Books *Ariſtotle* gave to *Theophraſtus*, when he made him his Succeſſor in the School, as *Strabo* affirmeth; adding, that *Ariſtotle* was the firſt we know of, that made a Library, which the Ægyptian Kings learned of him to do. *Theophraſtus* bequeathed all his Books to *Nelius* a Scepſian, who carried them to *Scepſis*, and dying, left them to his Heirs, men of no Learning, who only kept them confuſedly lock'd up: And when they underſtood what care was taken by the *Attaltick* Kings (in whoſe Juriſdiction *Scepſis* was) to make a Library in *Pergamus*, they hid them in a hole under ground [where they continu'd about 130 years] by which means they receiv'd ſome injury by the Wet and Worms. At laſt, ſome that were deſcended from *Ariſtotle* and *Theophraſtus*, ſold them to *Apellico* a *Teian*, [who, according to *Athenæus*, was made free of the City of *Athens*, a perſon very rich, who, beſides many other Libraries, bought this of *Ariſtotle* being himſelf a Lover of Peripatetick Philoſophy] for a great ſum of Money. This *Apellico* was more a lover of Books, than of Learning; ſo that becauſe they had received ſome injury, he cauſed them to be Tranſcibed, ſupplying the defects not rightly, and by that means put them forth full of faults. The Ancient Peripateticks that ſucceeded *Theophraſtus*, wanting Books, as having but very few, and thoſe Exoterick, could not treat exactly upon part of Philoſophy. They that lived later, after that theſe Books were publiſhed, had much greater helps to Philoſophy and the imitation of *Ariſtotle*, although by reaſon of the infinite faults they were forced to ſay many things by gueſs. Hereunto *Rome* conduced not a little; for (ſoon after the death of *Apellico*, *Sylla* taking *Athens*, in the fourth year of the 173 Olympiad, ſeiſed upon his Library. and cauſing it to be carried to *Rome*, *Tyrannio*, a Grammarian, a perſon ſtudious of *Ariſtotle*, obtained leave of the Library keeper to be permitted the uſe of them) the Bookſellers not having good Writers, and not comparing well the Copies, it occaſioned many faults, as well in thoſe Books that were at *Rome*, as in thoſe Tranſcribed and ſold into *Alexandria*. *Plutarch* adds, that from this *Tyrannio*, *Andronicus* the *Rhodian* had them, who firſt made them publick, ſetting forth thoſe Volumes, which, ſaith he, we have.

Thus *Strabo* and *Plutarch*; *Athenæus* ſaith, that *Nelius* ſold them to *Ptolemæus Philadelphius*, by whom they were Tranſlated to *Alexandria*, where how long they lay hid is uncertain, which Library was afterwards burned by *Julius Cæſar*.

CHAP. XVII.

His Commentators.

NO ſooner were the Writings of *Ariſtotle* communicated to the World, but they were entertained with general approbation, which ſome expreſſed, by employing themſelves in Commenting upon them, whoſe example was followed by many in all following Ages. To omit *Paſicrates* the *Rhodian*, Brother of *Eudemus* who wrote, as *Galen* affirmeth, upon the Book of *Categories*; we ſhall name in the firſt place,

Andronicus the *Rhodian*, who firſt publiſhed *Ariſtotle's* Writings, put forth a Paraphraſe or Comment upon the greateſt part of them.

Next, his Diſciple *Boethus*, a *Sidonian*, took much pains in the expoſition of *Ariſtotle*, whence he is often mentioned honourably by *Ammonius* and *Simplicius*.

Ariſto a *Coan*, Diſciple alſo to *Andronicus*, as a *Srabo* affirms, living in the time of *Nicias*, Tyrant of *Coos*, is reckoned by *Simplicius* amongſt the old Commentators upon *Ariſtotle's* Categories. [a *Geogr. lib.* 14.]

Nicolaus Damaſcenus, who lived in the time of *Auguſtus*, by whom much loved, is cited by *Simplicius* and *Averroes*, as an Expoſitor of *Ariſtotle*.

Athenodorus of *Tarſis*, a *Stoick*, who lived alſo under *Auguſtus*, as *Plutarch* affirms, is cited by *Simplicius*, as having written upon *Ariſtotle's Categories*; but rather by way of Confutation than interpretation, as did likewiſe *Alexander Ægeus*, *Nero's* Tutor, mentioned by *Simplicius*; *Cornutus*, who lived at the ſame time, cited by *Porphyrius* and *Simplicius*; *Lucius* and *Nicoſtratus* a *Macedonian*, who lived under *Antonius*.

Sotion of *Alexandria*, and *Achacius* ſeem to have written upon the *Categories*, being often cited by *Simplicius* upon that Subject.

Taurus the *Beriſian*, a *Platonick* Philoſopher, living under *Antonius*, wrote firſt concerning the difference between the Doctrines of *Plato* and *Ariſtotle*.

Adrastus the *Aphrodisæan*, wrote a Comment on *Aristotle*'s *Categories*, and of his Physick, and a Book concerning the Method of his Philosophy.

Aspasius wrote a Comment on all *Aristotle*'s Works, taking particular care to restore the Text, to which end he is often quoted by *Simplicius* and *Boetius*. There is Comment upon some Books of the *Ethicks* extant under his Name.

Herminus somewhat later, seems to have written upon all, or the greater part of *Aristotle*'s Works, cited by all the *Greek* Commentators that are extant, and by *Boetius*.

Alexander the *Aphrodisæan*, who lived under *Antonius* and *Severus*, wrote upon the *Analyticks*, *Topicks* and *Elenchs*, whence stiled by the latter Interpreters, Ἐξηγητὴς *the Expositor*.

Galen, who lived at the same time, wrote three Books upon *Aristotle* of *Interpretation*, four Books upon the first of the first *Analitick*, four upon the second of the first, six upon the first of the second *Analactick*, five upon the second.

[b] *Atticus* a *Platonick* Philosopher, besides seven Books, wherein he proved *Plato* and *Aristotle* to be of the same Sect, contrary to the Assertion of *Taurus*; he wrote also a Dialogue upon the *Categories* extant, seven Books upon the *Categories*, cited by *Simplicius*, a Comment upon the Book of *Interpretation*, cited by *Boetius*. Not to mention what he wrote upon *Aristotle de Anima*, since it appears from *Suidas*, that it was rather by way of Opposition than Exposition, which [c] *Theodoret* likewise confirms.

[b] Suid.

[c] Græ. affec. l. 12.

Jamblicus of *Calsis* in *Cœlosyria*, Master to *Julian* the Emperor, wrote in an abstruse way upon the Book of *Categories*.

Dexippus, by some thought to be Son of *Jamblicus*, wrote a Dialogue on the *Categories*, extant.

Maximus a *Byzantine*, Disciple of *Jamblicus*, wrote Commentaries on the *Categories*, and other Books of *Aristotle*, as *Simplicius* and *Suidas* affirm.

Plutarch the younger son of *Nestorius* flourishing under *Valentinian* the first, *Gracian* and *Theodosius* the first, according to *Suidas* and *Philoponus*, wrote Commentaries upon some Books of *Aristotle*.

Syrianus, surnamed the *Great*, of *Alexandria*, a Philosopher, who flourished under *Arcadius*, *Honorius*, *Theodosius* the second, and *Valentinian* the second, wrote Commentaries upon *Aristotle*'s Books of *Nature*, of *Motion*, of *Heaven*, and upon the *Categories*, cited by *Simplicius* and *Philoponus*. Likewise upon the Second, Fifth and Sixth Book of *Metaphysicks*, which are extant.

Olympiodorus an *Alexandrian*, who derived himself from *Ammonius Saccus*, and was contemporary to *Plutarch* and *Syrianus*, wrote upon *Aristotle*'s Meteors, extant. He was later than that *Olympiodorus*, who writ upon *Plato*.

Themistius, Living, according to *Suidas*, under *Julian* and *Jovian*, wrote a Paraphrase upon *Aristotle*'s *Physick*, eight Books; a Paraphrase on the *Analyticks*, two Books; upon his Books *of the Soul*, seven Books. Of the Scope and Title of the Book of *Categories*, one Book.

Proclus, Disciple of *Syrianus*, wrote two Books concerning Motions, wherein he made an abstract of *Aristotle*'s second Book of *Motion*. That he wrote also upon his Book of *Heaven*, and the *Elements*, may be conjectured from the frequent Citations of *Simplicius*.

Marinus, who succeeded *Proclus* in the School, seemeth to have written something upon *Aristotle*'s Book of the *Soul*, being often cited upon that Subject by *Philoponus*.

Ammonius Hermonæus wrote upon *Aristotle*'s *Categories*, and upon his Book of *Interpretation*, both which are extant; as likewise upon his Books of *the Soul*, cited by *Philoponus*.

Damascius, a *Platonick* Philosopher, Disciple to *Ammonius*, besides what he wrote in Confutation of *Aristotle* concerning *Time*, epitomiz'd the four first, and the eighth Book of his Physick, and the first Book of Heaven. To these add

Philoponus and *Simplicius*, and *Asclepius*, Disciple to *Ammonius*.

Johannes Damascenus, whose Compendium of *Aristotle*'s *Logick* and *Physick* are extant; he lived about the year 770.

Eustrathius wrote upon some of the *Nichomachian Ethicks*; and *Eustratius* upon his Book concerning Demonstration.

Michael Psellus, about the year 800. and *Michael Epesius*, upon the *parva naturalia*.

Magentinus upon the *Categories*, and the Book of *Interpretation*.

Nicephorus Blemmydes (under *Johannes duca*.) upon the *Logick* and *Physick*.

Georgius Plachymerius and *Theodorus Metochita* lived about the year 1080. and wrote Epitoms extant.

Of *Arabick* Commentators were *Avicenna* and *Averroes*; about the year 1216.

The later Writers it will be unnecessary to mention, there being a Catalogue of them annexed to *Aristotle*'s Works of the *Paris Edition*.

ARISTOTLE's Epistles.

To Philip 1.

THey who undertake a Command for the good of their Subjects, not preferred thereunto, either by Fortune or Nature, trust not in their own Power, which they know subject unto Chance, but grow great in Virtue, whereby they order the Commonwealth wisely. For there is nothing amongst men so firm and solid, but the rapid Motion of the Sun changeth it e'er the Evening. Nature, if we enquire into the truth, varieth all Lives, interweaving them like the action of a Tragedy with Misfortunes. Men, like Flowers, have a set time wherein they Flourish and Excel others. Wherefore behave not your self towards *Greece* Tyrannically or Loosely, for one argues Petulance, the other Temerity. Wise Princes ought not to be admired for their Government, but Governance; so that tho' Fortune change, they shall have the same Praise. As for the rest, do all things well, preferring the health of your Soul, by Philosophy, that of your Body by Exercise.

To Philip 2.

MOst Philosophers assert Beneficence to be something equal to God. To speak the truth, the whole Life of Mankind is comprised in conferring and returning Benefits. So as some bestow, others receive, others return. Hence it is just to commiserate all that are in Adversity, for Pity is the sign of a mild Soul, sternness of a Rude, it being dishonest and impious to neglect Vertue in Misfortunes. For this I commend our Disciple *Theophrastus*, who saith, we never repent of doing good; it brings forth good Fruit, the Prayers and Praises of the obliged. Wise Men therefore must study to oblige many, thinking that, besides the Praise, there may some advantage accrue from hence in the change of Affairs, and if not all, at least some one of those to whom he hath done good, may be in a capacity to requite him. For this reason, endeavour to be ready in doing good, but give not way to your Passions, for that is Kingly and Civil, this Barbarous and Odious. As you see occasion, practise and neglect not this useful Advice.

To Philip 3.

THE most excellent Princes, whose Honour toucheth the Stars, have conferred most Benefits, and not accommodating their sway only to the present, but considering the instability of Fortune, have treasured up good deeds as useful in either condition. In Prosperity it procures them Honour, for Honour is proper to Vertue; in Adversity Relief, for Friends are much better tried in bad Fortune, than in good. The sight of Benevolent Persons are like to that of Land to Men in a Storm. All Fortune apt to desert us, is the true scope which they propose to themselves, who war, or do unjustly, or comply dishonestly, only the clearness of virtuous persons is not unacquainted with the Instability of Fortune, but, by Reason sustaining all Accidents, and being, as *Plato* saith, above them, they are never disordered. Take heed therefore of the rapid motion of things; look upon them as a Circle which reverts into it self; cast up the Accounts of Life, for Chance imposeth many things upon Life, and maketh our Inclinations follow it. Pardon those that Offend Ignorantly; be ready to Acquit those that do Good. This, if you perform not once, but continually, your Court will be secure from all danger. This, considering the greatness of the things I have said, is but little, but, considering the Person to whom I write, All.

To Alexander 4.

I Am in doubt how to begin, for upon whatsoever I reflect, all seems great and wonderful, not fit to be forgotten, but proper for remembrance, and exhortation, not to be defaced by time. Good precepts and exhortations of Masters have Eternity for their Spectator. Endeavour to make use of your power, not to oppress, but to oblige others, than which nothing can be greater in Man's Life. Mortal Nature, which often yieldeth, and is overcome by Fate, obtaineth Eternal Memory by the greatness of such works. Consider this well; you are not unreasonable as some are, who think good advice ridiculous. Your Descent is Honourable, your Kingdom Hereditary, your Learning sound, your Glory Admirable; and as much as you exceed others in the Goods of Fortune, so ought you to be excellent among the Good in Vertue. In fine, do that which is profitable, and finish what you design.

To Theophrastus 5.

A Sudden Injury is better than a slow Benefit, for the remembrance and harm of that lasts but a while, but this groweth old, as if it hated to Build a Work to Perpetuity, and many times deferring what we intend to bestow upon another, he meets with a calm else-where, which allays the Tempest of his Mind. Wherefore I say, mutual Society ought not only to do no wrong, but if any be received, to be ready to forgive it, for perhaps to do no wrong is above the power of Man. As for him who hath erred, to make use of reproof, is the property of a good well-seated Judgment.

THE DOCTRINE OF ARISTOTLE.

The FIRST PALT.

CHAP. I.

Of Philosophy in General, and particularly of DIALECTICK.

THE Philosophy of *Aristotle* is well known, many abstracts thereof have been published, many are read daily in Universities by publick Professors: yet will it be requisite to our design, to give a short account thereof, that it may appear wherein the Doctrine and Method of the *Peripateticks* is different from that of the *Academicks* and *Stoicks*.

(*) *Laert.*

* *Philosophy*, according to Aristotle, *is twofold,* Practick *and* Theoretick. To the *Practick* belongs *Ethick* and *Politick*: *this, concerning the well ordering of a City: That, of a House.* To the *Theoretick* belongs *Physick* and *Logick*; but *Logick is not properly a part thereof, but a most expedient Instrument*.

Of *Logick* he asserted two ends, probable and true; for each he makes use of two Faculties, *Dialectick* and *Rhetorick* for the probable; *Analytick* and *Philosophy* for the true, omitting nothing towards Invention, Judgment and Use. For Invention, his *Topicks* and *Methodicks* afford a plentiful supply, out of which may be taken Problems for probable Arguments. For *Judgment*, his first and second *Analyticks*: in the first, Propositions are examined; in the second, he treats exactly of their composition, and the form of Syllogism. To *Use*, belongs his *Agonisticks*, and his Books concerning Interrogation, and his *Ericticks*, and his *Sophistick Elenchs*, and of *Syllogisms*, and the like. Hitherto *Laertius*.

Of his *Logick* we have only these Books remaining, *Of Categories, of Interrogation, Analyticks, Topicks,* and *Sophistick Elenchs*. The first considers *simple Terms*: The second, *Propositions*: The rest *Syllogisms, Demonstrative, Dialectick, and Sophistick*. The *Categories* are placed first by the general consent of all Interpreters: neither is it to be doubted, but that the rest are disposed according to the genuine Method of *Aristotle*. For, in the beginning of his [b] *Analyticks*, he faith, *We must speak of Syllogism before we come to speak of Demonstration, because*

[b] *Lib. c.* 2.

Syllogism is the more general. And in his [c] *Elenchs: Of Didascalick and demonstrative Syllogisms, we have spoken already in the Analyticks: Of the Dialectick and Pyractick, in the Book immediately preeeding these: We come now to speak of the Agonistick and Eristick.*

[c] *E. c. Cap.*

CHAP. II.

Of Terms.

[*] TErms are of three kinds, *Homonymous, Synonymous,* and *Paronymous*. *Homonymous*, whose name only is common, their Essence divers: *Synonymous*, whose name and definition are common to either: *Paronymous* have denomination from the same thing, but differ in case or termination.

[*] *Categ. c.* 1.

Synonymous, (or *Univocal*) terms, are reduced to ten general heads, called *Categories*.

1. [†] *Substance*, of two kinds: *First*, which is most properly Substance, is neither predicated of not inherent in a Subject. *Second, Substances* are Species and Genus's, which subsist in the first. The properties of first-substances are, 1. Neither to be in, nor predicated of a Subject. 2. To be all substances equally. 3. To signifie this particular thing. 4. To have no contrary. 5. To admit no degrees of more of more or less. 6. To be susceptible of contraries.

[†] *Cap.* 5.

2. [*] *Quantity*, of two kinds; *Discrete*, as Number; *Continuous*, as a Line. Their properties, 1. To have no contraries. 2. To admit no degrees of more or less. 3.d To denominate things equal or unequal.

[*] *Cap.* 6.

3. [†] *Relatives*, whose whole being is in some manner effected towards one another; their properties, 1. To have contraries, as Father and Son. 2. To admit degrees of more and less, as in kindled. 3. To follow one another mutually. 4. To be naturally together.

[†] *Cap.* 7.

5. *Quality,*

PART. VI.   ARISTOTLE.   245

e Cap. 8.   *e* 4. *Quality*, from which things are denominated *Qualited*: It hath four kinds. 1. *Habit* and *Disposition*. 2. *Natural Power* and *Impotence*. 3. *Passible Qualities* and *Passions*. 4. *Form* and *Figure*. The Properties, 1. To have contraries, as black and white. 2. To admit intension or remission. 3. To denominate things, like or unlike.

f Cap. 9.   *f* 5. *Action*. 6. *Passion*. Their Properties are, to admit contraries, to admit degrees of intension or remission.

7. *When*. 8. *Where*. 9. *Position*. 10. *Habit*. These admit not contraries, nor degrees of intension or remission.

Of those which cannot be reduc'd to any certain Category, are 1. *Opposites* and 2. *Precedents*. 3. *Coæquals*. 4. *Motion*. 5. *Possession*.

g Cap. 10.   *g* Of *Oppositions* there are four kinds, *Relatives*, *Contraries*, Extreams in the same kind, as black and white. *Privatives*, as privation and habit, light and darkness: *Contradictories*, which affirm and deny, as learned, not learned.

CHAP. III.
Of Proposition.

a De Interpret. cap. 1.   *a* Voice is a sign of the Notions of the mind, as in the mind are two kinds of Intellection, one simple, expert of truth and falsity, the other either true or false: So in voice, some is simple, some complex.

b Cap. 2.   *b* A *Noun* is a Voice signifying according to institution, whereof no part is significant by it self.

c Cap. 3.   *c* A *Verb* is a Voice implying time, whereof no part is significant by it self.

d Cap. 4.   *d* A *Speech*, λόγος, is a voice signifying according to institution, whose parts are significant separate.

Of Speech, the enunciative only (called proposition) belongs to Philosophy, the precatory and imperative, to Rhetorick, Poetry, &c.

e Cap. 5.   *e* Propositions are divided four ways; into *simple* and *complex*, into *affirmative* and *negative*, into *universal*, *particular*, *indefinite* and *singular*, into *pure* and *modal*; the modal is either *necessary*, *possible*, *contingent*, or *impossible*.

f Cap. 12.   *f* Propositions have three accidents, *Opposition*, *Consectation*, *Conversion*.

Opposition is either contradictory of a particular to an universal; or contrary, of an universal to an universal; or sub-contrary, of a particular Negative to a particular Affirmative.

Consectation, (ἀκολούθησις) or Æquipollens, is the Consideration of those Affections of a Proposition, in respect whereof, two Propositions signifie together the same thing, and are together true or false.

Conversion is a transposition of the Terms, preserving the Affirmation, Negation, and verity of the Proposition: It is either Absolute, which reserves the same quantity, but alters the quality; or Partial, which reserves not the same Quantity.

CHAP. IV.
Of Syllogism.

a A Syllogism is a Speech, in which some things *a Analyt.prior. lib. 1. cap. 1.* being laid down, another necessarily follows. *Perfect Syllogism* is that which requireth no other to shew its power, clearness, and efficacy. *Imperfect* requires another to that purpose, by Conversion, or transposition of the Propositions.

b The *Matter* of Syllogism is three Terms, *b Cap. 4.* the *Form* is the right Disposition of the Matter, according to Figure and Mood.

Figure is an apt disposition of the Medium with the extreams, apt for concluding a right. *Mood* is a disposition of Propositions, according to quantity and quality. There are three Figures.

The first, when the *Medium* is first *Subject*, then *Prædicate*. It hath nine Moods, four Useful, five Useless and Illegitimate: Of the Useful, two are Universal, two prticular.

The first. $\begin{cases} \text{Every A }is\text{ B.} \\ \text{Every C }is\text{ A.} \\ \text{Therefore every C }is\text{ B.} \end{cases}$

The second $\begin{cases} \text{No A }is\text{ B.} \\ \text{Every C }is\text{ A.} \\ \text{Therefore no C }is\text{ B.} \end{cases}$

The third. $\begin{cases} \text{Every A }is\text{ B.} \\ \text{Some C }is\text{ A.} \\ \text{Therefore some C }is\text{ B.} \end{cases}$

The fourth $\begin{cases} \text{No A }is\text{ B.} \\ \text{Some C }is\text{ A.} \\ \text{Therefore some C }is\text{ B.} \end{cases}$

c In the second Figure, the Medium is Prædicated of both the Extreams. It hath 16 Moods, *c Cap. 5.* 4 true, 12 false and Illegitimate. Of the true, two are universal, two particular.

The first. $\begin{cases} \text{No M }is\text{ N.} \\ \text{Every O }is\text{ N.} \\ \text{Therefore no O }is\text{ M.} \end{cases}$

The second. $\begin{cases} \text{Every M }is\text{ N} \\ \text{No O }is\text{ N.} \\ \text{Therefore no O }is\text{ M.} \end{cases}$

The third. $\begin{cases} \text{No M }is\text{ N.} \\ \text{Some O }is\text{ N.} \\ \text{Therefore some O }is\text{ not N.} \end{cases}$

The fourth. $\begin{cases} \text{Every M }is\text{ N.} \\ \text{Some O }is\text{ not N.} \\ \text{Therefore some O }is\text{ not M.} \end{cases}$

d In the third Figure, the Medium is Subjected to both Extreams. It hath 16 Moods, 10 *d Cap. 6.* false and Illegitimate; 6 Legitimate, which conclude particularly.

The first.
$$\begin{cases} \text{Every } P \text{ is } R. \\ \text{Every } P \text{ is } S. \\ \text{Therefore some } P \text{ is } S. \end{cases}$$

The second.
$$\begin{cases} \text{No } P \text{ is } R. \\ \text{Every } P \text{ is } S. \\ \text{Therefore some } S \text{ is not } R. \end{cases}$$

The third.
$$\begin{cases} \text{Some } P \text{ is } R. \\ \text{Every } P \text{ is } S. \\ \text{Therefore some } S \text{ is } R. \end{cases}$$

The fourth.
$$\begin{cases} \text{Every } P \text{ is } R. \\ \text{Some } P \text{ is } S. \\ \text{Therefore some } S \text{ is } R. \end{cases}$$

The fifth.
$$\begin{cases} \text{Some } P \text{ is not } R. \\ \text{Every } P \text{ is } S. \\ \text{Therefore some } S \text{ is not } R. \end{cases}$$

The fifth.
$$\begin{cases} \text{No } P \text{ is } R. \\ \text{Some } P \text{ is } S. \\ \text{Therefore some } S \text{ is not } R. \end{cases}$$

e Cap. 23. *e* Every Syllogism ought to be framed in one of these three Figures; but those of the second and third being imperfect, ought to be reduced to the first, which is the most absolute and perfect.

f Annal. Prior. lib. 2. c. 23, &c. f There are six other Forms of Argument, *Conversion of Terms, Induction, Example, Abduction, Instance, Enthymem.* All these have their Efficacy from the power of Syllogism, and are reducible to Syllogism.

As concerning the invention, power, and conversion of Syllogism, he is exact and curious to admiration.

CHAP. V.

Of Apodeictick (or demonstrative) Syllogism.

a Analyt. poster. lib. cap. 1. **A**LL *discursive* knowledge is made by a prænotion of the things themselves whereof we discourse; for ratiocination is not concerning things unknown. Demonstration is a discursive knowledge, and therefore requireth three præcognitions. First, that the Subject is, and what it is in a rude confused manner. Secondly, what the prædicate is, and what it signifieth. Thirdly, that the Principles are true.

b Cap. 2. *b To know,* is to understand that a thing is, that this is cause thereof, and that it cannot be otherwise. Demonstration is a scientifick Syllogism. *Demonstrative Science* is from true, first, immediate, more known causes of the conclusion *First,* as having none precedent, and being adæquate to, and convertible with the effect. *Immediate* or consectaneous, as having no term betwixt to joyn them. *More known,* as being præmises to the conclusion, not to be demonstrated by any thing.

c Cap. 4. *c Demonstrative Science* is of a thing necessaty, whence the demonstration it self consists of necessary propositions; which necessity requireth explication of that which is prædicated, *of all by by it self,* and which is *universal.*

Of all, is that which is attributed to every one, and at all times, as a living creature to a man:

By it self, as being of Essence, proper, competible *per se,* and compatible to it self, for it self.

An universal Attribute is that which is in every one by it self, in as much as it is it self.

d Demonstration is of conclusions of *eternal truth,* for they are universal propositions; whence it followeth, that neither demonstration nor Science are of perishable things; neither are definitions of such, which are the principles of demonstration. *d Cap. 8.*

That there is demonstration, it is not necessary to have recourse to *Plato*'s Idea's separate from singulars; it is enough that there are common natures which are in singulars, and are prædicated of them.

e It is one thing to know that a thing is so, another to know why it is so. Hence there are two kinds of demonstration, διότι, and ὅτι, the first is the true, and most perfect, of which hitherto. *e Cap. 11.*

f The other kind of demonstration, *viz.* ὅτι, is more imperfect; it is made two ways in the same Science: First, when the case is demonstrated by the effect thus, *Stars which do not twinkle are nearest to the Earth; but, the Planets do not twinkle, therefore they are earnest to the Earth.* Secondly, when the effect is proved by a cause remote, and not reciprocal, or by an effect of the remote cause, as this, *every thing that breatheth is a living creature; but no Wall breaths, therefore no Wall is a living Creature.* *f Cap. 13.*

To know διότι, is proper to subalternate principle Sciences, as Geometry and Arithmetick, which contemplate the first proper causes; to know ὅτι, is the subalternate and inferiour, as Optick and Musick.

g Of all Figures, the first is most accommodated to knowledge, for that only concludes with an universal affirmative, and therefore in that only is a demonstrative διότι. *g Cap. 14.*

h Thus far concerning Science; the opposite to Science is *Ignorance,* which is twofold: One of *pure negation,* as when a Boy or ignorant fellow knows not that the Sun is greater than the Earth, because he is ignorant of Astrology. The other, *of depraved disposition,* as when an Astrologer or ignorant Optick believes, that things are as they seem, this is error, which erroneous ignorance is in false propositions, or in a Syllogism through a false medium. *h Cap. 15, &c.*

Defect of Sense causeth Ignorance of pure negation; for if any sense be wanting, it is necessary that some science of sensibles be likewise wanting; for we learn all things either by induction or demonstration. *Induction* is made of singulars perceived by sense, *Demonstration* is of Universals, which are declared by Induction; wherefore the beginning of Science is from singulars, which are Sensibles. Hence it is Impossible for a Man born blind to have the science of Colours. Yet no Science is next and immediately from Sense, for Sense is of Singulars, which are here, and now; but Science and Demonstration is of Universals, which are every where, and ever, not subject to Sense. Yet, Sense conduceth to Science and Demonstration, for as much as an Universal is collected from Particulars known by Sense.

CHAP.

PART VI. ARISTOTLE.

CHAP. VI.
Of Dialectick Syllogism.

a Topic. lib. 1. cap. 1.

a **D**ialectick Syllogism is that which concludes from Probables; Probables are those things which appear such to all, or to most, or only to the Wise and most Eminent.

b Cap. 3.

b Dialectick is a conjectural Art, as Rhetorick and Medicine; therefore (like those) it attaineth not always its end; it is enough for a Dialectick, that he omit nothing of his Art for concluding probably.

c Cap. 4.

c All Disputation is of things controverted, either by Problem or Proposition. A Problem questions both parts, as *a living Creature, is it the Genus of Man or not?* A Proposition questions but one part, as, *is not living Creature the genus of Man?* Every Proposition and Problem is either *genus*, (under which is contained the difference) *definition, proprium*, or *accident*.

d Cap. 15, &c.

d Definition is a Speech, signifying what a thing is. *Proprium* is that which declareth, not what a thing is, but is in it only, and Reciprocal with it. *Genus* is that which is præcidated, *in quid*, of many that differ specifically. *Accident* is that which is neither Definition, nor Genus, nor Proprium, and may be, or not be in its subject.

e Cap. 10.

e Dialectick Proposition is a probable interrogation, received by all or many, or the most excellent, yet so as it is not wholly alienate from the common Opinion.

f Cap. 11.

f Dialectick Problem is threefold; *Practick* or *Moral*, pertaining to Election or Repulse; *Theoretick*, pertaining to Science; *neutral*, which conduceth to the rest. *viz.* Logick.

Thesis is a Paradoxal Sentence of some Eminent Philosopher, contrary to the vulgar Opinion.

g Cap. 12.

g Dialectick Argument is twofold, *Induction* and *Syllogism*.

h Cap. 13. &c.

h Arguments are gained by four *Instruments*, 1. Choice of Propositions. 2. Distinction of Æquivoques. 3. Invention of differences. 4. Consideration of Similitudes.

Problems are either universal or particular; the same places which confirm or confute one, confirm or confute the other. From *proprium*, *genus*, and *definition*, is immediately and simply made *Demonstration*, but not from *Accident*, because that is external, not necessarily and intimately inherent in the Subject. We shall not here say any thing of the multitude of places he hath invented, which are more necessary to those that will learn the Art, than suitable to this abridgment.

The Disputant must first find out a place (or medium) secondly, dispose and question it within himself; thirdly, propose it to his Adversary.

In Disputation against the Learned, Syllogism is to be used, against the Vulgar Induction.

i Lib. 8. Cap. 4.

i The Office of the *Opponent* is to compell his Respondent to this incredible and absurd consequent from his *Thesis*; of the *Respondent* to take care, that nothing absurd be collected from his *Thesis*.

CHAP. VII.
Of Sophistick Syllogism.

a Sophist. Elench. cap. 1.

a **A**N *Elench* is a Syllogism which contradicts the conclusion asserted by the Respondent. Of *Elenchs* some are true, some are false; that proper to a *Sophos*, whose Office is to pursue and defend Truth, and to discover and confute Falshood; this to a *Sophist*, who from seeming Wisdom acquireth gain, and had rather seem than be.

b Cap. 2.

b A *Sophist* hath five ends, whereto he endeavoureth to reduce his adversary; the first is *Elench*, or Redargution *c* of which there are two kinds; one in the word, the other out of the word.

c Cap. 3.

Sophisms in the word, are six. 1. *Homonymie*, as that ill is good, for τὰ δέοντα are good, but ills are τὰ δέοντα. The fallacy consists in the word τὰ δέοντα, which signifies sometimes necessarily inevitable, sometimes beneficial.

2. By *Amphibolie*, as βύλεσθαι λαβεῖν μὲ τὲς πολεμίους; which signifies either that the Enemies would take me, or that I would take the Enemies.

3. By *Composition*, as τὸ δυνασθαι καθημένον βαδίζειν, that he who sits can walk, which is true in a divided sense, not in a compounded.

4. By *Division*; as five are two and three, therefore even and odd.

5. By *Ascent*, which is not so easily done in Logick as in Poetry.

6. By *Figure of the word*, when things which are not the same, are Interpreted in the same manner, as a Male for a Female.

d Cap. 4.

d Sophisms out of the word are seven. 1. From *accident*, when that which is demanded is equally competent to the thing, and to the accident; for whereas many things are competent to the same, it is not necessary that they be all in the subject and Prædicate, as, *if Coriscus differs from a Man, he differs from himself, for he is a Man.*

2. *From that which is Simple*, or κατὰ πατί, when that which is said in part is taken as of all, as, *if that which is not, is imaginative, that which is not, is.*

3. *From Ignorance of the Elench*, when not understanding the true nature of a contradiction, they think that to be an absolute contradiction which is none, omitting either the same respect in the thing, or the same respect of the same thing, or the simplicicity, or the time. To this all Sophisms may be reduced.

4. *Of the Consequent;* when we allow those to be true Reciprocal Consequences which are not such, as, *it is yellow, therefore it is Honey*; and the contrary, *it is not yellow, therefore it is not Honey.*

5. *Of petition of the principle*, neither by requiring that to be granted, which was to be proved, or proving the same by the same, the terms only changed; as *the Soul is immortal because it is not subject to death.*

6. *Of a not-cause as a Cause*, as when that is taken to be the Cause of the thing or conclusion, which is cause of neither; as *Arms disturb Peace, therefore they are to be taken away.*

7. *Of Plurality of Interrogations as one*, when many things are asked in one; as *Justice and Impiety, are they Vertues or not?*

Hitherto

Hitherto of Elenchs; the four other Ends whereto a Sophist endeavours to reduce his adversary, are, *Falsity, Paradox, Solœcism,* and *Tautology.*

Sophisms are solved either by *distinction* or *negation.*

Thus much may serve for a slight view of his *Logick,* whereof we have but few Books left, in respect of the many which he wrote upon that part of Philosophy.

THE SECOND PART.

CHAP. I.

Of Physick.

NOT to question the method of *Aristotle's* Books of Physick, much less their Titles (as some, to make them better agree with *Laertius's* Catalogue, have done) and least of all their Authority, with *Patricius*; we shall take them in that Order which is generally received; according to which, next *Logick,* is placed *Physick.*

a Metaphys. 5. 1.

a Physick is a Science concerning that substance which hath the principle of Motion and Rest within it self.

The Physical Books of *Aristotle,* that are extant, treat of these nine general heads. *Of the Principles of natural things: Of the common affections of natural things: Of Heaven: Of Elements: Of the Action and Passion of Elements: Of Exhalation: Of Plants: Of Animals: Of the Soul.*

CHAP. II.

Of the Principles of Natural Bodies.

a Phys. lib. 1. cap. 3. 4.

THE *Principles* of Natural Bodies are not one, as *Parmenides* and *Melissus* held; nor *Homoiomerias,* as *Anaxagoras*; nor *Atomes,* as *Leucippus* and *Democritus*; nor *sensible Elements,* as *Thales, Anaximander, Anaximenes, Empedocles*; nor *Numbers,* or *Figures,* as the *Pythagoreans,* nor *Ideas,* as *Plato.*

b Cap. 5.

b That the Principles of things are *Contrary* (privately opposite) was the joynt opinion of the Ancients, and is manifest in Reason. For Principles are those which neither are mutually of one another, nor of others, but of them are all things. Such are, first, contraries; as being first, they are not of any other; as contrary, not of another.

c Cap. 6.

c Hence it follows, that being contrary they must be *more than one,* but *not Infinite,* for then natural things would not be comprehensible by Reason: yet more than two; for of contraries only nothing would be produced, but that they would rather destroy one another.

d Cap. 7.

d There are therefore *three* Principles of Natural Bodies; two contrary; *Privative* and *Form*; and one common subject of both, *Matter.* The constitutive Principles are Matter and Form; of privation Bodies consist not, but accidentally, as it is competent to Matter.

e Cap. 8.

c Things are made of that which is *Ens* potentially, *Materia prima,* not of that which is *Ens* actually, nor of that which is *Non ens* potentially, which is pure nothing. *f* Matter is neither generated nor corrupted. It is the first infinite subject of every thing, whereof it is framed primarily, in its self and not by accident, and into which it at last resolveth. To treat of Form in general, is proper to Metaphysicks.

f Cap. 9.

CHAP. III.

Of Nature, and the Causes of Natural Bodies.

a Phys. lib. 2. cap. 1.

a OF Being, some are by Nature, as Plants, others from other causes; those have in themselves the principle of their Motion, these have not. Nature is a Principle and Cause of the motion and rest of that thing wherein it is primarily, by it self, and not by accident. Material Substances have Nature; Natural Properties are according to Nature: Nature is twofold, Matter and Form; but Form is most Nature, because it is in Act.

b Cap. 3.

b Of Causes are four kinds; the Material, of which a thing is made; the Formal, by which a thing is made, or reason of its Essence; The Efficient, whence is the first Principle of its mutation or rest, as a Father; the Final, for which end it is made; as health is to walking. Causes are immediate *or* remote, principal *or* accidental; actual *or* potential; particular *or* universal.

Cap. 4. &c.

Fortune and Chance are Causes of many effects. Fortune *is* an accidental Cause in those things which are done by Election for some end; Chance is larger; an accidental cause in things which are done for some end, at least that of Nature. They are both efficient.

Nature

^{d Cap. 8.}   *d Nature acts for some end: not temerariously, or casually; for those things which are done by nature, are always or for the most part done in the same manner, yet sometimes she is frustrated of her end, as in Monsters, which she intends not.*

^{e Cap. 9.}   *e Necessity is twofold: absolute, which is from matter; Conditional, which is from the end or form: both kinds are in natural things.*

CHAP. IV.

Of the Affections of Natural Bodies, Motion, Place, Time.

^{Physic. lib. 3. cap. 2.}   Motion is of a thing which is not such, but may be such, the way or act by which it becometh such, as curing of a Body which is not in health, but may be in health, is the way and act by which it is brought to health. Neither is it absurd, that the same thing should be both in act and power, as to different respects; for the thing moved, as Water in warming is in act, as to the heat which it hath, in power, as to the greater heat which it is capable of.

^{b Cap. 7.}   *b Infinite* is that which is pertransible without end, such an *infinite in act* there is not: not amongst simple Bodies, for the Elements are confin'd to certain number and place: Neither amongst mixt Bodies, for they consist of the Elements which are finite. But, there are things *infinite potentially*, as *in addition*; Number, which may be augmented infinitely, *in division*; Magnitude, which may be divided infinitely; *in time*, and continued succession of Generation.

^{c Lib. 4. cap. 3.}   *c* The properties of place are, that it contains the thing placed: *that* it is equal to, and separable from the thing placed: *that* the place and the thing placed are together: *That it hath* upwards or downwards, and the like differences: *that* every Physical Body tends naturally to its proper place, and there resteth.

Place is the immediate immovable Superficies of a continent Body. Those things which are contained by another Body are in place: But those which have not any other Body above or beyond them, are not properly in place. Bodies rest in their natural places, because they tend thither as a part torn off from the whole.

^{d Cap. 8.}   *d Vacuum* is place void of Body: such a Vacuum there is not in Nature, for that would destroy all motion, seeing that in *Vacuum* there is neither *upwards* nor *downwards*, *backwards* nor *forwards*. Nor would there be any reason, why Motion should be to one part more than to another. Moreover it would follow, that it were impossible for one body to make another recede, if the triple dimension, which bodies divide, were vacuous. Neither is the motion of rare bodies upwards caused by vacuity, for that motion is as natural to light bodies, as to move downwards is too heavie.

^{e Cap. 10. 11.}   *e Time* is the number of motion by *before* and *after*. Those two parts of Time are conjoyned by (τὸ νῦν) the *present*, as the parts of a line are by a point. Time is the measure of rest as well as of motion: for the same measure which serves for the privation, serves for the habit. All motion and mutation is in time: for in every motion there is swiftness or slowness, which is defined by Time. The Heavens, Earth, Sea, and other sensibles, are in time, for they are movable.

f Time being a *numerate* number, exists not ^{f Cap. 14.} without a *numerant*, which is *the Soul*. The measure of time and other things, is that which measureth the first and most equal motion: this is the motion of the *Primum mobile*, for the first in every kind is the measure of the rest.

CHAP. V.

Of the Kinds and Properties of Motion.

a Motion appertains to three Categories, to ^{a Phys. l. 5.} Quantity, *accretion* and *diminution*; to ^{cap. 2.} Quality, *alteration*; to Where, *local motion*.

Rest is a privation of motion in a body, when, where, and how it is apt for motion.

b As all magnitude is primarily, and *per se*, ^{b Lib. 6. cap. 1.} continuous and divisible into infinite, so is all motion, by reason of magnitude, and time it self. For whatsoever is not composed of indivisibles, is divisible into infinite; but no continuous thing is composed of indivisible things, for it is quantitative, whereas indivisibles having no extreams or parts, can neither be conjoyned by continuous nor contiguous motion.

c Yet it followeth not, that if there be infi- ^{c Cap. 2.} nite magnitude, there can be no motion; for it is not infinite in act, but in power, as are likewise time and motion.

d Neither is there any motion in the instant, ^{d Cap. 3.} τὸ νῦν for nothing is moved or resteth, but in time.

e Motion therefore is divisible, as well in re- ^{c Cap. 4.} spect to the time, wherein it is made, as in respect to the thing wherein it inheres; as both these are always indivisible, so may motion it self be divided according to these.

f Whatsoever is changed, as soon as it is ^{f Cap. 5.} changed, must necessarily be in the (next) term *to which*, for it leaveth the state or form in which it was, and assumeth that to which it tendeth; yet tho' in motion, there is a first motion of perfection, wherein we may truly say, the mutation is made, yet there is no first motion of inception.

g Whatsoever is moved in any whole time, ^{g Cap. 6.} is necessarily moved in every part of that time.

h All motion is finite, for it is in time, which ^{b Cap. 7.} is finite.

Whatsoever is thus proper to motion, is to be applied also to rest and quiescence.

CHAP. VI.

Of the first Mover.

a Whatsoever is moved must necessarily be ^{a Lib. 7. cap. 1.} moved by another, either external or ^{2, 5, 6, 7.} internal. But lest this progression be into infinite, we must of necessity at last come to one first mover, which is not moved by another. This first mover, the Cause and Origen of all motion, is *Immoveable, one, eternal,* and *indivisible, void of all quantity*.

b *Immovable*, for whatsoever things are moved, are either immediately moved by a first immovable mover, or by some other which is likewise moved by another, until at last we come to some first mover, for nothing can move it self, unless there be a first mover: but of infinites there is no first.

b Lib.8.cap.6.

c *One*, for he is most perfect, as being Author of the most perfect and most simple motion, that of the *primum mobile*. Besides, the best in every kind is one: for good is simple, ill multiplicious.

c Cap. 6.

d *Eternal*, for motion it self is eternal, as appears thus: The mover and the moveable must either be from Eternity, or have had beginning in some time: if they began at any time, it must have been by motion, and consequently before the first motion there was another, by which the mover and moveable began, which were absurd. Again, if they were eternal, yet without motion, it must be either by reason of the inaptitude of the moveable, or of its remoteness from the mover. But neither could the moveable be made more apt, or brought nigher to the mover except by the motion, whence would follow that there was a motion before the first motion. Again, Time, the measure of motion, is eternal, therefore motion it self is such. That time is eternal (besides that it is the general agreement of Philosophers) is thus proved: it cannot be conceived without τὸ νῦν, the instant, which is intermediate betwixt the past and future, both the end of one, and the beginning of the other; but, if Time had a beginning, this τὸ νῦν would have been only a beginning, not end; if Time should have an end, this instant would be only an end, not a beginning, both which are repugnant to the nature of a moment.

d Cap. 7.

e *Indivisible, void of quantity*; the proof whereof is grounded upon three Theoremes. 1. That no finite mover can move in infinite time, therefore the first mover is infinite. 2. That there cannot be infinite power in finite quantity; therefore the first mover is incorporeal. 3. That there cannot be finite power in that wich is infinite, therefore the first mover is infinite in power. Hence may be collected, that it is impossible the first mover should be divisible, corporeal, or affected with quantity: for if he had any, it would either be infinite, of which kind actual there is none: or finite, wherein could not consist his infinite power.

e Lib.8.cap.10.

CHAP. VII.

Of HEAVEN.

Having treated of the Principles, Causes, and Affections of natural Bodies in general, he proceeds next to particulars.

a The World is perfect, because it consists of Bodies which are perfect, and comprehendeth all perfection, it self not being comprehended by any other.

a DeCælo.lib.1. cap. 1.

b Of Bodies, some are *simple*, others *compounded of the simple*. All natural bodies are moveable locally *per se*. There is a twofold local motion, *simple*, which is competible to simple bodies: and *mixt*, which is to the mixt.

b Cap. 2.

Hence it followeth, that there are so many kinds of simple bodies, as variations of simple motion: for of one simple body, there is one proper motion. Simple, local Motion is twofold: *circular*, about the center, and *right*: the right is either upwards from the center, or downwards to the center, and both these either simply, or κατὰ τὶ. This fourfold variation of right motion, evinceth that there are four simple bodies called *Elements*: circular motion must be proper to some other fift essence, different from the constitutions of the other four simple bodies, more divine and precedent to all the rest: This is *Heaven*.

c Heaven *hath neither gravity nor levity*: this is manifest from its motion which is circular, not from the center which is proper to light things, nor to the center, as is proper to heavie, but about the center.

e Cap. 3.

Heaven is *void of Generation, and Corruption*, and consequently of accretion, diminution and alteration, for it hath no contrary; it is therefore the first body, not to be consumed by time and age.

d No body can be infinite, therefore the world it self is not infinite, neither is there any body beyond it infinite, nor intelligible or mathematical.

d Cap. 5,7.

e There is but one World, for if there were more, the Earth of one would move to the Earth of the other (as being of one kind) and ascend out of its proper place.

e Cap. 2.

f The World is eternal; whatsoever is eternal is ingenerate and incorruptible. *Plato* therefore erred, in affirming the World to be generated, but incorruptible. If he meant that as it was generated, it is by nature corruptible, yet shall never be actually dissolved, because of the eternal cause of its conservation, God; he erreth also, for then there would be something that should be always, and yet could not be always.

f Cap. 12.

g Heaven is void of Labour (ἄπονος) for it hath no contrary to retard its motion.

g Lib.2.cap.3.

h Heaven hath *the threefold difference of position*, upwards and downwards, backwards, right and left, for these are proper to all animate things which have the principle of motion within themselves. The right side of Heaven is the *East*, for thence begins its motion; the left side the *West*; and consequently the Artick Pole is lowermost, the Antartick uppermost; forwards our Hemisphere, backwards the other.

h Cap. 2.

i Heaven *naturally moveth circularly*, but this circular motion is not uniform throughout all Heaven, for there are other Orbs which move contrary to the *primum mobile*; that there may be a vicissitude in sublunary things, and generation and corruption.

i Cap. 3.

k Heaven is *Sphærical*, for to the first Body the first figure is most proper. If it were quadrangular, triangular, or the like; the angles would sometimes leave a space without a body, and occupate another space without a body. The motion of Heaven is circular, as being the measure of all others, therefore most compendious and swiftest.

k Cap. 4.

l The motion of the *proprium mobile* is æquable and uniform, for it hath neither beginning, middle, nor end; the *primum mobile* and first mover being eternal in both, and subject to no variation.

l Cap. 6.

Stars

m *Cap. 7.* ᵐ *Stars* are of the same Body with that wherein they are carried, but more thick and compact; they produce warmth and Light in inferiour things through frication of the Air by their Motion; for swift motion fires Wood, and melts Lead, yet the Spheres themselves are not heated, but the Air only, and that chiefly by the Sphere of the Sun, which by his accession towards us, increaseth the heat, his Beams falling more directly, and with double force upon us.

n *Cap. 8.* ⁿ The Stars being infixed in the Heavens, are mov'd not by themselves with a proper motion, as Fishes in the Water, and Birds in the Air, but according to the motion of their Orbs. Otherwise those in the eighth Sphere would not be always be æquidistant from one another; neither would the Stars have always the same side turning towards us, as we see the Moon hath.

The *primum mobile* is carried about with the swiftest motion; the seven Orbs of Planets under it, as they are nearer to it, are carried so much the more swiftly about by the motion thereof; and as they are further distant, more slowly. Whence by how much the nigher they are to the *primum mobile*, so much the slower is their proper motion, because it is contrary to that of the *primum mobile*, as being from *East* to *West*.

o *Cap. 11.* ᵒ The Stars are round, for that figure is most unapt for Self-Motion: We see the Moon is round by her Orbicular Sections; therefore the other Stars are so likewise, for the reason is the same in all.

p *Cap. 13. 14.* ᵖ The Centre of Heaven is the *Earth*, round, seated immoveable in the midst; which together with the Sea makes up one Globe.

CHAP. VII.
Of Elements.

a *De Cælo. lib. 3. cap. 3.* ᵃ THE *Element* of Bodies is a simple Body, into which other Bodies are divided, in which it is either actually or potentially; as in Flesh, Wood, and the like, there is Fire and Earth potentially; for into these they are segregated, but actually they are not; for then should the flesh and wood be segregated.

Whereas every natural Body hath a proper motion. Motions are partly simple, partly mixt; the mixt proper to mixt Bodies, the simple to simple: It is manifest that there are simple Bodies, for there are simple motions; the circular proper to Heaven, the right to the Elements.

b *Cap. 5.* ᵇ The Elements are not Eternal; for they are dissolved with reciprocal mutations, and perish, and are mutually generated of one another.

c *Lib. 4. cap. 1.* ᶜ The motive qualities of the Elements are *Gravity* and *Levity*. Heavy is that which is apt to be carried downwards to the Center or midst of Heaven; *Light* is that which is apt to be carried upwards towards the extremities of Heaven. These are either simple or comparative. *Simply heavy* is that which is below all, as the Earth; *Simply light*, is that which is above all, as the Fire; *Comparatively, heavy and light* are those in which are both these; above some, below others, as Air and Water. From these have mixt things, gravity and levity, the heavy are carried downwards to a definite medium, the light upwards to a definite extream, for nothing tends to infinite. Whence it followeth, that two Elements are extreamly contrary, simply heavy, and simply light, Fire and Earth, which tend to contrary places. Betwixt these are two means, participating of the nature of each extream, Air and Water. Those Elements which are highest and lightest, are most perfect, and have the nature of Forms in respect of the Inferiour, because these are contained by those; to be contained, is the property of matter; to contain, of form.

d *Cap. 5.* ᵈ Hence it follows, that there are *four* kinds of particular second matter, differing by the accidental differences of heat, cold, humidity, siccity, levity and gravity, (simple and comparative) though there be but one common matter of them all; for they are made mutually of one another. The mean Elements are heavy in their proper places; for Earth being taken away, Water tending downwards, succeeds in its room; Air descends into the place of Water, but not contrariwise; for Water ascends not into its place of Air, unless by force. In the extream it is otherwise; for the Air being taken away, the Fire will not descend into its place, nor the Earth ascend into the place of Water or Air; for Fire is not heavy, nor Earth light in their natural place, because they are Extream Elements.

e *Cap. 6.* ᵉ Figure conduceth to the swiftness or slowness of motion either upwards or downwards, but is not simply, and in it self the cause of motion; so an acute Figure cuts the medium swiftly, a broad obtuse Figure slowly. Hence a thin plate of Lead or Iron will swim on Water, because it comprehends much of the subjected Body, which it cannot easily divide or penetrate.

CHAP. VIII.
Of Generation, Corruption, Alteration, Augmentation, and Diminution.

a *De gener. & corrup. lib. 1 cap. 3.* ᵃ THere is a perpetual succession of Generation, as well simple as accidental, which proceeds from two Causes; *Efficient*, the first mover, and the Heavens, always moving, and always moved; and *Material*, the first matter, of which, being *non-ens* actually, *ens* potentially, all things generable and corruptible consist. This is incorruptible in its self, susceptible of all forms, whereby the corruption of one natural substance becometh the generation of another, whatsoever matter remaineth upon the Corruption, being assumed towards the generation of another.

Generation and *Corruption* are two-fold, *simple*, of a substance, καθ ἀ τὶ, of an accident, generation of the less noble substance is called generation καθ ἀ τὶ in respect of the more noble, as that of Earth in respect of Fire.

Corruption always succeedeth Generation, because the Term, *to which* of Corruption (*viz. non-ens*) is the Term *from which* of Generation; and the Term *to which* of Generation (*viz. ens* in act) is the Term *from which* of Corruption. The matter of that which is Generated, and that which is corrupted is the same, forasmuch as they are and may be made reciprocally of one another, as Air of Water, Water of Air; but differently disposed.   Alte-

b *Alteration* and *Generation* are different mutations; in alteration the subject remaineth entire, the affections only are changed, as of sick, sound; in generation the whole is changed, not any sensible subject remaining. Alteration is a mutation according to quality, *augmentation* and *diminution*, according to quantity, *local motion* according to place.

c Augmentation and diminution differ from other mutations; first, in the object, generation and corruption concerns substances: Alteration, quality, lation, place; augmentation and diminution quantity. Again, in the manner, that which is generated, or corrupted, or altered, not necessarily changeth place, but that which augments or diminisheth, in some manner changeth place, for it is bigger or lesser.

Augmentation is an addition to præexistent quantity; *diminution* a detraction. Whatsoever is augmented or decreased, is augmented or decreased according to every part thereof, by reception of something throughout all parts; decretion on the contrary. The animate Body encreaseth, but not the aliment, for the living creature remaineth, the aliment is converted into the substance of the living creature. Hereupon that which is augmented is like unto that which is altered, for both of these remain. All parts of a living creature are augmented; the similar first, as bones and flesh; then the dissimilar, as consisting of the others.

Augmentation is made by accession, or something according to form, not according to matter; for by it the whole is augmented and made more such. Accession of parts, according to matter, is not augmentation, for by materials only (destitute of that form, which the parts to be augmented have) the whole living creature cannot encrease. Aliment therefore, whereby the living creature is augmented, must be the same potentially which the thing augmented is in act. At first, it is contrary, and dissimilar, being in power the part of a living creature, in act something else: at last it becometh assimilate to the living creature, taking the form of a part (by aggeneration) through the digestive power of the animate body, which changeth the aliment into its own substance.

For this reason augmentation presupposeth nutrition. *Nutrition* is, when the aliment as subance is converted into the same substance of the living creature. Augmentation, when the same aliment as quantitative, is added to the quantity of the living creature. Hence a living creature as long as it is sound, is always nourished, but not always augmented. As that which is added is potentially quantitative flesh, so it can augment flesh; as it is potentially flesh only, so it nourisheth; which when it can only do (as when so much Wine is poured into Water that it turns all into Water) then there is a diminution of the quantity, but the form remaineth.

b Cap. 4.

c Cap. 5.

CHAP. X.

Of Action and Passion.

a **C**Ontact is of several kinds, *Mathematical*, by contiguity; *Physical*, when the extreams of several Bodies meet, and mutually act and suffer; *virtual*, by power, and metaphorical.

b The mutual action and passion of Physical contact is betwixt things, partly unlike as to their form, partly like as to their genus (for they are contraries) matter; each endeavouring to reduce the patient to his own likeness, as fire, wood.

Every *Physical agent* in acting, suffers from the Patient; for both the Agent and Patient are active, endued with Forms Elementary, susceptible of contraries. But as the first mover is *immoveable*, so is the first agent *impassible*.

c Every thing acts, as it is such, actually suffers, as it is such, potentially. The conditions of Action and Passion are five: 1. What the Agent is in Act, the Patient is in Power. 2. The Patient is such according to each part. 3. That which is more disposed, suffers more, and so on the contrary. 4. Every Patient is continuous, and not actually divided. 5. The Agent must necessarily touch the Patient, either immediately or mediately.

a De gener. & corrup. l. 1.

b Cap. 7.

c Cap. 9.

CHAP. XI.

Of Mixtion and Temperament.

a **M**Ixtion is not Generation, for the matter is not fixt with the form; nor alteration, for the quality is not mixed with the subject; nor augmentation, for aliment, the matter of augmentation, is not mixed with, but converted into the animate body. Conjunction of small bodies is not true mixtion, but co-acervation, for those bodies remain actually in the same, according to their forms, not composing one third according to every part. Things which have not the same matter, are not mixt, because they cannot be active and passive reciprocally.

Those things which are properly said to be mixed, must have one common matter, they must mutually act upon, and suffer one from another; they must be easily divisible: yet so, as that one be not excessive in respect of the other, for then it is not mixtion, but mutation into the more predominant, as a drop of Wine into a great quantity of Water.

b The principles and differences of Elements (sensible tactile Bodies) are tactile qualities, in as much as by such qualities, sensible bodies, as such, are constituted and differ. Of tactile qualities there are seven Orders, Hot, Cold, Moist, Dry, Heavy, Light, Hard, Soft, Viscous, Arid, Rugged, Smooth, Thick, Thin. From the two first Orders are derived the differences of Elements, for by Heat and Cold, Humidity and Siccity, they act and suffer, and are mutually changed by alterative Passions. Of these first qualities two are active, Heat and Cold; two Passive, Humidity and Siccity. Heat is that which congregates homogneous

a De gener. & corrupt. lib. 1. *cap.* 10.

b De gener. & corrupt. lib. 2. *cap.* 2.

neous things; cold, that which congregates heterogoneous things; humid, that which is not easily contained in its own bounds; dry, the contrary.

c Cap. 3.   *c* As there are four Elements, there must be four conjunctions of the primary qualities, from each of which the Elements are severally collected. The first conjunction is of hot and dry, whence proceedeth fire; the second hot and moist, whence Air; the third of moist and cold, whence Water; the fourth of cold and dry, whence Earth. In each of these one quality is predominant: Earth is more dry than cold, Water more cold than moist, Air most moist than hot, Fire more hot than dry.

All these Elements may be mutually transmutated into one another; the Symbolical which agree in one primary quality, are more easily transmutated into one another than the assymbolical, because it is less difficult to change one than many. This Transmutation is not a Generation, but a kind of Alteration, whence it is manifest one Element cannot be the principle of another.

d Cap. 7.   *d Mixtion*, whereby the Elements concur to the composition of a mixt Body, is made by coacervation, as *Empedocles* held; but after such a manner, that their contrary qualities remain in the mixt, not potentially only, nor simply actually in their height, but in a mean kind of way, their extremities being reduced to some temper. From this contemplation come mixt Bodies, differing according to the various proportion of the temperament; and as they are compounded of the Elements, so they resolve into the same.

e Cap. 8.   *e* All these mixt Bodies consist of all the Elements; of Earth, for every thing participates of the nature of that thing whereof it is produced; of Water, because every mixt thing must be concrete and terminated; which properties Water best affordeth to Earth; of Air and Fire, because every perfect mixt Body is made by temperament of contraries, such is Air to Earth, Fire to Water. Again, the nature of all mixt Bodies, as well animate as inanimate, as to mixture is the same, but that the animate consists of all the Elements, is manifest in that they are nourished by them.

f Cap. 9.   *f* The causes and common principles of mixt bodies are three; material, formal, efficient. The *Material* is the power to be, and not to be, by which elementary things are generated and corrupted. The *formal* is the reason of the essence of every thing; *g* the *universal efficient* is the circular motion of Heaven, not only as being eternal, continual, and before generation, but chiefly because it bringeth nigh to us, and carrieth far from us that which hath the generative power of all things, that is, the Sun, and the other Stars, which by their accession and recession are the causes of generation and corruption.

g Cap. 10.

h Cap. 11.   *h* All these are so disposed according to the order of Nature, that because no natural being can be permanent in the same individual state, they may be at least preserved by a continual succession of many individuums of the same species. Whence the natural cause of generation is only conservation of the species.

CHAP. XII.

Of Imperfect mixt Bodies.

a Mixt Bodies are twofold, *imperfect* and *perfect*: Meteors are imperfect mixt Bodies produced according to Nature, but after a less orderly and constant manner. *b* The general matter thereof are the Elements; the efficient, the Cœlestial Bodies which act upon inferiors by a kind of coherence. *c* Heaven is highest; next Heaven the Element of Fire; next Fire, Air; under Air, Water and Earth. Clouds are not generated in the Sphere of Fire, nor in the Region of the Air, partly by reason of the heat which is there, partly by reason of the motion of the Heavens which carrieth along with it the Element of Fire, and the upper Region of the Air, by which motion heat is produced in inferior Bodies; for the Air being carried along by the Heaven, is heated by that motion, and by the proximity of the Sun and of the Element of Fire.

a Meteor. lib. 1. cap. 1.

b Cap. 2.

c Cap. 3.

d Flames that appear in the upper part of the Air, are made thus; The Sun by his warmth extracteth a kind of breath out of the Earth, which, if hot and dry, is called *exhalation*, and if hot and moist, *Vapour*. Exhalation ascends higher, as being higher, and being got into the upper Region of the Air, is there enkindled by the motion of the Air, and proximity of the Fire. Hence come those they call *Fire-brands*, *Goats*, *falling-stars*, and the like. *c* Hence are also *Phasmes*, such as are called *gulfs*, *chasmes*, *bloody colours*, and the like; the exhalation being variously coloured by reflection of the light, but chiefly seeming purple, which colour ariseth from the mixture of fire and white.

d Cap. 4.

e Cap. 5.

f The efficient cause of Comets are the Sun and Stars; the material, an exhalation, hot, dry, condensed, and combustible; so as it burns not much, nor is soon extinguished. It is called a *Comet*, or *airy Star*, when it is alike on every side: a *pogoneia* or *bearded star*, when it hath a long train. That it consists of Fire, is manifest, because at the same time, there is commonly great wind and drought. It appears seldom, and then single, and beyond the Tropicks, because Stars, especially the Sun, dissipate the matter whereof it consists.

f Cap. 6. 7.

g The *Galaxie* is not the light of many Stars together, as *Anaxagoras* held, but an exhalation hot and dry, kindled by the motion of many great stars, which are in that part where the Galaxie appeareth.

g Cap. 8.

h We come next to those Meteors which are in the middle and lower Region of the Air, they are there kept so long, until they are condensed by the cold of that place into drops of water, which if they come down very small, are called *misling*; if greater, *Rain*. This thick vapour, which is seen suspended in the Air, and changeth from Air to Water, is a Cloud. *Mist* is the superfluity of a cloud, condens'd into water.

h Cap. 9.

i Vapour attracted by a small heat not much above the Earth, and descending more condensed by the nocturnal cold, becometh either

i cap. 10.

Dew,

Dew or Frost: Frost, when it congealeth before it resolves into water; Dew, when it turns into water, so as the warmth cannot dry it up, nor the cold freeze it.

k Cap. 11.   *k* Snow is a congealed cloud; Rain, Dew, Frost and Snow differ almost only in bigness and smalness.

l Cap. 12.   *l* Hail, tho' it be of the same nature as Ice, yet is seldom produced in Winter, as being caused by *Antiperistasis*.

m Cap. 13.   *m* As the Air above the Earth condensed, becometh vapour, and vapour by cold becometh water, so doth it also in the caverns and receptacles of the Earth, by a continual mutation; first it turns into little drops, then those little into greater. Hence come all Springs and heads of Rivers, abundantly flowing out at one part of the Earth. Hence great Rivers and Fountains commonly flow from great Hills, which have greatest Caverns.

n Cap. 14.   *n* The parts of the Earth are in continual mutation, sometimes humid, sometimes dry, sometimes fertile, sometimes desert, by new eruptions or defections of Rivers, or access or recess of the Sea, according to certain periods of time. Thus have the parts of the Earth their youth and age, as well as Plants and living Creatures, by the heat and conversion of the Sun. Time and the World are Eternal; but Nilus and Tanais were not always, for those places whence they first issued, were once dry grounds.

o Lib. 2. cap. 2.   *o* The proper place of water is the concave superficies of the Air: This place the Sea, compassing the Earth, possesseth; for the swift and more rare water is drawn upwards by the heat of the Sun; the Salt, more thick and terrene, setleth downwards. For this reason all waters tend to the Sea, as to their proper place: Yet, hereby the Sea is not enlarged, for the Sun draweth out of it, by reason of its expansion, as great a quantity of water as it receiveth from Rivers.

p Cap. 3.   *p* The Sea is, as the World, Eternal, the saltness thereof proceedeth from admixtion of some terrene, adust, exhalation. From the top of the Sea is drawn up a fresh vapour; from the bottom, heated by the Sun, an exhalation, which passeth through the Sea, and cometh up with the vapour; but falling back into the Sea, bringeth that saltness with it, as water passed often through Ashes.

q Cap. 4.   *q* Winds are produced by the Sun and Stars, of a hot, dry exhalation, which ascending, is driven down again by the coldness of the middle Region of the Air, and by reason of the lightness of its nature, cannot go directly to the bottom, but is carried by the Air up and down. We call it a hot and dry exhalation, as being more dry than humid. Wind is weakest in the beginning, but gaineth strength, by taking along with it other light exhalations, which it meets with by the way.

r Cap. 5.   *r* Winds are laid by heat and cold, excessive heat consumeth the exhalations, as soon as it cometh out of the Earth: excessive cold binds up the pores of the Earth, so as it cannot pass.

s Cap. 8.   *s* Earthquake is a trembling of the Earth, caused by an exhalation hot and dry, inclosed in the bowels of the Earth, which striving to get forth, as its nature requireth, and not able, by reason of the solidity of the Earth, to pass, maketh the Earth shake, forcing a way through it, and bearing down whatsoever opposeth it. The more hot this included Spirit is, the more vehement.

Of the same nature is Lightning, Thunder, and the like. Thunder is, when an exhalation inclosed in a thick cold Cloud, rolleth it up and down, and at last breaketh through it with more or less noise, according to the thickness of the Cloud. By this eruption it acquireth a rare kind of heat and light, which is Lightning, subsequent to the noise of the eruption; yet seen before the other is heard, by reason of the quickness of the sight beyond the hearing.

t As of dry exhalations, the rare and dispersed produce Thunder and Lightning; so of the great and condensed is made ἐκνεφίας, τύφων, πρηστὴς, and Thunderbolts.   *b Cap. 9.*

u Of lucid Meteors appearing in the Clouds, are Haloes, Rain-Bows, Parelies, and Streaks: All these are caused by refraction, but differ according to the objects from which they are reflected. A Halo appeareth about some Star, when there hapneth a Cloud to be, the middle part whereof, by reason of its rarity, being dissipated the rest of the parts about, by reflection, represent the colour of the Star. Rainbow is a refraction of the Sun's beam upon a humid Cloud, ready to dissolve into Rain. In like manner are caused Parelies and Streaks.   *u Lib. 3. cap. 2.*

x There are likewise imperfect mixt Bodies, under, or within the Earth, and these also of two kinds; some caused by exhalation, called *Minerals*; others by vapour, called *Metals*, fusile or ductile.   *Cap. 7.*

CHAP. XIII.

Of perfect mixt Bodies.

a THE common affections of perfect mixt Bodies, are those which proceed from the primary qualities of the Elements, whereof two are active, Heat and Cold; two passive, humidity and siccity. The natural effect of these is *Generation*, when Heat and Cold overcome the Matter; otherwise it is *inquination* and *inconcoction*. The opposite to simple Generation is *Putrefaction*; every thing, unless violently dissolved, putrifieth. Hence those things that putrifie, become first humid, then dry; for the external heat expelleth the internal, and at last consumeth it. All things therefore putrifie except fire, for putrefaction is the corruption of the natural heat in every humid body, by the external. For this reason, things are less subject to putrifie in cold or in motion, and the hotter or greater they are; as a part of the Sea may putrifie, the whole cannot.   *a Meteor. lib. 4 cap. 1.*

Out of putrid things are bred living creatures; for the natural heat, whilst it is separating, endeavoureth as much as possible, that what is taken asunder and segregated by corruption, may gather together in some small parts, which afterwards, by help of the Sun, receive life. Thus are Worms, Beetles, Gnats, and other Insects bred.

b Concoction is the effect of heat, inconcoction of cold. Concoction is a perfection caused   *b Cap. 2.*

fed by natural heat of the opposite passive qualities, which are mixed with the matter, as being passive. The end of Concoction in some things is mutation of the Essence, as when food is converted into flesh and blood; in others only a mutation according to quantity or quality, as in fruits that ripen. Inconcoction is an Imperfection in the opposite passive qualities, proceeding from defect of heat.

Concoction is three-fold, πέπανσις, ὄψησις, ὄπ]ησις. Inconcoction is also three fold, ὠμόϊης, μόλυνσις, στάτευσις.

c Cap. 3.   *c* Πέπανσις is the Concoction of that Element which is in fruits; it is perfect, when the seeds that are within the fruit are capable of producing their like, hereto is opposite, ὠμόϊης, the Inconcoction of Fruits not able through want of heat to overcome the humidity.

Ἕψησις is a concoction of an humid interminate by external humidity and heat; hereto is opposite μόλυνσις, the inconcoction of a humid interminate, caused by defect of external humidity and heat.

Ὄπ]ησις is a concoction by dry and external heat, yet not excessive, for then it were adustion: to this is opposed στάτευσις, an inconcoction caused through defect of heat and fire, or excess of humidity in the Subject.

d Cap. 4.   *d* As concerning the two passive qualities; things are humid and dry, either actually, or potentially. Those things which are mixt of humid and dry, are terminate, for these qualities mutually terminate one another, whence bodies consist not without Earth and Water, this humid, that dry. And for this reason Animals can only live in Earth and Water, which are their matter.

The first affections of terminate bodies are hardness and softness; hard is that which yields not to the touch; soft the contrary. Both these are such, either absolutely, or relatively. They are made such by concretion, which is a kind of exiccation.

e Cap. 6.   *e* Exiccation is of things that are water, or of the nature of Water, or have water in them, either naturally insite, or adventitious. It is done principally by heat, accidentally by cold. Humectation (its contrary) is the concretion of a vapour into water, or liquefaction of a solid Body, as Metal. *Concretion* is, when the humidity being removed, the dry is reduced together, and condensed, either by cold, as in generation of Stones; or by heat, as in segregation of Salt from water. To Concretion is opposite, Resolution, which is effected by its contraries. Those things which are condensed by heat only, are resolved by cold only, and so on the contary.

f Cap. 8.   *f* Besides these principal affections, there are others secondary, chiefly competent to homogenous Bodies, some passive, some active.

Of passive qualities in mixt Bodies, there are eighteen differences, *Concretile, Eliquabile, Mollificable, Humectable, Flexible, Frangible, Impressible, Formable, Compressible, Tractile, Ductile, Fissile, Sectile, Unctious, Friable, Condensable, Combustible, Exhalable,* and their contraries. From these are thus denominated, *Homiomerious* mixt Bodies, as Metals, Gold, Brass, Silver, Stone and the like; and whatsoever is made out of these; as likewise similar parts in Animals and in Plants, as Flesh and Bone, whereof some are more cold, which consist most of Water others more hot, which consist most of Earth and Air.

CHAP. XIV.

Of Plants and Animals.

AT the end of *his Meteors he proposeth to speak of* Similar parts, *as* Blood, *and the like; what they are, and to what end, their matter and reason, but especially whence they have their motion; next to proceed to* dissimilar parts; *and lastly to speak of those which consist thereof, as* Men, Plants, *and the like.* Hence Patricius *conjectures that his Books* of the parts of living Creatures, *did immediately succeed those of the* Meteors, *wherein he treateth* (as he proposeth) *of* similar parts *unto the tenth Chapter of the second Book, and from thence of the Dissimilar. But to reduce his Books* of living Creatures *to this method, is the less certain, for as much as many of these (besides those which treated particularly of* Anatomy) *have been lost, of which perhaps were some which might better have cleared the series; for in the Books themselves concerning* Animals, *there is nothing to ground it upon.*

For the same reason, it is uncertain where his Books of Plants *ought to have been placed, which are lost. Perhaps they might precede those of* Animals; *for he asserts that* Plants have Souls, *(contrary to the* Stoicks) *endued with vegetative power; that they live even tho' cut asunder, as* Insects, *whereby two or more are made of one; that the substance they receive by aliment and the ambient Air, is sufficient for the preservation of their natural heat.*

As concerning Animals, we have, Of their Going, *one Book.* Of their History, *ten Books.* Of their parts, *four Books.* Of their Generation, *five Books. So exquisitely hath he treated upon this Subject, as cannot well be expressed by an abridgment, and therefore we shall omit it; the rather because little or nothing was done herein by the* Academicks *or* Stoicks, *a collation with whom is the principal design of this summary.*

CHAP. XV.

Of the Soul.

a THE knowledge of the *Soul* conduceth much to all Truth, and especially to Physick, for the Soul is as it were the principle of animate things. Animate things differ from inanimate chiefly by motion and sense.   *a De anima lib.* I. *cap* I.

b Whence the ancient Philosophers defined the Soul by these; *Democritus,* the *Pythagoreans, Anaxagoras* by *Motion; Empedocles* and *Plato* by *knowledge;* others by *both;* others by *incorporiety,* or a *rare body;* Thales, *something that moveth;* Diogenes, *Air;* Heraclitus, *Exhalation, an immortal substance;* Hippo, *Water;* Critas, *Blood,*   *b Cap.* I.

c The Soul doth not move it self, as *Democritus* held; for whatsoever, is moved, is moved by another. Again, if the Soul were moved *per se,* it would be in place, and it were capable of being   *c Cap.* 3.

being moved violently, and it would be of the same nature with the body, and might return into the body after the separation. Neither is the Soul moved by it self, but from its objects; for if it were moved essentially, it might recede from its essence. The Soul therefore is not moved *per se*, but by accident only, according to the motion of the Body.

d Cap. 4.   *d* The Soul is not *Harmony*, (a proportionate mixture of contraries) for then there must be more Souls in the same body, according to the different constitution of its parts. But tho' we commonly say, the Soul *grieveth, hopeth, feareth*, &c. we are not to understand that the Soul is moved, but only that these are from the Soul in the Body that is moved; some by local motion of the Organs, others by alteration of them. To say, the Soul is angry, is no more proper than to say she builds; for it is the man that is angry by the Soul, otherwise the Soul were liable to *age, decay*, and *infirmity*, as well as the Organs of the Body.

e Cap. 5.   *e* Neither is the Soul *a rare body*, consisting of Elements, for then it would understand nothing more than the Elements themselves; neither is there a Soul diffused through all things, as *Thales* held, for we see there are many things inanimate.

Some from the different functions of the Soul argue, that there are more Souls than one in man, or that the Soul is divisible, the supream intellectual part placed in the head, the irascible in the heart, concupiscible in the Liver: But this is false, for the Intellect is not confined to any part of the Body, as not being corporeal, nor organical, but immaterial and immortal.

f Lib. 2. cap. 2.   *f* The Soul is the first *Entelechy* of a natural organical body, having life potentially. *First, Entelechy.*] Entelechy is twofold, the first is the principle of Operation, as Science; the Second, *g Laert.* the Act it self. *Of a Natural,* [*g* not of an artificial body, as a Tower or Ship. *Organical Body.*] that is, endued with instruments for operation, as the eye for seeing, the ear for hearing; even Plants have simple Organs. *Having life potentially*] as it were in it self, for potentially is less than actually; actually, as in him that wakes; potentially, as in him that is asleep.

The Soul is otherwise defined, that by which we first live, feel, and understand; whence appeareth, there are three faculties of the Soul, *nutritive, sensitive, intellective*; the inferior comprehended by the superior potentially, as a triangle by a quadrangle.

CHAP. XVI.

Of the Nutritive Faculty.

a Cap. 4.   *a* THE first and most common faculty of the Soul, is the *Nutritive*; by which life is in all things, the acts and operation thereof are to be generated, and to take nourishment.

Nutriment is received either towards Nutrition or Augmentation. Nutrition is the operation of the Nutritive Faculty conducing to the substance it self of the animate being, augmentation is the operation of the nutritive faculty, whereby the animate Body encreaseth to perfect Magnitude. In nutrition are considered, the Soul nourishing, the Body nourished, and the food by which the nourishment is made; hereto is required a natural heat, which is in all living creatures. The aliment is both contrary, or unlike, and like, to the body nourished: as it is undigested, we say nourishment is by the contrary; as altered by digestion, like is nourished by its like.

CHAP. XVII.

Of the Sensitive Faculty.

a THE *Sensitive* Faculty of the Soul is that *a Cap. 5.* by which Sense is primarily in Animals. Sense is a mutation in the Organ caused by some sensible Object. It is not sensible of it self, nor of its Organ, nor of any interior thing. To reduce it to act, is requisite some external sensible object, for sense cannot move it self, being a passive power, as that which is combustible cannot burn it self.

b Of sensible Objects there are three kinds: *b Cap. 6. proper*, which is perceived by one Sense, without Error, as colour in respect of sight. *Common* which is not proper to any one, but perceived by all. *Accidental*, which, as such, doth not affect the Sense.

Sense is either *External or Internal*, the External are five, *Seeing, Hearing, Smelling, Touching, Tasting.*

c The Object of *Seeing* is Colour, and some- *c Cap. 7.* thing without a name that glistens in the dark, as the Scales of Fish, Glow-worms and the like. Colour is the motive of that which is actually perspicuous: nothing therefore is visible, without light. Perspicuous is that which is visible, not by it self, but by some other colour or light, as Air, Water, Glass. Light in the act of a perspicuous thing, as it is perspicuous. It is not fire, nor a body, for then two bodies would be in the same place.

To sight and all other senses is requisite a *medium* and convenient distance. The object first effects the *medium*, then the Organ.

d The object of *Hearing* is sound. Sound is *d Cap. 8.* made by collision of two Bodies, Hard, Smooth, and Hollow, in a *medium*, as Air or Water, swiftly and vehemently before the *medium* be dissipated.

Ecco is a reflex sound, when the Air, gathered together and forced into a vessel, or some place which hindereth its diffusion and progress, reverts as a Base against a Wall. Sound is always reflected, tho' not always perceptibly, as light also, otherwise all places would be dark, which were not directly opposite to the Sun, or some lucid body.

Sound is made by that which moveth the Air, and continually stirreth it, till it arrive at the organ, wherein there is an infite, connatural, animate, immovable Air, which being moved by the external Air, yieldeth the sense of hearing. Hence it cometh that we can hear under water, for the water cannot get into this air, because of the winding narrow passages in the Ear: If it do get in, or the membrane which containeth

Alteration.

this Air be otherwise broken, it causeth deafness.

Voice is the Impulsion of Air attracted by respiration, and forced against against the vocal Artery by the Soul, which is in the Lungs, with some intent of signification. Voice therefore is not proper to all Animals, but to such only as have Blood and Breath. Fishes therefore have not Voice.

c Cap. 9.

e The object of *Smelling* is Odour. This Sense is not so perfect in Men as in other Creatures, whence Men peceive not Odours, unless with delight or dislike, when they are so strong as to excite one of these. This defect proceedeth from the organ of Smelling, which in us is more obtuse. The *medium* of smelling is Air and Water, for Fishes smell. Hence all living Creatures smell not after the same manner; they which breathe, smell by drawing in the Air, the rest not so, because of the different accommodation of the Organ. Those therefore which smell by drawing in the Air, cannot smell under Water, Odour consists generally in dry, as *sapor* in humid. The Organ of Smelling is dry potentially, as the Object is actually.

f Cap. 10.

f The object of *Taste* is sapor. Whatsoever is gustable, is tactable, and humid, either actually, or at least potentially. Dry things are subject to taste, as they are potentially humid, and melt as Salt. The Taste perceiveth that which is gustable, and that which is ingustable, as the Sight Darkness, the Hearing, silence; for every Sense perceiveth the presence and absence of its object: That which is potable is perceived by the touch, as humid by the taste, as having Sapor. The Tongue tastes not that which is dry, because the organ of taste must be such potentially, as the object is actually; but without humidity nothing is gustable. The kinds of Sapors are sweet and bitter; to sweet are referred unctious; to bitter salt. The mean are sharp, piccant, acid, acute; gustable is that which moveth the Taste, and reduceth it to act.

g Cap. 11.

g The objects of *Touch* are the primary qualities, the Organ is that part which is potentially that which the object is in act; for that which is like, cannot suffer from its like. We feel not things of equal heat, cold, hardness, or softness. The Flesh is the *medium*; the first sensory is something more internal. Herein touch and taste differ from the other Senses, whose objects are at greater distance. Touch perceiveth things tactile and not tactile.

h Cap. 12.

h All these Senses receive sensible Species without matter, as Wax the Impression of a Seal without the Gold. The Organ or Sensory is that in which the sensitive faculty primarily exists; a vehement Object destroyeth the Organ.

i Lib. 3. cap. 1.

i That there are no more external Senses than these five, is manifest, in that there are no more in perfect Animals; neither is there any need of a sixth Sense to perceive common Objects, which every Sense discerns by accident, as motion, figure.

The act of the Object, and the act of the Sense it self, as Sonation and Audition, are really the same, differ only intentionally. This act is generally in the sensitive, not in the subject.

k De sensu. cap. 6.

k Sensible qualities are finite, as being bounded by Extreams and their Contraries, divisible by accident into infinite, according to the division of their continuous Subject.

l In Sensibles, some are potentially sensible, as a part joined to the whole; others actually, as the whole it self, or a part separated from the whole. But of separate parts some are so little, that Sense cannot actually perceive them, by reason of their want of due Magnitude.

l Ibid.

m Sounds and Odours are successively generated in the *medium*, and by degrees deduc'd to the Organ; but light is produced in an Instant in the medium, not carried thro' it by local motion.

m Ibid.

CHAP. XVIII.

Of Common Sense.

a Every external Sense perceiveth the differences of its own object, as Sight judgeth of black and white; but the differences of divers objects cannot be perceiv'd by the same Sense; there is therefore a *common sense*, which judgeth the actions of external Sense and the differences of sensible objects. The Judgment being of a sensible object, must be done by sense, and by one sense only; for, if there were more, one would object one object apart, the other another, and consequently could not judge between them. For that which judgeth must have knowledge of all that whereof it judgeth, which no exteriour Sense can afford, as being confined to its proper Object.

a Lib. 3. cap. 2.

Common Sense judgeth contrary or different Sensibles in the same instant, for it discerneth together sweet and black, bitter and sweet. Hence it is like the Center of a Circle, which in divers respects is called one, and many. It is one, as all the external Senses are united in it; many, as it is the Fountain and Judge of them.

b Sense differs from Intellect; for Sense is in all living Creatures; Intellect in few. Sense erreth not about its proper object, but is always true; Intellect often erreth by false Opinions and Habits.

b De Anima, lib. 3. cap. 3.

CHAP. XIX.

Of Phantasie and Cogitation.

a From *Sense* is derived *Phantasie* and *Cogitation*. Phantasie differs from Sense and Intellect, tho' it exist not without a previous knowledge of Sense, as neither doth Cogitation, which is in action of the Intellect, comprehending Science, Opinion, and Prudence.

a Cap. 3.

The act of *Phantasie* differs from *Cogitation*, for we fancy things false and at our own pleasure; but we think only what is true, and like unto truth, and that not as we please our selves, but as the thing seemeth. Moreover, when we think that things are ill or good, we are moved with Fear, Joy, Hope; but when we fancy only without application of Judgment, we are not mov'd no more than we are frighted at a Picture.

Phantasie is not properly *Sense*; Phantasie acteth in him that sleepeth, Sense doth not. Sense was with us from our Birth, Phantasie not. Sense is in all Animals, phantasie is not. Sense is true, phantasie often false. Sense is only of things present, phantasie of the absent likewise.

Phantasie is not *Science* or *Intellect*, for that is always

always of things true and real, Phantasie often is of things false. Phantasie is not *Opinion*, for Opinion is followed by Faith, Phantasie is not.

Phantasie is a motion in Animals from Sense in Act, by which motion they are variously affected, and conceive things sometimes true, and sometimes false. The Error of Phantasie ariseth from the Error of the Senses: Phantasie therefore is of near affinity with Sense; for though it be not sense, yet it exists not without Sense, or in things that have no sense. It is derived ἀπὸ τῦ φάος from light; for Sight, the most excellent of Senses, cannot act without Light.

Many things are done by Animals according to Phantasie, either because they have not Intellect, as Beasts, or that Intellect is obscured in them.

CHAP. XX.

Of Memory and Reminiscence.

<small>*a* Lib. de Memor. & Rem. cap. 1.</small>

a FRom *Phantasie* proceeds *Memory*, which is of things *past*, as Sense is of the *present* Opinion of the *future*. Sense and Intellection are necessarily previous to Memory. Hence those Animals only which have Sense of time, remember as Horses and Dogs; yet Memory is not without Phantasie, even not that Memory which is of intelligible things; for he that remembreth is sensible that he first saw, heard, or learned what he remembreth. Memory therefore is reducible *per se* to Phantasie, as being of Phantasms, to Intellect only by Accident. Hence in the same part of the Soul, wherein Phantasie exists, resideth likewise Memory, for if it were placed only in the Intellectual Faculty, it would not be competent to Beasts, which we see it is.

Memory is made by impression of some Image by the Sense upon the Soul. Hence they who retain not the Image and Figure of Sense, either by continual motion, or excessive Humidity, as Children, or Drought, as Old Men, remember not. To Memory therefore is required a moderate temperature of the Brain; yet more inclined to dry.

<small>*b Cap.* 2.</small>

b Reminiscence is not a Resumption or Assumption of Memory, but differs specifically from both these, for Beasts have not Reminiscence though they have Memory, Reminiscence being made by discourse and diligent disquisition collecting one thing from another by a continued Series and order, until at last we cal that to Mind which we had forgotten.

CHAP. XXI.

Of Sleep and Waking.

<small>*a* Lib. de Som. & Vigil. cap. 1.</small>

a TO Sense belongeth *Sleep* and *Waking*; for those animate things which want sense neither sleep nor wake, as Plants. Sleep is an immobility, and band as it were of Sense; Waking is a solution and remission of Sense.

<small>*b Cap.* 2.</small>

b The chief Seat of Sleep is the common Sense, which being bound up by Sleep, all the exterior Senses, whereof this is the common Centre, are bound up likewise and restrained for the rest and health of the Animal; which is the end of waking also.

<small>*c Cap.* 3.</small>

c Every impotence of Sense is not Sleep, but only that which is caused by evaporation of the Aliment. Hence we are most subject to sleep after Meat; for then much humid vapour ascends, which first maketh the head heavy by consistence there, then descends and repels the heat, whereby is induced Sleep. That Sleep is made in this manner, is evident from all soporiferous things, as Poppy, which causeth Heaviness in the Head by sending up vapours. Labour produceth sleep, by dispersing the Humours, whence produceth Vapour. Drunken Men and Children are subject to sleep much, melancholly Persons little, for they are so cold within, that the Vapour exhaleth not, especially they being of a dry Constitution. Sleep therefore is a recession of the heat inward, with a natural kind of Circumobsistence.

CHAP. XXII.

Of Dreams.

<small>*a* Lib. de insom.</small>

a DReaming is an affection of the sensory part, in as much as it is Fantastick. A Dream is an Apparition or Phantasm seen in Sleep.

After the Functions of the external Senses, there remain their motions and similitudes induced by their objects into their Organs. These occurring in sleep, cause Dreams, but not at all times, nor at every age, for their Species shew not themselves, but upon cessation of the Humours. Hence Dreams are not immediately after sleep, nor in Infants soon after their Birth, for then there is too great Commotion by reason of the Alimentary Heat. As therefore in troubled water no Image appeareth, or if any, much distorted; but when it is calm, the Image is rendred clearly; so when there is a tumult and agitation of the Humours, there are no Images presented, or those dreadful, such as are the Dreams of Melancholy and Sick Persons; but when the Blood passeth smoothly, and the Humours are setled, we have pure and pleasing Dreams; a Dream therefore is a Phantasm caused by motion of Sensibles already perceived by Sense, occurring to Animals in Sleep.

CHAP. XXIII.

Of the Intellective Faculty.

<small>*a* De Anim. lib. 3. cap. 4.</small>

a THE third faculty of the Soul is the Intellective, proper to Man. Intellect is that part of the Soul whereby it knoweth and understandeth. It is two-fold, *Patient* and *Agent*. *Patient Intellect* is that by which Intellect becometh all things, for Intellection is like Sense; Sense is by Passion from a sensible Object, Intellect from an Intellectual. The properties of patient intellect are these; it is void of corruptive passion; it is apt for reception of Species, it is that Species potentially; it is not mixt with the Body; it hath no Corporeal Organs; it is the place of Species.

<small>*b Cap.* 5.</small>

b That there is also an Agent Intellect, is manifest;

nifest; for in whatsoever kind, there is something that is potentially all of that kind, there is something likewise which is the efficient cause of all in that kind; this is the agent Intellect, a cognoscitive power which enlightneth *Phantasms* and the patient Intellect. The properties thereof are, that it is separable from the Body, Immortal and Eternal; that it is not mixt with the Body; that it is void of passion; that it is ever in act; but the patient Intellect is Mortal, which is the cause of forgetfulness.

c Cap. 6.   *c* The action of the Intellect is twofold, one, *Intellection of Indivisibles*, in which is neither Truth nor Falshood, as all *simple* apprehensions; the other *complex*, when we compound and unite notions by Affirmation or Negation. This is always either true or false; the other neither. The simple is precedent to the complex.

d Cap. 8.   *d* Intellect in act is either *Practick* or *Theoretick*. As a sensible Object reduceth the sensible faculy from power to act, so doth an intellectual faculty; and as the operation of Sense is three-fold, simple apprehension, Judgment if it be good or ill, and lastly, appetition or aversion according to that perception: So likewise is the operation of the *Practick Intellect* threefold: First, it is moved by phantasms, as Sense is by external Sensibles. Secondly, it judgeth the object to be good or ill, by Affirmation or Negation. Thirdly, it moveth the Will to pursue or shun it, whence it is called *practick*. This practick Intellect is moved as well when the sensible object is absent, as when it is present, only excited by the phantasie. The object of the *Theoretick Intellect*, is true or false; of the practick, good or ill.

e Ibid.   *e* The rational Soul in some manner is every thing; for that which actually knoweth, is in some manner the same with the thing known.

that is, *Will.* For Appetite is the principle of all Motion, Honest and Dishonest; Intellect only of honest motion.

In Man, Appetite is twofold: *Will*, which followeth the Judgment of Reason; and *sensual Appetite*, irascible or concupiscible, which followeth Sense and phantasie.

In the motion of Animals, three things are considered: First, that which moveth, and that is two-fold; the *Appetible Object*, which moveth the Appetite as a final Cause, not as an Efficient; and the *Appetite* it self, which being moved by the appetible Object, moveth the Animal. Secondly, by what it moves, which is the Heart of the Animal, by which Instrument the appetible object moveth it. Thirdly, that which is moved, the Animal it self perfect.

c Insects are moved locally, as *perfect* Animals are, and consequently by the same principles, Appetite and Phantasie; but this Phantasie is imperfect, diffused through the whole Body, as appeareth by their uncertain motion, only towards present occurrent objects. That they have Appetite is manifest, in as much as they are sensible of Pain and Pleasure.   *c Cap. 11.*

Beasts have *sensitive* Phantasie only; Rational Creatures, *deliberative*, which compareth many things conducing to some foreknown end, and chooseth the most expedient. Yet sometimes the Sensitive Appetite in Man overswayeth the rational; but by the order of Nature, the Will, which is Rational, ought, as being the Superiour to it, to oversway the Sensitive. Thus there are three motions, one of the Will commanding, another of the Sensitive Appetite resisting, and a third of the Body obeying. But when the sensitive over-ruleth, there are only two motions, for the Will resists not, but is deceived.

CHAP. XXIV.
Of the motive faculty.

a Cap. 9.   *a* BEsides the *nutritive, sensitive*, and *intellectiva* Faculties, there is also a *motive* Faculty in animate Creatures. That it is not the same with the *nutritive* is manifest, in as much as it proceeds from Imagination and Apprehension, which Plants had not, neither have they Organs fit for motion, which Nature would have given them if they have this power. That it is not the same with the *sensitive*, appears, in that some Animals which have sense, have not the power, as *Zoophytes*, which have not the organs fit for this motion. Neither is it the same with the Theoretick *Intellect*, for that judgeth not as to Action: But progressive motion is the action of an Animal flying ill, or pursuing good.

t Cap. 10.   *b* The Principles of *local Motion* in Animals, are the *practick Intellect* (under which is comprehended Phantasie) and *Appetite*. These two direct and impel the motive faculty to action: Intellect and Phantasie by directing what is to be shunned, what to be embraced; Appetite by shunning or embracing it. Appetite is the chief Principle thereof; for that may move without Intellect, as in Beasts, and many times in Men, who desert their reason to follow their pleasure: But Intellect never moveth without Appetite,

CHAP. XXV.
Of Life and Death.

a GEneration and Dissolution are common to all living Creatures, though all are not produced and dissolved in the same manner.   *a De vit. & Mort. cap. 23*

b The Generation of a Living Creature is the first Conjunction of the nutritive Soul with the natural heat.   *b Cap. 24.*

Life is the permanence of that Soul with the said heat.

Youth is the encrease of the first Refrigerative part, *Age* the decrease thereof, ἀκμή, the constant and perfect Life which is betwixt both.

As long as an animate Creature liveth, it hath natural heat within it self; and as soon as that faileth, dieth. The Principle of this Heat is in the Heart. If it be extinguished in any other part, the Animal may live; but if in the Heart, it cannot.

This Heat is extinguished two ways; first by *Consumption*, when it faileth of it self; Secondly, by *extinction*, from some contrary, as in violent Death; the cause is the same in both, defect of aliment, which in the living Creature is its Vital Moisture, as Fire wanting Refrigeration, groweth more violent, and soon consumeth the Humidity, which being gone, it self must of necessity go out.

Kk 2   Refrigeration

Refrigeration therefore is necessary to the conservation of the natural Heat. Plants are refrigerated by the ambient Air, and by Aliment: their natural heat is extinguished by excessive Cold, and dried up by excessive Heat. Animals which live in the Air, or in the Water, are refrigerated by the Air or Water, some by breathing, others without.

c *Cap.* 23, 24. c *Death*, according to the extinction of Natural Heat, is two-fold, *violent* or *natural*; violent, when the Cause is extrinsical; natural, when the Principle thereof is in the animate Creature. For that part whereon Life dependeth (the Lungs) is so ordered by Nature, that it cannot perform its Office for ever. Death therefore cometh from defect of heat, when through want of Refrigeration the Radical Humidity is consumed and dried up. Refrigeration faileth naturally, when by progress of time the Lungs in Creatures that have Breath, the Gills in Fishes grow so hard that they are unapt for Motion.

d *Cap.* 23. d Old Men die easily, as having but little natural heat; and without Pain, because their dissolution comes not from any violent affection.

e *Lib. de lon. & brevit. cap.* 4. e The Lives of living Creatures, as well of the same, as of divers species, differ in length; the longest Life, most commonly, is that of some Plants, as the Palm and Cypress; that of Creatures which have blood, rather than the Bloodless; that of Terrestrial Creatures rather than the Aquatile: That of those which have great Bodies, as of Elephants, rather than those of little.

f The causes of long Life are first the quantity and quality of the vital Moisture, if it be much and fat, not easily dried up nor congeal'd. Secondly, Natural Heat, which suffereth not that Humour to be congealed. Thirdly a due proportion betwixt this heat and that Moisture. Fourthly, fewness of Excrements, for Excrements are contrary to Nature, and sometimes corrupt Nature it self, sometimes a part. f *Cap.* 5.

Salacious Creatures, or Laborious, grow soon old by reason of Exsiccation. For the same reason Men are shorter lived than Women, but more active.

In hot Countries animate Creatures are larger and live longer than in cold. Those Animals which have little or no Blood, either are not at all produced in the Northern parts, or soon die.

Both Plants and Animals, if they take not Aliment, die; for the Natural Heat when the aliment faileth, consumeth the matter it self, wherein it is, the Vital Moisture.

Aquatile Creatures are shorter Liv'd than the Terrestrial, and the Bloodless than those that have Blood, because their Humidity is more waterish, and consequently more apt to be congealed and corrupted.

g Plants live long, as having less of waterish moisture, which therefore is not so apt to be congealed. The largeness of the upper parts as well in Plants as Animals, is a sign of long Life, because it argues much natural heat. The upper part of a Plant is the Root, not the Boughs. g *Cap.* 6.

THE THIRD PART.

CHAP. I.

ETHICK.

WE come next to the *Moral* part of Philosophy, including *Ethick*, *Oeconomick*, and *Politick*. Of the first, we have ten Books of *Aristotle*'s, written (to his Son) *Nichomachus*, two Books call'd his *great Ethick*; one of *Virtues*. Of *Oeconomick*, two Books: of *Politick* eight. We shall not have recourse to these for an account of his Doctrine in this kind, being furnished by *Stobæus* with a summary of what he and the rest of the Peripateticks asserted in Morality.

a *Eclog. Ethic.* *Ethick* a (saith he) is so called ἀπὸ τῦ ἔθος, from *Custom*, for those things, the Principles and Seeds whereof we receive from Nature, are to be perfected by Custom and right Institution. Hence Ethick pertaineth only to Living Creatures, and particularly to Man; for the rest acquire custom, not by Reason, but Necessity, Man by Reason.

Of the *Soul*, one part is *Rational*, the other *Irrational*; the rational part is *Judicative*, the irrational *Appetitive*; of the rational that which is *Theoretick*, conversant in divine things, is called *Science*; that which is *Practick*, conversant in Humane Actions, is called *Council*. Of the latter, one part is *concupiscible*, another *irascible*.

In like manner *Virtue* is twofold, rational and irrational, consisting in Theory and Practice. Ethick Vertue consisteth not in Science, but in Election of Goods.

Vertue is perfected by three things; *Nature*, *Custom* and *Reason*. For a Man differing from other Creatures both in Body and Mind, as being a Species a Species placed between divine Essences and irrational Creatures, hath some affinity to both; in what is rational, and agrees with the Soul, he is ally'd to the Divinity; in what is irrational, proper to the Body, he agrees with the irrational. Both these desire Perfection by Reason; and first he desireth to be, for this is naturally insite in him. Hence he affecteth things that are according to Nature, and is averse from things contrary to his Nature. He endeavoureth to preserve *Health, Pleasure, Life*, these being according to Nature, expetible in themselves, and good. On the contrary, he shunneth *Sickness, Pain*, and *Death*, as being repugnant to Nature, and therefore ill, and to be avoided. We love our own Bodies, we love our own Souls, their parts, their faculties, their acts: The principle of Appetite, Office, and Vertue is a providential care of these. If Error did not happen concerning thins expetible and avoidable, but that we lived continually participant of good, and void of ill, we should not enquire in these for a true Election. But being things expetible and avoidable, through Ignorance often deceived, sometimes rejecting the good, sometimes admitting the ill for good, we necessarily have recourse to *constancy of Judgment*, which having obtained convenient to Nature, we call it, from the excellency of its Function, *Virtue*, admiring and honouring it above all things. For Actions, and those which are call'd Offices, proceed from election of things according to Nature, and rejection of things repugnant to Nature. Herein consist *right actions* and *Sins*; even on these dependeth almost the whole reason of *Election*, as we shall briefly demonstrate.

That Children are *expetible* to Parents, not only *for use* or benefit, but also in *themselves*, is most evident. There is no Man so cruel and savage, who doth not rather desire his Children after his Death should live happily and well, than otherwise: By this affection dying persons make Wills, providing even for the unborn, choosing Tutors and Guardians to assist them. And as *Children* are loved for themselves, so likewise we love *Parents, Brethren, Wife, Kindred, Acquaintance, Countrymen*, for themselves, as having some interest in them by Nature. For, Man is a sociable communicative Creature; and tho' of Friendships some are more remote than others, it is nothing to the purpose, for all friendship is for its own sake, and not for use only. And if Friendship with Country-men be expetible in it self, it will likewise be expetible in it self with all Men; for all those who benefit others, are so affected towards them, that they do most actions for the Office sake. Who will not free any Man from a wild Beast, if he be in his Power? Who will not direct a Man that is out of his way? Who will not relieve a Man that is ready to starve, or direct a Man in a Desart to a Spring? Who desires not to be well spoken of after Death? Who abhors not these Speeches as unnatural?

When I am dead, let Earth be mix'd with Fire,
I care not, so I now have my desire.

It is manifest therefore, that we have a natural good-will and friendship towards all Mankind, as a thing being expetible in it self, and consonant to Reason.

The Race of Gods and Men is one,
From Nature both alike begun.

Love of all Mankind being thus common to us, much more evidently it is expetible in it self towards those whom Conversation hath made our Friends. A Friend, Friendship, and Good-will, are expetible in themselves.

In like manner *Praise* is expetible *in it self*; for we contract Society with those who praise us: And if Praise, *Glory* likewise, which is nothing but the praise of many Persons.

Now seeing that *external Goods* are expetible in themselves, much more are the goods of Soul and Body expetible in themselves. For, if Man be expetible in himself, the parts of Man must likewise be expetible in themselves. The parts of Man in general are *Soul* and *Body*; the Body therefore is expetible in it self. Why should the body of another Person be dear to us, and not our own? Or why should our Body be dear to us, and not the parts and functions thereof? *Health* therefore, *Strength, Beauty, Swiftness, sound Sense*, and the rest are expetible in themselves; for none of ordinary capacity would choose to be *deform'd* or maim'd, tho' no Inconvenience would happen thereupon; so that deformity, even without any Inconvenience, seemeth justly avoidable. And if deformity be avoidable in it self, Beauty is expetible, not for *use* only, but in *it self*. For, that Beauty pleaseth is manifest, in as much as all have a natural Inclination (besides that of conversation) to such as are Beautiful, and endeavour to confer benefits on them, so as it seemeth to procure Benevolence. In this respect therefore Beauty is judged expetible in it self, deformity avoidable in it self. It is the same in *Health* and *Sickness, Strength* and *Weakness, Activity* and *Heaviness, Sense* and *privation* of Sense.

And if *Corporeal* Goods are expetible in themselves, and their contrary evils avoidable, the Parts and Vertues of the Soul must necessarily be expetible also. For, Vertue beginning, as we said, from the Body, and external Goods, and reflecting upon it self, and considering how much more near relation it hath to the Soul, contracteth a nearer affinity with it. So that the Vertues of the Soul are much to be preferred before those of the Body, which is easily collected from what hath been said. For, if Corporeal Health be expetible in it self, much more is *Temperance*, which freeth us from the fury of the Passions. And if Corporeal *Strength* ought to be number'd amongst Goods, much more ought *Magnanimity*, by which the Soul is strengthened. And if Corporeal *Beauty* be expetible in it self, much more is that of the Soul, *Justice*.

In like manner is it with the Vertues. For, there are three kinds of *Goods*, which though different, have some kind of Analogy. That which in the Body is called *Health*, in the Soul is called *Temperance*, and in Externals, *Riches*. What in the Body is *Strength*, in the Soul is *Magnanimity*, in Externals, *Power*. What in the Body is *vigour of Sense*, in the Soul is *Prudence*, in externals, *Felicity*. What in the Body is *Beauty*, in the Soul is *Justice*, in Externals, *Friendship*.

There are three kinds of Goods expetible in themselves, those concerning the *Soul*, those concerning the *Body*, and the *External*; but especially

ally those of the Soul, for the Soul is more excellent than the Body.

Yet tho corporeal and external Vertues be inferiour to those of the Soul, they are not to be neglected, partly, as being expetible in themselves; partly, as conducing to civil, sociable and contemplative life, for life is defin'd by civil, sociable, and contemplative actions; *Vertue* (according to this *Sect*) not being a lover of it self, but communicative and civil. For when we say, Vertue is nearest allied to it self, the desire of the knowledge of Truth necessarily followeth it, so as wise Men may rightly part with their life, and Fools rightly preserve theirs; since that to those who are perfect, it is an equal thing to depart this Life or not.

The excellency of Vertue is much encreas'd by corporeal and external goods; yet, the end cannot any way be compleated by them. The function therefore of *Vertue* is *Beatitude*, by successful actions. Corporeal and External goods are said to be efficient of Beatitude, for as much as they confer something thereto, not that they compleat it; for Beatitude is Life. Life consists of actions, but those can neither be reckoned amongst actions nor functions.

Hereupon comes in *Beneficence, Grace, Humanity, Love of Children* and *Brethren*, of our *Country, Parents, Benevolence of Kinsfolk, Friendship, Equality*, and the whole company of Vertues; which who neglect, manifestly sin, as to expetible goods, and avoidable Evils; and also in the acquisition and use of Goods, they sin in election, by Judgment; in acquisition, by the manner; in use, by Ignorance; in election they Sin, as desiring that which is not good, or preferring the lesser good, as most prefer *pleasant* before *profitable*, profitable before *honest*. In acquisition, as not considering whence, nor in what manner, nor how far it ought to be acquired. *In use*, for as much as all use being referr'd either to it self or some other, in the former they observe no *moderation*, in the latter no *decency*.

In these things, though the wicked Sin, yet do the Just behave themselves uprightly, following Vertue as their Leader.

In all Vertues there is *Judgment, Election*, and *Action*; there is no Vertue without these; Prudence hath the first place, the rest follow.

Vertue is called the *best Affection*, which may be collected from Induction. The Vertue of a Shooemaker is that by which he knoweth how to make Shooes; and of an Architect, that by which he knoweth how to build a handsome House. Vertue therefore is the best of Affections.

Of Vertue there are two Principles as it were, *Reason*, and *Passion*, which sometimes agree, sometimes disagree; for Pleasure or Grief, where Reason gets the Mastery, is called *Temperance*, when Passion, *Intemperance*; The *Harmony* and *Concord* of both is *Vertue*, one rightly commanding, the other obeying.

Expetible is that which attracteth the *Appetite* to it self; avoidable, that which repelleth it, Reason consenting thereto. Expetible and good were by the Ancients esteemed the same; for they affirm'd Good to be that which all desire.

Of Goods, they say some are expetible *for themselves*, some for *others*; the first are either *honest* or *necessary*. Honest are the *Vertues* and their Functions; necessary, *Life*, and those things which pertain unto it, as the Body with its parts and uses; and those which are call'd External Goods; as *Riches, Peace, Glory, Liberty, Friendship*, for each of these conferreth to the use of *Vertue*.

Beatitude consisteth of Good and successful Actions; wherefore it is wholly good, as playing upon Pipes is wholly artificial; for the use of the matter doth not take away the Goodness from Beatitude; as the use of Instruments taketh not away from the Art of Medicine. Such things as are made use of towards this perfection, are not to be reckoned as Parts; for they, without which the Action cannot be, are not rightly parts thereof; for parts conduce to the whole, the rest conduce to the End.

Good is divided into *Honest, Profitable*, and *Pleasant*; these are the Scopes of all Actions. Beatitude consists of all these. It is *the use of perfect Vertue, in perfect Life, with prosperous Success*; and the *Function of perfect Life according to Vertue*; *and the use of Vertue according to Nature, without any Impediment.*

Tho' some assert that the *End* is to be happy, and Beatitude the *scope*, as Riches are good, and to be Rich that which is behoveful; yet is it better to follow the Antients, who assert the End to be that for whose sake all things are, it self not being for the sake of any other; or the ultimate of things expetible; or Life according to vertue, in corporeal and external goods, either in all or the most principal.

This being the greatest good, useth the Ministry of the rest; for as those things which confer hereunto are to be esteemed Goods, so those things which resist it, are indifferents; for every good Action doth not effect Beatitude.

They assert *Beatitude* to be the *use of perfect Vertue*, as holding some Vertues to be *perfect*, others *imperfect*. The perfect are *Justice* and *Integrity*; the Imperfect are *Ingenuity* and *Progression*. The perfect agreeth with the perfect, so as the end thereof is the function of that Vertue, whereof no part is wanting.

They added *perfect Life* to shew that Beatitude is in Men of full Age, for a young man is imperfect, and so is his Life. Beatitude therefore is in perfect time, the longest that is appointed for us by the Gods. As one verse makes not a Poem, nor one step a Dance, nor one Swallow a Summer; so neither doth a short time confer Beatitude, for Beatitude is perfect, and requireth a perfect Man and Time.

They added *successful Function of Vertue*, because the Goods of Nature are necessarily requisite to Beatitude; for a good Man may exercise vertue in misery, but cannot be happy. For as *Vertue* is the only Efficient of *honest* Actions, so is *Beatitude* of *honest, good and excellent*. Neither doth it abide amongst ill or unhappy things, but enjoyeth the good, nor is deprived of the contemplation of good, or the conveniences of Life.

Beatitude being the most pleasant and fairest of things, encreaseth like an Art by the multitude of its Instruments. It is not the same in God and Man, neither is it equal amongst good Men, for it may sometimes be taken away by oppression of miseries. Hence it is to be doubted whether a Man may be termed happy as long as he is alive;

alive, considering the uncertainty of Fortune; whence *Solon* said, *Consider the end of a long Life, whether it be happy.*

Those who sleep, are not participant of Beatitude, but after some manner, as the function of the Soul is capable of awaking.

Lastly, they added *Nature*, because every waking of good Men is not the use of perfect Vertue, but only that which is according to Nature, that is, free from madness; for madness as well as sleep depriveth Men of use, and of this Reason, and maketh them like Brutes.

As Beatitude is said to be the use of Vertue, so is Misery of Vice; yet not so, that as this sufficeth to Misery, so that doth to Beatitude.

Life is made sour and unpleasant to the Good by excessive Adversity, to the Ill even in Prosperity, because they sin more, nor can rightly be termed happy.

Having asserted Beatitude to be the chief Good, it followeth that we expound how many ways it is taken.

Good is understood *three* ways. First, for that which is the cause of Preservation to all beings; next, for that which is predicated of every good thing. Lastly, for that which is expetible in it self. The first is *God*; the second the *Genus* of Goods; the third, the *end*, to which all are referred, Beatitude.

That which is expetible in it self, is said *three* ways, either that for which something is done; or, for which all things are done; or, some part of these.

Again, of these, some are *final*, some *efficient* : Final, are the actions proceeding according to Vertue; efficient, the materials of expetible things.

Of Goods, some are *Honourable*, some *Laudable*, some *Faculties*, some *profitable*. Honourable, as *God*, our *Prince*, *Parent*: Laudable, as *Riches*, *Empire*, *Liberty*: Profitable, the efficient, as *Health*.

Again, of things good and expetible, some are expetible *in themselves*, some for others; in themselves, as the *Honourable*, *Laudable*, and *Faculties*; for others, as the *Profitable*, which effect and conserve other things.

Again, of things good in themselves, some are *ends*, others *not ends*; Ends, as *Justice*, *Vertue*, *Health*, and whatsoever consisteth of these; Not ends, as *Ingenuity*, *Memory*, *Learning*.

Again, of Goods, some are *wholly* perfect, others *not*; of the first are *Vertue* and *Prudence*, which benefit all; of the latter, *Riches* and *Power*, which require to be used by a good Man. The same things whereof a good Man maketh right use, a wicked Man abuseth, as the same which a good Musician useth well, he who is ignorant of Musick useth amiss. Whosoever maketh ill use of any thing, is hurt thereby; as, a good Horse, which is a help to him that knoweth how to Ride, hurts the unskilful Rider.

Again, of Goods, some are in the *Soul*, some in the *Body*, some *External*: In the Soul are *Ingenuity*, *Art*, *Vertue*, *Wisdom*, *Prudence*, *Pleasure*; in the Body, *Health*, *soundness of Sense*, *Beauty*, *Strength*, *soundness of Limbs*, and all *Parts*, with their *Faculties* and *Functions*. External are *Riches*, *Glory*, *Nobility*, *Power*, *Friends*, *Kindred*, *Country*. The goods of the Soul are either conferred by *Nature*, as *Wit* and *Memory*; or acquir'd by *diligence*, as the *Liberal Sciences*; or fall into perfection, as *Prudence*, *Justice*, and lastly, *wisdom*.

Again of Goods, some may be both *obtained* and *lost*, as *Riches*; some obtained, but not lost; as *Felicity* and *Immortality*: Some lost, but not obtained, as *Sense* and *Life*; some neither obtained nor lost, as *Nobility*.

Again, of Goods, some are *only* expetible in themselves, as Pleasure and Indolence, some efficient *only*, as Riches: Some *both* efficient and expetible in themselves, as Vertue, Friends, Health.

Goods are divided more ways than these, as not belonging all to one *Genus*, but to all the ten Categories.

These things laid down, we come next to speak moe accurately concerning Vertue, which they place in both parts of the Soul: In the *Rational* part, *Integrity*, *Prudence*, *Wisdom*, *Memory*, and the like: In the *Irrational* part, *Temperance*, *Justice*, *Fortitude*, and other Vertues. These (say they) may be extinguished by excess, which they prove by testimony of the Senses, as things obscure by manifest. For, as by excess or defect of Exercise, *Health* is corrupted, but by moderate exercise is preserv'd: In like manner is it in *Temperance*, *Fortitude*, and other Vertues. For, as we do call him who feareth the Thunder, mad, not valiant; so on the contrray, he who feareth Shadows is a Coward: But, he is valiant who neither feareth all things, nor nothing. These things encrease or extinguish Vertue: Being moderate, they encrease Courage: being too great, or too little, they extinguish it.

In like manner are all other Vertues extinguished by *excess* or *defect*, encreased by *mediocrity*.

Neither is Vertue only limited by these, but by *Pleasure* and *Grief* likewise, in as much as for pleasure we commit Wickedness, and for grief shun good. To explain this more fully, they unfold the nature of the Soul, wherein are seen three things, *Passions*, *Faculties*, *Habits*: *Passions*, as Anger, Fear, Hate, Love, Emulation, Pity, and the lik: To which is subsequent *Pleasure* or *Grief*. *Faculties*, by which we make use of passions, and are angry, do emulate, and the like. *Habits* are those from which the Functions of these proceedeth rightly, or otherwise. If any Man be so disposed, that he is any upon any occasion, he hath the habit of *Anger*; if so, as to be angry upon no occasion, he hath the habit of *Stupidity*, both which are blameable. The laudable Habit is that of *Meekness*, by which we are angry in due time and place. Vertues therefore are Habits, by which the Functions of passions become laudable.

All Vertue consisteth in Action; all action is continuous. Whatsoever things are continuous, like magnitude, have excess, defect, and mediocrity, either in relation to one another, or to us. The mean, relating to us, is in all the best, (this is not quantitative, but qualitative, and therefore is perfect; whereas the extreams, excess and defect, being contrary, are repugnant to one another, and to the mean. But the mean is to both extreams, (as equality is to inequality, greater than the least, less than the greatest.) Vertue therefore is a deliberative Habit, consisting in mediocrity, relating to our selves. *Theo-*

Theophrastus having laid down some qualities, (following his Master) endeavoureth to conclude from each of them: The examples he alledgeth are these: Temperance, Intemperance, Stupidity, Meekness, Wrath, Indolence, Fortitude, Boldness, Timidity, Justice, Liberality, Prodigality, Avarice, Magnanimity, Pusilanimity, Arrogance, Magnificence, Ostentation. For of these Habits, some are ill, through excess or defect. Others good through mediocrity. He is not *temperate* who desireth nothing, nor he who desireth all things; one like a Stone, desireth not even natural expetibles; the other thro' excessive desire, becommeth Intemperate. He only is temperate, who desireth honest things with reason, in due time and measure. He is not *meek* who is angry upon all occasions, nor he who is angry upon none; but he who is endued with the mean Habit. He is not *valiant* who feareth nothing, not God himself; nor he who feareth all things, even his own Shadow. Nor *Just* who either assumeth or derogateth too much from himself, but who observeth equality. He is not *liberal* who giveth away all, nor he who giveth nothing, nor *magnanimous*, who esteemeth himself worthy all great things, nor he who esteemeth himself worthy none; but he who observeth a Decorum. He is not *magnificent* who is splendid every where, nor he who no where; but who observes due time and place.

Thus the Genus of Vertues is placed in *Mediocrity*, and mutually consequent in it self; yet, not alike in all, for Prudence is consequent to the rest in its own proper nature; the rest are consequent to it by accession; for he who is just, must necessarily be wise, but not on the contrary.

Of Passions and Appetites, some are *good*, some *bad*, some *mean*; the good are *Friendship, benevolence, indignation, shame, confidence, compassion*; the bad, *envy, malevolence, contumely*; the mean, *grief, fear, anger, pleasure, desire*.

Every Passion is conversant in Pleasure and Grief, for which reason the Vertues depend upon them; but *love of Money, love of Pleasure, love-Melancholy*, and the like, are habits distinct from Vices.

Of *Love*, one kind is of *Friendship*, another of *Conjunction*, the third of *both*. The first is good, the second bad, the third mean.

Of Friendship there are *four* kinds: *Sodality, Affinity, Hospitality, Erotick*: Whether that of *Beneficence*, and that of *Admiration* be to be added to these, is doubtful. The first is derived from *conversation*; the second from *nature*; the third from *cohabitation*; the fourth from *affection*, the fifth from *good-will*; the last from some *faculty*. Of all these, there are in general three ends, honest, profitable, and pleasant: All Persons that are studious of Friendship aim at one or more of these ends. The first Friendship is that which every Man hath to himself; the next to his Parent; the rest to his Friends and Neighbours: Whence excess in the first, and defect in the rest ought to be avoided; that being esteemed *self-Love*, this *reservedness*.

χάρις is taken three ways, for a profitable benefit, or for the profitable return of a benefit, or for the remembrance of a benefit. It is placed likewise in the Face and Speech, whence a Man is termed *gracious*, ἐυχαρις, ἐπιχαρις:

A good Man must lead a Life conjoined with Vertue, whether according to the necessity of the times, he execute the office of a Magistrate, or cohabit with Princes, or impose Laws, or govern some other part of the Common-wealth. If he be not busied in any of these, he must addict himself to a popular Life, either by Contemplation, or Action, or (which is between both) Instruction. For tho' he ought to follow the Action and Contemplation of excellent things; yet if the time will not allow him to use both, he may make choice of one, and prefer the Contemplative life, yet not neglecting the Common-wealth. He shall therefore marry, to the end he may have issue, and addict himself to chaste Love, and as occasion requireth, drink Wine freely, and finally maintain his Life by due observance of Vertue, and be ready to resign it, if there be necessity, taking care to be buried in his own Country, according to the Rites thereof.

Thus there are three kinds of Life, the *active*, and *contemplative*, and that which consists of *both*. As the voluptuous is esteem'd beneath the dignity of a Man, so is the contemplative preferr'd before the rest. A good Man shall addict himself to the Government of the Commonwealth, by choice not chance; for the active Life is conversant in civil Affairs, That Life is best which is led according to Vertue and Nature; the next is that which is a mean condition, as to both; these are both expetible. But the life which is conjoyned with Vice is to be avoided. A *happy life* differs from a *Good* in this. The happy is always consonant to Nature, the good sometimes repugnant to Nature. To the first, Vertue only is not requisite; to the other, it is requisite. A *mean* Life is that which is placed in mediocrity, not destitute of Offices. *Rectitudes* in life are according to Vertue, *Sins* according to Vice: *Offices* in the mean kind of Life.

To these things thus declared we must add, that Vertue is a habit desiring mean Pleasures and Griefs, pursuing that which is honest, as it is honest: Vice is the opposite hereto.

Wisdom is the Science of the first Causes.

Prudence a habit examining and acting good things, as they are good.

Fortitude a habit betwixt *boldness* and *Fear*.

Meekness is a mean betwixt wrath and *stupidity*.

Liberality is a mean betwixt *Prodigality* and *Penuriousness*.

Magnanimity is in the mean betwixt *Arrogance*, and *Pusillanimity*.

* *Magnificence* is the mean betwixt *Ostentation* and *sordidness*.

Indignation is the mean betwixt *Envy* and *Malevolence*.

Gravity is the mean betwixt *Assentation* and *Contradiction*.

Modesty is the mean betwixt *Impudence* and *Bashfulness*.

Urbanity is the mean betwixt *Scurrility* and *Rusticity*.

† *Friendship* is the mean betwixt *dotage* and *enmity*.

Truth is the mean betwixt *detraction* and *boasting*.

Justice is the mean betwixt *excess* and *defect*.

There are other Vertues, part ranked by themselves, part under the former. As under Justice

* For the Text doubtless is defective, and thus to be supplied, μεγαλοπρέπειαν δὲ μεσότητα [ἑαυτοῦ] βαναυσίας κ̀ μικροπρεπείας. Νέμεσιν δὲ μεσότητα [αὐτὴν] φθόνου καὶ ἐπιχαιρεκακίας. See Arist. Nicom. 4. 2 and Mag. mor. 1.28.

† But Arist. otherwise placing Friendship betwixt Arrogation and Derogation.

Justice are, εὐσέβεια, ὁσιότης, χρησότης, εὐκοινωνησία, εὐσυναλλαξία, under Temperance εὐκοσμία, εὐταξία, αὐτάρκεια, εὐψυχία, φιλοπονία, defined thus.

Εὐσέβεια, is a habit of Worshipping the Gods and Demons, a mean betwixt *Atheism* and δαισιδαιμονία.

Ὁσιότης, a Habit of observing Right towards the Gods and the Dead, a mean betwixt ἀνοσιότης, and something that wants a name.

Χρησότης, a Habit of doing well voluntarily for their own sakes: a mean betwixt πονηρία, and something that wants a name.

Εὐκοινωνησία, a habit, rendring men grateful in Society, a mean betwixt ἀκοινωνησία, and something that wants a name.

Εὐσυναλλαξία, a habit avoiding injustice in Contracts: a mean betwixt ἀσυναλλαξία, and something that wants a name, which pertaineth to *extream right*.

Ἐυκοσμία, a habit of observing order, a mean between Ἀταξία, and something that wants a name.

Αὐτάρκεια, a habit liberally content with the present, a mean betwixt πλεονεξία, and πολυτέλεια.

Ἐυψυχία, a habit of sustaining grievous things unconquered, a mean betwixt ἀψυχία, and δεισμανιότης.

Φιλοπονία, a habit performing excellent things indefatigbaly, a mean betwixt μαλακία, and ματαιοπονία.

Lastly, *Probity* is a virtue consisting of all the rest; it is perfect, as well because it rendreth good things honest and profitable, as for that it desireth honest things for their own sake.

CHAP. II.

OECONOMICK.

Having thus explained the Virtues and the chief Heads of *Ethick*, it remaineth that we speak of *Oeconomick* and *Politick*, for as much as Man is by nature a *Civil Creature*. The first Commonwealth is the lawful congression of man and woman, for procreation of Children, and Society of Life. This is called Οἶκος, a *Family*, it is the ground and beginning of a City. A Family seemeth to be a little City, for Marriage being contracted, and Children growing up one under another, and joyn'd one to another, there is deduced another Family, and so a third, and a fourth. Of these is constituted Neighbourhood and a *City*, for many Neigbourhoods make us up a City. Thus as a Family hath in it the seeds of a City, so likewise of a Common-wealth, for in a Family there are the prints of *Monarchy*, an *Aristocracy*, and a *Democracy*. The Society between Parents and Children represents a Monarchy; that betwixt man and Woman an Aristocracy, as being contracted for issue, mutual comfort and assistance. To these is added a *Servant*, appointed to be such by Nature, able for Service; but not to live of himself, requiring therefore a Master to Govern him. Of all these reduced to a community is constituted a *Family*.

The Government of a Family is by Nature given to *Men*, for the Counsel of *Women* is weaker; *Children* are not yet arrived to it, *Servants* never can. The whole ordering therefore of a Family depends upon the Man; the whole prudence of *Oeconomy* therefore is in Man: This is partly *Paternal*, partly *Nuptial*, partly *Herile*, partly *Acquisitive*. For, as an Army requireth *Provision*, a City, *Merchandise*, Art, *Instruments*; so a Family Necessaries, as well for common life as convenience. Of these the Master of the Family takes the first care, how honestly to encrease his Revenues, and moderate his expences. He, as being the head of the Family, ought to be skilful in many things, as in *Agriculture*, *Grasing*, *Metals*, whereby he may advantage himself without doing injury to others. Of Acquisition there are two kinds, one better than the other; that by *Nature*, this by *Art*.

CHAP. V.

POLITICK.

Thus much concerning *Oeconomick*; we come next to speak in short of *Politick*.

First then, *Cities* are constituted as well for the natural propensity of man to society, as for utility. A City is the most perfect Society. A Citizen is he who is concern'd in the Magistracy. A City is a compleat number of such persons, which proceedeth so far, as that it be not a disagreeing within it self, not contemptible, but may conveniently provide for life, and defend it self against enemies.

Oeconomical prudence is one kind, *Legislative* anothe, *Political* a third, *Military* a fourth.

A City is Governed either by one man, or some few, or all; and each of these either rightly, or unjustly: Rightly, when the Princes respect the common good; unjustly, when they consider their own private Interest. The right are *Monarchy*, *Aristocracy*, *Democracy*; the unjust, *Tyranny*, *Oligarchy*, *Ochlocracy*. There is also a mixt Government, consisting of the good kinds. And whereas a Commonwealth is often changed into better or worse; that is best which is guided according to Virtue; that worst, which is according to Vice.

They who Command, or Advise, or Judge in *Democracy*, are taken out of *all*, either by Suffrage, or Lot: In *Oligarchy*, out of the *Richer*; in *Aristocracy*, out of the *Best*.

Sedition in Cities is either according to *Reason* or *Interest*; the first, when equals are reduced to unequal extremities; the second, for Honour, Power, or Gain.

Commonwealths are overthrown either by *Force* or *Fraud*. They last longest which respect the publick utility.

Courts of *Judicature*, *Processes*, *Pleas*, and *Magistracies*, are ordered according to the forms of every Commonwealth. The most general commands are *Priesthood, Generalship, Admiralty,* ναυαρχία, ἀγορανομία, γυμνασιαρχία, γυναικονομία, παιδονομία, ἀστυνομία, ταμιεία, νομοφυλακία, περιπολαρχία, whereof some relate to Cities, others to Havens and Traffick.

The Office of a Commonwealth's-man is to reform a Commonwealth, which is much harder than to erect one; and to divide the common people into two parts, one for necessary Offices, the other for convenient: *Mechanicks, Husbandmen,*

men, and *Merchants* are for the necessary sort, continually serving the Commonwealth; but *Soldiers* and *Councellors*, who are Servants for Virtue, and perform Noble things, are the more excellent.

Old Men are most proper to be Councellors, and also Priests to perform the Sacred Rites; young men for War. This order is exceeding ancient, first constituted by the *Ægyptians*, who, amongst other things excellently disposed, appointed the Temples of the Gods to be built in the highest places, and the Lands of private persons to be disposed, partly at the confines of the Country, partly near the City, whereby both parts of the Country should meet in Tribute and Tax. They likewise well ordered the institution of *Sodalities*, and a publick care for the Education of Children, and that those who are too young or too old, should not Marry, to prevent their having weak Children. Likewise, that nothing mixt be taken away, nothing perfect exposed, abortion not procured. Thus much of *Politick*.

THE FOURTH PART.

CHAP. I.

Of METAPHYSICKS.

THE *Fourth* and last part of *Philosophy*, which treateth of *Ens* in general, is by *Aristotle* termed sometimes, *First*, *Philosophy*, sometimes *Wisdom*, sometimes *Theology*, by his *Followers* and *Interpreters* called *Metaphysick*, from the order thereof, as *Alexander Aphrodisæus* and *Philoponus* affirm; being placed after *Physick*, as treating of a less known, and more Noble Object.

Upon this Subject there are fourteen Books of *Aristotle* Extant, which, saith *Alexander Aphrodisæus*, by the method of the discourse and style, are easily evinced to be his.

a Metaphyf. lib. 6. cap. 1.
b Lib. 4. cap. 2.

a *Metaphysick* considereth *Ens* as it is *Ens*, and the primary cause thereof. b *Ens* is Analagous, prædicated primarily of substance, which is one essence; of Accidents, not simply, but in regard of their common attribution to substance. *Ens* thus being one analogically, the Science thereof is one likewise; but it treateth chiefly of substance, because that is the first essence upon which the rest depend, and from which they are denominated.

CHAP. VI.

Of the first Principle.

Cap. 3.

Cap. 4. 5.

THE first most common Axiom, or complex principle is this, *It is impossible that the same thing should be, and not be, in the same, and according to the same respect.*

To this principle, all demonstrations and opinions are reduced. It is it self indemonstrable, as being the first; otherwise there would be an infinite progression in demonstration. There is nothing more known by which it may be proved, no greater absurdity than the denial of it, that an Adversary can be reduced to.

With the first negative principle, the first affirmative hath a near affinity. *It is necessary that every thing be predicated affirmatively or negatively of another.* It is not true in matter of a future contingent determinately, but only indeterminately. This affirmative principle therefore is not absolutely the first, yet it is true; neither can there be a medium betwixt contradictory propositions, no more than betwixt even and uneven number; every proposition either affirms or denies, therefore every proposition is either true or false; between these there is no medium.

a Cap. 7.

CHAP. III.

Of Substance and Accident.

a OF *Ens* in general there are three divisions; first, by *Accident* and *per se*; secondly, *Potentially* and *Active*; thirdly, *Intentional* and *Real*.

a Lib. 6. cap. 2.

Of *Ens by Accident*, there is no Science, for it is in a manner *Non ens*, it hath no cause *per se*, it is not generated or corrupted *per se*; it is not always, nor for the most part, nor necessary, whereas Science is of things contrary to these.

b *Ens per se*, is divided into ten *Categories*. The first is *Substance*, and the first *Ens*, and consequently the first *Category*, for it is predicated *in quid* of the first subject, whereas Accidents are predicated *in quale* or *quantum*. Again, Substance only is *Ens per se*, Accidents are *Ens*, as they are Affections of Substance. Substance is the first *Ens*, by *Reason* or *Definition*, because Accidents are defined by Substance. By *Knowledge*, because the Knowledge of Accidents depends on the Knowledg of Substance. By *Time*, for there is some Substance without Accident, as God and Intelligences, but there is no Accident without a Substance. Likewise material Substances are prece-

b Lib. 7. cap. 1.

precedent in Time, at least to some Accidents, which arrive unto them after they have sometime generated. And lastly, by *Nature*, for the Subject is, by Nature, before that which inhereth in it. Hence this part of Physick treateth only of Substance.

c Cap. 3.   *c* Subject or Substance is three-fold; *Matter, Form, Compositum.* The two latter are more *Ens,* than Matter, tho' Matter be truly Substance, as being the first and last Subject which remaineth, tho' all the Affections of a Body be taken away. This is first Matter, which in it self is neither compleat Substance, nor Quantitative, nor in any other *Category.* Neither is it first Substance, for that is separable, and may exist by its own power without others. That is likewise a determinate, perfect, singular Substance; but Matter cannot be separated from Form, neither is it singular or determinable.

d Cap. 4.   *d* Form is that which the thing it self is said to be, *per se*, τὸ τί ἦν εἶναι, *The being of a thing what it was,* the whole common Nature and Essence of a Thing, answerable to the Definition. Compound sensible Substances have a proper Definition; but *Ens by Accident*, consisting of Subject and Accident, hath not, tho' it may be by Accident described and explained. Even *Categorical* Accidents being one *per se*, and of one Nature, have a *Quiddity* and Definition, not simple, as Substances, but after their own manner.

e Cap. 8.   *e Matter* and *Form* are not properly generated, but the whole *Compositum*, whereto *Idea's* [separate Substances] confer nothing, neither as efficient, nor exemplary Causes.

f Cap. 10.   *f* The common substantial, or formal parts of the thing defined, are to be put into the Definition of the whole; but the material parts of the *Individuum* it self, must not.

CHAP. VI.

Of Power and Act.

a Lib. 9. cap. 9.   *a* Next *Substance*, we come to *Power* and *Act.* Power is either *Active* or *Passive:* Active Power is *the Principle of changing other Things, or acting on another, in as much as it is another.* Passive Power is in a manner the same with Active, for the motion of Passion and Action is really the same, neither can one be without the other, tho' simply they are diverse, being in different Subjects, Passive in the Patient, Active in the Agent.

b Cap. 2.   *b* Of Powers, some are void of Reason, as the Power of warming; some *Rational*, as Arts. The Rational are of Contraries, as Medicine is of Health and Sick; the Irrational of one only, as Heat produceth Heat.

c Cap. 3.   *c* The Power (contrary to the *Megarick* Philosophers, followers of *Zeno*) remains, although not reduced to Act; for we call a Man *Architect,* tho' he be not actually employed in Building. Again, Animals have Sense, even when they are not in Act. Thirdly, it were impossible any thing could be, which were not actually. *Possible* is that whose Power, if it were reduced to Act, would not imply any impossibility.

d They are mistaken, who think there is *d Cap. 6.* any thing possible, which shall never actually be, or that there are Powers whose Acts are impossible; for hence it would follow, that all things should be possible, nothing impossible. *Possible* is that which doth or may follow from some Power; if it never followeth, or cometh out of that Power, it is impossible. That which is possible therefore, must at some time or other be in Act.

e Of Powers there are three kinds, some *e Cap. 5.* *Natural*, as senses; some *acquired* by *Custom*, as playing on a Pipe; some by *Discipline*, as Arts. The two last require previous Operations; the natural do not. Natural and Irrational Powers are necessarily reduced to Act, when the Agent and Patient are at a due distance, and there is nothing betwixt to hinder them. The rational Powers are not so, for they are free to Act or not to Act as they please.

f Act is, when the thing that was in power *f Cap. 6.* is otherwise than when it was in power.

g All Act is before Power, and before all *g Cap. 8.* Nature which is contained under Power, by *Reason, Essence* and *Time. By Reason,* because Power is defined by Act. *By Time,* because tho Power be temporal before Act in the same numerical Object; for a Man may first be learned, before he actually be such; yet, in different things of the same species, Act is ever before Power in time; for nothing can be made or reduced from Power, unless by an Agent actually existent.

Lastly, Act is before Power *in Essence*; first, because it is later in Generation; for Generation beginneth from the imperfect State of a Thing, and proceedeth to the perfect. Now all Generation proceedeth from Power to Act. Secondly, Act is the end of Power; but the end, as it is later in Generation, so it is more perfect by Nature, and first in Intention.

CHAP. V.

Of True and False.

a The first Division of *Ens* is into Intentional *a Lib. 6. cap. 2.* and *Real.* *b* The Intentional is either *b Lib. 9. cap. 10.* *true* or *false.* The Intellect asserteth *truly*, if its judgment be conformable to the thing; *falsly*, if not conformable, for there is composition and division in the things themselves, as well as in the Intellect. Whence if the Intellect compound things by Affirmation, as they are really compounded; or divide them by Negation, as they are really divided, it asserteth truly, otherwise falsly. True and false are in the *simple* apprehension of things, but simply, not enunciatively, so as that truth is nothing but a simple perception of the Object: falshood a non-perception or ignorance thereof, tho' ignorance be not properly falsity. Whence simple apprehension may be true in it self, false it cannot be, for falsity requireth composition.

Complex Truth and Falshood may be of the same separate substances.

He cannot be deceived in the knowledge of things *immoveable*, whosoever hath once conceived them *immutable*; for either he will judge always truth, or always err, because things immovable are always in the same manner. The vicissitude and deception, and true and false judgment, is only in things contingent and mutable.

CHAP. XVI.

Of One, the Same, and Diverse.

Cap. 2. ONE is an affection of *Ens*, not a substance as *Pythagoras* and *Plato* affirmed, but a *Categoreme*, prædicated of every thing as it is *Ens*. To *one* is opposite *many*, by *privative* opposition, and therefore one is manifested by many, as indivisible by divisible, the privation by the habit. For divisible is more known to sense than indivisible, and multitude than unity. To *one* are referred *the same, equal, like*; to *many, divers, unequal, unlike*.

b Cap. 3. *b* Things are *diverse* either by *Genus* or *Species*: by *Genus* those which have not the same matter, or a mutual Generation; or whereof one pertains to *corruptible* substance, the other to *incorruptible*. By *Species*, those which have the same *genus*. Genus is that wherein those things that are diverse are said to be the same according to substance.

CHAP. VII.

Of Immortal, Eternal, and Immoveable Substances.

a Lib.12 or 14. cap. 6. *a* SUbstance is threefold, two kinds, *natural*, whereof one is *corruptible*, as *Animal*; the other *sempiternal*, as Heaven. The third is *immoveable*.

That there is a perpetual immoveable substance, is proved thus. Substances are first *Ens*, therefore if all substances are corruptible, all things likewise must be corruptible; which is false, for there is an eternal local *motion*, circular, proper to Heaven, which it is not possible should have had a beginning, or shall have a dissolution, no more than time. If therefore *Time* be eternal, as motion, there must necessarily be some incorruptible and eternal substance, not only that wherein that eternal motion exists, the Heaven it self; but one substance, which so moveth, that tho' it remain its self moveable, yet it moveth others from eternity to eternity, not having only the power of moving, but being continually in the act of motion. For *Plato* and the rest, who conceived God to have done nothing for a great while, err, because that power were frustraneous which were not reduced to act. Besides, motion would not have been eternal, unless the moving substance were not only eternal, and in perpetual actual motion; but such likewise, that it could not but it must move always, as being a pure act void of power.

Hence the substances which cause eternal motion, are void of matter, for they move from an eternal act, and are void of all power.

In things that sometimes are, sometimes are not, power is precedent to act, but simply and absolutely act is precedent to power. For, neither things natural or artificial are reduced from power to act, but by something that actually exists. Now if the same thing always return by a circular motion, it necessarily followeth, that there is something eternal which remaineth ever the same, and operateth in the same manner. Such an eternal first moving substance is the first Heaven. The vicissitude of *Generation* and *Corruption* is not caused by the first Heaven, for that moveth always in the same manner, but by the inferior Orbs, especially the Sun, which by his accession bringeth life, by his recession death to all things mortal.

Thus is the first Heaven *eternal*, for it is moved with eternal motion; besides which there is something which always moveth, and is never moved it self, and is *eternal*, and *substance*, and *act*.

CHAP. VIII.

Of GODS.

Cap. 7. THis *first mover*, moveth in the same manner as things appetible and intelligible, that is, it so moveth others, as it self remaineth immoveable. The motion of the first Agent, as it is the first efficient cause, consisteth in that influence thereof, whereby it concurreth effectively with the inferior intelligences in moving its own Orb. Wherefore the efficience of the first mover is an application of the powers of the inferior movers to their proper works, wherein he concurreth with them actively, and independently. Thus the intelligences move the Heavens, not for the generation of inferior things (for the end must be more noble than the means) but for that chief and amiable good, whereunto they endeavour to be like, as their ultimate end.

The first mover is void of *mutation*, an *Ens*, wholly and simply necessary, and consequently the principle of all. Upon this first principle depend Heaven and Nature, because without him, their ultimate end and first efficient, nothing can be, or be operated.

This first mover, *God*, enjoyeth the most perfect life: perpetual and most pleasant, which absolute felicity is proper to him: for as much as he understandeth and contemplateth himself with infinite delight. For, as we are happy in contemplation that lasts but a little while, so is God most happy, in the infinite and most per-contemplation of himself, who is of all things most admirable.

God is *an eternal living being, the best of beings, an immoveable substance, separate from sensible things, void of corporeal quantity, without parts, and indivisible*; for such must that principle or substance be which moveth in infinite time. Nothing finite hath infinite power. All magnitude must be either *finite* or *infinite*. Finite magnitude cannot move in infinite time; infinite magnitude there is not, as we proved in the *Physick*.

God is *impassible, not subject to alteration*; the first local motion, which is the circular, not being compatible to God, because he is immoveable, it followeth that other motions that induce passion or alteration, and are later than local motion, cannot likewise be competent to him.

CHAP.

CHAP. IX.

Of Intelligence.

a Cap. 8.

BEsides this *first Substance* the mover of the first Heaven, there must likewise be other substances separate from matter, eternal and immoveable, president over the motions of the inferior Orbs; so that after what number and order those Orbs are disposed, according to the same are these external moving, and immovable substances ordered.

From the number of the *motions* may be collected the number of the Spheres, and consequently of the substances moving, which according to *Aristotle* are 47.

Heaven is numerically *one*, because the first mover is one. It is an ancient Tradition that these first substances that move the Heavens are *Gods*. This Opinion is truly Divine; but what is added, that they had the shape of Men, or some other Animal, was only invented for perswasion of the common People, for the use of Laws, and the convenience of Life. Thus much may serve for a short view of his *Metaphysicks*.

THEOPHRASTUS.

CHAP. I.

His Country, Parents, Masters.

* De Exil.
a Lib. 13.

THeophrastus succeeded *Aristotle*, he was born at *Erestus*, (as ** Plutarch, Laertius*, and others affirm) a Sea-Town of *Lesbos*, seated upon a Hill, as *a Strabo* describes it, distant from *Sigrium* 18 *Stadia*.

b Laert.
c Suid.

His Father was named *Melantes*, as *b Athenodorus* affirmeth, according to *c* others, *Leo*, by profession a *Fuller*. *Theophrastus* was first called *Tyrtamus*. He heard *Leucippus* in his own Country, afterwards went to *Plato*, and lastly became an Auditor of *Aristotle*, who changing the roughness of his Name, called him, as *Suidas* saith, *Euphrastus*, afterwards *Theophrastus*, from the Divine Eloquence of his Speech, wherein (as *Cicero, d Pliny, Laertius, e Strabo*, and others aver) he excelled all the rest of his Disciples.

d Præf. lib. 1.
e Lib. 13.

f Laert.

f He was likewise so quick of apprehension, that what *Plato* had said of *Aristotle* and *Xenocrates*, *Aristotle* applied to him and *Calisthenes*. *Theophrastus* was acute to admiration, ready to apprehend every thing that he taught; *Calisthenes* was dull: So that one needed a Bridle, the other a Spur.

CHAP. II.

His Profession of Philosophy, and Disciples.

a Laert. Suid.

ARistotle retiring to *Chalcis*, in the 2d. year of the 114th. Olympiad *a* being importuned by his Disciples to appoint a Successor, made choice of *Theophrastus* (as hath been already related in the Life of *Aristotle*) who thereupon undertook the Government of the School, and *Aristotle* dying, lived in his Garden, *Demetrius Phalerius* cohabiting with him. This time wherein *Theophrastus* flourished, is reckoned by *b Pliny* to be about the 440th. Year from the building of *Rome*; *c* 390 Years, as *d Salmasius* rightly Reads, before that time wherein *Pliny* wrote.

b Lib.15.cap.1.
c Plin. 19. 2.
d Exerc. c. Prinian pag. 350.

e Hermippus saith, he went at certain hours to the School, neatly dressed, and there sitting down, discoursed in such manner, that he omitted no gesture suitable to the Argument whereupon he treated, so that once to express a Glutton he licked his Lips.

e Athen. lib. 1.

f In the fourth year of the 118th Olympiad, *Xenippus* being Archon, *Sophocles*, Son of *Amphiclides*, procured a Law to be made, forbidding all Philosophers to keep publick Schools, unless such only as the Senate and People should think fit to License; if any did otherwise, he should be put to Death. By this Decree, saith *Athenæus*, he Banished all the Philosophers out of the City, amongst the rest *Theophrastus*, who the year following returned, when as *Philo*, a Disciple of *Aristotle*, accused *Sophocles* for having done contrary to Law. Whereupon the *Athenians* revers'd the Decree, fined *Sophocles* five Talents, and called home the Philosophers; by which means *Theophrastus* returning, was reinstated in the School.

f Laert. Athen. deipn.

Laertius saith, there came to hear him 2000 Disciples; *Suidas* saith (if there be no mistake in the Number) 4470. of whom were *Strabo*, his Successor, *Demetrius Phalereus*, *Nichomachus*, Son of *Aristotle*, whom *Aristippus* saith, he much affected; *Erasistratus* the Physician, as some affirm, and *Menander* the Comick Poet.

CHAP. III.

His Vertues and Apothegms.

a **H**E was exceeding Learned and Studious, as *Pamphila* affirmeth.

a Laert.

b He was very liberal in conferring benefits; and a great cherisher of Learning.

b Laert.

c He made Collections of Money for the Conventions of Philosophers, not for Luxury, but for Temperance, and Learned Discourses.

c Athen. lib. 5.

d He

d Plut. adv. Colet.

d He twice freed his Country, being under the oppression of Tyrants.

e Laert.

e Cassander Son of *Antipater* much esteemed him, and *Ptolomy* the first wrote Letters to him.

f Laert.

f He was so much honoured by the *Athenians*, that *Agnonides* accusing him of Impiety, very hardly escaped from being fined himself.

a Laert.

a Of his Apothegms are remembred these. He said, It is more safe trusting to an unbridled Horse, than intemperate Speech.

b Laert.

b To a young Man at a Feast silent: If you hold your peace, saith he, because you are foolish, then you are wise; but, if you are wise, you do foolishly in holding your peace.

c Laert. Stob.

c He used to say, Of all things that are spent, time is the most precious.

d Plut. vit. Demost.

d Being demanded, as *Aristo* saith, what he thought of *Demosthenes*; he answered, he is worthy of this City; of *Demades*; he is above the City.

e Symp. l. 2.

e To *Philip* Son of *Cassander* he saith, I wonder your eyes do not make musick, the pipe of your nose coming so directly upon them.

f Plut. de Anar.

f To prove that Riches are not to be loved and admired, he instanced *Callias*, a Rich *Athenian*, and *Ismenias* a *Theban*; these saith he, use the same things, as *Socrates* and *Epaminondas*.

g Plut. de frat. amor.

g He saith we must not love Strangers, to the end we may make trial of them, but make trial of them to the end we may love them.

h Plut. de sanit. tuend.
i Stob.

h He said the Soul paid a dear Rent for her Habitation in the Body.

i He said Falshood raised from Calumny and Envy, endureth a little while, but soon perisheth.

k Stob. Ser 101.

k Seeing a young man blush, be of good comfort, saith he, that is the complexion of Virtue.

l Ser. 121.

l He used to say, stand in aw of thy self, and thou shalt not be ashamed before others.

m Ser. 136.

m He said, The good need but few Laws, for things are not accommodated to Laws, but Laws to things.

n Ser. 139.

n The Envious are more unhappy than others in this respect, that they are troubled not only at their misfortunes, but also at the good fortunes of others.

o Ser. 141.

o Being demanded what preserved humane life, he said, beneficence, reward, and punishment.

p Ser. 162.

p He said Honours are to be acquired, not by conversation and favour, but by action.

q Ser. 185.

q Being demanded what Love is, he answered, the passion of an idle Soul.

r Ser. 193.

r He said a Woman ought not to be seen her self, nor behold others richly attired, for both are inticements to dishonesty.

s Ser. 193.

s He said, Love is an excessive desire of something irrational, the entrance thereof easie, the dis-ingagement difficult.

CHAP.

CHAP. IV.

His Will and Death.

a His Will is thus delivered by Laertius,   *a Laert.*

BE all well; but if any thing happen otherwise, thus we give Order. All those Goods which belong to the House, I bequeath to Melantes and Pancreon Sons of Leo; Those which are set apart for Hipparchus, I Will be thus disposed. First, That the Study and Ornaments belonging thereunto be perfected, and if any thing may be added more to Beautifie them, that it be done. Next; that the Statue of Aristotle be set up in the Temple, and the other Donaries which were before in the Temple. Moreover, that the little Walk which is near the School be built new, not worse than it was before, and that the Maps of the World be placed in the lower Walk. That an Altar likewise be built, wanting nothing of Perfection and Splendor. I Will that the Statue of Nicomachus as big as the Life be finished; it is in Praxitele's hand; let him go on with it. Let it be placed wheresoever they shall think good, who have the disposal of the rest, and are named in my Will. Thus much for the Temple and Donaries. My Land at Stagira I bequeath to Callinus, all my Books to Neleus. The Garden and Walk, and all the Houses belonging to the Garden, I bequeath to my Friends hereafter named, that they may Exercise themselves, and Study Philosophy therein; for Men cannot always be abroad. But with Condition, that they do not Alienate it, nor pretend any Propriety thereto, but esteem it a thing Sacred in common Possessions, making use of all things therein as becometh just and loving Friends. The Persons to whom I Will that this be in Common, are, Hipparchus, Neleus, Strato, Callinus, Demotimus, Demaratus, Callisthenes, Melantes, Pancreon, and Nicippus. Let also Aristotle, Son of Midias and Pythias, if he desire to Study Philosophy, partake likewise of the same Priviledge; and let the most Ancient of the Overseers take great care of him, that he be instructed as well as is possible in Philosophy. Let us be buried in that part of the Garden, which they shall think most convenient, not erecting a Monument, or any thing that is Sumptuous over our Graves. Thus let all things be ordered according as is said; the Temple, Monument, Garden, and Walk repaired; let Pompylus, who dwelleth in them, take charge of them, and of other things as he did heretofore, for whose pains therein, let the Possessors thereof consider him. As for Pompylus and Threpta, who have been long since manumitted, and done us good Service, if there be any thing which we have bestowed upon them, or they themselves have required, as also the 2000 Drachms which I appointed to be given to them and Hipparchus, let them firmly possess it all, as I have often expressed to Melantes and Pancreon, who assented thereunto. Moreover I bestow on them Somatales and the Girl. Of my Servants, I manumit Molon and Cimon, and Parmenon; as for Manes and Callias, when they shall have lived four years in the Gardens, discharging their Office unbameably, I Will they be set at Liberty.

Of the Domestick Utensils, let the Overseers bestow on Pompylus *as many as they think fit, and sell the rest.* To Demotimus *I give* Cario; *to* Neleus, Donax; *let* Eubius *be Sold. Let* Hipparchus *give to* Callinus *3000 Drachms. And for* Melantes *and* Pancreon, *if we did not look upon* Hipparchus, *as having heretofore been very beneficial to us, and now quite Ship-wreck'd in his Fortunes, we should have appointed him a Joynt-Estate with* Melantes *and* Pancreon. *But because I conceive it were not easie for them to be joyned in the ordering of one Family with him, and that it would be more to their advantage to receive something certain from* Hipparchus, *for these Reasons let* Hipparchus *give to each of them,* Melantes *and* Pancreon, *a Talent. Let him likewise duly furnish the Overseers with all Charges necessary for the performance of the forementioned Works; which done, let* Hipparchus *be free and discharged from all Debts and Covenants to me. If any benefit come to* Hipparchus *from* Chalcis *on my behalf, let him wholly enjoy it as his own. Be these the Overseers of those things contained in my Will;* Hipparchus, Neleus, Strabo, Callinus, Demotimus, Calisthenes, Cresarchus.

Copies of the Will of Theophrastus, *Signed with his Ring, are kept; the first by* Hegesias *Son of* Hipparchus. *Witnesses,* Callipus *a* Pelanean; Philomelus, *an* Euonymean; Lysander, *an* Hybæan; Philion, *an* Alopecian. *The second* Olympidorus *hath attested by the same Persons. The third is in the hands of* Adimantus, *delivered to his Son* Androsthenes. *Witnesses,* Aimnestus *Son of* Cleobulus; Lysistratus *Son of* Phidion, *a* Thasian; Strabo *Son of* Arcesilaus, *a* Lampsacene; Thesippus *Son of* Thesippus, *of* Potters Street; Dioscorides, *Son of* Dionysius, *an* Epicephisian. *Thus (saith* Laertius*) was his Will.*

Laert.

He died old, having lived Eighty five years, his Spirits being wasted, as *Suidas* affirms, with continual Writing; and upon the Marriage of one of his Disciples, giving himself some intermission and rest, it occasioned his end.

* *Tuscul. l. 4.*

As he lay upon his Death-bed, * *Cicero* saith, *He blamed Nature for giving Harts and Crows so long Life that could do no good thereby, and to Man who could do most good, so short; whereas if Man had been allowed longer time, his life might have been adorned with the perfection of Arts and Learning.* Thus he complained, that as soon as he came within the view of these, he was taken away.

His Disciples came to him, and asked him if he had any thing to say to them; *Nothing,* saith he, *but that the life of man loseth many pleasures only for glory. When we begin to live, then we die: nothing is more unprofitable than the desire of glory. But be happy, and either give over study, for it is very laborious, or go perseverantly thro' it, for it is of great glory. The vanity of life is much greater than the benefit thereof. But, I have not time to advise you what to do; do you consider at leisure what is best for you:* In saying which words, he expired. The whole People of *Athens* followed his body on foot to the Grave.

CHAP. V.

His Writings.

HE left many *Writings,* whereof, saith *Laertius,* because they are full of all kind of Learning, I thought good to give this Catalogue.

First Analyticks 3.
Later Analyticks 7.
Of the Analysts of Syllogisms, 1.
Epitome of Analyticks 1.
Places of Deduction 2.
Agonisticks, concerning the Theory of *Eristick* Arguments.
Of the Senses 1.
To Anaxagoras 1.
Of Anaxagoras 1.
Of Anaximenes 1.
Of Archelaus 1.
Of Salt, Nitre, Allom, 1.
Of Combustibles: or, as the other Edition, of things that may be *petrified,* 2.
Of indivisible lines 1.
Of Auscultation 2.
Of Winds 1.
The differences of Virtue 1.
Of a Kingdom 1.
Of the Discipline of a King 1.
Of Lives 3.
Of old age 1.
Of the Astrology of Democritus 1.
Of Sublime things 1.
Of Apparitions 1.
Of Humour, Colour, Flesh 1.
Of the Description of the World 1.
Of Man 1.
A Collection of the Doctrines of Diog. 1.
Of Definition 3.
Erotick 1.
Another of Love 1.
Of Felicity 1.
Of Species 2.
Of the Epilepsie 1.
Of Divine Inspiration 1.
Of Empedocles 1.
Epichirems 18.
Instances 3.
Of Voluntary 1.
Epitome of Plato's *Commonwealth* 2.
Of the diversity of voice in Creatures of the same kind 1.
Of Subitaneous Apparitions 1.
Of Biting and Blows 1.
Of Animals that are said to have Wisdom 7.
Of those which dwell in dry places 1.
Of those which change colour 1.
Of those which dwell in Caves 1.
Of Animals 7.
Of Pleasure according to Aristotle 1.
Of Pleasure, another 1.
Theses 24.
Of hot and cold 1.
Of dizziness and dimness 1.
Of sweat 1.
Of Affirmation and Negation 1.

Calisthenes, or of Grief 1.
Of Labours 1.
Of Motion 3.
Of Stones 1.
Of Pestilence 1.
Of Fainting 1.
Megarick 1.
Of Melancholy 1.
Of Metals 1.
Of Honey 1.
Of the Collections of Metrodorus 1.
Sublime Discourse 2.
Of Drunkenness 1.
Of Laws Alphabetically 24.
Epitome of Laws 10.
To Definitions 1.
Of Odours 1.
Of Wine and Oyl.
First Propositions, 18.
Legislative 3.
Politick 6.
Politick according to severl occasions 4.
Politick Customs 4.
Of the best Commonwealth 1.
Collection of Problems 5.
Of Proverbs 1.
Of Congelation and Liquefaction 1.
Of Fire 2.
Of Winds 1.
Of the Palsie 1.
Of Suffocation 1.
Of Madness 1.
Of Passions 1.
Of Signs 1.
Sophisms 2.
Of the solution of Syllogisms 1.
Topicks 2.
Of Punishment 2.
Of Hair 1.
Of Tyranny 1.
Of Water 3.
Of Sleep and Dreams 1.
Of Friendship 3.
Of Ambition 2,
Of Nature 3.
Of Physick 17.
Of the Epitome of Physicks 2.
Physicks 8.
To Natural Philosophers 1.
Of Natural Histories 10.
Of Natural Causes 1.
Of Chyles 5.
Of false Pleasure 1.
Of the Soul 1. Thesis.
Of undoubted Faith 1.
Of simple dubitations 1.
Harmonicks 1.
Of Virtue 1.
Occasions or contradictions 1.
Of Sentence 1.
Of Ridiculous 1.
Meridians 2.
Divisions 2.
Of Differences 1.
Of Injuries 1.
Of Calumny 1,
Of Praise 1.
Of Experience 1.
Epistles 3.
Of Casual Animals 1.

Of Selection 1.
Encomiums of the Gods 1.
Of Festivals 1.
Of Prosperity 1.
Of Enthymemes 1.
Of Invention 2.
Moral Disputes 1.
Moral Descriptions 1.
Of Tumult 1.
Of History 1.
Of the judgment of Syllogisms 1.
Of Flattery 1.
Of the Sea 1.
To Cassander, of a Kingdom 1.
Of Comedy 1.
Of Meteors 1.
Of Speech 1.
Collection of Words 1.
Solutions 1.
Of Musick 3.
Of Meteors 1.
Megacles 1.
Of Laws 1.
Of things contrary to Law 1.
A Collection of the Doctrines of Xenocrates.
Confabulations 1.
Of an Oath 1.
Rhetorical Precepts 1.
Of Riches 1.
Of Poesy 1.
Problems, Politick, Ethick, Physick, Erotick 1.
Proverbs 1.
Collection of Problems 1.
Of Physical Problems 1.
Of Example 1.
Of Proposition and Narration 1.
Of Poesie, another, 1.
Of the wise men 1.
Of Advice 1.
Of Solecisms 1.
Of the Art of Rhetorick 1.
Of Rhetorical Arts, 71 kinds.
Of Hypocrisie 1.
Aristotelick, or Theophrastick. Commentaries 6.
Natural Sentences 16.
Epitome of Physicks 1.
Of Gratitude 1.
Ethick Characters.
Of Falshood and Truth 1.
Of the History of Divinity 6.
Of the Gods 3.
Geometrical Histories 4.
Epitome of Aristotle, concerning Animals 6.
Epichirems 2.
Theses 3.
Of a Kingdom 2.
Of Causes 1.
Of Democritus 1.
Of Calumny 1.
Of Generation 1.
Of the Prudence and Manners of Animals 1.
Of Motion 2.
Of Sight 4.
To Definitions 2.
Of being Given 1.
Of greater and lesser. 1.

Of

Of Greater and Lesser 1.
Of Musick 1.
Of the Divine Beatitude 1.
To those of the Academy 1.
Protreptick 1.
How a City may be best Inhabited 1.
Commentaries 1.
Of the Fiery Ebullition in Sicily 1.
Of things granted 1.
Of the ways of knowing 1.
Of the Lying Argument 3.
Ante-Topick 1.
To Æschilus 1.
Astrological History 6.
Arithmetical Histories of Increase 1.
Acicharus 1.
Of Judicial Orations 1.
Epistles concerning Astycreon *to* Phanias *and* Nicanor.
Of Piety 1.

Euias 1.
Of opportunities 2.
Of seasonable discourses 1.
Of the Institution of Children 1.
Another, different 1.
Of Institution, or of Virtues, or of Temperance 1.
Protreptick 1.
Of Numbers 1.
Definitions of Syllogistick speech 1.
Of Heaven 1.
Politick 2.
Of Nature 2.
Of Fruits and Animals. All which, saith *Laertius*, amount to 1182 Divisions: These Books, as *Theophrastus* had ordered in his Will, were delivered to *Neleus.* What afterwards became of them, hath been related in the Life of *Aristotle.*

STRATO.

CHAP. I.

His LIFE.

a Laert.
b Cicer. Laert. Suid.
c Laert. Suid.
d Suid.
e Laert.
f Cic. de finib. 5.
g Plut. adv. Nat. Colot. Cic. de Nat. deoe
i Cic. de Nat. deor. 1. *Laert.*
k Cic. de fin. 5.
l Laert.

STrato *a* was Successor to *Theophrastus*. He was of *b* Lampsacum, his Father *c Arcesilaus*, or, as some, *d Arcesius*, mentioned in his Will. *e* He was a Person of great worth, Eminent, saith *Laertius*, in all kinds of Philosophy, but *especially*, in that which is called *Physick*, the *most* ancient and solid part, *f* wherein he introduced many things new, *g* dissenting not only from *Plato*, but from his Master *Aristotle.* *h* From his excellency herein he was called the *Natural Philosopher*: *i* He prescribed all Divine Power to Nature. *k* Ethick he touched but little. *l* He took upon him the government of the School, according to *Apollodorus* in the [third year of the 123 Olympiad] and continued therein eighteen years. He instructed *Ptolomy* the Son of *Philadelphus*, who bestowed eighty Talents upon him.

CHAP. II.

His Will and Death.

His Will, saith *Laertius*, was to this Effect.

THUS I order, *against the time that I shall die. All these things which are in my House, I bequeath to* Lampyrian *and* Arcesilaus. *Out of the Money which I have at Athens, let my Executors first defray the Charges of my Funeral, and the Solemn Rites after my Enterment, doing nothing superfluously, nor Niggardly.* The *Executors of these things I appoint in my Will to be these;* Olympicus, Aristides, Mnesigenes, Hippocrates, Epicrates, Gorgylus, Diocles, Lyco, Athanes. *I leave the School to* Lyco, *for the rest are either too old, or otherwise employed. All the rest shall do well if they confirm this Choice that I have made. I bequeath likewise all my Books unto him, except those which are written by our own hand, besides all Utensils, Carpets and Cups for Feasting. Let the Executors give* 500. *Drachmes to* Epicrates *and one of the servants, which* Arcesilaus *shall think goood. Let* Lampyrion *and* Arcesilaus *discharge all the debts, which* Daippus *undertook for* Hiræus. *Let nothing be owing either to* Lampyrion, *or to the Heirs of* Lampyrion, *but let him be discharged of all, and the Executors bestow on him* 500: *Drachmes, and one of the Servants, as* Arcesilaus *shall think good; that having taken much pains with us, he may have sufficient for Food, and Rayment. I manumit* Diophantus, *and* Diocles, *and* Abus. *I give* Simmias *to* Arcesilaus. *I manumit* Dromo. *When* Arcesilaus *shall come, let* Hiræus *with* Olympicus *and* Epicrates, *and the rest of the Executors cast up the Accounts of the Charges of my Funeral and other things; whatsoever is over and above; let* Arcesilaus *take it of* Olympicus, *not pressing him upon the day of payment. Let* Arcesilaus *discharge the Covenants which* Strato *made with* Olympicus, *and* Aminias, *which are in the hands of* Philocrates *Son of* Tisamenus. *As for my Tomb, let it be ordered* as Arcesilaus and Olympicus, and Lyco shall think good.

This was his *Will*, preserved by *Aristo* the *Chian*. He was of so thin and low a constituion, that he felt not any pain at his death.
Of his Name *Laertius* reckons eight.
The *first*, a Disciple of *Isocrates*.
The *second*, this Philosopher.
The *third* a Physician, Disciple of *Erasistratus*.
The *fourth* an Historian, who wrote the Wars of *Philip* and *Perseus* with the *Romans*.
The *fifth* is wanting.
The *sixth*, an Epigrammatick Poet.
The *seventh*, an ancient Physician.
The *eighth*, a Peripatetick, who lived at *Alexadria*.

CHAP. III.

*S*Uidas saith, he wrote many Books: *Laertius* gives this Catalogue of them.

Of a Kingdom 3,
Of *Justice* 3.
Of God 3.
Of Good 3.
Of *Principles* 3.
Of Lives.
Of Felicity.
Of Philosophy.
Of Fortitude.
Of Vacuum.
Of Heaven.
Of Breath.
Of Humane Nature.
Of the Generation of Animals.
Of Mixtions.
Of Sleep.
Of Dreams.
Of Sight.
Of Sense.
Of Pleasure.
Of Colour.
Of Diseases.
Of Judgments.
Of Faculties.
Of Metallick Machines.
Of Hunger and Offuscation.
Of Light and Heavie.
Of Divine Inspiration.
Of Time.
Of Aliment and Augmentation.
Of uncertain Animals.
Of Fabulous Animals.
Of Causes.
Solutions of Questions.
Proems of Places.
Of Accident.
Of More or Less.
Of Unjust.
Of Priority and Posteriority.
Of Priority of Genus.
Of Proprinm.
Of Future.
Confutations of Inventions.
Commentrries, which are suspected.
Epistles; beginning thus, *Strato* to *Arsinoe*, Health.

LYCO.

CHAP. I.

His LIFE.

*S*TRATO, saith *Laertius*, was Succeeded by *Lyco*, Son of *Astyanax* of *Troas*, an Eloquent Person, and excellent for Eduction of Children. He heard also *Panthædus* the Dialectick.

He said, that as Horses need both Bridle and Spur, so in Children there must be joyned both Modesty and Ambition. Of his florid expression is alledged this instance. Of a poor Maid he said, Βαρὺ γὰρ φορτίον παρθὶ κόρη διὰ σπάνον προικὸς ἐκτρέχουσα τὸν ἀκμαῖον τῆς ἡλικίας. A Maid is a heavie Burden to her Parents when she outruns the flowry season of her youth for want of a dower. Whence *Antigonus* said of him, That as the fragrancy and pleasantness of an excellent Apple will not admit Transplantation, so whatsoever he said was to be heard only from himself. For this sweetness of Discourse some added the letter γ 'to his name, calling him Γλύκων, which implieth *sweetness*: so * *Plutarch*.   * De Exsulio.

In Stile he was very different from himself.
Upon those who were sorry they had not learned when time was, and wished it might be recalled, he jested thus; he said, that they who endeavoured to make amends by a late penitence for their past negligence, were conscious of the impossibility of their wishes. And of those that sought to bring it to pass, he said, they had lost all Reason, in applying the nature of a strait Line to a crooked Ruler, or beholding their Face in troubled Water, or a confused Mirror.

He said, that to the wreath of publick Games in the *Forum* many aspired, to the *Olympick*, few or none.

He many times by his Counsel much advantaged the *Athenians*.

In his Garments he affected Neatness so much, that as *Hermippus* saith, he wore an upper garment very precious and fine.

He was very expert in all Exercises, active and well made for a Wrestler, being thin-ear'd and well set, as *Antigonus Carystius* affirmeth: Whence in his own Country he practised the *Elean* Games, and played at Ball.

He was intimate with *Eumenes* and *Attalus* beyond all men, who supply'd him with many things. *Antiochus* also would have had him lived with him, but could not get him.

He was so great an Enemy to *Hieronymus* the *Peripatetick*, that upon a Solemn day (of which already in the Life of *Arcesilaus*) he only forbore to come to him.

He compared Orators to Frogs, these, saith he, croak in the water, those by the water of an hour-glass.

He was Master of the School forty years, succeeding *Strato* in the 127th Olympiad, as he had given Order by his Will.

CHAP. II.

His Will and Death.

Laertius produceth a Will of his to this effect.

THUS I dispose of my Estate, if I shall not recover of this Sickness. All that is in my House I bequeath to the Brethren, Astyanax and Lyco, out of which is to be paid whatsoever I owe at Athens to any Man, as also the Charges of my Funeral and Exequies. What is in the City, and Ægina, I bestow upon Lyco, because he is of our Name, and hath lived long with us, to our great content, as one that deserved the place of a Son. The Peripatum I leave to those Friends that will make use of it, as Bulo, Callinus, Aristo, Amphio, Lyco, Pytho, Aristomachus, Heraclius, Lycomedes, Lyco, my Kinsman. Let them put him in that place who they conceive will persevere in it, and discharge it best, which let the rest of my Friends confirm for my sake, and the places. My Funeral and the Burning of my Body be so ordered by Bulo and Callinus, it be not Prodigal nor Niggardly. Out of my Estate at Ægina, let Lyco after my Death give to the Young Men as much Oyl as will serve their turns, that thereby the Memory of me and him that Honours me, may be justly preserved. Let them set up my * Statue, and choose a fit place for the setting up of it, wherein let Diophantus and Heraclides, Son of Demetrius assist them. Out of my Rents in the City, let Lyco pay all that I have named after his departure; in the next place let Bulo and Callinus, and the Expenses of my Funeral be discharged. Let that Houshold-stuff be taken away which I have left as common betwixt them. Let likewise the Physicians Pasithemis and Midas be Honoured and Rewarded for their care of me, and for their skill. To the Son of Callinus I leave a couple of Thericlean Pots; and to his Wife a couple of Goblets, and a fine Carpet, and a shaggy Carpet, and a Coverlet, and two Couch-Beds, the best that are left, that we may not seem unmindful of their due respect towards us. As for those that served me, I order thus; Demetrius, who hath been long a Free-man, I forgive the price of his Redemption, and bestow upon him five Minæ, and a Cloak and a Coat; and, as having undergone many Labours with me, let him be decently supplied with necessaries. Crito the Chelcidonian, I forgive the price of his Redemption, and bestow further on him four Minæ. Micrus also I manumit, whom let Lyco bring up, and six years hence let him instruct him. In like manner I manumit Chares, whom let Lyco also bring up; I give him two Minæ, and my Books that have been Published: The rest that have not been Published, let them be given to Callinus, and let him take diligent care for the publishing of 'em. To Syrus the Free-man I give four Minæ, and Menodora, and if he oweth me any thing, I forgive it him. To Hilara I give five Minæ, a shaggy Coverlet, two Couch-beds, a Carpet, and which Bed he shall choose. I manumit likewise the Mother of Micrus and Noemones and Dion, and Theon, and Euphranor, and Hermias; as also Agatho, after he hath served two years more; as also Ophelio and Possidonius, the bearers of my Litter, after they have served four years more, I will that they be set at Liberty. I give moreover, to Demetrius, Crito, and Syrus, to each a Bed and Coverlet, such as Lyco shall think fit. This I bestow on them, for as much as they have expressed themselves faithful in the performance of such things as were committed to their Charge. As for my Burial, whether Lyco will have it here or at home, let it be as he will; for I perswade my self, he will do what is fitting, no less than if I had done it my self. When he shall have faithfully performed these things, let the bequests of my Will remain firm. Witnesses, Callinus, an Hermionean, Aristo the Chian, Euphronius a Pæaniean.

Thus, saith *Laertius*, having wisely managed all thing appertaining to Learning and Humanity, his Prudence and Diligence extended even to the making of his Will; so that in that respect, also he deserveth studiously to be imitated.

He died 74 years old, of the Gout.

There were four of his name.

The *first*, a Pythagorean, mentioned in the Life of *Aristotle*.

The *second*, this Peripatetick.

The *third*, an Epick Poet.

The *fourth*, an Epigrammatick Poet.

* *For Wrestling and other Exercises.*

ARISTO.

a Strabo l. 10.

ARISTO Succeeded *Lyco*. He was of the Island [a] *Ceos*, famous for a Law, That whosoever exeeded 60 years of age, should be put to Death, that there might be no want of Provision for those that were more Serviceable. In former time, saith *Strabo*, it had four Cities, now there remain but two, *Julis* and *Carthæa*, into which the rest were transferred. *Pacessa* into *Carthæa*, *Caressus* into *Julis*. In *Julis Aristo* was born. He was an Auditor of *Lyco*, and Succeeded him in the Government of the *Peripatetick* School as *Cicero*, *Plutarch* and *Clemens Alexandrinus* affirm.

He was a great imitator of *Bion* the *Boristenite*. *Cicero* saith, he was neat and elegant. He wrote a Treatise of *Nilus*, cited by *Strabo*, and *Amatory Similies*, frequenty cited by *Athenæus*.

b Athen. deipn. 10.

In the second Book of his [b] *Amatory Similies*, he saith, that *Polemo* the *Academick* advised to provide such entertainment at Feasts, as should be pleasant not only at the present, but also on the morrow.

c Athen. deipn. 12.

[c] In the same Book of his *Amatory Similies*, of an Athenian well in years, named *Dorus*, who would be thought handsome, he apply'd the words of *Ulysses* to *Dolo*,

Rich Presents sure may lead away,
And thy too easie Soul betray.

d Deipn. l. 15.

[d] in the second of his *Amatory Similies*, he saith, the Ancients first bound their heads, conceiving it good against the pain caused by the vapours of the Wine, afterwards for more ornament they used Garlands.

Laertius upon the testimony of *Panætius* and *Sosicrates* affirmeth, that all the writings ascribed to *Aristo* of *Chios* the *Stoick* (except the Epistles) belong to *Aristo* the *Peripatetick*; their Titles, these,

Protrepticks 2.
Of Zeno's Doctrine: Scolastick Dialogues 6.
Of Wisdom, Dissertation 7.
Erotick Dissertations.
Commentaries upon vain-glory.
Commentaries 15.
Memorials 3.
Chrys 11.
Against Orators
Against Alexinus's oppositions.
To the Dialecticks 3.
To Cleanthes, *Epistles* 4.

CRITOLAUS.

a Lib. 16.

CRitolaus was, according to *Plutarch*, of *Phaselis*, an eminent Sea Town of *Lycia*; described by [a] *Strabo* to have three Havens, and a Lake belonging to it. He was an Auditor of *Aristo*, and Succeeded him in the School, as *Cicero*, *Plutarch*, and *Clemens Alexandrinus* affirm.

He went to *Rome* on an Embassy from the *Athenians* in the 534th year, from the building of the City, which falleth upon the 2d year of the 140th Olympiad.

b Sext. Emper.

[b] He condemned *Rhetorick*, as being used rather as an *Artifice*, than an *Art*.

DIODORUS.

Diodorus was Disciple to *Critolaus*, and Succeeded him in the School, as is manifest from *Clemens Alexandrinus*, who adds, that in his assertion concerning our chief end, he joyned *Indolence* with *Honesty*. He is mentioned by *Cicero*; how long he taught, or who succeeded him, is unknown. Thus far we have an unintermitted account of the *Peripatetick* School.

THE

PART VI. 277

THE
HISTORY of PHILOSOPHY.

The Seventh Part.

Containing the *CYNICK* Philosophers.

ANTISTHENES.
CHAP. I.
His LIFE.

THE *Cynicks* are derived from *Antisthenes*, Disciple of *Socrates*, who, being most pleased with those discourses of his Master, which treated of Tolerance and Laboriousness, instituted this Sect. *a* He was born at *Athens*; his Father an *Athenian* named *Antisthenes* also, his Mother

a Laert.

ANTISTHENES.

Mother a *Thracian*, or, as *Plutarch*, a *Phrygian*, in whose defence, to those who reproached him that she was a Foreigner, he answered, *Cibele the Mother of the Gods was a* Phrygian. He likewise derided the *Athenians* for boasting of their being Natives, saying, they were nothing more Noble than Snails and Locusts. b Neither did *Socrates* the less esteem him; but on the contrary, hearing that he had behaved himself valiantly at the Fight at *Tanagra*, he said of him, *I knew two Parents both* Athenians *could not beget so excellent a person*. He first heard *Gorgias* the Orator, whence his Dialogues are written in a Rhetorical Stile, consisting chiefly in Verity and Exhortation. *Hermippus* saith, at the *Isthmian* meeting, he used to make Orations in praise and dispraise of the *Athenians*, *Thebans*, and *Lacedemonians*, before all the Assembly. But seeing many of the Citizens come thither, he refrained.

Next he applied himself to *Socrates*, and profited so much under him, that he counselled his Scholars to become his fellow Disciples under that Master. He lived in the *Piræum*, and went every day 40 *Stadia*, to hear *Socrates*.

He affected even whilst he was Disciple to *Socrates*, to go in poor habit, and c once having turned the torn part of his Garment outermost, *Socrates* spying it, said, *I see vain-glory through a hole*; or, as *Ælian*, *do you use this Ostentation before us also?*

d Upon the death of *Socrates* he was the occasion of Banishment to *Anytus*, and of Death to *Melitus*; for *Melitus* meeting with some young Men of *Pontus*, invited to *Athens* by the Fame of *Socrates*, he brought them to *Anytus*, telling them he was wiser than *Socrates*; whereupon the standers by in Indignation, turn'd 'em both out of the City; of which already in the Life of *Socrates*.

CHAP. II.
His Institution of a Sect.

*S*Ocrates being Dead, of whom he learned Tolerance and Apathy, he made choice of *Cynosarges*, a Gymnasium at *Athens* just without the Gates, as of the fittest place in which he might Discourse of Philosophy. b It was so called upon this occasion. *Didymus* the *Athenian* Sacrificing in his own House, a white Dog that was by, snatcht the Victim, and running away with it, laid it down in another place; *Dydimus* much troubled thereat, consulted the Oracle, which enjoyned him to erect a Temple in that place where the Dog had laid down the Victim, and to dedicate it unto *Hercules*, which was called *Cynosarges*, ὁ κυνὸς ἀργυναὸς, *The Temple of the white Dog.* c Hence *Antisthenes* and his Followers were called *Cynicks*, and by those that disapproved their Institution, *Dogs*; *Antisthenes* himself being termed Απλοκύων, *the sincere Dog*.

He first doubled his old sordid Cloak, and wore it alone [without a Coat] as *Diocles* affirmeth; he carried likewise a Staff and Satchel. *Neanthes* saith he first used a single Cloak. *Sosicrates* in the third of his *Successions*, saith, *Diodorus* the *Aspendian* wore a long Beard, and carri'd a Staff and Wallet.

d His Assertions are these, *That Virtue may be acquir'd by teaching; and those Persons Noble, who are Virtuous*. *That Virtue was Self-sufficient to Felicity, not needing any thing but a Socratick Courage*. *That Virtue consisteth in Actions, not requiring many Words nor much Learning, and is self-sufficient to Wisdom: for all other things have a reference thereto*. *That Infamy is good and equal to Labour, and that a wise man ought not to Govern the Common-wealth according to the Laws in Force, but according to Virtue*; *That a wise Man, to have Issue, may make choice of beautiful women, and Love, for a wise man only knoweth what ought to be loved*.

Diocles addeth these; *That nothing is new to a wise man*; *That a good man deserveth Love*, *That Virtuous Persons are Friends*; *That we ought to get assistance in War, Valiant and Just*; *That Virtue is an Armour that never can be taken from us*; *That it is better with some few good men to oppose all the wicked, than with many wicked men to contend with few good*. *Observe your Enemies, for they first find out your Faults*; *esteem a just man more than a neighbour*; *The same Virtue belongeth to man and to woman*; *Those things are good which are honest, ill which are dishonest*; *all things esteem strange*; *Wisdom is the safest Fortification, for it will neither fall away, nor can be betray'd*; *In these inexpugnable things we ought to build Forts, by Meditation*.

c *Agellius* saith, He esteemed *Pleasure the greatest Ill*, whence he used to say, *I had rather be Mad, than be addicted to Pleasure*.

f As to the Opinion of the *Cynicks* in general (not esteeming them, saith *Laertius*, a meer Form and Institution of Life, but a true Sect of Philosophy) they were these.

They took away, with *Aristo* the *Chian*, *Dialectick* and *Physick*, and only admitted *Ethick*; whence what some said of *Socrates*, *Diocles* applied to *Diogenes*, affirming he used the same Expressions. That we ought to enquire,

What Good and Ill
Our Houses fill.

They likewise rejected the Liberal Sciences; whence *Antisthenes* said, those who have acquired Temperance, ought not to study any Learning, lest by other things they be diverted. *Geometry* likewise, *Musick*, and the like, they wholly took away. Whence *Diogenes*, to one that shewed him a Watch, *It is an excellent Invention*, saith he, *against Supping too late*. And to one that entertain'd him with *Musick*,

Wisdom the greatest Cities doth Protect;
But Musick cannot one poor House direct.

They likewise, as the *Stoicks*, affirmed to be happy to live according to *Virtue*, as *Antisthenes* in his *Hercules*; for there is a kind of affinity betwixt these two Sects, whence the *Stoicks* asserted *Cynism* to be the nearest way to Virtue, and so lived *Zeno* the *Cittiean*.

Their Diet was slender, their Food only such as might satisfie Nature, their Cloaks sordid; they despised Riches, Glory, and Nobility: Some of them fed only on Herbs and cold Water, living under such shelters as they could find, or in Tubs, as *Diogenes* did, who affirmed, it was proper to the Gods to want nothing, and that those who stand in need of fewest things come nearest to the Gods.

They held also, according to *Antisthenes* in his *Hercules*, that Virtue may be acquired by Learning, and that it cannot be lost; that a wise Man

Man deserves to be loved, and never sinneth, and is a Friend to such as are like him, and trusteth nothing to Fortune.

They took away with *Aristo* the *Chian*, all things between Virtue and Vice.

CHAP. III.
His Apothegms.

Laert. OF his Apothegms are remembred these. He proved Labour to be good, by the Examples of *Hercules* and *Cyrus*, one a *Grecian*, the other a *Barbarian*.

He first defined Speech thus, *Speech is that which declareth that which is or was.*

To a young man of *Pontus* that came to be his Disciple, and asked him what he must bring with him, he answered, Βιβλιαειν καινῳ, ϗ γραφειῳ καινῳ, ϗ πινακιδιῳ καινῳ, a new Book, a new Pen, and a new Tablet, where the word is καινῳ is equivocal, and signifieth divided (divided καινῳ) *Wit*.

To one, demanding what kind of Wife he should take; *If a fair one*, faith he, *she will be common; if foul, a torment.*

Hearing that *Plato* spoke ill of him; *it is Kinglike*, faith he, *to do well, and be ill spoken of.*

Being initiated into the *Orphick* Solemnities, the Priest telling him, that they who were initiated into those Rights, were made partakers of many excellent things in the next World: *Why then*, said he, *do you not die?*

To one that reproached him that both his Parents were not *free*; *Neither*, faith he, *were they both Wrestlers, and yet I am a Wrestler.*

Being demanded why he had few Disciples, *I beat them away*, said he, *with a Silver Staff.*

Being demanded why he rebuk'd his Disciples so sharply; *So*, faith he, *do Physicians the Sick.*

Seeing an Adulterer running away, *unhappy Man*, said he, *how much danger might you have escaped for one half-penny.*

He said according to *Hecaton*, *It is better to fall among Crows than Flatterers; for those only devour the dead, these the living.*

Being demanded what was most happy for Man, he answered, *To die in Prosperity.*

To a Friend, complaining he had lost his Notes; *You should have writ them in your mind*, faith he, *and not in your Book.*

As Rust consumeth Iron, so Envy, faith he, *consumeth the Envious Man.*

Those who would never die, faith he, *must live Piously and Justly.*

He said, *Cities were then perishing, when they could not distinguish the good from the bad.*

Laert. Stob. Being commended by some wicked men; *I am troubled*, faith he, *to think what ill I have done.*

He said, *The cohabitation of concording Brethren is firmer than any Wall.*

He said, *We ought to carry such provision along with us, as if we should happen to be Shipwreck'd, we might swim away with.*

To those who reproached him for conversing with wicked Persons, *So do Physicians with the Sick*, faith he, *yet are not sick themselves.*

He said, *It is absurd to separate Corn from the Weeds, and in War to reject the unserviceable Person; yet in a Common-wealth, not to extirpate the Wicked.*

Being demanded what he had gain'd by Philosophy, he answered, *That I can converse with my self.*

At a Feast, to one that said to him, *Sing*; he reply'd, *Do you then Pipe.*

Diogenes demanding a Coat, he bad him double his Cloak.

Being demanded what Learning was most necessary, *that*, faith he, *which unlearneth ill.*

He advised those who were provoked by revilings, to bear it with greater Fortitude, than if Stones were cast at them.

He derided *Plato*, as being proud; and seeing at a Show a Horse going loftily, turning to *Plato*, *Methinks*, said he, *you would have acted the Part of this Horse very well.* This he said, because *Plato* at the same time had commended the Horse.

Another time visiting *Plato* as he lay sick, and looking into the Basin whereinto he had vomited, *I see here*, faith he, *the Choler, but not the Pride.*

He advised the *Athenians* to love Asses as well as Horses, which they conceiving absurd; and yet, faith he, you choose those for Generals, who know nothing, but how to stretch out the hand.

To one that said to him, many praise thee; *Why*, faith he, *what ill have I done?*

To one that demanded (as *Phanias* faith) what he should do to be a good and an honest man: *If you learn*, faith he, *of knowing Persons, that the Vices which you have, are to be avoided.*

To one that praised a life full of delicacies; *Let the Sons of my Enemies*, faith he, *live delicately.*

To a young man who desired his Statue might be made handsomer than himself; tell me, faith he, if the Brass it self could speak, what you think it would boast of? the other answered of its handsome Figure: *Are you ashamed then*, reply'd he, *to be proud of the same that an inanimate creature would be?*

A young man of *Pontus* promised to supply him, assoon as his Ship came home laden with Salt-Fish; hereupon he took him to a Meal-woman, and filling his Satchel, departed; she calling to him for Money, *This young man*, faith he, *will pay you as soon as his Ship comes home.*

When at any time he saw a Woman richly dressed, he went to her House, and bad her Husband bring out his Horse and Arms, that if he were so provided, he might allow her those freedoms, being better able to justifie the injuries it occasioned; otherwise, that he should take off her rich habit.

He said, *Neither a Feast is pleasant without Company, nor Riches without Vertue.* *Stob. Serm.* 1.

He said, *Those Pleasures which come not in at the door, must not go out by the door, but by Incision or Purging with Hellebore, or by* * *Starving, so to punish those Surfeits which we have incurred for a short pleasure.* *Stob. Ser.* 38. * *Ser.* 44.

He said, *Whosoever feareth others, is a Slave, though he know it not himself.* *Ser.* 50.

He said, *No Covetous Man can be a good Man, or a King, or a Free-man.* *Ser.* 53.

Being demanded what a Feast is, he answer'd, *The occasion of Surfeits,* *Ser.* 87.

He said, *We ought to aim at such pleasures as follow labour, not at those which go before labour.* *Ser.* 117.

He said *Common Executioners are better than Tyrants; those put only guilty Men to Death, Tyrants the innocent.* *Ser.* 148.

He

Ser. 171.	He said, *We ought to wish our Enemies all good things but Fortitude, for that they possess would fall into the hands of the Victor, not the owner.*
l Ser. 212.	*Him that contradicteth*, he said, *we must not again contradict, but instruct; for a mad man is not cured by another's growing mad also.*
Plut. rep. Stoic.	He said, *A man should always have in readiness his Wits or a Rope.*
Plut. vie. Lyc.	Seeing the *Thebans* much exalted with their success at the Luctrian Fight: he said, *They were like Boys that Triumph when they have beaten their Masters.*
Plut. vit. Per.	To some that commended a Piper; *But*, saith he, *he is an ill man; for else he would never have been so good a Piper.*

CHAP. IV.
His Writings.

OF his Books, saith *Laertius*, there are *ten* Tomes.

The *first* containing these.
Of Speech, or of Characters.
Ajax, of the Speech of Ajax.
Ulysses, or of Ulysses.
An Apology for Orestes.
Of Lawyers.
Isographe, or Desias, or Isocrates.
Against Isocrates's Ἀμάϱτυϱον.

The *second* Tome.
Of the Nature of Animals.
Of Procreation of Children, or of Marriage, Erotick.
Of Sophists, Physiognomick.
Of Justice and Fortitude, Protreptick 2, 3.
Of Theognis.

The *third* Tome.
Of Good.
Of Fortitude.
Of Law, or of Policy.
Of Law, or of Fair and Just.
Of Freedom and Servitude.
Of Faith.
Of a Guardian, or of Trusting.
A Victory, Oeconomicks.

The *fourth* Tome.
Cyrus.
Hercules *the greater*, or of Strength.

The *fifth* Tome.
Cyrus, or of a Kingdom.
Aspasia.

The *sixth* Tome.
Truth.
Of Dissertation, Anti-Logick.
Sathon, of Contradiction 3.
Of Dialectick.

The *seventh* Tome.
Of Discipline, or of Names 5.
Of Dying.
Of Life and Death.
Of things after Death.
Of the use of Names, or Eristick.
Of Interrogation and Answer.
Of Opinion and Science 4.
Of Nature 2.
Interrogation concerning Nature 2.
Opinions, or the Eristick.
Problems concerning Learning.

The *eighth* Tome.
Of Musick.
Of Interpreters.
Of Homer.
Of Injustice or Impiety.
Of Chalcas.
Of the Spie.
Of Pleasure.

The *ninth* Tome.
Of the Odysseis.
Of Minerva's wand, or of Telemachus, Helena and Penelope.
Of Proteus.
The Cyclops, or of Ulysses.
Of the use of Wine, or of Drunkenness, or of the Cyclops.
Of Circe.
Of Amphiaraus.
Of Ulysses and Penelope.
Of the Dog.

The *tenth* Tome.
Hercules, or Midas.
Hercules, or of Prudence, or of Strength.
The Master, or Lover.
The Master, or Spies.
Menexenus, or of Ruling.
Alcibiades.
Archelaus, or of a Kingdom.

These, saith *Laertius*, were his Writings, the great number whereof *Timon* derides, calling him an ingenious Trifler.

There is also among the *Socratick* Epistles one under his name to this effect.

Antisthenes *to* Aristippus.

IT *is not the part of a Philosopher to live with Tyrants, and to wast time at Sicilian Feasts, but rather to be content with a little in his own Country; but you esteem it the greatest excellence of a virtuous Person, to be able to acquire much Wealth, and to have powerful Friends. Riches are not good; neither if they were in themselves good, are they such, being thus obtained; nor can a multitude of unlearned persons, especially Tyrants, be true Friends. Wherefore I would counsel you to leave* Syracuse *and* Sicily; *but if, as some report, you are in love with Pleasure, and aim at such things, as beseem not wise persons, go to* Anticyra *and cure your self by drinking* Hellebore, *for that is much better for you than the Wine of* Dionysius; *this causeth Madness, that assuageth it. So that as health and discretion differ from sickness and folly, so much shall you be better than you are in these things which you now enjoy,* Farewel.

The answer to this Epistle, see in the life of *Aristippus*.

CHAP. V.
His Death.

HE died, saith *Laertius*, of sickness. As he lay on his death-bed, *Diogenes* came to him and asked him if he wanted a Friend. Another time he came to him with a Dagger; *Antisthenes* crying out, who will free me from this pain? He shewed him the Dagger, saying, *This shall. Antisthenes* reply'd, I say from my pain; not from my life: for he bore his Sickness somewhat impatiently through love of life.

Theopompus commends him above all the Disciples of *Socrates*, as being of such acute and sweet discourse, that he could lead any man to what he would.

There were three more of this name, one a Heraclitean Philosopher, the second of *Ephesus*, the third of *Rhodes*, an Historian.

PART VII. 281

DIOGENES.

CHAP. I.

His Country, Parents, Time, Banishment.

a Laert.

a DIOGENES was of *Sinopis*, a City of *Pontus*, his Father named *Icesius*, or, as others, *Icetes*; by Profession a Money changer.

He was Born (as appears by Computation from his Death, which was in the 90th Year of his Age, in the first year of the 114th Olympiad, *Hegesias* being *Archon*) about the third year of the 91st Olympiad. *Suidas* saith, he was first called *Cleon*.

Diocles saith, his Father trading publickly in Exchange of Money, was surprised, Coining false Money, and thereupon fled: But *Eubulides* saith, *Diogenes* himself did it, and fled together with his Father; even *Diogenes* in his *Podolus*, acknowledgeth as much. Some affirm, That being made overseer, he was perswaded by the Workmen to go to *Delphi* or *Delus*, the Country of *Apollo*, to enquire of the Oracle if he should do that whereto he was advised, παραχαράξει τὸ νόμισμα, which is of ambiguous

N n Significa-

Signification, implying to alter the courſe of Life, and to coin falſe Money. The Oracle aſſented: *Diogenes* not underſtanding it in the *Civil* Senſe, betook himſelf to Coining, and being taken in the Act, was Baniſhed, or, as others ſay, fled for Fear. Some affirm, he adulterated the Money he received from his Father, for which the Father was caſt into Priſon, and there died; the Son fled, and coming to *Delphi*, enquired of the Oracle by what means he ſhould become Eminent, whereupon he received that Anſwer.

b Ælian. var. Hiſt. 13. 28.

When he left his Country, one of his Servants followed him, named *Manes*, who not enduring his Converſation, ran away from him; ſome perſwaded *Diogenes* to enquire after him; who anſwered, Were it not a ſhame, ſince *Manes* doth not need *Diogenes*, that *Diogenes* ſhould need *Manes?* The Fellow wandring up and down, came at laſt to *Delphi*, where he was torn in pieces by Dogs.

CHAP. II.

How he lived at Athens.

a Ælian var. Hiſt. 10. 16.

COming to *Athens*, ſaith *Laertius*, he applied himſelf to *Antiſthenes*, following the Cynical Philoſophy inſtituted by him. *a Antiſthenes* having invited many to hear him, and but few coming, at laſt in anger would not ſuffer any to come to him, and therefore bad *Diogenes* be gone alſo. *Diogenes* continuing to come frequently, he chid and threatned him, and at laſt ſtruck him with his Staff: *Diogenes* would not go back, but perſiſting ſtill in his deſire of hearing him, ſaid, *Strike if you will, here is my Head, you cannot find a Staff hard enough to drive me from you, until you have Inſtructed me.* *Antiſthenes* overcome with his Perſeverance, admitted him, and made him his intimate Friend. From that time forward he heard him.

Some affirm, ſaith *Laertius*, he firſt wore a double Cloak, upon which he uſed to lie [at Night:] He likewiſe carried a Wallet, wherein was his Meat. He made uſe of all places for all things, Dining, Sleeping, and diſcourſing in any Place, inſomuch that pointing to *Jupiter's* walk, and the *Pompæum*, two publick places at *Athens*, he ſaid, The *Athenians* built them for his dwelling. Falling once Sick, he walked with a Staff, which afterwards he continually uſed, as likewiſe a Wallet, not in the City, but when he Travelled. He wrote to one to build him a little Houſe, which the other not doing ſo ſoon as he required, he made uſe of a *Tub* in the *Metroum* to live in, as he declareth in his *Epiſtles*. In Summer he uſed to roul in the burning Sand; in Winter to embrace Statues covered with Snow, accuſtoming himſelf continually to Sufferance. *b* A *Lacedæmonian* ſeeing him in this Poſture in the depth of Winter, asked him if he were not a cold; *Diogenes* ſaid, he was not: What you do then, replied the other, is no great matter.

b Plut.

At firſt he uſed to beg, of which there are many Inſtances: He one time begg'd of a Man thus, *If you have given to others, give alſo to me. If to none, begin with me.*

c Another time he begg'd of a Statue, whereof being demanded the Reaſon, *That I may the better,* ſaith he, *bear a Refuſal.*

c Laert.

He requeſted ſomething of a covetous Perſon, who delaying to give; *Man*, ſaith he, *I ask you εἰς τροφὴν not εἰς ταφὴν, Food, not a Grave.*

He requeſted ſomething of a perſon very obdurate, who anſwered, yes, if you can perſwade me to it; Nay, replied he, *If I were able to perſwade you to any thing, it ſhould have been to have hanged your ſelf.*

Of a Prodigal he begged a *Mina*; the other asked why he begged a *Mina* of him, and of others but an *Obolus*: Becauſe, ſaith he, *I hope to receive of others again; but whether I ſhall ever have any more of you, the Gods know.*

Being reproached that *Plato* begged not, but he begged: Yes, ſaith he, *he beggeth too; but*

*Cloſe in your Ear,
Leſt others hear.*

d Having received ſome little Money from *Dionyſius* the *Cariſian*, he ſaid,

d Ælian var. Hiſt. 4. 27.

*The Gods afford thee thy Deſire,
A Man and Houſe* ――

Alluding to his Effeminacy.

e For this Reaſon he ſaid, the Imprecations of *Tragedians* concurred in him, for he was without any City, without a Houſe, depriv'd of his Country, a Beggar, a Vagabond, having his livelihood only from day to day. And yet, adds *f Ælian*, he was more pleaſed with this Condition, than *Alexander* with the Command of the whole World, when having conquered the *Indians*, he returned to *Babylon*.

e Laert.

f Var. Hiſt. 3. 29.

g Seeing a Mouſe, as *Theophraſtus* ſaith, running up and down, he thence took occaſion of Comfort, conſidering it a Creature that looked not for Lodging, and was not diſpleaſed with Darkneſs, nor nice as to Diet.

g Laert.

He walked in the Snow bare-foot, and tried to eat raw Fleſh, but could not.

He ſaid, he imitated Singing-Maſters, who raiſe their Voice too high, thereby to teach others the juſt Tone.

The *Athenians* loved him much; for a Youth having bored Holes in his Tub, they puniſhed him, and gave *Diogenes* a new one.

He uſed to perform the Offices of *Ceres* and *Venus* in publick, arguing thus: *If it be not abſurd to dine, it is not abſurd to dine even in the Market-place; but it is not abſurd to dine, therefore it is not abſurd to dine even in the Market-place.*

h χειρέργον in the publick Forum; I would, ſaith he, *I could as eaſily ſatisfie my Hunger.*

h Laert. it is explained by Plutarch, de rep. Stoic.

i As he dined in the *Forum*, ſome that were preſent called him Dog; Nay, ſaith he, *you are Dogs that ſtand about me when I am at Dinner.*

i Laert.

Being reproached for feeding in the open Forum; *In the Forum,* ſaith he, *I grew Hungry.*

Being reproach'd that he drank in a Victualing-houſe; *And in a Barber's ſhop,* ſaith he, *I am ſhaved.*

He lived without any Servant. Being demanded by one whether he would have a Maid-Servant, or a Man, he ſaid, neither; Who then, anſwered the other, ſhall carry you out to your Grave

grave when you die? *Diogenes* replied, *he that wants a House?*

CHAP. III.
How he lived at Corinth.

a Laert.

a IN his old age he took a Voyage to *Ægina*, but was by the way taken by some Pirates, the name of whose Captain was *Scirpalus*. They carried him to *Creet*, and there exposed him to Sale; they asked him what he could do; he answered, *he could command Men*; and to the Cryer, he said, *If any Man wants a Master, let him buy me.* Offering to sit down, they would not suffer him, (it being the Custom of such as were to be sold for Slaves, to leap up and down) *'Tis no matter for that,* saith he, *Fishes are sold which way soever they lie*; adding, he wondred that Men, being to buy a Pot or Vessel, examine it curiously on the inside; but if a Man, they are satisfied with his look, and outside. Pointing to a *Corinthian* richly attir'd that passed by, named *Xeniades, Sell me,* saith he, *to that Man, for he wants a Master.* To *Xeniades* as soon as he had bought him, he said, *Be sure you do as I command you,* he answered in the common Proverbial Verse.

The Springs of Rivers upwards run.

Diogenes reply'd, if being sick you had bought a Physician, would you obey his advice, or would you say as before, *The Springs of Rivers upwards run.*

His Friends, according to *Cleomenes,* offered to redeem him; but he told them they were fools, for Lyons were not Slaves to their Keepers, but the Keepers to the Lyons, for the property of Servitude is to fear, and Men fear Beasts.

b Laert.
c Gell.

b Xeniades having bought him, carried him to *Corinth, c* asked him what he would do; he answered, he knew how to command free persons. *Xeniades* wondring at his answer, set him at Liberty, and delivered his Sons to his Charge, saying, *take then my Children, and command them.*

d Laert.

d He put the Government of his Family also into his hands, which he acquitted himself of excellently well in every thing, in so much that *Xeniades* said, *he had brought a good Genius into his House.*

He did not suffer the young men that were under his charge, to exercise themselves as Wrestlers, but only till they were warm, and for their health sake. He taught them many sayings of Poets by heart, and some of his own; and that they might more easily remember the full sum of Learning, he made a brief Collection thereof. He taught them at home to Minister, using thin Diet, and drinking Water, to go negligently in Habit, shaven, without Coats, without Shooes, and silent, looking upon themselves as they went. He brought them up likewise to Hunting. On the other side, they took great care of *Diogenes,* and recommended him to their Parents.

e Plut. vit. Alex.

e When *Alexander* was upon expedition against the *Persians,* many Philosophers came to salute him; the same duty he expected from *Diogenes,* who was at that time at the *Craneum,* a *Gymnasium* in *Corinth,* where he lived idly, not minding *Alexander. Alexander* therefore went and found him out, sitting in the Sun; he rose a little to look upon the great Crowd of People that came along with *Alexander,* who saluting him, asked *Diogenes* what he would desire of him, he answered, *that you would stand aside a little from betwixt me and the Sun.* Hereat *Alexander* was so surprised, and so much admired his high Mind, that his Attendants in returning laughing thereat; but I, said he, were I not *Alexander,* would choose to be *Diogenes.*

CHAP. IV.
His Philosophy.

a Laert.

a AND concerning Opinions, he said, there is a twofold *Exercitation,* one *Spiritual,* the other *Corporeal*; if in the first of these we employ our selves constantly, frequent phantasies will occur, which faciliate the performance of Vertue; the one cannot be without the other, a good habit and strength being necessary both in respect of the Soul and the Body.

That Virtue is easily acquired by exercitation, he argued, in as much as in the Mechanick Arts and others, that Artists by practice quickly arrive at an extraordinary readiness therein, and Wrestlers and Musicians excel one another according to the continual pains they take therein one more than another; and if they should have taken the same pains about their Souls, it would not have been unprofitably and imperfectly employed.

He said, Nothing in Life can be rightly done without exercitation; and that exercitation could master any thing; for whereas men should chuse Natural Labours, whereby they might live happily; they on the contrary make choice of the unprofitable, and through their own Folly are in continual misery. For even the contempt of Pleasure, if we accustom our selves thereto, will be most pleasant; and as they, who inure themselves to a voluptuous life cannot be taken off it without much trouble and grief; so they who exercise themselves in a contrary manner, with as great ease contemn even the pleasures themselves.

He ascribed not so much to Law as to Nature; he affirmed that he followed the same course of Life with *Hercules,* preferring nothing before Liberty.

He asserted that all things belong to the Wise; arguing thus; *All things belong to the Gods, the Gods are Friends to Wise Persons; all things are common amongst Friends;* therefore *all things belong the Wise.*

As concerning Law, he held that without it a Commonwealth could not be ordered; for, saith he, *Without a City there cannot be any profit of Civil things; a City is a Civil thing; of Law without a City there is no profit, therefore Law is Civil.*

He derided *Nobility, Glory,* and the like, saying, they were the Ornaments or Veils of Wickedness, and that only a right Commonwealth ought to be honoured.

He held that there ought to be a Community of Women, conceiving Marriage to be nothing, and

and that every Man and Woman might enjoy one another as they pleased themselves, and consequently that all Children should be in common.

He held that it was not unlawful to take any thing out of a Temple, or to feed upon living Creatures; neither was it impious to eat Man's Flesh, as appeared by the Practice of other Nations; adding that all things are in all and by all: In Bread there is Flesh, in Flesh Bread; the remainders of Flesh and Bread being insinuated by occult passages into other Bodies,and evaporating in like manner.This *Laertius* cites out of a Tragedy of his named *Thyestes*, if saith he, that Tragedy belong to him, and not rather to *Philiscus* or *Pasiphon*.

Musick, Geometry, Astronomy, and the like, he rejected as unprofitable and unnecessary.

CHAP. V.
His Apothegms.

a Laert.

a HE was very acute, saith *Laertius* in deriding others. He said *Euclid*'s School was not χολὴ, but χολὴ, not a *School*, but *Anger*, for the Dialecticks affected *Litigious* dispute. He said *Plato*'s School was not διατριβὴ, but καταριβὴ, not an Exercitation, but Consumption.

He said, when, he look'd upon *Pilots*, *Physicians* and *Philosophers*, Man was the wisest of all Creatures; but when he looked upon *Interpreters* of Dreams, *Prophets*, or Persons puffed up with Wealth or honours,nothing is more foolish than Man.

He said, that he often found it convenient in Life to have ready an Answer, or a Rope.

At a great Feast, seeing *Plato* eat Olives; Why, saith he, you being a Wise Man, and going to *Sicily* for such Entertainments,did you not enjoy them? He answer'd,by the Gods,*Diogenes*, I fed upon Olives there likewise as well as upon other things.*Diogenes* replied,why then needed you to have gone to *Syracuse*, were there no Olives at that time in *Attica*,? This *Phavorinus* ascribes to *Aristippus*, adding, that as he was eating Figs, he met him, and said, Taste; the other taking and eating; I bade you, saith he, taste, and not devour.

In the Presence of some Friends of *Plato*, sent to him by *Dionysius*, *Diogenes* trod under foot *Plato*'s Robe, saying I tread under foot *Plato*'s Pride: But *Diogenes*, answered *Plato*,how proud are you your self,when you think you contemn Pride? *Sotion* relates this as said to the *Cynick* by *Plato*.

b Stob. Ser. 133.

b Diogenes sent to *Plato* for Wine and Figs, he sent him a large Vessel of Wine and Figs; whereupon *Diogenes*, As you, saith he, being demanded how much two and two are, answer Twenty, so you neither grant what I request, nor answer what I demand; thus censuring his Verbosity.

Being demanded in what part of *Greece* he had seen good Men: Men, saith he, *no where, but good Boys at* Lacedæmon.

Making a serious Discourse, and perceiving that no Man came to hear him, he began to Sing, whereat a great many gathered together, whom he reproached for coming to trifles, being so backward to serious Things.

He said, Men contested in undermining or kicking, but none about Goodness.

He wondred at *Grammarians*, who enquiring after the misfortunes of *Ulysses*, forgot their own; and at *Musicians*, who whilst they *Tune* their Instruments, have discordant Affections in their Souls; and at the *Mathematicians*, that gazing upon the Sun and Moon, neglecting what was just at their Feet; and at *c Orators*,who studied to speak just things,and neglected to act them; and lastly, at *covetous* Persons, for dispraising Money, which they loved above all things.

c Stob. 29ʃ.

He reprehended those, who though they commended Just Men for thinking themselves to be above Money, yet esteem'd the Rich happy.

He was angry at those, who when they sacrificed to the Gods for their health, Feasted at the same time contrary to their health.

He wondred at Servants, who seeing their Masters eat excessively, did not take away their Meat.

He praised those, who being about to Marry, would not Marry; who being about to go to Sea, would not go to Sea; who being about to undertake some publick Office, would not undertake it; and who being about to bring up Children, forbore to bring them up; and who would compose themselves to live with great Men, yet never went to them.

He said,when we stretch out our hand to our Friend, we should never clutch our Fist.

One bringing him into a new house, and forbidding him to spit, he spit in his Face, saying,he could not find a worse place. Some ascribe this to *Aristippus*.

Crying out upon a time, *Men come hither,* a great many flocked about him, whom he fell upon with his Stick, and beat them, saying, *I called Men, not Varlets*. This *Hecaton* in his *Chriæ* relates.

Alexander said, If he had not been born *Alexander*, he would have desired to have been born *Diogenes*.

He said, They were not maimed who were Dumb and Blind, but they who had not a Wallet.

Going once half shaven to a Feast of young Men, as *Metrocles* relates, they beat him,whereupon he took their Names, and setting them down in a Parchment-Roll, he wore it at his Breast, whereby being known, they were reviled and beaten.

He said, he was the *Dog of the praised, but none of the Praisers durst go a hunting with him.*

To one saying, At the *Pythian* Games I overcame Men; No, saith he, *I the Men, you the Slaves.*

To those who said to him, You are now old, take your Ease; *What,* saith he, *if I were to run a Race, should I give over when I were almost at the end, or rather contest with greater Courage?*

Finding *Demosthenes* the Orator at Dinner in a common Victualling house,who asham'd would have stolen away; Nay, saith he, you are now the more *Popular. Ælian* relates it thus, *Diogenes* being at Dinner a common Victualling-house, and seeing *Demosthenes* pass by, invited him in, *Demosthenes* refusing; Do you think it, saith

saith *Diogenes*, a disparagement to dine here, when your Masters dine here every day? Meaning the common People, to whom Orators are but Servants.

To some Strangers who were desirous to see *Demosthenes*, pointing to him with his middle Finger; this, saith he, is he that leads the *Athenians*.

In reproof to one who had thrown away his Bread, and was ashamed to take it up again, he tied a string about the neck of a Bottle, and dragged it after him through the *Ceramick*.

He said most Men were mad *Præter digitum*, all but the Finger; if any man should walk pointing with his middle Finger, he will be thought mad; if his Fore-finger, not so.

He said the most precious things were sold cheapest, and so on the contrary; for a Statue will cost 3000 pieces of Silver, a peck of Wheat, two pieces of Brass.

To one who came to him to study Philosophy, he gave a Fish, and bid him follow him; the other ashamed, threw it away, and departed: Not long after, meeting the same Person, he laughing, said, *The Friendship betwixt you and me was broke off by a Fish*. *Diocles* relates it thus; One saying to him, Command me, *Diogenes*; he gave him a Penniworth of Cheese to bring after him, the other refusing to carry it, Our Friendship, saith he, a penny-worth of Cheese hath dissolved.

Seeing a Boy drink Water in the hollow of his hand, he took his little cup out of his Wallet and threw it away, saying, *The boy outwent him in Frugality*. He threw away his Dish also, seeing a Boy that had broken his, supping up his Broth in the same manner.

Seeing a Woman prostrate her self unhandsomly in Prayer, and desirous to reprove her superstition, as *Zoilus* the *Pergæan* reports, came to her, and said, Are you not ashamed, Woman, that God who stands behind you (for all things are full of him) should see you in this undecent posture?

He said, such as beat others, ought to be consecrated to *Æsculapius*, the God of *Chirurgery*.

He said, *Against Fortune we must oppose Courage; against nature, Law; against passion, Reason*.

In the *Craneum*, *Alexander* standing by him, as the Sun shone, said to him, Ask of me what thou wilt; he answered, *Do not stand between me and the Sun*.

One reading a long tedious Discourse, and coming at last near a Blank Leaf at the end of the Book, *Be of good Courage Friend*, saith he, *I see Land*.

To one proving by the *horned* Syllogism that he had Horns, he feeling on his Forehead, *But I*, saith he, *feel none*. In like manner another maintaining there was no such thing as motion, he rose up and walked. To one disputing concerning Meteors, *How long is it*, saith he, *since you came from Heaven*?

A wicked Man having written over the door of his House, Let no ill thing enter here: *Which way then*, saith he, *must the Master come in*?

He anointed his Feet with sweet Unguents, saying, the scent went from the crown of his head into the Air, but from his Feet to his Nostrils.

To some *Athenians*, that perswaded him to be initiated into some Religious Mysteries, alledging that such as were initiated had the chiefest places in the other World: It is ridiculous, saith he, if *Agesilaus* and *Epaminondas* live there amongst Bogs, and the common People that are initiated, live in the Blessed Islands. Or as *Plutarch*, hearing these Verses of *Socrates*:

—— *Thrice happy they*
Who do these Mysteries survey:
They only after Death are Blest,
All miseries pursue the rest.

What, saith he, *shall* Patœcion *the Thief be in better condition* (because he was initiated) *than* Epaminondas?

Mice coming to him as he was at dinner; *See*, saith he, *Diogenes also maintaineth Parasites*.

d *Diogenes* being present at a discourse of *Plato's*, would not mind it; whereat *Plato* angry, said, Thou Dog, why mindst thou not? *Diogenes* unmoved, answered, *Yet I never return to the place where I was sold, as Dogs do*, alluding to *Plato's* Voyage to *Sicily*. ^{d Ælian var. hist. 14. 33.}

Returning from a Bath, one asked him, if there were many Men there? He said, *No*: The other asking him, if there were much company; he said, *there was*.

Plato defining Man *a two-footed Animal without Wings*, and this definition being approved; *Diogenes* took a Cock, and plucking off all its Feathers, turned it into *Plato's* School, saying, This is *Plato's* Man; whereupon to the definition was added, *Having broad Nails*.

To one demanding at what time he should Dine, *If thou art Rich*, saith he, *when thou wilt; if Poor, when thou canst*.

At *Megara*, seeing their Sheep with thick Fleeces, and their Children almost naked; *It is better*, saith he, *to be the Sheep of a* Megaræan, *than his Son*.

To one, who hitting him with the end of a long Pole, bade him take heed, *Why*, saith he, *do you mean to hit me again*?

He said, *The Orators were the Servants of the Multitude*; *Crowns, the Boils of Glory*.

e He lighted a Candle at Noon, saying, *I look for a Man*. ^{e Stob. Ser. 4.}

He stood in the Rain without any shelter; some that were present pitying him, *Plato*, who was there likewise, said, *If you will shew your selves pitiful to him, go away*, reflecting upon his Vainglory.

One giving him a box on the Ear, *O Hercules*, saith he, *I knew not that I should have walked with a Helmet*.

Medias giving him many Blows with his Fist, saying, There are 3000 Drachms [alluding to the fines imposed upon such Outrages] ready counted for you upon the Table: The next day he got a *Cæstus*, and beat him with it, saying, *There are three Thousand Drachms ready counted for you*.

Lycias an Apothecary asked him, if he thought there were many Gods: *How* saith he, *can I think otherwise, when I take you to be their Enemy*? Others ascribe this to *Theodorus*.

Seeing one that had besprinkled himself with Water; *O unhappy Man*, saith he, *dost thou not know, that the Errors of Life are no more to be wash'd away by Water, than Errors in Grammar*?

He

He rebuked those who complained of Fortune, saying, *They did not request what was good, but that which seemed good to them.*

Of those who are terrified with Dreams, he said, *You never are concerned for the things you do waking, but what you fancy in your sleep you make your greatest business.*

f At the Olympick Games the Cryer proclaiming, *Dioxippus hath overcome Men*; he *Slaves,* saith he, *but I mean.*

f Et Plut. de curiositate,

Alexander sending an Epistle to *Antipater* at *Athens,* by one whose name was *Athlias, Diogenes* being present said, *Athlias* from *Athlias,* by *Athlias* to *Athlias,* alluding to the name, which implieth *Misery.*

Perdiccas threatning him with death unless he would come unto him; *that is no great matter,* saith he, *for a Cantharides or Spider may do as much; you should rather have threatned, that you would have lived well without me.*

He often said, the Gods had given to Men an easie Life, but that it was hidden from those who used choice diet, unguents, and the like; whence to one whose servant put on his Cloaths, *you will not be truly happy,* saith he, *until he wipe your nose also,* that is, *when you have lost the use of your hands.*

Seeing some that had the charge of the things belonging to the Temple, leading a Man to Prison, who had stoln a Cup out of the Treasury, *the great Thieves,* saith he, *lead Prisoners the lesser.*

To a young man that throwing Stones at a Gibbet, *Well done,* saith he, *you will be sure to hit the mark.*

To some young men that coming about him, said, take heed you do not bite us: *fear not boys,* said he, Diogenes *eats not Beets* [for so he termed effeminate persons.]

To one Feasting, cloathed in a Lion's skin, *do not,* saith he, *defile Virtues Livery.*

To one extolling the happiness of *Callisthenes,* in that living with *Alexander* he had plenty of all things; nay, saith he, *he is not happy, for he dines and sups when* Alexander *pleases.*

When he wanted Money, he said, he went to re-demand, not borrow of his friends.

Seeing a young man going along with some great persons to a Feast, he took him from them, and carried him to his own friends, bidding them to look to him better.

To one neatly dressed, who had asked him some question, *I cannot answer you,* said he, *unless I knew whether you were a Man or a Woman.*

g Of a young Man playing at *Cattabus* in a Bath, *By how much the better,* saith he, *so much the worse.*

Vit. Athenæ.

At a Feast one threw a Bone to him as to a Dog, which he like a Dog took up, and lifting his Leg, προσουρησεν αυτοις.

Orators, and all such as sought glory by speaking, he called τρισανθρωπους, thrice men, instead of τρισαθλιους, thrice wretched.

He called an unlearned Rich-man *a Sheep with a Golden Fleece.*

Seeing written upon the Gates of a Prodigal's House, to be Sold; *I knew,* saith he, *being so overcharged with Wine, it would Vomit up the Owner.*

To a young man professing himself much displeased at the many persons that courted him, *Let him see,* saith he, *that you are displeased, by casting off your effeminacy.*

Of a foul Bath, *where,* saith he, *shall they be washed that wash here?*

A big fellow that plaid on the Harp, tho' by all others discommended for playing ill, he praised; being asked why, *because,* saith he, *being an able fellow, he chooseth rather to play on the Harp than to Steal.*

A certain Harper who plaid so ill, that the Company always went away and left him, he saluted thus, *good morrow Cock*; the other asking why, *because,* saith he, *your Musick maketh every one rise.*

Seeing a young man doing something, which tho' 'twere ordinary, he conceiv'd to be unseemly, he filled his bosom with Beans, and in that manner walked through the People, to whom gazing upon him, *I wonder,* saith he, *you look at me, and not at him.*

Hegesias desiring to lend him some of his Writings, *You are a fool,* saith he, Hegesias, *who eat Figs not painted, but real; yet neglect true exercitation, and seek after the written.*

Seeing one that had won the Victory at the Olympick Exercises, feeding Sheep; *you have made hast,* saith he, *good man, from the* Olympick *Exercises to the Nemæan,* the word alluding to feeding of Sheep.

Being demanded how it cometh to pass that Wrestlers are for the most part stupid fellows, he answered, *because they are made chiefly of the skins of Oxen and Swine.*

To a Tyrant, demanding of him what Brass was best, he answer'd, *that whereof the Statues of* Harmodius *and* Aristogiton *were made.* This others ascribe to *Plato.*

Being asked how *Dionysius* useth his Friends, *as vessels,* saith he, *emptying the full, and throwing away the empty.*

A young man newly Married, having written upon his House, *the Son of* Jupiter, Hercules, Callinicus *dwelleth here, let nothing ill enter*; he added, *Assistance after a defeat,* implying it was too late, he being already Married.

He said Covetousness is the Metropolis of all Evil.

Seeing one that had wasted all his means, eating Olives, *If you had used to dine so,* said he, *you would not have supp'd so.*

He said, *Good men are the Images of the Gods, Love is the business of idle persons.*

Being asked what is the most miserable thing in Life, he said, *an old man in want.*

h Being demanded, the bitings of what Beasts were most dangerous; *of Wild Beasts,* saith he, *a Detractor; of Tame, a Flatterer.*

h Et Stob. Ser. 65,

Beholding a Picture of two Centaurs very ill painted, he said, *Which of these is* Chiron? the Jest consisteth in the Greek word, which signifieth *worse,* and was also the name of a Centaur, Tutor to *Achilles.*

He said, *the Discourse of Flatterers is a Rope of Honey.* He called the Belly the *Charybdis of Life.*

Hearing that *Didymo,* an Adulterer was taken; *he deserves,* saith he, *to be put out of his name* (meaning Emasculated.)

i Being asked why Gold looks pale; *because,* saith he, *many lie in wait for it.*

i Stob. Ser. 55.

Seeing a Woman carried in a Litter; *that is not*, saith he, *a fit Cage for such a Beast.*

Seeing a Servant that had run away from his Master, sitting upon the brink of a Well: *Young Man*, saith he, *take heed you do not fall in*: alluding to the punishment of Fugitive Servants.

Seeing one that used to steal Garments in the Bath; he said, ἐπ ἀλομμάτιον ἤ ἐπ ἄλλο ἱμάτιον, *Do you come for Unguents, or for another Garment?*

Seeing some Women hanged upon an Olive-tree; *I would*, saith he, *all Trees bore the same Fruit.*

Seeing a Thief that used to rob Tombs, he spoke to him in that Verse of *Homer*,

—— *What now of Men the best,*
Com'st thou to plunder the Deceas't?

Seeing a handsome youth all alone asleep, he awaked him, saying in the words of *Homer*, *Awake.*

Μή τίς σοι εὕδοντι μεταφρενῶ ἐν δόρυ πήξη.

To one that Feasted sumptuously, he said that Verse of *Homer.*

Son thou hast but a little time to live.

Plato discoursing concerning *Ideas*, and naming τραπεζότητα, and κυαθότητα, as if he should say, *Tableity* and *Cuppeity*, he said, *I see* Plato, *the Table and the Cup, but not the Tableity and Cuppeity.* Plato answered, it is true indeed, you have Eyes by which the *Table* and *Cup* are seen; but not an Intellect, by which *Tableity* and *Cuppeity* are seen.

Being demanded what he thought *Socrates*; he answered, *mad.* Being demanded at what time a Man should marry; *a young Man*, saith he, *not yet; an old Man not at all.*

To one that asked, what he should give him to let him strike him, he answered, *a Helmet.*

[l Stob. Ser. 161.] To a young Man dressing himself neatly, *if this*, saith he, *be for the sake of Men, you are unhappy, if for Women, you are unjust.*

Seeing a young Man blush; *Take Courage*, saith he, *that is the Colour of Vertue.*

Hearing two Men plead against one another, he condemned both, saying, *One had stolen, the other had not lost.*

Being demanded what Wine he thought most pleasant, he answer'd, *That which is drunk at anothers Cost.*

To one that said, many deride thee; he answered, *but I am not derided*: As conceiving, [m Vit. Fab. Max.] saith *Plutarch*, *m* those only to be derided, who are troubled at such things.

To one who said, Life is an ill thing: *Life*, saith he, *is not an ill thing, but an ill Life is an ill thing.*

[n Stob. Ser. 39.] *n* As he was Dining upon Olives, they caused a Tart to be set before him, which he threw away, saying,

Stranger, when Kings approach, withdraw.

The words of *Laius*'s Officers to *Oedipus.*

Being asked what kind of Dog he was, he answered, *When he was hungry, a Spaniel; when his belly was full a Mastiff*; one of those which many commend, but dare not take abroad with them a Hunting.

Being demanded whether Wise Men might eat Dainties; *All things*, saith he, *as well as others.*

o Being demanded why Men gave to Beggars, [b Stob. Ser. 77.] and not to Philosophers; *Because*, saith he, *they are afraid they may be Lame or Blind, but are not afraid they may be Philosophers.*

To one that reproached him as having counterfeited Money; *Indeed*, saith he, *there was a time when I was such a one as you are; but the time will never come that you will be as I am.*

Coming to *Mindus*, and seeing the Gates very large, the City small, *Mindinians*, saith he, *shut your Gates, lest your City run out at them.*

Seeing a Thief that was taken stealing Purple, he applied that Verse of *Homer* to him,

The Purple death, and potent Fate have seiz'd.

To *Craterus*, who invited him to come to him, he returned Answer, *I had rather lick Salt at Athens, than enjoy the greatest Delicacies with* Craterus.

Meeting *Anaximenes* the Orator, who was very Fat; *Give us*, saith he, *some of your Flesh, it will ease you, and help us.*

The same *Anaximenes* being in the midst of a Discourse, *Diogenes* shewing a piece of Salt-fish, diverted the Attention of his Auditors; whereat *Anaximenes* growing angry, *See*, saith he, *a hard Pennyworth of Saltfish hath broke off* Anaximenes's *Discourse.*

Some ascribe this to him. *Plato* seeing him wash Herbs, came and whispered thus to him; *If you had followed Dionysius, you would not have needed to wash Herbs*; to whom he returned this Answer in his Ear, *If you had washed herbs, you needed not to have followed* Dionysius.

To one that said to him, many laugh at you; *And Asses perhaps at them*, saith he, *but they care not for Asses, nor I for them.*

Seeing a young Man studying Philosophy: Well done, saith he, you will teach those who love your outward Beauty, to admire your Soul.

To one that admired the multitude of votive Offerings in *Samothracia*, given by such as had escaped Shipwrack: *There would have been far more*, saith he, *if those who perished had presented theirs.* Others ascribe this to *Diagoras* the *Melian.*

To a young man going to a Feast, he said, *You will come back Chiron*(alluding to the word which implyeth *worse*) the young man came to him the next day, saying, *I went and returned not Chiron*: No, saith he, *not Chiron but Eurition.*

Returning from *Lacedæmon* to *Athens*, to one that asked him from whence he came, and whither he went: *From Men*, saith he, *to Women.*

Returning from the Olympick Games, to one that asked if there were much People there; *Much People*, saith he, *but few Men.*

He compared Prodigals to Fig-trees growing on a Precipice, whose Fruit Men taste not, but Crows and Vultures devour.

Phryne

Phryne the *Curtezan* having set up a golden Statue of *Venus* at *Delphi*, he wrote on it, *From the Intemperance of the* Grecians.

Alexander coming to him, and saying, I am *Alexander* the great King : *And I,* saith he, *am* Diogenes *the Dog.*

Being asked why he was called *Dog*: *I fawn on those that give,* saith he, *I bark at those that will not give, and I bite the wicked.*

As he was gathering Figs, the Keeper of the Orchard spying him, told him, it is not long since a Man was Hang'd upon that Tree : *And for that Reason,* saith he, *I will cleanse it.*

p *Ael.* 12.58. p Observing *Dioxippus* the Olympick Victor, to cast many Glances upon the *Curtezan* : *See,* saith he, *a common Woman leads the martial Ram by the Neck.*

To two infamous Persons stealing away from him : *Fear not,* saith he, *Dogs eat not Thistles.*

To one that asked him concerning a Youth taken in Adultery, whence he was; he answered, *of* Tegea; *Tegea (a City of* Arcadia) *whereto he alluded,* is a publick Brothel.

Seeing one, that in former times had been an ill Wrestler, profess Medicine; *What is the matter,* saith he, *have you a design to cast those down that have thrown you?*

Seeing the Son of a common Woman throw Stones amongst a croud. *Take heed,* saith he, *you do not hit your Father.*

To a Youth shewing him a Sword, given him by one that loved him, he said, ἡ μὲν μάχαιρα καλὴ ἡ δὲ λαβὴ αἰσχρά.

To some that extolled one who had bestow'd something on him : *But you do not praise me,* saith he, *who deserved to receive it.*

To one that redemanded an old Cloak of him, *If you give it me,* saith, he, *I must keep it*; *if you lent it me, I must make use of it.*

To a supposititious Person that said to him, You have Gold in your Cloak, *Yes,* saith he, *and for that Reason I lay it* q *under me when I go to Sleep.*

q *The jest consisteth in the Allusion betwixt those two Greek Words ὑποβολιμαῖος & ὑποβεβλημένος.*

Being demanded what he had gained by Philosophy, *If nothing else,* saith he, *at least this, to be prepared for all Fortunes.*

Being demanded of what Country he was, he answered, *A Citizen of the World.*

To one that Sacrificed, praying he might have a Child, *You Pray for a Child,* saith he, *but never trouble your self what kind of Child it may prove.*

At an Ordinary, being demanded Money, he answered the Master in that Verse of *Homer*,

Ask others, but from Hector *hold thy Hand.*

r *Et Stob. Ser.* r He said, *The Mistresses of Kings were Queens,* for the Kings did whatsoever they would have them.

The *Athenians* having decreed to stile *Alexander, Bacchus*; *And make me,* saith he, *Serapis.*

To one reproaching him for living in filthy places, *The Sun,* saith he, *visits Kennels, yet is not defiled.*

Being at Supper in the Temple, they brought him course Bread, he threw it away, saying, *Nothing but what is pure must come within a Temple.*

To one that said; Why do you, who know nothing, profess Philosophy? He answered, *Tho' I should but pretend to study Philosophy, yet that were a Profession thereof.*

To one that recommended his Son to him, saying, he was very Ingenious, and exceeding well Educated; He answered, *Why then doth he need me?*

Those who speak good things, but do them not, differ nothing from a Lute, for that neither hears, nor hath Sense.

He went to the Theatre; as all the people were going out, being asked why he did so, *This* saith he, *is that I study all my Life time.*

Seeing an Effeminate young Man, *Are you not ashamed,* saith he, *to use your self worse than Nature hath done? She hath made you a Man, but you will force your self to be a Woman.*

ſ Seeing an Ignorant Man tuning a Lute, *Are* ſ *Stob. Ser.* *you not ashamed,* saith he, *to try to make a Lute* 104. *sound harmoniously, and yet suffer your Life to be so full of Discord?*

To one that said he was unfit for Philosophy, *Why do you live,* saith he, *if you care not for living Honestly?*

To one who despised his own Father, *Are you not ashamed,* saith he, *to despise him who is the cause you are so proud?*

Hearing a handsome Youth speak foolishly, *Are you not ashamed,* saith he, *to draw a Leaden Dagger out of an Ivory Sheath?*

Being reproached for accepting a Cloak from *Antipater,* he answered in those words of *Homer,*

The Gifts of Gods must not be thrown away.

One that hit him with a pole, and then bid him take heed, he struck with his Staff, and said, *and take you heed.*

To one that sued to a Curtesan, *What mean you Wretch,* saith he, *to sue for that which is much better to miss?*

To one that smelled sweet of Unguents, *Take heed,* saith he, *this Perfume make not your Life stink.*

He said, *Slaves serve their Masters, but wicked Men their Passions.*

Being demanded why Slaves are called Ἀνδράποδα *Footmen,* because saith he, *They have Feet like Men, but such Minds as you that ask the Question.*

Seeing an unskilful Archer going to shoot, he sat down at the Mark, *Lest* saith he, *he should hit me.*

He said, Lovers are unhappy in pleasure.

Being demanded whether Death be ill, *How,* saith he, *can that be ill, whereof when it cometh we have no Sense?*

Alexander coming to him, and saying, Do you not fear me? What saith he, are you Good or Ill? He answered Good : *Who,* replies *Diogenes, fears that which is Good?*

He said, *Learning is a Regulation to young Men, a Comfort to Old Men, Wealth to Poor Men, and an Ornament to Rich Men.*

To *Didymo* an Adulterer curing a Maids Eye, *Take heed,* saith he, *lest in curing the Eye you hurt not the Ball,* [the word κόρη signifying both Eyeball and Virginity.]

To one that said his Friends lay in wait for him, *What then is to be done,* saith he, *if Friends and Enemies must be used alike?*

Being demanded what is best amongst Men, he answered, *Freedom of Speech.*

Coming into a School, and seeing there many Statues

Statues of the Muses, but few Auditors, *By the help of the Gods, Master,* faith he, *you have many Auditors.*

Stob. Eth. Ser. 1
To one that asked him how he might order himself best, *By reprehending,* faith he, *those things in your self which you blame in others.*

Ser.
He gave good Counsel to a person very dissolute; being demanded what he was doing, he answered, *Washing an Æthiopian.*

Ser. 32.
He went backwards into the School of the Stoicks, whereat some laughing, *Are you asham'd,* faith he, *to do that in the whole course of your life, for which you deride me in walking?*

Ibid.
He said, *Men provide for their living, but not for their well living.*

Ser. 37 & 84.
He said, it was a shame to see Wrestlers and Singing-Masters observe temperate Diet, and moderate their Pleasures, one for Exercise, the other for his Voice, and yet no man would do so much for Vertue's sake.

Ser. 45.
He said, Pride, like a Shepherd, driveth men whither it pleaseth.

Ser. 48.
Seeing the high Walls of *Megara,* he said, *Unhappy People, mind not the height of your Walls, but the height of their Courages, who are to stand on the Walls,*

Ser. 53.
He compared Covetous Men to such as have the Dropsie, those are full of Money, yet desire more; these have Water, yet thirst after more: Passions grow more intense by enjoyment of what they desire.

Sea. 53.
Seeing a man make Love to an old Rich Widows: *This Love,* faith he, *is not blind but toothless.*

Ser. 54.
Being demanded what Beasts were the worst: *In the Field,* faith he, *Bears and Lions; in the City, Usurers and Sicophants.*

Ser. 64.
He compared Flattery to an empty Tomb, on which *Friendship* was inscribed.

Ser. 65.
Blaming *Antisthenes* for being too remiss in discourse, in regard that when he spoke loudest, he could hardly be heard, and calling himself the Trumpet of Reproof: *Antisthenes* reply'd, he was like a *Bee,* that makes no great noise, yet stings sharply.

Ibid.
He said, Reproof is the good of others.

Ibid.
A certain *Athenian* asking him why he lived not with the *Lacedemonians,* whom he praised so much: *Physicians,* faith he, *tho' they study Health, converse with the Sick.*

Ibid.
He said, other Dogs bark at their Enemies, I my Friends, that I may preserve them.

Ibid.
He asked *Plato* if he were writing Laws: *Plato* affirm'd he was. Did you not write a Commonwealth before, faith *Diogenes*? I did, answers *Plato.* And had not that Commonwealth Laws, said he? the other answering it had; *To what end* reply'd *Diogenes, do you write new Laws?*

Ser. 68.
He said, *To give Physick to a dead Body, or advise an old Man, is the same thing?*

Ser. 71.
To a bald Man that reviled him, *I will not return your Reproaches,* faith he, *yet cannot commend your Hair, for leaving so bad a Head.*

Ibid.
To an Informer that fell out with him; *I am glad,* faith he, *of the enmity betwixt us, for you hurt not your Foes, but your Friends.*

Sey. 72.
To one that reviled him; *No man,* faith he *will believe you when you speak ill of me, no more than they would me, if I should speak well of you.*

Ser. 77.
Alexander sent him a Dish full of Bones with this Message, it was meat for Dogs; he answered, *Yea, but not for a King to send.*

He said, *It was the same fault to give to them that deserved nothing, as not to give to them that do.* *Ibid.*

He said, *As Houses where there is plenty of Meat, are full of Mice, so the Bodies of such as eat much, are full of Diseases.* *Ser.* 87.

At a Feast, one giving him a great Cup full of Wine, he threw it away, for which being blamed, *If I had drunk it,* faith he, *not only the Wine would have been lost, but I also* *Ser.* 88.

Being demanded what was hardest, he answer'd, *To know our selves, for we construe most things according to our own Partiality.* *Ser.* 105.

He said, *Medea* was a wise Woman, and not a Witch, who by Labour and Exercise corroborated the Bodies of Effeminate Persons, whence arose the Fable, that she could renew Age. *Se.* 117.

To one that profess'd himself a *Philosopher,* but argued litigiously, he said, *Why do you spoil the best part of Philosophy, yet would be thought a Philosopher?* *Ser.* 126.

Questioning one of those young Men that followed him, he was silent; whereupon *Diogenes, Do you not think,* faith he, *it belongs to the same man to know when to speak, and when to hold his peace?* *Ser.* 133.

Being demanded how a man should live under the Authority of Superiors; *as we do by Fire,* faith he, *not too near, lest it burn; not too far off, lest we freeze.* *Ser.* 149, & 153.

Seeing some Women talk privately together: he said, *the Asp borrows Poyson from the Viper.* *Ser.* 183.

Being demanded what was the heaviest burden the Earth bears, he answered, *An ignorant Man.* *Ser.* 210.

An Astrologer in the *Forum,* discoursing to the People, and shewing them in a Tablet the *Errat*ick Stars: *No,* faith *Diogenes, it is not the Stars that err, but these,* pointing to the People. *Ser.* 211.

Being demanded what Men are the most noble: *They,* faith he, *Who contemn Wealth, Glory, and Pleasure, and over-master the contraries to these, Poverty, Ignominy, Pain, Death.* *Ser.* 216.

Seeing the Servants of *Anaximenes,* carrying many goods, he demanded to whom they belonged; they answered to *Anaximenes. Is he not ashamed,* replied *Diogenes, to have so much Houshold-stuff, and yet not be Master of himself?* *Ser.* 230.

He said, Vertue dwelleth neither in a rich City, nor a private House. *Ser.* 233.

He said Poverty is a self-taught help to Philosophy; for what Philosophy endeavours to perswade by words, Poverty enforceth in practice. *Ser.* 235.

To a wicked man reproaching him for his poverty; *I never knew,* faith he, *any man punished for Poverty, but many for Wickedness.* *Ibid.*

He called Poverty a self-instructing Virtue. *Ibid.*

To one that reproached him with Poverty: *What mean you,* faith he? *Poverty never made a Tyrant, Riches many.* *Ser.* 237.

Alexander seeing him asleep in his Tub, said, O Tub full of Wisdom: The Philosopher rising up, answerd, Great King, *Ser.* 248.

One drop of Fortune's better far
Than Tubs replete with Wisdome are.

To whom a stander by reply'd.

One drop of Wisdom Fortune's Seas excells;
In unwise Souls misfortune never dwells.

Ser. 270.	Seeing an old Woman painted, *If this be for the living, you are deceived,* saith he; *if for the dead, make haft to them.*
Ser. 271.	To one bewailing his own misfortune, as that he should not die in his own Country, *Be of comfort,* saith he, *the way to the next World is alike in every place.*
Æl. var. hift. 10, 11.	Having a great pain in his shoulder which troubled him much, one said to him in derision, why doft thou not die, *Diogenes,* and free thy self from this Misery? He answer'd, *It is fit they fhould live who know how to order their Life ; for you who know not what to do or fay, it is a convenient time to die.*
Plut. de Exul.	He used to say, *Ariftotle* Dineth when *Philip* pleafeth, but *Diogines* when it pleafeth *Diogenes*.
Plut. quorum. ger. Refp.	At *Corinth,* seeing *Dionyfius* the younger, who was depofed from the Kingdom of *Sicily, This is a Life,* faith he, *you deferve not, you merit rather not to live here freely and without fear,* but *at home in perpetual imprifonment.*
Plut. de vert. Moral.	To fome who commended *Plato,* he said, *What hath he done worthy commendation, having profeffed Philofophy fo long, yet never moved any to grief.*
Plut. aud. de Poet.	To one demanding how he might take the greateft Revenge upon his Enemy, he answered, *By being Good and Virtuous your felf.*
Macrob. Sat. 7, 3.	In commending his Mafter *Antifthenes,* he would say of him, *Of Rich, he made me Poor ; and instead of a fair Houfe, made me live in a Tub.*

CHAP. VI.
His Writings.

OF the *Writings* ascribed to him, are thefe.

Dialogues.	Of Death.
Ichthyas.	Epiftles.
The Geay.	Trgedies 7.
The Leopard.	
The Athenian People.	⎰ Helena.
Policy.	⎱ Thyeftes.
Ethick Art.	⎰ Hercules.
Of Riches.	⎱ Achilles.
Erotick.	⎰ Medea.
Theodorus.	⎱ Chryfippus.
Hypfias. Ariftarchus.	OEdipus.

Soficrates and *Satyrus* affirm, that none of thefe were written by *Diogenes*; the Tragedies *Statyrus* afcribes to *Philifcus* of *Ægina*, *Socion* affirmeth thefe only to have been written by *Diogenes.*

Of Vertue.	Cephalio.
Of Good.	Philifcus.
Erotick.	Ariftarchus.
The Poor.	Sifiphus.
The Tolerant.	Ganymede.
The Leopard.	Chria's, &
Caffander.	Epiftles.

CHAP. VII.
His Death.

HE Died, as *Demetrius* faith, at *Corinth* about 90 years old, the same day that *Alexander* died at *Babylon*; which according to *Ælian* was the feventh of *Thargelion,* in the firft year of the 114*th* Olympiad.

The manner of his death is varioufly related. *Eubulus* faith, he lived to his end with *Xeniades,* and was buried by his Sons. As he lay fick, *Xeniades* asked him how he would be buried; he anfwered, with his Face downward ; *Xenides* demanding the reafon, *Becaufe,* faith he, *all things will be turned upfide down*; alluding, faith *Laertius,* to the greatnefs of the *Macedonians,* who not long before were a poor inconfiderable People. Some report, that being near Death, he gave order that his Body fhould be left unburied, that the wild Beafts might partake of him, or be thrown into a Ditch, and a little duft be caft over it ; or thrown upon a Dung-hill, that he might benefit his Brethren.

Ælian faith, that being fick to Death, he threw himfelf down from a Bridg which was near the Gymnafium, and ordered the Keeper of the *Palestra* to take his Body and throw it into the River *Iliffus*. *Var. Hift. 8, 14.*

Others affirm he died of a Surfeit of raw flefh; others, that he ftop'd his own Breath ; others, that cutting a Cuttle-fifh in pieces to throw it to dogs, it bit afunder a Nerve in his Foot, whereof he died.

Others affirm he died as he was going to the Olympick Games: Being taken with a Fever, he lay down by the way, and would not fuffer his friends to carry him; but fitting under the fhade of the next Tree, fpoke thus to them; *This night I fhall be a Victor, or Vanquifhed; if I overcome the Fever, I will come to the Games; if not, I muft go to the other World, and drive it away by death.*

Antifthenes faith, his Friends were of opinion he ftopp'd his own breath ; for coming, as they conftantly used, to vifit him in the *Cranæum* where he lived, they found him covered : they did not imagine it was fleep, by reafon of his great wakefulnefs; but immediately putting back his Cloak, perceived he was dead. Hereupon there arofe a contention amongft them who fhould bury him ; they fell from words to blows; but the Magiftrates and great ones of the City, came themfelves and buried him by the Gate, which leads to *Ifthmus*. Over the Sepulchre they placed a Column, and upon it a *Dog,* cut out of *Parian* Stone. Afterwards his own Country-men honoured him with many brazen Statues, bearing this Inscription ;

> Time doth the ftrongeft Brafs decay ;
> Diogenes, thou ne'er canft dye,
> Who to content the ready way
> To following Ages didft defcry.

Laertius reckons *five* of this name ; the *firft* of *Apollonia,* a Natural Philofopher.
The *fecond* a Sicionian.
The *third* this.
The *fourth* a Stoick of *Seleucia.*
The *fifth* of *Tarfis.*

MONIMUS.

MOnimus was a *Syracufian,* Difciple to *Diogenes*; he was firft Servant to a Moneychanger, to whom *Xeniades* who bought *Diogenes,* often coming, he was fo taken with the Worth and Virtue of the Perfon, that he counterfeited himfelf Mad, and threw all the Money from off the Table, whereupon his Mafter turning him away, he betook himfelf to *Diogenes.* *Laert.*

He

He followed likewife *Crates* the Cynick, and others of that Sect, which confirm'd his Mafter in the Opinion that he was Mad. He was a Perfon Eloquent and Learned, mentioned by *Meander* in his *Hippocramus*; of fo great conftancy that he contemned all Glory for Virtue's fake. He wrote fome things, which at firft appearance feemed *Ludicrous*, but contained deep ferious Senfe : as of *Appetites* two Books, and a *Protreptick*.

ONESICRITUS.

Laert.

Onesicritus was of *Ægina*; or according to *Demetrius*, an *Aftypalæan*; he had two Sons : he fent the younger, named *Androfthenes*, to *Athens*, who hearing *Diogenes*, would not depart thence. Hereupon he fent the elder, named *Philifcus*, who ftayed there likewife for the fame reafon. Laftly, the Father himfelf went, and was fo much taken with *Diogenes*, that he became a fedulous Auditor of him, as his two Sons were.

He was efteemed amongft the moft eminent Difciples of *Diogenes*. *Laertius* compares him with *Xenophon*: One fought under *Cyrus*, the other under *Alexander*: One wrote the *Inftitution of Cyrus*, the other the *Praife of Alexander*: Their Stiles alfo were very like.

CRATES.

Crates was a *Theban*, Son of *Afcandas* : He was likewife reckoned amongft the moft eminent of *Diogenes*'s Difciples : yet *Hippobotus* faith, he was not a Difciple of *Diogenes*, but of *Bryfo* the *Achæan*.

He flourifhed about the 113*th* Olympiad : *Antifthenes*, in his *Succeffions*, faith, that being at a Tragedy where *Telephus* was reprefented, carrying a Basket in a fordid condition, he betook himfelf to the Cynical Philofophy, and felling all his Eftate, (for he was very Rich, having gotten together above two hundred Talents) he diftributed it amongft the Citizens, and was fo conftant a Profeffor of this Philofophy, that *Philemon*, the Comick Poet, takes notice thereof in thefe words.

By him in Summer a thick Coat was worn.
In Winter-time (fo temperate) a torn.

Diocles faith, *Diogenes* perfwaded him to part with his Eftate, and to throw all the Money he had left into the Sea : and that the Houfe of *Crates* was from *Alexander*, that of *Hipparchia* his Wife, from *Philip*. Some of his near Friends that came to him to diffwade him from this courfe of Life, he beat away, for he was of a refolute fpirit.

Demetrius the *Magnetian*, faith, he depofited fome Money in the hands of a Banquier, with this condition, that if his Sons betook themfelves to any Civil Employments, it fhould be repaid again ; but, if to Philofophy, it fhould be diftributed amongft the People, for as much as a Philofopher ftands in need of nothing.

Eratofthenes relates, that having a Son named *Pafícles*, By his Wife *Hipparchia*, as foon as he arrived at mans Eftate, he brought him to the houfe of a young maid that was his flave, faying, This is a hereditary matrimony to you : but thofe who commit adultery, are, according to the Tragedians, punifhed with banifhment or death ; Thofe who keep Concubines were, according to the Comedians, by luxury and drunkennefs, tranfported to madnefs.

Pafícles, the Difciple to *Euclid*, was his brother.

He faid, 'tis not poffible to find a man without a fault ; for, in every Pomgranat there is at leaft one grain corrupt.

Having difpleafed *Nicodromus* a Lutinift, he beat him black and blew ; whereupon he pafted a piece of paper on his Forehead, wherein was written, Nicodromus *did this*.

He was exceedingly invective againft common women.

He reproved *Demetrius Phalerius* for fending bread and wine to him, faying, *I wifh the fountains alfo produc'd bread* ; intimating, that he lived with water.

The Athenian Magiftrates blamed him for wearing a long robe ; *I will fhew you,* Theophraftus, fays he, *in the fame attire* ; which they not believing, he brought them to a Barber's fhop, where he was fitting to be trimm'd.

At *Thebes*, being beaten by the Mafter of the *Gymnafium* ; or, as others, at *Corinth* by *Enthicrates*, he laughed, faying,
He by the foot him drew,
And o'er the threfhold threw.

Zeno in his *Chrias* faith, he fowed a fheepskin upon his cloak, to appear the more deformed. He was of a very unhandfome look ; and whilft he difcourfed, laughed.

He ufed to lift up his hands and fay, *Be of good courage,* Grecians, *both for the eyes and all other parts, for you fhall foon fee thefe deriders furprifed by ficknefs, and proclaiming you happy, blame their own flothfulnefs.*

He faid, we ought fo long to ftudy Philofophy, until the leaders of the Army feem to be Horfe-drivers.

He faid, they who lived with Flatterers, were forfaken perfons, living like fheep amidft wolves, not with thofe who wifh'd them well.

Perceiving he drew nigh to death, he looked upon himfelf, faying,
———*And doft thou go, old Friend,*
To the next World, thou whom old age doth bend?
For he was Crooked through Age.

To *Alexander*, asking whether he would that his Country fhould be reftored, or not : *To what end,* faith he, *feeing there will come perhaps another* Alexander, *and Depopulate it.* He faid, Contempt of Glory and Want were his Country, which were not fubject to Fortune ; and that he was Countryman to *Diogenes*, not fearing any body.

Stob. Ser. 37.

Coming into the *Forum*, where he beheld fome buying, others felling : *Thefe,* faith he, *think themfelves happy in employments contrary to one another* ; *but I think my felf happy, in having nothing to do either way.*

Ser. 62.

To a young man followed by a great many Parafites : *Young Man,* faith he, *I am forry to fee you fo much alone.*

Ser. 77.

He faid, *We ought not to accept gifts from all men, for Virtue ought not to be maintained by Vice.*

Seeing at *Delphi* a golden Image of *Phryne* the

the Curtezan, he cried out, *This is a Trophy of the Grecian Intemperance.*

Seeing a young man highly fed and fat: *Unhappy youth,* saith he, *do not fortifie your Prison.*

He said, *He gained Glory, not by his Riches, but his Poverty.*

To one, demanding what he should get by Philosophy: *You will learn,* saith he, *to open your purse easily, and give readily, not as you do now, turning away, delaying and trembling, as if you had the Palsey.*

He said, *Men know not how much a Wallet, a measure of Lupines, and security of mind is worth.*

The Epistles of *Crates* are extant, wherein, saith *Laertius,* he writes excellent Philosophy, in stile resembling *Plato.* He wrote *Tragedies* likewise, full of deep Philosophy.

He died old, and was buried in *Bœotia.*

METROCLES.

Metrocles was Disciple of *Crates*, Brother to *Hipparchia*. He first heard *Theophrastus* the *Peripatetick*, &c. afterwards apply'd himself to *Crates*, and became an eminent Philosopher.

He burnt, as *Hecaton* saith, his Writings, saying, *These are the Dreams of Wild Phantastick Youth.*

He burnt likewise the dictates of his Master, *Theophrastus.*

Vulcan come hither, Venus *needs thy aid.*

He said, *Of things, some are purchased by money, as Houses; some by time and diligence, as Learning: Riches is hurtful, if not rightly apply'd.*

He died old, he strangled himself.

Of his Disciples are remembred *Theombrotus* and *Cleomenes. Demetrius* of *Alexandria* was Auditor of *Theombrotus: Timarchus* of *Alexandria*, and *Echicles* of *Ephesus*, were Disciples of *Cleomenes. Echicles* heard also *Theombrotus*, from whom came *Menedemus*, of whom hereafter. Amongst these was also *Menippus*, of *Sinopis.*

HIPPARCHIA.

Hipparchia was likewise taken with the Discourses of those *Cynicks*, she was sister to *Metrocles*; they were both *Marionites*. She fell in love with *Crates*, as well as for his Discourse as manner of Life, from which none of her Suitors by their Wealth, Nobility or Beauty, could divert her, but that she would bestow her self upon *Crates*; threatning her Parents, if they would not suffer her to Marry him, she would kill her self. Hereupon her Parents went to *Crates*, desiring him to disswade her from this Resolution; which he endeavoured, but not prevailing, went away, and brought all the little Furniture of his House and shewed her, *This,* saith he, *is your Husband, That the Furniture of your House; consider upon it, for yor cannot be mine unless you follow the same course of Life.* She immediately took him, and went up and down with him, and and in publick, συνεγίνετο, annd went along with him to Feasts.

At a Feast of *Lysimachus,* she met *Theodorus* the *Atheist,* with whom she argued thus; if that, which if *Theodorus* do, be not unjustly done, neither is it unjustly done if *Hipparchia* do the same: But *Theodorus,* if he strike himself, doth not unjustly; therefore *Hipparchia* doth not unjustly if she strike *Theodorus*; *Theodorus* answered nothing, only plucked her by the Coat, which she wore not like a Woman, but after the manner of the *Cynicks*; whereat *Hipparchia* was nothing moved; whereupon he said,

Her Webb and Loom
She left at Home.

I did, saith she, *Theodorus,* and I think have not erred in choosing to bestow that time which I should have spent in weaving, on Philosophy.

Much more saith *Laertius* is ascribed to her.

MENIPPUS.

Menippus was a *Cynick,* a *Phœnician,* by Birth, Servant by condition, as *Achaichus* affirms. *Diocles* saith, his Father was of *Pontus*, called *Bato Menippus* for acquisition of Riches went to *Thebes,* and was made free of that City. He wrote nothing serious, all his Books being full of Mirth, not unlike the writings of *Meleager. Hermippus* saith, he was named *Hemerodanista,* the daily Usurer, for he put out Money to Merchants upon Interest, and took pawns; at last being cheated of all his goods, he hanged himself.

Some say the Books that are ascribed to him, were writ by *Dionysius* and *Zopyrus, Colophonians,* which being ludicrous, they gave to him as a person disposed that way; they are reckoned thirteen.

Nænia's.
Testaments.
Epistles, in the persons of the Gods.
Two Natural Philosophers, Mathematicians and Grammarians.
Of Epicure.

Laertius reckons six of this name; the first wrote the *Lydian* story, and epitomiz'd *Xanthus.*
The *second* this.
The *third* a Sophist, of *Caria.*
The *fourth* a Graver.
The *fifth* and *sixth* Painters, both mention'd by *Apollodorus.*

MENEDEMUS.

Menedemus was Disciple of *Colotes,* of *Lampsacum*; he proceeded, as *Hippobotus* relates, to so great extravagance, that he went up and down in the habit of the Furies, declaring he was come from the World below to take notice of such as offended, and that he was to return thither to give an account of them.

He went thus attired, *A dark Gown to's heels, girt with a purple girdle; upon his head an Arcadian hat, on which were woven the twelve signs; tragick buskins, a long beard, in his hand an ashen staff.* Hitherto of the *Cynicks*.

THE

PART VI.   293

THE
HISTORY of PHILOSOPHY.

The Eighth Part.
Containing the *STOICK* Philosophers.

ZENON
CHAP. I.

His Country, Parents, First Studies.

THE Sect of *Stoicks* had its Original from the *Cynicks*, *Zeno* was the Author thereof, who having first been a Scholar of *Crates*, and afterwards a hearer of other Philosophers, at last instituted this new Sect. * He was born at *Cittium*, a Greek Sea-town, in the Isle of *Cyprus*, *b* with

Laert.

Strab. lib. *b* with a lock'd Haven, Inhabited by *Phœnicians*, *c* whence he sometimes was termed the *Phœnician*. His Father was called *Mnaseas*, by some *Demeas*, a Merchant, whence was objected to *Zeno*, the obscurity of his Birth and Country, as being *d* a Stranger, and of mean Parentage, whereof he was so far from being ashamed, that *e* he refused to be made a Citizen of *Athens*, as conceiving it to be an undervaluing of his own Country; in so much as *f* when he contributed to a Bath in *Athens*, and his Name was inscribed upon a Pillar with the Title of Philosopher, he desired they would add a *Cittiean*.

c Suid.

d Cit. de fin.

e Plut. de rep. Stoic.

f Laert.

g *Zeno* (as *Hecaton* and *Apollonius Tyrius* relate) enquiring of the Oracle what course he should take to lead the best course of Life, was answer'd, that he should converse with the dead; whereupon he addicted himself to the reading of ancient Authors.

g Laert.

h Herein he was not a little furthered by his Father, who, as *Demetrius* saith, trading frequently to *Athens*, brought him as yet but very young, many Socratical Books, which excited in him a great Affection to Learning.

h Laert.

i Being now 17. (or as *Perseus* 22) years old, he took a Voyage to *Athens*, carried thither as well by his particular inclination to Philosophy, as by his Business, which was to sell some Purple that he had brought out of *Phœnicia*. He took along with him a hundred Talents, and having sold his Merchandise, apply'd himself to Philosophy, yet continued to lend his Money out to Merchants upon Interest, so to improve his Stock.

i Laert.

Some affirm his Ship was cast away in the *Piræum*, which news being brought him to *Athens*, he seemed nothing at all moved, but only said, *Thou dost well Fortune*, *k* *to drive me into a Gown*; or as *Seneca*, Fortune commands me to Study Philosophy more earnestly.

k Plut. de util. cap. ex inimic.

l Others say, That being troubled at the loss of his Ship, he went up to the City of *Athens*, and sitting in a Booksellers Shop, read a piece of *Xenophon*'s Commentaries, wherewith being much pleased, he asked the Book-seller where such men lived; *Crates* by chance passed by, the Bookseller pointed to him, saying, *Follow that Man*; which he did, and from that time forward, became a Disciple of *Crates*.

l Laert.

CHAP. II.

Of his Masters.

a Laert.

ZENO thus changing the course of his Life, applied himself to *Crates*, *a* being apt to Philosopy, but more Modest than suited with the Cynical Sect. Which *Crates* to remedy, gave him a Pot full of Pottage to carry through the Ceramick; and perceiving him to hide it, as ashamed, with his Coat, he struck the Pot with his Stick and broke it. *Zeno* running away, all wet, *What*, said he, *are you running away, little Phœnician? No body hurt you*. He made a little hollow cover of a Pot, in which he carried the Money of his Master *Crates*, that it might be in readiness when he went to buy meat. Thus he lived a while with *Crates*, during which time he writ his Book of the *Commonwealth*, whence some jesting, said, it was written under the Dog's tail.

At last deserting *Crates* he applied himself to *b* *Stilpo* the *Megarick* Philosopher. *Apollonius Tyrius* saith, That taking hold of his Cloak to pluck him away from *Stilpo*, he said, *O Crates, the handles by which the Philosophers are to be taken hold of, are their Ears; lead me by those your way, or else, tho' you constrain my Body to be with you, my mind will be with* Stilpo. With *Stilpo* he remained ten years.

b Laert.

From *Stilpo* he went to *Xenocrates*, being so well satisfied with the Instruction of these two Masters, that he said, *He made a very good Voyage when he was Ship-wreck'd*; tho' others apply it to his living with *Crates*.

c He afterwards apply'd himself to *Diodorus Cronus*, as *Hippobotus* avers, under whom he studied Dialectick, to which Science he was so much addicted, that *d* when a certain Philosopher of that Sect had informed him of seven Species of Dialectick, in that fallacy which is called *the Mower*, he asked him what he was to give him for his reward, the Philosopher demanded an hundred pieces of silver; *Zeno* (so much was he affected to Learning) gave him two hundred.

c Laert.

d Laert.

e Lastly, notwithstanding that he had made a great progress in Philosophy, he heard *Polemon*, whose Doctrine was *against Pride*; whereupon *Polemon* told him, Zeno, *I am not Ignorant that you lie in Ambush, and come slily into my Garden* (as the *Phœnicians* use) *to steal away Learning*.

e Laert. Suid.

CHAP. III.

His School, and Institution of a Sect.

HAving been long a hearer of others, he at last thought fit to communicate the Learning which he had received and improved. To this end he made choice of the ποικίλη σοα, *the painted Walk*, so named from the Pictures of *Polygnotus*, otherwise called *Pisianactia*. Here he constantly walked and discoursed, resolving to settle there, and make the place as full of Tranquility as it had been before of Trouble: For, in the time of the thirty Tyrants, near 1400 Citizens were there put to Death.

a Laert.

Hither resorted a great many Disciples to him, who were at first called *Zenonians*, as *Epicure* affirmeth, from their Master, afterwards from the place where he taught, *Stoicks*, as *Eratosthenes* in his eighth Book of Antient Comedy; adding, that not long before, some Poets that lived there were called *Stoicks* also, upon which occasion the name was very well known.

He was subtil in Disquisition and Dispute.

He Disputed earnestly with *Philo* the Dialectick, and exercised himself together with him: so that *Zeno the younger* admired him no less than his Master *Diodorus*.

He first seemeth (saith *Laertius*) to have set a bound to the looseness and extravagance of Propositions: But of this more when we come to speak of his Philosophy, which by reason of its largeness, we remit to the end of his Life.

CHAP.

CHAP. IV.

What Honours were conferred upon him.

ZENO, by the Philosophy which he taught, and the practise of his Life conformable to that Doctrine, gain'd so high an Estimation amongst the *Athenians*, that *a* they deposited the Keys of the City in his Hands, as the only Person fit to be entrusted with their Liberties. His Name was likewise much Honoured by his own Country-men, as well those at *Cyprus*, as those who lived at *Sidon*.

a Laert.

Amongst those who honoured and favoured *Zeno*, was *Antigonus Gonotus* King of *Macedonia*, a Prince no less Eminent for his Vertue than his Greatness, much esteem'd him, and as often as he went to *Athens*, heard him. He sent many times to invite him to come to him, amongst the rest, one Letter to this Effect, alledged by *Apollonius Tyrius*.

King Antigonus *to* Zeno *the Philosopher, Health.*

I Think that *I exceed you in Fortune and Glory; but, in Learning and Discipline, and that perfect Felicity which you have attained, I am exceeded by you: Wherefore I thought it expedient to write to you, that you will come to me, assuring my self you will not deny it. Use all means therefore to come to us, and know, you are not to instruct me only, but all the* Macedonians. *For, he who teacheth the King of* Macedonia, *and guideth him to Vertue, it is evident that he doth likewise instruct all his Subjects in Vertue. For such as is the Prince, such for the most part are those who live under his Government.*

Zeno answered thus:

To King Antigonus, Zeno, *health.*

I Much esteem your earnest desire of Learning, in that you aim at Philosophy; not popular, which perverteth manners, but that true discipline which conferreth profit, avoiding that generally commended pleasure which effeminates the Souls of some young Men. It is manifest, that you are enclined to Generosity, not only by Nature, but by Choice. A generous Nature with indifferent exercise, assisted by a Master, may easily attain to perfect Virtue. But I am very infirm of Body, by reason of my Age, for I am fourscore Years Old, and therefore not able to come to you. Yet, I will send you some of my Con-Disciples, who, in those things that concern the Soul, are nothing inferior to me; in those of the Body, are much superior to me; of whom, if you make use, you will want nothing conducing to perfect Beatitude.*

Thus *Zeno* absolutely refused to go to *Antigonus*; but sent him his Disciple *Persæus*, Son of *Demetrius*, a *Cittiean*, (who flourished in the 130th Olympiad, *Zeno* being then very old) and *Philonides* a *Theban*, both mentioned by *Epicurus* in his Epistle to *Aristobulus*, as having been with *Antigonus*.

CHAP. V.

His Apophthegms.

OF his Apophthegms are remembred these: Of a Man very finely drest, stepping lightly over over a Kennel; *He doth not care for the Dirt*, saith he, *because he cannot see his Face in it.*

A certain *Cynick* came to him to borrow Oyl, saying he had none left: *Zeno* denied him, and as he was going away; *Now*, saith he, *Consider which of us two are the more Impudent.*

Laert.

Cremonides, whom he much affected, and *Cleanthes* sitting down beside him, he arose; whereat *Cleanthes* wondring, *I have heard good Physicians say*, saith he, *that the best remedy for Tumours is Rest.*

Laert.

Two sitting by him at a Feast, he that was next him hit the other with his Foot: *Zeno* hit him that was next him with his Knee, and turning him to him, *What then think you*, saith he, *that you have done to him that sits below you.*

To one that loved the company of Boys, *Neither have those Masters*, saith he, *any Wit, who converse always with Boys, nor the Boys themselves.*

He said, that Elegant Speeches were like *Alexandrian* Silver, fair to the Eye, and figured like Money, but not a whit of the more value. Speeches which are otherwise, he likened to *Attick* Tetradrachmes, which had a rough stamp, but were of greater value.

Aristo his Disciple discoursing many things foolishly, some petulantly, others confidently, *It cannot be*, saith he, *but your Father was drunk when you were begot*: Whereupon himself being very concise of Speech, he called him the *Talker*.

To a great Eater who left nothing for those that eat with him, he caused a great Fish to be set before him, and immediately to be taken away; the other looking upon him, *What*, saith he, *do you think your Companions suffer every day, seeing that you cannot suffer my Greediness once?*

Laert. Athen. deipn.

A yonng Man, who questioned something more curiously than suited with his Age, he brought to him a Glass, and bad him look in it, and then asked him, *whether he thought that Question agreed with that Face?*

Laert.

To one that said, he disliked many things of *Antisthenes*'s Writing, he brought his *Chria* of *Sophocles*, and asked him, if there were any thing therein excellent? The other answered, he knew not: *Are you not ashamed then* (replied *Zeno*) *if* Antisthenes *have said any thing ill, you select and remember that: but if any excellent, you are so far from remembring, as not to mind it?*

To one that said the Speeches of Philosophers were short: *You say very true*, saith he, *so should their very Syllables be, as much as is possible*

One saying of *Polemon*, that he proposed some things and said others: He frowning said, *What rate do you set upon things that are given?*

He said, that *a Disputant should have the voice and Lungs of a Comedian, but not the loudness.*

To those that speak well, he said, *we should allow a place to hear, as to skilful Artificers to see; on the other side, the hearer must so attend to what is spoken, that he take no time to censure.*

To a young Man that spoke much; *your Ears* saith he, *are fallen into your Tongue.*

To a handsome youth, who said, that he thought that in his Opinion, a wise man ought not to love: *Nothing*, saith he, *will be more unhappy to you that are handsome*.

He said, that *most Philosophers are in many things fools, in trivial and vulgar ignorant*.

He pronounced that of *Capecia*, who when one of his Disciples began to grow high, beating him, he said, *Right is not placed in Great, but Great in Right*.

To a young man discoursing with much confidence; *Young man*, saith he, *I should be loath to tell you my thoughts*.

A Youth of *Rhodes* Handsome and Rich, but refractory to him; not enduring, he bad him first sit in a dirty seat, that he might dirt his Gown; next placed him amongst the Beggars, that he might converse with them and their rags, until at last the young man went away.

He said, *that nothing is more unseemly than Pride, especially in young men*.

He said, that *we must not only commit to memory speeches and words, as those who make ready some dish of meat; but apply it, and make use of it in our minds*.

He said, that *young men must use all modesty in their walking, in their behaviour, and in their garments*; often repeating those Verses of *Euripides* concerning *Capaneus*.

He was not puft up with his Store,
Nor thought himself above the Poor.

He said, *nothing was more alienate from the comprehension of Sciences, than Poetry*: and, *that we need nothing more than Time*.

Being asked who is a friend? he answered, *My other self*.

Having taken his Servant in a Theft, he beat him; the fellow said, it was his destiny to steal; *and to be beaten*, said he.

He said, that *Beauty is the sweetness of the voice*, or, according to some, he called it, *the flower of Beauty*.

Seeing the Servant of one of his Companions black and blew with stripes; *I see*, saith he, *the fruits of your Anger*.

To one that smelt sweet of Oyntments; *Who is it*, saith he, *that smells so effeminately?*

To *Dionysius* sirnamed μεταθέμενος *the retractor*, who asked him, why he corrected all but himself; *because*, saith he, *I do not believe you*.

To a young man who spoke too freely, *For this reason*, saith he, *we have two Ears and but one Tongue, that we should hear much and speak little*.

Laert. Stob. Serm. 126.

He was invited to a Feast with other Philosophers by the Ambassador of *Antigonus* (according to *Laertius* of *Ptolomy*) and whilst of the rest every one amidst their Cups made Ostentation of their Learning, he alone sate silent; whereupon the Ambassadors asking him what they should say of him to *Antigonus*, *That which you see*, saith he; *for of all things, it's hardest to contain speech*.

Being demanded how he behaved himself when reviled, he said, *as an Ambassador dismiss'd without answer*.

He changed the Verses of *Hesiod*, thus,

Who good advice obeys, of men is best.
Next, he who ponders all in his own brest.

For that man (saith he) is better who can obey god advice, and make good use thereof, than he who finds out all things of himself; for the latter hath only understanding, but the other practice also.

Being demanded how it came to pass that being very austere, he notwithstanding was very cheerful and merry at a Feast; he answered, *Lupines, tho' in themselves bitter, being steeped, grow sweet*.

Laert. Athen. Deipn.

He said, it was *better to slip with the foot than with the tongue*.

He said, *That to do well is no small matter; to begin well, depended on a small moment*. This some ascribe to *Socrates*.

One of the young men in the Academy speaking of foolish studies, *If you do'nt dip your tongue in your mind*, saith *Zeno*, *you will speak many other foolish things*.

Stob. Serm. 33.

He accused many, saying, *when they might take pleasure in labour, they would rather go to the Cooks shop for it*.

Stob. Ser. 38.

He said, that *we should not affect delicacy of diet, not even in sickness*.

Stob. Ser. 33. citing Musonius.

Being demanded by one of his Friends, what course he should take to do no wrong; *Imagine*, reply'd he, *that I am always with you*.

Stob. Ser. 52.

Being demanded whether a man that doth wrong, may conceal it from God; *no*, saith he, *nor he who thinketh it*.

Stob. Ser. 52.

To some that excused their Prodigality, saying, that they had plenty, out of which they did it; *will you excuse a Cook*, saith he, *that should oversalt meat because he hath store of salt?*

Stob. Ser. 7.74.

He said that of his Disciples, *some were*, φιλόλογοι *lovers of Knowledge*; *others*, λόγοφιλοι, *lovers of speaking*.

Stob. Ser. 133.

He compared *the Arts of Dialectick to just measures filled, not with Wheat or any thing of value, but with Chaff and Straw*.

Stob. Ser. 212.

He said, *we ought not to enquire whether men belonged to great Cities, but whether they deserved a great City*.

Stob. Ser. 217.

Seeing a friend of his too much taken up with the business of his Land, *unless you lose your Land*, saith he, *it will lose you*.

Stob. Ser. 222.

He said, *a man must live not only to eat and drink but to use this life for the obtaining of a happy life*.

Stob. Ser. 297.

Antigonus being full of Wine, went to visit him, and kissing and embracing him as a drunken man, bad him demand whatsoever he would, swearing that he would give it him; *Zeno* answered, πορευθεὶς ἔμεσον, at once reproving his vice, and taking care of his health.

Ælian. var. hist. 9.26.

Stretching out the fingers of his right hand, he said, *such is phantasie*; then contracting 'em a little, *such is assent*; then closing them quite, and shutting his fist, *such is comprehension*; then putting to it his left hand, and shutting it close and hard, *such* (saith he) *is Science, of which none is capable but a wise man*.

Cic. Acad. quæst. 4.

CHAP. VI.
His Death.

a ZENO having continued according to *Apollonius*, Master of his School fifty eight years, and attained to the 98*th* of his age, by the computation of *Laertius* and b *Lucian*, (for that he lived but 72 years, as some affirm upon the testimony of c *Persæus*, seems to be a mistake, seeing that his Letter to *Antigonus* was written

a Laert.

written in his 80th year) *d* in all which time he was never molested by any Sickness; died upon this occasion; Going out of the School, he fell and broke his Finger, whereupon striking the Ground with his Hand, he said, as *Niobe* in the Tragedy, *I come, why do you call me?* Or as others, *Why do you drive me?* And going out, *e* some say, he immediately strangled himself; *f* others, that by little and little he famish'd himself.

d Laert.
e Laert.
f Suid.

g When the news of his Death came to *Antigonus*, he broke forth into these Words, *What a spectacle have I lost!* and being demanded why he so much admired him, *Because*, said he, *tho' I bestowed many great things upon him, he was never therewith exalted or dejected.* He sent immediately *Thraso* on Embassie to the *Athenians*, requesting that they would build him a Tomb in the Ceramick, which the *Athenians* performed, honouring him with this Decree.

g Laert.

A DECREE.

ARhenides *being Archon, the Tribe of Acamantis having the first place in the Phrytanæum, the tenth day of Maimacterion, the three and twentieth of the sitting of the Phrytanæum, the Congregation of Presidents decreed thus :* Hippo Son of Cratistoteles *a* Xympetean, *and the rest of the Presidents,* Thraso Son of Thraso, *an* Anacæan, *declared;*

Whereas Zeno Son of Mnaseas, *a Cittican, hath professed Philosophy many Years in this City, and in all other things performed the Office of a good Man, encouraging those young Men, who applied themselves to him, to Vertue and Temperance, leading himself a Life suitable to the Doctrine which he professed, a Pattern to the best to imitate; The People have thought fit (good Fortune go along with it) to do Honour to* Zeno Son of Mnaseas *the Cittiean, and to Crown him with a Crown of Gold according to the Law, in reward of his Vertue and Temperance, and to build a Tomb for him publickly in the Ceramick. For, the making of which Crown, and building of the Tomb, the People shall make choice of five Men of the* Athenians *to take charge thereof. This Decree the Scribe of the People shall write upon two Pillars, one whereof shall be placed in the Academy, the other in the Lyceum. The charge of the Pillars, he who is Overseer of the Publick Works shall undertake to defray, by way of Rate, that all may know, the* Athenian *People honour good Men both alive and dead. To take care of the bulding are appointed,* Thraso *an* Anacæan; Philocles, *a* Pyrean; Phædrus, *an* Amphistian; Medon, *an* Acarnean; Micythus *a* Sympalletean.

The *Athenians* caused likewise his Statue in Brass to be set up, as did also the *Cittieans* his Countrymen. *Antipater* the Sidonian bestowed this Epitaph upon him.

Here Zeno *lies, who tall* Olympus *scal'd,*
Not heaping Pelion *on* Ossa's *head,*
Nor by Herculean *Labours so prevail'd,*
But found out Vertue's Path which thither led.

Another Epigram was written upon him by *Xenodotus* the Stoick, Disciple of *Diogenes.*

Zeno *thy Years to hoary Age were spent,*
Not with vain Riches, but with self-content:
A stout and constant Sect deriv'd from thee
The Mother of nought-dreading Liberty:
Phœnicia, *whence thou issuedst, who can slight?*
Thence Cadmus *too, who first taught* Greece
to write.

CHAP. VII.

His Person and Vertues.

AS concerning his Person, *a* Timotheus saith, he was wry-neck'd: *Apollonius Tyrius*, that he was lean, tall, and of a swarthy complexion, whence stiled by some (as *Chrysippus*) the *Egyptian sprig*. *b* His look was sad, grave, severe and frowning; his Constitution not strong, for which reason *Perseus* saith, he forbore to feast much. His ordinary Diet consisted in raw food, especially Figs, both raw and dried, bread and honey, which he eat moderately, and a little sweet Wine.

a Laert.
b Laert.

His Continence was such, that when *Perseus*, who cohabited with him, brought a She-Minstrel to him, he immediately sent her back.

Laert.

Notwithstanding his Severity, he was very complaisant, and often feasted with King *Antigonus*, and meeting him sometimes drunk, went along with him to *Aristocles* the Musician, to nightly Banquets and Plays.

Laert.

Popular Ostentation he avoided, by sitting in the lowest place, whereby he freed himself from the troublesome importunity of the other part.

Laert.

He never walked with more than two or three at once: *Cleanthes* saith, he many times gave Money to People that they would not trouble him; and throng about him. Being on a certain time encompassed by a great Croud, he shewed them a wooden Ball on the top of the Cloyster, which formerly belonged to an Altar: This, saith he, was once placed in the middle; but, because it is troublesome, it is now laid aside: I desire you would in like manner withdraw your selves, that you may be less troublesome.

Laert.

He was so free from being corrupted by Gifts, that *Democharis* Son of *Laches*, desiring him to let him know what business he would have to *Antigonus*, promising to write about it, and assuring him, that *Antigonus* would furnish him with whatsoever he desired; he turned away from him, and would never after converse with him.

Laert.

He was so humble, that he conversed with mean and ragged Persons; whence *Timon*,

Laert.

And for Companions gets of Servants store,
Of all Men the most empty, and most poor.

He was most patient and frugal in his houshold-Expences, something inclining to the sordidness of the *Barbarians*. *Laertius* mentions one Servant that he had; *Seneca* avers he had none.

Whensoever he reprehended any, it was covertly and afar off, as may appear by many of his Apophthegms.

Laert.

His Habit was mean, whence it was said of him,

Laert.

Him nor the Winters rigid Frost or Rain,
The scorching Sun, or sharp Disease can pain:
Not like the common sort of People he;
But, Day and Night bent on Philosophy.

The Comick Poets unwittingly, intending to discommend him, praise him, as *Philemon*, in his Comedy of Philosophers,

He Water drinks, then Broth and Herbs doth eat,
To Live, his Scholars teaching, without Meat.

This some ascribe to *Possidippus*.

His Vertues were so Eminent that they grew at last into a Proverb, *More Continent than Zeno the Philosopher*; whence *Possidippus*,

——*He ere ten days were spent,*
Zeno in Continence out-went.

Indeed he excelled all men in this kind of Vertue, and in Gravity, and, by *Jove* (addeth *Laertius*) in Felicity likewise.

CHAP. VIII.

His Writings.

HE wrote many Books, wherein (saith *Laertius*) he so discoursed, as no *Stoick* after him: Their Titles are these:

Laert. de vit. Alex. Orat.

Of Common-wealth, written whilst he was an Auditor of *Crates*, and (as * *Plutarch* saith) much applauded; the Scope whereof was this, *That we should not live in several Cities and Towns by distinct Laws; but, that we should own all Men as our Countrymen and Fellow-Citizens; that there should be one manner of Life, and one Order, as one Flock which grazeth by equal right in one Pasture.*

Of Appetite; or, *of humane Nature.*
Of Passions.
Of Office.
Of Law.
Of the Discipline of the Grecians.
Of Sight.
Of the Universe.
Of Signs.
Pythagoricks.
Universals.
Of Words.
Homerical Problems 5.
Of hearing Poetry.
The Art.
Solutions.
Confutations.
Memorials.
The Morals of Crates.

* *Laert.*

* Some, amongst whom is *Cassius* a *Sceptian*, reprehended many things in the Writings of *Zeno*: First, that in the beginning of his Commonwealth, he affirmeth, *The Liberal Sciences to be of no use.*

Again, That *all wicked Men are Enemies among themselves, and Slaves and Strangers, as well Fathers to their Children, as Brethren to Brethren.* Again, That *only good men are Citizens, and Friends, and Kindred, and Children,* as he affirmeth in his Book of the *Commonwealth.* So that according to the *Stoicks*, Parents should be Enemies to their Children, because they are not wise.

That in his Commonwealth he would have *Women to be in common.*

That *no Temples, Courts of Judicature, nor publick Schools, should be built in a Commonwealth.*

That *Money is not necessary, neither for Exchange nor Traffick.*

That *Women should go in the same Habit as Men.*

CHAP. IX.

His Disciples.

ZENO (saith *Laertius*) had many Disciples, the most eminent these;

PERSEUS Son of *Demetrius*, a *Cittiean*; some affirm he was *Zeno*'s Scholar, others that he was one of the Servants which were sent by *Antigonus* to *Zeno* to transcribe his Writings; whence *Bion* seeing this Inscription on his Statue, PERSÆUS OF ZENO A CITTIEAN said, *The Graver mistook, for instead of ὁ κιτιεὺς, he should have put οἰκέτης, a Servant.*

Laert.

* *Athen.*

Afterwards he returned to *Antigonus* King of *Macedonia*; *Antigonus* to make a Tryal of him, caused a false Report to be brought him, that his Lands were spoiled by the Enemy; whereat appearing troubled, *Do you not see*, saith *Antigonus, that Riches are not to be reckoned amongst indifferent things?*

Antigonus so much favour'd him, that he preferred him to the Government of *Acrocorinthus*; on which Fort depended not only *Corinth*, but all *Peloponnesus*; in this charge he was unfortunate; for the Castle was taken by the cunning of *Aratus* a *Sicyonian* (* *Athenæus* saith, whilst *Persæus* was feasting) who turned out *Persæus*, whereupon afterwards to one that maintained *only a wise Man is a Governour*; *and I*, saith he, *was one of the same Mind, being so taught by Zeno, but now am of another Opinion*; *The Sicyonian young Man* (meaning *Aratus*) *hath taught me otherwise*; Thus *Plutarch*; But *Pausanias* saith that *Aratus* upon taking of the Fort, amongst others put *Persæus* the Governour to Death.

* *Deipn.*

He said, That *those were esteem'd Gods who had invented some things very useful to humane Life.*

Cic.

He wrote these Books; *Of a Kingdon*; *the Lacedæmonian Commonwealth*; *Of Marriage*; *Of Impiety*; *Thyestes*; *Of Love*, *Protrepticks*, *Exercitations*; *Chrya's* 4. *Commentaries, against Plato's Laws* 7. * *Symposiack Dialogues.*

ARISTO Son of *Miliades*, a *Chian*, Sirnamed the *Siren*; when *Zeno* fell into a long Sickness, he left him, and went (as *Diocles* saith) to *Polemo*: He was also a follower of *Persæus*, whom he flattered much, because of his favour with *Antigonus*; for he was much given to Pleasure, even unto his End. Thus revolting from his Master *Zeno*, he asserted,

* *Athen. Deip. Laert.*

That the end consists in those mean things which are betwixt Vertue and Vice; that is, in indifference; not to be moved on either side, nor to imagine the least difference to be in these things, but that they are all alike: For a wise Man is like a good Player, who whether he personate *Agamemnon* or *Thersides*, will act either part very well: Thus he took away the Dignity which *Zeno* held to be in these mean things betwixt Vertue and Vice; holding that there is no difference in them.

Cic. Acad. quest 4.

Cic. definit. 4.

He

PART VIII.   ZENO.

He took away *Physick* and *Logick*, affirming that one is above us, the other appertains nothing to us: *Ethick* only appertains to us; he compared Dialectick Reason to Cobwebs, which tho they seem artificial, yet are of no use.

He introduced not on any Virtues, as *Zeno*; nor one called by several names, as the *Megarick* Philosophers, but affirmed they have a Quodammodotative Relation to one another.

Professing these Tenets, and disputing in *Cunosarges*, he came to be called Author of a Sect; whence *Milciades* and *Diphilus* were called *Aristonians*.

He was very persuasive, and wrought much upon the common people, whence *Timon in Sillis*.

One of Aristo's *smooth persuasive Race*.

He defended eagerly this Paradox of the *Stoicks, That a wise man doth not Opinionate, but Know*; which *Perseus* opposing, caused of two like Twins, first, one to give a depositum to him, then the other to come and re-demand it; and by his doubting, if it were the same person, convinced him.

Laert. vit. Arces.

He inveigh'd against *Arcesilaus* [* calling him a corrupter of Youth.] On a time, seeing a Monster like a Bull, but of both Sexes, he said, *Alas! here is an Argument for* Arcesilaus *against Energy*. To an Academick who said, he comprehended nothing, (*do you not see* (saith he) *him who sitteth next you?* which he denying, *Who struck you blind* saith he, *or took your light away?*

He wrote these Treatises, *Protrepticks* 2. Of *Zeno*'s Doctrine: *Scholastick Dialogues* 6. Of *Wisdom Dissertations* 7. *Erotick Dissertations: Commentaries upon Vain-glory. Commentaries* 15. *Memorials* 3. *Chrias* 11. *Against Orators: Against* Alexinus *his Oppositions*; *To the Dialecticks* 3. *To* Cleanthes *Epist.* 4. But *Panætius* and *Sosicrates* affirm the *Epistles* only to be his, the rest to be *Aristo*'s the *Peripatetick*.

The Sun striking hot upon his head (which was bald) occasioned his death. There was another of the same name, a Juliite, a Peripatetick; another an Athenian, a Musician, a Tragick poet; a fifth, an Alæan, who writ *the Rhetorical Art*; a sixth of *Alexandria*, a Peripatetick.

Laert.

Erillus, (or as *Cicero*, *Herillus*) was a *Carthagenian*; when he was a Boy, he was Loved and Courted by many; which *Zeno*, by causing him to be shaved, diverted.

He held, That the end is Science, which is to live so, as to refer all things to Science, joyned with Life. That Science is a habit susceptive of phantasies, falling under Reason.

Yet, sometimes he said, there is no end; but, that the end it self is changed by the things, and those which are joyned to the things, as Brass, of which the Statues of *Alexander* and *Socrates* is made.

That τέλος the end, and ὑποτέλις differ, one is objected to unwise persons as well as wise, the other to wise only.

Those things which are betwixt Virtue and Vice, are indifferents.

His Books are written in a short Stile, consisting of few words, but very efficacious, wherein is contained what he held contrary to *Zeno*.

His Writings these, *Of Exercitation, Of Passion, Of Suspition, the Law-giver, Majeutick, Antipheron, The Master, The Preparative, The Directive,* Hermes, Medea, *Dialogues, Moral* Theses.

His Disciples were called *Herilians*, named by *Cicero* as a particular Sect amog the *Socriticks*.

Dionysius, Son of *Theophantus*, an Hracleot, from the change of his Opinion, sirnamed ὁ μεταθέμενος, *The Retractor*. He was from the beginning studiously addicted to Learning, and writ Poems of all kinds; then betook himself to *Aratus*, being much pleased with him. Of Philosophers he first heard, as *Diocles* affirms, *Heraclides* his Country-man; then *Alexines* and *Menedemus*, after these *Zeno*.

Laert.

Revolting from *Zeno*, he addicted himself to the *Cyrenæans*; he went to common houses, and addicted himself to other Pleasures.

He asserted the end to be Pleasure, and that by reason of his own pur-blindness; for being much grieved thereat, he durst not affirm Grief to be one of the indifferents.

He died eighty years old, starved.

His Writings are thus intituled, *Of Apathy* 2. *Of Riches and Favour, and Punishment*; *Of the use of Men*; *Of good Fortune*; *Of the Kings of the Ancients*; *Of things that are praised*; *Of the Customs of the* Barbarians.

Sphærus was of *Bosphorus*; he first heard *Zeno*, then *Cleanthes*, and having made a sufficient progress in Learning, went to *Alexandria* to *Ptolomy Philopater*, where there arising a dispute, Whether a Wise Man doth Opinionate, and *Sphærus* maintaining that he doth not, the King commanded some Quinces, *Athenæus* saith Birds, of Wax to be set before him, wherewith *Sphærus* being cozened, the King cried out, that he assented to a false phantasie; *Sphærus* presently answered, That *he assented not that they were Quinces, but that it was probable they were Quinces*; *but comprehensive Phantasie differs from probable,* * *for that is never false, but in probable matters sometimes a thing falls out otherwise than we imagined.* † *Menesistratus* accusing him that he denied *Ptolomy* to be King, he answered, that *he thought* Ptolomy, *or such a one was King*.

* *Athen.*
† *Laert.*

His Writings are these: *Of the World, of the Seed of Elements, of Fortune, of Beasts, against Atoms and Apparitions, of the Organs of Sense, upon* Heraclitus's *five dissertations*; *of Moral discription, of Office, of Appetite, of Passions* 2. *Dissertations of a Kingdom*; *of the Lacedemonian Commonwealth, of* Lycurgus *and* Socrates 3. *Of Law, of Divination, Erotick Dialogues, of the Eretriack* Philosophers, *of things like, of Definitions, of Habit, of Contraries* 3. *Of Reason, of Riches, of Glory, of Death, of the Art of Dialectick* 2. *Of Categorems, of Ambiguities, of Epistles*.

Cleanthes, whom *Zeno* compared to writing-tables, that are so hard, they will not easily admit an impression, but having once received it, keep it long. He succeeded *Zeno*, of him therefore apart.

Philon, a *Theban*.
Callippus, a *Corinthian*.
Possidonius, an *Alexandrian*.
Athenodorus of *Soli*; there were two more of the same name, Stoicks.
Zeno, a *Sidonian*.

Last in the Catalogue of his Disciples must be remembred an *Eretrian* youth (mention'd by * *Stobæus*) who heard *Zeno* till he came to be a man: then returning to *Eretria*, his Father asked him what he had learn'd all that time; he answered, he would shortly let him see, and did so: for, not long after, his Father in anger did beat him, which he took quietly, saying, *This I have learned, To bear with the Anger of a Father, and not to oppose it*.

* *Ethic. Serm. 198.*

In the Life of *Zeno* (for as much as he is Author of that Sect) it will be requisite to give account of the Doctrine of the Stoicks in general; wherein, if the terms seem harshly rendred, it will easily be forgiven by those, who consider the Stoicks were no less particular in their words, than in their Doctrines.

THE DOCTRINE OF THE STOICKS.

The *First* Part.

CHAP. I.

Of Philosophy in General, and Particularly of Dialectick.

a ... plac. Phil. 1.

Wisdom is the Science of things Divine and Humane; *Philosophy* is the exercitation of convenient Art. *Convenient* is the only and supream Virtue. Of *Virtues* in the most general Sense there are three kinds, *Natural, Moral, Rational*: For which cause Philosophy likewise hath three parts, *Physick, Ethick, Logick*: Physick, when we enquire concerning the World, and the things in the World: *Ethick* is employed about humane life: *Logick* is that part which concerns Reason, which is also called *Dialectick*. *b* Thus *Zeno* the *Citiean* first divided it in his Book *of Speech*; and *Chrysippus* in his first Book of *Speech*, and in his first of *Physicks*; and *Apollodorus Ephillus* in his first Book *of Introductions into Doctrines*; and *Eudromus* in his *moral Institutions*, and *Diogenes* the Babylonian, and *Possidonius*. These parts *Apollodorus* calleth *Places*; *Chrysippus* and *Euromus Species*; others *Genus's*.

b Laert.

That Logick is a part of Philosophy distinct from the rest, (wherein all the Stoicks agree) is proved by two Arguments, the first this: *e* Every thing which useth another, if that which the thing using, useth, be neither part nor particle, nor part of part of any other, it must be part or particle of the thing using; as Medicine useth the art of prescribing diet, which art being neither part nor particle of any other, is consequently a part or particle of Medicine; of part, as to the Cure; of particle, as to the Practice.

c Ammonius in Categ.

d Philop. in lib. 1. Anal. prior.

d Philosophy is conversant about Logick; Logick therefore is either a part or particle of Philosophy; but, a particle it is not, for it is not a part either of the Contemplative or the Active. That which is a particle of any thing, ought to have the same matter and scope with that whereof it is a part. Logick hath neither of these common with Active Philosophy, the matter whereof is humane things, and moderation of appetite, the common scope, what in them is to be embraced or shunned; but the matter of Logick is propositions; the scope, to demonstrate by a composure of propositions, that which necessarily falls out upon the Collection. Neither is Logick a part of the contemplative, the matter whereof is things Divine; the end, contemplation of them: now, if it be not a part, either of the contemplative or the Active, it is not a particle of Philosophy, but equally separate from both these, and consequently it must be a part of it.

e The second Argument is thus. No Art frameth its own Instruments; if therefore Philosophy make Logick, it is not its Instrument, but part thereof.

e Ammonius in Categor.

f Philosophy, is by some compared to a Field which produceth all manner of fruit: Physick to the soil and tall trees, Ethick to the mature pleasant fruit, Logick to the strong fence. Others liken it to an Egg: Ethick to the yolk, which some affirm to be the Chicken: Physick to the white, which is the nourishment of the Chicken, Logick to the outside or shell. *Possidonius*, (because the parts of Philos. are inseparable from one another, but plants are distinct from the fruits, as Walls from Hedges) chuseth rather to compare Philosophy to a living creature, Physick to Blood and Flesh, Logick to Bones and Nerves, Ethick to the Soul. (Thus *Sextus Empiricus*, by whom, perhaps, *Laertius* is to be corrected, who saith, *They likened Ethick to the Flesh, Physick to the Soul*) Lastly, they compare Philosophy to a City well Fortified and Governed according to Reason.

f Sext. Emp. adv. Log. 1.

g Some affirm, that none of these parts are distinct from the rest, but all intermingled with one another, for which reason they deliver them confusedly. The greater part place Logick first, Ethick next, Physick last; because the Mind ought first to be fortified for the keeping those things which are committed to it, so as it be not easily expugnable. The Dialectick place is a fortification for the Mind. Secondly, to describe the contemplation of Manners, that they may be reformed, which is safely undertaken, when the Logical power is first laid down. Lastly, to induce the contemplation of Nature, for that is more Divine, and requireth a more profound attention. This method *h* *Plutarch* affirms to have been observed by *Chrysippus*, adding that *of Physick, the last part, is that which treateth of God; for which reason they call the precepts of Religion τελεῖ*ᾶς. It seems therefore, that there is some mistake in *Laertius*, who of those who place Logick first, Physick next, and Ethick last, citeth *Zeno* in his Book *of Speech*, and *Chrysippus*, and *Archedemus*, and *Eudromus*. But *Diogenes* the *Ptolemæan* (continueth he) begins with Ethick: *Apollodorus* puts Ethick in the second place; *Panætius* and *Possidonius* begin with Physick, as *Phanias*, companion of *Possidonius* affirms in his first of *Possidonius's dissertations*.

g Laert.

h De Plac.

i Of Logick, *Cleanthes* assigneth six parts, Dialectick,

Dialectick, Rhetorick, Ethick, Politick, Physick, Theologick: Some affirm, these are not parts of Logick, but of Philosophy it self: So *Zeno* of *Tarsis*. The Logical part is by some divided into two Sciences, *Rhetorick* and *Dialectick*; some add *the definitive part*, some divide the definitive into that which concerns *invention* of truth (by which the differences of Phantasies are directed) and that which concerns *knowledge* of truth; for things are comprehended by notions.

k Laert.   *k* Rhetorick is the science of well speaking, by dilating upon the thing comprehended. *Dialectick* is the Science of well speaking, (that is true and consentaneous) or well disputing by Question and Answer. It is defined by *Possidonius*, the Science of *True, False, and Neuter*.

l Laert.   *l* Rhetorick is of three kinds, *Deliberative, Judicial, Demonstrative*: The parts of Rhetorick are *Invention, Stile, Disputation, Pronunciation*: *Rhetorical Speech* is divided into, *Proem, Narration, Confutation, Epilogue*.

m Laert.   *m* Dialectick is necessary, and a *virtue* within its species, containing other virtues, ἀπροπτωσία, a Science whereby we are taught when to assent, and when not; ἀνεικαιότης, a firm reason, whereby we resist appearances, and are not led away by them; ἀνελεγξία, a Fortitude of Reason which keeps us from being transported with the adverse opinion: ἀματαιότης a habit directing phantasies to right reason.

n Laert.   *n* Dialectick is a Science or certain comprehension, or a habit, not erring by reason in reception of phantasies; but without Dialectick, a wise man cannot be infallible in reason; for by this, we discern the true, false, and probable, and distinguish the ambiguous.

CHAP. II.

Of the Instruments and Rules of Judgment.

a Laert.   *a* IN the first place, they put the discourse concerning phantasies and sense, as a Judicatory, whereby the truth of things is discerned.

b Cic. Acad. 1.   *b* The Senses (according to *Zeno*, who made many alterations in Dialectick, and asserted many things of the Senses that were wholly new) are joyned by a certain kind of extrinsecal impulsion, termed phantasie. To these phantasies received by the senses, is added an assention of the mind, which is placed in us voluntary. The phantasie, when seen, is comprehensible, when received and approved, comprehension; and, if so comprehended, as that it cannot be plucked away by reason, science.

c Galen. hist. phil.   *c* Judgment is a perfection which discerneth a thing.

d Sen. Empir. adv. log.   *d* That which judgeth is taken two ways: 1. By which we say, some things are, others are not; these are true, those are false. 2. Of Essence only; and this is understood three ways, commonly, properly, and most properly. *Commonly*, for every measure of comprehension, in which sense, even those things which judge naturally, have this appellation, as sight, hearing, taft. *Properly*, for every artificial measure of comprehension; thus a cubit, a ballance, a ruler, a pair of compasses, are called things that judge; but sight and hearing, and the other common Instruments of Sense, are not. *Most properly*, for every measure of comprehension of a thing, uncertain, and not evident. In which sense, those things which belong to the actions of life, are not said to be things judging, but the logical only, and those which dogmatical Philosophers alledge for the invention of truth.

The Logical is subdivided into that *from which*, that *by which*, and *application* or habitude. *From which*, the man; *by which*, the sense: the third is the application of phantasie or sight. For as in the Staticks, there are three things which judg, the weigher, the ballance, and position of the ballance: The weigher is the judge from which, the ballance the judge by which, the position of the ballance, as it were a habitude. And again, as to discern right or oblique things is required an Artificer, a Ruler, and the application thereof; in like manner in Philosophy are required those three things mentioned to the discernment of true and false; the man from whom the judgment is made, is like the Weigher or Artificer; to the Ballance and Ruler answer Sense and Cogitation, by which the judgment is made: to the habitude of the forenamed instruments, the application of phantasie, by which a man cometh to judge.

e Laert.   *e* The *Judge* of Truth, they affirm to be *comprehensive Phantasie*, that is, proceeding from that which is; so *Chrysippus* in the 12th of his Physicks, and *Antipater*, and *Apollodorus*. But *Boethus* holds many Judicatories, the *Mind*, and *Sense*, and *Appetite*, and *Science*; from whom *Chrysippus* dissenting in his first Book of *Reason*, affirmeth the Judicatories to be *Sense* and *Anticipation*. Anticipation is a natural notion of Universals. Others of the more ancient Stoicks (as *Possidonius* saith in his Book of *Judgments*) assert right *Reason* to be the Judicatory.

CHAP. III.

Of Sense.

a St. Aug. Civ. dei. 8. 7.   *a* Dialectick is derived from corporeal senses; for, from thence, the Soul conceiveth *noterious* (ἔννοιας) of those things which are explained by definition, and from thence is propagated and connexed the whole reason of Learning and Teaching.

b Laert.   *b* Sense is a Spirit, proceeding from the supream part of the Soul, and permeating to the Organs.

c Orig. contra Cels. lib. 7.   *c* Whatsoever things are comprehended, are manifestly comprehended by Sense; all conceptions of the Mind depend upon Sense.

d Cic. Acad. quæst. 1.   *d* Comprehension made by the Senses is true and faithful, (according to *Zeno*) for as much as Nature hath given it as a rule for Science, and principle of her self.

e Cic. Acad. quæst. 8.   *e* Nothing is more clear than this ἐναργεία *evidence*, there cannot be any Speech more perspicuous:

f Sext. Empir. Pyrrh. hyp. 2. 8.   *f* Of Sensibles and Intelligibles, some are true, but, not directly sensible; but, by relation to those things which are next, as falling under Intelligence.

CHAP.

CHAP. IV.
Of Phantasie.

a Laert. IN the first place (saith *a Diocles* the *Magnesian*) they put the reason concerning phantasie and sense, as a judgment, whereby the truth of things is discerned. It is phantasie as to its genus, and likewise in as much as the reason of assent, comprehension, and intelligence (which is more excellent than the rest) consists not without phantasie; for phantasie goeth first, then the mind endued with elocution, declareth by words what it suffers from the phantasie.

b Plut. plac. Phil. 4. 12. *b* Phantasie is so called from φῶς light; for as light sheweth it self, and with it self all those things which are contained within it; so phantasie sheweth it self, and that which maketh it.

c Sext. Emp. Pyrrh. hyp. l. 2. *c* Phantasie is an impression in the Soul: *Cleanthes* adds, an impression by depression and eminence, as that impression which is made in Wax by a Seal.

Chrysippus conceives this to be absurd: For 1. saith he, when the Soul first apprehends a triangle and a square, it will follow, that the same body, at the same time, must have in it self several figures, which is absurd. Again, whereas many phantasies are together consistent in us, the the Soul must have diverse figures, which is worse than the former. He therefore conceived, that *Zeno* used the word Impression, for Alteration, meaning thus: Phantasie is an alteration of the Soul, whereby it is no longer absurd; that the same body (many several phantasies being at the same time consistent in us) should receive several alterations. For, as the Air receiving at once innumerable different percussions, hath presently many alterations: so the supream part of Soul, receiving various phantasies, doth something which hath proportion and conformity thereto.

Some object, that this exposition is not right: because, tho' every phantasie is an expression and and alteration in the Soul: yet, every impression or alteration of the Soul, is not phantasie; as when the finger smarts or itches, and the hand is rubb'd, there is then an impression or alteration in the Soul: but it is not phantasie, because it is not in the supream part of the Soul.

They answer, That in saying, an impression in the Soul, is implied as in the Soul as fully, as if we should say, phantasie is an impression in the Soul as in the Soul: as when we say, the white in the eye, we imply, as in the eye, that is, the white is in a certain part of the eye, which all men have so by nature. So when we say, Phantasie is an impression in the Soul, we imply the impression to be made in the supream part thereof.

Others more elegantly answer, that the word Soul is taken two ways, either for the whole, or for the principal part; when we say, man consists of Soul and Body; or, that death is a separation of the Soul from the Body; we mean properly the supream part, wherein properly consists the motions and goods of the Soul. When *Zeno* therefore calleth phantasie an impression in the Soul, he is not to be understood of the whole Soul, but of part thereof; as if he should say, phantasie is an alteration of the supream part of the Soul.

To this interpretation, some object thus: Appetition, Assention, and Comprehension, are alterations in the supream part of the Soul; but, these differ from phantasie, that being a certain kind of perswasion and affection, whereas this is more operation than appetition, therefore the definition is not good, being compatible to many other things.

They answer by recourse to συνέμφασεις (*impliancies*) that a definition is understood to be in all. As he who saith, Love is an application of the Soul towards procurement of Friendship, implieth amongst young people; so when we say, that phantasie is an alteration in the supream part of the Soul, we imply by perswasion; for, alteration is not made by operation.

d Of phantasies there are many kinds, some *d Laert.* are *sensible*, others *not sensible*. *Sensible* are those which are received through one or more of the senses: *Not sensible* are those which are received through the mind, as of incorporeals, and other things, comprehended by reason. The sensible formed from things that are, are made with concession and assent. There are also apparitions of phantasies, proceeding from things which are.

Again, some are *Rational*, others *Irrational*; *Rational*, those of Reasonable Creatures; *irrational*, those of Unreasonable. The Rational are intelligence, the Irrational have no name.

Again, some are *Artificial*, others *In-artificial*; for, an Image is considered by an Artist one way; by him that is not an Artist, another way.

e Again, some are *Probable*, others *Improbable*: *e Sext. E-pir. lib. 2.* The *Probable* are those which make an easie motion in the Soul; as, it is now day, I discourse, and the like. The *Improbable* are of a contrary nature, averting us from assent; as, it is day, the Sun is not above the Earth; if it is dark, it is day. Both *Probable* and *Improbable* are those, which, by relation to other things, are sometimes such as in doubtful speeches, neither probable are improbable nor, such, as these, The Stairs are even, the Stairs are odd.

Of probable and improbable phantasies, some are *true*, some are *false*, some are neither true nor false. *True*, are those, whose predication is true, as, It is day, 'tis light: *False*, whose predication is false; *Both true and false*, as happened to *Orestes* in his madness, meeting *Electra*; that he met something, it was true, for it was *Electra*; but, that it was Fury, was false. *Neither true nor false*, are those which are taken from the Genus; for the Genus is not such as the species in all respects: As, of men, some are *Grecians*, some are Barbarous; but, Man in general is not *Grecian*, for then all men must be *Grecians*; neither Barbarous, for the same reason.

Of true phantasies, some are *comprehensive*, others are *not comprehensie*. *Not-comprehensive* are those which happen through sickness, or perturbation of mind; many being troubled with Frensie or Melancholy, attract a true Phantasie which is not comprehensive, even from that which extrinsecally occurs casually, for which reason, they neither assert it often, not assent unto it. *Comprehensive* phantasie is that which is impressed and signed by that which is, and conformable to that which is, so as it cannot be of that which is not.

To comprehensive phantasie three *conditions* are requisite: 1. That it arise from that which is; for many phantasies arise from that which is not, as in mad men. 2. That it be conformable to that which is; for some phantasies are from that which is, but represents the similitude of that which is not: As *Orestes* derived a phantasie from that which was, *viz.* from *Electra*, but not according to that which was; for he thought her to be one of the Furies. Comprehensive phantasie must be conformable to that which is, and so impressed and signed, as that it may imprint artificially all the properties of the thing fancied, as Gravers touch all the parts of those things which they imitate, and the impression made by a Seal on Wax exactly and perfectly, beareth all its characters. Lastly, That it be without impediment; for sometimes comprehensive phantasie is not creditable, by reason of outward circumstances; as when *Hercules* brought *Alcestis* taken out of the Earth, to *Admetus*, *Admetus* drew from *Alcestis* a comprehensive phantasie, but did not credit it; for, he considered, that she was dead, and therefore could not rise again, but, that sometimes Spirits appear in the shape of the deceased.

f *Phantasie, Phantaston, Phantasticon,* and *Phantasm,* according to *Chrysippus,* differ thus: *Phantasie* is a Passion made in the Soul, which sheweth it self, and that which made it; as, when with our eyes we see white, it is a passion engendred by sight in the Soul, and we may call this a passion, because the object thereof is a white thing which moveth us: The like of smelling and touching.

Phantaston is that which maketh phantasie; as the white and the cold, and whatsoever is able to move the Soul, that is Phantaston.

Phantasticon is a frustraneous attraction, a passion in the Soul proceeding from nothing; as in those who fight with shadows, or extend their hands in vain: For, to phantasie is objected Phantaston, but Phantasticon hath no object.

Phantasm is that, to which we are attracted by that frustraneous attraction, which happens in Melancholy, or Mad persons; as *Orestes* in the Tragedy, when he saith,

Bring hither, Mother, I implore,
The Snaky Bloody Maids no more,
Whose very looks wound me all o're.

This he saith in his madness, for he saw nothing: wherefore *Electra* answers him,

Ah! quiet in thy Bed (unhapyy) lie,
Thou seest not what thou thinkst before thy eye.

CHAP. V.
Of True and Truth.

a T R U E (according to *Zeno*) is that which is impressed in the Mind from that whence it is, in such manner, as it cannot be from that which is not: Or, as others; b True is that which is, and is opposed to something. *False* is that which is not; yet, is opposed to something also.

Truth and True differ three ways, by *Essence*, by *Constitution*, by *Power*. By *Essence*, for Truth is a Body; but, True is incorporeal, for it is a dicible λεπτὸν, and therefore incorporeal. On the contrary, Truth is a Body, as being the enunciative Science of all true things. All Science is in some measure the supream part of the Soul, which supream part is a Body: therefore Truth in general is corporeal.

By *Constitution*; True is conceived to be something uniform and simple by nature; as, *It is day, I discourse*. Truth, as being a Science, consisteth of many things, by a kind of conservation. Wherefore as a People is one thing, a Citizen another; a People is a Multitude consisting of many Citizens; but, a Citizen is no more than one. In the same manner differeth Truth from True. Truth resembleth a People, True, a Citizen; for, Truth consisteth of many things collected, True is simple.

By *Power*; for True doth not absolutely adhere to Truth: A Fool, a Child, a Mad man, may speak something True, but, cannot have the Science of that which is True. Truth considers things with Science, insomuch that he who hath it, is wise; for, he hath the Science of true things, and is never deceived, nor lieth, altho' he speak false, because it proceedeth not from an ill, but good affection.

CHAP. VI.
Of Comprehension.

a Comprehension (κατάληψις) was first used in this sense by *Zeno*, by a Metaphor taken from things apprehended by the hand; b which allusion he exprest by action. For, shewing his hand with the fingers stretched forth, he said, such was phantasie; then bending them a little, said, such was Assent; then compressing them and clutching his fist, such was Comprehension.

c Comprehension is a firm and true knowledg, non-comprehension the contrary; for some things we only think that we see, hear, or feel, as in Dreams and Frenzies; other things we not only think, but truly do see, or hear, or feel. These latter, all but the Academicks and Scepticks) conceive to fall under firm knowledge; the other, which we imagine in Dreams or Frenzie, are false.

d Whatsoever is understood, is comprehended by the Mind, one of these two ways, either by *evident Incursion* (which *Laertius* calls by Sense) or by *Transition from evidence* (*Laertius*, Collection by Demonstration) of which latter there are three kinds, by *Assimulation*, by *Composition*, by *Analogy*.

By *Incurrent Evidence* is understood White and Black, Sweet and Sowr.

By *Transition* from evidents: By *Assimilation*, is understood *Socrates* by his Picture: By *Composition*, as of a Horse and Man is made a Centaur; for putting together the Limbs proper to both Species, we comprehend by phantasie that which was neither Horse nor Man, but a Centaur compounded of both.

By *Analogy*, things are understood two ways; either by *Augmentation*; or, when from common ordinary men, we by augmentation phancy a Cyclops, who not like

Men that with Ceres's gifts are fed,
But, some tall Hill erects his head.

Or by *Diminution*, as a Pigmy. e Likewise the Center of the Earth is understood by Analogy from lesser Globes.

To these kinds add, f Comprehension by *Transference*, as eyes in the breast; by *Contrariety*, as Death; by *Transference*, as dicibles, and place; by *Privation*, as a Man without hands; just and good are understood *Naturally*.

CHAP.

CHAP. VII.
Of Assent.

^{a cic. acad. quaest. 4.}

a These things being enough known, which we have already explained, let us now speak a little of *Assent*, and *Approbation*, term'd συνκαταθησις, not that, that is not a large place, but the grounds thereof have been already laid, For when we explained the power that was in the Senses, we likewise declared, that many things were comprehended and perceived by the Senses, which cannot be done without *Assent*. Moreover, seeing that betwixt an inanimate and an animate being, the greatest difference is, that the inanimate doth nothing, the animate doth something; we must either take away sense from it, or allow it assent, which is within our power. When we will not have a thing either to perceive or assent, we in a manner take away the Soul from it; for as it is necessary, that the scale of Ballance which is laden, should tend downwards; so is it that the Soul should yield to things that are perspicuous,

^{b cic. lib. de fato.}

b Altho' Assent cannot be made unless it be moved by phantasie, yet when that phantasie hath an immediate cause, it hath not (according to *Chrysippus*) this principal reason; not that it can be made without any extrinsecal excitation (for it is necessary that Assent be moved by phantasie) but it returns to its Cylinder and Cone, which move not by impulsion; then of their own nature the Cylinder seems to rowl, and the Cone to turn round. As therefore he who thrust the Cylinder, gave it the beginning of motion, but did not give it volubility; so the objected phantasie imprinteth, and as it were sealeth in the Soul its Species, yet the assent is in our power, and that (as he said in a Cylinder) extrinsecally impelled, the motion is continued by its own power and nature.

^{c Agell. 19. 9. and from him St. August. civit. dei. 9. 4.}

c Phantasies, wherewith the Mind of Man is presently affected, are not voluntary or in our own power, but infer themselves by a kind of violence, approbations (συγκαταθεσεις) by which these phantasies are known and judged, are voluntary, and made according to our arbitrement. So as upon any dreadful noise from Heaven, or by the fall of any thing, or sudden news of some danger, or the like; it is necessary that the mind of a wise Man be a little moved, and contracted, and appalled, not through opinion perceived of any ill, but certain rapid and inconsiderate motions, which praevert the office of the Mind and Reason. But presently the same Wise Man approveth not τας τοιαυτας φαντασιας, those dreadful phantasies, that is, ȣ συγκαταθετται ȣδε προσεπιδοξαζει, but rejects and refuses them; nor is there any thing in these, which seemeth to him dreadful. Thus differ the Souls of wise and unwise men: The unwise, when phantasies appear cruel and difficult at the first impulsion of the mind, think them to be truly such as they appear, and receiving them as if they were justly to be feared, approve them by their assent, ϗ προσεπιδοξαζει, (this word the Stoicks use upon this occasion:) But a wise man suddenly changing Colour and Countenance, ȣ συγκαταθετται, assents not, but retaineth the state and vigour of his judgment, which he always had of these phantasies, as nothing dreadful, but terrifying only with a false shew, and vain fear.

CHAP. VIII.
Of Notions.

a From Sense, the Rule of Science, Notions, ^{a cic. acad. 1.} are imprinted in the Soul, by which, not only principles, but larger ways to Reason are found out.

b A man when he is born, hath the supream ^{b Plut. de plac. phil. 4. 12.} part of his Soul, like unto clean paper, upon which every notion is inscribed. The first manner of inscription is by the Senses; as for example: They who perceive a thing that is white, after it is taken away, retain the memory thereof; but, when they have conceived many remembrances of one Species, then they say, they have experience, for experience is a multitude of similitudes.

Of *Notions*, some are *Natural*, which are in such manner as we have said, and without Art: Others *gained* by Learning and Industry: These are properly called *Notions*, the other *Anticipations*. The reason for which we are called rational, is said to be perfected by anticipations in the first seven years.

Intelligence is the phantasm of the Intellect of a Rational Creature; for phantasm, when it lighteth upon a rational Soul, is then called ἐννοημα, Intelligence, a word taken from the Intellect. For to other Creatures there happen not phantasms; to the Gods only, and to us these are incident. Those which belong to us, are phantasms, as to their genus; notions as to their species; as denaries and staters, when paid for transportation, are called *Naula*.

c Common Notions are planted in all men, ^{c Arrian. 1. 22.} (in which they all agree together) one is not repugnant to another; for, who holds not, that good is profitable, and ought to be chosen with utmost endeavours? Who holds not, that what is just, is fair and well beseeming? Whence then proceed contentions and differences? To wit, from the application of first notions to singular things.

d These Notions, and whatsoever is of this ^{d Simp. in Epic.} kind, which right reason conformeth in us, being long examined, are true, and suitable to the natures of things.

CHAP. IX.
Of Science and Opinion.

a That which is comprehended by Sense, Ze- ^{a Cicer. Acad. quaest. 1.} no called *Sense*; and if so comprehended, as not to be plucked away by reason, *Science*, otherwise *Ignorance*; from which proceedeth *Opinion*, which is weak and common, to the false and unknown.

b These three are joyned together, Science, ^{b Sext. Emp. adv. Logic.} Opinion, and Comprehension, which borders upon the other two. Science is a firm, stable, immutable comprehension with Reason. Opinion, an infirm, weak assent: Comprehension, which cometh between both, is an assent to comprehensive phantasie. Comprehensive phantasie

PART VIII.   ZENO.   305

tasie is true, in such a manner, that it cannot be false. Therefore Science is in wise Men only, Opinion in Fools; Comprehension is common to both, as being that by which Truth is judged; *c* and is for this Reason reckoned by *Zeno*, neither amongst the right (κατορθώματα) nor amongst the bad (ἁμαρτήματα) but betwixt Science and Ignorance, affirming, that this only is to be credited.

Cic. acad. quæst 1.

CHAP. X.

Of Voice, Speech, and Words.

a 'Sext. Emp. adv. Log. cap. de vero.

a THese three are joined to one another; that which is signified, that which signifieth, and the contingent. *That which signifieth*, is the Voice, as *Dion*; *That which is signified*, is the thing declared by the Voice; it is that which we apprehend, and is present in our Cogitation. *The contingent* is the outward Subject, as *Dion* himself.

b Laert.
c Laert.

b Dialectick being conversant about that which signifieth, and that which is signified, *c* is divided into two places: One, *Of Significats*, the other of *Voice*. The place of Significats is divided into *Phantasies, and subsistents on Phantasie, Dicibles, Axioms*, &c.

In the other place, concerning *Voice*, is declared literal *Voice*, the *parts of Speech*, the nature of *Solœcisms* and *Barbarisms, Poems, Ambiguities, Song, Musick*, and (according to some) *Definitions* and *Divisions*.

d Laert.

d The Phantasies of the Mind precede Speech, (*Of these therefore we have already treated*) then the Mind endued with the Faculty of speaking, declareth by Speech what it receiveth from the Phantasie: For this Reason, *e* the consideration of Dialectick, by the joint consent of all, seems as if it ought to be first taken from the place of Voice.

e Laert.

f Laert.

f Voice is Air percussed, the proper sensible object of Hearing, (as *Diogenes* the *Babylonian*, in his *Art of Voice*.) The Voice of a living sensitive Creature, is Air percussed with Appetite; the Voice of Man is Articulate, proceeding from the Mind: At his fourteenth year it is perfected.

g Laert.

Speech (as *g Diogenes* saith) is a literate Voice; as, it is Day. Word is a significative Voice proceeding from the Mind. *Language* is a Speech according to the variety of Nations, whereof each useth its peculiar Dialect; as the *Attick* saith, θάλαττα, the *Ionick* ἡμέρη. Voice and Speech differ, in that Voice is sound, but Speech articulate only. Speech and Word differ; for Word is always significative; but, Speech sometimes signifieth nothing, as *Blitiri*, which is no word. To speak and to pronounce differ; Voices are pronounced, but things only are spoken; *h* for, to speak, is to pronounce a significant Voice of a thing that is said.

h Sext. Emp. Adv. log. cap. de vero.
i Varro de ling. lat. lib.5

i Hence *Chrysippus* saith, That he who beginneth to speak and pronounce Words, before he can put them in their right place, doth not speak, but think that he speaks; as the Image of a Man is not a Man: So in Crows, Daws and Children, when they first begin to speak, the words which they say are not words. He only speaketh who knoweth to put a word in the right place.

They (particularly *k Zeno*) *l* took much pains in the Invention and Explication of words, *m* wherein they distinguished very subtilly. Hence *Cicero* calleth the *Stoicks* Architects of Words. *Ammonius*, the Grammarians, followers of the *Stoicks*.

k Cicero.
l Dionys. Halic.
m Hieronym.

n The *Elements* of Speech are the 24 Letters. *Letter* is taken three ways: First, for the Character or Figure which is formed. Secondly, for the Element or Power. Thirdly, for the Name, as *A*. Of the Elements, seven are *Vowels* α ε η ο υ ι ω, six *Mutes*, β γ δ κ π τ.

n Laert.

o Of Speech there are five parts, as *Diogenes* saith in his Book of *Voice*, and *Chrysippus p*. At first they reckoned but four, separating the *Articles* from the *Conjunctions*, afterwards the latter *Stoicks* dividing the *Appellatives* from the *Nouns*, made them five, *Noun, Appellation, Verb, Conjunction, Article*. (*Antipater* in his Book of *Speech* added the *medium*.) *Appellation* (as *Diogenes* saith) is a part of Speech signifying a common quality; as, Man, Horse. *Noun*, a part of Speech denoting a proper quality; as *Diogenes, Socrates*. *Verb*, (as *Diogenes* saith) a part of Speech signifying a thing, which is predicated of one or more things, incomposed; or, as some say, an Element of Speech without cases, whereby the parts of Speech are connected; as I write, I speak. *Conjunction* is a part of Speech without Cases, conjoining the parts of Speech. *Article* is an Element of Speech, having cases; distinguishing the kinds and numbers of Nouns; as, ὁ, ἡ τὸ, ὅι, αἱ, τά.

o Laert.
p Dionys. Halic.

q Every word, by reason of that which it signifieth, called four necessary things into question, its *Origin, Power, Declination, Ordination*.

q S. August de Dialect. cap.6.

As concerning the first, which the *Greeks* call Ετυμολογία, they conceiv'd that Names are given by Nature: the first pronounced Voices, imitating the things themselves, from which the Names were afterwards imposed, by which reason they derive Etymologies, conceiving that there is not any word, for which there cannot be given a certain Reason. They therefore studiously enquired whence words are deduced; much pains was taken, first by *Zeno*, then by *Cleanthes*, afterward, by *Chrysippus*, to give a reason of commentitious Fables, and to explain the causes of Words, why they are called so and so.

This beginning is to be sought, until we arrive so far, as that the thing agree in some Similitude with the sound of the word, as when we say *tinkling* of Brass, the *neighing* of Horses, the *bleating* of Sheep, the *gingling* of Chains: These words by their Sound, express the things which are signified by them.

But for as much as there are things which sound not, in these the Similitude of Touching hath the same Power: As they touch the Sense smoothly or harshly, the smoothness or harshness of Letters in like manner touches the hearing, and thereby occasioneth their Names. As when we say *smooth*, it sounds smoothly: So who will not judge *harshness* to be harsh by the very word? it is smooth to the Ear, when we say *Pleasure*; harsh, when we say *Crux, a Cross*; the things themselves make good the sound of the Words. *Honey*, as sweetly as the thing it self affects our Taste, so sweetly doth the name touch our Hearing,

Q q

ing: *Sour*, as harsh in both. *Wool* and *Bryers*, as the Words are to the hearing, the Things are to the touch. These are conceived to be the Infancy, as it were of Words, when the Sense of the thing concords with the Sense of the sound.

From hence proceeded the licence of Naming, according to the Similitude of the things among themselves; as when, for example, *Crux*, a *Cross*, is therefore so called, because the harshness of the word concords with the harshness of the Pain which the Cross affecteth. But, *Crura*, Thighs, are so called, not from harshness of pain, but, because in length and hardness, they are, in respect of other Limbs, like unto the Wood of a Cross. Hence it comes to abuse, that the Name is usurped, not of a like thing, but as it were near; for what likeness is there between the Signification of *little* and *minute*, when as that may be *little*, which not only is nothing *minute*, but is somewhat grown; yet, by reason of a certain nearness, we say *minute* for *little*. But, this abuse of the Word is in the Power of the Speaker; for he may use the word *little*, and not *minute*. This Example belongs to that which we will shew, when we call that a *Fish-pond* which hath no Fish in it, nor any thing like a Fish: It is denominated from Fishes, by reason of the Water wherein Fishes live. So the word is used by Translation, not from Similitude, but a certain kind of Vicinity. And if any one should say, That Men in Swimming resemble Fishes, and that from thence a Fish-pond is so named, it were foolish to refuse it, since that neither is repugnant to the nature of the thing, and both are occult. But, this is to the purpose, which we cannot dilucidate by one Example, how much the Origine of the Word, which is taken from Vicinity, differs from that which is derived from Similitude.

From hence there is a Progression to the contrary. *Lucus* is thought to be so named, *Quod minime luceat*; and *bellum, quod res bella non sit*; and *fœdus, quod res fœda non sit*. But if we derive *porcus*, as some do a *fœditate*, it returns to that Vicinity, when that which is made, is named that by which it is made.

For this Vicinity is very large, and divided into many parts; either by efficiency, as this word *porcus à fœditate*; from which likewise *fœdus*; or by effect, as *puteus*, so named, because the effect thereof is *potatio*; or by that it containeth, as *urbs ab orbe*, because in a place which they liked, they first made a track about it with a Plough, as *Virgil* saith of *Æneas*.

———*Urbem designat Aratro.*

Or by that which is contained, as if *horreum* were derived from *hordeum*; or by abuse, as *hordeum* for Wheat; or the whole from a part, as *mucro*, which is the point, for the whole Sword; or a part from the whole, as *capillus quasi capitis pilus*, What need we go any further? Whatsoever else can be reckoned, we may see the Origin of the word contained, either in the Similitude betwixt Things and Sounds, or in the Similitude betwixt Things themselves, or in Vicinity or Contrariety, which Origin we cannot pursue beyond Similitude.

But this we cannot do always; for there are innumerable Words, the Reason of which lie hid. To the Infancy, or rather Stock and Seed of such Words, beyond which no Origin is to be sought, neither if a Man do enquire can he find any, they proceed in this manner. The Syllables, in which *v* hath the place of Consonant, as in these Words, *venter, vafer, velum, vinum, vomis vulnus*, have a thick, and as it were, a strong sound, which the very custom of speaking confirmeth, which from some Words we take them away, lest they should burthen the Ear; for which reason we say *amasti*, rather than *amavisti*; and *abiit*, not *abivit*, and innumerable of the same kind. Therefore when we say *Vis*, the sound of the word having, as we said, a kind of force, suiteth. Now from this Vicinity, by that which they affect, that is, because they are violent, *vincula* seem to be named, and *vimen quod aliquid vinciatur*. Thence *vites*, because they clasp about those things by which they grow. Hence also by Similitude, *Terence* calls a crooked old Man *vietum*. Hence the Earth, worn into winding Paths by the Feet of Passengers, is call'd *via*; but if *via* be so named, *quasi vi pedum trita*, the Origin returns to the Vicinity: But let us suppose it derived from the Similitude it hath with *vitis* or *vimen*, that is, from its winding; one asketh me why it is call'd *via*? I answer, from the winding and crookedness thereof, which the Ancients called *vietum*; thence the Rounds of a Wheel *vietos*. He demands how *vietum* comes to signifie winding? I answer, from the Similitude of *Vitis* a Vine: He requires whence *vitis* is so named? I say, because it doth *vincire* those things which it comprehends. He questions whence *vincire* is derived? We say, *a vi*. He asks whence *vis*? We give this reason, because the word in its robust and forcible sound agreeth to the thing which it signifieth. He hath nothing more to demand.

t In like manner, in this word *Ego*: as *Chrysippus* observes, in pronouncing the first Syllable, we depress the under-lip, as if it were to point to our selves; then by motion of the Beard we point to our own Breasts; of which *u Nigidius* hath given more Instances, in his Grammatical Commentaries.

The second Question concerning Words, is of their Power, περὶ σημαινόντων, *of Significants*; whence *x Chrysippus* divided Dialectick into two parts, περὶ σημαινόντων καὶ σημαινομένων, *of Significants, and Significats*. Here they enquire how many ways every thing may be said, and how many ways a thing said may signifie?

Here is examined the Ambiguity of Words. *y* Ambiguity (or Amphiboly) is a word signifying two or more things, naturally and properly, according to the Language of the Nation, in such manner, that many Senses may be collected from the same Words, as αὐλητρὶς πέπτωκε, which one way signifies, *the Pot fell thrice*; another way, *the She-Minstrel fell.*

z Every word (according to *Chrysippus*) is by nature ambiguous, for the same may be taken two or more ways: *y* Neither is that any thing to the purpose which *Hortensius* Calumniates in *Cicero*, Thus, they affirm that they hear Ambiguities acutely, explain them clearly. The same persons hold, that every Word is Ambiguous; how then can they explain the Ambiguous by the

t Galen. de decret. Hipp. & Plat. lib. 2
u Agel. 10. 5.
x Laert.
y Laert.
z Agel. 9. 12.
y D. August. de Dialect.

the Ambiguous, that were to bring a Candle not lighted into the Dark? This is ingeniously and subtilly said, but like that of *Scævola* to *Antonius*, You seem to the wise to speak acutely, to Fools truly: For what else doth *Hortensius* in that place, but by his Ingenuity and Facetiousness, as an intoxicating Cup, bring Darkness upon the unlearned? For, when they say, Every Word is Ambiguous, it is understood of single Words. Ambiguities are explained by Disputation; no Man disputeth by single words, none therefore explaineth Ambiguous words by Ambiguous words. And yet seeing that every word is Ambiguous, no Man can explain the Ambiguity of words, except by words, but those conjoined and not Ambiguous. As when we say, Every Soldier hath two Feet, it doth not follow, that a whole Regiment of Soldiers that have two Feet, should have in all but two Feet. So when I say, every word is Ambiguous; I do not say, a Sentence, nor a Disputation, although they are woven of Words. Every Ambiguous word therefore may be explained by an inambiguous Disputation.

The third Question is concerning *Declination*, ἀνωμαλία and ἀναλογία. *a* Some follow *Analogy*, others *Anomaly*. *Analogy* is a like Declination of like, in Latin *Proportio*. *Anomaly* is an inequality, following the customs of Declinations. *a Chrysippus* wrote six Books περὶ τῆς ἀνωμαλίας, shewing, that like things are noted with unlike words, and unlike things with like words.

The last Question is concerning *Ordination*, σύνταξις. *b* Upon this Subject *Chrysippus* wrote two Books (*Laertius* reckons more) whose scope is not Rhetorical, but Dialectick, as will easily appear to the Reader: *Of the Syntax of Axioms: of true and false Axioms: Of possible and impossible: Of contingent, and transient, and ambiguous*, and the like, which confer nothing to single speech or pleasure, or grace to elocution.

c There are five *excellencies* of Speech, *Propriety, Perspicuity, Succinctness, Decorum, Elegance*. *Propriety* is a proper Phrase, according to Art, not after the common Expression.

Perspicuity is, when that which is intended is deliver'd clearly.

Succinctness is, when that only is comprised, which is necessary to the thing.

Decorum is a conformity to the thing.

Elegance is an avoiding of vulgar Phrase.

d Amongst the faults of Speech is *Barbarism*, a Phrase not in use with the best Persons; and *Solæcism*, a Speech incoherently framed.

z Agel. 2. 25.
a Varro de ling. lat.
b Dionys. Halicarn. de compos. verb.
c Laert.
d Laert.

CHAP. XI.

Of Definition and Division.

a Definition (according to *Antipater* in his book of *Definitions*) is Speech by *Analysis* pronounced adæquately; or (as *Chrysippus* in his Book of *Definitions*) an Answer to this Question, What a Thing is?

b Those Definitions are vicious which include any of those things which are not in the things defined, or not in all, or not in some; so as if we should say, *A Man is a Rational Creature*, or *a mortal Grammatical Creature*; seeing that no Man is Immortal, and some Men are not Grammarians, the Definition is faulty.

c We must therefore, when we take those things which are common to the things we wou'd define, and others, prosecute them so far until it become proper, so as not to be transferrable to any other thing; as this, *An inheritance is riches*, add *which by the Death of some Person falleth to another*, it is not yet a Definition, for Riches may be held many other ways, as well as by Inheritance; add one word, *by right of Law*; now the thing will seem disjoyned from community: So that the definition is thus explained. *Inheritance is Riches, which by the death of one person falleth to another by right of Law*: It is not yet enough, therefore add, *neither bequeathed by Will, nor detained by Possession*, and it is perfect.

d Of Definition there are two kinds: One of things *which are*: the other of things *which are understood*. Those *things which are*, we call such as may be seen or touched, as a Field, House, a Wall, and the like. On the other side, we say those things *are not*, which cannot be touched or shewn, as Possession, Guardianship, Nation, Kindred, which have not any body, yet there is some Conformity in the understanding, which we call notional, whereby in Argumentation they may be explained by definition. This latter kind is rather called Description, a Speech, which by the exteriour figure of the things bringeth us to the things themselves, or a Definition simply expressing the Power of a Definition.

e Again, of Definitions, some are of *partitions*, others of *Divisions*. Of *Partitions*, when the thing proposed is torn (as it were) into pieces, as if we should say, the Civil Law is that which consisteth in Laws, Senators, things judged, the authority of Lawyers, Edicts of Magistrates, Manners and Equity.

The definition *of Divisions* comprehendeth all Species which are under the Genus defined, thus. *Abalienation* is of that thing which is in our power, or a deliverance of it into the power of another; or a concession by Law, amongst whom those things may be done by Civil Right.

f Division is a Section of the Genus into its immediate Species, as, *of Living Creatures, some are rational, some irrational*. *g* This therefore is an ill division, *Of men some are Grecians, some Egyptians, some Persians, some Indians*; for the next Species are not desperate, but opposite. We must therefore say thus; *Of Men some are Grecians, some Barbarians*; and again, by subdivision *of Barbarians, some are Egyptians, some Persians, some Indians*, which likewise is in the division of things that are. For those which are good and bad, are different to us; those who are intermediate betwixt good and bad, are indifferent to us. The division therefore ought not to be so, but rather thus: *Of things that are, some are indifferent, others different; of the different, some are good, some are ill*; for this division is like unto that which saith, of Men, some are Grecians, others *Barbarians*; of Barbarians, some are Egyptians, some Persians, some Indians; the other is likewise; *Of Men, some Grecians, some Egyptians, some Persians, some Indians*.

Hence it followeth, that *h* perfect division hath an universal power; for he who divideth thus; *Of Men, some are Græcians*, others Barbarians,

c Cicer. Topic.
d Cic. Topic.
e Cic. Topic.
f Laert.
g Sext. Empir. adv. Math. 10. 2.
h Sext. Empi. adv. Moral. 10.

barians, saith as much as this, if there are any Men, they are either *Grecians* or *Barbarians*; for if there be any Man, who is neither *Greek* nor *Barbarian*, the division must necessarily be ill, the universal false. Wherefore when we say, Of things that are, some are good, some ill, some intermediate, it is as much (according to *Chrysippus*) as this universal; If there be any things that are, they are either good or ill, or indifferent. But this universal is false, if any thing false be subjected to it: For, if two things be subjected, one good, the other ill; or, one good, the other indifferent, in this Expression of those things which are, one kind is good, that is true; but this, these are good, is false, for they are not good; for one is good, the other ill. And again, These are ill, is false, for they are not ill, but only one of them. The like in indifferents; for it is false that these are indifferents, as that these are good or ill.

i There are three forms of division, *anti-division*, *sub-division*, *partition*. *Anti-division* is a distribution of the Genus into Species by the contrary; as for example, by negation, as of things that are, some are good, others not good.

Sub-division is division upon a division: as of things that are, some are good, others not good; of the not good, some are ill, others indifferent.

Partition is a distribution of the Genus into places (according to *Crinis*) as of goods, some belong to the Soul, others to the Body.

CHAP. XII.
Of Genus, Species, &c.

a GENUS is a comprehension of many Notions referred to one, as, a *Living Creature*, for this includes all Living Creatures. Notion is a phantasie of the Mind, not any thing existent or qualitative, but as it were, something existent, and qualitative; as the notion of an Horse, no Horse being present.

Species is that which is contained under the Genus; as under living Creature is contain'd Man.

Most general, is that which is a Genus, but hath no Genus: Most special, that which is a Species, but hath no Species.

To this place of Voice belong likewise, as we said, the consideration of *Poem* and *Poesy*. Poem (according to *Possidonius*, in his *Introduction to Speech*) is a Speech in Metre or Rhime, not Prose, as γαῖα μεγίση, and δῖος ἀιδής. *Poesy* is a significant Poem, with design, containing the imitation of things divine and humane.

CHAP. XIII.
Of Things.

NOtions, Words, and things, as we have said, are conjoyned together. From Notions we come to Words, from Words we come now to Things themselves: By Notions Things are perceived. *a* Those are said to be *Things* which are dicible. *b* The Stoicks by a new name call things τυγχάνοντα, *Contingents*, because we desire that things might befal us, and that we might obtain them. *c* *Contingents* therefore is subject it self, beyond the notion or word, as *Dion*.

d They comprehended all things under one common Genus: τὶ *somewhat*; *e* placing this Genus above all; the Reason this: In nature some things are, some things are not. For, those things which are not, but only incur in the mind, as Centaurs, Giants, and whatsoever else is formed by false cogitation, hath some image, although it hath no substance. Even negatives are in being. *Somewhat* is therefore more general than *Ens*, which is understood only of Corporeals.

f Things are subdivided ino four Genus's, *Subjects*, and *Qualitatives*, and *Quodammodotatives in themselves*, and *Quodammodotatives as to others*. *g* Thus the Stoicks treating more strictly and subtilly of these things, contract the Predicaments into a lesser number, taking some of those things which they diminished, but with some alteration.

CHAP. XIV.
Of Subjects.

a THere is not any thing besides τὸ ὑποκείμενον, a *Subject*: The differences concerning this are non-subsistent.

b *Subject* is two-fold; one which is called the first *Subject*; such is Matter expert of all qualities, which, *Aristotle* calleth a Body potentially. The other, that which is *effected with quality*, as *Brass*, and *Socrates*, with those things which are in them, or praedicated by them.

CHAP. XV.
Of Qualitatives.

a QUalitatives have a subsistence, and are separate from their subjects. For qualities (as all other accidents) are Bodies, seeing that according to *Zeno*, nothing can be effected by that which is incorporeal, nor can that which is incorporeal effect any thing; whatsoever effecteth is a Body. Effective quality therefore is a Body. Matter is expert of quality, but qualities are not expert of matter.

b *Quality* is the habit of that which is qualitative. *Qualitative* is taken three ways: First, for whatsoever hath difference, whether it be motion or habit, and whether hardly or easily separable. In this sense, not only he who is wise, but he who stretcheth out his hand, are qualitative. The second signification includes not motions, but habits only, which they define qualitative, that is, which hath a difference endued with habit, as a wise man, or an armed man. Of these, some are adaequate, to the measure of their pronunciation and consideration; others not adaequate. These they omit; those which are adaequate, equal, and permanent they call qualitative; as, a Grammarian, and a wise man; neither of these exceeds, or falls short of his quality. Likewise a lover of Meat, and a lover of Wine, being in act such, as a glutton, and a drunkard, because they make use of those parts which serve to this end, are so called: So that if any man be a glutton, he is consequently a lover of meat; but if he be a lover of meat, he is not therefore immdiately a glutton; for, being destitute of those parts which he useth in eating, he wanteth the act, but not the habit. Quality is adaequated to qualitative in this last sense.

c All qualities are either *causes*, and then they are called *forms*; or *effects*, and then they are generally called ἑκτὰ, *habituals*, which word *Antipater* extends as large as the common accident, both of things corporeal and incorporeal, τὶ *somewhat*

what. Of *habituals* there are four kinds, μελεκ]ὰ, that is, ἐννοήμα]α, when they reside in the mind; τευκ]ὰ, that is, πλάσεις, when they fall from the mind into the voice; καθηγορήμα]α, when by the motion of the mind, they are prædicated of any thing; συμβεβηκό]α, or, συμβάμμα]α, when they happen to subjects.

d Habits are only things united; but those which are conjoyned by contiguity, as a Ship, or by distance, as an Army; in these there can be no habit; nor one thing Spiritual above all, nor one reason, whereby they may come to subsist within one habit.

It is common to quality of corporeal things to be the difference of their substance, not taken severally, but contracted into one notion and property of the mind, nor by time or strength reduced to form, but by its own tality, according to which, the generation of the qualitative subsists.

Power (a Species of quality) is that which hath and giveth the faculty of exercising many accidents; as Prudence giveth the faculty of walking prudently, and discoursing prudently: or according to some, Power is that which the faculty of exercising many Accidents, and which Ruleth and Governeth the Acts subjected unto it. What *Aristotle* called natural *Power*, they name *Aptitude*.

Habits are intended and remitted: Dispositions cannot be intended or remitted. Thus the straitness of a Wand, altho it may easily be discomposed and bent, is a Disposition; for straitness cannot be intended or remitted. Likewise the Virtues are Dispositions, not in respect of their firmness and constancy, but because they cannot admit of degrees of more and less: but, Arts must either have firmness, or not be Dispositions. Thus *Habitude* is taken in the Latitude of the Species, *Disposition* is the chief perfection of the Species, and in that which is the most it can be, whether it be easily alter'd (as the straitness of a Wand) or not.

d Simplic. in Categ.

Ibid.

Ibid.

Ibid.

Ibid.

CHAP. XVI.

Of *Quodammodotatives.*

THE third kind of things are τὰ πῶς ἔχον]α, *Quodammodatives.* *a* They differ from Qualitatives, because matter is otherwise effected by habits, otherwise by *Quodammodotatives*, in this or that manner. Moreover, Qualitatives are *Quodammodotatives* as to matter, and conversant therein; but properly, *Quodammodotatives* are conversant in Qualitatives. *b* Again, as habituals may be said to extend farther than habits, so *Quodammodotatives* are larger than Qualitatives; for *Quodammodotatives* extend even to those things which are *Quodammodotatives* as to others, and include them; but Qualitatives consist only in those which make a difference.

c This place *Boethius* conceives to have the power of habit. Habit chiefly and universally is taken three ways: First, to be to it self, and according to it self: Secondly, in respect to another: Thirdly, of another to it. That which is considered *as to it self*, pertains to *Quodammodotatives*; as *armed*, for it is a habit of ones self, to ones self, That which is *to another*, pertains to Relation; for a Father, or a right Hand, are said, according to a Habit, not of themselves to themselves, but of them to another. But that which is of another to us, as of an Armed Man, being the Habit of another to us, pertains to Habit.

a Plotin 1.30.

b Simplic. in Categ.

c Simplic. ibid.

To this head they reduce *Quantitatives* and *Quantity*, and their Species, *Place, Time,* and some Species (according to *Aristotle*) of quality, *Figure* and *Form*; as also *Action, Passion, Site, Habit.*

CHAP. XVII.

Of *Quodammodotatives as to others.*

THE last genus of Things is πρὸς τὶ πῶς ἔχον]α, *Quodammodotatives as to others. a* Of these there are two kinds, *Relatives* and *Quodammodotative-Relatives.* The *Relatives* are opposed and distinguished from those which are by themselves, and absolute. The *Quodammodotative-Relatives* are opposed to those which have a difference; as for Example, sweet and Sowr, and whatsoever is of the like kind, are Relatives; but *Quodammodotative Relatives*, are as the right side, *Father*, and the like; for they have a difference, in that they are characteriz'd by differences, according to some Species. As therefore there is one notion of those which are by themselves, and absolute, and another of those which are consider'd with difference: So some things are *Relatives*, others *Quodammodotative-Relatives.* The consequence of Conjunctions in these is contrary; for, with those which are by themselves, co-exist those which have a difference; for, those which are by themselves, have some differences, as white and black. But those, which are by themselves, co-exist not with those which have a difference. Sweet and Bitter have differences, whereby they are characterized; yet they are not absolute, but *Relatives.* But, those which are *Quodammodotative-Relatives*, being contrary to those which have differences, are likewise *Relatives.* For, the right side, and a *Father*, besides that they are *Quodammodotative*, are likewise *Relatives*: But sweet and Bitter being *Relatives*, have a difference, whereby they are contrary, being *Quodammodotative-Relatives.* Those which are *Quodammodotative-Relatives*, it is impossible should be by themselves, and absolute, or by difference; for they depend solely upon Relative-habit. *Relatives* therefore are not by themselves, for they are not absolute; yet are they according to difference, because they are distinguished by some Character. To express this more clearly, *Relatives* are those, which by their proper Character respect another: *Quodammodotative-Relatives* are those which use to happen to another, but not without mutation and alteration of those things which are about them; yet, with respect of something external. If therefore any thing with difference respect another, it is only *Relative*, as Habit, Science, and Sense: but if it respect another, not out of inherent difference, but in pure habit, it is *Quodammodotative Relative.* For, a *Father*, and right side, to their consistence, require some external things, for as much as there being no Mutation made in them, he is no longer a *Father*, his Son being dead, and the right side is no longer, so, after he is risen, in respect of whom it was said to be such; but sweet

a Simplic. in Categ.

sweet and bitter will not alter, unless their power be likewise changed. If therefore *Quodammodotatives* are changed in habit to another, although they receive no Passion in themselves, it is manifest they have their being in the habit alone, not in difference.

a Laert. vit. Aristonis.
b Simplic. in Categ.

a This Genus was first introduced by *Aristo*, b who first defined *Quodammodotative-Relatives* to be those, *whose being is the same with their* Quodammodotative *being to one another*: And so also *Andronicus* defines them.

CHAP. XVIII.
Of Dicibles.

a Laert.

TO the place concerning things and significats, belongeth that concerning *Dicibles*, ϖεὶ λεκ-τῶν, to which true and false is common. a *Dicible* is that which consisteth according to rational phantasie. b *Rational Phantasie* is that, by which what is comprehended by Phantasie, may be expressed by Speech. Every thing that may be said, ought to be said, for from thence is derived the Denomination

b Sext. E-pir. Adv. log.

c Ammon. in proem. Arist. ϖεὶ ἑρμ.
d Busf. in Disl. Cic. 5. 1

c *Dicible* is a mean betwixt Notion and Thing. *Dicibles* are Notions, that is, νοήματα, but not meerly and simply Notions, d which in as much as they are the principles of Science, and are Intelligences, are called περλήψεις, and ἔννοιαι, but in as much as they reside in the mind, are called ἐννοήματα, and are Genus's and Species, in which manner, being ready for expression, they are called *Dicibles*, and pertain to the Enunciative faculty of the Soul. For whatsoever is said, if it be so considered as it is said of something, they are *Categorems*; if so, as it breaketh forth into Voice, and with Voice, they are Words; if retained in the Mind, ready to break forth, they are *Dicibles*. *Dicible* therefore is a Word, and yet signifies not a Word, but that which is understood in the Word, and is contained in the Mind.

e Laert.

e Of *Dicibles* there are two kinds, the *Defective* and the *Perfect*. The *Defective* are those which have an imperfect Enunciation, not compleating the Sentence, but requiring something to follow; as *writeth*, for we ask, who? To this kind belong *Categorems*, which are prædicated of other things.

The *Perfect* are such as have a perfect Enunciation: Of these are two kinds: The first peculiarly called *Perfect*, which tho' they compleat the Sentence, yet signifie neither true nor false. Of these there are many kinds, as *Interrogation, Percontation, Imperative, Adjurative, Optative, Imprecative,* or *Execrative, Substitutive, Hypothetical, Compellative, like* to, or *Transcending an Axiom,* and *Dubitative.*

Interrogation is that which is a perfect Sentence, but requireth an answer, as, *Is it day?* for this is neither true nor false; so that *it is day,* is an Axiom, *Is it day?* an Interrogation.

Percontation is a thing for which we cannot answer significantly, as Interrogation, *yes*: but as thus, *He dwelleth in such a place.*

Imperative is a thing, in speaking whereof, we command; as,

Go thou to the Inachian *Flood.*

f Ammon. in lib. ϖεὶ ἑρμ.

f *Adjurative*, as *Witness thou Earth*
Optative, which we speak wishing, as,
Great *Jove who dost in* Ida *Reign,*
The *Victory let* Ajax *gain.*

Imprecative, or *Execrative,* as,
As on the Ground this Wine I pour,
So may the Earth his Blood devour.

Substitutive, or Expositive, as, *Let this be a right Line.*

Hypothetical, as, *supposing the Earth to be the Center of the Globe of the Sun.*

Compellative, is a thing in speaking, which we call another, as,

Atrides, Agamemnon, *King of Men.*

Like to, or *Transcending an Axiom,* is that which hath an axiomatical manner of speaking; but because it superabounds in some Particle or Affection, it is not ranked amongst Axioms, as,

How Beauteous is thy Virgin Train!
How like to Priam's Son, that Swain!

Dubitative is a thing different from an Axiom, which whosoever speaks, maketh a doubt, as,
Then are not Life and Grief of Kin? All these are neither true nor false.

The other kind of perfect Dicibles which compleat the Sentence, affirmeth or denieth, and is either true or false. It is called *Axiom.*

CHAP. XIX.
Of Categorems.

a Laert.

a **C**Ategorem is that which is prædicated of another, or a thing construed with one or more, or as (*Apollodorus*) a defective *Dicible,* construed with the right case, to make an Axiom.

b Ammon. in Arist. ϖεὶ ἑρμ.

b Whatsoer is prædicated of another, is prædicated of the name of the Case; and both these are either *perfect,* as that which is prædicated, and together with the subject sufficient to make an Axiom. Or they are *defective,* and require some Addition to make thereof a perfect Prædicate.

If that which is prædicated of a Name, make an Axiom, it is a *Categorem*, or σύμβαμα, a Congruity, as *walketh,* for Example, *Socrates walketh.*

But if it be prædicated of the Case (whereby Transitions are made from one Person to another, wherein it is necessary that some oblique Case be likewise pronounced with the right) they are called ϖαρασυμβάματα, as an addition to the σύμβαμα, (or as c *Priscian* renders it, *less than Congruities*) as *Cicero saved his Country.*

c Lib. 3.

Again, if that which is prædicated of some Noun, require a Case of some other Noun to be added to make up the Axiom, so as the Construction be made of two oblique Cases, they are ἀσυμβάματα, incongruities, or according to *Ammonius, less than,* σύμβαματα, as, *it pleases me to come to thee*; whether the Nouns only, or the Words require it.

d Laert.

d Again, of *Categorems* there are four kinds, *Right, Supine, Neuter,* and reciprocally *Active,* and *Passive. Right* are those which have a motion tending to another, and are construed with one of the oblique Cases, for the making of a *Categorem,* as *Heareth, Seeth, Discourseth.*

Supine are those which are considered from Habit to an Agent, and is construed with a passive particle, as, I am heard, I am seen.

Neuter, as those which are neither way, as, to be wise, to walk.

Reciprocally, Active and *Passive* are those, which seem Supines, but are not, for they are
acts

acts, as κειρεῖαι, for therein is included ὁ κειρόμϘ⊙.

The *Right* (or *Nominative*) *Case*, is so called by the Stoicks, whom the Grammarians follow, because it falleth directly from the Notion which is in the Mind. *Oblique Cases* are the Genitive, Dative, and Accusative.

CHAP. XX.
Of Simple Axioms.

a Laert.

a **A**Xiom is that which is either true or false, or a thing perfect by it self, negative, or affirmative, as far as it extends; or, (or according to *Chrysippus*, in his *Dialectick Definitions*) axiom is that which affirmeth or denieth as far as it extends; as *Dion* walketh. It is called Axiom ἀπὸ τοῦ ἀξιοῦσθαι καθεστάναι, because Assent is either given to it or not: for he who saith, it is day, assenteth thereunto. If it be day, the Axiom is true; if it be not, false.

b Laert.

b Of Axioms, the first and most proper difference is of the *Simple*, and not *Simple* (thus divided by *Chrysippus*, and *Archidemus*, and *Athenodorus*, and *Antipater*, and *Crinis*.)

c Laert. Sext. Empir. adv. Log. cap. ae vero.
d Laert.

c Simple axioms are those which consist neither of one axiom twice taken, nor of different axioms, neither by one or more conjunctions; as, *It is day, 'tis at night* Socrates *Disputes. d* Of simple axioms there are many kinds, *Apophatick*, or *Negative*, *Arnetick*, or *Universally Negative*; *Steretick*, or *Privative*; *Categórick*, or *prædicative*; *Categoreutick*, or *Indicative*; *indefinite* and *mediate*.

e Laert. Apud. πρὸς ἑρμ.

e Negative axioms are those, in which a negative particle is proposed; as, *If this is, that is not*. But if the negation be of the latter part of the axiom, the other part not being negative, then the axiom is not negative, but *prædicative*; as, *It hapneth to some pleasure not to be good*. This therefore declareth what hapneth to the thing, and therefore is prædicative. *f* A Species of negative axiom, is the supernegative, when, between the parts connected and copulated by two affirmations, a preposition with a negation is interposed, and that very negation denied; as, *If it is day, it is not light*. Of the same kind are all those, wherein negation is proposed to negation; as, *It is not both day, and not day*.

f Boet. in Cic. Top.

g Laert.

g Universally negative axioms are those, which consist of an universal negative particle, and a Categorem; as, *no man walketh*.

h Laert.

h Privative are those which consist of a privative particle, and an axiom in power, as, *he is inhumane*.

i Laert.

i Prædicative are those, which consist of a right Case and Categorem; as, *Dion walketh*.

k Laert.
l Sext. Emp.

k Indicative, or *l Definitive* is that which consists of a demonstrative right Case, and a Categorem; as, *this man walketh*.

m Laert. Sext. Empir.

m Indefinite, is that, which consists of one or more indefinite particles; as, *a certain man walketh, he is moved*.

n Sext. Emp.

n Intermediate are of this kind, *a man sitteth, or a man walketh*: *a certain man walketh* is indefinite, for it determines no single person; *that man sitteth* is definite. *Socrates sitteth*, is intermediate; for it is not indefinite, because it determines the Species; nor definite, because it is not pronounced with demonstration, but it is intermediate betwixt both.

o An *indefinite axiom*, as, *some one sitteth*, is true, when the thing definite is true; as, *he sitteth*; but if none of the singulars do sit, the indefinite axiom is not true, that *some one sitteth*.

o Sext. Emp.

CHAP. XXI.
Of not-simple Axioms.

a Laert.
o Sext. Emp. adv. Log. de vero.

a **N**Ot-simple axioms are those, which are in a manner double, consisting of one axiom diversified, or of axioms: of one axiom diversified; as, *if it be day, it is day*: of axioms, as, *if it be day, 'tis light*.

b Sext. Empir. adv. Log. cap. d vero.

b In *not-simple* axioms, that which immediately followeth the conjunction, *if*, or *whereas*, is called the *Antecedent*, *the first*, or *the beginning*; the rest is called *the ending*, or *Consequence* or *second*. Notwithstanding that the axiom be pronounced by inversion; as, *It is light, if it be day*; for in this, the ending or consequence, is, *it is light*, altho it be spoken first: the antecedent, *it is day*, altho it be put in the second place; for it immediately followeth the conjunction *if*.

c Laert.

The Laws and Rules of Consequents are these: 1. *c* From True followeth True: as, *if it be day, it followeth that it is light*. 2. From False followeth False; as, if this be False *that it is night*, this is likewise, *it is dark*. 3. From False followeth True, as from this, *the Earth flieth*, followeth, *the Earth is*. 4. From True doth not follow False; for from this, *the Earth is*, it followeth not, *that the Earth flies*.

d Laert.

d Of *not-simple* propositions there are many kinds, *Connex*, *Adnex*, *Conjunct*, *Casual*, *Declarative of the more*, and *Declarative of the less*.

e Laert.

e Connex (according to *Chrysippus* in his *Dialectick*, and *Diogenes* in his *Dialectick Art*) is that which consists of the connective conjunction, *if:* which conjunction declareth, that the consequent is second to the first: as, *if it be day, it is light*. Of a diversified axiom, and the Conjunction *if*, consisteth this connex, *If it be day, it is day*, these are properly right axioms. Of different axioms, and the Conjunction *whereas*, this, *if it is day, 'tis light*. *f* Connex axioms are called also *Tropical*, because they turn from the antecedent to the consequent.

f Philosoph. in Anal. prior.

The Rules of connex axioms are these: *f* That is a *true* connex wherein the contrary of the consequent is repugnant to the antecedent, as, *if it is day, 'tis light*; for, *that it is not light*, the contrary to the consequent, is repugnant to, *it is day*, the antecedent. A *false* connex is that wherein the contrary to the consequent, is not repugnant to the Antecedent; as this, *if it is day, Dion walks*; for, that *Dion walketh not*, is not repugnant to, *it is day*.

g Laert.

h Laert.

h Adnex (which some reckon as a species of the connex) according to *Crinis*, in his Dialectick, is an axiom connected by the conjunction *whereas*, beginning with an axiom, and ending with an axiom; as, *whereas it is day, it is light*, the conjunction sheweth, that the second is a consequent of the first, and that the first is subsistent.

i Laert.

The Rules of adnex axioms are these: *i* That is a *true* adnex, which beginneth from true, endeth in that which is consequent; as, *whereas it is day, the Sun is over the Earth*. False is that which beginneth from False, or endeth not consequently; as, as, *whereas it is day, Dion walketh*, if this be said when it is not day.

l Laert.

i A *conjunct* axiom is that, which is knit together by Conjunctions copulative; as, *it is both day and it is light*. The Rules thereof are these: That is a *right* conjunction wherein all things are true; as, *it is day, and it is light*. That is *false*, which hath something false. An axiom which hath neither conjunction nor disjunction, is to be taken in the sense of the speaker; for conjunction is sometimes taken for disjunction; as, to me, and my heir.

Laert.

A *disjunct* axiom is that which is disjoyned, by a disjunctive conjunction; as, *either it is day, or it is night*. This conjunction sheweth, that one of the axioms is false.

Agell. 16.8.

All things that are disjoyned, are repugnant to one another, and their opposites likewise are repugnant. Of all things that are disjoyned, one must be true, the rest false, otherwise nothing at all is true, or all, or more than one are true, either those which are disjunct, will not be repugnant, or those which are opposite to them will not be contrary to one another, then the disjunct will be false, and is called διεζευγμένον, as this is, in which the opposites are not contrary; either thou runnest, or walkest, or standest, for they are repugnant to one another, but their opposites are not repugnant, because not to walk, and not to stand, and not to run, are not contrary in themselves; for those things are said to be contrary, which cannot be true together. But you may at the same time neither walk, nor run, nor stand. Every disjunction therefore is not only true, but necessary; for if of contraries there could be a false conjunction, no disjunction could be true.

A *Casual* axiom is that which is connected by this conjunction, *because*, as because it is day, 'tis light; for the first is, as it were cause of the second. The Rules thereof are these: A casual conjunction is *true*, when beginning from true, it endeth in the consequent, and cannot have the antecedent for its consequent; as because it is day, 'tis light: but this axiom, it is light, doth not follow from the other, it is day.

A *False* casual is that which either beginneth from false, or endeth in that which is not consequent, or whose Antecedent may be the consequent, as, because it is night, *Dion walks*.

An Axiom *declarative of the more*, is that which is construed with this conjunction, *more*, as *it is more day than night*. Declarative of the *less*, is contrary to the former, as, *it is less day than night*.

CHAP. XXII.
Of contrary Axioms.

Laert.

COntrary Axioms are those which are repugnant to one another, according to Truth and Falshood, whereof one affirmeth, the other denieth, as, *it is day, it is not day*. Only Negatives are contrary. ἀντικείμενα, and opposite, and repugnant, for only in contraries one proposition is true, the other false. The other three kinds of contraries alledged by *Aristotle*, are pronounced without a conjunction. Whatsoever is pronounced without a conjunction, is neither true nor false, for true and false belongeth to axiom. Axiom is a speech which consisteth in the conjunction of some thing, whereas, of *Aristotle's* other three kinds of contraries, none are conjunct but simple, as black and white, double and single, sight and blindness.

Adverse are (as likewise defined by *Aristotle*) those which in the same kind are most distant. Nothing that is pronounced by negation is adverse, (ἐναντίον) to another, for then the adverse to Virtue will be not Virtue, and to Vice not Vice, and under not Virtue will be included many other things besides Vice, even a Stone, a Horse, and whatsoever is besides Virtue; under not Vice, will be found Virtue, and all other things. Thus all things would be adverse to one, and the same the adverse to Virtue and Vice. Moreover, if Virtue were not adverse to Vice, but to not-vice, the intermediate will be adverse both to good and to bad, which is absurd.

The Rules of Contraries are these: 1. Contrariety is principally in Acts, Habits, and the like. 2. Categorems and Qualitatives are called as it were contrary. Prudently and Imprudently in some manner lead to things contrary, but contraries absolutely are in things: and Prudence is so immediately contrary to imprudence, not this to that.

Contraries are either *disjunctive* or *subdisjunctive*; *disjunctive*, as when we say, *it is either day or night*. *Subdisjunctives*, are of two kinds, either in *whole*, betwixt Universals, as, *every living creature either doth or suffereth*, *no living creature either doth or suffereth*; or in *part*, betwixt particulars; as *he either sitteth or walketh*; *he neither sitteth nor walketh*.

* Simplic.

The rules of contraries are these: Of Disjunctives one being asserted, the other is necessarily taken away; one being taken away, the other is necessarily asserted.

Of subdisjunctives in whole, both cannot be true, both may be false; both cannot be affirmative, both cannot be negative.

Of Subdisjunctives in part, both may be true, because they are taken in part.

CHAP. XXIII.
Of Possible and Impossible, Necessary and Unnecessary, probable, paradoxal and reasonable Axioms.

a Laert.

MOreover of Axioms, some are *possible*, others *impossible*; some *necessary*, others not *unnecessary*. A *possible* Axiom is that which is susceptible of a true prædication, without obstruction from those things, which though external, are yet contingent with the thing it self; as, *Diocles lives*. *Impossible* is that which can never be susceptible of truth, externals oppugning it, as *the Earth flies*. *Necessary* is that which is so true as that it cannot any way receive a false prædication, or, may receive it; but those things which are extrinsecal, will not permit that it be true, as *Virtue profiteth*. *Not-necessary* is that which may be either true or false, exterior things not obstructing it, as *Dion walks*.

b These future repugnants and their parts are according to the same manner, as the present and the past. For if it be true that the thing either shall be or shall not be, it must be either true or false, because futures are determined according to these; as, if a Navy is built to morrow, it is true to say that it shall be built; but if

b Simplic. in lib. Arist. de opposit.

it be not, it is false to say that it shall be built, because it will not be; therefore it will either be, or not be, and consequently one of the two is false.

Concerning possibles and necessaries, there is great difference betwixt *Diodorus* and *Chrysippus*. *c Diodorus* holds that only to be possible which either is, or will hereafter be. That which neither is, nor ever shall be, is impossible. As *for me to be at* Corinth is possible, if I ever were there or ever shall be there; but if I never was there, nor ever shall be there, it is impossible. That *a Boy shall be a Grammarian* is not possible, unless hereafter he come to be one. *d* On the contrary, *Chrysippus* held, that those things which neither are nor ever shall be, are yet possible to be, as, *to break a Gem*, tho it never come to be broken. *e* Moreover that from possibles an impossible may follow, as in this Axiom, which is a true connex: *If* Dion *be dead, He* (pointing to *Dion*) *is dead* : The antecedent, *if* Dion *be dead*, is possible, because it may at some time be true that he shall be dead; but this Axiom, *he is dead*, is impossible : For *Dion* being dead, the Axiom likewise is abolish'd, that *he is dead*, seeing he is no longer that Man, capable of being demonstrated by the Pronoun, *He*, for *he* is a demonstration of a living Creature. If therefore *Dion* being not yet dead, this word, *He* may be said of him, being dead, it cannot be said *he is dead*. So that in this place, *he is dead*, is impossible. For it were not impossible, if, some time after the death of *Dion*, of whom it was before prædicated in the connex whilst he lived, it might be again prædicated, *he is dead*; but because that cannot be, it is impossible, that, *he is dead*, should be prædicated of him.

To conclude, *d* some held with *Diodorus*, that whatsoever is past, is true of necessity. That to impossible there followeth not a possible, and that what cannot be done, neither is nor shall be true. Others (as *Cleanthes* and *Antipater*) that something is possible that neither is nor shall be; that to possible followeth not impossible; and that which is past, is not true of necessity. Others, that something is possible which is not true; that whatsoever is past, is true of necessity, and that to possible followeth also impossible.

Furthermore of Axioms, some are *e probable*, some *paradoxal*, some *reasonable*. A *probable* Axiom is that which perswadeth us by a specious show to assent unto it; as *whatsoever bringeth forth another, is a Mother*; which is false, for the Hen is not the Mother of the Egg.

f Paradoxal Axioms are those which seem true only to the wise, *g* contrary to the opinion of all others. These are likewise in other Arts, besides Philosophy; for what is stranger than to prick the Eyes for the recovery of Sight? If we say this to one ignorant of Chirurgery, will he not laugh at it? Is it not therefore strange, that such things as are true in Philosophy should seem paradoxes to the unlearned.

i A *reasonable* Axiom, is that which hath many conditions requisite to the Truth thereof, as, *I shall live to Morrow*.

Marginalia:
c Johan. Grammat. in Arist. de opposit.
d Cic. de fat.
e Alex. Aphrod. in Anal. prior.
d Epictet. 11. 19.
e Laert.
f Laert.
g Cic. Parad.
h Epictet. 1.
i Laert.

CHAP. XXIV.
Of Reciprocal Axioms.

Hitherto of the contrariety and repugnance of Axioms. Now of their consent and agreement, whereby one followeth and is correspondent to another, either according to Truth or falshood, by μετάπτωσις, reciprocation.

Of Reciprocation there are three kinds : The first ἀναςτροφὴ, *perversion*, a migration into false; the second ἀντιςροφὴ, *conversion*, a migration into true; the third ἰσοδυναμία, *equipollence*, into the same.

CHAP. XXV.
Of Signs.

To the place of Axioms appertain likewise Signs. *a* Sign is an Axiom antecedent, in a true connex, and having power to detect the consequent.

b Sign is taken two ways: Commonly, for whatsoever falleth under any Sense, and signifieth something that proceedeth from it: And properly, for that which declareth a thing, which is not manifest.

Things which are certain require no sign, for they are comprehended of themselves; neither those which are wholly uncertain, for they can no way be comprehended; but those only which are uncertain in time, or by nature, may be comprehended by signs, but not by the same. Things that are uncertain in time, are comprehended by commemorative signs; things uncertain by nature, are comprehended by demonstrative.

Of Signs therefore, some are *demonstrative*, others *communicative*. A *communicative* sign is that which is so near to the thing, that together with the sign the thing it self appeareth, into the knowledge whereof the sign bringeth us, as Smoak, which when we see, we know it proceeds from Fire. A *demonstrative* sign is that, which not being observed before with an evident sign, leads us by that to the knowledge of the thing; as when a Female hath Milk, we presently know that she hath brought forth.

Marginalia:
a Sext. Emp. hypot. 2. 1.
b Sext. adv. log. cap. de signs.
Sext. Emp. ibid & Pyrrh. hyp. 2. 10. Galen. Philos.

CHAP. XXVI.
Of Reasons or Arguments.

Dialectick is the discipline of Speech, concluded by Reason. *Reason*, λόγος, sometimes called also *Argument*, and *Interrogation*, is according to *a Crisis*, and that which consists of one or more sumptions, and an assumption, and an inference; as

If it be day it is light.	Sumption.
But it is day :	Assumption.
Therefore it is light.	Inference.

The *Reason* of the Stoicks differs from the *Syllogisms* of *Aristotle* in three respects : *b* First, a Syllogism, according to *Aristotle*, cannot have less than two propositions, a reason may have but one; as, *Thou livest, therefore thou breathest*: which kind *Antipater* calls μονολήμματα. Secondly, in Syllogisms, something besides that which is granted in the premises; but in Reasons, the conclusion

Marginalia:
a Laert.
b Alexand. Aphrod. in anal. prior.

conclusion may be the same with both, or either of the sumptions. The first are called διαφορόμενοι, as,

If it is day, it is it is day.
But it is day,
Therefore it is day.

c The second are called ἀδυνατως περαίνοντες, as

It is either day or not day.
But it is not day.
Therefore it is not day.

d Lastly, in Syllogisms, the conclusion must necessarily follow by reason of the premises, whereas there are three kinds of reasons which have not this property: The first, μονολήμματα, already mentioned: The second ἀμεθόδως περαίνοντες, not methodically conclusive reasons; as

The first is greater than the second.
The second greater than the third:
Therefore the first is greater than the third.

This concludes necessarily, but not Syllogistically, unless this proposition be put in the first place: *What is greater than another, is greater also than that which is less than that other.* Of the same kind is that Theorem in the first of Euclid's Elements, *This line is equal to that, therefore this line is likewise equal to that;* which is true indeed; but to conclude Syllogistically, requires this universal Proposition, *Those which are equal to a third, are equal to one another.*

The third kind of reasons, from which Syllogism differeth by this property, are (e) παρέλκοντες λόγοι redundant reasons, and those of two kinds. The first are such as have a superfluous sumption; as,

Every just thing is honest,
Every honest thing is good,
Every good thing is expetible in it self;
Therefore every just thing is good.

The second are those in which the proper conclusion is not infer'd, but something consequent, or accident, as that argument of *Epicure*:

Whatsoever is dissolved hath not sense,
Whatsoever hath not Sense pertaineth not to us.
Therefore death pertaineth not to us.

Whereas to conclude Syllogistically, we should say, *Therefore whatsoever is dissolved pertaineth not to us.*

In a reason or argument the *sumption* λῆμμα and the *assumption* f πρόσληψις (termed by *Aristotle* μετάληψις) are axioms received by consent of the Adversary, for construction of that which is called Inference ἐπιφορά (by *Aristotle* συμπέρασμα conclusion) because it is infer'd from the rest. g Of *Sumption* and *Assumption*, according to *Chrysippus*, there are four differences: The first *Scientifick*: The second *Exercitative*, or (as *Aristotle* calls it) *Dialectick*; The third *Probable* and *Rhetorical*; The fourth *Sophistick*.

CHAP. XXVII.
Of conclusive Reasons.

a OF Reasons there are two kinds, *conclusive*, and *not-conclusive*. *Conclusive* Reasons are those, in which the *sumptions* being granted, from the concession thereof, the *Inference* seemeth to follow.

Conclusive reasons, in respect of their matter, are of two kinds, *true* and *false*. *True* are those, which from true sumptions collect a true inference. *Not true*, the contrary.

The Laws and Rules of true and false Reasons are these: Truth is consequent to Truth: As, if it is Day, it is Light. 2. False is consequent to False, as if it be false that it is night, it is likewise false that it is dark. 3. False is consequent to true: As Earth, if it flies is Earth. 4. False is not consequent to true: For, because it is Earth, it is not therefore consequent that it flies.

Again, of true reasons, some are *demonstrative*, others *not-demonstrative*. A demonstrative reason is that which by things that are certain, or perspicuous, collecteth that which is uncertain and less perspicuous: *As if sweat issue through the Skin, we may understand pores; but sweat issues thro' the Skin, therefore we may understand pores.*

Not demonstrative are contrary: As, *If it is Day, it is Light; but it is day, therefore it is Light.* Herein the Inference, *It is Light*, is certain.

CHAP. XXVIII.
Of Syllogistick conclusive Reasons, or Syllogism.

Conclusive Reasons, as to their form likewise are of two kinds; *Syllogistically conclusive*, and *not Syllogistically conclusive*.

a *Syllogistically conclusive* Reasons (or Syllogisms) are those which either cannot be more concluded, or whereof one or more of the sumptions are reduced to those which cannot be concluded again; as, if *Dion* walks, he is moved.

Syllogisms (by which the *Stoicks* understand only the tropical, or hypothetical) are of three kinds, *connex, disjunct, conjunct*.

b A *connex* Syllogism is, when two are so connected in themselves, that one is the antecedent, the other the consequent, in such manner, as, if the antecedent be asserted, the consequent followeth, and the consequent being taken away, the antecedent is likewise taken away, as, if it be day, it is not night, this antecedent is true, therefore it followeth, it is Night. This kind of Syllogism pertains to the first and second Moods. In the first it is called from position of the antecedent, to position of the consequent; in the second, from negation of the antecedent, to negation of the consequent. The Laws concerning the Truth, or falshood of these Syllogisms are the same with those of connex Axioms.

Of connex Syllogisms there are two kinds; *connex in themselves*, as *if it is light, it is light; but it is light, therefore it is light*; and *connex by others*; as, *if it is day, it is light; but it is day, therefore it is light*.

A *conjunct* Syllogism, is c when we deny something conjunct, and to these add another negation, and of these take the first, that what remains be taken away, as d it cannot be that a Legacy is Money, and Money not a Legacy; but a Legacy is Money, therefore Money is a Legacy.

e A *disjunct* Syllogism is that in which there cannot be more than one thing true, or, that in which if one be, the other is not, or if one be not, the other is; as, *It is either day or night, but it is not night, therefore it is day*; for one being asserted, the other is taken away, and so on the contrary. f The Evidence of this Syllogism *Chrysippus* conceives to be so great, that even Dogs have knowledge thereof. For coming to a place where are three ways, if by the scent they find that the Beast

Be aft hath not gone in two of them, they run directly to the third without scenting, as if they argued thus, the Beast went either this way, or that way, but neither this way nor that way, therefore that way: The Laws of disjunct Syllogisms are the same as those of disjunct axioms.

CHAP. XXIX.
Of MOODS.

a Laert.

a SYllogistick, conclusive Reasons are disposed into *Moods*. Of *Moods* there are two kinds, the first *simple*, properly call'd a Mood, τρόπος, defin'd a kind of figure of the Reason, as thus,

If the first is, the second is,
But the first is,
Therefore the second is.

(It is observable by the way, that the *Stoicks* for Letters used Numbers:) The other *compounded*, called λογότροπος, as being consistent of both Reason and Mood, as,

If Plato liveth, Plato breatheth,
But the first,
Therefore the second.

This is used in a long Syntax, that it be not necessary to speak a long assumption, or a long Inference, but they abbreviate them thus, but the first, therefore the second.

Of *Moods* or Tropes there are two kinds, one of *Indemonstrables*, so term'd, not that they cannot be demonstrated, but because they conclude so evidently, that they need not be reproved; the other of *Demonstrables*.

Cic. Topic.
Martian. capel.

Of Indemonstrable *Moods*, there are (according to *Chrysippus*) five, according to * others more or less.

The first wherein every reason consists of a Connex, and an Antecedent from which beginneth the connex, and the consequent is inferr'd, as,

If the first, then the second,
But the first,
Therefore the second.

The *second* indemonstrable is, which, by the consequent of the Connex, and the contrary of the consequent, hath a conclusion contrary to the Antecedent, as,

If it is day, 'tis light,
But it is night,
Therefore it is not day.

The *third* is that which by a negative complication, and one of those which are in the complication, infers the contrary to that which remains, as,

Plato is not both dead and alive,
But Plato is dead,
Therefore Plato is not alive.

The *fourth* is that which by a disjunctive, and one of those which is in the disjunctive, concludeth the contrary to that which remains, as,

Either 'tis the first or second,
But it is the first,
Therefore it is not the second.

The *fifth* is that wherein the whole reason is connected by a disjunctive, and one of those which are in the disjunctive of the contrary, inferreth the rest, as,

Either it is Night, or it is Day,
But it is not Night,
Therefore it is Day.

CHAP. XXXI.
Of not-Syllogistick-conclusive Reasons.

a Laert.

a REasons *not-Syllogistically-conclusive* (which are likewise especially called (as their Genus) conclusive in opposition to Syllogisms) are those which conclude not by way of Syllogism, as,

It is false, that it is both Night and Day,
But it is day,
Therefore it is not Night.

And this of *Chrysippus*.

Whatsoever is good is laudable,
Whatsoever is laudable is honest,
Therefore whatsoever is good is honest.

These *not-Syllogistick*, or *Categorick*-Conclusives, are frequently used by the *Stoicks* (as by *Zeno* in *Cicero*) but immethodically, not reduc'd to Mood and Figure. Those they applied only to Tropical Reasons, as in which consisteth the sole way and order of Inference. The Categorical are not Syllogisms, because in them something is ever omitted, and therefore they are ἀμεθόδως περαίνοντες, immethodically conclusive; as in that Argument of *Chrysippus* last mentioned, two assumptions, and an inference are omitted, for it ought to be thus,

If it be good, it is laudable,
But it is good,
Therefore it is laudable.

And again,

If it be laudable, it is honest,
But it is laudable,
Therefore it is honest.

Hence are Derived those reasons which are called ἐπιβάλλοντες, and ἐπιβαλλόμενοι, Adjicient and Adject, consisting of propositions continually assuming without conclusions. *Adject* are those whose conclusion is omitted; *Adjicient*, those whose demonstrative proposition is omited, as,

The First of every second,
The Second of every Third,
The third of every fourth,
Therefore the first of every fourth.

In this adject, the conclusion is omitted, which is, therefore the first of every third.

CHAP. XXXI.
Of not-conclusive Reasons.

a Laert.
b Sext. Emp. adv. Logic.

a NOt-conclusive Reasons are those, whose opposite to the inference is repugnant to the connexion of the Sumptions: *b* they are four kinds. 1. By incoherence. 2. By redundance. 3. By being in an ill figure. 4. By defect.

By incoherence, when the Propositions have no conjunction or Communion with one another, nor with the Inference, as,

If it is day, it is light,
But corn is sold,
Therefore it is Light.

For neither, *it is day*, hath any communion with *Corn is sold*, nor both of them together, with, *it is Light*, but each dependeth upon something else.

By Redundance, when something is assumed to the proposition extrinsecal and superfluous, as,

If it is day, it is light,
But it is day, and Virtue profiteth,
Therefore it is light.

For *Virtue profiteth*, is superfluously assumed with the other proposition, the inference depending upon the other two.

By *being in an ill figure*, as this is a right figure,

If the first, the second,
But the first is,
Therefore the second.

But this,

If the first, the second,
But not the second.

Is not conclusive; not that in this Figure, there cannot be Reason which may collect Truth from Truth, for that it may do, as thus,

If three are four, six are eight,
But three are not four,
Therefore six are not eight.

But because there may be some ill reasons in it, as this,

If it be day, 'tis light,
But it is not day,
Therefore it is not light.

By *Defect*, when there wants one of the collective propositions, as,

Riches are either ill or good,
But Riches are not good,
Therefore they are ill.

For in the disjunct there wanteth this, or *indifferent*; so that to be perfect the sumption should be thus, Riches are ill, or good, or indifferent.

CHAP. XXXII.
Of fallacious Reasons or Sophisms.

BY Dialectick are discerned true and false Reasons: The latter are *Sophisms*, proper to *Sophists*, who dispute for vain-glory, or gain; as true Reasons are to *Logicians*, whose end is only to find out Truth.

Of *fallacious Reasons* there are many kinds; the *Quiescent* Reason, or *Sorites*, the *Lying*, the *Inexplicable*, the *Sluggish*, the *Dominative*, the *Vailed*, *Electra*, the *Horned*, the *Crocodilite*, the *Reciprocal*, the *Nullity*, the *Defective*, the *Mower*, the *Bald*, the *Occult*, the *Negative*.

a Suid.
b Ulpian. 48. ad Sabin.
c Laert. tho' the example be falsly applied, as Bursus and Casaubon have observed. d Laert. in Chrysip.
e Cic. acad. quæst. 4.

a *Sorites*, named from σωρός, a heap, is b when from things evidently true, by short mutations, the dispute is brought to things evidently false: c As, *are not two few? Are not three so likewise; And four, and so on to ten? But, two are a few, therefore ten.* d It is called also ἰσυχά- ζων λόγος, the *quiescente reason*, e because the way to understand it, is by stopping, and witholding the assent.

The *lying* reason, ψευδόμενος λόγος. is a captious Argument, not to be dissolved. Of this, see the Life of *Eubulides*.

f Augel. 9. 15.

f The *inexplicable* reason, ἄπορος λόγος, so called, from the intricate nature thereof, not to be dissolved; wherefore it seems to be the same with the lying, and perhaps the genus to most of those which follow.

The *sluggish* reason, ἀργὸς λόγος, is manifested by this example: g If *it be decreed that you shall recover of this Sickness, you shall recover, whether you take Physick or not: Again, if it be decreed you shall not recover, you shall not recover, whether you take Physick or not, Therefore it is to no purpose to take Physick.* This Argument is justly termed sluggish, saith *Cicero*, because by the same reason, all actions may be taken away from Life.

g Cicer. de Fato.

The *Dominative* Reason, κυριεύων λόγος: Of this already in the Life of *Diodorus*.

The *vailed* Reason, ἐγκεκαλυμμένος λόγος: Of this, and *Electra*, and the *Horned* Reason, κερατίνος λόγος, in the Life of *Eubulides*.

The *Crocodilite*, so named from this Ægyptian Fable: h A Woman sitting by the side of *Nilus*, a Crokodile snatch'd away her Child, promising to restore him, if she would answer truly to what he asked; which was, *Whether he meant to restore him or not?* She answer'd, *Not to restore him*, and challenged his promise, as having said the Truth. He reply'd, that *if he should let her have him, she had not told true*.

h Doxopat in Aphthog.

i Agel. 5. 10.

The *reciprocal* Reasons, μεταπίπτοντες, such was that of i *Protagoras* the Sophist, against *Evathlus*, a rich young man, his Disciple, who promised him a great sum of Money for teaching him, whereof half he paid in hand, the other half was to be paid the first that he should Plead before the Judges, and carry the Cause. Having learned long, and attained a great perfection in Rhetorick, he forbore to Plead in Publick, that he might defraud *Protagoras*. *Protagoras* sues him, and the Cause coming to a hearing, begins thus: *Know, foolish young man, that which way soever the Cause goes, whether for thee or against thee, thou must pay what I demand. If against thee, it will be given me by judgment; If for thee, thou must pay it according to our agreement.* *Evathlus* answers: *I might have been entrapped by your Subtilty, if I did not Plead my self, but had employ'd some other to Plead for me. Now I rejoyce doubly in the Victory, that I shall be too hard for you, not only in Cause, but in Argument. Know therefore, my most wise Master, that which way soever the Cause goeth, either with me, or against me, I will not pay what you demand. If it go with me, the judgment will acquit me; if aginst me, you are to have nothing by our agreement.* The Judges not able to determine it, dismissed them both.

k The *nullity*, ὄτις, used by *Ulysses*, who called himself ὄτις, no Body, when he hurt *Polypheme*, whence it came to be so named.

k Odyss.

The *defective* Reason, ἐλλιπὴς λόγος, mentioned by *Laertius* in *Zenone*: The *Mower* θερίζων λόγος, by *Lucian*: The *Bald*, φαλακρὸς λόγος, by *Laertius* in *Eubulide*: The *occult*, διαλανθάνων λόγος, by *Laertius* in *Eubulide*: The *negative*, ἀποφάσκων λόγος, by *Laertius* in *Chrysippo*, and by *Epictetus*. But of these enough.

CHAP. XXXIII.
Of Method.

THere are two kinds of Disputation: a One, when the Truth it self is subtilly polished in the dispute: The other, when every expression

a Cic. Offic. 2.

on is accommodated to the vulgar Opinion; for, we must use popular and usual words, when we speak of popular opinions, which *Panætius* in the like manner hath done.

b Cic. de fin. 3. *b* The first way was peculiar to the Stoicks, short, acute, and spinous, called likewise Logick most worthy of Philosophy; for this useth definition, divisions, and the lights which they afford, as likewise similitudes, dissimilitudes, and the nice acute distinction of them.

c Senec. Epist. 14.90. The vulgar way of dispute is likewise twofold, one by continued Oration; The other by Question and Answer: The first called *c Analytick*, or *d Cic. de fin. 2.* *d Rhetorical*; the other *e Topick*, or *f Dialectical*. *g* Tho' the first be delightful, yet the latter is more commodious, when we insist on particulars, and understand what every Man granteth, what every Man denieth, what we would have concluded from concessions, and brought to an and. For, when a Speech is carried on like a Torrent, altho it bears many things along with it; yet we can hold nothing, we cannot stop the rapid course of an Oration. *h* The *h Cic. de nat. deor. 2.* other, concluding as *Zeno* used, more shortly and narrowly, lieth more open to reprehension. As a River in its Course, cannot at all, or very hardly be corrupted, but water shut up, easily: So by a fluent Oration, the faults of the opposer are carried quite away; in a narrow Speech, they are not easily defended.

But each of these methods hath a several use; the first is proper for exposition of Arts and Sciences, the other for Disputation.

THE SECOND PART.

CHAP. I.

ETHICK and the Parts thereof.

a Laert. *a* THE Moral part of Philosophy is divided into these places; *Of Appetite, Of Good and Ill, Of Passions, Of Virtue, Of the End, of the first Estimation, Of Actions, Offices, Exhortations and Dehortations.*

Thus distinguisheth *Chrysippus, Archidemus, Zeno* of *Tarsis, Apollodorus, Diogenes* (the Babylonians) *Antipater* and *Possidonius*. But *Zeno* the Cittiean, and *Cleanthes*, as being more antient, were less accurate in their manner of treating upon these things.

CHAP. II.

Of Appetite.

a Stob. Eclog. Ethic. THE consideration of Ethick, beginneth properly from Appetite. *a* Appetite is moved by Phantasie of an Office, for it is the impulsion of the Soul to something.

Appetite in rational and irrational Creatures is different; ὄρεξις, is not rational appetite, but a species of rational appetite. Rational appetite is defined an impulsion of the Intellect to the doing of something. Ὄρεξις is a species of practick appetite, being an impulsion of the Intellect to something future. Hence appetite is taken four ways, for rational and irrational Inclination, and for rational and irrational aversion. To these may be added the habit of Appetition, which is likewise called Appetite, the Origine of all appetitive Acts.

Of practick Appetite there are many species, of which are

1. πρόθεσις, A Designation.
2. ἐπιβολή, An Appetite before Appetite.
3. παρασκευή, An Action before Action.
4. ἐγχείρησις, an Appetite to something now existent.
5. αἵρεσις; A Will by ratiocination.
6. προαίρεσις, A Will before a Will.
7. βούλησις, An Appetite joyned with Reason.
1. θέλησις, a spontaneous Will.

CHAP. III.

Of first Natural Appetite.

a THE first appetite of a living creature is *a Laert.* to preserve it self, this being from the beginning proper to it by nature, as *Chrysippus* in his first Book of Ends, who affirms that the care our selves, and the consciousness thereof, is the first property of all living Creatures. For, Nature producing a living creature, intended either to alienate it from it self, or to commend it unto its own care; but the first is not likely; it followeth therefore, that Nature commendeth to every thing the preservation of it self, whereby it repulseth whatsoever is hurtful, and pursueth what is convenient.

b As soon therefore as a living creature cometh into the World, it is conciliated to it self; *b Cic. de fin. 3* commended to the conservation of it self and its own state, and to the Election of such things as may preserve its state; but alienated from Destruction, and from all such things as may destroy it. This is manifest, in as much as before the accession of Pleasure or grief, young creatures desire those things which conduce to their welfare, and refuse the contrary; which would not be, if they did not love their own state, and fear destruction. Neither could they desire any thing without having some sense of themselves, whereby they love themselves, and what belong to them. Hence it is manifest, that the principle of this love is derived from themselves.

c Whereas some do hold the first appetite *c Laert.* of a living creature to be that of pleasure, that is false *d* The greater part of Stoicks conceive *d Cic. de fin. 3.* that pleasure is not to be placed amongst the natural principles of love to our selves; for if Nature had so ordered it, many dishonest things would have followed. *e* Pleasure is an after- *e Laert.* accession, when as Nature enquiring by it self into it self, receiveth those things which are agreeable to its constitution, after which manner living creatures are exhilarated, and plants sprout forth. Nature hath thus far made no difference betwixt plants and living creatures, that whereas plants are ordered without appetite or sense, there is in living creatures something according to the nature of plants: But, there being over and above in living creatures an innate appetite, whereby

whereby they go to those things that are proper for them, the natural part in them is governed by the appetitive.

f Cic. de fin. 3. *f* That we naturally love those things which are first proposed unto us by Nature, may be argued from hence, in that there is no man, if both were put to his choice, but had rather have all his Limbs able and sound, than useless and imperfect. These comprehensions we conceive fit to be acquired for their own sake, because they have in themselves something, as it were, complex, including Truth. This is discernable in young ones, whom we see delighted, tho it nothing concerns them, if they themselves find out any thing by reason. Even the Arts we conceive to be assumed for themselves, as well because in these there is something worthy assumption, as because they consist of knowledge, and contain somethings constituted by reason and power.

CHAP. IV.
Of Appetites consequent to the first.

a Cic. de fin. 3. THus according *a* to the first innate principles of Nature, those things which are according to nature being expetible in themselves their contraries avoidable in themselves, the first Office is to conserve it self in the state of nature; the next, to obtain those things which are according to nature.

Here beginneth good to be first understood, for it is the first conciliation of man to things according to nature. This good, as soon as man receiveth intelligence or notion thereof, and seeth the order and concord of Offices, he esteemeth far above those things which he formerly loved; and by rational knowledge collecteth, that herein is placed the chief good of man, laudable and expetible in it self. To this chief good, which consisteth in homologie or convenience, all honest actions having reference, honesty it self, which is reckoned amongst the good, tho it rise afterward, is notwithstanding alone expetible in its own power and dignity. But, of those which are the first objects of nature, none is expetible in it self.

Now whereas offices proceed from the first natural objects, they must necessarily be referred to the same; so as all Offices tend to the fulfilling of the first natural appetites; yet, not so, as if therein consisted the ultimate good. Honest action is in the first conciliation of nature, for it is consequent, and ariseth as we said afterward; yet, it is according to nature, and much more allective than all that go before it.

And seeing that all Offices proceed from the first natural appetites, even wisdom it self must be derived from thence likewise. But as it often happens, that he who is recommended to another, more esteemeth him to whom he is recommended, than the person which recommended him: so it is not strange, that we being recommended to wisdom by the first natural appetite, afterwards more esteem that Wisdom, than those things whereby we arrived at it. And as our Limbs are given to us for a certain reason of living, so the appetition of the Soul is given, not for every kind of life, but for one certain form of living; so likewise Reason and perfect Reason. For, as Action is proper to a Player, Motion to a Dancer; yet, not any, but one certain kind: so the life that is to be acted, is in one certain kind, not in any, which kind we call convenient and consentaneous. Wisdom is not like the Art of a Pilot, or a Physician; but rather to that Action we mentioned, and to Dancing, that the extream, that is, the effection of the Art be in the Art it self, and not extrinsecal. There is another similitude betwixt Wisdom and these Arts, for in them are those things which are done rightly; yet, are not all the parts, whereof they consist, contain'd therein. Things done rightly, or Rectitudes, contain all numbers of Virtue; for, only Wisdom is wholly converted into it self, which is not in other Arts. But improperly is the Art of a Pilot and a Physician, compared with the ultimate of Wisdom: For, Wisdom includeth Fortitude and Justice, and judgeth all things that happen to Man to be below it, which happeneth not in other Arts: but none can hold these Virtues which we last mentioned, unless he affirm there is nothing that's different, but honest and dishonest.

CHAP. V.
Of Good and Ill.

HItherto of Appetites; we come next to their Objects. *a* Things (according to *Zeno*) are whatsoever participate of Essence. Of Things, some are *good*, some *ill*, some *indifferent*. *a Stob.*

b Good is several ways defined by the Stoicks, but their definitions tend all to one end. *c* Good is Profit, or that which differeth not from Profit. Profit is Virtue, and a virtuous action; not different from Profit is a Virtuous Man, and a Friend. For Virtue being a *quodammodotative* Hegemoniack, and virtuous action being an operation according to Virtue, is plainly Profit. A Virtuous man and a Friend is not different from profit; for Profit is a part of Virtuous, as being the Hegemoniack thereof. Now the wholes are neither the same with their parts, for a man is not a hand; nor different from their parts, for they subsist not without parts; wherefore the whole is not different from its parts, and consequently, a virtuous man being the whole, in respect of his Hegemoniack, which is profit, is not different from profit. *b Cic. de fin. 3.* *c Sext. Em. pb. Porph. 3. 20.*

Good is by some defined, that which is expetible in it self; by others, that which assisteth to felicity, or compleateth it: by *e Diogenes*, that which is absolute by nature [or, *f* that which is perfect, according to the nature of a rational creature.] The consequent thereof is a beneficent motion, or state absolute in nature. *e Cic. de fin. 3.* *f Laert.*

Whereas things are known, either by use, or conjunction, or similitude, or collation, by this fourth kind is the knowledge of good; for when from those things which are according to nature, the Mind ascendeth by collation of Reason, then it attaineth the notion of good.

h Good is known and armed, not by accession, increase, or comparison with other things, but by its proper power. For as Honey, tho it be most sweet: yet, in its proper kind of tast, not comparative to any other, we perceive it to be sweet: So this good of which we speak, is that which is most to be esteemed; but that estimation consisteth in the kind, not the magnitude. For estimation being neither amongst the good nor ill, whatsoever *h Cic. de fin. 3.*

Part VIII.   *ZENO.*   319

whatsoever you apply it to, it will remain in its kind. Different therefore is the proper estimation of Vertue, which consisteth in the kind, not in increase.

i Laert. Stob. *i* To *Good* belongeth all Vertue, as Prudence, Justice, Temperance, Fortitude, and whatsoever participates of those, as Vertuous Actions, and Persons. *k* Accessions here are Joy, Cheerfulness, and the like.

k Laert.

l Laert. Stob. *l* *Ills* are the contrary Vices, as Imprudence, Injustice, Intemperance, Pusillanimity, and whatsoever participates of Vice, as Vicious Actions and Persons. *m* The accessions hereunto are discontent, affliction, and the like.

m Laert.

n Stob. *n* Of *Goods*, some, as we have said, are *Vertues*, others *not Vertues*, as Joy, Hope, and the like. In like manner of *Ills*, some are *Vices*, as those already mention'd; others *not Vices*, as Grief and Fear.

o Stob. Again, *o* Of *Goods*, some are *continual* in all the Vertuous, and at all times; such is all Vertue, sound Sense, wise appetition, and the like. Others are *intermissive*, as Joy, Hope, and prudent Counsel, which are not in all the wise, nor at all times.

In like manner of *Ills*, some are continual in all, and always in the Imprudent, as all Vice, and imprudent sense, and imprudent Appetite: Others intermissive, as grief, fear, and imprudent answer, which are not always in the wicked, nor at all times.

p Laert. Stob. Sext. Emp. Pyrrh. hypot. 3. 21. *p* Again, of *Good*, there are three kinds, The first *from which* Profit cometh, as from its first cause, such is Vertue: The second, *by which* profit cometh, as Vertue, and vertuous Action: The third, *that which may* profit, as Vertue, and Vertuous Actions, and a Vertuous Man, and a Friend, and the Gods and good Demons. *q* Thus the second signification includeth the first; and the third, both the first and second.

q Sext. Empir.

r Laert. Stob. *r* In like manner of *Ills*, there are three kinds: First, that from which hurt originally proceedeth, as Vice: Secondly, that by which hurt cometh, as vicious Actions: Lastly, and most largely, whatsoever is able to hurt.

f Laert. Stob. Sext. Emp. Pyrrh. hyp. 3. 23. *f* Again, of *Goods*, some are *in the Soul*, as Vertue, and vertuous Actions: Some *without the Soul*, as a true Friend, a good Country, and the like: Some *neither* within nor without the Soul: As good and Vertuous Men.

t Laert. Stob. *t* In like manner of *Ills*, some are *within* the Soul, as Vices, and vicious Actions; some *without* the Soul, as imprudent Friends, Enemies, and the like; some *neither* within nor without the Soul, as wicked Men, and all that participate of Vice.

u Laert. Stob. *u* Of *Goods within the Soul*, some are *habits*, some *affections*, some neither habits nor affections. The *Vertues* themselves are affections; their *studies* habits, not affections; theire *acts* neither habits nor affections.

x Laert. Stob. *x* In like manner of *Ills*, some are *affections*, as Vices; some habits only, as infirmities of mind, and the like; some *neither* habits nor affections, as vicious actions.

y Laert. Stob. Cic. de finib. 3. *y* Again, Of *Goods*, some are *final*, some *efficient*, some both final and efficient. A Friend, and the benefits arising from him, are *efficient* Goods. Fortitude, Magnanimity, Liberty Delectation, Joy, Tranquillity, and all Vertuous actions, are final Goods. Both efficient and final, as all Vertues, as they perfect Felicity they are efficient, as they constitute it as parts, thereof, final.

z In like manner of *Ills*, some are final, some efficient, some both. Fear, baseness, servitude, stupidity, frowardness, grief, and all vicious actions, are final: Participant of, are vices, as they procure misfortune they are efficient, as they constitute it as parts thereof, final.

z Laert. Stob.

a Again, Of *Goods*, some are *expetible in themselves*, not desired for the sake of any other: Others are *preparatory* to some other, called effectively expetible. The expetible in themselves are (according to *Diogenes*) of two kinds: 1. Ultimately expetible, as Beatitude. 2. Those which have in them the cause of being expetible, as every good hath.

a Stob.

b Again, Of Goods some are *necessary Beatitude*, as all Vertues and their Acts; others *not necessary*, as Joy, delectation, and study. In like manner of Ills, some are necessary to infelicity, as all the vices and their Acts; others not necessary thereunto, as all passions and infirmities of the Soul and the like.

b Stob.

c Again, Of *Goods*, some consist in motion, as Joy, delectation and the like; some in affection, as quiet, imperturbation; of those which consist in affection, some are likewise in habit, as the Vertues; others in affection only, as the former. Neither consist the Vertues only in habits, but other acts likewise, changed by a vertuous Man, in a manner into vertue. Of these Goods which are in habit, are those we call studies, as love of Learning, and the like. For these Arts by their affinity with Vertue lead directly to our chief end.

c Stob.

Again, *d* Of Goods, some are *absolute*, as Science; others *relative*, as honour, benevolence, friendship, and the like.

d Stob.

e Science is a certain infallible comprehension by reason. It is taken three ways. First, for a System of Sciences conjoyned together in a good Man; Secondly for a System of artificial Sciences, having a certainty. Lastly, for a demonstrative infallible habit of Phantasies by reason.

e Stob.

f Friendship, is a community of Life, and consent of studies. The kinds thereof are six.
1. γνωριμωΐαλη a Friendship amongst known persons.
2. συνήθεια, amongst Familiars.
3. ἡλικεία, Amongst those of the same age.
4. ξενία, towards Strangers.
5. συγγενική, amongst Kindred.
6. ἐρωτική, from Love.

f Stob.

g Again, of *Goods*, some are *simple*, as knowledg; others *mixt*, as, εὐτεκνία, a good use of Children conformable to Nature, as εὐγηρεία, good use of old Age conformable to Nature, εὐζωία, a good use of Life conformable to Nature. *Exemption from Grief*, ἀλυπία, and *conservation of Order*, εὐταξία, are the same with, as the mind is with prudence, and communion with goodness; yet are otherwise referred, which is observable likewise in the other vertues. Hence are the same distinctions appliable to ill.

g Laert. Stob.

h Every good is *beneficial, opportune, conducible, useful, commendable, fair, helpful, eligible, just*. *Beneficial*, συμφέρον, as conferring that whereby we receive Benefit.

h Laert. Stob.

Opportune, δέον, as comprising that whereof we stand in need.

Condu-

Conducible, λυσιτελὲς, as resolving in it self the means, as the gain acquired by Traffick exceeds the charge.

Useful, χρήσιμον, as conducing to our profit.

Commendable, εὐχρηστον, from the use.

Fair, καλὸν, as proportioned to the necessities of receivers.

Helpful, ὠφέλιμον, as it relieves us.

Eligible, αἱρετὸν, as being in reason to be preferr'd.

Just, δίκαιον, as being conformable to Law.

i On the contrary, every ill is unbeneficial, importune, inconducible, unuseful, uncommendable, foul, unhelpful, avoidable, and unjust.

k Perfect good, is called καλὸν, *Fair*, because it is absolute in all numbers required of Nature, and perfectly proportionate.

l Of *Fair*, (or *Honest*) there are four Species, *Just*, *Valiant*, *Temperate*, *Knowing*; in these are honest actions consummated.

m Likewise of αἰχρον, *foul*, (or *dishonest*) are four Species, *unjust*, *cowardly*, *dissolute*, *foolish*.

n Honest, is called καλὸν, *Fair*, first, because it renders those who are endued therewith, worthy of Praise; Secondly, because it is most suitable to its proper work; Thirdly, because 'tis an ornament; we say a wise Man is only good and fair.

o Only that which is good, is fair or honest: So *Hecato* in his third Book of Good; and *Chryfippus* of Fair. This is Virtue, and what participates thereof, which is all one as to say, that whatsoever is good, is honest likewise; and reciprocally whatsoever is honest, is good.

p That what is honest, only is good, is prov'd thus. Whatsoever is good, is laudable; Whatsoever is laudable, is honest; therefore whatsoever is good is is honest. Again, there is no good which is not expetible, nothing expetible which is not pleasant and amiable, therefore approvable, therefore laudable, therefore honest. Again, no Man can glory in a Life that is miserable or not happy, therefore to glory is proper to the happy, but to glory relateth only to that which is honest, therefore honest is happy. And as he who is laudable, hath some eminent mark of renown and glory, for which he is justly stiled happy, the same may be said of the life of such a Man, whence if a happy life consist in Honesty, only that which is honest is to be esteem'd good. Moreover, what Man can be termed constant, firm, magnanimous, unless we grant that pain is not an ill? For, he who reckoneth Death amongst the Ills, cannot but fear it; so no Man in any thing can neglect and contemn that which he accounteth ill. This being granted, the next assumption is this, he who is magnanimous and valiant, despiseth, as if they were nothing, all things that can arrive to Man; whence it followeth, that nothing is ill which is not not dishonest; and this sublime, excellent, magnanimous Person, accounting all humane things below him, confideth in himself and his own Life past and future, knowing that no Ill can happen to a Wife Man. Whereby we see that what is honest only is good, which is to live happily and honestly.

q On the other side, nothing is good, but what is honest; for who is, or ever was so feverishly covetous, and of such disordinate affections, that the same things, for the attainment whereof he would perpetrate any Wickedness, he had not much attain'd unto (setting aside all punishment) without all that wicked means? What advantage or fruit do we aim at, in desiring to know those things which are hidden from us, how they are moved, and by what causes agitated in Heaven? Who is so savage, so obdurate to natural Studies, that he abhors things worthy knowledg, receives them without Pleasure, or some benefit, and values them at nothing? Who is there, that when he heareth of the Actions, Speeches, Counsels of magnanimous Persons, eminent in all Virtue, is not affected with any Pleasure? Who is there, that being instituted in an honest Family, and ingenuously Educated, is not offended at dishonesty, though it bring no hurt to him? Who is there, that looks without trouble upon such as live impurely and flagitiously? Who doth not hate sordid, vain, light, frivolous Persons? If dishonesty were not in it self avoidable, why should Men, when they are in the dark, or in a Wilderness, abstain from any thing that is evil, but that the very deformity and dishonesty thereof deters them? Nothing therefore is more clear, than that honest things are expetible in themselves, and dishonest things avoidable in themselves.

Hence it followeth, that what is honest, is more estimable than those mean things which accrue by it. And when we say, that folly, temerity, injustice, and intemperance, are avoidable, in respect of those things which are consequent to them, it contradicts not the former assertion, that what is dishonest only is ill, because they relate not to the hurt of the Body, but to dishonest actions which proceed from Vice.

r All good is equal, and every good is highly expetible, and admits neither increase, nor decrease. *s* Here cometh in a great Controversie betwixt the *Stoicks* and the *Peripateticks*, which though *Carneades* affirms to be only verbal, *Cicero* holdeth to be more things than words.

t The *Peripateticks* hold, that all goods are requisite to happy Life; the *Stoicks*, that whatsoever is worthy estimation, comprehendeth happy life. Those holding pain to be an ill, it follows, that a wise Man cannot be happy upon the Rack. These who account not pain among the Ills, hold, that a wise Man continueth happy in the midst of Torments: For, if some bear those Pains with greater Courage for their Country, or some lighter cause, opinion, not nature increaseth or diminisheth the power of the Pain. Again, the *Peripateticks* asserting three kinds of good, affirm a Man to be so much the more happy, the fuller he is of external corporeal goods; or, in the *Stoicks* Expression, he who hath most corporeal estimables, is most happy, for as much as by them Beatitude is compleated. On the contrary, the *Stoicks* hold, that those goods which they call of Nature, make not by their frequency a life more happy, or are more expetible, or more estimable: For then wisdom being expetible, and health expetible, both together would be more expetible than Wisdom alone; whereas either being worthy estimation, both are not more worthy of estimation than wisdom alone. For the *Stoicks*, who held Health to be estimable, but place it not amongst the goods, hold likewise, that no estimation is to be preferr'd before Vertue,

tue. From this, the *Peripateticks* dissent, asserting that an honest action without Pain, is more expetible than the same action with pain; the *Stoicks* otherwise. For, as a Taper is darkned by the light of the Sun, and as a drop of Water is lost in the vastness of the *Ægean* Sea, and as in the riches of *Cræsus* the accession of one farthing, and one step in the way between this and *India*, so in that end of all good which the *Stoicks* assert, all the estimation of corporeal things must necessarily be obscur'd, overwhelm'd, and perish, by the splendor and magnitude of vertue. And as opportunity εὐκαιεία, is not made any thing greater by production of time, for whatsoever is opportune hath its measure; so right affection, κατόρθωσις, and the good it self placed in it, that it be conformable to Nature, admitteth no accession of increase. For as that opportunity, to those of which we speak, are not made greater by production of time, for which reason the *Stoicks* conceive, that a happy Life is not more to be desired, if it be long, than if it be short; and they use this Simily: As it is the praise of a shooe to fit the Foot, neither are many Shooes preferr'd before two, nor the greater before the less: So in those things, whose good is confin'd to opportunity and convenience, neither are the more to be preferr'd before the fewer, nor the longer before the shorter. Nor do they argue acutely, who say, if long health be more to be esteem'd than short, then likewise a long use of wisdom, more than a short; they understand not, that the estimation of Health is judged by space, that of vertue by opportunity; as if they should say likewise a good death, or a good labour to a Woman in Travel, is better long than short; so that they see not, that some things are more esteemed for their shortness, others for their length.

CHAP. VI.

Of Eupathies.

a Cic. Tusc. quæst. lib. 4.

a AS soon as any object is presented to us, which seemeth good, Nature [*as we said*] drives, us on to the acquisition thereof, which being done constantly and prudently, is call'd *Will*; imprudently and excessively, *Desire*.

b Cic. ibid.

b Moreover, while we are so moved, that we are in some good, that happeneth also two ways, when the Soul is mov'd quietly and constantly according to reason, this is called *Joy*; when vainly and excessively, *Pleasure*.

c Cic. ibid.

c In like manner, as we desire good things by nature, so by nature we decline the Ill: This declination, if done according to reason, is called *Caution*, if without reason, *Fear*. *d* Caution is only in a wise man, of Fear he is not capable.

d Cic. ibid. Laert.

Hence it appeareth, that there are three kinds of good affections of the Mind, called *e* *Eupathies*, or *f* *Constancies*; *Joy, Caution, Will*.

e Laert.
f Cic.
g Laert.

1. *g* *Joy* is contrary to Pleasure, as being a rational Elevation of the Mind.
2. *Caution* is contrary to Fear, as being a rational declination of ill.
3. *Will* is contrary to desire, as being a rational Appetite.

These are the primary Eupathies; and as under the primary Passions are comprehended many subordinate passions; so are there secondary Eupathies subordinate to those.

Under *Joy* are 1. *Delectation*. 2. *Cheerfulness*. 3. *Æquanimity*.
Under *Caution*, 1. *Respect*. 2. *Clearness*.
Under *Will* are, 1. *Benevolence*. 2. *Salutation*. 3. *Charity*.

Notwithstanding that Eupathies and Passions are contrary; yet are there but three Eupathies, though there are four Passions; for there is no Eupathy contrary to *Grief*. Cic.Tusc.quæst.4.

CHAP. VII.

Of Passions.

a From falsities proceedeth a perversity of Intellect, hence spring up several passions, and causes of disorder. *a* Laert.

b *Zeno* defineth passion, a præternatural motion of the Soul, (or as *c* Cicero renders it, a commotion of the Soul, averse from right Reason, against Nature.) Others more briefly, a more vehement Appetite. More vehement they call that, which recedeth from the constancy of Nature, and *d* is contrary to nature, wherefore all passion is an excessive stupid desire. *b* Laert. *c* Tusc. quæst.4. *d* Laert.

e The kinds of Passion arise from two opinionated goods, and two opinionated Evils, so they are four. From the good, *desire* and *pleasure*; pleasure from present good, desire from future; from the ill, *Fear* and *Grief*; fear from the future, grief from the present; from these things, whose coming we fear, when they do come, grieve us. Pleasure and desire arise from an opinion of good things, desire is fervently transported to that which seemeth good, pleasure rejoiceth when we have obtained what we desire. Thus *f* desire and fear go foremost, that to apparent good, this to apparent ill; *pleasure* and *grief* follows; pleasure, when we attain what we desire, * grief, when we incur what we fear. *e* Cic. ibid. *f* Stob. * λυπῶ ὅταν περιπέσωμεν &c. so supply the Text.

g All passions arise from *Judgment* and *Opinion*, whence they are more strictly defined, (that it may appear not only how vicious they are, but also that they are in our power) thus; *g* Cic. ibid.

h *Grief* is a fresh opinion of present ill, wherein it seemeth fit that the Mind be contracted and dejected, or *i* a contraction of the Soul caused by opinion of present ill. *h* Cic. *i* Stob.

k *Pleasure* is a fresh opinion of present good, wherein it seemeth good that the Mind be exalted, or *l* an irrational elevation of mind to something that seemeth eligible. *k* Cic. *l* Laert.

m *Fear* is an opinion of eminent ill, which seemeth to be intolerable; or a contraction of the Soul disobedient to Reason, caused by expectation of ill. *m* Cic.

n *Desire* is an opinion of good to come, that if it were present, it were fit for our use, or *o* an appetite disobedient to Reason, caused by the opinion of consequent good. *n* Cic. *o* Stob.

These four are, as *Hecato* saith, primary passions, under each of which there are subordinate passions, several species belonging to their proper genus.

Under *Grief* are these kinds,

p Envy, φθόνος, *invidentia*; a grief at the prosperity of others, *q* which doth no hurt to him that envieth, * for some Men desire to see their *p* Laert. Cic. *q* Cicer. * Plut. Cont. Stoic.

their neighbours suppressed, that themselves might be advanced above them. For if a Man grieve at the prosperity of another, whereby he is damaged, he is not properly said to envy, as that of *Hector* to *Agamemnon*; but he who is nothing damaged by the prosperity of another, yet grieveth thereat, truly envieth.

r Cic.   *r Æmulation*, ζῆλος, (not here taken for the imitation of Vertue, for that is laudable) a grief that another Man enjoyeth that which we desire and want, or as *Laertius*, a grief for another's felicity, which we wish to our selves, and an emulation thereof, as greater than our own.

s Laert.   *s Jealousie*, ζηλοτυπία, *obtrectation*, a grief
t Cic.   lest another enjoy what we *t* love and possess.

u Laert.   *u Compassion*, ἔλεος, *misericordia*, a grief for
x Cic.   the misery another suffers undeservedly. *y* for no Man compassionates the punishment of a Parricide or Traytor.

y Laert. Cic.   *y Anguish*, ἄχθος, *Anger*, an oppressive grief.
z Cic. Stob.   *z Mourning*, πένθος, *Luctus*, grief for the death of a Friend that was dear to us.

a Cic.   *a Wailing*, *Mæror*, a grief accompanied with Tears.

b Cic. Laert.   *b Trouble*, ὀδύνη, *ærumna*, a laborious piercing grief.

c Cic.   *c Sorrow*, *Dolor*, a vexatious grief, perhaps the same which in *Stobæus* is termed ἄση, a grief with conflict of Spirit.

d Cic.   *d Lamentation*, ἀνία, a grief with thoughtful-
e Laert.   ness, *e* proceeding from, and encreasing by consideration and discourse.

f Cic.   *f Molestia*, a permanent grief.
g Cic.   *g Affliction*, a grief with corporeal torment.
h Cic.   *h Desperation*, a grief without any hope of amendment.

i Laert.   *i* Ἐνόχλησις, an urgent grief attended by difficulty.

k Stob.   *k* Ἄχος, a grief taking away the voice.

l Laert.   *l* Σύγχυσις, an irrational Grief corroding, and hindring us from enjoying the present.

Under *Pleasure* are,

m Cic. Laert. whence supply *Stobæus* where (Pleasure being omitted) these are applied to a wrong Head.   *m Malevolence*, ἐπιχαιρεκακία, a Pleasure at another's Ill, without any good to our selves. This hath no real subsistence; for no good man was ever known to rejoice at the harm of another.
n Cic. Laert.   *n Delectation*, κήλησις, a Pleasure affecting and soothing the Mind by the Ear, and in like manner by the Eye, touch, smell, or taste, which are all of one kind.

o Cic.   *o Jactation*, a boasting Pleasure, with insolent, behaviour.

p Laert.   *p* Τέρψις, quasi τρέψις, an inclination of the Mind to dissoluteness.

q Laert.   *q* Διάχυμα, the Dissolution of vertue.

r Stob.   *r* Ἀσμενισμός, a pleasure from things not expected.

s Stob.   *s* Γοήτεια, a Pleasure caused by Sight, without Deceit.

Under *Fear*, are

t Laert. Stob.   *t Dread*, δεῖμα, a fear causing νέος.
u Laert. Stob.   *u Sloth*, ὄκνος *Pigritia*, a fear of future Action, or susception of Labour.

* Laert. Stob.   ** Shame*, αἰσχύνη, a fear of Ignominy.

y Laert.   *y* Ἔκπληξις, a fear of some unusual Phantasie.
z Laert.   *z* Θόρυβος, a fear with loss, or trepidation of voice.

a Laert.   *a* Ἀγωνία, a fear of something uncertain, or a fear of offending or falling.

b Stob.   *b* Δεισιδαιμονία, a fear of Gods or Demons.
c Stob.   *c* Δέος, a fear of some grievous thing.

d Terrour, a Fear, which by striking the Mind   *d Cic.* causeth redness, paleness, trembling, or gnashing of the Teeth.

e Timor, a fear of approaching ill.   *Cic.*
f Pavor, a Fear thrusting the Mind out of   *f Cic.* its Place.

g Exanimatio, a Fear consequent, and as it   *g Cic.* were companion to *Pavor*.

h Conturbatio, a fear, which disperseth all our   *h Cic.* Thoughts.

i Formido, a permanent Fear.   *i Cic.*

k The Passions subordinate to Desire, are generally two, *Anger* and *Love*.   *k Stob.*

l Anger is a desire of taking revenge upon   *l Laert.* those by whom we conceive our selves wrong'd.

m The Species thereof are,   *m Stob.*

n Θυμός, or as *Cicero*, θύμωσις, *excandescentia*, Anger beginning.   *n Laert.*

o Χόλος, Anger encreasing.   *o Laert.*

p Μῆνις, *odium*, Anger inveterate.   *p Cic. Stob.*

q Κότος, *Inimicitia*, anger watching the occasion of Revenge.   *q Cic. Stob.*

r Πικρία, anger breaking forth into action.   Μῆνις & κότος are confounded by *Laertius*
s Μῖσος, a desire whereby we wish ill to another, with continual progression.   *r Stob.* *s Laert.*

t Malice, *Discordia*, a bitter anger, with utmost hatred, conceived in the Heart.   *t Cic.*

u Φιλονεικία, a desire conversant in difference of opinions   *u Laert.*

* Love is an impulsion of good-will for apparent Beauty, *y* whereby it is distinguish'd from the love of the Vertuous, which is a voluntary susception of labour for true Beauty. The Species of love are,   ** Stob.* *y Laert.*

z Σπάνις, *indigentia*, an (inexpleble) desire of that which we want, and being separated from it, in vain incline to it.   *z Laert. Cic.*

a Πόθος, *desiderium*, a desire to see that which is not present. They *b* distinguish these two thus: Desire is of those things which are said, or prædicated of any thing which they call *Categorems*, as to have Riches, to take Honours; Indigence is of the things themselves; as of honours of money   *a Stob.* *b Cic.*

c Ἵμερος, desire of conversation of that which is absent.   *c Stob.*

d Φιληδονία, desire of Pleasure.   *d Stob.*
e Φιλοπλουτία, desire of Riches.   *e Stob.*
f Φιλοδοξία, desire of Glory.   *f Stob.*

g In all these Passions there is Opinion.   *g Stob.*
h Opinion is a weak assent. *i* Hence passions, (as *Chrysippus* in his Book of *Passions* affirms) are Judgments ; for Avarice is an opinion, or false Judgment that Money is good; Drunkenness and Intemperance, are the like. *k* Opinion is likewise sudden from the contractive motion of an unreasonable elation of the Mind, unreasonable and præternatural, in as much as it is not obedient to reason. For every passion is violent: Wherefore oftentimes, though we see in those that are transported by passion, the inconvenience thereof; yet notwithstanding, the same Persons that condemn it, are carried away by it, as by a headstrong Horse, and therefore properly may use that saying: *h Laert. Cic.* *i Laert.* *k Stob.*

Against my Judgment Nature forceth me, Meaning by Judgment, the knowledge of right things; for Man is carried beyond Nature by Passion, to transgress natural reason and right.

l All those who are led by Passion, are diverted from Reason, but in another manner than those   *l Stob.*

those who are deceived. For the deceived, as for example, They who think Atomes to be the principles of all things, when they come to know that they are not, change their Judgment: But, those that are in passion, although that they are taught not to grieve, or fear, or give way to any passion in the Soul, yet they do not put them off, but are lead on by their passions, until they come to be subject to their tyrannical sway.

CHAP. VIII.

Of Sickness and Infirmities.

a Cic. Tusc. quest. 4.

a THE Fountain of all passions is Intemperance, which is a total defection from the Mind, and from right reason, so averse from the prescription of Reason, that the appetites of the Soul can by no means be ruled, or contained. As therefore Temperance allayeth Appetites, and causeth them to obey right reason, and preserveth the considerate judgments of the Mind; so Intemperance, the Enemy thereto, enflameth, troubleth, and inciteth the state of the Soul. Thus Griefs and Fears, and the rest of the passions, all arise from this. For, as when the blood is corrupt, or flegm, or choler aboundeth, sicknesses or infirmities arise in the Body; So the disorder of ill opinions, and their repugnance to one another, divesteth the Soul of health, and troubleth it with Diseases.

b Laert. Stob. Cic.

b By passions the Mind becometh indisposed, and as it were sick. *Sickness* of Mind, νόσημα, is an opinion and desire of that which seemeth greatly expetible, but is not such, as love of Women, of Wine, of Money. These νοσήματα, have likewise their contraries in the other extream, as hatred of Women, of Wine, of Money.

c Laert. Stoi. Cic.

c This sickness of mind happening with imbecillity, is called ἀρρώστημα, *infirmity*. For, as in the body there are Infirmities, as Gouts, Convulsions, and the like; so are there infirmities in the Mind, as love of glory, love of pleasure. And as in Bodies there is a propensity to some particular Diseases; so in the Mind there is a proclivity ἐυεμπτωσία, or ἐυκαταφυεία, to some particular passions, as φθονεεία, *propensity to Envy*, ἀνελεημοσύνη, *propensity to unmercifulness*, and the like.

d Cic. Tusc. quest. 4.

d In this place, much pains hath been taken by the *Stoicks*, chiefly by *Chrysippus*, to compare the Sicknesses of the Mind with those of the Body.

Passion (for as much as opinions are inconstantly and turbulently tossed up and down) is always in motion; and when this fervour and concitation of the Mind is inveterate, and, as it were, setled in the Veins and Marrow, then ariseth Sickness and Infirmities, and those aversions which are contrary to those infirmities and diseases. These differ only intentionally, but really are the same, arising from desire and pleasure; for when Money is desir'd, and reason not immediately applied, as a Socratick Medicine to cure that desire, the evil spreadeth thro' the veins, and cleaveth to the Bowels, and becometh sickness and infirmity, which when they grow inveterate, cannot be plucked away. The name of this sickness is Avarice. In like manner arise other Sicknesses, as desire of Glory, desire of Women, φιλογυνεία, and the rest of Sicknesses and Infirmities. Their contraries arise from fear, as hatred of Women, μισογυνεία, hatred of Mankind, inhospitality, all which are infirmities of the Mind, arising from fear of those things which they fly and shun.

Infirmity of Mind is defined, a vehement opinion, inherent, and wholly implanted in us, of a thing not to be desired, as if it were exceedingly to be desired. That which ariseth from aversion, is defined a vehement opinion, inherent, and throughly implanted in us, of a thing that ought not to be shunned, as if it ought to be shunned. This opinion is a judging our selves to know what we have not.

Under *Infirmity* are these species, *Love of Money, of Honour, of Women, of curious Meats*, and the like. Love of Money, Avarice, is a vehement opinion, inherent, and throughly implanted in us, as if it were exceedingly to be desired. In the like manner are all the rest defined.

Aversions are defined thus, Inhospitality is a vehement opinion, inherent, and throughly implanted in us, that Guests ought to be shunn'd. In like manner is defined hatred of Womankind, such as was that of *Hippolitus*; and of Mankind, as that of *Timon*.

As some are more prone to one Sickness than to another; so are some more inclinable to fear, others, to other Passions; in some is anxiety, whereby they are anxious; in others choler, which differeth from anger; for it is one thing to be cholerick, another to be angry, as anxiety differs from grief; for all are not anxious who are sometimes grieved, nor are all that are anxious griev'd always: As there is a difference betwixt Ebriety and Ebriosity, and it is one thing to be a Lover, another to be Amorous.

This propensity of several Persons to several Sicknesses, is call'd from an Analogy to the Body, Infirmity, whereby is understood a propensity to be Sick: But in good things, because some are more apt to some goods than to others, it is stiled Facility, in ill things Proclivity, implying a lapsion; in neuters it hath the former name.

As there is sickness, infirmity, and defect in the Body, so in the Mind. Sickness is the corruption of the whole Body. Infirmity is Sickness, with some weakness. Defect is, when the parts of the Body disagree with one another, whence ariseth pravity, distortion, deformity of the Limbs; so that those two, sickness and infirmity, arise from the confusion and trouble of the health of the whole Body; defect is seen in perfect health. But, in the Mind, sickness is not distinguished from infirmity, but by cogitation only.

Vitiosity is a habit or affection, inconstant in it self, and oft differing in the whole course of Life; so that in one by the corruption of opinions, is bred sickness and infirmity; in the other, inconstancy and repugnance. For, every vice hath not disagreeing parts, as of them who are not far from Wisdom, that affection is different from self, as being unwise, but not distorted nor depraved.

Sickness and Infirmities are parts of Vitiosity; but, whether Passions are parts thereof also, it is a question. For Vices are permanent affections, Passions are moving Affections, so that they cannot be parts of permanent Affections.

And as in all things the Soul resembleth the Body, so in good likewise. In the Body, the chiefest are Beavty, strength, health, soundness, agility; so likewise in the mind. And as the good temper of the body is, when those things whereof we consist, agree well among themselves: so the health of the Soul is, when the Judgments and Opinions thereof agree. This is the virtue of the Soul, which some affirm to be Temperance; others, a Soul obedient to the precepts of Temperance, and obsequious thereunto, not having any speciousness of her own. But, whether one or other, it is only in a wise man; yet there is one kind of health of the Soul, which is common also to the unwise, when by the care of Physicians, the Distemper of the Mind is removed.

And as there is in the Body an apt figure of the Limbs, together with a sweetness of Colour, which is called Beauty; so in the Soul, equality, and constancy of Opinions, and Judgments following Virtue, with a certain firmness and stability, or, including the very power of Vertue, is called Beauty.

Likewise correspondent to the Powers, Nerves, and efficacy of the Body, in the same terms are named the Powers of the Soul. Agility of Body is called quickness; the same commendation is ascribed to Wit, in respect that the Soul overrunneth many things in a short time.

Only there is this difference betwixt Souls and Bodies: strong Souls cannot be Assaulted by Diseases, strong Bodies may. But the offensions of Bodies may happen without any fault; those of the Soul cannot, all whose Sicknesses and Passions proceed from contempt of Reason, and therefore are in Men only; for, tho' Beasts do some things like this, yet, they fall not into Passions.

Betwixt acute and obtuse Persons, there is this difference, the Ingenious, as *Corinthian* Brass rusteth, slowly falling into Sickness, and more quickly get out of it: the dull do not so; neither doth the Soul of an Ingenious Person fall into every Sickness and Passion; for, there are not many things extreamly Savage and Cruel, and some also have a shew of Humanity, as Compassion, Grief, Fear.

But the Infirmities and Sicknesses of the Mind are less easily rooted out, than those great Vices which are contrary to the Virtues; for, the sicknesses remaining, the Vices may be taken away, because the Sicknesses are no sooner healed, than the Vices are removed.

CHAP. IX.

Of Virtue and Vice.

a V**Irtue** is a convenient Affection of the Soul throughout all Life.

Of Virtues there are three kinds: The first *general*, taken for any perfection of a thing, as of a Statue: The second are *c Sciences*, or *Contemplative*, which, according to *Hecaton*, consist in speculation, as *Prudence* and *Justice*. *d* The third *not Sciences*, or *not Contemplative*, which are considered as consequent to the speculative; as, *Health, Strength, Hope, Joy*, and the like. Health is consequent to Temperance, a Theoretick Virtue, as Strength to the Building of an Arch. They are called *not-contemplative*, because they require no assent, but are by after-accession, and common even to the wicked, as health and strength.

Vice is the contrary to Virtue, *e* for the rational creature is perverted sometimes by the persuasion of exterior things, sometimes by the counsel of those with whom he converseth, contrary to nature, who gives us inclinations unperverted.

Of Vices therefore there are two kinds: The first, *f Ignorance* of those things whereof Virtues are the knowledge; as Imprudence, Intemperance, Injustice,: The second *not-ignorances*; as, Pusillanimity, Imbecillity.

g Panætius asserteth two Virtues, *Theoretick* and *Practick*: others three, *Rational, Natural, Moral*. *Possidonius* four; *Cleanthes, Chrysippus*; and *Antipater* more; *Apollodorus* one only, *Prudence*.

h Of Virtues, some are *primary*, others *subordinate*. The *primary* are four, *Prudence, Temperance, Fortitude, Justice*; the first conversant in Offices, the second in Appetite, the third in Tolerance, the fourth in Distribution.

i Prudence is the Science of things that are to be done, and not to be done, and neuter; or the knowledge of good, bad and neuter in civil life.

k The Virtues subordinate to Prudence are five.

Εὐβουλία, *l* The Science of things that are to be done, how they may be done beneficially.

Εὐλογιστία, The Science of comprehending things to be effected.

Ἀγχίνοια, The Science of finding out our office.

Νουνεχία, The Science of attaining the scope in every thing.

Εὐμηχανία, The Science of finding out the issues of things.

m Temperance, is the Science of things expetible, avoidable, and neuter. Under Temperance are these Species.

Εὐταξία, *n* The Science of time and order for the well-doing of things.

Κοσμιότης, *o* The Science of honest and dishonest motions.

Αἰδημοσύνη, *p* The Science of avoiding just blame.

q Fortitude, is the Science of things grievous, not grievous and neuter; the Species under it these:

Ἐγκράτεια, *r* A Science tenacious of right Reason.

Καρτερία, *s* a Science persisting in right judgment.

Θαρραλεότης, *t* A Science whereby we trust.

Μεγαλοψυχία, *u* The Science of overcoming those things which happen to the good and bad.

Εὐψυχία, * A Science of the Soul which renders her invincible.

Φιλοπονία, *y* The Science of going through to the attainment of that whcih we propose to our selves.

z Justice is the Science of distributing to every one according to his desert; under Justice are four subordinate Virtues.

Εὐσέβεια, *a* The Science of Worshipping the gods.

Χρηστότης,

χρησότης, The Science of well-doing.

Ἐυκοινωνησία, The Science of equality in community.

Ἐυσυναλλαξία, The Science of contracting honestly with others.

b Laert.   *b* In like manner of Vices, some are primary, others subordinate to the primary. The primary vices are, *Imprudence, Intemperance, Pusillanimity, Injustice.*

c Stob. Ἀφροσύνην δὲ ἀγνοιαν ἀγαθῶν, καὶ κακῶν, καὶ ἀδιαφόρων, ἀγνοιαν ὧν ποιητέον, καὶ ἀδιαφόρων; so supply the Text.

c Imprudence is the ignorance of things good, ill, and neuter; and the ignorance of things to be done, not to be done, and neuter.

Intemperance is the ignorance of things expetible, avoidable and neuter.

Pusillanimity is the ignorance of things grievous, not grievous and neuter.

Injustice is the ignorance of distributing to to every one according to his deserts.

d Stob.   *d* The subordinate vices to these are correspondent to the secondary Virtues, as, ἀκρασία, βραδύνοια, κακοβυλία, which are defined answerably to their opposite Virtues.

e Stob.   *e* These Virtues are perfect, and consist in contemplation; but, there are other virtues, which are not Arts, but Faculties, consisting in Exercise, as, health of the Soul, integrity and strength thereof, and pulchritude. For, as the health of the Body is a good temperature of hot, cold, dry, and moist; so the health of the Soul is a good temperature of the Doctrines in the Soul. And as the strength of the Body consisteth in a tension of the Nerves; so the strength of the Soul in a proper extension thereof to judgment and action. And as the Beauty of the Body is a symmetry of all the parts to one another, and to the whole: so the beauty of the Soul is the symmetry of the Reason and parts thereof, to the whole, and to one another.

f Stob.   *f* All those Virtues which are Sciences and Arts, have common theorems, and the same end, wherefore they are (as *g* Zeno saith) inseparable, connexed to one another, as *Chrysippus, Apollodorus* and *Hecaton* affirm. He who hath

g Plut. repugn. Stoic.

h Plut. repugn. Stoic. one, hath all, (saith *b Chrysippus*) and he who doth according to one, doth according to all. He who hath virtue, is not only contemplative, but also practick of those things which are to be done. Things which are to be done are either expetible, tolerable, distributible, or retainable; so that whosoever doth one thing wisely, doth another justly, another constantly, another temperately; and so is both wise, magnanimous, just, and temperate.

i Stob.   *i* Notwithstanding these Virtues differ from one another by their heads: For, the heads of Prudence are, to contemplate and do well; that which is to be done in the first place, and in the second, to contemplate what things are to be avoided, as obstructive to that which is to be done. The proper head of Temperance is to compose our own appetites in the first place, and to consider them; in the second, those under the subordinate virtues, as being obstructive and divertive of appeties. The heads of Fortitude are in the first place, to consider all that we are to undergo; in the second, other subordinate Virtues. The heads of Justice are in the first place, to consider what every one deserves; in the second, the rest. For all virtues consider the things that belong to all, and the subordinate to one another. Whence *Panætius* saith, it is in virtue as in many

Archers, who shoot at one Mark, distinguished by divers colours: every one aims at the mark, but one proposes to himself the white line, another the black, and so of the rest. For, all these place their ultimate end in hitting the mark, but every one proposes to himself a several manner of hitting: so all Virtues have Beatitude, which is placed conformably to nature for their end, but several persons pursue it several ways.

k As virtues are inseparable, so are they the   *k Stob.* same substantially with the supream part of the Soul, in which respect all virtue is said to be a Body, for the Intellect and Soul are a Body; for the Soul is a warm spirit innate in us. Therefore our Soul is a living creature, for it hath life and sense, especially the supream part thereof, called the Intellect. Wherefore all virtue is a living creature, because it is essentially the intellect. And therefore φρόνησις φρονεῖ, for that expression is consequent to this assertion.

l Between virtue and vice there is no medium   *l Stob.* (contrary to the Peripateticks, who assert a mean progression betwixt virtue and vice) for all men have a natural appetite to good: and as a stick is either straight or crooked, so man must be either just or unjust; but cannot be either more or less just or unjust.

m That Virtue may be learned, is asserted by *Chrysippus,* in his first Book of the End, and by   *m Laert.* *Cleanthes* and *Possidonius* in his Exhortations, and *Hecaton,* because men of bad are made good.

n That it may be lost, is likewise affirmed by *Chrysippus,* denied by *Cleanthes.* The first faith,   *n Stob.* it may be lost by Drunkenness or Madness: the other, that it cannot be lost, by reason of the firm comprehensions of the Soul.

o Virtue is in it self Virtue, and not for hope or fear of any external thing. It is expetible in   *o Laert.* it self; for which reason, when we do any thing amiss, we are ashamed, as knowing that only to be good, which is honest.

q In Virtue consisteth Felicity, for the end of Virtue is to live convenient to Nature. Every   *p Laert.* Virtue is able to make a Man live convenient to Nature: for, Man hath natural inclinations for the finding out of Offices, for the composure of Appetites, for tolerance and distribution. Virtue therefore is self-sufficient to Beatitude, as *Zeno Chrysippus,* and *Hecaton* assert. For it, saith he, Magnanimity, as conceiving all things to be below it self, is self-sufficient, and that be a part of Virtue, Virtue it self, which despiseth all things that obstruct her, must also be self-sufficient to Beatitude. But *Panætius* and *Possidonius* deny that Virtue is self-sufficient, affirming, that it requireth the assistance of health, strength, and necessaries; yet, they hold, that Virtue is always used, as *Cleanthes* affirms, for it cannot be lost, and is always practis'd by a perfect mind, which is good.

s Justice is not by nature, but by prescription, as Law and right reason: Thus *Chrysippus* in his   *s Laert.* Book of Honesty.

t Virtue hath many Attributes, it is called,   *t Stob.*
1. Ἀγαθόν, a good, because it leadeth us to right life.
2. Ἀρετόν, because it is approved without any controversie, as being most excellent.
3. σπουδαῖον, because 'tis worthy of much study.
4. Ἐπαινετόν, because it may justly be praised.
5. Καλόν, because it inviteth those that desire it.
6. Συμφέρον,

6. Συμφέρον, because it conduceth to goodness of Life.
7. χρήσιμον, because it is useful.
8. αἱρετόν, because it is rightly expetible.
9. ἀναγκαῖον, because being present it profiteth; being absent, it doth not.
10. λυσιτελές, because it hath an use that exceeds the labour.
11. αὔταρκες, because it is alone sufficient to him that hath it.
12. ἀνενδεές, because it takes away all want.
13. ἀπόχρων, because it is common in use, and extendeth to all the uses of life.

CHAP. X.
Of the End.

^{a Stob.} *a* THE End is that, for whose sake all Offices are done, but it self is not done for the sake of any : or that to which all things done conveniently in life are referred, it self is referred to nothing.

^{b Stob.} *b* The end is taken three ways: First, for the final good, which consisteth in rational conversation : Secondly, for the scope, which is convenient life, in relation thereto : Lastly, for the ultimate of expetibles, unto which all the rest are referred.

^{c Stob.} *c* Scope and end differ ; for Scope is the proposed Body, which they who pursue Beatitude aim at. Felicity is proposed as the scope, but the end is the attainment of that felicity. If a man throw a Spear or an Arrow at any thing, he must do all things that he may take his aim aright, and yet so, as to do all things whereby he may hit : So when we say, it is the ultimate end of Man to obtain the principles of Nature, we imply in like manner, he must do all things necessary to taking aim, and all things likewise to the hitting of the Mark ; but, this is the last, the chief good in life, that is to be selected, not desired.

Reason being given to rational creatures, for the most perfect direction, to live according to reason, is in them to live according to nature, that being the Artificer of Appetite. Hence *e* Zeno ^{e Stob.} first (in his discourse of humane nature) affirms, that the end is, to live conformably, that is, to live according to ones own Reason concordantly, as on the contrary, Savage Beasts that are always at difference, live miserably.

^{f Stob.} *f* The followers of Zeno, conceiving his expression not full enough, enlarged it. First *Cleanthes* his Successor, added *to nature*, making it up thus, *The End is to live conformably to Nature, which is to live according to Virtue*: for Nature leads us to Virtue. Thus *Cleanthes* in his Book of *Pleasure*, and *Possidonius*, and *Hecaton* in his Book *of Ends*.

^{g Stob.} *g* Chrysippus, to make the expression of *Cleanthes* more clear, expounds it thus, *To live according to expert knowledge of things which happen naturally*: For our natures are parts of the Universe, our end therefore is to live conformably to Nature, which *Chrysippus*, in his first Book of Ends, expounds, both our own proper humane Nature, and likewise the common nature of the Universe, But *Cleanthes* allows only common Nature to be followed, and not the particular. To live according to this knowledge, is all one, as to live according to Virtue, not doing any thing forbidden by our common Law. Right Reason, which is current amongst all, being the very same that is in God, the Governor of all. The virtue thereof, and the beatitude of a happy man, is, when all things are ordered according to the correspondence of a mans Genius, with the will of him who Governs the Universe.

h Diogenes defineth the End, *a good use of* ^{h Stob.} *Reason, in the election and refusal of natural things, chusing those that are according to nature, and refusing those that are repugnant to nature.* So likewise *Antipater*.

Archidemus defineth it, *To live, performing compleatly all offices, choosing of those things which are according to nature, the greatest and most principal, and not to be able to transgress them.*

Panætius, *to live according to the appetites given us by nature.*

Possidonius, *to live contemplating the truth and order of the Universe.*

i Thus by living according to nature, the Sto- ^{i Cic. de fin. 4.} icks understand three things : First, to live according to the knowledge of those things which happen by nature. This is *Zeno*'s End, to live convenient to nature. Secondly, to live, preserving all, or the greater part of mean Offices. This exposition differeth from the former ; for that is a Rectitude, proper only to a wise man, this is the office of a progressive, not perfect person, which may likewise be to the foolish. The third is, to live in enjoyment of all, or the greater part of those things which are according to nature. This is not constituted in our action, for it consisteth of that kind of life which enjoyeth virtue, and of those things which are according to nature, and are not in our power.

k The chief good therefore, is to live suitably ^{k Cic. de fin. 2.} to the knowledge of those things which arrive by nature, elective of those which are according to nature, and rejective of those which are contrary to nature. *l* This is to live conveniently ^{l Philo. Jud.} and conformably to nature, when the Soul entring into the path of Virtue, walketh by the steps and guidance of right reason, and followeth God. That which is in other arts is artificial, is here epigematick and consequent.

m This End is Beatitude. *Beatitude* by *Zeno*, ^{m Stob.} is defined *a good course of life*, which definition is used likewise by *Cleanthes* and *Chrysippus*, and all their followers, who affirm Beatitude to be nothing but a happy life.

Fair, and *good*, and *Virtue*, and that which *participates of Virtue*, are equivalent terms, whence it follows that *n* Beatitude is all one with living ^{n Stob.} according to Virtue. *o* And as Good, and Virtue ^{o Cic.} admit no degrees of increase or diminution, neither doth the ultimate end of all good and virtue increase or diminish. For, as they who are drowned, are no more able to breath, tho they are nearer to the top of the Water than they who are in the bottom ; nor a little Whelp, the time of whose sight approacheth, see any more than one that is newly littered ; so he, who hath made some little progress in Virtue, is no less in misery than he who hath made none.

CHAP.

CHAP. XI.

Of Indifferents.

a Cic. de fin. 3.

OF things, as we have said, some are good, some ill, some indifferent. *a* To deny this difference of things, would be to confound all life, as *Aristo* doth; neither could there be any function or act of Wisdom, since that, if amongst those things which appertain to life there were no difference, no election were requisite.

Laert.

Good and ill, as we said, are those things which are honest or dishonest. Of these hitherto. Betwixt both these, there are some things which confer nothing to happy or unhappy life, called Indifferents. *b* To profit is a motion or state proceeding from Virtue; to hurt is a motion or state proceeding from Vice; but Indifferents neither profit nor hurt; such are Life, Health, Pleasure, Beauty, Strength, Riches, Honour, Nobility, and their contraries; Death, Sickness, Grief, Deformity, Imbecillity, Poverty, Dishonour, Meanness, and the like. Thus *Hecaton* in his seventh Book of *Ends*, and *Apollodorus* in his *Ethicks*, and *Chrysippus*. These therefore are not goods, but indifferents. For, as the property of heat is to warm, not to cool; so is it of good to profit, not to hurt. But health and wealth do not hurt more than they profit, therefore health and wealth are not goods. Again, that which we may use ill as well as well, is not good; but health and wealth may be used ill as well as well, therefore health and wealth are not goods. Yet *Possidonius* reckons these amongst goods. But *Hecaton* in his 19th of Good, and *Chrysippus* of Pleasure, will not allow Pleasure a good: For Pleasures are dishonest, but nothing dishonest is good.

c Cic. de fin. 3.

c Moreover, Riches, as *Diogenes* conceiveth, have not only this power that they guide to Pleasure and good health, but that they comprise them. They do not the same in Virtue nor in other Arts, whereto Money may be a guide, but it cannot contain them. Thus if Pleasure or health were good, Riches likewise should be numbred amongst the good; but if wisdom be good, it followeth not that Riches likewise be good, nor that any thing which is not reckoned amongst the good; that which is good cannot be contained by any thing which is not amongst the good. And also for this reason, because Sciences and comprehensions of things, by which Arts are produced, move appetition; but if Riches are not reckoned among the good, it followeth that no Art can be contained in Riches, and much less any Virtue, for Virtue requireth far more study and exercise than Art, and compriseth the firmness, stability, and constancy of all life, which Art doth not.

d Sext. Emp. Pyrrh. hyp. 3. 22. whence supply Laertius and Stobæus.

d Things are said to be indifferent in three respects: First, if they move neither appetite nor aversion, as, if the Stars be of even number, or to have even or uneven hairs on our head, to stretch out the finger this way or that way, to take up a straw, and the like. Secondly, things are said to be indifferent which move appetite and aversion equally, not one more than the other; as in two pieces of Silver of equal value, no way different, which to him who comes to make choice of either, are indifferent. There is an appetition to the election of one, but not more of this than of that. The third kind of indifferents are those which are neither good nor ill, expetible nor avoidable, conducing neither to happiness nor unhappiness. In this Sense all things are called indifferent, which are betwixt Virtue and Vice, as Health, Wealth, Strength, Glory, and the like; for we may be happy without these, tho their use hath some relation to happiness, their abuse to unhappiness. In this sense whatsoever we may sometimes use well, other times ill, is indifferent, which kind appertaineth chiefly to Ethick.

e Again, of indifferents some are *Natural*, and move appetite, as health, strength, soundness of sense, and the like; some *Præternatural*, which move aversion, as sickness, infirmity, and the like; some *Neuter*, which move neither appetite nor aversion, as the constitution of the Soul and Body, one capable of receiving Phantasies, the other wounds. *e Stob.*

f Of Natural and præternatural indifferents, some are *primary*, others by *participation*. *Primary* natural indifferents are motions or affections convenient with reason, as health and strength. *Participant* are those by which that motion or affection is communicated, as a healthful Body, sound Sense. *g Præternatural* Indifferents are the contrary to these. *f Stob.* *g Stob.*

CHAP. XII.

Of Estimation.

EStimation, ἀξία, is a certain concurrence with convenient life, *a* which concerns all good. *b* Estimation is twofold; one, a mediate power or use concurring with life according to nature; such we call health or wealth, as far as they conduce to life, according to nature. The other is the valuation of the Estimator, imposed by him who is skilfull in such things. *a Laert.* *b Stob.*

c Again, *Estimation* is taken three ways: First, for absolute *donation*: Secondly, for *return of approbation*: Thirdly, as *Antipater* calls it, *Elective*, by which, when some things are proposed, we rather choose these than those; as health before sickness, life before death, and riches before poverty. In like manner, disestimation is taken three ways, the terms only changed to the contrary. *Donation* according to *Diogenes*, is a judgment, that a thing is according to nature, or conferreth use thereto. *Approbation* is in man, not in things. *Election* only in the good, not the indifferent. *c Stob.*

d Hence followeth another distinction of indifferents, whereof some are *preferred*, some *rejected*, some *neither preferred nor rejected*. *Preferred* are those, which tho they are indifferents, have nevertheless a sufficient reason why they are to be had in estimation, as health, soundness of sense, exemption from grief, glory, and the like. *Rejected* are those, which are not worthy any estimation, as poverty, sickness, and the like. *Neuter* are those, which are neither preferred nor rejected, as to extend or contract the finger. *d Laert. Stob. Sext. Empir. Pyrrh. hyp. 3.*

These terms preferred, προηγμένον, and rejected, ἀποπροηγμένον, were invented by *Zeno*, upon this ground: *e* As when we speak of the Court, *e Cic. de fin. 3.*

Court, no man faith, the King himself is preferred to Dignity, but those who are in some Honour, next and second to him in Rank: so when we speak of life, we call not those things which are in the first place, the preferred or promoted, but those which are in the second: and so likewise in the rejected. Now forasmuch as good hath the first place, it follows, that what is preferred, is neither good nor ill. No good is reckoned amongst the preferred, because that hath the greatest estimation; but the preferred having the second estimation, approacheth somewhat to the nature of good. It is called preferred, not that it conduceth to Beatitude, but in respect of the rejected. We define it thus: *An Indifferent with mean estimation*; for it could not be, that nothing should be left in mean things, that is according to, or contrary to nature, neither being left, that nothing should be placed in them, which is sufficiently estimable, this being granted, that there is not something preferred. Rightly therefore this distinction is made, and may more fully be explained by this simily. As if we should suppose our ultimate end, to be so to cast the Die that it may chance right, the Die that shall be so cast as to fall right, must have something preposed and preferred towards its end; and on the other side the contrary; yet the preposition of the Die, nothing conduceth to that end; so those which are preferred, relate indeed to the end, but nothing pertain to the power and nature thereof.

f *Laert. Stob.* f Of the *preferred*, some are in the *Soul*, as ingenuity, art, progression, and the like; some *in the Body*, as Life, Health, Strength, Ability, Soundness, Beauty; some *external*, as Riches, Honour, Nobility, and the like.

g *Laert. Stob.* g In like manner of the *rejected*, some are *in the Soul*, as Habitude, Ignorance; some *in the Body*, as Death, Sickness, Infirmity, Maim, Deformity. Some *external*, as Poverty, Dishonour and Meanness.

Likewise of the *Neuter*, some are *in the Soul*, as Imagination, Assent; some *in the Body*, as whiteness, blackness; some *external*, which having no estimation or use, are of little value.

Those which are preferred in the Soul, conduce more to living according to Nature, and are of more worth than those of the Body, or the external, as to have a good disposition of mind, is better than to have a good disposition of Body.

h *Stob.* h Again, of the *preferred*, some are preferred for *themselves*, as ingenuity, countenance, state, notion, and the like; some *for others*, because they effect something, as Riches, and Nobility; some *both for themselves and others*, as health, strength, soundness, ability: for themselves, as being according to Nature; for others, as affording no small benefit.

i *Cic. de fin. 3.* i As concerning *Reputation*, εὐδοξία, *Chrysippus* and *Diogenes* affirm, that being separated from utility, we should not so much as stretch out our finger for it. But those who followed them, not able to withstand *Carneades*, affirmed Reputation to be preferred for it self, and that it was proper for an ingenuous man freely educated, to desire to be well spoken of by his Parents, Kindred, and good men, and that for the thing it self, not for the use thereof; adding, that as we provide for Children, though to be born after our death; so we must provide for future Reputation after death, even for its own sake separated from all use.

k *Stob.* k In like manner of the *rejected*, some are rejected *for themselves*, some *for others*, some *both for themselves and others*, which appears by the Rule of Contraries.

CHAP. XIII.
Of Actions and Offices.

OF those *Actions* which proceed from appetite, some are *Offices*, some *præter Offices*, some *neuter*.

a *Laert. Cic. de fin. 3.* a *Office* is that which is preferred, and hath a good reason for the doing thereof, as being convenient to life; or, as others, Office is whatsoever Reason requireth to be done, as to honour our Brethren, Parents, Country, to relieve our Friends. *Zeno* first gave it this name, τὸ Καθῆκον, Office, ἀπὸ τοῦ κατά τινας ἥκειν. It is an action conformable to the dictates of nature, and extends even to Plants, and irrational living creatures, for Offices may even be observed in those.

Præter-office is an action, which reason acquireth that we do not, as, to neglect our Parents, to contemn our Brethren, to disagree with our Friends, to despise our Country, and the like.

Neuter are those Actions which Reason neither requireth nor forbiddeth, as the taking up of a Straw.

b *Stob.* b Of *Offices*, some are *perfect*, called κατορθώματα, *Rectitudes*, actions done according to Virtue; as, to do wisely, to do justly: others *not-rectitudes*, actions which have not a perfect office, but a mediate; as to Marry, to go an Embassie, to Discourse, and the like.

Of *Rectitudes*, some are *in things requisite*, others not: Of the first kind are, to be wise, temperate, and the like: Of the second, those which are not requisite to the being such. In like manner are *præter-offices*.

Again, of *Offices*, some are: *ordinary*, as, to have a care of our selves, of our limbs, and the like: Some *extraordinary*, as, to maim our selves, throw away our goods. Accordingly is it of *præter-offices*.

Again, of *Offices*, some are *continual*, as, to live vertuously: some *intermissive*, as, to question, answer, walk, and the like. Accordingly it is of *præter-offices*.

c *Cic. de fin. 3.* c Office is a mean thing, placed neither amongst the good, nor their contraries; for, there is something in this approvable, so as a right reason may be given for it, as done approvably. That which is so done is office. And forasmuch as in those things which are neither Virtues nor Vices, there is something which may be of use, it is not to be taken away. Again, it is manifest, that a wise man doth something in these mean things, he therefore, when he doth it, judgeth that it is his office so to do; but, a wise man is never deceived in judgment, therefore there is an office in mean things. Again, we see there is something which we call a thing rightly done, or Rectitude, but that is a perfect office; therefore there is an inchoat office; as, if it be a Rectitude *justly to restore a depositum*; to restore a depositum must

must be a simple Office. The Addition of *justly* makes it Rectitude, the simple Restitution without the additional term, is an Office.

(d) *Cic. de fin. 3.*

(d) And since it is not to be doubted, but that in mean things, some are to be performed, others rejected, whatsoever is done in that manner, is comprehended in common Office; whence it is manifest, that all men by nature loving themselves, as well the foolish as the wise, will take those things which are according to Nature, and reject the contrary. This is therefore one common Office of the wise and unwise, conversant in mean things.

All Offices proceeding from these, it is justly said, that to those are referred all our thoughts, even the forsaking of Life, or continuing in it. In whom most things are according to Nature, the Office of that Person is to remain in Life; in whom there are, or are foreseen to be more things contrary to Nature, his Offices is to forsake Life, altho' he be happy, and of a fool to continue in Life, altho' he be miserable; for that good, and that ill, as we have often said, are things that follow afterwards. The first Principles of natural Appetite, fall under the Judgment and Election of a wise Man, and is as it were the matter subjected to Wisdom. Thus the reason of continuing Life, or forsaking it, is to be measured by all those things we mentioned. For, neither are they who enjoy Vertue, obliged to continue in Life, nor they who live without Vertue to Die; and it is often the Office of a wise Man, to part with his Life, even when he is most happy, if it may be done opportunely, which is to live conveniently to Nature. This they hold, that to live happily, depends on opportunity; for Wisdom commandeth, that a wise Man, if it be required, should part with his Life. Wherefore Vice having not Power to bring a cause of voluntary Death, it is manifest, that the Office even of Fools, who are likewise wretched, is to continue in Life, if they are in the greater part of those things, which we hold to be according to Nature. And forasmuch as going out of Life, and continuing in it, be alike miserable, neither doth continuance make his Life more to be avoided; we say not therefore without cause, that they who enjoy most Naturals, should continue in Life.

Hitherto it appertains to know, that the love of Parents towards their Children is the effect of Nature, from which beginning we may track all Mankind, as proceeding from thence. First, by the Figure and Parts of the Body, which declare, that Nature carefully provided for Procreation. Neither can these two agree, that Nature orders Procreation, and takes no care that those which are procreated should be loved: For even in Beasts the Power of Nature may be seen, whose care when we behold in bringing up of their Young, methinks we hear the very Voice of Nature her self. Wherefore as it is manifest that we abhor Pain by Nature, so it is likewise apparent, that we are driven by Nature to Love those we have begotten.

Hence ariseth a common natural Commendation of Men amongst Men, that it behoveth a Man not to seem alienate from Man, for this very Reason, because he is Man. For, as among the Parts of the Body, some are made only for themselves, as the Eyes and Ears; others assist towards the use of other Parts, as the Thighs and Hands: so, tho' some huge Beasts are born only for themselves; yet, that Shell-Fish which is called *Patula prima*, and the *Pinnoteres*, so named from keeping its Shell, which shutteth it self up so close, as if it taught others to look to themselves; as also Ants, Bees, Storks, do something for the sake of others. Much nearer is the Conjunction of Mankind; so that we are inclined by Nature to Conventions, Counsels, Cities.

(e) Whatsoever is produced upon the Earth, is created for the use of Man; but Men are generated for Men that they may profit one another. In this we ought to follow Nature our Leader, and to bring forth common benefit to the publick by mutual Offices, by Giving, by Receiving, by Arts, by Endeavours, and by Faculties, to unite the Society of Man with Man.

(e) *Cic. offic. 1.*

(f) The World is governed by the Power of God; it is as it were, a common City of Men and Gods, and each of us is a part of the World; whence is followeth by Nature, that we should prefer the common Benefit before our own. For as Laws prefer the safety of the general before that of any particular; so a good and wise Man, conformable to Law, not ignorant of Civil Office, taketh more care for the Benefit of the general, than of any particular, or of his own. Nor is he who betrays his Country more to be condemned, than he who deserts the common Benefit or Safety. Whence it followeth, that he is to be commended who undergoeth Death for the Commonwealth, and teacheth us, that our Country is dearer to us than our selves. And because that Speech is esteemed inhumane and wicked of those who affirm, They care not when they are dead, if all the Earth were set on Fire; it is certainly true, that we are likewise to provide for those who shall hereafter be, even for their own sake. From this Affection of the Soul, whence proceed Wills and Commendations of dying Persons, as also, forasmuch as no Man will live Solitary in a Desart, even with the greatest abundance or plenty; it is easily understood that we are born for Conjunction, Congregation, or natural Community; we are impelled by Nature to benefit others the most that we can. All these are Offices, chiefly by teaching and communicating the Reasons of Prudence, so that it is not easie to find one, who will not communicate to some other what he knoweth himself. Thus we are not only inclined to learn, but also to teach. And as it is given to Bulls by Nature, to fight even with Lions, for their Heifers, with great force and impetuosity; so they who abound in Wealth, and are able to do it (as is related of *Hercules* and *Bacchus*) are incited by Nature to preserve Mankind. Likewise, when *Jupiter* is stil'd *Optimus* and *Maximus*, *Salutaris*, *Hospitalis*, *Stator*, we hereby express that the safety of Mankind is under his Tuition. But we cannot expect, if we our selves are vile, abject, and neglected amongst our selves, that we should be dear to the immortal Gods, and loved of them. As therefore we make use of our Limbs, before that we have learnt for what cause of Utility we have them; so are we conjoined and consociated

(f) *Cic. de finib. 3.*

T t

sociated amongst our selves by Nature to civil Community, which if it were otherwise, neither would there be any room for Justice or Goodness.

Yet tho' there are mutual Chains betwixt Man and Man, Man hath no common right with Beasts, [(g) *by reason of our dissimilitude, as both* Chrysippus *and* Possidonius *affirm*] for all other things, saith *Chrysippus*, were made for Men and the Gods; but they for Community and Society one with another; so that Men may make use of Beasts for their benefit, without doing any wrong.

(g) *Laert.*

Moreover, since the Nature of Man is such, that there is a certain civil Right betwixt him and all Mankind, he who preserveth that Right is just; who transgresseth it, unjust. But as in a Theater, tho' it be common, that room which a man possesseth, is justly said to be his place; so this civil Right in a City and the World, doth not repugn to the Propriety of particular Persons.

In order to the Conservation of all Society, Conjunction, and Dearness betwixt Man and Man, Emoluments and Detriments, ὠφελήματα and βλάμματα, which benefit or hurt, must be common amongst them, and not only common but equal. Convenients and Inconvenients, εὐχρηστήματα, and δυσχρηστήματα must be common, but not equal. Those which benefit or hurt, are either good or ill, and therefore must necessarily be equal; Convenient and Inconvenient are ranked amongst the preferred and rejected, and therefore cannot be equal: Emoluments and Detriments are common, but Rectitudes and Sins not common.

Herein Friendship is requisite, as being one of those things which benefit. Some affirm, That a good Man ought to be as much concern'd for his Friend as for himself; others, that every Man ought to be most concern'd for himself. Yet these latter confess, that it is contrary to Justice, whereunto we are born, to take away any thing from another, and assume it to our selves.

Neither can Friendship be contracted, nor Justice performed for private respects and advantages, for then these advantages might overthrow and pervert them. But neither could Justice, or Friendship be at all, unless they were expetible in themselves. Justice is by Nature; it is contrary to a wise man, not only to do an injury, but even to hurt. Neither can it be right to injure those who are our Friends, or have deserved well of us; Equity cannot be separated from Utility; whatsoever is equal and just, is likewise honest; and reciprocally, whatsoever is honest, is equal and just.

(h) *Cit. offic. lib.* 1. *and again, lib.* 3.
(h) *Panætius*, who discoursed most accurately of Offices, proposeth three kinds wherein Men use to deliberate or consult of Offices. First, when they doubt, whether that of which the question is, be Honest or Dishonest. Secondly, whether it be Profitable or Unprofitable. Thirdly, if that which hath the shew of Honesty, be Repugnant to that which seems Profitable.

(i) *Laert.*
(k) *Sext. Empir. Pyrrh. hypot.* 3. 25.
(i) Next the *Gods*, we are to reverence our Parents and Brethren. (k) As concerning the Burial of Parents, *Chrysippus* saith, it ought to be done in the most simple manner. For the Body, as the Nails, Teeth or Hair, thereof nothing pertaineth to us, and therefore ought not to be used with any curiosity or respect. Flesh, if it be useful, ought to be converted into Aliment (tho' it were a part of our own Body, as the Foot) as is proper to it; if useless, put under Ground, or thrown into some remote Place, without more respect than we have of our Nails or Hair when cut off.

(l) Concerning the Office of the *Buyer*, and the *Seller*, *Diogenes* the *Babylonian*, and *Antipater* his Disciple differ. *Antipater* holds that all must be laid open, that the Buyer be not ignorant of any thing that the Seller knoweth; *Diogenes*, that the Seller as far as is appointed by Civil Law, ought only to tell the Faults, and to conceal the rest, for as much as he in selling desireth to sell to his best advantage.

(l) *Cit. de offic. lib.* 3.

Hecaton in his sixth Book *of Offices*, is full of this Questions, as *whether a good Man in a dearth may give over House-keeping.* He disputes it on both sides, but concludes that the Office is directed rather by Profit than Humanity.

He questions, *Whether if at Sea a Ship be to be disburthen'd by the casting out of something, we should rather cast over board a Horse of great price, or a Slave worth little.* In this case, private Interest leads one way, Humanity another.

If a Fool in a Shipwrack catch hold of a Plank, may a wise Man wrest it from him, if he can? He saith, he may not, for it is injurious. What may the Master of the Ship? May not he take his own? No; no more than he may throw a Passenger out of the Ship, because it is his own, into the Sea. For until they come to the place to which they are bound, the Ship is not the Master's, but the Passengers.

What if two Shipwrack'd Persons light upon one Plank, and both pluck at it, should one give it over to the other? Yes; but to him, who, it is more expedient, should live, either for his own sake or the Commonwealth. But what if these be alike in both? There will be no Contention, but either as it were by Lot, or Mication with the Fingers (*giuoco della mora*) one will give place to the other.

What if a Father rob Temples, undermine the publick Treasury, should the Son reveal it to the Magistrates? It were a great Wickedness. On the contrary, he ought to defend his Father, if he be called into question. But is not our Country before all Offices? Yes, but it is for the good of our Country to have Citizens pious to their Parents.

What if a Father should aim at Possession of the Tyranny, or endeavour to betray his Country, shall the Son keep his Counsel? He shall beseech him not to do it. If that prevail not, he shall accuse him, yea, threaten; and lastly, if the matter shall tend to the destruction of the Country, he shall prefer the safety of the Country before that of his Father.

If a wise Man receive Counterfeit Money for good, if afterwards he know it to be Counterfeit Money, may he pay it where he owes any thing, for good? Diogenes saith he may, *Antipater*, that he may not.

If a Man sell Wine that will not last, and know it to be such, ought he to declare it or no? Diogenes thinks he is not obliged, *Antipater* conceives a good Man must. These are, as it were, Cases of Controversie amongst the Stoicks.

CHAP.

CHAP. XIV.
Of Præter-Offices.

(a) AS every perfect Office in a rational Creature is a Rectitude, and always compleat in all numbers; so every *Præter-office* in a rational creature is a sin. A sin is that which is done contrary to right reason, or in which something of Office is omitted by a rational Creature. (b) A good deed is the command of the Law. Sin the prohibition of the Law. Hence it is that the Law forbiddeth fools and madmen many things, but prescribeth them nothing, because they are not capable of doing any thing well.

(c) All sins are impiety, as being a resisting of the will of the Gods. The Gods love Virtue and its works; they hate Vice and its works. Every sin therefore displeaseth them, and consequently is impiety.

(d) All sins are equal (so *Chrysippus* in the first of his *moral questions*, and *Persæus*, and *Zeno*) though not alike, for they flow from one fountain, as it were of Vice, and the judgment is the same in all, but by the external object by which the judgment is made, they are rendred unlike. That they are equal, is evident from this: If there be not one truth more truth than another, nor one falshood more falshood than another, neither is one deceit more deceit than another, nor one sin more sin than another. He who is distant from *Canobus* a hundred furlongs, and he who is distant but one furlong, are both alike not at *Canobus*: So he who sins more, and he who less, are both alike not in the right way.

Yet, though sins are equal, there are some differences in them, forasmuch as some proceed from an obdurate incurable affection, others from an affection not obdurate nor incurable. And though every lie is equally a lie, yet all men do not lie equally; but, every sin is equally sin; for every sin consisteth in lying. Thus *Chrysippus*, *Persæus*, and *Zeno*. But *Heraclides* of *Tarsis*, friend to *Antipater*, and *Athenodorus*, hold, that sins are unequal.

CHAP. XV.
Of wise or vertuous Persons Paradoxes.

THere are (according to *Zeno*) two kinds of men, the wise or virtuous, and the vicious. The wise make use of Virtue through the whole course of their life, the vicious of Vice.

(a) Of the wise there are two sorts, one in perfection, consummate; the other in progression, procedent. Of the first are these following Paradoxes to be understood; (b) not that the Stoicks positively affirm there ever was such a one in nature, (for (c) *Zeno*, *Cleanthes*, and *Chrysippus*, were great and venerable persons, yet did not attain the height of human nature) but, that such a one might possibly be.

(d) A wise man is void of passion; for he cannot fall. There is another kind of Person void of passion likewise, a wicked man that is obdurate and inflexible.

(e) A wise man is void of pride; honour and dishonour are alike to him. There is another kind of person void of pride, a wicked man, equally inclinable to dishonour as to honour.

(f) A wise man is austere; for he neither speaketh for complaisance, nor admitteth any thing spoken in that kind. There is another sort of austere persons, which resemble sowre wine, not fit for drinking, but for medicines only.

(g) A wise man is sincere; for he taketh care, that he be not thought better than he is, by reason of some specious show, and withal to express whatsoever good he hath, without any Rhetorical gloss.

(h) A wise man is not pragmatical; for he declineth the doing of any thing that is beyond his office.

(i) A wise man is never drunk, for although he drink wine; for he never sinneth, but doth all things according to Virtue.

(k) A wise man is never mad; yet sometimes strange phantasies may occurr to him through melancholly or deliration, not according to the reason of eligibles, but præternatural.

(l) A wise man is never grieved; for grief, according to *Apollodorus*, is an irrational contraction of the Soul.

(m) A wise man is divine; for he hath God with himself; but a wicked man is an Atheist. An Atheist is taken two ways, for him who is an enemy to the Gods, and for him who believeth there are no Gods; which all wicked men do not.

(n) A wicked man is impious, because he doth all things according to Vice, as the good according to Virtue; and he who hath one Vice, hath all. He is an enemy to the Gods, for enmity is the discord of life, as amity the concord. The wicked differs from the Gods in his course of life, and therefore is an enemy to them, for they account all their enemies who are contrary to them. The wicked are contrary to the good; God is good, therefore the wicked are enemies to God.

(o) A wise man is religious; for he is skilful in all Divine rites. Religion is the Science of Divine worship. He sacrificeth to the gods, and is pure, detesting all sin, holy and just in Divine things.

(p) A wise man only is a Priest, skilful in Sacrifices, business of the Temple, Expiations, and other things proper to the Gods.

(q) A wise man is a Prophet, endued with the Science of those signs which are communicated by Gods or Demons which belong to humane life. In him therefore are all kinds of vaticination, as well by dreams, birds, and other things.

(r) A wise man revereneth and loveth his Parents and Brethren, next the Gods. He hath likewise an innate love of his Children, which the vicious hath not.

(s) A wise man ought to apply himself to some Office in the Commonwealth, (according to *Chrysippus*) unless otherwise diverted: For he will encourage Virtue, and suppress Vice, (t) especially in those Commonwealths which are far from perfection. He ought to make Laws, instruct Men, prescribe Rules. To which is opposite, study of Popularity, specious Deceit, prescription of things Unprofitable, which are not competible to a wise man.

(u) A wise man ought to marry (as *Zeno* in his Commonwealth) that he may have Children.

(x) *A wise man doth not opinionate* or think, but believe or know, for he never assents to any falsity. (y) Ignorance is an infirm assent; he thinks all firmly. There are two kinds of opinion, one an assent to things not comprehended, the other a weak belief. Neither of these are in a wise man, for he never assented without comprehension, and then always firmly; for nothing is hidden from him, otherwise he might have a false opinion. Therefore he is never diffident. Faith is proper to a wise man, for it is a firm existimation. A Science is a firm habit, therefore a wicked man doth neither know nor believe.

(z) *A wise man must imitate the Cynicks*; for Cynicism is the nearest way for virtue, as *Apollodorus* in his Ethick: (a) Others say, a wise man ought to continue in that Sect, if he have been thereof; but if he have not, not to enter into it.

(b) *A wise man may upon occasion eat man's flesh*. Of this already amongst the Offices.

(c) *A wise man is only free*, the wicked are slaves; for liberty is the power of doing according to our own Judgment. Servitude is a privation of the power of doing according to our own judgment. There is another kind of Servitude which consisteth in subjection, a third in being possest and subjected, to which is opposed vicious domination.

(d) *A wise man is only a King*; for Monarchy is a Principality subordinate to none, which only consists in the wise, as *Chrysippus* in his Treatise. *That Zeno used words properly*. For (saith he) a Prince must know both good and bad, which none of the wicked knoweth. (e) Dominion and the kinds thereof, Monarchy, Magistracy, Generalship, Admiralty, and the like, are only proper to a wise man; therefore the wise only command, though not actually, yet potentially.

(f) *A wise man is only proper to be a Magistrate, Judge, and Orator*; but not any of the wicked.

(g) *A wise man is void of sin*; for he cannot fall into error.

(h) *A wise man is innocent, and uninjurious*; for he cannot hurt either himself or others, (i) nor receive, nor do any injury: For injury is a hurtful injustice, which is not compatible to a wise man, although he may be unjustly assaulted: For he having within himself all good and virtue, is not capable of vice or harm.

(k) *A wise man is not merciful*, nor pardons any, remitting nothing of the punishments inflicted by Law, as knowing them to be proportioned to, not exceeding the offence; and that whosoever sinneth, sinneth out of his own wickedness. A wise man therefore is not benign; for he who is benign, mitigates the rigor of Justice, and conceives the punishments inflicted by Law to be greater than they ought: But a wise man knoweth the Law to be good, or a right reason, commanding what is to be done, and what not.

(l) *A wise man nothing wonders at those things which seem Paradoxal*, as *Charon's* Cave, the ebbing and flowing of the Sea, and hot Springs, and ebullitions of Fire.

(m) *A wise man will not live in a desart*; for he is communicative by nature, and practick, and will undertake exercise to strengthen his body.

(n) *A wise man will pray*, requesting good things of the Gods, as *Possidonius* affirms, in his first of Offices, and *Heccaton* in his Thirteenth of Paradoxes.

(o) *A wise man only is a friend*: Friendship is only amongst the wise, for in them only is an unanimity as to things that concern life and community, so as our friends may make use of them as freely, as we our selves. Unanimity is the Science of common good. A friend it expetible in himself. Plenty of friends is a good: But amongst the wicked, there is no friendship; for friendship being real and not feigned, it is impossible it should consist without faith and constancy. But, in the wicked, there is infidelity, and inconstancy, and hostility, and therefore not friendship, but some external connexions, whereby necessity or opinion ties them together.

(p) *A wise man doth all things well*; as we say, all Pipes play the *Ismenian* tune well. (q) He doth all things wisely, temperately, prudently, modestly, and according to the other virtues, throughout the whole course of his life. A wicked man doth all amiss, sinning in the whole course of his life, inconstant by nature, often grieved by his own ill actions, wretched and troubled, forasmuch as he is vexed at the thing done, so much is he angry at himself for being the Author of it.

(r) *A wise man loveth* (s) (*virtuously*) *those, whose beauty express their inward virtue*. Thus *Zeno*, *Chrysippus*, and *Apollodorus* affirm. For love is an impulsion of benevolence, raised from beauty, which love is not of conjunction, but of friendship. For this reason, *Zeno*, though he were in love with *Thrasonides*, a young woman that was in his power, yet supprest his affection because she was averse from him. This *Chrysippus* calls the love of friendship; it is no way discommendable, for beauty is the flower of virtue.

(t) *A wise man upon occasion will die voluntarily for his Country and friends*; or, in case he be seized by some excessive pain, loss of his senses, or incurable diseases.

(u) *A wise man is* μέγας, for he compasseth that which is proposed; ἀδρός, for he is every way augmented; ὑψηλός, for he hath attained the just height of wisdom; ἰσχυρός, for he is invincible, and insuperable. The wicked are the contrary.

(x) *A wise man profiteth the wise, and is mutually profited by all the wise*, though not friends or acquaintance; for betwixt them there is a concord and community of goods; and he who benefiteth another, benefiteth likewise himself. A wicked man neither conferreth nor receiveth benefits; for one is to move towards virtue, the other is to be moved towards virtue.

(y) *A wise man is a good Oeconomist*, skilful to acquire Wealth. Oeconomist is a habit Active, and Contemplative in the Business of a Family; Oeconomy is the ordering of Expences, Works and Possessions; the Science of Acquisition is a Reason, whereby Wealth is attained, which some account in indifferents, others in good. But no wicked Man is a good Oeconomist, since only a wise Man knoweth from whence, how, and how far gain may be acquired.

(z) *A wise Man only is perfect*, for he wanteth no Virtue; a wicked Man is imperfect, for he hath no Virtue. Therefore the wise are always happy,

happy, the wicked miserable; which happiness, according to *Chrysippus*, differs nothing from that of God, nor is less expetible. The wicked partake of no good, because Virtue, and that which partakes thereof, is good, and those things which are convenient and requisite are proper only to the wise, as the contraries to the wicked.

(*a*) *Stob.* (*a*) A wise Man is only Rich; for good is true Riches, and ill true Poverty; a wicked Man is Poor, not having the means to become Rich.

(*b*) *Stob.* (*b*) A wise Man is only Obedient; the wicked can neither Obey nor Command.

(*c*) *Stob.* (*c*) A wise Man only is honourable; for honour is the reward of Virtue, the wicked wanting this, are justly dishonourable.

(*d*) *Stob.* (*d*) A wise Man is only Ingenuous and Noble, according to some of the Stoicks; but others deny it, referring these not to Nature, but Institution only, according to the Proverb, Custom is a second Nature. So that Ingenuity is an habit of Nature or Institution, apt to Virtue; Nobility is a habit of Descent or Institution, apt to Virtue.

(*e*) *Stob.* (*e*) A wise Man is Pleasing, Perswasive, Opportune and Sincere; for he is expert in every thing, affable in Conversation, and helpful to the Publick: The wicked are the contrary.

(*f*) *Stob.* (*f*) A wise Man is the best Physician; for he hath considered his Constitution, and those things which are requisite for his Health.

(*g*) *Stob.* (*g*) A wise Man may lawfully part with his Life, the wicked cannot, because in their Life they never acquire Virtue, nor eschew Vice. But Life and Death are limited by Offices, and their contraries.

(*h*) *Stob.* (*h*) A wise Man will accept of Empire, and cohabit with Princes; but not unless he perceive it may be done without danger, and to much advantage.

(*i*) *Stob.* (*i*) A wise Man never lieth; for he who speaketh a falshood is not properly said to lie, unless it be with intent to deceive. A lie may be used many ways without assent, as in War against Enemies, or in the like necessity.

(*k*) *Stob.* (*k*) A wise Man neither deceiveth, nor is deceived; for he never sinneth, he useth not his sight, hearing, or any other Sense ill. He is not suspicious, nor repenteth, for both these are proper to fallacious Assent. He can no way be chang'd, or err, or opinionate.

(*l*) *Stob.* (*l*) A wise Man only (tho' not all wise Men) is happy in Children, in old Age, in Death.

(*m*) *Stob.* (*m*) A wise Man doth nothing contrary to his Appetite; for all such things are done with a Privation, and nothing adverse unforeseen happeneth to him.

(*n*) *Stob.* (*n*) But in the Primitive time, there was some wise Man that did not desire or will any thing, because that those things which were then present, were not sufficient to be required by him.

(*o*) *Stob.* (*o*) A wise Man is meek; for meekness is a habit whereby things are done meekly, not breaking forth into Anger.

(*p*) A wise Man is Peaceful and Modest; Modesty is the Science of decent Motion; Tranquillity the order of natural Motions. The contrary to these are seen in the wicked. (*p*) *Stob.*

(*q*) A wise Man is free from all Calumny; he Calumniates none, and is not Calumniated by any; for Calumny is a lying Imputation of feigned Friends, to which the wise are not liable, for they are true Friends; the wicked are, for they are feigned. (*q*) *Stob.*

(*r*) A wise Man delayeth nothing; for delay is an Omission of Office through Slothfulness, of which *Hesiod*, (*r*) *Stob.*

Nothing deferr a Year, a Month, a Day;
He fights against himself that doth delay.

(*s*) A wise Man can only incite, and be incited to Virtue, a Fool cannot; for he neglecteth Precepts, and goeth no further than the Words, not proceeding to Action. A wicked Man is not desirous to Hear or Learn, as not being capable by Reason of his Imprudence of what is rightly said; whence it followeth, that he can neither be incited nor incite to Virtue. He that is capable to be incited, or to incite, must be prepared by Philosophy, which is not competible to a wicked Man; for he who diligently heareth Philosophers, is not prepared to Philosophy, but he who expresseth their Doctrine in their Life and Actions. This no wicked Man can do, for he is prepossess'd by Vice. If he should be incited, Vice would pull him back; but none that is vicious incited to Virtue, as none Sick to Health. (*s*) *Stob.*

(*t*) Every wicked Man is an Exile, wanting Law and Country, for both these are good. That a City or Country is good, *Cleanthes* proveth thus. If there be a Habitation, where those, who fly for Succour, find Justice, it is Good; but a City is such a Habitation, therefore a City is Good. A City is taken three ways; for a Habitation, for a Convention of Men, and for both. In the two latter Significations it is called Good. (*t*) *Stob.*

(*u*) Every wicked Man is Rustick; for Rusticity is Ignorance of Laws and Civil Manners. A wicked Man refuseth to live according to Law, and is hurtful as a Savage Beast. (*u*) *Stob.*

(*x*) A wicked Man is Tyrannical, Cruel, Violent and Injurious, whensoever he gets an Occasion. (*x*) *Stob.*

(*y*) A wicked Man is Ungrateful, not obliging nor requiring; for he doth nothing by Friendship. (*y*) *Stob.*

(*z*) A wicked Man is not Perseverant; for Perseverance is the Science of obtaining our purpose, not being deterred by Labour. (*z*) *Stob.*

(*a*) A wicked Man is not capable of the right of Donation. Donation is the good bestowing of Estimation, but nothing that is good is competible to the wicked. (*a*) *Stob.*

(*b*) Every wicked Man is delighted with his Wickedness, which we may perceive not so much by his Discourse, as Actions, which shews that he is carried on to Wickedness. (*b*) *Stob.*

THE

THE THIRD PART.

CHAP. I.

Physick, and the parts thereof.

(a) *Physick* is divided into these places; *Of Bodies, Of Principles, Of Elements, Of Gods, Of Place, Of Vacuum:* Thus especially; but generally into three places; *Of the World, Of Elements, Aitiologick of Causes.*

That concerning the *World*, is divided into two parts; whereof one Contemplation, is common also to the Mathematicks, concerning fixed Stars and Planets; as whether the Sun be of the same Magnitude as he appears to be, and whether the Moon be so likewise; of their Periods and the like: The other, Contemplation, proper only to Physick, to enquire into the Essence of these; whether the Sun and Stars consist of Matter and Form; whether Generate or Ingenerate, whether Animate or Inanimate, whether Corruptible or Incorruptible, whether govern'd by Providence, or the like.

The Place concerning *Causes*, is likewise twofold; whereof one, Contemplation, is common also to the Medicinal Disquisitions, whereby they enquire concerning the principal part of the Soul, and those things which are produced in the Soul and Seed, and the like. The other is likewise usurped by the Mathematicks, as, in what manner we see, what is the cause of the visual Phantasie? How are made Clouds, Thunder, Rainbows, Halo's, Comets, and the like?

(a) *Laert.*

CHAP. II.

Of Bodies.

(a) Natural Philosophy beancheth into two parts, of Corporeals and Incorporeals.

A Body is that which doeth or suffiseth; (b) It is the Sense with Essence or Substance, and finite: (c) Whatsoever is, is a Body, for whatsoever is, either doeth or suffereth.

(d) Principles are Bodies void of Form. Elements are Bodies endued with Form.

(e) Causes are Corporeal, because they are Spirits.

(f) Qualities are Corporeal, for they are Spirits, and aerical Intentions, which affect the parts of all things, generated with Form and Figure.

(g) Virtues, Vices, Arts, Memory, Phantasies, Affections, Appetitions, Assents, are Bodies existing in the Supream part of the Soul.

(h) The Soul is a Body, because it maketh us to be living Creatures.

(a) *Senec. Epist. 89.*
(b) *Laert.*
(c) *Plut. cont. Stoic.*
(d) *Laert.*
(e) *Plut. plac. phil. 1. 11.*
(f) *Plut. cont. Stoic.*
(g) *Plut. cont. Stoic. Tertul. de anima, cap. 5.*
(h) *Sen. Ep. 114.*

(i) Night and Day are Bodies.

(k) Voice is a Body, for it maketh that which is heard; in a word, whatsoever is, is a Body and a Subject, ((l) for the Stoicks take away intellectual Substances, affirming all things that are, to be comprehended by Sense) only differences are not subsistent.

(m) A solid Body (according to *Apollodorus*) is divisible three ways, into length, breadth and depth.

A Superficies is the term of a Body, or that which hath only Length and Breadth, but no Depth; thus *Possidonius*.

A Line is the term of a Superficies, or a Length without Breadth, that which hath Length only.

A Point is the term of a Line, or the least mark.

(n) A Body is divisible into Infinite, yet it consisteth not of infinite Bodies.

(i) *Plut.*
(k) *Laert.*
(l) *Orig.*
(m) *Laert.*
(n) *Stob. Phys. 17.*

CHAP. III.

Of Principles.

(b) The place concerning Bodies, is divided into two degrees, into those which produce, and those which are produced; the first Principles, the second Elements.

(b) Principles and Elements differ: Principles are Ingenerate, Incorruptible: Elements shall perish by Conflagration. Moreover, Principles are Bodies, and void of Form; Elements have Form.

(c) There are two Principles of all things, the Agent, and the Patient: The Patient is a Substance void of Quality, called Matter: the Agent is the Reason which is in the Matter, God.

(d) Matter is sluggish, a thing ready for all things, but will cease if none move it. The Cause, that is, the Reason formeth matter, and moldeth it which way he pleaseth, out of which he produceth various Works. There must therefore be something out of which a thing is made, and also by which it is made. This is the Cause, that Matter. (e) The Cause or active Reason is God.

(f) In the Agent there is Power, in the Patient a certain Matter [or Capacity,] and in both, both; for Matter it self could not Cohere, if it were not kept together by Power, nor that Power without some Matter; for there is nothing, which is not compelled to be somewhere.

(g) Both

(a) *Senec. Ep. 79.*
(b) *Laert.*
(c) *Laert.*
(d) *Sen. Ep. 65.*
(e) *Ibid.*
(f) *Cic.*

(g) Both these, God and the World, the Artist and his Work, they comprehend within this term, *Nature*, as if Nature were God mixed through the World. (b) Sometimes they call that Nature which containeth the World, sometimes that which generateth and produceth things upon the Earth.

The Agent is, as we said, called the Cause. (i) A Cause, according to *Zeno*, is that by which there is an Effect, which is not a Cause; or, as *Chrysippus*, the Reason of the Effect; or, as *Possidonius*, the first Author of a thing. A Cause is a Body, a not-Cause a Categorem. It is impossible that the Cause being assigned, the Effect should not be present, which is to be understood thus: The Soul is the Cause through which we Live, Prudence the Cause by which we are Wise. It is impossible that he who hath a Soul should not Live, or he who hath Prudence should not be Wise.

(g) *Lactant.* 7. 3.
(h) *Laert.*
(i) *Stob. Phys.* l. 16.

CHAP. IV.

Of Matter.

(a) THE Substance of all [(b) qualitative] Beings, is first Matter, according to *Zeno* and *Chrysippus*, in his first of *Physicks*. (c) Matter is that of which every thing is made; it hath two Names, ὐσία Substance, and ὕλη Matter. Substance is of all things in general, Matters of particulars. (d) Universal Matter is [(e) according to *Zeno*, wholly Eternal] not admitting, as *Chrysippus* saith, encrease or decrease. (f) Particular Matter admitteth Augmentation and Diminution, (g) for it remaineth not always the same, but is separated and mixed, so that, according to *Chrysippus*, its parts perish by Separation, and exist by mutual Mistion. But those who call Fire, Air, Water and Earth, Matter, assert not a thing void of Form, but of a Body. (b) Matter is a Body, [(i) and Finite.] *Possidonius* saith, that the Substance and Matter of the Universe is void of Quality and Form, in as much as it hath not a certain Figure and Quality in it self; but it is always seen in some Figure and Quality. But the substantial Nature of the Universe differs from Matter intentionally only.

(k) Matter is passible; for if it were immutable, things could not be generated of it. Hence it followeth, that it is divisible into infinite; yet, it self, as *Chrysippus* saith, is not infinite; for nothing that is divisible is infinite, but Matter is continuous.

(l) Through this Matter, *Zeno* affirmeth, that the Reason of the World, which some call Fate, is diffused as Seed.

(a) *Laert.*
(b) *Stob. Phys.* 14.
(c) *Laert.*
(d) *Laert.*
(e) *Stob. Phys.* 14.
(f) *Laert.*
(g) *Stob. Phys.* 14.
(h) *Stob. Phys.* 14.
(i) *Laert.*
(k) *Laert.*
(l) *Stob. Phys.* 14.

CHAP. V.

Of the World.

OF this Matter was made *the World*. The World hath several Appellations, κόσμος, the World; τὸ πᾶν, the All; τὸ ὅλον the Whole.

(a) κόσμος, World, is taken three ways: First, for God himself, who is properly qualified with all Essence, Incorruptible and Ingenerate, who framed the Universe after a certain period of time, who resolved all Nature into himself, and again generated it out of himself. Secondly, for the starry Ornament: and thirdly, that which consists of both.

(b) The All, τὸ πᾶν, is one way taken, as *Apollodorus* saith, for the World, and another way for the System of the World, and the Vacuity beyond it. The World is Finite, the Vacuity Infinite.

(c) Thus likewise they distinguish betwixt τὸ πᾶν, and τὸ ὅλον: τὸ πᾶν, includeth also an infinite Vacuity, in which the World is: τὸ ὅλον signifies the World without that Vacuity, which neither is increased nor diminished; but its parts are sometimes extended, sometimes contracted. It began from the Earth as its Center, for the Center is the beginning of a Circle.

(d) The World is that which is properly qualited with the Essence of all things; or, as (e) *Chrysippus* and (f) *Possidonius* define it, a System of Heaven and Earth, and of the Natures therein contained; or a System of God and Men, and of all things that were made for them.

(g) The World was made by God; for if (saith *Chrysippus*) there be any thing which produceth such things as Man, tho' indued with Reason, cannot produce, that (doubtless) is greater and stronger, and wiser than Man. But a Man cannot make the Cœlestial things; therefore that which made them, transcendeth Man, in Art, Counsel, Prudence and Power, and what can that be but God?

(b) The World was made for those animate Essences which have the use of Reason, these are the Gods and Men, than whom nothing is better. (i) All things of which it consisteth, and which it produceth within it self, are accommodated to the use of Man.

The World was made in this manner; (k) God in the beginning being alone by himself, converted all Substance (which according to *Zeno*, was Fire) first into Air, then into Water. And as in the Plant the Seed is contained; so God, who is the prolifick Reason of the World, left such a Seed in the Humidity, as might afford easie and apt Matter for the Generation of those things that were to be produced.

(l) *Zeno* addeth, that one part tending downward, was condensed into Earth, another part remained pure Water, and partly, being exhal'd, Air, of a particle of which Air flashed out Fire.

(m) *Cleanthes* describeth it in this manner; The Universe being set on Fire, the middle part thereof first settled downwards, then the next parts by little and little were quenched. Thus the Universe being wet, the extream fire, (the middle part opposing it) sprang upward, and began the constitution of the World; and the revolution of this constitution shall never end. For as the parts of every thing are at certain times produced of Seed; so the parts of the Universe (amongst which are living Creatures and Plants) are produced in their Seasons; and as some reasons of the parts are mixed together in the Seed, which being composed, are again dissolved; so of one are all things made; and again, of one

(a) *Laert.*
(b) *Laert.*
(c) *Stob. Phys.* cap. 24.
(d) *Laert.*
(e) *Stob. t.* 24.
(f) *Laert.*
(g) *Lactant. de ira dei cap.* 10.
(b) *Cic. de nat.* 2.
(i) *Lactant. de ira dei cap.* 13.
(k) *Laert.*
(l) *Laert. Stob. Phys. cap.* 20.
(m) *Stob. Phys. cap.* 20.

is all compounded by an equal and perpetual revolution.

(n) Laert. (n) The World is *One*, of the same corporeal substance, and of a Sphærical figure, for this is of all figures most apt for motion. Thus *Zeno, Chrysippus, Possidonius,* and others.

(o) Laert. (o) The World is seated in an infinite incorporeal vacuity, which is beyond it, circumfused about it, *(p)* into which the World shall be dissolved by Conflagration. The World is finite, the vacuity infinite; yet *(q) Possidonius* saith it is no more than will suffice for the revolution of the World, when it shall perish. (r) By this argument they confute the motion of Atoms downward, introduced by *Epicure*; for in that which is infinite, there are no local differences of high or low.

(p) Plut. pl. Phil. 2. 9.
(q) Plut. pl. Phil. 2. 9.
(r) Plut. contra Stoic.

The World is not heavy, because the whole Fabrick thereof consisteth of heavy and light Elements, and being placed in the midst, whither such bodies tend, it keepeth its place.

(s) Laert. (s) In the World there is no vacuity, but it is compleatly one, for that necessitates a conspiration and harmony, betwixt Celestials and Terrestrials.

(t) Plut. contra Stoic. The World only is (t) self-sufficient, because it alone hath all in it self, whereof it standeth in no need. Of it self it is nourished and augmented, whereas the parts are transmuted and converted into one another.

(u) Plut. contra Stoic. The World is a (u) perfect body; the parts of the World are not perfect, because they are respective to the whole, and not of themselves. The Universe is by Nature apt to move it self in all Parts, to contain, preserve, and not break, dissolve and burn it self, the Universe sending and moving the same point, and the parts thereof having the same motion from the Nature of the body. Like it is that this first motion is naturally proper to all Bodies, namely, to incline towards the midst of the World, considering the World moveth so in regard of it self; and the parts likewise, in that they are parts of the whole.

(x) Laert. (x) The World is a living Creature, rational, animate and intellectual, (so *Chrysippus, Apollodorus* and *Possidonius*) and hath an animate sensible essence. For a living Creature is more excellent than that which is not a living Creature; but nothing is more excellent than the World, therefore the World is a living Creature. That it is animate is manifest from our Soul, which is a piece thereof taken out of it. (But *Boethius* denies that the World is a living Creature.)

(y) Laert. (y) The Mind or Providence passeth through every part thereof, as the Soul doth in us, but in some parts more, in others less; through some permeating, as a habit, as in the Bones and Nerves; through some as a mind, as through the principal (Hegemonick) part. In like manner the whole World is an animate rational Creature, the Hegemonical part thereof is the Æther, as *Antipater* the *Tyrian* in his Eighth Book of the World. But *Chrysippus* in his first of *Providence*, and *Possidonius of the Gods*, affirm, that Heaven is the Hegemonick of the World; *Cleanthes*, the Sun. But *Chrysippus* in the same Book (differing from what he said before) affirmeth it to be the purest part of the Æther, which they call the first God, sensibly, because it passeth through all in the air, and through all living Creatures and Plants, but through the Earth as a habit.

(z) The World, according to the greater part *(z) Laert.* of Stoicks, is corruptible, for it is generated in the same manner as things comprehensible by sense. Again, if the parts thereof be corruptible, the whole is also corruptible; but the parts of the World are corruptible, for they are daily changed into one another, therefore the whole it self is corruptible. And again, if any thing admit any change into the worse, it is corruptible; but the World doth, for it admitteth exsiccation, and inundation; therefore, &c.

(a) The World shall perish by fire, caused *(a) Phil. Jud. de Immortal. mundi.* by the power of fire which is in all things, which after a long time, consuming all the moisture, shall resolve all things into it self. The Moon, Stars and Sun, saith (b) *Cleanthes*, shall perish, but *(b) Plut. com. not.* God shall assimilate all things to himself, and resolve all into himself. (c) This opinion of the general Conflagration of the World, was held by *(c) Numen. apud. Euseb.* the first and most ancient of this Sect, *Zeno, Cleanthes* and *Chrysippus*.

(d) This first is the seed of the World; after *(d) Plut. com. not.* the Conflagration it diffuseth it self even into the Vacuity that was beyond the World. Afterwards, by order of the same reason which made the World, it shall withdraw and contract it self towards the generation of a new World, yet not be quite extinguished, but so as that some portion thereof remain, forasmuch as it is the cause of motion.

But (e) *Boethius, Possidonius,* and (f) *Panætius* *(e) Phil. Jud.* deny this Conflagration of the World, conceiving *(f) Cic. Stob.* rather that the World is eternal, to whom likewise *Diogenes* the *Babylonian* assents.

CHAP. VI.
Of Elements.

(a) GOD having converted, as we said, all *(a) Laert.* matter into moisture, and prepared it for the generation of future things, in the next place produced the four Elements, Fire, Water, Air, and Earth. Of these discourseth *Zeno* in his Book of the Universe, and *Chrysippus* in his first of Physicks, and *Archedemus* of Elements.

(b) Element is that of which generated *(b) Laert.* things are first made, and into which they are resolved. The four Elements are matter or substance endued with quality. Fire is hot, Water moist, Air cold, Earth dry; yet not so, but that in Air there is part of the same quality; for in the highest it is Fire, which is called Æther, in which is generated the first Sphere of Planets; next Air, then Water, the basis of all, Earth being placed in the midst of all.

(c) Of the four Elements, two are light, Fire *(c) Laert.* and Air; the other two, Earth and Water, heavy, which properly tend to the Center; but the Center it self is no way heavy.

CHAP.

CHAP. VII.
Of Fire.

(a) Stob.

(a) THE first Element is that of *Fire*, which as all Bodies tend to the middle, inclineth, as much as the lightness of its Nature permits, to the centre of the World, by a circular motion round about it.

(b) Stob.

(b) There are (according to *Zeno*) two kinds of Fire, one artificial, requisite to the use of life, which converteth nutriment into it self; the other inartificial (so (c) *Cicero* renders ἀτεχνικὸν)

(c) De Nat. deor. 2.
(d) Cic. de Nat. deor. 2.

by which all things grow, and are preserved; (d) for whatsoever is nourished and groweth, compriseth within it self the power of heat. This Fire is diffused through all the parts of the World, and they are all sustained by it. That it is in the Earth, appeareth by Seeds and Roots, which spring up and grow by the temperament of this heat. That it is in Water appeareth, forasmuch as Water is susceptible of greater cold, as by freezing. It is consequently in air also; that being a vapour extracted from Water, and supply'd by motion of the heat which is in the Water. But primarily, and originally, it is in the Element of Fire, a Nature absolutely hot, which dispenseth salutary vital heat to all other things.

(e) Stob. Phys. p. 47

(e) This is Nature, saith *Zeno*, and the Soul: Of Fire consist the Sun, Moon, and Stars.

CHAP. VIII.
Of the Stars.

(a) Cic. Nat. deor. 2.

(a) IN the *æther* are generated the Stars of the noblest and purest part thereof, without admixtion of any other Nature, wholly hot and pellucid, animate creatures indued with Sense and Intellect.

(b) Stob. Phys.

(b) *Possidonius* defineth a Star, a Divine Body, consisting of ætherical fire, splendid and fiery, never resting, but always moving circularly.

(c) Cic. Nat. deor. 2.

(c) That the Stars are wholly fiery, *Cleanthes* proveth by the testimony of two senses, touch and sight. For the Lustre of the Sun is brighter than of any fire, seeing that it shines so far and wide, to so vast a world; and such is its touch, that it not only warmeth, but oftentimes burneth, neither of which it would do if it were not fiery.

Now (saith he) the Sun being fiery, is either like that fire which is requisite to the use of life, or unto that which is contained in the bodies of living creatures; but this our fire, which the use of life requireth, is a consumer of all things, disturbeth and dispatcheth all things. On the contrary, the other is corporeal, vital, and salutary, it conserveth all things, it nourisheth, encreaseth, sustaineth, and affecteth with sense; therefore, saith he, there's no question to which of these fires the Sun is like, for he causeth all things to flourish and sprout up, according to their several kinds: Wherefore the fire of the Sun being like those fires which are in the bodies of living creatures, the Sun must be a living creature also, and so must be likewise the rest of the Stars in the cœlestial fire, which is called Æther or Heaven.

* For seeing that of living creatures, one kind is generated in the earth, other kinds in the water, others in the air, it were absurd to think, that in that part which is most apt for generation of living creatures, no living creature is generated. The Stars possess the Æther, which being most rare, and in perpetual agitation and vigor, it is necessary the living creature that is generated in it, be endued with most acute sense, quickest mobility. The Stars therefore have sense and intelligence; whence it followeth, that they are to be reputed Gods. For we say, that they who live in the purest air, are much more acute and understanding, than those who live in a thick climate: The diet likewise is thought to conduce not a little to the sharpening of the understanding. Whence it is probable, the Stars are endued with most excellent understanding, forasmuch as they dwell in the ætherial part of the World, and are nourished with exhalations from the Sea and Earth, extenuated by a long distance.

* Cic. Nat. deor. 2.

The sense and intellect of the Stars is chiefly manifest from their order and constancy, for nothing can be moved by proportion and number without providence, in which nothing is temerarious, nothing various, nothing casual. But the order of Stars, and constancy throughout all eternity, cometh neither from Nature, for that is void of Reason, nor from Fortune, which affecteth Variety, and disalloweth Constancy.

Again, all things are moved either naturally, or violently, or voluntarily. Those which move naturally, are carried either by their weight downward, or by their lightness upwards, neither of which is proper to the Stars, for their motion is circular. Neither can it be said, that they are moved violently against their own nature; for what power can be greater? It remaineth therefore that their motion be voluntary.

(d) No fire can subsist without some aliment, (e) the Stars therefore are nourished by the vapours of the Earth.

(d) Cic.
(e) Laert.

(f) Of Stars (according to *Chrysippus*) there are two sorts, both which are by nature divine, animate, and providential, the fixed and the Erratick. The multitude of the fixed is incomprehensible; the Erratick are lower than the fixed; The fixed are all ranked in one superficies, as is manifest to the sight; the Erratick in several. The Sphere of fixed Stars includeth that of the Erratick. The highest of the Erratick, and next to the fixed Stars, is the Sphere of *Saturn*, next, that of *Jupiter*, after which, that of *Mars*, then that of *Mercury*, then that of *Venus*, then that of the *Sun*, and lastly that of the *Moon*, which being nearest the air, seemeth therefore aerial, and hath greatest influence upon Terrestrial Bodies.

(f) Stob.

(g) *Saturn*, φαίνων, finisheth his course in almost thirty years; *Jupiter*, φαέθων, in twelve; *Mars*, πυρόεις, in twenty four Months wanting six days; *Mercury*, ςίλβων, in a year; *Venus*, φωσφόρος, (lowest of the five Planets) in a year.

(g) Cic. de Nat. deor. 2.

(h) The *Sun* and the *Moon* are properly called ἄςρα, Stars; but ἀςὴρ and ἄςρον differ; for every ἀςὴρ is ἄςρον, but not the contrary.

(h) Stob.

(i) The *rising* of a Star, *Chrysippus* defineth, its advancement above the Earth; and the *setting* thereof its occultation under the Earth. The same Stars at the same time rise to some, and set

(i) Stob.

set to others. The apparition of a Star, ἐπιτολὴ, is its rising together with the Sun; and the setting thereof, is its setting with the Sun: For setting is taken two ways, in opposition to rising, and in opposition to apparition. As the apparition of the Dog-star is its rising together with the Sun, and its setting is its occulation under the Earth together with the Sun, the same is said of the Pleiades.

CHAP. IX.
Of the Sun.

(a) Cic. Nat. deor. 2.
(b) Stob. p. 56, 57.
(c) Laert.
(d) Stob. p. 57.
(e) Laert.
(f) Cic.
(g) Stob. p. 56. Laert.
(h) Stob.
(i) Stob. p. 57.
(k) Laert.
(l) Laert.

(a) Next *Venus* (the lowest Planet) is the *Sun*, the (b) chief of all that consist of this ætherial fire. The *Sun* is defined by *Cleanthes* and *Chrysippus*, an intellectual Taper, gather'd and kindled from the vapours of the Sea. (c) *Possidonius* defineth the *Sun* a most pure fire, greater than the Earth, of a Sphærical figure (as (d) *Cleanthes* also affirms) answerable to that of the World.

(e) That the *Sun* is fiery, is manifest in that it hath all the operations of (f) fire; and forasmuch as he is fire, it followeth that he must be nourished. (g) The *Sun* is nourished by exhalations from the great Ocean.

(h) According to the expansion of this subjected aliment, faith *Cleanthes*, in his motion from Tropick to Tropick, removeth in a spiral line, from the Æquinoctial towards the North, and towards the South. (i) *Zeno* saith, he hath two motions, one with the World from *East* to *West*, the other contrary, through the Signs.

(k) That the *Sun* is greater than the Earth, appeareth in that it enlightneth, not only all the Earth, but Heaven also. Again, the shadow of the Earth being conical, argues the Sun to be greater than the Earth. Again, it is visible every where by reason of its magnitude.

(l) The *Sun* is Eclipsed by interposition of the *Moon* betwixt us and that part of the *Sun* which is toward us, (as *Zeno* in his Book of the Universe.) For meeting the *Sun*, and coming under him, she seemeth to darken his light, and afterwards to disclose it again, as will appear in a Bason of water.

CHAP. X.
Of the Moon.

(a) Stob. Phys. p. 59.
(b) Phys. Stoic. 2. 13.
(c) Laert.
(d) Plut. pl. 2. 25. Stob. p. 59. 2. 30.
(e) Pl. plac. Phil.
(f) Stob. p. 60.
(k) Pl. Phil. 2. 26.

(a) In the lowest part of the æther is the *Moon*: The Moon (according to *Zeno*) is an intellectual, wise, igneous Star, consisting of artificial fire. *Cleanthes* saith, she is of a fiery substance, and of a dirty figure. (b) *Lipsius* for πιλοειδῆ, dirty, substitutes πιλοειδῆ, as if of the same figure, as a Hat or Cap. But perhaps there needs no alteration, for they (c) affirmed, as she is nearer to the Earth than the *Sun*, so is she of a more terrene Nature. (d) *Possidonius* and most of the Stoicks affirm, she is mixt of fire and air, (e) by reason of which diversity of substance she is not subject to corruption. (f) To this mixtion of air in her composition, they impute likewise those spots which are seen in her face. (g) She is greater than the Earth, as well as the *Sun* is, and Sphærical as the *Sun*, yet appeareth in various figures, the Full Moon, First Quarter, New Moon, Last Quarter.

(h) *Chrysippus* saith, she is a fire collected after the *Sun*, from the exhalation of fresh Waters, for which cause she is likewise nourished by them, as (i) *Possidonius* also asserteth.

(k) Her motion is spiral; (l) *Zeno* saith, she hath two motions, as the one with the World from *East* to *West*, the other contrary through the Signs. (m) The period of her course is called a Month; μεὶς, is likewise that part of the Moon which appeareth to us, for one half of her is always turned towards us.

(h) Stob. p. 59.
(i) Laert.
(k) Laert.
(l) Stob. p. 57.
(m) Stob. p. 59.
Laert.

The Moon is Eclipsed when she falleth into the shadow of the Earth. For although every Month she is opposite to the Sun, yet she is then only eclipsed when she is fullest, by reason of the obliquity of her course, whereby her latitude is varied towards the North and South. When therefore she happens to be near the Ecliptick, and opposite to the Sun, she is Eclipsed; which happens (as *Possidonius* saith) in *Libra* and *Scorpio*, and in *Aries* and *Taurus*. Thus *Laertius*; but *Possidonius* seems to have been ignorant of, or not to have considered the motion of the Nodes of the Moon (commonly called *Caput & Cauda Draconis*) whereby the restitution or period of Eclipses is made in nineteen years, (κατὰ τὸ ὀλοσχερέστερον) which was the ground of *Meton*'s Period, and of the *Cycle of the Moon*, in the *Julian* Calender.

CHAP. XI.
Of Air.

(a) Next the sphere of the Moon (saith *Chrysippus*) is the Element of *Air*, interposed betwixt the Sea and Heaven ((b) spherical in figure) (c) consecrated by the name of (d) *Juno*, Sister and Wife of *Jupiter*, who is the Æther; betwixt these there is a near conjunction.

(a) Stob.
(b) Cic.
(c) Laert.
(d) Cic.

(e) The Air is divided into three Regions, the highest, the middle, and the lowest. The highest Region is the hottest, and driest, and rarest, by reason of the vicinity of the eternal fires. The lowest and nearest to the Earth is thick and caliginous; because it receiveth terrene exhalations. The middle Region is more temperate than the higher and lower, as to siccity and rarity, but colder than both. This, wherein the clouds and winds are generated, is, according to *Possidonius*, forty furlongs above the Earth. Next to it is the pure and liquid air of untroubled light. From the turbulent part to the Moon is twenty hundred thousand furlongs.

(e) Stob. Phys.

(f) To the Air is attributed the primitive cold.

(f) Laert.

(g) As concerning things in the Air, *Winter* is the rigor of the Air, next above the Earth, occasion'd by the remoteness of the Sun, and is the coldest of the Seasons of the year. *Spring* is the season succeeding *Winter*, preceding *Summer*, and is a good temperature of the Air, occasion'd by approach of the Sun. *Summer* is that season of the year, when the Air above the Earth is warmed, by the Sun's access towards the North. *Autumn*

(g) Laert.

Autumn that season of the year which followeth Summer, and precedeth Winter, is made by the return of the Sun from us.

(h) Laert. (*h*) Winter cometh, when the air is predominant in thickness, and is forced upward: Summer, when the fire is predominant, and driven downward.

(i) Plut. plac. Phil. 3. 7. (*i*) Wind is a fluxion of the air, having several names, from the variety of places; as for example: That which bloweth from the darkness of the night, and Sun-setting, is called *Zephyrus*: from the East and Sun-rising, *Apeliotes*; from the North, *Boreas*; from the South, *Lybs*.

(k) Laert. (*k*) It is occasion'd by the Sun's extenuation of the vapours.

(l) Laert. (*l*) The *Rain-bow* is a reflection of the Sun's beams from a humid Cloud: Or, as *Possidonius*, an apparition of part of the Sun or Moon in a Cloud, dewy, concave, and continuous to the phantasie, as in a Looking-glass, the representation of a Circle.

(m) Laert. (*m*) *Comets* are fires subsisting of thick air, carried up to the ætherial place.

(n) Laert. (*n*) Σέλας is an accension of sudden fire, swiftly carried through the air, appearing lengthways.

(o) Laert. (*o*) *Rain* is a conversion of clouds into water, when either from the Earth, or from the Sea, by the power of the Sun, the humour is drawn upwards ineffectually.

(p) Laert. (*p*) *Frost* is congealed rain.

(q) Laert. (*q*) *Hail* is a concrete cloud, dispersed by the wind.

(r) Laert. (*r*) *Snow* is humidity, from a concrete cloud, according to *Possidonius*.

(s) Laert. (*s*) *Lightning* is an accension of clouds, which are driven by the winds upon on another, and broken, according to *Zeno*.

(t) Laert. Plut. plac. Phil. 3. 3. Stob. p. 65. (*t*) *Thunder* is a noise occasion'd by the collision of clouds.

(u) Laert. (*u*) *Thunderbolt* is a strong inflammation rushing upon the Earth with great violence, when the clouds by impulsion of the winds are broken against one another. Some define it a conversion of fiery inflamed air, violently rushing down.

(x) Laert. (*x*) *Typho* is a violent Thunder, thrust down with a great force of wind, or a smoking wind, which rusheth down upon the breaking of the cloud.

Prester is a cloud inclosed with fire by wind in the concavity of the Earth: There are many kinds, *Earthquakes*, *Chasma*'s, and the like.

CHAP. XII.

Of Water and Earth.

(a) Stob. THat part of the World (saith (*a*) *Chrysippus*) which is the most solid support of Nature, as bones are in a living Creature, is called the Earth: About this the Water is evenly diffused. The Earth hath some uneven parts arising out of the Water, called Islands, or, if of large extent, Continents, from the ignorance of man, who knows not, that even those are Islands, in respect of the great Ocean.

(b) Plut. plac. Phil. 3. 9. Laert.
(c) Plut. plac. Phil. 3. 10.
The Earth is in the midst, being in the nature of a Center (*b*) one and finite, (*c*) spherical in figure. The Water is likewise spherical, having the same Center with the Earth.

The Earth hath five *Zones*, one Northern, beyond the Artick Circle, uninhabitable through extremity of Cold; another Temperate; a third not habitable by reason of extream Heat, whence it is called Torrid; a fourth Temperate; a fifth Southern, not habitable by reason of Cold. * But *Possidonius* conceiveth the Climate under the Equinoctial to be Temperate; for, saith he, under the Tropicks where the Sun dwells longest, the places are habitable, and why not then under the Æquator? Again, the Night being equal to the Day, affordeth leisure enough for refrigeration, which is assisted likewise by showers and winds.   ** Cleomed.*

* The generation of the world began from the Earth, as from the Center; for the Center is the beginning of a sphere.   *(*) Stob.*

(d) Plut. plac. Phil. 5. 56. (*d*) Plants have not any soul at all, but spring up of themselves, as it were by chance.

CHAP. XIII.

Of Mistion and Temperament.

(a) Stob. Phys. 20. CHrysippus asserteth a (*a*) Spirit moving it self to it self, and from it self, or a spirit moving it self backwards and forwards. He calleth it spirit, as being moved air, answering in some proportion to the Æther, so that it both meets in one; and this motion is only according to those who think, that all nature receiveth mutation, solution, composition, and the like.

Composition, *mixtion*, *temperament* and *confusion* are different. Composition is a contact of bodies, whose superficies are contiguous to one another, as in heaps of grain or sand. Mixtion if of two or more bodies, whose qualities are diffused through the whole, as we see in fire, and red hot iron, and in our own souls; for everywhere there is a diffusion through entire bodies, so as one body doth pass through another. Temperament is of two or more humid bodies, whose qualities are diffused through the whole. Mixtion is also common to dry bodies, as to fire and iron, to the soul and the body, temperament only to the humid. For qualities appear from the temperament of several humid things, as of Wine, Honey, Water, Vinegar, and the like; that in such temperament, the qualities of the things tempered remain, is evident from this, that oftentimes they are by some art separated from one another. For if we put a spunge dipped in oyl into wine mixt with water, the water, separating it self from the wine, will gather to the spunge. Lastly, confusion is the transmutation of two or more qualities into another of a different nature, as in composition of Unguents and Medicines.

CHAP. XIV.

Of Generation and Corruption.

(a) Stob. Phys. (*a*) POssidonius asserteth four species of Generation and Corruption, of things that are, into things that are; (for that of things that are not, and of things that are not to be rejected, conceiving there is none such.) Of transmutations into

into things that are, one is by division, another by alteration, a third by confusion, a fourth of the whole by resolution. Of these, alteration concerneth the substance, the other three are of the qualities which inhere in the substance. According to these are generations made. But the substance it self is neither augmented nor diminished by appolition or detraction, but is only altered as happeneth to numbers and measures. But in things properly qualited, as *Dion* and *Theon*, there is augmentation and diminution, wherefore the quality of each remaineth from the generation until the corruption thereof, in plants and living creatures which are capable of corruption. In things properly qualited, he asserted two susceptible parts; one according to the substance, another according to the quality. This, as we have often said, admitteth augmentation and diminution. Neither is the thing properly qualited, and the substance out of which it is, all one, nor divers, but only, not all one, because the substance is a part, and occupateth the same place; but things that are divers have distinct places, and are not consider'd in part. That as to the thing properly qualited, and as to the substance, it is not the same, *Mnesarchus* affirmeth to be evident, because it is necessary, that to the same happen the same things. For if, for example, a man having formed a horse, should break it, and make a dog, we would presently, beholding it, say, this was not before, but it is now: So are the qualited and the substance divers. Neither is it likely that we should all be the same as to substance; for it often happens, that the substance is preexistent to the generation, as the substance of *Socrates* was, before *Socrates* was; and after the corruption and death of *Socrates*, the substance remaineth, though *Socrates* himself be not.

CHAP. XV.

Of Motion.

(*a*) Stob.

(*a*) MOtion (according to *Chrysippus*) is a mutation of Parts, either in whole or in parts, or an excession out of place, either in whole or in part, or a change according to place, or figure. *Jaculation* is a vehement motion from on high. *Rest* is partly a privation of Motion in a Body, partly the same habit of a Body before and after. There are two first Motions, *right* and *oblique*; from the Mixtion of these ariseth great variety of Motions.

(*b*) Stob.

(*b*) *Zeno* affirms the parts of all things consisting by themselves, are moved towards the middle of the whole, and likewise of the World it self; wherefore it is rightly said, that all parts of the World tend to the middle thereof, and principally the heavy, and that there is the same cause of the *Rest* of the World, in the infinite vacuity, and of the *Rest* of the Earth, in the World, in the midst of which it is constituted as a point. All Bodies have not Gravity, as Air and Fire; yet these in some manner tend to the midst of the World.

CHAP. XVI.

Of Living Creatures.

(*a*) OF animate Creatures there are two kinds, (*a*) Plut. Pl. Ph. (for Plants, as we said, have no Souls) some are Appetitive and Concupiscible, others Rational. The *Soul*, according to *Zeno*, *Antipater*, and *Possidonius*, is a hot Spirit, for hereby we Breathe and Move. *Cleanthes* saith, we Live so long as that heat holdeth.

Every Soul hath Sense, and is a Spirit innate in us, wherefore it is a Body, and shall not continue after Death; yet is it by Nature corruptible, notwithstanding that it is a part of the Soul of the Universe which is incorruptible: Yet some hold, that the less firm Souls, such are those of the unlearned, perish at the Dissolution of the Body; the stronger, as those of the wise and virtuous, shall last even until the general Conflagration.

(*b*) The Soul hath eight parts, whereof five (*b*) Laert. are the Sences, the sixth Generative, the seventh Plut. plac. phil. Vocal, the eighth Hegemonick. 4. 4.

(*c*) The Supream or Hegemonick part of the (*c*) Plut. plac. Soul, is that which maketh Phantasies, Assent, phil. 4. 4. Sense, Appetite. This Supream part is called Rotiocination; (*d*) it is seated in the Heart, (*d*) Plut. plac. some say in the Head, as in its Sphere. phil. 4. 4.

(*e*) From the Hegemonick issue, are extend- (*e*) Plut. plac. ed to the Body the seven other parts, which phil. 4. 21. it guideth by their proper Organs, as a Fish its Claws.

Sense is an Apprehension by the Sensitive Organ, or a Comprehension. Sense is taken many ways: For the Faculty, Habit, Act, Phantasie, whereby the sensible Object is comprehended, and the Hegemonick parts of the Soul are called Sense. Again, the Sensories are intelligent Spirits diffused from the Hegemonick to the Organs. (*f*) The Senses are Sight, Hearing, Smell, (*f*) Plut. plac. Taste, Touch. phil. 4. 21.

(*g*) *Sight* is a Spirit extended from the Hege- (*g*) Plut. plac. monick part to the Eyes. *Sight* is made by Con- phil. 4. 21. traction of that Light which is between the Eye and the Object, into a Cone, according to *Chrysippus*. *Apollodorus* saith, that part of the Air which is Conical is next the Sight, the Base next the Object; so as that which is seen is pointed out to by the Air as by a stick.

Colour is the first Figuration or Habit of matter. *Darkness* is visible, for from the Sight there issueth a Splendor which passeth round about that Darkness. Neither is the Sight deceived, for it truly sees that it is Dark. *Chrysippus* saith, that we see according to the Intention of the mediate Air, which is struck by the visual Spirit, which passeth from the Hegemonick to the Apple of the Eye, and after that blow, falleth upon the Ear next, extending it self in a Conical Figure. Again, from the Eye are emitted fiery Rays, not black or dusky, and therefore Darkness is visible.

(*i*) *Hearing* is a Spirit extended from the He- (*i*) Plut. plac. gemonick part to the Ears. *Hearing* is made phil. 4. 21. when the Air betwixt the Speaker and Hearer is verberated in a Circulation, and at last by Agitation, passeth in at the Ears, as the circles that are made in a Pond, by casting in a Stone.

(*k*) Smel-

(k) *Smelling* is a Spirit extended from the Hegemonick to the Nostrils.

(*l*) *Tasting* is a Spirit extended from the Hegemonick to the Tongue.

(*m*) *Touching* is a Spirit extended from the Hegemonick part to the Superficies, so that it perceiveth that which is obliged to it.

(*n*) The sixth part of the Soul is the Generative, which is a Spirit proceeding from the Hegemonick to the *Parastatæ*; of this part, see *Laertius* from σπέρμα δὲ λέγουσιν εἶναι, *&c.* τὸ ὡς ὁ σφαῖρ., and *Plutarch de Philosoph. Plac. lib. 5. cap.* 4, 5, 9, 11, 12, 13, 15, 16, 17, 23.

(*o*) The seventh and last part of the Soul, is that which *Zeno* calls Vocal, commonly called the Voice. It is a Spirit proceeding from the Hegemonick part to the Throat, Tongue, and other proper instruments of Speech. (*p*) Voice is Air, not composed of little pieces, but whole and continuous, having no Vacuity in it. This Air being struck by the Wind, spreadeth into Circles infinitely, until the Air round about it be filled like the Water in a Pond by throwing in of a Stone, only the Water moves spherically, the Air circularly. Voice is a Body, for it acteth, it striketh upon, and leaveth an Impression in our Ears, as a Seal in Wax. Again, whatsoever moveth and disturbeth some Affection, is a Body; Harmony moveth with delight, Discord disturbeth. Again, whatsoever is moved is a Body, but Voice is moved and reverberated from smooth Places, as a Ball against a Wall. So in the *Egyptian* Pyramids, one Voice is redoubled four or five times.

CHAP. XVII.
Of GOD.

Hitherto of the material Principle, and that which is produced of it; we come now to the other Principle, the Agent, *God.*

(*a*) This question they divide into four parts; first, that there are Gods; secondly, what they are; thirdly, that they order the World; fourthly, that they take care of human Affairs.

Cleanthes saith, That the notions of God are imprinted in the minds of Men from four Causes. First, from Divination, for the Gods afford us signs of future things, wherein if there be any mistake, it is not from their part, but from the Error of humane Conjecture. The second is from the multitude of good things we receive by the temperature of Heaven, the fertility of the Earth, and abundance of other benefits. The third from the Terror of Thunder, Tempest, Rain, Snow, Hail, Devastation, Pestilence, Earthquakes, and sometimes Groanings, showers of Stones and Blood, Portents, Prodigies, Comets, and the like; with which men are affrighted into a belief, that there is a heavenly Divine Power. The fourth and greatest cause is the Æquability of the Motion and Revolution of Heaven, the Sun, Moon and Stars, their Distinctions, Variety, Beauty, Order, the very sight whereof declares that they were not made by chance.

That there are Gods, *Chrysippus* proveth thus: (*b*) If there is something in Nature, which the Mind, Reason, Power, and Faculties of Man could not make, that which did make it is better than Man; but Celestial things, and all those, whose order is Sempiternal, could not be made by Man; there is therefore something which made them, which is better than Man, and what is that but God? For if there are no Gods, what can there be in Nature better than Man? For in him only is reason, than which nothing is more excellent. But for a man to think that there is nothing in the World better than himself, is a foolish Arrogance. Therefore there is something better, and consequently there is a God.

(*c*) *Zeno* more concisely thus; That which is Rational, is better than that which is Irrational; but nothing is better than the World, therefore the World is Rational. In like manner may be proved that the World is wise, that it is happy, that it is eternal, for all these are better than the want of these: But there is nothing better than the World; whence it followeth that the World is God.

Again, he argues thus. No part of an insensible thing hath Sense; but the parts of the World have Sense, therefore the World hath Sense.

He proceedeth to urge this more strictly: Nothing, saith he, that is void of Mind and Reason, can of it self Generate that which is Animate and Rational; but the World generates animate and rational Creatures, therefore the World is animate and rational.

Likewise, according to his Custom, he concludeth his Argument with a Similitude: If out of an Olive-tree should come harmonious Pipes, that made Musick, you would not doubt, but that the Science of Musick were in the Olive-tree. What if a Plain-tree should bear Musical Instruments? You would think there were Musick in those Plain-trees: Why then should we not judge the World to be animate and wise, that produceth out of it self animate and wise Creatures?

There is nothing besides the World which wanteth nothing, and which is perfect and compleat in all its Numbers and Parts: For as the cover, saith *Chrysippus,* was made for the Shield's sake, and the Scabbard for the Sword's; so besides the World, all other things were made for the sake of something else. Fruits of the Earth were made for living Creatures, living irrational Creatures for the use of Man, Horses for Carriage, Oxen for Tillage, Dogs for Hunting and Defence; but Man himself was made to contemplate and imitate the World. Not that he is at all perfect, but only a part of that which is perfect. But the World it self, forasmuch as it comprehendeth all things, neither is there any thing which is not in it, is every way perfect. What therefore can be wanting to that which is best? But there is nothing better than the Mind and Reason, therefore these cannot be wanting to the World.

Chrysippus addeth this Comparison: As all things are best in the most perfect and mature Creatures, as in a Horse better than in a Colt, in a Dog better than in a Whelp, in a Man better than in a Child: So that which is best in all the World, must be in that which is perfect and absolute;
but

Marginal notes (left column):
(*k*) *Plac. Phil.* 4. 21.
(*l*) *Plut. ibid.*
(*m*) *Plut. ibid.*
(*n*) *Plut. ibid.*
(*o*) *Plut. ibid.*
(*p*) *Plut. Pl. Ph.* 4. 19.
(*a*) *Cic. nat. deor. lib. 2.*
Cic. ibid.
(*b*) *Cic. ibid.*

Marginal notes (right column):
(*c*) *Cic. ibid.*

but, than the World, nothing is more perfect, nothing better than Virtue, therefore the World hath proper Virtue. The Nature of Man is not perfect; yet in Man there is Virtue, how much more then in the World? The World therefore hath Virtue, therefore it is wise, and consequently God.

(d) *Plut. pl. Ph. 16.* (d) Thus the notion and apprehension men have of God, is, first, by conceiving the beauty of those things which are objected to their eyes, for no beautiful thing hath been made by chance and adventure, but composed and framed by some ingenious and operative art. Now that the Heaven is beautiful, appeareth by the form, colour, and bigness thereof, by the variety also of Stars disposed therein. Moreover, the World is round in manner of a Ball, which figure of all others, is principal and most perfect, for it alone resembleth all the parts; for being round it self, it hath the parts also round.

(e) *Laert.* As to the second part of the question, (e) God is an Immortal being, rational, perfect, or intellectual in Beautitude, void of all evil, provident over the World, and things in the World, not of humane form, maker of all, and as it were father of all.

(f) *Plut. pl. Ph. 1. 6.* (f) They define God a spirit full of intelligence, of a fiery nature, having no proper form, but transforming himself into whatsoever he pleaseth, and resembling all things.

We understand by God, saith *Antipater*, a living nature or substance, happy, incorruptible, doing good to mankind. All men acknowledge the Gods immortal. They who deprive the Gods of beneficence, have an imperfect notion of them, as they likewise, who think they are subject to generation and corruption.

(g) *Pl. contrad. Stoic.* (g) Yet are there some Gods, saith *Chrysippus*, generative and mortal, as well as there are others ingenerate: [The (h) World, Stars, and Earth are Gods, but the supreme God is the ætherial mind, *Jupiter*.] The Sun, Moon, and other such like Gods were begotten; but *Jupiter* is eternal. Other Gods use a certain nourishment, whereby they are maintained equally; but *Jupiter* and the World after another sort than the generated, which shall be consumed by fire. *Jupiter* groweth continually, until such time as all things be consumed in him, death being the separation of the soul and body; for seeing that the soul of the World never departeth at all, but augmenteth continually, until it have consumed all the matter within it self, we cannot say that the World dieth.
(h) *Stob.*

(i) *Laert.* (i) The substance of God, *Zeno* affirms to be the whole World and Heaven; so also *Chrysippus* in his 11th of the Gods, and *Possidonius* in his first of the Gods. But *Antipater* in his *Seventh of the World*, affirms his substance to be aerial. *Boethius* in his Book of Nature, saith, the substance of God is the Sphere of fixed Stars. Sometimes they call him a nature containing the World, sometimes a nature producing all upon Earth.

(k) *Plut.* As concerning the *third* part of the question, they affirm, that (k) God is an operative artificial fire, methodically ordering and effecting the Generation of the World, comprehending in himself all prolifick reason, by which every thing is produced according to Fate. God is a Spirit, diffused through the whole World, having several denominations, according to the several parts of the matter through which he spreadeth, and the (l) several effects of his power shewn therein. They call him Δία, as Δι ὂν πάντα, by whom all things are: ζωία, as the Author τῶ ζωῖ, of Life. *Minerva*, as diffused through the æther; *Juno*, as through the air; *Vulcan*, as through the (m) artificial fire; *Neptune*, as through the water; *Ceres*, as through the Earth. In like manner the rest of his Names were imposed with respect to some property. (n) This place was first discoursed upon by *Zeno*, after whom *Cleanthes* and *Chrysippus* dilated more largely upon it. (l) *Laert.*
(m) Perhaps it should be ἀτεχνικόν, tho' Æschylus ascribe this to *Vulcan*, παντεχνον πῦρ. (n) *Cic.*

(o) By this Providence, the World, and all parts of the World, were in the beginning constituted, and are in all time ordered. This disputation they divided into three parts: The first, from the same reason that teacheth us there are Gods, inferreth, that the World is ordered by them, seeing that there is nothing higher or more excellent than this administration. The second, from that reason which teacheth us, that all things are subjected to an understanding nature, and exquisitely ordered by it, inferreth, that it is generated of animate Principles. The third place is derived from admiration of Cœlestial and Terrestrial things. Upon these *Cicero* discourseth at large, according to the opinion of the Stoicks.
(o) *Cic.*

As to the fourth part of the question in general concerning the Gods, that they have a particular providential care of mankind, it is manifest, in that whatsoever is in this World was made for the use of man, and is conducible thereunto; and if for the whole species, they must consequently have the same care of particulars, which they express by many portents, and all those signs whereupon the Art of *Divination* depends, there was never any great person without some divine inspiration. But we must not argue from hence, that if the Corn or Vineyard of any man be hurt by a Tempest, or Fortune deprive him of any of the conveniencies of life, that he to whom this hath happened, may be judged to be hated or neglected of God. The Gods take care of great things, the little they neglect; but to great persons all things have always a happy issue.

(p) *Chrysippus* in his fourth Book of *Providence* saith, there is nothing more ignorant, nothing more sordid than those persons, who think, Good might have been without Ill. For Good and Ill being contraries, it is necessary that both consist together mutually, sustaining one another, as it were by opposition. For how could we understand *Justice*, unless there were *Injuries*? What is *Justice*, but a privation of *Injustice*? How can *Fortitude* be understood, but by opposition to *Fear*? How *Continence*, but from *Intemperance*? How *Prudence*, if there were not *Imprudence*? Why do not these Fools desire that *Truth* might be without *Falshood*? Such are *Good* and *Ill*, *Happiness* and *Misery*, *Grief* and *Pleasure*; one is ty'd to the other, as *Plato* says, by their contrary ends.
(p) *Agel. lib. 6. cap. 1.*

(q) Here followeth the Question, Whether that Providence which framed the World and Mankind, did make likewise those corporeal Infirmities and Sicknesses which Men suffer. *Chrysippus* affirmeth, it was not the intent of Nature to
(q) *Agel. ibid.*

to make Men obnoxious to Sickness: For this agreeth not with the Author of Nature, and Parent of all good things; but he having generated many great things, most apt and useful, other things also, incommodious to those which he made, were aggenerated together with them, coherent to them, made, not by Nature, but certain necessary consequence κατὰ παρακολούθησιν. As, saith he, when Nature framed the Bodies of Men, more subtle reason and the benefit of the World, would have required that the Head should have been made of the smallest and thin bones; but this utility would have been followed by another extrinsecal inconvenience of greater consequence, that the Head would be too weakly defended, and broken with the least blow. Sicknesses therefore and Diseases are engendred whilst health is engendred. In like manner, saith he, whilst *Virtue* is begotten in Man, by the counsel of Nature, Vices likewise are begotten by contrary affinity.

CHAP. XVIII.

Of Nature.

(a) *Plut. plac. l. 28. Laert.* (a) Next *Jupiter*, *Possidonius* placeth Nature. By Nature they sometimes understand that which containeth the World, sometimes that which produceth things upon Earth; both which, as we said, is to be understood of God. For that Nature which containeth and preserveth the World, hath perfect sense and reason, which power is the Soul of the World, the Mind and Divine Wisdom. (b) Thus under the term of Nature, they comprehend both God and the World, affirming that the one cannot be without the other, as if Nature were God permeating through the World, God the Mind of the World, the World the Body of God. (c) This *Chrysippus* calleth *Common-Nature* in distinction from particular Nature.

(b) *Lactant. lib. 7. cap. 3.*

(c) *Plut.*

(d) *Laert.* (d) Nature is defined by *Zeno* an artificial fire, proceeding in the way of Generation, which is the fiery spirit, the Artist of forms; by others, a habit receiving motion from it self, according to prolifick reason, and effecting and containing those things which subsist by it, in certain definite times, producing all things, from which it self is distinct by Nature, proposing to it self these two ends, Utility and Pleasure, as is manifest from the production of Man.

CHAP. XIX.

Of Fate.

(a) *Stob. l. 9. Plut.* (a) THE third from *Jupiter* (according to *Possidonius*) is Fate, for *Jupiter* is first, next Nature, then Fate.

(b) *Plut. pl. Phil. l. 28.* (b) They call Fate a concatenation of Causes, that is, an order and connexion which cannot be transgressed.

Fate is a cause depending on Laws, and ordering by Laws, or a reason by which the World is ordered.

(c) *Laert.* (c) Fate is, according to *Zeno*, the motive power of matter, disposing so and so, not much differing from Nature and Providence.

(d) *Panætius* affirmeth Fate to be God. (d) *Stob.*

(e) *Chrysippus* defineth Fate a spiritual power, governing the World orderly; or, (f) a sempiternal and indeclinable series and chain of things, it self rolling and implicating it self by eternal orders of consequence, of which it is adapted and connected; or, as *Chrysippus* again in his Book of *Definitions* hath it, (g) the reason of the World, or Law of all things in the World, governed by Providence; or the reason why things past have been, the present are, the future shall be. For Reason, he useth Truth, Cause, Nature, Necessity, and other terms, as attributed to the same thing in different respects. Fate from the several distributions thereof, is called *Clotho*, *Lachesis* and *Atropos*. *Lachesis*, as it dispenseth to every one, as it were by lot; *Atropos*, as it is an immutable dispensation, from all eternity; *Clotho*, in allusion to the resemblance it hath with spinning and twisting of Threads.

(e) *Stob.* (f) *Agel.*

(g) *Stob.*

(h) Necessity is a cause invincible, most violent, and inforcing all things. (i) Fortune is a Cause unknown and hidden to humane reason. For some things come by Necessity, others by Fate, some by deliberate Counsel, others by Fortune, some by Casualty.

(h) *Plut. pl. Phil. l. 27.*
(i) *Plut. ph. l. 29.*

(k) But Fate, being a connexion of Causes interlaced and linked orderly, compriseth also that cause proceedeth from us.

(k) *Plut. Phil. l. 27.*

(l) That all things are done by Fate, is asserted by *Zeno* in his Book of *Fate*, and *Possidonius* in his second Book of *Fate*, and *Boethus* in his 11th of *Fate*. Which (m) *Chrysippus* proves thus: If there is any motion without a cause, then every axiom is not either true or false; for that which hath not efficient causes, will be neither true nor false; but every axiom is either true or false, therefore there is no motion without a cause. And if so, then all things that are done, are done by precedent causes, and if so, all things are done by Fate. That all axioms are either true or false, *Cicero* saith, he labour'd much to prove, whereby he takes away, *Possibles*, *Indeterminates*, and other distinctions of the *Academicks*, of which see *Alcinous*, Chap. 26.

(l) *Laert.*

(m) *Cic. de Fato.*

(n) In answer to *the sluggish reason*, if it be your fate to die of this sickness, you shall die whether you have a Physician or no; and if it be your fate to recover, you shall recover whether you have a Physician or not. *Chrysippus* saith, that in things some are *simple*, some *conjunct*. Simple is thus, *Socrates* shall die on such a day; for whether he do any thing or not, it is appointed he should die on such a day. But if it be destin'd thus, *Laius* shall have a son *Oedipus*, it cannot be said, whether he accompany with a woman or not, for it is a *conjunct* thing, and *confatal*, as he terms it, because it is destin'd that *Laius* shall lye with his wife, and that he shall get *Oedipus* of her. As if we should say, *Milo* shall wrestle at the Olympick Games, and another should inferr, then he shall wrestle whether he have an adversary or no, he were mistaken; for that he shall wrestle is a conjunct thing, because there is no wrestling without an adversary. Thus are refelled all sophisms of this kind, (you shall recover whether you have a Physician or not) for it is no less determined by fate that you shall have a Physician, than that you shall recover. They are *confatal*.

(n) *Cic. de fin.*

Thus

Thus there being two Opinions of the old Philosophers; one, That all things are so done by Fate, that Fate inferreth a Power of Necessity, as *Democritus, Heraclitus, Empedocles* and *Aristotle* held; the other, That the motions of our Souls were voluntary without any Fate: *Chrysippus*, as an honourable Arbitrator, took the middle way betwixt these, but inclining most to those who conceive the motions of our Souls free from necessity. The Antients, who held all things to be done by Fate, said, It was by a violence and necessity; those who were of the contrary Opinion, denied that Fate had any thing to do with our Assent, and that there was no necessity imposed upon Assents. They argued thus: If all things are done by Fate, all things are done by an antecedent Cause; and if Appetite, then likewise those things which follow Appetite, therefore Assents also. But, if the cause of Appetite is not in us, neither is the Appetite it self in our Power; and if so, neither those things which are effected by Appetite are in our Power, and consequently neither Assents nor Actions are in our Power; whence it followeth, that neither Praise can be Just, nor Dispraise, nor Honour, nor Punishment; but this is false, therefore all things are not done by Fate.

But *Chrysippus* not allowing this necessity, yet maintaining that nothing happened without precedent Causes, distinguisheth thus. Of Causes, saith he, some are perfect and principal, others assistant and immediate. When we say, all things are done by Fate, from antecedent Causes, we understand not the perfect and principal Causes, but the assistant and immediate. He therefore Answers the former Objection thus: If all things are done by Fate, it followeth, that all things be done by antecedent Causes, but not by the principal and perfect, but by the assistant and immediate, which tho' they be not in our Power, it followeth not, that the Appetite likewise is in our Power. This Argument therefore concludes well against those who joyn Necessity with Fate, but nothing against those who assert antecedent Causes not perfect nor principal. What assent is, and how it cometh to be in our Power, we have already shewn in the *Logick*.

Hence it followeth, that (*o*) notwithstanding that all things are necessarily co-acted and connected by Fate, with a certain principal Reason; yet (saith *Chrysippus*) our Minds are so obnoxious to Fate, as their property and quality is. For, if at the first by nature they were formed soundly and profitably, all that Power which cometh upon them extrinsecally from Fate, they transmit easily and inoffensively: But if they are Harsh, Ignorant and Rude, not supported by any helps of good art, altho' they are pressed by little or no conflict of fatal incommodity, yet by their own Unluckiness, and voluntary Impulsion, they rush into continual Sins and Errors, which thing maketh that this natural and necessary Consequence of things, which is called Fate, be by this Reason. For it is as it were fatal, and consequent in its kind, that wicked Minds should not be without Sins and Errors, an instance whereof he bringeth not unapposite. As, saith he, a rolling Stone, if you turn it down a steep Place, you first give it the cause and beginning of its Precipitation, but afterwards it rolleth headlong of it self; not that you make it do so any longer, but because its Figure, and the Volubility of its form is such. In like Manner, Order, and Reason, and Necessity, moveth the beginnings of Causes; but the impetuousness of our Thoughts and Minds, and our own Actions, are guided by every Man's private Will and Mind. Thence, continueth he, the *Pythagoreans* say,

Men of their own accord their Ills procure.

As conceiving that all Ills proceed from themselves, and according to their own Appetites, when they Sin and Offend, and according to their own mind and design.

For this Reason he denieth, That we ought to suffer and hear such wicked, or idle, or noxious, or impudent Persons, who being taken in some fault and wickedness, have recourse to the necessity of Fate, as to a Sanctuary, affirming, that they have done wickedly, is not to be attributed to their timerity, but to Fate.

(*o*) *Agell.* 6. 2.

CHAP. XX.

Of Not-Bodies, or Incorporeals; and first of Dicibles.

Hitherto of Bodies; we come next to the second place of Physick, concerning Not-Bodies, or Incorporeals. Incorporeal is that which may be, but is not contained in Bodies. (*a*) Of those there are four kinds, Dicibles, Vacuum, Place and Time.

Dicible is that which consisteth according to rational Phantasie, a mean betwixt Notion and Thing. Of this already in the Logick.

(*a*) *Sext. Emp.*

CHAP. XXI.

Of Vacuum and Place.

THE second Incorporeal is *Vacuum*, which is the Solitude or Vacuity of a Body. In the World there is no Vacuum, neither in the whole nor in any part: Beyond it there is an infinite Vacuity, into which the World shall be resolved. Of this already in the Chapter concerning the World.

Next is Place: Place is that which is fully occupated by the Body; or, as *Chrysippus* defines it, that which is or may be occupated by one or more things. Thus it differs from Vacuity, which hath no Body, and from Space, which is occupated but in part, as a Vessel half full of Wine.

CHAP. XXII.

Of Time.

LAst of the Incorporeals is *Time*. Time is, according to many of the Stoicks, the motion of it self, not of Heaven, and had no beginning of Generation. *Chrysippus* saith, That Time is the measure of Slowness or Swiftness. *Zeno* defined it the interval of Motion, and measure of Slowness and Swiftness, according to which, all things were and are.

Possidonius saith, That some are wholly infinite, as all Time; some only in part, as the past and future; for they are joyned together by the present. He defined Time the interval of Motion, or the measure of Swiftness and Slowness, one part of it being present, the other future, the present connected to the future by something like a point. It is called τὸ νῦν, attributed to the least part of Time that falleth under Sense, subsisting according to the difference of past and future.

Chrysippus saith, That Time is the interval of Motion, the measure of Swiftness and Slowness, a consequent interval to the Worlds motion, according to which all things are, and are moved, unless rather there be a twofold Time, as the Earth, and Sea, and Vacuity, and Universe, have the same names with their parts. And as Vacuity is every way infinite, so Time is both ways infinite, for the present and future have no end. He likewise asserts, That no entire present is Time, for continuous things being divided into Infinite, Time likewise admitteth of the same Division; so that no Time is properly present, but so called, after a less accurate manner. The present only is subsistent, unless it be understood as of *Categorems*; as, walking is attributed to him that walketh, but not to him that sitteth or lieth. Thus much for the STOICAL *PHILOSOPHY*.

CLEANTHES.

CHAP. I.

His LIFE.

Laert. **C**Leanthes was of *Assus* an *Æolian* City (fortified, as *Strabo* describes it, both by Nature and Art) Son of *Phanias*. He was first according to *Antisthenes* a Wrestler, and coming to *Athens*, having no more than four Drachms, he applied himself first to *Crates* then to *Zeno*, whom he heard constantly, and persevered in his Philosophy and Opinions.

He was much commended for his Laboriousness, in as much as being poor, he went by Night to the Gardens to draw Water, and in the Day time studied Philosophy. Hence he was called φρεάντλης. *The Drawer of Water*.

Being cited to the Court to give an Account how he lived, being so Healthful and Lusty, he produced the Gardner, under whom he drew Water, and a Woman, for whom he ground Meal, to Witness how he subsisted. The *Areopagites* wondring hereat, allotted him 10 *minæ*, which *Zeno* would not suffer him to accept. *Antigonus* gave him 3000 *minæ*. On a time leading some young Men to a Spectacle, the Wind blew back his Cloak, and discovered that he had no Coat; whereupon the *Athenians* much applauded him, and, as *Demetrius* the *Laert. Plut. Magnesian* saith, bestowed a Coat upon him.

Antigonus, who was his Auditor, ask'd him why he drew Water, he answer'd, *Do I only draw Water? Do I not also dig and water the Ground, and all for the sake of Philosophy?* For *Zeno* brought him up to this, and bad him bring him an *Obolus* gained by his Labour. Upon a time he brought in his gains before all his Disciples, saying, *Cleanthes, if he would, could maintain another* Cleanthes; *but they who have wherewithal to maintain themselves, would be suppli'd by others; yet study Philosophy nothing the more diligently.* Hence *Cleanthes* was called *a second Hercules*. He was very Laborious, but dull and slow.

He used to write the Dictates of *Zeno* in Shells, and the Shoulder-blades of Oxen, for want of Money to buy Paper. He was his Auditor 19 years.

For these Reasons, tho' *Zeno* had many other eminent Disciples, yet he succeeded him in the School.

CHAP. II.

His Apophthegms.

(a) **H**IS Fellow-Disciples derided him, he took it patiently, and being called *Ass*, answered, he only could bear *Zeno*'s burthen. *(a) Laert.*

Another time being reproached as Timerous, *Therefore*, saith he, *I sin little*.

Preferring his own Poverty before the Plenty of the Rich; *Whilst they*, saith he, *Play at Ball, I Manure a hard barren Soil*.

He often chid himself, being all alone, which *Aristo* over-hearing; whom, saith he, do you chide? he smiling, answered, *A Grayheaded old Fellow without Wit*.

To one that said, *Arcesilaus* abrogated the Offices of Life ; Peace, saith he, dispraise him not, for tho' he take away Offices in Discourse, he commends them in his Actions ; To whom *Arcesilaus* saying, I cannot endure Flattery ; *I do indeed Flatter,* replies *Cleanthes, when I say, you speak one thing and do another.*

To one that asked what he should teach his Son ; he answer'd in the words of *Electra* ;
Peace, peace, a little Step.

A *Lacedemonian* saying, that Labour was good, he laughed, answering,

My Son, thou of a gen'rous Race art come.

Disputing with a young Man, he asked him whether he did feel ; the other answers he did ; he replied, *Why then do I not feel that you feel?*

Sosythius the Poet, saying in the publick Theatre when *Cleanthes* was present ;
Those whom Cleanthes *madness leads away*; he sat still, not changing his Countenance ; whereupon the Auditors applauding him, turned out *Sosythius*, who afterwards coming to *Cleanthes*, told him he was sorry that he had reproached him ; *Cleanthes* answer'd, *It were unfit I should behold unconcerned* Bacchus *and* Hercules *derided by the* Poets, *and be angry at a little word against my self.*

He compared the *Peripateticks* to *Lutes*, that make good Musick, but hear it not themselves.

Holding, according to *Zeno*, that the mind may be discerned in the Countenance, some merry young Men brought an effeminate Youth to him rustically Cloathed, desiring his Opinion of that Man's Disposition. He bad him depart, which the other going to do, sneezed ; *Cleanthes* presently cried out, *I have found out the Man, he is Effeminate.*

To one that was all alone talking to himself, *You Discourse,* saith he, *with a Man that is not Ill.*

To one that reproached him with his Age, *I would be gone,* saith he, *but when I consider that I am in Health, fit to Write and Study, I rather chuse to stay.*

(b) *Cic. de Finib. lib. 2.*
(*b*) *Cleanthes* bad those who came to hear him, to fancy Pleasure painted in a Tablet, richly habited and adorned, sitting on a Throne, the Virtues standing about her, as her Handmaids, doing nothing else but wait on her Commands, whispering in her Ear (if it can be fancied of a Picture) to bid her take heed of doing any thing imprudently, that may offend the Minds of Men, or any thing that may occasion Grief.

(c) *Stob. Ser.* 116.
(*c*) He said, Whosoever sweareth at the same time sweareth truly, or forsweareth himself : If he intend to do that which he sweareth, tho' he do it not, he sweareth truly ; if he intended it not, he is forsworn.

(d) *Ser.* 126.
(*d*) One observing him silent, said to him, why do you hold your Peace ? It is pleasant to talk to Friends ; *It is indeed,* answer'd *Cleanthes, but the more pleasant it is, the more we ought to allow them the freedom of it.*

(e) *Ser.* 210.
(*e*) He said, That unlearned Men differed from Beasts in their Figure.

(f) *Ser.* 212.
(*f*) Being demanded why amongst the Ancients, when there were fewest Philosophers, there were more Eminent than at this time ; he answer'd, *Because then they minded the thing it self, now only in Words.*

(g) *Ser.* 229.
(*g*) To one that asked him, how a Man might be Rich, he answered, by being Poor in Desire.

CHAP. III.

His Writings.

HE left behind him (saith *Laertius*) these excellent Books.
Of Time.
Of Zeno's Philosophy.
Explications of Heraclitus 3.
Of sense 4.
Of Art.
To Democritus.
To Aristarchus.
To Erillus.
Of Appetite 2.
Archæology.
Of God.
Of Giants.
Of Hymeneals.
Of a Poet.
Of Office 3.
Of right Consultation.
Of Gratitude.
Protreptick.
Of Virtues.
Of Ingenuity.
Of Gorgippus.
Of Envy.
Of Love.
Of Liberty.
The Art of Love.
Of Honour.
Of Glory.
The Politick.
Of Counsel.
Of Laws.
Of Judging.
Of the Reason of Living.
Of Speech 3.
Of the End.
Of honest Things.
Of Actions.
Of Science.
Of a Kingdom.
Of Friendship.
Of a Symposium.
That the Vertue of Man and Woman is the same.
That a wise Man may use Sophisms.
Of Chria's.
Dissertations 2.
Of Pleasure.
Of Properties.
Of Inexplicables.
Of Dialectick.
Of Tropes.
Of Categorems.
Besides these, are mentioned
(a) *Of Atoms.*
Of Brass.
(b) *Of Sumptions.*
Fabulous Traditions.
(c) *The Art of Rhethorick.*

(a) *Laert. vit. Zen.*
(b) *Athen. deipn.*
(c) *Cic. de fin. L 4.*

CHAP. IV.
His Death.

HE lived according to *Laertius* 80 Years, according to *Lucian*, 99. The occasion of his Death this, being troubled with a soreness of his Gums (*Stobeus* saith, an Ulcer under his Tongue) he was enjoyned by the Physicians to fast two days; which he did, and was well; then they told him he might eat again, but he would not, saying, he was now gone a great way on his Journey; (a) *would you have me*, saith he, *having past over the greatest part of my Life, return back again, and begin it anew?* (b) Having fasted two days more, he Died.

(a) *Stob.*
(b) *Laert.*

(c) *Simplicius* saith, he saw an exquisite statue of *Cleanthes* in *Assus*, an example of the magnificence of the Roman Senate, dedicated to his Honour.

(c) *In Epictet.*

CHRYSIPPUS.

CHAP. I.
His Life.

Laert.

CHrysippus was of *Soli*, (a City of *Cilicia*, afterwards called *Pompeiopolis*) his Father was of *Tarsis*, named *Apollonius*, or, as *Suidas*, *Apollonides*, who came and lived at *Soli*, which perhaps gave *Laertius*, and from him *Suidas*, occasion to doubt whether *Chrysippus* himself were not of *Tarsis*.

He first exercised in the *Hippodrome*. *Hecaton* saith, that having wasted his Patrimony in the King's service, he applyed himself to Philosophy. Coming to *Athens*, he heard, as some affirm, *Zeno*, or rather (as *Diocles* and others) *Cleanthes*, from whom whilst he was yet alive he dissented. He was an eminent Philosopher, Ingenious and Acute in every thing; so that in most opinions he differ'd from *Zeno* and *Cleanthes*, to whom he would only say, *tell me the Doctrines, and let me alone for Proofs*. If at any time he crossed *Cleanthes* in dispute, he was afterwards sorry for it, often saying,

Of happiness in all I am possess'd,
But in Cleanthes; there alone unbless'd.

He was so famous for *Dialectick*, that it was a common speech, *If the Gods themselves would use Dialectick, they would make use only of the Chrysippean*. But he more was plentiful in matter, than free in expression.

He was infinitely studious and industrious, as appeareth from the multitude of his Books. An old Woman that waited on him said, that he wrote every day 500 Paragraphs.

When any question'd him in private, he answer'd meekly and freely; but as soon as any company came, he grew eager and litigious, saying,

Brother, there hangs a cloud before your Eyes;
Cast quite away this madness, and be wise.

When he drunk at Feasts, he lay very still, only shaked his Legs; whereupon his Woman said, *Chrysippus*'s legs only are drunk.

He had so good an opinion of himself, that to one who asked him to whom he should commend his Son, he answered, *To me; for if I knew any better, I would hear Philosophy of him my self*: Whence it was said of him,

He is inspir'd by Jove,
The rest like shadows move.

As also that,

Had not Chrysippus been,
No Stoa we had seen.

Arcesilaus and *Lacydes* (as *Sotion* saith) coming into the *Academy*, he studied Philosophy with them, whence he disputed *against* Custom, and *for* Custom, and of *Magnitude* and *Multitude*, using the arguments of the *Academicks*.

Laert.

(b) He was a great despiser of Honours, for of all his Writings, he Dedicates none to any King. (c) He was content with little, for (d) he lived without any other attendants than one old Woman; and when *Ptolomy* wrote to *Cleanthes*, desiring he would come to him, or send some one of his Disciples, *Sphærus* went, but *Chrysippus* refused.

(b) *Laert.*
(c) *Stob.*
(d) *Laert.*

Having sent for *Aristocreon* and *Philocrates*, his sisters sons, he first taught in the *Lyceum* in the open Air, as *Demetrius* writes.

CHAP. II.

His Apophthegms.

(a) *Laert.* (a) To one that blamed him for not hearing *Aristo* as many did; *If I should follow many,* saith he, *I should not study Philosophy.*
To a Dialectick assaulting *Cleanthes* with Sophisms: *Leave,* saith he, *diverting an aged Person from serious things; propound those to us that are young.*

(b) *Stob.* (b) He said, meditation is the fountain of discourse.

(c) *Stob. Ser. 44.* (c) He said, drunkenness is a lesser madness.

(d) *Ser. 48.* (d) He said, a wise man grieveth, but is not troubled, for his mind yields not to it.

(e) *Ser. 71.* (e) To one that said to him, Your friend revileth you behind your back: *Blame him not,* saith he, *for he might do it before my Face.*

(f) *Ibid.* (f) To a wicked man that cast many aspersions upon him: *You have done well,* saith he, *not to omit any thing that is in your self.*

(g) *Ibid.* (g) Being told that some spoke ill of him; *It is no matter,* saith he, *I will live so, that they shall not be believed.*

(h) *Ser. 116.* (h) He said, there is a difference between swearing true, and swearing truly; and betwixt swearing false, and forswearing. That which is sworn, at the time that it is sworn, must necessarily be either true or false, seeing that the form of swearing is an *Axiom*: But he that sweareth, at the same time that he sweareth, is not necessarily perjur'd, or sweareth true, because the time is not yet arrived that must determine his Oath. For as a man is said to have covenanted truly or falsly, not when the covenant is made, but when the time whereby it is limited is come: So a man is said to swear truly or falsly, when the time comes wherein he promised to make good his oath.

(i) *Ser. 151.* (i) Being demanded why he did not undertake the government of the Commonwealth; *Because,* saith he, *If I govern ill, I shall displease the Gods; if well, the People.*

(k) *Ser. 249.* (k) He said, he who hath arrived at perfection, dischargeth all offices, omiting none, yet his life is not happy, for Beatitude is a post-accession thereto, when as the mean actions acquire a constancy, habit, and peculiar confirmation.

CHAP. III.

His Writings.

Because, saith *Laertius,* his Writings were very celebrious, we shall give an account of them digested according to their subjects: They were these.

Of the Logical place, Theses.
Logick.
Philosophick Commentaries.
Dialectick definitions, to Metrodorus, 6.
Of Dialectick names, to Zeno 1.
Dialectick art, to Aristagoras 1.
Of connex Probables, to Dioscorides 4.

The first Order of the *Logical* place of things.

Of Axioms 1.
Of not-simple Axioms 1.
Of Connex, to Athenades 2.
Of Negatives, to Aristagoras 3.
Of Catagoreuticks, to Athenodorus 1.
Of things spoken by privation, to Thearus 1.
Of best Axioms, to Dion 3.
Of Indefinites 4.
Of things spoken according to Time 2
Of perfect Axioms 2

The second Order.

Of true disjunct, to Gorgippides 1
Of true connex, to Gorgippides 4
Division, to Gorgippides 1
Of Consequents 1
Of that which is for three, to Gorgippides 1
Of Possibles, to Clitus 4
Of Significations, against Philo 1
What are false 1

The third Order.

Of Precepts 2
Of Interrogations 2
Of Percontation 4
Epitome of Interrogation and Percontation 1
Epitome of Answers 1
Of Question 2
Answer 4

The fourth Order.

Of Categorems, to Metrodorus 10
Of right and supine, to Philarchus 1
Of Conjunctions, to Apollonides 1
To Pasylus, of Categorems 4

The fifth Order.

Of the five cases 1
Of expressions defined according to the subject 1
Of Assimilation, to Stesagoras 2
Of Appellatives 2

Of the Logical place concerning words, and their reasons. The first Order.

Of singular and plural expressions 6
Of Words, to Sosigenes and Alexander 5
Of the anomaly of Words, to Dion 4
Of Sorites pertaining to voice 3
Of Solæcisms, to Dionysius 1
Of unusual speech 1
Words, to Dionysius 1

The second Order.

Of the elements of speech 5
Of the syntax of things said 4
Of the syntax and elements of speech, to Philip 3

Of the elements of speech, to Nicias 1.
Of Relative speech.

The third Order.

Of Not-dividents 2.
Of Amphibolies, to Apollas 4.
Of Tropical Amphibolies 1.
Of Connex Tropical Amphibolies 2.
Upon Panthœdus, *of Amphibolies* 2.
Introduction to Amphiboly 5.
Epitome of Amphibolies, to Epicrates 1.
Connex to the Introduction of Amphibolies 2.

Of Logical place concerning Reasons and Moods: The first Order.

The Art of Reasons and Moods, to Dioscorides 5.
Of Reasons 3.
Of the Composition of Moods, to Stesagoras 2.
Comparison of Tropical Axioms 1.
Of reciprocal Reasons and Connex 1.
To Agatho, *or of sequent Problems* 1.
Of Inferences, to Aristagoras 1.
Of placing the same Reason in diverse Moods 1.
Against those who oppose that the same Reason may be placed in Syllogistick and not Syllogistick Moods 2.
Against those who oppose the Reduction of Syllogisms 3.
Against Philo's *Book of Moods*, to Timostratus 1.
Logical Conjuncts, to Timocrates, *and* Philomathes.
Upon Reason and Moods 1.

The second Order.

Of conclusive Reasons, to Zeno 1.
Of first indemonstrable Syllogisms, to Zeno 1.
Of Reduction of Syllogisms 1.
Of Redundant Syllogisms, to Pasylus 2.
Theorems of Solæcisms 1.
Syllogistick Introductions, to Zeno 1.
Introductions to Moods, to Zeno 3.
Of Syllogisms false in Figure 5.
Syllogistick Reasons by Reduction in Indemonstrables 1.
Tropical Questions to Zeno *and* Philomathes *(suspected to be spurious)* 1.

The third Order.

Of Coincident Reasons, to Athenades 1. *spurious.*
Coincident Reasons as to the Medium 3. *spurious.*
Of Aminius's *Disjunctions* 1.

The fourth Order.

Of Hypotheses, to Meleager 3.
Hypothetick Reasons in Law, to Meleager 1.
Hypothetick Reasons for Introduction 2.
Hypothetick Reasons of Theorems 2.
Solution of Hedylus's *Hypotheticks* 2.
Solution of Alexander's *Hypotheticks* 3. *spurious.*
Of Expositions, to Leodamas 1.

The fifth Order.

Of Introduction to the lying Reason, to Aristocreon 1.
Lying Reasons to the Introduction 1.
Of the lying Reason, to Aristocreon 6.

The sixth Order.

Against those who think true and false are one, 1.
Against those who dissolve the lying Reason by Distinction 2.
Demonstration, that Infinites are not to be divided 1.
Upon that which hath been said against the Divisions of Infinites, to Pasylus 3.
Solutions according to the Ancients, to Dioscorides 1.
Of the Solution of the lying Reason, to Aristocreon 3.
Solution of Hedylus's *Hypotheticks*, to Aristocreon *and* Apollas.

The seventh Order.

Against those who say the lying Reason hath false Sumptions 1.
Of the Negative, to Aristocreon 2.
Negative Reasons, to Gymnasius 1.
Of the diminutive Reason, to Stesagoras 2.
Of opinionative and quiescent Reasons, to Onetor 2.
Of the veiled Reason, to Aristobulus 2.
Of the occult Reason, to Athenades 1.

The eighth Order.

Of the Nullity, to Menecrates 8.
Of Reasons consisting of Indefinite and Definite, to Pasyllus 2.
Of the Nullity, to Epicrates 1.

The ninth Order.

Of Sophisms, to Heraclides *and* Pollis 2.
Of insoluble Dialectick Reasons, to Dioscorides 5.
Against Arcesilaus's *method*, to Sphærus 1.

The tenth Order.

Against Custom, to Metrodorus 6.

Of the Logical place besides these four differences, there are dispersed, not containing in the Body of Logical Questions, 39

Of the *Ethick* place, for Direction of moral Notions: The first Order.
Description of Speech, to Theoporus 1.
Moral Theses 1.

Proba-

Probable Sumptions for Doctrines, to Philomathes 3.
Definitions of civil Persons, to Metrodorus 2.
Definitions of wicked Persons, to Metrodorus 2.
Definitions of mean Persons, to Metrodorus 2.
General Definitions, to Metrodorus 7.
Definitions of other Arts, to Metrodorus 2.

The second Order.

Of Things like, to Aristocles 3.
Of Definitions, to Metrodorus 7.

The third Order.

Of things not rightly Objected against Definitions, to Laodomas 7.
Probables for Definitions, to Dioscorides.
Of Species and Genus, to Gorgippides 2.
Of Divisions 1.
Of Contraries, to Dionysius 2.
Probables for Divisions, Genus's and Species.
Of Contraries 1.

The fourth Order.

Of Etymologicks, to Diocles 6.
Etymologicks, to Diocles 4.

The fifth Order.

Of Proverbs, to Zenodotus 2.
Of Poems, to Philomathes 1.
How Poems must be heard 2.
Against Criticks, to Diodorus 1.

Of the Moral place of common Speeches, according to Arts and Virtue: The first Order.
Against Rescriptions, to Timonax 1.
How we think and speak Singulars 1.
Of Notions, to Laodamus 2.
Of Suspition, to Pythonax 1.
Demonstration that a wise Man doth not Opinionate 1.
Of Comprehension, and Science, and Ignorance 4.
Of Speech 2.
Of the use of Speech, to Leptines.

The second Order.

That the Ancients approved Dialectick with Demonstration, to Zeno 2.
Of Dialectick, to Aristocreon 4.
Upon the Objections against Dialectick 3.
Of Rhetorick, to Dioscorides 4.

The third Order.

Of Habitude, to Cleon 3.
Of Art and Sloth, to Aristocreon 4.
Of the differences in Virtues, to Diodorus 1.
What Virtues are 1.
Of Virtues, to Pollis.

Of the Moral place concerning Good and Ill: The first Order.

Of Honesty and Pleasure, to Aristocreon 10.
Demonstration, that Pleasure is not the chief end 4.
Demonstration, that Pleasure is not Good 4.
Of those which are said ********

Thus concludes the seventh Book of *Laertius*; and who seeth not that the last of these Titles is defective, and moreover that the rest of the *Orders*, concerning this place *of Good and Ill*, (whereof this is but the first) are wanting. Doubtless the end of this Book is imperfect, and wanteth, if not the Lives of any Stoical Philosophers, who succeeded *Chrysippus* (whereof he mentions *Zeno*, and others elsewhere) yet at least a considerable part of his Catalogue, containing the rest of his *Ethick Writings*, and all his *Physick*, many of which are elsewhere cited even by *Laertius* himself, which as the learned *Casaubon* had observed, he would not have ascribed to *Laertius*'s neglect that *Chrysippus*'s Book of *Laws* is not mentioned. Of his *Ethick Writings*, besides those here named, were these,

(a) *Of Laws*. — (a) Ael. 14. 4.
(b) *Introduction to the Consideration of Things, Good or Ill*. — (b) Athen. deipn. 4. & 11.
(c) *Of Honest*. — (c) Deip. 4. & 8.
(d) *Of Consent*. — (d) Deipn. 6.
(e) *Of Things expetible in themselves*. — (e) Athen. Deipn. 7.
(f) *Of Things not expetible in themselves*. — (f) Ath.Deipn. 4.
(g) *Of Politick*. — (g) Laert. vit. Zen. Pl. rep. Stoic.
(h) *Of Ends*.
(i) *Of Passions*.
(k) *Of Ethick Questions*. — (h) Laert.Zen.
(l) *Of Lives*, whereof Plutarch cites the 4th Book. — Pl. Rep.
(m) *That Zeno used Names properly*. — (i) Laert. vit. Zen.
(n) *Of Justice, the first Book cited by Laertius*. — (k) Laert. (l) Plut. rep. Laert.
(o) *Of Life and Transaction*. — (m) Laert.
(p) *Of Offices*. — (n) Plut.repug. Laert.
(q) *Demonstration of Justice*. — (o) Laert.
(r) *Protrepticks*. — (p) Plut.repug.
(s) *Of the End*. — (q) Plut.repug.
(t) *Of a Commonwealth*. — (r) Plut.repug.
(u) *Of the Office of a Judge*. — (s) Plut. repug. & de com.nor.
(x) *Of Good*. — (t) Plut. repug.
(y) *Of Habits*. — (u) Plut. repug. (x) Plut.repug. (y) Plut.repug.

To Physick belong these.

(z) *Physicks*. — (z) Laert.
(a) *Of the Soul, the 12th Book cited by Laertius*. — (a) Laert. (b) Laert.
(b) *Of Providence, the first Book cited*. — (c) Plut.repug. Laert.
(c) *Of the Gods*. — (d) Plut. rep. Laert.
(d) *Of Fate*. — (e) Laert.
(e) *Of Divination*. — (f) Laert.
(f) *Of the Philosophy of the Ancients*. — (g) Plut. rep.
(g) *In Calumniation of the Senses*. — (h) Plut. rep. & com. nor.
(h) *Of Jupiter*. — (i) Plut.repug
(i) *Of Nature*. — (k) Plut. rep.
(k) *Physical Theses*.

(l) *Of*

(l) Of Substance.
(m) Of Motion.
(n) Physical Questions, the third Book cited
(o) Of Vacuity.
(p) Epistles.

The Number of all his Writings, according to *Laertius*, was 705. He wrote so much, that he had often occasion to Treat upon the same Subject, and setting down whatsoever came into his Mind, he often corrected and enlarged it by the Testimonies of others; whence having in one Book inserted all *Euripides*'s *Medea*, one having the Book in his hand, answer'd another, that asked him what Book it was, It is *Chrysippus*'s *Medea*. And *Apollodorus* the *Athenian*, in his Collection of *Doctrines*, asserting, that *Epicurus* had written many Books upon his own Strength, without using the Testimonies of others, and that he therein far exceed *Chrysippus*, adds these words ; *For if a Man should take out of* Chrysippus's *Writings, all that belongs to other Men, he would leave the Paper blank.*

(q) De Benef. l. 3.
Seneca gives this Censure of him : (q) He is most Subtile and Acute, penetrating into the depth of Truth. He speaks to the thing that is to be done, and useth no more words than are necessary to the understanding thereof; but adds,

(r) Sen. de Benef. l. 4.
that his (r) Acuteness being too fine, is many times blunted, and retorted upon it self; even when he seems to have done something, he only pricks, not pierceth.

(s) Laert.
(s) Some there are who inveigh against him, as one that wrote many obscene Things, not fit to be spoken, as in his *Commentary of the Ancient Physiologists* ; what he writes concerning *Jupiter* and *Juno*, is obscenely feigned, delivering that in 600 Paragraphs, which the most impudent Person would not have committed to Writing ; for, say they, he hath related the Story most unhandsomely ; and tho' he prais'd it as natural, yet it becometh Curtezans rather than Gods.

Moreover, what he saith of those that writ *of Tables*, is false, not to be found in *Polemo*, nor *Hipsicrates*, nor *Antigonus*, but forged by himself.

In his Book of *Commonwealth*, he allows Marriage with the Mother and a Daughter, and repeats the same in the beginning of his Book, *Concerning Things expetible in themselves*.

In his third Book of *Justice*, extending to a thousand Paragraphs, he advised to feed upon the very Dead.

In his second Book of *Life and Transaction*, he affirmeth, A wise Man ought to take care to provide himself Food ; but to what end must he provide himself Food ? For Livelihood? Life is an *indifferent*. For Pleasure ? Pleasure also is *indifferent*. For Virtue ? That is *Self-sufficient* for Beatitude. Such kinds of Acquisition of Wealth are very Ridiculous. If they proceed from a King, there is a necessity of complying with him ; if from a Friend, that Friendship is Venial ; if from Wisdom, that Wisdom is mercenary. For these things, saith *Laertius*, some have inveigh'd against him.

CHAP. IV.

His Death.

HE died, according to *Apollodorus*, in the 143d Olympiad, (to supply *Laertius*, in whom the centenary Number is wanting by *Suidas*) having lived 73 years.

The manner of his Death is differently related ; *Hermippus* affirms, That being in the *Odæum* (a kind of publick Theatre at *Athens*) his Disciples called him away to Sacrifice, and thereupon taking a draught of Wine he was immediately seized by a *Vertigo*, of which at the end of five days he died. Others report, he died of excessive Laughter : Seeing an Ass eat Figs, he bid his Woman offer it some Wine, and thereat fell into such extremity of Laughter, that it killed him.

As to his Person, he was very little, saith *Laertius*, as appeareth, by his Statue in the *Ceramick*, which is almost hid by the Horse that stands next it, whence *Carneades* called him κρυψίππος, *hid by a Horse*. The Posture of this Statue, *Cicero* saith, was Sitting, and stretching forth his Hand. *Pausanius* saith, It was set up in the *Gymnasium*, called *Ptolomæan* from the Founder, not far from the *Forum*.

Laertius reckons four more of this Name.

The *first*, a Physician, to whom *Erasistratus* acknowledgeth himself beholding for many things.

The *second*, his Son, Physician to *Ptolomy*, who, upon the Calumnies of some that maligned him, was publickly punished and beaten with Rods.

The *third*, Disciple to *Erasistratus*.

The *fourth*, a Writer of *Georgicks*.

ZENO.

(a) Suidas.
(a) ZENO was of *Tarsis*, or according to others, of *Sidon*, his Father named *Dioscorides*. He was Disciple to *Chrysippus*, and his Successor in the School. (b) He wrote few Books, but left behind him many Disciples.

(b) Laert. vit. Zen.

DIOGENES.

DIOGENES.

(a) Laert. vit. Diog.

(a) DIOGENES was born at Seleucia, he was Sirnamed the *Babylonian*, from the Vicinity of that place. He was Disciple of *Chrysippus*, and is stiled by *Cicero* an eminent and serious Stoick. (b) *Seneca* relates, That discoursing earnestly concerning Anger, a foolish Young Man standing by, spat in his Face, which he took meekly and discreetly, saying, *I am not Angry, but am in doubt whether I ought to be so or not*. He was one of the three that was sent from *Athens* on Embassy to *Rome*; of which already in the Life of *Carneades*, who learn'd Dialectick of him. *Cicero* saith, he lived to a great Age. Amongst other things, he wrote a Treatise *of Divination*.

(b) De ira 3.

ANTIPATER.

(a) Laert.
(b) De Offic. 3.
(c) Plut. de Garrul.

(a) ANTIPATER was of *Sidon*, Disciple to (b) *Diogenes* the *Babylonian*, *Cicero* calls him a most acute Person; *Seneca*, one of the great Authors of the Stoical Sect. (c) He declined to dispute with *Carneades*, but filled his Books with Confutations of him, whence he was called καλαμοβόας, *The clamorous Penman*. (d) He disputed much against those who asserted nothing. Besides other things, he writ two Books of *Divination*. (e) *Cicero* at the latter end of his second Book of *Offices*, saith, he then was lately dead at *Athens*.

(d) Cic. Ac. quaest. 4.
(e) Cic. de Divin. l. 1.

PANÆTIUS.

(a) Strab. l. 4.
(b) Cic. de Divin. lib. 1.
(c) Plut. Apoph.
(d) Acad. Q. 4.
Cic. Tusc. quaest. lib. 1.

(a) PANÆTIUS was of *Rhodes*, his Ancestors eminent for Martial Affairs and Exercises. He was (b) Disciple to *Antipater*, intimate Friend to (c) P. *Scipio Africanus*, whom he accompanied in his Journey to *Alexandria*. *Cicero* calls him, (d) *Almost Prince of the Stoicks, a Person extreamly Ingenious and Grave, worthy the familiarity of Scipio and Lælius*. He was a great Admirer of *Plato*, whom every where he calleth, *Divine, most Wise, most Holy, the Homer of Philosophers*. But his Opinion of the Immortality of the Soul, he approved not, arguing thus; Whatsoever is generated, dieth; but Souls are generated, as is manifest from the likeness of those that are begotten, to their Parents, not only in Body, but in Disposition. His other Argument was, There is nothing that is grieved or pained, but is subject to be Sick; whatsoever is subject to Sickness, is likewise subject to Death; Souls are subject to Grief, therefore they are subject to Death.

He alone rejected Astrological Predictions, and receded from the *Stoicks*, as to *Divination*; yet would not positively affirm there was no such Art, but only that he doubted it.

He wrote three Books *of Offices*, much commended by *Cicero*.

Lipsius Conjectures he died old, because *Cicero* affirmeth out of *Posidonius*, that he lived thirty Years after he had written his Books of Offices.

Cic. de divinat. lib. 2.
De divin. l. 1.

POSIDONIUS.

Strab. lib. 14.

Cic. Tusc. qu. l. 2.

POSIDONIUS was born at *Apamea* in *Syria*. He lived at *Rhodes*, and there managed civil Affairs, and taught Philosophy. *Pompey* in his return from *Syria*, went to *Rhodes* purposely to hear him, and coming to his Door, forbad the Lictor to knock, as was the Custom; but he (saith *Pliny*) to whom the *East* and *West* had submitted, himself submitted his *Fasces* at this Gate. But understanding that he was very Sick of a great Pain in his Joynts, he resolved only to give him a visit. At his first Coming and Salutation, he told him with much Respect, that he was extreamly sorry he could not hear him. *Posidonius* answer'd, *You may, for no corporeal Pain shall make me frustrate the coming of so great a Person*: And thereupon he discoursed seriously and copiously upon this Subject, as he lay in his Bed, *That nothing is good, but what is Honest*. And as often as his Pain took him, he would say, *Pain, it is to no purpose; tho' thou art troublesome, I will never acknowledge thou art Ill*.

He made a Spear, wherein were all the Conversions of the Sun, Moon and Planets, exactly as they moved in the Heavens every day and night.

Of his Writings are cited by *Cicero*, five Books *of Divination*; as also five Books *of the Nature of the Gods*.

Thus far we have a continued Succession of the *Stoick* Philosophers, the last School, according to *Laertius*'s Disposition, of those that were descended from *Thales*.

Cic. de nat. Deor. lib. 2.

De divinat.

The End of the Eighth Part.

Francis Lord Verulam

Advancement of Learning, Lib. 3. Sect. 5.

AS for the *Placits of Ancient Philosophers*, as were those of *Pythagoras, Philolaus, Xenophon, Anaxagoras, Parmenides, Leucippus, Democritus*, and others, (which men use disdainfully to run over); it will not be amiss to cast our eyes with more reverence upon them. For although Aristotle (*after the manner of the race of the Ottomans*) thought he could not safely reign, unless he made away all his Brethren; yet to those who seriously propound to themselves the inquisition and illustration of *Truth*, and not *Dominion* or *Magistrality*, it cannot but seem a matter of great profit, to see at once before them, the several Opinions of several Authors touching the Natures of things. Neither is this for any great hope conceiv'd, that a more exact truth can any way be expected from these or from the like Theories : For, as the same *Phœnomena*, the same *Calculations*, are satisfied upon the Astronomical Principles, both of *Ptolomy*, and *Copernicus*: So the popular experience we imbrace, and the ordinary view and face of things, may apply it self to many several Theories; whereas a right investigation of Truth requires another manner of severity and speculation. For as *Aristotle* saith Elegantly, *That Children at first indeed call all men Fathers, and women Mothers; but afterwards they distinguish them both*: So certainly experience in Childhood, will call every *Philosophy, Mother*; but when it comes to ripeness, it will discern the true Mother. In the mean time it is good to read over divers *Philosophies*, as divers Glosses upon Nature; whereof, it may be, one in one place, another in another, is more corrected: Therefore I could wish a Collection made, but with diligence and judgment, *De Antiquis Philosophiis*, out of the lives of Ancient Philosophers; out of the Parcels of *Plutarch*, of their *Placits*; out of the Citations of *Plato*; out of the Confutations of *Aristotle*; out of a sparsed mention found in other Books, as well of Christians, as of Heathens, (as out of *Lactantius, Philo, Philostratus*, and the rest): For I do not yet see extant a *work of this Nature*. But here I must give warning, that this be done distinctly, so as the *Philosophies*, every one sever'dly, be composed and continued, and not collected by titles and handfuls as hath been done by *Plutarch*. For *every Philosophy, while it is entire in the whole piece, supports it self; and the Opinions maintained therein, give light, strength, and credence mutually one to the other; whereas if they be simple and broken, it will sound more strange and dissonant*. In truth, when I read in *Tacitus* the Actions of *Nero*, or of *Claudius*, invested with Circumstances of Times, Persons, and Inducements, I find them not so strange, but that they may be true: But when I read the same Actions in *Suetonius Tranquillus*, represented by Titles and common Places, and not in order of Time, they seem monstrous, and altogether incredible. *So is Philosophy when it is propounded entire; and when it is sliced and articled into fragments*.

MONTAIGNE, *Essays*, Chap. 12.

How much do I desire, that, in my life-time, either some other, or Justus Lipsius, *the most knowing person that is left us, of a most polished and judicious wit, truly allied to my* Turnebus, *had both the will and the health, and leisure enough to collect in one Register, according to their divisions and their classes, sincerely and curiously, as much as we can see thereof, the opinions of the ancient Philosophy, upon the subject of our Being, and of our Manners, its Controversies, the credit and succession of its Sects, the application of the Life of the Authors and followers, to their precepts in memorable and exemplary accidents! What an excellent and profitable work would this be?*

THE
HISTORY of PHILOSOPHY.

The NINTH PART.
Containing the *ITALICK* Sect.

PYTHAGORAS.

CHAP. I.
The Country, Parents, and Time of Pythagoras.

THE *Italick* Sect was distinct from the *Ionick* in respect of the Author, Place, Discipline, and Doctrine; denominated from that part of *Ita*-ly, which from the frequency of Greek Colonies, was called *Magna Græcia*. Yet was not the Author, *Pythagoras*, an Italian; (*a*) for, tho' some (*a*) *Porphyr. vit. Pythag.*

Part IX.   PYTHAGORAS.

(b) Plut. Sympos.
(c) Porph.

some think, his Father was of *Metapontum*; (b) some, a Tyrrhene, of *Etruria* in *Italy*; yet (c) *Diogenes* and others report him a Tyrrhene, of the race of those who inhabited *Lemnus, Imbrus,* and *Scyrus*; and that coming upon Traffick to *Samus*, he setled there, and was made free. With these concurrs

(d) Porph.

(d) *Aristoxenus*, (to whom *Clemens Alexandrinus* joyneth *Aristarchus* and *Theopompus*) who

(e) Strom. lib. 1.
(f) Porp.

((e) in the life of *Pythagoras*) faith, (f) That he was born in one of those Islands which the *Athenians* won, and expelled thence the Tyrrhenians. Whence *Suidas* faith, that *Pythagoras was a Samian, but by birth a Tyrrhenian, brought over young by his father from* Tyrrhenia *to* Samus. And indeed his Country seems inscrutable to

(g) Porph.
(h) Contra. Appion.

(g) *Lycus*; to (h) *Josephus* no less difficult to find out, than that of Homer.

Nor is it strange, that the Country of his Father should be question'd, since it is not agreed concerning his name and quality:

(i) Lib. 20.

(i) *Justin* calls him *Demaratus*, (and *Johannes Sarisburiensis*, from *Justine, Maratus*)

(k) Laert.

(k) others, *Mamercus*: But the greater part of Writers agree,

(l) Laert. Suid. Apul.

that he was called (l) *Mnesarchus*; his profession, according to *Hermippus* and others, a Graver of Rings; according to others, a Merchant.

(m) Porph.

(m) Some there are who affirm, he was a *Phliasian*; *Pausanias* reports, that he was Son of *Euphron*, Grandson of *Hippasus*, who upon the taking of *Phlius* by the *Dorians*, fled to *Samus*.

(o) Laert.

(o) Others, that he was Son of *Hippasus*; *Hippasus* was Son of *Euthyphron, Euthyphron* of *Cleonymus*, who was banished out of *Phlius*; and that *Mamercus* (or rather *Mnesarchus*) lived in *Samus*, whence *Pythagoras* was said to be a *Samian*.

(p) Porph.

(p) *Cleanthes* relates he was a *Syrian*, of the City *Tyrus* in *Syria*, (or rather in *Phœnicia*) whence making a Voyage to *Samus* for Traffick, at such time as the *Samians* were much opprest with Famine, he furnished them with Corn, in requital whereof, they made him free of their Country.

(q) Clem. Alex. Strom.

(q) *Hippobotus* faith, that *Pythagoras* was a *Samian*.

Indeed, the most general and approved opinion is, that *Mnesarchus* was a *Samian*, descended from *Ancæus*, who first brought a Colony into *Samus*; and that *Pythagoras*, his Son, was born at *Sidon* in *Phœnicia*; but by education, as well as extraction, a *Samian* also. This is ratify'd by the authority of *Jamblichus*, who begins his life with this fabulous Narration.

(r) Jambl. vit. Pyth. cap 2.
(s) So read both here and afterwards, as appeareth by the Oracle, ἀντὶ Σάμης.

(r) It is reported, that Ancæus, who liv'd at (s) Same in Cephalenia, was descended from Jupiter, [others say from Neptune and Astypalæa] an opinion occasioned by his virtues, or some particular greatness of soul. In prudence and magnanimity he excelled all other Cephalenians. This Ancæus was commanded by the Pythian Oracle, to gather together a Colony out of Cephalenia, Arcadia, and Thessaly, augmenting it from Athens, Epidaurus, and Chalcis; and that having got them together under his command, he should people an Island, named from the richness of the soyl

(t) Strab. lib. 14.

Melamphyllos, (t) black-leaf) *and call the City which they built* Samus, *from* Same *in* Cephalenia. *The Oracle was thus:*

Instead of Same, Samus thou (an Isle)
Shalt plant Ancæus, which men Phyllas style.

That this Colony was drawn from those several places, appears not only from their religious rites and sacrifices, (which are derived from the Countries out of which those people came) but also from the affinities and mutual conventions made by the Samians. Mnesarchus and Pythais, the parents of Pythagoras, are said to be descended from the family of the same Ancæus, that planted this Colony there. [(u) Of Pythais, it is confirmed by Apollonius.] Which nobleness of their extraction, being much celebrated amongst their Country men, a Samian Poet declar'd him to be the son of Apollo, in (x) these words.

(u) Porphyr. pag.

(x) Cited also by Porphyrius.

Pythais of all Samians the most fair,
Jove-lov'd Pythagoras to Phœbus bare.

Which report was raised thus. This Mnesarchus the Samian being upon occasion of Traffick at Delphi, with his Wife, who was at that time newly with Child, and not known to be so; he enquired of the Oracle concerning his Voyage to Syria. The Prophetess told him, That his Journey should be according to his mind, very advantageous. That his Wife was already with Child, and should bring forth a Son that should exceed all men that ever were, in Beauty and Wisdom, and through the whole course of his Life conduce much to the benefit of Mankind. Mnesarchus considering, That the Oracle would not have spoken of his Son, seeing that he demanded nothing concerning him, if there were not something extraordinary to be expected from him, immediately hereupon changed the Name of his Wife, which before was Parthenis to Pythais, from the Prophetess; and as soon as She was delivered at Sidon in Phœnicia, they called the Child Pythagoras. For Epimenides, Eudoxus, Xenocrates, [and others mentioned by (y) Apollonius] are to be rejected, who affirm Apollo at that time lay with Pythais, (z) and got her with Child, (She not being so before) and thereupon foretold it by the Prophetess, this is not to be admitted. But that the Soul of Pythagoras, being of the Regimine of Apollo, (whether as a Follower, or some other way more near to him) was sent to men, none can doubt, since it may be evinc'd by these circumstances of his Birth, and the universal Wisdom of his mind. Thus much (faith Jamblichus) concerning his Generation. Whence we see the Greeks did so much admire his Wit, that they thought it could be nothing less than Divine, and thereupon fabled Apollo to be his Father.

(y) Porphyr. pag.
(z) Adding ζʹ κυέσθαι αὐτὴν ἐν μὴ ὅπως ἐξ ὅσης κατασ-

Pythagoras was the youngest of three Sons, the eldest (a) *Cleanthes*, calls *Eunestus*; *Laertius*, and *Suidas Eunomus*; the second, *Tyrrhenus*. He had likewise an Uncle, *Zoilus*, mentioned by *Laertius*.

(a) Porphyr.

The reasons for establishing the times concerning *Pythagoras's* life will hereafter be set forth, upon occasion of his going into *Italy*. In the mean time I shall desire it may be admitted, that he was born about the third year of the fifty-third Olympiad: That being eighteen years old, he heard *Thales* and others. Then he went to *Phœnicia*, thence into *Egypt*, where he staid twenty-two years; afterwards at *Babylon* twelve years, then returned to *Samus*, being fifty-six years old; and from thence went into *Italy*. The particulars whereof shall in their several places be more fully discoursed.

Yy 2   CHAP.

CHAP. II.

His first Education and Masters.

(a) Vit. Pyth. cap. 2.

MNesarchus (saith (*a*) *Jamblicus*) returning from *Syria* to *Samus*, with much wealth, and abundance of Merchandize, built a Temple, which he dedicated to Apollo the *Pythian*, and brought up his son in several excellent disciplines, committing him sometimes to Creophylus, sometimes to Pherecydes *of Syrus*, and to almost all the Præfects of the Temple; as being blest with the fairest and most divine son that ever man had.

(b) Laert.
(c) St. August. Ep. 9. ad Volus.

Some there are who affirm, that (*b*) he was first a Wrestler; and that (*c*) when Pherecydes first discoursed among the *Greeks*, concerning the immortality of the Soul, Pythagoras the *Samian*, moved at the novelty of the discourse, became of a Wrestler, a Philosopher. But these relations seem to have been occasion'd by confounding *Pythagoras* the Philosopher with a Wrestler of that name, his contemporary, of whom hereafter.

(d) Porph. p. 2.
(e) In Pythag.

(*d*) *Cleanthes* and (*e*) *Suidas* relate, That he first heard Pherecydes *the Syrian*, at *Samus*; and in the second place Hermodamas, τῷ Κρεοφύλῳ, the Creophylian, at the same *Samus*, then very old. (*f*) Hermodamas *was his name*, but he was sirnamed Creophylus. Wherefore perhaps

(f) Jambl.
(g) As once in Ritterhusius's Edition, or perhaps τῷ Κρεοφύλῳ.
(h) Jamb.
(i) Strabo.
(k) Florid. l. 2.

instead of τῷ Κρεοφύλῳ, should be (*g*) read, τῷ Κρεοφύλῳ; or else he was termed a *Creophylian*, as well as sirnamed *Creophylus*; (*h*) for that reported to be descended from Creophylus a (*i*) *Samian*, who, *in times past, entertained* Homer *as his guest, and was, as some say, his Master and his Rival in Poetry*. But (*k*) *Apuleius*, who saith, Hermodamas, or *Leodamas*, as he calls him, was disciple to that *Creophylus*, an error no less in Chronology, than when he saith, *Pythagoras* was Disciple to *Plato*, unless the whole Text be corrupted.

(l) Jam. continues.

(*l*) Pythagoras *his father dying, he grew up in prudence and temperance, being, whilst he was yet very young, generally much respected and honoured, even by the most aged. His presence and discourse attracted all persons; to every one on whom he looked, he appeared worthy admiration, insomuch that many averred, he was the son of a deity. He being thus confirm'd by the great opinions that were had of him, by the education of his infancy, and by his natural felicity, made himself daily more worthy of these advantages, adorning himself with Devotions, with Sciences, with excellent Conversation, with constancy of Mind, with grave Deportment, and with a sweet inimitable Serenity; never transported with anger, laughter, emulation, contention, or any other disorder; living like some good genius, come to converse in* Samus. Hereupon, tho' young, a great report was spread of him, to Thales at *Miletus*, to Bias at *Priene*, two of the Sages, and to all the Cities thereabout; many in all those parts commending the young man, made him famous, calling him by a Proverb, [The *Samian* Comer] or, [The fair-hair'd *Samian*.]

About this time began the tyranny of Polycrates, when Pythagoras *about eighteen years old, foreseeing the event, and how obstructive it would prove to his designs, and to the pursuit of Learning,*

which he intended above all things, [(*m*) being *(m) Laert.* young, and desirous of knowledge, left his Country to go to travel] *stole away privately by night, taking with him* Hermodamas, (*sirnamed* Creophylus, *and descended, as was reported, from that* Creophylus, *who was Host to* Homer) *and made a voyage to* Pherecydes, [at *Lesbus*, to whom, Laertius saith, he was recommended by his Uncle *Zoilus*] and to Anaximander, *the natural Philosopher*, and to Thales at *Miletus*. With each of these he conversed severally in such manner, that they all lov'd him, admired his parts, and communicated their learning to him. [(*n*) Under Anaximander the *Milesian*, he is said to have studied the knowledge of natural things] Thales entertain'd him kindly, and, wondring at his excellency above other youths, which much surpassed the report he had received, assisted him as far as he was able in Sciences; withal, accusing his own age and infirmity, he advised him to make a voyage to Egypt, there to get acquaintance with the Priests of Memphis and (*o*) Diospolis, since of *(o) Thebes.* them he had learned those things, for which he was by many esteemed wise, tho' he were not of such forwardness, neither by nature or education, as he saw Pythagoras to be. Whence he presaged, that, if he conversed with those Priests, he should become the most Divine and Wisest of Men.

(n) Apul. Florid. lib. 2.

This *Pherecydes* fell sick at *Delus*: That he outlived not the fifty-seventh Olympiad, is manifest from a (*p*) Letter which he writ the day before *(p) Laert. vit.* his death to *Thales*, who died the first year of *Thaletis.* the Olympiad following. And tho' the greater part of Authors write, that at the same time, when the *Cylonians* in *Crotona*, conspir'd against the *Pythagoreans*, which was not long before *Pythagoras* died) *Pythagoras* was gone from *Italy* to *Delus*, to visit and bury *Pherecydes*, yet *Dicæarchus* and other more accurate Authors (saith * *Porphyrius*) averr, that Pythagoras *was* * Pag. 38. *present when that conspiracy broke forth; and that* Pherecydes *died before* Pythagoras *departed from* Samus. The former relation hath imposed, among others, † upon the learned *Salmasius*, who, † *Plin. exercit.* to reconcile this with other circumstances concerning *Pherecydes*, is constrain'd to imagine another person of the same name. It was therefore before *Pythagoras* left *Samus*, that (*q*) Pherecydes, being desperately seized by a *Phthiriasis*, *(q) Porph. p.* he went to visit him, and attended him in his *10, 11.* sickness until he died, and then performed the *Jam. cap. 30.* rites of funeral, as to his *Master*. For Laertius *pag. 162.* and *Porphyrius* add, that *after the death and burial of* Pherecydes, *he returned to* Samus, *out of a desire to enjoy the society of* Hermodamas.

(*r*) *Phavorinus*, in the seventh Book of his va- *(r) Laert.* rious History, and (*s*) *Porphyrius*, relate, that *(s) Vit. Pyth.* after he had lived a while with *Hermodamas*, he first taught Wrestlers, and of them *Eurimenes*, to diet with flesh, (whereas other Wrestlers used to eat dry'd Figs, Cheese-curds, and Whey) whereby he became Victor at the *Olympick* Games. But *Laertius* and (*t*) *Jamblichus* observe, *(t) Cap. 5.* that this is falsly ascribed to *Pythagoras* the *Samian*, (for he allowed not the eating of flesh) but was indeed the invention of *Pythagoras*, son of *Eratocles*, of whom hereafter.

CHAP.

CHAP. III.

How he travelled to Phœnicia.

(a) *Jamb.* cap. 13.

(a) Having learn'd of *Thales* above all things to husband his time, and for that reason forbearing wine and flesh, and having before refrained from eating much, and accustomed himself to such meats as were light and easie of digestion, by which means he procur'd a habit of watchfulness, clearness of mind, and an exact constant health of body; he made a voyage to *Sidon*, as well out of a natural desire to the place it self, esteeming it his Country, as conceiving that he might more easily pass from thence into *Egypt*.

Here he conferred with the Prophets, successors of *Mocus* the Physiologist, and with others, and with the *Phœnician* Priests, and was initiated into all the mysteries of *Byblus*, and *Tyre*, and sundry

(b) Reading ὀξαι, ἐπως.

of the (b) principal sacred Institutions in divers other parts of *Syria*, not undergoing these things out of Superstition, as may be imagined; but out of love to knowledge, and a fear, lest any thing worthy to be known, which was preserved amongst them, in the miracles or mysteries of the gods, might escape him. Withal, not being ignorant, that the rites of those places were deduced from the *Egyptian* ceremonies, by means whereof he hoped to participate of the more sublime and divine mysteries in *Egypt*, which he pursued with admiration, as his Master *Thales* had advised him.

CHAP. IV.

How he travell'd to Egypt.

(a) *Jamblicus* continueth.

(a) Some *Egyptian* Mariners passing accidentally along that coast, which lyes under *Carmel*, (a *Phœnician* mountain, where he spent much of his time in private retirement at the Temple) willingly received him into their Ship. But observing, during the voyage, how temperately he liv'd, keeping his usual diet, they began to have a greater esteem for him. And perceiving some things in the excellency of his demeanour, more than human, they reflected within themselves, how that he appeared to them as soon as they landed, coming down from the top of the mountain *Carmel*, (which they knew to be more sacred than other Hills, and not trod upon by the vulgar) easily and directly, neither stones for precipices obstructing his passage; and how that

† For μόγοντε ἀπφθεγξάμε- νΘ, reading ἀπφθεγξά- μενΘ τε μὴν ἐις Ἀιγυπΐον ὁ ἀπόπλυς, &c.

coming to the side of the Ship, * he asked, Whether they were bound for *Egypt*; and they answering, That they were, he went into the Vessel, and silently sitting down in a place, where he might least disturb the Mariners, in case they should be in any stress, continued in the same posture two nights and three days, without meat, drink, or sleep, (except when none perceived he slumbred a little, sitting in the same unmovable posture, and this constantly to the end) and how that the voyage proceeded direct, beyond their expectation, as if assisted by the presence of some god. Laying all these things together, they concluded and perswaded themselves, that some Divine Genius did indeed come along with them from *Syria* to *Egypt*. The rest of the voyage they performed prosperously, observing a greater respect than formerly in their words and actions, as well to one another, as towards him, until they at last arrived upon the coast of *Egypt*, by a most fortunate passage, without any storm.

As soon as he landed, they reverently took him up, and seating him on the cleanest part of the Sand, rear'd an extemporary Altar before him, on which they laid part of all the sorts of provisions which they had, as the first-fruits of their lading, and drew up their Vessel in the same place, where they first put to Sea. *Pythagoras*, tho' weakned with long fasting, was not sick, either at his landing, or by their handing of him; nor did he, when they were gone, abstain long from the fruits which they had laid before him, but took them, and preserved his constitution therewith undisturbed, till he came to the next houses. (b) From thence he went to search after all the Temples with diligent and exact inquisition.

(b) cap. 4.

(c) *Antiphon*, in his Book concerning such as were eminent for virtue, extolleth his perseverance when he was in *Egypt*, saying, *Pythagoras designing to become acquainted with the institution of the* Egyptian *Priests, and diligently endeavouring to participate thereof, desired* Polycrates *the Tyrant to write to* Amasis *King of* Egypt, *with whom he had friendship*, (as appears also by (d) *Herodotus*) *and hospitality*, (formerly) *that he might be admitted to the aforesaid Doctrine. Coming to* Amasis, Amasis *gave him Letters to the Priests, and going first to those of* Heliopolis, *they sent him to the Priest of* Memphis, *as the more ancient, which was indeed but a pretence of the* Heliopolitans: [(e) *For the* Egyptians *imparted not their mysteries to every one, nor committed the knowledge of Divine things to profane persons, but to those only who were to inherit the Kingdom; and, of Priests, to those who were adjudged to excel the rest in education, learning, and descent.*] *From* Memphis, *upon the same pretence, he was sent to* Thebes. *They not daring, for fear of the King, to pretend excuses; but thinking, that by reason of the greatness and difficulty thereof, he would desist from the design, enjoyned him very hard precepts, wholly different from the institution of the* Grecians, *which he readily performed, to their so great admiration, that they gave him power to sacrifice to the gods, and to acquaint himself with all their studies, which was never known to have been granted to any forreigner besides.*

(c) *Prophyr. vit. Pythag.* pag. 5. cited also by *Laertius*.

(d) *Lib.* 3.

(e) *Clem. Alex. Strom.*

(f) *Clemens Alexandrinus* relates particularly that *he was disciple to* Sonchedes, *an* Egyptian *Arch-prophet*.

(f) *Strom.* 1.

(g) *Diogenes* saith, that *whilst he lived with these Priests, he was instructed in the Learning and Language* (as *Antiphon* also affirms) *of the* Egyptians, *and in their three kinds of writing*, Epistolick, Hieroglyphick, *and* Symbolick; *whereof one imitates the common way of speaking; the rest allegorical, by Ænigms:* (h) They who are taught by the *Egyptians*, learn first the method of all the *Egyptian* Letters, which is called *Epistilographick*; the second, *Hieratick*, used by those who write of Sacred things; the last and most perfect *Hieroglyphick*, whereof one is *Curiologick*, the other, *Symbolick*. Of the *Symbolick*, one is properly spoken by *Imitation*, another is written

(g) *Porph.* γ. 8.

(h) *Clem. Alex. Strom. lib.* 5.

written as it were *Tropically*; another on the contrary doth allegorize by *Ænigms*. For instance, in the *Kyriologick* way, to express the Sun, they make a Circle; the Moon, a Crescent. *Tropically* they do properly traduce, and transfer, and express by exchanging some things, and variously transfiguring others. Thus when they deliver the praises of Kings, in Theological Fables, they write by *Anaglyphicks*. Of the third kind, by *Ænigms*, let this be an example: All other Stars, by reason of their oblique course, they likened to the bodies of Serpents, but the Sun to that of a *Beetle*, because having formed a ball of Cow-dung, and lying upon its back, it rolls it about (from claw to claw.) They say moreover, that this creature liveth six months under ground, and the other half of the year upon the earth; and that it immits seed into the Globe (of the earth) and so generates, there being no female of that species. Hitherto *Clemens*.

(b) *Val. Max.* 8. 7.

Thus (b) being acquainted with the learning of that Nation, and enquiring into the Commentaries of the Priests of former times, he knew the observations of innumerable Ages, as *Valerius Maximus* saith. And (i) living admir'd and belov'd of all the Priests and Prophets with whom he conversed, he informed himself by their means accurately, concerning every thing; not omitting any person, eminent at that time for learning, or any kind of religious rites; nor leaving any place unseen, by going into which he conceived that he might find something extraordinary. [For (k) he went into the *Adyta* of the *Egyptians*, and, as (l) *Clemens* saith, permitted himself to that end to be circumcised) and learned things not to be communicated concerning the gods, mystick Philosophy.] He travelled to all the Priests, and was instructed by every one, in that wherein they were particularly learned. In Egypt he lived twenty-two years, in their Private Sacred Places, studying Astronomy and Geometry, and was initiated (not cursorily or casually) into all the religious Mysteries of the Gods.

(i) *Jam.cap.* 4. continuing.

(k) *Laert.*
(l) *Strom.* 1. pag. 302.

Laertius saith, He made three Cups of silver, and presented them to each [Society] of the Egyptian Priests; which, as we said, were three, of *Heliopolis*, *Memphis*, and *Thebes*.

CHAP. V.

How he went to Babylon.

(a) *Olymp.*

(a) A*Masis* dying in the third year of the sixty-third Olympiad, (which was the 223d. of *Nabonasser*) his son *Psamminitus* succeeded him, who is by *Cresias* named *Amistæus*, and seems to be the same whom (b) *Pliny* calls *Semniserteus*, (tho' (c) others interpret it of *Amasis* in whose Reign, saith he, *Pythagoras* was in *Egypt*. At this time *Cambysis* invaded and conquered *Egypt*, (d) by whom *Pythagoras* was taken prisoner, and sent to *Babylon*. There he lived [(e) with the most excellent among the *Chaldeans*, and] *with the Magi*, the *Persian* Magi, for so (f) *Cicero*, (g) *Apuleius*, and (h) *Eusebius* term them) in respect that *Babylon* was then under that Monarchy; which is the meaning also of (i) *Valerius Maximus*, and (k) *Lactantius*, who affirm, that he went from *Egypt* to the *Persians*, (not to *Persia*, as (l) some conceive) and resigned himself to the most exact prudence of the *Magi* to be formed.

(b) lib. 36. cap. 9.
(c) *Usher Annal.* 4167.

(d) *Jam.* cap. 4.
(e) *Clem.Stro.* 1. *Laert.*
(f) *de finib.* 5.
(g) *Florid.* 2.
(h) *Præp.* 10.
(i) lib.8.cap.7.
(k) lib.4.c.2.

(m) The *Magi* received him kindly, and instructed him in the most profound and sublime mysteries of the worship of the gods. By their means also he arrived at the heighth of Arithmetick, Musick, and other Mathematical Sciences. From them, saith (n) *Valerius Maximus*, he, with a docile mind, received the motions of the Stars, their power, property, and effects, (o) their states and periods; the various effects of both in the nativities of men, as likewise the remedies of diseases, which are purchased at vast rates by Sea and Land.

Of the *Chaldeans*, with whom he lived in *Babylon*, (p) *Diogenes* particularly instanceth *Zabratus*, by whom he was cleansed from the pollutions of his life past, and instructed from what things virtuous persons ought to be free; and learnt the discourse concerning Nature, (Physick) and what are the principles of the Universe. This *Zabratus* was probably the same with that *Zoroastres*, one of the *Persian* Magi, whom, (q) *Apuleius* saith, he chiefly had for Teacher, terming him, *Omnis divini arcanum antistatem*: And the same with *Mazaratus* the *Assyrian*, whom (r) *Alexander*, in his Book of Pythagorick Symbols, affirms to have been Master to *Pythagoras*; the same whom (s) *Suidas* calls *Zares*; *Cyril*, *Zaran*; *Plutarch*, *Zaratas*: Whence (t) some conceive, that they all mean *Zoroastres* the Magus, who was also called *Zarades*, as evidently appears from *Theodoret* and *Agathias*. Indeed he could not hear *Zoroastres* himself, as being some Ages later; yet it appears from the relation of *Apuleius*, that many conceived *Pythagoras* to have been a follower of *Zoroastres*. Perhaps him whose doctrine *Pythagoras* embraced, (for (u) *Clemens* saith, he explained Zoroastres the *Persian Magus*) posterity believed to have been his Master. This *Nazaratus* the *Assyrian*, was by some supposed to be the Prophet *Ezekiel*, which opinion *Clemens* oppugns; nevertheless (as Mr. *Selden* observes) the most accurate Chronology teacheth, that *Ezekiel* and *Pythagoras* flourished together, betwixt the 50th and 52d. Olympiad; and therefore the account of time hinders not, but that this *Nazaratus* might be *Ezekiel*.

(l) *Virgius de Philosoph.* Sectis cap. 6. sect. 4.
(m) *Jambl.* continueth.

(n) lib 3.
(o) *Apul.Florid.* lib. 2.

(p) *Porphy.* p.2.

(q) *Florid.* 2.

(r) *Porphyr.* p.

(s) *In voce Pythagorus.*
(t) *Selden de Diis Syris.*

(u) *Strom.* 1.

(x) *Diogenes* (in his Treatise of incredible things, beyond *Thule*) adds, that he went also to the *Hebrews*, which (y) *Lactantius* expresly denies. (z) *Eusebius* saith, He is reported to have heard the Persian Magi, and the Diviners of the Egyptians, at what time some of the *Jews* were gone to Babylon, others to Egypt. That he conversed with the Jews at *Babylon*, (saith the (a) Bishop of *Armagh*) may be argued, for that he transferred many of their Doctrines into his Philosophy, as *Hermippus* declares in his first Book of things concerning *Pythagoras*, cited by (b) *Josephus*; and in his first Book of Law-givers, cited by (c) *Origen*, which likewise is confirmed by (d) *Aristobulus* the Jew, a Peripatetical Philosopher, in his first Book to *Philometor*; who moreover was induced by the same reason to believe, that the Books of *Moses* were translated into Greek before the *Persian* Empire; whereas it is much more probable, that *Pythagoras* receiv'd that part of his Learning from the conversation which he had with the *Hebrews*.

(x) *Porphy.* p. 8.
(y) lib.4.c.2.
(z) *Præpar.* lib. 13.

(a) *Annal.* p. 151.

(b) *Contra Apion.* lib. 1.
(c) *Contra Celsum.* lib. 1.
(d) *Clem. Strom.* 1. *Euseb. Præpar.* lib. 13.

Alex-

(e) Clem. Alex. Strom. 1.

(e) *Alexander* adds, that he heard the *Galatæ* and the *Brachmanes*. From *Chaldea* (saith *Apuleius*) he went to the *Brachmanes*; *these are wise persons, a Nation of India, for which reason he went to their Gymnosophists. The Brachmanes conferred many things to his Philosophy; what are the documents of minds, what the exercises of bodies, how many are the parts of the soul, how many the vicissitudes of life; what torments or rewards, according to their merits, are allotted to men after death.*

(f) Porph.

(f) *Diogenes* adds, that *he went also to Arabia, and lived with the King there*; but it is not easie to find the name of the Court of the King of that wandring Nation.

(g) Clem. Strom. 1.
(h) Porph. p. 8.
(i) Porph. p. 4.

As concerning his Learning, it is generally said, that (g) *he learned many, and those the most excellent parts of his Philosophy, of the Barbarians.* (h) *Diogenes* affirms, *he gained the greatest part of his wisdom from these Nations.* (i) *The Sciences which are called Mathematical, he learnt of the Egyptians, and the Chaldeans, and the Phœnicians; for the Egyptians were of old studious of Geometry; the Phœnicians, of numbers and proportions; the Chaldeans, of Astronomical Theorems, divine rites, and worship of the gods; and other institutions concerning the course of life, he learned and received of the Magi. These are more generally known, as being committed to writing; but the rest of his institutions are less known.*

(k) Joseph. contra Appion. lib. 1.
(l) Vossius de Philos. Sect. cap. 6. sect. 2.

(k) *Hermippus* saith, *He embraced the opinions of the Thracians*; which (l) some interpret of *Pittacus*, whose Father *Hyrrhadius* was of that Country: But with more reason may it be understood of *Orpheus*, from whom *Jamblichus* acknowledgeth, that he derived much of the Theological part of his Science.

CHAP. VI.

How he returned to Samus.

Jambl. c. 2, 5. (for the Chapters are ill distinguisht.)

Having lived at *Babylon* twelve years, he returned to *Samus*, [for that he was redeemed by one *Gyllus* Prince of *Crotona*, *Apuleius* cites but for a less creditable relation] about the fifty-sixth year of his age, *where being known by some of the most ancient persons, he was looked upon with greater admiration than before, for he seemed to them more wise, more beautiful, and more divinely majestick. His Country summoned him to some publick employment, that he might benefit the generality, and communicate his knowledge*: Which he not refusing, endeavoured to instruct them in the symbolical way of learning, altogether resembling that of the Egyptians, in which he himself had been instituted. But the Samians not affecting this way, did not apply themselves to him.

Pythagoras, tho' he saw that no man came to him, or sincerely affected his learning, endeavoured nevertheless all possible ways to continue amongst them, not despising or undervaluing Samus, because it was his Country. And whilst he was very desirous that his Country-men should taste, tho' against their wills, the sweetness of his Mathematicks, he observed in a Gymnasium, a young man that play'd at Tennis dexterously and nimbly, but otherwise poor and indigent: And imagining that this Youth would be wholly guided by him, if without labour he should supply him with necessaries; when they had done washing, he called him, to him, and told him, That he would continually furnish him with all things, sufficient for his maintenance, if he would learn briefly, and without labour, and constantly (that he might not be over-burthened) some Mathematicks, which he himself, when he was young, had learned of the Barbarians, which had now left him, by reason of old age and forgetfulness. The Youth promising, and being allured by the hopes of maintenance, he endeavoured to initiate him in Arithmetick and Geometry, drawing the demonstration of each in a Table; and teaching him, he gave the young man for every Scheme (or Diagram) three Oboli, as a reward and compensation. And this he continued to do a long time, out of a love of glory, and industriously bringing him into the Theory by an exact method. But when the young man, having made a good progress, was sensible of the excellency, both of the pleasure and the consequences in Mathematicks, the wise man perceiving it, and that he would not now quit his learning, what inconvenience soever he might suffer, pretended, that he had no more Trioboli to give him. 'Tis no matter, 'saith the youth, I am able to learn and receive 'your Arithmeticks without it. He replied, 'But 'I have not sufficient to find food for my self, 'wherefore I must now give over, to acquire ne-'cessaries for every day, and daily food; nor is 'it fit now to be taken up with Tables and fruit-'less Studies. Whereupon the young man, loth to 'be hindred from continuing his learning, replied, 'I will supply you, and in some manner require 'you; for I will give you for every Scheme 'three Oboli. And from thence forward became so much in love with Mathematicks, that he alone of all the Samians *was commended with Pythagoras, being likewise of the same name, son of* Eratocles. *His Aleiptick Commentaries are extant, and his directions to the Wrestlers of that time, to eat flesh instead of dried Figs*; which by some are falsly ascribed to Pythagoras *the son of* Mnesarchus, [as is formerly intimated] but by * Pliny, to one of that name, who professed Exercises of the Body, which agreeth with the relation of Jamblichus.

* lib. 23. cap. 7.

CHAP. VII.

How he went to Delus, Delphi, Creet, *and* Sparta.

(a) Cap. 5. & cap. 7.
(b) Clem. Strom. 7.
(c) Laert.

NOT long after, according to the relation of (a) *Jamblichus*, Pythagoras *went to* Delus, *where he was much admir'd by the Inhabitants, for that he prayed only at the Altar of* Apollo Genitor, *called* (b) *unbloody*, [which stands behind the horn Altar] (c) *because at it were offered only Wheat, and Barley, and Cakes; but no Victim, as* Aristotle *saith, in his Treatise concerning the* Delian Commonwealth*) and applied himself to none but the attendants thereof.*

(d) cap. 5. p. 40.
(e) Porph. p. 10, 11.
(f) Reading ἐν τῷ καλυμένῳ Τρίοπη Hesych. Τείοψ, ὁ ὑπὸ τῶν Πυτίων Δελφοῖς τριπους.
(g) Laert.

From Delus, (d) *Jamblichus* saith, he went to all places of Oracle. (e) At *Delphi* he writ an Elegy upon the Tomb of *Apollo*, whereby he declared, that *Apollo* was son of *Silenus*, but slain by *Pytho*, and buried in the place called (f) *Triops*, which was so named, for that the three daughters of *Triopas* mourned there for *Apollo*. At *Delphi* also ((g) *Aristoxenus* saith) *he learned many moral documents of* Themistoclea.

He

He went also to *Creet* and *Sparta*, to acquaint himself with the Laws of *Minos* and *Lycurgus*, which at that time were much renowned, as (b) *Justine* and (i) *Jamblichus* affirm.

(b) Lib. 20.
(i) Cap. 5.

Neither was *Creet* less famous for religious Ceremonies, being esteemed the place where *Jupiter* was born, and brought up by the *Corybantes* or *Dactyli* Priests of *Cybele*, in a Cave of the Mountain *Ida*, which they so named after that of *Phrygia*, whence they came. They had also a Tradition, that *Jupiter* was buried there, and shew'd his Tomb. Here (k) *Pythagoras* addressed himself to the Priests of *Morgus*, one of the *Idæan Dactyli*, who purify'd him with the *Ceraunian* Stone, [so called, in that it is conceived to be a piece of *Jupiter*'s Thunderbolt, and therefore perhaps used by his Priests.] In the morning he lay stretch'd forth upon his Face by the Seaside; at night by a River, Crown'd with a Wreath, made of the Wooll of a black Lamb.

(k) Porphyr. p. 11.

He also apply'd himself to the *Cretan Epimenides*, that Eminent Southsayer, as *Apuleius* calls him. (l) He went [(m) down] with him into the *Idæan* Cave, wrapt in black Wooll, and stayed there three times nine days, according to the Custom; and to *Jupiter*, and saw the Throne which is made yearly there for him, and writ an Epigram upon his Tomb, beginning thus:

(l) Porph. p. 11.
(m) Laert.

Here Zan deceased lyes, whom Jove they call.

Thus was he (n) initiated into all religious rites, as well *Grecian* as *Barbarian*.

(n) Laert.

CHAP. VIII.

How he went to Olympia *and* Phlius.

(a) AFter he had made enquiry into the Laws and Customs of *Creet* and *Lacedæmon*, he went down to the Olympicks Games; and having given a proof of his multiplicious Knowledge, to the Admiration of all *Greece*, being demanded what his Appellation was, he answer'd, That he was not *Sophos*, Wise; (for excellent men had already possess'd that Name) but, *Philosophos*, A lover of Wisdom.

(a) Val. Max.

But (b) some relate this, as done at *Sicyon*, in Discourse with *Leon*, Tyrant of that place; others at *Phlius*, distant from *Sicyon* a hundred Furlongs. Of the latter are (c) *Heraclides*, in his Book of the breathless Woman; and (d) *Socrates* in his Successions. The Testimony of *Heraclides* is thus delivered by (e) *Cicero*. He went (as is reported) to *Phlius*, and discoursed upon some things learnedly and copiously with *Leo* Prince of the *Phliasians*. *Leo* admiring his Wit and Eloquence, demanded in what Art he did most confide? 'He answered, That he knew 'no Art, but was a Philosopher. *Leo* wondring 'at the Novelty of the Name, asked, Who were 'Philosophers, and what difference there is be-'tween them and others? *Pythagoras* answered, 'That human Life seem'd to resemble that pub-'lick Convention, which is celebrated with the 'Pomp and Games of all *Greece*. For, as there, 'some by bodily Exercises aim at the Glory and 'Nobility of a Crown; others are led away by 'Gain in Buying or Selling: But there is a certain

(b) Laert. in Proœm.
(c) Laert. in Proœm.
(d) Laert. vit. Pyth.
(e) Tuscul. quæst. 5.

'kind of Persons, and that those of the better 'quality, who seek neither applause nor gain, 'but come to behold, and curiously observe what 'is done, and how. So we coming out of ano-'ther Life and Nature, into this Life, as out of 'some City into the full throng of a Publick 'Meeting, some serve Glory, others Riches: On-'ly some few there are, who despising all things 'else, studiously enquire into the Nature of 'things. These he called Enquirers after Wis-'dom, that is, Philosophers.

Thus, whereas Learning before was called *Sophia*, Wisdom; and the Professors thereof, *Sophoi*, Wise-men, (as *Thales* and the rest, of whom we treated in the first Book) *Pythagoras*, by a more modest Apellation, named it *Philosophy*, Love of Wisdom; and its Professors, *Philosophers*; conceiving the Attribute of Wise not to belong to Men, but to God only; that which is properly termed Wisdom, being far above human Capacity. (f) 'For tho' the frame of the whole 'Heaven, and the Stars which are carried about 'in it, if we consider their order, is fair; yet 'is it such, but by Participation of the primary 'Intelligible, who is a Nature of Numbers and 'Proportions, diffusing it self through the Uni-'verse, according to which, all these things are 'ordered together, and adorn'd decently. Wis-'dom therefore is a true Knowledge, conversant 'about those fair things which are first, and 'Divine, and Incommixt, and always the same; 'by Participation whereof, we may call other 'things Fair. But Philosophy is an Imitation of 'that Science, which likewise is an excellent 'Knowledge, and did assist towards the Refor-'mation of Mankind.

Laert. Proœm.

(f) Jam. cap.

CHAP. IX.

How he lived at Samus.

(a) HAving been a diligent Auditor and Disciple of all these, he returned home, and earnestly addicted himself to enquiry after such things as he had omitted; and first, [as soon as he returned to *Ionia*] (saith *Antiphon*, cited by (b) *Porphyrius*, repeated and enlarged by *Jamblicus*) he built [in his Country] within the City, a School, which even yet is called the Semicircle of *Pythagoras*, in which the *Samians*, when they would consult about publick Affairs, Assemble; chusing to enquire after things Honest, Just, and Advantageous in that place, which he, who took care of them all, had erected. Without the City he made a Cave, proper for his Study of Philosophy, in which he lived for the most part Day and Night, [and discoursed with his Friends] and made enquiry into the most useful part of Mathematicks, taking the same course as *Minos* Son of *Jupiter*. And so far did he surpass all whom he taught, that they for the smallest Theorems were reputed great Persons.

(a) Jam. cap 5. pag. 40.

(b) Pag. 6.

Pythagoras now perfected the Science of the Celestial Bodies, and over-run it, with all Demonstrations Arithmetical and Geometrical. Nor this only, but he became much more admir'd for the Things he performed afterwards; for Philosophy had now received a great increase, and all *Greece* began to admire him; and the best

best and most studious Persons, for his sake, resorted to *Samus*, desiring to participate of his Institutions.

CHAP. X.

His Voyage to Italy.

Jamb. cap. 5, 6. (for these also are ill distinguisht.)

BUT *Pythagoras* being engaged by his Country-men in all Embassies, and constrained to be interested in their publick Negotiations, and perceiving that if he should comply with the Laws of his Country, and continue there, it would be hard for him to study Philosophy; for which Reason, all former Philosophers ended their Lives in foreign Countries. Weighing all these considerations, and to avoid civil Employments; or, as others say, declining the negligence of Learning, which at that time possess'd the *Samians*, departed into *Italy*, preferring that place before his Country, which contained most Persons, fervently desirous of Learning.

But before we speak of his Actions in *Italy*, it will be requisite, as well to settle the time of his coming, as the State of that Country, as it was at that time. It was a received Opinion amongst the more Ancient, but less Learned, *Romans*, That *Pythagoras* was Contemporary with King *Numa*. The occasion of that Tradition might perhaps arise from those Books, which were found in the Sepulcher of *Numa*, 805 years after his Death, as *Antius Valerius*, cited by *(a) Livy*; and *Cassius Hemina*, by *(b) Pliny*, relate; and supposed to contain Pythagorical Philosophy. But that Opinion is long since refuted, by the more Learned *Romans* and *Grecians*, *Cicero*, *Titus Livius*, *Dionysius Halicarnassæus*, *Plutarch*, and others.

(a) Decad. 4. lib. ult.
(b) Lib. 13. cap. 13.

They who have looked more strictly into the time of *Pythagoras*, seem to follow two different Accounts. *Jamblichus* saith, That he lived in *Egypt* 22 years, That he was carried from thence by *Cambyses*, That he lived in *Babylon* 12 years, That from thence he returned to *Samus*, being 56 years old; That from *Samus* he went into *Italy* in the 62d Olympiad, *Eryxidas*, a *Chalcidean*, being Victor at the Olympick Games: From whence it follows, that he went into *Egypt* about the third year of the 53d Olympiad; and that he was Born the second year of the 48th Olympiad; and that it was the 52d Olympiad, when he, in the 18th year of his Age, heard *Thales*, *Pherecydes* and *Anaximander*. This account seems to be followed by *Laertius*, *Porphyrius*, *Themistius*, *Suidas*, (from *Laertius*) and others, who affirm, he went from *Samus* into *Italy*, at what time *Polycrates* was Tyrant of *Samus*, conceiving it unfit for a Philosopher to live under such a Government: For by *(c) Diodorus*, *Pythagoras* is acknowledged in the 61st Olympiad, *Thericles* being Archon; by *(d) Clemens Alexandrinus*, about the 62d Olympiad, under *Polycrates*; and in the second year of the 64th Olympiad, *Polycrates* was betrayed and put to Death by *Oroetas*. This Account *Antilochus* also seems to follow, who reckons from the time of *Pythagoras* to the Death of *Epicurus* 312 years. *Epicurus* died in the second year of the 127th

(c) Excerpt. Vales, p. 241.
(d) Strom.

Clem. Strom. 1.

Olympiad; the 312th year upwards, is the first of the 49th Olympiad. Neither is *Livy* much different from this Computation, who makes him to come into *Italy*, *Servio Tullio regnante*, who died about a year or two before. And this Account might be the occasion of making him live to 90 years, as *Laertius* saith many do; and to 104 years, as the nameless Author of his Life in *Photius*, the year of his Death being according to *Eusebius*, the fourth of the 70th Olympiad.

But this Account may, with good Reason, be question'd; for if it be granted, (as by *Jamblichus* himself, and other good Authorities it is affirmed) that *Pythagoras* was in *Egypt* when *Cambyses* subdu'd it, and that he was carried away Captive by him into *Babylon*, the time of his going into *Italy* must of necessity be much later; for *Cambyses* invaded *Egypt* in the fifth year of his Reign, which is the third year of the 63d Olympiad, and the 223d year of *Nobonassar*, of which there is no question in Chronology. For that the seventh year of *Cambyses* is known to be the 225th year of *Nobonassar*; because *Ptolomy* in his *(e) Almegist* relates an Astronomical Observation, of a Lunar Eclipse at *Babylon*, on the 17th day of the Month *Pharenoth*, according to the *Egyptians*, which is with us the 16th of *July*, one hour before Midnight. From whence now it follows, that if he lived 22 years in *Egypt*, that then he went thither in the third year of the 58th Olympiad, and that if he staid in *Babylon* twelve years, he went into *Italy* about the end of the 66th Olympiad; and that if he were then 56 years old, he was not Born before the first year of the 53d Olympiad. And according to this Account, they who make him to live but 70 or 80 years, do not much differ in the time of his Death from them, who, according to the other Account, make him live so much longer; for they who give him most years, do not make him to dye later, but to be Born sooner.

(e) Lib. 5. c. 4

This Account they seem to follow, who affirm, *(f)* he went from *Samus* to *Italy*, for that he could not brook *Syloson* the Brother of *Polycrates*, on whom (being a private Person, after his Brother's Death) *Darius Hystaspis* afterward bestow'd the Tyranny of *Samus*, in requital of a Garment which *Syloson* had given him, before he came to the Empire. And thus perhaps is *(g) Strabo* to be understood, who saith, Pythagoras, *as they reported, in the time of* Polycrates, *seeing the Tyranny begun, forsook the City, and went from thence to* Egypt *and* Babylon, *out of Love to Learning; and returning home, and seeing that the Tyranny continued still, he went into* Italy, *where he ended his days*. By this Continuation of the Tyranny, seems to be meant the Reign of *Syloson*, who Ruled so Cruelly, that many Persons forsook the City, insomuch that it became a Proverb,

(f) Diod. in excerpt. Vales, pag. 241.

(g) Lib 14.

Strabo, ibid.

A Region vast
By Syloson laid waste.

With both these Accounts agree what *(h) Cicero* and *(i) Agellius* affirm, concerning his coming into *Italy*, that it was in the Reign of *Tarquinius Superbus*; but to neither can that of *(k) Pliny* be

(h) Tusc. quæst. 1.
(i) Lib. 17. cap. ult.
(k) Lib. 2. cap. 8.

be accommodated, who saith, That *Pythagoras observed the Nature of the Star* Venus *about the* 42d *Olympiad, which was of the City of* Rome *the* 142d *year*. There must therefore be either an Error in both the Numbers; or, which I rather believe, in *Pliny* himself, occasion'd, perhaps by mistaking *Tarquinius Priscus* (under whom they both fall) for *Tarquinius Superbus*, under whom *Pythagoras* flourished.

Tuſ. quæſt. lib. 4.

If therefore he came into *Italy* in the Reign of *Tarquinius Superbus*, the opinion of *Cicero* is to be received, that he was there when *Lucius Brutus* freed his Country; and upon the expulsion of *Tarquinius Superbus*, he and *Lucius Collatinus* were made the first Consuls, at which time the Dominion of the *Romans* extended not any way above six Miles from their City; and the Southern parts of *Italy* were chiefly inhabited by the *Grecians*, who at several times had there planted divers Colonies, whereof we shall only mention those which were more particularly concerned in the Actions of *Pythagoras*.

The most Ancient of these is *Metapontum*, seated in the Bay of *Tarentum*, betwixt *Heraclea* and *Tarentum*, built by *Nestor* and the *(l) Pylians*, a People of *Peloponnesus*. Long after were founded;

(k) Solin.

Catana, a City on the East-side of *Sicily*, betwixt *Messena* and *Syracuse*, Built by a Colony of *Chalcideans*, in the *(m)* 11th Olympiad.

(m) Euseb.
(n) Euseb.
(o) Strab.

Tarentum in *Italy*, in the *(n)* 18th Olympiad, Built *(o)* by the *Parthenians*, who were Children of the *Lacedæmonian* Women, Born in the absence of their Husbands, at the *Messanian* Wars; and therefore called *Parthenians* in reproach; which not brooking, they conspired against the *Lacedæmonian* People, but being betrayed and banished, came hither.

Crotona, a City in the Bay of *Tarentum*, Built in the *(p)* 19th Olympiad, *(q)* by a Colony of *Achæans*, under the Conduct of *Miscellus*, by whom named *Crotona*, at the Command of *Hercules*, in memory of *Croto*, his Host, whom having unwittingly Slain, he Buried there; This City, for being Built by the command of *Hercules*, engraved his Figure in their Coins.

(p) Euseb.
(q) Strab.

Sybaris, a City distant from *Crotona* 200 Furlongs, according to *Strabo*'s Account; but, as others conceive, more than twice so much; built at the same time *(r)* by a Colony of *Troezenians*, under the Conduct of *Iseliceus*, betwixt the two Rivers *Crathis* and *Sybaris*.

(r) Solin.

(s) Locri in *Italy*, built the 24th Olympiad, by the *Locrians*, a People of *Achaia*.

(s) Euseb.

(t) Agrigentum, an *Ionian* Colony, built by the *Geloans (u)* 108 years after their own Foundation. *(x) Gela* was built in the 45th year after *Syracusa*; *(y) Syracusa* in the 11th Olympiad: *Agrigentum* therefore in the 49th.

(t) Strab.l.6.
(u) Thucyd.l.6.
(x) Thucyd. ib.
(y) Euseb.

To these add, of less certain time, *Rhegium* in *Calabria*, built by the *Chalcedeans*. *Nimera* and *Tauromenium* in *Sicily*, Colonies of the *Zancleans*. Indeed so generally was the Pythagorical Doctrine received in these parts, that *(z) Jamblicus* affirms, *All* Italy *was filled with Philosophical Persons; and whereas before it was obscure, afterwards by Reason of* Pythagoras, *it was named* Μεγάλη Ἑλλὰς, Magna Græcia.

(z) Cap. 29.

CHAP. XI.

His Arrival at Crotona, *and upon what Occasion he first became Eminent there.*

HE came at first to *Crotona*, the State of which City in particular was this; *(a)* at the beginning, the *Crotonians* joyning with the *Sybarites* and the *Metapontines*, determined to expel the rest of the *Grecians* out of *Italy*. They first took the City *Syris*, and taking it ill that at their besieging *Syris*, the *Locrians* assisted the adverse Party, raised a War against them, related thus by *(b) Justin*: 'The *Locrians* being terrify'd, 'recurr to the *Spartans* for Refuge, and beg their 'aid. They opprest with a long War, bad them 'seek help of *Castor* and *Pollux*. Neither did the 'Ambassadors slight the Advice of the Associate 'City, but going into the next Temple, they 'sacrific'd, and implor'd the help of the Gods; 'having offered Victims, and obtained, as they 'thought, what they requested, no less joyful, 'than as if they were to carry the Gods them-'selves along with them, they made Couches 'for them in the Ship, and by a Fortunate Voy-'age, bring Comfort, instead of Relief, to their 'Country-men. This known, the *Crotonians* 'also send Ambassadors to the Oracle at *Delphi*, 'praying for Victory, and a happy Success of the 'War. Answer is made, that Enemies must be 'overcome in Vows first, before in Arms. They 'vow'd to *Apollo* the Tents of the Spoil. The '*Locrians* understanding the Vow of their Ene-'mies, and the Answer of the god, Vow'd the 'Ninths, and kept it secret, lest they might be 'out-done in Vowing. Being drawn forth into 'the Field, the *Crotonian* Army consisting of '120000 Soldiers; the *Locrians* beholding how 'small a Number they were, (for they had but '15000) gave over all hope of Victory, and 'unanimously resolved to die; and so great 'Courage did every Man take from Desparati-'on, that they conceived they should be Con-'querors, if they did not die unwillingly. But 'whilst they fought to die honourably, they 'overcame more fortunately; neither was there 'any

(a) Justin.l.20.

(b) Lib. 20.

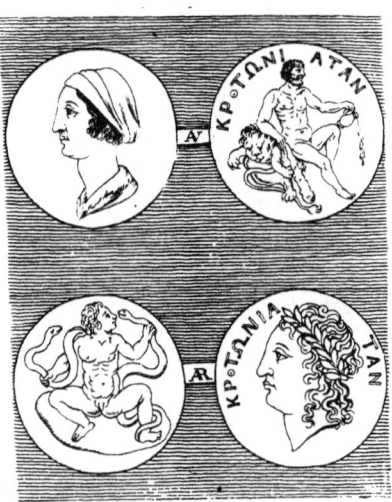

'any other cause of that Victory, than that they despaired of it. Whilst they were in sight, an Eagle never left the *Locrian* Army, but flew about it all the while, until they had gain'd the Victory. In the Wings of the Army also, two young men, armed after a fashion different from all the rest, of extraordinary bigness, on white Horses, in crimson mantles, were seen to fight; and, after the fight, were seen no more. This wonder was increased by the incredible swiftness of fame; for the very same day that this fight hapned in *Italy*, the Victory was reported at *Corinth*, *Athens*, and *Lacedæmon*. After this, the *Crotonians* used no military exercise, nor minded Arms; for they hated what they had taken up unsuccessfully, and would have changed their life into luxury, had it not been for *Pythagoras* the Philosopher. Hitherto *Justine*.

Porph. vit. Pythag. pag.

'As soon as he arriv'd in *Italy*, and came to *Crotona*, *Dicæarchus* saith, That upon the coming of a person, who was a great traveller, and excellent, and through a peculiar advantage of nature, prosperously guided by fortune, (for he was of a free presence, tall, graceful in his speech and gesture, and in all things else) the Citizens of *Crotona* were so taken with him, that having won the affections of the old men, who were the Magistrates of the City, and made an excellent and large discourse to the young men; he did the second time, by command from the Magistrates, make an exhortation to the young men, and afterwards to the boys, who came flocking out of the School to hear him; and lastly, to the Women, assembled to that purpose. The occasion and manner mentioned by *Plutarch* and *Porphyrius*, related thus by † *Jamblichus*.

* *Pag.*
† *cap. 8.*

'At this time, walking from *Sybaris* to *Crotona*, upon the Sea-side, he lighted upon some fisher-men; and whilst their Net was yet at the bottom loaden, he told them exactly the number of the fishes that they should draw up. And the men undertaking to do whatsoever he should command them, if it fell out accordingly, he required them to turn back again the fishes alive, after they had exactly numbred them; and which is more wonderful, not one of all the number, at that time, of the Fishes, whilst they were out of the water, died; he being present, and giving the Fishermen the price of the Fish, he departed to *Crotona*. But they divulged what was done, and, learning his name of the Boys, declared it to every one; which they hearing, desired to see the stranger, which was opportune to him; for he was of such an Aspect, that whosoever saw him could not but admire him, and conceive him to be the person that he really was.

CHAP. XII.

His Oration to the young Men.

Jambl. continueth.
‖ *The beginning of this Oration is in Laertius also.*

SOme few days after, he went into the publick Scool, and the young men flocking to him, it is said, that he made discourses to them, wherein in ‖ he exhorted them to respect their Elders, declaring, 'That in the World, and in Life, and in Cities, and in Nature, that which is precedent in time is more honourable than that which is subsequent; as, the East than the West, the Morning than the Evening, the Beginning than the End, Generation than Corruption; moreover, Natives than Strangers. In like manner, in Colonies, the Leader and Planter of Cities, and generally the Gods than Dæmons, Dæmons than Semi-gods, Heroes than Men: And of these (men) the causes of Generation, than the younger. This he said by way of induction, to make them have a greater esteem of their Parents, to whom, he said, they had as much obligation, as a dead man might owe to him that should raise him again to life. Moreover, that it was just to love above all, and never to afflict the first, and those who have done us greatest benefits: But Parents only, by the benefit of Generation, are the first, and Predecessors are the causes of all things that succeed rightly to their Successors; shewing, that they are nothing less beneficial to us than the gods, against whom it is not possible to offend in so doing; and the gods themselves cannot but in justice pardon those, who reverence their Parents equal to them; for it is from them that we learn to worship the Deity; whence *Homer* gives the King of the gods the same stile, caling him, *Father of gods and mortals*. And many other Fabulous Writers have delivered, that the chiefest of the gods were ambitious to make up the divided love of children, by a new Conjunction of Parents; and for this end, making a new supposition of Father and Mother, *Jupiter* brought forth *Minerva*; *Juno*, *Vulcan*, of a contrary sex to their own, that they might participate of that love which was more remote.

'Now all persons granting the judgment of the gods to be strongest, he demonstrated this particularly to the People of *Croto*, because that *Hercules* was of affinity with them, therefore they ought willingly to obey the injunctions of their Parents, since they understood, that this god, in Obedience to another elder than himself, underwent his labours, and presented to his father, as the Epinicium of his Actions, the Olympick Games.

'He declared likewise, that in their conversation to one another they should so behave themselves, that they might hereafter never become enemies to their friends, but might soon become friends to their enemies; as to their friends they should never become enemies, but to their enemies quickly become their friends. And that they should study in their behaviour towards their elders, their reverence towards their parents, and in their love to one another, their community towards their brethren.

This also is in Laertius.

'Furthermore he discoursed concerning Temperance, saying, That young men should make tryal of their nature at that time, in which they have their desires vigorous. Then he advised them, that it was worth their observation, that this only virtue was convenient both for Children, and Maids, and Women, and old Men, but especially for young Men. Further, this Virtue only declares, that they understand the goods of the Body and the Soul, seeing it preserves health, and a desire of the best Studies.

'This is manifest from the contrary; for the *Barbarians* and the *Grecians* contending about *Troy*, both parties, for the intemperance of one Man, fell into extraordinary Calamities; those in the War; these in their Voyage home. And God appointed ten years, and a thousand years, only for the punishment of this Injustice, foretelling by Oracle the taking of *Troy*, and the sending of the Virgins by the *Locrians*, to the Temple of *Minerva* the *Ilian*.

'He likewise exhorted the young Men to love learning, telling them, how absurd it were to judge Learning to be the most advantageous of all things, and to wish for it above all things, yet to bestow no time or pains in that Exercise: Especially, seeing the care of our Bodies is like evil Friends, which soon forsake us; but that of Institution, like the good, which stay with a Man till Death; procuring to some immortal Glory after Death.

'He framed many other things, partly out of History, partly out of Doctrines, shewing, that Learning was a common Nobility of those, who were first in every kind, for their Inventions were the Institutions of the rest. Thus is this naturally advantageous, that of other commendable things, some it is not possible to communicate to another, as Strength, Beauty, Health, Courage; some, whosoever imparts them to another, cannot have them himself, as Riches, Government, and the like: But for this, you may receive it of another, and yet the giver have nothing the less of it. Moreover some, a Man cannot gain if he would, he may receive Institution if he will: Then he may apply himself to the Affairs of his Country, not upon Self-confidence, but Institution; for by Education, Men differ from Beasts, *Greeks* from *Barbarians*, Freemen from Slaves, Philosophers from the Vulgar. Who have in general this advantage, that as of those who run swifter than others, there had been seven out of this their own City, at one Celebration of the Olympick Games; but of such as did excel in Wisdom, there had been found but seven in the whole World, and in the following times in which he lived, there was but one who did excel all others in Philosophy: For he called himself by that Name, (*Philosopher*) instead of *Sophos*, a wise Man.

Strab.

CHAP. XIII.

His Oration to the Senators.

Jamb. cap. 9.

THus he discoursed to the young Men in the School; but they relating to their Fathers what he had said, the Thousand-men summoned *Pythagoras* to the Court, and commending him for the advice he had given to their Sons, they commanded him, that if he had any thing which might benefit the People of *Crotona*, he should declare it to the Magistrates of the Commonwealth.

Lib. 8. cap. 18.

The *Crotonians* (saith *Valerius Maximus*) did earnestly entreat him, that he would permit their Senate, which consisted of a thousand Persons, to use his advice.

'Hereupon he first advised them to build a Temple to the Muses, that they might preserve their present Concord; for these Goddesses * have all the same Appellation, || and have a reciprocal communication and delight, chiefly in honours common to them all; and the *Chorus* of the Muses is always one and the same. Moreover, Concord, Harmony, Rythm, all those things which procure unanimity, are comprehended.

* Μοῦσαι q.
μοῦσαι Synef.
Dione, & Cass
dor. lib. 3. va
|| Ar. 1. Apost
ωπικοινωνία
πᾶσαι αἱ ἐν
ςήμαι ἀλλή
λαις.Cicer.qua
si cognation
quadam, &c.

'He likewise shewed them, that their power did not only extend to the excellent, but to the concord and harmony of Beings.

'Further he said, They ought to conceive, they received their Countrey as a *depositum* from their People: Wherefore they ought so to manage it, as being hereafter to resign up their trust with a just account to their own Children. That this will certainly be, if they be equal to all their Citizens, and excel other men in nothing more than in Justice; knowing, that every place requireth Justice. He show'd it out of the Mythology, that *Themis* hath the same place with *Jupiter*, as *Dice* with *Pluto*, and *Law* among Cities; so that he who did any thing unjustly in things under his charge, seemed to abuse the whole world, [*both above, below, and on Earth.*]

'That it is convenient in Courts of Judicature, that * none attest the Gods by Oath, but use to speak such things, as that he may be believed without Oath.

* To the same effect *Laertius*

'Moreover, That every one should so govern his Family, as that they should referr themselves to their own house, as to a Court of Judicature, and that they should be naturally affectionate to such as are descended of them, as having only of all creatures received the sense of this affection; and that they should converse with the Woman that is partner of their life: For, as some Men making Contracts with others, write them in Tables and Pillars; those with Wives, are in the Children. And that they should endeavour to be belov'd of those which come from them, not by Nature, of which they are not the cause, but by Election; for that kindness is voluntary.

'That they should likewise take care, that they know no Women but their Wives, and that the Wives do not adulterate the Race, through the carelessness and wickedness of their Husbands.

'Further, they must consider, they take the Wife from the Altar with Libations, as a Votaress, in the sight of the gods, and so to go in unto her, and that she become, in order and temperance, a pattern to those that live in the house with her, and to the Women of the City.

'And that they should see carefully that none transgress, lest, not fearing the punishments of Law, such as do unjustly lye hid; but having a respect to honesty in their carriage, they may be incited to justice.

'Further, he commanded, That in all their actions they should avoid Idleness; for there is no other good, than the opportunity in every action.

'He asserted, that it is the greatest of Injustices, to separate children and parents from each other.

'That he is to be thought the greatest Person, who can of himself foresee what is advantageous: The next to whom is he, who by those things which happen to other Men, observes what

'what is good for himself. The worst is he, who
'stays to Learn what is best, by the experience
'of suffering ill.

'He said, That they who are desirous of Glo-
'ry, shall not do amiss, if they imitate those
'who are crowned for Running; for they do no
'harm to their Adversaries, but desire that they
'themselves may obtain the Victory. And it be-
'seemeth Magistrates not to be rigid to those
'who contradict them, but to benefit those who
'obey them.

'He likewise exhorted every one that aimed
'at true Glory, to be indeed such, as he desired
'to appear to others; for it is not so sacred a
'thing to be advised by another, as to be praised
'for what is done; for one is only requisite
'to Men, the other much more used by the
'Gods.

'In Conclusion he said, That their City
'chanced to be built by *Hercules*. When he
'drove [*Gerion's*] Oxen through *Italy*, being
'injured by *Lacinius*, *Croto* coming to help him;
'not knowing him by reason of the Night, and
'thinking him to be one of his Enemies, he slew
'him; and then promising at his Grave, that he
'would build a City which should bear his Name,
'if ever he came to be a God; in gratitude for
'his kindness, he said, it behoved them to go-
'vern their Commonwealth justly.

'They hearing this, Built a Temple to the
'Muses, and put away the Concubines which
'they used to keep; and entreated him to Dis-
'course severally in the Temple of *Pythian Apol-*
* Mentioned by *lo* to the Boys, and in the Temple of * *Juno* to
Cicero and 'the Women.
others.

CHAP. XIV.

His Oration to the Boys.

Jamb. c. 10. HE being perswaded by them, discoursed to
the Boys in this manner; 'That they
'should neither begin Contumelies, nor return
'them to the Reproachers.

'And concerning παιδεία, (Institution) which
'is of the same Name as the time of their Youth,
'he commanded them diligently to pursue it; ad-
'ding, That to a well disposed Youth, it is easie
'to preserve honesty throughout all his Life;
'but to him that is not well disposed, it is
'hard at that time to continue it, but more
'difficult from an ill beginning to run to the
'end.

'Moreover he declared, That they are most
'beloved of the Gods, and for that reason in
'times of Death, they are sent forth to pray
'to the Gods for Rain, as if the Deity would
'soonest hear them. And they only being al-
'ways sanctified, had leave to live in the Tem-
'ple.

'For the same Reason, the Gods that are most
'kind to Men, *Apollo* and *Cupid*, are by all Pain-
'ters represented, as having that Age (of Boys.)
'It is likewise acknowledged, that the crowned
'Games were instituted for the sake of Boys;
'the *Pythian*, upon the Conquest of *Pytho* by a
'Boy; that in *Nemea*, for a Boy likewise; and
'that in *Isthmus*, upon the Death of *Archemorus*
'and *Melicertus*.

'Besides all this, at the building of the City
'*Croto*, *Apollo* told the Leader of the Colony,
'That he would give him a Progeny, if he con-
'ducted his Colony to *Italy*; whence they
'ought to reflect, that *Apollo* hath a particu-
'lar Providence for that Generation; and over
'Youth, even all the Gods. Wherefore they
'ought to study to be worthy of their Love,
'and employ themselves in hearing, that they
'may be able to speak. Moreover, if they
'would live to be old themselves, they should
'obey their Elders, and not contradict them;
'for by that means they will become esteemed
'worthy, not to be injured by those that are
'younger than themselves.

CHAP. XV.

His Oration to the Women.

IT is said, That he discoursed to the Women *Jamb.*cap.11.
concerning Sacrifices; first, that 'As when
'another Man were to pray for them, they
'would have him to be Honest and Good, be-
'cause the Gods hearken to such Men; in like
'manner ought they above all things so to behave
'themselves, as that they may indeed have the
'Gods attentive to their Prayers.

'Next, That they must present the Gods
'with such things, as they themselves make
'with their own hands; and without the help
'of Servants, offer them at the Altar; as Cakes,
'Wax and Incense: But that they present not
'the Deity with Slaughter and Death; nor that
'they offer so much at one time, as if they were
'never to come thither again.

'As concerning their Conversation towards
'their Husbands, he commanded them to con-
'sider, that Fathers did yield to their Daugh-
'ters, that their Husbands should be more
'beloved by them than their Parents. Where-
'fore it is fit, that either they contradict their
'Husbands in nothing, or then think they have
'the Victory, when they are over-ruled by them.

'Moreover he spared that celebrious Apoph-
'thegm concerning Coition, That for her who
'riseth from her own Husband, it is lawful to go
'to the Temples the same day; but for her who
'riseth from him that is not her Husband, never.

'He exhorted them likewise, throughout their
'whole life to speak well of others, and to take
'care that others speak well of them, and that they
'destroy not that good report which is given; nor
'confute those Mythographers, who (seeing the
'Justice of Women, in respect that they lend their
'Garments without witness, when any hath need
'of them, and that they made no Bargains and En-
'gagements) feigned three Women who made
'use of one Eye amongst them, because of their
'readiness to communicate. Which if ap-
'ply'd to Men, as if when one had received any
'thing, he should restore presently, or com-
'municate to his Neighbour, every one would
'say, there is no such thing, it being contrary to
'their Nature.

'Further, he who is said to be the wisest of all
'Persons, who disposed the Language of Men,
'and invented all Names, whether he were a
'God, or a Dæmon, or some divine Man, upon
consi-

'consideration, because the female Sex is most 'addicted to Piety) made every degree of Age 'synonymous with some God, and called the 'unmarried Woman, *Core*; her who is given to Man, * *Nympha*; her who hath Children, Mo- 'ther; her who hath Childrens Children, in the 'Dorick Dialect, *Maja*; to which respect of 'their Devotion) it agrees, that the Oracles at '*Dodona* and *Delphi*, are delivered by Wo- 'men.

*So supply the Text from Laertius, who cites something to the same purpose out of Timæus. Κόρη is a Name of Proserpina; Νύμφη, Bride, relates to the Nymphs; Μήτηρ, to Cybele mother of the Gods; Μαῖα, to Maja, mother of Mercury.

'Having thus commended their Devotion, he converted his Discourse to speak of Decency 'of Habit, that none should presume to wear any 'sumptuous Cloaths, but offer them all at *Juno*'s 'Temple (which amounted to) many millions of 'Garments.

'He is reported also to have said thus, That 'throughout the Country of the *Crotoniates*, the 'Virtue of a Man towards his Wife was much 'celebrated. *Ulysses* refusing Immortality at '*Calypso*'s hands, rather than to forsake *Penelope*. 'Let it be the part of the Wives to express their 'virtuous Loyalty towards their Husbands, that 'this praise may be Reciprocal.

CHAP. XVI.

His Institution of a Sect in Private and Publick.

Jamb. cap. 12.
Porphyr. p. 12.

BY this Discourse, *Pythagoras* gained no small Honour and Esteem in *Crotona*, and by means of that City, throughout all *Italy*.

Jamb. cap. 6.

At the first Oration which he made in *Crotona*, he attracted many Followers, insomuch that it is said, he gained six hundred Persons, who were by him not only won to the Philosophy which he profest, but following his Rules, became, as we call it, *Cœnobii*; and these were they who studied Philosophy. [They did put their Estates into one common Stock, and kept Silence five years, only hearing his Discourses, but not seeing him, until they were fully proved, and then they became of his Family, and were admitted to him.] There were the same *six hundred Persons*, who, *Laertius* saith, came to his nocturnal *Acroasis*, (perhaps meaning the Lectures through a Skreen during their Probation, for he adds) if any of them were thought worthy to see him, they wrote of it to their Friends, as having obtain'd a great matter. This Society *Laertius* calls, *his System*, (which *Cassiodorus* interprets, Colledge) *Agellius*, his Family.

Laert.

Besides these, there were many Auditors,

Jamb. cap. 6.
(a) Porp. p.13.

called *Acousmaticks*, whereof he gained [as (a) *Nicomachus* relates] two thousand by one Oration, which he made at his first coming into *Italy*, who [that they might not live from home] erected a large *Homacoceion*, [which *Clemens Alexandrinus* interprets to be the same as *Ecclesia*, Church, with us] whereinto were admitted also Boys and Women; and built Cities, and inhabited all that part of *Italy* which is called *Magno Græcia*, and received Laws and Statutes from him as divine Precepts, without which they did not any thing; they lived together unanimously, praised by all, and applauded as happy by such as lived round about them.

Strom. 1.

Thus *Pythagoras* distinguished those whom he admitted, according to their several merits; for it was not fit that all should partake alike, being not of a like Nature; nor fit that some should receive all the Learning, others none, for that would have been contrary to his Community of all, and to his Equality. He therefore, of the Discourses which he made, communicated to every one that part which was proper for him; and distributed his Learning so, as that it might benefit every one according to his Capacity; and observing the Rules of Justice, in giving to every one that share of the Discourse which they deserved; calling, upon this account, some *Pythagoreans* (those of the *System*) some *Pythagorites*, (those of the *Homacoceion*) as we call some *Atticks*, some *Atticists*. Dividing them thus aptly into two Names, he appointed one part to be γνήσιος, Genuine, the other he ordered to be Imitators of them. As to the *Pythagoreans* he decreed, that all their Estates should be in common, and that they should lead their whole Lives together in Community; but the others he ordered to keep their Estates to themselves, yet to meet together. Thus was this Succession of both Parties constituted by *Pythagoras*, The Discipline which was observed by the more Genuine, the *Pythagoreans*, we shall remit, together with his Doctrine, to the end of his Life.

CHAP. XVII.

His Authority in Civil Affairs.

Porphyr. p. 14. and from him Jamb. cap. 7.

WHatsoever Cities in his Travels through *Italy* and *Sicily*, he found subjected to one another, (whereof some had been so of a long time, others of late) he infused into them a Resentment of Liberty by his Disciples, of whom he had some out of every City, he restored them to Liberty. Thus he freed *Crotona*, *Sybaris*, *Catana*, *Rhegium*, *Himera*, *Agrigentum*, *Tauromenium*, and some others, to whom he sent Laws by *Charondas* the *Catanæan*, and *Zaleucus* the *Locrian*, by means whereof they lasted a long time well governed, and were deservedly envied by their Neighbours. He wholly took away Dissention, not only from among his Disciples, and their Successors for many Ages after, but also from all the Cities of *Italy* and *Sicily*, both intestine and external Dissention. For he did frequently pronounce to all manner of Persons every where, whether many or few, an Apophthegm, with resembles a monitory Oracle of God, which was a kind of Epitome or Recapitulation of all that he taught. The Apophthegm was thus, *That we ought to avoid with our utmost endeavour, and to amputate with Fire and Sword, and all other means from the Body, Sickness; from the Soul, Ignorance; from the Belly, Luxury; from a City, Sedition; from a Family, Discord; from all Things, Excess:* By which he did indulgently put every one in mind of his best Doctrines.

Yet is he reported to have been the occasion of the War between the *Sybarites* and the *Crotonians*, which ended in the total Subversion of the *Sybarites*; the manner is thus related by *Diodorus*, *Siculus* and *Jamblichus*.

* When the *Grecians* built *Sybaris* in *Italy*, it soon came to pass, that through the goodness of the Soil, [tho' † *Athæneus* deny it to be Fertile]

* Diod. lib.12.
† Deip. lib.12.

'the

PART IX. PYTHAGORAS.

'the City became in a short time very rich; for
'being seated betwixt two Rivers, *Crathis* and
'*Sybaris*, (from which it took its name) and the
'Citizens possessing a large Country, they soon
'gathered together great Riches; and admitting
'many to be free of their Country, they arrived to
'such height, that they seemed far to excel all the
'rest of the inhabitants of *Italy*. [* But so luxuri-
'ous that they become infamous even to a proverb;
'and no less addicted to all other vices, insomuch
'that they, out of insolence, put to death thirty Am-
'bassadors of the *Crotonians*, and threw their bo-
'dies from the walls to be devoured by beasts.]
'The City was so populous, that it contained no
'less than 300000 persons. At that time *Telys* was
'chief Magistrate, who, accusing the greatest men,
'procured of the *Sybarites* to banish 500 of the
'richest Citizens, and to confiscate their goods.
'These banished men went to *Crotona*, and
'there (after the manner of Suppliants) fled
'to the Altars erected in the *Forum*. Here-
'upon *Telys* sent Ambassadors to the *Crotonians*,
'to declare, that they should either deliver up
'the banished men, or expect war. [These
'*Sybarate*-Ambassadors had been instrumental in
'the murther of some friends of *Pythagoras*, per-
'haps some of the thirty *Crotonians* whom they
'flew.] 'Amongst them, one there was, who
'had killed some of them with his own hands;
'another was son to one of the same murtherers,
'who was dead. Moreover, he was of those
'kinds of persons, who, being opprest with
'want, stir up sedition, that they may take oc-
'casion thereby to fall on the goods of others.
'These *Sybarites* came to *Pythagoras*, and blamed
'him; and one of them (which was he that had
'a hand himself in the death of his friends) de-
'manding a reason of his reproof, he said, That
'he did not give Laws. Whereupon they ac-
'cused him, as if he had made himself *Apollo*,
'and especially for that before, upon a question
'being asked, Why these things were so, he asked
'him that propounded the question, Whether,
'when *Apollo* delivered his Oracles, he would
'require him to render a reason? The other de-
'riding, as he thought, those discourses, in
'which *Pythagoras* declared the return of the
'Soul, and telling him, That when he went in-
'to the other world, he would give him a Letter
'to carry to his Father, and desired him to bring
'an Answer of it when he came back. I shall
'not, replied *Pythagoras*, go to the place of the
'wicked, where murtherers are punished. The
'Ambassadors having thus reviled him, and he
'going to the Sea-side, and washing himself,
'many following him, one of those who advised
'the *Crotonians*, said, When he had sufficiently
'spoken against all the other things that they did,
'at last he accused them especially, for offering
'to oppose and abuse *Pythagoras*, of whom when
'heretofore, as fables report, beasts could speak,
'no one of them durst ever speak an ill word.
'*Diodorus* saith, that a Councel being called,
'and it being put to the question, Whether they
'should deliver up the † *Iraliotes* to the *Sybarites*,
'or undergo a War with an enemy more power-
'ful than themselves? The Senate and People
'made some doubt, and the People first inclined
'to the delivery of the Suppliants, rather than
'endure the War. But afterwards, *Pythagoras*

'the Philosopher advising them to protect the
'Suppliants, they changed their opinion, and
'determined to fight in their defence. The *Sy-
'barites* came into the Field, with an Army of
'three hundred thousand; the *Crotonians* had
'but one hundred thousand. They were led by
'*Milo* the Wrestler, who at the first onset himself
'put to flight that wing of the Army which was
'opposite to him; for he was of invincible
'strength. 'This man having Courage answera-
'ble to his Strength, had been six times Victor at
'the Olympick Games, and when he began this
'Fight, was crowned with Olympick Wreaths,
'wearing, like *Hercules*, a Lion's Skin, and a
'Club, and obtaining the Victory for his Coun-
'try-men, was much admired by them. [The
'*Crotonians* likewise made use of a Stratagem,
'whereby they got the day: * The *Sybarites* were
'so much addicted to Luxury, that they taught
'their Horses to dance at Feasts. This the *Croto-
'nians* knowing, (as *Aristotle* relates) in the midst
'of the Fight, they commanded some Pipers,
'whom, to that purpose, they had brought along
'with them, to play dancing Tunes. The Horses,
'as soon as they heard the Musick, not only fell
'a dancing, but carried their Riders violently
'over to their Enemies.] 'Thus the *Sybarites* be-
'ing put to Flight, the *Crotonians* spared none
'that they took, but put all to the Sword,
'whereby the greater part of the Army was Slain,
'and the City, after a dishonourable surrender,
'laid waste. This, according to *Diodorus*, hap-
'pened 63 years before the second of the 83d O-
'lympiad, which falls upon the first year of the 68th
'Olympiad.

Agrigentum was by his means freed from the
Tyranny of *Phalaris*, in this manner: '† When
'*Pythagoras* was detained by *Phalaris*, a most
'cruel Tyrant, [**with whom he stayed six*
'*Months*] and *Abaris* the *Hyperborean*, a wise
'Person, came to converse with him, and asked
'him Questions, particularly concerning sacred
'Rites, Images, Divine Worship, Providence of the
'Gods, as well of those in Heaven, as conver-
'sant about the Earth, and such like demands;
'*Pythagoras*, as being highly inspired, answered
'him with much Truth and Perswasion, inso-
'much as he drew the Standers by to his Opini-
'on. Whereupon *Phalaris* seeing the People
'taken with him, was angry with *Abaris* for
'praising *Pythagoras*. He grew fierce against
'*Pythagoras* himself, and at last came to that
'heighth, as to speak all Blasphemies against the
'Gods, as were possible for such a kind of Per-
'son. But *Abaris* acknowledged himself thank-
'ful to *Pythagoras* for these things. He learned
'next of him, that all things depend upon
'Heaven, and are disposed of from thence,
'which he collected, as from many other things,
'so especially from the efficacy of Sacrifices.
'Far therefore was he from thinking, that *Py-
'thagoras*, who taught him these things, was a
'deceiver, but he rather admir'd him, as a Per-
'son supernaturally inspir'd. *Phalaris*, in an-
'swer hereunto, deny'd plainly and openly all
'things that were done in sacred Rites. Where-
'upon *Abaris* transferred his Discourse from
'these things, to such as appear manifestly to all
'Men, and by the Divine Operations which are
'in all Extremities as in extraordinary Wars,
'and

Margin notes:
* *Athen. Deip. lib. 12.*
Jambl. cap. 30.
Lib. 12. Olymp. 83. 2.
† *So were the Greeks that inhabited Italy called, not the Natives. The same difference betwixt Siciliotes and Sicilians.*
* *Athen. Deip. lib. 12.*
† *Jamb. c. 32.*
* *Tzetzes Chiliad. 6. 31.*

'and in incurable Diseases, Destruction of Fruit, Transmission of Pestilence from Country to Country. By these difficult irremediable Causes, he endeavoured to prove, that there is a Divine Providence, which over-ruleth all human Hope and Power. But *Phalaris* impudently opposed it. Hereupon *Pythagoras*, knowing that that Day would be fatal to *Phalaris*, spoke very freely; and looking upon *Abaris*, said, That there is a passage from Heaven to the Aerial and Terrestrial parts; and did likewise Discourse scientifically, concerning the dependance of all things upon Heaven, and did irrefragably demonstrate the free Power of the Soul, and proceeded to shew the perfect Operation of the Reason, and of the Mind. Then he spoke boldly concerning Tyranny, and all excess of Fortune, all Injustice, all Covetousness, strongly maintaining that they are all nothing worth. After this, he made a Divine Exhortation concerning the best Life, and made a resolute Opposition against the worst, and did most plainly deliver the Doctrine, concerning the Power and Passions of the Soul; and which was more than all these, he demonstrated, that the Gods are not the causes of Ills; and that Diseases and Passions are Seeds of the Intemperance of the Body; and reprehended *Mythographers* and *Poets* for such things as they had falsly delivered; and sharply reproved *Phalaris*, and shewed what the Power of Heaven is, and how great, by its Operations. As concerning Infliction of Punishment by Law, he gave many instances thereof, and clearly shewed the difference betwixt Man, and other living Creatures. He likewise scientifically discoursed concerning intrinsical and enunciative Reason, and concerning the Mind, and the Knowledge proceeding from it, with many other moral Documents dependent thereon. He treated of what things are useful in Life, making an Exhortation to the pursuit of the useful, and dehorting from the hurtful; and that which is most of all, he made a distinction between the things done according to Fate, and according to the Mind, and of those which are done according to Necessity, and according to Decree. Moreover he discoursed concerning *Dæmons*, and the Immortality of the Soul, much and wisely; whereof we shall have occasion to speak elsewhere, and shew, that these things do conferr most to fortitude, seeing that he himself in the midst of all Dangers, did with a constant mind discourse Philosophy, and arm himself against Fortune; as also for that he slighted and contemned the Person that attempted to hurt him, and despised the fear of Death, and all human Contingencies, nor was he at that instant any thing concerned for them. Indeed (continues *Jamblichus*) it is manifest, that he was nothing troubled with the fear of Death, but had a far more noble design, the freeing of *Sicily* from the Oppression of Tyranny. That it was he who did it, is manifest from the Oracle of *Apollo*, which declared, That *Phalaris*, when his Subjects grew better and more Unanimous, should lose his Authority; which they did at the coming of *Pythagoras*, through his Exhortations and Instructions. But a clearer Evidence hereof is from the time: For that very day that *Phalaris* went about to bring *Pythagoras* and *Albaris* into danger of Death, he was himself Slain. The manner thus related by * *Tzetzes*: It chanced that a Hawk pursued a great flight of Pigeons; which *Phalaris* seeing, said to those that stood by him, Behold, Friends, how much an ignoble Fear can do; for if but one of all these Pigeons would turn again, it would presently give a stop to the Pursuer. This Speech an old Man that was present no sooner heard, when taking up a Stone he threw it at *Phalaris*; and the rest following his Example, did the like. Some say they stoned him to Death; others, that they put him into Chains, and wrapt him in a sheet of Lead, wherein he died miserably.'

* *Chil.* 6. 30.

To the *Locrians*, besides *Charondas* and *Zeleucus*, already mentioned, he sent † *Timarus* also, to make Laws for them.

† *Jam.* p. 103. and 154.

To the *Rheginenses* he sent upon the same Employment * *Theatetus*, *Helicaon*, *Aristocrates* and *Phytius*.

* *Jam.* p. 103.

Thus, as † *Porphyrius* saith, *Pythagoras* and his Friends were a long time so much admired in *Italy*, that many Cities committed themselves to be governed by them.

† Pag. 36.

CHAP. XVIII.

Wonders related of Him.

IF we may credit (saith (a) *Porphyrus*, and from him (b) *Jamblichus*) what is related of him, by ancient and creditable Authors, his Commands had an Influence even upon irrational Creatures, for he laid hold of the *Daunian* Bear, which did much hurt to the People thereabout, and having stroaked her awhile, and given her Maza and Fruits, and Sworn her, that She never more touch any living Creature, he let her go. She straightway hid her self in the Hills and Woods, and from thenceforward never assaulted any living Creature.

(a) Pag. 15. (b) Cap. 13.

Seeing an Ox at *Tarentum* in a Pasture, wherein grew several things, cropping green Beans, he came to the Neat-herd, and counselled him to speak to the Ox, that he should abstain from the Beans. But the Neat-herd mocking him, and saying, He could not speak the Language of Oxen; he himself went to him, and whispering in the Ear of the Ox, he not only refrained immediately from Beans at that time, but from thenceforward would never touch any, and lived many years after about *Juno*'s Temple at *Tarentum*, till he was very old; and was called the sacred Ox, eating such Meats as every one gave him.

Porphyr. p. 15. Jamb. cap.

An Eagle flying over his head at the Olympick Games, as he was by chance discoursing to his Friends concerning *Auguries* and *Omens*, and divine Signs, and that there are some messages from the Gods to such Men as have true Piety towards them; He is said [(c) *by certain Words to have stopt here, and*] to have caused her to come down; and after he had stroaked her awhile, he let her go again. This perhaps was that white Eagle, which *Jamblichus* reports he stroaked at *Croto*, and She endured it quietly. For the *Crotonians* instituted Games, which they called *Olympick*, in Emulation of the *Grecians*.

Porphy. pag. 16. Jamb. cap.

(c) Plin. in Na. ma.

A

† Pag. 18. A River (which † *Porphyrius* calls *Caucasus*, *Apollonius* Πόταμον κατὰ Σαμον; *Laertius* and *Jamblichus*, *Nessus*; *Ælian*, *Cosa*; St. *Cyril*, *Causus*) as he passed over it, with many of his Friends, spoke to him, and said with a plain clear voice, χαῖρε Πυθαγόρη. Hail *Pythagoras*.

Porph. pag. 18.
Jamb. In one and the same day, almost all affirm, that he was present at *Metapontum* in *Italy*, and at *Tauromenium* in *Sicily*, with the Friends which he had in both places, and discoursed to them in a publick Convention, when as the places are distant many *Stadia* by Sea and Land, and many days journeys asunder. *Apollonius* relates this, as done at *Croto* and *Metapontum*.

Plut. in Numa.
Laert.
Porph. p. 18. At the publick Solemnity of the Olympick Games, he stood up and shewed his golden thigh; as he did in private to *Abaris*, to confirm him in the opinion, that he was *Hyperborean Apollo*, whose Priest *Abaris* was.

Porphyr. p. 18. A Ship coming into the Harbour, and his Friends wishing they had the goods that were in it: Then (saith *Pythagoras*) you will have a dead body: And when the Ship came at them, they found in it the Body of a dead Man.

Jamb. cap. To one who much desired to hear him, he said, That he would not discourse until some sign appeared. Not long after, one coming to bring News of the Death of a white Bear in *Caulonia*, he prevented him, and related it first.

Anon. de vita Pyth. apud Phot.
† Laert. They affirm he foretold many things, and that they came to pass; insomuch that † *Aristippus* the *Cyrenæan*, in his Book of Physiologick, saith, He was named *Pythagoras*, from speaking things as true as *Pythian Apollo*. He foretold an Earthquake by the Water which he tasted out of a Well; and foretold, That a Ship, which was then under sail with a pleasant gale, should be cast away.

At *Sybaris* he took in his hand a Serpent of deadly biting, and let it go again. And at *Tyrrhenia* he took a little Serpent, and biting it, kill'd it with his Teeth.

Porph. p. 18, 19. A thousand other more wonderful and Divine things are related constantly, and with full agreement of him; so that, to speak freely, more was never attributed to any, nor was any more eminent. For his Predictions of Earthquakes most certain are remembred, and his immediate chasing away of the Pestilence, and his suppression of violent Winds and Hail, and his calming of Storms, as well in Rivers as upon the Sea, for the ease and safe passage of his Friends, from whom *Empedocles*, and *Epimenides*, and *Abaris* learning it, often performed the like, which their Poems plainly attest. Besides, *Empedocles* was sirnamed *Alexanemos*, the chaser away of Winds; *Epimenides*, *Cathartes*, the Lustrator; *Abaris*, *Æthrobates*, the Walker in the Air; for, riding upon an Arrow of *Hyperborean Apollo*, which was given him, he was carried in the Air over Rivers and Seas, and inaccessible places, which some believed to have been done by *Pythagoras*, when he discoursed with his Friends at *Metapontum* and *Tauromenium* upon the same Day.

In Nubes. pag. 169. To these add his trick with a Looking-glass, as the Scholiast of *Aristophanes* calls it, who describes it thus: The Moon being in the Full, he wrote whatsoever he pleased in blood upon a Looking-glass, and telling it first to the other party, stood behind him, holding the Letters towards the Moon; whereby he who stood betwixt him and the Moon, looking steadfastly upon her, read all the Letters which were written in the Looking-glass in the Moon, as if they were written in her.

But these things, some, even of the Ancients, have imputed to Goetick Magick, as *Timon*, who terms him, Γοητα, a Magician; others, to imposture, as appears by this Relation of *Heraclides*, and the Scholiast of *Apollonius*: † When he came into *Italy*, he made a Vault under ground, and charged his Mother [* to give out that he was dead, and] to set down in a Table-book all things that hapned, expressing the times punctually. Then he went down [and shut himself up in the Vault], and his Mother did as he ordered her, until such time as he came up again. After a while *Pythagoras* came up, lean and withered; and coming into the Congregation, declared, That he was returned from the *Inferi*, and related to them what was done there] and told them many prodigious Stories concerning the *Palingenesie*, and the things of the *Inferi*; telling the living news of their dead friends, with whom, he said, he met in the *Inferi*.] † *Hieronymus* relates, That he saw there the Soul of *Hesiod* bound with Brass to a Pilar, shrieking; and that of *Homer* hung up on a Tree, encompassed by Serpents, for the Fables which he had raised concerning the gods: Those likewise tormented who used not the company of their own Wives. For this he was much honoured by the *Crotonians*. They being much moved at what he said, wept and lamented, and hereupon conceived such an esteem of *Pythagoras*, as being a Divine Person, that they sent their Wives to him to be Instructed in his Doctrine, which Women were called *Pythagoreans*. Thus *Hermippus*. The Scholiast adds, [Hereby he raised an Opinion concerning himself, That, before the *Trojan* War, he was *Æthalides*, the Son of *Mercury*; then *Euphorbus*, then *Hermotimus*, then † *Pyrrhus*, a *Delian*; lastly, *Pythagoras*.] And, as *Laertius* saith, in his Writings he reported of himself, That he had come from the *Inferi* to Men, 207 years since. Of this more in his Doctrine, Part. 2. Chap. 5. Sect. 10.

† Heraclides apud Laertium.
* Schol. Apol.

† Laert.

† So read not *Pythius*.

CHAP. XIX.

His Death.

THE time of *Pythagoras* his Death hath been formerly touched; it was, according to *Eusebius*, in the Fourth year of the 70th Olympiad, after he had lived, as † *Justine* saith, at *Crotona* 20 years. The occasion is differently related. *Laertius* thus.

† Lib. 20.

Pythagoras died in this manner: As he sate in counsel together with his Friends, in the House of *Milo*, it happened that the House was set on fire by one who did it out of Envy, because he was not admitted. Some affirm, the *Crotonians* did it out of fear of being reduced to a Tyranny. *Pythagoras* running away, was overtaken; coming to a Place full of Beans, he made a stop, saying, It is better to be taken, than to tread; and better to be killed, than to speak.

speak. So the pursuers slew him. In the same manner died most of his Disciples, about Forty in number; some few only escaped, of whom were *Archytas* the *Tarentine*, and *Lysis*, of whom we spake before. *Dicæarchus* saith, That *Pythagoras* fled to the Temple of the Muses at *Metapontum*, and died † for want of Food, having lived there forty days without eating. *Heraclides*, in his Epitome of the Lives of *Satyrus*, relates, That having buried *Pherecydes*, he returned to *Italy*, where finding the Faction of *Cyclo* (prevalent), he departed to *Metapontum*, and there starved himself, not willing to live any longer. *Hermippus* saith, That the *Agrigentines* and *Syracusians* warring against one another, *Pythagoras*, with his Friends, went to the *Agrigentines*, and was Head of them: But they being vanquished, and he flying to a field of Beans, was there slain; the rest (being thirty-five) were burn'd at *Tarentum*, for intermeddling with the Governors and Rule of the Commonwealth.

† Ἀσιτήσαντα. So in *Porphyrius*, pag. 39. σωπεις τῶν ἀναγκαίων, ill rendred, *canicorum inopia*.

Jamblichus, from *Aristoxenus*, and others, gives a more particular account: There were (*saith he*) some, who oppugned these Men, and rose up against them. That this Conspiracy happened in the absence of *Pythagoras*, is acknowledged by all; but they disagree concerning his Journey: Some say, he was gone to *Pherecydes*, the *Syrian*; others, to *Metapontum*. The Causes of this Conspiracy are diversly related also; one is said to have proceeded from the Men, who were called *Cylonians*, thus: *Cylo*, a *Crotonian*, who, in Race, and Honour, and Wealth, excelled all the rest of the Citizens, but otherwise of a harsh, violent, turbulent, and tyrannical Humour, was exceedingly desirous to participate of the *Pythagorick* Institution; and coming to *Pythagoras*, who was now very old, he was repulsed for the Reasons aforesaid. Hereupon there arose a great Contest, *Cylo* and his Friends opposing *Pythagoras* and his Friends: And so eager and violent was the Malice of *Cylo* and his party, that it extended even to the last of the *Pythagoreans*. *Pythagoras* therefore for this reason departed to *Metapontum*, where it is said that he died. The *Cylonians* (so called) continued to exercise their hatred and enmity towards the *Pythagoreans*: For a while, the integrity of the *Pythagoreans*, and the kindness of the Cities (which was so great as to be governed by them) was prevalent; but at last they so plotted against the Men, as that surprising them, assembled in the House of *Milo*, at *Crotona*, consulting about Military Affairs, they burned them all, except two, *Archippus* and *Lysis*, who being youthful and strong, escaped out of doors. This falling out, and the Cities not taking any notice of the misfortune, the *Pythagoreans* gave over their business. This happened from two Causes, as well by reason of the unconcernment of the Cities (for they had no regard of the Murther, to punish the Authors thereof) as by reason of the Death of the most excellent Persons, two only of them were saved, both *Tarentines*; of whom, *Archippus* retired to *Tarentum*; but *Lysis*, out of hatred of the neglect they had received from the Cities, departed into *Greece*, and lived at *Achaia* in *Peloponnesus*: Thence, upon a particular design, he removed to *Thebes*, where *Epimanondas* heard him, and called him Father: There he died. The rest of the *Pythagoreans*, all but *Architas* the *Tarentine*, forsook *Italy*, and assembling at *Rhegium*, they lived there together. But in progress of time the management of publick Affairs decayed. The most eminent of these were *Phanto*, and *Echecrates*, and *Polymnastus*, and *Diocles* (both *Phliasians*), and *Xenophilus*, a *Chalcidean* of *Chalcis* in *Thrace*; these preserved the Customs and Doctrines from the beginning, but with the Sect it self at last they were wholly extinguished. This is related by *Aristoxenus*.

Nicomachus agreeth in all things with this Relation, except in that he saith, This Insurrection happened at what time *Pythagoras* was gone to *Delus*, to visit *Pherecydes*, who was sick of a *Phthiriasis*; then were they stoned and burned by the *Italiotes*, and cast forth without burial. Hitherto *Jamblichus*.

With these also agreeth the Relation of *Neanthes*, thus delivered by † *Porphyrius*. † Pag. 37.

Pythagoras and his Friends having been a long time so much admired in *Italy*, that many Cities committed themselves to them, at last they became envied, and a Conspiracy was made against them in this manner: *Cylo*, a *Crotonian* (who, in Extract, Nobility, and Wealth, exceeded all the rest of the Citizens, but otherwise was of a violent, rigid, and tyrannical Disposition, and one that made use of the multitude of his Friends to compass his unjust ends) as he esteemed himself worthy of all excellent things, so most particularly to partake of the Pythagorick Philosophy; he came to *Pythagoras*, and much extolled himself, and desired his Conversation. But *Pythagoras* presently observing the Nature and Manners of the Person, and perceiving by the signs which he observed in the bodies of such as came to him, what kind of disposition he was of, bad him depart, and go about his business. Hereat *Cylo* was not a little troubled, taking it for a great affront, being of himself a person of a rough violent Spirit. Therefore calling his Friends together, he began to accuse *Pythagoras*, and to conspire against him and his Disciples. Whereupon, as some relate, the Friends of *Pythagoras* being gathered together in the House of *Milo* the Wrestler, *Pythagoras* himself being absent (for he was gone to *Delus*, to visit *Pherecydes* the *Syrian*, formerly his Master, who was desperately fallen sick of a *Phthiriasis*, and to attend on him), they set the House on fire, and burned and stoned them all, except two who escaped the fire, *Archippus* and *Lysis*, as *Neanthes* relates, of whom, *Lysis* went into *Greece*, to *Epymanondas*, whose Master he had formerly been.

But *Dicæarchus*, and other more accurate Authors affirm, That *Pythagoras* himself was there present when this Conspiracy was perpetrated, for *Pherecydes* died before he left *Samus*. Of his Friends, Forty being gathered together, were beset in a House, most of them going dispersedly to the City, were slain. *Pythagoras*, his Friends being taken, first escaped to the *Caulonian* Haven, thence went to the *Locrians*. The *Locrians* sent some old men to the borders of their Countrey, who gave him this answer; We have heard, *Pythagoras*, that thou art a person wise, and of great worth; but

Porphyr. p. 38

but we have nothing in our Laws that is reprehensible, and therefore we will endeavour to preserve them. Go to some other place, taking of us whatsoever you have need of. Hereupon leaving the City of the Locrians, he sailed to *Tarentum*, where receiving the same entertainment he had at *Croto*, he went to *Metapontum*, for great Seditions were raised against him in every part, which are remembred by the Inhabitants at this day, who recount the Seditions against the *Pythagoreans*, as they call them; for all that Faction which sided with *Pythagoras* were called *Pythagoreans*. In the *Metapontine* Faction, *Pythagoras* is said to have died, flying to the Temple of the Muses, and staying there forty days, through want of necessaries.

Others relate, That when the house wherein his Friends used to meet, was fired, his Friends threw themselves into the fire, to make a way for their Master, spreading their Bodies like a bridge upon the first; and that *Pythagoras*, escaping out of the burning, destitute of all his Friends, for grief ended his days.

With these Men, oppressed with this Calamity, failed their Knowledge also, which till then they had preserved secret and concealed, except some things difficult to be understood, which the Auditors that lived without (*the Skreen*), repeated by heart. *Lysis* and *Archippus* escaping, and as many as were at that time in other parts, preserved some little sparks of Philosophy, obscure and difficult to be found out; for being now left alone, and much grieved at the perpetration of that wickedness, fearing lest the Name of Philosophy should be quite extinguish'd amongst Men, and that for this reason the gods would be angry with them, they made some summary Commentaries; and having reduc'd the Writings of the Ancients, and those which they remembred, into one Body, every one left them in the place where they died, charging their Sons, Daughters, and Wives, that they should not communicate them to any out of their own Family. Thus privately continuing it successively to their Successors, they observed it a long time. And for this reason, saith *Nicomachus*, we conjecture, that they did purposely avoid friendship with Strangers; and for many Ages they preserved a faithful constant friendship amongst themselves.

† *Porph*. p.36. † *Moderatus* saith, That this (Pythagorick Philosophy) came at last to be extinguished, first, because it was ænigmatical; next, because their Writings were in the *Dorick* Dialect, which is obscure, by which means, the Doctrines delivered in it were not understood, being spurious and misapprehended, because (moreover) they who publish'd them were not *Pythagoreans*. Besides, *Plato*, *Aristotle*, *Speusippus*, *Aristoxenus*, and *Xenocrates*, as the *Pythagoreans* affirm, vented the best of them, as their own, changing only some few things in them; but the more vulgar and trivial, and whatsoever was afterwards invented by envious and calumnious persons, to cast a contempt upon the *Pythagorean* School, they collected and delivered as proper to that Sect.

Jamb. cap. 35. pag. 211. But forasmuch as *Apollonius* gives a different Account of these things, and adds many things which have not yet been spoken, let us give his Narration also concerning the Insurrection against the *Pythagoreans*. He (therefore) saith, That the *Pythogoreans* were envied from their very Childhood; for the People, as long as *Pythagoras* discoursed with all that came to him, loved him exceedingly; but when he apply'd himself only to his Disciples, they undervalued him. That he should admit Strangers, they well enough suffered: But that the Natives of the Countrey should attribute so much to him, they took very Ill, and suspected their meetings to be Contrivements against them. Besides, the Young Men being of the best rank and estate, it came to pass, that after a while, they were not only the chief Persons in their own Families, but governed even the whole City, they becoming many, as to a Society, (for they were above three hundred Persons) but being a small part as to the City, which was not ordered according to their Manners and Institutions. Notwithstanding, as long as they possessed the place they were in only, and *Pythagoras* lived there, the City followed the Original Goverment thereof, though much perplexed, and watching an opportunity for change. But after they had reduced *Sybaris*, and that he departed, and they distributed the conquered Countrey into Colonies, as they pleased; at length, the concealed hatred broke forth, and the multitude began to quarrel with them. The Leaders of this dissention were those who were nearest ally'd to the *Pythagoreans*. Many things that had past, grieved them, according as they were particularly affected; but one of the greatest was, that he only should be thought capable of disrespect. For the *Pythagoreans* used never to name *Pythagoras*; but whilst he lived, they called him, *Divine*; after Death, *the Man*: As *Homer* introduceth *Eumæus* mentioning *Ulysses*.

I to pronounce his Name, though absent, fear;
So great is my respect, and he so dear.

In like manner, not to rise out of bed, after the Sun's up, nor to wear a Ring, whereon the Image of God is engraved; but to observe the Sun, that they may adore his rising; and not to wear a Ring, lest they might chance to have it on at a Funeral, or carry it into any unclean place. Likewise, not to do any thing without premeditation, nor any thing whereof they could not give a good account; but that in the Morning they should consider what they were to do, and at Night they should make a recollection thereof, as well to ponder the things themselves, as to exercise the Memory. Likewise, if any one of that Community had appointed to meet another in any place, he should stay there Day and Night until the other came. The *Pythagoreans* likewise accustomed themselves to be mindful of what is said, and to speak nothing rashly. But above all things, as an inviolable Precept, to be kept even until Death, he advised them not to reproach, but always to use good Words, as at Sacrifices. These things much displeased all in general, as I said, forasmuch as they admitted men to be educated in this singularity amongst them. But, in that they reached forth the hands to *Pythagoreans* only, and not to any of their own Family, except their Parents: Likewise, in that they had their Estates in common, wholly alienated from their own Domesticks: Hereat their Allies were much displeased. And they beginning the dissention, the rest readily joyned themselves, and engaged in it. And at the same time, *Hippasus*, and *Diodorus*, and *Theages* saying, That it was fit every one should partake of the publick Government and Convention; and that the Magistrates being chosen by lot, ought to give an Account. But on the other side, the *Pythagoreans*, *Alcimachus*, and *Dimachus*, and *Meto*, and *Democedes*, opposing it, and forbidding that the Government of the Countrey should be abrogated; these taking the part of the Commons, got the better. But afterwards, many of the common People understanding that there was a division in the publick Convention, *Cylo* and *Nino*, Orators, framed an Accusation against them; the first was one of the best quality; the other of the vulgar sort. To this effect, a long discourse being made by *Cylo*, the other continued it, pretending that he had found out the greatest Secrets of the *Pythagoreans*. But indeed having forged and writ such things, as thereby he might chiefly traduce them; and having delivered the Book to a Notary, bad him read it: The Title was, *The Sacred Discourse*: The Sum whereof this: *That Friends ought to be reverenced as the Gods themselves, but all other Men tyranniz'd over like Beasts. That the same Sentence of* Pythagoras *himself reduced to Verse, was thus rehearsed by his Disciples*:

Friends equal with the gods he did respect,
All others (as of no account) neglect.

And that he chiefly praised Homer, *for saying,* Ποιμένα λαῶν, *the Shepherd of the People, for that he tacitely imply'd, that the rest of Mankind were but Beasts. That he affected Oligarchy, and was an Enemy to unmarried Persons, as those who had been Chief in Election of Magistrates by lot. That he affected Tyranny, in as much as he saith, It is better to be a Bull, though but one day, than an Ox all our life time. That he praised the Laws and Customs of other People, and commanded, That whatsoever was decreed by them, should be used. In fine, he declared, That their Philosophy was a conspiracy against the People, and advised them, that they should not hearken to the Voice of their consultations, but rather think of forbidding them to meet in counsel at all, if they alledged, That they had a setled Assembly, consisting of a Thousand Voices. Wherefore it was not fit that they should, as far as in them lay, give ear to prohibited Persons, and permit them to speak; but to esteem their right hand which they held from them hostile, when they should offer to put in a stone for voting, conceiving it an unworthy thing, that three hundred thousand Men, who all lived about the River* Tetrais, *should be oppressed by Seditions, and overcome by the thousand part of them in that City*. This calumny so much exasperated the hearers, that some few days after, as they were sacrificing in the Temple of *Pythian Apollo*, they ran in tumultuously to do violence to them. But the *Pythagoreans* being informed beforehand thereof, fled to the publick Hall. *Democedes*, with the Young Men, went to *Platea*; but they dissolving the Laws, used Decrees, whereby accusing *Democedes* of stirring up the Young Men to Tyranny, they proclaimed, That whosever did kill him, should have in recompence Three Talents. And there being a Fight, wherein he, by the means of *Theages*, was overcome, they gave him Three Talents out of the publick Treasury. But there arising many misfortunes in the City and Countrey, the banished Persons being called to Judgment, and the Examination thereof being committed to Three Cities, *Tarentum, Metapontum* and *Caulon*, they that were put in Commission, thought good (as appears by the *Crotonian* Records) to banish them. So they banished the whole Generation, saying, That the Children ought not to be separated from their Parents, and seiz'd their Estates. But after many years, *Dimachus* and his Friends being slain in another Fight, and *Litago* also, who was head of this Faction, they took compassion on them, and resolved to call home those who were left. Wherefore sending for their Ambassadors from *Achaia*, they made an agreement with the banished Men by them, and hung up the Copies of their Oaths in the Temple of *Delphi*. The *Pythagoreans* who returned, were about Threescore, besides those who were very aged, of whom some addicted themselves to Medicine, and cured the sick, and so became Masters of that which is called Method. Those who were restored, grew into great favour with the People, at that time in which it was proverbially said, in opposition to those who violate the Laws, *These are not under the Government of* Nino.

CHAP. XX.

His Person and Virtues.

HIS Person (a) *Jamblichus* describes to have been in his Youth extraordinary beautiful, called, The fair-hair'd *Samian*; (b) and at 56 years of age, of a more comely and divine presence. (c) *Laertius* saith, *He is reported to have been of a most awful aspect, insomuch as his Disciples thought him* Hyperborean Apollo: Adding, That (d) *Timon* takes notice of the awfulness of his presence in his *Silli*, though he alledg'd it in disparagement of him.

(a) Cap. 2. p. 31.
(b) Cap. 5. p. 37.
(c) Pag.
(d) Pag. 590.

Pythagoras *skill'd in the Goetick Laws,*
Who courts by grave discourse humane applause.

So great an impression it made upon those with whom he conversed, that a Young Man being sharply reprehended by him, immediately went and hanged himself. Whereupon
Pythagoras

PART IX. PYTHAGORAS.

Pythagoras ever after forbore to reprove any Person.

(e) *Athen. Deipn. 10.*
(f) *Ibid.*

(e) *Lycon*, in the Life of *Pythagoras*, saith, That he used a spare Diet: (f) *Athenæus*, That he drunk very little, and lived so moderately, that he was often content only with Honey.

(g) *Porphyr.*

(g) *By his moderate Diet, he preserved his Body in the same constant state, not sometimes sick, sometimes well, sometimes fat, sometimes lean. It appeared by his Countenance, that the same Constancy was in his Soul also.* He was not subject to Joy (as *Cicero* likewise observes) *or Grief, no Man ever saw him rejoyce or mourn.* * Neither did any ever see him *alvum exonerantem, coeuntem*, or drunk. He refrained wholly from derision, and assentation, and scoffs, and detractive speeches. He never punished any in Anger, neither Servant nor free Person.

* *Laert.*

(h) *Laert. see also Jamb.cap. 21.*
(i) *Ælian. var. Hist.* 12, 22.

(h) He wore a white and clean Stole, (or Gown) and used white woollen Blankets, *for as yet linnen was not known in those parts*, and (i) *a gold Crown and Breeches*.

(k) *Porph.*

(k) *Diogenes* discoursing of his Daily Conversation, saith, He had Morning Exercitations at his own House, composing his own Soul to the Lyre, and singing some old Pæans of *Thales*. He likewise sung some Verses of *Homer* and *Hesiod*, whereby he rendred his Mind more sedate. Moreover, he used some Dances, which he conceived to conduce to Agility and Bodily Health. His Walks he used not with many, promiscuously, but with Two or Three, in the Temples or Groves, making choice of such places as were most pleasant, and remote from noise.

(l) *Jamb. cap. 30. pag. 153.*

(l) Having purchased the Estate of *Alcæus*, who, after his Embassy to *Lacedæmon*, died, he was no less admired for his Oeconomy than Philosophy.

Besides this *Pythagoras* the Philosopher, there were many others of the same Name, the most ancient a (m) *Laconian*, Contemporary with King *Numa*.

(m) *Plut. in Numa.*

Laertius reckons Four, all about the same time, or at least not long distant from one another; for, (besides the Philosopher) there was one a *Crotonian*, a tyrannical person; another a *Phliasian*, σωματομήτης αλειπίης, (*Exercitator*, as (n) *Pliny* renders it) one that professed to teach Corporeal Exercises, and to diet and order the Body for them. This seems to be the same *Pythagoras*, (o) Son of *Eratocles*, who writ *Aleiptick Commentaries*, and advised the Wrestlers, instead of Figs to eat Flesh; both which are ascribed by some to *Pythagoras* the Philosopher. The Third a *Lacynthian*, to whom are ascribed the Doctrines of Philosophy, which it was lawful to divulge, and the proverbial αὐτὸς ἔφα; both which were proper to *Pythagoras* the Philosopher. Some reckon another *Pythagoras* of *Rhegium*, a Statuary, who invented Rythm and Symmetry, and another of *Samus*, a Statuary also, (perhaps the same whom (p) *Pliny* placeth in the 67th Olympiad) and another, an Orator, of no Reputation; another, a Physician, who writ of σκύλλη, the Sea-Onyon, (ascribed by * *Pliny* to the Philosopher) and concerning *Homer*; and another, the History of the *Doreans*, as *Dionysius* relates. Hitherto *Laertius*.

(n) *Lib. 23. cap. 7.*

(o) *Jamb. c. 6. pag. 40.*

(p) *Lib. 34. c. 8.*

* *Lib. 19. c. 5.*

(q) *Suid.*

To these add (q) *Pythagoras* the *Ephesian*, who lived before *Cyrus*; another of the same Name, (r) Præfect under *Ptolemy*; a Third, a (s) Painter.

(r) *Plin. 37. 2.*
(s) *Plin. 34. 8.*

CHAP. XXI.

His Wife, Children, Servants.

HE took to Wife *Theano*. Some affirm, she was a (a) *Crotonian*; but (b) *Porphyrius*, a *Cretan*, Daughter of *Pythanax*, or (c) *Pythonax*. After the Death of *Pythagoras*, she took upon her the Tuition of their Children, and the (d) Government of the School, (e) marrying *Aristæus*, who succeeded him in that Dignity. *Laertius* saith, There were some Writings extant under her Name; whereof *Suidas* instanceth, *Philosophical Commentaries, Apophthegms*, and a *Poem in* Hexameter *Verse*. Of her Apophthegms are remembred these: (f) Being demanded how soon, after Coition, a Woman is pure, she answered, *If with her own Husband, at the same instant; if with a strange Person, never*. She advised every Woman, when she goeth to bed to her Husband, to put off her Modesty with her Cloaths, and when she riseth, to put it on again with them. Being asked (upon occasion perhaps of some ambiguous word) ποια; which of the two she meant? She answered, *That for which I am called a Woman*. To one, admiring her Beauty, and saying, *How white an Arm!* She answered, *But not common*. *Laertius*, who affirms, she was Daughter to *Brontinus*, a *Crotonian*, adds, That, according to some, *Theano* was Wife to *Brontinus*, and Disciple to *Pythagoras*. And with this Second, it seems, the former was frequently confounded, as particularly in the first of the precedent Apophthegms, which *Jamblichus* affirms to have been spoken by *Theano*, the Wife of *Brontinus*, though attributed by some (of whom is *Laertius*) to *Theano*, the Wife of *Pythagoras*.

(a) *Suid. in Theano.*
(b) *Pag.*
(c) *Suid.*
(d) *Theodoret. de princip. adv. gent. Serm. 2.*
(e) *Jamb. cap. ult.*

(f) *Laert.*

(g) Of his Sons by *Theano* are remembred *Telauges* and *Mnesarchus*: *Mnesarchus* seems to be the same whom (h) *Plutarch* calls *Mamercus*; for both these Names are given to the Father of *Pythagoras*, from whom that of his Son, doubtless, was derived. (i) By some he seems to be called *Damo*, if there be no mistake occasion'd by *Pythagoras* his Daughter, of the same Name. These Two, *Telauges* and *Mnesarchus*, were, upon their Father's Death, bred up under their Mother *Theano*, and afterwards governed the School, as *Jamblichus* attests of *Mnesarchus*, *Laertius* of *Telauges*, who adds, That he taught *Empedocles*, as some conceive, and *Hippobotus* cites, out of *Empedocles* himself, this:

(g) *Suid.*
(h) *In Numa.*
(i) *Suid. in Pythag.*

(k) Noble Telauges *from* Theano *sprung,*
And great Pythagoras——

(k) Perhaps Τηλαυγές, κλυτὲ κύρε, &c.

But of *Telauges* there is no Writing extant. Thus *Laertius*, who yet elsewhere cites an Epistle of *Telauges* to *Philolaus*. And *Jamblichus* affirms, That some ascribed to him the Sacred Discourse, which went under the Name of *Pythagoras*.

To

To these two Sons, add, (upon the authority of (*l*) *Duris* the *Samian*, in his second Book of Hours) *Arimnestus*, Master to *Democritus*, who returning from banishment, suspended a brazen Tablet in the Temple of *Juno*, the Diameter whereof was nigh two cubits, bearing this Inscription.

> Me Arimnestus, *who much learning trac'd,*
> Pythagoras *beloved Son here plac'd.*

His Daughters were *Sara, Muya, Arignota,* (whose Pythagorical Writings *Porphyrius* mentioneth, as extant in his time) and (*m*) *Damo*: With her, *Pythagoras* left his Writings at his death, charging her not to communicate them to any that were not within the Family. Whereupon she, though she might have had much money for the Books, would not accept it, preferring poverty, with obedience to her Father's command, before riches. One of his Daughters *Pythagoras* gave in Marriage to *Meno* of *Crotona*, whom he had educated so well, that when a Virgin, she went foremost in the company of the Virgins; and when a Wife, foremost among the married Women. The *Crotonians* made of her House a Temple to *Ceres*: The street they called *Musæum*.

Of his Servants are particularly remembered two, *Astræus* and *Zamolxis*: Of the first, thus (*n*) *Diogenes*, in his Treatise of incredible things beyond *Thule*; *Mnesarchus* being a *Tyrrhenian*, by extract of those *Tyrrhenians* who inhabited *Lemnus, Imber* and *Scyrus,* went from thence, and travelled to many Countries and Cities, found an Infant lying under a large tall Poplar, and coming to it, he perceiv'd that it lay with the face towards the sky, looking steadfastly upon the Sun without winking. In its mouth was put a little slender Reed like a Pipe. And seeing, to his great wonder, that the Child was nourished with the drops that distill'd from the Tree, he took the Child away, believing it to be of a Divine race. This Child when he grew up, was entertain'd by *Androcles,* a native of that Country, who adopted him into his own Family, and committed the management of his affairs to his trust. *Mnesarchus* afterwards growing very rich, brought up the Child, naming him *Astræus*, together with his own three Sons, *Eunostus, Tyrrhenus,* and *Pythagoras*: Which boy, as I said, *Androcles* being yet very young, adopted his Son. He put the Boy to a Lutenist, a Wrestler, and a Painter; but as soon he was grown up, he sent him to *Miletus* to *Anaximander,* to learn Geometry and Astronomy. *Mnesarchus* gave *Astræus* to *Pythagoras*, who receiving him, and considering his Physiognomy, and examining the motions and restings of his Body, Instructed him. For he first found out the way of discerning the nature of every Man; neither did he entertain any as his Friend or Disciple, before he had examined by Physiognomy his Disposition.

He had likewise another Servant whom he entertained in *Thrace*, named *Zamolxis*, for that as soon as he was born, they wrapped him in a Bear's skin, which skin the *Thracians* call *Zalmus*; whom *Pythagoras* affecting, Instructed in sublime Speculations, and concerning sacred Rites, and the Worship of the Gods. Some affirm, he was called *Thales*. The Barbarians worshipped him instead of *Hercules. Dionysiphanes* saith, he was servant to *Pythagoras*, and falling into the hands of Thieves, and being branded by them, when *Pythagoras* was disturbed by seditious factions, and banished, he bound his forehead about because of the scars. Some say, that the name *Zamolxis* signifies a strange Person. Hitherto *Diogenes*. To this *Zamolxis* (saith *Laertius*) the *Getes* Sacrifice, as *Herodotus* relates, conceiving him to be *Saturn*. But (*o*) *Herodotus* having delivered the Tradition of the *Grecians*, (that he served *Pythagoras* at *Samus*, bought out his Freedom at a great rate, and returning to his Country, reformed their manners) concludes with his own Opinion, that *Zamolxis* lived many years before *Pythagoras*.

CHAP. XXII.

His Writings.

SOme there are who hold, that *Pythagoras* left not any thing in Writing; of this Opinion are (*a*) *Plutarch*, (*b*) *Josephus*, (*c*) *Lucian*, (*d*) *Porphyrius*, (*e*) *Ruffinus*, and others: But (*f*) *Laertius* saith, that all such as affirm he wrote nothing, do but jest; for *Heraclitus* the Natural Philosopher said expresly of him, *Pythagoras* Son of *Mnesarchus* was skilful in History above all Men; and selecting those Writings, made up his own wisdom, and variety of learning and art. To which citation perhaps, (*g*) *Clemens Alexandrinus* referrs, who saith, *Heraclitus* being later than *Pythagoras*, mentioneth him in his Writings. The Books attributed to him are these.

in a good sense; Greg. Naz. adv. Jul. Orat. 3. ἐπεὶ κ̀ ἕτοι μιμεῖσθαι μὲν λέγονται τῆ ἀνθρωπίνων τινὰ δελεασμάτων μὲν τοι κακοτεχνῶς περσιδεμένων τόποις κ̀ ἁλίσκονται, the Text being so to be restored. (*g*) Strom.

(*h*) Three Treatises, *Pædeutick, Politick, Physick,* to which *Laertius* referrs the foresaid Testimony of *Heraclitus*, forasmuch as *Pythagoras*, in the beginning of his Physical Treatise, saith, *No, by the air which I breathe; no, by the water which I drink, I shall not* (*i*) *bear the blame of this Discourse.*

(*k*) Six Treatises, reckoned by *Heraclides*, Son of *Serapion*, in his Epitome of *Solion*, thus; *One concerning the Universe in Verse.* The second Intituled, *The sacred Discourse,* beginning thus:

Young Men in silence entertain all these.

[To the same perhaps belongs this;

Wretched, thrice wretched, Beans forbear to eat,
Your Parents heads as well may be your meat.

(*l*) And this cited by *Eustachius;*

Which way to Orcus *souls descend; which way*
Return, and the Sun's chearful light survey.]

The third, of the Soul. The fourth, of Piety. The fifth, *Helothales,* Father of *Epicharmus*. The sixth, *Crotona,* and others.

Two Treatises, a Discourse concerning Nature, and another concerning the gods; (*m*) both which

which he in a short time taught *Abaris* the *Hyperborean*. The first may possibly be the same with the Physical Treatise, mentioned by *Laertius*; the other, as *Jamblichus* saith, is intituled also, *The Sacred Discourse*, [but it is not the same with that Sacred Discourse, which *Heraclides* ascribes to him; for that was in Verse, this in Prose] as being collected out of the most mystical places of *Orpheus*, written either by *Pythagoras*, as most hold; or, as some eminent and creditable persons of that School assert, by *Telauges*, out of the Commentaries left by *Pythagoras* with *Damo* his Daughter, Sister of *Telauges*, which after her death they report to have been given to *Bitale*, Daughter of *Damo*, and to *Telauges* Son of *Pythagoras*, Husband to *Bitale*. What *Jamblichus* cites out of this work, see hereafter in the Doctrine of *Pythagoras*; it is cited also by (n) *Hierocles*, *Syrianus*, and others.

(n) In Aur.

An Oration to *Abaris*, mentioned by *Proclus*.
Orpheus, a Poem, as *Ion* the Chian (*in triagmis*) affirms. *Laert.*
The *Scopiads*, beginning thus, Μὴ ἀναιδῶ μηδ᾽ἑνί. (*Laert.*)
Hymns, out of which *Proclus* brings these Verses.

——— *Sacred Number springs*
From th' uncorrupted Monad, and proceeds
To the Divine Tetracties, she who breeds
All; and assigns the proper bounds to all,
Whom we the pure immortal Decad call.

(o) De Origin.

Arithmetick, mention'd by (o) *Isidore*, who affirms, *He was the first that writ upon this subject amongst the Grecians, which was afterward more copiously composed by Nicomachus.*

(p) Chil. 1. 58.

Prognosticks, of which thus (p) *Tzetzes*.

Pythagoras Samian, Mnesarchus Son,
Not only knew what would by fate be done,
But even for those who futures would perceive,
He of Prognosticks several Books did leave.

(q) Lib. 24. c. 17.

Of the Magical Virtues of Herbs, frequently cited by (q) *Pliny*, who saith, That though some ascribe it to *Cleemporus* a Physician; yet pertinacious fame and antiquity vindicate it to *Pythagoras*; and this very thing gives authority to the Volumes, that if any other thought his pains worthy the name of that Person, which that *Cleemporus* did, who can believe? Seeing that he hath put forth other things in his own name. To this work seems to belong that Volume, which *Pythagoras* wrote concerning the Sea-Onion, cited also by *Pliny*; but by *Laertius* ascribed to another *Pythagoras* a Physician.

The *Golden Verses* of *Pythagoras*, or, as others, of the *Pythagoreans*. But indeed their Author, as *Suidas* saith, is not certainly known, though some ascribe them to him. Of these is (r) *Proclus*, who styles him, *Father of the Golden Verses*. Even the Verses themselves seem to confirm it, there being amongst them some, which *Pythagoras* is known to have repeated to his Disciples, by the Testimonies of *Laertius*, *Porphyrus*, and others.

(r) In Timæum, lib. 3.

Nor suffer sleep at night to close thy eyes,
Till thrice thy acts that day thou hast o're-run;
How slipt? what deeds? what duty left undone?

Others, (as (s) *Chrysippus*) attribute them to his Disciples; some particularly to *Lysis* the *Tarentine*; some to *Philolaus*. St. *Hierom* conceives that the Sentences and Doctrines were of *Pythagoras*, but reduced to verse succinctly by *Archippus* and *Lysides* his Disciples, who had their Schools in *Greek*, and at *Thebes*, and having the precepts of their Master by heart, made use of their own ingenuity instead of Books. Or they might be compiled by *Epicarmus*, of whom *Jamblichus* saith, (t) coming to *Syracusa* in the reign of *Hiero*, he forbore to profess Philosophy openly, but did reduce the opinions of the *Pythagoreans* into Verse, thereby in sportive manner venting the Doctrine of *Pythagoras*.

(s) Agel. l. 9. c. 2.

(t) Cap. ult.

Epistles; of which are extant two only, one to *Anaximenes*, the other to *Hiero*.

Pythagoras to *Anaximenes*.

AND thou, O best of Men, if thou didst not excel Pythagoras *in extract and honour, wouldst have left* Miletus; *but now the honour of this Country detains thee, and would also detain me, were I like* Anaximenes. *But if you who are the most considerable Persons should forsake the Cities, their glory would be lost, and they become more infested by the* Medes. *Neither is it fit to be always busied in Astrology, but better to take care of our Country. Even I my self bestow not all my time in Study, but sometimes in the Wars, wherein the* Italians *are engaged one against another.*

This Epistle seems to have been written in answer to that of *Anaximenes* to *Pythagoras*, already produc'd in the Life of *Anaximenes*.

Pythagoras to *Hiero*.

MY life is secure and quiet, but yours will no way suit with me: A moderate and self-denying person, needs not a Sicilian Table. Pythagoras, wheresoever he comes, hath all things sufficient for the day; but to serve a Lord is heavy and intolerable for one unaccustomed to it. Αὐτάρκεια, self-sufficiency, is a great and safe thing, for it hath none that envies or conspires against it; whence that life seemeth to come nearest God. A good habit is not acquired by venereal pleasures, nor high feeding; but by indigence, which leadeth to Virtue; Various and intemperate pleasures enslave the souls of weak persons, but especially those which you enjoy, inasmuch as you have given your self over to them; for you are carried in suspence, and cannot be safe, because your reason opposeth not it self to those things which are pernicious. Therefore write not Pythagoras to live with you; for Physicians will not fall sick to bear their patients company.

These are mentioned as the genuine Writings of *Pythagoras*; others there were accounted spurious, as,

The *Mystick Discourse*, which (saith *Laertius*) they affirm to have been written by *Hippasus*, in detraction from *Pythagoras*.

(u) Many Writings of *Asto*, a *Crotonian*, were likewise ascribed to *Pythagoras*; as were also,

(u) Laert.

(x) *Aliptick Commentaries*, written indeed by another of that name, Son of *Eratocles*.

(x) Jambl. c. 5.

The Dialect used by *Pythagoras* and his Disciples, was the *Dorick*, which some conceive chosen by them as the most excellent, as *Metrodorus*, cited by (y) *Jamblichus*; *Epicharmus* (saith he) and before him *Pythagoras*, took the *Dorick*, the best of Dialects, as it is also the best musical Harmony; for the *Ionick* and *Æolick* partake of the *Chromatick*, the *Attick* is much more participant of the *Chromatick*; but the *Dorick* Dialect is *Enarmonick*, consisting of full sounding Letters. The Antiquity of the *Dorick* Dialect is testified by the Fable: For *Nereus* married *Doris*, Daughter of the Ocean, whom they feign to have had Fifty; of whom, one was the Mother of *Achilles*. Some (saith he) affirm, That *Deucalion*, Son of *Prometheus*, and of *Pyrrha*, Daughter of *Epimetheus*, begot *Dorus*; he, *Hellen*; he, *Æolus*. But in the *Babylonian* Sacred Records, *Hellen* is said to be the Son of *Jupiter*, and that *Hellen* begot *Dorus*, and *Xanthus*, and *Æolus*, by whose direction he went to *Rhodes*. Now it is not easie to speak exactly concerning the Ancients to those of later times, yet is it acknowledged by both these stories, That the *Dorick* is the most ancient of these Dialects. Next which the *Æolick*, so named from *Æolus*. The Third the *Ionick*, derived from *Io*, Son of *Xanthus*. The Fourth the *Attick*, founded by *Creusa*, Daughter of *Erechtheus*, so named Three Ages after the rest, according to the *Thracians*, and the Rape of *Orithuia*, which many Histories declare. *Orpheus* also, the most ancient of Poets, used the *Dorick* Dialect.

But perhaps the true Reason is, because it was the Dialect of the Countrey. For the *Pythagoreans* (z) admonished all Persons to use the Language of their own Countrey, what *Grecians* soever came into their Community; for to speak a strange Language, they approved not. The *Dorick* Dialect was common throughout *Magna Grecia*. *Crotona* and *Sybaris* were Colonies of the *Achaans*, *Syracuse* of the *Corinthians*; both which were originally *Dorick*, as being of *Peloponnesus*; (a) *Thucidides* alledgeth this as a Motive which induced the *Athenians* to war with the *Sicilians*, lest being *Doreans*, they should at some time or other assist the *Doreans*, by reason of their Affinity; and, being a Colony of the *Peloponesians*, should joyn with the *Peloponesians*. Hence, to the Stranger, in *Theocritus* his *Adoniazuzæ*, reproving the *Syracusian* Women thus,

(b) *Peace foolish babbling Women, leave your prate;*
Your wide-mouth'd Dorick *here is out of date.*

One of them answers,

Gup, whence are you? what is our talk to thee?
Correct your Maids, not us of Sicilie.
I would you knew't, we are from Corinth *sprung,*
As was Bellerophon, *our Mother-tongue*
Peloponesian is, nor is it scorn
That they speak Dorick *who are Dorick-born.*

For (saith the Scholiast) the *Syracusians* were originally *Corinthians*: *Peloponnesus* was inhabited by the *Doreans*, together with the *Heraclidæ*.

CHAP. XXIII.
His Disciples.

Many were the Persons, who from several parts resorted to *Pythagoras*, to be his Disciples, and lived with him in that Condition. Of these there were (as (a) *Aristoxenus* relates) *Leucanians*, *Messapians*, (or, as *Laertius*, *Peucetians*) and *Romans*.

(b) *Simichus*, Tyrant of the *Centoropians*, [a People of *Sicily*, the Town it self being called *Centorpa*] having heard him, laid down his Command, and distributed his Riches, part to his Sister, part to his Citizens.

(c) *Abaris* also of *Scythia*, a *Hyperborean*, came hither, who being unacquainted with the *Greek* Language, and not initiated, and withal advanced into Years, *Pythagoras* would not introduce him by various Theorems; but instead of the silence, and the long attention, and other trials, he made him presently fit to receive his Doctrines, and taught him in a short time to understand those Two Books concerning Nature, and concerning the Gods. For *Abaris* now in years, came from the *Hyperboreans*, a Priest of *Apollo* there, and converting the wisest things concerning Religion, from *Greece* to his own Countrey, that he might lay up the collected Gold to his God's use, in his Temple among the *Hyperboreans*; but coming by the way into *Italy*, and seeing *Pythagoras*, and likening him to the God whose Priest he was, and believing he was no other, not a man like him, but very *Apollo* himself, both by his Gravity, and by some Marks and Tokens which he knew, he gave *Pythagoras* an Arrow which he brought from the Temple, as necessary for his Journey, through so many different Contingencies, and such a long Travel: For riding upon that, and so passing over places that were otherwise impassible, as Rivers, Lakes, Marshes, Mountains, and the like, and coming to any place, as they say, he made Purifications, and expelled Pestilences and Storms from those Cities that desired his assistance. We are informed, that *Lacedæmon* being purged by him, never had the Pestilence afterwards, whereas it was formerly very subject to that sickness, by reason of want of free passage of the Air (the *Taygetan* Mountains, amongst which it is built, penning it up: For those Hills lye above it, as *Gnossus* to *Creet*) and other such Signs of the power of *Abaris* are reported. But *Pythagoras* accepting the Arrow, and not looking strangely upon it, or asking the cause why he gave it him; but, as if he were himself the true God, taking *Abaris* aside, he showed him his golden Thigh, as an assured mark that he was not mistaken, and then reckoning every particular of all those that were in the Temple, that he did not guess amiss, and adding, That he came for the benefit of men, and for this reason was in man's shape, that they might not be astonished at one so far above them, and so fly his Doctrine. And he commanded him to stay there, and to joyn with him in instructing them who came to him: And as for the Gold which

which he had gathered for his God, he commanded him to give it to those whom he had assembled; insomuch that he actually confirmed the Sentence, *All things are common amongst Friends*. *Abaris* thus staying with him (as we said), he gave him the Epitome of Physiology and Theology, and instead of the Art of guessing by Sacrifices, he taught him that kind of Prognostick which is by Numbers, as thinking that more Sacred and Divine, and more agreeable to the Celestial Numbers of the Gods. And other Doctrines he taught *Abaris*, such as were proper for him.

(e) *Stab. lib. 6. page 263.*

(e) *Milo* of *Crotona*, the most eminent Wrestler of those times, was Disciple to *Pythagoras*: He, when in the Hall of the Colledge a Pillar begun to yeild, went under it, and by that means saved all the Scholars, and at last got away himself; and it is probable that this confidence in his great strength was the occasion of his Death. For they report that as he was going through a thick Wood far from any way, finding a great Tree with Wedges in it, he set his Hands and Feet to it, trying to reive it asunder; whereupon the Wedges fell out, and he being caught, became a Prey to the Wild Beasts. In his House it was, that the *Pythagoreans* were surprized and burned by the *Cylonians*.

(f) *Joseph. contra Appion. lib. 11.*

(f) *Calliphon* of *Crotona*, is mentioned by *Hermippus*, as an intimate Friend of *Pythagoras*, who reported, when *Calliphon* was dead, That his Soul was continually present with him, and that the Soul commanded him that he should not pass the place where his Ass fell; and that he should abstain from impure Water, and avoid ill-speaking.

We only mention these here, as being most particularly interested in the Relation of *Pythagoras* his Life: A more perfect Account of the rest, receive in the following Catalogue.

CHAP. XXIV.

The Succession of his School.

Jamb. cap. ult.

THE Successor of *Pythagoras* is by all acknowledged to have been *ARISTÆUS*, Son of *Damophon*, a *Crotonian*, who lived in the time of *Pythagoras*, Seven Generations above *Plato*: Neither did he succeed in the School only, but in breeding the Children of *Pythagoras*, and in the Marriage of *Theano*, for his eminent understanding of his Opinions; for he is said to have taught the Doctrine of *Pythagoras* Forty Years together lacking one, living in all, near an Hundred; he essigned the School to *Aristæus*, as being the oldest.

Next him, *MNESARCHUS*, Son of *Pythagoras*.

He delivered it to *BULAGORAS*, in whose time the City of *Crotona* was sacked.

Him Succeeded *TIDAS*, a *Crotonian*, returning from travel which he began before the War, but he died with grief for the Calamity of his Countrey; whereas it was a common thing to others, when they were very old, to free themselves from the fetters of the Body.

Afterwards they took one of the *Lucanians*, saved by some strangers, to be President of the School, to whom came *DIODORUS* the *Aspendian*, who was taken by reason of the scarcity of Men in their Colledge.

As *Heraclea*, *CLINIAS* and *PHILOLAUS*.

At *Metapontum*, *THEORIDES* and *EURYTUS*.

At *Tarentum*, *ARCHYTAS*.

Of the External *Acroaticks* was *Epicharmus*, but not of the Colledge. Coming to *Syracusa*, in the time of the Tyranny of *Hieron*, he forbare publickly to profess Philosophy; but he reduced the Opinions of those Men, (the *Pythagoreans*) into Verse, sportively divulging the abstruse Doctrines of *Pythagoras*.

Of the *Pythagoreans* it is likely that many were obscure; the Names of such as were eminent, are these;

Crotonians.

Hyppostatus, Dymas, Ægon, Æmon, Silius, Cleosthenes, Agelas, Episylus, Phyciadas, Ecphanius, Timæus, Buthius, Eratus, Itanaus, Phodippus, Bryas, Evander, Millias, Antimedon, Ægeas, Leophron, Agylas, Onatus, Hyppusthenes, Cleophron, Alcmæon, Damocles, Milon, Meton.

Metapontines.

Brontinus, Parmiscus, Arestadas, Leo, Damarmenos, Æneas, Chilas, Melisias, Aristeas, Laphaon, Evander, Agesidamus, Xenocides, Euriphemus, Aristomenes, Agesarchus, Alcias, Xenophantes, Thraseos, Arytus, Epiphron, Eiriscus, Megisteas, Leocydes, Thrasymides Euphemus, Proclus, Antimedes, Lacritus, Damotages, Pyrrhon, Rhexibius, Alopecus, Astylus, Dacydus, Aliochus, Lacrates, Glucinus.

Agrigentine.
Empedocles.

Velian.
Pamenides.

Tarentines.

Philolaus, Arytus, Archytas, Theodorus, Aristippus, Lycon, Estiæus, Polemarchus, Asteas, Cænias, Cleon, Eurymedon, Arceas, Clinagoras, Archippus, Zopyrus, Euthynus, Dicæarchus, Philonides, Phrontidas, Lysis, Lysibius, Dinocrates, Echecrates, Paetion, Acusiladas, Iccus, Pisicrates, Clearatus, Leonteus, Phrinichus, Simicheas, Aristoclides, Clinias, Abroteles, Piserrydus, Brias, Evander, Archemachus, Mimnomachus, Achmonidas, Sicas, Caraphantidas.

Sybarites.

Metopus, Hippasus, Proxenus, Evanor, Deanax, Menestius, Diocles, Empedus, Timasius, Polemæus, Evæus, Tyrsenus.

Parians.

Ætius, Phenecles, Dexitheus, Alcimachas, Dinarchus, Meton, Timæus, Timesianax, Amcærus, Eumaridias.

Locrians.

Gyptius, Xenon, Philodamus, Euetes, Adicus,

Sthenonidas, Sosistratus, Euthynus, Zaleucus, Timares.

Posidonians.
Athamas, Simus, Proxenus, Cranius, Mayes, Bathylaus, Phædo.

Lucanians.
Ocellus and *Ocylus* (Brethren), *Oresander, Cerambus, Dardaneus, Malias.*

Ægæans.
Hippomedon, Timosthenes, Euelthon, Thrasydamus, Crito, Polyctor.

Laconians.
Antocharidas, Cleanor, Eurycratus.

Hyperborean.
Abaris.

Rhegians.
Aristides, Demosthenes, Aristocrates, Phytius, Helicaon, Mnesibulus, Hipparchides, Athosion, Euthycles, Opsimus.

Selinuntian.
Colæs.

Syracusians.
Leptines, Phintias, Damon.

Samians.
Melissus, Lacon, Archippus, Glorippus, Heloris, Hippon.

Caulonians.
Callibrotus, Dicon, Nastas, Drymon, Xentas.

Phliasians.
Diocles, Echecrates, Polymnastus, Phanton.

Sicyonians.
Paliades, Demon, Sostratius, Sosthenes.

Cyrenæans.
Prerus, Melanippus, Aristangelus, Theodorus.

Cyzicenes.
Pythodorus, Hypposthenes, Butherus, Xenophilus.

Catanæan.
Charondas.

Corinthian.
Lysiades.

Tyrrhene.
Chrysippus.

Athenian.
Nausitheus.

Of Pontus.
Neocritus, Lyramnus.
In all, 208.

The *Pythagorean* Women eminent, are,
Tymicha, Wife of *Millius* the *Crotonian.*
Philtes, Daughter of *Leophron,* a *Crotonian,* Sister of *Bindæcus.*
Oecelo and *Eccelo,* of *Luca.*
Chilonis, Daughter of *Chilo* the *Lacedæmonian.*
Theano, Wife of *Brontinus* the *Metapontine.*
Muya, Wife of *Milo* the *Crotonian.*
Lasthenia of *Arcadia,* Daughter of *Abroteles* the *Tarentine.*
Echecrates, a *Phliasian.*
Tyrsenes of *Sybaris.*
Pysirronde of *Tarentum,* Daughter of *Nistiades.*
Salacera.
Bio of *Argos.*
Babelyma of *Argos.*
Cleæchma, Sister of *Antocharides,* a *Lacedæmonian.*
In all, 15. Thus *Jamblichus.*

Laertius saith, His System (or, as *Cassiodorus,* Colledge) continued for Nineteen Generations; for the last of the *Pythagoreans* (whom **Aristoxenus** saw) were *Xenophilus* the *Chalcidean* of *Thrace,* and *Phanton* a *Phliasian,* and *Echecrates,* and *Diocles,* and *Polymnestus,* who also were *Phliasians.* They heard *Philolaus* and *Eurytus,* both of *Tarentum.*

THE
Discipline and Doctrine
OF
PYTHAGORAS.

CHAP. I.

The great Authority and Esteem of Pythagoras *amongst his Disciples.*

PYTHAGORAS, to render his Disciples capable of Philosophy, prepar'd them by a Discipline so strict and severe, as might seem incredible to have been undergone by free persons, were it not founded upon the great Authority and Reputation which he had amongst them.

(a) *Jamb. c. 28. p. 131.* (a) The Credit of their Opinions they conceived to be this, That he who first communicated them was no ordinary Person, but a God; and one of these Acousmata is, Who *Pythagoras* was: for they say, He was *Hyperborean Apollo*. (b) In confirmation hereof, they instance those Wonders related in his Life, and the like, which being acknowledged to be true, and it being impossible they should all be performed by one Man, they conceive it manifest, that these Relations are to be ascribed, not to a Humane Person, but to something above Mankind. This they acknowledge; for amongst them there is a saying, That,

(b) *Pag. 132.*

(c) Read Νίτις. See *Etymolog. magni.*

(c) *Two-footed Man, and Bird*
Is, and another Third.

by which Third they meant *Pythagoras*. And (d) *Aristotle*, in his Book of Pythagorick Philosophy, relates, That such a Division as this was preserved by the *Pythagoreans*, amongst their ineffable Secrets. Of Rational Animals, one kind is God; another, Man; a third between both these, *Pythagoras*.

(d) *Jamb. c. 6. p. 44.*

(e) *Jamb. c. 6. p. 43.*

(e) They esteemed *Pythagoras* in the next place to the Gods, as some good Genius indulgent to Mankind: some affirming, that he was *Pythian*; others, *Hyperborean Apollo*; some, one of those *Genii* which dwell in the Moon; others, one of the Celestial Deities, appearing at that time in a humane shape, for the benefit and direction of Mortal Life, that he might communicate the wholsome Illumination of Beatitude and Philosophy to Mortal Nature; than which, a greater good can never come, nor shall ever come, which is given by the Gods through the means of this *Pythagoras*. Whence to this day the Proverb of the Fair-hair'd *Samian* is used for a most reverend person.

(f) *Porphyrius* saith, They reckon'd him amongst the Gods; and therefore whensoever they went to deliver to others any excellent thing, out of the Secrets of his Philosophy, whence many Physical Conclusions might be deduced, then they swore by the *Tetractys*, and calling *Pythagoras*, as some God, to witness, said,

(f) *Pag. 18.*

Who the Tetractys *to our Souls exprest,*
Eternal Nature's Fountain I attest.

(g) Which Oath they used, as forbearing, through Reverence, to name him; for they were very sparing in using the Name of any God.

(g) *Jamb. cap. pag. 138.*

So great indeed was the respect they bare him, That (h) it was not lawful for any one to doubt of what he said, nor to question him further concerning it; but they did acquiesce in all things that he deliver'd, as if they were Oracles. And when he went abroad to Cities, it was reported, He went not to teach, but to cure.

(h) *Ælian. var. hist. 4. 27.*

Hence it came to pass, That (i) when they asserted any thing in dispute, if they were questioned why it was so, they used to answer, *Ipse dixit*, He said it, which *He* was *Pythagoras*. This (k) αὐτὸς ἔφα was amongst them the first and greatest of Doctrines, his Judgment being a Reason free from, and above all Examination and Censure.

(i) *Cic. nat. deor. lib. 1.*

(k) *Greg. Naz. Orat. 3.*

CHAP.

CHAP. II.

The two sorts of Auditors: and first of the Exoterick, how he explored them.

THE Auditors of *Pythagoras* (such I mean as belonged to the family) were of two sorts, *Exoterick* and *Esoterick*: the *Exotericks* were those who were under probation, which if they well performed, they were admitted to be *Esotericks*. For, of those who came to *Pythagoras*, he admitted not every one, but only those whom he liked: first, upon choice; and next, by tryal.

(a) *Jamb.*c.34. (a) *The Pythagoreans are said to have been averse from those who sell learning, and open their souls like the gates of an Inn, to every one that comes to them; and if they find not a vent or sale in this manner, then they run into Cities, and ransack the* Gymnasia, *and exact a reward from dishonourable persons: Whereas* Pythagoras *hid much of his speeches, so as they who were purely initiated might plainly understand them. But the rest, as* Homer *said of* Tantalus, *grieve, for that being in the midst of learning, they cannot taste of it. Moreover, they said, That they who for hire teach such as come to them, are meaner than Statuaries and Chariot-*
(b) *Apul.* in A-pol og. lib. 1. cites this sentence of *Pythagoras*. *makers; for, a Statuary, when he* (b) *would make a* Mercury, *seeks out some piece of wood fit to receive that form; but these, of every disposition endeavour to make that of Virtue.*

(c) *Jamb.*c.17. (c) When (therefore) any friends came to him, and desired to learn of him, he admitted them not, till he had made tryal and judgment of them. First, he enquired how they did heretofore converse with their parents and friends; next, he observed their unseasonable laughters, and unnecessary silence or discourse. Moreover, what their inclinations were,
(d) *Jamb.*c.20. [(d) whether possess'd with passion and intemperance, whether prone to anger or unchaste desires, or contentious, or ambitious, and how they behaved themselves in contention and friendship]
Jamb. c. 17. As likewise what friends those were, with whom they were intimate, and their conversation with them, and in whose society they spent the greatest part of the day; likewise upon what occasions they joyed and grieved.
(f) *Jamb.*c.20. (f) Moreover he considered their presence and their gaite, and the whole motion of their body: and, physiognomizing them by the symptoms, he discovered by manifest signs the occult dispositions
(g) *Porph.* pag. of their souls. For, (g) he first studied that Science concerning men, thereby discovering of what disposition every one was; neither did he admit any into his friendship and acquaintance, before he had physiognomized the man what he were. This word
(h) Lib.1. c.4. (faith (h) *Agellius*, upon the same occasion) signifieth to make enquiry into the manners of some, by some kind of conjecture of the wit by the face and countenance, and by the air and habit of the whole body.
(i) *Jamb.*c.20. (i) If upon exact observation of all these particulars, he found them to be of good dispositions, then he examined whether they had good manners, and were docile; first, whether they could readily and ingeniously follow that which he told them; next, whether they had any love to those things which they heard. For he considered what disposition they were of as to being made gentle, this is called κατάρτησιν; for he accounted roughness an enemy to his way of teaching,

because it is attended by impatience, intemperance, anger, obtuseness, confusion, dishonour, and the like; but mildness and gentleness by their contraries.

Likewise (k) in making the first tryal of them, (k) *Jamb.* ca he considered, whether they could ἐχμυθεῖν, (for pag. 95. that was the word he used) and examined, whether if they could learn that which they heard, they were able to be silent, and to keep it to themselves.

CHAP. III.

Purificative Institution by sufferings.

(a) THE chiefest scope which Pythagoras propos'd (a) Porph. was to deliver and free the mind from the ingagements and fetters, in which it is confin'd from her first infancy; without which freedom, none can learn any thing sound or true, nor can perceive by what that which is unsound in sense operates. For, the mind (according to him) seeth all, and heareth all, the rest are deaf and blind.

This he performed by many exercises which he appointed for purification of the mind, and for the probation of such as came to him, which endured five years before they were admitted.

(b) *If upon this examination* (which we de- (b) *Jamb.*c.1 clared *he judged any person capable, he then re-* pag. 77. *mitted him three years to be despised, making a test of his constancy and true love to learning, and whether he were sufficiently instructed as to despise glory, to contemn honour, and the like.*

(c) *He conceived it in general requisite, that* (c) *Jamb.* *they should take much labour and pains, for the acquisition of Arts and Sciences; and to that end he appointed for them some torments of cauterising and incision to be performed by fire and steel, which none that were of an ill inclination would undergo.*

CHAP. IV.

Silence.

(a) MOreover, he enjoyned those that came to (a) *Jamb.* him Silence for five years, making tryal how firmly they would behave themselves in the most difficult of all continencies; for such is the government of the tongue, as is manifest from those who have divulged mysteries.

This πεντετής σιωπή, a quinquennial silence, was called ἐχεμυθία, (and sometimes, but less frequently ἐχερημοσύνη) (b) ἀπὸ τοῦ ἔχειν ἐν ἑαυτῷ (b) Hesych. ἢ λόγον, *from keeping our speech within our selves.*

The reason of this silence was, (c) *That the* (c) Simplic. *soul might be converted into her self from external* Epictet. *things, and from the irrational passions in her, and from the body even unto her own life, which is to live for ever.* Or, as (d) *Clemens Alexandrinus* (d) Strom. expresseth it, *That his disciples, being diverted from sensible things, might seek God with a pure mind.* Hence (e) *Lucian* to the demand, how *Pythagoras* (e) In vit. could reduce men to the remembrance of the things which they had formerly known, (for he held Science to be only Reminiscence) makes him answer, First, by long quiet and silence, speaking nothing for five whole years.

Yet

(f) Lib.1.c.4. Yet (f) *Agellus* affirms, That he appointed not the same length of silence to all, but several to several persons, according to their particular capacities. And *Apuleius*, That for the graver sort of persons, this taciturnity was moderated by a shorter space; but the more talkative were punished, as it were, by exile from speech five years.

(g) Agel. ibid. (g) He who kept silence, heard what was said by others, but was not allowed either to question, if he understood not, or to write down what he heard. None kept silence less than two years. *Agellius* adds, That these within the time of silence and hearing, were called *Acoustici*. But when they had learned these things the most difficult of all, to hold their peace, and to hear, and were now grown learned in silence, which they called ἐχεμυθίαν, then they were allowed to speak, and to question, and to write what they heard, and what they conceived. At this time they were called *Mathematici*, from those Arts which they then began to learn and to meditate. Thus *Agellius*, how rightly, I question; for *Mathematici* and *Acousmatici* were distinctive appellations of the *Pythagoreans* not in probation, but after admission, as we shall see hereafter.

(h) Florid. Thus, (h) *Apuleius* saith, He taught nothing to his disciple before silence; and with him, the first meditation, for one that meant to be a wise man, was, wholly to restrain the tongue of words, those words which the Poets call Winged, to pluck off the fears, and to confine them within the walls of our teeth. This, I say, was the first rudiment of wisdom, to learn to meditate, and to unlearn to talk.

CHAP. V.

Abstinence, Temperance, and other ways of Purification.

(a) Jamb.c.16. p. 74. (a) MOreover, he commanded them to abstain from all things that had life, and from certain other meats also which obstruct the clearness of the understanding, (b) and for the same end (viz. in order to the inquisition and the apprehension of the most difficult Theorems) he likewise commanded them to abstain from wine, to eat little, to sleep little; a careless contempt of honour, riches, and the like; an unfeigned respect towards kindred, sincere equality and kindness towards such as were of the same age, and a propensity to further the younger without envy.

(b) Jamb.ibid.

(c) Jamb.ibid. (c) In fine, he procured to his Disciples a conversation with the gods by visions and dreams, which never happen to a soul disturbed with anger or pleasure, or any other unbefitting transportation, or with impurity and a rigid ignorance of all these. He cleansed, and purified the soul divinely from all these, and inkindled the divine part in her, and preserved her, and directed in her that intellectual

(d) For σωθῆναι reading ὡς φῆναι χρὴ τ Πλάτωνα. divine eye which is better, (d) as *Plato* saith) then a thousand eyes of flesh, for by the help of this only, Truth is apprehended; after this manner he procured purification of the Intellect: And such was his form of Institution as to those things.

(e) Excerpt. Vales. p. 245. (e) *Diodorus* saith, they had an exercise of temperance after this manner; there being prepared and set before them all sorts of delicate food, they looked upon it a good while, and after that their appetites were fully provoked by the sight thereof,

(f) Jambl. they commanded it to be taken off, [(f) and given to the servants] they themselves going away without dining; (this they did, saith *Jamblichus*) to punish their appetite.

CHAP. VI.

Community of Estates.

IN this time, all that they had (that is their whole estate) was made common [(a) put together and made one.] They brought forth, saith (b) *Agellius*, whatsoever they had of stock or money, and constituted an inseparable Society, as being that ancient way of association, which truly is termed Κοινοβίον (c) This was given up to such of the disciples, as were appointed for that purpose, and were called *Politici & Oeconomici*, as being persons fit to govern a family, and to give Laws.

(a) Jamb.c.17.
(b) Laert.
(c) Lib.

This was conformable to the precepts of *Pythagoras* (as (d) *Timæus* affirms) first κοινὰ τὰ φίλων εἶναι, All common amongst friends; and, φιλότης ἰσότης, friendship, equality; (e) and, esteem nothing your own. By this means (f) he exterminated all propriety, and increased community even to their last possessions, as being causes of dissention and trouble; for all things were common amongst them, no man had a propriety to any thing.

(d) Jamb.
(e) Laert.
(f) Jamb.

But what *Agellius* terms *an inseparable Society*, is to be understood only conditionally, provided that they misliked not at any time this community: for, whosoever did so, (g) *took again his own estate, and more than that which he brought into the community, and departed*.

(g) Laert.

CHAP. VII.

Admission or Rejection.

(a) THey who appeared worthy to participate of his doctrines, judging by their lives and moderation, after their five years silence, were made *Esotericks*, and were admitted to hear *Pythagoras* within the Screen, and to see him; but before that time they heard him discourse, being on the outside of the Screen, and not seeing him, giving a long time experiment of their proper manners by Hearing only. But if they were rejected, they received their estate double, and a tomb was made by the Disciples, as if they had been dead; for so all that were about *Pythagoras* spoke of them, and when they met them, behaved themselves towards them, as if they had been some other persons, but the men themselves they said were dead.

(a) Jamb.c.17.

CHAP. VIII.

Distinction.

(a) WHatsoever he discoursed to those that came to him, he declared either plainly or symbolically (for he had a twofold form of teaching:) and of those who came to him, some were called *Mathematici*, others *Acousmatici*. The *Mathematici* were those who learnt the fuller and more exactly elaborate reason of Science. The *Acousmatici* they, who heard only the chief heads of learning, without more exact explication.

(a) Porph. pag. 24.

Thus

Thus (b) as there were two kinds of Philosophy, so were there two sorts of those who studied Philosophy. The *Acousmatici* did confess that the *Mathematici* were *Pythagoreans*; but the *Mathematici* did not acknowledge that the *Acousmatici* were *Pythagoreans*; for they had their learning, not from *Pythagoras*, but from *Hippasus*; who, some say, was of *Crotona*, others of *Metapontium*.

The Philosophy of the *Acousmatici* consists of Doctrines without demonstrations and reasons, but that, So it must be done, and the like, which they were to observe as so many Divine Doctrines, and they did esteem those amongst them the wisest, who had most of these *Acousmata*. Now all these *Acousmata* were divided into three kinds; some tell, *what something is*, others tell, *what is most such a thing*; the third sort tell, *what is to be done, and what not*. Those that tell *what a thing is*, are of this kind, *as* What is the Island of the Blessed? The Sun? the Moon? What is the Oracle at *Delphi*? the Tetractys? What is the Musick of the Syrens?

Those which tell *what is most*, as, *What is most just? To sacrifice. What is the wisest? Number; and in the next place that which gave names to things. What is the wisest amongst us? Medicine. What the most beautiful? Harmony. What the most powerful? Reason. What the best? Beatitude. What the truest? That men are wicked.* For which (they say) he commended *Hippodamas*, a Poet of *Salamis*, who said,

O Gods! whence are you? How so good? so blest?
O Men! whence are you? How with ill possest?

These and such like are the *Acousmata* of this kind; for every one of these telleth, What is most. The same it is with that which is called the wisdom of the Seven Sages, for they enquired not what is good, but what is most good; not what is difficult, but what is most difficult, which is to know our selves; not what is facile, but what is most facile, which is the custom of Nations. Those *Acousmata* seem to follow this kind of wisdom, for those Sages were before *Pythagoras*. The *Acousmata* which tell *what is to be done, or what is not to be done*, are thus, *As that we ought to beget children, for we must leave behind us such as may serve the Gods in our room; or, that we ought to put off the right shooe first; or, that we ought not to go in the common Road*, and the like. Such were the *Acousmata*; but those which have most said upon them, are *concerning sacrifices*, at what times, and after what manner they are to be performed, and *concerning removal* from our place of habitation, and concerning *Sepulture*, how we must bury the Dead, for some whereof there is a *reason* given. As, *that we ought to get children, that we may leave in our room another servant of the Gods*. But of others there is no reason: and, in some, that which follows the precept seems to be allied to the words, but in others is wholly distant, as, *that we ought not to break bread, because it conduceth to judgment in Hell*. But the reasons that are applied to these, are not *Pythagorean*, but given by some other who studied *Pythagorean* Learning, endeavouring to apply some probable conjecture to them: As of the last mentioned, That [Bread is not to be broken; some say, He who gathers together, ought not to dissolve. For anciently all Friends used after a barbarous manner to meet at one Loaf; others, That you must not give so bad an omen, as when you are going about any thing; to break it off.

But there was one *Hippomedon*, an (c) *Agronean*, a *Pythagorean* of the Acousmatick rank, who said, That *Pythagoras* gave reasons and demonstrations of all these things; but because they were delivered by Tradition through many, and those still growing more idle, that the Reasons were taken away, and the Problems only left. Now the Mathematical *Pythagoreans* grant all this to be true, but the occasion of the difference they say was this: *Pythgoras* went from *Ionia*, and *Samus*, in the time of *Polycrates*'s reign, to Italy, which was then in a flourishing condition, where the chiefest persons of the Cities became conversant with him. To the most ancient of these, and such as had least leasure, (because they were taken up with publick employments, so that it would be very hard for them to learn Mathematicks and Demonstrations) he discoursed barely, conceiving it did nothing less advantage them, even without the causes, to know what they had to do: as Patients, not enquiring why such things are prescribed them, nevertheless obtain health. But to the younger, who were able to act and learn, he imparted by Demonstrations and Mathematicks. The *Mathematici* professed that they came from these; the *Acousmatici*, from the others, chiefly from *Hippasus*, who was one of the *Pythagoreans*. But because he published [their doctrine] and first wrote of the Sphear of twelve Pentagones, he died in the Sea as an impious person, not obtaining the fame at which he aimed.

CHAP. IX.

How they disposed the Day.

(a) WE shall next speak concerning those things which he taught them in the day; for, according to his directions, thus did they who were taught by him. These men performed their morning walks by themselves, and in such places where they might be exceeding quiet and retired, where were Temples, and Groves, and other delightful places; for they thought it was not fit they should speak with any one, till they had first compos'd their Souls, and fitted their Intellect, and that such quiet was requisite for the composure of their Intellect; for, as soon as they arose, to intrude among the people, they thought a tumultuous thing. Therefore all the *Pythagoreans* ever made choice of the most sacred places.

After their morning walk, they came to one another, chiefly in the Temples, or in some such places. They made use of these times for doctrines, and disciplines, and rectifications of their manners.

After they had studied a while, they went to their morning exercises; the greater part used to anoint themselves, and run races; the fewer, to wrestle in Orchards and in Groves; some, by throwing sledges, or by grappling hands, to make tryal of their strength; chusing such exercises

exercises as they judged most convenient for them.

At Dinner they used Bread and Honey. Wine after meals they drunk not. The time after Dinner they employ'd in Political affairs, as well foreign as domestick, according to the injunction of their Laws; for they endeavoured to manage every thing in the afternoons. As soon as the evening came, they betook themselves again, not singly, as in their morning walks, but two or three walked together, repeating the Doctrines they had learnt, and exercising themselves in virtuous employments. After their walks, they used baths and washing; having washed, they met together to eat; but they did not eat together more than ten Persons. As soon as they who were to come together were met, they used libations, and sacrifices of meal and frankincense. Then they went to supper, that they might end it before the Sun were set. They used Wine, and Maza, and Bread, and Broth, and Herbs, both raw and boiled: They likewise set before them the Flesh of such beasts as used to be sacrificed. They seldom eat Broths of Fish, because some of them are, in some respects, very hurtful; likewise (seldom) the Flesh of such Creatures as use not to hurt Mankind. After Supper, they offered libations, then had lectures. Their custom was, that the youngest amongst them should read, and the eldest should, as President, order what and how he should read. When they were to depart, he who filled the Wine poured forth to them in libation; and during the libation, the eldest of them declared these things, That none should hurt or kill a domestick plant or fruit; besides, that they should speak well, and think reverently of the gods, dæmons, and heroes; likewise to think well of Parents and Benefactors; to assist Law, and oppose Rebellion. This said, every one departed to his house.

(b) For ἱμαλίλινα, perhaps read καὶ ἱμαλιανα. Yet Laertius expresly saith, that linnen was not as yet used in those parts.

They wore a white and clean garment; they had also coverlets white and clean of (b) linnen, for they used not any of skins, because they approved not the exercise of Hunting.

These were the Traditions that were delivered to that society of Men, partly concerning diet, [of which hereafter more particularly] partly concerning the course of life.

CHAP. X.

How they examined their actions morning and evening.

(a) Jam. cap.

These and all other actions of the day, they contriv'd in the morning before they rose, and examined at night before they slept, thus, by a twofold act, exercising the memory. (a) They conceived that it was requisite to retain and preserve in memory all which they learnt, and that lessons and doctrines should be so far acquired, as until they are able to remember what they have learnt, for that is it which they ought to know, and bear in mind. For this reason they cherished memory much, and exercised it, and took great care of it; and in learning they gave not over, until they had gotten their lesson perfectly by heart. A Pythagorean rose not out of bed, before he had called to mind the actions of the day past, which recollection he performed in this manner: He endeavour'd to call to mind what he first, as soon as he rose, either had heard, or given in charge to his servants; and what in the second place, and what in the third, and so on in the same order. And then for his going forth, whom he met first, whom next; and what discourses he had with the first, what with the second, what with the third, and so of the rest; for he endeavoured to repeat in memory all that hapned throughout the whole day, in order as it hapned: And if at their up-rising they had more leisure, then after the same manner they endeavour'd to recollect all that hapned to them for three days before. Thus they chiefly exercised the memory; for they conceived, that (b) nothing conduceth more to science, experience, and prudence, than to remember many things.

(b) From Jamblichus restore Diodorus, in Except. Vales. pag. 245.

reading ουδὲν γὰρ μεῖζον πρὸς ἐπιστήμην καὶ φρόνησιν, ἔτι δὲ τῆς πάντων ἐμπειρίαν, τὸ δύνασθαι πολλὰ μνημονεύειν.

This was conformable to the Institution of Pythagoras; for, (c) He advised to have regard chiefly to two times, that when we went to sleep, and that when we rose from sleep; at each of these we ought to consider, what actions are past, and what to come. Of the past, we ought to require an account of our selves; of the future, we ought to have a providential care. Wherefore he advised every one to repeat to himself these verses [(d) so soon as he came home, or] before he slept.

(c) Porph. p. 26.

(d) Laert.

Nor suffer sleep at night to close thine eyes,
Till thrice thy acts that day thou hast o're-run,
How slipt? what deeds? what duty left undone?

And before they arose, these:

As soon as e're thou wak'st, in order lay
The actions to be done that following day.

To this effect *Ausonius* hath a *Pythagorical Acroasis*, as he terms it.

A good wise person, such as hardly one
Of many thousands to Apollo known,
He his own judge strictly himself surveys,
Nor minds the Noble's or the Common's ways:
But, like the World it self, is smooth and round,
In all his polisht frame no blemish found.
He thinks how long Cancer *the day extends,*
And Capricorn *the night: Himself perpends*
In a just ballance, that no flaw there be,
Nothing exuberant, but that all agree;
Within that all be solid, nothing by
A hollow sound betray vacuity.
Nor suffer sleep to seize his eyes, before
All acts of that long day he hath run o're;
What things were mist, what done in time, what
Why here respect, or reason there fergot; (not;
Why kept the worse opinion? When reliev'd
A beggar; why with broken passion griev'd;
What wish'd which had been better not desir'd;
Why profit before honesty requir'd?
If any by some speech or look offended,
Why nature more than discipline attended?
All words and deeds thus searcht from morn to
He sorrows for the ill, rewards the right. (night,

CHAP.

CHAP. XI.

Secrecy.

BEsides the Quinquennial silence, μυετης ἐχεμυθία, of the *Pythagoreans*, whilst they were Exotericks, there was another, termed παντελης ἐχεμυθία, a perpetual or compleat silence, (or secrecy) proper to the Esotericks, not amongst one another, but towards all such as were not of their Society.

(a) *Jambl. cap. pag.*

(a) The principal and most efficacious of their Doctrines they all kept ever amongst themselves, as not to be spoken, with exact *Echemythia* towards extraneous persons, continuing them unwritten and preserv'd only by Memory to their Successors, to whom they delivered them as Mysteries of the Gods; by which means, nothing of any moment came abroad from them. What had been taught and learnt a long time, was only known within the walls; and if at any time there were any extraneous, and as I may say, profane persons amongst them, the Men (so commonly were the *Pythagoreans* termed) signify'd their meaning to one another by Symbols.

(b) *Jambl. cap. 17. pag. 80.*

(b) Hence *Lysis* reproving *Hipparchus*, for communicating the discourse to uninitiated persons, void of Mathematicks and Theory, saith, They report, that you teach Philosophy in publick to all that come, which *Pythagoras* would not do, as you, *Hipparchus*, learnt with much pains. But you took no heed after you had tasted (O noble person) the *Sicilian* delicacies, which you ought not to have tasted a second time. If you are changed, I shall rejoyce; if not, you are dead to me; for he said, We ought to remember, that it is pious, according to the direction of divine and human exhortations, that the goods of wisdom ought not to be communicated to those, whose soul is not purify'd so much as in dream. For it is not lawful to bestow on every one that which was acquired with so much labour, nor to reveal the mysteries of the *Eleusian* Goddesses to prophane persons; for they who do both these, are alike unjust and irreligious. It is good to consider within our selves, how much time was employ'd in taking away the spots that were in our breasts, that after five years we might be made capable of his discourses. For as Dyers first wash and wring out the cloaths they intend do dye, that they may take the dye so as that it can never be washed out, or taken away; in like manner the Divine prepared those who were inclined to Philosophy, lest he might be deceived by those, of whom he hoped that they would prove good and honest. For he used no adulterate learning, nor the nets wherewith many of the Sophists intangle the young men; but he was skilful in things divine and human: Whereas they, under the pretence of his Doctrine, do many strange things, inveigling the young men unbeseemingly, and as they meet them, whereby they render their Auditors rough and rash. For they infuse free Theorems and Discourses, into manners that are not free but disordered. As if into a deep Well full of dirt and mire, we should put clear transparent water, it troubles the dirt, and spoils the water: The same is it, as to those who teach and are taught; for, about the minds and hearts of such as are not initiated, there grows thick and tall coverts, which darken all modesty, and meekness, and reason, hindring it from increasing there. Hence spring all kinds of ills, growing up, and hindring the reason, and not suffering it to look out. I will first name their Mothers, Intemperance and Avarice, both exceeding fruitful. From Intemperance spring up unlawful marriages, lust, and drunkenness, and perdition, and unnatural pleasures, and certain vehement appetites leading to death and ruin; for some have been so violently carried away with pleasures, that they have not refrained from their own Mothers and Daughters; but violating the Commonwealth, and the Laws, tyrannically imprison Men, and carrying about their (c) *Jails* (or Stocks) violently hurry them to destruction. From Avarice proceed rapines, thefts, parricides, sacriledges, poysonings, and whatsoever is allied to these. It behoves therefore first, to cut away the matter wherein these vices are bred, with fire and sword, and all arts of discipline, purifying and freeing the reason from these evils; and then to plant something that is good in it. Thus *Lysis*. Neither is that expression, [If you are not changed, you are dead to me] to be understood simply: For this *Hipparchus*, (d) because he communicated, and publickly set forth by writing, the *Pythagorick* Doctrines, was expelled the School, and a Tomb was made for him, as if he were dead, (according to the custom (e) formerly mentioned.) So strict were the *Pythagoreans* in observance of this Secrecy.

(c) Ἀγῶνας

(d) *Clem. Alex. Strom. 5.*

(e) *Chap.*

THE DOCTRINE OF PYTHAGORAS.

CHAP. I.

Sciences preparative to Philosophy.

(a) Porph. vit. Pyth. pag. 31.

THE mind being purify'd [by Discipline *(a)*] ought to be applied to things that are beneficial; these he procured by some contrived ways, bringing it by degrees to the contemplation of eternal incorporeal things, which are ever in the same state; beginning orderly from the most minute, lest by the suddenness of the change it should be diverted, and withdraw it self through its so great and long pravity of nutriment.

To this end, he first used the Mathematical Sciences, and those Speculations which are intermediate betwixt Corporeals and Incorporeals, (for they have a Threefold Dimension, like Bodies, but they are impassible like Incorporeals) as Degrees of Preparation to the Contemplation of the things that are; diverting, by an artificial Reason, the Eyes of the Mind from corporeal things (which never are permanent in the same manner and estate) never so little to a desire of aliment; by means whereof, introducing the contemplation of things that are, he rendred men truly happy. This use he made of the Mathematical Sciences.

(b) Dial. cum Tryph.

Hence it was, that *(b) Justin Martyr* applying himself to a *Pythagorean*, eminently learned, desirous to be his Disciple, he demanded, whether he were vers'd in Musick, Astronomy, and Geometry: Or do you think, saith he, you may be able to understand any thing that pertains to Beatitude, without having first learned these, which abstract the Soul from Sensibles, preparing and adapting her for her intelligibles? Can you without these contemplate what is honest and what is good? Thus, after a long commendation of these Sciences, he dismist him, for that he had confest himself ignorant of them.

CHAP. II.

Mathematick, its name, parts.

THese Sciences were first termed Μαθήματα by *Pythagoras* upon consideration that all *Mathesis* (discipline) is Reminiscence, which comes not extrinsecally to souls as the phantasies which are formed by sensible objects in the Phantasie; nor are they an advantageous adscititious knowledge, like that which is placed in Opinion; but it is excited from Phænomena's, and perfected intrinsecally by the cogitation converted into it self.

Procl. in Eucl. l. 25.

(b) The whole science of Mathematicks, the *Pythagoreans* divided into four parts, attributing one to *Multitude*, another to *Magnitude*; and subdividing each of these into two. For Multitude either subsists by it self, or is consider'd with respect to another; Magnitude either stands still, or is moved. *Arithmetick* contemplates Multitude in its self: *Musick* with respect to another: *Geometry*, unmoveable magnitude; *Sphærick*, moveable.

(b) Procl. in Eucl. l. 12.

These Sciences consider not Multitude and Magnitude simply, but in each of these that which is determinate: For Sciences consider this abstracted from infinite, that they may not (in vain) attempt in each of these that which is infinite. When therefore the wise persons say thus, we conceive it is not to be understood of that multitude which is in the sensible things themselves, nor of that magnitude which we perceive in bodies, for the contemplation of these I think pertains to Physick, not to Mathematick. But because the Maker of all things took Union, and Division, and Identity, and Alterity, and Station, and Motion to compleat the soul, and framed it of these kinds, as *Timæus* teacheth, we must conceive that the Intellect, consisting according to the diversity thereof, and the division of proportions and multitude, and knowing it self to be both one and many, proposeth numbers

Τὸ καθ' ἕ- κά τερον θεἰς- μένον. Baroci- us renders it otherwise.

Read ὡς ἐ τῆς καθ' ἑκάτερον ἀπειρίαν γνῶ- σι λαβεῖν κε- νόν.

to it self, and produceth them and the Arithmetical knowledge of them. According to the union of multitude and communication with it self, and colligation, it acquireth to it self Musick: For which reason Arithmetick excels Musick in antiquity, the soul it self being first divided by the Maker, then collected by proportions. And again establishing the operation within it self, according to its station, it produceth Geometry out of it self, and one figure, and the principles of all figures, but according to its motion, Sphærick: for she is moved by circles, but consists always in the same manner according to the causes of those circles, the straight and the circular: And for this reason likewise Geometry is precedent to Sphærick, as Station is to Motion.

But forasmuch as the Soul produced these Sciences, not looking on the excitation of Ideas, which is of infinite power, but upon the boundure of that which is limited (d) in their several kinds, therefore they say that they take infinite from multitude and magnitude, and are conversant only about finite: For the mind hath placed in her self all principles both of multitude and magnitude, because being wholly of like parts within her self, and being one and indivisible, and again divisible, and producing the world of Ideas, it doth participate essential finiteness and infiniteness from the things which it doth understand: But it understands according to that which is finite in them, and not according to the infiniteness of its life. This is the opinion of the *Pythagoreans*, and their division of the four Sciences. Hitherto *Proclus*.

(d) Read Καται γίνει.

SECT. I.

Arithmetick.

(a) OF these four methods, Which is that which ought necessarily to be learned the first, (*viz.* that which is by nature præexistent to the rest and chiefest, being as it were principle, and root, and mother of the rest)? *Arithmetick*: Not only for that it is præexistent before the rest in the Intellect of the efficient God, as an ornative and exemplary reason, according to which the Maker of the Universe caused all things to be made out of matter to its proper end, as after a περικεντημα and archetypal pattern: But also because being (b) naturally first generated, it together takes away the rest with it self, but is not taken away with them. Thus Animal is first in nature before Man: For taking away animal, we take away man, but not in taking away man do we take away animal. (Of this *Nicomachus* discourseth more largely.]

As concerning Arithmetick, *Timæus* affirms that *Pythagoras addicted himself chiefly to it*: (d) Stobæus, that *he esteemed it above all others, and brought it to light, reducing it from the use of Trading*. (e) Hence *Isidore*, and others, style him *the Inventer of Arithmetick*, affirming (f) *he was the first who writ upon this subject amongst the Græcians, which was afterwards more copiously composed* by Nicomachus. *He studied this Science exceedingly, and so much did he prefer it above all the rest, that he conceived, The ultimate good of man to consist in the most exact Science of Numbers*.

(a) Nicom. Ἀριθμητικῆς εἰσαγωγῆς, (so supply the Title, as a pag. 30, 35, 44, 62, 76.) cap. 4.

(b) Read περιγενέσεως ὑπαρχοντα, συναιρει, &c. viz. ἡ ἀριθμητικὴ.

Laert.
(d) *Physic.* 2.
(e) *Chron.*
(f) *Orig.* 3. 2.
Stob. *Phys.* 2.

CHAP. I.

Number, its kinds; the first kind, Intellectual in the Divine Mind.

(a) NUmber is of two kinds, the Intellectual, (or immaterial) and the Sciential. The Intellectual is that (b) *eternal substance* of Number, which *Pythagoras* in his Discourse concerning the Gods asserted to be the *principle most providential of all Heaven and Earth, and the nature that is betwixt them*. Moreover, it is *the root of Divine Beings, and of Gods, and of Dæmons*. This is that which he termed (c) *the principle, fountain, and root of all things*, and defined it to be *that which before all things exists in the Divine mind; from which and out of which all things are digested into order, and remain numbred by* (d) *an indissoluble series*.

For all things which are ordered in the world by nature according to an artificial course in part and in whole, appear to be distinguished and adorn'd by Providence and the All-creating Mind, according to Number; the Exemplar being established by applying (as the reason of the principle before the impression of things) the number præexistent in the Intellect of God, maker of the world. This only in Intellectual, and wholly immaterial, really a substance according to which as being the most exact artificial reason, all things are perfected, Time, Heaven, Motion, the Stars, and their various revolutions.

(a) Nicom. *Arith.*
(b) Jambl. vit. Pyth. cap. 38.

(c) Theon. Smyrn.

(d) Nicom. Arithm. cap. 5.

CHAP. II.

The other kind of Number, Sciential; its Principles.

SCiential Number is that which *Pythagoras* defines *the extension and production into act of the seminal reasons which are in the* (a) *Monad, or a heap of Monads, or a progression of multitude, beginning from Monad, and a regression ending in Monad*.

(b) The *Pythagoreans* affirmed the expositive terms, whereby even and odd numbers are understood, to be the principles of [Sciential] Numbers, as of three insensible things, the Triad; of four Insensibles, the Tetrad; and so of other numbers.

They make a difference betwixt the Monad and One, concerning the Monad to be that which exists in Intellectuals; One, in numbers [or as (d) *Moderatus* expresseth it, *Monad* amongst Numbers, One amongst things numbred, one body being divisible into infinite: Thus numbers and things numbred differ, as incorporeals and bodies] in like manner Two is amongst numbers. The Duad is indeterminate; Monad is taken according to equality and measure, Duad according to excess and defect: Mean and measure cannot admit more and less, but excess and defect (seeing that they proceed to infinite) admit it, therefore they call the Duad indeterminate (e) holding Number to be infinite, not that number which is separate and incorporeal, but that which is (f) not separate from sensible things.

(a) Moderat. ap. Stop.

(b) Theon. Mathem. cap. 4.
(c) Anon. Phot. vit. Pythag.

(d) Stob. Phys. 2.

(e) Themist. in Phys. 3.
(f) Arist. Phys. 3, 4.

CHAP.

CHAP. III.

The Two kinds of Sciential Number, Odd and Even.

(*a*) *Eustrat. in Ethic. 1. Serv.in Eclog.8.*
(*b*) *Nicom. Introd. Arithmet. cap. 6.*

(*a*) OF [Sciential] Numbers *Pythagoras* asserted Two Orders, one bounded, Odd, the other infinite, Even. (*b*) *Even Number*, (according to the Pythagorick definition) is that which at once admits division into the greatest and the least; into the greatest Magnitudes, (for halves are the greatest parts) the least in multitude (for Two is the least number) according to the natural opposition of these two kinds. *Odd* is that which cannot suffer this, but is cut into two unequals.

(*c*) *Themist. in Phys. 3.*

(*c*) Herein the *Pythagoreans* differ from the *Platonists*, in that they hold not all Number to be infinite, but only the Even: for even Number is the cause of section into equal parts, which is infinite, and by its proper Nature generates infinity in those things in which it exists. But it is limited by the Odd; for that being applied to the Even, hinders its dissection into two equal parts.

(*d*) *Macrob. Saturn. 1. 13.*
(*e*) *Serv. in Æned. 3.*
(*f*) *Plutarch de Hom. poesi.*
(*g*) *Serv. ad Æn. 3.*

(*d*) Odd Number is said to have been found by *Pythagoras*, and to be of Masculine Virtue, and proper to the Cœlestial Gods (*e*) to whom they sacrificed always of that Number,) and to be (*f*) full and perfect. Even, is indigent and imperfect, and Female, and (*g*) proper to the subterraneous Deities, to whom they sacrificed Even things.

(*h*) *Anon in Ptolem. Tert. bibl. lib. 1.*

(*h*) Moreover, whatever is generated of Odd Number is Male, whatsoever of Even is Female; for Even Number is subject to Section and Passion, Odd is void of both, and is efficacious; wherefore they call one the Male, the other the Female.

(*i*) *Anon. Theolog.*

(*i*) A Number, which ariseth out of the Power and Multiplication of Even and Odd, is called ἀρρενόθηλυς, *Hermaphrodite*.

(*k*) *Plut. de anima. procr.*

This Opinion *Pythagoras* seems to have derived from *Zarates*, his Master, (*k*) who call'd *Duad* the Mother of Number, *Monad* the Father; and therefore they said, that those Numbers which resemble *Monad* (*viz.* the Odd) are the best.

(*l*) *Simplic. in phys. lib. 3.*

(*l*) Odd Numbers they called *Gnomons*, because being added to Squares, they keep the same Figures; so *Gnomons* do in Geometry.

CHAP. IV.

Symbolical Numbers.

(*a*) *Porph. p.32.*

(*a*) THE *Pythagoreans* (saith *Moderatus* of *Gades*, who learnedly comprised their Opinions in Eleven Books) using the Mathematical Sciences as degrees of Preparations to the contemplations of the things that are, were studiously addicted to the business of Numbers, for this reason. Seeing they could not clearly explain the first Forms and Principles in discourse (those being the most difficult to understand and express) had recourse to Numbers for the better explication of their Doctrine, imitating Geometricians, and such as teach to read. For as these going about to explain Letters and their Powers, recurr to Marks, saying, That these are, as it were, the first Elements of Learning; nevertheless afterwards they tell us, That they are not the Elements, but that the true Elements are known by them. And as the Geometricians, not being able to express Incorporeal Forms in words, have recourse to the Description of Figures, saying, This △ is a Triangle, not meaning that this which falleth under the sight is a Triangle, but that which hath the same Figure, and which is by the help thereof, and representeth the knowledge of a Triangle to the Mind. The same did the *Pythagoreans* in the first Reasons and Forms; for, seeing they could not in words express incorporeal forms, and first principles, they had recourse to demonstration by Numbers. And thus they called the Reason of Unity, and Indentity, and Equality, and the cause of amicable Conspiration, and of Sympathy, and of the Conservation of the Universe, which continueth according to the same, and in the same manner, ONE. For the one which is in particulars, is such united to the parts, and conspiring by participation of the first cause. But the twofold Reason of diversity and inequality, and of every thing that is divisible and in mutation, and exists sometimes one way, sometimes another, they called *DUAD*, for the nature of the *Duad* in particular things is such. These Reasons are not only according to the *Pythagoreans*, and not (acknowledg'd by) others, but we see that other Philosophers also have left certain unitive powers, which comprize all things in the Universe; and amongst them there are certain Reasons of equality, dissimilitude and diversity. Now these Reasons, that the way of teaching might be more perspicuous, he called by the names of *Monad* and *Duad*; but it is all amongst them if it be called biform, or æqualiform, or diversiform.

The same Reason is in other Numbers, for every one is ranked according to some powers. In the Nature of things exists something which hath beginning, middle and end. To such a form and nature they attributed the number Three, saying, That whatsoever hath a middle is triform; so they called every perfect thing. And if any thing be perfect, they affirm it maketh use of this principle, and is adorned according to it; which, since they could not name otherwise, they made use of the term *Triad* to express it; and when they endeavour to bring us to the knowledge thereof, they lead us to it by the form of this *Triad*. The same in other Numbers.

These therefore are the Reasons, according to which the foresaid Numbers were placed; but these that follow are comprehended under one form and power, which they call *Decad*, q. *Dechad*, [from comprehension.] Wherefore they say, that Ten is a perfect number, even the most perfect of all numbers, comprehending in it all difference of Numbers, all Reasons, Species and Proportions. For if the nature of the Universe be defined according to the Reasons and Proportions of Numbers; and that which is produced, and increased, and perfected, proceed according to the Reasons of Numbers; and the *Decad* comprehends every Reason of Number, and every Proportion, and all Species: Why should not Nature it self be termed by the Name of Ten, the most perfect Number? Hitherto *Moderatus*.

Thus from the symbolical use of numbers proceeded a multiplicious variety of names, attributed to them by *Pythagoras* and his followers. Of which we shall speak more particularly, beginning with the *Monad*.

CHAP. V.

The Monad.

Moderatus apud Stob. Phys. 1. 2.

THE *Monad* is a quantity, which in the decrease of multitude, being deprived of all number, receiveth mansion and station; for below Quantity, *Monad* cannot retreat. The *Monad* therefore seems to be so called, either from standing, or from remaining (μένειν) always in the same condition, or from its separation (μεμονῶσθαι) from multitude.

To the *Monad* are attributed these Names.

Mind, (*Nicom. Phot. Anon. Theolog.*) because the Mind is stable, and every way alike, and hath the preheminence. (*Alex. Aphrod. in Metaph.*)

Hermaphrodite, (*Nicom.*) it is both Male and Female, Odd and Even, (*Macrob. in Somn. Scip. 1. 6.*) it partakes of both Natures; being added to the even, it makes odd, to the odd, even. (*Aristot. in Pythagorico*, cited by *Theon. Smyrn. Mathem.* cap. 5.)

God, because it is the beginning and end of all, it self having neither beginning nor end. (*Macrob.*)

Good, for such is the Nature of one. (*Porphyr. vit. Pyth.*)

Matter, receptacle of all, (*Nicom.*) because it produceth *Duad.* which is properly Matter. (*Anon. Theol.*)

Chaos, Confusion, Contemperation, Obscurity, Chasme, Tartarus, Styx, Horrour, Impermistion, Subterraneous Barathrum, Lethe, Rigid Virgin, Atlas, Axis, Sume, Pyralios, Morpho. (*Nicom. Anon.*)

Tower of Jupiter, (*Nicom.*) *Custody of Jupiter, Throne of Jupiter*, (*Simplic.*) from the great power which the Center hath in the Universe, being able to restrain the general Circular Motion, as if the Custody of the Maker of all things were constituted therein. (*Procl. in Timæum.* com. 4.

Seminal Reason, (*Nicom.*) because this one only is one to the Retractors, and is alone, and the rest are procreated of it, and it is the only Seminary of all Numbers. (*Mart. Capel.* 7.)

Apollo Prophet. (*Nicom.*)

Prometheus, as being Author of Life. (*Anon. Theol.*)

Geniture, because without it no number hath being. (*Anon. Theol.*)

Substance, (*Theolog.*) because Substance is primary. (*Alex. Aphr. Met.* 1.)

Cause of Truth, Simple Exemplar, Constitution of Symphony. (*Anon. Theolog.*)

In Greater and Lesser, *Equal*; in Intention and Remission, *Middle*; in Multitude, *Mean*, (*Theolog.*) in Time, *Now*, the present, (*Anon. Theolog.*) because it consists in one part of time which is always present. (*Macrob. in Somn.* 1. 6.

Ship, Chariot, Friend, Life, Beatitude. (*Anon. Theolog.*)

Form, (or *Species*) because it circumscribes, comprehends, and terminates, (*Anon.*) and because it produceth the rest of the effects. (*Mart. Capel.*)

Jupiter, (*Anon. Procl. in Tim.*) because he is Father and Head of the Gods, (*Mart. Cap.*) whence the Pythagorick Verse:

Hear noble Number, Sire of gods and men.

Love, Concord, Piety, Friendship, because it is so connected, that it cannot be divided into parts. (*Mart. Cap.*)

Proteus, as containing all forms. (*Anon.*)

Mnemosyne, (*Anonym.*)

Vesta, or *Fire*, (*Plut. in Numa.*) For the nature of *Monad*, like *Vesta*, is seated in the midst of the World, and keeps that Seat, enclining to no side.

Polyonymous. (*Hesych.*)

CHAP. VI.

The Duad.

THE Names of the *Duad* are these,
Genius, Evil, (*Plut. Plac. Phil.* 1. 3.)

Darkness, Sinister, Unequal, Unstable, Moveable, (*Porphyr. vit. Pythag.*)

Boldness, (*Nicom.*) *Fortitude*, (*Anon.*) *Contention*, (*Plut. de Isid. & Osirid.*) because it proceeds to action, and first separates it self from the *Monad.* (*Anon.*)

Matter, (*Nicom.*) because indefinite; indeterminate *Duad*, proceeds from *Monad* as Matter: The cause of tumour and division. (*Simplic. Phys.* 1.)

Cause of Dissimilars. (*Nicom.*)

Partition betwixt Multitude and Monad. (*Nicom.*)

Equal, because, in composition and permistion, this only maketh Equality. (*Nicom.*) Two and two are equal to twice two.

Unequal, Defect, Superfluity, (*Nicom.*) according to the motion of matter. (*Anon.*)

Only inform, Indefinite, Indeterminate, (*Nicom.*) because from a Triangle and Triad, Polygones are actually procreated to infinite; in *Monad* they exist all potentially together: But of two right Lines or Angles is made no Figure. (*Anon.*)

Only principle of Purity, yet not even, nor evenly even, nor unevenly even, nor evenly uneven. (*Nicom.*)

Erato, (*Nicom.*) because through love applying it self to *Monad*, as the species it procreated the rest of the effects. (*Anon.*)

Harmony, (*Nicom.*)

Tolerance, (*Nicom.*) because it first underwent separation. (*Anon.*)

Root, but not in act. (*Nicom.*)

Feet of Fountain-abounding Ida. (*Nicom.*)

Top, Phanes, (*Nicom.*)

Justice, because of its two equal parts. (*Anon. Mart. Cap.*)

Isis,

Isis, Nature, Rhea, Jove's mother, Fountain of distribution, Phyrgia, Lydia, Dindymene, Ceres, Eleusinia. (Nicom.)

Diana, (Nicom.) because the Moon takes many Settings from all the fixed Stars, and because she is forked, and called Half-moon. (*Anon.*)

Love, Dictinna, Aeria, Asteria, Disamus, Station, Venus, Dione, Micheia, Cythereia, Ignorance, Ignobility, Falsity, Permistion, Alterity, Contention, Diffidence, Fat, Death, (Nicom.) *Impulse.* (Anon.)

Opinion, because it is true and false. (*Anon. Alex. Aphrod. Met.* 1. *Philop. ibid.*)

Motion, Generation, Mutation, Division, Anon. (*Meursius* reads Διακρισις, Dijudication) *Longitude,* (Anon.) or rather, *first Longitude,* (Simplic.) *Augmentation, Composition, Communion.* (Anon.)

Misfortune, Sustentation, because it first suffered separation, (*Anon. Martian.*) *Discord.* (*Plut. de Isid. & Osirid.*)

Imposition, (Hesch.)

Marriage, Juno, Juno, being both Wife and Sister to *Jupiter.* (*Mart. Capel. Eulog. in Somn. Scip.*)

Soul, from motion hither and thither. (*Philop. Metaph.* 1.)

Science, for all demonstration, and all Credit of Science, and all Syllogism Collects from some things granted, the thing in question, and easily demonstrateth another; the comprehension of which things is Science. (*Plut. de Plac.* 1. 3.)

Maia. (Nicom. apud Phot.)

CHAP. VII.

The Triad.

(a) Anon. Theolog.

(a) THE Triad is the first number, actually odd, and the first perfect number, and middle, and proportion. It causeth the power of the Monad to proceed to act and extension; it is the first and proper Coacervation of Unities. (b) For which Reason Pythagoras said, Apollo gave Oracles from a Tripod; and he advised to offer Libation Three times.

(b) Jamb. vit. cap. 28.

The Names of the Triad are these:

First Latitude, not simply Latitude. (*Simp. de Anim.* 1.)

Saturnia, Latona, Cornucopiæ, Ophion, Thetis, Harmonia, Hecate, Erana, Charitia, Polyhymnia, Pluto, Arctus, Helice. Not descending to the Ocean, *Damatrame, Dioscoria, Metis, Tridume, Triton, President of the Sea, Tritogenia, Achelous, Nailis, Agyiopeza,* (perhaps ἀργυρόπεζα, as before, *Thetis*) *Curetis, Crataeis, Symbenia, Mariadge, Gorgonia, Phorcia, Trisamus, Lydius.* (Nicom.)

Marriage, Friendship, Peace, Concord, (Nicom.) because it collects and unites, not similars, but contraries. (Anon.)

Justice, (Nicom.)

Prudence, Wisdom; because men order the present, foresee the future, and learn Experience by the past. (Anon.)

Piety, (Anon.) *Temperance,* (Anatol.) All Virtues depend upon this number, and proceed from it.

It is the *Mind*; it is *cause of Wisdom and Understanding.* It is *Knowledge* which is most proper to number.

It is the *power and composition of all Musick,* and much more of *Geometry:* It hath all *power in Astronomy,* and the nature and knowledge of Celestials, containing and impelling it to the production of substance.

(c) The Cube of this number Pythagoras affirmed to have the power of the Lunar Circle, in as much as the Moon goeth round her Orb in 27 days, which the Number Ternio, in Greek Τειας, the Triad gives in its Cube.

(c) Agel. l. 20

CHAP. VIII.

The Tetrad.

(a) THE Tetrad was much honoured by the Pythagoreans, and (b) esteemed the most perfect number, the (c) primary and primogenious, which they called the Root of all things, and the Fountain of Nature.

(a) Protospath. in Hesiod dies.
(b) Lucian. pro lapf. in salutar. adm.
(c) Irenæus. lib. 1. cap. 1.

(d) The Tetrads are all Intellectual, and have an emergent Order, and (for that Reason) the Empyreal Præfecture; they go round about the World, as the *Empyreum* passeth through all.

(d) Simplic. ad Physi. 4.

Even God himself Pythagoras expressed by the Tetrad.

(e) How God is a Tetrad, you will clearly find in the Sacred Discourse ascribed to Pythagoras, wherein God is the number of numbers. For if all Beings subsist by his eternal Counsel, it is manifest, that number in every species of Beings depends upon their Causes; the first number is there, from thence derived hither: The determinate stop of number is the Decad, for he who would reckon further, must return to 1, 2, 3. and number a second Decad, in like manner a third, to make up 30, and so on, till having numbred the tenth Decad, he comes to a 100. Again, he reckons from a 100. in the same manner, and so may proceed to infinite, by revolution of the Decad. Now the Tetrad is the power of the Decad; for, before we arrive at the perfection of the Decad, we find an united perfection in the Tetrad, the Decad being made up by addition of 1, 2, 3, 4.

(e) Hierocl. in aur. carm.

Moreover, the Tetrad is an Arithmetical mean betwixt 1 and 7, equally exceeding, and exceeded in number. It wants 3 of 7, and exceeds 1 by 3. Monad, as being the Mother of numbers, contains all their powers within it self. The Hebdomad, as being motherless, and a Virgin, possesseth the second place, in dignity, for it is not made up of any number within the Decad, as 4 is of twice two, 6 of twice 3, 8 of twice 4, 9 of thrice 3, 10 of twice 5. Neither doth it make up any number within the Decad, as 2 makes 4, 3 makes 6, 5 makes 10. But the Tetrad lying betwixt the unbegotten Monad, and the motherless Hebdomad, comprehends all powers, both of the productive and produced numbers; for this of all numbers under 10, is made of a certain number, and makes a certain number; the Duad doubled makes a Tetrad, the Tetrad doubled makes 8.

Besides, the first solid figure is found in a Tetrad, for a point is correspondent to Monad, a line to Duad, [because drawn from one point to another] a Superficies to Triad, (because it is the most simple of all rectiline figures) but a solid properly agrees with the Tetrad. For the first Pyramis is in a Tetrad, the Base is triangular, so that at the bottom is 3, at the top 1.

Furthermore, the judicative power in things are Four, Mind, Science, Opinion, and Sense; for all Beings are dijudicated either by Mind, or (f) *Plut. plac.* Science, or Opinion, or Sense: [(f) for which phil. lib.1.cap. Reason *Pythagoras* affirmed, the Soul of Man to consist of a Tetrad.]

Finally, the Tetrad connects all Beings, of Elements, Numbers, Seasons of the Year, Coævous Society; neither can we name any thing, which depends not on the Tetractys, as its Root and Principle: For it is, as we said, the maker and cause of all things; intelligible God, Author of Celestial and Sensible Good. The knowledge of these things was delivered to the *Pythagoreans* by *Pythagoras* himself. Hitherto *Hierocles.*

For this Reason the Word *Tetractys* was used by *Pythagoras*, and his Disciples, as a great Oath, who likewise, out of respect to their Master, forbearing his Name, did swear by the Person that communicated the *Tetractys* to them,

Eternal Nature's Fountain I attest,
Who the Tetractys *to our Soul exprest.*

(g) In procr. (g) But *Plutarch* interprets this *Tetractys*, an. sec. *Tima-* (which he saith was also called κόσμῳ, World) um. to be 36, which consists of the first four odd numbers, thus:

$\begin{Bmatrix}1\\2\end{Bmatrix}3\quad \begin{Bmatrix}3\\4\end{Bmatrix}7\quad \begin{Bmatrix}5\\6\end{Bmatrix}11\quad \begin{Bmatrix}7\\8\end{Bmatrix}15\quad \begin{Bmatrix}3\\7\\11\\15\end{Bmatrix}36$

The Names of the Tetrad are these;
Another Goddess, Multideity, Pantheos, Fountain of natural Effects. (Nicom.)
Key-keeper of Nature, because the universal Constitution cannot be without it; to these Sciences it conferreth Constitution and Settlement, and reconcileth them: yea, it is Nature it self and Truth. (*Nicom.*)
Nature of Æolus. (Nicom.) from its various property. (Anon.)
Hercules, Impetuosity, most Strong, Masculine, Ineffeminate, Mercury, Vulcan, Bacchus, Soritas, Maiades, Erinnius, Socus, Dioscorus, Bassarius, Two-mother'd, of Feminine Form, of Virile Performance, Bacchation. (Nicom.)
Harmony. (Nicom.) because it hath a *sesquitertia.* (Anon.)
Urania the Muse. (Nicom.) *World.* (Plut.)
Body, as a Point is 1, a Line 2, a Superficies 3.
Soul, because it consists of Mind, Science, Opinion and Sense. (*Plut. Plac. Phil.* 1.3.)
First Profundity, as it is a body. (*Simplic. de Anim.* 1.)
Justice The Property of Justice is compensation and Equality. This Number is the first evenly even; and whatsoever is the first in any kind, is most that thing. This, they said, was the Tetrad, because being quadrate, it is divided into Equals, and is it self equal. (*Alex. Aphrod. Metaph.* 5.)

CHAP. IX.

The Pentad.

(a) THE Pentad is the first complexion of both (a) *Theon.* kinds of number, even and odd, two *Smyrn.* c. 44. and three: Its names these:

Ἀνεικία, *Reconciliation.* (Nicom.) because the fifth Element, *Æther,* is free from the Disturbances of the other four. (Anon.)
Alteration, Light, because it changed that which was separated threefold, into the Identity of its sphere, moving circularly, and ingenerating light. (Anon.)
Justice, (Nicom.) because it divides 10 into two equal parts. (*Johan. Port. in Hes.*)
The least and top of livelihood. (Nicom.)
Nemesis. (Nicom.) because it distributes conveniently Celestial, Divine, and Natural Elements. (Anon.)
Bubastia. (Nicom.) because worshipp'd at *Bubastus* in Ægypt. (Anon.)
Venus, Gamelia, Androgynia, Cytherea, Zoneia. (Nicom.) *Marriage.* (Anon.) because it connects a masculine and feminine number. (*Anon. Plut. de* Ἐῖ *delph.*) consisting of 2. the first even, and 3. the first odd (*Alex. Aphrod. in Metaph. Protosp. in Hesiod.*)
Κυκλιύχος, *President of Circles.* (Nicom.)
Semi-goddess, (Nicom.) not only as being the half of 10. (which is divine, but for that it is placed in the middle. (Anon.)
Tower of Jupiter.
Didymæa, or *Twin.* (Nicom.) because it divides 10 into two. (Anon.)
Firm Axis. (Nicom.)
Immortal, Pallas, implying the fifth Essence. (Anon.)
Καρδίαιης, *Cordial.* (Nicom.) from similitude with the heart. (Anon.)
Providence, because it makes unequals equal. (Anon.)
Τέζαρς, *Sound,* the fifth being the first diasteme. (*Plut. de An. procr. e Tim.*)
Nature, because multiply'd by it self, it returns into it self. For as Nature receiving Wheat in seed, and introducing many forms by altering and changing it, at last returns it Wheat, at the end of the whole mutation restoring the beginning; so, whilst other numbers multiply'd in themselves, are increased, and end in other numbers, only 5 and 6 multiply'd by themselves, represent, and retain themselves. (*Plut. de* Ἐῖ *delph.*)

This number represents all superiour and inferiour beings; for it is either the supreme God, or the Mind born of God, wherein are contained the Species of all things, or the Soul of the World, which is the Fountain of all Souls, or Celestials, down to us; or it is Terrestial Nature, and so the Pentad is repleat with all things. (*Macrob. in Somn. Scip.* 1.6.)

CHAP. X.

The Hexad.

THE Pythagoreans held the number Six to be perfect, respecting (as *Clem. Alexandrinus* conceives) the creation of the World according to the Prophet. The names of the Hexad, are these;

Form of Form, Articulation of the Universe, Maker of the Soul, Harmony; (Nicom.) because it hath the power to ingenerate a vital habit; Whence it is called *Hexad*, ἀπὸ τῆς ἕξεως: and *Harmony*, because all Souls are harmonick, (Anon.)

Ὀυλομέλεια, *perfection of parts*, (Nicom.) or (as Anon.) Ὁλομέλεια. The Pythagoreans called it thus, imitating *Orpheus*, either as being the only number under ten, which is whole and equal in its parts; or because the whole Universe is divided into parts by it. (Anon.)

Venus, (Nicom.) because it procreates harmony: 6, to 12. is a diapason concord; 6, to 9. hemiolos; 6, to 8. epitrites; that is a diatessaron concord: Whence it is named *Venus* who was the Mother of Harmony. (Mart. cap. 7.)

Ζύγια, (Nicom.) Γαμήλια, (Nic.) Γάμ@, *Marriage*, (Clem. Strom. 5.) because of the mixtion of the first even and first odd. (Plut. de An. procr. Sec. Tim.): For as Marriage procreates by a male and female; so this number is generated of 3. Which is odd and called male, and of 2. which is even and called female; for twice 3, make 6. (Clem. Alexand. Strom. 6.) It produceth Children like the Parents; (Theon. Smyr. Mathem. 45.)

Ζυγίτης, Φιλοτησία, (Nicom.) or Φιλίωσις *Conciliation*, because it conciliates the male and female: (Anon.

Ὑγίεια, *Health*; (Nicom. Anon.) a triple triangle which being alternately conjoyned within ✡ it self constituteth a figure of five lines; they used it as a Symbol to those of their own sect, and called it *Ὑγίεια, Health*. (Lucian. prolaps. in sal. admiss.)

Ἄκμων, *Anvile*; (Nicom.) qu. ἀκάματον, unwearied; because the principal triangles of the mundane Elements have share in it, being each of them Six, if measured by three perpendiculars. (Anon.)

Ἑκατηϐέλετις, being compounded of and as it were ϐολήσασαν, the triad, which is called Hecate, (Anon. Theol.)

Trioditis; from the nature of that Goddess, or because the Hexad first assumes the three motions of intervals, being divided into two parts, each of which is on each side. (Anon.)

Διχερνία, the distribution of all time, of things above the earth, and under the earth, which is done by the Hexad in the Zodiack, or because Time is of the nature of the Triad, consisting of three parts, and the Hexad consists of two Triads. (Anon.)

Persæa, Triform (Nicom.)

Amphitrite; (Nicom.) because it hath a Triad on each side. (Anon.)

Neighbour to Justice, (Nicom.) as being nearest to 5. (which is named Justice. (Anon.)

Thalia, the Muse; (Nicom.) because of the harmony of the rest. (Anon.)

Panacæa, (Nicom.) in respect to health mentioned already; or q. *Panarceia*, omni-sufficience, endued with parts sufficient for totality. (Anon.)

Μεσευθὺς, *Middle-right*, being in the midst betwixt 2, and 10, æquidistant from both. (Clem. Alexandr. Strom. 6.)

World, because the World, as the Hexad, is often seen to consist of contraries by harmony. (Anon.)

CHAP. XIV.

The Heptad.

(a) THE Heptad was so called, qu. σεπ[ὰς σεβασμοῦ ἄξι@ worthy of veneration; for (b) *Pythagoras* held this number to be most proper to Religion. (c) He also held, that it is perfect; (d) thence it was, (as the Pythagoreans conceived) that creatures born in the seventh month live.

The names of the Heptad, are these.

Fortune, Occasion; (Nicom.) because it occurrs casually and opportunely to every thing. (Anon.) Whatsoever is best amongst sensible things, by which the seasons of the year and their periods, are orderly compleat, participates of the Hebdomad, (Philo. de die sept.) the Moon having 7 days, measures all time. (Johan. Philop. in Metaphys. 7.)

Ἀμήτωρ, *Motherless, Virgin*, (Hieroc. in aur. car. Nicom.) *Minerva*, as being a Virgin, unmarried, not born of a Mother (odd number,) nor of a Father, (even number;) but out of the Crown or Top of the Father of all, Monad. (Anon. Chalcid. in Tim. Theon. Smyrn. c. 45.

Mars, Nicom. Anon. Ἀκρέωσις, (Nicom.)

Ageleia, (Nicom.) an epithet of *Minerva* (Heiych.)

Ἀτρυτώνη, (Nicom.)

Φυλακιτις, *Custody*, (Nicom.) because the Stars which guard the Universe are seven. (Anon.)

Ὀβριμοπάτρης, Τριτογενία, Γλαυκῶπις, Ἀλαλκιμένεια, Παντευχία, Ἐργάνη, Πολυαρήτη, Ὀυλομέλεια; *Stock of Amalphea, Ægis, Osiris, Dream, Voice, Sound*, *Clio* the Muse, *Judgment*, *Adrastia*. (Anon.)

Τελέσφορ@, *leading to the end*; (Anon.) because by it all are led to the end. (Philo. de Mund. opif.)

(a) Nicom. apud Phot.
Anon. Macrob. in Somn. Scip.
(b) Apud Metam. lib.11.
(c) Alex. Aphrod. Probl. 2. Quæst. 47.
(d) Jul. Paul. recept. sent. lib. 4. cic. 9.

CHAP. XII.

The Ogdoad.

THE Ogdoad, they said was the first Cube, and the only number evenly even under ten. (Anon.)

The Names of it.

Panarmonia, (Nicom.) because of its excellent convenience. (Anon.)

Cadmæa, Mother, Rhea, θηλύποπ@, *Cibele, Dindymene*, Πολύχ@, *Love, Friendship, Council, Prudence, Orcia, Themis, Law*, Ηλιτόμηνα, *Euterpe* the Muse, Ἀσφάλεια, Ἕδρασμα, (Anon.) *Neptune*. (Plut. de Isid. & Osirid.

Justice,

Justice, because it is first resolved into numbers, especially equal. (*Macrob.* in Somn. Scip. l. 5.)

CHAP. XIII.

The Ennead.

THE Ennead is the first square of an odd number. Its names, these:

Ocean, *Horizon*; because number hath nothing beyond it, but it revolves all within it. (Anon.)

Prometheus, because it suffers no number to out-go it; and justly, being a perfect ternary. (Anon.)

Concord, (*Nicom.* Anon.) *Perasia*, (Anon.) *Halius*, (*Nicom.* Anon.) because it doth not permit the consent of number to be dispersed beyond it, but collects it. (Anon.)

Ἀνακαία, because of the revolution to Monad. (Anon.)

Ὁμοίωσις, because it is the first odd Triangle, (Anon.)

Vulcan, because to it, as consistature and relation, there is no return. (Anon.)

Juno, because the sphear of the Air hath the ninth place. (Anon.)

Sister and Wife to Jupiter, from conjunction with unity. (Anon.)

Ἐκάεργος, because there is no shooting beyond it. (Anon.)

Pæan, *Nysseis*, *Agyica*, *Ennalios*, *Agelia*, *Tritogegenia*, *Suada*, *Curetis*, *Proserpina*, *Hyperion*, *Terpsichore* the Muse. (*Nicom.* Anon.)

Τελέσφορος, Τέλειος, because nine months compleat the Infant.

CHAP. XIV.

The Decad.

(a) *Athenag. apolog. pro Christ.*
(b) *Plut. plac. l. 3.*

(a) TEN, according to the Pythagoreans, is the greatest number, as well for that it is the Tetractys, as that it comprehends all arithmetical and harmonical proportions. (b) Pythagoras said, that ten is the nature of number: because all Nations, Greeks, and Barbarians, reckon to it; and when they arrive at it, return to the Monad.

Names of the Decad.

World; because according to the Decad, all things are ordered in general and particular. (Anon.) The Decad comprehends all numbers, the World all forms; (*Philop.* Metaph. 1.) for the same reason termed also *Sphear*. (Anon.)

Heaven, (*Nicom.*) because it is the most perfect term of number, as Heaven the receptacle of all things. (Anon.) The Decad being a perfect number, the Pythagoreans desired to apply to it those things which are contained in Heaven, where finding but 9, (the Orbs, the seven Planets, and the Heaven of fixed Stars, with the earth) they added an Antichthon, (another earth opposite to this) and made Ten; by this means they accommodated them to the Decad. (*Pachymer.* in Metaphys. 3.)

Fate, (*Nicom.*) because there is no property neither in numbers nor beings, according to the composition of number, which is not seminally contained in the Decad. (Anon.)

Age. (*Nicom.*)

Power, (*Nicom.*) from the command it hath over all other Numbers. (Anon.)

Faith, *Necessity*. (Anon.)

Atlas; for as *Atlas* is fabled to sustain Heaven with his shoulders, so the Decad all the Sphears, as the Diameter of them all. (Anon.)

Unwearied, *God*, *Phanes*, *Sun*, *Urania*, *Memory*, *Mnemosyne*. (Anon.)

First square, because made of the first four numbers, 1, 2, 3, 4. (*Chalcid.* in *Tim.*)

Κλειδοῦχος, as the magazine and confinement of all proportions; (Anon.) or, Κλαδοῦχος, because other numbers branch out of it. (*Cedren.*)

Παντέλεια, because it perfects all number, comprehends within it self all the nature of even and odd, moved and unmoved, good and ill. (Anon.)

CHAP. XV.

Divination by Numbers.

UPon the near affinity which *Pythagoras* (following *Orpheus*) conceived to be betwixt the gods and numbers, he collected a kind of Arithmonanty; not practised by himself only, but communicated to his Disciples, as is manifest from (a) *Jamblichus*, who cites this fragment of the *Sacred Discourse*, a Book ascribed to him: *Concerning the gods of Pythagoras, son of Mnesarchus, I learned this when I was initiated at Libeth in Thrace, Aglaophemus administring the rites to me; Orpheus son of Calliope, instructed by his mother, in the Pangæan mountain, said, That number is an eternal substance, the most provident principle of the Universe, Heaven, and Earth, and middle Nature; likewise the root of Divine beings, and of gods and dæmons.* (a) *Vit. Pyth. cap. 28.*

Hence (saith *Jamblichus*) it is manifest that Pythagoras *received of Numbers the determinate essence of the gods, from the traditions of* Orpheus. *By these Numbers he framed a wonderful divination and service of the gods, of nearest affinity to numbers, as may be evinced from hence, (for it is requisite to give an instance for confirmation of what we say,) whereas* Abaris *performed those kind of sacrifices to which he was accustomed, and practised diligently divination, after all the ways of the* Barbarians, by Victims, *principally of* Cocks, *(whose entrals they conceived to be most exact for inspection)* Pythagoras *willing not to take him off from his study of truth; yet to direct him by a safer way, without blood and slaughter, (moreover esteeming the Cock sacred to the Sun) taught him to find out all truth by the science of Arithmetick.* Thus *Jamblichus.* (b) *And elsewhere he saith, that* Pythagoras, *instead of the art of divining by sacrifices, taught him that kind of prediction which is by Numbers, as conceiving that to be more sacred and divine, and more agreeable to the celestial numbers of the gods.* (b) *Vit. Pyth. cap. 19.*

This hint some have taken to impose upon the world, under the name of *Pythagoras*, an Onomantick kind of Arithmetick, assigning particular numbers *to the letters of the Alphabet, to the Planets,*

Planets, to the days of the Week, and to the Signs of the Zodiack, thereby resolving questions concerning *nativities, victory, life, or death, journies, prosperity or adversity*; as is set down by (c) *Flud*, who adds, *Apollonius hath delivered another way of divination, according to the Pythagorick Doctrine; affirming, that future things may be prognosticated by virtue of a Wheel invented by* Pythagoras, *whereby is treated of life and death, of fugitives, of litigious business, of victories, of the sex of children unborn, and infinite others of the like kind. But concerning the exposition of the Wheel, and the true position of Numbers, therein the ancient Authors have written very inconstantly, so as the truth of its composition cannot be comprehended otherwise than by conjecture.* What ancient Authors he means, I know not; the citation of *Apollonius*, I doubt to be no less suppositious, than the Wheel it self, which (d) *Trithemius* and others acknowledge to be an invention of later times.

(c) Microcosm.

(d) Antip. Mal. l. 3.

SECT. II.

Musick.

(a) Theon. Smyrn. Math. cap. 1.

(a) THE *Pythagoreans* define Musick an apt composition of contraries, and an union of many, and consent of differents. For it not only co-ordinates rythms and modulation, but all manner of Systems. Its end is to unite, and aptly conjoyn. God is the reconciler of things discordant, and this is his chiefest work according to Musick and Medicine, to reconcile enmities. In Musick, say they, consists the agreement of all things, and Aristocracy of the Universe: For, what is harmony in the world, in a City is good Government, in a Family Temperance.

(b) Porphyr. in Harm. Ptolomai.
(c) Plut. de Mus. Porph. in Ptol. Harm. &c.
(d) Ptolem. Harmonic. c. 2.

(b) Of many Sects (saith *Ptolemais*) that were conversant about harmony, the most eminent were two, the *Pythagorick* and *Aristoxenian*; [(c) *Pythagoras* dijudicated it by reason, *Aristoxenus* by sense.] (d) The *Pythagoreans* not crediting the relation of hearing in all those things, wherein it is requisite, adapted reasons to the differences of sounds, contrary to those which are perceived by the senses; so that by this critery (reason) they gave occasion of calumny to such as were of a different opinion.

(e) Ptolemais loco citato apud Porphyr.

(e) Hence the *Pythagoreans* named that which we now call Harmonick, Canonick; not from the Canon or Instrument, as some imagine, but from rectitude, since reason finds out that which is right, by using Harmonical Canons or Rules. Even of all sorts of Instruments, framed by Harmonical Rules, (Pipes, Flutes, and the like) they call the Exercise, Canonick; which although it be not Canonick, yet is so termed, because it is made according to the Reasons and Theorems of Canonick. The Instrument therefore seems to be rather denominated from its Canonick affection. A Canonick in general is a Harmonick, who is conversant by ratiocination, about that which consists of Harmony. Musicians and Harmonicks differ; Musicians are those Harmonicks who begin from sense, but Canonicks are *Pythagoreans*, who are also called Harmonicks; both sorts are termed by a general name, Musicians.

CHAP. I.

Voice, its kinds.

(a) OF human voice, they who are of the *Pythagorean* School, said, That there are (as of one Genus) two Species. One they properly named Continuous, the other Diastematick, (intermissive) framing appellations from the accidents pertaining to each. The Diastematick they conceived to be that which is sung, and rests upon every note, and manifest the mutation which is in all its parts, which is inconfused, and divided, and disjoined, by the magnitudes which are in the several sounds, as coacerved, but not commixt; the parts of the voice being apply'd mutually to one another, which may easily be separated and distinguished, and are not destroy'd together. Such is the Musical kind of voice, which to the knowing, manifests all sounds, of what magnitude every one participates: For if a man use it not after this manner, he is not said to sing, but to speak.

(a) Nicom. Harm. cap. 2.

The other kind they conceived to be *Continuous*, by which we discourse one to another, and read, and are not constrained to use any manifest distinct tensions of sounds, but connect the discourse, till we have finished that which we intended to speak. For if any man in disputing, or apologizing, or reading, make distinct magnitudes, in the several sounds, taking off, and transferring the voice from one to another, he is not said to read, but to sing.

Human voice having in this manner two parts, they conceived, that there are two places which each in passing possesseth. The place of Continuous voice, which is by nature infinite in magnitude, receiveth its proper term from that, wherewith the speaker began, until he ends, that is the place from the beginning of his speech to his conclusive silence, so that the variety thereof is in our power. But the place of Diastematick voice is not in our power, but natural; and this likewise is bound by different effects. The beginning is that which is first heard, the end that which is last pronounced; for from thence we begin to perceive the magnitude of sounds, and their mutual commutations, from whence first our hearing seems to operate; whereas it is possible there may be some more obscure sounds perfected in nature, which we cannot perceive or hear. As for instance, in things weigh'd there are some bodies which seem to have no weight, as Straws, Bran, and the like; but when as by apposition of such bodies, some beginning of ponderosity appears, then we say, They first come within the compass of Statick. So, when a low sound increaseth by degrees, that which first of all may be perceived by the ear, we make the beginning of the place which musical voice requireth.

Ddd CHAP.

CHAP. II.

First Musick in the Planets.

(a) Nicom. Harm. cap. 3.

(a) THE names of Sounds, in all probability, were derived from the seven Stars, which move circularly in the Heavens, and compass the earth. *(b) The circumagitation of these bodies must of necessity cause a sound; for air being struck from the intervention of the blow, sends forth a noise; Nature her self constraining that the violent collision of two bodies should end in sound.*

(b) Macrob. in Somn. Scip. 2. 1.

(c) Nicom. ibid.

(c) Now (say the *Pythagoreans*) all bodies which are carried round with noise, one yielding and gently receding to the other, must necessarily cause sounds different from each other, in the magnitude and swiftness of voice, and in place; which (according to the reason of their proper sounds, or their swiftness, or the orbs of repressions, in which the impetuous transportation of each is performed) are either more fluctuating, or on the contrary more reluctant. But these three differences of magnitude, celerity, and local distance, are manifestly existent in the Planets, which are constantly with sound circumagitated through the ætherial diffusion; whence every one is called ἀνὴρ, as void of στάσις, station; and ἀεὶ θέων, always in course, whence God and Æther are called Θεός and Ἀιθήρ.

Macrob. ibid.

Moreover the sound which is made by striking the air, induceth into the ear something sweet and musical, or harsh and discordant: for, if a certain observation of numbers moderate the blow it effects a harmony consonant to it self; but if it be temerarious, not governed by measures, there proceeds a troubled unpleasant noise which offends the ear. Now in heaven nothing is produced casually, nothing temerarious, but all things there proceed according to divine Rules and setled Proportions: whence irrefragably is inferr'd, that the sounds which proceed from the conversion of the Cœlestial Spheres, are musical. For sound necessarily proceeds from motion, and the proportion which is in all divine things causeth the harmony of this sound. This Pythagoras first of all the Greeks conceived in his mind; and understood that the Spheres sounded something concordant, because of the necessity of proportion, which never forsakes Cœlestial Beings.

Nicom. ibid.

From the motion of *Saturn*, which is the highest and furthest from us, the gravest sound in the diapason concord, is called *Hypate*; because ὕπατον signifieth *highest*: but from the Lunary, which is the lowest and nearest the earth, *neate*; for νέατον signifieth *lowest*. From those which are next these, viz. from the motion of *Jupiter* who is under *Saturn, parypate*; and of *Venus*, who is above the *Moon, paraneate*, Again, from the middle, which is the *Sun*'s motion, the fourth from each part, *mese*, which is distant by a diatessaron, in the Heptachord from both extreams, according to the ancient way; as the Sun is the fourth from each extream of the seven Planets, being in the midst. Again, from those which are nearest the Sun on each side, from *Mars* who is placed betwixt *Jupiter* and the Sun, *Hypermese*, which is likewise termed *Lichanus*, and from *Mercury* who is placed betwixt *Venus* and the Sun, *Paramese*.

Plin. l. 2. c. 22.

Pythagoras by Musical proportion calleth that a Tone, by how much the *Moon* is distant from the Earth: from the *Moon* to *Mercury* the half of that space, and from *Mercury* to *Venus* almost as much: from *Venus* to the *Sun* sesquiple: from the *Sun* to *Mars* a Tone, that is as far as the *Moon* is from the Earth: from *Mars* to *Jupiter* half, and from *Jupiter* to *Saturn* half, and thence to the Zodiack sesquible: thus there are made seven Tones, which they call a Diapason harmony, that is an universal concent: In which *Saturn* moves in the *Dorick* mood, *Jupiter* in the *Phrygian*, and in the rest the like.

Porph. p. 21.

Those sounds which the seven Planets, and the Sphere of fixed Stars, and that which is above us, termed by them *Antichthon*, make, *Pythagoras* affirmed to be the Nine Muses: but the composition, and symphony, and as it were connexion of them all, whereof as being eternal and unbegotten, each is a part and portion, he named *Mnemosyne*.

CHAP. III.

The Octochord.

(a) Nicom. c.
(b) The Heptachord was made up of two Tetrachords, which being conjoined, the middle Note was the end of one, and the beginning of the other.

(a) NOW *Pythagoras* first of all, (b) lest the middle sound by conjunction, being it self compared to the two Extreams, should render only a Diatessaron concent, both to the Neate and to the Hypate: but that we might have greater variety, the two Extreams making the fullest concord each to other, that is to say, the concord of Diapason, which consists in a double proportion. Which inasmuch as it could not be done by two Tetrachords, he added an eighth sound, inserting it betwixt the Mese and Paramese, setting it from the Mese a whole Tone, and from the Paramese a Semitone; so, that which was formerly the Paramese in the Heptachord, is still the third from the Neate, both in name and place; but that which was now inserted is the fourth from the Neate, and hath a concent unto it of Diatessaron, which before the Mese had unto the Hypate; but the Tone between them, that is, the Mese, and the inserted, called the Paramese, instead of the former, to which soever Tetrachord it be added, whether to that which is at the Hypate, being of the lower; or to that of the Neate, being of the higher, will render Diapente concord; which is either way a system, consisting both of the Tetrachord it self, and the additional Tone, as the Diapente proportion (viz. sesquialtera) is found to be a system of sesquitertia, and sesquioctava, the Tone therefore is sesquioctava. (c) Thus the interval of four Chords, and of five, and of both conjoined together, called Diapason, and the Tone inserted between the two Tetrachords, being after this manner apprehended by *Pythagoras*, were determined to have this proportion in numbers.

(c) Meibonius seems to mistake the meaning of καταληφθῦναι ἔχειν, and therefore puts a Point after λεγομένη.

CHAP. VI.

The Arithmetical Proportions of Harmony.

(a) Theon. Smyrn.

(a) PYthagoras *is said to have first found out the proportion and concord of Sounds one to another, the Diatessaron in sesquitertia, the Diapente in sesqui-*

PART IX. PYTHAGORAS. 387

Sesquialtera, the Diapason in duple. The occasion and manner is related by (b) *Censorinus*, (c) *Boethius*, (d) *Macrobius*, and others; but more exactly by (e) *Nicomachus*, thus:

_{a) De die na-}
_{li. cap. 10.}
_{c) Muf.1.cap.}
_{c. 11.}
_{d) In Somn.}
_{cap. 2.}
_{e) Harm. en-}
_{hirid. cap. 6.}
_{repeated by}
_{Iamblichus de}
_{it. Pyth. cap.}

Being an intense thought, whether he might invent any instrumental help for the Ear, solid and infallible; such as the Sight hath by a compass and a rule, and by a dioptre; or the Touch by a Ballance, or by the invention of measures: As he past by a Smith's shop, by a happy chance he heard the Iron Hammers striking upon the Anvil, and rendring sounds most consonant one to another in all combinations except one. He observed in them these three concords, the Diapason, the Diapente, and the Diatessaron; but that which was between the Diatessaron and the Diapente, he found to be a discord in it self, tho' otherwise useful for the making up of the greater of them, (the Diapente). Apprehending this come to him from God, as a most happy thing, he hasted into a shop, and by various trials, finding the difference of the sounds to be according to the weight of the Hammers, and not according to the force of those who struck, nor according to the fashion of the Hammers, nor according to the turning of the Iron which was in beating out: Having taken exactly the weight of the Hammers, (f) he went straightway home, and to one beam fastned to the walls, cross from one corner of the room to the other, (lest any difference might arise from thence, or might be suspected to arise from the properties of several beams) tying four strings of the same substance, length, swiftness, and (g) twist, upon each of them he hung a several weight, fastning it at the lower end, and making the length of the strings altogether equal. Then striking the strings by two at a time interchangebly, he found out the aforesaid concords, each in its own combination; for that which was stretched by the greatest weight, in respect of that which was stretched by the least weight, he found to sound a Diapason. The greatest weight was of 12 Pound, the least of 6. Thence he determined, that the Diapason did consist in double proportion, which the weights themselves did shew. Next he found, that the greatest to the least but one, which was of eight pound, sounded a Diapente, whence he inferred this to consist in the proportion, called, Sesquialtera, in which proportion the weights were one to another. But unto that which was less than it self in weight, yet greater than the rest, being of nine pound, he found it to sound a Diatessaron; and discovered, that, proportionably to the weights, this concord was Sesquitertia, which string of nine pound is naturally Sesquialtera to the least, for 9 to 6 is so, (viz. Sesquialtera) as the least but one, which is 8, was to that which had the weight 6, in proportion Sesquitertia; and 12 to 8 is Sesquialtera; and that which is in the middle between Diapente and Diatessaron, whereby Diapente exceeds Diatessaron, is confirmed to be in Sesquioctava proportion, in which 9 is to 8. The system of both was called Diapente, that is, both of the Diapente and Diatessaron joined together, as duple proportion in compounded of Sesquialtera and Sesquitertia; such as are 2. 8. 6. Or on the contrary of Diatessaron and Diapente, as duple proportion is compounded of Sesquitertia and Sesquialtera, as 12. 9. 6. being taken in that order.

_{(f) Περὶ ἑαυ-}
_{τὸν ἀπηλλά-}
_{γη, Meibomius}
_{otherwise.}

_{(g) Ἰσοςρόφες,}
_{which Meibo-}
_{mius, contra-}
_{ry to all MSS.}
_{would change}
_{unnecessarily}
_{into ἰσοερό-}
_{πες, and ren-}
_{ders æque}
_{graves.}

Applying both his hand and ear to the weights which he had hung on, and by them confirming the proportion of the relations, he did ingeniously transfer the common result of the strings upon the cross beam, to the bridge of an instrument, which he called Χορδότον@; and as for stretching them proportionably to the weights, he did transfer that to an answerable screwing of the pegs. Making use of this foundation as an infallible rule, he extended the experiment to many kinds of Instruments, Cymbals, Pipes, Flutes, Monochords, Trigons, and the like; and he found, that this conclusion made by numbers was consonant without variation in all. That sound which proceeded from the number 6, he named *Hypate*; that which from the number 8, *Mese*, being Sesquitertia to the other, that from 9, *Paramese*, being a tone sharper than the *Mese*, viz. Sesquioctava; that from 12, *Neate*. And supplying the middle spaces according to the Diatonick kind, with proportionable sounds, he so ordered the Octochord with convenient numbers Duple, Sesquialtera, Sesquitertia, and (the difference of these two last) Sesquioctava.

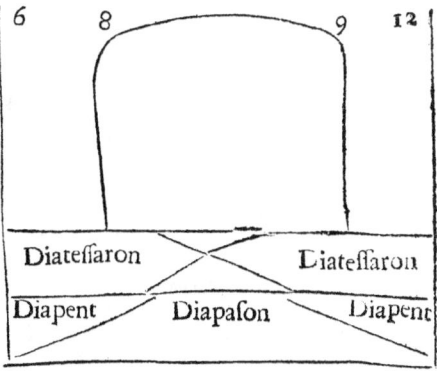

Thus he found the progress by a natural necessity, from the lowest to the highest, according to the Diatonical kind; from which again he did declare the Chromatick and Enarmonick kinds.

CHAP. V.

The Division of the Diapason, according to the Diatonick kind.

THIS Diatonick kind seems naturally to have these degrees and progresses, hemitone, tone and tone, (half note, whole note and whole note.) This is the system Diatessaron, consisting of two tones, and that which is called a hemitone; and then another tone being inserted, Diapente is made, being a system of three tones and a hemitone. Then in order, after this there being another hemitone, tone and tone, they make another Diatessaron, that is to say, another Sesquitertia. So that in the antienter Heptachord, all fourths from the lowest, sound a Diatessaron one to another, the hemitone taking the first, second, and third place, according to the progression in the Tetrachord. But in the *Pythagorical* Octochord, which is by a conjunction a system of the Tetrachord, and the Pentachord, and that either

Ddd 2 joinjoyntly of two Tetrachords, or disjoyntly of two Tetrachords, separated from one another by a tone, the procession will begin from the lowest, so that every fifth sound will make Diapente, the hemitone passing into four places, the first, the second, the third, and the fourth.

CHAP. VI.

The Canon of the Monochord.

(a) Laert.

(b) De Musica, lib. 3.

(c) Vit. Pyth.

(d) Mathemat.

(f) Manual. Music. lib. 1. p. 24.
(g) Sect. Canon.
(h) Mus. lib. 3. pag. 116.

(a) PYthagoras, as Timæus saith, found out the Canon of one Chord, that is the rule of the Monochord. (b) Aristides relates, that a little before he dyed, he exhorted his friends to play on the Monochord, thereby implying, that the heighth which is in Musick, is to be received rather by the Intellect through numbers, than by the sense through the ears.

Duris (cited by (c) Porphyrius) mentions a brazen Tablet, set up in the Temple of Juno, by Arimnestus son to Pythagoras, on which were graven, besides other arts, a Musical Canon; which was afterwards taken away by Simon a Musician, who arrogated the Canon to himself, and published it as his own.

(d) The division of the Canon, saith Theon, is made by the Tetractys in the Decad, which consists of a Monad, a Duad, a Triad, a Tetrad, 1, 2, 3, 4. For it comprehends a Sesquitertia, a Sesquialtera, a Duple, a Triple, and a Quadruple proportion. The Section of the Pythagorical Canon, according to the intention of Pythagoras himself, not as Eratosthenes misunderstood it, or, Thrasyllus, [whose operation Theon sets down] but as Timæus the Locreon (whom Plato also followeth) to 27. (f) Nicomachus mentions, as intending to deliver it in his larger Treatise of Musick. See also (g) Euclid, (h) Aristides, Quintilianus, and others.

CHAP. VII.

Institution by Musick.

(a) Jamb. vit. Pyth. cap. 15.

(a) COnceiving, that the first institution of men was to be made by sense, so that a man might see those fair figures and forms, and might hear the most excellent Musick, he first began by teaching Musick by Songs and Rythms, by which the cures of manners and passions were made, and by which the harmonies of the faculties of their souls were reduced to their primitive dispositions; and cures of distempers both of body and mind were invented by him. And that which was above all these, worthy to be taken notice of, that he made for his disciples those which were called ἐξαρτήσεις and ἐπαφαί, [of Musick] both by weight and by sound, and composed them harmonically, in a strange way making the commixtures of those tones which are called Diatonick, Chromatick, and Enarmonick, by which he changed all the passions of the mind, which were newly raised in them without reason, and which did procure griefs, and angers, and pities, and unseemly loves, and fears, and all kind of desires, and vexations, and appetites, and softnesses, and idlenesses, and impetuosities, correcting and directing every one of these towards virtue, by convenient harmonies, as by certain effectual medicines. And at night when his disciples went to sleep, he delivered them from all the noises and troubles of the day, and purified the perturbations of their minds, and rendred their sleeps quiet, with good dreams and predictions. And when they rose again from their beds, he freed them from the drousiness of the night, from faintness and sluggishness, by certain proper Songs, either set to the Lute, or some high Voice. As for himself, he never played on Instrument, or any thing, but he had it within him; and by an unconceivable kind of divinity, he applied his ears and mind unto the harmony of the world, which he alone did understand; and understanding the universal harmony and concent of the Spheres, and those Stars that move in them, which makes a more full and excellent musick than mortals by reason of their motion, which of unequal differing swiftnesses and bignesses overtaking one another, all which are ordered and disposed in a most musical proportion one towards another, beautified with various perfections, wherewith being irrigated, as having likewise orderly the discourse of his mind, as we may say exercising, he framed some representations of these, to exhibit them as much as was possible, imitating (that Musick) chiefly by Instruments, or the Voice alone. For he conceived that to himself only of all upon the earth, were intelligible and audible, the universal sounds, from the natural fountain and root, and thought himself worthy to be taught and to learn, and to be assimilated by desire and imitation to the celestials, one that was organized [in the parts of the body] by the deity which begot him. But it was sufficient for other men, that they, always looking upon him, and such things as they received from him, be benefited by images and examples, as not being able to lay hold on the first clear archetypes of all things: As to them, who cannot look upon the Sun, by reason of its splendor, we show the Eclipse either in a pond of water, or by some boared pitched thing, or by some dark-coloured glass, fearing the weakness of their eyes, and framing another way of perception, instead of looking on it, to those who love such things, tho' something inferior. This *Empedocles* seemeth to imply concerning his extraordinary and divine constitution above others, when he said:

> 'Mongst these was one in things sublimest skill'd,
> His mind with all the wealth of learning fill'd.
> He sought whatever Sages did invent;
> And whilst his thoughts were on this work intent,
> All things that are, he easily survey'd,
> And search through ten or twenty ages made.

Intimating by *sublimest things*; and, *He survey'd all things that are*; and, *The wealth of the mind*, and the like, the exquisite and acurate constitution of *Pythagoras* beyond others, both for body and mind, in seeing, hearing, and understanding.

CHAP.

CHAP. VIII.

Medicine by Musick.

a) *Jamb.c.*25. (*a*) Pythagoras conceived, that Musick conduced much to health, if used appositely; for he was accustomed to make use of this purification, not perfunctorily. This he called, *Medicine by Musick*, which kind of Melody he exercised about the Spring-time. He seated him who play'd on the Lute in the midst, and those who could sing sat round about him; and so he playing, they made a consort of some excellent pleasant Verses, wherewith they seemed exhilerated, and decently composed.

They likewise at another time made use of Musick as of a Medicine, and there were certain pleasant Verses framed, conducing much against the affections and diseases of the mind, and against the dejections and corrodings of the same. Moreover, he composed others against anger and malice, and all such disorders of the mind. There was also another kind of Musick and Song invented, against unlawful desires. He likewise used Dancing. He used no musical instrument but the Lute. Wind-Instruments he conceived to have an ignoble sound, and to be only fit for the common people, but nothing generous.

He likewise made use of the words of Homer and Hesiod, *for the rectification of the mind*. It is reported, that Pythagoras, *by a Spondiack Verse*

b) Reading ἐπὶ τῶν ἔργων. This example of Pythagoras seems to relate to Hesiod; the other of Empedocles to Homer.

(*b*) *out of the works* [perhaps of Hesiod, whose Poem bears that title, ἔργα] *by a Player on the Flute, assuaged the madness of a young man of* Tauromenium, *who being drunk, and having employ'd all the night lasciviously with his mistress, was going about to fire the door of his Rival's house, for he was exasperated and enflamed by the Phrygian mood. But* Pythagoras, *who was at that time busied in observing the Stars, immediately appeased and reclaimed him, by perswading the Piper to change his Air into the Spondiack mood. Whereupon the young man being suddainly composed, went quietly home, who but a little before would by no means hear the least exhortation from* Pythagoras, *but threatned and reviled him. In like manner* Empedocles, *when a young man drew his sword upon* Anchitus, *his Host,* (for that he had in publick judgment condemned his father to death) *and was about to have killed him, straightway changing his Tune, sung out of* Homer,

Nepenthe calming anger, easing grief:

and by that means freed Anchitus *his Host from death, and the young man from the crime of murther; who from thenceforward became one of his disciples, eminent amongst them.*

(c) See cap.

Moreover the whole School of Pythagoras made that which is called (*c*) ἐξάρτησις, and συναρμογὴ, and ἐπαφὴ, by certain Verses suitable thereto, and proper against the contrary affections, profitably diverting the constitutions & dispositions of the mind. For when they went to bed, and resigned themselves to rest, they purified their minds from the troubles and busie noises of the day, by some Songs and proper Verses, whereby they rendred their sleeps pleasant and quiet, and little troubled with dreams, and those dreams which they had were good. In the morning, when they arose from the common relief of sleep, they expelled drowsiness and sleepiness of the head with other Songs.

Sometimes also without pronouncing Verses, they expelled some affections and diseases, and reduced the sick to health, ἐπᾴδοντες, by charming them. And from hence it is probable, that the word Epode came to be used. After this manner, Pythagoras instituted a most profitable correction of manners and life by Musick. Hitherto Jamblichus. All which is ratify'd by other testimonies: That *they had Verses against the affections of the mind, grief, anger, lust,* is related also by (*d*) Seneca, who saith, that Pythagoras *composed the troubles of his soul by the Lute*. And (*e*) Cicero, That *the Pythagoreans used to deliver Verses, and some Precepts, and to reduce the mind from intenseness of thoughts to tranquillity, by Songs and Instruments*. To which effect, (*f*) Ælian relates of Clinius the Pythagorean, *that if at any time he perceived himself enclining to anger, he, before it took full possession of him, play'd upon the Lute; and to those who asked him, Why he did so, answered, Because I am calmed.*

(d) De ira. 3, 9.
(e) Tusc. quæst. 4. proem.
(f) Lib. 14. c. 23.

That he *danced*, (*g*) Porphyrius confirms, saying, *He danced some dances, which he conceived to confer agility and health to the body*.

(g) Pag. 21.

That he *disallowed Flutes and Wind-Instruments*, appears from (*h*) Aristides Quintilianus, who saith, *He advised his disciples to refrain from permitting their ears to be defiled with the sound of the Flute; but on the contrary, to purifie the irrational impulsions of the soul by solemn Songs to the Lute.*

(h) Lib. 2.

That *he made use of* Homer *and* Hesiod *for rectification of the mind*, is thus related by (*i*) Porphyrius; *he had morning Exercises at his own house, composing his soul to the Lute, and singing some old Pæans of* (*k*) Thales. *He likewise sung some Verses of* Homer *and* Hesiod, *whereby the mind seemed to be rendred more sedate.*

(i) Pag. 21.
(k) Not the Philosopher, but the Cretan. See the Life of Thales, cap.

The story of the young man is confirmed by (*l*) Ammonius, by (*m*) Cicero, related thus; *Whenas some young men being drunk, and irritated by the musick of Flutes, would have broken open the door of a modest Matron's house, he bad the woman-piper play a Spondiack tune; which as soon as she did, their raging petulancy was allayed by the slowness of the Mood, and solemnness of the Tune.*

(l) In quinque voc.
(m) Cited by Boethius.

(*n*) St. Basil relates another story to the same purpose, That Pythagoras *meeting with some that came from a feast drunk, bid the Piper* (the Musician at that feast) *to change his Tune, and to play a Dorick Air; wherewith they were so brought to themselves, that they threw away their Garlands, and went home ashamed.*

(n) Homil. 14.

That, evening and morning, they used Musick to compose their minds, is affirmed by many others. (*o*) Quintilian. *It was the custom of the Pythagoreans as soon as they waked, to excitate their souls with the Lute, that they might be the readier for action; and before they went to sleep, to soften their minds by it.* (*p*) Plutarch. *The Musick of the Lute the Pythagoreans used before they went to sleep, thereby charming and composing the passionate and irrational part of the soul.* (*q*) Censorinus. *Pythagoras, that his mind might be continually seasoned with Divinity, used* (as they say) *to sing before he went to sleep, and as soon as he waked.*

(o) Lib. 9. cap. 4.
(p) De Isid. & Osirid.
(q) Cap. 12.

As for the several moods, which, in musical compositions, were observed by the Ancients, for moving particular passions, there is a remarkable fragment of *Damon* the Musician, cited by (*r*) *Aristides*.

(*q*) *Muf.* lib. 2. pag. 95.

SECT. 3.

Geometry.

PYthagoras (saith (*a*) *Jamblichus*) *is reported to have been much addicted to Geometry; for, amongst the Egyptians [of whom he learned it] there are many Geometrical Problems, the most learned of them having been continually, for many ages of gods and men, necessitated to measure their whole country, by reason of the overflowing and decrease of Nilus; whence it is called Geometry.* (*b*) *Some there are who ascribe all Theorems concerning Lines, jointly to the Egyptians and the Chaldeans, and all these, they say, Pythagoras took, and augmenting the Science, explained them accurately to his Disciples.* (*c*) Proclus affirms that *he first advanced the Geometrical part of Learning into a Liberal Science, considering the Principles more sublimely* (than *Thales, Ameristus,* and *Hippias* his predecessors in this study) *and perscrutating the Theorems immaterially and intellectually:* (*d*) *Timæus* faith, *That he first perfected Geometry; the Elements whereof,* (as *Anticlides* affirms) *were invented by* Moeris. (*e*) Aristoxenus, that *he first introduced Measures and Weights amongst the Græcians.*

(*a*) Cap. 29. p. 144.

(*b*) Ibid.

(*c*) In *Euclid.* lib. 2.

(*d*) Laert.

(*e*) Laert.

CHAP. I.

Of a Point, Line, Superficies and Solid.

(*a*) PYthagoras afferted a Point to be correspondent in proportion to an unite; a Line, to 2; a Superficies, to 3; a Solid, to 4. (*b*) The *Pythagoreans* define a point, a *Monad* having position.

(*c*) A line being the Second, and constituted by the first Motion, from indivisible nature, they called *Duad.*

(*d*) A superficies they compared to the Number 3. for that is the first of all causes which are found in figures: for a Circle, which is the Principle of all round figures, occultly comprifeth a Triad in center, space, and circumference. But a Triangle, which is the first of all rectiline figures, is manifestly included in a Ternary, and receiveth its form according to that number.

(*e*) Hence the *Pythagoreans* affirm, that the Triangle is simply the Principle of generation, and of the formation of things generable; whereupon *Timæus* faith, that all proportions, as well natural, as of the constitution of Elements, are Triangular, because they are distant by a threefold interval, and are collective of things every way divisible, and variously permutable, and are replenished with Material infinity, and represent the natural conjunctions of bodies dissolved, as Triangles which are comprehended by three right Lines; but they have Angles which collect the multitude of Lines, and give an adventitious Angle and Conjunction to them. With reason therefore did *Philolaus* dedicate the Angle of a Triangle to four Gods, *Saturn, Pluto, Mars, Bacchus,* comprehending in these the whole quadripartite Ornament of Elements coming down from Heaven, or from the four quarters of the Zodiack. For *Saturn* constituteth an essence wholly humid and frigid: *Mars* wholly fiery, *Pluto* comprifeth all Terrestrial life, *Bacchus* predominates over humid and hot generation, of which Wine is a sign, being humid and hot. All these differ in their operations upon second bodies, but are united to one another, for which reason *Philolaus* collected their Union according to one Angle. But if the differences of Triangles conduce to generation, we must justly acknowledge the Triangle to be the Principle and Author of the constitution of sublunary things, for the right Angle gives them essence, and determines the measure of its being; and the proportion of a rectangle triangle causeth the essence of generable Elements; the obtuse Angle giveth them all distance, the proportion of an obtuse angled triangle augmenteth material forms in magnitude, and in all kinds of mutation; the acute Angle maketh their nature divisible, the proportion of an acute-angled Triangle prepares them to receive divisions into infinite; and simply, the Triangular proportion constituteth the essence of Material bodies, distant and every way divisible: Thus much for Triangles.

(*a*) Procl. in *Euclid.* lib. 2. def. 2.

(*b*) Procl. in *Eucl.* lib. 2. def. 1.

(*c*) Procl. lib. 2. def. 2.

(*d*) Procl. lib. 2. def. 5.

(*e*) Procl. in *Eucl.* lib. 2. def. 24.

(*f*) Of quadrangular figures, the *Pythagoreans* hold that the square chiefly representeth the divine essence, for by it they principally signifie pure and immaculate order; for rectitude imitateth inflexibility, equality firm power; for Motion proceedeth from inequality, rest from equality. The Gods therefore, who are Authors in all things of firm consistence, and pure incontaminate order, and inevitable power; are not improperly represented by the figure of a Square. Moreover, *Philolaus* by another apprehension calleth the Angle of a Square, the Angle of a *Rhea, Ceres,* and *Vesta*; for seeing that the Square constituteth the Earth, and is the nearest Element to it, as *Timæus* teacheth, but the earth it self receiveth Genital seeds and Prolifick power from all these gods; he not unaptly compareth the Angle of a Square to all these life-communicating Deities. For some call the Earth and *Ceres* her self *Vesta*; and *Rhea* is said wholly to participate of her, and that in her are all generative causes. Whence *Philolaus* faith, the Angle of a Square by a certain terrestrial power, comprehends one union of these divine kinds.

(*f*) Procl. *Eucl.* lib. : def. 34.

SECT. II.

Propositions.

OF the many Geometrical Theorems invented by *Pythagoras,* and his followers, these are particularly known as such.

(*a*) *Only these three Polygones fill up the whole space about a point, The æquilateral Triangle, and the Square, and the Hexagone æquilateral and æquiangle.* The æquilateral Triangle must be taken six times, for six two thirds make four right Angles; the Hexagone must be taken thrice, for every sex angular Angle is equal to one right Angle, and one third; the square four times, for every Angle of a Square is right. Therefore six æquilateral Triangles joined as the Angles, com-

(*b*) Procl. *Eucl.* lib. 3. Com. 20.

compleat four right Angles, as do also three Hexagones and four Squares. But of all other Polygones whatsoever, joined together at the Angles, some exceed four right Angles, others fall short. This *Proclus* calls *a celebrious Theorem of the Pythagoreans.*

(b) Procl. in Eucl. lib. 4. Prop. 32. Com. 6.

(b) *Every Triangle hath the internal Angles equal to two right Angles.* This Theorem *Eudemus* the Peripatetick, ascribes to the Pythagoreans; their manner of Demonstration see in *Proclus.*

(c) Euclid. lib. 1. Prop.

(c) *In rectangle Triangles the square which is made of the side that subtendeth the right Angle, is equal to the squares which are made of the sides containing the right Angle.*

(d) Vitruv. Archit. 9. 1.

(d) This Theorem *Pythagoras* found out; and by it shewed how to make a gnomon or square (which the Carpenters cannot do without much difficulty and uncertainty) not Mechanically, but according to Rule; for if we take three Rulers, one of them being three foot long, the Second four foot, the Third five foot, and put these three so together that they touch one another at the ends in a Triangle, they make a perfect Square: Now if to each of these Rulers be adscribed a Square, that which consisted of three foot will have 9; that which of 4, will have 16; that which of 5, will have 25. So that how many feet the area's of the two lesser squares of three and four make, so many will the square of 5 make.

(e) Laert.

(e) *Apollodorus* the *Logistick*, and others, relate, that *upon the invention of this Theorem,* Pythagoras *sacrificed a Hecatomb* (f) to the Muses, in confirmation whereof they alledge this Epigram,

(f) Vitruv. loco cit.

That noble Scheme Pythagoras *devis'd,*
For which a Hecatomb he sacrific'd.

(g) Non posse su. viv. sec. Epicur.
(h) Nat. deor. 3.
* Pag.
(i) Epist.

(g) *Plutarch* saith, it was only *an Ox*; and even that is questioned by (h) *Cicero*, as inconsistent with his doctrine, which forbad bloody sacrifices. *The more accurate therefore* (saith ** Porphyrius*) *say, he sacrificed an Ox made of Flower*; or, as (i) *Gregory Nazianzen*, *of Clay*.

(k) Non posse suaviter vivere. sec. Epicurum.

But (k) *Plutarch* doubts, whether it were for the invention of the forementioned Proposition, that *Pythagoras* sacrificed an Ox, or for *the Problem concerning the Area of a Parabola.* Indeed,

(l) Procl. in Eucl. lib. 4. prop. 44.

(l) *the application of spaces or figures, to lines, is,* as *Eudemus* his followers *affirm, an invention of the Pythagorick Muse, Parabole, Hyperbole, Elleipsis.* From them the later Writers taking these names, transferr'd them to Conical lines, calling one *Parabole*, another *Hyperbole*, another *Elleipsis*; whereas those ancient divine persons (the Pythagoreans) signified by those names the description of places, applied to a determinate right line.

(m) Reading ὅ τ' ἂν ᾖ εὐθείας ἐκκειμένης τὸ δοθὲν χωρίον παρὰ τῇ εὐθείᾳ συμπερατεῖναι τότε παρα-βαλεῖν ἐκεῖνο τὸ χωρίον φασὶν ὅταν δὲ μεῖζον, &c.

(m) For when a right line being proposed, the space given is wholly adæquate to the right line; then, they say, the space is applied, (παραβάλλειν) but when you make the length of the space greater than that of the right line, then, they say, it exceeds; (ὑπερβάλλειν) but when less, so as the space being described, there is some part of the right line beyond it, then it falls short. (ἐκλείπειν) In this sense *Euclid* useth *Parabole*, lib. 1. prop. 44. and *Hyperbole* and *Elleipsis*, in the 6th Book.

CHAP. III.

How he collected the Stature of Hercules.

(a) Agel. l. 1. c. 1.

(a) PLutarch in his Treatise, entituled, *How great difference there is in the souls and bodies of men, as to ingenuity and strength,* relates, that *Pythagoras* reasoned curiously and subtilly, in finding out and collecting the extraordinary stature and length of *Hercules* his body: for, it being manifest, that *Hercules* measured with his feet the running course of Olympian-*Jupiter* at *Pisa*, and that he made it 600 feet long; and that all the other running courses in *Greece*, instituted afterwards by other persons were 600 foot long, yet shorter than this; He easily understood the measure of *Hercules* his foot, considering that it was proportionably so much longer than that of other men, as the Olympick course was longer than all others. And having comprehended the size of *Hercules* his foot, he considered what length of body did suit with that measure, according to the natural proportion of all the members one to another; and so collected the consequent, That *Hercules* was so much taller in body than others, by how much the Olympick course was longer than the rest, which were made after the same number of feet.

SECT. IV.

Astronomy.

(a) Jamb. cap. 29. pag. 144.

(a) NEither did they superficially consider the speculation of celestial things, in which *Pythagoras was exquisite*, as appears by these few remains.

CHAP. I.

The System of the Spheres.

(a) Anon vit. Pyth. apud Phot.

(a) THE word οὐρανὸς, Heaven, is taken three ways; first, for the sphere of fixed Stars; secondly, for all that is betwixt the sphere of fixed Stars and the Moon; lastly, for the whole world, both Heaven and Earth.

(b) Apud Phot.

(b) The anonymous writer of the life of *Pythagoras* affirms, that *he said, there are twelve orders in Heaven, whereof the first and outmost is the fixed sphere, next to this is the Star of* Saturn, *and then the other six Planets,* Jupiter, Mars, Venus, Mercury, Sun *and* Moon; *next these, the sphere of Fire, then that of Air, then that of Water, last of all the Earth.*

But they who seem more strictly to follow the mind of *Pythagoras* and his disciples, averr, *They held the celestial spheres to be ten, whereof nine only are visible to us,* (the fixed Sphere, the seven Planets, and our Earth) *the tenth is* Antichthon, *an Earth above, or opposite to ours.* This Antichthon they (d) added, to make up the number of the moving bodies. For (e) *considering, that the affections and proportions of Musick consist in numbers, that all other things appear to be assimilated to numbers, that numbers are the first of all nature, that the elements of numbers are the elements of all beings;*

(d) Plut. Simplic.
(e) Aristot.

They

They asserted, that all Heaven is Harmony and Number, and that the affections and parts of Heaven are correspondent to number: and collecting these, they adapted them to the composition of the whole, wherein if any thing were wanting, they supplied it, that the whole might be alike compacted. As, because the Decad seems to be perfect, and to comprehend the whole nature of numbers, therefore they asserted the Celestial Spheres to be Ten. Now there being Nine only visible to us, hereupon they conceived the Tenth to be *Antichthon*, an Earth opposite to ours.

As concerning the Order and System of these, the *Pythagoreans* (*f*) held, *That in the middle of the world is fire*; or (as (*g*) *Stobæus*) *in the midst of the Four Elements is the fiery Globe of Unity,* (*h*) which they term *Vesta* and *Monad*. They (saith *Simplicius*) *who understand this thing more intimately, say, that this fire is the procreative, nutritive, and excitative power, which is in the midst of the Earth*. But *Simplicius* himself seems not to have apprehended the right meaning of the *Pythagoreans*, who by this *fire*, or *fiery Globe of Unity*, meant nothing else but the Sun, seated in the midst of the Universe, immoveable, about which the other parts of the World are moved. This Opinion *Pythagoras* seems to have derived from the Ægyptians, who Hieroglyphically represented the Sun by a Beetle, (*k*) because, as the Beetle having formed a Ball of Cow-dung, and lying upon its back, rouls it about from Claw to Claw; so the other parts of the World are moved and rouled by and about the Sun.

That by this immoveable fire in the midst of the Universe, they understood not (as (*l*) *Simplicius* conceiveth) the Earth, is manifest, forasmuch as they further held, that (*m*) the Earth is not immoveable, nor seated in the midst of the Globe, but suspended, as being (*n*) one of the Stars carried about the fire which is in the middle, and that thereby it maketh Day and Night. (*o*) The Reason why the Earth ought not to have the middle place, is, because the most excellent body ought to have the most excellent place: but Fire is more excellent than Earth, and the Center more excellent than all places without it; therefore they conceived, that not the Earth, but the Fire, is placed in the midst. (*p*) Moreover, because that which is the most excellent of the Universe, ought principally to be preserved, and the middle is such, therefore they term the Fire, Διὸς φυλακὴν, *the custody of* Jupiter.

(*q*) The same they held of the *Antichthon* also, [*viz.* That like our Earth it is suspended, as being one of the Stars carried about the Fire, and thereby maketh Day and Night.] By this *Antichthon*, *Clemens* saith, they understood *Heaven*: *Simplicius*, the *Moon*, as being a kind of æthereal Earth, as well for that it eclipseth the light of the Sun, which is proper to the Earth, as for that it is the bound of Cœlestials, as the Earth of Sublunaries. But the contrary is manifest, as well from the compleating of the number ten, (in respect whereof this *Antichthon* was imagined) as for that they held, (*r*) it is not visible to us, by reason, that following the motion of this Earth, it is always opposite to, or beneath us, and the bigness of our Earth hinders us from seeing it: And *Aristotle* affirms there were some who conceived the Antichthon to be the cause why there are more Eclipses of the Moon than of the Sun, which may likewise happen by reason of many other bodies invisible to us.

(*s*) *Laertius*, who saith *Philolaus* was the first that conceived the Earth to have a Circular Motion, seems to mean no more, than that he first committed this Opinion of *Pythagoras* to writing, and first made it publick; for *Eusebius* expresly affirms, that he committed to writing the dissertations of *Pythagoras*. His Opinion, as delivered by *Plutarch* and *Stobæus*, is exactly the same; for he placed fire in the midst, which he called the *Genius* of the Universe, and the Mansion of *Jupiter*, and the Mother of Gods, and Altar, and Ward, and Measure of Nature: he conceived that the Ten Celestial Bodies move about it. Heaven, of the sphere of fixed Stars, the five Planets, the Sun, the Moon, the Earth, and lastly the *Antichthon*.

From the same Fountain seems *Aristarchus* the *Samian* to have derived this Hypothesis, though some ascribe the invention thereof to him; for he supposed, that (*u*) the Sun and Planets move not, but that the Earth moveth round about the Sun, which is seated in the middle. (*x*) *Plutarch* adds, that *Plato* in his old age repented for that he had placed the Earth in the midst of the Universe, and not in its proper place.

This Opinion was of late revived by *Nicolaus Copernicus*, who considering how inconvenient and troublesome it is to understand, and maintain the motions of the Heavens, and immobility of the Earth, explained it with admirable Ingenuity, after the mind of the *Pythagoreans*. According to whose Hypothesis, the Sun (as we said) is settled in the midst of the World, immoveable: The sphere of fixed Stars in the extremity or outside of the World, immoveable also; betwixt these are disposed the Planets, and amongst them the Earth as one of them; the Earth moves both about the Sun, and about his proper Axis. Its diurnal Motion by one revolution, makes a night and a day; its annual motion about the Sun, by one revolution makes a year; so as by reason of his diurnal motion to the *East*, the Sun and other Stars seem to move to the *West*; and by reason of its annual motion through the *Zodiack*, the Earth it self is in one Sign, and the Sun seems to be in the Sign opposite to it: Betwixt the Sun and the Earth they place *Mercury* and *Venus*: Betwixt the Earth and the fixed Stars, *Mars*, *Jupiter*, and *Saturn*: The Moon being next the Earth, is continually moved within the great Orb betwixt *Venus* and *Mars*, round about the Earth, as its Centre: Its revolution about the Earth is compleated in a Month; about the Sun (together with the Earth) in a Year.

CHAP. II.

The Motions of the Planets.

AS concerning the Course and Revolution of the Planets, (*a*) they affirm the great year to be the Revolution of *Saturn*; for the rest of the Planets absolve their Periods in a shorter time; but *Saturn* in no less than Thirty Years, *Jupiter* in 12 Years, *Mars* in Two; the Sun [speaking according

PART IX. PYTHAGORAS. 393

ing to the *Phænomenon*] in One; *Mercury* and *Venus* as the Sun, [or to speak more exactly. *Mercury* in Three Months, *Venus* in Eight] the Moon, as being next the Earth soonest, in a Month.

According to this inequality, appears the motion of the Planets to our sight, by reason that the Eye is out of the Center of the Orb: But in the whole course of Astronomy (saith *Geminus*) are supposed the motions of the Sun, Moon, and five Planets, equal and circular, contrary to the diurnal Revolution of the World. The *Pythagoreans* first applying themselves to these disquisitions, supposed circular and equal motions of the Sun, the Moon, and the five Planets; for they admitted not such irregularity in eternal and divine bodies, that sometimes they should move swifter, sometimes slower, and sometimes stand still (as the stationary Points in the Planets. Neither in any sober, well-tempered person could we admit such irregularity of pace. Indeed, the necessities of life often cause men to move faster or slower; but in the incorruptible Nature of the Stars, there cannot be alledged any cause of swiftness and slowness. Wherefore the *Pythagoreans* proposed this question, how the *Phænomena*s might be salved by circular and equal motions.

That *Pythagoras* himself observed these Irregularities, and the ways to salve them, appears from *(b)* Cap. 6. *Jamblichus*, who saith, *(b)* he communicated a revelative right knowledge of all manner of motion of the Spheres and Stars; ἐπιπροσθήσεων τε, ὑπολείψεων, καὶ ἀνωμαλιῶν, ἐκκεντροτήτων τε, καὶ ἐπικύκλων. Ἐπιπρόσθησις is the anticipation of any Planet, either in respect to some other Planet, or to the fixed Stars. Ὑπόλειψις is the *falling later* of any Planet, either in respect to some other Planet, or to the fixed Stars, Ἀνωμαλία, *Inequality*, is, when the same Planet moveth slower and faster, according to its distance from the Sun, in the Pythagorick Hypothesis; (or in the Ptolemaick, from the Earth) slower in its *Aphelium*, faster in its *Perihelium*.

The two ways of salving these *Phænomena*'s, are by *Eccentricks*, or by *Epicycles*; for a Hemocentrick with an *Epicycle* (as *Eudoxus* first demonstrated) is equipollent to an *Eccentrick*. *Eccentricity* is, when the Center of their equal motion is distant from the Center of their apparent *(c)* Loc. cit. motion. Both these *(c) Jamblichus* ascribes to *Pythagoras*, from whom perhaps they were de-*(d) Laert.* rived to *Eudoxus*, to whose invention *(d)* others *Eudox.* ascribe them.

CHAP. III.

The Intervals and Harmony of the Spheres.

Pythagoras (saith *(a) Censorinus*) asserted, that *(a)* De die na-this whole World is made according to mu-tal. cap. 13. sical proportion, and that the seven Planets, betwixt Heaven and the Earth, which govern the Nativities of Mortals, have a harmonious motion, and Intervals correspondent to musical Diastemes, and render various sounds, according to their several heights, so consonant, that they make most sweet melody; but to us inaudible, by reason of the greatness of the noise, which the narrow passage of our Ears is not capable to receive. For, as *Eratosthenes* collected, that the largest Circumference of the Earth is 252000 *Stadia*, so *Pythagoras* declared how many *Stadia* there are betwixt the Earth and every Star. In this measure of the World, we are to understand the *Italick Stadium*, which consists of 625 Feet; for there are others of a different length, as the *Olympick* of 600 Feet, the *Pythick* of 500. From the Earth therefore to the Moon, *Pythagoras* conceived to be about 126000 *Stadia*, and that distance [according to musical proportion] is a *Tone*; from the Moon to *Mercury* (who is called στίλβων) half as much, as it were a *Hemitone*, from thence to *Phosphorus*, which is the star *Venus*, almost as much, that is, another *Hemitone*; from thence to the Sun twice as much, as it were a *Tone* and a half. Thus the Sun is distant from the Earth Three *Tones* and a half, which is called *Diapente*; from the Moon Two and a half, which is *Diatessaron*; from the Sun to *Mars*, who is called Πυρόεις, there is the same Interval as from the Earth to the Moon, which makes a *Tone*; from thence to *Jupiter*, who is called Φαέθων, half as much, which makes a *Hemitone*; from thence to the supream Heaven, where the Signs are a *Hemitone* also; so that the Diasteme from the supream Heaven to the Sun is *Diatessaron*, that is, Two *Tones* and a half: from the same Heaven to top of the Earth six *Tones*, a *Diapason* concord. Moreover he referred to other Stars many things, which the Masters of Musick treat of, and showed, that all this World is Enarmonick. Thus *Censorinus*. But *(b) Pliny* delivering this Opinion of *Pythagoras*, reckons seven *Tones* from the Earth *(b)* Lib. 9. cap. to the supream Heaven; for whereas *Censorinus* 21, 22. accounts but a *Hemitone* from Saturn to the Zodiack, *Pliny* makes it *Sesquiple*.

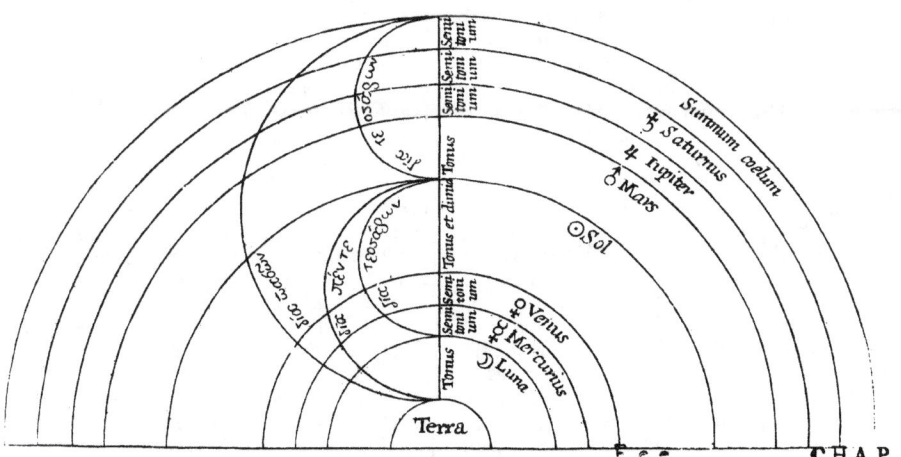

CHAP.

CHAP. IV.

Of the Planet Venus.

(a) Lib. 2. cap. 8.

(a) NExt the Sun (faith *Pliny*) there is a great Star, called *Venus*, alternately errant, in Names emulating both the Sun and Moon. For, preventing and rising before morning, he takes the Name of *Lucifer*, as another Sun bringing on day; on the other side, shining at Sun-set, it is called *Vesper*, as proroguing light, and performing the Office of the Moon, which its Nature *Pythagoras* the *Samian* first found out, about the XLII *Olympiad*, which was of *Rome* the 147th year. In magnitude it exceeds all the other Stars, and is of so great splendor, that this Star only casts a shadow; whence it hath diversity of Names; some call it *Juno*; others, *Isis*; others, *Mothers of the gods*. By the Nature hereof, all things are generated upon Earth; for, at either rising, it scattereth prolifick dew, supplying not only the Conceptions of Earth, but likewise stimulating all living Creatures. It performs the Revolution of the *Zodiack* in 348 days, never receding from the Sun more than 46 parts, according to *Timæus*. Thus *Pliny*. That there is a mistake in the time, hath been already shown; but the thing it self is confirmed by *Laertius*, who affirms, *Pythagoras* first said, that *Vesper* and *Lucifer* are the same star; yet elsewhere adds, that some ascribe this to *Parmenides*. But that it was a Doctrine of the *Pythagoreans*, appears from this account given by *Timæus*; the star *Juno* many call *Venus* and *Lucifer*. All persons are not skilful in the Rules of sacred Astronomy, and in the Sciences of rising and setting; for the same star is sometimes *Hesper*, when it followeth the Sun in such manner, that it is conspicuous to us when the Sun is set; and sometimes *Eous*, when it goeth before the Sun, and riseth before Sun-rising.

The Doctrine of *Pythagoras*.

CHAP. I.

Philosophy, its Name, Definition, Parts, Method.

(a) Agell. 1. 9.

(a) THE *Pythagoreans* being adorned with these studies of Science, from thence ascended to perfect the Works of the World, and the Principles of Nature.

(b) Jamb. cap. 29. pag. 144.

(b) *Pythagoras* first gave the Name to Philosophy, defining it, An Appetition, and Love to Wisdom. *Wisdom* is the Science of Truth in things that are. *Things that are*, he called Immaterials, and Eternals, and sole Agents, which are the Incorporeals; the rest are equivocally called such, by Participation with these, *viz.* Corporeals, Materials, and Corruptibles, which indeed are not. Now *Wisdom* is the Science of those things which are, but not of those which are equivocally; for Corporeals are not docible, nor admit certain knowledge, being infinite, and not comprehensible by science, and things which (as it were) are not, according to the difference of all things, neither can be rightly described by any definition. Of those whose Nature is such, as that they cannot be known, it is impossible to frame a Science; wherefore neither is it likely, that there can be a love of a Science which is not. But rather of that which is conversant about those things which properly are, and continue always the same, and like themselves, and co-exist always with a true appellation. Upon the knowledge of these followeth that which is of equivocal things, (tho' not sought after) as the science of Particulars follows the science of Universals: For, as *Architas* saith, They who know *Universals* well, will plainly see what *Particulars* are. Wherefore *things that are*, are not of one kind only and simply, but of many various kinds, Intelligibles and Incorporeals, whose appellation is τὰ ὄντα, *things that are*. Corporeal things, subject to sense, are those which are by participation of those that are. Concerning all these, he delivered most proper Sciences, leaving nothing unexcussed, and delivered also to men the common Sciences, as the demonstrative, the definitive, the divisive, as is manifest from the Commentaries of the *Pythagoreans*.

Hereupon he defined Philosophy, (c) the knowledge of things that are, as things that are, and (d) the knowledge of things divine and humane; as also (e) the meditation of death, daily endeavouring to free the soul from the prison of the body; and (f) the resemblance of God as far as is possible for man.

For (g) the scope of Philosophy is to free the mind, (the divine part of the soul) which is planted in us, and to set it at liberty, without which liberty none can learn or perceive any thing solid or true, by the help or benefit of sense; for the mind, according to him, seeth all things, and hears all things; all things else are deaf and blind.

In order hereunto it is, that Philosophy being of two kinds, Practick and Theoretick; the Practick, according to the method of the *Pythagoreans*, precedes the Theoretick. The Reason receive thus, explain'd by (h) *Hierocles*.

(c) Psell. compend. de 5000.
(d) Psell. loc. cit.
(e) D. Hieron. adv. Rufin.
(f) Stob. serm.
(g) Porph. pag.
(h) In aur. carm.

Philosophy is the purification and perfection of humane life; *purification, from material irrationality and the mortal body*; *perfection, from the recovery of its own excellent life, reducing it to the Divine Resemblance. Virtue and Truth are chiefly able to effect these, that taking away Excess of passions, this (rightly had) inducing the divine form.*

First are laid down the Instructions of Practick Virtue; for first we must compose the Irrationality which is in us, and then (so prepar'd) apply our selves to the knowledge of the more divine things. For as it is not possible for the Eye, being full of dirt, and not cleansed, to look upon things very bright; so neither can the Soul, not possessing Virtue, gaze upon the Beauty of Truth. For that which is not pure, is not capable of touching that which is pure. Practick Philosophy produceth Virtue; Theorick, Truth. As in these Golden Verses (of Pythagoras) we find the Practick Philosophy, called Humane Virtue, but the *Theoretick* celebrated as *Divine Virtue*, when closing the *Instructions of Civil Virtue*.

These labour (saith he) *study these, and these affect;*
To Divine Virtue, these thy steps direct.

First therefore a Man must be made good, then a God: good the Civil Virtues render a Man, but the Sciences conducing to the Divine Virtue divinifie. But to those who ascend, the lesser things precede the greater; for which reason in the Pythagorical Precepts, the Rules of Virtue are first delivered, teaching us to ascend from the greatest use of Life, to the Divine Resemblance.

* *Anon. Phot.*   * Three ways, say they, man may become better than himself; first by Conversation with the Gods; for it is necessary, that he who addresseth himself to them, at that time, sequester himself from all evil, assimilating himself as near as he can to God: Secondly, by well doing, for that is proper to God, and therein he imitates God: Thirdly, by death; for if the Soul in this Life, being a little separated from the Body, becometh better, and beginneth to divine in Dreams by Visions and Extasies of Diseases, it will be much better when it shall be wholly separated from the Body.

Hence he affirmed, that (*i*) the most considerable of all things Humane, is to inform the Soul concerning good and ill; That (*k*) men have perfect felicity when they have a good Soul, or that (*l*) the knowledge of the perfection of the Virtues of the Soul is the chief felicity; That (*m*) every man is appointed by God to know and to contemplate; That (*n*) Virtue is a Harmony, and so is all good, even God himself; That (*o*) the End or chief Good is to resemble God: whence he expresly said, Follow God, not visible to the Eye, but intelligible to the Understanding, by the harmony of the World; That (*p*) the most excellent things given by the gods unto men, are, to speak truth, and to benefit others, [Theoretick and Practick Virtue] and that each of these resembled the Works of God: to this latter *Strabo* alludes, commending those who said, (*q*) Men imitate the gods most when they benefit others: The former is confirmed by (*r*) *Porphyrius*, that he advised above all things to speak truth, for that only is able to make Men like to the gods; for God himself, as he learn'd of the *Magi*, who term him *Oromasdes*, in his Body resembles light, in his Soul truth. This is that Θεότης, (*Divinity*) which (*s*) *Jamblichus* reckons last in his Recapitulation of the Heads of the Pythagorick Philosophy; and is the same with which the Golden Verses conclude, thus,

Then stript of flesh up to free Æther soar,
A deathless god, divine, mortal no more.

(*i*) *Laert.*
(*k*) *Laert.* ibid. citing *Alexander*.
(*l*) *Clem. Strom.* 2. citing *Heraclides*.
(*m*) *Jamb.* protrept. cap. 9. pag. 58.
(*n*) *Laert.* loco cit.
(*o*) *Stob. Eth.* 2. pag. 163.
(*p*) *Porph.*

(*q*) Lib.

(*r*) Pag. 27. see also *Stob. Serm.* 11.

(*s*) Cap. 6.

SECT. I.

Practick Philosophy, its parts; and first of Pædeutick.

PRactick Philosophy seems to have been the Invention of *Pythagoras*; for *Aristotle* affirms that he first undertook to discourse concerning Virtue; That *Socrates* is generally esteemed the Author thereof, perhaps is only because, as *Aristotle* adds, coming after him he discoursed better and more fully thereupon.

To this part of Philosophy alludes (*b*) this Sentence of *Pythagoras*; That the discourse of that Philosopher is vain, by which no passion of a man is healed: for as there is no benefit of Medicine, if it expel not diseases out of bodies, so neither of Philosophy, if it expel not ill out of the Soul.

(*b*) *Stob. serm.* 80.

Virtues being of two kinds, *private*, which respect our selves, and *publick*, which have reference to others; *Pythagoras* seems to have comprehended the first under *Pædeutick*, the second under *Politick*. *Laertius* affirms he writ Three Treatises, *Pædeutick, Politick, Physick.* The Heads of *Pædeutick*, according to the general recapitulation of (*c*) *Jamblichus*, seem to have been these, *Institution, Silence, Abstinence from Flesh, Fortitude, Temperance, Sagacity.*

(*c*) Cap. 6.

CHAP. I.

Institution, Silence, Abstinence.

COncerning Institution, &c. there are these Sentences and Precepts of *Pythagoras*, preserved by *Stobæus* and others.

(*a*) We ought to make choice of the best course of life; for Custom will make it pleasant: Wealth is a weak Anchor, Glory a weaker: The Body, Magistracies, Honours, all these are infirm and unable. What are then able Anchors? Wisdom, Magnanimity, Fortitude; these no tempest shakes. This is the Law of God, that Virtue only is solid; all else are but trifles.

(*a*) *Stob. serm.* 1. mentioned also by *Plutarch,* de exilio.

(*b*) To take away bitterness from Wormwood, and liberty from Speech, are both alike.

(*b*) *Stob. ser.* 9.

(*c*) Endeavour not to conceal thy faults with words, but to amend them by reproof.

(*c*) *Stob.* ibid.

(*d*) It is not so hard to offend, as not to reprove an offending person.

(*d*) *Stob.* ibid.

(*e*) As the sickness of the body, if hid or praised, is not healed, so the soul cherished in its ways, or concealed, is not reformed.

(*e*) *Stob.* 13.

(*f*) Rejoice more in reprovers than in flatterers: fly from flatterers as Enemies.

(*f*) *Stob.* 14.

(*g*) We ought either to be silent, or to speak things that are better than silence.

(*g*) *Stob.* 24.

(*h*) It is better to throw a stone at random, than an idle word.

(*h*) *Stob.* 34.

(*i*) Comprehend not few things in many words, but many things in few words.

(*i*) *Stob.* 35.

(*k*) We must faithfully restore to him that entrusts us, the *Depositum*, not only of money, but of words.

(*k*) *Porph.* p. 25.

(*l*) Of Opinion, the *Pythagoreans* said thus: It is the part of a man void of understanding, to adhere to all mens Opinions, especially to that which is maintained by the greatest number: for to conceive and judge aright is proper to few, it only belongs to the knowing, who are not many: this power therefore extends not to many. On the other side, it is no less madness, to contemn all Conception and Opinion. Such a person must be unlearned and unrectifiable: for it is necessary, that he who is ignorant learn those where-

(*l*) *Jamb. cap.*

of he is ignorant; and that he who learneth, addict and resign himself to his Teacher. In a word, they said, It is necessary, that such young men as would be preserved, should addict themselves to the Conceptions and Opinions of their Elders, and such as lead a good life.

Now in the whole course of humane life, there are certain distinct Ages, which are not temerariously to be connected, for they are expelled by one another, unless a man be well and rightly ordered from his birth. It is requisite therefore, that from the institution of a Child in Goodness, Temperance, and Fortitude, a great part be transmitted to his Youth, when he arrives at that age; likewise of his Youth instituted in Goodness, Fortitude and Temperance, a great part be transmitted to his manly estate. Herein the course ordinarily taken, is ridiculous; for most think, that Children ought to be well ordered, instructed in Temperance, and to abstain from all things odious and undecent; but when they come to be Youths, most leave them to their own management, to do what they please; whereas at that Age they are subject to both sorts of Vices, of Children, and of Men. To shun Study and Order, and to follow Play and Wantonness, the Vice of Childhood is likewise most proper to Youth. Again, vehement Desires, Ambition, and the like, the Affections of Manhood, insinuate into Youth, for which reason, this Age requireth care above all the rest. In fine, a man should never be so given over, as to do whatsoever he pleaseth, but that there should always be some Overseer president over the rest, a legitimate sitting Magistrate, whom every Citizen ought to obey. For a living creature, as soon as ever it is neglected, falls into ill and wickedness.

They affirm, that they often have enquired and examined, for what reason we give Children food at set times, and moderately; the ordinary Answer is, That Order and Moderation are good; their contraries, Disorder and Immoderateness, ill, as is manifest, in as much as to be a Glutton or a Drunkard is esteemed a great reproach. For if none of these were useful and beneficial to us when we arrive at man's estate, it were needless to accustom our selves, whilst Children, to such Order. It is the same in other habits. We see it manifest also in all other kinds of living creatures, which are taught by man from the very beginning, as Whelps, and the like, those things which they are required to practise when they are come to full growth. Thus *Jamblichus*. Of *Silence*, *Abstinence*, and the whole course of his *Institution*, we have formerly treated.

CHAP. II.
Fortitude.

(*a*) Jamb. cap. 32. pag. 189.

(*a*) THE greatest Argument of the *Pythagoreans* for Fortitude, was, for that they fully perswaded themselves, that of all Humane Chances, nothing ought to happen unexpectedly to any, but that they should expect all things which were not within their own power. Precepts of *Pythagoras*, tending to this Virtue, are these.

(*b*) Stob. serm.

(*b*) Do those things which you judge to be good, although after you have done them, you shall be disesteemed; for the vulgar is an ill judge of all good things: As you despise their praise, so despise their dispraise.

(*c*) Cic. de senect.

(*c*) He forbad to forsake the protection and station of this life, without the command of our supream Lord.

CHAP. III.
Temperance and Continence.

(*a*) Porph. Jamb.

(*a*) HE often used this Apophthegm to all his Auditors, whether many or few, *We must avoid with our utmost endeavour, and amputate with Fire and Sword, and by all other means, from the Body, Sickness; from the Soul, Ignorance; from the Belly, Luxury; from a City, Sedition; from a Family, Discord; from all things, Excess.*

(*b*) Stob. serm. 4.

(*b*) It is better to live lying on the ground with a settled confidence, than to have a golden bed and be troubled.

(*c*) Stob. 5.

(*c*) Temperance is the strength of the Soul; for it is the light of the Soul clear from Passion.

(*d*) Stob. ibid.

(*d*) To serve Passions is more grievous than to serve Tyrants.

(*e*) Stob. ibid.

(*e*) It is impossible he can be free, who serves passions, and is governed by them.

(*f*) Stob. ibid.

(*f*) No man is free who doth not command himself.

(*g*) Stob. 14.

(*g*) The labour of Continence precedes all excellent things.

(*h*) Stob. 17.

(*h*) To possess Continence is the best strength and wealth.

(*i*) Stob. ibid.

(*i*) It is better to die, than to cloud the Soul by Intemperance.

(*k*) Stob. 18.

(*k*) He said, that Drunkenness is a little Madness; or, that it is the study of Madness; or, as *Laertius*, that it is the Canker of the flower of the Mind.

(*l*) Stob. 99.

(*l*) The Voice of the flesh is, No hunger, no thirst, no cold.

(*m*) Porph. p. 21.

(*m*) He admonished all men to shun Ambition and Vain-glory, because these chiefly excite Envy.

(*n*) Laert.

(*n*) He discommended all Excess, saying, that we ought not to exceed a due proportion in labour and food.

(*o*) Porph. p. 25.

(*o*) We must consider, there are three kinds of things which deserved to be pursued and acquired; the first is of those which are honourable and vertuous; the second, conducing to life; the last, pleasures: not the vulgar enchanting pleasure, for that he allowed not, but the solid and grave, free from blame. For, he said, there are two kinds of pleasure, whereof that which indulgeth to the belly, and to lasciviousness; by profuseness of wealth, he compared to the murtherous Songs of the *Syrens*; the other, which consists in things honest and just, as also in the necessaries of life, is sweet as well as the first, and withal it is not followed by repentance. Hither perhaps alludes (*p*) *Clemens*, who saith, *Pythagoras* advised to esteem the Muses sweeter than *Syrens*; teaching, that we should study Learning not with delight; whereby he condemned the other delight of the Mind, which is fallacious.

(*p*) Strom. 1. p. 294.

(*q*) Py-

(q) *Pythagoras* seeing one that made himself fat by exercising and eating: (r) *This man* (saith he) *will not cease to make a stricter Prison for himself.*

(s) The *Pythagoreans* exhorted such as came into their Society, to shun Pleasure as much as any thing that ought to be avoided; for nothing so deceives us, and draws into sin, as this passion. In general, as it seems, they endeavoured not to do any thing which might tend to pleasure, this scope being for the most part undecent and hurtful; but that they should aim at what is good and decent, to do what they ought. In the next place, to discern what is convenient and beneficial, it requireth a more than ordinary judgment.

As to that which is called Desire, they said thus: Desire is an impulsion and appetite of the Soul, either of some repletion, or derogation of some things belonging to sense, or the sensitive affection. This passion is various, and the most multiplicious of all that belong to man. Of humane desires many are acquired and framed by the persons themselves; wherefore this Passion requireth greatest care and observation, and corporeal Exercises more than ordinary. For the body, when its aliment is evacuated, to desire Repletion, is natural; and again, being repleat, to desire Evacuation, is natural also: But to desire superfluous Aliment, or superfluous and sumptuous Raiment and Lodging, or superfluous and various Houshold-stuff, and Utensils, and Cups, and Servants, and Herds of Cattel, bred for diet; in a word, of all humane passions, this is most such, that it never is at a stay, but proceeds to infinite. Wherefore from our very Childhood, care must be taken, that we desire such things as are needful, and shun vain and superfluous desires, being undisturbed, and clear from such appetites, and contemning those who deserve contempt, being fettered in their desires.

It is of most concernment to observe the vain, hurtful, superfluous desires of those, who are transported by their Power; there is nothing so absurd, whereto the Souls of such persons, Children, Men and Women, are not transported. The most various is that of Meats, infinite is the multitude of Fruits, infinite of Roots, used by Mankind. Besides this, all sorts of flesh making it their business to find, of terrestrial, volatile, and aquatile creatures, wherewith to satisfie their taste, and all variety of dressing them, with the mixture of all kind of Juices, whereby Mankind is really prophetick and multiform, as to the motion of the Soul; for every several sort of Meat is cause of a peculiar Constitution. Now men behold, that these produce great alteration, as Excess of Wine to such a degree exhilerates; further, causeth frenzy and disorder: But those things which discover not so much their force and efficacy, they are ignorant of, notwithstanding, that whatsoever food we take, is cause of some peculiar constitution. Wherefore it is a great part of Wisdom to know and understand, what kind and quantity of Meat is requisite for Nourishment. This Science was first communicated by *Apollo* and *Pæon*, afterwards by the *Æsculapians.*

Concerning Generation, (t) he said thus: We ought principally to observe that which is called περωρες, *precocious*: for neither too forward Plants nor Animals, before the due season, when they are in their full strength. Youths therefore and Virgins ought to be educated in labour, and exercises, and actions conducing to fortitude, using food convenient thereto, and in a laborious, temperant and tolerant life. Of the things in humane life there are many, in which to be late conversant is best; of this kind is Coition. A Youth ought so to be educated, as not to addict himself thereto before twenty years of age; and when arrived at those years, to use it seldom is best, if we esteem a good habit of body; for Intemperance and Good rarely meet in the same person.

They commended the Rites and Laws of the Ancients, in the *Greek* Cities, not to lye with Mothers, or Daughters, or Sisters, nor in a Temple, nor in Publick, for this is evil; and to procure all possible Impediments thereof, is very profitable.

They were of Opinion, That all unnatural ignominious Generations ought to be taken away, and those only preserved which were according to Nature, with Temperance, and Lawful.

They conceived, that such as go about to beget Children, ought to have much providence of their future Issue: The first and greatest providence is, to prepare himself for that action by a temperate healthful Life, not eating too much at unseasonable times, not using such meats as deprave the habits of the body; but above all things, not to perform it when drunk; for they thought that by ill, and discordant, and disturbed temperament, the Seed became adulterate. They also thought him a foolish inconsiderate person, who being desirous of Children, and taking a Wife to that end, should not with utmost study foresee by what means his Issue might be most advantaged. They who love dogs, are very careful of their breed, as of which they shall breed, and when, and accordingly the Whelps prove; the like do they who love birds. But tho' it be well known, that they who breed any other kind of living creature, use their utmost endeavour to procure a generous Race, yet men have no respect to their own Offspring, but beget them inconsiderately, and bring them up negligently. This is the chief and most manifest cause that so many men are evil and wicked, the greater part begetting their Children like Beasts, without any consideration.

Finally, (u) Pythagoras *discoursing concerning the benefit of venereal pleasures, advised, in the Summer-time to abstain wholly from Coition; in the Winter, to use it but rarely; for it is generally hurtful: but the continual use thereof causeth debility, and is most pernicious.* Laertius saith, *He advised, that in the Winter and Spring it should not be used at all, in Summer and Autumn but sparingly; for at all times it is pernicious and prejudicial to the Health. And being asked, At what time a man should use it? he answered, When he hath a mind to be weaker.*

CHAP.

CHAP. IV.

Sagacity and Wisdom.

TO *Wisdom* (the last general head of *Pædeutick*) belong the Sentences of *Pythagoras*.

(a) Stob.   (a) *The strength, wall, and armour of a wise man is wisdom.*

Call to mind, that most men acknowledge wisdom to be the greatest good, but few endeavour to possess this greatest good.

(b) Stob.   (b) *The sacrifices of Fools are the food of fire; their Donatives the subsistence of sacrilegious persons.*

(c) Stob.   (c) *A Horse is not to be guided without a Bridle, nor Riches without Wisdom.*

(d) Cic. Tusc. 1.   (d) *He conceived the imposition of names on things, to be the highest part of wisdom.*

SECT. II.

Of Politick, the other part of Practick Philosophy.

(a) Cap. 6.   THE heads of Politick (according to (a) *Jamblichus*) are these; *Common Conversation, Friendship, Worship of the Gods, Piety to the Dead,* and *Law-making*.

(b) Jamb. cap.   (b) They hold *Pythagoras* to be the Inventor of all Politick Discipline. He used to say, That amongst Beings, nothing is pure, but every thing partakes of some other, as Earth of Fire, Fire of Water and Air. In like manner, honest partakes of dishonest, just of unjust, and the like. Hence it is, that Reason is carried away to either side. There are two motions, one of the Body, the other of the Mind; one irrational, the other elective. Commonwealths he compared to a rectangle Triangle, wherein one side consists of Three Parts, the Base of Five, the other side of the mean between them, of four. In the Coincidence of these Lines with one another, and their Squares, we behold delineated the best Form of a Commonwealth, [and of Justice.]

CHAP. I.

Common Conversation.

TO common conversation belong these Maxims of *Pythagoras*.

(a) Stob.   (a) *A stranger just, is to be preferr'd not only before a Countreyman, but before a Kinsman.*

(b) Stob.   (b) *Esteem is a great part of good Education, to be able to suffer the want of Education in others.*

(c) Stob.   (c) *Desire that they who converse with you, should rather respect than fear you: for admiration accompanies respect; hatred, fear.*

(d) Jamb. cap.   (d) There being a Justice in the mutual conversation of men one towards another; of this also the *Pythagoreans* delivered this manner. There is in the common conversation of Men one opportune, another importune: they differ in diversity of Age, and in Dignity, and in nearness of Affinity, and Beneficence, and if there be any thing like these in mutual differences. For there is a kind of Conversation which appeareth, to the younger towards the younger, not to be importune; but, towards the elder, it is importune: for no kind, neither of Anger, nor of menacing, or boldness, but all such kind of importunity ought diligently to be avoided by the younger toward the elder. In like manner is the reason of Dignity; for coming to a person endowed with true Worth and Virtue, it is neither decent nor opportune to speak much, or to commit any of the fore-mentioned things. Like these also are those which concern such as have obliged and deserved well of others.

There is a various and multiplicious use of Opportunity. For of those that are angry and incensed, some do it opportunely, others importunely: and again, of those who covet, and desire, and have appetite, it may be opportune for some to pursue those things, not for others. The same Reason there is of other affections, and actions, and dispositions, and conversations, and intercessions, and discourses. But Opportunity is of such a Nature, that it is docible, and undeceivable, and capable of act, and generally, and simply, having nothing of all those in it. But the consequents are of such a kind, that they together, decent, and convenient, and the like, attend the Nature of opportunity.

They held that there is a Primacy in every thing, and that every-where there is one thing which is best; in Science, and in Experience, and in Generation; likewise in a Family, and in a City, and in an Army, and in all such like Constitutions: but it is difficult to discern and understand the Nature of the Primacy in all the aforesaid things; for in Sciences it is the part of more than ordinary intelligence, by clear intuition, to discern and judge the parts of the thing, which is the Primacy of them. But there is great difference, and almost of the whole and general a hazard, in not rightly taking the Primacy: For, in a word, nothing can afterwards be right, if the true Primacy be not known. The same Manner and Reason is in other kinds of Primacy; for neither can a Family be well governed, where there is not a true Master, and voluntary Government; for it is requisite, that both these be voluntary in the præfecture, as well he who is chief, as those who are subject to him. As Learning is then right, when there is such conformity betwixt the Masters and the Scholars, that they will teach, these will learn; for if either be refractory, it cannot be rightly performed. In this manner he conceived it to be fit for Inferiors to obey Superiors, Disciples their Masters.

CHAP. II.

Friendship.

(a) Jambl.   (a) *Pythagoras* evidently demonstrated that there is a friendship of all unto all; of god's towards men, by piety and religious worship; of doctrines to one another; of the soul to the body; of the rational part to the irrational, by Philosophy and its Theory; of men towards one another; betwixt Countrymen, by right observation of Laws; betwixt

betwixt Strangers, by right Physiology; of a Man to his Wife, or Children, or Brethren, and Servants, by unperverted Communion. In a word, of all towards all; moreover of some irrational Creatures, by Justice and natural Affinity and Communion; of the body, in it self mortal, a conciliation and combination of the contrary faculties, by health and wholesome diet, and temperance, in imitation of the good composure in the Elements. In all these, of one and the same, according to comprehension of the name Friendship, *Pythagoras* is acknowledg'd to be the Inventer and Lawgiver: And so admirable a Friendship did he deliver to those who enquired of him, that, unto this day, (saith *Jamblichus*) we say of those who are intimately joined together by Friendship, *they are of the Pythagoreans*.

We must add the Institution of *Pythagoras* herein, and the exhortations he used to his Disciples. They were advised to take away all contention, and love of controversie, out of true friendship; if possible out of all. But if that be not possible, at least out of that which is our own Country, and generally that towards Elders. Likewise out of that towards Benefactors; for to become Antagonists, or contest with such, when we are fallen into anger, or some other passion, is not consistent with the preservation of the amity we have with them. They said, that in Friendship there ought to be least scratches and cuts; and, if any happen, we should fly and subdue anger: It were best, that both should do so, but chiefly the younger, and that those exercises which they called παιδαρτήσεις, ought to be made from the elder towards the younger, with much commendation and benevolence. That there appear much care and tenderness in those who give the correction; for by this means the correction shall be profitable. That we do not extirpate Credit out of Friendship, neither in jest nor in earnest; for it is not easie to heal the friendship betwixt Men, if once a falshood hath incurred into the manners of those who call themselves Friends.

That we must not renounce friendship for adversity, or any other impotence which happens in life. That renunciation of friendship only is commendable, which is made by reason of some great wickedness and misdemeanour. But that we must not take away our friendship from them, unless they become absolutely wicked; and, before we take it off, we must ingeniously pause, to try, if by contestation and fight he may be diverted from this ill habit, and become rectified. We must fight, not in words, but actions; the fight is lawful and pious. Though difference of power be not a just ground for one man to fight with another, yet this is a just ground, even the most just that is possible.

They said, that to a friendship, that will prove true, are required many definitions and rules; these must be well discerned, and not confusedly: Moreover, it ought to be accommodated to the disposition of others, that no conversation be made negligently and vainly, but with respect and right order: Neither that any passion be excited vainly, and wickedly, and sinfully, as concupiscence, or anger. The same of the other passions and habits.

Much more admirable are those things which they defined concerning the community of the divine good, and those concerning the unanimity of the mind, and those concerning the divine mind. For they mutually exhorted one another, that they should not tear asunder the god which is in them. Thus their study of friendship by words and actions, had reference to some divine temperament, and, to union with God, and to unity with the mind, and the divine soul. Thus *Jamblichus*.

(b) *He conceived the extremity (or end) of friendship, to be the making one of two.* (c) *Man ought to be one.* This sentence (saith *Clemens*) is mystick. (d) He first said, κοινὰ φίλων, and φιλίαν ἰσότητα.

(b) Cic. off. 1.
(c) Strom. 4.
(d) Laert.

CHAP. III.

Worship of the Gods.

(a) THE principles of worshipping the gods, proposed by *Pythagoras* and his followers, are these.

(a) Jambl.

That all which they determine to be done, aim and tend to the acknowledgment of the Deity: This is the principle, and the whole life of man consists in this, that he follow God, and this the ground of Philosophy. For men do ridiculously, who seek that which is good anywhere else than from the gods. They do as if a man in a Country, govern'd by a King, should apply his service to some Citizen of inferior Magistracy, and neglect the supream Governour. In the same manner conceive they that such men do; for, since there is a God, we must confess, that good is in his power. Now all, to those whom they love and delight in, give good things; and to the contrary to these, their contratres. Therefore it is manifest, that such things are to be done in which God delights.

Thus he defined particularly of all things. To believe of the Divinity, that it is, and that it is in such manner as to mankind; that it over-looks them, and neglects them not; the *Pythagoreans*, taught by him, conceived to be profitable. For we have need of such a Government, as we ought not in any thing to contradict; such is that which proceeds from the Divinity; for the Divinity is such, that it merits the Dominion of all. Man they affirmed to be, rightly speaking, a creature reproachful and fickle, as to his appetites, affections, and other passions; he therefore hath need of such government and guidance, from which proceeds moderation and order. Now they conceived, that every one being conscious of the fickleness of his own nature, should never be forgetful of sanctity, and service towards the Divinity; but always have (the Divinity) in their mind, how it over-looks and observes human life.

In fine, they say, that *Pythagoras* was an imitator of the Orphean Constitutions, worshipping the gods after the manner of *Orpheus*, placed in brazen images, not representing the forms of men, but of the gods themselves, who comprehending and foreseeing all things, resemble in nature and form the whole. He declared their purifications and rites, which are called τελεταί, having the most exact knowledge of them.

Moreover they affirm, he made a composition of the divine Philosophy and Service, part whereof he had learned from the *Orpheans*, part from the

the *Ægyptian* Priests ; some from the *Chaldeans* and *Magi* ; some from the *Eleusinian* Rites, and those in *Imber*, and *Samo Thracia*, and *Delos*, and the *Celtæ*, and *Iberians*.

Amongst the *Latines* also is read the Sacred Discourse of *Pythagoras*, not to all, but to such as are admitted to the doctrine of excellent things, and are not addicted to ought that is dishonest.

It prescribes, that men offer libation thrice; and *Apollo* gives Oracles from a Tripod, because number first consists in a Triad.

That we must sacrifice to *Venus* on the sixth day, because that is the first common number of the number of universal Nature. Now after all ways, the thing divided in like manner, assumes as well the power of those things which are taken away, as of those which are left.

That to *Hercules* we ought to sacrifice on the eightth day of the Month, in respect of his being born at the end of seven Months.

It saith also, That we ought to enter into a Temple having a pure garment, and in which none hath slept the sleep of slothfulness; black and russet, testifying purity in ratiocinations of equality and justice.

It commanded, that if blood be shed unwillingly in a Temple, that it be either taken up in a dish, or scattered into the Sea; for that is the first element, and most estimable of all creatures.

It saith likewise, that a woman ought not to be brought to bed in a Temple, for it is religious; that the divinity of the soul should be annected to the body in a Temple.

It commanded, that upon Holy-days we cut not our hair nor pair our nails ; intimating, that the encrease of our goods ought not to be preferr'd before the empire of the gods.

That we must not kill a flea in the Temple, because to the Deity we ought not to offer any superfluous things, or vermine ; but that the gods are to be worshipped with Cedar, Lawrel, Cypress, and Myrtle, &c.

(b) *Cic. leg.* 2. (b) *He said, Piety and Religion is chiefly conversant in our minds, at such time as we attend the divine rites.*

(c) *Laert.* (c) *That the gods and Heroes are not to be worshipped with equal honours, but that the gods must always be worshipped with applause,* (or silence at the celebration of their rites) *we being white and pure; Heroes, only from noon,* [(d) He advised,

(d) *Diodor. excerpt. Valef. pag. 247.* that such as sacrifice should present themselves to the gods, not in rich, but in white and clean garments; and that not only the body be clear from all blemish, but that they bring also a pure mind.]
Purity is acquired by expiations, and bathings, and sprinklings ; and by refraining from murther, and adultery, and all pollution ; and by abstaining from the flesh of things that die of themselves, and from Mullets, and Melanures, and Sheep, and Oviparous Creatures, and Beans, and all other things which are commanded by those who have the care of sacred rites.

(e) *Laert.* (e) *He permitted not, that any man should pray for himself, because none knoweth what is good for himself.*

(f) *Laert.* (f) *An Oath is just, and therefore* Jupiter *is Sirnamed* Ὅρκιος.

(g) *Diod. excerpt. Valef.* (g) *He commanded his disciples to be very backward in taking an Oath; but that when they have taken it, they should be very forward and diligent to keep it.*

CHAP. IV.

Piety to the Dead.

Piety to the Dead was a part, not the least, of the *Pythagorick* doctrine : whence *Cicero* speaking of the Immortality of the Soul ; *More prevalent with me,* saith he, *is the authority of the Ancients, or our Ancestors, who afforded the dead so religious rites, which certainly they had not done, if they had conceived, that nothing pertains to them ; or of those who were in this Country, and instructed* Magna Græcia, *which now is abolisht, but then flourisht'd, with their institutions and precepts.*

(b) *Pythagoras* allowed not the bodies of the dead to be burned, herein imitating the Magi, as not willing that any mortal should participate of divine honour. The *Pythagorick* custom, as described by (c) *Pliny,* was, to put the dead into Earthen Barrels, amongst leaves of Myrtle, Olive, and black Poplar. (b) *Jamb.*

(c) *Lib. 35.*

(d) To accompany the dead at Funerals in white garments, he conceived to be pious; alluding to the simple and first nature, according to number, and the principle of all things. (d) *Jamb.*

(e) The *Crotonians* delighting to bury their dead sumptuously, one of the *Pythagoreans* told them, he heard *Pythagoras* discoursing of divine things, thus : The cœlestial gods respect the affections of the sacrificers, not the greatness of the sacrifice. On the contrary, The terrestrial gods, as to whose share the lesser things belong, delight in banquets, and mournings, and funeral litations, and costly sacrifices; whence *Hades* (the Inferi) from its making choice of entertainment, is named *Pluto* ; those who pay honours to him most sparingly, he permitted to continue longest in the upper world ; but of those who are excessive in mourning, he bringeth down ever and anon one, that thereby he may receive the honours which are paid in memory of the dead. By this discourse he wrought a belief in his Auditors, that they who do all things moderately upon such adverse occasions, further their own safety ; but as for those who bestow excessive charge, they will all die untimely. (e) *Jamb.*

(f) *They forbore to make Tombs of Cypress, forasmuch as* Jupiter's *Scepter was of that wood*; *as* Hermippus, *in his second Book of* Pythagoras, *affirms.* (f) *Laert.*

CHAP. V.

Reverence of Parents, and Obedience to the Law.

(a) NExt to gods and dæmons, we ought to reverence Parents and the Law, and to render our selves obedient to them, not feignedly, but really. Or, as (b) *Porphyrius,* He commanded to think and to speak reverently of gods and dæmons, to be kind to parents and benefactors, and to obey the law. (a) *Jamb.*

(b) *Pag.*

They held (saith (c) *Jamblichus*) that we ought to believe, there is no greater ill than Anarchy; for a man cannot be safe where there is no Governour. They held also, that we ought to persevere in the customs and rites of our own Country, though they be worse than those of other Countries. To revolt easily from settled laws, and to be studious of novelty, they conceived to be neither advantageous nor safe. (c) *Loco ci.*

(d) See-

(d) Seeing that contumelies, pride, and contempt of Law, often transport men to unjust actions, he daily exhorted, (e) *that the law should be assisted, and injustice opposed.* To which end he alledged this distinction: The first of ills, which insinuateth into Houses and Cities, is *Pride*; the second, *Contumely*; the third, *Destruction*. Every one therefore ought to expel and extirpate Pride, accustoming themselves from their youth to a temperate masculine life, and to be free from slanderous repining, contentious reproaching, and hateful scurrility.

Wickedness disobeys the Divine Law, and therefore transgresseth.

A wicked man suffers more torment in his own conscience, than he who is punished in body and whipped.

(d) Jamb. cap. 153.
(e) Mention'd by Laertius.

CHAP. VI.

Law-making.

Moreover, (saith (a) *Jamblichus*) he constituted another excellent kind of Justice, the Legislative part, which commandeth that which ought to be done, and forbiddeth that which ought not to be done, which is better than the Judicative part; for this resembles that part of medicine which cureth the sick, but the other suffers them not to fall sick, but takes care afar off of the health of the soul.

(b) *Varro* affirms, that *Pythagoras* delivered this discipline (of governing States) to his Auditors last of all, when they were now learned, now wise, now happy; for he saw so many rough waves therein, that he would not commit it, but to such a one as was able to shun the rocks, or, if all fail'd, might stand himself as a rock amidst those waves.

(c) They who punish not ill persons, would have the good injur'd.

(a) Cap.

(b) D. Augustin.

(c) Stob.

SECT. 3.

Theoretick Philosophy, its parts; and first of the Science concerning Intelligibles.

WE come next to the Theoretick part, to which more particularly belongs that saying of *Pythagoras*, That by Philosophy he had this advantage, *To admire nothing*; for, *Philosophical discourse takes away wonder, which ariseth from doubt and ignorance, by knowledge and examination of the facility of every thing.*

Theoretick Philosophy seems to have been divided by the *Pythagoreans* into two parts; They first (saith (b) *Jamblichus*) delivered *the Science of Intelligibles, and the gods*; next which, they taught *all Physick*. To the Science of Intelligibles belong these heads, wherewith (c) *Jamblichus* begins his recapitulation, *Of the gods, of heroes, of dæmons*.

(a) cap.

(b) cap. 6.

CHAP. I.

Of the Supream God.

Pythagoras defined what God is, thus, (a) *A mind which commeateth, and is diffused through every part of the World, and through all Nature; from whom all animals that are produced receive life,*

(a) Lactant.

(b) *God is one.* He is not (as some conceive) out of the world, but intire within himself, in a compleat circle surveying all generations. He is the Temperament of all ages, the Agent of his own powers and works, the Principle of all things, one, in heaven luminary, and father of all things; mind and animation of the whole, the motion of all circles.

(c) *God* (as *Pythagoras* learned of the *Magi*, who term him *Oromasdes*) *in his body resembles Light, in his soul, Truth.*

(d) He said, *that God only is wise.*

(e) He conceived that the first, (being) God, is neither sensible, nor passible; but invisible, and intelligible.

(b) Just. Mart.

(c) Porph. vit. Pyth.

(d) Clem. Alex. Strom. 4.

(e) Plut. in Numa.

CHAP. II.

Of Gods, Dæmons, Heroes.

NExt to the supreme God, there are three kinds of Intelligibles, *Gods, Dæmons, Heroes*; that *Pythagoras* thus distinguished them, is manifest from his (a) precept, that *We must in worship prefer Gods before Dæmons, Heroes before Men*: But in (b) *Jamblichus*, he seems either to observe a different method, or to confound the Terms; teaching first *of Gods*, then *of Heroes*, last *of Dæmons*; which order perhaps is the same with that of the *Golden Verses*,

First, as decreed, th' immortal Gods adore,
Thy Oath keep: next great Heroes, then implore
Terrestrial Dæmons with due sacrifice.

By *Terrestrial Dæmons* seems to be understood (not Princes, as *Hierocles*; but) the Dæmons themselves, confin'd to several offices upon earth; For,

(c) *All the air is full of Souls, which are esteemed Dæmons and Heroes*; from these are sent to men dreams and presages of sickness, and of health; and not only to men, but to sheep also, and to other cattel; to these pertain expiations and averruncations, and all Divinations, Cledons, and the like.

(a) Laert.

(b) cap 6.

(c) Laert.

CHAP. III.

Of Fate and Fortune.

(a) ALL the parts of the World above the Moon, are governed according to Providence and firm order, and εἱμαρμένη, the Decree of God, which they follow: but those beneath the Moon by four causes, by God, by Fate, by our Election, by Fortune. For instance, to go aboard into a Ship, or not, is in our power: Storms and Tempests to arise out of a calm, is by fortune; for the Ship being under water to be preserved, is by the Providence of God. Of Fate, there are many manners and differences: it differs from Fortune, as having a determination, order, and consequence; but Fortune is spontaneous and casual, as to proceed from a boy to a youth, and orderly to pass through the other degrees of age happens by one manner of Fate. [Here the Text seems deficient.]

(a) Anon. apud Phot.

(b) Man

*) Laert.

(b) Man is of affinity with the God's, by reason that he participates of Heat, wherefore God hath a Providential care of us. There is also εἱμαρμένη, a Fate of all things in general and in particular, the cause of their administration.

CHAP. IV.
Divination.

(a) Cap. 29.
(b) Jamb. cap. 28.

Forasmuch as by Dæmons and Heroes, all Divination is convey'd to men, we shall here add what *Pythagoras* held and practised therein, *Jamblichus* saith, that (a) *he honoured Divination not the least of the Sciences*; (b) *for what things are agreeable to God, cannot be known, unless a man hear God himself, or the Gods, or acquire it by divine art*. For this reason they diligently studied Divination, as being the only interpretation of the benevolence of the Gods. It is likewise an employment most suitable to those who believe there are Gods: but whoever thinks either, (belief of the Gods, or Divination) a folly, to him the other is such also.

(c) Plut. Plac. Phil. lib. 4.

(c) *Pythagoras approved all kinds of Divination, except that which is performed by the sacrifice of living Creatures.*

(d) Porph.
(e) Laert.

(d) *He first used Divination by Frankincense.* (e) This was the only burnt-offering by which he divined.

(f) Laert.
(g) Cic. divinat. I.
(h) Cic. ibid.

(f) *He also used Divination by Cledones, and by Birds,* which *Cicero* confirms, saying, that (g) *he would himself be an* Augur, and that (h) *the Pythagoreans observed not only the voices of the gods, but of men also, which they call Omens.* Cledones are observations of occurrent speeches, collecting from what is accidentally said upon some other occasion, the effect of what is sought: an instance whereof see in the Epigram of *Callimachus* upon *Pittacus*.

Life of *Pittacus* chap. pag. cap.

The Interpretation of Dreams, (*Porphyrius* saith) *he learned of the Hebrews:* He communicated it also to his Disciples; for *Jamblichus* relates, *he used means to procure them quiet sleeps, with good and prophetick dreams*: Out of this respect some conceive it was, that he forbad flatulent and gross meats, for that they obstruct the serenity which is requisite thereto. Such apparitions he held not to be fantastick, but real, (not ὄναρ but ὕπαρ) as is manifest from one who *told him, that he dreamed he had talked with his father, (who was dead) and asked him what it portended; Nothing,* (saith he) *for you did really talk with him; as my speaking now to you portends nothing, no more did that.*

Jamb.

Florid. lib. 2.

He was skilful likewise in Judicial Astrology, if we credit *Apuleius,* who affirms, *the Caldæans shewed him the Science of the Stars, the number of the Planets; their Stations, Revolutions, and the various effects of both, in the Nativities of men.*

(d) August. civ. Dei, lib. 7.
In Iliad. π.

(d) *Varro* relates him skilful in Hydromancy, which (saith he) *came from* Persia, *and was practised by* Numa, *and afterwards by* Pythagoras; *wherein they used blood, and invocation of Dæmons.* Hither perhaps alludes *Eustathius,* who saith, *the Pythagoreans affirm, that all brass doth sound by some diviner spirit, for which reason a Tripod of that metal is dedicated to* Apollo; *and when the Winds are all laid, the air calm, and all things else quiet, yet the hallow brass caldrons seem to quake*; the same may be the meaning of *Pythagoras,* when he saith, *The*

Porph. pag.

sound which is made by brass, is the voice of the voice of the Dæmon inclosed in the brass; reading (perhaps) ἐναπειλημμένη, for so *Psellus* describes a kind of Hydromancy practised by the *Assyrians*: *They take a bason full of water convenient for the Dæmons to glide into the bottom: The bason of water seems to make a noise as if it breath'd, the water in the bason in substance differs nothing from other water, but through the virtue infused thereinto by charms is much more excellent, and made more ready to receive a prophetick spirit This is a particular Dæmon, Terrestrial, attracted by compositions; as soon as he glideth into the water, he maketh a little sound inarticulate, which denotes his presence, afterwards the water running over, there are certain whispers heard with some prediction of the future: This kind of spirit is very wandring, because it is of the Solar order; and this kind of Dæmons purposely speak with a low voice, that by reason of the indistinct obscurity of the voice, their lies may be less subject to discovery.* Hitherto *Psellus*.

SECT. IV.
Physick.

THE general Heads of Physick are these, *Of the World, and of all things in the world, of Heaven, and of Earth, and of the Natures betwixt them.* Jamb. cap. The defect of the fragments concerning these we shall endeavour to supply, by adding the Treatise of *Timæus* the Locrian upon the same subject.

CHAP. I.
Principles.

Adv. Mat lib. 9.

THE most learned of the Naturalists (saith *Sextus Empericus*) attributed so great power to Numbers, that they thought them to be the principles and elements of all things. These were the disciples of *Pythagoras*: For, say they, such as treat of Philosophy aright, imitate those who study a Language; they first examine words, because language consists of words; then, because words consist of syllables, they first consider syllables; and because syllables consist of letters, they first examine letters. In like manner, say the *Pythagoreans*, Natural Philosophers, when they make enquiry into the Universe, must first examine into what the Universe is resolved.

Now to affirm, that something apparent to sense is the principle of all things, is repugnant to Physick; for whatsoever is apparent to sense, must be compounded of things not apparent; whereas a Principle is not that which consists of any thing, but that of which the thing consists. Therefore things apparent cannot be said to be Principles of the Universe, but those of which things apparent consist, themselves not being apparent.

They who maintain Atomes, or Homoiomeria's or bulks, or intelligible bodies, to be the principles of all things, were partly in the right, partly not: As conceiving the principles to be unapparent, they are in the right; as holding them to be corporeal, they err. For as intelligible unapparent bodies precede the sensible, so most incorpo-

incorporeals precede intelligible bodies. The elements of words, are not words; nor of bodies, bodies: but they must either be bodies, or incorporeal; therefore they are wholly incorporeal. Neither can we say, that Atomes are eternal, and therefore, tho' corporeal, the principles of all things; for first, they who assert Homoiomeria's, and bulks, and leasts, and indivisibles, to be elements, conceive their substance eternal, so as in that respect, Atomes are no more elements than they. Again, tho' it were granted, that Atomes were eternal; yet, as they who conceive the world to be unbegotten, and eternal, enquire by an imaginary way, the principles whereof it first consists; so we (say the *Pythagoreans*) treating of Physick, consider in an imaginary way, of what things these eternal bodies, comprehensible only by reason, consist. Thus the Universe consists either of bodies or incorporeals; we cannot say bodies, for then we must assign other bodies whereof they consist; and so proceeding to infinite, we shall remain without a principle. It rests therefore to affirm, that intelligible bodies consist of incorporeals, which *Epicurus* confesseth, saying, By collection of figure, and magnitude, and resistance, and gravity, is understood a Body.

Yet it is not necessary, that all corporeals pre-existent to bodies, be the elements and first principles of beings. Idea's (according to *Plato*) are incorporeals, pre-existent to bodies, and all generated beings have reference to them; yet they are not the principles of being: for every Idea, singly taken, is said to be one; when we comprehend others with it, they are two, or three, or four. Number therefore is transcendent to their substance, by participation whereof, one, two, or more, are predicated of them. Again, solid figures are conceived in the mind before bodies, as having an incorporeal Nature; yet they are not the principles. Superficies precede them in our imagination, for solids consist of superficies. But neither are superficies the elements of beings, for they consist of lines; lines precede them; numbers precede lines. That which consists of three lines, is called a Triangle; that which of four, a Quadrangle. Even line it self, simply taken, is not conceived without number: but being carried on from one point to another, is conceived in two. As to Numbers, they all fall under the Monad: for the Duad is one Duad, the Triad one Triad, and the Decad one summary of number.

This moved *Pythagoras* to say, That the principle of all things is the Monad; by participation hereof, every being is termed One; and when we reflect on a being in its identity, we consider a Monad: but when it receives addition by alterity, it produceth indeterminate Duad, so called, in distinction from the Arithmetical determinate Duads; by participation whereof all Duads are understood, as Monads by the Monad. Thus there are two principles of beings, the first Monad, and the indeterminate Duad.

That these are indeed the principles of all things, the *Pythagoreans* teach variously. Of beings, (say they) some are understood by difference; others by contrariety: others by relation. By *difference*, are those which are considered by themselves, subjected by their proper circumscription; as, a man, a horse, a plant, earth, water, air, fire; each of these is considered absolutely without any. By *contrariety*, are those which are considered by contrariety of one to the other; as, good and ill; just, unjust; profitable, unprofitable; sacred, profane; pious, impious; moving, fixt; and the like. By *relation*, those which are considered by relation to others; as, right, left; upwards, downwards; double, half. For right is understood by a relative habit to left, and left by a relative habit to right; upwards to downwards, and downward to upwards; and so of the rest. Those which are understood by contrariety, differ from those that are understood by relation. In contraries, the corruption of the one is the generation of another; as, of health, sickness, motion, and rest. The induction of sickness is the expulsion of health, and the induction of health is the expulsion of sickness; the same in grief and joy, good and ill, and all things of contrary Natures. But the relative exist together, and perish together; for right is nothing, unless there be left; double is nothing, unless we understand the half whereof it is the double: Moreover, in Contraries there is no mean, as between health and sickness, life and death, motion and rest. But betwixt Relatives there is a mean; as betwixt greater and lesser, the mean is equal: betwixt too much and too little, sufficient: betwixt too flat and too sharp, concord.

Above these three kinds, Absolute, Contrary, Relative, there must necessarily be some supream Genus; every Genus is before the Species which are under it. For if the Genus be taken away, the Species are taken away also; but the removal of the Species takes not away the Genus, the Species depending on the Genus, not the Genus on the Species. The transcending Genus of those things which are understood by themselves, (according to the *Pythagoreans*) is the *One*; as that exists and is considered absolutely, so they. Of contraries, equal and unequal, holds the place of a Genus, for in them is considered the nature of all Contrarieties; as of rest in equality, it admits not intension and remission; of motion inequality, it admits intension and remission. In like manner, natural inequality, it is the instable extremity; preternatural inequality, it admits intension and remission. The same of health and sickness, straightness and crookedness. The relative consists of excess and defect, as their Genus; great and greater, much and more, high and higher, are understood by excess: little and less, low and lower, by defect.

Now forasmuch as Absolutes, Contraries and Relatives, appear to be subordinate to other Genus's, (that is, to One, to Equality, and to Inequality, to Excess and Defect) let us examine, whether those Genus's may be reduc'd to others. Equality is reducible to One, for one is equal in it self; inequality is either in excess or defect; of unequals, one exceeds, the other is deficient: Excess and defect are reducible to the indeterminate Duad; or the first excess and defect is in two, in the excedent and the deficient. Thus the principles of all things appear in the top above all the rest, the first Monad, and the indeterminate Duad.

Of these is generated the Arithmetical Monad and Duad, from the first Monad, one; from the Monad and the indeterminate Duad, two; the Duad being not yet constituted amongst Numbers; neither was here two, before it was taken out of the indeterminate Duad, of which, together with the Monad, was produced the Duad which is in Numbers. Out of these, in the same manner proceeded the rest of the Numbers, one continually stepping forward, the indeterminate Duad generating two, and extending Numbers to an infinite multitude.

Hereupon they affirm, that, in principles, Monad hath the nature of the efficient cause, Duad of passive matter; and after the same manner, as they produced Numbers, which consists of them, they composed the World also, and all things in it. A Point is correspondent to the Monad; the Monad is indivisible, so is the Point; the Monad is the principle of Numbers, so is the Point of Lines. A Line is correspondent to the Duad, both are considered by transition. A line is length without breadth, extended betwixt two Points. A Superficies corresponds to the Triad; besides length, whereby it was a Duad, it receives a third distance, breadth. Again, setting down three Points, two opposite, the third at the juncture of the lines made by the two, we represent a superficies. The solid figure and the body, as a Pyramid, answer the Tetrad; if we lay down, as before, three points, and set over them another point, behold the Pyramidical form of a solid body, which hath three dimensions, length, breadth, thickness.

Some there are who affirm, that a Body consists of one point, the point by fluxion makes a Line, the Line by fluxion makes a Superficies, the Superficies moved to thickness makes a Body, three ways dimensurable. This Sect of the Pythagoreans differs from the former; they held, that of two principles, the Monad and the Duad were made Numbers, of Numbers were made Points, Lines, Superficies, and Solids: These, that all things come from one point, for of it is made a line, of the line a superficies, of the superficies a body.

Thus are solid Bodies produc'd of Numbers precedent to them. Moreover, of them consist Solids, Fire, Water, Air, Earth, and in a word, the whole World, which is governed according to Harmony, as they affirm again, recurring to Numbers, which comprize the proportions that constitute perfect Harmony. (*b*) Harmony is a system consisting of three Concords, the Diatessaron, the Diapente, the Diapason; the proportions of these three Concords are found in the first four Numbers, one, two, three, four. The Diatessaron consists in a sesquitertia proportion. The Diapason in sesquialtera, the Diapente in duple; four being sesquitertius to three, (as consisting of three and one third) hath a Diatessaron proportion; three being sesquialter to two (as containing two and its half) a Diapente; four being the double of the Monad of two, a Diapason. The Tetracties affording the analogy of these Concords, which make perfect harmony, according to which all things are governed, they stil'd it,

(*b*) Sext. Emp. adverf. Log. lib. 1.

The root and fountain of eternal Nature.

Moreover, whatsoever is comprehended by man, (say they) either is a body, or incorporeal; but neither of these is comprehended without the notion of Numbers: a body, having a triple dimension, denotes the number three. Besides, of Bodies, some are by connexion, as Ships, Chains, Buildings; others by union, compriz'd under one habit, as Plants, Animals; others by aggregation, as Armies, Herds. All these have numbers, as consisting of plurality. Moreover, of Bodies, some have simple qualities, others multiplicious, as an Apple, various colour to the sight, juice to the taste, odour to the smell; these also are of the nature of numbers. It is the same of Incorporeals; Time, an incorporeal, is comprehended by number, years, months, days, and hours. The like of a Point, a Line, a Superficies, as we said already.

Likewise to numbers are correspondent both naturals and artificials. We judge every thing by criteries, which are the measures of numbers. If we take away number, we take away the Cubit, which consists of two half cubits, six palms, twenty four digits; we take away the Bushel, the Ballance, and all other criteries, which consisting of plurality, are kinds of number. In a word, there is nothing in life without it. All art is a collection of comprehensions, collection implies number; it is therefore rightly said,

——*To Number all things reference have.*

that is, to dijudicative reason, which is of the same kind with numbers, whereof all consists. Hitherto *Sextus*.

(*c*) The sum of all (as by *Alexander* in his Successions, extracted out of the *Pythagorick* Commentaries) is this: *the Monad is the principle of all things. From the Monad came the indeterminate Duad, as matter subjected to the cause, Monad; from the Monad and the indeterminate Duad, Numbers; from Numbers, Points; from Points, Lines; from Lines, Superficies; from Superficies Solids; from these solid Bodies, whose Elements are four, Fire, Water, Air, Earth; of all which, transmutated, and totally changed, the World consists.*

(*c*) Laerc.

CHAP. II.

Of the World.

(*a*) THE World, or comprehension of all things, *Pythagoras* called Κόσμος, from its order and beauty.

(*b*) The World was made by God, (*c*) in thought, not in time; (*d*) He gave it a beginning from fire, and the fifth element: for there are five figures of solid bodies, which are termed Mathematical. Earth was made of a Cube, Fire of a Pyramis, Air of an Octaedre, Water of an Icosiedre, the Sphere of the Universe of a Dodecaedre. In these *Plato* followeth *Pythagoras*.

(*e*) The World is corruptible in its own nature, for it is sensible and corporeal; but it shall never be corrupted, by reason of the providence and preservation of God. (*f*) Fate is the cause of the order of the Universe, and all Particulars; (*g*) Necessity encompasseth the World.

(*a*) Plut. 2. 1. Sto phyf. 1.
(*b*) Plut. 2. 4.
(*c*) Stob. 1. 1.
(*d*) Plut. 2. 6.
(*e*) Plut 2. 4.
(*f*) Laer.
(*g*) Plut. 1. 25.

(*h*) The

(b) *Laert.*

(i) *Arist. phys.* 3. 4.

(k) *Plut. plac.* 2. 9.

(l) *Plut. plac.* 2.

(b) The World is animate, intelligible, spherical, enclosing the earth in the midst of it.
(i) The *Pythagoreans* affirm, That what is without Heaven is infinite; for (k) beyond the world there is a Vacuum, into which, and out of which, the world respires.
(l) The right side of the World is the East, whence motion begins; the left is the West.

CHAP. III.

Of the Superior or Ætherial parts of the World.

(a) *Anon. vit.*

(a) PYthagoras *first called Heaven* Κόσμον, *as being perfect in all kinds of animals, and adorned with all kinds of pulchritude.*

(b) *Anon. vit.*

(b) *In the fixed Sphere resides the first Cause; whatsoever is next him, that they affirm to be best, and firmly compounded and ordered; that which is furthest from him, the worst. There is a constant order observed as low as the Moon, but all things beneath the Moon are moved promiscuously.* For,

(c) *Laert.*

(c) *The air, which is diffused about the earth, is unmoved and unwholsome, and all things that are in it are mortal; but the air which is above is perpetually in motion, and pure, and healthful; and all that are in it are immortal, and consequently divine.*

(d) *Hierocl. in aur. carm.* pag. 313.

(d) This they call, *The Free Æther*, (immediately above the Moon:) *Æther, as being void of matter, and an eternal body; Free, as not being obnoxious to material disturbances.* Hence it followeth, that
The Sun, Moon, and the rest of the Stars, according to Pythagoras, *are gods.*

The *Pythagoreans* held, that every Star is a world in the infinite Æther, which containeth Earth, Air, and Æther. This opinion was also held by the followers of *Orpheus*, that every star is a world.

(f) *Plut.*

(f) The Sun is Spherical, eclipsed by the Moons coming under him.

(g) *Plut.*
(h) *Plut.*

(g) The body of the Moon is of a fiery nature; she receives her light from the Sun. (h) The Eclipse of the Moon is a reverberation or obstruction from the Antichthon.

(i) *Plut.*

(i) The *Pythagoreans* affirm, that the Moon seems earthly, because she is round-about inhabited as our earth; but the creatures are larger and fairer, exceeding us in bigness fifteen times, neither have they any excrements; and their day is so much longer.

(k) *Aristot. Meteor.* 1. 6.

(k) Some of the Pythagoreans *affirm, that a Comet is one of the Planets, but appears not in heaven but after a long time, and is near the Sun, as it happens also to* Mercury; *for, because it recedes but little from the Sun, often when it should appear it is hid, so as it appears not but after a long time.* Or, as (l) *Plutarch* expresseth it, *A Comet is one of those stars which are not always apparent, but rise after a certain period.* (m) Others hold, that it is the reflection of our sight on the Sun, like images in glasses.

(l) *Plac.*

(m) *Plut.*

(n) *Ælian. var.* 4. 27.

(n) The Rain-bow he asserted to be the splendor of the Sun.

SECT. IV.

Of the Sublunary parts of the World.

(a) *Apud Phot.*

OF the inferior Sublunary parts of the World, the (a) anonymous *Pythagorean* placeth first the sphere of Fire, then that of Air, next that of Water; last, that of Earth.

(b) *Plut. plac.* l. 14.

(b) The bodies of all the Elements are round, except that of Fire, which is conical.

(c) *Anon. apud Phot.*

(c) Below the Moon, all things move disorderly; evil therefore necessarily exists about the Region of the Earth; that being settled lowest as the basis of the World, the receptacle of the lowest things.

(d) *Laert.*

(d) The Air, which is diffused about the Earth, is unmoved and unwholesom, and all things in it are mortal.

(e) *Plut. plac.* lib. cap. 23.

(e) There is generation and corruption; for things are produced by alteration, mutation, and resolution of the Elements. Motion is a difference, or alterity in matter.

(f) *Laert.*

(f) In the world there is equally proportioned light and darkness, and heat and cold, and siccity and humidity; which when they are exuberant, the excess of heat causeth Summer; of cold, Winter: when they are equal, then are the best seasons of the year; whereof that which is growing up is the Spring, healthful; that which is decaying is Autumn, unhealthful. Even of the day, the morning is growing up, the evening decaying, and therefore more unwholesome.

CHAP. V.

Of Living and Animate Creatures.

(a) *Laert.*

(a) THere penetrates a beam from the Sun, through the Æther, which is cold and dry; (they call the Air cold Æther, and the Sun and humidity gross Æther) *this beam penetrates to the Abyss, and thereby all things vivificate; all things live in as much as they participate of heat; (wherefore even plants are* ζῶα, *living Creatures) but all things have not soul; the soul is a portion of Æther of heat and cold, for it participates of cold Æther; the soul differeth from life. She is immortal, because that from which she is taken is immortal.* Thus *Alexander* in his Successions, out of the Commentaries of the *Pythagoreans*.

CHAP. VI.

Of the Generation of Animate Creatures.

(a) *Laert.*

(a) ANimate Creatures are generated of one another by seed, (but of earth nothing can be generated.) *Seed is a distillation from the Brain,* [of the foam of the most useful part of the blood, the superfluity of the Aliment, as blood and marrow] *which being injected* τῇ μήτρα, *purulent matter, and moisture, and blood, issue from the Brain, whereof Flesh, Nerves, and Bones, and Hair, and the whole Body consists:* [the power of Seed is incorporeal as the motive mind; but the effused matter corporeal.] *From the vapour comes the Soul and*

and sense; it is *first compacted and coagulated in* 40 *days: and being perfected according to harmonical proportions in* 7, 9 *or* 10 *months (at the farthest) the Infant is brought forth, having all proportions of life; of which (aptly connected according to the proportions of harmony) it consists; all things happening to it at certain times.* Thus *Alexander,* out of the Pythagorick commentaries; the proportions themselves are more exactly deliver'd by (*b*) *Censorinus;* thus.

Pythagoras said, that generally there are two kinds of births, one lesser, of 7 months; which comes into the world the 207 day after the conception: the other greater, of 10 months; which is brought forth in the 274 day. The first and lesser is chiefly contained in the number 6: For that which is conceived of the Seed, (as he saith) the 6 first days, is a Milky substance; the next 8 days, Bloody; which 8 with the 6 make the first concord, Diatessaron: The third degree is of 9 days; in which time it is made flesh; these to the first 6 are in sesquialtera proportion, and make the second concord, Diapente: then follow 12 days more in which the body is fully formed; these to the same 6 consist in duple proportion, and make the Diatessaron concord: These four numbers, 6, 8, 9, 12. added together make 35 days; nor without reason is the number 6 the foundation of generation, for the *Greeks* call it τέλειον, we *perfect;* because its three parts, ½ and ⅓ and ⅙ (that is, 1, 2, and 3.) perfect it; now as the beginnings of the Seed, and that Milky foundation of conception, is first compleated by this number; so this beginning of the Man now formed, and as it were another foundation of maturity, which is of 35 days, being multiplied by 6, makes 220 days, in which this maturity is fulfilled.

The other (greater) birth, is contained in the greater number 7. And as the beginning of the former is in 6 days, after which the seed is converted into blood; so that of this is in 7. And as there the members of the Infant are formed; so here in (about) 40. These 40 days being multiplied by the first 7, make 280 days, that is, 40 weeks: but forasmuch as the birth happens on the first day of the last week, 6 days are substracted, and the 274th observed.

(*c*) He held that *Mankind had ever been; and never had beginning.*

(*b*) *De die natal. Cap.* 11.

(*c*) *Varro de re rust. lib.* 2. *cap.* 1. *Censor de die nat. cap.* 4.

CHAP. VII.

The Soul, its parts, and first of the irrational part.

(*a*) THE power of number being greatest in Nature, *Pythagoras* defined the Soul, (*b*) *A self-moving Number.*

(*c*) Of the *Pythagoreans* some affirm, that the Soul is the motes in the Air; others, that it is that which moves those motes.

(*d*) The soul is most generally divided into two parts, rational, and irrational, but more especially into three; for the irrational they divide into irascible and desiderative. * These are termed νῦς, φρὴν, θυμός. Νῦς and θυμὸς are in other living Creatures, Φρὴν only in man. [*Yet*]

(*e*) The soul of all Animate Creatures are rational, even of those which we term irrational, but they act not according to reason, because of the ill Temperament of the body, and want of speech, as in Apes and Dogs, λαλοῦσι μὲν γὰρ ἔτι, ὐ φράζουσι δὲ. *They talk, but cannot speak.*

The beginning of the soul, is from the heat of the brain, that part which is in the heart is θυμὸς, but φρένες and νῦς are in the Brain. The senses are distillations from these, the rational part is immortal, the rest mortal. The soul is nourished by blood, and the faculties of the soul are spirits. Both the soul and her faculties are invisible, for Æther is invisible: The fetters of the soul are Veins, Arteries, and Nerves; but when she is strong, and composed within her self, her fetters are Reasons and Actions.

(*g*) Every sense is derived from its proper Element; sight from Æther, hearing from Air, smelling from Fire, taste from Water, touch from Earth.

Sense in general, and particularly Sight, is a vapour very hot; and for this reason we are said to see through air, and through water, for the heat pierceth the cold; for if that which is in the eyes were a cold vapour, it would fight with the Air, which is like it, (hot.) In some places he calleth the eyes the gates of the Sun; the same he determined concerning Hearing, and the rest of the Senses.

(*i*) Sight is the judge of Colours. (*k*) Colour they call the superficies of a body. The kinds of Colour are Black, White, Red, Pale; or, as the anonymous writer delivers the opinion of *Pythagoras*) Ten, Black, White, and the rest between them, Yellow, Tawney, Pale, Red, Blew, Green, Bright, Grey. (**l*) The differences of Colours are derived from mixtions of the Elements, and in living Creatures from variety of place, and of Air.

(*m*) The image in a mirrour is made by reflection of the sight, which being extended to the * brass, and meeting with a thick smooth body, is repercussed, and returns into it self; as when the hand is stretch'd forth, and again brought back to the shoulder.

(*n*) Hearing, is the judge of Voice, sharp and flat. (*o*) Voice is incorporeal; for not air, but the figure and superficies of air, by a stroke becomes voice; but no superficies is a body. And tho' it followeth the motion of the body, yet it self hath no body; as when a rod is bent, the superficies suffers nothing, the matter only is bent.

(*p*) Smelling judgeth of Odors, good and ill, and the six between them, putrid, humid, liquid, vaporate.

Taste judgeth of savors, Sweet, Bitter, and the five between them, for they are in all seven, Sweet, Bitter, Sharp, Acid, Fresh, Salt, Hot.

Touching judgeth many things, Heavy, Light, and those that are between them; Hot, Cold, and those that are between them; Hard, Soft, and those that are between them; Dry, Moist, and those that are between them. The other four Senses are seated in the head only, and confined to their proper Organs; but Touching is diffused through the head, and the whole body, and is common to every sense; but exhibits its judgment most manifestly by the hands.

(*a*) *Nemes. de nat. hom.*
(*b*) *Plut.*
(*c*) *Arist. de anima* 1, 2.

(*d*) *Plut. plac.* 4. 4.
* *Laert.*

(*e*) *Plut. plac.* 10.

(*g*) *Stob. phys.* 1. pag. 150.

(*i*) *Anon. phot.*
(*k*) *Plut. plac.* 1. 15. for ῥοδέα perhaps δίκα
(**l*) *Plut.*

(*m*) *Plut. plac.* 4. 14.
* Of which the Ancients made their Mirrours. see *Callim. Hymn.* 5.
(*n*) *Anon. pho:*
(*o*) *Plut. plac.* 4. 20.

(*p*) *Anon. v.*

CHAP.

CHAP. VIII.

Of the Rational Part of the Soul, the Mind.

(a) Plac. phil. 4. 2.
(b) Stob. phys. I.
(c) Clem. Alex. strom. 5.
(d) Cic. de senect.
(d) Cic. nat. deor. I.
(f) Laert.
(g) Cicer. Tusc. quæst. I.

IN Pythagoras his Definition of the Soul, *A self-moving Number,* (a) Plutarch faith, he takes Number for Mind. (b) The Mind, νοῦς, is induced into the Soul, *ab extrinseco,* from without, (c) by divine participation, θεία μοίρα, (d) delibated of the Universal Divine Mind. For (e) there is a Soul intent and commeant through the whole Nature of things, from which our Souls are pluck'd. (f) She is immortal, because that, from which she is taken, is immortal; yet not a God, but the work of the eternal God. Thus (g) Pythagoras exceedingly confirmed the Opinion of his Master Pherecides, who first taught, that the Souls of Men are sempiternal.

(h) Anon.

(h) Our Souls (said he) consist of a Tetrad, Mind, Science, Opinion, Sense: from which proceeds all Art and Science, and by which we our selves are Rational. The mind therefore is a Monad, for the mind considereth according to a Monad. As for Example; There are many men; these one by one are incomprehensible by Sense, and innumerable, but we understand this, one Man, to which none hath Resemblance; and we understand one Horse, for the Particulars are innumerable. Thus every *Genus* and *Species* is according to Monad, wherefore to every one in particular they apply this Definition, A Rational Creature, or, A Neighing Creature. Hence is the mind a Monad, whereby we understand these things. The indeterminate Duad is Science: for all demonstration, and all belief of Science, and likewise all Syllogism from some things granted, inferrs that which is doubted, and easily demonstrateth another thing, the comprehension whereof is Science, therefore it is as the Duad. Opinion is justly a Triad, being of many. Triad implies a multitude, as, *Thrice happy Greeks——[The rest of the Text is wanting.*

(i) Anon. apud Phot. de vit. Pyth.

(i) The *Pythagoreans* assert Eight Organs of Knowledge, Sense, Phantasie, Art, Opinion, Prudence, Science, Wisdom, Mind. Of these, we have common with Divine Natures, Art, Prudence, Science, Mind; with Beasts, Sense and Phantasie; only Opinion is proper to us. *Sense,* is a deceitful knowledge through the Body; *Phantasie,* a motion in the Soul; *Art,* a Habit of operating with Reason. We add, *with Reason,* for a Spider also operates, but without Reason. *Prudence,* is a habit elective of that which is right in things to be done; *Science,* is a habit of those things which are always the same, and in the same manner; *Wisdom,* a knowledge of the first cause; *Mind,* the principle and fountain of all good things.

CHAP. IX.

Of the Transmigration of the Soul.

(a) Pag.

WHat he delivered to his Auditors (saith) (a) Porphyrius) none can certainly affirm, for there was a great and strict silence observed amongst them; but the most known are these: First, he said, that the Soul is immortal; then, that it enters into other kinds of living creatures. [Or, as *Laertius* expresseth it, *He first asserted, That the soul passing through the circle of Necessity, lives at several times in different living creatures.*] Moreover, that after some periods, the same things that are now generated, are generated again, and that nothing is simply New; and that we ought to esteem all animate creatures to be of the same kind with us. These Doctrines Pythagoras seems to have brought first into Greece. (b) *Diodorus Siculus* affirms, he learn'd them of the *Ægyptians:* (c) *They were the first who asserted, that the Soul of man is immortal, and the Body perishing, it always passeth into another Body; and when it hath run through all things terrestrial, marine, volatile, it again entreth into some generated humane body. Which circuition is compleated in three thousand years.* This Opinion (adds *Herodotus) some of the Greeks have usurped as their own, some more ancient, others later, whose Names knowingly I omit.*

(b) Cited by Euseb. præpar. Evang. 10.
(c) Herodot.

Pythagoras, (saith *Theodoret*) *Plato, Plotinus,* and the rest of that Sect, acknowledging Souls to be immortal, asserted, That they are præexistent to Bodies; that there is an innumerable company of Souls; that those which transgress, are sent down into bodies, so as being purify'd by such Discipline, they may return to their own place. That those which, whilst they are in bodies, lead a wicked life, are sent down farther into irrational creatures, hereby to receive punishment, and right expiation; the angry and malicious into Serpents, the ravenous into Wolves, the audacious into Lions, the fraudulent into Foxes, and the like.

(e) Upon this ground (as some conceive) it was, that he forbad to eat Flesh: for, (f) *We ought to esteem all animal creatures to be of the same kind with us,* and (g) *to have common right with us,* and (h) *to be allied (in a manner) to us.* Whence a Bean is by *Horace* stiled, *cognata Pythagoræ,* because he forbad it to be eaten upon the same grounds; (k) *for that Men and Beans arose out of the same putrefaction.*

(e) Anon. vit.
(f) Porph. loc cit.
(g) Laert.
(h) Jamb.
(k) Porph.

This Assertion he defended by many instances, particularly of himself. (l) *Heraclides* relates, that he said, *he had been in former times Æthalides,* esteemed the Son of Mercury, [(m) a powerful Orator, who wrote two Treatises, the one mournful, the other pleasant; so that, like *Democritus* and *Heraclitus,* he bewailed and derided the instability of life, and was said to die and live from day to day] *and that Mercury bad him request whatsoever he would, Immortality only excepted. That he desired, that he might preserve the remembrance of all actions, alive and dead: whereupon he remembred all things whilst he lived, and after death retained the same memory. That afterwards he came to be Euphorbus, and was slain by* Menelaus. *Now Euphorbus said, that he had been in former times Æthalides, and that he had received this gift from Mercury, to know the Migration of the Soul, as it past from one Body to another, and into what Plants and Animals it migrated, and what things his Soul suffered after death, and what other Souls suffered.* Euphorbus *dying, his soul passed into* Hermotimus, *who desiring to profess who he was, went to the Branchidæ, and coming into the Temple of Apollo, shewed the shield which* Menelaus *had hung up there,* [but (n) *Porphyrius* and (o) *Jamblichus* affirm, it was dedicated

(l) Laert.
(m) Tzetz. Chil. 249.
(n) Pag.
(o) Cap.

(toge-

together with other *Trojan* spoils) to Argive *Juno* in her Temple at *Mycenæ*) for he said, *That at his return from* Troy, *he had dedicated that Shield to* Apollo, *it being then old, and nothing remaining but the Ivory stock.* As soon as Hermotimus *died, he became* Pyrrhus, *a Fisherman of* Delus; *and again remembred all things, how he had been first* Æthalides, *then* Euphorbus, *then* Hermotimus, *and lastly* Pyrrhus. *When* Pyrrhus *died he became* Pythagoras, *and remembred all that we have said.* Others relate, that he said, he had been, *first*, Euphorbus; *secondly*, Æthalides; *thirdly*, Hermotimus; *fourthly*, Pyrrhus; *and lastly*, Pythagoras. (p) *Clearchus* and *Dicæarchus*, that *he had been first* Euphorbus; *then* Pyrander; *then* Calliclea; *then a beautiful Curtezan, named* Alce. (q) *For this reason, of all Homer's Verses, he did especially praise these, and set them to the Harp, and often repeat them as his own Epicedium.*

(p) *Agell.*4.11.
(q) *Porph. Jam.* cap. 14.

> As by some hand, a tender Olive set
> In a lone place, near a smooth Rivolet.
> Fair she shoots up, and, fann'd on every side
> By amorous winds, displays her blooming pride;
> Until some churlish unexpected gust
> Plows up her root, and buries her in dust.
> So by *Alcides* slain *Euphorbus* lay,
> Stretch'd on the ground, his Arms the Victor's (prey.

Hence in his person, (r) *Ovid.*

(r) Lib. 15.

(s) O you, whom horrors of cold death affright,
Why fear you *Styx*? vain names, and endless night,
The dreams of Poets, and feign'd miseries
Of forged Hell? Whether last flames surprize,
Or age devours your bodies, they not grieve,
Nor suffer pains. Our souls for ever live:
Yer evermore their ancient houses leave
To live in new, which them, as guests receive,
In *Trojan* Wars, I (I remember well)
Euphorbus was, *Pantheus* son, and fell
By *Menelaus* Lance: my shield again
At *Argos* late I saw in *Juno*'s fane.
All alter, nothing finally decays:
Hither and thither still the spirit strays,
Guest to all bodies, out of beasts it flies
To men, from men to beasts, and never dies.
As pliant wax each new impression takes,
Fixt to no form, but still the old forsakes,
Yet is the same: so souls the same abide,
Though various species their reception hide.
Then left thy greedy belly should destroy
(I prophesie) depressed piety,
Forbear t'expulse thy kindreds Ghosts with food
By death procur'd, nor nourish blood with blood.

(s) Englished by my Uncle, Mr. *Sandys*.

Neither did he instance himself only, but (t) put many others also in mind of the accidents of their former life, how they had lived, before their souls were confined the second time to the body. This he did (adds (u) *Porphyrius*) to those, whose souls were rightly purifi'd; such was (x) Millias of *Crotona*, whom he caused to call to memory, that he had been Midas son of Gordias. Whereupon Millias went to Epire, to perform some Funeral rites, as he appointed.

(t) *Porph.* p. 17. *Jamb.*cap. 14.
(u) Pag. 31.
(x) *Jamb.*cap. 28. pag. 132. See also Ælian. var. Hist.

CHAP. X.

The separate life of the Soul.

(a) THE Soul hath a twofold life, Separate, and in the Body; her faculties are otherwise *in anima*, otherwise *in animali*.

(a) *Stob.* phys.

(b) The Soul is incorruptible; for when it goes out of the body, it goes to the Soul of the world, which is of the same kind.

(b) *Plut.* plac. 4. 7.

(c) When she goeth out upon the earth, she walketh in the air like a body. *Mercury* is the keeper of souls, and for that reason is called Πομπεύς, and Πυλαῖος, and Χθόνιος, because he brings souls out of bodies in the Earth and the Sea; of which, those that are pure, he leadeth into an high place; the impure come not to them, nor to one another, but are bound by the Furies in indissoluble chains.

(c) *Laert.*

(d) The *Pythagoreans* affirmed, that *the souls of the dead neither cast a shadow, nor wink*; for that it is the Sun which causeth the shadow. But he who enters there, is by the law of the place deprived of the Sun's light which they signifie in that speech.

(d) *Plut.* quæ. græc.

(e) *Pythagoras* held, that *Earthquakes proceed from no other cause, but the meeting of the dead.*

(e) Ælian. var. hist. 4. 26.

SECT. V.

Medicine.

TO Physick we shall annex, as its immediate consequent, Medicine. *Apuleias* affirms, that *Pythagoras* learnt the Remedies and Cures of Diseases of the Chaldeans. *Laertius*, that he neglected not Medicine. (a) Ælian, that he studied it accurately. *Jamblichus*, that the *Pythagoreans* esteem it not the least of the Sciences. Lastly, (b) *Diogenes* relates of *Pythagoras*, that whensoever his friends fell into any indisposition of body, he cured them.

(a) Var. hist. 9. 22.
(b) *Porph.*

(c) Health *Pythagoras* defined, *The consistence of a form*. Sickness, *The violation of it*.

(c) *Laert.*

CHAP. I.

Diætetick.

(a) OF Medicine, the Pythagoreans chiefly applied themselves to the Diætetick part, and were most exact in that; and endeavoured first to understand the proportion, not only of labour, but likewise of food and rest. Then concerning the dressing of such meats, they were almost the first who endeavoured to comment and to define.

(a) *Jamb.* cap. 29. pag. 147, 148.

(b) Forasmuch as Diet doth much conduce to good Institution, being wholesom and regular. Let us examine what he decreed therein. Of meats, he absolutely disallowed such as are flatulent, and disorder the body; on the contrary, he approved and commanded those which confirm and unite the constitution; whence he judged Millets to be a convenient food.

(b) *Jamb.* cap. 24.

But he also wholly forbad such meats as are not used by the gods, because they separate us from the correspondence which we have with them.

Likewise he advised to abstain from such meats as are esteemed sacred, which deserve a respect, and are nothing convenient for the ordinary use of man.
What-

Whatsoever Meats *obstructed Divination, or were prejudicial to the purity and sanctity of the mind, or to Temperance,* and habitual *Virtue, be advised to shun: As also those which are contrary to Purity, and defile the Imaginations which occur in sleep, and the other Purities of the Soul, be rejected and avoided.*

These Rules concerning Diet he prescribed generally to (c) *all persons, but more particularly to Philosophers,* (d), *who are most addicted to contemplation of the sublimest things. He denied at once all superfluous meats as were unlawful to be eaten, not permitting them at any time to feed on that which had life, or to drink Wine, or to sacrifice to the Gods any living creature, or hurt any of them; but commanded with all exactness, to preserve the justice which belongs even to them. In this manner he lived himself, abstaining from the flesh of living creatures, and worshipping unbloody Altars, and both taking care, that others should not put tame beasts to death, and himself making the savage tame, and moderating and instituting them both by words and actions; but by no means would punish or kill them.*

He likewise commanded civil Law-givers to abstain from the flesh of living creatures, because it behoveth them who would make use of the heigth of justice, no way to injure living creatures, which are of Affinity with us. For how can they perswade other men to do just things, who themselves are transported by Avarice to feed on living creatures, which are of Affinity with us, allyed, in a manner, to us, through the community of life, consisting of the temperament and commixtion of the same Elements.

But to (e) *others, whose life was not extraordinary pure, and sacred, and Philosophical, he prescribed a certain time for Abstinence. To those he decreed, That they should not eat the Heart: That they should not eat the Brain. And these are prohibited to all* Pythagoreans; *for they are leaders, and, as it were, seats and houses of wisdom and life. But those were conjecrated by the nature of the divine word.*

In like manner he prohibited Mallows, as being the first Messenger and Interpreter of Celestial Affections, and (as I may say) Compassions towards men.

Likewise he commanded to abstain from the Melanure, [a fish so called from the blackness of its Tail] because it is peculiar to the Terrestrial Deities.

He forbad also the Erythrine, for the like Reasons.

Also to abstain from Beans, for many Reasons, divine and natural, referring to the Soul.

(f) The Pythagoreans at Dinner used Bread and Honey. Wine they drank not (betwixt Meals.) At Supper, Wine, and Maza, and Bread, and Broth, and Herbs, both raw and boiled. They likewise set before them the Flesh of Sacrificed Beasts. They seldome eat Broths of Fish, because some of them are in some respects very hurtful, likewise (seldom) the Flesh of such Creatures as use not to hurt Mankind.

(g) *As concerning the Diet of* Pythagoras *himself, his Dinner consisted* (h) *of Honey-Combs, or Honey, his Supper of Bread made of Millet, and* [(i) *his Opsonium] of boil'd or raw Sallads, very seldom of the flesh of sacrificed Victims, and that not promiscuously of every part,* (k) [*and seldom of Sea-fish.*]

(l) *When he designed to go into the private places of the Gods, and to stay there a while, he used for the most part such meats as expelled hunger and thirst. For the expelling of hunger, he made a composition of the seed of Poppy, and Sesame, and the skin of the Sea-Onyon well wash'd, till it be quite drain'd of the outward juice; of the Flowers of the Daffodil, and the leaves of Mallows, of Past of Barley and Pea: of all which taking an equal weight, and chopping them small, he made up into a Masse, with Hymettian Honey. Against thirst, he took of the seeds of Cowcumbers, and the fullest dried Raisins, taking out the kernels, and the Flower of Coriander, and the seeds of Mallows, and Purselain, and scraped Cheese, Meal and Cream; these he made up with wild Honey. This Diet, he said, was taught to* Hercules, *by* Ceres, *when he was sent into the* Lybian *desarts.*

CHAP. II.

Theraputick.

THE Theraputick part *Pythagoras* practised by Cataplasms, Charms, and Musick.

(a) *The* Pythagoreans (*saith* Jamblicus) *treated chiefly of Cataplasms; but Potions they less esteemed. And of those they used only such as were proper against Ulcerations; but Incision, and Cauterising they absolutely disallow'd.*

Magical Herbs, saith (b) Pliny, *were first celebrated in our part of the world by* Pythagoras, *following the Magi.* (c) *He first wrote a Treatise of their Virtues, assigning the Invention and Original to* Apollo *and* Æsculapius, *Immortal Gods.*

(d) *By* Coriacesia, *and* Callicia, Pythagoras *affirms, that water will be turned into ice, the mention whereof I find not, saith* Pliny, *in others, nor in him, any more concerning them.*

(e) *He likewise speaks of* Menais, *which he also calls by another name,* Corinthas; *the juice whereof boiled in water, he saith, immediately cures the biting of Serpents, fomenting the part therewith. The same juice being spilt upon the Grass, they who tread upon it, or are besprinkled therewith, die irrecoverably: a strange Nature of Poyson, except against Poyson.*

(f) *There is an Herb called* Aproxis, *by the same* Pythagoras, *the Root whereof takes fire at distance, as* Naptha, *of which, saith* Pliny, *we have spoken in the wonders of the Earth. The same* Phythagoras *relates, That if any Disease shall happen to men when the* Aproxis *is in its Flower, although they be cured, yet shall they constantly have some grudging thereof as often as it blows: and Wheat, and Hemlock, and Violet, have the same quality. I am not ignorant, adds* Pliny, *that this Book is by some ascribed to* Cleemporus, *the Physician; but pertinacious Fame, and Antiquity, vindicate it to* Pythagoras.

(g) Pythagoras *the Philosopher wrote also one Volume concerning the Sea-Onyon, collecting the Medicinal properties thereof, which* Pliny *professeth to have taken from him, lib.* 20. *And* (h) *again, he saith,* Pythagoras *affirms, that a Sea-Onyon, hung over the Threshold of the Gate, hinders all ill Medicaments from entring the house.*

Likewise, Coleworts (*as* (i) Pliny *relates*) *were much commended by* Pythagoras. *He adds* (k) *that concerning the white kind of the Eringo, (by the Romans*

mans call'd, Centum-capita) there are many vanities delivered, not only by the Magi, but by the Pythagoreans.

Besides the Pharmaceutick, Pythagoras practised two other ways of cure, one by Musick, the other by Charm. Of the first we have already spoken. Of the second, thus (*l*) *Jamblichus*: *There is also a way without the singing of birds, by which they expell'd some passions, and sicknesses, (as they say) indeed by Incantation, whence it seems was derived the word* ἐπῳδὴ, The way of cure by Charm, saith (*m*) the *Greek* Etymologist, *was of ancient use*; whence *Homer* :

—— *And staid the black blood by a Charm*.

And *Pindar, speaking of Æsculapius*, ἀμφέπων, *with soft Charms*.

That *Pythagoras* made use of *Epodes*, is also affirmed by (*n*) *Porphyrius*. He allayed, saith he the passions of the Soul and Body by Rythms, and Verses, and Epodes. And *Diogenes*, cited by the same *Porphyrius*, *if his Friends fell into any indisposition of body, he healed them*; *if they were troubled in mind, he assuaged their Grief, as we said, partly by Charms and Magick Verses, partly by Musick*. For he had some Verses proper to the cure of the indispositions of the Body, by singing which, he restored the sick to their former health: He had other Verses that procured forgetfulness of grief, assuaged anger, and suppressed inordinate desires.

Of these Charms we find an instance preserv'd by (*o*) *Pliny*, who prescribes, as *an Invention of Pythagoras, which seldom fails against Lameness, or Blindness, or the like Accidents, to apply to the part; if on the right side, an uneven number of Vowels of impositive words; if on the left, an even.*

l Cap.

m In ἐπῳδὴ.

n Pag.

o Lib. 23. c 4.

The Doctrine of PYTHAGORAS.

CHAP. I.

Pythagoras his Symbolical way of Teaching.

(*a*) PYTHAGORAS *had a twofold-manner of teaching: whatsoever he communicated to his Auditors, was delivered, either plainly or symbollically.* Hitherto of the plain way. We come now to the other, the symbolical.

(*b*) *He used by short sentences to vaticinate an infinite multiplicious signification to his Disciples, after a symbolical manner: no otherwise than Apollo by short Answers exhibits many imperceptible sentences; and Nature her self, by small seeds, most difficult effects. Of this kind is,*

—— *half, is the whole's beginning.*

an Apothegm of *Pythagoras* himself. *Neither in that Hemistick only, but in others of the same kind, the most divine Pythagoras wrapped up sparks of truth, for such as could enkindle them, in a short way of speech treasuring up concealed a most copious production of Theory: as in this,*

—— *to number all have reference.*

And again, φιλότης, ἰσότης, Friendship, Equality; and in the word Κόσμος, (World, or Heaven) and in the word Philosophy, and in ςὴν κρέντων, and in that celebrious word Tetractys. *All these, and many more, did Phythagoras invent, for the benefit and rectification of such as conversed with him.*

Some things likewise (saith (*c*) *Porphyrius*) he spoke in a mystical way symbolically, most of which are collected by *Aristotle*; as when he called the Sea (*d*) *a tear of Saturn*; the two Bears, *the hands of Rhea*; the Pleides, *the Lutes of the Muses*; the Planets, *the dogs of Proserpina* [the (*e*) *eyes, the gates of the Sun*.]

(*f*) He had also another kind of Symbols, as, *Go not over a ballance*; that is, *Shun avarice*, &c. Thus *Porphyrius*. Those are variously recited and interpreted by several Authors; we shall begin with *Jamblichus*, as being herein of greatest credit.

a Porph. pag.

b Jamb. cap. 89. pag. 146.

c Pag. 24.
d For, τὴν θάλατταν ἐ- καλεῖ ἔναι Κρόνου δάκρυον; read ἐκάλει Κρόνου δάκρυον, for so Clemens Alexandrinus, Strom. lib. 5. pag. 571.
e Laert.
f Porph. loco. cit.

CHAP. II.

The Symbols of Pythagoras, *according to* Jamblichus.

(*a*) THE last way of exhortation to Virtue, and dehortation from Vice, is that by Symbols; one way being proper to the Sect, not communicable to other Institutions; another vulgar and common to them; the third is betwixt both, neither absolutely Publick, nor wholly *Pythagorical*, nor quite different from either; such are those they term Symbols, of which, as many as deserve commemoration, in our opinion, of the adhortatory form, we shall communicate, and add a suitable interpretation; conceiving that hereby, the exhortation to Philosophy may be more prevalent on those that hear them, than if delivered more at large. And forasmuch as we shall insert some Exoterick solutions, common to all Philosophy, it is to be understood, as different from the meaning of the *Pythagoreans*. But inasmuch as we shall intermix some of the most particular opinions of the *Pythagoreans*, consonant to each; this is wholly proper to them, and dissonant from all other Philosophers, but most fit to be alledged. This will insensibly lead us from the Exoterick notions, bringing us to the others, and acquainting us with them. And to the exhortations framed according to this Sect, as a Bridg or Ladder,

a Jamb. protrept. cap. ult.

by

by which we ascend from a depth to a great heighth, guiding the minds of those, who addict themselves genuinely thereto. For to this end it was framed, according to imitation of the things already mentioned. For the most ancient, and such as were contemporary with, and disciples to *Pythagoras*, did not compose their writings intelligible, in a common vulgar style, familiar to every one, as if they endeavoured to dictate things readily perceptible by the hearer, but consonant to the silence decreed by *Pythagoras*, concerning divine mysteries, which it was not lawful to speak of before those who were not initiated; and therefore clouded both their mutual discourses and writings by Symbols; which, if not expounded by those that proposed them, by a regular interpretation, appear to the hearers like old wives proverbs, trivial and foolish; [(*b*) but being rightly explained, and instead of dark, rendred lucid and conspicuous to the vulgar, they discover an admirable sense, no less than the divine Oracle of Pythian *Apollo*, and give a divine inspiration to the Philologists that understand them.] That therefore their benefit may be known, and their adhortative use manifest, we will give the solutions of every Symbol, both after the Exoterick and the Acroatick way, not omitting those things which were preserved in silence, not communicable to uninitiated persons. The Symbols are these:

b Vit. cap 23.

1. *When you go to the Temple, worship, neither do nor say any thing concerning Life.*
2. *If there be a Temple in your way, go not in, no not though you pass by the very doors.*
3. *Sacrifice and worship barefoot.*
4. *Decline high-ways, and take the foot-path.*
5. *Abstain from the Melanure, for it belongs to the Terrestrial gods.*
6. *Above all things, govern your tongue, when you follow the gods.*
7. *When the winds blow, worship the noise.*
8. *Cut not fire with a sword.*
9. *Turn away from thy self every edg.*
10. *Help a man to take up a burthen, but not to lay it down.*
11. *Put on the shoo first on the right foot, but the left foot first into the bason.*
12. *Discourse not of Pythagorean things without light.*
13. *Pass not over a pair of Scales.*
14. *Travelling from home, turn not back; for the Furies go back with you.*
15. *Urine not, being turned towards the Sun.*
16. *Wipe not a seat with a Torch.*
17. *A Cock keep, but not sacrifice; for it is consecrated to the Moon and the Sun.*
18. *Sit not upon a Chœnix.*
19. *Breed nothing that hath crooked talons.*
20. *Cut not in the way.*
21. *Receive not a Swallow into your house.*
22. *Wear not a Ring.*
23. *Grave not the image of God on a Ring.*
24. *Look not in a glass by candle-light.*
25. *Concerning the gods, disbelieve nothing wonderful, nor Concerning divine Doctrines.*
26. *Be not taken with immoderate laughter.*
27. *At a sacrifice, pare not your nails.*
28. *Lay not hold on every one readily with your righs hand.*
29. *When you rise out of bed, disorder the coverlet, and deface the print.*
30. *Eat not the Heart.*
31. *Eat not the Brains.*
32. *Spit upon the cuttings of your hair, and the parings of your nails.*
33. *Receive not an Erythrine.*
34. *Deface the print of a pot in the Ashes.*
35. *Take not a woman that hath gold, to get children of her.*
36. *First honour the figure and steps, a figure and a Tribolus.*
37. *Abstain from Beads.*
38. *Set Mallows, but eat it not.*
39. *Abstain from living creatures.*

CHAP. III.

An Explication of the Pythagorick *Symbols, by* Jamblichus.

ALL these Symbols are in general adhortative to all virtue; and every one of them in particular conduceth to some particular virtue, and part of Philosophy, and Learning; as the first are adhortative to devotion, and divine knowledge.

SYMB. I.

FOr this, *When you go to the Temple, worship, neither do nor say any thing concerning life*, observes the Divinity after such manner, as it is in it self, pure and incommixt. He joyns pure to the pure, and takes care, that no worldly business insinuate it self into the divine worship; for they are things wholly different and opposite to one another. Moreover, this conduceth much to Science; for we ought not to bring to the divine Science any such thing as humane consideration, or care of outward life. Thus nothing is hereby commanded, but that divine discourses, and sacred actions, ought not to be intermixt with the instable manners of men.

SYMB. II.

TO that is consonant the next, *If a Temple lie in your way, go not in, not though you pass by the very doors.* For if like is delightful to its like, it is manifest that the Gods, having the chiefest essence of all things, ought to have the principal worship: but if any man doth it upon occasion of any other thing, he makes that the second, which is the first and chiefest of all; and by that means he subverts the whole order of worship, and science. The most excellent good, ought not to be ranked in the latter place, as inferior to humane good; neither ought our own affairs to have the place of the chief end and better things, either in our words or thoughts.

SYMB. III.

THat which follows is an exhortation to the same; for this, *Sacrifice and worship bare foot*, signifieth one way, that we ought to serve the Gods, and perform their knowledg decently and moderately, not exceeding the order in the earth. Another way that we ought to perform their service and knowledg; being free without Fetters This the Symbol commands to be observ'd, not in the body only, but in the acts of the soul, that they be not restrained by passions, nor by the infirmity of the body, nor by our external generation, but all free and ready for communication with the Gods.

SYMB. IV.

THere is another Symbol of this kind, exhorting to the same virtue; *Concerning the gods, disbelieve nothing wonderful, and concerning divine Doctrines.* This rule is religious, and declareth the superlative excellence of the Gods; instructing us, and putting us in mind, that we ought not to estimate the Divine power by our own Judgment. To us who are corporeal, and generated and corruptible, and transitory, and obnoxious to several diseases, and to narrowness of habitation, and to aggravation of motion towards the Center, and to sleepiness, and to indigence, and to abundance, and to imprudence, and to infirmity, and to impediment of soul, and the like some things will seem difficult, and impossible; yet have we many excellencies by Nature: but we are quite short of the Gods, neither have we the same power, or ability. This Symbol, therefore, chiefly adviseth to knowledge of the Gods as of those who are able to do all things; whence it admonisheth *to disbelieve nothing concerning the Gods.* There is added, *nor concerning divine Doctrines,* meaning those which are declared by the *Pythagorick* Philosophy; because they being setled by Mathematicks, and Scientifick speculation, will show by demonstration, strengthned by necessity, that there are true Beings existent void of fallaciousness.

These may also exhort to the Science concerning the Gods, and perswade that such a Science is to be acquired, as by which we shall not * disbelieve any thing concerning the Gods: The same may advise to divine Doctrines, and to proceed by Mathematicks; for they only clear the eyes, and are illuminative of all Beings, to him that will behold them; for by participation of Mathematicks, One thing is constituted before all; that we disbelieve not any thing, either concerning the nature of the Gods, or their Essence, or their Power: nor of those *Pythagorical* Doctrines, which seem monstrous to persons, not initiated into Mathematicks: Thus *disbelieve not,* is equivalent to, *acquire and possess* those things, by means whereof you shall not disbelieve; that is Mathematicks, and Scientifick Demonstrations.

* Perhaps ἀπιστήσομεν.

SYMB. V.

THE next Symbol tends (as I conceive) to the same effect; *Declining high-ways, walk in path-ways.* For it commandeth to leave the publick popular course of life, and to pursue that which is separate, and Divine: likewise that we despise the common opinions, and much esteem the private, which are not to be divulged; and to contemn the pleasure which tends towards men; but to value exceedingly that felicity, which is joyned with the divine will: And to leave humane customs as vulgar; but to apply our selves to the worship of the Gods, which far excels the ordinary course of life. Allied to this, is that which followeth.

SYMB. VI.

ABstain from the Melanure, for it belongs to the Terrestrial Gods. We shall say more upon it, in our explication of the adhortative Symbols: It adviseth to make choice of the Heavenly Journey, and to adhere to the Intellectual Gods, and to withdraw our selves from Material nature, and to direct our course to that life which is pure, void of matter, and to make use of the best way of Divine worship, and that which is most suitable to the chief deities. These Symbols are adhortative to the knowledge and worship of the Gods.

SYMB. VII.

THE following Symbols exhort to Wisdom; *Above all things govern your Tongue, following the Gods;* for the first work of Wisdom is to revert our speech into it self, and to accustom it not to pass forth, that it may be perfect within our selves, and in its conversion towards our selves; Moreover *in following the Gods:* For nothing renders the mind so perfect, as when a man, being reverted into himself, followeth the Gods.

SYMB. VIII.

THis Symbol likewise, *When the winds blow, worship the noise.* is an exhortation to Divine Wisdom; For it implieth that we ought to love the similitude of Divine Natures and Powers: and when they make a reason suitable to their efficacies, it ought exceedingly to be honoured and reverenced.

SYMB. IX.

THE next Symbol, *Cut not fire with a Sword,* exhorts to wisdom; for it excites in us a convenient knowledg, that we ought not to give sharp language to a man full of fire and anger, nor to contest with him; for you may often by words exasperate and trouble a rude and unlearned person. Of this *Heraclitus* witnesseth; *To contest with anger* (saith he) *is hard, for whatsoever it would have done, it will purchase tho at the expence of life.* And he said truly; for many, gratifying their own anger, have exchanged their Souls, and preferred death before them: but from continence of the Tongue, and peacefulness, this happens, that out of contention ariseth friendship, the wrathful fire being extinguished, and thou thy self wilt appear, not to be void of reason. This Symbol is confirmed by that which followeth.

SYMB. X.

TUrn away from thy self every edge; for towards whomsoever it shall be turned, it will hurt him. This Symbol commandeth to use prudence not anger; for that edg of the mind which we call anger, is void of reason and prudence;

dence; for anger boileth like a pot upon the fire, never dividing the mind to that which is past. You must therefore settle your mind in tranquillity, diverting it from anger, and often preventing your self; as a man maketh brass sound, not without touching it. This passion therefore must be suprest by reason.

SYMB. XI.

This, *Help to lay on a burthen, but not to take it off*, adviseth to fortitude; for, whosoever layeth on a burthen, signifieth labour and action; but he who taketh it off, rest and remisness. The meaning therefore of the Symbol is this, Be not the cause, either to thy self or any other, of remisness of mind, and soft life; for every useful thing is acquired by labour. This Symbol *Pythagoras* called Herculean, as being sealed by his labours; for whilst he lived amongst men, he passed frequently through fire, and many difficulties, shunning idleness. From actions and labour proceeds a right office, but not from sloath.

SYMB. XII.

This, *Pluck off your right shoo first, but put your left foot first into the bason*, exhorts to active prudence; that good actions, as right, are to be set round about us; but the ill, as left, to be laid aside and rejected.

SYMB. XIII.

This, *Discourse not of Pythagorean things without light*, is chiefly adhortatory, that the mind acquire prudence; for that resembles the light of the mind, which being indefinite, limits and reduceth it, as it were, out of darkness into light; It is therefore chiefly requisite to look upon the mind, as guide of all good actions in life; but in the Pythagorick doctrines, this is most particularly necessary; for it is not possible to understand what they are without light.

SYMB. XIV.

This, *Pass not over a ballance*, commands to do justly, and above all things, to respect equality and mediocrity, and to know justice, the most perfect Virtue, which compleats the rest, and without which, the rest profit nothing; neither must we know it superficially only, but by Theorems, and scientifick Demonstrations. This knowledge is the work of no Art and Science, but only of the Philosophy of *Pythagoras*, which preferreth Mathematicks before all things else.

SYMB. XV.

To the same purpose is this, *Travelling from home, turn not back, for the furies go back with you*. This Symbol exhorteth to Philosophy, and free action about the mind. It likewise manifestly teacheth thus, When thou studiest Philosophy, separate thy self from all corporeal and sensible things, and truly make a meditation of death unto things intelligible, which are always the same, and after the same manner; proceeding (without turning back) by Mathematicks, conduceing thereto. For travel is the change of Place, death is the separation of the Soul from the Body. But we must so study Philosophy, as to make use of the pure mind sincerely, without the acts of corporeal senses, to the comprehension of the truth which in things that are, which is acknowledged to be wisdom. But after you have once applied your self to study Philosophy, turn not back, nor be drawn back to the former corporeal things, in which you were bred up; for you will much repent hereof, being hindred from sacred comprehensions, by the darkness which is in corporeal things. Repentance they call *Erinys*, or *Fury*.

SYMB. XVI.

This, *Urine not being turned towards the Sun*, admonisheth, that we offer not to do any bestial action, but to study and practise Philosophy, looking upon Heaven and the Sun; and remember, that in the study of Philosophy, you never bear a low mind, but by the contemplation of heavenly things, ascend to the gods, and to wisdom. And having applied your self to study Philosophy, and to the light of truth that is in it, purifying your self, and converting your self wholly to that design, to Theology, and Physiology, and Astronomy, and Ætiologick, which is above all the rest, do nothing irrational or bestial.

SYMB. XVII.

The same meaning is of the next, *Wipe not a seat with a Torch*; for not only because a Torch is purificative, as partaking of much quick fire, like sulphur, it adviseth that this ought not to be defiled, its nature being such, as it dispelleth all things that defile; nor ought we to oppose natural habitude, by defiling that, whose nature is repugnant to defiling. Much less ought we to joyn and mix things proper to wisdom, with those which are proper to animality. For, *a Torch*, in respect of its brightness, is compared to Philosophy; *a Seat*, in respect of its lowness, to Animality.

SYMB. XVIII.

This, *Breed a Cock, but not sacrifice it*; *for it is sacred to the Moon and the Sun*; admonisheth us, to nourish and cherish (and not to neglect, so as to suffer them to perish and corrupt) the great evidences of the union, and coagmentation, and sympathy, and conspiration of the World. It therefore adviseth, to address our selves to contemplation of the Universe, and to Philosophy; for the truth of all things being by nature concealed, and hard to be found out, yet requisite to be sought, and investigated by man, chiefly through Philosophy, (for to do it by any other study is impossible) which receiving some little sparks from nature, blows them up, and makes them greater and more perspicuous by its Doctrines. Philosophy therefore ought to be studied.

SYMB. XIX.

This, *Sit not upon a Chœnix*, may appear to be more Pythagorical, from what was already said; for because aliment is to be measured by corporeity and animality, not by the Chœnix rest not, nor lead thy life uninitiated into Philosophy; but applying thy self thereto, take greatest care of that in thee which is most Divine, the Soul; and in the Soul, chiefly the mind, whose aliment is not measured by the Chœnix, but by contemplation and discipline.

SYMB. XX.

This, *Breed nothing that hath crooked talons*, adviseth to a thing which is yet more Pythagorical; be free and communicative, and endeavour to make others such also, accustoming thy self to give and receive without grudging or envy; not to take all things insatiably, and to give nothing. For the natural condition of those Fowls, which have crooked talons, is, to receive and snatch readily and quickly, but not easily to let go, or impart to others, by reason of the tenacity of their talons, being crooked, as the nature of Shrimps is such, that they quickly lay hold of a thing, but very hardly part with it, unless they be turned upon their backs. Now we having hands given us by nature, proper to communicate, and straight, not crooked fingers, ought not to imitate those which have crooked talons, unlike us; but rather mutually to communicate to, and participate from, one another, as being excited thereto by those, who first gave names to things, who named the more honourable hand δεξιὰν, *the right*, not only ἀπὸ τȣ̂ δέχεϑαι, *from receiving*: but likewise, ἀπὸ τȣ̂ δεκτὸν ὑπάρχειν ἐν τῷ μεταδιδόναι, *from being ready to receive in communicating*. We must therefore do justly, and for that reason Philosophise; for Justice is a return and remuneration, exchanging and supplying excess and defect.

SYMB. XXI.

This, *Cut not in the way*, that truth is one, falshood multiplicious; which is manifest from this, that what every thing is, speaking plainly, is expressed but one way; but what it is not, is expressed infinite ways. Philosophy seems to be a way; it therefore saith, Choose that Philosophy, and that way to Philosophy, in which thou shalt not cut (or divide) nor establish contrary Doctrines, but those which are constituted and confirmed by scientifick demonstration, by Mathematicks and contemplation; which is, *Philosophise Pythagorically*. It may be taken also in another sence, forasmuch as that Philosophy which proceeds by corporeals and sensibles, .(with which Philosophy the younger sort are satisfied, who conceive, that God, and Qualities, and the Mind, and Virtues, and in a word, all the principal causes of things, are Bodies) is easily subverted and confuted, as appears by the great disagreement amongst them, who go about to say any thing therein. But the Philosophy which is of incorporeals, and intelligibles, and immaterials, and eternals, which are always the same in themselves, and towards one another, never admitting corruption or alteration, is firmly established, and the cause of irrefragable demonstration. Now this precept adviseth us, when we Philosophise, and perfect the way which is manifest, that we shun the snares and entertainments of corporeals and divisibles, and intimately apply our selves to the substance of incorporeals, which are never unlike themselves, by reason of the truth and stability which they naturally have.

SYMB. XXII.

This, *Receive not a Swallow into your house*, adviseth, that you admit not a slothful person (who is not a constant lover of labour, neither will persevere to be a disciple) unto your Doctrines, which require continual labour, and patience, by reason of the variety and intricateness of the several disciplines. He makes use of the swallow to represent sloth, and cutting off times, because this bird comes to us but in one season of the year, and then stays but a short while with us; but is absent from us, and out of our sight, a much longer space.

SYMB. XXIII.

This, *Wear not a Ring*, is likewise adhortatory after the *Pythagorick* way, thus: Forasmuch as a Ring encompasseth the finger of the wearer, in nature of a chain, but hath this property, that it pincheth not, nor paineth, but is so fit, as if it naturally belonged to that part; and the body is such a kind of chain to the soul. *Wear not a Ring*, signifies, *Philosophise truly*, and separate your soul from the chain which goeth round about it. For Philosophy is the meditation of death, and separation of the soul from the body. Seriously and earnestly therefore apply your self to the *Pythagorick* Philosophy, which separates the soul, by the mind, from all corporeals, and is conversant about intellectuals and immaterials, by Theoretick doctrines. But unty and loose your fins, and all things that pluck you back and hinder philosophising, diversions of the flesh, excessive eating, unseasonable repletion, which as it were, fetter the body, and continually breed infinite diseases.

SYMB. XXIV.

This, *Grave not the image of God in a Ring*, adviseth thus, Philosophise, and, above all things, think, that the gods are incorporeal. This Symbol is, beyond all others, the Seminary of the *Pythagorick* doctrines; of it all things (almost) are fitly adapted, and by it are established to the end. Think not that they use forms that are corporeal, neither that they are received into material substance, fettered (as it were) to the body, like other living beings. The figures engraved in Rings, in the very Ring express a chain, and corporeity, and sensible form, as it were the figure of some animal, perceptible by sight, from which we must absolutely separate the gods, as being eternal and intelligible, and always the same in themselves, and towards one another; as is largely discoursed in the Treatise concerning God.

SYMB.

SYMB. XXV.

THis, *Look not in a glass by candle-light*, adviseth more *Pythagorically* thus: Philosophise, pursuing, not the phantasies of sense (which give a kind of light to comprehensions, like a candle, neither natural nor true) but those which procure Science, and are conversant in the mind, by which a most bright purity is constituted in the eye of the soul, of all Notions, and Intelligibles, and the speculation of them, but not of Corporeals and Sensibles; for they are in contiual fluxion and mutation, (as hath often been shown) no way stable or existing like themselves, whereby they might uphold a firm and Scientifick comprehension, as the others do.

SYMB. XXVI.

THis, *Be not seized with immoderate laughter*, showeth that we should vanquish passions: Put thy self in mind of right reason; be neither blown up in good fortune, nor cast down in bad; admitting no thought of change in either. He named *Laughter* above all other passions, because that is most apparently shown in the face it self; perhaps also, because this is proper to man only of all living creatures; whence some define man, A risible living Creature. This precept shows that we ought to take humanity only, as it were in our way, like guests; but to acquire the imitation of God, as far as we are able; by Philosophising, secretly withdrawing our selves from the property of men, and preferring the rational before the risible, in distinction from other Creatures.

SYMB. XXVII.

THis, *At a Sacrifice pare not your nails*, is adhortative to friendship: for of Domesticks and Allies, some being nearly relatd to us, as Brothers, Children, Parents, are like our Limbs and Parts which cannot be taken away without much pain and maim: others who are allied to us at a great distance, as the Children of Uncles, or of Cousins, or their Children, or such like, resemble those parts which may be cut off without pain, as Hair, Nails, and the like. Intending therefore to signifie those Allies, whom, by reason of this distance, we at other times neglect, he useth the word *nails*, saying, Cast not those quite away; but, in Sacrifices, (though at other times neglected) carry them along with you, and renew your Domestick familiarity with them.

SYMB. XXVIII.

THis, *Lay not hold on every one readily with your right hand*, saith, give not your right hand easily, that is, Draw not to you, nor endeavour to draw out improper and unitiated persons, by giving them your right hand: Moreover, to such as have not been long tried by Disciplines and Doctrines, nor are appoved as worthy to participate of temperance, and of the Quinquennial silence and other Trials, the right hand ought not to be given.

SYMB. XXIX.

THis, *When you rise out of bed, wrap the coverlets together, and confound the print of your body*; adviseth, that having undertaken to Philosophise, you should acquaint your self with Intellectuals, and Incorporeals: Therefore as soon as you rise from the sleep of Ignorance, and that darkness which resembles night, draw not to your self any corporeal thing, to the light of Philosophy which resembles the day; but blot out of your remembrance all prints of that sleep.

SYMB. XXX.

THis, *Eat not the heart*, signifieth, that we ought not to tear asunder the unity and conspiration of the whole; Moreover it implieth, Be not envious, but obliging, and communicative: hereupon it exhorted to Philosophise. For of all Arts and Sciences, only Philosophy envieth not the good of others, nor grieveth thereat, nor rejoyceth in the ill of a neighbour; but declareth that all men are by nature allied to one another, and friends, and alike affected, and subjected alike to fortune, and alike ignorant of the future; and therefore commands them to commiserate and love one another, as becomes a Creature, sociable and rational.

SYMB. XXXI.

Like that, is this, *Eat not the Brain*, for that is the principal instrument of Wisdom; it signifieth therefore that we ought not with reproaches to bite and tear in pieces things well intended, and Doctrines. Those are well intended, which are exactly donsidered by the principal reason of mind, like to things comprehended by Science; for these are beheld not by the organs of the irrational soul, that is, by the heart and the liver; but by the pure rational part of the soul: wherefore it is a folly to oppose them. This Symbol rather adviseth to worship the fountain of Minds, and next instrument of intellection, by whose means we acquire speculation and Science, and (in a word) all Wisdom, and truly Philosophise; and not to confound and deface the Prints that are therein.

SYMB. XXXII.

THis, *Spit upon the cuttings of thy Hair, and parings of thy Nails*, saith thus, those things are easily contemned which are born with thee, but are more distant from the Mind; as, on the other side, those are more esteem'd, which are nearer to the mind. So having addicted thy mind to Philosophy, above all, reverence those things which are demonstrated by the soul and mind, without the organs of sense, by speculative Science: But contemn and spit upon those things which are seen without the light of the mind, by the sensitive organs which are born with us: which are not capable of reaching the eternity of the mind.

SYMB.

SYMB. XXXIII.

This, *Receive not an Erythrine*, seems to respect the Etymology of the word; Entertain not an impudent blushless person; nor on the other side one over-bashful, ready to fall back from the mind, and firm intellection; whence is understood also, Be not such your self.

SYMB. XXXIV.

This, *Deface the print of a pot in the ashes*, signifieth, that he who applies his mind to Philosophy, must forget the Demonstrations of confusion and grossness, (that is, of corporeals and sensibles) and wholly make use of Demonstrations of Intelligibles; By *ashes* are meant the dust or sand in Mathematical Tables, wherein the Demonstrations and Figures are drawn.

SYMB. XXXV.

But *approach not her to get Children, who hath money*, is not meant of a woman, but of a Sect of Philosophy, which hath in it much corporiety and gravity tending downwards; for of all things in the Earth Gold is the most heavy, and aptest to move towards the Center, which is the property of Corporeal weight: to *approach*, means not only *coition*, but to apply our selves, and to be *assistant*.

SYMB. XXXVI.

This, *In the first place honour the figure and the degrees, the figure and the Tribolus*; adviseth to Philosophise, and study Mathematicks not superficially, and by them as by degrees of ascention arrive at our proposed end; but despise those things which others prefer before these; and chiefly reverence the *Italick* Philosophy, which considers Incorporeals in themselves, before the *Ionick*, which first looks upon bodies.

SYMB. XXXVII.

This, *Abstain from Beans*, adviseth to beware of every thing that may corrupt our discourse with the gods, and prescience.

SYMB. XXXVIII.

This, *Plant Mallows, but eat it not*, signifies that such things are turned with the Sun. *Plant*, that is, Insisting on its nature and application to the Sun, and Sympathy, neither abstain from it, nor wholly adhere to it; but transfer your mind and intellect, and transplant them as it were to plants and herbs of the same kind; and to Animals which are not of the same kind, and to Stones and Rivers, and in a word to all natures, for thou wilt find that which designeth the unity and conspiration of the World, to be fruitful and full of variety, and admirably copious, as if it sprung from a Mallows root: Therefore not only eat not, nor deface such observations, but on the contrary encrease them, and multiply them, as it were by transplantation.

SYMB. XXXIX.

This, *Abstain from living Creatures*, exhorts to Justice, and respect of alliance by a like kind of life, and the like.

By these is explained the Symbolical adhortative form; containing much that is common with the Customs of the Ancients, and *Pythagorical*. Thus *Jamblichus*.

CHAP. IV.

The same Symbols explained by others.

Most of these Symbols are mentioned also by others, with different explications. The first (*a*) *Olympiodorus* ascribes to *Philolaus*, delivering it thus, *When you come into a Temple, turn not back.* (*b*) *Jamblichus*, in the life of *Pythagoras*, cites it in the same words, adding this exposition, *That we ought not to perform divine Rites cursorily and negligently.* (a) In *Plat. Phædon.* (b) Cap.

Upon the Second, *Adore not the gods, as it were, in passing by*: (*c*) *Plutarch* saith, *We ought to go from home with that express intent. And for this reason the Cryers used, upon Festival days, to go before the Priests, and commanded the people to forbear working.* (c) In Num.

The same exposition (*d*) *Jamblichus*, in the life of *Pythagoras*, gives of the Third, *Sacrifice, and go to sacred rites barefoot*. (d) Cap.

To the Fourth, *Concerning the gods, disbelieve nothing wonderful, and concerning divine Doctrines*, may be applied to what *Jamblichus* saith in the life of *Pythagoras*: (*e*) *Many precepts were introduc'd into the practice of divine rites, forasmuch as they gave firm credit to these things, conceiving them not to be fantastick boasts, but to derive their beginning from some god. All this the Pythagoreans believe to be true, as the fabulous reports concerning Aristæus the Proconnecian, and Abaris the Hyperborean, and the like. And they did not only believe all these, but also endeavour themselves to frame many things that seem fabulous, derogating from nothing which relates to the Deity. In all such things he conceived not, that the persons themselves were foolish, but those only who gave no belief to it. For they are not of opinion, that the gods can do some things, others they cannot, as the Sophists imagine; but, that all things are possible. And the same is the beginning of the Verses which they ascribe to* Linus, *but perhaps were made by* Pythagoras. (e) cap. 28.

Hope all things, for to none belongs despair;
All things to God easie and perfect are.

The fifth, *Decline High-ways*, is mentioned by many; only *Laertius* delivers it quite otherwise, *Go not out of the high-way*; but, in the exposition, differs not from the rest, that *we ought not to follow the opinions of the vulgar, which are without judgment, and not indisputable; but those of the few and learned*.

The sixth, *Abstain from the Melanure, for it belongs to the Terrestrial gods*, (*f*) *Plutarch* interprets, as forbidding to converse with persons black in impiety. *Tryphon*, as forbidding falshood and lies, which are black in their close. The *Melanure* is a kind of fish, so named from the blackness of its tayl. (f) De Educ. lib.

The ninth, *Cut not fire with a sword*, is one of those Symbols which are ascribed to *Andocides*, the *Pythagorean*. (g) *Porphyrius*, (h) *Plutarch*, *Laertius*, and (i) *Athenæus*, interpret it, as advising, *not to exasperate an angry person, but to give way to him. Fire is anger, the sword contention.* St. *Basil* expounds it *of those who attempt an impossibility*.

The tenth, *Laertius* reads thus, *Turn away a sharp sword*; it is generally expounded, *Decline all things dangerous.*

The Eleventh, *Help to lay on a burthen, but not to take it off*, is expounded by *Porphyrius*, that *we ought to further others, not in sluggishness, but in virtue and labour.* Or, as *Jamblichus*, that *we ought not to be the cause of another's being idle*. *Laertius* and *Olympiodorus* cite it thus, *Lay not burthens down together, but take them up together*; expounding it, that *we must work together in the course of life, and co-operate with others in actions, tending not to idleness, but to virtue.*

The Twelfth, which is cited by *Suidas* out of *Aristophanes*, in verse, thus:

Into the shoo first the right foot,
The left first in the bason put.

He expounds it not as a Symbol, but a Proverb, *of those who perform things dextrously.*

The Fourteenth, *Pass not over a ballance*, is generally interpreted by (k) *Plutarch*, *Laertius*, (l) *Clemens Alexandrinus*, *Porphyrius*, and others, that *we ought to esteem Justice, and not to exceed it.* *Athenæus* and *Porphyrius* expound it, as dehorting *from avarice, and advising to pursue equality.*

The Fifteenth *Laertius* delivers thus, *When you go to travel, look not back upon the bounds.* (m) *Plutarch* thus, *When you come to the borders, return not back.* They both interpret it, that *when we are dying, and arrived at the bound or end of our life, we should bear it with an equal mind without grief, not to desire a continuance of the pleasures of this life.* So also (n) *Porphyrius*.

The Sixteenth *Laertius* reads thus, *Wipe not a seat with Oyl.*

The Seventeenth, *Laertius* and *Suidas* deliver thus, *Touch not a white Cock, for it is sacred to the Moon, and a monitor of the hours.*

The Nineteenth, *Sit not upon a Chœnix*, *Plutarch* and *Porphyrius* interpret, that *we ought not to live idly, but to provide necessaries for the future*. For, a Chœnix, according to *Laertius* and *Suidas*, is the same which *Clearchus* calls *Hemerotrophen*, a proportion of food daily spent. But *Clemens Alexandrinus* interprets it, as advising to consider not the present day, but what the future will bring forth: To be sollicitous, not of food, but prepar'd for death.

The Twentieth, *Breed nothing that hath crooked talons*, is ascribed to *Andocides* the *Pythagorean*.

The Twenty one, *Olympiodorus* delivers thus, *Cleave not wood in the way*; whereby, saith he, the Pythagoreans advised, *not to disquiet life with excessive cares, and vain solicitude.*

The Twenty second, *Entertain not a swallow under your roof*, (o) *Plutarch* interprets, *Take not unto you an ungrateful and unconstant friend and companion; for only this bird, of all the lesser kind, is reported to prey upon flesh.* (p) *Clemens Alexandrinus* and *Porphyrius* interpret it, as forbidding to admit into our society a talkative person, intemperate of speech, who cannot contain what is communicated to him.

The Twenty third, (q) *Plutarch* alledgeth thus, *Wear not a strait Ring*; that is, saith he, *Follow a free course of life, and fetter not your self.* Or, as St. *Hierom*, that we live not anxiously, nor put our selves into servitude, or into such a Condition of life, as we cannot free our selves from, when we should have a mind to do it.

The Twenty fourth, *Wear not the picture of the gods in Rings*, (r) *Porphyrius* expoundeth, *Discourse not of the gods inconsiderately, or in publick*. (s) *Jamblichus*, in the life of *Pythagoras*, delivers it thus, *Wear not the image of God in a Ring, lest it be defiled; for it is the image of God.* (t) *Clemens Alexandrinus* affirms the meaning to be, that *we ought not to mind Sensibles; but to pass on to Intelligibles*.

In the Twenty eighth, *Lay not hold on every one readily with your right hand*. *Plutarch* omits ῥαδίως, *Suidas* πάντα. It is generally expounded thus, *Be not hasty and precipitate in contracting friendship with any.*

The Twenty ninth, *When you rise out of bed, wrap the coverlet together, and confound the print of your body*; *Plutarch* referreth it to the *modesty and respect due to the bed*. (u) *Clemens Alexandrinus* saith it signifies, that *we ought not in the day-time to call to mind any pleasures, even of dreams which we had in the night.* Perhaps also, saith he, it means, that we ought to confound dark phantisie with the light of truth.

The 30th and 31, *Eat not the Heart and the Brain*, (x) *Jamblichus*, in the life of *Pythagoras*, saith, *he enjoyned; forsmuch as these two are the seats of life and knowledg*. *Porphyrius* to the first, and *Plutarch* to the second, give one interpretation, *Consume not your self with grief, Nor afflict your mind with cares.*

The Thirty second, *Laertius* delivers contrary to *Jamblichus*: *Upon the pairing of your nails or cuttings of your hair, neither urine nor tread.*

The Thirty fourth, *Deface the print of a pot in the ashes*; *Plutarch* and *Clemens Alexandrinus* expounds, as advising, *that upon reconcilement of enmity, we utterly abolish, and leave not the least print or remembrance of anger.*

The Thirty sixth concerning *the figure and three oboli*, seems to have reference to the story, related in the sixth Chapter of his life.

Of the Thirty seventh, *Abstain from Beans*, there are alledged many different reasons. (y) *Aristotle* saith, *He forbad them, for that they resemble* αἰδοῖα, *or the gates of the inferi*; or, for that they *breed worms*; [a little sort of Maggots called *Midæ*] or, for that they resemble the nature of the *Universe*; or, for that they are Oligarchick, being used in Suffrages. This last reason is confirmed by *Plutarch*, who explains this Symbol, *Abstain from Suffrages*; which of old were given by Beans. *Porphyrius* saith, *He interdicted Beans, because the first beginning and generation being confused, and many things being commixed, and concrescent together, and computrified in the earth by little and little, the generation and discretion broke forth together; and living creatures being produced together with plants, then out of the same putrefaction arose both men and beans*; whereof he alledged manifest arguments. For, if any one should chew a bean, and, having minced it small with his teeth, lay it abroad in the warm Sun, and so leaving it for a little time, return to it, he shall perceive the scent of humane blood. Moreover, if any one at the time when Beans shoot forth the flower, shall take a little of the flower which then is black, and put it into an Earthen vessel, and cover it close, and bury it in the ground ninety days, and at the end thereof take it up, and take off the cover; instead of the Bean, he shall find either the head of an Infant, or γυναικὸς αἰδοῖον. The same reason (z) Origen ascribes to *Zaratus*; from whom perhaps *Pythagoras*, being his Scholar, received them. Hence it is that *Pliny* saith, *He condemned Beans, because the souls of the Dead are in them.* And *Porphyrius* elsewhere, *Because they most partake of the nature of a living creature.* Some of whom, as *Cicero*, say, It was because they disturb the tranquility of the mind. *Wherefore to abstain from them*, saith *Porphyrius, makes our Dreams serene and untroubled.* (a) *Agellius* saith, he meant, *from venereal delights*. And *Plutarch* saith, He forbad Beans, because they conduce thereto. On the contrary, (b) *Clemens Alexandrinus* affirms they were prohibited out of no other reason, than that *women feeding on them, became barren.*

z In Philos.

a Lib.

b Strom. 5.

For the Thirty ninth, *Abstain from the flesh of living creatures*; the most general reason is, because they are of the same nature and temperament with us, and, in a manner, allied unto us. But of this, formerly.

CHAP. V.

Other Symbols.

TO the foregoing Symbols collected by *Jamblichus*, may be added these:

Take not up what falls from the Table; meaning, that men should not accustom themselves to eat intemperately. Or, alluding to some religious rite; for, *Aristophanes* saith, That which falls so, belongs to the Heroes; saying in his *Heroes*:

Tast not what from the Table falls. (*Laert.*)

Break not Bread; Divide not friends. Others refer it to the judgment in the Infernal places. Others, that it implieth fear in War. (*Laert.*)

Set down Salt, in remembrance of Justice; for Salt preserves all things, and is brought out of the purest thing, Water. (*Laert.*)

Pluck not a Crown; that is, Offend not the Laws, for Laws are the Crown of Cities. (*Porphyrius.*)

Offer libation to the gods, just to the ears of the cup; signifying, that we ought to worship and celebrate the gods with musick, for that passeth in at the ears. (*Porph.*) And drink not of that libation. (*Jamb.* cap. 18. pag. 87.)

Eat not (which are unlawful) *generation, augmentation, beginning, end, nor that of which the first basis of all things consists*, Meaning, we must abstain from the loins, διδύμων αἰδοίων, marrow, feet, and head of Victims. He called the loins, Basis, because living creatures are setled upon them as their foundation; διδύμα κỳ αἰδοῖα, Generation, for without the help of these, no living creature is engendred. Marrow he called Increase, it being the cause of augmentation in living creatures. The beginning, the feet; the head, the end; which have most power in government of the body. (*Porph.*)

Eat not Fishes. (*Laert.*) Some apply this to silence, (*Athen. Deipn.* Lib. 7.)

Others say, he disproved them, because not used in sacrifice to the gods.

Put not meat in a Chamber-pot; meaning, communicate nothing that is wise to a rude and foolish person. (*Plut.* de Educ. Lib.)

Sleep not at noon. For at that time the Sun sheweth its greatest force. (*Olympiad. in Plat. Phædon.*) We ought not to shut our eyes against the light, when it is most manifest.

Quit not your station without the command of your General: Our souls ought to be kept in the body, neither may we forsake this life without special leave from him who gave it us, lest we seem to despise the gift of God. (*Cicer. in Cat.* and *de Repub.*)

Roast not what is boiled; that is, change not meekness to anger. (*Jambl.*)

Heap not up Cypress; Of this wood they conceived the Scepter of *Jupiter* to be made. (*Laert.*)

Sacrifice even things to the Celestial deities, cal'd to the *Terrestrial*. Of this, already in his Arithmetick.

When it thunders, touch the earth, calling to mind our own mortality: (*Jambl.*) or, When a King is angry, the offender ought to humble himself.

Eat not sitting in a Chariot. (*Plut.*) Some expound it, that we ought to eat in quiet; or, that we ought not to give our selves to luxury in a time of business.

Go into the Temple on the right hand, go out on the left. Right and left seem to refer to the Ceremonial numbers; of which, already.

Where blood hath been shed, cover the place with stones; that is, abolish the very remembrance of any war or dissention. (*Jamb.*)

Hurt not a mild plant. (*Laert. Porph.*) Some expound it, Harm not the harmless.

Pray aloud; implying, not that God cannot hear such as pray softly, but that our prayers should be just (*Clem. Alex. Strom.* 4.) such as we need not care who hears.

Sail not on the ground; signifying, that we ought to forbear raising Taxes, and such revenues as are troublesome and unstable. (*Clem. Strom.* 5.)

Beget Children; For it is our duty to leave behind us such, as may serve the gods in our room. (*Jambl.* vit. cap. 18.)

Neither dip in a bason, nor wash in a bath. (*Jamb.* ibid.)

Put not away thy Wife, for she is a suppliant. (*Jamb.* ibid.)

Counsel nothing but what is best, for Counsel is a sacred thing: (*Jamb.* ibid.)

Plant not a Palm; (*Plut.* in Isid. and Osir.)

Lastly, Hither may be referred the Symbolical Letter Y. *They said that the course of humane life is like that Letter, for every one arriving at the first state of youth, where the way divides it self into two, stands at a gaze, not knowing which to take; if he meets with a guide that leads to the better, that is, if he learn Philosophy, Oratory, or some honest Art, which may prove beneficial, but cannot be attain'd without much labour, they affirm that he shall lead an Honourable and plentiful Life. But if not lighting upon such a Master, he takes the left hand way, which seems at first to be the better, and to lead to virtue, that is, if he gives himself over to sloath and*

and luxury, which seem pleasant at first to him who is ignorant of true good, he shall e're long lose both his Credit and Estate, and live thence forward ignominiously, and miserably. Thus (a) *Lactantius*, perhaps alluding to the old Verses.

(a) De vero cultu, lib. 6. cap. 31.

The Pythagorick Letter two ways spread,
Shows the two paths in which Mans life is led.
The right hand track to sacred Virtue tends,
Though steep and rough at first, in rest it ends;
The other broad and smooth, but from its Crown,
On rocks the Traveller is tumbled down.
He who to Virtue by harsh toyls aspires,
Subduing pains, worth and renown acquires:
But who seeks slothful luxury, and flies
The labour of great acts, dishonour'd dies.

The GOLDEN VERSES of *Pythagoras*.

A Summary of the *Pythagorick* Doctrine is extant in Verse, Entituled, *The Golden Verses of Pythagoras*: or as others, of the *Pythagoreans*. For that, saith *Hierocles*, *as Gold is the best and purest of Metals, so these are the best and most Divine of Verses*. They are these.

First, in their ranks, the Immortal Gods adore,
Thy Oath keep; next, great Heroes; then implore
Terrestrial Dæmons with due sacrifice.
Thy Parents reverence, and near Allies:
Him that is first in Virtue make thy Friend,
And with observance his kind speech attend:
Nor (to thy power) for light faults cast him by,
Thy pow'r is neighbour to Necessity.
These know, and with intentive care pursue;
But anger, sloth, and luxury subdue.
In sight of others or thy self forbear
What's ill; but of thy self stand most in fear.
Let Justice all thy words and actions sway;
Nor from the even course of Reason stray:
For know, that all men are to die ordain'd,
And riches are as quickly lost as gain'd.
Crosses that happen by divine decree,
(If such thy lot) bear not impatiently.
Yet seek to remedy with all thy care,
And think the Just have not the greatest share.
'Mong'st men, discourses good and bad are spread,
Despise not those, nor be by these misled.
If any some notorious falshood say,
Thou the report with equal Judgment weigh.
Let not mens smoother promises invite,
Nor rougher threats from just resolves thee fright.
If ought thou shouldst attempt, first ponder it;
Fools only inconsiderate acts commit;
Nor do what afterwards thou mayst repent;
First learn to know the thing on which th' art bent.
Thus thou a life shalt lead with joy repleat.
Nor must thou care of outward health forget.
Such temp'rance use in exercise and diet,
As may preserve thee in a setled quiet.
Meats unprohibited, not curious, chuse;
Decline what any other may accuse.
The rash expence of vanity detest,
And sordidness: A mean in all is best.
Hurt not thy self: Before thou act, advise;
Nor suffer sleep at night to close thine eyes,
Till thrice thy acts that day thou hast ore-run,
How slipt, what deeds, what duty left undone?
Thus thy account summ'd up from first to last,
Grieve for the Ill, joy for what good hath past.
These study, practise these, and these affect;
To sacred Virtue these thy steps direct.
Eternal Nature's fountain I attest,
Who the Tetractis on our souls imprest.
Before thy mind thou to this study bend,
Invoke the Gods to grant it a good end.
These if thy labour vanquish, thou shalt then
Know the connexure both of Gods and Men;
How every thing proceeds, or by what staid;
And know (as far as fit to be survey'd)
Nature alike throughout; that thou mayst learn
Not to hope hopeless things, but all discern;
And know those Wretches whose perverser wills
Drawn down upon their heads spontaneous Ills;
Unto the good that's nigh them, deaf and blind:
Some few the cure of these misfortunes find.
This only is the Fate that harms, and rolls,
Through miseries successive, humane souls.
Within is a continual hidden fight,
Which we to shun must study, not excite.
Great Jove! how little trouble should we know,
If thou to all men wouldst their Genius show?
But fear not thou; Men come of heav'nly race,
Taught by diviner Nature what t'embrace:
Which if pursu'd, thou all I nam'd shall gain,
And keep thy Soul clear from thy body's stain.
In time of Pray'r and cleansing, meat's deni'd
Abstain from; thy mind's reins let reason guide:
Then strip'd of flesh up to free Æther soar,
A deathless God, Divine, mortal no more.

TIMÆUS the *Locrian*.

Of the Soul of the World, and of Nature.

Principles. TIMÆUS, the *Locrian*, said these things: There are two Principles of all things: the *Mind*, of things effected according to Reason; *Necessity*, of those which are by Violence according to the powers of Bodies. Of these, one is of the nature of good, and is called *God*, and is principle of the best things; the consequent and concausals are reduced to *Necessity*. For all things are the off-spring of these, Idæa, Matter, Sensibles. The first is ungenerated, immovable, permanent, of the nature of Identity, intellectual, the exemplar of things that are made, and immutable. This is Idæa. Matter, is the print, mother, nurse, and productrix of the third essence; for, receiving likeness into it self, and being, as it were, characterised by them, it perfects all productions. This Matter he asserted to be eternal,

eternal, but not immovable, in form of it self, and without figure; but receiving all forms. In bodies it is divisible, and of the nature of Alterity: They call Matter, Place and Religion. These two principles are contrary. Form hath the nature of male and father; Matter, of female and mother; the Third is their off-spring. These being three, are known three ways; Idæa, by intellect, according to science; Matter, by spurious ratiocination, not being understood by direct comprehension, but by analogy; their Off-spring, by sense and opinion. Before Heaven was made, we must conceive, that there was Idæa, and Matter, and God, the maker of the better, [viz. Idæa.] Now forasmuch as the elder is better than the younger, and the orderly than the disorderly; God, being good, and seeing Matter receive Idæa, and become totally changed, yet disorderly, saw also it was needful to bring it into Order, and from indefinite transmutations, to fix it determinately, that bodies might have proportionate distinctions, and not receive promiscuous variations.

The World. Of all this Matter he framed the World, (making it the bound of the nature of Being, since it comprehends all other things) one only-begotten, perfect, animate, and rational, (for these are better than inanimate and irrational) and a spherical body, that being more perfect than other figures. Designing therefore to make the best production, he made this God, generate, not corruptible by any other cause, but by the same God only which compos'd it, if it should please him at any time to dissolve it. But he who is good, will not be carried on to the destruction of the fairest production. Wherefore it is permanent, and being such, incorruptible, unperishable, and blessed. It is the best of productions, being made by the best cause, who looked not upon patterns made by hands, but upon the Idæa, the intellectual essence; after which, this being exactly made, is the fairest of all, and not to be demolish'd. It is perfect, as to sensible things, for the exemplar comprehended in it self all intelligible creatures, left nothing out, it being the perfect bound of Intelligibles, as the World is of Sensibles; which being solid, tactile, and visible, is divided into Earth, Fire, and (betwixt these) Air, and Water. It consists of perfect bodies, which exist intirely in it, so as no part remains beyond it, that the body of the Universe might be self-sufficient, and not liable to dissolution by any external accidents; for there are no other things besides these, and what are contained in them, they being, after the most excellent analogy, connected in equal power, neither predominating over the other in any part, nor being predominated, that whereby some might encrease, others decrease; but it resteth in an indissoluble harmonious concord, according to the best proportion. For there being three bounds, and the intervals distant from each other in the same proportion, the middle is that to the first which the third is to it, and so reciprocal, according to disposure of place and order. But to number these without the help of another thing equal to them, is absolutely impossible. It is well ordered both for figure and motion: As to the first being round, it is every way like it self, and able to contain all other figures. As to its circular motion, it keepeth a perpetual Tenor: for, a sphear only, whether in rest or in motion, is so adapted to the same place, as that it never ceaseth nor removes; all its parts being equidistant from the Center. Now its outward superficies being exactly smooth, it needs not the weak organs, which are bestow'd on other living creatures, for their accommodation.

The Soul of the World God inkindled in the midst, but diffused beyond it, covering the Universe with it, and tempering it with a temperament of indivisible Form, and divisible Substance, so as these two make one temperament; with which he mingled two Powers, principles of the two motions of Identity and Alterity; which (Soul) being not easily miscible, was not without difficulty contemperated. *The Soul of the World.*

All these proportions are mixed according to harmonical numbers, which proportions he cunningly divided, that it might be known of what, and by what, the Soul consisteth. This Soul God did not ordain (as we affirm) after corporeal substance, (for that which is most honourable, is first both in power and time) but made it before the body, removing one, the first of four Monads, into eight Decads, and three Centuries. Of this, the duple and triple is easily collected, the first being setled. All these, with their complements, and sesquioctaves, will amount to thirty six. The whole sum will be one hundred and fourteen thousand six hundred ninety five. The divisions are one hundred and fourteen thousand six hundred ninety five. After this manner he divided the soul of the Universe.

The Mind only seeth the Eternal God, the Ruler and Father of all things. That which is generated we behold with our eyes, this World, and its parts; the Ætherial are twofold, some of the nature of Identity: others, of Alterity. Of these, some extrinsecally carry about all that is within them, from East to West, by an universal motion. The rest, being of the motion of Alterity, intrinsecally turn about from the West to the East, moved by themselves. They are carried round by accident, with the motion of Identity, having the greatest force in the World. The motion of Alterity, divided according to harmonical proportions, is disposed into seven Circles; the *Moon* being nearest the Earth, performeth her course in a Month: next her, the *Sun* perfects his course in a year. There are two of equal course with the *Sun, Mercury,* and the Star *Juno,* which many call *Venus,* and *Lucifer.* All persons not being skilful in the Rules of sacred Astronomy, and the observations of Rising and Setting. The same Star is sometimes *Hesper,* when it so followeth the *Sun,* that it is conspicuous to us when the *Sun* is set: sometimes *Eous,* when it goeth before the *Sun,* and riseth before him. *Lucifer* therefore, many times is the Star *Venus,* when she runs along with the *Sun:* and likewise is many of the fixed Stars and Planets; for any Star of visible magnitude, ushering the *Sun* above the Horizon, foretells day. The other three, *Mars, Jupiter,* and *Saturn,* have peculiar velocities, and unequal years: but they compleat their course in certain and comprehensible regularities, and appearances, and occultations, and Eclipses, and Risings, and Settings. They have, besides their *phases,* Rising and Setting in regard of the *Sun:* who maketh day in performing his Course from East to West: night, by Motion from West to East: *The Parts of the World.*

whilst

whilst he is carried about with the Motion of Identity, a year, by his own proper Motion. By these two Motions, the *Sun* performs a double course, one, as being carried about with the general Motion of Heaven, the other by an oblique Motion: One distinguisheth the times of the day and the seasons: The other, by which he is carried about after the rapid Motion of the fixed Stars, at every revolution maketh night day. These are parts of Time called Periods, ordained by God together with the World: for before the World there were no Stars, and consequently neither year nor seasons, by which this generable World is commensurated. This time is the image of that which is ingenerate, called Eternity: for as this Universe was formed after the eternal exemplar of the Idæal World, so was this Time ordained together with the World after its pattern, Eternity.

The Earth being established in the midst, the seat of the gods is the bound of night and day, of rising and setting, according to the Section of Horisons, as they are circumscribed by the sight, and by Section of the Earth. It is the most ancient of all Bodies in the Universe: for Water was not produced without Earth, nor Air without humidity: and Fire cannot subsist without humidity and matter, which it kindles. So that the Earth is setled upon its own weight, as the root and basis of all things. The principle therefore of generated things, as to the subject, is Matter ; as to form, Idæa. The productions of these are Bodies ; Earth, Water, Air, and Fire, whose generation is thus: Every body consists of superficies's; a superficies, of Triangles ; of which this is a rectangled equi-crural semiquadrangle ; the other unequilateral, having the greater Angle in power, Triple to the lesser. The least Angle in it is one third of a right angle: double to this is the middle Angle, consisting of two thirds, the greatest is a right Angle, sesquialter to the middle, Triple to the least. Now this Triangle is a sesquiquadrangle to an equilateral Triangle, the perpendicular from the Top to the Bottom, being divided into two equal parts; there are therefore in each two rectangled Triangles, but in one the two sides which include the right Angle are equal ; in the other, all the three sides are unequal. This figure is called *Scholion*. This semiquadrangle is the principle of which the earth was constituted ; for the quadrangle is compounded of these four semiquadrangles. Of the quadrangle is generated the Cube, the firmest and most setled of all bodies, having six sides, eight angles. For this reason Earth is the most heavy body, and unapt for motion, and not transmutable into any other, as being incommunicable with any kind of Triangle, for the Earth only hath a stable principle, which is the semiquadrangle, the element of the other bodies, Fire, Air, and Water: for the semiquadrangle being six times compounded, there ariseth an equilateral Triangle, of which a Pyramis, with four bases, and four equal Angles is compounded, the form of fire most apt to motion, and of rarest parts. Next, these Octaedron, with eight bases and six Angles, the element of Air. The Third, Icosiedron, of twenty bases, and twelve Angles, the element of Water, being fullest of parts, and heaviest. These being compounded of the same Element, are transmutated into one another. The Dodecaedron, he made the image of the Universe, as nearest to a Globe. Fire by reason of the rarity of its parts, penetrates all things ; Air, all things but Fire ; Water, Earth. All things therefore are full, and admit no vacuity. They are carried about by the circumvolution of the Universe, and by reason of their solidity, grate one another, rendring an unintermitted alteration to generation and corruption. These God used in framing the World, tactile by reason of Earth; visible by reason of Fire, the two extreams. By Air and Water, he connected it in a most firm band, proportion capable to contain both it self, and the things that are comprised in it. If then that which is connected be a Superficies, one Medium is sufficient ; if a solid, it requires two. To the two Mediums, he adapted the two Extreams, Fire to Air, Air to Water, Water to Earth ; and again, Fire to Air, Air to Water, and Water to Earth ; and again, as Earth to Water, Water to Air, and Air to Earth ; and reciprocally, as Earth to Air, Water to Fire. And forasmuch as all these are equal in power, their proportions are equal likewise. Thus is the World one, and by a happy connexure proportionable. Each of these four Bodies have divers species ; the Fire, flame, light, splendor, by reason of the inequality of the Triangles in each of these. The Air is partly clear and dry, partly humid and cloudy. The Water, fluid and concrete, as Snow, Frost, Hail, and Ice. Of Humid, one sort is fluid, as Honey, Oyl ; another compact, as Pitch, Wax. Of the compact are two kinds, one fusile, as Gold, Silver, Brass, Tin, Lead ; the other frangible, as Sulphur, Bitumen, Nitre, Salt, Allom, and Stones of that kind.

After he had made the World, he proceeded to the production of mortal creatures, that it might be perfect and compleatly wrought according to its pattern. Having contemperated and distributed the Soul of Man, by the same proportions and powers, he delivered it over to that Nature which had the power of changing. She succeeding him in the producing mortal transitory creatures, instilled their souls, some from the Moon, some from the Sun, some from the other Stars which wander in the Region of Alterity, excepting one soul in the power of Identity, which he mingled in the rational part, an image of wisdom, to those who make use of good Fate. For of the human soul, one part is rational and intellectual, the other irrational and foolish ; of the irrational, the better is of the nature of Identity ; the worse, of that of Alterity. Each of these is resident about the Head, that all the other parts of the soul and body may be subservient to it, according to the analogy of the body of the Universe. Of the irrational part, one is irascible, placed about the Heart ; the other desiderative, about the Liver.

As for the Body, the principle and root of Marrow is in the Brain, wherein is the Hegemonick of the Soul. From the brain issues a defluxion along the spohdyles of the back, from whence it is distributed into Seed and generative substance. The bones are the case of the marrow ; the flesh is the tegument of the bones, the joynts he connected by nerves for motion. Of the inward parts, some were made for nourishment,

Animals.

others

others for conversation. Of the Motions, those which come from without, and flow into the apprehensive part, are sensible; those which fall not under comprehension, are insensible, whether by reason that the affected bodies are more earthy, or that the motions are weaker. Whatsoever motions change nature, are painful; whatsoever comply with her, are named pleasures.

Of the Senses, God enlightned our sight for contemplation of Celestials, and apprehension of Science. Hearing, he framed perceptive of Discourse and of Musick. Of this, if any be destitute from his birth, he will also be uncapable of Speaking. Whence we say, This sense is nearest ally'd to reason. All that are termed affections of bodies, are denominated with reference to the Touch, and their inclinations to a place; for, the Touch dijudicates vital faculties; warm, cold; dry, moist; smooth, rough; yielding, resisting; soft, hard; but heavy and light, the Touch prejudicates, Reason defines by inclination to move to the middle, and from the middle; below, and the middle, they affirm to be the same thing, for the center of a Globe is below, whatsoever is betwixt that and the circumference is above. Heat seems to consist of rare parts, and disgregates bodies; Cold of more dense parts, and bindeth the pores. The Taste resembles the Touch in concretion and discretion, and in penetration of the pores, and in its objects, which are either harsh or smooth. Those which have an abstersive faculty, stupifying the tongue, are bitter; those which are moderately abstersive, salt; those which inflame and pierce further into the flesh, acid. Contrary to these, are smooth and sweet. The kinds of Odor are not distinct, for they insinuate through narrow pores, which are too solid to be contracted and dilated by putrefaction, and concoction of earth and earthly things. They are sweet or stinking. Voice is a percussion in the air, passing to the soul through the ears, whose pores extend to the Liver. In the ears is a spirit, whose motion is Hearing. Of voice and hearing some are swift, the sharp; some flow, the flat; the mean, are incommensurable. Again, one is much and diffused, the *loud*; another small and contracted, the *low*: one is ordered according to proportions, the *harmonious*; another disorderly and unproportionate, the *inharmonious*. The fourth kind of Sensibles is most various and multiform, termed Visibles, comprising all colours, and innumerable coloured things. The primary colours are four, White, Black, Bright, Purple; the rest are made by commixtion of these. White disperseth the sight, Black contracts it; as Hot diffuseth the touch, Cold contracts it; Bitter contracteth the taste, and Sweet dissipates it.

The bodies of creatures that breathe air, are nourished by aliment, distributed by the veins through the whole frame defluxively, as by channels, and irrigated by the spirit which diffuseth it to the utmost bounds. Respiration is made (there being no vacuity in nature) by influxion, and attraction of the air in the room of that which issueth forth at invisible vents, out of which also sweat evaporates. Now something of it being wasted by the natural heat, it is necessary something be introduced to supply that which was consumed; otherwise there would be a vacuity, which is impossible: For a living creature could not be restored by perpetual fluxion, and entire, if the body were disjoyn'd by vacuity. The like composition of Organs is likewise in inanimate things, with an analogical respiration; a Cupping glass and Amber are resemblances of respiration, for the spirits evaporate through the body, and enter again at the mouth and nostrils by respiration; then again, like *Euripus*, it is brought round into the body, which by these effluxions is extended. The cupping-glass, the air being consumed by fire, attracts moisture; the Amber, by emission of spirits, attracts the body that is like to it. All aliment is taken into the body from the root of the heart, and the fountain of the ventricle; if the accession be more than the defluxion, it is termed Growth; if the contrary, Decay. The *Acma* consists in the confine betwixt these two, and is conceived to be the equality of accession and defluxion. When the ligaments of the constitution are dissolv'd, so as there is no passage for the breath, or distribution of Aliment, the Animal dies. There are many things which are pernicious to life, and cause death; whereof one is termed, Sickness. The origines of sickness are the disproportions of the primary faculties: if the simple faculties, Heat, Cold, Humidity, Siccity, abound, or are Deficient, then follow Mutations, and alterations of the blood, by corruption, and depravations of the Consumptive flesh: If according to the changes into Sharp, or Salt, or Acid (humours) the turnings of the Blood, or Consumptions of the flesh be caused; for hence are generated Choler and Flegm. Unwholesome Chyles, and putrefaction of Humours, are inconsiderable except they be deep; but those whose causes lie in the bones, are not easily cur'd; these which arise out of the marrow are painful. The Extremities of Diseases are Wind, Choler, Flegm, increasing and flowing, into places not proper to them, or into the vital parts, for then obtaining a better place, they expel their neighbours, and settle there, and afflicting the bodies, they resolve them into themselves.

These are the Diseases of the Body. Out of these arise many sicknesses of the soul, several of several faculties; of the sensitive, stupidity; of the reminiscent, forgetfulness; of the desiderative, loathing, and excessive appetite; of the Pathetick, wild passions, and furious frensies; of the rational, indocility and indiscretion. The forces of Vice, are pleasures and griefs, desires and fears, raised out of the body, mingled with the soul, and express'd by various names, Loves, Desires, dissolute affections, impetuous Angers, deep Malices, various Longings, inordinate Delights. In a word, to behave our selves amiss as to passions, or to subdue them, is the bound betwixt virtue and vice; for to be excessive in them, or too hard for them, put us in a good or bad condition. To these inclinations the temper of the body may contribute much: if vehement, fervent, or any way extraordinary, it transports us to Melancholy and extravagant lusts. For the parts being overflown by these defluxions, make the constitution of the body rather hydropical than sound, whence arise sadness, forgetfulness, folly, and consternation. The customs also, whereunto a man hath conformed himself in the City, or Family, where

he

was born and bred, conduce much; as also the daily course of life, whether softning or corroborating the soul; for, living abroad, Diet, Exercise, and the manners of those with whom we converse, greatly avail to virtue or vice; and these occasions are derived rather from our Parents, and Elements, than from our selves; for they are not ineffectual, we our selves so easily receding from those * actions which are good.

*Ποθεικόντων perhaps is for πρεπικόντων Doricè.

To the well-being of an Animal, it is requisite that the body have the virtues competent to it, Health, perfect Sense, Strength, and Beauty. The principles of Beauty are a symmetry of the parts amongst themselves, and with the soul; for nature made the body as an instrument, obedient, and accommodate to all the businesses of Life. In like manner, the soul must be ordered to virtues answerable to those; to Temperance, as the body to Health; to Wisdom, as the body to perfect sense; to Fortitude, as the body to strength; to Justice, as the body to beauty. The principles of these are from Nature, their Means and Ends from industry; those of the body are attained by exercise and Medicine; those of the Soul by Institution and Philosophy. For these faculties nourish and strengthen both the soul and body, by Labour, Exercise, and pureness of Diet; these by Medicaments; those instituting the soul by chastisements and reprehensions, for they strengthen it, by exhortation, by exciting the inclination, and enjoyning those things which are expedient for action. The Aleiptick art, and, its nearest ally, Medicine, are design'd for the cure of Bodies, reducing the faculties to the best harmony; they purifie the blood, and make the spirits flow freely, so as if any thing unwholesome settle, the vigors of the blood and spirits being thus confirmed, overmaster it. Musick, and its director, Philosophy, ordained by the gods, and by the Laws, for reformation of the soul, inure, compel and perswade the irrational part to obey the rational, and in the irrational mollifie anger, and quiet desire; so as they neither move nor rest without reason, the mind summoning them either to action or fruition. The bound of Temperance is obedience and fortitude. Now science and venerable Philosophy, purifying the mind from false opinions, bring her to knowledge, and reducing her from great ignorance, raise her to contemplation of Divine things; wherein if a man be conversant with contentedness as to human things, and endeavour in a moderate way of living, he is happy. For he to whom God hath allotted this Estate, is undoubtedly guided to a most happy life. But if a man be stiff and refractory, he shall be pursued by punishment according to the Laws, and those discourses which declare things Cœlestial and Infernal. For irremissible punishments are prepar'd for the unhappy dead, and many other things, for which I commend the *Ionick* Poet, who makes men religious by ancient fabulous Traditions. For as we cure Bodies with things unwholesome, when the wholesome agree not with them; so we restrain souls with fabulous relations, when they will not be led by the true. Let them then, since there is a necessity for it, talk of these strange punishments, as if souls did transmigrate, those of the effeminate into the bodies of Women, given up to ignominy; of Murtherers, into those of Beasts, for punishment; of the Lascivious, into the forms of Swine; of the light and temerarious, into Birds; of the slothful, and idle unlearned, and ignorant, into several kinds of Fishes. All these in the second period, *Nemesis* decrees, together with the vindictive and Terrestrial Dæmons, the overseers of human affairs, to whom God, the disposer of all things, hath committed the administration of the World, replenisht with Gods, Men, and all other living Creatures; all which are formed after the best image, of the ungenerate and eternal Idæa.

An Explication of the *Pythagorick* Doctrine.

By * JOHN REUCHIN.

*è Cabalæ. libro 2.

CHAP. I.

Of Pythagoras *his way of Teaching, by Silence and Symbols.*

a Pag. 664.
b. Out of which *Paulus Scbalichius* collects his first Canon, de *Mysteriis Pythagoricus*: *Myst. Philos.* cap 7.
b *Florid.*

(*a*) THE Indocible and abstruse tradition of *Mysteries* and *Symbols*, is not to be investigated by acuteness of humane Wit, (which rather affects us with a doubtful fear, than an adherent firmness) it requires ample strength of thinking and believing, and above all things, faith and taciturnity. Whence *Pythagoras taught nothing* (as (*b*) *Apuleius* saith) *to his disciples before silence; it being the first rudiment of contemplative wisdom to learn to meditate, and to unlearn to talk.* As if the *Pythagorick* sublimity were of greater worth, than to be comprehended by the talk of Boys. This kind of learning (as other things) *Pythagoras* brought into *Greece* from the *Hebrews*, that the disciple being to ask some sublime question, should hold his peace; and being questioned, should only answer αὐτὸς ἔφα, *He said*. Thus the Cabalists answer אמר החכם *The wise said*; and Christians, πίστευον, *Believe.*

(*c*) Moreover, all the *Pythagorick* Philosophy (especially that which concerns divine things) is mystical, expressed by *Ænigms* and *Symbols.* The reasons, these: *First*, The Ancients used to deliver wisdom by Allegories; all their Philosophers and Poets are full of Riddles, avoiding, by obscurity, contempt of the vulgar; for the most apt interpreter of things, not preceptible

c Pag. 635.

by human infirmity, is Fable: *That befits Philosophers, which is declared under the pious veil of Fictions, hidden in honest things, and attired in honest words; for, what is easily found, is but too negligently pursu'd.* Secondly, It sometimes happens, that we cannot express abstruse things without much circumlocution, unless by some short Ænigm. *Thirdly,* as Generals use Watch-words to distinguish their own Soldiers from others; so it is not improper to communicate to friends some peculiar Symbols, as distinctive marks of a Society. These, among the *Pythagoreans*, were a chain of indissoluble love. (d) *Pythagoras* was studious of friendship; and if he heard of any that used his Symbols, he presently admitted him into his Society. Hereupon all became desirous of them, as well thereby to be acceptable to their Master, as to be known *Pythagoreans.* Lastly, As memorial notes; for, in treating of all things divine and human, the vastness of the subject requires short Symbols, as conducing much to Memory.

d *Laert.*

CHAP. II.

The Triple World.

(a) THE Pythagoreans reduce all *Beings,* subsistent or substant, immediately to *Idæa's* which truly are; and those to the *Idæa of Idæas.* Hereupon they asserted *three Worlds,* whereof the third is infinite, or rather not finite; and that all things consists of Three. *The Pythagoreans* (saith *Aristotle*) *affirm that the whole, and all things are terminated by Three: Some are bodies and magnitudes, others keep and inhabit bodies and magnitudes, others are the rulers and origines of the Inhabitants.* This we understand of the three Worlds, the *Inferior,* the *Superior,* and the *Supreme.* The *Inferior* containeth bodies and magnitudes, and their appropriate Intelligence, movers of the Sphears, overseers and guardians of things generable and corruptible, who are said to take care of bodies, each according to the particular task assign'd him; by the Anciets named sometimes *Angels,* sometimes *Gods,* and (in respect of the anxious sollicitude of things whereto they are confin'd) *Dæmons.*

a Pag. 664. g. Scalich. can. 4.

Next over it, immediately shineth the *Superior* World; this containeth the superior Powers, incorporeal essences, divine exemplars, the seals of the inferior World, after whose likeness, the faces of all inferior things are formed. These (b) *Pythagoras* calls, *Immortal gods,* as being the principles of things produc'd out of the divine Mind, essential ἀρχαὶ, *causes* of those forms which dwell in bodies, and inform the compounded substances of the lower World. There are also other gods, incorporeal beings, individual, differing (not by material, but) by formal number; spirits void of matter, simple, unmixt, seated beyond the sensible Heaven, confin'd neither to time nor place, neither suffering age nor transmutation, much less any alteration; In a word, not being affected with any passion, they lead a self-sufficient excellent life, and inhabit Eternity, which is αἰων ἀει ὤν, *always being,* because it always was, is, and shall be intemporally in the divine Mind; yet by the energy of God, it was created and placed beyond the convex of the visible Heaven, as being the lucid mansion of the blessed spirits, [whom the Pythagoreans believe gods] placed in the highest region of Æther, æviternal, invested in the immortal Ævum.

b Aur. carm.

The *third* World, *Supreme,* containing all other Worlds, is that of the Deity, consisting of one divine Essence, existent before *Ævum,* for it is the Age of Ages, the præexistent entity and unity of existence, substance, essence, nature.

These three Worlds are called *Receptacles,* in different respects; the first, of *Quantity*; the second, of *Intelligences*; the third, of *Principles.* The first, *circumscriptively*; the second, *definitively*; the third is not received, but receiveth, because it is every where, and is called a receptacle *repletively.*

Through the Superior world is communicated from the *Tetractys* to the inferior, life, and the being (not accidental, but substantial) of every species; to some, clearly; to others, obscurely. This the Pythagoreans collect from those words of their Master:

———(c) *the* Tetractys *to our Souls did send, The Fountain of Eternal Nature*———

c Carm.

The *Tetractys,* is the *Divine mind* communicating, the *Fountain* is the *exemplar Idæa* communicated, and *eternal Nature* is the *essential Idæa* of things received. *Idæa,* considered as to God, (say they) is his *knowledge*; as to the sensible World, *exemplar*; as to it self, *Essence.*

Now as in the Sensible World, the Superior sphear hath an influence on all the sphears beneath it; so in the Intelligible World, not only every superior Chorus of Angels, hath an influence upon all the inferior; but the whole superior world hath an influence upon the whole inferior, whereby all things are reduced according to their capacities, as far as possible, momentary to eternal, inferior to superior. But to the third World, nothing that is meerly a Creature can be reduced, incapable in its own nature of that sublimity which is proper only to God.

CHAP. III.

The Supreme World.

(a) THE Supream World, being (as we said) that of the Deity, is one divine, continual constant Essence of Sempiternity, poized, (as it were) with immovable weight; not unfitly termed, παντοκρατορικὴ ἕδρα, the *all-governing Throne.* It is not confined to Genus, Place, Time or Reason, but is the free unlimited President over all these; infinitely Supreme in Place, Power, Possession, Excellence, above all Essence, Nature, Ævum, Age.

a Pag. 666. g.

This Divine mind, the receptacle of principles, *Pythagoras* symbolically terms *Number,* saying, *Number is the Principle of all things.* (For none can believe so meanly of so wise a Person, as that he should conceive the ordinary Numbers by which we cast account, to be the Principle of all things, which are far from being antecedent to things, for they are consequential accidents) So (b) *Plutarch, by Number* Pythagoras *understands the Mind*; a Symbol not improper; in Incorporeals nothing more divine than the *Mind,* in Abstractions nothing more simple than *Number.*

b Plac. phil.

The

The divine Essence therefore, existent before Ævum and Age, (for it is the Age of Ages) the præexistent entity and unity of existence, substance, essence, nature, was by *Pythagoras* called τὸ *one*, by *Parmenides* τὸ *being*, both upon a like ground; because it is the super-essential Unite and Being, from which, and by which, and through which, and in which, and by which, all things are, and are ordered, and persist, and are contained, and are filled, and are converted.

Of this first *one*, and first *ens*, Aristotle thus; *Plato and the Pythagoreans* (saith he) *hold no other concerning Ens or One, but that this is their Nature, their essence is the same, to be One and a Being*. *Xenophanes* declared this *One* to be *God*, herein agreeing with *Pythagoras*, (c) who asserted *infinite*, and *one*, and *number*, to be the first Principles of things; by *infinite* signifying the *power*; for nothing can be imagined before power, which in God is infinite, or rather it is infinite God: in him *esse* and *posse* are not distinct, who containeth the essences, virtues and operations of all producibles. With *Pythagoras* agreeth (d) *Anaxagoras*, saying, *for all things were together*; Democritus, *for all things were in power*. This also is the *commixion of things* mentioned by *Empedocles*, and *Anaximander*; not confusedly in *Chaos, Erebus*, or *Night*, but distinctly and orderly in *full light*, in the most perfect splendor of the divine light intuitive knowledge, that is the *Idæa*, (from εἶδω γινώσκω) whose power is being; including all, whether Mental, Rational, Intelligible, Sensible, Vital, Substantial, Adhæsible or Adhæsive; and is not only all things that are, but those that are not: This is no other than the divine Essence, within which (before all things) *one* produced *two*. *Two* is the first number, *one* is the principle of Number, *One* is God; and the production of *two* being within the divine Essence, (for number is constituted of it self, and next *one* is naturally only the number *two*) this *two* must necessarily be God also, for within God is nothing but God. Thus these three, (*One* and *Two*) being the Principle and first, and not exceeding the Essence of God, are indeed one God: for his Essence is not divided by the production of *two* out of *one*. In like manner, it often happens in corporeals, that *one* being moved to *two*, proceeds to *three*, the substance of things continuing; as, in a Tree, of boughs and branches; in Man, the body, arms, and fingers. Of *one* therefore in the Divinity producing, and *two* produced, ariseth a *Trinity*, to which if there be added an essence formally distinct from them, there will be a formal *quaternity*, which is the infinite one and two, the Substance, Perfection, and end of all Number. *One, two, three, four*, by a collective progression make *Ten*; beyond ten there is not any thing. This *Pythagoras* meant, when he asserted the Principle of all things *Tetractis*; he understood God by it; for he swore by it, and seems to have transferr'd the Hebrew Tetragrammaton, into a Greek Symbol.

(e) Thus the most apt Symbol, of the Principles of things, is *one* and *two*; for when we make enquiry into the causes and origine of all things, what sooner occurs than one and two? That which we first behold with our Eyes, is the same, and not another; that which we first conceive in our mind is *Identity* and *Alterity*, One and Two. (*Alomæon*, contemporary with *Pythagoras*) affirmed *two* to be many, which he said were *contrarieties*, (perhaps the same with *Empedocles*' *Eers*) yet unconfin'd and indefinite, as White and Black, Sweet and Bitter, Good and Evil, Great and Small. These multiplicious diversities the *Pythagoreans* designed by the number *Ten*, as finite and infinite, even and odd, one and many, right and left, male and female, stedfast and moved, straight and crooked, light and darkness, good and ill, square and oblong. These pairs are two, and therefore contrary; they are reduced all into ten, that being the most perfect number, as containing more kinds of numeration than the rest, even, odd; square, cube; long, plain; the first uncompounded, and first compounded, than which nothing is more absolute, since in ten proportions, four cubick numbers are consummated, of which (according to the *Pythagoreans*) all things consist. By this all Nations reckon, (not exceeding it) as by the natural account of ten fingers; Heaven it self consists of ten Spheres. *Architas* includeth *all that is*, in the number *ten*; in imitation of whom *Aristotle* nameth ten kinds of Ens, *Categories*, reducible to two, *Substance* and *Accident*, both springing from one Essence; for *ten* so loves *two*, that from *one* it proceeds to *two*, and by *two* it reverts into *one*. The first *Ternary* is of *one* and *two*, not compounded, but consistent; *one* having no position, makes no composition; an unite whilst an unite hath no position; nor a point whilst a point. There being nothing before One, we rightly say, *one* is first; *two* is not compounded of numbers, but a co-ordination of unites only. It is therefore the first number, being the first multitude; not commensurable by any number, but by unite the common measure of all number; for one, two, is nothing but two; so that the multitude which is called *Triad*, Arithmeticians term *the first number uncompounded*, the *Dual* being not an uncompounded number, but rather *not-compounded*.

(a) Now the *Triad*, through its propensity to multiply, and communicate its goodness to all creatures, proceeds from power to operation, beholding with a perpetual intuition that fæcundity of multitude which is in it, productive (as it were) of number from number, and that essentiality which is one in it, the fountain of all production, the beginning of all progression, the permanence of all immutable substance; it reverts it self into it self, multiplying it self (as it were) by unity and duity, saying, *Once twice two, are four*. (b) This is the *Tetractys*, the Idæa of all created things; for all progression is perfected in four. Hence ariseth the *Decad*, the ten most general kinds of all things; *one, two, three, four*, going out of Omnipotency to Energy, (out of power to act) produce *ten*, the half whereof is *five*; now in the midst put *five*, on the right hand the next superior number *six*, on the left hand the next inferior *four*; these added, make *ten*. Again, the next superior *seven*, and the next inferior *three*, make *ten*. Again, the next superior *eight*, and the next inferior *two*, make *ten*. Lastly, *one* and *nine* make *ten*. This *ten* being carried up to *twenty*, comes again to *one*; and so on, in all the Cardinal numbers to a *hundred*: For, as twice one make two, thrice one three, four times one four, and so forward; so twice ten makes twenty, thrice ten thirty,

thirty, four times ten forty, and so on; the like in a hundred, a thousand, and forward. And because the Decad ariseth out of, and ends in a Monad, the *Greeks* express ten by *ι̃*, the *Hebrews* by a Point, which marks (as well amongst the Barbarians, as in *Latin*) denote one. (c) Hitherto alludes the *Pythagorick* Symbol, *One, Two*, by *Zaratas* (the Master of *Pythagoras*) used as the names of propagation; *one*, the father; *two*, the mother; one and two (in the divine essence) producing *four*, the *Tetractys*, the Idæa of all things, which are consummated in the number Ten. This *Pythagoras* styles ⸺⸺ *Eternal Nature's fountain* ⸺⸺ no other than *the knowledge of things in the divine mind, intellectually operating*. From this *fountain of eternal Nature*, floweth down the *Pythagorick* Number, One and Two, which from Eternity, in the fountain of the immense Ocean, was, shall be, or rather always is, plenteously streaming. This one was by the Ancients termed Ζεὺς, *Jupiter*; two, Ἥρη, *Juno*, wife and sister to *Jupiter*, of whom * *Homer*:

Golden-thron'd Juno, *with eyes full of love,*
Beheld her spouse and brother, sacred Jove,
Sitting on th' top of fount-abounding Ide.

In *Ida* (ἀπὸ τοῦ ἰδεῖν, from *prescience*) *Jupiter* and *Juno* sat as *one* and *two*, in the streaming Idæa of the *Tetractys*, whence flow the principles of all things, *Form* and *Matter*.

c Scalich. can. 11.

* Illiad. 14.

CHAP. IV.

The Intelligible World.

a Pag. 689. d.

(a) THE *Intelligible World* proceeds out of the Divine mind, after this manner: The Tetractys reflecting upon its own essence, (the first Unite, productrix of all things) and on its own beginning, (the first product) saith thus, Once one, twice two, immediately ariseth a *Tetrad*, having on its top the highest unite, and becomes a Pyramis, whose Base is a plain Tetrad, answerable to a Superficies, upon which the radiant light of the divine unity, produceth the form of incorporeal fire, by reason of the descent of *Juno*, (Matter) to inferior things. Hence ariseth essential light, not burning, but illuminating. This is the creation of the *middle world*, (which the *Hebrews* call the *Supream*, the world of the Deity, admitting no comparison.) It is termed *Olympus*, ὁλολαμπρὴς, *wholly lucid* and repleat with separate forms, where is the seat of the Immortal gods,

⸺⸺ *Deum domus alta*

whose top is Unity, wall Trinity, superficies Quaternity.

Number emanating from the divinity by degrees, declineth to the figure of creatures; instead of the Tatractys a Tetragone, in each of its angles a point, for so many unites, the unite at the top, which now begins to have position, elevated as much as is possible. Thus the former sides elevated will be four triangles, built upon their quadrangular latitude, and carried on to one high point. This is the Pyramis it self, *the species of fire, of which a Pyramis, having four bases, and equal angles, is compounded, the most immovable and penetrant form*, without matter essential separate light, next to God sempiternal life. The work of the Mind is *life*, the work of God is immortality, *eternal life*. God himself is not this created light, but the Author of all light, whereof in the divine Trinity, he containeth a most absolute Pyramid, which implieth the vigor of fire. Whence the *Chaldeans* and *Hebrews* affirm, that God is fire. But the Pyramid which this divine Tetractys produceth, is the fiery light of the immaterial world, of separate intelligences, beyond the visible Heaven, termed αἰών, *age*, eternity, *æther*. Having overcome these things (saith *Pythagoras*) thou shalt know εὐσίαν, *the cohabitation of the immortal gods, and mortal men*. In which words are imply'd three properties of this middle world, (which he terms the *free Æther*; *free*, as being separated from the power of matter; *Æther*, as receiving ardor from God, and heating all inferiors by an insensible motion) *Condition, Chorus, Order*.

Timæus, de Anima Mundi.

Aur. carm.

Condition, it is replenished with forms simple, immaterial, separate, both universal and individual, containing all ideated Idæa's of genus's and species, the exemplars imitated in lesser copies, their original being in the divine mind. Thus the world of the Deity is the absolute exemplar, in the intelligible world: the abstract example; and in the sensible world, not example, but contraction of exemplars, as seal, figure, and sealed wax.

Chorus, the infinite joy of the blessed spirits, their immutable delight, styl'd by *Homer* ἄσβεστος γέλως, *inextinguishable laughter*. For what greater pleasure, than to behold the serene aspect of God; and next Him, the Idæa's and forms of all things, more purely and transparently, than secondarily in created beings? and to communicate these visions to inferiors, the office of the gods called θεοὶ ἀπὸ τῆς θέας, *from speculation and vision*; Angels, from communicating their visions to others; not that we imagine them equal to the supreme God, who is ineffable. No Dæmons, how good soever, are admitted into this *Chorus*; so *Plotinus*, (the most exact follower of the *Pythagorick* Mysteries, as *Porphyrius* and *Longinus* attest.) (b) *The kind of gods we conceive to be void of passion; but to Dæmons we adjoyn passions, saying, They are sempiternal in the next degree after the gods. It is better to call none in the intelligible world Dæmon; rather, if a Dæmon be placed there, to esteem him a god.*

b De amore Deor.

Order, thus explained by *Pythagoras* (c): *If thou live according to right reason, grieving for what is ill done, and rejoycing in what is well done, and prayest the gods to perfect thy work:*

c Aur. carm.

Then stript of flesh, up to free Æther soar,
A deathless god, divine, mortal no more.

This is the order in the acquisition of man's beatitude. The incorporeal Heaven of the middle world, the invisible *Olympus* of the blessed, admits nothing impure; therefore vices are to be shun'd, and virtues to be embrac'd. The preservation of men is by the mercies of God; therefore the Divinity is to be worshipped, and the superior powers to be invocated, that they would perfect our work. Lastly, nothing material, corporeal, mixt, is received there. Therefore we must die, and holily put off the body, before we can be admitted to the society of the gods.

CHAP.

CHAP. V.
The Sensible World.

a Pag. 694. f.

(a) WE now come down to the *sensible World*. Its *exemplar* is the *world of the Deity*, its *example* the *intelligible world of Idæa's*, the αὐυσυπόσατον, subsistence of exemplars in *it self*. As *One* is the beginning of the intelligible world; so is *Two* of the corporeal, which were not corporeal, if it did not consist of these four, *point, line, superficies, solidity*, after the pattern of the Cube, made by *one, two, three, four*. *One*, fixed by position, creates a *point* ; a *line*, being protracted from one point to another, is made of the number *two*; a *superficies* ariseth from *three* lines ; a *solid*, from *four* positions, *before, behind, upwards, downwards*. *Two* multiplied in it self produceth *four*; retorted into it self (by saying twice two twice) makes the first *Cube*. Next *five* (the Tetragonical Pyramis principle of the intelligible World) is the cube of *eight* with six sides, architect of the Sensible World. Amongst principles, the *Heptad* hath no place, being a virgin, producing nothing, and therefore named *Pallas*. This first cube is a fertile number, the ground of multitude and variety, constituted of Two and of Four. *Zaratas* termed *two* the *Mother*; we the *cube* that proceedeth from it, *Matter*, the bottom and foundation of all natural beings, the seat of substantial forms.

b De Anima Mundi.

(b) *Timæus*, of the Tetragone *is generated the Cube, the most setled body, stedfast every way, having six sides, eight angles*. The form immers'd in this solid receptacle, is not received loosely, but fixtly, and singly it becomes individual and incommunicable, confin'd to time and place, losing its liberty in the servitude of Matter. Thus the two principles of temporal things, the *Pyramis* and *Cube*, *Form* and *Matter*, flow from one fountain, the *Tetragone*, whose Idæa is the *Tetractys*, the divine exemplar.

Now there is requisite some third thing to unite these two, *Matter* and *Form*, for they flow not into one another spontaneously, or casually; the matter of one thing doth not contingently receive the form of another. When the soul departs out of man, the body becomes not brass or iron, neither is wool made of a stone. There must then be a third thing to unite them, (not *privation*; privation and power act nothing substantively; nor *motion*, an accident cannot be the principle of a substance; but) *God*, as *Socrates* and *Plato* acknowledg, saying, *There are three principles of things, God, Idæa, and Matter*; symbolized before by *Pythagoras* in these three secret marks, *Infinite, One* and *two*; by *Infinite*, designing *God*; by *Unity, Form*; by *Alterity, Matter*. Infinite in the *Supreme* world; One, or Identity, in the *Intellectual*; Two, or Alterity, in the *Sensible*; for Matter is the mother of Alteration.

Scalich. can. 3.

The Tetragonal bases of these figures joyned together, make a *Dodecaedre*, the symbol of the Universe. * *Alcinous, The Dodecaedre God used in making the Universe*, this world. If upon an octangle Cube we erect a Pyramis, by four æqui-crural triangles, it makes a Dodecaedre, wherein the Cube is, as it were, mother, and the Pyramis father. Thus † *Timæus, Form hath the nature of male and father; Matter, of female and mother*; the compositions are their off-spring.

* *Doctor Plat.*

† *De Anima mundi.*

Of these are produced all thing in this world, by their seminal faculties, which things appear in a wonderful variety, by reason of the various commensuration of forms to their matter, and the admixtion of innumerable accidents, by excess and defect, discord and amity, motion and rest, impetuosity, and tranquility, rarity and density. Hence arise the Spheres, the Stars, the four Elements, out of which evaporate hot, moist, cold, dry, and all the objects of sense, the transmutation of forms, and variety of colours in several things.

The gods are natural, the gods of gods supernatural; those inhabit the inferior world, these the superior. The gods of gods are most simple and pure, as being no where; they are super-celestial, as being every where, they are with us; here strangers, there natives; never in our world but when sent, *Angels*, messengers from heaven, appearing in what form they please, kind and beneficial to us. The inferior spirits never ascend to the super-celestial, but are sent sometimes on embassie to us, whence termed *Angels*, as the others. God himself inhabits the lowest, the highest, and the middlemost, intimately; so that there is no being without God. Moreover the gods of this world are more excellent than the souls of men, though those assist, these inform bodies. Betwixt them, are placed *Dæmons* and *Heroes*; Dæmons next the gods, Heroes next souls; mentioned by *Pythagoras* in his *Golden Verses*, who assigns to each a peculiar worship.

CHAP. VI.
The state of the Soul after Death.

Pag. 675.

RAtional *man is more noble than other creatures*, as more divine, not content solely with one operation, (as all other things drawn along by nature, which always acts after the same manner) but endu'd with various gifts, which he useth according to his free will, in respect of which liberty,

b Aur. carm.

(b) *Men are of heavenly race,*
Taught by diviner Nature what t' embrace.

By *diviner Nature* is meant the Intellectual soul; as to intellect, man approaches nigh to God ; as to inferior senses, he recedeth from God: Reason teaching us *what to imbrace*, when it converts it self to the mind, renders us blessed; when perverted by the senses, wretched. For men often straying from the rule of right reason, precipitate themselves into misery , ἀυσαίρετα πήματ' ἔχοντες, in *Pythagoras's* word, *incurring ills voluntary*.

Thus is man placed between Virtue and Vice, like the stalk betwixt the two branches in the Pythagorical *Y*; or young *Hercules*, described by *Prodicus*. As therefore none can be called happy before their death, (as *Solon* said to *Crœsus*) so none is to be esteemed unhappy whilst he is in this life: *We must expect the last day of a man*. If when he hath put off his body, he remaineth burdened with vices, then begins he to be truly miserable. This misery after death, *Pythagoras* divides into two kinds. The unhappy are either near Beatitude, which though at the present they enjoy not; yet are they not oppressed with extream misery, being hereafter to be delivered from their punishment: Or, wholly distant from Beatitude, in endless infinite pains. Thus there are two mansions in the Inferi, *Elizium*, possest by those that are to ascend into blessedness; and *Tartarus*, by those who endure infinite torments, ἔστιν ὧντε ἐκβαίνειν, (as *Plato*, imitating *Pythagoras*, saith)

Xenoph. memor. lib. Herod. lib. Ovid Met.

whence they never come out. But when a man, who hath lived justly, dieth, his soul ascends to the pure Æther, and lives in the happy Ævum with the blessed, as a god with the gods.

Pag 697.f. Man is the image of the world; he, in many things, metaphorically, receives the name of the world. The *mind* of man (as the supreme mind) is termed God, by participation; the *rational soul*, if directed by the mind, it inclines the will to virtue, is termed the *good Dæmon* or *Genius*; if by phantasie and ill affections, it draweth the *Aur. carm* will to vices, the *evil Dæmon*. Whence *Pythagoras* desires of God, *to keep us from ill, and to shew every one the Dæmon he ought to use.* Leaving the body, the soul, if defiled with vices, becomes an evil Dæmon: Its life, δυσδαιμονία, *infelicity*; but if having forsaken vice, it retain a sollicitous affection to the good exercises and virtues which it practised in this life, it shall become a *good Dæmon*, and in the amænity of that world live happily, reflecting with joy upon the good actions it hath done, and retaining the same willingness to the right doing of them. This life is εὐδαιμονία, *Æneid. 6.* *felicity*, of which *Virgil*:

———— *the same care*
Which heretofore, breathing this vital air,
Of Chariots, Arms, and sleekt-skin'd Steeds they
Pursues them now in earth's cold bosom laid. (had,

These souls the Ancients termed *Lemures*; of these that which lives in, and takes care of any particular House, is *Lar-familiaris*; that which for its demerits in this life, wanders up and down in the air, a terror, vain to good men, but to the bad hurtful, is *Larva*; those which are not certainly known to be *Larvæ* or *Lares*, are called *Dii manes*; *Dii*, out of reverence, who having performed the course of their lives prudently and justly, died holily.

CHAP. VII.
Of the Pythagorical Transmigration.

Pag. 676. IT is commonly averred *Pythagoras* was of opinion, that the souls of men after death informed the bodies of beasts. We cannot imagin this of so knowing a person. This suspicion of this Transanimation, seems rather to have been raised by such, as were partly ignorant, partly envious, of the *Pythagorick* mysteries, as *Timon*, *Xenophanes, Cratinus, Aristophon, Hermippus*, and others, who have ascribed many things to *Pythagoras* which he never said nor wrote, and have *b Scalich.* perverted what he did say. (b) He holds, *that the* *can. 6.* *substantive unity of one number, is not the unity of another number. That the Monads in the Duad are inconnexive to those in the Triad. That the participate essence of every thing is One, which will not occupate the essence of another thing.* No Animal (then) can transmigrate into the life of a different animal; but must continue under the Law of its own nature in its proper office; ὥστε τὸ εἶδος εἶδει ἒ συνέρχεται, *species not being coincident with species*. One seal may make many impressions upon several pieces of wax; but one piece of wax cannot bear the form of many seals. * *Scalich.* * The seal of human form (the image of God) is *can. 5.* not permitted to set an impression upon inferior nature, implied by *Pythagoras* in this Symbol, *We must wear the image of God in a Seal-ring.* The image of God (man's soul) cannot seal or form the other natures that are near it. So *Hermes Trismegistus*, *Of man, one part is simple, which we* call, *The form of divine similitude.* And again, *There are two images of God, the World, and Man.*

This is the meaning of *Pythagoras* concerning the transmigration of souls after death, and their descention into life. Others thought the soul educed out of the power of Matter; *Pythagoras* asserted it infused by God into the body, and therefore before it, not in time, but in purity and dignity. This infusion he termed, *The descent of the soul,* not understood of its situation, or its motion from the intellectual world through the several sphears of the Elementary, as *Proclus* and others; but of the natural series or form, the rational soul being the ultimate perfection of human body.

(a) That *Pythagoras* said, he was in times past *a Scalich.* *Euphorbus*, the meaning is this: The Ancients call-*can. 8.* ed the inclinations and wills of men their *Minds*, whence such as are of one study, intention, inclination, motion, and sense, are termed *Unanimous*. Thus the ancient Philosophers call the motive and sensitive faculty, *The Soul*. *An animate differs from an inanimate* (saith *Aristotle*) *chiefly in two things, Motion and Sense.* Whosoever therefore are alike affected, and moved by the same object, are said to have *the same soul*. The *Metempsychosis* then is nothing else, but equal care, motion, and study of some dead person, appearing in some living person. Thus *Pythagoras* might arrogate the soul of *Euphorbus*; *Callicles, Hermotimus; Pyrrhus, Pyrander; Calidona, Alce;* as having an inclination to the several excellencies that were in those persons.

Again, in saying he was *Euphorbus*, *Pythagoras* *Pag. 681.* ænigmatically taught (not the transmigration of souls, but) the transmutation of bodies out of first matter; which is not only susceptible, but covetous of all forms, continually desiring, never satiated with any; as, *If a Comedy* (to use the comparison of *Aristotle*) *should say, I was first a Tragedy, De Gener.* *because both Tragedy and Comedy are form'd of the same Letters and Elements.* Thus *Apollonius*, deman-*Philost. vit.* ding of the Indian Bracmanes, what their opini-*Apollon.* on was concerning the Soul, *Jarchus* answered, ' *According as* Pythagoras *delivered to you, we to* ' *the Ægyptians.* Apollonius *replies,* ' Will you then ' *affirm you were one of the Trojan Captains, as* Py-' thagoras *said he was* Euphorbus? *Thespasian* warily askt, ' *Whom he thought the most worthy of* ' *them*? Achilles (saith *Apollonius*) *if we believe* ' Homer. *Then* Jarchus, ' *Look on him as my Pro-*' *genitor, or* προγονον σώμα, *progeniting body; for* ' *such* Pythagoras *esteemed* Euphorbus.

Or if he meant Historically, παλιγγενεσία, that is, The soul, separate from the body, may by the power of God, be brought again, the same into the same body: The body in which *Pythagoras* was so often revived, though called by several names, was one and the same, not in quantity, but substance, as the Sea is one and homogenious in it self, yet is here called *Ægean*, there *Ionian*; elsewhere, *Myrtæan* and *Colcan*; so one man often renate, is named *Æthalides, Euphorbus, Hermotimus, Pyrrhus,* and lastly *Pythagoras*. These Generations he ascribes not to the power of Nature, but to *Mercury*, God only; none can revive but by the Divine power of God, whom he acknowledgeth, ψυχὴ τοῦ ὅλου, *A-nimation of all things*. He infuseth soul into all men, and being infused, taketh it away; and being taken away, restores it, when, and as often as he pleaseth.

CHAP.

Part IX.

Empedocle's.

CHAP. I.

His Country, Parents.

IN the Catalogue of the *Pythagoreans*, we find *Empedocles*, not the least eminent amongst them. He was of *Agrigentum*, the most considerable City, next *Syracuse*, of *Sicily* ; built by a Colony (a) of *Geloans*, 108 years after their own foundation. *Gela* was built 45 years after *Syracuse*; *Syracuse* in the 11th Olympiad, *Gela* therefore in the 22d. *Agrigentum* in the 48th. It had its name from the River, and (b) grew in a short while to so vast an increase, that in the time of *Empedocles* it contained 800000 Inhabitants. Eminent it was for many things, but for none so much as the birth of *Empedocles*: Whence *Lucretius*:

(c) *An* Agrigentine *Citizen 'mongst these*
Is chief and principal, Empedocles :
Born on the shore of Sicil's *trpile bounds,*
Which the Ionian *in wide bayes surrounds.*
Laving its cliffs with azure waves, whose force
And rapid current Italy *divorce*

a *Thucid.*

b *Laert.* lib. 6.

c By Mr. *Evelin.*

By

By a small strait; Here's vast Charibdis *seat,*
And here the murth'ring Ætna's flames do threat
To re-inforce once more their dreadful ire,
And vomit yet again devouring fire;
Belching it forth out of his fiery jaws,
Which he at Heaven in lightning flashes throws.
Although this Isle for sundry things may seem
Famous, and many Nations it esteem,
Renown'd for wealth, and many gallant men;
Yet never had it ought more glorious, then
This Personage, nought more miraculous,
More holy, or which was more precious.
His Verse divine, and his Inventions rare;
The fruits of that rich breast do so declare
An universal knowledg, that some doubt
Whether or no he sprung from human root.

Of his Parentage, *Laertius* gives this account. *Empedocles,* as *Hippobotus* saith, was an *Agrigentine,* Son of *Meto,* son of *Empedocles,* which *Timæus* confirms in his Sixteenth Book of *Histories,* saying, that there was one *Empedocles* an eminent Person, Grandfather to the Poet. *Hermippus* saith the same. Likewise *Heraclides,* in his Treatise concerning Islands, affirms that his Grandfather was of a Noble family, and kept Chariot-Horses. And *Eratosthenes,* in his *Olympionicæ,* saith, that the Father of *Meto* was Victor in the 71 Olympiad, upon the testimony of *Aristotle.* But *Appollodorus* the Grammarian saith, it was that *Empedocles* who was son of *Meto. Glaucus* writes, that he came to the *Thurians,* at such time as they had newly built their City; and not long after adds, They, who relate that he was banished his Country, and came to *Syracuse* and fought with the *Syracusians* against the *Athenians,* seem to me to be quite mistaken. For either *Empedocles* at that time was dead, or very old: the latter is not likely, for *Aristotle* saith, that he and *Heraclitus* dy'd in the Sixtieth year of their age. But he who won the Race in the Seventy-first Olympiad, was of the same name, as *Appollodorus* hath set down the time. *Satyrus* in his *Lives,* saith, that *Empedocles* was son of *Exænetus,* and that he himself had a son named *Exænetus;* and that in the same Olympiad *Empedocles* won the Horse-race, and the son was Victor at wrestling, or, as *Heraclides,* won the Foot-race. But I find in the Commentaries of *Favorinus,* that in the Olympiac Games, *Empedocles* sacrific'd an Ox made of honey and flower, and that he had a Brother named *Callicratides.* But *Telauges* son of *Pythagoras,* in his Epistle to *Philolaus* saith, that *Empedocles* was son of *Archinomus:* That he was of *Agrigentum* in *Sicily,* he himself professeth in his *Lustrations,* beginning thus.

Friends, who in spacious Agrigentum
  dwell, &c.

Thus much (saith *Laertius*) of his descent.

CHAP. II.

His Masters.

a *Laert.*

(a) *Timæus,* in the Ninth book of his History affirms, he heard *Pythagoras;* adding, that he was taken stealing a dissertation of his, (as *Plato* also was) and thereupon expelled out of their Society, and that he mentions *Pythagoras* in his Verses, saying,

'Mongst these was one in things sublimest skill'd;
His mind with all the wealth of Learning fill'd.

But some there are who say, he meant this of *Parmenides. Neanthes* relates, that until *Philolaus* and *Empedocles,* the *Pythagoreans* communicated their Discourses; but, after that *Empedocles* divulged them in his Poems, they made an order not to communicate any thing to an Epick Poet. They say likewise, that *Plato* was prohibited in the like manner.

But which of the *Pythagoreans Empedocles* heard, he tells not; the Epistle which goes abroad under the name of *Telauges,* affirming, *Empedocles* was Disciple to *Hippasus* and *Brontinus,* deserves no credit.

Theophrastus saith, he was an Æmulator and Imitator of *Parmenides* in his Poetry; for he among other things writ a Discourse concerning Nature.

Hermippus saith he, he was not an Æmulator of *Parmenides,* but of *Xenophanes,* with whom he lived and imitated his Poetry, and afterwards applied himself to the *Pythagoreans.* But *Alcidamas,* in his Physick, relates, that *Zeno* and *Empedocles* heard *Parmenides* at the same time; at last both left him. *Zeno* went and studied Philosophy by himself; *Empedocles* went and heard *Anaxagoras* and *Pythagoras;* and imitated the one in his gravity of life and deportment; the other in his Physiology.

Empedocles, saith *Philostratus,* repeated by *Suidas,* is reported to have followed the *Pythagorean* Philosophy, which is confirmed by many Verses of his, as this.

Farewell, friends, mortal I shall be no more.

And this,

A Boy I was, then did a Maid become.

Besides the Ox which he made of meal, and sacrificed in *Olympia,* shews, that he approved the way of *Pythagoras.*

CHAP. III.

How he lived amongst the Agrigentines; his Power and Authority.

(a) *Neanthes* relates, that *Meto* dying, there began a Tyranny: But *Empedocles* perswaded the *Agrigentines* to give over sedition, and to endeavour a civil parity; and that he himself being very rich, bestowed Dowries upon many Virgins that had none, and thereupon clothed himself in Purple, and wore a Golden Girdle, as *Phavorinus* affirms, and a Delphick Crown, and had servants attending on him; his look severe and constant. After this manner he went. And the Citizens that met him paid such respect to him, as if those had been the marks of Regal Authority.

Nevertheless, he was, as *Aristotle* affirms, very free, and averse from taking any Government upon

a *Laert.*

upon him; for he refused a Kingdom which was offered him, (as *Xanthus* saith in his Book concerning him) preferring a moderate condition. *Timæus* relates the same, adding the reason of his being Democratically affected; for being invited by one of the Governours, and the company falling to drink, he commanded, that Supper should be brought in. He who had invited him, said, That he staid for the chief Magistrate. As soon as he came, he was made Symposiarch, Master of the Feast, for so it was ordered by him who invited them. He began to discover a tyrannical kind of humour, commanding, either that he should drink, or that it should be poured on his head. *Empedocles* for the present held his peace. But the next day citing them to the Court, he condemned them both to death, the Inviter, and the Symposiarch. Of so great authority was he in the Commonwealth.

Again, when *Acro* the Physician petition'd for a place, to build a Monument for his Father, *Empedocles* stood up and opposed it, and discoursed very largely of Parity; and withal asked, what Epitaph should be inscribed on the Tomb? This:

Ἄκρον ἰητρὸν Ἄκρων Ἀκραγαντῖνον πατρὸς Ἄκρα
Κρύπτει κρημνὸς ἄκρος πατρίδος ἀκροτάτης.

playing upon his name *Acro*. Others recite the second Verse thus:

Ἀκροτάτης κορυφῆς τύμβῳ ἄκρῳ κατέχει.

This, some ascribe to *Simonides*.

Afterwards *Empedocles* dissolved the Council of a thousand Senators, and constituted it Triennial; so that it consisted, not only of the rich, but of the ordinary sort.

But *Timæus*, in his first and second Books, (for he often mentions him) saith, that he seems to be of an opinion contrary to the Democracy; sometimes proud and self-conceited in his Poetry, as when he saith,

A deathless god am I, mortal no more.

CHAP. IV.

Wonders related of him.

HE was so excellent, not only in Natural Philosophy, but in Medicine also, that by his skill in both these, he performed many admirable things.

a *Laert.*

(*a*) *Timæus* relates, that the *Etesian* winds blowing very strongly, insomuch that they destroy'd the fruits; he gave order, that many Asses should be flead, and bottles made of their skins, and placed on the tops of the hills to receive the blasts; by which means the winds gave over: and upon him was conferred the attribute of *Colusanemos*, or *Alexanemos*, The chaser away of the winds.

Not unlike to this is that which *Plutarch* reports of him, that by stopping up a cleft in a Mountain, out of which there came an unwholsome Southern blast to the Plains, it is conceived, that he drove away the Plague out of that Country.

The same cure he wrought among the *Selinuncians*, by a different means; for they being, as *Diodorus* the *Ephesian* saith, infested by a plague, caused by the noisomness of the River, whereof the men died, neither could the women be, without much difficulty, delivered; *Empedocles* contrived, and at his own charge convey'd two other Rivers that ran near, into this Channel; by which mixtion, the water became sweet, and the plague ceased.

(*d*) Another time, a young man drawing a sword upon *Anchitus* his Host, (for that he had in publick judgment condemned his father to death) and being about to have killed him, *Empedocles* prevented it, and immediately changing his Tune, and singing out of *Homer*,

d *Jamb. vit. Pyth.*

Nepenthe *calming anger, easing grief.*

freed *Anchitus* his Host from death, and the young man from the crime of murder; who from thenceforward became one of his disciples, eminent amongst them.

(*e*) *Hermippus* saith, that he cured *Panthea*, a woman of *Agrigentum*, given over by all the Physicians.

e *Laert.*

But the most memorable cure was that which he performed upon a woman that had lain seven days dead, as *Pliny* terms it; but as *Galen* more exactly out of *Heraclides*, describes it, *breathless, and without pulse, differing in nothing from a dead body, saving that she had a little warmth about the middle parts of her body.* The Book of Heraclides was intituled, The breathless woman. And it was a controversie amongst the Physicians that were present, whether she were dead or alive? (*g*) *Heraclides* adds, that *Empedocles* acquainted Pausanias with the whole business, and that the breathless woman could preserve her self thirty days, without breathing or eating. Whence he terms *Empedocles* both a Physician and a Prophet, confirmed even by his own verses.

g *Laert. Suid.*

Friends, who in spacious Agrigentum *dwell,*
Busied in noble high designs, farewell.
A deathless god I am, mortal no more;
Honour'd by all, with Garlands cover'd o're:
Which, 'soon as e're I come to any Town,
Both men and women pay to me renown.
Thousands of men enquire the way to wealth,
Some would divine, others restore to health.

Some there were who ascribe these to *Goetick. Magick. Satyrus* in his *Lives* relates, that *Gorgias* the *Leontine*, who had been disciple to *Empedocles*, used to say, that he himself had been present with him, when he practised *Goetick*; and that *Empedocles*, makes a profession thereof in his Poems, when he saith:

Med'cines to strengthen age, and cure disease,
Thou shalt be taught, for I am skill'd in these;
The wrath of restless winds thou shalt assuage,
Which blast the corn in their pernicious rage.
And when thou call'st, they shall come back again,
Rain thou shalt change to drought, and drought to rain,
By whose kind moisture trees may sprout and thrive,
And make the dead quit Pluto, and revive.

In

In fine, he was so much admired for these things, that when he went to the Olympick Games, the eyes of all men were fixed on him; neither was their discourse of any thing so much as of *Empedocles*.

CHAP. V.

His Death.

His death, (saith *Laertius*) is variously reported. *Heraclides* having related the story of the breathless woman, how much *Empedocles* was admired for raising a dead woman to life, adds, that he appointed a Sacrifice in the field of *Pisianax*, and invited thither many of his friends, amongst whom was *Pausanias*. After the feast was done, the company withdrew themselves to rest, but he stir'd not out of the place where he lay at supper. The next morning when they arose, he alone was missing, which giving them occasion to enquire after him of the servants, they said they knew not what was become of him, only one of them said, that about Midnight he heard a great voice, calling *Empedocles*; whereupon rising up, he saw a heavenly light, and a splendor of Torches, but nothing else. They were all amazed at this accident, and *Pausanias* going down, sent forth others to enquire more strictly, but was at last perswaded not to trouble himself any further, saying, that the thing that had fallen out, deserved prayer, and that sacrifice should be made to him as to a god. *Hermippus* saith, that he made the Sacrifice upon the cure he wrought on *Panthea*, and that the Persons invited were eighty.

Hippobotus affirms, that he rose up from his place and went to *Ætna*, where he leaped into the fire, that he might leave behind him an opinion that he was a god; and that afterwards, it was discovered by one of his Sandals, which the fire cast up again, for his Sandals were of Brass. But this report *Pausanias* contradicts.

Diodorus the *Ephesian*, having told how he cured the *Selinuncians* of the Plague, adds, that the *Selinuncians* upon a time feasting by this River, *Empedocles* appeared to them, and they rising up, worshipped him, and prayed to him as a god: which opinion he desiring to continue, cast himself into the fire.

This relation *Timæus* contradicts, affirming, that he departed into *Peloponnesus*, and never return'd; whereby it came to pass, that the manner of his death is not known. He likewise in his fourth Book expresly confutes *Heraclides*, for he proveth that *Pisianax* was a *Syracusian*, and had not any estate or field at *Agrigentum*; that *Pausanias*, upon that report, erected in memory of his friend, either a little Image or Chappel, as to a god, for he was rich. And how, saith he, could he cast himself into the flames of *Ætna*, of which being so far distant, he never makes any mention? Indeed he died in *Peloponnesus*, and it is no wonder that his Tomb is not known, for it hath happened so to many others besides. Thus *Timæus*, adding, that *Heraclides* tells extraordinary things, as among the rest, the story of a man that fell out of the Moon.

Hippobotus affirms, that a Statue of *Empedocles* cover'd, which stood first at *Agrigentum*, was afterwards plac'd before the Senate-house at *Rome* uncover'd, being brought thither by the *Romans*, of which saith *Laertius*, there are yet some pictures.

Neanthes relates, that going in his Chariot to a great solemnity at *Messina*, he fell and broke his thigh; of which he died, being seventy seven years old. His Sepulcher is at *Megara*: but in the accompt of his years *Aristotle* differs, who saith he died at sixty. Yet others affirm, he lived to an hundred and nine years of age. He flourished in the 84th Olympiad.

But *Democritus* the *Træzenian* relates, in *Homer*'s words, that,

About his neck he knit a rope, and fell
From a high cliff; his soul went down to hell.

In the forementioned Epistle of *Telauges*, it is said, that being exceeding old, he fell into the Sea, and so died. Thus much for his death.

CHAP. VI.

His Writings.

Aristotle in his Sophist affirms, that *Empedocles* first found out Rhetorick, *Zeno* Dialectick; and in his Book concerning the Poets, that *Empedocles*'s style was *Homerical*, and that he was weighty in his expressions, using Metaphors much, and other Poetical figures; and that having written, among other Poems, the passage of *Xerxes* over the *Hellespont*, and a Hymn to *Apollo*, they were both burnt by a sister, or, as *Hieronimus*, a daughter of his, the Hymn upon mistake; the *Persian* Poem wittingly, for that it was imperfect. He adds, that he wrote Tragedies also, and Politicks: but *Heraclides*, son of *Serapion*, ascribes the Tragedies to another. *Hieronimus* saith, he lighted upon forty three of them; *Neanthes*, that he wrote Tragedies when he was young, and that he had a sight of them.

Moreover he wrote Books concerning *Nature* and *Lustrations*, which extended to 5000 verses, and a *Medicinal Discourse*, containing six hundred verses.

His *Lustrations*, *Clemens* the Rhapsodist collected, and sung at the Olympick Games, as *Poavorinus* saith in his Commentaries.

CHAP. VII.

His Opinions.

He held that there are (a) four Elements, Fire, Air, Water, Earth; and two principal powers, Amity and Discord; one unitive, the other discretive: for thus he writes:

To the four roots of all, attention give;
The Æther Jove; Juno, by whom we live;
Next these is Pluto; Nestis last, whose eyes
Afford the mortal fountain fresh supplies.

He calls the Heat and Æther, *Jupiter*; the Air, vital *Juno*; the Earth, *Pluto*; the Water, *Nestis*, and the Mortal Fountain, *Laertius* cites it thus:

White Jove, *and vital* Juno, Pluto *then,*
And Nestis *giving tears to th' eyes of men.*

The Fire, saith he, he calls *Jupiter*; the Earth, *Juno*; the Air, *Pluto*, the Water, *Nestis*. These are in an incessant mutation, whereby there is such an eternal production of things; whence he adds,

Sometimes by Friendship all are knit in one;
Sometimes by Discord sever'd and undone.

b *Plut. pl. 1. 13.*
c *Stob. Ecl. Phys. 1. 17.*
d *Plut. pl. 1. 5.*

(b) Before the four Elements, there are certain less fragments, (c) as it were Elements of Elements, of similar parts, and round.

(d) The World is one; the World is not the Universe, but a little part of the Universe; the rest is sluggish matter.

e *Plut. 1. 30.*

(e) Nature is nothing but the mixture and separation of the Elements; for so he saith in the first of his Physicks:

We otherwise; there's no such thing at all
As that which Mortals Death or Nature call.
To Mixtion and Discretion all we owe,
On which the names of Nature men bestow.

f *Plut. 2. 1.*

(f) The World is circumscribed by the circulation of the Sun, and that is the bound of it.

g *Plut. 2. 10.*

(g) The right side of the World is that which is towards the Summer Tropick, the left that which is towards the Winter Tropick.

h *Plut. 1. 24.*

(h) He, as all those who held the World to be made of little bodies, introduced Concretions and Discretions, but deny'd Generation and Corruption, saying, That compounds are not made by quality and alteration, but by quantity and coagmentation.

i *Plut. 2. 11.*

(i) Heaven is solid, being made of air condens'd by fire, like Crystal; it containeth a fiery and aerial nature in both Hemispheres.

k *Plut. 2. 13.*

(k) The Stars are fiery, consisting of that fire which the Æther containing in it self, struck forth in its first secretion.

l Ibid.

(l) The fixed Stars are fastned to the Crystal of the Heavens, the Planets are loose.

m *Laert.*

(m) The Sun is a great heap of fire, bigger than the Moon.

n *Plut. 2. 20.*

(n) There are two Suns, one an archetypal fire in the other Hemisphere of the World, filling this Hemisphere, which is continually opposite to its splendor. As for that which we see, it is the light in that other Hemisphere, replenished with air, mixed with heat; and the same is occasioned by refraction from the Earth, that is more round, entring into the Sun, which is of a Chrystaline nature, and yet is trained and carried away together with the motion of that fire. But to speak more plainly and distinctly, this is as much as to say, The Sun is nothing else, but the reflection of that light of the fire which is about the Earth.

(o) He ascribed the reasons of the Solstices, or Tropicks of the Sun, to the Sphere that containeth him, and hindreth him from passing further; as also to the two Tropicks.

o *Plut. 2. 23.*

(p) The Moon is in form like a dish.

(q) The Moon is twice as far from the Sun, as she is from the Earth.

p *Plut. 2. 27. Laert.*
q *Plut. 2. 31.*

(r) Winter cometh when the air is predominant in thickness, and is forced upward; Summer, when the fire is in like manner predominant, and is driven downward.

r *Plut. 3. 8.*

(s) The Sea is the sweat of the Earth, burnt by the Sun, which squeeseth the sweat out of it.

s *Plut. 3. 16.*

(t) The soul puts on the several forms of all living creatures, and plants; whence he said of himself:

t *Laert.*

A Boy I was, then did a Maid become:
A Plant, Bird, Fish, and in the vast Sea swom.

(u) The particular senses are affected according to the proportion of their pores and passages, namely, as the proper object of each sense is well disposed and fitted.

u *Plut. 4. 9.*

(x) Resemblances in Mirrours come by the means of certain defluxions gathered together, upon the superficies of the Mirrour, and accomplished by the fire that ariseth from the said Mirrour; and withal, transmuteth the air that is before it, into which those fluxions are carried.

x *Plut. 4. 14.*

(y) *Plutarch* saith, he mingled the visual images and beams together, calling that which is made thereof, The rays of a compound image.

y *Plut. 4. 13.*

(z) Hearing is perform'd by means of a wind within the hollow of the Ear, turned in manner of a screw, fitted and framed of purpose within the Ear, hanging up, and beaten upon in manner of a Bell.

z *Plut. 4. 16.*

(a) The Hegemonick is the consistence of the blood.

a *Plut. 4. 5.*

EPICHARMUS.

Laert.

EPICHARMUS also heard *Pythagoras*. He was of *Coos*, son of *Helothales*. At three months old; he was carried from *Sicily* to *Megara*, and from thence to *Syracuse*, as he himself saith in his *Commentaries*. On his Image was this Inscription:

As Stars exceeded by the radiant Sun,
Streams by the Ocean, into which they run;
So all by Epicharmus *are surpast,*
On whose head Syracuse *this Garland plac'd.*

He wrote Commentaries, in which he discoursed Physiologically, and Sententiously, and Medicinally: and added little Notes to his Commentaries, by which they are known to be his. He died ninety years old.

ARCHYTAS.

Laert.

ARCHYTAS was of *Tarrentum*, Son of *Mnesagoras*, or (as *Aristoxenes*) of *Hestyæus*. He also heard *Pythagoras*. This was he, by whose means *Plato*, when *Dionysius* had a mind to put him to death, was delivered. He was generally admired for all sorts of Virtue. He was seven times General of his own Country-men, whereas all others were but once, the Law prohibiting, that they should not be oftner. There is extant an Epistle of his to *Plato*, to this effect.

Archytas to *Plato*, Health.

IT is well that you are recovered of your sickneß; for, besides what you wrote, Damiscus hath informed us so. We took care of the Commentaries, and went to the Lucanians, where we discoursed with the Sons of Ocellus. Part, concerning Laws, and a Kingdom, and Piety, and the Generation of all things, we have; and part we have sent; the rest are not to be found at present: As soon as we find them, you shall have them.

Plato

Plato returned this Answer:

Plato to *Archytas*, Ἐυπραῆειν.

THE Commentaries which you sent, we received with much joy, and exceedingly admire the Author, who seems to us to be a person worthy his Ancestors, who were Myræans, some of those Trojans who went with Laomedon, good men, as the story speaks them. As for my Commentaries, concerning which you wrote, they are not polished, but as they are I have sent them; as for the custody of them, we are both agreed, so that I shall need to inquire nothing of you. *Farewel.*

Aristoxenus saith, He was never worsted in the Field; but once through the envy of others, resign'd his Charge, and then all his Soldiers were taken. It appears by * *Horace*, that he perished by Shipwrack, who brings in a Mariner Expostulating with him upon it, thus:

*Lib. 1. Ob. 28.

Thee the Surveyor of the Sea and Land,
 And the innumerous sand,
A little share of these small dusty grains,
 Archytas *now contains,*
Hard by the Marine shore: It nought avail'd,
 Since die thou must, t'have scal'd
Th' aerial Orbs, or that thy soaring soul
 O'rerun the wheeling Pole.

ARCHYTAS Answers,

And so dy'd Pelop's *father, at whose Feasts*
 The gods themselves were guests;
And Tithon, *who* Aurora *entertain'd;*
 Minos, *whom* Jove *design'd*
Admission to his counsels; and again
 Dark Tartara *detain,*
Panthous *son, who, by his Target known,*
 And from the shrine ta'ne down,
Attested, that in Trojan *Wars, he breath'd,*
 And to black death bequeath'd.
Nothing but skin and nerves, whom thou wilt yield
 In truth and nature skill'd.
But all men to one endless night are led,
 And once death's path must tread.
Some are stern Mars's *Trophies; Seas become*
 The greedy Sailor's Tomb.
The fates of young and old together croud,
 No head is disallow'd
By merciless Proserpina; *and me*
 Into th' Illyrian *Sea*
The wind, which doth Orion's *Star pursue,*
 Unruly Auster *threw.*
But grudg not thou, kind Mariner, to spread
 On my unburied head
And bones, some few of these loose sands; so may
 Fierce Eurus *turn away*
Whatever threatens the Hesperian *floods,*
 On the Apulian Woods,
Securing thee from harm; a swelling tyde
 Of wealth on every side
Flow on thee, by great Jove *and* Neptune *sent.*
 Tarentum's *President*
If thou neglect, thou maist in future age
 Thy guiltless sons engage
In this offence, perhaps fate may return
 What's due unto thy scorn.
Vengeance may on my poor petition wait,
 And thee nought expiate.
The stop is small, as thou sail'st on, thou maist
 Dust thrice upon me cast.

He invented Cranes and Screws, and made a Pigeon of wood that flew; but when she once rested, could not rise. Of the duplication of a Cube, I have spoken formerly in the Life of *Plato*. *Laert.*

Being angry with a Country-man, he said, What would I have done to thee, if I had not been angry? *Cic. de Amic.*

He was very modest, and abstained from obscene expressions; and if there were a necessity of any, he wrote it upon the wall. *Æl. var. Hist.*

He said, That if a man should go to heaven, and behold the nature of the World, and beauty of the Stars, he would find, that the admiration of them, otherwise the most pleasing thing in the world, would be very unpleasant to him, if he had not one to communicate it unto.

He said, That it is as hard to find a man without deceit, as a Fish without bones.

He said, That the Judg and Sanctuary is one; for he who hath received wrong, flies to both.

He said, That every Commonwealth consists of three things, the Ruler, the Ruled, and the Laws: whereof the best ought to command; the worst, to be commanded.

Cicero, in the person of *Cato*, gives an account of an Oration of *Archytas* to this effect: That there is no pestilence more capital given by nature to men, than corporeal pleasure, by which they are incited to run head-strong, and unbridled on, to enjoy the lust of that greedy pleasure. Hence proceed betrayings of our Country; hence, subversions of Commonwealths; hence, private Treaties with enemies. In fine, there is no wickedness, no mischief to the undertaking whereof, this lusting after pleasure will not impel us: Rapes, Adulteries, and all such leudness, are provoked by no other allurements than those of pleasure. And whereas Nature, or some god, hath not bestowed on man any thing more excellent than a mind, there is nothing so contrary to this divine gift, as pleasure; for, as long as pleasure rules, there is no place for Temperance, nor can virtue subsist under the jurisdiction of pleasure. Which to understand the better, he advised to fancy to our selves some man, provoked by corporeal pleasure the greatest imaginable; and he conceived, that no man will doubt, but that as long as he took joy therein, he could fix his reason, his mind, his thoughts, upon nothing else. Wherefore there is nothing so detestable, nothing so pestilent, as pleasure; for if it be great and long, it extinguisheth all the light of the mind. *De Senect.*

There were four of this name: the first, this Philosopher; the second, of *Mitilene*, a Musician; the third, wrote concerning Agriculture; the fourth, an Epigrammatick Poet. Some add the fifth, an Architect. *Laert.*

ALCMÆON.

Laert.   ALCMÆON was of *Crotona*; he also heard *Pythagoras*. He was chiefly addicted to Medicine, but studied Phisiology also, saying, There are many causes of humane things. *Phavorinus* thinks him the first that wrote a Physical Dissertation. He asserted, that the Moon hath an eternal nature. He was son of *Perithus*, as appeareth by the beginning of his Book; Alcmæon *a* Crotonian, *son of* Perithus, *saith thus to* Brontinus, *and* Leon, *and* Bathyllus, *of invisible and immortal things, the gods have a certain knowledg*; *men, conjecture*, &c. He asserted the soul to be immortal, and that it moveth perpetually like the Sun.

Plut. pl. phil. 2. 16.   He asserted, that the Planets hold an opposite course to the Fixed Stars, from West to East.

Plut. 4. 16.   We hear by the hollow of the Ear; that resoundeth when the wind entereth into it, because all empty things make a sound.

Plut. 4. 18.   By moisture and warmth in the Tongue, together with the softness thereof, all objects of taste are distinguished.

Plut. pl. 4. 17.   Reason, the principal part of the soul, is within the Brain, and that by it we smell, drawing in scents and smells by respirations.

Why Mules are barren, see *Plut. plac. phil. lib. 5. cap. 14.*

The Infant in the Womb feeds by the whole body; for it sucketh and draweth to it, like a spunge, of all the food, that which is good for nourishment. *Plut. 5. 16.*

The head is first made, as being the seat of reason. *Plut. 5. 17.*

Sleep is made by the return of blood into the confluent veins: Waking, is the diffusion of the said blood; Death, the utter departure thereof. *Plut. 5. 24.*

The equal distribution of the faculties of the body, moisture, heat, driness, cold, bitter, sweet, and the rest, is that which maintaineth health; the predominance of any of them causeth sickness, for the predominance of one is the corruption of all the other, and is the cause of indisposition; the efficient, in respect of excessive heat or cold; the material in respect of abundance, or defect of humours; as in some there is want of blood or brain; whereas health is a proportionable contemperation of all these qualities. *Plut. 5. 30.*

HIPPASUS.

Laert.
* De vit. Pythag.   HIPPASUS was a Metapontine, (or as some affirm a *Sybarite*) a *Pythagorean* also. * *Jamblichus* saith he was drown'd in the Sea, a just reward for his impiety, for that he had publisht the Doctrine of *Pythagoras*.

Laert.   He asserted that fire is the principle of all things, of which all things are made, and into which all things resolve. All things are made by extinction of this fire: first, the grosser part of it, being contracted, becometh Earth, then the Earth being loosened by the nature of the fire, becomes water; the water exhaled becomes air.

Again, the World and all Bodies shall be dissolved in a conflagration; fire therefore is the principle, for all things were made of it; and the end, because all things are resolved into it.

Likewise he held that there is a determinate time of the mutation of the World, and that the Universe is bounded, and always moved.

Demetrius saith, he left nothing extant in Writing.

There was another of this name, a *Lacedemonian*, who wrote five Books of the *Lacedemonian* Commonwealth.

PHILOLAUS.

PHILOLAUS was of *Crotona*, a *Pythagorean*: of him it was that *Plato* wrote to *Dion*, to purchase some *Pythagorean* Books; he was put to death upon suspicion, that he aimed at the Tyranny.

He asserted, that all things are made by Necessity and Harmony; and was the first that said the Earth moveth circularly: which some ascribe to *Hicetus* of *Syracuse*.

He

He wrote one Book, which *Hermippus* (citing some other Author) affirms that *Plato* when he went to *Sicily* to *Dionysius*, purchased of the Kinsmen of *Philolaus*, paying for it forty *Alexandrian* Minæ, and out of it took his *Timæus*. Others say that *Dionysius* gave it him, having taken it from a young man, Disciple to *Philolaus*, whom he freed out of Prison.

Demetrius faith, that *Philolaus* first published a *Pythagorick* Discourse concerning Nature, beginning thus, *Nature, and the whole world, and all things in it, are aptly connected of Infinites and Finites.*

Plutarch relates, that after the *Pythagorean* Associations were expelled the Cities, those who kept still together, being assembled in a house at *Metapontum*, the * *Cylonians* set the house on fire, and burnt them all except *Philolaus* and *Lysis*, who being young men, strong and active, escaped through the fire. *Philolaus* fled to the *Lucanians*, where some other friends came to him, who gathering themselves together, over-master'd the *Cylonians*. But of this formerly, in the Life of *Pythagoras*.

* So read here, and afterward.

He affirmed, that there is a twofold corruption: one while by fire falling from Heaven: another, by water out of the Moon, poured forth by the circumgyration of the Air; the exhalations whereof become the food of the World.

The substance of the Sun is, as it were of glass, receiving the reverberation of all the fire in the world, and transmitting the light thereof to us, as it were through a strainer, as that fiery light in Heaven resembleth the Sun; then that which proceedeth from it, is in form of a mirrour: and thirdly, there is a splendor, which by way of reflection from that mirrour, is spread upon us; and this we call the Sun, as it were the Image of an Image.

Plut. 2.40.

The earth moveth round about the fire in an oblique Circle, as the Sun and Moon do.

Plut. 3.13.

EUDOXUS.

Laert.

EUDOXUS was of *Gnidus*, son of *Æschines*: he was an Astrologer, Geometrician, Physician, and Lawgiver: He learnt Geometry of *Arthytas*; Medicine of *Philistio*, the *Sicilian*, as *Callimachus* affirms.

Sotion faith, he heard *Plato* also: for being 23 years old, and in a very mean condition, he was invited by the fame of the Socratick Philosophers to go to *Athens*, with *Theomedon* a Physician that maintained, and much affected him. He lived in the *Pyræum*, and went up every day to *Athens*, where he heard the Sophists, and return'd. Thus he lived two Months, and then went home; where his friends making a collection of money for him, he travelled to *Ægypt* with *Chrysippus* a Physician, carrying along with him Letters of reccommendation from *Agesilaus* to *Nectabis*, who recommended him to the Priests. There he lived a year and four months, shaving his Eye-brows; and wrote, as some think, his History of eight years. Thence he went to *Cyzicus*, and to *Propontis*, teaching Philosophy; and to *Mausolus*. At last, having gotten together many Disciples, he return'd to *Athens*, to vex *Plato*, as some conceive, for having formerly rejected him. Some say, that *Plato* making a Feast, he taught him the way of placing his Guests in the figure of a Semicircle.

Nicomachus, son of *Aristotle*, faith, he asserted pleasure to be the chief good.

He was much honoured in his own Country, as appears by the Decree made concerning him. He was very eminent also among the *Greeks*, for he gave Laws to some Cities, and taught them (as *Hermippus* affirms) Astrology and Geometry; and many other excellent things.

He had three Daughters, *Actis*, *Philtis*, and *Delphis*. *Eratosthenes* affirms, he wrote Κυνῶν διαλόγους; but others, that the *Ægyptians* wrote them in their own Language, and that *Aristoxenus* translated them into *Greek*.

From him *Chrysippus* the *Gnidian*, son of *Erineus*, received all that he wrote concerning the Gods, and the World, and Meteors.

He left many excellent Writings.

He had a son, *Aristagoras*, father to *Chrysippus*, the Disciple of *Aethlius*.

He flourished in the 103 Olympiad, died 53 years old. When he lived in *Ægypt* with *Ichonuphus*, a *Heliopolitane*, an Ox licked his Garment; whereupon the Priests foretold that he should be very eminent, but not long-liv'd. Thus *Laertius*.

If therefore he lived about the 103 Olympiad, and in the twenty third year of his age heard *Plato*, *Eusebius* seems to be mistaken, who affirms, he flourished in the beginning of the 97 Olympiad, which was seven years after the death of *Socrates*, at what time *Eudoxus* could not have attained any eminence, if he were Disciple to *Plato*, as *Cicero* also affirms he was; *Strabo*, that he went with *Plato* into *Ægypt*; *Suidas*, that he was Contemporary with him.

Of his Writings are mentioned *Octaeteres*; see *Censorinus*, de Die Natali, Cap. 18.

Γῆς περίοδος, cited by *Athenæus* and others; perhaps the same *Strabo* calls Τὴν περὶ τὸν Εὔδοξον ἱστορίαν; it consisted of many Books, the Seventh cited by *Stephanus* and *Porphyrius*.

Phænomena; mentioned by the Anonymous Writer of the Life of *Aratus*.

There were others of this Name; (a) one of *Rhodes*, a Historian; another of *Sicily*, a Comick Poet; another of *Gnidus*, a Physician; (b) another of *Cyzicus*. Hitherto of the *Pythagorean* Philosophers.

a Laert.
b Strabo. Plin 2 6,7.

THE HISTORY of PHILOSPOHY.

The Tenth Part, Containing the HERACLITIAN Sect.

HERACLITVS.

CHAP. I.
His Country, Parents, Masters.

AS the *Ionick* Sect, which was so named from the place of its Institution, commnicated that denomination in general to all the Sects that were descended from it, though founded in other places: So the *Pythagorean* Sect, being from the Country where it was planted termed *Italick*,

Italick, all the Sects that sprung out of it, though some of them had their beginning far from *Italy*, were included under the general notion of *Italick*. Of these there were four; the *Heraclitian*, the *Eleatick*, the *Septick* (or *Phyrronian*) and the *Epicurean*.

The Author of the first was *Heraclitus*, an (a) *Ephesian*, his Father, by *Laertius*, called *Flyso*, by *Clemens Bauso*, by *Suidas Blosso*, or *Pleuto*, or (saith he) as others *Heracion*: He had also an Uncle, *Heracleodorus*, whom he mentions in his (b) Epistles.

(c) *Aristonymus* saith, That whiles he was yet young, he was the wisest of all men, because he knew that he knew nothing; *Laertius*, that he was admirable from his Childhood; for, whilst he was young, he used to say, that he knew nothing; and when he was grown up, that he knew all things.

Laertius adds, That *he heard no man, but professid that he himself made inquiry, and sought out all things of himself*. But the learned *Casaubon* justly doubts, That *Laertius* mistakes the meaning of those words, and that they rather refer to a strict enquiry, which he used to make into himself, according to the *Delphian* Motto, *Know thy self*; to which effect, (d) *Plutarch* commends as a memorable saying of his, *I have been seeking out my self*. And *Laertius* himself acknowledgeth, upon the testimony of *Sotion*, that *some affirmed, he heard Xenophanes*; to whom *Suidas* adds, *Hippasus the Pythagorean*.

(e) He flourished about the 69th Olympiad, (f) in the time of *Darius Hystaspes*.

a *Cic. Laert. &c. Strom. 1.*
b *Ad Amphid.*
c *Stob. Serm. 21.*
d *Adv. Colot.*
e *Laert.*
f *Suid.*

CHAP. II.

How he lived at Ephesus.

*L*Aertius saith, *He was of a high spirit, contemning others, as appears by a Book of his* (perhaps the Fifth Book of Politicks, out of which (g) *Clemens* seems to cite the same Sentence) *wherein he saith*, "*Much Learning instructs not the Mind, for then it would have instructed Hesiod and Pythagoras, as also Xenophanes and Hecataeus, for there is but one wise thing; which is to know when to govern all by all: He also said, That Homer deserved to be thrown out of the Schools and beaten, as also Archilochus.*

As a further (h) Argument of the greatness of his Spirit, *Antisthenes* relates, That he gave the Kingdom to his Brother; *Laertius*, That being desired to take upon him the Supreme Power, he slighted it, because the City was prepossess'd with an ill way of Government; and retiring to the Temple of *Diana*, play'd at Dice there with the Boys, saying to the *Ephesians* that stood about him, "*Worst of Men, what do you wonder at! Is it not better to do thus, than to govern you?*

Much offended was he with the *Ephesians*, for that they had banished his Friend *Hermodorus*, in whose behalf he reproved them sharply, writing thus; *The Ephesians deserve to die all Children, and to leave their City to Children, for that they cast out Hermodorus, the most excellent amongst them, saying, Let not one of us be more excellent than the rest; and if there be any such, let him go to another place, and live amongst other People.*

g *Strom. 1.* where perhaps read πολυμαθίη νόον ἐχὴ διδάσκει.
h *Laert. ibid.*

Darius (i) King of *Persia*, wrote to the *Ephesians*, to repeal the Banishment of *Hermodorus*, and to restore him to his Patrimony. He wrote also to *Heraclitus*, inviting him to come and live with him; the Letter was to this effect:

(k) *I King Darius salute Heraclitus the Ephesian, a wise Person.*

*Y*OU have put forth a Book concerning Nature, hard to be understood and interpreted; but by so much as I understand of it, it seems to promise the Theory of the whole World, and of the things that depend hereon, which consists in Divine Motion; and by many Questions and Doctrines, as well to those who are skilful in the Greek Learning, as to others vers'd in Meteorology, and other Learning, to doubt what is the true meaning of what you have written. King Darius therefore, Son of Hystaspes, desires to participate of your Learning, and of the Greek Institution. Come as soon as you can to my Presence, and Royal Palace; for the Greeks, for the most part, are not obsequious to wise men, but despise the good things which they deliver. With me you shall have the first place, and daily Honour and Titles; your way of living shall be as noble as your Instructions.*

But *Heraclitus* refused his offer, returning him this Answer.

Heraclitus to Darius the King, Son of Hystaspes, Health.

*A*LL men living refrain from Truth and Justice, and pursue Unsatiableness and Vain-glory, by reason of their Folly; but I, having forgot all Evil, and shunning the society of imbred Envy and Pride, will never come to the Kingdom of Persia, being contented with a little, according to my own mind.*

(l) *Demetrius* affirms, he slighted the *Athenians* also, who had a great respect for him.

He continually bewailed the wicked lives of men, and *as often as he came abroad amongst them fell a weeping, considering that all things which are done, are misery.*

i *Epist. Graec.*
k *Epist. Graec. & Laert.*
l *Laert.*

CHAP. III.

His Retirement.

*A*T the last, saith *Laertius*, *growing into a great hatred of mankind, he retired to the mountains, and lived there, feeding upon Grass and Herbs*; the dislike which he had of the *Ephesians* being much exasperated by a disrespect they shewed to him; whence, (m) *Demetrius* affirms, that *the Ephesians slighting him, he betook himself to a private Life*; the occasion is related by himself in two Epistles to *Hermodorus*; the first is this,

Heraclitus to Hermodorus.

*B*E not angry any longer in your own Cause, *Hermodorus*; *Euthycles*, Son of that *Nychophon* who committed Sacrilege, hath Indicted me of impiety (overcoming me by his ignorance, who am excellent in Wisdom) for that upon the Altar by which I stood, I wrote my Name, making my self, of a Man, a God. Thus I shall be condemned of impiety by the impious. What think you? I shall seem impious to them for dissenting from them in opinion concerning the Gods. If blind Men were to judg of Sight, they would say, that Blindness were Sight: but, O ye ignorant Men, teach us first what God is, that when you declare us to be impious,

m *Laert.*

impious, you may be believed. Where is God, shut up in Temples? O pious Men, who place God in the dark! It is a reproach to a Man to tell him, he is a Stone; but of God you profess, as a truth and in his commendations, he is born of a Rock. You ignorant people! you know not, that God is not made with Hands, neither hath he any Basis from the beginning, nor hath one Circumference, but the whole World, adorned with living Creatures, Plants and Stars, is his Mansion. But if you your selves are unlearned, let not my Learning be construed impiety. Learn Wisdom, and understand; but you will not, neither do I force you. You grow old with ignorance, and rejoyce in your own Wickedness. *Hercules* was not, as *Homer* bely'd him to be, a Murtherer of Strangers. What was it that Deified him? his own Integrity and Fortitude, by which he perform'd so many Labours. Am not I then, O ye Men, good also? I was mistaken when I asked you; for though you should say the contrary, yet I am good, and have performed many difficult Labours. I have overcome pleasures; I have overcome Riches; I have overcome Ambition; I have master'd Cowardice; I have master'd Flattery: Fear hath nothing to object against me, Drunkeness hath nothing to object against me: Sorrow is afraid of me; Anger is afraid of me; I have won the Garland in Fighting against these Adversaries, a task which was imposed on me by my self, not by *Euristus*. Will you not give over to slander Wisdom, and to press your own Sins, and Crimes upon your selves? If you could return to life 500 years hence, you would find *Heraclitus* still alive, but not the least print of your Names. I shall equalize, by reason of my Learning, the lives of Cities and Nations, I shall never be silenc'd. If the City of the *Ephesians* were razed to the Ground, and all their Altars destroy'd, yet will the Souls of Men be the places to preserve my memory. I will also marry *Hebe*, not the *Hebe* of *Hercules*, he will always be with her Himself; mine is another. Vertue hath brought forth many, and bestow'd one upon *Homer*, another upon *Hesiod*, and to every good Man one, which is the renown of his Learning. Am not I wiser than *Euthycles*, who alone know God? But thou being bold and impious thy self, think'st him God, who is not God: If the Altar of God be not erected, there is not God; but if the Altar of one that is not God be erected, then he is God, as if stones were witnesses of the Gods. His works should bear witness of him, as those of the Sun, Night and Day, bear witness; the four seasons of the year are his witnesses; the whole fruitful Earth is his witness; the Moon is his work, a heavenly testimony.

The other Epistle is this.

To Hermodorus.

I Understand that the *Ephesians* are about to make a Law against me, most illegally; for it is not a Law which is made for a single person, but Judgment: the *Ephesians* know not that a Judge is different from a Law-giver, and this is so much the better, for that it is uncertain who shall transgress it: But the Judge seeth before his Eyes the Person that is to suffer. They know, *Hermodorus*, that I assisted you in the framing of Laws, and therefore will banish me, but not before they have confuted themselves. They decree, that he who laughs not, and hates mankind, shall depart the City before the Sun rise; this is the Law they would make. There is no Man, *Hermodorus*, but laughs, except *Heraclitus*; and so they banish me. O ye Men! Will ye not learn, why I never laugh? It is not that I hate Men, but their Wickedness; write your Law thus, Whosoever hateth Wickedness, let him depart the City, and I will be the first that shall go, willing to forsake, not my Country, but the malice of my Country-men. Write your decree over again. But if you grant there is Wickedness and Vice amongst the *Ephesians*, and that I hate you for it, why should not I make a juster Law, That they, who through their Wickedness are the occasion that *Heraclitus* never laughs, should depart this life? Or rather let them be fined great Sums, for the loss of Wealth will more afflict you, this is death to you. You have done me wrong in taking away that which God gave me, and banishing me unjustly. Shall I therefore love you? first, for that you have taken all joy away from me, and not ceasing there, oppress me with Laws and Exile; for whilst I live in the City, I am banished from you? With whom do I commit Adulteries? With what company do I commit Murther? with whom am I Drunk? With whom do I joyn in Wickedness? I corrupt none; I injure none; I am alone in the City. You have made it a Desart by your Wickedness. Hath *Heraclitus* made your *Forum* honest? No: but *Heraclitus* would have made you and the whole City good; but you would not. I would do it, and am a Law to others; I am the only Person that ought not to be punished by the City. Do you wonder, that I never laugh? I wonder at you, that you can rejoyce, and do wrong; for those that do unjustly ought to have a sower look. If you would give me an opportunity of laughter, live in peace; and contest not unjustly: You carry Swords in your Tongues, plunder Wealth, ravish women, poison friends, commit sacriledge, betray the Trust the People repose in you, take away Mens Lives by Torture; every Man is full of a several Wickedness. Shall I laugh, when I see Men do these things? Their Garments, Beards and Heads order'd with unnecessary care; a Mother deserted by a wicked Son, or young Men consuming their Patrimony, or a Citizen whose Wife is taken from him, or a Virgin ravish'd, or a Concubin entertained as a Wife, or one impudent young man courted by the whole City, or deadly Poisons by Unguents; or some at Feasts filling their Bellies more with Poison than with Dainties, or the People treating of Publick Affairs in the Theatre? Virtue, more rigid than Vice, would strike me blind, if I should laugh at your Ways. By Musick, Pipes, and Stripes, you are excited to things contrary to all Harmony. Iron, a Metal more proper for Ploughs and Tillage, is fitted for slaughter and death. You injure the Gods, warlike *Minerva*, and *Mars*, surnamed *Enyalius*: Men, raising Armies against Men, covet to kill one another, punish them who forsake the Field, for not being murderous; and honour, as valiant, such as are drunk with blood: But Lyons arm not themselves against one another;

ther; Horses betake not themselves to Swords; the Eagle buckles not a Breast-plate against an Eagle. No other Creatures use Instruments of War, their Limbs are their Weapons. Horns are the Arms of those, Beaks of these, Wings of others; Swiftness to some; Bigness, Smallness, Swimming to others; to many their Breath; no irrational Creature useth a Sword, but keeps it self within the Laws to which it is design'd by Nature; but Man doth not so, more blameable, because more understanding. You must with for an end of your Wars, if you would take me off from this severity. Nor worse than these internal Dissentions, is your Depopulations of Cities, tormenting aged Persons, ravishing Wives, taking away Children from their Mothers and Nurses, defiling Beds, Vitiating Virgins, abusing Boys, casting free persons into Bonds, demolishing the Temples of the Gods, digging up the Monuments of the Heroes, triumphing in wickedness, and offering gratulatory Sacrifices to the Gods for these unjust actions. About these, without laughing, you contest in Peace by Argument, and in War with Steel. You force away Justice by your Swords. *Hermodorus* is banished for writing Laws; *Heraclitus* is banished for Impiety; the Cities are deserted of Justice, the Desarts of Injustice. The People have built Walls, as Testimonies of the wickedness of the Inhabitants, shutting up your own Lives. You are all fenced with Houses; there are other walls of wickedness, Enemies within you, your own Countrey-men; Enemies without you. Strangers; All Enemies, no Friends. Can I laugh, seeing so many Enemies? You think the wealth of other men is your own; you think the Wives of other men are your own. You lay the yoke of servitude upon free Persons; you devour the Living; you violate the Laws; you ratifie wickedness by a Law; you do violence to all such as consent not to your Justice. Your Laws themselves convince you of injustice; for if they were not, you would go wholly unpunished, whereas now you are a little restrained, and, by fear of punishment, with-held from the utmost injustice.

There is a third Epistle of his to the same Person, expressing no less disaffection to the *Ephesians*.

Heraclitus to Hermodorus.

GIve me notice, *Hermodorus*, when you intend to go to *Italy*; may the Gods and Demons of that place receive you kindly. I dreamt, that I beheld all the Diadems of the whole World make their address to your Laws, and, shutting their mouths after the *Persian* manner, adore them, they being seated above all the rest. The *Ephesians* will adore thee when thou art dead, when thy Laws shall bear a general sway; then necessity will force them to use them, for God hath taken away the power from them, and they have acknowledg'd themselves worthy of servitude. This I learnt from the more Ancient. All *Asia* is reduced by the King [of *Persia*] and the *Ephesians* are spoiled. They are not accustomed to true Liberty and Dominion, and now it is very likely will be obedient, if they are commanded to lament and accuse the Gods for not giving them riches. It is the part of blind men, not of a good man, to value the goods of Fortune. The Sibyl frequently hinted this, that from *Greece* there should come a wise man into *Italy*. The Sibyl knew thee so many ages since, *Hermodorus*; even then thou wert in being: but the *Ephesians* will not yet see him whom Truth acknowledg'd by the mouth of a Woman divinely inspir'd. A testimony is given of your wisdom; but the *Ephesians* disallow the testimony of a God: they shall smart for their insolence, and even now do smart for it, having an ill opinion of us also. God punisheth not by taking away riches, he rather allows them to the wicked, as an aggravation of their crimes, that, abounding in wealth, their offences may be more notorious to all men; for poverty is a veil. I wish fortune may not forsake you, that all men may see your wickedness. But farewel they; as for you, acquaint me with the time of your departure, for I would by all means meet you, and discourse with you a little, amongst other things, concerning Laws. I had committed to writing, but that I thought it fit rather to be conceal'd: nothing is more conceal'd than when one man speaks to another alone, and especially when *Heraclitus* to *Hermodorus*. The ordinary sort of men differ not from broken Pitches, which can hold nothing, but let it run out by babling. The *Athenians*, being *Autochtones*, knew the nature of men, that being made of earth, they have crasie minds, and therefore instituted them in a secrecy and silence of Mysteries, that they might hold their peace through fear, not out of judgement, and that it might be no longer hard for them to practise silence.

CHAP. IV.

His Sickneß and Death.

THE diet which he used in the Mountains being nothing but Grass and Herbs, brought him into a Dropsie, whereupon he was constrained to return to the City. The account of his sickness receive from himself, in * two Epistles to *Amphidamas*. The first is this.

Laert.

* *Epist. Græc.*

Heraclitus to Amphidamas.

I Am fallen sick, *Amphidamas*, of a Dropsie. Whatsoever is in us, if it get the Dominion, it becomes a disease. Excess of heat is a Fever; excess of cold, a Palsie; excess of wind, Colick. My disease comes from excess of moisture. The Soul is something divine, that keeps all these in due proportion; the first thing is health, nature her self is health; we cannot foresee what is contrary to nature, but after that it happens. I know the nature of the World, I know that of man; I know diseases, I know health; I will cure my self, I will imitate God, who makes equal the inequalities of the world, committing it to the Sun. *Heraclitus* shall not dye of this disease; the disease of *Heraclitus* shall dye by good direction. In the Universe moist things are dried up, hot things are made cold. My wisdom knoweth the ways of nature; it knows the cure of sickness: but if my body be over-press'd, it must descend to the destin'd place; nevertheless my Soul shall not descend, but being a thing immortal, shall fly up on high to Heaven. The ætherial Mansions shall receive me, and I will accuse the *Ephesians*. I shall converse, not with Men, but with Gods; I shall not build Altars to others, but others to me. *Euthycles* shall not charge me with impiety; but I him of malice. They wonder, that *Heraclitus* look'd always sad; they wonder not that men are always wicked. Withhold from your wickedness, and perhaps I shall smile. My sickness is the more gentle to me, for that I am not amongst men, but alone; and perhaps for that my Soul presageth she shall shortly be freed out of this prison, and looking through her shatter'd body, calls to mind her own Country, from whence she came to encompass this transitory mortal body, which to others seems built up of flegm, choler, purulent matter, Blood, Nerves, Bones, and Flesh; for unless passions did contrive pains, we would never go out of it.

The second Epistle was to this effect.

To the Same.

THE Physitians, *Amphidamas*, met together, and were very diligent about the cure of my sickness, but knew neither Art nor Nature; they would have it to be this, and to be that, but knew neither. They did nothing but soften my belly with feeling it, as if it had been a Leather Bottle; yet some of them would have undertaken the cure, but I would not allow it, before I had required an account of the disease, which they could not give me; neither were they too hard for me, but I for them. How, said I, can you be masters of piping, when one that is not a piper hath over-match'd you? I shall cure my self sooner than you can, if you will but teach me how a drought may be made of a shower; but they, not understanding my question, held their peace, and were much at a loss in their own Science. I have known others cured, not by them, but by chance. These men, *Amphidamas*, do wickedly, professing Arts which they have not, and undertaking the cure of that which they understand not, bringing death to men under the pretext and name of Art, doing wrong both to Art and Nature. It is abominable to profess ignorance, but more abominable to profess an Art, of which we are ignorant. What delight take they in lying, but that by deceit they grow rich? It were better for them to beg, for then they would be pitied, but now they are hated for doing wrong, and lying. Other Arts are more fortunate; these are easily confuted, the better more hardly. These were the men that took compassion of me in the City; not a Physitian amongst them, but all Cozeners and Impostors, who sell cheats of Art for Money. They kill'd *Heracleodorus*, my Uncle, and took Money for it, and were not able to tell me the cause of my distemper, and how a drought might be made out of an excess of moisture. They are ignorant that God cures the great bodies in the World, reducing their inequality to an even temper; that he makes whole those that are broken, stops such as are falling, gathers the dispersed together into one body, polisheth the deformed, those which are taken, he puts into Custody; those which fly, he pursues, illuminates the dark with his light, terminates the infinite with certain bounds, gives form to those which have none, gives sight to things void of sense, perminates through all substance, Striking, Composing, Dissolving, Condensing, Diffusing; he dissolves the dry into moist, he condenseth the loose Air, and continually moveth the things above, setleth those beneath. This is the cure of the sickly World; This I will imitate in my self; to all the rest, I bid farewel.

Thus having demanded of the Physicians ænigmatically, whether they could of a shower make a drought, they not understanding him, he shut himself up in an Oxe-stall, hoping that the Hydropical humours would be extracted by the warmth of the dung; but that doing him no good, he dyed, having lived 60 years. *Laert.*

Hermippus relates, that he demanded of the Physitians, Whether they could squeeze the water out of the inward parts of his body; which they acknowledging they could not do, he lay'd himself in the Sun, and commanded his Servants to playster him all over with Cow-dung, in which posture he dyed the next day, and was buried in the Forum. *Neanthes* of *Cyzicum* saith, that they could not get off the Cow-dung, and not being known in that condition by the Dogs, they tore him to pieces.

But *Aristo* saith, he was cur'd of this dropsie, and dyed afterwards of some other disease, which *Hippobotus* confirms.

Laertius reckons five of this Name. This Philosopher the *first*.

The *second*, a Lyrick Poet, who writ an Encomium of the twelve gods.

The *third* an Elegiack Poet, of *Halicarnassus*; upon whom *Callimachus* hath an Epigram.

The *fourth* of *Lesbos*, who writ the Macedonick.

The *fifth* a Jester. To whom add, mentioned by *Athenæus*, another of *Mitylene*, a Jugler: and lastly, one of *Tarentum*, a Lutenist who, play'd at the marriage of *Alexander*.

It is reported of *Heraclitus* the Philosopher, that he perswaded *Melancomas* a Tyrant to lay down his Crown. *Clem. Alex. Strom. 1.*

CHAP. V.

His Apothegms.

OF his Apothegms, and moral Sentences, are remembred these: He said, That we ought to take more care to extinguish Contumely, than the Hottest Fire; And that a People ought to fight for their Laws, as well as for their Walls. *Laert.*

Deriding the Sacrifices, whereby they thought that the Gods were pacifi'd; These, saith he, cleanse themselves by polluting themselves with Blood, as if a Man should go into the Dirt to wash himself. *El. Cret. in Nazianz. Orat.*

He saith, that he wholly contemned his Body, and esteemed it more vile than Dross; yet would take care for the Cure of it, as long as God should command him to use it as an Instrument. *Suid.*

Of all the Discourses that ever I heard, none came so far as to prove, That Wisdom is something separate from all other things; A solitary Man is either a God or a Beast. *Stob. Ser 3.*

Even

PART IX. HERACLITUS.

Ser. 4. Even the Eyes and Ears of Fools that have rude Minds, are tainted with ill.

Ser. 5. It concerneth every Man to know himself, and to govern himself prudently.

Plut. de Garrul. Being desired by the Citizens, to make some discourse concerning Concord, he went up into the Chair, and taking a Cup full of water, sprinkled some Meal and Penny-royal into it, and having drunk it off, went away; giving them to understand, That Cities might be preserved in Peace and Concord, if the Inhabitants would be content with a little, and not affect costly Superfluities.

Stob. Ser. 18. It is hard to conceal Rudeness at any time, but especially in Wine.

Ser. 17. A Drunken Man reels, and is led by a Child; his Soul is wet, and knows not whither she goeth; a dry Soul is the wisest and best.

Ser. 102. He said, That the Wit of a Man is his Genius.

Laert. Being asked by one, why he held his peace? he answer'd, That you may speak.

Plut. de Pyth Orac. He said, That the King to whom the *Delphian* Oracle belongs, neither speaks, nor conceals, but gives signs.

Consol. ad Apollon. It is all one to be living and dead, waking and sleeping, young and old; for each of these alternately changeth into the other.

Clem. Strom. 5. He seemed to blame Generation, saying, That those who are born will live and dye, or rather rest, and leave behind them Children to dye also.

Strom. 2. Unless a Man hopeth that which is not to be hoped for, he shall not find that which is inscrutable, and hath no passage whereby he may come at it. This, *Clemens* calls a kind of Paraphrase upon that of the Prophet, (*Isa.* 6.) *Unless you believe, you shall not understand.*

Strom. 6. Reproving some incredulous Persons, he said, They can neither hear nor speak.

Strom. 2. How can that Light, which never sets, be hidden or obscured, (meaning God?)

Strom. 5. Justice shall seize upon the Framers and Witnesses of false things.

CHAP. VI.

His Writings.

THe Treatise (saith *Laertius*) which goeth abroad under his Name, is a continued discourse of Nature; it is divided into three Books; One, concerning the *Universe*; the Second, *Politick*; the Third, *Theologick*. This Book he deposited in the Temple of *Diana*, and, as some affirm, he affected to write obscurely, (whence called ακοτεινὸς, dark) that he might be read only by the more Learned, and not become contemptible, by being read by the Vulgar; which *Timon* implies, saying,

'Mongst these the great Confounder did arise,
Dark Heraclitus, he that doth despise
The Multitude ———

And perhaps it conduceth not a little to the obscurity of his Writings, that, through excess of Melancholy, as *Theophrastus* saith, he began many things, and left them unfinish'd, and many times wrote contrary things.

Aristo relates, that *Euripides* brought this Book of *Heraclitus* to *Socrates* to be read; and asking his opinion of it; "The things, said *Socrates*, which I understand in it, are excellent, "and so, I suppose, are those which I understand "not; But they require a *Delian Diver*, (one "that is able to explain Oracles.) But *Selucus* the Grammarian, citing one *Croto*, saith, That a certain person, named *Crates*, brought this Book first among the Grecians, and said, It required a *Delian Diver*, for only such a one could escape drowning in it. Some entitle it, *The Muses*; others, *Concerning Nature*; Diodotus, *An exact rule to steer Life by*; others, *The Judgment of Manners, the Ornament of one Institution above all.*

Yet *Laertius* gives this judgment of that Treatise, that sometimes he writes so clearly and plainly, that any Man may understand it, and discern the height of his Mind; adding, that his style was very short and sound.

There were many that explain'd and commented upon his Book: of whom were *Antisthenes*, and *Heraclides* of *Pontus*, and *Cleanthes* of *Pontus*, and *Sphærus* the Stoick; as also *Pausanias*, who was sirnamed the *Heracliti*, and *Nicomedes*, and *Dionisius*; and, of Grammarians, *Diodotus*, who denies the Book concerning *Nature* to be his; but admits that of *Politick*, alledging, that what he said of Nature, is only brought in by way of example.

Hieronymus saith, that *Scythinus*, an *Iambick* Poet, wrote against him in Verse.

CHAP. VII.

His Doctrine.

Laertius saith, That his Writings gained so great a Reputation, that the Followers of his Sect were, from him, called *Heraclitians*. His Assertions were these:

SECT. 1.

That Fire is the Principle of all Things.

HE held, that (a) Fire is the Principle of all things, for of Fire all things are made, and into Fire all things shall resolve; Or, as *Laertius*, That Fire is the Element, and the vicissitude of Fire generates all things by Rarefaction and Condensation, (but he delivers nothing plainly.) That all things are made by contrariety, and the whole flows like a River. That the Universe is bounded, and that there is one World, which was made of Fire; And shall again be set on Fire by certain Periods for ever, and that this is done by Fate. That, of the Contraries, that which conduceth to Generation is named War and Contention; That which to Conflagration, Concord and Peace. That Mutation is a way up and down, and that the World is made by it; For the Fire being condensed, groweth humid, and settles into Water; the Water condensed turns into Earth, this is the way down. Again, the Earth is diffused, of which is made Water; of the Water, almost all things else, meaning the exhalation out of the Sea, this is the way up. That there are made exhalations

a Plut. place. 1, 3.

from

from the Earth and from the Sea, some whereof are bright and pure, others dark: the Fire is augmented by the bright, the Water by the rest; but what that is which includes all, he declares not. Hitherto *Laertius*.

b Loc. cit. (*b*) *Plutarch* delivers it thus: That all things are made by extinction of this Fire; first the grosser part of it being contracted, becometh Earth, then the Earth being loosned by the nature of the Fire, becomes Water; the Water exhaled, becomes Air. Again, the World and all Bodies shall be dissolved in a Conflagration: Fire therefore is the Principle, for all things were made of it; and the End, because all things are resolved into it.

c Strom. This is further explain'd by (*c*) *Clemens Alexandrinus*, out of the words of *Heraclitus*. That he held, (saith *Clemens*) the Universe to be eternal, is manifest, for that he saith, *the Universe was not made by any, either God or Man, but was, is, and shall be an ever-living Fire, kindling measures, and quenching measures.*

That he held this World was generated, and shall perish, is manifest also from his saying, *The conversions of Fire, first Sea, then the half of Sea, Earth, the Half-prester*, meaning, that by the power of that Fire, the Word and God, who governeth all things, turneth by Air into moisture, the seed as it were of the disposer of the World, which he calleth Sea. Of this again is generated Heaven and Earth, and all things that are in them.

Lastly, how it returns to its first condition, and becomes Fire again, he shews thus. *The Sea is diffused, and measured according to the same proportion as it was first, before it was Earth, the like happens to the other Elements.* Thus *Clemens.*

d Plut. plac. 4 3.
e Plut. plac. 1. 28.
Moreover he held, (*d*) that the soul of the World is an exhalation of the humid parts thereof, and that (*e*) the essence of Fate is a reason (or proportion) permeating through the Universe, which Fate is an æthereal body, the seed of the generation of all things; for (*f*) all things are done by Fate.

f Laert.

This opinion (that Fire is the Principle of all things) was asserted also by *Hippasus* the *Pythagorean*; whom *Plutarch*, in the account which he gives of it, joins with *Heraclitus*; and it is probable, that *Heraclitus*, being his Disciple, received it from him.

g Plac. 1. 13. (*g*) *Plutarch* adds, that he introduced ψήγματα τινα ἐλάχιστα, *certain sharings, the least of things, and not divisible.*

SECT. 2.

Of the Stars, Sun, Moon, Day, Night, &c.

h Laert. IN the World (*b*) there are certain *Scaphæ*, things in the fashion of Boats, the hollow sides whereof are turned towards us, in which certain shining Exhalations are crowded, which cause flames. These Flames are the Stars, nourished by Exhalations, arising out of the Earth. Of these, the Flame of the Sun is the brightest and hottest, by reason that the other Stars are more distant from the Earth, and therefore shine and heat less.

(*i*) The Sun is just as big as it seems to be, (*k*) his Figure like that of a Boat, the hollow part turned downwards. (*l*) He is in a transparent and unmixt place, (*m*) (that is, in the purer Air) and keeps a proportionable distance from us, by which means he heateth and shineth more than the Moon. (*n*) He happens to be Eclipsed by reason of his Boat-like figure, when the hollow thereof is turned upwards, and the convex part downwards towards us.

i Laert.
k Plut. plac. 2. 22.
l Laert.
m Stob.
n Plut. plac. 2. 24. Laert.

(*o*) The Moon is a kind of Earth encompassed with a Mist, (*p*) in form like a Boat; (*q*) she is nighest the Earth, and moved in a place that is not pure, the grosser Air. (*r*) She is Eclipsed, when the hollow part is turned upwards; and the variety of appearances, which she hath in a Month, are caused by the turning of her hollow part upwards by degrees.

o Plut. plac. 2. 25.
p Plut. plac. 2 27.
q Laert.
r Plut. p.

(*s*) Day, Night, Months, Hours, Years, Showers, Winds, and the like, are caused by different Exhalations: for a splendid Exhalation, flaming in the circle of the Sun, makes it Day; the contrary, being predominant, makes it Night; the heat of the splendid increasing, maketh Summer; the moisture of the dark abounding, maketh Winter Suitably to these he explained the Causes of other things; but of the Earth he said nothing, nor of the *Scaphæ*.

s Laert.

SECT. 3.

Of the Ebbing and Flowing of the Sea.

THe Ebbing and Flowing of the Sea is caused by the Sun, which stirreth, raiseth and carrieth about with him the most part of the Winds, which coming to blow upon the Ocean, cause the *Atlantick* Sea to swell, and so make the Flux or High-Water; but when the same are allay'd, the Sea falleth low, and so causeth a Reflux and Ebb.

Plut. plac. 3. 17.

SECT. 4.

Of living Creatures.

OF the Nature (*a*) of the Soul, he said, It is so profound, as that it cannot by any means be found out: He only asserted, (*b*) That it is, as all other things are, an Exhalation; that which is without, and that which is within, being all of one Nature: it is incorporeal and always in fluxion. That it is moved, is evident from it's being moved; (*c*) Of Souls, the dry is the wisest and best.

a Laert.
b Plut. plac. 4. 3. Arist. de an 1, 3.
c Stob. se. 17.

(*d*) Man beginneth to be perfect about his second seventh year, at what time the generative vigour beginneth to move: for then Trees begin to be perfect, when they begin to bring forth; for as long as they bear no Fruit, they are immature, and imperfect. Moreover, at that time a Man comes to the knowledge of good and ill, and is capable of being instructed therein.

d Plut. plac. 5. 23.

THE

Part XI.   445

THE HISTORY of PHILOSPOHY.

The Eleventh Part,
Containing the ELEATICK Sect.

XENOPHANES.

CHAP. I.
His Life.

THE *Eleatick* Sect was denominated from *Ela* a City of *Magna Græcia*, founded in the time of *Cyrus* by a Colony of *Phocæans*; of whom, being besieged by *Harpagus*, some made their escape by night, and came into this part of *Italy*, where they built a City which they named

Elea-

Elea, Helea, or Hyela, either from *Elea* the River of that place, or, as (a) some conceive, in allusion to the Marshes round about it.

<small>a *Dionys. Halic.*</small>

Of this City were *Parmenides, Zeno,* and *Leucippus*; who being eminent Persons of one Sect, from them the Sect it self was termed *Eleatick.* But its first Institutor was *Xenophanes.* The *Eleatick Sect,* saith (b) *Clemens, was begun by* Xenophanes *the* Colophonian, *who (as* Timæus *affirms) lived in the time of* Hieron *King of* Sicily, *and of* Epicharmus *the Poet; But* Apollodorus, *that he was born in the fourth* Olympiad, *and his life extended to the times of* Darius *and* Cyrus. Parmenides *was Disciple to* Xenophanes; *Zeno to him;* then Leucippus; then Democritus. The *Auditors of* Democritus *were* Protagoras *the* Abderite, Metrodorus *the* Chian, *and* Diogenes *the* Smyrnæan, *whose Disciple was* Anaxarchus.

<small>b *Strom.*</small>

(c) Xenophanes *was (as was said) a* Colophonian, *Son of* Dexius, *or (as* Appollodorus) *of* Orthomenes, *praised by* Timon; *who saith of him,*

<small>c *Laert.*</small>

Zenophanes, *not wholly free from pride,*
The fictions *of old* Homer *did deride.*

Being banished his Country, he lived at Zencle and Catana *in* Sicily. Some affirm, he had no Master; others, that he heard Botho *the* Athenian; others Archelaus, [*which is least probable, for*] he *was (as* Sotion *relates)* contemporary with Anaximander. He wrote in verse Elegies and Iambicks *against* Hesiod and Homer, reprehending what they *deliver'd concerning the Gods.* He also wrote the building of Colophon, and the bringing of the Colony into Elea *in* Italy, *which consisted of two thousand verses.* But (d) Strabo, who affirms *he writ the* Silli *in verse,* seems to have ascribed to him what was indeed written by *Timon* the Sceptick, his mistake perhaps arising from hence, that (e) the second and third books of that Poem were written by way of Dialogue, wherein *Timon* questions *Xenophanes* about every thing, who gives answers to all.

<small>d *Lib.* 14.</small>

<small>e *Laert. in Timone.*</small>

Zenophanes *sung his own works. It is farther said, that he asserted doctrines contrary to* Thales *and* Pythagoras*, and somewhat against* Epimenides. *He flourish'd in the* 60th *Olympiad.* Demetrius Phalereus, *and* Panætius *the* Stoick *relate, that like* Anaxagoras *he buried his Sons with his own hands. He lived to a great age, for he saith of himself,*

Sixty seven years in *Greece* I now have told;
And when I came was twenty five years old.

Lucian *therefore reckons amiss, affirming he liv'd ninety one years; for this account of sixty seven and twenty five amounts to ninety two.* (f) Censorinus saith, *he lived above a hundred years.*

<small>f *De die nat. cap* 15.</small>

(g) Empedocles *saying to him, that he could not find a wise man; That may very well be,* saith he, *for you are not capable to know a wise man.*

<small>g *Laert.*</small>

He was redeemed by Parmeniscus *and* Orestades, Pythagoreans, *as* Phavorinus *relates.*

There was another Xenophanes *of* Lesbus, *an* Iambick-Poet.

CHAP. II.
His Opinions.

XEnophanes, (b) *as* Socion *affirms,* held all things to be incomprehensible, and (i) reproved the arrogance of those persons, who not capable of knowing any thing, durst say, they knew; Nevertheless he did maintain many dogmatical assertions; affirming,

<small>h *Laert.*</small>
<small>i *Cic.*</small>

(k) Not all at first the Gods to men reveal'd,
But by long search they find out things conceal'd.

<small>k *Stob.*</small>

Whence it is, that *Timon* the Sceptick calls him ὑπότυφον, not wholly free from pride, or dogmatical self-conceit.

He held, that God is one, and incorporeal, eternal, (l) in substance and figure round, no way resembling man; that he is all sight, and all hearing, but breathes not; that he is all things, the mind and wisdom, not generate, but eternal, impassible, immutable, and rational,

<small>l *Laert.*</small>

(m) Greatest of Gods and men, one God we find,
Like mortals not in body, not in mind.

<small>m *Clem. Alex.*</small>

Moreover, (n) he reproved and confuted the fabulous narrations of Homer and Hesiod concerning the Gods; and (o) the descriptions which the Grecians made of them, as that they are of human form, and subject to humane affections; every one fancying them after their own likeness, the Æthiopians black and flat-nos'd, the Thracians ruddy and grey-ey'd; and so for their minds or dispositions, the Barbarians believed them fierce and cruel, the Grecians more mild, yet obnoxious to passions.

<small>n *Laert.*</small>
<small>o *Clem. Alex.*</small>

Men think the Gods like them begotten were,
And that like them their form, shape, garments are.

(p) That this (God, or) One, is all things; the Universe consists of this eternal One. (q) Whatsoever is, is eternal; for it is impossible that something should be made of nothing. The World is eternal without beginning or end, [as being ingenerate, for] (r) he first asserted, that whatsoever is generated, is corruptible.

<small>p *Cic. Acad.*</small>
<small>q *quæst* 4. *Aristot. de Xenoph.*</small>
<small>r *Laert.*</small>

(s) That there are infinite Worlds, and those immutable.

<small>s *Laert.*</small>

(t) That there are four Elements.

<small>t *Laert.*</small>

(u) That the Stars are made of certain Clouds set on fire, which are extinguished every day, and kindled again at night: for the rising and setting of the Stars is nothing else, but their enkindling and extinguishing. (x) As for those lights which appear about ships, (commonly termed *Castor* and *Pollux*) these are little Clouds set on fire, and shining by reason of some motion; and that all Comets, Falling-stars, and the like, are Clouds kindled by motion.

<small>u *Plut. plac. Stob.*</small>
<small>x *Plut. plac.* 2. 18.</small>

(y) That the Sun consists of a collection of little fires made by a humid exhalation, or that it is a (z) fiery Cloud. (a) That the Eclipse of the Sun is caused by extinction, and that there riseth a new Sun in the East. He further avers, that the Sun hath been Eclipsed for a whole Month together.

<small>y *Plut. plac.* 2. 20.</small>
<small>z *Stob. phys.* 1. p. 55.</small>
<small>a *Plut. plac.* 2. 24.</small>

(b) That

(*b*) That the Moon is a close compacted Cloud; *Cicero* (*c*) saith, he held that she is habitable, containing many Cities and Mountains.

(*d*) That the Sun is requisite for the generation of the World and living Creatures, but the Moon of no use thereunto.

(*e*) That there are many Suns and many Moons, according to the several Climates and Zones of the Earth; and that when the Sun goeth sometimes to some part of the Earth unknown to us, he seemeth to be eclipsed; That the Sun goeth forward to infinite, but to us seemeth to move circularly by reason of the great distance.

(*f*) That the Clouds are a vapour drawn up by the Sun to the Heavens.

(*g*) That the Earth was first founded and rooted as it were in an infinite depth.

(*h*) That the Soul is a Spirit, and that there are many things beneath the mind.

(*i*) *Cicero* saith, that he was the only Philosopher that believed there were Gods, and yet denied Divination; but (*k*) *Plutarch* joyns *Epicurus* with him in this Assertion.

b *Plut. plac.* 2. 25.
c *Acad. quæst.* 4.
d *Stob.*
e *Stob. Phys.* 1.
f *Laert.*
g *Plut. plac.* 3. 11.
h *Laert.*
i *de Divinat.* 1.
k *Plac. Phil.* 5. 1.

PARMENIDES.

CHAP. I.

His Life.

Parmenides (*a*) was of *Ela*, son of *Pyrethus*; he heard *Xenophanes*: *Theophrastus*, in his Epitome, saith, that he heard *Anaximander*. But tho' he heard *Xenophanes*, yet he did not follow him. He conversed also with *Aminias*, and with *Diochætes* the Pythagorean, (as *Sotion* saith) a Person indigent, but good and honest, whom he chiefly follow'd, and when he died, built a Temple to him as to an Hero. *Parmenides* being of a noble family, and rich, he was reduced to privacy of life by *Aminias*, not by *Xenophanes*.

He flourished in the 69th Olympiad.

(*b*) *Athenæus* therefore, not without reason, blames *Plato* for supposing him contemporary with *Socrates*.

He is also said to have given Laws to his Countreymen, as *Spusippus* saith in his Book of Philosophers.

He wrote Philosophy in verse, as did also *Hesion*, *Xenophanes*, and *Empedocles*.

But *Callimachus* saith, that he wrote not any Poem.

There was another *Parmenides*, an Orator, who wrote concerning that Art.

a *Laert.*
b *Deipnos.* 11.

CHAP. II.

His Opinions.

HE (*c*) asserted, that Philosophy is twofold, one according to Truth, the other according to Opinion; wherefore he some where saith,

—— *All things I would that thou enquire,*
As well the heart that doth sweet truth pursue,
As mens opinions, whose beliefe's untrue.

That Reason is the Criterie, and that the Senses are not certain; whence he saith,

Trust not thy self into the various way,
Nor thy rash eye, or ear, or tongue obey;
But poise with reason every Argument.

c *Laert.*

That (*d*) the Principle of all things is *one*, and that it is immovable; that One is all, that *Ens* is infinite; whatsoever is besides *Ens*, is *non Ens*, and consequently nothing; but *Ens* is One, therefore, whatsoever is besides One, is nothing; therefore all is One.

(*e*) That hot and cold are the Principles or Elements of things; these he called Fire and Earth; one hath the office of Maker, the other of Matter.

That no things are generated and corrupted, but only seem so to us.

(*f*) That the Moon is of equal brightness with the Sun, yet borroweth her light from him.

(*g*) That the Galaxie is a mixture of dense and rare.

(*h*) He first asserted, that the Earth is round, and seated in the midst; and (*i*) first set out and limited the habitable parts of the Earth, betwixt the cold Zones and the Tropicks.

(*k*) That the Earth is every way equidistant, and evenly poised; so that there is no reason she should incline more to one side than to another; yet is she shaken, but not removed.

(*l*) That men were generated of (*m*) slime, and consist of hot and cold, whereof all things are compounded.

That (contrary to *Empedocles*) men (*n*) were first produced in the Northern parts of the World, those being most dense; the first woman in the Southern, those being most rare. That (*o*) Males now are generated on the right side of the Mother; Females, on the left. (*p*) That the Hegemonick is seated in the breast.

(*q*) *Phavorinus* ascribes to his Invention the Observation, That *Vesper* and *Lucifer* are the same Star; others attribute this to *Pythagoras*.

Phavorinus also saith, (*r*) he used the argument called *Achilles*, by others ascribed to *Zeno*.

d *Arist. Phys.* 1, 2, 3.
e *Laert.*
f *Plut. plac.* 2. 26.
g *Plut. plac.* 3. 1.
h *Laert.*
i *Plut. plac.* 3. 11.
k *Plut. plac.* 3. 15.
l *Laert.*
m *so read.*
n *Plut. plac.* 5. 7.
o *Plut. plac.*
p *Plut. plac.* 4. 5.
q *Laert.*
r *Laert.*

CHAP.

CHAP. III.

Of Idæa's.

But the Assertion for which he became most eminent, was that of *Idæas*, delivered by *Plato* in a Dialogue, which he entit'led *Parmenides*, or *of Idea's* ; the sum whereof is this :

All is One, and Many ; One the *Archetype*, *Idæa* ; Many the Singulars.

There are *Idæa's*, that is, certain common Natures, which include all Singulars, and are the Causes of them, from which they have both their Essence and Name. These are εἰδῆ *Species*, the Many exist, as they participate of One, in these *Species*.

The *Species* so include all Singulars, as that they may combine them, and difference them ; for there is a twofold power of specifick Differences, Compositive and Discretive.

The visible things shew the power of this One ; all Singulars are reduced to a One, that is, to their respective Communities ; and so particular things can neither subsist nor be apprehended, but in this community of *Species* ; therefore the *Species* is one thing, the *Individua* contained in the *Species*, another.

These *Idea's* subsist two ways ; in our Minds, as Notions ; in Nature, as Causes. In our Minds they exist, as they are variously comprehended by us, according to divers manifold respects. In Nature they exist, as they are Idæal forms, and have the power both of existence and denomination. All Beings are reduced to this unity of *Idæa*. Thus are they insensible visible things, and the kinds of them are Similitude, Dissimilitude, Unity, Multitude, Rest, Motion, &c. Things visible are, or are denominated Like, inasmuch as they participate of Similitude, which is the *Idæa* of things Like ; Great or Little, inasmuch as they participate of the *Idæa* of Greatness or Littleness, &c. The like of Man himself, for many Individual Men are such by participation of the *Idæa* of Man, (as if we should say Homineity) which hath a permanent Subsistence, whereas particular Men are in perpetual Fluxion and Mutation.

The same power of the one in *Idæa's*, is also in things comprehended by discourse : they likewise have a Form subsistent by and of it self ; so that to know the nature of Intelligibles, they must be recalled to the unite of *Idæa*. For instance ; if we would understand the nature of Good things, we must proceed in such manner as that we may arrive at the *Idæa* of Good, which is the very Form of Good, whence all things that participate thereof, are, and are called Good. So that there are two distinct things, the Form of things, which subsists of it self, and the Things themselves, sensible or intelligible

Idæa is twofold, αὐτὸ τὸ καλὸν ὅ ἔςι κ̀ τὸ ἀγαθὸν, *the fair, which is also the good,* and all the things which we understand as being *Idæa's* ; The first is God, the second the *Species* of things in the order of Nature.

As concerning the second *Idæa's*, there is a One, that is the foundation of all Singulars ; out of which, as from a Thread, the whole Web (as it were) of *Individuum's* is woven.

One and the same *Species* in many Individuals, which exist separately, is wholly together One, and not separate from it self, but whole in it self.

The Many (that is, Singulars) so participate of their *Idæa's*, in such manner as that the *Idæa's* are not divisible, but preserve their own Essence in themselves, over and above all the Singulars ; that is, they have their Essence in themselves, and not in reference to us.

Idæa's are notions of the Mind, and subsist in our Mind ; yet so, as that primarily, and of themselves, they exist in Nature. So as these Notions subsist no otherwise in our Minds, than as they resemble those eternal Forms of Nature, that is, not as real Beings, but as Similitudes and Images of Beings. So that from these *Idæa's*, which subsist of themselves, as a communication is derived to the Notions that are in our Mind ; for otherwise, if the *Idæa's* themselves, or the whole *Species*, were in our Minds, Notions would not be Notions, and *Ens, non Ens*, forasmuch as the things themselves are variously perceived by several Men.

Besides, there would follow a great confusion and disorder in the things themselves, if there were continually produced new Forms of things at Man's pleasure ; which must needs be, if the Mind of Man could form them, and that whatsoever a Man imagined in his Mind, became immediately a *Species*.

Again, by this means, the most excellent Science of all things, that is in God, would be denied to be in Him, whose Mind is the Original of all things ; so as it were a great absurdity to attribute to Man, a Mind procreative of *Species*, and to deny it to God, who governs all things.

Therefore *Species* have not their dependance on the Mind of Man ; on the contrary, they are unknown to human Nature, or Mankind. The *Genus* and Essence of every thing is of it self, not existing in the Singulars, but the support and foundation of the Singulars.

Moreover, if there were not certain *Species* of things, there would be a great confusion in all Sciences, they being of Universals ; for no Man comprehends in his Mind all Individuals ; it were infinite and full of disorder to take that course ; so that all Philosophy and dissertation would lose the truth and certain knowledge of things : whereas, on the contrary, in all Science, the true course of Learning is to reduce Particulars to their proper *Species*, whence may appear their Nature and Qualities.

Of the Primary Archetypal *Idæa*, the Essential Properties ; and they are these.

First, It is not Many, (that is, it is not intermingled with generated Beings, of which it is the Original ;) for it is void of Parts and Figure, being infinite.

Secondly. It is void of all Motions and Mutation, remaining always immovable and the same.

Thirdly, It is void of all Age and Time, being eternal, neither elder nor younger, nor any way partaking of Time, subject to no circumstances of Time, all things being always present to it.

Fourthly, It partakes not of that Essence by which Singulars are said to be, but communicates the power and faculty of Being to all Singulars, itself

itself being beyond all Essence. Essence is distributed amongst the many of Beings, and is not wanting in any Being whatsoever, neither least nor greatest.

Fifthly, The first *Idea* is so diffused into all things whereto it gives the power and faculty of Being, as that it circumscribes and limits the multiplicity, and almost infinity of Singulars, within the bounds of the *One*: So that the *One*, which of it self is infinite and void of parts, is as it were terminated in Singulars.

Of the secondary *Idæa's* (which are natural Causes, the Works of the primary *Idæa*) the Properties are these.

First, They, as well as the primary *Idæa*, are *One*; for all Singulars comprised within them are determinately reduced to their respective Classes; but in this they differ from the primary *Idæa*, that the *One* in secondary *Idæa's* is truly Finite, having beginning, middle and end.

Secondly, They consist entire in the Singulars, not as deriving their Essence from them, for they exist in the divine mind, yet they are conspicuous in Singulars, as if you would know what is Homeneity, or the *Species* of Man, you must look upon the Singulars of Men, in which the *Species* it self is visible. The secondary *Idæa's* in sensible things are ἐχηματισμέναι, figurate.

Thirdly, The secondary *Idæa's* are *the same* and *another*; the same, in Themselves; another, in the Singulars; and consequently both rest and move: Whereas the primary *Idæa* is void of all mutation, amidst the vicissitudes of transient things.

In the order of nature, the *One* in the *Species* is of it self, and derives not its Essence from Singulars, but is self-subsistent, as being a *Species*; by whose power all the Many (*i.e.* Singulars) subsist.

Fourthly, The others (*i.e.* Singulars) proceed from the *One*; but the One, which is seen in the Others, hath its Essence from a third; that is, Individuals exist by those secondary *Idæa's*, yet so as that the secondary *Idæa's* have from the primary *Idæa* their Essence, and the power by which they give to Singulars a Subsistence.

Fifthly, the secondary *Idæa's* act from contrary Principles, yet so as that those contraries are connected in one tye of similitudes, whence a third thing reflects. To the production of natural things three things concur, two ἄψεις, and the third that ties them together; ἄψεις are Beings mutually touching one another (that is, the natural things themselves.) The third is the Analogy betwixt the other two, the similitude of their proportions. There can be no ἄψεις without two things at the least; nor can they produce any thing without the third, Combination. The ἄψεις must be dissimilar, that *one* and *equal* may be introduced.

Sixthly, The secondary *Idæa's* are not without time, but what they do, they do in time; whereas (as we said) to the primary *Idæa* all things are present. Natural things exist and perish according to time, but their *Species* or *Idæa's* are constant and permanent.

MELISSUS.

CHAP. I.

His Life.

Laert.

MElissus was a *Samian*, Son of *Ithagenes*, he heard *Parmenides*, and conversed also with *Heraclitus*, at what time the *Ephesians* had such a misapprehension of him, as the *Abderites* had of *Democritus*. He was a Person conversant in Civil Affairs, and much honoured by his Countrymen, who made him their Admiral, and particularly admired him for his virtue. He flourish'd, according to *Apollodorus*, about the 84th Olympiad.

His Opinions.

a *Arist. Phys.* 1. 1, 2, 3.

HE asserted (as *Parmenides*) That (*a*) the Principle of things is One, which is immovable; That this One is All; That *Ens* is Infinite; arguing thus, That which is made, hath a Principle, therefore that which is not made hath no Principle: But the Universe, or that which is, is not made, therefore it hath no Principle, and therefore no End; Therefore it is Infinite, therefore One, for there cannot be more Infinites; therefore immovable, for it occupates all things, and hath not any thing whereby it may be moved.

(*b*) That the Universe is infinite and immutable, and immovable, and one like it self, and full. (*c*) He proved that it is immoveable thus; because, if it were moved, there must necessarily be a *Vacuum*, but there is not a *Vacuum* amongst Beings.

(*d*) That there is not Motion, but that it only seems to be; And (*e*) that things are not generated and corrupted, but only seem so to us.

(*f*) As for the Gods, he said, That we ought not to assert any thing concerning them, forasmuch as we have not any knowledge of them.

b *Laert.*
c *Arist. Phys.* 4. 8.
d *Laert.*
e *Arist. de Cæl.* 3. 1.
f *Laert.*

ZENO.

CHAP. I.

His Life.

a Laert.
b The Text seems to require to be thus supplied.

(a) Zeno was of *Elea*; *Apollodorus* faith, he was Son of *Pyrethus*; (b) but *Pyrethus* indeed was father to *Parmenides*. Zeno was by nature Son of *Teleutagoras*; by adoption, Son of *Parmenides*, whom he heard and was much beloved of him. *Plato* faith, he was tall, and calls him the *Eleatick Palamedes*. He was a Person excellent, as well for Philofophy as Politicks; his Writings being full of much Learning.

c Lib. 3. c. 3.

(c) *Valerius Maximus* faith, he forfook his own Country, where he could not enjoy security and freedom, and went to *Agrigentum*, which at that time was oppreffed with miferable fervitude, out of a confidence, that by his own wit and courage, he might deliver the People there from the favage tyranny of the Tyrant *Phalaris*; and perceiving, that he was carried on more by a cuftomary way of rule, than found Counfel, he excited in the young men of the City, a defire to free their Country: which being difcovered to the Tyrant, he called the People together into the *Forum*, and began to torture him feveral ways, demanding of him, Who were privy to the confpiracy, befides himfelf? Zeno would not difclofe them, but names one that was moft in favour with the Tyrant, and reproving the *Agrigentines* for their cowardice and timidity, raifed fuch a fudden courage in them, that they immediately fell upon the Tyrant, and ftoned him to death. Thus not a fuppliant Prayer, nor pitiful Crying out, but the valiant Exhortation of an old Man, ftretch'd upon the Rack, chang'd the minds and fortune of the whole City.

d Laert.

But others relate this after a different manner. (d) *Satyrus* in his Epitome of *Heraclides*, faith, that confpiring againft *Nearchus*, or, as others, *Diomedon*, a Tyrant, he was taken, and being queftion'd concerning the Confpirators, and the Arms he had convey'd into *Lipara*, he named all fuch as were friends to the Tyrant, as privy to the Plot, that thereby he might leave him deftitute of Affiftants; and further, telling him that he had fomething to fpeak in his ear, he bit him by the ear, and would not let go his hold, till they run him thorough, fuffering in the fame manner as *Ariftogiton*, who flew *Hipparchus* the Tyrant of *Athens*. *Demetrius* affirms, he bit off his Nofe; *Antifthenes* relates, that having named all the Tyrant's Friends, and being demanded by him, Whether there were any more? anfwered, Yes, Thou, that art the deftruction of the City. And then turning to the ftanders by, faid, I wonder at your Cowardice, that you can endure to be flaves to a Tyrant, only through fear of fuffering what I now fuffer; which faid, he bit off his Tongue, and fpit it in the Tyrant's Face: whereupon the Citizens unanimoufly fell upon the Tyrant and ftoned him. Thefe relate the ftory after this manner; but *Hermippus* faith, he was bray'd to death in a ftone-Mortar.

Befides his other Virtues, he had a magnanimous contempt of great Perfons, as well as *Heraclides*, and therefore preferred his own Country *Elea*, firft named *Hyela*, a Colony of the *Phoceans*, a little Town, only for that it brought forth honeft Men, before the pride and glory of the *Athenians*, never travelling thither, but living for the moft part at home.

It is reported of him, that being reviled, he appeared much troubled at it, anfwering one that reproved him for it, If I fhould be pleafed with reproaches, I could not delight in praifes.

He flourifhed in the 79th *Olympiad*.

CHAP. II.

His Invention of a Dialectick.

a Adv. Math.
b Hift. Phil.
c In Euclid.

Ariftotle (cited by *Laertius*, and (a) *Sextus Empiricus*) affirms, that Zeno *Eleates* was the Inventer of *Dialectick*, as *Parmenides* of *Rhetorick*; which (b) *Galen* likewife confirms, faying, Zeno *is remembred as Author of the Eriftick Philofophy*. But the names of *Eriftick* or *Dialectick* feem to have been later; for, as (c) *Laertius* defcribes the fucceffion of it, *Euclid* [who was of *Megara*] learning the *Parmenidean Philofophy*, his Difciples were called Megaricks, *afterwards* Eristicks, *laftly* Dialecticks; *which name* Dionyfius the Carthagenian *firft gave them, for that they made differtations by way of Queftion and Anfwer*; that by *the Parmenidean Philofophy*, he means no other than *Dialectick*, may be evinc'd from *Sextus Empiricus*, who alledgeth, that *Parmenides feemeth not to have been ignorant of* Dialecticks, *for that, as* Ariftotle *conceives*, Zeno, *his Difciple, invented it*. Hence perhaps may *Cicero* be explain'd, who, for this reafon feems to include the *Eleatick* Philofophers, under the title of (d) *Megaricks*, who had, faith he, *a noble Difcipline, of which as I find it written, the Prince (or Author) was* Xenophanes *lately mentioned. Then did* Parmenides *and* Zeno *follow him; fo they were named* Eleatick Philofophers, *from thefe. Afterwards* Euclid, *Difciple of* Socrates, *a* Megarean, *from whom the fame were called* Megaricks; *who held, That only to be good, which is one and the fame, and like, and always. Thefe alfo borrowed much from* Plato, *being called, from* Menedemus, Eretriacks, *for that he was an* Eretrian. Thus *Cicero*.

d Acad. 4.

CHAP.

CHAP. III.

His Opinions.

a Aristot. de Zenon.

HE held, (*a*) That it is impossible, that if there be any thing, it can be generated, or made; asserting this of God: For it is necessary, that whatsoever is generated, is generated either of things like, or of things unlike; but neither of these is possible: For a thing like may as well generate its like, as be generated of it, forasmuch as amongst things aqual and alike, all things are in a like respect to one another. But neither can an unlike be generated of a like; for whether a stronger be made of a weaker, or a greater of a lesser, or a worse of a better; or on the contrary, the better be made of the worse, of a *non Ens* will be made something, which can no way be. For this Reason, He asserted God to be Eternal: And if God be that which is the most excellent of all things, it is requisite, saith he, That he be *One*; for if there were two or more, he could by no means be the most excellent of all, forasmuch as every God of them, being like him, would be such as he. Now God, and the power of God is such, as that it governs, but is not governed; it governs all things, so that if there were any thing better than he, he could not be God. If therefore there were many, and of these some were better, others worse, they could not be Gods, for God cannot be inferior, or subjected, or governed. Neither if they were equal, could God be more excellent than all things else; for what is equal must neither be better nor worse than that to which it is equal; therefore if there be a God, and He be such, this God must be Onely One; otherwise, he could not do all things that he would; because, if there were more, the one could not be of absolute power. Now God being one, he further affirms, That he is every way like himself, as to seeing, and hearing, and all other senses; for otherwise, the parts of God would not be most excellent, but exceeded by one another, which is impossible. Now being every way alike, he must be round, for he must not be partly of one fashion, partly of another. Thus being eternal, and one, and round, he is neither finite nor infinite; infinite he is not, for that hath neither middle, nor beginning, nor end, nor any other part, but an *Ens* cannot be such as is a *non Ens*. If there were many, they would bound one another; but *One* is neither like to a *non Ens*, nor to many, for *One* hath nothing whereby it may be bounded. Moreover, God being such an *One*, is neither moved nor immovable, for that which is immovable is *non Ens*. Neither can any thing pass into it, nor it into another. Again, the Things which are moved are more than one; for a Thing must be moved into another; now if that which is not, is not moved, forasmuch as that which is not, is no where; and those things which are moved, must be more than one; hence he affirmeth, That those which are moved are two, or more than one; and that *non Ens* rests, for it is immovable, but *One* neither rests nor moveth, forasmuch as it is neither *non Ens*, nor many. Thus he asserted, That God is Eternal, and One, and Like, and Round; neither Infinite, nor Finite; neither Quiescent, nor Movable.

(*b*) Moreover he asserted, That there are many Worlds; that there is no *Vacuum*; That the Nature of all things consists of Hot and Moist, and Cold and Dry, mutually interchanged; That Man was made of Earth, and his Soul contemperated of those Four, neither of them being predominant.

b Laert.

(*c*) Against Place he argued thus; If every *Ens* be in a Place, there must be a Place of that Place, and so to Infinite.

c Aristot. Phys. 6.

Against Motion, he alledged four Arguments: The first, that Nothing is moved; for whatsoever makes a Progression, must come to the Middle, before it comes to the End. The second is that which is termed *Achilles*, that a slow Thing will never be overtaken by a swift; for the thing which followeth must necessarily come to the place from which that which went before departed, therefore that which went before makes a continual Progression as well as the other. The third, if every thing rests when it is in its just place, and, in every moment, every thing is in its just place, an Arrow flying is immovable. The fourth, that if Things were moved, as for Example, if equal Bulks were moved, one from the Beginning of the Race, another from the Middle, alike swiftly, it would come to pass, that the Half of Time would be equal to the Whole.

LEUCIPPUS.

Laert.

Leucippus was of *Elea*, or, as some say, an *Abderite*, or, as others, a *Melian*: He heard *Zeno*.

His Assertions are thus delivered by *Laertius*; That all things are Infinite, and transmutated into one another; That the Universe is *Vacuum* and Full, (that is, little Bodies, or Atoms.) That the Worlds are made by the falling of these Bodies into the *Vacuum*, and intangling with one another, from which Motion, by Coagmentation of them, the Stars were made. That the Sun is moved in a greater Circle about the Moon. That the Earth is moved about the Centre, and is in figure like a Drum. He first asserted Atoms to be the Principles of all things. This is the Sum of his Doctrine, the Particulars these.

He held, that the Universe, as we said, is Infinite; one part of it is Full, the other Vacuous; these are the Elements of which infinite Worlds are made, and resolve into them. The Worlds were generated after this manner: Out of the Infinite there were carried, by a kind of Abscission (from the rest) into a great *Vacuum* many Bodies of all sorts of Figures, which being crouded up together, caused a Circumgyration, by which means hitting against one another, and rolling about all manner of ways, those which were alike, separated themselves from the rest, and joined with their equal like; but being of equal weight, and not able, by reason of their multitude, to move round; those of them which were rare, leaped forth to the exterior *Vacuum*, the rest stayed together, and entangled themselves by running one within another, and made a first Compound round. This was like a kind of Membrane or skin containing all kinds of Bodies, which Bodies moving round about the middle, the Membrane that enclosed them became more thin, there flowing together continually more Bodies unto those in the middle, and engaging themselves in their motion. By this means was the Earth made, those which went to the middle being setled together. Moreover, the outer Circumference or Membrane, as it were, was continually increased by the accession of new Bodies from without, and, as it turned about, got hold of all that came at it. Some of these, entangling with one another, first made a Humid, and, as it were, a dirty kind of Mass; but being dried in their motion together with the whole, and afterwards enkindled, the Stars were made of them. The outmost is the Orb of the Sun, that of the Moon is next the Earth, the rest are betwixt these; the Stars are kindled or set on fire by the swiftness of their motion, the Sun by the Stars, the Moon borrows a little fire from the Sun. The Sun and Moon happen to be eclipsed, by reason that the Earth inclines towards the South; the Northern Parts are continually oppress'd with Snow and Frost; the Sun is seldome eclipsed, the Moon continually, because their Orbs are not equal. In the same manner as the World was made, it increased, will diminish, and perish, by a certain kind of necessity. Hitherto *Laertius*. What is more to be said of his Opinions, we shall insert amongst those of *Democritus*, who borrowed most of them

DEMOCRITUS.

THE HISTORY of PHILOSOPHY.

DEMOCRITVS.

CHAP. I.

His Country, Parents, Brethren, Time.

^a *Laert.* Democritus (*a*) is by some supposed to have been a *Milesian*; but the more general Opi-
^b *Laert.* nion is, that (*b*) he was of *Abdera* a Town of *Thrace*, noted for the (*c*) simplicity of the Inha- ^c *Cic.*
bitants, which grew even to a Proverb. He was ^d *Abderit*
of a Noble Family (*d*), being descended from the *Ep. ad*
Brother *Hippocr.*

Brother of *Hercules*. His Father is by (a) some called *Hegesistratus* ; by others *Athenocritus* ; by others (b) *Damasippus*. *Democritus* was the youngest of three Sons ; the other two, (o) *Herodotus* and *Damasus*, or (as (d) *Suidas*) *Damastees*.

(e) *Democritus* was born (according to *Apollodorus in his Chronology*) in the 80th. *Olympiad*; which is confirmed by what (f) he saith of himself in his little *Diacosmus*, that he was young when *Anaxagoras* was old, being forty Years younger than he. *Anaxagoras* was born in the first year of the 70th. Olympiad ; the 40th. year after it, exclusively, falleth upon the first of the 80th. Olympiad, *Thrasyllus* therefore is not to be followed, (g) who *affirms, he was born in the third year of the 77th. Olympiad, being a year elder than* Socrates.

(h) *Pliny* and (i) *Agellius* affirm he flourished chiefly in the time of the *Peloponnesian* War ; *Pliny* saith, after the building of *Rome* 300 years ; *Agellius*, 323 years ; by which it appears that he was contemporary, as *Agellius* adds, *with Socrates*, and perhaps (as *Laertius*) with *Achelaus the Disciple of* Socrates, *and with* Oenipodes, *for he mentions him, as likewise the opinion of* Zeno *and* Parmenides *concerning* One, *as Persons most eminent in his time, and* Protagoras *the* Abderite, *whom all acknowledge* (saith he) *to have been in the time of* Socrates. That he is said to have written his little *Diacosmus* 730 years after the taking of *Troy*, agrees with this accompt. For, according to *Eratosthenes*, from the taking of *Troy* to the first Olympiad are 407 years, to which add 323. years (to make up 730.) and it falls upon the 84th. Olympiad.

CHAP. II.

His first Education and Masters.

DEmocritus , (saith (k) *Valerius Maximus*) may well be reckoned amongst the rich, for his Father was able to entertain the Army of Xerxes. *Laertius* adds, from the testimony of *Herodotus*, that the King in requital left with him some Magi and *Chaldæans*, referring perhaps to (l) *that Text of* Herodotus, *where he relates, that* Xerxes, *in his return to* Asia, *came to* Abdera, *and was entertained by the* Abderites, *and bestowed on them a golden Scimiter, and the Tiara imbroidered with Gold; and, as the People there affirm, this was the first place where he untied his zone, since he fled from* Athens (which I believe not) *so great was his fear.* Abdera *is nearer to the* Hellespont *than the Bay of* Strymon, *so that he took Shipping from hence.* Thus *Herodotus*. From these *Magi* and *Caldæans*, *Democritus* first received Learning, (m) of whom, whilst yet a Boy, he learnt Theology and *Astronomy*.

(n) He next applied himself to *Leucippus*. (o) Some *affirm, he was Disciple also to* Anaxagoras ; but *Phavorinus, in his various History, relates, that* Democritus *said of* Anaxagoras, *that those opinions which he delivered concerning the Sun and Moon, were not his, but more Ancient, and that he stole them. He likewise undervalued his Assertions concerning the Fabrick of the Universe, and the Mind ; How then* (saith *Phavorinus*) *was he, as some hold, his Disciple ?*

No less doubted is the report of his going to *Athens*, where (p) *Valerius Maximus* saith, he dwelt many years, making use of every moment of time, towards the perception and exercise of Learning. He lived unknown in that City, as he himself attests in one of his Books. *Laertius* adds, *he kept himself undiscover'd, out of a contempt of Glory ; and knew* Socrates, *but was not known to him ; whereupon he said of himself,* " I went to Athens, and " no man knew me. If the *Rivals* (saith *Thrasyllus*) *be a genuine Dialogue of* Plato, *this is the Anonymous Person there, who, besides the two who were busied concerning* Oenipodes *and* Anaxagoras, *discourseth concerning Philosophy with* Socrates, (q) *to whom he said that a Philosopher resembles a Pentathlus*, (a Person skilful in five exercises) *and indeed he was,* (continues* Thrasyllus) *a Pentathlus in Philosophy, for he was skilful in Physick, Ethick, Mathematick, the liberal Sciences, and all Arts.* But *Demetrius Phalereus, in his Apology for* Socrates, *saith, he never went to* Athens ; *and this* (saith Laertius) *is far greater, that he could despise so eminent a City, desiring rather to give honour to a place, than to receive it from a place.*

More certain it is, that he heard some *Pythagorean* Philosopher. (r) *Thrasyllus affirms, that he imitated the* Pythagoreans, *and mention'd even* Pythagoras *himself, admiring him in a Treatise bearing his Name. He seems to have taken all from him, and might be thought to have heard him, but that the times agree not.* But *Glaucus of Rhegium, who lived at the same time, affirms, he heard one of the* Pythagoreans. *Apollodorus of Cyzicus conceives him to have been contemporary with* Philolaus. (s) *Duris, that he heard* Arimnæstus, *Son of* Pythagoras.

So studious was he even from his youth, that (t) *Demetrius* affirms , " he retir'd to a little " Summer-house belonging to the Orchard, and " shut himself up ; and on a time his Father " bringing thither an Ox to be sacrific'd, and " tying it there, he knew nothing of it a good " while, until his Father roused him up, and told " him the Business concerning the Ox.

CHAP. III.

His Travels.

HIs Father dying, the three Brothers divided the Estate. (u) *Democritus*, *the youngest, made choice of that part which consisted in Money, as being, though the least share, yet the most convenient for Travel. And notwithstanding it was the least, yet were they jealous of him, as if he had an intention to defraud them.* Demetrius *affirms, his Portion amounted to an hundred Talents, and that he spent it all, not gave it* (as *Valerius Maximus* relates) *to his Country.* Hence is it that *Cicero* saith, he neglected his Patrimony, left his Fields untilled, seeking nothing else but a happy Life.

(x) *Laertius* (citing *Demetrius*, and *Antisthenes*) relates, that *he travelled to* Egypt *to the Priests, to learn Geometry, to* Persia *to the Chaldæans, and went to the* Red-Sea ; *some affirm, he conversed with the* Gymnosophists *in* India, *and travell'd to* Æthiopia, *and* (y) *learnt the several Wisdoms of each of these Nations:* (z) With the *Ægyptians* he lived (as he himself affirms) 80 years.

For

PART XI. DEMOCRITUS. 455

a Lib. 4. c. 20.

For these things (saith (a) Ælian) Theophrastus commends him, because by his Travels he collected better things than either Menelaus or Achilles; for they went up and down no otherwise than like Phenæcian Merchants; they gathered money, and that was the occasion of their Travels by Sea and Land. Not without reason therefore was it,

b Clem. Strom.

that he said of himself, (b) Of any Man in my time, I have been the greatest Traveller, and made the furthest Enquiries, and seen most variety of Air and Earth, and heard the most Learned Persons; and in making Demonstrations by Lines, none yet have gone beyond me, no not those Ægyptians, who are called Arpedonaptæ.

CHAP. IV.

How he lived at Abder, after his return from Travel, and governed there.

Laertius saith, that *at his return from Travel he was in a very mean condition, having spent all his Estate; whereupon his Brother Damasus (in regard of his indigence) received him kindly, and maintain'd him. But after that he had foretold some things, which fell out accordingly, people from thenceforward, honour'd him as a God: moreover, there being a Law, that whosoever had consumed his patrimony, should not be allow'd burial in his own Country:* Antisthenes *relates, that to prevent being liable to some envious Persons and Sycophants, he read to the people his Book entituled the great* Diacosmus, *which was the most excellent of all his Writings, and for it was rewarded with 500 Talents; and not only so, but with brazen Statues also.* Hitherto Laertius.

a Lib. 18. Cap. 27.

Of these Predictions, (a) Pliny gives two instances. *It is reported,* saith he, *that Democritus, who first understood and demonstrated the correspondence betwixt Heaven and Earth, the most wealthy of the Citizens despising this his pains, foreseeing a future dearth of Olives, from the future rising of Pleiades, (after the same manner as we have mentioned, and shall declare more fully hereafter) with extraordinary profit, by reason of the expectation of Olives, bought up all the Olives in that Country, to the admiration of all those, who knew he chiefly affected Poverty, and the quiet of Learning. But assoon as the reason appeared, together with the great gain of money, he restor'd the Bargain to the anxious and greedy repentance of the Owners, contenting himself to have thus proved, that he could easily be Rich, whensoever he pleased.*

b Plin. 18. 35.

The other is this: (b) *His Brother Damasus being employ'd about Reaping in an extraordinary hot day, he desired him to let the rest of the Corn alone, and to Cock that which was already Reaped as fast as he could: within few hours, a terrible*

c Strom. 6. pag. 631. d.

Tempest ratifi'd his Prediction. (c) Clemens adds, *that he foretold it by some Stars; and that they, giving credit to him, cock'd their Crop, for, it being*

d Reading ἐν ᾧ ἄλλω οὐ κεῖτι ἦτα.

Summer, (d) *it was not yet Inned in the Barn; but the rest lost theirs by the great and unexpected Rain.*

(e) *By these (and the like) Predictions, he gained so great esteem amongst the People, that from*

e Laert.

thenceforward they honoured him as a God; Clemens saith, they called him σοφία, *Wisdom;* Ælian, *Philosophy;* as Protagoras *was termed* Logos,

f Suid.

Discourse. (f) *So much indeed was he reverenc'd*

for his extraordinary Wisdom, that they conferred the Supream Government of Abdera *upon him.*

CHAP. V.

His Retirement.

But being naturally more inclined to contemplation, than delighted with publick honours and employments, he withdrew himself from them, and (a) "endeavoured, as Antisthenes "relates, to make several Tryals of Phantasies "(meaning the impressions of things appearing to "the Phantasy, not the Phantasy it self) "often "living alone, and in Sepulchres. (b) Lucian adds, "that shutting himself up in a Tomb with-"out the Gates of the City, he continued there "writing and composing Night and Day: And "that some young Men intending to deride and "fright him, attired themselves like Ghosts, in "black Garments, with Vizards like Deaths-"heads, and came about him dancing and skip-"ping, whereat he was nothing moved, nor "would so much as look on them, but continu-"ed to write; Leave fooling, saith he; So firm-"ly, did he believe, that Souls are nothing after "they are out of the Bodies.

a Laert.

b Φιλοψευδῆ.

Such places he made choice of, as were most conducing to contemplation, by reason of their Solitude and Darkness. And (c) Agellius reports, "out of the Monuments of the Greek History "now not extant, that for the same reason he "put out his own Eyes, because he conceived "the cogitations and meditations of his Mind, "in contemplating the reasons of Nature, would "be more vigorous and exact, if free from the "allurements of Sight, and impediments of the "Eyes: which act, together with the manner "whereby he easily procured Blindness, by a most "subtle ingeniousness, Laberius described; feign-"ing another cause of his voluntary Blindness, "converting it to his own purpose.

c Lib.

Democritus, the *Abderite*, well skill'd
In natural Philosophy, a Shield
Plac'd to *Hyperion*'s rising opposite, (sight;
And with the Sun's beams thus put out his
That bad and impious Men he might not see,
Triumphant in their full prosperity.

The former Reason given by *Agellius* (that he might study Philosophy the better) is alledged also by (d) Cicero, Plutarch, and others. "For though, saith Cicero, having lost his Eyes "he could not discern Black and White, yet could "he Good and Ill, Just and Unjust, Honest and "Dishonest, Profitable and Unprofitable, Great "and Little; he might live happy without the "variety of Colours, but he could not without "the knowledge of things. Thus he concei-"ved, that the acuteness of the mind was ob-"structed by the sight of the Eyes. (e) Ter-"tullian alledgeth another Reason, because he could "not look on Women without inordinate desires. But Cicero (f) elsewhere speaks doubtfully concerning the truth of the thing it self; and not without reason, since the contrary appears manifest by this following Narration.

d Tusc. quæst. 5.

e Apolog. adv. gent.

f De finib. 5.

CHAP.

CHAP. VI.

His Communication with Hippocrates.

(a) *Epist. Græc.*

Democritus (a) thus neglecting all outward things, living Day and Night privately in Caves and solitary places, the *Abderites* imagined that he was melancholy even to Madness; which suspicion was confirmed by his continual Laughing upon all occasions whatsoever. Hereupon they sent *Amelesagoras*, one of the chief Persons of their City to *Hippocrates*, that most eminent Physitian who lived at *Cos*, with this Epistle.

The Senate and People of Abdera *to* Hippocrates, *Health.*

Our City, *Hippocrates*, is in very great danger, together with that Person, who, we hoped, would ever have been a great Ornament to it. But now, O the Gods! it is much to be feared, that we shall only be capable of envying others, since he, through extraordinary Learning and Study, by which he gained it, is fallen sick, so as it is much to be feared, that if *Democritus* become mad, our City *Abdera* will become desolate; for, wholly forgetting himself, watching Day and Night, laughing at all things Little and Great, and esteeming them as nothing, he after this manner leadeth his whole Life. One marries a Wife; another Trades; another Pleads; another performs the Office of Magistrate; goeth on Embassy, is chosen Officer by the People, is put down, falls sick, is wounded, dies; he laughs at all these, beholding some to look discontented, others pleas'd. Moreover, he enquireth what is done in the Infernal places, and writes of them, and affirms the Air to be full of Images, and that he understands the Language of Birds, and often rising in the Night singeth to himself, and saith, That he sometimes travels into the Infinity of Things, and that there are innumerable *Democritus*'s like him; thus, together with his Mind, he destroyeth his Body. These are the Things which we fear, *Hippocrates*; These are those which trouble us. Come therefore quickly, and preserve us by your Advice; And despise us not, for we are not inconsiderable; And if you restore him, you shall not fail either of Money or Fame: and though you prefer Learning before Wealth, yet accept of the latter, which shall be offered to you in great abundance.

To restore *Democritus* to health, if our City were all of Gold, we would give it; We think our Laws, *Hippocrates*, are sick; Come then, Best of Men, and cure a most excellent Person; Thou wilt not come as a Physitian, but as a Founder of all *Ionia*, to encompass us with a sacred Wall. Thou wilt cure not a Man, but a City, a languishing Senate, and prevent its Dissolution, thus becoming our Lawgiver, Judge, Magistrate, and Preserver. To this purpose we expect thee, *Hippocrates*; all these (if you come) you will be to us. It is not a single obscure City, but all *Greece*, which beseecheth thee to preserve the Body of Wisdom. Imagine that Learning Her self comes on this Embassy to Thee, begging, that Thou wilt free Her from this danger. Wisdom certainly is nearly allied to every one, but especially to us who dwell so near Her. Know for certain, that the next Age will own it self much obliged to Thee, if thou desert not *Democritus*, for the Truth which he is capable of communicating to all. Thou art allied to *Æsculapius* by thy Family, and by thy Art; he is descended from the Brother of *Hercules*, from whom came *Abderus*, whose name, as you have heard, our City bears; wherefore even to him will the cure of *Democritus* be acceptable. Since therefore, *Hippocrates*, you see a whole People, and a most excellent Person falling into Madness, hasten we beseech you to us. It is strange, that the exuberance of Good should become a Disease; *Democritus*, by how much he excelled others in acuteness of Wisdom, is now in so much the more danger of falling mad, whilst the ordinary unlearned People of *Abdera* enjoy their Wits as formerly; and even they, who before were esteemed foolish, are now most capable to discern the indisposition of the wisest Person. Come therefore, and bring along with you *Æsculapius*, and *Epione*, the Daughter of *Hercules*, and her Children, who went in the Expedition against *Troy*; bring with you the Receipts and Remedies against Sickness; the Earth plentifully affords Fruits, Roots, Herbs, and Flowers to cure Madness, and never more happily than now, for the recovery of *Democritus*. Farewel.

Hippocrates returned this Answer.

Hippocrates *to the Senate of* Abdera, *Health.*

Your Countryman, *Amelesagoras* arrived at *Cos* the same day on which with us was Celebrated the Susception of the Rod, which, as you know, is an annual Convention, and great Solemnity amongst us, held at a Cypress Tree, which are born by those who are particularly consecrated to the God.

But finding both by the Words and Countenance of *Amelesagoras*, that your Business required much haste, I read your Letter, and much wondred to find your City no less troubled for one Man, than if the whole City were but one Man. Happy indeed are the People who know, that wise Men are their Defence; not Walls or Bulwarks, but the sound Judgments of wise Persons. I conceive, that Arts are the dispensations of the Gods; Men the works of Nature: and be not angry, ye Men of *Abdera*, if I conceive, that it is not you, but Nature her self which calls me to preserve her work, which is in danger of failing.

Wherefore, obeying that which is the invitation of Nature and of the Gods, rather than yours, I shall make haste to cure the Sickness of *Democritus*, if it be a Sickness, and not, as I hope, an Error in you. And it would be yet a greater Testimony of your Good will, if you were troubled only upon suspition. Neither Nature nor the Gods have promised me any thing for my coming, and therefore (Men of *Abdera*) do not you force any thing upon me, but suffer the works of a free Art to be free. They who take Rewards compel Sciences to servitude, and make them Slaves, bereaving them of their former freedom. Besides, it is impossible that such may dissemble, in a great disease, and deny in a little; and when they have promised, not come; and come, when they are not sent for. Miserable indeed is Human Life, for that the unsatiate desire of Wealth continually invades it, as a Winter-Wind. I wish that all Physicians would rather joyn together to cure it of this Disease, which is worse than Madness, notwithstanding it is thought happy, but indeed a pestilential Sickness. All distempers of the Mind, are, as I conceive, High-madness, for they stir up in the Reason strange Opinions and Fantasies, which Reason must be purifi'd and cur'd by Vertue. As for me, if at all I made it my design to be Rich, I would not, ye men of *Abdera*, come to you for ten Talents, but would rather have gone to the great King of *Persia*, where there are vast Cities full of all kind of wealth, there I would have practis'd Physick. But I refused to cure a Nation which are Enemies to *Greece*, and, to the best of my power, have my self opposed the *Barbarians*. I thought it a dishonour to accept of the wealth of a King, Foe to our Country, by which means I might become a destroyer of *Greece*. To get Wealth by all means, is not to be Rich; the Rites of Vertue are sacred and just. Do you not think it an equal offence to cure our Enemies, as to take Money for the cure of our Friends? But this is not my Custom; I raise not Gain out of Sickness; nor did wish, when I heard that *Democritus* was Mad, that it might prove so indeed; if he be Well, he is a Friend; if he happen to be cured of his Sickness, more a Friend. I understand that *Democritus* is a person of firm and settled parts, the Ornament of your City.

In order to this Voyage, he sent to his Friend *Dionysius*, that he would take care of his Family in his absence; to *Damagetus*, that he would provide a Ship for him; to *Cratevas*, that he would furnish him with Simples. The day before he arrived at *Abdera*, he dreamt that *Æsculapius* appear'd to him, and told him, that he would have no need of his assistance, but only of the direction of a woman, whom he brought along with him; and having presented her to him, departed. The Woman promised, that she would meet him on the morrow at *Democritus*'s house; he asked her Name, she told him she was called *Truth*; and, pointing to another Woman that followed her, added, that her Name was *Opinion*, and that she lived with the *Abderites*. This was the Dream of *Hippocrates*. How he was received the next day at *Abdera*, he gives this account to his Friend *Damagetus*.

To *Damagetus*, Health.

It was, as I conjectur'd, *Damagetus*: *Democritus*, is not mad, but is extraordinary Wise, and hath taught us Wisdom, and by us all men. I have sent back, with many thanks, the *Æsculapian* Ship, on the Prow whereof, to the Picture of the *Sun*, may be added *Health*, for we made a quick Voyage, and arrived the same day that I had sent word I would be there at *Abdera*. I found all the people flocking together at the Gate, in expectation, as it should seem, of our coming; not only the Men, but the Women, the Old, the Young; and by *Jove*, the very Children; so much were they troubled at the Madness of *Democritus*, who, at that time, was seriously employ'd in Philosophy. As soon as they saw me, they seemed a little to be comforted, and to have some hope. *Philopœmen* offer'd to conduct me to my Lodging, as all of them likewise desired; but I told them, "Men of *Abdera*, I "will do nothing till I have seen *Democritus*; which as soon as they heard, they applauded and rejoyc'd, and brought me immediately along the *Forum*; some following, others running before, crying out, Great King *Jupiter*, help, heal; I advised them to be of comfort, for that it being the season of the *Etesian* Winds, I was confident that there was not any Sickness that would continue long; and in saying thus, on I went. The House was not far, nor indeed the City; we went to it, it being next the Walls, whither they brought me quietly. Behind the Tower there was a high Hill, very full of tall Poplars, from whence we beheld the habitation of *Democritus*. *Democritus* himself sat under a thick, but low, Plaine-Tree, in a thick Gown, all alone, squalid, upon a seat of Stone, wan and lean, with a long Beard, at his right hand ran a little Brook down the Hill, upon the Hill there was a Temple consecrated, as it should seem, to the Muses, encompassed round about with Vines, which grew there naturally. He sat very composedly, having a Book upon his knees, and round about him lay other Books, and the Bodies of many living Creatures dissected. Sometimes he wrote hastily, sometimes paused, seeming to revolve things within himself. Soon after he rose up and walked, and looked intently into the dissected Creatures; then laid down again, and return'd to his seat. The *Abderites*, standing about me, and hardly refraining from Tears, said, "You see, *Hippocrates*, "the life of *Democritus*, how mad he is, and "knoweth not either what he would have, or "what he doth. One of them, that would have given me a farther description of his Madness, on the sudden fell a sobbing, and howled like a Woman at the death of her son, and then began to lament like a Traveller robb'd of his Goods: which *Democritus* hearing, sometimes smiled, sometimes laughed, not writing any longer, but often shaking his head. "Men of "*Abdera*, (said I) stay you here, whilst I go "nigher to him, that by hearing him speak, and "observing his Constitution, I may judge the "truth of his Distemper; and in so saying, I went gently down: the place was very steep, so that I could hardly keep my self from falling. At such time as I came nigh him, it hapned; that he was writing something as in a Rapture, earnestly; whereupon I made a stand, waiting when he would give over. It was not long ere he did so; and seeing me coming towards him, said, "Hail, Stranger; I answer'd, "Hail also, "*Democritus*, the Wisest of Men. He, as I imagine, a little troubled that he had not saluted me by Name, reply'd, "What may I call "you? for my Ignorance of your Name is the "Reason that I styled you, Stranger. "My "Name, said I, is *Hippocrates*, a Physitian. "You are, reply'd he, the glory of the *Æscula-*
"*pian*,

"pians, the fame of whose Worth, and know-
"lege in Physick, is arrived as far as to me. What
"Business hath brought you hither? but first sit
"down. This seat you see, is pleasant, green,
"and soft, better than high Thrones, which are
"subject to the envy of Fortune. Assoon as I
"was set, Is it a publick or private business, *saith
"he*, which brought you hither? Tell me free-
"ly, and we shall to our utmost power assist you.
"I answered, It is for your sake that I come hi-
"ther, to be acquainted with you, a wise Per-
"son, the occasion being afforded me by an Em-
"bassy from your Country. He reply'd, Then
"let my House entertain you.

Having thus made Trial of him several ways,
and not finding any thing of madness in him,
"You know, *said I, Philopœmen*, one of this
"Town. Exceeding well, *answer'd he*; you
"mean the Son of *Damon*? He lives near the
"*Hermæan* Fountain. The same, *repli'd I*; he
"hath been my old Aquaintance, and received
"me for his Guest. But you, *Democritus*, I in-
"treat to afford me a better entertainment, and
"first tell me, What it is that you are writing?
"*He after a little pause answer'd*, Concerning
"Madness. Good *Jupiter*, said I, you write
"seasonably against the City! What City, *Hip-
"pocrates, answer'd he*? I replied, that I only
"spoke at random. But what is this that you
"write of Madness? What else, said he, but,
"What it is, and how it comes to be ingendred
"in Man, and How it may be cured. These
"Creatures which you behold, I have dissected
"for that end; not as *hating* the Works of the
"Gods, but to make inquiry into the nature and
"seat of Choler; for you know, that where
"this abounds too much, it most commonly cau-
"seth Madness in Men. It is in every Nature,
"but in some less, in others more; its excess
"causeth diseases, as being a matter partly
"good, partly bad. By Jove, said I, *Democritus*,
"you speak truly and wisely; and I judge you
"happy, who can enjoy such quiet, as I can-
"not partake of. And why cannot you, *saith
"he*? I answer'd, because either Travel, or
"Children, or Estate, or Sicknesses, or Deaths,
"or Servants, or Marriages, or the like, inter-
"cept my leisure.

Hereupon he fell into his usual passion, and
laughed a while exceedingly, giving over discourse. "Why, *said I, Democritus*, do you
"laugh? Whether is it, that I have spoken well
"or ill? Hereat he laughed more than before,
which the *Abderites*, who stood aloof off, seeing,
some beat their own Heads, others their Fore-
heads, others tore their Hair; for as they afterwards said, they observed him to laugh at that
time more than ever he had done. "*Democri-
"tus*, Thou best of wise men, *continued I*, I de-
"sire to know the reason of this Passion, where-
"in that which I said seems ridiculous? That if
"it proves such, I may reform it, but if other-
"wise, that you may desist from this unseaso-
"nable Laughter. By *Hercules*, said he, if you
"can convince me, *Hippocrates*, you will per-
"form a Cure greater than any you have yet
"done. And why, *said I*, should you not be
"convinced? Know you not, that you do ab-
"surdly in laughing at the Death of a Man, or
"at Sickness, or Madness, or Murther, or any

"thing that is worse than these; and on the
"other side at Marriages, at Assemblies, at the
"Birth of Infants, at Solemn Rites, at Magi-
"stracies, at Honours, and generally at every
"thing that hath the Name of Good? At those
"things which deserve to be pitied, you laugh;
"and at those things for which we should re-
"joyce, you laugh also; insomuch that you
"seem not to put any difference betwixt Good
"and Bad. *Then he*, You say well, *Hippocrates*,
"but you are not acquainted with the reason of
"my Laughing, which as soon as you know, I
"am confident, you will prefer it before the
"Cause for which you came hither, and carry
"it along with you as a Medicine to your Coun-
"try, thereby improving both your self and
"others: and in requital of it, perhaps will
"think your self obliged to teach me Physick,
"when you shall understand what pains all
"Men take for things that deserve not pains,
"but are of no value, and consume their Lives
"unprofitably in pursuit of things that deserve
"only to be laugh'd at. What, *said I*, Is all
"the World sick, and knows it not? If so, they
"can send no whither for help; for what is
"beyond it? *He repli'd*, There are infinite
"Worlds, O *Hippocrates*! Have not so mean an
"esteem of the Riches of Nature. Teach me
"this, *said I, Democritus*, at some other time;
"for I am afraid, that if you begin to talk of
"this Infinity, you will fall again into your Fit
"of Laughter; but now, tell me the Reason,
"why you Laugh at the accidents of Life.

Then, looking stedfastly upon me, "You
"think, *saith he*, there are two things, which
"occasion my Laughter, Good and Ill, where-
"as indeed I laugh but at one thing, Man, full
"of Folly, destitute of right Actions, playing
"the Child in all his Designs, undergoing great
"Toils for no Benefit, travelling to the ends of
"the Earth, and sounding bottomless Depths,
"to get Silver and Gold, never ceasing to hoard
"them up, and with their store increasing his
"own Troubles, lest, if he should want them,
"he might be thought not happy. He digs in-
"to the Bowels of the Earth, by the hands of
"Slaves, whereof some are buried by the Earth
"falling upon them, others dwell there, as if it
"were their Native Soil, searching for Gold and
"Silver, sifting one Sand from another, cut-
"ting and tearing their Mother-Earth, which
"they both admire and tread on. How ridi-
"culous is this, that they should love that part
"of the Earth that lies hid, and contemn that
"which lieth open unto them? Some buy Dogs,
"others Horses; some delight in having large
"Possessions, which they may call their own,
"and would command many others, when they
"are not able to command themselves. They
"marry Wives, and in a short time put them
"away; they love, and then hate; they take
"delight in their Children, and when they are
"grown up, disinherit them; They War, and
"despise Quiet; they conspire against Kings;
"they murther Men; they dig the Earth to
"find Silver; with the Silver, which they have
"found, they buy Land; what the Land which
"they have bought yields, of Corn, or Fruits,
"they sell, and receive Silver again. To what
"changes and mischances are they subject?
"When

"When they have not Riches, they desire them; when they have, they hide or scatter them; I laugh at their ill-designed Actions, I laugh at their Misfortunes. They violate the Laws of Truth, by Contention and Enmity with one another; Brethren, Parents, and Countrymen, fight and kill one another for those Possessions, of which, after Death, none of them can be Masters. They pursue an unjust course of Life; they despise the poverty of Their Friends and Country; Mean and Inanimate things they account for Riches; they will part with a whole Estate to purchase Statues, because the Statues seem to speak, but those who speak indeed they hate. They affect things hard to be got; they, who dwell in the Continent, covet the things of the Sea; they who dwell in the Islands, the things of the Continent, perverting all things to their own depraved desires. In War they praise Valour, whilst they are daily subdued by Luxury, Avarice, and all Passions, and in the course of his Life every man is a *Thersites*. Why did you, *Hippocrates*, reprove my Laughter? No Man laughs at his own Madness, but at the Madness of another. They who think themselves to be Sober, laugh at those who seem to them to be Drunk; some laugh at Lovers, whilst they themselves are sick of a worse distemper; some, at those who travel by Sea; others, at those who follow Husbandry, for they agree not with one another, neither in Arts nor Actions. All this, *said I, Democritus*, is true, neither is there any Argument that may better prove the unhappy Estate of Man: but these Actions are prescribed by Necessity, by reason of the government of Families, the building of Ships, and other civil Offices, wherein a Man must necessarily be employ'd, for Nature did not produce him to the end he might rest Idle. Again, Height of Ambition causeth many Men to go astray, who aim at all things, as if there were nothing amiss in them, not being able to foresee the darkness that attends them. For, *Democritus*, what Man is there, that when he marries, thinks of Divorce or Death? Who is there, that whilst he bringeth up his Children, thinketh of losing them? The like in Husbandry, Navigation, Dominon, and all other Offices of Life. No Man foresees that it may go amiss with him, but every one flatters himself with hopes of good success, and does not look upon the worst. Why therefore is this ridiculous?

Democritus replied, "You are yet far from understanding me, *Hippocrates*, neither perceive, through want of knowledge, the bounds of Indisturbance and Perturbation. For if they did order these things prudently, they might be easily discharged of them, and evade my Laughter; whereas now they are blind as to the Offices of Life, and, with Minds void of reason, are carried on by inordinate Appetites. It were enough to make them wise, if they would but consider the mutability of all things, how they wheel about continually, and are suddenly changed; whereas they looking upon these, as if they were firm and setled, fall into many inconveniencies and troubles, and coveting things harmful, they tumble headlong into many Miseries. But if a Man would rightly consider and weigh in his mind all things that he attempts, understanding himself and his own Abilities, he would not let his desires run to Infinite, but follow Nature, out of whose store all are plentifully nourished and supplied. As a fat Body is in greatest danger of sickness, so an high Estate is in greatest danger of falling; great minds are known in Extremities. Some there are, who, taking no warning at that which hapneth to others, perish by their own ill Actions, minding things Manifest no more than as if they were not Manifest, whereas yet they have a large Precedent by which to guide their Life, of things done and not done, by which we ought to foresee the future. This is the occasion of my Laughter, Foolish Men punished by their own Wickedness, Covetousness, Lust, Enmity, Treachery, Conspiracy, Envy. It is a hard thing to give a name to many of these Ills, they being innumerable, and practised so closely. Their Behaviour, as to Virtue, is yet worse; they affect Lies, they follow Pleasure, disobeying the Laws; my Laughter condemns their Inconsiderateness, who neither see nor hear, whereas the Sence of Man only, of all others, is able to foresee Futures. They hate all Things, and then again apply themselves to them; they condemn Navigation, and then they put to Sea; condemn Husbandry, and then fall a Ploughing; they put away their Wives, and then marry others; they bury their Children, and beget more, and bring them up; they wish to live long, and when old Age comes, are grieved at it; never remaining constant in any Estate whatsoever. Kings and Princes commend a private Life; private Persons, a publick; he that ruleth a State, praiseth the Tradesman's life, as free from danger; the Tradesman his, as full of Honour and Power. For they regard not the direct, sincere and smooth way of Virtue, in which none of them will endure to walk; but they take crooked and rough Paths, some falling down, others running themselves out of breath to overtake others. Some are guided by incontinence to the Beds of their Neighbours; others are Sick of a Consumption through unsatiate Avarice; some by Ambition carried up into the Air, and by their own wickedness thrown down headlong. They pluck down, and then they build; they do good, and oblige others, and then, repenting of it, break the laws of Friendship, and do wrong, and fall at enmity, and fight with their nearest Relations; of all which, Avarice is the cause. Wherein do they differ from Children that play, whose Minds, being void of Judgment, are pleased with every thing they light on? In their Desires they differ not much from brute Beasts, only the Beasts are contented with that which is enough. What Lyon is there, that hides Gold under ground? What Bull fights for more than he needs? What Leopard is unsatiately greedy? The Wolf, when he hath devoured as much as "serves for his necessary nourishment, gives over. But whole Nights and Days, put together, are not enough for Men to feast and riot. All brute Beasts have their yearly set-times of Coition, and then leave; but Man is continually transported with Lust. How can I, *Hippocrates*, but laugh at him that laments the loss of his Goods? And especially, if without regard to Dangers, he travels over Precipices, and on the Sea; how can I forbear to laugh exceedingly? Shall I not laugh at him, who drowns a Ship by lading it with rich Marchandize, and then blames the Sea for drowning it? If I seem wrongfully to laugh at these, there is at least in them something that deserves to be lamented. These stand not in need of the Physick or Medicines of your Predecessors *Æsculapius*, who, preserving Men, was himself requited with Thunder. Do you not see, that I also am partly guilty of Madness, who, to enquire into the causes of Madness, dissect these several living Creatures, whereas indeed I ought to search for it in Man himself? Do you not see, that the whole World is full of Inhumanity, stuffed as it were with infinite hatred against Man himself? All Man is from his very Birth a disease: when first born he is useless, and sues for relief from others; when he grows up, foolish, wanting Instruction; at full growth, wicked; in his decaying Age, miserable, toyling throughout all his time imprudently; such is he from the Womb. Some being of furious angry dispositions, are continually engaged in Broyls, others in Adulteries and Rapes, others in Drunkenness; others in coveting the Goods of their Neighbours; others in consuming their own; so that if the Walls of all Houses were transparent, we should behold some Eating, others Vomiting, others Wrongfully Beaten, others mixing Poisons, others Conspiring, others Casting Accounts, others Rejoycing, others Weeping, others Plotting against their Friends, others Raving mad with Ambition. Some actions there are more remote within the Soul, some young, some old, suing, denying, poor, rich, starved, luxurious, sordid, imprison'd, murther'd, buried, despising what they Enjoy, and aiming at what they have not; impudent, niggardly, insatiate, vain-glorious; some setting their minds on Horses, others on Men, others on Dogs, others on Stone or Wood; some affect Embassy, others the Command of Armies, others sacred Rites; some wear Crowns, others Armour; some fight at Sea, others at Land, others Till the Ground, some plead in the Forum, others act on the Theatre, every one is severally employ'd; some affect Pleasure and Intemperateness, others Rest and Idleness, how then can I but laugh at their Lives? And it is to be feared, that your Art of Physick will nothing please them, for Intemperance makes them froward, and they esteem Wisdom madness, and I doubt much that many things in your Art are openly reproached, either through Envy or Ingratitude; for the Sick, assoon as they are cured, ascribe the Cause either to the Gods, or to Chance; and many are of such a disposition, as to hate those that have obliged them, and can hardly refrain from being angry if they need their help; many also, being themselves ignorant, prefer Ignorance before Science; Fools give their Suffrages, neither will the Sick commend, nor they who are of the same Art give their approbation, through Envy. And it cannot be, but that you must have suffered wrong in this kind, for I know very well, that you have been often treated unworthily, and reproached by Malice and Envy."

There is no knowledge nor attestation of Truth in saying this; he smiled and seemed to put on a Divine Look, casting off that which he had before. "*Then I*, Excellent *Democritus*, I shall carry back with me to *Cos* the great Gifts of your Hospitality, full of your wise Instructions. I shall return to proclaim your Praises, for that you have made enquiry into humane nature, and understood it; I shall go away cured in Mind, it being requisite that I take care for the Cure of the Bodies of others. To morrow, and afterwards, we shall meet here again."

Which said, I arose, and he readily accompanied me. A man came to him, from whence I know not, to whom he delivered his Books. When I came to the *Abderites*, who all this while stayed for me; "Men of *Abdera, said I*, I return you many Thanks for the Message you sent me, for I have seen *Democritus*, the wisest of Men, who only is able to reduce men to sound understanding. This (*Damagetus*) is all, which I had to relate unto you with joy, concerning *Democritus*. Farewel."

This Account *Hippocrates* gives of *Democritus*; neither did their Acquaintance and Friendship end here, but continued after the departure of *Hippocrates* to *Cos*, as appears by the Correspondence of two Letters betwixt them. The first, from *Democritus* to *Hippocrates*, in these words.

You came to us, *Hippocrates*, as to give *Hellebore* to a mad Man, at the instigation of foolish People, who think Study madness; I was at that time busied in writing concerning the Fabrick of the World, and the Poles and the Stars of Heaven; assoon as you understood the nature of these things, how excellently they are framed, and how far from madness, you commended my Employment, and condemned Them as stupid and mad. All those things which pass to us through the Air by Images, and are seen in the World, and succeed one another, my Mind, making a scrutiny into these, hath clearly found out the Nature of them, and brought it to light, witness the Books that I have written. You ought not therefore, *Hippocrates*, to converse with such men, whose Minds are wavering and unconstant; For if, as those men desired, you had given me *Hellebore*, as being mad, you had, of Wise, made me Mad indeed, the Guilt whereof would have lain upon your Art; for *Hellebore*, administred to Sound Persons, clouds their Understandings; but to the Mad it doth good. I believe, that if you had found me not writing, but lying down or walking, revolving things in my mind, sometimes laughing,

and

and not minding such Friends as came to me, but wholly taken up with Contemplation of something, you would have inferred from what you beheld, that I was Mad. A Physitian therefore must not judge of the Affections or Passions by the sight only, but by the Actions themselves, and observe, whether they are in their Beginning, or in the Middle, or in the End, and to consider the difference of Time and Age, before he undertake to cure the Body; for by all these, the Disease will be discovered.

To which Hippocrates *return'd this Answer.*

In the art of Physick, that which happens Successfully, men for the most part commend not, but commonly ascribe to the Gods; but if any thing happen amiss in it, so as that the Patient dieth, they let the Gods alone, and accuse the Physician. And indeed, I perceive, that I gain more blame than credit by my art; for, tho' now very old, I have not yet arrived at the height of Medicine, neither did *Æsculapius* himself who invented it, as appears in that he many times dissents from those who have written hereupon. Your Letter to us condemns the administration of Hellebore; I was sent for indeed, *Democritus*, to cure a Mad-man, neither at that time could I guess in what condition you were: But assoon as I had conversed with you, I knew you to be far from madness, and worthy of all respect. I acknowledged you to be the most excellent Interpreter of Nature, and the World; and judged those that sent for me, mad, and to stand in need of Physick. But since this Accident hath begot an acquaintance betwixt us, you will not do amiss in writing oftner, and in communicating your works to me. I have sent you a Treatise concerning the use of *Hellebore*. Farewel.

Hence it is, that some held *Hippocrates* to have been the Disciple of *Democritus*, as *Cornelius Celsus* affirms; indeed, that *Hippocrates* learnt much Philosophy of him, as well by his Discourse, as communication of his Writings, is manifest from the precedent *Epistles*.

CHAP. VII.
His Death.

a *Cic. de senect.*
b *de die. nat. cap.*
c *Laert.*

HE (a) lived to a great age; *Laertius* saith, *above* 100. *years*; *Phlegon* and *Lucian* more expresly, 104. (b) *Censorinus*, 108. (c) *Hipparchus*, 109. Laertius saith, *he died of Age*; *Phlegon*, for want of food; the manner related thus by *Hermippus*. Being very old, and drawing nigh his end, his Sister was extreamly troubled, that he should dye within the time of the Festival of *Ceres*; but he bad her be of good comfort, and bring him every day some hot Bread, which holding to his nose, he prolonged his life, till the days of the Festival were past, which were three: and then without any pain gave up the Ghost,

d *Laert.*

(d) and was buried at the publick Charge.

CHAP. VIII.
His Writings.

a *Laert.*

THrasyllus, (a) who disposed the Writings of *Plato* according to Tetralogies, digested also those of *Democritus* into order; thus,

ETHICK.

Pythagoras.
Of the *Disposition of a wise man.*
Of the *things that are in the Inferi*, to which perhaps the *Abderites* alluded in their Epistle to *Hippocrates.*
Tritogenia; that all human things consist of Three.
Of *Goodness*, or *Virtue.*
Amalthæa's Horn.
Of *Tranquility of mind.*
Commentaries, or, of *Houses, Oeconomical.*
Felicity (εὐεστώ) not extant in the time of *Thrasyllus*.

PHYSICK.

The great *Diacosmus*, consisting of 12 Books, *Theophrastus* ascribes it to *Leucippus*: but *Antisthenes* affirms, *Democritus* recited it in publick as his own; and as His is it cited by *Epicurus*, in his Epistle to *Herodotus*. To this Work it was perhaps, that *Cicero* alludes, saying, *What shall I say of* Democritus? *Whom can we compare with him, who durst begin thus*, Hæc loquor de Universis? *He excepts nothing, whereof he professeth not to treat; for what can be beyond all things?*
The little *Diacosmus*.
Of *the Planets*; in which Treatise he proved that there are more than Seven.
Of *Nature*, the first.
Of the *Nature of Man*, or *of flesh*; the second, dedicated to *Hippocrates*.
Of *the Mind*. Of *the Senses*; these two, some put together, and entitled, Of *the soul*.
Of *Sapours*.
Of *Colours*.
Of *Different figures* (ῥυσμοί.)
Of *the reciprocation of figures* This and the fore-going Treatise, perhaps tended to shew the nature of Qualities, which according to him arise from the various disposure of Atoms, according to their particular figures.
Κρατυντήρια, or Of *the mixtures of the things aforesaid.*
Of *an Image*, or, Of *foresight*.
Of *Pestilences* (*Gassendus* reads περὶ λογικῶν, Of *Logicke*.) Canon. 1, 2, 3.
Of *Effluctions*.

EXTRAORDINARY.

Celestial Causes.
Aerial Causes.
(b) *Plain superficial Causes*; perhaps, what things are made of plain Atoms; for that which immediately followeth, is opposite to it.

b *Magnetica plane causæ*; See, *his interpretation, pag* 16.

Causes of Fire, and things in Fire, these consist of round Atoms.
Causes of Sounds.

Causes

Causes of Seeds and Plants and Fruits.
Causes of Animals, three.
Mixt Causes.
Of Stone.

MATHEMATICK.

Περὶ διαφορῆς γνώμης, or, of the contact of a Circle and a Sphear.
Of Geometry.
Geometrick.
Numbers.
Of surd lines, and solid, two, Ἐκπεταομαλα.
The great year, or, Astronomy.
Parapegma; *Salmasius* makes this all one with the other, reading, *The great year, or Parapegma of Astronomy.* Parapegma is a Table describing the rising and setting of the Stars, equinoxes, solstices, and the like.
The contention or examination of the Hour-glass.
Uranography.
Geography.
Polography.
Actinography.

MUSICK.

Of Rythms and Harmony.
Of Poetry.
Of the neatness of Verses.
Of sweet-sounding and harsh-sounding Letters.
Of Homer, or of right-versifying and speaking.
Of Songs.
Of Words, a Dictionary.

MECHANICK, or concerning ARTS.

Prognostick.
Of Diet, or Diætetick, or a Medicinal rule.
Causes of things seasonable and unseasonable.
Of Agriculture, or Geometrick.
Of Painting.
Tactick, and, of Armes.

To which some, cut of his Commentaries, annex these;

Of the sacred Letters in Babylon; to which perhaps (c) *Clemens Alexandrinus* alludes. *Democritus*, saith he, writ Babylonian Moral discourses, for he is said to have inserted into his own Writings the sense of the Pillar of *Acicarus*.
Of the things that are at Meroe.
A voyage on the Ocean.
Of History.
A discourse of Chaldæa.
A discourse of Phrygia.
Of the Fever and Cough in sickness.
Chernica, or Problems. Perhaps the same which (d) *Pliny* terms *Chirocineta*, (e) *Vitruvius*, *Chirotoniton*, adding, that *in it he made use of a ring, and drew the figures of the experiments in wax and red-lead*.

The rest (saith *Thrasyllus*) that go under his name, and partly made out of his Writings, partly acknowledged to be the Writings of other men. Of which kind perhaps in his Book *of the virtue of herbs*, mentioned by (f) *Pliny*, and that of (g) *Commentaries upon Apollonices*, *Capridenes*, and *Dardanus*, from whence he argues *Democritus* to have been skilful in Magick: But (h) *Agellius* much blames him for ascribing to *Democritus* such prodigious fables.

c *Strom.* 1
d 24. 17.
e 9 3 5.
f 25. 3.
g 30. 1.
h 10. 12.

(i) *Aristoxenus* affirms, that *Plato* had an intent to have burned all the writings of *Democritus*, and for that end had made a Collection of a great many of them: but was diverted by *Amyclas* and *Clinias*, Pythagoreans.

i *Laert.*

CHAP. IX.

Physick.

HE compleated the *Eleatick* Sect, and brought it to Perfection, insisting upon and improving the Principles of those that went before, but most particularly those of *LEUCIPPUS*. His Assertions these.

SECT. I.

Of the Principles of things, Atoms and Vacuum.

THE Principles of all things are Atoms (a) (solid (b). full) and Vacuum, (c) whereof one is *Ens*, the other *Non-ens*. (d) *Ens* is full and solid; *Non-ens* is Vacuous and rare; *Ens* participates no more of Being than doth *Non-ens*, nor of Body more than doth Vacuum, These are the causes and matter of beings.

(e) Bodies must either consist of Atoms, or of nothing; for if every body be divisible, let us suppose it actually divided, and then there will remain either Atoms or nothing; but of nothing, nothing is made, and nothing goes away into nothing.

(f) Neither of these Principles is made of the other, but the common body it self is the Principle of all things, differing only in magnitude and the figure of its parts.

They are both infinite: Atoms (g) in number, Vacuum in Maglitude.

(h) The Properties of Atoms are two, Figure and Magnitude; (i) as to Figure, they are infinite; (k) Angulous, not-angulous, strait, round; (l) some are smooth, others rugged; some pointed, some crooked, and as it were hooked.

As to their Magnitude, (m) they are by reason of their littleness, invisible; (n) by reason of their solidity, indivisible, (o) impassible, and unalterable.

To these two Properties ascribed to Atoms by *Democritus* (p) *Plutarch* saith, that Epicurus added a third, weight; but (q) *Aristotle* affirms, that Democritus held one Atom to be heavier than another, according as it exceeded that other in bigness.

Of all other qualities they are destitute; having neither native whiteness, nor blackness, nor sweetness, nor bitterness, nor heat, nor cold, nor any other quality.

(r) Cicero, who calls *Democritus* the Inventor and Author of this assertion of Atoms, elsewhere ascribes it to *Leucippus*, adding, that (s) Democritus *herein followed him, but was far more full in the rest.* But neither seems it to have been invented by Leucippus, for *Posidonius* the Stoick ascribes it to *Moschus* a Phœnecian; whom *Strabo* affirms to have lived before the Trojan War. But perhaps the Eleatick Philosophers derived it from *Pythagoras*: of which opinion (t) *Aristotle*

a *Arist. Phys.* l. 6.
b *Cic. Acad.* 4. *Arist. Met.* l. 4.
c *Arist. loc. cit.*
d *Arist. Met.* 14.
e *Aristot.*
f *Arist. Phys.* 3. 4.
g *Arist. de gen. & cor.* l. 1. & de calo 3.
4. *Laert.*
h *Arist. de gen. & cor.* l. 1.
i *Laert.*
k *Arist. Phys.* l. 6.
l *Cic. nat. deor.*
m *Philop. in* l. *Phys.*
n *Cic. de finib.* 1.
o *Plut. plac. phil.* l. 15. *Laert. Magnenus interprets this of the vulgar Elements, fire, water, earth,* pag. 41. 42. *adding as an assertion of Democritus, Atomis mutabiles esse figuras, and proves it out of Aristotle, as strangely,* pag. 42.
p *l Lac.*
q *De gen.* l. 8.
r *De fato.*
s *Acad.* 4.
t *De Cælo* 3.

ſtotle ſeems to be; *In ſome manner*, ſaith he, *they make all things that are, Numbers, and to conſiſt of Numbers: for tho' they ſay it not expreſly, yet this is their meaning.* Whence perhaps it is, that (*u*) *Automedon* gives them the Pythagorick denomination, *Monads*.

u *Anthol. 4.*

SECT. II.

Of the motion of Atoms in Vacuum, whereby all things are made.

These (*a*) Atoms, of firſt bodies, are continually moved in the infinite (*b*) Vacuum, in which there is neither high, nor low, nor middle, nor laſt, nor extream.

This motion had not any beginning, but was from all eternity.

(*c*) *This motion is but of one kind, oblique.* Herein *Epicurus* diſſents from him, aſſerting a two-fold motion, direct, and declining.

The little bodies being carried in this region or ſpace, are entangled with one another, or hit againſt one another, or rebound, or ſeparate, or aſſociate with one another, by whoſe concuſſions and complications all things are made. Thus (*d*) whatſoever is, or is made, is or is made by natural weights or motions.

Thus (*e*) *all things are done by a neceſſity, the rapid motion of the Atoms* (which he called *neceſſity*) *being the cauſe of the production of all things.* (*f*) This neceſſity is fate, and juſtice, and the providence which made the World, which is no other than (*g*) the reſiſtance, lation, and percuſſion of matter.

a *Ariſt. de cælo 3, 4. Cic. de finib. 1.*
b *Magnenus will have Democritus to underſtand by this vacuum, the air: and endeavours to prove it by Authorities of Ariſtotle, Galen, Virgil, which intimate the contrary, pag. 37. and 42.*
c *Stob. phyſ. 1. 23.*
d *Cic. Acad. queſt. 4.*
e *Laert. Cic. de fato. Plut. plac. l. 25.*
f *Stob. phyſ. r. 8.*
g *Plut. plac. l. 26.*

SECT. III.

Of the Generation, Corruption, Alteration, and Qualities of compounds.

The (*a*) Elements (as we ſaid) or Principles *of all things are two, Full, and Vacuum. One is Ens, the other non Ens; the full and ſolid is Ens, the Vacuous and rare, non Ens. Ens participates not more of being, than non Ens, nor a body more than Vacuum. Theſe are the cauſes and matter of beings.*

a *Ariſt. Metaph. 1, 4.*

" And (*b*) as they who aſſert a ſubject to be
" one, in ſubſtance, various as to its affections,
" make rare and denſe to be the Principles of
" thoſe affections; in like manner, they (*Leu-*
" *cippus* and *Democritus*) affirm, that the diffe-
" rences are the cauſes of all the reſt. Theſe
" differences they hold to be three, figure, order,
" and poſition; for they ſay that *Ens* differs
" only ῥυσμῷ and διαθιγῇ and τροπῇ. ῥυσμῷ is fi-
" gure, διαθιγῇ order, τροπῇ poſition: A. and N.
" differ in figure; A. N. and N. A. in order;
" Z. and N. in poſition.

b *Ibid.*

" Thus (*c*) they ſuppoſe figures of which
" they make Alteration and Generation: Gene-
" ration and Corruption, by Congregation and
" Segregation (*of Atoms*;) Alteration, by
" Order and Poſition.

c *Ariſt. de gen. & cor. 1, 2.*

" Now (*d*) foraſmuch as they conceived,
" that what is apparent to ſenſe is true, ſeeing
" that apparent things are contrary to one ano-
" ther, and infinite in number, they conceived
" that there are infinite figures, (*of Atoms*) ſo

d *Ibid.*

" that by ſeveral tranſmutations of the com-
" pound, the ſame thing ſeemeth contrary to an-
" other, and ſo another thing; and by immix-
" ture of ſome ſmall thing to be tranſmutated,
" and to appear quite different; and being tran-
" mutated, one thing to appear to be quite
" another thing; for a Comedy and Tragedy
" are made of the ſame Letters.

" Hence it is, that (*e*) Plutarch *and others aſ-*
" *firm*, he did reject Qualities, aſſerting that co-
" lour is νόμῳ, white νόμῳ, ſweet νόμῳ, hot νόμῳ, cold
" νόμῳ, and all other qualities; νόμῳ ᾗ *is here com-*
" *monly expounded* (*after the uſual acception of the*
" *word*) lege eſſe, *to be by law.* (*f*) Magnenus
" *interprets it*, that by a certain Law and pro-
" portion betwixt the Agent and Patient, the ſame
" thing is ſweet to one, which is bitter to an-
" other. (*g*) *The learned* Gaſſendus, *Metaphorical-*
" *ly, that as the juſtice, injuſtice, decency, inde-*
" cency, laudability, culpability, &c. of human
" actions, depend on the conſtitutions of Laws;
" ſo the whiteneſs, blackneſs, ſweetneſs, bitter-
" neſs, heat, cold, &c. of natural things, de-
" pend on the various poſitions and ordinations
" of Atoms. Whence you ſee (ſaith he) how
" in *Laertius* is to be underſtood, Ἀρχὰς ᾗ τῶν
" ὅλων ἀτόμους κ᾽ κενόν, τὰ δ᾽ ἄλλα πάντα νενομίσθαι,
" That Atoms and Vacuum are the Prin-
" ciples of all things, cætera omnia lege ſanciri.
" *Thus* Gaſſendus.

e *adv. Coloſ. lib. 1.*
f *Democr. revivi pag. 436.*
g *Animadv. pag. 231.*

But νόμῳ, which (as *Suidas* ſaith) is πολυώνυμος λέξις, *a word of various ſignifications*, ſeems here to be taken in oppoſition to ἐτῇ, in which ſenſe *Laertius* explicates it by νενομίσθαι, (from whence it ſeems derived) and νενομίσθαι by δοξάζεσθαι, for ſo perhaps ſhould the Text be diſtinguiſh'd, τὰ δ᾽ ἄλλα πάντα νενομίσθαι δοξάζεσθαι, cætera omnia cenſeri vel exiſtimari, the later being only a Gloſs and expoſition of the former. So that in the ſenſe of *Democritus*, (who affected a particular uſe of words, as appears by ῥυσμὸς, διαθιγή, τροπή, συν &c.) νόμῳ is no other than δόξη. Thus he ſeems to have oppoſed ἐτῇ and νόμῳ, as the Schools *Ens reale* and *rationis*; as if he ſhould ſay, there is nothing really exiſtent but Atoms and Vacuum, all things elſe are only *quoad nos*, viz. *in opinion*. This may be further confirmed by a noted place of (*h*) *Gallen*, who dilates upon it in this manner.

h *lib. 1. de Elem. cap. 1.*

" The firſt Element of things is void of Qua-
" lity, having not in its own nature whiteneſs,
" nor blackneſs, nor ſweetneſs, nor bitterneſs,
" nor heat, nor cold, nor any other quality;
" colour is (νόμῳ) in opinion, bitterneſs is in
" opinion, ſweetneſs is in opinion; but Atoms
" and Vacuum are indeed, ſaith *Democritus*, con-
" ceiving that all ſenſible Qualities are made by
" the concuſſion of Atoms, according as they
" are, as to us, who have the ſence of them; but
" that nothing is by nature white, or yellow, or
" red, or bitter, or ſweet. By νόμῳ he means
" as it were νομιςί, by opinion, and as to us; not
" in the nature of the things themſelves, for that
" on the other ſide he calls ἐτῇ, making the word
" from ἐτόν, which ſignifies True. The whole
" meaning of the ſentence is this, Men do opi-
" nionate or think (νομίζει) that white is
" ſomething, and black, and ſweet, and bitter;
" but truly and indeed (ἓν) One, and (μηδὲς)
" Nothing are all. All Atoms are little bodies,
" void

"void of Qualities, Vacuum is a region or space "in which all these bodies are carried upwards "and downwards everlastingly, or are intangled "within one another, or hit against one another, or rebound, or separate from, or associate with one another, whereby they make "all compounds, and especially our bodies, "and their passions and senses. *Hitherto* Galen.

Democritus (*i*) alone, contrary to the rest of the Philosophers, Asserted, that the Agent and the Patient must be the same and like; for he conceived it not to be possible, that things different and divers can suffer from one another: and if any different things act upon one another, this happens to them not as being different, but as they have something in them that is the same.

Broad (*k*) iron swims on the Water, because the atoms of heat, which ascend out of the Water, uphold the broad atoms even of things that are weighty; but the narrow slide down, because these which resist them are but few. But then, objects he, This will be done much more in the Air; whereto he Answers, that the *Soun* is not carried one way, meaning by *Soun* the motion of bodies ascending.

Things (*l*) become liquid or concrete, by conversion, or contaction.

SECT. IV.

Of the World.

THere (*a*) are infinite Worlds in the infinite space, according to all circumstances; (*b*) some of which are not only like to one another, but every way so perfectly and absolutely equal, that there is no difference betwixt them. (*c*) These all are generated and corrupted.

The World is (*d*) inanimate (*e*), round, (*f*) compassed about with a coat, as it were, interwoven with Stars.

(*g*) *The atoms being* (as we said) *rapidly carryed through the Universe; by this means all things were made, Fire, Water,* (*h*) *Air, Earth.*

To (*i*) the fire, He and *Leucippus* ascribed a round figure; but Air, Water, and the rest, he distinguished only by greatness and littleness, because their nature is the Pan-spermia, or universal dissemination of the Elements or Atoms.

SECT. V.

Of the Heavens.

THE (*a*) Sun and Moon consist of smooth little bodies which are carried round. (*b*) *Plutarch* affirms, He held, with *Anaxagoras*, that the Sun is a burning plate or stone; *Laertius* adds, *he said of* Anaxagoras, *that those opinions which he delivered concerning the Sun and Moon, were not his, but more ancient, and that he had stoln them.*

(*c*) He conceived the Sun to be very big: for, adds *Cicero*, he was exceeding skilful in Geometry.

(*d*) The Moon is a fiery Firmament; containing Plains, Mountains, Valleys.

(*e*) He placed the Stars in this order; first, the fixed Stars, then the Planets, then the Sun, *Lucifer*, and the Moon.

(*f*) All the Stars move from East to West. (*g*) Those which are nearest to the Earth are less apt to be carried about by the rapid circumvolution of Heaven. Whence it comes to pass, that the Sun and the inferior Stars, especially the Moon, move much slower than the rest.

(*h*) He held, as *Anaxagoras*, that Comets are the co-apparition of Planets, which coming near one another seem to be all one.

SECT. VI.

Of Air, Earth, Water.

WHen (*a*) in a narrow Vacuum there are many little bodies, there followeth wind; and contrary, the Air is quiet and calm, when in a great Vacuum there are but a few little bodies. For as in a Market-place or street, as long as the people are but few, they walk without any trouble, but when they run into some narrow place, they justle and quarrel with one another; so in this space which encompasseth us, when many bodies croud into one place, they must necessarily justle one another, and be thrust forward, and driven back, and entangled, and squeezed, of which is made the Wind, when they which contested yield; and, having been long toss'd up and down uncertainly, shrink; but when a few bodies stir up and down in a large space, they can neither drive, nor be driven impetuously.

(*b*) The Earth at first wandred up and down, as well by reason of its smallness as lightness; but in time growing thick and heavy, it setled down immovable. (*c*) Its breadth is the cause of its setledness, for (*d*) [*it is of the fashion of a dish, hollow in the midst, and*] it divides not but covers the Air, which is beneath it, as appears in broad bodies, which are not easily stirred by the Winds, but stick fast; Thus doth the Earth, by reason of its breadth, to the Air; and the Air, not having a place whereto it might go, sufficient to receive it, resteth underneath, as water within vessels which cover it. That the Air can uphold a great weight, they demonstrate many ways.

(*e*) Now by reason that this Air is weaker towards the South, the Earth, as it groweth and increaseth bendeth to that side; for the Northern parts are intemperate, the Southern temperate, whence they produce more and fairer fruits.

(*f*) He imputeth the cause of Earthquakes to water: for (*g*) the Earth being full of water, and receiving to it much rain-water, this causeth the Earthquake: For, there coming more, because it is not able to receive it, forcing its caverns, it maketh it shake, and being dryed and attracted into empty places from the more full, in its passage causeth that motion.

(*h*) The Sea continually decreaseth, and at last will dry up.

(*i*) The overflowing of *Nilus* is caused by the melting and diffusion of the Snow in the Northern parts under the Summer Tropick; from the vapours, Clouds are condensed, which being driven towards the South, and to *Ægypt*, by the Etesian winds, they are dissolved into great and vehement showers, wherewith are filled as well the Lakes, as the River *Nilus*.

SECT.

SECT. VII.

Of the generation of living Creatures.

MEN (*a*) were first generated of water and mud; from which opinion *Epicurus* little differs.

(*b*) The distinction of sexes, Male and Female, is made (*c*) in the womb, not by reason of heat or cold, but according to that party of the Two, whose seed proceeding from the part which distinguisheth Male and Female, is predominant; or of that party whose seed first takes up the place.

(*d*) The Infant in the womb is nourished at the mouth, wherefore assoon as it is born, it layeth the mouth to the dug.

SECT. VIII.

Of the Soul.

Democritus (*a*) held, That the Soul is a kind of Fire and Heat; (*b*) for there being infinite Figures of Atoms, he saith, the round make Fire, and the Soul, because that figure is most capable to permeate through the Universe; and to move the rest, the soul it self being moved also. Thus he and *Leucippus* held the Soul to be that which giveth motion to living Creatures. Hence it comes to pass, that respiration is the bound of Life, for when that which encompasseth the Bodies, compresseth them, and squeezeth out those Figures which give motion to living Creatures, forasmuch as they never rest, there is a relief by the coming in of others of the same kind through Respiration; for this hinders those which are in the Animals from being squeezed out, they driving forward together that which compresseth and fastneth. All Animals [*c* breathe, *and they*] live as long as they can do thus.

(*d*) The Soul is corruptible, and perisheth with the Body.

(*e*) The Soul hath Two parts; the rational, seated in the Breast; the irrational, diffused through the whole Body: but (*f*) the Soul and Mind are all one.

(*g*) There are more than five Senses of irrational Animals, God and Wise Men.

(*h*) Sensation and Intellection are made by the insinuation of Images from without, which flow from solid Bodies and certain Figures. (*i*) So the Image in a Looking-glass is made also.

He conceived, as *Aristotle* saith, that *all Sensibles are Tangibles*, that all Sensation is caused by a touch or stroke upon the Organ; and further affirmed, that (*k*) *Whiteness is smoothness*, [the Light being reflected from a smooth Superficies upon the Eye, exhibits a white colour.] (*l*) *Blackness is Roughness*; [the same light reflected from a rough Superficies, exhibits Blackness;] in like manner (*m*) He referred *Sapours to Figure*; (*n*) the round Atoms, and such as are of a bulk suitable [to the contexture of the Organ] make a *sweet* Sapor; the great, a *sower*; the Multangulous and Nothing-round, a *harsh*; the Acute, Conical, Crooked, not slender nor round, a *sharp*; the Round, slender, angulous, crooked, an *acrimonious*; the Angulous distorted equicrural, a *Salt*; the Round, light distorted small, a *bitter*; the slender round small, a fat or *luscious*.

(*o*) The Mind is the same with the Soul, consisting of smooth little Bodies. (*p*) The *Hegemonick* is seated in the whole Head, (*q*) Cogitation is made by incurrence of Images; (*r*) so also are Dreams.

SECT. IX.

Of the Gods.

Democritus (saith (*a*) *Cicero*,) in my opinion, wavers, and seems uncertain, concerning the nature of the Gods; for sometimes he conceives, that there are Images indued with Divinity in the Universe; sometimes he calleth the Principles and Minds in the same Universe, God; sometimes animate Images, which use either to profit or to harm us; sometimes certain vast Images, so great, that they extrinsecally embrace the whole World.

(*b*) *Sextus Empiricus* delivers his Opinion thus: There are certain Images which come to Men, some of which do good, others hurt; whence he wisheth, that he might light upon good Images; these are large and extraordinary vast, not easily perishable, nor absolutely unperishable. They foretel events to Men by Discourse and Speech, the Antients having received an Impression of these in their Fantasies, from thence imagined that there is a God, whereas besides these there is no God, or a Nature that is not subject to Dissolution.

(*c*) He approved the Pre-sention of future things, that is Divination; and Conceived, that (*d*) the Antients did wisely institute, that the entrails of sacrificed Victims should be looked into; from the Constitution and Colour whereof may be perceived signs of Health or Pestilence; sometimes also what Dearth or Plenty shall follow.

CHAP. X.

Ethick.

HE (*a*) asserted, the chief end or good to be ἐυθυμία: not placing it in Pleasure, as some have misunderstood him; but in a serene, secure state of Mind, not distracted with any fear, or superstition, or any other passion.

Of his Moral Sentences these have been preserved by *Stobæus* and others.

> *'Tis easie wickedness to circumvent:*
> *For whilst on gain alone it is intent,*
> *It blindly strays, and any way is bent.*

It is easy to praise what we ought not, and to blame; but both are signs of a depraved disposition.

Wisdom not admiring any thing, merits all things, being most Honourable.

The bounds of profitable and unprofitable are, pleasant und unpleasant.

It is the work of Prudence to prevent an injury; of Indolence, when done, not to revenge it.

There ariseth a great delight from beholding good actions.

Ser. 4.	From good things arise ill to Men, if they know not how to manage or bear the good.
Ser. 5.	To yield to the Law, the Magistrate, and a wise Person, is decent.
Ibid.	Temperance augments things that are pleasant, and maketh the pleasure it self greater.
Ser. 6.	Sleeps in the day signifieth either distemper of the Body, or grief of the Mind, or sloth, or dulness.
Ibid.	Coition is a short Apoplexy; One man is struck out of another.
Ser. 7.	Not he only is valiant who vanquisheth his Enemy, but he also who subdueth Pleasure; yet some there are, who Command Cities, and are slaves to Women.
Ser. 9.	It is good not only to do no harm, but not so much as to will it.
Ser. 10.	Where ill Actions acquire Wealth, the Infamy is the greater.
Ibid.	Hope of ill gain is the beginning of loss.
Ser. 12.	We ought to speak Truth where it is best.
Ser. 17.	It is better to blame our own faults, than those of others.
Ibid.	Freedom of Speech is proper to generosity, but the difference of occasions render it dangerous.
Ser. 14.	To praise good things is good, but to praise the ill is proper to a counterfeit deceitful Soul.
Ser. 17.	He is well disposed who grieves not for what he hath not, and rejoyceth for what he hath.
Ibid.	Of pleasant things, those which we have most seldome, delight most.
Ibid.	If a Man exceeds moderation, the sweetest things prove the most bitter.
Ibid.	He is valiant who vanquisheth, not Enemies only, but pleasures.
Ibid.	They who indulge to the pleasures of the Belly, consuming the time in eating, drinking, or wantonness; in all these there are short pleasures, which last as long as they are eating and drinking, but many griefs: For they are in a continual desire of these things, and when they have obtain'd them, the pleasure passeth away, and there is nothing in them but a momentany titillation; the pleasure is short, and they soon need the same again.
Ser. 20.	To resist Anger is difficult, but to vanquish it is proper to an understanding Person.
Ser. 22.	He who contends with his Superior, ends in Infamy.
Ser. 28.	Wicked Men, after they have escaped the danger, keep not the Oaths which they had made in their extremity.
Ser. 29.	More are made good by Exercitation, than by Nature.
Ibid.	All Labours are sweeter than Rest, when Men obtain that for which they labour; but if a Man be frustrate of his designs, there is one remedy, if all things are alike troublesome and difficult.
Ser. 31.	Neither say nor do ill, though alone; learn to stand more in awe of thy self than of others.
Ser. 36.	It is a defrauding of others, to desire to speak all, and to hear nothing.
Ser. 37.	A Man must either be good, or seem such.
Ibid.	They whose Manners are orderly, their Life is orderly.
Ibid.	A good Man cares not for the reproofs of ill Men.
Ibid.	The Laws would not have prohibited every Man from living according to his own Will, if one were not injurious to another, for Envy causeth the beginning of Sedition.
Ser. 38.	To live in foreign Countries teacheth Frugality; Maza, and a grassy Bed are sweet Cures of Hunger and Labour.
Ibid.	Every Country is pervious to a wise Man; for the whole World is the Country of a wise Soul.
Ser. 41.	The Law requires, that the Life of Man should do good to others; this may be done if they will suffer, for it declares its own Virtue to the Obedient.
Ibid.	Civil War hurts both Parties; the harm is equal to the Victor, and to the Vanquished.
Ibid.	By Concord, besides other great things, War may be undertaken by Cities; without it, not.
Ser. 42.	It is better for the Unwise to be Governed, than to Govern.
Ibid.	It is justice to do those things which ought to be done; Injustice not to do them, but to decline them.
	As concerning the killing and not killing of Animals, the business stands thus, Those who do, or would do injury, he who killeth is blameless; nay, such ought rather to be killed, than not.
Ibid.	We ought to kill all that do Injury and Injustices; and he who kills them, ought to have, throughout the whole World, esteem and privilege of his Desire, and Justice, and Courage, and Possession.
Ibid.	As it is written concerning Beasts and Serpents, that are in enmity with us, so also in my Opinion may we do with Men. According to the Laws of our Country, an Enemy may be kill'd in any part of the World, where no Law forbiddeth it; but Law forbiddeth sometimes, and they have sacred Rites, Covenants, and Oaths.
Ibid.	Any Man that either kills with his own hand, or causeth to be killed by Command or Vote, a Thief, is to be esteemed innocent.
Ibid.	It is a grievous thing to be ruled by a worse Person.
Ser. 43.	They who suffer Injuries are to be defended to the utmost, and not to be despised; for this is just and good, the other unjust and ill.
Ser. 44.	They who commit any thing deserving Banishment, or Bonds, or any other punishment, ought not to be acquitted, but condemned; if any Man should acquit them either for Gain or Favour, he doth unjustly.
Ser.	He hath the greatest part of Justice and Virtue, who Honors those that are Worthy.
Ser.	Stand not more in awe of other Men than of thy Self; nor commit more offences, though no Man were to know it, than if all Men: Imprint this Rule in thy Mind; and do no ill.
Ser.	Men are more mindful of Wrongs than of Benefits, and it is but just it should be so: as he who restores a *Depositum*, deserves no Commendation; but he who detains it, Blame and Punishment. The same case it is in a Ruler, who is chosen not to do ill, but good.
Ser.	To be naturally fitted for Command, is proper to the most excellent Persons.
Ser. 46	Boldness is the beginning of an Action, the end is guided by Fortune.
Ser 49	Make use of Servants, as of the parts of your own

Ser. 61.	own Body; appoint to each a several Office. She that is belov'd, easily forgiveth the Offence of her Lover.
Ibid.	A Woman is sharper-witted for mischief than a Man.
Ser. 62.	To speak little, becomes a Woman; plain Attire adorns her.
Ibid.	To obey a Woman is the greatest Ignominy to a Man.
Ser. 74.	I approve not the having of Children; for I see the troubles of them are many and great; the Comforts and Pleasures few and small.
Ibid.	A rich Man, in my opinion, shall do well to adopt the Son of some Friend; for, by this means, he may have such a one as he hath a mind to; for he may chuse where he pleaseth, and take such a one as may best agree with him. There is a great difference betwixt these two; he who Adopts a Son, hath the liberty to make choice out of many that are good, and will please him; he that begets one, runs the hazard whether he will prove such, or no.
Ibid.	The begetting of Children seemeth to come from a most ancient Institution, and instinct of Nature, as is manifest even from brute Beasts, who beget young ones, though without hopes of receiving any advantage by them; As soon as they are brought forth, they feed and bring them up, and are solicitous for them even in the least things: and if they come to any hurt, they grieve at it. Such is the disposition of all Animals; how much more of Man, who hopes for a benefit from his Off-spring.
Ser. 84.	The excellency of Sheep consisteth in being fat; of Men, in being virtuous.
Ser. 90.	As of Wounds, the worst is that which Gangrenes: so, of the Diseases of the Mind, is insatiate Avarice.
Ser. 92.	A prudent use of Money conduceth to the practice of liberality and relief of others; he that useth Money foolishly, makes it the Prey of all Men.
Ibid.	To get Money, is not ill; but to get it unjustly, is the worst of ills.
Ser. 95.	Poverty and Riches are the Names of Want and Sufficiency: He who wants, ought not to be called Rich; nor He who wants not, Poor.
Ibid.	If you desire many things, many things will seem but a few.
Ibid.	To desire little, makes Poverty equal with Riches.
Ser. 96.	Good things are hardly obtained by those that seek after them; the ill come without seeking.
Ibid.	We must consider that the Life of Man is brittle, and momentany, involved in many troubles.
Ser. 101.	He is happy who is chearful, though possessing little; he unhappy who is troubled, amidst much wealth.
Ibid.	He that will lead a secure quiet life, must not engage himself in many things, neither publick nor private; nor attempt any thing above his own Ability and Nature; but have such regard to himself, that he decline any exuberance of Fortune that is offer'd him, assuming no more than he is well able to bear; for the convenience of what we enjoy is more excellent than the largeness of it.
Ser. 102.	A publick calamity is greater than a private, for it affords no hope of relief.
Ser. 109.	The hopes of Wise Men may come to pass, but those of Fools are impossible.
Ibid.	The hopes of Fools are beyond reason.
Ser. 111.	They who rejoyce in the misfortunes of their Neighbours, know not that Fortune is common to all, and that they have not a Propriety in joy.
Ser. 112.	Strength and Beauty are the Goods of the Body; Temperance and Prudence the Crown of old Age.
Ibid.	It is certain, that the Old Man was once young; but whether the Young Man shall ever come to be Old, is uncertain. A good thing that is compleat, is better than that which is to come, it being uncertain.
Ser. 115.	Old Age is a universal imperfection; it hath all things, and yet wants all things.
Ser. 119.	Some Men, not understanding the nature of moral Dissolution, and being conscious of their own ill actions in Life, are, during the whole course of their Lives, miserably distracted with Fears, fancying and feigning to themselves many things that are false, as if they were to happen after death.

(a) His also was this saying, (b) Speech is the shadow of Action. [a Laert. b Magnentius mistakes it for the Title of a Book; but the contrary is manifest from Plut. de educ. liberis.]

(c) He held, that from publick Offices, and the favour of great Persons, accrue many Ornaments which grace and set off this Life.

(d) He said, that Nature thrust down Truth, and hid her quite in the bottom.

(e) He said, that none can be a great Poet without Madness.

To his Moral Sentences may be added, what is related of him by (f) *Julian* the Emperor, That not being able by Discourse to comfort *Darius*, who was extreamly afflicted at the death of his beautiful Wife, he promised him to restore her to Life, if he would supply him with such things as were requisite for performance thereof. *Darius* bad him not spare any thing, which he thought might help him to bring it to pass: Soon after he came to *Darius* and told him, that he had furnished himself with all things except only one, which he could not get, but that He, who was King of all *Asia* might haply procure it with little difficulty. *Darius* demanding what it was, that no Man could get but the King himself? *Democritus* told him, that if he could write on her Tomb the Names of three Persons that have never grieved, she would return to Life. *Darius* perplexed hereat, there being no Man to whom some occasion of Grief hath not happened; *Democritus*, after his usual manner laughed, saying, Can you then, the most unreasonable of all Men, Weep with such confidence, as if you were the only Person that ever suffer'd affliction, and yet are not able to find out, through all the ages of Mankind, one Person that hath not received some particular Cross?

[c Plut. : on passe juvo. vero. d Cic. Acad quæst. 4. e Cic. de divinat. f Lo.g]

PROTAGORAS.

CHAP. I.

His Country, Father, and the occasion upon which he studied Philosophy.

Laert.

PRotagoras, was an *Abderite*, Son of *Artemon*; or as *Apollodorus* and *Dinon*, of *Mæandrius*; but *Eupolis* saith, he was a *Teian*.

He was first a Porter, as *Epicurus* relates, and by that occasion came into favour with *Democritus*: Being young, saith *Agellius*, he was constrained, for his sustenance, to take upon him the Office of a Porter; and, from some places adjoining, carried burthens of Wood to *Abdera*, of which City he was. *Democritus*, who was also of the same City, a person eminent for his Virtue and Philosophy, going abroad into the fields, saw him coming nimbly along loaden with one of his usual burthens; and when he came near him, observing that the Wood was neatly placed, and handsomly bound up, spoke to him to rest himself a little; which he did, and *Democritus*, in the mean time, took great notice of the bundle, that it was tyed up as it were Geometrically. He asked him, who put his Wood in that order? and he answering, that it was he himself had done it; *Democritus* desired him to unty it, and put it into the same order again; which he did. *Democritus* admiring the ingenuity of a person wholly void of Learning; Young man, *saith he*, seeing you have the wit to know how to do well, there are better and greater things which you may do with me, and immediately carrying him home, kept and maintained him, and made him that which afterwards he was.

CHAP. II.

His Opinions, and Writings.

Laert.

HE first said, That every thing hath two reasons or arguments, one contrary to the other; which way of arguing, he first used.

He began one of his Books thus; *Man is πάντων χρημάτων μέτρον, the measure of all things: of beings as they are; of not beings, as they are not.* By μέτρον he means the critery, by χρημάτων, πραγμάτων, of things; which is as much as to say, Man is the Critery of all things, of Beings as they are, of not Beings as they are not. Hereupon he asserts the Phœnomena's to be particular to every one.

He saith, that Matter is fluid; and being in perpetual fluxion, appositions are made instead of substractions; and the senses are transmutated and changed, according to the several ages and constitutions of the body.

He saith also, the reason (or powers) of all Phænomena's are subjected in Matter; so that Matter in it self, is all things which it appears unto all. But men at different times perceive things different, by reason of their different habits. He whose Constitution is sound, of the things which are in Matter, perceiveth those which are capable of appearing to such persons; They who are otherwise disposed, perceive the things which are capable of appearing to persons of a contrary Constitution. The same reason there is in the difference of ages, in sleeping and waking, and in all kinds of habits. Man therefore is the Critery of things that are; for all things, which appear to men, are; those which appear not to any man, are not.

He held, that the Soul is nothing more than the senses, as *Plato* in his *Thætetus* affirms; and that all things are true.

Another of his Books he began thus; *Of the Gods I know nothing, neither that they are, nor that they are not; for there are many things which hinder us from this knowledge, the blindness and shortness of human life.* For the beginning of this Book he was banish'd by the *Athenians*, and his Books burnt in the open Market-place. After that they had been diligently exacted of all that had any of them, by the publick Cryer.

He was the first that took a hundred Minæ for a gratuity. He, and *Prodicus* the *Teian*, got Money by reciting Orations in publick.

He first defined the parts of time, and explained the power of opportunity, and instituted disputations by way of contest; and proposed sophisms to the disputants, slipping besides the sense and playing upon the word, introducing the light, superficial, eristick way, whence *Timon* saith of him,

Protagoras, well in contention read.

He first abrogated the Socratick way of disputation, and first examined the argument of *Antisthenes*, whereby he endeavours to demonstrate, that it could not be contradicted, as *Plato* saith in his *Euthydemus*; and first produced Epicheirems against Positions.

He first divided an Oration into four parts, Request, Interrogation, Answer, Command: Some say into seven; Narration, Interrogation, Answer, Command, Enuntiation, Request, Appellation; which parts he called the foundations of Orations. But, as *Alcidamas*, four; Affirmation, Negation, Interrogation, Appellation.

He first recited his discourse concerning the Gods (the beginning whereof we formerly mentioned) at *Athens*, in the House of *Euripides*, or, as some say, of *Megaclides*: Others say, in the *Lyceum*, and that *Archagoras*, his Disciple, Son of *Theodotus* spoke it for him. He was accused by *Pythodorus*, Son of *Polyzelus*, one of the 400 Senators; but *Aristotle* saith, that *Evathlus* accused him.

His Writings which are now extant, saith *Laertius*, are these;

The Eristick Art.
Of Wrestling.
Of Mathematicks.
Of Politicks.
Of Ambition.
Of Vertues.
Of Settlement of Government.
Of the things in the Inferi.
Of the things that are done amiss by men.
Preceptory.
Judgment upon reward.
Antilogicks. 2.

These were His Books. *Plato* wrote a Dialogue, and intituled it by his Name.

CHAP. III.

His Death.

PHilochorus relates, that, as he was sailing to *Sicily*, the Ship wherein he went was cast away; and this, he saith, is confirmed by *Euripides* in his Ixion. Others relate, that he dyed by the way, having attained to ninety years; *Apollodorus* saith, to 70. and that he had been a Sophist forty years; and that he flourish'd about the 74th Olympiad. *Laertius* hath this Epigram upon him.

And thee, Protagoras, *flying, they say,*
From Athens, *death did seize on by the way;*
Thou might'st escape from Pallas *and her Town,*
But Pluto *would not lose what was his own.*

ANAXARCHUS.

ANaxarchus was an *Abderite*; he heard *Diomenes* of *Smyrna*; or, as others, *Metrodorus* of *Chios*, who said he did not know so much as this, that he knew nothing. *Metrodorus*, as some say, heard *Nessus* a *Chian*; as others, *Democritus*. *Anaxarchus* lived with *Alexander*, and flourish'd about the 110th Olympiad, and was a great Enemy to *Nicocreon* King of *Cyprus*; insomuch that *Alexander* at a Feast demanding what he thought of the entertainment? he Answered, All things, great King, are very Magnificent; only there is wanting the head of some Satrapa, reflecting upon *Nicocreon*. After the King's death, *Nicocreon* bearing this Injury in mind, laid hold of *Anaxarchus*, (who against his will was cast upon the shore of *Cyprus*) and caused him to be put into a Mortar, and pounded with Iron Pestles: whilst he, despising the pain, often repeated this celebrious Speech, *Pound the case of* Anaxarchus, Anaxarchus *himself you hurt not.* Hereupon the Tyrant commanding them to cut out his Tongue, he bit it off, and spit it in his Face.

He, from his Apathy and the Tranquillity of his life, had the attribute of *fortunate* bestow'd on him. He likewise had an excellent faculty in reducing others to Moderation; as he reformed *Alexander*, who would conceit himself a God, by pointing to his finger when it bled, and saying, This is Blood, and not
——*The juice that from immortal Gods doth flow.*

Yet *Plutarch* relates, that *Alexander* himself said this to his friends.

Another time, *Anaxarchus* drinking to him, pointed to the Cup, saying,
A mortal hand one of the Gods shall wound.

When *Alexander* came near *Babylon*, the *Chaldeans* disswaded him from entring the City, affirming, that if he did, it would be fatal to him; whereupon he passed by, and went to *Bursia*, a City on the other side of *Euphrates*. But *Anaxarchus* and other Greeks perswaded him by Philosophical reasons to contemn the predictions of the Magi as false and uncertain; whose advice he following, brought back his Army to *Babylon*, where he died.

THE

470   PART XII.

THE HISTORY of PHILOSOPHY.

The Twelfth Part, Containing the SCEPTICK Sect.

PYRRHO.

CHAP. I.

His Country, Parentage, Time, Masters.

OUT of *Elia* there sprung another Sect, no less Eminent than the former, its Author was (*a*) *Pyrrho*, an *Elian*. His Father, as *Diocles* affirms, was named *Plistarchus*, of obscure and mean Quality, for such (*b*) *Antigonus* relates *Pyrrho* himself at first to have been; his Sister *Philista*, a Midwife.

a *Laert.*
b *Laert.*

PART XII.   PYRRHO.   471

Suidas saith, He was in the time of *Philip* King of *Macedon*, about the 101 Olympiad: But this seems rather to have reference to the time of his Birth, than to that wherein he flourished; for *Anaxarchus* (his Master) was Contemporary with *Alexander* the Son of *Philip*, and is, by *Laertius*, said to have flourished in the 110th. Olympiad; for which reason perhaps it is, that *Suidas* adds, *And thence forward*. (*c*) He was first (as *Apollodorus* relates) a Painter; *Aristocles* saith, An ill one; But (*d*) *Antigonus* affirms, That in the *Gymnasium* at *Elis*, was preserved a very good piece of his doing, representing Torch bearers.

(*e*) Afterwards (saith *Apollodorus*) he applied himself to Philosophy. *Aristocles* saith, he lighted upon some Writings of *Democritus*. *Alexander* in his Successions, That he heard *Dryso* Son of *Stilpo*, whom *Suidas* terms *Bryso*, adding, He was Disciple to *Glinomachus*, a Dialectick, Contemporary with *Stilpo*.

(*f*) Next he addicted himself to *Alexander*, Disciple of *Metrodorus* the Chian, whose Master was *Metrodorus* the *Abderite*.

(*g*) Afterwards he heard *Anaxarchus*, [the *Abderite*] whom he followed every where, insomuch as he conversed with the *Gymnosophists* in *India*, and with the *Magi*.

c Laert.
d Laert.
e Laert.
f Suid.
g Laert.

CHAP. II.

His Institution of a Sect.

'HE seemeth (saith (*a*) *Ascanius* the *Abderite*) to have found out a noble way of
' Philosophizing, introducing Incomprehension,
' and the way of Suspension. For he asserted
' nothing, neither honest nor dishonest, just nor
' unjust, and so of every thing. That there is
' nothing indeed such, but that Men do all things
' by Law and Custom; That in every thing,
' this is not rather than that.

(*b*) This was was called the *Zetetick* Philosophy, from its continual enquiry after Truth; *Sceptick*, from its continual Inspection, and never finding; *Ephectick*, from the Affection which follows upon this Inquisition, Suspension ; *Aporetick*, from doubting of all dogmatical Opinions ; (*c*) *Pyrrhonian*, from *Pyrrho*. But *Theodosius*, in his *Sceptick* Summary, saith, That the *Sceptick* Philosophy ought not to be called *Pyrrhonian*: For if the motion of another's Intellect be incomprehensible to us, we cannot know how *Pyrrho* was affected; and, not knowing it, we cannot be called *Pyrrhonians*. Besides, neither was *Pyrrho* the first that found out *Scepticism, to assert no Doctrine*. It should rather be called, *like the course of* Pyrrho. Thus *Theodosius*.

On the other side, *Numenius*, (and he only, as *Laertius* observes) affirmed, That *Pyrrho dogmatizeth*; But of this more hereafter.

a Laert.
b Laert.
c Reading πυρρώνειος. See ext. Empir. hypoc. 1. 3.

CHAP. III.

His Manner of Life.

COnformable (*a*) hereunto was his manner of Life; he shunned nothing, nor took any heed, but went straight on upon every thing; Chariots, if it so hapned, Precipices, Dogs, and the like, not turning out of the way, nor having any regard to Sense, being saved, as *Antigonus* saith, by his Friends that followed him. But *Ænesidemus* affirms, That though he discoursed Philosophically upon Suspension, yet all his Actions were not inconsiderate.

(*b*) He used to walk forth solitary, seldome shewing himself to those of his Family. This he did upon hearing a certain *Indian* reproach *Anaxarchus* for teaching, That no Man but himself was Good, and yet in the mean time he frequented the Courts of Princes.

(*c*) He was always in the same state, insomuch that if any Man in the midst of his Discourse went away, he nevertheless continu'd his Discourse till he had ended it. Though in his Youth he were fickle, he took many Journies, never telling any whither he went, and chose such Company as he pleased.

(*d*) *Anaxarchus*, falling into a Ditch, he went on, not offering to help him; which when some blamed, *Anaxarchus* himself commended his Indifference and want of Compunction.

(*e*) Being found talking to himself, and demanded, Why he did so? *I study*, saith he, *how to be good*.

(*f*) In Arguments he was slighted by none, forasmuch as he had an extraordinary way of speaking to the Question; with which he took *Nausiphanes*, being a very young Man. He said, that his Affection ought to be *Pyrrhonian*, his Words his own. *Epicurus*, often admiring the Conversation of *Pyrrho*, continually question'd him concerning himself; so much was he honor'd by his Country, as that they made him chief Priest, and, for his sake, made a Decree of Immunity for all Philosophers. He had many that imitated his Unconcernedness, whence *Timon* saith of him in his *Pytho*, and *Silli*;

a Laert.
b Laert.
c Laert.
d Laert.
e Laert.
f Laert.

How learnd'st thou (aged Pyrrho) *to untye*
The slavish bands of empty Sophistry?
The Air of Greece *thou mind'st not, nor to know*
Whence things are made, and into what they go.

And again in *Indalmis*,

Pyrrho *I long to be inform'd by Thee,*
How Thou, a Man, liv'dst like a Deity?

Diocles (cited by *Laertius*) affirms the *Athenians* made him free of their City, for killing *Cotis* the *Thracian*; But this, as the learned *Causabon* hath observed, seems to be a mistake, occasion'd by the nearness of the Names; for it was *Pytho*, Disciple to *Plato*, who slew *Cotis*, as is manifest from *Plutarch*.

(*g*) *Eratosthenes* relates, That he lived piously with his Sister, and often carried to Market Birds; or, as it hapned, Pigs to sell, and managed his Houshold-Affairs with the like indifference, insomuch as he is reported to have washed a Sow.

(*h*) But as once *Philista*, his Sister, was sacrificing, (who being disappinted by a Friend, who promised to give her things for the Sacrifice, *Pyrrho* himself was constrain'd to buy them)
he

g Laert.
h Arist. it is mention'd also by Laert.

he was very angry, and fell out with her for it; whereupon one of his Friends saying, "That "his Actions were not answerable to his Dif- "course, nor such as his profession of Apathy, "or Indifference, required; He answer'd, *In- "difference is not to be shewn towards Women.*

i *Arist.* and *Laert.*
(*i*) On a time, a Dog flying upon him, he was troubled at it, [and got to a Tree] for which they who were by, deriding him, and cavilling at it, he said, "It is hard to put off "Man quite, yet we must first strive as far as "possible, with action against things, and if not "so with reason.

k *Laert.*
(*k*) They say, that upon occasion of some Wound, he underwent corrosive Medicines, Incision and Cauterising. His greatness of Courage is attested by *Timon.*

Philo the *Athenian*, who was his Disciple, saith, He mentioned *Democritus* with greatest respect, and next him *Homer* with much admiration, continually saying,

Just like the race of Leaves, is that of Men; and for that he compared Men to Flies, and Birds. He used also to repeat these Verses,

But dye, my Friend, why should'st thou thus lament? Patroclus dy'd too, who Thee far out-went.

And all things whatsoever that declar'd the Inconstancy, Vanity, and Childishness of Mankind.

Posidonius relates of him, That, being at Sea in a Storm, his Companions dejected, he, with a quiet mind, shewed them a Pig feeding in the Ship, saying, *A wise Man ought to be settled in such Indisturbance.*

CHAP. IV.

His Death, and Disciples.

HE (*a*) dyed 90 years old, (*b*) leaving nothing behind him in writing.

a *Laert.*
b *Laert.*
c *Laert.*

(*c*) Of his Disciples, some were very eminent, of which number were these,

Eurylochus, of whom is related this Extravagance: On a time he was so far transported with Fury, that, snatching up the Spit with the Meat upon it, he pursued the Cook into the *Forum:* And at *Elis,* being weary of those that disputed with him, he threw off his Cloke, and swam cross the River *Alpheus.* He was a great Enemy to the *Sophists,* as *Timon* saith.

Philo, [an *Athenian*] who frequently talked to himself; whence *Timon* of him.

Of private, talking with himself alone, Not minding Glory, or Contention.

Hecataeus of *Abdera.*
Timon, the *Phliasian,* who writ the *Silli.*
Nausiphanes, a *Teian,* whom, they say, *Epicurus* heard.

These all were called *Pyrrhonians* from their Master; *Aporeticks,* and *Scepticks,* and *Epheticks,* and *Zeteticks,* from their (as it were) Doctrine.

THE

THE HISTORY of PHILOSOPHY.

TIMON.

CHAP. I.
His Life.

APollonides the *Nicean*, in his First Book of Commentaries upon the *Silli*, Dedicated to *Tiberius Cæsar*, saith, that the Father of *Timon* was named *Timarchus*, by Country a *Phliasian*; and that *Timon*, whilst in his Youth, taught to Dance; but afterward changing his Mind, he

took

took a Journey to *Megara*, to see *Stilpo*, and having had conversation a while with him, returned home and Married. Then he went to *Elis* to see *Pyrrho*, taking his wife along with him, who, during the time of his being there bare him Sons; the Elder he called *Xanthus*, whom he taught Physick, and left him his Successor in the course of Life he himself had led.

Sotion in his Tenth Book affirms, he was very eminent. Wanting necessary Provisions, he went to the *Hellespont*, and *Propontis*, and professing Philosophy at *Chalcedon*, was exceedingly honour'd. From thence having now gotten a good stock, he went to *Athens*, and lived there to his end, except that once he made a short journey to *Thebes*. He was known to *Antigonus* the King, and *Ptolomæus Philadelphus*, as he himself attests in his Iambicks.

He was, as *Antigonus* saith, a lover of Wine, and gave himself much diversion from Philosophical Studies, as appears by his Writings.

He took much delight in Gardens and Solitude, as *Antigonus* reports; whereupon *Hieronymus* the Peripatetick said, That *as the Scythians shoot both when they fly and when they pursue; so of Philosophers, some get Disciples by running after them, others by running from them, as* Timon.

He was of an acute apprehension, and quick in deriding; a great lover of Writing, very skilful in Composing Poetical Fables, and Drama's. In his Tragedies he had much of *Homer*, and of *Alexander*. When Servants or Dogs disturb'd him, he gave over, aiming above all things at a quiet life.

Aratus demanding of him by what means he might procure an uncorrupt Copy of *Homer*? he answer'd, If you can light upon old Copies, not those that have been lately corrected.

His own Poems were thrown up and down, confusedly, and many times torn; insomuch as when *Zopyrus* the Orator read something of his, he made it up out of his own Memory; but when he came to the midst, there was a great gap, which he was ignorant of.

He was so indifferent, that he observed no time for Dinner.

Seeing *Arcesilaus* walking amongst Flatterers, He said, What do you here, where we Freemen are?

Of those who judge by the Senses, and Mind, he continually said, *Attagas* and *Numinius* are met.

b *Laert.* (b) He often used to sport after this manner; To one that admired all things, *Why then*, saith he, *dost thou not admire, that we, being but three, have four Eyes*; for he, and *Dioscorides* his Disc *Laert.* ciple, had each of them but one Eye, [(c) whence he used to call himself *Cyclops*] the other to whom he spoke had two. And on a time, being demanded by *Arcesilaus*, Why he came from *Thebes* to *Athens*, he said, *That I might laugh to see you fly*. But though in his *Silli* he abused *Arcesilaus*, yet in his Treatise entituled, *The funeral Banquet of* Arcesilaus, he commends him.

CHAP. II.

His Death and Writings.

HE Died almost 90 years of age, as *Antigo-* Laert. *nus*, and *Sotion* in his 11th Book affirm.

There was another Timon, *the Man-hater*; of whom, see *Lucian* and *Suidas*.

He writ *Poems*, and *Verses*, and *Tragedies*, and *Satyrs*, *Comical Drama's* 30. and *Tragical* 60. and *Silli* and *Cinædi*. There were also several Writings of his in *Prose*, amounting to 20000 Paragraphs.

Of his *Silli* there are Three Books, in which, as a Sceptick, he reproached and derided all the Dogmatists: The *First* written in his own Person, in a continued way. The *Second* and *Third* by way of Dialogue. He questioned *Xenophanes* the *Colophonean* about every thing, who answers to all. In the *Second*, He Treats of the more Ancient; In the *Third*, of the Later Philosophers, whence some entitle it the *Epilogue*. The *First* Book contains the same things, only delivered in another way, the Poem having but One Person. It begins thus;

Now busie Sophists all, come follow me.

CHAP. III.

Succession of the School.

ALthough, as Disciples of *Timon*, are mentioned by *Laertius*, *Xanthus* his Son, and *Dioscorides*; and, by *Suidas*, *Pyrrho* a *Phliasian*, Son of *Timarchus*; yet (a) *Monodotus* affirms, a *Laert.* " That *Timon* had no Successor, but that the " Institution was intermitted, until *Ptolomy* a " *Cyrenæan* renew'd it; whose Auditors (according " to *Hippobotus* and *Sotion*) were *Dioscorides* " a *Cyprian*, *Niolochus* a *Rhodian*, *Euphranor* a *Se-* " *lucian*, and *Praylus* of *Troas*, who was of so " setled a constancy, that being accused of " Treason, he chose rather to undergo the punishment " unjustly, than to plead to his Countrymen.

" *Eubulus* an *Alexandrian*, heard *Euphranor*; " him, *Ptolomy*; him, *Sarpedon* and *Heraclides*, " Disciple to *Heraclides* was *Ænesidemus* a *Gnos-* " *sian*, [who flourished, as *Aristocles* saith, at " *Alexandria*] he wrote eight Books of *Pyrrhonian* " Discourses. Him, *Zeuxippus* of *Polis* heard; " Him, *Zeuxis*, sirnamed Γωνιοπὲς; him, *An-* " *tiochus*, a *Laodicean* of *Lycus*; him, *Meno-* " *dotus* of *Nicomedia*, an Empirical Physician, and " *Theodas* of *Laodicea*, Disciple to *Menodotus* was " *Herodotus* of *Tarsis*, Son of *Arieus*; to *Herodotus*, *Sextus Empiricus*, whose Ten Books of *Sceptick Philosophy* are extant, and other excellent *Treatises*. [This *Sextus* may probably be esteemed that *Sextus Chæronensis*, Nephew of *Plutarch*, whom *Marcus Aurelius* the Emperor so honoured, that he admitted him to sit in Judicature with him.] " Disciple to *Sextus* was *Saturninus* a *Cythenæan*, " who was also Sirnamed *Empiricus*. Hitherto *Laertius*.

Having

'Having spoken of the Author of the *Sceptick* Philosophy, and its Succession, our Method leads us to set forth the Doctrine it self; which being already excellently handled by *Sextus Empiricus*, I think it would be more for the Reader's advantage, to have it delivered in his Words than in my own. The Treatise, I confess, may seem long; and indeed I had some Thoughts of abridging it: But when I considered, how difficult it were so to prune it, as to please all Persons, and that itself was intended but as a Summary; and that if it had been my case to have received it from some other hand, I should rather have desired to have it entire, of what length soever, than mangled even by a skilful Artist: I hope I shall be excused, if I so deal with the Reader, as I should desire to have been dealt withal my self. Neither can I suppose it will be unpleasant to those, who have been conversant in the more severe and knotty Disquisitions of the Schools; for the Author is Learned and Acute, even beyond the Subject he handles, and hath many passages of the Antients, which are not elsewhere to be had. But if any who have accustomed themselves only to lighter Studies, shall think it tedious, it is no great pains to turn over some Leaves, and see if they can find something else more acceptable.'

A Summary of SCEPTICISM.

Sexti Empirici, Pyrrhoneæ Hypotyposes.

THE FIRST BOOK.

CHAP. I.

The Three Differences of Philosophers in General.

IT is likely, that they who seek, must either find, or *deny that they have or can find*, or *persevere in the enquiry*. Hence (it may be) some of those who profess Philosophy, declare, they have found the truth; others hold it impossible to be found; others still enquire. They who suppose they have found it, are called *Dogmatists*; such are the *Peripateticks*, the *Epicureans*, the *Stoicks*, and others; they who think it incomprehensible, are *Clitomachus, Carneades*, and other *Academicks*; they who still enquire, are the *Scepticks*. So as there seemeth to be three kinds of Philosophy, *Dogmatick*, *Academick*, *Sceptick*. The two first we leave to others, intending a summary of the *Sceptick*: professing before-hand, that we are not sure any thing we say is absolutely so, as we affirm; but we shall plainly discourse on every thing, as it appeareth to us for the present.

CHAP. II.

The Parts of Scepticism.

OF *Sceptick* Philosophy there are two parts, *General* and *Special*; The general is that, wherein we explain the Character of *Scepticism*, declaring (1) the Signification of it; (2) the Principles; (3) the Reasons; (4) the Criterie, (or Instrument of Judication;) (5) the End; (6) the Common-places of Suspension; (7) how the Sceptical Phrases are to be understood; (8) the difference of *Scepticism* from those Philosophies that are most like it. The *Special* is that, wherein we contradict every part of that which is called Philosophy. But first of the *General*.

CHAP. III.

The Names of Scepticism.

THE *Sceptick* Institution is called also *Zetetick*, (*Inquisitive*) from the Act of Enquiring; *Ephectick*, (*Suspensive*) from the Affection rais'd by enquiry after things; *Aporetick* (*Dubitative*) either (as some say) from doubting of, and seeking after all things, or from being in doubt whether to assent or deny; *Pyrrhonian*, in as much as *Pyrrho* delivered it to us more substantially and clearly than those before him.

CHAP. IV.

What Scepticism *is.*

SCepticism *is a faculty opposing* Phænomena's *(Appearances) and Intelligibles, all manner of ways; whereby we proceed through the Æquivalence of contrary Things and Speeches, first to Suspension, then to Indisturbance.*

We call it a *Faculty*, from the power thereof; by *Phænomena's* we understand Sensibles, which we oppose to Intelligibles. These words, *all manner of ways*, may be referred to Faculty, taking the word Faculty, (or Power) simply. (a) It may likewise be applied to the opposition betwixt *Phænomena's* and Intelligibles, since we oppose them several ways, *Phænomena's* to *Phænomena's*, or Intelligibles to Intelligibles, or

a Καὶ τῷ ἀντιτιθέναι, &c. M.S. ᾗ τῶν, read τῷ.

One

One to the Other. Wherefore, to include all Oppositions, we say, *all manner of ways.* Or, all manner of ways, of *Phænomena's* and Intelligibles, not enquiring how *Phænomena's* seem, or how Intelligibles are understood, but taking them simply. By *contrary Speeches*, we mean not only Affirmation and Negation, but simply those which are repugnant. *Æquivalence* we call an equality as to Belief or Unbelief; so as neither of the repugnant Speeches is preferred as more credible than the other. *Suspension* is a settlement of the Intellect, whereby we neither affirm nor deny any thing. *Indisturbance* is a composure and tranquility of Mind: how Indisturbance is induced by Suspension, we shall discourse when we come to speak of the End.

A *Pyrrhonian* Philosopher is wholly addicted to the *Sceptick* Institution; for he is such an one as participates of this Faculty.

CHAP. V.

The Principles of Scepticism.

THe final Cause *(End or Aim)* of *Scepticism* we hold to be, Hope of *Indisturbance* : for Man's Mind being troubled at the unsetledness in things, and doubting what to assent unto, enquireth what is true and what false, that by determination thereof it may be quiet. But the chief ground of *Scepticism*, is, *that to every Reason there is an opposite Reason equivalent*, which makes us forbear to dogmatize.

CHAP. VI.

Whether the Sceptick *dogmatizeth, and hath a Sect, and treats of Physick.*

WE say, *The Sceptick doth not dogmatize:* not understanding *Dogma* as some do in the general acceptation, an *assent to any thing* (for the *Sceptick* assenteth to those Affections [or Impressions] which are necessarily induced by Phantasie, as (being hot or cold) he will not say, *I think I am not heated or cool'd* ; but we say, he doth not dogmatize in their sense who take *Dogma*, for an *Assent to any of those non-manifest things which are enquired into by Sciences.* For a *Pyrrhonian* Philosopher assents to nothing that is not manifest: neither doth he dogmatize when he pronounceth the *Sceptick* Phrases concerning things not manifest, as, *Nothing rather*, or, *I assert nothing*, or any of the rest, of which hereafter. For he who dogmatizeth, asserteth the thing, which he is said to dogmatize, to be such; but a *Sceptick* useth these expressions not as positive, for he conceiveth that this Proposition, *All things are false*, (amongst the rest) declareth it self also to be false; in like manner this, *Nothing is true*; so this, *Nothing rather*, (amongst others) implies itself is nothing rather to be credited; so as (together with the rest) it circumscribeth it self. The same we hold concerning the rest of the *Sceptick* Phrases. Now if he who dogmatizeth, asserteth that which he dogmatizeth to be such; but the *Sceptick* delivers his expressions in such manner as they may be circumscribed by themselves, he cannot be said to dogmatize. Moreover, in these Expressions he speaketh that which appeareth so to him, and declareth how he is affected, without engaging his Opinion, (or Judgment) but ascertaining nothing concerning external objects.

The same course we observe, being demanded *Whether the* Sceptick *hath a Sect*; If a Man understand *Sect*, to be an inclination to many Dogma's or Tenents, which have a mutual consequence, and likewise *Phænomena's*, and take *Dogma* to be an assent to something not manifest; we say he hath not a *Sect*. But taking *Sect* to be an Institution, which according to the *Phænomenon*, adhereth to some kind of Reason, that Reason shewing how to live rightly (meaning rightly, not only according to Virtue, but more simply, and tending to Suspension of Assent) we say, he hath a *Sect* ; for we follow some certain reason according to the *Phænomenon*, which sheweth how to live according to the Rites, Laws, and institutes of our Country, and our own Affections.

The like we say to those who enquire, *Whether the* Sceptick *treats of Physick* ; as to Assention grounded on a firm belief of any Physical dogm, we have nothing to do with Physick: But, as to equal opposition of all Speeches, even in Physick, we obtain Indisturbance, and thus also we deliver the *Logick* and *Ethick* parts of that which is called Philosophy.

CHAP. VII.

Whether the Scepticks *take away* Phœnomena's.

THey who say, *the Scepticks take away* Phœnomena's, seem not to understand what we have said: For we subvert not those Patheticks in Phantasy, which force us against our Wills to an Assent, (as we said before) Such are *Phænomena's*; For, when we enquire whether the Subject be such as it appears, we grant that it appears; but we enquire (not of the *Phænomenon*, but) of that which is said concerning the *Phænomenon*. For instance, Honey seemeth to us to be Sweet; this we grant, for we find it such to our Sense; but whether Sweet come within the reach of Reason, we doubt: this is not the *Phænomenon*, but that which is said concerning the *Phænomenon*. Moreover, when we raise questions concerning the *Phænomenon*, we endeavour not to subvert the *Phænomena's* (these we presuppose) but only to discover the Temerity of the Dogmatists. For if reason be so fallacious, that it almost takes away *Phænomena's* from our Eyes, how can we but mistrust it in things not manifest, rather then precipitately follow it?

CHAP. VIII.

The Criterie of Scepticism.

THat we acquiesce in *Phænomena's*, is manifest from what we say concerning the Criterie of the *Sceptick* Institution. *Criterie* is understood two ways; *One is*, that whereby we believe a Thing to be, or not be, (of this hereafter,

after, when we come to refel the opinions of others concerning it;) the *other* is of Action, whereby we judge in the course of Life what things are to be done, what not; this last is that of which we now speak. We say the Criterie of *Scepticism* is the *Phænomenon*; so call we Phantasie in power; for when it proceeds to Perswasion and coactive Passion, it is not questionable. As to the appearance, whether the subject be such or such, perhaps none doubteth; but whether it be such as it appeareth, is questioned. Thus acquiescing in *Phænomena's*, we live (without engaging Opinions or Judgments) according to the ordinary course of life, in regard we cannot be free from acting [as we may from assenting.]

This course of Life seems to be four-fold; conversant partly in *natural Instruction*, partly in the *Impulsion of Passions*, partly in *giving Laws and Customs*, partly in *teaching Arts*. In *Natural Instruction*, by which we are naturally endued with Sense, and Intellect; in *Impulsion of Passions*, as Hunger leads us to meat, Thirst to drink; in *giving Laws and Customs*, by which we learn that to live Vertuously is Good, to live Viciously, ill; in *teaching Arts*, by which we are not idle in those Arts which we receive. All this we say, without engaging our Opinion (or judgment.)

CHAP. IX.

The end of Scepticism.

IT follows that we treat of the *End of Scepticism*. The End is, *That for which all things are acted or contemplated, but it self is not for any other;* or *the last of things appetible*. We say that the End of the *Sceptick* is ἀταραξία, *Indisturbance*, in whatsoever belongs to Opinion, and μετριοπάθεια *Moderation*, in whatsoever belongs to Compulsion. For beginning to study Philosophy, that he may descern and comprehend which Phantasies are True, which false, and by that means not to be disquieted, he lights upon an equivalent Contrariety, of which not being able to judge, he suspends; and whilst he is accidentally in this Suspence, there follows it an Indisturbance as to things Opinionative: For he who is of Opinion there is something Good or Bad in its own nature, is continually disturbed; when those things which seem to him good, are not present, he imagineth himself (*a*) tormented with things Ill in their own nature, and pursueth that he conceives to be Good; which having obtained, he falleth into more Troubles. For being unreasonably and immoderately transported, and fearing a change, he useth all endeavour that he may not lose those things which he conceives Good. Whereas he who defines nothing concerning Things naturally Good or Bad, neither flyeth nor pursueth any thing eagerly, so that he remains undisturbed.

a Perhaps ποιηλα-ϑῆθαι.

Thus it happens to the *Sceptick*, as to *Apelles* the Painter, who having drawn a Horse, and trying to Paint his Fome, it succeeded so ill, that in Despair he threw the Spunge, wherewith he used to blot out Colours, at the Picture; which lighting upon the place, made an exact representation of Fome. In like manner, the *Scepticks* hoped to obtain Indisturbance by judging of the Unsetledness in *Phænomena's* and Intelligibles; which not being able to do, they suspended, and whil'st they were in Suspence, as it were accidentally, Indisturbance overtook them, as a Shadow follows the Body.

Yet we conceive not the *Sceptick* to be absolutely free from trouble; we grant, he is troubled by external Impulsions, he suffers Cold, Thirst, and the like. But in these, the ordinary sort of men are doubly Affected, first with the Passions themselves; and again, no less that these things are naturally ill, whereas the *Sceptick*, taking away the opinion that they are naturally ill, undergoes them more moderately. Hence we say, that the *Sceptick's* end is, in Opinionatives, Indisturbance; in Impulsives, Moderation; to which some eminent *Scepticks* add *Suspension in disquisitives*.

CHAP. X.

The general Ways (or Places) of Scepticism.

IN Disturbance following Suspension, it is requisite that we declare how we attain Suspension.

It ariseth, (to speak generally) from the opposition of things; we oppose either *Phænomena's* to *Phænomena's*, or *Intelligibles* to *Intelligibles*, or the former to the latter. *Phænomena's* to *Phænomena's*, as when we say, the same Tower seemeth afar off, round, near, square: *Intelligibles* to *Intelligibles*, as when to him, who from the order of the Celestial Bodies, argues, there is a Providence, we oppose, that Good Men are often Unfortunate; Bad Men, Fortunate, and thence infer, there is no Providence: *Intelligibles* to *Phænomena's*, as *Anaxagoras*, to *Snow is white*, opposed that *Water is Snow concrete*; but Water is black, therefore Snow is black.

Again, we sometimes oppose things *Present* to the *Present*, as those we last instanced; sometimes the *Present* to the *Past*, or the *Future*, as when an Argument is proposed, which we are not able to resolve, we say; 'As before the Author of the 'Sect, to which you addict your self, was born, 'the reason thereof did not seem sound, and yet 'the thing was the same in nature; so it is like-'ly, that a Reason (or Argument) contrary to 'this which you have alledged, may be subsi-'stent in Nature, and not yet appear to us; 'wherefore we ought not to assent to any Ar-'gument, how convincing soever it seems.

To shew these oppositions more exactly, I will lay down the common places by which Suspension is collected, not asserting any thing of their Number or Power; for it is possible, they may be of no force, or more in Number than we reckon.

CHAP. XI.

The ten Common places of Suspension.

THe ancient *Scepticks* have delivered ten Moods, whence Suspension seems to be collected, which they call also *Reasons* and (*a*) *Places*.

a Reading perhaps τύπες, for so *Laert.* κατα διχα τύπες.

Places. They are these; the First, from the *variety of living Creatures*; the Second, from the *difference of Men*; the Third, from the *difference of the Organs of sense*; the Fourth, from *Circumstances*; the Fifth, from *Positions, and Distances, and Places*; the Sixth, from *Commissions*; the Seventh, from *the quantities and constitutions of Subjects*; the Eighth, from *Relations*; the Ninth, from *rare Accidents*: the Tenth, from *Institutions, Customs, Laws, Fabulous Perswasions, and Dogmatical Opinions*.

This is the Order which we lay down; but there are three moods which comprehend the rest; First, from the thing *judging*; Secondly, from the thing *judged*; Thirdly from *both*. Under that of the thing judging, are comprehended the first *four*, the thing judging is either an Animal, or a Man, or Sense, or in some circumstance; under the thing judged, the *Seventh*, and the *Tenth*; under that which consists of both, the *Fifth*, the *Sixth*, the *Eighth*, and the *Ninth*. Again, these three are comprehended in the Mood of *Relations*; so as the most *general* is, that of Relations; the *Special*, the other three, under which are comprehended the ten. Thus much we probably hold as to their Number; now as concerning their Power.

CHAP. XII.

The first Common-place.

THe first Common-place we hold to be that whereby, *through the difference of living Creatures*, Phantasies not the same are derived from them. This we collect both from the difference of their *Generations*, and from the difference of the *Constitutions* of their Bodies. Of their *Generations*, because of living Creatures, some have their Being *without Coition*; others *by Coition*. Of those which are produced *without Coition*, some come of Fire, as the Crickets in Chimneys; some of *Corrupted Water*, as Gnats; some of *sour Wine*, as Snipes; some of *Earth*, whereof some of *Slime*, as Frogs; some of *Dirt*, as Worms; some of *Ashes*, as Beetles; some of *Plants*, as Caterpillers; some of *Fruits*, as Maggots; some of *putrify'd Animals*, as of *Bulls*, Bees; and of *Horses*, Wasps.

Of those which are produced *by Coition*, some are begotten by creatures of the *same Species*, such are the greatest part; others by Creatures of *different Species*, as Mules. Again, of living Creatures, some are brought forth *alive*, as Man; others come from *Eggs*, as Birds; some from a *lump* of Flesh, as Bears. It is therefore probable, that the Dissimilitudes and Differences of these Generations effect great Antipathies, receiving thereby contrary Temperament, Discordance, and Repugnance.

Moreover the *difference of several parts* of the Body (especially of those which Nature made for Judgment and Sense) may cause a great repugnance of Phantasies, according to the diversity of living Creatures. Those things which to us seem White, they who have the *Yellow Jaundice* affirm to be Yellow, and they who have a *Hyphosphagme* in their Eyes, Red. As therefore, of living Creatures, some have Eyes Blood-red, others Whitish, others of other Colours, it is likely they perceive Colours after different manners. Even to us, if we gaze a while upon the Sun, and immediately after look upon a Book, the Letters will seem of Gold, and as if they moved round.

Forasmuch also, as some living Creatures have naturally a certain *Brightness* in their Eyes, and emit from them a quick rare light, so as they can see in the Night, we think it probable, that External Objects incur not into *their* Sense, like what they seem to *ours*.

Again, Juglers, by anointing Candles with a Liquor made of the rust of Brass, or with the Blood of the Fish *Sepia*, cause the Standers-by to seem either *of the Colour of Brass, or Black*, by that little insertion of Unguent; Much more (*a*) likely is it, that the humours, mixed in the Eyes of living Creatures, being different, they have different Phantasies, from the same Object.

a M. S. εὐλογίστ- ερν.

Again, if we pinch the Eye, the Forms and Figures of visible things seem *long* and *narrow*: It is therefore likely, that all living Creatures which have Eye-balls oblique and narrow (as Goats, Cats, and the like) have a peculiar phantasie of Objects, different from those which have round Balls.

Looking-glasses, according to their several Forms, sometimes represent the Object *less*, as when they are concave; sometimes *oblong and narrow*, as the convex; some there are that represent the head of the beholder *downward*, and his feet *upward*. As therefore of the Organs of Sight, some are extuberant, some hollow, some plain; it is likely the Phantasies are different, and that Dogs, Fishes, Lions, Men, Lobsters, behold not things as great, or in the same Form, as they are in themselves; but according to the various Impressions which the sight suffereth from the Object.

It is the same in other senses; for how can we say, That Creatures covered with Shells, with Flesh, with Prickles, with Feathers, with Scales, are alike affected as to the Touch? Or, that they which have the hole of their Ear narrow, and they which have it wide; those which have Ears full of hair, and those which have smooth Ears, receive sound alike? Seeing that we our selves, (*b*) pressing the Ear, hear it different from that which it seems otherwise.

b Perhaps ϖϱοσού]ες.

Moreover, the *Smelling* may differ according to the difference of living Creatures; for, since we our selves are affected one way, when we have caught Cold, and are oppress'd with Flegm; another way, when the Parts of, and near the Head, abound with Blood, (disliking those Scents which to others seem sweet, and thinking our selves, as it were, hurt by them:) And since of living Creatures, some are naturally flegmatick, others sanguine; some cholerick, others melancholick, it is possible, that from thence, Scents seem different to them.

The like, as to the *Taste*; some have a Tongue rough and dry, others very moist, (even we our selves having our Tongues drier than ordinary in Feavers, think, that such things as are given us taste earthy, unsavoury, or bitter.) This we suffer, through the different prevalence of Savours in us. Since therefore in living Creatures, the organs of Taste are different, and abound with different Humors; hence they

they may in Taste receive different Phantasies from the same Objects.

For, as Meat digested turns here into Veins, there into Arteries; here into Bone, there into Sinewes, and so of the rest; manifesting a different power, according to the difference of the parts which receive it. And as Water, one and the same specifically, being infused into Trees, here turns into Leaves, there into Boughs; here into Fruit, Figs, Pomgranats, and the rest. And as one and the same blast of a Musitian in a Pipe, here is Flat, there Sharp: and the touch of the hand upon the Lute, makes sometimes a high, sometimes a low sound: so is it likely, that external Objects are differently apprehended, according to the different constitutions of the living Creatures, to which the phantasies occur.

This we learn more evidently from the Appetite, and Aversion of living Creatures. Unguents seem sweet to Men, but to Beetles and Bees are intolerable: Oyl is wholesome to Men, but kills Wasps, and Bees, if sprinkled upon them: Sea-water, to Men, is unpleasant of taste and unwholesome; to Fishes sweet and potable. Swine delight more to wallow in filthy Mire, than in pure Water.

Moreover, of living Creatures, some eat Herbs, some Boughs, some Sperm, some Flesh, some Milk, some love putrified Meat, some fresh; some raw, some rosted. Generally, what is pleasant to some, is to others unpleasant, distastful, and poysonous; as Hemlock fattens Quails, Henbane Swine; Swine delight also to eat Salamanders, as Stags do Serpents, and Swallows Cantharides: Pismires and Snipes are unpleasant and unwholesome for Men to take down; but the Bear, if he fall sick, recovers his strength by feeding on them. The Viper, if it touch a Bough of a Beach Tree, is taken with a Giddiness; so the Bat, if it touch the Leaf of a Plain-tree; the Elephant flies from the Ram; the Lion from the Cock; Whales, from the crackling of bruised Beans; the Tiger from the sound of a Drum. We might instance many more, but not insist too long hereupon; if the same things are to some pleasant, to others distastful; but pleasant and distastful, consist in Phantasies; then different Phantasies are arrived to several living Creatures, from the same Object. Now if the same things seem different to several Creatures, what the Object appears to *us*, we can say, but as to what it is in its *own* Nature, we will suspend; for we are not competent Judges betwixt our own and other Creatures Phantasies, our selves being parties in the difference, and consequently requiring a Judge, rather than being in a capacity of judging.

Again, neither without Demonstration can we prefer our own Phantasies before those of irrational Creatures, nor with Demonstration; for, to prove, that there is no Demonstration, perhaps the Argument or Demonstration will either be apparent to us, or not apparent; if not apparent, we shall not entertain it with belief; but if apparent, seeing the question is concerning (*Phænomena's*) things apparent to living Creatures, and the Demonstration seems apparent to us, who are in the number of living Creatures, the Demonstration it self will be questioned, (forasmuch as it is apparent) whether it be true. But it is absurd, to endeavour to prove a thing in Question, by a thing which is likewise in Question, for so the same thing shall be Credible and Incredible; Credible as used in Demonstration; Incredible, as requiring to be demonstrated. We shall not therefore find a Demonstration, whereby to prefer our own Phantasies before those of other living Creatures, called Irrational. Now if Phantasies be different, according to the variety of living Creatures, and it be impossible to judge of them, it is necessary we suspend as to the external Objects.

CHAP. XIII.
Whether the Creatures, commonly termed Irrational, have Reason.

WE will (over and above) compare the Creatures termed Irrational, with Men, as to their Phantasie, that we may, after the more serious Reasons, sport with the self-conceited Opinion of the *Dogmatists*. Most of our party confer Irrational Creatures in general, simply with Men; but because the *Dogmatists* cavil hereat, we the better to deride them, will insist only upon one Creature, the *Dog*, than which none seemeth more contemptible. By this means we shall know, that the Creatures of which we now discourse, are nothing inferior to us, as to credit of *Phænomena's*.

Now that this Creature excelleth us in Sense, is acknowledged by the *Dogmatists*; it is of a much quicker Scent, whereby it pursueth beasts unseen; it discovers them sooner by the Eye than we, and is likewise more acute of Hearing.

Come we therefore to discourse, which is twofold, *Internal* and *Enunciative*. Let us first examine the *Internal*; This, according to (our greatest Adversaries amongst the Dogmatists) the *Stoicks*, seemeth to be conversant in these things; in Election of things convenient, and Evitation of their Contraries; in knowledge of the Arts conducing hereto; in comprehension of the Vertues belonging to their nature concerning Passions. Now the Dog, in whom we instance, chuseth things convenient, and flieth the hurtful; he pursueth his Food, and runneth away from the Whip; he hath likewise the Art of acquiring things proper for him. Neither is he destitute of Vertue; Justice being distributive to every one according to their merit; the Dog, who fawneth upon his Friends and Benefactors, and revengeth himself upon his Enemies, by whom he is injur'd, is not void of Justice. And if he hath this Virtue, all the Virtues being linked together, he hath all the rest, which the wisest allow not the ordinary sort of men. We see he is Valiant, in revenging Wrong; Prudent by the testimony of *Homer*, who makes *Ulysses*, not discovered by any of his Friends, owned by *Argus* the Dog; not deceived, either by the alteration in the Body of the Man, swerving from his own comprehensive Phantasie, (which is manifest) he hath in a degree above Man. But, according to *Chrysippus*, (who oppugns irrational Creatures with most eagerness) he partakes of their so much cryed up *Dialectick*; for he saith, When the Dog cometh into a way divided into three, he makes choice of the third by several (*a*) Indemonstrables;

a What Indemonstrables are, see afterwards, Lib. 2. cap. 13.

strables; for having scented the two ways by which the Beast did not pass, he runs strait upon the third, without scenting it; which is as much (saith the old Philosopher) as to discourse thus; *The Beast passed either this way, or this way, or this way; but neither this way, nor this way, therefore this way.*

Moreover, he apprehends and cures his own Sickness: If a Splinter get into his Foot, he presently strives to get it out, by rubbing his Foot against the Ground, and with his Teeth. If he be Wounded, (Wounds that are kept clean being easily cur'd, the putrid not easily) he continually licks the Hurt. He likewise strictly observes the rule of *Hippocrates*, the Cure of the Foot consisting in rest; he, if hurt in that part, holds it up, and stirs it as little as he can. If he be troubled with ill Humors, he eats Grass; by which means, vomiting up that which disagreed with him, he is cured. Now if this Creature can chuse what is convenient for him, and fly what is inconvenient; if he hath the art of acquiring things proper to him, and can apprehend and cure his own Sickness, and is not void of Virtue, in all which consists the perfection of intrinsecal Discourse, the Dog must be Perfect, as to that. For which Reason as I conceive (b) some Philosophers chose to be called by name of that Creature.

b The Cynick.

As to *Enunciative* discourse, it is not necessary to examine it; for there are (c) some Dogmatists who condemn it, as contrary to Virtue; whence they kept silence all the time of their Institution Besides, though we should suppose a Man to be Dumb, yet none will say, he is void of Discourse, (irrational;) and on the other side, we see many living Creatures which have the speech of Man, as Pyes, and the like. To omit which, though we understand not the Voices of Creatures (termed) Irrational, it is nevertheless likely they discourse among themselves. We understand not the Language of Foreigners, it seems a continued Sound without variety. But we hear that the Voice of the Dog is different; of one kind, when he assaults; of another, when he howls; of another, when he is beaten; of another, when he fawns. In a word, he who examines it curiously, will find a great variety of Voice, not only in this Creature, but in others, according to the diversity of Accidents. So that the Creatures, called Irrational, may justly be said to participate of Enunciative Discourse; and if they come not short of Men, in acuteness of Sense, nor in Intrinsecal Discourse, nor in Enunciative, (though that be not necessary) certainly they are no less creditable, as to Phantasy, than we.

c Pythag.

It is possible, perhaps, to shew the same discourse in all other Creatures; as, who will deny Birds to have a Sagacity, and Enunciative discourse, seeing they know not only things present, but the future, which they declare to such as are able to comprehend it, (amongst many other ways) by (d) Voice. But this Comparison is added, as I said before, more than necessary, without which, we have sufficiently, I conceive, declared, That our own Phantasies are not to be preferred before the Phantasies of Irrational Creatures. Now if Irrational Creatures are no less creditable than we, in dijudication of Phantasies, and Phantasies are different, according to the variety of the Creatures; what every object *appeareth* to me, I am able to say; but what it *is* in itself, (for the Reasons alledged) I Suspend.

d Augury.

CHAP. XIV.

The second Common place.

THe second Common place of Suspension we hold to be, *from the Diversity of Men*; for, though we should grant it were more reasonable to stand to the judgment of Men, than of any other living Creature; yet shall we find so much difference amongst our selves, as may well induce Suspension. Man, they say, consists of two parts, *Soul* and *Body*, in both these we differ one from another; in *Body*, by *Form* and *Constitution*; The Body of a *Scythian* differs in Form from the Body of an *Indian*. This difference ariseth, as we said, from the different prevalence of Humors, and from the different prevalence of Humors arise Phantasies, as we said upon the first ground; whence in Election and Evitation of external things, there is great difference among them. *Indians* delight in some things, we in others; but to delight in several things, argueth a reception of different Phantasies from the same Objects.

We differ also in *Constitution*; there are some who can digest Beef, easier than Anchovies; some, upon drinking of *Lesbian-Wine*, are troubled with Choler. It is reported of an old *Athenian* Woman, That she drank four drams of Hemlock without any hurt; And *Demophon, Alexander's* Sewer, whilst he was in the Sunshine, or in a Bath, was cold; in the Shade, was hot. *Athenagoras*, the *Argive*, felt no Pain at the biting of Scorpions, or Phalangies. The People called (a) *Psylli*, never take Hurt by the biting of Serpents or Asps. (b) The *Tintyritæ* of *Ægypt* take no Hurt by Crocodiles. The *Æthiopians*, that live opposite to *Meroe*, along the River *Hydaspes*, eat Scorpions, Snakes, and the like, without danger. *Rufinus* of *Chalcis* when he drunk *Hellebore*, never vomited, nor was purged any way by it, but digested it as ordinary drink. *Chrysermus*, the *Herophilian*, if at any time he eat Pepper, was taken with *the Passion of the Heart*, even to hazard of his Life. In *Soterius* the Chyrurgion, the smell of the Fish *Silurus* excited Choler. *Andron* the *Argive* was so little subject to Thirst, that when he travelled through the Deserts of *Lybia*, he did not need Drink. *Tiberius Cæsar* saw in the dark. *Aristotle* mentions a (c) *Thasian*, who thought the Apparition of a Man went always before him. Now there being so great diversity in the *Bodies* of Men, (it is sufficient that we instance these few, out of the multitude acknowledged by the *Dogmatists*) it is probable, that Men differ from one another in *Soul* also, for the Body is a kind of Image of the Soul, as the Physiogmony-Science sheweth. But the greatest evidence of the infinite difference of Men, as to Intellect, is the discordance amongst them in Election and Evitation, rightly expressed by the Poets; as *Pindar*,

Some joy in swift-heel'd Coursers; some,
In living wantonly at home;
And others on the Ocean roam.

a Procop. Hist. Mir. 19.
b The Text is defective; but Franciscus Mirandula renders it thus, Qui Tyntiritæ dicuntur incolæ, Ægypti, inter Crocodilos impunè versantur. de vanit. Gent. Lib. 2. cap 23.
c Antipheron Oretanus.

And

And the Poet.

In several Actions, several Men delight.

The *Tragedians* are full of this, as

*If all Men what is good did see
Alike, they would not Disagree.*

And again,

*Alas! that some Men take delight
In things which grieve another's sight.*

Since therefore Appetition and Aversion consist in Pleasure and Hatred, but Pleasure and Hatred consists in Phantasy; and since the same things are pursued by some, shunned by others; we may infer this Consequence, That they are not alike affected by the same things, otherwise they would all alike desire to shun them. Now if these things affect differently, according to the diversity of Men, there may justly be induced Suspension, since what every subject appeareth, every one perhaps according to his particular Apprehension may express; but what it is in its own Nature, we cannot assert. For we must either give Credit to all Men, or to some few; if to All, we undertake Impossibilities, and admit Repugnancies; if to some Few, let them tell us, which those Few are, The *Platonists* will say, we must assent to *Plato*; the *Epicureans*, to *Epicurus*; and by their confused Disagreement, reduce us again to Suspension. If any Man alledg, we ought to assent to the greater Number; he argues Childishly, since None can over-run all Men, and examine what every one thinks best; and it is possible that in Countries unknown to us, what things are rare to us, are there frequent; and what happens frequently to us, happens there very seldom. As for instance, in such a Country there are many who receive no Harm by the Biting of Phalangies, Few who receive Harm thereby. And so in all other Constitutions: wherefore it is also necessary to induce Suspension, by reason of the diversity of Men.

CHAP. XV.

The third Common-place.

FOrasmuch as *Dogmatists* are so self-conceited, as to affirm, That their Judgment in things ought to be preferred before all others; though we know how absurd this Postulation is, (for they are Parties in the Controversie, and having first prejudged themselves, if then they judge *Phænomena's*, even before they begin to judge, they seize on the *Phænomena's* as already judged:) yet that, in our Dispute, fixing the Discourse upon one Man (that wise Man they dream of) we may arrive at Suspension, let us examine the third Common-place.

This we derive *from the difference of the Senses*. That the Senses differ from one another is manifest. *Pictures* seem to the Eye rising and falling, but not such to the Touch. Many esteem *Honey* pleasant to the Tongue, unpleasant to the Eye; whence it is impossible to say, whether it is simply pleasant, or unpleasant. The like of *Unguents*, they please the Smell, displease the Taste. *Euphorbium* is hurtful to the Eyes, but not to any other part of the Body: therefore, whether it be simply hurtful to the Body, we cannot say. *Rain-water* is good for the Eyes, but frets the Arteries and Lungs; as Oyl doth also, though it smooths the Skin. The *Sea-Tortoise*, applied to the extream parts of the Body, causeth Numbness, but laid to any other part makes no alteration. Thus, what each of these things is in its own nature, we cannot affirm; but how it appears to others, we may. We might instance more; but, not to insist longer hereon than our design permits, let us say, Every sensible *Phænomenon* seemeth to incur a several way into our Senses, as an Apple smooth, fragrant, sweet, yellow. It is therefore unmanifest, whether it really hath these qualities, or whether it hath but one quality, which seemeth different, according to the diversity of the Senses; or whether it hath many more qualities, some of which incur not to our Senses. For, that it hath but one quality, may be argued from what was said before, concerning the Nutriment of living Creatures, the growth of Trees by Rain, the unequal sound of the Breath in Pipes, and other Instruments. It is therefore possible, the Apple may have but one quality, and yet be looked upon as different, by reason of the difference of the Organs of Sense, by which it is apprehended. Again, That it is possible, the Apple may have more qualities than appear to us, we argue thus: Let us suppose a Man, endued from his Birth with Touch, Smell, and Taste; but wanting Sight and Hearing, he will think there is nothing Visible, nothing Audible: So it may be, that we having Five Senses, of all the qualities of an Apple, perceive only those, whereof our selves have the apprehensive Faculty; yet in the mean time, it may have other qualities, incident to other Organs of Sense, which we have not. Therefore neither can we perceive what their sensible Operations are.

But Nature, may Some object, hath equally commensurated the Senses according to the Sensibles. What Nature? there being so confused a disagreement among the *Dogmatists* concerning her Essence? For if any Man judge what Nature is, if he be one of the Unlearned, he is, according to them, not worthy Credit; if a Philosopher, he is interess'd in the Difference, being one of the Parties to be judged, not the Judge. Now if it be nothing absurd to say, The Apple hath all the qualities we seem to apprehend, and more than these; or, on the contrary, that it hath not even those which incur to our Senses, it will be unmanifest to us, how the Apple is qualited. The same of other Sensibles. And if the Senses comprehend not External Objects, neither can the Intellect comprehend them. Thus Suspension may be induced from External Objects.

CHAP. XVI.

The fourth Common-place.

THat as well over-running in our Discourse every Sense, as receding from Sense, and receding from Sense, we may arrive at Suspension, we come to the fourth ground.

This is said to be *from Circumstances*, By περιστάσεις, (Circumstances) we understand Dispositions; we say it consists in being according *to Nature*, (sound;) or *contrary to Nature*, (unsound;) in *Waking* or *Sleeping*, in difference of *Age*, in *Motion* or *Rest*, in *Hate* or *Love*, in *Want* or *Satiety*, in *Drunkenness* or *Thirst*; in *Predispositions*, in *Courage* or *Fear*, in *Joying* or *Grieving*. According as we are Sound or Unsound, things occur variously to us; Frantick, and Divinely-inspired Persons, think they hear Spirits, we not; and those kind of Persons often say, they smell Perfumes of Storax or Frankincense, when we smell none. Again, the same water poured upon any Part that is Inflamed, seems scalding, to us lukewarm: The same Garment to those that have a Hyposphagm in their Eyes, seems bloody, to me not: The same Honey to me is sweet, to those that are troubled with the over-flowing of the Gall, bitter. If any shall alledge, that the admission of some humors, in those who are unsound, excites Phantasies not conformable to their Objects; we answer, Forasmuch as they, who are in health have commixed Humors, those Humors may cause external Objects (which perhaps appear to those who are unsound, such as they are indeed in themselves) to appear to the healthful, such as they are not in themselves. For, to attribute the power of changing Objects to the Humors of the one, and not to those of the other, is vain; since as they who are in health, are according to the nature of the healthful, but contrary to the nature of the sick; so they who are sick, are contrary to the nature of the healthful, and according to the nature of the sick: So that these also are to be credited, as being according to Nature.

From *Sleep* and *Waking* arise also different Phantasies; we have not the same Phantasies sleeping, which we have waking; nor the same waking, which we have sleeping; therefore their existence is not simple, but relative. Thus in Sleep we see things, which when we Wake, are inexistent; not that they are inexistent in themselves, for they exist in sleep, as well as these things which are said to exist when we are awake.

From *different Ages*; the same Air to old Men seems cold, to the youthful temperate; the same meat to old Men heavy, to the young light. So the same voice to some seemeth low, to others loud. In like manner are they, who differing in age, differently incline to desire, or abhor things. Children delight in Whips and Tops; they who come to Man's estate, prefer other things; old Men, others. Whence many be inferr'd, That different Phantasies are derived from the same object, according to the difference of ages.

From *Motion* or *Rest*, things appear unlike; that which seems unmoved to us, while we stand still, when we sail we think it moves.

From *Love* or *Hate*; some abhor Swines flesh, which others eat with much delight. Many that have deformed Mistresses, think them beautiful.

From *Hunger* or *Satiety*: The same meat to an hungry Man, seems pleasant; to a Man that is full, unpleasant.

From *Drunkenness* and *Sobriety*; Things, which when we are sober, ws esteem undecent; drunk, seem not such to us.

From *Predispositions*; The same wine to such as have eaten Dates or Figs a little before, seems sowre; to such as have eaten Nuts or Pulse, sweet. The *Parastas of a Bath warms those that go in, cools those who go out, if they have stay'd any while in it.

*See Vitruv. Architect. lib. 6. cap. 10.

From *Courage* or *Fear*; the same thing to a timorous Man seems dreadful, to a Valiant nothing so.

From *Sorrow* and *Joy*; the same things which trouble the sorrowful, delight the joyful.

Now there being so great difference and disproportion of Habits, and Men being constituted sometimes in one Habit, sometimes in another, what every Object *seems* to any, perhaps it is easie to declare; but what it *is*, is not easie, since the difference is indijudicable. For he that judgeth it, either is conversant in one of the forementioned Habits, or in none: To say he is in none, that is, he neither is Well nor Sick, neither moveth nor resteth, nor is of any age, and wholly void of the other habits, is most absurd: On the other side, if being in any of these habits, he judgeth Phantasies, he is himself a Party in the Controversie, and consequently cannot be a sincere Judge of external Objects, being infected with the habits in which he is. For he who is awake, cannot compare the Phantasies of those who are asleep, with the Phantasies of those who are awake; nor he, who is in health, compare the Phantasies of the sound and the sick: for we sooner assent to such things as are present, and move us, than to things not present.

Moreover, the difference of such Phantasies is indijudicable another way. He that prefers one Phantasie before another, and one circumstance (or habit) before another, either doth it without judgment and demonstration, or upon judgment and demonstration. Not without, for then he is of no credit; nor with, for if he judge Phantasies, he must do it by a Criterie, this Criterie must be either the true or false; if false, neither is it to be credited; if he say it is true, he affirms it, with demonstration or without. If without demonstration, it will be uncreditable; if with demonstration, it is absolutely necessary that the demonstration be true, otherwise neither will that be creditable. He will therefore say, the Demonstration alledged to prove the Judicatory creditable, is true. Whether doth he affirm this, as having judged, or not judged? If not having judged, he is not to be credited; if as having judged, he must acknowledge he hath judged it by a Criterie, of which Criterie we shall require a Demonstration, and then of that Demonstration a Criterie. Thus the Demonstration will continually require a Criterie to confirm it, and the Criterie a Demonstration to shew it is true: Therefore the Demonstration cannot be true, unless a true Criterie precede it; nor can the Criterie be true, unless the Demonstration be first credited. Thus the Criterie and the Demonstration fall into the *Alternate Common-Place*, wherein both will be found not creditable; for either wants credit, till the other afford its assistance to confirm it.

If therefore we cannot prefer one Phantasie before another, neither without a Demonstration and Criterie, nor with them, the Phantasies which different Habits produce, will be indijudicable. Thus Suspension is induc'd from the nature of external Objects.

CHAP. XVII.

The Fifth Common-place.

THE fifth Common place is from *Positions*, *Distances*, and *Places*: for through any of these, the same things seem different: the same Walk, to him that is entring into it, seems narrow at the further end; to him who is in the middle, equally broad. The same Ship, at a distance, seems little and fixt; near, great and in motion. The same Tower seems afar off, round; near, square. This for *Distance*.

From *Place*; the light of a Candle in the Sunshine seems dim; in the dark, bright: The same Oar under water, seems broken; above water, straight. An Egg in the Fowl is soft; in the Air, hard. The *Lyncurium* [a stone concrete of the *Lynx* his urine,] in the *Lynx* is humid, in the Air, hard. Coral is soft in the Water, hard in the Air. A voice sounds diversly through a Pipe, through a Flute, and in the open Air.

From *Position*; the same Image, laid flat, seems smooth, but inclining, seems to have Extuberances and Cavities; the Neck of a Pigeon, as it is variously turned, seems to have a different colour.

Since then all *Phænomena's* are seen in some *Place*, at some *Distance*, and in some *Position*, every one of which (as we said) causeth a great alteration in Phantasies, we shall be hereby reduced to Suspension. For he who would prefer one of these Phantasies before another, attempts an impossibility; for if he assert it of them simply, without Demonstration, he shall not be credited; if he would use Demonstration, and acknowledge that Demonstration to be false, he confutes himself: If he say it is true, it will be required he bring a Demonstration to prove it true, and a third to prove the second, because that also must be true, and so to infinite; but to alledge infinite Demonstrations, will be impossible. Therefore one Phantasie cannot be preferred before another by Demonstration. And if the aforesaid Phantasies can neither be judged with Demonstration, nor without it, there must be inferred Suspension; since what every thing *seems* according to this *Position*, this *Distance*, or in this *Place*, we may indeed affirm; but what in it self it *is*, (for these Reasons) we cannot.

CAAP. XVIII.

The Sixth Common-Place.

THe Sixth Place is, from *Commixtions*: Whence we infer, That no Object incurreth into our Sense simply, but together with some other; what this Mistion *is*, as well from the external Object, and from that together with which it is seen, it is perhaps possible to say, what it seems to us; but what the external Object is, purely in it self, we cannot say: For no external thing incurreth into our Sense, purely of itself, but with some other; whence, as I conceive, it seems different to beholders. Our Complexion seems of one Colour in warm air; of another in cold; neither can we say what our colour is naturally, but what it seemeth with these Circumstances. The same voice seems different in a thin Air, and in a thick. Perfumes are of stronger scent in a Bath, or in the warm Sun, than in the Cold; a Body surrounded with Water, is light; with Air, heavy.

Moreover, (setting aside external Commistion) even our eyes have in themselves tunicles and humors. Visible objects therefore, because we cannot see without these, are not perhaps perceived exactly and purely, for we perceive them with Admistion. Hence to those who have the Jaundies, all things seem yellow; to those who have a Hyposphagm, red. And forasmuch as the same voice seemeth different in open and strait places, from what it seems in narrow and crooked; in calm Air, from what it seems in tempestuous; it is probable, we perceive no Voice purely. For our Ears have narrow oblique holes, and are said to be troubled and prepossess'd by vapours from the parts next the Head.

Likewise by our Nostrils, and the Instruments of Taste, when Objects are presented, we perceive their Smell, and Taste, but not purely. Wherefore what external Objects are exactly in themselves, the Senses cannot perceive, by reason of Commistions. Neither can the Intellect, because the Senses, her Guides, err. Perhaps also, the Intellect alters that which it receiveth from the Senses, by intermixing something of its own. For in the parts wherein the Hegemonick, according to the Dogmatists, is placed, we see there are certain humors, as in the Brain, or the Heart, or what part soever they shall place it in. Thus, by this Common-place, seeing that we can determine nothing concerning the Nature of the external Objects, we Suspend.

CHAP. XIX.

The Seventh Common-place.

THe Seventh Place is, *from the Quantities and Constitutions* of Subjects, generally stiled *Compositions*. That we are inforced upon this ground to Suspension concerning the nature of things, is manifest; as, the shaving of Goats-horn seems white, but in the Horn it self black; filings of Silver seem black, but in the whole white; the pieces of the *Tænarian* Stone polish'd seem white, the whole seems yellow; Sands taken singly seem rugged; altogether in a heap, smooth; *Ellebore* eaten young and downy, suffocates, but at full growth it doth not; Wine drunk moderately, strengthens; excessively, weakens: Meat commonly shews a different power, according to the quantity; excess thereof, for the most part, oppresseth the Body with crudities, and Cholerick humors. Now as to these we are able to say, What the thin parts of the Horn seem separated, and what they seem compacted; what the minute parts of Silver, and what the whole consisting of those parts; what a little piece of the *Tæna-*

rian Stone, and what the whole : So likewise in Sands, *Hellebore,* Wine, Meat, we can express what they are relatively ; but the nature of the things themselves we cannot, by reason of the difference which happens in composition. Generally, healthful things are hurtful, if we take too much of them ; and hurtful things hurt not, if we take but little of them. This is most evident in Medicine ; a just measure in their Composition is beneficial; but sometimes, to put in ever so little more or less, is not only not beneficial, but destructive, and often deadly. Thus Quantities and Compositions confound the existence of external Objects, whereby we are justly reduced to Suspension, not being able to affirm any thing of the external Object.

CHAP. XX.

The Eighth Common-Place.

THe Eighth-Place is, *From Relation;* for every thing having relation to some other, what they are simply in their own Nature, we suspend from affirming. (The term [*Is,*] here and elsewhere we use improperly for Seems ; which is as much as to say, Every thing seems to have relation to some other.) This is said to be two ways ; one is to the thing judging, for the External Object appeareth such to the thing judging ; the other is to the things which are considered together with it, as Right to Left.

That all things are relative, we argued before, as well *to the thing judging ;* for the appearance of a thing is what it seems to this Animal, to that Man, to such a Sense, to such a Habit : As likewise *to the things seen together with it;* for every thing appears by such a Commistion, such a Manner, such a Composition, such a Quantity, such a Position.

That all things are Relative, may also be argued thus: Whether are different things different from Relatives, or not? If not different, then they are Relatives; if different, since every thing that differs from another is relative, (as implying a relation to that from which it differs) they are relative by difference.

Again, of things, some, according to the Dogmatists, are Supream Genus's ; others, most Special *Species* ; others, *Genus's* and *Species*: But all these are Relative, therefore there is nothing that is not Relative.

Moreover they say, that of things, some are manifest, some unmanifest. The manifest *(Phænomena's)* signify the unmanifest ; the unmanifest are signify'd by the *Phænomena's,* for they hold *Phænomena's* to be the sight of the unmanifest things ; but the significant and the significate are relatives, therefore all things are relative.

Besides, of things, some are like, some unlike ; some are equal, others unequal ; but these are relatives, therefore all things are relative.

Even he who saith, *All things are not relative,* confirmeth, that they *are relative* : For by the Arguments wherewith he oppugns us, he sheweth, that this Assertion, *All things are relative,* hath reference only to us, but not to all in general.

Thus all things being relative, what every object is in its own nature we cannot say, but only what it appears in relation: Whence it follows, that, as to the nature of the things, we suspend.

CHAP. XXI.

The Ninth Common-Place.

THe (*a*) Ninth Place is, *from frequent or rare Contingence,* thus deduced: The Sun is certainly much more wonderful than a Comet ; yet because one is seen every day, the other seldom, the Comet makes us wonder so much, as to think some strange thing is portended thereby, the Sun not so. But if we should imagine the Sun to appear but seldom, and as soon as he had enlightned all things, presently to withdraw, and leave all in darkness, we should therein find much cause of wonder. Earthquakes trouble us far more at first, than when we are us'd to them. How doth a man admire the Sea at first view ? Even corporeal Beauty strikes us much more at the first sight, than after we have been accustomed and acquainted with it. Moreover, things that are scarce are esteemed, the common not esteemed. If Water were hard to be got, how much would it be prized above all things, which we now value at so high rates ? If Gold were as common as Stones, who would hoard it up? Since therefore the same things are sometimes esteemed wonderful or precious, sometimes not such, according to their scarcity or commonness, we infer, that, How things seem according to their frequent or rare Contingences, we may perhaps say ; but simply, what these external Objects are in themselves, we cannot ; and therefore suspend.

a This Ninth place *Laertius* saith that *Phavorinus* reckons the eighth, and *Sextus* and *Ænesidemus* the tenth; and that which is the tenth, *Sextus* makes the eighth. *Phavorinus* the ninth. But in the Editions, and M. SS. of *Sextus* the ninth is the same as with *Laertius*; the tenth is with *Laertius* the fifth.

CHAP. XXII.

The Tenth Common-Place.

THe Tenth-Place chiefly concerns *Morals,* as being drawn from *Institutions, Customs, Laws, Fabulous Perswasions,* and *Dogmatick Opinions.*

Institution is the election of a course of life, or any other thing, which is done by one or many ; as by *Diogenes,* or the *Lacedemonians.*

Law is a covenant written by the Magistrate, which whosoever transgresseth is punished.

Custom (ἔθος or συνήθεια, they differ nothing) is the approbation of something by the common consent of many, which he who transgresseth is not punished ; as, it is a Law, that we commit not Adultery ; a Custom, that we lie not with our Wives in publick.

Fabulous Perswasion is the approbation of feigned things which never were ; such are the stories of *Saturn,* which yet some believe true.

Dogmatick Opinion is the approbation of something which seems to be confirmed by some Reason or Demonstration; as that Atoms, Homoiomeria's, Least-parts , or the like, are the Elements of things.

Of these, we oppose sometimes *one of the same kind to another of that kind* ; sometimes *one kind to another.* For example, *Custom* to *Custom,* thus ; Some *Æthiopians* paint the skins of their children, we do not so. The *Persians* think it decent to wear Garments stained like Flowers, we think it undecent. Some *Indians* lie with their Wives in publick, most people think it unseemly.

Law to *Law*, thus: Amongst the *Romans*, he who quits his Inheritance doth not quit his Fathers name; amongst the *Rhodians*, he is forced to quit it. At *Tauris* in *Scythia*, there was a Law, That strangers should be sacrific'd to *Diana*; amongst us, it is prohibited to put a Man to death in a Temple.

Institution to *Institution*; as, that of *Diogenes* to that of *Aristippus*; that of the *Lacedemonians* to that of the *Italians*.

Fabulous Perswasions to *Fabulous Perswasions*; as, when we say, that *Jupiter* is sometimes called Father of Men and gods; sometimes the Ocean is so called, as,

Ocean the Sire of gods, Tethys the Mother.

Dogmatick Opinions, one to another; as when we say, Some assert one Element, others infinite; and some hold the Soul to be mortal, others immortal; some hold the World to be governed by Providence, others not.

Again, we oppose *Custom* to something of different kind, as to *Law*; when we say, Adultery is forbidden amongst us, used amongst the *Massagetes*, as a thing indifferent; according to *Eudoxus* the *Gnidian*, in his first Book. It is prohibited amongst us to lie with our Mothers; in *Persia*, nothing so frequent as to marry them. The *Ægyptians* marry their Sisters, which we are forbidden by Law.

To *Institution*: as there are very few, who will lie with their Wives in publick; yet *Crates* did so with *Hipparchia*. *Diogenes* wore his upper Coat continually; it is not our use to do so.

To *Fabulous Perswasions*: As it is fabled, That *Saturn* eat his Children; but with us it is a custom to bring up our Children. Again, we use to worship the gods, as good, not subject to ill; but the Poets feign them to be wounded, to envy, and the like.

To *Dogmatical Opinion*: It is a custom with us, to pray to the gods for good things; but *Epicurus* denies the gods take any care of us. Again, *Aristippus* thought it an indifferent thing to wear a Woman's garment, we think it undecent.

We oppose *Institution* to *Law*, thus. There is a Law, that no Man shall strike a Free person; yet Wrestlers strike one another, following the institution of their life. *Homicide* is forbidden, yet *Gladiators* kill one another, upon the same ground.

Fabulous Perswasions to *Institution*; as when we say, Fables tell us that *Hercules* served *Omphale*, spun, and did other actions of a most effeminate person; but *Hercules* his institution of life was generous.

To *Dogmatick Opinion*; as Wrestlers addicted to the pursuit of Glory, as of a good thing, chuse a laborious kind of life; but many Philosophers assert Glory to be an ill thing.

We oppose *Law* to *Fabulous Perswasion*: as, The Poets introduce the gods committing Adulteries, and the like; but with us, the Law prohibits such things.

To *Dogmatick Opinion*; as, *Chrysippus* holds it a thing indifferent, to lie with Mothers or Sisters; the Law forbids it.

We oppose *Fabulous Perswasions* to *Dogmatick Opinion*. As, the Poets say, *Jupiter* came down on earth to lie with mortal Women; but the Dogmatists think this impossible. Again, the Poets say, that *Jupiter*, through excessive grief for *Sarpedon*, let fall drops of Blood, upon the earth; but it is a Tenent of Philosophers, that the gods are not subject to any Passion. Likewise the *Dogmatists* take away *Hippocentaures*, instancing them as examples of Inexistency. Many other Presidents might be alledged, but let these serve.

Now there being so great difference, (as appeareth also by this place) what the Subject *is* in its own Nature, we cannot say; but only what it *seems* as to that Institution, this Law, this Custom, *&c.* Wherefore, upon this ground also we suspend concerning the nature of External Objects.

CHAP. XXIII.

The Five Common-Places.

THE (*) later *Scepticks* deliver Five Common-Places of Suspension; the First *from Disagreement*; the Second *reducing to Infinite*; the Third *from Relation to something*; the Fourth, *Hypothetick*; the Fifth *Alternate*.

* *Laertius* ascribes these to *Agrippa*.

The First place, *from disagreement*, is that by which we find an indetermined disagreement concerning the thing in the practice of life, and amongst Philosophers; whence, not being able to prove or disprove either side, we are reduced to Suspension.

The second place, *from infinite*, consisteth in this; whatsoever is alledged in proof of the thing proposed, we say requireth something else whereby that may be proved; and that likewise something else, and so to infinite: So that not having a ground whereon to fix our Beginning, we suspend.

The Third, *from Relation*: Of this place, we have treated already.

The Fourth, *Hypothetick*, is when the *Dogmatists*, perceiving themselves reduc'd to Infinite, begin upon some ground which they prove not, but would have it simply granted without Demonstration.

The Fifth, *Alternate*, is when that by which we should prove a thing, requireth it self to be proved by that thing; then, because we cannot assume either to maintain the other, we suspend.

That all questions may be reduced to these places, we shew briefly thus. Whatsoever is propounded, is either sensible or intelligible; but which soever it be, there is disagreement concerning it. Some hold that sensibles only are true, some that Intelligibles only; others, that some Sensibles, and some Intelligibles. Whether will they say, the controversy is dijudicable, [capable of decision] or indijudicable? if indijudicable, it is fit we suspend; for in things indijudicably repugnant, it is not possible to assert: But if dijudicable, we ask, How it shall be judged? As a Sensible, (for we will first take that for instance) whether by a Sensible or by an Intelligible? If by a Sensible, forasmuch as we disagree concerning Sensibles, even that Sensible will require another for its proof; which other, if it be Sensible,

Sensible, will require another, and so to infinite: But if a Sensible require to be determined by an Intelligible, forasmuch as Intelligibles also are controverted, that (as being Intelligible) will require adjudication and proof; which way shall it be proved? If by an Intelligible, they run, as before, into Infinite. If by a Sensible, forasmuch as Intelligible was assumed for proof of a Sensible, and a Sensible for proof of an Intelligible, the *Alternate common-place* is brought in.

But if, to avoid this, the Disputant would assume something as granted, without demonstrating it, whereby to demonstrate the Consequent, *the hypothetical place* occurs, which is inextricable. For if he be creditable in things which he requires to be granted and supposed, we likewise may be creditable, in requiring their Contraries to be granted. If that be true which he supposeth, he renders it suspicious by supposing (not proving) it; if false, his foundation is unsound. Further, if such a supposition conduce any thing to proof, let him suppose the thing in question, rather than another thing by which he would prove it. If it be absurd to suppose the thing controverted, it is also absurd to suppose the ground upon which we build it. That all Sensibles are *Relatives*, is manifest, for (as such) they relate to those who have Sense. It is therefore evident, that whatsoever Sensible thing is proposed to us, may easily be reduced to one of these five Places.

So likewise we argue concerning Intelligibles. If the Controversie be indijudicable, we shall be allowed to suspend; if dijudicable by an Intelligible, it runs into *Infinite*; if by a Sensible we drive them to *the Alternate place*: For the Sensible being Controverted, as not capable of being judged by itself, because of running into Infinite, will require an Intelligible, as the Intelligible the Sensible. He who hereupon would assume any thing as granted, is as foolish on the other side. Further, an Intelligible is relative, for it is such in reference to the Intelligent; and if it were indeed such as it is named, it would not be controverted. Thus we reduce Intelligibles also to these five Places. Whereupon we are necessitated to suspend our Assent upon any proposition. These are the five Places introduced by the later *Scepticks*, not to exclude the other Ten, but more variously to refel the Temerity of the *Dogmatists*.

CHAP. XXIV.

The Two other Common-Places.

THey likewise deliver two Places more of Suspension; for seeing that whatsoever is comprehended, seems to be comprehended (or understood) either *through it self*, or *through some other*; they seem to introduce an absolute Inextricability of all things. That nothing is comprehended *through it self*, they say, is manifest, from the Controversie amongst Natural Philosophers, concerning (I think) all Sensibles and Intelligibles: which Controversie is indijudicable, (not to be determined) by reason that we cannot use either a Sensible or an Intelligible Criterie; for, whichsoever we take, it will be uncreditable, as being controverted.

For the same Reason they conceive that nothing can be comprehended *through some other*; for if that through which it is comprehended, will continually require to be comprehended through some other, they run into *the Alternate place*, or into *Infinite*. But if a man will assume any thing as comprehended through itself, by means whereof he would comprehend some other thing, to this it is repugnant, that nothing can be comprehended through itself, for the reasons before alledged. But how that which is repugnant can be comprehended either through itself, or any other, we doubt, since there appeareth no Criterie of Truth or Comprehension; but without Demonstration, signs are destroy'd, as we shall prove hereafter. Hitherto of the Places of Suspension.

CHAP. XXV.

The Places for Confutation of Ætiologicks.

IN like manner, as we have delivered these places of Suspension, some have laid down others, particularly against Ætiologies, (Allegations of Causes or Reasons) because the Dogmatists please themselves exceedingly therein. *Ænsidemus* delivers eight Places, whereby he conceives all Dogmatick Ætiology may be refelled, as defective.

The *First*, for that the kind of Ætiology, which is conversant in things not apparent, hath not an acknowledged proof from apparent things.

The *Second*, for that there are many great Reasons to induce an Inclination, and but one alledged.

The *Third*, for that of things done orderly, Reasons are given that shew no order.

The *Fourth*, for that taking *Phænomena's* as they are, they think they comprehend things not apparent, as they are likewise; for things not apparent are perhaps effected the same way as *Phænomena's*, perhaps some other peculiar way.

The *Fifth*, for that all (very nigh) give Reasons, according to their own particular supposed Grounds, not according to the general and universally received ways of disputation.

The *Sixth*, for that they often take for granted such things as are easily comprehensible; but omit their Contraries, tho' equally probable.

The *Seventh*, for that they alledge Reasons not only repugnant to *Phænomena's*, but even to their own Suppositions.

The *Eighth*, for that the things which appear, and those which are controverted, being equally dubious, they would prove their opinion concerning doubtful things, by things as doubtful.

He addeth, that it is possible, in Ætiologicks some may err by other places dependent upon these.

But perhaps, the five places of Suspension are sufficient against Ætiologicks. For a man must either alledge a Reason which agreeth with all Sects of Philosophy, and with *Scepticism*, and with *Phænomenon's*, or not: But to alledge such a Reason is impossible, for all *Phænomena's* and not-apparents disagree; and disagreeing, it will be required, that a cause or reason thereof be given. Now if he alledge a *Phænomenon* for reason of a *Phænomenon*, or a not-apparent for reason of a not-apparent, he runs into *Infinite*. If he prove one kind by the other, he incurs *the Alternate place*. If he make a stand any where, or say, that the cause (or reason) is such, as that it consists with the thing by him alledged, he falleth into the place of *Relation*, taking away that which is according to the proper nature of the thing; or if he assume something by way of supposition, we shall disallow it. Thus also may the Temerity of the *Dogmatists* in Ætiology be confuted.

CHAP. XXVI.

The Phrases of the Scepticks.

Forasmuch as in using these places of Suspension, we express ourselves by some particular Phrases, which declare the Sceptical affection, and our own passion, as *Not more, Not to be defined*, and the like, it follows, that we treat of these.

Let us begin with this, *Not more*, for which sometimes we say, *Nothing more*; not using (as some conceive) *not more* in particular questions; and *nothing more*, in the general; but both promiscuously. We therefore will treat of them both under one. It is an imperfect expression, as when we say διπλῆ, we imply ἐςία διπλῆ; and when πλείεια, we imply πλείεια ὁδὸς; so when we say, *Not more*, it is as much as to say, *Not more this than that*, upwards nor downwards. There are some Scepticks, who for the Interrogation ἢ, use τί, *Which more, this or that?* taking τί, casually, as if they should say, διὰ τί, *Why more this than that?* Interrogations are commonly used for * Axioms, as,

To what Man is the Wife of Jove unknown? and Axioms for Interrogations, as, *I would know where Dion dwells?* and, *I demand for what cause a Poet is admir'd*. Menander useth τί for διὰ τί, as, Τί γὰρ ἐγὼ καταλελοίπαμεν.

* What Axioms are, see in the doctrine of the *Stoicks*.

This Phrase, *Not more this than that*, declareth likewise our affection, by which we are brought, by reason of the equivalence of contrary things, to ἀρρεψία; we mean *Equivalence*, in that which appeareth probable to us. Contraries are those which generally oppugn one another; 'Αρρεψία is an inclining to neither. Now this Phrase, *Not more*, though it seem to imply assent or denial, we use not that manner, but indifferently and improperly, either by way of question, or for *I know not to which of these I should assent, and to which I should not assent*. But being required to declare what seemeth to us, we use the Phrase by which we declare it indifferently. Know likewise, that when we say, *Not more*, we assert not that the doubt is true, but only express what appeareth to us.

The next is *Aphasia*; *Phasis* is taken two ways, generally and particularly: generally for any speech, declaring assertion or denial, as, *It is day, It is not day*: particularly, for Assertion only; in which acception, the Negatives are not called φάσεις. *Aphasia* therefore is a renunciation of *Phasis*, in the general signification, which comprehends both Affirmation and Negation. It is that affection by which we neither assert a thing, nor deny it. We assume *Aphasia*, not because the nature of things is such, as necessarily move it; but declaring, that at present we are thus affected, as to these or those questions. Always remember, that we neither assert nor deny any thing unapparent, but yield to those which move us pathetically, and necessarily compel us to assent.

These Phrases, τάχα καὶ ὀυ τάχα, ἔξεςι καὶ ὀυκ ἔξεςι, ἐνδέχεῖ καὶ ὀυκ ἐνδέχεῖ, *Perhaps*, and *Not Perhaps*, we use for, *perhaps it is, perhaps it is not*. Thus, for brevity, we take, *not perhaps*, for, *perhaps it is not*. Here again we contest not about words, nor enquire what they naturally signifie, but take them indifferently. These Phrases declare an *Aphasia*, for he who saith, *Perhaps it is*, implies its contrary to be as probable, because he assents not that this is. The same of the rest.

Ἐπέχω, *I suspend*, we take for, *I cannot say whether I ought to believe or disbelieve the thing proposed*, declaring, That the things seem equal to us, as to Belief and Unbelief; whether they are equal in themselves, we assert not, but speak of the *Phænomenon*, as it incurs into our Sense. Ἐποχὴ, *Suspension*, is so called, ἀπὸ τῦ ἐπέχεσθαι τὴν διάνοιαν, *from the mind's being held in Suspense*, betwixt asserting and denying, through equivalence of the thing questioned. The same we say concerning,

Ὀυδὲν ὁρίζω, *I determine nothing*; ὁρίζειν, we conceive to be, not simply to speak a thing, but to pronounce an unmanifest thing with assent. Thus perhaps the *Sceptick* will be found to determine nothing, not so much as this, *I determine nothing*. For it is not a Dogmatical Opinion: (that is, an assent to something not manifest) but a Phrase declaring our affection. When therefore the Sceptick saith, *I determine nothing*, he meaneth, *I am so affected at the present, as not dogmatically to assert or deny any of the things controverted*. This he saith, as expressing how they appear to him, not pronouncing it enunciatively with perswasion.

Ἀορισία is a passion of the mind, whereby we neither assert nor deny things dogmatically controverted, that is, not-manifest. When therefore the *Sceptick* saith, *All are undefinable*, he taketh *are* for *appear* so to him; he saith *all*, not *beings*, but those *not manifest*, controverted by the *Dogmatists*. *Indefinable*, that is, *Not to be preferred before their Contraries, or common repugnants, by belief or disbelief*. And as he who saith, *Ambulo*, implieth, *Ego ambulo*; so he who saith, *All things are indefinite*, implieth, *as to us*, or, *as it seemeth to me*. The Meaning therefore is this, *All things controverted by the Dogmatists appear so to me, as that I think none of them more worthy belief than its contrary*.

The same is our meaning when we say, *All are incomprehensible*; we take [*all*] in the same sense, and imply [*to me*;] as if we should say, *All things controverted among the Dogmatists seem to me incomprehensible*. We affirm not, they are incomprehensible in their own nature, but declare our own affection, that we conceive we understand them not, by reason of the equivalence of Contraries.

Likewise the Phrase, ἀκαταληπῶ, and ὀυ καταλαμβάνω, declares our own affection, by which the *Sceptick*, for the present, neither asserts nor denies any of the things not-manifest that are in Controversie. This is evident from what hath been said upon the other Phrases.

When

When we say, *To every Speech an equal Speech is opposite*, we mean, to every Speech that we have examined. *Speech*, we take not simply, but for that which asserteth something dogmatically, that is, of a thing not manifest, not only by premises and conclusion, but any other way. *Equal*, we take not simply, but as to belief and disbelief. *Is opposite*, we take generally for is repugnant, implying, *as I think*. When therefore we say, *To every Speech, there is an equal Speech opposite*; the meaning is, *To every Speech that I have examined, which asserteth any thing dogmatically, there seemeth to me to be opposite another Speech, asserting likewise dogmatically, equal to it for belief or disbelief.* Thus this Expression is not dogmatical, but the signification of an human affection, which is that which appeareth to the person affected. Some there are who pronounce it thus, *To every Speech, to oppose an equal Speech*, laying this down as a Precept, That to every Speech dogmatically asserting any thing, we should oppose the Speech which dogmatically asserteth its contrary. Thus addressing their words to the *Sceptick*, they use the Infinitive for the Imperative, *To oppose*, for, *Let us oppose*. They advis'd the *Sceptick*, not to be deceived by the *Dogmatists*, nor to give over his Inquisition, for the indisturbance which they conceive accompanies those who suspend their assent in every thing, as we said before.

It is not necessary to alledge more of these Phrases, even of these alledged some might have been spared; but take it for a Rule, In all the Sceptical Phrases, we affirm not that the Phrases themselves are true; for we say, that some may be taken away by others, and are circumscribed by those very things of which they are spoken, as purgative Medicines expel not only Humors, but, together with the Humors, themselves out of the Body. Moreover, we say, that we use them not, as properly signifying the thing to which they are applied, but indifferently, or (if they will so call it) improperly; for, it becomes not the *Sceptick* to contest about words. This we may the better do, in that the words are said not to signifie any thing purely in themselves, but relatively, and therefore as well in reference to the *Scepticks*. Furthermore, it must be remembred, that we pronounce them not generally of all things, but of the not-manifest, and those which are dogmatically controverted. The *Phænomenon* (that which appeareth to us) we declare; but of the nature of the external Object, we affirm nothing. By what hath been said, I conceive, that all Sophisms brought against the Sceptical Phrases, may be resolved.

CHAP. XXVII.

Wherein Scepticism *differs from those Philosophical Sects which are most like it; and first wherein it differs from the Philosophy of* Heraclitus.

Having declared the *signification* of Scepticism, its *Parts*, its *Criterie*, its *End*, its *Places of Suspension*, its *Phrases*, and its *Character*; it followeth that we explicate briefly, *wherein it differs from those Sects which seem most like it*, that by this means we may the better understand it.

We will begin with the Philosophy of *Heraclitus*. That this differs from our Institution, is evident; for *Heraclitus* asserteth dogmatically concerning many things not manifest, which (as I said before) we do not. But forasmuch as the followers of *Ænesidemus* said, the *Sceptick* Institution is the way to the *Heraclitian* Pholosophy, Because that *Contraries appear in the same Thing*, is precedent to *Contraries are in the same Thing*: But the *Scepticks* say, *Contraries appear in the same Thing*, and the *Heraclitians* go on farther, affirming *Contraries are in the same Thing*; We answer, That Contraries appear in the same Thing, is not a Doctrine of the *Scepticks*, but a thing evident by Sense, not to the *Scepticks* only, but to all other Philosophers, and Men; as none dare deny, but Honey to the Sound is sweet; to such as have the overflowing of the Gall, Bitter. Hereupon, the *Heraclitians* begin from the common Prænotion of men, as we do also, and perhaps other Sects: Wherefore if they had taken this sentence, *There are Contraries in the same thing*, as from this saying, *All are Incomprehensible*, or from, *I determine nothing*, or some other of that kind, perhaps they might collect rightly what they say; but since they have some Principles incident not only to us, but to other Philosophers, and even to the course of Life itself, why should any say, our Institution is preparative to the Philosophy of *Heraclitus*, more than to any other Sect, or to the course of Life itself, seeing all of us use these in common? Neither know I whether the *Sceptical* Institution divert not from the Philosophy of *Heraclitus*, rather than conduce to it; since the *Sceptick* reprehends, as temerarious, all that *Heraclitus* asserted dogmatically, contradicting his *Conflagration*, contradicting also his Tenent, *That there are contraries in the same Thing*; and to every Doctrine of *Heraclitus*, (deriding the temerity of the *Dogmatists*) he saith, *I comprehend not, I determine not*, (as before) which oppugns the *Heraclitians*. But it is absurd to say, That an Institution, which oppugns another, is the way preparative to the Discipline it oppugns. Therefore it is absurd to say, That the *Sceptical* Institution is the way to the *Heraclitian* Philosophy.

CHAP. XXVIII.

Wherein Scepticism *differs from the Philosophy of* Democritus.

In the like manner, the Philosophy of *Democritus* is said to be all one with *Scepticism*, in that it seems to use the same matter; for from the appearance of Honey, to some Sweet, to some Bitter, *Democritus* argued, that in itself, it is neither Sweet nor Bitter, and thereupon used to say, *not more*, a Sceptick-phrase. But this Phrase, *not more*, is taken by the *Scepticks*, and by the *Democritians*, after a different manner. The *Democritians* signifie by it, that *neither is*, but we, that *we know not whether both of the* Phœnomena's *are, or whether neither is*: Herein we dissent from them. But far greater is the difference in that *Democritus* saith, *Atoms, and Vacuum, truly are*; That herein, he differs from us, (though he begin with the inequality, and disagreement of *Phænomena's*) I conceive it needless to prove.

CHAP. XXIX.

Wherein Scepticism *differs from the* Cyrenaick *Sect.*

SOme affirm the *Cyrenaick* Sect to be the same with *Scepticism*, for as much as it holds, *that the Affections themselves only are comprehended*. Nevertheless it is different from *Scepticism*; for it holds *Pleasure, and a light motion of the Flesh* to be the *End*; we, *Indisturbance*, to which the End they propose is contrary. For whether Pleasure be present or absent, he who asserts it to be the End, is disturbed, as we said * before. Besides, we suspend only from asserting any thing concerning external Objects; but the *Cyrenaicks* affirm they are of an incomprehensible Nature.

* *Chap.* 7.

CHAP. XXX.

Wherein Scepticism *differs from the Institution of* Protagoras.

PRotagoras will have Man to be πάντων χρημάτων μέτρον, *the measure of all things*; *of Beings, as they are*; *of not Beings, as they are not*. By μέτρον, he means the Criterie; by χρημάτων, πραγμάτων, *of things*; which is as much as to say, *Man is the Criterie of all things*; *of Beings, as they are*; *of not Beings, as they are not*. Hereupon, he asserts the *Phænomena's* to be particular to every one, and thus brings in the *relative Common place*, whereby he seems to have community with the *Pyrrhonians*; But he differs from them, as we shall easily find in explicating his Opinion. He saith, *Matter is fluid, and being in perpetual Fluxion, Appositions are made instead of Substractions, and the Senses are transmutated and changed, according to the several ages and constitutions of the Body*. He saith also, *The Reasons* (or Powers) *of all* Phænomena's *are subjected in Matter*; *so that Matter*, in it self, *is all things which it appears unto all*. *But Men at different times perceive things different, by reason of their different Habits*; *He whose Constitution is sound, of the things which are in Matter, perceiveth those which are capable of appearing to such Persons*; *they who are otherwise disposed, perceive the things which are capable of appearing to Persons of a contrary Constitution*. *The same Reason there is in the difference of Ages, in Sleeping and Waking, and in all kinds of Habits*. Man therefore, according to him, *is the Criterie of things that Are*; *For all things which appear to Men, Are*; *those which appear not to any Man, Are not*. Thus we see, he dogmatically asserted, *that Matter is fluid*, and that *the Reasons of all Phænomena's are subjected in it*, wherein we, as being things not manifest, suspend our assent.

CHAP. XXXI.

Wherein Scepticism *differs from the* Academick Philosophy.

SOme hold the *Academick* Philosophy to be the same with *Scepticism*, let us therefore examine it. It is said, there were more than three *Acamedies*; One, the most *Ancient*, instituted by *Plato*; the Second, and middle *Academy*, by *Arcesilaus*, Disciple of *Polemon*; the Third, and new *Academy*, by *Carneades* and *Clitomachus*; there are who reckon a Fourth, instituted by *Philo*, and *Charmides*; some also a Fifth, by *Antiochus*. We will begin with the most *Ancient*. Some hold *Plato* to be *Dogmatick*, others *Aporematick* (dubitative;) others in some things, *Dogmatick*, in some, *Aporematick*. For in his Gymnastick Discourses, where *Socrates* is introduced deriding or disputing with the *Sophists*, they say he hath a *Gymnastick*, and *Aporematick* Character; but when he declareth his own Opinion in the Person of *Socrates*, *Timæus*, or the like, a *Dogmatist*. As for those, who say he is a *Dogmatist*, or in some things *Dogmatick*, in others *Aporematick*, we shall not need to meddle with them; for they acknowledge, that he dissents from us. Whether he be purely *Sceptick*, we discourse at large in our *Hypomnemata*; we shall now only examine it briefly, according to *Permedotus*, and *Ænesidemus*, (for they chiefly undertook this Task) who say, that *Plato*, when he asserted *concerning Idea's*, or that *there is Providence*, or that *Life joined with Virtue, is to be preferred before Life joined with Vice*: If he assent to these as existent, he averreth dogmatically: if he assent as to the more probable, he differs from the *Sceptick* Character, in preferring one before the other, as to Belief and Disbelief, as is manifest from what hath been said already. Nor though he pronounce things *Sceptically* in his *Gymnasticks*, is he therefore a *Sceptick*, for he who asserteth any one thing dogmatically, or preferreth any Phantasie before another, for Belief, or Disbelief, of a thing not manifest, followeth the *Dogmatick* Character, as *Timon* sheweth, speaking of *Xenophanes*: For (having often commended him, insomuch that he writes his *Silli* in his Person) he maketh him to complain, and say;

I wish my Soul were subtle, and her Eye
*So sharp, as might * both sides at once descry.*
Lost in the doubtful way, I long have straid;
Even though (grown old) *I had with care essay'd*
Every opinion, search'd all Theory,
For unto which could I my mind apply?
All into one resolve, and this one ever
Drawn into one like Nature, doth persever.

Whence also he calls him ὑπόνοφον, and not absolutely, ἄνοφον, *void of Pride*, thus;

† *Xenophanes, not wholly free from Pride,*
The fixions of old Homer *did deride*;
*And fram'd a God, * whose Figure doth dissent*
From Men; *equal each way*: *Intelligent.*

He calls him ὑπόνοφον, as being not quite ἄνοφ©; and Ὁμηρεπάτην ἐπικοπτην, for that he reproached and blamed the † fabulous way of *Homer*. Now *Xenophanes* asserted, besides *prænotions* (as others also) that the *Universe is one*, and that *God is of the same Nature with all things*; that *He is Sphærical, Impassible, Immutable, and Rational*; Whence it is easie to shew that *Xenophanes* differs from us. Moreover, from what we

* M.S. Ἀμφοτερόβλεπτος.
† *Laert.* Ξεινοφάνης.
* M.S. Ἐκπίν, perhaps ξέσον. *Laertius* saith, He held, That God is of a Spherick Form, nothing like to men. This seems to be meant ἀπάνθρωπον, to the figure refer ἴσον ἁπάντα, such is a Globe.
† His Stories concerning the gods, *Laert. in Xenoph.*

we said, it is manifest that *Plato*, though of some things he doubt, yet because in others he asserts, concerning the Essence of things not manifest; and of things not manifest, preferreth some before others, is no *Sceptick*.

Those of the *new Academy*, though they say *all things are Incomprehensible*, differ from the *Scepticks*, perhaps in saying that all things are Incomprehensible; for they assert this, but the Sceptick *admits it possible that they may be comprehended*. But more apparently they differ from us in the dijudication of Good and Evil. For the *Academicks* say, that something is Good and Ill, not after our manner, but as being perswaded, it is more probable, that what they call Good is Good, than the contrary: Whereas we say not that any thing is Good or Ill, as thinking what we say is probable, but without Opinion, we follow the ordinary course of Life, or otherwise we should do nothing. Moreover we hold Phantasies to be equal, as to Belief and Disbelief; but they, that some are *Credible*, others *Incredible*. The *Credible* also, they subdivide into many kinds, some they hold to be *Credible* only, some to be *Credible* and *Circumcurrent*, some to be *Credible* and *Circumcurrent*, and *Undistracted*; as, a Rope lying loose in a dark Room, a Man receives a *Credible* Phantasie from it, and runs away; another considering it more exactly, and weighing the circumstances, as that it moves not, that it is of such colour, and the like, to him it appears a Rope, according to *Credible* and *Circumcurrent* Phantasie. *Undistracted* Phantasie is after this manner. It is reported that *Hercules* brought *Alcestis* back from the *Inferi*, after her Death, and shew'd her to *Admetus*. He received a true and *circumcurrent* Phantasie of *Alcestis*, but remembring she was Dead, his Phantasie was distracted from assent, and inclined to Disbelief. Now the new *Academicks*, before Phantasie which is simply *Credible*, prefer that which is *Credible* and *Circumcurrent*; and before both, that which is *Credible* and *Circumcurrent* and *Undistracted*. For though, both *Academicks* and *Scepticks* say they believe some things; yet herein is a manifest difference between their Philosophies: *To believe*, is taken several ways; sometimes for *not to resist*, as a Boy is said to believe his Master; sometimes for *assenting to another, with an earnest resolute desire of the thing*, as a Prodigal believes him who perswades him to live sumptuously: Now *Carneades* and *Clitomachus* using the word *Believe*, and *Credible*, as with vehement inclination, we only for yielding without propensity to any thing; herein also we differ from them.

We differ likewise from the *new Academy*, as to what belongs to the *End*: They use in the course of Life what is *Credible*, we following Laws, Customs, and natural Affections, live without engaging our Opinion. We might add more instances of the difference between us, if it were not too large for our design.

But *Arcesilaus*, Institutor and President of the *middle Academy* seems to me to participate so much of the *Pyrrhonian* Reasons, as that his Institution and Ours is almost the same. For neither is he found to assert concerning the Existence of Inexistence or any thing, neither doth he prefer one thing before another for Belief or Disbelief, but in all things he suspends, holding *Suspension* to be the *End*, which, as we said brings us to *Indisturbance*. He likewise holds particular Suspensions to be good, particular Assertions to be ill. But if we may believe what is related of him, they say, at first sight he appears a *Pyrrhonian*, but was indeed a *Dogmatist*; and that making trial, by doubts, of his Disciples, whether they were capable of *Plato*'s Doctrine, he was thought to be Aporetick, but that to his more ingenious Friends he taught the Doctrine of *Plato*, whence *Aristo* of him;

Pyrrho *behind,* Plato *before,*
And in the middle, Diodore.

For, though a *Platonick*, he used the Dialectick of *Diodorus*.

Plato saith, As to (the Stoical Criterie) *comprehensive Phantasie, things are incomprehensible; as to the natures of the things themselves, comprehensible*. *Antiochus* transferred the *Stoick* Sect into the *Academick*: whence it was said of him, That he taught the *Stoick* Doctrine in the Academy, for he shewed, that the *Stoical* Tenents were in *Plato*. Hereby it appears, the *Sceptick* Institution is different from the fourth and fifth *Academy*.

CHAP. XXXII.

Whether Empirical Medicine be the same with Scepticism.

SOme hold *Empirical Medicine* to be the same with the *Sceptick Philosophy*; but we must know, (notwithstanding it holds, that things not-manifest are incomprehensible,) it is not the same with *Scepticism*, neither is this Sect fit for a *Sceptick*, who, in my opinion, ought rather to pursue that which is called *Methodick*; which alone, of all the Sects of Medicine, seems to behave it self not temerariously in things not-manifest; nor arrogantly to determine whether they are comprehensible or incomprehensible; but following *Phænomena's*, it takes from them what seemeth profitable, according to the course of the *Scepticks*. For, as we said before, the common life of a *Sceptick* consists of four parts, conversant in the *Instruction of Nature*, in the *Impulsion of Passions*, in the *Constitutions of Laws and Customs*, and in the *Tradition of Arts*. As a *Sceptick* therefore, by the Impulsion of Passions, is brought from Thirst to Drink, from Hunger to Meat, and the like; so a Methodick Physician is guided by the Passions to that which is convenient, from Constriction of the Pores to Relaxation, as when we shun the condensation of Cold, by going into the Sun-shine; from Relaxation of the Pores to Constriction, as when sweating immoderately in a Bath, we retire to the cooler Air. That the things contrary to Nature lead him to those that are agreeable to Nature, is manifest even from a Dog, who having got a Thorn in his Foot, endeavours presently to get it out. Not to reckon up every thing, which were to exceed the scope of a Summary, I conceive, that all things said in this

manner

manner by the Methodicks, may be referred to the impulsion of our Passions, as well those which are agreeable to Nature, as those which are not. Herein indeed these two Institutions agree, both disclaim Opinion, and both use words indifferently; as the *Sceptick*, *I design nothing, I comprehend nothing*; the Methodick, κοινότης, διήκειν, and the like. The word ἔνδειξις also he takes without Opinion, for an Action, whereby we are deduced from apparent Passions, Natural and Preternatural, to those which seem convenient, as I shewed in Thirst and Hunger. The Methodicks therefore are nearer ally'd to the *Scepticks* than any other Medicinal Sect, as appears by comparing them. Thus having discoursed of those, which are of nearest resemblance to the *Sceptick* Institution, we conclude the general part of *Scepticism*, and the first Book of our Summary.

Of DIALECTICK.

THE SECOND BOOK.

CHAP. I.
Whether a Sceptick can examine and dispute against Assertions?

HAVING undertaken an inquisition of the Dogmatists, we will briefly, and by way of Summary, examine every part of that which they call Philosophy. But first, let us Answer them who cry, *A Sceptick is not capable to examine or comprehend Dogmatick assertions*. They argue thus, *A Sceptick either comprehends assertions, or not; if he comprehend them, how can he doubt of that, which by his own confession he comprehends? If he doth not comprehend them, he cannot discourse upon that which he comprehends not. For, As he who knows not (for example) what is* τὸ καθ᾽ ὃ μεταξυμίων, *or, a Theorem by two Topicks, is not able to say any thing of them: So, he who knows not the particular assertion of the Dogmatists, cannot dispute against that, of which he knows nothing; therefore a Sceptick cannot examine or dispute against the assertions of Dogmatists.*

Who argue thus, Let them say, in what sense they use the word [*comprehend*,] whether simply, for *to understand without affirming ought, concerning the beings of the things whereon we discourse*; or not only to understand, but to grant *the being of those things*. If they say, To comprehend, *is by discourse to assent to comprehensive phantasie*, forasmuch as comprehensive phantasie proceeds from a thing that hath being, impressed and sealed according to the being thereof, in such manner as cannot be derived from that which hath no being, perhaps even they themselves will not be capable of examining or disputing against that which they comprehend not: As when the *Stoick* disputes against the *Epicurean*, who affirms, that *Substance is divided*; or, that *God orders not the World by providence*; or, that *Pleasure is a good*; Doth he comprehend, or not? If he *comprehend*, he, in saying these things *are*, wholly subverts the *Stoick* Doctrine; if he comprehends not, neither can he say any thing against it. The same may be objected to those of all other Sects, when they offer to dispute against Opinions, which they conceive heterodox; so as none of them can dispute against another, upon any pretence whatsoever. Besides, (not to trifle) in a word, all their Dogmatick learning will be subverted, and the Sceptick Philosophy firmly established, if it be granted, that none can dispute of any thing, which is not thus comprehended. For whosoever asserts Dogmatically concerning a thing not certain, asserts, either as having comprehended it, or not; if he hath not comprehended it, what he saith will not be creditable; if he hath comprehended it, he must say, that he did it either through the very thing it self, and by some act incident to it, or by some inquisition and examination. If *through it self by some act incident to it* a thing not-manifest be comprehended, it cannot be said to be not-manifest, but equally apparent to all, granted and not controverted. But concerning every thing not-manifest, there is an irreconcilable difference amongst them; wherefore the Dogmatist, who asserts concerning the being of a thing not manifest, doth not comprehend it through it self, and by an Act incident to it. But, if *by some inquisition*, how is he capable of enquiring or disputing, before he comprehends the thing it self, according to the hypothesis proposed? For inquisition requiring, that the thing after which we enquire be exactly comprehended; and on the other side, the comprehension of the thing whereof we enquire, requiring first inquisition, by the *alternate Common-place* of Suspension, it will be impossible for them to enquire and assert Dogmatically, concerning things not-manifest. If they would begin from *comprehension*, we object, that they must first enquire before they can comprehend; if from *inquisition*, that they must comprehend before they can enquire. Wherefore they can neither comprehend, nor positively affirm concerning things not manifest. So that this foolish *Dogmatick*-flourish will be taken away, and, as I conceive, the *Ephectick* Philosophy come in of it self.

Now if they say, They conceive it not necessary, that such comprehension precede inquisition, but simple intellection only; it is not impossible but they, who suspend as to things not-manifest, may dispute also; for the Sceptick, as I think, is not excluded from intellection, which ariseth from Phænomena's that occur, and actually affect us. Neither doth this necessarily infer, that intelligibles are existent; for we understand not only things existent, but the inexistent; whence the Ephectick, whether enquiring or understanding, continueth in his Sceptick Institution. For, that he assents to things that occur to him by passive phantasie, as they appear to him, is manifest.

Let us now see, whether the Dogmatists themselves are not excluded from Inquisition. It is not Incongruous, that they who confess themselves ignorant of the nature of things, should yet enquire after them, but that they who think they know them exactly should do so; for these are arrived, as they think, at the end of Inquisition, the others still retain the ground of Inquisition, *to think they have not found*. We shall briefly enquire into every part of that which they call Philosophy. And forasmuch as there is great controversie among the Dogmatists, concerning the parts thereof; some asserting one, others two, others three, (which it is to no purpose here to enlarge,) we will explain the opinion of those who seem most perfectly conversant therein, and accommodate our discourse to that.

CHAP. II.

From whence the Inquisition against Dogmatists should begin.

THE Stoicks and some others say, The parts of Philosophy are three, *Logick, Physick, Ethick*; they begin with the Logick, teaching that first (yet there is no little controversie, which of them they should begin withal.) These we shall follow, without engaging our opinion. And because the assertions in these three parts require judgment and a Criterie, and the discourse concerning the Criterie seemeth to belong to Logick, we will begin with the Logical part; and first of the Criterie.

CHAP. III.

Of the Criterie.

WHereas they call a Criterie, *that whereby essence and existence* (as they say) *are judged*; as also, *that wherein we acquiesce in the course of life*: Our purpose now is to discourse of that which they call, *The Criterie of Truth*; for of Criterie in the other sense, we discoursed formerly * in the first Book.

* Chap. 8.

The *Criterie* of which we now discourse is taken three ways, *Commonly, Properly, Most properly. Commonly, for every measure of comprehension; in which sense, Naturals also are called Criteries, as, Sight. Properly, for every artificial measure of comprehension; as, a Ruler, a pair of Compasses. Most properly, for every artificial measure of comprehension of a thing not manifest; in which sense, those things which belong to the actions of life, are not called Criteries, but the rational only, and those which Dogmatick Philosophers* alledge for invention of truth. Our design is, as we said, to discourse of the *rational Criterie*; and of this also there are three kinds, *in which, by which, according to which*; as, *in which*, the man; *by which*, the sense, or the intellect; *according to which*, the application of the phantasie, according to which a man attempts to judge by one of the fore-named. This it was necessary first to lay down, for understanding the subject of the question. It remains we confute those, who unadvisedly affirm, they comprehend the Criterie of truth; we will begin with that.

CHAP. IV.

Whether there be any Criterie of Truth.

OF those who have discoursed concerning the Criterie, some hold, that it is, as the Stoicks and others; some, that there is none, as (among the rest) *Xeniades* of *Corinth*, and *Xenophanes* of *Colophon*, who saith,

——— *in every thing opinion's fram'd.*

But we suspend, whether there be, or be not. This controversie they must hold to be either dijudicable, (that is, determinable) or indijudicable, (indeterminable.) If indijudicable, they grant, we ought to suspend in it; if dijudicable, let them say whereby it shall be judged, whenas we have not a Criterie acknowledged by all, neither know we whether there indeed be one, but enquire.

Moreover, to judge this controversie of the Criterie, it is requisite we have a Criterie acknowledged, by which we may judge it; and to have a Criterie acknowledged, it is necessary, that the controversie concerning the Criterie be first judged. The dispute thus incurring *the alternate Common place*, it cannot be resolved whether there be a Criterie or no. For we grant them not a Criterie by supposition; and if they judge a Criterie by a Criterie, we force them to go on *into infinite*.

Again, Demonstration requiring a Criterie demonstrated, and the Criterie a Demonstration dijudicated, they fall into the *alternate Common-place*.

This we conceive sufficient to confute the confidence of the Dogmatists, in what they assert concerning a Criterie. It is not from the purpose to insist longer hereon, and to shew several other ways, whereby they may be confuted; but we shall not mention all their particular opinions herein, (for it cannot be expressed, how much they differ among themselves concerning it; and this would put us out of the right method in our dispute.) Because therefore the Criterie after which we enquire seems threefold, *in which, by which, according to which*, we shall examine every one of these apart, and shew its incomprehensibility. Thus our discourse will be most Methodical and perfect. We will begin with that *in which*, for the rest seem in some manner dubious by reason of it.

CHAP. V.

Of the Criterie, in which.

NOW *Man*, (in my opinion) by what the Dogmatists say, is not only not to be comprehended, but not to be understood; for we hear *Socrates* (in *Plato*) plainly confessing, *he knows not whether he is a man or some other thing*. And when they would declare the notion of *man*, they first disagree among themselves, next they speak foolishly; for *Democritus* saith, *Man is that which we all know*; by which we cannot know what Man is; for we know a Dog, and

and according to this, a Dog should be a Man; some men we know not, and therefore they should not be men. But indeed, according to this notion there will be no man at all; for if it be necessary that a man be known by all, there is no man known to all men, and consequently there is no man at all. That we say not this sophistically, but as a consequence to his Doctrine, is apparent; for he holds that, *nothing really exists but Atoms and Vacuum, which* (he saith) *exist not in Animals only, but in all compounded things*; by these we cannot understand the property of Man; for they are common to all, but there is in these nothing else within our capacity; we have nothing therefore whereby we may distinguish Man from other Creatures, and understand him simply.

Epicurus saith, that *Man is such a kind of figured animate Being*: Now, according to this, seeing Man is only such a kind of Being, as is shewn, (by him, who thus describes him) that person who is not such, as is thus shewn, is not a man: and if a man (in describing Man after this manner) shew a Woman, the Man himself will not be a Man; or if a Woman shew a Man, the Woman will not be of Mankind; The same we may argue from the difference of *circumstances* mention'd in the fourth Common-place of Suspension.

Others say, *a man is an Animal, Rational, Mortal, capable of Understanding and Science*: Now having shewn in the *first Common-place* of Suspension, that no Animal is irrational, but that all are capable of Understanding and Science, by their own confession, we know not what they mean. Again, the accidents which are inserted into a definition, are meant either actual or potential. If actual, he is no Man who hath not attained perfect Science, and hath not perfect Science or discourse, and is not in the state of death, for that is to be mortal actually. If potential, he who hath perfect reason, and hath attained Understanding and Science, is no man, which were more absurd than the former.

Plato, who will have a man to be *an Animal without feathers, with two feet, with broad nails, capable of political Science*, dares not affirm this positively. For if a man be, * as he holds, one of those things which are generated, but indeed, are not: It is impossible (as he acknowledgeth) to affirm positively concerning things that are not. Neither doth *Plato* himself lay down this position as certain, but discoursing, as he useth, according to the most probable.

* So *Plato* distinguisheth often, especially in *Timæo*, where he at large explained τὸ τὸ ὂν μὲν ἀεί, γινόμενον γ᾽ ἂ πώποτε, & τὸ γινόμενον μὲν, ὂν δ᾽ ἀπότε.

But though we should grant, that Man may be understood, we shall nevertheless find that he cannot be comprehended. For we consist of Soul and Body, but neither Soul nor Body (perhaps) can be comprehended, therefore not Man. That *the body is not comprehended*, appears from this; the accidents of a thing are distinct from the thing, to which they are accidents; now when colour, or the like, presents it self to us, the accidents of the Body are presented to us, but not the Body it self. A Body, they say, hath three dimensions; we must therefore, to comprehend the Body, comprehend the length, breadth, and depth; but if this did present it self to us, we might discern silver that is gilt: Therefore the Body cannot be comprehended.

Besides this, a Man shall be found to be incomprehensible, because *his soul is incomprehensible*. That his Soul is incomprehensible, is manifest, thus. Of those who have discoursed concerning the Soul, (to omit the great undetermined contest amongst them) some said, that *there is no Soul*, as the Followers of *Dicæarchus* the Messenian; others that *there is*; others *suspended*. This controversie therefore, if the Dogmatists acknowledge to be indijudicable, they grant the incomprehensibility of the Soul; if dijudicable, let them say, by what they judge and determin it. By Sense they cannot, for they hold the Soul to be intelligible; if by Intellect, we object, the Intellect is the most unmanifest thing in the Soul, as they shew, who agree in the Existence of the Soul, but disagree concerning her Intellect. If therefore they would comprehend the Soul, and determin the controversie concerning her by Intellect, they would determin that which is less in controversie, by that which is more in controversie, which is absurd. Therefore neither by Intellect can the question concerning the Soul be judged and determined, therefore by nothing; therefore it is incomprehensible, and consequently, Man cannot be comprehended.

But tho' we should grant, that Man may be comprehended, yet perhaps it cannot be proved, that things should be judged (and determined) by him. For he who saith, that things should be judged by Man, saith it either without demonstration or with demonstration. Not with demonstration, for demonstration ought to be true and adjudged; but, we knowing none, who by the consent of all, is able to judge the demonstration, (for the Criterie *in which* is in question) we are not able to judge the demonstration, and consequently cannot demonstrate the Criterie *in which*, the subject of our discourse. If it be said, that things may be judged by Man without demonstration, it will be increditable, because we have not any thing whereby to ascertain, that the Criterie *in which* is Man. From what shall it be judged, that the Criterie *in which* is Man? For if they say it without judgment and determination, it will not be admitted; if as determined by Man, the question is begged; if, as by any other Creature, how can any such be allow'd, to determin that Man is the Criterie? If without determination, it is no credit; if with determination, that Criterie must again be judged by some other, to be capable of determining; If by it self, the absurdity continues, for the thing in question is determin'd by the thing in question. If by Man, the *alternate Common-place* comes in. If by any other besides these, we shall again require a Criterie *in which*, and so to infinite. Therefore, we cannot say, things are to be determined by Man.

But if it be granted, that Man ought to determin things; yet seeing there is so great dissention amongst Men, the Dogmatists must agree among themselves, what one Man they ought to follow before they impose it upon us. Otherwise, if,

As long as streams shall flow, and tall Trees bloom,

they are like to disagree upon this, why do they press us so earnestly to assent to any one person?

If say they, We must believe a Wise man; we shall ask, What kind of Wise man, whether an *Epicurean*, or a *Stoick*, or a *Cynick*? They cannot agree Which. If any require us to lay down this Question concerning the Wise man, and simply to believe him who is wiser than all others; first, they will herein also disagree, Who is wiser than the rest; and, tho' they could agree in some one person, acknowledging him wiser than all that are, or ever were, yet neither will he be worthy to be credited; for there being a great, and, almost infinite intension and remission, as to Wisdom, we say, it is possible, there may be another wiser than this Man, whom they hold to be wiser than all, that either are or were. As therefore they require of us to give credit to him, that is said to be wiser than all that are or ever were, in respect of his Wisdom; so, if one comes after him wiser than he, this last is to be believed before him; and whilst this second lives, we may hope for another wiser than he; after whom, another; and so to infinite. Now whether these will agree with one another, no Man knows. So that tho' it were granted, that there is one Man wiser than all that are, or ever were; yet because we cannot affirm, there shall never be any one wiser than he; (for that is uncertain,) we ought always to expect the judgment of that future wisest person, and not assent to him who is wisest at present.

But tho' we should grant, that there is not, was not, nor ever shall be, any person wiser than him whom they suppose, yet neither is it convenient to believe him; for wise persons affect most (in the construction of things) to maintain Paradoxes, making the unsound seem sound and true. When therefore the sagacious person says any thing, we cannot tell whether he speaks it according to the nature of the thing it self, or alledgeth a falsity as if it were a truth, perswading us to believe it, he being wiser than all Men, and therefore we not able to contradict him. Thus ought we not to assent to him, as judging things rightly, because we may imagine, The things which he saith are not true, but represented as such, by the extraordinary advantage he hath over us in sagacity. For these reasons, we ought not in the judgment of things to believe him, who seemeth the most sagacious of all Men.

If any shall say, We ought to believe the agreement of many. We answer, That to do so is foolish; for first, Truth perhaps is rare, and therefore one may be wiser than many. Again, every Criterie hath more adversaries, than those who agree in defence thereof. For all those who maintain any other Criterie whatsoever, oppose them who agree in the defence of one, and are therefore of much greater number than the others. Besides, they who agree, either are in different affections, or in one. In different they are not, at least as to this, for then they would not agree in it. If in one, seeing that he who affirmeth any thing, different from this which they agree in, hath one affection, and all they who agree in it have but one; as to the affections which we follow, there is no advantage in the number: Wherefore we ought not to follow many rather than one. As also, because the difference of judgment, as to their multitude, is incomprehensible, as we shewed from the *fourth Common-place* of Suspension; for there are infinite Men, if we consider them singly, neither are we able to examine the judgments of all, and so to say what the greater part holds, what the fewest. It is therefore in this respect absurd also, to prefer some Judges before others, because of their number. And if the judgment of all in general is not to be followed, neither shall we find any at all by whom things may be judged, tho' we should grant never so much otherwise. Wherefore by all this, the Criterie *in which* all things are judged, appears to be incomprehensible; and the other Criteries being circumscribed by this, (for each of them is either a part, or a passion, or an action of Man) it followeth, * we need not perhaps speak of them, having here discoursed of them already. But lest we should seem to decline the confutation of every one in particular, we will say something over and above of them; and first of the Criterie called, *By which*.

* reading ἀκόλουθον μὴ ἰῶ.

CHAP. VI.

Of the Criterie, By which.

Great, almost infinite, is the disagreement amongst the Dogmatists concerning this; but we, observing our first method, shall only say; Forasmuch as, according to them, Man is the Criterie *in which* things are judged, but he hath nothing *by which* he can judge (as they all agree) besides Sense and Intellect; if we shew he cannot judge neither by *Sense* alone, nor by *Intellect* alone) nor by *both* together, we shall compendiously refute all their particular Assertions.

Let us begin with the *Senses*. Whereas some hold, that *the affections of the Senses are vain*, (and that none of those things which we think that we perceive, are subjected to them.) Others, that *all the things by which the Senses think they are moved, are subjected to them*. Others, that *some of them are subjected to the Senses, others not*. We know not to which of these we should assent, for we cannot determine the controversie, neither by Sense, (for the question is, whether that be vainly affected, or comprehend truly) nor by any other; for there is no other Criterie whereby it ought to be determined, (according to the Hypothesis) it will therefore be indeterminable and incomprehensible, whether Sense be vainly affected, or comprehendeth any thing. Whence it followeth, that we ought not to rely wholly upon Sense in the determination of things, when as we cannot say, that it comprehendeth any thing.

But let us grant the Senses to be comprehensive, yet will they be found to be nothing the less uncreditable, as to determination concerning external Objects. The Senses are contrarily moved by externals, as the taste by the same Honey is sometimes affected sweetly, sometimes bitterly. The Sight thinketh the same colour sometimes red, sometimes white. Neither doth the smell agree with it self. He who hath some kind of obstructions in the Head, thinketh Unguents not to be sweet; he who hath not, saith they are sweet. Persons Divinely inspired, and Fanatick,

natick, imagine they hear others difcourfing with them, whom we hear not. The fame water to thofe who are troubled with an Inflamation feems exceffive hot, to others moderately warm. Now whether fhall we fay, All thefe phantafies are true, or all falfe; or fome falfe, fome true? To fay, that all are falfe is impoffible, for we have not any Criterie uncontroverted, whereby to determine that which we prefer; neither have we any true determined demonftration, feeing that the Criterion of Truth, whereby true demonftration ought to be determined, is ftill in queftion, For this reafon, he who conceived we ought to give credit to thofe who are well, and not to thofe who are not, fpeaks abfurdly; for faying this without demonftration, he fhall not be believed; but a true adjudged demonftration, he cannot have, for the reafons alledged.

But though we fhould grant that the phantafies of thofe who are well, are creditable, others not; neverthelefs it will be found, that external Objects cannot be judged by the Senfes only. The Sight, in perfons that are well, judgeth the fame Tower fometimes to be round, fometimes fquare; the Tafte judgeth the fame Meats upon Repletion Sowre, in Hunger pleafant; the Hearing perceiveth the fame voice in the night loud, in the day low; the fmell, what moft Men declare to be ftinking, in Tanners commonly denies it; the fame touch when we enter a Bath is warmed by the Paraftas, when we come out cooled by it. Wherefore feeing the Senfes of fuch as are well, difagree amongft themfelves, and their difagreement is indeterminable, (for we have not any thing univerfally acknowledged, whereby they may be determined) the doubt muft neceffarily be infolvable. Many other things might be alledged out of the Common places of Sufpenfion. Thus perhaps it is not true, that Senfe alone can judge of external Objects.

Let us now come to *Intellect*. They who conceive, that Intellect only is to be followed in the judication of things; Firft, they cannot demonftrate it to be comprehenfible, that there is Intellect; for *Gorgias*, in faying, *There is nothing*, faith, that there is not Intellect. Others affert, *It exifts*. How will they determine this controverfie? Not by Intellect, (for that were to beg the queftion) nor by any other; for they fay, there is no other (according to the Hypothefis) by which the things may be judged. It remains therefore indeterminable and incomprehenfible, whether there be Intellect or not. Whence it followeth, that we ought not to relye upon Intellect only, in the dijudication of things, being itfelf is not yet comprehended.

But let us admit Intellect to be comprehended, and grant by way of fuppofition, that it exifts; notwithftanding, I fay, it cannot determine of things; for if it feeth not it felf exactly, but difagreeth concerning its own Effence, and the manner of its Generation, how then can it exactly comprehend other things? Befides, though we grant Intellect to be capable to determine of things; yet we fhall not find how to determine by it. For there being much difference as to Intellect; one Intellect of *Gorgias*, according to which he faith, *Nothing is*; another of *Heraclitus*, according to which he faith, *All things are*; another of thofe who affirm, *Some things are, others are not*: We fhall not find any way to dijudicate thefe differences of Intellects, nor be able to fay, This Intellect is to be preferred before that, or that not to be preferred before this. For if we would judge it by any Intellect, we yield to Parties in the difference, and beg the Queftion: if by any other than by Intellect, we are deceived, becaufe we ought to judge things by Intellect only. Moreover, from what we faid upon the Criterie *by which*, may be demonftrated, that we can neither find a Sagacity exceeding the Sagacity of others: Nor if we could find an Intellect more Sagacious, than any ever had, or have been; yet, (forafmuch as it is uncertain whether there will not be one more Sagacious than it) we ought not to follow it. And though we fhould fuppofe an Intellect more Sagacious, than any fhall ever be hereafter, yet ought we not to follow him who judgeth by it, left alledging fome falfe reafon, he perfwade us by the acutenefs of his Wit, that it is True. Therefore neither doth Intellect only judge things.

It remaineth we fay, that things are judged *by both*, which likewife is impoffible; for the Senfes are fo far from guiding the Intellect to comprehenfion, that they contradict one another. Honey feems fweet to fome, bitter to others; *Democritus* held, *it is neither fweet nor bitter*; *Heraclitus*, that *it is both*. 'Tis the fame in other Senfes, and other Senfibles. So as the Intellect, impelled by the Senfes, is conftrained to affirm things different and repugnant. But fuch a kind of Criterie is far from comprehenfive.

Moreover, they muft fay, That they judge things either by all the Senfes, and all * Intellects; or, by fome. By all, it is impoffible; there appearing fo great controverfie amongft feveral Senfes and Intellects, (likewife the Intellect of *Gorgias* declaring, that *neither the judgment of Senfe or Intellect ought to be followed*, the argument will be retorted:) If by fome, Who can judge, that we ought to adhere to the Senfes, and this Intellect, and not to thofe, not having an acknowledged Criterie, by which to judge different Senfes and Intellects. If we fay, that they judge Senfes and Intellects by Intellect and Senfe,† they beg the queftion, which is, Whether we can judge by thefe.

Again, either he judgeth Senfes and Intellects by Senfe; or Senfes and Intellects by Intellect; or Senfes by Senfe, and Intellects by Intellect; or Intellects by Senfe, and Senfe by Intellect. If they fay, they judge thefe by Senfes or Intellect, they judge not by Senfe and Intellect, but by one of them, which they make choice of, and confequently incur the difficulties alledged formerly. If Senfes by Senfe, and Intellects by Intellect, there being fo great repugnance of Senfes to Senfes, and Intellects to Intellects, which foever they take of the repugnant Senfes to judge the reft of the Senfes, they beg the queftion; for they affume part of the difference, as creditable, for dijudication of things equally controverted with it. It is the fame in Intellects. If they judge Intellects by Senfes, and Senfes by Intellects, the *alternate Common place* occurs, fhewing, that to judge Senfes we prejudge Intellects, and

*Read here and after, διανοίας.

†Betwixt νεύσμεν & νοῖ, there is a breach and defect, in the MSt. of Mr. Cafaubon and Sir Henry Savile; which the printed Edition not taking notice of, confounds the fenfe.

and to examin Intellects we must prejudge Senses. Wherefore seeing that Criteries of one kind cannot be judged by Criteries of the same kind, nor both kinds by one kind, nor reciprocally one kind by the other kind; nor can we prefer Intellect before Intellect, or Sense before Sense; it follows, That we have not any thing whereby to judge. For if we cannot judge by all Senses and Intellects, nor know by which we ought to judge, and by which not to judge, we shall not have any thing by which to judge things. Wherefore there is no Criterie *by which*.

CHAP. VII.

Of the Criterie According to which.

LET us next examine the Criterie *according to which* things are judged. In the first place we may hold that phantasie is unconceivable; for they say *Phantasie is an impression in the Hegemonick part of the Soul*. Seeing therefore that the Soul and the Hegemonick is a Spirit, or something more subtle than Spirit, as they themselves hold; no Man can conceive that there is in himself an impression, either by extuberance and depression, as we see in Scales; or by the wonderfully invented Heteræotick, for he could retain in memory so many Theorems, as make up an Art, because by succeeding Heteræoses, the precedent would be defaced.

But tho' there were such a thing as Phantasie, yet would it be incomprehensible, for it is a passion of the Hegemonick; the Hegemonick, as we shew'd, is not comprehended; therefore neither can we comprehend its affection.

Moreover, tho' we should grant that phantasie is comprehended, yet things cannot be judged according to it; for it doth not (say they) apply it self to externals, and conceive Phantasies in it self, but by the Senses. Now the Senses comprehend not the external objects, but their affections only; For Honey, and my being sweetly affected, are not all one thing; neither is Wormwood the same with my being bitterly affected; they differ. But if the affection differ from the External object, the Phantasie will not be of the External object, but of some other thing different from it. Therefore if the Intellect judge according to the Phantasie, it will judge amiss, and not according to the object; whence it is absurd to say, External objects are judicated according to the Phantasie.

Neither can it be said, that the Soul comprehends sensible objects by sensible affections, because the affections of the Senses are like their External objects; for how can the Intellect know whether the affections of the Senses are like the sensible objects, when as it self meddles not with External objects, neither do the Senses declare the natures of them to her, but only their own affections, as we argued in the *Common places of Suspension*. For as he who knows not *Socrates*, if he look upon his picture knows not whether it be like *Socrates*; so that Intellect, beholding the affections of the Senses, but not seeing the External objects themselves, cannot tell whether the affections of the Senses are like their External objects. Therefore neither by assimilation can it judge those things according to the Phantasie.

But let us grant, that the Phantasie cannot only understand and comprehend, but is able also to judge things of it self, (tho' we have proved the contrary) it follows, that either we must believe all Phantasies, (one whereof saith, that all Phantasies are incredible, by which means the argument will be retorted, that all Phantasies by their own acknowledgment, are not capable to judge things) or if we must believe only some, How shall we judge, Which Phantasies are to be believed, which not? If without Phantasie, then they grant, that Phantasie is not requisite to the judgment of things, in as much as they say they can judge things without it. If with Phantasie, How will they assume that Phantasie by which they mean to judge all other Phantasies? Or again, they will need another Phantasie to judge the Phantasie by which they judge all Phantasies, and another to judge that, and so to infinite; but it is impossible to judge to infinite; therefore it is impossible to find what Phantasies ought to be used as Criteries, what not. Since therefore, which way soever we grant that things ought to be judged according to Phantasies, the argument will be retorted, whether by all, or by some only. We conclude, that Phantasies ought not to be used as Criteries, to judge things.

This may serve for an Answer by way of Summary, to the Criterie *according to which*: But take notice that our purpose is not to prove there is no Criterie of truth existent (for that were Dogmatical) but because the Dogmatists seem probably to have evinced that there is a Criterie of truth, we have proposed arguments that seem probable against them; not that we think them true, or more probable than the contrary; but forasmuch as these arguments, and those of the Dogmatists, seem alike probable, we are driven to Suspension.

CHAP. VIII.

Of True and Truth.

THough we should grant, (by way of supposition) that there is some Criterie of truth, yet will it be useless and vain, if we prove, (even out of what the Dogmatists themselves say) that truth is not, neither can it be. We shew it thus: *True is said to differ from Truth three ways*; *by Essence, by Constitution, by Power*. *By Essence*, for True is Incorporeal, (as being an axiom and a dicible) but Truth is a Body, as being the enunciative Science of all true things; but Science is the Hegemonick *after such a manner, as the fist is the hand after such a manner*; but the Hegemonick is a Body, for *(according to them) it is a Spirit*.

By Constitution, for True is *something simple, as, I discourse*; but Truth consists of the knowledge of many True things.

By Power, for Truth adhereth to Science, True doth not absolutely; whence they say that Truth can only be in a *wise* person, but True in a *wicked*; for a wicked man may speak something that is True. Thus the Dogmatists.

But we cntinuing our first design, will discourse onely concerning *True:* For *Truth*, which is said to be *the Science of she knowledge of things True.*, is included therein. Again, forasmuch as of arguments, some are general by which we take away the substance of True; others particular, whereby we shew that Truth is neither in speech, nor in a dicible, nor in the motion of the Intellect, we conceive it sufficient to use onely the General. For, as when the foundation of a Wall is taken away, all the superstructures fall; so the subsistence of True being taken away, the particular conceits of the Dogmatists are thereby excluded also.

CHAP. IX.

Whether True be somthing in nature.

THere being a disagreement amongst the Dogmatists concerning Truth (some holding, that True is somthing, others that it is not) the controversie is not capable to be judged. For he who saith, that *True is somthing,* if he say it without demonstration, will not be credited, because of the disagreement; if he alledge a demonstration, and acknowledge it to be false, he is increditable; if he say, that it is True, he runs into the *alternate Common place.* It will be required of him, that he produce a demonstration to demonstrate that to be True, and another to prove this, and so to infinite; but it is impossible to demonstrate infinites, therefore it is impossible to know whether *True* be *somthing.*

Again, this *somthing,* which they hold to be the most General of all things, is either True or false or neither True nor false, or both True and false. If they say, it is false, they confess that all things are false; For as because an Animal is something Animate, therefore every Animal in particular is Animate; in like manner, if this *somthing,* being the most General of all things, be false, all things in particular will be false and nothing true. Whence also may be inferred that *nothing is false,* for this proposition *all things are false,* this other *somthing is false,* including all things, will be false. And if somthing be True, all things will be True, and consequently nothing will be True; for this proposition, *Nothing is true,* will be True.

If somthing be both True and false, every thing in particular will be both True and false, whence it will follow, that nothing is in its own nature True; for that which is True in its own nature, cannot by any means be false.

If something be neither True not false, they confess, that all things in particular being said to be neither True nor false, are not True, and therefore it is not manifest to us whether this be True.

Moreover, either things manifest onely are True, or onely things not manifest, or of True things, some are manifest, others not manifest; But neither of these, as shall be proved; therefore nothing is True. If onely things manifest are True, they must say that all the manifest are True, or some onely; if *all,* the argument will be retorted, saying *it is manifest, that no-*thing *is True;* if *some,* none can say, without dijudication, *this is True, that false.* If he use a Criterie, he must grant it to be either manifest or unmanifest; not unmanifest, for the manifest onely are now supposed True; if manifest, we demand, Which manifest things are True, which false? The thing manifest, assumed to judge things manifest, will it self require another Criterie, and that another, and so to infinite; but it is impossible to judge to infinite; therefore it is imossible to comprehend, which manifest things onely are True.

He who saith, *onely unmanifest* things are True, holdeth not that all things are True, (for he will not say, *that the stars are even and that they are odd, is alike True*) if *some,* by what shall we judge that these unmanifest things are True, those False? Not by any thing manifest, and it by any thing unmanifest, that unmanifest thing will require another to judge, and this another, and so to infinite. Wherefore, neither are onely things unaparent True.

It remains, that we say of the True, some are manifest, others unmanifest, which also is absurd. For either all things both manifest and unmanifest, are True, or some of the manifest, and some of the unmaitest. If all, the argument will be retorted, granting it to be True, that *nothing is True.* He likewise grants it to be True, *that the Stars are even, and that they are odd.* If of the manifest some onely are True, and of the unmanifest some onely, by what shall we judge that of the manifest, these are True, these False; if by a thing manifest, we run into infinite. If by an unmanifest, forasmuch as the unmanifest requires dijudication also, By what shall that unmanifest be judged? If by a manifest, the *alternate Common place* occurs; if by an unmanifest, the Common place of *infinite.* The same may be said of the unmanifest, for he who undertakes to judge it by an unmanifest, is forc'd to run into infinite; he who by a manifest, either assuming a manifest, runs into the Common place of *infinite,* or passing to an unmanifest, into the *alternate.* It is therefore false to say, that of the True some are manifest, others not manifest.

Now if neither the manifest onely are True, nor onely the unmanifest, nor some of the manifest, and some of the unmanifest, then nothing is True; and if nothing be True, the Criterie conducing to the judgment of Truth, would be useless and vaine, tho' we should grant it had a being. Now if we must suspend concerning this question, *whether True be somthing,* it will follow, that they who say, *Dialectick is the Science of things True, False, and Neuter,* speak rashly; since the Critery of Truth appears to be undeterminable; neither can we affirm any thing, either concerning those things which seem *evident* as the Dogmatists call them, or concerning the unmanifest; For since the later, (as the Dogmatists conceive) are comprehended by the former, if we are inforced to suspend concerning the Evident, how dare we assert concerning the Unmanifest?

But we shall (over and above) alledge our Arguments against particular things; and forasmuch as these seem to be comprehended by *Sign,* and *Demonstration,* we shall shew that we ought to suspend our Assent concerning Sign and Demonstration. We will begin with *Sign*, for Demonstration is a species of Sign.

CHAP. X.
Of Sign.

OF things (according to the Dogmatists) *some are* manifest, others unmanifest. *Of the unmanifest, some are* absolutely unmanifest, *others* unmanifest for a time, *others* unmanifest by nature. *Manifest they hold to be those things which of themselves come into our knowledge, as,* it is day. *Absolutely unmanifest, those which come not within the reach of our comprehension, as, that the number of the Stars is even. Unmanifest for a time, those which are manifest in their own nature, but by reason of some external circumstances, they are for a time not manifest to us, as the City of* Athens *is to me at this present. Unmanifest by nature, are those, which have a nature not subject to be manifest to us, as Pores; for these never appear to us of themselves, but are comprehended from some others, as by sweat or the like. Manifest things, say they, require not a sign,* (*for they are comprehended of themselves*) *neither those which are absolutely unmanifest, for they are no way to be comprehended; but the unmanifest for a time, and the unmanifest by nature, are comprehended by signs, yet not by the same; the unmanifest for a time, by the Hypomnestick* (admonitive) *the unmanifest by nature, by the Endictick* (indicative.) *Of Signes therefore, some are according to them, Hypomnestick, others Endictick. A Hypomnestick sign, they call that which being observed to be together with a significate, evident, assoon as ever the sign evidently incurreth to our sense, tho' the significate appear not, yet it causeth us to remember that which was concomitant to it, tho' at present not evident, as smoak and fire.*

An Endictick sign, (*say they*) *is that, which is not observed together with an evident *significate, but of its own nature and constitution signifieth that whereof it is a sign; thus the motions of the body are signs of the Soul.*

* M.S. ἐνδεικνύμενον

Hereupon they define Sign thus, *Sign is a demonstrative axiome, antecedent in a sound connex, detective of that which followeth.*

Of these two kinds of signs, we oppose not both, but onely the Enoictick, as seeming to be forged by the Dogmatists; the Hypomnestick is creditable in the course of life; for whosoever sees smoak, knows that fire is signified; and seeing a scar, saith, it had been a wound. So as we not onely not contradict the common course of life, but maintain it, assenting inopinionatively to that in it which is creditable, but opposing what is particularly forged by the Dogmatists. Thus much it was requisite to say for explication of the question. We now proceed to confutation, not endeavouring to shew that the Endictick sign is wholly inexistent, but the apparent equivalence of arguments on both sides, for its existence and inexistence.

CHAP. XI.
Whether there be any Endictick Sign.

A Sign therefore, by what the Dogmatists speak of it, is unintelligible. The *Stoicks*, who have discoursed with most exactness hereupon, to shew the notion of sign, say, "A Sign "is an Axiome antecedent in a sound Connex, "detective of that which follows. Axiome, they "say, "is a Dicible, Self-perfect, Enunciative "as it is within it self. A sound Connex is that "which beginneth not from true, and endeth "in false; for a Connex either beginneth from "true, and endeth in true; as, if it is day, it is "light; or, it beginneth from false, and endeth "in false, as, if the Earth flyeth, the Earth has "Wings: Or, it beginneth from true, and "endeth in false; as, if the Earth is, the Earth "flies: Or it beginneth from false, and endeth in "true; as, if the Earth flyeth, the Earth is. Of "these, they hold that only to be unsound, which "beginneth from true, and endeth in false, the "rest are all true. Antecedent they call that, "which goeth foremost in a Connex, beginning "from true, and ending in true; it is Detect- "ive of that which followeth, for in this Con- "nex, If she hath Milk, she hath Conceived; "These words, She hath conceived, are decla- "red by those, She hath Milk. *Thus they.*

Now we first say, That it is uncertain whether there be a *Dicible*: For seeing that of the Dogmatists, the *Epicureans* say, there is no *Dicible*; the *Stoicks*, that there is; when the *Stoicks* say, that a *Dicible* is something, either they use Assertion only, or Demonstration also. If Assertion only, the *Epicureans* will oppose it with the contrary Assertion, that a *Dicible* is nothing. If by Demonstration, forasmuch as Demonstration consists of Dicible Axioxms, nothing that consists of *Dicibles* can be assumed to prove that a *Dicible* is something. For he who allows not a *Dicible* to be, How will he grant a collection of *Dicibles* to be? Thus, whosoever shall endeavour by a collection of *Dicibles* to prove that there is a *Dicible*, goes about to prove a thing controverted, by a thing controverted. If therefore neither simply, nor by Demonstration it cannot be proved, that there is a *Dicible*, it is not manifest that there is a *Dicible*, and consequently that there is an Axiome; for, an Axiome is a *Dicible*.

Yet, though by way of supposition we should grant, that there is a *Dicible*; an Axiome will be found notwithstanding to be inexistent, which consists of *Dicibles* not coexistent with one another. As for example in these, *If it is day, it is light*, when I say, *it is day*, I have not yet said *it is light*; and when I say *it is light*, I had before said that *it is day*. If therefore whatsoever is compounded of any thing cannot exist unless its parts coexist with one another, but the parts whereof an Axiome is compounded coexist not with one another, therefore an Axiome will not exist.

But besides all this, *a sound Connex* will be found to be incomprehensible. For, *Philo* saith, *That is a sound Connex which beginneth not from True and endeth in False, as* (*it being day and I disputing*

disputing) *this*, *If it is day I dispute*. But Diodorus *saith*, *That beginning from True it neither could nor can end in False*, according to whom that *Connexion seemeth to be False*, for it being Day, and I being silent, it will begin in True and end in False. But *this is a True one*, *If the Elements of things are not indivisible*, *the Elements of things are indivisible*, for beginning always from False (*the Elements of things are not indivisible*) it will end in True, *the Elements of things are indivisible*. But they who introduce Synartesis, *say*, *That is a sound Connex*, *when that which is contrary to that which ends in it*, *is contrary to that which is antecedent in it*, according to whom *these Connexes which we have instanced are unsound*; but *this is a True one*, *If it is day it is day*. They who judge by Emphasis, *say*, *That is a true Connex whose Consequent is potentially contained in the Antecedent*, according to whom this, *If it be day it is day*, and every reduplicate connex'd Axiome perhaps will be false, for a thing cannot contain it self. Thus this controversie seems indeterminable, for neither shall we be creditable, if we prefer any of the fore-mentioned Propositions without Demonstration, nor with Demonstration: For the Demonstration seemeth then to be found, when its conclusion followeth the conjunction of its Sumptions or Premises, as the Consequent the Antecedent. As thus; If it is day it is light, but it is day, therefore it is light. But if we demand how the consequence of the conseqent to the antecedent shall be judged, they incur *the alternate* common place; for to demonstrate the Dijudication of the Connex, the Conclusion as we said must follow the Sumptions of the Demonstration. Again, that this may be credited, the Connex and the Consequence ought to be determined, which is absurd. Therefore a sound Connex is incomprehensible.

Likewise the antecedent is undeterminable. For *the antecedent*, (say they,) *is that which goeth foremost*, *in such a Connex as beginneth from True and endeth in True*. Now if it be a sign detective of the Consequent, either the Consequent is manifest or unmanifest; if manifest, it needs no detective, for it will be comprehended together with the other, neither is it a significate, and therefore this is not its sign; if unmanifest, forasmuch as there is an undetermined Controversie concerning things not manifest, which of them is true, which false, and whether any of them be true, it will be unmanifest whether the Connex speak true; whence it followeth, that it is also unmanifest, whether the antecedent in it precede (rightly.)

But besides this, Though there be a significate to the sign, yet it cannot be detective of the Consequent even for this reason, because it is comprehended together with it: For Relatives are comprehended together, as Right cannot be comprehended before Left, as being right in relation to left, not on the contrary Right without Left. The like in all other Relatives; so it is impossible that the sign can be comprehended before the significate; but if the sign be not comprehended before the significate, it cannot be detective of it, the significate being comprehended together with it, and not after it. Thus from their disagreeing Opinions, we may gather that a sign is unintelligible, for they say that it is relative, and detective of the significate to which it is relative; whence it followeth, That if it be relative to the significate, it must necessarily be comprehended together with the significate, as right with left, upwards with downwards, and the like: But if it be detective of the significate, it is necessary that it be comprehended before it, that, being first known, it may bring us to the notion of the thing which is known by it; but it is impossible to understand a thing which cannot be known but by the fore-knowledge of another thing which cannot be known before it. Therefore it is impossible to understand any thing which is not only relative to, but detective also of, that to which it is relative: But a sign, say they, is both relative to, and detective of the significate, therefore it is impossible to understand the sign.

Moreover, it was a controversie before our time, some affirming, that there is an Endeictick sign, others that there is none; now he who saith that there is an Endeictick sign, either affirmeth it barely without demonstration, or with demonstration. If with bare affirmation, he will not be creditable; if he would demonstrate it, he begs the Question. For the Genus of demonstration being sign, when we question whether there be sing, we question whether there is demonstration, as, If we question whether there be an Animal, we question whether there be a Man, for Man is an Animal; but to demonstrate a thing controverted by a thing controverted, or by it self, is absurd; therefore it cannot be demonstrated that there is a sign. And if it can neither be affirmed simply nor demonstratively, it is impossible to frame a comprehensive enunciation of it. Now if sign be not exactly comprehended, neither can it be said to be significant of any thing, it not being acknowledged it self; therefore there will be no sign. Whence, according to this argument, sign is unexistent and unintelligible.

Again, Signs either are apparent only, or unapparent only, or some apparent, others unapparent; but none of these is true, therefore there is no sign. That signs are not unapparent, is shewn thus. What is unapparent is not manifested by it self, according to the Dogmatists, but occurreth to us through some other; a sign therefore if it be unapparent will require another sign, which also will be unapparent (for according to the proposed Hypothesis, no sign is apparent) and that another, and so to infinite: But it is impossible to take infinite signs, therefore it is impossible to comprehend a sign, it being unapparent. For which reason it will be inexistent, not capable to signifie any thing, as to be a sign, because it cannot be comprehended. On the contrary, If all signs are apparent, forasmuch as the sign is relative to the significate, and relatives are comprehended together with one another, the significate being comprehended together with the apparent, will be also apparent. For as right and left incurring to us together, right is not said to be more apparent than left, or left than right; in like manner the sign and the significate being comprehended together, it cannot be said that the sign is more apparent than the significate: But if the significate be apparent, it is not a significate, as not needing any to signifie and detect it. Whence taking away right, we take away left also; so

taking

taking away the significate, the sign cannot exist. Thus the Sign will be found to be inexistent, if we say that Signs only are apparent. It remains, we say, that of Signs some are apparent, some unapparent, but this also incurs the same difficulties; for the Significates of apparent Signs will be apparent, as we said, not requiring any thing to signifie them, and consequently they will not be Significates. Whence neither will the other be Signs, as signifying nothing; The unmanifest Signs requiring something to detect them. If they say, they are signifi'd by Unmanifest, the Argument running into Infinite, they will be found to be Incomprehensible, and consequently Inexistent, as we said. If by apparent, they will also be apparent, as being comprehended together with their apparent signs, and consequently will also be inexistent, for it is impossible a thing should be by nature apparent and unapparent; but the Signs, of which our discourse is, being supposed unapparent, will be found to be apparent, by retorting the Argument. If therefore neither all Signs be apparent, nor all unapparent; nor some apparent, others unapparent; and that there be nothing more than this, as they acknowledge, what they call Signs will be inexistent. These few Arguments, alledged out of many, may suffice to shew, that there is no Endeictick Sign.

Let us now lay down the Arguments of those who hold a Sign to be, that we may shew the equivalence of contrary Reasons. Either the words alledged against Sign signifie something, or they signifie nothing; if insignificant, How can they take away the existence of Sign? If they signifie what Sign is, they are demonstrative against Sign, or not demonstrative; if not demonstrative, they do not demonstrate that Sign is not; if demonstrative, demonstration being a *Species* of Sign, detective of its conclusion, Sign will be. Whence is argued thus, If Sign be something, there is Sign; and if there be not Sign, there is Sign; for that there is no Sign must be proved by demonstration, which is a Sign. Now either Sign is, or it is not, therefore it is not.

Upon this Argument followeth another in this manner; If there be not some Sign, there is no Sign: and if a Sign be that which the *Dogmatists* hold it to be, it is no Sign; for the Sign of which we discourse, according as it is understood, and as it is relative to, and detective of, the significate, is found to be inexistent, as we shewed before. Now either Sign is, or it is not; therefore it is not.

As concerning the words which are spoken of Sign, let the *Dogmatists* answer, Whether they signifie any thing, or not; if they signifie nothing, they prove not that there is Sign; if they signifie, the Significate followeth them, which is, there is Sign; whence it followeth, as we shewed, that there is Sign, by retorting the Argument. Since therefore Reasons equally probable may be alledged, to prove there is Sign, and that there is not Sign, we ought not to say either rather than the other.

CHAP. XII.

Of Demonstration.

FRom what hath been said, it is manifest that neither is Demonstration a thing acknowledged. For if we suspend as to sign, and Demonstration be a Sign, we must necessarily suspend as to Demonstration; For we shall find that the Arguments alledged against Sign will serve also against Demonstration: It seemeth to be Relative to, and detective of, its Conclusion, upon which will follow almost all that we alledged against Sign. But if something must be said of Demonstration in particular, I will comprise the Discourse in a narrow compass, first laying down what Demonstration, according to them, is.

' Demonstration (as they say) is a Reason
' which, by Collection of acknowledged (indubi-
' tate) Sumptions, detecteth a thing unmanifest.
' *But clear wi'l it seem by this that followeth,* Reason
' (*or Argument*) is that which consists of Sumpti-
' ons and a Conclusion; Its Sumptions are said
' to be the Axioms taken suitably for constructi-
' on of the conclusion concordantly.
' Inference or Conclusion is the Axiom framed
' out of the two Sumptions, as in this, If it is
' Day, it is Light; but it is Day, therefore it is
' Light: Therefore it is Light, is the Conclusion,
' the rest are the Sumptions. Of Reasons, some
' are conclusive, others not conclusive: Conclu-
' sive, when the Connex, beginning from Com-
' plication of the Sumptions of the Argument,
' and concluding in the Inference thereof, is
' found; as the instanced Reason is Conclusive,
' because to this Complication of its Sumptions,
' It is Day; and, if it is Day it is Light; it is *con-*
' *sequent*, it is Light, in this Connex, if it is Day,
' and if it is Day, it is Light. Not conclusive are
' those, which are not after this manner.
' Of the Conclusive, some are true, others not
' true. True, when not only the Connex, as to
' Complication of the Sumptions and the Infe-
' rence, is, as we said, found; but the Conclusion,
' and that which is a Complication of the Sumpti-
' ons is true, which is the Antecedent, and the
' Connex. ' A *true* Complication is that which
' hath all true, as, It is Day, and, if it is Day it
' is Light. ' Not true, is, when they are not
' thus; for this Reason, if it is Night, it is dark;
' but it is Night; therefore it is dark, is indeed
' Conclusive, because the Connex is found, if it
' is Night, and, if it is Night it is dark; but it
' is not true, for the consequent complicate is
' false, it is Night, and if it is Night it is dark,
' it containing this falsity, for it is a false com-
' plicate whatsoever containeth in it self a falsi-
' ty. Whence they say, A true reason is that,
' which, from true Sumptions, inferreth a true
' Conclusion.
' Again, of true Reasons, some are (*Apodeictick*)
' Demonstrative, others not Demonstrative.
' Demonstrative, are those, which, from things
' manifest, collect something not manifest; not
' Demonstrative are those which are not so,
' as this reason, If it be Day it is Light; but it is
' Day, therefore it is Light, is not demonstra-
' tive, for its conclusion, it is light, is manifest.
' But this, if Sweat pierce through the Skin, there
are

'are Pores intelligible, but Sweat pierceth
'through the Skin, therefore there are Pores
'intelligible,is demonstrative; for its conclusion,
'therefore there are Pores Intelligible, is unma-
'nifest.

'Again, of those which collect something un-
'manifest, some bring us by the Sumptions to
'the Conclusion inductively only, others indu-
'ctively and detectively. Inductively, those which
'seem to depend upon Belief and Memory, as
'this; if one tell you, that such a Man shall grow
'rich, he shall grow rich; but this God (as sup-
'posing *Jupiter*) tells you, that such a Man shall
'grow rich, therefore he shall grow rich. We af-
'sent to the conclusion not so much for any ne-
'cessity of the Sumptions, as for that we believe
'what the God saith. Others not only induct-
'ively, but detectively also lead us to the Con-
'clusion; If Sweat issue through the Skin, Pores
'are intelligible; but the first, therefore the se-
'cond; for this, Sweat issueth forth, is detect-
'ive of the other, there are Pores; forasmuch
'as we preconceive, that moisture cannot pe-
'netrate through a Body not porous.

'Thus Demonstration must be a Reason con-
'clusive and true, and have an unmanifest Con-
'clusion detective by the power of the Sumpti-
'ons, and therefore Demonstration is said to be
'a Reason, having indubitate Sumptions, and by
'Collection detecting an unmanifest Inference.
By this we may understand the Notion of Demonstration.

CHAP. XIII.

Whether there is Demonstration.

THat Demonstration is not, may be argued from what they themselves say, by over-throwing every Particular that is included in the Notion. For Example; A Reason or Argument consists of Axioms, but a compound thing cannot exist, unless the things whereof it is compounded coexist one with another (as a Bed, and the like:) But the parts of a Reason are not coexistent one with another; for whilst we are speaking the first Sumption, the other Sumption nor the Inference do not yet exist; and while we are speaking the second, the first is no longer existent, and the Inference exists not yet; and when we pronounce the Inference, the Sumptions are no longer existent. Thus the parts of a Reason are not existent with one another, and therefore the Reason it self seemeth not to exist.

Besides, *A conclusive Reason* is incomprehensible; for, if it be judged from the consequence of the Connex, but the consequence of the Connex be undeterminably controverted, and perhaps is incomprehensible, (as we shewed in our discourse concerning a Sign;) conclusive Reason will also be incomprehensible.

Moreover the *Dialecticks* say, that 'A not-
'conclusive Reason is made, either by Incohe-
'rence, or by Defect, or by being in an ill Fi-
'gure, or by Redundance. By incoherence,
'when the Sumptions have no coherence with
'one another, nor with the Inference, as, If it
'is Day it is Light, but Corn is sold in the
'Market, therefore *Dion* walks.

'By Redundance; when there is found some
'redundant Sumption superfluous to collection
'of the Reason, as, If it is day it is light, but it
'is day, and *Dion* walks, therefore it is light.

'By being in an ill Figure; for these are as they
'call them *Syllogisms*. *If it is Day it is Light, but* So supply the
'*it is Day, therefore it is Light*; And *If it is not* Text.
'*Light it is not Day; But it is not Light, therefore
'it is not Day*. But this is an inconclusive reason,
'If it is Day it is Light, but it is Day, therefore
'it is Light; because the Connex promising that
'its Consequent is in its Antecedent, the Antece-
'dent being assumed, the Consequent is also as-
'sumed; and the Antecedent being taken away,
'the Consequent is also taken away; for if the
'Antecedent be, the Consequent must be also. But
'assuming the Consequent, the Antecedent is not
'always assumed also; for the Connex doth not
'promise that the Antecedent shall follow upon
'the Consequent, but only the Consequent upon
'the Antecedent. Hereupon a Reason, which
'collects the Consequent from the Connex of
'the Antecedent, is said to be Syllogistick; and
'that which from the Connex, and from the con-
'trary of the Consequent collects the contrary
'of the Antecedent: But that which from the
'Connex and the Consequent collects the An-
'tecedent, is inconclusive, as we said before.
'Whence its Sumption being true, it collects a
'Falsity, if it be spoken in the Night-time by
'the light of a Candle: for this, If it is Day it is
'Light, is a true Connex; and so is this Assum-
'ption, But it is Light; but the inference, There-
'fore it is Day, is false.

'By defect; a Reason is faulty, when there is
'omitted something of those which are requisite
'to Collection of the Conclusion; as this Reason,
'being, as they conceive, sound, Riches are either
'good or ill, or indifferent; but neither ill nor
'indifferent, therefore good. This other is un-
'sound by Defect, Riches are either good,
'or ill, or indifferent; but not ill, therefore
'good.

Now if I shall shew, that according to them, no difference of inconclusive Reasons can be judged by the Conclusive, I shall have cleared, that the Conclusive Reason is Incomprehensible, and that all their Ostentation in Dialectick is folly. I prove it thus, *A Reason Inconclusive by Incoherence, is said to be known from its sumptions, not having any coherence one with another, and with the Conclusion*; now forasmuch as the knowledge of coherents must precede the judgment of the Connex, the Connex will be indijudicable, (according to our usual Argument) and consequently so will the Reason, *Inconclusive by Incoherence*, be also. For he who saith, That a Reason is Inconclusive by Incoherence, if he do it by simple Enunciation, we oppose the contrary Enunciation; if he demonstrate it by a Reason, we shall tell him, he must first demonstrate that Reason to be Conclusive, and afterwards prove the sumptions of a Reason defective by Incoherence, to be Incoherent; but whether his Reason be demonstrative, we cannot know, not having a generally acknowledg'd Judgment of the Connex, whereby to judge, whether the Conclusion cohere with the Complication of the sumptions in the Reason. Therefore we have not whereby to judge the difference betwixt

the

the Conclusive Reason, and the Defective by Incoherence.

The same we object to him, who saith, that a Reason is faulty by *being in an ill Figure:* For he that goeth upon this Ground, that there is some Figure ill, will not have acknowledged conclusive Reason, whereby to collect what he saith.

In the same manner may those be confuted, who say, that a Reason is *Inconclusive by defect*; for if the Perfect be indijudicable, the Defective must be so also. Again, he who would prove by some Reason, that there is something wanting to Reason, unless he hath an acknowledged judication of the Connex, whereby he may judge the Coherence of the Reason which he alledgeth, he cannot judicially and rightly say, that the other is defective.

Likewise, that Reason which is said to be faulty by Redundance, is not dijudicable by the Demonstrative; for as to Redundance, even those very Reasons, which the *Stoicks* cry up as *Indemonstrable*, will be found to be inconclusive, which, if they should be taken away, all Dialectick will be overthrown. These are they, which (they say) need not Demonstration to establish them, but by them are demonstrated the other Conclusive Reasons. That these are redundant, will appear plainly if we lay them down and discourse upon them. They dream, 'that there are many Indemonstrables, but assert chiefly Five, whereto all the rest seem to 'be referred. The First, from the Connex and 'the Antecedent, collects the Consequent, as, 'If it is Day it is Light, but it is Day, therefore 'it is Light. The Second, from the Connex 'and the contrary of the Consequent, collects 'the contrary of the Antecedent, as, If it is 'Day it is Light, but it is not Light, therefore 'it is not Day. The Third, from the negative Complicate, and one of the Parts of the 'Complicate, collects the contrary of the other 'Part, as, It is not Day and Night also, but it 'is Day, therefore it is not Night. The Fourth, 'from the Disjunct and one of the Conjuncts, 'collects the contrary of the other, as, Either 'it is Day or it is Night, but it is Day, therefore it is not Night. The Fifth, from the 'Disjunct and the contrary of one of the Conjuncts, collects the other, as, Either it is Day 'or it is Night, but it is not Day, therefore it 'is Night. These are the Reasons which they cry up as Indemonstrable; but they all seem to me Inconclusive, by Redundance. For to begin with the First; Either it is acknowledged [as undoubted] that this part, *it is Day*, followeth upon this other, *it is Light*, which is the Antecedent in this Connex, *if it is Day it is Light*; or, it is not Manifest: If Unmanifest, we shall not allow the Connex as acknowledged; but if it be manifest that if this be, *it is Day*, this other must necessarily be also, *it is Light*, in saying, *it is Day*, we collect the other, *it is Light*, and this Connex, *it is Day, it is Light*, is Redundant.

The same may be said of the *second Indemonstrable*, for either it is possible the Antecedent may be, the Consequent not being, or it is not possible. If possible, it is not a sound Connex; if not possible, as soon as ever the word *Not* is spoken in the Consequent, it declareth the *Not* in the Antecedent, so as this is a redundant Connex, *It is not Light, therefore it is not Day.*

The same may be said of the *third Indemonstrable*; either it is manifest, that those which are in the Complication cannot possibly coexist, or not manifest; if not manifest, we shall not allow the Negative of the Complication; if manifest, as soon as one is laid down, the other is taken away, whereby the Negative of the Complicate is redundant thus, *It is Day, therefore it is not Night*.

The like we say of the *fourth and fifth Indemonstrables*; either it is manifest, that in the Disjunct one is true, the other false, with perfect opposition, (as the Disjunct promiseth,) or it is not manifest. If unmanifest, we shall not grant the Disjunct; if manifest, as soon as one is laid down, the other is taken away, and one being taken away, it is manifest that the other is, as, *It is Day, therefore it is not Night; It is not Day, therefore it is Night.*

The like may be said of the *Categorick Syllogisms* used chiefly by the *Peripateticks*, such as this, *Just is Honest, Honest is Good, therefore Just is Good*; either it is manifest that Honest is Good, or it is doubted and unmanifest; If unmanifest, it will not be granted upon this Argument, and consequently the *Syllogism* will not convince; if it be manifest, that *whatsoever is Honest is Good*, in saying, it is Honest, is implied, it is Good also; so that this were enough, *Just is Honest, therefore Just is Good*; and the other Sumption, in which *Honest* is said to be *Good*, is redundant. The like in this Reason, Socrates *is a Man, every Man is a living Creature, therefore* Socrates *is a living Creature*. If it be not manifest in it self, that whatsoever is Man is also a living Creature, the universal first Proposition will not be acknowledged, neither shall we grant it in the Argument. But if from being a Man it followeth, that he is a living Creature, and therefore the first Proposition, *Every Man is a living Creature*, is acknowledged true, then, as soon as ever *Socrates* is said to be a Man, it is imply'd, that he is *a living Creature*; and therefore the first Proposition is redundant, *Every Man is a living Creature*. The like method may be used against all Categorical Reasons, not to insist longer hereon: Seeing therefore these Reasons whereupon the Dialectick ground their Syllogisms are redundant, as to Redundance all Dialectick will be subverted, we not being able to judge the redundant inconclusive Reasons, from the conclusive, called Syllogisms. And if any will not allow *Monolemma*'s Reasons, (that have but one Sumption,) they will not be more creditable than *Antipater*, who allows them.

Thus a true Reason is impossible to be found, as well for the Causes alledged, as because it ought to end in true; for the Conclusion which is said to be true, must be either apparent or unapparent; not apparent, for then it would not require the Sumptions to detect it, it being of it self manifest to us, and no less apparent than the Sumptions themselves; If unapparent, forasmuch as there is an undeterminable Controversie concerning Unapparents, (as was said formerly) it is therefore incomprehensible. Thus the Conclusion of the Reason which they call true, will be incomprehensible, and if that be incompre-

incomprehensible, we shall not know whether that which is collected be true or false, therefore we shall not know, whether the Reason be true or false; and consequently the Reason which they call *true* cannot be found.

Moreover, that Reason which collects a thing unmanifest from a manifest, cannot be found out; for if the Inference follow the Complication from its Sumptions, that which followeth [the consequent] is relative to the antecedent; but relatives are comprehended together with one another, as we said before. If therefore the conclusion be unmanifest, the Sumptions will also be unmanifest: If the Sumptions are manifest, the Conclusion will also be manifest, as being comprehended together with the manifest, (Sumptions) So as nothing unmanifest can be collected from what is manifest. Hereupon the Inference cannot be detected by the Sumptions, whether it be unmanifest and not comprehended, or manifest and not needing detection. Now if *Demonstration* be said to be a' *Reason according to Connexion,* that is, *conclusive by some acknowledged true thing, detecting an unmanifest Inference;* and we have proved, that it neither is a Reason nor Conclusive, nor true, nor by some things manifest collecting an unmanifest, nor detective of the Conclusion; it appeareth there is no such thing as Demonstration.

Likewise we shall other-ways find Demonstration to be inexistent and unintelligible: For he who saith, there is Demonstration, asserts either general Demonstration or particular, but neither general nor particular Demonstration are possible, (as we shall prove;) and besides these, there is no other can be understood; therefore no Man can assert Demonstration to be existent.

That there is no general Demonstration, we prove thus. Either it hath Sumptions and an Inference, or it hath not; if it hath not, it is no Demostration; if it hath, forasmuch as every thing that is demonstrated, and also that which doth demonstrate is particular, it will be a particular demonstration, therefore there is no general demonstration.

But neither is there any particular demonstration. For either they must say, it consists of Sumptions and an Inference, or of Sumptions only, but neither of these, therefore there is no particular demonstration. That which consists of Sumptions and an Inference, is not a demonstration; First, as having one part unmanifest (the Inference) it will be unmanifest, which were absurd; for if the demonstration be unmanifest, it rather will require to be demonstrated by somthing, than be capable to demonstrate by somthing. Again, forasmuch as they say, the demonstration is relative to the Inference, and Relatives, as they also say, are different, from one another; the thing demonstrated must be different from the demonstration. If therefore the conclusion be the thing demonstrated, the demonstration will not be understood together with the conclusion. For either the conclusion confereth somthing towards demonstrating it self, or no; if it confer, it will be detective of it self; if it confer not, but be redundant, it will be no part of the demonstration, for such a demonstration will but fortifie redundance. Neither is that which consists of Sumptions only a demonstration; for, who will say that this, *If it is day it is light, but it is day, it is light,* either is a reason or indeed inferreth any thing? Wherefore neither is that which consists of Sumptions only a demonstration; whence it follows, that there is no particular demonstration. Now if there be no particular demonstration nor no general, and besides these is no demonstration intellgible; there cannot be demonstration.

Moreover, the inexistence of demonstration may be proved this way; If there be demonstration, either an apparent detects an apparent, or an unmanifest an unmanifest or an unmanifest an apparent, or an apparent an unmanifest; but none of these can be understood; it is therefore unintelligible. For if an apparent detect an apparent, the thing detecting will be at once apparent and unmanifest; apparent, or being supposed such; unmanifest, as requiring somthing to detect it, and not manifestly of it self incurring to us. If an unmanifest an unmanifest, it self will require somthing to detect it, rather than be capable of detecting another, which is inconsistent with the nature of a demonstration. Neither can an unmanifest be the demonstration of a manifest, nor a manifest of an unmanifest, for this reason, because they are relative. Relatives are comprehended together with one another; if that which is said to be demonstrated be comprehended together with the manifest demonstration, it is manifest it self. Thus the reason will be retorted, and it will not be found, that the manifest can demonstrate the unmanifest. If therefore there be not demonstration, neither of an unmanifest by an unmanifest, nor of an unmanifest by a manifest, nor of a manifest by an unmanifest, and more than these, they say, there is not any, we must say, that demonstration is nothing.

Moreover, there is controversie concerning demonstration; some say, that it is not, as they who hold, that there is none; others, that it is, as most of the Dogmatists; we say *neither rather* that it is, or that it is not. Again, demonstration must necessarily contain some Doctrine, but every Doctrine is controverted, and therefore every Demonstration must be controverted. For if, for example, the demonstration to prove Vacuum being acknowledged, Vacuum also be acknowledged, it is manifest, that they who doubt whether there be Vacuum, doubt also the demonstration thereof. It is the same in all other demonstrated Doctrines. Thus all demonstration is doubted and controverted. Since therefore demonstration is unmanifest, as appears by the controversie concerning it, (for things controverted, inasmuch as controverted, are unmanifest) it is not evident in it self, but must be evinced to us by demonstration. Now an acknowledged indubitate demonstration to prove demonstration, there cannot be (the Question being, Whether there be any demonstration at all?) but if it be controverted and unmanifest, it will require another demonstration, and that another, and so to infinite; but it is impossible to demonstrate Infinites, therefore it is impossible to prove, there is Demonstration.

Neither can it be detected by a sign; for it being questioned whether there be a Sign, and
the

the Sign consequently requiring a demonstration of it self, it runs into the *Alternate* common place; the demonstration requiring a sign, the sign a demonstration, which is absurd. Neither can the controversie concerning sign be judged, because dijudication wanteth a Criterie, it being controverted, as we shewed, whether there be a Criterie, and the Criterie consequently requiring a Demonstration to prove that there is a Criterie, it runs again into the Alternate place. If therefore neither by Demonstration, nor by Sign, nor by Criterie, it can be proved, that there is Demonstration, and it be not manifest of it self, as we have shewn, it will be incomprehensible whether there be Demonstration; therefore Demonstration is inexistent: For it is understood by demonstrating, but not being comprehended it cannot demonstrate, therefore there will be no Demonstration. This, by way of Summary, may serve against Demonstration.

But the Dogmatists, on the other side, say, The Reasons alledged against Demonstration, either are demonstrative, or not demonstrative; If not demonstrative, they are not able to prove there is no Demonstration; If demonstrative, they themselves, by Retortion, prove the subsistence of Demonstration. Hereupon they argue thus, If there is Demonstration there is Demonstration; if there is not Demonstration there is Demonstration, therefore there is Demonstration. Upon the same grounds they also propose this Reason, That which followeth from contraries, is not only True, but Necessary, but, there is Demonstration, and, there is not Demonstration, are opposite one to another, from both which it followeth, that there is Demonstration, therefore there is Demonstration.

But this may be contradicted, as for Example, if we say thus; Forasmuch as we conceive that there is not any Reason demonstrative, neither do we conceive that the Reasons alledged against Demonstrations are adsolutely demonstrative, but that they seem probable to us; but Probables are not necessarily demonstrative, therefore if the Demonstratives are (which we allow not) necessarily true, but true Reasons collect true from true, their Inference is not true, and if not, it is no Demonstration; therefore (by way of Retortion) there is no Demonstration. Besides, as purgative Medicines expel themselves, together with the Humors which they purge, it is possible that these Reasons may exclude themselves, together with those which are said to be Demonstratives. For this is not absurd, seeing that this Sentence, *That there is nothing True*, not only takes away all other things, but it self amongst the rest. Moreover, this Argument (If there be Demonstration there is Demonstration, if there is not Demonstration there is Demonstration, but either there is, or there is not, therefore there is) may many ways be shewn to be Inconclusive; but, for the present, we shall be contented with this Epicherem. If this Connex (If there is Demonstration there is Demonstration,) be not faulty, the contrary of its Consequent (that is, there is not Demonstration) must be repugnant to its Antecedent, there is Demonstration, for that is the Antecedent of the Connex: But, according to them, it is impossible that a Connex can be found, if it consists of contrary Propositions, for a Connex promiseth, that if its Antecedent be, its Consequent is also; but in Opposites quite contrary, which of them soever is, the other must not be. Therefore if this be a true Connex, If there is Demonstration, there is Demonstration, this other cannot be true, If there is not Demonstration, there is Demonstration

Moreover, If we grant by Supposition, that this is a sound Connex, If there is not Demonstration, there is Demonstration, this part, if there is not Demonstration, may coexist with the other, there is Demonstration: But if it may coexist with it, it cannot be repugnant to it, so that in this Connex, if there is Demonstration, there is Demonstration, the contrary of the Consequent is not repugnant to the Antecedent, therefore it is not found. Again, If this Connex, which, by way of Concession, is laid down for sound, and this part, there is no Demonstration, be repugnant to that part, there is not Demonstration, neither will this be a good Disjunct, either there is Demonstration, or there is not Demonstration; for a good Disjunct promiseth that one of its parts is true, and that the other is false and repugnant. Or if the Disjunct be found, this, if there is not Demonstration, there is Demonstration, will again be found to be faulty, a Connex consisting of Repugnants. Wherefore the Sumptions in the foresaid Reason are inconsistent, and destroy one another, therefore the Reason is not sound. But neither can they shew that somthing followeth upon Repugnants, not having a Criterie of the Consequents, as we argued before. But this is said over and above. Now if the Reasons for Demonstration be probable, and the Reasons against Demonstration be probable also, we must suspend, saying no more, that there is Demonstration, than that there is not.

CHAP. XIV.

Of Syllogisms.

COncerning those which they call *Syllogisms*, perhaps it were superfluous to discourse, as well for that they are subverted by taking away Demonstration, (for if there be no Demonstration, there is no Demonstrative Reason) as also, forasmuch as what we have already said may serve for Confutation of them, whereas we over and above delivered a Method, to shew, that all the Demonstrative Reasons of the *Stoicks* and *Peripateticks* are inconclusive. But perhaps it would not be amiss to say something in particular concerning these, especially, seeing they have a high conceit of them. But whereas many things might be alledged, to shew, they cannot exist; yet we, persuing our design of a Summary, will use our first Method.

Let us first speak of Indemonstrables; for if they be taken away, all other Reasons are overthrown, as being by them demonstrated to be Conclusive. Now this Proposition, *Every Man is a living Creature*, is inductively proved by particulars; because from *Socrates*'s being a Man, and a living Creature, and so *Plato*'s and *Dion*'s, and every one in particular, it seemeth possible to be proved, that every Man is a living Creature. For if there be but one particular, which seemeth contrary to the rest, the universal Proposition will not be found. As for Example, Although the greatest part of living Creatures move the lower Jaw, only the Crocodile the upper, this Proposition is not true; all living Creatures move the lower Jaw. When therefore they say, *Every Man is a living Creature, Socrates is a Man, therefore Socrates is a living Creature*; intending from this universal Proposition, *Every Man is a living Creature*, to collect this particular Proposition, *therefore Socrates is a living Creature*; this being one of those, by which the universal Proposition was (as I said) inductively proved, they fall into the *Alternate Common Place*, proving the universal Proposition by the Particulars, and the Particular by the Universal. In like manner in this Reason Socrates *is a Man*; but *no Man is Four-footed, therefore* Socrates *is not Four footed*. This Proposition, *No Man is Four-footed*, endeavoring to prove inductively by Particulars, and to prove every Particular syllogistically out of this, they run into the *Alternate Common Place* inextricably.

In like manner, let us examine the rest of the Reasons, which the *Peripateticks* call Demonstrable; for this. *If it be Day, it is Light*, they say, is conclusive of this, *it is Light*; and again, this, *it is Light*, together with the other, *It is Day*, is confirmative of this, *If it is Day, it is Light*: For the aforesaid Connex would not be thought sound, if the first part, *It is Light*, were not always coexistent with, *it is Day*. *If* therefore it must first be comprehended, that when there is Day, there is necessarily Light, for the framing of this Connex, *If it be Day, it is Light*, hence is inferred, that in these, *When it is Day, it is Light*; this Connex, *If it is Day, it is Light*, (as far as concerns the present indemonstrable Reason) proving the coexistence of this, *It is Day*, and of this, *It is Light*; and reciprocally their existence, confirming the Connex here again, by the *Alternate Common Place*, the existence of Reason is subverted.

The same may be said of this Reason, *If it is Day, it is Light; but it is not Light: therefore it is not Day*; For, inasmuch as there connot be Day without Light, this is conceived to be a sound Connex, *If it be Day, it is Light*; But if we should suppose some Day to be; and Light not to be, it will be said to be a false Connex. Now as to the foresaid Indemonstrable, that, *If there is not Day, there is not Light*, is collected from this, that, *If there is Day, there is Light*; so as either is requisite to the proof of the other, and incurs the *Alternate Common Place*.

Likewise, Forasmuch as some things are inconsistent one with the other, as Day and Night, and the Negative of the Complicate, (*It is not Day, and it is not Night*,) and the Disjunct is thought to be found; but that they are inconsistent, they conceive to be proved by the Negative of the Complicate, and by the Disjunct, saying, *It is not Day and Night; but it is Night, therefore it is not Day*. Or thus, *Either it is Day or Night; but it is Night, therefore it is not Day*. Or, *but it is not Night, therefore it is Day*. Whence we again argue, that if to Confirmation of the Disjunct, and of the Negation in the Complicate, it be necessary that we first comprehend the Axioms contained in them to be inconsistent; but that they are Inconsistent, seems to be collected from the Disjunct, and the Negative of the Complicate, they run into the *Alternate Common Place*, seeing that we can neither credit the foresaid Modals, unless we first comprehend the Inconsistence of the Axioms that are in them, nor can affirm their Inconsistence, before we can affirm the Coargution of the Syllogisms which is made by the Modals. Wherefore not having whereupon to ground our Belief first, (they being Reciprocal) we must say, that neither the Third, nor Fourth, nor Fifth, of the Indemonstrables (as far as appeareth by this,) have Subsistence. Thus much for Syllogisms.

CHAP. XV.

Of Induction.

INduction, as I conceive, may easily be overthrown; for, seeing that by it they would prove an Universal from Particulars, either they must do it, as having examined all Particulars, or only some. If some only, the *Induction* will not be valid, it being possible, that some of the omitted Particulars may be found contrary to the Universal Proposition. If they would examine all, they attempt Impossibles, for Particulars are infinite, and undeterminate. Thus it happens, that Induction cannot subsist either way.

CHHP. XVI.

Of Difinitions.

FOrasmuch as the *Dogmatists* are highly conceited of themselves, as to the framing of *Definitions*. (which they rank under the Logical part of Philosophy) let us discourse a little hereupon. The *Dogmatists* say, that *Definitions* conduce to many things, but perhaps all their necessary use may be reduced to two general Heads; they shew that *Definitions* are necessary, either to Comprehension, or to Instruction. Now if we prove they are useful to neither, we overthrow their vain Labor. We argue thus: If he who knoweth not that which is defined, cannot define that which he knoweth not, and he who knoweth first, and afterwards defineth, comprehends not, by the Definition, that which is defined, but applies the Definition to that which he already comprehends; then Definition is not necessary to the Comprehension of things. And forasmuch as if we would define all things. we cannot define any, because, we shall run into Infinite; and if we say, that some things may be comprehended without Definitions, we shew, that Definitions are not necessary to Comprehension: As those which are not defined are comprehended, so we might comprehend all the rest without Definitions; either we shall define nothing at all, because of proceeding to Infinite, or we alledge Definitions not necessary.

For the same Reasons shall we find, that neither are they necessary to Instruction: For, as he who first knoweth a thing, knoweth it without Definition; in like manner, he who teacheth it, may teach it without a Definition.

Moreover, from the things defined they judge Definitions, saying, Those are faulty Definitions, which include somthing which is not in the things defined, either in all, or in some. So as if we say, *A Man is a living Creature, Rational, Immortal*; Or, *A living Creature, Rational, Mortal, Learned*, forasmuch as there is no Man Immortal, and that there are some Men not learned, they say it is a faulty Definition Therefore Definitions, perhaps, are indijudicable, by reason of the Infinity of the Particulars, by which they ought to be judged. Besides, they cannot make us comprehend and learn the things of which themselves are dijudicated, inasmuch as they are already known and comprehended. Is it not therefore ridiculous to say, That Definitions conduce to Comprehension, or Instruction, or Declaration, when they involve us in such obscurity? As for Example, (to sport a little) If one Man meaning to ask another, Whether he met a Man on Horseback, with a Dog following him, should do it after this manner. *O Living Creature, Rational, Mortal, capable of Intellect and Science, Didst thou not meet a Living Creature, Visible, Broad-nail'd, capable of Political Science, mounted upon a living Creature that hath the faculty of Neighing, leading a four-footed living Creature that hath the faculty of Barking*. Who would not laugh to see a Man, that knows the things themselves, puzzled by their Definitions? We must therefore acknowledge Definitions to be unnecessary, whether it be a Speech, which, by a short Explication, brings us to knowledge of the thing, meant by the words, (which, by what we have said, it appeareth, that it doth not) or whether it be a Speech declaring what a thing is, τὸ τί ἦν ᾖ, or even what they please. For when they go about to shew what Demonstration is, they fall out among themselves irreconcileably, of which for Brevity's sake, we will not take Notice.

CHAP. XVII.

Of Division.

FOrasmuch as some of the Dogmatists say, That *Dialectick is a Science Syllogistick, Inductive, Definitive*; after our discourse of the *Criterie*, and of *Demonstration*, and of *Syllogisms*, and of *Inductions*, and of *Definition*, we will come to say somthing of *Division*, conceiving it not to be from our purpose.

They say, That of *Division*, there are four kinds; *Of the Word into Significations*; *Of the Whole into Parts*; *Of the Genus into Species*; *Of the Species into Individuals*. But that there is not a divisive Science of any of these, I think may easily be shewn, by examining them severally.

CHAP. XVIII.

Of the division of a Word into Significations.

THE Sciences they hold to be by Nature, not by Imposition; and justly, for Science must be a thing stable and unmoveable: But those things which are by Imposition, are very subject to Mutation, being varied according to the diversity of Impositions which are in our power. Now forasmuch as words signifie by Imposition, and not by Nature, (otherwise all Men would understand all Languages, both *Greeks* and *Barbarians*, besides it is in our power to declare our meaning by other words) how is it possible there should be a divisive Science of the word into Significations? Or how can *Dialectick* be (as some conceive,) the Science of Significants, and Significates?

CHAP. XIX.

Of Whole and Part.

COncerning *Whole* and *Part*, we shall discourse in that which they call *Physick*; at present, we shall only speak of the division of the Whole into its Parts. We say thus, When the *Decad* is said to be divided into *One*, and *Two*, and *Three*, and *Four*, it is not divided into these, for as soon as the first part (granting this by the way of supposition) is taken away, (as the *Monad*) there is no longer the *Decad*, but the *Ennead*, a thing quite different from the *Decad*; therefore the substraction and division of the rest concerns not the *Decad*, but other Numbers according to the several Substractions.

Let us now see, Whether it be possible to divide the Whole into those things, which they say are its Parts. If the Whole is divided into its Parts, the Parts before the division either are contained in the Whole, or not contained: To use our first Example, the *Decad*; They say, that 9 is one of its Parts, for it is divided into 1. and 9. so is 8 also, for it is divided into 8. and 2. So also is 7. and 6. and 5. and 4. and 3. and 2. and 1. Now if all these are contained in the *Decad*, and compounded with it, they making 55. the *Decad* must contain 55. which is absurd. Therefore are not the Parts, as they call them, contained in the *Decad*; neither can the *Decad* be divided into them, as a Whole into Parts, since they are not to be found in it. The same may be objected against Magnitudes, as if we should divide a Magnitude into ten Cubits; perhaps therefore it is not possible to divide the Whole into Parts.

CHAP. XX.

Of Genus and Species.

IT remains to treat of *Genus* and *Species*, of which elsewhere we shall speak more largely, but now compendiously. If *Genus* and *Species* are Notions, the Arguments which we brought against the Hegemonick, and Phantasie, subvert

vert them; but if they allow them to have a peculiar subsistence, What will they answer to this? If there are *Genus*'s, either there are as many as there are *Species*, or there is one common *Species*, or *Genus*, in all those which are called *Species*. If there be as many *Genus's*, as there *Species*, of them there will not be one common *Genus*, which is divided into them; but if it be said, there is one *Genus* in all its *Species*, then every *Species* must participate of the Whole *Genus*, or of Part thereof; but not of the Whole, for it is impossible, for one thing contained at once, in one, and another, to be wholly in one. If of Part only, first, the whole *Genus* will not follow the *Species*, as they conceive it doth, for Man will not be a living Creature, but part of a living Creature, as a substance, but neither animate nor sensible. Again, either all the *Species* will be said to participate of the same Parts of their *Genus*, or some of some Part, others of others. That they should participate of the same is impossible, for the Reason aforesaid. If some of some, others of others, the *Species* will not be like to one another, according to their *Genus*, (which they will not admit) and besides, every *Genus* will be infinite, being divided into infinite, not only as to *Species*, but as to Particulars, in which it is consider'd with those *Species*; for *Dion* is not only said to be a Man, but a living Creature. But if these things be absurd, neither do the *Species* participate of Part of their *Genus*, it being one; but if neither doth every *Species* participate of its *Genus* in Whole, nor in Part, how can one *Genus* be said to be in all its *Species*, so as to be divided into them. None sure can say any thing hereto, unless he frame some kind of Images; and yet even those will be subverted, according to the Sceptical Method, by their own indeterminate consequences.

We shall add this, *Species's* are either such or such, their *Genus's* are either such and such, or they are such and they are not such, or they are neither such nor such. As for Instance: Forasmuch as of these or those, some are Corporeal, others Incorporeal, and some True, others False, and some peradventure White, others Black, and some very Great, others very Little: This word *Thing*, for example, which some say is most general, will either be All, or Some, or Nothing; but if it be absolutely Nothing, neither will it be *Genus*, and so there is an end of the Controversie. If they say it is All, besides that it is impossible it should be so, it must be all the *Species*, and every particular in them. For because an Animal, as they say, is an Animate, Sensitive Substance, therefore each of its *Species* is said to be both a Substance, and Animate, and Sensitive: So if *Genus* be both Body, and Incorporeal, and False and True, and Black and White, and Little and Great, and all the rest, each of its *Species* and particulars will also be All, which we do not find to be so; therefore this also is False. But if it be only some, then that which is the *Genus* of those, will not be the *Genus* of the rest; as if *Thing* be Body, it will not be the *Genus* of Incorporeals; and if living Creature be Rational, not of Irrationals; so that neither will an Incorporeal be a Thing, nor Irrational a Creature. Therefore *Genus* is neither such and such, nor such and not such, nor neither such nor such: And if so, neither is *Genus* any thing at all.

If any shall say, that *Genus* is all Potentially; we answer, that what is any thing Potentially, must be somthing Actually also; as none can be a *Grammarian* Potentially, if he exist not Actually; now if *Genus* be all things Potentially, we demand of them what it is Actually, and thereupon occur the same inextricable difficulties, for it cannot be all Contraries Actually. Again, neither can it be some Actually, others Potentially, only as a Body Actually, Incorporeal Potentially; for a thing is Potentially, such as it may be Actually, but what is Actually a Body cannot be Actually Incorporeal; so as, for example, If it be a Body actually, it is Incorporeal Potentially, and on the contrary. Wherefore we cannot say that *Genus* is some things Actually, others Potentially, only. Now if Actually it be nothing at all, it exists not; and therefore the *Genus*, which they affirm to be divided into its *Species*, in nothing.

This likewise is worthy consideration, That as because *Alexander* and *Paris* are the same, therefore it is impossible, if it be true that *Alexander* walks, it should be false that *Paris* walks. In like manner, If to be Man, be the same thing in *Theon*, and in *Dion*, this Appellation, *Man*, alledged in the framing of any Axiom will make the Axiom either True or False in both, but this we find not to be so, for when *Dion* sitteth, and *Theon* walleth, this Axiom, *a Man sitteth*, spoken of one, is True; of the other, False; wherefore this Appellation, *Man*, is not common to both, not one and the same in both, but proper to each.

CHAP. XXI.

Of Common Accidents.

THe like may be said of *Common Accidents*. For if one and the same accident belong to *Dion* and *Theon*, for example, *Seeing*; if *Dion* die, and *Theon* survive and see, either they must say, that the sight of *Dion* is not subject to perish, which is absurd, or that the same sight is perished, and not perished, which is irrational also: Therefore the sight of *Theon* is not the same with the sight of *Dion*, therefore proper to each. For if the same Respiration happen to *Dion* and *Theon*, it cannot be that it should be in *Theon*, and not in *Dion*; but one may die and the other survive, therefore it is not the same. But of these, let what we have briefly said suffice.

CHAP. XXII.

Of Sophisms.

IT will not haply be absurd to insist a little upon *Sophisms*, in regard that they who cry up *Dialectick* so much, say, It is necessary for the Solution of them. For, say they, *If it discern Speeches True and False, and Sophisms be false Speeches; it is dijudicative of these, which corrupt Truth with an apparent likelihood.* Wherefore the *Dialectiks*, as assisting and underpropping the failing course of life, with much labour, teach the Inferences, and Solutions of Sophisms, saying, *A Sophism is a Reason probable and deceitful; so as it receives an Inference, either False, or like to False, or Uncertain, or otherwise not to be received.* False, as in this Sophism,

> No man giveth a Categorem to be Drunk,
> But this, to Drink Wormwood, is a Categorem,
> Therefore, No man giveth Wormwood to be drunk

Like to False, as in this;
> That which could not be, nor cannot be, is not absurd,
> But this, a Physician, as a Physician, kills; neither could, nor can be,
> Therefore this [Proposition,] a Physician, as a Physician, kills, is not absurd.

Uncertain, as this;
> I did not ask thee something first, and the Stars are not even in Number,
> But I did ask thee something first;
> Therefore, the Stars are not even in Number.

Not otherwise to be received, as those Speeches which are called Solœcisms, as,
> That which thou seest, is,
> But thou seest him Mad,
> Therefore he is Mad.

Again,
> That which thou seest, is,
> But thou seest many Houses burning,
> Therefore many Houses are burning.

Then they endeavour to shew their Solutions, saying, That 'in the first Sophism, one thing is 'granted by the Sumptions, another inferred; it 'is granted that a Categorem is not Drunk, and 'that to drink Wormwood is a Categorem, but 'not the Wormwood it self. So that, whereas the 'Inference ought to be, Therefore no Man drinks 'this [Categorem,] To drink Wormwood; 'which is true, it inferreth, Therefore no Man 'drinketh Wormwood, which is false, and is not 'collected from the granted Premises.

'As to the Second, It seems to lead to False, '(insomuch as they who mind it not well, doubt 'whether they ought to assent to it or not,) but 'it collects Truth, therefore this is not absurd. 'A Physician, as a Physician, killeth, for no Pro- 'position is absurd; but this, A Physician, as a 'Physician, killeth, is a Propsiotion; therefore 'it is not absurd.

'That which leadeth to Uncertainty, is, they 'say, of the Nature of reciprocal Reasons; for 'if nothing were asked before, then the Nega- 'tive of the Connex were true, the Connex it 'self being false, *because this*, [I asked thee som- 'thing first] which is false, is inserted into it; but 'after asking, (the Assumption being true, [I 'asked thee first] by reason the asking was be- 'fore the Assumption) the Negative of the Con- 'nex is false, so that a Conclusion cannot any 'way be gather'd, the Negative of the Connex 'being inconsistent with the Assumption.

'The last kind being by Solœcism, (some 'say,) infers absurdly, and contrary to common 'use.

Thus some *Dialecticks* discourse of *Sophisms*, (others otherwise) which may perhaps tickle the Ears of the lighter sort of Persons, but are indeed superfluous, and forged by themselves to no purpose. This perhaps may be observed from what was said formerly; for we shewed, that neither True nor False can be comprehended, according to the *Dialecticks*, as many other ways, so particularly, by overthrowing Demonstration, and indemonstrable Reasons, the props of their Syllogistick faculty. Many other things might be alledg'd against the Subject in hand, of which we shall only say briefly thus.

Of all those *Sophisms*, which *Dialectick* seems properly to confute, the Solution is unprofitable; but those, the Solution whereof is profitable, it is not within the power of a *Dialectick* to solve, but of those who are conversant in the particular Arts of each several thing. As for instance, If this *Sophism* were propounded to a Physician, 'in the remission of a Disease, there ought 'to be variety of Diet, and Wine allowed; But 'on the third day, there usually happens a Re- 'mission; Therefore before the third day, there 'ought to be variety of Diet, and allowance 'of Wine. A *Dialectick* can say nothing to all this, but the Physician can solve the *Sophism*, knowing that Remission is taken two ways, either of the whole Disease, or for any particular inclination towards amendment. Before the first third day it happens for the most part, that there is a Remission of some particular Intenseness; now we approve not variety of Diet in this Remission, but in the Remission of the whole Disease. Whereupon he will say, That one of the Sumptions of the Argument is disjoyned from the other, *viz.* that which concerns the whole Disease, from the other which concerns part; Again, to this Argument concerning an intense Feaver, 'Contraries are the 'remedies of Contraries; but Cold is contrary 'to the Heat of the Feaver, therefore cold things 'are convenient for the Cure of it; a *Dialectick* will not know what to say; but the Physician, knowing that some are Affections adherent to the Disease, others Symptoms of those Affections, will answer, that the Question is not to be understood of the Symptoms, (for it usually happens that Heat is encreased by pouring on cold things,) but of the adherent Affectedness, and that Constipation is an adherent Affection which requires not Condensation, but rather Opening; but the Heat which follows upon it, is not primarily adherent, wherefore that which is Cold is not convenient to be applied. Thus to Sophisms, whose Solution is profitable, the *Dialectick* will not know what to say; but to such as these, 'If thou hast not large Horns, and hast 'Horns, thou hast not Horns; but thou hast not 'large Horns, and hast Horns; therefore thou 'hast not Horns. *And*, If a thing be moved, either 'it is moved in the place wherein it is, or in that 'wherein it is not; but neither in that wherein 'it is, (For there it rests;) not in that wherein it 'is not, (for it cannot act, where it is not;) there- 'fore nothing is moved: *And*, Either that which 'is generated, or that which is not, but that 'which is not generated (for is is already) not 'that which it is not; for that which is gene- 'rated

'rated suffers something, that which is not, suffers 'not; *Again*, Snow is water congeal'd, but water 'is black, therefore Snow is black. And a great many such fooleries gathering together, he knits his Brows, and produceth his *Dialectick*, and with a great deal of gravity, endeavours to shews us by Syllogistick Demonstrations, that something is generated, and that something is moved, and that Snow is white, and that we have not Horns; when perhaps, if he did only oppose the evidence of the contrary to them, it would suffice to overthrow their *Theses* by the testimony of their Contraries, which are manifest. Whence a Philosopher, to whom the Argument against Motion was objected, said nothing, but walked. And Men, in the ordinary course of Life, travel by Sea and Land, build Ships and Houses, and beget Children, never minding the Arguments against Motion and Generation. There is also a facete Apothegm of *Erophilus* the Physician, (contemporary with *Diodorus*, who introduc'd into his foolish Logick many sophistical Arguments, as about other things, so particularly concerning Motion,) *Diodorus* having put his Shoulder out of joynt, *Erophilus* coming to set it, derided him, saying, 'Either the Bone slipt out of the place in 'which it was, or out of that in which it was not; 'but neither out of that in which it was, nor out 'of that in which it was not, therefore it is not 'slipt. So as the *Sophist* was fain to intreat him to let his Arguments alone, and to betake himself to the Cure. For it is sufficient (I conceive) to live experimentally, and inopiniatively, according to common observations and assumptions, suspending our assent in all dogmatical Superfluities, and especially those, which are besides the use of life. If therefore *Dialectick* cannot solve those *Sophisms*, whose Solution is useful; and of those which some think it doth solve, the Solution is unuseful, *Dialectick* is of no benefit in solving *Sophisms*.

Moreover, even from what the *Dialecticks* themselves say, it may be proved, that their Art concerning *Sophisms* is superfluous; they say, That they applied themselves to *Dialectick*, not only to learn what may be gathered from it, but proposing to themselves chiefly, to know how to judge true and false by demonstrative Reasons. Whence they affirm *Dialectick* to be the Science, of True, and False, and Neuters. When therefore they assert that to be a true Reason, which by true Sumptions collects a true Conclusion, as soon as any Reason, which hath a false Conclusion, is brought against us, we shall know it is false, and therefore will not assent to it; for of necessity, the Reason must either be not conclusive, or not have true Sumption, which is manifest from hence. The false Conclusion which is in the Reason, is either consequent to the Connexion made by its Sumption, or not Consequent; if not Consequent, the Reason is not Conclusive; for they say, a Conclusive Reason is that which followeth the Connexion made by its Sumptions; if Consequent, the Connexion which is made by its Sumptions must necessarily be false, by their own Rules; for they say, False is consequent to False, but not True. Now that a Reason which is neither conclusive nor true, is, according to them, not demonstrable, is manifest from what was formerly said. If therefore a Reason being propounded, in which there is a false Conclusion, we know even by itself, that it is neither True nor Conclusive, forasmuch as it hath a false Conclusion, we will not assent to it, though we do not know where the Fallacy lies. For, as we believe not the Tricks of Juglers to be true, but know that they deceive, though we know not which way they do it; so neither do we credit false Reasons, which seem true, though we know not which way they are fallacious.

Or because *Sophisms* lead us not only to one Falsity, but to many Absurdities besides, we may argue more generally thus: The Reason proposed either leadeth us to something unexpected, or to something that we must have expected; if to the later, we shall not do absurdly in assenting to it; if to something beyond our expectation, we ought not to assent to an Absurdity rashly, upon a Probability; but they rather ought to withdraw their Reason, which compelleth assent to an absurdity, if they intend not to trifle childishly, but to make a serious enquiry into the Truth, as they profess. For if there be a way leads to some Precipice, we will not run upon the Precipice, because there is a way that leads to it, but rather go out of the way, because of the Precipice; In like manner, if there be a Reason which bringeth us to something, acknowledged to be absurd, we must not assent to the Absurdity, because of the Reason, but reject the Reason because of the Absurdity. When therefore a Reason is objected to us, we will suspend to every Proposition; and then, when the whole Reason is laid down, we will bring in that which appeareth to us. For if the Followers of *Chrysippus*, being *Dogmatists*, upon a *Sorites* proposed, say, They must put a stop to the Progress of the Reason, and suspend their Assent, lest they fall into an Absurdity; certainly we, who are *Scepticks*, and jealous of Absurdities, ought much more to take heed, lest we be betray'd by Sumptions, and therefore suspend upon every one, until we hear the whole Argument. Besides, we, without Opinion, being only informed by the common observations of Life, thus avoid fallacious Reasons: But the *Dogmatists* cannot discern a *Sophism* from a true Reason, seeing they are constrained to judge dogmatically, whether the form of the Reason be conclusive, and whether the Sumptions be true or not; but we have formerly shewn, that they cannot comprehend what Reasons are Conclusive, nor judge Truth in any thing, as having neither a Criterie nor Demonstration, which we proved from their own words. Hence it appears, that the artificial forms of *Sophisms*, so much cry'd up by the *Dialecticks*, are superfluous.

CHAP. XXIII.

Of Amphibolies.

WE say the same concerning distinction of *Amphibolies*. For, if *Amphiboly* be a word which signifies two or more things, and words signifie by Imposition, it is fit they be distinguished by Those, who are of the several Arts to which they belong, they having had experience of the positive use of the words, which they applied to the things that they signified; but a

Dialectick hath not, as in this *Amphiboly*; *In the Remission of Diseases, variety of Diet, and Wine is allowed.*

Moreover, we see, that in Common Life, even Children distinguish those *Amphibolies*, the distinction whereof seemeth useful to them. For if a Man, having two Servants of the same Name, shall bid a Child, call *Manes*, to him, (let us suppose that to be the name of both) the Child would ask, Which? And if one having several sorts of Wine, shall bid a Child, Fill him some Wine, the Child will ask, Of which Sort? Thus in all things experience of that which is useful introduceth Distinction; but those *Amphibolies*, which come not within the experience of Life, and are perhaps only in the sayings of the *Dogmatists*, and nothing useful to living without opinion, the *Dialectick* being particularly employ'd in these, will be necessitated even in them to suspend after the *Sceptical* way, according as they are annexed to things uncertain, or incomprehensible, or inexistent. But of these we shall discourse again. Now if any *Dogmatist* attempt to say any thing against this, he confirms the *Sceptick* reason, and by the allegation of Arguments on both sides, and their indeterminable Difference, will settle *Suspension* as to the thing controverted: Having spoken thus much concerning *Amphibolies*, we close our Second Book of *Hypotyposes*.

Of Physick.

THE THIRD BOOK.

Hitherto by way of Summary we have spoken of the *Logical* part of Philosophy; we shall observe the same course in examining the *Physical* part, not confuting every particular, but endeavouring to overthrow the more general, wherein the others are comprehended. We will begin with the *Principles*. And forasmuch as the greatest part hold, that some of them are Material, others Efficient, we will first speak of the Efficient, those being said to be Principles more properly than the Material.

CHAP. I.

Of GOD.

Now seeing that most of the Dogmatists hold *God* to be the most Efficient cause, let us first enquire concerning *God*; professing, that, following the course of Life; we say, (without engaging our Judgment) that there are gods, and we worship the gods, and we say, that they have Providence. Only, to confute the temerity of the Dogmatists, we say as followeth.

Of the things which we understand, we ought to consider the Substances, as, whether they are Bodies, or Incorporeal; likewise their Forms. For none can understand a Horse, if he hath not first learnt what the Form of a Horse is. Likewise, that which is understood, must be understood as being somwhere. Now forasmuch as, of the Dogmatists, some say, That God is a Body; others, Incorporeal; some, that he hath a Human form; others, not; some, that he is in place; others, that he is not in place: And of those who say, he is in place, some, that he is in the World; others, that he is beyond it. How can we have a notion of God, not having an indubitate knowledge of his Substance, nor of his Form, nor of the Place wherein he is. Let them first agree amongst themselves, What God is? and then they may represent him to us, and require, that we receive such a notion of God; for, while they disagree irreconcileably amongst themselves, we cannot receive any thing from them as undoubtedly true. But, say they, conceive with your self somthing incorruptible and blessed, and think God to be such. This is foolish. For, as he who knoweth not *Dion*, cannot know the Accidents that are competent to him, as *Dion*; so, not knowing the Substance of God, neither can we know his Accidents.

Moreover, let them tell us what is Blessed: Whether that which acts according to Virtue, and hath a providence over the things subordinate to it; or that which is unactive, and neither hath any business it self, nor affords business to any other. For, differing irreconcilably even about this, they shew, that what they call Blessed is not to be found out, and consequently not God himself.

But though we should admit the notion of God, yet is it necessary we suspend, whether he is, or he is not, even from what the Dogmatists say, because it is not manifest that there is a God; for, if that were self-evident, the Dogmatists would have agreed, Who, and What, and Where he is; whereas on the contrary, there is an undeterminable controversie amongst them, whereby we see, that his Being is unmanifest to us, and requireth Demonstration. Now he who saith, that there is a God, must either demonstrate it by a thing manifest or by an unmanifest; not by a thing manifest, for it that were manifest which demonstrates there is a God, forasmuch as that which demonstrateth is relative to that which is demonstrated, and consequently is comprehended together with it, (as we have formerly proved) that there is a God will be manifest also, as being comprehended together with the unmanifest thing that demonstrates it. But this is not-manifest, therefore neither can it be demonstrated by a manifest thing.

But neither by an unmanifest, for the unmanifest that should demonstrate there is a God will require a Demonstration. If demonstrated by a manifest, it will no longer be unmanifest, but manifest, that there is a God. Therefore the unmanifest demonstrative cannot be demonstrated by a manifest. But neither by an unmanifest; for he who saith so, will be driven into *infinite*, we continually requiring a Demonstration of the unmanifest, that is alledged for Demonstration of the thing proposed. Therefore it cannot be demonstrated from any other, that there is a God; and if it neither be manifest in it self, nor demonstrable from any other, it will be incomprehensible whether there be a God.

Moreover, he who saith there is a God, holds either, that he is provident over the things in the world, or not provident. If provident, either over all, or over some. If over all, there would be no ill or wickedness in the World; but all things (as they confess) are full of ill; therefore God cannot be said to be provident
over

over all. If over some only, Why is He provident over these, and not over those? For either He both will, and can be provident over all; or He will, but cannot; or He can, but will not; or He neither will nor can. If He both will and can, then He would be provident over all; but He is not, as is manifest from what we last alledged; therefore that He both will and can provide over all, is not so. If He will, but cannot, His Power is exceeded by that Cause, which hinders Him from being provident over the things over which He is not provident; but it is absurd, to imagine God to be weaker than some other. If He can be provident over all, and will not, He may be thought envious: If He neither will nor can, both envious and infirm; which to affirm of God, were impious. Therefore God is not provident over the things of the World; and if He is not provident over them, neither performeth any Work or Effect, none can say by what means He comprehends there is a God, seeing that it neither is manifest in it self, nor comprehended by any Effects. For these Reasons therefore it is incomprehensible, Whether there be a God or No.

Hence we also argue, That perhaps they who say there is a God, cannot be excused from Impiety; for in affirming, That He is provident over all things, they say, that God is the Author of Evil; and in saying, that He is provident over some, and not over all, they will be forced to confess, That God is either Envious or Infirm; which cannot be said, without manifest Impiety.

CHAP. II.

Of Cause.

BUt that the *Dogmatists*, not being able to extricate themselves out of these difficulties, may not charge us with Blasphemy; we will in general examine *Efficient Cause*, first, endeavouring to lay down the Notion thereof.

From what the *Dogmatists* say, none can understand what *Cause* is. Some hold it to be a Body; others, Incorporeal. It seems to be, according to their most general Opinion, *That by which the Effect is operated*; as the Sun, or the Sun's heat is Cause that the Wax is melted, or Cause of the Liquefaction of the Wax; for even here they differ. Some will have the Cause to be of the Abstract, as Liquefaction; others of the Concrete, as to be Liquefied. Thus, as I said, according to the most general and received Opinion, a Cause is that by which the Effect is operated.

Of these Causes, they hold some to be Continent (or Solitary;) others, Con-causal; others, Co-operative. Solitary are those, which being present, the Effect is present; and being taken away, the Effect is taken away; and being Diminished, the Effect is Diminished. Thus, the knitting a Halter about the Neck is the cause of Suffocation. Con-causal is that which joineth with another Con-causal, towards production of the same Effect, thus, Every one of the Oxen that draw the Plough, is cause of the drawing thereof. Co-operative is that which affords Assistance, but very little to the Effect; as when two Men carry a Burthen, and a third helps them a little.

Some say, That things present are impulsive Causes of the future, as the vehement heat of the Sun is of a Feaver; but some will not admit these; for that a Cause, being relative to its Effect, cannot, as Cause, precede it.

CHAP. III.

Whether there be any Cause of a Thing.

IT is probable, there is such a Thing as Cause; For how can Augmentation, Diminution, Generation, Corruption, Motion of natural and spiritual Agents; in a word, the ordering of the whole World be, if not from some Cause, For, If none of these be really such in their own Nature, we must say; That they seem to us, by reason of some Cause, to be such as indeed they are not. Again, All Generations would be promiscuous, if there were no Cause; Horses, of Mice; Elephants, of Pismires. At *Thebes* in *Egypt*, there would be great showers of Rain and Snow; in the Southern Parts none, unless there were some Cause that produced extraordinary Cold in the Southern Parts, and made the Eastern dry and hot.

Again, he who saith, There is no Cause, is confuted either way: If he say it simply, without a Cause, (or Reason) he is not worthy credit; if upon any Cause, let him shew a Cause why there is no Cause, and by that very reason he will prove that there is a Cause.

That they likewise speak probably who deny Cause, we shall shew, by alledging some Reasons out of many; As thus. It is impossible to understand the Cause, before we comprehend the Effect as its Effect; but neither can we comprehend the Effect of the Cause as its Effect, if we comprehend not the Cause of the Effect as its Cause; for then we seem to know that it is its Effect, when we comprehend the Cause as its Cause. Now if to understand the Cause, it be necessary that we first know the Effect; and to know the Effect (as I said) it be necessary, that we first know the Cause, the *Alternate Common Place* comes in, to shew, that neither of them can be known; not the Cause as Cause, nor the Effect as Effect; for each of them requiring the other to its credit, we shall not know upon which to ground our knowledge first. Wherefore we are not able to assert, that there is any Cause of a Thing.

But though we should grant there is a Cause, yet will it appear to be Incomprehensible, from the Controversies about it. For he who saith, That there is Something Cause of Something, either saith it simply, not moved by any Cause or Reason, or else is moved to this Assent by some Cause. If simply, he will be nothing the more creditable, then he who simply saith, There is no Cause of any Thing. If he alledge any Cause, why he thinks there is a Cause, he endeavoureth to prove that which is in Question by that which is in Question. For the Question being, Whether there be any Cause of a Thing, he takes it for granted that there is a Cause,

when

when he alledgeth a Cause, why there is a Cause. Moreover, the Question being concerning the Existence of Cause, if we prove it by any Cause, it will be requisite to alledge another Cause to prove that, and so to Infinite; but to alledge infinite Causes, is impossible. It is therefore impossible to assert, That there is something Cause of another.

Moreover, a Cause produceth the Effect, either when it already is, and exists as Cause, or when it is not a Cause; not the later; and if when it already is, it must first exist, and be a Cause, and then produce the Effect, which is said to be the Effect thereof, the Cause already existing. But Cause being relative to the Effect, it is manifest, that, as Cause, it cannot exist before it. Therefore a Cause, even when it is already a Cause, cannot produce that whereof it is Cause. And if it produceth not any Thing, neither when it is not a Cause, nor when it is a Cause, then there is no Cause at all; for a Cause cannot be understood as Cause, unless it produce something.

Whence some argue also thus; A Cause must exist either together with the Effect, or before it, or after it; now to say, that the Cause begins to exist after the production of the Effect, were ridiculous. Neither can it exist before it, as being understood in relation to it; but Relatives, as Relatives, coexist, and are understood together; but neither can it coexist with the Effect, for if it be its Efficient, and that whatsoever is effected, must be effected by some other that hath a Being, it is necessary, that a Cause first be a Cause before it produce the Effect. Therefore if a Cause exist not either together with, or before, or after the Effect, it exists not at all.

Moreover, the Notion of a Cause may haply be overthrown thus. For if we cannot understand a Cause (forasmuch as it is relative,) before its Effect; and, to understand it, as Cause of the Effect, it be necessary to understand it, as being before the Effect: But it be impossible to understand any thing to be before that, before which we cannot understand any thing to be, then it is impossible to understand that there is Cause.

Hence we argue thus; Forasmuch as the Reasons by which we proved, that there must be a Cause, are probable; and those also are probable on the other side, which prove there is no Cause; and of these Reasons we cannot possibly know, which ought to be prefered, since we neither have a Sign, nor Criterie, nor Demonstration, ackowledged indubitate, (as we shewed formerly.) Therefore we must necessarily suspend, as to the Existence of Cause, saying, That from what the *Dogmatists* affirm of it, it appears *nothing rather* to be, than not to be.

CHAP. IV.

Of Material Principles.

Hitherto of the *Efficient*; we shall next speak briefly of those which are called *Material Principles*. That these are incomprehensible, is manifest, from the disagreement of the *Dogmatists* about them. *Pherecides* the *Syrian*, asserted Earth to be the Principle of all Things; *Thales*, the *Milesian*, Water; *Anaximander*, his Disciple, Infinite; *Anaximenes* and *Diogenes Appollionates*, Air; *Hippasus*, the *Metapontine*, Fire; *Xenophanes*, the *Colophonian*, Earth and Water; *Enopides*, the *Chian*, Fire and Air; *Hippo*, of *Rhegium*, Fire and Water; *Onomacritus*, in his Orphicks, Fire, Water, and Earth; not to speak of Matter void of quality, (which some have prodigiously fancied, but not understood;) the Followers of *Aristotle* (the *Peripateticks*,) a circular moving Body consisting of Fire, Air, Water, and Earth; *Democritus* and *Epicurus*, Atoms; *Anaxagoras*, the *Clazomenian*, Homoiomeria's; *Diodorus Cronus*, least and indivisible Bodies; *Heraclides*, of *Pontus*, and *Asclepiades*, of *Bithynia*, uncompounded Bulks (or little Bodies;) the *Pythagoreans*, Numbers; the *Mathematicians*, the Terms of Bodies; *Strato*, the Naturalist, Qualities.

Such, (or, yet greater) being the Controversy amongst them concerning the Material Principles, we must either assent to all their Opinions, or to some. To all is impossible, for we cannot hold with *Asclepiades*, that they are tangible and qualited, and with *Democritus*, that they are Atoms, and void of quality; and with *Anaxagoras*, who ascribes all sensible qualities to his *Homoiomeria's*. But if we must of our own judgments make choice of some of these Opinions, we must do it either without Demonstration, or with Demonstration. If without Demonstration, it will not be credited; if with Demonstration, that Demonstration must be true: But it will not be granted to be true, unless it be judged and determined by a true Criterie, but the Criterie must be proved to be true by an adjudged Demonstration. If therefore, to prove that which preferreth one Opinion before the rest to be true, it be requisite that its Criterie be demonstrated; and, to demonstrate that the Criterie is true, it be requisite that its Demonstration be first adjudged, it runs into the *Alternate Common Place*, which will suffer the Argument to proceed no further, the Demonstration continually requiring a Criterie; and the Criterie, adjudged Demonstration: But to judge a Criterie by a Criterie, and a Demonstration by a Demonstration, were to run into Infinite. Now if we cannot assent to all Opinions concerning the Elements, nor to some of them, we must necessarily suspend.

This perhaps is sufficient to shew the Incomprehensibility of the Elements and Material Principles. But to refute the *Dogmatists* more fully, we will insist longer hereupon. Their Opinions concerning Elements are so many, that to examine every one in particular is more than our design will allow, but what we shall alledge may serve to confute all: For seeing that in all Controversies concerning the Elements they are held either to be Bodies or Incorporeal, we conceive it sufficient to prove, that both Bodies and Incorporeals are incomprehensible; for thence it will follow, That the Elements must be Incomprehensible.

CHAP. V.

Whether Bodies be incomprehensible?

A Body (some of them say,) *is that which* (they think) *doth, or suffereth*: But according to this notion it is incomprehensible, as we have shewn. For not being able to say whether there be a Cause, we cannot say whether there be a Patient, for the Patient suffers from the Cause; Thus both the Cause and the Patient being incomprehensible, a Body also must be incomprehensible.

Some say, A Body is that which hath a triple dimension and resistence: For a point, (they say) is that which hath no part, a line is a length without breadth: Now when these have received depth also, and resistence, it then becomes the Body we speak of, consisting of length, breadth, depth, and resistence. But these are easily disproved; for, either they must say, that a Body is nothing but these, or that it is something else different from these: * That it is something else different from these, we cannot conceive; for we cannot conceive that there is a Body, where there is not length, breadth, depth, and resistence. But if a Body be these, and we prove that these are not existent, we take away Body; for the Whole, if you take away all its Parts, is taken away also. These may be confuted several ways, of which we shall only alledge this; If there are terms, either they are Lines, or Superficies, or Bodies; if they shall say, that there is Line or Superficies, they must grant that each of them can exist by it self, or is considered only in the Bodies. That a Line or Superficies exists by it self, none perhaps is so foolish as to imagine: If they say, that they exist not by themselves but in the Body: First, they must grant that Bodies are made of them, for then they must first have had a subsistence by themselves, and afterwards concur to the making of a Body. Again, neither do they exist in the things which are called Bodies, as, (to omit other Instances) we shall shew from Contract only: For if the Bodies which are clapt together, touch one another mutually, they must touch mutually by their terms, that is, by their Superficies; But the Superficies touch not each other in whole, for then they would be united one to the other by the act of touching, the touch would confound the substances; so as to divide two things that touch one another, would be a Divulsion. Neither doth a Superficies by some parts touch the Superficies of the Body which is applyed to it, and by others is united to the Body, whose term it is: certainly no Man can consider this to be without depth, and consequently, not a Superficies but a Body; In like manner, if we suppose two Superficies, laid one upon the other, according to their terms or bounds; It follows, that, according to that which is called their length, (that is, according to their lines,) those lines, by which the Superficies are said to touch one another, shall not touch one another totally, for then they would be confounded; Neither doth any one line of them touch, by some parts, the line to which it is applyed, and by others is united to the Superficies, whose bound it is, for then it would not be without breadth, and consequently no Line: Now if in a Body there is neither Line nor Superficies, there is neither length, breadth, nor depth in a Body.

* The Text seems defective, and to be thus supplied out of his Chapter concerning Body, *adversus Mathematicos.* Page 368.

If any shall say these Terms are Bodies; they may be confuted briefly thus: If length be a Body, it is divided into its three Dimensions, and each of those being a Body, is again divided into its three Dimensions, and so into Infinite. Thus a Body will be of infinite Magnitude, being divided into Infinite; but that is absurd: Therefore the foresaid Dimensions are not Bodies: And if neither Bodies nor Lines, nor Superficies, it may well be conceived that they are not at all.

Resistence likewise is not to be comprehended or understood; for if it might be comprehended, it would be comprehended from the Touch. Now if we shew that the Touch it self is incomprehensible, it will appear that it is impossible to comprehend Resistence; That Touch is incomprehensible, we collect thus; Whatsoever things touch one another, either touch one another mutually by their Parts; or the Whole, the Whole. Not the Whole, the Whole; for that were not to touch, but to be made one; neither the Parts, the Parts; for those Parts, though in respect of their Wholes they are Parts, yet in respect of their own Parts are Wholes, for they have Parts within themselves. But Wholes touch not Wholes, for the reason alledged; and consequently neither do Parts touch Parts; these Parts, in respect of their own Parts, being Wholes. Now, if we cannot comprehend, that Touch may be made either by Whole, or by Parts; Touch must be incomprehensible, and consequently so must a Body; for if it be nothing more than these three Dimensions and Resistence, and we have shewn that each of these is incomprehensible, Body also is incomprehensible. Thus therefore, as to the notion of Body it self, it is incomprehensible, whether there is a Body.

Moreover, of Bodies, say they, some are sensible, others intelligible; these are comprehended by Intellect, those by the Senses. The Senses are simply passible, but the Intellect cometh to the comprehension of intelligible things, through comprehension of Sensibles. If therefore a Body be something, it must either be sensible or intelligible: Sensible it is not, for it seemeth to be comprehended by collection of length, and breadth, and depth, and resistence, and colour, and such like, together with which it is considered; but the Senses they hold to be simply *passive*. If they say, a Body is Intelligible, there must be something in the nature of Sensible things, by which Bodies, being intelligible, may be understood: But there is nothing besides Body and Incorporeal, whereof the Incorporeal is it self intelligible, the Body therefore is not sensible, as we proved; and there not being in the nature of things any Sensible, by which Body might be understood, neither will Body be intelligible; and if neither sensible nor intelligible, and there be nothing besides these, we may say, a Body is nothing. Wherefore opposing these Reasons, which prove there is no Body, to those which prove that there is a Body, we Suspend.

Now, from the incomprehensibility of Body, will be inferred also, that Incorporeal is Incomprehensible; for privations are understood to be the privations of Habits, as, of Sight, Blindness; of Hearing, Deafness; and the like. Wherefore to comprehend the Privation, we must first comprehend the Habit, whereof it is a Privation; for, he who understands not what Sight is, cannot say, This Man hath not Sight, that is, he is blind. If therefore the Privation of a Body be Incorporeal, and the Habits being incomprehensible, it be impossible to comprehend their Privations; But Body, as we have shewn, is incomprehensible; Incorporeals also will be incomprehensible. For, either it is sensible, or intelligible; if Sensible, it is incomprehensible, by reason of the difference of living Creatures, and of Men, and of Senses, and of Circumstances, and by reason of Commixion, and the like, mentioned in the ten Common-places of Suspension; if Intelligible, there not being granted a comprehension of Sensible things, by which we may be carried to Intelligibles; neither will there be granted a Comprehension of things Intelligible, and consequently not of an Incorporeal. Besides, he who saith, that he comprehends an Incorporeal, must say, that he Comprehends it either by Sense or by Reason; not by Sense, for the Sense seemeth to perceive sensible things, by intromission and insinuation; as the Sight, (whether it be made by a conick impression, or by emission, or immission of Species, or by effusion of Raies and Colours) and the Hearing (whether it be that the Air is struck, or that the parts of the Voice are carried to the Ear, and strike the Sense, so as to cause a preception of the Voice;) likewise Odours to the Nostrils, and Sapours to the Tongue, and tangible things are derived to the touch in the same manner. But Incorporeals are not capable of receiving such impressions, therefore they cannot be comprehended by Sense. But neither by Discourse (or Reason;) for if Discourse be a Dicible and Incorporeal, (as the Stoicks hold) He, who saith Incorporeals are understood by Discourse, begs the Question; For when we demand, Whether an Incorporeal can be comprehended, He, taking Incorporeal simply, would thereby shew the Comprehension of Incorporeals; whereas Discourse itself, if it be Incorporeal, is a part of the thing controverted. How then can any shew that this Incorporeal (Discourse) is comprehended first? If by any Incorporeal, we shall require a demonstration of its Comprehension, and so to Infinite. If by a Body, the comprehension of Bodies is the thing in question. By What then shall we demonstrate, that a Body is comprehended, which is assumed to demonstrate the comprehension of Discourse and Incorporeal? If by a Body, we run into *Infinite*; If by an Incorporeal, we run into the *Alternate common-place*. Thus Discourse being, If Incorporeal, Comprehensible; none can say, that an Incorporeal may be comprehended by it. But if Discourse be a Body, forasmuch as there is Controversie concerning Bodies, whether they are comprehended or not, because of the continual effluxion (as they call it) of them; in respect whereof, they neither can admit Demonstration, nor are conceived to be; insomuch as *Plato* termeth Bodies, γινόμενα ὄντα δ ἐδέποτε, *Generated, Not being*. Hereupon I doubt which way the Controversie concerning Body determineth, since neither by a Body, nor by an Incorporeal, for the inconveniences alledged. Therefore neither is it possible to comprehend Incorporeals by Discourse, but if they neither incur to Sense, nor are comprehended by Discourse, they cannot be comprehended at all. Now if we can neither assert the existence of a Body, nor of an Incorporeal, we must suspend as to the Elements; and perhaps we must suspend also concerning those things, which are after the Elements; if, of them, some are Corporeal; others, Incorporeal, and both these are controverted. Moreover, seeing we ought to suspend concerning Efficient and Material Principles, for the precedent Reasons, the whole Discourse concerning Principles will be inextricable.

CHAP. VI.

Of Temperament.

BUT, setting this aside, how can they say, that Temperaments are made of the first Elements, whenas there is not any Touch, nor Contact, nor Temperament, nor Mixture at all? That Touch is nothing, we shewed lately, in discoursing concerning the Existence of Bodies. And that Temperament also, from what they say, is not possible, we shall briefly declare. They speak much concerning it, and almost innumerable are the controversies of the Dogmatists about it, so as from the Indijudicableness of the Controversie may be argued the Incomprehensibility of the Subject. To confute them all in particular, would be beyond our Design; this which we shall say, we conceive, may suffice.

All contemperated things consist, as they say, of Substance and Qualities. They must therefore either hold, that either the Substances are mingled, and not the Qualities; or the Qualities but not the Substances; or neither with the other; or both with one another. But if neither Substance nor Qualities are mingled one with the other, Temperament will be unintelligible; for how can one Sense be made of the things tempered, if the things tempered be not mingled together, by any of the foresaid ways? If they say, that the Qualities are simply adjacent one to another, but the Substance is mingled; this also is absurd, for we comprehend not Qualities in Temperaments, as separate, but we feel them as made one by the things tempered. If they say, that the Qualities are mingled, but not the Substances; it is impossible, for the subsistence of the Qualities is in the Substance. Wherefore it is ridiculous to say, that the Qualities are separated from their Substances, and so mingled with one another, and the Substances left deprived of their Qualities. It remains to say, that the Qualities and Substances of things tempered pass through one another, and being mingled, make the Temperament, which is more

more absurd than the former; for such a Temperament is impossible. For example, If with Ten pints of Water there be mixed one pint of Hemlock, the Hemlock will be said to be commixed with all the Water; for if a Man take never so little of this mixture, he will find it full of the power of the Hemlock. Now if the Hemlock be mixed with every part of the Water, and co-extended with it, the whole with the whole, by mutual Permeation of the Substances and Qualities one through another, that so the Temperament may be made; and things, co-extended with one another in every part, take up equal place, and consequently, are equal to one another, the pint of Hemlock shall be equal to the Ten pints of Water; so that the mixtion must either be Twenty pints or Two pints, according to this Hypothesis of the manner of Temperament. And again, One pint of Water being put to Twenty pints of Water, according to this Hypothesis, must make the measure either of Forty pints, or of Two only; because we may either conceive the pint to be Twenty pints, as being co-extended with so many; or the Twenty pints to be that One, with which they are co-equaliz'd. In like manner, a Man adding but one pint, may argue, that the Twenty pints, which we see, ought to be Twenty thousand, or more, according to this Hypothesis of Temperament, and that the same are but two only; than which, nothing is more absurd; Therefore this Hypothesis of Temperament is absurd. Now if Temperament neither be by mixing the Substances only, nor Qualities only, nor both, nor either; and besides these, nothing can be imagined; the manner of Temperament, and of all mixtures, is not to be understood. Wherefore if those things which are call'd Elements, are not capable of making Contemperations, neither by touching one another, nor by being blended or mingled, the Physiology of the Dogmatists, as to this thing, is unintelligible.

CHAP. VII.

Of Motion.

BEsides, what hath been said, the Physiology of the Dogmatists may be conceiv'd to be impossible, by discoursing upon Motions; for all Commixtions must be made by some Motion of the Elements, and the Efficient Principle. If therefore we prove, that there is no generally acknowledged Species of Motion, it will be manifest, that, though all which we formerly opposed, should, by way of supposition, be granted; yet that, which the Dogmatists call Physick, serves to no purpose.

CHAP. VIII.

Of Local-Motion.

THey who seem to have discoursed most exactly of Motion, say, there are six kinds thereof, Local-Motion, Alteration, Augmentation, Diminution, Generation, and Corruption. We shall examine each of these particularly, beginning with Local-motion. This, according to the Dogmatists, is, that, by which that which moveth, passeth from place to place, either according to its Whole, or according to Part; according to its Whole, as in them who walk; according to Part, as in a Sphear that moves about its Center; for the Whole remaineth in the same place, the Parts only change place.

Three, as I conceive, are the principal Controversies concerning Motion. *Bias*, and some other Philosophers, hold that there is Motion; *Parmenides, Melissus*, and others, that there is not Motion; the Scepticks *nothing rather* that it is, than that it is not. For as to the Phænomena's, it appeareth that there is Motion; but as to Philosophical Discourse, that there is not. If therefore, upon examination of the Arguments on both sides, we shall find them to be of equal weight, we shall not assent to either. Let us begin with those who hold, that it is.

These insist most upon Evidence: For if they say, there is no Motion, How doth the Sun appear now in the East, anon in the West? or How doth he make the Seasons of the year, which are according as he is nearer to, or further from us? Or How do Ships put off from one Port, and reach another far distant? Or how does he, who denies Motion, go abroad and come home? These they conceive cannot be answered, and therefore one of the Cynicks, an Argument being propounded to him to take away Motion, made no Answer, but rose up and walk'd, shewing by action and evidence, that there is Motion. Thus they endeavour to silence the contrary Party.

But they who take away the existence of Motion, argue thus. If a thing be moved, it must be moved either by itself, or by some other; but neither by itself, nor by any other. For that which is said to be moved not by itself, must be moved either by some Cause, or by none, by no Cause they say nothing is done; if by some Cause, the Cause by which it is moved, will be its Mover, and so they will run into Infinite, according to our usual way of Argument. Again, if that which moveth, effects, and that which effects, is moved, that will also require another to move it, and this a Third, and so to Infinite; so that Motion shall be without any Principle of first beginning, which is absurd. Therefore every thing that moveth, is not moved by another. But neither by itself; for every thing that moveth either impelleth forward, or draweth backward; or upward, or downward; therefore whatsoever moveth itself, must do it after one of these ways. If by Impelling forward, it must be behind itself; if by drawing back, before itself; if upwards, below itself; if downwards, above itself. But for a thing to be either above, or before, or below, or behind itself, is impossible; it is therefore impossible for any thing to be moved by itself. But if neither by itself, nor by any other, then nothing at all is moved. If any recur to Appetite and Election, we must let him know, that the Question is concerning *that which is in our power*, and that this Question is indeterminable, forasmuch as we have not yet found a Critery of Truth.

Again,

Again, if a thing be moved, it is either moved in the place in which it is, or in which it is not; but not in the place wherein it is, for if it be in it, it continues in it. Nor in the place in which it is not, for where a thing is not, there it can neither act nor suffer. This was the Argument of *Diodorus Cronus*. But it is answered several ways, of which we shall only alledge those which we conceive to be of greatest force, together with the Judgment which appeareth for the present to us. Some say, that a thing may be moved in the place where it is, for the Sphears which roll about their Centers are moved, and yet continue in their place. In Answer to whom, the Argument should be transferred to the several parts of the Sphear, and we must shew by this Argument, it is not moved as to its parts, if we will prove that nothing is moved in the place wherein it is.

The same Answer may be made to those, who say, that a thing moved must touch two places, that wherein it is, and that to which it goes; We shall ask them, seeing, that what is moved is carried from the place wherein it is to another, Whether this be when it is in the first place, or when it is in the second? But whilst it is in the first, it passeth not to another, for it is yet in the first; and when it is not in this, it passeth not out of it: Besides this, the Question is Begged. For in the place wherein it is not, it cannot act; for no Man will grant simply, that it is carried to any place who grants not that it is moved,

Some there are, who distinguish thus. Place is taken two ways, largely, as my House; strictly, as the Air, which encloseth the Superficies of a Body. Now when a thing that is moved, is said to be moved in Place, we mean not Place in the large sense but in the strict. To these may be answered, by subdividing Place largely taken; that in one part thereof, the Body is said to be moved properly, as being its exact Place; in the other, not so, this being the rest of the parts of Place largely taken. Then inferring, that nothing can be moved, neither in the Place wherein it is, nor in the Place wherein it is not, conclude, that neither in Place at large, improperly taken, can any thing be moved. For it consists of two Parts, of that wherein the thing exactly is, and of that in which exactly it is not; in neither of which can any thing be moved, as was proved.

It may be argued also thus: If any thing be moved either it is moved from some part of the space, and then another; or it is moved all at once, over the whole divisible Interval: But neither can any thing be moved from some first part of the space, and then another, not all at once, over the whole divisible Interval, therefore nothing is moved. That nothing is moved from some first part of the space, is manifest from hence; for that, if the Bodies, and the Places, and the Times, in which those Bodies are said to be moved, be divided into Infinite, there will be no Motion, it being impossible to find in Infinites a First, from which First (Part) that which is said to be moved shall be moved. But if the things aforesaid end in an indivisible, and every thing that is moved pass the first divisible Part of its Place, In like manner as the first indivisible Part of its Time, all things will be of equal Celerity; as the fleetest Horse, and a Tortoise; which is absurder than the former. Therefore Motion is not made from some first part of the space. But neither all at once over the whole divisible Interval: For if apparent things must, as they say, clear things unapparent; when a Man should go the space of a Stadium, it is requisite that he first perform the first part of the Stadium, and then the second, and so the other parts in order. So every thing that is moved according to the First, must first be moved; for if that which is moved be said to pass at once over all the parts of the place, in which it is moved, it will be in all its parts at once; and if one part of the place be cold, another hot; or one black, another white, so much as to qualifie the things that are in it; that which moveth will be at once hot and cold, and black and white. Besides, let them say, how much of the Place at once that which is moved passeth. If they say it is Indefinite, they grant, that somthing may be moved over the face of the whole Earth at once; if they deny that, let them define the quantity of the place; for to endeavour exactly to define such a place, than which the thing moved cannot pass, at once, any (though never so little) greater distance, besides that it is absurd and ridiculous, will perhaps incur the former inconvenience; for all things will be swift alike, seeing that every thing passeth alike through determinate places. But if they shall say, that what is moved all at once, is moved through a little, but not exactly determinate, Place, we shall confound them by a Sorites, continually adding to the supposed Magnitude, another very little Magnitude of Place. For if at any time they make a stand, then they fall into their former determination of the Place, and strange Conceits; but if they admit an increase, we shall force them to Grant, that a thing may be moved all at once over the whole Earth. Wherefore neither are those things which are said to be moved, moved at once over the whole divisible Interval; and if neither all at once, nor from some part, then nothing is moved. This and much more is alledged by those who take away local Motion: But we (not being able to disprove either these Arguments, or the Phænomenon which they follow, who say there is no Motion, as to the opposition betwixt the Phænomenas and the Arguments) suspend, Whether there be Motion or not.

CHAP.

CHAP. IX.

Of Augmentation and Diminution.

Upon the same Ground we suspend as to *Augmentation* and *Diminution*: For, Evidence seems to prove that they are, but Discourse (or Reason) to overthrow them; As thus, That is augmented, being already an *Ens* and *Subsistent*, must be moved further as to quantity (for if any shall say that by Apposition of one thing another is augmented; he speaketh falsly:) Since therefore Substance never is at a stand, but always in fluxion, and some are insinuated into others, that which is augmented hath not its first substance with the addition of some other, but a Substance wholly new; As therefore (for Instance,) If there being a piece of Wood three Foot long, some Man putting to it a piece ten Foot long, should say he hath augmented the piece of three Foot, he shall say falsly, (forasmuch as this is wholly another thing from the other:) So in every thing that is said to be augmented, the former matter flowing out, and new matter flowing in, If that be added which is said to be added, none will say that this is Augmentation, but Alteration of the Whole.

The same may be said of Diminution; for how can that which subsists not, be said to be diminished? Besides, If Diminution be made by Detraction, Augmentation by Addition; But neither Detraction nor Addition be any thing, neither is Diminution nor Augmentation any thing.

CHAP. X.

Of Detraction and Addition.

That Detraction is Nothing, they argue thus: If Somthing be detracted from another, either an Equal, is detracted from an Equal, or a Greater from a Lesser, or a Lesser from a Greater: But none of these; therefore Detraction is not possible. That Detraction is not made by any of these ways, is manifest: That which is detracted from another, before it is detracted, must be contained in that from which it is detracted, but an Equal is not contained in a Equal, as Six in Six; for that which containeth, ought to be greater than that which is contained; and that from which somthing is detracted, ought to be greater than that which is detracted, that after the Detraction there may be somthing remaining, for herein Detraction seems to differ from quite taking away. Neither is the Greater contained in the Lesser, as Six in Five; that were absurd. Neither is the Lesser contained in the Greater; for if Five were contained in Six, as the fewer in the more, by the same Reason, in Five will be contained Four, and in Four Three, and in Three Two, and in Two One; thus Six shall contain Five, Four, Three, Two, One, which being put together, make Fifteen, which must be contained in Six, if it be granted that the Lesser is contained in the Greater. In like manner, in the Fifteen which is contained in Six, will be contained Thirty five; and so, by Progression, infinite Numbers: But it is absurd to say, that infinite Numbers are contained in the Number Six, therefore it is absurd to say, that the Lesser is contained in the Greater. If therefore it be requisite, that what is Detracted from another, be contained in the thing from which it is Detracted, but neither Equal is contained in Equal nor the Greater in the Lesser, nor the Lesser in the Greater; Nothing certainly is Detracted from any Thing.

Again, if Somthing be Detracted from Somthing, either the Whole is Detracted from the Whole, or Part from Part or the Whole from the part, or part from the Whole. But to say, That the Whole is Detracted from the Whole or from Part, is absurd; it remains therefore to say, That the Part is Detracted from the Whole, or from Part, which is absurd also. We will instance (not to change our Example in Numbers, as being most perspicuous,) in the Number Ten, and let us suppose One to be substracted from it. This One cannot be substracted from the whole Ten, nor from the remaining part of it Nine, as I shall prove; therefore is it not substracted. For if One be substracted from the whole Ten, forasmuch as Ten is nothing else but Ten Unites, not any one of the Unites, but a Combination of all, this Unity to be substracted out of the whole Ten, must be substracted out of every Unite: But first, from an Unite nothing can be substracted, for Unites are indivisible, and therefore One cannot be substracted from Ten in this manner. But if we grant an Unite may be taken from every Unite, an Unite will have Ten parts, and having Ten Parts, will be an Unite; now there being Ten other Parts remaining, from which were substracted the Ten Parts of that which is called an Unite, those Ten will be Twenty: But it is absurd to say, that One is Ten, and that Ten is Twenty, and that what is Indivisible (according to them) is divided, therefore it is absurd to say, That an Unite is substracted from the whole Number Ten. But neither is the Unite substracted from the remaining Number Nine, for that from which a Thing is substracted remaineth not intire, but the Nine remaineth intire after the Substraction of the Unite. Besides, the Nine being nothing else but nine Unites, if the Unite be said to be taken away from the Whole, the Nine itself will be taken away; if from a part of the Nine, as from Eight, the same Absurdities will follow: If from an Unite, which is the last, they must say that an Unite, is divisible, which is absurd; therefore the Unite is not substracted out of the Nine. Now if it neither be substracted from the whole Ten, nor from a Part thereof, neither can a Part be substracted from the Whole, nor from a Part. If therefore neither Whole can be substracted from Whole, nor Part from Whole, nor Whole from Part, nor Part from Part, Nothing is substracted from another.

Likewise Addition is reckoned by them amongst Things impossible: For say they, That which is added, is either added to itself, or to some Subject præexistent, or to that which consists of both; but none of these is true, therefore

fore nothing is added to another. For Instance, suppose the quantity of four Pints, and thereto let be added one Pint, I demand, To what it is added? To it self it cannot, for that which is added, is diverse from that to which it is added, but nothing is diverse from it self. But neither is it added to that which consists of both, the measure of four Pints and one Pint, for how can any thing be added to that which is not yet? Besides, if to the four Pints, and to the one Pint, be added a Pint, it will make up six Pints, from the quantity of four Pints, and the one Pint, and the additional Pint. Now if to the four Pints only, be added one Pint, forasmuch as that which is coextended with another, must be equal with that to which it is coextended: if one Pint be coextended with four Pints, it will double the quantity of the four Pints, so as the whole measure will be eight Pints, which we see to be otherwise. If therefore that which is said to be added, be neither added to it self, nor to some other Subject, nor to that which consists of both these, and besides these, there be nothing; certainly there is no addition of one thing to another.

CHAP. XI.

Of Transposition.

TRansposition comes within the compass of Addition, and Detraction, and Local Motion, for it is Detraction from one thing, and Addition to another, transiently.

CHAP. XII.

Of Whole and Part.

THE like may be said of Whole and Part, for the Whole seemeth to be made by convention, and addition of the Parts; but by detraction of any one, or more of them, it leaveth to be Whole.

Besides, If there be a Whole, either it is a thing diverse from its Parts, or its Parts are the Whole, but it seems not to be diverse from its Parts; For, the Parts being taken away, nothing remaineth whereby we may think that the Whole is any thing besides them. Now if the Parts are the Whole, the Whole is only a word, and an empty name, but hath no proper subsistence, as Distance is nothing more than things distant, and Contiguity nothing but things contiguous; Therefore the Whole is not any thing. But neither the Parts also; for if there are Parts, either they are Parts of the Whole, or Parts of one another, or each is Part of it self. Not of the Whole, for that is nothing more than the Parts themselves. Besides, the Parts would then be Parts of themselves, because every Part is completive of the Whole. Neither of one another, for a Part seemeth to be contained in that whereof it is a Part, and it were absurd to say, that the Hand (for example) is contained in the Foot. Neither is each of them a Part of it self, for then, as containing, and contained by it self, a thing will be greater, and less than it self. Now if those which we call Parts, neither be Parts of the Whole, nor of themselves, nor of one another, they are not Parts of any thing, and if Parts of nothing, neither are they Parts, for Relatives are taken away together. This, by way of digression; for we treated of Whole and Part once before.

CHAP. XIII.

Of Alteration.

SOme also deny that there is any Alteration or natural Mutation, (as they term it,) arguing thus. If Something be changed, either that which is changed is a Body, or Incorporeal; but neither of these is determinable, therefore Alteration it self is indeterminable. If any thing alter by operating as a Cause, it alters as being the Patient; and the subsistence of it, as Cause, is subverted, together with which the Patient also is subverted, not having a thing from which to suffer, therefore nothing is altered.

Moreover, If there be Alteration, it is either of a Being, or of a Not-being; but a Not-being is insubsistent, and can neither suffer nor act, therefore it is not capable of Alteration. If that which is changed be a Being, it is either changed as a Being, or as a Not-being. As a Not-being it is not changed, for Not-beings are not. If it be changed as a Being, it becomes different from a Being, that is, it will not be a Being: But to say that a Being is a Not-being, is absurd. Therefore a Being is not changed. Now if neither a Being be changed, nor a Not-being, and besides these there is nothing, it remains to say, that nothing is changed.

Some argue thus. That which is changed, must be changed in some time, but neither is any thing changed in the time past, nor in the future, nor in the present, (as we shall shew;) therefore nothing is changed. In time past or future, nothing is changed; for neither of these is present, but it is impossible for any thing to act or suffer in a non-existent and not-present time. But neither in the present, for perhaps the present also is inexistent. This τὸ νῦν, Now, is indivisible: But it is impossible to imagine that Iron (for Example) can be changed from hard to soft, or that any other Alteration can be made in indivisible time, for they seem to require Succession. Now if nothing be changed either in the time past, nor in the present, nor in the future, nothing at all is changed.

Moreover, If there be Alteration, † either it is subject to Sense, or to Intellect; not to the Senses, for they receive only single Notions, but Alteration hath a twofold Respect, both to that out of which the Alteration is, and to that into which it is. If they say, It is Intelligible, forasmuch as there is an indeterminable Controversie concerning Intelligibles, as we have already said, we cannot assert the Being of Alteration.

† *The Text requires to be supplied to this effect.*

CHAP. XIV.

Of Generation, and Corruption.

Generation, and Corruption, are subverted together with Addition, and Detraction, and Alteration; for without these, nothing can be generated, nor corrupted: As for Example. Of the corruption of the Number Ten, say they, is generated the Number Nine, by Substraction of One; and of Nine corrupted is generated Ten, by addition of One; and Canker, (by alteration) of Brass corrupted; therefore the forenamed Motions being taken away, perhaps it necessarily followeth, that Generation and Corruption are also taken away.

Moreover, some argue thus. If *Socrates* were generated, he was generated either when he was not *Socrates*, or when he was *Socrates*: If when he was, he must have been generated twice; if when he was not, he was, and was not, at the same time. He was, as being generated; he was not, according to the *Hypothesis*. Again, if *Socrates* Dyed, either he Dyed when he Lived, or when he was Dead; not when he Lived, for so the same Person should be both Dead and Alive; neither when he was Dead, for so he should Dye twice. Therefore *Socrates* Died not. By this Argument, upon every thing that is said to be generated, or corrupted, Generation and Corruption may be subverted.

Some argue thus: If there be Generation, that which is generated, is either a Being, or a Not-Being; not a Not-Being, for to that, which *is not*, nothing can happen, not so much as to *be*. Neither a Being, for if a Being be generated, it is generated either as it is a Being, or as it is a Not-Being. As it is a Not-Being, it is not generated, and if it be generated as a Being, forasmuch as a thing is generated of somthing different from it, that which is generated must be different from a Being, that is, a Not-being. Therefore that which is generated shall be a Not-being, which is absurd. Now if neither a Being, nor a Not-being be generated, nothing at all is generated.

Upon the same grounds also nothing is corrupted. For if Something be corrupted, it is either a Being, or a Not-Being; not a Not-Being, for that which is corrupted must suffer Something; not a Being, for either it is corrupted, as continuing in the state of a Being, or as not continuing. If as continuing in the state of a Being, the same will be at once a Being and a Not-Being; because it is not corrupted as a Not-Being, but as it is a Being; and as it is corrupted, it is different from a Being, and consequently a Not-Being. But it is absurd to say, the same thing is a Being and a Not-Being; therefore a Being is not corrupted whilst it continueth in the state of a Being. But if a Being be corrupted, not whilst it is in the state of a Being, but first reduced to a Not-Being, and afterwards corrupted; it is not a Being, but a Not-Being, that is corrupted; which (as we said before) is impossible. If therefore neither a Being is corrupted, nor a Not-Being, and besides these there is Nothing, Nothing is corrupted. This may serve, by way of Summary, to say of Motions; whence it followeth, That the Physiologie of the *Dogmatists* is inexistent, and unintelligible.

CHAP. XV.

Of Rest.

In like manner some doubt as to the Nature of Rest, saying, That whatsoever Moves, Rests not; but every Body continually Moveth, according to the Opinions of the *Dogmatists*, who say, That Substance is Fluid, and hath continual Evacuations and Recruits; (Whence the *Platonicks* chuse rather to call Bodies, Things generated, than Beings; and *Heraclitus* compared the Mobility of our Matter, to the rapid course of a River.) Therefore no Body rests.

Again, that which is said to rest, seemeth to be contained by the things that are about it; that which is contained suffers, but there is no Patient; for, as we proved before, there is no Cause, therefore nothing Rests. Some argue thus: That which Rests Suffers, that which Suffers is moved; therefore that which is said to Rest is moved, and if moved, it Rests not. Hence also it is manifest, That an Incorporeal Rests not; for if that which Rests Suffers, and to suffer be proper to Bodies, and not to Incorporeals, no Incorporeal either Suffers or Rests; therefore nothing Rests.

Now forasmuch as none of the fore-named are understood without *Place* or *Time*, we must proceed to Disquisition of these; and if we prove, that these Exist not, the others will appear to be Inexistent upon that account also. Let us begin with *Place*.

CHAP. XVI.

Of Place.

Place is taken two ways, Properly, and Improperly; Improperly for Place at large, as a City; Properly, for that in which we are exactly contained. We inquire of Place in the proper exact Sense; some have asserted it, others deny'd it, others suspended. Of these; they who assert it, recur to Evidence: For who is there, say they, who will affirm, there is not Place, when they behold the parts of Place, as, Right, Left; Upwards, Downwards; Before, Behind? and that the same Person is at several Times in several Place? and that where my Master taught, there do I now teach? They argue also, That there is Place, because things are naturally light or heavy; and for that the Antients said, *Chaos was first*; for they hold, That Chaos is Place, because it contained all things that were made in it. And if a Body be any thing, say they, so is Place also; for without this, there will be no Body: And if there be a *from which*, there is also an *of which*, and an *in which*, that is, Place. The first is in either, the second therefore in both.

But neither do they who take away Place grant, that the Parts of Place are; for Place is nothing else but it's Parts: And he who asserts that Place is, if he takes for granted that it's Parts are, endeavours to make good the thing in Question, by itself. In like manner they do foolishly, who say, That something is In a Place, when as Place itself is absolutely deny'd to be: They take away together with it the existence of Place, which of itself is not granted, and the *of which*, and the *from which*, are proved to be inexistent, as well as Place; and disalow *Hesiod*, as not a competent Judge in Philosophy. And thus overthrowing the Arguments alledged, for the existence of Place, they, with greater subtlety, prove it to be inexistent, converting to their own use those Opinions of the *Dogmatists* concerning Place, which seem of greatest weight; as that of the *Stoicks*, and that of the *Peripateticks*, in this manner: The *Stoicks* say, *Vacuum is that which is capable of being contained by a Being, but is not contained: Or a Distance void of Body: Or a Distance not contained by a Body*. But Place is a Distance which is contained by a Being, and is adæquate to that which containeth it; they call a Body a Being; the Distance, which is partly contained by the Body, partly not contained Region. Whereas others by Region understand the Place of a great Body, so as *Place* and *Region* differ in Magnitude. Now it's objected, when they say, *Place is the Distance contained by a Body*; how do they mean it to be a Distance, (or Dimension) whether the Length of a Body, or the Breadth, or the Depth only, or whether all three together? If they mean but one of these, the Place will not be adæquate to that whose Place it is. Besides, that which containeth will be part of that which is contained, which were absurd. If all the three Distances, forasmuch as in that which is called Place, there is not *Vacuum*, nor any other Body that hath Dimensions; but that Body which is said to be in the Place, consists not of Distances, (for that is Length, and Breadth, and Depth, Resistence also comes within these) the Body itself will be it's own Place, and that which containeth will be the same with that which is contained, which were absurd. There is not therefore any Distance of the Place, and consequently Place is nothing.

There is also an Argument to this Effect. Forasmuch as in a thing that is said to be in Place, there are not seen double Dimensions, but one Length, and one Breadth, and one Depth; Whether are these Dimensions of the Body only, or of Place, or of both? If of Place only, then the Body will have no proper Length, Breadth, or Depth, and consequently it will not be a Body, which is absurd. If of both, forasmuch as *Vacuum* hath no subsistence besides the Dimensions, and those of the *Vacuum* subjected to the Body; of whatsoever Dimensions the Body consists, of the same will the *Vacuum* consist also. For of the existence of Resistence, nothing can be positively asserted, as we formerly shewed. Now seeing that the Dimensions which belong to the *Vacuum*, and are the same with the *Vacuum*, appear only in the Body, which is visible, the Body will be *Vacuum*, which is absurd. If the Dimensions are of the Body only, then there will be no Dimension of Place, and consequently no Place; if therefore the Dimension of Place be not found by any of the foresaid ways, there is no Place.

This is likewise alledged: When a Body enters into a *Vacuum*, which thereby becomes a Place, either the *Vacuum* suffers, or yields, or is destroyed; but if it suffers, the same will be full and vacuous; if it either yields, being ** moved locally, or is destroy'd by Motion, *Vacuum* will be a Body, for these are proper Affections of a Body. But it is absurd to say, the same is vacuous and full, or that *Vacuum* is a Body; therefore it is absurd to say, that a *Vacuum* may be occupied by a Body, and become Place. Whence it is also found, that *Vacuum* is absolutely inexistent, if it cannot be occupied by a Body, so as to become Place; for *Vacuum* was said to be that, which may be occupied by a Body.

** Reading χινυμενον.

Hereby also is subverted *Region*, for either it is a great Place, or is circumscribed with the Place; but if it be partly occupied by Body, and partly a vacuous distance or dimension, it is taken away with both. This, and much more, is alledged against the Opinion of the *Stoicks* concerning Place, wherein they dissent from others.

But the *Peripateticks* say, that *Place is the term* (or inmost *Superficies*) *of that which containeth, inasmuch as it containeth*; so that my Place is the *Superficies* of the air which incloseth my Body. But if this be Place, the same will be and not be; for when a Body is about to go into some Place, forasmuch as nothing can be in that which is not, it is necessary that Place first exist, and then that Body be in it; so that there must be Place, before there can be a Body that is said to be in Place. But inasmuch as Place is made, by accommodating of the *Superficies* of the thing containing, to the thing contained, Place cannot exist before there be a Body in it, and therefore will not have been before. But it is absurd to say, that the same is Something, and is not; therefore Place is not the term of a thing continent, inasmuch as it containeth.

Moreover, If Place be something, it is either Generate or Ingenerate; not Ingenerate, for they say it is made, whilst it is conformed to the Body which is in it; but neither is it Generate, for either when the Body is in Place, then is made the Place, in which that which is in Place, is now said to be; or when it is not in it: But neither when it is in it, (for it is already the Place of the Body that is in it) seeing that which containeth is adapted, as they say, to that which is contained, and so becometh Place. But nothing can be adapted round about that which is not in it. Now if Place be neither made when the Body is in it; nor when it is not in it; and besides these, we know not any way, then Place is not generated; but if it be neither Generated nor Ingenerated, it is not at all.

More generally may be argued thus: If there be Place, it is either a Body, or Incorporeal; but both these are doubtful, as we discoursed formerly, therefore Place itself is doubtful. Place is understood with reference to the Body whereof it is Place; but that which is alledged concerning the existence of a Body is uncertain, therefore that which is said of Place. The Place of every particular thing is not eternal, but if it be said to be Generated, it will be found to be Inexistent forasmuch as Generation itself is not. Much more might be said, but not to insist longer hereon, we shall, from what hath been said, infer, That the *Scepticks* ought not to assent to any thing, that is said by the *Dogmatists*, concerning Place, but to Suspend.

CHAP. XVII.

Of Time.

THe same we do in the Question concerning *Time*: For by *Phænomena's*, Time seemeth to be something; but by that which is said of it, it seems to have no Being; for some affirm, That Time is the Interval of the motion of Time, (by Time understanding the World;) others, That it is the motion of the World. *Aristotle*, or, as some, *Plato*, that it is the number of *Prius & Posterius* in motion. *Strato*, or, as some, *Aristotle*, that it is *the Measure of Motion and Rest*. *Epicurus*, (as *Demetrius* the *Lacedemonian* saith) that it is an Accident of Accidents, accompanying Days, and Nights, and Hours, and Affections, and Apathies, and Motions, and Rests. As to its Essence, some affirm it is a Body, as the Followers of *Ænesidemus*; for they hold, it differs nothing from Being, and from the first Body; others, that it is Incorporeal. Now therefore, either all these dissonant Opinions are true, or all are false; or some are true, some false. But all cannot be true, for most of them are repugnant to one another; neither will the *Dogmatists* yield that all are false. Besides, if we should grant it to be false, that Time is a Body; and false likewise, that it is Incorporeal, it must immediately be granted, that Time is not at all; for besides these, there can be nothing. Neither is it possible to comprehend which are true, which false, by reason of the equivalence of the Arguments on both sides, and the uncertainty of the Criterie and the Demonstration. For these Reasons therefore, we cannot assert any thing concerning Time. Moreover, seeing that Time exists not without Motion or Rest, if Motion and Rest be taken away, Time also is taken away. Nevertheless, some bring these Arguments against Time:

If Time be, either it is Determinate, or Infinite; if Determinate, it began from some Time, and will end in some Time; and consequently there was once a Time, when Time was not, that is, before it began to be; and there will be a Time, when Time shall not be, that is, when it shall have ceas'd to be, which is absurd; Therefore Time is not Determinate. Now if it be Infinite, forasmuch as one is said to be Past, another Present, another Future; the Future and Present either are or are not; but if they are not, seeing there only remains the Present, than which nothing can be shorter, Time will be Determinate, and consequently there will arise the same difficulties as at first. But if the Past exist, and the Future exist, they must both be Present; but it is absurd to say, That that which is Past and Future is Present, therefore Time is not Infinite. Now if it be neither Infinite nor Determinate, it is not at all.

Moreover, if Time be, 'tis either Divisible or Indivisible; Indivisible it is not, for it is divided, as they say, into Present, Past, and Future; but neither is it Divisible, for every Divisible is measured by some part of itself, that which measureth being applied to every part of the thing measured, as when we measure a Cubit with a Digit. But Time cannot be measured by any part of itself; for if the Present (for example) measureth the Past, it must be in the Past, and consequently Past; and, if the Future, it must be in the Future, and consequently Future. In like manner the Future, if it measure the others, must be Present and Past; and the Past must be Future and Present, which is a Contradiction; therefore it is not Divisible. Now, if it be neither Divisible nor Indivisible, it is not at all.

Again, Time is said to have three Parts, the Past, the Present, and the Future; of which, the Past and Future are not, (for if the Past and Future were now, each of them would be the Present) neither is the Present also. For if the Present Time be, it is either Indivisible or Divisible; Indivisible it is not, for things that are changed, are said to be changed in present Time; but nothing is changed in indivisible Time, as, I am softned, or the like. Therefore the present Time is not indivisible. But neither is it divisible; it cannot be divided into Presents; for by reason of the swift fluxion of things in the world, the Present is imperceptibly changed into the Past. Neither is it divided into Past and Future, for then it were inexistent, as having one part no longer existent, the other not yet existent. Whence neither can the Present be the end of the Past, and Beginning of the Future, for so it will be, and not be; it will be, as it is Present; and not be, because its parts are not: Therefore it is not divisible. Now if the Present be neither divisible nor indivisible, it is not at all. But if there be neither Present, nor Past, nor Future, Time is not; for that which consists of what is not, itself is not.

Against Time, is also brought this Argument: If Time is, it is either generate and corruptible, or ingenerate and incorruptible. Ingenerate and incorruptible it is not, for Part is Past, and hath no longer Being; Part is Future, and hath no Being yet: But neither is it generate and corruptible; for things that are generated, are generated of some Being, and Things that are corrupted, are corrupted into some Being, according to the Tenent of the *Dogmatists*. If therefore it be corrupted into the Past, it is corrupted into a Not-Being; and if it be generated of the Future, it is generated of a Not-Being, for neither of these is. But it is absurd to say, that a Thing is generated of a Not-Being, or corrupted into a Not-Being; therefore Time is not generate and corruptible. Now if Time be neither ingenerate and incorruptible, nor generate and corruptible, it is not at all.

Moreover, forasmuch as every thing that is generated, seems to be generated in Time; if Time be generated, it is generated in Time; it is therefore either generated in itself, or one
time

time in another: But if in itself, the same will be and not be; for since that in which any thing is generated, must be pre-existent to that which is generated in it; Time generated in itself, if it be generated, is not yet; and if it be generated in itself, it is already. Wherefore Time is not generated in itself. But neither is one Time generated in another; for if the Present be generated in the Future, the Future must be Present; and if in the Past, the Past. The same may be said of other Times; therefore one Time is not generated in another. Now if Time be neither generated in itself, nor one Time in another, it is not generate at all. But that it is not ingenerate, we shewed also. Therefore seeing it is neither generate nor ingenerate, it is not at all; for every Being must either be generate or ingenerate.

CHAP. XVIII.

Of Number.

Forasmuch as Time seemeth not to be considered without *Number*, it will not be from the purpose, to speak something briefly concerning Number. As to common Conversation, we say, without Opinion, that we Number something; and allow it to be said, that Number is something: But the superfluous Curiosity of the *Dogmatists* urgeth us to dispute against it. The *Pythagoreans* assert Numbers to be the Elements of the World, for they say, that *Phænomena's* must consist of something, but the Elements must be simple, therefore the Elements are unapparent. Now of things unapparent, some are Bodies, as Vapors, and little Bulks; others Incorporeal, as Figures, and Idea's, and Numbers, of which Bodies are compounded, consisting of Length, Breadth, Depth, Resistance, and Gravity. The Elements therefore are not only unapparent, but Incorporeal. Moreover, Number is considered in every Incorporeal, for it is either one, or two, or more; whence is gathered, that the Elements of all things are Numbers, which are unapparent and incorporeal, and consider'd in all things; and this not simply, but by the *Monad*, and the * indefinite *Duad*, made by composition of the *Monad*, by participation whereof, all particular *Duads* are *Duads*. Of these are made the other Numbers, which are considered in things numerate, and, they say, frame the World. For the Point is correspondent to the *Monad*, the Line to the *Duad*, (for it is considered, as lying betwixt two Points) the *Superficies* to the *Triad*, (for they say, it is the fluxion of a line into breadth to another point over against it.) The Body of the *Tetrad* to the *Tetrad*, for it is made by elevating the *Superficies* to a point over it. These Fictions they make of Bodies, and of the whole World, which they affirm to be governed according to the harmonical Propositions; the *Diatessaron*, which is *Sesquitertia*, as 8 to 6; the *Diapente* which is *Sesquialtera*, as 9 to 6; and the *Diapason*, which is duple, as 12 to 6. These things they dream, asserting Number to be something distinct from the things Numbred, arguing thus; If an Animal be in its own proper respect One, a Plant, not being an Animal, will not be One; but a Plant is One, therefore an Animal is not One in its own proper respect, but according to * something extrinsecal that is considered in it, whereof every thing partakes, and is made One by it. And if Number be the things numbred, forasmuch as the things numbred are (for example) Men, and Oxen, and Horses, Number must be Men, Horses, and Oxen; and Number must be white, and black, and bearded, if the things numbred happen to be such; but this is absurd, therefore Number is not the things which are numbred, but hath a peculiar existence distinct from them, according to which it is consider'd in the things Numbred, and is also an Element.

The *Pythagoreans* having thus collected, that Number is not the things Numbred, there comes in the insoluble doubt concerning Number; for Number is said to be Number, therefore is either the things numbred, or some extrinsecal thing distinct from them; but neither is Number the things numbred, as the *Pythagoreans* have demonstrated; nor is it any thing distinct from them, as we * shall declare; therefore Number is nothing. That Number is nothing extrinsecal, distinct from the things numbred, we shall prove, instancing in the *Monad*, for the better explication hereof. For if the *Monad* be Something in itself, by participation whereof, every thing that participates of it becomes One, either the *Monad* itself is but One, or it is as many as there are things which participate of it; but if it is One, Whether doth each of those Things which are said to participate of it, participate of the Whole, or of Part thereof? For if one Man (for example) hath the Whole *Monad*, there will be no more *Monad*, whereof one Horse, or one Dog, or any of those things which we affirm to be One, can communicate. For, supposing one Garment to be amongst many naked Men, if one of them put it on, the rest must remain naked, and without any Garment; now if every one participates of part thereof, first, a *Monad* will have a part, and consequently Infinite Parts into which it is divided, which were absurd. Again, as a part of the *Decad* (as a *Duad*) is not a *Decad*, so neither will a part of the *Monad* be a *Monad*, and therefore nothing participates of the *Monad*: Therefore there is not one *Monad*, of whose Parts all singulars participate. Now if the *Monads* are equal in number to all numerate things, of which the word *One* is predicated, by participation of which *Monads* every Particular is said to be One, there will be Infinite *Monads* thus participated. And these either participate of a transcendent *Monad*, or of *Monads* which are of equal Number with them, and are for that reason *Monads*; or they participate not, but are *Monads*, without any Participation. If these can be *Monads* without Participation, every Sensible Thing may in like manner be One without Participation; and then the *Monad*, which is consider'd in itself, is overthrown. But if these *Monads* also are by Participation, either they all participate of One, or there is One peculiar to each; if all participate

cipate of One, each participates of Part thereof, or of the Whole; whereupon follow the former Absurdities. But if each hath a peculiar to itself, we must consider over each of these another Monad, and over each of those another, and so to Infinite. If therefore to comprehend, that there are some Monads in themselves, by participation whereof every thing that is is One, it be requisite to comprehend infinitely infinite intelligible Monads; but it is impossible to comprehend infinitely infinite intelligible Monads; by consequence it is impossible to assert, that there are certain intelligible Monads, and that every Being is One, being made One by participation of its proper Monad. Therefore it is absurd also to say, there are as many Monads as there are things participant of them. Now if that which is said to be Monad in itself, neither is One, nor so many as are the things which participate of it, there is no such thing as a Monad in itself. In like manner, neither will there be any of the other Numbers in itself; for the same Argument which we have brought against the Monad, will hold against them all. But if Number be neither in itself, as we have shewn; nor Number be the things numbred, as the *Pythagoreans* approved; and besides these there is nothing; we must say, that Number is not.

Moreover, How do they, who conceive Number to be Somthing extrinsecal, distinct from the Things numbred, affirm, That the Duad is generated of the Monad? For when we add a Monad to another Monad, either Somthing extrinsecal is added to the Monads, or is substracted from them, or is neither added nor substracted; but if nothing be added or substracted, there will be no Duad. For neither will the Monads, being separate from one another, have a Monad considered as above them, according to their peculiar respects; neither is any thing added to them from without, (nor taken away, according to the *Hypothesis*.) So that the addition of a Monad to a Monad, there being no Addition nor Substraction from without, will not make a Duad; but if there be Substraction, there will not only be no Duad, but the Monads themselves will be diminished; and if from without a Duad be added to them, that of the two Monads there may be made a Duad, seeming to be Two they will be Four; for there is first laid down one Monad, and another Monad, to which a Duad from without being added, the number Four is made. It is the same as to all other Numbers, which are said to be made by Composition. If therefore those Numbers which are said to be compounded of transcendent Numbers, are made neither by Substraction nor Addition, nor without Substraction and Addition, the generation of that Number, which is said to be by itself, and about numerate things, will be insubsistent. But that the Numbers which are by Composition, are not ingenerate, they themselves declare, affirming, That they are compounded, and made of those which are transcendent, as of the Monad, and indefinite Duad; therefore Number hath not a subsistence of itself. And if Number hath not a Subsistence, neither considered in itself nor in things numbered, Number is not any thing, according to the superfluous curiosity of the *Dogmatists*. Thus much may serve for a brief Account, as to that which is called the *Physical* Part of Philosophy.

CHAP. XIX.

Of the Ethical part of Philosophy.

There remains the *Ethical* part, which seemeth conversant about *Goods*, and *Ills*, and *Indifferents*. That therefore we may treat of this also, by way of Summary, we will inquire into the existence of Goods, Ills, and Indifferents having first explained their Notions.

CHAP. XX.

Of Goods, Ills, and Indifferents.

THe *Stoicks* say, that *Good is Profit*, or, *that which differeth not from Profit*, calling *Profit*, Virtue; and virtuous Action, *that which is not different from Profit*, a virtuous Man, and a Friend; for Virtue being the *Hegemonick* part of the Soul, consistent after such a manner; and virtuous Action, being an Operation according to Virtue, is plainly Profit; and a virtuous Man and a Friend, is not different from Profit. For Profit is a part of virtuous, as being the *Hegemonick* thereof; now the Wholes, they say, are neither the same with their Parts, (for a Man is not a hand;) nor different from their Parts, for they subsist not without their Parts: Wherefore they say, the Whole is not different from it's Parts, consequently, a virtuous Man being the Whole in respect of it's *Hegemonick* (which they say is Profit) is not different from Profit.

CHAP. XXI.

That Good is taken Three ways.

HEnce, *Good*, they say is taken Three ways: One way, Good is said to be that from which Profit cometh; this is the most principal, and the Virtues: The Second, is that by which Profit cometh, as Virtue and virtuous Actions: The Third, is that which is able to Profit, as Virtue, and virtuous Actions, and a virtuous Man, and a Friend, and the Gods, and good Dæmons: Thus the Second Signification includes the first; and the Third, both First and Second.

Some say, *Good is that which is expetible for itself*; Others, *that which assisteth to Felicity, or compleateth it*. Felicity, according to the Stoicks, is Εὔροια βίου, *a good current of Life*.

These things are said to explain the Notion of Good; but whether a Man saith, Good is that which profiteth, or that which is expetible in itself, or that which co-operates towards Felicity, he declareth not what Good is, but something accident to it, which is frivolous. For the foresaid are either Accident to Good only, or to other things also. If to other things also, they are not Characteristicks of Good, forasmuch

much as they are made common. If to Good only, we cannot by these understand Good; for as he who understands not what a Horse is, knoweth not what Neighing is, nor can by that come to the Notion of a Horse, if he first light not upon a Horse Neighing: So, he who enquireth what is Good, forasmuch as he knoweth not what Good is, he cannot know what properly and solely belongs to it, that thereby he might come to understand Good itself. For first he must learn the Nature of Good itself, and then understand, that it profiteth, and that it is expetible for itself, and that it is effective of Felicity. But that the foresaid Accidents are not sufficient to declare the Notion and Nature of Good, the *Dogmatists* manifest in Effect. For, that Good profiteth, and that it is expetible, (whence called ἀγαθὸν qu. ἀγωγὸν) and effective of Felicity, all perhaps grant: But being demanded, What that is, to which these are Accident? they run into an incredible contest, some saying that it is Virtue, others Pleasure, others Indolence, others something else; whereas, if by the foresaid Definitions it were determined what Good is, they would not fall out among themselves, as ignorant of its Nature. Thus the most Eminent among the *Dogmatists* differ concerning the Notion of Good. They likewise differ about Ill, saying, that Ill is Hurt, or not different from Hurt; others, that which is avoidable for itself; others, that which is effective of Infelicity; whereby perhaps declaring not the Essence of Ill, but some of the things accident to it, they fall into the foresaid Inextricability.

CHAP. XXII.

Of Indifferent.

*I*Ndifferent *is taken Three ways: First, for that which moveth neither Appetite nor Aversion; as, that the Stars or the Hairs of our Head are of even Number. Secondly, for that which moves the Appetite or Aversion not one more than the other, as in two Tetradrachmes nothing different, when one of them is to be chosen. There is an Appetite to choose one of them, but not this more than that. The Third kind of Indifferent is, that which conduceth neither to Felicity nor Infelicity, as Health, Wealth; for that which sometimes may be used Well, sometimes Ill, this, they say, is Indifferent. Concerning this last chiefly they discourse in* Ethicks.

What to conceive of this Notion, is manifest from what we said before from Goods and Ills. They bring us not to the Notion of each of these things; but it is not strange, that they fail in things inexistent. That nothing by Nature is Good, Ill, or Indifferent, some argue thus.

CHAP. XXIII.

Whether there is any thing naturally Good, Ill, or Indifferent.

FIre being Hot by Nature, appeareth to all to be heating; Snow being Cold by Nature, appeareth to all to be cooling; all things which affect by their Nature, affect all that are according to Nature or well, after the same manner; but none of those which are called Good, affect all Men as Good (as we shall shew) therefore there is nothing Good by Nature. That none of those which are called Goods, affect all Men alike, is manifest; for (to pass by the ordinary People, whereof some think a good habit of Body to be Good; others, venereal Pleasures; others, Eating; others, Drinking; others, Dicing; others, Riches; others, somthings worse than these.) Some Philosopers, as the *Peripateticks* say, There are Three kinds of Goods, *some in the Soul, as the Virtues; some in the Body, as Health and the like; others, external, as Friends, Wealth, and the like*. The *Stoicks* also affect Three kinds of Goods, *some in the Soul, as the Virtues; some external, as a virtuous Man, and a Friend; some, neither in, nor without the Soul, as a virtuous Man as to himself*. But those which are in the Body or external, which the *Peripateticks* account Goods, they deny to be Goods. Some there are who hold Pleasure to be a Good; others on the contrary say, it is an Ill: Whence one of the Philosophers cried out, *I had rather be Mad, than be Pleased*. Now if all things, which move (or affect) by Nature, move all Men alike, but by those which are called Goods, all Men are not affected alike, nothing is good by Nature. For neither can we believe all the foresaid Opinions, by Reason of their Repugnance, nor some one of them; for he who saith we must believe this Sect, and not that, seeing he is opposed by the Reasons of the other side, becomes a Party in the Controversy, and will himself need a Judge, but shall not judge others. Now there neither being an acknowledged Criterie, nor a Demonstration, by Reason of the indijudicable Controversy concerning these, he must come to Suspension, and hereupon will not be able to assert what is good by Nature.

Moreover some argue thus. Good is either the desire itself, or that which we desire: The desire itself is not Good, in itself; for then we would not endeavour to obtain that which we desire, lest having obtained it we lose the desire. For example; if to desire Drink were Good, we would not endeavour to get Drink; for, assoon as ever we have obtained it, we leave to desire it. 'Tis the same in Hunger, Love, and the like; therefore the desire is not a thing expetible in itself; rather on the contrary, perhaps troublesome. For he who is Hungry, endeavours to obtain Meat, that he may be freed from the trouble of Hunger; the like doth he who Loves, and he who Thirsts. Neither is that which is desired, the Good itself; for either it is without us, or above us. If without us, either it causeth in us some pleasing Motion, and such a Constitution as we willingly embrace, and consequently is a delightful Affection, or it affects us not at all; but if it be not delightful, it is not Good, nor can incite us to it's Appetition, nor can be any way expetible. If there be ingenerate about us extrinsecally some delightful Constitution and Affection, which we willingly embrace, that which is without us, shall not be expetible in itself, but for the Affection which is raised in us through

through it ; but neither about us, for then it must either be about the Body, or about the Soul, or about both. If about the Body only, we cannot know it, for all knowledge they attribute to the Soul, the Body they say in it self is Irrational. Now if it be said to proceed as far as the Soul, it will seem to be expetible to the Comprehension of the Soul, and to it's delightful Affection: For that which is judged to be expetible, is judged (according to them) by the Intellect, not by the irrational Body. It remains therefore to say, that Good is about the Soul only, but even this, according to the Grounds of the *Dogmatists*, is impossible ; for perhaps the Soul it self is not existent, or if it exist, it is not (from what they themselves say) comprehended, as we have proved in the discourse concerning the Criterie. But how will any venture to say, that somthing is produced in a thing, which comprehends it not?

Besides all this, How do they say that Good is in the Soul? If *Epicurus* say, That Pleasure is the End, and that the Soul (for so do all things,) consists of Atoms, how Pleasure, and an assent or judgment, that this is expetible and Good, that avoidable and ill, can be in a heap of Atoms, is not possible to be resolved?

CHAP. XXIV.

What that is, which is called Art about Life.

AGain, the *Stoicks* say, That the Goods in the Soul are certain Arts, the Virtues. Art, they say, is a System of coexercised Comprehensions ; Comprehensions are made in the Hegemonick. Now, how in the Hegemonick, which, according to them, is a Spirit, there is a storing up of Comprehensions, and a Coacervation of them, so as to make an Art, is not possible to be understood ; forasmuch as the later impression still defaceth the forgoing, since they say it is a Spirit, and moved totally, according to every Impression. For to say that *Plato*'s ἀνειδωλοποιησις can demonstrate Good, I mean that temperament of divisible and indivisible substance, and of the nature of Alterity and Identity, or Numbers, is meerly to trifle ; whence neither can Good be in the Soul. Now if neither the desire be the Good, nor the extrinsecal Subject which is expetible for it self, nor in the Body, nor in the Soul, as I have proved, there is nothing naturally Good ; and for the same Reasons, neither is there any thing naturally Ill. For those things which to some seem Ill, are persued by others for Good, as Lasciviousness, Injustice, Covetousness, Intemperance, and the like. Whence if those which are naturally Good, affect all Men alike ; and those which are said to be Ill, affect not all alike, there is nothing Ill naturally.

Neither is there any thing naturally Indifferent, by reason of the Controversie about Indifferents, as for example : The *Stoicks*, of Indifferents, say, That *some are preferred, others rejected ; others neither preferred, nor rejected. Preferred are those, which have a sufficient dignity, as health, riches ; rejected, those which have not a sufficient dignity, as poverty, sickness. Neither preferred nor rejected ; as to stretch, or bend the finger*. But some hold, that, *of Indifferents none is absolutely preferred or rejected ; for every Indifferent, seemeth sometimes preferred, sometimes rejected, according to various circumstances*. For if (say they) a Tyrant plots against the Rich, whil'st the Poor are suffered to live quietly, there is none but had rather be poor than rich ; so as Riches in this case will be in the number of the rejected. Thus each of these which are called Indifferents, is by some held to be good, by others to be ill ; but if it were Indifferent by nature, all men would alike conceive it to be Indifferent. Therefore there is nothing Indifferent by Nature. Again, if some shall argue, that Courage is expetible by nature, because Lyons, and Bulls, Cocks, and some Men are naturally inclined to it, we reply, that for the same reason timidity ought to be reckoned amongst things expetible in their own nature ; for Harts, and Hares, and many other Creatures are addicted to it by nature. Even a great part of Mankind are such. For it seldom happens, that a man gives up himself to dye for his Country, or, couragiously attempts some bold Action, as being with-held by effeminate timidity ; the greater part of men decline all these. Whence the *Epicureans* conceive it to be proved, that pleasure is expetible in its own nature ; for living Creatures, say they, as soon as they are born, being yet unperverted, desire pleasure, and decline pain. To these may be objected, That whatsoever causeth ill, cannot be good by nature, but pleasure causeth ill, for to all pleasure is annexed pain, which, according to them, is ill in its own nature ; For example : A Drunkard hath pleasure in drinking, a Glutton in eating, a Luxurious person in wantoning ; but these cause Poverty and Sickness, which are painful and ill, as they conceive ; therefore pleasure is not good in its own nature. Besides, that which causeth good, cannot be naturally ill, but pains cause pleasures ; by Labour we attain Science and Riches ; by Labour a Man obtains the Enjoyment of his Love, by Pain is acquired Health ; therefore Labour is not ill naturally. For if Pleasure were good in its own nature, and Labour or Pain ill in its own nature, all Men would be alike affected with them : But we see many Philosophers embrace Labour and Pain, and contemn Pleasure.

In the same manner may they be overthrown, who say, that a Life conjoined with Virtue is good by nature, because some Philosophers have made choice of a voluptuous Life ; so as by the disagreement amongst them, is subverted, that a thing is such or such in its own nature.

It will not perhaps be from our purpose, to propose briefly some more particular opinions of things honest and dishonest, of the lawful and unlawful, Laws, and Customs, and devotion to the Gods, and piety to the dead, and the like ; for by this means we shall find a great difference amongst things to be done, and not to be done. With us ἀῤῥενομιξία is held dishonest and unlawful ; with the *Germans*, not dishonest, but an allowed custom. Neither did the *Thebans* of old esteem it dishonest ; and *Merione* the Cretan, they say, was so called, by Emphasis of the Cretan Nation. Some also refer to this *Achil-*

les's fervent friendship to *Patroclus*. And no wonder, when the *Cynicks*, and *Zeno* the Cittiean, and *Cleanthes*, and *Chryfippus* say, It is an Indifferent. Again, for a Man to lie with his Wife in publick, though we esteem it unseemly, yet some in the *Indies* do not so, for they make no distinction of places therein; as *Crates*, the Philosopher, is also said to have done. For Women to prostitute themselves, with us, is dishonest, and shameful, but with many of the *Egyptians* honourable; for it is said, that those who have lay n with many Men, used to wear a Bracelet about their Ancles as a mark of Honour. Moreover, amongst them, Virgins before Marriage gain'd a Dowry by prostituting themselves. The *Stocks* say, That it is no shame to cohabit with a common Woman, or to be maintained by what she gets. To be stigmatized, with us, is shameful and dishonourable; but many of the *Egyptians* and *Sarmatians* stigmatiz'd their Children. For men to wear Ear-Rings is, with us, accounted shameful, but with some *Barbarians*, as with the *Syrians*, it is a mark of Nobility; insomuch as some extending this mark of Nobility, bore holes in the Nostrils of their Children, in which they hang Rings of Silver or Gold, which none amongst us do. As neither to wear a Mantle stain'd and dy'd with Flowers, for though the *Persians* esteem this an Ornament, we think it undecent. When at a Feast made by *Dionysius* Tyrant of *Sicliy* such a kind of Robe was offered to *Plato*, and to *Aristippus* the Philosophers; *Plato* refus'd, saying,

I will not with a Female Robe myself disgrace,
Who am a Man, and of a Manly Race.

But *Aristippus* took it, with these words;

If she come pure, a Bacchanalian Feast
Never corrupts a modest Woman's breast.

Thus even of the wise Men, to some it seemed Decent, to others Indecent, With us it is Unlawful to marry our Mother, or Sister; but the *Persians* (and of them the *Magi*, who make greatest profession of Wisdom) marry their Mothers, and the *Ægyptians* their Sisters, and all; as the Poet,

Jove *to his Wife and Sister* Juno, *said.*

Zeno the Cittiean saith, That it is not dishonest, τὸ μόριον ᾖ μητρὸς ᾧ ἑαυτίω μόριον τρίψαι, no more than if it were to rub any other part of the Body. *Chryfippus*, in his Treatise of Policy, asserts, That the Father may lye with the Daughter, and the Mother with the Son, and the Brother with the Sister. But *Plato* more universally saith, That all Wives ought to be in common. With *us it is detestable, *ἀχρυρσεῖν Zeno approves it; and we are informed that some there are, who use this Evil as a Good. To eat Man's Flesh with us is unlawful; whereas amongst the *Barbarians* there are whole Nations which use it as a thing indifferent. What need we instance *Barbarians*, when *Tydeus* himself is said to have eaten the Brains of his Enemy? and the *Stoicks* say, it is not unfitting to eat not only the Flesh of other Men, but our own. Moreover to defile the Altar of God with Blood, with most People, as with us, is held impious; but the *Lacedæmonians*, at the Altar of *Orthosia*, and *Diana*, whipp'd themselves cruelly, so as much Blood run down upon the Altar of the Goddess. Besides, some sacrifice a Man to *Saturn*, as the *Scythians* do Strangers to *Diana*; but we, on the contrary, think the Temples are defiled with human Blood. With us, there is a Law for punishment of Adulterers; but some hold, that to lie with other Mens Wives, is a thing Indifferent: Even some Philosophers say, that, to lie with other Mens Wives, is Indifferent. With us, Children are found by Law to take care for their Parents; the *Scythians*, when they exceed Threescore years, cut their Throats, And what wonder, when *Saturn* himself with a Sickle emasculated his Father; *Jupiter* threw down *Saturn* into *Tartarus*; *Minerva* joined with *Jupiter*, and *Neptune*, to fetter her Father; *Saturn* devoured his own Children. Moreover, *Solon* the *Athenian* made a Law concerning indemnate persons, whereby any Man was permitted to kill his Son; but with us, the Laws forbid to kill our Sons. The *Roman* Lawgivers order the Children to be under the power of the Parents, and to be their Servants; and the Children not to be Masters of their own Estates, but the Parents, until they are manumitted after the same manner as purchased Slaves. Others reject this Custom as Tyrannical. There is a Law to punish Homicides, but *Gladiators*, when they kill a Man, are many times honoured for it. The Laws forbid to strike a free Person, but Wrastlers, beating Freemen, somtimes killing them, are rewarded with Honors and Garlands. The Law commands every Man to have but one Wife; but amongst the *Thracians* and *Getulians*, a People of *Lybia*, every one hath many. To rob is with us held unlawful and unjust; but with many of the *Barbarians*, not so: On the contrary, the *Cilicians* esteem it Honorable; whereupon such as die in Robbing, they judge worthy of Honor. *Nestor* in the Poet, after he had kindly received those who were with *Telemachus*, sayes

———*Do you uncertain stray*
As Thieves?

But if to Rob had been dishonorable, he would not have entertained Persons, that might be suspected for Thieves, with so much Humanity. Besides, to steal, is, with us, unjust and unlawful; but those who say *Mercury* is a Thievish God, do not conceive it unjust; for how can a God be wicked? Some also say, That the *Lacedæmonians* punish'd Thieves, not for Stealing, but for being Taken. A Coward that throws away his Shield, is in many Countries punished by Law, (whence the *Lacedaemonian* Woman giving her a Son a Shield, said to him, * Thou Son, or this, or upon this,) but *Archilochus* brags, that he had thrown away his Shield, and run away, writing of himself in his Poems thus:

*With Laertius, χειρυργεῖν. See the Life of Diogenes.

*Either Bring it home, or, Be brought home dead upon it.

Some

Some Sajan *doth perhaps himself adorn*
Now with the Shield which once by me was born
And left behind (though sore against my will)
To save my life ———

The *Amazons* maim their Male-Children, that they might not be fit for War, and they themselves underwent all Military Business; whereas we think the contrary to be the best order. The Mother of the Gods admits Eunuchs, which a God would never do, if it were ill by nature, not to be perfectly virile. Thus concerning things just and unjust, and virility, there is great disagreement.

Likewise; concerning Devotion, and the Gods, there is much Controversie; the greater part hold, that there are Gods; but some, that there are none, as the Followers of *Diagoras* the *Melian*, and *Theodorus*, and *Critias* the *Athenian*. Of those who affirm there are Gods, some worship the Gods of their Country, others those which the Sects of Dogmatists have framed; as, *Aristotle* held God to be incorporeal, the boundure of Heaven; the *Stoicks*, a Spirit, penetrating even through things horrible to behold; *Epicurus*, of humane Form; *Xenophanes*, an impassible Sphere; some, that he is provident over our Affairs; others, that he is not provident over them: For that which is blessed and incorruptible, saith *Epicurus*, neither hath any trouble itself, nor causeth any to others. Whence also, of those according to life, some say, that there is one God; others, that there are many, and of different forms; so as they run into the opinions of the *Egyptians*, who conceived the Gods to be faced like Dogs, and formed like Hawks, and Oxen, and Crocodiles, and what not. Whence also there hapned a great difference as to Sacrifices, and the worship of the Gods. Things that are sacred in some Temples, are profane in others; whereas this could not be, if there were any thing sacred or prophane in its own nature. For example, None sacrifice a Swine to *Serapis*, but to *Hercules* and *Æsculapius* they sacrifice them. 'Tis unlawful to sacrifice a Sheep to *Isis*, but to her who is called the Mother of the Gods, and to other Gods, they are sacrificed. To *Saturn* they sacrifice a man, which to most is impious. In *Alexandria* they sacrifice a Cat to *Hero*, a Moth to *Thetis*, which amongst us none do. To *Neptune* a Horse is sacrificed, but to *Apollo* the *Didymean* especially, this Creature is abominable. To sacrifice Goats to *Diana* is pious, but not to *Æsculapius*. Many others might be alledged, which, for brevity I omit. Now if there were any Sacrifice pious or impious in its own nature, all persons would have the same opinion of it.

Like to these we shall find the things that concern the diet of men, as to worship of the Gods. A *Jew* or an *Egyptian* Priest will dye, rather than eat Swine's flesh; a *Lybian* thinks it most unlawful to eat the flesh of Sheep; some of the *Syrians*, that of a Pidgeon; others, of Victims; in some Temples, it is lawful to eat Fish; in others unlawful. Of these who amongst the *Egyptians* were thought to be wise, some conceived it abominable to eat the head of a Creature; others, the shoulder; others, the foot; others, other parts. None eat Onions, who are initiated in the Rites of *Cacian Jupiter*, at *Pellusium*. The Priest of *Lybian Venus*, never eats Garlick. In some Temples, they abstain from Mint; in others, from Marjoram; in others, from Smallauge. Some affirm it better to eat the heads of our own Parents, than Beans; others hold the eating of these indifferent. We think it abominable to eat the flesh of Dogs, but some among the *Thracians* are reported to feed thereon; perhaps also it was in use amongst the *Crecians*, whence *Diocles*, following the *Æsculapians*, perscribed to some sick persons the flesh of Puppies. There are, who, as I said, eat Man's flesh indifferently, which we think unlawful. Now if these Rules of worship and things unlawful were by nature, all Men would have the like opinion of them.

The same may be said concerning Piety towards the Dead: Some cover the Bodies of the Dead with earth, thinking it impious to shew them to the Sun; The *Egyptians*, drawing out the Entrals, embalm them, and keep them amongst them above ground. Amongst the *Æthiopians* the *Ichthyophagi* throw them into Ponds, to be eaten by the Fishes; the *Hircanians* give them to be devoured by Dogs; some of the *Indians* to Vultures. It is reported, that the *Troglodytes* bring the dead Body to a hillock, tye it head and heels together, and threw stones at it, laughing, with which when they have covered it, they depart. There are some *Barbarians*, who sacrifice and eat those who out-live threescore years; but such as dye young, they bury in the Ground. There are who burn their Dead, of whom, some gathering their Bones, preserve them, others cast them away. The *Persians* it is reported, hang up their Dead, and Embalm them with Nitre, and then wrap Cloaths about them. We see with what Mourning some follow the Dead; some esteem Death horrible, and to be shunned; others, nothing such. *Euripides*,

If Life be Death who know,
And Death a Life below?

And *Epicurus* saith, *Death concerns us not. For what is dissolved in insensible, but what wants Sense, concerns us not.* They say moreover, *If we consist of Soul and Body, and Death be a Dissolution of the Soul and Body, then when we are, Death is not, for we are not dissolved; and when Death is, we are not; for this Composition of Soul and Body consisting no longer, neither are we.* *Heraclitus* saith, *That to Live is to Dye, and that whilst we Live we are Dead; for whilst we Live, our Souls are Dead; Buryed in us; but when we dye, our Souls revive and live.* There are who conceive, that to dye is better than to live; whence *Euripides*,

We New-born Infants rather should lament,
Pitying the miseries to which they'r sent :
But him who Dies, set from all Labours free,
Bear to the Grave with Joy triumphantly.

To the same effect, is also this?

*Of wretched Mankind, the most happy state
Were never to be Born nor see the day:
Next which, as soon as Born to pass the Gate
Of Pluto, and their Bones in dust to lay.*

We know the Story of *Cleobis* and *Biton*, related by *Herodotus*, concerning the *Argive* Priestess. It is said, amongst the *Thracians* there are some that mourn over a Child as soon as it is born. Therefore ought not Death to be reckoned amongst things horrible in their own nature, nor Life amongst things good in their own nature? Nor is there any of the forementioned things, such or such in their own nature, but all are such by Opinion and Reference. The same kind of Argument we might deduce from many other things, which, for brevity we omit. And if we cannot immediately instance a contrariety to somthing, we may say, It is possible, that in some Nations which we know not, there may be a different Opinion. For if we did not (for example) know, that the custom of the *Ægyptians* is to marry their Sisters, we might falsly affirm, that it is a thing acknowledged by all, that we ought not to marry our Sisters. In like manner, in such things as have not a difference known to us, it is not fit to affirm, that there is no Controversie concerning them, it being, as I said, possible, that some other Nations which we know not, may hold the contrary.

Hereupon the *Sceptick* observing so great difference of things, suspends as to what is Good or Bad in it's own Nature, or what is absolutely to be done or not to be done; herein declining the temerity of the *Dogmatists*; but he follows the common course of Life without being positive; whence it comes, that in things Opinionative, he remaines void of Passion; in things Compulsive, he is moderately affected: As being a Man, sensible, he suffers; but not taking the Opinion, that what he suffers is ill in it's own Nature, he is moderately affected; for to have such an Opinion is worse than the suffering itself, insomuch as they who suffer the amputation of some Limb or the like, many times bear it well, whil'st the standers by, out of an opinion that is ill, faint. For doubtless, he who proposeth to himself that somthing is good or ill in its own nature, and to be done or not to be done, is troubled many ways. When the things are present, which he conceives ill by nature, he seems to be tormented, and when he possesseth those which seem to him good, through his being exalted in mind for it, and his fear of losing it, and care lest he should fall again into those things which he conceives ill by nature, he is involv'd in no small trouble. For those who say, that Goods cannot be lost, are to be silenced by the Insolubility of the Question. Hence we argue. If what causeth ill be ill, and to be avoided; but the Persuasion, that some things are ill, some good, in their own nature, causeth troubles; then that Persuasion is ill, and to be avoided. Thus much of Goods, Ills, and Indifferents.

CHAP. XXV.

Whether there be an Art about Life.

FRom what hath been said it is manifest, That there is not an Art about Life; for it there be such an Art, it is conversant in the Contemplation of Goods, Ills and Indifferents, but these being inexistent, the Art about Life will be inexistent also. Besides, the *Dogmatists* not agreeing concerning this Art about Life, several of them being of several Opinions, they are subject to the Controversie and Argument from *Disagreement*, which we alledged in the Discourse concerning Good.

But though we should suppose all to agree in one Art about Life; as for example, That celebrated Prudence which the *Stoicks* dream of and seem to press more than the rest, many Absurdities will nevertheless follow. For seeing that Prudence is a Virtue, and *a wise Man only hath Virtue*, the *Stoicks* not being wise, will not have the Art about Life. And seeing, according to them, the Art cannot subsist, there will be no Art about Life, if we follow what they say. For they affirm, *Art to be a System of Comprehensions, Comprehension to be an assent to comprehensive Phantasie*; but comprhensive Phantasie cannot be found, for neither is all Phantasie comprehensive, nor can it be known, what Phantasies are comprehensive, and what not; but needing comprehensive Phantasie to discern what Phantasie is comprehensive, we run into *infinite*, another comprehensive Phantasie being required, for the discerning of the comprehensive Phantasie which we assumed. The *Stoicks* give such a notion of comprehensive Phantasie, as is not right; for, saying, *comprehensive Phantasie is that which ariseth from a Being, and a Being is that which is able to move comprehensive Phantasie*, they run into the *Alternate Commonplace*. If therefore, that there be an Art about Life, it is first requisite, that there be an Art; and that there be an Art, it is first requisite, that there be Comprehension; and that there be Comprehension, it is first repuisite, that there be an Assent to comprehensive Phantasie; but comprehensive Phantasie cannot be found; therefore the Art about Life cannot be found.

Again, every Art seems to be comprehended from those things which it properly delivers; but there is no work proper to that Art which is about Life; for whatsoever work shall be instanced, it will be found common with the Vulgar, as, to honour Parents, to restore a *Depositum*, and the like; therefore there is no Art about Life. Neither, as some maintain, from that which seemeth to be said or done through a prudent habit of mind, can we know what is the work of Wisdom; for a prudent habit of mind itself is incomprehensible, it neither being manifest in and by itself simply, nor by its words, for those are common with the Vulgar. And to say, that we comprehend him who hath the Art about Life, by the equability of his actions, is to speak above human nature, rather to be wished than asserted:

*For every man's endu'd with such a mind,
As several dayes are by the Gods assign'd.*

It remaineth to say, That this Art about Life is comprehended from their Writings; which being many, and all of one kind, we shall instance only some few. The Prince of their Sect, *Zeno,* in his *Exercitations concerning the Institution of Children,* amongst other things, saith thus, 'To
'distinguish nothing more or less, Childish or
'not Childish, Masculine or Feminine; for there
'is no difference between (*manners*) Childish
'and not Childish, Masculine and Feminine, the
'same become both. *Also,* of Piety towards
'Parents, *he saith, speaking of* Jocasta *and* Oedi-
'pus, That it was not abominable, &c. *With
'this agrees* Chrysippus, *in his Treatise of* Poli-
'cy, *saying,* These things in my Judgment
'ought so to be ordered as they are used not
'amiss with some, that the Mother should have
'Children by the Son, and the Father by the
'Daughter, and the Brother by the Sister. *In
'the same Book he alloweth* to eat Man's Flesh;
'*for he saith,* If any part be cut off from a Bo-
'dy Living, which is fit for Food, we should
'not bury it, nor carelesly throw it away, but
'so consume it, that it may become another
'part of us; *In his Books of* Office, *treating of
'the Burial of Parents, he expresly saith,* When
'our Parents are dead, we must provide for
'them the most simple Tombs; for the Body
'(no more than Nails, or Teeth, or Hair)
'pertaining nothing to us, we need not to have
'any respect or care of it. If the Flesh be
'sound, it may be converted into Aliment, (in
'like manner, as if some Limb of our own Bo-
'dy, wear cut off, as the Foot) but if unsound,
'it is to be buried, or burnt, or thrown away
'without any regard, as our Nails and Hair.
Much more of this kind is said by Philosophers, which they could not have the heart to do, unless they had been brought up among the *Cyclopes,* and the *Lestrigones.* Now if they do none of these, but their Actions are common with the vulgar, there is no particular work proper to them, who are thought to have the Art about Life. If therefore it be absolutely necessary, that Arts be comprehended from their proper works; but there is no work proper to the Art about Life, it is not comprehended. Wherefore none can say, that it is existent.

CHAP. XXVI.

Whether there is in Men an Art about Life.

NOW if there be in Men an Art about Life, either it is ingenerate in them by Nature, or acquired by Discipline and Doctrine. If by Nature, either it is ingenerate in them as they are Men, or as they are not Men. Not as they are not Men, for they are Men; If as they are Men, this wisdom would be in all Men, insomuch that all Men would be prudent, virtuous, and wise: but the greater part of Men, they say, are evil; therefore the Art which is according to Life is not in them, as they are Men, and therefore not by Nature. Besides, forasmuch as they hold an Art to be a System of unexercised Comprehensions, they seem rather to conceive both this and other Arts, to be comprehended by Experience and Discipline.

CHAP. XXVII.

Whether the Art about Life can be taught.

NEither is it understood by Doctrine and Discipline, for before these are, there must be three things acknowledged; the Thing taught, the Teacher, and He who learneth the manner of Discipline; but none of these are, therefore not the Doctrine.

CHAP. XXVIII.

Whether there be any thing taught.

FOR what is *taught,* is either true or false. If it be false, it cannot be taught, for that which is false, is not; that which is not, cannot be taught. But neither, if it be said to be true; for, that true is inexistent, we proved in our Discourse concerning the Criterie. If therefore neither false nor true is taught, and besides these there is nothing docible, (for these not being docible, no man will say that things indeterminable are docible) nothing is taught.

Again, that which is taught is either manifest, or unmanifest; if manifest, it needs not be taught, for things manifest are alike manifest to all. If unmanifest, forasmuch as things unmanifest, by Reason of the indijudicable Controversie concerning them, are incomprehensible, they cannot be taught; for how can any man learn, or teach, that which he comprehends not; Now if neither that which is manifest, nor that which is unmanifest is taught, nothing at all is taught.

Besides, that which is taught, is either a Body or Incorporeal; but neither of these, whether manifest or unmanifest, can be taught, for the foresaid Reason; therefore nothing can be taught.

Moreover, either that which is, is taught; or that which is not. If that which is not, be taught, forasmuch as Doctrines are conceived to be of things true, that which is not, will be true, and if true, it will be existent, for Truth, they say, is that which exists, and is opposed to some thing. But it is absurd to say, that which is not, exists, therefore that which exists not, cannot be taught. Neither can a Being be taught. For if a Being be taught, it must either be taught as a Being, or according to some other thing. If, as it is a Being, it is docible, it is a Being and consequently not docible; for Doctrines must be made of things indubitate and indocible, therefore a Being, as a Being, is not docible. But neither according to some other thing, for a Being hath nothing accident to it, which is not a Being. Therefore if a Being be not taught, as it is a Being, neither can it be taught according to any other thing, for whatsoever is accident to it, is a Being. Besides, whether the Being which they say is taught, be manifest, or unmanifest, it appears by the foresaid difficulties to be indocible. Now if neither that which is, nor that which is not, be taught, nothing is taught. CHAP.

CHAP. XXIX.

Whether there be a Teacher, and a Learner.

BY the foresaid difficulties are also subverted the *Teacher* and the *Learner*; nevertheless, we will question them more particularly. Either the Artist teacheth the Artist; or the Ignorant, the Ignorant; or the Ignorant, the Artist; or the Artist, the Ignorant. The Artist teacheth not the Artist, for, both being Artists, neither needs Teaching. The Ignorant cannot teach the Ignorant, no more than the Blind can lead the Blind. The Ignorant cannot teach the Artist, that were ridiculous. It remains to say, that the Artist teaches the Ignorant, which likewise is impossible. For there can be no such thing as an Artist, seeing that no Man is an Artist naturally, and Born such, neither is an Artist made of one that is not an Artist: For either one Theorem, and one Comprehension is sufficient to make an Artist of him that was not an Artist, or not; but if one Comprehension can make an Artist of him that was not an Artist, First, we may say, that Art is not a System of Comprehensions; for he that before knew nothing at all, if he have learnt one Theorem of Art, may thus be said to be an Artist. Next, if any shall say, that he who hath attained some Theorems of Art, but as yet wanteth one, and therefore being not an Artist, shall, as soon as he hath attained that one, be made an Artist of a Not-Artist, he holds that it is compleated by one Comprehension. But if he come to particulars, he cannot shew a Man that is yet no Artist, but shall be an Artist as soon as he hath attained one Theorem more; for no Man can number the Theorems of every Art, so as having numbred the Theorems known, he shall be able to say, how many there are behind to compleat the number of the Theorems of the Art: Therefore the knowledge of the Theorem maketh not a Man an Artist, who was not an Artist before. But if this be true, Forasmuch as a Man comprehends not all the Theorems of Arts together, but one by one, (as must be granted) he who attaineth every Theorem of Art distinctly by itself, cannot become an Artist, for we have shewed, that the knowledge of one Theorem cannot make him an Artist, who was not an Artist; therefore he, who is not an Artist, cannot be made an Artist. So as from hence it appeareth, that there is no Artist at all, and consequently no Teacher.

But neither can he who is said to Learn, not being an Artist, Learn and Comprehend the Theorems of Art, whereof he is ignorant: For as he who is blind from his Birth, as being blind, cannot comprehend Colours; nor he who is Deaf from his Birth, Sounds; So neither can he who is not an Artist, comprehend the Theorems of Art, whereof he is ignorant. Otherwise, the same Person might be both an Artist, and ignorant of Art; Ignorant of the Art, for he is supposed to be such; An Artist, for he comprehends the Theorems of the Art. Wherefore neither doth an Artist teach him, who is not an Artist: Now if neither the Artist teacheth the Artist; nor the Ignorant, the Ignorant; nor the Ignorant, the Artist; nor the Artist, the Ignorant; (and besides these there is nothing) neither is there a Teacher, nor a Learner; and there being neither a Teacher nor a Learner, the way of Learning likewise is superfluous.

CHAP. XXX.

Whether there is a Way of Learning.

NEvertheless, against this also are raised Doubts: For the way of Teaching is either by Evidence, or by Discourse; But neither by Evidence, nor by Discourse, as we shall prove; therefore the way of Teaching is inextricable. Learning is not acquired by Evidence; for Evidence is of things shewn, but that which is shewn is apparent to all, that which is apparent, inasmuch as it is apparent, is perceptible by all; that which is commonly perceptible by all, is not to be Learned; therfore nothing is to be Learn'd by Evidence.

But neither is there any thing learnt by Discourse; For Discourse either signifies somthing, or signifies nothing; but if it signify nothing, it teacheth nothing. If it signifies something, it signifies it either by Nature, or Imposition; By Nature it signifies not, for all Men understand not all Men, as *Greeks Barbarians*, and *Barbarians Greeks*. If it signifieth by Imposition, it is manifest, that the makers of these Words, first comprehending the things to which they accommodated them, understand them, not, as being taught by these Words the things which they knew not, but, as being put in mind of the things which they knew. Now they who have need to learn that which they know not, not knowing to what things the Words are accommodated, will understand nothing at all : Wherefore, there can be no way of Learning. For the Teacher ought to insinuate into the Learner, an understanding of the Theorems of the Art, which is to be learnt, that so he, comprehending the Collection of them all, may be made an Artist. But Comprehension, as we shewed already, is nothing, therefore there cannot be a way of Teaching. Now if there be nothing Taught, nor a Teacher, nor a Learner, nor a way of Teaching, there will neither be any Discipline nor Doctrine. These Arguments are in general alledged against Discipline and Doctrine.

Another difficulty may be raised against that, which is called, The Art concerning Life. Thus. The thing Taught, that is, Wisdom, we have formerly proved insubsistent; The Teacher likewise, and Learner are insubsistent: For either the Wise, teacheth the Wise, the Art concerning Life; or the Foolish the Foolish; or the Foolish the Wise; or the Wise the Foolish; but none of these teacheth another; therefore the Art concerning Life is not taught. To speak of the rest were superfluous. But if the Wise teach the Foolish Wisdom, and Wisdom be the Science of Good, and Ill, and Indifferent; the Foolish, not having Wisdom, will be Ignorant of the things Good, and Ill, and Indifferent; and, being Ignorant of them, whilst the Wise teacheth him

him things Good, Ill, and Indifferent, he can only hear the Things he saith, but not know them. For if he did understand them whilst he is in his Folly, Folly also might contemplate things Good, Bad, and Indifferent: But according to them, Folly contemplates not these, (otherwise a Foolish Person were Wise) therefore the Foolish understand not by Learning the things said or done by the Wise: but if he understands not, he cannot be taught by him any way, but by Evidence and Discourse, as we said before. Now if that which is called the Art concerning Life, is neither communicated by Learning and Discipline, nor by Nature, it is not to be found out by the Philosophers, who cry it up so much.

CHAP. XXXI.

Whether the Art concerning Life be profitable to him who hath it.

Moreover, though we should grant, that the Art which they dream of concerning Life, may be communicated, yet it will rather appear hurtful and troublesome to those that have it, than beneficial. We will take but one instance for brevity. The Art concerning Life may be profitable to a Wise Man in giving him Continence in Appetition of Good, and Aversion from Ill. For he, whom they call Continent, is said to be such, either for that he hath no Appetition to Ill, nor Aversion from Good; or for that he hath ill Appetitions and Aversions, but masters them by Reason: But as far as he is not in ill Judgments, he is not Continent; for he is not Continent in that which he hath not. And as no Man saith, an Eunuch is Continent in Venereal Pleasures; Or, he who hath no Appetite, Continent in Eating, (for they have not those things, that by Continence might be subdued) in like manner, a Wise Man cannot be said to be Continent, because he hath not in himself the Passion whereof he should be Continent. But if they will say, He is Continent, for that he is in ill Judgments, but overmasters them by Reason: First, they must Grant, that Wisdom hath profited him nothing; forasmuch as he is still in trouble, and needeth help: Next he will be found to be more unfortunate than those, who are said to be bad. For if he hath an Appetite towards any thing, he is wholly disturbed; if he overmasters it with Reason, he containeth the Ill within himself, and thereupon is more troubled than the Ill Person, who suffereth not this; for if he hath an Appetite to any thing, he is troubled; but if he obtain his Desire, the Trouble ceaseth. A Wise Man therefore, either is not Continent as to Wisdom; or if he be, he is of all Men the most unhappy; so that the Art concerning Life affords him not Benefit, but extraordinary Trouble. Now that he, who conceiveth that he hath the Art concerning Life, and thereby knoweth what things are Good and Ill in their own Nature, is exceedingly troubled, as well when the Good are present as when the Ill, we shewed heretofore. We must therefore say, If the subsistence of things Good, Ill, and Indifferent, be not undoubtedly a Knowledge, and the Art concerning Life be perhaps insubsistent also; and though it were granted by supposition to subsist, yet would it bring no profit to those who have it, but on the contrary, great Trouble; the Dogmatists look Superciliously, and take pride in vain, in the Ethical part of that which they call Philosophy. And with this Disputation (not to exceed the limits of a Summary,) we shall close our Third Book of *Pyrrhonian Hypotyposes*, adding only this.

CHAP. XXXII.

Why the Sceptick, sometimes on set purpose, alledgeth weak Arguments.

The *Sceptick*, by reason of his great Humanity, endeavours with Discourse to remedy, as far as in him lies, the Arrogance and rash Insolence of the Dogmatists. As therefore Physicians, in Corporeal Diseases, have Remedies of different sorts, applying violent to those who are violently sick, but gentle to those whose Disease is more gentle; In like manner, the Arguments proposed by the *Sceptick* are not all of equal force; but the more solid, which are best able to overthrow the affection of the Dogmatists, he useth against those who are most violently affected therewith, the lighter against those who have it more lightly and superficially; so as that they may be overthrown by lighter probabilities. Whence it happens that the *Sceptick*, somtimes, alledgeth stronger Probabilities and Arguments; somtimes, on set purpose, weaker, as often perceiving them sufficient to compass his Design.

THE

PART XIII. 533
THE HISTORY of PHILOSOPHY.

The Thirteenth Part,
Containing the EPICUREAN Sect.

EPICVRVS

CHAP. I.

His Country, Parents, Brethren.

(a) Lib. 10.   **E**picurus is by some conceived to have been a Samian; for *Timon* (in (a) *Laertius*) saith, he was the last of the Natural Philosophers that came out of *Samus*. And (b) *Constantinus Porphyrogeneta* conceives, that he derived his Original from *Samus*, as well as *Pythagoras*. But the   (b) Lib. 1. de Themat.

the occasion of this was, for that he passed the first part of his younger years at *Samus*, with his Father and Brethren; for thither came his Father, *Agripeta*, as (c) *Cicero* terms him, (that is, one who claimeth a portion in the division of Lands.) Upon the like ground (d) *Strabo* conceives him a *Lampsacene*, for he lived at *Lampsacum*, and conversed with the chief Personages there. But *Epicurus* indeed was by Country an *Athenian*, as (e) *Laertius*, (f) *Suidas*, and infinite other Writers affirm; whence (g) *Laertius*, about to praise him, begins thus.

(c) De Nat. deor. Lib. 1.
(d) Lib. 13.

(e) Loc. Cit.
(f) In voce *Epicurus*.
(g) Lib. 6.

First Ceres-gifts to Human-Indigence,
Renowned Athens did long since dispense,
And Mens disordered ways by Laws redrest,
And first our Life with greatest Comfort Blest,
When it produc'd a Person of such Worth, (forth.
Whose Breast contain'd, whose Lips all Truth brought

Now forasmuch as the *Athenian* People, being distinguished by Tribes, were dispersed into τοὺς δήμους, the adjacent Towns, which were made free Corporations, even from the time of *Theseus*; *Epicurus* was Born at *Gargettus*, a Town (as (b) *Hesychius* and *Phavorinus* describe it) belonging to the *Ægean* Tribe, where (saith (i) *Plutarch*) *Theseus* overcame the *Pallantidæ*, who conspired against him and *Ægeus*; and where *Eurystheus* (as (k) *Stephanus* relates) was buried. For this reason, he is said, by ((l) *Laertius*, to have been δῆμον Γαργήτιος; by (m) *Statius* termed, the *Gargettick Author*, and the *Gargettick old Man*; by (n) *Cicero* (o) *Ælian*, and others, simply the *Gargettian*.

(h) In *Lexicis*.

(i) In *Theseo*.

(k) De Urb.
(l) Loc. Cit.
(m) Silv. Lib. 1. and 2.
(n) Lib. 15. Ep. 16.
(o) Var. Hist. 4.
(p) Lib. 10.

Laertius (p) (out of *Metrodorus*, in his Treatise of *Nobility*) writes, that *Epicurus* was, of the Family of the *Philaidæ*; the *Philaidæ* were denominated from *Philæus*, the second Son of *Ajax*, who dwelt in *Melite*, and is mentioned by (q) *Plutarch*, who adds, that *Pisistratus* also was of the *Philaidæ*. Of this Family was the Father of *Epicurus*, (according to (r) *Laertius* and others) named *Neocles*, his Mother *Chærestrata*. He is also frequently cited, after the Greek fashion, *Epicurus Neoclis*, sometimes simply termed *Neoclides*, as when compared by (s) *Menander* with *Themistocles*, whose Father was named *Neocles* also. I omit, that his Father was (according to (t) *Strabo*) one of the Two thousand Citizens, whom the *Athenians* sent to *Samus* to share the Land by Lots, whither they had before sent *Pericles* and *Sophocles*, who strictly besieged the revolted *Samians*. I omit also, that he was a Schoolmaster, which (besides *Strabo*) (u) *Cicero* observes, when proceeding to reproach him, *But his little Farm*, saith he, *not being sufficient to maintain him, as I conceive, he became a Schoolmaster.*

(q) In *Solone*.

(r) Loc. Cit.

(s) In *Anthol.* Lib. 3.

(t) Lib. 14.

(u) De Nat. deor Lib. 1.

(w) In voc. *Epicur*.
(x) Loc. Cit.
(y) Adv. Colot. Lib. 2.

(z) De Amor. Frut.

(w) *Suidas* mentions only two Brethren of *Epicurus*, *Neocles* and *Chæredemus*; but (x) *Laertius* (out of *Philodemus* the *Epicurean*) adds a third, *Aristobulus*, whom (y) *Plutarch* sometimes seems to call *Agathobulus*. By what care and Benevolence *Epicurus* gained their Reverence and Affection, is excellently declared by (z) *Plutarch*, who conceives it worthy Admiration, how he came so to win them, and they to be won. That all these died before *Epicurus*, may be inferred from his Will, wherein he ordereth nothing, either to them, or of them, as alive; but only appointed a day to be Celebrated for his Brethren in the Month *Posidæon*. And though of *Chæredemus* there is no further Testimony, yet of *Aristobulus* it is more apparent from (a) *Plutarch* who writes, that *Epicurus* was wholly taken up about *Metrodorus*, *Polyænus*, and *Aristobulus*, Tending them in their Sickness, and Mourning for them when they Dyed. But of *Neocles* it is most manifest, from the same (b) *Plutarch*, relating, that *Epicurus* broke forth into a kind of Joy, mixt with Tears, upon the remembrance of the last Words of *Neocles*. Of how great and painful Sicknesses they died, is sufficiently aggravated by (c) *Plutarch* and (d) *Suidas*.

(a) Adv. Col. 2.

(b) Ibid.

(c) Ibid.
(d) Loc. Cit.

CHAP. II.

The Time of his Birth.

Epicurus was born (as (a) *Laertius* relates out of the Chronology of *Apollodorus*) in the 3d year of the 109th Olympiad, the 7th day of the Month *Gamelion*; at whose Birth, (b) *Pliny* saith, the Moon was Twenty days old. *Hecatombæon* (the First Month) this Year falling in the Summer of the Year 4372. of the *Julian* Period, (now used by Chronologers) it is manifest, that *Gamelion* the same Year, being the 7th Month from *Hecatombæon*, fell upon the beginning of the year 4373. which was before the ordinary Computation from Christ, 341 compleat Years. Now forasmuch as in *January*, in which Month the beginning of *Gamelion* is observ'd to have fallen, there hapned a new Moon in the Attick Horizon, by the Tables of Celestial Motions, the Fourth Day, in the Morning, (or the Third Day, according to the *Athenians*, who, as (c) *Censorinus* saith, reckon their Day from Sun-set to Sun-set) and therefore the Twentieth day of the Moon, is coincident with the Three and twentieth of *January*; It will follow, that *Epicurus* was Born on the 23 day of *January*, if we suppose the same Form of the Year extended from the time of *Cæsar*, upwards. And this in the old Style, according to which the Cycle of the Sun, or of the Dominical Letters for that Year, (it being Bissextile) was B. A. whence the 23 Day of *January* must have been Sunday. But if we suit it with the Gregorian Account, which is Ten days earlier, (now in use with us) we shall find that *Epicurus* was Born on the 2d of *February*, which was Sunday, (for the Dominical Letters must have been E. D.) in the Year before Christ, or the Christian Computation, 341. and consequently in the 1974th Year, compleat, before the beginning of *February* this Year, which is from Christ 1634. Some things here must not be passed by.

(a) Lib. 10.

(b) Lib. 35. Cap. 2.

(c) De Die Nat.

First, That (d) *Laertius* observes *Sosigenes* to have been Archon the same Year, wherein *Epicurus* was Born, and that it was the 7th Year from the death of *Plato*. Moreover, it was the 16th of *Alexander*, for it was, as the same (e) *Laertius* affirms, the Year immediately following that, in which *Aristotle* was sent for to come to him, then 15 Years old.

(d) Lib. 10.

(e) Lib. 1.

Secondly,

Secondly, That (f) *Eusebius* can hardly be excused from a Mistake, making *Epicurus* to flourish in the 112th Olympiad; for at that time, *Epicurus* scarce had pass'd his Childhood, and *Aristotle* began but to flourish in the *Lycæum*, being returned the foregoing Olympiad out of *Macedonia*, as appears from (g) *Laertius*.

(f) In Chron.

(g) Loc. Cit.

Thirdly, That the Error which is crept into (h) *Suidas*, and hath deceived his Interpreter, is not to be allowed, who reports *Epicurus* Born in the 79th Olympiad. I need not take Notice, how much this is inconsistent, not only with other Relations, but even with that which followeth in *Suidas*, where he extends his Life to *Antigonus Gonotas*; I shall only observe, that, for the number of Olympiads, *Suidas* having doubtless set down ϱ θ, which denote the 109th Olympiad, the end of the ϱ was easily defaced in the Manuscript, so as there remained only ο, by which means of ο θ, was made the 79th Olympiad.

(h) In voc. Epi.

Fourthly, That it matters not that the *Chronicon Alexandrinum*, *Georgius Sincellus*, and others, speak too largely of the time wherein *Epicurus* flourished, and that we heed not the Errors of some Persons, otherwise very Learned, who make *Aristippus* later than *Epicurus*, and something of the like kind. Let us only observe what (i) St. *Hierom* cites out of *Cicero, pro Gallio*; A Poet is there mentioned, making *Epicurus* and *Socrates* discoursing together, *Whose Times*, saith *Cicero*, *we know were disjoyned; not by Years, but Ages.*

(i) De vi. Cler.

Fifthly, That the Birth-day of *Epicurus*, taken from *Laertius* and *Pliny*, seems to argue, That amongst the *Athenians* of old, the Civil Months and the Lunary had different Beginnings. This indeed will seem strange, unless we should imagine it may be collected, that the Month *Gamelien* began only from the Full Moon that went before it: For, if we account the 14th day of the Moon to be the 1st of the Month, the 1st of the Moon will fall upon the 7th of the Month. Not to mention that *Epicurus* seems in his Will to appoint his Birth-day to be Celebrated on the First Decad of the days of the Month *Gamelion*, because he was Born in one of them; and then ordaineth something more particularly concerning the 20th of the Moon, for that it was his Birth-day, as we shall relate hereafter. Unless you think it fit to follow the *Anonymous Writer, who affirms, *Epicurus* was Born on the 20th Day of *Gamelion*; but I know not whether his Authority should out-weigh *Laertius*. Certainly, many Errors, and those very great, have been observed in him, particularly by *Meursius*. I shall not take Notice, that the δεκάς of *Gamelion* might perhaps be understood of the 20th of the Moon, hapning within the Month *Gamelion*, from *Cicero*, whose Words we shall cite hereafter. But this by the way.

*This Anonymous Writer is no other than *Scaliger*, whose mistakes for the most part, *Meursius* hath unhappily followed, and taken pains to confute the rest, conceiving him some antient Author.

CHAP. III.

Where he lived in his younger time.

LAertius, (a) out of *Heraclides*, in his Epitome of *Sotion* relates, that a Colony being sent by the *Athenians* to *Samus*, *Epicurus* was bred up there till the 18th year of his Age, in which he went to *Athens*; *Xenocrates* living in the Academy, *Aristotle* at *Chalcis*. (b) *Strabo* adds, that being first brought up, partly at *Samus*, partly at *Teos*, he spent the first part of his Youth at *Athens*, growing up together with *Menander*, the Comick Poet. (c) *Laertius* further relates, That *Alexander* dying, and the *Athenians* being opprest by *Perdiccas*, he went to *Colophon* to his Father, (about the 23 year of his age) and that he lived awhile there. And adds afterwards out of *Apollodorus*, that from the 32 year of his Age to the 37th he lived partly at *Mitylene*, partly at *Lampsacum*, (whither he made a dangerous Voyage, as (d) *Plutarch* observes.) (e) *Suidas* sets down how much time he bestowed in each of these places, One Year at *Mitylene*, Four at *Lampsacum*. *Laertius* adds, that he returned to *Athens*, when *Anaxicrates* was Archon. Now forasmuch as *Anaxicrates* (who succeeded *Charinus*, in the year of whose Magistracy, as (f) *Seneca* notes, *Epicurus* writ to *Polyænus*) was Archon in the 2d Year of the 118th Olympiad, and consequently the 36th of *Epicurus*'s Age, there must necessarily be here a Metachronism of one Year.

(a) Lib. 10.

(b) Lib. 14.

(c) Loc. Cit.

(d) Adv. Col. Lib. 2.
(e) In Epic.

(f) Epist. 18.

Hitherto of the places where *Epicurus* lived in his younger times, partly Learning, partly Teaching, before he setled at *Athens*, where he instituted a Sect.

CHAP. IV.

His Masters.

AS for the Masters which he had, we read, in (a) *Laertius*, that some relate, *Epicurus* was Auditor of *Pamphilus* the Platonick; (b) *Suidas* saith the same; (c) *Cicero* also mentions *Epicurus*, himself acknowledging, that he heard him at *Samus*, but exceedingly slighted his Doctrine. Others also report the same.

(a) Lib. 10.
(b) In Epic.
(c) De Nat. Deor. 1.

Moreover, (d) *Clemens Alexandrinus* and others, report *Nausiphanes* the Pythagorean, Disciple of *Pyrrho*, to have been his Master, though (e) *Sextus Empiricus* writes, That he himself deny'd he had been Disciple to *Nausiphanes*. *Apollodorus*, in his Chronology, reports, That *Epicurus* heard *Lysiphanes* and *Praxiphanes*; but this, saith (f) *Laertius*, he doth not himself acknowledge, in his Epistle to *Euridicus*.

(d) Strom. Lib. 1.

(e) Adv. Mat. 1.

(f) Loc. Cit.

He might indeed have heard *Xenocrates*, and some there are (saith (g) *Cicero*) who think, he did hear him, (as *Demetrius* the *Magnesian* in *Laertius*) but *Epicurus* himself will not allow it.

(g) De Nat. deor. Lib. 1.

I would mention *Democrates*, with whom, (h) *Plutarch* saith, *Epicurus* contested *about Syllables and Accents*; but that I suspect *Democrates* to be falsly read instead of *Democritus*, even from this, that *Plutarch* adds, That *Epicurus* stole all his Opinions from him, which was the common

(h) Adv. Col. 2.

Objection

Objection concerning *Democritus*, as shall be shewn hereafter.

(k) *Eccl. Phyf.* I should mention also *Metrodorus*, whom (k) *Stobæus* calls, καθηγητὴν, his Interpreter; *Doctorem, the Master* of *Epicurus*; and should suspect
(l) *Cap. 1.* he were the same with him, whom (l) *Solinus* makes contemporary with *Diogenes* the Cynick; did not the Opinion, attributed to him of the Infinity of Worlds, and of Atoms, argue, that this was *Metrodorus* the *Chian*, Disciple of *Democritus*, whom *Epicurus* might have, not as *Doctorem*, a Teacher by word of Mouth; but as *Ductorem*, a Leader, by Writing.

Thus also is *Lucian* to be taken, when he saith sportingly, that *Epicurus* was Disciple to *Democritus*, making him to be Disciple of *Aristippus* also, by reason of his Opinion of Pleasure, wherein yet there was a great difference between them, as we shall shew in its due place. But
(m) *Locis citatis.* notwithstanding all we have alledged, (m) *Cicero, Plutarch, Empericus,* and others, write, that *Epicurus* used to boast, That he never had any Master, but was αὐτοδίδακτος, his own Teacher, and attained Philosophy by his own Wit and Industry. And though they seem to mention this, not without some disparagement of him, yet it will easily be granted, that he found out many things of himself, since this was that wherein he took most delight at his last end; and withal, seeing he writ so many Books, filled only with his own Sayings, as we shall shew here-
(n) *Apud La-* after. And indeed (n) *Athenæus*, delivering in
ert. Lib. 10. an Epigram an excellent Sentence of his, concludes, as if *Epicurus* learnt it not from any other, than from the Muses and *Apollo*. Hither also conduce these commendations of *Laertius*:

Dispensing Gifts acquir'd by his own Breast.
And,
He rouz'd his Soul to break the narrow Bonds,
Which fetter Nature———

And others of the same kind.

As for those whom *Epicurus* particularly
(o) *Loc. Cit.* esteem'd, (o) *Laertius* (citing *Diocles*) affirms, he was chiefly addicted so *Anaxagoras*, (though in some things he contradicted him) and *Archelaus*, who was Master to *Socrates*. Of *Democritus* we shall speak hereafter. I only add, that *Epicurus* much admiring the conversation of *Pyrrho*, continually question'd his Disciple *Nau-*
(p) *Lib. 9.* *siphanes* concerning him; as (p) *Laertius* saith, in the Life of *Pyrrho*.

CHAP. V.

When, and upon what occasion, he addicted himself to Philosophy, and instituted a Sect.

(a) In *Epic.* *Suidas* (a) saith, That he began to apply himself to Philosophy in the 12th Year of his Age, which is confirmed by others, who
(b) *Lib. 10.* wrote his Life, as (b) *Laertius* relates. But
(c) *Ibid.* *Epicurus* himself (alledged by the same (c) *Laertius*) attesteth, That he did not addict himself to Philosophy till he was Fourteen Years
(d) *Ibid.* old. *Hermippus* (in (d) *Laertius*) saith, that, lighting accidentally upon the Books of *Democritus*, he betook himself to Philosophy; but *Apollodorus* the *Epicurean*, in the First Book of the Life of *Epicurus*, affirms, he applied himself to Philosophy upon dislike of the Sophists and Grammarians, for that they could not explain what *Hesiod* meant by *Chaos*. (e) *Sextus* (e) *Adv. Phys.* *Empiricus* having related this more fully, it will *Lib. 2.* not be amiss to transcribe his Words. Having proposed some Doubts concerning these Verses of *Hesiod*,

First, Chaos, next broad-Breasted Earth was made,
The seat of all———

He adds, and some affirm, That this was the occasion of *Epicurus*'s sudden applying himself to Philosophy; for being yet very young, He asked a Grammarian who read to him [*Chaos* was first made :] Of what was *Chaos* made, if it was first made? The other answering, That it did not belong to him to Teach such things, but to those who were called Philosophers. Then, saith *Epicurus*, I must go to those, for they are the Persons that know the Truth of Beings.

To omit, what some affirm, that he was, as *Hermippus* ((f) in *Laertius*) relates, before he (f) *Loc. Cit.* addicted himself to Philosophy, a Schoolmaster : And though the (g) *Stoicks*, who were much his (g) *Ibid.* Enemies, reproached him, that with his Father he taught Boys for a small stipend, and that with his Mother he went from House to House reading expiatory Prayers; I observe, that after he had applyed himself to Philosophy, he instituted a School, being Thirty two years old, as (h) *Laertius* relates, and this first (h) *Ibid.* at *Mitylene*, afterwards at *Lampsacum*, as may be collected from the relation of *Suidas*, but had Disciples also from *Colophon*, as (i) *Laertius* re- (i) *Ibid.* lates.

Returning to *Athens* in the 36th, or 37th Year of his Age, *He awhile Discours'd* (saith (k) (k) *Lib. 1.* *Laertius*) *of Philosophy in Publick with others, but afterwards instituted a Sect in Private, denominated from him.* At first indeed, admiring the Doctrine of *Democritus*, he professed himself a *Democritian*, as *Plutarch* (l) relates; but afterwards, (l) *Ad. Col. 1.* for that he changed or added many things, his Followers were from him called *Epicureans*.

CHAP. VI.

His School.

Whereas other Professors of Sects made choice of particular places in *Athens*, as the *Academy*, the *Lycæum*, and the like, he purchased a very pleasant Garden, for Fourscore *Minæ*, where he lived with his Friends and Disciples, and taught Philosophy. Thus, amongst others, (a) *Laertius* citing *Apollodorus*. (b) *Pliny* (a) *Loc. Cit.* writes, that *Epicurus* first brought into *Athens*, (b) *Lib. 19.* the Custome of having under the name of *Hortus* a Garden, the Delights of Fields and Country Mansions within the City itself, whereas, untill his Time, 'twas not the fashion to have those kinds of Mansions (*Rura*) in Towns.

Hence we may conjecture, that this was the place which (c) *Pausanias* reports to have been (c) *In Attic.* called, even in his time, *the Gardens*, adding, That there was in it a Statue of *Venus*, made by
Alcamenes,

(d) In Imag.

(e) Ad Attic. Eph. 2. 24.
(f) Sat. 14.

Alcamenes, one of the most eminent things in *Athens*, (as may be gathered also from *(d) Lucian*) and that the Temple of *Venus*, with the Statue of Celestial *Venus*, did joyn to it. This Garden is often mentioned in the Plural number by *(e) Cicero*, *(f) Juvenal*, and others, and sometimes diminutively, *Hortulus*, as *Virgil*; But, howsoever it be us'd, it is commonly taken for the Sect or Doctrine delivered in that place by *Epicurus* and his Scholars. When *Sextus Empiricus* calls the *Epicureans*, the *Philosophers of the Garden* (as the Stoicks, the Philosophers of the Stoa or Cloister,) and *Apollodorus* being in his time the Master of the Garden, was, as *Laertius* affirms, called κηποτύραννος the Garden King.

(g) In Lexic.

(h) In Lexic.

Besides this Garden, which, with Houses belonging to it, joyned upon the City, *Epicurus* had a House in *Melite*, which was a Town of the *Cecropian* Tribe, as *(g) Suidas* affirms, inhabited by *Philæus*, one of the Ancestors of *Epicurus*, as was formerly said. having (according to *(h) Phavorinus*) a famous Temple Dedicated to *Hercules*. Hither *Epicurus* sometimes retired with his Disciples, and at last bequeathed it to his Successors, as we shall declare hereafter.

CHAP. VII.

How he lived with his Friends.

(a) Lib. 10.

EPicurus after his return to *Athens*, at what time *Anaxicrates* was Archon, went only twice or thrice to *Ionia* to visit his Friends, but lived all the rest of his time at *Athens*, unmarried, nor would ever forsake his Country, though at that time reduc'd to great extremities, as *(a) Laertius* observes. The worst of which was, when *Demetrius* besieged *Athens*, about the 44th Year of *Epicurus*'s Age. How great a Famine at that time oppress'd the City is describ'd by *(b) Plutarch*. But it is observable, that having related a Story of the Contest between a Father and his Son, about a dead Mouse which had fallen from the top of a House; He adds, *They say, that* Epicurus *the Philosopher sustain'd his Friends with Beans, which he shared equally amongst them*.

(b) In Demetr.

(c) Loc. cit.

(d) De occ. viv.

Epicurus therefore lived all the rest of his time at *Athens*, together with so many Friends and Disciples, whom he conversed with, and instructed, as that whole Cities were not sufficient to contain them (they are the words of *(c) Laertius,*) who resorted to him, not only from *Greece* but all other parts, and lived with him in his Gardens, as he cites out of *Apollodorus*; but especially from *Asia*, and particularly from *Lampsacrum*, and from *Egypt*, as may be collected out of *(d) Plutarch*. Of the Temperance and Frugality of his Diet we shall speak hereafter. As to his living with his Friends, it is remarkable what *Diocles*, in *Laertius*, and others, relate, That *Epicurus* did not, as *Pythagoras*, who said the Goods of Friends ought to be in common, appoint them to put their Estates into one joint Stock, (for that imply'd a Distrust, not a Friendship) but that any one upon occasion should be freely supply'd by the rest. This will appear more manifest hereafter. In the mean time, we must not omit an eminent place of *(e) Cicero*; Neither (saith he) did *Epicurus* approve "Friendship in Discourse only, but much more "by Life, Actions, and Manners, which how "great a thing it is, the Fables of the Ancients "declare. For amongst the many various Sto- "ries repeated from utmost Antiquity, there "are hardly found three pair of Friends, from "*Theseus* his Time down to *Orestes*. But how "many great companies of Friends, and how "unanimously Loving did *Epicurus* keep in one "House, and that very little? Which is done "even unto this day by the *Epicureans*. Thus Cicero.

(e) P. De Sp. Lib.

Amongst the rest of his Friends, *(f) Laertius* mentions *Polystratus*, who seems to be the same, of whom together with *Hippoclides* another *Epicurean*, *(g) Valerius Maximus* gives a strange account. I shall insert the Words of *Valerius*, the rather because they will serve to illustrate part of *Epicurus*'s Will hereafter, concerning Communication of the Goods of his Disciple: They are these. "Hither may aptly "be referred *Polystratus* and *Hippoclides*, Philo- "sophers, who, born the same day, Followers "of the Sect of the same Master, *Epicurus*, joyn- "ed together in the common possession of E- "state and Maintenance of that School, died "very old, in the same moment of time. So "equal a Society of Fortune and Friendship, "who thinks not to have been begotten, bred, "and ended, in the bosom of Celestial Concord? Thus he.

(f) Loc. Cit. Cap. 8.

(g) Lib. 1. Cap. 8.

CHAP. VIII.

His Friends and Disciples.

BEing now to give a Catalogue of the chiefest of his Friends and Disciples, we must not in the first place pass by the Three Brethren of *Epicurus*, mention'd in the beginning, for they by his advice studied Philosophy with him, as *Philodemus* (in *(a) Laertius*) affirms. *(b) Plutarch* adds, That they took in the Philosophy of their Brother, as greedily as if they had been *Fra*. Divinely inspired, Believing and Professing from their first Youth, That there was not any Man wiser than *Epicurus*. The most eminent of the Three was *Neocles*: He declaring from a Boy, That his Brother was the wisest of Mortals; added, as a wonder, That his Mother could contain so many and so great Atomes, as, by their Convention, made up such a wise Man; as *(c) Plutarch* relates. Hence it appearing that *Neocles* followed not any Philosophy of his own, but that of his Brother, I know not why *(d)* some affirm, that he introduced a Sect like that of his Brother, unless perhaps they ground it upon that place of *(e) Suidas*, where he saith, that *Neocles* writ concerning his Sect. But who sees not, it may be understood, that he writ concerning the Sect which he himself professed, but was instituted by another, especially for that there is nothing said any where of the Sect of the *Neoclidæ*.

(a) Lib. 10.
(b) De Amor. Fra.

(c) Adv. Col. 2.

(d) As Genebr. Lib. 2. Chronol.

(e) In Epic.

Observe by the way, that this Saying (λάθε βιώσας, *Live closely*,) which *(f) Plutarch* oppugns, and is brought in *(g)* amongst the Pro-

(f) Lib. de Co.
(g) Erasm. Chil.

Proverbial Speeches) did belong to this *Neocles*, as the same (h) *Suidas* affirmeth. *(h) In Neocl.*

To his Three Brethren, may be added those Three Friends who, (as we read in (i) *Seneca*) became great Persons, through the Conversation of *Epicurus*. *(i) Epist. 6.*

Metrodorus is to be first nam'd; for he was, as (k) *Cicero* saith, almost another *Epicurus*. (l) *Strabo* plainly declareth, he was of *Lampsacum*. For whereas *Laertius* seems to say he was an *Athenian*, the place is very corrupt; especially seeing it is manifest he was not an *Athenian*, from this Antithesis of (m) *Cicero*, *How much was* Epicurus *happier for being in his Country, than* Metrodorus *for being at* Athens; because *Athens* was not the Country of *Metrodorus*: The Text of (n) *Laertius* is this " He had many Disciples " but the most eminent were *Metrodorus* Ἀθυναῖον " and *Timocrates*, and *Sandes* a *Lampsacene*, who " from his first acquaintance with the Man, ne- " ver left him, &c. For my part I am of opinion, that these words Ἀθυναῖον, ϰ Τιμοκράτην, ϰ Σάνδων should be quite expunged, for if you take them away, the rest joyns together very well; if you admit them, they will not hang together: for it was *Metrodorus* that was indeed a *Lampsacene*, and with whom all the rest that follows agreeth, not *Sandes*, whom, besides other things, it is false, that *Epicurus* should mention in his Will. And though (o) *Casaubon* conceives, that Ἀθυναῖον may be the proper name of a Man, yet is it strange that we hear nothing elsewhere, aswell of *Athenæus* as of *Sandes*, as *Epicureans*; Since *Laertius* in this place reckons up his most eminent Disciples; but taking these away, the Three, viz. *Metrodorus*, *Polyænus*, and *Hermachus* are described in a continued Series; who, as we said, are put together by *Seneca*, as most eminent. As for *Timocrates*, he is mentioned afterwards by the way, when he comes to name *Metrodorus* as his Brother, and seems here to be inserted amiss. The occasion upon which these Names crept into the Text I suspect to be, that perhaps some Transcriber had noted in the Margent, that what was delivered in the Text, was confirmed also by *Athenæus* (Author of the *Deipnosophistæ*: For in him there is something concerning the *Epicureans*) and by *Timocrates* (for he is also cited by *Laertius*,) and by one *Sandes* (perhaps *Suidas*, or some other.) That many things have heretofore been inserted out of the Margents into the Texts themselves, by carelesness of the Transcribers, is most manifest.

(k) De fin. Lib. 2.
(l) Lib. 13.

(m) Loc. Cit.

(n) Lib. 10.

(o) In Not. ad Laert.

Metrodorus therefore was by Country a *Lampsacene* (not the same with that Friend of *Anaxagoras*, whom (p) *Laertius* mentions of the same Name) born in the 12th Year of *Epicurus*'s age; for, dying in the 53 Year of his age, (the coherence of the Words and Sense makes me think it should be read Μιτρκοδώρον ἄγοντα) and that being the 7th before the death of *Epicurus*, who lived to the 72 Year, it is evident, that the Year of his Birth must fall upon the 12th of *Epicurus*'s. From the first time that *Metrodorus* became acquainted with *Epicurus*, (which might happen in the 22 Year of his age, at what time *Epicurus* lived at *Lampsacum*) he never (as we began to say out of *Laertius*) parted from him, but one six Months, in which time he was ab- *(p) Lib. 2.*

sent at home, and thence returned to *Epicurus*. He had a Sister, *Batis*, whom he Married to *Idomeneus*, and a Concubine named *Leontium*. He had Children, whom *Epicurus* recommended in his Will, and in the Epistle which he writ dying; and particularly a Son, named *Epicurus*. He was a very good Man, undaunted with Troubles, on Death it self, as *Epicurus* himself, in *Laertius* attests. He had the Dropsie; (q) for *Cornelius Celsus* writes, That whilst he was sick of that Disease, and could no longer abstain, as was convenient, from Drinking; he used, after he had forborn a great while, to Drink, and cast it up again. But whether it was of this Disease, or of some other, that he died, is not certain. The Books which he writ, are by *Laertius*, reckoned to be these; *Against Physicians* III. *Of the Senses*, to Timocrates. *Of Magnanimity*. *Of the Infirmity* of Epicurus. *Against the Dialecticks*, *Against the Sophists* IX. *Of the way to Wisdom*. *Of Alteration*. *Of Riches*. *Against* Democritus. *Of Nobility*. Besides which, (r) *Plutarch* cites his Books, *Of Philosophy*. *Of the Poets*. *Against* Timarchus. Likewise (s) *Clemens Alexandrinus* cites a Treatise, *That the cause of Felicity which comes from our selves is greater than that which comes from other things*. But of *Metrodorus*, enough. *(q) Lib. 3. Cap. 21.*

(r) Adv. Col.
(s) Strom. 2.

Polyænus was Son of *Athenodorus*, a *Lampsacene* also. He was *a great Mathematician*, (t) to use the words of *Cicero*, and to comprise much in little) Modest and Amiable, as *Philodemus* (in (u) *Laertius*) saith. *(t) Acad. 3.*
(u) Lib. 10.

Hermachus was Son of *Agemorchus*, a *Mitylenean*, his Father of mean quality. At first he studied Rhetorick, but afterwards became so knowing in Philosophy, that *Epicurus* dying, committed the Government of the School to him. He dyed at *Lyssas*. There is a great mention of him in *Epicurus*'s Will. His Writings, which *Laertius* commends for excellent these. *Epistolicks*, concerning Empedocles, XXII. *Of Disciplines*, (for *Casaubon* well reads not Μαθητῶν, but Μαθημάτων) Two Books. *Against* Plato. *Against* Aristotle.

To these must be added *Leontius*, a *Lampsacene*, whom (w) *Plutarch* calleth one of the most eminent Disciples of *Epicurus*; adding, That this was he who writ to *Lycophron*, that *Epicurus* honoured *Democritus*. *(w) Adv. Col. l. 1.*

Moreover, *Colotes* and *Idomeneus*, *Lampsacenes* also. Of the former we shall have occasion to speak oftner, especially, because of the Two Books which *Plutarch* writ against him. (x) *Laertius* elsewhere writes, that *Menedemus* the Cynick was his Disciple, (unless perhaps there were some other *Colotes* of *Lampsacum*) The same *Colotes* it is, who, cited by (y) *Macrobius*, argues, that *Plato* ought not to have invented the Fable of *Erus*, because no kind of Fiction agreeth with the Professors of Truth. The later, *Idomeneus*, *Epicurus* design'd to make famous by his Letters, as indeed he did, which appears from (z) *Seneca*: " I will alledge, saith he, *Epicurus* for an example, who writing to *Idomeneus*, (then a Minister of State employ'd in " great Affairs) to persuade him, from a specious kind of Life, to true settled Glory. If, saith he, you affect Glory, my Epistles will make you more famous, than all those things which *(x) Lib. 6*
(y) In Somn. Scip. Lib. 1.
(z) Epist. 21.

' which you esteem, and for which you are
' esteemed. Who would have known *Idomeneus*, if *Epicurus* had not graved his Name in his
' Letters? All those Magistrates and Princes,
' even the King himself, from whom *Idomeneus*
' derived his Title, are now suppressed by a deep
' Oblivion. Thus he, And these (saith *Laertius*)
' were the more eminent Disciples.

But to these may be added two out of *Valerius*, already mentioned, *Polystratus* and *Hippoclides*; especially seeing *Laertius* reckons *Polystratus* as Successor to *Hermachus*, unless the *Polystratus* who is joined to *Hippoclides*, were not the same with him that succeeded *Hermachus*.

We might add *Timocrates* of *Lapsacum*, Brother of *Metrodorus*; but he seems to have fallen off, not brooking the Reprehensions of his Brother. We shall therefore rather join to these *Mus*, the Servant of *Epicurus*, who, as *Laertius* affirms, became an eminent Philosopher, not omitted by (a) *Agellius*, and (b) *Macrobius*, in reckoning up those, who, of Servants, became famous for Philosophy.

(a) Lib. 1. cap. 12.
(b) Saturn. 1. 11.

To omit *Apelles*, somwhere derided by *Plutarch*, we must here mention three Women, who together with others of the same Sex, learnt Philosophy of *Epicurus*. One *Leontium*, who studied Philosophy under *Epicurus*, as (c) *Athenæus* recites, and may also be collected from (d) *Cicero*, who saith, she wrote a Book against *Theophrastus*, in an elegant Style, and in the *Attick* Dialect. The second, *Themista*, Daughter of *Zoilus*, a *Lampsacene*, Wife of the formentioned *Leontius*. Of her, besides the Testimonies which we shall hereafter alledge, (e) *Clemens Alexandrinus* taketh express notice. The third, *Philenis*, whom (f) *Athenæus* affirms to have written many things; adding that the obscene Books ascribed to her, were put forth under her Name, by *Polycrates* the Sophist, to discredit the Woman.

(c) Lib. 13.
(d) De Nat. deor.
(e) Strom. lib. 4.
(f) Lib. 8. and 10.

To these may be added *Herodotus*, to whom *Epicurus* writ a little Epitome of Physick, extant in *Laertius*; and who amongst other things according to the same *Laertius*, writ a Book *Of the youth* of *Epicurus*.

Pithocles, to whom *Epicurus* writ of Superior things; extant in *Laertius*, and who affirmed, that when he was but 18 years old, he had not his equal for Ingenuity in all *Greece*, as *Plutarch* relates.

Menœceus, to whom *Epicurus* writ that Epistle concerning *Morality*, which is extant in *Laertius*; its beginning recited also by *Clemens Alexandrinus*.

Timocrates, Son of *Demetrius*, a *Potamian*, and *Amynomachus*, Son of *Philocrates* of *Bate*, whom *Epicurus* made the Executors of his Will.

Nicanor, whom *Epicurus* recommended to the care of the said Executors.

Eurydicus, one of those to whom, as *Laertius*, saith, he writ Epistles.

Dositheus, and his Sons *Pyrrho*, and *Hegesinax*, to whom *Epicurus* wrote a consolatory Letter upon the death of their Father, as we find in *Plutarch*.

I omit *Polymedes*, *Antidorus*, and others, to be mentioned hereafter in treating of his Books.

CHAP. IX.

How much he writ.

NEither did *Epicurus* spend the time in giving his Disciples only Oral Instructions, but bestowed much pains in composing several Books. But to understand how much he labour'd herein, by comparison with other Philosophers, hear but *Laertius* in his (a) Preface; *Many things*, saith he, Zeno writ; *more*, Xenophanes; *more*, Democritus; *more*, Aristotle; *more*, Epicurus; *more*, Chrysippus. Where we see that *Epicurus*, as to multitude of Writings came short only of *Chrysippus*. But observe, that elsewhere (b) *Laertius*, to shew he may be thought to have exceeded *Chryssippus* herein, cites *Apollodorus* the *Athenian*, who, saith he, *to shew that what Epicurus writ of himself, not borrowed from any other, did far exceed the Books of* Chrysippus, *saith expresly thus: If a Man should take out of the Books of* Chrysippus, *the things which he hath borrowed of others, the Paper will be left blank*. But that this may not seem strange, the same (c) *Laertius* elsewhere relates, that *Chrysippus*, for his emulation of *Epicurus* in writing much, was called by *Carneades*, the *Parasite of his Books*, because, *if* Epicurus *writ any thing*, (read γεάψαι, not γεάψας) *he would affect to write as much*. Whence it came to pass, that he often wrote the same things over again, and whatsoever came next to hand, and presently thrust it in for haste, without correction; and brought in so many Testimonies of other Writers, that his Books were filled up only with them, as may be found in Zeno also, and Aristotle. Thus *Laertius* of *Chrysippus*, but of *Epicurus* not so: For (d) he relates, that his Volumes amounted to Three hundred, *in which*, saith he, *there is no testimony of any other Author, but they are all the very words of* Epicurus. Which I observe, to shew (seeing *Epicurus* wrote so many things, (e) *a great Writer*, as he terms him, and exceeding for multitude of Books, so as (f) *Origen* charging *Celsus* with temerity, objects as a thing he conceives impossible, *There is not any of us, who*, saith he, *knows all that* Epicurus *writ*) his fluent Vein, and how he was chiefly employ'd.

(a) Lib. 1.
(b) Lib. 17.
(c) Lib. 10.
(d) Ibid.
(e) Ibid.
(f) Adv. Cels. lib. 7.

CHAP. X.

What Writings of his are particularly mentioned by Authors.

HEre it is fit we give a kind of Catalogue of his Books, not of all he wrote, but of those whose Titles are extant in other Authors. I say their Titles, for the Books themselves have so miscarried by the injury of time, that besides some few Compendiums preserv'd by *Laertius*, and some Fragments scatter'd up and down amongst several Writers, there is not any thing of them remaining, at least, as yet known to us.

To begin with those, which *Laertius* accounts the best, they are ranked thus.

Zzz 2
Of

Of Nature, XXXVII. They are sometimes cited simply, *Of Nature*, somtimes with the number of the Books, as when *Laertius* hereafter in his Life, cites the I. the XI. XII. XIV. XV. (*a*) *Galen* also mentions the Title and number or the Books.

(*a*) Comment. in 1. lib. Hipp. de nat. hum.
(*b*) lib. 2. chap. 1.

Of Atoms and *Vacuum*, so usually cited, (*b*) *Cleomenes* seemeth to mean the same under another name, *Of the Principles of all things.*

Of Love.

An Epitome of things appertaining to Natural Philosophers. This Epitome was twofold, Great and Little; both are cited by *Laertius*; the Lesser, that which is written to *Herodotus.*

Against the Megarick (or *Dialectick*) *Philosophers, Doubts.* These *Doubts* seem chiefly to have concerned certain Moral Arguments, as concerning Justice, Marriage, and Dower: For this seems to be the same, which *Laertius*, and (*c*) *Plutarch* cite under the name of *Doubts*, without adding, *To the Megaricks.*

(*c*) Adv. col. lib. 1.

Κύριαι δόξαι, *Maxims*, or, as (*d*) *Cicero* interprets, *Maximè ratæ Sententiæ, because*, saith he, they are *Sentences briefly express'd, which conduce exceedingly to living happily.* He (*f*) elsewhere calls them *select*, and *short Sentences.* (*g*) *Sextus* seems to call them *Memorable Sayings. Laertius* hath put them at the end, and (*h*) *Lucian* somewhere commends them, as (*i*) *Cicero* the Book of *Crantor,* which is, saith he, *not Great indeed, but Golden, and*, as *Panætius advised Tubero, to be gotten by heart.* He was in Opinion different from *Suidas,* who calls them *wicked Notions.*

(*d*) Definit. lib. 2.
(*f*) De nat. deor. 2.
(*g*) Adv. Physs. lib. 2
(*h*) in Pseudon.
(*i*) Lib. 4. Acad.

Περὶ αἱρήσεων, *Of Elections*, so I conceive it ought rather to be rendred than of *Sects*; because in this Book *Epicurus* seems not to design a History of Sects, but Moral Institution, which is conversant about the Choice of things, as *Laertius* declares at the end of *Epicurus*'s Epistle to *Menæceus.* Not to mention that he teacheth the Ethick kind to consist only of Election and Avoidance. For which reason, the Book, which is ordinrily and next to this cited,

Περὶ φυτῶν, *Of Plants*, ought rather to be entituled, Περὶ φευκτῶν, *Of things to be avoided*; as well for coherence of the Title, as for that *Epicurus*, almost wholly taken up with Moral Philosophy, scarce treated of any particular subject in Physick, unless they were such as conduced to take away vain terrors from the minds of Men; of which kind, this of *Plants* could not be. Moreover, because in Manuscripts this Title is connexed to the former by the Conjunction &, we may conjecture, that the Inscription was, Περὶ αἱρήσεων & περὶ φυγῶν; or under a single Title, Περὶ αἱρήσεων, & φυγῶν; *Of Election and Avoidance.* Yet might the Inscription have been in the Plural number, forasmuch as it is afterwards said, *Elections and Avoidances are dijudicated from Pleasure and Grief.*

Of the End; So this Book is generally cited, as amongst others, by (*k*) *Plutarch.* Neither doth *Cicero* seem to mean any other, though he cite a Book *Of the ends of Good and Evil.*

(*k*) Adv. col. 2.

Of the Criterie, or the Canon; or, as (*l*) *Cicero* translates it, *Of the Rule, and of Judgment.* But if instead of Judgment we render it *Judicatory*, the force of the word will be more fully express'd.

(*l*) De nat. deor. 1.

Chæredemus; or, *Of the Gods.* This is one o those Books, which *Epicurus* entituled by the Names of his Brethren and Friends, that, being dead, their Names might not be forgotten, as (*m*) *Plutarch* observes.

(*m*) De occ. viv.

Of Sanctity, or, *Hegesianax.* This perhaps is he, whom (*n*) *Plutarch* terms, *Hegetoanax,* concerning whose Death, *Epicurus* wrote to his Parents; unless perhaps it were he who wrote Histories, and *Troica*, cited by (*o*) *Athenæus*; for he was of *Alexandria*, and *Epicurus* had Friends out of *Ægypt.*

(*n*) Adv. Col. 2.
(*o*) Lib. 3. & 9.

Of Lives, IV. Which is all one as if the Inscription had been, *Of Life and Manners.* Neither doth *Epicurus* seem in these Books to relate the Story of some eminent Persons, as *Plutarch* and *Laertius* have done in their Books of Lives, but to give Rules, whereby to lead a quiet Life, as may plainly enough be collected from the Catalogue of the Moral Treatises, and the Places cited out of this by *Laertius.* The word *Lives* seems here to be taken in the same Sense, as with (*p*) *Plutarch*, when he speaketh of *the Difference of Lives and Politicks*, which the Interpreter well renders, *Of Manners and Publick Institutes.* Of these Books, are hereafter cited by *Laertius* the first and second.

(*p*) Is Lycurgo.

Of Just Action.

Neocles to Themista. This seems to have been that *Neocles* who was Brother to *Epicurus*, not his Father; for in like manner he called other of his Books after the Names of his Brothers.

The Banquet, cited by (*q*) *Plutarch*, (*r*) *Athenæus*, and others, (*s*) *Plutarch* mentions Questions handled in it, concerning the heat of Wine, the time of Coition. *Laertius*, concerning troubles about Marriage, &c.

(*q*) Symp. quæst. 1. 1.
(*r*) Deipn. 5.
(*s*) Adv. Col. 1. Symp. quæst. 3. 3.

Eurylochus to Metrodorus. I guess, that this *Eurylochus* was the same with that *Eurydicus*, to whom, as we said formerly, *Epicurus* writ; but the thing is uncertain.

Of Seeing.

Of the Angle, which is in the Atome.

Of Touching; or perhaps, *Of the tangibility of Atoms*: for (*t*) *Epicurus* called *Vacuum* τὸ ἀναφές, *that which cannot be touched.*

(*t*) Apud Laert.

Of Fate.

Of Passions. Sentences to Timocrates.

Περιγνωστικὸν, *Præcognitorium*; so I render it, because he seemeth in this to have discoursed of the Precognitive Faculty.

Protreptick, (Exhortatory) that is, *Discourse*; for so *Isocrates* and *Clemens*, expresly.

Of Images, εἴδωλα, *Simulacra, Imagines, Species, Formæ, Spectra*; so several Persons variously interpret them, which are now commonly termed *Intentional Species.*

Of Phantasie, or the Impression thereof, which appeareth in the knowing Faculty; for neither did *Epicurus*, nor most of the ancient Philosophers, understand by this word, as we now for the most part do, the Faculty it self.

Aristobulus; this Book bears the Name of *Epicurus*'s third Brother.

Of Musick; viz. as it conduceth to Manners; for this may be collected from (*u*) *Plutarch* and (*w*) *Empiricus.*

(*u*) Adv. Col. 2
(*w*) Adv. Math.

Of

PART XIII.   EPICURUS.   541

Of Gifts and *Gratitude*, mentioned by (x) *Empiricus*, who cites somthing Grammatical out of it.   *(x) Adv. Gram.*

Polymedes, he seems to have been some Friend or Disciple of *Epicurus*.

Timocrates, III. Whether meaning the Brother of *Metrodorus*, or the Executor of his Will, or some other. Hence I should believe, that by *Laertius* was cited the third Book of *Timocrates*, or written by *Timocrates*; but that instead of Τιμοκράτης, I suspect it should be written by Τιμοκράτη, relating to the third Book, which, by *Epicurus*, was so intitled. This the Text seems to confirm.

Metrodorus, V. That this was the same *Metrodorus*, of whom we have spoken formerly, cannot be doubted. From the first Book, cited by *Laertius*, may be collected, that *Epicurus* related the Story of *Metrodorus*'s Life.

Antidorus, II. This *Antidorus* is mentioned by (y) *Plutarch*, and perhaps by (z) *Laertius* also, in the Life of *Heraclides*, if we there read *Antidorus* for *Autodorus*.   *(y) Adv. Col. 1.*   *(z) Lib. 5.*

Περὶ νόσων δόξαι περὶ Μίθρην, *Of the South-Winds, Sentences to Mithres*. But parhaps the Title ought rather to be read, περὶ νόσων, *Of Diseases*, as well for the reasons alledged about the Title περὶ φυτῶν, as for that these Sentences seem not to have been several Opinions, concerning some particular Winds, as Moral Sentences to moderate the pain of Diseases. This seems to be the same *Mithres* a *Syrian*, whom *Metrodorus* relieved, as (a) *Plutarch* hath several times delivered; and the same, whom (b) *Laertius* relates to have been the Steward of *Lysimachus*'s House; adding, that *Mithres* saying to *Theodorus*, Thou seemest not only not to acknowledge Gods, but Kings also. *Theodorus* repli'd, How can I but acknowledge Gods, who think thee an Enemy to the Gods?   *(a) Adv. Col.*   *(b) Lib. 10.*

Callistolas; who, it may be presumed, was some Friend of *Epicurus*'s.

Of a Kingdom, mentioned by (c) *Plutarch*.   *(c) Adv. Col. 2.*

Aneximenes; perhaps the same *Lampsacene* who is mentioned by (d) *Strabo*, and whom both (e) *Plutarch* and (f) *Laertius* seem to mean; for, though he were one of *Alexander*'s Masters, yet did he survive him, (for he wrote his Actions,) and was, according to *Suidas*, Disciple to *Diogenes* the *Cynick*, and consequently younger than he; whereas *Diogenes* died in the eighteenth year of *Epicurus*'s Age, viz. in the beginning of the 114th Olympiad.   *(d) Lib 14.*   *(e) in Pub.*   *(f) Lib. 2.*

Epistles. Of these, four are extant in *Laertius*; one, to *Herodotus*, which was, as we said, the lesser Epitome, and under that Name cited by (g) *Achilles Tatius*, *Of Natural things*. The second, to *Pythocles*, *Of Meteors*, or Superior things, as well Celestial, as all others above the Earth. The third, to *Menæceus*, *Of Manners*. The last is very short, which he writ Dying, to *Idomeneus*. That, besides these, he writ innumerable others, may be collected from (h) *Plutarch*, (i) *Laertius* and others. For *Plutarch*, for example, cites an Epistle of his, *To Anaxarchus*; (k) *Laertius* his Epistle, *To Aristobulus*; also an Epistle, *To his Friends at Mytilene*. This seems to be the same with that, which (l) *Sextus Empiricus* cites thus; *To the Philosophers at Mytilene*. But *Laertius* implyeth, there were more   *(g) in Phæn. Arat.*   *(h) Adv. Col. 1.*   *(i) Lib. 7.*   *(k) Lib. 10.*   *(l) Adv. Math. 1.*

which bore that Inscription, ἐν τῇ πρὸς τοὺς ἐν Μιτυλήνῃ φιλοσόφους; so as there might be one of them, Supposititious. In the same rank may be reckoned his Epistles, concerning several Institutions of Life hinted by (m) *Laertius* cited by (n) *Athenæus* and (o) *Eusebius*. I omit that the same (p) *Athenæus* mentions his Epistles to *Hermachus*; and not to enquire after any more, the highest in repute were those written to *Idomeneus*, as we may understand from (q) *Seneca*, who also citeth something excellent out of his Epistles to *Polyænus*. Amongst those to *Idomeneus* was that, out of which (r) *Michael Apostolius* cites a Fragment, containing the Original of the Proverb, *These shall be to thee both Pythian and Delian*, apply'd to those that shall die within a short time, though *Erasmus* affirms the Proverb it self to be cited out of *Menander*.   *(m) in Protag. Lib. 9.*   *(n) Deipn. 8.*   *(o) De Præpar Lib. 15.*   *(p) Deipn. 13.*   *(q) Epist. 18.*   *(r) Cent. 16. Paræm. 95.*

As to the Epistles, we shall by the way observe, that *Epicurus* used to write, by way of Salutation in the beginning of his Epistles, somtimes χαίρειν, Joy. somtimes εὖ πράττειν, well to to do; somtimes εὖ διάγειν, somtimes σπουδαίως ζῆν, well to live; ὑγιαίνειν, Health. For that which we read in (ſ) *Laertius*, ἢ ἐν τῇ ἐπιστολῇ αὐτὸς τῆς χαίρειν, ἐν πράττειν ἢ σπουδαίως ζῆν ἄριστον, is defective, there seems some word wanting to the Sentence; neither doth the word ἄριστον seem to belong to the form of Salutation. And besides, these words, ἀντὶ τοῦ, exclude χαίρειν from the Epicurean form of Salutation; whereas this word is not only put before his Epistles, extant in *Laertius*, but it is rendred by (t) *Cicero* also when he alledgeth that which he wrote at his Death. For this reason, when heretofore I would, in the room of these two words, have put ἐτίθη, (as a less Alteration, than if I should have substituted πρὸς ὑπνοῦ, or the like) the learned *Puteanus* approved it; but withal conceived, ἄριστον, ought to be retained; but the excellent *Menagius* was of Opinion, that since a word is wanting, for ἄριστον should be read ἔγραφεν, used on the like occasion by *Laertius* but that ἀντὶ τοῦ ought to be retained, forasmuch as *Epicurus* seemeth not to have used the word χαίρειν, it being mentioned as proper to *Cleon*, both by (u) *Lucian* and (w) *Laertius* himself. Or whether instead of ἄριστον might we not put ἀρέσκεται, or, with the least alteration, ἄρεσον, signifying, that for Salutation. he was best pleased with those words, εὖ πράττειν, and σπουδαίως ζῆν; or might not ἀντὶ τοῦ be retained, implying, that he did not quite cast aside the word χαίρειν, but instead of it somtimes used the other two, as if ποτὲ were either wanting or imply'd. Indeed, (x) *Lucian* seems not obscurely to hint as much, when relating, that *Epicurus* was extreamly delighted with the word χαίρειν; he adds, that somtimes he used other words, and that somtimes in his more Accurate and Profound Epistles, (which yet, he saith, were not many,) or when he writ to his most intimate Friends, he chiefly used ὑγιαίνειν. *Laertius* therefore attributing the word εὐπράττειν to him, may as well be thought to have intended χαίρειν as used by him: Since attributing εὖ διάγειν to him also, he makes εὖ πράττειν as peculiar to *Plato*, as χαίρειν to *Cleon*.   *(ſ) Lib. 10.*   *(t) De fin. 2.*   *(u) De lapſ. in Salut.*   *(w) Lib. 3.*   *(x) Ibid.*

This Catalogue of his Books is compiled by *Laertius*; but besides these, there are others, cited

cited both by *Laertius* himself, and other Writers. *Laertius* formerly cited his Book, *Of Rhetorick*, mentioned also by the Scholiast of *Hermogenes*. But that which is cited, *Of Perspicuity requisite to Discourse*, belongs to *Canonick*, which he substituted in the room of *Dialectick*.

He likewise seems to cite his Προηγμένα, *Antecedentia*, or *Præcipua*; things precedent or preferred, in the Sense of the *Stoicks*. I should think it meant of some of the Books before cited, if amongst them there were any, wherein that which is alledged were written by *Epicurus*.

There are cited also *Stœcheioses, Institutions* or *Elements*, XII.

There seems also to be cited, *Of Worlds*, XII. For, describing several Worlds, he is said to have done it in the XIIth περὶ τότε, or, as the Manuscripts, περὶ ουτε, upon this very Subject; the rather, because it seems not meant of those XXXVII which are constantly cited, *Of Nature*.

I should add his *Physical Problems*, and *Ethical Doctrines*; but that under these Names may be comprised, all that *Epicurus* wrote concerning *Nature* and *Morality*.

(*y*) *Tusc.* 3.

Moreover, (*y*) *Cicero* cites his Book, *Of the chief Good*; unless it be the same with that, *Of the End*, already mentioned.

(*z*) *De divin.* 2.

By the (*z*) same also is cited his Book, *Of Pleasure*; this perhaps *Laertius* meant, when he said, It was objected by some against *Epicurus*, that he usurped the Treatise of *Aristippus* concerning Pleasure, as if it had been his own.

(*) *De nat. deor.* 1.

Besides these, * *Cicero* cites his Book, *Of Piety towards the Gods*, distinct, as it seems, from that *Of Sanctity*, reckoned by *Laertius*. *Of Sanctity*, saith he, *Of Piety towards the Gods*, he wrote Books.

Again, *Plutarch* declares, that he wrote Books against *Theophrastus*: for the second of them, he saith, contained a discourse concerning Colours. Hitherto of his Books.

CHAP. XI.

His Will.

EPicurus having employed his Life in Teaching and Writing, and being now grown old, made, as the custom was, his Will, which being preserv'd entire by (*a*) *Laertius*, we shall not need to have recourse to those Fragments of it, which lie dispersedly in *Cicero*, and other Writers. It was in this Form.

(*a*) *Lib.* 10.

'Thus I bequeath; I give all my Estate to
'*Amynomachus*, Son of *Philocrates*, of *Batis*, (a
'Town of the *Ægean* Tribe, as (*b*) *Hesychius*
'describes it) and to *Timocrates* Son of *Demetrius*, a *Potamian*. (of *Potamus*, a Town belonging to the *Leontian* Tribe, (*c*) *Phavorin*.)
'according to the donation which hath already
'been made, and is Recorded among the Deeds
'in the *Metroum*, (a Temple of the great Goddess at *Athens*, seated upon the Haven, in
'which the Laws, Judgments, and other Acts
'were preserved, as *Athenæus*, *Suidas*, and
'others affirm) with this condition, that they
'bestow the Garden, and all that belongs to it,
'on *Hermachus*, Son of *Agemarchus*, a *Mitylenean*, and those that shall study Philosophy
'with him; and on those whom *Hermachus*
'shall leave his Successors in Philosophy, and to
'those who shall succeed us in the Profession of
'Philosophy, for ever. And that it may be
'preserved with all possible care, I assign the
'School to *Amynomachus* and *Timocrates*, and to
'their Heirs, according to the surest form of
'Law, that they may keep the Garden, and deliver it to those who shall profess Philosophy
'after us. The House which is at *Melite*, let
'*Amynomachus* and *Timocrates* deliver to *Hermachus*, and to those that study Philosophy with
'him, to dwell in it as long as he shall live. Of
'the Revenues made over by us to *Amynomachus*
'and *Timocrates*, let them set apart as much as
'shall be sufficient (advising with *Hermachus*,)
'to celebrate the Exequies of my Father, Mother, and Brethren; and to keep, as they have
'done hitherto, my Birth-day, in the first Decad of the month *Gamelion*; as also to provide
'a Feast for Entertainment of all those who study Philosophy with us, every month on the
'twentieth day of the Moon, in Commemoration of us, and of *Metrodorus*. Let them also
'keep a day in Memory of my Brethren in the
'month *Posideon*, as we used to do; and another
'to *Polyænus*, in the month *Metagitnion*. Let
'*Amynomachus* and *Timocrates* take care of
'*Epicurus*, Son of *Metrodorus*, and of the Son of
'*Polynæus*; and let them study Philosophy, and
'live with *Hermachus*. In like manner, let them
'take care of the Daughter of *Metrodorus*, and
'so soon as she shall be Marriageable, bestow
'her upon him of the Students of Philosophy,
'whom *Hermachus* shall chuse, provided she be
'modest, and obedient to *Hermachus*. Let *Amynomachus* and *Timocrates*, out of our Revenues,
'bestow yearly so much as shall be sufficient
'for their Maintenance, with the consent of
'*Hermachus*. For let them so esteem *Hermachus*,
'having an equal share in our Revenues, and
'grown old in studying Philosophy under us,
'and left by us Guide of those that studied Philosophy under us, that all things be done by
'his advice. As for her Portion, when she
'shall come to be Marriageable, let *Amynomachus*
'and *Timocrates* take as much as they shall think
'convenient, with the consent of *Hermachus*.
'Likewise, let them take the same care of *Nicanor* as we did, that all they, who, studying
'Philosophy with us, have communicated the
'use of their Estates, and expressing all Friendship, have chosen to grow old with us in Philosophy, want not any necessaries to the utmost
'of our Power. All my Books I bequeath to
'*Hermachus*; but if any thing of mortality happen to *Hermachus*, before the Children of *Metrodorus* arrive at full Age, let *Amynomachus* and
'*Timocrates* take care, that all necessaries be decently provided for them, as much as shall be
'necessary, out of the Revenues left by us. Let
'all the rest be ordered as we have appointed,
'as much as is possible. I manumit of my Servants, *Mus, Licias, Lycon*; *Phædria* also I set
'free.

CHAP.

CHAP. XII.

The Manner of his Death.

a) Laert. lib. 10.

AS concerning his last Sickness and Death, we must know that *Epicurus* was of a Constitution not very strong. This is implied even by the Title of the Book, written by (*a*) *Metrodorus*, *Of the Infirmity* (or Unhealthfulness) *of Epicurus*. It is implied also by the envious exaggeration of (*b*) *Suidas*, that *Epicurus* could not endure to put on his Cloaths, nor to rise out of Bed, nor to look upon the Sun, and the Fire, and the like. These may at least perswade, that *Epicurus* was of a Complexion not strong, and as in the whole course of his Life, he had not a constant health, so at last he died of a painful Disease, the Stone, whereof it is probable he had many Fits. (*c*) *Laertius*, out of *Hermachus*, in his Epistles, relates that he died of the Stone, stopping his Urine, having lain sick 14 days.

b) In Lex.

c) Loc. cit.

It is memorable, that being near death, he writ that Epistle which *Laertius* mentions, as written to *Idomeneus*; (*d*) *Cicero*, to *Hermachus*; perhaps it was sent to both, because of the τὸ ὑμῖν: or to *Idomeneus*, rather than to *Hermachus*, because the Children of *Metrodorus* were sufficiently recommended to *Hermachus*, by his Will. Moreover, it is not likely that *Hermachus*, his next Successor, was absent at that time, especially seeing he sent a relation of *Epicurus*'s death in Letters; not to press, that he from his Youth was more addicted to Rhetorick than Philosophy, as appeareth from *Laertius*. The Epistle is this.

d) De fin. lib. 2

'Leading a most happy life, and withal dying,
'we writ this to you, seized by the Stranguary
'and Dysentery beyond expression; but all these
'were counterpoized by the joy of mind, which
'I conceive in remembering our Discourses and
'Inventions. But thou, as becomes the good
'will which thou hast had from thy Youth to
'me, and Philosophy, take care of the Children
'of *Metrodorus*.

e) Loc. cit.

(*e*) *Laertius* adds, (out of *Hermippus*) that *Epicurus* went into a Bath of warm Water, called for Wine, drunk it off, and exhorting his Friends to be mindful of his Doctrine, whilst he was discoursing, died. Upon which *Laertius* hath this Epigram:

Farewel, and bear my Doctrine in your minds;
Said dying Epicurus *to his Friends:*
Into a warm Bath going, Wine he quaft,
And then from Pluto *took a colder draught.*

CHAP. XIII.

The time of his Death.

a) Lib. 10.

EPicurus died in the 2d year of the 127th Olympiad, *Pytharatus* being *Archon*. After δεύτερον ἔτος, which (*a*) *Laertius* cites out of *Apollodorus*'s Chronology, *Casaubon* rightly reads τ͂ εἰκοστῆς ἑβδόμης ᾗ ἑκατοστῆς Ὀλυμπιάδος, for in the ordinary reading εἰκοστῆς being wanting, who could imagine that *Epicurus*, born in the 109th Olympiad, could die in the 107th. And indeed, the 72d year of *Epicurus*, in which he is said to have died, falls upon the 127th Olympiad.

The month and day of the year, in which *Epicurus* died, is told by (*b*) *Clemens Alexandrinus*, who saith, that *Antilochus*, from the time of *Pythagoras* to the death of *Epicurus*, reckoned 312 years, adding, that the death of *Epicurus* hapned on the 10th day of the month *Gamelion*. Where observe, if the time of *Pythagoras* be reckoned from the 60th Olympiad, in which *Laertius* saith, he flourished; there will be found to be but 270 years from thence to the death of *Epicurus*, and consequently the account of *Antilochus* will fall short 42 years. Wherefore this ἡλικία must be taken from the birth of *Pythagoras*, who began to flourish in the 40th year of his age.

b) Strom. lib. 1.

Now whereas *Apollodorus* saith, that *Epicurus* lived 72 years, which is confirmed also by (*c*) *Cicero*, saying, *It always was true, that* Epicurus *shall dye, having lived 72 years;* Pytharatus *being* Archon, (whence some conjecture, *Epicurus* died in his Climacterical year, which is commensurated by 9.) the last, or 72d year, is not to be understood as compleat, for *Epicurus* had but newly entred into it, there being but three days over and above the 71 years; for he was born on the 7th, and dy'd on the 10th, of the month *Gamelion*, there being, between the time of his Birth, and his Death, 18 complete Olympiads, except one year. Wherefore, this is in the same manner, as when (*d*) *Pliny*, (*e*) *Lucian*, and (*f*) *Censorinus* affirm the *Sicilian* (or *Leontine*) *Gorgias* did live 108 years, whereas (*g*) *Cicero*, and (*h*) *Valerius Maximus* say, he compleated but 107. Here is observable, the comparison which (*i*) *Plutarch* makes between *Epicurus*, and *Gorgias*; for after he had said that *Alexis*, the Comick Poet, (Son of *Menander*, and Father of *Stephanus* the Comick Poet, as (*k*) *Suidas* relates) lived double the time of *Metrodorus*, that is 106 years. *Metrodorus* living according to (*l*) *Laertius*, 53. he adds, that *Gorgias* the Sophist outlived *Epicurus* πλέον ἢ ὁπότερον, more than one Third; for if we take the number 36, it will be the same which *Epicurus* lived double, *Gorgias* treble; and whereas *Plutarch* says *more*, perhaps he reflected upon the Opinion which (*m*) *Quintilian* and (*n*) *Suidas* afterwards followed, that *Gorgias* lived 109 years.

c) De fato.

d) Lib. 7. cap. 48.
e) In Macrob.
f) De die nat.
g) In Cat. Majore.
h) Lib. 8. cap. 13.
i) De orat. def.
k) In Lex.
l) Lib. 10.

m) Lib. 3. cap. 1.
n) In Lex.

I see not, why the (*o*) Interpreter of *Clemens Alexandrinus* should render *Gamelion* *October*; for though there be some Controversie about the order of the *Greek* months, yet shall we not find any but make *Gamelion* the 6th, 7th, or 8th, from *Hecatombæon*; which seeing it cannot begin higher than *June*, certainly *Gamelion* will be far distant from *October*. But since by many Arguments it is evinced, that *Gamelion* is the 7th from *Hecatombæon*, it ought rather to be reduced to *January*. Now because the 2d year of the 127th Olympiad began in Summer, in the 4443d year of the *Julian* period, the *Gamelion* of that year must fall upon *Janu-*

o) Hervetus.

ary, in the beginning of the 4444th Year of the *Julian* Period. Upon what day of *January*, the 10th of *Gamelion* might fall, it is not easie to determine. But if we may make *Gamelion* commence (as is done in the time of the Nativity,) from the 14th Moon, or from the 7th Full Moon, after the Summer Solstice, forasmuch as the new Moon hapned upon the 30th of *December*, and consequently the 14th Moon upon the 12th of *January*; Hereupon if we make that the 1st of *Gamelion*, the 10th will fall upon the 21st of *January*, upon which the death of *Epicurus* might fall. Where we must further observe, That whereas *Epicurus* is said to have lived 72 Years, it must be understood of the *Grecian* Years, not *Julian*, for so it would fall short two Days, it being already proved, he was born the 23d of *January*. Now, to reduce the Death of *Epicurus* to our Account is easie: For if we substract ten Days, and for the Cycle of the Sun that Year which is 20, and, for the Dominical Letter D, according to the Old Style, put G, according to our own, it will appear that *Epicurus* died the 31st of *January*, it being the 4th Day of the Week, or *Wednesday*, before the computation of Christ, 270 Years.

CHAP. XIV.
How dear his Memory was to his Followers.

IT remains, that we briefly tell how the Memory of *Epicurus*, after his death, was respected by his Followers. For, to omit, that his Country honoured him with brazen Statues, as (a) *Laertius* writes; I observe, that the Setdays and Ceremonies appointed in his Will were punctually kept by his Followers. (b) *Pliny*, (writing 350 years after upon this thing) *On his Birth-day*, saith he, *the twentieth Moon, they Sacrifice, and keep Feasts every Month, which they call Icades*; whence it may be conceived, that the *Epicureans* were by Greek Writers, as (c) *Athenæus*, termed εἰκαδίςαι, from observing εἰκαδὰς as *Rhodiginus* also takes notice. Although (d) some there are who think, they were called *Icadistæ*, from εἰκὼν an Image, because there was not one of them, but had the Picture of *Epicurus*. And of these Images, (*) *Pliny* also thus; *They keep* (saith he) *the Countenance of* Epicurus *in their Chambers, and carry it up and down with them*; And (e) *Cicero*, in the Person of *Atticus*, "Neither, saith he, can we forget *Epicurus* of "any Man; whose representation we have not "only in Pictures, but in Cups, and Rings also. (f) There are who add, that "some took great "care to have Pictures of *Epicurus*, not only in "Rings, but in Cups, as conceiving it a fortunate "Omen, to the Nation, and their own Name. As for the Affection which they bare to him, hear *Varro, Honour*, saith (g) *Cicero*, "Office, Right "of Wills, the Authority of *Epicurus*, the At"testation of *Phædrus*, the Seat, House, Foot"steps of excellent Persons, he saith, that he "must preserve; but especially (h) Torquatus, "Owe we not much to him, saith he, who, as if "he had heard the voice of Nature her self, did "so firmly and soundly comprehend her, as that "he brought all ingenious Persons into the way "of a peaceful, calm, quiet, happy Life? And (i) again, "Who, saith he, I think only saw "Truth, and freed the Minds of Men from the

(a) Lib. 10.
(b) Lib. 35. Cap. 2.
(c) Lib. 7.
(d) Rivier.
(*) Loc. Citat.
(e) De fin. 1.
(f) Alex. ab Alex. 2. 19.
(g) Epist. 15. 1.
(h) De fin. 1.
(i) Ibid.

"greatest Errors, and delivered all things apper"taining to well and happy living.

And because *Epicurus* dying, advised his friends to be mindful of his Doctrines, (k) *Cicero* saith, that all of them got by heart his *Maxims*, and some there were who learned without Book all his Doctrines, as particularly *Scyro*, mentioned in his Academicks. But let it suffice, to alledge some few Verses of (l) *Lucretius*, by which we may perceive how affectionate they were to the Memory and Doctrines of their Master. He begins his Third Book thus:

Who first from Darkness could'st a Light so clear
Strike forth, and make Life's Benefits appear,
Great Ornament of Græcia, I am lead
By thee, and in thy sacred Foot-steps tread:
Not to contend, but kindly imitate.
For how can chatt'ring Swallows emulate
The Swans? Or tender Kids keep equal pace
With the stout well-breath'd Steed's impetuous race?
From thee, O Father, every thing receives
Invention, thou giv'st Precepts, from thy Leaves,
As Bees skip up and down and sweetly suck
In flow'ry Groves, we Golden Sayings pluck:
Golden, deserving an Eternal Life.

And again;
By these a Pleasure I receiv'd from Thee
Divine; withal, a Reverence, to see
That Nature every way thou hadst unvail'd.

And afterwards,
Great Epicurus died, his Lives race run,
Whose Wit Mankind exceeded, as the Sun
Eclipseth by his Rising all the Stars.

CHAP. XV.
With what Constancy and Unanimity, the Succession of his School flourished.

IT deserves to be taken notice of, not only that the succession of his School was constant, but that his Successors and Followers did always so agree, as was indeed wonderful. As concerning the Constancy, it is known that the Presidents of the Gardens, or Masters of the School, from the death of *Epicurus*, to the times of *Julius Cæsar*, and *Augustus*, succeeding one another in a continued Series, were, according to (a) *Suidas*, XIV. and that for 237 Years: In which later times, How many *Epicureans* there were, eminent Persons, and of great account in the State, appears from *Cicero*. (b) *Lucian* also writes, that in his time there was a stipend allowed to the *Epicureans*, by the Emperor, no less than to other Philosophers; adding, that when any one of them died, he, whom they most approved of, was substituted in his room. (c) *Lærtius* who lived after *Lucian*, declares, that whereas the Successions of the other Philosophers did almost quite fail; yet the Succession of *Epicurus* did constantly persevere, so many succeeding one another in government of the Disciples, as could not be reckoned up. *Numenius* (cited by (d) *Eusebius*) adds, that this Succession lasted till his time, and that so perfectly, as it was likely to endure a great while after. After these (e) *Lactantius*; *The Discipline of* Epicurus, saith he, *was much more celebrious*. In a word, as long as Learning flourished in *Greece*, and *Rome* was preserved from the *Barbarians*, the School and Discipline of *Epicurus* continued eminent. As

(k) De fin.
(l) Lib. 4.

(a) In Epit.
(b) In Eun.
(c) Lib. 10.
(d) Præp. Lib. 14.
(e) Lib. 3. Cap. 17.

As for their unanimity, to omit that of Cicero, '*I will maintain the* Epicureans *who are so many, my Friends, Men that are so loving to one another*, and the like places; and shall rather observe, that whereas other Sects almost at their very beginning were distracted with intestine dissentions; the *Epicurean* was far from suffering any such thing. For (g) *Themistius* writes, that *the Opinions of* Epicurus *were kept by all the* Epicureans, *as Laws of* Solon *or* Lycurgus. And, as if they had all one Soul amongst them, saith (h) Seneca, *Whatsoever* Hermachus *affirm'd, whatsoever* Menodorus, *is referr'd to one. All things that any Man delivers in that Society, go under one Man's name*; This will appear more plainly, if we alledge the words of *Numenius*, the *Pythagorean*, in (i) *Eusebius*; who after he hath complain'd, that the Successors of *Plato* did not preserve that Unanimity, for which the *Pythagoreant* were esteemed, adds, " After this manner the *Epicureans* being instituted (though unworthy,) seeming not in any thing to dissent from *Epicurus*, and professing to have the same Tenents with their wise Master, have not unjustly attained their scope. Hence it hath hapned to the *Epicureans* for a long time, that they never, in any thing worth notice, contradicted either one another, or *Epicurus*. Amongst them it is an Offence, or rather Impiety, and Sin, to bring in any Innovation; wherefore none dares attempt it. Hence, by reason of their constant agreement among themselves, they enjoy their Doctrines peaceably and quietly; and this Institution of *Epicurus* resembles the true state of a perfect Common-wealth, which being far from Sedition, is governed by one Joynt Mind and Opinion. For which reason, there have not, nor are not, nor, in likelyhood, will be wanting, those, that shall willingly follow it, but amongst the Stoical Faction, &c. One would think there were nothing wanting to this Testimony, but, to say of all the *Epicureaus*, as (k) *Valerius* (before cited) did of two of them, that "Such a Society might be thought to have been begotten, nourish'd, and terminated in the bosom of Celestial Concord.

(g) Orat. 4.

(h) Epist. 35.

(i) Præp. lib. 14

(k) Lib. 1. Chap. 8.

CHAP. XVI.
The Successors and Followers of Epicurus.

IT remains, that we give a Catalogue of those who were eminent in that Sect, after the death of *Epicurus*. We have already said, that *Hermachus* succeeded *Epicurus*, and *Polystratus* *Hermachus*. It also is manifest from *Laertius*, that *Dionysius* succeeded *Polystratus*; and *Basilides*, *Dionysius*. But who those ten Successors were from *Basilides*, to him who govern'd the School in the time of *Augustus*, we cannot easily say. Perhaps after *Basilides*, succeeded *Protarchus Bargyleites*; whom (a) *Strabo* terms an Illustrious Person. The same *Strabo* saith, That Disciple to *Protarchus* was *Demetrius*, surnamed *Lacon*, who is mentioned also by (b) *Laertius*, and was, as (c) *Sextus Empiricus* saith, eminent amongst the Followers of *Epicurus*. Perhaps after him succeeded *Diogenes* of *Tarsus*, Author of the *Select Schools*, whereof *Laertius* mentions XX Books. He also cites an Epitome of Moral Doctrine, written by the same Person. *Laertius* menti-

(a) Lib. 14.

(b) Lib. 10.
(c) Adv. Log. 2

ons also (but whether they belong to this Series of Successors, is uncertain,) Two *Ptolomies* of *Alexandria*; whether from differences of Complexion, or some other Respect, one Sirnamed Black, the other White. He mentions also *Orion*, and seems to mention one *Democritus*, who, in his *Timocrates* takes notice of Pleasure after *Epicurus*'s Doctrine.

There follow Two out of this rank, named by (d) *Athenæus*; The First, *Diogenes* of *Seleucia* near *Babylon*, whom he describes to have been Eloquent, but of an ill Life; The other, *Lysias*, who, as he saith, Governed at *Tarsus*; and being chosen by the Country, *Stephanophorus* (Priest of *Hercules*) he enjoy'd the Supream Government, and wore Regal Ornaments. This is he, who distributed the Estates of the Rich amongst the Poor, and put many of them to death for refusing to part with them. At what time he lived, we cannot certainly determine; But *Diogenes* being contemporary with *Alexander* King of *Syria*, and *Antiochus* his Successor, may be referred to the 155th Olympiad.

(d) Deipn. 3.

About the same time seemeth to have flourished *Eucratidas*, to whom belongs this Inscription, recited by *Janus Gruterus*; *At* Brundusium, *before the Gate of* Diomedes Athenæus, *a Physician, on the Basis of*; EUCRATIDAS *Son* OF PISIDAMUS, A RHODIAN, AN EPICUREAN PHILOSOPHER. THIS PLACE APPOINTED FOR BURIAL BY THE SENATE OF BRUNDUSIUM.

Not long after seems to have flourished in the School that *Apollodorus*, whom *Laertius* termeth eminent, κηποτύραννον, for that (as I conceive) he bore such sway in the Garden, as *Demosthenes* is said to done in Courts of Judicature. He wrote about 300 Books, amongst which were some concerning the Life of *Epicuruss* cited by *Laertius*. It may be conjectured, that he was the same, whose Chronology is cited by *Laertius*, and others.

Auditor of *Apollodorus* was *Zeno* the *Sidonian*, according to (e) *Laertius*, who adds, that he wrote much, and that he was famous both for Philosophy and Rhetorick; whence I conjecture, it is the same *Zeno* of whom (f) *Cicero* saith, He spoke Distinctly, Gravely, and Neatly; and that he was Chief of the *Epicureans*; unless both He and *Apollodorus* lived earlier; which if it were so, this other belongs to the Times of the Emperors, for (g) *Cicero* heard him, and writing concerning him to (h) *Atticus*; *Zeno*, saith He, *I love as well as thou dost*.

(e) Lib. 7.

(f) De Nat. deor. 1.

(g) Ibid.
(h) Epist. 5. 11.

CHAP. XVII.
Laertius, *his Vindication of* Epicurus.

Diotymus the Stoick, much ma'igning *Epicurus*, traduced him exceedingly, producing Fifty Epistles, very lascivious, as written by *Epicurus*; to which he added, as *Epicurus*'s also, the short Epistles, commonly ascribed to *Chrysippus*. No less disaffected to him were *Posidonius* the Stoick, and *Nicolaus*, and *Sotion*, in the 12th of his Dioclean Confutations, (which are in all XXIV,) and *Dionysius Halicarnassaeus*. For they say, he went from House to House with his Mother reading expiatory Prayers; and that

'that with his Father he taught Children for a 'small stipend; that one of his Brothers was a 'Pandor; that he himself used the company of 'Leontium, a Curtezan; that he ascribed to him-'self the Books of *Democritus* concerning Atoms, 'and of *Aristippus* concerning Pleasure; that he 'was not a true Native of the City, as *Timo-*'crates acknowledgeth, and *Herodotus*, in his Book 'of the Youth of *Epicurus*; That he basely flat-'tered *Mithres*, Steward of *Lysimachus*, calling 'him in his Epistles, *Apollo* and *King*; That *Ido-*'meneus, *Herodotus*, and *Timocrates*, who pub-'lished some obscure Pieces of his, did commend 'and flatter him for the same. That in his Epi-'stles, he writes to *Leontium*, thus; O King 'Apollo, my dear little *Leontium*; How were we 'transported and filled with Joy at the reading 'of thy Letter! To *Themista* Wife of *Leontius*, 'thus; If you come not to me, I shall roll to you 'whithersoever you call me. And to *Pithocles*, 'a handsome Youth; I consume in expectation 'of your Amiable and Divine company. And 'again, writing to *Themista*, he thinks to per-'swade her: As *Theodorus* affirms, in his Fourth 'Book against *Epicurus*. That he wrote to ma-'ny other Curtezans, especially to *Leontium*, 'with whom *Metrodorus* also was in Love. That 'in his Book concerning the End, he writes thus, 'Neither know I what is this Good, If we take 'away the Pleasures of the Taste; If we take 'away those of Coition; If we take away those 'of Hearing; If we take away those of the Sight. 'That in his Epistle to *Pithocles* he writes; Hap-'py Youth, fly as fast as thou canst from all Di-'scipline. *Epicurus* calls him, Cinædologum, and 'rails at him exceedingly. *Timocrates*, Brother 'of *Metrodorus*, who was a while a Disciple of 'Epicurus, but at last forsook the School, saith; 'That he vomited twice a day, upon overchar-'ging his Stomach; and that he himself had much 'ado to get away from their Nocturnal Philoso-'phy, and Conversation in secret. That *Epi-*'curus, was ignorant of many things belonging 'to Discourse, but much more of those which 'belonged to Life. That he was of such a mise-'rable Constitution, that he was not able of him-'self for many years, to get out of Bed, or rise 'out of the Chair in which he was carried. That 'he spent every day a Mina at his Table, as he 'himself writeth in his Epistle to *Leontium*, and 'in his Epistles to the Philosophers at *Mitylene*. 'That he and *Metrodorus* also used the company 'of Curtezans; amongst others, *Marmarium*, '*Hedia*, *Erotium*, *Nicidium*. That in the Thirty 'Books which he writ concerning Nature, he 'saith most of the same things over and over; 'and that in them he writes against many Per-'sons, and, amongst the rest, against *Nausiphanes*, 'and that in these very words; But this Man, if 'ever any, had a way of teeming a Sophistick 'brag, like many other Slaves. And that in his 'Epistles, he writes thus concerning *Nausiphanes*; 'This so far transported him, that he railed at 'me, and called himself my Master. Likewise, 'that he called himself *Nausiphanes*, Lungs (as 'senseless,) and unlearned, and deceitful, and las-'civious. The Disciples of *Plato*, *Dionysius*'s Pa-'rasites; *Plato* himself, Golden; *Aristotle*, a Pro-

'digal, that, having wasted his Patrimony, was 'fain to turn Soldier, and Apothecary; *Preta-*'goras, a Basket-carrier, an *Amanuensis* to *De-*'mocritus, and a High-way Schoolmaster; *He-*'raclitus, κυκήτην, a causer of Confusion; *Demo-*'critus, Λημόκριτον, Purblind; *Antidorus*, Σαινίδωρον, 'a fawner upon Gifts; the *Cyrenaicks*, Enemies 'to *Greece*; the *Dialecticks*, Envious; *Pyrrho*, 'Unlearned and Unmanner'd.

'But these Men are mad; for, of the excellent 'Candor of *Epicurus* towards all Men, there are 'many witnesses; his Country, which honoured 'him with Statues of Brass; his Friends, who 'were so many, that whole Cities could not con-'tain them; his Disciples, who were also taken 'with his Sirenical Doctrine, except *Metrodorus* 'the *Stratonicean*, who, perhaps over-burdened 'with his excessive Goodness, revolted to *Car-*'neades; the Succession of his School, which, 'when all the rest were almost quite worn out, 'remained constant, and ordained so many Ma-'sters one after another, as cannot be numbred; 'his Piety towards his Parents, his Kindness to-'wards his Brethren, his Meekness towards his 'Servants, (as may appear by his Will, and their 'studying Philosophy with him, amongst whom '*Mus* formerly mentioned was most eminent;) 'and, in general, His Humanity towards all, His 'Devotion to the Gods, and Love to his Coun-'try, was beyond expression. He would not ex-'cept of any publick Office, out of an excessive 'Modesty; and, in the most difficult trouble-'some times, continued in *Greece*, where he lived 'constantly; except that twice or thrice he made 'a Journey to his Friends on the borders of *Ionia*. 'But to him they resorted from all parts, and 'lived with him (as *Apollodorus* relates) in the 'Garden which he purchased with 80 Minæ. '*Diocles* in his Third Book, *De Incursione*, saith, 'They used a most frugal spare Dyet, for they 'were contented with a pint of small Wine, and 'for the most part they drunk nothing but Wa-'ter. And that *Epicurus* would not have them 'to put their Estates into one common stock, as '*Pythagoras* ordained, saying, The Goods of 'Friends are common; for this argued distrust, 'and where there is distrust, there is no friend-'ship. As for himself in his Epistles, that he 'was contented with Water only, and course 'Bread; And send me, saith he, a little Cythe-'ridian Cheese, that I may Feast my self when I 'have a mind. Such was he, who professed, that 'Pleasure is the End, or chief Good; for which, '*Athenæus* in an Epigram, thus commends him:

Man's most unhappy Race for worst things toils,
For Wealth (unsatiate) raiseth Wars and Broils
Nature to Wealth a narrow bound allign'd,
But vain Opinions ways unbounded find.
Thus Neoclides; whom the Sacred Quire
Of Muses, or Apollo did inspire.

But this we shall understand better from his own Doctrine and Words. Hitherto *Laertius* in vindication of *Epicurus*; which Subject is more fully and Rhetorically handled by the Learned *Gassendus, De Vita & Moribus Epicuri*, in the six last Books.

THE DOCTRINE OF EPICURUS.

Of *PHILOSOPHY* in General.

(a) Sext. Emp. adv. Eth.

PHilosophy (*a*) (or the love of Wisdom,) "is an exercising of the Reason; by "which, in Meditating and Discoursing, 'it acquireth happy Life, and enjoyeth it. *For*

(b) Sext. Emp. adv. Math. 1.

'(*b*) Philosophy hath this propriety above other 'Arts, that its end is the end also of Reason 'which so tends to it, that it may rest in the en-'joyment of it.

Now happy Life consisting in the tranquillity of the Mind, and indolency of the Body, but especially in the former, (in regard, the Goods of the Mind are better than those of the Body, and the Ills thereof worse;) it comes to pass, that Philosophy is chiefly the Medicine of the Mind, in regard it both makes and preserves it sound, its Soundness or Health being nothing else but its tranquillity.

(c) Laert.

Hence it followeth, (*c*) That "neither ought a 'young Man to delay Philosophizing, nor an old 'Man to be wearied therewith; for, to rectifie 'and cure his Mind, no Man is too young; and 'he who pretends, that the time of Philosophi-'zing either is not yet, or is past, doth, as he 'who saith, the time to live well and happily 'either is not yet come, or is quite gone.

'Both young and old therefore must Philoso-'phize; the one, that whilst he is growing old, 'he may persevere to advance himself in good 'things to continue the excellence of his former 'actions; the other, that, though aged in years, 'he may yet be youthful in Mind, remaining 'secure from future eminent harms.

For it is Philosophy alone, which breeds in its Followers an assuredness and an immunity from all vain fears; whence we ought to devote our-selves to it, that we may be truly free.

Happy they, who are of such a disposition of Body or Mind, or Born in such a Country, as they can either of themselves, or by the instiga-tions of others, addict themselves to Philoso-phy, and persue Truth; by attainment whereof, a Man is made truly free or wise, and absolute Master of himself.

They who apply their Minds hereto, are of three sorts; Some address themselves to enquire after Truth, without the assistence of any; some require help, and would not go, if none had gone before, but follow well; some may be com-pelled to the Right, who need not so much a Leader, as an Assistent, and, as I may call it, a Driver.

The First are most to be commended; yet the ingenuity of the Second is excellent like-wise; and the Third not to be contemned. Of the Second was *Metrodorus*; Of the Third *Her-machus*. As I highly praise the fortune of the former, so I no less admire and value the later; but although both of them arriv'd at the same end, yet he deserv'd the greater praise, who, their performances being equal, broke through the greater difficulties.

Now whereas to a Philosopher nothing ought to be more valuable than Truth, let him proceed to it in a direct way, (*d*) and neither *(d) Laert.* feign any thing, nor admit any thing that is feign'd by another, for no kind of Fiction be-seemeth Professors of Truth. Neither is that perpetual Irony of (*e*) *Socrates* to be approved *(e) Cic. in Bru-*whereby he extolled to the Skies *Protagoras, Hip-* to. *pias, Prodicus, Gorgias*, and the rest, but pretend-ed himself rude and ignorant of all things.

(*f*) How much less was it becoming a (*g*) Phi- *(f) Macro. bin* losopher to have feign'd that Fable concerning Sumn. lib. 1. *Erus Armenius*: For why (if he had an intent Cap. 2. to teach us the knowledge of Celestial things, *(g) Viz. Plato* and the disposition of Souls,) did he not perform in Rep. Sib. 10. this by naked plain instruction, but rather chose to introduce a Person; by which carriage the newness of the Invention, and the formal Scene of a Fiction, represented on the Stage contami-nated the very way of seeking Truth with a Falshood?

For this reason (*h*) a Wise Man will neither *(h) Tacit.* hearken to the Fables of Poets, nor will himself labour in composing fabulous Poems; nay ra-ther, (*i*) he will have an aversion from the jug- *(i) Laert.* ling tricks and sophistications of Orators: And as he exacts no more from Grammar then Congruity, so neither will he exact more from Rhetorick than Perspicuity of Speech, but will use a plain familiar Style; whether he profess to Teach or Write Books, or explicate to the mul-titude any thing already written, he will be wa-ry that he do it not Panegerycally and Hyperbo-lically.

But seeing that of Philosophers there are some, who assert nothing of Truth, but doubt of all things, others, who imagine they know all things, and

and assert without any distinction: A wise Man ought not to behave himself so, as that he assert not all, but (k) only maintain some positive Maxims which are indisputable.

(l) Laert.

But when there are divers ways whereby some things may be performed, as the Eclipses of the Stars, their Rising, Setting, and other Superior things, so to approve one way as to disapprove the rest, is certainly ridiculous. But when we speak of things that cannot be any way but one, (such as are these Maxims) *Of nothing is made nothing; the Universe consists of Body and Vacuum; The Principles of things are indivisible,* and the like; then it is very absurd not to adhere firmly to them.

Hence, it is proper for a Wise Man to maintain both the manifold ways in those, and the one single way in these, and not to stagger nor recede from Science once obtained; not like those, who, as if prescribed by a Law, Philosophize concerning Nature, not in such manner as the things themselves require; but go out of the right way and run into Fables; never considering that to vent, or vainly boast our own Opinions, conduceth nothing to happy Life, but disturbeth the Mind.

(l) Senec. Epist.

Now whereas, (l) the principal parts of Philosophy are held to be Two; One *Physick*, consisting in contemplation of Nature; the other *Ethick*, which treats of directing of Manners in order to Happy Life, it is manifest, either that *Ethick* comprehends all Philosophy, or that *Physick* comes to be a part therefore, only inasmuch as it conduceth to Happy Life.

(m) Laert.

'For (m) if those things which we suspect 'and dread from the Superior Bodies, and even 'from death it self, breed no disturbance in us, 'as things unconcerning our condition; if also 'we could sufficiently comprehend what are the 'just bounds of our Desires, and to what degree 'the Grief which springs from them is to be assuaged, there were no need of Physiology, or 'the explication of Nature.

But because (n) it is not possible we should arrive at so great a Good, without having first surveyed the nature of things; but, (o) as Children in the dark tremble, and are afraid of every thing; so we miserably groping in the darkness of Ignorance, fear things that are fabulous, and no more to be dreaded than those which Children fear in the dark, and fancy to themselves will happen. It is therefore necessary, that this terror and darkness of the Mind be dispelled, not by the beams of the Sun, but by impressions from Nature and Reason, that is by Physiology. Whence all Physick is to be esteemed a part of Philosophy.

(n) Laert.

(o) Laert Lib 2. v. 53.

Dialectick, which some add as a third Part, is to be rejected, because as ordinarily taught it doth nothing but beget thorny Questions, being an empty bubbling and Forge of Cavils. Moreover, because it is superfluous to that end which they propose, that is, to the Perception and Dijudication of the Reasons of Naturalists: For there needs no more thereto, than, like the natural Philosophers themselves, to use terms ordinary and perspicuous.

If, besides this, there may seem any thing of use, it can be nothing but a collection of some few *Canons* or *Rules both concerning terms,* and the Criteries whereby we use to dijudicate.

Thus may this short Canonick, or Treatise of Rules, serve instead of a laborious and prolix Dialectick, and be reputed either a distinct part of Philosophy (though least considerable,) Or, (p) an addition to *Physick,* by way of Introduction.

(p) Senec. Ep. 89.

THE

The First Part OF PHILOSOPHY.

CANONICK of the CRITERIES.

(a) Laert.

FOrasmuch as (a) every question in Philosophy is either of the Thing or of the word, to Solution whereof many Canons may be given; hence the First part of Philosophy which compriseth them, may be termed *Canonick*.

(b) Laert

But because, of the Word, nothing more is sought then the Use or *Signification*; but of the Thing, the Truth, which is of an abstruse Nature; therefore we will, in the Second place, comprehend in a few Canons all that belongs to the use of the Words: But in the first place lay down those of Truth, and its Criteries (which in number exceed the other,) premising some few Notes concerning them.

CHAP. I.

Of Truth and its Criteries.

First then Truth is Twofold, one of *Existence*, the other of *Enunciation* or Judgment. Truth of *Existence* is that, whereby every thing which exists in the nature of things, is that very thing which it is, and no other. Whence it comes to pass, that there is no Falsity opposite to this Truth (for *Orichalcum*, for example, is not false Gold, but true *Orichalcum*,) and therefore *it is all one, whether we say a thing is Existent, or True*.

Truth of *Enuntiation*, or Judgment, is nothing else but a conformity of an Enunciation pronounced by the Mouth, or a Judgment made in the Mind, with the thing Enunciated or Judged.

(b) Emp. loc. cit.

This is that Truth to which Falshood is opposite; for as (b) *it is true that the thing is so as it is said to be, so is it false that it is not so as it is said to be*.

(c) Cic. de fato.
(d) Cic. Acad. 4.
(e) Cic. de fato. loc. cit.

As for that which they call a future Contingent, (c) those *Disjunctions which are made of Contraries* (or rather those Complexions which are made by disjunctive Particles.) *are true*; as if we should say, (d) Either *Hermachus* will live to Morrow, or will not live; but (e) *neither of the parts in this disjunctive Proposition, taken singly, is true*: for neither is there any necessity in Nature, that *Hermachus* shall live to Morrow; nor, on the contrary, that he shall not live.

Moreover, because as the thing, whose Truth is sought, belongs either to Speculation only, or to Action. (the first of which appertains to Physick, the later to Ethick;) we must for this reason have a Criterie, or instrument of Judging, whereby it may be examined, judged, and discerned, in order to both these.

But forasmuch as natural things affect the *Sense* or *Intellect*, and moral things the *Appetite* or *Will*; For this reason, Criteries are to be taken from both these.

From the *Sense*, nothing can be taken more then its Function, Sensation, which likewise is called Sense.

From the *Intellect*, forasmuch as besides the Function which it hath, whil'st like the Sense it contemplateth the thing, as if it were present and apparent, (whence the perception of a things appearing, which appeareth to be as well to the Intellect, as to the Sense, is called a Phantasie, or Appearance;) forasmuch, I say, as besides this Function, it is proper to the Intellect to ratiocinate or discourse; there is therefore required a Prænotion or Anticipation, by looking upon which, somthing may be inferred.

Lastly, From the *Will* or *Appetite*, whose Property it is to persue or shun somthing, nothing else can be taken, but the Affection or Passion itself; and that either *Allective*, as Pleasure; or *Aversive*, as Pain or Grief.

(f) There are therefore in all three Criteries; Sense, or Sensation; Prænotion, or Anticipation; and Affection, or Passion. Concerning each of these, some Canons are to be prescribed.

(f) Laert. Cic. Acad. 4.

CHAP. II.

(a) Canons of Sense, the First Critery.

TO begin with the Canons which concern Sense; of these there may be laid down Four.

(a) Quales Epicurus videtur posse instituisse; collected by Gassendus, ne Canonica censeatur id nomen haud jure adepta. p. 157.
(b) From Laertius and Plutarch adv. Col.

CANON I.

(b) Sense is never deceived; and therefore every Sensation, and every Perception, of an Appearance is true.

This is proved, First, because (c) ' All Sense 'is void of Ratiocination, and wholly incapable 'of Reminiscence. For neither being moved by 'itself, nor by any other, is it able to add or 'detract any thing; or to joyn or disjoyn by 'enunciating or concluding, so as thereby it 'might think any thing, and be mistaken in that 'Thought. The Intellect indeed can do this,

(c) Laert.

but

but the Sense cannot, (d) *whose property it is only, to apprehend that which is present, and moveth it; as the sight, colour presented to it: but not to discern, that what is here presented is one thing; what there, another.* Now where there is a bare apprehension, not pronouncing any thing, there is no error or falshood.

(d) *Sext. Emp.*

Next, because (e) 'there is nothing that can 'refel or convince the Senses of Falshood, (for 'neither can Sense of a like kind refel Sense of 'a like kind; as, the sight of the Right Eye 'the sight of the Left, or the sight of *Plato* the 'sight of *Socrates*; and this, by reason of the 'equality of their credits) or that there is 'the same reason for both. For a pur-blind Man doth not less see that which he sees, than *Lynceus* seeth that which he seeth. 'Neither 'can that which is of an unlike kind refel that 'which is of an unlike kind, as the Sight the 'Hearing, and the Taste the Smelling; 'be-'cause they have different objects, and serve 'not to give judgment of the same things. Nei-'ther can one sensation of the same Sense refel 'another, because there is not any sensation 'wherewith we are not affected; and to which, 'whil'st we are affected with it, we do not ad-'here, and assent: as whil'st we see a Staff one 'while strait, out of the Water; another time, 'part under Water, crooked, for we cannot by 'any means see it crooked in the former condi-'tion, or strait in the later. Lastly, 'neither 'can Reason or Ratiocination refel the Senses; 'because all Ratiocination depends upon pre-'vious Senses, and it is necessary the Senses first 'be true, before the reason which is founded on 'them can be true.

(e) *Laert.*

This is confirmed; forasmuch as Sense is the first of the Criteries, to which we may appeal from the rest, but itself is self-evident, and of manifest truth. For (f) if we say every Sense is deceived, you will want a Criterie to determine and make good even that very saying upon any particular Sense; or, (g) if some one only, you will entangle yourself in an intricate Dispute, when you shall be demanded, Which Sense, how, and when it is deceived, or not deceived? So as the Controversie not being determinable, you must necessarily be deprived of all Criterie. Whence may be inferred, that, if any appearance to Sense be false, nothing can be perceived, or, (to express it in other terms) unless all appearances and bare preceptions of a thing be true, there were no credit, constancy, and judgment of truth. For, (h) 'they who 'alledge the contradiction of appearances one 'with another, can never prove even this con-'tradiction of them, or, that some are true, 'others false; they cannot prove it by any 'thing that is apparent, for the Question is of 'things apparent; nor by any thing unapparent, 'for that which is unapparent is to be demon-'strated by something else that is apparent.

(f) *Laert.*

(g) *Laert.*

(h) *Sext. adv. Log.* 2.

Again, this is confirmed; because, taking away the certainty of the Senses, and by that means the genuine knowledge of things, we take away all rule of Life and Action. (i) For as in a Building, if the first Rule be amiss, the Square untrue, the Plummet faulty, all things must necessarily be defective, and awry, and disproportioned; so must all things in life be preposterous, and full of trouble and confusion, if that which is to be esteemed, as it were, the first Rule, Square, and Plummet, for the discerning things good and bad, done or not to be done, be unsincere or preverse, that is, if it want the certainty which is, as it were, its rectitude. Whence it cometh to pass, that though Reason (for example,) cannot explain the cause why things near at hand are square, but seem round afar off; yet is it better to hesitate and alledge some wrong cause, rather than to overthrow the first faith and foundations whereon the constancy and security of life is so grounded, that unless you dare credit Sense, you will not have any way to shun precipitation and destruction.

(i) *Lucret. lib.* 4.

Thirdly, (k) 'Because the truth of the Sen-'ses is manifest even from this, in that their 'functions exist in nature, or really and truly 'are. For that we see and hear, is as truly some-'thing indeed existing, as our very feeling pain; 'and there is no difference (as even now we 'said,) between saying, a thing is existent, and 'true.

(k) *Laert.*

To speak more fully, (l) 'As the first Af-'fections, Pleasure and Pain, depend upon some 'Causes which produce them, and are by rea-'son of those Causes existent in Nature, (that 'is, Pleasure depends on pleasant things, Pain on 'painful, and it neither cometh to pass, that, 'what produceth Pleasure is not pleasant, nor 'that what causeth Pain is not painful, but that 'which produceth Pleasure, must necessarily be 'pleasant; that which Pain, painful and offen-'sive to Nature,) in like manner, as to the af-'fections of the appearances produced in us, 'whatsoever is the efficient Cause of them, is 'undoubtedly such as makes this appearance; 'and being such, it cannot come to pass, that 'it can be any other than such as that is con-'ceived to be, which makes this appearance: 'The same is to be conceived of all the rest in 'particular, for that which is visible not only 'seems visible, but is such as it seems; and that 'which is audible, not only seems audible, but 'is indeed such, and so of the rest: Wherefore 'all appearances are true, and conformable to 'Reason.

(l) *Sext. Emp. Adv. Log.*

(m) 'Hence it is manifest, that the Phan-'tasies even of those who doat and dream, are, 'for this Reason, conceived to be true, for that 'they truly and really exist, seeing that they 'move the Faculty, whereas, that which is not 'cannot move any thing. So that there is a ne-'cessity in Nature, that the *species* of things which 'are received in the Intellect, or Imagination, be-'ing in this manner moved, mingled, and di-'sturbed, that such Phantasies cannot but be, what-'soever Opinion follows them, whereby things 'are judged to be such in themselves, of which 'we are to speak next.

(m) *Laert.*

CANON 2.

(n) *Opinion follows upon Sense, and is super-added to Sensation, and capable of Truth or Falshood.*

(n) *From Laertius.*

This is proved, because when a Tower (for example) appeareth round to the Eye, the Sense indeed is true, for that it is really affected with the

the *species* of roundness, which *species* is truly such, and hath a necessary cause for which it is such, at such a distance ; and withal it is not deceived, for it does not affirm that the Tower is such, but only behaves itself passively, receiving the *species*, and barely reporting that which appeareth to it. But Opinion, or the Mind, whose Office it is to conceive or judge, inasmuch as it adds, as it were from itself, that what appeareth to the Sense is a Tower, or that the Tower really and in itself, is round ; Opinion, I say is that which may be true or false.

Whence may be inferred, that (*o*) ' all Phantasies (or Sensations,) whereby *Phænomena*'s ' (things apparent,) are perceived, are true, ' but Opinions admit a difference ; for some are ' true, others false, inasmuch as they are our ' own Judgements superadded to the Appearances ; and we judge some things aright, others ' amiss, by reason that something is added, and ' imputed to the Appeartances, or something detracted from them : And generally Sense which ' is incapable of Ratiocination charged with ' falshood.

' But some are deceived by the diversity of ' those Apearances, which are derived from ' the same sensible Object, as in a thing visible, ' (for example) according as the Object seemeth to be either of another Colour, or of another Figure, or some other way changed ; for ' they conceive, that of contrary Appearances, ' one must necessarily be true, and the other ' which is opposite thereto false. Which certainly is very foolish, and proper to such men ' as consider not the nature of things, For (to ' continue our instance of things visible,) it is ' not the whole Solid, or the whole Solidity of ' the Body which we see, but the colour of the ' soild Body. Now of the colour, that which is ' in a soild Body, and appeareth in those things ' which are seen nigh at hand, is one ; that ' which is without the solid Body, as a *Species*, ' or Image flowing from it, and is received ' into places scituate one beyond another, such ' as appeareth in those things which are beheld ' at a great distance, is another. This later ' being changed in the intermedite space, and ' assuming a peculiar Figure, exhibits such an ' appearance as itself indeed is.

' Whence, neither the Sound which is in the ' Brass that is struck, nor the Voice which is in ' the Mouth of him who cryeth aloud, is heard, ' but that sound of Voice which lights upon our ' Sense ; for the same thing cannot be in two ' distant Subjects. And as no Man saith, that ' he hears falsly, who perceiveth the sound to be ' but small at distance, because coming nigher, ' he perceiveth it as if it were greater, so neither can we say, that the Sight is deceived, ' for that afar off it seeth a Tower, little and ' round ; near, great and square ; but rather that ' it is true. For when the sensible Object appeareth to it little, and of such a Figure, it is ' in that place little indeed, and of such a Figure, the extremities of those Images being ' broke off, whilst they are conveighed through ' the Air and thereupon coming into the Eye ' in a lesser Angle. And again, when it appeareth great and of another Figure, there it is ' great and of another Figure, it not being the

(*o*) Sext. Emp. adv. Log. 1.

' same in both places ; for here the extremities ' of the Images are more entire, nnd come into ' the Eye in a greater Angle : but it is a great ' mistake to think, that it is the same thing which ' appeareth to Sight, and affecteth the Eye near ' and afar off.

(*p*) Neither can we say, that the Sight is deceived, when we see a Shadow in the Sunshine to move, to follow our Footsteps, and imitate our Gestures. For Shadow being but Air deprived of Light, and the Earth, as we go, being now here, now there, successively deprived of the Sun's Light, and successivly recovering that whereof it was deprived, it comes to pass that the Shadow seems to change place, and to follow us ; but the Eyes are not therefore deceived, it being only their office to see the Light, and to see the Shadow in whatsover place it is. But to affirm, that the very Light or Shadow which is here, is the same, or distinct from that which even now was there, this belongs not to them, but to the Mind, whose office it is to determine and judge. So that whatsoever of falsity happens to be here, it is to be attributed to Opinion, not to Sense.

(*p*) Lucret.

(*q*) The same Answer may be given to a thousand other Objections, as of a Ship which seems to stand still, and the Land to move ; of the Stars, which seem to rest ; of Mountains far asunder, which yet seem to be nigh ; of Boys, who, having made themselves giddy by turning, think the Roof itself runs round ; of the Sun appearing to be near the Mountains, when as so great spaces divide them ; of the appearance of a Space under Water; as large, as from above it to the Sky ; of a River, which to those who pass over it, seemeth to flow back towards the Spring ; of a Gallery, which seems narrow at the further end ; of the Sun, who seems to rise out of the Water, and to go down into the Water ; of Oars, which seem crooked or broken : of Stars in the Night, which seem to glide over the Clouds ; of Things, which, by drawing the Eye on one side, double.

(*q*) Lucret. loc. cit.

CANON 3.

(*r*) *All Opinion attested, or not contradicted by the evidence of Sense, is True.*

(*r*) From Sext. Emp.

Evidence of Sense, I here call that kind of Sensation, or Appearance, which, all things obstructive to Judgment being removed, as distance, motion, indisposition of the Medium, and the like, cannot be contradicted. Whence to the Question, Whether a thing be such as it appears ? We ought not to give a sudden Answer, but to observe (*s*) that which I call προσ- μενόμενον *expectable*, in regard that we must stay, until the thing be fully examined and sifted out, according to all the ways that it can possibly happen.

(*s*) Laërt.

'(*t*) Attestation I call Comprehension, made ' by Evidence, that the thing conceivable is such ' as we before conceived it ; as *Plato* coming towards me, from afar off ; I conjecture, and , think, as far as I can guess at such a distance, , that it is *Plato* ; but when he draws nigher, and , the distance is taken away, by the evidence of , the thing, then, is there made an Attestation ' that it is *Plato*.

(*t*) Sext. Emp.

Not-

'Not contradiction is said to be the finding
'out of a thing not manifest, which we suppose,
'and conceive by reflecting on somthing manifest
'or evident; as when I say, there is *Vacuum*,
'which indeed is unmanifest, I am induced there-
'to by somthing manifest, that is, by Motion,
'for if there were no *Vacuum*, there would be
'no Motion, seeing the Body that should be mo-
'ved, would not have any place to go into, all
'things being full, and close pack'd together.
'Whence that which is apparent or manifest
'doth not contradict that which is unmanifest,
'since indeed there is Motion.

The Attestation and Not-contradiction is the Criteries, whereby a thing is proved to be true.

CANON 4.

(a) Out of Sext. Empir.

(a) *An Opinion, contradicted or not attested by evidence of Sense, is false.*

(b) Sext. Ibid.

In which words, (b) Contradiction is som-
'thing opposite to Not-attestation, it being the
'joint destruction of a manifest thing together
'with another supposed unmanifest; as for in-
'stance, Some affirm, there is not *Vacuum*; but
'together with this supposition must be subver-
'ted a thing manifest, *viz.* Motion. For if there
'be no *Vacuum*, Motion likewise cannot be, as
'we have already shewed.

'In like manner, Contradiction is opposed to
'Attestation; for it is a subversion, whereby it
'appeareth that the thing conceivable is not such
'as it was conceived in the opinion; as a Man
'coming towards us from afar off, we at that
'distance guess he is *Plato*, but the distance being
'taken away, it appeareth to us by evidence that
'he as not *Plato*. This is contradiction, for the
'thing manifest contradicts the preconceived
'Opinion. Thus an Attestation and Not-con-
'tradiction is the Critery, by which a thing is
'proved to be true; so Contradiction and Not-
'attestation is the Critery by which a thing is
'evinced to be false; Evidence being the Basis
'and Foundation upon which all right Opinion of
'Truth and False is grounded.

To omit, that Evidence is somtimes had by one Sense, and about some proper Sensible; somtimes by many, as when the Sensible is common, as Magnitude and Figure, Distance and Position, Rest and Motion, and such like, which may be perceived both by the Sight and Touch, and become manifest, if not to one Sense, at least to the other. Whereupon it somtimes happens, that by reason of several Qualities, several Senses may be summoned, that the Evidence which cannot be got by one, may be obtained by the other; as when we cannot discern by Sight, whether the Bread that is offer'd us be true or counterfeit, we may summon our Taste, whereby it will evidently appear, which of the two it is

But this I advise, that, after we have exactly considered all, we adhere to those things which are obvious to us; using our Senses, either the common about common Sensibles, or the proper about the proper. Since we must hold general-ly to all Evidence which is freely presented to us by every Critery, but especially by this: 'and tenaciously stick to it, as to an infallible Princi-'ple, lest either the Criteries which are esta-'blished by Evidence be overthrown, or Error, 'being established as strong as Truth, turn all 'things upside down.

I need not repeat or give particular Advice, what is to be done about the Instance alledged of a Tower, which at distance seems Round, but nearer, Square: for, from what is deduced it is manifest, that before we assert any thing, we must expect or pause, and approach neither, and examine and learn, whether the Tower be such when we come at it, as it appeared far off.

I shall only give this general Rule. That unless (the truth of the Senses being preserved after the manner aforesaid,) you distinguish that which is opinable or conceivable into that which is expectable or requireth time, before it be asserted what it is, as being not yet duely perceived, and into that which is present and proposed to us, and throughly examined, it will come to pass, that you will perpetually be disquieted with deceitful or vain Opinions. But if, when the things opinable are agitated in your Mind, you firmly esteem all that is here called expectable as such indeed, and pass not lightly by it, as if that which is false, not having the Attestation of any Evidence, were firm and allowable; in this Case you will behave your self as one that is cautious of all Ambiguity, and solicitously takes heed to every Judgment, which is rightly or falsly passed of an opinable thing.

CHAP. III.

Canons of Prænotion or Anticipation; the Second Criterie.

OF Prænotion or Anticipation may be given Four Canons;

CANON I.

(a) *All Anticipation or Prænotion, which is in the Mind, depends on the Senses, either by Incursion, or Proportion, or Similitude, or Composition,*

(a) Out of Laert.

I mean, that the Notion (or Idea, and Form as it were, which being anticipated is called Prænotion) is begotten in the Mind by *Incursion* (or Incidence,) when the thing incurreth into the Sense directly and by itself, as a man just before our eyes. By *Proportion*, when the Prænotion is amplified or extenuated, but the Number, Scituation and Figure of the Parts, with a convenient bigness of each, is retain'd; as when having seen a Man of due magnitude, we from thence form in our mind the *Speices* of a Giant, by Amplification; or of a Pigmy, by Extenuation. By *Similitude*, when according to a thing first perceived by the Sense, we fancy another like it; as when we imagine a City unseen, like to some that we have seen. Lastly, by *Composition*, when we put as it were into one the distinct Notions which we have of two or more things; as when we so unite the Notions of a Horse and a Man, as that the Notion of a Centaure ariseth out them, but (b) *not without some assistence of Ratiocination.*

(b) Laert.

CANON

CANON 2.

Anticipation is the very Notion, and (as it were) Definition of the Thing; without which, we cannot Enquire, Doubt, Think, nor so much as Name any Thing.

For by the word *Anticipation*, or Prænotion, I understand a Comprehension of the Mind, or a suitable Opinion or Understanding fixed in the Mind, and, as it were, a certain Memory or Monument of that Thing which hath often appeared from without, (which the Mind hath represented in itself after some one of the forementioned manners:) Such for example is the Idea, or Form and Spices, reflecting upon which, we say to our selves that Thing is Man. For assoon as ever we hear this word Man pronounced, immediatly the Image of a Man is understood, according to the Anticipation formed in the Mind by the foregoing Sensations.

'Wherefore that Thing which is primarily 'and chiefly meant by and coucht under every 'word, and so apprehended by the Mind, is som-'thing perspicuous and manifest: For when we 'enquire after any thing, or doubt of it, or think 'somthing; we should not do it, unless we al-'ready had a Prænotion of that thing; as when 'we enquire, whether that which appeareth afar 'off, be an Horse or an Oxe, it is requisite that 'we should first have seen and known by Antici-'pation the Figure of an Horse and Oxe. In-'deed we could not so much as name any thing, 'unless we first had some image thereof known 'by Anticipation.

Hence it comes to pass, that, if it be demanded what any thing is, we define or describe it in such manner as it is, according to the Anticipation thereof which we have in our Mind. Neither do we thus only, being demanded what some singular thing is, as what *Plato* is, but also what an Universal is, as Man, not this or that, but considered in general; this is brought to pass according as the Mind, having seen many Singulars, and set apart their several Differences, formeth and imprinteth in herself the Anticipation of that which is common to them all, as an Universal Notion; reflecting upon which, we say, Man (for example) is somthing animate, and endued with such a Form.

CANON 3.

Anticipation is the Principle in all Discourse, as being that to which we have regard, when we infer that one is the same or divers, conjoined with or disjoined from another.

(d) Laert.

For, (d) whil'st we conceive any thing, either by Enuciation or Ratiocination, *it depends upon somthing first evident, unto which thing we having regard, and referring our thought, infer that thing of which the Question is, to be such, or not to be such*; that is, the same, or another; coherent, or not coherent with it. Thus, if we are to prove that this thing which we behold is a Man, we so look back upon the Prænotion which we have of Man, as that without any stop we say, Man is somthing animate and endued with such a Form; this that I see, is animate and endued with such a Form, therefore this that I see is Man; Or, it is not animate, nor endued with such a Form, therefore it is not Man.

But it is not necessary to confirm all things with exquisite Reasons or Arguments, and scrupulous forms of Reasoning, which are cried up by the Dialecticks; For there is this difference betwixt an Argument and the Conclusion of the Reason, and between a slender Animadversion and an Admonition; that in one, some occult, and (as it were,) involved things are unfolded and opened; in the other, things ready and open are judged. But where there are such Anticipations as ought to be, then what will follow or not follow from them, or what agrees or disagrees with them, is perspicuously discerned, and naturally inferred, without any Artifice, or Dialectick Construction; wherefore we need only take care, that the Anticipation which we have of Things be clear and distinct.

CANON 4.

That which is Unmanifest ought to be demonstrated out of the Anticipation of a Thing Manifest.

This is the same we said even now, That the Anticipations of Things from which we infer Somthing, and thinking upon which we make Sumptions or Propositions, which are Maxims or Principles, by which that which is inferred or concluded is conceived to be demonstrated, be perspicuous and manifest. For, (e) *Demonstration is a Speech, which collecting by granted Sumptions (or Propositions,) brings to light a Truth not manifest before.* Thus, to demonstrate that there is *Vacuum*, which is not manifest, supposing the Anticipation of *Vacuum*, and the Anticipation of a manifest thing (Motion,) these Sumptions are premised, If there is Motion, there is *Vacuum*, but there is Motion, and then is inferred, therefore there is also *Vacuum*. (e) Sext. Emp.

In this place, Motion is taken for the Argument, Medium, or Sign, which properly ought to be a sensible thing: For the sense is that, according to which it is necassary to make a conjecture by Ratiocination, ultimately to that which is unmanifest, although such a Sign or Medium hath not always a necessary Connexion with that which is inferr'd, but is somtimes only contingent, or probable, and might be otherwise.

Of this kind are many, from which we argue chiefly in superior things, those being such as may be brought to pass, not one way only, but many, as was hinted formerly.

Hither also may be (f) referred that which I use to term ἰσονομίαν, Equivalence, by which it is inferred, that one of the contraries being, the other also must be: and when I argue thus, if the multitudes of Mortals be so great, that of Immortals is no less; and if those things which destroy be innumerable, those which preserve ought also to be innumerable. (f) Cic. de nat. l.

Against those who deny there is any Demonstration, may be brought this Argument: (g) Either you understand what Demonstraion is, or you understand in not? if you understand and have the Notion thereof, then there is Demonstration (g) Sext. Emp.

stration; but if you understand it not, Why do you talk of that, whereof you have not any knowledg?

(b) Lucret. lib. (b) They who take away the Credit of the Senses, and profess that nothing can be known being in the same Ranks, do they not, when they confess that they know nothing, imply they know not this very thing, Whether any thing can be known? We should not therefore contend against them, that they walk backwards upon their Head: Yet if they affirm they do, and I thereupon grant, that this is known by them, I have a fair occasion to ask them, how, since before they saw nothing true in the things themselves, they came to understand what it was to know, and what to be ignorant?

CHAP. IV.

Canons of Affection or Passion; the Third Criterie.

Lastly, concerning Affection (or Passion,) which is, as I said, Pleasure and Pain, there *(a) Out of La-* may be Four (a) Canons.
ertius.

CANON 1.

All Pleasure, which hath no Pain joined with it, is to be embraced.

CANON 2.

All Pain, which hath no Pleasure joined with it, is to be shunned.

CANON 3.

All Pleasure, which either hindreth a greater Pleasure, or procureth a greater Pain, is to be shunned.

CANON 4.

All Pain, which either putteth away a greater Pain, or procureth a greater Pleasure, is to be embraced.

Of these we shall speak more largely in the *Ethicks*. In the mean time, I shall give this general Advertisement concerning Pleasure: Pleasure is desirable of it self, because it is Pleasure; Grief or Pain is alwayes abhorred and avoidable, because it is Pain; whence I conceive, a wise Man will have an Eye to this exchange or recompence, that he shun Pleasure, If it procure a Pain greater than it self; and undergo Pain, if it produce a greater Pleasure. As for my own part, I should forsake Pleasure, and covet Pain, either if Remorse were annexed to the Pleasure, or a lesser Pain might be taken instead of a greater.

CHAP. V.

Canons concerning the use of Words.

I Shall add somthing concerning the use of Words, (which I design'd to speak of last) and especially that which concerns Discourse; for which, two Canons may seem sufficient, one for the Speaker, the other for the Hearer: They are these;

CANON 1.

When thou speakest, make use of Words Common and Perspicuous, lest either thy Meaning be not known, or thou unnecessarily waste the time in Explication.

CANON 2.

When thou hearest, endeavour to comprehend the Power and Meaning of the Words, lest either their Obscurity keep thee in Ignorance, or their Ambiguity lead thee into Errour,

Above all, (a) ' we must know what Things (a) *Laert.* ' the Words signifie; that we may have som- ' thing, reflecting upon which, we may safely ' discern whatsoever we either conceive, or seek, ' or doubt; otherwise, if all things should es- ' cape us undetermined, they who would de- ' monstrate any thing to us, will proceed to in- ' finite, and we our selves gain nothing by our ' Discourse, but Words and empty Sounds. For ' it is necessary, we have regard to the Notion ' and primary Signification of every Word, and ' that we need not any Demonstration to under- ' stand that thing, in case we can pitch upon ' any thing, to which we may refer that point, ' about which our Enquiry, Doubt, or Opinion ' are busied.

Hence it is, that the Method of enquiring after Truth, which is performed by a certain orderly Procedure, ought first to prescribe certain Rules, by which that Affair may be performed, that so the Discoursers may agree, what it is concerning which they discourse. So that if any Man shall not first agree to this, but hath a mind rather to cavil and trifle in wordish Equivocation, he is not to be discoursed with, or still to be prest to explain himself, what 'tis he would be at; for by this means his Juggling will be discovered, and his Cavils will solve themselves: Nor will he be able to intangle his Adversary, but rather discover himself a ridiculous Sophister.

The Second Part
OF
PHILOSOPHY.

PHYSICK; or of, NATURE.

WE now come to *Physick*: Which I usually term *Physiology*, for that it is a Discourse and Ratiocination about the nature of things, in the contemplation whereof it is wholly employ'd.

We have already said our scope to be, that, through Perspection of the nature of things, nothing of disturbance, either from Meteors, or from Death, or from the unknown ends of Desires, or any other way, may arise unto us. Now the things which this Contemplation fathoms being so many, and so various, it seems very profitable, that (some being engag'd in the more profound Study of the liberal Disciplines, or, through some other business, not having leisure to know every thing particularly and exactly,) we have ready at least (*a*) 'some proper compendium of the whole Science of Nature, that 'whensoever they will apply their Minds to the 'chief arguments of things, they may be assistent 'to themselves, according to the measure of their 'Knowledg, in contemplation of Nature.

'Besides, to those who have made a greater 'progress in the speculation of all things, whereof Physiology treateth, it is very useful, by some 'compendious Idea, to preserve the memory 'of the things themselves digested under heads. 'For it often happens, that we need a general 'inspection of things but not a particular disquisition. This way therefore is to be observed, and this kind of study continually used in 'exercising the Memory, that our attention to 'things may be constant and ready, and in the 'forms of things or notions, generally comprehended and imprinted in the Mind, and elsewhere throughly examined, according to the 'first Principles, and the terms whereby they 'are explained; if any thing be particularly inquired, in may be found, for where such a constancy and readiness is gotten, and the Mind is 'endu'd with a general and exquisite Information, we are able to understand of a suddain 'whatsoever we please. I add, *according to the 'words*; Forasmuch as it not possible, that a coherent sum of general heads can be frequently 'repeated by Heart, unless it so contain every 'thing, as that it may be explicated in few 'words, even if any thing come to be examined 'particularly.

'Hence it is, this course being most profitable 'to those, who are inclined and addicted to Physiology, that I would advise them therein, (especially if they enjoy a happy Life,) that they 'frame to themselves some such Epitome, and 'Information by general heads. But if they are not able of themselves, that they get one elsewhere, of which kind we have freely composed, for the benefit of the studious; hoping, that if what we have laid down be exactly remembred, as much as possible, although a Man runs not out into all particular Arguments that may be discussed, yet shall he obtain a copious knowledge of Physiology, incomparably beyond other Men; for he will of himself understand many things in the more general work, and, committing those to Memory, will help himself, and continually profit.

For these are of such a kind, that such as have made no little discussion of particulars, and addicted themselves perfectly to these contemplations, may thereby be enabled to raise and compleat more dissertations of all Nature; and whosoever of them are throughly vers'd in these, revolving them taictly within themselves, may be able in a moment, and quietly, to over-run whatsoever is most considerable in Physiology.

But not to stay longer in the entry, there being so many (as I say,) and various things contained in Physiology, it will be convenient to divide them into some principal *Sections*, which may afterwards be persued particularly; and every thing which especially belongs to any one of them, may be referred to it.

These Sections may by four. The first, of the *Universe*, or the nature of things which compriseth this World, and all other things that are beyond it. The Second, of the *World*, this wherein we are, and by which we may conjecture of the innumerable others. The Third, of *Inferior things*, the Earth, to which we adhere, and of the things in it. The Fourth, of *Sublime things*, which are seen and produced above the Earth, and upwards from it.

SECT. I.

Of the Universe, or the Nature of things.

TO begin then with the *Universe*, it is manifest, that it is so named, forasmuch as it containeth all things, even others besides this World; Whence it is also termed, *the Whole*, and, *the All*; And we usually call it, the Sum of things, and the Nature of things.

(*a*) *Laert.*

We must first speak generally of *the things where the Universe consists*; Next, of what *the so many things in the Universe are made*; Thirdly, *By what they are made*; Fourthly, *What kind they are of, when made*; Fifthly, *How they are made*; Lastly, *How they perish*.

CHAP. I.

That the Universe consists of Body, and Vacuum, or Place.

(a) Laert.
(b) Laert.

First therefore, (*a*) *The Universe consists of Body and* Vacuum (*b*); neither can there be conceived any third Nature besides these.

(c) Sext. Emp.

Now, (*c*) *Body is is understood by conceiting a certain vast heap (as it were)of Magnitude (or Bigness,) likewise of Figure, Resistence, (that is Solidity, and Impenetrability) and gravity*; withall, to be such, as it only can touch and be touched.

(d) Laert.

(*d*) *Emptiness, or Uacuum*; which is opposed to Body, and *only or properly, and in it self, is incorporeal*, is understood by Negation of these, and cheifly from being of an intactile Nature, and void of all Solidity, and *can suffer nor all any thing, but only afford a most free motion to Bodies passing though it*,

(e) Plut. Plac. l. 20.

For this is (*e*) *that Nature which being destitute of Body, is called* Vacuum; *taken up by a Body, Place; passed though by a Body, Region*, considered as diffused, Interval or Space,

(f) Laert.

(*f*) *That there are Bodies in the Universe, Sense attests*; *whence it is necessary to deduce Conjecture from other Principles, to that which is unmanifest, as I formerly touched.* Certainly, all these things which we behold, which we touch, which we turn up and down, whch we ourselves are, are nothing but Bodies.

But *that there is* Vacuum *also, is hence manifest, that if it were not in Nature, Bodies would neither have where to be, nor any way to perform their Motions*; *whereas that they are moved, is evident*.

(g) Lucret. lib. 1.

(*g*) Doubtless if all were full, and the matter of things crouded, as it were, together, it could not be, but that all things must be immoveable; for neither would any thing be moved, but it must thurst forward all things; nor would there be place left, whereinto any things might be thrust. For whereas some answer, that Fishes therefore can move, because they leave a place behind them, into which the Water, being thrust forward, and giving place, are received, they observe not, that the first impulsion forward could never begin, because there is not yet any place, neither behind, nor beside, whereinto the Water may by received. So as it is necessary, there should be little empty intervals of space within things, especially the fluid; into which the little Particles being driven may be so received, that, by the compression, place may be made, towards which, the impelling Body may be moved forward, and, in the interim, leave place behind, into which the compressed fluid may dilate it self, and, as it were, flow back.

(b) Lucret. loc. cit.

(*b*) I pass by other Arguments, as, That Thunder or Sound were not able to pass through Walls, nor Fire to penetrate into Iron, Gold, and the rest of Metals; unless in these there were some vacuous little Spaces intermingled. Besides, forasmuch as Gravity is proper to Bodies, the weight of things could not be made greater or lesser, if it were not according to their having more or less Vacuity intermixed.

Now *Vacuum*, being incorporeal, is so penetrated by Bodies, whether existing in it, or gliding by it, that it remains unchang'd, and preserves the same Dimensions to which it is adequate. Whence a streight Line, taken in *Vacuum*, is indeed streight, but not so, that it becomes crooked with the Body which fills it, because *Vacuum* is neither moveable in whole nor in part.

Whence it comes, that wheras the Notion of place is, to receive the things placed to be coextended with it; not to be moved with it, nor to forsake it; left either the Body be moved, yet not change place; or change place, yet not be moved: It therefore is only competible to *Vacuum*, to have the nature of place, forasmuch as it only, both by its corporeal Dimensions, length, breadth, and depth, is coextended with the thing placed in length, breadth, and depth, and exactly adjusted to it. Besides it is so immoveable, that whether the Body come to it, or go from it, or stay in it, it continueth the same and unvariable.

(i) Laert.

That I said, (*i*) *No third Nature beside can be conceived*, it is for this reason, that whether we take to be conceived *comprehensively*, (in which manner the things, which, by themselves and directly fall into our knowledg are perceived,) *or comparatively to those things which are conceived*, (after which manner those things are understood, which are known only by proportion, as was said about Anticipation,) whatsoever it be that is conceived, either it hath some Bulk and Solidity, and so is a Body; or it is void of all Bulk and Solidity, and so it is *Vacuum*; which is to be understood, *in case you conceive it a certain by it-self existent, subsistent, coheren Nature*; *and not as some adjunct or accident thereof*.

(k) Lucret. lib. 1. v. 450.

For since (*k*) and Adjunct is a property, which cannot be taken from the thing to which it belongs, without destruction of the thing; as Tactility from Body, Intactility from *Vacuum*; and in a more familiar Example, as weight from a Stone, heat from Fire, moisture from Water: But an Accident is that, whose presence or absence violates not the integrity of the Nature, ae Liberty and Servitude, Poverty and Riches, War and Peace, &c. Therefore they constitute not some third Nature, distinct from corporeal and incorporeal, but only are as somthing appertaining to one of these.

CHAP. II.

That the Universe is Infinite, Immoveable, and Immutable.

(a) Laert.

Now (*a*) *the Universe*, consisting of *Vacuum* and Body, *is* Infinite; *for that which is Finite hath a Bound, that which hath a Bound, is seen from some other thing*; or *may be seen from out of an interval beyond, or without it*. But *the Universe is not seen out of any other things beyond it*; *for there is no Interval, or Space, which it containeth not within it self, otherwise it could not be an Universe, if it did not contain all Space*

Space; *therefore neither hath it any Extremity. Now, that which hath no Extremity hath no End, and that which hath no End doubtless is not Finite, but Infintie.*

(b) Lucret. 1.

This is confirmed; (b) for if you imagine an Extremity, and suppose some Man placed in it, who with great force, throws a Dart towards it's utmost Surface, the Dart will either go forward, or not, but be forced to stay. If it go forward, there is place beyond, wherefore the Extremity was not there, where we desin'd it: If not, therefore there is somthing beyond, which hinders the Motion, aud so again, the Extremity was not in the fore-designed place.

(c) Laert. 968.

Moreover, (c) *this infinity belonging to the Universe is such, both in the multitude of Bodies, and the magnitude* of Vacuum; nay, in Infinites thrusting themselves forward mutually, alternately, or in order. 'For if *Vacuum* were Infinite, ' and Bodies Finite, then Bodies, *which are in* ' *perpetual Motion*, (*as we shall anon declare*,) ' would rest no where, but be dispersedly carried ' through the infinite *Vacuum*, as having no-' thing to stop them, and restrain them, by va-' rious Repercussions. But if the *Vacuum* were ' Finite, the Bodies Infinite, then there would ' not be place large enough for the Infinite Bo-' dies to exist in.

(d) Laert.

' *Hence* (*d*) we ought not so to attibute to ' the *Universe*, or Infinite Space, the being above ' or below, as if there were any thing in the ' Universe highest, or any thing lowest; the ' former, by conceiving the space over our Head, ' not to be extended to Infinite; the later, by ' imagining that which is under our Feet not to ' be of Infinite extent, as if both that which is ' above and that which is below, were termi-' nated with some one and the same point, as ' it happens with us, or the middle of this World, ' one of its extream parts being imagin'd high-' est, the other lowest; for in Infinite, which ' hath neither extreams nor middle, this cannot ' be imagin'd.

' Wherefore it is beter to assume some one ' Motion, which may be understood to proceed ' upwards into Infinite, and in like manner ano-' ther which downwards; although that movea-' ble, which from us is carried up towards the ' places over our Heads, meet a thousand times ' the Feet of those who are above, *and* (*con-*' *ceiting other worlds,*) *think it comes from below*; ' or which from us is carried towards that quar-' ter, which is under our Feet, to the Heads of ' those who are below us, *and who are thence apt* ' *to imagin, that it comes from above:* Notwith-' standing which Imagination of theirs, either ' of these opposite Motions, taken intirely, is ' rightly conceived to be of infinite extent.

(e) Laert.

' To these is consentaneous, 'that (*e*) the Uni-' verse was ever such as it now is, and such as ' it now is shall ever be, for there is nothing ' into which, *losing the Nature of the Universe,* ' it may be changed; and besides the Universe, ' *which containeth all things,* there is nothing, ' which by assaulting it, can cause an alteration ' in it.

(f) Eufeb.

Rightly therefore is the Universe esteemed as (*f*) *immoveable, there being no place beyond it, into which it may be moved:* So also Immutable, forasmuch as it admits neither Decrease nor Increase, and is void of Generation and Corruption, and therefore is eternal, not having beginning, nor end of Duration.

And indeed, many things in it are moved and changed, but whatsoever Motions and Mutations you conceive, they bear no proportion, if compared with the immensity of the Universe it self. Nor is therefore the whole Universe either moved into any other place, or changed into any other thing; does it therefore not persevere to be ever the same, which it ever was? For the Motions and Mutations in it were always alike, so as in may by said, *that* (*g*) *there is nothing new done in the Universe, more than what was already done in the infinity of time.*

(g) Eufeb. prap.

CHAP. III.

Of the Divine Nature in the Universe.

BUt before we speak of things in the Universe, which are generated and corrupted, and of the Principles whereof they are made, it is fit to premise, and put, as a By discourse, a Treatise concerning Divine Nature; as well for the Excellency of that Nature, as for that, although it be of the same with corporeal Nature, yet is it not so much a Body, as a certain thing like a Body, as having nothing common to it with other Bodies, that is, with transitory, or generated, and perishable things. Now it first being usually question'd concerning the Divine Nature, whether there be any in the Universe, yet the thing seems as if it ought not at all to be called in question, forasmuch as Nature herself hath imprinted a Notion of the Gods in our Minds: For what Nation is there, or what kind of Men, which without Learning have not some Prænotion of the Gods?

Wherefore, seeing it is an Opinion not taken up by any Institution, Custom, or Law, but the firm consent of all Men, none excepted, we must necessarily understand, that there are Gods; because we have the knowledg of them ingrafted, or rather innate in us. But that, concerning which the Nature of all men agreeth, must necessarily be true; therefore it is to be acknowledged, that there are Gods.

(*a*) Indeed men may seem, when they beheld the course of the Heavens, and the various Seasons of the year, to wheel about, and return in certain order, and were not able to know by what Causes it were performed, to have recurr'd to this Refuge, to attribute all things to the Gods, and make them obey their Beck, placing them withall in Heaven, for that they beheld in Heaven the Revolution of Sun, Moon, and Stars; but how could they attribute these to the Gods, unless they had first known, that there were Gods?

(*a*) Lucret.

(*b*) 'Did they not rather derive a knowledg ' of the Gods from the Apparitions of Dreams? ' certainly, they might by some great Images ' incurring to them under human Forms, by ' Dreams, conceive that there are indeed some ' Gods endued with such a human From; they ' might, I say, not so much in Sleep, as when ' Awake they called to mind, that those excellent Images had appeared to them in Sleep, so

(b) Sext. Emp. adv. Math.

Majestick of so subtle a composure, and so well proportion'd in shape, conceive that there is no repugnance, nay, that there was a necessity, that somwhere there should be things of like nature with these, capable also of Sense or Understanding, (c) because they fancied them moving their Limbs, and speaking. And those also immortal, because their shape was always present to their apprehensions because their Form remain'd still the same, and was of such grandeur, that they seem'd not easy convincible, but there were such; moreover Blessed, forasmuch as they neither fear death, nor take any pains in effecting their Works.

(c) Lucret.

(d) They might also by discourse use that ἰσονομία, or *quivalence*, by which when we treated of the Criteries, we affirmed it was concluded, that *if the multitude of Mortals were so great, that of Immortals was not less, and if those things which destroy be innumerable, those which preserve ought also to be innumerable.*

(d) Cic. de nat. deor. 1.

(e) Which way soever it came, we have this certainly by Prenotion, That we think the gods are blessed and immortal: 'For the same Nature 'which gave us information of the gods themselves imprinted also in our Minds, that we 'esteem them Blessed and Eternal; Which if it be so, our Opinion is truly laid down, (f) 'What is Eternal and Blessed, neither is troubled with any business it self, nor troubles any 'other; therefore not possessed with Favour or 'Anger; for all such are weak.

(e) Cic. de nat. deor. 1.

(f) Laert.

And if we sought no further than to Worship the gods piously, and to be free from Superstition, what we have said were sufficient; for the excellent Nature of the gods is worshipped by the Piety of Men, as being Eternal, and most Blessed. For to whatever is excellent, Veneration is due, and all Fear, proceeding from the Power and Anger of the gods, would be expelled; for it is understood, that Anger and Favour are far separate from a Blessed immortal Nature; which being removed, no fears hang over us as to the gods. But for confirmation of this Opinion, the Soul enquires after the Form and the Life, and the action of Mind, and agitation in God.

(*) 'As to the Form, Nature partly instructs 'us, partly Reason; for by Nature, all of us, of 'all Nations, have no other Form, but Human, 'of the gods. For what other Forms ever occur 'to any Man, waking or sleeping? But not to 'reduce all things to their first Notions, Reason 'it self declares the same. For seeing it is proper to the most excellent Nature, either because it is Blessed, or because it is Sempiternal, 'that it be most beautiful, What composition 'of Limbs, What conformity of Lineaments, 'What Figure, What Form can be more beautiful, than the Human?

(*) Cic. de nat. deor. 1.

'Now if the Figure of Men excelleth the Form 'of all things Animate, and God is Animate, certainly he is of that Figure which is the most 'beautiful of all. And forasmuch as it is manifest, that the gods are most Blessed, and none 'can be Blessed without Virtue, nor Virtue consist without Reason, nor Reason consist in any 'Figure but that of Man; we must acknowledge, that the gods are of Human Form.

But when I say, that the gods are of the Form of a Man, and of an animate Being, Do I therefor attribut such a Body to them, as ordinarily Men and animate Beings have? By no means; For 'God is not a thing, as *Plato* says, meerly Incorporeal; because what kind of thing that is, 'cannot be understood, for then he must necessarily want Sense, he must want Prudence, he 'must want Pleasure; all which we comprehend 'together with the Notion of the gods. But neither is he therefore a gross Body, no not the most subtle that can be coagmentated of Atoms; but he is altogether a Body of his own kind, which indeed is not seen by Sense, but by the Mind; nor is he of a certain Solidity, nor composed of Number, but consists of Images, perceived by Comparison; and which, compared with those that ordinarily occur, and are called Bodies, may be said 'to be (not Body, but) as before I said, 'resemblance of Body, and (for example) not 'to have Blood, but a certain resemblance of 'Blood.

In the mean time, I must intimate by the way, that (g) he is not such a kind of Body as is coagmented of Atoms, for then he could not be Sempiternal, and upon his Generation would follow Corruption: upon his Concretion, Dissipation, and so he could not be Sempiternal. Thus, there are four things to be esteemed *Eternal* and *Incorruptible*; the *Universe*, which hath no place into which it can fall; *Vacuum*, which cannot be touch'd, nor receive any blow; the *Matter* of things, which unless it did subsist unchanged, those things which are dissolved would go away into nothing; and the *Divine Nature*, which is inconcrete, and, by reason of its Tenuity, cannot be touched nor struck.

(g) Lactant.

Hence one of the Natural Philosophers was in a great error, when he said, That the Nature of the gods is such, as to diffuse, and send forth Images out of it self; for in this manner, somwhat might be so taken out of it, as that it might be admitted dissolvable. But (h) some have misinterpreted our meaning, when, upon our admitting many Worlds, and saying, that there are *Intermundia*, that is Intervals between the Worlds, they affirm we place the gods in the *Intermundia*, lest they should receive any injury by the Worlds ruine. For as (i) *Vacuum*, so is the nature of the gods more subtle, then to fear any harm from Bodies; which if it did fear, in no place were it more to be feared than in the *Intermundia*, when the World should come to be dissolved.

(h) Seneca de benef. 4. 19.

(i) Lucret. 5.

Neither can we design in what places the gods live, seeing that this our World is not a seat worthy of them; but we can only say in general, such as the Poets describe *Olympus*, such are, wheresoever they be, the blessed and quiet Seats of the gods.

(k) *Where Showers not fall, nor Winds unruly blow,*
Where neither blasting Frost, nor hoary Snow
Rifle the place; but Heaven is ever bright,
Spreading his Glorious Smiles with chearful Light.

(k) Lucret. 3.

(l) 'Hereupon it being further demanded, 'what kind of Life that of the gods is, and what 'state of age they enjoy, it may be answered, 'That certainly, than which nothing can be more 'Happy, nothing more abundant in all Goods,

(l) Cic. loc. cit:

'can be imagined. For God doth nothing, he is
'not intangled in any Employments, he under-
'takes no Works, but joyeth in his own Wisdom
'and Virtue. He knows for certain that he shall
'ever be in Pleasures, both Greatest and Eternal.
'This God we justly style Blessed, who ourselves
'place a blessed Life in security of Mind, and in
'disengagement from all Business; but not, such
'as others do describe him, Laborious, invol-
'ved in great and troublesome Employments.

CHAP. IV.

Of First Matter, or, of the Principles of Compound things in the Universe.

NOw to resume and persue our Discourse, forasmuch as in the first place 'tis manifest by Sense, that in Nature many things are generated, and many corrupted; therefore we must conclude, that hereto is required Matter, of which things may be generated, and into which they may be resolved; For (*a*) *of nothing, nothing is made; and into nothing, nothing goes away. For if something were made of nothing, every thing might be produceing from any thing, as not required Seeds; and if that which perisheth did go into nothing, all things would perish absolutely, there not remaining those things into which they were dissolved.*

(*a*) *Laert.*

Besides, forasmuch as we affect to know the nature of any thing, generated or made, it is first demanded, whether it be some thing one and simple, or compounded of some things which themselves are simple and precedent. It is manifest, that nothing generated or made can be one and simple, seeing that it hath parts of which it was made up, and into which again it may be dissolved, which therefore are precedent and more simple; and if they still be compounded, they may be conceived to consist of those, which at length are the first and most simple.

(*b*) *Laert.*

Thus again it appear, *that* (*b*) *of Bodies, some are Concretions*, or (if you like it better,) concrete or compounded Bodies; *others, of which Concretions*, or compounded Bodies, *are made*. These, if first and simple, are the first matter of things, and are termed Principles, and, by the later Authors, Elements also.

These *Principles*, or first things of all, must be simple uncompounded Bodies, (or rather Atoms) and *indivisible*, or not resolvable by any force, and consequently *immutable*, or in themselves void of all mutation. I mean, *if it shall so come to pass*, as that in the dissolution of Compounds, *all things go not into nothing, but that there consist and persevere a certain Nature, full, or void of vacuity,* and therefore solid; *which being such, it cannot in any part, or by any means, admit a diversion, and so be dissolved.*

Wherefore *it is necessary*, that those which are called the Principles of compounded *Bodies, be,* as *of a Nature*, full, solid, and *immutable*, so wholly *indivisible*; whence we use to call them *Atoms*. We term it an Atom, not as being the least, that is, as it were a point, (for it hath a Magnitude) but for that it cannot be divided, it being incapable of suffering, and void of vacuity. So that he who saith, *Atom*, names that which is free from a blow, and can suffer nothing; and which is invisible indeed by reason of its littleness, but indivisible by reason of its Solidity.

CHAP. V.

That there are Atoms in Nature, which are the Principles of Compound Bodies.

THat (*a*) there are Atoms, the Reason alledged sufficiently convinceth; For, seeing that Nature makes nothing of nothing, and reduceth nothing to nothing, there must remain in the dissolution of compound Bodies somthing that is incapable of further dissolution. Certainly if you say that it is still dissolvable, or divisible, it will be necessary, by subdividing, to come at last to somthing that is solid, and incapable of division; since that neither Nature itself doth dissolve things infinitely, but stays in some last things; nor can Body admit of an infinite division.

(*a*) *Laert.*

(*b*) 'In a finite Body, doubtless there can-
'not be parts of infinite either multitude or
'magnitude; wherefore there cannot be under-
'stood to be performed in it, not only that di-
'vision into infinite which is made into less, or
'by parts always lesser, and proceeds ever ob-
'serving the same proportion of division; but
'also that progression into infinite, which is
'made by proceeding not always by lesser, but
'by equal for those which are called determinate
'parts. For since infinite parts must needs be
'admitted to serve for an infinite division, how
'can there be infinite of them in a finite
'Body?

(*b*) *Laert.*

'He certainly who once hath said, that in eve-
'ry thing there are parts infinite in number, is
'not able further to understand and declare how
'that magnitude, whereof he speaks, comes to
'be finite. For whether the parts that a divi-
'sion or progression may be made into infinite
'be determinate, (that is, equal among them-
'selves,) or indeterminate, (that is, always les-
'ser) it is manifest that the magnitude, whose
'parts they are, and which consists and is com-
'pounded of them, must indeed be infinite.

'And since on the other side, a finite mag-
'nitude manifestly hath an extreme *or last* part, *easie to be perceived and shewn*, 'unless this part
'may by seen by itself, and as the last, we cannot, *although we should subdivide it,* 'understand any
'other part, which should be thought the last *rather than this; for that with as much reason will be divisible.* 'Whence *it will come*, that by pro-
'ceeding *further*, and consequently towards an
'extreme part into infinite, we can never ar-
'rive, not even by thought, to that part which
'is the last, *nor be able to over-run, by progression, even the least space.*

(*c*) Add to this, That unless in Dissolutions there did remain little Bodies, so solid as that they cannot be dissolved by any force, the difference between Body and *Vacuum* could not be sufficiently understood, inasmuch as nothing of Body, by infinite attenuation, would be capable to resist; by which means too all things would become weak or soft, and nothing could be made hard, seeing that Solidity only is the foundation of hardness. Neither need we scruple, as if be-

(*c*) *Lucret.*

cause

cause Atoms are solid, soft things cannot be made of them, for they may be made soft by intermission only of *Vacuum*, into which the compressed parts retire, and yeild to the touch.

(*d*) (*d*) add also the diverse sorts of constancy in nature, as in carrying on Animals always to certain bounds of strength, augmentation and life; in imprinting always the same distinctions and marks of every particular kind; which she could not do, if she did not use Principles certain and constant, and therefore not obnoxious to Dissolution and Mutation.

d) *Lucret. etc. cit.*

CHAP. VI.

Of the Properties of Atoms; and first, of their Magnitudes.

Although all Atoms, by reason of this solidity, may seem to be of one and the same nature, yet have they some Adjuncts or Properties, and certain (*a*) Qualities, by which they may differ among themselves, such only are *Magnitude, Figure, and Weight*. and if there be any beside which are necessarily ally'd to Figure, as roughness, and smoothness; for *Colour, Heat, Cold,* and the rest of the Qualities *are not such as are proper to Atoms*, but to Compounds, and arising partly out of the Adjuncts, partly the Accidents of Atoms, of which we shall speak hereafter.

(*a*) *Laert.*

This in brief, at present; (*b*) If Colour (for example) were in the Atoms themselves, it would be as intransmutable as they are; and so the things consisting of Atoms, that are of one Colour could not change that, and appear under another, whereas we observe the contrary happens; for the Sea foaming looks white, it being otherwise of a green Colour, which doubtless if it were in it by reason of green Atoms, could not be changed into a white Colour. For whereas some say, That Contraries are made of Contraries, it is so far from being so, that White will sooner be produced out of no Colour at all, than out of Black. Better they, who conceive the matter of things, that it may undergo variety of Colours and other Qualities, ought to be void of them; as we chuse that Oil which is most free from any scent to make Perfumes of.

(*b*) *Lucret.*2.

But to touch a little every property of the Atoms : Whereas in the first place I attribute magnitude to them, I mean not any magnitude; for the largest Atom is not so great as to be perceptible by sight, but that magnitude which, although it be below the reach of Sense, yet is of some bigness, (for if Atoms were points void of all magnitude, no body of any magnitude could be made up of them.) Whence I use to say of an Atom, that it is some small thing, thereby, as it were, not excluding all magnitude from it, but the larger size only.

(*c*) Neither can it be objected, That the magnitude of Atoms is not perceived by the Senses, since we must necessarily confess, there are innumerable things invisible; for can we see the Wind, Heat, Cold, Odor, Sound, or the little Bodies, by whose arrival to the Sense these are perceived ? Can we see the little Bodies of moisture, by which Garments hung by the Water-side are moistned, yet being spread abroad are dried ? Can we see those which are rubb'd off from a Long Ring-worm, from a Wheel that turns round, from a Plough-share in ploughing, from a Stone which a drop hollows, which a Tread diminisheth, or those by which a Plant or Animal grows in its youth, decays in its old age, and the like ?

(*c*) *Lucret*

(*d*) 'Yet we must not think that all Atoms 'are of the same magnitude, it is more conso-'nant to Reason, that amongst them there be 'some greater, others lesser; and, this admit-'ted, a Reason may be given of most things that 'happen about the passions of the mind, and 'about the senses.

(*d*) *Laert.*

(*e*) That there may be an incomprehensible variety of Magnitudes beyond the reach of Sense, may also be understood even from this, forasmuch as there are some little Animals, whose third part, if we imagine them divided, would be invisible; nevertheless, to the composition of them an incomprehensible number of parts is necessary. For how many must there be to make the Entrails, the Eyes, the Joints, the Soul; to constitute all parts, without which we cannot understand there should be any living, sensitive, moving Animal ?

(*e*) *Lucret.*4.

Whether may not (to use a gross Example,) this variety be comprehended from those dusty motes which the beams of the Sun, coming in at a Window, discover ? For whereas without such beams all things are alike dark, yet they coming in, there appeareth an innumerable company of little bodies, in such manner, as that there is an evident difference between the greater and the lesser; nevertheless, I say not, (as some conceive) that these kinds of litle Bodies are Atoms, for in the least of them are contained many Myriads of Atoms; I only use them by way of comparison, that whereas the whole Nation (as in were,) of Atoms is impervious, and dark, even to the sharpest sight, yet we may understand it to be so illustrated by the beams of Reason, that the Atoms may be perfectly seen by the mind, and that we may conceive there are several degrees of magnitudes in them.

(*f*) Hence it happens, that as in a great and measurable magnitude we take somthing, which, that it may be the common measure, must have the proportion of the least, as a Foot, a Digit, a Barly-corn; and in sensible magnitude we take also somthing which is accounted the least as to Sense, as the little Creature called *Acaris*; so in intelligible magnitude, such as is that of the Atom, we may take somthing which in it is esteemed (as it were,) the least; such as in an Atom may be conceived, the very point in which a sharp angle is terminated.

(*f*) *Laert.*

(*g*) But this difference there is between the least, under the notion of measure, and the least of those which are sensible and intelligible, that the former, by its repetition, may be understood to be adæquated to the whole magnitude; but these later are conceiv'd as certain individual points, which either are bounds of magnitudes, or certain Connexures (as it were,) so interpos'd between the parts, as that they have only certain respects to the parts connected on each side, though they are such, that a beginning of men-

(*g*) *Laertib.*

mensuration cannot be made from them. For nothing hinders but that we may, by the mind, frame some dimensions in an Atom.

Although, when as we say, there are parts or connexures in an Atom, it is not so to be understood, as if at any time they were disjoined, and afterwards united; but we do it, to declare that in an Atom there is a true magnitude consisting of parts, though withal they have that difference from compound things, that their parts can only be distinguished by designation, not by separation; forasmuch as they cohere by a natural, indivisible, and perpetual Connexion.

CHAP. VII.

Of the Figure of Atoms.

(*a*) Lucret. lib. 2.

AS (*a*) concerning *Figure*, which is the bound of magnitude, it is first necessary, that in Atoms it be manifold; or, that Atoms amongst themselves be variously figured. This is proved, forasmuch as all natural things framed of them, Men, Beasts, Birds, Fishes, Plants, *&c.* are variously figured, not only in respect of their *Genus*, but of every particular *Species* or *Indiuiuum*; for there are not any two so like one another, but that if you mind them exactly, you will find some defferences by which they are distinguished.

(*b*) Laert.

Again, (*b*) *Forasmuch as the kinds of Figures in Atoms are incomprehensible for number*, for they are round, oval, lenticular, flat, gibbous, oblong, conical, hooked, smooth, rough, bristly, quadrilateral, *&c.* as well regular as irregular, without any determination possible to the Intellect, yet are they not to be esteemed simply infinite in number: *For there would not be so many and so great differences in concrete things, if in the Atoms, of which they are compounded, there were such a diversity of Figure as could be comprehended by the mind. Yet the diversities of Atoms cannot be absolutely infinite, unless a man conceive in Atoms a magnitude*, which is not only so small as to escape Sense, but is in reality infinitely little: *For in magnitude, or the superficies of magnitude, which is finite, cannot be understood diversities, which are infinite.*

But thirdly, although the kinds of Figure be not infinite, *yet are there in every Figuration, or kind of Figure, Atoms simply infitite in number*; that is, there are infinite round Atoms, infinite oval, infinite pyramidal; *for otherwise the Universe would not be infinite in multitude of Atoms*, as was already declared, *unless the Atoms which are like to one another in Figure, were absolutely infinite in number.*

(*c*) Plut. plac. l. 4. Lactant. instit. 3. 17.

(*c*) But take notice, That though there are Atoms corner'd and hooked, yet can they not be conceiv'd to be worn away or broken, because both the corners and hooks, as also the middle little bodies themselves are of one nature, and kept together with equal solidity and necessity, insomuch as no force whatsoever can compress on Atom, either as to the whole, or as to its parts, even to its very points.

CHAP. VIII.

Of the Gravity (or Weight,) and manifold Motions of Atoms.

LAstly, I attribute to Atoms *Gravity*, or *Weight*; for, whereas they are perpetually in motion, or striving to move, it is necessary that they be moved by that internal Impulse which is called Gravity, or Weight.

(*a*) There first presents itself to us in the Atoms a twofold motion, one of the gravity or weight itself, whereby the Atom is carried after its own way; the other, bo percussion or reflection, whereby one Atom, being driven upon another, is beaten back again. And as for the motion of gravity or weight, that motion is first conceived, whereby the Atom is carried on in a *streight* or perpendicular line. By this motion are all heavy things moved. But because if all Atoms should be moved in a streight line, or downwards, and, as it were, streight on, it should come to pase, that one could never overtake the other; It is therefore necessary, that Atoms should go a little *aside*, the least that may be, that so may be produced the complications, and adhesions, and copulations of Atoms to one another, of which may be made the World, and all the parts of the World, and all things in it.

(*a*) Lucret.

(*b*) When I say, That otherwise the Atoms would not overtake one another, and consequently not meet, the reason is, That the Universe being infinite hath no middle or centre towards which they may tend, and so meet; but only there may be conceived, according to what hath been said, some Region above, out of which, without any beginning, all Atoms, by there Gravity, would descend like drops of Rain, that is, by motions in themselves parallel; the other below, into which all, without any bound, would be carried by the same motions.

(*b*) Lucret. ib.

(*c*) Motion from reflection may be understood to be made, as well when the Atom rebounds by great leaps, as when being impell'd and repell'd within short spaces, it doth, as it were, quake and tremble. Whence also (*d*) it comes to pass, that while it hapneth that the Atoms run into certain meetings and complications of many obviating to, and entangling one another, (which is chiefly done in those Compounds where they seem to rest,*j*) yet then they are still unquiet, and, as much as they can, *and according as they are further from, or nearer to one another, they get an agitaion, or kind of palpitation, being bent down, or repressed by the rest, which make up that association.*

(*c*) Plut. plac. 1. 12.

(*d*) Laert.

The cause of this not only longer rebounding, but also shorter agitation, or, as it were, inward palpitation, cotinuing still in those Compounds is partly the nature of *Vackuum*, which, being intercepted even within the must compact Bodies plucks all the Atoms asunder from one another, either in whole or in part, not having power to stay or fix them; partly the Solidity connatural to the Atoms, which by collision and repercussion cause a trembling, as much as that complication will suffer that motion to be kept still continued by the stroke of the descending Atoms.

Atoms. Now since Weight or Gravity is a certain Vigour, or Energy, as it were ingenerate in Atoms; and as I said, an Impulsion, whereby they are fitted for Motion, we must therefore take it for certain, *that* (*) *Atoms are moved* (even with both kinds of Motion, of Weight, and Reflection,) *continually, and through all eternity*, because there is no first instant, since which they began to be made; not only Atoms, but also *Vacuum*, which serves for both Motions, being eternal.

(*) *Laert.*

We must also take it for certain, 'that † 'that Motion of Atoms, to which nothing oc- 'curs, which may divert it by beating against 'it, is of so great swiftness, as it over-runs any 'imaginable Space *in a moment, that is* in time 'unimaginably short; *for they ought in Velocity to 'out-run those Beams of the Sun, which make not 'their Course through pure Vacuum; I say, to 'which nothing occurs that beats it back*; for other- 'wise, this frequent Reverberation makes a 'kind of Slowness, as want of Reverberation 'makes a kind of Swiftness.

(†) *Laert.*

'Yet doth not hereupon the Atom, which 'suffers several Repulsions, arrive at divers pla- 'ces in such times as may be discerned by the 'Mind, for to discern those times is not within 'the power of the Mind. Besides, it may so 'happen, that the same Atom, though diverted 'by several Repulses, may be so carried, as that 'from whencesoever it comes, out of that immen- 'sity of Space, we shall not be able to assign 'any place or term, which in that time it hath 'not over-passed. For the Repercussion may be 'such, (*that is, so little frequent, and so little 'diverting,*) that it may in some measure equal 'the Swiftness of that Motion which is free from 'Repercussion.

Ibid.

'We must lastly take it for certain, That 'Atoms are equally swift, forasmuch as they are 'carried through *Vacuum*, neither is there any 'thing that resists their Progress: For neither 'are the heavy carried on more swiftly than 'those which are conceived light, seeing nothing 'occurs that may hinder either; nor the lesser 'more than the greater, forasmuch as the pas- 'sage is equally free to all, according to their 'several magnitudes. Neither do the Motions 'which are made, either upwards, or obliquely 'by Collisions, or downwards by their natural 'Gravity, differ in Swiftness; since an Atom, 'as long as it is not thrust on either side, so 'long keeps on its way, and that by a swift- 'ness equal to thought, untill being driven on, 'either extrinsecally, or by its own Gravity, it 'meets with the Resistence or Assault of the 'Atom that strikes it.

Laert.

'Moreover, as concerning compound Bodies, 'forasmuch as Atoms are in their own Nature 'equally swift, therefore one cannot be said to 'be swifter than another; as if the Atoms that 'are in compounds, and hurried away by the 'common Motion of them, were carried away, 'sometimes into one place by a sensible Motion, 'and that continuous, and in successive time, as 'whilst such Motion is slow; sometimes whe- 'ther into one or more places, they should be 'carried in times so short, as can only be con- 'ceived by reason, as when the Motion is most 'rapid. But we shall only say, that which way

Ibid.

'soever the Atoms are carried with the com- 'pounds, they are all the while exagitated with 'intestine, most frequent, or rather innumera- 'ble, and therfore not-sensible, Repercussions, 'untill the Perpetuity or Succession of the Mo- 'tion of the whole Body come to be such, as 'that it may fall under the reach of Sense.

'For what we fancy concerning the imper- 'ceptible Motion of Atoms, as if Times con- 'ceived by reason might reach the most swift 'Succession of their Parts, is no way true; but 'rather, whatsoever our Mind, attending to 'the very Nature of the thing, apprehends, 'that is to be esteemed true.

Ibid.

CHAP. IX.

That Atoms (not the vulgar Elements or Homoiomera's,) are the first Principles of things.

THis premised concerning Atoms, we now must shew how they are the Principles, or first Matter of things; but because that cannot be done without Treating at the same time of Generation and Corruption; and that cannot be performed, unless we first speak of the Qualities of things, and even before that, of the first Causes which produce these; it is sufficient in this place to take notice, that Atoms are the Principles and first Matter of things, because they are that first and most simple, of which all generated things are compounded; as also the last and most simple, into which all corruptible things are resolved.

I say, the first and the last; for besides other greater Bulks, of which that which is generated may more nearly be compacted, and into which that which is corrupted may be resolved, there are little Lumps, or certain small thin Compounds, which being made by some more perfect and indissoluble Coalitions, are, as it were, long durable Seeds of things; so that things may also be said to be generated of Seeds, not as of first Principles, because even these Seeds are generated of things precedent, that is, of Atoms. And likewise things may be said to be resolved into Seeds, but not ultimately, because even these may still further be dissolved into Atoms.

In like manner, the four vulgar Elements commonly admitted, Fire, Air, Water, Earth, may be called Principles, but not the first; they may also be called Matter, but not the first Matter; forasmuch as they have Atoms precedent to them, of which even they themselves are compounded.

Lucret. lib. 1.

And they who assign one Element only for Principle, will, that of it, by Rarefaction and Condensation, the three other be made, and of these afterwards, the rest of things. But how if it be one, and nothing mixt with it, can any thing be generated? For of Fire, (for instance,) rarefied, nothing else will be produced, but a more languid, or a stronger Fire.

Ibid.

And besides, that they who teach this, admit not *Vacuum*, without which, neither Rarefaction nor Condensation can be made; they seem not to observe, that Fire cannot be said to be changed by Extinction into some other thing;

Ibid.

because

because that which is simple cannot be changed, unless by going away into nothing. Or at least, if they admit that somthing common remains, which is first Fire, afterwards Air; since this somthing is the first and common Matter, the first Matter is not of itself, either Fire or Air, but rather those Atoms which being put together on one Fashion, may make Fire; being put together after another Fashion, may make Air.

Ibid. They who admit many, or all things, to be equally first, run moreover into this inconvenience, that making them contrary to one another, they by consequence make them such, as either can never join to make one Compound, or, if they do, must destroy one another.

Ibid. There was a natural Philosopher, who conceived that all things are generated of tenuious little Bodies. which he called *Homoiomera's, similar,* or *like Parts* (as it were,) *viz.* to the things generated ; so as those (for Example,) of which hot things are made; are hot ; those of which fleshy things, fleshy ; those of which bloody thing, bloody ; and so of the rest. But if Principles were of the same Nature with the things generated, they might, as well as they, be altered and lose their Qualities, and so be changed, and being of a simple Nature go into nothing.

Ibid. Not to press, that if the things, whereby somthing is made hot, must be hot ; as if things alike be not generated but of their like ; there must also be things laughing, that a laughing Animal may be made of them ; and things weeping, that a weeping Animal ; and the like.

CHAP. X.

Of the first and radical Cause of Compounds, that is, of the Agent, or Efficient.

IT followeth, That we speak of *Causes*, since to the making of any thing, is necessary, not only Matter, *of which*, but a Cause, *by which* it may be made; wherefore to say a Cause is no other, than to say, that which in the production of a thing is the Agent, or Efficient.

Now of the things that are made, no other first and radical Cause is to be required, than the same Atoms themselves as they are endued with that vigour, by which they are moved, or continually tending to Motion. Neither is it absurd to make Matter active, it is rather absurd to make it unactive, because they, who make it such, and yet will have all things to be made out of it, cannot say, from whence the things that are made, have their Efficient power, since they cannot have it elsewhere than from Matter.

Therefore, as the first little Compounds made up of Atoms have in themselves a certain Energy, or power to move themselves, and to act, consisting of the vigours of each several Atom, but variously modifi'd ; as some of them mutually entangling one another are carried hither, others thither ; so the greater Compounds made up of the lesser have some power also, and that modified according to their Variety ; and every natural Body consisting of those greater and lesser Compounds, and Atoms, have a particular Energy, or power of moving themselves, and acting, modified by a certain Reason. Thus, Motion or Action ascends to and proceeds from it's very Principles.

Yet we must observe, That though all Atoms are moved alike swiftly, yet within the Compounds themselves, those which are more corner'd and hooked, are intangled and hindred, and so made as it were more sluggish and dull, than the smoother and rounder. Wherefore the Energy, or power of acting, which is in compound Bodies, chiefly comes of these. And because those, of which Fire, the Soul, and those which are more generally termed Spirits, consist, are of this nature, hence it comes, that the chiefest Energy in Bodies, is from those very Spirits ; which, as they have Liberty of running up and down, so they have also Dominion within those Bodies.

But forasmuch as all Effection, or Action, whereby somthing is made, is either from an internal, or external Principle, it is manifest, that artificial things whose Nature is sluggish, and meerly passive, own all their Production to the Efficient, or external Agent. But natural things, although they borrow some part of themselves, or some Principle of acting from an extrinsecal Cause, yet they owe their Production to the Principles contained within themselves, as from which intrinsically, according to all their Parts, they are ordered and co-apted. *Lucret. 2, 133.*

Moreover, the very Action of the external Agent is from its own internal Principles, which always so turn and direct the Action, as that it may with greater Strength sustain the Violence of most things. For even in sensitive Creatures, where there is a kind of voluntary Action, it is therefore such, and carried rather this way than that way, because there occurs to the Mind a *Species* inviting it, rather this way than that way ; and the Mind, through the Dominion whereby it ruleth the Spirit contained in the Body, leads them this way and not that way, and together with them, the Members in which they are.

CHAP. XI.

Of Motion, which is the same with Action, or Effection ; and of Fortune, Fate, End, and sympathetical and antipathetical Causes.

IN the mean time, I shall not need to make any Excuse, for that I confound the Action or Effection of a Cause with Motion ; since it is known, that both of these are one with Motion, and only add the Connotation, and for that it must be terminated to the thing done or effected.

I understand here no other Motion, than that which is Migration from place to place, which for the most part it called Lation, and transient Motion, and local Motion. For thus they name it in Distinction from that Motion, which some use to call Mutation and Alteration ; that wereby a thing remaining unmoved, according to its internal Nature, is, as they conceive, changed or altered through Acquisition, or loss of some Quality, as Heat, or Cold.

This

This Mutation or Alteration is not a *Species* of Motion, distinct from that which is called local Motion or Transition. Local Motion or Transition is the *Genus*, this Mutation or Alteration is nothing but a *Species* thereof, to wit, that whereby moveables are carried through short and undiscernable intervals. *For whatsoever compound Body is changed according to Quality, is changed altogether by the local and transitive Motion of the Atoms and little Bodies, creating a Quality*; whether they be transposed in Place and Scituation in the Body itself, or come into it, or pass out of it.

<small>Sext. Emp. adv. Phys. 2.</small>

For Example: *That of sweet, something bitter be made; or of white, black; it is requisite, the little Bodies which constitute it be transposed, and one come into the rank of another. But this could not happen, unless those little Bodies themselves were moved by transient Motion. Again, that of hard, somthing soft be made; and of soft, hard? it is requisite, those Particles whereof it consists, be moved locally, forasmuch as by Extension of them it is softned, and by Condensation hardned; whence the Motion of Mutation is not generically different from the Motion of Transition.*

<small>Ibid.</small>

But to return to that Motion, which is proper to the Cause or Efficient, we may observe, that to some things the name of Cause is attributed, for that they excite Motion. For *Fortune*, which is a Cause of some things, can no other way be admitted, than as it is the same with the self-moving and Agent Cause, and only denotes Ignorance of the Effect connexed with it, and intended by it, Otherwise, so far is it from being fit to make it a Goddess, as the ordinary sort of Men do, (for by God nothing is done disorderly,) that it is not to be esteemed so much as an unstable Cause.

Even *Fate* also is no other than the self-moving Causes, that act by themselves, as they are connected among themselves, and the later depend of the former, albeit this Connexion and Dependance be not of that Dependance and Necessity which some natural Philosophers would persuade; for there is no such Necessity in Nature, since the Motion of the Declination of Atoms, of which we already spoke, breaks it off, so as it intercurs neither in a certain Line, nor in a certain Region of Place.

Likewise an *End* is said to be a Cause, forasmuch as it produceth somthing, or not produceth it, no otherwise than because it moveth. It moveth, I say, by sending a *Species* into the Soul, which draws and allures it by invisible, yet Physical little Hooks and Chains, as it were, by which, for the most part, together with the Soul, the Body also is attracted. Certainly, no such Attraction can be understood to be made, unless by some reboundings, and intanglings of Atoms.

Insomuch as even all those things, which are said to be done by Sympathy or Antipathy, are perform'd by Physical Causes, that is, by some (unseen indeed, but) very small Organs, which intervening, some things are as truly attracted to or repelled from one another, as those things which are wrought upon by sensible and grosser Organs are attracted and repelled.

<small>Lucret.</small>

For to explain this by an Example. How think we comes it to pass, that a Lyon is not able to endure the sight of a Cock, but, assoon as he sees him, runs away? unless there are some little bodies in the body of the Cock, which being, as in Looking glasses, immitted into the Eyes of the Lion, so pierce his Eye balls, and cause so sharp pain, that he is not able to withstand or endure it, how fierce and furious soever he be. But in our Eyes, those Bodies produce nothing like this, being they of a different contexture, as shall be shewed when we come to discourse of the Senses.

CHAP. XII.
Of the Qualities of Compound things in general.

AS concerning the Qualities belonging to Compound things, it is known, that under this term are comprehended all, as well Adjuncts as Accidents of things, but chiefly the Adjuncts, whether they be properly Adjuncts, that is, constantly abiding in a Compound Body, as long as it perseveres, and not separable from it without destroying; or more properly and largely taken, that is, as a mean between Adjuncts, properly so termed, and Accidents, forasmuch as, like these, they exist in them; but in those they come and go, may be with or from a Body, without the corruption thereof.

The most obvious Question concerning them, is, How it comes to pass, that they are in Compound things, when, as we said before, they are not in Atoms, of which Compound things consist? That they are not in Atoms, is already shewn; forasmuch as every Quality that exists in Atoms, as Magnitude, Figure, and Weight, is so natural to them, that it can no more be changed, than the very substance of the Atoms; and this, because in the dissolution of Compound things, there must needs remain somthing solid and undissolved; whence it comes, that all motions which are made, are neither into nothing, nor out of nothing.

We answer, that Qualities arise in Compound things, as well from the transposition that is made of the Atoms, now fewer, now more; which in one position afford one quality; in another, another; as from the accession that is made of some Atomes wholly new, and the discession of some pre-existent. Whence these Qualities again are varied, or seem different from what they were at first.

For as Letters give a divers representation of themselves, not only those which are of different Figure and Form, as *A* and *N*, but even the same Letters, if their Position or Order, be changed; Position, as in *N* and *Z*; Order, as in *A N*, and *N A*: So, not only Atoms, which are of divers Figures, (as also of different bulk and motion,) are naturally apt to effect divers Senses, and, in one, to exhibit Colour; in another Odour; in a third, Sapor; in a fourth, another: But also those which are of the same, if they change the Position or Order among them, affect the Senses in such manner, that those (for example,) which now exhibit one Colour, presently exhibit another, as we before instanc'd in the water of the Sea, which, being still, seemeth green; troubled, white; and, as is ordinarily instanc'd, the neck of a Pigeon, which, according

cording as it is variously placed towards the Light, receiveth a great variety of Colours.

And as there is made a diversity, not only when the same Letters which compose one word are so transposed, as that they exhibit divers Forms, but much more, when some are added to them, and some taken away from them; in like manner it is necessary, that Colours, Odours, and other Qualities, be changed, not only when the same Atoms change their Position and Order, but likewise when some come to them, some depart from them, as is manifest from the softning, hardning, crudefaction, ripening of things, and the like.

Briefly, as it is of great concernment amongst Letters, with what other Letters they are joyned, and in what Position and Order they are among themselves, since, by so small a unmber of Letters, we signify the Heaven, the Earth, the Sun, the Sea, Rivers, Fruits, Shrubs, living Creatures, and innumerable such like; so is it of great concernment amongst Atoms, with what others they are joyned, and in what other Position, and in what Intervals and Connexions, what Motions amongst one another they give or receive; forasmuch as by this means they are able to exhibit the variety, as of all things, so of all Qualities in them.

To speak more particularly, some Qualities first seem to arise out of Atoms, as consider'd according to Substance; and being in such Position amongst themselves, as that they have a greater or lesser *Vacuum* intercepted or excluded. Other Qualities are made of them, as they are endued with their three Properties, some from a single Property, others from a conjuncture of more.

CHAP. XIII.

Qualities from Atoms considered, according to their Substance, and interception of Vacuum.

And after the first manner arise *Rarity* and *Density*; for it is manifest, that no Dense thing can be made Rare, unless the Atoms thereof, or the parts of which it is Compounded (they themselves being compounded of Atoms,) be so put asunder from one another, that, being diffused into a larger place, they intercept within it more and larger Vacuities. Neither can any thing Rare be made Dense, unless its Atoms or parts be so thrust up together, as that, being reduced into a narrower place, they comprehend it in fewer, or more contracted Vacuities. Moreover, it is manifest, that, according to the more or lesser Vacuity which is intercepted, the Air (for example,) or Light is said to be Rare; but a Stone, Iron, and the like, said to be Dense.

Together with these seem to arise *Perspicuity* and *Opacity*; for every thing is so much more Perspicuous, (other respects being equal,) by how much more it is too Rare, so much more Opacous, by how much is is more Dense: Because the more Rare is the more patent to lucid and visible beams; the more Dense, the more obstructive of them. But I say, (other respects being equal,) a more thick Body, as Glass, may have little vacuous passages placed in so streight a line, that the beams may pass more easily through it, than through a rarer Body; as a leaf of Colewort, whose small Pores are pester'd with little Bodies variously permixt; even the beams themselves are cut off, unless they pass through strait holes, such as are in Glass.

Again, there ariseth also *Fluidity*, *Liquidity*, and *Firmness*; For a Body seemeth to be fluid for no other reason, than because the Atoms, or Parts whereof it consists, have little vacuities lodg'd within them, and are withal so dissociated from one another, as that they are easily moveable, one in order to another, through the not-resistence of the little Vacuities: Neither doth any thing seem to be firm from any other cause, than the contrary hereof; that is, the Atoms and Parts touch one another so closely, and are so coherent to one another, that for the same reason they cannot be moved out of their situation; for such Atoms there may be, as, being more hooked, and as it were, more branching, may hold the Body more closely compacted, How Water, in particular, being liquid, becomes hardned into Ice, shall be said hereafter.

Likewise, those Qualities which depend of these, *Humidity* and *Siccity*. *Humidity* is a kind of fluidness, only it superadds this, That the parts of a Humid thing, touching some Body, or penetrating into it, are apt to stick to it, thereby rendring it moist. *Siccity* is a kind of firmness, adding only this, that a dry Body is void of Humidity.

Moreover, *Softness* and *Hardness*, which cohere with these, and, upon another account, agree also with Rarity and Density, inasmuch as (other respects being equal,) every Body is so much the more soft, by how much the more rare; and so much the more hard, by how much the more compact; I say, (other Respects being equal,) because Dirt is soft, and a Pumice hard, by reason of the greater cohesion of the parts, which pester the Cavities, and resist the Touch, and cannot retire into the hindermost Cavities, as otherwise they would.

There are others which depend upon these; as *Flexility*, *Tactility*, *Ductility*, and others, from Softness; their opposites, from Hardness; but 'tis enough to have hinted them.

CHAP. XIV.

Qualities springing from Atoms, considered according to the Properties peculiar to each.

In the second manner, and as far as the Properties of Atoms are considered particularly; In the first place, the Magnitude, Quantity, or bulke of every thing, ariseth no other way than from the coacervate Magnitude of the Atoms, of which it is compounded. Whence it is manifest, that *Augmentation* and *Diminution* of Bodies is therefore made, because Atoms, wheresoever they arrive, give to the things an increase; wheresover they go away, they diminish them.

Not to mention, that, according as the Atoms are greater or lesser, may be made that which we call *Bluntness* and *Acuteness*. And thence a reason may be given, Why the Fire of Lightning

ning is more penetrative than that of a Taper: Or how it comes, that Light passeth through Horn, which resists Rain, and the like.

Besides, the very Figure of things, though it did not depend upon the Figure of Atoms, (whereas it seems to depend upon them, in all things which are constantly produced in the same Figure,) yet it is generally at least true, that every Body is therefore figured, because it consists of Parts terminate and figurate; for Figure is a Term, or Bound.

Thus, though out of smoothness, and roughness (which, as I said, are allied to the Figure of Atoms,) it doth not necessarily follow, that things smooth are made of smooth, rough things of rough: Yet in general nothing can be conceived to be smooth, but whose parts, to the least of them, are smooth; nor rough, but whose parts are rough.

Here observe, That as well from the Figure, as from the Magnitude, the Reason may be given, why Wine floweth easily through a Strainer, but Oil more slowly, which is, that the Oil may consist not of greater Atoms only, but also of more hooked, and much intangled among themselves.

Lastly, *Weight*, or the Motive-Faculty, which is in every thing, can arise no other way, than from the weight or Mobility of Atoms. But that being declared formerly, we shall here only observe, that all Atoms, are heavy, and none light; wherefore every compound Body is heavy, there is none that is light; or that is not of itself ready to tend downwards. Here presently comes in Fire for on Objection; but although it foregoeth not its propension downwards, yet it therefore tendeth upwards; forasmuch as it is driven that way by the ambient Air; After the same manner, as we see with great force the Water resist Logs and Beams, things otherwise heavy; and the deeper we plunge them, the more eagerly it casts them up, and sends them back. Whence it comes, that those things, which we call light, are not absolutely light; as if, of their own accord, they did tend upwards, but only comparatively, that is, as they are less heavy, and extruded by the more heavy, which press themselves down before them. So as Earth being the most heavy, Water less heavy, Air yet less heavy than that, and Fire least of all; the Earth drives the Water upwards, and far from the middle; Water the Air; Air the Fire: But if we suppose the Earth to be taken away, the Water will come to the middle; if the Water, the Air; if the Air, the Fire.

CHAP. XV.

Qualities from Atoms, considered according to their Properties taken together.

BUt Properties of Atoms, being taken together, and those things, especially of which we have hitherto spoken, Rarity, Density, and the rest, being commixt and varied, there arise faculties of things, which, being active and motive, have it from the Weight and Mobility of the Atoms. And whereas some act one way, some another, they must of necessity have it, as well from the peculiar Magnitude, and Figure of the Atoms, as from their various Order and Position amongst themselves, as from their looseness, compactedness, connexion, sejunction, &c.

Of this kind, are not only, in Animals, the faculties of Sense, Sight, Hearing, Smelling, Tasting, Touching, wherewith they can perceive sensible things; but also, in the things themselves, those very qualities which are called Sensible. These are, in things, the faculties of striking, and affecting the Senses, after a certain manner, to the end they may be preceived by them; as colour and light, the Sight; sound, the Hearing; odor, the Smell; sapor, the Taste; heat and cold (above the rest,) the Touch. Whence it comes, that being to speak of those hereafter, we ought not here to omit these: To treat of which, will be worth our pains.

To begin from Heat: We cannot treat of it, without joyning Light to it, for without Light there are no Colours, the variety of Colours being taken away by night; whence in the Infernal Region, all things are said to be black. But though in darkness, all things are alike discolour'd, nevertheless, in themselves, or in their Superficies, there are dispositions of extreme Particles, by reason of which the affused Light is so variously modify'd, that, together with this Modification reflected on the Eye, it exhibits various Colours in the Eye, as White, for example, when the Ball receiveth into itself one kind of blow or stroke; Black, when another, &c.

For though Colours are not coherent to Bodies, but generated according to some respective Sites, Orders, and Positions, yet are they not generated, unless Light also be adjoyned to the disposure of their Superficies, to compleat or make up the perfect nature of Colour. Neither, setting this aside, do I see how it can be said, that Bodies, which are in the dark invisible, have Colour.

And indeed, since not only a Pigeon's Neck, a Peacock's Train, and the like, exhibit several Colours, according to their several Positions to the Light; but also even all other things appear somtimes in some Colours, somtimes in others, according as they are placed in several degrees of Light, what else should we concive, but that generally it is Light, by whose coming things put on Colours, and by its departure lose them.

In the mean time, Light itself, being nothing else but a substantial effluxion from a lucid Body, is not visible of itself, but only in Colour, as that is a part of it; for neither is it seen through a pure or liquid medium; neither when we imagine that we see it, either in a lucid or an illuminate Body, is it beheld as a thing distinct from the colour of the thing lucid or illuminate. In fine, neither is Shadow (the privation thereof,) in any other manner, than as because it is withal the privation of Colour in a thing shadowed, which loseth Colour always by the same proportion as it loseth the Light. How it comes to pass, that Shadow, though it be a meer privation, yet seems to be moved, was declared in the Canonick. *Chap. 20.*

Sound is nothing but an effluxion of tenuious little Bodies, sent out from the thing speaking, sounding

sounding, or what way soever making a noise, and apt, by entring into the Ear, to affect the Hearing.

That it is a corporeal effluxion, is proved, in that it moveth the Sense, and that either by touching it smoothly and delightfully, or roughly and unpleasantly, according to the smoothness or roughness of the little Bodies. Also in that it is moved through the Air, and being driven against solid Bodies, leaps back, whence Eccho is made, *viz.* by reason of the solidity of the little Bodies. Also in that it is diminished, and becomes confused, in regard of the long train of little Bodies, when it goes forward, or their swerving while they go overthwart, through some thicker partition, and the like.

If you demand, why Sound can pass, where Light and the species of Colour cannot, as when we speak, the Doors being shut; the reason is, because Light, or the Images of Colour, cannot pass but in a direct line; but Sound can insinuate it self through oblique Tracts. For being excited, it leaps forward in little Bodies, which turn upwards, downwards, forwards, backwards, on the right Side, and every way; in like manner as a spark of Fire, sometimes scatters it self into little sparkles, which take a direct course towards all sides.

The same may be said of *Odor*. For this also is an effluxion, which going out of the odorous thing, is diffused every way, and, arriving at the Nostrils, moveth the Sense of Smelling, either by stroaking or pricking it. This is corporeal also, even more than Sound, in that it passeth more slowly through space, and cometh not from so great a distance, and penetrates not through those partititions, through which Sound doth penetrate.

As concerning *Sapor*, there is this difference, That tho it consist in little Bodies, contained in the thing styled Sapid; yet they issue not forth into the Tongue and Palate at a distance, but then only, when the thing Sapid is applied to the Tongue, they so insinuate themselves into it, that they affect the contexture, of it, either mildly, and then make a sweet Taste; or roughly, and so they make a sower Taste.

As for *Heat* and *Cold*, that Sensation which they cause, is to be referred to the *Touch*. But tho many of the foresaid Qualities properly appertain to the Touch, as Hardness, Softness, Humidity, Siccity, and the rest, which require application of the thing touched to the Hand, or to some other part of the Body; yet these two may be felt, not only when the Hot or Cold thing is applyed to the Hand, or some other part; but also when it is remote, and at such a distance, as it can transmit some little Bodies out of it self into it.

Heat indeed is chiefly an effluxion of little Bodies or Atoms, in Bulk slender, in Figure round, in Motion swift. For as they are slender, there is no Body compacted, that they find not little Pores, through which they insinuate into it; as they are round, they are easily moved, and insinuate themselves every where; As they are swift, they rapidly are impelled, and enter into the Body, and more and more still succeeding one another, they are so pressed, as that they penetrate through the whole; and if they proceed in acting, they sever and dislocate the parts thereof, and at last dissolve the whole. Such are the effects of Heat, and chiefly the fiery (for Fire is nothing but intense Heat,) towards all Bodies, and in a living Creature is only added the Sense of the Heat, which is from the plucking asunder, and loosening what before was continued.

Cold is an effluxion also, but of Atoms, whose Bulk is greater, their Figure more corner'd, their Motion slower; for, the Effects being contrary, the Principles must also be contrary. So that whereas Heat disgregates and disperses, Cold compresseth and constipates: And in a sensitive Creature, it doth this with a particular kind of Sensation; for, entring into the Pores of the Skin, it keeps back, and drives in again the little bodies of Heat, by opposing the bodies of Cold, and with its little sharp corners it tears and twingeth all things wheresoever it passes.

CHAP. XVI.

Of those Qualities which are esteemed the Accidents of Things; and particularly, of Time.

IT remains, that we a little touch those Qualities which are not so much Adjuncts as Accidents, and therefore affect not the thing internally, but externally only, and qualifie them with a certain kind of respect to some extrinsecal thing. Not but that within the things themselves also there are some Accidents, (such as Position, Orders, Intervals of parts or particles, and the like,) but that being such, they are Accidents of the parts themselves, not of the whole, which consists of them.

Accidents of this kind, are all those generally out of which ariseth some relation, for which every thing is said to be such or such, in order to another; as like, unlike; greater, lesser; many, few; superior, inferior; right, left; cause, effect; giving, receiving; and innumerable of the same kind.

But it is known, that Relation is a work of the mind, referring and comparing one to another; so that, setting aside the Mind, every thing is that only which it is in it self, but not that which it is in respect of another. Whence, to Accidents we formerly referred Liberty and Health, Riches and Poverty, &c. because, setting the Mind aside, a Man is nothing but a Man; not free, or subject; rich, or poor, &c.

Now of all Accidents, there is one which may be termed the *Accident of Accidents*, that is, *Time*, from which all things are denominated, either present, or past, or future; lasting, or little durable, or momentary; sometimes also swift or slow.

For first, That Time is an Accident, is manifest, in that it is not any thing by it self, but only attributed to things by Cogitation, or the Mind, as they are conceived to persevere in the state in which they are, or to cease to be, and to have a longer or shorter existence, and to have it, or to have had it, or be to have it. Whence it comes, that *Time is not to be enquired after the same manner as we enquire after other things, which are in some subject, setting aside the mind; and therefore* *Laert.*

therefore neither to understand what it is, must it be referred to the prænotions of things which occur to our sight; but we ought to discourse of it according to evidence, using familiar speech. And not entangling ourselves in Circumlocutions, we say, Time is long or short.

Moreover, we call it the *Accident of Accidents*, because, whereas some things cohere by themselves as a Body, and as a *Vacuum* or Space; others happen, or are accident to the Coherent, as Days, Nights, Hours; as also passions and exemptions from them, as Motion, Rest, &c. Time, by the assistence of the mind, presupposeth all these Accidents, and supervenes to them.

For Day and Night are Accidents of the ambient Air; Day happens by the Sun's illumination; Night by privation of the solar illumination. Hour being a part of Night or Day, is an Accident of the Air also, as likewise are Night and Day; But time is coextended with every Day, and Night, and Hour; and for this reason a Day or Night is said to be long or short, whil'st we are carried by thought to time that supervenes to them, according to the former Notions.

In the same manner happen Passions, and Indolencies, and Griefs, and Pleasures to us; and therefore they are not Substances, but Accidents of those things which are affected by them; to wit, by sense, of delectation, or of trouble. But these Accidents happen not without time.

Moreoverer, Motion and Rest, as we have already declared, are Accidents of Bodies, neither are they without time; wherefore we measure the swiftness and slowness of motion by time, as also much or little rest. And forasmuch as none understand time by it self, or seperate from the motion and rest of things; therefore by understanding things done, as the *Trojan* War, and the like, which are done with motion, and are Accidents partly of the men acting, partly of the places in which they are acted; together with them is understood their time, as they are compared to our affairs, and the existence of the things intervening betwixt those and us.

CHAP. XVII.

Of the Generation and Corruption of Compounds.

IT remains that we add, how things are *generated* and *corrupted*, either of which is some kind of mutation or alteration; but whereas by other mutations, a Body is not made and exists new, but only that which now is acquires a new quality, and a new denomination from it. *Generation* is a mutation, whereby every Body is first produced, and begins in nature to be, and to be denominated such. *Corruption* is a mutation, whereby it is at last dissolved, and ceases to be in nature, and to be denominated such; for thus Fire, a Plant, an Animal, and whatsoever is in a determinate *Genus* of Bodies, when it first ariseth into the light, and beginneth to be denominated such, is said to be *generated*; when it goeth out of the light, and can no longer be denominated such, to be *corrupted*.

When I say, that a Body is first produced, or beginneth to be, I mean not, but that whatsoever is in it of Substance, Body, or Corporeal, was before; for all the Atoms, and little Bulks or Seeds, of which it is compounded, were before. As when a House is said to be made, the Stones, Wood, and the rest, whereof it is said to be built, are understood to be pre-existent. But I only mean, that the Atoms and Seeds thereof are so commixt, and so united, as that they are in a new manner, or in a new form, wherein they were not before; and therefore a Body resulting thence, then first begins to be, and be denominated such.

Hence, because there ariseth not so much a new substance, as a new quality in compounds, it cometh to pass, that Generation is a *Species* of Mutation or Alteration; and so is Corruption likewise, but in a contrary manner. Wherefore also it comes to pass, that Generation and Corruption are performed only by conjoining and disjoining those Principles, and not by changing them, because the Atoms, as we said, are incapable of change.

'And indeed, seeing all change, (as we have 'already said, and shall shortly say again,) is *Laert.* 'perform'd either by Transposition, adding, or 'taking away of parts; it followeth, that Atoms, 'being so compact and solid, as that none of 'their Particles can be transposed, added, or 'taken away, are immutable and incorruptible, 'and such also are their Properties, of which 'sort are those little Magnitudes, and little Figures peculiar to them, for it is necessary that 'these also remain with the substance of the 'Atoms when the Compounds are dissolved; and 'with good reason, seeing that also in things 'which we trasform at our pleasure, as when a 'Man, of standing, or upright, becomes sitting, 'or bowed, (or, if you will, is made black or 'hot,) it is ever understood, that the same Magnitude, Figure, and Order of parts are in them. 'But the qualities that are not in them, nor proper to them, as Standing, Straightness, White, 'Cold, &c. remain not in the Subject, after its 'Transmutation, as the others do, but perish, or 'are lost to the whole body, or to the part 'wherein they were.

Since therefore, Principles are intransmutable, and, in Generation, are no other than mingled and put together, it follows that no such mixture can be made, as is a perfect Confusion by Coalition, but only that which is a compounding by Apposition; and this, whether those little Bulks made up of Atoms are only mingled, or whether also the Atoms themselves be mingled with those little Bulks resolved into their Atoms, or first Principles; whence it follows, that the destruction of those little Bulks, and of the Bodies consisting of them, as Wine, and Water, Honey, and the like, goeth accompanied with the generation of the mixt Body, and of the other little Bulks, which are proper to it; not as if Water and Wine, (for example,) but as if aquifying, and vinifying Atoms (as I may say,) were mingled together.

And to the Generation, which is made in an infinite *Vacuum*, we must conceive, that the Atoms severed from one another, and differing amongst themselves in Figure, Magnitude, Position,

sition and Order, are carried through the *Vacuum*, and, where they concur, being mutually entangled, are condens'd; whence it happens, that a different temperature of the thing results, for they are conjoined according to proportion of Magnitude, Figures, Positions, Order, and by this means the generation of compound things comes to be perfected.

But where the Generation of one is made out of the Corruption of another, that usually happens after a threefold manner, which we touched, speaking of alteration; either only by *Transposition* of the Parts or Atoms, as when a Frog is generated of Dirt, a Mite of Cheese; or by *addition* of things accessory, as when, by accession of the Seed to a greater mass, (as of Rennet into Milk, or of Leaven into Dough,) there is begotten a Plant, or Animal; after which manner also Augmentation is made, by which the generated thing becomes bigger: Or lastly, by *taking away* somthing pre-existent, as when Fire is generated by the severing of watery, ashy, or other parts which were in Wood; Wax, by the severing of Honey which was in the Comb; and so of the rest.

Here the former comparison of Letters will serve to make us understand two things. One, that the particular manners of generation, and their opposite corruptions, which may be comprehended under any of these three manners, are (if not infinite, at least) innumerable, inexpressible, and incomprehensible, since of Four and twenty Letters only, which are in the Alphabet, there may be produced a multitude of words almost incomprehensible.

The other is, that as words, accommodated to Pronunciation and Reason, are not made of every combination of Letters; so in natural things, all things are not made of all things; nor are all Atoms fit, by being joined together, to constitute any *Species* of compound things. For every thing requires such a disposition, as that the Atoms constituting it match, and, as it were, associate themselves with those which are agreeable to them, but pass by, and, as it were, reject others. Whence again it comes to pass, that when a thing is dissolved, all the agreeing Atoms draw one another mutually, and disengage themselves from those which are disagreeing. This is manifestly seen in Nutrition, which is Aggeneration, and is evident even from this, that otherwise Monsters would be ordinarily generated, as Half-men, Half-beasts; Chimera's, and Zoophyts.

In a word, certainly he never had the least taste of Physiology, who conceiveth, that any thing which is generated can be eternal; for what Composition is there, which is not dissolveable? Or what is there, that hath a Beginning, and no End? Though there were no external Causes to destroy its Frame, yet wants there not an intestine motion, and, even within the most compact and durable Bodies, an unvanquishable inclination of Atoms downwards, whence their dissolution must necessarily follow.

Yet, this dissolution is not always immediately made into Atoms, but for the most part into little bulks, or parts compounded of them; which are certain kinds of compound bodies, as when there is a dissolution of Wood, partly into fire, partly into smoke, partly into some waterish moisture, partly into ashes. But what way soever it be done, we must always hold, that in Generation there is no new Substance made, but præexistent Substances are made up into one; so in Corruption, no Substance absolutely ceaseth to be, but is dissipated into more Substances, which remain after the destruction of the former.

CHAP. XVIII.

Whence it comes, that a generated Body is in a certain kind of things, and distinguished from other things.

Moreover, seeing that every Body is generated only of the aggregation of Matter, or of material and substantial Principles, knitting together in a certain Order and Position; therefore, that which is concrete or generated, is understood to be nothing else but the Principles themselves, as they are knit together in such an order or position, and thereupon are exhibited in such a form or quality.

This form or quality, whereby a thing generate, is established in such a certain kind of things, as of Metal, or of Stone, or of Plant, or of Animal, and is distinguished from all the *Species* and *Individuums* of the *Genus* wherein it is; this form, I say, is not one and simple, but rather, as it were, an aggregation and collection of many, which collection cannot be found in any thing, but in this.

' Wherefore we must here observe, that the *Laert.*
' figures of things, their colours, magnitude,
' gravity, and (in a word,) all other qualities
' which are usually predicated of a compound
' Body, as its Accidents, (whether perceived by
' sight, or by other senses,) are so to be under-
' stood; not as if they were certain natures or
' substances, existent by themselves, (for our
' understanding cannot reach this;) nor, on the
' other side, as if truly they did not exist, or
' were absoutely nothing; neither again, as if
' they were such, as are those other incorporeal
' things, which are accident to it; nor, lastly, as
' if they were parts of the Body. But they are
' thus to be esteemed, that whereas a Body may
' be disposed after several manners, the whole
' complex gains, by the aggregation of them,
' a certain nature proper and peculiar to its
' kind.

' ' Not that a Body comes to be such, as is a
' greater bulk made up out of a lesser, whether
' those be the first, least, greatest, or in general
' made up of others more minute; but only, as
' I said, that of all these joined together, and
' by this conjunction differencing it from others,
' it possesses a nature proper to itself, and distinct
' from any other.

' All these are comprehended by certain spe-
' cial Notions and Conceptions, but so, that still
' the Body, which results out of them as a certain
' whole, and is not divided in itself, but conceived
' as one undivided thing, obtains the denomina-
' tion of a Body, which is reckon'd up in such a
' certain kind of things.

The same may, in a manner, be conceived to happen, by the concurrence of certain accidents, which are found the same in no other body; that is, the things indeed to which those accidents agree, may be distinguished and denominated from the notions of them, but yet only then, when each of those accidents is conceived to be there. For these are not of that kind of accidents, which, existing in the thing, become therefore necessary and perpetually conjoin'd to it, and consequently bestow on it a perpetual denomination.

Here it may be demanded, Whether, if we were dissolved by death, it might happen in process of time, that the very same Principles, of which we consist, might, by some odd chance, be ranged and ordered again in the same manner as they are now, and so we come to be denominated the same which we are at this present? To which we answer, That it is doubtlesly true, but still so, that, to have been formerly would nothing appertain to us, because in our very dissolution, every disposition which we had, and all memory of those things which compounded us, and which we were, would utterly be lost; by which means, all our remembrance too would so have been totally decay'd, that it were impossible it should come into our minds that we had ever had a Being. Thus much concerning the Universe.

SECT. 2.

Of the World.

IT followeth that we speak of the World, which is a Portion of the Universe, or Infinity of things, and may not unfitly be described, *The whole Circumference of Heaven, containing the Stars, the Earth, and all things visible.*

When I say, the *Circumference of Heaven*, I imply, That Heaven is the outmost part of the World, which may also be called *Æther*, and the Region of Fire, from the Stars which it containeth, and are, as it were, Fires lighted there.

When I say the *Earth*, I mean the lowest, or, as it were, the middle part of the World, in which also there is the Water, and next over it the Air, immediate to the Region of Fire. And, because the things which we see created of these, and in these, are various; therefore we comprehend them under the name of *things visible*.

But seeing it may, and useth to be demanded concerning the World, what Form it hath within, what Figure without? Whether it be Eternal, or had a Beginning? Whether it require any other Author, than Nature or Fortune? In what manner was the production of the Whole, and of its Parts? Whether it require any Ruler, or perform its vicissitudes by it self? Whether, How, and When it shall perish? Whether it be One, or, besides it, there be Innumerable? We must therefore speak a little of each.

CHAP.

CHHP. I.

Of the Form and Figure of the World.

AND as to the first Head, the World, by its internal form or constitution, is not animate, much less a God, as some think; but whereas what is conceived to be one in its form or constitution, is such, either for that its parts are contained under one disposition, as a Plant or Animal; or, that they are artificially joined one to another, without mingling their tempers, as a House, or Ship; or, that they are discreetly distinguish'd from one another, yet have some mutual relation to each other, as an Army, and a Common-wealth; the World is only to be conceived One, partly the second way, partly the third.

The second way it may be esteemed one, in regard between the Sun, the Moon, and the rest of the more solid and compacted parts of the World, there is intercepted either Air or *Æther* diffusive, whereby a kind of Coherence is made. It may also be esteemed one the third way, in regard the Sun, Moon, Earth, and other compacted Bodies, are so separated from one another, that, after a determinate order, they possess the Scituations or Seats of Superiors and Inferiors, Antecedents and Consequents, things Illustrating, and things Illustrated.

But to say, that the World is one the first way also, How can it be made good? Since that if it were so, that the World, as some will, were animate, nothing could be thought inanimate; not a Stone, not a Carkass, not any thing whatsoever; that same disposition, called Soul, being diffused through all things.

Neither do they, who assert, the World to be animate and wise, sufficiently mind and understand, what kind of nature that must be to which such expressions are proper, since as a Tree is not produced in the air, nor a Fish on dry ground, nor Blood in Wood, nor Moisture in a pumice; so neither can the Mind or the Soul be produced, or be, indifferently, in any kind of Body. But seeing it must be determinately ordered where every thing shall grow and inexist, the nature of the Soul must be looked for about the Nerves and Blood, not in putrid Globes of Earth, in Water, in the Sun, in the Sky, &c.

Now whereas some hold, That the World is not only endued with Mind and Senses, but that also it is a round burning God, and ever-moving with restless Circumvolutions; these are Prodigies and Monsters, not of Philosophers discoursing, but dreaming. For who can understand, what this ever-moving and round God is, and what Life is ascribed to him, to be turned about with so great swiftness, as is unimaginable to be equall'd? With which I see not how a constant Mind and a happy Life can consist.

But granting the World to be a God, not only the Sun, Moon, and the rest, are parts of God, but even the Earth it self, as being a part of the World, must be also a part of God. Now we see, there are very great Regions of the Earth unhabitable, and uncultivated, part of them being burnt up by the approach of the Sun, part
being

being oppressed with Snow and Ice through his distance from it. If then the World, be God, these, being the Parts of the World, are to be termed, some, the Burning; some, the frozen Members of God.

As to its external Form or Figure, it seems, in the first place, certain, that there is some extremity of the World, because the World is a kind of Segment of the infinite Universe; but what that is, who is able to tell, unless he came thence?

For whereas it seems to be Heaven, there is nothing in all apparent things hinders, but that it may be Rare, nor nothing hinders but that it may be Dense; Rare, forasmuch as the Stars which are in it, and appear to be moved, perform their Motions through it; Dense, forasmuch as itself is able to move the Stars fixed in it,

Again, nothing hinders, but that it may be either Quiescent, if the Stars are moved through it; or Circularly moved, if the Stars are carried round about with it.

Besides, nothing hinders, but that it may be round, oval, or lenticular, especially if it be moved. Again, nothing hinders, but that it may be triangular, pyramidal, squar, hexaedrical, or of any other plain Figure, especially if it be unmoved.

As for them, who, being persuaded by some Arguments, assert the World so to have one determinate Figure, as that it can have no other, we cannot but wonder at their Stupidity. For most maintain the world to be, as Immortal and Blessed, so also Round, because *Plato* denieth any Figure to be more Beautiful than that. But, to me, that of the Cylinder, or the Square, or the Cone, or the Pyramid, seem, by reason of the Variety, more Beautiful.

CHAP. II.

Of the late Beginning of the World.

AS for the second Head. The world is not Eternal, but began to be at some time.

For first, Seeing that the Nature of the whole and of the Parts is the same; And we observe, that the Parts of the World are obnoxious both to Generation and Corruption, it follows, That the whole World must be subject to Generation and Corruption. That the Parts of the World are generated and corrupted, is demonstrated even by the Sense, and shall be proved hereafter.

Neither let any say, that the Mutations which are made in the Parts of the world are not of the more Principal parts, as of the Sun, the Moon, the Earth, and the rest; but of the lesser only which are but Particles, whereof the Principal consist; for he ought to conceive, that if the Principal parts consist of parts subject to Mutation, those whole parts themselves are subject to Mutation; and though ordinarily there occur not Causes so powerful as to change them, nevertheless nothing hinders, but that such may sometimes occur, as even among the lesser parts, some continue safe a great while, which, at last, in progress of time, find causes of Mutation.

Besides, seeing that the most ancient Histories of all things exceed not the *Theban* and *Trojan* Wars, what is the reason of this, but because the world is not old, so far is it from being eternal? For if eternal, why did not other Poets celebrate other things? How came the memorable Acts of so many eminent Persons to perish? Why are the Records of Eternal Fame no where extant?

In like manner, seeing that we have all Arts newly invented, and their Inventors are not unknown, (for, that daily many Arts are advanced and receive increase, is very manifest,) how comes this to pass, but because the World had not its beginning long ago? for the World could not be so long without Arts, which are of so great importance to life

If you believe, that in times past there were such Records and Arts as now, which perished by some great Conflagrations, Deluges, Earthquakes, being subverted together with the Cities and Nations themselves, do you not acknowledge it necessary, that there must be at some time to come a destruction of Earth and Heaven, as it had happened, if in those cases some greater Causes had lighted? For we ourselves think ourselves mortal, for no other reason, but for that we perceive ourselves to fall into the same diseases, as they whom we see die.

The World therefore had a Beginning; nor was, as may appear by what we said, of very great Antiquity. But whensoever it begun, it is most probable it begun in the Spring, because then all things sprout, flourish, and bring forth; and the newness of the World required a temperate heat and cold for the cherishing of its young Brood, before it should pass to either of the Extreams

CHAP. III.

Of the Cause of the World.

AS to the next Head: We must first acquit the Divine Power from the solicitude and labour of framing the World, for it could not be a Cause blessed and immortal that made it.

With what Eyes could *Plato* look upon the Fabrick of so great a Work, as to conceive the World made and built by God? What Designs, What Tools, What Beams, What Engines What Ministers, in so great a task? How could Air, Fire, Water, Earth, obey and serve the will of the Architect? Whence sprung those five Forms, of which the rest also are framed, lighting aptly to make up Mind and Senses? It were too long to repeat all, which are rather in our Wish, than in our Power to find out.

Again, this God, of whom he speaks, either was not in the former age, wherein Bodies were either immoveable, or moved without any order; or he then slept or wak'd; or did neither. The first cannot be admitted, for God is Eternal; nor the second, for if he slept from Eternity he was dead, Death being an Eternal Sleep. But neither is God capable of Sleep, for the Immortality of God, and a thing near Death, are far asunder. Now if he were awake, either something was wanting to his Felicity, or he was perfectly

perfectly happy. But the first would not allow him to be Happy; for he is not Happy who wants any thing to make up his Felicity; the later is absurd, for 'twere a vain action for him who wants nothing, to trouble himself with making any thing.

To what end then, should God desire to adorn the World with fair Figures and Luminaries, as one that dresseth and sets out a Temple? If, to the end that he might better his Habitation, it seems then, that for an infinite time before, he lived in darkness as in a dungeon. Again, can we think, that afterwards he was delighted with the variety, wherewith we see the Heaven and the Earth adorned? What delight can that be to God, which, were it such, he could not so long have wanted it?

But some will say, That these were ordained by God for the sake of Men. Do they mean of the Wise? Then this great Fabrick of things was made for a very few persons. Or, of the Foolish? There was no reason, he should do such a Favour to the Wicked. Again, What hath he got by doing so, since all Fools are even in that regard most miserable; for what more miserable than Folly? Besides, there being many inconveniences in Life, which the Wise sweeten by compensation of the conveniences; Fools can neither prevent the future, nor sustain the present.

Or, Did he make the World, and, in the World, Men, that he might be worshipped by Men? But what doth the worship of Men advantage God, who is happy, and needeth nothing? Or, if he respect Man so much, as that he made the World for his sake, that he would instruct him in Wisdom, that he would make him Lord over all living Creature, that he would love him as his Son; Why did he make him Mortal and Frail? Why did he subject him, whom He loveth, to all evils? Seeing rather a Man ought to be Happy, as conjoyned with, and next unto God, and Immortal, as he himself is, whom he is made to worship, and contemplate.

For these reasons ought we to say, that the World rather was made by Nature; or, as one of the Natural Philosophers said, by Chance.

By Nature, for such is the nature of the Atoms, running through the immensity of the Universe, that in great abundance running against one another, they can lay hold of, entangle, and engage one another; and variously commixing themselves, First roll up a great kind of Chaos, in manner of a great Vortex, (clue or bottom,) and then after many Convolutions, Evolutions, and making several Efforts, and as it were Attempts. trying all kinds of Motions and Conjunctions, they came at last into that Form, which this World bears.

By Chance, for the Atoms concur, cohere, and are co-apted, not by any design, but as Chance led them. Wherefore, as I said, Chance is not such a Cause, as directly, and of itself, tends to mingle the Atoms, and dispose them to such an Effect; but the very Atoms themselves are called Chance, inasmuch as meeting one another, without any premeditation, they fasten on one another, and make up such a Compound, as chanceth thence to result.

CHAP. IV.

Of the Generation of the World.

BUt to discuss this Matter more narrowly, and to come to another Head; the World seemeth to have been elaborated and molded into this round Figure, by a certain kind of Reason, without Billows, Anvile, or other Instruments.

First, whereas the Atoms, by an inconsiderate and casual Motion, were continually and swiftly carried on, when they began to run in multitudes into this immense place, in which the World now is; and to fasten upon one another, they presently became heaped into one rude and indigested Mass, in which great things were mingled with small, round with corner'd, smooth with hooked, others with others,

Then in this confused Croud, those, which were the greatest and most heavy, began by degrees to settle down; and such as were thin, round, small, slippery, these, in the concurrence of the others, began to be extruded, and carried upwards; as in troubled water, until it rests and groweth clear, the Earthy parts settle downwards, the Watry are as it were thrust upwards; but after the impulsive force, which drove them upward, grew languid; nor was there any other stroke, which might toss them that way, the Atoms themselves, endeavouring to go down again, met with obstacles from others; whereupon they flew about with greater activity to the utmost bounds; as also did others, which were reverberated by them, and repressed by others that closely followed them, whence was made a mutual Implication, which did generate Heaven.

But those Atoms, which were of the same nature, (there being, as we said, many kinds of them,) and carried round about in heaps, whil'st they were thrust upwards, made the Sun, and Moon, and other Stars. These were chiefly called Signifying Atoms; those which they left, as not able to rise so high, produced the Air.

At length, of those which setled down the Earth was generated; and seeing there yet remained much Matter in Earth, and that condensed by the beatings of the Winds and Gales from the Stars, that Figuration of it which consisted of least Particles, was squeezed forth and produced maisture. This being fluid, either run down into hollow places, fit to receive and contain it, or, standing still, made hollow Receptacles for itself. And after this manner, were the Principal parts of the World generated.

To say somthing of the less Principal, the Particles as it were of the former part; there seems in that first Commistion, to have been made the divers Seeds of generable and corruptible things, of which, Compounds of divers Natures were first framed, and afterwards in a great degree propagated.

Stones, Metals, and all other Minerals were therefore generated within the body of the earth at the same time it was formed, because that Mass was heterogeneous, or consisting of Atoms and Seeds of different Natures; and in that the bulks of Stones did diversly swell out to the very Superficies. Whereupon Mountains came to be made, and consequently Vallies, and Plains must needs have been between them.

Soon after, about the Mountains and the Hills, and in the Valleys, and in the Fields grew up Herbs, Shrubs, Trees, almost in the same manner, as Feathers, Hair, Bristles, about the Bodies and Members of Birds and Beasts.

But as concerning Animals themselves, it is likely that the Earth, retaining this new genital Seed, brought out of it self some little bubbles, in the likeness of little Wombs, and these when they grew mature (Nature so compelling,) broke, and put forth young little Creatures. Then the Earth it self did abound in a kind of Humor, like to Milk, with which Aliment living Creatures were nourished.

Which Creatures were so framed, that they had all parts necessary for nutrition, and all other uses. For as when *Nilus* forsakes the Fields, and the Earth beginneth to grow dry, through heat of the Sun, the Husbandman, turning up the Glebe, finds several living Creatures, part begun, part imperfect, and maimed; so that in the same Creature one part liveth, the other is mere Earth: In like manner, amongst those first efforts of the Earth, besides the living Creatures perfectly formed, there were some produced, wanting Hands, Feet, Mouth, and other parts; without which, there is no way to take nourishment, or to live long, or to propagate their Kind.

What I say of other living Creatures, I hold also in Man, that some little Bubbles and Wombs, sticking to the Roots of the Earth, and warmed by the Sun, first grew bigger, and by the assistence of Nature afforded to Infants sprung from it a connatural moisture, called Milk; and that those thus brought up, and ripened to perfection, propagated Mankind.

Two things I add; One, that it is by no means to be allowed, what some affirm, that at that time were produced *Centaures*, *Scyllaes*, *Chimaeraes*, and other Monsters consisting of Parts, of different kinds. For how in a *Centaur* (for example,) could the Limbs of a Man, and of a Horse be joyned together, when at the third Year of his Age, at what time a Child is hardly weaned, a Horse is in full vigor? And at what time a Horse languisheth with Age, a Man flourisheth in the prime of his Youth.

The other, That in the Earth there were created new living Creatures, and more and greater than now, by more and more vigorous Seeds, and amongst those, Men too; so as that race of Men was more hardy, as consisting of greater and more solid Bones and Nerves: And so at last the Earth, her Seeds being exhausted, like a Woman too old to bear Children, left off to produce voluntarily such living Creatures. Whence it comes to pass, that now Men are no where generated on this fashion; but both they, and other more greater and perfect Animals, spring up only by way of Propagation.

CHAP. V.
Of the Vissitudes in the World.

There followeth a Question, Whether the World be Governed by it self, or by the Providence of any Deity?

First therefore, we ought not to think, that the Motion of Heaven, or the Summer and Winter, Course of the Sun, or the Eclipse of the Sun and Moon, or the Rising and Setting of the Stars, or the like, happen, because there is some Ruler over them, who disposeth, and hath disposed of them; and withal possesseth Beatitude and Immortality; for with Felicity agree not Business, Solicitude, Anger, and Favour; these happen through Imbecillity, Fear, and want of external Help.

Neither ought we (it being a troublesome employment, and wholly averse from a happy state,) to think, that the Nature which possesseth Felicity is such, as that (knowing and willing,) it undergoes these Commotions or Perturbations of Mind; but rather to observe, out of respect to it, all veneration, and to use some kind of address to it, suggesting such Thoughts, as out of which arise no Opinions contrary to Veneration.

We should rather think, that, when the World was produced, there were made those Circumplexions of Atoms, involving themselves about one another, that from thence the Celestial Bodies being framed, there was produced in them this necessity, whereby they are moved in such a manner, and perform such Periods; and after the same manner all the rest perform their tasks, in order to the course of things once begun.

And why should we not rather think thus? For whether the World it self is a God, as some conceive, What can be less quiet, than uncessantly to roll about the Axis, with admirable swiftness; But unless it be quiet, nothing is happy. Or whether there be some God in the World, who rules, governs, conserves the courses of the Stars, the mutations of Seasons, the vicissitude and order of things, who is present in all places, and at all times; and, how great soever is the variety, or rather innumerability of all particular things, is distracted by so many cares, by taking order that they be done this way, and no other; indeed he is, as I before objected, involved in businesses troublesome and laborious.

Besides, tho it were but only supposed, that God doth not take care of things, Shall we not find, that all things happen no otherwise, than as if there were no Providence? For some fall out well, but the most ill, and otherwise than they ought. To omit the rest, if *Jupiter* himself did Thunder, or guide the Thunder, he ought at least to spare Temples, tho it were only not to give occasion of doubting, whether it proceed from Fortune, or Divine Counsel; that is, all things, in a manner, holding on their course, as it was at first begun.

This also is of no little weight, that they assert a special Providence in respect of Men. For, (not to repeat what I even now said, That a happy and immortal Nature cannot be possess'd with Anger or Favour,) put case, That God

takes

takes no care of the Affairs of Men, How can they come to be otherwise than they are? In them there is an equal, or rather greater Imbecility, than in other Creatures, equal inconveniences, equal ills: Some of them, making Vows, are preserved from Shipwrack; How many have made Vows, and yet perished? Many pray for Children, and obtain them; How many pray for Children in vain?

But, to be brief, why, if God takes care of the Affairs of Men, is it ill with the Good, well with the Bad? Truly it is an Argument with me, when I see Crosses always happen to the Good, Poverty, Labours, Exile, loss of Friends; on the other side, wicked Persons to be Happy, to increase in Power, to be honoured with Titles; That Innocence is unsafe, wicked Actions go unpunished; That Death exercises his Cruelty without observing Manners, without order and distinction of Years; Some arrive at old Age, others are snatch'd away in their Infancy, others in their full strength; others in the flower of their Youth are immaturely cut off; In War, rather the best are vanquished and perish. But that which prevails most with me, is, That the most Religious Persons are afflicted with the greatest Ills; but to them, who either wholly neglect the Gods, or worship them not Religiously, happen either the least Misfortunes, or none at all.

Moreover, I think it may not be ill argued thus: Either God would take away Ills and cannot, or he can and will not, or he neither will nor can, or he both will and can. If he would and cannot, he is impotent, and consequently not God; if he can and will not, envious, which is equally contrary to God's Nature; if he neither will nor can, he is both envious and impotent, and consequently not God; if he both will and can, which only agrees with God, Whence then are the Ills? Or, why does he not take them away?

CHAP. VI.

A Digression, concerning Genii *or* Dæmons.

IT is all one, whether God takes care of things by Himself, as some will have it, or (as others hold,) by Ministers, whom they generally call *Genii* and *Dæmons*; for things happen no otherwise, than as if we should suppose no such Ministers; and tho it were granted, that there are some, yet can they not be such as they feign them, that is, of a Human Form, and having a Voice that can reach to us: To omit, since for the most part they are said to be ill and vicious, they cannot be happy and long-liv'd, since both much Blindness and a Proneness to Destruction perpetually attends Wickedness.

How much were it to be wished, that there were some who might take care of us, and supply what is wanting to our Prudence, and to our Strength? Especially, how much were it to be wished, by such as are Leaders in War of most Pious and Honest Attempts, that they might confide not only in Arms, Horses, Ships, but also in the assistence of the Gods themselves?

And indeed, some are said to appear sometimes to some Persons; and why may it not be, that they who affirm *Dæmons* to have appeared to them, either lye and feign, or are melancholy, and such, that their distemper'd Body either strangely raiseth, or diverts their Imagination to extraordinary conceits. It is well known, that nothing is more apt to be moved and transformed into any Species (altho there be no real ground,) than Imagination. For the impression made upon the Mind is like that in Wax, and the Mind of Man having within it self that which represents, and that which is represented, there is such a power in it, that, taking even the very least of things seen or heard upon some occasion, it can of it self easily vary and transfigure the Species, as is manifested by the commutations of Dreams which are made in Sleep, from which we perceive, that the imaginative Faculty puts on all variety of Affections and Phantasies; so that it is no wonder, if, where the Faculty is unsound, they seem to see *Dæmons*, or other things, of which they have had any foretaken conceit.

Moreover, they use to alledge Divination as an argument to prove both Providence and the existence of *Dæmons*; But I am ashamed at Humane Imbecillity, when it fetcheth Divinations even out of Dreams, as if God walking from Bed to Bed did admonish supine Persons, by indirect Visions, what shall come to pass; and out of all kinds of Portents and Prodigies; as if Chance were not a sufficient Agent for these Effects; but we must mix God, not only with the Sun, and with the Moon, and several other living Creatures, but also with all Brass and Stone.

But to instance in Oracles only: Many ways may it be evinced, that they are meer Impostures of Priests, as may particularly be discover'd, for that the Verses which proceed from them are bad, being, for the most part maimed in the beginning, imperfect in the middle, lame in the close; which could not be, if they came from Divine Inspiration, since from God nothing can proceed, but what is well and decent.

And I remember, that, when in my younger days I lived at *Samus*, that Oracle was much cried up, by which (as they reported,) *Polycrates* King of that Island, celebrating the *Pythian* and *Delian* Games, sent at the same time to *Delus*, demanding of *Apollo*, Whether he should offer Sacrifice at the appointed time? *Pythius* answered, *These to thee are the Pythian and the Delian*; whereby (said they,) it was signify'd, that those should be his last, for soon after he happen'd to be slain. But how could it be signify'd by that Answer, that these Sacrifices should be the last rather than the middle? But that the vulgar sort of Men are most commonly led by Hearsay, and are greedy of strange Stories.

CHAP.

CHAP. VII.

Of the End, or Corruption of the World.

THat the World shall perish and have an end, is consequent, Forasmuch as it was generated, and had beginning; for it is necessary, that all compounded things be also dissipated, and resolved into those things of which they are compounded, some by some Causes, others by others; but still all from some Cause, and at some time or other. Whence it is the more to be admired, that there should be some, who, not only broaching the Opinion, that the World was generated, but even in a manner made by hands, thence define, that it shall be ever. For as I argued before, What Coagmentation can there be indissoluble? or, what is there that hath a Beginning, but no End?

Certainly, the World seems like an Animal, or Plant, as generated so subject to corruption, as well because, no otherwise than they, it consists of Atoms, which by reason of the intestine Motion, wherewith they are incessantly moved, at length must cause a dissolution; as also because, there may happen both to them, and the World, some extrinsecal Cause, which may put them to destruction: Especially it being known that every thing is produced but one way, but may be destroyed many; As also, because, there are three Ages in them, Youth, Middle State, and Old Age; so the World first began to grow up; (as also after the time of its generation, there came extrinsecally from the Universe Atoms, which insinuated into the Pores as it were of the World, and by which Heaven, the Stars, the Air, the Sea, the Earth, and other things were augmented, the congruous Atoms accommodating themselves to those that were congruous to them) then, because there ought to have been some end of growing, it rested in a kind of perfect state; and at last began so to decay, as plainly shews, that it declines towards its last Age.

This is first proved, because, as we see, in progress of time, Towers fall, Stones moulder, Temples and Images decay, whereby at last they come to be dissolved; So we may perceive the parts of the World sensibly to moulder, and wear away; a great part of the Earth goes away into Air, (not to say any thing of those greater Concussions, which make us fear somtimes, lest the whole should fall, and sinking from under our Feet sink, as it were, into an Abysse,) the Water also is partly exhaled into Air, partly so distributed through the Earth, that is will not all flow back again: The Air is continually changed, many things going forth into it, and many produced again out of it. Lastly, the Fire (not only ours, but the Starry Fire, also, as that which is in the Sun,) sensibly decays by the emanation, and casting forth of Light. Wherefore, neither is there any reason to think, that these Bodies of the World will continue ever.

Again, because we see there is a continual Fight amongst the Bodies of the World themselves, through which somtimes happen Conflagrations, somtimes Deluges, as it were with equal strength. But, as in wrastling, so is it necessary, that in the World one of the Contraries prevail at last, and destroy all things. If any shall demand, which of the two is the more likely to prevail, it may be answer'd, The Fire, as being the more active, and reciving particular recruits from the Sun, and Heaven; so as, at last, it will come to get the upper hand, and the World thereupon perish by Conflagration.

Lastly, because there is nothing indissolvable, but either as it is solid, as an Atom; or intactile, as Vacuum; or hath nothing beyond it, whence either a dissolving cause may come, or whither itself may go forth, as the Universe. But the World neither is solid, by reason of Vacuum intermix'd; nor intactile, by reason of corporeal Nature; nor hath nothing without it, by reason of its extremity: Whence it follows, that a destruction may happen extrinsecally, by Bodies incurring to it, and breaking it; but, both extrinsecally and intrinsecally, it is capable of being dissolved.

This I add because the World may perish, not only by Conflagration, or, if you will, by Inundation also, but by many other ways; amongst which the chief is, that, as a living Creature, (to which I already compar'd it,) the frame of the Soul being unty'd, is dissolved into several parts, and these at length are quite dissolved also, either by being dissipated, and turning into Air, and the most minute Dust, or serving again for the production of some other living Creatures; So the Walls, as it were, of the World decaying, and falling, the several pieces of it are dissolved, and go at length into Atoms, which, having gotten into the free space of *Vacuum*, rush downwards in a Tumult, and recommence their first motions; or run forward, far and long; or soon fall upon other Worlds; or meeting with other Atoms, joyn with them to the production of new Worlds.

And though indeed, as a living Creature may be sooner or later dissolved by departure of the Soul, so may either of these happen to the World: Yet it is more probable, that it will so come to pass, as that in a moment of time, nothing thereof shall remain except Atoms, and a desolate space; for which way soever the gate of death, as it were, shall be first opened, thither will all the crowd of Matter throng to get out.

That the World, as I said, is declining towards its last age, is probable, for that the teeming Earth, as I lately touched, scarce bringeth forth even little Animals, when as formerly she produced large; and that she, not without extream labour, brings forth Corn and Fruits, whereas at first she brought them forth of her one accord, in great plenty. Whence it comes, that there are frequent complaints, praising the former ages, and accusing the present, for that they perceive not that it is the course of things, that all things should decay by little and little, and, wearyed with long space of age, tend as it were to destruction. I wish Reason, rather than the thing itself did persuade, that within a short tim, we shall see all things shatter'd in pieces.

CHAP. VIII.

Of Infinite Worlds.

Moreover, as to demand, Whether there are, besides this, not only other Worlds but many, even infinite: This seems to be the Answer, That there are infinite Worlds. For (a) the Atoms being infinite, as we formerly shewed, are carried through infinite spaces; and that several ways in far distances from this World, and there meeting one another in Multitudes, may joyn to the production of infinite Worlds. Since the Atoms, being of this nature, that a World may be made up, and consist of them, cannot, by reason of there Infinity, be consumed, or exhausted by one, nor any determinate number of Worlds; whether these Worlds be supposed, framed after one fashion, or after divers. It is not impossible therefore, but that there may be infinite Worlds,

(a) Laert.

Lucret. 2.

And indeed it is as absurd for a single World to be made in an infinite Universe, as for one Ear of Corn to sprout up in the vast Field, sowed with many Grains; For as in the Field there are many Causes, to wit, many Seeds apt to grow up, and places to produce them; So in the Universe, besides Places, there are Causes, not many, but infinite, namely Atoms, as capable of joyning, as those of which this World was made up.

Lucret. loc. cit.

Besides, we see not any generable thing, so one, as that it hath not many like itself, in the same kind, (for so Men, so Birds, so Beasts, so Fishes, are multiplied each under their particular Species.) Wherefore, seeing that not only the Sun, the Moon, the Earth, the Sea, and the rest of the parts of the World were generated; but even the whole World it self, which consists of them; we must acknowledge, that not only the Parts, but the World itself, are not single, but many, as to number, and (for the Reasons alledged) infinite.

Now there being nothing to hinder, but that some Worlds may be like this of ours, others unlike it; for there may be equal, there may be greater, there may be lesser; there may be, that have the same Parts, disposed in the same Order; there may be, that have different Parts, or disposed in a different Order; there may be, that have the same Figure; there may be, that have a different, (for though Atoms cannot have an infinite variety of Figures, having a determinate space in their Superficies, yet may they be of more Figures than we can number, as Round, Oval, Pyramidal, &c.) Although, I say, there be no repugnance in this, yet all these diversities are only certain kinds of conditions, which vary the common Quality, and Nature of the World.

But it seems, that each of the other Worlds, as this of ours, and every compound which is made in that vast Vacuity, and hath any resemblance with those things which fall under our Observation, is generated apart, and after a fashion peculiar to itself, *By certain Convolutions, and Intertextures of Atoms proper to it*; And this, whether it be generated in the *Intermundia*, (so we term the interval, included betwixt two or more Worlds, not far distant from one another,)

Laert.

or in a multivacuous place, (that is in which, though there be great and little Bodies, yet vacuities take up the greater share of it,) or Lastly, in a great unmixt and pure *Vacuum*, though not as some (who assert such a *Vacuum*,) describe it.

For we are to understand, contrary to them, that *there floweth together, if not from infinite, at least from one, or more Worlds, or intermundia, some apt Seeds, that is, a congruous heap of Atoms, or little Bodies, which are by degrees mutually adjoyned here and there, and variously formed, and change place diversly, according as it happens, and withal receive from without some Irriguous, as it were, Accretions; untill a bulk, consisting of the whole Assembly of all these, be made up, and gain a consistency, as much as the Principles, of which it was made, can well bear.*

Laert.

For it is *not sufficient, for the generation of a World, that a great heap of Atoms be thrown together in a* Uacuum *and by the accession of others, grow bigger, till it roll into another Vacuum: In the same manner, as a heap of Snow, being tumbled upon Snow, gathers still more, and grows bigger, as was the Opinion of a certain Philosopher, holding the necessity of such a Method: Since this is repugnant to our daily Experience.* For a heap, whose innermost kernel, as it were, is solid, and its outermost shell solid also, can neither be rolled up and down, nor increased, if the part intercepted betwixt the kernel and the Shell be fluid, as in the World it is.

Ibid.

Finally, That the other Worlds also are, because generated, subject to Corruption, is too manifest to be mentioned; that some may be dissolved sooner, others later; Some by some Causes, Others by others, is a thing necessarily consequent to the peculiar diversity of every one.

CHAP. IX.

Of inferior Terrestrial things.

But that (omitting the rest,) we may speak more particularly of this our World, since all things in it are either contained within the compass of the Earth, or exceed not the height of the ground, or are placed on high, that is, raised above the Earth's Superficies, and therefore may generically be divided into the low or Terrestrial sort of things, and those which are Sublime, Celestial, or Aerial; Let us then so order our Discourse, as to speak first of the former, in regard, that as they are nearer, and more familiar to us; so we may thence ascend by orderly degrees to discourse, and define, what we should most rationally conjecture of the later, which are more remote from us, and less visible to us.

In the first place, we are to take a general view of the body of the Earth, next of the Water, a considerable part of this Masse, and mingled diversly with the Earth, partly in its Superficies, partly in its very Bowels; Afterwards of these lesser Bodies, with which we see that whole Masse replenished, whether inanimate, as Minerals, Stones, and Plants; or animate, usually called Animals.

CHAP. I.

Of the Earth situate in the middle of the World.

First then, as to the Earth, we have already said, how it was framed together with the other parts of the World ; for it had been to no purpose to form it first, beyond the utmost Surface of the World and then convey it into the World already framed, since it was sufficient for that Effect, that there were such Seeds found in the Universal Mass, of which it, with the other parts of the World, might be generated ; in the same manner as it would be unnecessary, that living Creatures should first be seperated from, and carried beyond this Infinity of things, and be formed there, that, being now perfected, they might be brought thence into this our Region. Nor was it needful, that they should first be exactly wrought in Heaven, and thence transmitted to our Earth ; seeing no Man can shew, why there must needs be found such Seeds there, of which Animals, Plants, and other visible Compounds are made up, and could as well be found here ; Or, whence Heaven hath this priviledge, of having sufficient conveniences for their Generation and Nutrition, more than our Earth.

It is already said, That the Earth, when the Heaven, and other higher Bodies, did fly, as it were, upwards setled into the middle of the World, and there rested as in the lowest place. We add now, That as it is the middle part of the World, towards which all heavy things fall ; it follows not, that there is also a middle part of it, called the Center, towards which, all things that ponderate are directed in a streight line ; for all heavy things fall in parallel Motions, without any endeavour to meet in any Angle, there being, as in the Universe, so also in our World, one Region above, from which all heavy things come, and only one below, towards which they tend.

Whence, as they are not to be approved of, who say, there are Antipodes, or Men so situated in a strange region of the Earth, that they walk with their Feet Diametrically opposite to ours, in like manner as we see the Images of Men, or other things, either stand or go with their Heads downwards under the Water ; for these Philosophers endeavours to maintain, contrary to the Laws of Nature and of heavy things, That Men, and other Terrestrial Bodies placed there, tend upwards, or towards the Earth ; and that it is equally impossible, they should fall down from the Earth, to the inferior places of the Sky ; as that Bodies amongst us here should unimpell'd mount up to Heaven. However, upon another account they speak consequently to their Hypothesis, that 'tis day with the Antipodes when 'tis night with us, and night with them when 'tis our day.

The Earth then is framed indeed after a circular Figure, but yet as a Dish or a Drum is, not like a Sphear or Bowl ; for this Surface of it which we inhabit, and which indeed is only habitable, is flat or plain, and not globous, and such as all heavy things are carried to it in a streight line, or perpendicularly, as was formerly declared.

This being so, here ariseth a great difficulty, How it can then be, that it should stand steady, and not fall downwards into that Region, into which the Antipodes would slide ? But, *the reason why the Earth falls not, is, because it rests upon the Air, as ally'd to it in Nature ; Nor doth it any more burthen the Air than Animals, which are of like Nature with the Earth, burthen the Earth.*

Nor is it hard to conceive, that in the Air beneath there is a power to sustain the Earth, because the Air and the Earth, by the general contexture of the World, are things not of different extraction, but ally'd to one another by a certain affinity. Whence, as being Parts of the same Whole, one cannot be burthensom to the other, but are held by a mutual embrace, as if they had no Gravity at all ; especially since this Earth, however in this upper part of it more compacted and heavy, may, descending lower, be, by degrees, less solid, and so less weighty ; till at length, in its lowest part of all, it approach very near the nature of the Air which supports it.

And for this reason I said, that the Earth was not made in some place out of the World, and thence brought into it, because then it would have pressed the Air with its weight, as our Bodies are sensible of the least weight, if imposed from without ; Whereas, neither the Head, nor other Parts are heavy to one another, by reason that they are agreeable to one another in Nature, and knit to one another by the Common Law of the same Whole.

And that it seem not incredible, a thing so tenuious as is Air should be able to uphold so gross a Bulk ; do but consider, how subtle a thing the Soul or Animal Spirit is, and yet how gross and weighty a Bulk of the Body it upholds and governs, and that only by this means, because it is a thing joyned to it, and aptly united to it, as the Air is to the Earth.

But we must not therefore conceive the Earth to be Animate, much less a Goddess, for we have formerly proved the contrary ; The Earth indeed many times brings forth several living Creatures, yet not as being herself Animate, but because, containing various Atoms and divers Seeds of things, she produceth many things many ways ; of which, Animate Beings are formed. Some there are, who call the Earth, The *Great Mother of the Gods*, and *Berecynthia*. That to the Earth these Names be attributed, if it be lawful to make use of Divine things, thereby to signify Natural things, may perhaps seem tolerable ; but to believe, that there is a Divinity in the Earth, is no way allowable.

CHAP. II.

Of Earth-Quakes, and the Flames of Ætna.

It seems wonderful, how it comes to pass, That the Earth is somtimes shaken, and trembles ; but this is an Effect which may happen from divers Causes, supposing that the Earth, as I see no reason to doubt, is in all parts alike, and that below as well as above, it hath Caverns, Breaches,

Breaches, and Rivers, rolling great Billows, vast Stones, &c.

For the Water may move the Earth, if it hath wash'd or worn away some parts, which being made hollow, it can no longer be held up, as it was whilst they were entire; or if some Wind drive upon Chanels, and Lakes, or standing Waters within the Earth and the [blow] impulsion either shake the Earth from thence, or the agitation of the Wind increasing with its own motion, and stirring up it self, be carried from the bottom to the top; as a Vessel cannot stand stedfast, untill the water which hath been troubled in it give over moving

Likewise the Earth may receive a shock, by some part thereof suddainly falling down, and thereby be moved; seeing that some of its parts are upheld, as it were, with Columns and Pillars, which decaying and sinking, the wheight that is laid on them quakes: For we see whole Houses shake, by reason of the jumbling, and succussion of Carts and Chariots.

Also the very Wind it self may move the Earth, either if the Earth (its interior and lower parts being full of crannies and chinks,) be shaken by some Wind variously dispers'd, and falling into those hollow Caverns, and so tremble in such manner, as our Limbs by insinuation of Cold tremble, and are moved, whether we will or no; Or, if the Wind getting in at the top, and driving downwards, the Earth is driven upwards by the Air under it; which is somewhat gross and watery, (for it sustains the Earth,) and shaken as it were from beneath, leaps up, which happens to all things: Not only to those which are forc'd against any thing, hard or firm; or so stretched or bent, that being prest upon it recoils; but also against a fluid thing, if it be able to strike it back, as when Wood is plung'd into Water.

The force of this Wind, if we conceive it turned into Fire, and resembling Thunder, may be carried on with a great destruction of all things that oppose its passage. For as Lightning, engendr'd in a Cloud, breaks thorow it, and shakes the Air with wonderful violence; in like manner, may the Fire, generated within the Caverns of the Earth of a coacervate and exagitated Wind, break thorow it, and make it tremble.

Now as there appears not any Cause, more likely than that which is taken from the Wind, and chiefly in this last manner, either by distributing itself into many several Cavities of the Earth; it causeth a trembling only, and (as if there were a transpiration through the looser Earth,) the Earth is not so broken thorow, as that there is a breach made, or somthing overthrown, or turn'd awry; or else by its being heaped up together in greater Caverns, there may follow such a succussion and impulsion, as may heave up, and cleave asunder the Earth, and make Gaps big enough to entomb whole Cities, as in divers paces it hath often hapned.

What I say concerning the force of the Wind, which being turned into Fire breaks thorow and shakes the Earth, may serve to make us understand, that the eruptions of Fire which often happen in the same places, as at Ætna, proceed from the same Cause.

For this Mountain is all hollow within, and so underpropped with Vaults of Flint, that the Wind shut up in them groweth hot, and being enkindled, forceth its way thorough the breaches which it finds above, and eats into the sides of those Caverns; whence (together with Flame and Smoke,) it casts up sparkles and pumices.

And the better to bring this to pass, the Sea lies at the foot of the Mountain, which rolling its Waves to and from the Shore, unto which the Caverns of the Hill extend, thrusts in, and drives forward the Air, whereby the Fire is augmented, and cherish'd, as with the blowing of Bellows.

CHAP. III.

Of the Sea, Rivers, Fountains, and the overflowing of Nilus.

AS for those Waters which are on the (Earth, for of those which are generated on high, and thence fall down in Rain, we shall speak more opportunely hereafter;) First, there is a vast body of them, which we call the Sea: For besides those in-land Seas which wash our Shores, there is also an extern Sea, or Ocean, which flowing about all the habitable Earth, is believed by some to be so immediately placed under the Arch of Heaven, that the Sun and other Stars Rise from it, and Sett in it, as we shall have occasion to shew elsewhere.

And indeed, the Vastness of the Sea being such, it may be esteemed not the most inconsiderable Reason, Why the Sea seems not to be increased by the flowing of so many Rivers into it; for all the Rivers are hardly like a Drop, compared to so immense a Body. And withal the Sun, who with his beams so soon dries wet Garments; although he suck not up much moisture from every place, yet from so large a compass cannot but take away a great deal. Not to mention how much the Winds, which in one night many times dry up the Ways, and harden the Dirt, may in sweeping along the Sea, consume of it.

But, the chiefest reason seems to be this. The Earth being a rare Body, and easily penetrated, and withal, washed on all sides by the Sea, the Waters, as well as they are poured from the Earth into the Sea, so must they also soak down from the Sea into the Earth, that they may rise up in Springs and flow again.

Neither need it trouble us, that the water of the Sea is salt, and the waters of Springs and Rivers fresh; because the water, passing out of the Sea into the Earth is strained in such manner, that it puts off the little bodies of Salt, and returns quite stripp'd of them. For, the body of the Sea being commixed of Salt, and of Water; forasmuch, as the Seeds of Salt, are more hooked, and those of Water more smooth, therefore, these glide easily away, whilst the others cannot but be entangled, and are all along left behind.

Hence appeareth the Cause (which seemeth the Principal,) of the perpetual flowing of Springs: Where they rise up, there may indeed be some great quantity of water gather'd together, which may serve for supply: But upon another

other account, they may be supplied, forasmuch as there is somthing continually flowing from beneath into them. And though these subterraneous Rivulets (as it were,) might be made up of the several Seeds, which are dispersed through the Earth, yet must these Seeds be supplied by the Sea, which soaks into the Earth.

Whence it comes to pass, as was said, that those Rivulets, dispersing themselves into lesser streams, and running down into lower hollow Receptacles, and meeting there, at last joyn together in great Channels, and make large Rivers, which continually renew and supply the immense Sea.

But since, there is not any River more wonderful than *Nilus*, for that every Summer it overfloweth and watereth *Ægypt*, we must not therefore omit to say, that this may happen by reason of the *Etesian* Winds which at that season blowing towards *Ægypt*, raise up the Sea to the mouths of *Nilus*, and drive up Sands thither, so as *Nilus* cannot but stop, and swell, and rising above its Channel, overflow the Plain which lies beneath.

Perhaps also it happens, for that the *Etesian* Winds blowing from the North carry the Clouds into the South beyond *Ægypt*, which, meeting at some very high Mountains, are there crouded together, and squeeze forth Rain, by which *Nilus* is increased.

It may happen also, that the exceeding high Mountains of *Ethiopia*, may be cover'd with Snow, which being dissolved by the Sun's excessive heat, fills the Channel of *Nilus*.

CHAP. IV.

Of the Properties of some Waters, and of Ice.

BUt that we may select besides some properties of Water, which seem wonderful to the Vulgar, I omit at present that Property, which is of kin to those we last mentioned; That although the Water so easily dissolves Salt, and admits to be imbued by it; yet there are some sweet Fountains, which spring out of the midst of the Sea. For this plainly happens hence, That the Water bursting forth from the bottom of the Sea, riseth up with so great vehemency, that it drives away on all sides the Sea-water, and neither suffers it, nor its Salt to be mingled with it.

Wonderful is that Fountain in *Epirus*, over which Flax or a Taper is no sooner put, but it is presently set on fire and flames. It seems, that from the Earth which is beneath it, so many Seeds of Heat are breathed forth, as that, though they are not able to heat the Water in their passage through it; yet as soon as ever they get out of it into the open Air, running into the Flax and Tapers, they associate themselves with the fiery Seeds, wherewith such things abound, and break forth into flame; in the same manner, as when putting flame to a Candle newly extinguish'd, you may see it light before the flame touches it.

But what shall we say of that Fountain, which is reported to be at the Temple of *Jupiter Hammon*, cold in the day-time, and hot in the night?

Certainly, the Earth about this Fountain, tho' it be looser than other Earth, yet being compress'd by the cold of night, it striks out, or squeezeth forth, and trasmits into the Water, many Seeds of Fire which it contains, whereby the Water groweth hot; but being loosened by the Heat of Day, it sucks back again, as it were the same Seeds, whereby the Water becometh cold.

It may likewise come to pass, that the Water which is made hot through the same Seeds, which are repressed in the night-time, by reason of the cold Air, may become cold in the day-time, the beams of the Sun passing so through the Water, that they afford to those Seeds a free vent into the Air. Just as Ice is dissolved by the same piercing and rarifying Beams; and though the Effects are contrary, yet may they proceed from the same Cause, as the melting of Wax, and hardning of Clay.

'Tis from the same Cause, that Water in Wells is Hot in the Winter, Cold in the Summer. For in Summer, the Earth is rarify'd by Heat, and exhaleth the Seeds of Heat which are in her; by which means the Water, which is kept close within her, becomes colder. But in Winter the Earth is compress'd and condens'd with Cold; whence, if she hath any Heat, she squeezeth it forth into the Wells.

These put me in mind to speak of Ice, by which the Water, forgetting, as it were, its natural fluidity, grows solid and hard. Here we must conceive, that those Bodies only are capable of being made solid, which are made up of Parts of little Bodies, that have plain Surfaces; because, by exclusion of Vacuity, the Parts cohere best with one another; whereas if those little Bodies be round, or joyned to round, or intermingled with plain, there is a *Vacuum* contained round about them, into which the round may roll, and the plain bend; whence followeth softness, and (unless there be some hooks that stay it,) fluxibility.

Ice therefor is made, either when the round little Bodies, which cause Heat, are thrust out of the Water, and the plain which are in the same Water (part weereof are acute-angled, part obtuse-angled,) are thrust up close together; Or, when those little Bodies are brought thither from without, (and that for the most part from the Air, when it is made cold by them,) which being closely pressed, and thrusting out all the round that they meet, bring solidity into the Water.

CHAP. V.

Of things Terrestrial Inanimate.

OUr Method leading us to speak of those things which are generated of Earth and Water; it is in the first place manifest, that those things are either Animate or Inanimate. Animate things are those which have Sense, and are vulgarly called Animals; Inanimate things are those which want Sense, whence, under this Name are comprehended all those, to which the Name of Animal is not applyed.

Of this sort are, First, certain moist things which are grown consistent, as we see Salt, Sulphur, and ill-scented Bitumen generated in the Earth. Now these are the chief cause, not only of subterraneous Heat, and ignivomous Eruptions, as that of *Ætna*, already spoken of; but also of pestiferous Exhalations, which being carried on high cause Avernous Lakes and Diseases. Wherefore we will speak more amply of these, when we treat of Meteors. Concerning Amber, which attracteth Straws, we shall say something hereafter.

Of this sort also are Metals, which were first found out upon occasion of some Woods being burnt by Lightning, or some other Fire, which being quite burnt up, the Metals were melted and stuck to the roots, and thereupon dazled the Eye with their splendor, and were observ'd to retain the same Figure with the things in which they flowed. Whence Men conjectured, That the some Metals, being melted by the force of Fire, might be formed into any Figure, even, acute, or pointed; and by reason of the solidity they had acquired, might be made fit to malleate, or to strike, or for other uses.

Moreover, not only Lead, but also Gold and Silver lay neglected, as being found less commodious for those uses, and Brass only was in esteem, of which were made Darts, Swords, Axes, Ploughshares, and the like; until Iron came to be found out; of which then, they chose rather to make these things, by reason it was of greater hardness.

Of this sort also are Stones, whereof many are daily generated, many broke off from Rocks, but the man bodies of Rocks and Stones were made from the beginning; for by this means, as we said formerly, Mountains were first occasion'd; and somtimes we find, that the Earth encloseth in her Bowels, Caverns, Rocks, and broken Stones, as well as Rivers, Channels, and Winds.

Now as Stones are ordinarily discerned by their hardness and solidity, so in the first rank, as it were, may be reckoned Adamants, not damnifi'd by blows, (for a tryal of them being made upon Anvils, they split the Iron,) and huge Flints, out of which, by the stroke of Iron, Fire flyeth, for they contain Seeds of Fire close hidden in their Veins; neither doth the cold force of the Iron hinder, but that being stirred up by its stroke, they meet together in one Body or Spark.

Lastly, of the inanimate kind are Plants, that is, Herbs and Trees; for the Soul is not without Sense. And we see, that of animate Beings, which from thence are called Animals and living Creatures, some have a moving and desiderative Soul; others a discursive; But Plants neither have Sense, nor either of those Souls, and therefore cannot be called Animate things.

Somthing indeed they have common with living Creatures, that is, Nutrition, Augmentation, Generation; but they perform these things by the impulse of Nature, not by the direction of a Soul, and therefore are only Analogically, or for resemblance-sake, said to live and die as Animals. Whence also whatsoever may be said of them, may be understood by Parity, and in some proportion, by those things which shall be said of living Creatures.

I would add, that the original of Sowing and Grafting was, upon the observation Men took, that Berries and Acorns shedding, and falling to the ground, sprung up again, and begot new Plants, like those of which sort they themselves were. But it is enough to have hinted this.

CHAP. VI.

Of the Loadstone in particular.

BUt we must insist a little longer upon a thing inanimate indeed, yet very admirable; I mean the *Herculean* Stone, which we call also Magnet, for that it was first found in *Magnesia*. It is much wondred at, by reason of its singular Power (or Virtue,) in attracting Iron.

To explicate this Power, we must suppose three or four Principles; One is, That there is a continual effluxion of little Bodies out of all things: As, out of coloured and lucid Bodies, flow such as belong to Colour and Light; From hot and cold Bodies, such as belong to heat and cold Bodies; From odorous Bodies, such as belong to smell; and so of the rest.

A Second is, That there is no Body so solid, but hath little vacuities contained within it, as is manifest by all Bodies, through which passeth Moisture, (or Sweat,) Light, Sound, Heat, or Cold.

The Third, That these effluent little Bodies are not alike adaptable to all things. The Sun, by emission of his Beams, hardens Clay, melts Snow; Fire resolves Metal, contracts Leather; Water makes hot Iton harder, Leather softer; The Olive-tree is bitter to the Taste of Man, pleasing to Goats; Marjoram is sweet to the smell of Man, hateful to Swine, *&c.*

The Fourth, That the little Vacuities are not of the same compass in all things, wherefore neither can the same be accommodated to all little Bodies. This is manifest from the contextures of the Sense, for the little Bodies which affect these, move not those; or those which affect some one way, affect others another; as also from the contextures of all things else, for what will penetrate one, will not penetrate another.

From these it is understood, that the Loadstone may attract Iron (and Amber, Straw,) upon a double account. For First, We may imagine the Atoms that flow out of the Stone, so to suit with those which flow out of the Iron, that they easily knit together; wherefore being dashed on both sides on the Bodies of the Iron and the Stone, and bounding back into the middle, they entangle with one another, and draw the Iron along with them.

But forasmuch as we see, that the Iron, which is attracted by the Stone, is itself able to attract other Iron; Whether shall we say, that some of the particles flowing out of the Stone, hitting against the Iron, bound back, and these are they which catch hold of the Iron. Others, insinuating into it, pass with swiftness through the empty Pores, and being dashed against the Iron that is next, into which they could not all enter, although they had penetrated it; from thence leaping back to the first Iron, they made other compilcations like the former; and if any happened

ned to penetrate farther, they likewise might attract another Iron, and that another, upon the same ground.

Moreover, it may be conceived in this manner, that there flow certain little Bodies, as well out of the Magnet, as out of Iron, but more and stronger out of the Magnet; whereby it comes to pass, that the Air is driven away much farther from about the Magnet, than from about the Iron; whereupon there are many more little vacuities made about it than about the Iron. And because the Iron is placed within the compass of the dispelled Air, there is much *Vacuum* taken up betwixt it and the Magnet. Whence it happens, that the little Bodies leap forward more freely, to be carried into that place, and thereupon run towards the Magnet; but they cannot go thither in a great and extraordinary company, without enticing along the things that cohere with them; and so the whole mass, consisting of such coherent things, goes along with them.

It may also be said, that the motion of the Iron is assisted by the Aire, through its continual motion and agitation. And that first from the outward Air, which continually pressing, and pressing more vehemently where it most abounds, cannot but drive the Iron into that part where there is less, or which is more vacuous, as towards the Magnet. Next from the inward, which in the same manner continually agitating, moving, and deriving, cannot but give it a motion into that part, where there is greatest Vacuity.

CHAP. VII.

Of the Generation of Animals.

WE come now to speak of Animals, which are of so diffierent Natures, some Walking, others Flying, others Swimming, others Creeping; some being Greater, some Lesser; some more Perfect, some less Perfect, (even we Ourselves also being Animals,) and yet withal still of one Nature; that Nature discovers an admirable Power in the composure of them.

For since Nature is, as it were, instructed by the things themselves, and from their orderly procedure, and compelled by a kind of necessity, or by the concatenation of Motions, to perform these so many and so different Effects, which we call the Works of Nature; this especially appears in Animals, because the concatenation of Motions shews itself to be Artificial, chiefly in them, although proceeding from a substance utterly void of Reason.

And although the Atoms themselves be not endued with Reason, nor their motion govern'd by a rational Conduct; yet the nature of every living Creature in the beginning of the World grew to be such, that, according to the temperature of those Motions, which the Atoms then had, other Motions still, and others followed, which being caused after the same manner still produced their Like. By which means those motions, which, in the beginning were merely casual, in process of time became artificial, and succeeded after a constant and determinate Order.

But to discourse more fully hereupon, Divers kinds of Animals being produced in the beginning of the World, it came to pass, first by their receiving congruous Aliment, that those Atoms, which are adaptable to one another, were attracted and intangled by their fellow-Atoms, which were already in the Animal, (those which were not adaptable being cut off,) so that a peculiar Nature to every one of them, *viz.* Such a compound of such Atoms grows up first, and at length becomes confirmed.

Next, That by the perpetual motion of Atoms, and their intrinsecal Ebullition, some of them being still thrust out of their place, and running into the genital parts, meet there from all places; and, there being a distinction of Sexes, after mutual Appetition and Coition, are received in the Womb.

After this, that the Atoms, or seminal Bodies compounded of them, and flowing from all parts, (whence therefore, *the Seed may be conceived as somthing incorporeal*, not in rigour indeed, because only *Vacuum* is truly such, but *in the most familiar Sense of the Word, by which we term any thing incorporeal, which easily penetrates through the most solid Bodies,*) that the Atoms, I say, are those seminal little Bodies, which thus flowed from all parts, did therefore (this Motion continuing,) withdraw them from the tumult of others, and, like Atoms, drawing their Like; therefore those that come from the Head, would betake themselves to one place; those from the Breast into the next place; and those which come from every other part, each rank themselves in their distinct situation; and so at length, a little Animal is formed like that, whence the Seed was taken. *Laert.*

Moreover, that this little Animal is nourished, and increaseth by the attraction of like Atoms, or little Bodies meeting together in the Womb; until the Womb being wearied, and no longer fit to nourish them, slackens its motions, or rather opens the door, and gives them leave to go out.

Further, that this Animal being after the same manner fully grown up, and the continual agitation of the Atoms persuing one another, not ceasing, it begetteth another like thing, and that other consequently another.

At length, that Nature, being by little and little accustomed hereunto, learneth, as it were, so to propagate Animals like in their kinds, as that from the motion, and perpetual Series of Atoms, it derives a necessity of operating continually in this manner.

Thus much for the generation of those Animals, which are made by Propagation; As for those which we somtimes see produced otherwise, they may be generated after the same manner, as all things at first were; whether some Seeds of them were remaining, formed from the very beginning; or whether daily formed, either within, or without, the Animals themselves; and if within, then thrust out, (as in the generation of Worms, and Flies, leaving behind them some remainders, either in the Earth, or elsewhere; of which, other Animals, of the same kinds, are begotten.)

What I said of the defluxion of Seed, I mean not only, on the parts of the Male, but of the
Female

Female also, seeing that she likewise emitteth, having *Parastatæ* or Testicles, though placed in a contrary way, and therefore is she desirous of Coition.

And this indeed seems necessary to be granted towards giving the Reason, why a Male or Female is formed; for nothing can be alledged more proper than this, that whereas the young One consists of the Seeds, both of its Sire and Dam, if that of the Sire predominate, it proves Male, if that of the Dam, Female.

Hence also may be given a cause of the resemblance which it hath to either, or both its Parents; for if the Female with a sudden force attracts, and snatcheth away the Seed of the Male, then the young One becometh like the Dam; if both alike, it becometh like both, but mixtly.

If you demand, Why Children are somtimes like their Grandfathers, or Great Grandfathers? The Reason seems to be this; the Seed is made up of many little Bulks, which are not always all of them dissolved into Atoms, or nearest to Atoms, in the first or next Generations, but at length in some one of the following Generations, they unfold themselves in such manner, as that, what they might have done in the Immediate, they exhibite only in the Remote.

But whence comes Barrenness? From the Seed's being either thinner than it ought, so as it cannot fasten one the place; or thicker, so as it cannot easily be commixed: For there is requisite a due proportion betwixt the Seeds of the Male, and of the Female; whence it happens, that many times the same Man or Woman who are incapable of having Children by one, may yet have them by another. I omit other Reasons, as from the Aliment, since it is manifest, that Aliment, by which Seed is increased, differs from that whereby it is attenuated and wasted.

CHAP. VIII.

Of the use of Parts in Animals.

HEnce follows, That the parts of Animals were not from the very beginning of things framed, after the fashion they have now, for those ends and uses whereto we see them now serve, (for there was no cause to foresee this end, nor any things precedent to which that cause attending, and thence taking a conjectural aim might design any such fashion,) but because it hapned that the parts were made, and did exist as we now see them; therefore they came to be applied to these uses rather than to others, and being first made, themselves became afterwards the occasion of their own usefulness, and insinuated the knowledge of it into the minds of the Users.

The Eyes therefore were not made to see, nor the Ears to here, nor the Tongue to speak, nor the Hands to work, nor the Feet to go, for all these Members were made before there was Seeing, Hearing, Speaking, Working, Going; but these became their Functions after they had been made.

For the Soul being formed together with and within the Body, and moreover being capable of Sense, the Eye hapned to be made of such a Cotexture, that the Soul, being applied unto it, could not but produce the sensitive act of Seeing; and the Ear of such, as that being joined to it, it could not but produce Hearing; and there being within the Body, made together with it, an Animal Spirit capable to impel and move, the Tongue hapned to be framed after such a Contexture, as that this Spirit coming to it, could not but move it, and break the Air (which at the same time it breathed forth,) into words. In like manner, the Hands, the Feet, and the rest of the Limbs were so fashioned, as that this Spirit rushing into them could not but give this motion to one, and that to the other.

As for the Tendons, which are plainly the Organs, by which the Parts are stirred, it is evident that the Actions are not strong, because these are big; nor remiss, because they are small; but the Actions are such or such; according to the occasions of frequent or seldom using them: But the bigness of the Tendons follows the quantity of the Motion, so that those which are exercised are in good plight, and grow conveniently bigger, those which lie idle thrive not, but waste away.

Wherefore the Tendons were not so formed by Nature, as if it were better, that they should by strong and big for the discharge of vehement Functions; weak and slender for the weaker, (for we see even Apes have Fingers fashioned like ours,) but, as was said before, those which are exercised, must of necessity be big, because they are well nourished; and those which are not exercised, small, because they are less nourished.

For Confirmation hereof may be alledged, that most Parts are somtimes directed to those uses for which no Man will say they were design'd; and this, when either Necessity or Occasion, or some Conjecture taken elsewhere, lays them open to us, Men would not so much as dream of fighting with Weapons, if they had not first fought with their Hands; nor of holding Shields before them, if they had not first felt Wounds that were to be avoided; nor of making soft Beds, if they had not first slept on the Ground; nor of making Cups, if they had not drunk Water first out of their Hands; nor of making Houses, if they had not been acquainted with the use of Caves; And so of the rest.

CHHP. IX.

Of the Soul, the intrinsecal Form of Animals.

LET us now come to the Soul, by which Animals are, and from it have their denomination. In the first place we must conceive it to be Corporeal, *some most tenuious or subtile Body, made up of most subtile Particles.* Doubtless *they who affirm it is Incorporeal, besides that they abuse the Word,* play the Fools exceedingly; For, except it were such, it could neither act nor suffer; it could not act, for it could not touch any thing; it could not suffer, for it could not be touch'd by any thing, but *would be as a meer Vacuity, which, as I said before, is such that it can neither act nor suffer any thing, but only affords a free motion to Bodies passing thorow it.*

Now that the Soul acts and suffers somthing, is manifestly declared by those things which happen about its Senses and Affections; as also by the motions wherewith it impels the members, and, from within, governeth the whole Animal, turneth it about, transports it with Dreams; and, in general, by its union and consent, to mix in one compound with this grosser matter, which usually, upon this occasion, is more particularly termed the Body.

I say, it is a most tenuous and subtle Body, for that *it is made up of most tenuious or most subtle little Bodies; which, as they are, for the most part, exceeding smooth, so are they very round*; otherwise they could not permeate, and cohere intrinsecally with the whole Body, and with and its parts, as with Veins, Nerves, Entrals, and the rest. Which is manifest even from hence; for that when the Soul goeth out of the Body, we find not that any thing is taken off from the Whole, neither as to its Figure nor Weight; but like Wine, when its flower or spirit is gone; or Unguent, that hath lost its scent; for the Wine and Unguent retain the same quantity, as if nothing of them were perished, So that the Soul, if you should imagine her to be rolled up together, might be contained almost in a point, or the very least of places.

Nevertheless, though it be of such a subtle Contexture, yet is it mixed and compounded of four several Natures: for we are to conceive it a thing made up and contemperated of somthing fiery, somthing aerial, somthing flatuous, and a fourth which hath no name; by means whereof, it is endued with a sensitive faculty.

The Reason is this, because when a thin Breath departs out of the Body of a dying person, this Breath is mixed with Heat, and Heat attracts Air, there being no Heat without Air. Thus we have three of those things which make up the Soul; and because there is none of these three from which the sensitive motions can be derived, we must therefore admit a fourth, though without a name, whereunto the sensitive Faculty may be attributed.

This may be confirmed from hence, for that there is a certain Breath or Gale, as it is were, and Wind, which is cause of the Body's motion; Air, of its Rest; somthing Hot cause of the Heat that is in it; there must likewise be some fourth thing, the cause of its Sense.

Now the necessity of this fourth being manifest, upon another account, Anger, by which the Heart boils, and Fervor sparkles in the Eyes, convinceth, that there is Heat in it; Fear, exciting Horror throughout the Limbs, argues a Cold, or copious Breath or Wind; and the calm state of the Breast, and serenity of the Countenance, demonstrates there is Air.

Whence it comes to pass, that those Animals in which Heat is predominant are angry, as Lions; those in which a cold Breath, are timorous, as Harts; those in which an aerial portion, are more quiet, and, as it were, of a middle condition between Lions and Harts, as Oxen. The same difference is also to be observ'd amongst Men.

Lastly, Although the Soul be a mixt and compounded thing, and this fourth nameless thing, or sensitive faculty, be the chief of its parts, (it being, in a manner, the Soul of the Soul, for from it the Soul hath, that it is a Soul, and it distinguishes Animals from other things, as their intrinsecal form and essential difference,) nevertheless these parts are so perfectly contemperated, as that of them is made one substance, and that most subtle and most coherent; neither, as long as the Soul is in the Body, can these four be separeated from one another any more than Odor, Heat, or Sapor, which are natural to any inward part of the Body, can be separated from it.

Now this substance being contained in the Body, and coherent, as it were, with it, is, in a manner, upheld by it, and is likewise the cause of all the Faculties, Passions, and Motions in the Body, and mutally containeth the Body, and governeth it, and is moreover the cause of its Health and preservation, and can no more be severed from the Body, without the dissolution thereof, than Scent can be divided from Frankincense, without destruction of its nature.

I shall not need to take notice, that one of the Natural Philosophers seems, without any reason, to conceive, that there are as many parts of the Soul, as of the Body, which are mutually applied to one another. For the substance of the Soul being so subtle, and the bulk of the Body so gross, doubtless its Principles must be more subtle and fewer than those of the Body; so that every one of these coheres not with another, but each of them to little bulks and heaps, as it were, that consist of a greater number. Whence it comes to pass, that somtimes we feel not when Dust, or a Gnat lights upon the Body, nor a Mist in the Night, nor the Spiders thread, nor Feathers, nor Thistle-down, or the like, when we meet with them; it being requisite, that more of the little Bodies which are mingled with the parts of the Soul be stirred up, before they can feel any thing that toucheth or striketh them.

We must further observe, that there is some internal part of the Body of such a temperature, as that where the Soul adheres to it, it receives an extraordinary Perfection. This Perfection is the Mind, the Intellect, or that which we call the Rational part of the Soul; because (the other part diffused through the whole Body being irrational,) this only discourseth.

Now forasmuch as the Irrational part is twofold, Sense and Affection or Appetite, and the Intellect is between both, for it hath the Sense going before it to judge of things, and the Appetite coming after it, that by its own judgment it may direct it. We shall therefore, being to speak of each, begin with the Sense.

CHAP. X.

Of Sense in general, which is the Soul (as it were) of the Soul.

TO speak therefore first of Sense in general; We must observe, that the Soul possesseth it after such a manner, as that both to have it, and to use it, it requireth the Body, as being the thing wherein it is contained, and with which it operates. *Now the Body affording this to the Soul, viz. That it hath a Principle of Sensation, and is able to use it, becometh itself also participant of this Effect, which dependeth upon that Principle,* (that is to say, it feeleth or perceiveth,) *but not of all things that belong thereto*, as of Tenuity, and the like.

Wherefore it is not to be wondred at, that *the Body, when the Soul is departed, remaineth void of Sense; for it did not of it self possess this Faculty, but only made it ready for the Soul, which was congenius with it ; Which Soul, by means of the Faculty coeffected in the Body, exercising, by a peculiar motion of hers, the Act of Sensation, giveth Sense, not only to it self, but to the Body also, by reason of their Neighborhood, Cohæsion, or Union with one another.*

Ibid.

Thus it comes to pass, that not the Soul alone, nor the Body alone, perceive or feel, but rather both together ; and though the Principle of Sensation be in the Soul, yet whoever holds, that the Body doth not perceive or feel together with the Soul ; and believeth that the Soul, intermingled with the whole Body, is able of herself to perform this motion of Sensation, he oppugus a thing most manifest.

Lucret.

And they who say, (as some do,) that the Eyes see not any thing, but it is the Soul only that seeth through them, as through open doors, observe not, that if the Eyes were like doors, we might see things much better if our Eyes were out, as if the doors were taken away.

Now that which here seems the greatest difficulty being this, How it comes to pass that a thing Sensitive, or capable of Sense, may be generated of Principles that are wholly Insensitive, or void of Sense, we are to take notice, that this is to be ascribed to some necessary and peculiar Magnitude, Figure, Motion, Position, and Order of those Principles, as was before declared when we treated of Qualities, for the Faculty of Sense is one of the Qualities, which, that it appear where it was not, requireth that there be some Adition, Detraction, Transposition, and, in a word, a new Contexture, able to do that which the former could not.

Yet we must not therefore belive, that Stones, Wood, Clods of Earth, and such like Compounds, perceive, or feel ; for, as other Qualities, so this also is not begotten of every mixtion, or of the mixtion of any kind of things, but it is wholly requisite, that the Principles be endued with such a Bigness, such Figures, Motions, Orders, and the like Accidents ; whence it comes to pass, that even Clods of Earth, Wood, and the like, when putrifi'd by Rain, and heated by the Sun, the Position and Order of their Parts being changed, turn into Worms, and other sensitive things, This may be understood from the several Aliments, which being applied to the Bodies of living Creatures, and variously altered, do, in like manner, of Insensitive become Sensitive ; as Wood applied to Fire, of Not-burning becometh Burning.

And that it may appear, how much some are mistaken, who assert, that the Principles whereof Sense and Sensitive things consist, must be sensitive; consider, that if they were such, they must be soft, forasmuch as no hard, or solid thing is capable of Sense, and consequently, as we argued before, they must be corruptible ; because, unless they are solid, they may be diminished, and so lose their Nature, whereas the Principles of Things, as we have often heretofore alledged, must be incorruptible and permanent.

It may otherwise be proved thus, If we allow the Principles to be Incorruptible, we cannot conceive them to be Sensitive ; neither as Parts, for Parts severed from the Whole feel not ; neither as Wholes, for then they would be Animals, and consequently Mortal, or Corruptible, which is contrary to the *Hypothesis*. Moreover, if we should admit, that they are both Animals, and Immortal, it would follow, that no such Animals as we now behold, (that is, of a peculiar kind, and agreeing in one *species*,) could be generated, but only a heap of several little Animals.

Furthermore, If sensitive Things must be generated of sensitive, that is, like of like, it will be necessary, as we said before, that a Man (for Example,) consist of Principles that laugh, weep, ratiocinate, discourse of the mixture of Things, and of themselves, enquiring of what Things they consist, and these being like to corruptible Things must consist of others, and those likewise of others, into infinite.

Now it being well known, that in the Bodies of Animals there are five distinct Organs of Sense, by which the Soul (or the sensitive Faculty in Her,) apprehends, or perceives sensible Objects several ways, that is by Seeing, Hearing, Smelling, Tasting, Touching ; nothing hinders, but that we allow Five Senses, the Sight, the Hearing, the Smell, the Taste, and the Touch.

All this diversity ariseth from hence, that on one side the *species* of Colours, and visible Things, as also Sounds, Odors, Sapors, and other Qualities, are made up of little Bodies, endued with particular Magnitudes, Figures, Positions, Orders, and Motions. On the other side, the Organs of Sight, Hearing, and the rest of the Senses, are of such Contextures as contain little Vacuities, or Pores, which have likewise peculiar Magnitudes, Figures, Positions, and Orders, and these Organs being various have several Aptnesses and Proportions, to which the several little Bodies of the Qualities are commensurated, so as some can receive into themselves these, others those, whence it happens, that only these little Bodies, of which the *species* of Colour consist, are capable of penetrating into the Organ of Sight, and to move and affect it after that manner ; But so are not the little Bodies, which are only capable of piercing, moving, and affecting the Organ of Hearing, or those which can only affect that of the Touch, and so of the rest.

Hence also, when we observe, that not only Animals of different kinds, but even amongst Men themselves, some are not affected with the same sensible Objects, we may understand that there is not in them the same kind of Contexture. And since in all little Bodies blended and mingled together, some will naturally agree with others, some not, therefore neither can the impression and apprehensions, or sensation of the same quality be made in all Animals, neither can a sensible Object affect all Animals alike with all its parts, but each one with those qualities only which are suitable to their Senses, and convenient to affect them.

I shall add nothing concerning the common Objects of Sense, as Magnitude, Figure, Motion, and the like, which are perceptible by more Senses than one; for what we said of them in the Canonick, is sufficient.

CHAP. XI.

Of Sight, and of the Images which glide into it.

BEing to speak something of every Sense, we must begin with Sight, whose Organ manifestly is the Eye; nor is it less evident, that *the external Appearances, and Forms of Things, are therefore seen by us; because something glides from without, or from the Objects into us, that is, into our Eye,* But before we undertake to shew, that this is far more probable than what others assert, we must declare whether there be any thing which comes from the Things themselves into our Eye, and of what nature it is.

First then we affirm, that nothing hinders but that certain ' Effluxions of Atoms, perpetually ' flying in an uninterrupted course, are sent from ' the Surfaces of Bodies, in which also the same ' Position and same Order may be preserved, ' which was found in the Superficies and Solids of ' the very Bodies themselves, whence such Ef' fluxions are as it were Forms, Figures, or Ima' ges of these Bodies from which they are deri' ved, and resembling them in all their Linea' ments; and, moreover, are far more subtle than ' any of the things themselves, which by them ' are made visible to us. This then is the na' ture of those forms or figures, which we use to ' call Idols, or Images.

' Nor is it difficult, that such kind of contex' tures should be found in the middle Aire, or ' ambiently diffused space; nor, that there should ' be in the things themselves, and especially in the ' Atoms, certain dispositions rendring them apt ' to make representations, which are only meer ' empty cavities, and superficial tenuities of no ' determinable depth. * But in this place, we speak of those effluviums, which are as it were thin films, or skins stript from the remaining Bodies.

Nor yet is it difficult, that images of this nature should flow from the out-sides of bodies, as is hence proved, that there flowing ever something from the inner parts of bodies, as smell, heat, cold, (as we hinted formerly,) it is far more easie, that something should flow, or be carried away from their out-most parts; since the Atoms, as well in one as the other, are in a perpetual endeavour of disentangling themselves to get away, but in the former case, being covered with other Atoms, they find resistence, whereas in the later, being placed in the fore-front of the body, they find none. Add, that hence also they gain the advantage of flying out from the superficies in the same order and rank, which they held there; whereas those which comes from within, cannot but change their postures, being often disturbed in the way, by their anfractuous passages.

Now that there are indeed such effluviums, may hence be proved, that if the Sun-beams pass thorough Curtains, red (for example,) or of any other colour, drawn before the Theaters, such subtle emissions are sent from them, as make all things behind them apear so coloured. But the experiment from Looking-glasses is more than sufficient; for these clearly shew, that there are indeed such effluviums emitted from bodies, in regard, the bodies being present, they light upon the glass; If any thing intervene, they are hindred from coming thither; if the bodies be moved, they move also; if inverted, they also are inverted; if the bodies retire, they also goe back; if they are taken away, they wholly disappear.

But ' forasmuch as there is no point of time, ' in which these Images flow not into the Medium, ' doubtless, their production must be made in a ' poin of time, and be perpetually flowing out ' at the superficies, in a continued stream. For ' the reason, why they cannot be discerned apart, ' is, because, when one Image goes away, ano' ther coherently succeeds, and supplies its room; ' and instantly preserves the same order and po' sition of Atoms, which is in the superficies of ' the solid Body, and that for a long time, and ' at a great distance, (although at last they are ' confounded.) Whence it comes to pass, that the Body always appeareth with the same accidents, and in the same form.

I mean here, that form which is proper to the Body, and is conceived to be a collection (as it were,) of parts, disposed in a certain order, or (as it were,) the superficies left behind by the Image, which flies away from it.

It may here seem strange, that the Body seemeth no more to be diminish'd, than as if nothing at all were taken off from it; but this is by reason of their extraordinary tenuity, which cannot be understood, without first conceiving the tenuity of the Atoms. Concerning this, we instanc'd formerly, in an animal so small, as if we supposed it divided into three parts, each of them will be indiscernable; and yet for performance of those animal functions which it dischargeth, it must necessarly be made up of such parts and particles as can hardly be formed, without innumerable myriads of Atoms.

Not to mention, in confirmation of the probability hereof, that there are many odorous things, out of which, though something incessantly flow, yet for a long time nothing appeareth to be diminished, either as to their figure or weight, notwithstanding that the effluviums out of them are far grosser, and more numerous than these Images, which flow out along with them; yet are so inconsiderable a part of the things that flow out, as no man can express.

Wonderful also may seem their celerity in flying out; but this must be understood by the celerity of the Atoms, formerly declared; for these Images, by reason of the tenuity we spoke of, being nothing else but certain contextures of simple Atoms, ' have a celerity beyond all ima' gination, and their passage through the tran' sparent place which is round about them is ' like that which is through the infinit spaces, ' there being not much difference, because they ' meet few or no obstacles in the space which sur' rounds them. Certainly, if the light of the Sun and other Stars can come so swiftly (as we observe,) from Heaven, the celerity of these Images ought to be, if not greater yet not less, by reason of the Atoms which stand in the surface of the body, ready for motion, and have nothing to retard them.

CHAP. XII.

That Seeing is perform'd by means of those Images.

Laert. THese things presupposed, some conceive, that 'external and distinct things are 'therefore seen by us, because they imprint in 'our eye the Image of their colour or figure, the 'Air intervening between them and us, per-'forming the Office of a Seale, by means of 'which, this impression is made. Others think, 'that this is effected by the rays or effluviums 'sent from us or our eyes to the object; it is 'far more probable, that it is performed by 'these Images we spoke of, which coming from 'the things, or their colour and figure, flow 'into us, and preserving a congruous magni-'tude, enter into our eyes, and strike our sight 'with a very swift motion.

This sigillation (or impression,) indeed is a thing extream hard, and perhaps impossible to be explicated; and as for the emission of rays out of our eyes, it is unimaginable what the Looking-glasses send out of them, that they also should have Images painted in them; or what that is, which in a moment is sent from the eye, into the whole vast circumference of the Heavens.

To omit, that since in hearing, smelling, tasting, touching, we send nothing out of ourselves, but receive somthing from without, which causeth a sensation of itself, (for of itself a voice comes into the Ears, odors into the nostrils, sapors into the palate, and things which may be touched are applied to the body,) it is obvious to be conceived, that neither is any thing sent out from our eyes, but that somthing (*viz.* those Images,) comes into our eyes from the things themselves.

But the soul, inasmuch as it is in the eyes, cannot but see, that is, apprehend the colour and outward form of that thing which is presented to it: For by reason of the polite and perspicuous contexture of the Organ, it receiveth the Image of the thing, and is struck by it according to all the presented parts.

Lucret And forasmuch as those things are beautiful which delight the sight, those deformed which offend it; how should we imagine this to be, but that the Images which come from the one consist of bodies, which, by their smoothness, are gently accommodated to the contexture of the eye; but those which come from the other consist of such, as by their ugly figure rend the contexture?

Ibid. And when the eye is troubled with the Jaundice, how comes it, that all things seem yellow? but that the Images, in their application to the eye, receive a tincture; or they may be strain'd also without the eye, coming amongst the yellow little bodies or Images, which proceed in like manner from the eye.

Ibid. But how happens it, that we see not only the colour and form of a body, but we discern its distance also? This proceeds from the Air, which the Image drives on before, it For though it comes to the eye exceeding swiftly, and in imperceptible time; yet it comes thither, and touches upon it orderly; and by how much the longer it is in doing so, so much the more distant the thing appears to be; by how much the sooner, so much the nearer.

Hence also may be given a reason, why an I- *ibid.* mage seems to be beyond the Looking-glass; for as when a man, from any place within a house, looks upon a thing that is without doors, the Air cometh to him imprinted, as well that without to the door, as that within from the door: So to him who looketh in a glass, commeth successively as well that Air which is from the glass to the Eye, as that which is from the object to the glass.

Hence also may be given a reason, why, be- *ibid.* ing in the dark, we can see the things that are in the light; but being in the light, cannot see those that are in the dark. For the enlightned Air succeeding the dark, the Eye informed by it is enabled to see; but not when the dark succeedeth the enlightned.

How comes it, that the Images in a glass seem to walk as we do? This happens, by reason of *Ibid.* the varied parts of the glass, from which several parts there must necessarily be made a reflection upon the Eye, and thereupon the Images seem to walk as we.

If you ask, Why the Image which goeth from *ibid.* us to the glass represents not the back-side, but the fore-side, and that so, as that the right part is on the left side, and the left on the right; take notice, that this happens on the very same fashion, as if the Image of a man made of chalk or clay, not quite dried, should be clapt to a ball or pillar.

But if the Image be reflected from one glass to another, and thence to the Eye, the scitua- *ibid.* tion of the parts is restored, so as the right parts appear on the right side, and the left on the left, (and by this means it may be brought to pass, especially if there be many glasses, that such things as are hidden behind somthing, and out of sight, may be brought to view,) which may also happen even in one glass, if it hath little sides, whereof one reflects the Image to the other.

Thus much concerning the Sight; to which also some things, formerly hinted in our discourse of the Criteries and of Qualities, have reference.

CHAP. XIII.

Of Hearing.

COncerning Hearing, we must repeat what we have touched formerly, that, it being confess'd, the Ear is the Organ of the Hearing, As Seeing is perform'd by the coming of somthing into the Eye; so *Hearing* also 'is perform'd *Laer.* 'in the Ear by an emission of somthing, convey'd 'thither from the thing that speaks, sounds, 'makes a noise, or is some other way disposed 'to stir up the sense of hearing. This kind of effluvium, as it affects this sense, is called Sound.

More-

Moreover, this *effluvium*, either in the mouth of the Speaker, or generally in the thing struck upon and making a noise, is shatter'd there by motion into iunumerable little pieces of the same figure, (* round, if the whole effluvium were round ; inequilateral and triangular, if the first effluvium were such,) in like manner as we observe, that little drops are made when we pour any thing out of bottles, or when Cloath-workers spurt water upon their cloaths.

Laert. loc. cit.

* *Plut. plac. Phil.*

'These little pieces, or small bulks, are thereupon dispersed in such manner, as that they preserve a certain mutual conformity to one another, (and strike the hearing of several persons alike, so as they all seem to hear one and the same sound, though it be not the same, but like onely,) and keep fast also within themselves, each by a particular coherence, whereby it comes to pass that they are known to have reference to that thing, from which they were sent forth, and for the most part make such a sensation, as was first made by that which sent forth the sound, (as when the sound comes not from far into the Ear, and passeth through a free space.) But otherwise, (as by reason of a great distance, or some partition,) somthing from without bringeth in the sound confusedly onely. For without a kind of conformity and coherence, deduced and preserv'd from the very thing sounding, there could never be any distinct hearing.

Laert. ib.

'Yet must we not imagine, that when the voice (*for example,*) is once sent forth into the Air, the Air is presently imprinted or formed, either by that voice, or by some others made by it, into like voices. which (as * one expresseth it, flye away together, as one Jay with another, as saith the proverb,) 'It were too great a task, that the Air should be designed for any such employment ; but as soon as ever the blow is made within us when we speak, the voice being articulated out of certain little pieces, of a most spiritual and nimble effluxion, fit for the Office, and arriving at the Ear, causeth hearing in us.

ibid.

* *Democr.*

That these little pieces which insinuate into the Ear have a figure, may be argued, by reason that Sound could not affect the hearing pleasantly and unpleasantly, if it had not such a smoothness as suits with the contexture of the Organ, not such a roughness as rends the Organ. This may better be understood, by comparing the grating of a Saw with the sweetness of a Lute, or the hoarse cawing of a Crow with the sweet melody of a dying Swan.

Lucret.

Nor to repeat some things spoken heretofore, which seem to conduce hereunto, I shall onely touch this difficulty, How it comes to pass, that sounds in the night-times are both louder and clearer than in the day ? To solve this, we must assume what is manifest from our discourse formerly, That Motion is made through Vacuum, and that there is much of Vacuum scattered up and down through the little bodies, or bulks of Air, which are made up of Atoms ; and that in the day-time it being hot, and these little bodies rarifyed, and the Atoms diffused, the little Vacuities contained in them must necessarily become narrower and straiter ; but in the night, it being cold, and these little bodies prest up

Plut. Symp. quæst. 8. 37.

close, and the Atoms crowded together, the Vacuities become larger. This is evident from all things, which in a Vessel are boiled, softned, and melted ; but if they take up a larger place, they cool, return to their temper, and become contracted.

Hence therefore it happens, that the Sound in the Day-time passing thorough the dilated Air, and lighting upon many Bodies in its way, is either quite stopp'd, or torn, and much knock'd and worn away. But when in the Night it passeth thorough a space free from Bodies, it arrives at the hearing by a full, ready, and uninterrupted carriere, and with that swiftness preserves its clearness and distinction.

Ibid.

From the same ground it springs, that empty Vessels being struck, sound ; the full sound not ; and that the more small Bodies, as Gold, make a low dull noise ; the less compact, as Brass, a greater and clearer.

Ibid.

CHAP. XIV.
Of Smelling.

AS concerning *Smelling*, we must understand, that *Odor* (*as was in proportion declared concerning sound or voice, when we treated of Hearing*) *would not make any impression or stamp of itself, unless from the odorous thing there were deduced some little Bodies or Bulks, so commensurated to the organ of Smelling,* (*the Nostrils,*) *as to be able to move and affect it.*

Laert.

That Odors flow and come out of things, is manifest, forasmuch as all things esteemed odorous have a stronger Scent, being broken pounded, or dissolved by Fire, than whilst they are whole. For the stock of these little Bodies, which are fit to move the Smell, is pent up, as it were, within the odorous Body, and bound, but, the Body being broken, pounded, or burnt, it leaps forth, and spreads itself like a Vapor or Cloud, and affects the Smelling, if it can light upon it.

It useth to affect the Smell two ways, either *unquietly and unsuitably,* whence proceed unpleasant Odors; or *smoothly and aptly,* whence pleasant Odors. For some of the little Bodies of Odor having a smooth and even Surface ; others, more or greater Angles than is fit ; thence it happens, that some Odors affect the Organ with delight, as touching it smoothly ; others, with a kind of Pain, as if they tore it.

Laert.

There must needs be a difference betwixt the penetrations of these little Bodies into the Nostrils, when Carkasses are burnt, and when the Theatre is newly strew'd with Saffron. And it may be conceived after this manner. As the Hand, if we put Down to it, presseth upon it ; but if a Nettle, snatcheth itself back, (for the smoothness of the One, and the roughness of the Other by its Prickles, affect two different ways,) in like manner the little Bodies which proceed out of the Saffron, are smooth ; those which out of the Carkass, prickly : so as the first gently stroke and delight the Nostrils, the other prick them, and make them draw back.

Lucret. lib. 2.

Moreover, there being so great variety of tempers amongst Animals, (even amongst Men one in respect of another) and the Contexture of the organ of Smelling being different in several

Lucret. lib. 4.

ral Persons, it ough not to seem strange, that some Scents please Some; Others, Others; by reason of the dissimilitudes of the Figures of the little Bodies, of which they consist; nor that Bees delight in Flowers, Vultures in Carrion; or that Dogs find out by the Scent which way Beasts have gone, which we cannot perceive; as if in passing, they left a Steam which cannot strike our Smell.

CHAP. XV.

Of Tasting.

Lucret.

WE come next to speak of *Tasting*: Whereas it is manifest, that the Organ thereof is the Tongue and Palate; and that * we then taste and perceive the Sapor in our mouth, when chewing the Meat, we squeeze out the Juice (as when we press with the Hand a Sponge full of Water) and thereupon, the Juice which is squeezed forth, is distributed thorough the Pores, or complicated Holes of the Tongue and Palate, we may in general assert the Sapor to be sweet, the little Bodies whereof are accommodated to the Organ, gently and smoothly; on the contrary, that to be Bitter, Salt, Sharp, Acid, Sower, Hot, &c. which roughly and unsuitably. For neither could Hony or Milk affect the Tongue pleasantly, nor Wormwood or Centory unpleasantly, if it were not that those consist of smoother and rounder little Bodies, these of more harsh and hooked; so as those touch it gently, these prick and rend it.

Theophrast. lib. 4. de sens & sens.

He therefore not defines the thing amiss, who saith, That the Atoms, which make a sweet Sapor, are round, and of a convenient size; Those which a sower, large; Those which a harsh, multangular, and nothing round; Those which a sharp, acute, conical, crooked, not slender, nor round; Those which an acid, round, slender, corner'd, crooked; Those which a salt, corner'd, distorted, æquicrural; Those which a bitter, round, smooth, distorted, little; Those which a fat, slender, round, little.

Lucret

But, more particularly, seeing that the tempers, not only of Animals, but even of Men among themselves, are so various, and that as they differ in the outward lineaments of their Bodies, so they cannot but differ also in their inward Contextures, hence we may say, that the Sapors. that are pleasing to some Animals or Men, are displeasing to others, by reason that the little Bodies, of which they consist, are suitable, and accommodated to the Contexture of the Organs of those, but unsuitable and unaccommodate to the Contexture of the Organs of these; since the round Pores, that in the Organ, can receive the round Atomes smoothly, but the triangular difficultly; and the triangular Pores can receive the triangular smoothly, but the round difficultly.

Ibid.

Hereby also is understood, how it comes to pass, that the things which were formerly pleasant to us, are in a Fever distasteful, for the texture is so disorder'd, and the Figures of the Pores so alter'd, that the Figures of the little Bodies which insinuate into them, though formerly they were adaptable, now become unsuitable and incongruous.

From the same Reason it is, that the Meat which agreeth with one Animal, is Poison to another; as Hemlock, or Hellebore, is destructive to a Man, yet it fattens Goats, and Quails. This happens, by reason of the interior Contextures, which differing from one another, that which is accommodate, and adaptable to one, is inadaptable to another. *Ibid.*

CHAP. XVI.

Of Touching.

LAstly, Concerning the *Touch*, I mean not that *Lucret.* which is common to all Bodies, as they are said to touch one another by their *Superficies*, (contrary to the Nature of *Vacuum*, which can neither touch, nor be touched,) but that which is proper to Animals, not performed without perception of the Soul; and hath not one, but all parts of the Body for its Organ. Concerning this *Touch*, I shall only declare, that what is perceived by it, is perceived three ways:

For first, A thing is perceived by the *Touch*, *Ibid.* when it is extrinsecally applied, or, from without insinuates itself; applied, as when the Hand feels a Stone clapp'd to it; insinuated, as when a hot thing emitting Heat, or a cold thing Cold, certain little Bodies get into the Pores, which, according to the state wherein the Body is, either refresh or disturb it.

Secondly, When a thing which is within, is *Ibid.* driven out, which somtimes happens with Pleasure, especially when the thing itself was burthensom and incommodious, *ut dum semen excernitur*; somtimes with Pain, as when by reason of the angles of the little Bodies, it excoriates the Passage, as by the Strangury, or Difficulty of Urine.

Lastly, When some things within the Body *Ibid.* take some of these motions, as by Impulsion, Diduction, Distraction, Convulsion, Compunction, Rasure, Excoriation, Inflation, Tension, Breaking, and innumerable other ways, it disturbs the Natural Constitution, and confounds and troubles the Senses. Thus all Aches and Pains of the Head, and other parts within, are caused; and the Animal doth in such manner affect itself, as if a Man should with his own hand strike a part of his Body.

CHAP. XVII.

Of the Intellect, Mind, or Reason, and its Seat.

HItherto of the *Sense*. We must now speak of the *Intellect*, which is also usually called, *Mind, Reason*. The Rational and Hegemonick part; somtimes Cogitation, Imagination, Opinion, Counsel: Its property is, when the Sense strikes it, to think, apprehend, understand, revolve, meditate, discourse, or deliberate somthing.

The Contexture of the *Intellect* consists of little Bodies, the most subtle, smooth and round of all, forasmuch as nothing can be more subtle, nor of quicker motion. Neither is there any thing that can stir up itself sooner, or perform any thing

thing quicker than the Intellect, which if it design or begin any thing, brings it to pass in a moment; whence all acknowledge, that nothing can be swifter than (her action) Thought.

And certainly, as Water is much apter to move, and more fluent than Honey, by reason that is made up of little Bodies, which are smoother, lesser, and rounder; nothing consequently can consist of rounder, lesser, and smoother, than the Mind, for nothing can be readier for motion, quicker, or more pliant.

And in whatsoever part of the Body the Intellect inheres, it so cohereth to the Soul, or to that portion of the Soul which coexists with it in that part, as that it is indivisibly conjoined to it, and constitutes one Nature with it, yet it always so preserves and retains its own Nature, as that it is the property of the Intellect, to think; of the Soul, to undergo affections; though, by reason of their Cohæsion, it be conceived, that the Soul thinks, and the Intellect is affected.

Indeed, the Intellect is void of Affection or Passion; but (because, as the Passions depending on Sense, are stirred up in the Soul about those parts wherein the Sense is seated; so those which depend on Cogitation, are stirred up in the Soul about that part where Cogitation is, and in which part the Soul is one thing with the Intellect thinking:) Hence it cometh to pass that, as if the aggregate or compound of the Intellect and the Soul residing in that part, made up only Intellect, the Passions come to be attributed to the Intellect itself.

Thus, whether the Intellect be taken distinctly or jointly, it hath this property beyond the other part of the Soul, that, As when the Head or Eye aketh, we are not thereupon pain'd all over the Body; so somtimes the Intellect is affected with Grief or Joy, when the other part of the Soul, which is diffused through the Body, is free from this affection. I say, *somtimes*, because it may happen, that the Intellect be seis'd with a Fear so vehement, as that the rest of the Soul may be struck together with it, and thereby may be caused Sweating, Paleness, stopping of the Speech, the Eyes grow dim, the Ears possessed with a humming, the Joints grow faint, and, in a word, the Man may fall into a Swoon.

Moreover, the Intellect may be conceived to partake of life more perfectly than the Soul, or the other part of the Soul, forasmuch as the Soul cannot subsist never so little in the limbs, without the Intellect; but the Intellect, though the limbs round about it were cut off, and thereby a great part of the Soul taken away, would nevertheless subsist and preserve life: Like the Ball, which conduceth more to Sight than all the rest of the Eye, because the Ball being hurt, though the rest of the parts be sound, the Sight is destroy'd; but as long as the Ball is sound, though the other parts be destroy'd, the Sight continueth.

It seemeth not, that there can be any other seat assign'd for the Intellect, or rational part of the Soul, than the middle part of the Breast, and consequently the Entrails, or the Heart, which is in the midst of the Breast. This is manifest from the affections of Fear and Joy, proceeding from Cogitation, (or the Intellect thinking,) which we preceive to be in the Breast.

CHAP. XVIII.

That the Soul thinketh by Images, which glide into it.

THere is only this difficulty, How the Intellect can be stirred up to think somthing? But it being manifest, that things are thought by the Intellect, in the same manner as they are seen by the Eye; it is also evident, that as Sight, so Thinking or Cogitation is made by Images which glide into it. *Lucret.*

For besides those Images which glide into the Eye, and being of somthing a grosser bulk, are accommodated to the contexture of the Eye, and produce in it the act of Seeing, there must necessarily wander through the Air an innumerable company of others, far more subtle, and those either peel'd off from Bodies, or form'd in the Air itself, as was formerly said; which penetrating through the Body, and being adaptable to the contexture of the Intellect, as soon as they arrive as it, move it to Think. *Ibid.*

Whence it comes to pass, that as we see (for example,) a Lion, because the image thereof glides into our Eyes; so we think a Lion, because the image of a Lion, glides into our Mind. That we think or imagine Centaurs, Sylla's and the like, which neither are, nor ever were; this may happen, not so much by Images framed on purpose, as for that when the Images (for example) of a Man and of a Horse are presented to us, they, by reason of their Tenuity or Subtlety, like a Cobweb, or a Leaf of Gold, are joined together, and made one, such as is attributed to a Centaur. *Ibid.*

But take notice, that when somtimes we persevere in the same thought, whether waking or sleeping, this happens not, for that we use some one image of the same thing, but that we use many images succeeding in a continual fluxion, which if they come to us in the same posture, the thing thought or imagined seemeth unmoved; if in a varied, it seems moved. Which is the reason, why, in dreams especially, images seem to us to be moved, and to stir their arms and other limbs one after another. *Ibid.*

But how comes it to pass, that whatsoever any Man would, his Mind or Intellect thinks that very thing? Because, though there are every where Images of all sorts, yet the greatest part passeth by unthought of, and those only move the Mind which she herself takes notice of, or would observe, or frames herself to think of. And, observe we not, that the Eyes, when they begin to have a sight of somthing very little, bend and fix themselves upon it, and, till they see somthing plainly, all other things are as if they were not, although they receive their images also. *Ibid.*

Now as there is some Intentiveness requisite to the Mind, that it may apprehend things distinctly, so much more that it may simply think or give some judgment, by affirming or denying? but most of all, that it may discourse of them as if its greatest care were not to be deceived.

But this we declared formerly, in treating of the Criteries. It will be sufficient, as to the speculation of natural things, here to observe, that

Laert. *Human Discourse first admireth the things that are produced by Nature, and next enquires into them, and finds out their Causes ; but in some sooner, in others later ; and somtimes evinceth this, or arrives at the full knowledge in a longer times, somtimes in a shorter.*

CHAP. XIX.

Of the Affections or Passions of the Soul.

THere is besides Sense another part of the Irrational Soul, which may be called Affectuous, or Passionate, from the Affections or Passions raised in it. It is also termed the Appetite or Desire, from the chief Affection which it hath, called Appetite or Desire ; some distinguish it into Concupiscible and Irascible.

Now whereas it was already said, that the affections which follow Sense, are produced in the organs of Sense, those which follow opinion in the Breast ; hereupon there being two principal affections, Pleasure, and Pain ; the first, familiar, and suitable to the Soul ; the other, incommodious, and unsuitable to Nature. It is manifest, that both these are excited, not in the Breast only, where Pleasure, for the most part, comes under the name of Joy, Gladness, Exultation, Mirth ; and Pain, under that of Grief, Sorrow, Anguish, &c. but also in the other parts, in which, when they are removed from their natural state, there is raised Pain or Grief ; when they are restored to that state, Pleasure.

If all the parts could continue in their natural state, either there would be no affection, or if there were any, it must be called Pleasure, from the quiet and calmness of that state. But because either by reason of the continual motion of principles in the Body of an Animal, some things depart from it, others come to it ; some are taken asunder, others put together, &c. or by reason of the motion which is in the things round about, some things are brought which insinuate into them, change, invert, disjoin, &c. pain is caused, (from the first occasion, as by Hunger, Thirst, Sickness ; from the second, as by burning, bruising, wresting, wounding,) therefore the affection of pain seems to be first produced : And withal, because it is of an opposite nature, that of aversation or avoidance of it, and of the thing that bringeth it, to which, for that reason, is attributed the name of Ill.

Hereupon followeth a desire of exemption from pain, or of that state which is void of pain, and consequently of the thing by which it may be expelled, and to which, for that reason, is given the name of Good ; and then the pain being taken away, and the thing reduced into a better, that is, into its natural state, pleasure is excited, and goeth along with it ; so as there would not be pleasure, if some kind of pain did not go before, as is easily observable even from hunger and thirst and the pleasure that is taken in eating and drinking.

For this pleasure is only made, because (most of the parts being dissipated by the action of the intrinsecal heat, by which means the body itself becomes rarify'd, all Nature destroy'd, and the stomach especially grip'd, or otherwise some little Bodies of heat rolling about it, make it glow, whereby is caused pain) because, I say, meat cometh, and supplieth the defect, supports the limbs, stoppeth the desire of eating, which gapeth throughout the members and the veins ; Drink comes and extinguishes the heat, moistneth the parts which before were dry, and reduceth them to their first state. And besides, both are made with a smooth and pleasing sense of Nature, which, it is manifest, is then absent, when a Man eats, not being hungry ; or drinks, not being athirst.

Thus the general affections of the Soul seem to be these four, Pain and Pleasure, the Extreme ; Aversion and Desire, the Intermediate. I say, General, because the rest are kinds of these, and made by opinion intervening, and may be reduced principally to Desire and Avoidance.

For Desire is particularly called Will, when the Mind wills that which it thinks, and conceiveth it to be good ; and Avoidance is called Aversion, when it turneth away from that which it thinketh, or conceiveth to be ill. Hereupon, Love (for Example) is a Will, whereby we are carried to the enjoyment of something. Hate is an Aversion, whereby we withdraw ourselves from conversing with something. Again, Anger is nothing but Desire, whereby we are carried on to vengeance. Fear is an Avoidance, by which we shrink at some future Ill, and retire, as it were, within ourselves ; and so of the rest.

But forasmuch as Desire (as also in proportion Avoidance too,) is partly excited by Nature, and by reason of some Indigence, which must necessarily be supplied, that Nature may be preserved ; partly is begotten by Opinion, which is sometimes conformable to the design of Nature, and so tends to remove her Indigence, as that yet it is not necessary it should be quite taken away. Lastly, it sometimes conduces nothing either to Nature, or to the taking away of its Indigence. Hence is comes to pass, that of Desires, some are Natural and Necessary ; others Natural, but not Necessary ; others, neither Natural nor Necessary, but Vain.

Natural and Necessary are those, which take away, both the Indigence, and the Pain proceeding from the Indigence ; such is that of Meat, of Drink, of Cloathing, to expel the Cold. Natural, but not Nncessary, are those which only vary the Pleasure, but are not absolutely Necessary to the taking away of the Pain, as those which are of delicate Meats, even that which is of Venereal Delights, to which Nature gives a Beginning, but from which a Man may abstain without Inconvenience. Lastly, neither Natnral nor Necessary are those, which contribute nothing to the taking away of any Pain, caused by some indigence of Nature, but are begot only by Opinion ; such are for Instance, those of Crowns, Statues, Ornaments, Rich Cloathing, Gold, Silver, Ivory, and the like.

Moreover, it is to be observed, That whereas Pleasure consists in the fruition of Good, Pain in suffering Ill ; for this Reason, the first is produced with a kind of dilatation and exaltation of the Soul, the other with a contraction and depression thereof ; and therefore it is not to be wondred at, if the Soul dilates herself as much as she can, to make way for the Good to come into her, and contracts herself to prevent the Ill.

There is a Diffusion, or Dilatation; for as soon as ever the Form of a good and pleasing thing strikes the Sense, or moveth the Mind, the little Bodies, of which it consists, so insinuate into the organs of Sense, or into the Heart itself, as that being accommodated as well to the Soul, as to the Body, they, in a more particular manner, gently stroke and delight the Soul, and, like little Chains, allure and draw it towards that thing out of which they were sent; Whereupon the Soul being turned towards, and intent upon that thing, gives a great leap, as it were, towards it, with all the strength it hath, that it may enjoy it.

On the other side there is Cantraction, because as soon as ever the Form of a painful thing strikes the Sense, or the Mind, the little Bodies of which it consists, as so many little Darts or Needles, prick the very Soul together with the Organ, in such manner, that they loosen its Contexture, while she, to prevent them as much as she can, shuts herself up, and retires to her very Centre or Root, where the Heart or Intellect is placed.

It will not be necessary to repeat what we formerly said, that it depends upon the contexture of the Soul, why one Animal is more inclined to Anger, another to Fear, a third to calm smooth Motions; nor to add, that this difference is found in Men also, according as their Souls participate more of a fiery, or a flatuous, or of an aerial Principle. Or we may observe even in Men that are polished by Learning, these Seeds cannot be so rooted out, but that one is more propense to Anger, another more subject to Fear, a third more prone to Clemency than he ought. Moreover, the difference of manners, which is observed to be so great, not amongst Animals only, but in Men from one another, is plainly enough derived from the various commistion of these Seeds.

CHAP. XX.

Of Voluntary Motion, and particularly, of Speaking, and Imposition of Names.

NOW the Soul being naturally stirring, and ready for motion, and able to move the Body wherein it exists, and the Members thereof; it is well known, that whensoever she moveth the Body, or its Members with any motion whatsoever, she therefore doth it, because she hath a Will to move them, and that this Will is stirred up by the Intellect, imagining; and that this Imagination is caused by the Image that strikes it: for the Intellect, or Mind, never doth any thing, but first she foreseeth it; nor foreseeth it, unless she first have the Image of that thing.

Lucret. 4. 879. Thus, when we move (for Example) the Thighs, and walk, this is therefore done, because first the Images of walking coming to the Mind, strike it, thence proceeds a Will to walk; then when the Mind hath so mov'd itself, as that it wills to walk, it instantly strikes the Soul in that part whereto it is joined; that part strikes the rest of the Soul, which is diffused through the whole Body, and especially through the Thighs and Feet. Thus the whole Frame is by degrees thrust forwards, and moved; Not to mention that the Air conduceth somthing thereto, by reason that as the whole Body becomes rarity'd, the Air insinuates into its parts. The Body therefore is moved from two causes, like a Ship, which is driven on by Oars and Wind.

That the beginning of Motion proceeds from the Heart, where the Mind is seated, is manifest, for that we see somtimes Horses (for Example) cannot, as soon as ever the Barrier is let down, break forth, nor start away so suddenly, as their Will prompts them; because the whole substance of the Soul diffused, thorough all the Limbs, must first be summoned, that, being stirred up, it may follow the design of the Mind. Thus it proceeds first from the will of the Mind, and then thorough the Body and Limbs. *Lucret.*

It may perhaps seem strange, that so little *Lucret. 4. 896.* Bodies as those, whereof the Mind consists, should be able to move, wrest, and turn about so great a weight, as is that of the Body. But what wonder, when the Wind, a thing so subtle, can with so great a force drive forward a vast Ship; and one Hand, one Rudder, turn it about and guide it, though under full Sail? And are there not Engines, which by Pullies and Screws, move and draw up huge Weights, and that with no great force?

But forasmuch as of the motions, with which we move the parts of the Body, as we will ourselves, that of the Tongue is most considerable, which is called Speaking, it seems requisite to say somthing of this in particular.

The Tongue being framed in breathing Animals *Lucret. 5. 1028.* after such a manner, as that it can break, and, as it were, mould the Air, which is vehemently breathed forth, and thereupon causeth a Sound; hence it happeneth, that, as because every Animal perceiveth its own power, by which it can do somthing, and hereupon the Bull butts with his Horns, the Horse strikes with his Heels, the Lyon teareth with his Teeth and Claws, the Bird trusts to her Wings; hence it hapneth, I say, that Animals, and chiefly Men, perceiving the ability of their Tongue to express the affections of the Mind, (even when they would signifie somthing, that is without them,) they send out a Sound which is called Voice, and by the interposition of the Tongue, and other parts serving for that variation, bend and mould it in several Fashions.

I instance Animals also, because we see that *Lucret. ibid.* they likewise send forth several Voices, according as they are joy'd or griev'd, or fear, or persue any thing; Dogs, for Example, make several Noises, when they assault furiously, when they bark, when they play with their Whelps, when they fawn, when they are hurt, and cry or howl; a Horse neigheth after a different manner, when he rouzeth himself, when he followeth a Mare, and when he is spurr'd by his Rider. And Birds make different Cries, when they strive about their Prey, and when they perceive Change of Weather, and when they sit idly, still.

Now

Lucret. ib.

Now Man, above the rest, perceiving the great power of his Tongue, and how he can bend it various ways, so as to make divers articulate Sounds, which may be accommodated to signifie several things, hence proceeds Speech, by which Men ordinarily discourse with one another, expressing the passions of the Mind, and other things, no otherwise than as by nodding the Head, or pointing with the Finger.

Laert.

Here, because it is usually demanded, How Men came at first impose Names on things? We must know, that *Names were not imposed merely by Invention of Man, nor by some Law; but the very Natures, or natural Dispositions of Men, which were in several Nations, being, upon the presentment of things to them, affected with particular motions of the mind, and compelled by images proper to the things, sent forth the Air out of their mouths, after a peculiar fashion, and broke and articulated it, according to the impulsion of the several affections or phantasies, and sometimes according to the difference of places,* as the Heaven and the Earth is various in different Countries. The words which were thus pronounced, and particularly with a will of denoting things to others, became the names of things.

Laert.

Some also desiring to mention some things to others, which were out of their sight, pronounced certain sounds or words, and then were constrained to repeat the same words; whereupon the hearers finding out the thing by some discourse and conjecture, at last, with much use, understood what the others meant.

And because several Men used several Names, to signifie the same things to others, and thereupon there was a variety of Names; for this Reason, *Names proper to signifie things were in every Nation by degrees, and, as it were, with common consent chosen and appointed, so as their mutual significations might be less ambiguous, and things might be explicated by a more compendious way of speaking.*

Laert.

Lucret. 5. 1040.

For this Reason I conclude, That the first Man imposed Names on things, not out of certain Science, or by the Command or Dictate of any one Man; for how should he come by that Science, or have power to compel many Men to use the words which he dictated? But rather, that they imposed them, being moved by a certain natural Impulsion, like those who cough, sneeze, bellow, bark, sigh. And therefore we may say, that Names are not by Institution, but by Nature, seeing they are the Effects and Works, as it were, of Nature; for, to see and hear things (which are certain Effects and Works of Nature,) are of the same kind, as the giving of Names to Things.

CHAP. XXI.

Of Sleep and Dreams.

IT rests, that we add something concerning *Sleep*, and the *Death of Animals*, two things near of Kin; for one is an Intermission, the other the Extinction of Sense, and Death is ordinarily termed an Everlasting Sleep.

Laert.

Sleep is caused, when the parts of the Soul, which are diffused thorough the whole composition of the Body, are either repressed or segregated; or else some little Bodies, either from the Air or from Food, light upon the dispersed parts, which partly drive them away from the Body, partly crowd them into the Body, and discompose them. For hereupon the Body, as destitute of its ordinary support and government, becometh weak, and all the limbs grow feeble, the Arms and Eye-lids hang down, the Knees sink, and, in a word, there is no more Sense.

Lucret. 4. 918.

Lucret. 4. 918.

For it being certain, that Sense proceeds from the Soul, it is no less evident, that when Sleep hindereth the Sense, the Soul is disturbed, and thrown out of doors; not the whole Soul, for then it were not Sleep, but Death; but a part only, and yet so, as that which is left behind is oppressed within, and buried like Fire rak'd up in ashes. And as, if we stir up the Fire, it wakes, as it were, and a flame arises from it, in appearance extinguished; so the Senses are restored throughout the Members, and raised again out of a thing in appearance dead.

Lucret.

When I say, that little Bodies coming from the Air cause this disturbance, I mean, partly the exterior Air, which never ceaseth to beat and drive against the Body, (whereby it comes to pass, that the outward part of every Animal becomes solid and hard,) partly the interior, or that which is drawn in at the mouth, and blown out again. For the stroke of each of these passing through the little vacuities, to the principles and first elements of the Body, their Positions are so disordered, that part are cast out, part thrust in, and the rest, which is diffused through the limbs, are not able to discharge their office, by reason that they are intercepted, and not joined one to another.

Lucret.

I add, that this happens from the Food also, because the Food, being convey'd inwardly by the Veins, performs the same thing as the Air, and that with more abundant and greater force. Whence it comes to pass, that the Sleep which is caused by Meat, by reason of the greater disturbance of those Particles, is more sound than ordinary, as is that also which proceeds from excessive weariness, by reason of their greater dissipation.

Lucret.

Now forasmuch as it may seem strange, that Dreams should come to us in Sleep, we must observe what was said not long since, that every where there are Images of innumerable things, continually roving up and down, which, by reason of their subtlety, are able to penetrate into the Body, and able to strike and affect the Mind, which is seated in the midst of the Breast, so as it is stirred up to think of those things whereof they are the Images, Hereupon, forasmuch as these penetrate and strike the Mind no less in sleep, than in waking, it comes to pass that we seem to behold things as well in sleep as awake.

Lucret.

But it happens, that we receive the things which appear to us in this manner as true, because our Senses being stupified, nothing can occur to us, that may give us notice of the Error, and convince the Falsity by true things; and besides, our Memory being laid asleep, we esteem (for example,) those Men to be alive who are dead, because their Images are present to us, and we remember not their death.

Lucret.

If you demand, why we dream most of those things in which we chiefly delight, or to which we are most particularly addicted when awake, (for Orators plead, Solders fight, Mariners contest with the winds, Gamesters play, and so of others; Neither is it thus with men only, but amongst other Animals also; Horses sweat and blow, as if they were running a race; Hounds stretch their legs, cry, and snuff up the Air; and so of the rest,) We must say, that this happens; forasmuch as by reason of the impression lately made in the mind, the passages are left open, into which the same Images insinuate, and above the rest, move the soul again.

Lucret.

From the same ground it seems to proceed, that he who is thirsty dreams of a fountain, and that he is drinking; he that hath need to Urine dreams of a chamber-pot, and that he is using it. For the intrinsecal motions open as it were, the wayes, into which the Images of things of the same nature insinuating, strike the mind. Hence also it comes to pass, that many Images of the same thing meeting together, there are produced certain great motions in the mind, and then he who dreameth, imagines that he possesseth great knowledge, performeth great actions, speaketh excellent things; and sometimes cryeth out as if his throat were about to be cut, or himself to be devoured by a Lion or Panther, and is no less affrighted, than if he had cast himself down from a high Mountain, so as when he awakes, he has scarce the use of his reason.

CHAP. XXII.

Of Death.

AS for Death, it is nothing but a privation of sense, by reason of the departure of the Soul. By sense here, I understand not only the action, of which sleep also is the privation; but the faculty likewise of feeling or perceiving, which perisheth with the soul, and together with these, the mind also; so that the soul going forth, the mind which is joyned with it goeth forth also.

Laert.

For, 'as long as the soul exists in the body, 'although some other part fail, yet there is not 'a privation of sense: but sense perishes together 'with the soul, as soon as ever that wherein it is 'contained, whether it be the whole body, or 'some part in which it is seated, happens to be 'dissolved. Neither can it be objected, that the 'body remaineth a while undissolved, either in 'whole or in part: For it is nevertheless void 'of sense, as soon as such a company of Atoms, 'as is necessary to constitute the nature of the 'soul, goeth out of it.

Ibid.

'Moreover, the body being dissolved, the soul 'itself is dissipated, and hath no longer the same 'faculties, nor any longer is moved, nor any long-'er hath sense; for we cannot imagine, that the 'same thing doth any longer feel or perceive, 'when it no longer useth the same motions, when 'it no longer is in the same compound, when 'those things no longer are by which it was che-'rished and preserved, and in which existing it 'performed such kind of motions. It is the same 'with the soul as with the eye; which, being out,

'and divided from the body in which it was, 'cannot see any thing.

When I say, The soul is dissipated, I imply the mind also; since the mind is indivisibly joyned with it, neither can it subsist if the soul perish. So that here it is all one to say, the mind and the soul, for the same dissipation happens to both. Now this dissolution is made, not into nothing, (as they must necessarily affirm, who hold the soul to be harmony, or such a contemperation as health,) but into the Principles and little bodies, of which its contexture is made; and this not so much like water, which runneth about when the vessel is broken, as like smoke, or a mist, which goes away into Air, but much more easily; its contexture being more subtle, since it is capable of receiving impressions from the Images of smoke and mist.

That the soul is dissipated and perisheth, is manifest; for that it is compounded and hath a beginning. Some indeed there are, who conceive it to be Eternal, denying it to have a beginning, to avoid its dissolution; and assuming for granted, that it was before the Body, and came from without into it, that they may maintain, that it survives after the body, out of which it goes intire. I shall omit, that they seem not it observe, that nothing can be durable for ever, unless it be such, either by reason of its solidity as an Atom; or for that it is uncapable of being struck, as Vacuum: or for that it wants place whereinto it might remove, as the Universe. Neither do they reflect how great a madness it is to conceive, that things so different as immortal and mortal, may be joyned together.

I omit this, I say, and demand onely, How it is possible the soul can, from without, be insinuated into the body, and diffused through its parts, and yet not be divided and dissolved, as meat distributed through the limbs; And must it not dwell in the Body, as a Bird in a Cage, rather than be thought to grow, and be coextended with the Body? And how then arrives it together with the Body, at the flower of age? And why it is, that in old age it fears, not rejoyceth, to go out of the Body as out of her prison, and like the serpent to cast her decay'd skin? And if forsaking the Body, it leaves some relicks of it self behind, is it not dissolvable? But if it leaves none, how comes it, that so many worms are generated in a carkass?

For to say, that so many souls flow thither from without, and fly up and down like shadowes, and chuse their own matter, and frame their own Bodies, and the like, How absurd is it? Neither is it less ridiculous, that there should be a swarm, as it were, of Souls, hovering round about at the coition and birth of Animals, contesting with one another which shall enter into the Body.

And if Souls did so often shift Bodies, would not their natures, by degrees, become changed, and so the Lion in time not be fierce, the Hart not timorous, the Fox not crafty, the Dog afraid of the Hare, the Hawke of the Dove? And if any shall say, that human souls only pass into human Bodies, he cannot give a reason, Why the soul, of wise, becomes foolish? why no children are wise? why we, as the first Author of these Opinions feigned of themselves, never remem-

Gggg ber

ber our past life, and the actions performed in it.

The soul therefore hath a beginning, from which, as it groweth up and flourisheth, with the Body, so must it necessarily tend to an end, growing old, and decaying by degrees, together with it.

This I say likewise of the Mind, which by degrees is perfected, and decayeth; seeing that it not only bears a share in the diseases, and pains of the Body, but suffers diseases, and pains of her own, and is cured by Medicine: which could not be, if somthing were not added to, or taken from, or transposed in her contexture. We need not instance, what happens to her by drunkenness, the falling sickness, or dotage.

We must observe, that she is affixed to some certain part of the Body, no otherwise than the ear to the eye, so that, accordingly she begins and ends with the whole; and this is manifest, forasmuch as every thing, (Thees, Fishes, &c.) hath a certain determinate place in which it is produced, liveth, and at last ceaseth to be, and cannot exist out of it.

And forasmuch, as a man dieth limb by limb, and expireth by degrees, the soul being as it were divisible; who can say, that the Mind (or Intellect) doth not evaporate out of the mid'st of the brest, but goeth entire out at the throat and mouth? For that the soul her self goeth out, sifted as it were, and sever'd thorough the whole Body, is argued, even for that the stench which after her departure is in the dead carkass, preceedeth from no other cause, than that its several parts are got into that place, which was taken up by the several parts of the soul. Not to mention, that, otherwise, when the Body is suddenly cut asunder, into two or more pieces, the soul could not be cut into two or more pieces as the Body.

As therefore, the soul was not before the generation, so neither will it be after the dissolution, or death; and as, before that, we did not feel any pain; so neither shall we no any, after this; as well, for that there will be no longer Touch, or any other Sense, which cannot exist in a separate soul; as for that, it is now without those Organs, in which only the senses reside, and with which only, they can act and suffer.

Hence it is manifest, that all fears of the Inferi are vain; *Ixion* is not roll'd upon a wheel; *Sisiphus* does not thrust a stone up hill continually; *Prometheus*'s liver cannot be devoured and renew'd every day. These are but Fables, as are also those which are reported of *Tantalus*, of *Cerberus*, of the *Danaides*, of the Furies, and the like; which if they are made good any where, it is in this life, through the depraved manners of men.

SECT. IV.

Of Superiour things, as well Cælestial, as Aerial.

Hitherto, of *Inferiour* things; we come now to the *Superiour*, which appear in the Region above the Earth; such are the Sun, the Moon, and other Stars, and all that belongs to them, as Risings, Settings, Tropicks, Eclipses, and the like. Moreover Clouds, Rain, Wind, Lighting, Thunder, Thunder-bolts, and the like. For tho' some make a distinction, and call these later only Μετέωρα, *Superiour things*, yet is it convenient, to call the former also Meteors, and to include both within Meteorology, that is, a Treatise of superiour things.

Here we must repeat what was said at first, that 'we must not propose any other end of *Laert.*
' the knowledge of Superiour things, whether
' they be treated of jointly with others, as here,
' or separately, and by themselves, as else where
' we do, than an undisturbed state of mind, and
' unwavering Judgement; as also in the rest of
' the things, of which we use to discourse.

' For Superiour things being such, as that they *Ibid.*
' either have, or may have a manifold cause of
' generation, and declaration of their being,
' conformable to that which we perceive by the
' sense; we ought not to adhere to one particular
' way, as we do in Moral Maxims, or some in Physick, such as are, The Universe is Body and Vacuum; the Principles of things are indivisible, ' and the like' which agree onely one way
' with the Phænomena's: But firmly hold, that
' these things are indeed explicable, not one, but
' many ways, neither ought we to attempt any
' thing above the reach of human power, by defining one certain way, after which only the
' thing may be performed.

This, I say, we must repeat; forasmuch as *Laert.*
' it is requisite to conceive, that it is the Office
' of Physiology, accurately, to examine the causes
' of the chief things which are in nature, and
' that from hence proceedeth all the felicity
' which consisteth in knowledge of superiour
' things, and in that especially, that we examine,
' what kind of things those are, which are discovered in those superiour ones, and whatever
' has affinity with them. And withal, inviolably
' to observe this rule, that it is competent to
' those things, to be done many ways, *and not necessarily* one way onely; *but*, that they may be brought some other way also.

This, I so expresly inculcate; lest, if we adhere onely to one way, and that happen to displease us, we presently recur, not to some other natual cause, but to the divine; for this were to acknowledge a manifold manner, where there is but one. Thus to the divine nature we should attribute trouble and business, whereas ' it is simply and absolutely necessary, that in
' an Immortal and Blessed Nature, there be none
' of those things which cause dissolution and trouble; for the mind immediately apprehends, and
' concludes from the consideration of an immortal and blessed condition, that it is absolutely
' impossible, any such thing should happen to it.

And doubtless, for want of this consideration, it comes to pass, that ' the contemplation and
' observation of rising, setting, solstices, eclipses
' and the like, make our knowledge nothing the
' happier, but they who have considered these
' things (yet know not what are the nature of
' those Bodies, and what are their chief Causes,)
' fear as much, and perhaps more, than as if they
' had not contemplated them at all; by reason, that
the

'the admiration which ariseth from their consideration, cannot be satisfied, as to the disposition and manner, whereby they performed. For this reason we endeavour to find out, and alledge many several causes of solstices, settings, risings, eclipses and the like, conformable to things of the like kind, which happen amongst us on the earth.

Ibid.

'Besides we must not think, that an accurate enquiry after these things, conduceth to acquisition of tranquillity and felicity. In superiour things, and others that are obscure, we ought to seek out causes, according to the several ways by which the like things happen amongst us, despising those who neither know one certain way by which a thing is effected, nor a manifold way, but content themselves only with the appearance of things as presented at that distance, and yet are ignorant in what consists or not consists imperturbation. Truly, if we conceive it may fall out, that a thing may be done one certain way, and thereupon we are not troubled; truly I say, knowing on the other side, that the same thing may be effected many several ways, we shall be no less undisturbed, than if we knew it could be done by a certain way.

Laert.

'But whensoever one has a mind to adhere to, or defend any thing that is likely in itself, that explication is sufficient in this present subject which runs congruously, according to the manifold ways the Phænomena's afford us. Yet is it necessary to derive our conjectures concerning superiour things, from those which are done amongst us; from those, I say, which are observ'd to resemble those in those which are seen above: For those things are effected several ways; wherefore also that which appeareth in every superiour thing, is to be considered by those thing, which agree with it, and which may be effected several ways amongst us, as several things may happen.

But I insist too much hereupon. To come therefore to the business. Although the whole Region above Earth is sometimes called Heaven, for even the nearer part of it, the Air, is sometimes called so too; yet by the word Heaven and Æther we will understand the superiour part of the Region, which containeth the Stars; and, by Air, the inferiour, in which Clouds, Lightning, and the like are generated. We shall begin with the celestial superiour things, and speak afterwards of the Aerial.

CHAP. I.

Of the Substance and Variety of the Stars

Laert.

WE must first lay down what was formerly touched, that *the Sun, Moon, and other Stars, were not made apart, and afterwards brought into the World, but received their figure, augmentation, and magnitude, immediately, and together with the World,* (*as the Earth, the Sea, and whatsoever is in the World,*) *by the coagmentations and convolutions made within it, of some more tenuious natures, and those either aerial, or fiery, or both; for this our sense suggests to us.*

Hence some Stars seem to be of more fiery substance, especially the Sun, whose heat is so manifest to sense; but withal, they seem not so much to be pure fires, as some mixed concretions, to which fire is annext.

Or, it may be, they are, as it were, certain glassy smooth dishes, capable to receive the bright, fiery little Bodies, which, coming from the ætherial Region thorough which they run, light upon them, and so reflect them, and shew them to us in that form wherein they appear: For the like is done amongst us. Or that they may be clouds, enlightned, and, as it were, enkindled; for those Meteors, called the Parelii, are caused no other way.

Or, it may be, they are, as it were, deep vessels, containing fire in their hollow part, like a Lanthorn, or a Chafing dish, which holdeth coles, or melting metals. Or, they may be, as it were, glowing plates, or, as it were, stones burning in a furnace; for there is nothing in all these that implies a contradiction.

In like manner, the Sun in particular may be nothing else, but a thick kind of clod, which being like a pumice, or a spunge ful of pores, and little holes, may, containing fire, dart light out of them.

Onely the most impossible thing seems to be what some assert, that the Stars are animate, or so many Animals, and moreover, so many gods. For though we should grant, that each of them is a kind of World, or rather, as it were, an Earth, which hath not onely an Air, but an æther peculiar to itself. Nevertheless, as this our Earth, though it produceth Animals, is not therefore itself an Animal; so neither would the Stars be, although we should grant that some Animals may be generated in them,

But if we should admit this, yet what they further press, that there are such a kind of round and rolling gods, needs to be repeated onely; for we formerly proved that these are prodigious fancies, not of discoursing but dreaming Philosophers, when expressing inmortal beings by the language proper to mortal, they prouounce things so contrary to the felicity of the gods, and which seem so far beneath their excellent nature.

The Stars have been already distinguished into two kinds; some are fixed, which observe the same position from one another, and keep the same course from East to West, never altering it. Others are wandring, whence called Planets or erratick Stars, because they never observe the same position, either towards one another, nor to the rest; and sometimes perform their courses nigher the North, sometimes nigher the South.

If you demand from whence this diversity proceeds, I shall say, that *it may be the Stars were from the beginning moved round, with such a necessity, that some took a circular motion uniform and even; others, an irregular and unequal one.*

Laert.

It may also be, that, in the places thorough which they move, there may be some even diffusion of spaces, which may carry them on the same way one after another, whereby they may move evenly, but that elsewhere they may be uneven for the same reason; varieties which we observe in their motions proceeding from hence.

To alledge one onely cause for these, seeing that the Phænomena's argue that the causes may be many, is madness, and not rightly considered by those, who dote *on vain Astrology, and trivially explain the cause of some things, and in the mean time will not allow the divine nature (to which they ascribe most of these) to be free from the task of several troublesome offices.*

CHAP. II.

Of the Magnitude and Figure of the Stars.

AS concerning the magnitude of the Sun, and of the rest of the Stars, it may be considered, either as to us, or in itself. *As to us, it is so much as it appeareth to be,* for the sense is not deceived; and whatsoever magnitude the eye seeth in them, is such in them, for they have not any other thing immediately encompassing them without, which is visible; nor any thing of their own, which falls not within view of the eye.

But this magnitude considered it itself, or *as to the thing itself, may be either somwhat greater, or somwhat lesser, or exactly so much as it appears to be.* For with such variety are fires presented to our senses; seen at a distance, in the day-time, or by night. For either they are just so big as they seem, as the light of a candle if we look near it; or lesser, as when we see the same light in the day-time at distance; or greater than indeed they are, as when the same light is seen in the night-time afar off.

I say, somwhat greater or lesser, in regard this diversity betwixt the appearance and the true compass cannot be very great, as may be evinced from our ordinary fires; for, from what distance soever we perceive the heat of any fire, from the same its just form appeareth to us. In like manner, since we perceive the heat of the Sun here from the place where he seemeth to us to be, his just magnitude cannot be sensibly different.

That nothing perceivable is taken off from the Stars by this distance, is confirmed; because those things which we behold at a great distance, and much Air mediating between, are presented to us with a confused circumference; but the Sun, to those who can look upon him, appears to be of an exact compass; nor can any thing be seen more distinctly than the circumference of the Moon. There are indeed same Stars which twinkle, and seem to shoot forth trembling beams; but upon another account, this argues they are so near, as to be seen exactly. For fires amongst us seem, in like manner, to wave and tremble, when we behold them at a distance, which, near at hand, seem fixed and constant.

Again, this is confirmed, because, if the Stars did lose their due magnitude by reason of distance, they would much more lose their colour; for we know, that a thing at distance ceaseth to be seen in its native colour, sooner than by reason of its littleness it totally disappears, or comes not to be seen at all. But though there be no distance more capable to effect this, (for there is not any length greater,) yet the Stars do not therefore lose their true colour.

Many things may be objected against this, but they are easily solv'd, if a man stick close to those things which are manifest to us, as we have shewed in our Books concerning Nature, where we bring in this distinction of magnitude, considered in itself, and, according to us, we declared, that neither he did absurdly, who said, The Sun is a foot broad; nor he that said, It was many times bigger than *Peloponnesus*; nor he who said It is of equal bigness with the Earth, forasmuch as of things, which in themselves are greater and lesser, there may be as to us one magnitude, according as they are nearer or farther off.

As for the figure, I shall onely say, that since it appeareth round to us, it is globous and plain like a Plate, and therefore the Stars are either as dishes, or as cylinders, or as cones and tops, or as certain nails fixed in the Sky. For none of these hath any thing that implyeth a contradiction, nor dissonancy from the phænomena.

CHAP. III.

How the Stars move, out-run one another, and are turned round.

HAving said, not long since, that, of the Stars, some are fixed, others erratick, and that this difference proceeds from their having different motions; we must now say, in general, that the motions of both may be made *either by the turning about of the whole Heaven,* in which one or more of them are, supposing it to be solid, and carying them about with it, like nails fastned into it; or else, the Heaven standing still, as a fluid or pervious thing, by their being whirled about, and moved thorough it.

Now forasmuch, as whether it be the motion of the Heaven, or of the Stars, it may have begun from a necessity made at the very time that the World was generated, and impress'd east-wardly; it might in the first case, (that is, if it be in the whole Heaven,) both have begun, and be continued by the hurry of some Air. For there may be a two-fold extrinsecal Air ; one, pressing from above, and driving the Heaven towards the West ; the other lifting it up as it were, and carrying it on, and that otherwise than the former, which on all sides presses and fixes the Poles. In the second case, (that is if the motion be in the Stars themselves,) it may have been, either by hurry of Air, or by the course of the fire.

For it may have been from the very beginning, that a great company of little Bodies, evaporating, and diffusing themselves, might break the Air, and force their passage thorough it ; and the Air, receiving this motion of the Wind, and hurrying the Stars along with it, might carry them about, and cause that continual circular Motion, which is still seen above in them. It might also be, that the proper fire of every Star, either being shut up close and seeking a vent, might begin to turn about, and continue still as it began ; or, being at greater liberty, might move in this fashion that way, unto which the food or aliment of each invites them, and so go on, *thorough its heat and desire of aliment to the next Bodies which were fuel* convenient to nourish it.

None of all these is repugnant to the Phænonena's, ; but otherwise, we canot easily determine

mine from what cause the motion of the Stars should proceed.

But, How comes it to pass, that some Stars anticipate, or get before others, so as that we see the other left behind them; This may happen, either because the others performing the same diurnal revolution with them are moved more slowly, as the Moon, which moving more slowly than the rest, towards the West, is left as it were behind them East-ward. Or because, being carried about by the diurnal motion towards the West, they are in the mean time slowly carried on, by a contrary motion towards the East, whereby the Moon may not have been left by the rest, East-ward, but rather have left them West-ward. Or because, all things being carried about only with a diurnal revolution, and equal motion, yet some perform a longer, others a shorter course; and so the Moon, if she be a-above the fixed Stars, as some conceive, will perform its revolution more slowly, and be observed to be left behind.

Certainly, to assert any thing absolutely in these matters, becomes those, who affect to make ostentation of something magnificent, and prodigious before the multitude.

Again, How comes it to pass, that the Sun, Moon, and Planets, when they come to the Tropicks, or Solstices, turn about and go back again? This may happen, either because, such a kind of circular motion was at the beginning impress'd upon these Stars, as that they should be carried round about after a spiral manner, limited on each side at the Solstices. Or that they go according to the obliquity of Heaven, which in process of time acquired a necessity of that indirect position. *Or because, they are repell'd by the Air, which driveth them back on,* now to this side, now to that, by reason of its coldness, density, or some other quality. *Or because, their aliment is conveniently disposed all along that way, kindling backward,* and failing forwards.

And these, and those which are like these, have in them nothing reugnant to the evidence of things ; if a man, adhering only to the possibility that is in these things, can reduce each of them to that, which agreeth with the Phænomena's, not fearing the groundless contrivements of Astrologers, who forbear not to build upon and in them a vast company of concentrick Orbs.

CHAP. IV.

Of the Rising and Setting of the Stars, and of the alternate length of dayes and nights,

THe Rising and Setting of the Sun, Moon, and the rest of the Stars may happen three ways.

First, *by appearance above, and occultation beneath:* For that the Stars being always bright and never extinguish'd, are so carried about, above, and below the Earth, that sometimes they rise, somtimes they go down, or set; and the Sun, in particular, when he goeth down causeth darkness with us; but returning, he enkindleth as it were the Heaven with his morning-beams. There is not any thing amongst the Phænomena's which contradicts this.

Again, *by being enkindled* in the East quarter, *and extinguished* in the West: For, *there may be such a disposition of the Medium in both these places, as that,* whilst the Stars pass through it, *what I affirm may be effected, there being nothing in the Phænomenas that contradicts it*; seeing, there are not only fountains that extinguish, but such also, as enkindle Tapers, as that at *Epire,* formerly mentioned. So that the Ocean compassing the Earth, the Sun may be extinguished by it in the West quarter, and return all along it, passing along the North into the East quarter, and from thence arise re-enkindled.

Thirdly, by a new production every day; for nothing hindreth, but that there may every day arise new Suns; for example, there flowing together to the East, several fires, or seeds of fire, which joyn in one round Body, and shine, and are carried on impetuously towards the West. For it is reported, that the like happens in the Mountains of *Ida,* and chiefly about the rising of the Dog-star; and that fires may meet in great Bodies together at certain seasons, may be understood from what is observed to be done at some determinate time in all other Bodies. For, from the confluxion and defluxion of seed, Trees at a certain time bring forth leaves and fruits, at a certain time shed them; at a certain time Teeth are bred, at a certain time cast; and so in other things, which it were too long to instance.

Now the Sun's continuance above the Earth making day, and his absence night; How comes it to pass, that all daies are not equal, and all nights equal, but that in Summer the days are longer, the nights shorter; in Winter alternately, the nights longer and the days shorter? This also may happen three ways.

First, *For that the revolutions of the Sun above and beneath the Earth, are sometimes performed faster, sometimes slower, according the the alternate lengths of the paces,* or ways in which the Sun passeth: And this by reason of the position of the Orb called the *Zodiack,* through which the Sun passeth obliquely, and in two Signs of it makes the nights and the days equal. But when from thence he declineth to the North or South, as much of his journey as he taketh off from one part, either above or below the Earth, so much he adds to the other.

Secondly, *Because there may be certain places in the Æther, which, by reason of their grossness, and the resistance which happens thereupon, cannot be passed through so swiftly as others.* Such are those which make the Sun stay long beneath the Earth in the Winter, whereby they make the night longer and the day shorter than in Summer. *Some things of the same kind may be observed amongst us, according to which it is convenient to explicate superiour Bodies.*

Thirdly, that in the alternate parts of the year, the fires, or seeds of fire aforesaid, flow together in such manner, as that they make a Sun sooner or later; and the Sun rises out of that part from which he begins a longer or shorter course above the Earth.

They who insist and fix upon but some one particular way, to explicate these effects, both contradict things apparent, and deviate from that which falls under human comtemplation.

CHAP. V.

Of the light of the Stars, and of the changes and Spots in the Moon.

Let us now say something of the light, not onely of the Sun, but of the rest of the Stars, and particularly of the Moon. First, men admire, that the Sun, being so little, should pour forth so much light out of himself, as sufficeth to enlighten and warm the Heaven, the Earth, the Sea, and yet not be itself exhausted. But the Sun is a kind of fountain, into which there flow together from beneath on very side perpetual rivulets; for the seeds of heat throughout the whole world flow so into the Sun, as that immediately from him, as from one fountain or head, both heat and light overfloweth every way.

Moreover, the substance of the Sun, may be of such thickness, and the light and heat which floweth from him of such thinness, that as a little current or a rivulet, streaming from a spring, watereth the meadows and fields round about it, without any loss to itself; so that of the Sun may be sufficient to irrigate, as it were, the whole world, without any sensible diminution of the Sun.

Moreover, the Air may be of such a nature, as that it may be kindled, as it were, by a little light, diffused from the Sun; as a whole field of corn may be set on fire by one spark.

Likewise, the Sun may have his aliment round about him, which may supply what he loseth, as the flame of a lamp is fed by the oyl which is put to it. It may happen also many other ways.

Laert. As to the rest of the Stars, especially the Moon, it may be, that they have their light from themselves, *it may be they borrow it from the Sun; for amongst us we see, that there are many things which shine of themselves, many things which borrow light from others; and there is nothing appearing in the superiour things themselves, which hinders, but that either of those opinions may be true.*

If a man perserve stedfast in his mind the manifold ways, and the suppositions conformable to it, and consider the causes together with it, lest minding things that are incoherent, he grow vainly proud, and sometimes fall into one particular way, sometimes into another.

As for the Moon, it is in the first place wonderful, How she comes to have so many changes, or increase or decrease of light. It may be, that being round, and receiving light from the Sun, she is sucessively so figured, (after the same manner as the Air, when the Sun riseth, is enlightned, and when he setteth is dardened succcessively,) as that going away from the Sun, she seemeth every day to encrease, because she sheweth more and more of her enlightned face to us, until she persents it at full ; and then going towards the Sun, decreaseth every day, because she sheweth less and less of it, until at last she turneth no part of it towards us, but is quite unseen.

Moreover, it may be, that the Moon being round, one part of her may be bright, another dark, and as she turneth her Body about, may discover to us, alternately, more or less of each part.

It may also be, that being bright of itself, she may be obscured by an interposition of some opacous Body coming under her, which is hemispherical and hollow, and, moved along with her, is continually rolled about her.

Neither doth any thing hinder, but that there may every day (according to what we formerly said,) be made a new Moon of a several form and figure ; as in like manner the seasons of the Spring, Summer, Autumn, and Winter, and many things in them, come and go, are produced and perish, at set times.

In fine, it may be any way, wherein those things which appear to us may be applyed to explication of that manner, unless some man, being much in love with one singular way, shall vainly reject the rest, not considering what things it is possible for a man to know, and thereupon aims at the knowledge of those things which man cannot attain.

Moreover, they admire in the Moon, that there *Laert.* appear spots in her face ; but *her face may appear so, either from the various and diferent nature of the parts of the Moon, or from the interposition of some body,* not so much opacous as dusky ; not rolling about her, but perpetually adhering to her, and not solid all over, but full of holes like a Racket.

Or, it may be any other way of all those which are *Laert.* *observed to be conformable to things apparent. This is the course to which we must adhere, concerning superiour things ; for no man, if he contest against apperent things, can ever partake of true tranquillity.*

CHAP. VI.

Of the Eclipses of the Stars, and their set Periods.

But there is nothing which useth to strike a greater terrour into men, than that sometimes they observe Eclipses, and defects of light in the Sun and Moon, to happen on a suddain. Yet why may not this also happen many several ways ?

For first, the Sun may be Eclipsed, for that the Moon, being interposed, puts her dark Orb or opacous Body before him, and keeping away his light from the Earth, causeth darkness in her, until by her removal the light is restored. The Moon may be Eclipsed, for that the Earth, being interposed betwixt her, and the Sun, takes the Sun off from her, and darkens her, while she comes within the cone of the shadow, until, passing from out of it, she recovereth light.

Again, the Sun may be Eclipsed, for that some part of Heaven, or some other opacous Body, such as is the Earth, may move along with the Sun, and at certain times come underneath him, and intercept his light. And the Moon in like manner, for that some other opacous Body passing betwixt her and the Sun, keeps off the beams of the Sun from her, or moving together with her, doth not onely perform its phases slowly, but sometimes overcasts her with a suddain darkness. Not to mention, that if she be dark on one side and bright on the other, it may happen, that she may sometimes on a suddain turn her dark side towards us.

Moreover, both the Sun and Moon may suffer Eclipse, for that they may pass thorough places pernicious to fire, and thereby their light become
exting-

extinguished, until going beyond them they renew and recover it.

Thus ought the several ordinary wayes to be heeded, and some of them also put together, it being possible, that many causes may concur.

Laert. The *periodical order*, by which Eclipses happen at certain times, *is conceived to be kept in like manner as amongst us in some things, as in the vicissitude of seasons. There is no need of recurring to the divine nature for the bringing of these to pass; let us allow that to be free from all business, and exquisitely happy.*

Unless this be done, all discourse of Causes in superiour things will be vain; as hath already happened to some, who taking an impossible course became frivolous for that they approved only one, and rejected all the rest, though they were possible, and were transported to dream of that which exceeds the capacity of the Intellect, and were neither able to admit, as they ought, apparent signes, nor understand, as they say, how to rejoyce with God.

CHAP. VII.

Of the Presignifications of the Stars.

IT remains, we speak of the Presignifications of the changes of the Air attributed to the Stars, as rain, wind, drought, heat, and the like, which happen according to the time of the rising or setting of certain Stars, as of the Dog, Orion, the Pleiades.

Laert. *These Presignifications may be made either according to the condition of the Seasons, as it happens in those living creatures which being seen at one time with us, at another with others, passing hither and thither, are signs not causes of the seasons for the rising and setting-Stars may be not causes but signs of those mutations; or as it happens not certainly, but casually, at what time the Stars rise or set, there are causes of some mutation in the Air.*

For neither of those is repugnant with things apparent; and what cause there may by, besides these agreeable with things apparent, we cannot perceive.

It is not without some reason what I hinted of Presignifications; which are observed in some Animals, to be made according to the condition of the season which at that time comes in, so as the motions observed in Animals only declare tempests but make them not. As those for example, which depart from us in Autumne induce not any necessity of the Winters being at that time; Neither is there any divine nature which sits and marks the departure of living creatures; that it may make good what is foretold by them.

This is a kind of folly that cannot fall upon any Animal, in which there were the least grain of wit; so far is it from being in that nature which possesseth all felicity.

CHAP. VIII.

Of Comets, and those which are called Falling Stars.

WHat hath been hitherto spoken of the Stars, belongs to the Sun and Moon, and Stars, which having been made from the beginning of the World constantly inhere and appear in Heaven. But besides these, there are other Stars, which somtimes are generated or newly appear, and after some few dayes or Months either perish or lye hid. They are called Comets, *quasi Comatæ Stellæ* hairy-stars, for that they have a long train, like hair.

Some also there are, that last but for a moment, vanishing almost assoon as they appear; and, seeming in some kind of excursion to fall down, they are ordinarily termed falling-Stars.

As for the Comets, ' they may be generated, *Laert.* ' Either for that some fire is sometimes kindled in ' some of those superiour places, and being kind-' led is for a time nourish'd and moved, accord-' ing to the abundance and disposition of the ' matter. Or else they appear, for that Heaven, ' as to that part which is over our heads, hath ' some peculiar motion according to several vi-' cissitudes, so as these Stars are driven to be ' made manifest. Or else, they come forth by ' reason of a certain disposition at some times; ' and, assoon as they come lower towards us, ' they become manifest.

' Comets disappear to our sight through the ' causes contrary to these. Either the matter con-'venient for them is not placed all along, as it is in ' that place where they are observed to in-' here, so as by degrees through want of ali-' ment, they consume as it weir and go out, or ' that some thing opposeth there motion. And ' that may happen, not only for that this part of ' the World, round about which the rest is turn-' ed, remaineth unmoved, as some affirm; but al-' so, for that there may be in the Air some im-' petuous gyration, which may hinder their ' moving round, and drive it another way, as ' may also happen to the other Stars which are ' called Planets at the Tropicks.

' Moreover this may happen many other ' wayes, if we discourse upon that which is con-' formable to things apparant.

As for those which are called falling-Stars, ' they may be made either by pieces broken off ' from the true Stars or from the falling down ' of that matter whereof there is a kind of dif-' flation, as may happen also in lightning; or ' from a company of ignifying Atoms, meeting ' and joyning together to effect it; the motion ' being made, according as the force of meet-' ing together was from the beginning. Or ' from the driving of wind up together within ' certain cloudy bottoms or windings, and set-' ting it a-fire whilst it is rolled up and down, ' and breaking thorough the bottoms which ' restrain them, and moving to that part to-' wards which that impulsion carries them.

' There are other wayes not fictitious, by ' which this may be done. But of cælestial Meteors, enough.

CHAP.

CHAP. IX.

Of Clouds.

Next these are the aerial Meteors, which are made nearer us in the Air. We shall begin with the Clouds; than which nothing is generated above in the Air, or seen more frequently.

A Cloud therefore may be generated and have its being, by some accumulation as it were of the Air, the Winds driving it, so as that a Cloud is nothing but a thickning of the Air. Again by implication of some Atoms cohering mutually to one another, and fit to produce such a compound; and this when they first come together into little Bodies of Clouds, and those are gathered together into greater bulks, so as at last they become greatest of all.

They most commonly seem to rise at the tops of Hills, for that the first little compounds are so subtle as that they escape the sight, and are carryed on by the wind, until being by little and lettle condensed, they appear on the tops of the Hills which by reason thereof seem to smoak.

If any shall doubt, From whence there can come so great a conflux of Atoms as is sufficient to make such great bulks of Clouds, let him consider, that if no other way, yet they may at least come from without, out of the immensity of the Universe were there is an infinite multitude of them. And this because there is allowed to the principles a free passage in and out, thorough the vents of the World, as was formerly declared.

Moreover, a Cloud may be generated *by the gathering together of effluxions and exhalations, out of the Earth and Water,* and carried upwards. For, that there are many little Bodies drawn out of the whole Sea, appeareth by Garments which being hung upon the shore grow moyst. Besides we see, that every where out of Rivers, arise mists and exhalations and vapours, in such abundance, as that being carried upwards they darken the Skye, and by little and little meeting together turn into Clouds.

Neither doth any thing hinder, but that these coagmentations may be made many other ways,

CHAP. X.

Of the Winds, and of Presters.

Wind may be generated, first, *when the Atoms or little Bodies leap out of some convenient places and fly thorough the Air, there being a more vehement effusion made from some heaps which are proper for such kind of emissions;* * When in a narrow Vacuum there are many little Bodies, there followeth Wind; and contrary, the Air is quiet and calm, when in a great Vacuum there are but a few little Bodies.

For, as in a market place or street, as long as the people are but few, they walk without any trouble; but when they run into some narrow place, they justle and quarrel with one another; so in this space which encompasseth us, when many Bodies crowd into one little place, they must necessarily justle one another, and be thrust forward, and driven back and entangled and sqeezed; of which as made the wind, when they which contested yeeld and having been long toss'd up and down uncertainly, shrink. But when a few Bodies stir up and down in a larg space, they can neither drive nor be driven impetuously:

Again, Wind may be caused when the Air is driven on and agitated either by exhalations coming from the Earth and Water, or by the Sun's pressing upon it from above; for it is manifest, that where the Air is agitated and stirred, there is caused wind, so as wind seems to be nothing else but the waves of the Air. Whence we may conceive, that the wind somwhat resembles water troubled, and that the more violent winds come from being stirred by some more vehement cause, after the same manner as torrents rage and make waste, when there happens a vast defluxion of waters by great showers falling upon the Mountains.

Presters are windy whirlings (for the fiery, and those which burn, from which the name is taken, are a kind of Thunder.) They ' may be gene-'rated either from the depression of a Cloud after various fashions towards inferiour places, 'whilst ' it is carried down and driven on by abundance ' of wind, which rouls itself about, and tears ' away the sides of the Clouds, the wind also ' driveth on the Cloud immediately from with-'out, or from the wind standing round about, ' whereas the Air pressing upon it from above, ' and withal the Air which is driven on and dif-'fused round about hindring by reason of its ' density, the great abundance of wind knoweth ' not which way it may spread itself, and being driven back, as well by the sides as from above, it necessarily thrusts the Cloud downwards.

When this Prester is thrust down upon the land, it causeth whirl-winds; when upon the Sea, whirl-pools. Whirle-winds are less frequently seen, because the mountains snatch them away before they come within our sight; whirl-pools more frequently, by reason of the wide smoothness of the Sea, into which we may behold a Cloud like a pillar descend from Heaven, and push it down, as it were with the force of an arm or fist, untill the violence of the wind breaking thorough it, the Sea works and boils, and the ships incur a danger almost inevitable.

CHAP. XI.

Of Thunder.

It was not without reason that I said, there are also fiery Presters, which are not different from Thunder. For, *Thunder seems to be caused by the manifold conglomeration of blasts, swelling with fiery little Bodies, within the bulks of the Cloud; and by the evolution and strong enkindling of them, and breaking of the Clouds by the fire, which is so forcibly darted to inferiour places, according as that breaking forth is somtimes directed towards a high mountain,* (which kind of places are oftnest struck *with Thunder,*) *somtimes towards other things.*

For that the nature of Thunder is fiery is manifest, even because it often burneth the houses upon which it is darted, and for that it leaveth behind it a stench like brimstone. That it is generated within the Clouds, is evident for that it never Thunders when the sky is clear; but the Clouds first gather together all along the Air, and darken the sky, and there ariseth a foul night, as it were, of showers. Lastly, that many little Bodies or seeds, as it were, of fire, are contained within a Cloud may be argued, as well from the effect, as for that amongst the little Bodies of a Cloud rising up from beneath, are intermingled, not only watery, but fiery also, and of other sorts. Withal, it cannot be, but that the Cloud must receive many things from the beams of the Sun.

When therefore the blast or wind, which drove the Clouds together, hath intermingled itself with the seeds of fire, that are in the bosom, as it were, and cavity of the Clouds, there is caused a whirling or vortex within it, which being carried about very rapidly, groweth hot by motion; and either by intension of this heat, or the contagion of some other fire, breaketh out into perfect Thunder, and tearing the Cloud is darted forth. Now the Cloud is cleft and broken, by reason that the places round about the whirling or vortex are taken up, and stuffed thicker with the part of the Cloud; neither, by reason of their being squeezed up so close together, is there any chink open, whereby whilst it is spread with the wind may insinuate itself, and retire, by penetrating into it by degrees. Whereupon it is necessary, that the fire lately made, being dilated by the wind, breaks thorough the Cloud with violence, which makes the noise of Thunder; and coming forth, shineth and filleth all parts with a glitting light.

It may also be, that the force of the wind may light from without upon the Cloud, at such time as the Thunder is mature and perfect, and rending the Cloud, make way for the fiery vortex to break thorough.

It may also be, that the fiery vortex, though not set on fire when it breaks forth, may be kindled afterwards in its passage thorough the Air; after the same manner as a leaden slugg passing thorough the Air grows hot, and takes fire. It may also be, that the fire is made in the very dashing against the thing which it hits, the seeds of fire being struck out of both, in the same manner as they are struck by a Flint out of Steel.

Laert. ' There are many other ways by which this ' fire may be kindled, or Thunder made, only ' let us cast away all fiction; and cast away it ' will be, if we take our conjecture of things un- ' seen, from that which is conformable to things ' apparent.

Hence may be given the reason, Why it comes to pass, that it Thunders oftner in the Spring and Autumn, than in other seasons. In Winter, there wants the seeds of fire; in Summer, the blasts and heaps of Clouds; in the Spring and in Autumn, all things convenient are ready.

But how comes it to pass, that the motion of Thunder is so swift, and its stroke so violent? This proceeds from the great violence of the eruption, and the tenuity; by reason of which, nothing in the way resists them, and force, which is, as it were, doubled by gravity, and encreaseth by motion.

How comes it to penetrate thorough the walls of Houses, to melt metals in a moment, to draw out all the Wine out of full vessels? This proceeds from the tenuity, and quick motion, and violent force of the little Bodies, whereby it can in a moment dissipate and disperse those things, which the ordinary fire of the Sun cannot under a long time.

CHAP. XII.

Of Lightning and Thunder-claps.

ALthough I hinted by the way how Lightning and how Thunder are generated; yet nothing hinders, but that they may be generated many ways besides.

For ' Lightning may be made either by the *Laert.* ' rubbing or striking of the Clouds against one ' another, such a kind of figure issuing from ' them; or by such a disposure and conformation of Atoms heaped up together, as causeth fire, and generates lightning; after the same manner as we observe it to be done, when Iron and a Stone are hit against one another.

Or by the winds stirring up out of the Clouds those Bodies, or little Bodies, that is, Atoms, *which cause this glittering brightness;* for that the wind (and especially if it grow hot like a leaden slugge,) strikes off the same little Bodies, which are struck by the mutual attrition of the Clouds.

' Or by squeezing forth; there being made a ' compression either by the Clouds one with a- ' nother, or by the winds driving them, which is caused over and above the force of collision.

' Or by interception of the light which is ' diffused by the Stars, which thereupon is dri- ' ven by the motion of the Clouds and winds, ' and falleth out of the Clouds.

' Or by the falling down of some most tenui- ' ous light out of the Clouds, whilst the Clouds ' are intrinsecally gather'd together by the fire; ' and withal, Thunder is caused like a kind of ' bounce by their motion.

' Or by the enkindling of a wind, which is ' caused, as well by a vehement intenseness, as ' convolution of motion.

' Or by a breaking of the Clouds by the winds, ' and falling down of fiery Atoms, which cause ' lightning to shine.

That lightning may be generated many other ways, he will easily perceive, who adheres to things ' apparent, and is able to understand ' what suits with them.

Thunder-claps may be made thus, ' Either by ' the rolling of a wind within the cavities of the ' Clouds, as in ordinary vessels, when somthing ' is rolled in them.

' Or making a crack by the very difflation and ' ebullition, as it were, of the fire, within the ' same Clouds.

Or by the breaking and tearing of the same Clouds, as when a swollen bladder cracks, paper is torn, or a shrowd rent.

' Or by the same Clouds, rubbing and driving ' against one another, having acquired an icy kind ' of concretion, *and this by reason of the winds * *Lucret* ' driving them; as tall Woods crackle at the blowing of the East-wind, waves unbroken murmur, garments hung up, and papers carried away and beaten, as it were, by the winds, make a clattering noise.

Or by extinction of the fire of Thunder, breaking out of one Cloud, and lighting upon another which is waterish, whereupon it hisses like red-hot Iron, taken out of the fire, and cast into the water.

Or by the burning of some dry Cloud, which crackles like a branch in the fire.

'In a word, that this also may be explained 'several ways, the things which appear evince 'and teach us, that we think not, with ignorant and superstitious persons, that the noise of Thunder denotes the appearance of some god, since other Bodies, being struck against one another, make a sound also, as Mill-Stones in grinding, or the hands clapped together.

Lest any wonder how it comes to pass, that Lightning is seen before the Thunder is heard, this may happen, ' either for that in some cer-'tain disposition of the Clouds, as soon as the 'Wind lights upon them, there leaps forth such 'a configuration of little Bodies, as causeth light-'ning; and thereupon the wind, by rolling up 'and down, maketh this sound.

'Or for that they being both generated toge-'ther, the lightning is brought to us with a quick-'er nimbleness; the Thunder cometh later, as 'happeneth in some things which are seen at 'distance and make a sound by blowes; for it is manifest, that the stroak is seen before the sound is heard.

CHAP. XIII.

Of Rain and Dew.

WE must now speak of watery concretions, whereof some continue fluid, others acquire some solidity by the impression of cold; those which continue fluid are Rain and Dew, whereof one is made, the Heaven being cloudy; the other, when it is clear.

Laert.   Rain may be made of the Clouds, either when being thinner than ordinary, the wind driving them, or they pressing upon one another, are squeezed together, and knit into drops; or when being thicker than ordinary, they are rarifi'd and changed by heat or by the wind? or, like Wax, melt so, that they fall down in drops.

That there are seeds of Water contained in the Clouds, is so well known, that we need not speak of it. They ascend together with Clouds, they encrease together with them, and are dispersed thorough them, as blood through the parts of our Body. Neither doth there ascend moisture into the Clouds from all Rivers only, but the Clouds also which hang over the Sea receive moisture, like a fleece of wool.

Lucret.   Wherefore Rain may flow from the Clouds, either when the force of the wind thrusteth the Clouds up together, and great store of showers being raised above them, presseth and thrusts them; or when the Clouds by the power of the winds are rarifi'd, and suffer their moisture to flow abroad; or by the heat of the Sun are so dissolved, that they fall down in drops, and, as I said, like melting wax.

It may happen, that Rains somtimes last a long while, because it then happeneth, that many seeds of waters, rising up to several Clouds, and dispersed every way, may supply the Rain. Somtimes also the Earth reeking, exhales back again all the moisture which she receiveth.

Dew is made, either by the meeting together of the little Bodies in the Air, which are of such a nature, as to be fit to generate this kind of moisture; or by the bringing forth of little Bodies, which chiefly generate Dew above, when they so meet together as to make that moisture, and flow down into the places beneath. Many things of this kind are done amongst us, especially in stoves.

CHAP. XIV.

Of Hail, Snow, and Frost.

OF watery Concretions, which by impression of cold are congealed into some solidity, there are two things which are made when the Heaven is Cloudy, Hail and Snow; one, when it is clear, Frost.

Hail is generated, either when the congelation is stronger, by reason of the setling of a cold wind which is on every side, and presseth the drippings or drops of the Clouds, which otherwise would go away into Rain, or when the congealed bulk cleaveth asunder in many pleaces, and by a moderate liquefaction, watery drops insinuating into the chinks by compression of the parts, and breaking the whole frame into pieces, they cause that the parts exist compacted severally by themselves, and make a heap of fragments, which are thereupon dispersed.

That these fragments be in a manner round, nothing hindreth, either, for that the outmost corners are cut off on every side, by reason of their long falling; or, for that in their very forming, somthing either watery or windy surrounds all the parts evenly, as we said, so that their surface is round, and not uneven.

Snow happeneth to be made either by thin water poured out of the Clouds, so that it froaths, (some Clouds fit for that purpose pressing, and the winds blowing them abroad,) and is afterwards congealed in the very Motion, by reason of some more vehement cold in the lower places of the Clouds.

Or by some smooth congealing, caused in the Clouds; unto which, whilst the little watery Bodies, compressed by, and neighbouring to, one another, arrive, there is caused an aggeneration of such loosness, as the flocks of Snow have, whereas, the same driving one another cause Hail, which two things chiefly are made in the Air.

It may also be, that a kind of ejaculation of the Snow, which falleth down in heaps, may be made, the Clouds, which were first congealed, breaking in asunder.

Lastly, Frost is made of the same little Bodies as Dew, whenas the little drops of Dew made either way, are by the cold temperament of the Air congealed, and in congealing, receive a light compactedness.

CHAP.

CHAP. XV.

Of the Rain-bow, and Halos.

WE must not here pass by two remarkable things, which appear in the Clouds or above; The Rain-bow, an Arch of various colours, over against the Sun; and Halos, which somtimes like a White Crown compasseth the Moon.

The Rain-bow is made either, for that the moist Air shineth by the opposite splendor of the Sun, or for that it is the particular nature of light, and of the Air, to present such kind of colours either all of them, or one only, from which (shining forward,) the neighbouring parts of the Air are so coloured; in like manner, as we observe to be don, when the parts of any thing, which is enlightned, make the parts of other things next to it shine also.

As to the roundness of its figure, this is caused by reason, that it is only convey'd to the beholders eye, from a distance every way equal; or, for that the Atoms, which are carried out of the Air into the Cloud, are so compelled, that every concretion made of them is formed into this roundness.

A Halos is made about the Moon, either by the carrying up of a somewhat gross or lightly-cloudy Air towards the Moon, whilst in the mean time, some effluxions derived from her do as it were sift it, (for they do not absolutely disperse it,) in such manner, that they are formed into a circle about her in this cloudy figure.

Or by the Air, compelled about the Moon, after such a manner, as to make this round and grosser figure about her; which some conceive to happen according to some of her parts, or by some effluxion driving together from without, or, by insinuation of heat from beneath, fit to effect this.

CHAP. XVI.

Of Avernal places.

IT rests, that we speak some things of Avernal places, so termed, for that they are pernicious to Birds; for when Birds attempt to flye over them, they instantly fall down and dye: As also concerning the causes of Pestilence, as far as they depend on the Air.

I must here only repeat, that the Earth containeth all kinds of little Bodies so diversly figured that same are suitable to the natures of Animals, others hurtful; and by reason that the contextures of Animals are so unlike to one another, some of these are convenient and wholsome to some Animals, which to others are inconvenient and pernicious. And why not? when the contexture and temper of the same person being changed by a Feaver, the same wine, which before did him much good, is now as deadly to him as to be stabb'd to the heart.

It is manifest, that many things unpleasant, troublesome, and pernicious ordinarily come into the taste, the smell, the touch, and all the senses, not to mention some Trees which either cause a heaviness to those who sleep in their shade or by an ill scent kill them; nor strong Wine, or the fume of coles and the like. How many places are there, which exhale strong and hurtful scents of Brimstone and sulphur? They who dig in Mines, who look so whan, and dye so soon, how many noisome vapours do they find to breath out of the inmost parts of the Earth?

Thus there are some places out of which these vapours breathe, which being carried up into the Air, diffused round over it, in some manner poyson it, and infect it with a deadly quality; so as that, when Birds come to pass over it, *Veluti si Mulier mensium tempore Castoreum olfaciat*, they become stupefy'd, and immediately fall down dead.

It may also be, that the Air which lies between the Birds and the Earth, being cleft asunder by the force of a vapour breaking forth, and the place becoming almost Vacuous; the Birds may not have a support, upon which to rest their spreading wings, and centinue their flight, so that they sink and fall, over-burthen'd by the weight of their own Body. Thus much for Avernal places.

CHAP. XVII.

Of Pestilence.

THough Pestilence, or a mortal affection of the Air may come from above, like a Cloud or dew, yet it is most commonly caused, when the Earth is putrify'd by unseasonable rains and heats, and such a vapour ariseth out of it, as infects the Air, and killeth far and neer, not only men but other living Creatures.

That the Air easily entertains the affection (or quality,) of the vapour breathed immediately out of the Earth into it, is manifest, from the diseases that are particular to Coutries, as here with us, the Gout is frequent; among the *Achæans*, soreness of Eyes; among the *Ægyptians*, the Leprosie; As also for that Travellers find it by experience, acknowledging that the Air in several places is very different.

That this affection is somtimes propagated by the Air, the nature of the Pestilence declareth, as That especially, which, in the memory of our Ancestors beginning in *Æthiopia*, ran on into *Libia* and *Ægypt*, and almost over all the Dominions of the King of *Persia*, so as it came into our City and Country also, and quite laid it waste.

This propagation is made, when the poisonous vapour intermingling its little Bodies with the Air, doth so disorder, and pervert the scituation of the little Bodies thereof, that whatsoever of them are like its own, it formeth into the same contexture: As when fire insinuating with its little Bodies into wood, so altereth its composition, that it striks forth all the fiery little Bodies that are in it; and, out of it, maketh a new fire like to itself. Moreover, as fire running along in its swift motion, is able to spread it self thorough a whole Wood; so this Pestilent affection, by reason of the little Bodies, of which it consists, creepeth forward by Degrees, and changeth the Air a great way, until it be repress'd by an affection quite different, in like manner, as when a Cloud or mist creeps thorough the Air, and by little and little, changeth and disturbeth it all along as it goeth.

Not to mention, that when men by breathing, draw the Air into their Bodies, they suck in at the same time, the little Bodies of this affection; wherewith, those which are like them in the Body are transposed, and perverted in the same manner, as we said of the Air; and by contagious afflation, they are transmitted on to others, which cause the same perversion, whereby the disease spreads every where.

Thus much concerning not Meteorology only, but all Physiology: Of which the few things that we have said are such, as that by contemplating them, we may throughly understand the things that are done, whereby the things that are of affinity with them, may be comprehended; and the causes of particular effects in Nature, known. For they, who persue not these with all possible diligence, are far from understanding them, as they ought, and from obtaining the end, for which those are to be understood.

And never must we cast out of Mind the Criteries, (nor the evidence that belongs to every one of them,) because, if we forsake not these, we shall with right reason find out from whence perturbation ariseth, and what it is that causeth fear, and shall quit ourselves from it, understanding the cause of superiour things, and of all others which ordinarily happen, and strike great fear into others.

But, presupposing the Criteries, it avails most to apply ourselves to speculation of the Principles, of which all things consist, and of the infinity of Nature, and other things coherent with these, and with constant remembrance to preserve the chiefest and most general Maxims concerning them. For by this means, we shall be farthest off From Fables, and obtain that undisturbed state of mind, which is the true and only mark, at which, in all this discourse, we have aimed.

THE

The Third Part OF PHILOSOPHY.

ETHICK, or MORALS.

IT resteth that we speak of *Ethick*, or the Philosophy of *Manners*; neither is it without cause that we said at first, that this is to be esteemed the principal Part of Philosophy, because that which is of Nature would be useless, unless it conferr'd to the End of Life with an Ethical Consideration, Even Prudence itself, which belongs to this Part, therefore excels Natural Philosophy, because it rules it, and useth it as a means to Moral Philosophy.

In saying this Part concerns the *End of Life*, I shew why it is commonly called the Philosophy *concerning Life and Manners*, or concerning the Institution of the Actions of Life, (for Manners are no other than the customary Actions of Human Life ;) likewise concerning the *End*, that is, the extream or greatest of the Goods which we pursue ; and concerning things eligible and avoidable, inasmuch as it prescribeth the election of such things as conduce to that End, and the avoidance of such as divert from it.

For the *End* of Life, by the tacit Consent of all Men, is *Felicity*; and since almost all miss of that End, must it not happen either, for that they propose not to themselves that Felicity which they ought, or for that they use not the right means to attain it?

When we behold so many, who, abounding in all things necessary to the use of Life, (swimming in Wealth, adorn'd with Titles, flourishing in a hopeful Issue ; in Fine, possess'd of all things commonly esteemed desirable,) are notwithstanding anxious and querulous, full of cares and solicitudes, distracted with terrors, in a word, leading a miserable life; thence we may infer, that they know not wherein true Felicity consists, and by what means it may be attained : Their Hearts resembling a Vessel, which either being leaky and full of holes, can never be filled ; or being tainted with ill liquor, corrupts and spoils whatsoever it receives.

It is therefore worth our pains, by the benefit of this Philosophy, (which treats of the *End* and of *Felicity*,) to cleanse and mend our heart, that it may be satisfi'd with a little, and be pleased in the enjoying of any thing, *we must Philosophize not for shew, but seriously ; for it is requisite, not that we seem sound, but that we be found* : *Senec. Ep.* 13. We must Philosophize forthwith, and not defer it to the morrow; for even to day it concerns us to live happily, *and it is a mischief of Folly that it always begins to live*, or defers to begin, but in the mean time liveth never.

A strange thing, it is ! *We have been born once, we cannot be born twice, and Age must have an End ; Yet thou, O Man, though the Morrow be not in thy power, in confidence of living to Morrow, put'st thyself off to the future, and losest the present : So mens lives waste with delay, and hence it is that some of us die in the midst of business* : Every man leaves the World as if he had but newly entred it ; and therefore old men are upbraided with Infancy, because, as if employed in business that concerns them not, they do not take notice that they live, and so their whole life passeth away without the benefit of life.

Let us therefore endeavor so to live, that we may not repent of the time past ; and so enjoy the present, as if the morrow nothing concerned us. He most sweetly attains the morrow, who least needs or desires the morrow ; and that hour overtakes a man most welcom, whereof he had framed to himself the least hope. And since *it is troublesom always to begin life*, let life be always to us as it were perfect and obsolute, and as if there wanted nothing to its measure. *The life of a Fool is unpleasant, it is timorous, it is wholly carried on to the future*; let us endeavor that ours be pleasant, secure, not only present, but even now setled in safety.

Doubtless the way to flie Folly, is to ascend that Watch-tower (as it were) of wise men, from whence we may behold the rest wandring, and, in life, vainly seeking life. If you think it pleasant, from Land to behold Mariners striving with Storms ; or, without endangering yourself, see Armies joining Battel ; certainly nothing can be more delightful, than from the calm Throne of Wisdom, to view the Tumults and Contentions of Fools, Not that it is pleasant that others be afflicted, but it pleaseth that we are not involved in the same evils.

But that we may in some measure, to our ability, help those who desire to attain this height of Wisdom, we will collect our meditations upon these things, treating first of *Felicity*, which is man's greatest good, and then of those things which conduce to the making and preserving it, which are nothing else but the *Virtues* themselves.

CHAP. I.

Of Felicity, or the End of Good, as far as Man is capable of it.

OF *Felicity* we must first take notice, it is termed the *End*, that is, the last, the extreme and greatest of Goods; because since those things are called Good which allure the Appetite to persue them, and of these Goods some are desired for themselves, some for other things, Felicity is such a Good as all Goods ought to be referred unto, itself to none.

And though *Felicity*, or *Beatitude*, and *Happy Life* be the same thing, yet that doth not hinder us, but that we sometimes mention the End of Happy Life, which we do, according to the Vulgar Phrase, taking the End of Happy Life, and Happy Life, for the same thing; but not implying any farther End, to which Happy Life, may be thought to be referred.

This premised, we must first distinguish Felicity into two kinds; one Supreme, incapable of Intension and Remission; the other Subalternate, in which there may be Addition and Detraction of Pleasure.

The first is conceived to be a state, than which none can be imagined, better, sweeter, more desirable, in which there is no Ill to be feared, no Good wanting: There is nothing that would and may not be done; and which is so sure, that it can at no time be lost.

By the other we understand a state, in which it is as well as may be, or in which there are very many necessary Goods, very few Ills, and in which it is permitted to lead a Life so sweetly, so quietly, and constantly, as the Company, Course of Life, Constitution of Body, Age, and other Circumstances will allow.

Nor without Reason is it I make this Distinction and Definition. For, though it seem manifest, that the first kind is proper only to Good; yet there are, who, having a high opinion of themselves, and of their own Wisdom, dare promise and arrogate it to themselves, and therefore affirm, that they are equal to God; and modest amongst them are they, who repute themselves inferior to none but *Jupiter*.

But these truly seem forgetful of their own Mortality and Weakness, whenas all, who are conscious thereof, cannot but acknowledge, that Men are capable only of the later, and that Wisdom doth much, if, all Men being in some manner miserable, it place thee in a state, wherein thou shalt be the least miserable of all Men. Or, if among the several degrees of miseries, to which thou art obnoxious by Birth, it place thee in that wherein thou shalt be least miserable. For that is to be happy, to be free from those Ills wherewith thou mightest be afflicted; and in the mean time to enjoy such Goods, than which, greater cannot be had in the condition wherein thou art.

This indeed is the Reason, why I conceive a Man, though deprived of Sight and Hearing, may nevertheless partake of Happy Life, because he will yet persevere in as many Goods as he can, and be free from those Ills, if not of Body, at least of Mind, which otherwise might have afflicted him.

I further declare, that a wise Man, though he should be cruelly tormented, will yet be happy, by Felicity not Divine but Human; which in a wise Man is always as great as can be for the condition of the time.

For in Torments he feels the Pain indeed, sometimes groans and cries out; but because there is a necessity of suffering them, he exasperates not or makes them greater, by Impatience or Despair, but rather, with as great constancy of Mind as is possible, mitigates and renders them somewhat more easie. Herein certainly he is more happy than if he sunk under them, like those, who, being under the same Torment, bear them not with equal Courage and Constancy, nor have the like assistence from Wisdom (which confers at least innocence of Life, and security of Conscience,) to lighten them.

Therefore neither is there any Reason to cavil, that the Bull of *Phalaris*, and a Bed of Roses, are all one to us; and the wise Man, burning in that Bull, must cry out, *How pleasant is this! How unconcern'd am I! How little care I!* Since there are some things, which a wise Man had rather should happen to him, as rest of Body, free from all Disturbance, and leisure of Mind, rejoycing in contemplation of its own good. There are other things, which though he would not have them, yet when they do come, he bears them constantly, even commends and approves them, inasmuch as they give him occasion to please himself in his own constancy, and to say, I burn, but yield not. Why may it not be wished, not indeed to be burnt, but to be vanished?

This I say, in regard a wise Man is obnoxious both to the Pains of Sickness, and the Tortures of Tyrants, although he neither invites those, nor provokes these, so far as decently he may. Besides, the times are not such always to all Men, as that they may by Indolence live happy.

CHAP. II.

That Pleasure, without which there is no Notion of Felicity, is in its own Nature Good.

SEeing that to live without Pain is sweet or pleasant, and to enjoy good things, and be recreated by them; it follows that Felicity cannot consist without both, or at least one of these; (by Pleasure, Suavity, Jucundity, and the like terms, I understand the same thing:) Yet some there are, who, with great flourishes, have so discoursed against Pleasure itself, as if it were something ill in its own Nature, and consequently not appertaining to Wisdom and Felicity.

Therefore, before we enquire whether Felicity really consists in Pleasure, we must shew, that Pleasure is in its own Nature good, as its contrary, Pain, is in its own Nature ill.

Certainly since that is good which delighteth, pleaseth, is amiable, and allures the Appetite; that, consequently, ill which harmeth, is unpleasant and therefore excites Hate and Aversion: That is nothing pleaseth more than Pleasure, deligteth more, is lov'd more, is desired more; as on the contrary, nothing incommodes more than Pain, displeaseth, is abhorred, and shunned.
So

So as Pleasure seems not only to be a good, but the very essence of good, it being that by which any thing is good or desirable: Pain not only an ill, but the very essence of ill, as being that by which any thing is ill or hateful.

For though we sometimes shun Pleasure, yet it is not the Pleasure itself which we shun, but some Pain annexed accidentally to it; as, if at any time we persue Pain, it is not the Pain itself that we persue, but some Pleasure accidentally joined to it.

For, (to express this more plainly,) no man slights, hates, or shuns Pleasure as Pleasure, but because great Pains overtake those who know not how to follow Pleasure with reason. Nor is there any who loves, persues, would incur Pain simply as Pain, but because sometimes it so happens, as that with Labour and Pain he must persue some great Pleasure.

For to instance in the least things; Who amongst us undertakes any laborious exercise of Body, unless that some Commodity arise by it? Who can justly blame him, who desires to be in that Pleasure which hath no Trouble? Or him, who shuns that Pain which procures no Pleasure? But we accuse and esteem those worthy of Contempt, who, blinded and corrupted with the blandishments of present Pleasures, foresee not the Troubles that must ensue. Alike faulty are they, who desert their Duties out of softness of Mind, that is, the avoidance of Labour and Pains.

Of these things, the Distinction is easie and ready. For at a free time, when our Election is at liberty, and nothing hinders, but that we may do what pleaseth us most, all Pleasure is to be embraced, all Pain to be expelled. But at some times it often falleth out, that Pleasures are to be rejected, and Troubles not to be declined.

Thus, although we esteem all Pleasures a good, and all Pain an ill, yet we affirm not, that we ought at all times to persue that, or to avoid this; but that we ought to have regard as to their quantity, so also to their quality; since it is better for us to undergo some Pains, that we may thereby enjoy the more abundant Pleasures; and it is expedient to abstain from some Pleasures, lest they prove the occasion of our incurring more grievous Pains.

Hereupon this was, as it were, the Fountain, from which, in treating of Criteries, we deduced several Canons concerning Affection or Passion, esteeming Pleasure or Pain the Criterie of Election and Avoidance. And not without reason, forasmuch as we ought to judge of all these things, by the commensuration and choice of things profiting or hurting, since we sometimes use a good as an ill; and, on the contrary, sometimes an ill as a good.

Hence therefore, to press this further, I say, that no Pleasure is ill in itself, but some things there are which procure some pleasures, but withal bring Pains far greater than the Pleasures themselves. Whereupon I add, that if every Pleasure might be so reduced within itself, as that it neither should comprise within it, nor leave behind it any Pain; every Pleasure, by this reduction, would be no less perfect and absolute than the principal works of Nature, and consequently there would be no difference amongst Pleasures, but all would be expetible alike.

Moreover, if those very things which afford Pleasure to luxurious Persons, could free them from the fear of Meteors, and of Death, and Pain, and could instruct them what are the bounds of desires, I could not find any fault, forasmuch as they would be every way replete with Pleasures, and have nothing grievous or painful that is ill.

CHAP. III.

That Felicity consists generally in Pleasure.

NOW to come to what was proposed, Felicity seems plainly to consist in Pleasure. This is first to be proved in general, then we must shew, in what Pleasure particularly it consists.

In general, Pleasure seems to be, as the Beginning, so the End also of Happy Life, since we find it to be the first good, and convenient to our, and to all animal, Nature; and is that from which we begin all election and avoidance, and in which at last we terminate them, using this affection as a Rule to judge every Good.

That Pleasure is the first and connatural good, or (as they term it,) the first thing suitable and convenient to Nature, appeareth; for that *every Animal, as soon as born, desireth pleasure, and rejoiceth in it, as the chief good*; *shunneth pain as its greatest ill, and to its utmost ability, repels it.* Cic. de fin. We see that * even *Hercules* himself, tormented * Laert. by a poisonous Shirt, could not with-hold from tears;

Crying and howling whil'st the *Locrian* Stones,
And high *Eubœan* Hills, retort his Groans.

Thus doth every undepraved Animal, its own Cic. ibid. *nature judging incorruptly and entirely.*

There needs not therefore any reasoning to prove, that Pleasure is to be desired, Pain to be shunned; for this is manifest to our Sense, as that Fire is hot, Snow white, Honey sweet. We need no Arguments ibid. *to prove this, it is enough that we give Notice of it. For since that if we take away from Man all his Senses, there is nothing remaining, it is necessary that what is convenient or contrary to Nature, be judged by Nature herself, and that Pleasure be expetible in itself, and Pain in itself to be avoided: For what perceives, or what judgeth, either to persue or avoid any thing, except Pleasure and Pain?*

That Pleasure, as being the first thing convenient to Nature, is also the last of Expetibles, or the end of good things, may be understood even from this, Because it is Pleasure only for whose sake we so desire the rest, that itself is not desired for the sake of any other, but only for itself; for we may desire other things to delight or please ourselves, but no man ever demanded a Reason, why we would be delighted and pleased? Certainly no more, than for what cause we desire to be happy; since Pleasure and Felicity ought to be reputed, not only in the same degree, but to be the very same thing, and, consequently, the end, or ultimate and greatest good, on which the rest depend, but itself depends on none.
This

This is further proved, for that *Felicity* is, as we hinted formerly, no otherwise, than becauſe it is that ſtate, in which we may live moſt ſweetly and moſt pleaſantly, that is, with the greateſt pleaſure that may be. For, take from life this ſweetneſs, jucundity, pleaſure; and where, I pray, will be your Notion of *Felicity*, not of that *Felicity* only which I termedDivine,but even of the other, eſteemed Human; which is no otherwiſe capable to receive degrees of more and leſs, or intenſion and remiſſion,than becauſe addition or detraction of pleaſure may befal it.

Cic. de fin.

To underſtand this better,by comparing Pleaſure with Pain, ‘ let us ſuppoſe a man enjoying ‘ many great inceſſant pleaſures, both in mind ‘ and body, no Pain hindring them, nor likely ‘ to diſturb them; What ſtate, can we ſay, is ‘ more excellent, or more deſirable than this? ‘ For in him who is thus affected, there muſt ne‘ceſſarily be a conſtancy of mind, fearing nei‘ther death nor pain, becauſe death is void of ‘ ſenſe; pain, if long, uſeth to be light; if ‘ great, ſhort, ſo as the ſhortneſs makes amends ‘ for its greatneſs, the lightneſs for its length. ‘ When he arrives at ſuch a condition, as he ‘ trembles not with horror of the Deity,nor ſuf‘fereth the preſent pleaſures to paſs away, ‘ whil'ſt his mind is buſied with the remembrance ‘ of paſt, or expectation of future, good things, ‘ but is daily joyed with the reflecting upon ‘ them? What can be added to better the con‘dition of this perſon?

‘ Suppoſe, on the other ſide, a man afflicted ‘ with as great pains of body, and griefs of mind, ‘ as man's nature is capable of, no hope that they ‘ ſhall ever be eaſed, no pleaſure paſt, preſent, ‘ or expected; What can be ſaid or imagined ‘ more miſerable than he?

‘ If therefore a life full of pains be of all ‘ things moſt to be avoided, doubtleſs the great‘eſt ill is to live in pain; whence it followeth, ‘ that the greateſt good is to live in pleaſure. ‘ Neither indeed hath our mind any thing elſe, ‘ wherein,as its Centre, it may reſt; all ſickneſſes ‘ and troubles are reduced to pain, nor is there ‘ any thing elſe which can remove Nature out ‘ of her place, or diſſolve her.

CHAP. IV.

That the Pleaſure, wherein conſiſts Felicity, is Indolence of Body, and Tranquillity of Mind.

THere being (as before is intimated,) two kinds of Pleaſures; one in ſtation or reſt, which is a placabiltity, calmneſs, and vacuity, or immunity from trouble and grief; the other in motion, which conſiſts in a ſweet movement, as in gladneſs, mirth, and whatſoever moveth the Senſe delightfully, with a kind of ſweetneſs and titillation, as to eat and drink out of hunger and thirſt: It may be demanded, Whether in both, or in either, and in which, conſiſt Felicity?

We ſay, that Pleaſure, wherein Felicity conſiſts, is of the firſt kind, the ſtable, or that which is in ſtation; and ſo can be no other than Indolence of Body, and Tranquillity of Mind.

When therefore we ſay in general terms,Pleaſure is the end of happy Life, we are far from meaning the pleaſures of luxurious perſons, or of others, as conſidered in the motion or act of fruition, by which the Senſe is pleaſantly and ſweetly affected; as ſome, either through ignorance, diſſent, or ill will, interpret, We mean no more but this, (to repeat it once more,) *Not pained in Body, nor troubled in Mind.*

For it is not perpetual Feaſting, and Drinking, not the Converſation of beautiful Women; not Rarities of Fiſh, nor any other Dainties of a profuſe Table, that make a happy Life; but Reaſon, with Sobriety,and a ſerene Mind,ſearching the cauſes,why this Object is to be preferr'd, that to be rejected; and expelling Opinions, which occaſion much trouble to the mind.

The better to underſtand why this Pleaſure only is the End, we may obſerve, that Nature tends to no other Pleaſure primarily, as to her end, but to the ſtable, which followeth upon removal of pain and trouble. The Moveable ſhe propoſes not as the end, but provides only as a means conducing to the ſtable, to ſweeten (as it were) that operation of hers which is requiſite to the extirpation of pain and trouble. For Example, Hunger and Thirſt being things troubleſom and incommodious to an Animal,the primary end of Nature is to conſtitute the Animal in ſuch a ſtate, as that it may be free from that trouble and inconvenience; and becauſe this cannot be done but by eating and drinking, ſhe therefore ſeaſons with a ſweet reliſh the action of eating and drinking, that the Animal may apply himſelf more readily thereto.

Moſt Men,indeed,live prepoſterouſly; tranſported inconſiderately and intemperately, they propoſe for their end the pleaſure which conſiſts in motion; But Wiſdom ſummon'd to our relief reduceth all pleaſures into decent order, and teacheth that pleaſure is to be propoſed as the end; but that which is the end according to Nature,is no other than that which we have ſpoken of. For while Nature is our Guide, whatſoever we do tends to this, that we neither be pained in Body, nor troubled in Mind; And as ſoon as we have attained this, all diſturbances of the Mind are quieted, and there is nothing beyond it,that we can aim at to compleat the good both of our Soul and Body. For we then want pleaſure when its abſence excites pain in us: But as long as we are not pained, we want not pleaſure.

Hence comes it,that a motion of pain, or the ſtate which follows upon that one word is the furtheſt bound or height of pleaſures; for,whereever pleaſure is, as long as it is there, there is nothing painful or grievous, or both together. Hence alſo it comes, that the higheſt pleaſure terminated in privation of pain may be varied and diſtinguiſhed, but not increaſed and amplified: For Nature,until ſhe hath quite taken away the pain,increaſeth the pleaſure; but when the pain is quite removed,ſhe permits not the pleaſure to increaſe in greatneſs, but only admits ſome Varieties which are not neceſſary, as not conducing to our not being pained.

Moreover, hence it apears, that they inſult without cauſe, who accuſe us, that we mean not by want of pain,ſome middle thing betwixt pain and

and pleasure, but so confound it with the other part (in the division,) as to make it not only a pleasure, but the very highest of pleasures. For, because when we are delivered out of Pain, we rejoice at that very freedom and exemption from all trouble, but every thing whereat we rejoice is pleasure, as every thing whereat we are offended, pain; the privation of all pain is rightly named pleasure. For, when hunger and thirst are expelled by eating and drinking, the very detraction of the trouble brings pleasure; so in every thing else, the removal of pain causeth succession of pleasure.

Hence also may be shewn the difference, when they object, that there is no reason why this Middle state should rather be esteemed a pleasure than a pain. For discontent ensues not immediately upon detraction of pleasure, unless some pain chance to succeed in the room of the pleasure: But on the contrary, we rejoice at the loss of pain, though none of those pleasures which move the sense succeed. By this we may understand, how great a pleasure it is, not to be pained; which if any doubt, let them ask those who are oppressed with sharp sicknesses.

Some laugh hereat; they object, that this pleasure is like the condition of one that sleeps, and accuse us of sloth, never considering that this constitution of ours is not mere stupidity, but rather a state wherein all actions of life are performed pleasantly and sweetly. For, as we should not have the life of a wise man to be like a torrent or rapid stream, so we would not it should be like a standing dead-pool: But rather like a river gliding on silently and quietly. We therefore hold his pleasure is not unactive, but that which reason makes firm to him.

But to omit these, and return to our Subject, there are two good things of which our chiefest Felicity consists; That the mind be free from trouble, the body from pain; and so as that these goods be so full, and all trouble taken away, that they admit not increase. For how can that increase, which is full? If the Body be free from all pain, what can be added to this indolence? If the mind from perturbation, what can be added to this tranquility? As the serenity of Heaven being refin'd to the sincerest splendor, admits no greater splendor; so the state of a man who takes care of his Body and Soul, and connects his good out of both, is perfect, and he hath attained the end of his desires, if his Body be neither subject to pain, nor his mind to disturbance. If any external blandishments happen, they increase not the chief good, but, as I may say, season and sweeten it; for that absolute good of human nature is contained in the peace of the Soul and the Body.

CHAP. V.

Of the means to procure this Felicity; and of Virtues, the chief.

Now seeing this peace of Body and mind, tranquility in one, indolency in the other, is the compleat felicity of man; nothing more concerns us than to consider what things will procure and preserve it; for when we have it, we want nothing, while we want it, all we do is to obtain it, and yet (as we said,) for the most part we fail of it.

First, therefore, we must consider of Felicity no otherwise than as of Health; it being manifest, that the state, in which the mind is free from perturbation, the Body from pain, is no other than the perfect health of the whole man. Whence it comes, that as in the Body, so in the Mind also, those things which produce and conserve health are the same with those which either prevent diseases, or cure and expel them.

Now seeing that to provide against the diseases of the Body belongs to the art of Medicine, as well for the prevention as cure of them, we shall not need to say much hereupon, but only give two cautions which may be sufficient.

One, that for the driving away all diseases, or at least making them lighter and easier to be cured, we use Temperance and a sober continent life.

The other, that when there is a necessity of our suffering them, we betake our selves to fortitude, and undergo them with a constant mind, not exasperating them by impatience, but comforting our selves with considering, that, if great, they must be short; if long, light.

Against the diseases of the Mind, Philosophy provides, when we justly esteem it the medicine of the mind: But it is not with equal facility consulted, nor applyed, by those who are sick in Mind. For we judge of the diseases of the Body by the Mind; but the diseases of the Mind, we neither feel in the Body, nor know or judge as we ought by the Mind, because that whereby we should judge is destempered. Whence we may understand, that the diseases of the Mind are more pernicious than those of the Body; as amongst those of the Body, the worst and most dangerous are such as make the patient insensible of them; as the Apoplexcy, or a violent Feaver.

Moreover, that the diseases of the Mind are worse than those of the Body, is evident from the same reason which demonstrates that the pleasures of the Mind are better than those of the Body; *viz.* because in the Body we feel nothing but what is present, but in the Mind we are sensible also of the past and future. For, as the anxiety of the Mind which ariseth from pain of the Body, may be highly aggravated, if we conceit, (for instance,) that some eternal and infinite Evil is ready to fall on us; so (to transfer the instance, (pleasure is the greater, if we fear no such thing; it being manifest, that the greatest pleasure or trouble of mind doth more conduce to a miserable or happy life, than either of the other two, though they should be equally lasting in the Body.

Now forasmuch as there are two principal diseases of the mind, *Desire*, and *Fear*, with their several off-springs, and accompany'd with discontent and trouble, in the same manner as pain is joyned to the diseases of the Body; it is therefore the office of Philosophy to apply such remedies as may prevent them from invading the Mind, or, if they have invaded it, expel them. Such briefly, are the vain desires of health, of honours, fear of the gods, of death, and the like, which having but once taken possession of the Mind they leave no part thereof sound.

The remedies which Philosophy applyeth, are the *Virtues*, which, being deriv'd from reason, or the more general prudence, easily drive away and expel the affections. I say, from Reason, or the more general prudence; because, as there is a more particular prudence, serving for the directions of all the particular actions of our life; so is there a more general prudence, which is no other than reason itself, or the dictate of reason, and is by most esteemed the same with wisdom; whereas, Virtue is only a perfect disposition of the mind, which reason or prudence doth create and oppose to the diseases of the Mind, the *Vices*.

CHAP. VI.

Of Right-reason, and Free-will, from which the Virtues have all their praise.

BEing therefore to proceed in our discourse to Virtue and its several kinds, we must premise something concerning Reason itself, and likewise concerning the Free-will which is in it; for thence is derived all the praise belonging to Virtue; as also its opposite, the reproach due to Vice.

Forasmuch as Reason generally is nothing but the faculty of ratiocinating, or judging and inferring one thing from another, we here take it particularly for that which judgeth, inferreth, and ratiocinates in things of action, subject to election or avoidance.

But whereas, judgment or reasoning may be either right or wrong, that reason, whose judgment is false, is not properly reason, and therefore we term it *opinion*; yet in respect it is the common phrase, you may call it also reason if you please, meaning *wrong reason*; as right reason may be termed *Opinion*, meaning *sound Opinion*.

Right reason ariseth either from ingenuity, or experience, and sedulous observation. Being grounded upon firm and correct principles, our ratiocination becomes solid; and justly do we appeal to the judgment of him, who is expert and knowing in things. But of this already in the Canonick part, concerning the Criteries, which need not repetition.

When, I say, things subject to election and avoidance; I take for granted that there is in us a free or arbitrary power or reason, that is, a faculty elective and protective of that which reason hath judged good, and of avoiding, and shunning what it hath judged ill.

That it really is in us, is proved even by experience, and by common sense, which manifests, that nothing is worthy of praise or dispraise, but what is done freely, voluntarily, deliberately, and by election; and therefore must depend on something within us which is beyond compulsion, and in respect whereunto, all rewards and punishments are rightly ordained by the Laws: Than which nothing were more unjust, if the actions of men were to be imputed to that rigid Necessity, which some assert, derived from Fate, as the sole commandress of all things, declaring, that whatsoever comes to pass floweth from an eternal truth, and continuation of causes.

Truly it is much better to be addicted to the fabulous (that is, the common,) opinion of the gods, than to be slaves to the belief of Fate, according as some Naturalists hold it, imposing it upon our necks as an everlasting Lord or Tyrant, whom we are to stand in awe of, night and day. For the other opinion hath some comfort in it, that the gods will be moved with our prayers; but this, imports an inexorable necessity.

True indeed it is, that, in things void of reason, some effects are necessary, (yet not so necessary, but that they might have been prevented, as we declared in the Canonick; and where we treated of causes,) but, in Man, endu'd with reason, and as far as he makes use of that reason, there can be no Necessity. Hence it was, we endeavoured to assert the declination of motions in Atoms, that we might from thence deduce, how Fortune might sometimes intervene, and put in for a share amongst human affairs, yet, that which is in us, our Will not be destroy'd.

It behoves us to employ all our wit and endeavours to maintain our own free-will against that sempiternal motion, and not to suffer wickedness to escape unculpable.

But what I say of fortune, implies not that we ascribe any divinity to it, not only as the vulgar, but even as those Philosophers, who esteeming her an unstable Cause, though they conceive not, that she bestows on men any thing of good or ill that may conduce to happy life, yet think that she gives occasion of very considerable goods and ills. We imply not this, I say, but only mean, that, as many things are affected by necessity and counsel, so also by Fortune; and therefore, it is the duty of a wise man to arm himself against Fortune.

Now seeing, whatever good or ill there is in human actions, depends only upon this, that a man doth it knowingly, and willingly, or freely; therefore the mind must be accustomed to know truly, that is, to use right reason; and to will truly, that is, to bend the free will to that which is truly good, from that which is truly ill. Forasmuch, as this accustoming begets that disposition in the mind, which we described to be Virtue; as the accustoming of it to the contrary, begets that disposition which we may justly define Vice.

Not to mention, that what produceth pleasure, sincere without any pain, trouble or repentance attending or ensuing thereupon, is truly good; that which produceth pain, sincere without any pleasure, or joy succeeding upon it, is truly ill; I only give this hint of both to distinguish each of them from what is only apparent and dissembled: Such as that good which begets present pleasure, and afterwards introduceth pain and trouble; and that ill which procures pain or trouble, but afterwards pleasure and cheerfulness.

CHAP.

CHAP. VII.

Of the Virtues in General.

FOrasmuch as all *Virtue* is either *Prudence*, or the Dictate of *Right Reason*, as we accustom ourselves to it, or is directed by, and dependent on Prudence, and the Dictate of Right Reason; it is manifest, that to this later kind belongs, as well, that whereby a man is affected toward himself, as that, whereby he is affected towards another: For by Prudence, a Man is made capable to govern not only himself, but others.

The Virtue which relates to others, is generally called *Justice*; that which concerns ourself, is ordinarily distinguished into *Temperance*, and *Fortitude*. But we use to comprize both under the term *Honesty*, as when we say, to act Virtuously, is no other than to act Prudently, Honestly, Justly; they who live Soberly and Continently, are said to live Honestly or Decently; they who do Valiantly, are thought to behave themselves Honestly or Decently.

Hereupon we (as others,) distinguish Virtue into four kinds. *Prudence Temperance, Fortitude,* and *Justice*; but so, as that we oppose not *Prudence* to any affection so much as to *Incogitance Ignorance, Folly,* (except by accident, inasmuch as perturbation blinds Reason, and causeth a Man to act imprudently;) nor *Justice*, to any affection in so much as to *Malice*, whereby a Man is prone to Deceits, (unless by accident, in as much as anger, hatred, covetousness, or some other passion may cause a Man to do unjustly; (*Temperance*, we oppose to *Desire*; *Fortitude*, to *Fear*.

Hence is manifest, when I formerly said, A sober or well ordered Reason procures a pleasant or happy Life; we are to understand, that it procures it by means of the Virtues which it ingenerates and preserves. And whereas I added, that it searched out the Causes, why things are to be embraced or avoided, and chaseth away Opinions which occasion great trouble in the mind, we are to understand that is all one with general prudence, the principle of all things expetible and avoidable, and consequently the greatest, because the Virtues which arise from it appease Perturbations, teaching, that we cannot live pleasantly, unless prudently, honestly, and justly; not prudently, honestly, and justly, unless pleasantly.

By this you find why I conceive, that the Virtues are connatural to a happy life, and that it is impossible to separate happy life from them. All other things, as being frail and mortal, are transitory, separable from true and constant pleasure; only Virtue, as being a perpetual and immortal good, is inseparable from it.

By this also you may understand, that all the Virtues are connected within one another, and that by one; because to the principal Prudence, all the rest are conjoined, as the Members to the Head, or as Rivers to the Spring from which they flow; the other, because as well Prudence, as all the rest cohere with happy life, there cannot be a happy life where the Virtues are not; neither can the Virtues be there, where the life is not happy.

Notwithstanding that the Virtues are all connected within one another, yet are they not therefore all equal, as some conceive, who hold that all Vices and Faults are also equal. For a man may be more inclin'd to Justice, than to Temperance; and Temperance may be more perfect in one, than in another. As for instance, (without Envy be it spoken,) myself by length of time, have made so great a progress in Sobriety, as less than an *Obolus* serves me for a meal; *Metrodorus*, who hath not yet made so great progress, a whole *Obolus*. And it is evident, that, of men, one is wiser than another; and of them, who do rightly according to Virtue, equal Rewards are not allotted to all, as neither equal Punishments to all Offenders. Even Sence and Manners confute them, who make all equal, and hold that they offend alike, he who beats his Servant wrongfully, and he who his Parent; seeing, some there are who make no difference betwixt eating a Bean, and the head of our Father.

Others condemn, and exclaim on us, for affirming, that the Virtues are of such a nature, as that they conduce to Pleasure or Felicity, as if we meant that Pleasure which is obscene and infamous, but let them rail as they please. For as they make Virtue the chief good, so do we: If the discourse be of the means conducing to happy life, neither is there any of so great power as *Virtue*, therefore not more excellent, (not Wealth, not Honour, not Friends, not Children, *&c.*) But if the discourse be of living happily, or Felicity, why should not this be a good superior to Virtue, to the attainment whereof Virtue itself is but subservient?

They exclaim again, that we enervate Virtue, in not allowing her so much power, as to render a wise man free from all passion or affection, but to permit him to be moved therewith, (as for instance) to grieve, weep, and sigh at the death of Friends: But as we set a high value upon Virtue, as being able to deliver us from vain terrors and superfluous desires, the chief heads of all greivous Perturbations; so likewise not a little esteem it, for that it reduceth the rest of the affections to such a mediocrity, in which there remains some sense as it were of humanity.

Certainly, that total exemption from Grief, which these men boast of, proceeds from some greater ill, cruelty, and immoderate ambition of vain-glory, and a kind of madness. So that it seems much better to feel some passion, to be affected with some grief, to shed some tears, such as proceed from persons touched with love and tenderness, than to be wise as these would have us, and grin like brute Beasts.

CHAP. VIII.

Of Prudence *in general.*

WE must now say somthing of every Virtue in particular, beginning with *Prudence*, whose office being to govern the life, and so to provide for every occurrent in life, as to direct it to happiness, it seems alone to comprize the offices of all Virtues.

That the propriety of Prudence, is to dispose all accidents and actions of life to felicity, or pleasure, is most manifest. As we value Medicine, not for the Science it-self, but for Health; and the Art of steering, not for its Ingenuity, but use in Navigation; so Prudence, the Art of living, would never be desired, if it were nothing efficacious in life; but being so, it is desired, as the Art, by which Pleasure is sought and obtained.

For Prudence, or (if you like the word better) Wisdom, alone it is, which not only provides that nothing happen which may afflict the Body, but likewise above all, expels sadness from the mind, not permitting us to be daunted with fear; Under which Governess we may live in tranquility, extinguishing the ardor of all desires. For desires are insatiable, they subvert not only single Persons, but Families, many times a whole Commonwealth. From Desires arise Hatreds, Dissentions, Discords, Seditions, Wars; neither do these only revel abroad, or with blind fury assault others only, but likewise, shut up in the breast, they disagree and quarrel with one another, which must necessarily make life exceeding bitter. Only the prudent and wise person, cutting off all vanity and error, content with the limits of nature, can live without discontent, and without fear.

Now seeing Life is disturbed by error and ignorance, and that it is Prudence alone which rescues us from the violence of Lusts and Fears, teacheth us temperately to sustain the injuries of Fortune, and sheweth us all the ways that lead to quiet and tranquillity, Why should we stick to affirm, that Prudence is expetible in order to pleasure, and Imprudence to be shunned for trouble's sake?

That we say, a Prudent Person temperately sustains the injuries of Fortune, the reason is, that he foresees them, if not in particular, at least in the general; Neither, if any thing happen contrary to his expectations or designs, is he troubled, for that he knoweth it not to be within the reach of human industry, sagacity, or power, either to foresee, or to prevent, that nothing adverse or troublesome happen. He judgeth it better to be, with well ordered reason (as far as human frailty will admit,) unfortunate, than with inconsideration fortunate; and thinks nothing more handsome, than if Fortune bring about a thing fairly and prosperously, that was not undertaken without judgment and deliberation.

But indeed, a wise man orders so himself, that cutting off vain desires, he contracts himself within necessaries, which are so few and small, as hardly any Fortune can snatch them from him. Thus, since none, or very little fortune can intervene to a wise man, he may say to her, I have seized on thee, (Fortune,) and intercepted thee, so as thou canst not come at me.

Concerning the cutting off all Desires, we shall speak hereafter. Now forasmuch as prudence may be considered, either as it governs ourselves, or a House, or a Family, or a City, or a Commonwealth, and so is distinguished into Private, Domestick, Civil, let us say something upon each.

CHAP. IX.

Private Prudence.

PRivate Prudence consisteth almost wholly in this, that a man understand his own *Genius*, and undertake nothing whereto his nature is averse, that he deliberately pre-examin the state in which he is to spend his whole life, and to which he must so accommodate all the actions of life, as that, as much as possible, he may live in indolence and tranquility.

For he ought to have the end or scope of life fixt, and constantly set before his eyes, and consult with right reason, according to all evidence, whereby we use to weigh whatsoever we think or determine. For unless this be done, all will be full of indiscreet temerity and confusion, and our designs and enterprizes will be overtaken by too late repentance.

Besides, if upon every emergent occasion, you refer not each of your actions both to this kind of scope, and to that end of nature which you proposed to yourself in designing it, but turn aside to pursue or flie some other thing, the actions of you life will not correspond to your own words. For example, you extol tranquility in words, but in actions discover yourself busie and obnoxious to trouble.

He understands the bounds prescribed by Nature, to those who enter the course of life, who knows how easily procurable that is which is necessary to life, or what is sufficient to remove any thing that afflicts the body with indigence. Thereby he knows so well to order the whole series of life, as never to need such things or business as are contentious, and consequently full of hazard and danger.

Hence it is, that a wise man is not much afraid of poverty, it hapning seldom, that any man wants the things necessary to life. Yet if those should chance to be wanting, and he not have money to procure them, he will not betake himself to beg, as the *Cynick*, but rather apply himself to instruct some persons in learning: thus taking an employment not misbecoming Wisdom, and at the same time supplying himself with necessaries from those who have full estates.

Whilst we are obliged to this or the like employment; 'If necessaries fail us, and our bu- *Porp. de non* 'siness be, to entertain daily occurrences with a *esu carn.* 'settled courage, we must have recourse to Wis-'dom or Philosophy for relief. To an ill Coun-'sellor we resign the ordering of the things that 'concern us, if, what is necessary to nature, we 'measure and provide without Philosophy.

'It therefore imports a Philosopher to be-'stow time in looking after these things, until 'by diligent care he hath furnished himself with 'them. But as long as he hath so much of these, 'as that he can spend of them, yet retain per-'fect confidence, he is not to apply himself to 'acquisition of wealth and provisions.

'Thus is Philosophy to be our Guide in these 'things, by which we shall soon perceive, what 'a Vertue, and how great a Good it is, to require 'only what is simple, light, and very small; be-'cause what is most sweet and free from trou-'ble in all a man's life, depends upon our being
'con-

'contented with the least. But, by those impe-
'diments which a sollicitous acquisition of things
'draws upon us, being quickly discover'd, either
'by the pains and toil of the Body, or by the
'difficulty of their procurement, or by their
'drawing the mind away from the most advan-
'tageous speculations, (which we ought ever-
'more highly to esteem,)or by some other cause;
'we shall clearly find, that it is altogether fruit-
'less, and not of countervalue with the troubles
'which follow it.

I advised, that every man should examine his own genius, and advise with himself, that he may apply himself to that which is proper for him, because otherwise, nothing can be more miserable, and more at a distance with tranquility, than to be engaged in a course of life, for which nature hath rendred thee unfit.

For neither is an active life to be undertaken by an unactive person, nor an unactive life by an active person. To one, rest is quiet, and action labour; to the other, rest is labour, and actions quiet. A timerous and soft person must avoid the military life; a bold and impatient, the easie; for one cannot brook War, nor the other Peace. The same it is in all the rest. So that nothing can be more safe, than to undertake that course only which thou canst run through, without any reluctance or repugnance of nature.

I shall only add this, That every man, as far as lies in his power, to the end the state of life which he chooseth may be the more secure and quiet, ought to choose it mean, neither very eminent, nor very abject. For it behoves him to live in a Civil society, neither as a Lion, nor as a Gnat, lest, resembling the one, he be cast out; the other, caught in a snare.

CHAP. X.

Domestick Prudence.

Domestick Prudence being either conjugal and paternal, or dominative and possessory; we shall, in the first, only consider that which ariseth from what hath been said, concerning the Institution of life.

If you find, that you cannot, without much trouble, live single; that you can patiently bear with a cross wife, and disobedient children; that you will not so much as vex, to behold your children crying before you; that you shall not be perplexed and distracted with various sollicitudes, how to provide all things requisite to a married life, how to prevent all inconveniences, and the like: In this case, to marry a wife, and to beget children, for whom you may provide with a conjugal and fatherly prudence, is lawful. But unless you know yourself to be such, you see, by Marriage and Issue, how much you hinder the happiness of your life, True tranquility.

Presume you may, of having a loving wife, dutiful children, cares neither great nor many; but you can only presume it, there is not any God will warrant the success of your presumption. Since therefore the case is hazardous, it is no wisdom voluntarily to undergo the venture, and throw yourself into a condition, out of which, should you afterwards repent, you can never retire.

I say, voluntarily; for some circumstance of life may exact, that, though unwilling, you marry and beget children; as if your condition be such, as that it requires you to serve your Country herein. For whereas some pretend propagation of the species, to which we are in a manner oblig'd, certainly there is no danger, that there should be wanting such as will marry and procreate; so that some few wise men may be allowed to abstain from this employment.

But if some case, or certain counsel, or necessity, enforce you to marry, you must so dispose your wife, as that she may be loving to you, and a partner in your cares. You must take such care for your children, as is partly prescribed by Nature, which instigates us to love them as soon as born, (common also to sheep, wolves, and other living creatures;) partly by prudence, which adviseth so to bring them up, as they may be obedient to the Laws of their Country, and desirous themselves may become wise.

Neither is this care to be taken for our own children only, but likewise for the children of our friends, especially if they are our Pupils, there being nothing more beseeming friendship, than to be a Guardian in the room of a parent to those, whom our deceased friend entirely loved, and hath left Orphans needing protection.

For the other kind, as having slaves and servants under us, (a possession, though necessary, yet for the most part not very pleasant,) a wise man must take order, they grow not insolent and froward, that he may behave himself mildly (as far as is fitting,) towards them, and chastise the disobedient, remembring they are men, with a kind of unwillingness, being ever ready to forgive, especially if they are diligent, not of an ill disposition. And not only this, but if he find any inclined to learning, (such as we had, particularly *Mus*,) let him delight to further them, call them Friends, and study Philosophy with them.

As to his Estate, he must take care of it, and provide for the future, but so, as without covetousness, and the desire of growing rich, of which hereafter. A wise man must not neglect his estate, because it is his livelihood; lest, if that be consumed, and he want the necessaries of life, his study of Philosophy be hindred, whilst he either gains by labour what might with little or no pains have been preserved; or begs, and by importunity extorts from another, what every one with little endeavour might provide for himself; or, gowing old, fall sick, and die in want, which not a little hinders the tranquility of the mind.

Besides the things necessary to the uses of life, there may be others, which, according to the condition of the person, place, time, must be esteemed necessary, and therefore not to be neglected. But our chiefest care must be for things requisite, to the prevention of natural indigence, without which, nature herself would suffer; such is the provision of corn. Those who store their houses with corn, are to be commended above those, who adorn them with rich furniture. I rejoyce exceedingly, that lately in a strict Siege, when many perished in our City by Famine, we were able to sustain so many good friends with

food

food (no delicacies, but a provident quantity of Beans,) which we destributed daily to every one by tale.

CHAP. XI.

Civil Prudence.

Lastly, as to Civil prudence we must likewise repeat what we insinuated concerning the choice of a course of life.

They who are naturally ambitious, desirous of honour, active withal, and fit to manage publick affairs; as also they, whom the quality of their birth, or fortune, and opportunity invite by an easie accession to publick government; those men may decline quiet, and comply with their own nature, by addicting themselves to publick government, and an active life. For their disposition is such, that a quiet life gives them trouble and molestation, whilst they obtain not what they desire.

But they, who either are naturally inclined to quiet, or have suppress'd ambition and vanity by the power of reason; or, having made tryal hereof, have escaped, as out of a storm, or took warning by many eminent precedents; these will justly conceive, that quiet is much the best for them, and that it is not convenient to exchange it for an active life, unless by chance some accident intervene in the Common wealth, requiring their industry. Whence we conclude, that a wise man must not involve himself in publick affairs, unless upon some intervening necessity.

What else? Since he in pursuing quiet, may far more easily and safely attain to that end, which the ambitious aim at by dangers and by labours.

For to speak of their scope, there never wanted some, who, to procure security of men, (according to the condition of Soveraignty and Rule, by which they commonly think it gained,) have affected to excel in honour, and to become illustrious, thinking that by this means to attain a secure and quiet estate. But if their life be secure and quiet, they have acquired the chief good of nature; if not secure and quiet, (as indeed it can hardly be,) then have they lost it, because they sought that which is convenient to nature in Dominion.

But the wise mans scope being the same, security and tranquility of life, by how much nearer a way doth he arrive at that end, when flying the troubles of civil life, he directly and immediately settles himself in a most profound quiet, as in a still calm Haven? Happy indeed, who knows, The chief good and a blessed life consists not in Soveraignty or power, not in numerous wealth or plenty, but in indolence, composure of affection, and such a disposition of mind, as, circumscribing all things by the boundaries of nature, makes him, in being content with little, obtain that which they, who rule over many, and possess great Treasures, despair ever to arrive at.

Truly, if it be fit to speak of my self, I esteem it a great happiness that I was never engaged in the factions of our City, and never studied to flatter and please the people. To what end should I? when as, what I know, the people approve not; what the people approve, I know not. That *Metrodorus* and I lived private, How far was it from doing us harm, when among the large goods enjoyed in narrow gardens, and in obscure *Melite*, *Greece* was so far from knowing us, that she had scarce ever heard of us.

I said, unless something intervene as to the Common-wealth: Because, if the Commonwealth should summon and really need our assistance, we should be inhuman, where we might benefit many, not to do it: Injurious also to ourselves; for unless the Common wealth be safe, we cannot be what we most desire, quiet.

A wise man therefore doth not like some, who, professing wisdom, have, through excessive pride so great an opinion of their own judgment in civil government, that they think they could equalize *Lycurgus* and *Solon*.

But if he be desired to make Laws, and to prescribe a form of government, and the offices of Magistrates, he will not refuse it; knowing that they, who first made laws and ordinances and constituted Government and Magistracy in Cities, setled life in a secure and quiet condition: For if that be taken away, we shall live like Beasts, and every man devour the next he meets with.

And if he be called to the supeam power to govern the Common wealth according to the laws and form of Government already established, he shall not refuse; knowing that though the thing itself is for the most part full of hazard, yet a wise man may have such regard to all things, and such a provident care of all, as that little of fortune, as I said before, shall intervene to him; but the greatest things, and such as are of most concernment be managed by his advice and conduct. He will first take care, that the weaker sort of men, discharging their duty towards the more powerful, be neither oppressed by them, nor permitted to want those necessaries of life wherewith the others abound; it being the end of every Society and Common wealth, that by mutual assistance the lives of all be safe, and as happy as is possible.

Lastly, if he be summoned by his Prince, and some occasion require, that he serve him either with his advice or help, neither shall he refuse this, knowing that as it is, not only more honourable, but more pleasant to give than to receive a benefit: It is as the most honourable, so the most pleasant thing to oblige a Prince who confers so many obligations on others. Hitherto of Prudence.

CHAP. XII.

Of Temperance in general.

Next follows Temperance, the first part, as we said, of honesty, and which seems to contain the greatest share of what is honest and decent. For it being the office of Temperance to suppress the mind when it desires, as of Fortitude to exalt it when it fears; it is esteemed less undecent to be dejected by pusillanimity, than exalted by desire; and therefore to resist desire, is more decent than to oppose fear.

Concerning Temperance, we must first observe, that it is desired not for its own sake, but for that it procureth pleasure, that is, brings peace to the minds of men, pleasing and soothing them with a kind of concord. For it being employed in moderating desires, and consequently in advising that in things to be pursued or avoided we follow reason, it is not enough that we judge what is to be done or not to be done, but we must fix upon that which is judged.

But most men, not able to hold and keep to what they have resolved on, being vanquish'd and debilitated by the appearance of a present pleasure, resign themselves to the fetters of Lust, not foreseeing what will follow; and hereupon for a small unnecessary pleasure, which might otherwise have been procured, or wholly wanted without incurring pain, they fall into great sicknesses, losses, and infamy, and many times into the penalties of Law.

But they who so enjoy pleasures as that no pain shall ensue, and who preserve their judgment constant, nor are overcome by pleasure, to the doing of what they know ought not to be done; these men obtain the greatest pleasure, by pretermitting pleasure: They also many times suffer some pain to prevent falling into greater.

Hence is it understood, that Temperance is to be desired, not for that it avoids some pleasures, but because he who refrains from them declines troubles; which being avoided, he obtains greater pleasures. Which it so doth, as that the action becomes honest and decent, and we may clearly understand, that the same men may be Lovers both of pleasure and of decency, and that such as esteem and practise all virtues, perform for the most part those actions, and attain those ends, as that by them it is manifest, how odious to all men cruelty is, and how amiable, goodness and clemency; and that those very things which ill men most desire and aim at, happen also to the good.

Now forasmuch as of the desires about which Temperance is employ'd, some are natural, others vain; and of the natural, some necessary, others not necessary, (to omit, that, of the necessary) some pertain simply to life, as that of meat and drink, and the pleasure which consists in motion; others to felicity itself, (as that of indolence and tranquility or stable pleasure:) It is manifest, that not without good cause we in our Physiology distinguished desires into three kinds, some both natural and necessary; others natural but not necessary; others neither natural nor necessary, but vain, or arising from vain opinion.

And forasmuch as we said, that those are natural and necessary, which unless they be satisfied, cause damage and pain in the Body; it is evident, that those which infer no damage nor pain, though not satisfi'd, yet are accompanied with earnest and vehement instigations, are such not by necessity, but vain opinions, and though they have some beginning from nature, yet their diffusion and excess they have not from nature, but from the vanity of opinions, which render men worse than beasts, that are not obnoxious to such diffusion or excess. Likewise, that such desires are not only not necessary, but not natural may be proved, for that they have a diffluent excessive appetition, very hardly or never to be satisfi'd; and are, for the most part, justly esteemed causes of harm.

But to discourse of some chief kinds of Temperance, according to some chief kinds of desires, we may make choice of Sobriety opposed to Gluttony, or the excessive desire of meat and drink; Continence, to Lust, or the unbridled desire of coition; Mildness, to Anger or desire of Revenge; Modesty, to ambition or desire of honour; Moderation, to Avarice or desire of riches; and lastly, in respect of the affinity betwixt desire and hope, Mediocrity, which consists betwixt hope and desperation of the future.

CHAP. XIII.

Of Sobriety opposite to Gluttony.

IT can hardly be expressed, how great a good Sobriety is, which reduceth us to a thin simple and spare dyet, teaching us how little that is which Nature requires, and clearly shewing, that the necessities she lies under may be abundantly satisfi'd with things light, and easily provided, as Barly-cakes, Fruits, Herbs, and Water.

For these things being every where to be had, and having the simple nature of moist and dry, moist aliments sufficiently remove the trouble of the Body arising from want of sustenance. Whatever is more than this amounts to Luxury, and concerns only the satisfaction of a desire, which neither is necessary, nor occasion'd by any thing, the want whereof doth necessarily infer any offence to nature, but partly for that the want of somewhat is born with impatience; partly, for that there is presumption of an absolute delight without mixture of any trouble; partly, (to speak in short,) for that there are vain and false opinions inherent in the mind, which serve neither for the supplying of any natural defect, nor tend to the acquisition of any thing, by the want of which, the frame of the Body would be dissolved. Porph. de non esu carn.

Those very things which are ready at hand, abundantly suffice to supply all nature's wants, and they are such as partly for their simplicity, partly for their slightness, are easily made ready. He, for example, who feeds on flesh, needs other things inanimate to eat with it; whereas he, who is content with inanimate, needs but half so much as the other, and sustains himself with what is easily got, and cheaply dress'd.

There are four benefits arising from Sobriety; Laërt. the first, that to accustome ourselves to a simple diet *brings and preserves health*: For it is sumptuous feasting and variety of meats, which begets, exasperates, and continues crudities, head-aches, rheums, gouts, feavers, and other diseases; not plain and simple food, which nature makes both necessary and wholsome, and not only to other Animals but even to man himself, who yet depraves

praves them by his exuberancy, and corrupts them by such delicates, as which while he affects he affects only his own destruction.

Porph. loc. cit.

Therefore if we are wise, *let us beware of that meat which we much desire and long for, but assoon as we have had it, find it was pleasant to us only to our harm.* Such are all costly and luscious meats; whence the eating flesh is less to be approved, as being rather prejudicial to health than wholsome, as may be argued, because * *health is preserved by the same means whereby it is recovered; but it is manifest that it is recovered by a thin dyet and abstinence from flesh.*

Porph. loc. cit.

Neither is it any wonder, that the ordinary sort of men conceive the eating of flesh to conduce much to health; for, they in like manner think, that the way to preserve health is to wallow in pleasures, even the Venereal; whereof nevertheless there is none benefits any man, and it is well if it hurt not.

Porph.

The second is, that *it makes a man ready and quick in the offices necessary to life.* For if you look upon the functions of the mind, it preserves her serenity, acuteness, vigour; if upon the functions of the Body, it keeps it sound, active, and hardy. But repletion, over-satiety, surfeiting and drunkenness cloud the mind, make it blunt and languid; the Body diseased, unactive, and burdensome. What, I pray, can you expect extraordinary from that man, whose limbs are unweildy, his knees feeble, his tongue faltring, his head swimming, his eyes full of rheum, his mouth of the hic-up, brawling, and clamour; and all this, through excess of Wine.

Laert.

Certainly, a wise man, who ought to content himself with a *hemina* of small Wine, or to esteem the next water he comes at to be the most pleasant of all drinks, will be far from spending the night in drunkenness; and as far from stuffing himself with meats that are high, or burthening his stomach with such as are luscious and gross, who ought to be content with the most simple, even the very free, gifts of Nature.

' Indeed such simple and slender dyet will not
' make a man as strong as *Milo*, nor conduceth
' absolutely to an intense corrobation of the
' Body; but neither doth a wise man need such
' intense strength, seeing his employment con-
' sists in contemplation, not in an active and
' petulant kind of life.

The third benefit is, that 'if somtimes the
' Table happen to be more plenteously furnish'd,
' we shall come much better prepared to taste
' what it yeilds. Not but that homely fare affords as much delight as sumptuous feasts; when hunger, which, in want of food, troubleth us, is satisfied, (for Barley-cakes and water are highly pleasant, if taken only when we hunger and thrift;) but because they who are daily accustomed to more costly viands are not so sensible of their sweetness, by reason of their being almost continually cloyed with them; as a wise man is, who the better to relish them brings along with him a taste prepared by mean dyet: In like manner it comes to pass, that he, if at any time he chance to be present at publick spectacles, is taken with them more sensibly than are others.

What I affirm concerning the coursest meat and drink, that it affords no less pleasure than the greatest delicates, cannot be deny'd by any but by him who deceiveth himself with vain opinions; who observes not, that they only enjoy magnificence with greatest pleasure, who least need it; who never hath tasted course bread and water, pressed with hunger and thirst. For my own part, when I eat course bread and drink water, or sometimes augment my Commons with a little *Cytheridian-Cheese*, (when I have a mind to feast extraordinarily,) I take great delight in it, and bid defiance to those pleasures which accompany the usual magnificence of feasts; so that if I have but bread, or barley-cakes and water, I am furnish'd to contend even with *Jove* himself in point of Felicity.

Shall I add, that ' magnificence of feasts, and
' variety of dishes not only not free the Mind
' from perturbation, but not so much as augment the pleasure of the Body, forasmuch as
' this also, when that trouble is removed, hath
' found its end ? For example, the eating of
' flesh (which we lately instanc'd,) neither takes
' away any thing particularly that is a trouble
' to nature, nor performs any thing which would
' occasion trouble, if not fulfilled. But it hath
' a forc'd delight, and perhaps mingled with
' that which is contrary to these, for it conduceth little to long life, and serveth only to
' variation of pleasures, like Venereal pleasures,
' and the drinking of foreign Wines, without
' which nature or life may well subsist: For
' those things, without which it cannot subsist,
' are most compendious, and may be obtained
' easily without breach of Justice, Liberality and
' Tranquility.

' Neither is it any matter, whether the ordinary sort of men be of this belief or not; since
' petulancy and intemperance abound in such
' persons, so that we need not fear, but there
' will be those who will feed on flesh. For though
' all men had the best and right judgment of
' things, yet would there be no need of Fowling
' or Fowlers, or Fishers, or Swine-herds; these
' Animals, living by themselves, free and without a keeper, would in a short time be destroy'd by others preying upon them, and suppressing the vastness of their increase, as happens to infinite others which men eat not. But
' since there reigneth always a multiplicious, or
' rather universal, folly amongst men, there will
' never be wanting an innumerable company of
' gluttons to feed on these.

Lastly, the fourth benefit is, that 'it renders
' us fearless of Fortune. For they only must stand in awe of Fortune, who being accustom'd to live sumptuously, conceive their lives cannot be otherwise than most miserable, unless they are able to spend Pounds, and Talents every day. Whence it happens, that such men are for the most part subject to a troublesome life, and often commit Rapines, Murthers, and the like villaines. But he, who is content with course food, as fruits and sallads, who is satisfy'd with bread and water; who hath confin'd his desire within these, what can he fear from Fortune ? For, who is there so poor as to want these ? Who so distress'd, that he cannot easily meet with beans, pulse, herbs, fruits ? As for water, what need I mention it ?

For

For my own part, truly (that I may with modesty instance my self) I am content, and highly pleas'd with the Plants and Fruits of my own little Gardens; and will, that this Inscription be set over the Gate, *Stranger, here you may stay; here the Supreme Good is Pleasure; the Master of this little house is hospitable, friendly, and will entertain you with polenta, and afford you water plentifully, and will ask you, How you like your entertainment? These little Gardens invite not hunger, but satisfie it; nor encrease thirst with drinks, but extinguish it with the natural and pleasant remedy.*

In this pleasure I have grown old, finding by account, that my diet amounts not fully to an *obolus* a day, and yet some days there are, in which I abate somwhat even of that, to make trial, whether I want any thing of full and perfect pleasure, or how much, and whether it be worth great labour.

CHAP. XIV.

Of Continence, opposite to Lust.

Moreover, Continence or Abstinence from Venereal Pleasures is a great Virtue; for the use of them, as I said formerly, doth never benefit, and it is well if it hurts not.

Certainly, to abuse them intemperately, is to make a man destitute of vigor, anxious with cares, painful with diseases, and of short continuance. Wherefore a wise man must stand upon his guard, and not suffer himself to be caught with love, far from conceiving love to be somthing sent from the Gods above, and therefore to be cherished.

And that a man may be least subject thereto and want the chief excitements to venereal delights, nothing more avils than spare diet, of which we lately treated: for excess in eating, causeth abundance of that humor, which is the food and fuel of love's fire. The next antidotes are, an honest employment, (especially the study of wisdom,) and meditation upon the inconveniences to which they, who suffer themselves to be transported with love, are liable.

The general incoveniences which attend love of Women and Boys, are consumption of strength, decay of industry, ruin of estate, mortgages and forfeitures, loss of reputation. And while the feet wear *Sicyonian* buskins, the fingers Emeralds, the body other ornaments, the mind, in the mean time, conscious to it self, is full of remorse, for that she lives idly, and suffers good years to be lost, and the like, which it were easie to instance.

But as to Particulars, What ill doth it not draw upon a Man to desire the company of a Woman prohibited to him by the Laws? Doubtless, a wise Man will be very far from thinking of such a thing; it being enough to deter him from it, to reflect upon the vast solicitude, which is necessary to precaution, of those many and great dangers which intervene; it hapning, for the most part, that they who attempt such things are wounded, murthered, imprison'd, banish'd, or suffer some great punishments. Whence it comes, that (as we said before) for a pleasure, which is but short, little, and not necessary, and which might either have been obtained otherwise, or quite let alone, men expose themselves to great pain, and sad repentance.

Besides, to be incontinent, to resign up our selves to this one kind of pleasure, were to defraud our selves in the mean time of other pleasures, many and great; which he enjoys, who lives, continently according to the Laws. He so applies himself to wisdom, as that he neither blunts his mind, nor excruciats it with cares, nor disturbs it with other affections; and for his body, he neither enervates it, nor vexeth it with diseases, nor torments it with pains. And thus he attains the chief good, which (as I said,) is not gotten by keeping company with Boys or Women, not having a Table plenteously furnished with choice of Fish or Fowl.

Yet there is no reason, any one, from this commendation of general abstinence from venereal delights, should infer, that therefore a man ought to abstain even from lawful marriage. What our judgment is of that Particular, we have formerly declared. I shall only add, that whereas I said, Love is not sent from the gods, it gives us to understand, that if a man hath no Children by his wife, he must not attribute it to the anger of *Cupid* or *Venus*, or hope to become a Father by Vows, Prayers, and Sacrifices, rather than by natural Remedies.

I shall add, that a wise man ought not to live after the manner of the *Cynicks*, or to behave himself with such immodesty as they shew in publick. For whilst they plead they follow Nature, and reprehend and deride us, for esteeming it obscene and dishonest to call things which are not dishonest by their names, but things which are indeed dishonest we call by their proper Names; as to rob, to cozen, to commit adultery, are dishonest indeed, but not obscene in name; whereas to perform the act of generation, is honest in deed, but obscene in name, and alledge divers other arguments against modesty: they seem not sufficiently to consider, that they live in a civil Society, not in the Fields, like wild Beast, and therefore ought not to follow Nature exactly.

For, from the time that we enroll'd our names in a Society, Nature commands, that we observe the Laws and Customs of that Society; to the end, that participating of the common goods, we draw no evil upon our selves: such as is (besides all other punishments,) the very infamy or ignominy which attends Impudence, or the want of such Modesty as is prescribed by the customs and manners of the Society wherein we live, and from which, in the Voice, the Countenance, and Behaviour, that modest Respect, which is deservedly commneded by all, is denominated.

Lastly, I add, that it not a little conduceth as to Modesty in particular, so to all kinds of Continency, to abstain from Musick and Poetry, for that their pleasing Songs and Airs are no other than Incentives to Lust.

Hence is our Maxim, That a wise Man only can treat of Musick and Poetry aright, and according to virtue. For others, easily taken with the allurements of both, indulge to both; only the wise Man duely foreseeing the harm that would

would ensue, cast them away; declaring that Musick is, amongst other things, an allurement to drink, an exhauster of Money, a friend to idleness, conducing nothing to good, honest, and generous works; that Poetry hath always made men prone to all sorts of vices, especially to lust, even by the examples of the Gods themselves, whom it introduceth, inflamed with anger, and raging with lust, and represents not only their Wars, conflicts, wounds, hatred, discords, dissentions, birth, deaths: But also their complaints, lamentations, imprisonments, coiton with mortal children of immortal Parents, and the like; which certainly sober men would abhor.

CHAP. XV.

Of Meekness opposite to Anger.

Moreover Lenity or Meekness, whereunto are reduced Clemency and Pity, is so excellent an antidote against anger, or desire of revenge, that it is esteemed a most eminent virtue; in as much as anger, especially if excessive, causeth madness for the time. For by anger, the mind is heated and darkned, the eyes sparkling with fire, the breast ready to burst with rage, the teeth gnashing, the voice choaked, the hairs standing on end, the face glowing, and distorted with menacing looks, horrid, and ugly to behold, so that the mind seems to have lost the command of herself, and to have forgotten all decency. But, lenity cures the mind, or rather preserves it sound, so that it is neither moved in itself, nor is there any eruption of passion into the Body, that may cause the least undecency.

Now anger being commonly kindled, and set on fire, by opinion of some injury receiv'd; but men are injur'd through hatred, envy, or contempt; how can a wise man so bear an injury, as to behave himself with Lenity, and sweetness towards those who did it? By submitting himself to the government of right reason; whereby (as I formerly said,) he must fortifie himself against fortune. For, he accounts an injury among things of chance, and discreetly considers, it is not in his power to make other men just, and free from passion; and therefore, is as little moved at injuries done to him by men, as at the incommodities, or losses which happen by accidents of fortune, or by any other cause above, beyond his own power.

He is not, for example, troubled at the great heates or colds of the seasons of the year, because it is the nature of the seasons in their vicissitudes, which he connot alter! In like manner, neither is he troubled at the injuries, which dishonest and malicious men do to him, because in doing so, they act according to their own natures, and to make them do otherwise, and to change their natures, is not in his power. Besides, he conceives it not agreeable to Reason, and Wisdom, to add ill to ill, (to add, unto the harm which happens to him from without, perturbation within by opinion,) or, because another man would afflict his mind with vexation he should be so foolish as to admit that vexation, and further the ill designs of his enemy upon him.

Yet is it fit, that a wise man take such care of his reputation, as not to become contemptible, since there are some pleasures that arise from a good Name, some troubles from an Ill, and the contempt that follows it; but he must take care of his reputation, not so much by revenging injuries, or being offended at those that do them, as by living well, and innocently, giving no man a just cause of contumely or malediction. To do thus, is in our power; not, to hinder another from exercising his one malice.

Whence, if one that bears you ill-will, and is your profes'd enemy, shall demand any thing of you, you must not deny him, provided what he demand be lawful, and you are nothing the less secure from him; he differs not from he Dog, and therefore must be appeased with a morsel. Nevertheless, nothing is better or safer, than to confront his malice with innocence of life, and the security of your own Conscience, and withal to shew that you are above injury.

Especially, seeing it may so happen, that a wise man (as I said before,) may be arraign'd and suffer not only injury, but calumny, accusation, condemnation: Even then he considers, that to live well and virtuously, is in his power, but, not to fall into the hands of envious unjust persons; not to be unjustly accused by them; not to be sentenced by unrighteous Judges, is not in his power. He therefore is not angry, either with the accusers, witnesses, or judges but confiding in a good conscience, loseth nothing of his lenity and tranquillity, and esteeming himself to be above this chance, he looks upon it undanuted, and behaves himself in his tryal boldly, and with courage.

Let not any object, that what I here advise concerning lenity, is repugnant to what I formerly said of the chastising of servants; for I limited castigation, only to the refractory and perverse. It is manifest, that punishment ought to be inflicted on offenders, as well in a private family, as in a Common-wealth; and that, as a Prince or Magestrate punisheth the offences of his subjects, without anger; so the Father of a family may without anger, punish the faults of his servants.

Moreover, a wise man must not only bear injuries, nor only pardon them mildly, but even kindly encourage, and congratulate him, who betakes himself to a better course. For since the beginning of reformation is to know our fault; therefore must this gratulation, and encouragement be given to the penitent offender, that, as he is affected with horrour at this knowledge of his crime, so the excellence, and beauty of that which he ought to have done, and thenceforward must do, may be fully represented to him, and the love of it increase daily in him.

CHAP.

CHAP. XVI.

Of Modesty, opposite to Ambition.

AS concerning *Modesty*, there needs little more to be said, than what we formerly declared, when we shew'd it was not the part of a wise man to affect high Offices, or Honours in a Common-wealth, but rather so to contain himself, as to live in some private corner: Wherefore, here I shall once more give the same counsel, which I give to all my friends. Live close, or private, (provided no necessities of the Common-wealth require otherwise,) for even experience teacheth, that he hath lived well, who hath well concealed himself.

It is but too frequently seen, that they who climb up to the top of Honour, are cast down by envy, as with a Thunder-bolt, and then too late acknowledge that it is much better, quietly to obey, than by laborious climbing up the narrow path of ambition, to aim at command and sovereignty, and to arrive there, where nothing can be expected, but a great and dangerous precipitation. Besides, are not they, whom the common people gaze upon with admiration, glittering with Titles and Honours, the most unhappy of all men, for that their breasts are gnawn with weighty and troublesome cares? You must not imagine that such persons live quiet and secure in mind; for it is impossible, but that they who are feared by many, should themselves fear many.

And though you see them send out great Navies, command Legions, compassed with Guards, yet you must not think they live all quiet, or indeed do at all partake of any true pleasure, for all these things are ridiculous pageantry and dreams: Fears and cares are not afraid of the noise of Arms, nor stand in awe of the brightness of gold, or splendor of purple, but boldly intrude amongst Princes and Potentates, and, like the Vulture, which the Poets talk of, gnaw and prey on their hearts.

Neither must you think, that the Body is any thing the better for this, since you see that Fevers go away nothing the sooner, if you lye in a bed of *Tyrian* purple, in a chamber furnished with rich Tapistry, than under a plain homely coverlet; and that we take no harm by the want of purple robes, embroidered with Gold and pearl, as long as we have a course plain Garment sufficient to keep away the cold. And what, if, being cheerful and contented with rags and a bed of straw, you should instruct men how vain those are, who with astonish'd and turbulent minds gape and thirst after the trifles of magnificence, not understanding how few and small those things are which make a happy life? Beleive me that which you shall say will appear far more magnificent and high, being delivered from a Mattress covered with course cloath; for it is not only spoken but practised.

Though your house shine not with Silver and Gold, resound not with musick, hath not any Golden Images of Boyes holding tapers to light you at your nightly Revels and Banquets; truly, it is not a whit less pleasant to repose yourself on the soft grass by a purling stream, underneath a spreading tree and especially in the spring, at what time the fields are besprinked with flowers, the Brids entertain you with their musick, the West wind fans you, and Nature herself smiles on you.

Why therefore should any man, that may live thus in his own fields and garden, persue honour, and not rather modestly restrain his desires within this compass; For to aim at glory by ostentation of Virtue, Science, Eloquence, Nobility, Wealth, Attendants, Attire, Beauty, Meen, and the like, is a ridiculous vanity: In all these, Modesty requires no more than that we transgress not decency through rusticity, stupidity, or negligence. It is (as I said,) equally base and abject, to grow insolent, upon possession of these, as to be cast down at their loss.

Hereupon a wise man, if he happen to have the Images or statues of his Ancestors or other persons, will be far from taking pride in them, or shewing them as badges of honour; yet on the other side, he will not neglect them, but place and keep them carefully in his gallery.

In like manner, neither will he be solicitous about his own Funeral, or give order that it be performed Magnificently. He will only consider what may be beneficial and pleasant to his successours, knowing that as for himself or his dead Body, it is all one what becomes of it. For to propagate vanity even beyound death is madness, and such also is the fancy of those, who would not that their dead Bodies should be devoured by wild beasts. For, if that be well, must it not be very bad to have them burnt, embalmed, and immersed in honey, to grow cold and stiff under a Marble-stone, to be pressed and consumed with Earth?

CHAP. XVII.

Of Moderation, opposite to Avarice.

THe next is Moderation, or that disposition of mind by which a man is contented with little, and than which he cannot have a greater Good. To be content with little is the greatest wealth in the world, forasmuch as a mean estate proportion'd to the the Law of Nature is great riches. To have wherewithal to prevent hunger, thirst, and cold, is a felicity equal to that of the Divinity; and who possesses so much, and desires no more, however the world may esteem him poor, is the richest man.

How sweet a thing is this poverty, cheerful and contented with what is enough, that is, with those riches of nature which suffice to preserve from hunger, thirst, and cold? Truly, seeing the riches of nature are finite and easie to be had, but those that are coveted out of vain opinions, are without measure and infinite, we ought to be thankful to kind Nature, for making those things necessary, that are easie to be had, and those that are hard to be got, unnecessary.

' And since it behoves a wise man to hope he
' shall never, as long as he lives, want necessaries,
' doth not the easie acquisition of these cheap
' and common things abundantly cherish that
' hope? Whereas, on the contrary, things of
' magnificence afford him not the like hope. And
' this is the reason, why ordinary men, though
' they have great possessions, yet as if they feared
' those might faile them, labour still to heap up
' more, never thinking their store compleat.

' This may teach us to content ourselves with
' the most simple things, and such as are easily
' gotten, remembring that not all the wealth in
' the World put together is able in the least mea-
' sure to allay the perturbation of the mind,
' whereas things that are mean, ordinary, and ea-
' sie to be had remove that indigence which is in-
' commodious to the Body, and besides are such
' that the thought of parting with them is noth-
' ing grievous to him who reflects upon death.

Miserable indeed are the minds of men and their hearts blind, in as much as they will not see that Nature dictates nothing more to them than this, that they supply the wants of the Body, and withal enjoy a well pleased mind, without fear or trouble; not that they should employ their whole life in scraping together that which is necessary to life, and that with such greediness as if they were to out-live death, never thinking how deadly a cup, from our very birth, we are design'd to pledge.

What though those things which are purely necessary, and in respect whereunto no man is poor, yield not the delights which vulgar minds dote on? Nature wants them not, and yet she ceaseth not to afford real and sincere pleasures, in the fruition of those mean and simple things, as we already have declared. Whence a wise man is so indifferently affected towards those things, for whose sake mony is coveted, (to supply the dayly expences of love, and ambition,) as that being at a great distance from them all, he hath no reason either to desire or care for mony.

Whereas I said, that the riches which are coveted through opinions, have not any measure or bound, the reason is, that though Nature is satisfied with little, yet vain opinion, ushering in desire, always thinks of somthing which we have not, and, as if it were really needful, directs the desire to that thing. Whence it happens, that he who is not satisfied with a little, can never have enough; but the more wealth he hath, the more he conceives himself to be in want.

Wherefore seeing there can never be want of a little, a wise man, possessing that little, ought to esteem it great riches, because therein is no want; whereas other riches, how great soever in esteem, are indeed small, because they want multiplication to infinity. Whence it follows, that he who thinks not what he possesseth is sufficient and plenteous, though he were master of the whole World, would yet be miserable. For misery is the companion of want, and the same vain opinion which first perswaded him, that his own estate was not sufficient, will continue to perswade him, that one World is not sufficient, but that he wants more and more to infinity.

Would you then make a man rich? Know, that it must be done, not by adding to his riches, but by detracting from his desires. For when, having cut off all vain and superfluous desires, he shall compose himself to the rules of Nature, and covet no more than she requires, then shall he find himself to be rich indeed, because he shall then find that he wants nothing. Whence this also should be inculcated to him, if you live according to Nature, you shall never be poor; but if according to Opinion, never rich. Nature desires little, Opinion infinite.

Certainly this disposition or faculty of the mind, whereby a man, moderating himself, cuts off from his desires whatsoever is not necessary to nature, and contents himself with such things as are most simple and easie to be got; this disposition, I say, begets that security which is found in a quiet retirement, and avoidance of the multitude; moreover, by it, even he who lives with much company wants no more, than he who lives alone.

Hence also it proceeds, that whosoever endeavours to beget a confidence and security to himself out of external things, the best way that may be, seeks after things possible to be got, as being not unsuitable to him: But the impossible he esteems unsuitable. Besides, even of the possible, there are many which he attains not; and all those which it is not necessary for him to attain, he renounceth.

Now for want of this renouncing or detraction, how great misery is it for a man, to be continually pouring into a bored Vessel, never able to fill his mind? For not to mention, that many, who have heaped up wealth, have therein found only a change, not an end, of their misery; either because they run themselves into new cares, to which they were not subject before, or because they made way for snares, in which they were entangled and taken. Not to mention this, I say, the greatest misery is, that the more thou feedest, the more thou art tormented with hunger.

CHAP. XVIII.

Of Mediocrity, betwixt Hope and Despair of the Future.

Lastly, seeing that all desire whatsoever is carried to that which is not possessed, but proposed as possible to be attained, and accompany'd with some hope of obtaining it; which hope, cherishing the desire, is accompany'd with a certain pleasure; as its contrary Despair, fomenting a fear that what is desired cannot be obtained, is not without trouble. Somthing therefore must be added concerning *Mediocrity*, which is of great use, as well in the general concerning things hoped or despaired, as in the particular, concerning the duration, or rather perpetuity of life, whereof, as there is a desire kindled in the breasts of men, so the despair of it torments them.

In the first place therefore we must look upon this as a general Rule; In contingent things, that which is to come is neither absolutely ours, nor absolutely not ours; so that we are neither to hope for it, as if it must certainly come to pass, because it may be diverted by some accident intervening; *nor to despair of it, as if it must certainly not come to pass,* because it may fall out, that no accident may intervene to divert it. Thus, not being destitute of all hope, we shall not be without some pleasure; nor being quite frustrated of our hope, we shall not receive any trouble.

This difference there is betwixt a wise Man and a Fool; the wise Man expects future things, but depends not on them, and in the mean time enjoys the present, (by considering how great and pleasant they are,) and remembers the past with delight. But the life of a Fool (as I said before,) is unpleasant and timorous, for that it is wholly carried on to the future.

How many may we see, who neither remember the past good, nor enjoy the present? they are wholly taken up with expectation of future things, and, those being uncertain, they are perpetually afflicted with anguish and fear, and are exceedingly grieved when they too late perceive, that they have in vain addicted themselves to the getting of Riches, or Honours, or Power, or Glory; for they fail of obtaining those Pleasures, with the hopes whereof being enflamed, they had undergone many and great labours. Nor to say any thing of those others, who being abject and narrow-hearted despair of all things, and are, for the most part, malevolent, envious, morose, shunners of the light, evil speakers, monstrous.

I say a wise Man remembers the past goods with delight and gratitude; but indeed it cannot sufficiently be lamented, that we are too ungrateful towards the past, in not calling to mind, nor accouting amongst pleasures all the good things we have received; forasmuch as no pleasure is more certain, than that which cannot now be taken from us. The present goods are not yet consummate and wholly solid, some chance or other may intervene, and cut them off in half; the future are dependent and uncertain, what is already past is only safe, and out of all danger to be lost.

Among the past goods I reckon, not only such as we have enjoyed, but even the avoidance of the Ills that might have befall'n us; as also, our deliverance out of such Ills as did fall on us, and mihgt have lasted longer, likewise the remembrance and delight that we sustained them constantly and bravely,

As to the desire of prolonging Life to a vast extent, I already hinted, that a wise Man must cut off that desire, because there would immediately upon it follow Desperation, which is never without trouble and anguish. Hither it conduceth to consider, that no greater pleasure can be recived from an age of infinite duration, than may be received from this which we know to be finite, provided a Man measure the bounds of it by right reason.

For seeing that to measure the bounds of Nature by right reason, is nothing else but to consider, (as I said before,) that the supreme pleasure is no other, than an exemption from pain and trouble, it is manifest, that it can neither be made greater by length; nor lesser, or more remiss, by shortness of time.

And though the hopes of a more prolonged pleasure, or of a longer age, seem to render the present pleasure more intense; yet it is only so with those, who measure the bound of pleasure, not by right reason, but by vain desires; and who look upon themselves so, as if, when they die and cease to be, they should yet be troubled at the privation of pleasure, as if they had been alive. Whence it happens, that, as I hiuted formerly, to understand fully, that Death nothing concerns us, much conduceth to our enjoyment of this mortal life, not by adding any thing of uncertain time, but by casting away the desire of Immortality.

Wherefore seeing that since Nature hath prescribed bounds to corporeal pleasure, and the desire of eternal duration takes them away, it is necessary that the mind or reason interpose, that, by discoursing upon those bounds, and extirpating the desire of Sempiternity, it may make life every way perfect, so that we being content therewith, shall not want a longer duration.

Moreover, neither shall we be deprived of pleasure, even then when Death shall summon us, forasmuch as we have attained the perfect and delightful end of the best life, departing like Guests full and well satisfied with life, and having duly discharged that Office, to acquit ourselves of which we received life.

CHAP. XIX.

Of Fortitude in general.

WE come next to *Fortitude*, which I affirmed to be the other part of *Honesty*, because it withstands Fear, and all things that use to cause Fear; whereby, they who behave themselves not timorous and cowardly, but valiantly and stoutly, are said to behave themselves honestly and beseemingly. This may be manifested many ways, especially from War, wherein they who behave themselves with courage and honesty, get honour above the rest. Whence Honest is almost the very same with that, which in the common esteem is Honourable.

That this virtue conduceth also to pleasure, may be inferred from hence, for that neither the undergoing of Labours, nor the suffering of Pains, are things in themselves allective, nor patience, nor assiduity, nor watching, nor industry, though so highly commended, nor Fortitude itself; but we persue these, to the end we may live without care and fear, and so (as much as possible) free both the body and mind from molestation.

For as by the fear of death (for example,) all the quiet of life is disturbed; and as to sink under pains, and to bear them with a dejected and weak mind, is a great misery, and by such lowness of spirit, many have quite undone their Parents, Friends, Country, and even themselves: so on the other side, a strong and gallant mind is free from all care and anguish, for it contemns death,

death becaufe they who fuffer it, are in the fame cafe, as before they were born; and is fo fortify'd againft all pains, as to remember, That the greateft are determined by death, the leaft have many intervals of eafe, the middle fort we ourfelves can mafter; if they are tolerable we can endure them, we can contentedly quit this life, when it no longer pleafeth us, as if we went off from a ftage.

Hence is it manieft, that Timidity and Cowardlinefs are not difpraifed, nor Fortitude and Patience praifed, for their own fakes, but, thofe are rejected, for that they caufe pain; and thefe defired, for that they produce pleafure.

Whereas I faid, that Fortitude withftands Fear, and all things that ufe to caufe Fear, it tends to let us underftand, that they are the very fame ills, which torment when they are prefent, and are feared, when expected as future; and therefore, we muft learn not to fear thofe ills, which we either fancy to ourfelves, or any ways apprehend as future, but to bear thofe which are prefent with conftancy and patience.

Of the Ills, which we fancy to ourfelves, but are not really future, the chiefeft are thofe which we fear either from the Gods, as if they were ill to us; or from death, as if that brought along with it, or after it, fome fempiternal ill. Of the Ills which we fear, for that they may happen, and yet in the mean time are fo prefent, that they afflict and trouble us, are, thofe which either caufe pain in the body, or difcontent in the mind.

Thofe which caufe pain are, Sickneffes, Stripes, Fire, Sword and the like: Thofe which caufe difcontent, are fuch as are termed external Ills; and of thefe fome are publick, as Tyranny, War, deftruction of our Country, Peftilence, Famine, &c. Others private, of which fort are Servitude, Banifhment, Imprifonment, Infamy, Lofs of Friends, and the like.

The difference betwixt all thefe things on one part, and pain and difcontent on the other, is this, that pain and difcontent are abfolute Ills in themfelves, the others are not fo, but only inafmuch as they relate to pain and difcontent, as caufes; for if they did not caufe pain and difcontent, there were no reafon why we fhould fhun them.

We fhall fay fomthing, in order, upon thefe: But firft take notice, that Fortitude is not to Be looked upon as if ingenerate in us by nature, but acquired by reafon. Fortitude is different from Audicity, Ferocity, inconderate Temerity, for thofe are found even in brute Animals alfo, but this is proper to Man, and to fuch Men only as act advifedly and prudently; and therefore it is to be meafured not by the ftrength and violent carriage of the Body, but by the firmnefs of the Mind, conftantly adhering to an honeft intention or purpofe.

CHAP. XX.

Of Fortitude, as to Fear of the Gods.

WE muft firft treat of a twofold fear, far tranfcending the reft. For it any thing ever produced the ultimate good, and chief pleafure, proper to the mind; it was the expunction of thofe opinions, (and all allied to them,) which have imprefs'd the greateft fear upon the mind. Such is the condition of miferable Mortals, that they are not led by found opinions, but by fome affection void of reafon; fo that not difcerning what is ill indeed, by reafon they fuffer an equal and no lefs intenfe pertur bation, than as if thefe things, for which they are troubled, were indeed fuch.

That, which in the firft place, ufeth to poffefs men with greateft fear, and, confequently caufes in them the greateft perturbation, is this, that, conceiving there are certain bleffed and immortal Natures, they do yet think them to have wills, paffions, and operations, plainly repugnant to thofe attributes, (of beatitude and immortality,) as perpetual Solicitude, Bufinefs, Anger, Favour; whereby it comes to pafs, that Ill men receive great harms by way of punifhment; the Good protection and benefits, from thefe Natures, that is from the Gods. Thus men being nurfed up in their own, that is, in human affections, fancy and admit Gods like to themfelves; and whatfoever fuits not with their own difpofitions, that they conceive incompetent to them.

Hereupon, it cannot be exprefs'd, how great unhappinefs mankind hath drawn upon itfelf, by attributing fuch things to the Gods, efpecially Anger, and Severity; by reafon whereof, Mens minds being dejected, every one trembles with fear, when the Heaven Thunders, or the Earth quakes, or the Sea is Tempeftuous, or any other thing happens, whereby he is perfwaded, that the Gods intend to punifh him, miferable man.

But it is not fo with thofe, who, inftructed by reafon, have learnt, that the Gods live in perpetual fecurity and tranquillity, and that their nature is too far remov'd from us, and our affairs, for them to be either pleafed or difpleafed with us. Truly if they were, and did hear the prayers of men, how foon would all men be deftroy'd, who continually imprecate mifchief on one another?

Therefore, when you conceive God to be an immortal and bleffed Animal, (as the common notion concerning God fuggefts,) take heed of attributing any thing to him, which is either incompetent with immortality, or repugnant to beatitude; but let all your conceptions be fuch, as may confift with immortality and beatitude.

Gods indeed there are, for the knowledge of them is evident, as we formerly proved; but fuch as men commonly conceive them, they are not. For firft, they defcribe them by fome adjuncts or properties, as when they fay, they are immortal and bleffed, and then overthrow what they afferted, by applying other attributes to them, repugnant to the former; as when they fay, that they have bufinefs, or create bufinefs for others;

that

that they are affected with anger or favour, which, as I hinted formerly, imply imbecillity, fear and want of external assistance.

Neither need you fear, that this will make you esteemed impious; for he is impious indeed, not, who denies the vulgar Gods of the multitude, but he who ascribes to the Gods the opinions of the multitude. For those things which are commonly delivered concerning the Gods, are not genuine prænotions, but false opinions.

By the same reason likewise, he is not pious, who out of fear to the Gods addresseth himself to every stone, to every Alter, besprinkles every Temple with the blood of Victims: But he, who contemplating all things with a serene and quiet soul, conceiveth aright of the Gods, and worshipping them in his mind, not induced thereto by hope or reward, but for their excellent Majesty and supreme nature, observes all kind of veneration towards them, and useth expressions suggesting such thoughts, as out of them arise no opinions repugnant to veneration, and consequently, suffereth not that which others suffer, in whose minds, this contrariety causeth an extraordinary perturbation.

CHAP. XXI.

Of Fortitude, as to fear of Death.

THat which next striketh greatest terrour into the minds of men is *Death*, for that they expect, and fear, I know not what everlasting ill, as Fables tell them, (and which is strange, in the very privation of sense which then happens, as if they should still have being,) not knowing that all stories concerning the infernal places (which we spoke of formerly,) and mere fictions of Poets; or if they contain any thing of truth, it is made good in this life, by vain fears, superfluous cares, insatiable desires, and other violent passions, which torture unhappy men in such manner, that their life is worse than hellish.

That you may exempt yourself, therefore, from these terrours, accustome *your self to this thought, That death nothing concerns us*; and to this argument, That *all good or ill that happen to us is with sense; but death is a privation of sense,* for death is a dissolution, and what is dissolved remains without sense. So that death seems easie to be contemn'd, because it is an ineffectual Agent, and in vain threatens pain, when the patient is not.

Indeed the ordinary sort of men abhor death, because they look upon it somtimes as the greatest of pains, somtimes because they apprehend it as the cessation of all things that we enjoy in life; but without cause is it, that not to live, or not to be, is fear'd; for when it comes to that, we shall not have any faculty left whereby to know, that, not to live, is ill.

Hence we may conclude, that they are very foolish who abhor, amongst other things, to think, that after death their Bodies should be torn by wild Beasts, burnt by fire, devoured by worms; for, they do not consider, that then they shall not be, and so not feel nor complain, that they are torn, burnt, devoured, turned into corruption. As also, those who are troubled to think, that they shall no longer enjoy the conversation of their Wives, Children, Friends; no longer do them good offices nor assist them; for these consider not, that they shall have no desire of such things.

Death therefore, which is esteemed the most horrid of Ills, doth (as I said,) nothing concern us, because while we are, Death is not; and when Death is, we are not: So that it concerns neither the living nor the dead; the living it toucheth not, the dead are not.

Now the assured knowledge that Death nothing concerns us, makes us enjoy this mortal life, not adding uncertain time to it, but casting away the desire of immortality. For, in life, there can be nothing of ill to him, who perfectly understand that there can be nothing of ill in the privation of life. Whence, as we make choice not of the most meat, but of the best, so should we covet, not the longest, but most pleasant life.

Neither can he be acquitted of folly, who says, he fears death, for that, when it comes, it brings not any trouble, but because it afflicts the mind with grief before it comes: For, that which brings no trouble with it, when it comes, ought not to make us sad with expectation. Certainly, if there be any thing of inconvenience or fear in this business, it is the fault of him that is dying, not of Death: Nor, is there any trouble in death, more than there is after it, and it is no less folly to fear death, than to fear old age, since as old age follows youth, so death follows old age.

Moreover, we are to hope at least, that either we shall feel no pain at the point of death; or if any, so short, as the very consideration of that may comfort us; for no great pain lasts long, and every man ought to believe, that, though the dissolution of his Soul and body be accompanied with some torment, yet that being past he shall feel no more pain.

He also who advised young man to live well, and old to dye well, was very ridiculous, for these are not to be parted; the meditation of living well and of dying well is one and the same, seeing that a young man may dye suddenly, and an old man hath somthing more of life behind: Besides, the last act is a part, even the crown, of life.

Both young and old ought to consider, that though men may provide for their security in other things; yet as to death itself, all men live as it were in a City without walls or bulwarks.

Besides, a young man may dye happy, if he consider, that he should find nothing more in a longer life, than what he hath already seen and experienc'd; and an old man may live unhappy, if, like a vessel full of holes, he suffer the goods of life only to run thorough him, and so is never full of them, nor, as a sober guest of Nature, after a plentiful feast of life, is willing to go away, and take his repose.

Think not any old man happy for dying old, but for dying full and well satisfi'd with goods.

Lastly, far more foolish and ridiculous is he, who saith, It is good either not to be born at all; or as soon as born to pass the gates of death. For, if he speak this in earnest, why does he not presently rid himself of life, it being very easie for him so to do, if he hath well deliberated upon it? If in jest, he is perfectly mad, because these are things that admit not of jesting. Again, in life there is somthing amiable in itself; and therefore they are no less to be reproved who desire death, than they who are afraid of it. What can be so ridiculous as to desire Death, having made your own life unquiet by fear of death? Or, out of a weariness of life, to run to death, when your own imprudent and constant course of life is the cause of that weariness.

You must rather take care to make life not tedious to you, that you be not willing to part with it, unless either nature, or some intolerable chance summon you to surrender it. And in that respect we ought seriously to consider, whether it be more commodious, that death come to us, or that we go to death. For though it be an evil indeed to live in necessity, yet is there no necessity we should live in necessity; since Nature, though she hath given us but one way into life, yet hath furnish'd us with many to get out of it.

But though it may somtimes so fall out, that it behoves us to hasten and flye to death, before some greater power intercept and rob us of the liberty to quit life; yet ought we not to attempt any thing, but when it may be attemped conveniently and opportunely, and when that long waited for time comes, then to leap out of life resolutely. For neither is it fit for him, who thinks of flight, to sleep; nor ought we to despaire of a happy exit even out of the greatest difficulties, if we neither hasten it before the time; nor, when the time is come, delay it.

CHAP. XXII.

Of Fortitude aginst Corporeal pain.

Corporeal pain is that, which alone would deserve the name of ill, even of the greatest ill, did we not of our selves add to it the pain of the Mind, which is worse than that of the Body. For discontent of mind, taken at the loss of riches, honours, Children, and the like, many times becomes more intolerable than the greatest corporeal pains; but this is by reason of our own opinion, which if it were right and found, we should not be moved by any such loss, in regard that all such things are without or beyond us, and touch us not indeed, but only by mediation of that opinion which we frame to our selves. And thereupon we may infer, that there is no real ill, but the pain of the Body, and that the mind ought not to complain of any thing, which is not joyned to some pain of the Body, either present or to come.

He therefore who is wise, will be very cautious that he draw not any corporeal pain upon himself, or do any thing upon which corporeal pain may ensue; unless it be done either for avoidance of some greater pain, or accquisition of some greater pleasure, as we formerly declared. Hence we may well wonder at those Philosophers, who, accounting health, which is the state of indolence, a very great good, as to all other respects, do yet, as to this, hold it to be a thing indifferent? as if it were not a trivial playing with words, or rather a high folly, to affirm, that to be in pain, and to the free from pain, is all one thing.

But if any necessity either of the natural constitution, whereby the Body is obnoxious to diseases, or of any external violence done to him, which, as human affairs stand, cannot somtimes be avoided, (for that a wise and innocent person may somtimes be arraigned, condemned, beaten and tortur'd, is manifest,) if either of these shall bring pain upon him, then is it his part to endure that pain, with a constant and valiant mind, and patiently to expect, either the solution or relaxation of it.

Certainly, Pain never continues long in the Body, but that which is great, or highly intense soon ceaseth, for either it is determined of itself, and succeeded, if not by absolute indolence, yet by very great mitigation, or is taken away by death, in which there is no Pain. And as for that Pain which is lasting, it is not only gentle, but hath many lucid intervals; so that it will not be many days, nay, not hours, ere the Body hath not only ease, but pleasure.

And may we not observe, that long or Chronical Diseases have more hours of ease, and quiet intervals, than of pain and trouble ? For (not to mention that the thirst, which they raise, increaseth the pleasure of drinking,) they allow us time for repast, strength to talk, some recreation and sports, and for the most part have many long intermissions, in which we may apply ourselves to studies and business. Whence it is evident, that as great pain usually is short, so long pain is light : thus the shortness makes amends for the greatness, the remissness for its length.

Let us therefore often reflect, that Pain either is not intolerable, or not perpetual ; for if it be long, it is light ; if great, short. Provided, that you remember the bounds prescribed to the things themselves by nature, and add nothing through your own opinion, whereby you may think, and make it greater than it is; and oppressing yourself with complaints, and impatient exasperations, help only to render it more insupportable: Whereas, on the other side, nothing doth asswage Pain more than constancy, and inurance to suffering. Whence it comes that a wise man, accustom'd to Pain, can many times rejoyce and smile, even in the height of his sickness.

Thus much we can testifie of our friend *Metrodorus*, who hath at all times behaved himself undauntedly, as well against death, as pain. For concerning myself, I need not say any thing, who frequently suffer such pain in the bladder and bowels, as none can be greater: And yet full amends, for all these, is made by the alacrity of mind which redounds to us, from the remembrance of our dissertatians and inventions, and by our constant patience ; whereby we forbear not to esteem those very days, in which we are tormented with those diseases and pains, happy.

And this indeed is the reason, why we formerly said, that a wise man, though in torments, may yet be happy ; because he both softens, by his patience, the necessity which he cannot break; and, as much as possible, withdraws his mind from his suffering Body, conversing no otherwise with it, than as with a weak and querulous part. He bethinks himself, what he hath at any time done honestly and generously ; and fixing his memory upon those things, which he hath most admired, and have most delighted him, cheers himself with the past goods, for which he is far from shewing himself, as fools usually do, unthankful.

He

He also considers, that he can do nothing more worthy that virtue and wisdom which he professeth, than not to yield the victory to pain, though the most hard to be sustained of all things; to bear up couragiously, to repulse by patience so dangerous an enemy; and at length to make so perfect a conquest, as that the very remembrance of it will be most delightful, and especially through absolute indolency, which will be so much the more pleasing, as a quiet Haven is most welcome after a Tempest.

Now if a wise man is not without his alleviations and conforts in the greatest pain, what shall we say of him in remiss and gentle pains, or at the loss of some limb or sense? Truly, it was not without reason, that I said formerly, a wise man, though depriv'd of the best of Senses, Sight, would yet be happy: For if the Night doth not diminish the happiness of life, why should blindness, that so nearly resembles Night? However he may want some pleasures that depend upon the light, yet are there several others left him, and what is much above all the rest, he may delight his mind with many things, and many ways without Seeing.

For since to a wise man, to live is to think, certainly his thoughts are not oblig'd to his eyes in the business of searching into truth. And that man, to whose Doctrine I gave up my name, could live long and happy, without being able to distinguish colours: But without the knowledge of things, he could not have lived happy. Moreover, he was of opinion, that the perspicacity of the mind was very much dimm'd by the sight of the eyes; and while others could scarcely be said to see things that were before them, he travelled abroad into all infinity, not stopping at any bounds.

CHAP. XXIII.

Of Fortitude, against Discontent of Mind.

I Said, that Discontent of Mind is commonly taken at such things as are conceived to be external Ills, and the Contraries to those Goods which we most love and desire. For men call some things adverse, others prosperous: And we may generally observe, that the Mind, which is elevated, and insolent with prosperity, and cast down with adversity, is abject and base. Hence is it, that all we should here say, concerning the Ills which cause Discontent, and against which we have need of Fortitude, may be sufficiently inferred from what we formerly said, touching those Goods which are the general objects of our desires or inclinations, and in respect whereof we have need of Temperance.

Let it suffice in general to repeat what we formerly said, That Discontent of Mind is not grounded upon Nature, but merely upon opinion of Ill. Wherefore, who ever conceives himself to lie under som Ill, whether only foreseen and expected, or already come upon him, must of necessity be discontented. For how comes it, that a Father whose Son is kill'd, and he knows it not, is not a whit less chearful or merry, than if he were alive? Or that he, who hath lost much of his good Fame abroad, or all his Goods, and Cattel, by Robbery at home, is not at all sensible of either loss till he hear of it? Is it not Opinion only which discontents him? For, if Nature did it, at the same minute wherein the Son was slain, the Father's mind would be struck with a sense of his death; the like would be perceived in the loss of Honours or Goods.

Therefore, to raise Discontent in the Mind, it is necessary that Opinion, not Nature, intervene. And that you may doubt the less of this, observe, that a Man who thinks a supposititious Child his own, and his own suppositions; if News be brought him of the death of his own Son, he will not be moved, but if of his supposititious, he will be exceedingly afflicted; and this comes not from Nature, but Opinion.

But that those things which afflict us are not indeed Ills to us, appears even from this, that they are without or beyond us, and cannot reach us of themselves, but only by our own opinion are made Ills to us. And hence it was that I said, it is reason which makes Life happy or pleasant, by expelling opinions, for which the mind is possess'd with trouble. For it is discontent alone which disturbs the mind, and its quiet and content.

But how can reason expel these opinions? By teaching a wise Man to arm his mind against Fortune. For the external things which we think Goods, and the loss of which causeth discontent in our minds, are termed the Goods of Fortune, because indeed they are not ours, but come and go, as Fortune pleaseth.

For this reason, a wise Man esteems them no more belonging to him, than to others; nor possesseth them so, as not to be ready to part with them. He hath cast off that opinion which tells us, Such Goods are our own, and can never be lost; and hath put on the right opinion, which assures him they are uncertain and transitory, as indeed they are. And hereupon he considers with himself before-hand, what he shall do if he chance to lose them; he considers, I say, before-hand, that when it happens he may not be afflicted with vain grief, but take it quietly, that Fortune redemands what she gave not, but only lent,

Certainly to those who think, that to be deprived of these Goods is an Ill, the most unhappy thing of all is, that Premeditation encreaseth the Ills which it might have much diminished, if not wholly prevented; and thus becomes only a foolish consideration of Ill to come, and which perhaps will never come. Every Ill is of itself troublesom enough when it comes; and if it chance never to come, we draw a voluntary misery upon ourselves to no purpose, and by that means shall never be free from trouble, either by receiving or apprehending some Ill; for he who always thinks that some Ill or adversity will befall him, to him that very thought is a continual Ill.

Now if it shall happen also to a wise man, that, by being long accustomed to the possession and use of the goods of Fortune, he hath not quite blotted that opinion out of his mind, and so some little of Fortune intervene, and give him a blow, by reason whereof, he falls into some

some discontent, and perhaps grieves: In this case, the asswagement of his discontent consists in two things, formerly prescribed as remedies against corporeal pain; *viz.* Diversion of his thoughts from his loss, or the cause of it: and an application of them to those things, which he knows to be grateful and pleasant to his mind.

For the mind of a wise man is conformed to reason, and follows the conduct thereof; but reason forbids to look on those things, which create and nourish discontent; and thus he abstracts the mind from bitter thoughts, to convert it to think upon goods, either future or past, especially those which he knows please him most.

Those sad and importune thoughts indeed are very apt to return, but he must insist upon that diversion and application of the mind whereby it is brought by little and little to wear out, and deface its sorrow. Neither doth time diminish discontent any other way, than by exhibiting various occasions of divertisement, which, by degrees, take the mind off, and make her forget, as it were, the things that caused her discontent.

CHAP. XXIV.

Of Justice in general.

It rests, we speak of Justice, which, as I said before, wholly relates to others, and therefore belongs to a man, as living in a civil society. And certainly it is a common tye, without which, no Society can subsist, it being a virtue which gives to every one that which is his, and takes care that none receive injury.

And to begin with that, with which I used to begin, in treating of the other virtues, truely not unlike are the things that may be said of this. For, as I shewed, that Prudence, Temperance, Fortitude, are inseparably Joyned to pleasure, the same may be said of Justice, which not only never hurts any one, but, on the contrary, always preserves and nourisheth something, that calms and quiets the mind; and this aswell by its own power and nature, as by hope, that none shall ever want any of those things, which pure undepraved Nature desires.

Now forasmuch as temerity, lust, and cowardise, always excruciate the minds alway, perplex and trouble it; it is impossible, that a mind in which Injustice dwells, should, for that very reason, because Injustice dwells in it, be otherwise than unquiet: Because though such a mind should attempt any unjust action with the greatest secrecy imaginable, yet can it not perswade itself, but that it will at last come to light. And though some men may think their consciences sufficiently barricado'd and fortifi'd by their wealth, yet they dread the divine power, and imagin, that those very solicitudes and troubles, which torture their souls day and night, are sent by the immortal Gods for their punishment.

But, how can we expect, that unjust actions should diminish the troubles of life, so much as remorse of conscience, penalties of the Law, and the being hated by our country-men encrease them? And yet, in some men, there is not any bound or moderation of wealth, of honour, of power, of lust, of gluttony, and other desires, which nothing that is unjustly gotten diminisheth, but rather encreaseth and emflameth, so that they are fitter for restraint than instruction.

All sound and Judicious persons therefore, are, by right reason, induced to Justice, equity, honesty; but neither can unjust actions benefit a Child or impotent person, for such can neither easily effect what they endeavour, nor obtain their ends when they have effected it, Besides, riches are more suitable to fortune, or a noble genius, which they who enjoy, procure to themselves a general respect and goodwill, and (what most conduceth to quiet living,) an endearment from others, especially there being no cause of offending.

For the desires which proceed from Nature are easily satisfied, without injuring any man; those which come from vain opinions are not to be followed, for they aim at nothing which is desirable, and there is more detriment in the injury itself, than advantage or benefit in the things that are gained by the injury.

Nevertheless, no man can say rightly, that Justice is a virtue, expetible only for itself, but because it brings great pleasure along with it, For to be belov'd, and to be dear to others, is pleasant, because it renders life more safe, and pleasure more full. We therefore conceive, that Injustice ought to be avoided, not only for the inconveniences which happen to the unjust; but much more, for that as long as it is in the mind, it never suffers it to take breath, never to be at rest.

These considerations might perhaps be sufficient, yet I shall add somthing, partly concerning *Right* or *Just*, from which *Justice* is denominated, that we may come the better to understand what is its original, among whom it is practised, what are its benefits; and partly concerning some other virtues nearly allied to Justice, as, *Beneficence*, *Gratitude*, *Piety*, *Observance*, and *Friendship*.

CHAP. XXV.

Of Jus (Right,) or Just, whence Justice is denominated.

First therefore, forasmuch as *Justice* is so named, for that it preserves the *Jus* or Right, due to one another, or performs that which is *Just*; it is worth our knowing what that is, which ought to be esteemed *Right* or *Just*.

Now in regard Justice was instituted in order to the common good, necessary it is, that Right or Just, to which Justice hath respect, should be such a good, as is common to all and every member of the Society. And because every one, by the direction of nature, desires what is good for himself; it is also necessary, that what is right or Just be conformable to Nature, and therefore termed Natural.

It is not without cause that I hint this; for sometimes it happens, that in a Society, somthing is prescribed as Right and Just, which is not good for the Society, and so being not Natural, or contrary to Nature, it cannot, but by abuse, and only in name, be reputed Right or Just, since that

that which hath the true reason of Natural right or juſt, is ſuch, as that it is not only preſcribed as profitable and good, but is really ſuch.

Wherefore to ſpeak properly, Natural right or juſt is no other, than a ſymbol of utility, or ſuch an utility agreed upon by concurrence of votes, as may keep men from hurting, or being hurt by one another, ſo that they may live ſecurely ; A good, which every man is taught by Nature to deſire.

I here take Profitable and Good for the ſame thing ; and I conceive, that, to a thing's being juſt or rightly kept, two things are requiſite ; One, That it be profitable, or reſpect the common utility, that is, ſecurity : The other, That it be preſcribed by the common conſent of the Society ; For nothing is compleatly juſt, but what the Society, by common conſent or agreement, hath decreed to be obſerved.

Hence it is, that the name of Right or Juſt is uſually given to both theſe, ſince not only what is profitable is ſaid to be juſt, but alſo the very common Covenant or preſcription of the Society, which is Tearmed Law, as being that which Preſcribes to very one what is profitable or juſt.

Some there are, who conceive all things that are juſt, to be juſt of their own proper and unalterable Nature, and that Laws do not make them to be juſt, but only declare and preſcrib, according to the Nature which thoſe things have. But it is not ſo, but rather after the ſame manner as is obſerved in other things, which are profitable, as in thoſe which concern health, and many others of the like Nature, which are beneficial to ſome men, hurtful ta others ; by which means they often fail of their mark, as well in common as in private.

And ſeeing that every thing is apprehended every where, always, and by all men, to be really ſuch as it is in its own Nature, becauſe its Nature is unalterable, whether are thoſe things, which theſe men call juſt, juſt in all places and always, and amongſt all men ? Ought they not to have obſerved, that many of thoſe things that are conſtitured by Laws, and Conſequently accounted lawful and juſt, are not conſtituted and received amongſt all Nations alike, but are neglected by many as things indifferent, rejected by others as hurtful, and condemned as unjuſt? And are there not ſome, who account things not generally profitable, to be neverthelefs ſuch ; and accordingly embrace thoſe things which are not generally approv'd, if they find them advantageous in reſpect of their own Society, and ſeem but to promiſe ſome general benefit ?

In fine, that is univerſally juſt, or hath the Nature of juſt, which is profitable or conformable to the prenotion of right or juſt even now deſcribed : For particularly, according as utility is various amongſt ſeveral Nations, ſo alſo is right or juſt, various ; inſomuch as what is eſteemed juſt in one, is unjuſt in another. Whence, if it be demanded, whether juſt or right be the ſame among all men ? I anſwer, that, as to the general, it is the ſame, for it is ſomthing that is profitable in mutual ſociety : But the differences of ſeveral Countries, and various cauſes amongſt them being conſidered in particular, it comes to paſs that it is not the ſame amongſt all.

And, (to deduce ſome few particulars hence,) whatſoever is by experience found profitable to a mutual Society, or the common participation of ſuch things as are eſteemed juſt, that thing hath the nature of juſt or right, if it be ſuch as its utility extends unto all. But if any man ſhall eſtabliſh ſuch a thing for juſt, and yet it ſhall happen not to be profitable to mutual Society, it hath not the true nature of juſt or right.

Again, though ſomtimes the utility of that which was eſteemed juſt may fail, neverthelefs, if there be ſomtimes ſome utility in it, ſo that it correſponds to the prenotion of juſt or right, it is truly juſt for that time : They certainly will eſteem it ſo, who confound not themſelves with vain loquacity, but look more generally into human affaires.

Laſtly, where, no new circumſtance of things intervening, thoſe very things, which were eſteemed juſt in the actions of men, are found nor to correſpond with the notion of juſt, they are not juſt at all : But where, upon innovation or change of affairs, thoſe things, which we formerly decreed to be juſt, ceaſe to be profitable, they were juſt, as long as they continued profitable to mutual Society, but as ſoon as ever they ceaſed to be profitable they ceaſed to be juſt.

CHAP. XXVI.

Of the Original of Right and Juſt.

BUt that we may go higher and deduce the thing from its original, it appears that Right and Juſt are as ancient, and Juſtice hath been kept amongſt men, as long as they have had ſocieties amongſt themſelves.

For, in the beginning, Men wandring up and down like wild beaſts and ſuffering many inconveniences, as well from beaſts as from the injuries of weather, a certain natural agreement amongſt them (by reaſon of their likeneſs in form and ſoul or manners,) perſwaded them to joyn together in ſeveral companies, and to make ſome proviſion againſt thoſe inconveniences, by building huts or Cottages, and Furniſhing themſelves with other Shelters, as well againſt Wild Beaſts as the Weather. But in regard every one was deſirous to be in a better condition than another, hereupon there aroſe frequent conteſtations about food, women, and other conveniences, which they took away from one another ; until at length they perceived, that they could not live ſecure and commodiouſly, unleſs they made a covenant not to injure one another, and that in caſe any one did harm and injure another, the reſt ſhould puniſh him.

This was the firſt band of Society ; which, ſuppoſing that every one might have ſomthing proper to himſelf, or which he might call his own, as being his, either by firſt poſſeſſion, or by purchaſe, or by acquiſition through his own induſtry, or otherwiſe, decreed, that it ſhould remain in the poſſeſſion and diſpoſal of that perſon. Now this band or covenant was no other than a common law, which all were equally bound to obſerve, and which did confirm to every one a certain right or faculty of uſing whatſoever was his own. Whereupon that very law also came to be (as I formerly intimated,) the common right as it were of the Society.

I need not mention, how the whole Society transferr'd their power of restraining or punishing, upon some few wise and good persons, or else on one, who was reputed the wisest and best amongst them. I shall only observe, that in the Society those were accounted just or favourers of justice, who being content with their own rights invaded not those of other men, but did injury to none; those unjust, or doers of injustice, who being not content with their own rights, did assault the rights of other men; and, harming them by rapine, personal violence or some other way, became injurious to them.

Thus men lived a while peaceably and happily, especially being under one or more Kings or Princes, the wisest and best, who being wholly intent upon the conservation and utility of the publick, made, and, with consent of the people, established divers Laws, to prevent dissentions from rising, or, if any did arise, to compose them. But, such is the corruption of mens manners, in process of time the government fell into the hands of Princes or Kings that were not good; and those being either deposed or slain, it reverted to the people, whereupon tumults were raised by the factions of such as aspired to the supream power, until at length, the people languishing under enmities and dissentions, and weary of living by force and hostility, became willing to submit again to the Government of Magistrates or Princes. But because the Wills of Princes had formerly pass'd for absolute laws, they made a covenant with their Governours, about those Laws, according to which they desired to be governed; and thus brought themselves again under Laws, that is, under strict Rights.

But not to descend to later times, but to touch only upon that chief head, which concerns the preservation of life, for whose security (as being the most precious of all things,) care was taken from the beginning that it might be established by common Covenant or Law; * *It appears, that those most wise and good founders of Laws, having regard to the Society of life, and to those things, which men usually do each to other, declared it a wicked act to kill a man, and decreed, that the Murtherer should be punish'd with more than common ignominy, and loss of life.* And to this they seem to have been induced, partly by considering the conciliation of men among themselves, (of which I treated even now,) in respect whereof men ought not to be as forward to destroy an animal of their own kind, as one of different kind, which it is lawful to kill; partly, indeed chiefly, by considering, that *men ought to abhor, what is no way advantageous to life, but tends only to evil.*

Indeed from the beginning, to those who had regard to the utility of that constitution, there needed not any other cause to make them contain themselves from doing any such act; But they, who could not sufficiently comprehend of what great concernment it was, abstained from murthering one another, only out of a fear of those great punishments; both which we may observe to have happened even in our own days. They, who consider the great advantages of such a constitution, are sufficiently disposed for a constant observance thereof; but they, who are not capable of understanding it, conform themselves to it out of fear of the punishments threatned by the Laws, and ordained by the more prudent, again such as had no regard to this utility, the greater part of the multitude admitting them as legal.

For none of the Laws written or not written that have been derived to us, and shall be transmitted to our posterity, did at first subsist by any force or violence, but (as I said) merely by the consent of those who used it. For it was prudence, not strength of Body or imperious sway, wherein they, who setled these Laws upon the People, Transcended the Vulgar; and this, by inducing some men to consider, what would be profitable, (especially when they did not before so well understand it as they ought,) and by Terrifying others with the greatness of the Punishments. Nor could they indeed make use of any other remedy for cure of the peoples ignorance of this utility, than fear of the punishment prescribed by the Law; for even now also, it is fear alone, that keeps the ordinary sort of men within the bounds of their duty, and hinders them from committing any thing against either the publick or private good.

Now if all men could alike understand, and bear in mind what is truly profitable, they should need no Laws at all, but would of their own accord beware of doing such things as the Laws forbid, and do what they enjoyn: since only to know what is profitable and what hurtful, is more than sufficient, to induce them to avoid this, and persue that. But as for those, who discern not what is beneficial, what hurtful, doubtless the commination or punishment against such is highly necessary; insomuch, as the fear of the punishment impendent causeth them to suppress and bridle those heats of their passions, which instigate them to unjust actions, and in a manner compel them, though against their wills, to do what is right.

Hereupon was it, the Law-makers ordained, that even involuntary killing of a man should not be free from all mulct and punishment. Not that they might not, to such as were apt to commit wilful murder, give any occasion of pretext or excuse, to imitate that on set purpose which the others did unwittingly; but lest they might seem not to have used sufficient caution, and diligence as to this particular, whereupon many things would fall out, which indeed were not involuntary. Nor could this course but prove beneficial for the same causes, for which men were expressely prohibited to kill each other. So that considering, that, of these actions, of this kind, that are done involuntarily, some happen from a cause, that could not before seen, nor prevented by human nature, others meerly through our negligence, and heedlesness of the imminent danger; therefore to prevent negligence, which might tend to the destruction of others, they provided, that even the involuntary action should not pass altogether unchastised, but took away the frequency of this sin, by the fear of Law.

Moreover I conceive, that even those slaughters of men, which were permitted by the Law, were made liable to those accustomed expiations, by publick Lustrations, (and that by order of the same persons, who first ordained them,) for no other cause but this, that they had a mind to deter men from involuntary slaughter, which was too too frequent.

For the vulgar sort of men stood in need of something, to restrain them from doing any thing rashly, which might not conduce to the publick utility; which these first Law-makers understanding, not only decreed severe punishments, but withal strook another fear

*Parph. de non esu carnium.

fear into their minds, the reason of which was not so manifest as the other, declaring that such as had killed a man, by what means or accident soever, should be impure until they had used lustrations.

Thus the brutish part of the Soul, in which the affections and passions reside, being instructed and reform'd, came at length to that Gentleness which now flourisheth amongst us, by applying the arts of taming and civilizing our savage affections, which were invented, and practised at first, by those who ruled the multitude; of which, this is one chief act among the rest, that men should not destroy one another without any distinction.

CHAP. XXVII.

Between whom, Right and Justice is to be exercised.

NOw since, it may be demanded, Betwixt what Persons, as well Right, and the violation of it, which is Injury, as Justice, and what is opposite to it, Injustice, properly consist? We shall therefore explicate this, by comparing men with other living Creatures.

As therefore, there is no reason of Right or injury, or just and unjust betwixt Animals, that could not make a common agreement, not to hurt nor be hurt by mutual invasion: So neither, is there between those nations which neither would not, or could not, enter into a mutual engagment, not to hurt, nor be hurt by one another.

For just, or right, the conservation whereof is Justice, hath no being at all, but in mutual Society; whence Justice is the good of a Society, insomuch as by it, every one of the said associated Persons live securely, free from that anxiety, which is caused by the continual fear of harm. Whence it follows, that whatever Animals, or what Men soever, either cannot, or will not make an association, nor enter into Covenant among themselves, must want this good, not being reciprocally oblig'd by any bond of right or Justice, whereby they might live securely. And so to them, there can remain no other reason of security, than only this, to do harm to others, that they be not harmed themselves.

As therefore, when one of those brute Animals, amongst which there hath past no such agreement or pact, doth hurt another, though it may be said that one hurts the other, yet it cannot be said that one doth an injury to the other, because one was not bound by any right, compact, or Law, not to hurt the other: In like manner, if one man of that nation, among whom there is no Covenant, or association, hurt another, it may be said that he hurts him, but not that he wrongs or doth him an injury; because he was not obliged by any compact or Law, not to hurt him.

I speak of brute Animals, not as if there were any even of those who live in heards or flocks, that are capable of entring into Covenant, not to harm or be hurt by each other, and so might be conceived to be just if they do not hurt each other, and unjust if they do; but only to the end, that from thence it may be the better understood, that, even among men, justice in itself is nothing, for that it is found only in mutual Societies, according to the amplitude of every Country, in which the inhabitants may conveniently enter into agreements, and Cavenants of not doing, or receiving any hurt; since otherwise, and in a man singly considered, there is no Justice at all; and what is Justice in one Society of men, many times is in respect of contrary Covenants, Injustice in another.

But can there be Justice betwixt Men and other Animals? Certainly not. For if men could make a covenant with brute Animals, as they can with other men, that they should not kill, nor be killed by them, without any distinction: then indeed, might the reason of Just or right be founded betwixt them and us, since the end of that covenant would be the security of both parties: But, because it is impossible, that Animals void of reason should be obliged by one Law with us, it must also be impossible, for us to obtain more assurance of security from Animals, than even from inanimate beings. So that, there is no other way for us to secure ourselves from brute Beasts, but only to execute that power of destroying them, which Nature hath given us.

Perhaps you will, by the way, demand, why we kill even such Animals, as can give us no occasion of fear? This we may do either through intemperance, and a certain natural savageness or cruelty, as we exercise cruelty even upon men, who live out of our Society and cannot give us any fear. But it is one thing, to break the rules of Temperance, or any of its kinds, as Sobriety, Lenity, or Mansuetude, or, (if you please,) mere humanity or goodness of nature; another, to violate Justice, which presupposeth Laws and Covenants established by mutual consent.

* *Nor can it be alledg'd, that we have a power* * *Porphyr.* *granted us by Law, to destroy any such Animals, as are not offensive or destructive to mankind. I confess, there is not any kind of living Creatures, among all those we are allowed to destroy, which being permitted to increase to vast multitudes, would not prove pernicious to mankind, but being preserved in such number as ordinarily they are, are not some ways useful to life.*

For sheep, kine, and all such like, as long as they are preserv'd to a moderate number, afford us many necessaries for life: But if they were suffered to multiply in a far greater manner; certainly, they could not but prove very hurtful to us, as well in regard of their strength, as for that they would devour the fruits of the earth, that should serve for our subsistence. And for this very cause is it, that we are not prohibited to destroy such Animals, yet preserve so many of them as may be useful to us, and easily ruled by us.

For, of Lyons, Wolves, and all such as are called wild Beasts, (whether little or great,) we cannot take a certain number, which being preserved, may afford us any relife necessary to life, as we may of kine, horses, and the rest, that are called tame Creatures. Whence it comes to pass, that we endeavour wholly to exterminate those, and of these cut off only so many as are over and above a Competent stock.

Hereupon, (to touch briefly on this also,) we may conceive, that even among those Nations who make their choice of certain sorts of Animals for food, *the matter was determined and prescribed by certain Laws, grounded upon reason correspondent to those we have now given. And as for those Animals that were not to be eaten, there was respect had to their utility and inutility, and for some*

reason

reason Peculiar to each Country; to the constitutious whereof there is no necessity for us to adhere, who live not in those places.

Hence we come to understand, that from the very beginning a difference was put betwixt the killing of Men, and the killing of all other Animals * ; for as to other Animals it is manifest, that those primitive wise persons who prescribed what we should do, and what not, did not forbid to kill any of them, because the profit that ariseth from them is perfected by the contrary action, that is, by killing them. For it could not be, that men living promiscuously amongst beasts, could preserve themselves in safety otherwise, than by expelling or destroying them.

* Porph.

But as concerning Mankind, * Some, who at that time were more gracious than the rest, (these perhaps were they that perswaded men first to enter into the Covenant we spoke of) remembred, that in those places where men lived promiscuously, they had somtimes abstained from slaughter, out of a respect to that utility which conduced to their safety, as also represented to others in their meetings what had hapned, that refraining from slaughter of an Animal of the same kind, they might defend the society of life, which is generally the cause of every man's particular safety. And it was profitable at first to quit the society of either other Animals, or Men meeting together, at least not to hurt any, to avoid the incensing of, not only other Animals of several kinds, but also Men, who are all of the same, and apt enough of themselves to do harm. Whence, upon this account, Men refrained laying hands upon an Animal of their own Species, that offer'd itself to the communication of things necessary, and contributed some benefit to society.

* Porph.

But in process of time, there being a great encrease on both sides, and Animals of different Species being forc'd away, Men began to make use of their reason, (whereas before that time they had trusted altogether to memory,) and to enter into consultation what was to be done in order to their safety, when they should come together, and conjoin their habitations. For they endeavor'd strongly to restrain those who rashly and imprudently would murder one another, and thereby made the mutual assistence, that Men were able to afford each other, daily the weaker; and this chiefly, because those great inconveniences which had frequently fallen out in former times upon the like cases, were utterly forgotten. Now whilst they endeavoured to bring this to pass, they at length introduced the Laws and Constitutions which continue in all Cities and Nations even to this day, the Common people of their own accord consenting to them, as I said; being sensible how much greater utility would from thence accrue to them, living in mutual society. In like manner, it conduceth also to security, both to destroy without any pity what is pernicious, and to preserve whatever is useful to exterminate it.

Thus it is probable, that upon these Considerations, the slaughter of all other Animals came to be permitted, and that of Men prohibited. But I insist too long hereupon.

CHAP. XXVIII.

With what Right Justice is to be exercised.

JUstice being established by a mutual agreement, it remains, that every Man, whether a Native or Alien, ought, from the time he hath given up his Name to a Society, to account himself a Member of that Society, upon this condition, either expresly or tacitly, that he hurt non of his Fellow-members, nor be hurt by any other. Wherefore he must either stand to the Covenant, or depart out of the Society; for he is not to be suffer'd to live in the Society upon any other terms. Whence it follows, since by nature no Man is willing to receive harm from another, that he do not that to another which he would not should be done to himself.

Hereupon it may be imagined, that the Laws in all Societies were made in favour of the wise, not to prevent wise Men from doing unjustly, but that others should not injure them : For as for them, they are so well disposed, as that, if there were no Laws, yet would they not do harm to any. They have prescribed bounds to their desires, and accommodate them to Nature, which requires nothing that must be obtained by ways of Injustice; nor indeed is there any of Nature's pleasures which induceth a Man to do injury to another, but some exorbitant desire arising from vain opinion.

For Nature having (for Example,) provided Herbs, Corn, Fruits, for Food, competent and useful, and Water for Drink, things easie to be had, it cannot be the pleasure of satisfying Hunger and Thirst, that should cause a Man to rob his Neighbour, or commit any of those Injuries which they usually do : But the vain desire of living at a higher rate, more splendidly and wantonly, that so he may acquire wealth enough to discharge the expences of his Luxury. The same may be said also of those, who not content with plain Apparel, a plain House, a plain Match, and the like, through Ambition, Pride, Lust, and other Passions, desire more than Nature needs.

Moreover, seeing that a wise Man, as I hinted formerly, doth all things for his own sake, nothing certainly can more conduce to his advantage, than to observe Justice exactly. For in giving to every one his due, and harming no Man, he, to his utmost, preserves and keeps safe that Society, which, unless it be safe, he cannot be safe himself; nor doth he provoke any Man to revenge an injury suffered at his hand, or fear any mulct or punishment to be inflicted upon him by publick Decree. Thus being conscious to himself of no ill done, he remains free from all perturbation, which is the greatest benefit and fruit of Justice; and while he reaps that, what can be more to his own advantage ?

Neither ought you to think, that he, who, though secretly, and without the knowledge of any Man, violates Right, or the Covenants ratifi'd by general consent, to prevent the commitmitting and suffering of wrong, can live in the same security and indisturbance as the Just Man doth, because (as I said,) he cannot assure himself that his Injustice shall never be brought to light: For Crimes, though they may be secret, can never be secure; nor doth it avail an Offender to be concealed from others, while he can never be concealed from himself.

Truly, though his Offence were never so well concealed for a time, yet it is very uncertain, whether it will continue so concealed till his death. For first, there is a jealousie and suspicion, that follows upon ill actions; and again, there have been many who have detected themselves, some in Dreams, others in raving Fits, others in Drink, others through Incogitancy. S that a wicked Man, though he may for a tim lie hid both from gods and men, (as they say,) yet he hath reason to mistrust that he will not be concealed for ever.

Hence is it, that notwithstanding Injustice is not an Ill in itself, because what is reputed unjust in one place, may be Just in another; yet it is an Ill in respect of that fear, which, stinging the Conscience, creats in it a continual suspition, that at some time or other his unjust deeds will come to the ears of the avengers of Unjustice, and so he be called to a severe account for them. Thus there is nothing that more conduceth as to security, so likewise to a quiet and pleasant life, than to live innocently, and upon no occasion to violate the common Covenants of Peace.

Wherefore since the Just and unjust are in this opposition, that the Just, of all men, are the most fee from Perturbations, What can be more profitable to those, than Justice? What more hurtful to these, than Injustice? For how can any anguish of mind, solicitudes, dayly and nightly fears, be profitable to any man?

Justice therefore being so great a good, and Injustice so great an ill, let us embrace one, and abhor the other. And if at any time our mind seem to stagger, and we are in suspence what to do, let us fix on some grave good Man, and suppose him to be always present with us, that we may live and do all things as if he looked upon us.

By this means we shall not only avoid the doing of any thing openly against Justice, but also of offending in secret against the Rules of Honesty. This good man will be to us in stead of a Guardian or Tutor, whom, because we reverence, we fear to offend. Following this counsel therefore, thus argue; If he were present, I would not do it; Why do I do it in his absence? He would find fault with it, becuse it is Ill; Why do not I shun ill, of my self? Thus, do all things, as if some such person looked on; for if you in this manner reverence another, you will soon come to be reverenced your self.

CHAP. XXIX.

Of Beneficence, Gratitude, Piety, Observance.

WE come next to the Virtues which we said were allied to Justice, for that they have regard to other persons; and though they are not (as Justice is,) prescribed by Laws and Covenants, yet they import, out of decency, a certain obligation like that of Justice.

The first is *Beneficence,* or the doing good to others, whereunto those are obliged, who are able to assist or relieve others, either with their hand or purse. If they deny the assistence of their hands, they are censured as barbarous, cruel, inhomen; if that of their purse, they are thought the same, as also sorbid, tenacious, covetous, and the like. But if they assist others, they are accounted courteous, civil, kind; as also liberal, munificent, magnificent, *&c.* So that they are obliged for their own sakes to do good to others, so far as may be without prodigality.

For those who practise this Virtue, procure to themselves good will, and (what most of all conduces to quiet living) dearness or tender estimation from others: They who use it not, illwill, and (what most occasions troublesom life) contempt and hatred. Take heed therefore you omit not to be beneficent, at least in small matters, that so you lose not the advantage of being accounted ready to gratifie others, even in great.

Not without reason did I say formerly, It is not only more honourable, but also more delightful to give than to receive a benefit; because, the giver thereby makes himself superior to the receiver, and reaps moreover the interest of Thanks; and there is not any thing that Joys a man more than Thanks. A beneficent person is like a Fountain, which if you should suppose it to have a reasonable Soul, what Joy would it not have at the sight of so many Cornfields, and Pastures, which flourish and smile as it were with plenty and verdure, and all by the diffusion of its streams upon them?

The second is *gratitude,* to which every man that receives a benefit is reciprocally obliged, unless he would incur the greatest hatred and ignominy. For Ingratitude is worthily hateful to all men; because seeing nothing is more suitable to nature, than to be propense to receive a good, it is highly contrary to nature, not to be readily grateful towards the Author of that good.

Now since no man is more gratefully affected towards his Benefactors than the wise man, we may Justly affirm, that only the wise man knows how to fulfil the duty of gratitude, because he alone is ready upon all occasions to express his thankfulness to his Friends, both present and absent, even to those that are dead.

Others pay thanks only to present Friends, when present, and this perhaps for their own farther ends, to encourage them to some new favour; but how few are there, who gratefully commemorate their absent Benefactors? Who requite the good they did them upon their Children, or other Relations? How few who honour their memory after death; who rejoyce not rather, as if their obligations were cancelled? Who love those that were dear to them, respect them, and as far as in them lies, do good to them?

The third is *Piety,* the most sacred species of gratitude. It looks upon our parents in the first place, to whom every man is more obliged than to all the World besides: For to others he may
owe

owe other things; but to his parents he owes himself. Therefore if ingratitude to others be hateful, that which is shewn to parents must certainly be the most horrid and detestable.

We say, in the first place; because piety in the second place extends to kindred, and chiefly to our Brothers and Sisters, to whom we are obliged by the interest of our parents; in such manner as that we cannot shew ourselves disrespectful and unkind to them, but we must be at the same time highly ungrateful to our parents, and all our progenitors, who in the circle of their love and benevolence comprehended all that were, and should afterwards be derived from them.

Nor is this piety distinct from that dearness we are to bear towards our native Country, which comprehends our Parents and all our kindred, and receives us at our Birth, brings us up and protects us. And as by the interest of our parents we are obliged to our kindred, so by the interest of our Country we are obliged to respect all our Countrymen; but more especially the Magistrates and Princes, who defend the Country itself, and the laws of it, and give us this benefit in particular, that under their protection we may live securely and peaceably.

The fourth is *observance*, or that reverence which we owe to all persons of eminency in any kind. This is accompany'd partly with gratitude and piety, (for we cannot any way better express the gratefulness of our minds, than by giving due veneration and worship to our Benefactors, Parents, Governours, Princes, and all men of dignity and power,) and partly with honour and respect, as it is the best testimony we can give of our internal sentiments of their deservings, who excel in Age, Wisdom, Learning, and Virtue, the most honourable of all things.

To this observance belongs that which men call *Religion* and *Sanctity* toward the Gods, whom we are bound to reverence and honour no otherwise than our parents, nor through hope of any reward, but (as I said before,) for their transcendent majesty and the supremacy of their nature. Because, whatever is excellent deserves a Just veneration, and no excellency is greater than that of the divine Nature, for it is immortal and most blessed.

Thus understanding, that the Gods neither create troubles themselves, nor give to others, we piously and holily reverence their most excellent nature.

CHAP. XXX.

Of Friendship.

THE last is *Friendship*, to which all are mutually obliged, who love and are reciprocally belov'd. And well may it be the close and crown of this Discourse; for amongst all the means procured by wisdome, to make life happy, there is not any thing more full and pleasant than Friendship; and the same reason that confirms the mind not to fear any lasting or eternal ill, doth also assure, that, in life, there is no Sanctuary so safe, no protection so secure as that of Friendship, which together with that security, conferreth also very great pleasures.

For as hatreds, envies, despites are enemies to pleasure; so are friendships, not only most faithful conservers, but effectual causers of pleasures, aswell to our friend as to ourselves: By which, men not only enjoy present things more fully, but are cheer'd with hopes of those to come. And a solitary life destitute of friends being full of fears, and subject to treacheries, reason itself adviseth us to procure friendships, by which the mind is confirmed, and possessed with hopes of enjoying future pleasures.

Now though friendship is contracted in respect of use and utility, in like manner as we sow the earth in hope of a crop hereafter; and the first meetings and conversations of friendship are made in respect of the utility and pleasures which are hoped from thence; Yet when this custom hath gone on to intimacy, then love so flourisheth, that though there were not any benefit of friendship, yet friends would be loved for their own sakes. If we love Places, Temples, Cities, Academies, Plains, Horses, Dogs, Sports, out of an habitual custome of exercising or hunting, how much easier and more Justly may we do this in conversation with men?

But in the choice of our friends, we must be exceeding cautions and prudent; for it concerns us to be more circumspect with whom we eat, than what we eat. And though to eat alone without a friend, be to lead the life of a Lion or Wolfe, yet we must be careful to choose such a friend, whose conversation may be the best sauce to our meat. We must seek one to whom nothing is more in esteem, than candor, simplicity, and sincerity; one that is not morose, querulous, and murmuring at all things, but who by his complacency, alacrity, and pleasantness may render our life sweet to us.

Friendship, I grant, consists in, and is kept alive by, the mutual participation of pleasures or goods which we may enjoy whilst we live; yet is it not necessary that the goods of friends should be put into one common stock, as he conceived, who said, *Amongst Friends all things are common.* This implies a diffidence, (that all their wills may not continue constant,) and they who are diffident are not friends; such only are friends, who can with full confidence, and freedom take and use so much of their friends goods or estate as they need, although kept in several not in one Joyntstock, no otherwise than as if it were their own, esteeming them to be no less their own, than if they had them in their own possession and keeping.

This sounds strange in the ears of the vulgar: But what are they to us? There is no faith or constancy in their kindness and friendship, they being uncapable of these things and of the least part of commendable Wisdom.

Moreover, he that is one of the vulgar understands not, what is profitable in private or publick, nor can distinguish betwixt good manners and bad.

I speak therefore of the wise only, amongst whom there is a kind league, and covenant not to love their friends less than themselves, which we know may be done and see it often comes to pass; whence is it manifest, that there can be nothing more conducing to pleasant living than such a conjunction.

Whence also we understand, that the placing of the chief good in pleasure is so far from being obstructive hereunto, that without it there can be no institution of friendship.

For it being impossible for us to conserve the sweetness and security of our lives firm and lasting without friendship, and to preserve friendship, unless we love our friends as much as ourselves; this therefore and pleasure are the inseparable adjuncts of friendship; for, we rejoyce in our friends joy as much as if it were our own, and are concern'd equally in his grief.

A wise man therefore will be alike towards his friend as towards himself; what labour and pains he undergoes for his own pleasure, the same will he undergo for the pleasure of his friend. And as he would rejoyce to think, that he hath one that will sit by him, if he should be sick, and relieve him if he were cast into prison, or fallen into want; so will he rejoyce, as having one, by whom, if he should fall sick, he may sit, and whom if imprisoned, or fallen into want, relieve. And not only this, but his love will be so great, as to undergo the greatest torments, even death itself, for his friend's sake.

We have known it certainly happen, (and that within the memory of our parents,) that many, who had the happiness of procuring to themselves full confidence and security in the Society of men, living in the same opinion and the same affections with them, have, in the assurance of this comfortable league, lived most sweetly together, and been conjoyned with so absolute a nearness, as that one could without the least reluctancy, wish to suffer for the other, condemned to dye.

This is all I had to say concerning ETHICK, which in the beginning I asserted to be the chiefest part of Philosophy. You, who ever you are, that aspire to true wisdom, practise and meditate upon these rules, considering them as the grounds of honest, well, and happy living.

Meditate, I say, upon them day and night, as well when you are alone, as when in company of some faithful companion who is like yourself, and to whom you may say, We are indeed alone, but by this means we have the greater opportunity of making inquisition into truth without prejudice. I speak not to many, but to you; and you speak not to many, but to me; and that's enough, since each to other is a theatre large enough.

Do you not now grant, that no man can be compared to him, whose mind is rightly informed as concerning the Gods, and is fearless of Death and who hath so reasoned concerning the end of nature, and the ultimate good, as to understand, that it may be compleated and attain'd with the greatest facility imaginable, and that whatever ill he must endure, either is short, if vehement; if long, gentle; and telleth himself, that there is no such thing as an inevitable necessity of fates concerning him, but that he hath an absolute freedom of will, and that nothing at all or very little of Fortune can at any time intervene to cross him; and the rest which we have laid down?

Certainly when you shall come to be such a man as this, you will never be troubled waking *Laert.* nor sleeping (for even in sleep you will be just as you are when awake, by reason of the wellcom posedness of your mind,) but shall live like some Deity among men. For that man who spends his life in the enjoyment of immortal goods, is far different from a mortal creature. Hitherto *Gassendus.*

CHAP. XXXI.

Wherein Epicurus, *asserting Pleasure to be the ultimate good, differs from the* Cyrenaicks.

Though *Epicurus* agrees with the *Cyrenaicks* in asserting Pleasure to be the ultimate good yet * *concerning this Pleasure, they disagree.* *Laert. The* Cyrenaicks *admit not pleasure, to consist in rest, but in motion only*, Epicurus *allowed both, as well that of the Soul as of the Body, as he asserts in his Book* Of Election and Avoidance, *and in his Treatise of the End, and in his first book of* Lives *and in his Epistle to the Philosophers at Mitylene. Likewise* Diogenes *in the eleventh of his Select Rules, and* Democritus *in his* Timocrates, *for thus; Whereas pleasure is twofold, one consisting in motion, the other in rest,* &c. *And* Epicurus *in his Treatise* Of Elections, *expresly thus; Of pleasures, indolence and imperturbation consist in rest; and delight, in motion.*

Moreover he differs from the Cyrenaicks, *for that they conceived the pains of the Body to be worse than those of the mind; whence it comes to pass, that, upon Malefactors, Corporal punishment is inflicted as being the most grievous. But* Epicurus *held, that the pains of the mind are the greatest, for that no ill can afflict the Body longer than whilst it is present; but besides the present, the past and future also torment the Mind; and by the same reason, the pleasures of the Soul are the greatest. Thus much of the* Epicurean, *the last of all the* Italick *Sects.*

FINIS.

A
CHRONOLOGICAL
TABLE.

Olymp.	Archons.	Olympick Victors.
XXX 2 3 4		
XXXI 2 3 4		
XXXII 2 3 4		
XXXIII 2 3 4		
XXXIV 2 3 4		
XXXV 2 3 4	*Damasias*. See Life of *Thales*. Chap. 2.	*Sphærus*. Dion.
XXXVI 2 3 4	*Epænetus*. Antig. Carist. Hist. Mir. 133.	*Phryno*. Euseb. probably the same with whom *Pittacus* fought. Pitt. c. 1. but *Antigonus Caristius* calls the Victor this year, *Arytamas*.
XXXVII 2 3 4		
XXXVIII 2 3 4		
XXXIX 2 3 4	*Draco*. Clem. Alex. Strom. 1. Tatian. Suid.	
XL 2 3 4		

1. *Thales*

	1. *Thales* born. See *Thales*, chap. 2. 2. *Solon* born about this time.	2. *Ancus Martius* King of *Rome*. *Dion. Halic. lib.* 3.
	4. *Periander* begun to Reign at *Corinth*. *Periand.* chap. 2.	
	Arion. See *Periand.* chap. 4.	

Olymp.	Archons.	Olympick Victors.
XLI 2 3 4	*Heniochides.* Halic. lib. 3.	*Cleonidas.* Dion.
XLII 2 3 4		
XLIII 2 3 4	*Aristocles,* (perhaps.) Marm. Arund.	
XLIV 2 3 4		
XLV 2 3 4	*Megacles* (perhaps.) Plut. in Solon.	
XLVI 2 3 4	*Philombrotus.* Plut. in Solone. *Solon.* Laert. in Solone. *Dropides.* Philostr. in Critia.	
XLVII 2 3 4	*Eucrates.* Laert. in Amachars. *Simon.* Marm.	
XLVIII 2 3 4	*Philippus.* Clem. Strom. 1. Euseb. Chron. 1.	*Glaucias.* Pausan. *Glycon.* Euseb.
XLIX 2 3 4	*Damasias* the Second. *Marm.* See *Thales* Life, Chap. 2.	
L 2 3 4	*Archestratides.* Dionys. Halic. lib. 4.	*Epitelides.*

Anaximander

		2. *Tarquinius Priscus*, King of *Rome. Dionyſ. Halic. lib.* 3. 3. *Allyattes*, King of *Lydia*, begun to Reign.
	Anaximander born. *Leart.*	
ÆRA PHILOSOPHICA	1. *Epimenides* luſtrates the City of *Athens. Laert.* 3. *Solon* made *Archon. Laert.*	
	1. *Anacharſis* came to *Athens* to viſit *Solon, Laert.*	
	4. *Periander* died. *Laert.*	
1 2	In the third year, *Damaſias* being Archon, the Attribute of *Wiſe* was conferred on *Thales* and the reſt, from which the Philoſophical Æra begins. *Thal chap.* 5.	
3 4 5 6	*Theſpis* preſents Tragedies; reproved by *Solon, Sol. cap.* 10 *Anaximander* found out the obliquity of the Zodiack, *Plin.*	4. *Servius Tullus*, King of *Rome.*

Olymp.

Olymp.	Archons.	Olympick Victors.
LI 2 3 4	Aristogenes. Laert.	
LII 2 3 4		
LIII 2 3 4	Hippoclides. Marcellin. in vita Thucyd.	
LIV 2 3 4	Comias. Plut. in Solone. Marm.	
LV 2 3 4	Hegestratus. Plut. in Solone.	
LVI 2 3 4	Euthydemus. Marm. Laert. See Life of Chilon.	
LVII 2 3 4		
LVIII 2 3 4	Erixiclides. Pauf. in Phoc. See Thal.	Diognetus.
LIX 2 3 4		
LX 2 3 4		

Æra

Æra Phil.		
7 8 9 10	Pittachus dies.	
11 12 13 14		
15 16 17 18	Pythagoras born.	
19 20 21 22		
23 24 25 26		1. Cyrus began his Reign over Persia. 4. Crœsus King of Lydia.
27 28 29 30	Chilon Ephorus, *Laert.*	
31 32 33 34		
35 36 37 38	Pythagoras went into Ægypt.	
39 40 41 42		1. Cyrus vanquisheth Crœsus.
43 44 45 46		

Olymp.	Archons.	Olympick Victors.
LXI 1	--- næus 1. Marm.	Agatharcus.
2	Theribles, Diod. excerpt. p. 241.	
3	Heraclides, Dionyſ. Halic, 4. rather	
4		
LXII 1		Eryxidas.
2		
3		
4		
LXIII 1		
2		
3		
4		
LXIV 1	Miltiades, Halic. 7.	
2		
3		
4		
LXV 1		
2		
3		
4		
LXVI 1		
2		
3		
4		
LXVII 1		
2		
3		
4		
LXVIII 1	Iſagoras, Halic. 1. & 5.	Iſchomachus.
2		
3		
4		
LXIX 1	Aceſterides, Hal. 5.	Iſchomachus.
2		
3		
4		
LXX 1	Mynus, Hal. 5.	Nicæas.
2		
3		
4		

Æra

Æra Phil.		
47 48 49 50		4. *Tarquinius Superbus*, King of *Rome. Halic.* 4.
51 52 53 54	(years. *Arist. Pol.* 5. *Pisistratus* died, having Reigned 17.	
55 56 57 58	*Cambyses* conquers *Ægyt*, and sends *Pythagoras* prisoner to *Badylon*.	2, *Amasis* King of *Ægypt* dies, *Psammeticus* his Son succeeds him.
59 60 61 62		4. *Darius Hystaspis*, King of *Persia*.
63 64 65 66		
67 68 69 70	*Pythagoras* went into *Italy*.	
71 72 73 74		
75 76 77 78		
79 80 81 82		
83 84 85 86	*Anaxagoras* born. *Pythagoras* died. *Euseb.*	

Olymp.	Archous.	Olympick Victors.
LXXI 2 3 4	*Hipparchus*, Halic. 6. *Pythocritus*, Marm.	*Tisicrates*.
LXXII 2 3 4	*Diognetus*, Hal. 6. *Phænippus* 2. Plut. in Aristide. *Hybrilides*, Hal. 7. Pauf. El. 2. *Aristides*, Plut. ibid. Marm. *Themistocles*, Thuc. 1. Pauf. lib. 27.	*Tisicrates*.
LXXIII 2 3 4	*Anchises* Hal. 8. *Lacratides*, Schol. Arist. Suid. *Phædon*, Plut. *Philocrates*, Marm.	*Astylus*.
LXXIV 2 3 4	*Leostratus*, Hal. 8. *Nicodemus*, Hal. 8. *Calliades*, Marm.	*Astylus*,
LXXV 2 3 4	*Xantippus*, Marm. *Cal.* Hal. 9. Diod. *Timosthenes*, Marm. *Xantippus*, Diod. *Idimantus*, Marm. *Timosthenes*. Diod. *Adimantus*, Diod.	
LXXVI 2 3 4	*Phædon*, Hal. Diod. *Dromoclides* Diod. *Acestorides*, Diod. *Menon*, Diod.	*Scamandrus*.
LXXVII 2 3 4	*Chares*, Mamr. Halic. Diod. *Praxiergus*. Diod, (Socr. chap. 1. *Apsephion*, Mar. *Demotion*, Diod. see *Theagenides*, Marm.	*Dates*.
LXXVIII 2 3 4	*Theagenides*, Hal. Diod. *Lysistratus*, Diod. *Lysanias*, Diod. *Lysithens*, Diod.	*Parmenides*.
LXXIX 2 3 4	*Archedemides*, Diod. *Archim.* Pauf. *Euthippus*, Marm. *Thepolemus*, Diod. *Conon*, Dion. *Euippus*, Diod.	*Xenophon*.
LXXX 2 3 4	*Phasiclides*, Diod. *Phrasides*, Hal. *Philocles*, Diod. *Bion*, Diod. *Callias* 1. Marm. *Mnesithides*, Diod.	*Torymbas*.

Æra

(645)

Æra Philo.		
87 88 89 90		
91 92 93 94		2. The Fight at *Marathon*.
95 96 97 98		3. *Darius* dies, *Xerxes* succeeds.
99 100 101 102		
103 104 105 106	*Anaxagoras* went to *Athens*. *Laert*.	1. *Xerxes* croſt the *Hellespont* The Fight at *Salamis*.
107 108 109 110		
111 112 113 114	*Socrates* born. A Stone fell from Heaven, foretold by *Anaxagoras*.	
115 116 117 118		
119 120 121 122		1. *Artaxerxes Longimanus* King of *Perſia*.
123 124 125 126	*Democritus* born, *Anaxagoras* being 40 years old. *Laert*.	

Olymp.

Olymp.	Archons.	Olympick Victors.
LXXXI	Collias, Diod. Hal.	Polymnestus.
2	Sosistratus, Diod.	
3	Ariston, Diod.	
4	Lysicrates, Diod.	
LXXXII	Chærophanes, Halic.	Lycus.
2	Antidotus, Diod.	
3	Euthydemus, Diod. lib. 12.	
4	Pedieus, Diod.	
LXXXIII	Philiscus, Diod. Halic.	Crison.
2	Timarchides, Diod.	
3	Callimachus, Diod.	
4	Lysimachides, Diod.	
LXXXIV	Diphilus, Marm. Praxiteles, Diod.	Crison.
2	Lysanias, Diod.	
3	Diphilus, Diod. Halic.	
4	Timocles, Diod.	
LXXXV	Munichides, Diod.	Crison.
2	Glaucides, Diod.	
3	Theodorus Diod.	
4	Euthemenes, Diod.	
LXXXVI	Nausimachus, Diod.	Theopompus, or, as Plato, Diopompus.
2	Antilochides, Diod.	
3	Chares, Diod.	
4	Apseudes, Diod.	
LXXXVII	Pythodorus, Diod.	Sophon.
2	Euthydemus, Diod.	
3	Apollodorus, Diod.	
4	Epaminondas, Diod.	
LXXXVIII	Diotimus, Diod. Life of Eucl. c. 3.	Symmachus.
2	Euclides, Diod. Euclees, Arist. See	
3	Euthydemus, Diod.	
4	Stratocles, Diod.	
LXXXIX	Isarchus, Diod.	Symmachus 2.
2	Amintas, Diod.	
3	Alcæus, Diod.	
4	Astyphilus, Marm. Ariston, Diod.	
XC	Aristophilus, Diod.	Hyperbius.
2	Archias, Diod.	
3	Antiphon, Diod.	
4	Euphormus, Diod.	

Æra Phil.		
127128129130		
131132133134	*Xenophon* born about this time.*Anaxagoras* condemned, and Banished *Athens*.	1. From the building of *Rome*300. *Italic*.
135136137138		
139140141142		
143144145146		
147148149150		
151152153154		1. *Archelaus* King of *Macedon*.2. The Peloponnesian War; year 1 2 3
155156157158	*Anaxagoras* died.	4567
159160161162	The Fight at *Delium*, in which were *Socrates* and *Xenophon*. The *Clowds* of *Aristophanes* acted.The *Clowds* of *Aristophanes* acted the second time.The time of *Xenophon's* Symposium.	891011
163164165166		12131415

Olymp.

Olymp.	Archons.	
XCI	Aristomnestus, Diod.	
2	Chabrias, Diod.	
3	Pisander, Diod.	
4	Cleocritus, Diod.	
XCII	Callias, Diod. Halic.	
2	Theopompus, Diod.	
3	Glaucippus, Diod. Halic.	
4	Diocles, Diod.	
XCIII	Euctemon, Diod.	
2	Antigenes, Diod.	
3	Callias, Diod.	
4	Alexias, Diod.	
XCIV	Pythodorus.	
2	Euclides, Diod.	
3	Micion, Diod.	
4	Exenætus, Diod.	
XCV	Laches, Diod.	
2	Aristocrates, Diod.	
3	Pithycles, Diod.	
4	Iysiades, Diod.	
XCVI	Phormio, Diod.	
2	Diophantus, Diod.	
3	Eubulides, Diod.	
4	Demostratus, Diod.	
XCVII	Philocles, Diod.	Terires.
2	Nicoteles, Diod.	
3	Demostratus, Diod.	
4	Antipater, Diod.	
XCVIII	Pyrrhion, Diod. Pyrgion, Halic.	Sosippus.
2	Theodotus, Diod.	
3	Mystichides, Diod.	
4	Dexitheus, Diod.	
XCIX	Diotrephes, Diod.	Dicon.
2	Phanostratus, Diod.	
3	Menander, Diod.	
4	Demophilus, Diod.	
C	Pytheus, Marm. Diod.	Dionysiodorus.
2	Nicon, Diod. Halic.	
3	Nausinicus, Diod. Halic.	
4	Callias, Marm. Diod.	

Æra

Æra Phil.			Olymp.
167			16
168			17
169			18
170			19
171		*Thucydides* ends: *Xenophon* begins.	20
172			21
173			22
174			23
175			24
176		2 The first ascent of *Cyrus* into *Asia*.	25
177		3 *Dionysius* made King of *Syracuse*.	26
178			27
179	The 30 Tyrants at *Athens*. See *Socr* chap. 9.		
180			
181	(put down.		
182	*Xenopeon's* retreat. The 30 Tyrants	4 The ascent of *Cyrus* into *Asia*.	
183	*Socrates* put to death. End of *Xenophon's* retreat.		
184			
185			
186			
187		1 *Agesilaus* goes into *Asia* against the Persian.	
188		2 *Agesilaus* call'd him, fights with the Bœotians at *Coronea*.	
189		3 *Conon* re-edifies the Walls of *Athens*.	
190			
191			
192			
193			
194			
195			
196			
197			
198			
199	*Aristotle* born. *Laert.*		
200			
201			
202			
203			
204			
205			
206			

Olymp.	Archons.	Olympick Victors.
CI 2 3 4	Chariander, Diod. Hippodamus, Diod. Socratides, Diod. Asteius, Marm. Diod.	Damon.
CII 2 3 4	Alcisthenes, Diod. Demosth. Halic. Phrasiclides, Marm. Diod. Dem. Pauf. Dysnicetus, Diod. Dyscinctus, Pauf. Lysistratus, Diod.	Damon.
CIII 2 3 4	Nausigenes, Marm. Diod. Polycelus Diod. Polyzelus, Halic. Cephisodorus, Marm. Diod. Chion, Diod.	Pithostratus.
CIV 2 3 4	Timocrates, Diod. Halic. Chariclides, Diod. Molon, Diod. Halic. Nicophemus, Diod. Halic.	Phocides.
CV 2 3 4	Callimedes, Diod. Halic. Eucharistus, Diod. Halic. Cephisodorus, Diod. Halic. Agathocles, Mar. Diod. Halic. Pauf.	Porus.
CVI 2 3 4	Elpinus, Diod. Halic. Callistratus, Marm. Diod. Halic. Diotymus, Diod. Halic. Eudemus, Diod. Halic.	Porus.
CVII 2 3 4	Aristodemus, Diod. Halic. Thessalus, Diod. Halic. Apollodorus, Diod. Halic. Callimachus, Diod. Halic.	Suierinas.
CVIII 2 3 4	Theophilus, Diod. Theomnestus, Halic. Themistocles, Diod. Halic. Archias, Diod. Halic. Eubulus, Diod. Eudorus, Halic.	Polycles.
CIX 2 3 4	Lyciscus, Diod. Halic. Pythodorus, Diod. Pythodotus, Halic. Sosigenes, Diod. Halic. Nicomachus, Diod. Halic.	Aristolochus.
CX 2 3 4	Theophrastus, Diod. Halic. Lysimachides, Diod. Halic. Charondas, Diod.. Chæronidas, Halic. Phrynichus, Diod. Halic.	Anticles.

Æra

Æra Philo.		
207		
208		
209		
210		
211		
212		
213		
214		
215	Eudoxus flourished. *Laert.*	1. *Dionysius* the Elder dieth, succeeded by his Son.
216		
217		
218		
219		
220		
221		
222		
223		
224		
225		
226		
227		
228		
229		3. *Dion* murdered.
230		
231		
232		
233		
234		
235	*Plato* died 82 years old, *Athen.*	
236	*Aristotle* went to *Hermias* at *Atarne.*	
237		
238	*Aristotle* went to *Mysilene. Laert.*	
239		
240	*Aristotle* went to King *Philip*, *Alexander* being 15 years old. *Laert.*	
241		
242		
243		
244		
245		
246		

Olymp.	Archons.	Olympick Victors.
CXI	Pythodorus, Diod. Pythodemus, Halic.	Cleomantis.
2	Euænetus, Diod. Halic.	
3	Cteficles, Diod. Halic.	
4	Nicocrates, Diod. Halic.	
CXII	Niceratus, Diod. Nicetes, Halic.	Gryllus.
2	Aristophanes, Diod. Halic.	
3	Aristophon, Diod. Halic.	
4	Cephisophon, Diod.	
CXIII	Euthycritus, Diod. Halic.	
2	Chremes, Diod. Hegemon, Halic.	
3	Anticles, Diod. Chremes, Halic.	
4	Soficles, Diod. Anticles, Halic.	
CXIV	Agafias, Diod.	Micinas.
2	Cephifodorus, Diod. Halic.	
3	Philocles, Diod. Halic.	
4	Archippus, Halic.	
CXV	Neæchmus, Diod.	Dinomenes.
2	Apollodorus, Diod. Halic.	
3	Archippus, Diod. Halic.	
4	Demogenes, Diod. Halic.	
CXVI	Democlides, Diod. Halic.	Parmenio.
2	Praxibulus, Diod. Halic.	
3	Nicodorus, Diod. Halic.	
4	Theophrastus, Diod. Halic.	
CXVII	Polemon, Diod. Halic.	Apollonides.
2	Simonides, Diod. Halic.	
3	Hieromnemon, Diod. Halic.	
4	Demetrius Phalereus, Diod. Halic.	
CXVIII	Charinus, Diod. Cærimus, Halic.	Andromenes.
2	Anaxicrates, Diod. Halic.	
3	Corybus, Diod. Coræbus. Halic.	
4	Xenippus, Diod. Euxenippus, Halic.	
CXIX	Pherecles, Diod. Phericles, Halic.	
2	Leostratus, Diod. Halic.	
3	Nicocles, Diod. Halic.	
4	Calliarchus, Halic.	
CXX	Hegemachus, Halic.	
2	Euclemon, Halic.	
3	Mnefidemus, Halic.	
4	Antiphanes, Halic.	

Æra

Æra Phil.		
247 248 249 250	*Aristotle* teacheth in the *Lycæum* 13 Years.	1. *Alexander* begun to Reign. 3. *Alexander*'s Expedition in to *Asia* against *Darius*.
251 252 253 254		
255 256 257 258		
259 260 261 262	*Aristotle* went to *Chalcis*, and died there, 63 years old. *Laert*	
263 264 265 266		
267 268 269 270		
271 272 273 274		
275 276 277 278		
279 280 281 282		
283 284 285 286		

Olymp.

Olymp.	Archons.	Olympick Victors.
CXXI	*Nicias*, Halic.	
2	*Nicostratus*, Halic.	
3	*Olympiodorus*, Halic.	
4	*Philippus*, Halic.	
CXXII		
2		
3		
4		
CXXIII		*Idæus*, Pausan. Eliac. 2.
2		
3		
4		
CXXIV		
2		
3		
4		
CXXV		
2		
3		
4		
CXXVI		
2		
3		
4		
CXXVII	*Pytharatus.* Cic.	
2		
3		
4		
CXXVIII		
2		
3		
4		
CXXIX	*Diognetus.*	
2		
3		
4		
CXXX		
2		
3		
4		

Æra

(655)

Æra Phil.		Olymp.
287		
288		
289		
290		
291		
292		
293		
294		
295		
296		
297		
298		
299		
300		
301		
302		
303		
304		
305		
306		
307		
308		
309		
310		
311		
312		
313		
314		
315		
316		
317		
318		
319		
320		
321		
322		
323		
324		
325		
326		

Olymp.	Æra Philo.		
CXXXI	327		
2	328		
3	329		
4	330		
CXXXII	331		
2	332		
3	333		
4	334		
CXXXIII	335		
2	336		
3	337		
4	338		
CXXXIV	339		
2	340		
3	341		
4	342		
CXXXV	343		
2	344		
3	345		
4	346		
CXXXVI	347		
2	348		
3	349		
4	350		
CXXXVII	351		
2	352		
3	353		
4	354		
CXXXVIII	355		
2	356		
3	357		
4	358		
CXXXIX	359		
2	360		
3	361		
4	362		
CXXXX	363		
2	364		
3	365		
4	366		

Olymp.	Æra Philo.		
CXLI	367		
2	368		
3	369		
4	370		
CXLII	371		
2	372		
3	373		
4	374		
CXLIII	375		
2	376		
3	377		
4	378		
CXLIV	379		
2	380		
3	381		
4	382		
CXLV	383		
2	384		
3	385		
4	386		
CXLVI	387		
2	388		
3	389		
4	390		
CXLVII	391		
2	392		
3	393		
4	394		
CXLVIII	395		
2	396		
3	397		
4	398		
CXLIX	399		
2	400		
3	401		
4	402		
CL	403		
2	404		
3	405		
4	406		
CLI	407		
2	408		
3	409		
4	410		

Olymp.	Æra Philo.		
CLII	411		
2	412		
3	413		
4	414		
CLIII	415		
2	416		
3	417		
4	418		
CLIV	419		
2	420		
3	421		
4	422		
CLV	423		
2	424		
3	425		
4	426		
CLVI	427		
2	428		
3	429		
4	430		
CLVII	431		
2	432		
3	433		
4	434		
CLVIII	435		
2	436		
3	437		
4	438		
CLIX	439		
2	440		
3	441		
4	442		
CLX	443		
2	444		
3	445		
4	446		
CLXI	447		
2	448		
3	449		
4	450		
CLXII	451	*Clitomachus* flourished.	
2	452		
3	453	*Carneades* died	
4	454		

A TOPOGRAPHICAL TABLE.

A

Abdera, a City of *Thrace*, situate next beyond the River *Nestus*, toward the East; Founded and Named by *Abdera*, Sister to *Diomedes*, in the 104th. year after the taking of *Troy*: And afterwards, (*Olymp.* 31.) re-edifi'd by a Colony of Clazomenians.

Ægina, an Island over against *Epidaurus*, in the Saronian Bay.

Ægos potamos, a River in the Thracian *Chersonesus*, distant from *Sestos* 15 Furlongs.

Ægypt, a Kingdom of *Africa*, most Eminent; divided into the Upper and Lower: It had Twenty Thousand Cities, the Principal were *Memphis*, *Diospolis*, and *Heliopolis*; Its River, *Nilus*.

Agrianes, a People of *Thrace*, dwelling upon the River *Agrianes*, betwixt the Mountains *Rhodope* and *Hæmus*. Of this Country perhaps was *Hippomedon* the Pythagorean, mentioned by *Jamblichus*. [*Doctr. Pyth.* p. 1. chap. 8.]

Agrigentum. See *Pythag.* Chap. 10.

Ambracia, an Eminent City of *Epirus*, in the bottom of the Abracian Bay, upon the River *Aracthus*, not far from the Sea. The Ambracion Bay parts *Epirus* from *Acarnania*.

Atarna, a City of *Mysia*.

Athens, the chief City of *Greece*, seated in *Attica*; founded by *Cecrops*.

Attica, an Eminent Region of *Greece*, bounding on the Territory of *Megara*, on the Shore over against *Salamis*; and on the Territory of the Bœotians, by Sea, at *Orpus*; by Land, at *Panactum*, at *Oenœ*, at *Hysiæ*.

B.

Bœotia, a Region of *Greece*, between *Attica* and *Phocis*; reaching from the Ægean Sea to the Corinthian Isthmus.

Brachmanes. See *Pythag. ch.* 5:

Branchidæ, a Town where there was a Temple to *Apollo*, on the Milesian Shore, between the Promontory of *Posideum*, and the City *Miletus*.

Byzantium, a City of *Thrace*, situate at the entrance of the *Bosphorus*, over against *Chalcedon*; *Constantine* afterwards enlarg'd it, from whom it is now called *Constantinople*.

C.

Caria, a Region of *Asia* bounded on the North by *Ionia*, on the East by *Lycia*, on the West by the Carpathian Sea, on the South by the Rhodian: Its principal Cities were *Miletus*, *Mindus*, *Halycarnassus*, and *Cnidus*.

Catana. See *Pythag. chap.* 10.

Chalcedon, a City of *Bythinia*, over against *Byzantium* in the Mouth of *Pontus Euxinus*. From its nearness to *Byzantium*, which is less than a Mile, it was termed (*Pliny* saith,) *The City of the Blind*.

Chene, an obscure Village, either belonging to *Octæa*, or *Lacedæmonia*; not mentioned (that I know of,) by any Geographer.

Chios, an Island and City of the Ionians, distant from *Lesbos* about 400 Furlongs, and 900 Furlongs in Circuit.

Cilicia, an Eminent Kingdom of *Asia*, denominated from *Cilix*, Son of *Rhea*; lying betwixt *Pamphylia* to the West, and *Syria* to the East, and Mount *Taurus* to the North, and the Cilician Sea to the South.

Cirrha, a Maritime City of *Phocis*, seated in the Corinthian Bay, at the Foot of the Mountain *Parnassus*, over against *Sicyon*, distant from *Delphi* 60 Furlongs. From *Delphi* to *Cirrha* runs the River *Pustus*; It is the Haven or Town of Shipping for *Delphi*. It bordereth on *Locris*.

Clazomene, an Ionick City in *Lydia*, situate in the Chersonesus of *Erythræ*, confining on the Erythræans, these being within the Chersonesus, the Clazomenians without it: In the narrowest part of the Isthmus.

Cnidus, a City of the Dorians in *Asia*, by the Sea, called *Tropium*; on the North is the Ceraunian Bay; on the South, the Rhodian Sea.

Cnossus, a City of *Creet*.

Corcyra, an Island in the Ionian Sea, over againg *Epirus*, from which it is but 12 Miles distant.

Corinth, an Eminent City near the Isthmus of *Peloponnesus*, governed Democratically.

The TABLE.

Cos, an Island of the *Carpathian* Sea, with a City in it of the same Name, opposite to *Tarmerium*, a Promontory of the *Myndians*. It belonged to the Dorians of *Asia*, called *Cos Meropidis*, because inhabited of old by the Meropians. It was most eminent, for being the Country of *Hippocrates* the Physitian. [*Heraclit.* chap. 3.]

Cranon, a City of *Thessaly*, bordering upon *Macedonia*, distant from *Crato* an 100 Furlongs.

Creet, an Island in the Mouth of the Ægean Sea, between *Rhodes* and *Peloponnesus*; famous for the Birth and Priests of *Jupiter*, and Laws of *Minos*; for both which visited by many Philosophers.

Crotona. See *Pythag.* chap. 10.

Cyclades, islands in the Ægean Sea; so called, for that they lye round about the Island *Delos*; their Number and Order, according to *Strabo*, is this, *Helena, Ceos, Cythnos, Seriphus, Melos, Siphaus, Cimolis, Prepesinthus, Olearus, Naxus, Parus, Syrus, Myconus, Tenus, Andrus, Gyarus.*

Cyprus, an Island in the *Carpathian* Sea, situate betwixt *Syria* and *Cilicia*.

Cyrene, a City of *Africk*, the Metropolis of the *Cyrenaick* Province, which contained besides, *Apollonia, Barce, Teuchira* and *Berenice*.

Cythera, an Island in the Ægean Sea, opposite to *Malea*, a Promontory of *Laconia*, and distant from it 40 Furlongs, opposite directly to the City *Bœa*.

Cyzicus, an Island and City of *Mysia* in *Asia*, seated on the *Propontis*, at the Mouth of the River *Æsopus*; built after *Rome* 70 years, at the same time as *Miletus*.

D.

Delium, a little Town in *Bœotia*, by the Sea-side, in the Territory of *Tanagra*, opposite to *Chalcis* of *Eubœa*. Here there was a Temple of *Apollo*.

Delos, an Island in the Ægean Sea, the chiefest of these that were called *Cyclades*, and in it a City, with a Temple of *Apollo*. It is distant from *Andros* 15 Miles, and as many from *Mycomus*; from *Eubœa* 30 Miles to the West.

Delphia, a City of *Phocis* in *Achaia*, at the Foot of the Mountain *Parnassus*, on the South part of the Hill; Famous for the Temple and Oracle of *Apollo*; Threescore Furlongs from the Sea.

E.

Elia, a City of *Magna Græcioa*. See *Xenophanes*, chap. 1.

Elis, a Region on the West part of *Peloponnesus*, bounded on the North by the Promontory *Araxus*, and divided from *Messenia* in the parts towards the Sea, by the River *Neda*; the principal City thereof bore the same Name, distant from the Sea 120 Furlongs, from *Olympia* almost 300.

Ephesus, a Maritime City of *Ionia*, built by the Amazons, 40 years after the taking of *Troy*. It was famous for the Temple of *Diana*, burnt by *Herostratus*, after it had stood 385 years.

Epidaurus, a City of *Argia* in *Peloponnesus*, seated by the Sea, in the inmost part of the Saronian Bay.

Eressus, a City of *Lesbos*, between *Pyrrha* and the promontory *Sigrium*.

Eretria, a Maritime City of *Eubœa*, between *Chalcis* and *Gerestus*, opposite to *Oropus* in *Attica*; distant from *Chalcis* 20 Miles to the East.

Eubœa, a great Grecian Island, opposite to the Continent of *Attica*, and *Bœotia*, and *Locris*, extending from *Sunium* as far as *Thessaly*; the length of it is reckoned to be 150 Miles: Its principal Cities, *Chalcis, Carystus*, and *Eretria*.

G.

Galatæ, Galli.

H.

Hellas, first signified only a City of *Thessaly*, betwixt *Pharsalus* and *Melitæa*, named from *Hellen* Son of *Deucalion*, *Thucydides* lib. 1. *Stephanus*: Whence *Eustathius*, throughout *Homer*, interprets ἑλλάδα and ἕλληνας, only that City of *Thessaly* and *Thessalians*. Afterwards the word extended to all that Tract of Land, which is from the *Sinian* Promontory to *Acarnania* and *Athamena* on the East, and to *Thessaly* on the North, unto the *Melian* Bay. This is the *Hellas* of *Ptolomy*, who excludes *Thessaly*, which first gave that Name to *Greece*, out of the Name *Hellas*. Thirdly, in a larger acceptation, besides that Tract, it includes also *Thessaly* and *Peloponnesus*, and most of the Islands in the Ægean Sea; and this is the *Greece* of *Strabo*. Lastly, besides those Countrys, it implies *Asia* the Lesser, and some parts of the African Shore; and, in a Word, all Places inhabited by the *Grecians*: In which sense, it is most commonly used by the later Authors.

Heraclea of *Pontus*, a City of *Bithynia*, the Metropolis of the *Mariandyni*, seated upon the Euxine Sea. See *Xenoph.*

Himera. See *Pythag.* chap. 10.

Hyperboreans, a People of *Scythia*, so named from the *Hyperborean*-Mountains.

I.

Imbros, an Island in the Ægean Sea, not far from the Thracian Chersonesus, distant from *Lemnos* 22 Miles.

Ionia, a Region of *Asia*, lying upon the Ægean Sea, inhabited by the Grecians, reaching from *Posideum*, a Promontory of *Miletus*, on the South, to *Phocea*, and the Mouth of the River *Hermus* on the North; its chief Cities, *Miletus* and *Ephesus*.

L.

Lacedæmon, the chief City of *Laconia*, on the West side of the River *Eurotas*, remote from the Sea, lying beneath the Mountain *Taygetus*; to which was ascribed its unhealthfulness. *Pyth.*

Lampsacum, a City of *Mysia*, seated on the *Hellespont*, at the Mouth of the River *Granicus*; having *Parius* on the North, and *Abydus* on the South.

Larissa; there were two Citys in *Thessaly* of this Name.

Lebedus, a Maritime City of *Ionia*, between *Colophon* to the South, and *Teos* to the North; distant from each, 120 Furlongs.

Lesbos, an Island in the Ægean Sea, over against Æolis in *Asia*, distant from *Lemnos, Tenedos*, and *Chios*, almost equally; less than 500 Furlongs from the

The TABLE.

the fartheſt of them. Cities, *Mitylene* and *Methymne*. Promontories; to the North, *Sigrium*; to the Eaſt, *Melea*.

Lindus, one of the three chief Cities of the Iſland *Rhodes*, ſituate on the right hand to them that ſail from the City of *Rhodes* Southward.

Locri in *Italy* : See *Pythag. chap.* 10.

Lydia, a Kingdom of *Aſia*, lying betwixt *Ionia* to the Weſt, and *Phrygia magna* to the Eaſt.

M.

Magna Græcia. Ovid. Faſt. 4.
For the Italian *Land was* Greater Greece.
Hither Evander *did his Navy Steer*,
Hither Alcides *Sail'd* ; *both Grecians were*.
The Club Arm'd Traveller, whoſe Herd did ſtray
On Aventine, *here drunk of* Albula.
That here Ulyſſes *was*, Leſtrigons *beſt,*
And the Shore nam'd from Circe, *can atteſt*.
Not long ago, of Telegone *appear'd*
The Walls, and Tiber, *both by Grecians rear'd*.
Hither Haleſus *forc'd* Atrides *Death,*
Who to Faliſca *did his Name bequeath.*
Antenor *add, who for* Troy's *peace did plead* ;
And (Son t' Apulian Daunus, *)* Diomed.
Hither Æneas, *ſince* Antenor, *came,*
And brought his Gods, reſcu'd from Ilion's *Flame:*
Him Solimus *from* Ida *did attend,*
From whom to Sulmo *did that Name deſcend*.

But though *Ovid* takes it for *Italy* in general, yet *Pliny* more cautiouſly ſaith, it comprehended *a great part thereof,* (*quotam partem.*) *Athenæus, almoſt all* Italy. And perhaps no otherwiſe is *Feſtus* to be underſtood, than as of a great part, when he ſaith, Italy *was called* Major Græcia, *becauſe the Sicilians poſſeſſed it, or becauſe many great Cities thereof were derived from the Greeks*. And *Servius*, Italy *is called* Μεγάλη Ἕλλας *becauſe from* Tarentum *to* Cumæ, *all the Cities were built by the Greeks*. More expreſly *Seneca, all that ſide of* Italy *which lies upon the low Sea, was called* Major Græcia. And ſo indeed is it ſet out by Geographers, but including alſo *Sicily*.

Mantinea, a City of *Arcadia* in *Peloponneſus*, confining on *Argia, Tegea, Methydrium*, and *Orchomenes*, near to *Megalopolis*.

Marathon, a Town of *Attica*, over againſt *Eratria* of *Eubœa*, between *Rhamnus* and *Brauron*; diſtant from *Athens* Ten Miles, and as much from *Caryſtus* in *Eubœa*.

Media, the greateſt Kingdom in *Aſia*, lying betwixt *Armenia* the Greater, to the Weſt, and *Parthia* and *Hyrcania* to the Eaſt ; extending Northward to the *Caſpian* Sea, and Southward to *Aſſyria* and *Suſiana*.

Megara, a City confining with *Attica* at *Eleuſis*, diſtant from the Sea 18 Furlongs.

Memphis, a City of *Egypt*, built by *Oſiris* at the point of *Delta*, over againſt *Babylon*.

Metapontum. See *Ppthag. chap.* 10.

Miletus, an Ionick City of *Caria*, the furthermoſt towards the South, next to *Poſideum*, ſituate 12 Furlongs from the Mouth of the River *Mæander* ; built by *Miletus*, Son of *Apollo*.

Mitylene, the chief City of *Lesbos*, ſituate between *Methymna* and *Malea*, diſtant from *Malea* 70 Furlongs, from *Canæ* 120 Furlongs. *Cicero* much commends it for ſituation, beauty of the Buildings, and fruitfulneſs of the Soil; *Cic. de leg. agr.* 2.

Munychia, a Promontory of *Attica*, which, with *Piræus*, made the Harbour of the Athenian Shipping, with three fair Havens within it. At the Mouth of the River *Iliſſus*, on the Weſt is *Piræus*; on the Eaſt, the Promontory *Sunium*.

O.

Oetœa, a City of *Thaſſay*, named from the Mountain *Oeta*.

Olympia, a place in *Elis*, with a Temple dedicated to *Jupiter*, upon the ſide of the River *Alpheus*, diſtant from the Sea 80 Furlongs. Here were celebrated the Games called *Olympick*.

P.

Parnes, a Mountain of *Attica*.

Paros, an Iſland in the Ægean Sea ; one of the *Cyclades*.

Peloponneſus, a Grecian Peninſula, within the Iſthmus of *Corinth*, containing many Regions, whereof the principal, *Achaia, Elis Meſſenia, Laconica*, and *Argia* ; the moſt Eminent Cities, *Meſſena, Corinth, Tegea, Lacedæmon, Argos*.

Phœnicia, a Region of *Syria* lying next the Sea ; it contained four Eminent Cities, *Tripolis, Byblus, Tyre*, and *Sidon*. The Phœnicians were Inventors of Navigation and Arithmetick; great Merchants, but Subtle, Deceitful, and Thieviſh to a Proverb, *Phœnicum more*. Whence *Polemo* ſaid of *Zeno, He came to ſteal Learning* (φοινικῶς,) *like a Phœnician*, (not *Phœniceo amictu*, as rendered,) *Zen. chap.* 2.

Phologondros, an Iſland to the Weſt of the Iſland *Ios*, of very mean account, as appears by *Solon's* expreſſion, *chap.* 2.

Piræus a Town and Haven of *Attica*, ſerving for the Shipping of *Athens*, in the midſt betwixt *Pegæ* and *Sunium*, diſtant from *Athens* 40 Furlongs.

Piſa, a City of the *Peloponneſus*, ſituate at the River *Alpheus* and the *Piſæan* Mountain.

Poſidonia, Pæſtum, a Maritime City of *Lucania* in *Italy*, betwixt *Salernus* to the Weſt, and *Velia* to the Eaſt ; built by the *Darians* and *Sybarites*.

Priene, a Maritime City of *Caria* in *Ionia*, between the Mouth of *Mæander*, and the Mountain *Mycale*.

Pylus, a City of *Meſſenia*, in the Promontory *Coryphaſium*, diſtant from *Methone* 100 Furlongs.

R.

Rhegium. See *Pythag. chap.* 10.

S.

Salamis, an Iſland in the Saronick-Bay, bewixt *Peloponneſus* and *Attica* ; adjacent to *Eleuſis* of *Attica*, and to *Ægina*.

Same, a City in the Iſland *Cephalonia*, at the paſſage between it and *Ithaca*. From hence went *Ancæus*, who wrſt planted a Colony in the Iſland *Samus*, which he ſo named from *Same*. See *Pythag. chap.* 1.

Samus, an Ionian Iſland, and a City of the ſame Name; the Iſland is 600 Furlongs about, and *Poſideum*, a Promontory thereof, not above Seven Furlongs from the Continent. The City ſtandeth on the South part of it, at the Sea-ſide. It

was

The TABLE.

was first called *Melamphylos*, as *Strabo*; or *Melamphyllos*, as *Jamblichus*. See *Pythag. chap.* 1.

Sardes, the Metropolis of *Lydia*, situate under the Hill *Tmolus*, upon the River *Pactolus*.

Scepsis, a City of *Troas* in *Asia*, seated on *Cotylus*, the highest part of Mount *Ida*, whence floweth the River *Scamander*.

Sicinus, an Island not far from *Melos*, on the West of the Island *Ios*, obscure, and of no esteem, as appears by *Solon*'s expression, *chap.* 2. and *Aristophanes* in his *Clouds*, *Act.* 1. *Scen.* 2.

Sicyen, a City of *Peloponnesus*, Metropolis of the Kingdom of *Sicyenia*, between *Corinth* and *Achaia*, distant 100 Furlongs from *Phlius*.

Sinope, a Maritime City of *Paphlagonia*.

Sparta, all one with *Lacedæmon*.

Stagyra, a City of *Thrace*, seated in the Bay of *Strymon*, between *Argilus* and *Acanthus*. See *Arist. chap.* 1.

Sunium, a Promontory in *Attica*, together with a Town of the same Name, between the Saronean Bay, and the Sea towards *Eubœa*.

Sybaris. See *Pythag. chap.* 10.

Syrus, an Island in the Ægean Sea, one of the *Cyclades*, 20 Miles distant from *Delus*, to the North. The Adjective is *Syrius*; as on the contrary, the Adjective of *Syria* in *Syrus*: Which the Interpreters of *Clemens Alexandrinus*, *Eusebius*, *Theodoret*, *Diogenes Laertius*, and others, not observed, who, render Φερεκύδην τὸν Σύριον *Pherecidem Syrum*; much less they, who, as an argument to prove, that Learning was brought out of *Syria* into *Greece*, instance *Pherecydes*, Master to *Pythagorus*, the first Philosopher.

T.

Tænarus, a Promontory of *Laconia* in *Peloponnesus*, parting the Laconian and Messenian Bays.

Tarentum. See *Pythag. chap.* 10.

Tauromenium. See *Pythag. chap.* 10.

Taygetus, a Mountain of *Laconia*, at the River *Eurotas*, and the City *Sparta*; which City was subject to Diseases, by reason of that Mountain's hanging over it.

Thebes, a City of *Bœotia*, seated at the River *Asopus* and *Ismenus*; built by *Cadmus*.

Thyatira, a City of *Lydia*, seated upon the River *Lycus*, betwixt *Sardes* and *Pergamum*.

Troas, a Territory of *Asia* the Less, upon the side of the Ægean Sea, between *Æolis* and *Hellespont*; having a City of the same Name.

A TABLE

Of some Memorable Passages in the Lives of the Philosophers.

A.

Abaris the Hyperborean, *Pyth. chap.* 23.
Academy. *Plat. cap.* 5.
Achillean Field contested for by the Mytelenæans and Athenians *Pit. cap.* 1.
Achilleum founded. *Pit. cap.* 1.
Acroatick Doctrine of the Peripateticks. *Arist. cap.* 6.
Ægyptian Priests. *Sol. cap.* 8. *Pyth. cap.* 2, 3.
Ægyptian Priests. *Thal. cap.* 3.
Ægyptian kind of Writing. *Pyth. cap.* 4.
Ægyptian year introduced into *Greece*. *Thal. cap.* 8. §. 4.
Æthiops of *Ptolemais*, a Cyrenaick Philosoper. *Aristip. cap.* 9.
Agesilaus warreth against the Persian, returns to *Greece*, overcomes the Thebans at *Coronea*. *Xen. cap.* 5.
Adomena, what. *Thal. cap.* 11.
Alcibiades. *Socr.* 1. 17.
Alexander taught by *Aristotle*, *Arist. cap.* 5. began to Reign, *Ibid.* sends all Rarities to *Aristotle*, *Arist. cap.* 8. visits *Diogenes*, *Diog. cap.* 3. dies, *Arist. cap.* 8.
Alters erected to *Anaxagoras*. *Anaxag. cap.* 5.
Amasis King of Ægypt. *Thal. cap.* 3.
Amasis his contest with the King of Æthiopia. *Thal. cap.* 9.
Amasis his Correspondence with *Bias*. *Bias, cap.* 1.
Amphibolis taken by *Brasidos*. *Socr. cap.* 8.
Analysis, what. *Plat. cap.* 7.
Annicerians. *Annis. cap.* 2.
Anniversary of *Anaxagoras*. *Anaxag. cap.* 5.
Antigonus. *Arces. cap.* 3.
Antigonus Gonatas invites *Zeno*. *Zen. cap.* 4.
Antipater receives *Xenocrates* Ambassador from *Athens*. *Xenocr. cap.* 3.
Antipodes, the word by whom first used. *Plat. cap.* 7.
Anytus accuseth *Socrates*. *Socr. cap.* 10.
Appelles the Painter, relieved by *Arcesilaus*. *Arces. cap.* 3.
Apocarteron, a Book of *Hegesias* against Life. *Heges. cap.* 1.
Archelaus King of Macedonia. *Socr. cap.* 15.
Areopagus, when instituted, and when reformed. *Sol. cap.* 5.
Arete, Daughter to *Aristippus*, educated in Philosophy, *Aristip. cap.* 8.
Arginusæ, a Sea-fight there, *Socr. cap.* 9.
Arymnesius, Son of Pythagoras, *Pyth.* 21.

Arion.

The TABLE.

Arion. *Per. cap.* 4.
Aristophanes his *Clowds* acted. *Socr. cap.* 10.
Aristotle, downed not himself. *Arist. cap.* 11.
Arithmetick, *Pyth. doctr. p.* 2, *Sect.* 1.
Artaxerxes Mnemon. *Xen. cap.* 2.
Aspasia, Mistress to *Pericles. Socr. cap.* 3
Astrological Predictions of *Thales. Thal. cap.* 8. sect. 5.
Astronomy. *Thal. c.* 8. *Doct. Pyth. part.* 2 *sect.* 2.
Astu of Athens. *Per. cap.* 2.
Athens lustrated. *Sol. cap.* 3.
Atlantick Language or Story. *Sol. cap.* 8. 13. *Plat. cap.* 15.
Attalus, Lacydes:
Axes and Cyrbes. *Sol. cap.* 7.

C.

Cleobule, a Comedy of *Cratinus. Cleob. cap.* 1.
Callisthenes put to Death by *Alexander. Arist. cap* 5
Carneades sent on Embassy to *Rome. Carn cap.* 3.
Cato moves the Senate against the Philosophers. *Carn. cap.* 3.
Charicles, one of the 30 Tyrants. *Socr. cap.* 9.
Chersonesus Thracian, reduc'd by the Athenians. *Sol. cap.* 2.
Chio bestows a Talent upon *Speusippus. Speus. cap.* 1.
Chirisophus. *Xen. cap.* 4.
Chreocopidæ, Who ? *Sol. cap.* 4.
Cirrha reduc'd by the Athenians by a Stratagem. *Sol. cap.* 2.
Cleander Governor of *Byzantium. Xen. cap.* 4.
Cleobis and Bito. *Sol. cap.* 11.
Cleobulina. *Cleob. cap.* 1.
Cleombrotus kills himself, upon reading of *Plato's Phædo. Plat. cap.* 15.
Commentaries upon *Aristotle. Ar. cap.* 17.
Connus a Lutinist. *Socr. cap* 3.
Corinth, the Wise Men meet there. *Sol. cap.* 8.
Creet, *Sol. cap.* 1. *Pyth. cap,* 6. famous for Religious Mysteries. *Thal. cap.* 3.
Critias, one of the 30 Tyrants. *Socr. cap.* 9.
Crito, his Discourse with *Socrates. Socr. cap.* 11.
Critolaus sent on Embassy to *Rome. Carn. cap.* 3.
Crœsus diverted from his expedition, &c. *Bias. cap.* 1. *Pitt. cap.* 1.
Crœsus his Discourse with *Solon. Sol. cap.* 11.
Crœsus taken Prisoner by *Cyrus*, and set at Liberty. *Sol. cap.* 11.
Crœsus, how he passed his Army over *Halys. Thal. cap.* 10.
Crotonians instituted Games in Emulation of those at *Olympia. Pyth. cap.* 18.
Cube duplicated. *Plat. cap.* 7.
Cylonian Impiety. *Sol. cap.* 3.
Cynosarges, whence so named. *Antisth. cap.* 2.
Cynosura, the lesser Bear. *Thal. cap.* 3. by whom found out. *Thal. cap.* 8. *sect.* 2.
Cypsalus, Son of *Periander, Periand. cap.* 6. at what time he Reign'd. *Per. cap.* 1.
Cyrus, his first Ascent into *Asia* confounded with his second. *Xenoph. cap.* 2.

D.

Dæmon of *Socrates. Socr. cap.* 2, 6, 8.
Damasias, two of that Name, Archons, confounded one with the other. *Thal. cap.* 2.
Decree of the Athenians, concerning *Zeno. Zen. cap.* 6.

Delium, a Fight there. *Xenoph. cap.* 1.
Delphi, the Wise Men meet there. *Sol. cap.* 8.
Delium, a Fight there. *Socr. cap.* 7.
Dialectick invented. *Zeno Eleat. chap.* 2.
Diogenes the Babylonian, bent on Embassy to *Rome. Diog.*
Dionysius King of *Sicily* entertains *Xenophon. cap.* 9. entertains *Æschines. Æsch. cap.* 1.
Dionysius, the Carthaginian. *Euclid. cap.* 2.
Dionysius, the Elder, entertains *Plato. Plat. cap.* 9.
Dionysius, the Younger, entertains *Plato. Plat. cap.* 9.
Dionysius entertains *Aristippus, Aristip. cap.* 5.
Diogenes the Stoick sent on Embassy to *Rome. Carn. cap.* 3.
Dion, Friend to *Plato. Plat. cap.* 9.
Diotyma, a Learned Woman. *Socr. cap.* 3.
Distinctions of *Plato*, collected by *Aristotle. Plat. cap.* 8.
Divination, *Pyth. doct.* 2. *p.* 3. *sect.* 3. *cap.* 4. *p.* 2. *sect.* 1, *cap.* 15.
Divine Providence, the expression by whom first used. *Plat. cap.* 7.
Dogmatise, what; and, whether *Plato* doth Dogmatise *Plat cap.* 15.
Dorick Dialect, why used by the Pythagoreans. *Pyth. cap.* 22.

E.

Eclipse, by whom first foretold. *Thal. cap.* 8. *sect.*
Eclipse parted the Armies of Medes and Lydians. *Thal. cap.* 8. *sect.* 3.
Elatus, when *Ephorus. Chil. cap.* 1.
Ephori, when first chosen. *Chil. cap.* 1.
Epigrams of *Plato. Plat.* 1. 15.
Epimenides, his long Sleep. *Epim.*
Euthydemus, when Archon. *Chil. cap.* 1.
Exoterick Doctrine of the Peripateticks. *Arist. cap.* 6.

F.

Feast, made by *Periander* for the Wise Men. *Anachar. cap.* 1.
Furies, their Habit. *Menedem.*

G.

GeographickMap, by whom first set out. *Anaximand. cap.* 1.
Geometry, by whom first introduced into *Greece. Thal. cap.* 7.
Geometry. *Pyth. doct. p.* 2. *sect.* 3.
Geometrical Proportions. *Thal. cap.* 7. *sect.* 1, 2.
Gnomonick, by whom invented. *Anax. cap.* 1.
GOD, from whom the Grecians first received the Names of God. *Thal. cap.* 6. *sect.* 2.
Golden Verses, by whom made. *Cap.* 22.
Gorgias, a Sophist. *Socr. cap.* 10.
Grecian army brought off by *Xenophon. Xen. cap.* 3
Gryllus Son of *Xenophon* slain. *Xen. cap.* 6.

H.

Hectemori. *Sol. cap.* 3.
Hegesistratus, Son of *Pisistratus. Pit. cap.* 1.
Heraclides, Friend to *Plato. Plat. cap.* 9.

Hermes

The TABLE.

Hermes Trismegistus the Books ascribed to him supposititious. Plat. ch. 4.
Hermias King of *Atarna*. Arist. ch. 4.
Hermodamas, firnamed *Creophilus*. Pyth. ch. 2.
Hermolaus and others conspire against *Alexander*. Arist. ch. 5.
Herpylis, Wife of *Aristotle* Arist. ch. 12.
Hippias a Sophist. Socr. ch. 10.
Homacocion of *Pythagoras*, distinct from his private School. Pyth. ch. 16.
Horoscopes, of what use first. Anax ch. 1.

I.

Jeremy the Prophet, not contemporary with *Plato*. Plat. ch. 1.
Jews, *Pythagoras* conversed with them. Pyth. ch. 5.
Immortality of the Soul, by whom first held. Thal. ch. 6. sect. 4.
Immortality of the Soul, by whom. Pherec.
Immortality of the Soul, of whom. *Plato* learnt it. Plat ch 3.
Indifference. Theod. ch. 2.
Induction, Socr. ch 4. how used by Socrates. Ibid.
Induction, its kind; how used by Plato. Plat. 15.
Ionian Common-Council-Hall, *Thales* advised to be built in *Teos*. Thal. ch. 10.

L.

Labynitus King of *Babylon*. Thal. ch. 8 sect 3.
Lacydæan-Gardens. Lac.
Lais. Aristip. ch. 3.
Laws of *Solon*. Sol. ch. 6.
Laws of *Draco*. Sol. ch. 5.
Laws of *Pittacus*. Pit. ch. 1.
Laws given by *Plato* Plat. ch. 10, 14.
Library of *Aristotle*. Arist. ch. 16.
Lycæum, School of the Peripateticks. Arist. ch. 6.

M.

Magna Græcia. Pyth. ch. 10.
Manes, servant to *Diogenes*. Diog. ch. 1.
Mantinea, a Battle there. Xen. ch. 6.
Marius entertains *Theodorus*. Theod. ch. 1.
Marks affixed to *Plato*'s Writings. Plat. ch. 15.
Mathematick. Pyth. doct. p. 2. ch. 2.
Medicine. Pyth. Doct. p. 3. sect. 4.
Megacles. Sol. ch. 3.
Magarenses contest with the *Athanians*, concerning *Salamis*. Sol. ch. 2.
Megarenses recover *Salamis*, Sol. ch. 2. take *Nysæa*. Ibid. ch. 3.
Megarenses prohibited by decree to come within the *Athenian* Jurisdiction. Euclid. ch. 1.
Nelitus accuseth Socrates. Socr. ch. 11.
Metro Carn ch. 4.
Middle Academy, Arcef. ch. 2. upon what occasion *Lacydes* betook himself to it. Lac.
Mill-Song. Pitt. ch. 1.
Milo. Pyth. ch. 23.
Mind, *Anaxargorus* so termed. Anax. ch 1.
Mnesarchus, Son of *Pythagoras*. Pyth. 21
MoralPhilosophy, by whom invented. Archelaus
Moses afforded light to *Plato*. Plat. ch. 4.
Munychia, the Haven of *Athens*. Epim.
Muses. Pyth. ch. 13.
Musick. Pyth. Doct. p. 2. sect. 2.

N.

Neleus long before *Thales*. Thal. ch. 1.
New-Academy, Carn. ch. 2.
Nichomachus, Son of *Aristotle*. Arist. ch. 13.
Noumenia. Sol. ch. 7.

O.

Oath taken by the Senate of *Athens*. Sol. ch. 7.
Oblong-Number, what Plat. ch. 7.
Olympia, Mother to *Alexander*. Arist. ch. 5.
Olympids instituted by *Iphitus*, long before *Corœbus*, who is commonly conceived the first Victor. Thal ch. 2.
Olympick Sect design'd by *Alexinus*. Alex.
Oracle mistaken by *Diogenes*. Diog. ch. 1.
Oracle. Pyth. ch. 2.

P.

Palamedes, a Tragedy of *Euripides*. Socr. ch. 14.
Panionium, one common Temple belonging to 12. Ionian Cities. Bias, ch. 1.
Peloponnesian War. Socr. ch. 7.
Periander, at what time he began to Reign. Per. ch. 2.
Pericles. Anaxag. ch. 5.
Peripateticks, whence so called Arist. ch. 6.
Phalaris kill'd. Pyth. ch. 17.
Pherecides, at what time he died. Pyth. ch. 2.
Philip receives *Xenocrates* Ambassador from *Athens*, Xenocr. ch. 3. sends for *Aristotle*. Arist. ch. 5.
Philistus. Plat. ch. 9.
Philocyprus, King of *Cyprus*. Sol. ch. 8.
Philosophers banished *Athens*. Theophr. ch. 2.
Philosophy, why so called. Pyth. ch. 8.
Phryne, an *Athenian* Curtezan. Xenocr. ch. 2.
Phryno slain by *Pittacus*. Pit. ch. 1.
Phthiriasis. Pherec.
Pisistratus gains the Tyrany of *Athens*. Sol. ch. 10, 12.
Pisithanatos Death's Orator, *Hegesias*: Who so called. Heg. ch. 1.
Pittaceian Sentence. Pit. ch. 1.
Pittaceian Field. Pit. ch. 1.
Plato fought not at *Delium*. Plat. ch. 2.
Plato not supplanted by *Aristotle*. Arist. ch. 3.
The word [Poem] by whom first used. Plat. ch. 7.
Pompey visits *Posidonius*. Posid.
Potidæa besieged. Socr. ch. 7.
Predictions of *Anaxagoras*. Anax. ch. 3.
Predictions of *Thales*. Thal. ch. 13.
Predictions of *Epimenides*. Epim.
Predictions of *Anaximander*. Anax. ch. 1.
Predictions of *Chilon*. Chil. ch. 1.
Priene conquer'd. Bias, ch. 1.
Principle and Element, by whom first distinguished. Plat. ch. 7.
Principle and Element confounded by the first Philosophers. Thal. ch. 6. sect. 1.
Prodicus the Sophist. Socr. ch. 3.
Protagoras a Sophist. Socr. ch. 10.
Proverb, Samian Comet. Pyth. ch. 2.
Proverb, These are under the Government of *Nino*. Pyth. ch. 18.
Proxenus accompanies *Cyrus* in his Expedition. Xen. ch. 2.
Proxenus Educated *Aristotle*. Arist. ch. 2.

Psamminitus,

Psamminitus, the same with *Amiſlæus* and *Semniſerteus*. *Pyth. ch.* 5.
Ptolomy Son of *Lagus*, entertains *Theodorus* the Atheist. *Theod. ch.* 1.
Potlomy's Question to *Eucild*. *Eucl. ch.* 3.
Pyramid's height, how taken by *Thales*. *Thal. ch.* 7. *ſect.* 2.
Pythagoras his time. *Pyth. ch.* 10.
Pythagoras the Wrestler. *Pyth. ch.* 2. *bis, ch.* 6. *ch.* 22.
Pythagoras esteemed a god. *Pyth. doct. p.* 1. *ch.* 1.
Pythagoreans Exoretick. *Pyth. doct. p.* 1. *ch.* 2, 3, 4, 5, 6, 7.
Pythagoreans Esoterick. *Pyth. doct. p.* 1. *ch.* 8, 9, 10, 11.
Pythagoreans and Pythagorists, how distinguish'd. *Pyth. ch.* 16.
Pythais, Wife of *Ariſtotle*. *Ariſt. ch.* 13.
Pythais, Daughter of *Ariſtotle*. *Ariſt. ch.* 13.

R.

Resurrection of the Body. *Thal. ch.* 6. *ſect.* 4.
Retiarii, Roman-Gladiators. *Pitt. ch.* 1.

S.

Saitick Province in *Egypt*. *Plat. ch.* 3.
Salamis reduc'd by the Athenians by a stratagem. *Sol. ch.* 1.
Saulius, or *Cadovides*, Brother to *Anacharſis* King of *Scythia*. *Anachar. ch.* 1.
Scylla, the Sea-Onyon, a Book concerning it; written by *Pythagoras* the Physician. *Pyth. ch.* 22.
Scilluns, a Town bestow'd on *Xenophon* by the Lacedæmonians. *Xen. ch.* 6.
Sentences of the wise Men, set up at *Delphi*. *Chil. ch.* 2.
Scuthes, King of *Thrace*, entertains the Grecian Army to fight for him. *Xen. ch.* 4.
Sisacthia, what. *Sol. ch.* 4.
Skin of *Epimenides*, a Proverb. *Epim.*
Socratick way of discourse, abrogated by whom, *Arceſ. ch.* 2.
Soleis in *Cilicia* built. *Sol. ch.* 11.
Soli in *Cilicia*. *Chryſ. ch.* 1.
Soli in *Cyprus* built. *Sol. ch.* 8.
Solæcism, whence so termed. *Sol. ch.* 11.
Sophocles's judgment of *Polemo*. *Pol.*
Stagyra re-edified by *Alexander*. *Ariſt. ch.* 8.
Superficies, the word by whom first used. *Plat. ch.* 7.
Superstition, arising from ignorance of Physical Causes, confuted. *Anaxag. ch.* 4.
Style of *Plato*. *Plat. ch.* 15.
Stoe, Ποικίλη, the School of the Stoicks. *Zen. ch.* 3.
Stone fell from the Sun at *Ægos*. *Anax. ch.* 3.

Sun's apparent Diameter. *Thal. ch.* 8. *ſect.* 2.
Sybarites and Crotonians fight. *Pyth. ch.* 17.
Syenneſes, King of *Cilicia*. *Thal. ch.* 8. *ſect.* 3.
Xen. ch. 4.

T.

Tarquinius Priſcus, mistaken by *Pliny* for *Tarquinius Superbus*. *Pyth. ch.* 10.
Telauges. *Pyth. ch.* 21.
Tellus. *Sol. ch.* 11.
Temple of *Diana* at *Scilluns*, in imitation of that at *Epheſus*. *Xen. ch.* 6.
Thales the elder, confounded with the younger. *Thal. ch.* 2.
Thales Contemporary with the later Prophets. *Thal. ch.* 2.
Thargelion the sixth, a day fortunate to the Athenians. *Socrat. ch.* 1.
Theano, many of that Name. *Pyth. ch.* 21.
Theon Smyrnæus. *Plat. ch.* 7.
Theramenes accuseth the six Commanders. *Socr. ch.* 9.
Theramenes put to death. *Socr. ch.* 9.
Theſpis, when he first presented Tragedies. *Sol. ch.* 10.
Thetis. *Sol. ch.* 3.
Thirty Tyrants. *Socr. ch.* 9.
Thraſibulus's advice to *Periander*. *Per. ch.* 2.
Thraſimachus a Sophist. *Soc. ch.* 10.
Toxaris a Scythian. *Anachar. ch.* 1.
Triops, a place at *Delphi*. *Pyth. ch.* 6.
Tripod of Gold. *Thal. ch.* 5.
Tropicks imply also Equinoxes. *Thal. ch.* 8. *ſect.* 1.
Tinondas King of *Eubæa*. *Sol. ch.* 3.

W.

Water, the Principle of all things, held by the Phœnicians and Indians. *Thal. ch.* 6. *ſect.* 1.
Wise Men, when first so called. *Thal. ch.* 5.

X.

Xantippe, Wife of *Socrates*. *Socr. ch.* 16.
Xeniades buys *Diogenes*. *Diog. ch.* 2.
Xenophon's Armour. *Xen. ch.* 3.
Xerxes his expedition into *Greece*. *Anaxag. ch.* 1.

Z.

Zamolxis. *Pyth. ch.* 21.
Zeno consults the Oracle. *Zen. ch.* 1.
Zodiack's Obliquity, when found out. *Anaximand. ch.* 1.
Zoroaſtres. *Pyth. ch.* 5.

Authors that have Written the Lives and Doctrine of Philosophers.

Damastes (of *Sigeum*, a Promontory of *Troas*,) Son of *Dioxippus*, Disciple of *Hellanicus*, wrote *Of Sophists*, (*Suid.*) He lived before the Peloponesian War. (*Dionys. Halicar. de Thucyd. Charact.*)

Xenophon, the Philosopher, wrote first, *Of the Lives of Philosophers*; (*Suid.*) perhaps meaning his Socratical-Apology and Commentaries.

Anaximander the Younger, of *Miletus*, Contemporary with *Xenophon*, for he lived in the time of *Artaxerxes Mneon*, wrote, *An Explication of the Pythagorick Symbols*.

Theopompus, of *Chios*, the most eminent of all *Isocrates* his Disciples, (*Dionys. Halic. Epist. ad Pomp.*) in the time of *Artaxerxes Ochus*, King of *Persia*, and of *Philip* King of *Macedon*, wrote, *Concerning the Exorcitations of Plato*. *Athen. Deip. 11.*

Timæus the Locrian, a Pythagorean Philosopher, wrote *the Life of Pythagoras*, (*Suid.*)

Speusippus wrote, *Of Philosophers*, 1 Book. (*Laert.*)

Xenocrates, the Philosopher, wrote Books, *Of Lives*. (*Laert.*)

Theophrastes wrote of the *Wise Men*. (*Laert.*)

Aristoxenus of *Tarentum*, Disciple of *Aristotle*, wrote, *Of the Lives of Eminent Persons*; amongst whom were *Pythagoras*, *Archytas*, *Socrates*, *Plato*.

Heraclides, of *Pontus*, heard *Speusippus* and *Aristotle*; wrote, *Of the Pythagoreans*, and, *Of Lives*: Which last tho reckoned by *Laertius* amongst Physical Writings, yet, as *Vossius* (*de Histor. Græc. 1. 9.*) conceives, they seem to have been rather Historical, because *Eutocius* cites his *Life of Archimedes*, (*in Archim.*)

Dicearchus of *Messene*, Disciple also to *Aristotle*, (*Athen. Deipn. 11.*) wrote of *Lives. Laert in Plat.*

Glearchus of *Soli*, Disciple also to *Aristotle*, wrote, *Of Lives*, (*Athen. Deipn. 6.*) Of this work, *Atheneus* cites the First, Fourth, and Fifth Book; and out of it, *Agellius* takes what he writes of *Pythagoras*. ch. 11.

Phanias of *Enessus*, Disciple also to *Aristotle*, wrote, *Of the Socraticks*. (*Laert. in Antisth.*)

Epicurus wrote, *Of Lives*, Four Books: (*Laert.*) But *Gassendus* conceives, they contained not the Stories of any Eminent Persons, but Moral Rules, whereby to lead a quiet Life. (*Laert.*)

Apollodorus, Sirnamed *Cepotyrannus*, Disciple of *Epicurus*, wrote, *His Life*, (*Laert.*)

Bardesanes, a Babylonian, living in the time of *Alexander Severus*, wrote, *Of the Brachmanes* and *Samanæans*, Indian Philosophers, whom the Grecians term Gymnosophists.

Idomenæus of *Lampsacum*, Disciple to *Epicurus*, wrote Books, *Of the Socraticks*. (*Laert. in Socrates.*)

Antigonus of *Caristus*, Lived in the time of *Ptolemæus Lagis*, and *Ptolemæus Philadelphus*; wrote, *Of Lives*, (*Laert.*) of which were particularly mentioned those of *Polemo*, *Menedemus*, *Dyonysius*, *Metathemenus*, *Lyco*, *Zeno*, *Pyrrho*, *Timon*, by *Athenæus* and others.

Callimachus of *Cyrene*, a Poet, Lived in the time of *Ptolemæus Philadelphus*; wrote a *Table or Description of those, who were eminent in any kind of Learning, and of their Writings*. (*Athen. Deipn. 6. & 14.*)

Neanthes, of *Cyzicus*, an Orator, (Disciple of *Philiscus* the Milesian, the Orator, (who learnt of *Isocrates*, wrote, *Of Eminent Persons*, cited by *Stephanus*, *Clemens Alexandrinus*, *Laertius*, *Porphyrius*, and *Hesychius Milesius*.

Hermippus of *Smyrna*, about the time of *Ptolemæus Euergetes*, wrote Books, *Of Lives*, of which are particularly cited the Lives of *Plato*, *Arcesilaus*, *Aristotle*, *Theophrastus*, *Lyco*, and others; by *Laertius*.

Spherus, in the time of *Ptolemeus Euergetes*, Disciple to *Zeno* the Cittean, and to *Cleanthes*, wrote, *Of the Eretriack Philosophers*, and *of Lycurgus and Socrates*, Three Books. (*Laert.*)

Chrysippus, the Philosopher, wrote, *Of Lives*; to which, perhaps appertained that which he wrote, *Of ancient Physiologists*.

Sotion wrote a *Succession of Philosophers*, wherein, as *Eunapius* declares, he gave an account of the Lives of the Philosophers, as they succeeded one another. *Laertius* cites the third Book.

Heraclides, Son of *Serapion*, lived under *Ptolomy Philometor*, wrote a *Succession* in Six Books, doubtless *of Philosophers*; perhaps the same with his Epitome of *Sotion*: *Laertius* cites both Titles.

Apollodorus an Athenian, Son of *Asclepiades*; he was a Grammarian, flourished under *Ptolomæus Euergetes*, heard *Aristarchus* the Grammarian, and *Panætius* the Stoick, (*Suid.*) He wrote, *Of the Sects of Philosophers*; and (if it were not the same work,) a *Collection of Doctrines*, both cited by *Laertius* in *Solone*, & *in Chrysippo*.

Clitomachus, Disciple to *Carneades*, flourished about the 162 Olympiad; wrote, *Of Sects*. (*Laertius in his Life.*)

Alexander Cornelius, Sirnamed *Polyhistor*, flourished in the 173 Olymp. wrote *Successions*. (*Laert.*)

Damis the Assyrian, wrote the Life of *Apollonius Tyanæus*. (*Hierocles*, cited by *Euseb.*)

Maximus the Ægiean, Contemporary with *Damis*, wrote the Life of the same *Apollonius* (*Hierocl. Ibidem.*)

Mocragenes wrote Four Books of the life of the same *Apollonius*; descredited by *Philostratus*, lib. 1. cap. 4.

Plutarch (who flourished under *Trajan* and *Hadrian*,) wrote of the *Opinions of Philosophers*, Five Books extant.

Diogenes Laertius, or, as *Tzetzes* terms him, *Diogenianus*, whose Ten Books, *Of the Lives of Philosophers*, are extant; out of which *Photius* affirms, that *Sopater* borrow'd much, (*Timem.* 161.) *Diogenes* therefore lived before *Constantine* the Great, who put *Sipater* to Death, (*Suid.* in 'Αλεξανδρὸς,) but later than *Trajan*; for he mentions *Plutarch*, and *Sextus Empriricus*, and *Saturninus* Disciple of *Sextus*. Whence *Vossius* collects, he lived under *Antoninus Pius*, or somewhat later, *De Natura & constit. Rhetor. cap. 9.*

Lucian of *Samosata*, under *Aurelius* and *Commodus*, wrote the life of *Demonax*, a Philosopher of that time.

Philostratus, flourishing from *Severus* to *Philippus* (*Suid.*) wrote the Life of *Apollonius Tyanæus*, comprising

prising all that *Maximus* and *Damis* had written before; it consists of Eight Books extant.

Philostratus, Uncle and Father-in-Law to the other, living under *Macrinus* and *Heliogabalus*; wrote the *Lives of the Sophists*.

Porphyrius, living from *Galienus* to *Probus*, wrote Φιλοσόφω ἱστορίαν, *Historian Philosophican*, concluding about the time of *Plato*, (*Eunap. Proem.*) It is mentioned by *Theodoret* and *Tzetzes* under the Title of, *The Lives of Philosophers*. The third Book of it is cited by *Suidas*; part of the Life of *Pythagoras* belonging to it is extant, first set forth by *Ritterhusius*, afterwards by *Lucas Holstenius*.

Soterichus lived under *Dioclesian*, wrote the Life of Apollonius Tyanæus. (*Suid.*)

Jamblichus, Master to *Julian* the Emperor, wrote the *Life of Pythagoras*, put forth by *Joannes Arcerius*.

Eunapius, living under *Valentinian*, *Valens*, and *Gratian*, an Eminent Sophist, Physician, and Historian, wrote, at the request of *Chrysantius*, The Lives of the Philosophers and Sophists, extant.

Marinus, a Neapolitan, a Philosopher and Orator, Disciple to *Proclus*, lived about the times of *Zeno* and *Anastasius*; wrote, *the Life of Proclus*, his Master and Predecessor in the School, in Prose and Verse. That in Prose only is extant.

Hesychius illustris, a Milesian, wrote a *Nomenclator*, or *Index of such as were Eminent for Learning*, extant.

Damascius, of *Damascus* in *Syria*, lived under *Justinian*, was a Stoick, Disciple of *Simplicius* and *Elamita Phrygians*; wrote a *Philosophical History* (*Suid.* in Δωρός.)

Of more uncertain time are these following.

Amphicrates, who writ a Book of Eminent Persons, cited by *Laertius* and *Athenæus*.

Andron of *Ephesus*, who wrote a Treatise *of the Seven Wise Men*; perhaps the same with his *Tripod*, the subject of which was the Story of the Golden Tripod. *Laert. in the Life of Thal.*

Antisthenes, a Peripatetical Philosopher, writ the *Successions of Philosophers*. (*Laert.*)

Apollodorus, who wrote a *Collection of Doctrines*. (*Laert.*)

Aristocles of *Messena*, a Peripatetical Philosopher, wrote Ten Books, *Of Philosophy*, in which he gave account of all the Philosophers and their Opinions. (*Suid.*)

Damas wrote, *The Life of Eudemus*; *Eudemus* was a Rhodian, Disciple to *Aristotle*.

Damon, a Cyrenæan, wrote a Book of *Philosophers*. (*Laert.*)

Didymus lived in the time of *Julius* the Dictator; wrote, *Of the Pythagorick Philosophy*. (*Suid.*)

Diocles wrote the *Lives of Philosophers*. (*Laert.*)

Eubulides wrote a Book of *Diogenes*; and perhaps of *Socrates*. (See *Laert. Socr.*)

Herodotus wrote, *Of the Youth of Epicurus*, (*Laert. Dionys. Halic.*)

Heron, Son of *Cotys*, an Athenian Orator, wrote an *Epitome of the Histories* of Heraclides. (*Suid.*)

Hippobotus wrote, *Of Sects*, (*Laert.*) not only of the Doctrines, but Lives, of Philosophers; for there is cited also his Book, *Of Philosophers*, perhaps the same. (*Laert.*)

Jason wrote, *Successions of Philosophers*. (*Suid.*)

Lycon of *Jasia* wrote, *The Life of* Pythagoras. (*Athen.* 14.)

Meleager wrote, *Of Opinions*. (*Laert. in Aristip.*)

Nicander of *Alexandria* wrote, *Of the Disciple* of Aristotle. (*Suid.* in αἱρέων.)

Nicias of *Nice*, wrote the *History*, or *Succession of Philosophers*. (*Athen.*)

Panætius wrote, *Of Sects*. (*Laert. in Aristippo.*)

Satyrus, a Peripatetick, wrote, *The Lives of Eminent Persons*; Epitomiz'd by *Heraclides*.

Socrates wrote, *Successions*, cited by *Laertius*, *in Diogene*; but perhaps it should be,

Sosicrates, a Rhodian, who wrote the *Successions of Philosophers*.

Theodorus wrote, *Of Sects*. (*Laert. in Aristip.*)

Timotheus an Athenian, wrote, *Of Lives*, (*Laert.*)

CONJECTURES

UPON

Some Passages of the said AUTHORS.

Aristotle.

DE anima, lib. 1. cap. 2. ἀπείρων γὰρ ὄντων χρημάτων κ᾽ ἀτόμων (Pacius, *cum enim infinitæ sint figuræ & atomi*;) perhaps, χρημάτων ἢ ἀτόμων. (*Democr. chap.* 9. *Sect.* 8.)

De generatione animalium, lib. 4. cap. 9. ἐν μὲν τ᾽ μητει (perhaps μήτρᾳ) γίνεσθαι φυσὶ τὴν διαφορὰν τῷ θήλεος κ᾽ τοῦ ἄρρενος. (*Democr. chap.* 9. *Sect.* 7.)

Basil.

Homil. 24. de legend. lib. Gentil. οὕτως ἔφη· ἃ παύσει χαλεπώτερόν σεαυτῷ κατασκευάζων τὸ δεσμωθήσῃ· perhaps, ὅτῳ, ἔφη, ἃ παύσῃ χαλεπώτερον σεαυτῷ, &c. (*Pythag. doctr. part.* 3. *Sect.* 1. *chap.* 3.)

Ibid. Διὸ δὴ κ᾽ Πλάτωνα φασὶ τὴν ἐν σώματι βλάβην περισόμενον, &c. perhaps περιισόμενον. (*Plat. chap.* 5.)

Clemens Alexandrinus.

Stromat. lib. 1. ἤδη δ᾽ οἶμαι, ὡς ἄρα ἤδη πολυμαθὴν νόον ἔχειν ὁ διδάσκει κατὰ Ἡράκλειτον (rendred, *sciebat enim, ut existimo, eum multarum rerum scientem jam habere mentem, quod docet, ut est*, Heracliti *sententia*,) perhaps, πολυμαθίην νόον οὐχὶ διδάσκει. (Heracl. *chap.* 1.)

Lib. 5. for Εὐρύσου πυθαγορείω, perhaps read Εὐρύτω. (*Pyth. chap.* 24.)

Lib. 6. κ᾽ γὰρ ὧδε θέμις, ἐν ταῖς ἄλωσιν ἔμπεσεν, the sense seems to require ἐκεῖ ἦσαν. (*Democr. chap.* 4.)

Diodorus Siculus.

Hist. lib. 6. ἐπ᾽ ἄρχοντ@ δ᾽ Ἀθήνησι * φαινος, supply, ἀ᾽ϕεσίου. (Socrat. *chap.* 1.)

Excerpt. Vales. pag. 245. supply the Text (out of Iambl. de vit. Pyth. cap. 29.) thus, ὑδὲν γὰρ μεῖζον πρὸς ἐπιστήμην κ᾽ φρόνησιν, ἔτι δὲ τῆς πάντων ἐμποιεῖν, τῷ δυνατῷ πολλὰ μνημονεύειν, (*Pyth. doctr. part.* 1. *chap.* 10.)

Diogenes Laertius,

More frequently.

Etymologicum Magnum.

Pag. Σολοικοὶ οἱ βάρβαροι ἀπὸ Σόλωμ@ κιλικ@, perhaps ἀπὸ σόλων κιλικίων. (Solon. *chap.* 11.)

Gregory Nazianzen.

Adverf. Julian. Orat. 3. Ἐπεὶ κ᾽ ὅτοι μιμεῖσθαι μέν λέγονται τῶν ἀνθρωπίνων τινὰ δελεασμάτων, κακοτέχνως περιεδεμένων τέλοις μέν τοι κ᾽ ἁλίσκουσαι μὴ δυναμένης ἐξίκεσθαι τῆς ἡμετέρας σοφίας τῆς μιμήσεως, perhaps transpose; δελεασμάτων μὲν τοι κακοτέχνως περιεδεμένων τέλοις κ᾽ ἁλίσκουσαι. (*Pyth. chap.* 22.)

Herodotus.

Lib. 4. ἴσω ὑπὸ τ᾽ ἀδελφιδέω ὑποθανών. (Valla & Stephen. *a patruele,*) perhaps ἀδελφοῦ. (Anacharf. *chap.* 1.)

Iamblichus, his Life of Pythagoras,

Set forth corruptly by *Arcerius*; and corrupted yet more by his Translation and Castigations, restored a little by the *Anonymus* Writer at the end of his Edition, and by *Desiderius Heraldus* at the end of his *Animadversions*; and by *Rittereusius* upon *Porphyrius*: But generally requires much more; as,

Cap. 2. for τὴν Σάμον τὴν ἐν τῇ Κεφαληνίᾳ, read Σάμην, and afterwards, pag. 27. ἀντὶ τῆς Σαμίης read Σάμης· For so the Oracle immediately following.

Ἀγκαῖ᾽, (not Ἀγκαῖε,) εἰναλίαν νῆσον Σάμον ἀντὶ Σάμης σὺ

Οἰκίζειν κέλομαι φυλλάς (Hesych. φυλλὶς,) δ᾽ ὀνομάζεται αὔλη. (Pyth. c. 1.)

Pag. 29. κ᾽ κυέσης αὐλὴν, εἰ μὴ οὕτως ἐχούσης κατέσαι, read, κ᾽ κυέσαν αὐτὴν ἐκ (for so the MS.) μὴ οὕτως ἐχούσης. (*Pyth. chap.* 2.)

Pag. 32. περὶ γὰρ ἐκείνων κ᾽ ἑαυτὸν ἐφωδιάζεσθαι ταῦτα· διὸ σοφὸς παρὰ τοῖς πολλοῖς νομίζεται, read, περὶ γὰρ ἐκείνων κ᾽ ἑαυτὸν ἐφωδιάζεσθαι ταῦτα, διὰ ἃ (for the MS. had διὰ,) σοφὸς, &c. and immediately, for ὅσα τοῦ Πυθαγόραν κατορθ᾽, read, ὅσων and κατορθᾷ. (*Pyth. ibid.*)

Chap. 3. κἂν τέλον ὀλιγουπνίαν, read, κἂκ τέλε· (*Pyth. chap.* 3.)

Pag. 32. κ᾽ τοῖς ἄλλοις, κ᾽ φοινικοῖς ἱερογλύφαις, κ᾽ πάσαις τελεταῖς τελεσθεὶς ἐν τε Βύβλῳ κ᾽ τύρῳ, κ᾽ κατὰ πολλὰ τῆς Συρίας μέρη ἐξ αἱρέσεως ἱεργασμένα, read and distinguish, κ᾽ τοῖς ἄλλοις τῆς φοινίκης (or φοινικικοῖς) ἱερογλύφαις, κ᾽ πάσας τελετὰς τελεσθεὶς ἐν Βύβλῳ κ᾽ τύρῳ. κ᾽ κατὰ πολλὰ τῆς Συρίας μέρη, ἐξαιρέτως ἱεργασμένα. (*Pyth. ibid.*)

Pag. 34. μετὸν τὸ ἐπιφθεγξάμεν@, εἰς Αἴγυπτον ὁ ἀπόπλευς, perhaps, ἐπιφθεγξάμενον τὸ, μὲν εἰς Αἴγυπτον ὁ ἀπόπλευς, (*Pyth. chap.* 4.)

Cap. 5.

Conjectures.

Cap. 5. for κατ' ἐπαιδεύθη, read καθᾶς. (Pyth. chap. 6.)

Pag. 38. ἐνδιαδέξατο αὐτόν, read ἦν διαδέξαιτο αὐτός. (Pyth. ibid.)

Pag. 39. διὰ νοῶν χολάζειν, read νῶν. (Pyth. ibid.)

Cap. 8. pag. 50. ἐν οἷς (read θεοῖς,) οὐδενὸς ἐλάττον, &c. (Pyth. chap. 12.)

Pag. 51. for ἐνθυμίας read ἐπιθυμίας. (Pyth. Ibid.)

Cap. 9. ἰδὲ πρῶτον μὲν αὐτοῖς συμβουλεύει ἰδύεσθαι μυσῶν, (read μυσῶν,) ἵνα πρώσιν τὴν ὑπάρχα (read ὑπάρχυσαν,) ὁμόνοιαν. (Pyth. chap. 13.)

Cap. 10. μετὰ ἄρχειν λοιδοεῖαν, read λοιδοεῖας, and afterwards, καὶ μόνοις διὰ τέλους ἁγνεύυσιν ἐξυσίαι, &c. (Ibid.)

Pag. 60. for ἐληλυθόσιν, read περεληλυθόσιν (Ibid.)

Cap. 11. ὅτως αὐτὰς περὶ πλεῖςα ποιῶνδε ἐπιεικείαν, perhaps ἐπιμέλειαν. (Pyth. chap. 14.)

Cap. 15. for ἀευροῶσι, read ἀπὶ ἐφορῶσι. (Pyth. doctr. part. 1. Sect. 2. chap. 7.)

Cap. 18. pag. 89. ἱππομέδων ἄγει© Αἰνεύς, perhaps Ἀγειανεύς. (Pyth. doct. part. 1. chap. 8.)

Cap. 19. ἀκεσάσατο πρὸς τὴν ἀκεσάσιν, perhaps ἀπειργάσατο. (Pyth. chap. 23.)

Pag. 93. for χρὶ τὰ ἄβαλα διαβαίνειν, read καὶ, and afterwards, for ἄλλα τοιαῦτα τέχνη, perhaps ἴχνη: (Ibid.)

Cap. 21. pag. 99. παρατίθεσθαι δὲ κρέα ζώων θυσιμῶν ἱερέων, expunge ἱερέων, which seems a gloss. (Pyth. doct. part. 1. chap. 9.)

Cap. 25. ἐπὶ (read ἀπό.) τῆς ἔργων. (Pythag. doctr. part. 1. Sect. 2. chap. 8.)

Cap. 26. ἐςὶ μὲν τοὶ ἴσως ἐκείνων) perhaps ἐκείνῃ, Ἐλπεσθαι χρὴ πάντ' ἐπεὶ ἐκ ἐς' ἐδὲν ἀέλπτον. (Pyth. doctr. part. 4. chap. 4. Symb. 4.)

Pag. 135. θέαν * οἱ τῇ μητεὶ, read θεανοῖ. (Pyth. chap. 21.)

Ibid. ὀργιαθεὶς ἐν Λιβήθροις, read ὀργιαθεὶς. (Pyth. doctr. part. 2. Sect. 1. chap. 15.)

Marmora Arundeliana.

Pag. 10. line 38. ἄρχον©- Ἀθήνησι τῇ δήμῳ, (Mr Selden, archonte Athenis populo,) read Ἐυθυδήμου: (Chilon. chap. 1.)

Nicomachus, his Introduction to Arithmetick.

(So supply the Title, ἀριθμητικῆς εἰσαγωγῆς; see pag. 30, 35, 44, 62, 76.)

Pag. 7. ἀλλὰ καὶ ὅτι φύσει προγενέστερο© ὑπάρχων ὅσῳ συναναιρεῖ μὲν ἑαυτῇ τὰ λοιπὰ, read, προγενεστέρα ὑπάρχυσα· συναναιρεῖ μέν, &c. (Pythag. doct. part. 2. Sect. 1.)

His Enchiridion of Musick, set forth by Meibomius.

Pag. 10. continue the fifth Section, and distinguish thus, ὁ ἄρα τόν©- ἑπόγδο©-. τὴν δὲ κατ' ἀριθμὸν ποσότητα ταύτην, ἥτε διὰ πέντε, καὶ ἡ κατ' ἀμφοτέρων σύνοδον, διὰ πασῶν λεγομένη, καὶ περισκεπιθ©- μεταξὺ τῆς δύο τετραχόρδων τόν©-, τρόπῳ τινι ταῦτα ὑπὸ τοῦ Πυθαγόρου καταληφθέντα ἔχειν ἐβεβαιώθη. (Sect. 6.) Ἐν φερτίδι ποτέ ἢ διαλογισμῷ, &c. (Pyth. part. 2. Sect. 2. chap. 3.

Pag. 11. ἰσόςρεφυς, not ἰσορρόπως as Meibomius: (Pyth. part. 2. Sect. 2. chap. 4.)

Porphyrius, his Life of Pythagoras,

Set forth by Lucas Holstenius: p. 2. and p. 10. Ἑρμοδάμαντι τῷ Κρεοφυλίῳ, perhaps τῷ Κρεοφύλῳ· οἱ τῇ Κρεοφύλε. (Pyth. chap. 2.)

Pag. 11. ἐν τῷ καλυμένῳ τείποδι, perhaps τέλσαι. (Pyth. chap. 7.)

Pag. 27. τὴν θάλατταν μὲν ἐκάλει εἶναι read Κρόνυ, δάκρυον. (Pyth. doctr. part. 4. chap. 1.)

Ibid. φαυλὼ εἶναι τινὸς τῆς δαιμόνων ἐναπειμμόλυ τῷ χαλκῷ, perhaps ἐναπειλημμένη. (Pyth. doctr. 3. Sect. 3. chap. 4.)

Proclus, upon Euclid.

Lib. 1. chap. 12. τοῦτο γὰρ ἀφελύσας (read ἀφελέσας,) τῆ ἀπείρων τὰς ἐπισήμας κατανοεῖν, ὡς ἐ κενόν τὴν καθ' ἑκάτερον ἀπειρίαν γνῶσιν λαβεῖν, transpose, ὡς ἐ τὴν καθ' ἑκάτερον ἀπειρίαν γνῶσιν λαβεῖν κενόν. (Pyth. doctr. part. 2. chap. 2.)

Ibid. καὶ τ' ἀριθμητικὴν χρὴ δὲ τὴν ἕνωσιν τῇ πλήθους, καὶ τὴν πρὸς ἑαυτὸ κοινωνίαν, καὶ τὴν νοήσασα ἑαυτῇ ἓν καὶ πολλὰ ἕσαν τῆς τε ἀριθμὸς περιβάλλει, καὶ τὴν τέλων γνῶσιν, καὶ συνδεσμὸν * τῇ μυσικὴν, transpose the lines, καὶ νοήσασα ἑαυτὴν ἓν καὶ πολλὰ ἕσαν, τῆς τε ἀριθμὸς περιβάλλει, καὶ τὴν τέτων, γνῶσιν τῆς ἀριθμητικὴν. χρὴ δὲ τῆ ἕνωσιν τῇ πλήθους, καὶ τὴν πρὸς ἑαυτὸ κοινωνίαν καὶ συνδεσμὸν, τῆ μυσικὴν. (Pythag. Ibid.)

Ibid. for καταγενῆ read χρὴ γένη. (Pyth. Ibid.)

Lib. 3. chap. 4. ἀπὸ αἰσθήσεως δὴν εἰς λογισμὸν, καὶ ἀπὸ τ' ἡ μετάβασις γίνοιτ' ἂν εἰκότως, supply καὶ ἀπὸ τῷ λογισμῷ εἰς τ' νοῶν ἡ μετάβασις, &c. and presently after, for ὃς ἐφαψόμεν©-, read ὡς ἐφαψάμεν©-. (Thal. chap. 7.)

Ibid. καὶ μέν τοι καὶ φασὶν ὅτι Πτολεμαῖ©- ἤρετο ποτὲ αὐτὸν εἴ τις ἐςὶ περὶ γεωμετρίαν, νεώτερος μὲν ἓν, &c. supply, εἴ τις ὁδὸς περὶ γεωμετρίαν τῆς ςοιχειώσεως βραχίων μέθοδ©-, οὐδεμία (φησίν,) ὦ βασιλεῦ, περὶ γεωμετρίαν βασιλικὴ ὁδὸς νεώτερ©-, &c.

Pag. 31. τρῆς γραμμαῖς ὅτι πέντε τομαῖς εὑρὼν τὰς * σπενκὰς, read, τὰς σπενεικας εὑρών. (Thal. chap 7. Sect. 1.

Lib. 4. pag. 109. ὅτ' ἂν γὰρ ἐυθείας ἐκκειμένης τὸ δοθὲν χωρίον πάσῃ τῇ εὐθείᾳ συμπαραβάλειν ἔκεῖνο τὸ χωρίον φασίν, ὅτ' ἂν μεῖζον δή ποιῆτης, &c. supply πάσῃ τῇ ἐυθείᾳ συμπαραβληθέντος, τότε παραβαλεῖν ἐκεῖνο τὸ χωρίον φασὶν ὅπαν δὲ μεῖζον, &c. (Pythag. doctr. Sect. 3. chap. 2.)

Sextus Empiricus, his Pyrrhonean Hypotuposes.

Lib. 1. c. 4. καὶ τὰ, αὐλιθελικὴν φαινόμενόν τε καὶ νοεμέ νων. καὶ τ', perhaps τῷ. (Sext. Ibid.)

Cap. 14. ὃς καὶ λόγυς καὶ τύπυς συωνύμως καλῦσιν. perhaps τόπυς, (chap. 11.)

Ibid. p. 10. πολὺ δήπυ ἀλογώτερόν ἐςι. MS. ἐυλογώτερον. better. (chap. 12.)

Chap. 33. pag. 46. in the Verses of Xenophanes, for ἀμφότερα βλέπλα MS. ἀμφοτέρῃ βλέπλ©-. for ὅπη read ὅππη. for ἴσαδ' MS. ἴσαδ'. for Ἐα τ. MS. Εκ]ον· perhaps ξίσον· (chap. 31.)

Lib. 2. cap. 5. pag. 61. ἀκόλυθον μὴ ἦν ἴσως perhaps μὴ ἦν. (Ibid.)

Cap. 6. p. 64. τῇ διανοίᾳ καὶ ταῖς αἰσθήσεσι κενῶμεν, τισὶ δὲ μή, in the MS of Sir Henry Savile and Mr Casaubone there is a breach, to shew the defect, thus, ταῖς αἰσθήσεσι κενῶμεν * τισὶ δὲ μή. presently after for διὰ τῶτο κεῖνειν, read τέλων. (Ibid.)

Ibid. lin. 36. ποῖ ἀγαθὸς ἐςὶν ὁ πλῶτ©-, ἢ κακὸς, supply, ἢ ἀδιάφορ©-· otherwise it is not a defective reason. (Ibid.)

Cap. 13. pag. 82. lin. 4. εἰ ἡμέρα ἐςί, οὐχὶ δὲ φῶς ἐςιν, ἐκ ἄρα ἡμέρα ἐςίν. supply, εἰ φῶς ἐκ ἐςιν ἐχὶ ἡμέρα ἐςί. οὐχὶ δὲ φῶς ἐςίν· ἐκ ἄρα, &c. (Ibid.)

Cap. 22. pag. 101. lin. 18. ἐρώτηκα δέ τί σε πρότον, εἰ ἄρα ἀςέρες ἀρτιοὶ εἰσιν, read ἐκ ἄρα. (Ibid.)

Cap. 23.

Conjectures.

Cap. 23. pag. 102. perhaps τὸ ὑποφαλικὸν ᾗ συμπλοκῆς should be expunged; and is but a repetition of the next line. (Ibid.)

Lib. 3. cap. 8. line 30. for ἀλλ' εἰ μὲν ὑφ' ἑτέρῳ. perhaps read, ἀλλ' ὑδὲ ὑφ' αὑτῷ ὑδευρ' ἑτέρῳ. (Ibid.)

Cap. 16. pag. 136. lin. 40. εἰ δὲ ὑπαρχεῖ, κενέμετον μεταβαλικῶς. perhaps κινέμενον. (Ibid.)

Cap. 18. * ἄεισϑ᾽ δυσί· read ἀσεισϑ᾽. (Ibid.)

Pag. 141. lin. 3. ἐκ ἄρα τὸ ζῶον ἓν ὅτιν, add, κτι ᾗ ἑαυτῆ λόγον. (Ibid.)

Lin. 30. ὡς ὑπεμνήσαμῳ, rea ὑπεμνήσομῳ. (Ibid.)

Socrates and the *Socraticks*, their Epistles.
Set forth by *Leo Allatius*.

Epist. 1. pag. 2. ὁπόσης ὁμοίως ἀκύειν τῷ ἀεὶ ὅτι τε, κ̀ μή. perhaps τῷ ἀιόντι τε, κ̀ μή, (*Socrat. Epist.* I.)

Pag. 2. ὡς ὑμῖν περιάξ. perhaps ὡς ὑμῆς ἡμῖν περὶ δαι. (Ibid.)

Pag. 5. ἀλλὰ τῶν μὲν ἑτέρων ἔχειν τὴν αἰτίαν, τῶ δὲ καθάπαξ αὐτός. M.S. τῷ μὲν ἑτέρων. perhaps ἀλλὰ τῷ μὲν ἑτέρ' ἂν ἔχοι τὴν αἰτίαν, τῷ δέ, καθάπαξ αὐτός. (Ibid.)

Pag. 9. ὅτι ἐκ ἀλλάττομαι τῶν ἐκεῖ πυνθάδε, ἀμείνω δοκῶν. perhaps, ἄμεινον ἔιναι δοκέων, οι ἐμμένειν δοκεῖν. (Ibid.)

Epist. 5. Περιέξενον δὲ καταλαβεῖν εἰς τὴν Ἀσίαν. perhaps, καταλαβεῖν τὴν Ἀσίαν, or διαβαλεῖν εἰς τὴν Ἀσίαν. (*Socr. Epist.* 5.)

Pag. 15. κ̀ μακαειεωτάτῳ ὑπάρχειν. read μακαειότατον. (Ibid.)

Pag. 16. περὶ οἷς ἡ τύχειν ἤδη κ̀ τῶν ὄντως ἀνθρωπίνων ἀγαθῶν περιαπεστερῆλαι, τὴν ὑπὲρ τῶν μελλόντων χρηστὴν ἐλπίδα. perhaps, περὶ τῇ ἐπιτύχωσιν ἤδη γε τῶν ὄντως ἂν θεραπίνων ἀγαθῶν, περιαπεστέρηνται, &c. or, περὶ οἷς ἀνυχ..., ...τῶν ἁπλως ἀνθρωπίνων ἀγαθῶν περιαπεστέρηνται ᾗ ὑπὶ τῶν μελλόντων, &c. (Ibid.)

Ibid. κ̀ λόγοις μόνον, ἀλλὰ κ̀ ἔργοις δηλώσαντες. MS. ἑαν ὁ λόγοις. which I choose, reading afterwards δηλῶσαι τις. (Ibid.)

Pag. 18. περὶ ἂν μὲν ὅσω τιμῆς τυγχάνει· read, ἀξίων.

Epist. 7. pag. 22. τῇ μὲν γὰρ ἐξεῖναι ἔρη οἱ κρατήσασι πεποιηκέναι ἐβόλοντο τῶν συμμάχων, &c. perhaps, τουτο μὲν γὰρ ἐξεῖναι σφίσι γε κρατήσασι πεποιηκέναι οἱ ἐβόλοντο. (Ibid.)

Epist. 8. 'Οὐκ ἔσι τοῦτο φιλοσόφου, τὸ παρὰ τυράννοις, ἀνδράσι. perhaps add, ζῆν. (*Amisth.* chap. 4.)

Epist. 9. ταῦτα γὰ δοκέει ἀμείνω τὰ χρώματ᾽ εἶναι. perhaps χρώματ᾽. Dorice, for χρήματ᾽. (*Aristpi. cap.* 7.)

Pag. 26. ἥδειν ὅτι κακοδαιμονήσα ταῦτα πάσχων, καθάπερ σύ μοι γράφεις νῦν. ἐλεοῦντές με περιβλέπονται Συρακούσιοι, &c. read and distinguish, καθάπερ σύ σοι γράφεις. νῦν δὲ ἐλεοῦντές με περιβλέπονλὶ, &c. Dorice. (Ibid.)

Ibid. τὰς δὲ μανίας ἃς ἐμάνλω, read, τᾶς δὲ μανίας ῳὲι ἃς ἐμάνλω. (Ibid.)

Ibid. ὅτι δὲ ἐγὼ γεγονώς, &c. read, ὅτι δὲ, &c. (Ibid.)

Epist. 13. Ἀκύω σε θαυμάζειν ἡμᾶς· perhaps, ταράξειν. (*Simon.*)

Ibid. μέμνησο μὲν τοι ἀεὶ μηθ᾽ κ̀ δίψης Ταῦτα γὰρ δύναται μέγα τοῖς σωφροσύνη διάκυσιν. read, μέμνησο μὲν τοι λιμῷ κ̀ δίψης ταῦτα γὰρ δύναται μεγάλα τοῖς σωφροσύνω διάκυσιν. for so *Stobæus* Serm. 17. citing this fragment, *ex Simonis Epistola ad Aristippum*: whence supply the Inscription also. (Ibid.)

Stobæus.

Serm. 82. citing *Hierocles*, πολὺ δὲ διαφέρωνος ἐπ᾽ ἀδελφῷ, τῷ τῆ Σωκρατικῆς, perhaps τοῦ Σωκρατικοῦ. (*Euclid. chap.* 3.)

Themistius.

Orat. 4. ἐκ Κέϕτουϑ δὲ εἰς Λόκρους. διὰ γυλῶνα read (as also in *Laertius*, vit. *Pyth.* for Κύδωνα.) Κυλῶνα and in *Plutarch de Gen. Socr.* for Κυκλωνείος, Κυλώνειοι, twice. (*Pyth. chap.* 19.)

Synes: Hymn. 4.

Πάτερ ἄγνωστε,
Πάτερ ἀρρήτε,
Ἄγνωστε νόῳ,
Ἄρρητε λόγῳ,
Νόϑ ἐπὶ νόυ,
Ψυχᾶν ψυχᾶ,
Φύσις εἰ φυσίων.

FINIS.

THE HISTORY OF THE CHALDAICK Philosophy.

BY THOMAS STANLEY.

LONDON,

Printed for *A.* and *J. Churchill* at the *Black Swan* in *Pater-Noster-Row,* MDCCI.

TO
Sir John Marſham, Kt.

SIR,

I Send this Book to you, becauſe you firſt directed me to this Deſign. The Learned *Gaſſendus* was my Precedent; whom neverthelefs I have not follow'd in his Partiality: For he, tho' limited to a Single Perſon, yet giveth himſelf Liberty of Enlargement, and taketh occaſion from his Subject to make the World acquainted with many excellent Diſquiſitions of his own. Our Scope being of a greater Latitude, affords leſs Opportunity to favour any Particular; whilſt there is due to every one the Commendation of their own Deſerts. This Benefit I hope to have received from the variety of the Subject; but far more are thoſe I owe to your Encouragement, which if I could wiſh leſs, I ſhould upon this Occaſion, that there might ſeem to have been expreſſed ſomething of Choice and Inclination in this Action, which is now but an inconſiderable Effect of the Gratitude of,

Dear Uncle,

Your Moſt Affectionate Nephew,

and Humble Servant,

THOMAS STANDLEY.

PREFACE.

WE are entring upon a Subject which I confess, is in it self harsh, and exotick, very unproper for our Tongue; yet I doubt not but they will pardon this, who shall consider, that other Philosophies and Sciences have been lately well received by several Nations Translated into their own Languages, and that this, as being the first, contributes not a little to the understanding of the rest.

Another disadvantage this Subject incurs far more considerable: There is not any thing more difficult to be retrieved out of the Ruins of Antiquities than the Learning of the Eastern Nations, and particularly that of the Chaldæans. What remains of it is chiefly transmitted to us by the Greeks, of whom, some converted it to their own use, intermixing it with their Philosophy, as Pythagoras and Plato; others treated expresly of it, but their Writings are lost. Of its first Authors nothing remains; what others took from it, is not distinguishable from their proper Philosophy. The Greeks were first made acquainted with it by Osthanes, and, long after, by Berosus; the former living in the time of Xerxes, the other, under Ptolomæus Philadelphus. Whence it may be inferred, that the Discourse, which Democritus writ of Chaldæa, and his Commentary of the Sacred Letters at Babylon, either came short of these Sciences, or were so obscure, that they conduced little to their discovery. Neither seems the Treatise, entituled Magicum, ascribed by some, to Aristotle, by others, to Rhodon, but indeed written by Antisthenes, to have considered the Learning and Sciences, so much as the History of the Professors. Of which kind were also the Writers concerning the Magi, cited, under that general Title, by Diogenes Laertius.

But there wanted not those, who further explained to the Greeks what Osthanes and Berosus had first communicated. Hermippus (to use Pliny's Words) wrote most diligently of Magick, and Commented upon the Verses of Zoroaster. About the time of Antonius Pius flourished the two Julians, Father and Son, Chaldaick Philosophers: the first wrote concerning the Chaldaick Rites, the latter, Theurgick Oracles in Verse, and other Secrets of that Science. Afterwards wrote Symbulus and Pallas, concerning the Magi; and the latter Platonick Philosophers more frequently: Amelius, 40 Books of Confutation; Porphyrius 4 on the History of Julian the Chaldæan; Jamblichus, 28 intituled, Of the most perfect Chaldaick Theology; and Syrianus 10 upon the Oracles.

Of all these, there's nothing extant, unless (which we shall have occasion hereafter to prove) the few Oracles, dispersed among the Platonick Writers, be part of those, which were, by the Greeks, (Hermippus, Julian the Son, and others) translated out of the Chaldaick. Some of these Pletho and Psellus have explained with a Comment, adding two brief obscure Summaries of the Chaldaick Doctrine, which we have endeavoured to supply and clear, by adding and digesting the few Remains of those Sciences which lie dispersed amongst other Authors; taking care to reject such as are supposititious, or of no credit, as in the Historical Part, Annius Viterbiensis, Clemens Romanus, and the like: in the Philosophical, the Rabbinnical Inventions, which tho' incuriously admitted by Kircher, Gaulmin, and others) manifestly appear to have been of later Invention.

PART XIV.

THE HISTORY OF THE CHALDAICK PHILOSOPHERS.

The First BOOK.

Of the Chaldæans.

PHilosophy is generally acknowledged even by the most Learned of the *Grecians* themselves, to have had its Original in the East. None of the Eastern Nations, for Antiquity of Learning, stood in Competition with the *Chaldæans* and *Ægyptians*. The *Ægyptians* pretended that the *Chaldæans* were a Colony of them, and had all their Learning and Institutions from them; but they who are less interessed, and unprejudiced Judges of this Controversie, assert that *a* The *Magi* (who derived their Knowledge from the *Chaldæans*) were more ancient than the *Ægyptians*, that *b* *Astrological Learning passed from the Chaldæans to the Ægyptians, and from them to the* Grecians, and, in a word, that the *Chaldæans* were *c antiquissimum Doctorum genus,* the most ancient of Teachers.

a The Author of the Treatise Μαγικὸν, cited by Laertius in Proœm.
b Joseph. 1. 8.
c Cic.

Chaldæa is a part of *Babylonia* in *Asia*, the Inhabitants termed *Chasdim*, (as if *Chusdim*) from *Chus* the Son of *Cham*. But the Philosophy of the *Chaldæans*, exceeded the Bounds of their Country, and diffused it self into *Persia* and *Arabia*, that Border upon it; for which reason the Learning of the *Chaldæans, Persians* and *Arabians* is comprehended under the general Title of CHALDAICK.

Of these therefore we shall begin with That, from which the other two were derived, and is more properly termed CHALDÆAN, in respect of the Country. In treating of which (as likewise of the other two) the first part of our Discourse shall consider the Authors or Professors, and their Sects; the Second their Doctrine.

THE FOURTEENTH PART.

The Chaldæan Philosophers, Institution, and Sects.

SECT. I.

Of the Chaldæan Philosophers.

CHAP. I.

The Antiquity of the Chaldaick Learning.

THE Antiquity of the *Chaldaick* Learning, though such as other Nations cannot equal, comes far short of that to which they did pretend. When *Alexander*, by his Victories against *Darius*, was possessed of *Babylon*, (in the 4383d year of the *Julian* Period) *Aristotle*, a curious promoter of Arts, requested his Nephew *Calisthenes*, who accompanied *Alexander* in the Expedition, to inform him of what Antiquity the Learning of the *Chaldæans* might with reason be esteemed. The *Chaldæans* themselves pretended, that, from the time they had first begun to observe the Stars until this Expedition of *Alexander* into *Asia*, were 470000 years. But far beneath this number were the Observations, which (as *Porphyrius* cited by *Simplicius* relates) *Calisthenes* sent to *Aristotle*, being out of 1903 years, preserved to that time, which from the 4383d year of the *Julian* Period upward, falls upon the 2480th. And

a In lib. 2. de cælo, p. 123. line. 18.

[Bbbb] even

ven this may with good Reason be questioned, for there is not any thing extant in the Chaldaick Astrology more ancient than the Æra of *Nabonaſſar*, which began but on the 3967th of the *Julian* Period. By this Æra they compute their Astronomical Observations, of which if there had been any more ancient, *Ptolomy* would not have omitted them. *b* The firſt of theſe is the firſt year of *Merodach*, *c* (that King of *Babylon* who ſent the Meſſage to *Ahaz* concerning the Miracle of the Dial) which was about the 27th of *Nabonaſſar*. The next was in the 28th of *Nabonaſſar*. *d* The third Obſervation is in the 127th of *Nabonaſſar*, which is the 5th year of *Nabopolaſſar*. This indeed is beyond all exception; for we have them confirmed by the Authority of *Ptolomy*, who ſhews the Reaſons and Rules for the Obſervations. What is more than this, ſeems to have been only hypothetical. And if we ſhall imagine a canicular Cycle, which conſiſts of 1461 years (and are 1460 natural years) to have been ſuppoſed by *Porphyrius* to make up his Hypotheſis, then there will want but 18 years of this number.

b Ptol. lib. 4. cap. 6. 7.
c Ezek.

d Lib. 5. p. 125

CHAP. II.

That there were ſeveral Zoroaſters.

THE Invention of Arts among the *Chaldeans* is generally aſcribed to *Zoroaſter*. The name *Zoroaſter* (to omit thoſe who give it a Greek Etymology from ζῶον and ἄςειν) *Dinon* cited by *a Laertius* Interprets ἀςεροθύτην, Rendred by his Tranſlators, a Worſhipper of the Stars. *b Kircher* finds fault with this Etymology as being compounded out of two ſeveral Languages, from the Greek ἄςειν, and the Chaldee *Zor*, and therefore endeavours to deduce it from *c tſura*, a figure, or *d tſajar*, to faſhion, and *e as* and *f ſtar*, hidden fire, as if it were *g Zairaſter*, faſhioning Images of hidden fire, or, *h Tſuraſter, the Image of ſecret things*, with which the *Perſian Zaraſt* agreeth. But it hath been obſerved, that *Eſter* in the Perſian Language ſignifieth a Star. The former Particle *Zor*, *i Bochartus* derives from the Hebrew *Schur*, to contemplate, and thereupon, for ἀςεροθύτης, (in *Laertius*) Reads ἀςεροθεάτης, a contemplater of the Stars. But we find *Zor* uſed among other words (by compoſition) in the name *Zorobabel*, which we Interpret, *Born at Babylon*: *Zoroaſter* therefore properly ſignifies *the Son of the Stars*.

a In Præm.
b Obeliſc. Pamphil, l. 1. c. 2. Sect. 1.

צורא
d צור
e עם
f סטר
g זאירסטר
h צוראסתר

i Geor. Sacr. l. 1. c. 1.

The ſame name it is which ſome call *Zabratas*, others *Nazaratas*, others, *Zares*, others *Zaran*, others, *Zaratus*, others *Zaradas*; all which are but ſeveral corruptions from the Chaldee or Perſian Word, which the Greeks moſt generally render *Zoroaſter*.

That there were ſeveral *Zoroaſters* (except *Goropius* who paradoxically maintains there was not any one) none deny; but in reckoning them up, there is no ſmall diſagreement amongſt Writers, grounded chiefly upon *k Arnobius*, whom they differently interpret; his words are theſe, *Age nunc veniat quis ſuper igneam zonam Magus interiore ab orbe Zoroaſtres, Hermippo ut aſſentiamur Authori: Bactrianus & illi conveniat,*

k Cont. gent.

cujus Cteſias res geſtas hiſtoriarum exponit in primo; Armenius, Hoſtanis nepos, & familiaris Pamphilius Cyri. *l Patricius*, *m Naudæus*, *n Kircher*, and others, conceive that *Arnobius* here mentions four *Zoroaſters*; the firſt a *Chaldæan*, the ſecond a *Bactrian*, the third a *Pamphilian* (named alſo *Erus*) the fourth an *Armenian*, Son (as *Kircher* would have it) of *Hoſtanes*. *o Salmaſius* alters the Text thus, *Age nunc, veniat quæſo per igneam Zonam Magus interiore ab orbe Zoroaſtres, Hermippo ut aſſentiamur Authori, Bactrianus. Et ille conveniat, cujus Cteſias res geſtas hiſtoriarum exponit in primo, Armenius, Hoſtanis nepos, & familiaris Pamphilus Cyri.* Which words thus altered by himſelf, imply, as he pretends, but three *Zoroaſters*, the firſt according to ſome, an Æthiopian, (a Country near the torrid Zone) but according to Hermippus, a *Bactrian*; the ſecond, Armenius, Nephew of Hoſtanes, of whoſe Actions Cteſias gives account in the *firſt Book of his Hiſtories*; the third named Pamphilus, Friend to Cyrus. *p Urſinus*, from the ſame reading of the words, infers that *Arnobius* mentions only two, that *he manifeſtly explodes the Bactrian Zoroaſter of Hermippus, and that Cteſias confuting the fabulous Relation of Eudoxus, proved Zoroaſter to have lived in the time of Cyrus.* But the words of *Arnobius* ſeem not to require ſuch alteration; which will appear more, if we mention particularly all thoſe on whom the name of *Zoroaſter* was conferred.

l Mag. Phil.
m Apol. Mag. 8.
n Obeliſc. Pamphil.

o Plin. Exercit.

p In Zor.

The firſt a *Chaldean*, the ſame whom *q Suidas* calls the *Aſſyrian*, adding that he died by fire from Heaven; to which Story perhaps *Arnobius* alludes, or to that other Relation mentioned by *r Dion Chryſoſtom*, that *Zoroaſter* the Perſian (for their Stories are confounded) *came ſtih. to the People out of a fiery Mountain*; or elſe by *fiery Zone*, he means the Seat of the *zoned Deities* juſt above the Empyreal or Corporeal Heaven, according to the Doctrine of the *Chaldeans*; for I find not any where that *Zoroaſter* was eſteemed an Æthiopian, or of interiour *Lybia* as *Salmaſius* expounds. Concerning this *Zoroaſter*, Arnobius cites Hermippus: who, as *f Pliny* ſaith, *wrote in explication of the Verſes, and added Tables to his Volumes.*

q In Zor.

r Orat. Borl.

ſ Lib. 36. c 1.

The ſecond a *Bactrian*; *t Juſtin* mentions *Zoroaſtres*, King of *Bactria* contemporary with *Ninus* the *Aſſyrian*, by whom he was ſubdued and ſlain; adding, *He was ſaid to be the firſt that invented Magical Arts, and obſerved the beginnings of the World, and the Motions of the Stars* Arnobius ſaith, *u he conteſted with Ninus, not only by ſteel and ſtrength, but likewiſe by the Magical and abſtruſe Diſciplines of the Chaldeans.* The Actions of this *Zoroaſter*, *Cteſias* recorded in the firſt Book of his *Perſica*; for ſo *Arnobius*, *Bactrianus & ille conveniat, cujus* Cteſias *res geſta hiſtoriam exponit in primo*. The firſt ſix Book of that Work treated (as *y Photius* ſhews) only of the *Aſſyrian* Hiſtory, and paſſages that preceded the *Perſian* Affairs. Whereupon, I cannot aſſent to the conjecture of *Salmaſius*, who applies the citation of *Cteſias* to the Nephew of *Hoſtanes*, ſince *Hoſtanes* (as *z Pliny* affirms) lived under *Darius*. But *a Diodorus* names the King of *Bactria*, whom *Ninus* conquered, *Oxyartes*; and ſome old Mss. of *Juſtin* (atteſted by *Ligerius*) *Oxyatres*, others *Zeoraſtes*:
perhaps

t Lib. 1.

u Cont. gent.

x Loc. cit.

y Biblioth.

z Lib. 36. c. 1.
a Lib.

The Chaldaick Philosophy.

perhaps the nearness of the Names and Times (the *Chaldean* living also under *Ninus*, as (b) *Suidas* relates) gave occasion to some to confound them, and to ascribe to the *Bactrian* what was proper to the *Chaldean*; since it cannot be imagined, that the *Bactrian* was Inventer of those Arts, in which the *Chaldean*, who lived contemporary with him, was so well skilled. *Elichmannus*, a Persian Writer, affirms the Arabians and Persians to hold, that *Zoroaster was not King of the Bactrians, but a Magus or Prophet; who by perswasions having wrought upon their King, first introduced a new Form of Superstition amongst them, whereof there are some remainders at this day.*

The third a *Persian*, so termed by c *Laertius* and others; the same whom *Clemens Alexandrinus* styles a *Mede*; *Suidas* a *Perso-Mede*; Institutor of the Magi, and Introductor of the *Chaldaick* Sciences amongst the *Persians*. Some confound this *Zoroaster* with the *Chaldean*, and both of them (as d *Kircher* doth) with *Cham* the Son of *Noah*, not without a very great Anachronism: for we find the word *Persian* no where mentioned before the Prophet *Ezekiel*, neither did it come to be of note till the time of *Cyrus*. The occasion of which mistake seems to have been; for that *Zoroaster* the *Persian*, is by *Pliny*, *Laertius*, and others, styled Institutor of Magick, and of the *Magi*, which is to be understood no otherwise than that he first introduced them into *Persia*. For e *Plutarch* acknowledgeth, *Zoroaster instituted Magi amongst the Chaldæans, in imitation of whom the Persians had theirs also*: And the f *Arabick* History that *Zaradussti not first instituted, but reformed, the Religion of the Persians and Magi, being divided into many Sects*.

The fourth a *Pamphylian*, commonly called *Er*, or *Erus Armenius*. That he also had the Name of *Zoroaster*, g *Clement* witnesseth: *The same Author* (saith he, meaning *Plato*) *in the 10th of his Politicks, mentioneth* Erus Armenius, *by descent a Pamphylian, who is* Zoroaster; now this *Zoroaster writes thus*, h ' *This wrote I,* Zoroaster Armenius, *by descent a Pamphylian, dying in War, and being in Hades, I learned of the Gods.* This *Zoroaster*, i *Plato* affirmeth to have been raised again to Life, after he had been dead ten days, and laid on the Funeral Pyle, repeated by k *Valerius Maximus*, and l *Macrobius*. To this *Zoroaster*, doubtless the latter part of *Arnobius's* Words, with which Interpreters are so much perplexed, ought to be preferred, *Armenius Hostanis nepos & familiaris Pamphylius Cyri*. Some conjecture he mentions two *Zoroasters*; I rather conceive the words, relate only to this one, and perhaps are corrupt, thus to be restored and distinguished, *Armenius Hostanis nepos & familiaris, Pamphilius Erus: Armenius*, Nephew and Disciple (in which sense γνώριμος is usually taken) of *Hostanes*, *Erus Pamphylius*.

The fifth a *Proconnesian*, mentioned by m *Pliny*; *such as are more diligent* (saith he) *place another* Zoroaster, *a Proconnesian, a little before* Hostanes. This *Zoroaster* might probably be *Aristeas* the *Proconnesian*, who, according to n *Suidas*, lived in the time of *Cyrus* and *Crœsus*. He adds, that *his Soul could go out of his Body, and return as often as he pleased.* o *Herodotus* relates an Instance hereof, not unlike that of *Erus*

Armenius, that *he died suddenly in a Fuller's Shop at* Proconnesus, *and was seen the same time at* Cyzicus: *his Friends coming to fetch his Body, could not find it. Seven years after he returned home, and published the Verses which were afterwards called* Arimaspian, *a Poem describing a happy Life, or rather an Imaginary Civil Government after such a manner as he conceived most perfect.* This we may gather from p *Clemens Alexandrinus*, who saith, that *the Hyperborean and Arimaspian Cities, and the Elizian Fields are Forms of Civil Governments of just Persons*; of which kinds Plato's Common-wealth.

To these may be added a sixth *Zoroaster*, (for so q *Apuleus* calls him) who lived at *Babylon*, at what time *Pythagoras* was carried Prisoner thither by *Cambyses*. The same Author terms him *omnis Divini arcanum Antistitem*, adding, that *he was the chief Person whom* Pythagoras *had for Master*; probably, therefore, the same with *Zabratus*, by whom r *Diogenes* affirms, *he was cleansed from the Pollutions of his Life past, and instructed from what things Virtuous Persons ought to be free; and learn the discourse concerning Nature* (Physick) *and what are the Principles of the Universe*; the same which *Nazaratas* the *Assyrian*, whom *Alexander* in his Book of Pythagorick Symbols, affirms to have been Master to *Pythagoras*; the same whom *Suidas* calls *Zares*; *Cyril*, *Zarn*; *Plutarch*, *Zaratus*.

That there should be so many *Zoroasters*, and so much confusion amongst Authors that write of them, by mistaking one for another, is nothing strange; for, from extraordinary Persons, Authors of some Publick Benefit, they who afterwards were Eminent in the same kind, were usually called by the same name. Hence it is, that there were so many *Belus's*, *Saturns*, *Jupiters*; and, consequently, so much confusion in their Stories. The like may be said of *Zoroaster* the *Chaldean*, who being the inventer of Magical and Astronomical Sciences, they who introduced the same into other Countries, as *Zoroaster* the *Persian* did, in imitation (as *Plutarch* saith) of the *Chaldæans*, and such likewise as were eminently skilful in those Sciences, as the *Bactrian*, the *Pamphylian*, and the *Proconnesian*, are descibed to have been, were called by the same Name.

CHAP. III.

Of the Chaldean Zoroaster, *Institutor of the Chaldaick Philosophy.*

The first of these *Zoroasters* term'd the *Chaldean* or *Assyrian*, is generally acknowledged the inventer of Arts and Sciences amongst the *Chaldeans*, but concerning the time in which he lived, there is a vast disagreement amongst Authors.

Some of these err so largely, as not to need any Confutation; such are a *Eudoxus*, and the Author of the Treatise entituled Μαγικὸν, commonly ascibed to *Aristotle*, and so b *Pliny* cites it,) who asserts he lived 5000 years before *Plato*. Such likewise are *Hermippus*, *Hemodorus* the *Platonick*, *Plutarch* and *Gemistus Pletho* (following *Plutarch*,) who place him 5000 years before the destruction of *Troy*.

Others

Others conceive *Zoroaster*, to be the same with *Cham*, the Son of *Noah*; of which Opinion (not to mention the *Pseudo-Berosus* of *Annius Viterbiensis*) were *Didymus* of *Alexandria*, *Agathias*, *Scholasticus*, and *Abenephi*: *Cham* (saith the last) was the Son of *Noah*; he *first taught the Worshipping of Idols, and first introduced Magical Arts into the World, his Name is* Zuraster, *he the second Adris, a perpetual fire.* Hither also some refer the Rabbinical stories concerning *Cham*, that c *by Magick he emasculated his Father*, &c. d *That Noah being by this means disabled from getting a fourth Son, Cursed the fourth Son of* Cham; *That* e *this Curse* (which was, that he should be a Servant of Servants) *implied strange Service, viz. Idolatry*; *That* f *hereupon the Posterity of* Chus *became Idolaters*, Cham *himself being the first that made Idols, and introduced strange Service into the World, and taught his Family the Worshipping of Fire*.

c *R. Levi in Gen. R. Samuel. in fortalitio fidei.*
d *Rassi.*
e *Aben Ezra in Gen.*
f *R. Hanasse in scuto fortium*

The greater part of Writers place him later. *Epiphanius* in the time of *Nimrod*, with whom agree the Observations g said to be sent by *Calisthenes* to *Aristotle* of 1903 years before *Alexander*'s taking *Babylon*, for from the year of the *Julian* Period, in which *Babylon* was taken, the 1903. upward falls on the 2480 of the same *Æra*; about which time *Nimrod* laid the Foundations of that City, and there setled his Empire.

g *Simplic.*

Suidas relates him contemporary with *Ninus* King of *Assyria*; *Eusebius*, with *Semiramis* wife of *Ninus*; *Ninus* is placed by Chronologers above the 3447. of the *Julian* Period.

Suidas (elsewhere) reckons him to have lived 500 years before the taking of *Troy*; *Xanthus*, 600 years before *Xerxes*'s Expedition into *Greece*. *Troy*, according to the *Marmor Arundelianum* was taken 444 years before the first Olympiad. *Xerxes*'s Expedition was on the first of the 75th Olympiad, viz. the of the *Julian* Period. The Account of *Suidas* therefore falls on the 3030. that of *Xanthus* on the 3634th. of the *Julian* Period. The latest of these seemeth to me most Historical, and agreeable to Truth.

Of his Birth, Life, and Death, there is little to be found; and even that uncertain, whether appliable to him, or to the *Persian*. *Plato* styles *Zoroaster* the Son of *Oromases*; but *Oromases* (as *Plutarch* and others shew) was a Name given to God by *Zoroaster* the *Persian*, and his Followers: whence I conceive that *Plato* is to be understood of the *Persian Zoroaster*, who perhaps in regard of his extraordinary knowledge, was either Allegorically styled, or fabulously reported to be the Son of God, or of some good Genius, as *Pythagors*, *Plato*, and many other Excellent Persons were.

b *Pliny* reports, that *Zoroaster* (not particularizing which of them) *laughed the same day he was born*; and that *his Brain did beat so hard that it heaved up the hand laid upon it, a presage of his future Science*; and that *he lived in the Desarts twenty years upon Cheese so tempered, as that it became not old*. The *Assyrian* Zoroaster, (saith *Suidas*) *prayed he might die by fire from Heaven, and advised the Assyrians to preserve his Ashes, assuring them that as long as they kept 'em, their Kingdom should never fail*; but *Cedrenus* attributes the same to the *Persian*.

b *lib. 36. cap. 1.*

Of Writings attributed to him, are mentioned, i *Verses*, two *Millions*, upon which *Hermippus* wrote a Comment, and added Tables to them.

i *Plin. lib. 36. cap. 1.*

Oracles, perhaps part of the foresaid Verses; upon these *Syrianus* wrote a Comment in twelve Books.

Of Agriculture, or, *Mechanicks*; *Pliny* alledgeth a Rule for Sowing; and the Author of the *Geoponicks*, many Experiments under his name: but this was either spurious, or written by some other *Zoroaster*.

Revelations; suppositious also, forged (as *Porphyrius* professeth) by some *Gnosticks*.

To these add, cited by the *Arabians*, a *Treatise of Magick*; and another *of Dreams, and their Interpretations*, cited by *Gelaldin* frequently; Inventions doubtless of latter times.

Some ascribe the Treatises of the *Persian Zoroaster* to the *Chaldæan*; but of those hereafter.

CHAP. IV.

Of Belus, *another reputed Inventer of Sciences amongst the* Chaldeans.

Some there are who ascribe the Invention of Astronomy to *Belus*, of which Name there were two Persons, one a *Tyrian*, the other an *Assyrian*, who Reigned in *Babylonia* next after the *Arabians*, about the 2682 year of the World according to the accompt of *Africanus*; for whose Inventions the *Babylonians* honoured him as a God. There is yet standing, (saith a *Pliny*) *the Temple of* Jupiter Belus; *he was the Inventer of the Sciences of the Stars*, and b *Diodorus*, speaking of the *Ægyptians*, *They affirm that afterwards many Colonies went out of* Ægypt, *and were dispersed over the Earth, and that* Belus *reputed to be Son of* Neptune *and* Lybia, *carried one to* Babylon; *and making choice of the River* Euphrates, *to settle it, instituted Priests after the manner of those in* Ægypt, *exempt from all publick Charges and Duties, which the* Babylonians *call Chaldæans*; *these observed the Stars, imitating the Ægyptian Priests, Naturalists and Astrologers.* Thus *Diodorus*. But that *Belus* was Son of *Neptune* and *Lybia*, is nothing but Greek Mythology; that he brought a Colony out of *Ægypt* into *Babylon*, is Fabulous. For the *Ægyptians* had not any Correspondence with Foreigners for a long time after. But to confirm that he was skilful in those Sciences, c *Ælian* gives this Relation.

a *Lib.*
b *Lib. 1.*

Xerxes Son of Darius, *breaking up the Monument of ancient* Belus, *found an Urn of Glass, in which his dead Body lay in Oyl*; *But the Urn was not full, it wanted a hand-breadth of the top*: *next the Urn there was a little Pillar, on which it was written, That whosoever should open the Sepulcre, and did not fill up the Urn, should have ill Fortune, which* Xerxes *reading grew afraid, and commanded that they should pour Oyl into it with all Speed; notwithstanding it was not filled*: *Then he commanded to pour into it a second time*; *but neither did it increase at all thereby. So that at last failing of Success, he gave over; and shutting up the Monument, departed very sad. Nor did the*

c *Var. Hist.*

the Event foretold by the Pillar, deceive him: for he led an Army of 50 Myriads against Greece, where he received a great Defeat, and returning home, died miserably, being Murdered by his own Son, in the Night-time, a-bed.

To this *Belus, Semiramis* his Daughter *d erected a Temple* in the middle of *Babylon*, which was exceeding high, and by the help thereof the *Chaldeans*, who addicted themselves there to Contemplation of the Stars, did exactly observe their Risings and Settings.

d Diod. l. 2.

CHAP. V.

Other Chaldean Philosophers.

FRom *Zoroaster* were derived the Chaldean *Magi* and Philosophers his Disciples; amongst whom, *a Pliny* mentions one *Azonaces* Master of *Zoroaster*, which doubtless must have been meant of some later *Zoroaster*, there being many of that name, as we shewed formerly.

a Lib. 36.

By the same *b* Author are mentioned of the Ancient *Magi, Marmaridius* a *Babylonian,* and *Zarmoceniadas* an *Assyrian*; of whom nothing is left but their Names, no Monuments extant of them.

b Loc. cit.

To these add *c Zoromasdres* a *Chaldæan Philosopher*, who wrote Mathematicks and Physicks; and *Teucer* a Babylonian, an ancient Author, who wrote concerning the *Decanates*.

c Suid.

The Mathematicians also, saith *d* Strabo, mention some of these, as Cidenas, and Naburianus, and Sudinus, and Seleucus of Seleucia a Chaldean, and many other Eminent Persons.

d Lib.

CHAP. VI.

Of Berosus, who first introduced the Chaldaick Learning into Greece.

AFter these flourished *Berosus*, or, as the Greeks call him Βηρωσὸς, which name *a* some interpret *the Son of Oseas*: for as is manifest from *Elias*, ביר with the *Chaldees* is the same with בר in *Syriack*; whence *Bar-Ptolemeus*, as if the Son of *Ptolemy, Bar-Timæus,* and the like: *Gorionides* and other Rabbins call him *b Bar-Hosea*, The Arabians *Barasa*; so *Abenepei*, and others.

a Jos. Scal. in Euseb.

b בר הושע

c Barthius saith, that there are some who assert him contemporary with *Moses*, which Opinion justly he condemns as Ridiculous; *d Claudius Verderius* in his Censure upon the *Annian Berosus* affirms, he lived a little before the Reign of *Alexander* the Great; upon what Authority, I know not. That he lived in the time of *Alexander,* we find in the Oration of *Tatian* against the *Gentiles*; but the same *Tatian* adds, he dedicated his History to that *Antiochus,* who was the third from *Alexander*. But neither is this Reading unquestionable; for *e Eusebius* cites the same place of *Tatian* thus, Berosus *the* Babylonian, *Priest of* Belus *at* Babylon, *who lived in the time of* Alexander, *and dedicated to* Antiochus, *the third after* Seleucus, *a History of the* Chaldæans *in three Books, and relates the Actions of their Kings,* mentions one of them named *Na*

c Voss. de hist. Græc. lib. 1. c. 31.
d Adversar. 51. 7

e Præpar. Evang. l. 10.

buchodonosor, &c. Here we find μῂ Σέλευκον, but in the Text of *Tatian*, μετ' αὐτὸν after *Alexander*. And indeed this Reading seems most consonant to the Story. The next to *Alexander* was *Seleucus Nicanor*: the next to him, *Antiochus* Σωτῂρ; The third, *Antiochus* Θεός, who began his Reign 61 years after the Death of *Alexander*: Now, it is possible that *Berosus* at the time of *Alexander's* taking *Babylon* might be thirty years old or less; and at the 90th year, or somewhat younger, might dedicate his History to *Antiochus* Θεός. Or we may say, that by *Antiochus* the third from *Alexander* is meant *Antiochus* Σωτῂρ, reckoning *Alexander* himself inclusively for one, *Seleucus,* the second *Antiochus* Σωτῂρ the third; to whom from the death of *Alexander* are but 44 years: And in approving this Account we may retain the Reading of *Eusebius,* supposing the first to be *Seleucus,* the second *Antiochus* Σωτῂρ, the third *Antiochus* Θεός: Neither is this inconsistent with *Gesner's* Translation of the Words of *Tatian*, κτ' Ἀλέξανδρον γενόμεν⸗, as in *Stephen's* Edition of *Eusebius*; or κτ' Ἀλέξανδρον γεγονώς, as in *Tatian* himself, *qui Alexandri ætate vixit*: which Interpretation *f Onuphrius Panvinius* also follows. But considering these words more intently, it came into my Mind (saith *Vossius*) that it might better be rendred, *qui Alexander ætate natus est,* whereby all scruple may be taken away, supposing *Berosus* to have been born but two years before *Alexander's* death; by which account he must have been but 64 years old when *Antiochus* Θεός, to whom he dedicated his Book, began to Reign: which way soever it is, *Berosus* Published his History in the time of *Ptolemæus Phiadelphus*; for he Reigned 38 years, and in the sixth year of his Rein *Antiochus Soter* began to Reign in *Syria* in the 22d of *Antiochus* Θεός, to one of whom *Berosus* dedicated his Book. But by no means we can assent to the Learned *g Conradus Gesnerus*, who by *Alexander* conceives to be meant not he who was surnamed the Great, Son of *Philip*, but that *Alexander* who succeeded *Demetrius Soter*, in the Kingdom of *Syria,* and was Succeeded by *Demetrius Nicanor*; by *Antiochus* understanding *Antiochus Sedetes* who Reigned next after *Demetrius Nicanor*: for if it were so, *Berosus* must have been a whole Age later than *Manetho*; but *Manetho* flourished under *Philadelphus,* (as *Vossius* elsewhere proves.) *Philadelphus* died in the third year of the 133d Olympiad; but *Antiochus Sedetes* invaded *Syria* in the first of the 160th Olympiad: How then could *Berosus* live so late, who was a little precedent to *Manetho*, as *Syncellus* expressly affirms? Again, we may assert the time of *Berosus* another way. *h Pliny* saith, he gave account of 480 years, which doubtless were of *Nabonassar*: Now the Æra of *Nabonassar* began in the second year of the 8th Olympiad; from which if we reckon 480, it will fall upon the latter end of *Antiochus Soter's* Reign; wherefore *Berosus* dedicated his Book either to him or to *Antiochus* Θεός his Son. These Arguments will not suffer us to doubt of the time *Berosus*.

f Lib. de Sibyl

g Tatian.

This *Berosus* is mentioned by many of the Ancients *i Vitruvius* faith, he *first settled in the Island* Coos, *and there opened Learning*. *k Josephus*

i Lib. 9. c. 7.
k Contr Apion. lib. 1.

sephus that *he introduced the Writings of the Chaldæans concerning Astronomy and Philosophy among the Grecians.* *l Pliny*, that *the Athenians, for his Divine Predictions, dedicated to him publickly in their Gymnasium a Statue with a golden Tongue.* He is mentioned likewise by *m Tertullian*, and the Author of the *n Chronicon Alexandrinum.*

l Lib. 7. c. 37.
m In Apologet. cap. 19.
n P. 48.

He wrote *Babylonicks* or *Chaldaicks*, in three Books: for they are cited promiscuously under both these Titles: *The Babylonicks of Berosus o Athenæus* cites; but *Tatian* saith, *he wrote the Chaldaic History in three Books.* And *p Clemens Alexandrinus* cites *Berotius*, *his third of Chaldaicks*; and elsewhere, simply his *Chaldaick Histories.* And *Agathias* affirms, *he wrote the Antiquities of the Assyrians and Medes*; for those Books contained not only the *Assyrian* or *Chaldæan* Affairs, but also the *Median, q Agathias, , as somewhere* Berosus the *Babylonian*, and *Athenocles*, and *Simacus*, relate, who have *Recorded the Antiquities of* the *Assyrians* and *Medes.* Out of this work *r Josephus* hath preserved some excellent Fragments; but the suppositious *Berosus* of *Annius* is most trivial and foolish, of the same kind as his *Megasthenes* and *Archilochus*: Many Kings are there reckoned which are no where to be found; and scarce is there any of those fragments which *Josephus* cites out of the true *Berosus*; on the contrary, some things are plainly repugnant, as when he saith, *Semiramis* built *Babylon*, whereas *Josephus* saith *Berosus* wrote, that it was not Built by *Simeramis*.

o Deipn. l. 14.
p Strom. 1.

q Lib. 2.

r Antiquit. Jud. l. 5. con tra Apion. Lib. 1

A Daughter of this *Berosus* is mentioned by *s Justin Martyr* a Babylonian *Sibyl*, who prophesied at *Cumæ*; this cannot be understood of that *Cumæan Sibyl*, who lived in the time of *Tarquinius Priscus*; for betwixt *Tarquinius Priscus*, and the first Pontick War, (in which time *Berosus* lived) are 245 years; but some other *Cumæan Cibyl*, of much later time. That there were several *Cibyls*, who Prophesied at *Cumæ t Onuphrius* hath already proved out of the *Treatise of wonderful things* ascribed to *Aristotle*; and out of *Martianus Capella*, and other Writers.

s Paræn.

t Lib. de Sibyl.

Berosus being the Person who introduced the *Chaldaick* Learning into *Greece*, we shall with him close the History of the Learned Persons of or Philosophers amongst the *Chaldeans*.

SECT. II.

The Chaldaick Institution and Sects.

CHAP. I.

That all Professors of Learning were more peculiarly termed Chaldæans.

PHilosophy or Learning was not taught and propagated by the *Chaldeans* after the Grecian manner, communicated by publick Professors indifferently to all sorts of Auditors; but restrained to certain Families. These were by a more peculiar compellation termed *Chaldæans*, addicted themselves wholly to study; had a proper habitation allotted for them; and lived exempt from all publick Charges and Duties.

Of these is a *Diodorus* to be understood, who relates, that *Belus Instituted Priests exempt from all publick Charges and Duties, whom the Babylonians call* Chaldæans. *Strabo* adds, that *there was a peculiar Habitation in* Babylonia *allotted for the Philosophers of that Country, who were termed* Chaldæans, *and that they inhabited a certain Tribe of the* Chaldæans, *and a portion of* Babylonia, *adjoyning to the* Arabians, *and the* Persian Gulf.

a Lib. 1.

There were those *Chaldæans* who, as *Cicero* saith, *were named not from the Art, but Nation.* And of whom he is elsewhere to be understood, when he affirms that *in* Syria *the* Chaldæans *excell for knowledge of the Stars, and acuteness of Wit*; and *b Q. Curtius*, who describing the Solemnity of those two who went out of *Babylon* to meet *Alexander*, saith, *Then went the Magi after their manner*; *next whom, the* Chaldæans *Non vates modo, sed Artifices Babyloniorum*: Where tho' some interpret *Artifices*, those *Astrologers who made Instruments for the practice of their Art*; yet *Curtius* seems to intend no more than the *Chaldæans* of both sorts, the Plebeian Tradesmen, and the Learned.

b Lib.

Of these *Chaldæans* peculiarly so termed, is *c Laertius* likewise to be understood, when he cites as Authors of Philosophy *amongst the* Persians *the* Magi, *amongst the* Babylonians *or* Assyrians *the* Chaldeans. And *Hesychius*, who interprets the word *Chaldæans, a kind of Magi that know all things.*

c In proœm.

CHAP. II.

Their Institution.

THese *Chaldæans* preserved their Learning within themselves by a continued Tradition from Father to Son. *They learn not*, (saith *a Diodorus*) *after the same fashion as the* Greeks: *For amongst the* Chaldæans, *Philosophy is delivered by Tradition in the Family, the Son receiving it from the Father, being exempted from all other Employment; and thus having their Parents for their Teachers, they learn all things fully and abundantly, believing more firmly what is communicated to them: and being brought up in these Disciplines from Children, they acquire a great habit in Astrology, as well because that Age is apt to Learn, as for that they imploy so much time in Study. But among the* Greeks, *for the most part they come unprepared, and attain Philosophy very late*; *and having bestowed some time therein, quit it to seek out means for their Livelihood: and tho' some few give themselves up wholly to Philosophy, yet they persist in Learning only for gain, continually innovating some things in the most considerable Doctrines, and never follow those that went before them*; *whereas the Barbarians persevering always in the same, receive each of them firmly: But the* Greeks *aiming at gain, by this Profession erect new Sects, and contradicting one another in the most considerable Theorems, make their Disciples dubious*; *their minds, as long as they live,*

a Lib. 1.

live, are in suspense and doubt, neither can they firmly believe any thing: for if a Man examine the chiefest Sects of the Philosophers, he will find them most different from one another, and directly opposite in the principal assertions.

CHAP. III.

Sects of the Chaldæans *distinguished according to their several Habitations.*

As all Professors of Learning among the *Chaldæans*, were distinguished from the rest of the People by the common denomination of the Country, *Chaldæans*; so were they distinguished among themselves into Sects, denominated from the several parts of the Country, wherein they were seated: Whereof *a* Pliny and *b* Strabo mention *Hipparenes* from *Hipparenum*, a City in *Mesopotamia*; *Babylonians*, from *Babylon*; *Orchenes*, *c* (a third *Chaldaick Doctrine*) from *Orchoë* a City of *Chaldæa*; and *Borsippenes*, from *Borsippe*, another City of *Babylonia* dedicated to *Apollo* and *Diana*. And though *d Diodorus* prefer the *Chaldæans* before the *Grecians*, for the perseverance in the same Doctrines without Innovations; yet we must not infer thence, that there was an universal consent of Doctrine amongst them; but only, that each of them was constant in belief, and maintenance of his own Sect, without introducing any new Opinion. For, that amongst these Sects there was no absolute agreement, is manifest from *Strabo*, who adds that *e they did (as indifferent Sects) assert contrary Doctrines*; *f some of them calculated Nativities, others disapproved it;* Whence *g Lucretius*,

a Lib. 6. c.26.
b Lib. 16. p. 739.
c Lib.

d Suprà citat.

e Loc. citat.
f Loc. citat.

g Lib.

The Babylonick Doctrine doth oppose
The Chaldee, and Astrology o'rthrows.

CHAP. IV.

Sects of the Chaldæans *distinguished according to their several Sciences.*

Another (more proper) distinction of Sects amongst the Learned *Chaldæans*, there was, according to the several Sciences which they profest. The Prophet *a Daniel* relating how *Nebuchadonosar* sent for all the Learned Men, to tell him his Dream, takes occasion to name the principal of them, which were four; *Hbartumim, Ashaphim, Mecashphim, Chasdim*.

a Chap. 2. v. 2.

Hbartumim, are by *Abrabaniel*, expounded *Magi*, skilful in *Natural Things*; and by *Jachiades*, *those Magi who addicted themselves to contemplative Science*, which interpretation suits well with the derivation of the Word; not as some would have from *Charmini, Burnt-Bones*, (for that the *Magi* performed their Rites with Dead Mens Bones) nor from *Charat*, a *Pen* or *Scribe*) in regard the *Egyptians* used to call their wise Persons Scribes,) for the Word in *Chaldee*, is not taken in that Sense; but from *Charad* a *Persian* Word, (by Transmutation of ר into ש) signifying *to know*, whence *Elmacinus* instead of this *Persee-Chaldeee*, useth two *Arabick* Words, *Albochamaon, Walarrathaon*; *Wise and Knowing Persons*. The *Hbartumim*, therefore were not (as commonly rendered) *Magicians*, but rather such as studied the Nature of all things, under which Contemplation is comprehended Theology, and Physick, the Knowledge of Beings, Divine and Natural.

Ashaphim b Jachiades expounds those *Magi qui scientiam activam excolebant*: So *Constantinus* renders him, but adds, *that* Jachiades *is mistaken, and that the* Ashaphim *were rather the same as* Souphoun *in Arabick,Wise,Religious Person*. This indeed, is the more probable; *Souphoun* is an Attribute, proper to all those who delivered all Theology, Mystically, and Allegorically, deriv'd from *Souph, Wool*; either for that the Garments of these Professors of Theology, were made only of *Wool*, never of Silk; or from *attiring*, and *vailing* the things which concern the Love of God, under the figures of visible things: whence is derived the Word *Hatseviph*, *Mystick Theology*; and perhaps from the *Hebrew* Root, *Ashaph*, comes to the *Greek* σοφὸς, the first Attribute given by the *Greeks* to Learned Persons, afterwards changed into φιλόσοφ⊙. These *Ashaphim*, the ordinary Interpretation of the Text in *Daniel* stiles *Astrologers*: And *Eben Ezra* derives the Word from בשף *twy-light, because they observe the Heavens at that time*; but the Astrologers are meant afterwards by the Word *Chasdim*, (last of the four.) The *Ashaphim* of the *Chaldæans* seem rather to be the same with the *Magi* of the *Persians*, Priests, the Professors of Religious Worship, which they termed *Magick*.

b In Dan. p. 34.

Mecashphim, properly signifieth *Revealers*, (that is,) of abstruse things: The Word is derived from *Chashaph*, which the *Arabians* still use in the same sense of *Revealing*: *Mecashphim* are generally taken, (as by R. *Moses*, *Nachmarides*, *Abrabaniel*, and others) for such as practised Diabolical Arts: Not improperly rendered, *Sorcerers*.

Chasdim, (or *Chaldæans*) was an Attribute (as we shewed formerly) conferred in a particular sense upon the Learned Persons of the *Chaldæans*: Amongst whom, by a restriction yet more particular, it signified the professors of Astrology, this being a Study, to which they were more especially addicted, and for which most eminent; these are those *Chasdim*, whom *c Strabo* stiles χαλδαίους ἀςρονομικὰς, *Astronomical Chaldæans*.

c Lib. 16. p. 739.

Besides these four kinds (which seem to have been the principal,) there are several others mentioned, and prohibited by the Levitical Law. *Deut.* 18. 10. *Choser, Casmim, Megnonenim, Menacheshim, Hhober, Hhaber, Shel, Ob, Jideoni, Doresh el Hammetim,* R. *Maimonides* reciting them all, adds, *that they were sveeral sorts of Diviners sprung up of old amongst the* Chaldæans. *Jachiades* mentions them, as particular kinds of the *Mecashphim*.

THE

THE FIFTEENTH PART.

The Chaldaick Doctrine.

From the four general kinds of the Professors of Learning amongst the *Chaldæans*, mentioned by the Prophet *Daniel*, (of which we *a* last treated) may be inferred, of what parts or Sciences the *Chaldaick* Doctrine did consist. The *Hhartumim* were employed in *Divine* and *Natural Speculation*; The *Ashaphim*, in *Religious Worship, and Rites*; The *Mecashphim*, and *Chasdim* in *Divination*: these by *Astrology*, those by other *Arts*: which two last, *Diodorus*, speaking of the Learned *Chaldæans*, comprehends under the common name of *Astrologers*; the other two, under that of *Natural Philosophers*, and *Priests*: for he saith, *they imitated the* Egyptian *Priests, Naturalists, and Astrologers*.

In treating therefore of the *Chaldaick* Doctrine, we shall first lay down their *Theology*, and *Physick*, the proper Study of the *Hhartumim*; Next, their *Astrology*, and other Arts of *Divination*, practised by the *Chasdim*, and *Mecashphim*: Thirdly, their *Theurgy*, and Lastly, their *Gods*. Which Contemplation and Rites were peculiar to the *Ashaphim*.

a Part. 1. Sect. 2. cap. 4.

SECT. I.

Theology and Physick.

The *Chaldaick* Doctrine, in the first place considers all Beings, as well Divine, as Natural: the Contemplation of the first, is Theology; of the latter, Physick.

a Zoroaster *divided all things into three kinds; the first Eternal; the second had a beginning in time, but shall have no end; the third Mortal*: the two first belong to Theology. The Subject of Theology, (saith *b* Eusebius, speaking doubtless of the Followers of *Zoroaster*) *they divided into four kinds; the first is God, the Father and King: next him, there followeth a multitude of other Gods; in the third place they rank Dæmons; in the fourth Heroes*, or, according to others, Angels, Dæmons, and Souls.

The third, or Mortal kind is the Subject of *Physick*: It comprehends all things material; which they divide into seven Worlds, one *Empyreal*, three *Ætherial*, three *Corporeal*.

a Psell. in Or[a]. p. 51.

b Præp. Evang. lib. 4. cap. 3.

CHAP. I.

Of the Eternal Being, God.

The first kind of things (according to *Zoroaster*) is Eternal, the Supream God. In the first place (saith *Eusebius*) they conceive that God the Father and King ought to be ranked. This the *Delphian* Oracle (cited by *Porphyrius*) confirms.

Chaldees and Jews wise only, Worshipping Purely a self-begotten God and King.

This is that Principle of which the Author of the Chaldaick Summary saith, *They conceive there is one Principle of all things, and declare that it is one and good.*

a God (as Pythagoras *learnt of the Magi, who term him* Oromasdes)*in his Body resembles Light, in his Soul truth*; That God (according to the Chaldaick Opinion) is Light, besides the Testimony of *Eusebius*, may be inferred from the Oracles of *Zoroaster*, wherein are frequently mentioned *the b Light, Beams, and Splendor of the Father.*

a Porphyr. [de] Pythag.

b φάος ἀυγὴ καὶ ἐγγὺς, φάτεϊς.

In the same sense they likewise termed God *a Fire*; for *Ur* in Chaldee signifying both *Light* and *Fire*, they took Light and Fire promiscuously (as amongst many others *Plato* doth when he saith that *God began to compound the whole Body of the World out of Fire and Earth*: by which Fire he afterwards professeth to mean *the Sun*, whom he Styles *the brightest and whitest of things*, as if Light and Fire, Brightness and Whiteness were all one;) this is manifest from the *Zoroastrean* Oracles also; wherein he is sometimes called simply *Fire*, sometimes the *Paternal Fire, the one Fire, the first Fire above*.

Upon this Ground (doubtless) was the Worship of Fire instituted by the Ancient *Chaldæans*, and *c* from them derived to the *Persians*, of which hereafter, when we shall ce[ase] to speak of their Gods and Religious Rites.

c Agath.

CHAP. II.

The Emanation of Light or Fire from God.

God (as we have shewn) an Intellectual Light or Fire *did not* (as the Oracle saith)*shut up his Fire within his Intellectual Power*, but communicated it to all Creatures; first and immediately to the first Mind (as the some Oracles assert) and to all other æviternal and incorporeal Beings, (under which notion are comprehended a multitude of God's Angels, good Dæmons, and the Souls of Men:) The next Emanation is the Supramundane Light, an Incorporeal Infinite luminous Space, in which the intellectual Beings reside; The Supramundane Light kindles the first Corporeal World, the Empyreum or Fiery Heaven, which being immediately beneath the Incorporeal Light, is the Highest, Brightest, and Rarest of Bodies. The Empyreum diffuseth it self through the Æther, which is the next Body below it, a Fire less refined than the Empyreum: But that it is Fire, the more condensed parts thereof, the Sun and Stars sufficienty evince; from the Æther this Fire is transmitted to the Material and Sublunary World; for though the Matter whereof it consists be not Light but Darkness, (as are also the Material or bad Dæmons) yet this *a vivificative Fire* actuates and gives Life to all its Parts,

a Ζωογόνιον πῦρ, Orat.

Parts, insinuating, diffusing it self, and penetrating even to the very Center: *passing from above* (saith the Oracle) *to the opposite Part, through the Center of the Earth*. We shall describe this more fully, when we treat of the Particulars.

CHAP. III.

Of things Æviternal and Incorporeal.

THe Second or middle kind of Things (according to *Zoroaster* is that which) is begun in time, but is without end (commonly termed æviternal.) To this belong that *multitude of Gods*, which *Eusebius* saith, they *asserted next after God the Father and King*; and the Souls of Men: *Psellus* and the other Summarists of the *Chaldaick* Doctrine, name them in this order; *Intelligibles*; *Intelligibles and Intellectuals*; *Intellectuals*; *Fountains*; *Hyperarchii, or Principles*; *Unzoned Gods*; *Zoned Gods*; *Angels*; *Dæmons*; *Souls*. *a* All these they conceive to be light, (except the ill Dæmons which are dark.)

b Over this Middle kind *Zoroaster* held *Mithra* to preside, whom the Oracles (saith *Psellus*) call the Mind. *c* This is employed about secondary things.

a Euseb.
b Plut.
c Plut.

CHAP. IV.

The First Order.

IN the first place are three Orders, one *Intelligible*, another *Intelligible and Intellectual*, the third *Intellectual*. The first Order which is of Intelligibles, seems to be (as the Learned *Patricius* conjectures; for *Psellus* gives only a bare accompt, not an Exposition of these things) that which is only understood: This is the highest Order: The *second* or middle Order is of Intelligibles and Intellectuals, that is, those which are understood, and understand also; as *Zoroaster*,
There are Intelligibles and Intellectuals, which understanding are understood.
The *third* is of Intellectuals; which only understand: as being Intellect, either essentially or by participation. By which distinction we may conceive that the higest Order is above Intellect, being understood by the middle sort of Minds. The middle Order participates of the Superiour, but consists of Minds which understand both the Superiour and themselves also. The last Order seems to be of Minds, whose Office is to understand not only themselves but Superiors and Inferiours also.

Of the first of which Orders, the *Anonymus* Author of the Summary of the *Chaldaick* Doctrine, thus: *Then* (viz. next the one and good) *they Worship a certain paternal Depth consisting of three Triads; each Triad hath a Father, a Power, and a Mind: Psellus somewhat more fully; Next the one they assert the paternal Depth compleated by three Triads: each of the Triads having a Father first, then a Power middle, and a Mind the third amongst them: which* (Mind) *shutteth up the Triad within it self, these they call also Intelligibles.*

This Tripple Triad seems to be the same with the Triad mentioned in the Oracles of *Zoroaster*. What *Psellus* terms *Father*, he calls *Father* also.

The Father perfected all things, and *Paternal Monad.*

Where the paternal Monad is. ———

The second which *Psellus* calls Power, he terms also *the Power of the Father.*
Neither did he shut up his own Fire in his Intellectual Power.
And ———*The strength of the Father.*
And the *Duad* generated by the Monad, and resident with him:
The Monad is enlarged, which Generates two.
And again,
The Duad resides with him.
This is also *the first paternal Mind*: for the third of this Triad, which *Psellus* terms the Mind, he saith is the second Mind.
The Father perfected all things, and delivered them over,
To the second Mind, which all Mankind calls the first,
And as *Psellus* saith, that this Mind shuts up the Triad and paternal depth within it self: so *Zoroaster*;
It is the Bound of the paternal Depth and Fountain of Intellectuals.
And again,
It proceeded not further, but remained in the paternal Depth.

CHAP. V.

The Second Order.

NExt these (saith *Psellus*) *there is another Order of Intelligibles and intellectuals*; This also *is divided three-fold, into Jynges Synoches, and Teletarchs*. With him agrees the Anonymous Summarist. *Then is the Intelligible Jynx; next which are the Synoches, the Empyreal, the Ætherial and the Material; after the Synoches are the Teletarchs.*

The first are Jynges, of which the Oracle;
Intelligent Jynges do themselves also understand from the Father
By unspeakable Counsels being moved so as to understand;

Psellus saith, *they are certain Powers next to the paternal Depth consisting of three Triads* (I would rather read, *the paternal Depth which consists of three Triads,* for so it is described in the foregoing Chapter, by the same Author) *which, according to the Oracle, understand by the paternal Mind, which contains the cause of them singly within it self*: Pletho, *They are Intellectual Species conceived by the Father, they themselves being conceptive also, and exciting Conceptions or Notions by unspeakable Counsels*; These seem to be the Idea's described by the Zoroastræan Oracle;

The Mind of the Father made a jarring noise, understanding by vigorous Counsels
Omni-form Idea's, and flying out of one Fountain,

They sprung forth, for from the Father was
  the Counsel and End;
But they were divided, being by Intellectual
  Fire distributed
Into other Intellectuals, for the King did set
  before the multi-form World
An Intellectual incorruptible pattern, the Print
  of whose Form
He promoted through the World, and accord-
  ingly the World was framed,
Beautified with all kind of Idea's, of which
  there is one Fountain.
Out of which came rushing forth others undi-
  stributed,
Being broken about the Bodies of the World,
  which through the vast Recesses,
Like Swarms, are carried round about every
  Way,
Intellectual Notions from the paternal Foun-
  tain, cropping the Flower of Fire.
In the point of sleepless Time, of this
Primigenious Idea, the first self-budding Foun-
  tain of the Father budded.

Upon which Words, *Proclus* having cited them as an Oracle of the Gods, adds, *Hereby the Gods declared as well where the subsistence of Idea's is, as who that God is who contains the one Fountain of them, as also, after what manner the multitude of them proceeded out of this Fountain, and how the World was made according to them. And that they are movers of all the Systems of the World, and that they are all Intellectual essentially: Others may find out many other profound things, by searching into these Divine Notions; but for the present, let it suffice us to know, that the Gods themselves ratifie the Contemplations of Plato, for as much as they term those Intellectual Causes Idea's; and affirm that they gave pattern to the World, and that they are Conceptions of the Father: for they remain in the Intellections of the Father: and that they go forth to the making of the World, for, ἴσχνσις implies their going forth, and that they are of all forms, as containing the Causes of all things divisible: and that from the Fountainous Idea's there proceeded others, which by several parts framed the World, and are said to be like Swarms* (of Bees) *because they beget the secondary Idea's*: Thus *Proclus*.

The second are *the Synoches, which are three, the Empyreal, the Æthereal, the Material*: answerable to the several Worlds, which they Govern: For they seem to be Minds, which receiving from *Hecate* the influence of that Fire which dispenseth life, infuse it into the Empyreal, Æthereal, and Material Worlds, and Support and Govern those Worlds, and give them vital Motion. The Oracle termeth them *Anoches*.

Each World hath Intellectual *Anoches* inflexible, where *Psellus* interprets them *the most Excellent of Intelligible Species, and of those that are brought down by the Immortals in this Heaven, in the head of whom is conceived to be a God, the second from the Father.*

The last of this Order are the *Teletarchs*, joyned with the *Synoches* by the Oracle.

The Teletarchs are comprehended with the Synoches.

This second Order or Triad, *Proclus* and *Damascius* often mention, styling it by the double name of *Intelligent and Intellectual*.

CHAP. VI.

The third Order.

THe last Order is of *Intellectuals*; a *Psellus*, *a Epist.* *After the middle Order is the Intellectual having one paternal Triad, which consists of the once above, and of Hecate and of the twice above; And another* (Triad) *which consists of the Amilicti, which are three; And one, the Hypezocos. These are seven Fountains.* Anonymus Summarist, *After these are the fountainous Fathers called also Cosmagogues; the first of whom is called the once above; next whom is Hecate; then the twice above, next whom three Amilicti; and last, the Hypezocos.*

Of the *Cosmagogues Psellus* interprets the *Zoroastrean* Oracle.

Oh how the World hath intellectual Guides, inflexible!

The *Chaldæans*, saith he, *asserts Powers in the World, which they term Cosmagogi,* (guides of the World) *for that they guide the World by provident Motions. These Powers the Oracle calls* ἐνοχῆσας, *Sustainers, as sustaining the whole World. The Oracle saith, they are immoveable, implying their setled Power; sustentive, denoting their Guardianship. These Powers they design only by the Causes and immobility of the Worlds.* Pletho *interprets them the most excellent of Intelligible Species, and of those that are brought down by Immortals in this Heaven. The* Coryphaus *of whom, he conceives to be a God, the second from the Father.*

The *Amilicti* also, and the *Hypezocos* are mentioned by the Oracle.

—— ——*for from him*
Spring forth all the implacable (Amilicti) *Thunders.*
And the Recesses (*suscipient of Presters*) *of the omni-lucent Strength.*
Of Father-begotten Hecate, and Hypezocos the Flower of Fire.

The *Amilicti* [implacable] are Powers so termed, for that they are firm, and not to be converted towards these inferiour things; and also cause that Souls be not allured by affections. *Psell. in Orac.*

CHAP. VII

Fountains, and Principles

BEsides this last Order of Intellectuals, which *Psellus* styles *seven Fountains*, and the Anonymous Summarist *fountainous Fathers*, the latter gives account of many other Fountains, *They reverence also* (saith he) *a Fountainous Triad* *Ἀρχικὴ. *of Faith, Truth, and Love; they likewise assert a Principiative Son from the Solar Fountain, and Archangelical, and the Fountain of Sense, and fountainous Judgment, and the Fountain of Perspectives, and the fountain of Characters: which walketh on unknown Marks, and the fountainous Tops of Apollo, Osyris, Hermes, they assert material Fountains of Centers and Elements, and a* Συνθήματα. *Zone of Dreams, and a fountainous Soul.*

Next the Fountains, saith *Psellus*, are the *Hyperarchii*; the Anonymous more fully, *Next the* Ἀρχαί. *Fountains*

Fountains, they say, are the Principalities, for the Fountains are more principal than the Principles; Both these names of Fountains and Principles are used by *Dionysius Areopagita*, frequently; even in the third Triad, he puts the name of Principles, ἀρχῶν (or Principalities) after whom the Arch-Angels.

In Orac.

Of the Animal-productive Principles, (continues the Anonymus) *the top is called Hecate, the middle principitative Soul, the bottom principitative Virtue*. This seems to be that *Hecate*, whom *Psellus* saith, they held to be the Fountain of Angels and Dæmons, and of Souls, and of Natures; The same which the Oracle means, saying,

On the left side of *Hecate*, is the Fountain of Vertue: for *the Chaldæans*, (as *Psellus* saith,) *esteem Hecate a Goddess, seated in the middle rank, and possessing as it were the Center of all the powers; in her right parts they place the Fountain of Souls, in her left the Fountain of Goods, or of Vertues; Moreover they say, the Fountain of Souls is prompt to propagations, but the Fountain of Vertues continueth within the bounds of its own Essence, and is as a Virgin incorrupted; which setledness and immobility, it receives from the power of the Amilicti, and is girt with a Virgin Zone*. What *Psellus* here calls the Fountain of Souls, and the Fountain of Vertues, is the same which the Anonymous styles, principiative Soul, and Principiative Virtue.

CHAP. VIII.

Unzoned Gods, and Zoned Gods.

a Reading ἀζώναι.
b Σειρά.

Next (the Hyperarchii, according to *Psellus*) are the *Azoni*, (Unzoned Gods) there are amongst them, (saith the Anonymus) Summarist) *a unzoned Hecates, as the Chaldaick, the Triecdotis, Comas, and Ecclustick: The unzoned Gods are Sarapis and Bacchus, and the b Chain of Osyris, and of Apollo*, (continu'd Series of Geniusses, connected in the manner of a Chain) *they are called unzoned, for that they use their power freely* (without restriction) *in the Zones, and are enthroned above the conspicuous Deities*: These conspicuous Deities are the Heavens and the Planets, (perhaps of the same kind as the Intelligences, which the Peripateticks asserted Movers of the Spheres;) and whereas he saith, *they live in Power*, ἐν ἐξουσίᾳ, it is the same Attribute which *Dionysius* gives the third of the second Hirarchy, τῶν ἁγίων ἐξουσίαν.

c Psell.
d Amon.

c The Zoned Gods are next: d These are they which have (confinement to) *particular Zones, and are rouled freely about the Zones of Heaven, and have the Office of Governing the World; for they hold, there is a Zoned kind of Deity, which inhabits the parts of the sensible World, and girdeth* (or circleth) *the Regions about the material place according to several distributions*. The same Office *Dionysius* seems to assign to the second and third Hierarchies.

e Σειρά.

These *Azoni*, and *Zonæi*, are mentioned also by *Damascius*; This (saith he) *sendeth out of her self the Fountain of all things, and the fountainous e Chain; but That* (sendeth out of her self the fountainous Chain) *of Particulars; and passeth on to Principles and Arch-Angels, and Azoni, and Zonæi, as the Law is of the Procession of the renowned particular Fountains*. And by *Proclus, The Sacred names of the Gods delivered according to their Mystical Interpretation, as those which are celebrated by the Assyrians,* * *Zonæi,* * *and Azoni, and Fountains, and Amilicti, and Synoches, by which they Interpret the Orders of the Gods*.

In Proæm. Parmenid.
* Read. Ζω-
* voices.

CHAP. IX.

Angels and Immaterial Dæmons.

Psell.

Next (the *Zonæi*) are the Angels. *Arnobius* saith of *Hosthanes*, (one of the Persian Magi, who receiv'd their Learning from the Chaldæans) that *he knew the Angels, Ministers, and Messengers of God* (the true God) *did wait on his Majesty, and tremble as afraid, at the Beck and Countenance of the Lord*; the Zoroastrian Oracles mention *reductive Angels, which reduce Souls to them, drawing them from several things*.

In Orac.

The next are Dæmons; of these the *a Chaldæans* hold some to be good, others bad. *b* The good they conceive to be Light; the bad Darkness. That there are good Dæmons, natural Reason tells us; Oracle:

a Psell. in Orac.
b Euseb.

Nature perswades that there are pure Dæmons. The bourgeons even of ill matter are beneficial and good.

Nature, or natural Reason, saith *Pletho*, *perswades, that the Dæmons are holy, and that all things proceeding from God, who is good in himself, are beneficial: if the bloomings of ill matter* (viz. of last Substances) *are good, much more are the Dæmons such, who are in a more excellent rank, as partaking of Rational Nature, and being mixed with Mortal Nature*.

CHAP. X.

Souls.

Next to Dæmons, *Psellus* (in his Epitome of the Chaldaick Doctrine) placeth Souls, the last of æviternal Beings.

a Pletho in Orac.

a Of Forms, the *Magi*, (and from them the Pythagoreans and Platonists) assert three kinds; One wholly separate from matter, the superceleftial intelligences; Another inseparable from matter, having a substance not subsisting by it self, but dependent on matter, together with which matter, which is sometimes dissolved by reason of its nature, subject to mutation, this kind of Soul is dissolved also, and perisheth. This they hold to be wholly Irrational.

b Ibid.

b Betwixt these, they place a middle kind, a Rational Soul, differing from the Superceleftial Intelligences, for that it always co-exists with matter; and from the irrational kind, for that it is not dependent on matter, but on the contrary, matter is dependent on it; and it hath a proper substance potentially subsistent by it self. It is also indivisible, as well as the Superceleftial Intelligences, and performing some Works in some manner ally'd to theirs, being it self also busied in the knowledge and contemplation of Beings, even unto the Supreme God, and for this reason is incorruptible,

c This

c Psel. in Orac.   *c* This Soul is an Immaterial and Incorporeal Fire, exempt from all Compounds, and from the Material Body; it is consequently Immortal: for nothing Material or Dark is commixed with her, neither is she compounded so as that she may be resolved into those things of which she consists.

d In Orat.   *d* This Soul hath a self-generate and self-animate Essence; for it is not moved by another: For if according to the Oracle, it is a portion of the Divine Fire, and a Lucid Fire, and Paternal Notion, it is an immaterial and self-subsistent Form, for such is every Divine Nature, and the Soul is part thereof.

e Epit.   *e* Of Humane Souls they alledge two Fountainous Causes, the Paternal Mind, and the Fountainous Soul: the particular Soul, according to them, proceeds from the Fountainous, by the Will of the Father.

f Psel. in Orac   *f* Now whereas there are several Mansions, one wholly bright, another wholly dark; others betwixt both, partly bright, partly dark, the place beneath the Moon is circumnebulous, dark on every side; the Lunary, partly Lucid, and partly Dark, one half Bright, the other Dark, the place above the Moon circumlucid, or Bright throughout; the Soul is seated in the circumlucid Region.

g Psel. Epit.   *g* From thence this kind of Soul is often sent down to Earth, upon several occasions, either by reason of the flagging of its Wings (so they term the Divination from its Original Perfection) or in Obedience to the Will of the Father.

h Pletho in Orac   *h* This Soul is always co-existent with any Æthereal Body as its *Vehiculum*, which she by continual approximation maketh also Immortal. Neither is this her *Vehiculum* inanimate in it self, but is it self animated with the other Species of the Soul, the irrational (which the Wise call (εἴδωλον) the Image of the Rational Soul) adorned with Phantasie and Sense, which seeth and heareth it self whole through whole, and is furnished with all the Senses, and with all the rest of the Irrational Faculties of the Soul.

i Loc. cit.   *i* Thus by the principal Faculty of this Body Phantasie, the Rational Soul is continually joyned to such a Body, and by such a Body sometimes the Humane Soul is joyned with a Mortal Body, by a certain Affinity of Nature, the whole being enfolded in the whole enlivening Spirit of the Embryon; this *Vehiculum* it self being of the nature of a Spirit.

k In Orac.   *k* The Image of the Soul, viz. that part which being it self void of irrational, is joyned to the Rational Part, and depends upon the Vehicle thereof, hath a part in the circumlucid Region; for the Soul never layeth down the Vehicle adherent to her.

l Pletho in Orac.   *l* The Soul being sent down from the Mansion wholly bright, to serve the Mortal Body, that is, to operate therein for a certain time, and to animate and adorn it to her power, and being enabled according to her several Virtues, do dwell in several Zones of the World, if she perform her Office well, goes back to the same place, but if not well, she retires to the worst Mansions, according to the things she hath done

m Psel. in Epit.   in this Life. *m* Thus (the Chaldæans) restore Souls to their first condition, according to the measure of their several Purifications, in all the Regions of the World; some also they conceive to be carried beyond the World.

CHAP. XI.

The Supramundane Light.

ALL these æviternal and incorporeal Beings are seated in the Supramundane Light, which it self also is incorporeal, placed immediately above the highest Corporeal World, and from thence extending upwards to infinite.

Proclus (cited by *Simplicius* on this Oracle of *Zoroaster*.
Abundantly animating Light, Fire, Æther, Worlds.)

saith, This Light is above all the seven Worlds, as a Monad before or above the Triad of the Empyreal Æthereal, and Material Worlds: adding, that *this primary Light is the Image of the Paternal Depth, and is therefore supramundane, because the paternal Depth is supramundane.* And again, *this Light,* saith he, *being the supramundane Sun, sends forth Fountains of Light; and the Mystick Discourses tell us, that its generality is among supramundane things, for there is the Solar World, and the Universal Light,* as the Chaldaick Oracles assert.

And again, *The Centers of the whole World, as one, seem to be fixed in this : for, if the Oracles fixed the Centers of the Material World above it self, in the Æther, proportionably ascending, we shall affirm that the Centers of the highest of the Worlds are seated in this Light. Is not this first Light the Image of the Paternal Depth, and for that reason supramundane also, because that is so?*

CHAP. XII.

Of Things Temporal (or Corruptible) and Corporeal.

THe third and last kind of things, according to *Zoroaster*, is Corruptible or Temporal; which as it began in time, so shall it likewise in time be dissolved: the President over these is *Arimanes.*

Under this third kind are comprehended the Corporeal Worlds, the Empyreal immediately below the Supramundane Light, the Æthereal next the Empyreal, and the Material the lowest of all, as the Oracle Ranks them.

Abundantly animating Light, Fire, Æther, Worlds.
These Corporeal Worlds are seven; *Orac.*
For the Father formed seven Firmaments of Worlds,
Including Heaven in a round Figure,
He fixed a great company of inerratick Stars,
He constituted a Heptad of Erratick Animals,
Placing the Earth in the middle, but the Water in the bosom of the Earth;
The Air above these.

Psellus explaining how they are seven, saith, They

They affirm that there are *seven Corporeal Worlds*; one *Empyreal* and *first*; then three *Æthereal*; and lastly three *Material*, the *fixed Circle*, the *Erratick*, and the *Sublunary Region*: But this enumeration seems to fall short; for he mentions but two Æthereal Worlds (the Orb of fixed Stars, and the Planetary Orb) and one Material, (the Sublunary Region;) as the Learned *Patricius* observes, who therefore reckons the seven thus; one Empyreal, three Æthereal, (the fixed Orb, the Planetary Orb, the Orb of the Moon) and three Elementary, (the Aereal, the Watery, and the Terrestrial;) but perhaps it will better suit with the Oracle (which includes the Moon within the Planetary Orb, and placeth the Water under the Earth,) as also with *Psellus* (who calls the last three Worlds, Material,) to dispose them thus,

Corporeal Worlds Seven,
- One *Empyreal* World.
- Three *Æthereal* Worlds;
  - The Supreme Æther next the Empyreum,
  - The Sphere of fixed Stars,
  - The Planetary Orb.
- Three *Material Sublunary* Worlds;
  - The Air,
  - The Earth,
  - The Water.

Neither can it seem strange that the three last only should be called Material; for the Chaldæans conceiving Matter to be a dark substance or rather darkness it self, the Empyreal and Æthereal Worlds, which, (as we shall shew) consist of Light or Fire, cannot in their sense be said to be Material, though Corporeal.

Epitom. 1. The Empyreal or *First* of these, saith *Psellus*, they attributed to the Mind, the Æthereal to the Soul, the Material to Nature.

CHAP. XIII.

The Empyreal World.

* *Psel.*

THe * *First* of the Corporeal Worlds, is the Empyreal; (by *Empyræum* the Chaldæans understand not, as the Christian Theologists, the Seat of God, and the Blessed Spirits, which is rather analagous to the Supreme Light of the Chaldæans, but the outmost Sphere of the Corporeal World.) It is round in Figure, according to the Oracle,

Inclosing Heaven in a round Figure.

It is also a *solid Orb*, or *Firmament*: for the same Oracles call it ςερέωμα. It consists of Fire, whence named the Empyreal, or, as the Oracles *the Fiery World*; which Fire being immediately next the Incorporeal supramundane Light is the rarest and subtilest of Bodies, and by reason of this Subtily penetrates into the Æther, which is the next World below it, and, by Mediation of the Æther, through all the Material World: *This may be evinced more particularly*, saith *Proclus*, *from the Divine Tradition* (meaning the Zoroastrian Oracles:) *for the Empyræum penetrates through the Æther, and the Æther through the Material World*; and tho' all the *Intellectual Tetrads* and *Hebdomads* have a *Fountainous Order*, and consequently an *Empyreal President*, nevertheless they are contained in the Worlds, since the Empyreal passeth, through all the Worlds.

Nevertheless, the Empyræum it self is fixed and immoveable; as *Simplicius*, further explicating the Chaldaick Doctrine, acknowledgeth, by this Similitude; *Let us imagine to our selves* (saith he) *two Spheres, one consisting of many Bodies, these two to be of equal bigness, but place one together with the Center, and put the other into it; you will see the whole World existing in place, moved in immoveable Light, which World according to its whole self is immoveable, that it may imitate place, but is moved as to its Parts, that herein it may have less than Place*.

CHAP. XIV.

The Æthereal Worlds.

AFter the Empyræum, the Oracle names the Æther, *Fire, Æther, Worlds*; confirmed by *Psellus* and the *Anonymos Summarist*, who assert, that next the Empyræum are the three Æthereal Worlds; but of these three they mention only two, (and those misapply'd to the Material Worlds) *The Sphere of fixed Stars, and the Planetary Sphere*: The third (perhaps implied though not express'd) might be the Æther which is betwixt the Empyræum and the Sphere of fixed Stars.

The Æther is a Fire (as its name implies) less subtile than the Empyræum, for *the Empyræum penetrates through the Æther*: yet is the Æther it self so subtile, that *it penetrates through the Material World*.

The second Æthereal World is the Sphere of fixed Stars, which are the more compacted or condensed parts of the Æthereal Fire; as *Patricius* ingeniously interprets this Oracle.

He compacted a great number of inerratick Stars.
Forcing (or pressing) *Fire to Fire*.

The third Æthereal World is that of the Planetary Orb, which contains the Sun, Moon, and five Planets; stiled by the Oracles, *Erratick Animals and Fire*,

He constituted a Heptad of Erratick Animals.
And again, *He constituted them six; the seventh was that of the Sun,*
Mingling Fire in them.

CHAP. XV.

The Material Worlds.

THe last and lowest are the Material Worlds; which *Psellus* and the other Summarist assert to be three, meaning doubtless the Air, Earth, and Water, for so the Oracle ranks 'em.

Placing

Placing the Earth in the middle, but the Water in the Bosom of the Earth, The Air above them.

This is that last Order of Worlds, of which the Chaldaick Summary saith, *it is called Terrestrial, and the hater of Light: it is the Region beneath the Moon, and comprehends within it self matter, which they call the bottom.* By which Words it appears upon what ground the Chaldæans asserted only these Sublunary Worlds to consist of Matter, but the Empyreal and Æthereal to be Immaterial though Corporeal: for Matter they understand to be the hater of Light, Darkness, and the bottom of a Nature quite different from the Empyræum and Æther, whose very substance is Light it self, yet it is actuated by their vivificative Fire which penetrates quite through it even to the Center, as we shewed formerly.

Lib. 1.

Concerning the Earth, *Diodorus Siculus* saith, they held Opinions peculiar to themselves, asserting that *it is in Figure like a Boat, and hollow*, for which, as likewise for other things concerning the World, they abound with probable Arguments.

Psellus adds, that *they sometimes call this Sublunary Hades.*

CHAP. XVI.

Of Material Dæmons.

OF Dæmons, as we said, they asserted two kinds, some good, others ill; the good, light, the ill dark. The former are those whom * *Hostanes* calls the *Ministers and Messengers of God, dwelling in his Presence*; But these, he describes as *Terrestrial, wandring up and down, and Enemies to Mankind.* Of the first we have treated already; of the latter *Psellus* in his Discourse upon this Subject, gives a large account from one *Marcus* of *Mesopotamia*, who having been of this Religion, and well acquainted with their Institutions, was afterwards converted to Christianity: What he relates, as well from the Doctrine it self, as from the place, sufficiently appears to be of the *Chaldaick* Tradition. It is to this effect.

* *Arnob.*

These Dæmons are of many kinds, and various sorts, both as to their Figures and Bodies, insomuch that the Air is full of them, as well that which is above us, as that which is round about us. The Earth likewise is full, and the Sea, and the most retired Cavities and Depths.

There are six general kinds of these Dæmons. The first named *Leliurius*, which signifies Fiery. This kind dwelleth in the Air that is above us: for from the places next about the Moon, as being Sacred, all kinds of Dæmons, as being Prophane, are expelled. The second kind is that which wandreth in the Air contiguous to us, and is by many peculiarly called Aereal. The third, Terrestrial. The fourth, Watery and Marine. The fifth, Subterraneous. The sixth, Lucifugous, and hardly sensible.

All these kind of Dæmons are haters of God, and Enemies of Man. Moreover, of these ill Dæmons, some are worse than others. Aquatile, and Subterraneous, and Lucifugous, are extreamly malicious and pernicious: For these do not hurt Souls by Phantasms and Delusions, but by Assault, like the most Savage Beasts, accelerate the Destruction of Men. The Watery Drown those who are Sailing upon the Water. The Subterraneous and Lucifugous, insinuating into the Entrails, cause Epilepsies and Frenzy. The Aereal and Terrestrial circumvent Men by Art and Subtilty, and deceive the Minds of Men, and draw them to absurd and illegal Passions.

They effect these things not as having Dominion over us, and carrying us as their Slaves whithersoever they please, but by Suggestion; for applying themselves to the phantastick Spirit, which is within us, they themselves being Spirits also, they instill Discourses of Affections and Pleasures, not by Voice verberating the Air, but by whisper, insinuating their Discourse.

Nor is it impossible that they should speak without voice, if we consider that he who speaks, being a far off, is forced to use a greater sound; being near, he speaks softly into the ear of the Hearer, and if he could get into the Spirit of the Soul, he would not need any Sound, but what discourse soever he pleaseth, would, by a way without sound, arrive there where it is to be received, which they say is likewise in Souls, when they are out of the Body, for they discourse with one another without noise. After this manner the Dæmons converse with us, privately, so that we are not sensible which way the War comes upon us.

Neither can this be doubted, if we observe what happens to the Air. For, when the Sun shineth it assumeth several colours and forms, transmitting them to other things, as we may see in Looking glasses. In like manner the Dæmons, assuming Figures and Colours, and whatsoever Forms they please, transmit them into our animal Spirit, and by that means afford us much business, suggesting Counsels, representing Figures, resuscitating the remembrance of pleasures, exciting the images of passions, as well when we sleep, as when we wake, and sometimes, titillating the genital parts, inflame us with frantick and unlawful desires, especially if they take, co-operating with them the hot humidities which are in us.

The rest of the Dæmons know nothing that is subtile, nor how to breed disturbance, yet are they hurtful and abominable, hurting in the same manner as the spirit or vapour in *Charon*'s Cave: For as that is reported to kill whatsover approacheth it, whether Beast, Man, or Bird; in like manner these Dæmons destroy those upon whom they chance to fall, overthrowing their Souls and Bodies, and their natural Habits, and sometimes by Fire, or Water, or Precipice, they destroy not Men only, but some irrational Creatures

The Dæmons assault Irrational Creatures, not out of Hate, or wishing them ill, but out of the love they have of their Animal heat: For dwelling in the most remote Cavities, which are extreamly cold and dry, they contract much coldness, wherewith being afflicted, they affect the humid and animal heat, and, to enjoy it, they insinuate themselves into irrational Creatures, and go into Baths and Pits; for they hate the heat of Fire and of the Sun, because it burns and drieth up.

But they most delight in the heat of Animals, as being temperate, and mixt with moisture, especially that of men, being best tempered, into which insinuating themselves, they cause infinite disturbance, stopping up the pores in which the Animal Spirit is inherent, and streightning and compressing the Spirit, by reason of the grossness of the Bodies with which they are indued. Whence it happeneth, that the Bodies are disorder'd, and their principal Faculties distemper'd, and their Motions become dull and heavy.

Now if the insinuating Dæmon be one of the Subterraneous kind, he distorteth the possessed Person, and speaketh by him, making use of the Spirit of the patient, as if it were his own Organ. But if any of those who are called Lucifugous, get privately into a Man, he causeth relaxation of the Limbs, and stoppeth the Voice, and maketh the possessed person in all respects like one that is dead. For this being the last of Dæmons is more Earthly, and extreamly Cold and Dry, and into whomsoever it insinuates, it hebetates and makes dull all the Faculties of his Soul.

And because it is Irrational, void of all Intellectual Contemplation, and is guided by irrational Phantasie, like the more Savage kind of Beasts, hence it comes to pass, that it stands not in aw of Menaces, and for that reason most Persons aptly call it Dumb and Deaf, nor can they who are possessed with it by any other means be freed from it, but by the Divine Favour obtaintained by Fasting and Prayer.

That Physicians endeavour to perswade us, that these Passions proceed not from Dæmons, but from Humours, and Spirits ill affected, and therefore go about to cure them, not by incantations and Expiations, but by Medicines and Diet, is nothing strange, since they know nothing beyond Sense, and are wholly addicted to Study the Body. And perhaps not without reason are some things ascribed to ill affected Humours, as Lethargies, Melancholies, Frenzies, which they take away and cure, either by evacuating the Humours, or by replenishing the Body, if it be empty, or by outward applications. But as for Enthusiasms, ragings, and unclean Spirits, with which whosoever is possessed is not able to act any thing, neither by Intellect, Speech, Phantasie nor Sense; or else there is some other thing that moves them unknown to the Person Possessed, which sometimes foretelleth future Events; how can we call these the Motions of depraved Matter?

No kind of Dæmon is in its own Nature Male or Female, for such Affections are only proper to Compounds: but the Bodies of Dæmons are simple, and being very ductile and flexible, are ready to take any figure. As we see the Clouds represent sometimes Men, sometimes Bears, sometimes Dragons, or any other Figures: So is it with the Dæmoniack Bodies. Now the Clouds appear in various Figures according as they are driven by exteriour Blasts or Winds: But in Dæmons, who can pass as they please into any Bodies, and sometimes contract, sometimes extend themselves like Worms on the Earth, being of a soft and tractable Nature, not only the Bulk is changed, but the Figure and Colour, and that several ways; for the Dæmoniack Body being by Nature capable of all those, as it is apt to recede, it is changed into several Forms; as it is Aerial, it is susceptible of all sorts of Colours, like Air, but the Air is coloured by something extrinsecal.

The Dæmoniack Body, from its intrinsecal Phantastick Power and Energy, produceth the Forms of Colours in it self, as we sometimes look Pale, sometimes Red, according as the Soul is affected either with Fear or Anger. The like we must imagine of Dæmons: for from within they send forth several kinds of Colours into their Bodies. Thus their Bodies being changed into what Figure, and assuming what Colour they please, they sometimes appear in the shape of a Man, sometimes of a Woman, of a Lyon, of a Leopard, of a Wild Boar, sometimes in the figure of a Bottle, and sometimes like a little Dog fawning upon us.

Into all these Forms they change themselves, but keep none of them constantly: for the Figure is not solid, but immediately is dissipated; as when we pour something coloured into Water, or draw a Figure in the Air. In like manner is it with Dæmons, their Colour, Figure, and Form presently vanish.

But all Dæmons have not the same Power and Will, there is much inequality amongst them as to these. Some there are Irrational, as amongst compound Animals; for, as of them, Man participating of Intellect and Reason, hath also a longer Phantasie, extending also to all sensibles, as well in the Heavens, as on Earth and under the Earth; but Horses, Oxen, and the like, have a narrower, and more particular phantasie, yet such as extends to the knowledge of the Creatures that feed with them, their Mangers and their Masters; Lastly, Flies, Gnats, Worms, have it extreamly contracted and incoherent; for they know neither the hole out of which they came, nor whither they go, nor whither they ought to go, they have only one phantasie, which is that of Aliment. In like manner there are different kinds of Dæmons. Of these some are Fiery, others Aereal; these have a various phantasie which is capable of extending to any thing imaginable: the Subterraneous and Lucifugous are not of this nature; whence it comes to pass, that they make not use of many figures, as neither having variety of phantasms, nor a Body apt for Action or Transformation. But the Watry and Terrestrial being of a middle kind betwixt these, are capable of taking many Forms, but keep themselves to that in which they delight. They which live in humid places, transform themselves into the shapes of Birds and Women, whence termed by the Greeks *Naiades* and *Nereides* and *Dryades* in the Feminine Gender. But such as are conversant in dry places, have also dry Bodies, such as the *Onosceles* are said to be. These transform themselves into Men, sometimes into Dogs, Lions, and the like Animals, which are of a Masculine Disposition.

The Bodies of Dæmons are capable of being struck, and are pained thereby, though they are not compounds, for Sense is not only proper to Compounds. That thing in Man which feeleth,

eth, is neither the Bone nor the Nerve, but the Spirit which is in them: Whence if the Nerve be pressed, or seized with cold, or the like, there ariseth pain from the Emission of one Spirit into another Spirit: for it is impossible that a Compound Body should in it self be sensible of pain, but in as much as it partaketh of Spirit, and therefore being broken into pieces, or dead, it is absolutely insensible, because it hath no Spirit. In like manner a Dæmon being all Spirit, is of his own nature sensible in every part; he immediately seeth, and heareth, he is obnoxious to suffering by touch; being cut asunder, he is pained like Solid Bodies, only herein, differing from them, that other things cut asunder can by no means or very hardly be made whole again, whereas the Dæmon immediately cometh together again, as Air or Water parted by some more Solid Body. But though this Spirt joyns again in a moment, nevertheless, at the very time in which the dissection is made, it is pained.

Hitherto the Theology and Physick of the Chaldeans.

THE SECOND SECTION.

Astrology, and other Arts of Divination.

THe Second Part of the *Chaldaick* Learning consists in Arts of Divination; the chief whereof is Astrology. This as it is generally acknowledged to have been their proper Invention, so were they most particularly addicted to it, for which *Ptolomy* gives a Reason out of the Art it self; *because they are under Virgo and Mercury*; but *Cicero* one much better; that *the plainness and evenness of the Country* did invite them to Contemplation of the Stars.

It consists of two parts; 1. *Meteorologick*, which considers the Motions of the Stars; the other *Apotelesmatick*, which regards Divination: The first was known to the Ancient *Græcians* by the common names of *Astronomy* and *Astrology*; until the other being brought into *Greece* also, they for distinction called the former more particularly *Astronomy*, the latter *Astrology*. The excellent a *Joseph Scaliger* to advance the Credit of the *Greek* Learning, constantly avers that the Chaldæans had only a *gross and general, not exact knowledge of Astronomy*; ὁλοσχερῆ, tantum, non etiam ἀκριβῆ, and that the Greeks learned nothing therein of the Chaldæans: when as *Aristotle* ingenuously acknowledgeth the contrary, *the Ægyptians and Babylonians*, saith he, *from whom we have many Informations concerning each of the Stars*. Though doubtless they were far short of that height in this Art, to which the *Greeks*, who brought it out of the East, improved it: for *Diodorus Siculus* affirms

a Proleg. in *Manil.*

that b *they alledged very weak Reasons for the Eclipses of the Sun, which Eclipses they neither durst foretell, nor reduce to certain Periods.*

b Lib. 1.

But of the *Apotelesmatick* part they boasted themselves not only the Inventors, but Masters; insomuch that all the Professors of it, of what Country soever, were (as we formerly shewed) called after them, *Chaldæans*.

CHAP. I.

Of the Stars fixed and Erratick, and of their Præsignification.

THey first lay down for a Ground, *That Terrestrials Sympathize with the Cælestials, and that every one of those is renewed by the influence of these.*

Sext. Emp.

*For evey Man's indued with such a Mind,
As by the Sire of God's and Men's assign'd.*

Above all things they hold that our Act and Life is subjected to the Stars, as well to the Erratick as the Fixed, and that Mankind is governed by their various and multiplicious course; * *That the Planets are of the kind of efficient Causes in every thing that happens in Life, and that the Signs of the Zodiack co-operate with them:* † *That they confer all good and ill to the Nativities of Men*, and that by contemplation of their Natures may be known the chief things that happen to Men.

Censor.

* Sext. Emp. loco cit.

† Diod. lib.

They held the Principal Gods to be twelve, to each of which they attributed a Month, and one of the Signs of the Zodiack.

Diod. lib. 1.

Next the Zodiack they assert twenty four Stars, whereof half they say are ranked in the Northern Parts, the other half in the Southern: Of these they which are apparent they conceive to be deputed to the Living, the inapparent congregated to the Dead: These they call *Judges of all things*.

Diod. loc. cit.

But the greatest Observation and Theory they hold to be that concerning the five Stars termed Planets, which they call the Interpreters, * because the rest of the Stars being Fixed, and having a setled Course, these only having a peculiar Course, foretell things that shall come to pass, interpreting and declaring to Men the Benevolence of the Gods: for some things (say they) they presignifie by their rising, some things by their setting, some things by ther colour, if observed; sometimes they foretel great Winds, sometimes extraordinar Rains, or Droughts. Likewise the rising of Comets, and Eclipses of the Sun, and of the Moon, and Earth-quakes, and in a word, all Alterations in the Air signifie things advantagious or hurtful, not only to Nations or Countries, but even to Kings and private Persons.

* Ibid.

Beneath the course of these, they hold that there are placed thirty Stars, which they call *Consiliary Gods*; that half of these oversee the places under the Earth, the other half oversee the Earth and the Business of Men, and what is done in the Heavens, and that every ten days one of these is sent to those below as a Messenger, and in like manner one of the Stars under the Earth is sent to those above, and that they have this certain Motion setled in an Æternal Revolution.

Diod. loc. cit.

CHAP.

PART XV.   *The Chaldaick Philosophy.*   17

CHAP. II.

Of Planets.

Diod. Lib. 1. The greatest Theory they hold (as we said) to be that which concerns the Planets: These they call the *Interpreters*, because, whereas the rest of the Stars are *Fixed*, & have a setled Course, these having their proper Courses foretell what things shall come to pass, Interpreting and declaring to Men the Benevolence of the Gods.

Sext. Em. Of the Seven, they hold the Sun and Moon to be the chief, and that the other five have less Power than they, as to the causing Events.

Sext. Em. loc. cit. Of the five, they affirm there are three which agree with, and are assistant to the Sun, viz. Saturn, Jupiter and Mercury; these they call diurnal, because the Sun, to whom they are assistant, predominates over the things that are done in the day.

Sext. Emp. loc. cit. As concerning the Powers of the five, some they say are Benevolent, others, Malevolent, others Common; the Benevolent are Jupiter and Venus; the Malevolent, Mars and Saturn; the Common, Mercury, who is Benevolent with the Benevolent, and Malevolent with the Malevolent.

CHAP. III.

The Divisions of the Zodiack.

Sext. Emp. The Chaldæans having at first no certain Rule of Observation of the other Stars, in as much as they contemplated not the Signs as within their proper circumscriptions, but only together with their observation of the seven Planets, it came at length into their minds to divide the whole Circle into twelve Parts: The manner they relate thus; they say that the Ancients having observed some one bright Star of those in the Zodiack, filled a Vessel (in which they boar'd a hole) with water, and let the water run into another Vessel placed underneath, so long until the same Star rose again; collecting that from the same Sign to the same, was the whole revolution of the Circle; Then they took the twelfth part of the water which had run out, and considered how long it was in running, affirming that the 12th part of the Circle past over in the same space of time; and that it had that proportion to the whole Circle which the part of water had to the whole water: By this Analogy (I mean of the Dodecatemorion or 12th part) they marked out the extream term from some signal Star which then appeared, or from some that arose within that time, Northern, or Southern; the same course they took in the rest of the Dodecatemoria.

That to each of these Dodecatemoria, the Ancient Chaldæans apply'd a particular Figure and a Character, (as for instance to the first, the Figure of a Ram, and this Character ♈.) tho' denied by the Learned * *John Picus Mirandula*, seems manifest enough from what we find ascribed peculiarly to them, by *Ptolomy*, *Sextus Empyrius* and others, which we shall cite in their due places.

Contra Astrol. lib.

Diod. lib. 1. To each of these Signs they appropriated one of the principal Gods which they held to be twelve, and One of the Months; the Zodiack it self they termed the Circle *Mazaloth*, which the Septuagint render μαζερθ, interpreted by *Suidas*, the Constellations which are commonly termed Ζωδια, Signs, for *Mazal* Signifieth a Star. That they ascribed several Gods to them agreeth with what is said of the followers of *Baal* (whom Rabbi *Maimonides* conceives the same with these Chaldæans) *they burnt Incense to Baal, to the Sun, and to the Moon, and to the Mazaloth, and to all the Host of Heaven.* Hence some are of Opinion that *Homer* received this Doctrine from the Ægyptians, as the Ægyptians from the Chaldæans, alluding to it in the first of his Iliads, where he mentions the entertainment of *Jupiter* and the rest of the Gods in *Æthiopia* twelve days, with the several Houses built for them by *Vulcan*; and better deserve they to be credited than those Ancients, who (according to *Eustathius*) writ that *Homer* first gave the Hint of this Opinion to the Mathematicians. Neither is what he adds in Explication of this Mythology dissonant from the Chaldaick Doctrine, that the making those Mansions for the Gods or Stars, is ascribed to Vulcan *in respect of the Ætherial heat of the Celestial Orb.*

2 Kings 23. 5

In Iliad. 1.

In Iliad 1.

Of the Signs some they call Masculine, others Feminine; some Double, others Single; some Tropical, others Solid.

Sext. Emp.

The Masculine or Feminine are those which have a Nature that co-operates towards the Generation of Males or Females; Aries is a Masculine Sign, Taurus a Feminine, Gemini a Masculine; in like manner the rest alternately are Masculine and Feminine. In imitation of whom as I conceive the Pythagoreans call the Monad Masculine, the Duad Feminine, the Triad Masculine, and so on thro' all Numbers, Odd and Even. Some there are who divide every Sign into 12 Parts, observing almost the same order; as in Aries they call the first 12th part Aries and Masculine, the second Taurus and Feminine, the third Gemini and Masculine, and so of the rest.

Double Signs are Gemini, and its diametrically opposite Sagittarius; Virgo and Pisces: The rest are single.

Tropical are those to which when the Sun cometh he turneth back, and maketh a Conversion: Such is the Sign Aries, and its opposite Libra, Capricorn and Cancer; In Aries is the Spring Tropick, in Capricorn the Winter, in Cancer the Summer, in Libra the Autumnal. The Solid are Taurus and its opposite Scorpio, Leo, and Aquarius.

Sext. loc. cit.

Some Chaldæans there are who attribute the several parts of Man's Body to particular Signs, as sympathizing with them; To Aries the Head, to Taurus the Neck, to Gemini the Shoulders, Cancer the Breast, Leo the Sides, Virgo the Bowels and Belly, Libra the Reins and Loins, Scorpio the Secret Parts and Womb, Sagittarius the Thighs, Capricorn the Knees, Aquarius the Legs, Pisces, the Feet. This did they not without consideration, for if any Star shall be in any Ascension of these Malignant Signs, it will cause a Maim in that Part which bears the same Name with it. Thus much in brief of the Nature of the Signs in the Zodiack.

* *Sext. Emp.*

Besides this Division of the Zodiack into Signs * they *Subdivided* every Sign into 30 Degrees, every Degree into 60 Minutes, so they call the least indivisible Parts, (as *Empyrius* affirms; whence it may be argued, that the Chaldeans made not any lower Divisions into Seconds, or the like.) The Degrees being in every Sign 30. are

Censorin. de die natali.

[Dddd]

are in the whole Zodiack 360. in some one of these the Sun must necessarily be at the time of the Nativity, which Degree the Chaldæans properly call the place of the Birth. Hence the Greeks call these Degrees μοιραι, in allusion to the μοιραι Goddesses of Destiny, these being our Fates; for it is of greatest Importance which of these Degrees is Ascendant at the time of Birth.

Ptol. Three other ways there are of dividing of the Zodiack ascribed to the *Chaldæans*, which are *Triplicities, Terms, Decanates.*

The Trigons or Triplicities are these four. The *first* is Aries, Leo, Sagittarius, *the second* Taurus, Virgo, Capricorn, *the third* Gemini, Libra, Aquarius, *the last* Cancer, Scorpio, Pisces; That the *Chaldæans* divided the Zodiack according to these Triplicities is manifest from their way of collecting the Terms of the Planets described by *Ptolemy*.

* *Ptol.* Every Sign hath five *Terms.* * The Chaldaick *way of finding out the quantity of the Terms in every Sign is one, and that very plain, for their Quantities differ by an equal Diminution, every Term is less than the precedent by one Degree,* for they made the first Term of every Sign to be eight Degrees, the second seven, the third six, the fourth five, the fifth four, which makes up 30 Degrees.

Lastly, the Signs are divided into *Faces,* for so the Ancients called them, in Hebrew *Phanim,* in Arabick *Mageah,* in Greek πρόσωπα; but the latter Astrologers *Decanates* δεκάνοι. Decanos a *In Manil.* word (as *Scaliger* observes) deriv'd from the *Roman* Militia, of these in every Sign there are three, each of which comprehends ten Degrees. That the *Chaldæans* were not ignorant of these is manifest, in as much as *Temer* the *Babylonian,* an Author of great Antiquity, wrote concerning them.

CHAP. IV.

Of the Planets considered in respect to the Zodiack.

Sext. Emp. THE *Chaldæans* held *that the Planets have not always* Power *alike, as the procuring of Good and Ill; but that in some Places [or Signs of the Zodiack]* they are more efficacious, *Sext. Emp. loc. cit.* in others less; *and that same Stars have greater Power being in their proper Houses, or in their Exaltations [or Triplicities,] or Terms, or Decanates.* All which the later Astrologers call their Essential Dignities.

Sext. Emp. ibid. The most Efficacious is that of Houses. They hold the Sun's House to be Leo, the Moon's Cancer, Saturn's Capricorn and Aquarius, Jupiter's Sagittarius and Pisces, that of Mars Aries and Scorpio, that of Venus Taurus and Libra, that of Mercury Gemini and Virgo.

They call the Exaltations and Depressions of *Sext. loc. cit.* the Planets, when they are in Signs wherewith they are delighted, or when they are in those in which they have little (or no) Power : For they are deligted in their Exaltations ; but have little (or no) Power in their Depressions. As the Sun's Exaltation is in Aries, when he is exactly in the 19th Degree thereof, his Depression in the Sign and Degree diametrically opposite to it. The Moon's Exaltation is in Taurus, her Depression (or Detriment) in the Sign diametrically opposite. That of Saturn is in Libra, of Jupiter in Cancer, of Mars in Capricorn, of Venus in Pisces, and their Depressions are in the Signs diametrically opposite to their Exaltations:

The Trigones or Triplicities of Planets are order'd by the *Chaldæans* after this manner.* The * *Ptol.* Lord of the first Triplicity (of the Zodiack) is Jupiter, of the second Venus ; the same Order they observe in the other two Triplicities, except that the third is said to have two Lords, Saturn and Mercury : The first part of the Day is assigned to Saturn, the Night to Mercury. The Lord of the last Triplicity is Mars. How much this differs from the Vulgar Way (which takes in the Sun and Moon) will easily appear to those who will take the pains to compare them. The latter way see in *Firmicus.*

They call the Terms of the Planets in every *Sext. Emp.* Sign, those in which any Planet from such a Degree to such a Degree is most powerful or prevalent.* The Chaldaick way of Terms is gather- * *Ptol.* ed from the Lords of the Triplicities, (which is plainer and more effectual than that of the Ægyptians from the Lords of the Houses) yet neither in their Orders nor Quantities do they always follow those Planets which govern the Triplicities. In the first Triplicity, their Division of Terms in every Sign thereof is one and the same. The first Term they give to the Lord of the Triplicity Jupiter, the second to the Lord of the following Triplicity, Venus, the third and fourth, to the two Lords of the Triplicity of the Gemini, which are Saturn and Mercury ; the fifth, to the Lord of the last Triplicity Mars. In the second Triplicity they divide every Sign alike, and allot the first Term to Venus, by reason of her Dominion in that Triplicity, the second and third to the two Lords of the Triplicity of the Gemini, which are Saturn and Mercury ; the fourth to Mars ; the last to Jupiter. To Saturn are attributed in the day 66 Degrees, in the night 78, to Jupiter 72, to Mars 60, to Venus 75, to Mercury in the Day, 66, in the Night 78.

The

The Terms of the Chaldæans or Babylonians.

Aries	Jupiter	8	Venus	7	Saturn	6	Mercury	5	Mars	4
Taurus	Venus	8	Saturn	7	Mercury	6	Mars	5	Jupiter	4
Gemini	Saturn	8	Mercury	7	Mars	6	Jupiter	5	Venus	4
Cancer	Mars	8	Jupiter	7	Venus	6	Saturn	5	Mercury	4
Leo	Jupiter	8	Venus	7	Saturn	6	Mercury	5	Mars	4
Virgo	Venus	8	Saturn	7	Mercury	6	Mars	5	Jupiter	4
Libra	Saturn	8	Mercury	7	Mars	6	Jupiter	5	Venus	4
Scorpio	Mars	8	Jupiter	7	Venus	6	Saturn	5	Mercury	4
Sagittarius	Jupiter	8	Venus	7	Saturn	6	Mercury	5	Mars	4
Capricorn	Venus	8	Saturn	7	Mercury	6	Mars	5	Jupiter	4
Aquarius	Saturn	8	Mercury	7	Mars	6	Jupiter	5	Venus	4
Pisces	Mars	8	Jupiter	7	Venus	6	Saturn	5	Mercury	4

The *Decanates* or *Faces* of the Planets, have reference to those of the Zodiack; the first Face is that Planet whose Sign it is: the second, the next Planet; and so on. That these were of Ancient *Chaldaick* Invention is manifest, not only in regard that *Teucer* the *Babylonian* wrote concerning them, but likewise they were observed by the *Egyptians*, who, (as *Josephus* saith) derived this Learning from the *Chaldæans*. *Nicipso* King of Ægypt, *a most Just Governor, and excellent Astrologer*, did (if we credit *Julius Firmicus*) collect all Sicknesses from the Decanates; shewing what Diseases every Decanate caused; because one Nature was overcome by another, and one God by another. The same Author adds, that *Ptosiris touched this part of Astrology but lightly; not as being ignorant of it, but not willing to communicate his Immortal Learning unto Posterity.*

CHAP. V.

Aspects of the Signs and Planets.

Censor.
Sext. Emp.

Every Sign of the Zodiack hath a mutual Aspect to the rest; in like manner the Planets have several Aspects; * They are said to be in mutual Aspect or Configuration, when they appear either in Trine or Square. They are said to behold one another in Trine, when there is an Interposition of three Signs between them: In Square or Quartile, when of two.

Censor.

The Sun passing into the Sign next to that wherein he was at the time of Birth, regards the place of Conception either with a very weak Aspect, or not at all; for most of the *Chaldæans* have absolutely denied, that the Signs which are next to one another behold one another; but when he is in the third Sign, that is, when there is a Sign betwixt them, then he is said to behold the first place whence he came, but with a very oblique and weak light, which Aspect is termed Sextile; for it subtends the sixth part of a Circle: for if we draw Lines from the first Sign to the third, from the third to the fifth, and from thence to the seventh, and so on, we shall describe an æquilateral Hexagone. This Aspect they did not wholly rely on for that it seemed to conduce the least to the Nativity of the Child, but when he comes to the fourth Sign, so that there are two betwixt, he looks on it with a *Quarterly Aspect*: for that Line which his Aspect makes, cuts off a fourth part of the Circle. When he is in the fifth, there being three betwixt it, is a *Trine Aspect*, for it subtends a third part of the Zodiack: which two Aspects the *Quartile* and *Trine*, being very efficacious, afford much encrease to the Birth. But the Aspect from the sixth place is wholly inefficacious, for the Line there makes not a side of any Polygone, but from the 7th Sign which is the opposite to the Aspect is most safe and powerful, and bringeth forth some Infants already mature, termed *Septimestres*, from being born in the 7th Month: But if within that space it be not mature, in the 8th Month it is not born, for from the 8th Sign as from the sixth the Aspect is inefficacious, but either in the 9th Month, or in the 10th for the Sun from the 9th Sign beholds again the Particle of the Conception in a *Trine Aspect*, and from the 10th in a *Quartile*; which Aspects, as we said, are very efficacious: But in the 11th Month they hold it cannot be born, because then, the Light being weak, sends forth his languishing Ray in a *Sextile Aspect*, much less in the 12th which Aspect is not at all valid.

CHAP. VI.

Schemes.

Sext. Emp.

The way by which the *Chaldæans* from the very beginning observed the Horoscope of any Nativity, corresponds with that of their Division of the Zodiack (mentioned formerly;) For a *Chaldæan* sate in the night time on some high Promontory contemplating the Stars; another sate by the Woman in Travail until such time as she were delivered. As soon as she was Delivered, she signified it to him on the Promontory, which as soon as he heard, he observed the Sign then rising for the Horoscope, but in the Day he attended the Ascendants and Sun's Motion.

Sext. Emp. loc. cit.

Of the twelve parts or Houses into which the Zodiack is divided, those which are predominant in every Nativity, and chiefly to be considered in Prognosticks, are four, by which one common Name they

they term *Centers* (or *Angles*) *but more particularly, they call one the* Horoscope, *or* Ascendent, *another the* Medium Cœli, *(the tenth House,) another the* Descendant, *(the seventh House, another the* Subterrestrial *and opposite to the* Medium Cœli, *(the fourth House.) The* Horoscope *is that which happens to be Ascendant at the time of the Birth, the* Medium Cœli *is the fourth Sign inclusively from it. The* Descendant *is that which is opposite to the* Horoscope. *The* Subterrestrial *and* Imum Cœli, *that which is opposite to the* Medium Cœli: *as (to explain it by an Example) if* Cancer *be the* Horoscope, Aries *is the* Medium Cœli *Capricorn* Descendant, *and* Libra *Subterrestrial. That House which goes before either of these Houses they call* cadent, *that which followeth,* succedent; *now that which goeth before the* Horoscope *being apparent to us, they affirm to be of the ill* Genius, *that next which followeth the* Medium Cœli *of the good* Genius, *that which is before the* Medium Cœli, *the inferior Portion and single Lot, and God. That which is before the* Descendant, *a Slothful Sign, and the beginning of Death; that which is after the Ascendant, and is not apparant to us, the Fury and ill Fortune; that which cometh under the Earth good Fortune, oppositethe to the good Genius: that which is beyond the* Imum Cœli *towards the East,* Goddess; *that which followeth the Horoscope slothful, which also is opposite to the Slothful.*

Sext. loc. cit.

Or more briefly thus: *The cadent of the Horoscope is called the ill* Genius, *the Succedent slothful, the Cadent of the* Medium Cœli, God, *the Succedent good* Genius, *the Cadent of the* Imum Cœli *Goddess, the Succedent good Fortune, the Cadent of the Descendant ill Fortune, the Succedent Slothful. These, as they conceive, ought to be examined not superficially.*

Sext. loc. cit.

Upon these Grounds the *Chaldæans* made their Apotelesmatick *Prædictions, of which there is a difference; for some of them are more simple, others, more acurate: the more simple, those which are made from any one Sign, or the simple force of a single Star, as that a Star being in such a Sign shall cause such kind of Men: the more accurate, those which are made by the Concourse, and as they say, the Contemporation of many. As if one Star be in the* Horoscope, *another in the Mid-heaven, another in the opposite Point to the Mid-heaven, others thus or thus posited, then these or these things will come to pass.* These are all the Remains of this Art, which can be attributed to the Ancient *Chaldæans.*

CHAP. VII.
Other Arts of Divination.

THe *Chaldæans*, besides Astrology, invented and used many other ways of Divination, of which *a Diodorus Siculus* instanceth, *Divination by Birds, Interpretation of Dreams, Explication of Prodigies, and Hieroscopy.* b *R. Maimonides* likewise affirms, that *among the* Chaldæans *anciently there arose several sorts of Diviners,* in particular these, *Megnonemim, Menacheshim, Mecashephim, Chober chaber, Shel ob, Fideyoni, Doresh el hammetim*; all which are mentioned, Deut. 18. 10, 11.

a Lib. 1.
b Mor. Nev.

The first ascribed by *Diodorus* to the *Chaldæans*, is Divination of Birds, οἰωνῶν μαντικὴ, or Augury: neither is it probable, that they who were so great Inquisitors into the several kinds of Divination, should be ignorant of this, which after-Ages esteemed one of the most considerable. But they who understand the Word *c Menacheshim* in this Sense, seem to have been drawn to it by a mistake of the Latine Word *augurari*, by which it is rendred.

The next, *Interpretation of Dreams*, ἐξήγησις ἐνυπνίων, *d Philo Judæus* affirms to have been invented by *Abraham*. That it was profess'd by the ancient *Chaldæans* appears from their Answer to *Nebuchadnezzar*, e *Tell thy Servants the Dream, and we will shew the Interpretation.* There are extant many onirocritical Verses, under the name of *Astrampsychus*, collected out of *Suidas*, and digested by *Joseph Scaliger*: *Astrampsychus* is mentioned among the Magi by *Laertius*: and f there are who conceive the name to be only an Interpretation of the *Chaldæan* or *Persian* Zoroaster, which some render, *a living Star.*

d Suid.
e Dan. 2.
f Ursin. Zor.

The third, *Explication of Prodigies*, ἐξήγησις τεράτων, this kind the *Greek* Interpreters conceive included in the Word *Jydgoni*, for they render it ἐπαοιδὸς καὶ τερατοσκόπος.

The last that *Diodorus* mentions, is *Hieroscopie*, by which I conceive to be meant *extispiciam*, Divination by inspection into the Entrails (ἱερῶν) of Sacrificed Beasts. That the *Chaldæans* used this kind, may be argued from the Prophet *Ezekiel*, who saith of the King of *Babylon* (using Divination) g *he looked into the Liver.* These seem to be the *gazrin*, reckoned by h *Daniel* among the *Chaldæan* Diviners; from *Gazar*, *to cut*; for they cut open the Beast and Divined by his Entrails.

g Chap. 21. v. 21.
h Chap. 2.

Ob, is rendred *Pytho*, or (rather) *Pythonicus Spiritus*; the Word Originally signifieth *a Bottle*; and thereupon is taken for that Spirit which speaketh *ex utero Pythonissæ*: The Sacred Text calls the Woman *Esheth Baalath Ob*, which the Septuagint render, γυναῖκα ἐγγαστρίμυθον, and where *Saul* saith, i *I pray thee Divine to me in Ob*; they Translate, μαντεύσαι δή μοι ἐν τῷ ἐγγαστριμύθῳ. R. *Maimonides* saith, she that was *initiated held in her hand a Myrtle Wand, and received Suffumigations*, R. *Abraham ben David*, that *these Rites were usually performed at some dead Man's Tomb.*

i 1 Sam. 22. v. 8.

Doresh el hammetim, is properly (as rendred) a *Necromancer*; k some affirm this kind of Divination had its Original in *Chaldæa*.

k Fran. Mirand. de ver. prænot. lib. 4. p. 328.

These and the rest of this kind are all comprehended under the general name *Mecashphim*, of which formerly.

THE
THIRD SECTION.

Magick, Natural and Theurgick.

THe third Part of the *Chaldaick* Doctrine was *Magick*: for though the Name is conceived to be *Persian* (by some derived from

from *Mog*, *a* a Sirname of the *Persian Zoroaster*, *b* by others from the *Magussæans*) yet this Science it self was originally *Chaldæan*, and properly the Study of the *Ashaphim*; of whom *Laertius* is to be understood, when he saith that the *Chaldæans were the same with the Babylonians as the* Magi *with the* Persians: Hence it is also that the Term *Magi* is sometimes extended to the *Chaldæan* Philosophers.

a Salmas.
b Suid.

Pliny indeed saith, that *c* Magick *had its beginning in* Persia *from* Zoroaster, but adds, that *whether this* Zoroaster *was one, or afterwards a second also, is not certain*: And that he rather meant the *Chaldæan*, than the *Persian*, may be inferred from his citing those Authors who placed this *Zoroaster* 6000 years before *Plato*, or 5000 years before the *Trojan* War; which Accounts (though extravagant) were doubtless intended of the most Ancient *Zoroaster*, the *Chaldæan*. He likewise instanceth *d* as skilful in this Art *Marmaridius a Babylonian*, and *Zormocenidas an Assyrian* both so ancient as that *there are not any Monuments of them extant*.

c Lib. 30. c. 1.

d Loc. cit.

The few Remains we find of the *Chaldæan Magick* may be reduced to two Kinds, *Natural* and *Theurgick*.

CHAP. I.

Natural Magick.

THE first part of the *Chaldaick* Magick is that which we commonly term *Natural*, because it contemplates the Vertues of all Natural Beings, Cœlestial and Sublunary, *a* makes Scrutiny into their Sympathy, and mutual Application of them, produceth extraordinary Effects.

a Psel.

By this kind of Magick the *Chaldæans* professed *b to perform many admirable things, not only upon particular Persons, but upon whole Countries*. R. Maimonides instanceth *c the expelling Noxious Animals, as Lions, Serpents, and the like, out of Cities*; *the driving away all kind of harms from Plants, prevention of Hail, the destroying of Worms that they hurt not the Vines*; concerning these (saith he) *they have written much in their Books*; and some there are who boast they can cause that *no Leaves or Fruit shall fall from the Trees*.

b Maimon. Mor. Ne.
c Mor. Ne.

CHAP. II.

Magical Operations, their Kinds.

THeir Operations *a* R. Maimonides reduceth to three Kinds. *The first of those which deal in Plants, Animals, and Metals. The Second consists in Circumscription and Determination of some time, in which the Operations are to be performed. The third consists in Humane Gestures and Actions; as in clapping the Hands, Leaping, Crying aloud, Laughing, Lying Prostrate on the Earth, Burning any Thing, Kindling of Smoak, and lastly, in pronouncing certain Words Intelligible or Unintelligible*; these are the Kinds of their Magical Operations.

c Mor. Ne.

b Some there are which are not performed but by all these Kinds: As when they say, take *such a Leaf of such an Herb, when the Moon is in such a Degree and Place*: Or, take of *the Horn of such a Beast, or of his Hair, Sweat or Blood, such a quantity, when the Sun is in the middle of Heaven, or in some other certain Place. Or, take of such a Metal, or of many Metals, melt them under such a Constellation, and in such a Position of the Moon*; *then pronounce such and such Words*; *make a suffumigation of such and such Leaves, in such and such a Figure, and this or that thing shall come to pass*.

b Loc. cit.

c Other Magical Operations there are which they conceive may be performed by one of the forementioned Kinds, only these (say they) *are performed for the most part by Women*, as we find amongst them: *For the bringing forth of Waters, if ten Virgins shall adorn themselves, and put on red Garments, and leap in such manner that one shall thrust on the other, and this to be done going backwards and forwards, and afterwards shall stretch out their Fingers towards the Sun, making certain Signs, this Action being finished, they say that Waters will issue forth. In like manner they write, that if four Women, &c. using certain Words and certain Gestures, by this Action they shall divert Hail from falling down*. Many other such like Vanities they mention all along their Writings, which are to be performed by Women.

c Loc. cit.

d But none of these (as they imagine) *can be performed without having respect and consideration* of the Stars; *for they conceive that every Plant hath its proper Star*: *They ascribe also certain Stars to all living Creatures and Metals*; *Moreover these Operations are peculiar Worships of the Stars, and that they are delighted with such an Action, or Speech, or Suffumigation, and for its sake afford them what they wish*. Hitherto R. Maimonides, who only hath preserved these Remains of the Ancient *Chaldaick* Superstition.

d Maim. Mor. Ne.

CHAP. III.

Of the Tsilmenaia (or Telesmes) used for Averruncation.

MOreover the *Chaldæans* are by the Rabbies reported to have been the first that found out the secret power of Figures; neither was there any thing more celebrious than the Images of this kind made by them.

They are called in *Chaldee* and *Persian Tsilmenia*, from the Hebrew Tselem, an Image: in *Arabick*, Talitsmam, or Tsalismam, perhaps from the same Root; rather than as some conjecture from the Greek word, τελεσμα τελεσμωυν τι.

These Images were prepared under certain Constellations, for several purposes; some for Averruncation, others for Prædiction.

Those that serve for *Averruncation*, some conceive to have been of later invention, and ascribe them to *Apollonius Tyanæus*; he indeed was the first amongst the *Grecians* that was famous for them: but it is most probable that he brought this Art out of the East, there being yet to be seen many of these Figures or Telesms throughout the whole Eastern part of the World; and some of them very Ancient, which *a Gaffarel* alledgeth to confirm, that *the Persians, or if you will the Babylonians, were the first that found 'em out*.

a Curios. inouyes.

These

These the *Greeks* term also στοιχεῖα, and στοιχειώσεις; and the makers of them *Stoicheiomaticks*, [b] Ptolemy, *The generable and corruptible Forms are affected by the Celestial Forms: for which reason the Stoicheiomaticks make use of them, considering the entrance of the Stars into them:* On which words *Hali Aben Rodoan* (or as the Hebrew Translation *Aben Giafar*) writes thus. *In this Chapter* Ptolemy *means to discover many secrets of Images, and that the Figures which are here below are corespondent to the like Figurations above, which predominate over them: as for instance, the Celestial Scorpion predominates over the Terrestrial Scorpions, and the Celestial Serpent over the Terrestrial Serpents; and the skilful in Images* (Stoicheiomaticks) *observed, when a Planet was out of his combustion, and entred into any of these Figures, then placing the Planet in the Horoscope, they engraved the Figure upon a Stone, and having added what else was necessary, they fitted it for preservation, or destruction, as they pleased; and this Power continued in the Stone a long time after.*

[b] *Centiloq.*

CHAP. IV.

Of the Tsilmenaia, used for Prediction.

Another kind there was of *Tsilmenaia* or *Telesmes*, used for Prediction: These Images (according to the Description of a [a] R. *Maimonides*) they did erect to the Stars: of Gold to the Sun, of Silver to the Moon, and so distributed the Metals and Climates of the Earth among the Stars, for they said, that such a Star is the God of such a Climate. There they built Temples, and placed the Images in them, conceiving that the Power of the Stars did flow into those Images, and that those Images had the faculty of understanding, and did give to Men the gift of Prophecy, and in a word, did declare to them what things were good for them. So also they say of Trees, which belong to those Stars, every Tree being dedicated to some Star, and planted to its Name, and Worshipped for this or that Reason, because the Spiritual Virtues of the Stars are infused into that Tree. So that after the manner of Prophecy they discourse to Men, and speak to them also in Dreams.

[a] *Mr. Ne.*

The word *Teraphim* in the Sacred Scripture, among other significations, is sometimes taken for these Images, whence [b] *Onkelos* the *Chaldee* Paraphrast renders it *Tsilmenaia*, with which the *Syriack* Version agrees; the Septuagint δήλους and ἀποφθεγγομένους, and φωτισμούς, implying by all these Interpretations, that they were indued with the Gift of Prediction: which is no more than the Text it self confirms; For [c] *Ezekiel* saith of the King of *Babylon* using Divination, that *he consulted the Teraphim*.

[b] *Gen.* 3.

[c] *Ch.* 21. 21.

Of this kind are those *Teraphims* conceived to be, which *Rachel* stole from her Father *Laban*; for he calls them his [d] *Gods*; the *Coptick* Version renders it, *the greatest of his Gods*: R. D. *Kimchi* conceives they were made by Astrologers to foretel things to come, and that they were Images whose Figures we know not, by which the Ancients were informed of future Events, they being in some manner like the Oracles, which often spake by the mouth of the Devil. R. *Eliezer*, that they were Statues made in the Figure of Men under certain Constellations, whose influences (which they were capable of receiving) caused them to speak at some set hours, and give an answer to whatsoever was demanded of them. *Aben Ezra*, that they were made after the Shapes of Men, to the end they might be capable of Celestial Influence (and in the same manner interprets he the *Teraphim* placed by *Michol* in *David*'s Bed.) Adding, that *the reason why* Rachel *took them away, was not to take her Father off from Idolatry; for if it were so, why then did she take them along with her, and not rather hide them in the way near his House? But by reason that her Father was skilful in Astrology, she feared lest by consulting those Images and the Stars, he should know which way* Jacob *was gone*. And S. *Austin*, that Laban saith, *why hast thou stoln my Gods? It is perhaps in as much as [*] if he had said be Divined,* * *I divined the Lord because of thee*;] for so the more antient Expositors interpret the word *nicashti*, and the Jews understand that place, of Prescience, Divination, or Conjecture, as Mr. *Selden* observes.

[d] *Gen.* 31.

In Gen. quæst. 94.

* *Gen.* 30.

De Diis Syriis.

Philo Judæus speaking of the * *Teraphim* of *Micah*, fancies *that* Micah *made of fine Gold and Silver three Images of young Lads, and three Calves and one Lion, one Dragon, and one Dove; so that if any had a mind to know any Secret concerning his Wife, he was to have recourse to the Image of the Dove, which answered his demands; if concerning his Children, he went to the Boy; if concerning Riches, to the Eagle; if concerning Power and Strength, to the Lion; if it any thing concerned Sons and Daughters, he went then to the Calves; and if about the length of years and days, he was to consult the Image of the Dragon.* This, how light soever, shews that he also understood the *Teraphim* to be Prophetical.

* *Judg.* 17.

CHAP. V.

Theurgick Magick.

The other part of the *Chaldaick* Magick is *Theurgick*: to which perhaps *Plato* more particularly alluded, when he defined a [a] the *Magick of* Zoroaster, *the Service of the Gods*. This they called also [b] *the Method of Rites*; *the works of Piety*, and (as rendred by the Greeks) τελεστικὴν ἐπιστήμην, *the Telestick Science and Telesiurgick*. It what it did consist may be gathered from what *Suidas* saith of the two *Julians*; *Julian* (saith he) the Chaldæan, *a Philosopher, Father of* Julian *Sirnamed the* Theurgick; *he wrote of Dæmons four Books*; they treat of *Preservatives of every part of Man's Body*, of which kind are *the Chaldaick Telesiurgicks*. And again, Julian *Son of the aforementioned, lived under* Marcus Antonius *the Emperor*; he also wrote Theurgick *Initiatory Oracles in Verse*; and all other Secrets of the Science.

[a] *Alcibiad.* 1.

[b] *Psel. in Orac*

Thus the Telestick Science was conceived to procure a Conversation with Dæmons by certain Rites and Ceremonies, and [c] *to initiate or perfect the Soul by the power of Materials here on Earth*; for *the supream faculty of the Soul cannot by its own guidance aspire to the sublimest Institution, and to the comprehension of Divinity, but the work of Piety leads it by the hand to God*

[c] *Psel. in Orac.*

by

by illumination from thence; Plato indeed holds, that we may comprehend the ungenerate Essence by Reason and Intellect; but the Chaldæan asserts, that there is no other means for us to arrive at God, but by strengthning the Vehicle of the Soul by material Rites; for he supposeth that the Soul is purified by Stones, and Herbs, and Charms, and is rendred expedite for Ascent.

It is likewise beneficial to the Body, as well as to the Soul, for * *if a Man shall give his mind to these, he shall not only render his Soul unvanquishable by Passions, but shall also preserve his Body the better in health: for the usual effect of Divine Illumimations is to consume the matter of the Body, and to establish Nature by Health, that we be not seized either by Passions or Diseases.*

* Psell. in Orac.

CHAP. VI.

Theurgick Rites.

BY Theurgick or Telestick Rites they conceived that they could procure a Communication with the good Dæmons, and Expulsion or Averruncation of the bad.

The chief of these Rites was Sacrifice; concerning which there is a remarkable passage in a *Jamblichus*, who delivers the *Chaldaick* Opinion thus: *The Gods give those things that are truly good, to such as are purified by Sacrifices; with whom also they converse, and by their communication drive away Wickedness and Passion far from them; and by their brightness chase from thence the dark Spirit; for the evil Spirits, when the light of the Gods cometh in, fly away as Shadows at the light of the Sun: Neither are they able any longer to disturb the Pious Sacrificer, who is free from all Wickedness, Perversness, and Passion: But such as are pernicious, and behave themselves insolently in opposition to sacred Rites and Orders, these by reason of the imbecillity of their Action, and want of Power, are not able to attain to the Gods, but because of certain Pollutions are driven away from the Gods, and associated with ill Dæmons, by whose bad Breath they are inspired, and depart thence most wicked, profane and dissolute; unlike the Gods in desire, but in all things resembling the bad Dæmons with whom they converse daily. There Men therefore being full of Passion and Wickedness, by the Affinity that is betwixt them, draw the evil Spirits to them, by whom being quickly possest, they are again excited to all Iniquity, one assisting and strengthning the other, like a Circle whose beginning and end meet.*

a De Myster. Ægypt.

Several other Rites they used also, which they conceived to be prevalent in evocation of these Dæmons. They are allowed (saith b *Gregorius Nicephoras*) *out of the Air and Earth by certain Stones or Pulse, or certain Voices or Figures, which they call Characters, invented by the Chaldæans and Egyptians who first found out the proper dignoscitive sign of every Dæmon.*

b In Synes.

Some few of these are mention'd in the *Chaldaick* Oracles, as,

When thou seest the Terrestrial Dæmon approach, Sacrifice the Stone Mnizuris, using Invocation.

The Dæmons (saith *Psellus*) *that are near the Earth are by Nature lying, as being far off from the Divine Knowledge, and filled with dark matter. Now if you would have any true Discourse from these, prepare an Altar, and Sacrifice the Stone Mnizuris. This Stone hath the Power of Evocations, the other greater Dæmon who invisibly approacheth to the material Dæmon will pronounce the true Relation of Demands, which transmits to the Demandant the Oracle the vocative name with the Sacrificing of the Stone.*

Another of these Rites mentioned by the same Oracles, is that of the *Hecatine Strophalus*.

Labour about the Hecatine Strophalus.

The Hecatine Strophalus (saith *Psellus*) *is a Golden Ball, in the midst whereof is a Saphire; they fold about it a Leather Thong, it is beset all over with Characters; thus whipping it about they made their Invocations. These they use to call Jynges whether it be round or triangle, or any other Figure, and whilst they are doing thus they make insignificant or brutish cries, and lash the Air with their Whips. The Oracle adviseth to the performance of these Rites, or such a Motion of the Strophalus, as having an expressible Power. It is called* Hecatine *as being dedicated to* Hecate. Hecate *is a Goddess amongst the Chaldæans, having at her right side the Fountain of Vertues.*

No little Efficacy was attributed to certain Words used in these Rites, which the *Chaldaick* Oracles expresly forbid to be changed.

Never change Barbarous Names.

There are certain Names (saith *Psellus*) *among all Nations delivered to them by God, which have an unspeakable Power in Divine Rites, change not these into the Greek Dialect; As* Seraphim *and* Cherubin, *and* Michael *and* Gabriel: *These in the Hebrew Dialect have an unspeakable Efficacy in Divine Rites; but changed into Greek Names are ineffectual.*

CHAP. VII.

Apparitions.

THE Apparitions procured by these Rites are of two Kinds.

a The first is called ἐπόπτεια *Super-inspection* (in respect to the initiated Person.) When he who orders the Divine Rites seeth a meer Apparition, (as for instance) of Light in some Figure or Form, concerning which the *Chaldaick* b Oracle adviseth, that if any one sees such a Light, he apply not his Mind to it, nor esteem the voice proceeding from thence to be true. c *Sometimes likewise too many initiated Persons there appears whilst they are sacrificing some Apparitions in the shape of Dogs, and several other Figures. These are Apparitions of the Passions of the Soul in performing Divine Rites, meer Appearances, having no Substance, and therefore not signifying any thing true.*

a Psel. in Orac. 15.
b Psel. in Orac. 14.
c Psel. in Orac. 19.

The Second is called d αὐτοψία, *self-inspection*, this is *when the initiated Person seeth the Divine Light it self without any Figure or Form*: This the Oracle calls ἐνεργὸν, e *Sacro-sanct*, for

d Psel. in Orac. 15.
e Loc. Cit.

that

f Loc. cit.

that it is seen with a Beauty by Sacred Persons, and glides up and down pleasantly and graciously through the Depths of the World. *f* This will not deceive the initiated Person, but whatsoever question you shall propose, the answer will be most true,

> When thou seest (saith the Oracle) a
> Sacred Fire without
> Form, shining flashingly thro' the Depths
> of the whole World,
> Hear the voice of Fire.

g Psel. in Orac. 21.

g When thou beholdest the Divine Fire void of Figure, brightly gliding up and down the World, and graciously smiling, listen to this voice, as bringing a most perfect Prescience.

h Psel. in Orac. 25.

But *h* these things which appear to initiated Persons, as Thunder, Lightning, and all else whatsoever, are only Symbols or Signs, not the Nature of God.

CHAP. VIII.

Material Dæmons how to be repulsed.

AS it is one property of *Theurgy* to evocate and procure a Conversation with good Dæmons, so is it another, to repulse and chase away the Material Dæmons, which, as they conceive may be effected several ways; either by Words or Actions.

a Psel. de Dæmon.

By *Words*: For as *a Marcus* delivers the *Chaldaick* Opinion) *these material Dæmons fearing to be sent to Abysses and subterraneal Places, and standing in awe of the Angels who send them thither, if a Man threaten to send them thither, and pronounce the names of those Angels whose Office that is, it is hardly to be expressed how much they will be affrighted and troubled; so great will their astonishment be, as that they are not able to discern the Person that menaces them, and tho' it be some old Woman, or a little old Man that threatens them, yet so great is their fear, that they depart as if he that menaces were able to kill 'em.*

b De Dæmon.

By *Actions*: For *the Bodies of Dæmons* (saith the same *b* Author) *are capable of being struck, and are pained thereby; Sense is not the Property of Compounds, but of Spirits; That thing in a Man which feeleth, is neither the Bone, nor the Nerve, but the Spirit which is in them: whence, if the Nerve be pressed or seized with cold, or the like, there ariseth pain from the Emission of one Spirit into another; for 'tis impossible that a compound Body should in it self be sensible of Pain, but in as much as it partakes of Spirit, and therefore being cut into pieces, or dead, it is absolutely insensible; because it hath no Spirit. In like manner a Dæmon being all Spirit is of his own Nature sensible in every part; he immediately seeth and heareth; he is obnoxious to suffering by touch; being cut asunder he is pained like solid Bodies; only herein differing from 'em, that other things being cut asunder can by no means or very hardly be made whole again, whereas the Dæmon immediately comes together again, as air or water parted by some more solid Body. But tho' this Spirit joyn again in a moment, at the time in which the dissection is made 'tis pain'd; for this reason they are much afraid of Swords;* which they who chase 'em away knowing, stick up pointed Irons or Swords in those places where they would not have them come, chasing them away by things Antipathetical to them, as they allure them by things Sympathetical.

* Psel. de Dæmon.

From these Material Dæmons, *** *upon those that worship them, descend certain fiery Irradiations, like those they call falling Stars, gliding up and down, which those mad Persons term Apparitions of God;* but there is nothing true, firm, or certain in them, but cheats, like those of *Juglers*, which the common People term Wonders, because they deceive the eye, *** for being removed far from the Beatitude of Divine Life, and destitute of Intellectual Contemplation, they cannot presignifie futures, but all that they say or shew is false and not solid, for they know Beings μορφωτικῶς, by their outsides, but that which knoweth futures particularly, useth Notions indivisible and not figured.

* Psel. in Orc. 23.

THE FOURTH SECTION.

Of the Gods, and Religious Worship of the Chaldæans.

IN the last place, as to the Explication of the *Chaldaick* Doctrine, especially of that part which concerns their *Ashaphim*) it is necessary we give account of the Gods of the *Chaldæans*, and of their Religious Worship.

And tho' Mr. *Selden* hath reduced all the *Asiatick* Gods under the common name of *Syrian*, in his excellent Treatise upon that Subject; yet we shall take notice of such only as were proper to *Assyria*, (whether as being Worshipped no where else, or from thence brought into *Syria* and other Countries) conceiving the rest nothing pertinent to the *Chaldæans* or *Babylonians*.

The Religious Worship of the *Chaldæans* may be reduced to three Kinds; The first, a Worship of the true God, but after an Idolatrous manner: The second, of Dæmons, or Spirits: The third, of the Celestial Bodies, and Elements.

CHAP. I.

Of their Idolatrous Worship of the True God.

THe first kind of the *Chaldaick* Worship was of the True God, tho' after an Idolatrous manner: The Author of the *Chaldaick* Summary affirms, that *they held one Principle of all things, and declare that it is one and good.* That by this *one* and *good* they meant the True God, (to whom alone those Attributes belong) may be gathered from *a Eusebius*, who saith, (speaking doubtless of the Followers of *Zoroaster*) that in the first place they conceive God the Father and King ought to be ranked; for this reason the *Delphian* Oracle attested by *Porphyrius*, joyns them with the Hebrews;

a Præpar. Evang.

> *Chaldees* and *Jews* wise only, Worshipping
> Purely a Self-begotten God and King.

But

But (notwithstanding the Oracle) that this Worship, though of the True God, was Idolatrous, is beyond doubt: so as to them might be applied what St. *Paul* saith of the *Romans*, a *when they knew God they Glorify'd him not as God, but* b *changed the Glory of the uncorruptible God into an Image made like to corruptible Man.*

a Rom. 1. 20.
b Verse 23.

The Name and Image whereby they represented the supream God was that of *Bell*, as appears by the prohibition given by God himself, not to call him so any more: c *Thou shalt call me no longer Baali*; *Bell* with the *Chaldæans* is the same as *Baal* with the *Phœnicians*, both derived from the *Hebrew Baal*, *Lord*; this *Bell* of the *Babylonians* is mentioned by the Prophets *Esay* and *Jeremy*: They who first translated the Eastern Learning into *Greek*, for the most part interpret this *Bell* by the word Ζεὺς, *Jupiter*. So *Herodotus, Diodorus, Hesychius,* and others: *Berosus* (saith *Eusebius*) *was Priest of Belus, whom they interpret (Δία) Jupiter*; the reason of which seems to be, for that *Bell* was the chief God with the *Chaldæans,* as *Jupiter* with the *Grecians*, who by that name meant the True God, as the *Chaldæans* by the other; for to him St. *Paul* applies that Hemistick of *Aratus* τοῦ γὰρ καὶ γένος ἐσμέν, (for we are also his off-spring,) which hath reference to the first Verse, ἐκ Διὸς ἀρχώμεσθα. And upon these words of St. *Peter*, *Worship ye God, but not as the Grecians*. *Clemens Alexandrinus* observes, *that he saith not, Worship not the God whom the Grecians, but as the Grecians: he changed the manner of the Worship, but Preached not another God.*

c Hos. 2. 16.

Acts 17. 28.

Strom. 6.

The Temple of this *Jupiter Belus* at *Babylon*, is exactly described by *Herodotus* an Eye-witness in whose time it was yet extant, thus: *the gates were of Brass: the Temple it self square; every side two furlongs broad. In the midst of the Temple there was a solid Tower* (not hollow) *of thickness and height of a Stadium; upon which there was set another, and another upon that, and so on to eight: on the outside of these were stairs, by which to go up every one of them; in the midst of the stairs were seats for such as went up, to rest themselves: in the highest Tower there was another Temple* (or *Chappel*,) *and in it a Bed sumptuously furnish'd, and a Table of Gold; but neither in this was there any Statue, nor doth any Person lie here a nights except one Woman, a Foreigner, of whom the God makes choice above all other, as the* Chaldæans *who are Priests of this God aver: for they (say tho' I hardly credit it) that the God himself comes into this Temple, and rests in this Bed: There is moreover in this Temple another lower Chappel, in which there is a great Statue of* Jupiter *all of Gold, sitting; and beside it a Table and Bench all of Gold also: insomuch that the* Chaldæans *value it at* 800 *Talents: Likewise without the Chappel there is an Altar of Gold, and another Altar very great, upon which are Sacrificed Sheep of full growth, for upon that of Gold, it is not lawful to Sacrifice any but Sucklings; On this greater Altar the* Chaldæans *burn yearly of Frankincense to the value of* 100000 *Talents, in Sacrifice to their Gods. There was also at the same time in this Temple a Statue* 12 *Cubits high, of massie Gold,* which I saw not, but take upon the report of the *Chaldæans*: this Statue *Darius* Son of *Hystaspes* had a great mind to take, but durst not; but his Son *Xerxes afterwards took it, and slew the Priest which forbad him to stir it*: Thus was this Temple Built and Beautified, beside infinite Gifts and Presents. Hitherto *Herodotus*: he terms the Priests of *Belus Chaldæans*; and R. *Maimonides* asserts the *Chaldæan* Idolaters to be the same with the Prophets of *Baal.*

Lib. 1.

The Festival of *Bell* is mentioned, 2 *King* 10. 20. his Oracle by *Arrian*; the same which *Stephanus* means, saying, *The Chaldæans had an Oracle which was no less in esteem with them, than that at* Delphi *was with the* Græcians*.*

CHAP. II.

Worship of other Gods, Angels and Dæmons.

THe second kind of their Religious Worship, was that of other Gods, Angels and Dæmons; Next the Supream God (saith *Eusebius,* delivering their Opinion) *there followeth a multitude of other Gods,* Angels, and Dæmons. These Gods they distinguished into several Orders, *Intelligibles*; *Intelligibles and Intellectuals*; *Intellectuals*; *Fountains*; *Principles*; *Unzoned Gods*; *Zoned Gods*; *Angels and Dæmons*. To the Worship of these belongs what we have already delivered concerning their Theurgy.

CHAP. III.

The Chaldæan Worship of the Cœlestial Bodies.

THe third kind of Idolatrous Worship used by the *Chaldæans* and *Babylonians* was of the Celestial Bodies; into which, *Maimonides* saith, *they fell soon after the Flood*: perhaps occasioned by their continual addiction to Contemplation of them; and grounded upon Observation of the great Benefits communicated to Mankind by their Influence.

Mor. Nev.

The Levitical Law, in prohibiting this Idolatry, sets down the particulars of it, *Lest thou lift up thine eyes unto Heaven, and when thou seest the Sun, and the Moon, and the Stars, even all the Host of Heaven, should be driven to Worwip them and Serve them.* And of the Jewish Idolaters put down by *Josiah* (besides *those that burn Incense to* Baal, of whom already) are reckoned those that burnt Incense *to the Sun and to the Moon and the Planets* (or Signs, *Mazaloth*) *and to all the Host of Heaven.* This doubtless they learned of their Neighbours the *Assyrians*, of whom the Prophet *Ezekiel* complains that they doted.

Deut. 4. 19.

2 Kings 23. 5.

CHAP. IV.

Of the Sun.

THe Sun and Moon are first named and distinguished from the rest; with them perhaps this kind of Idolatry began, before it came to be apply'd to any of the other Stars; for the most ancient mention of it, (which is by *Job* a Neighbour to the *Chaldæans*) we find these two only named: That the *Chaldæans* esteemed these the principal is confirmed by R. *Maimonides,* who saith, *They held the rest of the seven Planets*

Cap. 31. v. 26.

Mor. Ne.

to be Gods, but the two Luminaries the greatest. But of these (adds *Maimonides*) they held the Sun to be the greatest God. What he farther relates in confirmation hereof, out of the Books of the *Sabæans* concerning *Abraham*, and the like, was delivered formerly. Of the *Assyrian* Idols dedicated to the Sun, *Macrobius* mentions three, *Adad*, *Adonis* and *Jupiter Heliopolites*.

More. Ne.

Adad signifieth one; this God they adore as most powerful, but they joyn with him a Goddess named Atargates, ascribing to these two an absolute power over all things; by these they mean the Sun and the Earth; that hereby they understand the Sun, is manifest, for the Image of Adad is very fair and hath beams bending downwards, to shew that the Power of Heaven consists in the beams of the Sun, sent down upon the Earth. The Image of Atargates hath beams erected, to shew that the Earth produceth all things by the power of the beams sent from above: Thus *Macrobius*; but whereas he saith that *Adad* signifieth one, either he himself is mistaken, or his Text depraved, for (as Mr. *Selden* observes) with the *Syrians*, and *Chaldæans* or *Assyrians*, *Chad*, from the Hebrew *Achad*, signifieth one; but *Adad* or *Adod* which in the Scripture is *Hhadad*, is of a different spelling; *Drusius* reads (in *Macrobius*) *Hhada*, which signifies *One* in *Syriack*. Of this Idol perhaps is the Prophet *Isaiah* to be understood, *they that sanctifie and purifie themselves after One in the midst of the Gardens*, dedicated to that Idol behind the Temple; *Subintelligendum enim Templum, pone Templum*, saith *Joseph Scaliger*.

Saturn. 1. cap.

Cap. 66. v. 17.

Adonis is derived from *Adon*, *Lord*. That *Adonis* is the Sun (saith *Macrobius*) is not doubted, upon view of the Religion of the Assyrians, with whom *Venus Architis* (now worshipped by the Phenicians) and *Adonis* were held in great veneration: For the Naturalists Worshipped the Superiour Hemisphere of the Earth, in part whereof we dwell, by the name of *Venus*, the inferior they called *Proserpina*. Hereupon among the Assyrians or Phoenicians the Goddess is introduced mourning, because the Sun in performing his annual Course passeth thro' the 12 Signs of the inferior Hemisphere; for of the Signs of the Zodiack, six are esteemed *superior*, *six inferior*; and when he is in the inferior, and consequently makes the days shorter, the Goddess is believ'd to mourn, as if the Sun were snatch'd away by death for a time, and detained by *Proserpina* the Goddess of the inferior part, and of the *Antipodes*: Again, they conceive that *Adonis* is restor'd to *Venus* when the Sun surmounting the six Stars of the inferior Order begins to illuminate our Hemisphere, and lengthen the light and days.

Saturn. 1. 21.

Saturn. 1. 17.

The last is *Jupiter Heliopolites*; the Assyrians (saith the same Author) under the name of *Jupiter Worship the Sun* (whom they style Διὶ ἡλιοπολίτῃ) *with extraordinary Ceremonies*: The Image of this God was taken from a Town in Ægypt, named Heliopolis *also, at what time Senemus, perhaps the same as Senepos, Reign'd over the Ægyptians; it was brought thither by Oppias Ambassador of Delebois King of the Assyrians, and by the Ægyptian Priests, the chief of whom was Parmetis, and having been a long time kept by the Assyrians, was afterwards removed to Heliopolis (in Ægypt) the reason of which, and why being carried out of Ægypt it was brought back into the place where now it is, and where it is Worshipped with Rites that are more Assyrian than Ægyptian, I forbear to relate*, as being nothing pertinent to our purpose. That this Jupiter *is the same with the Sun, appears as well by their Religious Rites, as by the fashion of the Image, for its being of Gold* (of which Metal *Maimonides* describes those Telesmes to have been which the *Chaldæans* made to the Sun) *and without a Beard, is sufficient Argument hereof. The right hand is lifted up, holding a Whip like a Charioteer, the left holds a Thunderbolt and some Ears of Corn, all which denote the consociate powers of* Jupiter *and the Sun. Moreover the Religion of this Temple is excellent for Divination, which is ascribed to the power of* Apollo, *who is the same with the Sun: Likewise the Image of the Heliopolitane God is carried on a Bier, as the Image of the Gods are carried at the Solemnity of the Games of the* Circensian *Gods; Many Nobles of that Country follow, their Heads shaved, they themselves pure by a long Chastity; they are driven by Divine inspiration, not as they will themselves, but whither the God carries them. This God they consult even absent, by sending Table-books Sealed up, and he writes back in order to the Questions inserted in them: Thus the Emperor* Trajan *being to go out of that Country into* Parthia *with his Army, at the request of his Friends zealous in this Religion, who having had great experiments in this kind, perswaded him to enquire concerning the success of his Expedition, proceeded with Roman prudence, lest there might be some deceit of Man in it, and first sent the Tablebooks Sealed up, requiring an answer in writing: The God commanded Paper to be brought, and ordered that it should be sent to him blank, to the astonishment of the Priests.* Trajan *received it with admiration, for that he also had sent a blank Table-book to the God. Then he took another Table-book, and wrote in it this Question, whether having finished this War, he should return to* Rome; *This he Sealed up; The God commanded a Centurial Vine, one of those Gifts that were in the Temple, to be brought, and to be cut into two pieces, and wrapt up in a Napkin and sent. The event appeared manifest in the death of* Trajan, *his Bones being brought back to* Rome: *For by the Fragments, the kind of Reliques* (his Bones) *by the token of the Vine, the future chance was declared.* Hitherto *Macrobius*.

To these add *Bell* or *Belus* a name tho' more peculiar to the Supreme Deity, yet common to many of the *Chaldæan* Gods, and among others to the Sun, as *Servius* witnesseth. *In Punick Language* (saith he) *God is named* Baal; *but amongst the Assyrians he is called* Bell, *and by a certain mystical reason*, Saturn *and the Sun*.

In Æneid. 1.

CHAP. V.

The Chaldæan *Worship of the Moon.*

THe Moon was Worshipped by the *Chaldæans* under many names, all which are Feminine; and the greater part answerable to those of the Sun (last mentioned) which seems to confirm what R. *Maimonides* delivers of them, that *they held the seven Planets to be Gods and Goddesses, Male and Female, Married to one another*.

Pag. 18.

Now the *Chaldæans* (or rather they who first Translated the *Chaldaick* Learning into Greek) among other names applyed to the *Sun* those of

Jupiter

Jupiter and *Adonis*, in like manner did they give to the *Moon* the correspondent Attributes of *Juno* and *Venus*.

To *Juno* belong *Ada* and *Belta*, for so interpreted by *Hesychius*; a *Ada*, *Juno*, with the *Babylonians*; b *Belthes*, *Juno*, or *Venus*. Both which are doubtless no other than the Feminine names answerable to *Adad* and *Bell*, two names of the Sun. That by *Juno* Mythologists sometimes understand the Moon, the Learned c Mr. *Selden* confirms by the old Form of incalation which the *Roman* Priests used at the Nones of every Month, *dies te quinque calo Juno novella* (or *covella, Cœlestis*) to this *Juno* perhaps may more properly be referred what *Julius Firmicus* applies to the Air; The *Assyrians* (saith he) *ascribed the Principality of the Elements, to the Air, the Image whereof they Worshipped, styling it by the name of* Juno *or* Venus *the Virgin; whom the Quires of their Priests Worshipped with effeminate Voices and Gestures, their skin smoothed, and their habit after the fashion of Women*; thus he, but that the *Assyrians* worshipped the Element of Air is not elsewhere easily found; what he adds concerning their immodest Rites, seems rather of Affinity with those of *Venus*, as described by other Authors.

To *Venus* (taken for the Moon) belong the names *Mylitta* and *Alilat*. They *learnt* (saith *Herodotus* speaking of the *Persians*) *of the Assyrians and Arabians to Sacrifice to* Urania: *the Assyrians call* Venus Mylitta, *the Arabians* (our *Sabæans*) Alilat. Thus *Herodotus*; who indeed seems to make this *Mylitta* distinct from the Moon, (of whom he had spoken a little before) but that by *Alilat* was meant no other, is evident from its Etymology from *Lail* Night. The Ancients (saith *Sihal Assemon*) *among many other false Gods, Served one* whom they called Alilath, *and affirmed that she is the Moon, as being the Mistris and Queen of the Night*.

margin: a In Ada, b In Belthes. c De diis Syr. Lib. 1.

CHAP. VI.

The Chaldæan *Worship of the Planets*

THe rest of the seven Planets (as a *Maimonides* saith) they held to be Gods also. To *Saturn*, whom *Diodorus* (if the Text be not depraved, which I suspect) affirms they held to be the chiefest of the five, they gave the common name of *Bell*. *Eusebius* in the 28th year of *Thara*; *Belus the first King of the Assyrians died; whom the* Assyrians *styled a God*; others call him Saturn; and Servius cited elsewhere, b *In the* Punick Language God is named Baal; *but among the* Assyrians *he is called* Bell, *and by a certain Mystical Reason*, Saturn *and the Sun*. c Whence *Theophilus* Patriarch of *Antioch, some Worship* Saturn *as a God; and call him* Bell, *and* Baal; *this is done chiefly by those who dwell in the Eastern Climates, not knowing who* Saturn *is, and who* Belus.

Some conceive that the more particular name of this Planet was *Chium* or *Remphan*: of which the Prophet *Amos*, *but ye have born the Tabernacle of your* Moloch *and* Chiun *your Images, the Stars of your God which ye made to yours selves*: Which Text St. *Stephen* renders thus, d *Yea, ye took up the Tabernacle of your God* Remphan,

margin: a Mor. Ne. b In Æneid. lib. c Ad Antolic. lib. 3. Chap. 5. d Acts 6. 43.

Figures which ye made to Worship them; what is the Hebrew *Chiun*, the Greek renders *Remphan*. By *Chiun Aben Ezra* understands the Planet *Saturn*, whom *Plautus* also, as *Petitus* observes, calls *Chiun* : *Rephan* (as *Kircher* attests) is used in the *Coptick* Language for the same Planet.

Of *Jupiter* (having spoken already in treating of *Bell* and the Sun, to both which this name was applied,) there is little more to be said.

Mars (as the Author of *Chronicon Alexandrinum* relates) was first owned as a Deity by the *Assyrians* : *the* Assyrians, saith he, *were the first who did erect a Column to* Mars, *and adored him as a God*; They gave him the common name of *Belus*, whence the *Babylonian Belus* is by *Histiæus* interpreted Ζεὺς ἐνυάλιΘ *Jupiter Martius*.

But a more particular name of *Mars* was that of *Azizus*, under which he was worshipped together with *Mercury* in the Temple of the Sun at *Edessa*, a City of *Mesopotamia*. They who inhabit *Edessa* (saith *Julian*) *a Region of a long time Sacred to the Sun, place together with him in the Temple* Monimus *and* Azizus. *That by* Monimus *they understood* Mercury, *by* Azizus, Mars, and *that both these were Assessors to the Sun*, *Julian* acknowledgeth to have learned of his Master *Jamblicus*.

Some there are who refer the Idol *Negal* (brought by the *Samaritans* out of *Assyria*) to this Planet, for the Rabbies fancy this Idol to have been in the form of a Cock : Now the Cock being * Sacred to *Mars*, and *styled his Bird in regard of his Courage*, † hence they infer that *Mars* was represented under that form, as *Venus* under that of the Hen by the Idol *Succoth Benoth*.

*margin: 2 Kings 17. 30. * Aristoph. † Aristoph. Scal. Kircher.*

Venus was Worshipped by the *Assyrians* and *Chaldæans* under many names : Three of which we find in *Hesychius* : The first *Belthes* (or rather *Belta*) which he interprets *Juno* and *Venus*. This was a name common to the Moon also, and spoken of formerly.

The next *Delephat*, a name more appropriate to *Venus* than the former, as appears by its Etymology, from the Syriack word *Delpha*, coition.

The last *Myleta*, as *Hesychyus* reads, who adds, the *Assyrians* (so called) *Urania*. *Herodotus* writes it *Mylitta*: *They Learned* (saith he, speaking *of the* Persians) *from the* Assyrians *and* Arabians, *to Sacrifice to* Urania : *The* Assyrians *call* Venus Mylitta, *the* Arabians Alilat. Of which two names, tho' *Alilat* (as was observed heretofore) was given to the Moon also; yet that of *Mylytta* seems peculiar to *Venus*, it being no other (as *Scaliger* observes) than the plain *Syriack* Word *Mylidtha*, generative or prolifick : *Venus genetrix*. With this Etymology well suit the Rites belonging to the Idol; of which thus *Herodotus*: *The* Babylonians *have one abominable Law, every Woman of that Country, must once in her life sit in the Temple of* Venus, *and accompany with a Stranger. Some of the Richer sort disdaining to associate themselves with the rest of ordinary quality, are carry'd thither in covered Chariots, and stand before the Temple, a Train of Attendants coming after them; the greater part do in this manner; there are Women sitting in the Temple of* Venus *Crowned with Garlands of Flowers, some coming, others going: There are also several Passages distinguished by Cords, which guide the strangers*

margin: Lib. 1.

[Eeee 2]

gers to the Women; of whom they made choice as they best like; *No Woman being once set there, returns home, until some Stranger have cast Money in her lap, and taking her aside, lain with her. The Stranger who offers this Money must say, I Invoke the Goddess* Mylitta *for thee; the* Assyrians *call* Venus Mylitta; *the Money she must not refuse whatever it be; for it is Sacred. Neither may the Woman deny any Man, but must follow him that first offers her money, without any choice on her part. Assoon as she has lain with him, and performed the Rites of the Goddess, she returns home, nor from thenceforward can be allured by any price whatsoever. Such as are handsome are the soonest dismiss't; but the deformed are forced to stay longer before they can satisfie the Law; sometimes it happens that they attend a whole year, or two, or three in expectation.* Hitherto *Herodotus,* of which Custom some interpret the Words of the Prophet *Baruch* concerning the *Chaldæan* Women, *The Women sit in the ways girded* (or rather surrounded) δεσμεναι χοινια) *with Rushes and burnt Straw; and if one of them be drawn away and lie with such as come by, she casteth her Neighbour in the Teeth, because she was not so worthily reputed, nor her Cord broken.*

2 Kings 17. 30.

To these add *Succoth benoth,* an Idol made by the Men of *Babylon*: the signification of the Word being *the Tents of the Daughters.* Some conceive that hereby were meant those Tents or Partitions by Cords described by *Herodotus,* in which the Women sate to perform the Rites of *Venus Mylitta*; *Venus* being, as Mr. *Selden* is of Opinion, derived from *Benoth*: but from the Words of the Sacred Text, it is manifest, that by *Succoth Benosh* was meant rather an Idol, than Temple or Tents. The Rabbies fancy it to have been in form of a Hen and Chickens; For as they called a Hen Succus, *that is covering,* so they called Hens Succoth, *as brooding and covering,* and Benosh *they Interpreted her Chickens, which she useth to cover with her Wings.* Whence Kircher expounds it of *Venus Mylitta.*

Radak.

CHAP. VII.

Of the other Stars.

2 Kings

NOr were the Planets only but the Signs, and all the rest of the Stars esteemed Gods by the *Chaldæans*: for they burnt Incense *to the Mazaloth, and to all the rest of the Host of Heaven. Mazal* is a Star: they called the Signs the twelve *Mazaloth*: the Zodiack the Circle *Mazaloth*; and sometimes changing ת into ר *Mazaroth*; the Septuagint renders it μαζυρωθ, which *Suidas* interprets, *the Constellations called* ζωδια, *Signs.* This agrees with what *Diodorus* reports of the *Chaldæans*, that *they held the principal Gods to be* 12, *to each of which they attributed a Month, and one of the Signs of the Zodiack.*

Lib. 1.

That they worshipped the rest of the fixed Stars as Gods also, is imply'd by the Sacred Text last cited, which adds, *and to all the Host of Heaven*; and is more expresly asserted (among others) by *Diodorus,* who in his account of their Doctrine affirms, that as they called the Planets *Interpreters,* so of the other Stars, they called *some the judges of all things, others consiliary gods; as we shall shew more particularly, when we come* to speak of their Astrology: Neither is it to be doubted, but that as they owned some of the fixed Stars by these common Titles of Dignity *Judges* and *Counsellors,* so to the principal of them they attributed particular names and Idols, as well as to the Planets. And since the *Chaldaick* Polytheism was not (like that of the *Greeks*) founded upon an imaginary Mythology, (tho' later Writers treat of it after the same manner) but had reference to the Celestial Bodies, which they Worshipped under several Names and Idols; it is no less probable than Consonant to the Chaldaick Doctrine, that those other Assyrian Idols, (*Ashim, Nibhaz, Tartak, Adrammelek, Anammelek, Nisroch,*) mentioned in the Scripture, were of the same kind with the rest, and belonged to several other of the Stars; but this conjecture is not easily evinced, in regard that there is little extant of those Idols more than the bare mention of their names.

Lib. 1.

CHAP. VIII.

Of Fire.

THere are who reckon the Elements among the Gods which the *Chaldæans* worshipped: That they had a particular Devotion to the Fire, is certain; by it as some conceive they represented the supreme God; as others, the Sun; the ground of which Analogy we deliver'd formerly.

Concerning this Idolatry of the *Chaldæans* there is a memorable passage related by *a Rufinus*; *The Chaldæans in the time of* Constantine *the Great Travelled all over the Earth to shew all Men that their God excelled all other Gods, for they destroyed all the Statues of other Gods by their Fire; at length coming into* Ægypt, *and making this Challenge, the Ægyptian Priests brought forth a large Statue of* Nilus, *filling it with water, and stopping up the holes it had (which were many) with Wax, so artificially, that it kept in the Water, but could not hold out against the Fire.* b *Suidas* relates this something differently, as performed by a Priest of *Canopus,* who taking off the head of an old Statue, put it upon a water-pot, which (stopping the holes with wax) he painted over, and set up in the room of *Canopus.*] *The Chaldæans began the Contest with much rejoycing, and put fire round about the Statue; the wax melted, the holes opened, the water gushing forth, put out the fire, and the Chaldæans were laughed at for their God.*

a Hist. Ecclesiast. lib. 2.

b In voce Κανωπ G.

CHAP. IX.

Of the Air and Earth.

OF the Air thus *a Julius Firmicus*: *The Assyrians ascribed the Principality of the Elements to the Air, the Image whereof they Worshipped, stiling it by the name* Venus *the Virgin; whom the Quires of their Priests Worshipped with effeminate voices and gestures; their skins smoothed, and their habit after the fashion of Women.*

a De error. profan. Relig.

As for the Earth, b *Macrobius* saith, *They worshipped the Superior Hemisphere of it, in part whereof*

b Saturn. lib. 1. cap. 21.

whereof we dwell, by the name of Venus; the inferiour Hemisphere of the Earth they called Proserpina; more of this Mythology, rather Phœnician than Assyrian, and perhaps more Græcian than either, see in *Macrobius.* Thus much concerning the Doctrine of the *Chaldæans.*

THE SECOND BOOK.
Of the Persians.

BEyond *Chaldæa*, to the South, on one hand lies *Persia*, on the other, *Arabia.* Philosophy (or Learning) was communicated to both these Countries by their Neigbours, the *Chaldæans.* *Zoroaster*, saith *a* Plutarch, instituted Magick among the Chaldæans, *in imitation of whom, the Persians had theirs also.* Persia is the most considerable Kingdom of *Asia*; bounded, on the North, by *Media*, on the East by *Cilicia*, on the West, by *Susiana*; on the South, by part of the *Persian* Gulf.

a De Isid.

THE SIXTEENTH PART.
The Persian Philosophers, their Sects and Institutions.

SECT. I.
Of the Persian Philosophers.

CHAP. I.
Of the Persian Zoroaster, *Institutor of Philosophy among the* Persians.

THE *Persian* Learning is generally acknowledged to have been instituted by *Zarades*, *Zaradusht*, or *Zoroaster*: but this name, (as we observed formerly,) seems to have been commonly attributed to such Persons as were eminently Learned. Who therefore this *Zoroaster* was, or *a* about what time he lived, is uncertain. *b Laertius* stiles him a *Persian*; *c Clemens Alexandrinus*, a *Mede*; *d Suidas*, a *Perso-Mede*: whence it may be argued, that he was not of so great Antiquity, as most Authors conceive. For we find the word *Persian* no where used before the Prophet *Ezekiel*; neither did it come to be of any note, until the time of *Cyrus.* The later *Persians*, saith *e Agathias*, affirm, *he lived under Hystaspes, but simply, without any addition. so as it is much to be doubted, nor can it be certainly known, whether* this *Hystaspes were the Father of* Darius, *or some other.* *Hystaspes* the Father of *Darius* was contemporary with *Cyrus*, neither doth it appear that the Persian *Zoroaster* lived much earlier.

a Agath.
b In Proem.
c Strom. lib.
d Zor.

e Lib. 2.

But at what time soever he lived, saith *f Agathias, he was the Author, and Introducer of Magical Religion among the Persians, and changing their old Form of Sacred Rites, he Introduced several Opinions.* So likewise *g* the *Arabick* Historiographer, *Zaradusht not first Instituted, but Reformed the Religion of the Persians and Magi, it being divided into many Sects.*

f Loc. cit.
g Elm.

A fabulous Tradition of the occasion and manner thereof related by the *Persians* themselves, receive from *h Dion Chrysostom.* They say, *that through love of Wisdom, and Justice, he withdrew him from Men, and lived alone in a certain Mountain; That afterwards leaving the Mountain, a great fire coming from above, did continually burn about him; That hereupon the King, together with the Noblest of the Persians came nigh him, intending to pray to God; that he came out of the Fire unharmed, appeared propitiously, bidding them be of good cheer, and Offered certain Sacrifices, as if God had come along with him into that place; that from thenceforward he conversed not with all men, but with such only as were naturally most addicted to truth, and capable of the knowledge of the Gods, whom the Persians called Magi.*

h Borislhen.

To this Persian *Zoroaster i Suidas* ascribes, *Of Nature, four Books; of precious Stones, one; Astroscopick Apotelesmes, five; k Eusebius,* a *Sacred Collection of Persicks*, which by the Fragments he cites, seems to have treated of the *Persian Religion.* These some attribute to the *Chaldæan Zoroaster*; others, to some other, nor any with greater certainty that the rest.

i In Zor.
k Præp. Evang. l. 1. c. 7.

CHAP. II.
Of Hystaspes, *as a great improver of the* Persian *Learning.*

THe Doctrine of the *Persian Magi* was much augmented by *Hystaspes.* He was (according to *a Herodotus*) of *Achæmenia*, a Region of *Persia*, Son of *Arsames*, or, (as other Editions) *Arsases*; he lived in the time of *Cyrus*, whose Dream concerning *Darius*, the eldest Son of *Hystaspes*, prognosticating his being King of *Persia*, together with the discourse betwixt *Cyrus Hystaspes* concerning it, is related by *b Herodotus.* *Darius* the Son of this *Hystaspes* was born in the 4165th year of the *Julian* period, and was almost twenty years old a little before *Cyrus* died. About the same time also *c Hystaspes* and *Adusius* joyning together, Conquered all *Phrygia* bordering upon the *Hellespont*, and taking the King thereof, brought him Prisoner to *Cyrus.*

a Lib. 1.

b Loc. cit.

c Xenoph. Institit. Cyr. lib. 7.

Hystaspes was, (as *d Ammianus Marcellinus* affirms) *a most wise Person*, who adds, *that boldly penetrating into the inner parts of the upper India, he came to a woody Desart, whose calm silence was possessed by those high Wits the Brachmanes. Of these he learnt the discordant Concord of the motions of the Stars, and of Heaven, and of pure Rites of Sacrifices*, which, returning into *Persia*, he contributed as an addition and complement to *Magick.*

d Lib. 23.

CHAP.

CHAP. III.

Of Osthanes, who first introduced the Persian Learing into Greece.

[a Lib. 30. 1.] THE *Persian* Learning, (as *a Pliny* affirms,) was first communicated to the *Græcians* by *Osthanes*. *The first*, saith he, *that I find to have commented on this Art* (Magick) *is Osthanes who accompanied* Xerxes *King of the Persians in the War which he made upon Greece.* Xerxes set out from *Susa* upon this Exposition in the beginning of the fourth year of the 74 Olympiad, though *Diodorus Siculus*, confounding the Transactions of two years in one, relates this done in the first [b Lib. 7. c. 21.] year of the Olympiad following. *b Herodotus* affirms, that this Provision was in making the three whole years before this year; but with a note premised in the precedent Chapter, which cannot consist with the exact course of the times. For, saith he; From the subduing of *Ægypt*, he was full four years in gathering an Army, and in making his Preparations, and in beginning of the fifth year, he began to March with a huge Army; for indeed he set out from *Susa*, in the beginning of the 5th year, not from his subduing [c Lib. 2. c. 20.] of *Ægypt*, but from his coming to the Crown. So that both *c Justin* out of *Trogus*, and *Orosius* following him do unadvisedly attribute five years: but most absurdly, doth *Julianus*, in his first Oration of the praises of *Constantine*, say that he was ten years in making this preparation. But [d In Βασιλικῳ.] more Ingenuous than all those, (yet not over exquisite in his account) (is *d Libanius*, where he saith, that, between *Darius* and *Xerxes* there was ten years time spent in make this preparation against *Greece*, since we have formerly shewed out of *Plato*, that from the Fight at *Marathon*, to the Fight of *Salamis*, which was fought in the first year of the 75 Olympiad (almost a full year after *Xerxes* his setting out from *Susa*) there were only ten years run out.

Hence it appears that *Pythagoras* and *Plato* who were precedent in time to *Osthanes*, and in their Travels conversed with the *Persian* Magi, were not fully acquainted with the depth of their Sciences, or else being more reserved forbore to communicate them, otherwise than as intermingled with those which they appropriated to themselves.

[e Loc. cit.] *e Pliny* adds, that *Osthanes*, whilst he accompanied Xerxes *into* Greece, *scattered the seeds as it were of his portentous Art* (Magick) *wherewith he infected the World, all the World whithersoever he went*; and *'tis certain, that this Osthanes chiefly made the Græcians not desirous, but mad after his [f Laertius proœm.] Art.* Thus *Pliny*, alluding to *Goetick Magick*, of which the Author of the *f* Treatise μαγικὸν, [g Cont. gent.] asserts the *Magi* to have been *wholly ignorant.* And *g Arnobius* affords him a better Character, *that he was chief of the Magi, both for Eloquence and Action; that he made address to the true God with due Veneration; that he knew the Angels did wait upon the true God,* and the like.

By *Osthanes* (as we said) the *Persian* Learning was brought into *Greece*, and therefore we shall not proceed farther in our enquiry after the professors of it among the *Persians*.

SECT. II.
The Institution, and Sects of the Persians.

CHAP. I.
The Persian Magi their Institution.

ALL Professors of Learning among the *Persians* were termed Magi. *a Laertius.* [a Proœm.] *It is said that Philosophy had its Original from the Barbarians, since among the Persians were Magi; among the Babylonians, or Assyrians, the Chaldæans; and Gymnosophists among the Indians; among the Celtæ and Gallatæ, where those who were called the Druides, or Seninothei, as* Aristotle, *in his Treatise* Magicum, *and* Sotion, *in the 23d Chap. of his Succession, affirms,* Hence, *b* [b In voce Mag.] *Suidas, Magi among the Persians were Philosophi and Philothei.* But their principal Study and Employment consisting in Theology and Religious Rite, *Magus* is more frequently Interpreted a *Priest.* Among the *Persians*, saith *Porphyrius, those wise Persons who were employed about the Divinity, and served him, were called Magi; this is the signification of* Magus *in their Dialect.* And *d* Apuleius, Magus *in the Persian Lan-* [d Apolog. 1.] *guage, signifieth the same as* Priest *in ours.* Hesychius, *A Worshipper of God, and a Theologist, and a Priest, is by the Persians styled* Magus.

Some conceive they were so termed by *Zoroaster*, at their first Institution. *e* Suidas, *Zoro-* [e In Zor.] *aster the Perso-Mede, who first began the name of* Magi *celebrious among them.* *f* Others derive [f Salmas.] the Word from *Mog* a Sirname of *Zoroaster*, or from *Mije Gush*, one that hath *short ears*, affirming that *Zoroaster* was such.

The Author of the *Arabick History* relates, that the *Religion of the Persians being before Zoroaster's time divided into many Sects, he reformed it;* Agathias, *that he changed their old Form of Sacred Rites, and introduced many new Opinions, and was the Author and Introducer of Magical Religion among the Persians.*

k The *Magi delivered their Learning succes-* [k Ammian. Marcellin.] *sively in their Families from one Age to another,* whence, *after the Succession of many Ages, at this present,* saith *Ammianus Marcellinus, a multitude sprung from one and the same Race, is dedicated to the Rites and Worship of the Gods. For, increasing by degrees, they grew at last to the largeness and name of a compleat Nation dwelling in Towns not fortified with any Walls, and, being permitted to use their own Laws, they were honoured in respect of their Religion.*

The Country of the Magi in *Persia*, is mentioned by *l Clemens Alexandrinus*, who takes no- [l Strom. 6.] tice of three wonderful Mountains in it. And *Solinus* mentions, as belonging to them, the City *Pasargada.* *Suidas* and *Cedrenus* call them *Magusæans*, and affirm, that they were called *Magog* by those of their own Country.

So great was the esteem which the Magi had among the *Persians*, that *Cicero* saith, the Kings of *Persia*, before they undertook the Government, were always *initiated in the Sacred Mysteries*

Mysteries of the Magi, which *q* Plato describes thus: *At fourteen years old they whom they call the Royal Pædagogues take charge of the Youth. These are four Men chosen out of the most excellent of the Persians, in the prime of their age. The most wise, the most just, the most temperate, and the most valiant. The first of these teacheth him the Magick of* Zoroaster *the Son of* Horomases *(this is the Service of the Gods) and teacheth him also the Royal Institutions.* Dyon Chrysostom saith, that *the Magi were admitted to the King's Counsels, and were Assessors with him in Judicature, as being well acquainted with the natures of things, and knowing after what manner the Gods are to be Served. All publick Affairs* (saith Agathias) *were managed by their direction and advice. They adjudged Rewards or Punishments.* Dion elsewhere relates, that *Cambyses, upon his Expedition into Ægypt, resign'd the Government of the Persians into the hands of the Magi.* ſ Constantius Manasses styles them *the Guardians of the Royal Palaces*, and *t* Pliny, speaking of Magick, saith, *it grew up at last to so great height, that even at this day it is exceeding prevalent with many Nations, and in the East it beareth Sway over the King of Kings*: King of Kings was the proper Title of the *Persian* Monarch.

q Alcib.

t 30. 1.

CHAP. II.

The Sects, Discipline and Manners of the Magi.

EUbulus, *a* who wrote the History of Mythra in many Volumes, affirms, that amongst the Persians there were three kinds of Magi: the first, who were the most Learned and Eloquent of them, did eat no other food but Meal and Oyl. Thus *Eubulus* cited by St. *Hierom.* More of the distinction of the Magi into three Sects we meet not elsewhere; but, probably, it had reference (as among the *Chaldæans*) to their several Studies, of which hereafter.

b Dinon and *Aristotle*, or rather the Author of the Treatise of Magick cited by *Laertius*, relate of the Magi, that *they renounce rich attire, and to wear Gold. Their Rayment is white upon occasion, their Beds, the ground, their Food, nothing but Herbs, Cheese, and Bread; instead of a Staff, they carry a Cane, in the top whereof they put their Cheese, which as occasion served they did eat.*

They had one their Society chief among 'em, called by *Zozomene, the Prince of the Magi.*

d Their chief Employment was Religious Worship, they being conceived to be the only Persons whose Prayers the Gods would hear.

e They made discourses concerning Justice, and esteemed it impious to burn the Bodies of the dead, and Lawful to lie with a Mother or a Daughter, as *Solion* in his 23d Book.

ƒ *Herodotus* saith, *they differ, as from others, so from the Ægyptian Priests, in this, that these pollute themselves with the death of nothing but their Sacrifices, whereas the Magi, with their own hands, kill any thing, except a Man and a Dog; yea they esteem it a great exploit, if they have killed very many Ants, or Serpents, or other creeping or flying things.*

a D. Hieron. adverſ. Jovin. li. 2.

b Laert. in proœm.

d Laert.

e Laert. proœm.

ƒ Lib.

THE SEVENTH PART.

The Doctrine of the Persians.

THat which is delivered to us of the *Persian* Doctrine and Opinions, is so little and so imperfect, as it will not easily admit of being knit together by any Method; yet, in regard of the near affinity their Learning is conceived to have had with the *Chaldæans*, we shall observe the same course in collecting and digesting the few remains of it: First, to alledge what concerns their Theology and Physick; Next, their Arts of Divination; Thirdly, Their Religious Worship and Rites, particularly termed Magick; And lastly, to give a Catalogue of all their Gods.

CHAP. I.

Theology and Physick.

THat the *Persian* Magi were not unacquainted with Theology and Physick, is confirm'd by *a* Suidas. *Magi*, saith he, *among the Persians are Philosophers and lovers of God.* b Laertius affirms, *they discoursed concerning the Substance and Generation of the Gods*; and *c* Dion Chrysostom, *that they were skilful in Natures.*

d Zoroaster *the Magus in his Sacred Collection of Physicks, saith expresly thus.* 'God hath 'the Head of a Hawk: he is the first Incorrupti-'ble, Eternal, Unbegotten, Indivisible, most like 'himself, the Charioteer of every good, one that 'cannot be Bribed: the best of things Good; the 'wisest of things Wise: Moreover, he is the Fa-'ther of Equity and Justice: self-taught, Natu-'ral and Perfect, and Wise, and the sole Inventor 'of Sacred Nature.

e Plutarch *relates of* Zoroaster, *that he divided all things into three kinds. Over the first kind he conceived* Horomazes *to be President, the same whom the Oracles call* the Father. *Over the last*, Arimanes; *over the middle kind*, Mythra, *whom the Oracles call* the second Mind. *And that* Horomazes *made himself 3 times as big as the Sun (who in the Persian Language is called* Cyrus.) Mythra *made himself twice as big (as the Sun) who was next to* Horomazes. *To which these Platonick assertions are correspondent, That all things are about the King of all, and that all things are for him. That he is the cause of all good things, The second is employed about the secondary things, The third is employed about the third kind of things. The three parts into which* Zoroaster *and* Plato *divided all things, are these*; *The first is Eternal; The second had a beginning in Time, but is Eternal; The third is corruptible.* Thus *Pletho* citing *Plutarch*, whose own words are these.

ƒ *Some are of Opinion there are two Gods, one opposite in operation to the other*; *one, working good, the other ill. Others call him who is the good, God, the bad, Dæmon: of this Opinion was* Zoroaster *the Magus, whom they report to have preceded the*

a Voc. Magi
b In Proœm.

d Euseb. Præp. Evang.

e Pletho in Orac. ad fin.

g Isid. & Oſirid.

the *Trojan War* 5000 *years. This Zoroaster declared the names of the good, to be* Oromazes, *of the bad,* Arimanius, *adding, that, of sensible things the one did most resemble Light, and Knowledge, the other Darkness and Ignorance. Wherefore the Persians call* Mythra *the Mediator. He further taught, that, to one, we ought to offer votives and gratulatory Sacrifices, to the other, averruncative and dismal Oblations. For, pounding a certain Herb called* Omomi, *in a Mortar, they invoke* Hades *and Darkness, then mixing it with the blood of a slain Wolf, they carry it forth and throw it into a place where the Beams of the Sun come not: for, of Plants, they hold, that some belong to the good God, others, to the ill Dæmon, and that of Animals, some, as Dogs, Birds, and Porcupines, belong to the good, the aquatile, to the bad; for which reason they esteem him blessed who killed most of that kind.*

g *Loc. cit.*

g *They likewise relate many fabulous things concerning the gods, of which kind is this I will alledge, That* Oromazes *was produced of purest light,* Arimanes *of darkness, and that these two war against one another; That* Oromazes *made six Gods, The first, of Benevolence; the second of Truth; The third, of Equity; the rest of Wisdom, Riches, and Pleasure, which good things are attendant upon the Maker; That then* Oromazes *tripled himself, and removed himself so far from the Sun, as the Sun is distant from the Earth, and adorned the Heaven with Stars, appointed one the Dog-Star as Guardian and Watch for the rest; That he made* 24 *other gods, and put them in an Egg, and that* Arimanius *having made as many more they broke the Egg. Whence it comes, that good is intermingled with ill. That the fatal time approacheth, in which these shall be destroyed by Famine and Pestilence, and* Arimanius *utterly destroyed, and the Earth made even and smooth; There shall be one Life and one City (or common Society) of all men living, and one Language.*

CHAP. II.

Arts of Divination.

AMong the other parts of the *Persians* Learning, are to be reckoned their Arts of Divination and *Prædiction*, which a *Laertius* affirms were *practised by the Magi*. b *Cicero* adds, that *they assembled in (fana) in Temples or consecrated places, to consult about Divination.*

a *In Proæm.*
b *De Divinat.*

Hence c *Strabo* saith, that, *by the Ancients, Diviners were much esteemed, such as among the Persians, were the Magi, and Necromancers, and Lecanomancers, and Hydromancers:* d *Ælian*, that *the Wisdom of the Persian Magi, besides all other things which it was lawful for them to know, did consist also in Divination;* And e *Lucian* styles the Magi a *kind of Persons skilful in Divination, and dedicated to the Gods.* Of their Divination f *Cicero* giveth an instance concerning *Cyrus*; g *Ælian*, another concerning *Ochus*.

c *Lib.*
d *Var. Hist.*
e *Macrob.*
f *Divinat. lib.* 1.
g *Var. Hist.* 2. 17.
b *Lib.* 2.
i *In Zor.*

Among other kinds of Divination, h *Velleius Paterculus* affirms, they foretold by the marks of the Body. They seem to have been skilful likewise in Astrology, for i *Suidas* ascribeth to the *Persian Zoroaster* five Books of *Astroscopick Apotelesmes*. That they were also consulted concerning the presignification of Prodigies, is manifest firm the Relation of k *Valerius Maximus*, concerning that which hapned to *Xerxes*.

k *Lib.* 1. *c.* 6.

CHAP. III.

Of the Religious Rites, or Magick of the Persians.

THe chief Science and Employment of the *Persian Magi*, was termed *Magick*, from the Professors, *Magi*, and is defined by *Plato*, a *the service of the Gods*, called also Μαγαγίεια. The *Magi*, saith b *Laertius*, are employed in the *Service of the Gods, and about Sacrificing and Praying, as being the only Persons whom the Gods will hear.* So c *Dion Chrysostom*, the *Persians call them Magi, who are skilful in the Worship of the Gods, not like the Greeks who, ignorant of the meaning of the Word, call them so who were skilful in Goetick Magick*; of which that the *Persian Magi were ignorant,* d *Laertius* alledgeth the Testimonies of *Aristotle*, in *his Treatise entituled Magick*, and *Dinon* in the first Book of his Histories.

a *Alcibiad.*
b *Proæm.*
c *Borysthen.*
d *Proæm.*

As concerning their Religious Rites, e *Herodotus* and f *Strabo* affirm that *they had no Temples, Altars, or Images, but did impute it to madness in such as had;* the reason whereof g *Herodotus* conceives to have been, *for that they did not believe as the Grecians, that the Gods were of humane form;* or as i *Cicero, for that they conceived the Gods, to whom the whole World was but a Temple or House, could not be shut up within Walls;* upon which ground the *Magi perswaded* Xerxes to burn the *Grecian Temples*.

e *Lib.*
f *Lib.*
g *Loc. cit.*
h *De leg.* 2.
i Ἀνθρωποφύεις, *i. e.* ἀνθρωπόμορφοις.

But *Strabo* frequently elsewhere mentions their *Temples, Altars, and Images*; whence it may be argued, either that in the time of *Herodotus* they had not any, and that *Strabo*, in affirming the same, with *Herodotus*, is to be understood only of their Primitive Institution, which when the *Macedonians* afterwards Conquered them, became corrupted with *Græcian* Rites; Or that there were different Sects among them from the beginning; whereof some allowed Altars, Images, Temples, others disallow'd them.

Herodotus and *Strabo* further add, that *they Sacrificed in High Places*; their Rites and Sacrifices *Herodotus* describes thus. *When they go about to Sacrifice, they neither erect an Altar, nor kindle Fire, nor use Libation, nor Flutes, nor Garlands, nor Cakes, but when any Man intends to Sacrifice to one of these Gods, he drives the victim to a clean place, and invocates that God; his Tyara being Crown'd with Myrtle; 'tis not Lawful for him who Sacrificeth to pray for good things for himself alone, but he must pray for all Persians in general, and in particular for the King: for in praying for all Persians he includes himself. Having cut the victim into little pieces, he boils the flesh, and strewing soft herbs, especially* Trifoly, *he lays the flesh on them; the Magus standing by sings a Theogonal Hymn; for this they conceive to be a powerful incantation. Without a Magus it is not lawful for them to Sacrifice. Soon after, he who Sacrificeth taks the flesh and disposeth of it as he pleaseth.*

m *Strabo* adds, that *when the Magus who declares the Sacrifice, hath distributed the pieces of flesh, every one taking his piece they depart home, leaving no part for the Gods; for they say the Gods require*

m *Lib.* 15.

require nothing but the Soul of the victim: Yet some (it is said) lay part of the Fat upon the Fire.

CHAP. IV.

The Gods of the Persians.

a Lib. 1.
b Lib. 15.

HErodotus *a* and *b* Strabo reckon the Gods of the *Persians* thus, *Jupiter*; the *Sun*; the *Moon*; *Venus*; the *Fire*; the *Earth*; the *Winds*; the *Water*. *c* Laertius not so fully, the *Fire*, the *Earth*, and not the *Water*.

c Proæm.

By *Jupiter*, as *d* Herodotus and Strabo affirm, they understood *the whole Circuit of Heaven*: *Agathias* adds, that *they Worshipped* Jupiter *under the name of* Bell, which sufficiently argues they derived this God from the *Chaldæans*.

d Loc. cit.

To the *Sun* (as both *e* Herodotus and Strabo witnesses) *they Sacrificed*: Strabo adds, that *they called him* Mithra. This was the greatest of their Gods, as *Cyrus* (introduced by *f* Xenophon) acknowledgeth; swearing by him: *Hesychius* likewise affirms it was the greatest of their Gods, and that the greatest Oath which the King himself took was by *Mithra*.

e Loc. cit.

f Oeconom.

They represented him with the face of a Lion, in a *Persian* Habit, with a Tiara, holding with both hands a Bull by the Horns, which seemed to strive to get from him; signifying, that the Moon begins to receive her Light from him when she leaves him.

g Porphyr.
in antr. Nymph.

g Zoroaster *first among the Persians* (as Eubulus *affirms, who wrote many Volumes of the History of* Mithra) *did Consecrate a natural Cave in the Mountains next* Persia, *in honour of* Mithra, *the King and Father of all: signifying by this Cave the World framed by* Mithra; *by the other things disposed within it, in fit distances, the Elements and Quarters of the World.* The Cave of *Mithra* is mentioned by many others.

In *the Mithrean Rites* (for so *Lampridius* terms them) *Celsus* (cited by *h* Origen) saith, *the twofold Motion of the Stars, Fixed and Erratick, was represented; and the passage of the Soul through them: in sign whereof there was set up a high pair of Stairs, having seven Gates, the first of Lead, the second of Tin, the third, of Brass, the fourth of Iron, the fifth of Leather, the sixth of Silver, the seventh of Gold; the first belongs to Saturn, the Lead signifying the slowness of that Planet; the second to Venus, to whom they compare Tin, for its brightness and softness; the third to Jupiter, as being most solid, with Brazen Steps; the fourth to Mercury, for they hold him to be the stoutest undertaker of all Businesses, Cunning, and Eloquent, the fifth to Mars, in regard of its unequal and various commixture; the sixth to the Moon, of Silver; the seventh to the Sun, whose colour, as also that of the Stars resembles Gold.*

h Lib. 6. contra Cels.

He who was *initiated into these Rites proceeded*, as *Suidas* relates, *through several degrees of contumely. i Nonnus upon Gregory Nazianzen* saith *twelve k and of pain, as burning, blows, and the like, by which trial he was to give testimony of his Sanctity, and of his being void of Passion.*

i In Stelicut.
k Gregor. Naz.

Of the Rites of the Moon there is nothing said in particular.

Concerning those of *Venus*, *l Herodotus* saith, *They Sacrifice also to* Urania, *which they learnt of the Assyrians and Arabians; the Assyrians call* Venus, Militta, *the Arabians* Alilat, *the Persians* Metra. And as *Militha* in Syriack signifieth *generative, prolifick, Venus genetrix*, so *mader*, or *mater*, with the *Persians* signifies, (as *Raphelengius* observes) a *Mother*. This perhaps was that *Mother of the Gods*, which *Cicero* affirms to have been *Worshipped by the Persians, Assyrians, and all the Kings of* Europe *and* Asia, *with great Devotion.*

l Lib. 1.

The Fire, n *Julius Firmicus* saith, *they preferred before all the other Elements*; o *Agathias affirms they learnt to Worship it of the Chaldeans*: *p* Strabo relates, that *in* Cappadocia *there was a great number of Magi, called* Pyrethi, *and many Temples of the Persian Gods; they kill not the Victim with a Knife, but strike it down with a Club: Here also there are Pyrethia Chappels, in the midst of which is an Altar, covered with great store of Ashes; where the Magi preserve a fire that never goes out; and coming in every day sing almost the space of an hour, holding a bundle of Rods before the Fire,* (with which, as *q* M. Selden observes, they stirr'd it up whilst they sung,) *Their Heads are covered with Woollen Tiara's, which being tied on both sides hide their Lips and Cheeks*: Thus *Strabo*, an eye-witness. These *Pyratheia* (or as *Suidas* terms them *Pyreia*) were those *sempiternal Fires of the Magi* mentioned by *r Ammianus Marcellinus*. Neither in Temples only did they use these Rites, but in private Caves, where *s Julius Firmicus* reports, they Worshipped the Fire with many extraordinary Ceremonies, as among other things using to pronounce these Words, Μιϰλαβῶ μυσαϰῶ ὁ ϰλοπίης σύνδιε παϊδες ἀγάνα. Nor did this Worship extend to Fire only, but *t to all things that resembled it*, as *Dyonisius* reports, whereof, *u* Strabo instanceth *the Pyropus*. *Julius Firmicus* adds, that *they called the Fire Mithra*, by which, as also by their Worshipping it in Caves, it is manifest, that (sometimes at least) they took it for the Sun, their greatest Deity.

n De error. prof. Relig.

p Lib. 15.

q De Diis Syr. synt. 2. c. 7.

r Lib.
s Lib. 1.

t Perieg.
u Lib.

Concerning the Worship of the *Earth* and *Winds* nothing particular is delivered; That of the *Water* was performed in this manner, *x They go to a Lake, River, or Spring, where they make a Trench, and kill a Victim; taking care that none of the Blood come at the Water; then laying Myrtle and Laurel on it they burn it with Rods and making some Prayers, sprinkle Oyl mixed with Milk and Honey, not in the Fire or Water, but on the Earth.*

x Strab. lib. 15.

Other Gods the *Persians* had, though not reckoned among these, whether as less principal, or of later date; of these are mentioned by the same Author (*Strabo*,) and by others, *Anaitis* (Venus) *Amandatus Sacæa, Sandes,* and *Nannæa* (Diana.)

Hitherto of the Doctrine of the Persians.

Ffff   THE

THE THIRD BOOK.

Of the Sabæans.

ARABIA the Noblest Peninsula (if we may so term it) of *Asia*, is terminated by the Persian, the Indian, and the Red Sea, except that on one side it is conterminous to *Syria*, by which vicinity was occasioned so near a correspondence betwixt those Nations, that as the Chaldæan Learning overspreading all *Mesopotamia*, *Syria*, and *Assyria*, did on one side extend to their Neighbours the *Persians*, so on the other it reached to the *Arabians*, from which nearness perhaps it was (not only of Situation, but Religion and Opinions,) that *Pliny* useth their names promiscuously, calling a great part of *Mesopotamia*, *Arabia*; and the *Arabians* themselves *Syrians*. And the later Eastern Writers (especially the *Arabians*) under the appellation of *Chasdim* or *Chaldanin* (*Chaldæans*,) comprehended not only the *Babylonians* but the *Nabathæans*, *Charanæans*, and *Sabæans*, as (among others) *Muhamed Isacides* takes *Chasdanin* and *Nabathæa* to be synonimous, and *Ahmedus*, to his Book concerning the Religion of the *Sabæans*, gives this Title, *Of the Rites of the Charanean Chaldæans commonly known by the name of Sabæans*, he adds; *commonly known by the name of Sabæans*; because the *Sabæans* being the most considerable of these, they likewise under the appellation of *Sabæans* included all the rest; even the *Chaldæans* of *Mesopotamia*: using the terms of *Chaldæa* and *Sabæa* no less promiscuously than *Pliny* those of *Arabia*, *Mesopotamia*, and *Syria*: for which R. *Maimonides* (who doth so throughout all his Writings) gives this reason, because the Doctrine of the *Chaldæans* extend thither, and that the Religion of all these Nations was the same.

Now whereas *Arabia* is commonly distinguished into the *Stony*, the *Desart*, and the *Happy*, we here mean not that part which is styled the *Desert*, lying on the North of *Sabæa*, and first planted by *Ismael*, whose Posterity afterwards, having learned the Language of the *Sabæans* (*Arabick*) were called *Arabians* also, or more properly, *Hagarens*, as descended from *Hagar*, and *Aarab Mastiaarabah*, *the made Arabians*, (that is, made such by cohabitation and conversation with the true *Arabs*,) but those other true *Arabs* the Inhabitants of the *Desart* and the *Happy*, whereof the former came from *Nebaiothus*, Son of *Ismael*, and are by *Pliny*, *Strabo*, and *Ptolomy* called *Nabatæans*, as the Country it self *Nabatæa*, the later from *Saba*, Son of *Chus*, the Son of *Cham*, after whom stiled *Sabæans* (as the Country *Sabæa*) and (in distinction from *the made Arabians* of *Arabia*, the *Desert*) the native *Arabians*. The *Charanæans* mentioned together with these, were the Inhabitants of *Cara*, a City of *Arabia*, mentioned by *Pomponius Mela*, whose Inhabitants the *Carræans*, *Pliny* placeth next the *Sabæans*, distinct from *Hara* or *Caran* in *Mesopotamia*.

THE EIGHTEENTH PART.

The Sabæan Philosophers

CHAP.

Of the Institutors of the Sabæan Sect.

CONcerning the first Institutor of Learning and Religion among the *Sabæans*, there is not any certain agreement of Authors. *Patricides*, an *Arabian* Writer, attribute; this Invention to *to a certain Persian named Zoroaster, contemporary with Tera Father to Abraham*; *Zerodast* and *Zoroaster* are the same; wereby it appears, that *Patricides* means one of these two *Zoroasters*, whereof one was the first Author of Sciences among the *Chaldæans*, the other introduced the same Sciences among the *Persians*; and tho' he calls this *Zerodast* a *Persian*, yet by the Antiquity of the Time in which he conceives him to have lived, it is probable he rather intended the *Chaldæan*.

Others (adds *Patricides*) are *of Opinion that Tachmurat King of Persia gave beginning to this Religion*. The same perhaps whom *Elmacinus* (another *Arabian* Historian,) calls *Tachurith*: *Others* (saith he) *conceive that the Religion of the Sabæans was manifested by a certain King of the Persians, whose name was* Tachurirth.

Elmacinus mentions another *Persian*, to whom the same invention was attributed, *In those days* saith he, *came forth* Nazarib *a Persian, who, as is reported, was Author of the Religion of the Sabæans*.

Others (continues *Patricides*) *derive the Infancy of the Sabæans From a certain Græcian named* Juvan *or* Javan, *Son of* Berkley, *and him they will have to be of the City of* Zaiturra, *which was built in* Attica. Thus he; where *Hottinger* for *Berkley* reads, *Mercolim*, *Mercury*, confirmed by *Elmacinus* upon the same Subject. *Others*, saith he, *affirm, that the Religion of the* Sabæans *was brought forth by a man whose name was* Juvan, *Son of* Markoli, *a* Græcian, *who first found out the Science of the Stars*.

To these *Patricides* adds the Opinion of some *others, who held that the Authors of this Sect were some of those who were at the building of the Tower of* Babel. Thus the *Arabians*.

Some attribute the Institution of the *Sabæans* to *Cham*, Son of *Noah*, who, *being banished from his Father's sight*, *fled thither*, and (to use the words of *Lactantius*) *setled in that part of the Earth, which is now called* Arabia. *This was the first Nation that knew not God, because the principal Founder thereof had not received the Worship of God by Tradition from his Father*: Thus *Lactantius*, with whom many agree in attributing the Original of Idolatry to *Cham*, and to his Son *Chus* the first Planter of *Chaldæa*, from whose Son *Saba* the *Sabæans* were named, and, upon this ground, some have laboured to prove *Cham* and *Chus*, to be the same with the first and second *Zoroasters*, of which formerly.

Others (as *Damascene*) ascribe the Original of Idolatry to *Zerug*. *Epiphanius*, and the Author of the *Chronicon Alexandrinum*, affirm that *Hellenism* began in the time of Zerug. This *Hellenism* some conceive the same with the *Sabæan* Superstition; what the *Greek* Fathers call *Hellenism*, the Rabbins term *Goth*, the *Arabians*, *Algiabeleiton*, the time of Ignorance and Paganism. And tho' to determine any thing of those early and obscure times be very difficult, yet we cannot doubt, but that the Idolatrous Worship of Fire, and of the Sun (ascribed to the *Sabæans*) was of great Antiquity among them, since mentioned by the most ancient Authors, *Job*, who lived near them, as appears by the inroad which ^a the *Sabæans* made upon him. ^b If I beheld (saith he) *the* ^c *Sun when it shined, and the Moon walking in brightness, and my heart hath been secretly enticed, or my mouth hath kissed my hand, this also were an Iniquity to be punished by the Judge, for I should have denied the God that is above*; where by kissing of the hand is implied the ancient manner of Veneration.

a Chap. 1. v. 15.
b chap.
c The word is Ur, which signifieth as well Fire.

CHAP. II.
Others of the Sabæan Sect.

That *Tera* Father of *Abraham* was bred up in this Doctrine, might be conjectur'd from *Joshua* 24. 2. where he is reckoned among those *that Served Strange Gods*. *Philo* terms him an Astronomer, one of those that are versed in Mathematicks.

a De Nobilit.

Of *Abraham* Son of *Terah*, ^b R. *Maimonides* expresly saith, *It is well known that our Father Abraham was Educated in the Faith of the Zabians, who held, there is no God but the Stars*; indeed ^c *Berosus* acknowledgeth *he was skilful in the Cœlestials*, and *Eupolemus*, cited by *Eusebius*, ascribes to him the Invention of *Astrology* and *Chaldaick*. The *Zabians* themselves in their Annals give this account of his departure out of *Chaldæa*. *Abraham*, say they, *being Educated in* Ur, *but dissenting from the Vulgar, and asserting that there was another Creator besides the Sun, they began thus, and objected against him, and among other Objections, they alledged the evident and manifest operations of the Sun in the World*; but Abraham answered them, *You are right, which Sun is like the Ax which is in the hand of him that striketh therewith*. Then they recite some of the Objections which he brought against them, and at last, they say, *that the King cast him in Prison, nevertheless, he persisted in Prison to oppugn them; whereupon, the King fearing lest he might do some hurt to his Kingdom, and seduce Men from their Religion, Confiscated all his Estate, and Banished him to the utmost Borders of the East*. Thus the *Zabians*: from which Relation *Josephus* differs not much, who saith, that ^c *Abraham first undertook to convince the received Erroneous Opinion of Men, concerning the Deity, and that he first taught and proved that there is but one God, but seeing the Chaldæans and Mesopotamians begin to Mutiny against him for it, he thought it Expedient to forsake the Country*.

b Mor. Nev.

c Joseph. Antiquit. 1. 8.

d Mor. Nev.

e Lib. 1. c. 3.

The Rabbinical Traditions, are more particular herein: R. *Solomon Hiarki* reports from an Ancient Commentary, that *Tera* fell out with his Son *Abraham*, in the Presence of *Nimrod*, for breaking his Idols, and that *Abraham* was thereupon cast into a Fiery Furnace. *Moses Gerundensis* confirms the same Story, but R. *Chain* relates it otherwise; *Abraham*, saith he, met with a Woman holding a Dish in her hand, and the Woman asking him whether he would offer any thing to the Gods, he took a Staff, and broke the Images which the Woman had, and threw away the Staff; his Father coming thither at the same time, demanded what was the matter? *Abraham* answered, she had asked him to make an Offering, and upon his answering that he would first eat something, there arose a dispute betwixt them: but his Father urged that the business was otherwise, and that he was heard to say many reproachful things of *Nimrod*. The Controversie was brought before *Nimrod* the King of *Babel*: he commanded *Abraham* to Worship the Fire that was set before him; *Abraham* answered, If so, then adore you the Water, Water which quencheth Fire. *Nimrod* said to him, Worship the Water; *Abraham* answered, If so, Worship the Clouds which distil the Water. *Nimrod* said, Then Worship the Clouds; whereupon *Abraham*, If it be so, then the Wind is to be Worshipped, which agitates and scatters the Clouds. Again, *Nimrod*, Worship the Wind; but *Abraham*, If so, then is Man much more to be worshipped who understands the Wind. At length *Nimrod* growing angry, You talk, saith he, idly, I Worship none but the Fire, into the midst of which I will cast thee. Let the God whom thou Worshippest come and free thee by his right hand. *Aran* stood by and talked; they asked of which Opinion he was; he answered, if *Abraham* get the better, I will be for him, if *Nimrod* for *Nimrod*. After *Abraham* had gone into the Fiery Furnace and was freed, they said to *Aran*, of which side art thou; he said, of *Abraham*'s; then they took him, and cast him into the Fire, and all his Bowels were Burned, and he was taken out dead in the Presence of his Father. Thus R. *Chain* but *Cedrenus* affirms, that *Abraham* throwing his Father's Idols into the Fire, his Brother *Aran* endeavouring to Rescue them, was Burned.

The *Arabians* who imitate the Jews in Relations of this kind, and fancy Superstructures of their own upon Fables of the Rabbins, give a further accompt of what happen'd to *Abraham* after his departure from *Nimrod*, as appears by a fragment of a Mahumetan Writer, of which I shall cite only so much as most particularly concerns the *Sabæans*. *Edris*, on whom be Peace, was the first who after Enoch, the Son of Seth, the Son of Adam, on whom Peace, wrote with a Pen. This thing afterwards Edris taught his Sons, and said to them, O Sons, know that you are Sabæans, learn therefore to read Books in your Youth. Now Sabæans are Writers, of whom the High, he means, *Mahumet*, said (Alk. Sur. 2.) *The Sabæans and the Nazarenes*. The Author adds, that *they ceased not to possess the Books of Seth and Edris by Hereditary Right among themselves, until the times of Noah, and of Abraham, after that the High God aided him against Nimrod, on whom be malediction. But in that day wherein Abraham went out of the Land of Irack, and would go into Syria, into the Land of his Fore-fathers, he went to the Land of Charan, and Ghesira, and there he found a People*

ple of the Zabians, who read old Books, and believed such things as were contained in them. But Abraham said, 'O my God, I did not think that besides my self, and those that are with me, there had been any of the Faithful who believed thee to be One; and God breathed to Abraham this Answer. O Abraham, the Earth is never destitute, but that there are some in it that dispute for God: But God commanded him to call them to his Religion, and he called them, but they would not, saying, how shall we believe thee, when thou readest not a Book? and God sent among them a forgetfulness of those things which they knew of Sciences and Books, for they conceived the Books which they used, to be from God, and some of them Believed, others not. Afterwards the Zabians were divided, and some of them believed, viz. the Barhameans, who did not separate themselves from Abraham of Blessed Memory, but the rest followed their own Religion very eagerly, viz. those who were in the Land of Charan, who went not with Abraham into Syria, and said, we follow the Religion of Seth, Edris, and Noah; Thus, according to Kissæus, the Religion of the Sabæans was the same with that of the Haranæans, or Mesopotamians. What he relates of Abraham's being sent to the Sabæans, is all borrowed from the Rabbinical Traditions.

But that there were anciently Learned Persons in Arabia, skilful in Natural Philosophy, Astronomy, and other Sciences, is manifest from Testimonies far more authentick; (as particularly) from the Discourses betwixt Job and his Friends; of the Arabian Philosophers it is understood, that Solomon's Wisdom is said to have Excelled the Wisdom of all the Sons of the East. Tacitus, describing Judæa, the Land and Bounds to the East are terminated by Arabia. And that the Jews called Arabia the East County is evident from several places in Scripture, as Gen. 10. 30. and 25. 6, 18. Job 1. 3. Judges 6. 3, 1. &c. Pliny also mentions the Magi of Arabia (of whom he instanceth Hippocus.) Ptolomy, the Gulf of the Magi, in Arabia; and Porphyrius (citing Diogenes) relates that Pythagoras (among other Countries to which he Travell'd for Learning) went also to Arabia, and lived with the King there.

30. 1.

CHAP. III.

Their Writings.

THE Sabæans pretended (as was lately shewed out of Kissæus,) to have had the Books of Seth and Edris, and not only those, but some also written by Adam; for the same Author continuing the Story of Abraham's coming among the Sabæans, adds, that aftewards Abraham opened the Chest of Adam, and behold, in it were the Books of Adam; likewise the Books of Seth, and of Edris; as also the names of all the Prophets that were to be sent after Abraham; But Abraham said, Happy indeed are the Lins out of which all these Prophets shall come: And God Breathed to him (this Answer) Thou, O Abraham art the Father of them all, and they thy Children; and for this reason Abraham deserved to be called the Father of the Prophets, upon whom be Peace.

Of the same allay *a* Maimonides conceives the Book of Healings to have been, which was hid by Ezekiel.

a Mor. Nev. lib.

The same *b* Maimonides cites many other Books of the Sabæans, Translated into Arabick, of which the chiefest is entituled, *of the Agriculture of the* c *Nabateans, Translated by* Aben Vachschijah: *full of Idololatrical extravagancies, it treats of the making of* Tisilmenaias, *of the descent of Familiar Spirits, of Conjurations of Dæmons, of Devils, of such as dwell in Desarts* (as Satyrs were thought to do) *many other things it contained very ridiculous, by which nevertheless they conceived that they could confute the manifest Miracles* (of *Moses*, and the Prophets.)

b Mor. Nev. lib.

Another entituled, *the Worship, or of the Worship of the* Nabatæans, out of which, *d* Maimonides cites a Story concerning *Abraham* related formerly.

d Lib.

e The Book Haistanchus, *ascribed to* Aristotle, *but falsly.*

e Maim. Mor. Nev. lib.

f The Book Hattelesmaoth, *of Tsilmenaias*; Buxtorfus renders it, *of speaking Images*; the reason we have given formerly.

f Ibid.

The Book Tamtam.
The Book of Hassearab.
The Book of the Degrees of the Cœlestial Orbs and the Figures that are ascendent in evey degree
Another Book concerning Tsilmenaias, *which also is attributed to* Aristotle.
Another Book ascribed to Hermes.
The Book of Isaak *the Zabian, wherein he argues in defence of the Laws of the* Zabians.
A great Book of the Customs and Particularities of the Law of the Zabians, as of their Feasts, Sacrifices, Prayers, and other things concerning their Beliief: All these (saith *Maimonides*) *are Books which treat of Idololatrical things, and are Translated into the Arabick Tongue.*

Besides these, (as *Maimonides* acknowledgeth,) there are many others, *g* Hottinger cites, (n his own Possession) *A Treatise of* Mahomet *the Elder, Son of* Isaak, who is otherwise called *Abulfark*, the Son of *Abi Jakub*.

g Histor. Oriental. lib. 1. cap. 8.

THE

NINETEENTH PART.

The Doctrine of the Sabæans.

WHat is left to us of the Doctrine of the Sabæans is delivered upon later Authorities, than those from which we have the Chaldaick: and therefore perhaps is but an account of what it was it later times, degenerated from their Primitive Doctrine, which was immediately derived for the Chaldaick. Nor is it impossible, but that this Corruption might be somewhat aggravated by the eager opposition of the Talmudists, and some Arabick Writers that follow them, from whose hands only we receive it. However, we conceive it necessary to be annexed to the former, of which, tho' depraved, it pretends at least to be the continued Succession.

CHAP.

CHAP. I.

Of the Gods and Rites of the Sabæans.

THE [a] Sabæans *held* (as the *Chaldæans*) that the Stars are Gods, but the Sun the greatest God; for they plainly assert, that the Sun Governs the *superiour* and *inferiour* Worlds; [b] and call him the great Lord, the Lord of good. What they relate concerning *Abraham*, refusing to Worship the Sun, is delivered elsewhere, what they further fable of the Patriarchs, that *Adam*, (not being the first Man, but begotten by a Man and Woman) was a Prophet of the Moon, and, by Preaching, perswaded Men to Worship the Moon, and composed Books of Husbandry; That *Noah* was an Husbandman likewise, but believed not in Idols, for which they discommended him in all their Writings; That *Seth* also dissented from *Adam*, as to Worshipping the Moon; see delivered more fully by [c] *Maimonides*.

a Maimon.
b Idem.
c Mo. Nev.

Their Forms of Worshipping these Gods was twofold, daily, and Monthly; the daily, is by *Said Vahed* described thus: *They make the first day Sacred to the Sun; the second to the Moon, the third, to Mars; the fourth to Mercury; the fifth to Jupiter; the sixth, to Beltha Venus; the seventh, to Saturn.*

The description of their Monthly Worship receive from a Ms. of *Mahumed ben Isaac*, cited by *Hottinger*; They begin the year from the Month *Nisan*, of which they keep holy the first, second, and third days; adoring and praying to their Goddess *Beltha*: they go to her Temples, Sacrificing Sacrifices, and burning living Creatures: On the sixth day of the same Month they kill a Bull to their Goddess the Moon; and towards the Evening of the same Day eat it. On the eighth day they keep a Fast, and likewise celebrate (at Night) a Feast in honour of the seven Gods, and of the Dæmons; Offering a Lamb to the God of the Blind (*Mars*:) On the fifteenth day is the Festival of *Sammael*, (by this name the *Talmudists* understand the Devil) Celebrated with many Sacrifices, Holocausts, and Offerings; On the twentieth they visit a *Cænobium* of the *Haranæans*, called *Cadi*, where they kill three Oxen, one to *Saturn*; another to *Mars*, the blind God; the third to the Moon: they kill likewise nine Lambs, seven to their seven Gods (the Planets) one to the God of the Geniusses, and one to the God of the Hours. They likewise burn many Lambs and Cocks. On the 28th day they go into the Temple which they have in the City *Saba*, at a certain Gate of *Charran*, called the Gate *Assarah*; and kill to *Hermes* their God, a great Bull; as also seven Lambs to their seven Gods; one to the God of the Dæmons, and to the God of the Hours, eating and drinking; but they burnt nothing of any Beast that day.

The second Month which is *Jiar*, they begin also with Sacrifices, celebrating the Consecration of *Sammael*, and Feasting; The second day they keep in honour of *Aben Salem*; drinking, and filling their hands with Tamarik and other Fruits.

The 23d day of the third Month they keep in honour of *Sammael*, whom they affirm to be the God that maketh the Arrows fly; the *Cumar*, or Priest, makes an Arrow take fire twelve times, by rubbing another stick against it: the last time he creeps upon the ground, and puts Flax to it; if their Flax kindle, they conceive their Rites well accepted of the Gods, otherwise not.

The fourth Month *Thammuz*, had a peculiar Solemnity about the middle of it, called the Festival *Albukal*, of the *Weeping Women*: The Original of which is thus related by R. *Maimonides*: In the same Book, faith he, they tell a Story of a certain Idolatrous Pseudo-Prophet, named *Thammuz*: who calling upon the King to Worship the seven Planets, and the twelve Signs of the Zodiack, and being by the King put to an ignominious death, the same night in which he was slain, all the Images from all parts of the Earth met in the Palace which was erected at *Babylon* to the great Golden Image of the Sun, suspended betwixt Heaven and Earth: There this Image of the Sun fell down prostrate in the midst, and (all the rest of the Images standing round about it) bewailed *Thammuz*, and began to relate what hapned to him; whereupon the rest of the Images fell a weeping, and lamented all that Night: But assoon as the Morning appeared they all flew away and returned home to their several Temples. Hence came the Custom, that on the first day of the Month *Thammuz* (*June*) they Weep, Lament, and Bewail *Thammuz*. This Custom of *Women-Weeping* for Thammuz, is mentioned also by the Prophet [d] *Ezekiel*, as imitated by the Jews the 29th day of this Month they consecrate to *Sammael*, and to other Gods and Dæmons; Sacrificing nine Lambs to *Hanan*.

d Chap. 8 v. 14.

In the fifth Month, which, as the *Syrians*, they call *Ab*, they press new Wine to their Gods, and give it several Names; this they do the eight first days. They likewise kill a new born Infant to their Gods, which they beat all to pieces; then they take the flesh and mix it with Rye-meal, Saffron, Ears of Corn, Mace, and little Cakes like Figs; they bake this in a new Oven, and give it to the People of the Congregation of *Sammael* all the year long; no Woman eats of this, nor Servant, nor Son of a Bond-woman, nor Man that is Possessed, or Mad.

The Rites of the sixth Month, named *Eloul*, are thus described by the same Author; Three days they boil Water to wash themselves, that they may perform the Rites of *Sammael*, who is the Prince of the Dæmons, and the greatest God; into this water they cast some Tamarisk, Wax, Olives, Spice, &c. and when it is hot, take it before Sun-rise, and pour it upon their Bodies, as an Amulet: The same day also they kill eight Lambs, seven to their Gods, and one to the God *Sammael*; they eat also in their Congregations, and drink every Man seven Cups of Wine; The Prince exacts of every one of them two Drachms to be paid into his Exchequer. On the 26th day of the same Month, they go forth to a Mountain, celebrating the Rites of the Sun, *Saturn* and *Venus*; burning eight Hen-Chickens, eight Cocks, and as many Hens; He who made a Prayer and Request to Fortune takes an old Cock, or a Cock-chicken, to the wings of which he ties two strings; and sets their ends on fire,

fire, and gives up the Chickens to the Goddess Fortune; If the Chickens are quite consumed by the fire, his Prayer is heard, but if the fire of those strings goes out before the Chickens be quite burnt, the Lord of Fortune accepts not his Prayer, nor Offerings, nor Sacrifices. On the 27th and 28th they have their Mysteries, Sacrifices, Offerings, and Holocausts to *Sammael*, (who is the greatest Lord:) to the Dæmons and Geniusses, which compass them about, defend them, and bestow good Fortune on them.

The seventh Month, which the *Syrians* and *Sabæans* call *the first Tischri*, hath peculiar Rites, thus described by the same Author: About the middle of this Month, they burn Meat to the Dead, in this manner: Every one buys of every sort of Meat that is in the Market; of all kind of Flesh, Fruits, green and dry; they likewise dress it several ways; all which they burn in the night time to the Dead, and wish it the Thigh-bone of a Camel; they also pour mixed Wine upon the Fire for the Dead to drink.

In the eighth Month, which is called the *later Tischri*, they Fast on the 21st day, and so on, for nine days, the last of which is the 29th, this day they do in honour of the Lord of Fortunes, &c.

The ninth Month, called *the first Canun*, is chiefly Sacred to *Venus*; on the fourth day they set up a Tabernacle, which they call the Bed of *Beltha*; adorning it with several Leaves, Fruits, Roses, &c. Before they offer their Sacrifices of Beasts and Birds, they say, Let these Sacrifices be Destined to our Goddess *Beltha*; this they do for seven days: all which time they burn many Beasts to their Gods and Goddesses. On the 30th day of the same Month, the Priest sits in an high Chair, to which he gets up by nine steps; and, taking in his hand a stick of Tamarisk, stretcheth it out to them all, and striketh every one of them with it three, or five, or seven times. Afterwards he makes a Discourse to them, wherein he declareth to the Congregation their continuance, multitude, places, and excellency above all other Nations; he likewise tells them the largeness of their Empire, and the days of their Reign: After which he comes down from the Chair, and they eat of the things Offered to the Idols, and drink: and the Prince exacts of every one of them this day two Drachms to the Exchequer.

The tenth Month, called *the other Canun*, seems particularly devoted to the Moon; for on the 24th day thereof is the Nativity of the Lord, that is, the Moon, at what time they celebrate the Rites of *Sammael*, Sacrificing, and Burning fourscore living creatures, four-footed Beasts and Fowl; they also eat and drink and burn *Badi*, sticks or canes of Palm, slender at the bottom, to their Gods and Goddesses.

In the eleventh Month, *Sijubat*, they Fast seven days together, beginning from the 9th day, upon which they proclaim a Fast to the Sun, who is the great Lord, the Lord of Good: They eat not in all this time any thing of Milk; nor drink Wine; nor pray during this Month to any but *Sammael*, the Genii, and Dæmons.

In the Month *Adar*, which is the twelfth and last, they Fast also to the Moon, especially on the 28th day; The President distributes a Barley Loaf to the Congregation, in honour of *Mars*; the Prince exacts of every one of them towards his Exchequer two Drachms.

CHAP. II.

Other Rites of the Sabæans *contrary to the Levitical Law.*

a R. *Maimonides* mentions several other Rites of the *Sabæans*, which were expresly repugnant to the Levitical Law, adding, that *he was acquainted with the Reasons and Causes of many of the Laws of* Moses, *by means of knowing the Faith, Rites, and Worship of the* Sabæans. The Examples alledged by him and others are these. a *Mor. Nev.*

They Offered Levened Bread only, and, *for their Offerings, made choice of sweet things only, and anointed their Sacrifices with Honey;* prohibited, *Levit.* 2. 11.

They used on a certain day to feed on Swines Flesh; prohibited, *Levit.* 11. 7.

They held it unlawful to kill and feed on some Beasts permitted to the Jews; as the Ox, which *Maimonides* saith, *they much honoured for the great Profit he brings by Agriculture, and therefore held it unlawful to kill him, as also the Sheep;* neither of which they killed.

Some of the Sabæans *worshipped Devils, believing they had the Shapes of Goats, and therefore called them* Seirim; On the contrary, the Levitical Law prohibits *to Offer Sacrifices* le Seirim, *unto Goats*, that is to say, Devils, appearing in the Forms of Goats, *Levit.* 17. 7.

Though they did abominate Blood, as a thing exceeding detestable, yet they did eat it, believing it to be the Food of the Dæmons, and that he that did eat of it should become a Brother, or Intimate Acquaintance of the Dæmons, insomuch that they would come to him and tell him future Events; prohibited, *Levit.* 17. 10, 23.

They worshipped the Sun at his Rising, for which Reason, as our Rabbins exresly teach in Gemara, saith *Maimonides*, Abraham *our Father designed the West for the place of the* Sanctum Sanctorum, *when he Worshipped in the Mountain* Moria. Of this Idolatry they Interpret what the Prophet b *Ezekiel* saith, of the *Men with their Backs toward the Temple of the Lord, and their Faces towards the East, Worshipping the Sun towards the East.* b *Chap.* 8. 16.

Mahummed Ben-Isaac relates, that *they shaved themselves with Razors, and branded themselves with fire*; *there were also Married Women among them who shaved themselves in the same manner*; forbidden, *Levit.* 21. 5.

c They had a Custom of *passing their Children, as soon as they were born, through the Fire, which they Worshipped, affirming, that such Children as were not so passed would die.* This was also expresly forbidden by the Levitical Law. c *Maimon. Mor. Nev.* 3.

Another most obscene Custom they had of Engrafting, described by d *Maimonides*, to which he conceives the Levitical Prohibition to allude. d *Mor. Nev.* 3. 37.

Others there are of the same kind cited by the same e Author, who concludes, that *as concerning those particular Laws, the reasons whereof are concealed* e *Mor. Nev.* 3. 44.

concealed, and the benefit unknown to me, it proceeds from hence, that the things which we hear are not such as those which we see and perceive with our eyes. For this cause, those things concerning the Rites of the Sabæans, which I have learnt by hearing, and from their Writings, are not so solid and certain, as with those who have seen them practised, especially seeing that their Opinions and Sects perished 1000 years since, and their Names were abolished.

With the *Sabæans*, we conclude the *Chaldaick* Philosophy.

THE CHALDAICK ORACLES OF ZOROASTER. and his Followers.

The most considerable Remains of the *Chaldaick* Philosophy are those Oracles which go under the name of *Zoroaster*; some indeed condemn them as suppositious, *a* Forged by some *Pseudo-Christian Greek*; (perhaps the rather, because *b* The followers of *Prodicus* the Heretick, boasted that they had the secret Books of *Zoroaster*.) But this seems less probable, in regard they lie dispersed among several Authors; nor are they to be neglected, in that they have been held in great veneration by the Platonick Philosophers. Which sufficiently also argues, that they are none of the Writings charged by *c Porphyrius* upon the *Gnosticks*, as *Forged by them under the name of* Zoroaster, since those (as he acknowledgeth) were by the Platonick Philosophers, (of whom he instanceth *Plotinus* and *Amelius*) rejected and *demonstrated to be spurious and suppositious*.

a Beza.
b Clem. Strom.
c Vit. Plot.

Some argue that they are not *Chaldaick*, because many times accommodated to the Greek Style; but there are in them many so harsh and exotick Expressions, as discover them to be Originally foreign; and where they agree in Terms with that which is proper to the Greek Phylosophy, we may say of them as *d Jamblichus* upon another occasion, (On the Writings that go under the Name of *Hermes Trismegistus*) as they are published under the name of *Zoroaster*, so also they contain the Doctrine of *Zoroaster*, though they frequently speak in the Style of the Greeks; for they were Translated out of *Chaldee* into *Greek* by Persons skilful in the Greek Philosophy.

d De Myst. Ægypt.

To perswade us that they are genuine, and not of Greekish Invention, *e Mirandula* professeth to *Ficinus*, that he had the *Chaldee* Original in his possession, *I was* (saith he) *forcibly taken off from other things, and instigated to the Arabick and Chaldaick Learning by certain Books in both those Languages, which came to my hands, not accidentally, but doubtless by the disposal of God, in favour of my Studies. Hear the Inscriptions, and you will believe it. The Chaldaick Books, (if they are Books, and not rather Treasures) are the Oracles of Aben Esra, Zoroaster and Melchior, Magi: in which those things which are faulty and defective in the Greek, are Read perfect and entire. There is also,* (adds he) *an Exposition by the Chaldæan Wise-men upon these Oracles, short and knotty, but full of Mysteries; There is also a Book of the Doctrines of the Chaldaick Theology, and upon it a Divine and Copious Discourse of the Persians, Grecians and Chaldeans*; Thus *Mirandula*, after whose Death these Books were found by *Ficinus*, but so worn and illegible that nothing could be made out of them.

e Epist.

Further, to confirm that these Oracles were (as we said) Translated into Greek by Persons skilful in the Greek Phylosophy, let us call to mind that *Berosus f* introduced the Writings of the *Chaldæans* concerning Astronomy and Philosophy among the Grecians; and that *Julian* the Son, a *Chaldaick* Philosopher, *g* wrote the *ur-gick Oracles in Verse*, and other Secrets of that Science: and probably, if these were no part of that *Chaldaick* Learning which *Berosus* first rendred in *Greek*, they yet might be some of the *Theurgick Oracles* (for such the Title speaks them) of *Julian*; for some of them are cited by *Proclus* as such. From the account which *Mirandula* gives of those in his Possession, to which were added a Comment, and a Discourse of the Doctrines of the *Chaldaick* Theology, it might be conjectured, that what is delivered to us by *Pletho* and *Psellus*, who, besides the Oracles, give us a Comment on them, together with a Chaldaick Summary, was extracted out of that Author which *Mirandula* describes to have been of the same kind and Method, but much more perfect and Copious.

f Joseph. contra opian 1.
g Suid. in voce Julianus.

This Title of *Oracles* was perhaps not given to them only Metaphorically to express the Divine Excellence of their Doctrine, but as conceived indeed to have been delivered by the Oracle it self; for *h Stephanus* testifies that *the Chaldæans had an Oracle which they held in no less Veneration than the Greeks did theirs at* Delphi: This Opinion may be confirmed by the high Testimonies which the Platonick Philosophers give of them, calling them *i the Assyrian Theology revealed by God, and the Theology delivered by God.* And *Proclus* elsewhere having cited as from the Gods, one of those Oracles which speaks of the Ideas, a (Platonick Doctrine) adds, *that hereby the Gods declared the Subsistence of Idea's*, and acquiesceth as *satisfied that the Gods themselves ratifie the Contemplation of* Plato.

h De urb.
i Procl. in Tim.

Some of these Oracles which escaped the Injuries of Time, were first published by *Ludovicus Tiletanus*, Anno 1563. at *Paris*; together with the Commentaries of *Gemistus Pletho*, under the Title of *the Magical Oracles of the Magi descended from* Zoroaster, the same were afterwards Translated and put forth by *Jacobus Marthanus*, and lastly, together with the Comment of *Psellus* also, by *Johannes Opsopæus* at *Paris*, 1607.

These by *Franciscus Patricius* were enlarged with

with a plentiful Addition out of *Proclus, Hermius, Simplicius, Damascius, Synesius, Olympiodorus, Nicephorus,* and *Arnobius*: encreasing them *k* by his own account, to 324. and reducing them for the better perspicuity to certain general heads, put them forth, and Translated them into Latin, *Anno* 1593.

They were afterwards put forth in Latin by *l Otho Hurnius, Anno* 1619. under the Title of *The sincere Magical Oracles of* Zoroaster *King of* Bactria, *and Prince of the Magi*; but *Heurrius* under the pretence of *m putting them into good Latin,* as he calls it) *and polishing them with a rougher File,* hath patch'd up and corrupted what *Patricius* delivered faithfully and sincerely, endeavouring to put these Fragments into a continued Discourse, which in themselves are nothing coherent, but dispersed among several Authors.

Patricius indeed hath taken much Learned pains in the Collection of them; but with less Regard to their Measures and Numbers, and, (as from thence may be shown) sometimes of the Words themselves: nor is there any certain means to redress this Omission by comparing them with the Authors, out of which he took them, since few of those are extant, neither doth he, (as he professeth to have done) affix the Names of the Authors to the several Fragments, except to some few at the beginning; However, we shall give them here according to his Edition, that being the most perfect; together with such Additions as we meet withal elsewhere, and some conjectures to supply the defect we mentioned.

And whereas many of these Oracles are so broken and obscure, that they may at first sight seem rather Ridiculous than Weighty, yet he who shall confider, that as many of them as are explained by *Pletho, Psellus,* and others, would without those Explications seem no less absurd than the rest, but being explained, disclose the Learning of the *Chaldæans* in a profound and extraordinary manner, will easily believe all the rest, even those which appear least intelligible) to be of the same kind, and consequently ought no more to have been omitted than any of the rest,

Φ P.

ΦP. ΠΑΤΡΙΚΙΟΥ | FRANCISCI PATRICII
ΤΑ ΤΟΥ ΖΩΡΟΑΣΤΡΟΥ ΛΟΓΙΑ. | ZOROASTRI ORACULA

ΜΟΝΑΣ, ΔΥΑΣ, ΚΑΙ ΤΡΙΑΣ. | MONAS, DYAS, TRIAS.

Ψελ. Ὅπε παλεική μονάς ἐςι.
UBi paterna Monàs est. *Psel.*

Δαμ. Ταναή ὅτι μονάς ἣ ϑ δύο γεννᾶ.
Ampliata est Monàs, quæ duo generat. *Dam.*

Πρχ. Δαμ. Δυάς γὸ ῶρα τῷ ϑ κάθηται, καὶ νοεραῖς ἀςεράπ]ε τομαῖς.
Duitas enim apud hunc sedet, & intellectualibus *Proc. Dam.* fulget sectionibus.

Καὶ τὸ κυβερνᾶν τὰ πάντα, καὶ τάτίειν ἕκαςον ὁ ταχθέν.
Et gubernare cuncta, & ordinare quodcunque non ordinatum.

Δαμ. Πάντι γὸ ἐν κόσμῳ λάμπει τειάς, ἧς μονάς ἄρχει.
Toto enim mundo lucet Triàs, cujus Monàs est *Dam.* princeps.

Ἀρχὴ πάσης τμήσεως ἥ ϑ ἡ τάξις.
Principium omnis sectionis hic est ordo,

Πρχ. Εἰς τεία γὸ νῦς εἶπε πατρὸς τέμνεσθαι ἅπαντα,
In tria namque Mens dixit Patris secari omnia, *Proc.*

Οὗ τὸ θέλειν κατένευσε, καὶ ἤδη πάντα ἐτέτμητο.
Cujus voluntas annuit, & jam omnia secta fuëre.

Εἰς τεία γὸ εἶπε νῦς πατρὸς αἰδίς,
In tria namque dixit Mens patris æterni,

Νῷ πάντα κυβερνᾶν.
Mente omnia gubernans.

Δαμ. Καὶ ἐφάνησαν ἐν αὐτῇ ἥ τ᾽ ἀρετὴ καὶ ἡ σοφία,
Et apparuerunt in ipsâ Virtus & Sapientia, *Dam.*

Καὶ ἡ πολύφρων ἀτρέκεια.
Et Multiscia Veritas.

Τῇ τῶνδε ῥέει τριάδος δέμας πρὸ τῆς οὔσης,
Hinc fluit Triadis vultus ante essentiam,

Οὐ πρώτης, ἀλλ᾽ ᾗ τὰ μετρεῖται.
Non primam, sed eam quæ mensuratur.

Ἀρχαῖς γὸ τρισὶ ταῖς δὲ λάβοις δωλεύειν ἅπαντα.
Principiis tribus hisce capias servire cuncta.

Ἱερὸς πρῶτος δρόμος, ἐν δ᾽ ἄρα μέσῳ
Ἥλιος, τρίτος ἄλλος, ὃς ἐν πυρὶ τὴν χθόνα θάλπει.

Καὶ πηγὴ πηγῶν, καὶ πηγῶν ἁπασῶν.
Et fons fontium, & fontium cunctorum.

Μήτρα συνέχουσα τὰ πάντα.
Matrix continens cuncta.

Πρχ. Ἔνθεν ἄρδην θρώσκει γένεσις πολυποικίλα ὕλης.
Indè affatim exilit generatio multivariæ materiæ. *Proc.*

Ἔνθεν συρόμενος πρηστὴρ ἀμυδροῖο πυρὸς ἄνθος,
Indè tractus prester exilis ignis flos,

Κόσμων ἐνθρώσκων κοιλώμασι. Πάντα γὸ ἔνθεν.
Mundorum indens cavitatibus. Omnia namque indè.

Ἄρχεται εἰς τὸ κάτω τείνειν ἀκτῖνας ἀγητάς.
Incipit deorsum tendere radios admirandos.

ΠΑΤΗΡ ΚΑΙ ΝΟΥΣ. | PATER ET MENS.

Ψελ. Ἑαυτὸν ὁ πατὴρ ἥρπασεν οὐδ᾽ ἐν ἑῇ
Δυνάμει νοερᾷ κλείσας ἴδιον πῦρ.
Seipsum rapuit pater neque suæ *Psel.* Potentiæ mentali claudens propriam ignem.

Ψελ. Οὐ γὸ ὑπὸ πατρικῆς ἀρχῆς ἀτελές τι τροχάζει.
Non enim a paterno Principio imperfectum quid *Psel.* rotatur.

Πάντα γὸ ἐξετέλεσε πατὴρ,
Cuncta namque perfecit pater,

Καὶ νῷ παρέδωκε δευτέρῳ,
Et menti tradidit secundæ,

Ὃν πρῶτον κληίζεται πᾶν γένος ἀνδρῶν.
Quam primam vocat omne genus hominum.

Πρχ. Πατρογενὲς φάος, πολὺ γὸ μόνος
Ἐκ πατρὸς ἀλκῆς δρεψάμενος νόου ἄνθος.
Patrogenia lux, multum namque sola *Proc* E partis robore decrepens mentis florem.

Ἔργα νοήσας, γὸ πατρικὸς νόος αὐτογένεθλος,
Opera enim intelligens paterna mens è se genita,

Πᾶσιν ἐνέσπειρε δεσμὸν πυριβριθῆ ἔρωτος.
Cunctis inseminavit vinculum igni gravis amoris.

Ὄφρα τὰ πάντα μένῃ, χρόνον εἰς ἀπέραντον ἐρῶντα.
Quo omnia maneant, tempus in interminatum amantia.

Μήτε πᾶσι τὰ πατρὸς νοερῶς ὑφασμένα φέγγη.
Neque omnibus quæ patri mentaliter contexta monstret.

Ὡς ἐν ἔρωτι μένῃ κόσμου ςοιχεῖα μένοντα.
Ut in amore maneant mundi elementa manentia.

Ἔχει τῷ νοεῖν πατρικὸν νοῦν ἐνδιδόναι
Habet ipsa intelligentia paternam mentem indere

Πάσαις πηγαῖς τε καὶ ἀρχαῖς.
Omnibus fontibus & principatibus.

Ἔςι γὸ πέρας τοῦ πατρικοῦ βυθοῦ, καὶ πηγὴ τῶν νοερῶν.
Est enim finis paterni profundi, & fons mentalium.

Μὴ ϑ προῆλθεν, ἀλλ᾽ ἔμενεν ἐν τῷ πατρικῷ βυθῷ,
Neque progressus est, sed mansit in paterno profundo,

Καὶ ἐν τῷ ἀδύτῳ, κατὰ τὴν θεοθρέμμονα σιγήν.
Et in adyto, per Deo-nutriens silentium.

Οὐ γὸ εἰς ὕλην, πῦρ ἐπέκεινα τὸ πρῶτον
Ἑὴν δύναμιν κατακλείει ἔργοις, ἀλλ᾽ ἀνῷ.
Non enim in materiam, ignis trans primus Suam potentiam claudit operibus, sed mente.

Σύμβολα γδ παΐρικὸς νός ἔσπειρε κτ κόσμον.	Symbola enim paterna mens seminavit per mundum
Ὃς τὰ νοητὰ νοεῖ καὶ ἄφραςα καλλύνεται,	Quæ intelligibilia intelligit, & ineffabilia exornat.
Dam. Ὁλοφυὴς μερισμὸς, καὶ ἀμέρεισος.	Tota partitio, & impartibilis. *Dam.*
Νῷ μὲν κατέχει τὰ νοητὰ, αἴσθησιν δ᾽ ἐπάγει κόσμοις.	Mente quidem continet intelligibilia, sensum verò inducit mundis.
Νῷ μὲν κατέχει τὰ νοητὰ, ψυχὴν δ᾽ ἐπάγει κόσμοις.	Mente quidem continet intelligibilia, animam verò inducit mundis.

ΝΟΥΣ, ΝΟΗΤΑ, καὶ νοερὰ

MENS, INTELLIGIBILIA, & Mentalia.

Dam. Καὶ τῇ ἑνὸς νοῦ τῇ νοητῇ.	Et unius mentis intelligibilis. *Dam.*
Psell. Οὐ γὰρ ἄνα νοῦς ὅτι νοητῇ· ὐ χωρὶς ὑπάρχει.	Non enim sinè intelligibili mens est: non seorsum existit. *Proc.*
Τὰ μὲν ὅτι νοερὰ καὶ νοητὰ, ὅσα νοοῦντα νοεῖται.	Quædam sanè sunt mentalia & intelligibilia, quæcunque dùm intelligunt intelliguntur.
Τροφὴ ἢ τῷ νοοῦντι τὸ νοητόν.	Cibus verò intelligenti est intelligibile.
Μάνθανε τὸ νοητὸν ἐπεὶ νόε ἔξω ὑπάρχει.	Disce intelligibile, quandoquidem extra mentem existit.
Καὶ τῇ νῦ, ὃς τὸν ἐμπύρειον κόσμον ἄγει.	Et mentis, quæ Empyreum mundum ducit.
Νοῦ γὰρ νοῦς ἔτιν ὁ κόσμου τεχνίτης πυρός.	Mentis enim mens est quæ mundi est artifex ignei.
Οἱ τὸν ὑπέρκοσμον παΐρικὸν βυθὸν ἴτε νοοῦντες.	Qui supermundanum paternum profundum estis intelligentes.
Ἡ νοητὴ πάσης τμήσεως ἄρχει.	Intelligibilis omnis sectionis princeps est.
Ἔστι γάρ τι νοητὸν, ὃ χρή σε νοεῖν νόε ἄνθει.	Est enim quoddam intelligibile, quod oportet te intelligere mentis flore.
Dam. Ἢ γὰρ ἐπεγκλίνῃ, ὡς ἂν νοῦν, κἀκεῖνο νοήσῃ,	Vel enim inclines, ut mentem, & illud intellexeris. *Dam.*
Ὡς τὶ νοῶν, ὐ κεῖνον νοήσεις.	Ut aliquid intelligens, non illud intelliges.
Ἔστι γὰρ ἀλκῆς ἀμφιφαὴς δύναμις,	Est enim roboris circumquaque lucidi potentia,
Νοεραῖς ςραπῇῃσα τομαῖς, ὐ δὴ χρὴ	Mentalibus fulgens sectionibus, non sanè oportet
Σφοδρότητι νοεῖν τὸ νοητὸν ἐκεῖνο.	Vehementià intelligere intelligibile illud,
Ἀλλὰ νόε ταναᾷ ταναᾷ φλογὶ	Sed mentis amplæ amplà flammà
Πάντα μετρούσῃ, πλὴν τὸ νοητὸν ἐκεῖνο.	Omnia metiente, præterquam intelligibile illud.
Χρεὼ δὴ τοῦτο νοῆσαι· ἢ γὰρ ἐπεγκλίνῃς	Opus ergò est hoc intelligere; nam si inclina. veris
Σὸν νοῦν, κἀκεῖνο νοήσεις ἐκ ἀκλινῶς.	Mentem tuam, etiam illud intelliges non parùm.
Ἀλλ᾽ ἁγνὸν ἐπίστρεφον ὄμμα,	Sed purum converte oculum,
Φέροντα σῆς ψυχῆς τεῖναι κενεὸν νόον	Ferentem tuæ animæ tendere vacuam mentem
Εἰς τὸ νοητὸν, ὄφρα μάθῃς τὸ νοητόν·	In intelligibile; ut discas intelligibile,
Ἐπεὶ ἔξω νόε ὑπάρχει.	Quandoquidem extra mentem existit.
Τὸν ἢ νοεῖ πᾶς νῦς θεόν, ὐ γὰρ ἄνα	Deum hunc intelligit omnis mens, non enim sinè
Νοός ὅτι νοητῇ, καὶ τὸ νοητὸν ὐ νῦ χωρὶς ὑπάρχει.	Mente est intelligibili, & intelligibile non sinè mente existit.
Τοῖς ἢ πυρὸς νοεροῦ νοεροῖς πρηστῆρσιν ἅπαντα	Ignis mentalis mentalibus præsteribus cuncta
Εἴκαθε δουλεύοντα, παρὸς πιθοῖ ἰδὶ βουλῇ.	Cedunt servientia, Patris persuasorio consilio.
Καὶ τὸ νοεῖν, ἀεί τε μένειν ἀόκνῳ ςροφάλιγγι.	Et intelligere, sempérque manere impigrà vertigine.
Πηγάς τε καὶ ἀρχὰς, δινεῖν, ἀεί τε μένειν ἀόκνῳ ςροφάλιγγι.	Fronte & principii, vertere, sempérque manere impigrà vertigine.
Ἀλλὰ δ᾽ ὄνομα σεμνὸν ἀκοιμήτῳ ςροφάλιγγι	Sed nomen venerandum insomni vertigini
Κόσμοις ἐνθρώσκων, κραιπνὸν διὰ παρὸς ἐνιπλώ.	Mundis indens, terribiles ob patris minas.
Ὑπὸ δύο νόων ἡ ζωογόνος πηγὴ περιέχεται ψυχῶν.	Sub duabus mentibus vitigenius fons continetur animarum.
Καὶ ὁ ποιητὴς, ὃς αὐτεργῶν τεκτήνατο τὸν κόσμον.	Et facta, qui per se operans fabrefecit mundum.
Ὃς ἐκ νόε ἔκθορε πρῶτος.	Qui ex mente exiliit primus.
Ἑσσάμενος πυρὶ πῦρ, συνδέσμον ὄφρα κεράσῃ	Indutus igne ignem, Vinculorum ut temperet
Πηγαίες κρατῆρας, ἑοῦ πυρὸς ἄνθος ἐπίσχων.	Fontanos crateras, sui ignis florem sustinens
Νοεραῖς ἀςράπῇει τομαῖς, ἔρωτι δ᾽ ἀνέπλησε τὰ πάντα.	Mentalibus fulget sectionibus, amoréque implevit omnia.
Τὰ ἀτύπωτα τυπῶσθαι.	Infigurata figurans.
Σμήνεσιν ἐοικυῖαι φέρονται, ῥηγνύμεναι	Examinibus similes feruntur, perrumpentes
Κόσμου περὶ σώμασι.	Per mundi corpora.
Ἃ νῦς λέγει, τῷ νοεῖν δή πε λέγει.	Quæ mens dicit, intelligendo sanè dicit.
Ἡ μὲν γὰρ δύναμις σὺν ἐκείνοις, νῦς δ᾽ ἀπ᾽ ἐκείνε.	Potentia quidem cum illis, Mens verò ab illà.

ΙΥΓΓΕΣ, ΙΔΕΑΙ, ΑΡΧΑΙ.

Πολλαὶ μὲν αἷδε ἐπεμβαίνουσι φαεινοῖς κόσμοις.
Ἐκθρώσκουσι, κ᾽ ἐν αἷς ἀκρότητες ἔασι τρεῖς,
Ὑπόκειται αὐταῖς ἀρχικὸς αὐλών.
Ἀρχὰς, αἱ πατρὸς ἔργα νοήσασαι νοητὰ

Αἰσθητοῖς ἔργοις, κ᾽ σώμασιν ἀπεκάλυψεν.
Διαπόρθμιοι ἑστῶτες φάναι τῷ πατρὶ κ᾽ τῇ ὕλῃ.
Καὶ τὰ ἐμφανῆ μιμήματα τῶν ἀφανῶν ἐργαζόμενοι,
Καὶ τ᾽ ἀφανῆ εἰς τὴν ἐμφανῆ κοσμοποιΐαν ἐγγράφοντες.

Νοῦς πατρὸς ἐρροίζησε, νοήσας ἀκμάδι βουλῇ
Παμμόρφους ἰδέας· πηγῆς δ᾽ ἀπὸ μιᾶς ἀποπτᾶσαι.
Ἐξέθορον. πατρόθεν γὰρ ἔην βουλή τε τέλος τε.
Δι᾽ ὧν συνάπτεται τῷ πατρὶ, ἄλλην κατ᾽ ἄλλην

Ζωὴν, ὑπὸ μεριζομένων ὀχετῶν.
Ἀλλ᾽ ἐμερίσθησαν, νοερῷ πυρὶ μοιρηθεῖσαι,
Εἰς ἄλλας νοερὰς· κόσμῳ γὰρ ἄναξ πολυμόρφῳ

Περύθηκεν νοερὸν τύπον ἄφθιτον, ὃν κατὰ κόσμον
Ἴχνος ἐπειγομένου μορφῆς καθ᾽ ὃ κόσμος ἐφάνθη.

Παντοίαις ἰδέαις κεχαρισμένος, ὧν μία πηγή.
Ἐξ ἧς ῥοιζοῦνται μεμερισμέναι ἄλλαι,
Ἄπλατοι, ῥηγνύμεναι κόσμου περὶ σώμασι.
Αἳ περὶ κόλπους σμερδαλέους, σμήνεσιν ἐοικυίας,
Φορεῦνται τραπεῖσαι περὶ δ᾽ ἀμφὶ ἀλλυδὶς ἄλλῃ.
Ἔννοιαι νοεραὶ πηγῆς πατρικῆς ἀπὸ
Πουλὺ δραττόμεναι πυρὸς ἄνθος
Ἀκοιμήτου χρόνου. ἀκμὴ ἀρχεγόνους ἰδέας
Πρώτη πατρὸς ἔβλυσε· τάς δ᾽ αὐτοθαλὴς πηγή.

Νοούμεναι ἴυγγες πατρόθεν νοέουσι κ᾽ αὐταί.
Βουλαῖς ἀφθέγκτοισι κινούμεναι ὥστε νοῆσαι.

ΕΚΑΤΗ, ΣΥΝΟΧΕΙΣ, ΚΑΙ Τελετάρχαι.

Ἐξ αὐτοῦ γὰρ πάντες ἐκθρώσκουσι
Ἀμείλικτοί τε κεραυνοί, κ᾽ πρηστηροδόχοι κόλποι
Παμφεγγέος ἀλκῆς πατρογενοῦς Ἑκάτης.
Καὶ ὑπεζωκὸς πυρὸς ἄρθος, ἢ δ᾽ κραταιὸν
Πνεῦμα πόλων, πυρίων ἐπέκεινα.
Φρουρεῖν αὖ πρηστῆρσιν ἑοῖς ἀκρότητας ἔδωκεν.
Ἐγκεράσας ἀλκῆς ἴδιον μένος ἐν συνοχεῦσιν.
Ὦ πῶς ἔχει κόσμῳ νοερὰς ἀνοχῆας ἀκαμπεῖς.

Ὅτι ἐργάτις, ὅτι ἐκδότις ἐστὶ πυρὸς ζωηφόρου.
Ὅτι κ᾽ τὸ ζωογόνον πληροῖ τῆς Ἑκάτης κόλπον.
Καὶ ἐπιρρεῖ τοῖς Συνοχεῦσιν ἀλκὴν ζείδωρον πυρὸς
Μέγα δυναμένοιο.
Ἀλλὰ κ᾽ φρεσὶ τῶν ἔργων εἰσὶ τοῦ πατρός.
Ἀφομοιοῖ γὰρ ἑαυτόν, ἐκεῖνος ἐπειγόμενος
Τὸν τύπον περιβάλλεσθαι τῶν εἰδώλων.
Οἱ τελετάρχαι συνείληπται τοῖς συνοχεῦσι.
Τοῖς δ᾽ πυρὸς νοεροῦ νοεροῖς πρηστῆρσιν
Ἅπαντα εἴκαθε δουλεύοντα.
Ἀλλὰ κ᾽ ὑλαίοις ὅσα δουλεύει συνοχεῦσι.

Ἑσσαμένω πάνθαλκον ἀλκὴν φωτὸς κελάδοντος.
Ἀλκῇ τριγλύχῳ, νόον ψυχὴν δ᾽ ὁπλίσαντα.
Πανθοῖον σύνθημα βάλλειν φρενί.
Μηδ᾽ ἐπιφοιτᾶν ἐμπυρίοις σποράδην ὀχετοῖς,
Ἀλλὰ σιβαρηδόν.
Οἱ δ᾽ τὰ ἄτομα, κ᾽ αἰσθητὰ δημιουργοῦσι,
Καὶ σωματοειδῆ, κ᾽ καταταταγμένα εἰς ὕλην.

IYNGES, IDEÆ, PRINCIPIA,

Multæ quidem hæ scandunt lucidos mundos.
Insilientes, & in quibus summitates sunt tres.
Subjectum ipsis est principale pratum.
Principia; quæ patris opera intelligentes intelligibilia
Sensibilibus operibus, & corporibus revelârunt.
Transvectrices stantes dicere patri & materiæ.
Et manifesta imitamina latentium operantes.
Et latentia in manifestam Cosmopœiam inscribentes.

Mens patris stridit, intelligens vigente consilio
Omniformes Ideas. Fonte vero ab uno evolantes
Exilierunt. A patre enim erat consilium & finis.
Per quæ conjunguntur patri, per aliam atque aliam
Vitam, à compartitis canalibus.
Sed partitæ sunt, mentali igne dispositæ,
In alias mentales: mundo namque rex multiformi
Proposuit mentalem typum incorruptibilem, non per rotundum
Vestigium promovens formæ per quæ mundus apparuit.
Omnifariam ideis gratiosus, quarum unus fons.
Ex quo strident dispertitæ aliæ,
Immensæ, perrumpentes mundi circa corpora:
Quæ per sinus immensos, examinibus similes,
Feruntur conversæ: circumque alibi alia.
Conceptiones mentales fonte à paterno
Multum decerpentes ignis florem
Insomnis temporis. Vigor principigeniæ ideæ
Prima, è patris missa est: cujus per se florens fons.
Intellectæ Iynges à patre intelligunt & ipsæ.
Consiliis ineffabilibus moventur ut intelligant.

HECATE, SYNOCHES, ET Teletarchæ.

Ex ipso enim omnes exiliunt
Amilictique fulmines, & presterocapaces sinus
Omnilucidæ vigoris patrogenii Hecates.
Et Hypezocus ignis flos, & fortis
Spiritus polorum, igneos trans.
Custodire presteribus suis summitates dedit.
Immiscens vigoris proprium robur in Synochis.
Quo mundus habeat mentales sustentatores inflexibiles.

Quia operatrix, quia largitrix est ignis vitiferi.
Quia & vitigenium implet Hecates sinum.
Et influit Synochis vigorem vitidonum ignis
Magni potentis.
Sed & Custodes operum sunt patris.
Assimilat enim se ipsum; ille urgens
Typum induere idolorum.
Teletarchæ comprehensi sunt cum Synochis.
His vero ignis mentalis mentalibus presteribus
Omnia parent servientia.
Sed & quæcunque materialibus serviunt Synochis.

Induti armorum vigorem luminis resonantis.
Vigore Triglicho, mentem animamque armantem.
Pervarium Synthema jacere ratiocinio.
Neque super incedere empyreis sparsim canalibus,
Sed collectim.
Hi vero individua, & sensibilia efficiunt,
Et corporiformia, & destinata in materiam.

ANIMA,

ΨΥΧΗ, ΦΥΣΙΣ.

Ὅτι ψυχὴ πῦρ δυνάμει πατρὸς ἶσα φαινὸν,

Ἀθάνατίς τε μένει, κ̀ ζωῆς δεσπότις ἐςί·
Καὶ ἴχει κόσμε πολλὰ πληρώμαλα κόλπων.
Νοῦ γ̀ μίμημα πέλει τὸ ἢ τεχθὲν ἔχει τι σώμαζ⸖.

Μιγνυμένων δ' ὀχετῶν, πυρὸς ἀφθίτα ἔργα τελῦσα.

Μετὰ ἢ παλρικὰς διανοίας ψυχὴ, ἐγὼ, ναίω·

Θερμὴ, ψυχῦσα τὰ πάνλα, καλέϑετο γ̀
Νῦν μὲν ἐπὶ ψυχῆ, ψυχῶ δ' ἐπὶ σώματι ἀργῷ.

Ἡμέων ἐγκαθέθηκε παλὴρ ἀνδρῶν τε θεῶν τε.
Ἀρδίω ἐμψυχῶσα φάος, πῦρ, αἰθέρα, κόσμυς.
Συντῳίσαλαι γ̀ τὰ φυσικὰ ἔργα τῷ νοερῷ φέγγει

Τῶ παλρός· Ψυχὴ γ̀ ἡ κοσμήσασα τ̀ μέγαν
Οὐρανὸν, κ̀ κοσμῶσα μί τῶ παλρός.
Κέρατα ἢ κ̀ αὐτῆς ἐσήεικ]αι ἄνω.
Νώτοις δ' ἀμφὶ θεᾶς φύσις ἄπλεζ⸖ ἠώρηλαι.

Ἄρχει δ' αὖ φύσις ἀκαμάτη κόσμων τε κ̀ ἔργων·

Οὐρανὸς ὄφρα θέει δρόμον ἄδιον καλασύρων·
Καὶ ταχὺς ἥλιος περὶ κέντρον, ὅπως ἐθὰς ἔλθη.
Μὴ φύσεως ἐμβλέψεις εἱμαρμένον ὄνομα τῆσδε.

ΚΟΣΜΟΣ.

Ὁ ποιηλὴς ὃς αὐτυργῶν τεκλήνατο τ̀ κόσμον.
Καί τις πυρὸς ὄγκος ἔλω ἕτερος· τὰ ἢ πάνλα

Αὐτυργῶν, ἵνα σῶμα τὸ κοσμικὸν ἐκλολυπευθῆ.
Κόσμος ἴν' ἔκδηλος, κ̀ μὴ φαίνηλαι ὑμενώδης.

Τὸν ὅλον κόσμον ἐκ πυρὸς, κ̀ ὕδαζ⸖, κ̀ γῆς,
Καὶ πανοτρόφε αἰθέρης.
Τ' ἄρρητα, κ̀ τὰ ῥητὰ συνθήμαλα τῶ κόσμε.
Ἄλλω κατ' ἄλλω ζωὴν, ὑπὸ μεμερισμένων ὀχετῶν.
Ἄνωθεν διήκονος ἐπὶ τὸ κατ' ἀντικρὺ
Διὰ τῶ κέντρε τ̀ γῆς, κ̀ πέμπλον μέσον, ἄλλον
Πυρίοχον, ἔνθα κατῆσι μέχει ὑλαίων ὀχετῶν.

Ζωηφόρον πῦρ.
Κέντρῳ ἐπισπέρχων ἑαυτὸν φωτὸς κελαδόνζ⸖.
Πηγαῖον ἄλλον, ὃς ἐμπύρειον κόσμον ἄγει.
Κέντρον ἀφ' ὗ πᾶσαι μέχρις ἂν τυχὸν ἴσαι ἔασι.

Σύμβολα γ̀ παλρικὸς νόος ἔσπερε κτ̀ κόσμον.

Μέσον ἢ̀ πατέρων ἑκάστης κέντρον φορῆται.
Νῶ γ̀ μίμημα πέλει· τὸ ἢ τεχθὲν ἔχει τι σώμαζ⸖.

ΟΥΡΑΝΟΣ.

Ἑπτὰ γ̀ ἐξόγκωσε πατὴρ στερεώματα κόσμων

Τὸν οὐρανὸν κυρτῷ σχήματι περικλείσας.
Πῆξε ἢ πολὺν ὅμιλον ἀστέρων ἀπλανῶν,
Ζώων ἢ πλανωμένων ὑφέστηκεν ἑπτάδα.
Γῆν δ' ἐν μέσῳ τιθείς, ὕδωρ δ' ἐν γαίας κόλποις,

Ἠέρα δ' ἄνωθεν τέτων.
Πῆξε ἢ κ̀ πολὺν ὅμιλον ἀστέρων ἀπλανῶν.
Μὴ τάσει ἐπιπόνῳ πονηρᾷ.

ANIMA, NATURA.

Quoniam anima ignis potentiâ patris existens lucidus,
Immortalísque manet, & vitæ domina est:
Et tenet mundi multas plenitudines sinuum.
Mentis enim imitamen est, partum verò habet quid corporis.

Mistis verò canalibus, ignis incorruptibilis opera efficiens.

Post verò Paternas conceptiones anima, ego, habito:

Calida, animans omnia, reposuit enim
Mentem sanè in animâ, animam verò in corpore inerti.

Nostri imposuit pater hominúmque Deúmque.
Affatim animans lucem, ignem, æthera, mundos.
Coexistunt namque naturalia opera mentali splendori

Patris. Anima enim est quæ ornavit magnum
Cœlum, & quæ ornat simul cum patre.
Cornua & ipsius firmata sunt sursum.
Humeros verò circa Deæ natura immensa attollitur.

Imperat rursus natura infatigabilis mundisque operibúsque:

Cœlum ut currat sursum æternum trahens:
Et celer sol circa centrum, ut assuetus veniat.
Non naturæ inspicias fatale nomen ejus.

MUNDUS.

Factor qui per se operans fabrefecit mundum.
Etenim quædam ignis moles erat altera: hæc Omnia

Per se efficiens, ut corpus mundanum———
Mundus ut manifestus, & non videatur membraneus.

Totum mundum ex igne, & aquâ, & terrâ,
Et omni-alente aere.
Ineffabilia, & fabilia synthemata mundi.
Aliam per aliam vitam, à partitis canalibus.
Desuper permeantis in oppositum
Per centrum terræ, & quintum medium, alium
Igneum, ubi descendit usque ad materiales canales.

Vitifer ignis.
Centro incitans seipsum lumine resonante.
Fontanum alium, qui Empyreum mundum ducit.
Centrum à quo omnes usque quo fortè æquales fuerint.

Symbola enim paterna mens seminavit per mundum.

Medium inter patres singulæ centrum fertur.
Mentis enim imitamen est: quod verò partum est habet quid corporis.

COELUM.

Septem enim in moles formavit Pater firmamenta mundorum:

Cœlum rotundâ figurâ circumcludens.
Fixítque multum cœtum astrorum inerrantium,
Animaliúmque errantium constituit septenarium.
Terram in medio posuit, aquámque in terræ sinibus.

Aerémque supra hæc.
Fixítque multum cœtum astrorum inerrantium.
Tensione, non laboriosâ malâ.

Sed

Πῆξεν ᾗ πλάνην ἐκ ἐχούσῃ φέρεθαι.
Ἔπηξε δὴ καὶ πολὺν ὅμιλον ἀςέρων ἀπλανῶν.
Τὸ πῦρ πρὸς τὸ πῦρ ἀναγκάσας.
Πῆξεν πλάνην ἐκ ἐχούσῃ φέρεθαι.
Ἐξ αὐτοῦ ὑπέςησεν, ἕξδομον ἥλιον,
Μεσεμβολήσας πῦρ.
Τὸ ἄτακλον αὐτῶν διατάκλοις ἀνακρεμάσας ζώναις.

Τίκτει γὰρ ἡ θεὰ, ἥλιόν τε μέγαν, καὶ λαμπρὰν σελώνην.

Αἰθὴρ, ἥλιε, πνεῦμα σελώνης ἀέρος ἄγοι,
Ἡλιακῶν τε κύκλων, καὶ μηναίων καναχισμῶν,
Κόλπων τε ἠερίων.
Αἴθηρος μέλος, ἡλίη τε καὶ μήνης ὀχετοῦ, ἡ τε ἠέρος

Καὶ πλατὺς ἀὴρ, μηναῖός τε δρόμος, καὶ πόλος ἡελίοιο.
Συλλέγει αὐτὸ, λαμβάνουσα αἴθηρος μέλος,
Ἡλίῳ τε, σελήνῃ τε, καὶ ὅσα ἠέρι συνέχονται.
Πῦρ πυρὸς ἐξοχέτευμα, καὶ πυρὸς ταμίας.
Χαίται γὰρ ἐς ὀξὺ πεφυκότι φωτὶ βλέπονται,

Ἔνθα Κρόνος.
Ἡλίῳ πάρεδρος ἐπισκοπέων πόλον ἁγνόν.
Αἰθέριός τε δρόμος, καὶ μήνης ἄπλετος ὁρμὴ,
Ἠέριοί τε ῥοαί.
Ἡλιόν τε μέγαν, καὶ λαμπρὰν σελώνην.

ΧΡΟΝΟΣ.

Θεὸν ἐγκόσμιον, αἰώνιον, ἀπέραντον.
Νέον, καὶ πρεσβύτην, Ἑλικοειδῆ.
Καὶ πηγαῖον ἄλλον, ὃς τὸν ἐμπύρειον κόσμον ἄγει.

ΨΥΧΗ, ΣΩΜΑ, ΑΝΘΡΩΠΟΣ.

Χρή σε σπεύδειν πρὸς τὸ φάος καὶ πατρὸς αὐγάς,
Ἔνθεν ἐπέμφθη σοι ψυχή, πολὺν ἑσαμένη νοῦν.

Ταῦτα πατὴρ ἐννόησε, βροτὸς δ' οἷ ἐψύχωτο.

Σύμβολα γὰρ πατρικὸς νόος ἔσπειρε ταῖς ψυχαῖς.
Ἔρωτι βαθεῖ ἀναπλήσας τὴν ψυχήν.
Καθέζετο γὰρ νῦν ἐν ψυχῇ, ἐν σώματι δὲ
Ὑμέας ἐγκατέθηκε πατὴρ ἀνδρῶν τε θεῶν τε.
Ἀσώματα μὲν ὅτι τὰ θεῖα πάντα.
Σώματα δ' ἐν αὐτοῖς ὑμῶν ἕνεκεν ἐνδέδεται.
Μὴ δυνάμενος κατέχειν ἀσωμάτους τῶν σωμάτων,
Διὰ τὴν σωματικὴν, εἰς ἣν ἐνεκεντρείθητε, φύσιν.

Ἐν δὲ θεῷ κεῖνται πυρσοὺς ἕλκουσαι ἀκμαίους.
Ἐκ πατρόθεν κατιόντες, ἀφ' ὧν ψυχὴ κατιόντων

Ἐμπυρείων δρέπεται καρπῶν, ψυχοτρόφον ἄνθος.

Διὸ καὶ νοήσαται τὰ ἔργα τοῦ πατρὸς
Μοίρης εἱμαρμένης τὸ πτερὸν φεύγουσιν ἀναιδές.
Κἂν γὰρ τήνδε ψυχὴν ἴδῃς ὑποκαταβᾶσαν,
Ἀλλ' ἄλλην ἐνίησι πατὴρ, ἐναρίθμιον εἶναι.
Ἦ μάλα δὴ κεῖναί γε μακάρταται ἔξοχα πασέων
Ψυχάων, ποτὶ γαῖαν ἀπ' οὐρανόθεν προχέονται.
Κεῖναι ὄλβιαί τε, καὶ ἃ φατὰ νοήματα ἔχουσαι.
Ὅσσαι ἀπ' αἰγλήεντος, ἄναξ, σέθεν, ἠδὲ καὶ αὐτῆς
Ἐκ Διὸς ἐξεγένοντο. Μίτου κρατερῆς ὑπ' ἀνάγκης
Ἡγείσθω ψυχῆς βάθος ἄσβεστον, ὄμματα δ' ἄρδην

Πάντα ἐκπέτασον ἄνω.
Μήτε κάτω νεύσῃς εἰς τὸν μελαναυγέα κόσμον.

Sed fixione errorem non habente in motu.
Fixítque multum cœtum astrorum inerrantium.
Ignem ad ignem cogens.
Fixione errorem non habente in motu.
Sex eos constituit, septimum Solis,
In medium jaciens ignem.
Inordinationem eorum bene-ordinatis suspendens zonis.

Parturit enim Dea Solémque magnum, & splendidam Lunam.

Æther, Sol, spiritus Lunæ, aeris ductores,
Solariúmque circulorum, & lunarium est crepituum,
Sinuúmque aereorum.
Ætheris cantus, Solísque, & Lunæ canalium, & aeris.

Et latus aer, lunarísque cursus, & polus Solis.
Colligit ipsum, accipiens ætheris harmoniam,
Solísq; Lunæque, & quæcunque aere continentur.
Ignis ignis derivatio, & ignis penu.
Crines enim in acutum nato lumini conspiciuntur,

Ubi Saturnus.
Sol assessor intuens polum purum.
Æthereúsque cursus, & Lunæ ingens impetus,
Aeriíque fluxus.
Solémque magnum, & splendidam Lunam.

TEMPUS.

Deum mundanum, æternum, infinitum.
Juvenem, & senem———
Et fontanum aliud, quod empyreum mundum ducit.

ANIMA, CORPUS, HOMO.

Oportet te festinare ad lucem & patris lumina,
Unde missa est tibi anima, multam induta mentem.

Hæc pater mente concepit, mortalísque ei est animatus.

Symbola enim paterna mens seminavit in animis
Amore profundo replens animam.
Reposuit enim mentem in animâ, in corpore verò
Vos reposuit pater hominúmque deúmque.
Incorporea quidem sunt divina omnia.
Corpora verò in ipsis vestrî causâ sunt alligata;
Non potentes continere incorporeos corpora,
Ob corpoream, in quam concentrati estis, naturam.

Inque deo jacent faces trahentes validas.
A patre descendentes, à quibus anima descendentibus

Empyreos carpit fructus, animam· alentem florem.

Ideóque mente concipientes opera patris
Parcæ fatalis alam fugiunt inverecundam.
Et si hanc animam videris redeuntem,
At aliam imittit pater, ut in numero fit.
Certè valdè illæ sunt beatissimæ supra omnes
Animas, ad terram à Cœlo profusæ.
Illæque divites, & ineffabilia stamina habentes.
Quæcunque à lucente, ô rex, à te,. vel ipso
Jove sunt progenitæ. Miti validâ à necessitate
Ducatur animæ profunditas immortalis oculósque affatim

Omnes sursum extende.
Nec deorsum pronus sis in nigricantem mundum.

Ὦ βαθὸς αἰὲν ἄπιστ⸗ ὑπέςρωταί τε, κỳ Ἅδης

Ἀμφικνεφὴς, ῥιπόων, εἰδωλοχαρὴς, ἀνόητ⸗,

Κρημνώδης, σκολιὸς, πωρὸν βάθ⸗ αἰὲν ἑλίσσων,

Λεπυμφάων ἀφανὲς δέμας, ἀργὸν, ἄπνοͅμον.

Καὶ ὁ μισοφανὴς κόσμ⸗, κỳ τὰ σκολιὰ ῥέεθρα
Ὑφ᾽ ὧν πολλοὶ καταςύρονται.
Ζήτησον παράδεισον.
Δίζεο σὺ ψυχῆς ὀχετὸν, ὅθεν, ἢ τίνι τάξει
Σώματι τιθύσας, ἐπὶ τάξιν ἀφ᾽ ἧς ἐρρύης
Αὖθις ἀναςήσεις, ἱερῷ λόγῳ ἔργον ἐνώσας.
Μήτε κάτω νεύσης, κρημνὸς, κατὰ γῆς ὑπόκειται,

Ἑπταπόρου σύρων κατὰ βαθμίδ⸗· ἣν ὑπὸ
Δεινῆς ἀνάγκης θρόν⸗ ἐςί.
Μὴ σὺ αὔξανε τὴν εἱμαρμένην.
Ψυχὴ ἡ μερόπων θεὸν ἄγξει πῶς εἰς ἑαυτήν.

Οὐδὲν θνητὸν ἔχουσα, ὅλη θεόθεν μεμέθυσται.
Ἁρμονίαν αὐχεῖ γὰρ, ὑφ᾽ ἧ πέλε σῶμα βρότειον.

Ἐκτείνας πύρινον νοῦν ἔργον ἐπ᾽ εὐσεβίης,
Ῥευςὸν κỳ σῶμα σαώσεις.
Ἔςι κỳ εἰδώλῳ μερὶς εἰς τόπον ἀμφιφάοντα.
Παντόθεν ἀπλάςῳ ψυχῇ πυρὸς ἡνία τεῖνον.
Ὁ πυριθαλπὴς ἔννοια πρωτίςην ἔχει τάξιν.

Τῷ πυρὶ γὰρ βροτὸς ἐμπελάσας θεόθεν φάος ἕξει.

Δηθύνοντι γὰρ βροτῷ κραιπνοὶ μάκαρες τελέθουσι.
Αἱ ποῖναι μερόπων ἄγκτειραι.
Καὶ τὰ κακῆς ὕλης βλαςήματα χρηςὰ, κỳ ἐσθλά.
Ἐλπὶς τρεφέτω σε πυρείοχ⸗ ἀγγελικῷ ἐνὶ χώρῳ.
Ἀλλ᾽ οὐκ εἰς δέχεται κείνης τὸ θέλειν πατρικὸς νοῦς,
Μέχρις ἂν ἐξέλθῃ λήθης, κỳ ῥῆμα λαλήσῃ

Μνήμην ἐνθεμένη πατρικοῦ συνθήματ⸗ ἁγνοῦ.
Τοῖς δὲ διδακτὸν φάος ἔδωκε γνώρισμα λαβέσθαι.

Τοὺς δὲ ὑπνώοντας ἑῆς ἐνεκάρπισεν ἀλκῆς.

Μὴ πνεῦμα μολύνῃς, μήτε βαθύνῃς τὸ ἐπίπεδον.

Μήτε τὸ τῆς ὕλης σκύβαλον κρημνῷ καταλείψῃς.
Μὴ ἐξάξῃς, ἵνα μὴ ἐξιοῦσα ἔχῃ τι.
Βίῃ ὅτι σώματι λιπόντων ψυχαὶ καθαρώταται.
Ψυχῆς ἐξωςῆρες, ἀνάπνοοι, εὔλυτοί εἰσι.

Λαιᾷ δ᾽ ἐν λαγόσιν Ἑκάτης ἀρετῆς πέλε πηγή,
Ἔνδον ὅλη μίμνουσα, τὸ παρθένον οὐ περιοῦσα.
Ὦ τολμηροτάτης φύσεως, ἄνθρωπε, τέχναςμα!
Μὴ τὰ πελώρια μέτρα γαίης ὑπὸ σὴν φρένα βάλλε.

Οὐ γὰρ ἀληθείης φυτὸν ἐπὶ χθονί.
Μήτε μέτρει μέτρα ἡελίῳ κανόνας συναθροίσας,

Ἀϊδίῳ βουλῇ φέρεται, οὐχ ἕνεκα σοῖο.
Μηναῖον μὲν δρέμημα, κỳ ἀςέριον προπόρευμα
Μήνης ῥοῖζον ἔασον, ἀεὶ τρέχει ἔργῳ ἀνάγκης

Ἀςέριον προπόρευμα, σέθεν χάριν οὐκ ἐλοχεύθη.
Αἰθέρι⸗ ὀρνίθων ταρσὸς πλατὺς οὔ ποτ᾽ ἀληθής.
Οὐ θυσιῶν σπλάγχνων τ᾽ ὀτόμαι· τάδ᾽ ἀθύρματα πάντα,
Ἐμπορικῆς ἀπάτης ςηρίγματα· φεῦγε σὺ ταῦτα

Μέλλων εὐσεβίης ἱερὸν παράδεισον ἀνοίγειν.

Cui profunditas semper infida substrata est, & Hades

Circumquaque caligans, squalidus, idolis gaudens, Amens,

Præcipitosus, tortuosus, cæcum profundum semper involvens,

Semper desponsus obscuram faciem, inertem, Spiritu-carentem.

Et Osor luminis mundus, & tortuosi fluxus
A quibus vulgus attrahitur.
Quære paradisum.
Quære tu animæ canalem, unde, aut quo ordine
Corpori inservieris, in ordinem à quo effluxisti
Rursus restituas, sacro sermoni operam uniens.
Neque deorsum sis pronus, præcipitium in terrâ subest,
Septemvios trahens per gradus: quo sub
Horribile necessitatis Thronus est.
Nè tu augeas fatum.
Anima hominum Deum coget quodammodo in seipsam :
Nihil mortale habens, tota à Deo est ebria facta
Harmoniam resonat namque, sub quâ est corpus mortale.
Extendens igneam mentem ad opus pietatis,
Et fluxile corpus servabis.
Est & idolo portio in loco circumlucente.
Undique inficta animâ ignis habenas tende.
Igne calens cogitatio primissimum habet ordinem.
Igni namque mortalis propinquans à Deo lumen habebit.
Immoranti enim mortali præstò Dii aderunt.
Pœnæ hominum sunt angores.
Et malæ materiæ germina utilia sunt, & bona.
Spes nutriat te ignea Angelicâ in regione.
Sed non recipit illius velle Paterna mens,
Donec non exeat ex oblivione, & verbum loquatur.
Memoriam indens Paterni Synthematis puri.
His quidem discibile lucis dedit notitiam suscipere.
Hos verò & somnolentos sui fructum dedit roboris.
Ne spiritum macules neque profundum fac superficiem.
Neque materiæ quisquilias præcipitio relinquas.
Nè educas, nè exiens habeat quidpiam.
Vi corpus relinquentium animæ sunt purissimæ.
Animæ expulsores, respiratores, & faciles solutu sunt.
Sinistris in lumbis Hecates virtutis est fons,
Intùs tota manens, virgineum non abjiciens.
O audacissimæ naturæ, homo, artificium!
Neque ingentes mensuras terræ in tuam mentem pone,
Non enim veritatis planta est in terrâ.
Neque in mensuris mensuras Solis regulas congregans,
Æterno consilio fertur, non gratiâ tui.
Lunarem quidem cursum, & astreum progressum
Lunæ strepitum dimitte, semper currit operâ necessitatis
Astreus progressus, tui gratiâ non est partus.
Æthereus avium pes latus nunquam verus est.
Non sacrificia visceráque cupio : hæc sunt omnia ludi,
Mercatoriæ deceptionis firmamenta; fuge tu hæc
Si vis pietatis sacrum paradisum aperire.

Ubi

Ἔνθ' ἀρετή, σοφία τε, καὶ ἐννομία συνάγονται.

Σὸν γὰρ ἀγγεῖον θῆρες χθονὸς οἰκήσουσι.
Αὐτὰς δὲ χθὼν καθώρικται ἐς τέκνα μέχρις.

ΔΑΙΜΟΝΕΣ, ΤΕΛΕΤΑΙ.

Ἡ φύσις πείθει εἶναι τὰς δαίμονας ἁγνούς.
Καὶ τὰ κακῆς ὕλης βλαστήματα χρηστὰ, καὶ ἐσθλά.
Ἀλλὰ ταῦτα ἐν ἀβάτοις σηκοῖς διανοίας ἀνελίττω.
Πῦρ ἴκελον σκιρτηδὸν ἐπ' ἠέρος οἶδμα τιταῖνον,

Ἢ καὶ πῦρ ἀτύπωτον, ὅθεν φωνὴν προθέουσαν,

Ἢ φῶς πλούσιον ἀμφιγυῶν, ῥοιζαῖον, ἑλιχθέν·

Ἀλλὰ καὶ ἵππον ἰδεῖν φωτὸς πλέον ἀστράπτοντα,
Ἢ καὶ παῖδα θοοῖς νώτοις ἐποχούμενον ἵππου,

Ἔμπυρον, ἢ χρυσῷ πεπυκασμένον, ἢ πάλιν γυμνόν,
Ἢ καὶ τοξεύοντα, καὶ ἑστῶτα ἐπὶ νώτοις.
Πολλάκις ἢν λέξῃς μοι, ἀθρήσεις πάντα λέοντα,
Οὔτε γὰρ οὐρανίου κυρτὸς τότε φαίνεται ὄγκος.
Ἀστέρες οὐ λάμπουσι, τὸ μήνης φῶς κεκάλυπται,
Χθὼν οὐχ ἕστηκε, βλέπεταί τε πάντα κεραυνοῖς.
Μὴ φύσεως καλέσῃς αὐτόπτεον ἄγαλμα,
Οὐ γὰρ χρὴ κείνους σε βλέπειν πρὶν σῶμα τελεσθῇ.

Ὅτε τὰς ψυχὰς θέλγοντες ἀεὶ τῶν τελετῶν ἀπάγουσι.
Ἐκ δ' ἄρα κόλπων γαίης θρώσκουσι χθόνιοι κύνες,
Οὐ ποτ' ἀληθὲς σῆμα βροτῷ ἀνδρὶ δεικνύντες,

Ἐνέργει περὶ τὸν Ἑκατικὸν στρόφαλον.
Ὀνόματα βάρβαρα μήποτ' ἀλλάξῃς,
Εἰσὶ γὰρ ὀνόματα παρ' ἑκάστοις θεόσδοτα
Δύναμιν ἐν τελεταῖς ἄρρητον ἔχοντα.
Ἡνίκα βλέψῃς μορφῆς ἄτερ εὔϊερον πῦρ,
Λαμπόμενον σκιρτηδὸν ὅλου κατὰ βένθεα κόσμου,

Κλῦθι πυρὸς φωνήν.

Ubi Virtus, sapientiáque, & bona lex congregantur.
Tuum enim vas bestiæ terræ habitabunt.
Ipsas autem terra sepeliit ad filios usque.

DÆMONES, SACRIFICIA.

Natura suadet esse Dæmonas puros.
Et mala materiæ germina, utilia, & bona.
Sed hæc in abditis septis mentis evolvo.
Ignis simulacrum saltatim in aëre in tumorem extendens,
Vel etiam ignem infiguratum, unde vocem currentem,
Vel lumen abundans radians, streperum, convolutum:
Sed & equum videre luce magis fulgurantem,
Vel etiam puerum suis humeris inequitantem equo,
Ignitum, vel auro distinctum, vel spoliatum,
Vel etiam sagittantem, & stantem super humeris.
Multoties si dixeris mihi, cernes omnia leonem,
Neque enim cœlestis curvitas tunc apparet moles.
Astra non lucent, Lunæ lux opertum est,
Terra non stat, cernuntur verò cuncta fulminibus.
Neque naturæ voces per se visibile simulacrum,
Non enim oportet illos te spectare antequam corpus Sacris purgetur.
Quando animas mulcentes semper à Sacris abducunt.
Ergo ex finibus terræ exiliunt terrestres canes,
Nunquam verum corpus mortali homini monstrantes.
Operare circa Hecaticum turbinem.
Nomina barbara nunquam mutaveris,
Sunt enim nomina apud singulos à Deo data
Potentiam in Sacris ineffabilem habentia.
Quando videris formâ sine Sacrum ignem,
Collucentem saltatim totius per profundum mundi,
Audi ignis vocem.

THE ORACLES OF ZOROASTER;

Collected By

FRANCISCUS PATRICIUS.

MONAD. DYAD. TRIAD.

Where the Paternal Monad *is*.
The Monad *is* enlarged, which generates Two.
For the Dyad *sits by him, and glitters with Intellectual Sections.*
And to Govern all things, and to Order all things not Ordered,
For in the whole World *shineth the* Triad, over which the Monad Rules.
This Order *is* the beginning of all Section.
For the Mind of the Father *said*, that all things be cut into three.
Whose Will assented, and then all things were divided.
For the Mind of the Eternal Father said into three, Governing all things by Mind.
And there appeared in it (the Triad) Virtue and Wisdom,
And Multiscient Verity.
This way floweth the Shape of the Triad, being præ-existent.
Not the first (Essence) but where they are measured.
For thou must conceive that all things serve these three Principles.
The first course is Sacred, but in the middle.
Another the third, aerial; which cherisheth the Earth in Fire.
And Fountain of Fountains, and of all Fountains.
The Matrix containing all things.
Thence abundantly springs forth the Generation of multivarious Matter.
Thence extracted a prester the flower of glowing Fire,
Flashing into the Cavities of the World: for all things from thence
Begin to extend downwards their admirable Beams

FATHER. MIND.

The Father hath snatched away himself; neither hath he shut up his own fire in his Intellectual Power.
For the Father perfected all things, and delivered them over to the second Mind,
Which the whole Race of Men call the first
Light begotten of the Father; for he alone
Having crop'd the Flower of the Mind from the Fathers Vigour.
For the Paternal self-begotten Mind understanding [his] Work,
Sowed in all the fiery bond of Love,
That all things might continue loving for ever.
Neither those things which are intellectually context in the light of the Father in all things.
That being the Elements of the World they might persist in Love.
For it is the Bound of the paternal Depth, and the Fountain of the Intellectuals.
Neither went he forth, but abode in the paternal Depth,
And in the Adytum according to Divinely-nourished Silence.
For the Fire once above, shutteth not his Power
Into Matter by Actions, but by the Mind.
For the paternal Mind hath sowed Symbols thro' the World,
Which understandeth Intelligibles, and beautifieth ineffables.
Wholly Division and Indivisible.
By Mind he contains the Intelligibles, but introduceth Sense into the Worlds.
By Mind he contains the Intelligibles, but Introduceth Soul into the Worlds.

MIND. INTELLIGIBLES. INTELLECTUALS.

And of the one Mind the intelligible (Mind.)
For the Mind is not without the intelligible; it exists not without it.
These are Intellectuals, and Intelligibles, which being understood, understand.
For the Intelligible is the Aliment of the Intelligent.
Learn the Intelligible, since it exists beyond the Mind.
And of the Mind which moves the Empyreal Heaven.
For the Framer of the fiery World is the Mind of the Mind.
You who know certainly the supermundane paternal Depth.
The intelligible is predominant over all Section.
There is something Intelligible, which it behooves thee to understand with the flower of the Mind.
For if thou enclinest thy Mind, thou shalt understand this also;
Yet understanding something [of it] thou shalt not understand this wholly; for it is a Power
Of Circumlucid Strength, glittering with Intellectual Sections (Rays).
But it behooves not to consider this intelligible with Vehemence of Intellection,
But with the ample flame of the ample Mind, which measureth all things,
Except this Intelligible: but it behooves to understand this.
For if thou enclinest thy Mind, thou shalt understand this also,
Not fixedly, but having a pure turning Eye [thou must]
Extend the empty mind of thy Soul towards the Intelligible,
That thou mayst learn the Intelligible, for it exists beyond the Mind.
But every mind understands this God; for the Mind is not
Without the Intelligible, neither is the Intelligible without the Mind.
To the Intellectual Presters of the Intellectual fire, all things

By yielding are subservient to the perswasive Counsel of the Father.
And to understand, and always to remain in a restless whirling.
But insinuating into Worlds the Venerable Name in a sleepless Whirling.
Fountains and Principles; to turn, and always to remain in a restless Whirling.
By reason of the terrible menace of the Father.
Under two Minds the Life generating Fountain Souls is contained;
And the Maker, who self-operating framed the World.
Who sprung first out of the Mind.
Cloathing Fire with Fire, binding them together, to mingle
The Fountanous Craters, preserves the flower of his own fire.
He glittereth with Intellectual Sections, and filled all things with Love.
Like Swarms they are carried, being broken, About the Bodies of the World.
That things unfashioned may be fashioned.
What the Mind speaks, it speaks by understanding.
Power is with them, Mind is from Her.

JYNGES. IDEÆ'S. PRNICIPLES.

These being many ascend into the lucid Worlds. Springing into them, and in which there are three Tops.
Beneath them lies the chief of Immaterials.
Principles which have understood the intelligible Works of the Father.
Disclosed them in sensible Works as in Bodies;
Being (as it were) the Ferry-men betwixt the Father and Matter.
And producing manifest Images of unmanifest things,
And inscribing unmanifest things in the manifest frame of the World.
The Mind of the Father made a jarring Noise, understanding by vigorous Counsel,
Omniform Idea's; and flying out of one Fountain They sprung forth; for, from the Fathers was the Counsel and End,
By which they are connected to the Father, by alternate
Life from several Vehicles.
But they were divided, being by Intellectual fire distributed
Into other Intellectuals: for the King did set before the multiform World
An Intellectual incorruptible Pattern; this Print through the World he promoting, of whose form
According to which the World appeared
Beautified with all kind of Idea's, of which there is one fountain,
Out of which come rushing forth others undistributed, being broken about the Bodies of the World, which through the vast Recesses,
Like Swarms, are carried round about every way.
Intellectual Notions from the paternal Fountain cropping the flower of Fire.
In the point of sleepless time, of this Primigenious Idea.
The first self-budding fountain of the Father budded.
Intelligent Jynges do (themselves) also understand from the Father:
By unspeakable Councils, being moved so as to understand.

HECATE. SYNOCHES. TELETARCHS

For out of him spring all
Implacable Thunders, and the Prester-receiving cavities
Of the Intirely-lucid strength of Father-begotten Hecate.
And he who begirds (viz.) the flower of Fire, and the strong
Spirit of the Poles fiery above.
He gave to his Presters that they should guard the Tops.
Mingling the power of his own Strength in the Synoches.
O how the World hath intellectual guides inflexible!
Because she is the Operatrix, because she is the Dispensatrix of Life-giving fire.
Because also it fills the Life-producing Bosom of Hecate.
And instils in the Synoches the enlivning strength Of potent fire.
But they are guardians of the works of the Father.
For he disguises himself, professing
To be cloathed with the Print of the Images.
The Teletarchs are comprehended with the Synoches,
To these Intellectual Presters of intellectual fire, All things are subservient.
But as many as serve the Material Synoches,
Having put on the compleatly-Armed Vigour of resounding Light.
With tripple strength fortifying the Soul and the Mind.
To put into the Mind the Symbol of Variety.
And not to walk dispersedly on the Empyræal Channels;
But stiffly
These frame Indivisibles, and sensibles,
And Corporiforms, and things destin'd to Matter

SOUL NATURE.

For the Soul being a bright fire, by the power of the Father
Remains Immortal, and is Mistress of Life;
And possesseth many Complexions of the Cavities of the World:
For it is in imitation of the Mind; but that which is born hath something of the Body.
The Channels being intermixed, she performs the Works of incorruptible Fire.
Next the paternal Conceptions I (the Soul) dwell, Warm, heating all things; for he did put
The Mind in the Soul, the Soul in the dull Body.
Of us the Father of Gods and Men imposed,
Abundantly animating Light, Fire, Æther, Worlds.
For natural Works co-exist with the Intellectual Light of the Father, for the Soul which adorn'd the great
Heaven, and adorning with the Father,
But her Horns are fixed above,
But about the shoulders of the Goddess, immense Nature is exalted.
Again, indefatigable Nature commands the Worlds and Works.
That Heaven drawing an eternal course may run.
And the swift Sun might come about the Center as he useth.
Look not into the fatal name of this Nature.

THE WORLD.

The Maker who operating by himself framed the World.
And there was another Bulk of fire,
By it self operating all things that the Body of the World might be perfected,
That the World might be manifest and not seem Membranous.
The whole World of Fire, and Water, and Earth, And all-nourishing Æther,
The unexpressible and expressible Watch-words of the World.
One Life by another from the distributed Channels Passing from above to the opposite Part,
Through the Center of the Earth; and another fifth Middle. :
Fiery Channel, where it descends to the material Channels.
Life-bringing fire.
Stirring himself up with the Goad of resounding Light.
Another fountainous, which guides the Empyreal World.
The Center from which all (Lines) which way soever are equal.
For the paternal Mind sowed Symbols through the World.
For the Center of every one is carried betwixt the Fathers.
For it is in imitation of the Mind, but that which is born hath something of the Body.

HEAVEN.

For the Father congregated seven Firmaments of the World;
Circumscribing Heaven in a round Figure,
He fixed a great company of inerratick Stars,
And he constituted a Septenary of erratick Animals.
Placing Earth in the middle, and Water in the middle of the Earth.
The Air above these.
He fixed a great Company of inerratick Stars,
To be carri'd not by laborious and troublesome Tension,
But by a settlement which hath no Error.
He fixed a great Company of inerratick Stars,
Forcing Fire to Fire,
To be carried by a settlement which hath not Error
He constituted them six; casting into the midst
The fire of the Sun,
Suspending their Disorder in well-ordered Lones.
For the Goddess brings forth the great Sun, and the bright Moon.
O Æther, Son, Spirit, Guides of the Moon and of the Air;
And of the solar Circles, and of the Monthly clashings,
And of the Aerial Recesses.
The Melody of the Æther, and of the Passages of the Sun, and Moon, and of the Air,
And the wide Air, and the Lunar Course, and the Pole of the Sun.
Collecting it, and receiving the Melody of the Æther,
And of the Sun, and of the Moon, and of all that are contained in the Air.
Fire, the Derivation of fire, and the Dispenser of fire;
His Hair pointed is seen by his native Light;
Hence comes Saturn.
The Sun Assessor beholding the pure Pole;
And the Ætherial Course, and the vast Motion of the Moon,
And the Aerial fluxions,
And the great Sun, and the bright Moon.

TIME.

The Mundane God, Æternal, Infinite, Young, and Old, of a Spiral form.
And another fountainous, who guides the Empyræal Heaven.

SOUL. BODY. MAN.

It behoves thee to hasten to the Light, and to the Beams of the Father;
From whence was sent to thee a Soul cloathed with much Mind.
These things the Father conceived, and so the mortal was animated.
For the paternal Mind sowed Symbols in Souls;
Replenishing the Soul with profound Love.
For the Father of Gods and Men placed the Mind in the Soul;
And in the Body he established you.
For all Divine things are incorporeal.
But Bodies are bound in them for your sakes:
Incorporeals not being able to contain the bodies.
By reason of the Corporeal Nature in which you are concentrated.
And they are in God, attracting strong flames.
Descending from the Father, from which descending the Soul
Crops of Empyræal fruits the Soul-nourishing flower.
And therefore conceiving the Words of the Father
They avoid the audacious wing of fatal Destiny;
And though you see this Soul manumitted,
Yet the Father sends another to make up the Number.
Certainly, these are superlatively blessed above all Souls; they are sent forth from Heaven to Earth,
And those rich Souls which have unexpressible fates;
As many of them (O King) as proceed from shining Thee, or from
Jove Himself, under the strong power of (his) Thread.
Let the immortal Depth of thy Soul be predominant; but all thy eyes
Extend upward.
Stoop not down to the dark World,
Beneath which continually lies a faithless Depth, and Hades
Dark all over, squalld, delighting in Images, unintelligible,
Precipititious, Craggy, a Depth; always Rolling,
Always espousing an opacous, idle-breathless Body,
And the Light-hating World, and the winding currents,
By which many things are swallowed up.
Seek Paradise;
Seek thou the way of the Soul, whence or by what Order
Having served the Body, to the same place from which thou didst flow.
Thou maist rise up again, joyning Action to sacred speech,
Stoop not down, for a Precipice lies below on the Earth;

Drawing

Drawing through the Ladder which hath seven steps, Beneath which
Is the Throne of Necessity.
Enlarge not thou thy Destiny.
The Soul of Man will in a manner clasp God to her self;
Having nothing Mortal, she is wholly inebriated from God:
For she boasts Harmony, in which the mortal Body exists.
If thou extend the fiery Mind
To the work of Piety, thou shalt preserve the fluxible Body.
There's a room for the Image also in the circumlucid place.
Every way to the unfashioned Soul stretch the Reins of Fire.
The Fire-glowing Cogitation hath the first Rank.
For the Mortal approaching to the Fire, shall have Light from God.
For to the slow Mortal the Gods are swift.
The Furies are Stranglers of Men.
The bourgeons, even of ill Matter, are profitable good.
Let Hope nourish thee in the fiery Angelic Region.
But the Paternal Mind accepts not her Will,
Until she go out of Oblivion, and pronounce a Word, Inserting the remembrance of the pure paternal Symbol.
To these he gave the docible character of Life to be Comprehended.
Those that were asleep he made fruitful by his own strength.
Defile not the Spirit nor deepen a Superficies.
Leave not the Dross of Matter on a Precipice.
Bring her not forth, lest going forth she have something.
The Souls of those who quit the Body violently, are most pure.
The ungirders of the Soul, which give her breathing, are easie to be loosed.
In the side of sinister Hecate, there is a Fountain of Vertue;
Which remains entire within, not omitting her Virginity.
O Man the Machine of Boldest Nature!
Subject not to thy Mind the vast measures of the Earth; For the Plant of Truth is not upon Earth.
Nor measure the Measures of the Sun, gathering together Canons;
He is moved by the Eternal Will of the Father, not for thy sake.
Let alone the swift Caurse of the Moon: she runs ever by the impulse of Necessity.
The Progression of the Stars was not brought forth for thy sake.
The ætherial wide flight of Birds is not veracious,
And the Dissections of Entrails and Victims all these are toys,
The supports of gainful Cheats; fly thou these
If thou intend to open the Sacred Paradise of Piety
Where Virtue, Wisdom, and Equity, are assembled.
For thy Vessel the Beasts of the Earth shall inhabit.
These the Earth bewails, even to their Children.

DÆMONS. RITES.

Nature perswades there are pure Dæmons;
The bourgeons, even all ill matter, are profitable and good,
But these things I revolve in the recluse Temples of my Mind,
Extending the like Fire sparklingly into the spacious Air
Or Fire unfigur'd, a Voice issuing forth.
Or Fire abundant whizzing and winding about the Earth,
But also to see a Horse more glitering than Light.
Or a Boy on [thy] shoulders riding on a Horse,
Fiery or adorned with Gold, or divested,
Or shooting and standing on [thy] shoulders.
If thou speak often to me, thou shalt see absolutely that which is spoken:
For then neither appears the Cœlestial concave Bulk, nor do the Stars shine: The light of the Moon is covered,
The Earth stands not still, but all things appear Thunder.
Invoke not the self-conspicuous Image of Nature;
For thou must not behold these before thy Body be initiated.
When soothing Souls they always reduce them from these Mysteries.
Certainly out of the Cavities of the Earth spring Terrestrial Dogs.
Which shew no true sign to mortal Man.
Labour about the Hecatick Strophalus.
Never change Barbarous Names;
For there are Names in every Nation given from God, which have an unspeakble power in Rites.
When thou seest a Sacred Fire without Form,
Shining flashingly through the depths of the World,
Hear the Voice of Fire.

PLETHO

HIS

EXPOSITION

Of the more obscure Passages in these ORACLES.

Seek thou the way of the Soul, whence or by what Order.
Having served the Body, to the same Order from which thou didst flow.
Thou mayst rise up again; joyning Action to Sacred Speech.]

The *Magi* that are Followers of *Zoroaster*, as also many others, hold, that the Humane Soul is immortal; and descended from above to serve the Mortal Body, that is, to operate therein for a certain time; and to animate, and adorn it to her power; and then returns to the place from which she came. And whereas there are many Mansions there for the Soul, one *wholly bright*, another *wholly dark*; others betwixt both *partly bright, partly dark*: The Soul being descended from that which is wholly bright, into the Body, if she perform her Office well, runs back into the same place; but if not well, she retires into worse Mansions, according to the things which she hath done in Life. The Oracle therefore saith, *Seek thou the Soul's Path*, or the way by which the Soul floweth into thee; or by what course (*viz.* of Life) having performed thy Charge toward the Body, thou may'st mount up to the same place from which thou didst flow down, *viz.* the same Track of the Soul, *joyning Action to Sacred Speech*. By Sacred Speech, he understands that which concerns Divine Worship; by *Action*, Divine Rites. The Oracle therefore saith, that to this Exaltation of the Soul, both Speech concerning Divine Worship (Prayers,) and Religious Rites (Sacrifices) are requisite.

Stoop not down, for a Precipice lies below on the Earth,
Drawing through the Ladder which hath seven steps; beneath which
Is the Throne of Necessity.]

He calls the Descension into wickedness, and misery, a Precipice; the Terrestrial and Mortal Body, the Earth: for by the Earth he understands mortal Nature, as by the Fire frequently the Divine; by the Place with seven Ways, he means Fate dependant on the Planets, beneath which there is seated a certain dire and unalterable Necessity: The Oracle therefore adviseth, that thou stoop not down towards the mortal Body, which being subject only to the Fate, which proceeds from the Planets, may be reckoned among those things which are at our Arbitrement: for thou wilt be unhappy if thou stoop down wholly to the Body, and unfortunate and continually failing of thy Desires, in regard of the Necessity which is annexed to the Body.

For thy Vessel the Beasts of the Earth shall Inhabit.]

The *Vessel* of thy Soul, that is this mortal Body, shall be *inhabited* by Worms and other vile Creatures.

Enlarge not thou thy Destiny.]

Endeavour not to encrease thy Fate, or to do more than is given thee in charge, for thou wilt not be able.

For nothing proceeds from the Paternal Principality imperfect.]

For from the Paternal Power, which is that of the Supream God, nothing proceedeth imperfect, so as thou thy self mightest compleat it; for all things proceeding from thence are perfect; as appears, in that they tend to the Perfection of the Universe.

But the Paternal Mind accepts not her Will, Until she go out of Oblivion, and pronounce a Word, Inserting the remembrance of the pure paternal Symbol.]

The Paternal Mind, (*viz.* the Second God and ready maker of the Soul) admits not her Will or Desire until she come out of the Oblivion, which she contracted by Connexion with the Body; and until she speak a certain word, or conceive in her thoughts a certain Speech, calling to remembrance the Paternal Divine Symbol or Watch-word; this is the pursuit of the good which the Soul calling to remembrance hereby becomes most acceptable to her Maker.

It behoves thee to hasten to the Light, and to the Beams of the Father:
From whence there was sent to thee a Soul endued with much Mind.]

The Light and Splendor of the Father is that Mansion of the Soul which is circumlucid, from whence the Soul arrayed with much of the Mind was sent hither, wherefore we must hasten to return to the same Light.

These the Earth bewails, even to their own Children.]

Those who hasten not to the Light, from which their Soul was sent to them, the Earth or Mortal Nature bewails, for that they being sent hither to adorn her, not only not adorn her, but also blemish themselves by living wickedly; moreover the wickedness of the Parents is transmitted to the Children, corrupted by them through ill Education.

The ungirders of the Soul, which give her breathing, are easie to be loosed.]

The Reasons which expell the Soul from Wickedness, and give her breathing, are easie

PART XIX.   *The Chaldaick Oracles.*   53

to be untied; and the Oblivion which keeps them, is easily put off.

In the side of the sinister Bed there is a Fountain of Virtue:
Which remains entire within; not emitting her Virginity]

In the left side of thy Bed, there is the Power or Fountain of Virtue, residing wholly within, and never casting off her Virginity, or Nature void of Passion: for there is always in us the power of Virtue without passion which cannot be put off; although her Energy or Activity may be interrupted: he saith the power of Virtue is placed on the left side, because her Activity is seated on the right: By the Bed is meant the Seat of the Soul, subject to her several Habits.

The Soul of Man will, in a manner, clasp God to her self.
Having nothing Mortal, she is wholly inebriated from God;
For she boasts Harmony, in which the Mortal Body consists.]

The Humane Soul will in a manner clasp God, and joyn him strictly *to her self,* (who is her continual Defence) by resembling him as much as we can possibly; *having nothing mortal* within her, *she is wholly drenched in Divinity,* or replenished with Divine Goods; for though she is fetter'd to this mortal Body, yet she *glories in the Harmony* or Union *in which the Mortal Body exists*; that is, she is not ashamed of it, but thinks well of her self for it; as being a cause, and affording to the Universe, that, as Mortals are united with Immortals in Man, so the Universe is adorned with one Harmony.

Because the Soul being a bright fire by the power of the Father,
Remains Immortal, and is Mistress of Life,
And possesseth many completions of the cavities of the World.]

The second God, who first before all other things proceeded from the Father and supream God, these Oracles call all along, *The Power of the Father,* and his *intellectual Power,* and the *paternal Mind.* He saith therefore, that *the Soul procreated by this power of the Father, is a bright fire*; that is, a Divine and Intellectual Essence, and *persisteth immortal* through the Divinity of its Essence, *and is Mistress of Life,* viz. of her self, possessing Life which cannot be taken away from her, for, how can we be said to be Masters of such things, as may be taken from us, seeing the use of them is only allowed us? but of those things which cannot be taken from us, we are absolute Masters: The Soul according to her own Eternity, *possesseth many Rooms in the* Receptacles of the World, or divers places in the World, which according as she hath led Life past is allotted to every one.

Seek Paradise.]

The circumlucid Mansion of the Soul.

Defile not the Spirit, nor deepen a Superficies]

The followers of *Pythagoras* and *Plato* conceive the Soul to be a Substance not wholly separate from all Body, nor wholly inseparate; but partly separate, partly inseparate; separable potentially, but ever separate actually. For they assert three kinds of Forms, one wholly separate from matter, the Supercelestial Intelligences, another wholly inseparable from Matter, having a Substance not subsistent by it self but dependent on Matter; together with which Matter, which is sometimes dissolved by reason of its nature subject to Mutation, this kind of Soul is dissolved also and perisheth: this kind they hold to be wholly irrational. Betwixt these they place a middle kind, the rational Soul, differing from the Supercelestial Intelligences, for that it always co-exists with Matter; and from the irrational kind, for that it is not dependant on Matter; but, on the contrary, Matter is dependent on it, and it hath a proper substance potentially subsistent by it self; it is also indivisible, as well as the supercelestial Intelligences, and performing some works in some manner allyed to theirs, being it self also busied in the knowledge and contemplation of Beings even unto the supreme God; and for this reason is incorruptible. This kind of Soul is always co-existent with an Æthereal Body as its *Vehiculum,* which she by continual approximation maketh also Immortal: neither is this her *Vehiculum* inanimate in it self, but it is it self animated with the other species of the Soul, the irrational (which the Wise call the Image of the rational Soul) adorned with Phantasie and Sense, which seeth and hears it self whole through whole; and is furnished with all the Senses and with all the rest of the irrational Faculties of the Soul. Thus by the principal Faculty of this Body, Phantasie, the rational Soul is continually joyned to such a Body, and by such a Body sometimes the humane Soul is joyned with a mortal Body by a certain affinity of Nature, the whole being infolded in the whole enlivening Spirit of the Embryon. This *Vehiculum* it self being of the nature of a Spirit. The Dæmons Souls differ not much from the humane, only they are more noble and use more noble Vehicles. Moreover, they cannot be mingled with corruptible Nature. Likewise the Souls of the Stars are much better than the Dæmons, and use better Vehicles; are Bodies splendid by reason of the greatness of the operative faculty: These Doctrines concerning the Soul the *Magi,* followers of *Zoroaster,* seem to have used long before. Defile not this kind of Spirit of the Soul, saith the Oracle, nor deepen it being a superficies; he calls it superficies, not as if it had not a triple dimension, for it is a Body; but to signifie its extraordinary Rarity: nor make it become gross by accession of more matter to its Bulk: for this Spirit of the Soul becomes gross, if it declines too much towards the mortal Body.

There is a room for the Image also in the circumlucid place.]

He calls the Image of the Soul that part which being it self void of irrational, is joyned to the rational

rational part, and depends upon the Vehicle thereof: now he saith that this kind of *Image hath a part in the circumlucid Region*; for the Soul never layeth down the Vehicle adherent to her.

Leave not the drofs of Matter on a Precipice.]

He calls the Mortal Body *the drofs of Matter*, and exhorteth that we neglect it not being ill affected, but take care of it whilst it is in this life, to preserve it in Health as much as possible, and that it may be pure, and in all things else correspond with the Soul.

Carry not forth, left going forth she have something.]

Carry not forth, meaning the Soul, out of the Mortal Body, *left by going forth thou incur some danger*, implying as much as to carry her forth beyond the Laws of Nature.

If thou extend the fiery Mind to the work of Piety, thou shalt preserve the fluxible Body.]

Extending up thy Divine Mind to the Exercife of Piety or to Religious Rites, and thou *shalt preserve the Mortal Body* more sound by performing these.

Certainly out of the Cavities of the Earth spring Terrestrial Dogs,
Which shew no true sign to Mortal Man.]

Sometimes to many initiated Persons there appear, whilst they are Sacrificing, some apparitions in the shape of *Dogs*, and several other Figures. Now the Oracle faith, that these *issue out of the Receptacles of the Earth*; that is, out of the terrestrial and mortal Body, and the irrational Passions planted in it, which are not yet sufficiently adorned with Reason; these are apparitions of the Passions of the Soul in performing Divine Rites: meer appearances having no substance, and therefore *not signifying any thing true*.

Nature perfwadeth that Dæmons are pure;
The bourgeons, even of ill matter, are profitable and good.]

Nature or natural Reason *perfwadeth that Dæmons are Sacred*, and that all things proceeding from God, who is in himself good, *are beneficial*; and the *very bloomings of ill Matter*, or the forms dependent upon Matter are such: also he calls Matter *ill*, not as to its substance, for how can the substance be bad, the bloomings whereof are beneficial and good? but for that it is ranked last among the substances, and is the least participant of good, which littleness of good is here exprest by the Word ill: now the Oracle means, that if the bloomings of ill Matter, *viz.* of the last of substances are good, much more are the Dæmons such, who are in an excellent Rank as partaking of rational Nature and being not mixed with mortal Nature.

The Furies are Stranglers of Men.]

The Furies or the Vindictive Dæmons clasp Men close, or restrain and drive them from Vice and excite them to Vertue.

Let the immortal depth of the Soul be predominant; but all thy Eyes
Extend quite upward.]

Let the *divine depth of thy Soul* govern and lift thou all thy Eyes or all thy knowing faculties *upward*.

O Man, the Machine of boldest Nature!

He calls Man the *Machine of boldest Nature!* because he attempts great things.

If thou speak often to me, thou shalt see absolutely that which is spoken:
For there neither appears the celestial concave bulk
Nor to the Stars shine: the light of the Moon is covered,
The Earth stands not still, but all things appear Thunder.]

The Oracle speaks as from God to an initiated Person, *If thou often speak to me*, or call me, *thou shalt see that which thou speakest, viz.* Me whom thou callest every where: for then thou shalt perceive nothing but *Thunder* all about, fire gliding up and down all over the World.

Call not on the felf-confpicuous Image of Nature.]

Seek not to behold the self-seeing *Image of Nature, viz.* of the Nature of God, which is not visible to our Eyes: but those things which appear to initiated Persons, as Thunder, Lightning, and all else whatsoever, are only Symbols or Signs, not the *Nature of God*.

Every way to the unfashioned Soul stretch out the Reins of Fire.]

Draw unto thy self every way *the Reins of Fire*, which appear to thee when thou art Sacrificing, with a sincere Soul; *viz.* a simple, and not of various habits.

When thou feest a Sacred Fire, without Form,
Shining flashingly through the depth of the World,
Hear the voice of Fire.]

When thou beholdest the divine fire void of figure brightly gliding up and down the World and graciously smiling, listen to this Voice as bringing a most perfect Præscience.

The Paternal Mind hath implanted Symbols in Souls.]

The *Paternal Mind, viz.* the Sedulous Maker of the substance of the Soul, *hath ingrafted Symbols* or the Images of Intelligibles *in Souls*, by which every Soul possesseth in her self the reasons of Beings.

Learn the Intelligible, for as much it exists beyond the Mind.]

Learn the Intelligible, because it exists beyond thy Mind, viz. actually; for, tho' the Images of
Intellectual

intellectual things are planted in thee by the Maker of All; yet they are but potentially in thy Soul; but it behoves thee to have actually the knowledge of the Intelligible.

There's a certain Intelligible which it behoves thee to comprehend with the flower of thy Mind.]

The Supream God, who is perfectly One, is not conceived after the same manner as other things, but *by the flower of the Mind*, that is, the Supream and Singular part of our Understanding.

For the Father perfected all things and delivered them over to the
Second Mind, which the Nations of Men call the First.]

The Father perfected all things, *viz.* the Intelligible Species, (for they are absolute and perfect) *and delivered them over to the second God*, next him to rule and guide them: whence, if any thing be brought forth by this God, and formed after the likeness of Him, and the other Intelligible Substance, it proceeds from the Supream Father; This other God, *Men esteem the First*, that is, they who think him the Maker of the World, to whom there is none Superiour.

Intelligent Jynges do themselves also understand from the Father;
By unspeakable Counsels being moved so as to understand]

He calls *Jynges* the Intellectual Species which are *conceived by the Father*; *they themselves also being conceptive*, and exciting Conceptions or Notions, *by unspeakable* or unutterable *Counsels*: by *Motion* here is understood Intellection, not Transition, but simply the Habitude to Notions so as unspeakable Counsels is as much as unmoved, for speaking consists in Motion; the meaning is this, That these Species are immoveable and have a habitude to Notions not transiently as the Soul.

Oh how the World hath Intellectual Guides inflexible.]

The most excellent of the Intelligible Species, and of those which are brought down by the Immortals in this Heaven, he calls *the Intellectual Guides of the World*; the Coryphæus whom he conceives to be a God, which is the Second from the Father. The Oracle saying that *the World hath inflexible Guides*, means that it is incorruptible.

The Father hath snatched away himself;
Neither hath he shut up his own Fire in his Intellectual Power.]

The Father hath made himself exempt from all others; *not including* himself neither *in his own Intellectual Power*, nor in the Second God who is next him; or limiting *his own Fire* his own Divinity; for it is absolutely ungenerate, and it self existing by it self; so that his Divinity is exempt from all others; neither is it communicable to any other, although it be loved of all: That he communicates not himself, is not out of Envy, but only by reason of the Impossibility of the thing.

The Father infuseth not Fear but Perswasion.]

The Father makes no impression of Fear, but infuseth Perswasion or Love; for he being extreamly good, is not the cause of ill to any, so as to be dreadful; but is the cause of all good to all; whence he is loved of all.

These Oracles of Zoroaster many Eminent Persons have confirmed by following the like Opinions; especially the Pythagoreans and Platonists.

PSELLUS.

PSELLUS
HIS
EXPOSITION
of the ORACLES.

There is a Room for the Image also in the Circumlucid place.]

Images, εἴδωλα, with the Philosophers, are those things which are connatural to things more Excellent than themselves, and are worse than they; as the Mind is connatural to God, and the Rational Soul to the Mind, and Nature to the Rational Soul, and the Body to Nature, and Matter to the Body: The Image of God is the Mind; of the Mind, the Rational Soul; of the Rational Soul, the Irrational; of the Irrational, Nature; of Nature, the Body; of the Body, Matter. Here the *Chaldaick Oracle* calleth the Irrational Soul the Image of the Rational, for it is connatural to it in Man, and yet worse than it. It faith, moreover, that there is a part assigned to the Image in the circulucid Region, that is to say, the Irrational Soul, which is the Image of the rational Soul, being purified by Virtues in this Life, after the dissolution of the humane Life, ascends to the place above the Moon, and receives its Lot in the *Circumlucid place*, that is, which shineth on every side, and is splendid throughout; for the place beneath the Moon is circumnebulous, that is, dark on every side: but the Lunary, partly Lucid, and partly Dark, that is, one half bright, the other half dark; but the place above the Moon is circumlucid or bright throughout. Now the Oracle saith, that the circumlucid Place, is not design'd only for the rational Soul, but for its Image also, or the irrational Soul is destin'd to the circumlucid place, when as it cometh out of the Body bright and pure, for the Græcian Doctrine asserting the irrational Soul to be Immortal, also exalts it up to the Elements under the Moon; but the *Chaldaick Oracle*, it being pure and unanimous with the rational Soul, seats it in this circumlucid Region above the Moon. These are the Doctrines of the *Chaldæans*.

Leave not the Dregs of Matter on a Precipice.]

By *the Dregs of Matter*, the Oracle understands the body of Man consisting of the four Elements, it speaks to the Disciple by way of Instruction and Exhortation, thus; not only raise up thy Soul to God, and procure that it may rise above the confusion of Life; but, if it be possible, leave not the Body wherewith thou art cloathed, (and which is *Dregs of Matter*, that is, a thing neglected and rejected, the sport of Matter) in the inferiour World: for this place, the Oracle calls a *Precipice*. Our Soul being darted down hither from Heaven, as from a sublime place. It exhorteth therefore, that we refine the Body (which he understands by the dregs of Matter) by divine, or that, being stripped, we raise it up to the Æther; or that we be exalted by God to a place Immaterial and Incorporeal, or Corporeal but Æthereal or Cœlestial, which *Elias* the *Tisbite* attained; and, before him, *Enoch*, being Translated from this Life into a more Divine Condition, not leaving the dregs of Matter, or their Body, in a Precipice; the Precipice is, as we said, the Terrestrial Region.

Bring not forth, lest going forth she have something.]

This Oracle is recited by *Plotinus* in his Book of the Eduction of the irrational Soul; it is an excellent and transcendent Exhortation. It adviseth, that a Man busie not himself about the *going forth of the Soul*, nor take care how it shall go out of the Body; but remit the Business of its Dissolution to the course of Nature; for, Anxiety and Sollicitude about the Solution of the Body, and the Eduction of the Soul out of it, draws away the Soul from better Cogitations, and busieth it in such cares that the Soul cannot be perfectly purified; for if Death come upon us at such time as we are busied about this Dissolution, the Soul goeth forth not quite free, but retaining something of a Passionate Life. Passion the Chaldæan defines, a Man's sollicitous thinking of Death; for we ought not to think of any thing, but of the more excellent illuminations; neither concerning these ought we to be follicitous: but resigning our selves to the Angelical and Diviner Powers, which raise us up and shutting up all the Organs of Sense in the Body and in the Soul also without distractive Cares and Sollicitudes, we must follow God who calls us.

Some interpret this Oracle more simply; *Bring it not out lest it go forth, having something*: that is, Anticipate not thy natural Death, altho' thou be wholly given up to Philosophy; for as yet thou hast not a compleat Expiation; So that if the Soul pass out of the Body by the way of Educting, it will go forth retaining something of Mortal Life: for if we Men are in the Body, as in a Prison, (as *Plato* saith) certainly no Man can kill himself, but must expect till God shall send a Necessity.

Subject not to thy Mind the vast Measures of the Earth;
For the Plant of Truth is not upon the Earth.
Nor measure the Measures of the Sun, gathering together Canons:
He is moved by the Eternal Will of the Father, not for thy sake.
Let alone the swift course of the Moon: she runs ever by the impulse of Necessity.
The Progression of the Stars was not brought forth for thy sake.
The Ætherial broad-footed flight of Birds is not voracious.
And the Dissections of Entrails and Victims, all these are Toys.
The supports of gainful Cheats. Fly thou those,
If thou intend to open the Sacred Paradise of Piety.

Piety. Where Virtue, Wisdom, and Equity are assembled.)

The *Chaldæan* withdraws the Disciple from all Græcian Wisdom, and teacheth him to adhere only to God, *Subject not* (saith he) *to thy Mind the vast measures of the Earth; for the Plant of Truth is not on Earth;* that is, enquire not sollicitously into the vast Measures of the Earth, as *Geographers* use to do, Measuring the Earth; for the Seed of Truth is not in the Earth. *Nor measure the measures of the Sun, gathering together Canons; he is moved by the Eternal Will of the Father, not for thy sake*: That is, busie not thy self about the Motion and Doctrine of the Stars, for they move not for thy sake, but are perpetually moved according to the Will of God; *Let alone the swift course of the Moon, she runs ever by the impulse of Necessity*: That is, enquire not anxiously the rolling motion of the Moon, for she runs not for thy sake, but is impelled by a greater necessity. *The Progression of the Stars was not brought forth for thy sake*; that is, the Leaders of the fixed Stars, and the Planets received not their Essence for thy sake. *The Æthereal broad-footed flight of Birds is not veracious*; that is, the Art concerning Birds flying in the Air, called Augury, observing their Flight, Notes, and Pearching, is not true. By *broad feet*, he means the walking or pace of the Foot, in respect of the extention of the Toes in the skin. *And the Dissections of Entrails and Victims, all these are Toys*: that is, the Art of Sacrificing, which enquireth after future Events, as well by Victims, as by inspection into the Entrails of Sacrificed Beasts, are meerly Toys. *The supports of gainful Cheats: fly thou those*, that is, fraudulent acquisitions of gain. *If thou intend to open the Sacred Paradise of Piety, where Virtue, Wisdom, and Equity are assembled.* (Thou (saith he) who art under my Discipline, enquire not curiously after these things, if thou wouldst that the Sacred Paradise of Piety be open to thee. The Sacred Paradise of Piety, according to the *Chaldæans*, is not that which the Book of *Moses* describes, but the Meadow of sublimest Contemplations, in which there are several Trees of Vertues; and the Wood, (or Trunk) of knowledge, of good and evil, that is, Dijudicative Prudence which distinguisheth Good from Evil; likewise, the Tree of Life, that is, the Plant of Divine Illumination, which bringeth forth to the Soul the fruit of a more holy and better life; in this Paradise, therefore, grow Vertue, Wisdom, and Equity; Vertue is one in General, but hath many Species; Wisdom comprehendeth within it self all the Vertues, which the Divine Mind pronounceth, as only unspeakable.

Seek thou the way of the Soul, whence or by what Order
Having served the Body, to the same order from which thou didst flow,
Thou maist rise up again; joyning Action to Sacred Speech.)

That is, *Seek the Origin of the Soul*, from whence it was produced and served the Body, and how Men cherishing and raising it up by the Exercise of Divine Rites, may reduce it to the place whence it came. *Uniting Action to Sacred Reason*, is to be understood thus. *Sacred Reason* (or discourse) in us is the Intellectual Life, or rather the supream faculty of the Soul, which the Oracle elsewhere styles the Flower of the Mind; but this Sacred Reason cannot by its own guidance aspire to the more sublime Institution, and to the comprehension of Divinity; the work of Piety leads it by the hand to God, by assistance of Illuminations from thence: but the *Chaldæan* by the Telestick Science, perfects (or initiates), the Soul by the power of Materials here on Earth. To this Sacred Reason, saith he, when thou hast united Action, that is, joyned the work of Initiation to the Sacred Reason, or better Faculty of the Soul.

Our Theologist *Gregory* raiseth the Soul to the more Divine things by Reason and Contemplation: by Reason which is in us the best and most intellectual Faculty; by Contemplation, which is an Illumination coming from above: But *Plato* affirms, that we may comprehend the ungenerate Essence by Reason and Intellect. But the *Chaldæan* saith, that there is no other means for us to arrive at God, but by strengthning the Vehiculum of the Soul by Material Rites; for it supposeth that the Soul is purified by Stones and Herbs, and Charms, and is rendred expedite for Assent.

Stoop not down; for a Precipice lies below on the Earth.
Drawing through the Ladder which hath seven steps, beneath which
Is the Throne of Necessity.)

The Oracle adviseth, the Soul which is next to God, that she adhere only to him with her whole Mind, and bend not downwards; for there is a great *Precipice* betwixt God and the Earth which draweth Souls down the *Ladder* which hath *seven Steps*: The *Ladder of seven Steps* signifies the Orbs of the seven Planets; if therefore the Soul decline, she is carried to the Earth through the seven Orbs: but that passage thro' the seven Circles leads her as by so many steps to the Throne of Necessity, whither, when the Soul arriveth, she is necessitated to suffer the terrestrial World.

Never change barbarous Names.)

That is, there are certain *Names* among all Nations delivered to them by God, which have an unspeakable Power in Divine Rites: change not these into the Greek Dialect; as *Seraphim* and *Cherubin*, and *Michael* and *Gabriel*: These in the Hebrew Dialect have an unspeakable Efficacy in Divine Rites; but changed into Greek Names, are ineffectual.

The World hath intellectual Guides inflexible.)

The *Chaldæans* assert Powers in the World, and call them (*Cosmogogi*) *Guides of the World*, for that they guide the World by provident Motions: These Powers the Oracles call ἀνοχῆας *Sustainers*, as sustaining the whole World. Unmoveable

moveable implies their setled Power; sustentive, their Guardian-ship; these Powers they design only by the Cause and Immobility of the Worlds: There are also other Powers (*amilicti*) implacable, as being firm and not to be converted towards these inferiour things, and cause that Souls be never allured with Affections.

Labour about the Hecatine Strophalus.]

The *Hecatine Strophalus* is a Golden Ball, in the midst whereof is a Sapphire; they fold about it a Leather-Thong; it is beset all over with Characters: thus whipping it about, they made their Invocations: these they use to call *Jynges*, whether it be round or triangular, or any other Figure; and whilst they are doing thus, they make Insignificant or Bruitish Cries, and lash the Air with their Whips. The Oracle adviseth to the performance of these Rites or such a Motion of the *Strophalus*, as having an expressible Power. It is called *Hecatine*, as being dedicated to *Hecate*: *Hecate* is a Goddess among the *Chaldæans*, having at her right side the Fountain of Virtues.

If thou speak often to me, thou shalt see absolutely that which is spoken.
For then neither appears the Cœlestial Concave Bulk, nor do the Stars shine; the light of the Moon is covered,
The Earth stands not still, but all things appear Thunder.]

The Lion is one of the twelve Signs of the Zodiack, and is called the House of the Sun, whose Fountain or the cause of his Lion-formed Constellation the *Chaldæans* calls λεόντουχον: now he saith, that amidst the Sacred Rites thou call this Fountain by its Name, thou shalt see nothing else in Heaven but the apparition of a Lion, neither will the *Concave Bulk*, or the Circumference of Heaven appear to thee, neither shall the Stars shine, even the Moon her self shall be covered, and all things shall be shaken; but this Lion-having Fountain takes not away the Essence of those, but their own predominating Existence hides their View.

Every way to the unfashioned Soul, extend the Reins of Fire.]

The Oracle calls the Soul ἄπλασον, that is, *without Form and Figure*, or most simple, and most pure. Reins of Fire of such a Soul are the expeditious activity of the Theurgick Life, which raiseth up the Fiery Mind to the Divine Light: therefore by stretching the Reins of Fire to the inform Soul, he means, endeavour that all the Faculties consisting both in the Intellect, Cogitation, and Opinion, may receive Divine Illuminations suitable to themselves. This is the meaning of *stretch the Reins of Fire*; but Nature useth to fail, and busie it self in the second or worse Life.

Oh Man, the Machine of boldest Nature!]

Man is called a *Machine* as being framed by God with unspeakable Art: The Oracle likewise calleth him *audacious Nature*, as being busied about excellent things, sometimes measuring the Course of the Stars, sometimes enquiring into the Orders of the supernatural Powers; contemplating also the things which are far above the Cœlestial Orb, and extending to discourse something of God. For these endeavours of the Mind in Disquisition proceed from an audacious Nature: he calls it boldness, not by way of Reproach, but to express the forwardness of Nature.

In the side of the sinister Hecate *is a Fountain of much Vertue; which remains entire within, not emitting her Virginity.*]

The *Chaldæans* esteem *Hecate* a Goddess, seated in the middle rank, and possessing as it were the Center of all the Powers; in her right parts they place the Fountain of Souls, in her left the Fountain of *Goods*, or of *Vertues*; and they say, that the Fountain of Souls is prompt to Propagations, but the Fountain of Vertues continues within the bounds of its own Essence, and is as a Virgin incorrupted: this settledness and Immobility it receives from the power of the *Amilicti*, the Implacables, is girt with a Virgin-Zone.

When thou seest a Sacred Fire without Form Shining flashingly through the depths of the whole World,
Hear the Voice of Fire.]

The Oracle speaks of *Divine Light*, seen by many Men, and adviseth, That if any one see such a Light in some Figure and Form, he apply not his Mind to it, nor esteem the Voice proceeding from thence to be true; but if he see this without any Figure or Form he shall not be deceived: and whatsoever Question he shall propose, the Answer will be most true, he calls this ἐυίερον *Sacrosanct*, for that it is seen with a Beauty by Sacred Persons, and glides up and down pleasantly and graciously through the Depths of the World.

Invoke not the self-conspicuous Image of Nature.]

Αὐτοψία, *Self-inspection*, is, when the initiated Person (or he who performs Divine Rites) seeth the Divine Lights: but if he who orders the Rites seeth an Apparition, this, in respect of the initiated Person is ἐπόψια, *super-inspection*. The Image which is evocated at Sacred Rites, must be Intelligible and wholly seperate from Bodies: But the Form or Image of Nature is not every way intelligible: for Nature is for the most part an Administrative Faculty. *Call not*, saith he, in the Rites *the self-conspicuous Image of Nature*; for it will bring thee nothing along with it but only a crowd of the four Natural Elements.

Nature perswades that Dæmons are pure.
The bourgeons even of ill matter are profitable and good.

Not that Nature her self perswades this, but that being called before her presence there floweth in a great Company of Dæmons and many
Dæmonious

Dæmonius forms of several shapes appear raised up out of all the Elements, compounded and shaped from all the parts of the Lunar Course, and many times appearing pleasant and gracious, they make shew of an Apparition of some good to the initiated Person.

The Soul of Man will in a manner clasp God to her self.
Having nothing Mortal she is wholly inebriated from God.
For she boasts Harmony, in which the mortal body exists.]

He saith that the Soul *forceth*, (for that is the meaning of ἄγχιν,) the Divine Fire into her self, through Immortality and Purity, for then she is *wholly inebriated*, that is, she is replenished with the more excellent Life and Illumination, and exists as it were out of her self: the Oracle saith to her, *boast of Harmony*; that is, Glory in the obscure and unintelligible Harmony by which thou art tied together in Arithmetical and Musical Proportions: for under this unintelligible Harmony even the Mortal and compounded Body is composed, having its compositions derived from thence.

Let the Immortal depth of the Soul be predominant, but all thy Eyes
Extend upward.]

The *depth of the Soul* is her three-fold powers; the intellectual, the intelligent, the opinionative. Her Eyes are the three-fold cognoscitive operations of these; for the Eye is the Symbol of Knowledge, as Life is of Appetite. Open therefore, saith he, the immortal depth of the Soul, and extend thy cogniscitive Powers upwards, and even thy own self (to use our own Expression) *transfer to the Lord*.

Defile not the Spirit, nor deep not a Superficies.

The *Chaldæans*. Cloath the Soul with two Garments: one they call Spiritual, woven for it by the sensible World; the other Lucí-form, tenuious and intangible, which is here termed *Superficies*: *Defile not*, saith he, the Spiritual Garment of thy Soul with impurity; neither cause its Superficies to grow deep by certain material additions: but preserve both in their own Natures, one pure, the other undipt.

Seek Paradise.]

The *Chaldaick* Paradise is the whole Chorus of Divine Powers about the Father, and the fiery Beauties of the creative Fountains: The opening thereof by Piety is the participation of the Goods; the flaming Sword is the implacable Power which withstands those that approach it unworthily; to such Persons it is shut, for they are not capable of its felicity. To the Pious it is open: To this place tend all the Theurgick Vertues.

This Vessel the Beasts of the Earth shall inhabit.]

The *Vessel* is the compounded mixture of the Soul, the Beasts of the Earth are the Dæmons which rove about the Earth: our life therefore being full of Passions shall be inhabited by such Beasts: for such kinds are essentiated in Passions, and have a material Seat and Order. Wherefore such as are addicted to Passions are glued to them by assimilation, for they attract what is like them, having a motive-faculty from the Passions.

If thou extend the fiery Mind to the work of Piety, thou shalt preserve the fluxible Body.]

That is, *If thou extend thy illuminated Mind* upwards, and the work of fire *to the works of Piety*, (the works of Piety, with the *Chaldæans*, are the Methods of Rites,) thou shalt not only render the Soul unvanquishable by Passions, but shalt also preserve thy Body the more healthful; for this ordinarily is the effect of Divine Illuminations, *viz.* to consume the Matter of the Body, and to establish Health, that it be not seized either by Passion or Diseases.

Certainly out of the Cavities of the Earth spring terrestrial Dogs,
Which shew no true sign to mortal Man.]

The Speech is of material Dæmons: These he calls *Dogs*, for that they are Executioners of Souls; *Terrestrial*, for that they fall from Heaven, and are rolled about the Earth. These, saith he, being removed far from the Beatitude of Divine Life, and destitute of Intellectual Contemplation, cannot pre-signifie Futures; whence all that they say or show is false, and not solid: for they know Beings μορφοδικῶς, by their out-sides; but, that which knoweth figures μερικῶς, particularly, useth Notions indivisible and not figured

For the Father perfected all things, and deliver'd them over to the second
Mind, which all Nations of Men call the first.]

The first *Father of the Triad*, having made the Universal Frame, deliver'd it over to the *Mind*; which Mind the whole Race of Mankind (being ignorant of the paternal Excellency) call the *first God*: but our Doctrine holds the contrary, *viz.* that the first Mind, the Son of the Great Father, made and perfected every Creature; for the Father, in the Book of *Moses*, declareth to the Son the Idæa of the production of Creatures, but the Son himself is the Maker of the Work.]

The Furies or Stranglers of Men.]

(Ἀναγωγοὶ ἄγγελοι) The reductive Angels reduce Souls to them, drawing them from general things; but the *Furies* (ποιναὶ) being the Tormentors of the Natures which are dispersed, and enviours of humane Souls, entangle them in material Passions; and as it were strangle them: and not only torture such as are full of Passions, but even those that are converted towards the immaterial Essence, for these also coming into Matter and into Generation, stand in need of such purification; for we see many Persons even of those who live holily and purely, fall into unexpected Miseries.

The Paternal Mind hath implanted Symbols in Souls.]

As the *Mosaick* Book saith, that Man was formed after the Image of God; so the *Chaldæan* saith, that the Maker and Father of the World *sowed Symbols* of his Essence in the Souls thereof. For out of the paternal Seed, not only Souls, but all superiour Orders sprung. But in Incorporeal substances there is one kind of signs, *viz.* incorporeal, and individual; in the World, there are other Signs and Symbols, the unspeakable properties of God, which are far more Excellent than the Vertues themseves.

The Souls of those who quit the Body violently are most pure.]

Whosoever shall take this saying rightly, will find that it contradicts not our Doctrine; for the Crowned Martyrs who in time of persecution leave their Bodies by a violent End, purifie and perfect their Souls: but this is not that which the *Chaldæan* means. He praiseth all violent Death, because the Soul, which leaveth the Body with Trouble, abhors this Life, and hateth conversation with the Body, and, rejoycing, flyeth up to the things above; but those Souls which forsake this Life, their Bodies being naturally dissolved by sickness, do regret its propension and inclination to the Body.

*Because the Soul being a bright Fire, by the Power of the Father
Remains immortal, and is Mistress of Life,
And possesseth many Completions of the Cavities of the World.*]

The Soul being an immaterial and incorpereal *Fire*, exempt from all compounds, and from the material Body, is immortal; for nothing material or dark is commixed with her, neither is she compounded, so as that she may be resolved into those things of which she consists; but she is the Mistress of Life, enlightening the Dead with Life, she hath the Complements of many Recesses, that is, susceptive of the Government of Matter, for she is enabled according to her different Vertues to dwell in different Zones of the World.

The Father infuseth not Fear, but instead of perswasion.]

That is, the Divine Nature is not stern and full of Indignation, but sweet and calm; whence it doth not cause Fear in the Natures subjected to it, but attracts all things by *perswasion* and graciousness; for if it were formidable and minacious, every Order of Beings would have been dissolved; none of them being able to endure his Power. And this Doctrine, is in part esteemed true amongst us, for God is a Light, and a Fire consuming the wicked; The Menaces and affrightings of God are the Intermission of the Divine Goodness towards us, by reason of our ill management of our Affairs.

*The Father hath snatched away himself:
Neither hath he shut up his own fire in his Intellectual fire.*]

The meaning of which Oracle, is this, The God of all things, who is also termed Father, hath made himself Incomprehensible, not only to the first and second Natures, and to our Souls, but even to his own Power; for the Father, saith he, hath snatch'd himself away from every Nature: But this Doctrine is not Orthodox; for with us the Father is known in the Son, as the Son in the Father, and the Son is the Definition of the Father, and the Divine supernatural World.

For the intelligible is somethinng, which it behoves thee to comprehend with the flower of the mind.]

The Soul hath a power correspondent to every thing that is conceivable by the Mind; As to Sensibles, Sense; to Cogitables, Cogitation; to Intelligibles, Mind. Now the *Chaldæan* saith, that although God is an Intelligible, yet he is not Comprehensible by the Mind, but only by the *Flower of the Mind*. The Flower of the Mind is the (ἰδέα) singular power of the Soul: since therefore, God is properly one, endeavour not to comprehend him by the Mind, but by the singular power: for that which is first one, can only be apprehended by that which is one in us, and not either by cogitation or Mind.

The ungirders of the Soul which give her breathing are easie to be loosed.]

Lest any one should say, I would free my Soul from my Body, but I cannot; the Oracle tells us, that the Powers, which *thrust the Soul* out of the natural Body, and give her breathing, as it were, from the toil and trouble of the Body, are easily *loosed*; that is, these Faculties are free and not restrained by any Nature, and able to set the Body at Liberty generously from corporeal Bonds.

*It behooves thee to hasten to the Light, and to the Beams of the Father,
From whence was sent to thee a Soul cloathed with much Mind.*]

Seeing that the Soul hath not its Being from Seed, neither consists of corporeal mixtures but had its Essence from God above; therefore she ought to turn towards Him, and to make her return to the *Divine Light*: for she came down *cloathed with much Mind*; that is, she was furnished by the Maker and Father, with many Remembrances of the Divine sayings, when she came hither, whence she should endeavour to return by the same Remembrances.

All things are produced out of one Fire.]

This is a true Doctrine, conformable to our Religion; for all Beings, as well intelligible, as sensible, received their Essence from God above, and are converted to God alone; those which have Being only Essentially; those which have
Being

Being and Life, Essentially and Vitally; those which have Being, and Life and Mind, Essentially, and Vitally, and Intellectually. From *One* therefore *all things came*, and to One is their return: This Oracle is not to be condemned, but is full of our Doctrine.

What the Mind speaks, it speaks by Intellection.]

When (saith he) thou shalt hear an articulate Voice, Thundering from above out of Heaven, think not that the Angel or God who sends forth that Voice, did articulate it after our manner Enunciatively; but that He, according to his own Nature, conceived it only inarticulately: but thou, according to thy own Impotence, hearest the Notion syllabically and enuntiatively. For as God heareth our Voice not vocally, so Man receiveth the Notions of God vocally, every one according to the operation of his Nature.

These the Earth bewails, even to their Children.]

It is meant of *Atheists*, that God extends his Vengeance even to their Posterity: for the Oracle, to express the Torments which they shall receive under the Earth, saith, *It howls beneath for them*: that is, the Place under the Earth bellows to them, and roareth like a Lion. Whence *Proclus* also saith, The composition of Souls that are of Affinity with one another, is of like Nature; and those which are not yet loosed from the Bands of Nature, are entangled and detained by like Passions. These therefore must fulfil all Punishments, and since by Natural Affinity they are infected with Pollutions, must again be cleansed from them.

Enlarge not thy Destiny,]

The wisest of the Greeks call Nature or rather the Completion of the Illuminations which the Nature of Beings receiveth (ἑμαρμένην) Fate. Providence is an immediate Beneficence from God. But Fate is that which Governs all our Affairs, by the concatenation of Beings. We are Subjects to Providence, when we act Intellectually; to Fate, when Corporeally. Encrease not therefore, saith he, thy Fate, nor endeavour to surmount it, but commit thy self wholly to the Government of God.

For nothing proceeds from the paternal Principality imperfect.]

The Father (saith he) produceth all things perfect and self-sufficient according to their Order, but the Imbecillity and Remission of the things produced sometimes causeth a Defect and Imperfection, but the Father calleth back again that defect to Perfection; and converts it to its Self-sufficience. Like this, is that which *James* the Brother of our Lord pronounceth in the beginning of his Epistle, *Every perfect Gift cometh down from above, from the Father of Lights*. For nothing proceeds Imperfect from the Perfect, and especially when we chance to be ready to receive that which is primarily distilled from him.

But the Paternal Mind accepts her not until she come forth.]

The Paternal Mind doth not admit the Impulsions of the desires of the Soul, before she hath excluded the forgetfulness of the Riches which she received from the most bountiful Father, and called back to her Memory the Sacred Watchwords which she received from him, and pronounce the good Speech imprinting in her remembrance the Symbols of the Father who begot her. For the Soul consists of Sacred Words and Divine Symbols, of which those proceed from the Sacred Species, these from the Divine Monads; and we are (εἰκόνες) Images of the Sacred Essences, but (ἀγάλματα) Statues of the unknown Symbols. Moreover we must know that every Soul differs from another Soul specifically, and that there are as several Species of Souls as there are Souls.

When thou seest the Terrestrial Dæmon approach, Sacrifice the Stone Mnizuris, using Invocation.]

The Dæmons that are near the Earth are by Nature lying, as being far off from the Divine knowledge, and filled with dark Matter. Now if you would have any true discourse from these, prepare an Altar, and *Sacrifice the Stone Mnisuris*: this Stone hath the power of evocating the other greater Dæmon, who, invisibly approaching to the material Dæmon, will pronounce the true solution of demands, which he transmits to the demandant. The Oracle joyneth the evocative Name with the Sacrificing of the Stone. The Chaldeans assert some Dæmons good, others ill; but our Religion defines them to be all ill, as having by a premeditated defection exchanged good for ill.

Learn the Intelligible, forasmuch as it exists beyond the Mind.]

For though all things are comprehended by the Mind, yet God the first Intelligible exists *without* or *beyond the Mind*. This *without* you must not understand distantially, nor according to intellectual alternity, but according to the intelligible excess alone, and the propriety of the existence, it being without, or beyond all Mind, whereby the superessential is manifested. For the first intelligible Mind is Essence, beyond which is the Self-intelligible. Besides these is God, who is beyond the Intelligible, and Self-intelligible: for we assert the Divinity to be neither intelligible nor self-intelligible, it being more excellent than all Speech and Notion, so as that it is wholly unintelligible, and unexpressible, and more to be Honoured by Silence, than Reverenced by wonderful Expressions. For it is more Sublime than to be Reverenced, Spoken, and Conceived.

Intelligent Jynges do themselves also understand from the Father,
By unspeakable Counsels being moved so as to understand.]

Jynges are certain (Vertues or) Powers, next
the

the Paternal Depth, consisting of three Triads. These understand according to the Paternal Mind, which containeth their Cause solely in himself. Now the Counsels of the Father in regard of their intelligible Sublimity, are not vocal; but the Intellectual Marks of abstract things, though understood by Secondaries (or Inferiours) are understood as without speaking, and as it were abstracted from Intelligible Prolations. For as the Conceptions of Souls, they understand Intellectual Orders, yet understand them as Immutable: So the Acts of the Intellectuals understanding the Intellectual Signs, understand them as not a vocal subsisting in unknown Existences.

CONJECTURES

Upon the Greek Text of the

ORACLES.

WHO it was that rendred these Oracles in Greek is (as we said) uncertain; much more certain is it that they were all composed in Hexameter Verse: though they are sometimes cited indistinctly and abruptly by *Patricius*, seeming wholly irreconcileable with Poetick Numbers; yet that the greater part of them are Hexameters, none can deny; and whosoever shall look more cautiously upon the rest, will find Prints enough, by which they may be traced and demonstrated to have been of the same kind, though confounded in the manner of Citations, sometimes by the Authors out of which *Patricius* took them, sometimes by *Patricius* himself, who was far more diligent to Collect and Digest, than Curious to Distinguish them, or to regard their Numbers: which Defect we shall endeavour, in some measure, to supply.

ΜΟΝΑΣ, ΔΥΑΣ, ΚΑΙ ΤΡΙΑΣ.

Ὅπε πατεικὴ μονάς ἐςι.]

The latter part of the Hexameter, ——— ὅπε πατεικὴ μονάς ἐςι. as is that also which immediately follows,

——— Ταυτὴ [ἐςι] μονάς, ἢ δύο ἠνώα.

and the next,

——— Δυὰς [γδ] παρὰ τῆδε κάθηται. That which follows is cited again by it self afterward.

Καὶ τὸ κυβερνᾶν]

This seems to be a loose Citation of two several Hemistichs, with reference to the Phrase (infinitively) not to the Verse.

Ἀρχὴ πάσης τμήσεως ἢ δὲ ἡ τάξις]

Read, perhaps,

Ἀρχή τοι πάσης τ̓ τήσεως, ἥδε δὲ τάξις.

Οὐ τὸ θέλειν κατένδωσε, κὴ ἤδη πάντα ἐτέτμητο.]

The Verse requires ——— πάντ᾽ ἐτέτμητο.

Εἰς τέλα γδ ἔιπε νῦς πατερὸς.]

Before,

Εἰς τέλα γδ ἢυς ἔιπε πατερὸς.

Καὶ ἐφάνησαν ἐν αὐτῇ ἥ τ᾽ ἀρετή.]

Perhaps [κὴ]

——— ἐφάνησαν ἐν αὐτῇ
Ἥ τ᾽ ἀρετὴ σοφίη τε, κὴ ἡ πολύφρων ἀτρέκεια.
Ἱερὸς πρῶτος δεσμὸς, ἐν δ᾽ ἄρα μέσω]

Read μέσῳ.

Καὶ πηγὴ πηγῶν.]

Perhaps,

Καὶ πηγὴ πηγῶν, μήτρα συνέχουσα τὰ πάντα·

The rest being a Gloss.

Ἔνθεν ἄρδην.

It should be Ἔνθ᾽ ἄρδην.

Ἔνθεν συρομόν⊙ πρηστῆς ἀμυδροῖο πυρὸς ἄνθ⊙.]

Proclus reads ἀμυδροῖ in Theolog.

ΠΑΤΗΡ ΚΑΙ ΝΟΥΣ.

Ἑαυτὸν ὁ πατὴρ ἥρπασεν, ἐδ᾽ ἐν ἑῇ.]

Pletho reads,

Οὐδ᾽ ἐν ἑῇ δυνάμει νοερᾷ κλείσας ἴδιον πῦρ·
Πάντα γδ ἐξετέλεσε.]

Pletho,

Πάντα γδ ἐξετέλεσε πατήρ, κὴ Νῷ παρέδωκε
Δευτέρῳ, ὃν πρῶτον κληίζεται (perhaps κληίζετο)
πᾶν γέν⊙ ἀνδρῶν.

Πολὺ γδ μόν⊙]

Distinguish,

——— πολὺ γδ μόν⊙ ἐκ πατρὸς ἀλκῆς]
Δρεψάμεν⊙ νόκ ἄνθ⊙.
Πᾶσιν ἐνέσπειρε] ἐνέσπειρεν· and afterwards, ἔσπειρεν κατὰ κόσμον.
Μήτε πᾶσι τὰ πατρὸς νοεραῖς ὑφασμένα φέγγει.]

Perhaps,

Μήδεα πᾶσι πατρὸς, &c.

Ἔχει τῷ νοεῖν πατρικὸν νοῦν ἐνδιδόναι.]

Perhaps, ——— ἔχει τὸ νοεῖν πατρικὸν νοῦν

Ἐνδιδόναι πάσαισιν (ὁμᾶ) πηγαῖς τε κὴ ἀρχαῖς·
Οὐ γδ εἰς ὕλην, πῦς ἐπέκεινα τὸ πρῶτον]

Distinguish,

——— ὦ γδ ἐς ὕλην
Πῦρ ἐπέκεινα τὸ πρῶτον ἑὴν δύναμιν κατακλείει
Ἔργοις, ἀλλὰ νόῳ ———
Νῷ μὲν κατέχει.]

Distinguish,

——— νῷ μὲν κατέχει τὰ νοητὰ,
Αἴσθησιν δ᾽ ἐπάγει κόσμοις ———

ΝΟΥΣ, ΝΟΗΤΑ, ΚΑΙ ΝΟΕΡΑ.

Οὐ γδ ἄνευ νό⊙ ἐςὶ νοητὸν ἐ χωρὶς ὑπάρχει.]

Afterwards cited thus,

Οὐ γδ ἄνευ νό⊙ ἐςὶ νοητοῦ, κὴ τὸ νοητὸν
Οὐ νῦ χωρὶς ὑπάρχει.
Μάνθανε τὸ νοητὸν.]

Afterwards,

Ὄφρα μάθῃς τὸ νοητὸν ———
Νῦ γδ νῦς ἐςὶν ὁ κόσμε τεχνίτης πυρὸς.]

Distinguish,

——— νῦ γδ νῦς ἐςὶν ὁ κόσμε
Τεχνίτης πυρὸς ———
Ἔςι γάρ τι νοητὸν] Ἔςιν.
Ἡ γδ ἐπεγκλίνη, ὡς ἂν νῦν.]

Read and distinguish,

Ἡ γδ ἐπεγκλίνη, σὸν νῦν, κἀκεῖνο νοήσῃ,
Ὥς τι νοᾶν, ὁ κεῖνο νοήσῃς ἔςι τὸ ἀλκῆς
Ἀμφιφαῆς δύναμις νοεραῖς ςραπῆλυσα τομαῖσι.
Οὐ δὴ χρὴ σφοδρότητι νοεῖν τὸ νοητὸν ἐκεῖνο,
Ἀλλὰ νόκ ταναᾶ ταναᾶ φλογὶ, πάντα μετρούσῃ

Πλὴν

Πλίω τὸ νοητὸν ἐκεῖνο· χρεὼ δὴ τᾶτο νοῆσαι.
Η γὰρ ἐπεγκλίνης σὸν νῶν, κἀκεῖνο νοήσεις
Οὐκ ἀτενῶς, ἀλλ' ἁγνὸν ἐπίςροφον ὄμμα, φέρονΊα
Τῆς ψυχῆς τεῖναι κενεὸν νόον εἰς τὸ νοητόν.
Ὄφρα μάθης τὸ νοητὸν, ἐπεὶ νόε ἔξω ὑπάρχει.

And presently after,
———— ἐ γὰρ ἄνὰ νός ἐςὶ νοητᾶ, κὶ τὸ νοητόν
Οὐ νᾶ χωρὶς ὑπάρχει————

ΙΥΓΓΕΣ, ΙΔΕΑΙ, ΑΡΧΑΙ.

Πολλαὶ μὲν·
Distinguish,
———— πολλαὶ αἵδε ἐπεμβαίνεσι φαενοῖς
Κόσμοις, ἐνθρώσκεσαι, ἐν αἷς ἀκρότητες ἔασι,
Τρεῖς.
Νᾶς παΐρὸς ἐρροίζησε.]
cited elsewhere by *Patricius* clearly, without
[Δι' ὧν συνάπΊεται τῷ παΊρὶ, ἄλλω κατ' ἄλλω Ζωὼ, ὑπὸ μεειζομθυίων ὀχεΊῶν.] which belong to some other place,
Ἐξ ἧς ῥοιζῶνΊαι.]
Distinguish,
———— μεμερισμθυῶαι ἄλλαι,
Ῥηγνύμθυαι κόσμε τεὶ σώμασι. αἱ τεὶ κόλπες
Σμερδαλέες, σμιλύεσιν ἐοικύαι, φορέονΊαι.
Πολύ δραΊΊόμθυαι πυρὸς ἄνθος.]
Distinguish,
———— πολὺ
ΔραΊΊόμθυαι πυρὸς ἄνθος ἀκοιμήτε χρόνε.
ἀκμή
Ἀρχεγόνε ἰδέας πρώτη παΊρὸς ἔβλυσε· τὰς δ'
Αὐτοθαλὴς πηγή.

ΕΚΑΤΗ, ΣΥΝΟΧΕΙΣ, ΤΕΛΕΤΑΡΧΑΙ.

Ἐξ αὐτῆς γὰρ πάνΊες ἐνθρώσκεσι.]
Distinguish,———— ἀμείλικΊοί τε κεραυνοί,
Καὶ πρηςηρεσδόχοι κόλποι παμφεγγές ἀλκῆς
ΠαΊερογλῶς Ἑκάτης· κὶ ὑπεζωκὸς πυρὸς ἄνθος,

Ἡ δ' κραΊαιὸν πνεῦμα πόλων, πυείων ἐπέκεινα.
Ὅτι κὶ τὸ ζωογόνον.]
Distinguish,
Τῆς Ἑκάτης κόλπον· κὶ ὀπιρρεῖ τοῖς Συνοχεῦσιν
Ἀλκὼ ζείδωρον πυρὸς μέγα δυναμένοιο.
Ἀλλὰ κὶ φρουρεί.]
Distinguish,
Ἔργων εἰσὶ παΊρὸς. ἀφομοιοῖ γὰρ ἑαυτόν,
Κεῖνος ἐπιγόμθυος.
ΠανΊοίαδος σύνθημα βάλλειν.]
Distinguish,
ΠανΊοίαδος σύνθημα βαλλεῖν φρενὶ, μηδ' ἐπιφοιΊᾶν
Ἐμπνείοις σποράδλω ὀχεΊοῖς, ἀλλὰ ςιβαρηδόν·

ΨΥΧΗ, ΦΥΣΙΣ.

Ὅτι ψυχή.]
Pletho, Ὅτι.
ΜεΊὰ ῇ παΊρικὰς διανοίας.]
Distinguish,
———— μεΊὰ δὴ παΊρικὰς διανοίας,
Ψυχὴ, ἐγὼ, ναίω, θερμοψυχᾶσα τὰ πάνΊα.
Μὴ φύσεως ἐμβλέψεις.]

Proclus in Theolog.
Μὴ φύσιν ἐμβλέψης, εἱμαρμθυὸν ὄνομα τῆς δε.

What follows under the Title of ΟΥΡΑΝΟΣ is very confused, the same Fragments being often repeated.

ΨΥΧΗ, ΣΩΜΑ, ΑΝΘΡΩΠΟΣ.

Most of these are perfect, being put forth by *Pletho* and *Psellus*.
Δίζεο σὺ ψυχῆς ὀχετὸν, ὅθεν, ἢ τίνι τάξει
Σώμαΐι θηΊάσας (so *Pletho*) ἐπὶ τάξιν ἀφ' ἧς ἐρρύης
(read ἐρρύθης.)
Αὖθις, &c.

The rest may be corrected by the Edition of *Pletho* and *Psellus*.

FINIS.

Books Printed for, and Sold by A. and J. Churchil, at the Black Swan in Pater-noster-Row, 1701.

FOLIO.

Talent's Chronological Tables,
Dr. Whitby's Comment on the Epistles,
Camden's Britannia in English, with Maps,
Leybourn's Dialling with Figures,
———— Surveyor with Cuts,
———— Cursus Mathematicus,
Sir P. Ricaut's Lives of the Popes,
Titus Livius's Roman History, English,
Sir Roger L'Estrange's Æsop's Fables,
Dr. Brady's Introduction to English History,
———— Compleat English History, 2 Vol,
Machiavel's Works compleat,
Buchanan's Chronicle or History of the Kings of Scotland,
Baker's Chronicle of the Kings of England,
Mr. Lock's Essay on Human Understanding,
Riolanus }
Vellingus } Anatomy

State-Tracts, a Collection of private Pamphlets,
Usher's Body of Divinity,
Cambridge Concordance, Enlarged,
Sir George Wheeler's Travels into Greece,
Diodorus Siculus's History, English,
Sir R. Blackmore's Prince Arthur,
———— King Arthur,
———— Paraphrase on *Job*,
Bishop Usher's Life and Letters,
———— Sermons,
Bishop Sanderson's Sermons,
Bishop Brownrigg's Sermons,
Common-Prayer, Welsh
Van Helmont's Works
Wing's Astronomia Britannica,
Galilæus's System of the World,
Davilla's History of France,
Hammond's Sermons,
Speed's Maps,

www.ingramcontent.com/pod-product-compliance
Lightning Source LLC
Chambersburg PA
CBHW081141230426
43664CB00018B/2765